# Politics in America

## Members Of Congress In Washington And At Home

Alan Ehrenhalt, Editor

Robert E. Healy, Associate Editor

**Congressional Quarterly Press**
a division of
CONGRESSIONAL QUARTERLY INC.
1414 22nd Street N.W., Washington, D.C. 20037

# Congressional Quarterly Inc.

Wayne P. Kelley  *Publisher*
Peter A. Harkness  *Executive Editor*
Robert E. Cuthriell  *Director, Research and Development*
Robert C. Hur  *General Manager*
I. D. Fuller  *Production Manager*
Maceo Mayo  *Assistant Production Manager*
Sydney E. Garriss  *Computer Services*

## Book Department

David R. Tarr  *Director*
Jean L. Woy  *Deputy Director*

**Production Supervisor**  Maceo Mayo
**Cover Design**  Richard Pottern

Printed in the United States of America

**Library of Congress Cataloging in Publication Data**

Main entry under title:

Politics in America.

Includes index.
1. United States. Congress — Biography. 2. United States. Congress — Committees. 3. Election districts — United States — Handbooks, manuals, etc. I. Ehrenhalt, Alan, 1947—    . II. Congressional Quarterly, inc.

JK1010.P64          328.73          81-9848
ISBN 0-87187-208-0                  AACR2

| | |
|---|---|
| *Editor* | Alan Ehrenhalt |
| *Associate Editor* | Robert E. Healy |
| *Major Contributors* | In Washington:<br>Martha Angle<br>Alan Ehrenhalt<br>Shirley Elder<br>Mary Russell | At Home:<br>Christopher Buchanan<br>Rhodes Cook<br>Phil Duncan<br>Larry Light<br>Warden Moxley |

*Other Contributors*

Robert A. Benenson
Nadine Cohodas
Harrison Donnelly
John Felton
Gail Gregg
Bill Keller
Kathy Koch
Norman Kurz

Andy Plattner
Stuart Rothenberg
Judy Sarasohn
Dale Tate
Pat Towell
Elizabeth Wehr
Richard Whittle

*Research*

Judy Aldock
Dan Elmer
Eugene J. Gabler
Carolyn Goldinger
Michael L. Koempel
Kyung S. Lee
David Long
Kathy McDonald
Mary McNeil
Barbara L. Miracle
John L. Moore
Mary M. Neumann
Jed Newman

Patricia Ann O'Connor
Doug M. Podolsky
Patricia M. Russotto
Debra F. Sessoms
Beth Summers
David Tarrant
Wayne Walker
Ricka P. Wolf
Michael D. Wormser

*Maps*

Richard Pottern
Robert O. Redding
Cheryl Rowe
David A. Seldon

*Photographs*

Karen Ruckman
Jim Wells

Alan Ehrenhalt has written about Congress since 1970, for Congressional Quarterly and as a reporter for the Washington Star. Born in Chicago, he graduated from Columbia University School of Journalism in 1969, and was a Nieman Fellow at Harvard in 1977-78. He is currently political editor of CQ, and contributes a regular column, *Congress and the Country*, to the CQ Weekly Report.


Robert E. Healy is a senior editor of Congressional Quarterly books. He has edited Congressional Quarterly's *Washington Information Directory* and its companion, the *Federal Regulatory Directory*. Born in Winfield, Kansas, he majored in American studies at George Washington University, graduating in 1972. studies.

# Preface

This book is concerned with influence. Its most important purpose is to assess members of Congress in a way that official biographies and interest group ratings never do. We are interested in what each individual member has tried to accomplish in his career, the approach he uses, the allies he has on the inside and the interests he works with on the outside.

It has been a difficult task. Evaluating members of Congress is even harder than evaluating ordinary people; often there is a collision between public record and personal impression, and one has to decide which to trust. But we have worked hard to sort out all 535 of them as best we could. It has been a subjective process — we would not pretend otherwise. We might have written this book by asking all the members a series of multiple choice questions and quantifying the result, but that would have produced a mountain of irrelevant numbers. We were not interested in making a list of the ten smartest, dumbest, best or worst. Real life is more complicated than that. What we wanted to do was understand them.

So we have spent a year interviewing members of Congress about each other, with the understanding that nothing would be attributed to them. We have gone back into the public record for speeches, news releases, amendments and floor votes. And we have sought to portray things we have seen as reporters covering Congress over the past decade and longer. Most of the descriptions of members in Washington were written by people who spent the 1970s writing about the institution for Congressional Quarterly or for the daily press.

We have been in touch with every congressional office, House and Senate. Most have been gracious about providing us with material to use in doing our work. No effort was made, however, to interview any member at length about his own career. Some will surely feel that they might have made us understand better if they had had a chance to sit down and talk to us about their work. But asking people to evaluate themselves, or describe their style, is a precarious business, and we felt talking to peers was a more fruitful way to proceed.

Washington is only part of a legislator's life, probably a smaller part than it was a generation ago. The current group goes home more often, and spends more time on constituent interests, than any in congressional history. So we have marked off a separate section of each profile for politics "at home." We wanted to explain who these people were before they came to Washington, what they have done to keep themselves in office, and what groups or pressures at home they seem to respond to. We added short profiles of each district to make the situation clearer. These are profiles of the current constituencies, not the ones that will be created by redistricting for 1982. Where we felt reasonably sure what a district will look like next year, we mentioned that.

To add some extra perspective, the book summarizes politics and voting patterns in all 50 states, searching for the separate elements that seem to define elections in each of them in the 1980s. Sometimes this was easy; in Alaska, for example, issues of growth and conservation seem more important these days than partisan loyalties. In other places things are more complicated, and we have tried to reflect that, rather than reaching for a glib judgment.

The core of the book, however, remains its effort to portray the members of Congress as others see them. Our goal has been to evaluate them by their own standards. We do not try to decide where a politician ought to stand on a controversial issue — our interest has been to assess how he goes about expressing his views, and how effective he is at it.

The Reagan regime and the new era in budget politics have complicated our task somewhat. We were preparing most of these profiles just as the administration was fostering important changes in many of the ways Congress does business. With a few exceptions, we were able to cover the important congressional events of the first half of 1981. Those after July 1 we will catch up with in later editions.

Washington, D. C.
July 1981

# TABLE OF CONTENTS

**Table of Contents**

**Table of Contents**

## Table of Contents

# Explanation of Statistics

## Committees

Standing and select committees are listed for Senate and House members, as are joint committees. Subcommittee memberships are included below. Seniority ranking is as of May 1, 1981. No seniority is given for the House Budget Committee, which does not operate under normal seniority rules.

## Elections

### House

General election returns are given for House members for 1980 and 1978; returns include candidates receiving 5 percent of the vote or more. Primary returns are given for all House members for 1980. 1978 primary returns are included only for those members first elected in that year. No primary results are given if a candidate ran unopposed or was nominated by caucus or convention.

### Senate

Primary and general election returns are given for each senator's most recent election. No primary results are given if a candidate ran unopposed or was nominated by caucus or convention.

### Key to Party Abbreviations

AM I - American Independent
C - Conservative
D - Democrat
DFL - Democrat Farmer-Labor
I - Independent
IP - Independent American
L- Liberal
LIB - Libertarian
LRU - La Raza Unida
R - Republican
RTL - Right to Life
SOC - Socialist

### Previous Winning Percentages

Winning election percentages are given for each member's entire congressional career. Any year for which a percentage is not given indicates that the member either did not run or lost the election that year. Percentages are given for both general elections and special elections. Percentages have been rounded to the nearest whole number. For senators with previous service in the House, elections to the House are indicated with a footnote.

### District Vote for President

The vote presidential candidates received in each congressional district is given for 1972, 1976 and 1980. (No 1972 district vote is given for California because the 1972 districts were temporary and differ from the districts as they existed in 1976 and 1980, making comparisons impossible.) Data for the district vote for president was compiled by Congressional Quarterly using official results supplied by the secretaries of state or boards of election of the 50 states. The vote totals included for independent (I) are for John Anderson in 1980 and Eugene McCarthy in 1976. The independent vote is included only if the candidate received at least 2 percent of the vote in the district.

## Campaign Finance

Figures are given for all members of Congress and their general election challengers, if they filed reports with the Federal Election Commission (FEC). If no figures are listed, the candidate either did not file a report (reports are not required if receipts and expenditures are less than $5,000) or the reports listed receipts and expenditures of zero.

For House members, figures are given for the 1978 and 1980 elections. For senators, figures are given for the most recent election.

Campaign finance data covers the total receipts and expenditures of each candidate during the two-year election cycle ending on Dec. 31 of the year the election was held. 1980 data covers the period Jan. 1, 1979 - Dec. 31, 1980. 1978 data covers the period Jan. 1, 1977 - Dec. 31, 1978.

Data for 1980 was compiled by Congressional Quarterly from information in the files of the Federal Election Commission. Adjustments have been made in the 1980 receipts and expenditures data for those campaigns with more than $5,000 in loan repayments, rebates or refunds of expenditures, returned contributions, transfers between affiliated committees, contributions to other candidates, purchases and redemption of certificates of deposit and transfers of excess campaign funds. Debts owed to or by the campaign at the end of the election year are not included. Also excluded are repayments of prior election loans or debts and transfers out of prior election excess campaign funds.

Data for 1978 is contained in FEC Reports on Financial Activity 1977-78, published by the Federal Election Commission.

# Voting Studies

Scores of members in voting studies prepared by Congressional Quarterly are given for all years since 1961 (87th Congress). Scores represent the percentage of the time a member of Congress has supported or opposed a given position. An explanation of the voting studies follows.

### Presidential Support

CQ tries to determine what the president personally, as distinct from other administration officials, does and does not want in the way of legislative action. This is done by analyzing his messages to Congress, press conference remarks and other public statements and documents.

In borderline cases where an issue reaches a vote in a different form from the original on which the president expressed himself, CQ analyzes the measure to determine whether, on balance, the features favored by the president outweigh those he opposed or vice versa. Only then is the vote classified.

Occasionally, important measures are so extensively amended on the floor that it is impossible to characterize final passage as a victory or defeat for the president. These votes have been excluded from the study.

Votes on motions to recommit, to reconsider or to table often are key tests that govern the legislative outcome. Such votes are necessarily included in the presidential support tabulations.

Generally, votes on passage of appropriation bills are not included in the tabulations since it is rarely possible to determine the president's position on the overall revisions Congress almost invariably makes in the sums allowed. Votes on amendments to cut or increase specific funds requested in the president's budget, however, are included.

In tabulating the support or opposition scores of members on the selected presidential-issue votes, CQ counts only "yea" and "nay" votes on the ground that only these affect the outcome. Most failures to vote reflect absences because of illness or official business. Failure to vote lowers both support and opposition scores equally.

All presidential-issue votes have equal statistical weight in the analysis.

Presidential support is determined by the position of the president at the time of a vote, even though that position may be different from an earlier position or may have been reversed after the vote was taken.

### Party Unity

Party unity votes are defined as recorded votes in the Senate and House that split the parties, a majority of voting Democrats opposing a majority of voting Republicans. Votes on which either party divides evenly are excluded.

Party unity scores (S - support) represent the percentage of party unity votes on which a member votes "yea" or "nay" in agreement with a majority of his party. Failure to vote, even if a member announced his stand, lowers his score.

Opposition-to-party scores (O - opposition) represent the percentage of party unity votes on which a member votes "yea" or "nay" in disagreement with a majority of his party. A member's party unity and opposition-to-party scores add up to 100 percent only if he voted on all party unity votes.

### Conservative Coalition

As used in this study, the term "conservative coalition" means a voting alliance of Republicans and Southern Democrats against the Northern Democrats in Congress. This meaning, rather than any philosophic definition of the "conservative" position, provides the basis for CQ's selection of coalition votes.

A conservative coalition vote is any vote in the Senate or the House on which a majority of voting Southern Democrats and a majority of voting Republicans oppose the stand taken by a majority of voting Northern Democrats. Votes on which there is an even division within the ranks of voting Northern Democrats, Southern Democrats or Republicans are not included.

The Southern states are defined as Alabama, Arkansas, Florida, Georgia, Kentucky, Louisiana, Mississippi, North Carolina, Oklahoma, South Carolina, Tennessee, Texas and Virginia. The other 37 states are grouped as the North in the study.

The conservative coalition support score (S - support) represents the percentage of conservative coalition votes on which a member voted "yea" or "nay" in agreement with the position of the conservative coalition. Failures to vote, even if a member announces a stand, lower the score.

The conservative coalition opposition score (O - opposition) represents the percentage of conservative coalition votes on which a member voted "yea" or "nay" in disagreement with the position of the conservative coalition.

## Key Votes

A series of significant votes has been selected from the roll-call votes taken during the 96th and 97th Congresses. The following captions give the number of the bill, the primary sponsor, a brief description of the bill, a breakdown of the vote, the date the vote was taken and the president's position on the issue, if he took one. The following symbols are used: Y, voted for (yea); N, voted against (nay); #, paired for; +, announced for; X, paired against; -, announced against; P, voted "present"; C, voted "present" to avoid possible conflict of interest; ?, did not vote or otherwise make a position known.

### SENATE KEY VOTES

**96th Congress**

**S 245. Taiwan Relations.** Charles H. Percy, R-Ill., amendment to declare that hostile action against Taiwan would be a threat to the "security interests of the United States." Rejected 42-50: R 35-5; D 7-45, March 8, 1979. A "nay" was a vote supporting the president's position.

**S 932. Synthetic Fuels.** William Proxmire D-Wis., amendment to substitute the Banking Committee version of Title I of the bill for the Energy Committee version. The Banking Committee approved only $3 billion in funds, rather than the $20 billion called for by the Energy Committee. In addition, the Banking Committee opposed government ownership of plants and refused to set up a special corporation to administer the plan. The substitute was rejected 37-57: R 24-15: D 13-42, Nov. 7, 1979. A "nay" was a vote supporting the president's position.

**S 562. Nuclear Regulatory Commission.** Gary Hart, D-Colo., amendment to defer issuance of any new construction permits for nuclear power plants in the first six months of fiscal 1980. Rejected 35-57: R 8-31; D 27-26, July 17, 1979.

**HR 3939. Windfall Profits Tax.** Russell Long, D-La., motion to table (kill) the Abraham Ribicoff, D-Conn., amendment to set a 20 percent tax on three types of oil: 1) newly discovered, 2) tertiary and 3) heavy oil. Motion rejected 44-53: R 34-6; D 10-47, Dec. 12, 1979.

**HR 5860. Chrysler Loan Guarantees.** Passage of the bill to authorize $1.5 billion in federal loan guarantees, to be matched by $2.1 billion from other sources, and to establish a $175 million employee stock ownership plan. Passed 53-44: R 12-27; D 41-17, Dec. 19, 1979. A "yea" was a vote supporting the president's position.

**H J Res 521. Draft Registration Funding.** Passage of the bill to transfer $13.3 million from the fiscal 1980 Department of the Air Force personnel account to the Selective Service System to register 19- and 20-year-old males for a possible military draft. Passed 58-34; R 25-16; D 33-18, June 12, 1980. A "yea" was a vote supporting the president's position.

**HR 7112. Revenue Sharing.** Robert Dole, R-Kan., motion to table (kill) the George J. Mitchell, D-Maine, amendment to authorize an appropriation of $2.3 billion for revenue sharing payments to state governments during fiscal 1981. Motion agreed to 47-44: R 16-23; D 31-21, Dec. 9, 1980. A "yea" was a vote supporting the president's position.

**HR 7584. State, Justice, Commerce, Judiciary Appropriations, Fiscal 1981.** Strom Thurmond, R-S.C., motion to table (kill) the Appropriations Committee amendment to delete a provision prohibiting the Justice Department from using money appropriated under the bill to bring any action that directly or indirectly required busing a student to school, except for students requiring special education. The purpose of the motion was to restrict federal involvement in busing cases. Motion agreed to 49-42: R 25-12; D 24-30, Sept. 25, 1980.

**97th Congress**

**S Con Res 9. Budget Reconciliation Instructions.** John H. Chafee, R-R.I., amendment to lessen cuts recommended by the Budget Committee by restoring $1.2 billion in fiscal 1982 budget authority and $973 million in fiscal 1982 outlays to various committees for elementary and secondary education, low-income fuel aid, urban development action grants, urban mass transit, community health centers and the energy weatherization program. The Reagan administration had called for the cuts as part of its program to reduce federal spending. Rejected 40-59: R 11-42; D 29-17 (ND 26-5: SD 3-12), March 31, 1981. A "nay" was a vote supporting the president's position.

## HOUSE KEY VOTES

### 96th Congress

**HR 3919. Windfall Profits Tax.** James R. Jones, D-Okla., substitute amendment to provide a tax rate of 60 percent, discontinuation of the windfall tax at the end of 1990 and other changes. The plan originally proposed by President Carter called for a permanent tax. The Jones substitute was adopted 236-183: R 146-10; D 90-173, June 28, 1979.

**HR 2626. Hospital Cost Control.** Richard A. Gephardt, D-Mo., substitute amendment, to the Commerce Committee substitute, to establish for three years a National Study Commission on Hospital Costs, and to authorize $10 million in fiscal 1980 and sums as needed for fiscal 1981-82 to state hospital cost control programs. Adopted 234-166: R 135-8; D 99-158, Nov. 15, 1979. A "nay" was a vote supporting the president's position. (The Commerce Committee substitute, as amended by Gephardt, was adopted subsequently by voice vote.)

**HR 111. Panama Canal Treaties Implementation.** John M. Murphy, D-N.Y., amendment to the George Hansen, R-Idaho, amendment, to restore the original language in the bill dealing with annual payments to Panama from canal revenues, property transfers to Panama and U.S. costs in implementing the 1978 canal treaties. Adopted 220-200: R 25-132; D 195-68, June 20, 1979. A "yea" was a vote supporting the president's position.

**HR 2444. Education Department.** Passage of the bill to establish a separate Department of Education. Passed 210-206: R 35-117; D 175-89, July 11, 1979. A "yea" was a vote supporting the president's position.

**H J Res 74. School Busing Amendment.** Passage of the joint resolution to propose an amendment to the Constitution to prohibit compelling students to attend a school other than the one nearest their home to achieve racial desegregation. Rejected 209-216: R 114-40; D 95-176, July 24, 1979. A two-thirds majority vote (284 in this case) is required for passage of a joint resolution proposing an amendment to the Constitution. A

"nay" was a vote supporting the president's position.

**HR 5860. Chrysler Loan Guarantees.** Passage of the bill, as amended to authorize $1.5 billion in federal loan guarantees, for the Chrysler Corp. to be matched by $1.93 billion from other sources, including $400 million in wage concessions by the company's unionized workers and $100 million by other employees. Passed 271-136: D 62-88; R 209-48, Dec. 18, 1979. A "yea" was a vote supporting the president's position.

**H J Res 521. Draft Registration Funding.** Appropriations Committee amendment to transfer $13.3 million from the Air Force to the Selective Service System, an independent agency, to start draft registration of 19- and 20-year-old males in 1980. Adopted 218-188: R 83-66; D 135-122, April 22, 1980. A "yea" was a vote supporting the president's position.

**HR 6081. Nicaragua Aid.** Passage of the bill to authorize $80 million in supplemental economic assistance in fiscal 1980 to the Central American countries of Nicaragua ($75 million) and Honduras ($5 million). Passed 202-197: R 28-119; D 174-78, Feb. 27, 1980. A "yea" was a vote supporting the president's position.

**HR 5200. Fair Housing Act Amendments.** Mike Synar, D-Okla., substitute amendment, to the F. James Sensenbrenner Jr., R-Wis.-Harold L. Volkmer, D-Mo., amendment, to: 1) give the Justice Department authority to appoint administrative law judges (ALJs) to handle housing bias cases; 2) prohibit appointment as an ALJ of anyone who had worked as an investigator or prosecutor for the Department of Housing and Urban Development within the previous two years; 3) prohibit dismissal of ALJs without a merit system protection board hearing; and 4) require the HUD secretary to refer all land-use control cases to the attorney general. Adopted 205-204: R 25-128; D 180-76, June 11, 1980. A "yea" was a vote supporting the president's position. (The original Sensenbrenner-Volkmer amendment would have eliminated administrative proceedings to enforce the housing laws and required cases to be handled by federal magistrates or judges.)

### 97th Congress

**H Con Res 115. Fiscal 1982 Budget Targets.** Delbert Latta, R-Ohio, substitute, to the resolution as reported by the Budget Committee, to decrease budget authority by $23.1 billion, outlays by $25.7 billion and revenues by $31.1

billion, resulting in a $31 billion deficit for fiscal 1982. Adopted 253-176: R 190-0; D 63-176, May 7, 1981. A "yea" was a vote supporting the president's position.

# Interest Group Ratings

Ratings of members of Congress by four different interest groups are given since 1961 (87th Congress). The groups were chosen to represent liberal, conservative, business and labor viewpoints. In addition, groups were selected that have been rating members of Congress for at least ten years. Following is a description of each group along with notes regarding their ratings for particular years.

## Americans for Democratic Action (ADA)

Americans for Democratic Action was founded in 1947 by a group of liberal Democrats that included the late Sen. Hubert H. Humphrey and Eleanor Roosevelt. In 1981, the president was former Rep. Patsy T. Mink, D-Hawaii (1965-77).

ADA ratings are given for every year except 1963. The 1964 ratings cover both 1963 and 1964 (88th Congress).

## Americans for Constitutional Action (ACA)

Americans for Constitutional Action was formed in 1958 at the request of a group of conservative senators to help elect more "constitutional conservatives" to Congress. In 1981, the chairman was Charlene Baker Craycraft.

ACA ratings are given for every year except 1961. The 1962 ratings cover both 1961 and 1962 (87th Congress).

## American Federation of Labor-Congress of Industrial Organizations (AFL-CIO)

The AFL-CIO was formed when the American Federation of Labor and the Congress of Industrial Organizations merged in 1955. With affiliates claiming more than 16 million members, the AFL-CIO accounts for approximately three-quarters of national union membership. In 1981, the president was Lane Kirkland.

Prior to 1980, the AFL-CIO ratings of members of Congress were issued by the AFL-CIO Committee on Political Education (COPE).

AFL-CIO ratings are given for every year except 1961, 1963 and 1965. Prior to 1966 the ratings were biennial rather than annual, the 1962 ratings cover both 1961 and 1962 (87th Congress), the 1964 ratings cover both 1963 and 1964 (88th Congress) and the 1966 ratings cover both 1965 and 1966 (89th Congress).

## Chamber of Commerce of the United States (CCUS)

The Chamber of Commerce of the United States represents local, regional and state chambers of commerce as well as trade and professional organizations. It was founded in 1912 to be "a voice for organized business." In 1981 the president was Richard Lesher.

Before 1972 the Chamber of Commerce did not always rate members of Congress every year. No ratings were issued in 1971, 1969, 1968, 1966 and 1964 and before.

In 1979, there are two Chamber of Commerce scores given for members of the Senate. The CCUS originally calculated scores based on 11 votes and excluded several procedural votes. After considerable criticism, much of it from senators who had received low scores, the chamber revised its ratings using 16 votes instead of 11. The score under CCUS-1 is the original score, revised scores are listed under CCUS-2.

# Politics in America

## Members Of Congress In Washington And At Home

# Congress in the 1980s

## Facing Outside

*By Alan Ehrenhalt*

There was major news in the House of Representatives on October 2, 1980. For the first time since 1861, the House expelled one of its members: Michael (Ozzie) Myers, the Philadelphia Democrat convicted in the Abscam bribery probe.

It was a story important enough to fill the press galleries above the chamber. But to sit in the gallery and watch the event unfold was to be struck by something more interesting than the decision itself: the way the House was doing it. The first expulsion since the Civil War was being carried out in a few hours on the last day of the session, with the participants ready to leave for home and most of them not even present in the chamber.

That was what struck Lee Hamilton, the Indiana Democrat who argued for a postponement. "Members sit here," he said, "with airplane tickets in their pockets, with bags packed and poised for the rush to the airport which will begin in a matter of minutes ... the political pressures on members to vote to expel are simply overwhelming."

Whatever one thinks of Abscam or Ozzie Myers, his expulsion is a symbol of the modern Congress, an institution that faces outside. Less than 15 years ago, the House agonized for weeks over whether to exclude New York Democrat Adam Clayton Powell, charged with misusing committee funds. The Senate twisted itself into contortions in 1967 over the censure — no one ever mentioned expulsion — of Connecticut Democrat Thomas J. Dodd for diverting campaign contributions to personal use.

Something has happened in that time to change a Congress protective of its own rules and privileges into one where expelling a colleague becomes entangled with running for re-election. A generation ago, William White wrote *Citadel* and *Home Place*, books about the Senate and House, respectively, and focused on a kind of member now virtually extinct: a senior member with no political problems at home, steeped in the traditions and camaraderie of congressional life.

In the House, he devoted admiring attention to George Mahon of Texas,

3

chairman of Defense Appropriations and later of the full Appropriations Committee. "A Mahon at work in the House," he wrote, "is a thousand miles removed from any partisan political stump." He singled out Mahon because he regarded him a symbol of a small, necessary elite: nationally minded members who made most of the important decisions.

The Senate, to people at that time, was a place where personal relations meant everything, a "club," to use the old cliché. White felt there was a word for what successful senators had to have and that the word was character. "Character," he said, "in the sense that the special integrity of the person must be in harmony with ... the special integrity of the institution — the integrity of its oneness."

Contrast that "inner club" idea with what Edmund S. Muskie wrote toward the end of his career: "You don't see the other senators very often and you rarely get a chance to discuss serious issues with them. . . . Days go by when you don't run into more than one or two senators."

There are all sorts of reasons why Congress faces outside these days, reasons ranging from the cosmic to the mundane. At the most mundane level, there is air travel. Thirty years ago, Congress often went home by Labor Day, but during the part of the year when members were in Washington, they stayed in Washington. It was not possible to take weekend trips to the Pacific Coast on the train. It used to be said, in fact, that congressmen from the Northeast forfeited some of their influence by dabbling in local politics all the time rather than focusing on legislation.

"The New York delegation is always running for office up there," California Democrat Don Edwards said early in his House career, which began in 1963. "The constituents expect them to be activists, proving themselves over and over again and competing with local politicians. Thank God we don't have to go through that."

It is hard to imagine any Californian saying that today. Home is accessible every week, whether home is New York or Hawaii, and it is rare for any junior House member not to be publicly visible in his district two weekends a month — weekends that can last five days most of the year. House allowances now permit every member travel expenses sufficient to pay for 32 trips home every year, regardless of distance, and it is easy to finance more by saving on other expense items, such as stationery or telephone calls. Going home, of course, is only part of the package of constituent service and public relations that members use to get themselves re-elected these days. But it is the part that most affects a member's attitude toward his work, as is clear to readers of *Home Style,* the 1978 book by Richard Fenno that has re-focused attention on a neglected aspect of congressional life.

Meanwhile, Congress has changed its rules in ways that all but force members to face outside in doing legislative business. A decade ago, nearly all congressional committees wrote their bills in private, symbolized by the Ways and Means Committee, whose members sat casually around a table for months, then reported a "consensus" bill and took it to the floor under rules that precluded amendment. Today, Ways and Means and most other committees make their decisions in the open, a triumph for the people's right to know, perhaps, but a special triumph for the interest groups back home that want to know whom to support and finance next time.

Senators and representatives may choose to keep their heads down in committee. But there is no place to hide on the floor of either chamber. Until 1971, votes on major House amendments were taken by an "unrecorded teller" system, in which members filed past a clerk who counted only bodies, not names. Liberal pressure groups fought hard for the change to recorded voting, hopeful that it would move members toward popular consumer, environmental and anti-war causes. And the first such vote in the House seemed to confirm their hopes: The chamber reversed itself and voted to kill the subsidy for a supersonic transport plane environmentalists had been fighting for years.

There is no doubt that open voting has made members more responsive to local opinion. But local opinion is fleeting; the more that members feel compelled to go home and defend themselves, the more likely they are to accept the role of messengers for their constituents. It is not hard to find members of Congress today who say proudly that they poll their districts on every important issue and vote the way the polls tell them to.

Hundreds of interests are now organized into political action committees rating, rewarding and punishing various forms of congressional behavior. In early 1981, six and a half years after the Federal Election Commission had approved the creation of PACs by business, labor and other interest groups, there were 2,551 of them giving money to congressional candidates, contributing about a quarter of the money for House and Senate elections.

One can argue for days over whether PACs represent legitimate free speech or incipient control of Congress by special interests. But it seems clear that PACs have a psychological importance to members of Congress, especially senior ones. There are no limits on the amount a wealthy challenger can contribute to his own campaign, and an incumbent without personal resources of his own often comes to consider PAC money as his only weapon against the youthful newcomer who, next time or the time after, will be spending $500,000 or more to discredit him. Not only do PACs represent a form of security for these members, they represent an easy one. Any House Democrat with an important subcommittee chairmanship can raise a fortune in a crisis, but at the price of turning his focus to the pressure groups of the outside rather than the demands of the institution itself.

It was clear by the early 1970s that some of these changes were taking place, but they seemed at that point to apply mainly to the House, which has always been supposed to reflect swings of opinion in the outside world. Six-year Senate terms seemed to provide at least a modest cushion from outside pressures. Twenty-five senators had run for re-election in 1974, and 23 of them had won. A senator could be statesman for the first half of his term, it was still said in 1975; there was time enough for politics in the last couple of years.

But the election returns since 1976 have pretty much forced senators to rival House members as permanent candidates. There were nine incumbents beaten in 1976, more than a third of those running. That was only the beginning. Ten senators were beaten in 1978, counting primaries and the general election, and 13 in 1980, when the odds were only marginally better on re-election than on defeat.

The reasons for the change are a catalogue of contemporary politics: voter frustration, voter mobility, weak parties and television. But the important point is that most senators now can expect a re-election challenge next time out from a candidate with the money and skill to make himself known statewide. Statesmanship is as perilous in the Senate as it has always been considered in the House. The constituency requires courting all the time, whether it is the year before election or the year after.

On the numbers alone, the House seems a much safer place for incumbents nowadays. Despite all the concern about voters' feelings, or perhaps because of it, the re-election rate in the House has been above 90 percent in every recent election except one. But the figures are misleading, as political scientist Thomas Mann showed in his 1978 book, *Unsafe at Any Margin*. House members win more by escaping serious challenge than by overcoming it; in an average year, there simply are not 400 competent and well-financed challengers to go around. But the opposing party knows it can cause trouble in a given district if it makes that district one of its priorities. Or at least so the members believe.

"The Republicans could have beaten me this time," a House chairman insisted early in 1981, despite his easy re-election in what nearly everyone else considers a safe Democratic district. "They could have made my voting record look ridiculous. It's just a matter of where they want to spend the money." What about Jim Wright, the majority leader, he was asked. A Republican challenger spent $500,000 against Wright and failed to draw 40 percent of the vote. "What that shows," he said, "is that they probably needed to spend a million."

Southern Democrats might seem an exception to such a rule. Most of them win by as much as Mahon and Mills did in the 1950s. The Deep South states are full of districts that returned Democratic incumbents with little or no opposition in 1980 while giving a presidential majority to

Reagan. But few of those incumbents feel they would be invulnerable to a well-financed challenger running to their right, either in a primary or general election. That was the main reason so many Southern Democrats voted with Reagan on budget issues in early 1981.

"You don't have many people in the House any more who are truly independent beings," says Phil Gramm, the conservative Texas Democrat. "They've got to feel the pressure to do things." Gramm helped apply the pressure in 1981 as he cosponsored the Reagan budget, giving it a nominal bipartisan status.

Beyond that, the outside focus has meant more members concerned not only with whether they are re-elected, but by how much. The House is full of people who drew 58 percent last time and wanted 60, or got 60 but wanted 70, or have their eyes on a free ride in 1982.

House Speaker Thomas P. O'Neill Jr. singled out these kinds of people as the ones who frustrated him most in his unsuccessful lobbying against the Reagan budget: "It's the fellow who comes up to me and says, '. . . I didn't have any opposition the last time, I think if I voted against Reagan I'm apt to breed opposition.' "

Finally, there is turnover. It takes a few years to build a sense of loyalty to the institution, even in those who want to build one, and most of the current Congress has simply not been serving very long. In the current Senate, a majority of the majority party (27 of 53 Republican senators) had been serving two years or less when they took control of the 97th Congress. A member of the House who arrived in 1975 is well into the upper half of the chamber in seniority.

In part, the turnover is a phenomenon of the 1970s. As the decade began, the House and Senate were both top-heavy with senior members who stayed because it was as easy as leaving and the pay was reasonably good. "Few die," they used to say of House members, "and none retire." That began to change in 1970 with the enactment of much more generous congressional pensions, an idea that Rep. Morris K. Udall promoted in part because he saw that encouraging the elderly to leave was the simplest way to attack the seniority system.

The "deadwood revolution" has now happened; nothing like it will take place in the 1980s. But another important reason for turnover remains. Facing outside is hard work for a member of Congress. The weekend flying, town meetings and constituent pressures lead even some secure veterans to decide that the job is not as much fun as it was in the beginning. And that is not likely to change. Being a member of Congress in the 1980s is a job for someone willing to work more or less full-time at keeping it. That will mean members whose minds are on the outside world — whether they are writing legislation, disciplining a colleague, addressing a town meeting, or racing to the airport on a Thursday afternoon.

# Reagan and Realignment

*By Rhodes Cook*

Ronald Reagan's landslide victory has fueled new speculation that a realignment in American politics may be under way.

More than a decade ago, Republican thinkers felt that by projecting conservative themes on economic and social issues, the party could fashion a ruling coalition built on the Sun Belt and blue-collar ethnics. But Watergate and the election of Jimmy Carter in 1976 quenched that optimism, and it looked even to Republican partisans as though the GOP had wasted a golden opportunity.

Now the emerging Republican majority does not seem so farfetched. In the wake of Reagan's sweeping victory — in concert with the Republican takeover of the Senate and the substantial GOP gains in the House — it is at least arguable that realignment was not canceled by the events of the 1970s, only postponed.

It will take several national elections to determine whether realignment really has taken place. But in 1980, Reagan accomplished much of what Republican strategists had been hoping for in the previous decade.

Reagan made deep inroads into the blue-collar vote that had gone for Nixon in 1972 but had returned to the Democratic column in 1976. He wooed back rural white voters whom Republicans had been cultivating in the early 1970s but who had defected in large numbers to Carter in 1976.

Reagan showed particular appeal among rural whites in the South and Southern-oriented portions of Northern industrial states. Many of these were strongholds of George C. Wallace in 1968. Reagan's strength among rural whites was pivotal in enabling him to run substantially better than Ford had across the heart of the Sun Belt, from southern Florida to southern California.

It remains to be seen, however, whether the 1980 presidential vote reflected new Republican muscle, Democratic flabbiness or a confusing mixture of both.

The Democratic coalition clearly fragmented in 1980. With the exception of blacks, Carter failed to halt defections from any major Democratic constituencies. In spite of incumbency, the Georgian was not the same fresh face he was in 1976, when he emphasized traditional small-town

8

values and anti-establishment themes. While he seemed the perfect antidote for the Watergate era, by 1980 he was an embattled incumbent saddled with a series of economic failures and an image as a weak leader.

Compared to 1976, Carter's share of the total vote dropped in every state. His best showing — a 2 percent decline — came in Mississippi. Elsewhere, his share decreased at least 4 percentage points, with huge declines west of the Mississippi River.

Carter ran poorly west of the Mississippi in 1976, but he did little during his administration to mend fences. Instead, through policies like the Russian grain embargo and curtailment of water projects, he antagonized much of the Western part of the nation.

The result in 1980 was an atrocious showing. In virtually all the states of the West and agricultural Midwest, the Democratic share of the presidential vote plummeted even below the level established by George McGovern in 1972. In eight Plains and Western states, Carter did not draw even 30 percent of the vote.

Some political observers doubt that any realignment took place in 1980 because there was a declining turnout. The turnout rate in 1980 dropped for the fifth consecutive election, from 54.4 percent of the voting age population in 1976 to 53.9 percent in 1980.

But in most of the states where the Republican percentage of the presidential vote went up significantly in 1980, there was an *increase* in the turnout rate. In many states the increases were modest — less than 2 percentage points. But in 12 of the 19 states where Reagan ran at least 5 percentage points ahead of Ford, the participation rate was higher than 1976. Eight of these strong Reagan states were in the South, an indication of the intensive activity of fundamentalist groups like the Moral Majority on behalf of Reagan and the return of many Southern white voters to the GOP banner.

But there was hardly a perfect correlation between higher turnouts and the Reagan vote. In South Dakota, Reagan ran 10 percentage points better than Ford and the participation rate was up. In North Dakota, Reagan ran 12 percentage points better than Ford and the turnout rate was down.

Blue-collar and rural white voters are the keys to realignment, as well as the ingredients of Reagan's 1980 victory. Industrial workers, many of them ethnic Catholics, have been an integral part of the ruling Democratic coalition since the New Deal. But in the last decade, blue-collar voters have been the prime Republican target.

With economic issues failing the Democrats in 1980, the GOP was able to make breakthroughs among "lunch-pail" Democrats by emphasizing popular anti-busing, anti-abortion positions and their own economic solutions. In every region of the country, Reagan carried blue-collar suburban and small urban industrial counties that Nixon in 1960 and 1968

9

and Ford in 1976 were unable to win.

Many of the counties where Reagan made breakthroughs have a large ethnic population, such as Coos County (Berlin), N.H., with its sizable French-Canadian element, heavily Slavic Luzerne County (Wilkes-Barre and Hazleton), Pa., and Lucas County (Toledo), Ohio, with German, Irish and Eastern European elements. The ability of Reagan to carry the latter was particularly noteworthy, since it was among the few predominantly blue-collar counties won by McGovern in 1972.

Even in working-class counties that Reagan did not win, he generally ran better than Ford. Typical were Galveston County, Texas, a Gulf Coast shipping center where the Republican presidential vote was up 7 percentage points over 1976 and Pueblo County, Colo., a major steel-producing center, where the GOP vote increased 4 percentage points.

The upturn in the GOP presidential vote was just as dramatic among rural white voters in the Midwest farm states and Southern Wallace strongholds. In each case, the percentage increase from 1976 was frequently in double digits.

Reagan's attraction of rural white voters in the South and the southern portions of major electoral vote states like Illinois and Ohio was crucial to the outcome of the election. These rural voters had helped Carter win four years earlier, and their defection in large numbers to Reagan helped turn a close election into a rout.

More conservative than the Democratic Party nationally, Southern whites had been drifting away from the party of their grandfathers since Strom Thurmond's Dixiecrat movement in 1948. Many found Wallace's third-party candidacy in 1968 a convenient resting place before voting for Nixon in 1972. With a populist, native son appeal, Carter briefly interrupted the Republican trend in 1976. But it resumed in 1980.

Throughout the South, the Republican vote surged upward dramatically in rural counties that were leading bastions of Wallace support. In Geneva County, Ala., for instance, which Wallace carried in 1968 with an almost unanimous 92 percent of the vote, Reagan ran 19 percentage points better than Ford, carrying the county. In Hickman County, Ky., a Wallace stronghold along the Mississippi River, Reagan lost but increased the Republican vote by 21 percentage points.

While these gains were unusually large, it was commonplace in rural Wallace hotbeds for the Republican vote to be at least 10 percentage points higher than it was in 1976. Coupled with normal GOP strength in Southern urban centers, that was enough to cancel strong black support for Carter and swing most of the South back into the Republican column.

In Wallace bastions outside the South, the increases in the GOP presidential vote were smaller but still significant. In counties in southern Delaware, Maryland, Ohio, Indiana and Illinois — portions of those states where the former Alabama governor had made his best showings — the Republican vote generally rose 5 to 10 percentage points above 1968.

In population centers of the South and West, Republican majorities generally crept upward. Throughout the fast growing counties of the Sun Belt — from Pinellas County (St. Petersburg), Fla., to San Diego, Calif. — Reagan often ran up to 10 percentage points ahead of Ford.

Basically, Reagan trailed Ford only in Sun Belt urban centers with a large minority population, such as Jefferson County (Birmingham), Ala., Hinds County (Jackson), Miss., and Bernalillo County (Albuquerque), N.M.

While Reagan scored breakthroughs among a number of voting blocs, his landslide victory obscured the fact that his share of the national popular vote was only 3 percentage points better than Ford's showing four years earlier. He ran behind Ford in a number of bastions of moderate Republicanism — prosperous white-collar suburbs, Yankee New England and traditional Republican urban centers of the Frost Belt.

All four constituencies were more comfortable with mainstream GOP standard-bearers like Eisenhower and Ford. While conservative on economic issues, Republicans in these places traditionally have been more liberal on social issues than Reagan and his supporters from the Moral Majority and the "New Right." Many moderate Republicans found an acceptable alternative to Reagan in independent candidate John B. Anderson. In two decades as a Republican congressman from Illinois, he had planted his roots firmly in the party's moderate wing. Anderson made his best showing nationally in white-collar suburbs, academic communities and Yankee New England.

The Anderson candidacy symbolizes a likely side effect of realignment, the exodus of many moderate Republicans to the Democratic Party. Liberal Democrats and independents provided Anderson with much of his support. But just as George Wallace in 1968 acted as a vehicle for many blue-collar and Southern white voters to begin their movement from the Democratic Party, it may turn out that in 1980 Anderson served as a vehicle for many moderate Republicans to finally exit the GOP. The volume of moderate Republican defections will not be apparent for a while. But they could prove large enough to provide at least a partial counterweight to GOP inroads among traditional Democratic voting blocs.

Reagan carried virtually all the white-collar suburban counties and traditional GOP urban centers of the Frost Belt. But with Anderson a significant factor, Reagan often drew a smaller share of the vote than Ford had. Typical was Fairfield County, Conn., which contains affluent New York City bedroom communities like Darien and New Canaan. There, the GOP presidential vote dropped 3 percentage points, from a 58 percent share in 1976 to 55 percent in 1980. Anderson received 10 percent of the

Fairfield County vote, well above his national share.

More severe declines in the GOP presidential vote were evident in moderate Republican strongholds in upstate New York. In Onondaga County (Syracuse), Reagan ran 9 percentage points behind Ford. In Monroe County (Rochester), he was down 13 percentage points. Monroe was one of the few counties in the country to vote for Ford in 1976 and for Carter in 1980.

In New England, the decline in the GOP presidential vote was nearly as dramatic. Reagan won every state in the region except Rhode Island, but he ran behind Ford in four of the six states. In Yankee Vermont, the Republican presidential vote skidded downward 11 percentage points from 1976, the largest falloff in the GOP vote in any state in the nation.

Major exceptions to the Republican decline in Frost Belt population centers were the Long Island suburbs of Nassau and Suffolk counties. Both have substantial ethnic elements, and Reagan increased the GOP share of the presidential vote in each by at least 3 percentage points.

Blacks provided Carter with some of his heaviest 1980 majorities and enabled him to make a respectable showing in most Southern states, even though he carried only Georgia. Reagan generally ran behind Ford in predominantly black counties, and in some of them he did not receive even 20 percent of the vote.

With few exceptions, Reagan also was unable to increase the Republican vote in large, traditionally Democratic urban centers across the country. Many of these cities have a heavy black population, which remained loyal to Carter, and several actually provided the incumbent with a higher share of the vote than in 1976. Among them were Baltimore, New Orleans, Richmond and St. Louis.

Reagan did run better than Ford in New York City and Dade County (Miami), Fla. In Dade County, the Republican vote soared 11 percentage points, bolstered by voter dissatisfaction with Carter's handling of the Cuban refugee problem. In New York City, Reagan registered increases in every borough except Manhattan and ran 5 percentage points ahead of Ford citywide.

Although Democratic percentages remained high in many major Northern urban centers, declining populations and turnouts in recent years have diminished Democratic chances of carrying key industrial states.

A major example is Illinois. In 1960, John F. Kennedy drew 63 percent of the vote in the city of Chicago and won the state by 8,858 votes. In 1980, Carter swept Chicago with 67 percent of the vote but lost the state by 376,681 votes. In 20 years, the turnout in Chicago had declined by more than a half-million votes. The city had remained a Democratic stronghold, but its impact on statewide voting had diminished as its population shrunk.

# Alabama

## ... Life After Wallace

Politics in every state has gone through a postwar and a post-Watergate era. But only in one state is it necessary to talk about a post-Wallace era.

For most of the past two decades, George Wallace dominated Alabama elections. He won the governorship in 1962, 1970, and 1974, and when he was ineligible to succeed himself in 1966, his late wife Lurleen ran as his surrogate and won.

Wallace had a unique ability to combine two of the most popular themes in Alabama politics — race and populism. The Wallace years brought down the curtain on a long era of personality politics in Alabama, in which campaigns were waged under a broad, one-party (Democratic) umbrella, with factions forming around dominant individuals.

Historically, Alabama's major rivalries have been sectional, with the large planters of the Black Belt aligned against the small farmers of north Alabama. With a malapportioned Legislature and with blacks effectively disfranchised from 1901 until the mid-1960s, the Black Belt was usually able to dominate.

But north Alabama remained a bastion of populism and spawned most of the state's more liberal politicians. Among them was Wallace's early mentor, Gov. James E. Folsom (1947-51, 55-59), who championed both poor whites and blacks, while railing against the ruling interests of the Black Belt and "the big mules" of Birmingham.

For a long time, the base of the small Republican Party was the mountainous north. But that began changing when the GOP veered rightward in the 1960s. In 1962, Republican James D. Martin came within 7,000 votes of upsetting veteran Democratic Sen. Lister Hill with a segregationist appeal. Two years later, the GOP rode Goldwater's long coattails in Alabama to victory in five of eight House races, the party's first congressional triumphs since Reconstruction.

But the Republican groundswell was terminated abruptly. Unable to match Wallace's populism or to compete with him on the racial issue,

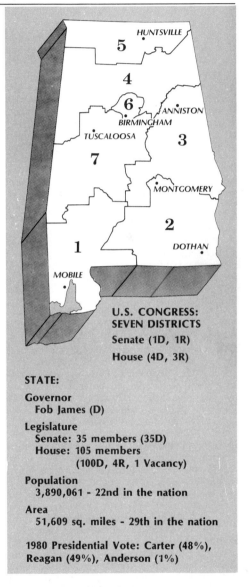

**U.S. CONGRESS:
SEVEN DISTRICTS**

Senate (1D, 1R)

House (4D, 3R)

**STATE:**

**Governor**
Fob James (D)

**Legislature**
Senate: 35 members (35D)
House: 105 members
(100D, 4R, 1 Vacancy)

**Population**
3,890,061 - 22nd in the nation

**Area**
51,609 sq. miles - 29th in the nation

**1980 Presidential Vote: Carter (48%),
Reagan (49%), Anderson (1%)**

the GOP lost two House seats in 1966. During the later Wallace years they did not win a major statewide office nor any more House seats.

When the post-Wallace era opened in 1978, the GOP looked no stronger. A member of the

13

state Republican executive committee, Forrest "Fob" James abandoned the GOP to run successfully as a Democrat for governor, handing the Republicans a moral victory and an insult at the same time.

But just two years later, Republican Jeremiah Denton shattered the popular conception that a candidate had to be a Democrat to win major statewide office in Alabama by winning a Senate seat.

# A Political Tour

**Northern Hill Country.** This region has had more in common with neighboring Tennessee, where its first settlers came from, than with the planter aristocracy of central Alabama. Northern Alabama never had a widespread plantation economy, so there were fewer blacks. Today they are less than 10 percent of the populace in 13 northern counties.

The dominance of poor whites in this area has made the hill country a haven for populism. For decades politicians railed against the "special interests" of the planters and their Birmingham big business allies. In recent years, utility companies have become a target.

The most heavily populated part of this region and one of the most prosperous areas of Alabama is the industrialized Tennessee River Valley, centered on Huntsville at the extreme northern end of the state. In the 1930s the Tennessee Valley Authority (TVA) provided abundant, cheap electricity that brought more industry into the valley. During World War II, Huntsville landed a chemical warfare plant, which was later taken over by the Army for research in rocketry. Then the National Aeronautics and Space Administration (NASA) located its major research and development center in Huntsville. As the space program burgeoned in the 1960s, Huntsville's population doubled. But with retrenchment in the space program, the city has had to diversify its economy in recent years, and now there are fewer high paying, high technology jobs.

The rest of the Valley has prospered from a mixture of agriculture (extensive cotton-growing) and heavy industry, including large aluminum, chemical and textile plants. Industry has been attracted in the 1970s to Decatur and the Quad cities of Florence, Sheffield, Tuscumbia and Muscle Shoals.

One of the most heavily unionized parts of Alabama, the valley has remained loyally Democratic. In 1980, the Reagan-Denton team carried only one of eight counties along the Tennessee

River — Madison (Huntsville) — and that by a narrow margin.

The rest of northern Alabama is less prosperous, although it has some of the richest coal deposits in the South. Tuscaloosa is the home of the University of Alabama. Gadsden and Anniston are steel-producing cities.

Like the Tennessee Valley area, most of the rest of northern Alabama is normally Democratic turf. However, Reagan and Denton carried Anniston and most of the counties around Birmingham, including Tuscaloosa. The Democrats held heavily-unionized Etowah County (Gadsden) and most of the rural areas.

**Birmingham and Environs.** Birmingham is Dixie's steel-making center, favorably located near iron, coal and limestone deposits. Although it was not founded until after the Civil War, Birmingham outstripped Mobile as the state's major population center by 1900.

Although whites and blacks worked side by side in the steel mills, Birmingham was the scene of much racial violence during the 1960s. And the city's police commissioner, Eugene "Bull" Connor came to epitomize the overt resistance of local government to integration efforts. But resistance began to crack with the development of the black vote. In 1967 the first black was elected to the City Council, and by 1979, when blacks made up more than half the population, Birmingham elected its first black mayor — Richard Arrington.

While blacks account for 56 percent of the city, they comprise only 17 percent of the population in the rest of Jefferson County. Suburban communities compose more than half the county population and provide the votes that regularly keep Jefferson County in the Republican column.

Birmingham today has serious economic troubles, brought about by the decline in heavy industry. It did not attract as much new business as other Southern cities during the Sun Belt boom of the 1970s, and in many ways has inherited the problems of the urban North.

**Black Belt.** No part of Alabama was more affected by the civil rights movement than the Black Belt, a strip about 30 miles wide that spans the south central part of the state.

While the term "Black Belt" is said to refer to the color of the rich, sticky soil and not the racial composition, the rural counties of the region are predominantly black. The Black Belt was the centerpiece of Alabama's cotton-based, plantation economy. With a Legislature apportioned to distort their power, the region's wealthy white landowners were able to hold the reins of state government much of this century.

But their world was turned upside-down by the civil rights legislation and court decisions of the 1960s. The enfranchisement of blacks not only stripped the planters of statewide authority, but also relegated them to a back seat in much of their own region. In 1964, when few blacks could vote, Goldwater won the region by a landslide margin. In 1972, the only six Alabama counties that McGovern carried were in the Black Belt.

But new-found black political clout has not stopped the region's long population drain. Not only is the Black Belt an area of extreme poverty, but mechanization and a change in emphasis from cotton to beef and dairy cattle has reduced farm employment. Of the eight Alabama counties that lost population in the 1970s, six were in the Black Belt.

The region's major city and oasis of Republicanism is Montgomery. The state capital and a cotton and cattle market town, Montgomery has been helped economically by a large influx of state and federal government projects. Unlike the surrounding countryside, Montgomery and its suburbs are growing quickly. Two Air Force bases are located in the city, including the Air University at Maxwell Air Force Base.

**Mobile and the South.** South Alabama is a diverse region stretching from the cosmopolitan port city of Mobile to the poor farming country where George Wallace grew up.

Mobile is a vestige of the Old South. It has a strong Catholic influence and in some ways resembles New Orleans. At the southwest corner of the state, Mobile is a booming international port favorably located 31 miles from the Gulf of Mexico along Mobile Bay.

At the southeast corner is another boom town, Dothan. Since the Army located an airfield nearby in World War II, it has been steadily growing and attracting new industry — most recently Michelin Tire and Sony plants. In the 1970s, Dothan's population increased 33 percent — the largest, except for Montgomery, of any city in the state with a population more than 25,000.

Much of the rest of rural south Alabama is an area of mediocre soil called the Wire Grass. Near the Mississippi border, the land is heavily timbered. Eastward are some of the top peanut growing counties in the country.

In pre-Wallace politics, rural southeast Alabama — with few blacks — was usually aligned with the northern populists. Mobile and the rest of the region voted with Birmingham and the Black Belt. In recent years, Republican strength in south Alabama has been limited to the major population centers in Mobile and Baldwin counties along the Gulf, and Houston (Dothan). But in 1980, Reagan and Denton expanded the GOP's base by carrying much of rural south Alabama, one-time strongholds of Wallace support.

## Redrawing the Lines

The 6th District, centered on Birmingham, needs to gain population. Democrats in the state Legislature are taking advantage of that fact to go after 6th District Rep. Albert Lee Smith, a Republican elected in 1980. Early speculation centered on a plan to remove a bloc of white conservatives from the 6th and replace them with blacks and Democratic-leaning blue-collar workers. Smith is the only Alabama representative substantially affected by the redistricting proposals that were being seriously discussed.

## Governor
## Fob James (D)

**Born:** Sept. 15, 1934, Lanett, Ala.
**Home:** Opelika, Ala.
**Education:** Auburn U., B.S. 1955.
**Military Career:** Army.
**Profession:** Manufacturer of consumer and industrial products.
**Family:** Wife, Bobbie; three children.
**Religion:** Episcopalian.
**Political Career:** Elected governor 1978; term expires Jan. 1983.

# Howell Heflin (D)

**Of Tuscumbia - Elected 1978**

**Born:** June 19, 1921, Poulan, Ga.
**Education:** Birmingham-Southern College, B.A. 1942; U. of Ala., J.D. 1948.
**Military Career:** Marine Corps, 1942-46.
**Profession:** Lawyer, judge.
**Family:** Wife, Elizabeth Ann Carmichael; one child.
**Religion:** Methodist.
**Political Career:** Chief Justice, Alabama Supreme Court, 1971-77.

**In Washington:** This former Alabama chief justice is still called "the judge" by colleagues and staff, and his self-image as jurist rather than politician has shaped his congressional career. It has been both a help and a hindrance.

Largely because of his background, Heflin was made chairman of the Senate Ethics Committee in 1979, the first freshman senator since 1910 to head a committee in his first year. While he ran the panel, Heflin reinforced his judicial reputation, seeking bipartisan consensus and keeping a tight lid on confidential committee proceedings.

But life in the Senate — where issues come up on a moment's notice — required considerable adjustment from life in the courtroom — where cases are scheduled well in advance to allow for lengthy preparation. In his first year, Heflin seemed to have trouble making up his mind on issues, hindered in part by the fact that virtually all of his top staff came directly from Alabama and had little Washington experience.

As he grew more accustomed to the legislative process in 1980, Heflin found ways to promote his legislative specialty — bills to improve court operations. He is a tireless advocate of more federal money for state courts.

In 1980, the Senate passed one Heflin bill to create a State Justice Institute which would provide grants to help states improve their legal systems. It stalled in the House. Another bill, yet to become law, would direct the Chief Justice of the United States to address Congress annually about the needs of the federal courts.

The most conspicuous Heflin campaign — and a rather quixotic one — was in behalf of the Law Enforcement Assistance Administration, the main source of federal money for local law enforcement. Budget cutters have long criticized it as a wasteful subsidy that has no effect on crime, but Heflin is a believer in it, and when the Senate Budget Committee took LEAA grant money out

of the 1981 budget, he waged a successful floor fight to have $100 million transferred to that category out of foreign aid, citing a speech from "Julius Caesar" as part of his argument. Conferees took the money out again, however, and Heflin found himself outnumbered when he sought to delay final approval of the $613 billion budget compromise until LEAA got its money.

As a former judge, Heflin sometimes seems preoccupied with the constitutional implications of any proposed legislation. Citing potential constitutional problems, he vigorously opposed one bill — now a law — that provides a method for disciplining federal judges short of impeachment by the House.

The senator earned points with Southern colleagues when he lobbied hard in 1980 to provide money for the Tennessee-Tombigbee inland canal. He lost some when he unsuccessfully challenged the appointment of a Tennessee man, Bob Clement, to the Tennessee Valley Authority (TVA). Sen. Jim Sasser, D-Tenn., who supported the nominee, accused Heflin of trying to block the nomination because Clement would not agree to move TVA headquarters from Knoxville, Tenn. to Muscle Shoals, Ala.

Reversing a previous Judiciary Committee vote, Heflin joined other Southern Democrats late in 1980 to help defeat a bill that would have strengthened open housing enforcement.

Although Heflin had helped draft the bill that emerged from the committee, he cast a floor vote against cutting off a filibuster by its opponents. He objected to a proposed compromise measure, aimed at resolving the dispute, because he said it would place too much power in the hands of U.S. magistrates.

**At Home:** Heflin demonstrated some remarkable personal popularity en route to the Senate in 1978, but he did more than that. He marked a symbolic end to the Wallace era in Alabama politics.

When 79-year-old Democratic Sen. John J. Sparkman announced his retirement, Gov. George C. Wallace was poised to replace him. But although the governor campaigned unofficially throughout 1977, he never announced as a candidate, and for good reason. Polls showed Heflin far ahead of him. Wallace, bound to a wheelchair and damaged politically by his recent divorce, was not the figure he had been in Alabama even two years earlier. He chose not to run.

One Democrat who did run against Heflin and came to regret it was Rep. Walter Flowers, a five-term House member. In a primary runoff that turned angry and unpleasant, Heflin took all but five counties. Better organized and financed than the congressman, he blasted Flowers for being "part of the Washington crowd." The general election was a formality; Republicans did not even have a candidate.

Heflin was simply the strongest candidate in the state. As chief justice of the Alabama Supreme Court, he had streamlined the state judicial system, which had been hampered by a huge case backlog. To accomplish the task, he needed adoption of a state constitutional amendment, and the voters gave it to him. When political opponents criticized him because the amendment made him eligible for a $30,000 annual pension, Heflin pointed out that he could not receive the money if he served in the Senate or practiced law.

## Committees

**Agriculture, Nutrition and Forestry** (8th of 8 Democrats)
Agricultural Credit and Rural Electrification; Agricultural Research and General Legislation; Soil and Water Conservation.

**Commerce, Science and Transportation** (8th of 8 Democrats)
Science, Technology and Space; Surface Transportation.

**Judiciary** (8th of 8 Democrats)
Courts; Separation of Powers.

**Select Ethics** (Vice chairman)

## Elections

**1978 General**

| | |
|---|---|
| Howell Heflin (D) | 547,054 (94%) |
| Jerome Couch (PROHIB) | 34,951 (6%) |

**1978 Primary Runoff**

| | |
|---|---|
| Howell Heflin (D) | 556,685 (65%) |
| Walter Flowers (D) | 300,654 (35%) |

**1978 Primary**

| | |
|---|---|
| Howell Heflin (D) | 369,270 (43%) |
| Walter Flowers (D) | 236,894 (28%) |
| John Baker (D) | 191,110 (22%) |

## Campaign Finance

| | Receipts | Receipts from PACs | Expenditures |
|---|---|---|---|
| 1978 | | | |
| Heflin (D) | $1,107,015 | $124,400 (11%) | 1,059,113 |

## Voting Studies

| | Presidential Support | | Party Unity | | Conservative Coalition | |
|---|---|---|---|---|---|---|
| Year | S | O | S | O | S | O |
| 1980 | 54 | 44 | 59 | 39 | 66 | 28 |
| 1979 | 55 | 40 | 48 | 47 | 75 | 12 |

S = Support      O = Opposition

## Key Votes

**96th Congress**

| | |
|---|---|
| Maintain relations with Taiwan (1979) | N |
| Reduce synthetic fuel development funds (1979) | N |
| Impose nuclear plant moratorium (1979) | N |
| Kill stronger windfall profits tax (1979) | Y |
| Guarantee Chrysler Corp. loans (1979) | Y |
| Approve military draft registration (1980) | Y |
| End Revenue Sharing to the states (1980) | N |
| Block Justice Dept. busing suits (1980) | N |

**97th Congress**

| | |
|---|---|
| Restore urban program funding cuts (1981) | N |

## Interest Group Ratings

| Year | ADA | ACA | AFL-CIO | CCUS-1 | CCUS-2 |
|---|---|---|---|---|---|
| 1980 | 39 | 50 | 63 | 63 | |
| 1979 | 26 | 46 | 53 | 18 | 47 |

# Jeremiah Denton (R)

### Of Mobile — Elected 1980

**Born:** July 15, 1924, Mobile, Ala.
**Education:** U.S. Naval Academy, B.S. 1946; George Washington University, M.A. 1964.
**Military Career:** Navy, 1946-77.
**Profession:** Retired Navy Admiral.
**Family:** Wife, Kathryn Jane Maury; seven children.
**Religion:** Roman Catholic.
**Political Career:** No previous career.

**The Member:** Denton has a fair amount in common with his Biblical namesake, the prophet Jeremiah, who warned the people of Israel against moral and religious decadence.

Like the prophet, Denton sees his nation on the verge of decline and fall. He claims that the United States has grown soft at home and abroad, with a weakened defense structure and an erosion of the American family. To Denton, the federal government has lost sight of its credo — "one nation under God."

This stark view of America was molded by more than three decades in the Navy, including seven and one-half years as a prisoner of war in North Vietnam, some of them in solitary confinement.

When Denton arrived in the Senate, the GOP leadership put him at the head of a new Security and Terrorism panel on the Judiciary Committee. Denton held hearings that pursued the theme of international terrorism promulgated by the Soviet Union and its surrogates. When Denton cautioned that Soviet-sponsored terrorism threatened domestic security, critics warned of a return to the politics of the McCarthy-era. But the hearings produced little drama; Denton seemed mainly interested in consciousness-raising.

Denton also introduced a measure — dubbed the "teen-age chastity bill" by one of his aides — to allocate $30 million in federal money for local programs to promote sexual self-discipline among unmarried teenagers. After striking any reference to chastity, the Labor and Human Resources Committee passed the bill.

As a certified war hero, Denton was able to make a spectacular political debut in 1980. In the Republican primary he overwhelmed the handpicked choice of the state party establishment, former Democratic Rep. Armistead I. Selden.

The general election was closer, but Denton defeated Democrat Jim Folsom Jr. to become Alabama's first Republican senator in the last century. While Reagan's coattails helped elect several GOP senators, that was not the case in Alabama. Denton received a larger share of the vote than Reagan.

Although a Catholic, Denton won support from many fundamentalist Protestant members of the state's Moral Majority. Sensitive to the criticism that he was merely a flag-waving moralist, Denton stressed his graduate degrees in international affairs and economics.

## Committees

**Armed Services** (9th of 9 Republicans)
Manpower and Personnel; Military Construction; Sea Power and Force Projection.

**Judiciary** (9th of 10 Republicans)
Security and Terrorism, chairman; Juvenile Justice; Separation of Powers.

**Labor and Human Resources** (8th of 9 Republicans)
Aging, Family and Human Services, chairman; Alcoholism and Drug Abuse; Education.

**Veterans' Affairs** (5th of 7 Democrats)

## Elections

**1980 General**

| | |
|---|---:|
| Jeremiah Denton (R) | 650,362 (50%) |
| Jim Folsom Jr. (D) | 610,175 (47%) |

**1980 Primary**

| | |
|---|---:|
| Jeremiah Denton (R) | 73,710 (64%) |
| Armistead Selden (R) | 41,823 (36%) |

## Campaign Finance

| 1980 | Receipts | Receipts from PACs | Expenditures |
|---|---|---|---|
| Denton (R) | $862,057 | $214,408 (25%) | $799,521 |
| Folsom Jr. (D) | $330,510 | $29,050 (9%) | 356,647 |

## Key Votes

**97th Congress**

| | |
|---|---|
| Restore urban program funding cuts (1981) | N |

# 1 Jack Edwards (R)

**Of Mobile — Elected 1964**

**Born:** Sept. 20, 1928, Birmingham, Ala.
**Education:** U. of Ala., B.S. 1952, LL.B. 1954.
**Military Career:** Marine Corps, 1946-48, 1950-51.
**Profession:** Lawyer.
**Family:** Wife, Jolane Vander Sys; two children.
**Religion:** Presbyterian.
**Political Career:** No previous office.

**In Washington:** Highly regarded for his intelligence and judgment, Edwards argues the case for military preparedness with a thoroughness and balance that even critics of the Pentagon find difficult to ignore. He is a somewhat gentler version of Sam Nunn, the Georgia Democrat who argues defense issues with similar skill in the Senate.

On some occasions, as senior Republican on the Defense Appropriations Subcommittee, Edwards has argued that the best way to help the defense effort in general is to challenge specific Pentagon requests. He has frequently criticized the services for insisting on the purchase of new equipment rather than better maintenance of the equipment they already have. In 1979 and 1980 he opposed congressional moves to finance a nuclear-powered aircraft carrier and a revised version of the B-1 bomber.

Edwards' effort to play the role of friendly critic toward the Defense Department has drawn him some opposition from fellow-conservatives. In 1979, the conservative weekly *Human Events* condemned him for lining up too frequently with Joseph P. Addabbo of New York, the Democrat who chairs Defense Appropriations, in favor of trimming the Pentagon budget. He has insisted that the programs he has tried to cut were not cost effective.

In overall terms, Edwards' record of support for a higher defense budget is clear. In 1980 he said that if the political traffic would have borne it, he could have supported a defense budget $10 billion to $15 billion above the appropriated amount — which already was several billion higher than the Carter request.

By then the "combat readiness" of U.S. forces had become a focus of national defense debate, and Edwards could claim a good part of the credit for raising the issue. He attacked the Carter administration — and the military services — for shortchanging the budget accounts for

spare parts and maintenance to buy more new hardware than otherwise would have been possible under Carter's budget limits. The result, he said, was a large number of planes and ships that could not perform as advertised.

In the course of his subcommittee's 1980 hearings, Edwards argued the issue — particularly as it affected combat airplanes — in meticulous detail.

In the near term, he insisted, he would not support funding for weapons without evidence that the current and projected budgets would buy the parts and maintenance needed to keep them operable. For the long term, he began moving toward the idea that the military services must restrain their quest for technical sophistication, on the theory that it has bred spiraling weapons costs and low reliability.

Some of Edwards' other issues are related to his concern for readiness. He regularly blasted the Carter administration for buying Navy combat planes at an annual rate that was not equal to the loss through age and accident. He warned that aircraft missile stockpiles were too small to allow for realistic training or for plausible wartime needs.

A former Marine, he has been particularly interested in the welfare of that service. During the Carter years, he felt the administration was jeopardizing the Marines' ability to shoot their way ashore by refusing to replace amphibious

---

**1st District: Southwest — Mobile.**
Population: 563,140 (15% increase since 1970).
Race: White 382,295 (68%), Black 174,607 (31%), Others 6,238 (1%). Spanish origin: 5,881 (1%).

---

**19**

landing ships and airplanes that were wearing out. He played a key role in forcing the administration to give the Marines a new class of landing ships and a new vertical-takeoff jet bomber.

Edwards has been quietly mindful of the interests of his district's only sizable defense contractor — a manufacturer of tank engines. The firm, Teledyne Continental, designed a diesel engine alternative to the novel gas turbine which powers the Army's new M-1 tank. The turbine engine had problems in its initial stages, and Edwards supported development of the Teledyne engine as an insurance policy.

He has backed another Pentagon move that would benefit his state (though not his district) — the proposed movement of a Navy helicopter school from Pensacola, Fla. to Fort Rucker, near Dothan, Ala. As in the case of the tank engine, Edwards' position has had the support of many defense specialists. But Congress has never been willing to make the move.

Edwards' Defense Subcommittee assignment dominates his legislative work. The only other national issue to receive a significant amount of his personal effort is the system of federally funded waterways that is economically crucial to Alabama. Such matters fall under the aegis of another Alabamian, Energy and Water Appropriations Chairman Tom Bevill, through whom Edwards works on the issue.

Edwards has a position of some importance in the Republican leadership as vice chairman of the party conference. He won it without opposition in 1979, and again in 1981. But he has never tried to move higher. The conference chairmanship was vacant in 1981, and he was a logical contender, but he did not run, and the post went to Jack Kemp of New York.

**At Home:** Edwards' personal reputation and his district's growing Republican tilt have made him one of the most solidly-entrenched Republican congressmen in the South. Swept into office in 1964 on the crest of the Alabama landslide for Barry Goldwater, he has easily won re-election eight times. Only twice — in 1968 and 1974 — has he been held to less than 60 percent of the vote.

Edwards was general attorney for the Gulf, Mobile and Ohio Railroad when he decided to run for the House in 1964. He had never sought any office before, but his timing was excellent. Redistricting had created an open seat in an increasingly Republican area, and Goldwater provided the perfect name for the top of the ticket.

Edwards was not shy about tying himself to Goldwater's coattails, explaining that his philosophy could be summed up in the words: "Thank God for Barry Goldwater." He urged a straight ticket vote for what he called "the Goldwater team." With the Arizonan collecting nearly three-quarters of the district vote, Edwards cruised past Democratic state Sen. John M. Tyson by 18,000 votes.

Democratic candidates have challenged Edwards repeatedly since then, but none have come any closer than Tyson. Democrats made their most extensive effort in 1978, when they ran state Sen. R. W. "Red" Noonan. A well-respected member of the Mobile social elite, Noonan had been a football star at the University of Alabama and was vice president of one of the two leading banks in the city.

But to many observers, the congenial, hard-working Noonan appeared to be a virtual clone of Edwards. The incumbent emphasized that he had 14 years of seniority, while Noonan was three years older and had no seniority. Starting early and tapping his traditional backers — home builders, doctors and lawyers — Edwards raised about twice as much money as Noonan. The results were nearly as one-sided, with Edwards winning by more than 31,000 votes.

Discouraged by the results, the Democrats did not offer a candidate in 1980.

**The District:** Although the Alabama 1st includes seven counties, it is dominated by the port city of Mobile, Alabama's second-largest city. Mobile County casts about two-thirds of the district vote, and like the neighboring Mississippi Gulf Coast, it is now almost always Republican in national elections.

Mobile has sizable shipbuilding, aluminum, chemical, lumber, paper and pulp industries. It also has a large Catholic element, which includes Jeremiah Denton, the first Republican senator to be elected from Alabama in the last century.

The Mobile area outvotes the rural, heavily black counties to the north. Democrats have not carried the district in a presidential election since 1960, and in closely contested Senate races in 1962 and 1980, the Republican nominee won district-wide.

In Democratic politics, the district has been strongly conservative and supportive of Gov. George C. Wallace. The 1st was a keystone in Wallace's dramatic 1970 runoff victory over Gov. Albert Brewer, which enabled him to regain the governorship and maintain a major role in national politics. In that Democratic contest, Wallace won all but one county in the 1st, carrying Mobile County alone by 15,000 votes.

## Committees

**Appropriations** (3rd of 22 Republicans)
Defense; Transportation.

## Elections

**1980 General**

| | |
|---|---|
| Jack Edwards (R) | 111,089 (95%) |
| Steve Smith (LIB) | 6,130 (5%) |

**1978 General**

| | |
|---|---|
| Jack Edwards (R) | 71,711 (64%) |
| L.W. (Red) Noonan (D) | 40,450 (36%) |

**Previous Winning Percentages**

| | | | |
|---|---|---|---|
| 1976 (63%) | 1974 (60%) | 1972 (77%) | 1970 (61%) |
| 1968 (57% | 1966 (66%) | 1964 (60%) | |

**District Vote For President**

| | 1980 | | 1976 | | 1972 |
|---|---|---|---|---|---|
| D | 77,758 (41 %) | D | 81,012 (48%) | D | 33,232 (24%) |
| R | 107,679 (56 %) | R | 83,622 (50%) | R | 101,960 (74%) |

## Campaign Finance

| | Receipts | Receipts from PACs | Expenditures |
|---|---|---|---|
| **1980** | | | |
| Edwards (R) | $37,675 | $28,788 (76%) | $26,661 |
| **1978** | | | |
| Edwards (R) | $158,770 | $45,046 (28%) | $166,456 |
| Noonan (D) | $85,775 | $3,150 (37%) | $85,773 |

## Voting Studies

| Year | Presidential Support | | Party Unity | | Conservative Coalition | |
|---|---|---|---|---|---|---|
| | S | O | S | O | S | O |
| 1980 | 43 | 44 | 56 | 20 | 76 | 9 |
| 1979 | 40 | 55 | 68 | 27 | 85 | 10 |
| 1978 | 38 | 61 | 78 | 20 | 88 | 10 |
| 1977 | 41 | 46 | 63 | 25 | 80 | 9 |
| 1976 | 80 | 14 | 80 | 15 | 85 | 9 |
| 1975 | 73 | 17 | 72 | 15 | 80 | 8 |
| 1974 (Ford) | 50 | 35 | | | | |
| 1974 | 83 | 13 | 60† | 20† | 79 | 10 |
| 1973 | 73 | 23 | 78 | 16 | 82 | 15 |
| 1972 | 59 | 22 | 79 | 9 | 93 | 1 |
| 1971 | 75 | 14 | 83 | 9 | 87 | 4 |
| 1970 | 63 | 26 | 69 | 18 | 82 | - |
| 1969 | 60 | 30 | 73 | 11 | 80 | 7 |
| 1968 | 45 | 50 | 80 | 11 | 82 | 8 |
| 1967 | 37 | 55 | 73 | 11 | 80 | 9 |
| 1966 | 20 | 52 | 73 | 3 | 73 | 0 |
| 1965 | 19 | 71 | 90 | 4 | 96 | 0 |

† Not eligible for all recorded votes.

S = Support          O = Opposition

## Key Votes

**96th Congress**

| | |
|---|---|
| Weaken Carter oil profits tax (1979) | Y |
| Reject hospital cost control plan (1979) | Y |
| Implement Panama Canal Treaties (1979) | N |
| Establish Department of Education (1979) | N |
| Approve Anti-busing Amendment (1979) | ? |
| Guarantee Chrysler Corp. loans (1979) | N |
| Approve military draft registration (1980) | Y |
| Aid Sandinista regime in Nicaragua (1980) | ? |
| Strengthen fair housing laws (1980) | N |

**97th Congress**

| | |
|---|---|
| Reagan budget proposal (1981) | Y |

## Interest Group Ratings

| Year | ADA | ACA | AFL-CIO | CCUS |
|---|---|---|---|---|
| 1980 | 17 | 83 | 11 | 84 |
| 1979 | 11 | 78 | 21 | 94 |
| 1978 | 20 | 89 | 11 | 78 |
| 1977 | 5 | 72 | 35 | 76 |
| 1976 | 0 | 81 | 23 | 94 |
| 1975 | 5 | 92 | 14 | 94 |
| 1974 | 9 | 71 | 0 | 88 |
| 1973 | 16 | 84 | 9 | 91 |
| 1972 | 0 | 78 | 10 | 100 |
| 1971 | 8 | 81 | 17 | - |
| 1970 | 4 | 83 | 0 | 89 |
| 1969 | 7 | 86 | 11 | - |
| 1968 | 0 | 100 | 0 | - |
| 1967 | 0 | 96 | 0 | 100 |
| 1966 | 0 | 100 | 0 | - |
| 1965 | 0 | 100 | - | 100 |

# 2 William L. Dickinson (R)

### Of Montgomery — Elected in 1964

**Born:** June 5, 1925, Opelika, Ala.
**Education:** U. of Ala. Law School, LL.B. 1950.
**Military Career:** Navy, 1943-46; Air Force Reserve.
**Profession:** Lawyer, judge, railroad executive.
**Family:** Wife, Barbara Edwards; four children.
**Religion:** Methodist.
**Political Career:** Opelika city judge, 1951-53; Lee County Court of Common Pleas and Juvenile Court judge, 1954-58; 5th Judicial Circuit judge, 1958-63.

**In Washington:** If and when Republicans take over the House, Dickinson stands to become chairman of its Armed Services Committee. For now, however, he is essentially a political gadfly on the committee, more than sympathetic to its pro-defense majority but not part of the panel's leadership.

Dickinson is recognized on Armed Services as a man of intelligence, one who shows flashes of brilliance when questioning witnesses. But he is not one of the committee's hardest workers, or a frequent builder of coalitions in favor of his point of view.

Dickinson suffered a defeat in 1980, when he launched one of his periodic drives to merge all military helicopter training into one program — at Fort Rucker in his district. Many Armed Services specialists concede the logic of this approach, and Dickinson was thought to have a good chance in 1980, but he lost a lobbying fight to a freshman Democrat from Florida whose district stood to lose under the change.

Although he can be a militant partisan on some issues, Dickinson has generally gone along with the bipartisan approach that has predominated at Armed Services over the years. His one significant quarrel has been with Samuel Stratton of New York, one of the committee's senior Democrats. In 1981, Stratton became eligible for the chairmanship of the Research and Development Subcommittee. Dickinson told a reporter that if Stratton took over the subcommittee, he would leave it. Chairman Melvin Price, D-Ill., stepped in, took the subcommittee himself and achieved at least temporary peace.

Dickinson has used his Armed Services position to travel around the world and to direct federal military spending into his district. As a traveler, he achieved distinction early. In his first

six years in Congress, he visited 29 countries. He has managed to keep up the pace since then.

As for his district, Dickinson takes pride in the comprehensive five-year development plan for Maxwell-Gunter Air Force complex in Montgomery and in the millions of dollars that have gone into flight training at Fort Rucker, even though the long-sought helicopter training expansion has never taken place.

Dickinson also is the senior Republican in years of service on the House Administration Committee. Under party rules, however, he could only be "ranking" on one panel, so he yielded that position on House Administration to Bill Frenzel of Minnesota, who has been more active than Dickinson in the committee's housekeeping work.

Outside his committee assignments, Dickinson tries to involve himself in measures of interest to the cotton and peanut farmers of his district. He sometimes testifies at the Agriculture Committee in favor of peanut price-support programs.

Dickinson's good-natured personal style does not always come through in his rhetoric. During his early years in Congress, strong words caused him a considerable amount of trouble.

In his first term, Dickinson took to the House floor and denounced civil rights marchers in his home state as "human flotsam" and "communist dupes," stirred up by outside agitators and a

---

**2nd District: Southeast — Montgomery, Dothan.** Population: 549,505 (12% increase since 1970). Race: White 376,259 (69%), Black 168,913 (31%), Others 4,333 (1%). Spanish origin: 5,731 (1%).

biased press. Some members, offended at the tone of his remarks, pointedly walked out of the House chamber as he spoke. His hometown newspaper criticized him publicly; Dickinson conceded he may have erred.

Dickinson chooses his words a little more carefully these days, at least in public, but his basic political conservatism remains solid.

He warns against the spread of international communism and speaks out for the nationalist Chinese government on Taiwan. And, as he notes in his own list of accomplishments, Dickinson "fights radical liberal efforts to further lower moral standards in the U.S. with such schemes as abortion on demand and so-called homosexual 'civil rights.' "

**At Home:** Like fellow-Republican Jack Edwards in the neighboring 1st District, Dickinson has worked his 1964 upset victory into a long-term congressional career.

But while Edwards has had an easy time holding his seat, Dickinson has rarely escaped serious opposition. Five times he has won re-election with less than 60 percent of the vote; three times, he has been held under 55 percent.

Unlike Edwards, Dickinson represents a primarily rural, traditionally Democratic area of Alabama. Some of his Democratic opponents have drawn the active support of former Gov. George C. Wallace, whose original home base is Barbour County, at the eastern end of the 2nd District.

But Dickinson has been able to establish a solid base of support in the population centers, Montgomery and Dothan, and he has embellished his conservative credentials with blessings from prominent figures like Jerry Falwell, the national leader of the Moral Majority.

A Democratic circuit judge in Lee County for four years, Dickinson quit the bench in 1963 to become assistant vice president of the Southern Railroad. But his stay in the business world was brief. He filed for the House just as Barry Goldwater was launching his presidential campaign, and when Goldwater swept Alabama in November 1964, Dickinson easily unseated Democratic Rep. George M. Grant.

Grant had a conservative record, but Dickinson managed to associate him with the national Democratic ticket, which was not only unpopular in the state but was excluded from an official position at the top of the ballot.

Dickinson has had a series of close re-election campaigns since then, with state Sen. "Walking" Wendell Mitchell offering the strongest challenge, in 1978. Mitchell said Dickinson had done little for the district and had missed too many House roll calls. Dickinson was held to 54 percent.

In the following two years, the Republican devoted increased attention to his constituency. From his position on the Armed Services Committee, he was able to win increased funding for Maxwell-Gunter. In 1980, with Republicans running well statewide in Alabama, Dickinson won re-election with a comfortable 61 percent of the vote.

**The District:** The 2nd District covers the southeast corner of Alabama. Most of the district is rural, but about one-third of the population lives in Montgomery County, which includes the state capital and Alabama's third-largest city.

Montgomery has considerable white-collar government employment, both state and federal, and is the site of the adjacent Maxwell and Gunter bases. It was also the site of the bus boycott that marked the beginning of the modern civil rights movement.

At the other end of the district, near the Florida and Georgia borders, is Dothan, an old cotton and peanut market town which has attracted new industry in recent years and has been growing rapidly. The presence nearby of Fort Rucker has enhanced the economy of the area.

Both Montgomery and Dothan have emerged as Republican strongholds. The rest of the 13-county district contains part of the state's Piney Woods section and a portion of the Black Belt. The latter extends across the northern part of the district and is loyally Democratic. But as one moves south toward the Florida border, the black population decreases. The south Alabama rural counties were Wallace strongholds, and they have been increasingly receptive to conservative Republicans in recent years.

## Committees

**Armed Services** (Ranking Republican)
Military Installations and Facilities; Readiness; Research and Development.

**House Administration** (2nd of 8 Republicans)
Services.

## Elections

**1980 General**

| | |
|---|---|
| William Dickinson (R ) | 104,796 (61 %) |
| Cecil Wyatt (D ) | 63,447 (37 %) |

**1978 General**

| | |
|---|---|
| William Dickinson (R ) | 57,924 (54 %) |
| Wendell Mitchell (D ) | 49,341 (46 %) |

**Previous Winning Percentages**

| | | | |
|---|---|---|---|
| **1976** (58 %) | **1974** (66 %) | **1972** (55 %) | **1970** (61 %) |
| **1968** (55 %) | **1966** (55 %) | **1964** (62 %) | |

**District Vote For President**

| | 1980 | | 1976 | | 1972 |
|---|---|---|---|---|---|
| **D** | 83,720 (44 %) | **D** | 88,208 (53 %) | **D** | 31,603 (22 %) |
| **R** | 99,283 (53 %) | **R** | 75,528 (46 %) | **R** | 107,821 (76 %) |

## Campaign Finance

| | Receipts | Receipts from PACs | Expenditures |
|---|---|---|---|
| **1980** | | | |
| Dickinson (R ) | $175,225 | $66,160 (38 %) | $116,504 |
| Wyatt (D ) | $29,071 | $300 (1 %) | $27,952 |
| **1978** | | | |
| Dickinson (R ) | $137,003 | $39,007 (28 %) | $139,313 |
| Mitchell (D ) | $115,823 | $12,519 (11 %) | $115,372 |

## Voting Studies

| | Presidential Support | | Party Unity | | Conservative Coalition | |
|---|---|---|---|---|---|---|
| **Year** | **S** | **O** | **S** | **O** | **S** | **O** |
| **1980** | 32 | 56 | 80 | 11 | 79 | 5 |
| 1979 | 20 | 72 | 82 | 11 | 88 | 5 |
| 1978 | 21 | 62 | 74 | 12 | 84 | 5 |
| 1977 | 32 | 56 | 74 | 12 | 81 | 4 |
| 1976 | 76 | 18 | 88 | 6 | 92 | 1 |
| 1975 | 64 | 27 | 78 | 10 | 85 | 4 |
| **1974 (Ford)** | 50 | 33 | | | | |
| 1974 | 60 | 28 | 77 | 8 | 82 | 2 |
| 1973 | 70 | 22 | 78 | 14 | 89 | 3 |
| 1972 | 43 | 24 | 74 | 8 | 77 | 2 |
| 1971 | 74 | 19 | 82 | 12 | 93 | 3 |
| 1970 | 52 | 32 | 71 | 18 | 89 | - |
| 1969 | 60 | 32 | 73 | 18 | 82 | 2 |
| 1968 | 35 | 48 | 67 | 9 | 78 | 2 |
| 1967 | 28 | 51 | 76 | 4 | 74 | 2 |
| 1966 | 15 | 46 | 61 | 0 | 59 | 0 |
| 1965 | 22 | 66 | 79 | 3 | 80 | 2 |

S = Support    O = Opposition

## Key Votes

**96th Congress**

| | |
|---|---|
| Weaken Carter oil profits tax (1979) | Y |
| Reject hospital cost control plan (1979) | Y |
| Implement Panama Canal Treaties (1979) | N |
| Establish Department of Education (1979) | N |
| Approve Anti-busing Amendment (1979) | Y |
| Guarantee Chrysler Corp. loans (1979) | N |
| Approve military draft registration (1980) | Y |
| Aid Sandinista regime in Nicaragua (1980) | N |
| Strengthen fair housing laws (1980) | N |

**97th Congress**

| | |
|---|---|
| Reagan budget proposal (1981) | Y |

## Interest Group Ratings

| Year | ADA | ACA | AFL-CIO | CCUS |
|---|---|---|---|---|
| 1980 | 11 | 83 | 10 | 81 |
| 1979 | 5 | 88 | 6 | 93 |
| 1978 | 5 | 96 | 16 | 81 |
| 1977 | 5 | 92 | 23 | 100 |
| 1976 | 0 | 96 | 17 | 100 |
| 1975 | 5 | 89 | 9 | 100 |
| 1974 | 4 | 92 | 0 | 88 |
| 1973 | 4 | 96 | 9 | 100 |
| 1972 | 0 | 95 | 0 | 100 |
| 1971 | 3 | 86 | 17 | - |
| 1970 | 8 | 94 | 0 | 89 |
| 1969 | 0 | 69 | 0 | - |
| 1968 | 0 | 96 | 0 | - |
| 1967 | 0 | 96 | 0 | 100 |
| 1966 | 0 | 100 | 0 | - |
| 1965 | 0 | 96 | - | 100 |

# 3 Bill Nichols (D)

**Of Sylacauga — Elected 1966**

**Born:** Oct. 16, 1918, Becker, Miss.
**Education:** Auburn U., B.S. 1939, M.A. 1941.
**Military Career:** Army, 1942-47.
**Profession:** Fertilizer and cotton gin executive.
**Family:** Wife, Carolyn Funderburk; three children.
**Religion:** Methodist.
**Political Career:** Ala. House, 1959-63. Ala. Senate, 1963-67,

**In Washington:** Normally slow to anger and reluctant even to speak out on public issues, Nichols was a man enraged in 1980, when President Carter vetoed his bill to increase bonuses for military doctors. As chairman of the Armed Services Subcommittee on Military Compensation, he had worked two years to pass it.

He had negotiated a compromise bonus bill acceptable to the Senate and to the Pentagon. But its passage came immediately after the administration announced its election-year austerity drive. Carter said it was too generous.

Nichols, who had thought his bill was supported by the White House, was privately devastated by the veto. But characteristically, he did not publicly challenge or criticize the president. Instead of trying to override the veto, as many of his colleagues suggested, Nichols went back to work and modified the bill the following month. Carter signed it.

Nichols has viewed himself as a protector of the nation's military personnel, particularly those of lower rank. He has proposed some additional benefits and larger pay raises, but has been reluctant to reform the military's complex pay system as has been suggested by the last several administrations and the General Accounting Office. In 1977, for example, he opposed a floor amendment to change the military retirement system, saying his committee was studying the issue. It still is. The uniformed services, which have vehemently opposed change, appreciate this. A huge man, tall and shaped like a barrel, Nichols lost a leg in combat as a World War II Army officer. His fervent patriotism has led him to support a series of presidents on military issues, regardless of party. He supported the Vietnam War policies under both Johnson and Nixon far longer than most other members of Congress.

Outside his compensation issues, Nichols is no legislative activist, even within Armed Ser-

vices. But he has always been comfortable within the panel's conservative, pro-military environment. He has had no other major assignment, although he pays close attention to farm issues. He was involved in an Armed Services junket controversy in 1976, when it was reported that legislators and Pentagon officials had been entertained by defense contractors at Maryland hunting lodges. Nichols had been a lodge guest of the Northrop Corp.

**At Home.** Of the seven Republicans that were elected to congressional seats in the 1964 Goldwater landslide, only one was defeated for re-election. That was in the Alabama 3rd, recaptured for the Democrats by Nichols. The GOP has not threatened there since then.

Nichols was a star football player at Auburn University, before the war in Europe cost him his left leg. After the war he returned to his hometown of Sylacauga, started farming, and became an officer in local gin and fertilizer companies.

He made his political debut in 1958 by winning a seat in the state House. Four years later he was elected to the state Senate, where he became a floor leader for Gov. George C. Wallace. Nichols handled education and agriculture legislation for Wallace, and gained widespread attention by promoting bills to provide free school textbooks. Nichols was well known across eastern Alabama when he ran for Congress in 1966, and he had little trouble winning the seat. In the Democratic

---

**3rd District: East — Anniston, Phenix City.** Population: 565,749 (15% increase since 1970). Race: White 396,659 (70%), Black 165,940 (29%), Others 3,150 (1%). Spanish origin: 5,252 (1%).

## Bill Nichols, D-Ala.

primary he easily defeated a labor-backed opponent, Public Service Commissioner Ed Pepper. In the general election, Nichols ousted one-term Republican Glenn Andrews with 58 percent of the vote. When Andrews tried to regain his seat in 1970, Nichols embarrassed him by nearly 6-1.

**The District.** The 3rd District sweeps north from the outskirts of Montgomery into the hills of eastern Alabama. It is mostly rural, although there is industry in Anniston, Phenix City and Opelika. Textiles are a major product.

Except for the counties of the black belt in the southern portion of the district, the 3rd was a conservative Wallace stronghold in the 1960s and 1970s. However, most people here still vote the straight Democratic ticket. In 1980, the 3rd District went narrowly for both Jimmy Carter and the unsuccessful Democratic Senate candidate.

## Committees

**Armed Services** (5th of 25 Democrats)
Military Personnel and Compensation, chairman; Research and Development.

## Elections

**1980 General**

| | |
|---|---|
| Bill Nichols (D ) | Unopposed |

**1980 Primary**

| | |
|---|---|
| Bill Nichols (D ) | 49,323 (85 %) |
| Charley Baker (D ) | 8,608 (15 %) |

**1978 General**

| | |
|---|---|
| Bill Nichols (D ) | Unopposed |

**Previous Winning Percentages**

| | | | |
|---|---|---|---|
| 1976 (99 %) | 1974 (96 %) | 1972 (76 %) | 1970 (84 %) |
| 1968 (81 %) | 1966 (58 %) | | |

**District Vote For President**

| | 1980 | | 1976 | | 1972 |
|---|---|---|---|---|---|
| D | 90,330 (50 %) | D | 93,766 (58 %) | D | 33,724 (25 %) |
| R | 81,575 (46 %) | R | 63,819 (40 %) | R | 100,199 (74 %) |

## Campaign Finance

| | Receipts | Receipts from PACs | Expenditures |
|---|---|---|---|
| **1980** | | | |
| Nichols (D ) | $106,892 | $42,920 (40 %) | $33,572 |
| **1978** | | | |
| Nichols (D ) | $17,162 | $15,000 (87 %) | $13,212 |

## Voting Studies

| | Presidential Support | | Party Unity | | Conservative Coalition | |
|---|---|---|---|---|---|---|
| **Year** | **S** | **O** | **S** | **O** | **S** | **O** |
| 1980 | 49 | 44 | 34 | 52 | 82 | 4 |
| 1979 | 36 | 55 | 32 | 60 | 90 | 6 |
| 1978 | 32 | 59 | 29 | 60 | 84 | 5 |
| 1977 | 44 | 46 | 31 | 62 | 88 | 7 |
| 1976 | 49 | 37 | 30 | 59 | 82 | 6 |
| 1975 | 48 | 47 | 32 | 62 | 84 | 11 |
| 1974 (Ford) | 46 | 39 | | | | |
| 1974 | 51 | 40 | 28 | 57 | 82 | 7 |
| 1973 | 52 | 38 | 36 | 58 | 91 | 4 |
| 1972 | 35 | 22 | 27 | 34 | 52 | 6 |
| 1971 | 65 | 19 | 28 | 60 | 86 | 3 |
| 1970 | 45 | 37 | 39 | 43 | 66 | 2 |
| 1969 | 40 | 47 | 27 | 49 | 71 | 9 |
| 1968 | 32 | 42 | 18 | 54 | 65 | 4 |
| 1967 | 45 | 43 | 34 | 62 | 91 | 4 |

S = Support          O = Opposition

## Key Votes

**96th Congress**

| | |
|---|---|
| Weaken Carter oil profits tax (1979) | N |
| Reject hospital cost control plan (1979) | Y |
| Implement Panama Canal Treaties (1979) | N |
| Establish Department of Education (1979) | N |
| Approve Anti-busing Amendment (1979) | Y |
| Guarantee Chrysler Corp. loans (1979) | N |
| Approve military draft registration (1980) | Y |
| Aid Sandinista regime in Nicaragua (1980) | N |
| Strengthen fair housing laws (1980) | N |

**97th Congress**

| | |
|---|---|
| Reagan budget proposal (1981) | Y |

## Interest Group Ratings

| Year | ADA | ACA | AFL-CIO | CCUS |
|---|---|---|---|---|
| 1980 | 17 | 59 | 26 | 67 |
| 1979 | 11 | 73 | 45 | 61 |
| 1978 | 5 | 83 | 25 | 67 |
| 1977 | 5 | 74 | 26 | 76 |
| 1976 | 5 | 84 | 33 | 82 |
| 1975 | 5 | 81 | 17 | 59 |
| 1974 | 4 | 64 | 25 | 75 |
| 1973 | 8 | 74 | 36 | 82 |
| 1972 | 0 | 92 | 17 | 89 |
| 1971 | 3 | 72 | 33 | - |
| 1970 | 8 | 73 | 29 | 70 |
| 1969 | 7 | 82 | 30 | - |
| 1968 | 0 | 86 | 0 | - |
| 1967 | 7 | 68 | 17 | 60 |

# 4 Tom Bevill (D)

**Of Jasper — Elected 1966**

**Born:** March 27, 1921, Townley, Ala.
**Education:** U. of Ala., B.S. 1943, LL.B. 1948.
**Military Career:** Army, 1943-46.
**Profession:** Lawyer.
**Family:** Wife, Lou Betts; three children.
**Religion:** Baptist.
**Political Career:** Ala. House, 1959-67; sought Democratic nomination for U.S. House, Alabama 7th District, 1964.

**In Washington:** Much of north Alabama was brought to health in the 1930s by the public works projects of the Tennessee Valley Authority, and Bevill, who represents part of TVA country in the House, has always treated public works as a personal creed.

Today, as chairman of the Energy and Water Subcommittee on Appropriations, Bevill is in a good position to determine the amount of money spent not only for the TVA, but for the Army Corps of Engineers and water projects all over the country. He approaches all these issues as a true believer.

"There is no question," Bevill says, "that water resources projects have helped develop the nation." He says every dollar invested in flood control has reaped benefits many times over. A fiscal conservative on most issues, he does not believe in judging public works on a rigid budget-cutting basis.

In 1977, when the new Carter administration decided to cancel 18 water projects it said were too expensive and environmentally damaging, Bevill and his committee went to war. They agreed to kill only one of the projects and took the battle to the floor. Against heavy administration lobbying, they won, but the vote was close, 218-194, not enough of a margin to override the veto Carter threatened.

After a long summer of wrangling between Congress and the administration, there was a compromise: nine of the 18 projects would survive. Carter agreed not to veto the bill.

The next year, however, Bevill resurrected six of the nine projects, contending he had only committed himself to a one-year moratorium on their funding. The administration accused him of bad faith, and the fight resumed.

This time the House vote in favor of the projects was greater, amid talk that Bevill planned to cut off money for favorite projects of members who voted with Carter on the issue.

One member explained it bluntly: "I have two projects in my district," he said. "They're small projects, but last year when I voted with Carter I didn't get those projects funded. This year, I think I'll vote with the committee."

Carter vetoed that bill, and the House eventually upheld the veto, largely because 62 Republicans voted with the president. The veto vote was 223-190. In the long run, however, Bevill was the winner. The effort to cut back on a small number of projects cost Carter enough political capital to make any president think hard about slashing the public works budget.

By 1980, in fact, Carter had agreed to resurrect two Oklahoma projects from among the rejected nine, and Bevill was calling the administration's water project request "reasonable." The Reagan White House takes a generally skeptical approach to massive new public works spending, but it has made few specific suggestions for projects to be cut.

These days, Bevill talks mostly about the future of the Tennessee-Tombigbee waterway, a planned $1.7 billion barge canal that will cut through Alabama on its way to the Gulf of Mexico. Bevill defends it emotionally against critics who question the cost and even the need for such a project.

---

**4th District: North central — Gadsden.** Population: 549,974 (21% increase since 1970). Race: White 548,655 (92%), Black 44,456 (7%), Others 1,863 (0.3%). Spanish origin: 3,391 (1%).

## Tom Bevill, D-Ala.

It is an issue that demands his eternal vigilance; opponents have offered numerous amendments to delete money for Tennessee-Tombigbee, and in June of 1980 came within 20 votes of passing one in the House. "I don't believe I have ever seen such misinformation," Bevill said of the tactics of his opposition that day.

Besides his public works ideology, Bevill has always carried with him a hint of north Alabama populism. He voted against deregulation of natural gas in 1977, for instance, and has spoken of "the big oil companies ripping off the people of the country." He went with the AFL-CIO on nearly half of its key test votes in 1980.

This populist streak has kept Bevill closer to the national Democratic leadership than most of his Deep South colleagues have been willing to venture.

Bevill fought hard for Hale Boggs of Louisiana in Boggs's successful campaign to become majority leader in 1971, and soon struck up a good relationship with the man Boggs chose as his whip, Thomas P. O'Neill Jr. In 1980, when Southern Democrats demanded a bigger role in House policy, Speaker O'Neill placed Bevill and three other members of the group on the Democratic Steering and Policy Committee. In May of 1981, however, Bevill voted against O'Neill and for the combined budget and tax cut proposal favored by President Reagan.

**At Home:** Bevill's political career parallels that of his 3rd District neighbor, Bill Nichols. Both were elected to the Alabama Legislature in 1958, served as floor leaders for Gov. George C. Wallace, and won election to Congress in 1966.

But while Nichols had a fairly clear path to the House, Bevill's route was difficult. He lost his first congressional race in 1964, when incumbent Carl Elliott defeated him in the Democratic primary by a margin of more than 3-to-2.

Two years later, the district was open. Republican James D. Martin, who had won it in November of 1964, was running for governor. Elliott was not interested in trying again.

Bevill entered a four-way Democratic primary that included a popular state representative, Gary Burns, and a former Wallace press secretary, Bill Jones. He led the first round with 36 percent of the vote, and his strength in the western part of the district gave him a runoff victory over Burns with 56 percent.

The general election was much simpler. Bevill beat Republican Wayman Sherrer, the little-known Blount County solicitor, by nearly 2-1 — a margin similar to the one by which Martin was losing the governorship to Lurleen B. Wallace.

Since then, Bevill has won every Democratic primary with at least 80 percent of the vote and every general election with at least 70 percent. Generally, his opposition has come from political novices. His only prominent challenger was Jim Folsom Jr., son of the colorful ex-governor, who made his political debut in 1976 by opposing Bevill for renomination. It was a flop. Bevill drew more than 80 percent of the vote.

**The District:** The 4th District runs across the north central part of the state, from the rolling hill country along the Mississippi border eastward into the mountains.

The district is rural, poor and overwhelmingly white. Poultry, cotton and livestock are the major farm products. Gadsden, an iron and steel center, is the largest city.

The area has a history of moderate politics, generally free of extreme race-baiting. Populism flourished here, producing political characters like James E. Folsom Sr., who won two terms as governor (in 1946 and 1954) as a champion of the "little man" and critic of the power structure in Birmingham and south Alabama.

In recent years, the 4th District has been loyally Democratic. Carter carried it by comfortable margins in both 1976 and 1980. But the political complexion of the 4th may be undergoing a subtle change. The district was the fastest growing in Alabama in the last decade, with much of the growth in areas near Birmingham where Republican strength has increased.

## Committees

**Appropriations** (11th of 33 Democrats)
Energy and Water Development, chairman; Military Construction.

## Elections

**1980 General**

| | |
|---|---|
| Tom Bevill (D ) | 129,365 (98 %) |

**1978 General**

| | |
|---|---|
| Tom Bevill (D ) | Unopposed |

**Previous Winning Percentages**

| | | | |
|---|---|---|---|
| 1976 (80 %) | 1974 (100%) | 1972 (70 %) | 1970 (100%) |
| 1968 (76 %) | 1966 (64 %) | | |

## District Vote For President

| 1980 | | 1976 | | 1972 | |
|---|---|---|---|---|---|
| D | 107,847 (52 %) | D | 124,601 (65 %) | D | 34,316 (22 %) |
| R | 95,900 (46 %) | R | 66,263 (34 %) | R | 118,055 (77 %) |

## Campaign Finance

| | Receipts | Receipts from PACs | Expenditures |
|---|---|---|---|
| **1980** | | | |
| Bevill (D ) | $59,988 | $30,650 (51 %) | $16,495 |
| **1978** | | | |
| Bevill (D ) | $18,480 | $8,800 (48 %) | $8,413 |

## Voting Studies

| | Presidential Support | | Party Unity | | Conservative Coalition | |
|---|---|---|---|---|---|---|
| Year | S | O | S | O | S | O |
| 1980 | 55 | 34 | 56 | 34 | 78 | 13 |
| 1979 | 42 | 50 | 53 | 40† | 84 | 12 |
| 1978 | 45 | 52 | 48 | 47 | 77 | 19 |
| 1977 | 54 | 42 | 47 | 49 | 75 | 19 |
| 1976 | 43 | 43 | 39 | 51 | 73 | 17 |
| 1975 | 42 | 55 | 45 | 53 | 79 | 19 |
| 1974 (Ford) | 56 | 41 | | | | |
| 1974 | 49 | 38 | 44 | 46 | 66 | 19 |
| 1973 | 46 | 50 | 49 | 46 | 80 | 18 |
| 1972 | 54 | 24 | 48 | 27 | 52 | 24 |
| 1971 | 65 | 25 | 40 | 45 | 70 | 14 |
| 1970 | 51 | 40 | 47 | 36 | 68 | 23 |
| 1969 | 45 | 43 | 33 | 56 | 78 | 13 |
| 1968 | 44 | 43 | 32 | 56 | 78 | 12 |
| 1967 | 51 | 47 | 34 | 63 | 87 | 7 |

S = Support    O = Opposition

†Not eligible for all recorded votes.

## Key Votes

**96th Congress**

| | |
|---|---|
| Weaken Carter oil profits tax (1979) | N |
| Reject hospital cost control plan (1979) | Y |
| Implement Panama Canal Treaties (1979) | N |
| Establish Department of Education (1979) | Y |
| Approve Anti-busing Amendment (1979) | Y |
| Guarantee Chrysler Corp. loans (1979) | N |
| Approve military draft registration (1980) | Y |
| Aid Sandinista regime in Nicaragua (1980) | N |
| Strengthen fair housing laws (1980) | N |

**97th Congress**

| | |
|---|---|
| Reagan budget proposal (1981) | Y |

## Interest Group Ratings

| Year | ADA | ACA | AFL-CIO | CCUS |
|---|---|---|---|---|
| 1980 | 22 | 35 | 44 | 68 |
| 1979 | 26 | 52 | 50 | 50 |
| 1978 | 15 | 67 | 35 | 44 |
| 1977 | 15 | 56 | 64 | 47 |
| 1976 | 25 | 64 | 50 | 69 |
| 1975 | 16 | 67 | 43 | 47 |
| 1974 | 13 | 64 | 56 | 57 |
| 1973 | 24 | 54 | 80 | 40 |
| 1972 | 19 | 65 | 82 | 44 |
| 1971 | 16 | 61 | 55 | - |
| 1970 | 20 | 56 | 43 | 30 |
| 1969 | 7 | 69 | 30 | - |
| 1968 | 8 | 64 | 25 | |
| 1967 | 7 | 76 | 8 | 80 |

# 5 Ronnie G. Flippo (D)

**Of Florence — Elected 1976**

**Born:** Aug. 15, 1937, Florence, Ala.
**Education:** U. of North Ala., B.S. 1965; U. of Ala., M.A. 1966.
**Profession:** Accountant.
**Family:** Wife, Faye Cooper; six children.
**Religion:** Church of Christ.
**Political Career:** Ala. House, 1971-75; Ala. Senate, 1975-77.

**In Washington:** Coming from one of the few Deep South districts with a history of moderate representation, Flippo has balanced an overall tilt to the right with a concern for the views of labor and an occasional gesture to the Democratic leaders. He combines a "good old boy" Southern manner with a fondness for conservative three-piece suits and a low-key style in public.

He quickly secured the two committee assignments he needed — Public Works and Science and Technology. His spot on Public Works allows him to promote the goals of the Tennessee Valley Authority, a dominant economic interest in north Alabama. His is among the most solid of the committee's votes in favor of water projects nearly anywhere in the country, but especially close to home. In this fight, he is an ally of his influential 4th District neighbor, Tom Bevill, who chairs the Appropriations subcommittee that funds water projects.

On the Science Committee, he has fought for subsidies for research into solar satellites. Much of this work would be done in his district, in Huntsville, where the U.S. space program is a crucial local industry. Flippo steered a $25 million solar satellite subsidy bill through the House in both 1978 and 1979, his most conspicuous congressional achievement. But the Senate did not pass it in either of the last two Congresses.

A former ironworker, Flippo had labor support in his first campaign, and has occasionally broken with orthodox Southern Democratic thinking to return the favor, although he has not been as union-oriented as his predecessor in the district, Democrat Robert E. Jones 1947-77). Shortly after he arrived in the House, Flippo opposed the common-site picketing bill labor badly wanted. Jones had voted for the bill.

Flippo's most quixotic effort in the labor field was a 1978 amendment to restore 100,000 public service jobs to a CETA employment bill after a bipartisan compromise had removed them. All parties to the debate insisted on sticking with the compromise, and Flippo was beaten 335-1, his own vote the only one cast in favor of the amendment.

**At Home.** It was a 55-foot fall that started Flippo on the way to Congress. When he was a 23-year-old ironworker, he fell from a building site and broke his arms, legs and pelvic bone. During his recovery he became interested in accounting, and eventually he went back to school and got an advanced degree.

After establishing a successful accounting business, Flippo went into politics, served four years in the state House, and moved to the state Senate in 1974.

When the veteran Jones decided to retire in 1976, Flippo entered a 10-man race to succeed him. With the backing of organized labor and a strong base in the tri-cities of Florence, Muscle Shoals and Sheffield, he ran first in the primary with 25 percent of the vote, then took the runoff by 16,000 votes over John Eyster, a conservative Baptist and corporate lawyer.

Flippo has had an easy time since then. The Republicans have never run an opponent against him, and his primary opposition has been weak.

**The District.** The 5th District, seven counties in the valley of the Tennessee River, may be the least typical of Alabama.

It is relatively prosperous, thanks to nearly a

---

**5th District: North — Huntsville.**
Population: 549,802 (12% increase since 1970).
Race: White 466,809 (85%), Black 78,639 (14%), Others 4,354 (1%). Spanish origin: 4,270 (1%).

half century of resource development by the TVA and to federal installations like the Army's Redstone Arsenal and the Marshall Space Flight Center, both in Huntsville. Labor unions are active in the metals, automobile and chemical industries. Fourteen percent of the district's residents are black, a smaller proportion than in most of the state.

In most years, the 5th District registers overwhelming support for the entire Democratic ticket. Carter easily carried it in 1980 as well as 1976. He also brought the small town of Tuscumbia into the national spotlight by opening his 1980 general election campaign there. In an off-the-cuff comment after Carter's appearance, Ronald Reagan mistakenly described the town as the birthplace of the Ku Klux Klan. His controversial remark drew a firestorm of criticism in Alabama and nearly cost Reagan the state in November balloting.

## Committees

**Public Works and Transportation** (15th of 25 Democrats)
Economic Development; Investigations and Oversight; Water Resources.

**Science and Technology** (10th of 23 Democrats)
Space Science and Applications, chairman; Energy Research and Production.

## Elections

**1980 General**

| | |
|---|---|
| Ronnie Flippo (D ) | 117,626 (94 %) |
| Betty Benson (LIB) | 7,341 (6 %) |

**1978 General**

| | |
|---|---|
| Ronnie Flippo (D ) | 68,985 (97 %) |

**Previous Winning Percentage**

1976 (100%)

**District Vote For President**

| | 1980 | | 1976 | | 1972 |
|---|---|---|---|---|---|
| D | 96,169 (54 %) | D | 106,191 (67 %) | D | 34,515 (25 %) |
| R | 72,831 (41 %) | R | 50,039 (32 %) | R | 99,447 (73 %) |
| I | 3,746 (2 %) | | | | |

## Campaign Finance

| | Receipts | Receipts from PACs | Expenditures |
|---|---|---|---|
| **1980** | | | |
| Flippo (D ) | $169,051 | $57,595 (34 %) | $77,827 |

| | | | |
|---|---|---|---|
| **1978** | | | |
| Flippo (D ) | $72,037 | $32,825 (46 %) | $41,660 |

## Voting Studies

| | Presidential Support | | Party Unity | | Conservative Coalition | |
|---|---|---|---|---|---|---|
| Year | S | O | S | O | S | O |
| 1980 | 56 | 33 | 55 | 36 | 77 | 13 |
| 1979 | 53 | 43 | 53 | 39 | 83 | 8 |
| 1978 | 44 | 52 | 47 | 50 | 80 | 15 |
| 1977 | 42 | 16 | 38 | 24 | 44 | 16 |

S = Support          O = Opposition

## Key Votes

**96th Congress**

| | |
|---|---|
| Weaken Carter oil profits tax (1979) | Y |
| Reject hospital cost control plan (1979) | Y |
| Implement Panama Canal Treaties (1979) | N |
| Establish Department of Education (1979) | Y |
| Approve Anti-busing Amendment (1979) | Y |
| Guarantee Chrysler Corp. loans (1979) | Y |
| Approve military draft registration (1980) | Y |
| Aid Sandinista regime in Nicaragua (1980) | N |
| Strengthen fair housing laws (1980) | N |

**97th Congress**

| | |
|---|---|
| Reagan budget proposal (1981) | Y |

## Interest Group Ratings

| Year | ADA | ACA | AFL-CIO | CCUS |
|---|---|---|---|---|
| 1980 | 28 | 42 | 42 | 70 |
| 1979 | 16 | 46 | 35 | 56 |
| 1978 | 10 | 74 | 42 | 56 |
| 1977 | 5 | 38 | 50 | 50 |

# 6 Albert Lee Smith Jr. (R)

**Of Birmingham — Elected 1980**

**Born:** Aug. 31, 1931, Birmingham, Ala.
**Education:** Auburn University, B.S. 1954.
**Military Career:** Navy, 1954-55.
**Profession:** Insurance agent.
**Family:** Wife, Eunie Walldorf; three children.
**Religion:** Baptist.
**Political Career:** Unsuccessfully sought Republican nomination for U.S. House, 1978.

**The Member:** Smith has sponsored the Family Protection Act, a bill to halt what he sees as the federal government's "wholesale destruction of rights that have always been reserved for families." Its provisions include a ban on Legal Services Corporation suits seeking abortion funding, homosexual rights and busing for desegregation. Smith's bill allows prayer in schools and offers tax breaks to individuals caring for dependents age 65 or older.

Smith's 1980 campaign received active support from two black Birmingham businessmen, something a bit unusual for a former John Birch Society member who tied himself closely to Reagan and the GOP platform. The two men, Lige Richardson and Pete Gresham, thought Smith's "self-help" philosophy might lead to more productive jobs for blacks than had traditional government welfare and jobs programs.

Smith brought the pair onto his congressional staff, but fired them after less than a month in office. He said they had failed several times to clear their public statements with him. Richardson and Gresham said Smith had lost interest in his campaign commitment to ease black unemployment.

Contending that Rep. John Buchanan was too liberal, Smith tried to unseat him in the 1978 GOP primary, but failed. Smith's victory in the 1980 rematch came with the aid of the Moral Majority, conservative Democratic crossovers, and his own large grass-roots organization.

In the general election, Smith narrowly defeated Democrat W. B. "Pete" Clifford, a city councilman not considered a strong candidate.

**The District:** The Birmingham district is like many other urban centers in the Deep South: Republican at the presidential level but loyally Democratic in most state and local contests. The presence of the steel industry and its unions gives it an old-fashioned industrial flavor that the newer white-collar Southern cities lack. Blacks are about 30 percent of the electorate. The Republican vote is concentrated in the suburbs.

## Committees

**Budget**
Task Forces: Economic Policy and Productivity; Energy and the Environment; Tax Policy.

**Veterans' Affairs** (11th of 14 Republicans)
Compensation, Pension and Insurance; Hospitals and Health Care.

## Elections

**1980 General**

| | |
|---|---|
| Albert Lee Smith Jr. (R ) | 95,019 (51 %) |
| W. B. Clifford (D ) | 87,536 (47 %) |

**1980 Primary**

| | |
|---|---|
| Albert Lee Smith Jr. (R ) | 25,857 (55 %) |
| John Buchanan (R ) | 20,855 (45 %) |

**District Vote For President**

| | 1980 | | 1976 | | 1972 |
|---|---|---|---|---|---|
| **D** | 83,112 (42 %) | **D** | 70,995 (43 %) | **D** | 41,262 (27 %) |
| **R** | 106,576 (53 %) | **R** | 91,928 (55 %) | **R** | 106,082 (70 %) |

## Campaign Finance

| | Receipts | Receipts from PACs | Expenditures |
|---|---|---|---|
| **1980** | | | |
| Smith (R ) | $258,335 | $65,843 (25 %) | $257,990 |
| Clifford (D ) | $42,979 | $11,500 (27 %) | $41,812 |

## Key Vote

**97th Congress**

| | |
|---|---|
| Reagan budget proposal (1981) | Y |

---

**6th District: Birmingham.** Population: 518,032 (5% increase since 1970). Race: White 348,174 (67%), Black 167,111 (32%), Others 2,747 (1%). Spanish origin: 3,531 (1%).

# 7 Richard C. Shelby (D)

### Of Tuscaloosa - Elected 1978

**Born:** May 6, 1934, Birmingham, Ala.
**Education:** U. of Ala., A.B. 1957; LL.B. 1963.
**Profession:** Lawyer.
**Family:** Wife, Annette Nevin; two children.
**Religion:** Presbyterian.
**Political Career:** Ala. Senate, 1971-79.

**In Washington:** Viewed as a progressive Democrat during most of his Alabama political career, Shelby surprised some of his colleagues by compiling a consistent conservative voting record in his first Washington term. Appointed by senior Democrats to a coveted place on the Commerce Committee — and its crucial Energy and Health subcommittees — he cast most of his votes in alliance with the panel's Republican minority. Once sought by House leaders as a possible vote for President Carter's hospital cost containment plan, he ultimately opposed it both in committee and on the floor.

Shelby's has been an inconspicuous conservatism, both on the Commerce Committee and on the floor. "My job is to represent the interests of the people back home," he once told a reporter. "I think of myself as a worker here rather than as an activist."

Some of Shelby's first-term work was in behalf of the Tennessee-Tombigbee Waterway, the controversial $1.7 billion barge canal that would run through his district on its way from the Tennessee River to the Gulf of Mexico. He also lobbied for federally subsidized research into coal production, especially at an experimental coal refining plant in Wilsonville, a few miles south of Birmingham.

Shelby remains a close ally of Walter Flowers, his House predecessor and former law partner, who now works for Wheelabrator-Frye, an engineering firm that makes pollution control equipment. Flowers was involved with the effort in behalf of synthetic fuels legislation, which Shelby supported. Shelby also served a year on the Judiciary Committee, Flowers' old House committee, but left it in the spring of 1980.

Some of Shelby's early votes disappointed old Alabama supporters, such as the state director of Common Cause, who accused him of bending to corporate campaign support, especially from drug companies. But the local business community sounded more satisfied. "Shelby is a good man," a Selma Chamber of Commerce official said in the middle of his first term.

**At Home.** Flowers' decision to try for the U.S. Senate in 1978 opened the door for Shelby's move to Washington.

After eight years in the Alabama Legislature, he was ready to move on to something. Initially he wanted the lieutenant governorship, but more than a dozen other Democrats had the same idea, and when Flowers left the 7th District open, Shelby was easily persuaded to change course and campaign for Congress.

He had already begun gathering resources for a statewide campaign, and he had a good base in the district's largest city, Tuscaloosa, where he had served as prosecuting attorney. That combination brought Shelby 48 percent of the primary vote, almost but not quite enough to win without a runoff.

Shelby's runoff opponent turned out to be Chris McNair, a black state legislator. McNair was the chairman of the Jefferson County (Birmingham) delegation in the Legislature, and the father of one of the children killed in the 1963 Birmingham church bombing. In a campaign strikingly free of the racial tensions common to Alabama politics in the past, Shelby won the nomination by a margin of about 3-2. The runoff victory was tantamount to election. Shelby easily won the seat over token Republican opposition

---

**7th District: West central — Tuscaloosa.** Population: 548,859 (12% increase since 1970). Race: White 350,837 (64%), Black 195,957 (36%), Others 2,065 (0.4%). Spanish origin: 5,044 (1%).

that fall, and had little trouble winning re-election in 1980.

During his years in the state Legislature, Shelby worked to strengthen laws against child abuse and child pornography, and was strict on the issue of government ethics. Often at odds with Gov. George C. Wallace, he introduced a resolution to ratify the Equal Rights Amendment. But it did not move far in the Legislature and Shelby rarely mentioned it in later campaigns.

**The District.** The 7th District moves southward from the outskirts of Birmingham, past the small industrial city of Bessemer and the college town of Tuscaloosa into the heart of the Alabama

black belt, one of the poorest areas in the nation.

Most of the district's population is concentrated around Birmingham — in the southern portion of Jefferson County (Bessemer and some Birmingham suburbs) and neighboring Shelby and Tuscaloosa counties. This is the part of the district where Republicans run best.

The city of Tuscaloosa has plants making rubber, chemicals and fertilizer, but is more often identified as the home of the University of Alabama. The black belt counties south of Tuscaloosa are the district's most loyally Democratic areas. In the midst of the region is Selma, the scene of violent civil rights struggles in the 1960s but now racially calm.

## Committees

**Energy and Commerce** (19th of 24 Democrats)
Energy Conservation and Power; Fossil and Synthetic Fuels; Health and the Environment; Oversight and Investigations.

**Veterans' Affairs** (11th of 17 Democrats)
Hospitals and Health Care; Housing and Memorial Affairs.

## Elections

**1980 General**

| | |
|---|---|
| Richard Shelby (D ) | 122,505 (73 %) |
| James Bacon (R ) | 43,320 (26 %) |

**1978 General**

| | |
|---|---|
| Richard Shelby (D ) | 77,742 (96 %) |
| Fulton Gray (C ) | 3,285 (4 %) |

**1978 Primary Runoff**

| | |
|---|---|
| Richard Shelby (D ) | 75,329 (59 %) |
| Chris McNair (D ) | 52,659 (41 %) |

**1978 Primary**

| | |
|---|---|
| Richard Shelby (D) | 46,706 (48%) |
| Chris McNair (D) | 36,312 (38%) |
| Goodloe Sutton (D) | 13,361 (14%) |

**District Vote For President**

| 1980 | | 1976 | | 1972 | |
|---|---|---|---|---|---|
| D | 97,518 (50 %) | D | 93,693 (56 %) | D | 47,789 (33 %) |
| R | 89,998 (46 %) | R | 70,799 (42 %) | R | 92,850 (64 %) |

## Campaign Finance

| | Receipts | Receipts from PACs | Expenditures |
|---|---|---|---|
| **1980** | | | |
| Shelby (D ) | $237,041 | $148,635 (63 %) | $126,936 |

**1978**

| | | | |
|---|---|---|---|
| Shelby (D ) | $181,573 | $34,125 (19 %) | $181,405 |

## Voting Studies

| | Presidential Support | | Party Unity | | Conservative Coalition | |
|---|---|---|---|---|---|---|
| Year | S | O | S | O | S | O |
| 1980 | 48 | 49 | 38 | 59 | 89 | 5 |
| 1979 | 36 | 63 | 35 | 64 | 97 | 3 |

S = Support          O = Opposition

## Key Votes

**96th Congress**

| | |
|---|---|
| Weaken Carter oil profits tax (1979) | N |
| Reject hospital cost control plan (1979) | Y |
| Implement Panama Canal Treaties (1979) | N |
| Establish Department of Education (1979) | Y |
| Approve Anti-busing Amendment (1979) | Y |
| Guarantee Chrysler Corp. loans (1979) | N |
| Approve military draft registration (1980) | Y |
| Aid Sandinista regime in Nicaragua (1980) | N |
| Strengthen fair housing laws (1980) | N |

**97th Congress**

| | |
|---|---|
| Reagan budget proposal (1981) | Y |

## Interest Group Ratings

| Year | ADA | ACA | AFL-CIO | CCUS |
|---|---|---|---|---|
| 1980 | 11 | 67 | 21 | 76 |
| 1979 | 5 | 68 | 40 | 83 |

# *Alaska*

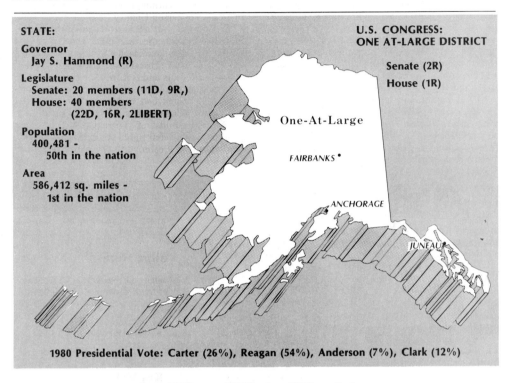

STATE:

**Governor**
Jay S. Hammond (R)

**Legislature**
Senate: 20 members (11D, 9R,)
House: 40 members
(22D, 16R, 2LIBERT)

**Population**
400,481 -
50th in the nation

**Area**
586,412 sq. miles -
1st in the nation

**U.S. CONGRESS:**
**ONE AT-LARGE DISTRICT**

Senate (2R)

House (1R)

One-At-Large

FAIRBANKS •

ANCHORAGE

JUNEAU

**1980 Presidential Vote: Carter (26%), Reagan (54%), Anderson (7%), Clark (12%)**

## . . . *At War With Washington*

Although oil dominates the economic life of Alaska these days, for most of the past decade, the dominant political issue has been land. And on that issue Alaska has fought a continuing war with Washington. The Alaska lands debate that occupied Congress in the late 1970s all but obsessed the state. The argument was resolved in 1980 with passage of a compromise bill restricting development on 104 million acres of the state's territory. But the result did not satisfy the thousands of Alaskans who resented the federal government telling them how to use their land.

The lands debate deepened the new cleavage in Alaska politics between pro-development "boomers" and environmentalist "greenies." The state's rapid population growth (32 percent in the 1970s, to a total of 400,000) has meant a vastly increased labor force looking for jobs following completion of the oil pipeline. Development would help solve some of those problems. But

Alaska still has a vocal political bloc which sees the state as the last frontier and wants that status disturbed as little as possible. At the congressional level, there was no doubt what most Alaskans wanted done. They wanted a minimum of interference from Washington in their land use decisions. Democratic Sen. Mike Gravel built much of his career out of his ferocious opposition to any Alaska lands bill, even a compromise with concessions to state interests.

Time finally ran out for Gravel in 1980, when he was beaten for renomination amid the public perception that his intransigence was doing Alaska more harm than good. Gravel's defeat, and the subsequent election of Republican Frank Murkowski to succeed him, marked a triumph for senior GOP Sen. Ted Stevens, who despised Gravel for undercutting his own efforts to broker a land bill fair to the state.

At the state level, things have been more

complicated. Republican Gov. Jay Hammond argued against federal interference along with the entire congressional delegation, but at home he has had a reputation as a man with sympathies toward environmental protection. When he won nomination to a second term in 1978, it was as the "greenie" vs. "boomer" Walter Hickel, the former governor and Nixon interior secretary. Hammond said he was for controlled growth; Hickel said that amounted to no growth at all.

The growth issue defines Alaska politics better than any partisan distinctions. The state comes closer than any in the country to having no organized parties at all. In primaries, voters can choose among Democrats for one office and among Republicans for the next. The primaries are dress rehearsals for the general election.

# A Political Tour

**Anchorage.** Established in 1916, Anchorage today has nearly 175,000 people, compared to less than 50,000 a decade ago.

The arrival of the U.S. military in World War II and the discovery of oil on the nearby Kenai Peninsula 15 years later turned Anchorage into a boom town. The continuing military presence, the fast-growth mentality of the oil industry, and an influential conservative newspaper have combined to make Anchorage a GOP stronghold.

**Fairbanks.** More than 300 miles north of Anchorage, at the end of the Alkan Highway, is Fairbanks, the traditional trading center for the hamlets of inland Alaska. In the 1970s, the city grew from 15,000 to 23,000, largely because of its role as supply center for the oil pipeline.

Republicans usually do as well in Fairbanks as in Anchorage. In 1978, Hammond trounced Hickel there in the primary and easily carried the area in November over Democrat Chancy Croft.

**Southeast: Juneau and the Panhandle.** Southeast Alaska is separated from the rest of the state by two time zones, the St. Elias Mountains and the Gulf of Alaska. Juneau, the state capital, is inaccessible by land. Many of the state legislators say they feel "claustrophobic" amid the towering mountains and ever-present clouds that loom over the city.

In 1976, Alaska voters chose to move the capital to a site near Anchorage, but as of 1980, the Legislature had not appropriated funds to relocate. Losing the capital would devastate the Panhandle's economy, which apart from government, relies on lumber products and fishing.

Government employees and a large native Indian population, give Juneau and the other Panhandle towns — Sitka, Ketchikan, Skagway — a distinctly Democratic slant. While losing statewide, both Croft in 1978 and Democratic Senate nominee Clark Gruening in 1980 carried the Panhandle.

**The Bush.** The great wilderness of Alaska, at least twice the size of Texas. With road building virtually prevented by harsh terrain and climate, the only access to the bush towns that dot the area is by air.

Native Indians and Eskimos predominate in remote Alaska, which includes the Aleutian Islands. Poverty is endemic, even with the state oil boom. Most of the native residents back Democrats. The Republican voters are mainly whites who work in the oil fields north of Fairbanks.

# Governor
# Jay S. Hammond (R)

**Born:** July 21, 1922, Troy, N.Y.
**Home:** Lake Clark, Alaska.
**Education:** Attended Penn. State U., 1940-42; U. of Alaska, B.S. 1948.
**Military Career:** Navy, 1942-46.
**Profession:** Bush pilot and guide, commercial fisherman.
**Family:** Wife, Bella; two children.
**Religion:** Protestant.
**Political Career:** Alaska House, 1959-65; manager (mayor) of Bristol Bay, 1965-67; Alaska Senate, 1967-72, president of Senate, 1971-72; Bristol Bay manager, 1973-74; elected governor 1974, 1978; term expires Dec. 1982.

# Ted Stevens (R)

**Of Anchorage — Elected 1970**
Appointed to the Senate 1968
**Born:** Nov. 18, 1923, Indianapolis, Ind.
**Education:** U. of Calif., Los Angeles, B.A. 1947;
Harvard Law School, LL.B. 1950.
**Military Career:** Army Air Corps, 1943-46.
**Profession:** Lawyer.
**Family:** Catherine Chandler; five children.
**Religion:** Episcopalian.
**Political Career:** Alaska House, 1965-68; Republican nominee for U.S. Senate, 1962; unsuccessful candidate for U.S. Senate nomination, 1968; appointed to U.S. Senate 1968.

**In Washington:** With the historic Alaska lands bill finally out of the way, Majority Whip Stevens began to seem like a changed man in 1981 — much to the relief of friends and colleagues, who had found him difficult to live with recently.

Acknowledged as one of the Senate's best parliamentary strategists, Stevens was tense and temperamental during the long dispute over how to apportion his state's land for development and environmental protection. The "new" Stevens has had more time and energy to devote to his role as the second-ranking senator in the Republican leadership, behind Majority Leader Howard H. Baker Jr. of Tennessee.

There was more to this transformation than the enactment of the lands bill. The defeat of his home-state nemesis, Democratic Sen. Mike Gravel, cheered Stevens immeasurably. And late in 1980 he remarried, two years after his first wife was killed and he was hurt in a plane crash.

The Stevens-Gravel feud was largely a question of style and tactics. Both wanted to keep the government from barring development in much of Alaska, but they disagreed vehemently on how to do so. Stevens felt the legislation was inevitable and wanted to make it as acceptable to Alaska as he could; Gravel sought to block the passage of any bill through filibusters and similar dilatory tactics, fighting with a showmanship Stevens regarded as pure demaguery.

"It's hard to do anything about Alaska with Mike Gravel in the Senate," Stevens once complained. In 1980, he took the unusual step of backing Gravel's Democratic primary opponent, who defeated him. The seat later went Republican.

It was a Gravel filibuster threat in late 1978 that prevented Senate passage of an earlier Alaska lands bill Stevens had helped craft in the Energy Committee, where he had been invited to sit for its deliberations even though he was not a member. Stevens later blamed Gravel's action for his wife's death, saying that if the bill had passed as planned, the lobbying mission that led to their ill-fated flight would never have been necessary.

In 1979, Stevens gave up the Commerce seat he had held for 10 years in order to join the Energy Committee as a voting member and draft a second version of the Alaska lands bill. Although he shifted back to Commerce in 1981, the previous move cost him his seniority and with it, an option on the Commerce chairmanship.

Through all this maneuvering, Stevens was struggling to play a central role in the leadership. For several months, while Baker was off campaigning for president, he acted as leader himself.

It has taken some time for Baker and Stevens to establish themselves as a team. Baker never served as whip himself before becoming leader in 1977, and he began his tenure by spending most of his time mastering procedure on the Senate floor, a job usually left to the whip. Later, Baker began to delegate more responsibility, but Stevens was too busy with the Alaska issue to help much. In late 1979, with Baker campaigning, Stevens was in full charge and he generally drew praise for his performance. But within a few months Baker was back, his campaign ended, and they had to sort out their roles all over again.

Baker has stuck with Stevens all the way; both men were re-elected without opposition in 1978 and at the start of the 97th Congress. They share a preference for compromise and conciliation. Stevens can be hot-tempered, which Baker rarely is, but he is no bully. "I've never even once threatened to punish a member," he has said. "We probably don't even have the power to do so if we wanted to."

Stevens has a reputation for delivering votes in a crunch. In 1979, during the fight over President Carter's standby gas rationing plan, he rounded up an estimated 8 to 10 GOP votes that proved critical for final approval. A moderate by GOP standards, he can deal effectively with Democrats as well as members of his own party.

Stevens is one of the few Republicans in the Senate to draw sizable campaign help from organized labor. He is popular with public employee unions grateful for his unflagging support for federal workers, an important constituency in Alaska. As the new chairman of the Civil Service, Post Office and General Services Subcommittee at Governmental Affairs, he is now ideally positioned to look out for those workers.

Stevens was once a federal employee himself, in the Interior Department, and he fights regularly against the imposition of "caps" on federal pay raises, saying it is unfair to make government workers suffer in a period of rampant inflation. In 1980, he argued for approval of the first increase in five years in the travel allowance for government employees. He also managed to secure one month's severance pay for Senate staffers, most of them Democrats, who lost their jobs as a result of the 1980 elections.

Stevens' concern for public employees extends to members of Congress as well. Unlike his colleagues, who generally scurry for cover whenever the subject comes up, he has not been afraid to champion the cause of congressional pay raises. In 1980, he persuaded the Appropriations Committee to lift a cap on top-level federal salaries, which would have meant 17 percent higher pay for members of Congress. But the cap was restored on the floor.

But his great achievement in this field came in 1979, when he single-handedly persuaded the Senate to accept a 5.5 percent congressional pay raise most of its members did not want to vote for. The raise was a final point at issue in a conference between the House and Senate; the House wanted the money; the Senate was against it. The issue was holding up an emergency appropriation needed to keep several federal agencies in business, and to guarantee the next round of paychecks to millions of federal employees.

When House and Senate conferees met, Stevens unilaterally conceded on behalf of the Senate, even though a show of hands had just revealed four out of five Senate conferees opposed to the raise. Then he took the deal to the floor, where it was promptly rejected, 62-26. Within an hour, Stevens turned it around. "If you do not want your pay raise now," he told the Senate, "vote on whether or not you want your constituents to get paid." The second time, twisting every arm he could find in the chamber, Stevens got the compromise approved, 44-42.

That argument was complicated by a second House-Senate dispute, over abortion. The House wanted to block all federal abortion funding except to save the life of the mother. The Senate did not. Over the years, Stevens has tried, usually without success, to prevent strict House anti-abortion language from becoming law. Abortion, he said, is a question for a woman and her doctor, not for "99 middle-aged men in the Senate."

Stevens has never had much use for parts of the tough ethics code the Senate adopted in 1977. In 1979, he joined New York Democrat Daniel P. Moynihan in a lightning move, made with just six senators on the floor, to postpone for four years the code's limit on outside earnings. The coup succeeded, and was later confirmed by a roll-call vote.

"Service in the Senate," Stevens said, "should not require a sacrifice."

Regardless of how they feel about the ethics code, few senators like to buck the chamber's Ethics Committee. Stevens, again, is an exception. When the committee recommended in 1979 that veteran Georgia Democrat Herman E. Talmadge be denounced for financial misconduct, Stevens was one of just 15 senators opposing the move on the floor.

In the 97th Congress, much of Stevens' legislative attention has been focused on Appropriations, where he is chairman of the Defense Subcommittee and second senior Republican on the full committee.

In his subcommittee, Stevens generally supports President Reagan's defense increases but he has been skeptical of the mobile basing modes proposed for the MX missile. He lost a battle in 1981 over plans to begin modernizing the battleship *New Jersey*, now in mothballs. He said the $90 million the House wanted to spend on the project was a waste of money. But conferees voted to spend it.

**At Home:** Stevens' careful defense of Alaska interests has made him invulnerable politically. Although he has not had his way on every issue, he has always seemed to be in the right spot politically — stubborn but pragmatic.

Stevens, who had been majority leader in the Alaska House, made it to Washington by appointment when Democratic Sen. E. L. Bartlett died in 1968. He owed his promotion to Walter J. Hickel, the state's Republican governor. Only months before, Stevens had campaigned for the Senate on his own and lost the Republican primary. Six years earlier, he had been nominated and drawn only 41 percent of the vote.

Once in Washington, however, Stevens began digging in politically. In the 1970 contest to fill the final two years of Bartlett's term, he won with almost 60 percent of the vote while Republicans were losing the statehouse. In that campaign, against liberal Democrat Wendell P. Kay, Stevens favored greater oil and mineral development; Kay was a firm conservationist.

Running for a full term in 1972, Stevens crushed Democrat Gene Guess, the Alaska House Speaker, whom he linked to presidential nominee George McGovern. Stevens also appealed to Alas-

ka's hunters by labeling Guess as pro-gun control.

By 1978 Stevens had been elected to the Senate Republican leadership and no prominent Democrat even considered a serious campaign against him. An electrical contractor and an economics professor fought for the Democratic nomination, and the contractor, who got it, managed to capture less than a quarter of the vote.

## Committees

**Majority Whip**

**Appropriations** (2nd of 15 Republicans)
Defense, chairman; Interior; Labor, Health and Human Services, Education; Legislative Branch; State, Justice, Commerce, and the Judiciary.

**Commerce, Science and Transportation** (8th of 9 Republicans)
Aviation; Communications; Merchant Marine.

**Governmental Affairs** (3rd of 9 Republicans)
Civil Service, Post Office, and General Services, chairman; Congressional Operations and Oversight; Oversight of Government Management.

## Elections

**1978 General**

| | |
|---|---|
| Ted Stevens (R ) | 92,783 (76 %) |
| Donald Hobbs (D ) | 29,574 (24 %) |

**Previous Winning Percentages**

1972 (77 %)    1970* (60 %)
* *Special election. Stevens was appointed in 1968 to fill the vacancy caused by the death of Sen. E. L. Bartlett. The 1970 election was to fill the remainder of Bartlett's term.*

## Campaign Finance

| | Receipts | Receipts from PACs | Expenditures |
|---|---|---|---|
| **1978** | | | |
| Stevens (R ) | $366,895 | $170,724 (47 %) | $346,837 |
| Hobbs (D ) | $15,527 | $100 (1 %) | $21,234 |

## Voting Studies

| | Presidential Support | | Party Unity | | Conservative Coalition | |
|---|---|---|---|---|---|---|
| Year | S | O | S | O | S | O |
| 1980 | 38 | 47 | 68 | 21 | 75 | 14 |

| | | | | | | |
|---|---|---|---|---|---|---|
| 1979 | 46 | 42 | 60 | 28 | 67 | 21 |
| 1978 | 28 | 64 | 71 | 20 | 68 | 21 |
| 1977 | 52 | 38 | 65 | 22 | 79 | 15 |
| 1976 | 57 | 25 | 64 | 25 | 74 | 14 |
| 1975 | 71 | 17 | 57 | 27 | 55 | 31 |
| 1974 (Ford) | 65 | 26 | | | | |
| 1974 | 43 | 47 | 44 | 50 | 49 | 48 |
| 1973 | 57 | 34 | 62 | 30 | 71 | 22 |
| 1972 | 43 | 43 | 38 | 51 | 36 | 51 |
| 1971 | 60 | 24 | 50 | 38 | 56 | 33 |
| 1970 | 58 | 20 | 38 | 36 | 36 | 31 |
| 1969 | 67 | 15 | 55 | 18 | 59 | 14 |

S = Support          O = Opposition

## Key Votes

**96th Congress**

| | |
|---|---|
| Maintain relations with Taiwan (1979) | Y |
| Reduce synthetic fuel development funds (1979) | X |
| Impose nuclear plant moratorium (1979) | N |
| Kill stronger windfall profits tax (1979) | Y |
| Guarantee Chrysler Corp. loans (1979) | Y |
| Approve military draft registration (1980) | Y |
| End Revenue Sharing to the states (1980) | Y |
| Block Justice Dept. busing suits (1980) | Y |

**97th Congress**

| | |
|---|---|
| Restore urban program funding cuts (1981) | N |

## Interest Group Ratings

| Year | ADA | ACA | AFL-CIO | CCUS-1 | CCUS-2 |
|---|---|---|---|---|---|
| 1980 | 39 | 71 | 50 | 86 | |
| 1979 | 21 | 43 | 35 | 78 | 86 |
| 1978 | 10 | 61 | 33 | 65 | |
| 1977 | 20 | 50 | 47 | 72 | |
| 1976 | 25 | 45 | 36 | 44 | |
| 1975 | 33 | 38 | 70 | 53 | |
| 1974 | 52 | 21 | 91 | 30 | |
| 1973 | 15 | 57 | 60 | 44 | |
| 1972 | 35 | 38 | 86 | 11 | |
| 1971 | 48 | 36 | 60 | - | |
| 1970 | 25 | 19 | 83 | 29 | |
| 1969 | 28 | 17 | 56 | | |

# Frank H. Murkowski (R)

**Of Fairbanks — Elected 1980**

**Born:** March 28, 1933, Seattle, Wash.
**Education:** Seattle U., B.A. 1955.
**Military Career:** Coast Guard, 1955-56.
**Profession:** Banker.
**Family:** Wife, Nancy Gore; six children.
**Religion:** Roman Catholic.
**Political Career:** State commissioner of economic development, 1967-70; unsuccessful Republican nominee for U.S. House, 1970.

**The Member:** With the exception of three years in state government and a yearlong campaign for the House, Murkowski has spent all his adult life in banking. His father was a banker as well.

Ten years ago, Murkowski won a Republican primary for Alaska's at-large House seat, defeating a member of the John Birch Society. But he lost the general election. That experience left Murkowski with a desire to try again. After serving for nine years as president of the Alaska National Bank of the North, at Fairbanks, he quit banking and announced for the Senate.

Murkowski, who moved to Alaska while in high school, says he is a "conservationist," but not an "environmentalist or a preservationist." Those last two, pejoratives to many Alaskans, he reserved for the man he beat in the 1980 general election, Democrat Clark S. Gruening.

Gruening, the grandson of the late Sen. Ernest Gruening, ousted incumbent Democrat Mike Gravel in an acrimonious primary that diverted publicity from the GOP primary, which Murkowski won with ease. With Gravel removed as the central campaign issue, Murkowski was able to focus attention in the fall on Gruening's record in the state Legislature. Aided by a strong Reagan vote, Murkowski's anti-Gruening campaign was enough to give him a solid 10-point victory.

In the Senate, Murkowski has specialized in energy issues, and especially in the future of the Strategic Petroleum Reserve. He wants to stock the reserve with Alaskan royalty oil — the oil Alaska receives from companies that drill there.

Although President Reagan requested $3.8 billion for the SPR in fiscal 1982, some in the administration have suggested cutting SPR funds in order to pressure the government into finding a private financing mechanism for the reserve. Murkowski thinks the reserve is needed for national security, and he opposes cuts in the pro-

gram. "If we can afford to add $30 billion for the defense budget," he says, "we can afford $3.8 billion for the Strategic Petroleum Reserve."

## Committees

**Energy and Natural Resources** (8th of 11 Republicans)
Water and Power, chairman; Energy and Mineral Resources; Public Lands and Reserved Water.

**Environment and Public Works** (9th of 9 Republicans)
Regional and Community Development, chairman; Toxic Substances and Environmental Oversight; Water Resources.

**Veterans' Affairs** (6th of 7 Republicans)

## Elections

**1980 General**

| | |
|---|---|
| Frank Murkowski (R) | 84,159 (54%) |
| Clark Gruening (D) | 72,007 (46%) |

**1980 Primary**

| | |
|---|---|
| Frank Murkowski (R) | 16,292 (59%) |
| Arthur Kennedy (R) | 5,527 (20%) |
| Morris Thompson (R) | 3,635 (13%) |

## Campaign Finance

| | Receipts | Receipts from PACs | Expenditures |
|---|---|---|---|
| **1980** | | | |
| Murkowski (R) | $624,194 | 294,148 (47%) | $472,704 |
| Gruening (D) | $512,411 | $2,218 (0.4%) | $507,445 |

## Key Votes

**97th Congress**

| | |
|---|---|
| Restore urban program funding cuts (1981) | N |

# AL Don Young (R)

**Of Fort Yukon — Elected in 1973**

**Born:** June 9, 1933, Meridian, Calif.
**Education:** Chico State College, Calif., B.A. 1958.
**Profession:** Teacher, riverboat captain.
**Family:** Wife, Lula Fredson; two children.
**Religion:** Episcopalian.
**Political Career:** Fort Yukon City Council, 1960-64; mayor of Fort Yukon, 1964-68; Alaska House, 1967-71; Alaska Senate, 1971-73; unsuccessful Republican nominee for U.S. House, 1972.

**In Washington:** Being Alaska's only representative in the House demands a certain single-mindedness, and Young has more than passed that test in the years since he came to Washington to replace Nick Begich, killed in an airplane crash in 1972.

The single thing Young has had on his mind is defending his state from what he sees as a predatory federal government. In the marathon debate over apportionment of Alaska's lands, and in dozens of debates over bills less publicized, Young has demanded bluntly and emotionally that Washington leave his state alone.

He is a former riverboat captain, and often he has sounded like one, an individualist willing to go it alone and resentful of the attitude of those who want to interfere. His sentences do not always parse, but when he gets worked up about something, he may be the most articulate inarticulate man in Congress.

"People can sit on this floor," he said in May of 1979, "and say it is all right to take what is already the people's of Alaska. That is immoral."

Young was complaining that day about the Alaska lands bill, reserving portions of the state's territory as wilderness and closing them to development. Young and other pro-development forces agreed some of Alaska should be wilderness; what they objected to was the plan brought to the House floor by Interior Chairman Morris K. Udall of Arizona, setting aside 67 million acres of Alaska as wilderness. Young was reluctantly backing an alternative version with 53 million acres of wilderness, and allowing energy exploration in several mineral-rich parts of the state.

To Young, the Udall proposal was not just interference. It was an outrageous violation of his state's rights by a federal government thousands of miles away. When Udall won easily, Young told

his colleagues angrily that "none of you has to go home to unemployment created by national legislation." Then he broke down in tears.

For Young, the vote that day represented an unsuccessful climax to the most important debate of his House career. When the Alaska lands bill first came up in an Interior subcommittee in 1978, he offered 82 amendments. Sixty six were accepted, eight were defeated and eight were withdrawn. By the end he had succeeded in whittling down the wilderness acreage considerably. But no Alaska bill became law that year, and at the end of 1978 President Carter set aside 50 million acres of the state as wilderness, placing environmentalists in the controlling position and forcing Young and the Alaskans to accept what they could get.

The ultimate Alaska lands bill, as enacted in 1980, had been shifted in a developmental direction by the Senate. But it still left Young feeling angry and outnumbered.

Before the Alaska lands issue came to dominate his time in the House, Young worked on oil pipeline legislation and on fishing rights as a member of the Interior and Merchant Marine committees. In 1981, with the lands issue decided, he spent much of his effort on oil spill cleanup legislation. As a bill moved through the Merchant Marine Subcommittee, Young introduced several amendments reducing the liability of the oil industry.

**At Home:** A native of California, Young

---

**At-Large District: Entire State.** Population: 400,481 (32$^c_c$ increase since 1970). Race: White 308,455 (77$^c_c$), Black 13,619 (3$^c_c$), Indian 64,047 (16$^c_c$), Others 14,360 (4$^c_c$). Spanish origin: 9,497 (2$^c_c$).

moved to Alaska to teach and then went native. He became a licensed riverboat captain and a member of the Dog Mushers Association.

He also went into politics, winning election to the Alaska House in 1966 and the state Senate in 1970. In 1972, he decided to challenge Begich, a popular freshman Democratic congressman. It was an uphill battle, with Begich a strong and popular campaigner. But in October, a plane carrying Begich and House Majority Leader Hale Boggs from Anchorage to Juneau disappeared in flight. Begich was re-elected over Young by almost 12,000 votes, but his body was never found, and his seat was declared vacant in December.

A special election was held early in 1973, and Young easily won the Republican nomination. Democrats selected Emil Notti, their former state chairman, who was the son of an Italian-born gold miner and an Athabascan Indian woman. The contest turned out to be close, with Notti running strongly in southeastern Alaska and in the bush country. But Young, who by then had been campaigning for almost a year, pulled out his winning margins in the Anchorage and Fairbanks areas. Overall, he beat Notti by 2.8 percentage points. Since then, he has been re-elected easily, although an aggressive challenger came within 13,000 votes in 1978.

## Committees

**Interior and Insular Affairs** (3rd of 17 Republicans)
Mines and Mining; Public Lands and National Parks.

**Merchant Marine and Fisheries** (5th of 15 Republicans)
Coast Guard and Navigation; Fisheries and Wildlife Conservation and the Environment; Merchant Marine.

## Elections

**1980 General**

| | |
|---|---|
| Don Young (R) | 114,089 (74%) |
| Kevin Parnell (D) | 39,922 (26%) |

**1978 General**

| | |
|---|---|
| Don Young (R) | 68,811 (55%) |
| Patrick Rodey (D) | 55,176 (44%) |

**Previous Winning Percentages**

1976 (71%)    1974 (54%)    1973* (51%)
*Special Election*

**District Vote For President**

| | 1980† | | 1976 | | 1972 |
|---|---|---|---|---|---|
| D | 41,228 (26%) | D | 44,058 (36%) | D | 32,967 (35%) |
| R | 85,364 (55%) | R | 71,555 (58%) | R | 55,349 (58%) |
| I | 10,988 (7%) | | | | |

† *In addition, Ed Clark, the Libertarian Party candidate, received 18,389 votes, 12% of the total.*

## Campaign Finance

| | Receipts | Receipts from PACs | Expenditures |
|---|---|---|---|
| **1980** | | | |
| Young (R) | $289,259 | $57,155 (20%) | $285,518 |
| Parnell (D) | $55,037 | — (0%) | $51,065 |
| **1978** | | | |
| Young (R) | $259,897 | $74,902 (29%) | $270,359 |
| Rodey (D) | $150,279 | $26,016 (17%) | $149,211 |

## Voting Studies

| | Presidential Support | | Party Unity | | Conservative Coalition | |
|---|---|---|---|---|---|---|
| Year | S | O | S | O | S | O |
| 1980 | 26 | 43 | 53 | 12 | 55 | 5 |
| 1979 | 28 | 49 | 59 | 17 | 65 | 5 |
| 1978 | 13 | 44 | 50 | 16 | 58 | 8 |
| 1977 | 39 | 37 | 59 | 20 | 72 | 10 |
| 1976 | 49 | 27 | 54 | 17 | 62 | 8 |
| 1975 | 49 | 34 | 67 | 19 | 79 | 7 |
| 1974 (Ford) | 33 | 35 | | | | |
| 1974 | 72 | 19 | 59 | 18 | 64 | 16 |
| 1973 | 57 | 39† | 72 | 23† | 8 | 15† |

S = Support          O = Opposition
† *Not eligible for all recorded votes.*

## Key Votes

**96th Congress**

| | |
|---|---|
| Weaken Carter oil profits tax (1979) | Y |
| Reject hospital cost control plan (1979) | ? |
| Implement Panama Canal Treaties (1979) | N |
| Establish Department of Education (1979) | Y |
| Approve Anti-busing Amendment (1979) | N |
| Guarantee Chrysler Corp. loans (1979) | Y |
| Approve military draft registration (1980) | N |
| Aid Sandinista regime in Nicaragua (1980) | N |
| Strengthen fair housing laws (1980) | N |

**97th Congress**

| | |
|---|---|
| Reagan budget proposal (1981) | Y |

## Interest Group Ratings

| Year | ADA | ACA | AFL-CIO | CCUS |
|---|---|---|---|---|
| 1980 | 22 | 70 | 31 | 67 |
| 1979 | 11 | 71 | 22 | 93 |
| 1978 | 5 | 73 | 53 | 54 |
| 1977 | 5 | 64 | 55 | 56 |
| 1976 | 0 | 75 | 53 | 75 |
| 1975 | 5 | 71 | 19 | 88 |
| 1974 | 9 | 75 | 30 | 75 |
| 1973 | 12 | 74 | 64 | 64 |

# Arizona

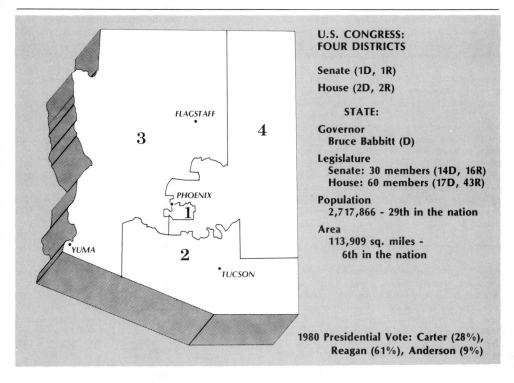

**U.S. CONGRESS:
FOUR DISTRICTS**

Senate (1D, 1R)

House (2D, 2R)

**STATE:**

Governor
Bruce Babbitt (D)

Legislature
Senate: 30 members (14D, 16R)
House: 60 members (17D, 43R)

Population
2,717,866 - 29th in the nation

Area
113,909 sq. miles -
6th in the nation

1980 Presidential Vote: Carter (28%),
Reagan (61%), Anderson (9%)

## ... A Generation in the Sun

As its desert bloomed green from irrigation in the years after World War II, Arizona led the way in turning the Southwest from rural and Democratic to developed and Republican. Retirees lured by Arizona's climate and engineers attracted by high-technology industries — both Republican by habit — made Arizona the prototypical Sun Belt state. Some of the changes occurring now in Deep South states took place in Arizona a generation ago.

On the presidential level, the state has not voted Democratic since 1948. It began going Republican in statewide contests in 1950, when Howard Pyle won election as governor in a campaign masterminded by a young Phoenix city councilman, Barry Goldwater. Two years later, Goldwater was elected to the Senate.

That contest marked the end of traditional dominance by "pinto Democrats" — rural conservatives whose base was the malapportioned state Legislature. From 1950 on, Phoenix became the single most important factor in state elections, and Republicans nearly always carried it. Since 1950, the GOP has won the governorship eight out of 13 times — although a Democrat Bruce Babbitt, has it now. They have won seven of 11 contests for the Senate.

Goldwater's hard-line foreign policy and distrust of big government found a receptive audience in the newcomers. Even his hobby, piloting airplanes, fits in with the independent-minded, technologically-oriented Arizona. Goldwater, Pyle and their generation built something new in a land grown used to stodgy, sometimes corrupt, government.

It took Democrats nearly 20 years to recover from the Republican advances. By 1970, the governorship, both U.S. Senate seats and two of three U.S. House seats were in Republican hands. Rep. Morris K. Udall of Tucson was the only major

Democratic officeholder in the state. Since then, however, a new generation of Democrats has emerged as a competitive force in state politics.

Raul H. Castro was elected governor in 1974, a Democrat and the first Hispanic chief executive in Arizona history. Bruce Babbitt built on his reputation as an anti-corruption attorney general to retain the governorship for the Democrats four years later. In 1976, bitter Republican feuding allowed a Democrat, Dennis DeConcini, to take a Senate seat. And in 1980, Goldwater himself came within 10,000 votes of losing re-election to a wealthy apartment developer, Bill Schulz.

As elsewhere in the West, water holds an almost sacred place on the Arizona agenda. It made possible the growth that transformed the state. All major statewide political candidates back the Central Arizona Project, the major piece of uncompleted irrigation work. If Arizona harbors any of the ambivalence about growth now associated with Colorado and other Mountain states, this has not shown up in recent election returns. Development still has a good reputation in Arizona.

But development has brought with it an organized crime problem. Periodically, amid the real estate speculation, land fraud scandals surface. When Joe Bonanno, the reputed underworld boss, moved to Arizona from New York in the 1960s, the state began to develop a reputation it did not particularly want. Following the 1976 bombing murder of *Arizona Republic* investigative reporter Don Bolles, a team of journalists identified what they saw as an extensive Mafia web operating in the state.

# A Political Tour

**Phoenix and Maricopa County.** In 1911, when Theodore Roosevelt dedicated a dam on the Salt River, he began the transformation of the Arizona desert into a citadel of Sun Belt capitalism.

Sitting in the Valley of the Sun, Phoenix today is a thicket of high-rise office buildings and palm-lined streets. Motorola, the electronics firm, is the largest employer in the area and provides a symbol of its scientific bent.

Most of the time, Republicans capture the city, doing best in the prosperous east side. The still-developing west side — Interstate 10, its connecting link to downtown, has not been completed yet — also displays Republican inclinations.

The south side of Phoenix is the Democratic part of the city and also the poorest. Blacks (5 percent of the Phoenix population) and Hispanics (15 percent) live there, but have yet to organize for maximum political strength.

Outside the city limits, Republicans have a firm hold on almost everything. Wealthy Scottsdale and Paradise Valley, to the east of Phoenix, are predictably Republican. The well-to-do retirement community of Sun City turns out close to 90 percent of its voters, most of whom normally pull the GOP lever.

With its concentration of electronics plants, the one-time Mormon farming hamlet of Mesa nearly tripled in population in the last decade. Republicans also carry nearby Chandler, another electronics center.

The only exceptions to the Republican domination of the county are in Tempe, home of Arizona State University, which is marginal politically, and the Democratic strongholds of Buckeye, an old-time farming community, and the Gila Bend Indian Reservation.

Casting more than half the state's vote, Maricopa County often determines how Arizona will go. Internal feuding in the county GOP gave Maricopa — and the state — to DeConcini in 1976. Four years later, Goldwater survived only because of his 50,000-vote plurality in the county.

**Tucson and Pima County.** Hugging the Mexican border and holding a fifth of the state's electorate, Pima County ranks second in electoral influence. It is more ethnically diverse than Maricopa County and much more Democratic.

With its Spanish adobe architecture and large Hispanic population (25 percent), Tucson has stronger ties to Mexico than does Phoenix. There are as many liberal Democrats as conservative "pinto" Democrats. The site of the University of Arizona, Tucson has an academic vote that sometimes helps Democratic candidates.

Of the 10 Arizona counties that voted against favorite son Goldwater in the 1964 presidential election, Pima was the only one of any size. The rest were rural counties, and the state as a whole went Republican that year.

Since then, however, Pima has begun to favor the GOP on the national level — signaling a change in the county's demographics. The same influx of retirees and technical people seen earlier in Phoenix has gradually come to Tucson. Retired military personnel from Davis-Monthan Air Force Base help feed the Republican vote.

Pima grew 51 percent between 1970 and 1980, causing problems for Udall, who continually has to woo new blocs of voters, and other Democratic incumbents. A 1980 survey by Udall's office found that one in four of his district's residents had been there five years or less.

The foothills of the scenic Santa Catalina Mountains, in the northern section of Tucson, are dotted with the homes of the wealthy and furnish Republican votes. The growing east side of the city also is turning Republican.

Outside Tucson, the San Xavier and Papago Indian reservations vote for the Democrats. Ajo, a copper mining center, has a Democratic background, too. But the large retirement community of Green Valley has become a major force for the Republicans.

**Desert.** Forming an upside-down U around the Maricopa-Pima growth core, the desert counties are an amalgam of ranchers, Indians, miners and, of late, retirees. Largely, this remains a "pinto" Democratic region, although signs of Republican inroads are appearing.

Yuma County, in the state's southwestern corner, is an old pinto Democratic stronghold that now favors Republicans on the presidential level. The city of Yuma, famous as America's hottest city, has a large Mexican-American population and a Democratic heritage.

In Mohave County, occupying the northwestern corner of the state, tension exists among Indians, pinto Democrats in Kingman, and Republican retirees in Lake Havasu City. The county leans Democratic in national and statewide contests.

Coconino County contains a Republican bastion, "the Arizona Strip" — a Mormon region on the Utah border. Sedona, in the south of the county, is filled with retirees and Republicans. Flagstaff, the county's largest city, has old-time Democratic loyalties.

The Democrats' most faithful county happens to have the smallest population. It is agricultural Greenlee, bordering New Mexico. It was the only Arizona county Carter carried in 1980.

More typical pinto Democratic counties — typical because they at times defect to the Republicans — are Pinal, Gila and Graham, where copper mining takes place.

Heavily Hispanic (74 percent) Santa Cruz County, next to Mexico, and the Old West county of Cochise (home of Tombstone, "the town too tough to die") go Democratic. In Navajo and Apache counties the Navajo and Hopi Indian tribes make up almost half the population. Of the two, the Navajos are the more Democratic tribe.

## Redrawing the Lines

Arizona today has nearly a million more people than it did in 1970, and will gain a fifth House district as a result. The Republicans in control of the state Legislature are trying to make certain their party gets the new district, which they may build around a group of southern counties, including some pinto Democrat areas.

Growing 55 percent during the past decade, Maricopa County now has a population of 1,508,030 — enough for nearly three full districts.

Pima County, with 531,263 people, is almost populous enough to constitute its own district, but in early redistricting discussions, some GOP legislators talked about trying to unseat Democrat Udall by splitting up his Pima County home base.

The Legislature's plan will meet resistance unless it satisfies Democratic Gov. Babbitt. Though Republicans dominate the state House, they have only a narrow margin in the Senate and probably could not override his veto.

## Governor
## Bruce Babbitt (D)

**Born:** June 27, 1938, Los Angeles, Calif.
**Home:** Phoenix, Ariz.
**Education:** U. of Notre Dame, B.A. 1960; U. of Newcastle, England, M.A. 1962; Harvard Law School, LL.B. 1965.
**Profession:** Lawyer.
**Family:** Wife, Hattie; two children.
**Religion:** Roman Catholic.
**Political Career:** Arizona attorney general, 1975-78; assumed governorship March 1978, upon death of Gov. Wesley Bolin; elected governor 1978; term expires Jan. 1983.

# Barry Goldwater (R)

**Of Scottsdale — Elected 1952**
Did not serve 1965-1969.

**Born:** Jan. 1, 1909, Phoenix, Ariz.
**Education:** Attended U. of Ariz., 1928.
**Military Career:** Army Reserve and Air Force
Reserve, 1930-67; Army Air Corps, 1941-45.
**Family:** Wife, Margaret Johnson; four children.
**Religion:** Episcopalian.
**Political Career:** Phoenix City Council, 1949-
52; Republican nominee for president, 1964.

**In Washington:** The conservative prophet who led Ronald Reagan into politics has been relegated to the periphery of the Reagan regime.

Reagan acknowledges his personal and philosophical debt to the Arizona Republican, but has shown little inclination to include him in the inner circle. And Goldwater, whose influence has always been greater outside the Senate than within it, has seen younger Republicans seize legislative control under a GOP majority.

He is not totally without power, of course; he is chairman of the Intelligence Committee, the Tactical Warfare Subcommittee of Armed Services and the Communications Subcommittee of Commerce.

But Goldwater is not inclined to activism in these assignments, even though they fit his personal interests. He has little appetite for the daily drudgery of Senate business, and he genuinely believes in reducing government.

He announced on taking over the Communications Subcommittee that his goal would be to get the bureaucracy out of broadcasting. What broadcasters need, he said, "is more freedom — and that's what I want to give them."

Goldwater's main job as Intelligence chairman is congressional oversight of U.S. intelligence activities, a type of work he has never even believed in. "There are many bits of information I would just as soon not know," he said once. He has expressed the wish that U.S. intelligence agencies enjoyed the sort of secrecy which shields their Soviet counterparts.

Whatever Goldwater chooses to do with his chairmanships, it is all but certain he will attract national attention the way he has for years — with his startling and sometimes profane candor. There is hardly an interest group or a colleague whom he has not offended at some point. He offended much of the Republican right with his criticisms of President Nixon during the Water-

gate era, especially his characterization of the affair at a relatively early stage as "one of the most scandalous and stupid in the history of the country." The unfolding events left Goldwater looking rather statesmanlike, however, especially after he played a critical role in convincing the president he stood no chance of winning a Senate trial if impeached by the House.

Unlike most of his colleagues, Goldwater expresses some of his bluntest opinions right on the Senate floor, as he did one day in 1980, when the Senate continued voting past midnight on a Thursday so it could take Friday off. "I am getting a little sick and tired of having to jam the work of this Senate into three days," he complained, "to take care of the senators who are running for re-election."

Roll-call votes at inconvenient times have not usually been a big problem for Goldwater; he is willing to skip them. He missed 42 percent of the votes in 1980, which was a campaign year for him, and has had similar percentages of absenteeism in some non-election years. Part of it has been unavoidable; Goldwater has had to have frequent treatment over the years for chronic bone ailments. But part of it reflects his disdain for the tedious side of Senate life.

Goldwater's colleagues in the Senate generally enjoy his crusty humor, even if he has used it against them or their ideas at times in the past. But such affection has evolved slowly. At the time of his 1964 presidential bid, he was regarded with considerable suspicion by his more liberal colleagues in both parties.

Goldwater denies that he has mellowed, but admits that he has become "a little bit more forgiving. As you grow older I think you come to understand that there are more than just two sides to a question."

Indeed, Goldwater is now viewed as an "establishment" Republican by many on the right. There were early complaints about his support for President Nixon's opening to the People's Republic of China, and they grew louder when he decided to back President Gerald Ford in the primary battles against Reagan in 1976.

That undercurrent of skepticism on the far right did not disappear when Goldwater voted against the Panama Canal transfer treaties in 1978, in part because he had once praised Ford for seeking to negotiate the treaties. Nor was it erased by his lawsuit challenging President Carter's right to abrogate unilaterally the mutual defense treaty between the United States and Taiwan.

But it seemed all but gone in the summer of 1980, when Reagan acknowledged him as a man who had been ahead of his time, and the Republican National Convention hailed him as a hero in Detroit.

In fact, Goldwater has changed very little since his presidential aspirations of 1964 ended in a landslide defeat of historic proportions. When he talks about giving the Pentagon the tools it needs to carry on its work, or about the need to get the federal government out of the affairs of small business, it is the same Goldwater talking, and it generates the same response it evoked from conservatives 20 years ago.

"I have little interest in streamlining government or in making it more efficient," he wrote in 1960, "for I mean to reduce its size. . . . My aim is not to pass laws, but to repeal them." That could stand as a summary of Goldwater's congressional career.

**At Home:** There is still a soft spot in Arizona hearts for Goldwater, but it has grown faint with time and his own inattention. Overconfidence and a wealthy Democratic challenger nearly unseated him in 1980 as conservative Republicans were winning easily all around him.

Actually, Goldwater's 49-48 escape in 1980 was only a modest departure from form. Legend though he may be, he has never drawn as much as 60 percent of the vote in a re-election campaign. Goldwater's defenders like to attribute that to a series of pretty good Democratic opponents in a state that still has a nominal Democratic registration advantage. But it also represents fallout from his national image — since Goldwater became a renowned symbol of national conservatism, Arizona has never seemed as important to him as national politics. After his narrow escape in 1980, he answered a question about why he had done so poorly by saying "I don't know, and I don't

particularly care."

Goldwater's 1968 challenger had labeled him a "part-time senator" who used the Senate only as a "forum for his political philosophy." In 1980, Democrat Bill Schulz remodeled that issue by criticizing him for not appearing in rural parts of the state and for missing more than 30 percent of the votes during the preceding 95th Congress. Goldwater pointed out that he had undergone surgery for his hip ailment.

Arizona has grown and changed dramatically since Goldwater got his political start by winning election to the Phoenix City Council in 1949. He was already well-known then as manager of his family's department store, and he was a charter member of a group of young conservatives that took the city government over from its sleepy Democratic caretakers in the postwar years. He made his first mark statewide in 1950 by managing a successful Republican campaign for governor.

Two years later, as Eisenhower was taking Arizona into the Republican presidential column for the first time since 1928, Goldwater narrowly defeated Senate Majority Leader Ernest W. McFarland, castigating the Truman administration over the Korean War. In their rematch six years later, Goldwater defeated McFarland by a more comfortable margin.

Goldwater had to leave the Senate to run for president in 1964, because his Senate term expired that year. But he made a successful comeback in 1968, defeating Roy Elson, the quietly influential aide to retiring Democratic Sen. Carl Hayden, Senate Appropriations chairman. In 1974, Goldwater survived the Watergate election with relative comfort against Jonathan Marshall, a newspaper publisher at least a shade more liberal than most of the state's voters.

Goldwater had hinted in 1974 that he would retire after one more term, but GOP leaders prevailed on him to run again in 1980. They were leery of a divisive primary struggle that might hand his seat to the Democrats. Goldwater turned out to be a surprisingly weak candidate.

Schulz, a millionaire developer, used a slogan of "Energy for the 80s," and asked voters when they had seen Goldwater last. He spent freely to publicize his views, favorable to abortion and the Equal Rights Amendment but conservative on fiscal and defense policy. Other Democrats found it convenient to kill Goldwater with kindness, implying that he had served the state well and was entitled to the retirement he seemed to want. It came within 10,000 votes of working.

## Committees

**Armed Services** (3rd of 9 Republicans)
Tactical Warfare, chairman; Preparedness; Strategic and Theater Nuclear Forces.

**Commerce, Science and Transportation** (2nd of 9 Republicans)
Communications, chairman; Aviation; Science, Technology, and Space.

**Select Indian Affairs** (2nd of 4 Republicans)

**Select Intelligence** (Chairman)

## Elections

**1980 General**

| | |
|---|---|
| Barry Goldwater (R) | 432,371 (49%) |
| Bill Schulz (D) | 422,972 (48%) |

**Previous Winning Percentages**

| | | | |
|---|---|---|---|
| 1974 (58%) | 1968 (57%) | 1958 (56%) | 1952 (51%) |

## Campaign Finance

| | Receipts | Receipts from PACs | Expenditures |
|---|---|---|---|
| 1980 | | | |
| Goldwater (R) | $989,055 | $288,432 (29%) | $949,992 |
| Schulz (D) | $2,084,069 | $280 (.01%) | $2,073,232 |

## Voting Studies

| | Presidential Support | | Party Unity | | Conservative Coalition | |
|---|---|---|---|---|---|---|
| Year | S | O | S | O | S | O |
| 1980 | 32 | 41 | 45 | 11 | 62 | 4 |
| 1979 | 24 | 51† | 69 | 7† | 76 | 4† |
| 1978 | 14 | 62 | 74 | 4 | 75 | 8 |
| 1977 | 33 | 41 | 64 | 5 | 71 | 3 |
| 1976 | 72 | 2 | 44 | 2 | 40 | 2 |
| 1975 | 61 | 10 | 73 | 2 | 80 | 1 |
| 1974 (Ford) | 41 | 25 | | | | |
| 1974 | 61 | 27 | 71 | 10 | 75 | 2 |
| 1973 | 45 | 9 | 54 | 2 | 60 | 1 |

| | | | | | | |
|---|---|---|---|---|---|---|
| 1972 | 59 | 9 | 47 | 3 | 53 | 2 |
| 1971 | 55 | 10 | 58 | 3 | 63 | 3 |
| 1970 | 29 | 9 | 40 | 7 | 45 | 7 |
| 1969 | 39 | 19 | 47 | 2 | 45 | 1 |
| 1964* | 10 | 23 | 25 | 1 | 37 | 2 |
| 1963 | 14 | 55 | 81 | 0 | 81 | 0 |
| 1962 | 21 | 50 | 60 | 1 | 68 | 3 |
| 1961 | 15 | 52 | 72 | 1 | 57 | 3 |

† Not eligible for all recorded votes.
S = Support     O = Opposition
*Goldwater did not run for re-election in 1964 because of his run for the U.S. Presidency.

## Key Votes

**96th Congress**

| | |
|---|---|
| Maintain relations with Taiwan (1979) | Y |
| Reduce synthetic fuel development funds (1979) | Y |
| Impose nuclear plant moratorium (1979) | N |
| Kill stronger windfall profits tax (1979) | Y |
| Guarantee Chrysler Corp. loans (1979) | - |
| Approve military draft registration (1980) | Y |
| End Revenue Sharing to the states (1980) | Y |
| Block Justice Dept. busing suits (1980) | ? |

**97th Congress**

| | |
|---|---|
| Restore urban program funding cuts (1981) | N |

## Interest Group Ratings

| Year | ADA | ACA | AFL-CIO | CCUS-1 | CCUS-2 |
|---|---|---|---|---|---|
| 1980 | 0 | 100 | 18 | 83 | |
| 1979 | 5 | 95 | 6 | 90 | 85 |
| 1978 | 10 | 95 | 12 | 100 | |
| 1977 | 0 | 100 | 20 | 94 | |
| 1976 | 0 | 94 | 8 | 89 | |
| 1975 | 6 | 100 | 14 | 100 | |
| 1974 | 5 | 100 | 10 | 90 | |
| 1973 | 0 | 90 | 29 | 100 | |
| 1972 | 5 | 87 | 0 | 100 | |
| 1971 | 4 | 100 | 10 | - | |
| 1970 | 3 | 92 | 20 | 100 | |
| 1969 | 0 | 90 | 0 | - | |
| 1964 | 0 | 90 | 0 | - | |
| 1963 | - | 100 | - | - | |
| 1962 | 0 | 100 | 0 | - | |
| 1961 | 0 | - | - | - | |

# Dennis DeConcini (D)

**Of Tucson — Elected 1976**

**Born:** May 8, 1937, Tucson, Ariz.
**Education:** U. of Ariz., B.A. 1959, LL.B. 1963.
**Military Career:** Army, 1959-60; Army Reserve, 1960-67.
**Profession:** Lawyer
**Family:** Wife, Susan Hurley; three children.
**Religion:** Roman Catholic.
**Political Career:** Pima County Attorney, 1973-76.

**In Washington:** Nothing DeConcini did before or has done since can match the inadvertent show he put on during the Senate's bruising 1978 debate over the Panama Canal treaties.

Just a year into his freshman term and lacking any claim to foreign policy expertise, the Arizona Democrat wound up, to his own bemusement and to the astonishment of his colleagues, playing the pivotal role in ratification of the two pacts. It was through his reservations to the treaties, assuring the United States the right to intervene to keep the canal open in case of trouble, that the leadership finally drew enough support to assure their approval by the Senate.

DeConcini had brooded about possible internal threats to the canal's operation ever since he visited Panama in December 1977 — at his own expense — to inspect the canal and question Panamanian leaders. He became one of the crucial "swing" votes as the Senate debate progressed, and the object of intensive lobbying and wooing by President Carter and various administration officials.

Carter finally won DeConcini's support — and enough other wavering votes to assure ratification — but only at the price of accepting the reservations that almost sank the treaties in Panama. Ironically, while treaty supporters were accusing DeConcini of jeopardizing the acceptability of the pacts, treaty opponents back in Arizona were launching a recall campaign to strip him of his Senate seat. The idea never went anywhere.

If DeConcini practices what he preaches, he is likely to impose his own limits on his Senate tenure. He has sponsored a proposed constitutional amendment to limit members of the Senate to either two terms or a maximum of 14 years, and House members to seven terms or a maximum of 15 years. After that period, he said, those who have served in Congress should "return to real life and live under the laws that they helped make."

DeConcini's proposal will not win much support on Capitol Hill, but that is unlikely to dissuade him. He has more than once shown a penchant for acting on his own.

In March 1979, for instance, he was one of only three senators to object to an unannounced voice vote which postponed until 1983 the previously-passed limit on their outside earnings. DeConcini called the attempt a "slick trick," but the Senate acted anyway — later confirming its decision with a recorded vote.

On another occasion, DeConcini, a member of the Judiciary Committee, received an angry phone call from Supreme Court Chief Justice Warren Burger, who objected to provisions of a bill which DeConcini and others had worked on in a House-Senate conference. The Arizona senator told a reporter that the chief justice had screamed at him — a charge that embarrassed Burger.

In October 1980, less than two weeks before the presidential election, DeConcini insisted on holding public hearings into charges that the Justice Department had bungled a probe of fugitive financier Robert Vesco's alleged efforts to influence Carter White House aides and Democratic Party officials.

As a former prosecutor and ex-administrator of the Arizona Drug Control District, DeConcini has frequently criticized government efforts to control narcotics traffic. He has urged appointment of a drug enforcement "czar" in the executive branch, and the creation of a select committee in the Senate to address the narcotics control problem.

**At Home:** As the only Democrat to win a Senate election in Arizona since 1962, DeConcini has spent much of his first term trying to secure himself against the coming challenge from the right.

His relatively conservative voting record is no

**49**

certain protection. In his first year in the Senate, when he voted for the Panama Canal treaties, billboards sprang up in Arizona decrying him.

DeConcini had campaigned for the Senate as a conservative in 1976, when he beat Republican congressman Sam Steiger. He emphasized his law-enforcement background as Pima County district attorney, and called for a crackdown on organized crime in Arizona.

But neither crime nor any other policy issue had a great deal to do with DeConcini's victory that year in the contest to succeed retiring Republican Paul J. Fannin. He was mainly the beneficiary of a vicious Republican primary quarrel between Steiger and Rep. John Conlan, long-time personal enemies. Supporters of Steiger, who is Jewish, accused Conlan of pandering to anti-Semitism in a pitch for fundamentalist Christian votes. When Steiger won the primary, Conlan refused to endorse him, and Democrats rallied behind DeConcini in anticipation of a rare statewide victory. DeConcini even carried the Phoenix area, normally a Republican stronghold.

DeConcini has his base in Tucson, the state's No. 2 population center, where his father made a fortune in real estate. The father was also a state Supreme Court justice, and his mother a member of the Democratic National Committee. A brother, Dino, is former Democratic chairman in Tucson.

## Committees

**Appropriations** (13th of 14 Democrats)
Foreign Operations; Interior; State, Justice, Commerce, and the Judiciary; Treasury, Postal Service and General Government.

**Judiciary** (5th of 8 Democrats)
Constitution; Immigration and Refugee Policy.

**Select Indian Affairs** (3rd of 3 Democrats)

**Veterans' Affairs** (4th of 5 Democrats)

## Elections

**1976 General**

| | |
|---|---|
| Dennis DeConcini (D ) | 400,334 (54 %) |
| Sam Steiger (R ) | 321,236 (43 %) |

**1976 Primary**

| | |
|---|---|
| Dennis DeConcini (D ) | 121,423 (53 %) |
| Carolyn Warner (D ) | 71,612 (32 %) |
| Wade Church (D ) | 34,266 (15 %) |

## Campaign Finance

| | Receipts | Receipts from PACs | Expenditures |
|---|---|---|---|
| **1976** | | | |
| De Concini (D ) | $598,668 | $100,433 (17 %) | $597,405 |
| Steiger (R ) | $722,691 | $106,524 (15 %) | $679,384 |

## Voting Studies

| | Presidential Support | | Party Unity | | Conservative Coalition | |
|---|---|---|---|---|---|---|
| Year | S | O | S | O | S | O |
| 1980 | 64 | 31 | 59 | 28 | 49 | 37 |
| 1979 | 57 | 34 | 56 | 36 | 58 | 36 |
| 1978 | 44 | 48 | 47 | 46 | 60 | 33 |
| 1977 | 68 | 19 | 55 | 35 | 51 | 40 |

## Key Votes

**96th Congress**

| | |
|---|---|
| Maintain relations with Taiwan (1979) | Y |
| Reduce synthetic fuel development funds (1979) | N |
| Impose nuclear plant moratorium (1979) | Y |
| Kill stronger windfall profits tax (1979) | N |
| Guarantee Chrysler Corp. loans (1979) | N |
| Approve military draft registration (1980) | Y |
| End Revenue Sharing to the states (1980) | Y |
| Block Justice Dept. busing suits (1980) | Y |

**97th Congress**

| | |
|---|---|
| Restore urban program funding cuts (1981) | N |

## Interest Group Ratings

| Year | ADA | ACA | AFL-CIO | CCUS-1 | CCUS-2 |
|---|---|---|---|---|---|
| 1980 | 67 | 39 | 67 | 56 | |
| 1979 | 26 | 64 | 42 | 36 | 50 |
| 1978 | 35 | 39 | 58 | 47 | |
| 1977 | 40 | 36 | 65 | 33 | |

# 1 John J. Rhodes (R)

**Of Mesa — Elected 1952**

**Born:** Sept. 18, 1916, Council Grove, Kan.
**Home:** Mesa, Ariz.
**Education:** Kan. State College, B.S., 1938; Harvard Law School, LL.B, 1941.
**Military Career:** Air Force, 1941-46.
**Profession:** Lawyer.
**Family:** Wife, Mary Elizabeth Harvey; four children.
**Religion:** Methodist.
**Political Career:** No previous office.

**In Washington:** John Rhodes became a rank and file Republican again in 1981 after eight terms in the party hierarchy, a voluntary refugee from the leadership post that was bringing him more trouble than influence.

Rhodes's unusual decision to retire as minority leader — but not as a member of the House — related to his unending dream of being back in the majority, where he was when he entered in 1953. He did not want to risk leaving town in a year when Republicans might take over the House, so he decided to seek re-election once more in 1980 and retain his presumptive right to a Republican Speakership, just in case. But there is no Republican majority in the House, and Rhodes is left in a delicate position somewhere between elder statesman and backbencher. He is near the party's strategy center as a brand-new member of the Rules Committee, but he is not making the strategy.

Still, it is a less frustrating role than the one he played during most of his seven-year tenure as minority leader, a job he won when Gerald R. Ford left it to become vice president of the United States in 1973. Rhodes immediately was in the middle of one of the GOP's most trying times, the last days of the Nixon administration. Rhodes tried hard to remain loyal to Nixon while quietly urging White House aides to prepare Nixon for the worst — impeachment. "The idea of resigning should be pretty high up in his mind," Rhodes said in December, 1973.

Rhodes had entered the party leadership along with Ford seven years earlier, as GOP policy chairman, and he adopted the Ford policy of roasting the Democrats occasionally in public without straying too far from bipartisan comity in private. He is a personal friend and occasional golfing partner of Speaker O'Neill.

But each election during Rhodes's tenure as leader brought in more Republicans who preferred a different strategy against the Democrats: relentless in public and often belligerent behind the scenes as well. Rhodes responded with a 1976 book, "The Futile System," in which he was as harsh toward Democrats as his nature would allow. He singled out O'Neill, then majority leader, as principal architect of a rigidly partisan attitude that unfairly left Republicans out of House legislative strategy. "Tip," Rhodes wrote, "can be impossible to deal with if you are in the minority."

Junior Republicans still were not satisfied. The 37 elected in 1978 summoned Rhodes to a meeting in Washington before the 96th Congress opened and demanded more activist leadership. Some of the freshmen, especially the younger ones, used terms like "partisan theater" to describe their concept of proper minority conduct in the House, and charged that Rhodes and other party leaders had grown acquiescent in the minority.

Some of the dispute was ideological as well. Raised in Council Grove, Kansas, Rhodes reflects Midwestern, mid-century values rather than any of the New Right sentiments of some of his Sun Belt conservative colleagues.

He made much of his legislative reputation fighting for higher defense spending on the House Appropriations Committee and against the wishes of organized labor as a spokesman for the Arizona

---

**1st District: Southern Phoenix, Tempe, Mesa.** Population: 624,551 (41% increase since 1970). Race: White 515,917 (83%); Black 31,054 (5%); Native American 11,620 (2%); Other 65,960 (11%). Spanish origin 97,944 (16%).

business community. But for years, his greatest legislative efforts were bipartisan, working with homestate Democratic colleague Morris K. Udall to fund the Central Arizona Project, a billion-dollar plan to divert water from the Colorado River to the arid land around Phoenix and Tuscon.

By the time he became minority leader, Rhodes seemed to be taking on the coloration of a moderate Republican.

He initially backed President Carter's proposal for Election Day voter registration, but reversed himself amid widespread complaints that it was a scheme to promote Democratic candidates. He tried to negotiate with O'Neill the next year on a compromise bill for public financing of congressional elections, but this, too, had to be abandoned when it provoked massive Republican mutiny. He initially denounced the idea of a constitutional amendment to balance the federal budget, but bowed to rank and file pressure and switched on that too.

By mid-1980, Rhodes was not often seen on the House floor. Much of the party's legislative strategy, even on crucial issues, was in the hands of Robert E. Bauman of Maryland, then the leading conservative parliamentary expert in the House. The minority leader spent most of his time in his office in the Capitol, working to promote Republican House challengers. He was not a major figure in the legislative process.

Rhodes's leadership status was more evident in the string of press releases and series of news conferences he scheduled to criticize President Carter and the Democratic leadership. Occasionally, in response to the new conservative generation, Rhodes took on the left within his own party. When 29 Republicans voted for a 1979 bill to limit contributions from political action committees, Rhodes accused them of "placing loyalty to labor unions or Common Cause" ahead of their party. Rep. Paul N. McCloskey Jr., a California Republican, accused Rhodes of impugning his motives and threatened to resign from the party. But the quarrel was quickly smoothed over and in Rhodes's last year as minority leader, after he announced his decision to step down, his relations with both wings of his party seemed amiable.

**At Home:** A small-town Kansas boy, but a Harvard law graduate, Rhodes chose fast-growing Phoenix as the place for his law practice when he left the Air Force after World War II. Seven years later the city had changed enough to trade in its traditional populist Democratic representation for postwar Republican conservatism. In 1952 Rhodes was the House nominee on the ticket with Senate candidate Barry Goldwater and national hero Dwight D. Eisenhower, the Republican presidential candidate. Even though Rhodes was on such a strong ticket, his unseating of the aging Democratic representative, John R. Murdock, came as a surprise.

There was enough latent Democratic sentiment in the district to keep Rhodes in the marginal category throughout the 1950s, but his pro-military record on the House Appropriations Committee and his strong anti-labor stand went over well, and by the end of the sixties he had what appeared to be a safe seat. The 1972 redistricting changed that. Because metropolitan Phoenix had grown far too large for one district, much of its suburban territory was placed in a new one, leaving Rhodes with a substantial minority population based in the central city. The effect was immediate. In 1970 Rhodes had been re-elected with 69 percent of the vote. Two years later, in his first campaign within the new district lines, he was down to 57 percent; in 1974, after he had won the minority leadership, a liberal Democrat held him to 51 percent. That forced Rhodes to spend a bit more of his first leadership term mending fences than he would have chosen, but he was back to 57 percent by 1976 and has drawn only minor opposition since then.

**The District:** A postwar Sun Belt metropolis like Houston, greater Phoenix has shown few signs of shedding the conservatism that has now controlled its politics for a generation. Maricopa County, in which it is located, has more than half the state's population, and is its most reliably Republican territory. When the Democrats win statewide, it is in spite of this area, not because of it. The current Democratic governor, Bruce Babbitt, had to wipe out a 9,000-vote deficit in Maricopa to win election in 1978.

Slightly more than half the voters in Rhodes's district as it has existed since 1972 live outside the city of Phoenix, and despite the inner-city minority population, they should be enough to keep it Republican in most years. But Arizona is gaining a House seat in the 1980 reapportionment, leaving the Republican Legislature and a Democratic governor a variety of options as they create five new districts out of the four old ones.

## Committees

**Rules** (5th of 5 Republicans)

## Elections

**1980 General**

| | |
|---|---|
| John Rhodes (R) | 136,961 (74%) |
| Steve Jancek (D) | 40,045 (21%) |

**1978 General**

| | |
|---|---|
| John Rhodes (R) | 81,108 (71%) |
| Ken Graves (D) | 33,178 (29%) |

**Previous Winning Percentages**

| | | | |
|---|---|---|---|
| 1976 (57%) | 1974 (51%) | 1972 (57%) | 1970 (69%) |
| 1968 (72%) | 1966 (67%) | 1964 (55%) | 1962 (59%) |
| 1960 (59%) | 1958 (59%) | 1956 (55%) | 1954 (53%) |
| 1952 (54%) | | | |

**District Vote For President**

| | 1980 | | 1976 | | 1972 |
|---|---|---|---|---|---|
| D | 51,119 (27%) | D | 66,632 (37%) | D | 46,573 (31%) |
| R | 118,001 (62%) | R | 99,375 (59%) | R | 98,436 (65%) |
| I | 16,930 (9%) | | | | |

## Campaign Finance

| | Receipts | Receipts from PACs | Expenditures |
|---|---|---|---|
| **1980** | | | |
| Rhodes (R) | $242,977 | $61,717 (25%) | $191,809 |
| **1978** | | | |
| Rhodes (R) | $200,661 | $112,661 (56%) | $201,177 |
| Graves (D) | $6,411 | — (0%) | $6,306 |

## Voting Studies

| | Presidential Support | | Party Unity | | Conservative Coalition | |
|---|---|---|---|---|---|---|
| Year | S | O | S | O | S | O |
| 1980 | 41 | 38 | 57 | 23 | 53 | 18 |
| 1979 | 39 | 46 | 69 | 19† | 77 | 10 |
| 1978 | 32 | 49 | 63 | 14 | 62 | 10 |
| 1977 | 41 | 47 | 71 | 17† | 77 | 10 |
| 1976 | 76 | 6 | 66 | 20 | 71 | 17 |
| 1975 | 84 | 11 | 69 | 17 | 76 | 12 |
| 1974 (Ford) | 59 | 15 | | | | |
| 1974 | 68 | 8 | 61 | 20 | 64 | 15 |
| 1973 | 76 | 16 | 71 | 21 | 79 | 17 |
| 1972 | 73 | 11 | 67 | 11 | 73 | 7 |
| 1971 | 86 | 7 | 66 | 17 | 81 | 10 |
| 1970 | 74 | 8 | 61 | 21 | 59 | 16 |
| 1969 | 66 | 30 | 69 | 22 | 82 | 11 |
| 1968 | 49 | 36 | 66 | 12 | 76 | 14 |
| 1967 | 43 | 45 | 71 | 15 | 80 | 9 |
| 1966 | 40 | 56 | 83 | 14 | 97 | 3 |
| 1965 | 38 | 54 | 82 | 9 | 86 | 2 |
| 1964 | 29 | 63 | 85 | 3 | 92 | 0 |
| 1963 | 37 | 52 | 72 | 19 | 80 | 7 |
| 1962 | 40 | 52 | 72 | 19 | 94 | 6 |
| 1961 | 37 | 60 | 79 | 14 | 87 | 13 |

S = Support   O = Opposition

† Not eligible for all recorded votes.

## Key Votes

**96th Congress**

| | |
|---|---|
| Weaken Carter oil profits tax (1979) | Y |
| Reject hospital cost control plan (1979) | ? |
| Implement Panama Canal Treaties (1979) | Y |
| Establish Department of Education (1979) | N |
| Approve Anti-busing Amendment (1979) | Y |
| Guarantee Chrysler Corp. loans (1979) | N |
| Approve military draft registration (1980) | Y |
| Aid Sandinista regime in Nicaragua (1980) | N |
| Strengthen fair housing laws (1980) | N |

**97th Congress**

| | |
|---|---|
| Reagan budget proposal (1981) | Y |

## Interest Group Ratings

| Year | ADA | ACA | AFL-CIO | CCUS |
|---|---|---|---|---|
| 1980 | 0 | 86 | 8 | 80 |
| 1979 | 11 | 81 | 11 | 100 |
| 1978 | 15 | 70 | 13 | 80 |
| 1977 | 5 | 88 | 17 | 100 |
| 1976 | 0 | 67 | 9 | 100 |
| 1975 | 11 | 88 | 5 | 100 |
| 1974 | 4 | 62 | 10 | 86 |
| 1973 | 4 | 73 | 0 | 100 |
| 1972 | 6 | 67 | 30 | 89 |
| 1971 | 11 | 92 | 19 | - |
| 1970 | 24 | 72 | 0 | 90 |
| 1969 | 0 | 69 | 10 | - |
| 1968 | 8 | 75 | 0 | - |
| 1967 | 7 | 88 | 0 | 80 |
| 1966 | 0 | 84 | 0 | - |
| 1965 | 0 | 85 | - | 100 |
| 1964 | 0 | 94 | 0 | - |
| 1963 | - | 82 | - | - |
| 1962 | 13 | 78 | 0 | - |
| 1961 | 0 | - | - | - |

# 2 Morris K. Udall (D)

**Of Tucson — Elected 1961**

**Born:** June 15, 1922, St. Johns, Ariz.
**Education:** U. of Ariz., J.D. 1949.
**Military Career:** Army Air Corps, 1942-46.
**Profession:** Lawyer.
**Family:** Wife, Ella Royston; six children.
**Religion:** Mormon.
**Political Career:** Pima County attorney, 1952-54.

**In Washington:** Unfailing grace and a few good jokes have allowed Udall to evolve from brash reformer to elder statesman in little more than a decade without making a real enemy in the House. Watching him on the floor today, one forgets that only 12 years ago he was the Young Turk challenger to John W. McCormack for Speaker of the House. He was a youthful and bold 46 then; today he is a mellow and frail-looking 58, slowed down physically by Parkinson's Disease.

But he is the same Udall, blessed with the even-tempered patience that has always made him a popular man on both sides of the aisle. Udall's patience has sustained him through one of the more remarkable careers in modern congressional history, one marked by enormous creativity but also by frequent and disappointing defeat.

Losing his challenge to McCormack, even by a vote of 178-58, was no great shock; Udall had wanted mainly to publicize the complaints of his generation about McCormack's weak leadership, and he had even promised to step aside for someone else if he somehow out-polled the Speaker.

Two years later, Udall and many of his liberal allies expected him to be elected majority leader over Hale Boggs of Louisiana, who had only recently recovered from the effects of a 1969 nervous collapse. But Boggs offered no threat of disruption in the traditional power structure, and Udall, a critic of seniority, did. Boggs won on the second ballot, 140 to 88. "I assumed that because a man was with me ideologically, he would be with me when it counted," Udall said later. "I'm a lot tougher and more realistic now."

That defeat marked the end of Udall's leadership hopes. It drove him deeper into the legislative process, in which he had come to excel.

Udall's legislative career is striking evidence that a member of Congress can find important work to do anywhere in the committee system. He has never had anything resembling a major assignment — he joined Interior in 1961 to work on Arizona land and mining issues, and also went on Post Office at the leadership's request.

Post Office serves as a resting place for many of the less ambitious members. Udall found it a perfect vehicle for his interests. In his first decade there, he worked to revise the federal pay system, including the one for Congress, and to make the Post Office a semi-private corporation.

Much later, he won passage of President Carter's civil service reforms, designed to promote merit incentives and give managers more flexibility.

The federal pay legislation sought to end in-house control over congressional salaries, creating a federal commission to deal with the subject. That has never quite been accomplished, but the law had a greater effect rarely talked about now: It raised congressional pensions to the point where members began retiring at earlier ages. It was a benign way to attack seniority.

The semi-private Postal Service has never pleased its creators, including Udall, who has said "the way to slow down inflation is to turn it over to the Post Office." But there has been little support for a return to the old system.

The years since 1971 have fixed Udall's reputation as a dominant force on environmental issues, but he has not always been able to win.

When he has won, it has been difficult.

---

**2nd District: South — Tucson.** Population: 658,936 (49% increase since 1970). Race: White 547,936 (83%), Black 18,713 (3%), Indian 16,498 (3%), Others 75,789 (12%). Spanish origin: 156,873 (24%).

The House had to pass strip mine control legislation three times, and twice failed to override Ford vetoes before a bill reasonably close to what Udall wanted became law in 1977, the first year of the Carter administration. It took four years for Congress to enact legislation dividing Alaska lands between development and wilderness. Two years of struggle ended in deadlock on the last day of the 95th Congress in 1978; a compromise bill finally passed in 1980.

But other Udall ideas have run out of steam. His scheme to provide federal aid for local land-use planning as a solution to urban sprawl failed on the House floor amid charges that it smacked of socialism. His committee's efforts to restrict nuclear power have run into a stubborn pro-nuclear bloc in the rest of the House.

Udall took over the Interior Committee in 1977 and has managed it relatively smoothly since then, staying on good terms with pro-development Republicans as well as environmentalists.

The one frequent complaint against Udall as a chairman is that he is too "soft," good at winning through persuasion but less effective when something stronger is needed. Democrats on Interior know they can cross Udall on a major issue without fear of retribution; other chairmen are not always so generous.

Outside his committees, Udall has spent 20 years pushing for changes in the political system, again with mixed results. He was chief sponsor of the 1971 bill that made the first real national rules for campaign finance, limiting expenditures and contributions and providing for voluminous disclosure. But he has failed repeatedly with legislation to establish public financing of congressional campaigns, and none seems likely.

Udall's own campaign for the 1976 Democratic presidential nomination, as the leading liberal alternative to Jimmy Carter, left a curious record: He built wide respect within his party and survived through to the convention in New York without ever winning anything.

He never took a single primary, although he finished second seven times and was declared the Wisconsin winner prematurely by two networks. He would almost certainly have won in New Hampshire had former Sen. Fred Harris not drawn off liberal votes, but by the time Harris withdrew the next month, Carter was too strong to be headed off.

Udall eventually made his peace with Carter and was not one of the more outspoken critics during Carter's presidential term, but he endorsed Edward M. Kennedy in 1980. Eventually he receded into the elder statesman's role that allowed him to give the convention keynote address.

**At Home.** Udall came to politics as a member of one of Arizona's best-known families. His father was a justice of the Arizona Supreme Court; his mother was a local Democratic activist.

A professional basketball player for the old Denver Nuggets despite the handicap of a glass eye, Udall entered private law practice with his brother Stewart in 1949 and later was Pima County attorney while Stewart served in Congress. When Stewart Udall resigned from Congress in 1961 to become President Kennedy's interior secretary, Morris ran for the seat in a special election that drew attention as a test of Kennedy's first 100 days in office. Udall backed such Kennedy programs as federal aid to education and medical care for the aged. He won, but with only 51 percent. He was hurt by Stewart Udall's call for evacuation of farmers squatting on federal land along the Colorado River.

For years after that, Udall won easily. But in 1976 he drew less than 60 percent for the first time in a decade. His unsuccessful campaign for the Democratic presidential nomination that year gave him high visibility to his liberal views.

In 1977, copper mine operators in the district, upset with his effort to revise federal mining laws, began a recall drive. Udall responded by withdrawing his support for the measure. In January 1978, the recall effort was dropped.

Still, Republicans mounted an intensive challenge. The district's GOP county chairmen coalesced early in the year behind Tom Richey, a former army colonel and state legislator. The race was bitter. One Richey ad carried a statement by Udall, apparently uttered in jest, in which the congressman said that he was a socialist. Even though he outspent Richey by more than 2-to-1, Udall won by less than 10,000 votes.

Although the GOP continued its attack on Udall's record in 1980, the charges had less impact. As keynoter at the Democratic Convention, he portrayed himself as a healing force in the party. He noted his role in reversing Carter's opposition to the Central Arizona Project.

The campaign was expensive, with Udall and GOP real estate developer Richard H. Huff together raising more than $1.4 million. Udall's disclosure that he was suffering from Parkinson's Disease, a chronic neurological disorder, did not seem to hurt him. He won by nearly 40,000 votes.

**The District.** In recent years, the 2nd has been a congressional Democratic outpost in a generally Republican state. The district has been represented by a member of the Udall family since 1955, and in state elections it regularly turns in majorities for the Democratic candidate.

## Morris K. Udall, D-Ariz.

The heart of the district is Pima County (Tucson), where more than 80 percent of the ballots are cast. Settled by the Spanish, Tucson still has a sizable Hispanic population, a large academic community and a Democratic tradition.

But voting patterns are being altered by the population boom. In 1979, one out of 10 households had lived in Tucson less than a year. The result of the turnover has been an increase in conservative Republican voting.

## Committees

**Interior and Insular Affairs** (Chairman)
Energy and the Environment, chairman; Insular Affairs; Water and Power Resources.

**Post Office and Civil Service** (2nd of 15 Democrats)
Civil Service; Investigations.

## Elections

**1980 General**

| | |
|---|---|
| Morris Udall (D ) | 127,736 (58 %) |
| Richard Huff (R) | 88,653 (40 %) |

**1978 General**

| | |
|---|---|
| Morris Udall (D ) | 67,878 (53 %) |
| Thomas Richey (R ) | 58,697 (45 %) |

**Previous Winning Percentages**

| | | | |
|---|---|---|---|
| 1976 (58 %) | 1974 (62 %) | 1972 (64 %) | 1970 (69 %) |
| 1968 (70 %) | 1966 (60 %) | 1964 (59 %) | 1962 (58 %) |
| 1961* (51 %) | | | |

*Special Election*

**District Vote For President**

| | 1980 | | 1976 | | 1972 |
|---|---|---|---|---|---|
| D | 75,694 (35 %) | D | 85,224 (46 %) | D | 65,926 (42 %) |
| R | 111,164 (51 %) | R | 91,113 (50 %) | R | 89,052 (56 %) |
| I | 27,721 (13 %) | | | | |

## Campaign Finance

| | Receipts | Percent of Receipts from PACs | Expenditures |
|---|---|---|---|
| **1980** | | | |
| Udall (D ) | $860,395 | $182,558 (21 %) | $763,650 |
| Huff (R ) | $548,152 | $156,336 (29 %) | $528,477 |
| **1978** | | | |
| Udall (D ) | $295,268 | $60,350 (20 %) | $294,849 |
| Richey (R ) | $139,491 | $58,026 (42 %) | $134,130 |

## Voting Studies

| Year | Presidential Support S | O | Party Unity S | O | Conservative Coalition S | O |
|---|---|---|---|---|---|---|
| 1980 | 63 | 19 | 72 | 7 | 19 | 58 |
| 1979 | 75 | 17 | 81 | 10 | 22 | 68 |
| 1978 | 71 | 15 | 81 | 10 | 14 | 80 |
| 1977 | 75 | 18 | 88 | 6 | 10 | 85 |
| 1976 | 16 | 41 | 50 | 1 | 3 | 44 |
| 1975 | 11 | 31 | 44 | 2 | 8 | 35 |
| 1974 (Ford) | 46 | 39 | | | | |
| 1974 | 42 | 45 | 78 | 7 | 9 | 70 |
| 1973 | 38 | 57 | 82 | 12 | 19 | 74 |
| 1972 | 43 | 41 | 85 | 7 | 5 | 88 |
| 1971 | 23 | 63 | 85 | 3 | 5 | 82 |
| 1970 | 62 | 26 | 75 | 14 | 11 | 77 |
| 1969 | 64 | 34 | 85 | 13 | 11 | 82 |
| 1968 | 83 | 6 | 79 | 5 | 8 | 78 |
| 1967 | 76 | 9 | 82 | 4 | 7 | 81 |
| 1966 | 81 | 6 | 90 | 1 | 3 | 84 |
| 1965 | 80 | 9 | 85 | 7 | 10 | 86 |
| 1964 | 88 | 2 | 90 | 5 | 8 | 92 |
| 1963 | 96 | 3 | 93 | 5 | 13 | 87 |
| 1962 | 90 | 7 | 84 | 14 | 25 | 75 |
| 1961 | 89 | 7† | 90 | 7† | 12 | 88 |

S = Support    O = Opposition

†Not eligible for all recorded votes.

## Key Votes

**96th Congress**

| | |
|---|---|
| Weaken Carter oil profits tax (1979) | N |
| Reject hospital cost control plan (1979) | Y |
| Implement Panama Canal Treaties (1979) | Y |
| Establish Department of Education (1979) | Y |
| Approve Anti-busing Amendment (1979) | N |
| Gaurantee Chrysler Corp. loans (1979) | Y |
| Approve Military draft registration (1980) | N |
| Aid Sandinistas regime in Nicaragua (1980) | ? |
| Strengthen Fair Housing Laws (1980) | Y |

**97th Congress**

| | |
|---|---|
| Reagan budget proposal (1981) | N |

## Interest Group Rating

| Year | ADA | ACA | AFL-CIO | CCUS |
|---|---|---|---|---|
| 1980 | 61 | 14 | 67 | 61 |
| 1979 | 74 | 9 | 79 | 18 |
| 1978 | 70 | 13 | 83 | 25 |
| 1977 | 85 | 0 | 90 | 17 |
| 1976 | 45 | 0 | 88 | 6 |
| 1975 | 47 | 13 | 92 | 8 |
| 1974 | 65 | 8 | 100 | 0 |
| 1973 | 84 | 8 | 82 | 40 |
| 1972 | 100 | 0 | 100 | 0 |
| 1971 | 81 | 4 | 82 | - |
| 1970 | 76 | 0 | 83 | 22 |
| 1969 | 67 | 0 | 80 | - |
| 1968 | 92 | 0 | 100 | - |
| 1967 | 93 | 4 | 100 | 10 |
| 1966 | 82 | 8 | 85 | - |
| 1965 | 74 | 12 | - | 20 |
| 1964 | 88 | 0 | 82 | - |
| 1963 | - | 6 | - | - |
| 1962 | 63 | 18 | 88 | - |
| 1961 | 100 | - | - | - |

# 3 Bob Stump (D)

**Of Tolleson — Elected 1976**

**Born:** April 4, 1927, Phoenix, Ariz.
**Education:** Ariz. State U., B.S. 1951.
**Military Career:** Navy, 1943-46.
**Profession:** Farmer.
**Family:** Divorced; three children.
**Religion:** Seventh Day Adventist.
**Political Career:** Ariz. House, 1959-67; Ariz. Senate, 1967-77, president of Ariz. Senate, 1975-77.

**In Washington:** For years, Republican officials have been urging Stump to cross the aisle, and run for office the way he votes — 82 percent against the majority Democratic position in 1980. "I've told him," fellow-Arizonan John Rhodes, the former House GOP leader, has said, "any time he wants to switch parties, I can guarantee him the Republican nomination."

Democratic leaders do not think that is so amusing. Although they are happy to have Stump's vote to organize the House at the beginning of each Congress, they grouse in private about his habit of siding with the opposition.

Stump says he has no intention of leaving the Democratic Party. He has been a Democrat all his life — a traditionally conservative one from the Arizona desert, but still a Democrat, and insists there should be room in the party for his views.

Because he is still a Democrat, Stump is much in demand as a board member for national conservative organizations, to whose efforts he lends a trace of bipartisanship. He is currently on the advisory boards of the National Right to Work Committee, the Gun Owners of America and the American Conservative Union.

When the 1980 election brought House Republican strength up to 192 seats, Stump became a charter member of the Democratic Forum, organized by conservative Democrats to place political pressure on the leadership.

By implying that the group could make life miserable for Democratic leaders by forming an informal alliance with the GOP, the 44-member forum won important concessions from Speaker O'Neill at the start of the 97th Congress. Stump, despite his record of party-bolting, got two prizes of his own — new memberships on the Veterans' Affairs and Intelligence committees. For most other members, those memberships would be routine. But in Stump's case, they symbolized a reluctant acceptance of his renegade voting.

Both of those new committees fit neatly into Stump's principal area of interest: national defense. He has been on the Armed Services Committee since 1978, and is on its Readiness and Research and Development subcommittees. But he is not one of the more active members.

Like all Arizonans in Congress, Stump protects the state on water issues. When the Carter administration tried to impose on Western landowners the stringent federal water controls of a long-ignored 1902 law, Stump simply introduced a bill to repeal major portions of the law. The Stump bill was never taken up, but the administration retreated and under pressure from other Westerners, a compromise bill failed.

**At Home.** A cotton farmer with roots in rural Arizona, Stump is a "pinto" Democrat, a conservative of the type that dominated state politics before the postwar population boom.

A veteran of 18 years in the state Legislature, Stump rose to the presidency of the state Senate during the 1975-76 session. When Republican Rep. Sam Steiger tried for the U.S. Senate in 1976, Stump decided to run for his House seat.

In the Democratic primary, he defeated a more liberal, free-spending opponent, former Assistant State Attorney General Sid Rosen. Stump drew 31 percent to Rosen's 25 percent, with the rest scattered among three others. In the fall campaign, Stump's GOP opponent was fellow

---

**3rd District: Western Phoenix, Glendale, Yuma.** Population: 745,653 (68% increase since 1970). Race: White 621,678 (83%), Black 17,835 (2%), Indian 31,187 (4%), Others 74,935 (10%). Spanish origin: 123,107 (17%).

state Sen. Fred Koory, the Senate minority leader. Stump wooed back many conservative Democrats who had supported Steiger by attacking the Democratic vice presidential nominee, Walter Mondale.

Stump may have been helped in the election by a third candidate, state Sen. Bill McCune, a Republican running as an independent. McCune drained GOP votes away from Koory, allowing Stump to win a 9,700-vote plurality.

Since 1976, Stump's toughest decision has been whether to remain a Democrat, at odds with his party, or to join the GOP. An effort against him by the AFL-CIO and the state Education Association in the 1978 primary failed badly.

**The District.** About 60 percent of the 3rd District population lives in the western portion of Maricopa County, which includes part of the city of Phoenix and suburbs like Glendale and Sun City, the latter a major retirement community.

The rest of the population lives in rural and small-town areas of northern and western Arizona. Copper and silica mining are important, and cotton and vegetables grow in the limited farmlands of the vast, dry region. The Grand Canyon provides a tourist boost to the economy.

Flagstaff is the closest town to the Grand Canyon and the trading center for northern Arizona. In the mountains to the southwest is Prescott, the former territorial capital. At the extreme southwest corner of the district, in the desert along the California border, lies Yuma, one of the hottest places in the nation.

Although Stump has been elected to Congress three times, the district is a Republican bastion in presidential and state elections.

## Committees

**Armed Services** (15th of 25 Democrats)
Readiness; Research and Development.

**Select Intelligence** (9th of 9 Democrats)
Program and Budget Authorization.

**Veterans' Affairs** (14th of 17 Democrats)
Oversight and Investigations.

## Elections

**1980 General**

| | |
|---|---|
| Bob Stump (D ) | 141,448 (64 %) |
| Bob Croft (R ) | 65,845 (30 %) |
| Sharon Hayse (LIB) | 12,529 (6 %) |

**1978 General**

| | |
|---|---|
| Bob Stump (D ) | 111,850 (85 %) |
| Kathleen Cooke (LIB) | 19,813 (15 %) |

**Previous Winning Percentage**

**1976 (48 %)**

**District Vote For President**

| | 1980 | | 1976 | | 1972 |
|---|---|---|---|---|---|
| D | 60,656 (26 %) | D | 74,467 (39 %) | D | 41,012 (27 %) |
| R | 148,411 (65 %) | R | 111,116 (58 %) | R | 104,197 (69 %) |
| I | 15,468 (7 %) | | | | |

## Campaign Finance

| | Receipts | Receipts from PACs | Expenditures |
|---|---|---|---|
| **1980** | | | |
| Stump (D ) | $145,211 | $71,290 (49 %) | $88,979 |
| Croft (R ) | $3,120 | — (0 %) | $2,799 |

| 1978 | | | |
|---|---|---|---|
| Stump (D ) | $200,305 | $62,082 (31 %) | $198,085 |

## Voting Studies

| | Presidential Support | | Party Unity | | Conservative Coalition | |
|---|---|---|---|---|---|---|
| Year | S | O | S | O | S | O |
| 1980 | 32 | 65 | 15 | 82 | 93 | 4 |
| 1979 | 19 | 73 | 8 | 85 | 92 | 1 |
| 1978 | 20 | 65 | 14 | 74 | 82 | 4 |
| 1977 | 29 | 61 | 16 | 76 | 91 | 3 |

S = Support    O = Opposition

## Key Votes

**96th Congress**

| | |
|---|---|
| Weaken Carter oil profits tax (1979) | Y |
| Reject hospital cost control plan (1979) | Y |
| Implement Panama Canal Treaties (1979) | N |
| Establish Department of Education (1979) | N |
| Approve Anti-busing Amendment (1979) | Y |
| Guarantee Chrysler Corp. loans (1979) | N |
| Approve military draft registration (1980) | Y |
| Aid Sandinista regime in Nicaragua (1980) | N |
| Strengthen fair housing laws (1980) | N |

**97th Congress**

| | |
|---|---|
| Reagan budget proposal (1981) | Y |

## Interest Group Ratings

| Year | ADA | ACA | AFL-CIO | CCUS |
|---|---|---|---|---|
| 1980 | 0 | 83 | 17 | 71 |
| 1979 | 0 | 96 | 10 | 100 |
| 1978 | 5 | 100 | 10 | 82 |
| 1977 | 5 | 100 | 9 | 100 |

# 4 Eldon Rudd (R)

**Of Scottsdale — Elected 1976**

**Born:** July 15, 1920, Camp Verde, Ariz.
**Education:** Ariz. State. U. at Tempe, B.A. 1947;
U. of Ariz., J.D. 1949.
**Military Career:** Marine Corps, 1942-46.
**Profession:** Lawyer, FBI agent.
**Family:** Wife, Ann Merritt; two children.
**Religion:** Roman Catholic.
**Political Career:** Maricopa County Board of
Supervisors, 1972-76.

**In Washington:** Eldon Rudd has pursued his fiscal conservatism quietly but with utter consistency on Budget and Appropriations.

A man of limited debating skill, he played only a passive role in most of the partisan Budget Committee debates in recent Congresses. But when his more articulate Republican colleagues on Budget worked out a "balanced budget" compromise with the committee's Democrats in 1980, he believed that it was a sham, and that the resolution would never produce a balanced budget. He cast the only GOP vote against the package as it cleared committee. A few weeks later, when it was clear that the budget would be in deficit, the other Republicans opposed it too. That episode may have been the highlight of Rudd's two-year stint on Budget, which ended in 1981. His only real crusade on the committee was for reductions in food stamp spending; he offered a string of unsuccessful food stamp amendments in committee in 1980, then tried to get the Rules Committee to allow them on the floor.

None of the amendments were approved for a floor vote. Later in the year, when the House took up a bill to appropriate more money for the food stamp program, Rudd did get a vote on his amendment to limit eligibility for food stamps to families who have gross incomes below the federally defined poverty level, with a 15 percent reduction for earned income. The amendment lost, 297-106.

Rudd's committee work now is confined to Appropriations, where he has a chance to support Arizona water projects on the Energy and Water Subcommittee. Earlier in his House career, working on water issues as a member of the Interior Committee, he opposed a coal slurry pipeline bill on the grounds that it would open the door to intrusion on state water rights.

Outside his committees, Rudd devoted special attention to a change in federal pension law

that has applied, so far, only to him.

Rudd is a former FBI agent who retired from the bureau in 1970, after 20 years of service. Federal pension law puts a five-year freeze on an individual's right to participate in a federal pension plan if the person retires, then returns to government service. The law is aimed at "double dipping" — collecting on one federal pension while holding a second federal job.

Rudd quietly had members of Congress exempted from the law, though he is the only member affected. He argued that if he waited five years to participate, he would have to make enormous contributions after that, in order to have his pension cover his entire service.

**At Home.** An Arizona columnist once described Rudd as having "the charisma of a broomstick," but his conservatism has well satisfied the electorate in Phoenix and outlying rural areas.

Following his career as an FBI agent and a legal attaché in Latin America, Rudd returned home and was elected to the Maricopa County Board. There he vigorously opposed what he regarded as unnecessary spending and frills.

When Republican Rep. John B. Conlan tried for the U.S. Senate in 1976, Rudd ran for the House with Conlan's strong backing. Drawing 52 percent of the primary vote, he defeated his nearest competitor, Arizona Corporation Commissioner Ernest Garfield, by a wide margin.

---

**4th District: East — northern Phoenix, Scottsdale.** Population: 688,744 (55% increase since 1970). Race: White 554,502 (81%), Black 7,432 (1%), Indian 93,552 (14%), Others 33,258 (5%). Spanish origin: 62,991 (9%).

## Eldon Rudd, R-Ariz.

But the general election was surprisingly close in what is supposed to be a solidly Republican district. The GOP feuding throughout the state over the Senate primary between Conlan and arch-rival Sam Steiger cost Rudd much of his normal support. He lost the rural areas of the seven-county district to Democrat Tony Mason, a former chairman of the Phoenix Planning and Zoning Commission, but carried populous Maricopa County by enough to win by 719 votes.

Rudd's Democratic rival in 1978, Michael L. McCormick, complained that the incumbent was so rigidly conservative "that a robot could do the job and do it cheaper." But with a reputation as a hard-working congressman who provided good constituent service, Rudd easily won re-election in both 1978 and 1980 with 63 percent.

**The District.** Although the 4th includes Indian reservations and mining towns, all reliably Democratic, its political core is the well-populated northern portion of Phoenix and its adjoining suburbs, which return huge GOP margins. The city and surrounding Maricopa County cast about 70 percent of the vote.

The district was created by the Republican Legislature in 1971, when reapportionment gave Arizona an extra seat. But it has been something less of a GOP bastion than expected. It went for Democratic Sen. Dennis DeConcini in 1976, and Democratic Gov. Bruce Babbitt carried it in 1978.

The 4th is the second-fastest growing district in a rapidly growing state, with a population increase of 55 percent in the 1970s, as electronics and scientific industries flocked to the Phoenix area.

## Committees

**Appropriations** (14th of 22 Republicans)
Energy and Water Development; Treasury-Postal Service-General Government.

## Elections

**1980 General**

| | |
|---|---|
| Eldon Rudd (R ) | 142,565 (63 %) |
| Les Miller (D ) | 85,046 (37 %) |

**1980 Primary**

| | |
|---|---|
| Eldon Rudd (R ) | 35,515 (88 %) |
| Richard Rosberg (R) | 4,718 (12 %) |

**1978 General**

| | |
|---|---|
| Eldon Rudd (R ) | 90,768 (63 %) |
| Michael McCormick (D ) | 48,661 (34 %) |

**Previous Winning Percentage**

**1976 (49 %)**

**District Vote For President**

| | 1980 | | 1976 | | 1972 |
|---|---|---|---|---|---|
| **D** | 58,941 (25 %) | **D** | 72,578 (37 %) | **D** | 45,029 (28 %) |
| **R** | 151,495 (65 %) | **R** | 116,475 (60 %) | **R** | 111,127 (69 %) |
| **I** | 16,784 (7 %) | | | | |

## Campaign Finance

| | Receipts | Receipts from PACs | Expenditures |
|---|---|---|---|
| **1980** | | | |
| Rudd (R ) | $277,432 | $94,808 (34 %) | $228,663 |
| Miller (D ) | $153,290 | $11,850 (8 %) | $153,345 |

| 1978 | | | |
|---|---|---|---|
| Rudd (R ) | $227,908 | $77,283 (34 %) | $178,134 |
| McCormick (D ) | $23,548 | $4,921 (21 %) | $23,548 |

## Voting Studies

| | Presidential Support | | Party Unity | | Conservative Coalition | |
|---|---|---|---|---|---|---|
| Year | S | O | S | O | S | O |
| 1980 | 26 | 62 | 88 | 5 | 91 | 1 |
| 1979 | 17 | 74 | 87 | 6 | 90 | 3 |
| 1978 | 13 | 61 | 76 | 5 | 82 | 2 |
| 1977 | 32 | 63 | 92 | 5 | 97 | 0 |

S = Support          O = Opposition

## Key Votes

**96th Congress**

| | |
|---|---|
| Weaken Carter oil profits tax (1979) | Y |
| Reject hospital cost control plan (1979) | # |
| Implement Panama Canal Treaties (1979) | N |
| Establish Department of Education (1979) | N |
| Approve Anti-busing Amendment (1979) | Y |
| Guarantee Chrysler Corp. loans (1979) | N |
| Approve military draft registration (1980) | Y |
| Aid Sandinista regime in Nicaragua (1980) | N |
| Strengthen fair housing laws (1980) | N |

**97th Congress**

| | |
|---|---|
| Reagan budget proposal (1981) | Y |

## Interest Group Rating

| Year | ADA | ACA | AFL-CIO | CCUS |
|---|---|---|---|---|
| 1980 | 6 | 95 | 11 | 71 |
| 1979 | 0 | 100 | 5 | 100 |
| 1978 | 0 | 96 | 0 | 87 |
| 1977 | 5 | 100 | 17 | 100 |

# Arkansas

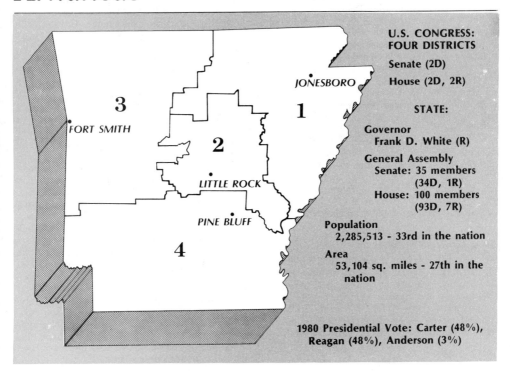

**U.S. CONGRESS:**
**FOUR DISTRICTS**

Senate (2D)

House (2D, 2R)

**STATE:**

Governor
Frank D. White (R)

General Assembly
Senate: 35 members
(34D, 1R)
House: 100 members
(93D, 7R)

Population
2,285,513 - 33rd in the nation

Area
53,104 sq. miles - 27th in the nation

**1980 Presidential Vote: Carter (48%), Reagan (48%), Anderson (3%)**

## ...Sudden Competition

For most of the 1970s, Arkansas seemed to be living in a different world from most of its Southern neighbors. While other states were flirting with Republicanism and rejecting the views of the national Democratic Party, Arkansas was electing avowed national Democrats to its highest offices. Its Republicans, seemingly on the verge of a breakthrough in 1966, had been virtually wiped out a decade later.

That political situation ended abruptly on Nov. 4, 1980, when "sacrificial" Republican candidate Frank White stunned the state's Democratic gubernatorial prodigy, Bill Clinton, who was seeking a second term at age 34.

Clinton's loss can be explained on narrow and personal grounds: the massive influx of Cuban refugees into the state had upset many Arkansans, and Clinton's badly timed increase in automobile license fees had compounded the situation.

But it can also be explained as the political reaction that was bound to come after a decade in which Arkansas had elected only national Democrats to the governorship and the Senate. From 1964, when segregationist Gov. Orval Faubus won his last term, to 1980, when White won, only one conservative Democrat was elected to either office. That was Sen. John L. McClellan, re-elected without serious opposition in 1966 and winning his sixth Senate term in 1972, after being forced into a runoff by David Pryor. All the others have been moderate-to-liberal. Dale Bumpers won two terms as governor and then went to the Senate. So did Pryor, following his loss to McClellan. Clinton was an easy winner for governor in 1978.

Meanwhile, the Republican Party was moribund. Winthrop Rockefeller won two terms as governor in the 1960s, but Rockefeller and his money were about all the GOP had, and when he lost to Bumpers in 1970, there was no structure to build on. The one lasting contribution from the GOP era was an end to the race politics that had predominated under Faubus. Rockefeller discredited and all but destroyed the older generation of conservative Democrats in Arkansas, leaving a vacuum for Bumpers, Pryor and Clinton to take advantage of in the following decade.

By 1980, it seemed reasonable to many people that Arkansas simply did not vote like a Southern state. But it is one. It has many of the demographic ingredients that have helped the GOP elsewhere in the South in recent years: an influx of corporate business and its managers, a growing suburban vote around Little Rock and numerous retirees arriving from other states. After decades of low population growth that cost it two House seats in 1960, the state began to show the results of its in-migration during the 1970s. It grew by 19 percent and in 1978 Little Rock elected its first Republican congressman in the 20th century.

All of that made White's breakthrough in 1980 reasonable, if not exactly predictable. But whether it will continue is hard to tell. While the governorship was going Republican and Reagan was eking out a victory over Carter, Bumpers was winning a second Senate term with nearly 60 percent of the vote. White is certain to have strong Democratic opposition in 1982, and the results of that contest may be a clue to the future of Arkansas politics.

# A Political Tour

**Little Rock.** Located in the center of the state on the Arkansas River, Little Rock is the capital, the largest city and the industrial center for Arkansas. It is also the home of the only newspapers with statewide circulation. One of them, *The Arkansas Gazette*, has a decidedly liberal editorial tone which has influenced politics both on the local and state level.

At close to 160,000 people, Little Rock is more than twice the size of the state's next largest city. With surrounding parts of Pulaski County, it accounts for 15 percent of the state's population.

Now one-third black, Little Rock is remembered as an early battleground in the fight to integrate public education in the South. But the efforts by Faubus in 1957 to keep nine black students from enrolling in Little Rock's Central High School are now dim memories. The city's racial tensions have subsided, thanks in part to governors in the post-Faubus era who have taken an open-minded attitude toward racial questions. And the city's attention has turned to other

matters, such as rebuilding the downtown area and eradicating the remaining slum areas.

The voters in Pulaski County recently have shown little partisan consistency. In 1968, the county split its vote evenly in thirds among Humphrey, Nixon and Wallace. Four years later, Nixon won 63 percent, which was the same figure Carter received in 1976.

But by 1980, both Carter and Clinton had lost nearly as much support in Little Rock as they had in the rural areas of the state. Carter's percentage fell 14 points; Clinton, still supported by many blacks and state government workers, dropped nine points from his 1978 mark. While Carter and Clinton barely edged out their GOP opponents in this area, Republican congressman Ed Bethune racked up a whopping 80 percent in Pulaski County.

**Republican Ozarks and Ouachita Mountains.** Highway 67, which enters Arkansas in the northeast corner and leaves via Texarkana in the southwest, divides the state in two.

To the north and west of that line are the Ozarks, spilling over from southern Missouri, and the Ouachita Mountains, coming from eastern Oklahoma. Bisected by the broad Arkansas River, this is hilly country that is less suited to the large scale farming found south and east of Route 67 Anti-secessionist during the Civil War, the small-scale farmers of the region blamed the hardships of the war on the plantation east and have been voting Republican ever since.

For decades after the Civil War, Republicans in Arkansas were cloistered in a few counties in the northwest. For the first 60 years of the 20th century, Newton and Searcy counties were the only two that would consistently vote Republican.

But in the last two decades, Republicans have begun to spread their influence. The 3rd District, covering the entire northwestern quarter of the state, has been in GOP hands since 1966. In 1980, White carried virtually every county north and west of U.S. 67.

Fort Smith, with 71,000 people, is the only city of any size in the area. Sitting on the Oklahoma border, it has a Western flavor that comes in part from its large livestock business. The local citizenry rose up in anger in 1980 when thousands of Cuban refugees were housed at nearby Fort Chaffee. Blaming both President Carter and Gov. Clinton for imposing this burden, area voters gave Carter his lowest mark in the state (27 percent) and Clinton his second lowest (33 percent).

The Ozark region is best known for its cattle, poultry and lumbering, but is traditionally a poor area. In the Ouachita Mountains, harvesting pine has been a chief source of income.

Recently, however, an infusion of small industry and the arrival of retirees have brought a population boom to northwest Arkansas. Nearly every county north of the Arkansas River grew by at least 30 percent in the last decade.

It is an overwhelmingly white part of the South. There are no more blacks in this half of Arkansas than in rural parts of Minnesota or Wisconsin. The 1980 census found two counties — Searcy and Madison — where there were no black people at all.

**The Mississippi Delta and Southern Plains.** While the 1980 election brought out Republican votes in the north and west, it also confirmed that the Mississippi Delta and the Southern Plains are still steadfastly Democratic.

Closer in appearance to Mississippi and Louisiana, this is large-scale farming and oil-drilling country. Although rice and soybeans now enjoy wide popularity with the farmers of the area, the cotton fields still stretch for miles along the Delta.

This was plantation Arkansas in the early 19th century, and secessionist territory prior to and during the Civil War. Since Reconstruction the region has been consistently Democratic, and among white voters, conservative.

Today, the strongest cotton areas are also those with the greatest black population and the largest Democratic vote. Along the Mississippi River from West Memphis to the Louisiana border, every county is at least 40 percent black; three of them — Lee, Phillips and Chicot — have black majorities. The cotton economy, however, is not healthy and the population has declined.

In 1970, many black Delta voters stayed loyal to Republican Gov. Winthrop Rockefeller, in recognition of his many black appointments. Ten years later, while nominal Democrats elsewhere were abandoning the Carter-Clinton ticket, the Delta counties remained firm in their support for both incumbents with percentages in the 50s for Carter and the 60s for Clinton.

Moving west and south from the Delta, the black population drops to between 20 and 30 percent and the white voters, still ostensibly Democrats, assume a more "redneck" Southern style. George Wallace carried the entire area in his 1968 presidential campaign. Carter did well here even in 1980, but Clinton was too liberal for many Democrats in south Arkansas. He lost every county in the south central part of the state.

This is the oil producing section of Arkansas. El Dorado in Union County, center for oil workers, has become increasingly Republican.

Poultry, cattle and cotton predominate in far southwestern counties, but the land grows more wooded closer to Pine Bluff, the largest city in the southern region. Nearly 50 percent black, Pine Bluff is a solidly Democratic town.

# Redrawing the Lines

Arkansas became the first state to establish new districts following the 1980 census when the Legislature March 18 approved a plan that made only minor shifts among the state's four districts. In all, only seven counties were moved, bringing no political harm to incumbents of either party.

The Republican 3rd District grew 33 percent over the last decade and was forced to give up the most territory. Some 3rd District residents of Garland County objected to being transferred from Republican Hammerschmidt to Democrat Anthony, but the new plan stirred few other complaints. Gov. Frank D. White allowed the bill to become law without his signature.

# Governor
# Frank D. White (R)

**Born:** June 4, 1933; Texarkana, Ark.
**Home:** Gordon, Ark.
**Education:** U.S. Naval Academy, 1956.
**Military Career:** Air Force, 1956-61.
**Profession:** Savings and loan association president.
**Family:** Wife, Gay; three children.
**Religion:** Protestant.
**Political Career:** Elected governor 1980; term expires Jan. 1983.

# Dale Bumpers (D)

**Of Charleston — Elected 1974**

**Born:** Aug. 12, 1925, Charleston, Ark.
**Education:** U. of Ark.; Northwestern U., LL.B.
1951, J.D. 1965.
**Profession:** Lawyer, farmer.
**Military Career:** Marine Corps, 1943-46.
**Family:** Wife, Betty Flanagan; three children.
**Religion:** Methodist.
**Political Career:** Ark. governor, 1971-75.

**In Washington:** Despite a pronounced iconoclastic streak and an initially cool reception from his colleagues, Bumpers has gradually won both respect and popularity in the Senate.

The initial resentment came from his primary victory in 1974 over Sen. J. William Fulbright, renowned chairman of the Foreign Relations Committee. But he dissolved it with hard work and the same sense of humor that helped him in Arkansas politics.

Like most former governors who make the shift to Capitol Hill, Bumpers chafed at the slow pace of legislative action and the inefficiency of Senate operations. Much of what transpired on the Hill, he complained publicly, was pure "charade."

Those public complaints stamped Bumpers as a budding Senate "outsider," but unlike genuine outsiders, Bumpers followed up on his frustrations. Early in his first term, he commissioned a Library of Congress study that turned out to be a key step toward the 1977 overhaul of the Senate's committee structure, the first of its kind in 30 years.

One of the panels eliminated in that 1977 reform was the Aeronautics and Space Committee, to which Bumpers had been assigned as a freshman. With few regrets, he shifted first to Armed Services and later to Appropriations. But his real mark has been made on the Energy Committee, where he is now the third-ranking Democrat.

Over the last several years, Bumpers has emerged as one of the Senate's foremost advocates of energy conservation and as a stubborn, sometimes lonely proponent of mandatory gasoline rationing. Arguing that nothing less will "get our energy appetite under control," Bumpers contends that when energy shortages make it necessary to restrict gasoline consumption, rationing is more equitable than higher taxes and soaring pump prices. He admits that rationing is "about as popular as leprosy in this country," but his

support for the concept did him little harm at the polls in 1980. Considerably more popular is another conservation measure which Bumpers successfully promoted — the requirement that all states permit right turns on red lights, or else face the loss of federal highway funds.

When it comes to the price of oil, Bumpers' streak of mountain populism reasserts itself. Both within the Energy Committee and on the Senate floor, he has repeatedly battled the oil industry — unsuccessfully in most cases, but with unflagging vigor. He joined other liberals during the 96th Congress in fighting deregulation of oil and natural gas prices, and favored a stiff windfall profits tax on the oil companies.

Bumpers is also a critic of nuclear power. He fought to block funding for the Clinch River breeder reactor, opposed the neutron bomb and voted against deployment of large nuclear-powered aircraft carriers. He supported the ill-fated SALT II treaty.

While no more than moderately liberal by the standard interest group litmus tests, Bumpers is clearly to the left of most of his Southern colleagues in the Senate. But his iconoclastic streak makes him difficult to label and still catches colleagues by surprise. In 1978, for instance, Bumpers was the only senator to vote against popular "sunset" legislation to force periodic review of all federal programs. He called it "a classic bureaucratic response to bureaucracy."

And in 1979, Bumpers startled and dismayed his usual liberal allies by pushing through the Senate a proposal that would change the traditional legal presumption that all federal regulations are valid. Bumpers' amendment would shift to government agencies the burden of proving that regulations they draft are within the intent of Congress in passing the underlying law. The measure died with other aspects of regulatory reform legislation in the waning days of the 96th Congress, but is likely to arise again.

When Bumpers first arrived in the Senate, he was frequently touted as a prospect for presidential politics. As a Southern moderate with considerable personal charm, he looked like a natural for the second spot, at a minimum, on a national Democratic ticket. But while Bumpers was learning the Senate ropes, another Southerner got the jump on him politically. Allies occasionally argued with some vehemence that their man was "the real Jimmy Carter," but Bumpers was left stranded on Capitol Hill. Even the most charming of campaigners would have found it difficult to persuade the Democratic electorate in 1980 that it should replace a moderate former governor of Georgia with a moderate former governor of Arkansas.

**At Home:** "A smile and a shoeshine" was the phrase Winthrop A. Rockefeller used to describe the political phenomenon that removed him from the Arkansas governorship in 1970. It was a slur on Dale Bumpers' intellectual substance, but it was not a bad description of the campaign that lifted Bumpers from a small-town law practice to the Little Rock statehouse in only a few months.

The Republican Rockefeller had made Bumpers possible by discrediting and retiring most of the segregationist "old guard" that dominated the Democratic Party in Arkansas over the previous two decades. After four years of Republican rule under Rockefeller, the state was ready to go Democratic again under a modern leader. Bumpers was so clearly the right man that a smile, a shoeshine and a sophisticated set of television commercials were more than enough to give him a primary victory over the legendary race-baiter Orval E. Faubus in a Democratic runoff, and an easy win over Rockefeller in the fall. Issues were beside the point.

Bumpers' gubernatorial campaign was so vague that the state had little reason to know exactly what it was getting when he took office in January 1971. In fact, it was getting a man with a fair degree of liberal Yankee influence, a graduate of Northwestern University law school and a long-time admirer of Adlai E. Stevenson, who was governor of Illinois when Bumpers got his law degree there in 1951. Bumpers came to the governorship without any political experience beyond the school board in Charleston, Ark., but with a clear sense of where he was going — the same one Jimmy Carter had in Georgia during the same four years.

Over four years in office, Bumpers presided over a modernization of state government, closing down many of the bureaucratic fiefdoms that old-guard Democrats had controlled for a generation before. By early 1974, he was ready for national politics and as popular as he had been on Inauguration Day. Arkansas Democrats braced themselves for a titanic struggle between the governor and Fulbright, who had helped raise money for Bumpers in 1970.

As it turned out, the struggle was less than titanic. Bumpers decided to run only after political consultant Deloss Walker showed him polls guaranteeing he could not lose. Bumpers defeated Fulbright by nearly 2-1 in the Democratic primary without offering a word of criticism or a divisive issue — just a smile, a shoeshine, and four years of carefully managed state government.

The 1980 election was nothing to worry about. While other Arkansas Democrats were finally paying the price for a decade of too-easy liberal politics, Bumpers was winning a second term over a weak Republican opponent by 150,000 votes.

## Committees

**Appropriations** (14th of 14 Democrats)
District of Columbia; Interior; Legislative Branch; State Justice, Commerce, the Judiciary.

**Energy and Natural Resources** (3rd of 9 Democrats)
Energy and Mineral Resources; Energy Research and Development; Public Lands and Reserved Water.

**Small Business** (3rd of 8 Democrats)
Government Regulation and Paperwork.

## Elections

**1980 General**

| | |
|---|---|
| Dale Bumpers (D) | 477,905 (59%) |
| Bill Clark (R) | 330,576 (41%) |

**Previous Winning Percentage**

**1974 (85%)**

## Campaign Finance

| | Receipts | Receipts from PACs | Expenditures |
|---|---|---|---|
| 1980 | | | |
| Bumpers (D) | $299,465 | $430 (0.14%) | $220,861 |
| Clark (R) | $118,521 | $3,730 (3%) | $199,196 |

## Dale Bumpers, D-Ark.

## Voting Studies

| | Presidential Support | | Party Unity | | Conservative Coalition | |
|------|----|----|----|----|----|----|
| Year | S | O | S | O | S | O |
| 1980 | 69 | 19 | 66 | 20 | 42 | 47 |
| 1979 | 67 | 24 | 72 | 18 | 45 | 43 |
| 1978 | 70 | 17 | 69 | 21 | 46 | 42 |
| 1977 | 68 | 18 | 69 | 17 | 26 | 64 |
| 1976 | 42 | 51 | 67 | 17 | 27 | 59 |
| 1975 | 46 | 38 | 69 | 20 | 36 | 55 |

S = Support          O = Opposition

## Key Votes

**96th Congress**

| | |
|---|---|
| Maintain relations with Taiwan (1979) | N |
| Reduce synthetic fuel development funds (1979) | N |

| | |
|---|---|
| Impose nuclear plant moratorium (1979) | Y |
| Kill stronger windfall profits tax (1979) | N |
| Guarantee Chrysler Corp. loans (1979) | N |
| Approve military draft registration (1980) | Y |
| End Revenue Sharing to the states (1980) | Y |
| Block Justice Dept. busing suits (1980) | N |

**97th Congress**

| | |
|---|---|
| Restore urban program funding cuts (1981) | Y |

## Interest Group Ratings

| Year | ADA | ACA | AFL-CIO | CCUS-1 | CCUS-2 |
|------|-----|-----|---------|--------|--------|
| 1980 | 56 | 35 | 56 | 41 | |
| 1979 | 53 | 35 | 63 | 9 | 31 |
| 1978 | 45 | 35 | 26 | 44 | |
| 1977 | 75 | 15 | 67 | 27 | |
| 1976 | 70 | 19 | 79 | 0 | |
| 1975 | 56 | 18 | 44 | 15 | |

# David Pryor (D)

### Of Camden — Elected 1978

**Born:** Aug. 29, 1934, Camden, Ark.
**Education:** U. of Ark., B.A. 1957, LL.B. 1964.
**Profession:** Lawyer.
**Family:** Wife, Barbara Lunsford; three children.
**Religion:** Presbyterian.
**Political Career:** Ark. House, 1961-67; U.S. House, 1967-73; Ark. Governor, 1975-79; unsuccessfully sought Democratic nomination for U.S. Senate, 1972.

**In Washington:** Pryor is promoting fiscal conservatism these days with the same exuberance he showed in his House crusade for senior citizens a decade ago, and struggling to make the case that the two are compatible.

In the 97th Congress, Pryor joined a group of the Senate's most conservative Democrats to support President Reagan's budget cuts. He has taken up the cause of eliminating frills and "reckless spending" in government. He insists that the budget can be trimmed without crippling support for the elderly and other social programs if Congress tightens the rules on hiring outside consultants and buying supplies.

"We are not talking about small potatoes," Pryor said early in 1981 as he tried to sell the Senate on one of his belt-tightening amendments. "We are not talking about a few boxes of Kleenex here or there. We are talking about one of every eight tax dollars that the American people invest in their country."

Pryor's amendment would have required the Appropriations Committee to take a "long hard look" at the procurement budgets of each federal agency, $100 billion worth of spending. Pryor lost that vote. Opponents argued his plan was too vague. But he managed to create an issue for himself, and he does not intend to let it go away.

Pryor discovered the consultants-and-supplies issue accidentally, but he has nurtured it carefully. Riding in a taxi one day in 1979, he overheard two men discussing how much to charge the government on a consulting contract — $25,000 or $12,000. They chose the larger figure on the theory that no one could tell the difference.

Pryor, then chairman of a General Services Subcommittee at Governmental Affairs, instructed his staff to look into the entire question of federal contracting. He concluded that millions of dollars were wasted each year, and that a prime offender was the new Department of Energy. "We are

literally seeing our nation's energy policy set by private consultants," he said, "...private consultants who are in no way responsible to the people of this country."

Pryor is a man who needs a cause. Over six years in the House, before he left for an unsuccessful Senate campaign in 1972, he showed an inspired talent for attracting public attention to social problems. When he was not engaged in a crusade, he tended to lose interest in legislative business.

In the House, Pryor's issue was the plight of the elderly. During his second House term, he worked four weekends in Washington area nursing homes, without identifying himself, and emerged with a report that he was shocked at conditions. He tried and failed to get the House to set up a committee on the aging. So he formed his own "special" aging committee in a trailer parked at a nearby gas station, and began issuing news releases.

Pryor has also drawn attention for his repeated warnings about unsafe conditions around Air Force Titan II missile silos, many of them in his state. In September of 1980, he persuaded the Senate to adopt his amendment requiring alarm sirens near any silo in a populated area. Three days later, fuel exploded at a silo in Damascus, Arkansas, killing an Air Force sergeant.

**At Home:** Pryor has always had a talent for picking issues that can bring favorable exposure in Arkansas. He was still in his twenties, struggling outnumbered against the segregationist "old guard" in the state Legislature, when he began investigating abuses in nursing homes. That issue helped him win a House seat in 1966, when the 4th District was left vacant with the departure of veteran Democrat Oren Harris. Once settled in Washington, he ran unopposed in 1968 and 1970.

**67**

## David Pryor, D-Ark.

In 1972, Pryor took on a challenge virtually every Democrat in the state told him he could not win — a primary campaign against the venerable senior senator, John L. McClellan. Pryor was determined, and campaigned intensely all over the state for months, raising the issue of McClellan's age, which was 76. When he held the senator to 44 percent in the initial primary in May, forcing a runoff, Arkansas' startled Democrats assumed he had McClellan on the run.

That was the second wrong assumption of the spring. The veteran fought back with surprising vigor in the runoff, seizing on Pryor's labor support to argue that union bosses wanted to get even for past McClellan corruption probes. On runoff night, Pryor found himself beaten by 18,000 votes.

Two years after his defeat, Pryor was elected governor, spoiling a comeback effort by Gov. Orval Faubus in that year's runoff. Faubus' once-vaunted political power had faded, along with the race issue that had fueled it, and his allies in the Arkansas business establishment deserted him for Pryor. Faubus called Pryor the "candidate of 52 millionaires" seeking to influence state policy, but the result was not even close. Pryor had no

trouble winning the general election that fall, or a second two-year term in 1976.

Late in 1977, McClellan died. Pryor appointed Kaneaster Hodges to fill the remaining year of the late senator's term. Under state law, Hodges was ineligible to succeed himself, and Pryor moved in on the seat in 1978.

This time he was no longer fighting the old guard. His competition in the primary came from two moderate congressmen, Jim Guy Tucker of Little Rock and Ray Thornton, Pryor's own successor in southern Arkansas' 4th District.

Pryor's pro-labor image had long since faded. As governor, he lost union support by sending in the National Guard to replace striking Pine Bluff firemen. In the two man runoff, Tucker got the labor endorsement; Pryor made an issue of it.

Pryor also ran on his record as governor. pointing to an improved economic climate and a surplus in the state treasury. He won the runoff by a surprising 47,000 votes, picking up much of the southern Arkansas support that had gone at first to Thornton, a close third in the initial primary. The general election against Republican Thomas Kelly was easy.

## Committees

**Agriculture, Nutrition and Forestry** (5th of 8 Democrats)
Agricultural Research and General Legislation; Foreign Agricultural Policy; Rural Development, Oversight, and Investigations.
**Governmental Affairs** (7th of 8 Democrats)
Congressional Operations and Oversight; Civil Service, Post Office and General Services; Oversight of Government Management.
**Select Ethics** (2nd of 3 Democrats)
**Special Aging** (4th of 7 Democrats)

## Elections

**1978 General**

| | |
|---|---|
| David Pryor (D) | 399,916 (77 %) |
| Tom Kelly (R) | 84,722 (16 %) |
| John Black (I) | 37,488 (7 %) |

**1978 Primary Runoff**

| | |
|---|---|
| David Pryor (D) | 265,525 (55%) |
| Jim Tucker (D) | 218,026 (45%) |

**1978 Primary**

| | |
|---|---|
| David Pryor (D) | 198,039 (34 %) |
| Jim Tucker (D) | 187,568 (32 %) |
| Ray Thronton (D) | 184,095 (32%) |

**Previous Winning Percentages**

1970* (100%)  1968* (100%)  1966* (65%)

* House elections

## Campaign Finance

| | Receipts | Receipts from PACs | Expenditures |
|---|---|---|---|
| **1978** | | | |
| Pryor (D ) | $802,861 | $97,280 (12 %) | $774,824 |

| | | | |
|---|---|---|---|
| Kelly (R ) | $16,210 | $300 (2 %) | $16,208 |

## Voting Studies

| Year | Presidential Support | | Party Unity | | Conservative Coalition | |
|---|---|---|---|---|---|---|
| | S | O | S | O | S | O |
| 1980 | 66 | 24 | 63 | 27 | 59 | 37 |
| 1979 | 64 | 32 | 63 | 33 | 71 | 21 |

S = Support          O = Opposition

## Key Votes

**96th Congress**

| | |
|---|---|
| Maintain relations with Taiwan (1979) | N |
| Reduce synthetic fuel development funds (1979) | Y |
| Impose nuclear plant moratorium (1979) | ? |
| Kill stronger windfall profits tax (1979) | N |
| Guarantee Chrysler Corp. loans (1979) | N |
| Approve military draft registration (1980) | Y |
| End Revenue Sharing to the states (1980) | N |
| Block Justice Dept. busing suits (1980) | N |

**97th Congress**

| | |
|---|---|
| Restore urban program funding cuts (1981) | N |

## Interest Group Ratings

| Year | ADA | ACA | AFL-CIO | CCUS-1 | CCUS-2 |
|---|---|---|---|---|---|
| 1980 | 44 | 46 | 42 | 59 | |
| 1979 | 42 | 42 | 58 | 27 | 56 |

# 1 Bill Alexander (D)

Of Osceola — Elected 1968

**Born:** Jan. 16, 1934, Memphis, Tenn.
**Education:** Southwestern at Memphis, B.A.
1957; Vanderbilt U., LL.B. 1960.
**Military Career:** Army, 1951-53.
**Profession:** Lawyer.
**Family:** Divorced; one child.
**Religion:** Episcopalian.
**Political Career:** No previous office.

**In Washington:** Alexander has always shown a fondness for the inside politics of the House floor, and he has had ample opportunity to indulge it in the 97th Congress as chief deputy whip, the fifth ranking position in the Democratic leadership.

When the House began debating the budget in May 1981, and Democratic leaders found alarming numbers of Southern Democrats defecting to the Reagan alternative, Alexander came up with an interesting strategy: give the House a chance to vote on a balanced budget for 1982 without the massive Reagan-sized tax cut or any tax cut at all. The theory was that some of the Southerners who liked the spending cuts in Reagan's budget more than the tax cuts would like a balanced budget even better.

The scheme turned out not to attract many new votes, and the leadership never did offer it. By that time, most of the House was already committed one way or another, for Reagan or against him, and it would have made little difference.

It was also Alexander who revealed that Southern Democrats were being pressured by the Reagan White House through their campaign contributors, who were calling to threaten a cutoff in funds for 1982 if the members did not vote with Reagan on the budget. Alexander and Speaker O'Neill both called this unreasonable pressure, but that did not prevent the administration from using it. It appeared to be an effective tactic.

Alexander's leadership job is a direct result of his support for Jim Wright, D-Texas, in the 1976 contest for majority leader. After the election was over, Alexander took Wright's old post in the middle ranks of the Democratic whip structure. In early 1981, when Chief Deputy Whip Dan Rostenkowski of Illinois took the chairmanship of the Ways and Means Committee, Wright chose Alexander to replace him.

A 12-year House veteran at age 47, Alexander shares the majority leader's enthusiasm for public

works spending, especially water projects. He was one of the most outspoken House critics of President Carter's plan to cut back on such spending. "It boils down to a question of who is going to decide water policy," Alexander complained at one point in 1979. "Is it going to be the Congress or a few self-appointed people within the administration?"

As a member of the Agriculture Appropriations Subcommittee, Alexander gets a chance to speak up for his district's rice growers, a large and politically significant group. He has worked to expand export markets and trade assistance for agricultural products, especially rice, soybeans and cotton. He also has sought a role as a spokesman for rural areas in general; he has moved to change community development block grant formulas to give more money to small towns, and he led a successful fight early in the 1970s to make it easier for rural areas to obtain health planning subsidies.

The Appropriations Committee has given Alexander an opportunity to promote a variety of other projects. He fought a long-term battle to include language in foreign aid funding bills penalizing countries delinquent in payment of their debts to the United States. Another idea, less successful, would have brought the U.S. Postal Service back under congressional control.

Alexander floated plans in 1980 for a primary challenge to Dale Bumpers, Arkansas' popular senior senator. He questioned Bumpers' skepticism about some public works projects and occa-

---

**1st District: East — Jonesboro.** Population: 521,904 (9% increase since 1970). Race: White 417,319 (80%), Black 101,057 (19%), Others 3,528 (1%). Spanish origin: 4,383 (1%).

sional votes against military spending. But Alexander chose to run for re-election instead.

Alexander's most publicized battle in Washington was one he would just as soon forget — a fight with a policeman outside National Airport in 1973. The policeman claimed Alexander bumped him with his car, and he charged the congressman with assault. Alexander said he had been "brutalized" by the officer. After a series of newspaper articles, no one pressed any charges.

**At Home:** Alexander was a young lawyer in the small town of Osceola when he entered the free-for-all 1968 Democratic primary to succeed Rep. Ezekiel "Took" Gathings, who was retiring.

There were nine candidates for the nomination, and Alexander had never held office before. But he started campaigning early, and his residence in the most populous county in the district gave him an advantage. His main competition came from Jack Files, a former aide to Sen. J. William Fulbright. Alexander got 38.1 percent of the vote, not enough to avoid a runoff but almost 25 percentage points more than Files. In the runoff, he drew 62.2 percent.

The newly resurgent Arkansas Republicans attempted to give Alexander a fight in November. Their candidate was Guy Newcomb, a pharmacist and farmer, also from Osceola. It was the first real inter-party contest in the district since Reconstruction. The Republican came out with a more-or-less respectable 31.1 percent of the vote but never threatened Democratic control. Alexander sailed through the next three elections.

In 1976, Republicans decided to make another major attempt to take the district, which by then had been expanded to include several less Democratic counties. This time the GOP candidate was Harlan (Bo) Holleman, a seed merchant from Wynne. Holleman raised a sizable campaign treasury and concentrated on the district's prime issue, agriculture. He had good contacts throughout the district from his work as state Republican finance director and as director of the oilseeds division of the U.S. Department of Agriculture. But the result was exactly what it had been eight years before: 31.1 percent of the vote. In 1978 and 1980, Alexander was unopposed in both the primary and general election.

**The District:** The eastern area of Arkansas is the part of the state with the strongest Deep South tradition, the one whose rich Mississippi Delta lands were tied to cotton long before the Civil War. It is still primarily an agricultural region, with small market-towns and a large black population. Some industry has come into the district, including electronics plants at Forrest City and Paragould, and Arkansas State University is at Jonesboro, but the 1st is still the least prosperous of the four Arkansas districts.

In 1972, the district was underpopulated and had to expand further west, taking in non-Delta counties in the northern part of the state. Many retirees from outside the South have been settling in that area, and often they vote Republican.

In the 1980 redistricting, the 1st was underpopulated by about 50,000, but no drastic changes were made in its borders. Three counties have been added for 1982 — Arkansas, Prairie and Cleburne. The largest new town in the district is Stuttgart, with about 10,000 people.

## Committees

**Appropriations** (13th of 33 Democrats)
  Agriculture; Commerce, Justice, State, and Judiciary; Military Construction.

**Standards of Official Conduct** (3rd of 6 Democrats)

## Elections

**1980 General**

| | |
|---|---|
| Bill Alexander (D ) | Unopposed |

**1978 General**

| | |
|---|---|
| Bill Alexander (D ) | Unopposed |

**Previous Winning Percentages**

| | | | |
|---|---|---|---|
| 1976 (69 %) | 1974 (91 %) | 1972 (100%) | 1970 (100%) |
| 1968 (69 %) | | | |

### District Vote For President

| | 1980 | | 1976 | | 1972 |
|---|---|---|---|---|---|
| D | 93,654 (52 %) | D | 120,799 (70 %) | D | 45,355 (31 %) |
| R | 79,426 (44 %) | R | 52,491 (30 %) | R | 98,979 (68 %) |
| I | 3,588 (2 %) | | | | |

## Campaign Finance

| | Receipts | Receipts from PACs | Expenditures |
|---|---|---|---|
| **1980** | | | |
| Alexander (D ) | $121,712 | $47,475 (39 %) | $50,289 |
| **1978** | | | |
| Alexander (D ) | $50,015 | $28,475 (57 %) | $37,844 |

## Voting Studies

| Year | Presidential Support S | O | Party Unity S | O | Conservative Coalition S | O |
|------|------|----|------|----|------|----|
| 1980 | 64 | 16 | 68 | 9 | 39 | 48 |
| 1979 | 58 | 19 | 70 | 11 | 34 | 46 |
| 1978 | 57 | 26 | 65 | 18 | 33 | 51 |
| 1977 | 58 | 34 | 70 | 23 | 49 | 43 |
| 1976 | 37 | 39 | 54 | 31 | 53 | 30 |
| 1975 | 42 | 48 | 56 | 32 | 54 | 34 |
| 1974 (Ford) | 37 | 44 | | | | |
| 1974 | 42 | 42 | 53 | 32 | 61 | 27 |
| 1973 | 33 | 53 | 60 | 27 | 53 | 32 |
| 1972 | 41 | 38 | 44 | 38 | 55 | 24 |
| 1971 | 44 | 32 | 50 | 20 | 31 | 32 |
| 1970 | 57 | 29 | 50 | 35 | 57 | 25 |
| 1969 | 64 | 30 | 42 | 47 | 60 | 24 |

S = Support        O = Opposition

## Key Votes

**96th Congress**

| | |
|---|---|
| Weaken Carter oil profits tax (1979) | Y |
| Reject hospital cost control plan (1979) | Y |
| Implement Panama Canal Treaties (1979) | Y |
| Establish Department of Education (1979) | Y |
| Approve Anti-busing Amendment (1979) | N |
| Guarantee Chrysler Corp. loans (1979) | ? |
| Approve military draft registration (1980) | Y |
| Aid Sandinista regime in Nicaragua (1980) | ? |
| Strengthen fair housing laws (1980) | Y |

**97th Congress**

| | |
|---|---|
| Reagan budget proposal (1981) | N |

## Interest Group Ratings

| Year | ADA | ACA | AFL-CIO | CCUS |
|------|-----|-----|---------|------|
| 1980 | 44 | 33 | 56 | 80 |
| 1979 | 37 | 4 | 50 | 53 |
| 1978 | 25 | 41 | 59 | 44 |
| 1977 | 25 | 24 | 61 | 50 |
| 1976 | 30 | 41 | 59 | 60 |
| 1975 | 21 | 54 | 62 | 47 |
| 1974 | 17 | 57 | 60 | 67 |
| 1973 | 44 | 38 | 63 | 44 |
| 1972 | 19 | 44 | 40 | 63 |
| 1971 | 27 | 42 | 75 | - |
| 1970 | 20 | 50 | 20 | 67 |
| 1969 | 13 | 27 | 50 | |

# 2 Ed Bethune (R)

### Of Searcy — Elected 1978

**Born:** Dec. 19, 1935, Pocahontas, Ark.
**Education:** U. of Ark., B.S. 1961; U. of Ark. Law School, J.D. 1963.
**Military Career:** Marine Corps, 1954-57.
**Profession:** Lawyer.
**Family:** Wife, Lana Douthit; two children.
**Religion:** Methodist.
**Political Career:** Republican nominee for Arkansas Attorney General, 1972.

**In Washington:** This soft-spoken former FBI agent strikes people as an unlikely firebrand, but he was at the center of internal Republican ferment in the House throughout his first term.

Chosen as president of the incoming GOP class of 1978, Bethune drew the assignment of summoning Minority Leader John Rhodes and Whip Robert Michel to a pre-session meeting with the group in a Washington, D.C., motel. It was more of a demand than a request. He and the other freshmen told both leaders to be more outspoken in their partisanship. "It was mostly a question of style," Bethune said afterward. "A question of aggressiveness and image."

A few months later Bethune helped persuade Henry Hyde of Illinois, a third-term conservative, to run for GOP conference chairman as the "freshman" candidate. When Hyde came within three votes of upsetting veteran Samuel Devine of Ohio for the No. 3 leadership position, the freshmen claimed a moral victory, and savored their influence.

Rarely seen as an aggressive partisan in Arkansas, Bethune quickly became one of the most consistent Republican partisans on the House floor, roasting Democratic economic policy and expressing an almost personal outrage at the majority's decision to hold a "lame duck" congressional session after the 1980 election.

Beyond the partisan speeches and press releases, however, lies a streak of independence. Bethune was one of five House Republicans to support President Carter in a key test vote on Carter's gas rationing proposal in 1980. He cast one of only 35 GOP votes for the bill to implement the Panama Canal treaties, although he muted criticism in Arkansas by calling the treaties themselves "the worst mistake we have made in 20 years." He and Ron Paul of Texas were the only Republicans from the South to vote for an amendment that would have blocked spending for

chemical warfare. There is a substantial chemical weapons stockpile at an Army arsenal in Pine Bluff, just south of the 2nd District.

On the House Banking Committee, Bethune shared the skepticism of most of his GOP colleagues about the Chrysler loan guarantee; he not only voted against it but testified against it, and became a public critic of loan guarantees of various sorts. As a new member of the Budget Committee in 1981, he worked on efforts to ensure that the money the federal government spends guaranteeing loans is included in estimates of federal spending.

Bethune also spent several months of his first term on his own investigation of the purchasing practices of international oil companies. He attributed the time-consuming effort, which paralleled existing committee work, to a "bloodhound instinct" from his days at the FBI.

**At Home:** Bethune's surprising 1978 victory followed a decade of political and governmental activity, and an upbringing in a political family. His father was a candidate for state auditor in the 1940 Democratic primary.

After retiring from the FBI in 1968, Bethune returned to Arkansas and joined the Republican Party. He set up a law practice with the Republican state chairman, and Republican Gov. Winthrop Rockefeller appointed him to an unexpired

---

**2nd District: North — Little Rock.**
Population: 595,768 (24% increase since 1970). Race: White 488,287 (82%), Black 101,480 (17%), Others 6,001 (1%). Spanish origin: 4,711 (1%).

---

term as a prosecuting attorney in 1970. In 1972, Bethune ran for attorney general. He did not win, but he established a statewide reputation and nearly carried the 2nd District. The next year, he got an appointment as district chairman of the Federal Home Loan Bank Board. President Ford nominated him for a federal judgeship in 1976, but Democratic Sen. Dale Bumpers blocked the appointment.

When Bethune announced for the House in 1978, he was a decided underdog, even though the seat was open with the Senate candidacy of Democratic Rep. Jim Guy Tucker. But Democrats had a divisive primary to choose a new nominee, and Bethune was able to tag labor-backed Doug Brandon, the eventual winner, as too liberal for the district. Bethune carried Pulaski County (Little Rock), the largest county in the district, by a wide majority and overcame Democratic margins elsewhere in the district to win by 3,145 votes. By

1980, Bethune had a solid grip on the district, and neither Tucker nor any other well-known Democrat wanted to take him on.

**The District:** Centered around Little Rock, the 2nd combines that city's traditional district with rural areas to the north which once formed part of another. Wilbur D. Mills began his congressional career in the old rural constituency and represented it for more than 20 years. When the two were merged in 1962, Mills took over both, until his retirement in 1976.

Pulaski County makes up about half the district. With growing business migration from the north, the Little Rock area prospered during the 1970s, and has an increasing Republican base. The rural counties remain largely Democratic, and there is a politically active labor movement. Included in the 2nd District are plants manufacturing aluminum, telegraph equipment, and watches and cameras.

## Committees

**Banking, Finance and Urban Affairs** (9th of 19 Republicans)
  Economic Stabilization; Financial Institutions Supervision, Regulation and Insurance; Housing and Community Development.

**Budget**
  Task Forces: Economic Policy and Productivity; Enforcement, Credit and Multi-year Budgeting; Reconciliation.

## Elections

**1980 General**

| | |
|---|---|
| Ed Bethune (R ) | 159,148 (79 %) |
| James Reid (D ) | 42,278 (21 %) |

**1978 General**

| | |
|---|---|
| Ed Bethune (R ) | 65,285 (51 %) |
| Doug Brandon (D ) | 62,140 (49 %) |

**District Vote For President**

| | 1980 | | 1976 | | 1972 |
|---|---|---|---|---|---|
| D | 103,040 (50 %) | D | 126,790 (68 %) | D | 56,514 (36 %) |
| R | 95,148 (46 %) | R | 60,457 (32 %) | R | 100,761 (64 %) |
| I | 7,317 (4 %) | | | | |

## Campaign Finance

| | Receipts | Receipts from PACs | Expenditures |
|---|---|---|---|
| **1980** | | | |
| Bethune (R ) | $262,714 | $73,136 (28 %) | $193,207 |
| Reid (D ) | $14,918 | — (0 %) | $14,919 |

| | | | |
|---|---|---|---|
| **1978** | | | |
| Bethune (R ) | $255,176 | $44,074 (17 %) | $255,098 |

## Voting Studies

| | Presidential Support | | Party Unity | | Conservative Coalition | |
|---|---|---|---|---|---|---|
| Year | S | O | S | O | S | O |
| 1980 | 40 | 50 | 82 | 12 | 89 | 4 |
| 1979 | 28 | 70 | 82 | 14 | 86 | 7 |

S = Support          O = Opposition

## Key Votes

**96th Congress**

| | |
|---|---|
| Weaken Carter oil profits tax (1979) | Y |
| Reject hospital cost control plan (1979) | Y |
| Implement Panama Canal Treaties (1979) | N |
| Establish Department of Education (1979) | N |
| Approve Anti-busing Amendment (1979) | N |
| Guarantee Chrysler Corp. loans (1979) | N |
| Approve military draft registration (1980) | Y |
| Aid Sandinista regime in Nicaragua (1980) | N |
| Strengthen fair housing laws (1980) | N |

**97th Congress**

| | |
|---|---|
| Reagan budget proposal (1981) | Y |

## Interest Group Ratings

| Year | ADA | ACA | AFL-CIO | CCUS |
|---|---|---|---|---|
| 1980 | 11 | 74 | 11 | 69 |
| 1979 | 16 | 84 | 25 | 82 |

# 3 John Paul Hammerschmidt

**Of Harrison — Elected 1966**

**(R)**

**Born:** May, 4, 1922, Harrison, Ark.
**Education:** Attended the Citadel, 1938-39; U. of Ark., 1940-41; Okla. State U., 1945-46.
**Military Career:** Army, 1942-45; Air Force Reserve.
**Profession:** Lumber company executive.
**Family:** Wife, Virginia Sharp; one child.
**Religion:** Presbyterian.
**Political Career:** No previous office.

**In Washington:** Hammerschmidt had to learn how to court Democrats to survive in Arkansas politics, and he has made ample use of his skill in the House, where his folksy conservatism marks few differences from his Southern Democratic allies. Partisanship is rarely much of an issue on Hammerschmidt's two committees, Public Works and Veterans' Affairs, where benefits and water projects are equally popular on both sides of the aisle. As ranking member of the Veterans' Affairs Committee, Hammerschmidt has allied himself with Southern Democrats to maintain high benefit levels for World War II veterans, to the occasional frustration of those who served in Vietnam. That stance in part reflects his district, a mountain retirement mecca with an estimated 66,000 World War II veterans.

Hammerschmidt has, however, cosponsored a bill to set up a comprehensive treatment and rehabilitation program for narcotics addicts, both veterans and those still on active duty.

Hammerschmidt joined Public Works in his first House term, after campaigning for Congress on a promise to work for creation of a national park along the Buffalo River. In 1972, the Buffalo National River area was created.

Since then, like others on Public Works, he has been diligent in getting projects for his district. He obtained money for a four-lane highway from Fayetteville to the Missouri state line, and for two bridges across Lake Norfolk.

He has opposed moves on Public Works to open up more of the highway trust fund for mass transit. "What Arkansas needs now," he has said, "are good four-lane primary roads."

**At Home:** In 1966, Hammerschmidt became the first Republican elected to Congress from Arkansas in the 20th century.

His timing was perfect. Two years earlier, Democratic Rep. James Trimble had been held to 55 percent of the vote by a Republican challenger,

while Barry Goldwater was drawing a respectable 44 percent of the presidential vote in the district. The 1966 election promised national Republican gains, and Hammerschmidt was in the right district to take advantage of them.

Hammerschmidt had been Arkansas Republican chairman for two years, as the state GOP made its ultimately successful move to elect Winthrop A. Rockefeller governor. He also ran a lumber firm that had been in his family three generations.

Trimble had held the seat since 1944, when he succeeded J. William Fulbright. He was a moderate Democrat, closely identified with Arkansas River and Ozark development projects.

Trimble was 72 years old in 1966, and had to fight off two strong primary challengers. He never really recovered politically. In November, Hammerschmidt beat him by almost 10,000 votes.

Only one Democrat has gotten more than a third of the vote against Hammerschmidt. That one was Bill Clinton, who as a 28-year-old law professor in 1974, put on a yearlong campaign that came within 6,300 votes of a complacent Hammerschmidt in an election dominated by Watergate. Four years later, Clinton won the governorship, but he lost it after one term in 1980.

**The District:** Northwestern Arkansas is hill

> **3rd District: West — Fort Smith, Fayetteville.** Population: 638,607 (33% increase since 1970). Race: White 614,468 (96%), Black 14,382 (2%), Others 9,757 (2%). Spanish origin: 4,813 (1%).

country, with an overwhelmingly white, traditionally poor population, based for most of this century in small, not very productive farms. That has been changing in the past decade, however, as Northern retirees have moved in, major corporations have found the area attractive, and the traditional small poultry farms have given way to large broiler operations financed by corporate interests.

The area has long been the only part of the state with appreciable GOP strength, though the district-wide vote was nearly always Democratic. Now the influx of industry and retirees are making the 3rd more Republican. Local government and party registration are still heavily Democratic, but Reagan carried the 3rd by 57,000 votes in 1980, wiping out pluralities by Carter elsewhere in the state.

## Committees

**Public Works and Transportation** (3rd of 19 Republicans)
Aviation; Economic Development; Water Resources.

**Select Aging** (3rd of 23 Republicans)
Housing and Consumer Interests; Human Services.

**Veterans' Affairs** (Ranking Republican)
Compensation, Pension and Insurance; Hospitals and Health Care, Oversight and Investigations.

## Elections

**1980 General**

| | |
|---|---|
| John Hammerschmidt (R ) | Unopposed |

**1978 General**

| | |
|---|---|
| John Hammerschmidt (R ) | 130,086 (78 %) |
| William Mears (D ) | 35,748 (22 %) |

**Previous Winning Percentages**

| | | | |
|---|---|---|---|
| 1976 (100%) | 1974 (52 %) | 1972 (77 %) | 1970 (68 %) |
| 1968 (67 %) | 1966 (53 %) | | |

**District Vote For President**

| | 1980 | | 1976 | | 1972 |
|---|---|---|---|---|---|
| D | 96,831 (37 %) | D | 128,322 (56 %) | D | 47,922 (26 %) |
| R | 150,405 (58 %) | R | 99,178 (44 %) | R | 138,541 (74 %) |
| I | 8,365 (3 %) | | | | |

## Campaign Finance

| | Receipts | Receipts from PACs | Expenditures |
|---|---|---|---|
| **1980** | | | |
| Hammerschmidt (R) | $80,864 | $32,700 (40%) | $42,037 |
| **1978** | | | |
| Hammerschmidt (R ) | $64,368 | $20,500 (32 %) | $47,521 |

## Voting Studies

| | Presidential Support | | Party Unity | | Conservative Coalition | |
|---|---|---|---|---|---|---|
| Year | S | O | S | O | S | O |
| 1980 | 33 | 57 | 77 | 20 | 91 | 5 |
| 1979 | 26 | 71 | 83 | 13 | 88 | 6 |
| 1978 | 25 | 71 | 83 | 14 | 93 | 4 |
| 1977 | 38 | 58 | 77 | 17 | 89 | 5 |
| 1976 | 65 | 33 | 81 | 18 | 91 | 7 |
| 1975 | 63 | 37 | 78 | 19 | 89 | 6 |
| 1974 (Ford) | 33 | 44 | | | | |
| 1974 | 70 | 26 | 74 | 20 | 84 | 7 |
| 1973 | 62 | 32 | 74 | 19 | 85 | 7 |
| 1972 | 68 | 30 | 79 | 19 | 91 | 7 |
| 1971 | 77 | 19 | 71 | 19 | 84 | 8 |
| 1970 | 71 | 28 | 72 | 24 | 86 | 9 |
| 1969 | 66 | 30 | 85 | 11 | 96 | 2 |
| 1968 | 50 | 43 | 84 | 12 | 90 | 4 |
| 1967 | 49 | 50 | 84 | 15 | 93 | 7 |

S = Support     O = Opposition

## Key Votes

**96th Congress**

| | |
|---|---|
| Weaken Carter oil profits tax (1979) | Y |
| Reject hospital cost control plan (1979) | Y |
| Implement Panama Canal Treaties (1979) | N |
| Establish Department of Education (1979) | N |
| Approve Anti-busing Amendment (1979) | Y |
| Guarantee Chrysler Corp. loans (1979) | N |
| Approve military draft registration (1980) | ? |
| Aid Sandinista regime in Nicaragua (1980) | N |
| Strengthen fair housing laws (1980) | N |

**97th Congress**

| | |
|---|---|
| Reagan budget proposal (1981) | Y |

## Interest Group Ratings

| Year | ADA | ACA | AFL-CIO | CCUS |
|---|---|---|---|---|
| 1980 | 6 | 77 | 11 | 73 |
| 1979 | 16 | 92 | 16 | 82 |
| 1978 | 10 | 88 | 11 | 78 |
| 1977 | 5 | 89 | 18 | 94 |
| 1976 | 0 | 85 | 26 | 87 |
| 1975 | 5 | 78 | 19 | 82 |
| 1974 | 9 | 79 | 18 | 100 |
| 1973 | 4 | 71 | 11 | 100 |
| 1972 | 6 | 74 | 9 | 100 |
| 1971 | 14 | 79 | 17 | - |
| 1970 | 16 | 84 | 14 | 80 |
| 1969 | 0 | 60 | 20 | - |
| 1968 | 0 | 87 | 0 | - |
| 1967 | 0 | 83 | 8 | 100 |

# 4 Beryl Anthony Jr. (D)

### Of El Dorado — Elected 1978

**Born:** Feb. 21, 1938, El Dorado, Ark.

**Education:** U. of Ark., B.S. and B.A. 1961, J.D. 1963.

**Profession:** Lawyer, timber company executive.

**Family:** Wife, Sheila Foster; two children.

**Religion:** Episcopalian.

**Political Career:** Prosecuting attorney, Ark. 13th Judicial District, 1971-79.

**In Washington:** Timber is Beryl Anthony's business in Arkansas, and has occupied much of his time in Washington, where he is a frequent industry spokesman on the Agriculture Committee's Forests Subcommittee. He remains on the board of directors of his family business, Anthony Forest Products. Anthony is also friendlier to the oil industry than some of his Arkansas Democratic colleagues; during his first term he backed legislation to exempt independent producers and royalty holders from the windfall profits tax. Much of Arkansas' limited oil production has come from the area around his hometown of El Dorado.

Southern Arkansas has a history of moderate Democratic representation in the House, at least in recent years, and Anthony has been careful to keep his ties as a national Democrat while building a conservative voting record on most issues. When the Carter-Kennedy contest developed for the 1980 Democratic presidential nomination, Anthony led a delegation of 22 freshman House Democrats to the White House to meet privately with the president, and expressed his support for Carter. He also complained to Carter about delayed funding of a water project in Hope, Arkansas. "It's a quid pro quo," Anthony explained afterward. "They know they need help from Congress and I know, as a freshman, I need help."

Anthony tried another type of bargain on the House floor early in 1979, seeking to trade the votes of a bloc of Democratic freshmen for a promise by House leaders that legislation to balance the federal budget would come up later.

The leaders made a loose promise, and Anthony voted to raise the debt ceiling. Later in the year, he also voted with the leadership to accept the House Budget Committee's proposal calling for a $29 billion deficit.

In 1981, House leaders gave him an important second committee assignment, on the Budget Committee. There he went along with the Democratic alternative proposed by Chairman James R. Jones of Oklahoma. One of his projects on the committee was to try to restore money for the Farmers' Home Administration, but this was unsuccessful. On the House floor, he reversed himself and voted, like most Southern Democrats, for the Reagan-backed substitute budget.

**At Home:** When the 4th District opened up in 1978, with Rep. Ray Thornton's Senate candidacy, five major candidates entered the Democratic primary to succeed him. The overwhelming favorite was Arkansas Secretary of State Winston Bryant, who had already been on district ballots several times before, and whose vote-getting record was impressive.

Bryant had a 10,000-vote lead in the initial primary, but he was forced into a runoff against Anthony, then a businessman and prosecuting attorney in El Dorado, who portrayed himself as the "businessman's candidate" and campaigned against Bryant's identification with labor and teachers' associations. Personal wealth from the family's lumber company and ties with the district's oil and gas producers gave Anthony a strong fund-raising edge over Bryant, and he

---

**4th District: South — Pine Bluff.**
Population: 529,234 (10% increase since 1970). Race: White 369,928 (70%), Black 156,273 (29%), Others 3,033 (1%). Spanish origin: 3,966 (1%).

came from behind to defeat him in the runoff by 5,500 votes.

During his years as prosecuting attorney for a five-county district in southern Arkansas, Anthony had a reputation for taking a hard line against offenders. He chaired a study commission that recommended reinstating the death penalty in Arkansas.

**The District:** The 4th District stretches across southern Arkansas from the Mississippi River to the Texas border. In the east, it takes in some of the delta area along the Mississippi and Arkansas rivers. In the central portion lies a profitable wood and paper industry.

Pine Bluff, the district's major city, has several pulp and paper mills. It is also a railroad center. But most of the district is rural, with county courthouse politicians still influential.

The district has been Democratic throughout the past century. Republicans rarely even have bothered to put up congressional candidates. Even when the district was open in 1978, no Republican entered.

## Committees

**Agriculture** (20th of 24 Democrats)
Conservation, Credit, and Rural Development; Cotton, Rice and Sugar; Forests, Family Farms, and Energy.

**Budget**
Task Forces: Entitlements, Uncontrollables and Indexing; Reconciliation; Tax Policy.

## Elections

**1980 General**

| Beryl Anthony (D ) | Unopposed |

**1978 General**

| Beryl Anthony (D ) | Unopposed |

**1978 Primary Runoff**

| Beryl Anthony (D ) | 67,380 (52 %) |
| Winston Bryant (D ) | 61,619 (48 %) |

**1978 Primary**

| Winston Bryant (D ) | 50,835 (33 %) |
| Beryl Anthony (D ) | 40,326 (26 %) |
| Bill Elder (D ) | 23,275 (15 %) |
| Tom Wynne (D ) | 19,978 (13 %) |
| Don Smith (D ) | 17,952 (12 %) |

**District Vote For President**

| | 1980 | | 1976 | | 1972 |
|---|---|---|---|---|---|
| D | 104,516 (55 %) | D | 122,693 (69 %) | D | 49,108 (31 %) |
| R | 78,185 (41 %) | R | 55,777 (31 %) | R | 107,470 (68 %) |
| I | 3,198 (2 %) | | | | |

## Campaign Finance

| | Receipts | Receipts from PACs | Expenditures |
|---|---|---|---|
| **1980** | | | |
| Anthony (D ) | $112,992 | $22,400 (20 %) | $101,235 |

| **1978** | | | |
| Anthony (D ) | $374,165 | $57,315 (15 %) | $372,652 |

## Voting Studies

| | Presidental Support | | Party Unity | | Conservative Coalition | |
|---|---|---|---|---|---|---|
| Year | S | O | S | O | S | O |
| 1980 | 56 | 31 | 63 | 27 | 61 | 25 |
| 1979 | 59 | 35 | 64 | 28 | 65 | 26 |

S = Support          O = Opposition

## Key Votes

**96th Congress**

| Weaken Carter oil profits tax (1979) | Y |
| Reject hospital cost control plan (1979) | Y |
| Implement Panama Canal Treaties (1979) | N |
| Establish Department of Education (1979) | Y |
| Approve Anti-busing Amendment (1979) | N |
| Guarantee Chrysler Corp. loans (1979) | N |
| Approve military draft registration (1980) | ? |
| Aid Sandinista regime in Nicaragua (1980) | N |
| Strengthen fair housing laws (1980) | N |

**97th Congress**

| Reagan budget proposal (1981) | Y |

## Interest Group Ratings

| Year | ADA | ACA | AFL-CIO | CCUS |
|---|---|---|---|---|
| 1980 | 22 | 36 | 44 | 76 |
| 1979 | 26 | 29 | 37 | 65 |

# California

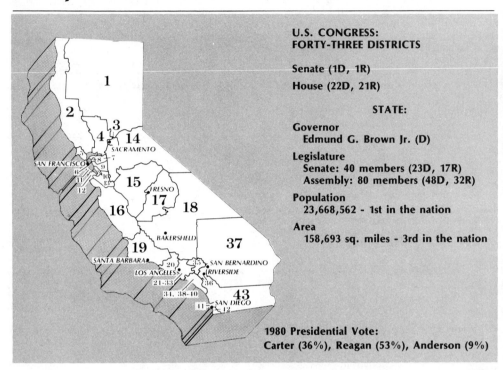

**U.S. CONGRESS:
FORTY-THREE DISTRICTS**

Senate (1D, 1R)
House (22D, 21R)

**STATE:**

Governor
Edmund G. Brown Jr. (D)

Legislature
Senate: 40 members (23D, 17R)
Assembly: 80 members (48D, 32R)

Population
23,668,562 - 1st in the nation

Area
158,693 sq. miles - 3rd in the nation

1980 Presidential Vote:
Carter (36%), Reagan (53%), Anderson (9%)

## ... A Different Country

California is not embarrassed about being unusual. It thrives on its reputation for setting trends in American culture and politics. From tax rebellion to the skateboard, from electing celebrities to establishing communes, California is often months, sometimes years, ahead of the rest of the nation.

California is seen from the outside as different; it sees itself as different. "We like to be viewed as a land of fruits and nuts," says Ed Salzman, its veteran political writer and editor of the *California Journal.* "We enjoy our status as the breeding ground for weirdo politicians."

One does not have to describe any current office holder as a weirdo to document the state's penchant for entrusting public office to people with unorthodox backgrounds. In the last two decades California has elected not one movie actor but two (former Republican Sen. George Murphy is the second), a 70-year-old Japanese-

American semanticist (GOP Sen. S.I. Hayakawa), and a record promoter (Lt. Gov. Mike Curb). Its current governor is a man who succeeded in politics almost overnight out of a background in Jesuit study, social activism and part-time Zen contemplation.

These men have been successful largely because of the weak party system that has existed in the state for most of the 20th century. Reacting against the railroad barons' domination of state politics in the late 19th century, political reformers eviscerated the political parties, introduced widespread use of referendum and set the stage for generations of politics dominated by personality rather than party.

The boom of the post-World War II years, when the population was increasing by a thousand people per day, turned the state into a quasi-nation. On its own, California's gross national product would be topped by only five nations in the world.

Massive waves of immigrants from the East, Midwest and South also have given a unique flavor to California politics. Nearly half of the state's current congressional delegation was born outside California. Whether seeking a fortune in real gold, green gold (lettuce), black gold (oil), or pure tinsel (motion pictures), millions have come to California trying to assimilate their local values and political beliefs into the so-called California culture.

Throughout the 1930s and 1940s, the political beliefs of the newcomers were predominantly Democratic. Registered Democrats have outnumbered Republicans in every general election since 1934, when Socialist Upton Sinclair nearly got himself elected governor on a tide of Depression discontent.

But the early wave of newcomers has grown conservative with prosperity, probably changing more than most generations elsewhere in the United States. It no longer makes much sense to talk about parts of the state being Democratic by registration; the people do not vote that way any more.

But by any measure, the latest group of newcomers is overwhelmingly Democratic. It is the Hispanic population that has moved into the state across the Mexican border and from other parts of Latin America in recent years. It is potentially a crucial force in state politics; the state's Hispanic population rose over the 1970s from 15 percent to 19 percent. But it has not realized its potential so far. A large but impossible-to-estimate number of these Hispanics are illegal aliens and cannot vote; others simply do not vote. No Hispanic has held major statewide office in recent years.

California's congressional delegation is almost evenly divided at the moment between Democrats and Republicans. Democrats control the state Legislature, although by decreasing margins. But in presidential voting over the last 30 years, none of the ten largest states have supported Republican candidates more often than California. Since 1948, only Lyndon B. Johnson among Democratic presidential candidates has carried the state.

# A Political Tour

**The Rural North and Sierra Nevadas.** Covering all the distance from the Oregon border down to Death Valley, this is the most scenic and least populated part of the state. Although partisan labels are largely ignored, voters in most of the region usually back conservatives. Six of the seven counties that Republican Paul Gann carried in his devastating loss to liberal Democratic Sen. Alan Cranston in 1980 were in this area. They included such lightly populated counties as Modoc, Sutter, Mono and Inyo, which usually give the Republican right its highest percentages in the state.

The only Democratic strength in the region is along the Pacific Coast north of the San Francisco Bay, in Humboldt, Mendocino and Sonoma counties. Environmentalist voters have become highly organized in local fights with the area's developers and lumber interests, and are beginning to make their presence felt in elections for state and federal office as well.

The light population density dictates spacious congressional and state legislative districts in which challengers find it difficult to develop enough name recognition to unseat an incumbent. In contests without incumbents, however, virtually any district in the region can go to either party.

The forests, including the majestic redwood stands, are a major part of the economic base in northern California, along with the grape vineyards from California's wine region in the Napa Valley. North of Sacramento, between the Coastal Range and the southern part of the Cascades, lies the fertile Sacramento River plain, forming the northern part of the Central Valley. The rice and barley farmers around Yuba City tend to be more Republican than the fruit and vegetable farmers of the San Joaquin Valley directly to the south. Further east and south in the Sierra Nevadas, ski resorts and other recreational pursuits provide a large percentage of the local income, as well as controversy between local vendors and Sierra Club activists bent on keeping development to a minimum.

**The Central Valley.** From Sacramento on the north to the foothills of the Tehachapi Mountains on the south, the Central Valley forms a figurative fruit basket for the nation. The valley's rich soil, sun and extensive irrigation provide a suitable growing climate for virtually every species of fruit, vegatable and field crop found in the Temperate Zone.

Naturally, agricultural issues play a paramount role in the region's politics, with irrigation and farm labor being the thorniest matters in recent decades. Agribusiness interests have tried to cut costs by keeping wages low for farm workers and taking advantage of federally subsidized irrigation. Mexican-American migrant workers — few of whom vote — have fought for unionization and better working conditions, while others have sought to break up the land holdings of the farming conglomerates by reimposing an acreage limit on federally subsidized water.

Many of the farm managers and small farm owners migrated to California from southern states. They retain a pro forma allegiance to the Democratic Party, but often find Republicans more sympathetic to their interests.

Alternating bands of Democratic and Republican strength work their way down the valley from north to south.

The most Democratic part of the region is at its northern end in Sacramento and Yolo counties. Sacramento has thousands of state government professionals and a large minority population — two groups which tend to favor greater government involvement in social problems. Yolo County is dominated by the University of California's Davis campus, the third largest branch of the massive state system. As with nearly all the state campuses in California, there is a strong liberal tilt. Yolo County gave George McGovern his second highest percentage in the state and was one of only three counties that opposed tax-cutting Proposition 13 in 1978. It rejected Ronald Reagan in the 1980 general election.

The farming areas around Stockton and Modesto, just south of the Sacramento area, tend to be more Republican. The farms are not as large as in other parts of the valley and are often devoted to dairy farming, fruits and vegetables.

One band further south is the Fresno area — the unofficial capital of the Central Valley. Fresno is the largest and most economically diverse city in central California. It is more Democratic than the surrounding area.

The southernmost portion of the Central Valley, around Bakersfield, tends to be the most Republican area. Oil wells and cotton produce a political environment akin to parts of Texas, from which some of the older residents of the area originally came.

**The San Francisco Bay Area.** Most Democrats run better here than anywhere else in the state, but it is not highly partisan territory. Only parts of San Francisco and a few of its nearby communities are true Democratic strongholds. The bulk of the area — much of it middle-class suburban — exhibits a high degree of independence in its voting behavior. While Cranston had no trouble winning 69 percent of the Bay area vote in 1980, Reagan still carried the region, despite losing San Francisco and Alameda counties. Nearly a third of the state legislators from the Bay area are Republicans.

San Francisco is the most liberal — some would say radical — part of the area. It was the only county in the state to vote against the death penalty in 1978. Homosexuals take an active role in San Francisco politics and are easily accepted by the city's liberal power structure, notwithstanding the assassination of a homosexual member of the city's board of supervisors by a former board member in 1978. The large Chinese and Japanese communities and the strong labor movement add to the city's Democratic tendency.

But San Francisco itself accounts for only 14 percent of the Bay Area population. Ringing the San Pablo and San Francisco bays are six counties which cover a wide spectrum of political values and life styles.

Moving in a clockwise direction from the Golden Gate Bridge, one first encounters the "mellow" affluent voters of Marin County, liberal but independent in their politics. Then come the blue-collar workers who labor in the shipyards and refineries of Vallejo and Richmond, and after that the student community in Berkeley and the poor black neighborhoods of Oakland. These provide Democratic majorities equal to those found in San Francisco. But further south, along the eastern shore of San Francisco Bay, are new suburbs and pockets of older ethnic neighborhoods, where the population is solidly middle-class and increasingly conservative.

At the southern end of the bay is the Democratic city of San Jose, once a quiet farm center that has seen rapid expansion and soon will have more people than San Francisco.

Turning north and moving up the western shore of the bay, one comes to the "Silicon Valley" — a center of modern electronic technology spurred on by its proximity to Stanford University — followed by some exclusive, wealthy Republican areas, and finally, blue-collar suburbs, such as Daly City, just south of San Francisco.

**Central Coast.** As in the Central Valley, the political cast of the Pacific Coast region becomes increasingly Republican the further south one travels. Beginning in Santa Cruz, on the northern shore of Monterey Bay, the region extends south along the coast for 335 miles to the Los Angeles County border.

Most of the region's population resides in coastal urban areas where the mountains have receded enough to allow communities to develop. But while most of the region's voters are urban, agriculture is a vital part of the area's livelihood, particularly around the Salinas Valley in the north and in the citrus groves around Oxnard and Ventura in the south.

Once a predictably Republican area, the central coast has become marginal in the last decade, in part because of the 18-year-old vote and the large student concentrations in Santa Cruz and Santa Barbara, where state universities are located.

Santa Cruz students and others who have been drawn to the area for its scenery and relaxed pace make Santa Cruz County the most liberal area along the coast. It is also the only county in the region where the Democratic registration percentage has increased during the last decade.

Around the rest of the Monterey Bay and in the Salinas Valley exists a strange admixture of beach communities, exclusive Monterey Peninsula estates, military enclaves around Fort Ord and agricultural centers, such as Castroville, which bills itself the "Artichoke Capital of the World."

As the farm land gives way to ranch land farther south, the population becomes more Republican, with the one exception of Santa Barbara. Over the last two decades, the expansion of exurban Los Angeles has gradually consumed Ventura County. Although few actually commute into Los Angeles from as far away as Ventura, it marks the northern edge of the urban conglomeration that continues almost uninterrupted to the Mexican border, nearly 200 miles south. The voters who live in the new housing developments of this area usually support statewide GOP candidates.

**Los Angeles County.** It has become almost axiomatic that a statewide candidate has to carry Los Angeles County in order to win. In the 26 statewide contests held over the last 14 years, only two have won without it — Republicans Gerald R. Ford for president and S. I. Hayakawa for the Senate, both in 1976.

Few places in the country can boast of having such great social, economic and ethnic diversity in such a compact space. In less than an hour, one can drive from the middle-class San Fernando Valley to the palatial homes on the Palos Verdes bluffs and pass through a demographic potpourri that includes the extravagant homes of Beverly Hills liberals, the West Side apartments of the elderly, ocean-front condominiums and yacht clubs, an Oriental community and a black ghetto.

Most of the city itself, which accounts for 3 million of the county's 7.5 million people, sits in a smog-enshrouded basin, surrounded by water or mountains. Living in relatively close proximity are the affluent liberal Jews of west Los Angeles, the burgeoning Hispanic community in east Los Angeles, and the black Watts neighborhood to the south of the central business district. Not surprisingly, the eight congressional districts from Long Beach north to the Santa Monica Mountains are all in Democratic hands. Since 1973, the city has

elected a black Democrat, Tom Bradley, to the mayor's job.

But conservative suburban voters of all occupations and social classes surround this area, living in and over the various mountain ranges and along the Pacific Coast. Except for areas where the Hispanic vote has drifted to the east and the black vote moved southward, Republicans are dominant in suburban Los Angeles.

This diversity has resulted in a number of very close elections in the county over the last decade. With the political spectrum swinging back and forth, particularly in the marginal areas such as the San Fernando Valley and Long Beach, Los Angeles County has gone for both liberals and conservatives, often in the same election.

**Orange County.** This county, located between Los Angeles and San Diego, was once synonymous with the militant right. Democrats had little chance of winning, and membership in the John Birch Society was considered an advantage. For 17 years, voters in Orange County returned to Congress Republican James B. Utt, who likened government to a "child molester who offers candy before his evil act."

Orange County's conservative image has often been attributed to the homogeneity of its population. White, middle-class engineers and technicians who work in the area's aerospace firms have long been committed to a less-government-is-better philosophy, although that attitude was tested by recession in the aerospace industry in the early 1970s.

While Orange County still is predominantly Republican, working-class Democrats have begun to fill in the spaces Republicans left open. In 1978, Edmund G. Brown Jr. became the first Democratic gubernatorial candidate to carry the county since its orange groves were plowed under to make way for suburban annexation in the years after World War II. The Santa Ana-Garden Grove area regularly elects Democrats now to the state Legislature and Congress.

The southern and coastal areas of Orange County, however, remain overwhelmingly Republican. San Clemente, the location of Richard M. Nixon's Western White House, gave more than 70 percent of its votes to Ronald Reagan in 1980.

**San Diego County.** With one of the best natural harbors on the West Coast, San Diego is the home base of the Navy's Pacific fleet. That fact plays a vital role in the area's political leanings. Ranked with Norfolk, Va., as one of the two predominant Navy cities in the U.S., San Diego owes much of its economic prosperity to the military — the city's major employer. Not only is the military payroll enormous, but there are also thousands of civilian jobs dependent on Naval contracts, and the city has become a haven for retired Naval officers.

Overall, the state's second largest city tends to follow a pro-military, Republican line. The last Democratic presidential candidate to carry San Diego County was Franklin D. Roosevelt in 1944. (In 1964 Republican Barry Goldwater edged out Lyndon B. Johnson in the county by less than 3,000 votes.) The Republican trend is likely to continue as thousands of retirees and skilled professional workers are drawn to the area by its warm climate and strong economy. In the last decade, San Diego was one of the fastest growing parts of the state.

Low-income black and Mexican voters, however, keep the GOP percentages lower in San Diego County than in neighboring Orange County. Concentrated in the city and close to the Mexican border, these blue-collar workers from the shipyards provide the core of Democratic support in San Diego. But to win, a Democrat must attract many Republican voters.

**The Imperial Valley.** Irrigation in the Imperial Valley in the early 20th century turned desert into some of the most productive farm land in the nation, specializing in melons and winter vegetables. The politics of this self-proclaimed "Inland Empire," center around the booming twin cities of San Bernardino and Riverside, both centers for packing and shipping of the region's enormous citrus crop.

Once solidly Republican territory, the area east and south of Los Angeles has gradually turned into a competitive two-party area within the last decade. In Imperial and Riverside counties in particular, the increase in Democratic registration has clearly outdistanced Republican growth. But the farmers in the Imperial Valley tend to be a conservative lot and often abandon their stated party preference at election time.

The industrial character of Riverside, along with a large steel mill at nearby Fontana, provides a base of Democratic votes on the edge of the desert. But it is sometimes offset by the voters in San Bernardino, a nearby metropolis devoted more to agriculture and the many military establishments in the immediate vicinity.

## Redrawing the Lines

California is entitled to two more seats as a result of its 18 percent population growth during the last decade. Although Democrats control the redistricting process, the population shifts clearly favor the GOP.

Most of the districts represented by Democrats are clustered in the two major metropolitan areas — San Francisco and Los Angeles. The major growth areas, however, have been in the strongly Republican areas around Orange County and San Diego County, which is where one of the new districts will have to be located. As for the other district, there was some talk among Democrats in the Legislature about putting it in the San Joaquin Valley. No formal action was taken on redistricting in the first half of 1981.

With some room to maneuver in the Los Angeles area, the Democrats should have little difficulty protecting their seats. In the San Francisco Bay area, however, there are eight Democratic districts clustered about the bay and hemmed in by Republican strongholds. All but two of those districts are badly underpopulated.

# Governor
# Edmund G. Brown Jr. (D)

**Born:** April 7, 1938, San Francisco, Calif.
**Home:** Los Angeles, Calif.
**Education:** U. of Calif., B.A. 1961; Yale Law School, J.D. 1964; attended Sacred Heart Novitiate, Calif.
**Profession:** Lawyer.
**Family:** Single.
**Religion:** Roman Catholic.
**Political Career:** California secretary of state, 1971-75; unsuccessful presidential nomination campaigns, 1976, 1980; elected governor 1974, 1978; term expires Jan. 1983.

# Alan Cranston (D)

**Of Los Angeles — Elected 1968**

**Born:** June 19, 1914, Palo Alto, Calif.
**Education:** Stanford U., A.B. 1936.
**Military Career:** Army, 1944-45.
**Profession:** Journalist, real estate executive.
**Family:** Wife, Norma Weintraub; one child.
**Religion:** Protestant.
**Political Career:** Calif. Controller, 1959-67; un-
successfully sought Democratic nomination
for U.S. Senate, 1964.

**In Washington:** Cranston would sooner
walk onto the Senate floor without his tie than
without his tally sheet. Covered with scribbled
pluses, minuses and question marks, the narrow
roll call list is his trademark, the tool that brought
him to the inner circle of power and influence.

Cranston's talent for vote counting made him
Democratic whip in 1977, and it keeps him in the
job now in a much different political situation.
With the tally sheet, Cranston and Minority
Leader Robert C. Byrd can tell at a glance who is
for a bill, who is against it, and who remains
undecided, and can plan their strategy accord-
ingly — although their options are sharply restricted now that Republicans control the scheduling of Senate business.

Cranston started nose-counting in 1969, his
first year in the Senate, when he was given a
chance to help manage a Job Corps bill on the
floor. He liked being at the center of the action,
and soon started helping to round up votes on
other measures crucial to his fellow liberals.

Cranston had discovered a vacuum in the
party's leadership of the early 1970s: Majority
Leader Mike Mansfield was no arm twister, and
Byrd, then the whip, was no liberal. Cranston was
a certified liberal with a rare skill at building
bridges to Senate moderates and conservatives. In
the years that followed, he put together numerous
winning coalitions.

In 1977, when Byrd moved up to majority
leader, Cranston easily won election as his deputy.
Despite their ideological differences, which have
narrowed considerably over the years, the two
have worked together with little friction. Cranston, a self-effacing man with little need for ego
massage, defers to Byrd in public and quietly
carries out the tasks Byrd assigns him.

Cranston also continues to function as a
pipeline to and from the dwindling band of liberals in the Senate. But he is more a mediator than

a point man, more absorbed by process than by
ideological questions. Others operate at the cutting edge of issues; Cranston is most comfortable
finding and enlarging the middle ground, and
forcing opponents to the extremes.

He is taking the middle ground now in the
discussion over the future of the Democratic
Party. Shortly after Republicans took over the
Senate in early 1981, he began putting together a
new fund-raising and strategy group to help Senate Democrats up for re-election in 1982. His
message has been that the party cannot afford to
stray too far from popular opinion.

By early 1980, for example, Cranston was
solemnly warning that the Democrats would lose
to "right-wing radicals" unless they were prepared to "face the fact that government has
gotten too big and far too expensive." He followed
up the rhetoric by voting for cuts in some of the
very programs — such as public service jobs — he
had helped to create a few years earlier.

He did not, however, go so far as to advocate
reductions in veterans' benefits. Cranston became
chairman of the Veterans' Affairs Committee in
1977, and in the four years he held that job,
aggressively sought expanded benefits for ex-ser-
vicemen, especially Vietnam era veterans. When
the time came for his 1980 re-election campaign,
most veterans' groups were on his side, whatever
their views about his overall voting record.

Cranston is no doctrinaire foe of business; he
regularly casts at least a few votes, and drafts at
least a few bills, pleasing to the multitude of
special interests — from winegrowers to Realtors
— in the California economy. In 1978, for instance, he was virtually alone among Senate liberals in supporting the B-1 bomber, which would
have been built in California. But he has opposed
the supersonic transport plane, which also has
homestate ties.

**83**

## Alan Cranston, D-Calif.

Cranston's "something for everyone" approach has backfired on occasion. In 1979, for example, he was caught between longtime liberal allies and his agribusiness supporters.

The Carter administration and many environmentalist friends of Cranston wanted to restrict the amount of federally subsidized water available to the large growers. Cranston took up the growers' cause but failed to deliver all that they wanted; several large California farms would have lost water rights under the bill that passed the Senate. The legislation never became law, but by the time the dust cleared, both sides were upset and Cranston wound up voting against the legislation he had worked so hard to shape.

If there is one cause to which Cranston has demonstrated a lasting and passionate commitment, it is world peace. From his early work as a member of the United World Federalists in California to his leadership role in the aborted struggle for Senate ratification of the SALT II Treaty, he has never wavered from his course.

"Those of us who believe in the dire necessity for arms control and the dire dangers of a world without it have a responsibility to try to make that case whenever we can," he once said. Not surprisingly, it was Cranston who took up and won the battle for Senate confirmation of President Carter's controversial arms control negotiator, Paul Warnke, after Byrd had indicated some reservations about the choice.

Until 1981, when he took a seat on Foreign Relations, Cranston was an active member of the Labor and Human Resources Committee. For four years, he chaired its Subcommittee on Children and Youth. Like Walter F. Mondale, his predecessor in that job, he pressed in vain for expanded federal support for child care.

He has been a strong supporter of Head Start, and of legal services to the poor and bilingual education, and was a sponsor of the Comprehensive Employment and Training Act (CETA) of 1973.

Cranston has also been a sponsor of so-called "shield" legislation to protect the confidentiality of news sources. He was a foreign correspondent himself, and author of a book, "The Killing of the Peace," an account of the struggle that kept the United States out of the League of Nations after World War I.

In more recent years, Cranston has put his journalistic talents to use in other ways. During the early months of the Carter administration, he regularly took detailed notes at White House meetings and then briefed the congressional press corps afterwards. To the regret of reporters, he dropped the practice after White House staffers started complaining.

**At Home:** Without the benefit of a dynamic personality or speaking style, Cranston has retained the allegiance of most of California's demanding liberal Democrats while gradually expanding his base into a stable majority. His careful combination of idealism and interest-group politics has brought him three terms, the last two by overwhelming margins.

After World War II started, Cranston left his journalism career to become head of the Foreign Language Division of the Office of War Information. After the war, still haunted by the League of Nations fiasco, he became involved with the United World Federalists and other peace groups.

While involved in the family real estate business in Palo Alto in the late 1940s, Cranston helped form the liberal California Democratic Council (CDC) and served as its first president. The group was vital to launching his early electoral career.

In 1958, Cranston became the first Democrat elected state controller in 72 years. Four years later, he won re-election by a record margin. Thus emboldened, he ran for the Senate in 1964, but narrowly lost the Democratic primary to former White House press secretary Pierre Salinger, who charged that state inheritance tax appraisers had been forced to give to the Cranston campaign. Salinger went on to lose to Republican George Murphy.

The voters dealt Cranston another blow in the Republican year of 1966. They turned him out of his controller's post. But two years later, he tried for the Senate again. He won a five-way primary over a field that included state Sen. Anthony C. Beilenson, now a U.S. House member. That contest was gentle, as the top contenders all were liberals and Vietnam doves.

The general election, however, pitted Cranston against conservative Max Rafferty, the state superintendent of public instruction. Rafferty punched hard, attacking Cranston for ties to "left-wing radical groups" like the CDC and for advocating a Vietnam bombing halt — which he said would endanger U.S. troops.

The GOP was badly divided, however, following an angry primary in which Rafferty had unseated moderate incumbent Thomas H. Kuchel, the Senate minority whip. In addition, a newspaper series tarnished Rafferty's super-patriot reputation by alleging that he was a World War II draft-dodger.

In 1974, Cranston had an easy time against state Sen. H. L. "Bill" Richardson, a former John Birch Society field worker. At one point, when the Birch Society announced plans to circulate material linking Cranston to communists, it drew a rebuke from Gov. Ronald Reagan.

Cranston was similarly blessed with weak Republican opposition in 1980, from tax revolt leader Paul Gann. Gann had become famous in 1978 as the co-author, with Howard Jarvis, of Proposition 13, which cut state property taxes.

But the tax issue had faded in two years, and Gann, two years older than Cranston, was an inarticulate candidate.

## Committees

**Banking, Housing and Urban Affairs** (3rd of 7 Democrats)
Economic Policy; Financial Institutions; Housing and Urban Affairs.

**Foreign Relations** (7th of 8 Democrats)
Arms Control, Oceans, International Operations, and Environment; East Asian and Pacific Affairs; Near Eastern and South Asian Affairs.

**Veterans' Affairs** (Ranking Democrat)

## Elections

### 1980 General

| | |
|---|---|
| Alan Cranston (D) | 4,705,399 (57%) |
| Paul Gann (R) | 3,093,426 (37%) |

### 1980 Primary

| | |
|---|---|
| Alan Cranston (D) | 2,608,746 (80%) |
| Richard Morgan (D) | 350,394 (11%) |
| Frank Thomas (D) | 195,351 (6%) |

### Previous Winning Percentages

1974 (61 %)    1968 (52 %)

## Campaign Finance

| | Receipts | Receipts from PACs | Expenditures |
|---|---|---|---|
| 1980 | | | |
| Cranston (D) | $3,144,399 | $421,984 (13%) | $2,823,462 |
| Gann (R) | $1,762,102 | $26,289 (1%) | $1,705,523 |

## Voting Studies

| | Presidential Support | | Party Unity | | Conservative Coalition | |
|---|---|---|---|---|---|---|
| Year | S | O | S | O | S | O |
| 1980 | 63 | 10 | 81 | 6 | 6 | 89 |

| Year | S | O | S | O | S | O |
|---|---|---|---|---|---|---|
| 1979 | 77 | 16 | 83 | 28 | 15 | 81 |
| 1978 | 87 | 13 | 88 | 8 | 11 | 87 |
| 1977 | 80 | 16 | 81 | 10 | 20 | 74 |
| 1976 | 34 | 58 | 84 | 6 | 11 | 79 |
| 1975 | 40 | 57 | 92 | 7 | 13 | 86 |
| 1974 (Ford) | 44 | 56 | | | | |
| 1974 | 33 | 63 | 87 | 9 | 6 | 90 |
| 1973 | 32 | 56 | 82 | 5 | 13 | 76 |
| 1972 | 35 | 61 | 86 | 8 | 7 | 87 |
| 1971 | 35 | 60 | 80 | 13 | 8 | 86 |
| 1970 | 47 | 43 | 73 | 17 | 16 | 72 |
| 1969 | 47 | 32 | 78 | 9 | 13 | 74 |

S = Support          O = Opposition

## Key Votes

### 96th Congress

| | |
|---|---|
| Maintain relations with Taiwan (1979) | N |
| Reduce synthetic fuel development funds (1979) | Y |
| Impose nuclear plant moratorium (1979) | Y |
| Kill stronger windfall profits tax (1979) | N |
| Guarantee Chrysler Corp. loans (1979) | Y |
| Approve military draft registration (1980) | N |
| End Revenue Sharing to the states (1980) | Y |
| Block Justice Dept. busing suits (1980) | N |

### 97th Congress

| | |
|---|---|
| Restore urban program funding cuts (1981) | Y |

## Interest Group Ratings

| Year | ADA | ACA | AFL-CIO | CCUS-1 | CCUS-2 |
|---|---|---|---|---|---|
| 1980 | 83 | 5 | 83 | 22 | |
| 1979 | 79 | 4 | 88 | 27 | 33 |
| 1978 | 85 | 8 | 89 | 28 | |
| 1977 | 80 | 4 | 79 | 12 | |
| 1976 | 75 | 4 | 88 | 0 | |
| 1975 | 89 | 11 | 90 | 6 | |
| 1974 | 90 | 0 | 91 | 10 | |
| 1973 | 85 | 8 | 90 | 0 | |
| 1972 | 90 | 5 | 100 | 0 | |
| 1971 | 89 | 0 | 92 | - | |
| 1970 | 91 | 0 | 100 | 0 | |
| 1969 | 72 | 0 | 100 | - | |

# S. I. ''Sam'' Hayakawa (R)

Of Mill Valley — Elected 1976

**Born:** July 18, 1906, Vancouver, B.C., Canada.
**Education:** U. of Manitoba, B.A. 1927; McGill U., M.A. 1928; U. of Wis., Ph.D. 1935.
**Profession:** Professor of semantics.
**Family:** Wife, Margedant Peters; three children.
**Religion:** Methodist.
**Political Career:** No previous office.

**In Washington:** Nearly five years into his Senate career, this irrepressible semanticist is still doing and saying pretty much what he pleases, and leaving it to others to figure out exactly what he means. He is not one of the Senate's more important legislators, but at age 75, he may be its freest spirit.

A firm believer in the work ethic and middle-class values, he shares the standard conservative disdain for federal social programs. He has a strong faith in the free enterprise system. But his bluntness not only startles people but frequently offends them.

In 1979, he was asked what would happen to the poor if gasoline went to more than $2 per gallon, which he had suggested as the only solution for energy shortages. "The poor don't need gas," he said, "because they're not working."

During the hostage crisis in Iran, Hayakawa managed to infuriate his fellow Japanese-Americans by suggesting that President Carter round up and detain all Iranians living in this country "the way we did the Japanese in World War II."

If Hayakawa's conservatism is intense on many issues, it is not predictable. An internationalist at heart, he has supported foreign aid as a member of the Foreign Relations Committee. He voted for the Panama Canal transfer treaties in 1978, despite having said two years earlier that the U.S. should keep the canal because "we stole it fair and square."

A longtime student of African culture and art, he brings an informed interest in the Third World to the Foreign Relations Committee, where he now chairs the Subcommittee on East Asia and Pacific Affairs. He was deeply involved in efforts to force a lifting of U.S. sanctions against Rhodesia (now Zimbabwe), and has argued that this country should use trade relations and "quiet diplomacy" — not aid cut-offs and similar sanctions — to promote human rights around the world.

Hayakawa also serves on the Agriculture Committee and the Select Small Business Committee, but he has left less of a mark on those panels. One of his prime legislative interests, outside of foreign affairs, has been the promotion of a sub-minimum wage for teen-agers, which he considers a key to drawing young people into the labor force and inculcating them with the work ethic.

Despite his belief in the virtues of honest labor, Hayakawa is something less than a workaholic himself. He is notorious for catnapping in committee, on the Senate floor, at White House meetings and elsewhere, although he insists that "I don't fall asleep around here nearly as much as I did at San Francisco State. Things were really boring there."

The senator is not lacking for outside interests when he finds his official duties growing dull. He is a gourmet cook, harmonica player, scuba diver, fisherman, fencing enthusiast, collector of African sculpture, Chinese ceramics and old jazz records, a disco fancier and a tap dancer. Of the latter, he says, "It's not that I dance well, but I dance with a lot of confidence."

**At Home:** When Hayakawa announced in early 1981 that he planned to run for a second term, no matter how vulnerable he seemed to be, he was displaying the same combative spirit that got him into politics in the first place at an age when most people have retired.

In 1968, as president of San Francisco State College, he became a conservative hero by putting down a student strike. Campus radicals had attempted to shut the college, so he called in city police, who arrested many of the protesters. Eight years later, when he ran for the Senate, voters still remembered him wearing his trademark tam-o'-shanter, ripping out the wires of the militants' sound truck.

The San Francisco State episode marked Hayakawa's transformation from a respected but little-known semanticist to a public figure. His 1949 book, *Language in Thought and Action*, is a classic in the field. It is an eloquent argument in favor of rational debate, political tolerance and free thought. But it never made him familiar to a mass audience.

Born in Canada of Japanese parents, Hayakawa spent most of his adult life as a liberal Democrat. He kept a picture of Hubert H. Humphrey on his wall. But his moment of glory in the 1960s seemed to change him. He switched to the Republican Party in 1973 and attempted to run for the Senate the next year, but could not get on the ballot.

In 1976, he tried again. With the advantage of his name recognition, he won the party nomination from former Lt. Gov. Robert H. Finch, the ex-secretary of health, education and welfare; former Lt. Gov. John L. Harmer; and Rep. Alphonzo Bell.

In the general election, he unseated Democrat John V. Tunney by nearly 250,000 votes. Tunney characterized him as a man of outdated views who was too old to begin a Senate career. But the Democrat had serious weaknesses that Hayakawa exploited — a reputation as a playboy and a politician willing to trim his liberalism to hold power.

Hayakawa's campaign had its bizarre moments, such as the one in which he responded to a question on dog racing by saying he did not "give a good god damn" about it. But this only seemed to improve his standing among an electorate that has often shown a weakness for the unusual.

## Committees

**Agriculture, Nutrition and Forestry** (3rd of 9 Republicans)
Forestry, Water Resources and Environment, chairman; Agricultural Research and General Legislation; Nutrition; Soil and Water Conservation.

**Foreign Relations** (4th of 9 Republicans)
East Asian and Pacific Affairs, chairman; African Affairs; Western Hemisphere Affairs.

**Select Small Business** (4th of 9 Republicans)
Advocacy and the Future of Small Business, chairman; Export Promotion and Market Development.

## Elections

**1976 General**

| | |
|---|---|
| S. I. "Sam" Hayakawa (R ) | 3,748,973 (50 %) |
| John V. Tunney (D ) | 3,502,862 (47 %) |

**1976 Primary**

| | |
|---|---|
| S. I. "Sam" Hayakawa (R ) | 886,743 (38 %) |
| Robert Finch (R ) | 614,240 (26 %) |
| Alphonzo Bell (R ) | 532,969 (23 %) |
| John Harmer (R ) | 197,252 (9 %) |

## Campaign Finance

| 1976 | Receipts | Receipts from PACs | Expenditures |
|---|---|---|---|
| Hayakawa (R ) | $1,218,485 | $115,125 (9 %) | $1,184,624 |
| Tunney (D ) | $1,903,527 | $263,644 (14 %) | $1,940,988 |

## Voting Studies

| | Presidential Support | | Party Unity | | Conservative Coalition | |
|---|---|---|---|---|---|---|
| Year | S | O | S | O | S | O |
| 1980 | 45 | 45 | 75 | 16 | 89 | 8 |
| 1979 | 50 | 43 | 75 | 19 | 78 | 19 |
| 1978 | 54 | 36 | 62 | 29 | 68 | 23 |
| 1977 | 43 | 52 | 75 | 4 | 82 | 1 |

S = Support          O = Opposition

## Key Votes

**96th Congress**

| | |
|---|---|
| Maintain relations with Taiwan (1979) | Y |
| Reduce synthetic fuel development funds (1979) | N |
| Impose nuclear plant moratorium (1979) | N |
| Kill stronger windfall profits tax (1979) | Y |
| Guarantee Chrysler Corp. loans (1979) | N |
| Approve military draft registration (1980) | Y |
| End Revenue Sharing to the states (1980) | N |
| Block Justice Dept. busing suits (1980) | Y |

**97th Congress**

| | |
|---|---|
| Restore urban program funding cuts (1981) | N |

## Interest Group Ratings

| Year | ADA | ACA | AFL-CIO | CCUS-1 | CCUS-2 |
|---|---|---|---|---|---|
| 1980 | 22 | 92 | 22 | 88 | |
| 1979 | 11 | 65 | 11 | 67 | 79 |
| 1978 | 15 | 68 | 24 | 82 | |
| 1977 | 5 | 96 | 20 | 94 | |

# 1 Gene Chappie (R)

**Of Roseville — Elected 1980**

**Born:** March 28, 1920, Sacramento, Calif.
**Education:** High school graduate.
**Military Career:** Army, 1942-46.
**Profession:** Rancher.
**Family:** Wife, Paula DiBenedetto; five children.
**Religion:** Roman Catholic.
**Political Career:** El Dorado County supervisor, 1950-64; Calif. Assembly, 1965-81.

The Member: Chappie is an affable, irreverent man who spent 15 years in the state Legislature loyally voting the party leadership position.

In Congress he is trying to persuade federal agencies to loosen their hold on areas of his district that have potential for development.

Chappie introduced a bill to allow construction of a privately owned and operated ski area on 1,090 acres of public land in Mt. Shasta National Forest. The forest is being considered for designation as a wilderness area, which would limit development of the land. Chappie says a new ski area would boost the local economy, which has faltered since a 1978 avalanche destroyed the main chairlift at another ski area.

During three decades in public life, Chappie has never lost an election. Careful not to spoil that record, he held off for several years challenging gradually-weakening Democratic Rep. Harold T. Johnson. But after 1978, when the incumbent's vote fell below 60 percent for the first time, Chappie decided to make his move.

He cited Johnson's age and claimed the incumbent had lost his effectiveness. Chappie campaigned relentlessly in the remote counties at the northern end of the district, far from his state legislative constituency. He rarely missed a sheep shearing contest or a 4-H Club bull sale. By contrast, Johnson ran a passive campaign until the final weeks.

The District: Covering 34,000 square miles in the northern third of the state, this is geographicaly the largest district in California. Although the registration favors Democrats, most of the farmers, ranchers and lumbermen who vote here have an individualist conservative streak.

The district has shown considerable loyalty to its incumbents; the last time one was defeated before Johnson was in 1910. Since then the district has had just one Republican and three Democratic representatives, including former Sen. Clair Engle, who served 15 years before running for the Senate in 1958.

## Committees

**Agriculture** (19th of 19 Republicans)
Cotton, Rice and Sugar; Domestic Marketing, Consumer Relations and Nutrition; Forests, Family Farms and Energy.

## Elections

**1980 General**

| | |
|---|---|
| Eugene Chappie (R ) | 145,585 (54 %) |
| Harold Johnson (D ) | 107,993 (40 %) |
| Jim McClarin (LIB) | 17,497 (7 %) |

**District Vote For President**

| | 1980 | | 1976 |
|---|---|---|---|
| **D** | 88,189 (32 %) | **D** | 110,186 (49 %) |
| **R** | 158,846 (57 %) | **R** | 106,842 (48 %) |
| **I** | 22,249 (8 %) | | |

## Campaign Finance

| | Receipts | Receipts from PACs | Expenditures |
|---|---|---|---|
| **1980** | | | |
| Chappie (R ) | $383,348 | $83,150 (22 %) | $375,721 |
| Johnson (D ) | $307,091 | $189,260 (62 %) | $378,764 |

## Key Vote

**97th Congress**

Reagan budget proposal (1981)    Y

---

**1st District: North — Chico.** Population: 652,219 (41% increase since 1970). Race: White 608,345 (93%), Black 7,382 (1%), Others 36,492 (6%). Spanish origin: 25,264 (4%).

# 2 Don H. Clausen (R)

**Of Crescent City — Elected 1963**

**Born:** April 27, 1923, Ferndale, Calif.
**Education:** Attended San Jose State College, Calif. Polytechnic State U., Weber State College, St. Mary's College.
**Military Career:** Navy, 1943-47.
**Profession:** Insurance executive.
**Family:** Wife, Ollie Piper; two children.
**Religion:** Lutheran.
**Political Career:** Del Norte County supervisor, 1955-62.

**In Washington:** A genial man who prefers to avoid confrontation, Clausen has managed to avoid it most of the time during recent years as a senior Republican on the House Interior Committee. Chairman Morris K. Udall has taken care to bring Clausen in on much of his legislative planning, and Clausen has responded by giving Udall his support or muting his opposition on key environmental issues.

In 1980, he joined Udall in trying to create a limited-purpose Energy Mobilization Board to speed up approval of high-priority energy projects. When the bill emerged from conference with a board powerful enough to override some state and local laws, he joined Udall and most environmentalist Democrats in voting against it.

The previous year, he and the chairman were on opposite sides of the Alaska lands issue, as Clausen agreed with most Republicans that Udall's bill provided for too much wilderness and not enough development. But he cast a quiet vote against it and generally stayed out of the frantic strategy sessions opponents held as they tried to block the bill.

Clausen is a cautious man, one who broods over the political implications of a vote before he casts it. Often he is pondering the views of the environmentalists and the timber companies who want to send him in opposite directions.

Sensitive to the environmental side in his "Redwood Empire" district, Clausen tuned in to clean air and clean water issues early in his career, and argued long ago that the 1970s should be known as "the environmental quality decade." He sided with environmentalists — and against most Republicans — through much of the marathon strip mining battle that ended with enactment of a control law in 1977.

But on the most sensitive issue to his district,

the Redwood National Park, Clausen has been on the other side, if somewhat hesitantly. When the idea of a new national park in his district was first discussed in the 1960s, Clausen fought it, arguing for the jobs it would cost his constituents then working in the timber industry.

"Are we to ruin their lives and businesses," he once asked, "merely to permit interested visitors to view the redwoods from the edge of the highway?" He offered his own "Redwoods to the Sea" proposal, to convert state park land into a national park area, without adding any new territory, but when the new 58,000-acre park was created anyway in 1968, he voted for the final bill on the House floor.

A decade later, he was arguing the issue again, fighting the Interior Committee's bill to add another 48,000 acres of private land to the park. His motion to drop 34,000 of those acres was badly beaten, but Democrats did give Clausen a useful plum to take back to his district, a six-year wage guarantee for workers who lost their jobs through the conversion from timberland to parkland. Meanwhile, on the Public Works Committee, Clausen was pushing for a Redwood Park bypass highway to ease traffic congestion caused by expansion of the park.

Seniority gave Clausen a choice in 1981 between the top-ranking GOP position on either

---

**2nd District: North coast — Santa Rosa, Eureka.** Population: 622,027 (34% increase since 1970). Race: White 573,832 (92%), Black 5,532 (1%), Indian 14,320 (2%), Others 28,343 (5%). Spanish origin: 39,415 (6%).

Interior or Public Works; he chose to become ranking Republican on Public Works, although the GOP remains dominated on that committee by Kentucky's M. G. "Gene" Snyder. Clausen is still second ranking among Republicans on Interior.

Fishing is an important district interest for Clausen, and he began pushing early for the 200-mile limit legislation that was passed in 1976, vastly expanding the zone in which U.S. fishermen have exclusive fishing rights. In 1978, Clausen introduced a bill limiting foreign investment in the U.S. fishing industry.

But the issue also has caused him trouble. When the federal government banned salmon fishing along the Klamath River in his district, critics accused Clausen of not doing enough to save the the the sport fishing industry. He promised to work with federal officials for a compromise.

**At Home:** It was aviation that led Clausen into politics, and wrote a bizarre script for his first election.

Clausen was a Navy flier in 1948 when Del Norte County decided it needed an "aviation director." He held that job for seven years, then filled a vacancy on the county supervisors' panel and successfully won re-election twice.

He was called the "flying supervisor," and he even made aviation a part of his political philosophy when he ran for the House in 1962. "Aircraft," he wrote in a campaign brochure, "can win peace as well as war by bringing together the peoples of the world to discuss their mutual problems."

Clausen lost that election to a man who had been killed a month earlier — in an airplane crash. Democratic Rep. Clem Miller was re-elected to a third term posthumously because Democrats did not have enough time to slot a replacement after his death.

Undaunted by losing to a dead man, Clausen immediately entered the special election held the next year to fill Miller's seat. He already had considerable recognition from his first campaign, and he enhanced it by continuing to fly around the elongated district. Democrats chose an aide to Miller as their nominee, but he had a difficult time making himself known in the short special election campaign. Clausen was elected by a comfortable margin.

He survived his first decade in the House with little political trouble back home, but since 1974 life has been difficult for him. He has continued to win partly because Democrats have never been able to unite behind a strong candidate.

In 1974, charging that Clausen had a "do-nothing" record, Democrat Oscar Klee reduced the incumbent's percentage nearly 10 points and came within 18,700 votes of defeating him. The eccentric challenger used a song he wrote, "The Ballad of Oscar Klee," — as a vehicle for telling of his opposition to all federal taxes. Between his 1974 campaign and his second try in 1976, Klee served a brief time in prison for failing to file a federal tax return.

Clausen prepared a more active re-election campaign for 1976, and voters became more aware of Klee's eccentricities. The incumbent won by 32,400 votes. But for the second time in a row, Clausen's margin was one of the smallest in the state for a Republican winner.

A similar scenario was repeated in 1978 and 1980. Both times, Clausen faced a speech pathologist, Norma K. Bork. A native of Ohio, Bork had been a Republican until a year before she started campaigning against Clausen. Her claim that she had been a "closet Democrat" for years was not convincing to many of the district's Democratic loyalists, but her non-stop campaigning twice brought her the Democratic nomination.

Bork reduced the incumbent's margin to less than 15,000 votes the first time, and she defeated two veteran officeholders to win the nomination against him in 1980. But even though Bork more than doubled her campaign treasury over 1978, Clausen still outspent her by two-to-one in 1980, and waged his strongest effort yet. Once again, the incumbent's margin bounced back above 30,000 votes.

**The District:** Vast redwood stands and Napa Valley vineyards make this one of America's most scenic districts, but behind the scenery there are fierce tensions between longtime residents who have made their living harvesting trees and younger immigrants who want nature preserved.

The district's 34 percent growth since 1970 reflects in large part an influx of young professionals looking for a serene life in the country. To find it they often are forced to fight political battles with the development-minded old-timers. Campaigns to block the construction of dams and expand the Redwoods National Park have changed the district's politics. The political impact of the newcomers exceeds their actual numbers.

Democratic candidates usually do well in the northern counties of Humboldt and Mendocino. But more than 60 percent of the vote is cast in Sonoma and Napa counties, where the slant is slightly more Republican and where Clausen is usually able to build his winning margins.

## Committees

**Interior and Insular Affairs** (2nd of 17 Republicans)
Insular Affairs; Public Lands and National Parks; Water and Power Resources.

**Public Works and Transportation** (Ranking Republican)

## Elections

**1980 General**

| | |
|---|---|
| Don Clausen (R ) | 141,698 (54 %) |
| Norma Bork (D ) | 109,789 (42 %) |

**1978 General**

| | |
|---|---|
| Don Clausen (R ) | 114,451 (52 %) |
| Norma Bork (D ) | 99,712 (45 %) |

**Previous Winning Percentages**

| | | | |
|---|---|---|---|
| 1976 (56 %) | 1974 (53 %) | 1972 (62 %) | 1970 (63 %) |
| 1968 (75 %) | 1966 (65 %) | 1964 (59 %) | 1963* (54 %) |

*Special Election

**District Vote For President**

| | 1980 | | 1976 |
|---|---|---|---|
| D | 95,971 (36 %) | D | 111,043 (50 %) |
| R | 132,531 (49 %) | R | 106,197 (47 %) |
| I | 27,880 (10 %) | | |

## Campaign Finance

| | Receipts | Receipts from PACs | Expenditures |
|---|---|---|---|
| **1980** | | | |
| Clausen (R ) | $453,197 | $176,575 (39 %) | $451,056 |
| Bork (D ) | $248,456 | $71,297 (29 %) | $190,689 |
| **1978** | | | |
| Clausen (R ) | $213,598 | $56,281 (26 %) | $200,924 |
| Bork (D ) | $81,745 | $14,580 (18 %) | $80,437 |

## Voting Studies

| Year | Presidential Support S | O | Party Unity S | O | Conservative Coalition S | O |
|---|---|---|---|---|---|---|
| 1980 | 48 | 46 | 64 | 30 | 71 | 25 |
| 1979 | 31 | 59 | 73 | 20 | 85 | 8 |
| 1978 | 33 | 63 | 71 | 18 | 77 | 15 |
| 1977 | 42 | 48 | 76 | 13 | 81 | 5 |
| 1976 | 63 | 33 | 73 | 19 | 82 | 10 |
| 1975 | 58 | 33 | 74 | 15 | 83 | 9 |
| 1974 (Ford) | 48 | 44 | | | | |
| 1974 | 58 | 28 | 65 | 26 | 82 | 11 |
| 1973 | 52 | 39 | 69 | 26 | 80 | 15 |
| 1972 | 76 | 22 | 62 | 24 | 79 | 10 |
| 1971 | 82 | 12 | 74 | 17 | 82 | 8 |
| 1970 | 70 | 17† | 68 | 10 | 80 | 2 |
| 1969 | 62 | 31† | 65 | 20† | 87 | 9 |
| 1968 | 50 | 33 | 51 | 23 | 65 | 18 |
| 1967 | 38 | 46 | 72 | 13 | 80 | 4 |
| 1966 | 41 | 43 | 63 | 23 | 78 | 11 |
| 1965 | 35 | 50 | 71 | 10 | 82 | 8 |
| 1964 | 37 | 48 | 74 | 15 | 92 | 0 |
| 1963 | 17 | 70† | 84 | 7 | 73 | 7 |

S = Support          O = Opposition

†Not eligible for all recorded votes.

## Key Votes

**96th Congress**

| | |
|---|---|
| Weaken Carter oil profits tax (1979) | Y |
| Reject hospital cost control plan (1979) | Y |
| Implement Panama Canal Treaties (1979) | N |
| Establish Department of Education (1979) | Y |
| Approve Anti-busing Amendment (1979) | Y |
| Guarantee Chrysler Corp. loans (1979) | Y |
| Approve military draft registration (1980) | N |
| Aid Sandinista regime in Nicaragua (1980) | N |
| Strengthen fair housing laws (1980) | N |

**97th Congress**

| | |
|---|---|
| Reagan budget proposal (1981) | Y |

## Interest Group Ratings

| Year | ADA | ACA | AFL-CIO | CCUS |
|---|---|---|---|---|
| 1980 | 22 | 64 | 28 | 72 |
| 1979 | 11 | 71 | 22 | 88 |
| 1978 | 10 | 89 | 24 | 82 |
| 1977 | 0 | 68 | 29 | 71 |
| 1976 | 10 | 79 | 27 | 67 |
| 1975 | 5 | 77 | 38 | 65 |
| 1974 | 13 | 64 | 0 | 70 |
| 1973 | 8 | 81 | 20 | 90 |
| 1972 | 0 | 75 | 27 | 100 |
| 1971 | 3 | 85 | 33 | - |
| 1970 | 16 | 72 | 14 | 90 |
| 1969 | 7 | 56 | 22 | - |
| 1968 | 0 | 82 | 25 | - |
| 1967 | 7 | 89 | 0 | 89 |
| 1966 | 0 | 71 | 0 | - |
| 1965 | 0 | 81 | - | 90 |
| 1964 | 4 | 94 | 18 | - |

# 3 Robert T. Matsui (D)

**Of Sacramento — Elected 1978**

**Born:** Sept. 17, 1941, Sacramento, Calif.
**Education:** U. of Calif., Berkeley, A.B. 1963;
Hastings College of Law, J.D. 1966.
**Profession:** Lawyer.
**Family:** Wife, Doris Okada; one child.
**Religion:** Methodist.
**Political Career:** Sacramento City Council,
1971-78.

**In Washington:** A quiet, courteous man who carries an ever-present briefcase, Matsui quickly earned a reputation in the House as a man willing to pay his dues.

One of the dues he paid was a stint on the Judiciary Committee, a once-glamorous panel that now carries so few political rewards that it cannot fill its quota of members. While there, Matsui took an interest in antitrust issues and cast the deciding vote in subcommittee in favor of the "Illinois Brick" bill, making it possible for consumers and small businesses to sue corporations for price fixing. The bill never made it to the House floor.

After a year on Judiciary, House leaders gave Matsui the assignment he really wanted, on the Commerce Committee. He had made his initial bid for Commerce at a bad moment — North Carolina's Richardson Preyer and California's Henry Waxman were competing for chairman of the panel's Health Subcommittee. Every vote counted, and House leaders, who tilted toward Preyer, realized Matsui was a likely vote for Waxman. The place went to Alabama's Richard Shelby instead. Waxman won anyway.

After a year on Judiciary, Matsui's loyalty was rewarded. He headed for Commerce and its Communications Subcommittee, which was busy trying to rewrite the 1934 Communications law. Matsui joined the committee faction fighting that part of the revision which would ease anti-trust laws and allow the American Telephone & Telegraph Co. (AT&T) to enter computer-related fields. One compromise proposal was to force AT&T to set up an independent subsidiary to operate the new ventures.

Matsui and ally Edward J. Markey, D-Mass., argued that was not enough, claiming it simply amounted to "cloning" the corporate giant. They said the plan would not only make AT&T bigger, but also give it a powerful competitive edge in the field. Matsui ultimately cast one of the dissenting

votes as the committee approved the bill 34-7. It did not reach the floor in the 96th Congress.

**At Home:** Matsui has been a loyal member of Sacramento's Democratic political community for more than a decade. He made it to Congress the same way he is succeeding in it — with patience and a willingness to play by the party's rules. Being able to raise a lot of money from friends in the community also helped.

As an infant, Matsui was one of 100,000 Japanese-Americans interned in detention camps during World War II. He used that experience to establish a strong bond with Sacramento's large Asian community, and he won two elections for the city council.

In 1972, the year after Matsui began his service on the council, he chaired Congressman John E. Moss' re-election campaign. Matsui's excellent fund-raising connections made him a perfect choice, and he took the job again in 1974 and 1976 as Moss won easily.

In 1978, Matsui was preparing to run for the county board of supervisors when Moss announced his retirement after 26 years. Matsui abruptly switched to a congressional campaign, building strong support in the area's business community and among the Japanese and Chinese voters.

Two other prominent Sacramento Democrats also filed for the House, but Matsui's $225,000 primary campaign budget gave him a clear advan-

---

**3rd District: Most of Sacramento, suburbs.** Population: 585,264 (26% increase since 1970). Race: White 469,280 (80%), Black 43,994 (8%), Others 37,950 (6%). Spanish origin: 54,204 (9%).

tage. He ran televison commercials identifying himself as "Citizen Matsui," setting himself apart from his rivals, both of whom had been heavily involved in state politics.

Matsui won the primary and then took the general election comfortably against Republican Sandy Smoley, considered the strongest candidate Sacramento Republicans had run for the House in many years. Moss repeatedly proclaimed his support for Matsui in a series of television commercials.

Republicans made no similar effort to capture the district in 1980. Their nominee was all but invisible most of the year, and Matsui drew more than 70 percent of the vote.

**The District:** The 3rd District is almost evenly split between Sacramento and its suburbs. Although it has gone Democratic in every House election since 1952, it is at least potentially a marginal district. The suburban voters to the east of the city sometimes favor Republican candidates in statewide contests; Republican S. I. "Sam" Hayakawa carried the district when he won his U.S. Senate seat in 1976.

The city of Sacramento is the liberal Democratic stronghold. The state government community consists of thousands of highly educated professionals, many of whom have chosen to live in the inner city. Sacramento also has substantial black, Asian and Hispanic communities.

## Committees

Select Narcotics Abuse and Control (11th of 11 Democrats)

Ways and Means (22nd of 23 Democrats)
Public Assistance and Unemployment Compensation; Select Revenue Measures.

## Elections

**1980 General**

| | |
|---|---|
| Robert Matsui (D ) | 170,670 (71 %) |
| Joseph Murphy (R ) | 64,215 (26 %) |

**1980 Primary**

| | |
|---|---|
| Robert Matsui (D ) | 95,565 (89 %) |
| Ivaldo Lenci (D ) | 11,967 (11 %) |

**1978 General**

| | |
|---|---|
| Robert Matsui (D ) | 105,537 (53 %) |
| Sandy Smoley (R ) | 91,966 (47 %) |

**1978 Primary**

| | |
|---|---|
| Robert Matsui (D ) | 37,314 (36 %) |
| Eugene Gualco (D ) | 30,159 (29 %) |
| Phil Isenberg (D ) | 29,341 (28 %) |

**District Vote For President**

| 1980 | | 1976 | |
|---|---|---|---|
| D | 99,225 (40 %) | D | 110,313 (52 %) |
| R | 118,814 (48 %) | R | 98,706 (46 %) |
| I | 23,357 (9 %) | | |

## Campaign Finance

| | Receipts | Percent of Receipts from PACs | Expenditures |
|---|---|---|---|
| **1980** | | | |
| Matsui (D ) | $223,284 | $81,697 (37 %) | $181,035 |

| **1978** | | | |
|---|---|---|---|
| Matsui (D ) | $468,263 | $63,050 (14 %) | $468,028 |
| Smoley (R ) | $328,049 | $25,600 (8 %) | $329,408 |

## Voting Studies

| | Presidental Support | | Party Unity | | Conservative Coalition | |
|---|---|---|---|---|---|---|
| Year | S | O | S | O | S | O |
| 1980 | 79 | 16 | 90 | 4 | 6 | 89 |
| 1979 | 86 | 14 | 94 | 5 | 10 | 89 |

S = Support          O = Opposition

## Key Votes

**96th Congress**

| | |
|---|---|
| Weaken Carter oil profits tax (1979) | N |
| Reject hospital cost control plan (1979) | N |
| Implement Panama Canal Treaties (1979) | Y |
| Establish Department of Education (1979) | Y |
| Approve Anti-busing Amendment (1979) | N |
| Gaurantee Chrysler Corp. loans (1979) | Y |
| Approve Military draft registration (1980) | N |
| Aid Sandinistas regime in Nicaragua (1980) | Y |
| Strengthen Fair Housing Laws (1980) | Y |

**97th Congress**

| | |
|---|---|
| Reagon budget proposal (1981) | N |

## Interest Group Rating

| Year | ADA | ACA | AFL-CIO | CCUS |
|---|---|---|---|---|
| 1980 | 94 | 13 | 79 | 58 |
| 1979 | 89 | 12 | 90 | 11 |

**93**

# 4 Vic Fazio (D)

**Of West Sacramento — Elected 1978**

**Born:** Oct. 11, 1942, Winchester, Mass.
**Education:** Union College, B.A. 1965.
**Profession:** Public official.
**Family:** Separated; two children.
**Religion:** Episcopalian.
**Political Career:** Calif. Assembly, 1975-79.

**In Washington:** Like many state legislative "stars" who come to Congress, Fazio has had to adjust to a less conspicuous role in Washington than he played at home.

After two years in the House, he was still far from becoming one of its familiar names, but he had secured a place on Appropriations, and even found himself with a subcommittee chairmanship — overseeing the money Congress spends on itself.

In his first year, while waiting for a spot on Appropriations to open up, Fazio put in an apprenticeship on Armed Services, quietly siding with the panel's minority of Democrats skeptical about many Pentagon funding requests. He made one effort on the House floor, to eliminate money for a nuclear aircraft carrier and replace it with funds for a new conventional carrier, at what he said would be an eventual savings of $1 billion. His amendment to do that was easily defeated.

Fazio also spent a term on House Administration, pursuing some of the political reform goals he worked on in California. He was a strong supporter of a bill to establish partial public financing of congressional campaigns, but the committee defeated it decisively in early 1979.

Later in the year, he supported legislation to limit contributions by political action committees, and added his own amendment to block wealthy candidates from lending their campaigns huge sums, then holding fund-raisers to reimburse themselves after election. The amendment passed, but the bill died in the Senate.

Fazio began campaigning for Appropriations early in his first term, and he had the California delegation behind him. The state had lost one of its seats on the committee in 1979, and Fazio was the delegation's vehicle for getting it back. When a vacancy came up in 1980, he got it easily. A year later he was chairman of the Legislative Branch Subcommittee, a politically unrewarding job but a good test of a member's management skills. He presided quietly over the panel's hearings early in 1981, then brought out of his subcommittee a bill

allowing only modest increases in funding for legislative branch activities.

**At Home:** During the years Fazio worked in the California State Capitol — as a journalist, aide to the assembly Speaker, and later as an assemblyman himself — he always seemed to be a few steps ahead of most of the other people there. Even while he was a staff aide, he was drafting bills and putting together coalitions.

His skills as a candidate were tested in 1975, when he ran for the Assembly to fill a vacancy. He won by just 472 votes, but he quickly established a strong political base in Sacramento and Yolo counties, and took a high profile on energy, consumer and environmental issues. After less than a year in office he was elected to a full term with 74 percent of the vote.

That same day, Democratic Rep. Robert Leggett survived by just 651 votes against Albert Dehr, a retired railroad worker. Leggett had been accused of taking bribes from South Korean government officials, and had acknowledged going into debt to support a Capitol Hill secretary and their two illegitimate children. It was clear he would draw a more substantial challenge the next time.

But Leggett managed to keep most Democratic aspirants out of the 1978 primary by insisting he would run again. His retirement announcement, made two weeks before the filing deadline, seemed a surprise to nearly every politician in the

---

**4th District: Lower Sacramento Valley — Vallejo.** Population: 581,198 (25% increase since 1970). Race: White 457,485 (79%), Black 44,541 (8%), Asian and Pacific Islander 30,034 (5%), Others 49,138 (8%). Spanish origin: 69,023 (12%).

district except one — Fazio. The blond-haired assemblyman was the only candidate ready with a campaign, and he coasted to the nomination.

The general election campaign was not particularly close. Republican Rex Hime, a former Reagan aide and state party staffer, could not match Fazio's fund-raising skills. The Democrat lost two agricultural counties in the northern part of the district, but carried the remaining territory, most of which he represented in the Assembly. In 1980, he won all five counties against Dehr, who was making his third try.

**The District:** The 4th District has very little social or economic cohesiveness. On its northern border are sparsely populated Colusa and Sutter counties, which grow rice, tomatoes and peaches, and provide a strong Republican vote. Just below that area is the academic com-

munity around the University of California at Davis, the liberal heart of the district. Further east, the district takes in part of Sacramento, whose state government workers are generally Democrats. In the south are blue-collar Democrats in Vallejo, a defense-oriented city on San Pablo Bay.

These disparate regions usually combine to produce majorities for almost any candidate with a Democratic label — as long as the Republican is not Ronald Reagan. In Democratic primaries, however, the diversity is quite evident, as shown by the 1976 Senate primary between incumbent John V. Tunney and former anti-war activist Tom Hayden. Tunney, the "establishment" Democrat, won Vallejo by almost three-to-one. Hayden, the insurgent, carried Davis by an equal margin. And the two evenly divided the vote in Sacramento.

## Committees

**Appropriations** (27th of 33 Democrats)
Legislative, chairman; Energy and Water Development.

## Elections

**1980 General**

| | |
|---|---|
| Vic Fazio (D ) | 133,853 (65 %) |
| Albert Dehr (R ) | 60,935 (30 %) |
| Robert Burnside (LIB) | 10,267 (5 %) |

**1980 Primary**

| | |
|---|---|
| Vic Fazio (D ) | 71,344 (80 %) |
| Wayne Cowley (D ) | 18,100 (20 %) |

**1978 General**

| | |
|---|---|
| Vic Fazio (D ) | 87,764 (55 %) |
| Rex Hime (R ) | 70,733 (45 %) |

**1978 Primary**

| | |
|---|---|
| Vic Fazio (D ) | 47,319 (57 %) |
| David Hansen (D ) | 20,591 (25 %) |
| Gordon Colby (D ) | 7,748 (9 %) |
| Larry Asera (D ) | 7,213 (8 %) |

**District Vote For President**

| | 1980 | | 1976 |
|---|---|---|---|
| **D** | 86,427 (40 %) | **D** | 96,028 (55 %) |
| **R** | 103,541 (48 %) | **R** | 76,230 (43 %) |
| **I** | 20,295 (9 %) | | |

## Campaign Finance

| | | Receipts from PACs | Expenditures |
|---|---|---|---|
| | Receipts | | |
| **1980** | | | |
| Fazio (D ) | $213,018 | $76,925 (36 %) | $142,511 |

| **1978** | | | |
|---|---|---|---|
| Fazio (D ) | $235,605 | $95,949 (41 %) | $235,600 |
| Hime (R ) | $138,479 | $36,090 (26 %) | $138,085 |

## Voting Studies

| | Presidental Support | | Party Unity | | Conservative Coalition | |
|---|---|---|---|---|---|---|
| **Year** | **S** | **O** | **S** | **O** | **S** | **O** |
| 1980 | 79 | 12 | 88 | 4 | 13 | 83 |
| 1979 | 81 | 17 | 92 | 5 | 20 | 77 |

S = Support          O = Opposition

## Key Votes

**96th Congress**

| | |
|---|---|
| Weaken Carter oil profits tax (1979) | N |
| Reject hospital cost control plan (1979) | N |
| Implement Panama Canal Treaties (1979) | Y |
| Establish Department of Education (1979) | Y |
| Approve Anti-busing Amendment (1979) | N |
| Guarantee Chrysler Corp. loans (1979) | Y |
| Approve military draft registration (1980) | Y |
| Aid Sandinista regime in Nicaragua (1980) | Y |
| Strengthen fair housing laws (1980) | Y |

**97th Congress**

| | |
|---|---|
| Reagan budget proposal (1981) | N |

## Interest Group Rating

| Year | ADA | ACA | AFL-CiO | CCUS |
|---|---|---|---|---|
| 1980 | 89 | 23 | 79 | 59 |
| 1979 | 84 | 8 | 79 | 33 |

# 5 John L. Burton (D)

### Of San Francisco — Elected 1974

**Born:** Dec. 15, 1932, Cincinnati, Ohio.
**Education:** San Francisco State U., B.A. 1954;
    U. of San Francisco, LL.B. 1960.
**Military Career:** Army, 1954-56.
**Profession:** Lawyer.
**Family:** Separated; one child.
**Religion:** Roman Catholic.
**Political Career:** Calif. Assembly, 1965-74; un-
    successful Democratic candidate for Calif.
    Senate, 1968 special election.

**In Washington:** It is not easy to tell, listening to John Burton on the floor of the House,
whether he is a man to be taken seriously. When
he assumes the microphone, he is liable to do just
about anything — complain about pay toilets,
exult that no one was killed in a minor grease fire
in the House restaurant, or make one-sentence
speeches utterly irrelevant to the debate, such as
"She wore a glove because she had warts."

Sometimes Burton's floor remarks amount to
high comedy, appreciated by all sides as a way of
relieving tension or tedium. Sometimes they
merely sound bizarre. When Burton announced
his intention to vote "present" on a budget
amendment in 1979, a colleague asked him
whether he was sure he was present. "I know I am
present here," Burton answered, "or I would not
be here. I would be somewhere else."

But if there is an Alice in Wonderland quality
to most of what Burton says, there is a reservoir of
intelligence and wit lying beneath it. Numerous
members have taken the floor to poke fun at their
strange colleague and found themselves embarrassed by the result. The sometimes abrasive
Harold Volkmer, D-Mo., once asked Burton how
long he planned to speak, because Volkmer had
chores to do in his office. "I am sure that the
gentleman could get unanimous consent," Burton
said, "to go back to his office for the rest of the
evening."

Burton says there is method to what he does.
"Half the time," he said in 1979, "you serve a
better purpose coming off the wall than with all
the so-called serious stuff. But people can take it
out of context and make it look certifiable."

Burton has seemed a little less eccentric on
the Government Operations Committee, where he
has investigated safety standards at the Federal
Aviation Administration and purchasing practices
at the General Accounting Office.

In the 96th Congress, as chairman of the
Transportation Subcommittee at Government
Operations, Burton held well-publicized hearings
into the causes of the DC-10 crash that killed 273
people in Chicago a few weeks before. Burton was
rough on FAA administrator Langhorne Bond —
abusive, some felt — but he came off as a man
seriously concerned about the quality of the aircraft millions of people were flying in. "The
FAA's yo-yo actions have caused chaos, confusion
and widespread lack of confidence," he lectured
Bond.

**At Home:** Burton's personality was a central
issue in 1980, when a well-financed Republican
novice came within 12,000 votes of defeating him,
denying him a majority in Marin County for the
first time in his House career. Until the final
weeks of the campaign, Republican Dennis
McQuaid was threatening to use videotape of
Burton in committee and on the House floor.

Ever since he graduated from law school and
joined his brother Phillip's San Francisco law
firm, he has been part of "the Burton machine," a
dominant force in San Francisco politics.

When Phil was elected to Congress in 1964,
John took his seat in the state Assembly. During
six terms in the Legislature he built a solidly
liberal record, focusing on environment and consumer protection. In the middle of his Assembly
career he narrowly lost a special election for the

---

**5th District: Northwest San Fran-
cisco — Marin County.** Population: 467,013
(1% increase since 1970). Race: White 360,680
(77%), Black 37,776 (8%), Asian and Pacific
Islander 54,465 (12%), Others 14,092 (3%).
Spanish origin: 21,909 (5%).

state Senate — his only electoral defeat. In 1973, he was elected state Democratic chairman.

In 1974, he joined his brother in Congress. Republican Rep. William S. Mailliard resigned to become ambassador to the Organization of American States, setting up a special election. Although San Francisco Mayor Joseph Alioto was cool to the idea of a Burton monopoly developing in his city, pro-Alioto labor unions backed Burton, and in the special election primary, Burton won a majority with just 40 votes to spare. That avoided a runoff against his nearest competitor, the officially endorsed Republican, Thomas Caylor, who received just a fifth of the vote.

By the time Burton ran for election to a full term five months later, his district had been changed to include more Democrats in San Francisco, and he won with little difficulty.

**The District:** Marin County has been stereotyped in fiction and journalism as the place with the "mellow" side of suburban living that San Franciscans looked for when they moved out of the city across the Golden Gate Bridge. It is rich, culturally permissive, and more or less liberal politically. It has half the district population.

The other half is in San Francisco. The city dominated the district when Burton was first elected, but its population has gradually fallen. The part of San Francisco currently in the 5th District includes the Pacific Heights, Richmond and Haight-Ashbury districts. It is slightly more liberal than the remaining portion of the city.

## Committees

**Government Operations** (8th of 23 Democrats)
Government Activities and Transportation, chairman; Government Information and Individual Rights.

**House Administration** (8th of 11 Democrats)
Accounts; Office Systems; Policy Group on Information and Computers.

**Select Aging** (5th of 31 Democrats)
Retirement Income and Employment, chairman.

## Elections

**1980 General**

| | |
|---|---|
| John Burton (D ) | 101,105 (51 %) |
| Dennis McQuaid (R ) | 89,624 (45 %) |

**1978 General**

| | |
|---|---|
| John Burton (D ) | 106,046 (67 %) |
| Dolores Skore (R ) | 52,603 (33 %) |

**Previous Winning Percentages**

**1976 (62 %)**   **1974 (60 %)**   **1974* (50 %)**
*Special election.

**District Vote For President**

| | 1980 | | 1976 |
|---|---|---|---|
| D | 91,480 (43 %) | D | 94,329 (48 %) |
| R | 80,930 (39 %) | R | 95,721 (48 %) |
| I | 26,904 (13 %) | | |

## Campaign Finance

| | Receipts | Receipts from PACs | Expenditures |
|---|---|---|---|
| **1980** | | | |
| Burton (D ) | $334,829 | $122,935 (37 %) | $369,237 |
| McQuaid (R ) | $416,103 | $169,016 (41 %) | $484,140 |
| **1978** | | | |
| Burton (D ) | $128,772 | $44,850 (35 %) | $88,923 |

## Voting Studies

| | Presidental Support | | Party Unity | | Conservative Coalition | |
|---|---|---|---|---|---|---|
| Year | S | O | S | O | S | O |
| 1980 | 51 | 40 | 72 | 18 | 13 | 81 |
| 1979 | 49 | 23 | 62 | 13 | 10 | 77 |
| 1978 | 63 | 21 | 73 | 12 | 7 | 79 |
| 1977 | 70 | 18 | 73 | 11 | 7 | 85 |
| 1976 | 20 | 71 | 81 | 6 | 6 | 83 |
| 1975 | 24 | 67 | 82 | 9 | 7 | 85 |
| 1974 (Ford) | 33 | 59 | | | | |
| 1974 | 14 | 86† | 88 | 4† | 2 | 88† |

†Not eligible for all recorded votes.

S = Support          O = Opposition

## Key Votes

**96th Congress**

| | |
|---|---|
| Weaken Carter oil profits tax (1979) | ? |
| Reject hospital cost control plan (1979) | N |
| Implement Panama Canal Treaties (1979) | Y |
| Establish Department of Education (1979) | ? |
| Approve Anti-busing Amendment (1979) | N |
| Guarantee Chrysler Corp. loans (1979) | Y |
| Approve military draft registration (1980) | N |
| Aid Sandinista regime in Nicaragua (1980) | Y |
| Strengthen fair housing laws (1980) | Y |

**97th Congress**

| | |
|---|---|
| Reagan budget proposal (1981) | N |

## Interest Group Ratings

| Year | ADA | ACA | AFL-CIO | CCUS |
|---|---|---|---|---|
| 1980 | 94 | 33 | 88 | 63 |
| 1979 | 84 | 14 | 100 | 12 |
| 1978 | 80 | 13 | 100 | 6 |
| 1977 | 100 | 20 | 86 | 13 |
| 1976 | 90 | 4 | 86 | 0 |
| 1975 | 95 | 16 | 96 | 18 |

# 6 Phillip Burton (D)

**Of San Francisco — Elected 1964**

**Born:** June 1, 1926, Cincinnati, Ohio.
**Education:** U. of Southern Calif., A.B. 1947; Golden Gate Law School, LL.B. 1952.
**Military Career:** Navy World War II, and Air Force, Korean War.
**Profession:** Lawyer.
**Family:** Wife, Sala Galant; one child.
**Religion:** Unitarian.
**Political Career:** Calif. Assembly, 1957-64.

**In Washington:** The qualities that brought Phil Burton within one vote of the majority leadership in 1976 are the same ones that kept him from winning it. Brilliant, passionate, obsessive and given to abusing even his friends when they do not go along with him, Burton is a San Francisco version of Lyndon Johnson.

Given the complexities of his character and House career, it is difficult to say which is more remarkable — that he did not become majority leader, or that he almost did.

Burton lives and breathes politics. His computer-like memory is filed with data on every House district and the political problems of every member. When he is excited, he flails the air with his gestures. He can be as clear as the four letter words that dot his speech, or as obscure as a Delphic oracle. An admirer once said, "If it weren't for the dirty words, I wouldn't know what he was saying."

He is willing to use virtually any method, deceptive or otherwise, to win. Yet he has never been accused of doing anything to enrich himself, and he is uninterested in publicity. What he likes is power, and he likes to use it to fulfill the liberal goals he brought with him from the California Legislature in 1964.

Burton's campaign for majority leader was the climax of years spent carefully creating a constituency among House Democrats. As chairman of the Democratic Study Group, he raised campaign money and signed the checks himself, making it clear who the benefactor was. As chairman of the Democratic Caucus in 1975 and 1976, and in earlier reform struggles, he fought to spread legislative power down to the subcommittee level, where junior Democrats could share it. As a senior member of Interior, he placed countless parks, monuments and trails in colleagues' districts, leaving many in debt to him whether they agreed with his politics or not.

But for every strength there was a weakness.

Burton's credentials as a reformer were tarnished somewhat by his close alliance with Wayne Hays, the bullying Ohio Democrat who was forced to resign in a 1976 sex scandal. The leadership contest, only months after Hays' downfall, came at an unfortunate time from Burton's point of view. Burton also carried scars from a 1974 battle over House committee reform, in which he led the fight to stop the reorganization drafted by Richard Bolling, D-Mo., infuriating Bolling and provoking him to challenge Burton for the leadership. And there was the attitude of Thomas P. O'Neill Jr., about to become House Speaker, who insisted he was neutral but who disliked Burton. He told reporters Burton had tried to "plea bargain" in Hays' favor, an embarrassing charge that Burton denied.

It was essentially a three-way contest: Burton, Bolling and Jim Wright of Texas. Most observers assumed Burton would lead on the early ballots, but that if Wright were eliminated, Bolling would win the showdown. On the second ballot, however, Wright knocked Bolling out of the contest, 95-93. Bolling's allies have always believed that Burton threw votes to Wright at a decisive moment, on the theory Wright would be easier to defeat in the end. Burton denies that. In any case, Burton came up short. Many Bolling loyalists defected to Wright on the third ballot, and the Texan became majority leader, 148-147.

---

**6th District: Eastern and southern San Francisco.** Population: 441,257 (5% decrease since 1970). Race: White 346,778 (56%), Black 54,237 (12%), Asian and Pacific Islander 98,513 (22%), Others 41,729 (9%). Spanish origin: 71,015 (16%).

Burton did not sulk. He promptly entered on one of his most productive legislative crusades, the massive "park barrel" bill authorizing $1.2 billion for more than 100 parks and preservation projects in 44 states. It was the largest single parks bill in U.S. history.

It was also vintage Burton. As he had done on past Interior projects, he all but bought bipartisan support, spreading federal generosity into the districts of dozens of legislators who might otherwise have opposed him. Interior, whose favors tend to be tangible items like parks, has been the perfect place for Burton to practice his political skills. When he brought his park bill to the floor in 1978, it passed by a 341-61 vote. But the Senate failed to act, so he attached most of it to a minor Senate-passed bill and the House went along by voice vote in the final frantic hours of the 95th Congress.

Meanwhile, Burton was the unofficial "governor" of Guam, American Samoa and other American territories, determining their legislative fate as chairman of the Interior Subcommittee on Insular Affairs. Nearly all these territories send delegates to Congress who cannot vote on the House floor but can vote in committee, and they have traditionally provided solid support for Burton.

For much of his career, though, Burton's focus was on the Education and Labor Committee, where he has been a traditional liberal and friend of organized labor. In the years before 1976 he worked to expand black lung benefits, raise the minimum wage and welfare benefits for the aged and disabled, and establish a cost of living escalator for Social Security recipients.

Here too, Burton often accomplished his legislative goals with trade-offs among Republicans and Southern Democrats. On one occasion, he lined up liberal Democratic votes for higher cotton price supports in return for Southern help on black lung payments. Another time, he persuaded allies to vote against a strict limit on farm subsidies, so that rural legislators would support his effort to preserve food stamp eligibility for strikers.

In 1981, as Reagan took office, Burton gave up his Interior Subcommittee and took over the chairmanship of the Labor-Management Subcommittee on Education and Labor. He wanted to protect unions during what he saw as a hostile era. He announced that any Reagan attempt to enact a reduced minimum wage for teen-agers would be met by a demand for an increase in the basic minimum wage itself.

Burton's change in committee focus brought him back to the causes he talked about as a House freshman in 1964 — the same ones for which many liberals have admired him over the years, even when they could not accept his style or tactics. "Phil uses power for better ends than 99 percent of the people in this institution," former California colleague Jerome Waldie once said in his defense., "Even when he makes his shabby little deals. . . . There's only one constituency he gives a damn about, the poor, the elderly, the black and the disabled."

**At Home:** Burton is as obsessed with politics in San Francisco as he is with politics in Washington. His high-pressure style has earned him enemies at home as well as friends, but he has always had more than enough friends — wealthy liberals and less privileged minorities — to re-elect him by overwhelming margins.

The son of a Cincinnati doctor who moved to California before World War II, Burton put himself through law school at night. At age 28 he made his first campaign for the Assembly, losing the primary to a man who had died before the election. He never stopped campaigning and in 1956, despite the heavy Eisenhower landslide, defeated a 32-year Assembly veteran, the only Democrat in the state that year to unseat a Republican assemblyman that year. He did it, he said, by personally meeting nearly a third of the district's voters.

When Democratic Rep. John Shelley was elected mayor of San Francisco in 1963, Burton was one of four Democrats who sought to replace him. After seven years of fighting over social welfare and civil rights legislation in the Assembly, Burton was not on good terms with Speaker Jesse Unruh, and Unruh opposed his House candidacy. So did Shelley, who thought Burton was too liberal.

But they were unable to come up with a strong alternative. Former White House press secretary Pierre Salinger wanted to run, but had not shifted his residence from Virginia in time to qualify. The only major figure backing Burton was Gov. Edmund G. Brown Sr.

Burton announced his candidacy in the office of a local black newspaper, and he ran a non-stop campaign that focused on registering the young, the elderly and the poor rather than on making speeches. He campaigned for strong civil rights legislation, government-supported medical care, and the abolition of the House Un-American Activities Committee. He took 54 percent of the vote, easily avoiding a runoff. Since then, Burton has had little trouble staying in office.

**The District:** The 6th District, covering two-thirds of San Francisco, is the most heavily Democratic in northern California. It is concen-

## Phillip Burton, D-Calif.

trated entirely within the city limits, and includes all but the northwest corner, which is in the 5th District.

In a relatively short distance, one can move from elegant Nob Hill to the largest Chinese community on this side of the Pacific. Farther from the center of the city's business section is the largely-Spanish Mission District, black Fillmore and Hunters Point. On the western side of the city, still in Burton's district, are white, middle-class neighborhoods with row upon row of neatly kept single-family homes.

A large and politically active homosexual community has added a new dimension to the city's already diverse political scene. The gay population of San Francisco has been variously estimated at between 80,000 and 200,000 out of a total of 674,000 people.

## Committees

**Education and Labor** (4th of 19 Democrats)
Labor-Management Relations, chairman; Labor Standards.

**Interior and Insular Affairs** (Ranking Democrat)
Insular Affairs; Public Lands and National Parks.

## Elections

**1980 General**

| | |
|---|---|
| Phillip Burton (D) | 93,400 (69 %) |
| Tom Spinosa (R ) | 34,500 (26 %) |
| Roy Childs (LIB) | 6,750 (5 %) |

**1980 Primary**

| | |
|---|---|
| Phillip Burton (D) | 57,463 (81 %) |
| Bob Barnes (D ) | 8,128 (12 %) |
| Tibor Uskert (D ) | 5,223 (7 %) |

**1978 General**

| | |
|---|---|
| Phillip Burton (D) | 81,801 (68 %) |
| Tom Spinosa (R ) | 33,515 (28 %) |

**Previous Winning Percentages**

| | | | |
|---|---|---|---|
| 1976 (66 %) | 1974 (71 %) | 1972 (82 %) | 1970 (71 %) |
| 1968 (73 %) | 1966 (71 %) | 1964 (100%) | 1964 (54 %) |

* Special election.

**District Vote For President**

| | 1980 | | 1976 |
|---|---|---|---|
| D | 81,691 (53 %) | D | 83,668 (54 %) |
| R | 50,967 (33 %) | R | 62,223 (40 %) |
| I | 16,502 (11 %) | | |

## Campaign Finance

| | Receipts | Receipts from PACs | Expenditures |
|---|---|---|---|
| **1980** | | | |
| Burton (D ) | $138,787 | $57,625 (42 %) | $129,373 |
| **1978** | | | |
| Burton (D ) | $96,039 | $42,050 (44 %) | $96,933 |

## Voting Studies

| Year | Presidential Support S | O | Party Unity S | O | Conservative Coalition S | O |
|---|---|---|---|---|---|---|
| 1980 | 53 | 22 | 73 | 4 | 1 | 77 |
| 1979 | 74 | 17 | 92 | 3 | 3 | 90 |
| 1978 | 71 | 17 | 83 | 6 | 4 | 82 |
| 1977 | 73 | 15 | 85 | 4 | 3 | 87 |
| 1976 | 18 | 76 | 88 | 5 | 4 | 90 |
| 1975 | 25 | 66 | 89 | 2 | 2 | 86 |
| 1974 (Ford) | 35 | 61 | | | | |
| 1974 | 30 | 49 | 82 | 4 | 2 | 86 |
| 1973 | 25 | 72 | 92 | 4 | 5 | 91 |
| 1972 | 43 | 54 | 83 | 10 | 7 | 87 |
| 1971 | 21 | 74 | 83 | 6 | 2 | 89 |
| 1970 | 58 | 35 | 78 | 11 | 2 | 80 |
| 1969 | 47 | 36 | 78 | 13 | 13 | 78 |
| 1968 | 81 | 12 | 93 | 0 | 0 | 92 |
| 1967 | 81 | 15 | 92 | 3 | 2 | 96 |
| 1966 | 78 | 11 | 89 | 3 | 0 | 92 |
| 1965 | 90 | 5 | 90 | 4 | 0 | 92 |
| 1964 | 85 | 4 | 89 | 2† | 0 | 100 |

S = Support          O = Opposition

† Not eligible for all recorded votes.

## Key Votes

**96th Congress**

| | |
|---|---|
| Weaken Carter oil profits tax (1979) | N |
| Reject hospital cost control plan (1979) | N |
| Implement Panama Canal Treaties (1979) | Y |
| Establish Department of Education (1979) | Y |
| Approve Anti-busing Amendment (1979) | N |
| Guarantee Chrysler Corp. loans (1979) | # |
| Approve military draft registration (1980) | N |
| Aid Sandinista regime in Nicaragua (1980) | Y |
| Strengthen fair housing laws (1980) | Y |

**97th Congress**

| | |
|---|---|
| Reagan budget proposal (1981) | N |

## Interest Group Ratings

| Year | ADA | ACA | AFL-CIO | CCUS |
|---|---|---|---|---|
| 1980 | 83 | 25 | 89 | 50 |
| 1979 | 95 | 0 | 89 | 0 |
| 1978 | 95 | 4 | 94 | 18 |
| 1977 | 90 | 0 | 87 | 6 |
| 1976 | 90 | 0 | 87 | 0 |
| 1975 | 89 | 0 | 95 | 6 |
| 1974 | 91 | 0 | 100 | 0 |
| 1973 | 100 | 8 | 100 | 0 |
| 1972 | 100 | 5 | 100 | 0 |
| 1971 | 92 | 7 | 91 | - |
| 1970 | 96 | 6 | 100 | 10 |
| 1969 | 93 | 6 | 100 | - |
| 1968 | 100 | 0 | 100 | - |
| 1967 | 93 | 4 | 100 | 10 |
| 1966 | 94 | 9 | 92 | - |
| 1965 | 100 | 0 | - | 10 |
| 1964 | 100 | 0 | 27 | - |

# 7 George Miller (D)

**Of Martinez — Elected 1974**

**Born:** May 17, 1945, Richmond, Calif.
**Education:** San Francisco State College, B.A.
1968; U. of Calif. Law School, J.D. 1972.
**Profession:** Lawyer.
**Family:** Wife, Cynthia Caccavo; two children.
**Religion:** Roman Catholic.
**Political Career:** Unsuccessful Democratic
nominee for California Senate, 1969.

**In Washington:** Miller's voting record places him among the most consistent House liberals, but he has an independent streak that makes it dangerous to label him.

Long before the Reagan budget reductions, he showed a willingness to cut the school lunch program, an article of faith for Democrats on his Education and Labor Committee. He surprised the Carter administration in 1980 by fighting its only new domestic initiative that year, a youth jobs bill. Miller said it was a "shell game" aimed at getting Carter re-elected, with "no evidence it would have any impact on unemployment.

And in one of the more striking floor speeches of the 96th Congress, he announced he would support a balanced budget — on the grounds that defense is the only category that benefits when the deficit goes up.

Miller has moved into a leadership position on Education and Labor in recent years as senior Democrats have given the panel less of their time. Arguing that American education is "in a shambles," he has tried to pursue new approaches, but has complained that most members are more interested in programs like school lunch.

Miller has, however, won enactment of bills providing federal support for adoption programs, thus reducing the number of children under foster care, and federal money to help school districts end asbestos poisoning in classrooms.

One new approach Miller found unexpectedly controversial was his scheme to provide federal support to shelters for battered wives. He had little trouble moving it through Education and Labor in two consecutive Congresses, but when he brought it to the floor he was caught up in two separate conservative protest movements.

In 1978, floor consideration of the measure was scheduled just weeks after California voters approved tax-cutting Proposition 13. The House, reflecting the national anti-spending mood, defeated it. In 1980 Miller moved a scaled down version through the House, only to run into

trouble in the Senate, where it was described as "government interference in family life."

On Interior, his second committee, Miller has battled doggedly to change a 1902 reclamation law that has allowed agribusiness companies to buy large amounts of cheap federally subsidized water. His attempt to get large users to pay the full cost of the water failed. As a result of his criticisms, the committee later agreed to place a cap on the amount of land a company could own or lease and still get subsidized water, but Miller said the cap was so high as to be meaningless. The bill never reached the House floor.

**At Home:** Not only is Miller a "third-generation Contra Costan" — a fact that sets him apart in California's mobile culture — he is also the third George Miller in his family to make a living in government.

Miller's grandfather, George Sr., was the assistant civil engineer in Richmond. His father, George Jr., served 20 years from a state Senate constituency that resembled the current 7th. A football and swimming star in school, George Miller III was a first-year law student in 1969 when his father suddenly died. Only 23, Miller won the Democratic nomination to fill the vacancy, but lost later in the year to Republican John Nejedly. Miller went to work in the state Capitol anyway, as a legislative aide to then-state Sen. George Moscone, the Democratic floor leader. In 1974, when Democratic Rep. Jerome Waldie

---

**7th District: Most of Contra Costa County.** Population: 555,306 (20% increase since 1970). Race: White 444,667 (80%), Black 57,314 (10%), Asian and Pacific Islander 24,132 (4%) Others 29,193 (5%). Spanish origin: 52,384 (9%).

decided to run for governor, Miller left his job in the Legislature and ran for Congress, challenging a local labor leader and the mayor of Concord, the largest city in the district.

Miller had the family name identification, plus the strong support of Assemblyman John T. Knox, who put his organization to work for him in Richmond, the second-ranked city. He won the primary with 38 percent. In the general election, against a moderate Republican named Gary Fernandez, Miller exploited the Watergate issue, diclosing his campaign finances twice a month and chiding his opponent for not doing likewise. It was a hard-fought election, but Miller won by more than 15,000 votes, and has increased his margin since then.

**The District:** The 7th includes all but the most Republican parts of Contra Costa County. It is a mixture of bedroom communities, agricultural tracts, and heavy industry. Large oil and sugar refineries along the bay from Richmond to Pittsburg give parts of the district the appearance of northern New Jersey. But rugged Wildcat Canyon and Mount Diablo, 3,849 feet above sea level, quickly reorient the visitor to the California topography.

The western part of the district, centered around Richmond and San Pablo, is divided between white-collar and blue-collar voters and is solidly Democratic. The eastern side is more suburban in appearance, and often backs Republicans, although not recently for the House. Walnut Creek, the district's most affluent community and third largest city, is the only one where Republicans outnumber Democrats by registration.

## Committees

**Education and Labor** (10th of 19 Democrats)
Labor Standards, chairman; Elementary, Secondary and Vocational Educatin; Select Education.

**Interior and Insular Affairs** (9th of 23 Democrats)
Water and Power Resources.

## Elections

**1980 General**

| | |
|---|---|
| George Miller (D ) | 142,044 (63 %) |
| Giles St. Clair (R ) | 70,479 (31 %) |

**1980 Primary**

| | |
|---|---|
| George Miller (D ) | 81,956 (85 %) |
| Alexander Malick (D ) | 14,253 (15 %) |

**1978 General**

| | |
|---|---|
| George Miller (D ) | 109,676 (63 %) |
| Paula Gordon (R ) | 58,332 (34 %) |

**Previous Winning Percentages**

1976 (75 %)    1974 (56 %)

**District Vote For President**

| | 1980 | | 1976 |
|---|---|---|---|
| D | 90,975 (39 %) | D | 104,664 (51 %) |
| R | 113,690 (49 %) | R | 95,241 (47 %) |
| I | 21,827 (9 %) | | |

## Campaign Finance

| | Receipts | Percent of Receipts from PACs | Expenditures |
|---|---|---|---|
| **1980** | | | |
| Miller (D ) | $127,517 | $25,141 (20 %) | $129,089 |
| St. Clair (R ) | $42,973 | $9,860 (23 %) | $38,434 |

| 1978 | | | |
|---|---|---|---|
| Miller (D ) | $70,435 | $21,220 (30 %) | $65,404 |
| Gordon (R ) | $57,805 | $8,050 (14 %) | $57,786 |

## Voting Studies

| | Presidental Support | | Party Unity | | Conservative Coalition | |
|---|---|---|---|---|---|---|
| Year | S | O | S | O | S | O |
| 1980 | 61 | 30 | 80 | 13 | 7 | 84 |
| 1979 | 76 | 17 | 80 | 10 | 8 | 79 |
| 1978 | 48 | 12 | 65 | 8 | 4 | 67 |
| 1977 | 68 | 22 | 82 | 11 | 8 | 82 |
| 1976 | 24 | 76 | 86 | 11 | 15 | 78 |
| 1975 | 28 | 71 | 87 | 12 | 9 | 91 |

S = Support        O = Opposition

## Key Votes

**96th Congress**

| | |
|---|---|
| Weaken Carter oil profits tax (1979) | N |
| Reject hospital cost control plan (1979) | N |
| Implement Panama Canal Treaties (1979) | Y |
| Establish Department of Education (1979) | Y |
| Approve Anti-busing Amendment (1979) | N |
| Gaurantee Chrysler Corp. loans (1979) | Y |
| Approve Military draft registration (1980) | N |
| Aid Sandinistas regime in Nicaragua (1980) | Y |
| Strengthen Fair Housing Laws (1980) | Y |

**97th Congress**

| | |
|---|---|
| Reagan budget proposal (1981) | N |

## Interest Group Rating

| Year | ADA | ACA | AFL-CIO | CCUS |
|---|---|---|---|---|
| 1980 | 94 | 27 | 88 | 65 |
| 1979 | 84 | 8 | 94 | 6 |
| 1978 | 85 | 6 | 94 | 30 |
| 1977 | 85 | 19 | 83 | 18 |
| 1976 | 95 | 15 | 86 | 13 |
| 1975 | 100 | 14 | 96 | 12 |

# 8 Ronald V. Dellums (D)

**Of Oakland — Elected 1970**

**Born:** Nov. 24, 1935, Oakland, Calif.
**Education:** San Francisco State U., B.A. 1960; U. of Calif., Berkeley, M.S.W. 1962.
**Military Career:** Marine Corps, 1954-56.
**Profession:** Psychiatric social worker.
**Family:** Wife, Leola Higgs; three children.
**Religion:** Protestant.
**Political Career:** Berkeley City Council, 1967-71.

**In Washington:** Dellums has expressed the outrage of the left for a decade in the House, offering visions of world peace and charges of racism while presenting a personal image of elegance and high fashion. His late-60s rhetoric often sounds out of place in the early 80s, but he still offers it the way he did in the beginning: with a great deal of vigor, flashes of eloquence and a casual disregard for orderly procedure. It is the oratorical flourishes of the floor that have always attracted him, rather than the tedious work of committee business.

In his first year on Capitol Hill, Dellums ignored the niceties of congressional politics and staged his own "unofficial" hearings into charges of atrocities in Vietnam and racism in the military. He was not yet a member of the Armed Services Committee, but he blithely challenged its old pro-war leadership. He made it as a committee member in 1973, and he has been the angriest outsider at Armed Services ever since.

Every year, he makes a futile but flamboyant effort to cut the defense authorization. He does this emotionally and at enormous length, repeatedly exceeding his allotted time but obtaining unanimous consent to go on. In 1979 and 1980, his move was to end funding for the MX missile; the second time, he got 82 votes. But he always puts on an impressive show.

"What is the military challenge of the Soviet Union that prompts this stupendous sum?" he asked in 1980 debate on the overall bill. "No one . . . really gives much credence to the possibility of an attack on the United States, our allies, or areas of U.S. strategic interest."

Those speeches and amendments are the core of Dellums' participation on Armed Services matters. Badly outnumbered at the committee, he has never played an effective role in its deliberations.

Dellums' speeches on social issues are studded with references to "brothers and sisters," and pleas for the unity of minority groups in America: "I hear you scream in outrage and despair and as a black man I understand outrage and despair. . . ."

He urges protest politics by the disadvantaged of all kinds: "America is a nation of niggers. If you're black, you're a nigger. If you're an amputee, you're a nigger. Blind people, the handicapped, radical environmentalists, poor whites, those too far to the left are all niggers."

In 1979, Dellums acquired a new forum — the chairmanship of the District of Columbia Committee. That panel no longer dominates D.C. affairs as it once did, but it still has some leverage over the city's politics and its chairman attracts valuable attention in the local media. Upon becoming chairman, Dellums laid out an agenda aimed at eventual full autonomy for the city. It included federal payments to help meet the huge D.C. pension liability, authority for city officials to impose a commuter tax on suburbanites who work in the district and an end to congressional review of the D.C. budget.

Dellums' relations with other black House members has sometimes been strained. He served as vice-chairman of the Congressional Black Caucus, but was rejected for chairman of the group in 1979 because some felt he was too militantly independent.

Such problems have never slowed Dellums down or quenched his ambitions. The nation

---

**8th District: Northern Alameda County — Oakland.** Population: 439,310 (5% decrease since 1970). Race: White 272,045 (62%), Black 105,356 (30%), Asian and Pacific Islander 40,415 (9%), Others 21,494 (5%). Spanish origin: 28,592 (7%).

could do worse, he has said, than to have him as president or vice president. In 1976, he was touted briefly for president by the National Black Political Assembly. In 1980, he offered himself to the Democratic National Convention as a symbol of protest — a "desperate attempt," he said, to raise issues he thought needed to be discussed.

**At Home:** Dellums was a social worker in San Francisco in 1967 managing federally assisted poverty programs when friends convinced him to pursue his ideas about poverty and discrimination by running for the Berkeley City Council. Since then, he has never lost an election.

He will never satisfy the conservative elements of his district, but he has always had more than enough constituency to get himself elected without them. In five elections, Dellums has never won more than 40 percent of the vote among his upper-income Contra Costa County constituents. But in the much larger Alameda County portion, which includes Berkeley and part of Oakland, he has won well over 60 percent in every election since 1974.

In 1970, when Dellums launched his primary challenge to six-term Democratic Rep. Jeffery Cohelan, the East Bay region was in a state of turmoil. Student protest over the war in Vietnam was becoming increasingly violent and the Black Panther movement was gaining strength in Oakland's ghettos. Although his credentials as a liberal were solid, Cohelan was considered "old-fashioned" in his approach to politics. Dellums, by contrast, was usually descibed in the press as "angry and articulate" or "radical and militant."

Dellums put together the coalition of blacks, students and liberal intellectuals that has been the core of his support ever since. His major issue was Cohelan's tardiness in opposing the Vietnam War. He registered nearly 15,000 new voters in the district and easily ousted Cohelan with 55 percent of the vote.

In the general election, attacks by Vice President Spiro T. Agnew only brought out more support for Dellums among the district's Democrats, and he easily defeated a 25-year-old political neophyte.

Dellums wanted to be a professional baseball pitcher when he grew up, but he has said that encounters with racial prejudice spoiled that dream, leaving him with little ambition after high school. After two years in the Marines, he went to college with the help of the GI Bill and six years later took a degree in psychiatric social work.

**The District:** Except for the exclusive Contra Costa communities of Lafayette, Orinda and Moraga, this district is so far to the political left that many of its Democrats consider the term "liberal" an insult.

The birthplace of the Black Panther Party, the "free speech" student protest movement and the Symbionese Liberation Army, the 8th District has been relatively quiet in recent years. But the poverty in Oakland that spawned the black power movement of the 1960s remains. And the political values of the intellectual community at the University of California's enormous Berkeley campus have changed little. These two cities account for about three-fourths of the district's population and dominate its politics.

Nearly all Democratic candidates, radical or merely liberal, manage to carry the district easily. Even Jimmy Carter, who was crushed by Edward M. Kennedy here in the 1980 Democratic presidential primary, carried the district by a comfortable margin in the general election against Ronald Reagan.

## Committees

**Armed Services** (11th of 25 Democrats)
Research and Development.

**District of Columbia** (chairman)
Fiscal Affairs and Health, chairman.

**Post Office and Civil Service** (12th of 15 Democrats)
Human Resources; Postal Operations and Services; Postal Personnel and Modernization.

## Elections

**1980 General**

| | |
|---|---|
| Ronald Dellums (D ) | 108,380 (56 %) |
| Charles Hughes (R) | 76,580 (39 %) |
| Tom Mikuriya (LIB) | 10,465 (5 %) |

**1978 General**

| | |
|---|---|
| Ronald Dellums (D ) | 94,824 (57 %) |
| Charles Hughes (R ) | 70,481 (42 %) |

**Previous Winning Percentages**

| | | | |
|---|---|---|---|
| 1976 (62 %) | 1974 (57 %) | 1972 (56 %) | 1970 (57 %) |

**District Vote For President**

| | 1980 | | 1976 |
|---|---|---|---|
| D | 106,500 (52 %) | D | 115,361 (57 %) |
| R | 65,088 (32 %) | R | 79,368 (39 %) |
| I | 22,813 (11 %) | | |

## Campaign Finance

| | Receipts | Receipts from PACs | Expenditures |
|---|---|---|---|
| **1980** | | | |
| Dellums (D ) | $356,661 | $26,050 (7 %) | 312,128 |
| Hughes (R ) | $83,474 | $5,650 (7 %) | $82,500 |
| **1978** | | | |
| Dellums (D ) | $76,577 | $7,930 (10 %) | $75,945 |
| Hughes (R ) | $7,185 | $400 (6 %) | $7,933 |

## Voting Studies

| Year | Presidential Support | | Party Unity | | Conservative Coalition | |
|---|---|---|---|---|---|---|
| | S | O | S | O | S | O |
| 1980 | 61 | 30 | 79 | 10 | 8 | 84 |
| 1979 | 72 | 17 | 83 | 5 | 1 | 89 |
| 1978 | 76 | 17 | 83 | 6 | 5 | 86 |
| 1977 | 73 | 25 | 85 | 10 | 5 | 90 |
| 1976 | 24 | 73 | 86 | 9 | 8 | 85 |
| 1975 | 30 | 70 | 87 | 8 | 5 | 91 |
| 1974 (Ford) | 35 | 61 | | | | |
| 1974 | 32 | 57 | 84 | 6 | 1 | 87 |
| 1973 | 23 | 72 | 86 | 9 | 6 | 91 |
| 1972 | 49 | 49 | 88 | 7 | 2 | 91 |
| 1971 | 14 | 74 | 82 | 9 | 2 | 87 |

S = Support          O = Opposition

## Key Votes

**96th Congress**

| | |
|---|---|
| Weaken Carter oil profits tax (1979) | N |
| Reject hospital cost control plan (1979) | N |
| Implement Panama Canal Treaties (1979) | Y |
| Establish Department of Education (1979) | Y |
| Approve Anti-busing Amendment (1979) | N |
| Guarantee Chrysler Corp. loans (1979) | Y |
| Approve military draft registration (1980) | N |
| Aid Sandinista regime in Nicaragua (1980) | Y |
| Strengthen fair housing laws (1980) | Y |

**97th Congress**

| | |
|---|---|
| Reagan budget proposal (1981) | N |

## Interest Group Ratings

| Year | ADA | ACA | AFL-CIO | CCUS |
|---|---|---|---|---|
| 1980 | 100 | 23 | 89 | 36 |
| 1979 | 95 | 4 | 95 | 6 |
| 1978 | 95 | 8 | 95 | 19 |
| 1977 | 95 | 19 | 86 | 12 |
| 1976 | 100 | 11 | 87 | 0 |
| 1975 | 100 | 11 | 95 | 24 |
| 1974 | 96 | 7 | 90 | 0 |
| 1973 | 92 | 11 | 91 | 0 |
| 1972 | 88 | 9 | 100 | 10 |
| 1971 | 97 | 11 | 83 | - |

# 9 Fortney H. ''Pete'' Stark (D)

**Of Oakland — Elected 1972**

**Born:** Nov. 11, 1931, Milwaukee, Wis.
**Education:** Massachusetts Institute of Technology, B.S., 1953; U. of Calif., M.B.A., 1960.
**Military Career:** Air Force, 1955-57.
**Profession:** Banker.
**Family:** Divorced; four children.
**Religion:** Unitarian.
**Political Career:** Unsuccessfully sought Democratic nomination for state senate, 1969.

**In Washington:** A man of personal sophistication and proven business sense — he made a fortune in banking by the time he was 40 — Stark has never quite shaken his early House reputation as a dabbler with a talent for investing his resources in the wrong issue at the wrong time.

Never short of ideas, Stark proposed a novel one during the Ways and Means Committee's 1979 oil windfall profits tax debate. He wanted to replace the complicated excise tax with a flat 10 percent levy on oil company profits. By the time he offered his plan, however, the panel had finished work and was ready to send the bill to the floor.

"This is legislation in its most ludicrous form," said Chairman Al Ullman of Oregon. Stark seemed to have the votes, but Ullman angrily gaveled him down, ending the debate.

It is unlikely that any banker in the history of Congress has played quite the role Stark has, taking a frequent anti-business posture and occasionally browbeating corporation executives as they testify before his committee. He has put his knowledge of finance to use on the Ways and Means Social Security Subcommittee, but here too, he has often found himself battling uphill against leaders in committee and in the House.

He has long been an advocate of solving the problems of the Social Security system with general revenues, rather than increased payroll taxes. In 1978, he persuaded the House Democratic Caucus to adopt a resolution asking Ways and Means to look into such a change. When the committee ignored this, Stark threatened to take the issue back to the caucus and launched an assault on the caucus itself for being too weak. That brought a statement from Speaker O'Neill. "I don't like any of these matters coming from the caucus on a direct vote," the Speaker said.

In 1981, Stark took over the Ways and Means Public Assistance Subcommittee just as President Reagan demanded substantial cuts in welfare spending. The panel reluctantly reported out its own reductions to comply with the Reagan budget.

Stark's reputation as a liberal House maverick was reinforced in 1979 when he led an effort to draft Edward Kennedy for president and in 1980 when he was a leader in the "open convention" drive against Carter after the primaries. One open-convention meeting was held at his home.

For most House members, however, nothing typifies Stark like his 1975 effort to join the Black Caucus. Stark argued that although he was white, his constituency and personal sympathies made him eligible. The caucus said it had to "respectfully decline" the request.

**At Home:** When Stark put an 8-foot high neon peace symbol atop his bank in conservative Walnut Creek, people knew he was no ordinary banker. Ordinary California bankers did not protest the war in Vietnam or join the consumer movement. But Stark, who left Wisconsin to go to business school in California, relished his role as a maverick banker. And having founded his second bank at age 31, he had the money to play it.

Stark made his first political move in 1969, running for the state Senate. He finished third, losing the nomination to George Miller, now his colleague in the California delegation.

Three years later, Stark decided to take on another George Miller — the crusty old conservative Democrat who had represented Oakland in

---

**9th District: Oakland — Eastern Alameda County.** Population: 474,611 (2% increase since 1970). Race: White 334,268 (70%), Black 88,561 (19%), Asian and Pacific Islander 25,787 (5%), Others 25,995 (5%). Spanish origin: 49,122 (10%).

Congress for 28 years. Stark spent his money generously and used one of the state's top political consultants to convince the voters that they did not "have to settle for the 81-year-old Congressman George P. Miller anymore," as a campaign brochure put it. Miller's support for the Vietnam War was a major issue.

Stark swept him aside easily and won by 11,000 votes in the fall. His only close contest since then was in 1980, when free-spending Republican William Kennedy held him to 55 percent.

**The District:** The East Bay's 9th Distri.

includes some of the less Democratic parts of Alameda County. Only a largely black section of Oakland can be counted on for solid Democratic majorities. San Leandro, a once-predominantly Portuguese enclave that still maintains its conservative, working-class flavor, goes Democratic by modest margins.

The suburbs east of the San Leandro Hills are the most rapidly growing parts of the district, and the most Republican. In the last two decades, Livermore has tripled in size; Pleasanton has increased its population eight-fold. In 1980, Reagan carried both by well over 2-to-1.

## Committees

**District of Columbia** (3rd of 7 Democrats)
Government Operations and Metropolitan Affairs.

**Select Narcotics Abuse and Control** (4th of 11 Democrats)

**Ways and Means** (6th of 23 Democrats)
Public Assistance and Unemployment Compensation, chairman; Select Revenue Measures.

## Elections

**1980 General**

| | |
|---|---|
| Fortney Stark (D ) | 90,504 (55 %) |
| William Kennedy (R ) | 67,265 (41 %) |

**1978 General**

| | |
|---|---|
| Fortney Stark (D ) | 88,179 (65 %) |
| Robert Allen (R ) | 41,138 (31 %) |

**Previous Winning Percentages**

1976 (71 %)    1974 (71 %)    1972 (53 %)

**District Vote For President**

| | 1980 | | 1976 |
|---|---|---|---|
| D | 75,961 (44 %) | D | 91,871 (55 %) |
| R | 77,897 (45 %) | R | 72,063 (43 %) |
| I | 15,400 (9 %) | | |

## Campaign Finance

| | Receipts | Receipts from PACs | Expenditures |
|---|---|---|---|
| **1980** | | | |
| Stark (D ) | $40,651 | $26,200 (64 %) | $62,905 |
| **1978** | | | |
| Stark (D ) | $45,194 | $25,460 (56 %) | $24,697 |
| Allen (R ) | $7,236 | $1,835 (25 %) | $7,234 |

## Voting Studies

| | Presidential Support | | Party Unity | | Conservative Coalition | |
|---|---|---|---|---|---|---|
| Year | S | O | S | O | S | O |
| 1980 | 62 | 30 | 79 | 10† | 4 | 84 |
| 1979 | 67 | 14 | 74 | 7 | 3 | 75 |
| 1978 | 75 | 13 | 81 | 12 | 4 | 87 |
| 1977 | 66 | 23 | 85 | 8 | 4 | 89 |
| 1976 | 16 | 76 | 87 | 6 | 5 | 87 |
| 1975 | 30 | 64 | 83 | 4 | 2 | 85 |
| 1974 (Ford) | 33 | 63 | | | | |
| 1974 | 32 | 58 | 82 | 8 | 5 | 86 |
| 1973 | 24 | 71 | 88 | 6 | 5 | 87 |

st

**S = Support          O = Opposition**

†Not eligible for all recorded votes.

## Key Votes

**96th Congress**

| | |
|---|---|
| Weaken Carter oil profits tax (1979) | N |
| Reject hospital cost control plan (1979) | N |
| Implement Panama Canal Treaties (1979) | Y |
| Establish Department of Education (1979) | Y |
| Approve Anti-busing Amendment (1979) | N |
| Guarantee Chrysler Corp. loans (1979) | X |
| Approve military draft registration (1980) | N |
| Aid Sandinista regime in Nicaragua (1980) | Y |
| Strengthen fair housing laws (1980) | Y |

**97th Congress**

| | |
|---|---|
| Reagan budget proposal (1981) | N |

## Interest Group Ratings

| Year | ADA | ACA | AFL-CIO | CCUS |
|---|---|---|---|---|
| 1980 | 94 | 17 | 83 | 53 |
| 1979 | 84 | 5 | 88 | 0 |
| 1978 | 95 | 17 | 95 | 19 |
| 1977 | 80 | 0 | 83 | 6 |
| 1976 | 95 | 0 | 87 | 7 |
| 1975 | 89 | 0 | 95 | 13 |
| 1974 | 91 | 0 | 100 | 0 |
| 1973 | 92 | 16 | 100 | 0 |

# 10 Don Edwards (D)

**Of San Jose — Elected in 1962**

**Born:** Jan. 6, 1915, San Jose, Calif.
**Education:** Stanford U., A.B. 1936, LL.B. 1938.
**Military Career:** Navy, 1942-45.
**Profession:** Lawyer, FBI agent, title company executive.
**Family:** Divorced, five children.
**Religion:** Unitarian.
**Political Career:** No previous office.

**In Washington:** The self-doubt that has afflicted House liberals in recent years has stopped somewhere short of Edwards, whose belief in social change has all the gentle passion it had 20 years ago. With him, there is no hesitation, no retrenchment. "We're absolutely right, you know," he says quietly.

For Edwards, liberalism means civil rights and civil liberties, for blacks, Mexican-Americans, women, children, and dissenters of all kinds. He is a liberal first and a Democrat second. He has never minded opposing his party's congressional leadership or its president on what he sees as a moral issue, such as Vietnam. But he has fought with a soft voice and a bemused tolerance, reflecting a feeling that even those he sees as unenlightened are not beyond persuasion.

Edwards has the perfect forum for carrying out his mission, the Judiciary Subcommittee on Civil and Constitutional Rights. His most important action there has been the avoidance of action. He has stalled some of the most sensitive legislation of the day — constitutional amendments to ban abortions and busing, permit school prayer and require balanced budgets.

Edwards' subcommittee has quietly stifled all these measures, backed up by liberal majorities on the full Judiciary Committee. He can be forced to act only through a petition signed by at least half the House membership. That has happened only once in recent years, on a busing amendment, and Edwards fought that successfully on the floor.

Occasionally, under pressure from conservatives, Edwards has scheduled brief hearings on various of these proposals, but never any committee votes. When criticized for his intransigence, Edwards is unmoved. "Every member should use the rules any way he can," he has said.

In 1981, when the Senate created a new Subcommittee on Security and Terrorism, Edwards complained that it resembled the old House Un-American Activities Committee, which he fought to abolish. "Sadly, alarmingly," Edwards wrote in *The New York Times*, "momentum appears to be on the side of those who savor the bad old days."

Edwards' fears of a new "witch-hunt" were strong enough for him to pass up the chairmanship of the full Veterans' Affairs Committee in the 97th Congress to stay with his Judiciary panel.

Edwards is always watching for conservative end-runs around his "watchdog" subcommittee. The most common is the discharge petition, which was used in 1979, as Ohio Democrat Ronald Mottl forced a floor vote on his anti-busing constitutional amendment.

Edwards coordinated the floor opposition, hoping to defeat Mottl decisively and put the busing issue aside. He was helped by Mottl's clumsy drafting, which produced language barring busing to a distant school even for reasons unrelated to race. But Edwards also activated the outside civil rights coalition he had used successfully in past years, and invoked the help of the traditional Republican civil rights bloc on Judiciary, especially Robert McClory of Illinois, the committee's senior GOP member.

The anti-busing amendment got 207 votes, not only far short of the two-thirds it needed for passage but short of a simple majority. The result

---

**10th District: Bay Area — San Jose, Fremont.** Population: 586,818 (27% increase since 1970). Race: White 415,944 (71%), Black 29,946 (5%), Asian and Pacific Islander 55,408 (9%), Others 85,520 (15%%). Spanish origin: 146,120 (25%).

embarrassed anti-busing forces and left Edwards glad the issue had come up the way it had.

The following year, Edwards managed an intricate fair housing bill in committee and on the floor, finally getting it passed largely intact after approval of a crucial amendment by one vote. The bill, described by President Carter as the most important civil rights legislation of the decade, was drafted to give the 1968 open housing law new enforcement language. It allowed the Justice Department to seek penalties against alleged violators, rather than having to wait for private lawsuits, as in the original act.

Edwards kept the bill alive on the floor by agreeing to shift enforcement from HUD to the Justice Department, which numerous members said would give the accused more legal rights. That change was made on a 205-204 vote, with House leaders switching the decisive vote in the final seconds. But the bill itself fell victim to a Senate filibuster and did not become law.

In earlier years, Edwards played a similar role on the Equal Rights Amendment. In 1971, he had to move ERA out of Judiciary over the objections of the committee's strong chairman, Emanuel Celler, who never did agree to vote for it. A 1978 bill, extending the time period for state ratification of ERA, passed only after Edwards agreed to reduce the length of the extension from seven years down to 39 months. On the floor, he had to fight efforts to allow states that had approved ERA in the early 1970s to rescind their decision. Edwards was crucial to extension of the Voting Rights Act in 1975, and a decade before, was active on passage of the bill that gave full voting privileges to the District of Columbia.

When he has not been promoting civil rights bills or blocking conservative change, Edwards has been watching the FBI, for which he once worked as an agent.

Looking at the issue as a civil libertarian, Edwards says his subcommittee has "helped the FBI get back on track" and out of the domestic surveillance business. His subcommittee spent some of the 96th Congress working on a new FBI charter, spelling out its duties and limits, but the measure never cleared committee.

Edwards was furious when the FBI's Abscam corruption probe resulted in indictments of seven members of Congress. He questioned whether they had committed a crime or been entrapped into one. His subcommittee began a yearlong investigation into FBI undercover operations, trying, as Edwards explained, to determine the "proper limits" of such tactics. Edwards thinks there should be strict limits.

**At Home:** Stories about Edwards inevitably

emphasize his FBI background, citing it as rather unusual preparation for a career as a civil libertarian. Actually, Edwards was not only an FBI agent as a young man — he was a Republican. He did not join the Democratic Party until he was 35, and on his way to a fortune as owner of the Valley Title Insurance Company in San Jose.

Wealth only seemed to make Edwards more liberal. He said he gave up on Republicans because they did not seem interested in the international agreements needed to preserve peace.

At the time, Edwards was beginning his long journey into activism. He joined the United World Federalists, the National Association for the Advancement of Colored People, the American Civil Liberties Union, and the Americans for Democratic Action. He was national ADA chairman in 1965 and still speaks at the group's annual meetings.

Most people in Edwards' district seem to care little about the causes that have preoccupied him all his life. What matters to them is that he is a friendly, open man whose staff promptly takes care of their problems. With that combination, Edwards has been able to overcome a long string of challengers who have questioned his patriotism and warned voters he is too liberal for them.

Edwards had never run for any office before 1962, devoting most of his time to his business. But when a new district was drawn that year to include part of his home city of San Jose, Edwards decided to run.

His two major opponents for the Democratic nomination both had more political experience, but less personal charm. They fought bitterly with each other and Edwards won the Democratic primary by 726 votes, edging Fremont Mayor John Stevenson. It was an overwhelmingly Democratic district, and Edwards easily won in the fall.

Edwards' outspoken support for Eugene McCarthy's presidential campaign, and early reports of his possible retirement, gave him a difficult time in 1968. He faced two Santa Clara city councilmen, one in the Democratic primary and one in the general election. But Edwards still won both elections by comfortable margins.

The district was altered substantially in 1972, but Edwards has continued to win easily.

**The District:** About half of the 10th District is in southern Alameda County, centered around the Fremont area, a major West Coast automobile manufacturing center. The district's other half lies in northern Santa Clara County, and includes about a third of San Jose.

Although both sections sport large Democratic registration advantages, Fremont votes more conservatively than San Jose. In 1980, Reagan won the Alameda County part of the district; Carter carried the Santa Clara County part. Overall, Reagan carried the district narrowly, a sign of the gradual shift among voters here away from the New Deal Democratic traditions. Eight years before, McGovern had won the district.

## Committees

**Judiciary** (4th of 16 Democrats)
Civil and Constitutional Rights, chairman; Criminal Justice; Monopolies and Commercial Law.

**Veterans' Affairs** (2nd of 17 Democrats)
Education, Training and Employment; Hospitals and Health Care.

## Elections

**1980 General**

| | |
|---|---|
| Don Edwards (D ) | 102,231 (62 %) |
| John Lutton (R ) | 45,987 (30 %) |
| Joseph Fuhrig (LIB) | 11,904 (7 %) |

**1978 General**

| | |
|---|---|
| Don Edwards (D ) | 84,488 (67 %) |
| Rudy Hansen (R ) | 41,374 (33 %) |

**Previous Winning Percentages**

| | | | |
|---|---|---|---|
| 1976 (72 %) | 1974 (77 %) | 1972 (72 %) | 1970 (69 %) |
| 1968 (57 %) | 1966 (63 %) | 1964 (70 %) | 1962 (66 %) |

**District Vote For President**

| | 1980 | | 1976 |
|---|---|---|---|
| **D** | 71,937 (41 %) | **D** | 92,239 (57 %) |
| **R** | 78,689 (45 %) | **R** | 65,121 (40 %) |
| **I** | 18,622 (11 %) | | |

## Campaign Finance

| | Receipts | Receipts from PACs | Expenditures |
|---|---|---|---|
| **1980** | | | |
| Edwards (D ) | $29,406 | $9,480 (32 %) | $29,151 |
| Lutton (R) | $2,491 | $350 (14 %) | $1,542 |
| **1978** | | | |
| Edwards (D ) | $33,531 | $8,530 (25 %) | $31,740 |
| Hansen (R ) | $25,128 | $400 (2 %) | $25,124 |

## Voting Studies

| | Presidential Support | | Party Unity | | Conservative Coalition | |
|---|---|---|---|---|---|---|
| Year | S | O | S | O | S | O |
| 1980 | 69 | 22 | 91 | 4 | 2 | 91 |
| 1979 | 76 | 17 | 83 | 5 | 2 | 90 |
| 1978 | 79 | 14 | 88 | 6 | 4 | 88 |
| 1977 | 82 | 16 | 92 | 5 | 3 | 95 |
| 1976 | 20 | 78 | 94 | 3 | 5 | 91 |
| 1975 | 30 | 65 | 95 | 3† | 2 | 95† |
| 1974 (Ford) | 37 | 56 | | | | |
| 1974 | 40 | 57 | 91 | 5† | 2 | 97† |
| 1973 | 21 | 70 | 86 | 4 | 3 | 88 |
| 1972 | 49 | 49 | 82 | 6 | 2 | 90 |
| 1971 | 26 | 72 | 86 | 9 | 3 | 93 |
| 1970 | 51 | 38 | 63 | 14 | - | 68 |
| 1969 | 23 | 38 | 62 | 9 | 7 | 69 |
| 1968 | 68 | 9 | 68 | 5 | 2 | 82 |
| 1967 | 73 | 12 | 79 | 4 | 2 | 81 |
| 1966 | 78 | 7 | 78 | 3 | 0 | 89 |
| 1965 | 83 | 4 | 87 | 1 | 0 | 94 |
| 1964 | 90 | 4 | 92 | 2 | 0 | 92 |
| 1963 | 89 | 4 | 91 | 0 | 0 | 80 |

S = Support    O = Opposition

†Not eligible for all recorded votes.

## Key Votes

**96th Congress**

| | |
|---|---|
| Weaken Carter oil profits tax (1979) | N |
| Reject hospital cost control plan (1979) | N |
| Implement Panama Canal Treaties (1979) | Y |
| Establish Department of Education (1979) | Y |
| Approve Anti-busing Amendment (1979) | N |
| Guarantee Chrysler Corp. loans (1979) | ? |
| Approve military draft registration (1980) | N |
| Aid Sandinista regime in Nicaragua (1980) | Y |
| Strengthen fair housing laws (1980) | Y |

**97th Congress**

| | |
|---|---|
| Reagan budget proposal (1981) | N |

## Interest Group Ratings

| Year | ADA | ACA | AFL-CIO | CCUS |
|---|---|---|---|---|
| 1980 | 100 | 17 | 89 | 63 |
| 1979 | 95 | 0 | 95 | 6 |
| 1978 | 80 | 4 | 84 | 22 |
| 1977 | 95 | 12 | 78 | 12 |
| 1976 | 95 | 0 | 87 | 14 |
| 1975 | 100 | 0 | 96 | 6 |
| 1974 | 100 | 0 | 100 | 0 |
| 1973 | 100 | 12 | 100 | 0 |
| 1972 | 100 | 9 | 100 | 10 |
| 1971 | 95 | 4 | 92 | - |
| 1970 | 88 | 12 | 100 | 11 |
| 1969 | 100 | 17 | 100 | - |
| 1968 | 100 | 5 | 100 | - |
| 1967 | 93 | 0 | 100 | 10 |
| 1966 | 100 | 9 | 92 | - |
| 1965 | 100 | 0 | - | 10 |
| 1964 | 100 | 0 | 100 | - |
| 1963 | - | 0 | - | - |

# 11 Tom Lantos (D)

**Of Hillsborough — Elected 1980**

**Born:** Feb. 1, 1928, Budapest, Hungary.
**Education:** U. of Wash., B.A. 1949; M.A. 1950; U. of Calif., Berkeley, Ph.D. 1953.
**Profession:** Economist.
**Family:** Wife, Annette Tilleman; two children.
**Religion:** Jewish.
**Political Career:** Millbrae Board of Education, 1958-66.

**The Member:** Few freshmen can match Lantos' range of experiences. Born in Hungary, Lantos left his native Budapest in 1947 at age 19, after fighting in the anti-Nazi underground. He won a scholarship to the University of Washington and six years later had a Ph.D. in economics.

Liberal on many domestic issues, Lantos cites his background in warning of the need for a tougher American attitude toward totalitarian regimes. "We have been confronted by Ayatollahs from the Mideast," he has said, "and pretended they were accountants from the Midwest."

Lantos has urged Congress to grant honorary American citizenship to Raoul Wallenberg, a Swedish diplomat who during World War II helped thousands of Jews escape the Nazis.

He has opposed Interior Secretary James G. Watt's plans to permit offshore oil drilling along the northern and central California coast. Lantos fears that an oil spill would ruin San Mateo County's tourist and fishing industries.

When testifying before the Government Operations Committee in 1981, Watt said he had a better perception of the national interest than California Gov. Jerry Brown, who opposes the drilling; Lantos ridiculed Watt's attitude of "self-righteousness."

Lantos was one of only three Democrats to unseat a Republican House member in 1980. He defeated incumbent Bill Royer by uniting the local Democratic Party, which was badly split following the 1978 assassination of Democratic Rep. Leo J. Ryan in Jonestown, Guyana.

**The District:** The most Democratic areas of the 11th are working class suburbs, Daly City and South San Francisco, which adjoin San Francisco. Farther south are liberal, more affluent communities such as Belmont and San Carlos. The strongest Republican area is the exclusive community of Hillsborough. Overall, Democrats outnumber Republicans 57 to 32 percent, but many Democrats split their tickets. In 1972 and 1976, Ryan won more than 60 percent, while the Democratic presidential candidates lost the district.

## Committees

**Foreign Affairs** (20th of 21 Democrats)
Asian and Pacific Affairs; Europe and the Middle East.

**Government Operations** (23rd of 23 Democrats)
Environment, Energy and National Resources; Government Activities and Transportation.

**Select Aging** (27th of 31 Democrats)
Housing and Consumer Interests; Retirement Income and Employment.

## Elections

**1980 General**

| | |
|---|---|
| Tom Lantos (D ) | 85,823 (46 %) |
| Bill Royer (R ) | 80,100 (43 %) |
| Wilson Branch (P&F) | 13,723 (7 %) |

**District Vote For President**

| | 1980 | | 1976 |
|---|---|---|---|
| D | 72,391 (37 %) | D | 85,027 (45 %) |
| R | 96,100 (49 %) | R | 94,646 (51 %) |
| I | 22,081 (11 %) | | |

## Campaign Finance

| | Receipts | Receipts from PACs | Expenditures |
|---|---|---|---|
| **1980** | | | |
| Lantos (D ) | $492,285 | $61,331 (12 %) | $554,718 |
| Royer (R ) | $798,043 | $254,576 (32 %) | $781,795 |

## Key Vote

**97th Congress**

Reagan budget proposal (1981)        N

---

**11th District: Most of San Mateo County.** Population: 498,238 (7% increase since 1970). Race: White 390,913 (78%), Black 20,350 (4%), Asian and Pacific Islander 53,422 (11%), Others 33,553 (7%). Spanish origin: 66,915 (13%).

# 12 Paul N. McCloskey Jr. (R)

**Of Menlo Park — Elected 1967**

**Born:** Sept. 26, 1927, San Bernardino, Calif.
**Education:** Stanford U., B.A. 1950, LL.B. 1953.
**Military Career:** Navy 1945-47; Marines 1950-52.
**Profession:** Lawyer.
**Family:** Divorced; four children.
**Religion:** Presbyterian.
**Political Career:** No previous office.

**In Washington:** Over nearly 15 years in Congress, McCloskey has been a rebel with a dozen causes — the Vietnam War, Richard Nixon, jet noise pollution, campaign finance abuses, labor corruption, civil rights, conservation, a national land use plan, the draft, nuclear power, and others almost certainly yet to come.

It has nearly all been against the grain, not only of public opinion, but of House Republican thinking. McCloskey has never had any shortage of friends in GOP ranks, but he has never really had the political trust of his party either, before or after his 1972 challenge to Nixon's renomination. As recently as 1979, he was threatening to quit the party, although that quarrel passed quickly, as previous ones have.

If it has been a quixotic career, though, it has had its successes, especially in recent years on the Merchant Marine Committee, where McCloskey was ranking Republican, sitting opposite Democrat John M. Murphy of New York, its chairman.

Soon after he assumed that position, McCloskey became an open critic of Murphy's close ties with maritime interests, and argued publicly that both the industry and maritime unions were getting special favors on legislation handled by the committee. He was a constant irritant to Murphy, challenging committee bills and defeating some.

In 1977, Murphy promoted a bill to require that nearly 10 percent of U.S. oil imports be shipped in American-built and operated tankers. He said it was needed to shore up the ailing U.S. merchant marine. McCloskey began fighting it in committee, arguing that it was a "political payoff" to maritime interests which had helped President Carter and congressional Democrats in 1976. He called on several Carter administration officials to testify about the bill, but they refused and Murphy refused to subpoena them.

When the bill reached the floor, McCloskey managed to add seveal weakening amendments. Murphy then moved it through on an initial voice vote, but Republicans insisted on a roll-call, and it was decisively defeated.

McCloskey fought Murphy on a variety of conservation issues at Merchant Marine, renewing the environmentalist reputation he brought with him to the House. In 1977, when the committee approved a bill limiting the quota of dolphins that could be killed in tuna fishing, McCloskey tried to reduce it further, but lost. He has also been involved in a variety of environmental issues outside the committee, such as the first Earth Day in 1970, which he sponsored.

The cold war on Merchant Marine continued until 1980, when McCloskey stepped down from his senior position to devote more time to his 1982 Senate campaign, and Murphy lost his seat.

On some of his Merchant Marine issues, McCloskey has had a majority of his party with him. But on most foreign policy and domestic social questions, he has been a minority within a minority. He has not been able, for example, to obtain the Ways and Means assignment that, as a former tax lawyer, he has long coveted. He has not been able to make things happen easily. So he has focused mostly on calling attention to things he thinks are wrong.

---

**12th District: Parts of San Mateo, Santa Clara counties.** Population: 472,813 (2% increase since 1970). Race: White 388,471 (82%), Black 23,430 (5%), Asian and Pacific Islander 35,896 (8%), Others 24,016 (5%). Spanish origin: 45,055 (10%).

---

In his second term, he defended Supreme Court Justice William O. Douglas against an attack from then-GOP leader Gerald R. Ford, who had called for Douglas' impeachment on charges that he advocated revolution. It was a well-argued legal brief, favorably received outside Congress, but it furthered McCloskey's maverick reputation.

Meanwhile, McCloskey was becoming more outspoken on Vietnam. A few days after he took the oath of office in 1967, McCloskey was in Vietnam proclaiming that he had "grave doubts that what we do here is right." By September, 1968, he was flatly opposed to the war and said so in a formal position paper. The level of his anti-war rhetoric gradually escalated between then and 1972, when he challenged Nixon's renomination.

Backed by a corps of anti-war volunteers, McCloskey entered the 1972 New Hampshire primary. He was philosophical. "I may get licked," he said, "but I can't keep quiet." Nixon beat him by better than 3-to-1, and McCloskey dropped out three days after the primary.

The challenge chilled McCloskey's relations with congressional Republicans for years to come. In the early aftermath of the campaign, he considered shifting his party affiliation to Democratic, but in the end he chose a different course. He began campaigning for Republicans all over the country to restore his party reputation. By 1980, he had mended fences enough to support Ronald Reagan for president, even though the two had exchanged insults over the years (Reagan once said McCloskey was fit only to represent the San Andreas earthquake fault and McCloskey suggested Reagan should raise his cattle there).

On economic matters, McCloskey has always been market-oriented. "I believe in the free enterprise system," he once said as he voted against a corporate loan guarantee, "and that includes the right to succeed if you're good and to fail if you're mismanaged." But on abortion, civil rights, and foreign policy he remains considerably to the left of most Republicans. He voted with his party against a majority of Democrats less than a fourth of the time in 1980.

**At Home:** For most of his political career, McCloskey has had to fight off attacks from primary opponents who claim he is not a "real" Republican. But in general elections, GOP voters have always found him better than the Democratic alternative, and he has begun to win easily in recent years as the Vietnam issue has faded.

But McCloskey's safe seat, achieved after a decade of struggle, has not made him content. He plans to leave the House in 1982 to run for the Senate seat held by Republican S. I. Hayakawa. McCloskey was the first challenger to set up a fund-raising committee for the campaign, partly because he has a long way to go. Both his liberal image and his lack of name recognition in Southern California will work against him. Republican primaries are usually decided by the conservatives in the southern part of the state.

McCloskey has won against the odds before. As a San Mateo County lawyer, running for Congress in a 1967 special election, he was obscured in the media by his leading primary rival, movie star Shirley Temple Black. But McCloskey had a political base in the environmental movement he had worked with, and he proved to be a dogged campaigner. He easily outdistanced Black in the special primary, then won the runoff against Democrat Roy Archibald, a San Mateo city councilman. McCloskey continued to call for an end to the U.S. military involvement in Vietnam, while Archibald campaigned as a "dawk," trying to steer a middle course between the hawks and doves. McCloskey took the first office he had ever sought with nearly 60 percent of the vote.

For nearly a decade after that, McCloskey lived on the edge of defeat in every Republican primary, even though no Democrat in the district had a chance against him.

His 1972 campaign against Nixon was about as popular in his newly redrawn California district as it had been in New Hampshire. He won renomination, however, because conservatives could not decide on a single opponent to him.

His two strongest challengers both accused McCloskey of tearing down the president while neglecting his duties as a congressman. The two won 56 percent between them, but McCloskey slipped through to the nomination by 8,000 votes. In the fall, disgruntled Republicans ran a write-in campaign for Gordon Knapp, an Atherton businessman, but McCloskey won by 37,000 votes.

Knapp continued his attack on McCloskey two years later in the GOP primary, this time with the unified backing of the district's conservatives. But McCloskey again survived, this time by 832 votes, thanks to a large registration drive among Stanford students and a visit from a former colleague, Vice President Gerald R. Ford.

In 1980, McCloskey took 80 percent of the primary vote — a clear indication that he had finally nailed down support within his own party.

**The District:** By registration, this is the closest thing to a Republican district in northern California, although even here Democrats still have a slight majority.

A large segment of the economy is centered around computers and high technology, symbolized by the offices and laboratories that line the highway south of San Francisco. Stanford University in Palo Alto plays a large role in both the district's economy and its politics. Its 12,000 students and 1,600 faculty members provide a significant liberal tilt. Democrats like Edward Kennedy and Tom Hayden do better in the Stanford area than ones like Jimmy Carter and John Tunney.

But in areas like Portola Valley and Los Altos Hills, the voters are wealthy and Republican. Santa Clara and Sunnyvale, the two largest cities in the district, are Democratic on paper, but often support Republican candidates.

## Committees

**Government Operations** (4th of 17 Republicans)
Manpower and Housing.

**Merchant Marine and Fisheries** (2nd of 15 Republicans)
Fisheries and Wildlife Conservation and the Environment; Merchant Marine.

## Elections

**1980 General**
| | |
|---|---|
| Paul McCloskey (R ) | 143,817 (72 %) |
| Kirsten Olsen (D ) | 37,009 (19 %) |
| Bill Evers (LIB) | 15,073 (8 %) |

**1980 Primary**
| | |
|---|---|
| Paul McCloskey (R ) | 51,688 (80 %) |
| Royce Cole (R ) | 13,302 (20 %) |

**1978 General**
| | |
|---|---|
| Paul McCloskey (R ) | 116,982 (73 %) |
| Kirsten Olsen (D ) | 34,472 (22 %) |

**Previous Winning Percentages**
1976 (66 %)   1974 (69 %)   1972 (55 %)   1970 (78 %)
1968 (79 %)   1967* (58 %)
*Special Election

**District Vote For President**
| | 1980 | | 1976 |
|---|---|---|---|
| D | 72,649 (35 %) | D | 89,818 (45 %) |
| R | 95,588 (46 %) | R | 103,233 (52 %) |
| I | 32,296 (16 %) | | |

## Campaign Finance

| | Receipts | Receipts from PACs | Expenditures |
|---|---|---|---|
| **1980** | | | |
| McCloskey (R ) | $96,371 | $29,510 (31 %) | $84,141 |
| Olsen (D ) | $6,866 | — (0 %) | $7,016 |
| **1978** | | | |
| McCloskey (R ) | $85,663 | $18,180 (21 %) | $56,144 |
| Olsen (D ) | $54,572 | $21,610 (40 %) | $54,203 |

## Voting Studies

| | Presidential Support | | Party Unity | | Conservative Coalition | |
|---|---|---|---|---|---|---|
| | S | O | S | O | S | O |
| **Year** | | | | | | |
| 1980 | 57 | 21 | 23 | 48 | 24 | 58 |

| | S | O | | S | O | | S | O |
|---|---|---|---|---|---|---|---|---|
| 1979 | 58 | 23 | | 31 | 52 | | 36 | 53 |
| 1978 | 71 | 20 | | 36 | 53 | | 35 | 57 |
| 1977 | 61 | 23 | | 33 | 55 | | 31 | 54 |
| 1976 | 37 | 49 | | 30 | 55 | | 29 | 52 |
| 1975 | 64 | 26 | | 48 | 40 | | 44 | 46 |
| 1974 (Ford) | 48 | 37 | | | | | | |
| 1974 | 47 | 30 | | 32 | 51 | | 25 | 55 |
| 1973 | 45 | 48 | | 38 | 58 | | 35 | 61 |
| 1972 | 49 | 27 | | 21 | 43 | | 18 | 52 |
| 1971 | 46 | 40 | | 28 | 45 | | 21 | 55 |
| 1970 | 77 | 12 | | 54 | 35 | | 43 | 39 |
| 1969 | 62 | 23 | | 29 | 56 | | 22 | 69 |
| 1968 | 65 | 23 | | 52 | 44 | | 43 | 49 |
| 1967 | 75 | 25† | | 50 | 50 | | 50 | 50 |

S = Support          O = Opposition
†Not eligible for all recorded votes.

## Key Votes

**96th Congress**

| | |
|---|---|
| Weaken Carter oil profits tax (1979) | Y |
| Reject hospital cost control plan (1979) | N |
| Implement Panama Canal Treaties (1979) | Y |
| Establish Department of Education (1979) | ? |
| Approve Anti-busing Amendment (1979) | N |
| Guarantee Chrysler Corp. loans (1979) | N |
| Approve military draft registration (1980) | N |
| Aid Sandinista regime in Nicaragua (1980) | Y |
| Strengthen fair housing laws (1980) | Y |

**97th Congress**

| | |
|---|---|
| Reagan budget proposal (1981) | Y |

## Interest Group Ratings

| Year | ADA | ACA | AFL-CIO | CCUS |
|---|---|---|---|---|
| 1980 | 78 | 35 | 35 | 73 |
| 1979 | 58 | 48 | 39 | 59 |
| 1978 | 65 | 32 | 58 | 59 |
| 1977 | 55 | 21 | 55 | 53 |
| 1976 | 45 | 27 | 35 | 27 |
| 1975 | 68 | 32 | 48 | 50 |
| 1974 | 74 | 15 | 91 | 44 |
| 1973 | 76 | 15 | 64 | 36 |
| 1972 | 50 | 8 | 71 | 13 |
| 1971 | 65 | 23 | 63 | - |
| 1970 | 64 | 59 | 14 | 70 |
| 1969 | 67 | 18 | 80 | - |
| 1968 | 33 | 43 | 75 | - |
| 1967* | | | | |

*Not available because member did not serve full term.

# 13 Norman Y. Mineta (D)

**Of San Jose — Elected 1974**

**Born:** Nov, 12, 1931, San Jose, Calif.
**Education:** U. of Calif., Berkeley, B.S. 1953.
**Military Career:** Army, 1953-56.
**Profession:** Insurance agent.
**Religion:** Methodist.
**Political Career:** San Jose City Council, 1967-71; mayor of San Jose, 1971-75.

**In Washington:** A flair for political brokerage has made Mineta one of the more influential members of his 1974 House class almost from the day he arrived in Washington. He proclaimed himself an "activist" early in his first term and worked to depose three veteran House chairmen, but he took most of his complaints to the leadership rather than the press, and helped set up regular meetings of the freshmen with then-Speaker Carl Albert. "A lot can be accomplished if you stick them with a hot poker," he said privately after one of the meetings.

Mineta's role in those sessions brought him the presidency of his 1974 class, a job that lasted only six months but established permanent ties to the members of what remains the largest group of its kind in the House. It also made him something of a leadership favorite. When Thomas P. O'Neill Jr. became Speaker in 1977, he supported Mineta for a spot on the Budget Committee. For several years after that, Mineta was the man O'Neill counted on to sell budget resolutions to junior Democrats skeptical about the size of the deficits. Many of those lobbying efforts failed, but Mineta's reputation with the leadership remained intact.

Mineta has been quiet during some of the Budget Committee's most acrimonious public debates, but he has left a few significant imprints on the budget process. One is a "credit budget," approved in 1980, that makes the first formal accounting of the money the federal government spends by guaranteeing private loans.

Mineta also has used his Budget Committee position to promote higher mass transit funding — or more recently, to limit the reductions in funding. In past budget conferences with the Senate, he has managed inconspicuously to nudge the final product a few hundred million dollars higher in the overall category of transportation. In 1981, he successfully insisted that the Budget Committee's resolution restore some initial cuts in airport construction money. But the resolution itself lost out on the House floor to a Reagan alternative.

On the Public Works Committee, his other assignment, Mineta has fought a far more conspicuous fight against aircraft noise, a serious problem in his district. In 1979, when Aviation Subcommittee Chairman Glenn Anderson, D-Calif., accepted a relatively weak noise control provision in conference with the Senate, Mineta helped form a coalition to fight the agreement. They persuaded Anderson to change his mind, and lobbied President Carter to threaten a veto. The conferees went back and drew up an agreement with somewhat tougher regulations.

In 1981, Mineta became chairman of the Aviation Subcommittee himself. The panel had to confront Reagan recommendations that federal funding be reduced for large airports. Mineta reluctantly accepted most of the cuts, although he argued that the money remaining was insufficient to meet national airport needs.

Mineta has played a public role as the only Japanese-American member of Congress who was interned by the U.S Government during World War II. He won passage of a bill in 1978 to grant retirement benefits to Japanese-American civil servants for the time they were interned, and helped with another in 1980 creating a federal commission to study the internment question.

**At Home:** San Jose's Japanese-American community was the springboard to Mineta's po-

---

**13th District: Most of Santa Clara County.** Population: 618,770 (33% increase since 1970). Race: White 506,756 (82%), Black 17,053 (3%), Asian and Pacific Islander 37,776 (6%), Others 57,185 (9%). Spanish origin 97,724 (16%).

---

litical career. Running an insurance businesss with his father in the 1960s, he became active in the city's Japanese-American citizens league. That led him to San Jose's human relations commission, its housing authority and City Council, and to the mayoralty in 1971.

The San Jose area was coming out of a decade of unprecedented suburban growth during Mineta's years as mayor, and he allied himself with those calling for limits on further development.

The 13th District was open in 1974; it had been Republican in every election since World War II, but Charles Gubser's retirement allowed Mineta to slip in by 15,000 votes against a Republican state legislator. Mineta drew two-thirds of the vote in 1976, and a still comfortable 57 percent in 1978, a much weaker Democratic year in California. In 1980, as Reagan took California easily, Mineta was up to 58.9 percent.

**The District:** Fifty miles from San Fran-cisco and 42 miles from Oakland, San Jose moved closer to the economic and political orbit of the Bay Area during the last two decades, all but shedding its earlier identity as a packing and trading center for the separate fruit and wine growing area to the south.

Mineta represents most of the city of San Jose, although not its most Democratic areas, and the less dense parts of Santa Clara County below it. Santa Clara is now California's fifth biggest county. Suburbanization has made some of this district's communities more Democratic, rather than less, but a substantial Republican vote remains.

The county was solid for Jerry Brown in the 1978 gubernatorial campaign, giving him more than 60 percent of the vote. It was never that kind to the governor's father, Edmund G. "Pat" Brown, in the days when San Jose was still a prune packing town and the elder Brown was trying to carry it in his gubernatorial campaigns.

## Committees

**Budget**
Task forces: Enforcement, Credit and Multi-year budgeting, chairman; Reconciliation.

**Public Works and Transportation** (5th of 25 Democrats)
Aviation, chairman; Investigations and Oversight; Public Buildings and Grounds.

**Select Intelligence** (5th of 9 Democrats)
Program and Budget Authorization.

## Elections

**1980 General**

| | |
|---|---|
| Norman Mineta (D) | 132,246 (59%) |
| W. E. Gagne (R) | 79,766 (36%) |

**1978 General**

| | |
|---|---|
| Norman Mineta (D) | 100,809 (58%) |
| Dan O'Keefe (R) | 69,306 (40%) |

**Previous Winning Percentages**
1976 (67%)    1974 (53%)

**District Vote For President**

| | 1980 | | 1976 |
|---|---|---|---|
| D | 73,035 (32%) | D | 91,620 (45%) |
| R | 121,122 (53%) | R | 108,664 (53%) |
| I | 29,470 (13%) | | |

## Campaign Finance

| | Receipts | Receipts from PACs | Expenditures |
|---|---|---|---|
| **1980** | | | |
| Mineta (D) | $260,904 | $81,208 (31%) | $221,552 |
| Gagne (R) | $5,517 | $550 (10%) | $9,439 |
| **1978** | | | |
| Mineta (D) | $195,359 | $55,025 (28%) | $176,628 |
| O'Keefe (R) | $54,956 | $6,075 (6%) | $54,741 |

## Voting Studies

| Year | Presidential Support | | Party Unity | | Conservative Coalition | |
|---|---|---|---|---|---|---|
| | S | O | S | O | S | O |
| 1980 | 76 | 20 | 93 | 4 | 11 | 87 |
| 1979 | 81 | 14 | 89 | 6 | 15 | 79 |
| 1978 | 81 | 19 | 90 | 8 | 9 | 89 |
| 1977 | 77 | 20 | 88 | 5 | 8 | 85 |
| 1976 | 20 | 76 | 93 | 3 | 8 | 88 |
| 1975 | 38 | 61 | 92 | 6 | 5 | 94 |

S = Support          O = Opposition

## Key Votes

**96th Congress**

| | |
|---|---|
| Weaken Carter oil profits tax (1979) | N |
| Reject hospital cost control plan (1979) | N |
| Implement Panama Canal Treaties (1979) | Y |
| Establish Department of Education (1979) | Y |
| Approve Anti-busing Amendment (1979) | N |
| Guarantee Chrysler Corp. loans (1979) | Y |
| Approve military draft registration (1980) | N |
| Aid Sandinista regime in Nicaragua (1980) | Y |
| Strengthen fair housing laws (1980) | Y |

**97th Congress**

| | |
|---|---|
| Reagan budget proposal (1981) | N |

## Interest Group Ratings

| Year | ADA | ACA | AFL-CIO | CCUS |
|---|---|---|---|---|
| 1980 | 83 | 21 | 68 | 59 |
| 1979 | 79 | 13 | 85 | 29 |
| 1978 | 80 | 4 | 84 | 22 |
| 1977 | 80 | 4 | 87 | 12 |
| 1976 | 95 | 0 | 82 | 6 |
| 1975 | 95 | 7 | 100 | 13 |

# 14 Norman D. Shumway (R)

**Of Stockton — Elected 1978**

**Born:** July 28, 1934, Phoenix, Ariz.
**Education:** Stockton Junior College, 1954; U. of Utah, B.S. 1960; U. of California, J.D. 1963.
**Profession:** Lawyer.
**Family:** Wife, Luana June Schow; six children.
**Religion:** Mormon.
**Political Career:** San Joaquin County Supervisor, 1975-79.

**In Washington:** A deeply religious man, reserved and serious, Shumway confined himself to a small number of traditional conservative issues in his first House term.

He introduced a floor amendment that would have ended the state "outreach" part of the food stamp program — the one by which states seek to publicize the program for potential new recipients. "They know what's available to them," Shumway said, "and they know how to have access to the program." He won a partial victory when the House accepted a milder version of the amendment, offered by Agriculture Chairman Thomas S. Foley of Washington, dropping the requirement that states use outreach programs, but allowing them to use them if they desire.

That amendment was Shumway's only conspicuous action on the House floor during the 96th Congress. On the Banking Committee, he took his place as a backbench Republican member. He was on the subcommittee that drafted the loan guarantee for the Chrysler Corp., and voted against it both there and on the floor.

Shumway was delighted in 1980 when the Interior Committee voted not to give "wild and scenic" status to the Stanislaus River in his district, thus allowing completion of the New Melones Dam, which he strongly favored. Shumway had brought constituents to testify at Interior against the wilderness designation.

Shumway introduced a bill calling for abolition of the federal estate tax, and spoke against the federal Legal Services Corporation. "Poor people are used as pawns," he said, "by legal services lawyers attempting to reform society."

**At Home:** Shumway's serious demeanor was a major asset in 1978 when he defeated 11-term Democratic Rep. John J. McFall, the former majority whip.

Less than a month before the general election, the House voted to reprimand McFall for taking $3,000 from South Korean rice merchant Tongsun Park. Shumway only indirectly mentioned McFall's involvement in "Koreagate," letting the extensive news coverage of the story do most of his work. But by emphasizing his own personal strictness, Shumway was able to capitalize on McFall's troubles.

Shumway's more overt campaign approach was to convince voters that the 60-year-old McFall had served too long and was not "as alert or energetic as he used to be." Favoring a 12-year limit on House service, Shumway said McFall had overstayed his welcome and was paying for it.

Shumway had been involved in elective politics only four years at the time of his election to Congress. But as chairman of the San Joaquin County Board of Supervisors, he had established enough name recognition by 1978 to win a seven-candidate GOP House primary. More than half the Republican primary vote was cast in his home county, where he opened a 5,000-vote margin over his nearest competitor.

After the primary, Shumway received financial and campaign help from the national GOP and was able to match McFall dollar-for-dollar. The Republican invested heavily in television advertising.

Shumway's victory was impressive. McFall carried San Joaquin County, but with only 49 percent of the vote. Two years earlier the veteran

---

**14th District: Lower San Joaquin Valley — Stockton.** Population: 634,718 (37% increase since 1970). Race: White 528,280 (83%), Black 21,130 (3%), Asian and Pacific Islander 23,414 (4%), Others 61,894 (10%). Spanish origin: 94,116 (15%).

Democrat had taken 75 percent there. In the rest of the district, the incumbent received scarcely more than a third of the vote, as Shumway attracted the support of longtime McFall supporters in the district's agricultural areas. By 1980, Shumway had a firm hold on the district. He outspent his Democratic opponent by more than three times, and comfortably carried every county.

**The District:** The 14th District is divided between the rich, agricultural San Joaquin Valley and the lightly populated counties in the Sierras, where winter and summer recreation pursuits are a major industry.

The most conservative parts of the district are in the mountains, along the Nevada state line, but they are so lightly populated that they rarely effect the outcome in the district.

The heart of the constituency is San Joaquin County. Stockton, the county seat, is the major canning center for the district's produce growers. Just under half of the district's registered voters live in the county, and they are mostly traditional Democrats. But that has not helped Democratic candidates much lately; the district supported Republican S. I. Hayakawa for the Senate in 1976, and Ronald Reagan for president in 1980. In 1976 Carter and Ford came out nearly even in every county in the district.

## Committees

**Banking, Finance and Urban Affairs** (10th of 19 Republicans)
Economic Stabilization; Financial Institutions Supervision, Regulation and Insurance; International Trade, Investment and Monetary Policy.

**Merchant Marine and Fisheries** (12th of 15 Republicans)
Coast Guard and Navigation; Fisheries and Wildlife Conservation and the Environment; Merchant Marine.

**Select Aging** (8th of 23 Republicans)
Human Services; Retirement Income and Employment.

## Elections

**1980 General**

| | |
|---|---|
| Norman Shumway (R) | 133,979 (61%) |
| Ann Cerney (D) | 79,883 (36%) |

**1978 General**

| | |
|---|---|
| Norman Shumway (R) | 95,962 (53%) |
| John McFall (D) | 76,602 (43 %) |

**1978 Primary**

| | |
|---|---|
| Norman Shumway (R) | 21,508 (37%) |
| James Pinkerton (R) | 12,278 (21%) |
| Fred Van Dyke (R) | 10,438 (18%) |
| Others (R) | 13,286 (23%) |

**District Vote For President**

| | 1980 | | 1976 |
|---|---|---|---|
| D | 79,120 (34%) | D | 92,328 (49%) |
| R | 128,907 (56%) | R | 92,163 (49%) |
| I | 17,939 (8%) | | |

## Campaign Finance

| | Receipts | Receipts from PACs | Expenditures |
|---|---|---|---|
| **1980** | | | |
| Shumway (R) | $216,188 | $95,794 (44%) | $235,364 |
| Cerney (D) | $67,190 | $26,237 (39%) | $65,486 |

| | | | |
|---|---|---|---|
| **1978** | | | |
| Shumway (R) | $272,282 | $58,876 (22%) | $251,948 |
| McFall (D) | $215,428 | $124,775 (58%) | $240,114 |

## Voting Studies

| | Presidential Support | | Party Unity | | Conservative Coalition | |
|---|---|---|---|---|---|---|
| Year | S | O | S | O | S | O |
| 1980 | 32 | 57 | 79 | 6 | 84 | 4 |
| 1979 | 22 | 75 | 95 | 3 | 96 | 1 |

S = Support          O = Opposition

## Key Votes

**96th Congress**

| | |
|---|---|
| Weaken Carter oil profits tax (1979) | Y |
| Reject hospital cost control plan (1979) | Y |
| Implement Panama Canal Treaties (1979) | N |
| Establish Department of Education (1979) | N |
| Approve Anti-busing Amendment (1979) | Y |
| Guarantee Chrysler Corp. loans (1979) | N |
| Approve military draft registration (1980) | Y |
| Aid Sandinista regime in Nicaragua (1980) | ? |
| Strengthen fair housing laws (1980) | N |

**97th Congress**

| | |
|---|---|
| Reagan budget proposal (1981) | Y |

## Interest Group Ratings

| Year | ADA | ACA | AFL-CIO | CCUS |
|---|---|---|---|---|
| 1980 | 0 | 95 | 7 | 69 |
| 1979 | 5 | 100 | 10 | 94 |

# 15 Tony Coelho (D)

**Of Merced — Elected 1978**

**Born:** June 15, 1942, Los Banos, Calif.
**Education:** Loyola U., B.A. 1964.
**Profession:** Congressional aide.
**Family:** Wife, Phyllis Butler; two children.
**Religion:** Roman Catholic.
**Political Career:** No previous office.

**In Washington:** House Democrats entrusted Coelho with a massive task in 1981 when they made him their campaign chairman at the start of his second term, something they previously had done only for one person — Lyndon B. Johnson.

There was no doubt that they were giving the job to a fund-raising prodigy. In his first year in Congress, Coelho sold more tickets to the party's congressional dinner than anyone else in the House. In his second year, he built a huge campaign treasury for himself against a weak Republican opponent and when the opponent gave up, began raising money for his colleagues.

A longtime aide to his predecessor, Democrat B. F. Sisk, (1955-79), Coelho made it clear in his first term that he had learned many of Sisk's old tricks and a few more besides. Sisk was a canny veteran who used every tactic he could think up to accumulate influence, such as his chairmanship of the panel that handed out parking spaces to other members. Coelho lacks the homespun style of his retired mentor, but he showed up in 1979 with the habits and ambitions of a senior member.

It did not take long for him to put them to use. One of the major environmental fights of the 96th Congress was over a reclamation bill — favored by the Carter administration — that would have placed strict new limits on the amounts of cheap, federally subsidized water available to large farm operators. Some of the nation's most influential agribusiness companies operate within the 15th District; Sisk took care of their interests for years on the Agriculture Committee, and Coelho, who had been Sisk's aide on farm matters, played the same role.

When the reclamation bill came up in the Interior Committee, Coelho was the chief in-House lobbyist for softening it, even though he was not a member of the committee. He teamed up with Gordon Nelson, another ex-Sisk aide, who was working for an agribusiness group. Coelho presided over a strategy session the night before a crucial vote.

When the panel met the next day, it voted against placing any limit on the amount of land any farmer could lease and still receive federally subsidized water. It was a defeat for the administration and for the Interior Committee chairman, Morris Udall, D-Ariz. It was a victory for California agribusiness and for Coelho. The limit was later modified, but not enough to please Udall, and it never came to the floor.

Coelho's water policies have brought him into frequent conflict with one of his California neighbors, Democrat George Miller of the 7th District. Nearly a million acre-feet of water flows through Miller's district every year on its way to the Westlands water area in Coelho's district. Miller, who fought for Udall's bill on the Interior Committee, wanted to charge Westlands water users higher prices, or failing that, to keep some of the water in his own Contra Costa water district. Coelho responded that users in Miller's area had been getting lenient treatment from the federal government for years.

Coelho is also able to look out for agribusiness on the Agriculture Committee. He was staff director of its Cotton Subcommittee in the 92nd Congress, when Sisk served on it, and he is on it now himself. Cotton is important in the district.

Outside the agriculture field, Coelho has worked to restrict immigration into the U.S. He favored a proposal to require that for every two

---

**15th District: Mid-San Joaquin Valley — Fresno, Modesto.** Population: 578,064 (24% increase since 1970). Race: White 442,061 (76%), Black 30,099 (5%), Others 105,904 (18%). Spanish origin: 145,018 (25%).

refugees admitted to the country over 50,000 a year, one person would be deducted from the regular immigration quota. He also complained that lax enforcement of immigration laws had brought a flood of illegal aliens into his district.

**At Home:** Côelho's life has revolved around the San Joaquin Valley and B. F. Sisk. Coelho was 12 years old, growing up on his family's dairy farm, when Sisk first went to the House. After college, Coelho began working for the Fresno Democrat he would one day succeed.

By the time Sisk was ready to retire in 1978, he knew he wanted his young aide to take his seat. Coelho had spent so much time in the district as a surrogate for Sisk that he had established his own ties with the district's political leaders. Only one Democrat, Vincent Lavery, dared to challenge the Sisk/Coelho forces in the 1978 primary, and Coelho handed Lavery his third congressional defeat, rolling up 79 percent.

Against anyone but Coelho, Republican Chris Patterakis might have stood a chance of winning

that November. A former stunt pilot with the Air Force Thunderbird team, Patterakis was a local hero of sorts in Modesto, where one supporter termed him a "Greek Joe Namath." But Modesto was the only town he carried against Coelho.

**The District:** This is the most Democratic of the four Central Valley districts in California. It includes the part of the nation's "fruit basket" between Fresno and Modesto, and takes in sections of both cities. Fresno is one of the most important agribusiness centers in the nation. Modesto is remembered for its restless teenagers in the film "American Graffiti" and for its winery run by the Gallo brothers.

In the 90 miles between Fresno and Modesto are hundreds of miles of irrigation ditches. The wide variety of fruits and vegetables grown in the district make it second only to the 18th, directly to the south, in farm production. Many of the farmers here have their roots in the Oklahoma dust bowl, which gave them a Democratic heritage that has been slow to change.

## Committees

**Agriculture** (18th of 24 Democrats)
Cotton, Rice and Sugar; Domestic Marketing, Consumer Relations and Nutrition; Livestock, Dairy and Poultry.

**Interior and Insular Affairs** (21st of 23 Democrats)
Oversight and Investigations; Water and Power Resources.

## Elections

**1980 General**

| | |
|---|---|
| Tony Coelho (D) | 108,072 (72%) |
| Ron Schwartz (R) | 37,895 (25%) |

**1978 General**

| | |
|---|---|
| Tony Coelho (D) | 75,212 (60%) |
| Chris Patterakis (R) | 49,914 (40%) |

**1978 Primary**

| | |
|---|---|
| Tony Coelho (D) | 48,253 (79%) |
| Vincent Lavery (D) | 12,926 (21%) |

**District Vote For President**

| | 1980 | | 1976 |
|---|---|---|---|
| D | 73,088 (44%) | D | 81,797 (54%) |
| R | 79,871 (48%) | R | 66,972 (44%) |
| I | 11,593 (7%) | | |

## Campaign Finance

| | Receipts | Percent of Receipts from PACs | Expenditures |
|---|---|---|---|
| **1980** | | | |
| Coelho (D) | $106,835 | $89,610 (84%) | $140,382 |
| Schwartz (R) | $4,823 | — (0%) | $5,136 |

| **1978** | | | |
|---|---|---|---|
| Coelho (D) | $304,513 | $75,852 (25%) | $266,094 |
| Patterakis (R) | $105,707 | $5,749 (5%) | $104,164 |

## Voting Studies

| | Presidental Support | | Party Unity | | Conservative Coalition | |
|---|---|---|---|---|---|---|
| Year | S | O | S | O | S | O |
| 1980 | 74 | 16 | 82 | 7 | 15 | 72 |
| 1979 | 72 | 22 | 77 | 13 | 38 | 55 |

S = Support          O = Opposition

## Key Votes

**96th Congress**

| | |
|---|---|
| Weaken Carter oil profits tax (1979) | Y |
| Reject hospital cost control plan (1979) | ? |
| Implement Panama Canal Treaties (1979) | Y |
| Establish Department of Education (1979) | Y |
| Approve Anti-busing Amendment (1979) | N |
| Gaurantee Chrysler Corp. loans (1979) | Y |
| Approve Military draft registration (1980) | N |
| Aid Sandinistas regime in Nicaragua (1980) | Y |
| Strengthen Fair Housing Laws (1980) | N |

**97th Congress**

| | |
|---|---|
| Reagan budget proposal (1981) | N |

## Interest Group Rating

| Year | ADA | ACA | AFL-CIO | CCUS |
|---|---|---|---|---|
| 1980 | 72 | 9 | 71 | 60 |
| 1979 | 58 | 13 | 65 | 41 |

# 16 Leon E. Panetta (D)

**Of Carmel Valley — Elected 1976**

**Born:** June 28, 1938, Monterey, Calif.
**Education:** U. of Santa Clara, B.A. 1960, J.D. 1963.
**Military Career:** Army, 1963-65.
**Profession:** Lawyer.
**Family:** Wife, Sylvia Marie Varni; three children.
**Religion:** Roman Catholic.
**Political Career:** No previous office.

**In Washington:** Panetta has been a Democrat for nearly a decade now, since shortly after he was fired from the HEW Office of Civil Rights in the Nixon administration for complaining about slowed-down desegregation policies. But in many ways, it is easiest to understand him as the liberal Republican he once was. He keeps an autographed picture of Chief Justice Earl Warren on his office wall, and mixes liberal social policy and fiscal conservatism in a combination that would still gain Warren's approval.

It is the fiscal side of Panetta that has dominated lately, especially as a member of the Budget Committee in the last two Congresses. Panetta has added a voice of calm reason and pragmatism to the highly political act of deciding how federal money should be raised and spent. Much of his commitment has been to the budget process itself.

When he joined the Budget Committee in 1979, Panetta immediately became a protégé of former Chairman Robert N. Giaimo — the two men traveled to Italy together on an interparliamentary visit —and Giaimo assigned Panetta some sensitive tasks in the budget-writing process.

Panetta's most important assignment has been as chairman of a Budget Committee task force to promote the process known as "reconciliation," a word that connotes peace but in the House is more likely to mean war. It is the way Congress translates budget decisions into specific spending cuts, ordering committees to make the cuts to comply with the budget.

Panetta had the thankless job in 1981 of developing the Democratic reconciliation package —the spending cuts House leaders hoped to enact in an effort to head off more drastic reductions favored by the Reagan administration. Under prodding from Panetta and Budget Chairman James R. Jones, House committees did cut $35 billion in spending for fiscal 1982. But the full House overruled them in June and voted with the Reagan administration, taking Panetta's carefully developed concept of reconciliation far beyond anything he ever intended.

In the 96th Congress, Panetta already had seemed to be the proponent of virtually every unpopular scheme, such as efforts to cut back on veterans' benefits, reduce school lunch subsidies, and limit cost-of-living adjustments for federal pensioners. It was not easy. "You've got constituencies built into these programs," he said during one 1980 debate. "The reality of it is that you aren't going to cut them off.... Any time you see the words 'school lunch,' that obviously raises a red flag."

Panetta insisted on bringing his message of discipline to the Agriculture Committee, where he also serves. When the committee approved a variety of bills in 1980 that would increase crop price supports, Panetta told the members that any extra money for farmers would be "difficult in the context of a balanced budget." It was Panetta who moved to adjust the level of food stamp benefits once a year instead of twice — and save $300 million.

Panetta's first efforts at reconciliation, in 1979, were ignored by most House committees and resulted in only a fraction of the savings he had hoped to achieve. But in May 1980, amid national political pressure for a balanced budget, he won House approval of a $9.2 billion package

---

**16th District: Central coast — Salinas, Monterey.** Population: 612,618 (32% increase since 1970). Race: White 481,631 (79%), Black 22,816 (4%), Asian and Pacific Islander 27,075 (4%), Others 81,096 (13%). Spanish origin: 121,975 (20%).

*Leon E. Panetta, D-Calif.*

of spending cuts. It was the largest such reduction in the history of the budget process. It took six more months and a horrendously complex conference with the Senate, but Panetta and the Budget committees ultimately got the reconciliation bill enacted into law, although the balanced budget goal was still out of sight.

The socially liberal side of Panetta still turns up frequently on civil rights-related issues. He spoke out vehemently in 1979 against a constitutional amendment to outlaw busing, "not just because it is wrong morally, constitutionally, or educationally," he said, "but because these kinds of amendments try to fool the American people into believing that they will stop enforcement of the 14th Amendment."

Panetta is equally intense in his approach to the Democratic Party and what he sees as a need for unity of purpose. Panetta feels the party has neglected defects in programs and ideas going back to New Deal days — leaving the way open for Republicans. "We need to combine a sense of compassion for legitimate needs that exist in our society," he has said, "with a kind of efficiency that most programs simply have not had."

**At Home:** Panetta's centrist politics and a healthy degree of attention to his constituents have proved to be a formidable combination. Since he defeated Republican incumbent Burt Talcott by 13,000 votes in 1976, Panetta has increased his plurality to over 100,000 votes.

Panetta's accomplishments for his district are numerous, and usually made quite visible by his staff. When there was not enough rain one year, he secured drought relief money. The next year, when it rained too much, he obtained flood relief. He brought the Army Corps of Engineers in to get rid of a sand drift that was closing off Santa Cruz harbor, and took credit for winning a higher price support for his district's sugar beet farmers.

Although Panetta had been close to politics all his adult life — as an aide to Republican Sen. Thomas Kuchel, then with HEW, and later as an adviser to New York Mayor John V. Lindsay — he had never run for public office until 1976.

By that time, Talcott had been in Washington for 14 years. In the previous two elections a Hispanic candidate, Julian Camacho, had whittled Talcott's margin down to just 2,000 votes, making the incumbent a prime target for Democrats in 1976. Camacho opted against a third try that year, allowing Panetta to battle two other

Democrats for the party's nomination.

Panetta was attacked for being a latecomer to the Democratic Party. But his most active primary opponent, John R. Bakalian, had serious problems of his own. He was viewed outside liberal Santa Cruz as being a bit too unconventional for the district's tastes. Bakalian wanted to impeach President Ford for allowing Secretary of State Henry Kissinger to threaten an invasion of Cuba. He also wanted to distribute bricks for residents to place in their toilets as a water-conservation measure.

Although Bakalian carried Santa Cruz County, Panetta won the nomination with a strong showing in Monterey. In the general election, Panetta kept Talcott on the defensive, saying the incumbent had little to show for his years in Congress. Stressing his roots in the Monterey area, Panetta narrowly defeated Talcott there, and beat him more decisively in Santa Cruz and San Luis Obispo counties, running far ahead of the Democratic ticket.

Two years later Republicans spent a lot of money trying to prevent Panetta from becoming entrenched in the district, but it was already too late.

**The District:** Following the Pacific Coast for 170 miles from Santa Cruz in the north to San Luis Obispo in the south, this is a district devoted to agriculture and recreation. It is also one that either party can win.

The Monterey Bay, at the northern end of the district, is one of Northern California's favorite playgrounds. A broad variety of California life styles is visible along its shores. On the northern shore of the bay, a vibrant counter-culture has emerged in Santa Cruz, drawn there by the the community's permissive University of California campus.

Further south along the bay is Castroville — artichoke capital of the world — and Fort Ord, a major military installation that employs numerous civilians.

At the southern tip of the bay is the exclusive and picturesque Monterey Peninsula, dominated by upper income Republicans and liberal Democrats.

The inland agricultural vote is centered around Salinas in Monterey County. A city with a Democratic registration advantage, Salinas has favored the Republican presidential candidate in the last four elections.

## Committees

**Agriculture** (14th of 24 Democrats)
Conservation, Credit, and Rural Development; Domestic Marketing, Consumer Relations and Nutrition; Forests, Family Farms, and Energy.

**Budget**
Task Force: Enforcement, Credit and Multi-year Budgeting.

## Elections

**1980 General**

| | |
|---|---|
| Leon Panetta (D) | 158,360 (71%) |
| W. A. Roth (R) | 54,675 (25%) |

**1978 General**

| | |
|---|---|
| Leon Panetta (D) | 104,550 (61%) |
| Eric Seastrand (R) | 65,808 (39%) |

**Previous Winning Percentages**

**1976** (53%)

**District Vote For President**

| | 1980 | | 1976 |
|---|---|---|---|
| D | 79,073 (34%) | D | 95,482 (48%) |
| R | 116,525 (50%) | R | 97,003 (49%) |
| I | 25,921 (11%) | | |

## Campaign Finance

| | Receipts | Percent of Receipts from PACs | Expenditures |
|---|---|---|---|
| **1980** | | | |
| Panetta (D) | $12,407 | $40,060 (39%) | $55,475 |
| Roth (R) | $12,046 | $475 (4%) | $11,995 |

| **1978** | | | |
|---|---|---|---|
| Panetta (D) | $227,374 | $51,080 (22%) | $219,357 |
| Seastrand (R) | $184,543 | $43,030 (23%) | $184,169 |

## Voting Studies

| | Presidential Support | | Party Unity | | Conservative Coalition | |
|---|---|---|---|---|---|---|
| Year | S | O | S | O | S | O |
| 1980 | 74 | 25 | 80 | 18 | 33 | 66 |
| 1979 | 70 | 28 | 71 | 28 | 41 | 59 |
| 1978 | 68 | 28 | 69 | 28 | 31 | 64 |
| 1977 | 68 | 29 | 68 | 26 | 36 | 60 |

S = Support          O = Opposition

## Key Votes

**96th Congress**

| | |
|---|---|
| Weaken Carter oil profits tax (1979) | N |
| Reject hospital cost control plan (1979) | N |
| Implement Panama Canal Treaties (1979) | Y |
| Establish Department of Education (1979) | Y |
| Approve Anti-busing Amendment (1979) | N |
| Gaurantee Chrysler Corp. loans (1979) | N |
| Approve Military draft registration (1980) | N |
| Aid Sandinistas regime in Nicaragua (1980) | N |
| Strengthen Fair Housing Laws (1980) | Y |

**97th Congress**

| | |
|---|---|
| Reagan Budget proposal (1981) | N |

## Interest Group Rating

| Year | ADA | ACA | AFL-CIO | CCUS |
|---|---|---|---|---|
| 1980 | 67 | 29 | 58 | 79 |
| 1979 | 84 | 23 | 68 | 33 |
| 1978 | 50 | 50 | 63 | 33 |
| 1977 | 75 | 36 | 70 | 29 |

# 17 Charles Pashayan Jr. (R)

**Of Fresno — Elected 1978**

**Born:** March 27, 1941, Fresno, Calif.
**Education:** Pomona College, B.A. 1963; U. of
Calif. Hastings Law School, J.D. 1968.
**Military Career:** Army, 1968-70.
**Profession:** Lawyer.
**Family:** Single.
**Religion:** United Church of Christ.
**Political Career:** No previous office.

**In Washington:** Brand new to politics when he won his House seat in 1978, "Chip" Pashayan had a sensitive adjustment to the legislative process, quickly developing a reputation as one of the Interior Committee's more stubborn members.

There was an important issue for him to argue about in 1980 — a bill aimed at limiting the use of federally subsidized water by farms beyond the traditional family size. Pashayan's Central Valley district is dominated by such farms, and he had a clear role to play at Interior, defending their continued right to the cheap water.

Pashayan served as an agribusiness spokesman during consideration of the measure, which was meant to place a cap on the number of acres a farmer could own or lease and still receive the water. He introduced several amendments designed to help Central Valley producers. But he proved quick to anger during committee debate, and his loner style limited his role in some of the more sensitive bipartisan negotiations conducted by the producers' coalition.

The committee initially rejected a 1,600-acre cap on the amount of federally irrigated land a farmer could own or lease. It later reversed itself and approved a more lenient limit, but the bill containing the provision never reached the House floor. Pashayan described the 1,600-acre limit as "a step backward to the age of feudalism."

Pashayan attracted valuable attention early in his first term with an amendment to the legislation implementing the Panama Canal transfer treaties. The amendment, accepted by the managers of the legislation, provided that the United States could suspend its annual payments to Panama if that country is "interfering in the internal affairs of any other state." The amendment was dropped in conference, but Pashayan stuck with the legislation on final passage, opposing the positon of most House Republicans.

**At Home:** Pashayan's interest in politics grew out of five years in Washington working for

the Pentagon and the Department of Health, Education and Welfare. Having seen close up how the federal government operated, Pashayan returned to California determined to curb "the growing threat of an uncontrolled federal bureaucracy." To do that, he ran for Congress.

At the time, most observers thought Democratic Rep. John Krebs was in good political shape: he had won his second term in 1976 with 66 percent of the vote. But Pashayan turned out to be a strong campaigner with good financing and a series of effective issues. Over two terms Krebs had gradually alienated many of his supporters. Some viewed him as self-righteous; others thought he was vindictive. His vote against common-site picketing and his environmental objections to the development of a year-round resort at Mineral King in the Sierras had cost him important allies in organized labor.

By contrast, Pashayan had the valuable help of the district's "mega-farmers," and the loyal backing of the small but influential Armenian community in Fresno, where his family's tire business was already well known. Outspending Krebs by more than $100,000, Pashayan put on a sophisticated television campaign in the closing weeks and won by 13,000 votes.

Although Democrats had hopes of recapturing the seat in 1980, Pashayan quickly put that idea to rest. An easygoing 62-year-old farmer and

---

**17th District: Upper San Joaquin Valley — Fresno, Visalia.** Pop.: 607,690 (31% increase since 1970). Race: White 467,023 (77%), Black 12,956 (2%), Asian and Pacific Islander 16,150 (3%), Others 111,561 (18%). Spanish origin: 163,877 (27%).

Fresno County supervisor, Willard "Bill" Johnson, spent a futile year trying to convince voters Pashayan was a "do-nothing" legislator whose only strength was raising money.

Pashayan's fund-raising talents were beyond question, as he amassed and spent nearly half a million dollars to Johnson's $75,000. But the other part of Johnson's argument made little impression on the voters. Pashayan's overwhelming plurality of 74,000 votes appeared to settle the district's future for some time to come.

**The District:** The 17th District is the agricultural heart of the nation's most agriculturally-productive state. The three counties in the district produce virtually every kind of fruit and vegetable grown in the temperate zone.

The farmland reaches almost to the eastern border of the district, where the Sierra Nevada Mountains climb steeply into Sequoia National Park, stopping just short of 14,500-foot Mount Whitney.

Although the district's voters may travel to the Sierra range to ski and hike, they live and work in the dusty crossroads farm towns and small-sized cities like Visalia and Tulare. The wealthier, northeastern side of Fresno is also included in the district.

Many of the farmers in the district are registered Democrats, but they tend to vote Republican. The same is true for many of the people who live in the cities but are economically dependent on agriculture. Since the district's creation in 1974, it has supported Republican presidential candidates both times. In 1976, Sen. John V. Tunney lost the district to Republican S. I. Hayakawa.

## Committees

**Interior and Insular Affairs** (8th of 17 Republicans)
Public Lands and National Parks; Water and Power Resources.

**Post Office and Civil Service** (6th of 11 Republicans)
Civil Service; Investigations.

## Elections

**1980 General**

| | |
|---|---|
| Charles Pashayan (R) | 129,159 (71%) |
| Willard Johnson (D) | 53,780 (29%) |

**1978 General**

| | |
|---|---|
| Charles Pashayan (R) | 81,296 (54%) |
| John Krebs (D) | 67,885 (46%) |

**1978 Primary**

| | |
|---|---|
| Charles Pashayan (R) | 32,696 (65%) |
| Lee Mirigian (R) | 17,605 (35%) |

**District Vote For President**

| | 1980 | | 1976 |
|---|---|---|---|
| D | 69,479 (36%) | D | 75,605 (46%) |
| R | 108,148 (56%) | R | 87,145 (53%) |
| I | 11,492 (6%) | | |

## Campaign Finance

| | Receipts | Receipts from PACs | Expenditures |
|---|---|---|---|
| **1980** | | | |
| Pashayan (R) | $488,329 | $93,847 (19%) | $482,896 |
| Johnson (D) | $73,823 | $5,455 (7%) | $73,755 |

| **1978** | | | |
|---|---|---|---|
| Pashayan (R) | $268,247 | $26,619 (10%) | $260,412 |
| Krebs (D) | $142,865 | $24,435 (17%) | $156,932 |

## Voting Studies

| | Presidential Support | | Party Unity | | Conservative Coalition | |
|---|---|---|---|---|---|---|
| Year | S | O | S | O | S | O |
| 1980 | 41 | 45 | 67 | 15 | 73 | 13 |
| 1979 | 34 | 54 | 77 | 13 | 82 | 8 |

S = Support          O = Opposition

## Key Votes

**96th Congress**

| | |
|---|---|
| Weaken Carter oil profits tax (1979) | Y |
| Reject hospital cost control plan (1979) | Y |
| Implement Panama Canal Treaties (1979) | N |
| Establish Department of Education (1979) | N |
| Approve Anti-busing Amendment (1979) | Y |
| Guarantee Chrysler Corp. loans (1979) | Y |
| Approve military draft registration (1980) | Y |
| Aid Sandinista regime in Nicaragua (1980) | X |
| Strengthen fair housing laws (1980) | N |

**97th Congress**

| | |
|---|---|
| Reagan budget proposal | Y |

## Interest Group Rating

| Year | ADA | ACA | AFL-CIO | CCUS |
|---|---|---|---|---|
| 1980 | 11 | 77 | 21 | 75 |
| 1979 | 11 | 79 | 35 | 82 |

**125**

# 18 William M. Thomas (R)

### Of Bakersfield — Elected 1978

**Born:** Dec. 6, 1941, Wallace, Idaho.
**Education:** San Francisco State U., B.A. 1963, M.A. 1965.
**Profession:** Political science professor.
**Family:** Wife, Sharon Lynn Hamilton; two children.
**Religion:** Baptist.
**Political Career:** Calif. Assembly, 1975-79.

**In Washington:** One of the shrewdest and most strategically-minded of the Republicans elected in 1978, Thomas spent a good deal of his first term measuring the pulse of his fellow freshmen and plotting strategy for them as a group.

He was involved early in 1979 in the freshman effort to demand more aggressive partisanship out of the House GOP leaders, and in the drive later in the year to win a leadership post for the relatively junior Henry Hyde of Illinois. But he turned out to be less militant than many members of his 1978 freshman class, and began disassociating himself from those who wanted to pursue a course of permanent partisan warfare.

In 1980, as Michigan Rep. Guy Vander Jagt sought to build his campaign for Republican leader with support from junior members, Thomas began quietly talking with other freshman members and urging them to keep their options open, waiting to see how things developed later in the year. Although Thomas was not promoting a specific candidate, his strategy probably slowed Vander Jagt's momentum against Robert Michel, R-Ill., the eventual winner.

Thomas was an activist during a term on the House ethics committee, arguing for strong measures against Charles C. Diggs Jr., D-Mich., who had been convicted on kickback charges in 1978, and Charles H. Wilson, D-Calif., charged with financial misconduct.

In the Wilson case, Thomas provoked a storm of Democratic protest by presenting evidence on the floor that had not been part of the committee report recommending censure. Just moments after the House had rejected a move to delay the issue until after Wilson's 1980 primary, Thomas introduced material he had obtained from the California secretary of state indicating Wilson had paid off a personal loan with campaign funds.

Democrats argued Wilson should be able to rebut the charge, and moved again for a postponement. Thomas offered to strike the new charges

from the record, but the mood had changed and the issue was delayed. When it came up again, after Wilson's primary defeat, the House censured him by voice vote.

On the Agriculture Committee, Thomas is generally a voice for the cotton, fruit and vegetable growers who dominate the district. When the House voted in 1979 to impose new controls on lending by the Farmers Home Administration, which critics said was offering too much money to wealthy agribusiness concerns, Thomas introduced an amendment softening the restrictions. It provided that a farmer's overall financial condition, rather than any arbitrary measure of his assets, determine his eligibility for a loan.

**At Home:** Thomas says he is a pragmatic conservative, and he has proved it at critical times in his relatively brief political career.

In 1974, running for the state Assembly in one of the most conservative districts in the state, he responded to local support for the death penalty by making it the focus of his campaign.

Four years later, when three-term Republican Congressman William Ketchum suddenly died after the June primary, Thomas positioned himself as the moderate in a heated convention held to nominate a replacement. Although Thomas was the ranking GOP legislator in the area and the presumed front-runner for the nomination, it took him seven ballots to defeat two more conservative but more obscure opponents.

Thomas' difficulty winning what should have been an easy nomination resulted from differ-

---

**18th District: South central — Bakersfield.** Population: 572,865 (24% increase since 1970). Race: White 454,023 (79%), Black 26,244 (5%), Others 92,598 (16%). Spanish origin: 108,849 (19%).

ences with GOP leaders in Kern County. He was acknowledged to be a skillful campaigner, but his bluntness sometimes hurt him within the party.

In the fall campaign, Thomas was successful in convincing voters that he would follow Ketchum's philosophy, if not his style, once elected. The two men had had their differences; Thomas backed Gerald R. Ford in the California primary in 1976 and Ketchum supported Ronald Reagan. But Thomas won an endorsement from Ketchum's widow and had little difficulty winning the general election against Democrat Bob Sogge, a former aide to a popular state senator. Sogge put on one of the strongest campaigns the district had seen by a Democrat in recent years, but he came close to Thomas only in Tulare County, which casts a small fraction of the vote.

**The District:** This is the most Republican of the four San Joaquin Valley districts. Located at the southernmost end of the valley, it is centered on Kern County (Bakersfield), which accounts for about two-thirds of the electorate.

Kern County has been described as a place with "a vested interest in keeping people where they are, especially racially, and instituting minimal change." For the district's black and Mexican-American population, the status quo means limited political representation. The real power in the district is in the agribusiness community, outspoken in its conservative views, and the aerospace industry, also Republican.

About a quarter of the voters live in northern Los Angeles County, between the Tehachapi and San Gabriel mountains. Culturally and politically distant from Los Angeles, they are even more Republican than the rest of the 18th. In 1980, Reagan won 71.1 percent in the Los Angeles County part, and 59.6 percent elsewhere.

## Committees

**Agriculture** (8th of 19 Republicans)
Cotton, Rice and Sugar; Department Operations, Research and Foreign Agriculture.

**House Administration** (5th of 8 Republicans)
Accounts; Office Systems; Policy Group on Information and Computers.

## Elections

**1980 General**

| | |
|---|---|
| William Thomas (R) | 126,046 (71%) |
| Mary Timmermans (D) | 51,415 (29%) |

**1980 Primary**

| | |
|---|---|
| William Thomas (R) | 48,215 (86%) |
| Michael Berry (R) | 8,127 (14%) |

**1978 General**

| | |
|---|---|
| William Thomas (R) | 85,663 (59%) |
| Bob Sogge (D) | 58,900 (41%) |

**District Vote For President**

| | 1980 | | 1976 |
|---|---|---|---|
| D | 55,531 (30%) | D | 70,093 (43%) |
| R | 114,504 (63%) | R | 89,166 (55%) |
| I | 9,068 (5%) | | |

## Campaign Finance

| | Receipts | Receipts from PACs | Expenditures |
|---|---|---|---|
| **1980** | | | |
| Thomas (R) | $243,642 | $74,611 (31%) | $174,586 |
| Timmermans (D) | $11,528 | $125 (1%) | $13,183 |
| **1978** | | | |
| Thomas (R) | $186,836 | $58,963 (32%) | $166,534 |
| Sogge (D) | $143,998 | $42,698 (30%) | $142,280 |

## Voting Studies

| | Presidential Support | | Party Unity | | Conservative Coalition | |
|---|---|---|---|---|---|---|
| Year | S | O | S | O | S | O |
| 1980 | 34 | 55 | 79 | 12 | 83 | 7 |
| 1979 | 26 | 72 | 87 | 7 | 91 | 2 |

S = Support          O = Opposition

## Key Votes

**96th Congress**

| | |
|---|---|
| Weaken Carter oil profits tax (1979) | Y |
| Reject hospital cost control plan (1979) | Y |
| Implement Panama Canal Treaties (1979) | N |
| Establish Department of Education (1979) | N |
| Approve Anti-busing Amendment (1979) | Y |
| Guarantee Chrysler Corp. loans (1979) | N |
| Approve military draft registration (1980) | Y |
| Aid Sandinista regime in Nicaragua (1980) | N |
| Strengthen fair housing laws (1980) | N |

**97th Congress**

| | |
|---|---|
| Reagan budget proposal (1981) | Y |

## Interest Group Ratings

| Year | ADA | ACA | AFL-CIO | CCUS |
|---|---|---|---|---|
| 1980 | 0 | 91 | 17 | 86 |
| 1979 | 5 | 100 | 5 | 100 |

# 19 Robert J. Lagomarsino (R)

Of Ventura — Elected 1974

**Born:** Sept. 4, 1926, Ventura, Calif.
**Education:** U. of California, Santa Barbara, B.A. 1950; U. of Santa Clara, LL.B. 1953.
**Military Career:** Navy, 1944-46.
**Profession:** Lawyer.
**Family:** Wife, Norma Smith; three children.
**Religion:** Roman Catholic.
**Political Career:** Ojai City Council, 1958; Mayor of Ojai, 1958-61; Calif. Senate, 1961-74.

**In Washington:** Elected in 1974 in a district still shaken by the oil spill that had blackened its beaches five years earlier, Lagomarsino came to Congress as an environmentalist and has remained one despite a hard-line conservatism on most other issues.

On the Interior Committee, he has generally cooperated with the two liberal Democratic leaders, Chairman Morris K. Udall of Arizona and fellow-Californian Phillip Burton. Lagomarsino stuck with Udall through the long battle over strip mining legislation, even when most Republicans were going the other way, as they did on the decisive 1977 amendment that restricted mining on river valley floors. Later, he backed an Alaska land bill that closed more land to development than energy companies and most GOP members liked.

He has worked closely with Burton on national park and territorial issues, and in return has received help on projects in his district. Only on nuclear power is he consistently at odds with the committee's environmentalist Democrats.

In 1980, he fought Udall to a tie vote on an amendment calling for completion of a feasibility study on reprocessing fuel from nuclear reactors. Udall and most committee Democrats were worried about use of the fuel for nuclear weapons.

On the Foreign Affairs Committee, Lagomarsino is a more orthodox Republican. In 1980 he fought to prevent the United States from helping the Nicaraguan government that took over after the overthrow of Anastasio Somoza.

He was one of six members who visited Nicaragua after the revolution, but was the only one who came back opposing any aid, saying it was going to be a "Marxist country" for the foreseeable future. "If it looks like a Cuba and walks like a Cuba and quacks like a Cuba ... it is probably a Cuba," he said.

Lagomarsino lost on that issue, but he did get an amendment adopted directing the president to cut off aid if the Nicaraguan government is engaged in totalitarian practices. He has also criticized ties with Peking, and backed Taiwan.

**At Home:** Lagomarsino began mixing conservatism and environmental values early in his career, and this has been his key to success. In 1965 he was the first recipient of the Legislative Conservationist of the Year award from the California Wildlife Federation. That was four years before Santa Barbara's beaches were polluted by a blowout on an offshore oil rig.

When Republican Rep. Charles M. Teague died in 1973 after serving 10 terms in Congress, Lagomarsino was the Republican heir apparent. He had served 13 years in the state Senate from a district that included most of Teague's old 13th Congressional District, and he shared Teague's strong opposition to offshore oil drilling.

The special election came in March 1974, at a time when Republicans had just lost three U.S. House seats in special elections, mostly because of anger over the Nixon administration's involvement in Watergate. Lagomarsino deftly steered the focus of the campaign away from the "mess in Washington" to the mess along the California coast. At the time, clumps of oil were still washing up on the sandy beaches, and the Republican called for a 400,000-acre sanctuary, free of oil

---

**19th District: South central coast — Santa Barbara.** Population: 565,413 (22% increase since 1970). Race: White 445,927 (79%), Black 15,322 (3%), Asian and Pacific Islander, 17,533 (3%), Others 86,631 (15%). Spanish origin: 129,544 (23%).

wells, near the Santa Barbara Channel islands.

As the only Republican against seven Democrats, Lagomarsino won 54 percent and avoided a runoff against second-place finisher James Loebl, the Mayor of Ojai, who had 19 percent.

Eight months later, in the regular general election, Lagomarsino and Loebl had a rematch. Loebl had two new advantages. He was the only Democrat on the fall ballot, and the district, redrawn as the 19th, had lost conservative areas of Ventura County and gained the liberal academic community in Santa Barbara, as well as Mexican-American sections of Oxnard.

But Lagomarsino had used his first few months in office to build support within the district, and he won a larger percentage of the vote than he had in the special election. After one

more serious effort to unseat him in 1976, Democrats have given Lagomarsino virtually a free ride.

**The District:** Like the incumbent, the district itself is torn between a desire for economic growth and a concern for the environment. Voters living closest to the oil rigs around Santa Barbara are environmentalists; oil workers in Oxnard, ranchers in the north and military families near Vandenberg Air Force Base are pro-growth.

Social activist Tom Hayden and President Ronald Reagan both have ranches in the district, symbolic of the district's divisions. Santa Barbara County, which has 60 percent of the population, was one of only four counties Hayden carried against Sen. John V. Tunney in the 1976 Democratic primary. Four years later, it backed Reagan overwhelmingly in the general election.

## Committees

**Foreign Affairs** (6th of 16 Republicans)
Inter-American Affairs; International Economic Policy and Trade.

**Interior and Insular Affairs** (4th of 17 Republicans)
Insular Affairs; Public Lands and National Parks.

## Elections

**1980 General**

| | |
|---|---|
| Robert Lagomarsino (R) | 162,854 (78%) |
| Carmen Lodise (D) | 36,990 (18%) |

**1978 General**

| | |
|---|---|
| Robert Lagomarsino (R) | 123,192 (72%) |
| Jerry Zamos (D) | 41,672 (24%) |

**Previous Winning Percentages**

| | | |
|---|---|---|
| 1976 (64%) | 1974 (56%) | 1974* (54%) |

*Special election.*

**District Vote For President**

| | 1980 | | 1976 |
|---|---|---|---|
| D | 72,903 (33%) | D | 95,297 (48%) |
| R | 119,582 (54%) | R | 98,614 (50%) |
| I | 22,713 (10%) | | |

## Campaign Finance

| | Receipts | Receipts from PACs | Expenditures |
|---|---|---|---|
| **1980** | | | |
| Lagomarsino (R) | $131,314 | $39,733 (30%) | $97,504 |

| | | | |
|---|---|---|---|
| **1978** | | | |
| Lagomarsino (R) | $126,841 | $24,149 (19%) | $95,044 |
| Zamos (D) | $14,196 | $400 (3%) | $14,042 |

## Voting Studies

| | Presidential Support | | Party Unity | | Conservative Coalition | |
|---|---|---|---|---|---|---|
| Year | S | O | S | O | S | O |
| 1980 | 36 | 63 | 92 | 8 | 92 | 8 |
| 1979 | 28 | 72 | 92 | 8 | 92 | 8 |
| 1978 | 32 | 68 | 88 | 12 | 94 | 6 |
| 1977 | 41 | 59 | 92 | 8 | 94 | 6 |
| 1976 | 67 | 31 | 77 | 22 | 83 | 16 |
| 1975 | 67 | 33 | 90 | 10 | 92 | 8 |

S = Support          O = Opposition

## Key Votes

**96th Congress**

| | |
|---|---|
| Weaken Carter oil profits tax (1979) | Y |
| Reject hospital cost control plan (1979) | Y |
| Implement Panama Canal Treaties (1979) | N |
| Establish Department of Education (1979) | N |
| Approve Anti-busing Amendment (1979) | Y |
| Guarantee Chrysler Corp. loans (1979) | N |
| Approve military draft registration (1980) | N |
| Aid Sandinista regime in Nicaragua (1980) | N |
| Strengthen fair housing laws (1980) | N |

**97th Congress**

| | |
|---|---|
| Reagan budget proposal (1981) | Y |

## Interest Group Ratings

| Year | ADA | ACA | AFL-CIO | CCUS |
|---|---|---|---|---|
| 1980 | 11 | 83 | 16 | 79 |
| 1979 | 26 | 96 | 20 | 78 |
| 1978 | 5 | 96 | 5 | 89 |
| 1977 | 0 | 85 | 17 | 94 |
| 1976 | 10 | 79 | 17 | 44 |
| 1975 | 11 | 93 | 22 | 65 |

# 20 Barry M. Goldwater Jr. (R)

**Of Woodland Hills — Elected 1969**

**Born:** July 15, 1938, Los Angeles, Calif.
**Education:** Ariz. State U., B.A. 1962.
**Profession:** Stockbroker.
**Family:** Divorced; one child.
**Religion:** Episcopalian.
**Political Career:** No previous office.

**In Washington:** Goldwater loves aviation, like his famous father, and he represents a district largely dependent on it. He has spent a decade pursuing it across the House committee system. Aviation research is handled in the Science Committee, and Goldwater has focused much of his attention there, voting regularly for more money for the U.S. space program. But the authority over commercial flying has shifted around over the years, and Goldwater has shifted with it.

Early in his career, the issue was in the Commerce Committee, and Goldwater moved from Government Operations to Commerce to deal with it. But in 1974, aviation was shifted to the Public Works Committee, and Goldwater went there. He is now firmly implanted on the Public Works Aviation Subcommittee, where he tried to soften the airline deregulation bill written in the 95th Congress, and argued for better treatment for commuter and cargo airlines.

But he has paid a price for the committee hopping. If he had stayed on Commerce, he would now be fourth in seniority on what may be the most powerful legislative committee in the House.

Rarely active on the floor, Goldwater played his most conspicuous role there early in his career, when Lockheed, the crucial California defense contractor, was arguing for a $250 million loan guarantee to help it stay in business.

Goldwater made the rounds of the entire California delegation seeking support for the Lockheed bill. He showed undecided members lists of contracts they would lose in their districts if the bill failed.

Outside his science-related interests, Goldwater has not been one of the more active legislators, or a leader within his party. But he has drawn attention with an issue few other conservatives have taken up — privacy.

With Democrat Edward Koch, now the mayor of New York City, Goldwater introduced a package of bills to protect citizens' control over their credit reports, medical files and employee records. Much of the legislation was adopted in a series of actions between 1974 and 1977. Since then, Goldwater has worked to secure the privacy of IRS records, and prevent the Social Security number from becoming a national identity device.

**At Home:** Goldwater's congressional career is more a result of heredity than life ambition. Until he ran for Congress in 1969, he had shown little interest in politics; he seemed to be heading for a career in corporate finance.

President Nixon's 1968 election, however, set in motion a chain of events that lifted Goldwater into the House. Nixon appointed California Lt. Gov. Robert Finch as HEW secretary, and Gov. Ronald Reagan in turn named Rep. Ed Reinecke to take Finch's place, vacating Reinecke's district. Some 16 candidates filed for the special election, all running on the same ballot under California law. That situation was perfect for a candidate whose name guaranteed him favorable recognition, even if he was new to politics. Promising to use his "Washington connections" to keep aerospace and defense contracts in the district, Goldwater won with 57 percent.

Three years later, after Goldwater had won re-election easily, his district was substantially changed, with only the western part of the San Fernando Valley retained. His first vote in the new district marked a career low. But by 1974, with district lines changed again, Goldwater's margin was back above 60 percent.

---

**20th District: Southern Ventura County, West Los Angeles County.** Population: 640,635 (37% increase since 1970). Race: White 569,800 (89%), Black 9,457 (1%), Asian and Pacific Islander 20,055 (3%), Others 41,323 (6%). Spanish origin: 72,365 (11%).

In late 1979, when Republican Rep. John H. Rousselot was backing out of his challenge to Sen. Alan Cranston in the 1980 Senate contest, conservatives turned to Goldwater. But he refused. In 1981, however, he began preparing a primary campaign for 1982 against GOP Sen. S. I. Hayakawa.

**The District:** The predominantly Republican 20th is a combination of three areas — the western, upper-class end of the San Fernando Valley; the Malibu Coast, where the rich and famous try to avoid the surfers; and middle-class southern Ventura County.

The Ventura County portion of the district has been steadily growing over the last decade, and now provides over 45 percent of the vote. The 20th was one of seven districts in the state carried by Republican Paul Gann over Cranston in 1980.

## Committees

**Public Works and Transportation** (5th of 19 Republicans)
Aviation; Investigations and Oversight.

**Science and Technology** (2nd of 17 Republicans)
Energy Research and Production; Transportation, Aviation and Materials.

## Elections

**1980 General**

| | |
|---|---|
| Barry Goldwater Jr. (R) | 199,681 (79%) |
| Matt Miller (D) | 43,025 (17%) |

**1978 General**

| | |
|---|---|
| Barry Goldwater Jr. (R) | 129,714 (66%) |
| Pat Lear (D) | 65,695 (34%) |

**Previous Winning Percentages**

| | | | |
|---|---|---|---|
| 1976 (67%) | 1974 (61%) | 1972 (57%) | 1970 (67%) |
| 1969* (57%) | | | |

* Special election

**District Vote For President**

| 1980 | | 1976 | |
|---|---|---|---|
| D | 67,044 (26%) | D | 86,610 (39%) |
| R | 166,697 (64%) | R | 129,113 (59%) |
| I | 20,802 (8%) | | |

## Campaign Finance

| | Receipts | Receipts from PACs | Expenditures |
|---|---|---|---|
| **1980** | | | |
| Goldwater (R) | $219,257 | $50,490 (23%) | $193,063 |
| Miller (D) | $15,371 | — (0%) | $15,420 |
| **1978** | | | |
| Goldwater (R) | $151,582 | $53,731 (35%) | $122,120 |
| Lear (D) | $236,643 | — (0%) | $229,306 |

## Voting Studies

| | Presidential Support | | Party Unity | | Conservative Coalition | |
|---|---|---|---|---|---|---|
| Year | S | O | S | O | S | O |
| 1980 | 34 | 56 | 71 | 13 | 71 | 13 |
| 1979 | 23 | 63 | 76 | 8 | 83 | 3 |
| 1978 | 29 | 60 | 81 | 8 | 85 | 4 |
| 1977 | 32 | 52 | 78 | 7 | 87 | 4 |
| 1976 | 69 | 20 | 80 | 7 | 83 | 6 |
| 1975 | 60 | 27 | 81 | 5 | 82 | 5 |
| 1974 (Ford) | 37 | 43 | | | | |
| 1974 | 53 | 23 | 73 | 12 | 74 | 5 |
| 1973 | 71 | 19 | 76 | 12 | 83 | 8 |
| 1972 | 59 | 22 | 70 | 6 | 73 | 2 |
| 1971 | 65 | 14 | 66 | 12 | 74 | 7 |
| 1970 | 55 | 9 | 70 | 9† | 82 | — |
| 1969 | 49 | 29† | 67 | 7† | 74 | 0† |

S = Support          O = Opposition

†Not eligible for all recorded votes.

## Key Votes

**96th Congress**

| | |
|---|---|
| Weaken Carter oil profits tax (1979) | Y |
| Reject hospital cost control plan (1979) | Y |
| Implement Panama Canal Treaties (1979) | N |
| Establish Department of Education (1979) | X |
| Approve Anti-busing Amendment (1979) | Y |
| Guarantee Chrysler Corp. loans (1979) | N |
| Approve military draft registration (1980) | N |
| Aid Sandinista regime in Nicaragua (1980) | N |
| Strengthen fair housing Laws (1980) | N |

**97th Congress**

| | |
|---|---|
| Reagan budget proposal (1981) | Y |

## Interest Group Ratings

| Year | ADA | ACA | AFL-CIO | CCUS |
|---|---|---|---|---|
| 1980 | 22 | 82 | 6 | 83 |
| 1979 | 21 | 100 | 5 | 88 |
| 1978 | 5 | 100 | 0 | 100 |
| 1977 | 0 | 96 | 10 | 88 |
| 1976 | 5 | 88 | 14 | 86 |
| 1975 | 0 | 88 | 18 | 93 |
| 1974 | 4 | 79 | 0 | 100 |
| 1973 | 4 | 96 | 9 | 90 |
| 1972 | 0 | 86 | 10 | 100 |
| 1971 | 14 | 96 | 25 | |
| 1970 | 0 | 88 | 14 | 100 |
| 1969 | 0† | 91 | 11 | |

†Member did not serve for entire period covered by voting study.

# 21 Bobbi Fiedler (R)

**Of Northridge — Elected 1980**

**Born:** April 22, 1937, Santa Monica, Calif.
**Education:** Attended Santa Monica City College
and Santa Monica Technical School.
**Profession:** Pharmacy owner.
**Family:** Divorced; two children.
**Religion:** Jewish.
**Political Career:** L.A. School Board, 1977-80.

**The Member:** As a parent volunteer in an elementary school in 1976, Fiedler learned of a proposed mandatory busing plan for the Los Angeles area. With a few other parents she founded BUSTOP, an anti-busing organization that has gained considerable political influence. In 1977, Fiedler defeated an incumbent school board member in a city-wide election. Three years later, she challenged Rep. James C. Corman, the chairman of the House Democratic campaign committee. She tried to move beyond the busing issue by mentioning her efforts to cut school costs and curb drug abuse in the schools.

But busing was the dominant issue. Corman said he did not support "massed forced busing," but could not overcome Fiedler's criticism that he was "out of touch" with voters on that issue.

In 1981, she backed an amendment to block the Justice Department from intervening on the pro-busing side in court cases.

Fiedler is one of four freshmen Republicans on the Budget Committee. During the 1981 budget debate, Fiedler criticized Democrat Bill Hefner of North Carolina for proposing an amendment on the floor that he had failed to support in the Budget Committee. Hefner wanted to raise defense spending in the Democratic budget alternative. Fiedler implied that Hefner's amendment was a partisan, last-ditch effort to entice conservatives from the Reagan-backed proposal. Majority Leader Jim Wright interrupted debate to tell Fiedler that House tradition discourages a member from "...impugning the honor or the integrity or the intentions ..." of another member.

**The District:** Based in the heart of the San Fernando Valley, the 21st is a mixture of upper middle class white suburbs, working class areas, and older, decaying communities with growing black and Latino populations. The district's 2-to-1 Democratic registration edge belies its conservatism on many social and economic issues. Tax-slashing Proposition 13 received 76 percent here in 1978, and an anti-busing amendment won 82 percent a year later.

## Committees

**Budget**
Task Forces: Enforcement, Credit and Multi-year Budgeting; Entitlements, Uncontrollables and Indexing; National Security and Veterans; Reconciliation.

## Elections

**1980 General**

| | |
|---|---|
| Bobbi Fiedler (R) | 74,843 (49 %) |
| James Corman (D ) | 74,091 (48 %) |

**1980 Primary**

| | |
|---|---|
| Bobbi Fiedler (R ) | 23,980 (74 %) |
| Patrick O'Brien (R ) | 8,580 (26 %) |

**District Vote For President**

| | 1980 | | 1976 |
|---|---|---|---|
| **D** | 60,172 (38%) | **D** | 80,681 (51%) |
| **R** | 80,766 (51%) | **R** | 73,773 (47%) |
| **I** | 12,634 (8%) | | |

## Campaign Finance

| | Receipts | Receipts from PACs | Expenditures |
|---|---|---|---|
| **1980** | | | |
| Fiedler (R) | $577,748 | $108,526 (19%) | $560,942 |
| Corman (D) | $850,248 | $294,915 (35%) | $896,590 |

## Key Vote

**97th Congress**

| | |
|---|---|
| Reagan budget proposal (1981) | Y |

---

**21st District: Northwest Los Angeles County.** Population: 489,475 (5% increase since 1970). Race: White 370,322 (76%), Black 24,571 (5%), Asian and Pacific Islander 18,896 (4%), Others 75,686 (15%). Spanish origin: 146,786 (30%).

# 22 Carlos J. Moorhead (R)

**Of Glendale — Elected 1972**

**Born:** May 6, 1922, Long Beach, Calif.
**Education:** U. of California at Los Angeles, B.A. 1943; U. of Southern California, J.D. 1949.
**Military Career:** Army, 1942-45.
**Profession:** Lawyer.
**Family:** Wife, Valery Joan Tyler; five children.
**Religion:** Presbyterian.
**Political Career:** Calif. Assembly, 1967-73.

**In Washington:** A minor player during the House Judiciary Committee's presidential impeachment debate in 1974, Moorhead has generally remained in that role over four terms at Judiciary and three on the crucial Energy Subcommittee of the Commerce Committee.

During his brief period in the Watergate spotlight, Moorhead was a defender of President Nixon, remarking early in 1974 that the president "has done a good job considering Congress has spent a million dollars trying to impeach him." When the time came for a vote, Moorhead backed Nixon on every impeachment count, changing his mind only with the release of the "smoking gun" tape two weeks later.

He has remained on Judiciary through its quiet years since then, frequently seeking to point out the negative side of the "good government" reforms the committee has drafted.

In 1976, when the House considered legislation to require public access to most federal government meetings, Moorhead tried to amend it to require that an individual protesting secrecy show he would be harmed if the meeting remained closed. When his subcommittee worked on a bill allowing federal agencies to pay for public participation in their work, he left the meeting at one point to block a quorum from approving it.

Moorhead argued against tight restrictions on executives moving back and forth from government to private lobbying, and opposed coverage of so-called "grass-roots lobbying" in a broad Judiciary lobby disclosure bill. By the end of the 1970s, some of these issues seemed to be moving Moorhead's way; lobby disclosure never came to a vote in the 96th Congress.

On Commerce, Moorhead is a backbench Republican, voting almost automatically with the Republican leadership and taking frequent cues from the oil and gas industries. One display of independence came on consideration of an Energy Mobilization Board to speed up priority energy projects. Sensitive to constituent fear of water diversion for such projects, he persuaded Commerce to accept language barring federal waiver of state or local water rights laws.

Like other California Republicans, Moorhead is also sensitive to his district's worries about massive numbers of Hispanic refugees. In 1980, he won floor approval of his amendment providing for a legislative veto of any presidential decision to admit more than 50,000 refugees per year. But the idea was dropped in conference.

**At Home:** Moorhead's electoral career has been a consistent success, although about as uneventful as his service in the House. His popularity in Glendale and Burbank is hard to shake, and few Democrats have tried.

A lifelong Glendale resident, Moorhead was a lawyer in the area for 15 years before entering the state Assembly. When eight-term Republican Rep. H. Allen Smith decided to retire from Congress in 1972, former Nixon adviser Robert H. Finch thought about running. But he opted against it, and nine candidates entered the GOP primary.

The contest quickly was narrowed to just two: Moorhead and Dr. Bill McColl, a Covina surgeon who had once played end for the Chicago Bears. Moorhead, who had carried the west side of the district three times in Assembly elections, was the favorite of the local party apparatus over McColl, who had narrowly lost to John H.

---

**22nd District: Central Los Angeles County — Glendale.** Population: 467,466 (0.6% increase since 1970). Race: White 370,308 (79%), Black 43,712 (9%), Asian and Pacific Islander 19,982 (4%), Others 33,464 (7%). Spanish origin: 71,870 (15%).

---

## Carlos J. Moorhead, R-Calif.

Rousselot in the neighboring 24th District in 1970. The result was an easy nomination for Moorhead, and an even easier general election.

Moorhead's service on the impeachment panel reduced his margin to 55.8 percent in 1974, but since then it has been comfortably above 60 percent. In 1980, Democrat Pierce O'Donnell waged a lavish campaign, spending nearly as much as all of Moorhead's previous opponents combined. The result, however, was about the same as the one in 1978, when the Democrat hardly campaigned at all.

**The District:** Democratic registration is growing in the 22nd, but Moorhead and virtually all Republican candidates continue to win with

very little difficulty. Reagan won with ease here in 1980, as did Paul Gann, the inarticulate GOP tax crusader who challenged Sen. Alan Cranston.

"Beautiful downtown Burbank," on the western side of the district, lives up to the middle-to-upper-class reputation it has received from West Coast comedians, such as Johnny Carson. It is not much different, however, from its larger neighbor to the east, Glendale. Both are solidly conservative and vote Republican.

Pasadena, most of which is in the 22nd District, has a significant middle-class black population, as does Altadena, to the north. As a result, both tend to be slightly more favorable to Democratic candidates than the rest of the district.

## Committees

**Energy and Commerce** (6th of 18 Republicans)
Energy Conservation and Power; Telecommunications, Consumer Protection, and Finance.

**Judiciary** (5th of 12 Republicans)
Administrative Law and Governmental Relations; Monopolies and Commercial Law.

## Elections

**1980 General**

| | |
|---|---|
| Carlos Moorhead (R) | 115,241 (64%) |
| Pierce O'Donnell (D) | 57,477 (32%) |

**1978 General**

| | |
|---|---|
| Carlos Moorhead (R) | 99,502 (65%) |
| Robert Henry (D) | 54,442 (35%) |

**Previous Winning Percentages**

| | | |
|---|---|---|
| 1976 (63%) | 1974 (56%) | 1972 (57%) |

**District Vote For President**

| | 1980 | | 1976 |
|---|---|---|---|
| D | 56,067 (29%) | D | 71,648 (38%) |
| R | 116,851 (61%) | R | 115,665 (61%) |
| I | 13,815 (7%) | | |

## Campaign Finance

| | Receipts | Receipts from PACs | Expenditures |
|---|---|---|---|
| **1980** | | | |
| Moorhead (R) | $156,227 | $69,730 (45%) | $116,853 |
| O'Donnell (D) | $176,494 | $16,659 (9%) | $171,977 |
| **1978** | | | |
| Moorhead (R) | $72,403 | $26,274 (36%) | $56,371 |
| Henry (D) | $13,714 | $4,600 (34%) | $13,368 |

## Voting Studies

| Year | Presidential Support | | Party Unity | | Conservative Coalition | |
|---|---|---|---|---|---|---|
| | S | O | S | O | S | O |
| 1980 | 35 | 62 | 86 | 8 | 85 | 7 |
| 1979 | 27 | 72 | 95 | 3 | 95 | 3 |
| 1978 | 29 | 65 | 93 | 4 | 92 | 4 |
| 1977 | 29 | 66 | 93 | 5 | 92 | 5 |
| 1976 | 69 | 31 | 91 | 7 | 93 | 4 |
| 1975 | 60 | 34 | 82 | 7 | 86 | 7 |
| 1974 (Ford) | 44 | 35 | | | | |
| 1974 | 66 | 25 | 82 | 9 | 81 | 9 |
| 1973 | 70 | 22 | 88 | 9 | 88 | 9 |

S = Support    O = Opposition

## Key Votes

**96th Congress**

| | |
|---|---|
| Weaken Carter oil profits tax (1979) | Y |
| Reject hospital cost control plan (1979) | Y |
| Implement Panama Canal Treaties (1979) | N |
| Establish Department of Education (1979) | N |
| Approve Anti-busing Amendment (1979) | Y |
| Guarantee Chrysler Corp. loans (1979) | Y |
| Approve military draft registration (1980) | N |
| Aid Sandinista regime in Nicaragua (1980) | N |
| Strengthen fair housing laws (1980) | N |

**97th Congress**

| | |
|---|---|
| Reagan budget proposal (1981) | Y |

## Interest Group Ratings

| Year | ADA | ACA | AFL-CIO | CCUS |
|---|---|---|---|---|
| 1980 | 11 | 96 | 16 | 71 |
| 1979 | 11 | 96 | 20 | 89 |
| 1978 | 5 | 100 | 0 | 88 |
| 1977 | 0 | 96 | 9 | 94 |
| 1976 | 5 | 89 | 18 | 88 |
| 1975 | 5 | 96 | 15 | 88 |
| 1974 | 9 | 87 | 0 | 100 |
| 1973 | 4 | 96 | 0 | 100 |

# 23 Anthony C. Beilenson (D)

**Of Los Angeles — Elected 1976**

**Born:** Oct. 26, 1932, New Rochelle, N.Y.
**Education:** Harvard U., B.A. 1954; Harvard Law
School, LL.B. 1957.
**Profession:** Lawyer.
**Family:** Wife, Dolores Martin; three children.
**Religion:** Jewish.
**Political Career:** Calif. Assembly, 1963-67;
Calif. Senate, 1967-77; sought Democratic
nomination for U.S. Senate, 1968.

**In Washington:** An intellectual with the
soft, resonant voice of an FM radio announcer,
Beilenson has maintained a liberal voting record
while demonstrating a pronounced skepticism
about much of what government does.

His clearest personal protest came in 1980,
when he cast the only vote in the House against
two separate and very popular bills. The first,
which passed the House 384-1, was a non-binding
resolution reassuring Social Security recipients
Congress would not tax benefits. A Social Security advisory council, looking for ways to ease the
system's financial troubles, had recommended,
among other things, that income taxes be applied
to half of each retiree's benefits. The report set off
protests from all over the country and congressmen were anxious to shoot it down. The only
exception was Beilenson, who said all ideas deserved consideration.

The second vote, 383-1, came on a bill to give
Veterans Administration doctors and dentists a
65 percent pay increase. "I've not believed in the
continuing buildup of this parallel health system," Beilenson explained, "especially since the
majority of what the VA treats is not battle
injuries." He said "a lot of conservative colleagues
who would not vote for medical care for anyone
else in the country have no hesitation in voting for
veterans."

In his quiet, studious way, Beilenson asks
similar questions about a variety of government
programs as a member of the Rules Committee.
Beilenson was named to the committee in 1979
following a round of infighting in the House
leadership and the California delegation. He was
not the delegation's first choice, but he was endorsed by Rules Chairman Richard Bolling.

Bolling soon gave Beilenson a difficult assignment, as head of a task force to review various
proposals for a spending limit on the federal
budget. The chairman himself was dubious about

the idea, agreeing to examine it because Majority
Leader Jim Wright had promised to do so.

Beilenson took his time with the project, but
emerged rather sympathetic. "It's a difficult,
complicated question with no easy answers," he
said at one point, adding that maybe "you need
some sort of forced discipline."

Beilenson brought a couple of legislative interests with him from the California Assembly —
family planning and elephants. Concerned over
world population problems, he has worked to
increase federal funds for family planning clinics.
He has also tried to ban trade in the ivory from
elephant tusks, because the African elephant is
endangered. His anti-ivory bill passed the House
in 1979 but died in the Senate.

**At Home:** Beilenson is well-suited for his
district, which includes Beverly Hills and some of
the most liberal and heavily Jewish parts of Los
Angeles. He has never been seriously challenged
in either the primary or the general election,
including the ones in 1976, when he replaced
retiring Democrat Thomas M. Rees.

Beilenson's way was cleared that year when
Howard Berman, the Assembly's majority leader,
chose to remain in the Legislature. Berman had
been seen as Rees's likely successor, and he would
have had access to an organization difficult for
Beilenson to match. But running against five
other candidates, none of whom held public office, Beilenson was the clear front-runner.

Wallace Albertson, who headed the state's

---

**23rd District: Los Angeles — North
Hollywood.** Population: 464,582 (0.1% increase since 1970). Race: White 412,339 (89%),
Black 15,670 (3%), Asian and Pacific Islander
18,264 (4%), Others 18,309 (4%). Spanish
origin: 35,387 (8%).

---

leading liberal organization, the California Democratic Council, criticized Beilenson for not being active enough in his support for Proposition 15, which would have restricted the development of nuclear power plants in the state. But Proposition 15 fared almost as poorly in the district as it did statewide, drawing 38 percent, and Albertson did even worse, finishing second with 21 percent to Beilenson's 58 percent.

Since he moved to the West Coast to practice law at age 25, Beilenson has met with only one political defeat. He was in the middle of his first state Senate term in 1968 when he decided to run for the U.S. Senate as a peace candidate, criticizing former state Controller Alan Cranston for what he said was a lukewarm anti-war position. Beilenson was second among five candidates, but more than a million votes behind Cranston.

**The District:** The 23rd is geographically and psychologically split by the Santa Monica Mountains. About 40 percent of the voters live north of the mountains, in the San Fernando Valley. Although Democratic, this area went for Ronald Reagan in 1980. The other 60 percent live in the lush foothills of Bel Air and Brentwood or along curving, palm-shaded boulevards in communities like Beverly Hills and Westwood. It is because of these areas that this is the wealthiest district in the state. Here volunteer work for liberal candidates is a social activity.

Large numbers of senior citizens are scattered in apartment buildings throughout the district, and on the eastern edge of the district is West Hollywood, where a growing homosexual population gives the district its most radical politics.

## Committees

**Rules** (8th of 11 Democrats)
Rules of the House.

## Elections

**1980 General**

| | |
|---|---|
| Anthony Beilenson (D ) | 126,020 (63 %) |
| Robert Winckler (R ) | 62,742 (32 %) |
| Jeffrey Lieb (LIB) | 10,623 (5 %) |

**1980 Primary**

| | |
|---|---|
| Anthony Beilenson (D ) | 67,432 (85 %) |
| Eileen Anderson (D ) | 11,588 (15 %) |

**1978 General**

| | |
|---|---|
| Anthony Beilenson (D ) | 117,498 (66 %) |
| Joseph Barbara (R ) | 61,496 (34 %) |

**Previous Winning Percentage**

1976 (60 %)

**District Vote For President**

| | 1980 | | 1976 |
|---|---|---|---|
| D | 89,053 (41 %) | D | 119,138 (52 %) |
| R | 100,601 (46 %) | R | 106,129 (46 %) |
| I | 22,521 (10 %) | I | 3,729 (2 %) |

## Campaign Finance

| | Receipts | Receipts from PACs | Expenditures |
|---|---|---|---|
| **1980** | | | |
| Beilenson (D ) | $72,945 | $500 (1 %) | $46,180 |
| Winckler (R ) | $9,368 | $2,290 (24 %) | $9,865 |

| 1978 | | | |
|---|---|---|---|
| Beilenson (D ) | $68,700 | — (0 %) | $47,776 |

## Voting Studies

| | Presidential Support | | Party Unity | | Conservative Coalition | |
|---|---|---|---|---|---|---|
| Year | S | O | S | O | S | O |
| 1980 | 80 | 15 | 86 | 8 | 7 | 88 |
| 1979 | 77 | 21 | 88 | 6 | 5 | 90 |
| 1978 | 76 | 12 | 81 | 9 | 5 | 80 |
| 1977 | 66 | 22 | 83 | 7 | 4 | 90 |

S = Support          O = Opposition

## Key Votes

**96th Congress**

| | |
|---|---|
| Weaken Carter oil profits tax (1979) | N |
| Reject hospital cost control plan (1979) | N |
| Implement Panama Canal Treaties (1979) | Y |
| Establish Department of Education (1979) | N |
| Approve Anti-busing Amendment (1979) | N |
| Guarantee Chrysler Corp. loans (1979) | N |
| Approve military draft registration (1980) | N |
| Aid Sandinista regime in Nicaragua (1980) | Y |
| Strengthen fair housing laws (1980) | Y |

**97th Congress**

| | |
|---|---|
| Reagan budget proposal (1981) | N |

## Interest Group Ratings

| Year | ADA | ACA | AFL-CIO | CCUS |
|---|---|---|---|---|
| 1980 | 94 | 21 | 68 | 39 |
| 1979 | 100 | 8 | 83 | 12 |
| 1978 | 80 | 8 | 79 | 31 |
| 1977 | 90 | 11 | 78 | 24 |

# 24 Henry A. Waxman (D)

**Of Los Angeles — Elected 1974**

**Born:** Sept. 12, 1939, Los Angeles, Calif.
**Education:** U. of Calif. at Los Angeles, B.A. 1961, J.D. 1964.
**Profession:** Lawyer.
**Family:** Wife, Janet Kessler; two children.
**Religion:** Jewish.
**Political Career:** Calif. Assembly, 1969-75.

**In Washington:** The political skill that made Waxman chairman of a key subcommittee after only two terms has not been sufficient to give him control over it in a time of liberal eclipse. Through mid-1981, at least, his chairmanship of the Commerce Subcommittee on Health has meant frustration as often as it has meant influence.

Waxman is a small, soft-spoken man with a thick mustache and a shy smile, one who looks like a Charlie Chaplin character bumbling through a chaotic world. That is the last thing he is. Few members of the House can match his ability to assemble and use power. A California reporter once wrote that Waxman "entered politics with a firm grasp of two simple theories: two votes are more than twice as good as one if they stick together, and God never meant liberals to be stupid."

When he wanted to run for Health Subcommittee chairman in 1979 against the highly respected Richardson Preyer of North Carolina, Waxman raised money from his own wealthy campaign contributors, and distributed it to Democrats on the full Commerce Committee who would be making the decision. It led to the charge that Waxman was buying himself a chairmanship, but he prevailed, 15-12.

Even Waxman, however, cannot turn a free enterprise conservative into a regulatory liberal. There are 18 votes on the subcommittee, and when it comes to using the power of the federal government on health and environmental issues, Waxman can assume no more than eight solid votes on his side. On an early test in 1981, he beat efforts to weaken the Consumer Product Safety Commission on a 10-10 tie, but given the even more conservative makeup of the full committee, seemed to feel the result had not been worth the effort. "Perhaps the best thing to do at this point," he said, "would be not to authorize the CPSC at all."

In 1978 and 1979, Waxman's most notable battle was a stubborn but unsuccessful attempt to pass President Carter's bill requiring hospitals to hold down cost increases below 11 percent a year. Hospitals lobbied heavily against the bill, arguing that their rates only reflected accelerating costs for supplies and labor.

In 1978, before he took over the Health panel, Waxman got the bill to the full committee, where, despite personal calls from President Carter, it lost by one vote, 22-21. In the 96th Congress, Waxman tried again and provided a graphic demonstration of the limited powers of his chairmanship by losing in his subcommittee, 8-4.

But he went on to the full committee anyway, and it passed 23-19. On the floor, however, it fell victim to a substitute by Missouri Democrat Richard Gephardt, making the entire program voluntary and essentially killing it. Waxman tried to delay a vote on the measure, hoping for a last-minute rally in its support, but the Carter administration insisted on going ahead in November 1979, and the substitute was approved, 234-166.

Waxman also worked in the 96th Congress to produce a new Child Health Assurance Program (CHAP). It was an ambitious effort to guarantee free health care to as many as five million poor children, at a cost of up to $2 billion a year by 1984.

Carter had made the bill one of his initiatives in 1977, but it was dormant until 1979, when Waxman moved it through the Commerce Committee and got it passed on the House floor,

---

**24th District: Los Angeles — North Hollywood.** Population: 539,132 (16% increase since 1970). Race: White 338,477 (63%), Black 44,819 (8%), Others 87,771 (16%). Spanish origin: 143,274 (27%).

---

fighting off criticism of it as another "entitlement" program with no limit on spending and enormous costs further down the road. But Waxman could not prevent the House from adding a controversial anti-abortion amendment, and that was one reason the bill died later in the Senate Finance Committee.

Waxman began his second term as chairman in 1981 with a frankly defensive agenda — trying to protect controversial federal health programs up for renewal amid Reagan efforts to cut them back. He no longer talks as often about his personal priority — national health insurance, which he cosponsored along with Sen. Edward M. Kennedy.

Foremost among the programs for Waxman to protect was the Clean Air Act. It pitted him and the environmentalists against Reagan and the national business community, for whom the law had become a symbol of costly over-regulation.

Waxman fought for tough environmental standards when the law was updated in 1977, and he pledged to keep it alive in the '80s. But that guaranteed a showdown between him and the full Commerce chairman, John Dingell of Michigan, an ally of the auto industry on air pollution issues. In the past, Dingell has been a tenacious fighter against the act's auto emissions standards.

On health issues, Waxman found himself in an equally difficult situation. Reagan proposed a cap on federal Medicaid spending for the poor. Reagan Budget Director David Stockman, a former member of Waxman's subcommittee, favored withdrawing the government from the health care field almost completely and promoting more competition in the private health industry.

Waxman accepted the Reagan administration positions as a challenge. "The president has warned of 'special interests' working to unravel his entire economic package," he said. "But if the term 'special interest' under the Reagan administration has become the sick, the poor, and the helpless, I am proud to defend them."

To add to the workload in 1981, Waxman decided to spend more time looking into the work of the National Institutes of Health, whose programs never before had been authorized by Commerce. NIH objected, but Waxman said he simply was advocating the standard authorization process applied to other federal agencies. He won his point.

Very few members identify themselves as liberals in the 97th Congress. Waxman does. He sticks by a statement in his first congressional campaign brochure from 1974. "I am a proud, self-confessed, unapologetic liberal."

**At Home:** One reason Waxman never has any trouble winning in this district is that its heavily Jewish, liberal constituency fits him ideally. The other reason is the so-called "Waxman-Berman machine."

Although this is not a machine in the sense that it can reward friends with patronage jobs, it is an efficient, smoothly functioning operation that pools resources, makes extensive use of computer technology and has substantial political power.

The "machine" label was fixed in 1972, when Waxman, then a two-term assemblyman, teamed up with the Berman brothers — Howard and Michael — to win a seat for Howard Berman in the Assembly. But the Waxman-Berman alliance was originally forged during college days at UCLA, when Waxman and Howard Berman each took a turn presiding over the state's Federation of Young Democrats.

The first visible success for the Waxman-Berman team came in 1968, when Waxman challenged Democratic Assemblyman Lester McMillan in a primary. McMillan had been in office 26 years and was nearing retirement. But rather than wait until the seat opened up and drew a large field of competitors, Waxman decided to take on the incumbent. With massive volunteer help, much of it recruited from the ranks of the Young Democrats, Waxman beat McMillan with 64 percent of the vote.

That election saw the beginning of what has since become the Waxman-Berman trademark — computerized mailings. Each voter is identified by a variety of socio-political characteristics, contacted by a precinct canvasser or by letter and given a campaign pitch specifically tailored to his or her interests.

By 1974 the operation was functioning so smoothly that Waxman had little trouble winning a newly-drawn U.S. House seat created with him in mind. He has had even less trouble retaining it.

Waxman does not rely on computers alone to keep up his popular image in the district. He shares his district office with the man he handpicked to take his Assembly seat in 1974, providing a "one-stop shop" for solving problems on the state as well as federal level. Waxman holds informal, unscheduled meetings with voters in the district's delicatessens.

**The District:** The heavily Jewish "bagel boroughs" of Los Angeles form the political core of this district, whose center includes the intersection of Hollywood and Vine.

The neighborhoods become more affluent as one travels north across the Santa Monica Mountains into the Studio City and North Hollywood sections of the San Fernando Valley. But the concentration of Jewish voters is the same at both ends and so is the Democratic tradition. The district also has a substantial gay population and an Asian-American community, including one of the largest concentrations of Korean voters out-side Seoul.

Liberal Democrats have always run well here. In the 1980 Democratic presidential primary, Edward M. Kennedy carried the district by a 54-31 margin over Jimmy Carter. In the general election, the district was one of only nine in the state that Carter carried over Ronald Reagan.

## Committees

**Energy and Commerce** (4th of 24 Democrats)
Health and the Environment, chairman; Telecommunications, Consumer Protection and Finance.

**Government Operations** (13th of 23 Democrats)
Government Information and Individual Rights; Legislation and National Security.

**Select Aging** (21st of 31 Democrats)
Retirement Income and Employment.

## Elections

**1980 General**

| | |
|---|---|
| Henry Waxman (D) | 93,569 (64%) |
| Roland Cayard (R) | 39,744 (27%) |

**1978 General**

| | |
|---|---|
| Henry Waxman (D) | 85,075 (63%) |
| Howard Schaefer (R) | 44,243 (33%) |

**Previous Winning Percentage**

1976 (68 %)    1974 (64%)

**District Vote For President**

| | 1980 | | 1976 |
|---|---|---|---|
| D | 74,435 (47%) | D | 93,650 (55%) |
| R | 65,890 (41%) | R | 74,042 (43%) |
| I | 13,545 (9%) | | |

## Campaign Finance

| | Receipts | Receipts from PACs | Expen-ditures |
|---|---|---|---|
| **1980** | | | |
| Waxman (D) | $32,948 | $18,150 (55%) | $32,391 |
| Cayard (R) | $9,264 | — (0%) | $8,288 |
| **1978** | | | |
| Waxman (D) | $18,472 | $22,945 (124%) | $26,019 |
| Schaefer (R) | $46,138 | $1,200 (3%) | $48,400 |

## Voting Studies

| | Presidental Support | | Party Unity | | Conservative Coalition | |
|---|---|---|---|---|---|---|
| Year | S | O | S | O | S | O |
| 1980 | 65 | 21 | 78 | 6 | 4 | 79 |
| 1979 | 68 | 19 | 78 | 5 | 5 | 85 |
| 1978 | 75 | 14 | 80 | 6 | 5 | 78 |
| 1977 | 72 | 22 | 84 | 4 | 3 | 90 |
| 1976 | 18 | 75 | 86 | 1 | 2 | 82 |
| 1975 | 30 | 60 | 82 | 4 | 3 | 85 |

S = Support          O = Opposition

## Key Votes

**96th Congress**

| | |
|---|---|
| Weaken Carter oil profits tax (1979) | N |
| Reject hospital cost control plan (1979) | N |
| Implement Panama Canal Treaties (1979) | Y |
| Establish Department of Education (1979) | N |
| Approve Anti-busing Amendment (1979) | N |
| Guarantee Chrysler Corp. loans (1979) | Y |
| Approve military draft registration (1980) | N |
| Aid Sandinista regime in Nicaragua (1980) | ? |
| Strengthen fair housing laws (1980) | Y |

**97th Congress**

| | |
|---|---|
| Reagan budget proposal (1981) | N |

## Interest Group Ratings

| Year | ADA | ACA | AFL-CIO | CCUS |
|---|---|---|---|---|
| 1980 | 83 | 22 | 89 | 50 |
| 1979 | 95 | 8 | 94 | 11 |
| 1978 | 90 | 13 | 90 | 29 |
| 1977 | 80 | 0 | 76 | 12 |
| 1976 | 80 | 0 | 86 | 6 |
| 1975 | 89 | 0 | 96 | 6 |

# 25 Edward R. Roybal (D)

**Of Los Angeles — Elected 1962**

**Born:** Feb. 10, 1916, Albuquerque, N.M.
**Education:** Attended U. of Calif, Los Angeles; Southwestern U.
**Military Career:** Army, 1944-45.
**Profession:** Social worker, public health educator.
**Family:** Wife, Lucille Beserra; three children.
**Religion:** Roman Catholic.
**Political Career:** Los Angeles City Council, 1949-62; unsuccessful Democratic candidate for Calif. lieutenant governor, 1954.

**In Washington:** Roybal is a loyalist Democrat who sees most issues from the vantage point of his Hispanic heritage.

Over the years, he has used his seat on Appropriations mainly to push for more spending on programs benefiting Hispanics, migrant workers and the elderly. In 1980, for example, Roybal persuaded the House to restore $5 million in funds for a senior citizens' public housing program, and $10 million for a community-based alternative to nursing homes.

He has offered numerous amendments on the House floor to add extra funding for causes like these. Most of them have been small, and most have prevailed, although Roybal is a reserved, almost dour man, little given to vote-trading with his colleagues.

Often Roybal talks of poverty and discrimination against his Hispanic constituents. He is an outspoken advocate of federal help for bilingual education programs.

Roybal's record as an ethnic spokesman was a help to him in 1978, when he and two other California colleagues were disciplined by the House in connection with the Korean vote-buying investigation. The ethics committee had recommended reprimands for Charles H. Wilson and John J. McFall, but urged that Roybal be censured, a more serious penalty, for lying to the committee about a $1,000 gift from Korean lobbyist Tongsun Park.

Many of Roybal's allies considered the distinction a race-related insult. "Two of our white colleagues are brought down here to be slapped on the wrist," complained the black California Democrat, Ronald V. Dellums, "And one of my brown brothers is down here to be totally wiped out in the process."

Rep. Phillip Burton, D-Calif., offered a fist-clenching defense of Roybal as a man of total personal integrity. "You can't buy Ed Roybal," Burton thundered, "for money, marbles or chalk."

At the same time, Roybal was calling in chits from Hispanic leaders outside Congress, asking them to help reduce the penalty to a reprimand. When the House agreed to do that, Roybal described the action as "not only a personal victory for me, but for all Hispanics throughout the nation.... [It] shows the potential strength of the Hispanic community when it unifies behind a cause."

A censured member must stand in the well of the House and face his colleagues to hear the charges against him read publicly. A reprimand simply passes into the *Congressional Record* and into history without further ado.

The ethics committee had reported that Roybal lied under oath when asked about $1,000 that Tongsun Park handed him in a brief 1974 meeting in the office of former Rep. Otto Passman, D-La.

At first, Roybal denied to committee investigators that he had received anything of value from Park or from any other "Oriental." Later, he acknowledged receipt of the money as a campaign donation.

"It never dawned on me," he said during the House floor debate, "that the man there was someday going to be the much-publicized

---

**25th District: Central Los Angeles.**
Population: 524,997 (13% increase since 1970). Race: White 265,063 (50%), Black 19,942 (4%), Asian and Pacific Islander 43,996 (8%), Others 195,996 (37%). Spanish origin: 373,241 (71%).

Tongsun Park." He said he used the money to invite senior citizens to a banquet. Earlier, however, Roybal told the House committee he had passed the money on to his campaign secretary. But she said she knew nothing about it.

Roybal spent the early part of his career on the Interior and Post Office committees, then switched to Foreign Affairs in 1965 and to Veterans' Affairs in 1969. In 1971, he gave up all his assignments for Appropriations. He is currently chairman of the subcommittee that handles the budget for the Treasury Department and Postal Service. He also serves on the Labor-Health and Human Services Subcommittee, which fits in more directly with his major interests of jobs and education, and on the Select Aging Committee.

**At Home:** Roybal is a durable man. Despite a style few would call dynamic, he has become an accepted part of the political landscape in the Hispanic ghettos of East Los Angeles.

Lately, Roybal has campaigned relatively little. The noisy Pomona Freeway that runs just a few yards from his Los Angeles home does not bother him, an aide once said, "because he is hardly ever there." But while there are younger, more aggressive Hispanic leaders in the East Los Angeles area, none has so far been willing to take on Roybal, who is viewed as a sort of community "elder."

Roybal has not shown any political weaknesses during his long House career. Beginning with his first re-election in 1964, he has never received less than 66 percent in a general election. He has won more than 80 percent the three times he has been challenged in a primary (1970, 1972 and 1976). Even Roybal's reprimand in 1978 had little political impact in his district.

When Roybal was four, he moved from New Mexico to the ethnically-mixed Boyle Heights section of Los Angeles. He has resided there since, as the neighborhood has turned almost entirely Hispanic.

During the Depression he worked in the Civilian Conservation Corps, and later he became involved in public health work for the California Tuberculosis Association. He won election to the Los Angeles City Council from a Hispanic east side district, served four terms, and ran for the House in 1962. In between he made an unsuccessful try for lieutenant governor.

The 1962 campaign was his only truly challenging contest. The state Legislature had just redrawn the congressional boundaries, pushing the district of nine-term Republican Rep. Gordon L. McDonough far into East Los Angeles. Given the lopsided Democratic registration in the district, McDonough looked so vulnerable that five Democrats, including Roybal, entered the 1962 primary.

Roybal had major primary opposition from William Fitzgerald, a Loyola University government professor, and G. Pappy Boyington, a World War II Marine flying ace who had become a hero as the commander of the "Black Sheep Squadron." But with a solid base in the Hispanic neighborhoods, Roybal won three-fifths of the primary vote and went on to defeat McDonough easily in the general election.

**The District:** Ten different expressways cut through the 25th District, and they are named for the communities to which many of the district's daytime residents flee every evening at rush hour: Glendale, Pasadena, Pomona, and San Bernardino.

Roybal's constituents are the people who remain behind at night in the barrios of East Los Angeles, just beyond the city limits, or in the Boyle Heights section of the city.

The recent influx of immigrants, legal and illegal, has kept the district's population growth nearly even with the state's average. But voting participation is very low. There are fewer registered voters here than in any other district in the state. Only 21 percent of the population was registered in 1980, compared to more than 40 percent statewide. And the trend is toward fewer voters, not more. Substantially fewer people voted for president here in 1980 than in 1972.

For the most part, those who do vote are Democrats. In the southern part of the district, nearly all of them are Hispanics. The Anglo vote increases as one moves north into the Highland Park and Eagle Rock sections. But the political base of the district is unquestionably in the Hispanic areas, just east of the towering buildings of downtown Los Angeles.

---

## Committees

**Appropriations** (9th of 33 Democrats)
Treasury - Postal Service - General Government, chairman; Labor, Health and Human Services, Education and Related Agencies.

**Select Aging** (2nd of 31 Democrats)
Housing and Consumer Interests, chairman.

## Elections

1980 General

## Edward R. Roybal, D-Calif.

| | |
|---|---|
| Edward Roybal (D ) | 49,080 (66 %) |
| Richard Ferraro (R ) | 21,116 (28 %) |
| William Mitchell (LIB) | 4,169 (6 %) |

**1978 General**

| | |
|---|---|
| Edward Roybal (D ) | 45,881 (67 %) |
| Robert Watson (R ) | 22,205 (33 %) |

**Previous Winning Percentages**

1976 (72 %)   1974 (100 %)   1972 (68 %)   1970 (68 %)
1968 (67 %)   1966  (66 %)   1964 (66 %)   1962 (57 %)

**District Vote For President**

| | 1980 | | 1976 |
|---|---|---|---|
| D | 44,131 (56 %) | D | 52,234 (62 %) |
| R | 27,630 (35 %) | R | 30,106 (36 %) |
| I | 5,013 (6 %) | | |

## Campaign Finance

| | Receipts | Receipts from PACs | Expenditures |
|---|---|---|---|
| **1980** | | | |
| Roybal (D ) | $46,467 | $17,520 (38 %) | $44,411 |
| Ferraro (R ) | $18,860 | $910 (5 %) | $14,751 |
| **1978** | | | |
| Roybal (D ) | $76,920 | $8,190 (11 %) | $41,232 |

## Voting Studies

| | Presidential Support | | Party Unity | | Conservative Coalition | |
|---|---|---|---|---|---|---|
| Year | S | O | S | O | S | O |
| 1980 | 67 | 23 | 84 | 4 | 6 | 80 |
| 1979 | 77 | 14 | 86 | 5 | 7 | 81 |
| 1978 | 77 | 21 | 88 | 5 | 7 | 90 |
| 1977 | 72 | 20 | 90 | 4 | 8 | 86 |
| 1976 | 20 | 73 | 92 | 5 | 8 | 90 |
| 1975 | 33 | 65 | 87 | 7 | 8 | 87 |
| 1974 (Ford) | 41 | 59 | | | | |
| 1974 | 34 | 58 | 82 | 9 | 8 | 87 |
| 1973 | 26 | 67 | 83 | 8 | 8 | 86 |
| 1972 | 41 | 54 | 81 | 10 | 6 | 87 |
| 1971 | 26 | 63 | 80 | 6 | 1 | 87 |

| Year | S | O | S | O | | O |
|---|---|---|---|---|---|---|
| 1970 | 43 | 38 | 76 | 14 | - | 84 |
| 1969 | 47 | 43 | 80 | 7 | 2 | 84 |
| 1968 | 71 | 10 | 74 | 2 | 4 | 67 |
| 1967 | 79 | 9 | 83 | 2 | 2 | 85 |
| 1966 | 81 | 8 | 81 | 5 | 0 | 92 |
| 1965 | 83 | 5 | 84 | 3 | 2 | 84 |
| 1964 | 85 | 4 | 79 | 3 | 0 | 83 |
| 1963 | 83 | 6 | 89 | 3 | 0 | 73 |

S = Support          O = Opposition

## Key Votes

**96th Congress**

| | |
|---|---|
| Weaken Carter oil profits tax (1979) | N |
| Reject hospital cost control plan (1979) | N |
| Implement Panama Canal Treaties (1979) | Y |
| Establish Department of Education (1979) | Y |
| Approve Anti-busing Amendment (1979) | N |
| Guarantee Chrysler Corp. loans (1979) | Y |
| Approve military draft registration (1980) | N |
| Aid Sandinista regime in Nicaragua (1980) | Y |
| Strengthen fair housing laws (1980) | Y |

**97th Congress**

| | |
|---|---|
| Reagan budget proposal (1981) | N |

## Interest Group Ratings

| Year | ADA | ACA | AFL-CIO | CCUS |
|---|---|---|---|---|
| 1980 | 89 | 14 | 89 | 50 |
| 1979 | 84 | 5 | 94 | 0 |
| 1978 | 85 | 15 | 79 | 24 |
| 1977 | 85 | 0 | 91 | 6 |
| 1976 | 100 | 7 | 87 | 13 |
| 1975 | 95 | 4 | 95 | 18 |
| 1974 | 100 | 0 | 100 | 0 |
| 1973 | 92 | 8 | 91 | 10 |
| 1972 | 100 | 10 | 100 | 0 |
| 1971 | 92 | 8 | 90 | - |
| 1970 | 100 | 6 | 100 | 11 |
| 1969 | 100 | 7 | 100 | - |
| 1968 | 100 | 5 | 100 | - |
| 1967 | 93 | 0 | 100 | 11 |
| 1966 | 94 | 9 | 92 | - |
| 1965 | 89 | 0 | - | 10 |
| 1964 | 96 | 6 | 100 | - |
| 1963 | - | 6 | - | - |

# 26 John H. Rousselot (R)

**Of San Marino — Elected 1970**
Also served 1961-63.

**Born:** Nov. 1, 1927, Los Angeles, Calif.
**Education:** Principia College, B.A. 1949.
**Profession:** Public relations executive, management consultant.
**Family:** Wife, Vyonne LeMasters; three children by previous marriage.
**Religion:** Christian Scientist.
**Political Career:** U.S. House, 1961-63; unsuccessful Republican candidate for re-election from 25th District, 1962.

**In Congress:** Like many of his conservative Republican allies, Rousselot has spent much of the past decade practicing guerrilla warfare on the House floor, savaging Democrats with sarcasm and procedural objections to their business routine. But unlike some of them, he has managed to do it without making many enemies on either side of the aisle. Close observers of Rousselot have always professed to see a twinkle in his eye at the moment of attack, and they watch him follow up his verbal assaults with a stroll across the aisle, a private joke and an arm around the enemy's shoulder. He is the nice guy of the Republican right.

Rousselot always has been hard to ignore, delivering his broadsides in a loud voice that attracts attention even from the unwilling. Since the advent of cable television coverage of House floor action, however, he has become even more theatrical, speaking directly to his audience and once even encouraging spectators in the gallery to applaud — a violation of House rules.

Rousselot's favorite oratorical gimmick is mock naiveté, a question asked in a tone of earnest innocence meant to provoke a straight answer that reveals a fallacy in the opponent's approach. Smart Democrats usually handle this without much trouble, but it has been known to trap aging and inarticulate committee chairmen in verbal disasters.

Rousselot's assaults have usually been ad hoc, rarely part of a long-term legislative strategy. The choice of guerrilla warfare has made him a generalist rather than a specialist; he moves wherever he sees an opening, and his conservatism is pure enough to be applicable to most subjects.

He has always been active on budget issues. Since the mid-1970s, he has offered a balanced budget amendment to every budget resolution on the House floor. Initially he drew less than 100 votes, but by 1980, with federal spending a hot issue, he was moving closer to 200. One problem, however, is that Rousselot's amendments have sometimes undercut other Republican substitutes. Some Democrats, feeling the political need to vote for some form of budget-cutting proposal, have chosen the drastic Rousselot approach, then confidently voted against more moderate Republican amendments that otherwise would have had a chance to pass.

Rousselot joined the Ways and Means Committee in 1979 and tried to find time to follow committee business while still playing his time-consuming watchdog role on the House floor. He became ranking Republican on the subcommittee dealing with welfare issues and proposed his own substitute to a major 1979 welfare bill. It would have deleted the bill's minimum national welfare standard and cut out new aid to states. Rousselot's version would have given the states primary responsibility for welfare programs. It failed on a surprisingly close 205-200 vote. The program was not enacted anyway.

Another favorite Rousselot target is foreign aid, and here he has been more successful. In 1980, he won House passage of his amendment cutting funds for the Asian Development Bank by more than half.

**At Home:** After a stormy political beginning two decades ago, Rousselot has finally settled into

---

**26th District: East central Los Angeles County.** Population: 469,700 (1% increase since 1970). Race: White 382,368 (81%), Black 10,094 (2%), Asian and Pacific Islander 26,647 (6%), Others 50,591 (11%). Spanish origin: 120,366 (26%).

## John H. Rousselot, R-Calif.

a comfortable situation in which his conservative views closely match his constituency. Charges of extremism no longer echo through the San Gabriel Valley with the ferocity that once made Rousselot national news.

It was Rousselot's longtime membership in the John Birch Society that sparked the controversy in his early political career. The son of a successful chemist, Rousselot began his career in public relations work. Before he decided to become a candidate himself, he spent two years as public information director for the Federal Housing Administration in Washington and managed 11 political campaigns, winning nine of them.

His first campaign for himself was in 1960, against first-term Democratic Rep. George A. Kasem. Rousselot put together the best organization in the state that year, defeated three better-known primary opponents and then ousted Kasem as well.

Once in office, Rousselot earned considerable attention for his outspoken views, such as suggesting to President John F. Kennedy that the United States simply invade Cuba. Statements like that brought him a primary challenger in 1962 who charged he was "taking his instructions from Belmont, Massachusetts," the home of Birch Society founder Robert Welch.

Rousselot won the primary with little difficulty, but his Birch Society membership became an even larger issue in the fall when he was joined by two other John Birch members running for Congress from California. Already viewed as a little too extreme even for conservative Los Angeles County Republicans, Rousselot also had to contend with a district substantially altered by the Democratic Legislature. Part of Whittier, plus San Marino and San Gabriel — all heavily Republican — had been removed.

The areas that remained closely resembled the state legislative district of Ronald B. Cameron, a strong Kennedy supporter, and Cameron became Rousselot's Democratic opponent. Rousselot was beaten, along with the other two Birch Society candidates.

During four of the next eight years, Rousselot worked for the John Birch Society, trying to purge it of what he felt were its more exotic obsessions. According to one account, Rousselot "nudged the overt racists and anti-Semites into the background and emphasized the Society's folksy, good-neighbor image."

That effort paid off in 1970, when Rousselot saw an opportunity to re-enter the House. A 16-year veteran from the neighboring 24th District, Republican Glenard P. Lipscomb, died in office in February, and Rousselot quickly entered the contest to succeed him. His two major opponents were former Rep. Patrick Hillings — Richard M. Nixon's successor in the House — and Dr. Bill McColl, a former wide receiver for the Chicago Bears. Both Hillings and McColl were conservatives, but they tried to paint Rousselot as an extremist.

The special election primary, in which candidates of all parties ran together on the ballot, took place the same day as the the regular primary for a full term, which was open only to Republicans. In the regular primary, Rousselot was able to edge McColl by just 127 votes. In the special election primary, he led McColl by 2,263 votes, winning support from Democrats who did not like their one candidate, Myrlie B. Evers, the wife of slain civil rights worker Medgar Evers. She was running almost exclusively on an anti-Vietnam War platform.

Evers and Rousselot opposed each other twice more that year, in the special election runoff in late June and four months later in the general election. In both those contests, Evers received the support of nationally-known Democrats and considerable media attention. But Rousselot had no trouble winning both elections.

Since then, the extremism issue has disappeared. Rousselot has never encountered any primary opposition since his successful comeback more than a decade ago. And he has never been seriously challenged in a general election.

Rousselot planned to run against Democratic Sen. Alan Cranston in 1980, and even quit the Birch Society to make the race. But he had difficulty raising money and was forced to drop out when party leaders turned their attention to tax protester Paul Gann. Gann proved to have no more success raising money against Cranston than Rousselot had, and most Republicans now feel Rousselot would have provided a more substantive challenge to Cranston.

**The District:** The 26th extends through 20 miles of solidly conservative suburbs just east of Los Angeles.

Rousselot's base is in the northwestern corner of the district, where it is hard for a candidate to be too conservative. This part of the district is unswervingly loyal not only to Rousselot, but to California's "godfather" of conservative politics, veteran state Sen. H. L. (Bill) Richardson. The towns here — San Marino, South Pasadena and Arcadia — are the wealthiest in the district. All voted heavily in 1980 for Gann, who carried the district with his second highest plurality in the state.

Farther east, in more middle-class, white-collar communities, voters still support Republicans but not by the same margins.

The Democratic vote comes largely from the Mexican-American population concentrated in the southwestern corner of the district, in Alhambra and San Gabriel, and on the east side of the San Gabriel River, in Baldwin Park and Azusa. But it is too small, usually, to make much of a dent in the solid Republican majorities.

## Committees

**Ways and Means** (11th of 12 Republicans)
Public Assistance and Unemployment Compensation; Social Security.

**Joint Economic**
Trade, Productivity and Economic Growth.

## Elections

**1980 General**

| | |
|---|---|
| John Rousselot (R ) | 116,715 (71 %) |
| Joseph Lisoni (D ) | 40,099 (24 %) |

**1978 General**

| | |
|---|---|
| John Rousselot (R ) | Unopposed |

**Previous Winning Percentages**

| | | | |
|---|---|---|---|
| 1976 (66%) | 1974 (59%) | 1972 (70%) | 1970 (65%) |
| 1970* (68%) | 1960 (54%) | | |

*\* Special Election*

**District Vote For President**

| | 1980 | | 1976 |
|---|---|---|---|
| D | 47,638 (27 %) | D | 66,151 (37 %) |
| R | 111,196 (64 %) | R | 108,532 (61 %) |
| I | 11,573 (7 %) | | |

## Campaign Finance

| | Receipts | Receipts from PACs | Expenditures |
|---|---|---|---|
| **1980** | | | |
| Rousselot (R ) | $165,136 | $113,861 (69 %) | $92,824 |
| Lisoni (D ) | $41,589 | $3,075 (7 %) | $41,082 |
| **1978** | | | |
| Rousselot (R ) | $115,864 | $37,290 (32 %) | $54,386 |

## Voting Studies

| | Presidential Support | | Party Unity | | Conservative Coalition | |
|---|---|---|---|---|---|---|
| Year | S | O | S | O | S | O |
| 1980 | 23 | 64 | 81 | 6 | 79 | 8 |
| 1979 | 21 | 68 | 81 | 3 | 82 | 1 |

| | | | | | |
|---|---|---|---|---|---|
| 1978 | 22 | 73 | 87 | 5 | 87 | 4 |
| 1977 | 23 | 68 | 83 | 4 | 92 | 3 |
| 1976 | 67 | 25 | 84 | 6 | 85 | 4 |
| 1975 | 58 | 30 | 85 | 7 | 86 | 6 |
| 1974 (Ford) | 33 | 46 | | | | |
| 1974 | 60 | 34 | 82 | 9 | 81 | 8 |
| 1973 | 58 | 34 | 85 | 11 | 86 | 11 |
| 1972 | 35 | 38 | 62 | 16 | 73 | 11 |
| 1971 | 53 | 28 | 71 | 12 | 70 | 12 |
| 1970 | 45 | 29† | 71 | 7† | 55 | † |
| 1962 | 17 | 68 | 75 | 2 | 75 | 0 |
| 1961 | 20 | 72 | 91 | 2 | 91 | 0 |

† Not eligible for all recorded votes.

st

S = Support        O = Opposition

## Key Votes

**96th Congress**

| | |
|---|---|
| Weaken Carter oil profits tax (1979) | Y |
| Reject hospital cost control plan (1979) | Y |
| Implement Panama Canal Treaties (1979) | N |
| Establish Department of Education (1979) | N |
| Approve Anti-busing Amendment (1979) | Y |
| Guarantee Chrysler Corp. loans (1979) | N |
| Approve military draft registration (1980) | N |
| Aid Sandinista regime in Nicaragua (1980) | N |
| Strengthen fair housing laws (1980) | N |

**97th Congress**

| | |
|---|---|
| Reagan budget proposal (1981) | Y |

## Interest Group Rating

| Year | ADA | ACA | AFL-CIO | CCUS |
|---|---|---|---|---|
| 1980 | 11 | 95 | 10 | 68 |
| 1979 | 5 | 100 | 12 | 100 |
| 1978 | 5 | 100 | 5 | 94 |
| 1977 | 0 | 96 | 9 | 94 |
| 1976 | 5 | 88 | 9 | 100 |
| 1975 | 0 | 96 | 9 | 100 |
| 1974 | 4 | 93 | 0 | 100 |
| 1973 | 8 | 96 | 9 | 100 |
| 1972 | 0 | 94 | 38 | 100 |
| 1971 | 8 | 96 | 18 | - |
| 1970* | 29 | 100 | 0 | 100 |
| 1962 | 0 | 100 | 0 | - |
| 1961 | 0 | - | - | - |

* Not eligible for all votes.

# 27 Robert K. Dornan (R)

**Of Santa Monica — Elected 1976**

**Born:** April 3, 1933, New York, N.Y.
**Education:** Attended Loyola U., 1950-53.
**Military Career:** Air Force, 1953-58.
**Profession:** Broadcast journalist and producer.
**Family:** Wife, Sallie Hansen; five children.
**Religion:** Roman Catholic.
**Political Career:** Republican nominee for mayor of Los Angeles, 1973.

**In Washington:** For passion, bombast, and sheer volume, there is no one in Congress to match this former TV talk show host, who often seems to focus on the occasional moments of drama the chamber offers, rather than on its routine legislative work.

When he speaks on the abortion issue, shouting hoarsely of babies "murdered in their mothers' wombs," he is as uncompromising as he is strident. He refused to go along in 1979, for example, when anti-abortion leader Henry Hyde agreed not to fight compromise language allowing federally funded abortions in cases of rape and incest. The deal was negotiated to allow passage of an appropriation bill providing paychecks to the unemployed and the handicapped, as well as federal workers. "I don't care if two million paychecks are held up," Dornan said, "if it means two million babies are being killed."

In 1980, Dornan managed to win House passage of an amendment preventing the District of Columbia from paying for abortions with public money. But the amendment was later dropped.

Dornan's impassioned rhetoric and die-hard attitude have made him a favorite of some New Right groups outside Congress, but inside the institution he is not one of the more effective conservative legislators. He spent his first four years in Congress on two minor committees, Science and Technology and Merchant Marine, then switched to Foreign Affairs in 1981. So far, his committee work has been limited. An impulsive man with a short attention span, he has never had the temperament to hammer out detailed legislation.

Dornan is as militant against communism and the Soviet Union as he is against abortion, and he is an argumentative supporter of Israel. In 1980, he got into an angry quarrel on the House floor over an amendment requiring that the U.S. Embassy in Israel be moved to Jerusalem, where the State Department has refused to place it out of deference to Arab views. "The Jewish people plead to have it recognized by their friends as

their holy capital," Dornan said. "If we lose some gasoline over it, so be it."

**At Home:** Dornan's flamboyance has turned all three of his House campaigns into close and costly affairs. Since 1976, when Alphonzo Bell gave up this district, Dornan and his Democratic opponents have spent a combined total of more than $4 million wrestling for control.

Dornan entered politics after an eclectic career that included five years as a pilot in the Air Force, various journalism jobs, numerous parts as an "extra" in television dramas, and several years as the host of TV talk shows. He spent much of his time on the road, registering black voters in Alabama in the 1960s and trying to ban objectionable textbooks in West Virginia in the 1970s. The prisoner of war issue also occupied a lot of his time. He boasts of inventing the POW bracelet.

By 1976 Dornan had been off the air for three years and lost an election for mayor of Los Angeles. Six Republicans and eight Democrats entered the House election to succeed Bell, with the GOP front-runners being former Peace Corps head Joseph Blatchford and Michael C. Donaldson, treasurer of the Republican State Central Committee. But they split the moderate primary vote, allowing Dornan to win the nomination on the strength of his conservative support.

The general election between Dornan and Gary Familian, a wealthy Marina del Ray businessman, was an exercise in name-calling. Dornan called Familian a "warmed-over McGovernite." Familian said Dornan was a "paid propagandist"

---

**27th District: Pacific Coast — Santa Monica.** Population: 463,584 (0.1% decrease since 1970). Race: White 409,520 (88%), Black 11,406 (2%), Asian and Pacific Islander 21,566 (5%), Others 21,092 (4%). Spanish: 42,794 (9%).

---

linked to the John Birch Society and Ku Klux Klan. When it was over, Dornan had won by nearly 20,000 votes.

In the two elections since then, Dornan's opponent has been Carey Peck, son of actor Gregory Peck. As in 1976, personalities have been more important than issues. Peck was an inexperienced and awkward candidate in 1978, but he came within 3,500 votes of Dornan, charging that the incumbent had little to show for all the sound and fury he had created in Washington.

Dornan countered that Peck was simply a rich young man playing at politics. He also won some points with defense workers by telling of his efforts to save the B-1 bomber.

Dornan was determined to trounce Peck in their 1980 rematch, and he spent nearly $2 million in the effort. Although Peck improved his campaign style somewhat in the rematch, Dornan pulled through once again.

**The District:** The district ranges across the political spectrum as it follows the coast from Pacific Palisades to Rolling Hills.

In the north, beach-oriented young people have settled in Venice and among the elderly, middle-class residents of Santa Monica. Democrats usually carry those parts of the district. In the center of the district, Westchester and El Segundo are the middle-class and politically divided. To the south are yacht-club Republicans and young singles living in Marina Del Ray and Manhattan Beach condominiums. And on the southern tip of the district are the most exclusive Republican enclaves in the Los Angeles area.

## Committees

**Foreign Affairs** (10th of 16 Republicans)
  Africa; Asian and Pacific Affairs; Human Rights and International Organizations.

**Select Aging** (6th of 23 Republicans)
  Housing and Consumer Interests.

**Select Narcotics Abuse and Control** (5th of 8 Republicans)

## Elections

**1980 General**

| | |
|---|---|
| Robert Dornan (R ) | 109,807 (51 %) |
| Carey Peck (D ) | 100,061 (47 %) |

**1978 General**

| | |
|---|---|
| Robert Dornan (R ) | 89,392 (51 %) |
| Carey Peck (D ) | 85,880 (49 %) |

**Previous Winning Percentage**

1976 (55 %)

**District Vote For President**

| | 1980 | | 1976 |
|---|---|---|---|
| D | 66,220 (30 %) | D | 82,854 (39 %) |
| R | 125,736 (57 %) | R | 125,254 (59 %) |
| I | 20,616 (9 %) | | |

## Campaign Finance

| | Receipts | Receipts from PACs | Expenditures |
|---|---|---|---|
| **1980** | | | |
| Dornan (R ) | $1,947,190 | $154,680 (8 %) | $1,947,209 |
| Peck (D ) | $564,582 | $129,476 (23 %) | $559,315 |

| 1978 | | | |
|---|---|---|---|
| Dornan (R ) | $292,615 | $62,923 (24 %) | $291,762 |
| Peck (D ) | $308,573 | $42,173 (14 %) | $308,017 |

## Voting Studies

| | Presidential Support | | Party Unity | | Conservative Coalition | |
|---|---|---|---|---|---|---|
| Year | S | O | S | O | S | O |
| 1980 | 33 | 52 | 73 | 14 | 75 | 16 |
| 1979 | 30 | 59 | 78 | 10 | 82 | 9 |
| 1978 | 26 | 63 | 84 | 10 | 84 | 10 |
| 1977 | 30 | 61 | 86 | 7 | 88 | 6 |

S = Support          O = Opposition

## Key Votes

**96th Congress**

| | |
|---|---|
| Weaken Carter oil profits tax (1979) | Y |
| Reject hospital cost control plan (1979) | Y |
| Implement Panama Canal Treaties (1979) | N |
| Establish Department of Education (1979) | Y |
| Approve Anti-busing Amendment (1979) | Y |
| Guarantee Chrysler Corp. loans (1979) | N |
| Approve military draft registration (1980) | N |
| Aid Sandinista regime in Nicaragua (1980) | N |
| Strengthen fair housing laws (1980) | N |

**97th Congress**

| | |
|---|---|
| Reagan budget proposal (1981) | Y |

## Interest Group Ratings

| Year | ADA | ACA | AFL-CIO | CCUS |
|---|---|---|---|---|
| 1980 | 11 | 73 | 12 | 77 |
| 1979 | 16 | 88 | 10 | 83 |
| 1978 | 5 | 92 | 5 | 81 |
| 1977 | 0 | 96 | 9 | 94 |

# 28 Julian C. Dixon (D)

**Of Culver City — Elected 1978**

**Born:** Aug. 8, 1934, Washington, D.C.
**Education:** Calif. State U., Los Angeles, B.S. 1962; Southwestern U., LL.B. 1967.
**Military Career:** Army, 1957-60.
**Profession:** Lawyer.
**Family:** Divorced, one child.
**Religion:** Episcopalian.
**Political Career:** Calif. Assembly, 1973-79.

**In Washington:** Dixon was given a California seat on the Appropriations Committee when he arrived in 1979, and barely a year later he was chairman of one of its subcommittees, on the District of Columbia.

The D.C. chairmanship has no political advantage for most members, and few seek it. But for Dixon, a black member born in the capital city, it offered not only local influence but increased visibility in the national black community.

The initial expectation among local officials was that Dixon would be a refreshing change for them from predecessor Charles Wilson of Texas, who expressed little sympathy with D.C. financial problems. And Dixon said on taking the job that his priorities were to eliminate the city's deficit, and eventually to phase out congressional control of its budget affairs.

But Dixon proved quickly that he was no soft touch for the city government. By the end of 1980, when D.C. Mayor Marion Barry lobbied to transfer the city's judicial system from federal to local authority, Dixon accused Barry of hoarding power. "A large concentration of power is accumulating in one person," Dixon said, "and I don't know if that is necessarily healthy."

While parceling out money to the district, Dixon was struggling with foreign aid issues on his other Appropriations subcommittee. Here too, he met the early expectation of being sympathetic to the plight of Third World countries, but skeptical about the way they use money.

Outraged in 1980 when the Haitian government spent lavish amounts of government funds on the wedding of the country's president, Jean-Claude Duvalier, Dixon persuaded his subcommittee to reduce American aid to Haiti by 30 percent. "There is a real question whether the money is really going to the people," Dixon said. Later the House voted to give $1 million of the money back, but through an international development fund.

Dixon also was one of six committee members who fought President Carter's proposal to send $20 million in military aid to Somalia in 1980, in exchange for U.S. rights to use facilities there. But he fought to raise the Carter request for military aid to Liberia, and succeeded in getting $3 million appropriated for a nutrition project in Nigeria.

**At Home:** Dixon has made a career of following in the path of Yvonne Brathwaite Burke. When she left the state Assembly in 1972 to run for the House, Dixon quit his job as an aide to then-state Sen. Mervyn Dymally and captured her Assembly seat. Six years later, when she left Congress to run unsuccessfully for attorney general of California, Dixon beat back eight opponents in the Democratic primary to win her House seat.

The primary turned into a struggle for power among political brokers in Los Angeles' black community. Dixon's closest competitor, state Sen. Nate Holden, was backed by Los Angeles County Supervisor Kenneth Hahn, a white man with considerable popularity in the black South Los Angeles area. Another rival, City Councilman David S. Cunningham, was supported by Mayor Thomas Bradley.

The strongest power bloc, however, was lined up behind Dixon, the candidate of U.S. Rep. Henry A. Waxman and state Assemblyman How-

**28th District: Western Los Angeles — Inglewood.** Population: 469,346 (1% increase since 1970). Race: White 157,698 (34%), Black 236,907 (50%), Asian and Pacific Islander 27,048 (6%) Others 47,693 (10%). Spanish origin: 90,500 (19%).

ard L. Berman. The Waxman-Berman machine is strong throughout the city, and it delivered 50 percent of the vote for Dixon in the primary, to 38 percent for Holden. Dixon ran unopposed in the general election, and had no trouble winning a second term in 1980.

Dixon's six years in the Legislature were productive. As a freshman in Sacramento, he was elected chairman of the assembly's Democratic Caucus, the third-ranking position in the leadership. He specialized in criminal justice matters, and pushed through a bill revising the juvenile justice system. He also fought to ban throwaway beverage containers, sponsored creation of the California Arts Council, and favored higher retirement benefits for women in the state public employee system.

**The District:** This racially mixed district is predominantly middle-class and firmly Democratic. Middle-income blacks have been moving in over the past two decades, gradually increasing their political influence among the whites, Hispanics and Asians who also live in the area.

The district includes most of Los Angeles west of the poorer Watts area, plus Culver City — home of the MGM studios — and Inglewood.

The black population in Inglewood has increased substantially in the last decade; Richard Nixon carried the city in 1968 and 1972, but Jimmy Carter defeated Gerald Ford there by a 2-1 margin in 1976, and won it over Ronald Reagan by nearly 3-to-1 in 1980. Culver City, still largely white, is the only Republican holdout in the district.

## Committees

**Appropriations** (26th of 33 Democrats)
District of Columbia, chairman; Foreign Operations.

## Elections

**1980 General**

| | |
|---|---|
| Julian Dixon (D ) | 108,725 (79 %) |
| Robert Reid (R ) | 23,179 (17 %) |

**1978 General**

| | |
|---|---|
| Julian Dixon (D) | Unopposed |

**1978 Primary**

| | |
|---|---|
| Julian Dixon (D ) | 42,988 (50 %) |
| Nate Holden (D ) | 30,162 (35 %) |
| Merle Mergell (D ) | 6,604 (8 %) |

**District Vote For President**

| | 1980 | | 1976 |
|---|---|---|---|
| D | 102,516 (69 %) | D | 104,135 (70 %) |
| R | 36,354 (24 %) | R | 42,972 (29 %) |
| I | 7,733 (5 %) | | |

## Campaign Finance

| | Receipts | Receipts from PACs | Expenditures |
|---|---|---|---|
| **1980** | | | |
| Dixon (D ) | $93,064 | $49,650 (53 %) | $63,822 |

**1978**

| | | | |
|---|---|---|---|
| Dixon (D ) | $233,910 | $56,050 (24 %) | $231,444 |

## Voting Studies

| | Presidential Support | | Party Unity | | Conservative Coalition | |
|---|---|---|---|---|---|---|
| Year | S | O | S | O | S | O |
| 1980 | 63 | 20 | 75 | 4 | 8 | 79 |
| 1979 | 76 | 15 | 84 | 3 | 6 | 84 |

S = Support          O = Opposition

## Key Votes

**96th Congress**

| | |
|---|---|
| Weaken Carter oil profits tax (1979) | N |
| Reject hospital cost control plan (1979) | N |
| Implement Panama Canal Treaties (1979) | Y |
| Establish Department of Education (1979) | Y |
| Approve Anti-busing Amendment (1979) | N |
| Gaurantee Chrysler Corp. loans (1979) | Y |
| Approve Military draft registration (1980) | N |
| Aid Sandinistas regime in Nicaragua (1980) | Y |
| Strengthen Fair Housing Laws (1980) | Y |

**97th Congress**

| | |
|---|---|
| Reagan budget proposal (1981) | N |

## Interest Group Rating

| Year | ADA | ACA | AFL-CIO | CCUS |
|---|---|---|---|---|
| 1980 | 94 | 10 | 88 | 54 |
| 1979 | 79 | 0 | 95 | 12 |

# 29 Augustus F. Hawkins (D)

**Of Los Angeles — Elected in 1962**

**Born:** Aug. 31, 1907, Shreveport, La.
**Education:** U. of Calif., Los Angeles, B.A. 1931.
**Profession:** Real estate executive.
**Family:** Wife, Elsie Taylor.
**Religion:** Methodist.
**Political Career:** Calif. Assembly, 1935-63.

**In Washington:** While other black political leaders have made fiery speeches and demonstrated for civil rights, gentle Gus Hawkins has plodded along, working through the legislative system for jobs, equal opportunity and education bills.

Hawkins is so light-skinned he is frequently mistaken for a white man, and so calm and dispassionate that he sometimes frustrates the more aggressive members of the Congressional Black Caucus. When he has been able to get results by making deals with his opponents, or letting white liberals carry the ball, he has been willing to do so. "Racializing an issue," he once said, "defeats my purpose — which is to get people on my side."

In the 1960s, when his own Watts area erupted in riot, he criticized those who thought militancy was the only approach. "We need clearer thinking and fewer exhibitionists in the civil rights movement," he said.

Hawkins' style has left him as one of the least-recognized members of the Black Caucus, even though he is its senior member. But in any measurement of legislative activity, he ranks as high as any caucus member in recent years.

He is best known for being the second half of the Humphrey-Hawkins full employment bill, a kind of last gasp of the New Deal, which originally set a fixed goal of 4 percent unemployment by 1983 and required the government to become employer of last resort to meet that goal.

But by 1978, when it was passed, public opinion was already moving against public jobs, and the legislation made it through Congress essentially as a memorial to Hubert Humphrey, who had died that year. It was stripped of almost all its strong provisions, including the requirement that the government be the employer of last resort, and its unemployment goals were diluted with the competing objectives of reducing inflation and balancing the budget.

But there is a more substantial monument to Hawkins' legislative work: Title VII of the 1964 Civil Rights Act, which mandated fair employment practices and created the Equal Employment Opportunity Commission.

Hawkins has fought to protect and strengthen the commission ever since, using his place as chairman of the Education and Labor Subcommittee on Employment Opportunities.

In 1972, Hawkins tried to give the commission power to issue cease and desist orders where it found job discrimination. Business groups opposed his bill, and fought to substitute one allowing the commission only to file suit in federal courts. Hawkins also wanted to extend coverage to state and local employees; business did not.

Hawkins won the fight on the liberal Education and Labor Committee, but lost it on the floor. Republican John Erlenborn of Illinois introduced the business bill as a floor amendment, and won by a close vote of 200-194. But Hawkins' supporters conceded that even the substitute strengthened the hand of the EEOC.

On most Education and Labor issues, Hawkins has been a close ally of Phillip Burton, his fellow California Democrat and the panel's chief liberal horse-trader. They have worked together repeatedly on minimum wage and other welfare-related bills, with Hawkins occasionally lobbying other black members to cast votes they otherwise would not cast in exchange for Southern Democratic help on other legislation.

---

**29th District: South Los Angeles — Watts.** Population: 488,347 (5% increase since 1970). Race: White 160,436 (33%), Black 239,578 (49%), Others 88,333 (18%). Spanish origin: 191,229 (39%).

---

In 1972, Hawkins and three other blacks voted against an amendment that would have put a $20,000 lid on subsidies farmers could receive. In return, three Southern Democrats, W. R. Poage and George Mahon of Texas and Jamie Whitten of Mississippi, backed Burton and Hawkins by opposing a prohibition on food stamps for strikers. The deal worked and both amendments failed. The next year Poage and other Southerners helped the Education and Labor bloc raise the minimum wage to an immediate $2.00 an hour, in exchange for farm bill votes later in the year.

In 1981, after 18 years in the House, Hawkins became a full committee chairman. He took over House Administration, the chamber's housekeeping panel, after an Abscam indictment forced New Jersey Democrat Frank Thompson to step down.

The committee normally manages to stay out of controversy, except when it is dealing with election finance. In 1981, however, Hawkins faced an immediate controversy over the budgets of all the other House committees. The new GOP Senate had reduced committee funds by 10 percent, and Republicans demanded the House do the same.

House Administration proposed initially to decrease funding for some committees but increase others. Republican pressure, however, forced the leadership to cut the budgets by 10 percent.

Interestingly, Hawkins had already cut his own House Administration budget by a whopping 19.4 percent, indicating to some that he was an advocate of streamlined House procedures, and to others that his major interest is still labor issues, not the congressional payroll.

When the Congressional Black Caucus was founded in 1971, Hawkins became vice chairman, but he has never played a leadership role and never chaired the group. He did not engage in a suit against President Nixon to stop the Vietnam War, for instance, though he voted against the war. He rarely joined in criticism of President Carter, though Carter's support of Humphrey-Hawkins was an issue in his 1976 campaign, and most black members felt Carter's administration did little to help it get through Congress.

**At Home:** For nearly half a century, Hawkins has been representing black voters in south central Los Angeles. But during all that time — first in the state Assembly, then in Washington — he has always campaigned on economics rather than race. "Race is just not an issue where I am concerned," Hawkins once told a reporter.

It was not much of a subject for Hawkins even in 1962, when he became California's first black member of Congress. "The Negro votes according to his economic interests," Hawkins maintained after that election.

His style had changed little in the 28 years since he had unseated a veteran Republican member of the Assembly. When Hawkins won his first legislative term, in 1934, he said "it wasn't I but the times that beat him." Hawkins won 13 more terms, in good times and bad, before his chance at Congress finally came.

Hawkins' father Nyanza had been a "Hoover Republican" until his son was elected. A British-born adventurer, Nyanza Hawkins had explored Africa before coming to the United States at the turn of the century. After a few years in Louisiana, the Hawkins family moved to California, where Augustus spent a few years in the real estate business, then plunged into Depression-era Democratic politics.

As a member of the Legislature, Hawkins wrote more than 100 pieces of legislation, including a bill to establish child-care centers, which he said was his proudest accomplishment. During his last three years in Sacramento, he was chairman of the Assembly's Rules Committee, a job he was given after he lost the Speakership by two votes. By then he was growing tired of state politics and was looking for a way out.

It came in 1962, when a new, mostly black district was created in Los Angeles. Yielding his Assembly seat to Mervyn Dymally, then a teacher and now a colleague in the House, Hawkins easily won both the primary and the general election. He was the first black member of Congress from any Western state, a fact he characteristically omits from his formal biography.

Although his district has changed its shape three times since then, Hawkins' margins have remained constant. Since he won the 1962 primary by a 54-24 margin over his nearest rival, Hawkins has had only four primary challenges. He has won each with more than 80 percent.

**The District:** The Watts riots of 1965 put Hawkins' district in the headlines. The poverty, unemployment and housing shortage of those days have for the most part remained, although federal and state money began to flow into the district at a much faster pace after the riots.

This is the most secure Democratic district in the state, with 85 percent of its voters registered Democrats. In 1980, Jimmy Carter won nearly 80 percent of the vote in the district, easily his best showing in the state.

There are a few conservative pockets. Several lower-income white communities immediately to the east of Watts — Bell, Cudahy, Huntington Park and South Gate — all supported Ronald

**151**

Reagan in 1980. They currently contribute only about a quarter of the district's vote, but could become more significant after redistricting when the 29th will gain about 35,000 residents.

## Committees

**House Administration** (Chairman)
Task Force on Committee Organization, chairman.

**Education and Labor** (2nd of 19 Democrats)
Employment Opportunities, chairman; Elementary, Secondary and Vocational Education.

**Joint Library** (Chairman)

**Joint Printing**

## Elections

**1980 General**

| | |
|---|---|
| Augustus Hawkins (D ) | 80,095 (86 %) |
| Michael Hirt (R ) | 10,282 (11 %) |

**1978 General**

| | |
|---|---|
| Augustus Hawkins (D ) | 65,214 (85 %) |
| Uriah Fields (R ) | 11,512 (15 %) |

**Previous Winning Percentages**

| | | | |
|---|---|---|---|
| 1976 (85 %) | 1974 (100%) | 1972 (83 %) | 1970 (95 %) |
| 1968 (92 %) | 1966 (85 %) | 1964 (90 %) | 1962 (85 %) |

**District Vote For President**

| | 1980 | | 1976 |
|---|---|---|---|
| D | 80,696 (80 %) | D | 83,291 (80 %) |
| R | 17,564 (17 %) | R | 19,596 (19 %) |
| I | 2,255 (2 %) | | |

## Campaign Finance

| | Receipts | Receipts from PACs | Expenditures |
|---|---|---|---|
| **1980** | | | |
| Hawkins (D ) | $39,784 | $20,900 (53 %) | $33,711 |
| **1978** | | | |
| Hawkins (D ) | $20,925 | $10,675 (51 %) | $13,887 |
| Fields (R ) | $6,609 | $400 (6 %) | $6,602 |

## Voting Studies

| | Presidential Support | | Party Unity | | Conservative Coalition | |
|---|---|---|---|---|---|---|
| Year | S | O | S | O | S | O |
| 1980 | 62 | 24 | 69 | 4 | 2 | 79 |
| 1979 | 75 | 14 | 81 | 2 | 3 | 84 |
| 1978 | 63 | 15 | 75 | 3 | 7 | 74 |

| | | | | | | |
|---|---|---|---|---|---|---|
| 1977 | 57 | 18 | 74 | 4 | 6 | 69 |
| 1976 | 20 | 65 | 73 | 3 | 8 | 68 |
| 1975 | 34 | 61 | 81 | 5 | 5 | 82 |
| 1974 (Ford) | 26 | 33 | | | | |
| 1974 | 28 | 34 | 60 | 3 | 2 | 62 |
| 1973 | 20 | 63 | 78 | 6 | 5 | 77 |
| 1972 | 35 | 32 | 58 | 3 | 0 | 62 |
| 1971 | 30 | 53 | 66 | 11 | 7 | 76 |
| 1970 | 29 | 18 | 57 | 10 | 7 | 66 |
| 1969 | 36 | 47 | 71 | 7 | 2 | 87 |
| 1968 | 46 | 4 | 49 | 1 | 0 | 47 |
| 1967 | 75 | 10 | 84 | 1 | 2 | 85 |
| 1966 | 54 | 4 | 56 | 0 | 3 | 65 |
| 1965 | 79 | 5 | 82 | 2 | 2 | 86 |
| 1964 | 88 | 0 | 89 | 0 | 0 | 92 |
| 1963 | 80 | 3 | 84 | 0 | 0 | 93 |

S = Support     O = Opposition

## Key Votes

**96th Congress**

| | |
|---|---|
| Weaken Carter oil profits tax (1979) | ? |
| Reject hospital cost control plan (1979) | N |
| Implement Panama Canal Treaties (1979) | Y |
| Establish Department of Education (1979) | Y |
| Approve Anti-busing Amendment (1979) | N |
| Guarantee Chrysler Corp. loans (1979) | Y |
| Approve military draft registration (1980) | N |
| Aid Sandinista regime in Nicaragua (1980) | Y |
| Strengthen fair housing laws (1980) | Y |

**97th Congress**

| | |
|---|---|
| Reagan budget proposal (1981) | N |

## Interest Group Ratings

| Year | ADA | ACA | AFL-CIO | CCUS |
|---|---|---|---|---|
| 1980 | 89 | 6 | 88 | 59 |
| 1979 | 74 | 0 | 93 | 0 |
| 1978 | 75 | 16 | 82 | 18 |
| 1977 | 60 | 4 | 90 | 0 |
| 1976 | 70 | 8 | 96 | 6 |
| 1975 | 84 | 12 | 100 | 13 |
| 1974 | 87 | 0 | 100 | 0 |
| 1973 | 88 | 14 | 91 | 20 |
| 1972 | 81 | 6 | 90 | 13 |
| 1971 | 81 | 5 | 100 | - |
| 1970 | 84 | 0 | 100 | 0 |
| 1969 | 100 | 7 | 100 | - |
| 1968 | 92 | 0 | 100 | - |
| 1967 | 93 | 4 | 100 | 0 |
| 1966 | 94 | 6 | 92 | - |
| 1965 | 95 | 0 | - | 10 |
| 1964 | 96 | 0 | 100 | - |
| 1963 | - | - | - | - |

# 30 George E. Danielson (D)

**Of Monterey Park — Elected in 1970**

**Born:** Feb. 20, 1915, Wausa, Neb.
**Education:** U. of Neb., B.A. 1937, J.D. 1939.
**Military Career:** Navy, 1944-46.
**Profession:** Lawyer, FBI agent.
**Family:** Wife, Candy Ohanian.
**Religion:** Protestant.
**Political Career:** Calif. Senate, 1967-71; Calif. Assembly, 1963-67.

**In Washington:** Danielson is like a good sergeant in the Army — he complains a lot, but when the big battles come up, he can be counted on to back the brass and provide leadership to his platoon.

He has offered yeoman service to his party for more than a decade in Congress, chairing the Democrats in his state's delegation, serving on the Democratic Steering Committee as a leadership loyalist, and lining up votes for leadership positions as a deputy whip.

At one point in 1977, that required him to stand in the well of the House and physically prevent Democrats from reaching a table where they could change their votes on a congressional pay raise. Many members had second thoughts and wanted to reverse their support of the raise to avoid criticism back home. But if many of them did that, it would be defeated. Danielson helped the leadership prevent it.

Danielson's own vote is one the party can reliably count on getting. In 1980, he ranked fourth among all members in support for President Carter. He voted with a majority of the Democrats 90 percent of the time.

On Judiciary, where he is a senior member, Danielson has often been asked to promote bills that are controversial, unpopular, or even futile. At times, mired in marathon debate over legal technicalities that few outside the committee understand, he has complained that service on Judiciary is itself no prize. "I went home and tried talking about my committee work," he once told a reporter, "making changes in the federal copyright law. After everybody fell asleep, I started talking about swine flu," Danielson said.

He said, "The Judiciary Committee is possibly the lousiest committee in Congress for raising campaign funds," adding that lawyers are about the only people interested in its work.

As chairman of the Judiciary Subcommittee on Administrative Law, Danielson has the worst of both worlds. His legislation is not only boring to the average citizen, it is controversial within the House and difficult to pass. A visitor to his office during one of these long legislative arguments is likely to hear him say he wishes only that they could be finished so he could move on to something else. But he rarely manages to extricate himself from his legalistic chores.

For three years in a row Danielson worked hard to produce a lobby disclosure bill. It has yet to become law, and seems unlikely to in the foreseeable future. In the 96th Congress he worked hard for the Carter administration to produce a bill streamlining the federal regulatory process. But it never reached the floor.

Danielson did push through to enactment a 1978 ethics in government bill, designed to prevent the "revolving door" effect produced by bureaucrats who leave federal employment, then go to work for the private sector to lobby the agency they just left.

But the bill placed such severe restrictions on contact between the ex-bureaucrats and their agencies that it produced a backlash of resentment. Danielson agreed to go back and modify the law in 1979.

He got the modification passed, but found himself in a delicate controversy involving Speaker O'Neill. The Speaker wanted the effec-

**30th District: Los Angeles County — El Monte.** Population: 504,331 (9% increase since 1970). Race: White 331,037 (65%), Black 6,092 (1%), Asian and Pacific Islander 37,728 (7%), Others 129,474 (27%). Spanish origin: 314,709 (62%).

**153**

tive date of the original law moved back three months —reportedly at the request of two ex-Carter Cabinet officers, Joseph Califano and Brock Adams, both highly popular in the House.

Danielson got this provision through Judiciary, and was ready to bring it to the floor when newspaper publicity led to demands that it be removed. Finally Danielson dropped it, letting it be known it was O'Neill's idea, not his.

Meanwhile, Danielson was working on his third version of a bill requiring lobbyists to report more on their activities and their sources of funding.

Danielson produced a strong bill from his subcommittee, but it was drastically weakened in the full committee. "I feel like I came with a steak, but left with a hamburger," he said. The bill died in the Rules Committee amid a shortage of enthusiasm on all sides of the issue.

The bill to ease regulatory procedures, Danielson's other major project of the 96th Congress, died amid controversy over a congressional veto of federal regulations. The Carter White House adamantly opposed this provision, and preferred no bill at all rather than one with a veto in it. Most House members, on the other hand, wanted the veto.

Danielson got the bill out of committee by compromising, providing for a veto only by both chambers of Congress, with the president's signature required at the end. This did not satisfy veto champion Elliott Levitas, D-Ga., who at one point had threatened to prevent Danielson's committee from even meeting unless he was promised a chance to offer his one-house veto on the floor. Danielson promised, but that caused the White House to back away from the bill and it died in the lame-duck session of 1980.

As much as Danielson complains about his legislative fate, the Judiciary Committee is the perfect place for him. A lawyer and ex-FBI agent, he has always been a stickler for detail. He can prolong Judiciary meetings for hours by going over legal arguments and objections. Liberal by instinct but politically cautious, he will frequently give a "yes, but" endorsement to a bill, then work on it until he is happy with the fine print, not just the broad outlines that would satisfy most members.

He is for the Equal Rights Amendment, but he is worried about drafting women, so he supported a Republican proposal to exempt them from the draft. On the floor, however, ERA supporters expressed the fear that any amendments might cripple the proposal, so he agreed to drop his objection. He voted several times to create a consumer protection agency, but against giving it

power to sue other agencies or represent consumers in hearings.

One issue on which he does not split hairs is the Legal Services Corporation. Even before President Reagan proposed cutting off its funding, Danielson had been one of its strong Judiciary Committee defenders. He has offered past amendments to add to the legal services budget.

**At Home:** Danielson is not personally invincible here, but the district's Democratic nature and the absence of serious opposition granted him routine re-election throughout the 1970s. In the last three campaigns, he has been unopposed for the Democratic nomination and has consistently taken more than 70 percent of the vote in the fall.

Those figures, however, mask a potential problem for him in the district's huge Hispanic community, now more than half the population. Earlier in his career, Danielson faced spirited Hispanic primary competition, especially from Richard Calderon, a Chicano political activist from Monterey Park. When Danielson campaigned for promotion from the Assembly to the state Senate in 1966, Calderon came within 501 votes of beating him. Two years later, Danielson ran for re-election, and Calderon held him to 51 percent. When Democrat George E. Brown Jr. left the House in 1970 to run for the Senate, the stage was set for another Danielson-Calderon battle. Calderon was a protégé of Brown, and he again dominated the Mexican-American vote. But Danielson had the advantage of already representing most of the constituency in the Legislature, and held on for a third triumph, 47 percent to 43.

Danielson had to wage his first three congressional campaigns in three different districts. The 1972 redistricting took out some Mexican-American parts of East Los Angeles and added middle-class Democrats in Baldwin Park. That was enough to discourage Calderon from trying again. But in 1974, when more Chicanos were added from the district of retiring Democrat Chet Holifield, Danielson had another major challenge, this time from Esteban Ed Torres, a United Auto Workers organizer. Once again Danielson's weakness in the Mexican-American precincts held him to barely 50 percent, but Torres could not win enough Anglo votes to unseat him.

**The District:** This is industrial suburban territory with a predominant Mexican-American influence. Small tract houses and rows of palm trees sit alongside acres of land devoted to building rocket motors, automobile parts, and electronic components.

The Chicano vote is strongest in the southern

part of the district, in Commerce and Pico Rivera. Democrats amass large majorities in this area, part of which is represented by a Hispanic in the state Legislature.

To the north and east, abutting the southern side of Republican John Rousselot's 26th District, are ethnically mixed towns like Monterey Park, Rosemead and El Monte, ones which register Democratic but which Republicans sometimes carry. Ronald Reagan took all three in 1980.

## Committees

**Judiciary** (7th of 16 Democrats)
Administrative Law and Governmental Relations, chairman; Courts, Civil Liberties and Administration of Justice.

**Post Office and Civil Service** (12th of 15 Democrats)
Civil Service; Compensation and Employee Benefits; Human Resources.

**Veterans' Affairs** (3rd of 17 Democrats)
Compensation, Pension and Insurance; Oversight and Investigations.

## Elections

**1980 General**

| | |
|---|---|
| George Danielson (D ) | 74,119 (72 %) |
| J. Arthur Platten (R ) | 24,136 (24 %) |

**1978 General**

| | |
|---|---|
| George Danielson (D ) | 66,241 (71 %) |
| Henry Ares (R ) | 26,511 (29 %) |

**Previous Winning Percentages**

| | | | |
|---|---|---|---|
| 1976 (74 %) | 1974 (74 %) | 1972 (63 %) | 1970 (63 %) |

**District Vote For President**

| | 1980 | | 1976 |
|---|---|---|---|
| D | 52,905 (48 %) | D | 69,424 (59 %) |
| R | 48,350 (44 %) | R | 46,152 (39 %) |
| I | 6,550 (6 %) | | |

## Campaign Finance

| | Receipts | Receipts from PACs | Expenditures |
|---|---|---|---|
| **1980** | | | |
| Danielson (D ) | $113,100 | $51,725 (46 %) | $79,852 |
| Platten (R ) | $5,060 | $1,615 (32 %) | $5,006 |
| **1978** | | | |
| Danielson (D ) | $82,516 | $25,770 (31 %) | $98,834 |
| Ares (R ) | $50,820 | $11,211 (22 %) | $50,823 |

## Voting Studies

| Year | Presidential Support | | Party Unity | | Conservative Coalition | |
|---|---|---|---|---|---|---|
| | S | O | S | O | S | O |
| 1980 | 83 | 12 | 90 | 3 | 20 | 77 |
| 1979 | 86 | 12 | 92 | 3 | 15 | 81 |
| 1978 | 77 | 17 | 84 | 7 | 14 | 79 |
| 1977 | 72 | 25 | 90 | 7 | 21 | 78 |
| 1976 | 29 | 67 | 85 | 11 | 22 | 71 |
| 1975 | 45 | 48 | 73 | 15 | 28 | 62 |
| 1974 (Ford) | 39 | 54 | | | | |
| 1974 | 45 | 43 | 75 | 8 | 18 | 68 |
| 1973 | 22 | 47 | 70 | 4 | 12 | 64 |
| 1972 | 51 | 41 | 75 | 11 | 21 | 71 |
| 1971 | 49 | 49 | 83 | 11 | 15 | 80 |

S = Support        O = Opposition

## Key Votes

**96th Congress**

| | |
|---|---|
| Weaken Carter oil profits tax (1979) | N |
| Reject hospital cost control plan (1979) | N |
| Implement Panama Canal Treaties (1979) | Y |
| Establish Department of Education (1979) | Y |
| Approve Anti-busing Amendment (1979) | N |
| Guarantee Chrysler Corp. loans (1979) | Y |
| Approve military draft registration (1980) | Y |
| Aid Sandinista regime in Nicaragua (1980) | Y |
| Strengthen fair housing laws (1980) | Y |

**97th Congress**

| | |
|---|---|
| Reagan budget proposal (1981) | N |

## Interest Group Ratings

| Year | ADA | ACA | AFL-CIO | CCUS |
|---|---|---|---|---|
| 1980 | 67 | 18 | 88 | 64 |
| 1979 | 84 | 0 | 85 | 11 |
| 1978 | 60 | 4 | 85 | 18 |
| 1977 | 60 | 15 | 91 | 6 |
| 1976 | 75 | 19 | 96 | 13 |
| 1975 | 68 | 23 | 91 | 12 |
| 1974 | 74 | 0 | 100 | 13 |
| 1973 | 60 | 5 | 88 | 20 |
| 1972 | 75 | 29 | 91 | 20 |
| 1971 | 73 | 15 | 92 | - |

# 31 Mervyn M. Dymally (D)

**Of Compton — Elected 1980**

**Born:** May 12, 1926, Cedros, Trinidad.
**Education:** Calif. State U., Los Angeles, B.A.
1954; Calif. State U., Sacramento, M.A. 1969;
U.S. International Univ., Ph.D. 1978.
**Profession:** Teacher.
**Family:** Wife, Alice Gueno; two children.
**Religion:** Episcopalian.
**Political Career:** Calif. Assembly, 1963-67;
Calif. Senate 1967-75; Calif. lt. gov., 1975-79,
unsuccessfully sought re-election, 1978.

**The Member:** Dymally's smashing victory
over Democratic Rep. Charles H. Wilson resurrected a political career whose future looked bleak
after a humiliating statewide loss in 1978.

Glib and gregarious, Dymally had become
California's leading black officeholder over a 15-
year career that was not derailed by a series of
unproven corruption charges. In 1974, running
with Democratic gubernatorial nominee Edmund
G. Brown Jr., he was elected as the state's first
black lieutenant governor. But four years later,
seeking a second term in a job he himself said was
not very enjoyable, Dymally received only 43
percent against Republican Mike Curb.

His 1980 comeback was aided by Wilson's
legal problems, which stemmed from alleged financial misconduct as a member of the House.
Wilson had won renomination to his last two
terms only because of split primary opposition.

In 1980, the opposition was divided again
between Dymally and former Democratic Rep.
Mark W. Hannaford. But Dymally had solid
backing from blacks and strong support from the
liberal political machine run by U.S. Rep. Henry
A. Waxman and Assemblyman Howard Berman.

When a State Department lawyer told a
House subcommittee that the federal government
should be able to override District of Columbia
zoning laws to provide land for foreign embassies,
Dymally accused him of harboring a "colonial
attitude" toward the district.

**The District:** The 31st District is a collection of suburbs in southern Los Angeles County,
without much local political identity but with
strong Democratic leanings. In recent years the
black population has increased substantially,
much of it in nearly all-black Compton. The
district also includes Gardena, a sizable Asian-
American enclave, and the blue- and white-collar
suburbs of Hawthorne and Torrance, where defense-related industries provide many of the jobs.

## Committees

**Foreign Affairs** (18th of 21 Democrats)
Asian and Pacific Affairs; Human Rights and International Organizations.

**Science and Technology** (23rd of 23 Democrats)
Science, Research and Technology; Transportation, Aviation
and Materials.

## Elections

**1980 General**

| | |
|---|---|
| Mervyn Dymally (D ) | 69,146 (64 %) |
| Don Grimshaw (R ) | 38,203 (36 %) |

**1980 Primary**

| | |
|---|---|
| Mervyn Dymally (D ) | 29,916 (49 %) |
| Mark Hannaford (D ) | 14,512 (24 %) |
| Charles Wilson (D ) | 9,320 (15 %) |
| B.E. Henschel (D ) | 4,953 (8 %) |

**District Vote For President**

| | 1980 | | 1976 |
|---|---|---|---|
| D | 68,544 (59 %) | D | 72,775 (65 %) |
| R | 39,927 (35 %) | R | 38,052 (34 %) |
| I | 5,242 (5 %) | | |

## Campaign Finance

| | Receipts | Receipts from PACs | Expen-ditures |
|---|---|---|---|
| **1980** | | | |
| Dymally (D ) | $494,254 | $82,230 (17 %) | $540,807 |
| Grimshaw (R ) | $3,642 | — (0 %) | $3,750 |

## Key Vote

**97th Congress**

| | |
|---|---|
| Reagan budget proposal (1981) | N |

> **31st District: Southern Los Angeles
> County — Compton.** Population: 463,513
> (No change since 1970). Race: White 182,082
> (39%), Black 168,685 (36%), Asian and Pacific
> Islander 32,153 (7%), Others 80,593 (17%).
> Spanish origin: 123,947 (27%).

# 32 Glenn M. Anderson (D)

### Of Harbor City — Elected 1968

**Born:** Feb. 21, 1913, Hawthorne, Calif.
**Education:** U. of Calif., Los Angeles, B.A. 1936.
**Military Career:** U.S. Army, 1943-45.
**Profession:** Savings and loan executive.
**Family:** Wife, Lee Dutton; three children.
**Religion:** Episcopalian.
**Political Career:** Mayor of Hawthorne, 1940-43; Calif. Assembly, 1943-51; Calif. lt. gov., 1959-67.

**In Washington:** A mild-mannered fellow who likes to avoid confrontations, Anderson was unable to escape them in his six years as chairman of the heavily lobbied Public Works Subcommittee on Aviation. He ended his tenure there voluntarily in 1981, switching to the Surface Transportation chairmanship, which allows him to work on a subject of personal interest to him, but one which could bring him nearly as much controversy.

The aviation panel makes basic decisions about how American airports should be financed and run and about which planes should land there. Airlines and aircraft companies are its clients, and within the industry, the major commercial carriers compete for favorable treatment with those who make and use private planes. Anderson, with a strong aircraft industry in his own district, has had to steer his way among the interests. But he tends to be less than forceful in his approach.

After a two-year crusade against airport noise, Anderson drafted a noise control bill in his subcommittee in 1979. But when the bill reached the full committee, it fell victim to a more industry-oriented substitute backed by Chairman Harold (Bizz) Johnson of California, that would have allowed noisier small planes to land at large airports.

Anderson said the bill had been ruined "at the behest of the airline industry and the airframe and engine manufacturers." It never reached the House floor, but the Senate added its own noise control language to an unrelated bill. In the complex conference that followed, a majority of the conferees voted for relatively mild standards. After weeks of urging by anti-noise Democrats, Anderson agreed to oppose that. President Carter promised to veto it. The conferees went back and drew up a slightly tougher bill.

Anderson took the second agreement back to the House floor, saying "it's not what I would have liked, but it's the best we could get." It became law early in 1980.

Anderson had had similar problems on the issue of airline deregulation, which was one of President Carter's initial legislative priorities. Lukewarm about deregulation, Anderson tried at first to tie it to a noise control bill, hoping to draw Carter's support on the noise issue. Then he went along with the concept and worked 10 weeks on it in subcommittee, only to have the panel switch at the last minute to a weaker version allowing far more government supervision of airline routes. But a compromise was ultimately reached, the subcommittee reconvened and a measure acceptable to the Carter administration became law.

Meanwhile, Anderson kept his hand in the issue of mass transit, which the Surface Transportation Subcommittee wrestles with. Early in his career, Anderson was a strong supporter of efforts to "bust" the Highway Trust Fund in order to make its money available for mass transit. He clashed frequently with the trust fund's main defender of that era, Rep. Gerald R. Ford of Michigan. Ford won most of the early skirmishes, but the fund was eventually opened up on a limited basis, although not to the extent mass transit advocates preferred.

In 1981, Anderson went along with full Public Works Chairman James J. Howard, D-N.J., in

> **32nd District: Southern Los Angeles — Part of Long Beach.** Population: 474,215 (2% increase since 1970). Race: White 292,975 (62%), Black 66,606 (14%), Asian and Pacific Islander 43,332 (9%), Others 71,302 (15%). Spanish origin: 123,690 (26%).

**Glenn M. Anderson, D-Calif.**

rejecting Reagan efforts to make drastic revisions in federal highway programs. Reagan wanted to shift the emphasis away from new construction and toward repairs and eliminate the federal share in costs for many urban and rural highways. The committee basically continued existing programs for another year, although it did agree to changes reducing the cost of completing the Interstate Highway System.

**At Home:** Anderson comes across at home as the quiet, successful businessman more than content to stay out of the limelight. And except for one traumatic moment, when he was lieutenant governor, he has stayed out of the limelight successfully throughout his political career.

Anderson entered politics early. At age 27 he was elected mayor of Hawthorne, a Los Angeles suburb which then had 8,000 people. (It now has 56,000.) At that point, Anderson already was a prosperous businessman. After getting his college degree in political science and psychology, he had embarked on a profitable career selling automobiles, running a car repair shop and operating a service station.

Anderson went from the Hawthorne city hall to four terms in the state Assembly, where he wrote legislation abolishing segregated schools in California. He was defeated for a state Senate seat in 1950 and spent most of the 1950s expanding his home construction business. He sserved two years as state Democratic chairman.

In 1958, Anderson returned to public office on the coattails of Edmund G. (Pat) Brown, who was elected governor. For two terms as Brown's lieutenant governor, Anderson quietly and efficiently carried out the thankless tasks Brown gave him to do. He specialized in education and urban problems and was a ceaseless cheerleader for Brown's programs in the Legislature, where he presided benignly over the Senate. He differed with Brown on only a few issues, one of which was Brown's support of John F. Kennedy for the 1960 Democratic nomination. Anderson was for Adlai Stevenson.

Brown frequently traveled outside California, leaving Anderson in charge, and that caused no problems until August of 1965, when race riots broke out in the Watts area of Los Angeles while Brown was vacationing in Greece. Anderson was not quick to respond and by the time he sent in the National Guard the situation was out of control with 35 dead, hundreds injured and millions of dollars in damages. Anderson's hesitancy to act was used against him the next year as he and Brown lost the statehouse to Republicans

Ronald Reagan and Robert H. Finch.

Once again, however, Anderson came back, and this time it took only two years. In 1968, Democrat Cecil R. King retired after serving more than 26 years in the House from the Torrance-San Pedro area.

In both the Democratic primary and the general election, Anderson tried to convince voters he was "a conservative in economic matters and a liberal in human matters." His major primary opponent, Los Angeles city Councilman John S. Gibson Jr., and his Republican opponent, Joseph Blatchford, both sought to persuade voters Anderson was too liberal on all matters.

Anderson won the primary with 35 percent and was helped in the fall by a strong presidential vote in the district for Hubert H. Humphrey. The local Democratic strength allowed Anderson to edge past Blatchford with less than 4,000 votes to spare.

By 1970 the exciting days of Anderson's political career were past. He was able to win re-election over GOP nominee Michael C. Donaldson by a comfortable margin.

Although subsequent redistricting has removed Anderson's boyhood home and original political base from the district, he has had little trouble keeping Democratic support firmly behind him.

**The District:** Driving through the 32nd District on either the San Diego or Harbor Freeway, it is easy to see what fuels the economy of the area. Aerospace and automobile plants extend for miles, large tracts of flat, brown land are given over to fuel storage tanks, and closer to the San Pedro Harbor, shipyards and fishing fleets clutter the horizon.

Symbolic of the district's devotion to all forms of transportation, the Goodyear blimp makes its home at the intersection of the district's two major expressways. And the Queen Mary rests at the foot of the Long Beach Freeway.

Set back from these transportation arteries are the homes of the black, Asian, Hispanic and other ethnic voters who live and work in the district. In most years, they are Democratic. Ronald Reagan won nearly every section of the district in 1980, but he is the only presidential, senatorial or gubernatorial candidate on the GOP side who has carried the district under its current boundaries.

Besides Carson, with its heavy minority vote, the district includes about half of Long Beach, the poorer third of Torrance and the San Pedro section of the city of Los Angeles.

## Committees

**Merchant Marine and Fisheries** (3rd of 20 Democrats)
Fisheries and Wildlife Conservation and the Environment; Merchant Marine.

**Public Works and Transportation** (2nd of 25 Democrats)
Surface Transportation, chairman; Aviation; Water Resources.

## Elections

**1980 General**

| | |
|---|---|
| Glenn Anderson (D ) | 84,057 (66 %) |
| John Adler (R ) | 39,260 (31 %) |

**1980 Primary**

| | |
|---|---|
| Glenn Anderson (D) | 43,475 (85 %) |
| Edward Jamison (D ) | 7,911 (15 %) |

**1978 General**

| | |
|---|---|
| Glenn Anderson (D) | 74,004 (71 %) |
| Sonya Mathison (R ) | 23,242 (22 %) |
| Ida Bader (I ) | 6,363 (6 %) |

**Previous Winning Percentages**

1976 (72 %)    1974 (88 %)    1972 (75 %)    1970 (62 %)
1968 (51 %)

**District Vote For President**

| | 1980 | | 1976 |
|---|---|---|---|
| D | 58,065 (43 %) | D | 72,386 (54 %) |
| R | 64,967 (48 %) | R | 58,147 (44 %) |
| I | 8,728 (7 %) | | |

## Campaign Finance

| | Receipts | Receipts from PACs | Expenditures |
|---|---|---|---|
| **1980** | | | |
| Anderson (D ) | $137,564 | $66,897 (49 %) | $153,001 |
| Adler (R ) | $30,720 | $500 (2 %) | $33,878 |
| **1978** | | | |
| Anderson (D ) | $91,260 | $25,950 (28 %) | $109,228 |

## Voting Studies

| | Presidential Support | | Party Unity | | Conservative Coalition | |
|---|---|---|---|---|---|---|
| Year | S | O | S | O | S | O |
| 1980 | 67 | 30 | 73 | 22 | 41 | 55 |
| 1979 | 60 | 39 | 69 | 26 | 38 | 58 |
| 1978 | 63 | 36 | 75 | 21 | 26 | 71 |
| 1977 | 63 | 34 | 68 | 26 | 30 | 64 |
| 1976 | 25 | 71 | 81 | 15 | 26 | 71 |
| 1975 | 26 | 69 | 75 | 22 | 29 | 67 |
| 1974 (Ford) | 31 | 56 | | | | |
| 1974 | 45 | 45 | 76 | 13 | 21 | 69 |
| 1973 | 30 | 64 | 80 | 13 | 11 | 83 |
| 1972 | 49 | 38 | 80 | 10 | 9 | 77 |
| 1971 | 44 | 53 | 79 | 16 | 14 | 81 |
| 1970 | 57 | 37 | 76 | 17 | 11 | 82 |
| 1969 | 51 | 47 | 91 | 7 | 9 | 89 |

†Not eligible for all recorded votes.

S = Support          O = Opposition

## Key Votes

**96th Congress**

| | |
|---|---|
| Weaken Carter oil profits tax (1979) | Y |
| Reject hospital cost control plan (1979) | N |
| Implement Panama Canal Treaties (1979) | N |
| Establish Department of Education (1979) | Y |
| Approve Anti-busing Amendment (1979) | Y |
| Guarantee Chrysler Corp. loans (1979) | Y |
| Approve military draft registration (1980) | N |
| Aid Sandinista regime in Nicaragua (1980) | Y |
| Strengthen fair housing laws (1980) | Y |

**97th Congress**

| | |
|---|---|
| Reagan budget proposal (1981) | N |

## Interest Group Ratings

| Year | ADA | ACA | AFL-CIO | CCUS |
|---|---|---|---|---|
| 1980 | 72 | 33 | 67 | 53 |
| 1979 | 63 | 38 | 61 | 40 |
| 1978 | 60 | 41 | 80 | 11 |
| 1977 | 65 | 35 | 77 | 24 |
| 1976 | 85 | 25 | 91 | 13 |
| 1975 | 58 | 42 | 83 | 25 |
| 1974 | 70 | 7 | 100 | 0 |
| 1973 | 92 | 8 | 91 | 18 |
| 1972 | 75 | 10 | 91 | 0 |
| 1971 | 89 | 14 | 100 | - |
| 1970 | 84 | 12 | 100 | 10 |
| 1969 | 87 | 18 | 100 | - |

# 33 Wayne Grisham (R)

**Of La Mirada — Elected 1978**

**Born:** Jan. 10, 1923, Lamar, Colo.
**Education:** Long Beach City College, A.A. 1947;
Whittier College, B.A. 1949.
**Military Career:** Army Air Corps, 1942-46.
**Profession:** Real estate broker.
**Family:** Wife, Millie Watt; three children.
**Religion:** Methodist.
**Political Career:** La Mirada City Council,
1970-78; Mayor of La Mirada, 1973-74; 1977-
78; GOP nominee for Calif. Assembly, 1976.

**In Washington:** A genial real estate man who reached Congress after a decade in local politics, Grisham has occupied his safe seat quietly and with a minimum of independent action.

Saddled in his first term with two secondary committee assignments — Government Operations and Veterans' Affairs — he traded them in at the beginning of 1981 for Public Works and Post Office and Civil Service.

While on Government Operations, he was involved in one important decision, over whether to give President Carter the new Department of Education he badly wanted. Grisham, like most Republicans, was unequivocally against it. When Vice President Mondale noted that every country in Europe had a national ministry of education, Grisham said it was a "wonderful thing that we don't have a national ministry of education."

On the House floor, Grisham has spoken only on rare occasions, mainly to echo GOP support for popular conservative causes. He endorsed a constitutional amendment against busing, arguing that the American people will not "sit in silence while miles away a handful of 'experts' move their children as if they were merely pawns in a master chess game."

Grisham joined fundamentalist church officials in a rally at the Capitol in support of a constitutional amendment to restore prayer in the public schools, and signed a petition to move a prayer amendment out of the House Judiciary Committee. He spoke up in defense of the tax exempt status of private academies accused by the Internal Revenue Service of violating federal desegregation standards.

**At Home:** Grisham won the right to succeed popular Republican Del Clawson by convincing voters he would represent them in the conservative manner they had become accustomed to. Now in his second term, he has not disappointed them.

A native of Colorado, Grisham moved to Southern California as a boy and has lived ever since in suburban Los Angeles. After World War II, in which he was a prisoner of war of the Germans, he returned home and settled in La Mirada, a comfortable middle-class suburb adjoining Whittier on the southeast side of Los Angeles County. At first Grisham taught school; then he switched to real estate. He was 47 years old when he entered politics in 1970, winning election to the La Mirada City Council. During eight years on the council he twice served as mayor.

By 1978, Clawson was ready to retire after 15 years in the House. Even though Grisham had won another term on the council just three months before the June congressional primary, he was not well-known in the district's major communities — Norwalk, Downey and Whittier. But with seven Republicans competing to succeed Clawson, loyalties in the other towns were divided. Grisham had unified support from La Mirada, and his 24 percent took the primary.

In the general election, Grisham contrasted his staid image against that of his much younger Democratic opponent, Dennis Kazarian. Seeking to exploit resentment toward Kazarian's personal wealth and brief residency in the district, Grisham stressed that as a fellow homeowner, he shared the concerns of the average voter. He rarely discussed issues other than his support for

---

**33rd District: Eastern Los Angeles County — Norwalk.** Population: 521,986 (12% increase since 1970). Race: White 426,804 (82%), Black 10,210 (2%), Asian and Pacific Islander 31,519 (6%), Others 53,453 (10%). Spanish origin: 137,204 (26%).

the Kemp-Roth tax cut and the recently-passed tax-cutting Proposition 13. But that was the most popular message of the year. Voters elected Grisham with 56 percent in a district where Democrats still slightly outnumber Republicans.

**The District:** It was assumed for years that this district would go Democratic once Clawson departed. A figure of wide personal respect, Clawson himself fell below 55 percent in his last two campaigns, and much of the area is under Democratic representation in the Legislature.

But that belief ignored the area's growing Republican sentiment, which was demonstrated dramatically again in 1980 with Reagan's 63 percent showing and Grisham's own 71 percent re-election.

The 33rd wanders about 25 miles, from the southern edge of Pomona to Cerritos along the southern border of Los Angeles County. About 80 percent of the voters and most of the political action are concentrated in the western end, in the collection of suburbs that includes Whittier, Downey, Norwalk and Cerritos.

Cerritos and Whittier — which was the childhood home of Richard Nixon — are largely upper-middle class Republican communities. The district's Democratic vote is concentrated in Norwalk and heavily Mexican-American Santa Fe Springs. Downey, the home of a large North American Rockwell plant, has a working class neighborhood similar to Norwalk's, but also has many more white-collar workers and generally votes Republican.

## Committees

**Post Office and Civil Service** (9th of 11 Republicans)
Census and Population; Investigations; Postal Personnel and Modernization.

**Public Works and Transportation** (13th of 19 Republicans)
Aviation; Water Resources.

## Elections

**1980 General**

| | |
|---|---|
| Wayne Grisham (R ) | 122,439 (71 %) |
| Fred Anderson (D ) | 50,365 (29 %) |

**1980 Primary**

| | |
|---|---|
| Wayne Grisham (R ) | 39,301 (76 %) |
| Mike Manicone (R ) | 12,736 (24 %) |

**1978 General**

| | |
|---|---|
| Wayne Grisham (R ) | 79,533 (56 %) |
| Dennis Kazarian (D ) | 62,540 (44 %) |

**1978 Primary**

| | |
|---|---|
| Wayne Grisham (R ) | 14,013 (24 %) |
| William Greene (R ) | 12,113 (21 %) |
| Albert Zapanta (R ) | 11,711 (20 %) |
| Others (R ) | 20,885 (36 %) |

**District Vote For President**

| | 1980 | | 1976 |
|---|---|---|---|
| D | 53,102 (29 %) | D | 75,709 (43 %) |
| R | 114,894 (63 %) | R | 99,127 (56 %) |
| I | 11,464 (6 %) | | |

## Campaign Finance

| | Receipts | Receipts from PACs | Expenditures |
|---|---|---|---|
| **1980** | | | |
| Grisham (R ) | $104,330 | $54,690 (52 %) | $97,778 |

| **1978** | | | |
|---|---|---|---|
| Grisham (R ) | $162,707 | $51,774 (32 %) | $162,423 |
| Kazarian (D ) | $124,901 | $14,323 (11 %) | $109,248 |

## Voting Studies

| | Presidential Support | | Party Unity | | Conservative Coalition | |
|---|---|---|---|---|---|---|
| Year | S | O | S | O | S | O |
| 1980 | 36 | 56 | 79 | 12 | 82 | 9 |
| 1979 | 23 | 76 | 90 | 9 | 92 | 7 |

S = Support       O = Opposition

## Key Votes

**96th Congress**

| | |
|---|---|
| Weaken Carter oil profits tax (1979) | Y |
| Reject hospital cost control plan (1979) | Y |
| Implement Panama Canal Treaties (1979) | N |
| Establish Department of Education (1979) | N |
| Approve Anti-busing Amendment (1979) | Y |
| Guarantee Chrysler Corp. loans (1979) | N |
| Approve military draft registration (1980) | Y |
| Aid Sandinista regime in Nicaragua (1980) | N |
| Strengthen fair housing laws (1980) | N |

**97th Congress**

| | |
|---|---|
| Reagan budget proposal (1981) | Y |

## Interest Group Ratings

| Year | ADA | ACA | AFL-CIO | CCUS |
|---|---|---|---|---|
| 1980 | 6 | 90 | 6 | 74 |
| 1979 | 5 | 92 | 15 | 94 |

# 34 Dan Lungren (R)

Of Long Beach — Elected 1978

**Born:** Sept. 22, 1946, Long Beach, Calif.
**Education:** U. of Notre Dame, B.A. 1968; Georgetown U., J.D. 1971.
**Profession:** Lawyer.
**Family:** Wife, Barbara Kolls; three children.
**Religion:** Roman Catholic.
**Political Career:** Republican nominee for U.S. House, 34th District, 1976.

**In Washington:** From the beginning of his first term, Lungren has been one of the loudest of the junior Republicans on the House floor, lashing out at the opposition and its policies in a style that begins at a near-shout and sometimes ends closer to a scream. Nearby listeners sometimes wonder whether there is something in the sound of his own voice that makes him angry.

But it is a somewhat different Lungren who has emerged in two terms on the Judiciary Committee, a serious, earnest conservative who carries a briefcase full of documents, plays an active role on most of the panel's legislative issues, and even visits judges to get their opinion on legislation.

In the 96th Congress, Lungren served on the Judiciary subcommittee that wrote a new federal criminal code, and he showed an independent streak that made it difficult to label him a partisan ideologue. On one occasion, he offered an amendment backed by the Carter Justice Department, giving the government the right to appeal sentences in federal criminal cases. He won in subcommittee, but lost in the full committee, 16-15. The code never went to the House floor.

On other Judiciary issues, he showed the skepticism of most of the panel's Republicans about new federal incursions into local legal issues. When the committee brought to the floor a bill expanding the controversial Law Enforcement Assistance Administration, Lungren fought to drop plans for a new office of Justice Assistance. He called it a "bureaucratic monster child that we know will grow greater." He also fought the committee's bill to provide federal aid to local communities to help them resolve minor criminal cases out of court.

On the floor, Lungren made an issue early in his first term of Charles Diggs, the Michigan Democrat who had been convicted in federal court of payroll padding. Lungren wrote to Speaker O'Neill asking that the Democrats permit a vote on whether to expel Diggs, rather than simply censure him, as they wanted to do. When O'Neill refused, Lungren introduced his own resolution of expulsion, but it was tabled on a vote of 205-197, far short of the two-thirds it needed.

**At Home:** Lungren has put his aggressive personal style to use in all his political campaigns, and has learned how to harness it for results. The son of Richard M. Nixon's White House physician, Lungren was practicing law in Long Beach in 1976 when he decided to try for Congress. The 34th had unexpectedly gone Democratic in 1974 for schoolteacher Mark Hannaford.

Hannaford's 1974 opponent, former state legislator Bill Bond, wanted a second chance. But many Long Beach Republicans blamed their 1974 defeat on Bond's halfhearted campaigning, and were ready for a new face. Lungren had most of the party regulars on his side. He won the primary by a solid 49-36 percent margin.

Lungren's fall campaign was made more difficult by lingering intraparty bitterness and by his own strident excesses, attributed to inexperience at running for office. Hannaford eked out a second-term victory by less than 3,000 votes.

Before starting his second campaign, Lungren went to national GOP campaign school. His 1978 effort against Hannaford stressed person-to-person contacts. Lungren spent days

---

**34th District: Los Angeles, Orange counties — Long Beach.** Population: 475,676 (2% increase since 1970). Race: White 419,481 (88%), Black 10,013 (2%), Asian and Pacific Islander 19,100 (4%), Others 27,082 (6%). Spanish origin: 51,542 (11%).

knocking on doors, visiting bowling alleys, and meeting as many voters as he could.

The challenger knew he would be strong in the Orange County part of the district, and spent little time there. He focused on the Los Angeles County section, talking about Proposition 13 to the usually-Democratic homeowners in Long Beach and Lakewood. Hannaford had been unyielding in his opposition to the June ballot measure, which Lungren and 72 percent of the district's voters supported.

As it turned out, Lungren carried both portions of the district, ousting Hannaford by nearly 17,000 votes.

He had an easy time two years later, running for re-election against Simone, a candidate who had no last name and could not raise enough money to publicize her first one. Simone's outspoken feminism helped her win a four-candidate Democratic primary, but she was overmatched and thoroughly trounced by Lungren.

**The District:** Straddling the Los Angeles-Orange County border, this district has two distinct personalities. In the larger Los Angeles County portion, Democrats easily outnumber Republicans. The straight streets of Long Beach and Lakewood have housed the same blue-collar families for years.

Across the county line, there are as many registered Republicans as Democrats. But in Orange County, even the Democrats support Republican candidates. Paul Gann demonstrated that in 1980, when he carried the Orange County portion of the 34th in his hopeless Senate campaign. The income level is slightly higher here than in the Los Angeles County part, especially in Rossmore.

During the last decade, the population shift has been out of Long Beach and Lakewood and into Orange County, specifically Huntington Beach. As a result, the district will probably gain more Orange County territory in redistricting, which will make it even more Republican.

## Committees

**Judiciary** (10th of 12 Republicans)
Civil and Constitutional Rights; Immigration, Refugees and International Law.

**Select Aging** (10th of 23 Republicans)
Health and Long-term Care; Human Services.

## Elections

**1980 General**

| | |
|---|---|
| Daniel Lungren (R ) | 138,024 (72 %) |
| Simone (D ) | 46,351 (24 %) |

**1978 General**

| | |
|---|---|
| Daniel Lungren (R ) | 90,554 (54 %) |
| Mark Hannaford (D ) | 73,608 (44 %) |

**1978 Primary**

| | |
|---|---|
| Daniel Lungren (R ) | 42,967 (68 %) |
| Art Jacobson (R ) | 19,828 (32 %) |

**District Vote For President**

| | 1980 | | 1976 |
|---|---|---|---|
| D | 58,974 (29 %) | D | 84,977 (42 %) |
| R | 123,748 (61 %) | R | 112,251 (56 %) |
| I | 15,573 (8 %) | | |

## Campaign Finance

| | Receipts | Receipts from PACs | Expenditures |
|---|---|---|---|
| **1980** | | | |
| Lungren (R ) | $232,105 | $81,248 (35 %) | $235,834 |
| Simone (D ) | $12,099 | $2,590 (21 %) | $12,082 |

**1978**

| | | | |
|---|---|---|---|
| Lungren (R ) | $270,917 | $79,741 (29 %) | $268,604 |
| Hannaford (D ) | $326,710 | $143,791 (44 %) | $329,904 |

## Voting Studies

| | Presidential Support | | Party Unity | | Conservative Coalition | |
|---|---|---|---|---|---|---|
| Year | S | O | S | O | S | O |
| 1980 | 38 | 60 | 90 | 9 | 89 | 9 |
| 1979 | 23 | 77 | 96 | 2 | 97 | 3 |

S = Support      O = Opposition

## Key Votes

**96th Congress**

| | |
|---|---|
| Weaken Carter oil profits tax (1979) | Y |
| Reject hospital cost control plan (1979) | Y |
| Implement Panama Canal Treaties (1979) | N |
| Establish Department of Education (1979) | N |
| Approve Anti-busing Amendment (1979) | Y |
| Guarantee Chrysler Corp. loans (1979) | N |
| Approve military draft registration (1980) | Y |
| Aid Sandinista regime in Nicaragua (1980) | N |
| Strengthen fair housing laws (1980) | N |

**97th Congress**

| | |
|---|---|
| Reagan budget proposal (1981) | Y |

## Interest Group Ratings

| Year | ADA | ACA | AFL-CIO | CCUS |
|---|---|---|---|---|
| 1980 | 6 | 100 | 11 | 74 |
| 1979 | 0 | 100 | 10 | 100 |

# 35 David Dreier (R)

**Of LaVerne — Elected 1980**

**Born:** July 5, 1952, Kansas City, Mo.
**Education:** Claremont Men's College, B.A. 1975; Claremont Graduate School, M.A. 1976.
**Profession:** Marketing and government relations consultant.
**Family:** Single.
**Religion:** Christian Scientist.
**Political Career:** Unsuccessful Republican nominee for U.S. House, 1978.

**The Member:** Using the Claremont Colleges as his political base and training ground, Dreier waged a four-year campaign against Democratic Rep. Jim Lloyd and defeated him on the second try. From the start, he had the support of the influential Claremont College Republican establishment. As a former Midwest chairman of Youth for Nixon, he had made a name for himself with his smooth style and obvious ambition even in his first year as an undergraduate in 1971.

On his first try he came within 12,000 votes of beating Lloyd. His second campaign was marked by greater maturity and a more substantive effort to discuss issues.

Dreier's traditional "free economy" Republican stance developed from college internships with Sen. S. I. Hayakawa and Rep. Barry M. Goldwater Jr., and from seeing his father's Kansas City construction firm crippled by costly labor disputes. He attacked Lloyd for his support of new governmental agencies. A firm supporter of President Reagan's efforts to cut government spending and regulation, Dreier sees a very limited task for the federal government. "Its prime role," he says, "is the protection of U.S. borders."

**The District:** Created from the leftovers of four Los Angeles-area districts in 1974, this constituency has little geographic cohesion of its own. It is divided in two parts by a modest-sized mountain, named after the corn flake king, W. K. Kellogg. To the west are the blue-collar suburbs of Covina and West Covina. On the eastern side of Kellogg Hill lie the more affluent university communities of Claremont and Pomona.

Although the two parts of the district interact very little, their voting behavior is similar. In recent statewide contests, the district has tended to favor Republicans, but the area elects a roughly equal number of Democrats and Republicans to the state Legislature.

## Committees

**Government Operations** (14th of 17 Republicans)
Environment, Energy and Natural Resources; Manpower and Housing.

**Small Business** (15th of 17 Republicans)
Export Opportunities and Special Small Business Problems; General Oversight.

## Elections

**1980 General**

| | |
|---|---|
| David Dreier (R ) | 100,743 (52 %) |
| Jim Lloyd (D ) | 88,279 (45 %) |

**1980 Primary**

| | |
|---|---|
| David Dreier (R ) | 32,189 (53 %) |
| Russ Blewett (R ) | 8,720 (14 %) |
| Frances Livingston (R ) | 8,036 (13 %) |
| Others (R ) | 11,597 (19 %) |

**District Vote For President**

| | 1980 | | 1976 |
|---|---|---|---|
| D | 58,017 (29 %) | D | 72,664 (44 %) |
| R | 124,297 (62 %) | R | 90,929 (55 %) |
| I | 14,318 (7 %) | | |

## Campaign Finance

| | Receipts | Receipts from PACs | Expenditures |
|---|---|---|---|
| **1980** | | | |
| Dreier (R ) | $414,859 | $117,058 (28 %) | $379,325 |
| Lloyd (D ) | $240,304 | $120,625 (50 %) | $237,886 |

## Key Vote

**97th Congress**

| | |
|---|---|
| Reagan budget proposal (1981) | Y |

---

**35th District: Los Angeles County — Covina, Pomona.** Population: 610,041 (31% increase since 1970). Race: White 491,965 (80%), Black 35,978 (6%), Asian and Pacific Islander 19,743 (3%), Others 62,345 (10%). Spanish origin: 129,140 (21%).

# 36 George E. Brown Jr. (D)

**Of Riverside — Elected 1962**
Did not serve 1971-73.

**Born:** March 6, 1920, Holtville, Calif.
**Education:** U.C.L.A., B.A. 1946.
**Military Career:** Army, 1944-46.
**Profession:** Engineer.
**Family:** Wife, Rowena Somerindyke; four children.
**Religion:** Methodist.
**Political Career:** Monterey Park mayor, 1954-58; California Assembly, 1959-63; sought Democratic U.S. Senate nomination, 1970.

**In Washington:** Brown has pursued his liberal principles through two very different careers in the House, punctuated by a two-year absence following his defeat for the Senate in 1970.

Watching Brown in action today, as he listens patiently to testimony on the budget for science research, or ponders amendments to a farm bill, it is easy to forget the militant anti-war crusader of the 1960s. At first glance, it seems to be a different man. On reflection, it turns out to be a mellower version of the same man.

Never a radical on domestic issues, Brown became a peace advocate during his days as a scientist, and argued his cause from the start of his first term, in 1963, when he opposed extension of the draft as it passed 388-3. He voted against money for civil defense, charging that it "created a climate in which nuclear war becomes more credible," and in 1966 cast the only vote in the House against a $58 billion defense funding bill.

He was already speaking out against the Vietnam War in the spring of 1965, when he accused Lyndon B. Johnson of pretending "that the peace of mankind can be won by the slaughter of peasants in Vietnam." He continued to talk that way through the next five years in the House, both on the floor and at outside rallies. He refused to vote for any military spending bill while the war continued, and once boasted that he had opposed more federal spending than any member in history.

Brown's anti-war work gave him a national reputation during those years, but much of his legislative time was devoted to environmental issues. He introduced a bill in 1969 to ban offshore oil drilling along the California coast, and backed federal land use planning. He proposed outlawing the production of internal combustion engines after a three-year period.

That environmentalism is the link between Brown's two House careers. When he returned as a freshman in 1973, U.S. participation in the war was ending. He settled quietly into the Agriculture and Science committees, and followed his issues without seeking much public attention. Since 1973, he has not been one of the more visible members of the House.

But he has been busy. Much of his work has been in defense of the Environmental Protection Agency, whose programs are authorized through the Science Committee. Brown has continually fought against cuts in the EPA budget; he has regularly introduced floor amendments adding extra money to fight air or water pollution. In 1980, when the committee voted to cut $10.5 million from EPA funds, Brown accused it of "criticizing the EPA and then cutting its budget in precisely the areas where in the past EPA has been criticized for not doing enough." Brown has strongly supported more money for research into alternative energy sources, especially solar and geothermal.

Brown also has been a vehement opponent of the controversial Clinch River nuclear breeder reactor. He sought to kill it in committee in 1977, joined the Carter administration in trying to deny funds for it in 1979, and was on the winning side

---

**36th District: Cities of Riverside, San Bernardino. Population:** 559,239 (21% increase since 1970). Race: White 431,812 (77%), Black 43,823 (8%), Others 83,604 (15%). Spanish origin: 123,149 (22%).

as the Science Committee voted against it in early 1981.

As chairman of the Science Subcommittee on Research and Technology in the 96th Congress, Brown managed basic research authorizations on the floor. He argued consistently for new efforts against various kinds of environmental damage; he managed one bill authorizing $5 million for a new program to fight pollution of the oceans.

Brown also has been an environmentalist on the Agriculture Committee. In 1976, he introduced a National Forest Timber Reform Act, one that would have restricted "clear cutting" — the harvesting of large stands of timber at one time.

Meanwhile, on other domestic issues, Brown has been casting the same liberal votes as during the 1960s, when he had a national reputation.

But he does not vote against defense spending any more, and on a few occasions, has cast pragmatic pro-military votes he might have denounced a decade ago. In 1980, he backed production of the B-1 bomber. "If the B-1 was being built in some other state," he explained afterward, "and I didn't have two Air Force bases and a lot of retired military people who feel strongly about the B-1, I'd probably have voted the other way."

**At Home:** Brown's 1970 Senate race divides his electoral career the same way it has split his Washington career. The first several chapters of Brown's political life took place in the heavily Hispanic area around Monterey Park. The more recent phases have focused on middle-class politics in San Bernardino, 50 miles to the east.

Brown moved to Los Angeles to attend college, then settled in Monterey Park after getting his physics degree. While working for the Los Angeles city government, he began to dabble in Monterey Park politics, and moved from the Monterey Park Democratic Club to the town's mayoralty. After four years on the City Council and in the mayor's office, he was elected to the state Assembly, where he focused on housing issues.

In 1962, the new 29th Congressional District was created on Brown's home turf. He easily defeated two strong primary opponents and Republican H. L. "Bill" Richardson in the general election.

Once he developed his reputation as an antiwar leader, Brown attracted a series of opponents — Democrats and Republicans — who challenged him on the Vietnam issue. His closest call came in 1966 against Republican Bill Orozco, who capitalized on his Mexican-American heritage and support for the gubernatorial campaign of Ronald Reagan. Brown won by 3,000 votes out of 135,000 cast.

In 1968, Orozco ran again. But redistricting had added territory on the district's east side, giving Brown more Anglo voters, and even though Republicans made it a high priority contest, Brown doubled his plurality. Still, it was clear Brown would have tough contests in future years.

Rather than run again for what had become a marginal seat, Brown decided in 1970 to take on GOP Sen. George Murphy. But to do that he had to oppose fellow U.S. Rep. John Tunney in a primary.

After American troops invaded Cambodia that spring, polls began to show Brown moving into a slight lead over Tunney, who had been much less outspoken in his opposition to the war. Brown called for the impeachment of President Nixon because of the invasion. Tunney then turned his aim on Brown, accusing him of being a radical and advocating student violence. Brown attempted to deflect what he termed Tunney's "dirty" tactics, but failed and lost by a 42-33 percent margin.

Brown's political resurrection came two years later and 50 miles east of Monterey Park, in another newly created district in the San Bernardino-Riverside area. There it was middle-class white conservatives, not Mexican-Americans, who caused initial problems for Brown.

The 1972 Democratic primary in the new district was one of the fiercest battles in the state that year. Brown was attacked as an extreme liberal and as a carpetbagger by David Tunno, a Tunney protégé, and by the conservative chairman of the San Bernardino County Board, Ruben Ayala. But Brown won the eight-candidate primary by finishing second in all three parts of the district. His 28 percent was not very impressive, but it was enough to get him on the November ballot as the Democratic candidate. The district was then about 63 percent Democratic in registration, and he was an easy winner in November.

The 1974 redistricting put more of Riverside County into the district and removed the Los Angeles County portion. Since then, as the vote in Riverside has grown, Brown has done progressively worse there. In 1980, facing a challenger whose organization came largely from the Campus Crusade for Christ, Brown was held below a majority in Riverside for the first time. But his vote in San Bernardino County remained safely above 55 percent, and his re-election was not threatened.

**The District:** Initially a safe Democratic district, the 36th has become competitive as Riverside County has grown.

Voters from Orange County have moved across the Riverside line, and new houses have gone up at a rapid rate in the towns of Norco and Corona, both of which voted for Ronald Reagan in 1980 by better than 2-1 margins. Overall, River-side County now accounts for more than 60 percent of the district vote.

The San Bernardino County part of the district, with a higher percentage of Mexican-American and working-class families, is still reliably Democratic.

## Committees

**Agriculture** (5th of 24 Democrats)
Department Operations, Research, and Foreign Agriculture, chairman; Forests, Family Farms, and Energy.

**Science and Technology** (3rd of 23 Democrats)
Natural Resources, Agriculture Research and Environment; Science, Research and Technology; Space Science and Applications.

## Elections

**1980 General**

| | |
|---|---|
| George Brown Jr. (D) | 88,634 (53 %) |
| John Stark (R) | 73,252 (43 %) |

**1980 Primary**

| | |
|---|---|
| George Brown Jr. (D) | 51,494 (73 %) |
| Gary Wedge (D) | 17,657 (27 %) |

**1978 General**

| | |
|---|---|
| George Brown Jr. (D) | 80,448 (63 %) |
| Dana Carmody (R) | 47,417 (37 %) |

**Previous Winning Percentages**

| | | | |
|---|---|---|---|
| 1976 (62 %) | 1974 (63 %) | 1972 (56 %) | 1970 (- %) |
| 1968 (52 %) | 1966 (51 %) | 1964 (59 %) | 1962 (56 %) |

**District Vote For President**

| | 1980 | | 1976 | |
|---|---|---|---|---|
| D | 65,274 (37 %) | D | 82,538 (55 %) | D |
| R | 92,118 (53 %) | R | 64,801 (43 %) | R |
| I | 13,171 (8 %) | | | |

## Campaign Finance

| | Receipts | Receipts from PACs | Expenditures |
|---|---|---|---|
| **1980** | | | |
| Brown (D) | $70,340 | $13,060 (19 %) | $66,917 |
| Stark (R) | $36,734 | $5,000 (14 %) | $38,094 |
| **1978** | | | |
| Brown (D) | $40,562 | $12,450 (31 %) | $39,914 |
| Carmody (R) | $11,183 | $400 (4 %) | $11,179 |

## Voting Studies

| Year | Presidential Support | | Party Unity | | Conservative Coalition | |
|---|---|---|---|---|---|---|
| | S | O | S | O | S | O |
| 1980 | 69 | 15 | 82 | 5 | 8 | 77 |
| 1979 | 74 | 13 | 83 | 5 | 10 | 75 |
| 1978 | 76 | 13 | 74 | 9 | 7 | 79 |
| 1977 | 70 | 14 | 81 | 4 | 6 | 78 |
| 1976 | 31 | 59 | 73 | 8 | 18 | 69 |
| 1975 | 37 | 60 | 81 | 10 | 11 | 76 |
| 1974 (Ford) | 33 | 46 | | | | |
| 1974 | 28 | 47 | 70 | 8 | 11 | 68 |
| 1973 | 30 | 61 | 82 | 8 | 10 | 80 |
| 1972 | - | - | - | - | - | - |
| 1971 | - | - | - | - | - | - |
| 1970 | 29 | 31 | 39 | 15 | 2 | 36 |
| 1969 | 17 | 36 | 64 | 9 | 7 | 69 |
| 1968 | 41 | 16 | 43 | 7 | 4 | 39 |
| 1967 | 54 | 14 | 55 | 13 | 11 | 65 |
| 1966 | 42 | 11 | 46 | 8 | 5 | 43 |
| 1965 | 78 | 4 | 85 | 1 | 2 | 86 |
| 1964 | 81 | 2 | 73 | 2 | 0 | 67 |
| 1963 | 75 | 6 | 77 | 2 | 0 | 60 |

S = Support      O = Opposition

## Key Votes

**96th Congress**

| | |
|---|---|
| Weaken Carter oil profits tax (1979) | N |
| Reject hospital cost control plan (1979) | N |
| Implement Panama Canal Treaties (1979) | Y |
| Establish Department of Education (1979) | Y |
| Approve Anti-busing Amendment (1979) | N |
| Guarantee Chrysler Corp. loans (1979) | Y |
| Approve military draft registration (1980) | N |
| Aid Sandinista regime in Nicaragua (1980) | Y |
| Strengthen fair housing laws (1980) | Y |

**97th Congress**

| | |
|---|---|
| Reagan budget proposal (1981) | N |

## Interest Group Ratings

| Year | ADA | ACA | AFL-CIO | CCUS |
|---|---|---|---|---|
| 1980 | 94 | 10 | 82 | 52 |
| 1979 | 84 | 0 | 74 | 12 |
| 1978 | 70 | 8 | 79 | 13 |
| 1977 | 80 | 4 | 90 | 6 |
| 1976 | 80 | 19 | 79 | 13 |
| 1975 | 89 | 4 | 100 | 24 |
| 1974 | 91 | 0 | 100 | 0 |
| 1973 | 88 | 13 | 91 | 18 |
| 1972 | - | - | - | - |
| 1971 | - | - | - | - |
| 1970 | 88 | 17 | 100 | 13 |
| 1969 | 87 | 25 | 89 | - |
| 1968 | 83 | 16 | 100 | - |
| 1967 | 87 | 11 | 100 | 11 |
| 1966 | 82 | 11 | 100 | - |
| 1965 | 95 | 0 | - | 10 |
| 1964 | 92 | 0 | 100 | - |
| 1963 | - | 0 | - | - |

# 37 Jerry Lewis (R)

**Of San Bernardino — Elected 1978**

**Born:** Oct. 21, 1934, Seattle, Wash.
**Education:** U.C.L.A., B.A. 1956.
**Profession:** Life insurance executive.
**Family:** Divorced; four children.
**Political Career:** San Bernardino School Board, 1965-68; Calif. Assembly, 1969-79; unsuccessful GOP candidate for Calif. Senate, 1973.

**In Washington:** Water is the main political issue in the desert-dominated district Lewis represents, and it is the issue he has concentrated on in the House.

If the Public Works Committee is a routine assignment for some freshman members, it was a helpful one for Lewis. He headed immediately for the Public Works Water Resources Subcommittee when he arrived and pushed his area's demands for flood control. In 1981 he moved to Appropriations, where he can pursue many of the same issues.

One of the first bills he introduced was one in behalf of the Palo Verde Irrigation District, allowing it to build a new hydroelectric power facility; currently the federal government has exclusive rights to build there.

On other occasions, Lewis has argued the other part of the water issue, trying to pry loose as much federal money as possible for flood control. On one occasion, when the House Appropriations Committee used some of its limited emergency money for relief to victims of the Mount St. Helen's volcano, Lewis took the floor to make sure it would not come out of a promised $7-million for flood control along the Colorado River in his district. When urban Public Works members began talking of the need to spend Public Works money on preservation of their older water installations, he took a trip to New York to inspect its sewer system for himself.

Actually, Lewis' interest in some of his committee work is technological as well as political. Something of a tinkerer in science, he used his secondary assignment to the House Administration Committee in 1979 to move into the issue of computerization of legislative business, and began filling his office with computer terminals and other electronic gadgetry. By the end of his first House term, he was working on plans to computerize both the sending of Dear Colleague letters and the scheduling of subcommittee meetings.

The only controversial issue at House Administration during Lewis' first term there was public financing of congressional campaigns; he voted against it, along with all his GOP colleagues on the panel.

**At Home:** Lewis' political career has followed a steady course from school board to state Legislature to Congress. Each time he has methodically used his existing electoral base to move up the political ladder.

He started a successful insurance business in San Bernardino, entered Republican politics, and developed the contacts that won him a place on the school board. After three years in that office, he ran for a state Assembly seat in the county, winning the five-candidate primary with 36 percent. Lewis was elected to five Assembly terms with a vote that ranged from 59 to 100 percent.

In late 1973, with a major redistricting about to take place, Lewis ran in a special election for the state Senate. He finished first in the special primary, winning 49 percent of the vote. Just 463 more votes would have given Lewis a majority and, by California law, elected him. But instead he was forced into a runoff with Democrat Ruben S. Ayala, who more than doubled his own vote in the runoff and won the seat with 54 percent.

Lewis was re-elected to the Assembly in 1974 in a redrawn district, and in 1976, even managed to win the Democratic nomination on a write-in,

---

**37th District: San Bernardino, Riverside counties.** Population: 650,999 (41% increase since 1970). Race: White 554,032 (85%), Black 22,429 (3%), Others 74,538 (11%). Spanish origin: 101,235 (15%).

the first Republican assemblyman to do so since state law barred candidates from filing in both parties.

Lewis' new Assembly constituency covered more than half the 37th Congressional District, so he was the obvious successor in 1978 when Republican Rep. Shirley N. Pettis retired. Earlier in his career, Lewis had worked as a field representative for Jerry Pettis, Shirley's husband, who represented the district for eight years before he was killed in a plane crash in 1975. Declaring himself a candidate in the "Pettis tradition," Lewis won the five-candidate GOP primary with 55 percent of the vote. In the general election, Lewis campaigned virtually as the incumbent, ignoring his Democratic opponent and spending three times as much money to win handily.

**The District:** Dominated by mountains and deserts, the 37th relies heavily on irrigation projects to support an economy based on agriculture and leisure. Palm Springs and Rancho Mirage, playgrounds of the rich, are both located in the district, as are several Indian reservations and many large irrigated farming tracts.

The district's population is about evenly split between vast San Bernardino County and the eastern four-fifths of Riverside County, although there is little political difference between the two. Both are solidly Republican.

The district was prime Republican territory in the 1976 and 1980 presidential elections, but strong statewide Democrats can sometimes carry it by slim margins, as Sen. Alan Cranston did in 1980 and Gov. Edmund G. Brown Jr. did in 1978.

## Committees

**Appropriations** (20th of 22 Republicans)
Agriculture; Foreign Operations; Legislative.

## Elections

**1980 General**

| | |
|---|---|
| Jerry Lewis (R ) | 166,640 (72 %) |
| Donald Rusk (D ) | 58,462 (25 %) |

**1980 Primary**

| | |
|---|---|
| Jerry Lewis (R ) | 67,694 (83 %) |
| Bud Mathewson (R ) | 5,802 (7 %) |
| George Beardsley (R ) | 4,876 (6 %) |

**1978 General**

| | |
|---|---|
| Jerry Lewis (R ) | 106,581 (61 %) |
| Dan Corcoran (D ) | 60,463 (35 %) |

**1978 Primary**

| | |
|---|---|
| Jerry Lewis (R ) | 40,101 (55 %) |
| John Joyner (R ) | 10,619 (15 %) |
| Danney Ball (R ) | 8,574 (12 %) |
| Other (R ) | 13,875 (19 %) |

**District Vote For President**

| | 1980 | | 1976 |
|---|---|---|---|
| D | 69,594 (29 %) | D | 84,725 (45 %) |
| R | 149,780 (63 %) | R | 101,935 (54 %) |
| I | 14,706 (6 %) | | |

## Campaign Finance

| | Receipts | Receipts from PACs | Expenditures |
|---|---|---|---|
| **1980** | | | |
| Lewis (R ) | $132,550 | $63,654 (48 %) | $54,488 |
| Rusk (D ) | $47,505 | $1,000 (2 %) | $47,382 |

**1978**

| | | | |
|---|---|---|---|
| Lewis (R ) | $159,553 | $63,166 (40 %) | $159,433 |
| Corcoran (D ) | $50,035 | $20,175 (40 %) | $50,005 |

## Voting Studies

| | Presidential Support | | Party Unity | | Conservative Coalition | |
|---|---|---|---|---|---|---|
| Year | S | O | S | O | S | O |
| 1980 | 31 | 62 | 67 | 22 | 72 | 20 |
| 1979 | 30 | 66 | 81 | 17 | 90 | 6 |

S = Support        O = Opposition

## Key Votes

**96th Congress**

| | |
|---|---|
| Weaken Carter oil profits tax (1979) | Y |
| Reject hospital cost control plan (1979) | Y |
| Implement Panama Canal Treaties (1979) | N |
| Establish Department of Education (1979) | Y |
| Approve Anti-busing Amendment (1979) | Y |
| Gurantee Chrysler Corp. loans (1979) | N |
| Approve military draft registration (1980) | N |
| Aid Sandinista regime in Nicaragua (1980) | N |
| Strengthen fair housing laws (1980) | N |

**97th Congress**

| | |
|---|---|
| Reagan budget proposal (1981) | Y |

## Interest Group Rating

| Year | ADA | ACA | AFL-CIO | CCUS |
|---|---|---|---|---|
| 1980 | 11 | 75 | 21 | 61 |
| 1979 | 5 | 88 | 15 | 94 |

# 38 Jerry M. Patterson (D)

**Of Santa Ana — Elected 1974**

**Born:** Oct. 25, 1934, El Paso, Texas.
**Education:** Long Beach State U., B.A. 1960;
UCLA Law School, J.D. 1966.
**Military Career:** Coast Guard, 1953-57.
**Profession:** Lawyer.
**Family:** Wife, Sally Sandoval; three children.
**Religion:** Congregationalist.
**Political Career:** Santa Ana City Council,
1969-73; Mayor of Santa Ana, 1973-74.

**In Washington:** Patterson found himself fighting two very different battles at once during the 96th Congress, trying to maintain federal water subsidies for his district's agribusiness community and struggling to reform the House committee system at the same time. He did much better on water policy.

One fight was in the Interior Committee, over changes in the 1902 Reclamation Act. A coalition of environmentalists, allied with the Carter administration, wanted to enforce tight limits on the size of farms eligibile for cheap, federally subsidized water. Patterson, initially receptive to this argument, ended up a leading spokesman against it and for his area's large farmers. It was his proposal, to place no limits on the amount of leased land eligible for cheap water, that marked the crucial agribusiness victory. Eventually the committee did reverse itself and imposed a relatively lenient lid of 2,400 acres, considerably larger than initially proposed by the Carter administration. Patterson criticized the 2,400-acre limit as too low. In the end, the bill did not make it to the House floor.

Meanwhile, Patterson was learning just how difficult it can be to change the way the House operates. He was the leadership's surprise choice in 1979 to head a new panel aimed at redrawing the committee lines, the first since an attempt by Richard Bolling, D-Mo., failed in 1974.

The job went to Patterson largely because no senior Democrats wanted it in the wake of the earlier defeat. It was in part a consolation prize for him; his bid for a place on the Rules Committee had just been unexpectedly turned down. Still, he set about the chore with enthusiasm and a sense of public relations.

Patterson decided to go for one big substantive change: a new House Energy Committee to replace the current jurisdictional sprawl. Speaker Thomas P. O'Neill Jr. favored the plan. But by

the time Patterson had moved it through his panel — a difficult job in itself — he found himself up against a powerful coalition: environmentalists who thought a new committee would be too pro-industry; Republicans who thought Democratic leaders would control it; and virtually the entire Commerce Committee, possessor of the largest share of energy jurisdiction under the existing arrangement. Patterson lost on the floor by a nearly 3-1 margin.

Patterson also serves on the Banking Committee, but has played a quiet role there in the last couple of years, supporting California banks, especially the statewide Bank of America.

**At Home:** In Orange County — a name synonymous with Republicanism — it is not easy to find a Democrat with a relatively safe political office. But Patterson seems to have one.

He represents the working-class part of Orange County, the only section of it where Democrats outnumber Republicans. He was elected as a moderate, conciliatory Democrat and has done little in the House to change that image.

Patterson lost his first election, in 1968, for a seat on the Orange County Board of Supervisors. But the following year he was elected to the Santa Ana City Council, his springboard to Washington. Patterson decided to run for the House in 1974 when Democrat Richard T. Hanna retired and the

---

**38th District: Orange County — Santa Ana, Garden Grove.** Pop.: 531,321 (15% increase since 1970). Race: White 415,886 (78%), Black 10,748 (2%), Asian and Pacific Islander 32,418 (6%), Others 72,269 (14%). Spanish origin: 130,280 (25%).

area's other leading Democrat, state Assemblyman Kenneth Cory, chose to run for statewide office instead. Patterson's major opposition in the primary came from Hanna's district aide, Howard Adler. But while Adler had most of Hanna's workers and contributors behind him, Patterson had a better electoral base and won the primary with 46 percent to Adler's 36 percent. Speaking out for the free enterprise system and in support of the building trades, Patterson did not present a threatening picture to many Republicans in the district.

Patterson won the general election easily, defeating David Rehmann, a former prisoner of war in Vietnam. Since then he has run far ahead of the Democratic ticket in the district. In 1980,

although his percentage fell slightly, he won nearly twice as many votes as Carter.

**The District:** This is a ticket-splitting suburban district, Democratic by registration but often Republican in statewide elections. GOP nominee Paul Gann carried it in his 1980 Senate campaign — one of seven districts he took in the state. But the entire area has been in Democratic hands at the congressional and state legislative level for most of the past decade.

Garden Grove and Santa Ana each provide about a quarter of the district's vote, with Santa Ana slightly larger and more Democratic. Farther north, nearer to Los Angeles County, are smaller suburban communities such as Democratic Buena Park and Republican Cypress.

## Committees

**Banking, Finance and Urban Affairs** (7th of 25 Democrats)
International Development Institutions and Finance, chairman; Housing and Community Development; International Trade, Investment and Monetary Policy.

**Interior and Insular Affairs** (17th of 23 Democrats)
Oversight and Investigations; Water and Power Resources.

## Elections

### 1980 General

| | |
|---|---|
| Jerry Patterson (D ) | 91,880 (56 %) |
| Art Jacobson (R ) | 66,256 (40 %) |

### 1978 General

| | |
|---|---|
| Jerry Patterson (D ) | 75,471 (59 %) |
| Don Goedeke (R ) | 53,298 (41 %) |

**Previous Winning Percentages**

**1976 (64 %)**    **1974 (54 %)**

### District Vote For President

| | 1980 | | 1976 |
|---|---|---|---|
| D | 47,995 (28 %) | D | 67,994 (43 %) |
| R | 109,167 (63 %) | R | 85,873 (55 %) |
| I | 11,375 (7 %) | | |

## Campaign Finance

| | Receipts | Receipts from PACs | Expenditures |
|---|---|---|---|
| **1980** | | | |
| Patterson (D ) | $215,648 | $115,145 (53 %) | $199,521 |
| Jacobson (R ) | $39,260 | $250 (6 %) | $39,195 |
| **1978** | | | |
| Patterson (D ) | $136,668 | $68,420 (50 %) | $134,557 |
| Goedeke (R ) | $61,769 | $18,225 (30 %) | $61,319 |

## Voting Studies

| | Presidential Support | | Party Unity | | Conservative Coalition | |
|---|---|---|---|---|---|---|
| Year | S | O | S | O | S | O |
| 1980 | 66 | 25 | 84 | 6 | 17 | 72 |
| 1979 | 72 | 17 | 77 | 5 | 15 | 65 |
| 1978 | 76 | 17 | 84 | 9 | 15 | 81 |
| 1977 | 62 | 20 | 77 | 8 | 12 | 76 |
| 1976 | 25 | 67 | 83 | 10 | 15 | 76 |
| 1975 | 29 | 65 | 85 | 9 | 15 | 78 |

S = Support        O = Opposition

## Key Votes

### 96th Congress

| | |
|---|---|
| Weaken Carter oil profits tax (1979) | ? |
| Reject hospital cost control plan (1979) | N |
| Implement Panama Canal Treaties (1979) | Y |
| Establish Department of Education (1979) | Y |
| Approve Anti-busing Amendment (1979) | N |
| Guarantee Chrysler Corp. loans (1979) | Y |
| Approve military draft registration (1980) | N |
| Aid Sandinista regime in Nicaragua (1980) | Y |
| Strengthen fair housing laws (1980) | Y |

### 97th Congress

| | |
|---|---|
| Reagan budget proposal (1981) | Y |

## Interest Group Ratings

| Year | ADA | ACA | AFL-CIO | CCUS |
|---|---|---|---|---|
| 1980 | 72 | 18 | 67 | 56 |
| 1979 | 63 | 5 | 73 | 8 |
| 1978 | 60 | 24 | 94 | 11 |
| 1977 | 65 | 8 | 90 | 13 |
| 1976 | 60 | 14 | 82 | 19 |
| 1975 | 79 | 7 | 95 | 15 |

# 39 William E. Dannemeyer (R)

**Of Fullerton — Elected 1978**

**Born:** Sept. 22, 1929, Long Beach, Calif.
**Education:** Valparaiso U., B.A. 1950; U. of Calif.,
Hastings Law School, J.D. 1952.
**Military Career:** Army, 1952-54.
**Profession:** Lawyer.
**Family:** Wife, Evelyn Hoemann; three children.
**Religion:** Lutheran.
**Political Career:** Calif. Assembly, served as a
Democrat, 1963-67; served as a Republican,
1977-79; unsuccessful Democratic nominee
for Calif. Senate, 1966; unsuccessful Republi-
can nominee for Calif. Assembly, 1972.

**In Washington:** "Dynamiter" is the name
some GOP colleagues give to this bull-headed
Californian who sometimes seems to prefer crash-
ing head-on into legislative obstacles rather than
steering his way around them.

It was Dannemeyer who conducted a one-
man conservative crusade in 1979 against a new
child health program in the Commerce Committee. Declaring the entitlement program "ridiculous," he blocked its progress with a series of
quorum calls and recorded vote demands that
kept it in committee for weeks. In part he was
angry over the way he had been treated while the
bill was still in subcommittee. After a barrage of
criticism from Dannemeyer, subcommittee Chairman Henry Waxman had waited until his antagonist left the meeting to make a telephone call,
then called for a vote on the bill without him.

It was also Dannemeyer who objected to the
1979 and 1980 budgets of most of the House
standing committees, forcing individual roll-call
votes on many of them. On one occasion the
House spent nearly two hours in consecutive votes
on these budgets, the longest such uninterrupted
period in recent memory. "This institution is
literally out of control," he complained, arguing
against the escalating costs of committee staffing.
"It is obvious," he said, "that a staff explosion has
taken place in the House, at least since 1974, if
not before."

Other floor work by Dannemeyer has tended
to concentrate on the same issue of trimming
government costs, if only by marginal amounts.
His amendment to cut virtually the entire federal
subsidy for nurses' training was beaten on a vote
of 341-12. But another effort, calling for a 10
percent reduction in the salaries of people working for the international development banks,
came within eight votes of being adopted, 189-

197. He also came within eight votes on a drive to
reduce the appropriation for the National Commission on Air Quality.

**At Home:** Dannemeyer has run for office as
a Democrat, and he has run as a Republican. But
he has never claimed to be anything but a conservative. In 1978, when he won his first congressional term amid the statewide furor over tax-
cutting Proposition 13, he left no doubt where he
stood on government spending. And he was on the
successful side of the issue.

Even before 1967, when Dannemeyer left the
Democratic Party, he had been on the political
right. He won two assembly terms in Republican
Orange County during the 1960s, but when he
tried to move up to the state Senate in 1966, he
was soundly defeated by a Republican
assemblyman. That was the end of Dannemeyer's
Democratic career.

He first ran as a Republican in 1972, challenging Assemblyman Ken Cory, one of the few
popular Democrats in Orange County. Cory easily
defeated him.

But in 1976, Dannemeyer was able to take
back the Assembly seat he had won as a Democrat
14 years before, defeating an aide to the Republican who had replaced him. His strong showing
convinced Orange County Republicans of
Dannemeyer's strength as one of their own.

When Republican Rep. Charles E. Wiggins
retired from Congress two years later, nobody

---

**39th District: North Orange County
— Anaheim.** Population: 592,845 (28% increase since 1970). Race: White 518,217 (87%),
Black 6,174 (1%), Asian and Pacific Islander
22,473 (4%), Others 45,981 (8%). Spanish
origin: 89,587 (15%).

tried to challenge Dannemeyer for the GOP nomination. His Democratic opponent, William Farris, had run twice before against Wiggins, whittling away at the Republican's base. But Dannemeyer defeated him easily, and by 1980 performed like a well-entrenched senior Republican.

**The District:** Covering the northeast quarter of Orange County, this district includes Disneyland, the California Angels' baseball stadium and hundreds of thousands of Republicans.

The middle-to-upper-class citizens of Anaheim and Fullerton, and of fast-growing Yorba Linda and Orange, vote a straight Republican ticket with more frequency than almost any other residents of the state. In the seven contests for president, governor and senator that have taken place within the district's boundaries, Republicans have lost only one — to Gov. Edmund G. Brown Jr. in 1978. In 1980, Ronald Reagan and GOP Senate nominee Paul Gann both won their highest statewide percentages in the 39th District.

## Committees

**Energy and Commerce** (11th of 18 Republicans)
Fossil and Synthetic Fuels; Health and the Environment.

**Post Office and Civil Service** (7th of 11 Republicans)
Compensation and Employee Benefits; Postal Personnel and Modernization.

## Elections

**1980 General**

| | |
|---|---|
| William Dannemeyer (R ) | 175,228 (76 %) |
| Leonard Lahtinen (D ) | 54,504 (24 %) |

**1978 General**

| | |
|---|---|
| William Dannemeyer (R ) | 112,160 (64 %) |
| William Farris (D ) | 63,891 (36 %) |

**District Vote For President**

| | 1980 | | 1976 |
|---|---|---|---|
| D | 51,811 (21 %) | D | 73,263 (35 %) |
| R | 170,015 (70 %) | R | 131,577 (63 %) |
| I | 16,328 (7 %) | | |

## Campaign Finance

| | Receipts | Receipts from PACs | Expenditures |
|---|---|---|---|
| **1980** | | | |
| Dannemeyer (R ) | $186,583 | $67,738 (36 %) | $154,849 |
| Lahtinen (D) | $16,837 | $1,150 (7 %) | $16,369 |
| **1978** | | | |
| Dannemeyer (R ) | $161,204 | $64,117 (40 %) | $161,151 |
| Farris (D ) | $49,760 | $11,184 (22 %) | $47,172 |

## Voting Studies

| | Presidential Support | | Party Unity | | Conservative Coalition | |
|---|---|---|---|---|---|---|
| Year | S | O | S | O | S | O |
| 1980 | 32 | 64 | 91 | 8 | 92 | 7 |
| 1979 | 25 | 74 | 94 | 5 | 94 | 6 |

S = Support          O = Opposition

## Key Votes

**96th Congress**

| | |
|---|---|
| Weaken Carter oil profits tax (1979) | N |
| Reject hospital cost control plan (1979) | Y |
| Implement Panama Canal Treaties (1979) | N |
| Establish Department of Education (1979) | N |
| Approve Anti-busing Amendment (1979) | Y |
| Guarantee Chrysler Corp. loans (1979) | N |
| Approve military draft registration (1980) | Y |
| Aid Sandinista regime in Nicaragua (1980) | N |
| Strengthen fair housing laws (1980) | N |

**97th Congress**

| | |
|---|---|
| Reagan budget proposal (1981) | Y |

## Interest Group Ratings

| Year | ADA | ACA | AFL-CIO | CCUS |
|---|---|---|---|---|
| 1980 | 6 | 100 | 10 | 70 |
| 1979 | 5 | 100 | 10 | 89 |

# 40 Robert E. Badham (R)

**Of Newport Beach — Elected 1976**

**Born:** June 9, 1929, Los Angeles, Calif.
**Education:** Attended Occidental College, 1948-49; Stanford U., A.B. 1951.
**Military Career:** Navy, 1951-54.
**Profession:** Hardware executive.
**Family:** Wife, Anne Carroll; five children.
**Religion:** Lutheran.
**Political Career:** Calif. Assembly, 1963-77.

**In Washington:** Badham, good humored and popular, is an insider in the affairs of his state's GOP delegation and in Republican politics at home.

He was president of his GOP freshman class, the 95th Club. He is a member of the Republican Policy Committee, and secretary of the California Republican delegation. As a second-termer, he helped organize the Travel and Tourism Caucus, a bipartisan collection of more than half the House, concerned that energy conservation measures would hurt the travel industry.

And he is relatively close to Ronald Reagan, whom he served as a loyal ally in the California Legislature during eight gubernatorial years.

So far, at least, Badham has been known more for his access to power than for his use of it. He has not been associated with many legislative issues in his early terms. On the Armed Services Committee, Badham has earned a reputation as a thoughtful student of military systems, interested in new technology. He votes with the panel's hard-line GOP bloc, but he rarely shows the stridency often associated with that group; he is a consistently courteous questioner.

Badham's first important floor duty came in early 1981, on a subject close to the hearts of Republican budget-cutters — committee spending allowances. As senior Republican on the Accounts Subcommittee at House Administration, Badham led the debate on a GOP move to slice all committee budgets 10 percent below the previous year's spending. "Do we have a better Congress than we did four years ago or 10 years ago?" Badham asked, paraphrasing Reagan's 1980 campaign question.

Democrats hesitated and delayed a vote and finally came up with a compromise, to cut the budgets by 10 percent below what was authorized for 1980, rather than what was actually spent. That left the budgets a bit higher than 1980 but lower than many chairmen wanted. Badham did

not win, but the Democrats had to take an action they wanted to avoid — making any cuts at all.

**At Home:** Badham comes from a part of Orange County where candidates still campaign by invoking the name of Barry Goldwater. That is exactly what Badham did in 1976 to win his House seat, taking it away from a GOP incumbent who had been convicted of bribery.

Saying he shared the pro-defense views of his "good friend, Barry Goldwater," and describing himself as an "inflation-fighting legislator in the Goldwater mold," Badham easily defeated Rep. Andrew J. Hinshaw and seven other Republicans who wanted Hinshaw's seat, then coasted in November.

His campaigns since then have been routine. Badham's views appear perfectly matched for his upper-class Orange County district.

Badham spent his childhood in Beverly Hills, took a degree in architecture and ran a hardware business in Newport Beach before entering Orange County politics at age 33. He won a seat in the Assembly and spent 14 years dividing his time between Sacramento and the hardware business.

He ran his office like a small-scale congressional operation, handling constituent problems with state government and sending out a newsletter three times a year. When it came time to run for the U.S. House in 1976, Badham was well-known and well-liked in his Assembly district,

---

**40th District: Southern Orange County — Costa Mesa.** Population: 774,539 (67% increase since 1970). Race: White 686,618 (89%), Black 17,901 (2%), Asian and Pacific Islander 30,297 (4%), Others 39,723 (5%). Spanish origin: 74,296 (10%).

---

which covered about half the 40th.

Hinshaw had been convicted that January and sentenced to a 1-to-14-year prison term. Admitting his chances of winning renomination were "mediocre," Hinshaw nevertheless ran in the primary. He finished in fourth place with less than 7 percent of the vote. The real contest was between Badham and John G. Schmitz, who had won a special election in the district in 1970, only to be defeated in 1972 by Hinshaw.

Most party officials thought Schmitz was too extreme in his conservative views. The year he lost his House seat he ran for president on the American Party ticket, accusing President Nixon of liberalism. But Schmitz was a more vibrant campaigner than Badham and he was at least as familiar to the voters. The decision went to Badham, but by fewer than 2,000 votes.

**The District:** By party registration as well as by reputation, this is the most Republican district in California. When a Democrat was elected to the state Assembly here in 1976, largely because the Republican nominee disappeared before the election, the winner did not even seek a second term two years later.

The 40th includes a series of wealthy seafront communities, notably Newport Beach and San Clemente, solid one-party towns. There are a few pockets of marginal Democratic strength, such as Costa Mesa and trendy Laguna Beach, but these have little effect on the overall result.

## Committees

**Armed Services** (11th of 19 Republicans)
Procurement and Military Nuclear Systems; Research and Development.

**House Administration** (3rd of 8 Republicans)
Accounts; Task Force on Committee Organization.

## Elections

**1980 General**

| | |
|---|---|
| Robert Badham (R ) | 213,999 (70 %) |
| Michael Dow (D ) | 66,512 (22 %) |
| Dan Mahaffey (LIB) | 24,486 (8 %) |

**1980 Primary**

| | |
|---|---|
| Robert Badham (R ) | 90,706 (76 %) |
| Richard Gardner (R ) | 23,938 (20 %) |

**1978 General**

| | |
|---|---|
| Robert Badham (R ) | 147,882 (66 %) |
| Jim McGuy (D ) | 76,358 (34 %) |

**Previous Winning Percentage**

1976 (59 %)

**District Vote For President**

| | 1980 | | 1976 |
|---|---|---|---|
| D | 68,255 (21 %) | D | 79,649 (32 %) |
| R | 225,599 (69 %) | R | 167,203 (67 %) |
| I | 24,575 (8 %) | | |

## Campaign Finance

| | Receipts | Percent of Receipts from PACs | Expenditures |
|---|---|---|---|
| **1980** | | | |
| Badham (R ) | $127,505 | $42,873 (34 %) | $123,492 |
| Dow (D ) | $16,790 | $1,300 (8 %) | $15,863 |

| 1978 | | | |
|---|---|---|---|
| Badham (R ) | $95,770 | $22,542 (24 %) | $51,719 |
| McGuy (D ) | $5,147 | $1,700 (33 %) | $5,182 |

## Voting Studies

| Year | Presidential Support | | Party Unity | | Conservative Coalition | |
|---|---|---|---|---|---|---|
| | S | O | S | O | S | O |
| 1980 | 28 | 55 | 75 | 6 | 82 | 4 |
| 1979 | 21 | 66 | 82 | 5 | 83 | 4 |
| 1978 | 19 | 55 | 75 | 7 | 82 | 4 |
| 1977 | 32 | 57 | 84 | 6 | 91 | 3 |

S = Support          O = Opposition

## Key Votes

**96th Congress**

| | |
|---|---|
| Weaken Carter oil profits tax (1979) | Y |
| Reject hospital cost control plan (1979) | Y |
| Implement Panama Canal Treaties (1979) | N |
| Establish Department of Education (1979) | N |
| Approve Anti-busing Amendment (1979) | Y |
| Guarantee Chrysler Corp. loans (1979) | N |
| Approve military draft registration (1980) | Y |
| Aid Sandinista regime in Nicaragua (1980) | N |
| Strengthen fair housing laws (1980) | N |

**97th Congress**

| | |
|---|---|
| Reagan budget proposals (1981) | Y |

## Interest Group Ratings

| Year | ADA | ACA | AFL-CIO | CCUS |
|---|---|---|---|---|
| 1980 | 0 | 95 | 11 | 74 |
| 1979 | 0 | 96 | 11 | 94 |
| 1978 | 10 | 100 | 21 | 100 |
| 1977 | 0 | 96 | 10 | 94 |

**175**

# 41 Bill Lowery (R)

**Of San Diego — Elected 1980**

**Born:** May 2, 1947, San Diego, Calif.
**Education:** San Diego State College, no degree.
**Profession:** Public relations and advertising consultant.
**Family:** Wife, Kathleen Brown; one child.
**Religion:** Roman Catholic.
**Political Career:** San Diego City Council, 1977-81.

**The Member:** Described as a "Republican regular" since the age of 12, Lowery began laying the groundwork for a House race long before Republican Rep. Bob Wilson announced his retirement in early 1980. A friend of President Ford's son, Jack, Lowery lined up $90,000 in commitments before the campaign began. With help from the Republican National Committee, he narrowly survived a tougher-than-expected primary challenge.

In the general election, Lowery's biggest problem was that his opponent had the same name as the retiring incumbent — Bob Wilson. Lowery attacked the conservative Democratic state senator for running on the "good name" of the incumbent. He also formed a committee called "Wilsons for Bill Lowery," of other San Diegans named Wilson who supported Lowery.

Much of the credit for Lowery's victory goes to one of those Wilsons — the San Diego mayor, Pete. Lowery has been a protégé of the popular mayor since his election to the City Council in 1977. Lowery was made deputy mayor in 1980, and Mayor Wilson arranged to have him address the GOP convention in Detroit.

In 1981, when the U.S. announced it planned to sell a World War II destroyer to the Ecuadorean navy, Lowery interceded on behalf of tuna fishermen in his district who opposed the sale. In the past, Ecuador has seized U.S. tuna boats it claims have violated its territorial limits. The ship transaction was canceled.

**The District:** Covering the northern half of San Diego, this district includes the more affluent, white-collar and Republican parts of the state's second largest city, although Democrats have a nominal registration advantage. Republican Bob Wilson rarely had a difficult time winning re-election during the 28 years he held the seat. In statewide contests, the district tends to vote about 6 to 10 points more Republican than its southern neighbor, the 42nd District, which includes the rest of San Diego.

## Committees

**Banking, Finance and Urban Affairs** (17th of 19 Republicans)
Domestic Monetary Policy; Financial Institutions Supervision, Regulation and Insurance; Housing and Community Development.

**Science and Technology** (17th of 17 Republicans)
Energy Research and Production; Space Science and Applications.

## Elections

**1980 General**

| | |
|---|---|
| Bill Lowery (R ) | 123,187 (53 %) |
| Bob Wilson (D ) | 101,101 (43 %) |

**1980 Primary**

| | |
|---|---|
| Bill Lowery (R ) | 37,066 (50 %) |
| Dan McKinnon (R ) | 34,236 (46 %) |

**District Vote For President**

| | 1980 | | 1976 |
|---|---|---|---|
| D | 68,347 (28 %) | D | 90,795 (42 %) |
| R | 138,300 (57 %) | R | 122,469 (56 %) |
| I | 27,803 (12 %) | | |

## Campaign Finance

| | Receipts | Receipts from PACs | Expenditures |
|---|---|---|---|
| **1980** | | | |
| Lowery (R ) | $541,216 | $110,556 (20 %) | $212,099 |
| Wilson (D ) | $366,214 | $1,000 (0.2 %) | $395,946 |

## Key Vote

**97th Congress**

| | |
|---|---|
| Reagan budget proposal (1981) | Y |

---

**41st District: San Diego — North.**
Population: 509,713 (10% increase since 1970). Race: White 449,804 (88%), Black 16,084 (3%), Asian and Pacific Islander 20,607 (4%), Others 23,218 (4%). Spanish origin: 39,691 (7%).

# 42 Duncan L. Hunter (R)

**Of Coronado — Elected 1980**

**Born:** May 31, 1948, Riverside, Calif.
**Education:** Western State U., B.S.L. 1976; J.D. 1976.
**Military Career:** Army, 1969-71.
**Profession:** Lawyer.
**Family:** Wife, Lynne Layh; one child.
**Religion:** Baptist.
**Political Career:** No previous office.

**The Member:** Hunter has an unusual background for a conservative Republican newcomer. For the three years before his House campaign, he lived and worked in the Hispanic section of San Diego. Running his own storefront law office, Hunter often gave free legal advice to poor people. He was one of those disagreeing when President Reagan called for abolition of the Legal Services Corporation.

Hunter's work in the usually-Democratic inner city was one of the reasons for his surprising 1980 upset of Democrat Lionel Van Deerlin, a nine-term House veteran. Another reason was Hunter's ceaseless campaigning. He was shaking 1,000 hands every day while Van Deerlin remained in Washington, assuming he would win by his usual comfortable margin.

Hunter, who won a Bronze Star for flying 25 helicopter combat assaults in Vietnam, blasted away at Van Deerlin's so-called "anti-defense" voting record. He promised his own pro-Pentagon stance would help prevent America from becoming a second-rate country, while keeping jobs in the district, where the nation's largest naval base and numerous defense industries are located.

In the House, Hunter pushed successfully for a $13.3 million authorization to build the Otay Mesa border station in his district. Hunter said Otay Mesa was needed because traffic passing between Mexico and the U.S. faced long delays at San Diego's single border station.

**The District:** When San Diego was divided into two congressional districts for the 1962 elections, Republican incumbent Bob Wilson chose the northern district, leaving this one, with a higher blue-collar population, for his older brother Dick. But Van Deerlin beat Dick Wilson and kept winning for 18 years.

With twice as many registered Democrats as Republicans, the 42nd is usually a sure bet for statewide Democratic candidates. Close to the Mexican border, it has witnessed a large influx of immigrants in the last decade, and the black and Hispanic population now forms a large minority.

## Committees

**Armed Services** (17th of 19 Republicans)
Military Personnel and Compensation; Procurement and Military Nuclear Systems.

## Elections

**1980 General**

| | |
|---|---|
| Duncan Hunter (R ) | 79,713 (53 %) |
| Lionel Van Deerlin (D ) | 69,936 (47 %) |

**1980 Primary**

| | |
|---|---|
| Duncan Hunter (R ) | 15,870 (52 %) |
| Michael McGuillen (R) | 14,681 (48 %) |

**District Vote For President**

| | 1980 | | 1976 |
|---|---|---|---|
| **D** | 55,380 (37 %) | **D** | 69,939 (52 %) |
| **R** | 79,670 (53 %) | **R** | 62,460 (46 %) |
| **I** | 12,636 (8 %) | | |

## Campaign Finance

| | Receipts | Receipts from PACs | Expenditures |
|---|---|---|---|
| **1980** | | | |
| Hunter (R) | 203,647 | $22,750 (11 %) | $191,396 |
| Van Deerlin (D ) | $105,367 | $44,810 (43 %) | $140,557 |

## Key Votes

**97th Congress**

| | |
|---|---|
| Reagan budget proposal (1981) | Y |

---

**42nd District: San Diego — South.**
Population: 549,981 (19% increase since 1970). Race: White 358,534 (65%), Black 70,141 (13%), Asian and Pacific Islander 43,752 (8%), Others 77,554 (14%). Spanish origin: 73,750 (13%).

---

**177**

# 43 Clair W. Burgener (R)

**Of La Jolla — Elected in 1972**

**Born:** Dec. 5, 1921, Vernal, Utah.
**Education:** Calif. State U., A.B. 1950.
**Military Career:** Army Air Corps, 1943-45; Air Force, 1951.
**Profession:** Real estate executive.
**Family:** Wife, Marvia Hobusch; two children.
**Religion:** Mormon.
**Political Career:** San Diego City Council, 1953-57; Calif. Assembly, 1963-67; Calif. Senate, 1967-73.

**In Washington:** Burgener is a quiet, friendly man, one his California colleagues confide in and sometimes try to thrust into the role of a leader. He rarely seeks such a role on his own, but when he does he can be effective; he agreed to run for secretary of the House Republican conference in 1979, and won overwhelmingly. He still holds the job, a largely honorary one but an entree into the leadership for California, which has been shut out of such posts before.

What has differentiated Burgener from most members is something that does not show up in the *Congressional Record*. As the father of a retarded child, Burgener has spent a great deal of his House career working on behalf of the handicapped and retarded. He has switched committees and subcommittees several times, but frequently has found a way to pursue his personal cause.

While he was on the D.C. Appropriations Subcommittee, he looked into complaints about conditions at Forest Haven, the District of Columbia's facility for the retarded. When the Commerce Committee wrote a disability development bill, Burgener warned that too broad an expansion of benefits would dilute funding for the more severely retarded and handicapped.

Most of Burgener's day-to-day Appropriations work now involves two of his district's most intense interests: water and military spending. On the Energy and Water Subcommitee during the Carter administration, he helped Chairman Tom Bevill fight off Carter's plans to drop funding for 18 water projects, including a major one in California. In 1981 he joined the Military Construction Subcommittee, where he can seek money for San Diego's naval facilities.

Burgener also served a term on the Budget Committee, which he severely criticized. He said it was an "adding machine," unwilling to set overall spending targets and live within them.

"Unless we're willing to deal with aggregates initially," he said, "we're condemned to a meat ax approach when we're done."

The district Burgener represents has had a large influx of illegal aliens in recent years. He has argued for tighter immigration enforcement and was one of the plaintiffs in an unsuccessful 1980 suit which sought to bar the aliens from being counted for reapportionment purposes.

**At Home:** Burgener drew more votes in 1980 than any House candidate in history — 299,037. That is not exclusively a tribute to his popularity. It is also a matter of population growth — the 43rd District is the third largest in the country — and the nature of the opposition. Burgener's Democratic opponent was a leader of the state Ku Klux Klan, repudiated by top statewide Democrats. Whatever the opposition happens to be in a given year, however, Burgener is always safe. He has never really faced a serious challenge, and has taken every election with at least 60 percent.

Burgener is a part of the San Diego boom generation that returns him to office. After moving to the area from Utah to attend college, he opened a real estate business that has provided homes for new residents ever since.

He served four years on the San Diego City Council and a decade in the state Legislature, where he helped shepherd through Gov. Ronald Reagan's welfare bill, reducing the number of recipients but increasing their benefits. In the

---

**43rd District: Parts of San Diego, Imperial counties.** Population: 866,687 (87% increase since 1970). Race: White 747,702 (86%), Black 13,203 (2%), Asian and Pacific Islander 23,716 (3%), Others 82,066 (9%). Spanish: 129,298 (15%).

middle of Burgener's second state Senate term, a new congressional district was created in the north San Diego area he was already representing in Sacramento. As the only candidate from either party who had held elective office, he had little trouble winning the four-way primary with 78 percent and the general election with 68 percent.

Two years later the district was redrawn, moving inland through back-county San Diego, and east through rural Imperial County to the Arizona border. But it remained safe for Burgener.

**The District:** The 43rd District is at the southern tip of California, along the Mexican border. Its agricultural heartland is in the heavily-irrigated Imperial Valley, but the major political activity and population growth has been in its coastal plain north of San Diego and, to a lesser extent, in Riverside County. Both are white-collar areas and heavily Republican.

The district's registration is closely divided between Democrats and Republicans, but low turnout among Mexican-Americans and high GOP voting guarantee solid Republican margins.

## Committees

**Appropriations** (11th of 22 Republicans)
Energy and Water Deveopment; Legislative; Military Construction.

## Elections

**1980 General**

| | |
|---|---|
| Clair Burgener (R ) | 299,037 (87 %) |
| Tom Metzger (D ) | 46,383 (13 %) |

**1978 General**

| | |
|---|---|
| Clair Burgener (R ) | 167,150 (69 %) |
| Ruben Brooks (D ) | 76,308 (31 %) |

**Previous Winning Percentages**

1976 (65 %)    1974 (60 %)    1972 (68 %)

**District Vote For President**

| | 1980 | | 1976 |
|---|---|---|---|
| D | 83,335 (24 %) | D | 106,706 (39 %) |
| R | 232,808 (66 %) | R | 159,799 (59 %) |
| I | 28,281 (8 %) | | |

## Campaign Finance

| | Receipts | Receipts from PACs | Expenditures |
|---|---|---|---|
| **1980** | | | |
| Burgener (R ) | $259,217 | $63,436 (24 %) | $175,009 |
| Metzger (D ) | $26,004 | — (0 %) | $26,003 |
| **1978** | | | |
| Burgener (R ) | $93,368 | $24,485 (26 %) | $90,072 |
| Brooks (D ) | $8,720 | — (0 %) | $8,511 |

## Voting Studies

| Year | Presidential Support | | Party Unity | | Conservative Coalition | |
|---|---|---|---|---|---|---|
| | S | O | S | O | S | O |
| 1980 | 37 | 49 | 70 | 15 | 81 | 9 |
| 1979 | 29 | 67 | 88 | 9 | 94 | 5 |
| 1978 | 33 | 59 | 77 | 17 | 84 | 10 |
| 1977 | 35 | 53 | 80 | 10 | 81 | 4 |
| 1976 | 75 | 22 | 84 | 13 | 90 | 6 |
| 1975 | 62 | 35 | 87 | 9 | 92 | 4 |
| 1974 (Ford) | 43 | 46 | | | | |
| 1974 | 75 | 21 | 72 | 16 | 82 | 8 |
| 1973 | 67 | 25 | 88 | 8 | 89 | 9 |

S = Support          O = Opposition

## Key Votes

**96th Congress**

| | |
|---|---|
| Weaken Carter oil profits tax (1979) | Y |
| Reject hospital cost control plan (1979) | Y |
| Implement Panama Canal Treaties (1979) | N |
| Establish Department of Education (1979) | N |
| Approve Anti-busing Amendment (1979) | Y |
| Guarantee Chrysler Corp. loans (1979) | N |
| Approve military draft registration (1980) | Y |
| Aid Sandinista regime in Nicaragua (1980) | N |
| Strengthen fair housing laws (1980) | N |

**97th Congress**

| | |
|---|---|
| Reagan budget proposal (1981) | Y |

## Interest Group Ratings

| Year | ADA | ACA | AFL-CIO | CCUS |
|---|---|---|---|---|
| 1980 | 6 | 86 | 11 | 77 |
| 1979 | 16 | 96 | 20 | 89 |
| 1978 | 10 | 88 | 11 | 88 |
| 1977 | 5 | 92 | 19 | 94 |
| 1976 | 10 | 85 | 23 | 88 |
| 1975 | 0 | 100 | 17 | 82 |
| 1974 | 9 | 79 | 0 | 88 |
| 1973 | 4 | 92 | 10 | 100 |

**179**

# Colorado

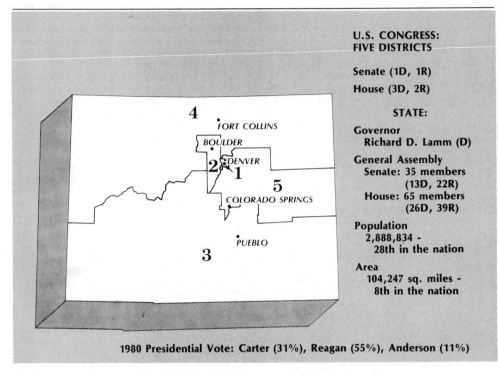

U.S. CONGRESS:
FIVE DISTRICTS

Senate (1D, 1R)
House (3D, 2R)

STATE:

Governor
  Richard D. Lamm (D)

General Assembly
  Senate: 35 members
    (13D, 22R)
  House: 65 members
    (26D, 39R)

Population
  2,888,834 -
    28th in the nation

Area
  104,247 sq. miles -
    8th in the nation

**1980 Presidential Vote: Carter (31%), Reagan (55%), Anderson (11%)**

## ... A Politics of Indecision

In just one decade, flourishing, energy-rich Colorado has been transformed from a bastion of conservative Republicanism into one of the nation's prime examples of political schizophrenia.

In 1971, pro-growth Republicans controlled the state. But after a turbulent decade of population growth, environmental activism and a second conservative reaction, political power has been effectively split between the two major parties.

Democrats now hold the governorship, a U.S. Senate seat and a majority of the congressional delegation. Republicans control the other U.S. Senate seat and the state legislature.

With little patronage to offer, the state parties have traditionally been weak in Colorado. But never so weak as now. One of the few states where there are more registered independents than Democrats or Republicans, Colorado has entered an era of unpredictable politics.

The face of the state has been changed by its rapid growth. Between 1945 and 1970, the population doubled. And in the 1970s, it grew by another 31 percent. Thousands of newcomers have been drawn by the scenery and job opportunities offered by "clean" industries that have grown up in the shadows of the Rocky Mountains.

But the populous Front Range of the Rockies has a limited water supply, and the strain of a booming population in the early 1970s led to a slow-growth movement concerned about protecting the state's landscape and natural resources.

In 1972, pro-growth politics suffered a striking defeat. Voters rejected a measure to hold the 1976 Winter Olympics in Colorado and turned out part of the "Old Guard." Republican Sen. Gordon Allott was unseated by Democrat Floyd K. Haskell and the pro-development House Interior Chairman Wayne Aspinall was upset in a Democratic primary. Democrat Patricia Schroeder won the Denver House seat from a GOP incumbent.

The pro-environment tide crested in 1974. Democrat Gary Hart overwhelmed conservative Republican Sen. Peter H. Dominick, Democrat Richard Lamm won the governorship and Democrat Timothy E. Wirth captured a House seat in the Denver suburbs.

Since then, the signals have been mixed, as if Colorado cannot decide from year to year what it thinks about its dominant political issue. In national elections, Republicans are as strong as ever; Carter lost convincingly in 1976, and in 1980 he drew less than a third of the vote.

But environmentalist Democrats still run remarkably well at the state level. In 1978, Gov. Lamm, a leader in the environmental movement, was re-elected by the landslide margin of 167,000 votes. At the same time, conservative Republican William L. Armstrong was sent to the Senate with a 150,000-vote majority over Haskell, the incumbent. Two years later, as Colorado was voting overwhelmingly for Reagan, it re-elected Hart.

# A Political Tour

**The Front Range.** Most of Colorado's rich supply of natural resources lies on the Western Slope of the Rockies. But most of the population, commerce and energy operations are on the eastern side of the mountains along the Front Range.

More than 80 percent of Colorado's population lives in the narrow strip extending from the Wyoming border to Colorado Springs.

Anchoring the south flank, Colorado Springs was originally a resort. After World War II it became a major center of military operations in the Rocky Mountains. Recently, electronics firms have come to the area. While it economic base has changed, the politics of Colorado Springs have remained consistent — conservative Republican.

Along the northern flank of the Front Range are the cities of Fort Collins and Greeley. Both are educational and trade centers for agricultural northern Colorado, and tend to be swing areas in major statewide races.

**The Denver Area.** In the center of the Front Range population corridor is metropolitan Denver, a five-county area that is home for 1.6 million of the state's 2.9 million residents.

With the Rockies looming in the west, the area has gained a reputation as one of the more relaxed and livable places in the nation. But it has not been able to escape air pollution. Even though there are few major industrial plants, a brown cloud of automobile pollutants frequently rests at the base of the mountains and engulfs the Denver area. In an effort to reduce pollution, an annual auto emission inspection law was passed in 1980.

Unlike the booming suburbs, the city of Denver is losing population. In 1970, Denver comprised 42 percent of the metropolitan population. In 1980, its share was down to 31 percent. But Denver's national prominence has increased as regional energy operations have joined federal government establishments in making the city a focal point of commerce in the Rocky Mountains.

Liberal white-collar voters and a sizable minority population have enabled the Democrats to maintain their dominance in Denver politics. Blacks make up 12 percent of the Denver population. Hispanics make up 19 percent.

The suburbs are middle-class and white. As electronics and engineering firms have moved into the area, the population has taken a big jump and Republicans have thrived. Every county around Denver grew by at least 32 percent in the 1970s.

Arapahoe County, to the south and east of Denver, grew 81 percent during the 1970s. With some of the most affluent communities in Colorado, Arapahoe provides the backbone for conservative Republicanism in the Denver suburbs.

Jefferson County to the west usually votes Republican, but is less uniform in its conservatism. The county mixes business executives and factory workers. Many are employed by the Coors Brewery or at the Martin-Marietta plant.

Boulder and Adams counties on the north are more Democratic. The University of Colorado is located in the city of Boulder and several government research firms are in the area. The university vote in Boulder helped give John B. Anderson a solid 16 percent in 1980. Democratic strength in Adams County is based on a large blue-collar and minority population. Hispanics alone comprise 16 percent of the county population. But party loyalty appears to be weakening. Reagan carried the county by a comfortable margin.

**Western Slope.** The western side of the state has a reputation as a swing area in state politics, although in 1980 it went heavily for Reagan and the GOP Senate candidate.

While the gold and silver deposits of the 19th century have petered out, Colorado ranks among the top 12 states in coal reserves and oil and natural gas production. It also is a leading supplier of tin, uranium, zinc and molybdenum.

Most of the oil and mineral wealth is located in the northwest part of the state, with the oil shale reserves centered in the counties along the Utah border. The promise of an energy boom has fueled a modest population influx into an area that was previously a vast, dry wasteland. Grand Junction, about 30 miles east of the Utah border, has emerged as the trade center for the local energy operations. It is the only city on the Western Slope with more than 25,000 people.

Grand Junction is connected to Denver by Interstate 70. The substantial completion of the route has opened up the development of more ski resorts in Glenwood Springs, Vail and Dillon. Every county along Interstate 70 between Denver and Grand Junction showed a population increase of at least 50 percent in the 1970s. The scenic, heavily timbered mountain counties of southwest Colorado showed more modest population growth.

**Southern Colorado.** The vibrant growth of the Front Range and the Western Slope has not been shared by southern Colorado, a triangular-shaped region that extends roughly from Durango near the Utah border on the west to Pueblo on the north and La Junta on the east.

Southern Colorado lacks the natural resources of the Western Slope and the strategic location of the cities of the Front Range. Pueblo County, the most populous in the region, grew by only 6 percent in the 1970s. Other southern Colorado counties had a similarly small growth or actually lost population.

Industrial Pueblo and the declining coal-mining communities of Trinidad and Walsenburg to the south all have large East European and Italian elements. A steel-producing center, Pueblo is the hub of union activity in Colorado and a Democratic stronghold.

To the southwest across the Sangre de Cristo Mountains is the San Luis Valley, which includes portions of the two heavily Hispanic counties, Costilla and Conejos. Both are more than 50 percent Hispanic and are in the poorest part of the state. Many residents of the dry, isolated valley live on small, unproductive farms and maintain their old cultural customs. Most of them also maintain loyalty to the Democratic Party. Costilla County regularly turns in higher percentages for Democratic candidates than any other county in Colorado.

**Eastern Plains.** The Great Plains of the agricultural Midwest extend across the eastern third of Colorado. Like neighboring Kansas and Nebraska, the region is conservative in outlook.

Sparse rainfall and high winds made the Plains part of the 1930s "dust bowl." But more mechanization and the discovery of an underground aquifer have helped the region's economy.

The South Platte River in the northern part of the area and the Arkansas in the south also provide water for irrigation. Wheat, vegetables and livestock are major agricultural pursuits. These lightly populated farm areas usually vote Republican.

# Redrawing the Lines

Colorado's 31 percent growth in the last decade brings it another House seat. Democrats are at a disadvantage in redistricting, since population has declined or grown little in most areas where they are strongest, such as Denver, Pueblo County and the southern region. With rapid growth in the Denver suburbs and other Republican-voting areas of the Front Range, the GOP has plenty of room to maneuver.

The Republican-controlled legislature passed a plan that created a new 6th District favorable to their party, but Gov. Lamm vetoed the map in June because it also weakened Democratic Reps. Ray Kogovsek and Wirth.

# Governor
# Richard D. Lamm (D)

**Born:** Aug. 3, 1935, Madison, Wis.
**Home:** Denver, Colo.
**Education:** U. of Wisconsin, B.B.A. 1957; U. of California, LL.B. 1961.
**Military Career:** Army.
**Profession:** Lawyer, certified public accountant.
**Family:** Wife, Dottie; two children.
**Religion:** Unitarian.
**Political Career:** Colorado House, 1967-75; House assistant minority leader, 1971-75; elected governor 1974, 1978; term expires Jan. 1983.

# Gary Hart (D)

### Of Denver — Elected 1974

**Born:** Nov. 28, 1937, Ottawa, Kan.
**Education:** Bethany College, B.A. 1958; Yale U., B.D. 1961, LL.B. 1964.
**Profession:** Lawyer.
**Family:** Wife, Lee Ludwig; two children.
**Religion:** Protestant.
**Political Career:** No previous office.

**In Washington:** Hart is not now and probably never was a "McGovern liberal," in the sense that phrase normally implies, but his entire Senate career has been measured against the backdrop of his role as manager of the South Dakota senator's 1972 presidential campaign.

From the moment he came to the Senate, Hart has generated debate among colleagues about how much of his call for liberal reappraisal represented personal philosophy, and how much represented an adjustment to Colorado politics.

By 1980, his mixture of environmentalism, balanced-budget voting and gentle skepticism toward the Pentagon had brought him re-election while McGovern himself was being swamped in South Dakota. Hart's name began showing up in speculation about future contenders for national office.

Hart was relatively quiet during his first few years in the Senate, but he involved himself in a complex variety of issues. "To me," he once said, "the legislative process is a big kind of smorgasbord. And I don't want to just eat the desserts or the salad. I want the whole thing."

On the Armed Services Committee, he has been a proponent of more mobile and flexible weapons systems, especially for the Navy. He contends the United States, using its superior technology, should seize the initiative against the Soviet Union with a revamped fleet that features small, fast carriers and other ships equipped with planes that can take off and land vertically.

He charges there are serious deficiencies in the "big carrier" approach favored by the Reagan administration. "Even with substantial increases in the Navy's shipbuilding budget," he said in 1981, "we can never have enough ships if each ship we build is extremely expensive." He appeared to win a small victory by attracting the sympathy of Maine Republican William S. Cohen, chairman of the Armed Services Sea Power Subcommittee in the 97th Congress.

Hart was a leading advocate of the now-derailed SALT II treaty and perhaps the most knowledgeable senator on his side of the issue about its detailed provisions.

Hart's defense views still show recognizable traces of the Vietnam dove of the early 1970s. But his domestic approach has little in common with earlier liberalism. Instead of relying on regulation and federal programs to achieve economic objectives, Hart has consistently urged greater attention to the market and its incentives. "Government regulations are often ill-conceived, unneeded and result in the opposite of the intended result," he has said. Regulation ought to be limited, he contends, primarily to the protection of health and safety —not economic goals.

By 1978, Hart was proposing his own program for balancing the budget and tackling inflation through a series of spending cuts and tax incentives — a plan not terribly different from some put forward by Senate Republicans.

He was an early and ardent advocate of policies to reduce U.S. dependence on imported oil; in 1980, he was one of just 10 senators supporting President Carter's effort to impose an oil import fee. Perhaps more surprising, he was one of just eight Democrats (and the only one remotely identifiable as a liberal) to vote against Carter's windfall profits tax, contending it would dampen incentives for exploration and production of new oil. In its place, Hart proposed a stiff severance tax on already-discovered "old oil." He said this would raise about the same revenue and preclude excessive oil company profits from price decontrol. Colorado's independent oil companies find considerable amount of new oil; they do not hold very much old oil.

Hart joined other Western senators in opposing Carter's attempts to trim water projects in the region. He opposed the Chrysler loan guarantee in 1979. He voted against the shipment of nuclear fuel to India, and against the 1978 Middle East arms sales package. He opposed resuming regis-

**183**

tration for the draft.

Some of these votes were "liberal" and others "conservative" by the usual definitions; such labels, however, are not easy to apply to Hart, despite his prominent position on the 1980 "hit list" of conservative interest groups. By his own account, he has "tried to occupy as much of the party spectrum as possible without compromising principle."

As chairman of the Nuclear Regulation Subcommittee of the Environment and Public Works Committee, Hart led the Senate's investigation into the Three Mile Island nuclear power plant accident. While he unsuccessfully sought a six-month moratorium on the licensing of new reactors pending a study of safety measures in all plants, he never advocated abandoning nuclear power. Saying there is no viable alternative to nuclear energy for the next quarter-century, Hart recommended improved safety precautions and a permanent solution to the disposal of nuclear wastes.

This tendency to thread a middle course was also evident in his performance as chairman of the National Commission on Air Quality, established by Congress in 1977 to analyze the effects of the Clean Air Act. The panel's report, released in March, 1981, drew fire from environmentalists and business groups alike, but it was used by chairmen of the House and Senate committees in reviewing the law in the 97th Congress.

On the Environment Committee, Hart has worked closely with Robert Stafford of Vermont, the moderate Republican who assumed control in 1981. But he has sought to get along with the Republican right as well. He and Barry Goldwater of Arizona worked together to produce a report on the problem of false alerts in the nation's missile attack warning system.

Hart is regarded as personable by his colleagues, although he often seems reserved to the point of aloofness. "I'm a disciple of the school that says a lot of people in public life are really shy, reticent people," he once said. "They manage to succeed in spite of their personality rather than because of it."

**At Home:** Hart has made few political mistakes as a candidate. From the early days of his Senate effort in 1974, when he assured Colorado voters that his generation of Democrats were not "a bunch of little Hubert Humphreys," to the beginning of his second term, when he obtained a commission in the U.S. Naval Reserve, he has avoided any damaging liberal stigma.

On election night, 1980, when McGovern was going down to overwhelming defeat in South Dakota, Hart was surviving by 19,000 votes. He was helped considerably by dissension among his state's Republicans, but he had also helped himself by finding issues that worked in Colorado — including support for a higher defense budget.

Hart was a college student during John F. Kennedy's presidential campaign, and he signed up to work in the Kennedy campaign. Later, after graduating from Yale Law School, he was a lawyer in the Justice Department and special assistant to Interior Secretary Stewart Udall. He worked for Robert Kennedy in the 1968 primaries. Hart moved to Denver at the end of the Johnson administration to practice law. In 1969, he met McGovern, who had stepped in as a substitute candidate the previous year after Robert Kennedy's assassination. The South Dakota senator impressed Hart with his intelligence, and the young attorney concluded McGovern had a chance to win in national politics.

Signed on as McGovern's presidential campaign manager, Hart orchestrated the movement of liberals and anti-war Democrats that all but locked up the 1972 nomination for their candidate in the months before most of the party was looking. Good field work at the precinct level and a thorough understanding of the new Democratic Party rules, which McGovern largely wrote, gave Hart a reputation as a political genius.

It was a reputation that did not survive the fall. After the election defeat, Hart went home to Denver, wrote a book about the McGovern experience, called *Right From the Start*, and decided to run for the Senate.

Intimately familiar with the world of 3x5 cards, phone banks and door-to-door canvassing, Hart successfully transferred his political organizing skills to the state level. He attracted more than 3,000 workers and deployed them to all corners of Colorado.

In the 1974 primary, Hart faced strong competition from Herrick S. Roth, a former state senator who had been ousted as Colorado AFL-CIO President for backing McGovern in 1972. Roth won the top-line ballot listing at the state party convention, and still had broad labor support. He was also a locally known talk show host in Denver.

But Hart eked out a primary victory on the strength of his superior organization. The contest was largely free of rancor, and Democrats unified behind him.

It was a strong Democratic year, and Republican Sen. Peter H. Dominick had major weaknesses. One was his health. Dominick suffered from a back problem that left him in obvious pain much of the time.

Ethics became a crucial issue when Hart accused Dominick, as chairman of the National Republican Senatorial Committee, of having "laundered" donations from a dairy cooperative in 1972 and channeled them to the Nixon re-election committee.

Dominick protested that he had done nothing illegal, but the issue kept him on the defensive in a year in which Watergate made any ethical controversy a serious liability.

Hart managed to play down ideology. Although he had worked for liberal politicians, he had no public record himself and thus had the freedom to sound more conservative themes. His margin over Dominick was a substantial 146,183 votes.

In 1980, Hart found himself rated among the most vulnerable Democratic senators. But he was fortunate once more.

Republicans nominated a candidate most of

the party did not like — Secretary of State Mary Estill Buchanan. A GOP convention denied her a place on the primary ballot, but she sued her way onto it, and the active minority of moderate Republicans gave her 30 percent of the vote, just enough to win the nomination against a divided field of three conservatives.

Buchanan had considerable appeal to Democrats, and began the fall campaign substantially ahead of Hart. But she was ill-informed on many national questions, and her late start put her at a disadvantage against the always-efficient Hart organization. Although she campaigned as a balanced-budget conservative sympathetic to Ronald Reagan, disgruntled GOP conservatives continued to call her "the Republican Gary Hart."

In the end, Reagan's huge statewide plurality nearly pulled Buchanan through. But Hart ran well enough in Denver to win a second term by a narrow margin.

## Committees

**Armed Services** (6th of 8 Democrats)
  Military Construction; Sea Power and Force Projection; Strategic and Theater Nuclear Forces.

**Budget**

**Environment and Public Works** (4th of 7 Democrats)
  Environmental Pollution; Nuclear Regulation; Toxic Substances and Environmental Oversight.

## Elections

**1980 General**

| | |
|---|---|
| Gary Hart (D) | 590,501 (50%) |
| Mary Buchanan (R) | 571,295 (49%) |

**Previous Winning Percentage**

1974 (57%)

## Campaign Finance

| | Receipts | Receipts from PACs | Expenditures |
|---|---|---|---|
| 1980 | | | |
| Hart (D) | $1,184,979 | $243,452 (21%) | $1,142,304 |
| Buchanan (R) | $1,150,558 | $339,685 (30%) | $1,085,445 |

## Voting Studies

| Presidential Support | Party Unity | Conservative Coalition |
|---|---|---|

| Year | S | O | S | O | S | O |
|---|---|---|---|---|---|---|
| 1980 | 66 | 23 | 68 | 19 | 25 | 63 |
| 1979 | 79 | 17 | 79 | 18 | 23 | 71 |
| 1978 | 84 | 9 | 87 | 8 | 20 | 76 |
| 1977 | 74 | 25 | 80 | 14 | 19 | 73 |
| 1976 | 40 | 55 | 84 | 9 | 10 | 84 |
| 1975 | 45 | 51 | 85 | 7 | 13 | 80 |

S = Support          O = Opposition

## Key Votes

**96th Congress**

| | |
|---|---|
| Maintain relations with Taiwan (1979) | N |
| Reduce synthetic fuel development funds (1979) | Y |
| Impose nuclear plant moratorium (1979) | Y |
| Kill stronger windfall profits tax (1979) | Y |
| Guarantee Chrysler Corp. loans (1979) | N |
| Approve military draft registration (1980) | N |
| End Revenue Sharing to the states (1980) | Y |
| Block Justice Dept. busing suits (1980) | N |

**97th Congress**

| | |
|---|---|
| Restore urban program funding cuts (1981) | Y |

## Interest Group Ratings

| Year | ADA | ACA | AFL-CIO | CCUS-1 | CCUS-2 |
|---|---|---|---|---|---|
| 1980 | 61 | 36 | 47 | 39 | |
| 1979 | 58 | 15 | 89 | 9 | 27 |
| 1978 | 65 | 17 | 78 | 22 | |
| 1977 | 90 | 4 | 75 | 11 | |
| 1976 | 75 | 8 | 84 | 0 | |
| 1975 | 94 | 11 | 82 | 6 | |

*Colorado - Junior Senator*

# William L. Armstrong (R)

**Of Aurora — Elected 1978**

**Born:** March 16, 1937, Fremont, Neb.
**Education:** Attended Tulane U. and U. of Minn., 1954-56.
**Military Career:** Army National Guard, 1957-63.
**Profession:** Broadcasting executive.
**Family:** Wife, Ellen Eaton; two children.
**Religion:** Lutheran.
**Political Career:** Colo. House, 1963-65; Colo. Senate, 1965-73; U.S. House, 1973-79.

**In Washington:** Armstrong has always displayed a canny ability to place himself in the center of events, and he did it in the 97th Congress by taking places on the Banking, Budget and Finance committees at the key moments of controversy over the Reagan economic proposals.

On Budget, he emerged early in 1981 as a pivotal conservative vote, frustrated by the discrepancy between his own low-deficit views and the deficit spending required to enact a Reagan-sized tax cut. He refused to vote for the overall Reagan budget at first, until the administration promised to outline spending cuts for future years, then decided to go along.

When Democrat Ernest Hollings of South Carolina chided him for compromising his philosophical purity to accept the Reagan program despite its deficit, he replied solemnly, "I'm still a purist." He said Reagan economists convinced him the tax cuts would bolster the economy, providing new tax revenues to offset revenue losses.

On Banking, where he is chairman of a subcommittee on economic policy, Armstrong became one of the most aggressive backers of the Reagan agenda for deep cuts in subsidized housing programs, particularly public rental housing.

On Finance, he started out pushing his own version of a tax cut, one which would not include the massive personal reductions of Kemp-Roth, but would index income taxes to inflation, to protect taxpayers from being pushed into higher brackets by cost-of-living pay raises, and offer businesses faster depreciation. He ultimately did vote in committee for the Reagan-approved 25 percent tax cut over three years.

During his first Senate term, in the 96th Congress, Armstrong focused on the issue of military pay, and lobbied for an across-the-board salary increase large enough to attract more recruits into the volunteer army, which he strongly

believes in. On this issue, he had to fight the Senate's dominant voice on military personnel matters, Georgia Democrat Sam Nunn, who believes in the draft and wants to target pay increases more to the officer level.

In 1980, Armstrong tried to persuade the Senate to vote for a 3.4 percent military pay increase across-the-board, on top of the 7 percent Carter had already granted all federal employees in 1980. He called the Army a "sweatshop," and said enlisted personnel were living on food stamps and working at checkout counters in order to survive. His amendment came within four votes, 44-40, but the Nunn approach eventually won out.

On military pay, as on other economic issues, Armstrong has proved to be one of the best media entrepreneurs among the younger conservatives in the Senate. He provided a regular flow of information on the extent of poverty in the Armed Forces, backed up by letters he had received in his office. A former radio announcer himself, he knows how to contribute quotable and resonant comment for broadcast news.

**At Home:** Armstrong's boyish good looks and crisply-stated conservatism made him a man of the future among Colorado Republicans from the day he entered the Legislature in 1963 at the age of 25. He was already a successful businessman. At 22, Armstrong bought a Denver radio station and turned it into a multimillion-dollar operation.

Politically, his life also was charmed. Armstrong was sent to Congress in 1972 from a new district in the eastern suburbs of Denver. At the time, there was speculation that he had a hand in creating the district for himself. Whether he did or not, it was perfect for him. Even though Democrats and independents outnumber Republicans there, Armstrong was an easy winner three times.

He angered the party's influential right wing only once — when he backed President Ford over Reagan for the 1976 Republican presidential nomination. But the Reagan forces forgave him, and the incident faded away when he made his long-planned campaign for the Senate two years later.

Democratic Sen. Floyd Haskell was an obvious Republican target when he came up for re-election in 1978. Haskell had upset three-term Republican Gordon Allott in 1972 with an environmentalist campaign. By 1978, the state was in a far more conservative mood.

There was little doubt that Armstrong would be the Republican nominee. He easily disposed of

a primary challenge from astronaut Jack Swigert, who tried to rally the Reagan elements from two years before. Armstrong had mended fences with the party's right wing and drew 73 percent of the primary vote. That set the stage for an ideological debate with Haskell.

Armstrong criticized the incumbent for favoring the Panama Canal treaties, and denounced him as ineffective, citing Haskell's inability to dissuade President Carter from moving to cancel Colorado water projects. Haskell tried to soften his liberal image by advocating a balanced budget, and countered the charges of ineffectiveness by importing Vice President Mondale, who called Haskell "a national treasure." But it was no contest.

## Committees

**Banking, Housing and Urban Affairs** (4th of 8 Republicans)
Economic Policy, Chairman; Housing and Urban Affairs; International Finance and Monetary Policy.

**Budget** (2nd of 12 Republicans)

**Finance** (9th of 11 Republicans)
Social Security and Income Maintenance Programs, Chairman; International Trade; Taxation and Debt Management.

## Elections

**1978 General**

| | |
|---|---|
| William Armstrong (R ) | 480,596 (59 %) |
| Floyd Haskell (D ) | 330,247 (40 %) |

**1978 Primary**

| | |
|---|---|
| William Armstrong (R ) | 108,573 (73 %) |
| Jack Swigert (R) | 39,247 (27 %) |

**Previous Winning Percentages**

1976* (66 %)   1974* (58 %)   1972* (62 %)
* House elections.

## Campaign Finance

| | Receipts | Receipts from PACs | Expenditures |
|---|---|---|---|
| **1978** | | | |
| Armstrong (R ) | 1,163,790 | 310,930 (27 %) | 1,081,944 |
| Haskell (D ) | 658,657 | 213,435 (32 %) | 664,249 |

## Voting Studies

| | Presidential Support | | Party Unity | | Conservative Coalition | |
|---|---|---|---|---|---|---|
| Year | S | O | S | O | S | O |
| Senate service | | | | | | |
| 1980 | 29 | 64 | 90 | 2 | 91 | 3 |
| 1979 | 32 | 60 | 86 | 6 | 79 | 8 |
| House service | | | | | | |
| 1978 | 15 | 47 | 62 | 6 | 60 | 7 |
| 1977 | 30 | 62 | 89 | 7 | 91 | 6 |
| 1976 | 78 | 14 | 87 | 8 | 87 | 8 |
| 1975 | 65 | 31 | 86 | 8 | 89 | 9 |
| 1974 (Ford ) | 41 | 35 | | | | |
| 1974 | 65 | 29† | 78 | 15† | 74 | 16 |
| 1973 | 74 | 23 | 81 | 18 | 82 | 16 |

† Not eligible for all recorded votes.

S = Support          O = Opposition

## Key Votes

**96th Congress**

| | |
|---|---|
| Maintain relations with Taiwan (1979) | Y |
| Reduce synthetic fuel development funds (1979) | Y |
| Impose nuclear plant moratorium (1979) | N |
| Kill stronger windfall profits tax (1979) | Y |
| Guarantee Chrysler Corp. loans (1979) | N |
| Approve military draft registration (1980) | N |
| End Revenue Sharing to the states (1980) | N |
| Block Justice Dept. busing suits (1980) | Y |

**97th Congress**

| | |
|---|---|
| Restore urban program funding cuts (1981) | N |

## Interest Group Ratings

| Year | ADA | ACA | AFL-CIO | CCUS-1 | CCUS-2 |
|---|---|---|---|---|---|
| Senate service | | | | | |
| 1980 | 17 | 92 | 5 | 88 | |
| 1979 | 11 | 100 | 0 | 90 | 87 |
| House service | | | | | |
| 1978 | 5 | 92 | 6 | 81 | |
| 1977 | 0 | 100 | 17 | 94 | |
| 1976 | 0 | 93 | 13 | 82 | |
| 1975 | 16 | 93 | 4 | 82 | |
| 1974 | 9 | 100 | 9 | 100 | |
| 1973 | 8 | 92 | 0 | 100 | |

**187**

# 1 Patricia Schroeder (D)

**Of Denver — Elected 1972**

**Born:** July 30, 1940, Portland, Ore.
**Education:** U. of Minn, B.A. 1961; Harvard U.,
    J.D. 1964.
**Profession:** Lawyer.
**Family:** Husband, James Schroeder; two
    children.
**Religion:** Congregationalist.
**Political Career:** No previous office.

**In Washington:** Schroeder came to town riding the waves of the New Politics and has remained to stake her claim to the fruits of the Old Politics — seniority, a safe seat and a subcommittee chairmanship.

Along the way she has been outrageous and outspoken, a political gadfly with a sharp irreverence and a sense of humor that some find refreshing and others find annoying.

Schroeder's good looks and coquettish manner have made it difficult for her to prove herself to some of her older male colleagues. And that has made her angry. She has always demanded to be judged on her credentials as a Harvard-trained lawyer and on her accomplishments in the House. But that effort has been undermined somewhat by her frequent temptation to make fun of the entire process, even at the risk of seeming a little goofy.

It was Schroeder who staged a "sit-in" with a colleague to protest closed-door conference sessions on defense spending, and Schroeder who wore a rabbit suit during an Armed Services trip to China at Eastertime and handed out jelly beans and candy eggs to the startled Chinese.

When she arrived in Washington in 1973, Schroeder asked for and received assignment to the Armed Services Committee. She wanted to protest the war in Vietnam and the pro-military thinking that dominated defense spending decisions in Congress.

She joined a small band of doves on the committee who wanted to influence it in their direction, but who over the years have failed to do much more than offer dissenting views to the majority decisions.

In 1980, she was one of three dissenters as Armed Services recommended a $53.1 billion defense authorization bill. "The military budget has become the tool of vested economic interests," she said. "Serving these interests rarely results in obtaining military preparedness in the most eco-

nomical manner." She suggested a moratorium on procurement of all new weapons systems, diverting part of the money to improved maintenance and higher pay levels.

When the bill reached the House floor, she joined in an effort to block the new MX missile system, reflecting not only her skepticism about arms spending but the fears of Colorado that the MX would use vast quantities of its precious water. "I do not see why we run out and commit megabucks to this system that seems to change monthly," Schroeder said. But the MX survived that round.

Schroeder also has fought the draft. In 1979, when Armed Services wrote a bill providing for a registration system for 18-year-olds, she offered a floor amendment to take the provision out and won decisively. The next year, however, President Carter endorsed a similar system himself. Schroeder remained opposed to it, but it passed the House and became law.

Given her minority position on Armed Services, she has been able to accomplish more on the Post Office and Civil Service Committee, normally a secondary assignment but one she has seized on to pursue subjects that interest her.

She now is chairman of the Civil Service Subcommittee. Government employee problems are important to her home district — Denver is the regional headquarters for many federal agencies. She has held hearings on racial bias in civil

---

**1st District: Denver.** Population: 426,794 (3% decrease since 1970). Race: White 323,173 (75%), Black 58,250 (14%), Others 45,371 (11%). Spanish origin: 62,050 (15%).

---

service exams, the excessive use of consultants on federal projects and retirement rights for women.

One of Schroeder's achievements on the committee was a law to liberalize pension rights of foreign service spouses. She is one of the more active supporters of women's rights in general. She co-chairs the Congressional Women's Caucus.

She is now working on the most ambitious and technically complex project of her career — a bill called the "Government Cost Reduction Act," which aims to reduce costs by tackling what Schroeder sees as the basic problem of government: the lack of incentive to do a better job. Initial studies convinced Schroeder government efficiency suffers in part from a lack of continuity from year to year. Her bill would set goals, provide employee bonuses for cost-savings, and cut down on paperwork and outside contractors.

In the 97th Congress, Schroeder joined a third committee, Judiciary, at the request of Democratic leaders who sought to build strength against growing conservative pressure for action to stop busing and abortion. Schroeder has always voted for the use of federal funds to pay for abortions and opposed an anti-busing amendment to the Constitution in 1979.

There has been little change in Schroeder's overall liberal voting record over the years, but her frustration with bureaucracy has led her in a few different directions from some of the liberal pressure groups that were most enthusiastic about her in the beginning. She has been denounced regularly by consumer activist Ralph Nader for her refusal to back legislation creating an independent consumer protection agency.

**At Home.** Schroeder was in the vanguard of the Democratic resurgence in Colorado in the early 1970s, scoring upset victories in the 1972 primary and general election to wrest the Denver House seat from Republican control.

Although she had been a practicing attorney and women's rights activist, Schroeder was a political neophyte at the time. She was encour-

aged to make the race by her lawyer husband, who had unsuccessfully sought a state House seat himself in 1970.

Cultivating support from liberals in Denver and feminists and environmentalists at the national level, Schroeder put together an effective grass-roots organization. She drew 55 percent of the vote against state Senate Minority Leader Clarence Decker in the primary, and 52 percent in the general election to oust freshman GOP Rep. James (Mike) McKevitt. McKevitt had been (and still is) the only Republican winner in the 1st District since 1950.

The GOP has fielded a variety of candidates against Schroeder since 1972 — an anti-busing leader, a veteran state legislator, a wealthy political newcomer and a woman school board member.

The legislator, state Rep. Don Friedman, came the closest, in 1976. Friedman sharply criticized the incumbent's liberal voting record and put together a campaign treasury that exceeded Schroeder's. He held her to 53 percent of the vote.

Since then, the Republican threat has subsided. Population movements have made the district more minority-oriented, and Schroeder has been able to draw on a coalition of liberals, young professionals, blacks and Hispanics. In 1978 and 1980, she averaged 60 percent of the vote.

**The District.** The urban 1st contains nearly all the city of Denver — the financial, trading and cultural center for the Rocky Mountain region.

It is the most Democratic district in Colorado and one of the party's few strongholds in the Rockies. It regularly gives Democratic state and national candidates a higher share of the vote than any other district in the state.

Early in the 1970s, Republican state legislators had hoped to develop the 1st into a GOP enclave. Their redistricting effort in 1972 transferred about 73,000 residents of the city's heavily Democratic west side into the suburban 2nd District. But when Republicans lost the seat to Schroeder that fall, it was apparent that their strategy had failed.

## Campaign Finance

| | Receipts | Receipts from PACs | Expenditures |
|---|---|---|---|
| **1980** | | | |
| Schroeder (D) | $180,788 | $56,088 (31 %) | $181,299 |
| Bradford (R) | $111,972 | $28,867 (26 %) | $118,417 |
| **1978** | | | |
| Schroeder (D) | $145,556 | $57,182 (39 %) | $119,930 |
| Hutcheson (R) | $154,739 | $34,083 (22 %) | $146,210 |

## Committees

**Armed Services** (12th of 25 Democrats)
Readiness; Research and Development.

**Judiciary** (12th of 16 Democrats)
Civil and Constitutional Rights; Immigration, Refugees and International Law.

**Post Office and Civil Service** (4th of 15 Democrats)
Civil Service, chairman.

*Patricia Schroeder, D-Colo.*

# Elections

**1980 General**

| | |
|---|---|
| Patricia Schroeder (D ) | 107,364 (60 %) |
| Naomi Bradford (R ) | 67,804 (38 %) |

**1978 General**

| | |
|---|---|
| Patricia Schroeder (D ) | 82,742 (62 %) |
| Gene Hutcheson (R ) | 49,845 (37 %) |

**Previous Winning Percentages**

1976 (53%)     1974 (59%)     1972 (52%)

**District Vote For President**

| | 1980 | | 1976 | | 1972 |
|---|---|---|---|---|---|
| D | 71,863 (40 %) | D | 93,764 (48 %) | D | 82,578 (43 %) |
| R | 77,299 (43 %) | R | 93,723 (48 %) | R | 105,608 (55 %) |
| I | 25,638 (14 %) | I | 4,700 (2 %) | | |

# Voting Studies

| | Presidential Support | | Party Unity | | Conservative Coalition | |
|---|---|---|---|---|---|---|
| Year | S | O | S | O | S | O |
| 1980 | 59 | 34† | 53 | 36† | 30 | 60† |
| 1979 | 61 | 34 | 60 | 34 | 33 | 62 |
| 1978 | 68 | 27 | 75 | 23 | 19 | 81 |
| 1977 | 65 | 35 | 75 | 24 | 19 | 81 |
| 1976 | 27 | 71 | 76 | 21 | 24 | 73 |
| 1975 | 31 | 67 | 76 | 22 | 24 | 74 |

†Not eligible for all recorded votes.

| | | | | | |
|---|---|---|---|---|---|
| 1974 (Ford) | 31 | 54 | | | |
| 1974 | 40 | 60 | 80 | 9 | 7 | 89 |
| 1973 | 29 | 71 | 87 | 11 | 5 | 90 |

S = Support          O = Opposition

# Key Votes

**96th Congress**

| | |
|---|---|
| Weaken Carter oil profits tax (1979) | Y |
| Reject hospital cost control plan (1979) | ? |
| Implement Panama Canal Treaties (1979) | Y |
| Establish Department of Education (1979) | N |
| Approve Anti-busing Amendment (1979) | N |
| Guarantee Chrysler Corp. loans (1979) | N |
| Approve military draft registration (1980) | N |
| Aid Sandinista regime in Nicaragua (1980) | Y |
| Strengthen fair housing laws (1980) | Y |

**97th Congress**

| | |
|---|---|
| Reagan budget proposal (1981) | N |

# Interest Group Ratings

| Year | ADA | ACA | AFL-CIO | CCUS |
|---|---|---|---|---|
| 1980 | 94 | 25 | 56 | 55 |
| 1979 | 79 | 42 | 65 | 35 |
| 1978 | 85 | 37 | 85 | 33 |
| 1977 | 90 | 22 | 65 | 35 |
| 1976 | 65 | 22 | 65 | 25 |
| 1975 | 84 | 25 | 77 | 18 |
| 1974 | 96 | 7 | 91 | 0 |
| 1973 | 96 | 20 | 91 | 18 |

# 2 Timothy E. Wirth (D)

**Of Denver — Elected 1974**

**Born:** Sept. 22, 1939, Sante Fe, N.M.
**Education:** Harvard U., A.B. 1961, M.Ed. 1964;
Stanford U., Ph.D. 1973.
**Military Career:** Army Reserve, 1961-67.
**Profession:** Education official.
**Family:** Wife, Wren Winslow; two children.
**Religion:** Episcopalian.
**Political Career:** No previous office.

**In Washington:** Wirth's career has been a struggle to play a leadership role in Congress while charting his away among the diverse interests of his Colorado district.

Survival in a constituency of conservative homeowners, university liberals, oilmen and inner-city Hispanics has generally been a matter of a few thousand votes, and that margin has helped to define Wirth's style.

He has been a cautious legislator, determined to find consensus on major issues and then operate from the center. His caution has led some exasperated colleagues to brand him indecisive, but it has also given him a key role to play in legislative bargaining and building coalitions in the House.

Wirth's skill and caution have both been evident in his years on the Energy and Commerce Committee, which he joined as a freshman in 1975. Like most of the other members of his Democratic class, he was initially against lifting price controls on energy.

He changed that view over the next several years, responding to free market arguments in the House and to the energy-producing interests of his state. By mid-1977, when the Commerce Committee worked on portions of President Carter's comprehensive energy bill, Wirth supported deregulation of natural gas. When that failed, he joined Republicans and oil-state Democrats in offering partial deregulation on the House floor. That lost, but the bill that finally emerged from conference in 1978 did include a gradual phase-out of gas price controls.

The next year, when President Carter lifted controls on crude oil prices, Wirth was with him, voting against a move to block the action, even though two-thirds of the Commerce Committee Democrats voted for it.

Early in his career, Wirth introduced his own legislation providing federal assistance for synthetic fuels development. And he voted for the scaled-down synfuels bill that finally became law in 1980. But he has grown increasingly hostile to massive energy exploration in the West.

In 1979, Commerce began drafting a bill to establish an Energy Mobilization Board designed to speed up approval of new high priority energy exploration projects. Energy Subcommittee Chairman John Dingell tried to add a provision allowing the board to waive local, state and federal laws if necessary to get the projects under way.

Western states, fearing a loss of state control of water rights, vigorously opposed the waiver, and Wirth led the fight on the Commerce Committee. He gave a masterful demonstration of his coalition-building skills, convincing state and local officials, labor unions and even civil rights groups that the waiver could be applied to anything from union contract negotiations to equal employment opportunities and local ordinances.

Dingell responded by specifically exempting labor, civil rights and water rights from the waiver, and he managed to get it through the committee. When it got to the House floor, Wirth's side forced him to fall back even further, exempting all state and local laws, leaving the waiver to apply only to federal laws.

In conference with the Senate, the bill was changed further, to require both houses of Congress and the president's signature for any proposed waiver of federal law. By that time even

---

**2nd District: Western Denver suburbs, Boulder.** Population: 629,034 (43% increase since 1970). Race: White 583,815 (92%), Black 4,738 (1%), Others 40,481 (6%). Spanish origin: 58,246 (9%).

## Timothy E. Wirth, D-Colo.

some of the oil companies were skeptical of the idea, arguing that it had become mired in the sort of red tape it had set out to cut. The conference report was beaten on the House floor — one of the significant triumphs of Wirth's career.

In 1981, a combination of retirements and political defeats gave Wirth an important chairmanship, of the Commerce Subcommittee on Telecommunications.

Under its earlier chairman, Lionel Van Deerlin of California, the subcommittee spent the entire 96th Congress working on a massive bill to deregulate the communications industry.

Wirth was a key player in those sessions, trying to work out a compromise over the role of the giant American Telephone & Telegraph Co. (AT&T) in a deregulated industry.

Smaller companies and consumer groups feared deregulation because it would give AT&T the ability to crush struggling competitors. Wirth drafted language allowing AT&T to enter deregulated fields like data processing, but only by setting up a separate subsidiary and keeping telephone rate money out of the new venture.

The compromise moved the bill through the Commerce Committee, but it never reached the floor, leaving Wirth the job of managing the issue as chairman in the 97th Congress.

Meanwhile Wirth has been an important figure on the Budget Committee in both the 96th and 97th Congresses. In 1980, he worked closely with Chairman Robert N. Giaimo in trying to draft a balanced budget with a Democratic label on it and helped put together a coalition with the panel's Republicans that moved the budget through committee against liberal Democratic opposition.

When that budget went to conference no longer carrying any hopes of balance, Giaimo was willing to yield to Senate demands for higher figures for defense and less for social programs. Wirth was reluctant to commit himself. He first went along with Giaimo, then turned against the agreement and joined with other Budget Committee Democrats in a "gang of five" that fought the deal and defeated it on the House floor, calling it too blatant a surrender of traditional party goals.

In 1981, with the Reagan administration applying pressure in Congress for its spending cuts, Wirth was no longer in a very bipartisan mood on the Budget Committee. He worked on the Democratic alternative budget, ultimately defeated on the House floor, and at committee sessions he frequently baited Republican members about the Reagan tax cut. He also sought to protect Colorado-related funds, arguing against an amendment that would have reduced federal revenue

sharing for states that collect energy severance taxes and supporting more money for science and energy research.

**At Home.** The 1974 election marked the peak of the modern Democratic resurgence in Colorado, and Wirth was one of its beneficiaries. Like the party's successful candidates for Senate and governor, he rode to victory on a wave of enthusiasm for environmental safeguards and reaction against Watergate.

It was Wirth's political debut. A former White House fellow with a Ph.D. in education from Stanford, he began his campaign early and organized skillfully. He combined an expertise on land, water and energy issues with sharp jabs at Republican Rep. Donald G. Brotzman for supporting President Nixon. Building large margins in west Denver and Boulder, Wirth was able to offset Brotzman's lead in Denver's Jefferson County suburbs to win the seat by 7,000 votes.

But he has had little time to relax since then because the district has remained difficult for him. Republican candidates have consistently criticized him as a big-spending liberal, and they have spent about $1 million themselves since 1974 in an effort to defeat him. Wirth did not draw more than 53 percent of the vote until 1980.

He almost lost in 1976, when former state senator and Denver television personality Ed Scott mounted an unexpectedly strong challenge that came within 2,500 votes of victory.

But muting his liberalism and building ties to business leaders in the district, Wirth rebuffed Scott by more than 10,000 votes in an expensive rematch two years later. Scott spent more than $550,000; Wirth over $400,000.

In 1980, Wirth had a weaker GOP challenger, and he attracted broad support with his campaign against massive energy development in the Rockies. He surprised his critics and some of his friends, winning by more than 40,000 votes.

**The District.** The 2nd District is one of the most diverse in the West, including the University of Colorado and the Joseph Coors Brewery, the low-income apartment houses of west Denver and the affluent residential suburbs of Jefferson County.

While Republican presidential candidates have carried it easily in recent elections, the 2nd has been marginal in state and congressional contests.

Democratic candidates usually run ahead in the academic community of Boulder and in west Denver, with its large Hispanic population. Republicans can frequently offset that advantage with majorities in Jefferson County, which contains nearly 60 percent of the district vote.

## Committees

**Budget**
Taskforces: Energy and Environment, chairman; Reconciliation.

**Energy and Commerce** (5th of 24 Democrats)
Telecommunications, Consumer Protection, and Finance, chairman; Fossil and Synthetic Fuels.

## Elections

**1980 General**

| | |
|---|---|
| Timothy Wirth (D) | 153,550 (56%) |
| John McElderry (R) | 111,868 (41%) |

**1978 General**

| | |
|---|---|
| Timothy Wirth (D) | 98,889 (53%) |
| Edward Scott (R) | 88,072 (47%) |

**Previous Winning Percentages**

1976 (51%)    1974 (52%)

**District Vote For President**

| | 1980 | | 1976 | | 1972 |
|---|---|---|---|---|---|
| D | 81,064 (30%) | D | 100,539 (41%) | D | 72,473 (35%) |
| R | 145,045 (54%) | R | 137,590 (55%) | R | 131,507 (63%) |
| I | 35,369 (13%) | | | | |

## Campaign Finance

| | Receipts | Receipts from PACs | Expenditures |
|---|---|---|---|
| **1980** | | | |
| Wirth (D) | $527,982 | $121,224 (23%) | $548,261 |
| McElderry (R) | $170,888 | $21,325 (12%) | $169,139 |

| | | | |
|---|---|---|---|
| **1978** | | | |
| Wirth (D) | $416,585 | $99,447 (24%) | $396,798 |
| Scott (R) | $560,325 | $100,255 (18%) | $554,538 |

## Voting Studies

| | Presidential Support | | Party Unity | | Conservative Coalition | |
|---|---|---|---|---|---|---|
| Year | S | O | S | O | S | O |
| 1980 | 79 | 16 | 81 | 13 | 20 | 76 |
| 1979 | 74 | 18 | 82 | 11 | 22 | 73 |
| 1978 | 71 | 21 | 71 | 19 | 20 | 71 |
| 1977 | 70 | 24 | 76 | 17 | 17 | 76 |
| 1976 | 27 | 67 | 79 | 11 | 24 | 69 |
| 1975 | 33 | 64 | 82 | 13 | 19 | 76 |

S = Support          O = Opposition

## Key Votes

**96th Congress**

| | |
|---|---|
| Weaken Carter oil profits tax (1979) | Y |
| Reject hospital cost control plan (1979) | N |
| Implement Panama Canal Treaties (1979) | Y |
| Establish Department of Education (1979) | Y |
| Approve Anti-busing Amendment (1979) | N |
| Guarantee Chrysler Corp. loans (1979) | N |
| Approve military draft registration (1980) | Y |
| Aid Sandinista regime in Nicaragua (1980) | Y |
| Strengthen fair housing laws (1980) | Y |

**97th Congress**

| | |
|---|---|
| Reagan budget proposal (1981) | N |

## Interest Group Ratings

| Year | ADA | ACA | AFL-CIO | CCUS |
|---|---|---|---|---|
| 1980 | 78 | 22 | 50 | 67 |
| 1979 | 74 | 16 | 63 | 39 |
| 1978 | 50 | 23 | 65 | 33 |
| 1977 | 70 | 12 | 83 | 35 |
| 1976 | 75 | 12 | 78 | 25 |
| 1975 | 79 | 18 | 91 | 13 |

# 3 Ray Kogovsek (D)

**Of Pueblo — Elected 1978**

**Born:** Aug. 19, 1941, Pueblo, Colo.
**Education:** Adams State college, B.S. 1964.
**Profession:** State government official.
**Family:** Wife, Eulice Kroschel; two children.
**Religion:** Roman Catholic.
**Political Career:** Colo. House, 1969-71; Colo.
Senate 1971-79, minority leader, 1973-79.

**In Washington:** Elected by the narrowest of margins in 1978, Kogosvek has moved carefully to provide at least something for all of his district's major constituent groups.

His pro-labor votes suit the strong organized labor movement in the steel mills of Pueblo. His defense of minority jobs and education programs appeals to the district's large Spanish-speaking population. He has a bill to ease the regulatory burden on small mining companies.

It has been a successful combination. Thought to be in serious trouble in 1980, he was re-elected by more than 20,000 votes.

On the Interior Committee, he stands somewhere between the environmentalist and pro-development factions. His Colorado wilderness bill, a major priority in his first term, protected 1.3 million acres from development — about half of what the Carter administration and environmental groups were seeking. Kogovsek's version carefully drew wilderness boundaries to allow mining and lumber operations in several areas and to permit ranchers to use motor vehicles in the wilderness. Early in 1979, Kogovsek voted with Interior Chairman Morris K. Udall of Arizona for an environmentally oriented Alaska lands bill, closing more land to drilling than energy companies wanted. He said he did so to ensure Udall's support later for the Colorado wilderness bill. He got it.

Kogovsek was active during the Interior Committee argument in 1980 over changing the 1902 federal reclamation act. That law limits the size of farms which can receive cheap, federally subsidized water, but has been easily evaded by farming interests which simply *lease* larger amounts of land. The Carter administration wanted to tighten the law to place an acreage limit on leasing as well.

Kogovsek sided with Republicans and Western landholders to block that effort. He introduced some major exemptions for the landholders and helped provide a narrow margin of victory on

all of them.

Kogovsek attracted notice as a freshman by applying for the Judiciary Committee. He is not a lawyer, but he had worked as a paralegal aide in a law firm and had been cited by the Colorado Bar Association for oustanding work on grand jury issues. Senior Judiciary members objected, however, insisting on their tradition as an all-lawyer committee. Kogovsek accepted Interior and Education and Labor without fuss. He added a third commitee, Public Works, in 1981.

**At Home.** Kogovsek rose quickly from the clerk's office in Pueblo County to the minority leadership of the Colorado Senate and then waited patiently for a chance to run for Congress.

He made his move in 1978 as Democratic Rep. Frank Evans was talking of retirement. Evans, who barely survived a GOP challenge in 1976, ultimately did retire, leaving Kogovsek as the logical successor.

But while the Democratic primary was easy for Kogovsek, the general election was unexpectedly difficult. His lightly regarded Republican foe, state Sen. Harold L. McCormick, mounted an energetic campaign that came within 400 votes of victory. Kogovsek's large lead in industrial Pueblo County and the traditionally Democratic Hispanic counties along the New Mexico border barely offset McCormick's advantage in the rest of the sprawling district.

The near-upset encouraged national GOP

---

**3rd District: South — Pueblo.** Population: 516,680 (17% increase since 1970). Race: White 443,653 (86%), Black 15,335 (3%), Others 57,692 (11%). Spanish origin: 107,698 (21%).

leaders to make the Colorado 3rd a higher priority in 1980. But Kogovsek was able to neutralize increased Republican support for McCormick by skillfully using two years of incumbency to expand his name identification throughout the district. He won the rematch by nearly 22,000 votes, carrying a number of rural farm and Western Slope counties he had previously lost.

The son of a Pueblo steelworker, Kogovsek started out in politics as an ally of the local Democratic organization, which helped boost him into the state Senate before his 30th birthday. He had served there only two years when he was chosen Democratic leader in 1973.

**The District.** The 3rd is one of the largest districts in the country, covering about half the state of Colorado. It extends from the semi-arid agricultural plains along the Kansas border to the mountainous mining and grazing country adjoining Utah.

Redistricting in 1972 gave the Democrats a narrow advantage. In part to keep Evans from challenging Republican Sen. Gordon Allott, the GOP Legislature favorably redrew his district. Most of strongly Republican Colorado Springs was removed, while 19 southwest counties — generally rural and sparsely populated — were added.

That made Pueblo the district's population center. Although beleaguered economically with problems in the local coal and steel industries, Pueblo is the center of organized labor in Colorado and a Democratic stronghold. With the Hispanic counties to the south, it has helped Democratic candidates carry a majority of the district vote in most state and congressional races.

## Committees

**Education and Labor** (17th of 19 Democrats)
Health and Safety.

**Interior and Insular Affairs** (18th of 23 Democrats)
Mines and Mining; Public Lands and National Parks: Water and Power Resources.

**Public Works and Transportation** (25th of 25 Democrats)
Surface Transportation.

## Elections

**1980 General**

| | |
|---|---|
| Ray Kogovsek (D) | 105,820 (55%) |
| Harold McCormick (R) | 84,292 (44%) |

**1978 General**

| | |
|---|---|
| Ray Kogovsek (D) | 69,669 (49%) |
| Harold McCormick (R) | 69,303 (49%) |

**1978 Primary**

| | |
|---|---|
| Ray Kogovsek (D) | 26,881 (66%) |
| Tom Watkinson (D) | 13,759 (34%) |

**District Vote For President**

| | 1980 | | 1976 | | 1972 |
|---|---|---|---|---|---|
| D | 69,185 (36%) | D | 85,881 (47%) | D | 57,152 (34%) |
| R | 107,289 (55%) | R | 91,136 (50%) | R | 102,569 (62%) |
| I | 13,293 (7%) | | | | |

## Campaign Finance

| | Receipts | Receipts from PACs | Expen-ditures |
|---|---|---|---|
| **1980** | | | |
| Kogovsek (D) | $276,423 | $141,125 (51%) | $271,167 |
| McCormick (R) | $256,831 | $126,894 (49%) | $255,896 |

| | | | |
|---|---|---|---|
| **1978** | | | |
| Kogovsek (D) | $121,678 | $35,080 (29%) | $121,323 |
| McCormick (R) | $86,277 | $13,250 (15%) | $81,500 |

## Voting Studies

| | Presidental Support | | Party Unity | | Conservative Coalition | |
|---|---|---|---|---|---|---|
| Year | S | O | S | O | S | O |
| 1980 | 68 | 25 | 68 | 23 | 51 | 44 |
| 1979 | 79 | 17 | 84 | 10 | 26 | 72 |

S = Support       O = Opposition

## Key Votes

**96th Congress**

| | |
|---|---|
| Weaken Carter oil profits tax (1979) | N |
| Reject hospital cost control plan (1979) | N |
| Implement Panama Canal Treaties (1979) | Y |
| Establish Department of Education (1979) | Y |
| Approve Anti-busing Amendment (1979) | N |
| Guarantee Chrysler Corp. loans (1979) | Y |
| Approve military draft registration (1980) | Y |
| Aid Sandinista regime in Nicaragua (1980) | Y |
| Strengthen fair housing laws (1980) | N |

**97th Congress**

| | |
|---|---|
| Reagan budget proposal (1981) | N |

## Interest Group Ratings

| Year | ADA | ACA | AFL-CIO | CCUS |
|---|---|---|---|---|
| 1980 | 56 | 22 | 72 | 55 |
| 1979 | 68 | 8 | 80 | 24 |

# 4 Hank Brown (R)

**Of Greeley — Elected 1980**

**Born:** Feb. 12, 1940, Denver, Colo.
**Education:** Univ. of Colo., B.S. 1961, J.D. 1969.
**Military Career:** Navy, 1962-66.
**Profession:** Beef company executive.
**Family:** Wife, Nan Morrison; three children.
**Religion:** United Church of Christ.
**Political Career:** Colo. Senate, 1973-77.

**The Member:** Brown's easy victory in the contest for Republican James P. Johnson's open House seat solidified his position as a rising star in the Colorado Republican Party, and he quickly began making a name for himself among congressional newcomers as well. He attracted attention with his speech in December supporting Guy Vander Jagt of Michigan for House Republican leader, and even though Vander Jagt lost, Brown was chosen president of the 52-member House GOP freshman class. Brown has represented his class in strategy sessions with President Reagan.

Brown favors hefty tax cuts, a constitutional amendment to balance the federal budget and an extensive transfer of power from federal to local governments. But to the chagrin of many Colorado Republicans, he also favors ratification of the Equal Rights Amendment, and disapproves of the GOP platform plank on abortion.

Brown made his political debut in 1972 when he won a state Senate seat, and his career has been on the upswing ever since. In 1974 he was selected assistant majority leader, and four years later was the Republican nominee for lieutenant governor.

Although the GOP ticket was defeated in 1978, Brown won high marks for his vigorous campaigning and established solid name identification in the state's sprawling 4th District. Johnson's decision to retire at age 50 set the stage for Brown's promotion, and the outcome was never really in doubt. He routed Democrat Polly Baca Barragan in 1980 by a more than 2-1 margin.

**The District:** The 4th is one of the largest districts in the country, stretching from the ranch country of northeastern Colorado to the desert landscape of the western part of the state. It also includes the northern suburbs of Denver and the resort community of Aspen.

But it is not diverse politically; it is solidly conservative and Republican. Since the district lines were radically redrawn in 1972, the 4th has been represented only by Johnson and Brown.

## Committees

**Interior and Insular Affairs** (13th of 17 Republicans)
Oversight and Investigations; Public Lands and Natinal Parks.

**Standards of Official Conduct** (5th of 6 Republicans)

## Elections

**1980 General**

| | |
|---|---|
| Hank Brown (R) | 178,221 (68%) |
| Polly Baca Barragan (D) | 76,849 (30%) |

**District Vote For President**

| | 1980 | | 1976 | | 1972 |
|---|---|---|---|---|---|
| **D** | 73,750 (28%) | **D** | 93,022 (40%) | **D** | 62,649 (32%) |
| **R** | 153,779 (58%) | **R** | 130,713 (57%) | **R** | 127,961 (65%) |
| **I** | 28,711 (11%) | | | | |

## Campaign Finance

| | Receipts | Receipts from PACs | Expenditures |
|---|---|---|---|
| **1980** | | | |
| Brown (R) | $287,771 | $110,759 (38%) | $233,857 |
| Barragan (D) | $116,938 | $38,099 (33%) | $116,186 |

## Key Vote

**97th Congress**

| | |
|---|---|
| Reagan budget proposal (1981) | Y |

---

**4th District: North — Fort Collins, Greeley.** Population: 664,563 (50% increase since 1970). Race: White 622,422 (93%), Black 2,854 (0.4%), Others 39,287 (6%). Spanish origin: 63,725 (10%).

# 5 Ken Kramer (R)

### Of Colorado Springs — Elected 1978

**Born:** Feb. 19, 1942, Chicago, Ill.
**Education:** U. of Ill., B.A. 1963; Harvard U., J.D. 1966.
**Military Career:** Army, 1967-70.
**Profession:** Lawyer.
**Family:** Wife, Nancy Pearson; two children.
**Religion:** Jewish.
**Political Career:** Colo. House, 1973-79.

**In Washington:** Kramer came to Washington acting and sounding as if he hoped to dismantle most of the edifice of liberal government by the end of his first term. He was ready with speeches and amendments by the basketful, fighting President Carter's proposals to create a new Department of Education and improve relations with mainland China. Few of his amendments passed.

In the time since then, Kramer has grown less excitable and more selective, apparently willing to wait for the best moments to offer his legislative ideas. But the ideas themselves have not changed.

Kramer favors eliminating the Education and Energy departments and cutting back the role of the Environmental Protection Agency, Occupational Safety and Health Administration and Federal Trade Commission. He wants to restrict federal court jurisdiction over busing and abortion.

"We are strangled by government red tape," he has said, "and drowned by government regulations administered by an ever-growing insensitive, unaccountable bureaucracy."

The issue of U.S. relations with China came up in the early weeks of Kramer's first term, and it was an issue that excited him. He offered an amendment to reverse the entire direction of U.S. friendship toward the Peoples' Republic of China, and retain a mutual defense treaty with Taiwan, calling for American involvement if Taiwan was attacked. It lost 221-149. He also offered an amendment guaranteeing Taiwan access to American weapons "incorporating the highest available technology." A modified version of this passed.

Later in the year, Kramer fought the legislation implementing U.S. transfer of the Panama Canal. He had an amendment to that bill which attempted to block any U.S. role in a new Canal Commission until after "free elections" in Panama.

Kramer was equally vehement against the Education Department. House leaders brought the issue to the House floor under procedures allowing open amendment, and Kramer was one of several Republicans who staged a sort of filibuster by amendment, proposing one change after another and prolonging the debate for weeks.

Kramer spent his first term on the Education and Labor Committee, where as an advocate of right-to-work laws, he was a sort of gadfly against the panel's solid pro-union majority. But much of his legislative interest was in military issues, and he joined the Armed Services Committee in 1981. As a defense hard-liner representing the hometown of the Air Force Academy, Kramer has differed with most of his Western-state colleagues on the MX missile. He has favored the mobile MX basing system, even though the planned sites were in the Mountain states.

"I'm certainly ready for Colorado to bear its share of that kind of responsibility," Kramer said of the MX. "I know there are some concerns about that, but the greater concern is having an adequate defense."

**At Home:** Once he survived a bruising primary to win the Republican nomination in 1978, Kramer was set for what is likely to be a long congressional stay. He has no re-election problems in a district designed to be reliably Republican.

Kramer was stubborn and sometimes strident

---

**5th District: East, South Denver area, Colorado Springs.** Population: 651,763 (48% increase since 1970). Race: White 597,552 (92%), Black 20,525 (3%), Others 33,686 (5%). Spanish origin: 47,581 (7%).

---

## Ken Kramer, R-Colo.

in the Colorado Legislature, where he gained notoriety for his efforts to push the more moderate GOP leadership in a conservative direction. He was active in promoting anti-pornography and state right-to-work legislation.

When Republican William Armstrong left the House seat in 1978 to run for the Senate, Kramer campaigned for it against another equally determined conservative Republican, state Rep. Bob Eckelberry. They waged a bitter primary struggle, with Eckelberry calling himself a rational conservative and portraying Kramer as a wild man. When each candidate claimed the other had distorted his voting record, a representative from the national GOP was sent in to cool things down. Kramer emerged with a 2,700-vote victory.

Although there was lingering bitterness, it did not prevent Kramer from capturing an easy general election victory over a liberal Democrat. He coasted to re-election in 1980 with no primary challenge and a weak Democratic opponent.

Born in Chicago and educated at Harvard Law School, Kramer moved to Colorado Springs to practice, and soon entered GOP politics on the precinct level. Only two years after he opened his law office he had a seat in the Legislature.

**The District:** The 5th was created not only for Republican representation, but specifically for Armstrong, the only person besides Kramer who has ever represented it.

The bulk of the population lives in the predominantly white-collar Arapahoe County suburbs east and south of Denver, and the military-oriented city of Colorado Springs (El Paso County). Part of Colorado Springs is in the neighboring 3rd District, but most of it belongs to the 5th. The Air Force Academy and several military installations are located nearby.

Arapahoe and El Paso counties are among the fastest growing in the state, and both are solidly Republican. Both went for Reagan in 1980 by margins of more than 2-to-1.

The district also includes four large, sparsely populated rural counties to the east, which are as Republican as the rest of the district.

## Committees

**Armed Services** (16th of 19 Republicans)
Military Installations and Facilities; Procurement and Military Nuclear Systems.

**Education and Labor** (6th of 14 Republicans)
Health and Safety; Labor-Management Relations.

## Elections

**1980 General**

| | |
|---|---|
| Ken Kramer (R) | 177,319 (72%) |
| Ed Schreiber (D) | 62,003 (25%) |

**1978 General**

| | |
|---|---|
| Ken Kramer (R) | 91,933 (60%) |
| Gerry Frank (D) | 52,914 (34%) |
| L. W. Bridges (I) | 8,933 (6%) |

**1978 Primary**

| | |
|---|---|
| Ken Kramer (R) | 19,493 (54%) |
| Bob Eckelberry (R) | 16,822 (46%) |

**District Vote For President**

| | 1980 | | 1976 | | 1972 |
|---|---|---|---|---|---|
| D | 65,236 (26%) | D | 80,765 (39%) | D | 47,634 (29%) |
| R | 153,698 (61%) | R | 121,504 (58%) | R | 113,375 (68%) |
| I | 24,695 (10%) | | | | |

## Campaign Finance

| | Receipts | Receipts from PACs | Expenditures |
|---|---|---|---|
| **1980** | | | |
| Kramer (R) | $251,692 | $77,378 (31 %) | $225,183 |
| Schreiber (D) | $3,834 | $175 (5%) | $3,152 |

| 1978 | | | |
|---|---|---|---|
| Kramer (R) | $162,156 | $67,914 (42%) | $161,413 |
| Frank (D) | $63,462 | $15,544 (24%) | $63,325 |

## Voting Studies

| | Presidential Support | | Party Unity | | Conservative Coalition | |
|---|---|---|---|---|---|---|
| Year | S | O | S | O | S | O |
| 1980 | 28 | 56 | 87 | 6 | 88 | 4 |
| 1979 | 21 | 78 | 93 | 6 | 94 | 3 |

S = Support          O = Opposition

## Key Votes

**96th Congress**

| | |
|---|---|
| Weaken Carter oil profits tax (1979) | Y |
| Reject hospital cost control plan (1979) | ? |
| Implement Panama Canal Treaties (1979) | N |
| Establish Department of Education (1979) | N |
| Approve Anti-busing Amendment (1979) | Y |
| Guarantee Chrysler Corp. loans (1979) | Y |
| Approve military draft registration (1980) | Y |
| Aid Sandinista regime in Nicaragua (1980) | ? |
| Strengthen fair housing Laws (1980) | N |

**97th Congress**

| | |
|---|---|
| Reagan budget proposal (1981) | Y |

## Interest Group Ratings

| Year | ADA | ACA | AFL-CIO | CCUS |
|---|---|---|---|---|
| 1980 | 0 | 91 | 13 | 72 |
| 1979 | 5 | 96 | 10 | 94 |

# Connecticut

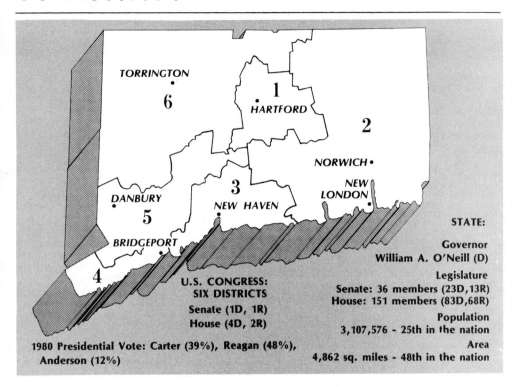

TORRINGTON

6

1

HARTFORD

2

NORWICH •

NEW
LONDON

NEW HAVEN

DANBURY

5

3

BRIDGEPORT

4

U.S. CONGRESS:
SIX DISTRICTS
Senate (1D, 1R)
House (4D, 2R)

1980 Presidential Vote: Carter (39%), Reagan (48%),
Anderson (12%)

STATE:

Governor
William A. O'Neill (D)

Legislature
Senate: 36 members (23D,13R)
House: 151 members (83D,68R)

Population
3,107,576 - 25th in the nation

Area
4,862 sq. miles - 48th in the nation

## ... An Ethnic Museum

It takes barely two hours to drive east across Connecticut from the affluent New York City suburb of Greenwich to the Portuguese fishing town of Stonington, but that drive is a demographic odyssey. On the edge of Long Island sound are the ethnic factory towns, picturesque Yankee villages, and shipbuilding communities heavily reliant on defense contracts. Inland, the ethnic and political mix is almost as great.

For its small geographic size — only Rhode Island and Delaware are smaller — Connecticut covers an enormous social and political spectrum. Through the early part of this century it was dominated by village Yankees, Republican by conviction and conservative by association with the Congregationalist church.

But the massive influx of immigrants from Ireland, Italy and Poland gave a heavy Democratic flavor to towns such as Hartford, New Haven, Bridgeport and Waterbury. As in other states, it nourished a political system that relied heavily on party bosses. By 1920, 70 percent of the people were first or second generation immigrants, and Connecticut was on its way to becoming one of the nation's most urbanized states. Today, less than a quarter of its people still live in rural areas, compared with two-thirds in Vermont and half in New Hampshire.

From the Depression until the mid-1950s, rural Republicans and urban Democrats fought to a virtual standoff as the governorship and the congressional delegation switched back and forth between parties every few years. The 1954 election of Abraham Ribicoff as governor marked a clear swing to the Democrats. Ever since, the Democratic Party has dominated state politics, and Republicans have held the governor's office for only four of the last 26 years. With the

199

beginning of the 97th Congress in 1981 the Democrats held one Senate seat and four of the state's six House seats.

Nearly all that Democratic success occurred under state party chairman John M. Bailey, who controlled nominations to Congress and all major state offices, awarding them at well-orchestrated conventions that provided balanced candidate slates without the inconvenience of the primary process. The machine began to lose its hold in the last few years before Bailey's death in 1975, and since then the Democratic Party has been as wide-open and unmanageable in Connecticut as it had become in most other states many years earlier.

# A Political Tour

**Urban Industrial Crescent.** More than half of Connecticut's votes come from Hartford and New Haven counties, located in mid-state. The two areas form the core of a crescent that includes the state's major industrial cities and most of its Democratic votes. Within it are Hartford, the nation's leading insurance city, and New Haven, home of Yale University, but also less-heralded places such as Waterbury, New Britain, Bristol, Meridan, Middletown and the state's most populous city, Bridgeport.

Danbury, once the hat center of the nation, and New London, where all U.S. submarines are built, are the only largely industrialized towns outside the crescent. The economy in nearly all the cities inside it is centered on manufacturing — usually metal parts. Connecticut has specialized in making precision equipment, such as aircraft engines, weapons, helicopters, office machines and typewriters. From the Revolutionary War through World War II its Colt and Winchester factories were the county's arsenal. Today the crescent areas suffer from the economic stagnation common to much of the northeast.

The people who work in the factories come from a variety of ethnic backgrounds. Since 1928, when Alfred E. Smith carried most of the state's major cities, Democrats have been able to count on the allegiance of nearly all the urban Catholic groups, although Italians have strayed occasionally.

Hartford, New Haven and New Britain are the three most solidly Democratic cities, the only major ones in Connecticut to support George McGovern's presidential bid in 1972. In 1980 Jimmy Carter received his largest margins from those towns. Waterbury, Bridgeport and Danbury are still firmly Democratic in local and statewide elections, but show signs of moving away from the Democrats at the presidential level. Waterbury, known for the brass manufacturing skills of its many Italian and Irish immigrants, favored Ronald Reagan in 1980. Danbury, the only large town to gain population in the last decade, has given small majorities to the last three GOP presidential candidates.

In general, the northern half of the crescent is the most solidly Democratic part of the state. Closer to Long Island Sound, voters are more likely to register as independents and split their tickets.

**"The Gold Coast."** The comfortable Fairfield County towns nearest New York City bear little resemblance to the rest of the state. They are centers of moderate Republican strength.

The "Gold Coast" towns of Greenwich, Darien, New Canaan, Weston and Westport are among the wealthiest in the country. New York executives, lured by the absence of a state income tax in Connecticut, have lived in these towns for most of the century. More recently, corporations also have started moving out of the city to large park-like headquarters in suburban Connecticut. Fairfield was the only county carried by former New York Sen. James L. Buckley in his 1980 Republican campaign. That is testimony not only to the area's conservatism but to the fact that it faces Manhattan.

The 4th Congressional District, which includes most of the fancier parts of Fairfield County, has stayed firmly in Republican control in all but three House elections since World War II.

Ribicoff and Ella T. Grasso, who was governor from 1975 to 1980, were the only major statewide candidates in the 1970s to carry Fairfield County. But because the county casts only a quarter of the state's vote, it is difficult for a large Republican tide there alone to swing an election to the GOP. To win, a GOP candidate also needs either an overwhelming vote in rural Connecticut or an unusual support in the cities, where ethnic voters have begun to break away from their traditional Democratic loyalties.

**Berkshire Highlands.** After Fairfield County, the next most Republican area is immediately to the north, in Litchfield County. Located in the northwestern corner of Connecticut, this is the state's last outpost of old-fashioned Yankee civilization: town greens, white clapboard houses, church spires and wooded Berkshire hills.

Although usually favoring Republican candidates in statewide contests, Litchfield County has been represented by Democrats in the House for most of the past 20 years, thanks mostly to the presence of New Britain and other industrial areas in the eastern corner of the 6th Congressional District.

**Eastern Connecticut.** The eastern third of the state is as poor and Democratic as the western third is rich and Republican. Unlike the elite at the other end of the state, the people here are hard-scrabble farmers working marginal land, mill workers in aging industrial towns, and craftsmen whose lives are focused on the sea.

New London and Groton, which together form the region's only significant metropolitan area, are shipbuilding towns. Their livelihood is largely dependent on orders from the Navy and Coast Guard. Democrats carry these cities unless, like George McGovern in 1972, they are perceived to be weak on defense issues. McGovern won 36 percent in the New London/Groton area. In 1980 Democrat Christopher J. Dodd, running for the Senate as a liberal but avoiding anti-military rhetoric, won 66 percent.

The only sizable pocket of Republican strength in the east is at the mouth of the Connecticut River, where the Yankee domination in towns such as Old Lyme and Essex has lasted for over two centuries.

In the northeast are Tolland and Windham counties, both Democratic but sparsely populated. The University of Connecticut campus at Storrs provides a boost for liberal candidates. In the 1980 Republican presidential primary, John B. Anderson won the Storrs area easily. He captured 20 percent in the general election, far above his statewide average. This was also the only part of the state McGovern carried in 1972.

# Redrawing the Lines

In the last decade population growth in Connecticut slacked off markedly. Earlier in the century the state gained a half-million people every 10 years, but between 1970 and 1980 it grew by fewer than 65,000 people. The growth was evenly spread, giving the Democrats, who control the redistricting process, a fairly easy chore in adjusting the state's six district boundaries.

Over the last two decades, Democrats have held a majority of the state's congressional delegation in every election except 1972, when there was a 3-3 split. Republicans gained one seat in the 1980 elections, giving them two out of six.

It appears unlikely that Democrats can recapture through redistricting the New Haven-based 3rd District, which they lost at the polls in 1980. The major task for the Democratic mapmakers is to shore up their vulnerable two-term Democrat, William R. Ratchford in the 5th.

Only two districts — the 1st, centered on Hartford, and the 4th, in Fairfield County — will need to grow in geographic size to make up for lost population. The 4th District, already solidly Republican, is likely to take on an additional group of Republican towns that have been unfriendly territory for Ratchford. By building up the population of the 4th District with Republican areas from the 5th, Democrats may be able to solidify Ratchford, who nearly lost the 5th in both 1980 and 1978.

Bringing the 1st District up to equal population size can be done by taking towns from either the 2nd or 6th, without hurting the Democratic nature of either significantly.

# Governor
# William A. O'Neill (D)

**Born:** Aug. 11, 1930, Hartford, Conn.
**Education:** New Britain Teacher's College, U. of Hartford.
**Military Career:** Air Force, 1950-53.
**Profession:** Restaurateur.
**Family:** Wife, Natalie.
**Religion:** Roman Catholic
**Political Career:** Conn. House, 1967-79, majority leader, 1975-77 and 1977-79. Lt. Governor, 1979-80; became Governor Dec. 31, 1980 when Gov. Ella Grasso resigned due to ill health. Term expires January 1983.

# Lowell P. Weicker Jr. (R)

## Of Greenwich — Elected 1970

**Born:** May 16, 1931, Paris, France.
**Education:** Yale U., B.A. 1953; U. of Va., LL.B 1958.
**Military Career:** Army, 1953-55; Army Reserve, 1959-64.
**Profession:** Lawyer.
**Family:** Wife, Camille DiLorenzo Butler; seven children.
**Religion:** Episcopalian.
**Political Career:** Conn. House, 1963-69; first selectman of Greenwich, 1963-67; U.S. House, 1969-71.

**In Washington:** Weicker, the "excitable kid" of the Senate Watergate Committee, is older and grayer than he was in those heady days, but only marginally calmer. The hulking Connecticut Republican has elevated righteous indignation to a political art form; it is his stock in trade. Others simply become frustrated; Weicker becomes outraged.

In the Watergate era, it was the sins of the Nixon White House that provoked him. Democrats on the Watergate Committee were positively soft-spoken in comparison with Weicker, who was the panel's junior member. As committee spectators applauded and a national television audience watched, Weicker accused the Nixon administration of trying to smear him.

His tirades rarely attract that much attention these days, but they are available for any visitor to watch on the Senate floor. The subjects vary widely, from a children's television probe by the Federal Trade Commission ("national nanny") to the Senate investigation of South Korean influence buying ("a resounding cover-up") to a congressional pay raise insisted on by the House.

When he starts pacing the Senate floor, arms waving and microphone in hand, it seems to make little difference to Weicker what the hour is or whether there is anyone else on his side. Once he winds himself up, it takes a long time for him to wind down.

A decade of this has not made Weicker popular among his fellow senators, many of whom see it as grandstanding. Sometimes it forces them to change their schedules, as it did during the summer of 1980, when Weicker held up passage of the fiscal 1981 budget for several days by demanding roll calls on string of amendments, few of which drew more than 20 votes.

A self-styled idealist, Weicker relishes a good fight — even a losing one. "I look for trouble, and I'll look for the underdog," he once said.

Most of his conspicuous battles have been losing ones. He tried and failed to block entry into the United States by the supersonic *Concorde* airplane. He fought in vain against federal loan guarantees for Lockheed, Wheeling-Pittsburgh Steel and the Chrysler Corporation. He has tried without success to preserve federal funding for abortions for poor women. And he was utterly unsuccessful in his brief bid for the 1980 Republican presidential nomination, one he concluded in May of 1979, citing polls which showed him running third in his home state.

In March 1981, Weicker was the only Republican in the Senate to vote against President Reagan's $36.9 billion package of budget cuts. He tried to amend the package to add $143 million for small-business loans and got 28 votes on that proposal, all but eight of them from Democrats.

But his objections went far beyond that. "I am not against great experiments," he argued, "but this has the makings of a great mistake.... This is a mean-spirited venture by a great nation."

At the end of the 96th Congress, Weicker led the successful struggle to strip an anti-busing rider from an emergency appropriation bill — a cause that many other traditional civil rights supporters in Congress had abandoned. The following year, when the same amendment showed up as a rider to a different bill, he spoke against it for 2½ days, charging that "demagoguery is once again afoot."

Several times since Watergate, Weicker has publicly threatened to bolt the GOP and run as an independent. "I'm tired of being kicked in the tail by the party I've sought to serve in the best way possible," he said once, "which is not in a partisan sense but by being intelligent and in the right place on the issues."

Now that the GOP has gained control of the Senate, however, Weicker would have considerably more to lose by making such a change. He is chairman of one committee, the Select Committee on Small Business, and is the third-ranking majority member of three others — Appropriations, Energy, and Labor and Human Resources.

**At Home:** Weicker is as iconoclastic in Connecticut as he is in the Senate.

He has fought the state GOP for years, interspersing his denunciations of it with his threats to become an independent. At one point, he called the state party "almost extinct" and its leaders "a bunch of losers."

Some of the differences stem from ideology; party regulars tend to be more conservative than Weicker. But much of the problem is simply Weicker's combative nature. In 1980, Weicker refused to endorse the Republican Senate nominee in Connecticut, James L. Buckley, a former senator from New York. The party convention had endorsed Buckley, and Weicker favored his primary rival.

Weicker's defiance could cause him trouble when he seeks renomination in 1982, although it never has in years past. Up until now, his reputation as a general election winner has spared him intraparty opposition.

After a political career as a state legislator and as first selectman (mayor) of Greenwich, Weicker unseated Democratic Rep. Donald J. Irwin in 1968. The affluent Fairfield County district had traditionally been Republican, and Weicker exploited growing dissatisfaction over the Johnson administration's Vietnam policies, which Irwin backed.

Two years later, Weicker had the good fortune to be appearing on a general election ballot against two Democrats. The Democratic state convention had never even considered renominating Sen. Thomas J. Dodd, who had been censured in 1967 for misusing campaign funds. The convention endorsed zipper magnate Alphonsus Donahue, who then lost a primary to the liberal Joseph D. Duffey, national chairman of the Americans for Democratic Action. Meanwhile, Dodd decided to run as an independent. By the time of the fall campaign, the Democratic Party was in a shambles.

Weicker ran as a supporter of President Nixon, but added that he was not "a rubber stamp" and stressed his moderate credentials. He drew only 41.7 percent of the vote, but under the circumstances, it was more than enough. Duffey was nearly 100,000 votes behind.

The Watergate hearings cemented Weicker's popularity in Connecticut, winning him bipartisan backing that his 1976 Democratic rival, state Secretary of State Gloria Schaffer, could not crack. Though a formidable vote-getter in her own right, Schaffer found Weicker, with his amalgam of liberal and conservative positions, difficult to campaign against. He ran as a public official with a conscience and was rewarded with a second term by a wide margin.

## Committees

**Appropriations** (3rd of 15 Republicans)
State, Justice, Commerce, and the Judiciary, chairman; Defense; District of Columbia; HUD-Independent Agencies; Labor — Health and Human Services — Education.

**Energy and Natural Resources** (3rd of 11 Republicans)
Energy Conservation and Supply, chairman; Energy Research and Development; Water and Power.

**Labor and Human Resources** (6th of 9 Republicans)
Handicapped, chairman; Aging, Family and Human Services; Education.

**Small Business** (Chairman)
Government Procurement; Urban and Rural Economic Development.

## Elections

**1976 General**

| | |
|---|---|
| Lowell Weicker (R ) | 785,683 (58 %) |
| Gloria Schaffer (D ) | 561,018 (41 %) |

**Previous Winning Percentages**

| | |
|---|---|
| 1970 (42 %) | 1968* (51 %) |

*House Election.*

## Campaign Finance

| 1976 | Receipts | Receipts from PACs | Expenditures |
|---|---|---|---|
| Weicker (R ) | $500,955 | $52,834 (11 %) | $480,709 |
| Schaffer (D ) | $312,394 | $28,156 (9 %) | $306,104 |

## Voting Studies

| | Presidential Support | | Party Unity | | Conservative Coalition | |
|---|---|---|---|---|---|---|
| Year Senate service | S | O | S | O | S | O |
| 1980 | 69 | 25 | 30 | 59 | 16 | 71 |
| 1979 | 59 | 29 | 32 | 52 | 31 | 56 |
| 1978 | 66 | 18 | 25 | 64 | 28 | 63 |
| 1977 | 60 | 28 | 39 | 42 | 51 | 34 |
| 1976 | 51 | 38 | 30 | 46 | 38 | 40 |

| | | | | | | |
|---|---|---|---|---|---|---|
| 1975 | 57 | 39 | 42 | 56 | 34 | 61 |
| 1974 (Ford) | 29 | 53 | | | | |
| 1974 | 45 | 31 | 32 | 58 | 31 | 60 |
| 1973 | 51 | 40 | 53 | 39 | 63 | 35 |
| 1972 | 65 | 24 | 56 | 31 | 57 | 30 |
| 1971 | 67 | 20 | 61 | 25 | 61 | 22 |
| **House service** | | | | | | |
| 1970 | 46 | 18 | 31 | 21 | 25 | 20 |
| 1969 | 60 | 34 | 55 | 35 | 49 | 42 |

S = Support          O = Opposition

## Key Votes

**96th Congress**

| | |
|---|---|
| Maintain relations with Taiwan (1979) | Y |
| Reduce synthetic fuel development funds (1979) | Y |
| Impose nuclear plant moratorium (1979) | N |
| Kill stronger windfall profits tax (1979) | N |
| Guarantee Chrysler Corp. loans (1979) | N |
| Approve military draft registration (1980) | Y |
| End Revenue Sharing to the states (1980) | N |
| Block Justice Dept. busing suits (1980) | N |

**97th Congress**

| | |
|---|---|
| Restore urban program funding cuts (1981) | Y |

## Interest Group Ratings

| Year | ADA | ACA | AFL-CIO | CCUS-1 | CCUS-2 |
|---|---|---|---|---|---|
| **Senate service** | | | | | |
| 1980 | 72 | 43 | 81 | 44 | |
| 1979 | 68 | 41 | 63 | 27 | 33 |
| 1978 | 60 | 20 | 87 | 53 | |
| 1977 | 60 | 39 | 65 | 38 | |
| 1976 | 75 | 25 | 65 | 29 | |
| 1975 | 72 | 32 | 75 | 69 | |
| 1974 | 67 | 39 | 80 | 50 | |
| 1973 | 55 | 50 | 50 | 56 | |
| 1972 | 30 | 42 | 50 | 44 | |
| 1971 | 30 | 57 | 18 | - | |
| **House Service** | | | | | |
| 1970 | 40 | 41 | 50 | 50 | |
| 1969 | 40 | 41 | 70 | - | |

# Christopher J. Dodd (D)

**Of Norwich — Elected 1980**

**Born:** May 27, 1944, Willimantic, Conn.
**Education:** Providence College, B.A. 1966; University of Louisville, J.D. 1972.
**Military Career:** Army 1969-75.
**Profession:** Lawyer.
**Family:** Wife, Susan Mooney.
**Religion:** Roman Catholic.
**Political Career:** U.S. House, 1975-81.

**The Member:** A member of the Class of 1974 in the House, Dodd has been more liberal than most members of that group, but reflects its general distrust of bureaucracy and its interest in "good government" issues.

On the House Judiciary Committee, he supported gun control and lobby disclosure bills. Later he was given a seat on the powerful Rules Committee, and was made an at-large whip. Arguing for his energy-poor Northeast constituency, Dodd opposed oil decontrol and tried to increase emergency fuel aid for the poor.

On Senate Foreign Relations in 1981, Dodd has been a human rights activist. He was one of the most vigorous critics of Ernest Lefever, Reagan's choice for assistant secretary of state for human rights, who he said was insufficiently sensitive to human rights. Lefever eventually withdrew his name.

Dodd tried to attach to the fiscal 1982 foreign aid authorization a provision allowing the Congress to veto military aid to El Salvador. State Department officials argued against Dodd's proposal, and he agreed to drop it if committee Republicans would accept a requirement that the president submit periodic reports certifying that the Salvadoran government is respecting the human rights of its citizens. Republicans agreed to Dodd's terms and passed his proposal.

From the day in 1979 when Democratic incumbent Abraham A. Ribicoff declared his retirement, Dodd campaigned for the Senate like an underdog, even though he was widely viewed as Ribicoff's heir apparent.

An affable and hard-working campaigner, the former Peace Corps volunteer was an ideal candidate with a popular name. His father, the late Thomas J. Dodd, served two terms in the Senate. He is still revered by many in the state despite his 1967 Senate censure and his defeat in 1970. His son was able to draw votes from liberal Democrats on an issue basis and from older ethnic voters out of family nostalgia.

Young Dodd's GOP opponent, former New York Sen. James L. Buckley (1971-77), called him a "big spender" in the House and said Dodd wanted to "bust local zoning." Such attacks, according to pre-election polls, increased Buckley's unfavorable rating, not Dodd's.

Dodd ran far ahead of President Carter, particularly in the more Republican towns in the western part of the state. By carrying the major cities by margins of 2- and 3-1, he accumulated a plurality larger than his father amassed in winning a first Senate term in 1958.

## Committees

**Banking, Housing and Urban Affairs** (6th of 7 Democrats)
Consumer Affairs; International Finance and Monetary Policy; Rural Housing and Development.

**Foreign Relations** (8th of 8 Democrats)
African Affairs; International Economic Policy; Western Hemisphere Affairs.

**Special Aging** (7th of 7 Democrats)

## Elections

**1980 General**

| | |
|---|---|
| Christopher Dodd (D) | 763,969 (56%) |
| James Buckley (R) | 581,884 (43%) |

## Campaign Finance

| | Receipts | Receipts from PACs | Expenditures |
|---|---|---|---|
| **1980** | | | |
| Dodd (D) | $1,374,674 | $298,713 (22%) | $1,394,197 |
| Buckley (R) | $1,559,507 | $221,236 (14%) | $1,595,970 |

## Key Vote

**97th Congress**

| | |
|---|---|
| Restore urban program funding cuts (1981) | Y |

# 1 William R. Cotter (D)

**Of Hartford — Elected 1970**

**Born:** July 18, 1926, Hartford, Conn.
**Education:** Trinity College, B.A. 1949.
**Profession:** State official.
**Family:** Single.
**Religion:** Roman Catholic.
**Political Career:** Hartford City Council, 1953-55.

**In Washington:** This quiet House veteran did not stand out in the crowd of Democrats added to Ways and Means in its major expansion in 1975. But he managed to carve out a politically useful role for himself as a New England consumer advocate and as a specialist in the problems of the insurance industry, which he regulated at the state level for more than a decade.

Cotter has been ill during most Ways and Means deliberations in the 97th Congress. Treated early in 1981 for cancer of the pancreas, he spent the early months of the year at home in Connecticut, keeping in touch with committee work by phone.

In the previous Congress, Cotter played an active role in consideration of President Carter's hospital cost control program. Like the insurance companies, Cotter favored it, although he expressed little confidence either in it or in the ability of the Department of Health, Education and Welfare to run it. In one hospital cost control debate, he called HEW "the lousiest agency of any government in the world."

Cotter fought a 1979 proposal for federal certification of private "medigap" insurance policies sold to elderly people to supplement Medicare. On that he spoke for the industry, afraid that the certification would lead to a further federal role in the insurance business. Later, Cotter accepted a compromise that kept the certification process but put more of it in the hands of state insurance commissioners, a group he once belonged to.

On other issues, Cotter's interests have been regional. He was one of the most militant critics of the oil industry during the 1979 windfall profits tax debate, arguing that the companies would be keeping profits that should be used to lower heating oil costs in New England. He introduced his own legislation to raise the basic windfall tax rate to 85 percent — considerably above the president's proposed 50 percent — but lost in committee 21-12. Two years earlier, he threatened a mass rebellion in New England if Ways and Means omitted a 3-cent-a-gallon heating oil rebate from the 1977 comprehensive energy bill. The committee had voted 20-4 to strip the rebate from the bill, but after Cotter wrote to House leaders with his threat, the provision was restored by voice vote.

The most visible moment of Cotter's career came early in his second term, when he called for a consumer boycott to protest high meat prices. Cotter asked people throughout the country not to eat meat for a week and even distributed a sample menu showing them how to get along without it. The boycott reduced meat sales by an estimated 50 percent during the first week of April 1973, but had no immediate impact on beef prices.

**At Home:** As an insurance specialist representing the nation's insurance capital, Cotter has kept the Hartford area well satisfied.

His electoral showings have improved in recent years even though he has not campaigned with much vigor. He won his sixth term in 1980 by his highest percentage ever and for the first time carried all 17 cities and towns in the district.

Cotter's political base has been the city of Hartford itself, where he has won about three-fourths of the vote. The only elective office he held before 1970 was a seat on on the City Council, but both his father and grandfather served as the city's registrar of voters, and the

---

**1st District: Central — Hartford.**
Population: 495,351 (2% decrease since 1970). Race: White 409,017 (83%); Black 59,228 (12%); Others 27,106 (5%). Spanish origin: 32,464 (7%).

Cotter name was familiar.

To make it to Washington in 1970, Cotter defeated a party-endorsed candidate in a Democratic primary and then edged out the city's Republican mayor, Ann Uccello, carrying Hartford by just enough to survive defeat in nearly all the surrounding suburbs. That was his only close election.

**The District:** The most Democratic district in the state, the 1st has elected a Republican only once since 1948. That was in 1956, when the second Eisenhower sweep brought in a all-GOP congressional delegation. Two years later, it was back in Democratic hands.

Hartford makes up only about an eighth of the district's vote but is the political and economic nucleus of the district. It also accounts for most of the district's black population, which is the highest in the state.

Glastonbury and a handful of small towns in the southeastern corner of the district are the only traditionally Republican areas.

## Committees

**Ways and Means** (5th of 23 Democrats)
Select Revenue Measures, chairman; Social Security.

## Elections

**1980 General**

| | |
|---|---|
| William Cotter (D ) | 137,849 (63 %) |
| Marjorie Anderson (R ) | 80,816 (37 %) |

**1978 General**

| | |
|---|---|
| William Cotter (D ) | 102,749 (60 %) |
| Ben Andrews (R ) | 67,828 (39 %) |

**Previous Winning Percentages**

| | | | |
|---|---|---|---|
| 1976 (57 %) | 1974 (63 %) | 1972 (57 %) | 1970 (49 %) |

**District Vote For President**

| | 1980 | | 1976 | | 1972 |
|---|---|---|---|---|---|
| D | 105,401 (46 %) | D | 120,874 (52 %) | D | 114,473 (48 %) |
| R | 89,511 (39 %) | R | 108,585 (47 %) | R | 121,196 (51 %) |
| I | 33,452 (14 %) | | | | |

## Campaign Finance

| | Receipts | Receipts from PACs | Expenditures |
|---|---|---|---|
| **1980** | | | |
| Cotter (D ) | $140,479 | $63,955 (45 %) | $127,447 |
| Anderson (R ) | $27,906 | $1,513 (5 %) | $27,713 |
| **1978** | | | |
| Cotter (D ) | $114,320 | $47,140 (41 %) | $96,791 |
| Andrews (R ) | $55,340 | $2,282 (4 %) | $54,733 |

## Voting Studies

| | Presidental Support | | Party Unity | | Conservative Coalition | |
|---|---|---|---|---|---|---|
| Year | S | O | S | O | S | O |
| 1980 | 62 | 26 | 63 | 20 | 41 | 44 |
| 1979 | 72 | 20 | 71 | 15 | 35 | 58 |
| 1978 | 66 | 21 | 66 | 21 | 66 | 21 |
| 1977 | 56 | 14 | 67 | 13 | 56 | 14 |
| 1976 | 29 | 61 | 74 | 14 | 29 | 61 |
| 1975 | 34 | 62 | 83 | 13 | 34 | 62 |
| 1974 (Ford) | 41 | 46 | | | | |
| 1974 | 43 | 49 | 73 | 11 | 43 | 49 |
| 1973 | 29 | 65 | 78 | 16 | 29 | 65 |
| 1972 | 51 | 38 | 73 | 19 | 51 | 38 |
| 1971 | 46 | 46 | 68 | 19 | 46 | 46 |

S = Support    O = Opposition

## Key Votes

**96th Congress**

| | |
|---|---|
| Weaken Carter oil profits tax (1979) | N |
| Reject hospital cost control plan (1979) | N |
| Implement Panama Canal Treaties (1979) | Y |
| Establish Department of Education (1979) | Y |
| Approve Anti-busing Amendment (1979) | N |
| Guarantee Chrysler Corp. loans (1979) | Y |
| Approve military draft registration (1980) | N |
| Aid Sandinista regime in Nicaragua (1980) | N |
| Strengthen fair housing laws (1980) | Y |

**97th Congress**

| | |
|---|---|
| Reagan budget proposed (1981) | ? |

## Interest Group Ratings

| Year | ADA | ACA | AFL-CIO | CCUS |
|---|---|---|---|---|
| 1980 | 44 | 25 | 68 | 63 |
| 1979 | 68 | 12 | 82 | 18 |
| 1978 | 50 | 28 | 63 | 33 |
| 1977 | 55 | 16 | 91 | 20 |
| 1976 | 60 | 13 | 90 | 27 |
| 1975 | 89 | 19 | 83 | 18 |
| 1974 | 57 | 21 | 100 | 71 |
| 1973 | 60 | 27 | 100 | 54 |
| 1972 | 63 | 18 | 91 | 40 |
| 1971 | 70 | 19 | 91 | - |

# 2 Sam Gejdenson (D)

**Of Bozrah — Elected 1980**

**Born:** May 20, 1948, Eschwege, Germany.
**Education:** U. of Conn., B.A. 1970.
**Profession:** Farmer.
**Family:** Wife, Karen Flemming; one child.
**Religion:** Jewish.
**Political Career:** Conn. House, 1975-79.

**The Member:** The son of Lithuanian Jews, Gejdenson (pronounced Gay-den-son) was born in a refugee camp in Germany. That heritage helps explain the vigor with which he opposed Warren Richardson, Reagan's choice to be assistant secretary of health and human services.

From 1969-73, Richardson was general counsel for Liberty Lobby, an organization Gejdenson charged was anti-Semitic. As evidence that Richardson was unfit to work at HHS, Gejdenson cited a 1971 *New York Times* article in which Richardson wrote critically of the "pro-Zionist" American press.

Richardson vehemently denied he was anti-Jewish, but subsequent disclosures about the Liberty Lobby did not boost his stock: the group's publications warned of the international influence of Jewish bankers.

When the Anti-Defamation League of B'nai B'rith and other civil rights groups announced their opposition to Richardson's appointment, it became clear that confirmation hearings would be divisive. Richardson later withdrew.

When Democratic Rep. Christopher J. Dodd announced plans to run for the Senate, few thought that Gejdenson could capture the 2nd District seat. His campaign, waged by a zealous staff all younger than he, was a crusade against the party's old guard. But Gejdenson won a primary against the party choice and then overcame a strong GOP candidate.

**The District:** Covering the eastern third of the state, the 2nd is Connecticut's largest and least urbanized district. On Long Island Sound are Democratic fishing and shipbuilding towns and Republican villages sporting fashionable country inns. In the hilly central and northern parts of the district are small industrial centers which tend to vote Democratic, plus several college towns and Yankee farming areas.

The 2nd may be the state's most marginal district. Between 1934 and 1950 it switched parties every two years. Gejdenson's victory marked the first time in nearly 50 years that the district changed hands without changing parties.

## Committees

**Foreign Affairs** (17th of 21 Democrats)
Human Rights and International Organizations; Inter-American Affairs.

**Interior and Insular Affairs** (23rd of 23 Democrats)
Energy and the Environment; Oversight and Investigations; Public Lands and National Parks.

## Elections

**1980 General**

| | |
|---|---|
| Sam Gejdenson (D ) | 119,176 (53 %) |
| Tony Guglielmo (R ) | 104,107 (47 %) |

**1980 Primary**

| | |
|---|---|
| Sam Gejdenson (D ) | 18,746 (62 %) |
| John Dempsey (D) | 11,654 (38 %) |

**District Vote For President**

| | 1980 | | 1976 | | 1972 |
|---|---|---|---|---|---|
| D | 89,252 (38 %) | D | 111,161 (50 %) | D | 85,382 (40 %) |
| R | 108,219 (46 %) | R | 110,616 (50 %) | R | 127,923 (59 %) |
| I | 33,388 (14 %) | | | | |

## Campaign Finance

| | Receipts | Receipts from PACs | Expenditures |
|---|---|---|---|
| **1980** | | | |
| Gejdenson (D ) | $210,667 | $51,467 (24 %) | $206,973 |
| Guglielmo (R ) | $144,998 | $29,750 (21 %) | $141,463 |

## Key Vote

**97th Congress**
Reagan budget proposal (1981)      N

---

**2nd District: East — New London.**
Population: 537,988 (6.4% increase since 1970). Race: White 513,209 (95%); Black 15,373 (3%); Other 9,406 (2%). Spanish origin 9,107 (2%).

# 3 Lawrence J. DeNardis (R)

**Of Hamden — Elected 1980**

**Born:** March 18, 1938, New Haven, Conn.
**Education:** Holy Cross College, B.S. 1960;
N. Y. U., M.A. 1964.
**Military Career:** Navy Reserve, 1960-63.
**Profession:** Political science professor.
**Family:** Wife, Mary Lou White; four children.
**Religion:** Roman Catholic.
**Political Career:** Conn. Senate, 1971-79; unsuccessful Republican nominee for Conn. Senate, 1966 and 1968.

**The Member:** DeNardis calls himself a "creative Republican." During his decade in the state Senate, he built a moderate reputation focusing mainly on state finance issues.

In his early months in Washington, DeNardis spent much time pulling together people and money on behalf of two New Haven buildings, the Union Station train depot and the Schubert Theatre. DeNardis lobbied federal railroad officials to spend $15 million for renovations to the station and he worked to line up $1 million to reopen the Schubert.

In his 1980 campaign to succeed Democratic Rep. Robert N. Giaimo, who retired, DeNardis talked mostly about cutting back government programs. On social issues he differed little with his liberal Democratic opponent, Joseph I. Lieberman. Both were seen by voters as being intelligent, thoughtful and, at times, rather dull.

Throughout the campaign, DeNardis emphasized his Italian heritage, serving pizza at his headquarters to appeal to the district's large Italian-American community. He made some inroads in Democratic New Haven, but the key to his victory lay in the more Republican suburbs, which are nearly as heavily Italian as the city.

**The District:** Centered around New Haven, the 3rd has both working-class and suburban white-collar voters. New Haven, which accounts for about a quarter of the district's vote, is the home of Yale University. But Yale plays a relatively minor role in the district's politics. The dominant influence is ethnic. Every election since 1952 has given the district a representative of Italian background.

Although there are twice as many registered Democrats as Republicans, unaffiliated voters outnumber both and have shown a strong tendency to split their tickets. While Reagan carried the district by nearly 30,000 votes in 1980, Democrat Christopher J. Dodd won handily here in his successful Senate bid.

## Committees

**Education and Labor** (12th of 14 Republicans)
Elementary, Secondary and Vocational Education; Employment Opportunities; Postsecondary Education.

**Government Operations** (16th of 17 Republicans)
Intergovernmental Relations and Human Resources.

**Select Narcotics Abuse and Control** (6th of 8 Republicans)

## Elections

**1980 General**

| | |
|---|---|
| Lawrence DeNardis (R ) | 117,024 (52 %) |
| Joseph Lieberman (D ) | 103,903 (46 %) |

**1980 Primary**

| | |
|---|---|
| Lawrence DeNardis (R ) | 8,749 (61 %) |
| Henry Povinelli (R ) | 5,679 (39 %) |

**District Vote For President**

| | 1980 | | 1976 | | 1972 |
|---|---|---|---|---|---|
| **D** | 90,454 (39 %) | **D** | 105,602 (46 %) | **D** | 87,766 (38 %) |
| **R** | 117,043 (50 %) | **R** | 121,685 (53 %) | **R** | 142,569 (61 %) |
| **I** | 23,103 (10 %) | | | | |

## Campaign Finance

| | Receipts | Receipts from PACs | Expenditures |
|---|---|---|---|
| **1980** | | | |
| DeNardis (R ) | $186,924 | $39,817 (21 %) | $185,799 |
| Lieberman (D ) | $302,062 | $60,730 (20 %) | $302,054 |

## Key Vote

**97th Congress**

| | |
|---|---|
| Reagan budget proposal (1981) | Y |

---

**3rd District: South — New Haven.**
Population: 513,057 (1.5% increase since 1970). Race: White 447,448 (87%); Black 53,730 (10%); Others 11,879 (2%). Spanish origin 15,082 (3%).

# 4 Stewart B. McKinney (R)

### Of Fairfield — Elected 1970

**Born:** Jan. 30, 1931, Pittsburgh, Pa.
**Education:** Yale U., B.A. 1958.
**Military Career:** Air Force, 1951-55.
**Profession:** Tire company executive.
**Family:** Wife, Lucie Cunningham; five children.
**Religion:** Episcopalian.
**Political Career:** Conn. House, 1967-71.

**In Washington:** At a time when most House Republicans have become increasingly partisan in their rhetoric and voting behavior, McKinney has stuck firmly to his career-long course of working with the majority and reaping as many benefits as he can. It is a role that has left him largely isolated on his own side of the aisle, but it gave him a broker's position in some of the most important legislative arguments of the late 1970s.

Strategically situated as ranking Republican on the crucial Economic Stabilization Subcommittee, McKinney helped draw up the loan guarantees to New York City and Chrysler Corp., and the national synthetic fuels program. In each case he allied himself with William Moorhead of Pennsylvania, the panel's nervous and beleaguered chairman, allowing Moorhead to sell the legislation as a bipartisan effort. It was the Moorhead-McKinney substitute that broke a long stalemate on the Chrysler loan and led to passage of the $3 billion guarantee.

Those alliances fit in well with McKinney's own political thinking; he is one of the few Republicans left in the House who is not uncomfortable with a liberal label. In 1979 he voted against a Republican majority more often than all but two other GOP members. He is a consistent supporter of legalized abortion, and of home rule for the mostly-black District of Columbia, reflecting his own description of himself as an "urbanist."

Ranking Republican on the District of Columbia Committee for most of the past decade, he supported the city government so often that Walter Fauntroy, the district's non-voting delegate to the House, described him as "my vote on the floor." McKinney's interest in Washington, D.C., is more than ideological, however; he began investing in city real estate shortly after his election, and after eight years had purchased 19 properties for $612,000 and sold them all for $1,737,000. But he insisted after it was over that heavy restoration costs had saddled him with a net loss. "I was an absolute jerk," he said in 1979.

"You can't do it the way I did it."

In recent years, the range of McKinney's legislative involvements has been limited both by his business investments and by a serious heart condition. He suffered two heart attacks while still in his forties, then underwent heart bypass surgery in 1979.

One of his few crusades outside D.C. and economic stabilization issues has been opposition to the export of Alaskan oil to Japan. Time after time, he introduced amendments to block it. One of them was finally attached to an Export Administration Act in the 96th Congress and became law. McKinney insisted that Americans would never learn to take the energy crisis seriously as long as the United States was exporting oil.

**At Home:** McKinney's moderate Republican style seems well-suited for his affluent suburban district. In spite of vigorous challenges by youthful opponents, he has won six terms with little difficulty.

McKinney's health problems have actually been a more serious factor in his political career than challengers have been. In fact, it was a bout with hepatitis in 1969 that helped derail his plans to run for governor and steered him toward the House instead. He easily won the GOP nomination and was elected to the seat held by Lowell P.

---

**4th District: Southwest — Bridgeport, Stamford.** Population: 478,265 (5.4% decrease since 1970). Race: White 397,794 (83%); Black 57,810 (12%); Other 22,661 (5%). Spanish origin 39,552 (8%).

Weicker Jr., who was elected to the Senate in 1970.

A tire dealer in Fairfield, McKinney married into a wealthy family and has substantial stockholdings in major American corporations. He became involved in politics in 1965 when a friend dared him to run for town selectman. Although he lost that election, the next year he won a state House seat. In his second term he became House minority leader, and began learning the trick of working with Democratic majorities.

**The District:** This is the most Republican and most affluent district in the state. Apart from industrial Bridgeport and some working-class sections of Stamford and Norwalk, the district's towns are mostly bedroom communities for wealthy New York City commuters. Growth is limited; many residents fight aggressively to maintain restrictive zoning laws.

Republicans have long dominated the region. In the last four decades only one Democrat has been elected from the 4th District. He served one term in the 1950s and was returned in the 1960s for two more.

## Committees

**Banking, Finance and Urban Affairs** (3rd of 19 Democrats)
Economic Stabilization; Financial Institutions Supervision, Regulation and Insurance; Housing and Community Development.

**District of Columbia** (Ranking Republican)
Fiscal Affairs and Health; Government Operations and Metropolitan Affairs.

## Elections

**1980 General**

| | |
|---|---|
| Stewart McKinney (R ) | 124,285 (63 %) |
| John Phillips (D ) | 74,326 (37 %) |

**1978 General**

| | |
|---|---|
| Stewart McKinney (R ) | 83,990 (58 %) |
| Michael Morgan (D ) | 59,918 (42 %) |

**Previous Winning Percentages**

| | | | |
|---|---|---|---|
| 1976 (61 %) | 1974 (53 %) | 1972 (63 %) | 1970 (57 %) |

**District Vote For President**

| | 1980 | | 1976 | | 1972 |
|---|---|---|---|---|---|
| D | 76,564 (36 %) | D | 91,058 (43 %) | D | 81,802 (37 %) |
| R | 110,273 (53 %) | R | 118,716 (56 %) | R | 138,496 (62 %) |
| I | 20,723 (10 %) | | | | |

## Campaign Finance

| | Receipts | Receipts from PACs | Expenditures |
|---|---|---|---|
| **1980** | | | |
| McKinney (R ) | $175,048 | $41,664 (24 %) | $173,413 |
| Phillips (D ) | $157,049 | — (0 %) | $155,631 |
| **1978** | | | |
| McKinney (R ) | $125,012 | $547 (0 %) | $123,628 |
| Morgan (D ) | $50,784 | $7,600 (15 %) | $51,744 |

## Voting Studies

| | Presidential Support | | Party Unity | | Conservative Coalition | |
|---|---|---|---|---|---|---|
| Year | S | O | S | O | S | O |
| 1980 | 48 | 24 | 29 | 46 | 27 | 49 |
| 1979 | 63 | 23 | 21 | 61† | 28 | 60 |
| 1978 | 60 | 27 | 38 | 52 | 34 | 57 |
| 1977 | 44 | 11 | 21 | 42 | 22 | 36 |
| 1976 | 53 | 39 | 34 | 53 | 39 | 48 |
| 1975 | 58 | 35 | 45 | 47 | 43 | 49† |
| 1974 (Ford) | 52 | 41 | | | | |
| 1974 | 49 | 42 | 35 | 60 | 27 | 66 |
| 1973 | 47 | 45 | 44 | 45 | 39 | 47 |
| 1972 | 57 | 16 | 35 | 48 | 33 | 48 |
| 1971 | 67 | 28 | 52 | 40 | 43 | 47 |

†Not eligible for all recorded votes.
S = Support    O = Opposition

## Key Votes

**96th Congress**

| | |
|---|---|
| Weaken Carter oil profits tax (1979) | Y |
| Reject hospital cost control plan (1979) | Y |
| Implement Panama Canal Treaties (1979) | Y |
| Establish Department of Education (1979) | N |
| Approve Anti-busing Amendment (1979) | N |
| Guarantee Chrysler Corp. loans (1979) | Y |
| Approve military draft registration (1980) | N |
| Aid Sandinista regime in Nicaragua (1980) | Y |
| Strengthen fair housing laws (1980) | ? |

**97th Congress**

| | |
|---|---|
| Reagan budget proposal (1981) | Y |

## Interest Group Ratings

| Year | ADA | ACA | AFL-CIO | CCUS |
|---|---|---|---|---|
| 1980 | 78 | 41 | 57 | 57 |
| 1979 | 53 | 30 | 65 | 41 |
| 1978 | 55 | 26 | 55 | 65 |
| 1977 | 35 | 13 | 40 | 64 |
| 1976 | 50 | 23 | 50 | 43 |
| 1975 | 72 | 28 | 67 | 53 |
| 1974 | 70 | 21 | 64 | 30 |
| 1973 | 52 | 40 | 82 | 45 |
| 1972 | 63 | 28 | 60 | 75 |
| 1971 | 49 | 54 | 50 | - |

# 5 William R. Ratchford (D)

## Of Danbury — Elected 1978

**Born:** May 24, 1934, Danbury, Conn.

**Education:** U. of Conn., B.A. 1956; Georgetown U. Law Center, J.D. 1959.

**Military Career:** National Guard, 1959-65.

**Profession:** Lawyer.

**Family:** Wife, Barbara Carpenter; three children.

**Religion:** Unitarian.

**Political Career:** Conn. House, 1963-75; unsuccessful Democratic nominee for U.S. House, 1974.

**In Washington:** Ratchford, once Speaker of the Connecticut House, came to Congress saying he would like to be Speaker of the U.S. House someday. But he has not been very obtrusive about it. Although he won the presidency of his freshman Democratic class, he has not been one of the more visible figures in the internal politics of Congress so far.

Much of Ratchford's work has been more mundane, focused on the details of federal aid to education. As a member of the Educaton and Labor Committee, he worked on developing a special program of college courses for older persons. A Ratchford bill, the Lifelong Learning Act, became part of a new Title I in the 1980 version of the Higher Education Act.

In the 97th Congress, he switched roles slightly on Education and Labor, joining the Labor Standards Subcommittee to help fellow liberal Democrats defend existing labor laws against expected Reagan attacks.

On the House Administration Committee, Ratchford tried in 1979 to help the leadership push through a bill to provide public financing for congressional elections. The attempt failed, despite Ratchford's argument in committee that the existing system, with no spending limits, was "like a reactor gone wild." He contended that newcomers attempting to challenge incumbents faced enormous problems in raising money to mount successful campaigns.

Ratchford also fought a losing battle in the 96th Congress to retain tariff protection for a latex foam rubber manufacturer in his district. He enlisted his Connecticut Democratic colleague William Cotter, a Ways and Means Committee member, in an attempt to keep it. But the effort failed after opponents argued that the firm could not supply enough of the latex foam to warrant protection.

**At Home:** Ratchford's political hold on his district has been tenuous. He won the seat on his second try in 1978 by a narrow margin, which was reduced further in 1980 even though his Republican opponent was neither well-known nor well-financed.

Ratchford is strong only in the three most urbanized parts of the district. His native Danbury, which he represented in the Legislature for a dozen years, is his best area. It took several years for him to win acceptance in Waterbury, the key to a Democratic victory in the district. When Ratchford ran in 1974, resentment from his primary victory over Waterbury's party boss resulted in a low Democratic turnout in the city that November, and this cost him the election.

In 1980, Ratchford won Waterbury by more than 6,000 votes — just enough to compensate for his weak showing in the wealthy Republican areas of Fairfield County. In spite of his likeable style, Ratchford is considered too liberal for some of those areas.

Ratchford has developed a following among the district's elderly population. After losing in 1974, he served on a state nursing home panel before becoming commissioner on aging for a

---

**5th District: Southwest - Danbury, Meriden, Waterbury.** Population: 542,298 (7.3% increase since 1970). Race: White 507,881 (94%); Black 21,899 (4%); Other 12,518 (2%). Spanish origin 17,497 (3%).

year. Both jobs sparked his interest in the problems of older citizens and also put him in touch with many who later provided a base for his political efforts.

**The District:** Located in the southwestern part of the state, this is the most marginal of the state's six districts.

Once strongly Democratic, the 5th has been losing its partisan identification steadily in recent years. In 1980 all but one of its 26 cities and towns supported Ronald Reagan. Losing Republican, Senate candidate James L. Buckley narrowly carried the district.

This is partly because redistricting after 1970 added four solidly Republican towns, which were enough to end Democratic Rep. John Monagan's career in 1972. It took Republican Ronald A. Sarasin three terms to gain a solid hold on the district. When Sarasin left in 1978 to run unsuccessfully for governor, Ratchford returned the seat to Democratic hands.

Ratchford's almost-victorious challenger from 1980 vows to try again. But it is likely that Democratic redistricting will pare some of the more Republican towns from the southwestern end, making it more difficult to unseat Ratchford in 1982.

## Committees

**Education and Labor** (16th of 19 Democrats)
Elementary, Secondary and Vocational Education; Labor Standards.

**House Administration** (9th of 11 Democrats)
Accounts; Personnel and Police.

**Select Aging** (19th of 31 Democrats)
Health and Long-Term Care; Human Services.

## Elections

**1980 General**

| | |
|---|---|
| William Ratchford (D ) | 117,316 (50 %) |
| Edward Donahue (R ) | 115,614 (50 %) |

**1978 General**

| | |
|---|---|
| William Ratchford (D ) | 96,738 (52 %) |
| George Guidera (R ) | 88,162 (48 %) |

**District Vote For President**

| | 1980 | | 1976 | | 1972 |
|---|---|---|---|---|---|
| D | 83,705 (34 %) | D | 104,081 (43 %) | D | 87,747 (37 %) |
| R | 133,228 (54 %) | R | 133,654 (56 %) | R | 144,149 (61 %) |
| I | 26,998 (11 %) | | | | |

## Campaign Finance

| | Receipts | Receipts from PACs | Expenditures |
|---|---|---|---|
| **1980** | | | |
| Ratchford (D ) | $140,066 | $52,450 (37 %) | $140,037 |
| Donahue (R ) | $52,514 | $6,032 (11 %) | $52,740 |

| | | | |
|---|---|---|---|
| **1978** | | | |
| Ratchford (D ) | $139,970 | $38,900 (28 %) | $139,778 |
| Guidera (R ) | $245,653 | $28,918 (12 %) | $245,933 |

## Voting Studies

| | Presidential Support | | Party Unity | | Conservative Coalition | |
|---|---|---|---|---|---|---|
| Year | S | O | S | O | S | O |
| 1980 | 65 | 24 | 70 | 9 | 15 | 72 |
| 1979 | 83 | 15 | 88 | 10 | 13 | 86 |

S = Support          O = Opposition

## Key Votes

**96th Congress**

| | |
|---|---|
| Weaken Carter oil profits tax (1979) | N |
| Reject hospital cost control plan (1979) | N |
| Implement Panama Canal Treaties (1979) | Y |
| Establish Department of Education (1979) | Y |
| Approve Anti-busing Amendment (1979) | N |
| Guarantee Chrysler Corp. loans (1979) | Y |
| Approve military draft registration (1980) | N |
| Aid Sandinista regime in Nicaragua (1980) | ? |
| Strengthen fair housing Laws (1980) | Y |

**97th Congress**

| | |
|---|---|
| Reagan budget proposal (1981) | N |

## Interest Group Ratings

| Year | ADA | ACA | AFL-CIO | CCUS |
|---|---|---|---|---|
| 1980 | 83 | 19 | 72 | 61 |
| 1979 | 95 | 12 | 90 | 6 |

**213**

# 6 Toby Moffett (D)

**Of Litchfield — Elected 1974**

**Born:** Aug. 18, 1944, Holyoke, Mass.
**Education:** Syracuse U., A.B. 1966; Boston College, M.A. 1968.
**Profession:** Social worker.
**Family:** Wife, Myra DeLapp; one child by previous marriage.
**Religion:** Roman Catholic.
**Political Career:** No previous office.

**In Washington:** Vestiges of Moffett's early reputation for bomb-throwing persist in the House, but they are gradually yielding to the reality of his role as a serious legislator who plays the game at least as well as most Democrats in his House generation.

The slow change in perception is understandable, given Moffett's arrival in early 1975, when he implied that some committee chairmen were senile and complained of members watching soap operas in the cloakroom. Moffett's activist style led to so many newspaper stories that colleagues seemed to agree his ambitions were outside the institution.

So it surprised many of them four years later when he won the chairmanship of the Energy Subcommittee on Government Operations with a quietly personal campaign that attracted no attention from anyone until it succeeded.

Actually, however, Moffett had been showing marked "go-along" tendencies for most of his House career, especially in his relations with Speaker Thomas P. O'Neill Jr., with whom he shares a fondness for sports and a concern about the high price of home heating oil in New England.

When Moffett argues with the leadership these days, it is usually about energy policy and how far to go in supporting consumers against the energy industry. One of his few conspicuous arguments with O'Neill came in 1980, when he formed an alliance with conservative Republicans to fight President Carter's proposed dime-a-gallon oil import fee. O'Neill, although privately skeptical about the fee, was committed to support it and was visibly angry that Moffett had organized against it without keeping him informed. But the fee was rejected, and there seemed to be no lasting rupture.

Earlier in the 96th Congress, Moffett was less successful in fighting the president's decision to decontrol the price of oil. He easily won a test vote in the Democratic Caucus, but the issue never came to the House floor.

Even on energy, Moffett often sounds less militant in his anti-business rhetoric than he did earlier in his career. At the height of the 1979 gasoline shortage, he told constituents that the crisis was real, not a ploy by the oil companies, which he said were fundamentally honest.

As a member of the Energy and Commerce Committee, he has pushed hard for a variety of energy conservation schemes, especially one that would require drivers to stay out of their cars one day a week. This idea attracted little support and noisy opposition when Moffett brought it to the floor in 1979. He also has professed a growing disenchantment with rationing as a solution, admitting that Commerce Committee Republicans have "educated" him on the issue.

As he has moved closer to a traditional legislative role, Moffett has kept up his ties on the Democratic left with consumer groups and with labor, especially the Machinists and the United Auto Workers. He fought hard for a federal consumer agency in the 95th Congress. Like most of his allies in liberal pressure groups, he was openly critical of Carter for the first three years, then backed Sen. Edward M. Kennedy's challenge for the Democratic presidential nomination in 1980. Even after Kennedy had failed in the primaries, Moffett lobbied for an "open" convention, giving up only at the very end in New York.

---

**6th Distict: Northwest — Bristol, New Britain.** Population 540,617 (7.0% increase since 1970). Race: White 524,071 (97%); Black 9,393 (2%); Other 7,153 (1%). Spanish origin: 10,797 (2%).

**At Home:** Moffett's commitment to social activism began long before his 1974 election to the House. Immediately after college he taught in Boston's inner-city schools. In the late 1960s, he worked with urban street gangs around the country trying to start storefront schools and job training programs. He directed youth programs for the Nixon White House before resigning in protest after the Cambodian invasion and Kent State University killings in 1970.

His most active consumer involvement came as the executive director of the Connecticut Citizen Action Group, a Ralph Nader-style organization. In three years, Moffett brought considerable public attention to the group, whose interests ranged from studying the state Legislature's operations to exposing manufacturers of unsafe toys.

When Ella T. Grasso left her House seat to run for governor, Moffett overwhelmed all comers with a strong organization and a consumer-oriented campaign. By blasting the Nixon administration and "gluttonous multi-national firms," Moffett won the party's endorsement, defeated the mayor of New Britain in a primary and overwhelmed the Republican nominee. He has had no trouble since.

Republicans have put up token challengers who have managed to carry only a few small towns on the western and northern fringes of the district.

Moffett's political ambition has been no secret ever since his first term. By extending his campaign appearances to cover the state, he has managed to expand his reputation far beyond the bounds of his district. To the irritation of some party leaders, Moffett has made a practice of endorsing fellow liberals in primaries elsewhere in Connecticut.

But he won points for party unity in 1979 with his early decision to back Rep. Christopher J. Dodd for the seat of retiring Sen. Abraham Ribicoff. The alternative was to challenge Dodd in what could have been a bloody and expensive Democratic primary. Most observers interpreted Moffett's decision as a sign he would wait until 1982, when he would either run for the Senate seat held by Republican Lowell P. Weicker Jr. or go for the governor's chair.

**The District:** Winning election in the politically diverse 6th District is a good test for any politician. The western third is dominated by solidly Republican New England villages. On the eastern side, closer to Hartford, are the Democratic cities of New Britain and Bristol where ball bearings and other metal parts are made. Part of the industrial corridor between Hartford and Springfield, Mass., also lies in the 6th District and usually provides lopsided Democratic majorities.

## Committees

**Energy and Commerce** (8th of 24 Democrats)
Commerce, Transportation and Tourism; Energy Conservation and Power; Fossil and Synthetic Fuels; Health and Environment.

**Government Operations** (12th of 23 Democrats)
Environment, Energy and Natural Resources, chairman.

## Elections

**1980 General**

| | |
|---|---|
| Toby Moffett (D ) | 142,685 (59 %) |
| Nicholas Schaus (R ) | 98,331 (41 %) |

**1978 General**

| | |
|---|---|
| Toby Moffett (D ) | 119,537 (64 %) |
| Daniel Mackinnon (R ) | 66,664 (36 %) |

**Previous Winning Percentages**

1976 (57 %)    1974 (63 %)

**District Vote For President**

| 1980 | 1976 | 1972 |
|---|---|---|
| D 96,351 (38 %) | D 115,119 (48 %) | D 98,328 (41 %) |
| R 118,936 (47 %) | R 126,005 (52 %) | R 136,430 (58 %) |
| I 34,143 (13 %) | | |

## Campaign Finance

| | Receipts | Receipts from PACs | Expenditures |
|---|---|---|---|
| **1980** | | | |
| Moffett (D ) | $168,048 | $31,490 (19 %) | $171,509 |
| Nicholas (R ) | $127,343 | $3,360 (3 %) | $125,137 |
| **1978** | | | |
| Moffett (D ) | $168,174 | $26,947 (16 %) | $162,006 |
| Mackinnon (R ) | $86,011 | $9,139 (11 %) | $83,896 |

## Voting Studies

| | Presidential Support | | Party Unity | | Conservative Coalition | |
|---|---|---|---|---|---|---|
| Year | S | O | S | O | S | O |
| 1980 | 65 | 24 | 77 | 11 | 5 | 85 |
| 1979 | 73 | 17 | 84 | 7 | 5 | 85 |
| 1978 | 71 | 20 | 79 | 16 | 13 | 81 |
| 1977 | 81 | 18 | 82 | 12 | 11 | 84 |

*Toby Moffett, D-Conn.*

| | | | | | | |
|---|---|---|---|---|---|---|
| 1976 | 22 | 75 | 80 | 12 | 16 | 75 |
| 1975 | 25 | 74 | 86 | 10 | 8 | 90 |

S = Support          O = Opposition

## Key Votes

**96th Congress**

| | |
|---|---|
| Weaken Carter oil profits tax (1979) | N |
| Reject hospital cost control plan (1979) | N |
| Implement Panama Canal Treaties (1979) | Y |
| Establish Department of Education (1979) | Y |
| Approve Anti-busing Amendment (1979) | N |
| Guarantee Chrysler Corp. loans (1979) | Y |
| Approve military draft registration (1980) | N |
| Aid Sandinista regime in Nicaragua (1980) | Y |

| | |
|---|---|
| Strengthen fair housing laws (1980) | Y |

**97th Congress**

| | |
|---|---|
| Reagan budget proposal (1981) | N |

## Interest Group Ratings

| Year | ADA | ACA | AFL-CIO | CCUS |
|---|---|---|---|---|
| 1980 | 94 | 15 | 89 | 55 |
| 1979 | 100 | 4 | 95 | 0 |
| 1978 | 95 | 16 | 89 | 22 |
| 1977 | 95 | 11 | 83 | 18 |
| 1976 | 95 | 13 | 86 | 14 |
| 1975 | 100 | 7 | 96 | 12 |

# Delaware

U.S. CONGRESS:
ONE AT-LARGE DISTRICT
Senate (1D, 1R)          House (1R)

STATE:
Governor
Pierre S. "Pete" du Pont IV (R)

General Assembly
Senate: 21 members (12D, 9R)
House: 41 members (16D, 25R)

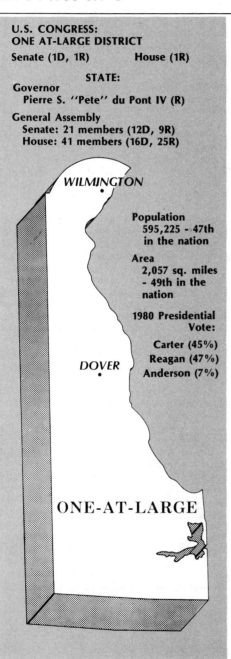

WILMINGTON

Population
595,225 - 47th
in the nation

Area
2,057 sq. miles
- 49th in the
nation

1980 Presidential
Vote:

Carter (45%)
Reagan (47%)
Anderson (7%)

DOVER

ONE-AT-LARGE

## ... Still the du Pont State

Delaware likes to think of itself as the "First State" — the earliest one to ratify the constitution — but it has always been better known as the home of E. I. du Pont de Nemours and Company.

The du Ponts settled in Delaware in the early 19th century and built up a small gunpowder business that, after World War I, became an economic giant. The family has played an important role in the government and politics of Delaware, and this fact has not escaped the notice of Ralph Nader. In the early 1970s a group of Nader activists issued a report that was extremely critical of the family, charging that the state was controlled by and for the corporation.

Whether or not it is a one-company state, Delaware has traditionally been a business state. Its liberal incorporation laws have led almost half of the Fortune 500's largest industrial companies to incorporate there. But there is another side to this issue. By the end of the 1970s, much of Delaware's business community was complaining about the state's personal income tax rates and environmental laws. Delaware is 30 percent marshland and has one of the nation's oldest and strictest coastal zoning laws. There is, in fact, a prohibition against any additional heavy industry in the coastal area.

In the 1980s, Delaware has once again adopted policies to attract business to the state. Under the direction of Governor Pierre "Pete" du Pont, the state Legislature passed legislation to eliminate usury limits on loan interest rates and to provide tax incentives for large banking operations.

Delaware is a swing state in national politics. It has voted with the winning party in every presidential election since 1952. In seven gubernatorial contests between 1948 and 1972, Democrats won four and Republicans three, and no candidate from either party drew more than 53.7 percent of the vote. Du Pont seems to have ended that tradition; after winning a first term with 56.9 percent in 1976, he soared to 70 percent in 1980. That was the highest figure in a century.

**217**

# A Political Tour

**North of the Canal.** Delaware is divided by the Chesapeake and Delaware Canal. North of the canal at the top of the Delmarva (Delaware-Maryland-Virginia) Peninsula is Wilmington, in New Castle County, the state's only real metropolitan area.

Wilmington has a black majority and problems typical of Northern inner cities. Its suburbs are affluent Republican areas similar to suburban areas anywhere. Nearby in northern New Castle County is the so-called Chateau Country, a wealthy area of rolling hills and huge estates located northwest of the city.

Forty years ago, almost half of the state's people resided in Wilmington, but the city itself now accounts for less than 12 percent of the state's total population. Over half of Wilmington's population is black, but it continues to have large numbers of Italians, Irish and Poles who vote Democratic. A Democratic candidate who hopes to win a state-wide election must carry Wilmington by at least 10,000 votes. This means doing well among all segments of the city's electorate.

While the city has been shrinking, the suburban areas around Wilmington have been growing steadily. As a result about 70 percent of Delaware's vote continues to be cast in New Castle County. When the ethnic voters of the city move to the suburbs, they frequently change their voting habits. As in many areas, economic status seems to override traditional ethnic voting patterns. The Republican voting habits of suburban New Castle County are frequently strong enough to overcome the solid Democratic margin turned in by Wilmington's voters.

**South of the Canal.** Moving south from the Chesapeake and Delaware Canal, one notices a change in values, language and attitudes toward those of the border South. Kent and Sussex counties are rural and agricultural.

Dover, the state capital, has some light industry, but the largest industries in the two southern counties are poultry and tourism. In fact, Sussex is the largest poultry-producing county in the United States. It also has Rehoboth Beach, which attracts thousands of sunbathers every summer and whose year-round residents are firmly Republican.

Kent and Sussex may have similar cultures, but they have noticeably different voting habits. Sussex' tendencies are toward conservative Republicans. Kent, in pure partisan terms, is the most Democratic part of Delaware. But these Democrats are conservative and gave Nixon a large margin in his 1972 race against George McGovern. On the county level, Kent County has the strongest Democratic organization in the state, and that organization does an effective job on election day. The same goes for the GOP organization in Sussex county.

# Governor
# Pierre S. du Pont IV (R)

**Born:** Jan. 22, 1935, Wilmington, Del.
**Home:** Rockdale, Del.
**Education:** Princeton U., B.S.E. 1956; Harvard Law School, LL.B. 1963.
**Military Career:** Navy, 1957-60.
**Profession:** Lawyer.
**Family:** Wife, Elise; four children.
**Religion:** Episcopalian.
**Political Career:** Delaware House, 1969-71; U.S. House, 1971-77; elected governor 1976, 1980; term expires Jan. 1985.

# William V. Roth Jr. (R)

**Of Wilmington — Elected 1970**

**Born:** July 22, 1921, Great Falls, Mont.
**Education:** U. of Ore., B.A. 1944; Harvard U.,
  M.B.A. 1947, LL.B. 1949.
**Military Career:** Army, 1943-46.
**Profession:** Lawyer.
**Family:** Wife, Jane Richards; two children.
**Religion:** Episcopalian.
**Political Career:** U.S. House, 1967-71.

**In Washington:** Roth has not always taken easily to being the second half of the nation's most famous tax cut. As far as he is concerned, it has always been Roth-Kemp, even if most people give the emphasis and the publicity to the younger, more dynamic congressman from Buffalo.

Actually, the media tendency to pronounce the two names together obscures a significant policy difference between the two men. Kemp has never felt a balanced budget was sacred or even necessary, as long the tax rate was sufficiently low. Roth has always worried about the effect a huge tax cut would have on the federal deficit if there were no accompanying reduction in spending. In the 1979-80 version of the proposal, (which he referred to as son of "Roth-Kemp"), Roth added a title to impose tight spending restraints.

But he has been selective and independent in deciding what to cut. When the first package of Reagan spending reductions reached the Senate floor in March of 1981, Roth voted against three of them: for the Conrail transportation system, trade adjustment assistance to unemployed workers, and energy subsidies for the poor.

Broad-stroke tax cuts are Roth's preoccupation at the Finance Committee. The panel is involved in health, welfare, and a variety of other issues, but Roth's participation in some of them is limited. When the committee wrote a complicated windfall profits tax on the oil industry in 1979, Roth showed up mainly to press his case on an unrelated issue: his amendment to cancel the Social Security tax increase scheduled for 1981. He was given a chance to offer it and it failed on a tie vote.

One personal crusade for Roth is college tuition tax credits. He is the the leading proponent of such a tax credit system in the Senate, and almost got it enacted in the 95th Congress. It passed the Senate without controversy, but died in the House after a dispute over whether it should also apply to tuition for private elementary and secondary schools.

Even when faced with setbacks, Roth is a patient and persistent legislator who can pursue an issue for years without giving up. For more than a decade, he has been pressing for the creation of a panel like the old Hoover commissions of 1947-49 and 1953-55 to study the executive branch and recommend a sweeping government reorganization. He has a better chance than before to press that case as Governmental Affairs chairman, a position he inherited with the Republican takeover of the Senate in 1980.

Roth believes the bureaucracy needs to be streamlined, and wants to use his committee to find ways of reducing the number of federal regulations in effect. He did, however, support creation of the government's two newest Cabinet departments — Energy and Education — and strongly advocates the creation of yet another one, a Department of Trade.

Roth has joined his Delaware colleague, Democrat Joseph R. Biden Jr., in pushing anti-busing legislation in the Senate, seeking among other things to limit the power of federal courts to require busing for racial balance. As a member from a small state, he has also joined Biden in opposing direct election of the president and abolition of the electoral college.

Roth's focus these days is primarily on domestic issues, but he served on the Foreign Affairs Committee during his two terms in the House, from 1967-71, and remains active in the Trilateral Commission, the private group that seeks ways to strengthen ties among the industrialized nations.

**At Home:** Born in Montana and educated at Harvard, Roth came to Delaware to work as a lawyer for a chemical firm, and got involved in politics. After an abortive 1960 bid for lieutenant governor, he became state Republican chairman.

In 1966, he went to the House by ousting veteran Democrat Harris B. McDowell. He talked

**219**

## William V. Roth Jr., R-Del.

about open housing legislation, saying he was opposed to it but willing to endorse state GOP convention language in favor of it.

With the retirement of Republican Sen. John J. Williams in 1970, Roth became the uncontested choice of the party to face the Democratic state House leader, Jacob W. Zimmerman, for the seat. Zimmerman, a Vietnam dove, had little money or statewide name recognition, and the contest was never in much doubt.

In 1976, Roth had a strong Democratic challenger — Wilmington Mayor Thomas C. Maloney. But Roth's efforts against busing had given him an excellent issue to run on, and Maloney was hurt by the coolness of organized labor, which was upset over his frugal approach to municipal pay raises. One state labor leader openly called Maloney a "union buster." Roth's margin was down from 1970, but he was too strong in the suburbs for Maloney to have any chance to beat him statewide.

## Committees

**Governmental Affairs** (Chairman)
Permanent Subcommittee on Investigations, chairman.

**Finance** (3rd of 11 Republicans)
Economic Growth, Employment, and Revenue Sharing; International Trade; Savings, Pensions, and Investment Policy.

**Select Intelligence** (7th of 8 Republicans)
Budget.

**Joint Economic**
Trade, Productivity and Economic Growth, chairman; Investment, Jobs and Prices.

**Joint Taxation**

## Elections

**1976 General**

| | |
|---|---|
| William Roth (R ) | 125,502 (56 %) |
| Thomas Maloney (D ) | 98,055 (44 %) |

**Previous Winning Percentages**

| | | |
|---|---|---|
| 1970 (59 %) | 1968* (59 %) | 1966* (56 %) |
| | | * House elections. |

## Campaign Finance

| 1976 | Receipts | Receipts from PACs | Expenditures |
|---|---|---|---|
| Roth (R ) | $321,292 | $71,600 (22 %) | $322,080 |
| Maloney (D ) | $211,281 | $71,275 (34 %) | $211,258 |

## Voting Studies

| | Presidential Support | | Party Unity | | Conservative Coalition | |
|---|---|---|---|---|---|---|
| Year | S | O | S | O | S | O |
| Senate service | | | | | | |
| 1980 | 41 | 55 | 85 | 12 | 87 | 10 |
| 1979 | 46 | 47 | 72 | 22 | 67 | 23 |
| 1978 | 32 | 62 | 82 | 14 | 80 | 15 |
| 1977 | 58 | 39 | 81 | 14 | 87 | 8 |
| 1976 | 66 | 28 | 70 | 24 | 75 | 19 |
| 1975 | 63 | 33 | 65 | 29 | 64 | 28 |
| 1974 (Ford) | 54 | 46 | | | | |
| 1974 | 71 | 27 | 68 | 28 | 76 | 19 |
| 1973 | 71 | 25 | 76 | 22 | 79 | 20 |
| 1972 | 83 | 17 | 79 | 19 | 84 | 14 |
| 1971 | 85 | 15 | 84 | 15 | 79 | 21 |
| House service | | | | | | |
| 1970 | 72 | 26 | 69 | 25 | 75 | 25 |
| 1969 | 70 | 30 | 85 | 15 | 73 | 24 |
| 1968 | 54 | 35 | 74 | 15 | 71 | 16 |
| 1967 | 52 | 48 | 84 | 16 | 87 | 13 |

S = Support  O = Opposition

## Key Votes

**96th Congress**

| | |
|---|---|
| Maintain relations with Taiwan (1979) | Y |
| Reduce synthetic fuel development funds (1979) | N |
| Impose nuclear plant moratorium (1979) | N |
| Kill stronger windfall profits tax (1979) | Y |
| Guarantee Chrysler Corp. loans (1979) | Y |
| Approve military draft registration (1980) | N |
| End Revenue Sharing to the states (1980) | N |
| Block Justice Dept. busing suits (1980) | Y |

**97th Congress**

| | |
|---|---|
| Restore urban program funding cuts (1981) | N |

## Interest Group Ratings

| Year | ADA | ACA | AFL-CIO | CCUS-1 | CCUS-2 |
|---|---|---|---|---|---|
| Senate service | | | | | |
| 1980 | 22 | 73 | 21 | 80 | |
| 1979 | 21 | 70 | 21 | 64 | 73 |
| 1978 | 15 | 83 | 11 | 89 | |
| 1977 | 20 | 88 | 16 | 88 | |
| 1976 | 10 | 84 | 26 | 56 | |
| 1975 | 33 | 57 | 25 | 80 | |
| 1974 | 38 | 74 | 18 | 80 | |
| 1973 | 40 | 83 | 9 | 67 | |
| 1972 | 25 | 73 | 10 | 80 | |
| 1971 | 19 | 67 | 8 | · | |
| House service | | | | | |
| 1970 | 20 | 79 | 29 | 100 | |
| 1969 | 7 | 65 | 30 | · | |
| 1968 | 8 | 86 | 33 | · | |
| 1967 | 7 | 90 | 8 | 90 | |

# Joseph R. Biden Jr. (D)

### Of Wilmington — Elected 1972

**Born:** Nov. 20, 1942, Scranton, Pa.
**Education:** U. of Del., B.A. 1965; Syracuse U., J.D. 1968.
**Profession:** Lawyer.
**Family:** Wife, Jill Jacobs; three children.
**Religion:** Roman Catholic.
**Political Career:** New Castle County Council, 1970-72.

**In Washington:** Still one of the youngest members of the Senate after a decade in it, Biden is gradually living down an early reputation as an *enfant terrible* and gaining influence on key committees.

Not yet 40, he has emerged as the ranking Democrat on the Senate Judiciary Committee, the second in line on Foreign Relations and third on both Budget and Select Intelligence — an extraordinary array of committee plums for any senator, let alone one so young. If he remains in the Senate, he seems all but certain to become chairman of one or more of these major panels when and if the Democrats regain control.

Biden may not be content to serve indefinitely in the Senate, however, even if Delaware voters elect him a third time in 1984. Although he does not discuss his plans much anymore, he has demonstrated unmistakable national ambitions in the past. Asked once how he reacts when people suggest that he run for president, he said "I write their names down."

Biden nearly abandoned his Senate career before it even started. Just weeks after he was elected in 1972, his wife and daughter were killed and his two sons injured in an automobile crash. Biden at first said he did not want to take the oath of office, but then-Majority Leader Mike Mansfield talked him into assuming his seat. Sworn in at his son's hospital bedside, he became at age 30 one of the youngest popularly elected senators ever seated.

For much of his first year, Biden was distracted by family problems, dividing his time between Washington and his home in Delaware. But as time went on, he became more absorbed by the Senate and emerged as a rather brash and markedly ambitious maverick. "Why should I be here to be just one of 100 who vote?" he asked. "I want to be one of those guys who change people's minds."

On occasion, Biden was so eager to "change people's minds" that his mouth outran his thought processes. Once when he was in the middle of explaining one of his own amendments to the Judiciary Committee, a staff assistant passed him a copy of the proposal, which brought Biden to a stammering halt. "Obviously I don't know what the hell I'm talking about," he admitted cheerfully.

Biden, who once participated in sit-ins to desegregate restaurants along U.S. Route 40, startled his colleagues in 1975 when he broke liberal ranks to win Senate approval of an anti-busing amendment. Suddenly, he was allied with Southern conservatives on an emotional national issue. "It is not a comfortable feeling for me," he said. "I mean, I've never been there before." But it was time, he argued, to admit that "busing does not work" regardless of how ardently it might be supported by traditional civil rights groups. He has continued his opposition since then, coming within two votes in 1978 of gaining Senate approval of an amendment restricting the power of courts to order busing for racial balance.

He has had some trouble devising a position he can accept on abortion. As a Catholic, he is basically opposed to it. But he has conceded there is a rational argument for abortion in special cases. He votes against federal funding for abortions but also against legislation to ban them entirely.

Biden has moved away from traditional liberal positions on some domestic spending issues. He has proposed, for example, an end to all federal entitlement programs except Social Security and Medicare. He would force all programs except those two to compete for money from the regular appropriations pie. "I have an extreme aversion to the proposition that if we spend enough money we'll solve all our problems," he has said.

To help control federal programs, he has also

joined Delaware GOP Sen. William V. Roth Jr. in pushing "sunset" legislation, which would bring federal programs to an end after a specified number of years unless they were specifically renewed.

In 1977, Biden began working on an issue that eventually produced a new law, on "graymail." He was then chairman of an Intelligence subcommittee concerned that defendants could force prosecutors to abandon espionage cases by threatening to disclose classified information in their own defense. To avoid jeopardizing national security, charges were sometimes being dropped. It was a form of legal blackmail, Biden said. Cases at the time concerned illegal acts connected with U.S. covert operations in Chile. A Biden bill finally was enacted allowing judges to screen classified information before a trial to see if the data could be used.

One of the few senators to serve on both Foreign Relations and Intelligence, Biden used his role on them to press hard for approval of the SALT II treaty during the Carter administration. As chairman of the Foreign Relations Subcommittee on Europe, he traveled extensively in 1980 and 1981, meeting with key leaders in Moscow and Bonn to discuss SALT and other topics. In October, 1979, he released a committee report contending ratification of SALT II was essential to the well-being of NATO countries. Although the treaty never got beyond the committee, a Biden amendment was included to protect Europe from a buildup of Soviet missiles aimed its way in the future.

With SALT dead, Biden shifted to a similarly futile effort to hold the line on defense spending in the Budget Committee. "I'm not at all convinced the national interest requires (the increases)," he said at one point.

In early 1981, Biden was fighting the Reagan administration on Foreign Relations over a proposal to sell sophisticated AWACS surveillance planes to Saudi Arabia. He objected that the sale threatened the security of Israel and, by extension, the security of the United States.

Biden was considered a swing vote on Judiciary under Edward M. Kennedy's Democratic chairmanship in the 96th Congress. He was unwilling to go along with Kennedy, for example, on legislation to overturn the Supreme Court's 1977 *Illinois Brick* decision and give consumers the right to sue corporations for price-fixing. He went along reluctantly with a bill by Democrat Howard Metzenbaum of Ohio to block major U.S. oil companies from acquiring other large corporations. "I'd be willing to go this way (with Metzenbaum)," he said, "just to stick it in their

left ear, I'm so angry with the way the oil companies treat us here."

As chairman of Judiciary's Criminal Justice Subcommittee in the 96th Congress, Biden had responsibility for defending the 1974 "speedy trial" act requiring judges to dismiss any federal criminal case where prosecutors failed to go to trial within 100 days of arrest. When the Justice Department protested it could not get the necessary machinery in place to meet the law's deadlines, Congress enacted a one-year extension, but Biden warned, "As far as I'm concerned, the critics of the Speedy Trial Act have had their day in court and it is time for judges and prosecutors to get together and make this act work."

**At Home:** Biden was 29 years old when his celebrated brashness pushed him into the 1972 Senate race against GOP incumbent J. Caleb Boggs. With service on the New Castle County Council his only electoral credential, Biden seemed a sure loser.

But he ran hard on a dovish Vietnam platform and accused the Republican of being a do-nothing senator. He called for more spending on mass transit and health care services. The Biden campaign was essentially a family operation, without state-of-the-art media management, but it was sophisticated enough to cover a state with an electorate as small as Delaware's. Boggs awoke to the threat too late, and watched helplessly on election night as his "safe" seat went down the drain by 3,162 votes. Being an institution in Delaware Republican politics was not sufficient insurance against a personable and energetic challenger.

Delaware Democratic leaders, certain that a challenge to Boggs was hopeless, had given Biden little support in 1972. And he gave them little attention for most of his first term. At the 1976 Democratic National Convention in New York, he even stayed in a separate hotel from the state delegation.

By 1978, however, Biden had made up with the party. More important, however, was his opposition to busing. As he ran for re-election, a long disputed busing plan was taking effect in New Castle County, outraging voters in the white suburbs of Wilmington.

With this anti-busing position offsetting his liberalism on some other social issues, Biden seemed unbeatable in 1978, and big-name Delaware Republicans refrained from taking him on. The task fell to an obscure southern Delaware poultry farmer, James H. Baxter, who gamely tried to paint the Democrat as too far left for the state. Biden easily beat him.

An early 1976 Jimmy Carter backer, Biden

often claimed his friendly connections to the Carter administration helped the state win fed-

eral grants. With Carter gone, he no longer has that advantage.

## Committees

**Budget** (3rd of 10 Democrats)

**Foreign Relations** (2nd of 8 Democrats)
European Affairs; International Economic Policy.

**Judiciary** (Ranking Democrat)
Criminal Law; Security and Terrorism.

**Select Intelligence** (3rd of 7 Democrats)
Collection and Foreign Operations.

## Elections

**1978 General**

| | |
|---|---|
| Joseph Biden (D ) | 93,930 (58 %) |
| James Baxter (R ) | 66,479 (41 %) |

**Previous Winning Percentages**

1972    (51%)

## Campaign Finance

| 1978 | Receipts | Receipts from PACs | Expen- ditures |
|---|---|---|---|
| Biden (D ) | $487,637 | $126,100 (26 %) | $487,504 |
| Baxter (R ) | $207,637 | $9,923 (5 %) | $206,250 |

## Voting Studies

| | Presidential Support | | Party Unity | | Conservative Coalition | |
|---|---|---|---|---|---|---|
| Year | S | O | S | O | S | O |
| 1980 | 72 | 9 | 70 | 15 | 23 | 67 |
| 1979 | 66 | 12 | 68 | 14 | 14 | 68 |
| 1978 | 71 | 17 | 67 | 22 | 28 | 68 |
| 1977 | 77 | 15 | 72 | 14 | 13 | 76 |
| 1976 | 28 | 49 | 71 | 9 | 10 | 68 |
| 1975 | 27 | 56 | 77 | 13 | 14 | 74 |
| 1974 (Ford) | 28 | 66 | | | | |
| 1974 | 30 | 65 | 73 | 18 | 19 | 75 |
| 1973 | 30 | 49 | 75 | 10 | 9 | 81 |

†Not eligible for all recorded votes.

S = Support          O = Opposition

## Key Votes

**96th Congress**

| | |
|---|---|
| Maintain relations with Taiwan (1979) | N |
| Reduce synthetic fuel development funds (1979) | N |
| Impose nuclear plant moratorium (1979) | Y |
| Kill stronger windfall profits tax (1979) | N |
| Guarantee Chrysler Corp. loans (1979) | Y |
| Approve military draft registration (1980) | ? |
| End Revenue Sharing to the states (1980) | Y |
| Block Justice Dept. busing suits (1980) | Y |

**97th Congress**

| | |
|---|---|
| Restore urban program funding cuts (1981) | Y |

## Interest Group Ratings

| Year | ADA | ACA | AFL-CIO | CCUS-1 | CCUS-2 |
|---|---|---|---|---|---|
| 1980 | 67 | 18 | 76 | 31 | |
| 1979 | 53 | 20 | 87 | 0 | 8 |
| 1978 | 50 | 27 | 61 | 44 | |
| 1977 | 70 | 13 | 84 | 11 | |
| 1976 | 75 | 17 | 82 | 13 | |
| 1975 | 78 | 14 | 72 | 23 | |
| 1974 | 81 | 5 | 64 | 0 | |
| 1973 | 80 | 8 | 80 | 0 | |

# AL Thomas B. Evans Jr. (R)

**Of Wilmington — Elected 1976**

**Born:** Nov. 5, 1931, Nashville, Tenn.
**Education:** U. of Va., B.A. 1953, LL.B. 1956.
**Military Career:** National Guard, 1956-60.
**Profession:** Insurance and mortgage broker.
**Family:** Wife, Mary Page Hilliard; three children.
**Religion:** Episcopalian.
**Political Career:** No previous office.

**In Washington:** Ronald Reagan could hardly have made a more pragmatic choice than Evans to serve as his House spokesman and liaison during the 1980 presidential campaign. A wealthy and sophisticated Wilmington insurance broker, Evans could claim close ties to the moderate Eastern Republicans who had been suspicious of Reagan for more than a decade.

Evans' House voting record through 1979 placed him firmly in the moderate camp. But while many of his like-minded colleagues were stumping his country for George Bush in the spring of 1980, Evans was quietly assuring people that Reagan was within the party's mainstream and worthy of their trust.

It was the Reagan staff that thought up the liaison assignment for Evans. A longtime party activist, Evans worked his way up to the cochairmanship of the Republican National Committee (RNC) in 1971 during the Nixon administration. In that role he got to know Richard V. Allen, Reagan's foreign policy adviser, and Lyn Nofziger, his media specialist. Evans left his party post in 1973, and came to Congress in 1977, but maintained his contacts.

During the 1980 campaign, Evans joined top Reagan aides at a weekly strategy session. He arranged to have members of Congress travel with the candidate in the fall, briefing him on the local political terrain. When Reagan decided to give a speech to an Italian-American dinner, Evans saw that it was routed through Silvio O. Conte of Massachusetts, the senior House Republican of Italian descent.

When the 97th Congress began, Evans was conspicuously rewarded — with a new post as vice-chairman of the Republican National Committee for presidential liaison.

All those successes made Evans especially conspicuous when he became involved in a scandal early in 1981 involving lobbyist Paula Parkinson, who claimed that she had influenced Repub-

lican votes on a crop insurance bill by offering sexual favors. Newspapers reported that Evans had had an affair with Parkinson. He replied that she was a troubled woman who was "using my name in an effort to gain publicity." But he also asked "the Lord to forgive me."

Evans made no public appearances in Delaware for several weeks after the Parkinson scandal broke. Then he began surfacing again, talking about political issues and promising to run for another term in 1982.

Over the years, Evans has drawn more attention for his Reagan contacts than for his legislative work as a junior member of the House Banking Committee. On that panel he has specialized in foreign banking questions, generally taking the internationalist position traditional for moderate Republicans.

He is a supporter of the Export-Import Bank, and worked in 1978 for a compromise that allowed corporations doing business in South Africa to receive help from the bank, provided they approve a code of ethics for their dealings with employees. "If American companies withdraw from South Africa," he said at one point, "severe economic problems will result and South African blacks will be the first to suffer."

Evans caused some controversy in Delaware early in 1980 when he changed his position on credit legislation in the Banking Committee. The bill was designed to allow consumers, when a

---

**District: At-Large — All of Delaware.** Population: 595,225 (9% increase since 1970). Race: White 488,543 (82%), Black 95,971 (16%), Others 10,711 (2%). Spanish origin: 9,671 (2%).

credit card company changes its interest rate, to continue paying off the remaining balance at the old rate. Evans was an early sponsor of this idea, but turned against it, and offered the unsuccessful motion to send it back to subcommittee. He said it would create too many bookkeeping problems for creditors. The bill was opposed intensely by the financial community.

**At Home.** Although Evans had been a leading figure in national Republican politics for nearly a decade, he had not tried for elective office before Republican Pierre S. du Pont vacated Delaware's one House seat to run for governor in 1976. Backed by state party leaders, Evans won the nomination without a primary fight.

Democrat Samuel Shipley, a Wilmington advertising executive, tried to make an issue of Evans' role as operating head of the RNC during the early days of Watergate. But Evans denied any link to the scandal, claiming that he "did not raise one nickel for Richard Nixon in 1971 and 1972."

As a former member of the Republican National Finance Committee, Evans knew how to raise money. He collected more than $200,000 and outspent Shipley by a margin of more than 3-1. He needed most of that money, because his margin over Shipley was only 8,240 votes out of nearly 215,000 cast.

Democratic challengers since then have criticized Evans for being an affluent pawn of business interests. But his fund-raising ability has helped fend off serious opposition. In 1980 he won re-election with 62 percent of the vote, the second-highest share for any Delaware congressional candidate in the last half century.

Whether the Parkinson scandal will change that is an open question.

## Committees

**Banking, Finance and Urban Affairs** (7th of 19 Republicans)
Consumer Affairs and Coinage; Housing and Community Development; International Development Institutions and Finance.

**Merchant Marine and Fisheries** (8th of 15 Republicans)
Coast Guard and Navigation; Fisheries and Wildlife Conservation and the Environment.

## Elections

**1980 General**

| | |
|---|---|
| Thomas Evans Jr. (R ) | 133,783 (62 %) |
| Robert Maxwell (D ) | 81,227 (38 %) |

**1978 General**

| | |
|---|---|
| Thomas Evans Jr. (R ) | 91,689 (58 %) |
| Gary Hindes (D ) | 64,863 (41 %) |

**Previous Winning Percentage**

**1976 (52 %)**

**District Vote For President**

| | 1980 | | 1976 | | 1972 |
|---|---|---|---|---|---|
| D | 105,700 (45 %) | D | 122,596 (52 %) | D | 92,283 (39 %) |
| R | 111,185 (47 %) | R | 109,831 (47 %) | R | 140,357 (60 %) |
| I | 16,275 (7 %) | | | | |

## Campaign Finance

| | Receipts | Receipts from PACs | Expenditures |
|---|---|---|---|
| **1980** | | | |
| Evans (R ) | $369,590 | $99,400 (27 %) | $340,383 |
| Maxwell (D ) | $87,699 | $30,886 (35 %) | $86,038 |

**1978**

| | | | |
|---|---|---|---|
| Evans (R ) | $242,546 | $62,175 (26 %) | $241,410 |
| Hindes (D ) | $57,329 | $23,950 (42 %) | $57,252 |

## Voting Studies

| | Presidential Support | | Party Unity | | Conservative Coalition | |
|---|---|---|---|---|---|---|
| Year | S | O | S | O | S | O |
| 1980 | 50 | 39 | 63 | 27 | 56 | 33 |
| 1979 | 38 | 57 | 66 | 27 | 72 | 23 |
| 1978 | 39 | 57 | 74 | 21 | 78 | 18 |
| 1977 | 56 | 41 | 67 | 26 | 69 | 22 |

S = Support          O = Opposition

## Key Votes

**96th Congress**

| | |
|---|---|
| Weaken Carter oil profits tax (1979) | Y |
| Reject hospital cost control plan (1979) | Y |
| Implement Panama Canal Treaties (1979) | N |
| Establish Department of Education (1979) | N |
| Approve Anti-busing Amendment (1979) | Y |
| Guarantee Chrysler Corp. loans (1979) | Y |
| Approve military draft registration (1980) | N |
| Aid Sandinista regime in Nicaragua (1980) | Y |
| Strengthen fair housing laws (1980) | N |

**97th Congress**

| | |
|---|---|
| Reagan budget proposal (1981) | Y |

## Interest Group Ratings

| Year | ADA | ACA | AFL-CIO | CCUS |
|---|---|---|---|---|
| 1980 | 56 | 65 | 21 | 81 |
| 1979 | 26 | 81 | 15 | 83 |
| 1978 | 15 | 76 | 21 | 82 |
| 1977 | 20 | 83 | 27 | 88 |

# Florida

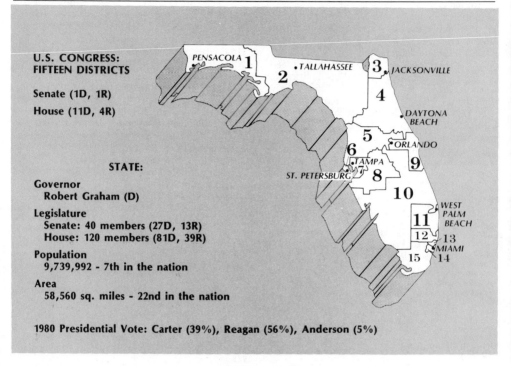

**U.S. CONGRESS:**
**FIFTEEN DISTRICTS**

Senate (1D, 1R)

House (11D, 4R)

**STATE:**

Governor
Robert Graham (D)

Legislature
Senate: 40 members (27D, 13R)
House: 120 members (81D, 39R)

Population
9,739,992 - 7th in the nation

Area
58,560 sq. miles - 22nd in the nation

1980 Presidential Vote: Carter (39%), Reagan (56%), Anderson (5%)

## ... A Climate of Change

Florida's ascent into national political significance has been dramatic. Twenty years ago it had eight congressional districts. After 1982 it will have 19. Its delegation will be the seventh largest in the House.

The rapid population growth shapes the style and agenda of Florida politics. Elections are often expensive, media-oriented battles of advertising consultants scheming for the votes of millions of newcomers who have not developed local political allegiances.

Once elected, all Florida officeholders must respond to the challenge of managing an explosion of population and economic activity that threatens to squander natural resources and lower the quality of life that is the state's allure.

From Reconstruction until the 1940s, politics in Florida was effectively limited to the Democratic Party. Two-party competition began after World War II when new arrivals from Northern states imported their Republican voting habits.

Eisenhower started a trend of "presidential Republicanism" by winning the state in 1952 and 1956. In 1954, the retirees who had moved in large numbers to Pinellas County (St. Petersburg) helped elect Florida's first GOP congressman since 1875, William C. Cramer. He was joined in Congress in 1963 by Edward J. Gurney, an Orange County Republican, and in 1967 by J. Herbert Burke, from Broward County, north of Miami.

Only in the past 15 years have Republicans become competitive in Florida gubernatorial and senatorial elections. The GOP success stems partly from the maturing of their metropolitan county organizations. But Republicans owe some thanks to the Democrats, who have squabbled away several chances for victory.

In the 1966 gubernatorial race and the 1968 senatorial race, bitter Democratic primaries gave Republicans their first statewide openings.

Claude Kirk won the governorship, and Gurney was promoted to the Senate.

In 1970, Democrats came back unexpectedly with two fresh faces, Reubin Askew for governor and Lawton Chiles for the Senate. Both won, and Democratic dominance continued through the 1970s. But in 1980, Republicans again exploited Democratic disunity to win the Senate election.

Democratic Sen. Richard Stone, seeking a second term, was defeated for renomination by former U.S. Rep. Bill Gunter. Former state Public Service Commissioner Paula Hawkins then defeated Gunter in the general election to become the second woman member of the Senate.

The Gunter-Stone contest revolved around regional rivalries, still a factor in Florida politics. Resentment against Miami has traditionally made it difficult for the city's candidates to win statewide. Stone challenged that tradition successfully in 1974, partly because he courted north Florida voters assiduously, diluting his Miami image. Graham won as a Miami-based candidate in 1978. But identification with the city is still a liability. It was Stone's biggest problem in the 1980 primary. He won Dade County which includes Miami, by about 2-to-1. But he lost 54 of the other 66 counties.

# A Political Tour

**North Florida.** Most of the counties along Florida's Panhandle are geographically and politically closer to Montgomery, Ala., than to Miami. Few tourists picture Florida as piney woods and farms, but the northern third of the state is mostly that. Its voting behavior is Deep South Democratic conservatism.

In the late 1960s, when Democrats outside of North Florida supported moderates for statewide office, the Panhandle registered its displeasure by bolting to the GOP in general elections. But Democrats usually held the region during the past decade; in 1980, Gunter won all but two Panhandle counties against Republican Paula Hawkins.

Traditional ties to the Democratic Party were even strong enough to help Carter carry a swath of central Panhandle counties in 1980. But to a majority of north Floridians, Reagan's conservatism was more alluring than partisan devotion to Carter.

White-collar and academic pockets in the rural areas are Tallahassee, the state capital and home of two major universities, and Gainesville, where the University of Florida is located.

From Pensacola to Jacksonville, defense installations are major economic forces in north Florida's port cities and surrounding coastal areas. The military presence can be traced in part to two longtime congressmen: Panhandle Democrat Robert L. F. Sikes and Democrat Charles E. Bennett. Sikes, who served 37 years, chaired the Appropriations Subcommittee on Military Construction for more than a decade. Bennett, now in his 17th term, ranks second on Armed Services and is Seapower Subcommittee chairman.

When Jacksonville was developing into a major Atlantic port and land transportation hub earlier this century, its jobs lured farm boys from south Georgia and the central Panhandle. In recent years, Jacksonville has become a financial and insurance center, but the population has not expanded as quickly as it has in cities further down the peninsula. Because of its slow growth and the Southern origin of many in its workforce, Jacksonville has more Southern ambience than those faster-growing cities to the south.

The Gulf Coast cities of Panama City and Pensacola attract more tourists and retirees than they used to, but the rate of population growth in North Florida, while high, has been modest by comparison with the rest of the state. Franklin County citizens have taken steps to limit development along the Appalachicola River in order to preserve the fishing industry that is central to the area's economy.

**Central Florida.** As the Florida Turnpike angles through the central part of the state toward the Atlantic, orange groves flank the road for mile after mile. In its early days, most Florida citrus was grown in the northern part of the state, around St. Augustine. But ruinous freezes in 1894 and 1895 drove growers south, and today Central Florida is the heart of a citrus industry producing annually upwards of 200 million boxes of oranges and grapefruit, more than two-thirds the national supply.

As the industry expanded during this century, the city of Orlando developed into a commercial and financial hub of citrus country. Starting about 1960, the Orlando economy was supplemented with aerospace and electronics firms serving the Cape Canaveral NASA facilities east of the city. Most recently, Walt Disney World, located west of Orlando, touched off a surge of tourist-related economic activity.

Central Florida has always been conservative. Some smaller, inland counties like Sumter, Hardee and Okeechobee still vote in concert with the rural, traditionally Democratic parts of northern Florida. But prosperity has brought most of the area into the Republican camp, especially Orange County (Orlando), which has nearly 475,000 residents and is now Florida's 7th-largest county. Orange gave Reagan 61 percent of its vote in 1980, a higher percentage than any other of Florida's metropolitan counties.

**St. Petersburg and Tampa.** These cities are separated only by Tampa Bay, but their political preferences could hardly be further apart. St. Petersburg, a retirement mecca and winter resort, spawned the Florida Republican Party. Democratic-voting Tampa is Florida's closest approximation to the blue-collar, industrial cities of the North.

People from Georgia, Alabama, South Carolina and other Southern states moved to Tampa to find factory jobs, joining a Cuban community that had worked in the city's cigar factories for many years. Those blue-collar workers have helped influence Tampa and surrounding Hillsborough County to vote Democratic in most elections. Kennedy won it in 1960 and Carter in 1976, and Humphrey would likely have won it in 1968 but for George Wallace's 33 percent, two points less than Nixon.

The city of Tampa lost population during the 1970s, while population in some of its suburbs expanded more than 120 percent. Relying on decisive margins in the outlying areas, Reagan took Hillsborough County in 1980.

Thanks to the influence of its conservative retirement community, St. Petersburg in 1954 elected Florida's first 20th century Republican congressman. Since then, the city and surrounding Pinellas County have rarely parted from the GOP fold. (One departure came in 1964, when Pinellas saw Barry Goldwater as a threat to Social Security and voted against him.)

**The Sun Coast.** Not too many years ago, much of the southwest coast of Florida was as undeveloped as the northern coastal region. Today, however, the Sun Coast ranks near the top on the list of Florida's fastest-growing areas. The six counties between St. Petersburg and the southern tip of the Florida peninsula grew by an average of 79 percent in the last decade.

Retirees are largely responsible for the influx. People from all over the country have come to the Sun Coast, but the largest number are natives of the Midwest. For them, southwestern Florida has seemed friendlier territory than the East Coast, where there is a large concentration of Hispanics and ethnics from the Northeast. Sun Coast cities like Bradenton, Sarasota, Fort Myers and Naples profited from their image as less crowded and less expensive than East Coast cities like Ft. Lauderdale and Palm Beach.

The political impact of the retirees has been a padding of Republican margins. For example, in Sarasota County and Lee County (Ft. Myers),

Nixon in 1960 and Reagan in 1980 won about two-thirds of the presidential vote. In those 20 years, the number of presidential ballots cast in Sarasota County jumped 71 percent, and in Lee County the vote increased nearly six-fold.

**The Gold Coast.** Condominiums, mansions, motels and private homes line the Gold Coast, which runs from North Palm Beach down through Boca Raton and Ft. Lauderdale to Hollywood. The bulk of population and commerce is concentrated along a narrow strip of land that reaches inland just a few miles.

During the past decade, population in both Palm Beach and Broward counties on the Gold Coast grew 64 percent. Many of the new residents have roots in the urban Northeast, where they were steadfast and active Democrats. Transplanted to Florida, these people continued their political involvement and made the "condo vote" an important political force. The task of Republican candidates has been to convince these lifelong Democrats that they are more conservative than they are Democratic.

To a significant degree, Republicans have succeeded. Broward County was one of the first places in Florida where Republicans organized. Broward and Palm Beach counties have given consistent support to GOP presidential candidates in the last two decades. In the seriously contested presidential elections of 1960, 1968, 1976 and 1980, both counties voted for Republicans all but once. (Broward narrowly chose Carter over Ford in 1976.)

**Miami (Dade County).** An isolated outpost in the early 1900s, Miami and metropolitan Dade County today teem with 1.6 million people. Beachfront overcrowding has impugned the city's reputation as a vacation resort, and Miami is wrestling with problems of illegal drug trafficking, drug-related violent crimes and racial tension.

The Cuban, Jewish and black communities are important actors in Dade County politics. The first wave of Cuban immigrants arrived after the Castro revolution in 1959. Many in this group were white-collar professionals in their homeland and quickly prospered in America. With middle-class values and fierce contempt for communism, they preferred the Republican philosophy and have voted with the GOP. The latest wave of refugee arrivals were generally not so well-off in Cuba. In the U.S., they compete with blacks for unskilled jobs in a swollen labor pool.

The large Jewish community that gave Miami Beach its New York flavor usually prefers candidates who are moderately liberal on social issues, conservative on defense and strongly supportive of Israel.

For years, blacks have joined with Jews and native-born Democrats to put Dade in the Democratic column regularly. The county went easily to the Democrats in the presidential elections of 1960, 1968 and 1976. But in 1980, Reagan narrowly won the Dade presidential vote.

# Redrawing the Lines

Parceling out four new congressional districts would seem an enviable opportunity, but the big redistricting task strains already-tense relations in the Florida Legislature. Democrats have a majority in both houses, but actual influence is closely divided among mainstream Democrats, Republicans and conservative Democrats, especially in the state Senate.

Only northeast Florida's 3rd District and the Miami-area 14th District have populations below the new ideal district size of 512,631. Ten other districts grew from 20 to 60 percent during the 1970s, and three districts — the 5th, 10th and 11th — nearly doubled in population.

Much of the north-central 5th District is friendly territory for Republicans, and the same is true of the 10th District, which takes in prosperous oceanside communities on both the East Coast and the Gulf Coast. A new district created of condominium-dwellers in north Dade and south Broward counties could favor the Democrats. Another current district with more than 200,000 too many people is the 4th, which is now represented by Democrat Bill Chappell Jr.

In its 1981 session, the Florida Legislature squabbled over state legislative reapportionment and other matters and put off congressional redistricting until later.

## Governor
## Robert Graham (D)

**Born:** Nov. 9, 1936, Miami, Fla.
**Home:** Miami Lakes, Fla.
**Education:** U. of Florida, B.A. 1959; Harvard Law School, LL.D. 1962.
**Profession:** Developer.
**Family:** Wife, Adele; four children.
**Religion:** Protestant.
**Political Career:** Florida House, 1967-71; Florida Senate, 1971-78; elected governor 1978; term expires Jan. 1983.

# Lawton Chiles (D)

Of Lakeland — Elected 1970

**Born:** April 3, 1930, Lakeland, Fla.
**Education:** U. of Fla., B.S. 1952, LL.B. 1955.
**Military Career:** Army, 1952-54.
**Profession:** Lawyer.
**Family:** Wife, Rhea Grafton; four children.
**Religion:** Presbyterian.
**Political Career:** Fla. House, 1959-67; Fla. Senate, 1967-71.

**In Washington:** The open government theme that dominated Chiles' first Senate campaign remains the focus of his legislative career, even though "government in the sunshine" has probably passed its peak as a political issue.

Chiles was the chief sponsor of a 1976 federal "sunshine" law requiring regulatory commissions and other government agencies to hold their meetings in public, and the driving force behind similar rules reforms affecting Senate committees.

Neither the law nor the rules change has totally succeeded; in 1978, Chiles said his sunshine crusade "looks like a lifelong job" after he discovered that only about half of all government agency meetings required by law to be open were actually being conducted in public.

Nonetheless, he has continued to press for openness in the conduct of official business, in the campaign and personal finances of federal officeholders, and in lobbying. He helped write disclosure requirements for the first two, and has been the chief sponsor in recent years of lobby disclosure legislation, although none has been enacted by Congress.

All this has made him one of the more active members of the Governmental Affairs Committee, whose Subcommittee on Federal Spending he chaired through 1980. In that capacity, he pursued abuses ranging from mismanagement to outright theft in a variety of federal programs and agencies, including the military, anti-poverty programs, the Small Business Administration and the General Services Administration (GSA).

The GSA, responsible for government space and equipment purchases, was a special target of oversight scrutiny during Chiles' tenure as subcommittee chairman, which included the 1978-79 period of major contracting fraud scandals at the agency.

Chiles was instrumental in the creation of the Office of Federal Procurement Policy, an agency designed to help control government procurement practices, and in the passage of a law to reform the way the government settles disputes with private contractors. He was the key sponsor of the 1980 Federal Paperwork Reduction Act, and of "sunset" legislation, yet to be passed, which would set a time limit on the life spans of federal agencies.

Chiles was in a particularly strong position to affect government spending practices during the past two Congresses because he was chairman not only of the Governmental Affairs subcommittee but also of the Appropriations Subcommittee on the Treasury, Postal Service and General Government.

He is also second-ranking Democrat on the Budget Committee, where he is conservative on most fiscal matters that do not involve the elderly — a normal exception for a Florida Democrat. He has been one of the most vigorous Democratic critics of federal jobs programs, especially the Comprehensive Employment and Training Act (CETA), which he has repeatedly sought to reduce in magnitude and cost. In the 96th Congress, he generally followed the lead of Budget Chairman Ernest F. Hollings (D S.C.) in voting to tip the balance of federal spending toward defense.

In the 97th Congress, he also joined Hollings in approving more of the Reagan budget cuts than most other Senate Democrats were willing to accept. He did make an effort on the floor in March to restore $300 million Reagan wanted to cut from veterans' programs, but failed on a 56-44 vote.

**At Home:** Chiles was the first politician in recent years to employ a campaign gimmick that since has become commonplace — the walking tour.

As a state legislator from rural Polk County, Chiles began his 1970 Senate campaign with little money and a narrow political base. So he put on baggy khaki pants and hiking boots and set off on a 1,003-mile, 92-day trek from the Panhandle town of Century to Key Largo at the southern tip of the state. Chiles talked with an estimated 40,000 people and filled nine notebooks with the concerns they voiced.

Long-distance walking was as fresh then as it is stale now. Voters who had previously never heard of Chiles saw him as a youthful, energetic newcomer, and responded favorably to his pleas for open government. In the Democratic primary, he finished second to former Gov. Farris Bryant (1961-65), who began with statewide name recognition, strong ties to the business community and significant support from the organization of retiring Sen. Spessard Holland. In the runoff, Chiles handily defeated Bryant.

Chiles' GOP opponent, U.S. Rep. William Cramer, was the senior Florida Republican in Congress but an enemy of Gov. Claude Kirk, who tried to dump him in a primary in favor of G. Harrold Carswell, recently turned down for the U.S. Supreme Court. Cramer tried to portray Chiles as a liberal, but the Democrat left little record to shoot at and avoided controversy during the campaign. Conservative Democrats were not frightened.

"Walkin' Lawton" has retained his casual manner and populist image in his home state relations over the past decade, and has remained popular. His 1976 re-election bid was made easy by his controversial GOP opponent, physician John Grady, who served on the national board of the John Birch Society and had been the American Party candidate for the Senate just two years before. Grady won 37 percent of the vote against Chiles.

## Committees

**Appropriations** (7th of 14 Democrats)
  Agriculture and Related Agencies; Defense; Labor-Health and Human Services-Education; Transportation

**Budget** (2nd of 10 Democrats)

**Governmental Affairs** (3rd of 8 Democrats)
  Federal Expenditures, Research, and Rules; Permanent Subcommittee on Investigations.

**Special Aging** (Ranking Democrat)

## Elections

**1976 General**

| | |
|---|---|
| Lawton Chiles (D ) | 1,799,518 (63 %) |
| John Grady (R ) | 1,057,886 (37 %) |

**Previous Winning Percentage**

1970 (54 %)

## Campaign Finance

| | Receipts | Receipts from PACs | Expenditures |
|---|---|---|---|
| **1976** | | | |
| Chiles (D ) | $362,477 | — (0 %) | $362,235 |
| Grady (R ) | $408,616 | $31,700 (8 %) | $394,574 |

## Voting Studies

| | Presidential Support | | Party Unity | | Conservative Coalition | |
|---|---|---|---|---|---|---|
| Year | S | O | S | O | S | O |
| 1980 | 75 | 23 | 65 | 31 | 68 | 24 |
| 1979 | 74 | 17 | 76 | 15 | 51 | 37 |
| 1978 | 66 | 30 | 63 | 34 | 61 | 37 |
| 1977 | 67 | 25 | 43 | 54 | 80 | 17 |
| 1976 | 45 | 34 | 54 | 38 | 59 | 33 |
| 1975 | 65 | 26 | 50 | 44 | 75 | 20 |
| 1974 (Ford) | 46 | 50 | | | | |
| 1974 | 46 | 46 | 55 | 37 | 55 | 37 |
| 1973 | 39 | 52 | 71 | 18 | 33 | 53 |
| 1972 | 61 | 33 | 53 | 34 | 47 | 39 |
| 1971 | 45 | 44 | 53 | 26 | 52 | 34 |

S = Support      O = Opposition

## Key Votes

**96th Congress**

| | |
|---|---|
| Maintain relations with Taiwan (1979) | N |
| Reduce synthetic fuel development funds (1979) | N |
| Impose nuclear plant moratorium (1979) | N |
| Kill stronger windfall profits tax (1979) | N |
| Guarantee Chrysler Corp. loans (1979) | Y |
| Approve military draft registration (1980) | Y |
| End Revenue Sharing to the states (1980) | Y |
| Block Justice Dept. busing suits (1980) | Y |

**97th Congress**

| | |
|---|---|
| Restore urban program funding cuts (1981) | N |

## Interest Group Ratings

| Year | ADA | ACA | AFL-CIO | CCUS-1 | CCUS-2 |
|---|---|---|---|---|---|
| 1980 | 50 | 38 | 53 | 50 | |
| 1979 | 42 | 26 | 47 | 45 | 47 |
| 1978 | 35 | 36 | 32 | 72 | |
| 1977 | 35 | 50 | 32 | 61 | |
| 1976 | 45 | 48 | 84 | 25 | |
| 1975 | 39 | 44 | 29 | 50 | |
| 1974 | 43 | 44 | 30 | 44 | |
| 1973 | 60 | 38 | 73 | 33 | |
| 1972 | 35 | 45 | 11 | 43 | |
| 1971 | 56 | 37 | 50 | - | |

# Paula Hawkins (R)

**Of Winter Park — Elected 1980**

**Born:** Jan. 24, 1927, Salt Lake City, Utah.
**Education:** Attended Utah State University, no degree.
**Profession:** Businesswoman; public official.
**Family:** Husband, Walter Hawkins; three children.
**Religion:** Mormon.
**Political Career:** Florida Public Service Commission, 1973-79, chairman, 1977-79; unsuccessful Republican nominee for Florida House, 1970; unsuccessfully sought Republican nomination for U.S. Senate, 1974; unsuccessful Republican nominee for lieutenant governor, 1978.

**The Member:** To her admirers, Paula Hawkins is an independent-minded iconoclast who tries, as she says, "to make government relate to the man on the street." To her critics, she is a sharp-tongued publicity hound. Both sides agree that Hawkins is a skillful politician who knows how to draw the spotlight.

During two terms on the Florida Public Service Commission, Hawkins gained a statewide reputation as a consumer watchdog by consistently opposing rate increases by telephone and utility companies. In 1980, she took advantage of that favorable exposure to win a Senate seat.

In Washington, Hawkins' unique style continues to win publicity. During confirmation hearings for Agriculture Secretary John R. Block, Hawkins advised him to watch over the work habits of his department's employees. She said she had taken a walk through the Agriculture buildings and seen people loitering in the halls and cafeteria.

Hawkins staged a luncheon to announce her proposal for mandatory imprisonment of food-stamp cheaters; guests were served a hearty fare of sirloin steak, asparagus and fresh strawberries. Her proposal did not make it through the Agriculture Committee.

After assuming the chair of the Investigations and Oversight Subcommittee at Labor and Human Resources, Hawkins announced she would find out why the National Cancer Institute had not discovered a cure for cancer with the approximately $8 billion Congress has given it since 1971. Hearings on the issue, however, produced little new information.

Hawkins' narrow 1980 victory over Democrat Bill Gunter makes her the second Republican senator from Florida since Reconstruction. She

capitalized on Reagan coattails, large contributions from the Republican Party and divided Democratic opposition. Gunter had ousted incumbent Sen. Richard Stone in a bitterly contested Democratic runoff and was unable to win the support of many of Stone's backers.

Although she is the first woman ever elected to the Senate without the help of a political relative, Hawkins is not a standard feminist. A Utah-born Mormon who likes to call herself a housewife, she opposes the Equal Rights Amendment and federal funding for abortions.

## Committees

**Agriculture, Nutrition, and Forestry** (8th of 9 Republicans)
Agricultural Credit and Rural Electrification, chairman; Agricultural Production, Marketing and Stabilization of Prices; Foreign Agricultural Policy; Nutrition.

**Labor and Human Resources** (4th of 9 Republicans)
Investigations and General Oversight, chairman; Employment and Productivity; Labor.

**Joint Economic**
Agriculture and Transportation; Economic Goals and Intergovernmental Policy.

## Elections

**1980 General**

| | |
|---|---|
| Paula Hawkins (R) | 1,822,460 (52%) |
| Bill Gunter (D) | 1,705,409 (48%) |

**1980 Primary**

| | |
|---|---|
| Paula Hawkins (R) | 209,856 (48%) |
| Louis Frey (R) | 119,834 (27%) |
| Ander Crenshaw (R) | 54,767 (13%) |
| Ellis Rubin (R) | 19,990 (5%) |

## Campaign Finance

| | Receipts | Receipts from PACs | Expenditures |
|---|---|---|---|
| **1980** | | | |
| Hawkins (R) | $704,830 | $211,520 (30%) | $660,969 |
| Gunter (D) | $2,021,468 | $172,534 (9%) | $2,019,299 |

## Key Votes

**97th Congress**
Restore urban program funding cuts (1981)                    N

# 1 Earl Hutto (D)

### Of Panama City — Elected 1978

**Born:** May 12, 1926, Midland City, Ala.
**Education:** Troy State U., Ala., B.S. 1949.
**Military Career:** Navy, 1944-46.
**Profession:** Advertising and broadcasting
executive.
**Family:** Wife, Nancy Myers; two children.
**Religion:** Baptist.
**Political Career:** Fla. House, 1973-79.

**In Washington:** Hutto will never be able to bring his district as much new military hardware as his predecessor, longtime Military Construction Chairman Robert L. F. Sikes, if only because he would have a hard time finding a place to put it. But he did prove in his first term that he has some of Sikes's skill at helping the Pentagon help Florida.

Early in the 96th Congress, it seemed likely that the Defense Department would close the helicopter training school at Pensacola, in the 1st District, and merge it with one in Alabama. Hutto, who did not have burdensome committee assignments in his first year, devoted much of his time to making the case for keeping the program at Pensacola. Personally popular among his fellow freshmen, he was able to bring most of them around to his side in a dispute peripheral to their interests. Even Democrats who preferred less defense spending were willing to agree that if the Navy was going to train helicopter pilots, it might as well do it in Florida.

By the time the fiscal 1980 Military Construction Appropriations bill came to a vote in committee, Hutto had won his fight. The committee bill made no mention of the transfer. When Alabama Republican William L. Dickinson tried to add it on the House floor, he was beaten on a 244-131 vote.

Hutto had wanted a place on Armed Services when he came to the House in 1979, but did not get one, and was temporarily sidetracked to Public Works and Merchant Marine. On Merchant Marine, he spoke for the sport fishermen who operate off the Florida Gulf Coast and bring money into the district.

By mid-1980, he had his place on Armed Services, and quickly showed a streak of independence. Shortly after President Carter had vetoed a bill increasing pay for military doctors because it was too expensive, the Armed Services Committee reported a bill considered likely to provoke a second veto.

The second bill contained a new provision containing extra pay for military dentists. Hutto, casting his first vote as a member of the committee, refused to go along, insisting there was no shortage of military dentists.

**At Home:** Before his election to the state Legislature in 1972, Hutto was a television sportscaster in both Panama City and Pensacola, at opposite ends of the 1st District. So when he began his 1978 congressional campaign, aiming to succeed the retiring Sikes, his face was already familiar to much of the constituency.

That was an enormous help to him in the Democratic primary against Curtis Golden, prosecuting attorney in Escambia County (Pensacola), which casts about 40 percent of the district vote. Rated no higher than third out of four candidates before the voting, Hutto finished a comfortable first in the initial primary, then dispatched Golden easily in the runoff.

With Sikes out of the picture, Republicans were optimistic that their candidate, former Pensacola Mayor Warren Briggs, could take the district in the fall. But Hutto gave Briggs no opening on the right. The two men matched vows to protect the district's military facilities, and Hutto stressed strict law enforcement and economy in government.

Hutto's involvement in Baptist church affairs was of special help in the district's rural areas,

---

**1st District: Northwest — Pensacola, Panama City.** Population: 555,343 (23% increase since 1970). Race: White 465,517 (84%), Black 76,350 (14%), Others 13,476 (2%). Spanish origin: 9,286 (2%).

---

where Briggs's close identification with Pensacola business interests was not an advantage. Hutto won 63.3 percent.

Briggs protested afterward that he was hampered by a late start in 1978. So he decided on a second campaign in 1980, and began it nearly two years in advance. But Hutto was untouchable. Even though Reagan won the district's presidential vote, Briggs improved his showing only 2 percentage points, to 39 percent.

**The District:** Most of Florida's westernmost district is Deep South rural country, heavily dependent on several large military installations. Two major urban concentrations cast well over half the district's vote in 1980. At the western end, about 275,000 people live in Pensacola and its metropolitan area. Another 90,000 live in Panama City and surrounding Bay County in the eastern part of the district.

The district consistently prefers the most conservative-talking presidential choice — Goldwater in 1964, Wallace in 1968, Nixon in 1972, Ford in 1976 and Reagan in 1980.

But Democrats still compete successfully, as they do in similar areas of Alabama and Georgia. Democrat Bill Gunter carried the district in his unsuccessful 1980 Senate campaign, winning Escambia and five of the seven other counties in the district.

## Committees

**Armed Services** (18th of 25 Democrats)
Military Installations and Facilities; Research and Development; Seapower and Strategic and Critical Materials.

**Merchant Marine and Fisheries** (14th of 20 Democrats)
Coast Guard and Navigation; Fisheries and Wildlife Conservation and the Environment.

## Elections

**1980 General**

| | |
|---|---|
| Earl Hutto (D ) | 119,829 (61 %) |
| Warren Briggs (R ) | 75,939 (39 %) |

**1978 General**

| | |
|---|---|
| Earl Hutto (D ) | 85,608 (63 %) |
| Warren Briggs (R ) | 49,715 (37 %) |

**1978 Primary Runoff**

| | |
|---|---|
| Earl Hutto (D) | 58,352 (62%) |
| Curtis Golden (D) | 35,721 (38%) |

**1978 Primary**

| | |
|---|---|
| Earl Hutto (D ) | 39,982 (42 %) |
| Curtis Golden (D ) | 29,692 (31 %) |
| Jerry Melvin (D ) | 21,186 (22 %) |

**District Vote For President**

| | 1980 | | 1976 | | 1972 |
|---|---|---|---|---|---|
| D | 75,955 (36 %) | D | 89,170 (49 %) | D | 24,864 (16 %) |
| R | 127,118 (60 %) | R | 91,674 (50 %) | R | 127,762 (83 %) |

## Campaign Finance

| | Receipts | Receipts from PACs | Expenditures |
|---|---|---|---|
| **1980** | | | |
| Hutto (D ) | $86,190 | $8,400 (10 %) | $63,451 |
| Briggs (R ) | $216,094 | $13,177 (6 %) | $227,563 |

**1978**

| | | | |
|---|---|---|---|
| Hutto (D ) | $119,866 | $12,550 (10 %) | $118,847 |
| Briggs (R ) | $192,916 | $20,634 (11 %) | $186,711 |

## Voting Studies

| | Presidential Support | | Party Unity | | Conservative Coalition | |
|---|---|---|---|---|---|---|
| Year | S | O | S | O | S | O |
| 1980 | 56 | 39 | 57 | 39 | 85 | 15 |
| 1979 | 48 | 39 | 53 | 40 | 81 | 15 |

S = Support          O = Opposition

## Key Votes

**96th Congress**

| | |
|---|---|
| Weaken Carter oil profits tax (1979) | Y |
| Reject hospital cost control plan (1979) | N |
| Implement Panama Canal Treaties (1979) | N |
| Establish Department of Education (1979) | Y |
| Approve Anti-busing Amendment (1979) | Y |
| Guarantee Chrysler Corp. loans (1979) | Y |
| Approve military draft registration (1980) | Y |
| Aid Sandinista regime in Nicaragua (1980) | Y |
| Strengthen fair housing laws (1980) | N |

**97th Congress**

| | |
|---|---|
| Reagan budget proposal (1981) | Y |

## Interest Group Ratings

| Year | ADA | ACA | AFL-CIO | CCUS |
|---|---|---|---|---|
| 1980 | 22 | 48 | 50 | 81 |
| 1979 | 21 | 36 | 35 | 56 |

# 2 Don Fuqua (D)

### Of Altha — Elected in 1962

**Born:** Aug. 20, 1933, Jacksonville, Fla.
**Education:** U. of Fla., B.S. 1957.
**Military Career:** Army, 1953-55.
**Profession:** Farmer.
**Family:** Wife, Nancy Ayers; two children.
**Religion:** Presbyterian.
**Political Career:** Fla. House, 1959-63.

**In Washington:** Fuqua heads a committee born to promote the space program, and much of his time is given to preserving that program — a task that, until the 1981 space shuttle, at least, had been growing more and more difficult.

The Science and Technology Committee has jurisdiction over the NASA budget, and it has been Fuqua's task to defend it from attack. He has done that in a quiet, unemotional and cautious manner. Because he is conservative about asking for space money, he has managed to avoid drastic funding cutbacks on the House floor. But some of the program's strongest supporters feel he does not ask for enough.

Fuqua rarely talks about space exploration as the next human adventure or a quest into the mysteries of the universe. His interest in the space shuttle is in the benefits it can bring to businesses on Earth. His major personal effort in his committee is a bill to provide financial assistance to private companies undertaking high risk ventures in orbit. The bill would provide $50 million annually for two years. He also supported a bill to provide $25 million in research for solar satellites in space.

In the years since space passed its legislative peak, the Science Committee has broadened into a source of other research money with a clientele among the aerospace, energy and high technology companies competing for government support. Millions of dollars are at stake; most of the projects find a sympathetic ear on the committee.

One project that the committee has argued endlessly over in recent years is the Clinch River nuclear breeder reactor in Tennessee.

President Carter wanted to kill the project because he considered the technology obsolete, and because he feared the plutonium it generated would lead to a spread of nuclear weapons.

When Fuqua became chairman of the committee in 1979, he tried to help the administration's cause. Although he did not accept Carter's anti-proliferation arguments, he did agree that the technology of Clinch River was obsolete. Fuqua combined with Democrat George Brown of California to offer a compromise allowing Carter to terminate Clinch River, but requiring another project, with updated technology.

"The Clinch River project is dead," Fuqua insisted. "We are wasting our time if we think we can keep resurrecting this project every year." Through 1980, Congress kept up a steady flow of funding. In 1981, however, with 13 new members voting, the committee cast a surprising vote in May against Clinch River. Fuqua sided with the project at that session, but reiterated his skepticism about the ultimate future of the project.

The committee's expansion into energy research in recent years has brought it into occasional conflict with other energy-related committees, especially Energy and Commerce. In 1975, Science and Technology brought out a synthetic fuels bill and saw it killed on the House floor, largely because it trampled the turf of both the Commerce and Banking committees. Fuqua has generally opposed attempts to concentrate energy jurisdiction in one committee — largely because Science would not be that committee and would lose the research side of the issue it now controls.

Fuqua does not always have a great deal of time for his other assignment, Government Operations, but he made his presence felt there in past years in support of inspectors general to monitor

---

**2nd District: North — Tallahassee, Gainesville.** Population: 612,964 (35% increase since 1970). Race: White 454,730 (74%), Black 150,749 (25%), Others 7,485 (1%). Spanish origin: 10,888 (1%).

bureaucratic waste, against a strong consumer protection agency, and against creation of a Consumer Product Safety Commission. He did favor giving strong powers to the new Department of Energy created in 1977.

Outside his committees, Fuqua has always been a conservative Democrat, but he has voted increasingly with the party's leadership in recent years. Early in his career, he opposed the 1964 Civil Rights Act and the 1965 Voting Rights Act. He voted for the Equal Rights Amendment, but with two universities in his district, voted to exempt undergraduate admissions from the amendment. In 1979, he voted against extending the deadline for passage of the amendment.

**At Home:** Fuqua has met only four Republican opponents in 18 years; the most successful one held him to 70.6 percent of the vote. He faced serious primary challenges in 1966 and 1976, but his general election campaigns have always been cakewalks.

Fuqua is a native of Altha, a small town near the district's western border. He was working on his family's 600-acre dairy farm when he campaigned in 1958 for the Florida House of Representatives. At 25, he became the youngest member of the House.

In 1962, Fuqua and five other Democrats ran for the central Panhandle congressional seat created after the 1960 census. All the contenders were conservative, but Fuqua was seen as more moderate because he said he wanted to support President Kennedy "when I can."

Fuqua finished first in the initial primary, ahead of attorney Hal Davis, his former college roommate. The two met in a runoff, and Davis accused Fuqua of being a liberal advocate of Kennedy's New Frontier programs. Fuqua held conservatives' support by pointing to his voting record in favor of states' rights and segregation in the Legislature. Fuqua won 58 percent of the runoff vote and defeated his GOP opponent in the general election by a 3-to-1 margin.

Fuqua's first serious re-election challenge came in his second term, after the state Legislature in 1965 rearranged congressional districts to balance their populations. Fuqua was thrown into the same district with Democratic Rep. D. R. "Billy" Matthews, a six-term veteran.

Matthews spoke in favor of Medicare, while Fuqua criticized it and other aspects of President Johnson's anti-poverty campaign. Against the more moderate Matthews, Fuqua found much of his support among white, middle-aged, middle-class voters in the business and professional sectors. He was weaker among blacks, students and blue-collar workers. Fuqua defeated Matthews in the primary with 53.8 percent of the vote.

Fuqua coasted through the next four elections, although some blacks, liberals and students grumbled that he was too conservative. The dissatisfaction centered in the district's two largest cities, Tallahassee and Gainesville, which both have sizable university communities.

Fuqua's last serious threat came in 1976, from former Tallahassee Mayor Russell R. Blevis. Not until absentee ballots were counted was it clear that Fuqua had won a bare majority in the Democratic primary and thus escaped a runoff with Blevis. Blevis' near-miss was expected to encourage other Democrats to oppose Fuqua, but no significant challengers came forward in 1978 or 1980.

**The District:** Together, Leon County (Tallahassee) and Alachua County (Gainesville) cast more votes in the 2nd District than the other 21 counties combined. Tallahassee is the state capital and home to more than 27,000 students at Florida State and Florida A & M. Close behind in population is Gainesville, site of the University of Florida (31,000 students).

State government and the universities generate white-collar employment in the metropolitan areas, but most of the district is rural, with an economy based on agriculture and a political outlook similar to nearby south Georgia and Alabama.

The 2nd District's longstanding Democratic tradition shows no signs of abating. In his unsuccessful 1980 Senate bid, Democrat Bill Gunter won the 2nd with ease, taking eight rural counties by margins exceeding 2-to-1. The district also chose Carter over Reagan in the presidential race.

The district's population grew by more than 30 percent since 1970, less than Florida's overall 41.1 percent growth rate, but enough to provoke discussion that Gainesville will be the center of a new North Florida district to be created before the 1982 election.

## Committees

**Government Operations** (5th of 23 Democrats)
    Legislation and National Security.

**Science and Technology** (Chairman)
    Energy Development and Applications, chairman.

## Elections

**1980 General**

| | |
|---|---|
| Don Fuqua (D ) | 138,252 (71 %) |
| John La Capra (R ) | 57,588 (29 %) |

**1978 General**

| | |
|---|---|
| Don Fuqua (D ) | 112,649 (82 %) |
| Peter Brathwaite (R ) | 25,148 (18 %) |

**Previous Winning Percentages**

| | | | |
|---|---|---|---|
| 1976 (100%) | 1974 (100%) | 1972 (100%) | 1970 (100%) |
| 1968 (100%) | 1966 (76 %) | 1964 (99 %) | 1962 (75 %) |

**District Vote For President**

| | 1980 | | 1976 | | 1972 |
|---|---|---|---|---|---|
| D | 116,268 (51 %) | D | 120,425 (61 %) | D | 50,857 (31 %) |
| R | 102,716 (45 %) | R | 71,806 (37 %) | R | 110,887 (68 %) |
| I | 9,107 (4 %) | | | | |

## Campaign Finance

| | Receipts | Receipts from PACs | Expenditures |
|---|---|---|---|
| **1980** | | | |
| Fuqua (D ) | $119,776 | $68,310 (57 %) | $131,165 |
| La Capra (R ) | $47,786 | $400 (1 %) | $47,786 |
| **1978** | | | |
| Fuqua (D ) | $101,759 | $51,150 (50 %) | $88,381 |
| Brathwaite (R ) | $20,081 | $1,120 (6 %) | $19,379 |

## Voting Studies

| | Presidential Support | | Party Unity | | Conservative Coalition | |
|---|---|---|---|---|---|---|
| Year | S | O | S | O | S | O |
| 1980 | 62 | 30 | 64 | 29 | 72 | 22 |
| 1979 | 52 | 36 | 61 | 29 | 72 | 17 |
| 1978 | 41 | 42 | 49 | 41 | 70 | 20 |
| 1977 | 51 | 34 | 46 | 43 | 73 | 16 |
| 1976 | 47 | 45 | 42 | 43 | 67 | 17 |
| 1975 | 44 | 51 | 51 | 38 | 68 | 22 |
| 1974 (Ford) | 44 | 54 | | | | |
| 1974 | 66 | 28 | 49 | 43 | 72 | 17 |
| 1973 | 41 | 39 | 43 | 42 | 67 | 15 |
| 1972 | 54 | 35 | 33 | 52 | 73 | 10 |
| 1971 | 61 | 26 | 45 | 43 | 73 | 18 |
| 1970 | 55 | 35 | 42 | 54 | 91 | 7 |
| 1969 | 47 | 45 | 35 | 49 | 80 | 4 |
| 1968 | 61 | 31 | 40 | 50 | 80 | 12 |
| 1967 | 50 | 35 | 43 | 44 | 78 | 7 |
| 1966 | 36 | 29 | 23 | 36 | 57 | 3 |
| 1965 | 47 | 40 | 33 | 51 | 84 | 4 |
| 1964 | 62 | 35 | 52 | 37 | 92 | 8 |
| 1963 | 58 | 25 | 53 | 22 | 67 | 7 |

S = Support     O = Opposition

## Key Votes

**96th Congress**

| | |
|---|---|
| Weaken Carter oil profits tax (1979) | Y |
| Reject hospital cost control plan (1979) | Y |
| Implement Panama Canal Treaties (1979) | N |
| Establish Department of Education (1979) | Y |
| Approve Anti-busing Amendment (1979) | Y |
| Guarantee Chrysler Corp. loans (1979) | Y |
| Approve military draft registration (1980) | Y |
| Aid Sandinista regime in Nicaragua (1980) | Y |
| Strengthen fair housing laws (1980) | N |

**97th Congress**

| | |
|---|---|
| Reagan budget proposal (1981) | Y |

## Interest Group Ratings

| Year | ADA | ACA | AFL-CIO | CCUS |
|---|---|---|---|---|
| 1980 | 33 | 29 | 44 | 73 |
| 1979 | 32 | 18 | 39 | 40 |
| 1978 | 20 | 58 | 30 | 56 |
| 1977 | 10 | 50 | 48 | 71 |
| 1976 | 20 | 58 | 41 | 57 |
| 1975 | 37 | 56 | 38 | 31 |
| 1974 | 17 | 64 | 30 | 50 |
| 1973 | 20 | 60 | 40 | 80 |
| 1972 | 13 | 68 | 22 | 88 |
| 1971 | 19 | 58 | 56 | - |
| 1970 | 16 | 63 | 29 | 70 |
| 1969 | 7 | 77 | 22 | - |
| 1968 | 17 | 57 | 25 | - |
| 1967 | 0 | 68 | 0 | 80 |
| 1966 | 0 | 84 | 8 | - |
| 1965 | 0 | 65 | - | 70 |
| 1964 | 28 | 59 | 36 | - |
| 1963 | - | 40 | - | - |

# 3 Charles E. Bennett (D)

**Of Jacksonville — Elected 1948**

**Born:** Dec. 2, 1910, Canton, N.Y.
**Education:** U. of Fla., B.A., J.D. 1934.
**Military Career:** Army, 1942-47.
**Profession:** Lawyer.
**Family:** Wife, Jean Fay; three children.
**Religion:** Disciples of Christ.
**Political Career:** Fla. House, 1941.

**In Washington:** Bennett has spent more than 30 years in the House insisting that he does not consider himself better or purer than his colleagues, and finding them a little reluctant to believe him.

Bennett's sense of duty seems to set him apart from most other politicians, and most other people. He answered 3,808 consecutive House roll calls over a quarter century despite having to wear a leg brace that makes it difficult for him to walk. He has returned more than $200,000 worth of wartime disability checks. He began making financial disclosure statements in the 1950s, long before disclosure was a political issue.

But it is not Bennett's personal principles that have always raised questions about him in the House. It is the fear that he would like to apply them to others.

While Bennett is a senior member of the Armed Services Committee and a likely chairman in the future, he is not known to other members primarily for his expertise in sea power. He is known by his reputation as an ethical purist.

Bennett is the author of the current code of ethics for federal employees, one that, among other things, asks them to report to their superiors on the misdeeds of co-workers. He was the driving force behind creation of a House ethics committee in 1967, and then failed to win a place on it — because House leaders were afraid of what he might do there. It was not until 1979 that Bennett became ethics chairman, and presided as the committee recommended censure for two members and expulsion for two others.

Bennett takes great pains to say that he avoids moral judgments about his colleagues, and that he feels subject to the same temptations they are. To some, however, his mere preoccupation with moral issues makes him different.

No one can dispute the basic fact that Bennett is the model of propriety. "I don't drink, smoke or run around," he once said matter-of-factly. "I'm a pretty simple guy."

Bennett was so simple when he first came to Congress, in fact, that he returned some of his federal pay to the U.S. Treasury. He said he was a bachelor and did not need all the money. Interviewed about this, he told a reporter, "I don't talk about it very much . . . I'm afraid fellow congressmen will consider me such a goody-goody or pantywaist they won't speak to me."

So far as is known, no one has ever refused to speak to Bennett. Trusting him as an ethical watchdog has been another matter.

During his early years in the House, Bennett introduced dozens of resolutions calling for an ethics committee to police congressional behavior. In 1957, following scandals in the Eisenhower administration, Bennett drafted his ethics code for government workers. It remained in force through the 85th Congress, then lay dormant for 20 years — until Bennett introduced legislation requiring that it be posted in prominent places in all federal office buildings. That bill became law in 1980.

There was little movement toward an ethics committee until 1966, when controversy over the spending habits of New York Democratic Rep. Adam Clayton Powell Jr. led Speaker John W. McCormack to set up a select panel to study the issue. Bennett was placed in charge. To no one's surprise, the committee promptly recommended that a permanent ethics panel be established.

The next year, the House voted to create a

---

**3rd District: Northeast — Jacksonville.** Population: 469,156 (4% increase since 1970). Race: White 327,076 (70%), Black 134,641 (29%), Others 7,439 (1%). Spanish origin: 8,241 (2%).

permanent new Committee on Standards of Official Conduct. When Bennett was left off, he called it the "heaviest rebuke ever given in the Congress." Melvin Price of Illinois, a man much closer to the Democratic leadership, was placed in charge of the committee.

Another eight years passed before Bennett finally was named to the committee, not as chairman, but at the bottom of the list behind senior members known to be loyal to House leaders. In two more years, however, after some retirements and surprise election defeats, Bennett found himself installed as chairman.

At that point, House leaders amended the rules to set two-term limits for ethics committee members. By 1981, Bennett was off the committee again after having performed, as expected, in a strict manner that resulted in a series of reprimands, two censures and an expulsion.

The committee's performance cannot fairly be attributed to any personal attitude of Bennett's; his chairmanship coincided with rising public attention to congressional ethics, and a newly zealous attitude approach by federal prosecutors toward taking on public officials, symbolized by Abscam. In fact, many House Republicans accused Bennett of being too soft when he recommended censure — rather than expulsion — for Michigan Democrat Charles C. Diggs Jr., convicted on kickback charges in federal court.

But Bennett did prove by far the toughest ethics chairman in House history. When he left the committee in 1981, Speaker O'Neill replaced him as chairman with Louis Stokes, an Ohio Democrat who had opposed some of the committee's actions under Bennett as unfair to the accused.

Bennett's legislative work has focused primarily on the Armed Services Committee, where he ranks second behind 76-year-old Melvin Price, and could become chairman before he retires.

As head of the Armed Services Sea Power Subcommittee, he plays an important role in determining long-term naval policy. Bennett has supported a Navy built around large ships, especially nuclear power submarines and aircraft carriers of the sort advocated by Admiral Hyman G. Rickover. Bennett and Rickover have maintained a close relationship over the years.

Though he has continually complained that defense has been shortchanged in competition with domestic programs, Bennett is careful to point out that he is no militarist. He likes to talk of the work he did toward creation of an arms control agency in the 1950s. On his office wall is one of the pens President Kennedy used to create such an agency in 1961.

Bennett speaks in terms of national priorities rather than pork for his constituents, but in fact he has served his Florida district well on Armed Services. The Jacksonville harbor has been deepened, three Navy bases have been expanded, the Atlantic fleet has been berthed and federal money has been poured into a dozen hospital and health facilities. The list of federal projects for Bennett's district is several pages long.

**At Home:** If World War II had not intervened, Bennett might now be serving his 20th term in Congress, rather than just his 17th. He launched his first campaign in late 1941, hoping to build on his political base as a state representative from Jacksonville. But he abandoned the race in 1942 to enlist in the Marines as a private, ignoring the draft deferment granted to legislators.

When he returned home to practice law five years later, he was a war hero, leader of 1,000 guerrillas in the Philippines. But he was also crippled, a victim of polio he contracted during the jungle and mountain fighting.

He was no less determined to run for Congress. In 1948, he challenged Democratic Rep. Emory H. Price, who had been elected instead of him in 1942. Bennett ran on a platform of support for a military draft and opposition to the Truman civil rights program. He won the primary by less than 2,000 votes out of more than 75,000 cast, and took the general election with 91.1 percent.

Price challenged Bennett in the 1950 primary, but his comeback attempt fell short. That year and throughout the 1950's, Bennett had no general election opposition.

Republicans fired their best shot in 1964, when prominent Jacksonville businessman William T. Stockton Jr. opposed Bennett. Stockton drew 27 percent of the vote, higher than any GOP percentage before or since, but low enough to convince the party to forget the idea after that.

Bennett was mentioned twice as a possible Senate candidate. In 1956, there was talk he would oppose first-term Democrat George A. Smathers. When Smathers retired in 1968, Bennett was again considered as a successor. Neither rumor lasted long; his sphere has never been statewide.

**The District:** For many years, Bennett represented all of Duval County, which is now coextensive with Jacksonville's city limits. Redistricting in 1967, however, attached the southeast corner of Duval to another district. In 1972 redistricting, Nassau County, a rural area directly north of Duval, was added to Bennett's territory. It is still a traditional Southern Democratic district and Jimmy Carter carried it in by over 10,000 votes in 1980, but a GOP candidate would have good chance to win Bennett's congressional seat if he retired.

Jacksonville has long been a major Atlantic port and land transportation hub, and in recent years it has become a banking and insurance center. Military installations are important to the economy. There is a relatively even mixture of blue-collar and white-collar workers, and blacks account for more than one-fourth of the residents. The population of metropolitan Jacksonville is about 700,000, but since 1970, the 3rd has grown less than any area in Florida.

## Committees

**Armed Services** (2nd of 25 Democrats)
Seapower and Strategic and Critical Materials, chairman; Military Installations and Facilities; Military Personnel and Compensation.

## Elections

**1980 General**

| | |
|---|---|
| Charles Bennett (D ) | 104,672 (77 %) |
| Harry Radcliffe (R ) | 31,208 (23 %) |

**1978 General**

| | |
|---|---|
| Charles Bennett (D ) | Unopposed |

**Previous Winning Percentages**

| | | | |
|---|---|---|---|
| 1976 (100%) | 1974 (100%) | 1972 (82 %) | 1970 (100%) |
| 1968 (79 %) | 1966 (100%) | 1964 (73 %) | 1962 (100%) |
| 1960 (83 %) | 1958 (100%) | 1956 (100%) | 1954 (100%) |
| 1952 (100%) | 1950 (100%) | 1948 (91 %) | |

**District Vote For President**

| | 1980 | | 1976 | | 1972 |
|---|---|---|---|---|---|
| **D** | 75,575 (53 %) | **D** | 87,760 (64 %) | **D** | 39,980 (31 %) |
| **R** | 64,148 (45 %) | **R** | 48,756 (35 %) | **R** | 90,008 (69 %) |
| **I** | 2,900 (2 %) | | | | |

## Campaign Finance

| | Receipts | Receipts from PACs | Expenditures |
|---|---|---|---|
| **1980** | | | |
| Bennett (D ) | $33,262 | — (0 %) | $39,318 |

## Voting Studies

| | Presidential Support | | Party Unity | | Conservative Coalition | |
|---|---|---|---|---|---|---|
| Year | S | O | S | O | S | O |
| 1980 | 59 | 41 | 56 | 44 | 89 | 11 |
| 1979 | 57 | 43 | 47 | 53 | 79 | 21 |
| 1978 | 48 | 52 | 42 | 58 | 79 | 21 |
| 1977 | 59 | 41 | 37 | 63 | 71 | 29 |
| 1976 | 57 | 43 | 36 | 64 | 78 | 22 |
| 1975 | 47 | 53 | 50 | 50 | 58 | 42 |
| 1974 (Ford) | 37 | 63 | | | | |
| 1974 | 62 | 38 | 53 | 47 | 68 | 31 |
| 1973 | 43 | 57 | 47 | 53 | 62 | 38 |
| 1972 | 57 | 43 | 37 | 63 | 79 | 21 |
| 1971 | 53 | 47 | 55 | 45 | 61 | 39 |
| 1970 | 58 | 42 | 39 | 61 | 70 | 30 |
| 1969 | 51 | 49 | 40 | 60 | 82 | 18 |
| 1968 | 64 | 36 | 37 | 63 | 76 | 24 |
| 1967 | 57 | 43 | 38 | 62 | 87 | 13 |
| 1966 | 57 | 43 | 44 | 56 | 76 | 24 |
| 1965 | 55 | 45 | 39 | 60 | 90 | 10 |
| 1964 | 52 | 48 | 44 | 56 | 92 | 8 |
| 1963 | 73 | 27 | 67 | 33 | 73 | 27 |
| 1962 | 88 | 12 | 82 | 18 | 37 | 63 |
| 1961 | 83 | 17 | 78 | 22 | 39 | 61 |

S = Support          O = Opposition

## Key Votes

**96th Congress**

| | |
|---|---|
| Weaken Carter oil profits tax (1979) | N |
| Reject hospital cost control plan (1979) | Y |
| Implement Panama Canal Treaties (1979) | Y |
| Establish Department of Education (1979) | N |
| Approve Anti-busing Amendment (1979) | Y |
| Guarantee Chrysler Corp. loans (1979) | N |
| Approve military draft registration (1980) | Y |
| Aid Sandinista regime in Nicaragua (1980) | N |
| Strengthen fair housing laws (1980) | N |

**97th Congress**

| | |
|---|---|
| Reagan budget proposal (1981) | Y |

## Interest Group Ratings

| Year | ADA | ACA | AFL-CIO | CCUS |
|---|---|---|---|---|
| 1980 | 22 | 42 | 47 | 62 |
| 1979 | 42 | 54 | 50 | 50 |
| 1978 | 30 | 85 | 25 | 61 |
| 1977 | 15 | 70 | 52 | 59 |
| 1976 | 25 | 86 | 26 | 63 |
| 1975 | 37 | 57 | 57 | 24 |
| 1974 | 35 | 60 | 45 | 40 |
| 1973 | 36 | 70 | 45 | 64 |
| 1972 | 13 | 78 | 45 | 60 |
| 1971 | 32 | 59 | 42 | - |
| 1970 | 24 | 68 | 43 | 70 |
| 1969 | 20 | 82 | 50 | - |
| 1968 | 17 | 78 | 0 | - |
| 1967 | 13 | 66 | 25 | 70 |
| 1966 | 6 | 63 | 15 | - |
| 1965 | 5 | 68 | - | 80 |
| 1964 | 32 | 74 | 64 | - |
| 1963 | - | 28 | - | - |
| 1962 | 63 | 17 | 82 | - |
| 1961 | 60 | - | - | - |

# 4 Bill Chappell Jr. (D)

### Of Ocala — Elected 1968

**Born:** Feb. 3, 1922, Kendrick, Fla.
**Education:** U. of Fla., B.A. 1947, LL.B. 1949.
**Military Career:** Navy, 1942-47.
**Profession:** Lawyer.
**Family:** Wife, Marguerite Gutshall; four children.
**Religion:** Methodist.
**Political Career:** Fla. House, 1955-65 and 1967-69, speaker, 1961-63.

**In Washington:** Unswerving support for defense in general and the Navy in particular has been the focus of Chappell's congressional career.

When it comes to the military, he is an old-style Southern Democrat: attentive to the judgments of senior officers and wary of budgetary limits that he thinks would cripple U.S. forces.

What sets Chappell apart from others who agree with him, however, is his mastery of the technical details. He was a naval aviator himself, and a captain in the Navy Reserve, and he has always remained in touch with changing technology.

In his earlier years on the Defense Appropriations Subcommittee, Chappell was a loyal ally of Florida's Robert L. F. Sikes, who consistently fought to give the Pentagon all it requested and more. When subcommittee Chairman George Mahon of Texas sought to cut defense spending bills, Chappell joined Sikes in fighting him.

When Sikes and several of his allies retired at the end of the 95th Congress, Chappell was left as senior Pentagon spokesman on the subcommittee. He seemed a lonely figure at first, outnumbered on the Democratic side and totally opposite in his views to the new chairman, Joseph Addabbo of New York, who replaced Mahon in 1979.

But by the end of that year, Chappell's war clearly was being won in the broader political arena, as concern over global Soviet adventurism was producing a much more defense-oriented Congress.

In 1980, for the first time in 13 years, the full Appropriations Committee added money to a president's defense budget request, although not as much as Chappell wished. As second-ranking Democrat on Defense Appropriations, Chappell was spending much of his time trying to prove that Carter's own military chiefs found the administration's spending requests inadequate. His typical approach at hearings was to press senior officers to give the panel their personal, professional judgments about how much money to spend on a program, without reference to administration-imposed constraints.

In 1979 and 1980, Chappell was in the forefront of members fighting for reversal of Carter's two big symbolic victories over the services: cancellation of the B-1 bomber in 1977, and the veto of a nuclear aircraft carrier in 1978.

Chappell had fought Carter's 1977 B-1 decision, and in early 1978 joined a congressional effort to keep the program alive a little longer. The move failed, narrowly, largely because of opposition from the Air Force itself. By 1980, however, thanks in part to Chappell, it was clear that Congress would vote for a new bomber, with or without Carter's support.

But Navy issues are Chappell's special forte. In 1978 and 1979, he was the Appropriations Committee's best-informed and most energetic advocate of a new nuclear-powered carrier. To him, the Carter administration's preference for a smaller ship was a clear case of civilian budgeteers sacrificing needed combat power for savings. By 1979, amid mounting concern over the U.S. position in the Persian Gulf, Congress was moving in Chappell's direction on this issue as well; money for a nuclear carrier was added to the defense budget.

Chappell has been a tireless critic of the F-18, a carrier-borne jet intended to serve as both a

---

**4th District: Northeast — Daytona Beach.** Population: 715,027 (58% increase since 1970). Race: White 622,888 (87%), Black 84,393 (12%), Others 7,746 (1%). Spanish origin: 12,271 (2%).

fighter and a light bomber. Here too, he has argued against what he considers a cheap substitute for more copies of the F-14, the Navy's front-line carrier fighter.

Chappell has complained constantly about technical flaws in the F-18 program and presented evidence he says proves the plane is inferior to the F-14. And he has highlighted the F-18's escalating cost: he says it is no longer much cheaper than the more sophisticated plane.

His reserve membership has been the source of one of his most intense crusades, against what he sees as Navy refusal to equip its reserve units with front-line combat ships. For several years in the late 1970s, Chappell blocked Navy plans to scrap the World War II-vintage destroyers that were the only large combatants assigned to reserve units.

The Navy said these ships were too old to maintain, and did not want to provide new ones. Chappell pointed to the high level of combat-readiness maintained by air squadrons as evidence of what a reserve unit could do if it was given good equipment and supported by a large enough full-time maintenance staff. In 1981, the Pentagon accepted Chappell's position, promising to transfer some relatively modern frigates to reserve control by the mid-1980s.

Chappell is a specialist. He is on the Military Construction Subcommittee as well as the Defense panel, and while he has one other subcommittee assignment, Energy and Water, he is rarely heard on issues outside his field. He has a solidly conservative overall record; in 1980, he ranked 17th among 273 House Democrats in his support for the "conservative coalition" of Republicans and Southern Democrats on the House floor.

**At Home:** Chappell was a 12-year veteran of the Legislature and a former state House Speaker when he ran for Congress in 1968 on a law-and-order platform. In a year of urban riots, he

blamed the unrest on a "lunatic fringe" and called for stricter law enforcement. He favored escalation of military activity in Vietnam to win the war there. Criticizing some Supreme Court rulings as based "on whim and sociological argument," Chappell advocated "restraints" on the court to prevent erosion of states' rights.

Chappell's resolute conservatism brought him the Democratic nomination by a narrow margin over state Sen. Douglas Stenstrom. His GOP general election opponent was William F. Herlong, a nephew of the district's retiring Democratic congressman, A. Sydney Herlong. It was a good Republican year in Florida, with Richard M. Nixon at the top of the ticket, but Chappell pulled through with 52.8 percent of the vote.

Herlong's near-miss in a traditionally Democratic district kept Republicans in pursuit of Chappell, and GOP candidates won 42.2 percent in 1970 and 44.1 percent in 1972. But Chappell was up to nearly 70 percent in 1974 and has glided easily through the past three elections.

**The District:** Although Chappell keeps this nine-county resort-and citrus district in the Democratic column without much effort, other Democrats have to struggle here. In 1980, only Putnam County voted uniformly Democratic — Chappell for Congress, Gunter for Senate and Carter for president.

More than a third of the district's 1980 vote was cast in Volusia County (Daytona Beach). Another 20 percent came from southeast Duval County, just below downtown Jacksonville. These metropolitan coastal areas went Democratic for the Senate but chose Reagan over Carter for president.

The population of the 4th District has grown 58 percent since 1970, the fourth fastest rate in the state. Clay County, which has grown 70 percent since 1970, voted for Reagan by a margin exceeding 2-to-1.

## Committees

**Appropriations** (12th of 33 Democrats)
   Defense; Energy and Water Development; Military Construction.

## Elections

**1980 General**

| | |
|---|---|
| Bill Chappell Jr. (D ) | 147,775 (66 %) |
| Barney Dillard Jr. (R ) | 76,924 (34 %) |

**1978 General**

| | |
|---|---|
| Bill Chappell Jr. (D ) | 113,302 (73 %) |

| | |
|---|---|
| Tom Boney (R ) | 41,647 (27 %) |

**Previous Winning Percentages**

| | | | |
|---|---|---|---|
| 1976 (100%) | 1974 (68 %) | 1972 (56 %) | 1970 (58 %) |
| 1968 (53 %) | | | |

**District Vote For President**

| | 1980 | | 1976 | | 1972 |
|---|---|---|---|---|---|
| D | 103,440 (41 %) | D | 115,332 (53 %) | D | 41,298 (24 %) |
| R | 137,667 (55 %) | R | 100,991 (46 %) | R | 134,211 (76 %) |
| I | 8,221 (3 %) | | | | |

## Campaign Finance

| | Receipts | Receipts from PACs | Expenditures |
|---|---|---|---|
| **1980** | | | |
| Chappell (D ) | $125,399 | $53,125 (42 %) | $110,668 |
| Dillard (R ) | $10,704 | — (0 %) | $8,750 |
| **1978** | | | |
| Chappell (D ) | $112,243 | $46,500 (41 %) | $87,346 |
| Boney (R ) | $9,520 | - (0 %) | $9,118 |

## Voting Studies

| | Presidential Support | | Party Unity | | Conservative Coalition | |
|---|---|---|---|---|---|---|
| Year | S | O | S | O | S | O |
| 1980 | 47 | 47 | 44 | 50 | 84 | 8 |
| 1979 | 30 | 61 | 30 | 56 | 78 | 8 |
| 1978 | 25 | 52 | 30 | 57 | 77 | 12 |
| 1977 | 38 | 44 | 29 | 58 | 83 | 8 |
| 1976 | 43 | 39 | 28 | 51 | 74 | 7 |
| 1975 | 49 | 40 | 33 | 54 | 79 | 10 |
| 1974 (Ford) | 52 | 37 | | | | |
| 1974 | 58 | 28 | 34 | 54 | 74 | 13 |
| 1973 | 53 | 39 | 41 | 56 | 86 | 10 |
| 1972 | 51 | 38 | 19 | 76 | 91 | 4 |
| 1971 | 63 | 23 | 26 | 59 | 79 | 5 |
| 1970 | 51 | 45 | 33 | 53 | 80 | 7 |
| 1969 | 38 | 43 | 22 | 64 | 91 | 0 |

S = Support          O = Opposition

## Key Votes

**96th Congress**

| | |
|---|---|
| Weaken Carter oil profits tax (1979) | Y |
| Reject hospital cost control plan (1979) | Y |
| Implement Panama Canal Treaties (1979) | N |
| Establish Department of Education (1979) | N |
| Approve Anti-busing Amendment (1979) | Y |
| Guarantee Chrysler Corp. loans (1979) | Y |
| Approve military draft registration (1980) | Y |
| Aid Sandinista regime in Nicaragua (1980) | Y |
| Strengthen fair housing laws (1980) | N |

**97th Congress**

| | |
|---|---|
| Reagan budget proposal (1981) | Y |

## Interest Group Ratings

| Year | ADA | ACA | AFL-CIO | CCUS |
|---|---|---|---|---|
| 1980 | 6 | 63 | 26 | 76 |
| 1979 | 11 | 77 | 21 | 100 |
| 1978 | 5 | 84 | 25 | 76 |
| 1977 | 5 | 75 | 33 | 88 |
| 1976 | 5 | 91 | 41 | 69 |
| 1975 | 5 | 82 | 32 | 67 |
| 1974 | 9 | 57 | 30 | 86 |
| 1973 | 8 | 61 | 30 | 90 |
| 1972 | 0 | 95 | 10 | 78 |
| 1971 | 8 | 73 | 50 | - |
| 1970 | 8 | 83 | 29 | 75 |
| 1969 | 7 | 93 | 10 | - |

# 5 Bill McCollum (R)

### Of Altamonte Springs — Elected 1980

**Born:** July 12, 1944, Brooksville, Fla.
**Education:** U. of Fla., B.A. 1965, J.D. 1968.
**Military Career:** Navy, 1969-72.
**Profession:** Lawyer.
**Family:** Wife, Ingrid Seebohm; two children.
**Religion:** Episcopalian.
**Political Career:** Chairman, Seminole County Republican Executive Committee, 1976-80.

**The Member:** McCollum has a considerably more virtuous image than Republican Rep. Richard Kelly, who was caught up in the Abscam bribery scandal, but the new congressman's philosophy differs little from his predecessor's. Voters discarded Kelly but did not repudiate his conservative approach.

McCollum launched his challenge to Kelly prior to the Abscam revelations and did not stress them as a campaign issue. Instead, McCollum pointed to a "leadership vacuum" in the district, while stressing his image as a morally upstanding family man. Kelly finished third in the GOP primary, and McCollum went on to win the runoff and general election comfortably.

One campaign promise that McCollum seems particularly serious about is his pledge to limit congressional tenure. He has introduced a constitutional amendment to allow representatives six two-year terms, and another to lengthen and limit terms in the House. He would restrict senators to two six-year terms.

In June of 1981, McCollum won passage of his amendment restricting the use of Legal Services funds for representing illegal aliens. He is the only Floridian on the Judiciary Committee, which has jurisdiction over immigration issues important to a state trying to cope with a massive refugee influx.

McCollum is also vice president of the 52-member GOP freshman class.

**The District:** The 5th is a wedge between north and south Florida. From the Gulf of Mexico on the west, it stretches all the way to eastern Seminole County, near the Atlantic. Created after the 1970 census as likely GOP territory, it was held by Democrats for one term before Kelly won it in 1974. Because nearly three-quarters of the the total vote is cast in two widely separated media markets — Orlando in the east and Tampa in the west — the cost of campaigning is high.

## Committees

**Banking, Finance and Urban Affairs** (13th of 19 Republicans)
Domestic Monetary Policy; Financial Institutions Supervision, Regulation and Insurance; General Oversight and Renegotiation; Housing and Community Development.

**Judiciary** (12th of 12 Republicans)
Criminal Justice; Immigration, Refugees and International Law.

## Elections

**1980 General**

| | |
|---|---|
| Bill McCollum (R ) | 177,603 (56 %) |
| David Best (D ) | 140,903 (44 %) |

**1980 Primary Runoff**

| | |
|---|---|
| Bill McCollum | 34,875 (54 %) |
| Vince Fectel | 29,229 (46 %) |

**1980 Primary**

| | |
|---|---|
| Bill McCollum (R ) | 26,152 (43 %) |
| Vincent Fechtel Jr. (R ) | 23,942 (39 %) |
| Richard Kelly (R ) | 10,889 (18 %) |

**District Vote For President**

| | 1980 | | 1976 | | 1972 |
|---|---|---|---|---|---|
| D | 125,393 (37 %) | D | 124,927 (49 %) | D | 49,673 (22 %) |
| R | 201,113 (59 %) | R | 125,067 (49 %) | R | 179,976 (78 %) |
| I | 13,127 (4 %) | | | | |

## Campaign Finance

| | Receipts | Receipts from PACs | Expenditures |
|---|---|---|---|
| **1980** | | | |
| McCollum (R ) | $271,578 | $49,800 (18 %) | $265,014 |
| Best (D ) | $181,771 | $52,950 (29 %) | $177,121 |

## Key Vote

**97th Congress**

| | |
|---|---|
| Reagan budget proposal (1981) | Y |

> **5th District: West Central — Clearwater, Orlando.** Population: 880,070 (94% increase since 1970). Race: White 773,148 (87%), Black 95,195 (11%), Others 11,727 (1%). Spanish origin: 21,527 (2%).

# 6 C. W. Bill Young (R)

**Of St. Petersburg — Elected 1970**

**Born:** Dec. 16, 1930, Harmarville, Pa.
**Education:** Attended Pa. public schools.
**Military Career:** National Guard, 1948-57.
**Profession:** Insurance executive.
**Family:** Wife, Marian Ford; three children.
**Religion:** Methodist.
**Political Career:** Fla. Senate, 1961-71, minority leader, 1967-71.

**In Washington:** The House has become increasingly suspicious and stingy about multilateral foreign aid in recent years, and Young is the man who has done most to seize on the mood and intensify it.

Young does not oppose U.S. participation in institutions like the World Bank and International Monetary Fund, but he has insisted the United States should have more say in how its money is spent. He has bitterly opposed attempts to loan money to communist countries.

Young began to develop his reputation as a scourge of foreign aid in 1977, when he took over as senior Republican on the Foreign Operations Subcommittee. He shocked the House with his successful amendment to ban indirect U.S. aid to Cambodia, Laos, Vietnam or Uganda.

The vote caused a dispute between the House and Senate, which did not go along with the ban. It ended only when President Carter agreed to a compromise instructing U.S. officials of the programs to vote against loans to those nations.

In 1978, Young tried to attach the same amendment to the foreign aid appropriations bill. But Democratic leaders conducted a massive lobbying campaign, one in which church groups and even the U.S. Chamber of Commerce applied pressure from the outside. Young lost, 203-198.

But the trend was clearly the other way and since then, backers of multilateral aid have been in full retreat. In 1979, World Bank president Robert McNamara agreed there would be no new loans to Vietnam in fiscal 1980. In return Young dropped an amendment to restrict aid to the Asian Development Bank and U.N. Development program.

In 1980, Young's threats of numerous amendments killed a bill authorizing a $3.24 billion contribution to the International Development Agency, the "soft loan" arm of the World Bank. The U.S. became the only nation to fall behind in its commitments to the World Bank. Congress also refused to authorize full U.S. contributions to two other international banks.

Young left the Foreign Operations Subcommittee in 1981 for a seat on the Defense Subcommittee, which he had coveted. There he plays a different role, pressing for more rather than less.

Young has made committee alliances across ideological lines. When some Appropriations conservatives wanted to block liberal Silvio Conte, R Mass., from becoming the panel's ranking Republican, Young put ideology aside and helped round up votes for Conte. Later Conte supported Young over others for the Defense vacancy.

Young is equally willing to play down ideology when it comes to money for his district. On the Appropriations subcommittee dealing with housing matters, he regularly tries to increase housing funds for the elderly, a prime concern in his St. Petersburg constituency. In 1978, Young tried to add $100 million for housing for the elderly on the House floor, but was defeated. In 1980, after a ship ran into the Sunshine Skyway bridge, near St. Petersburg, Young managed to wrest $50 million for repairs from the highway trust fund.

**At Home:** A high school dropout from a Pennsylvania mining town, Young worked his way to success in the insurance business before going into politics in 1960. Ten years later, he inherited Florida's most dependable Republican seat from Rep. William C. Cramer, who left it to him when

---

**6th District: West — St. Petersburg.**
Population: 600,088 (33% increase since 1970). Race: White 547,364 (91%), Black 47,237 (8%), Others 5,487 (1%). Spanish origin: 8,809 (1%).

---

he ran for the U.S. Senate in 1970.

Young had known Cramer a long time; he had met the congressman at a Rotary Club barbecue in 1955, worked in his 1956 campaign, and was hired as Cramer's district aide in 1957. In 1960, the Pinellas County GOP organization urged Young to challenge a veteran Democratic state senator. He won, and took office as the only Republican in the state Senate. By 1967, he had more than 20 others as company, and was minority leader.

When Cramer announced for the Senate in 1970, there was little question who would replace

him. Young won 76 percent of the primary vote, and 67 percent in the general election. Since then it has been even easier. In 1980 Young was unopposed in both the primary and general election.

**The District:** The 6th takes in two-thirds of Pinellas County, including all of St. Petersburg, some northern suburbs, and part of Clearwater. Its median age is highest in the nation.

Pinellas is the birthplace of modern-day Republicanism in Florida. The retirement community exerts a conservative influence that has been growing ever since Cramer first won.

## Committees

**Appropriations** (8th of 22 Republicans)
Defense; HUD-Independent Agencies.

**Select Intelligence** (5th of 5 Republicans)
Oversight and Evaluation; Program and Budget Authorization.

## Elections

**1980 General**

| | |
|---|---|
| C. W. Bill Young (R ) | Unopposed |

**1978 General**

| | |
|---|---|
| C. W. Bill Young (R ) | 150,694 (79 %) |
| James Christison (D ) | 40,654 (21 %) |

**Previous Winning Percentages**

1976 (65 %)     1974 (76 %)     1972 (76 %)     1970 (67 %)

**District Vote For President**

| | 1980 | | 1976 | | 1972 |
|---|---|---|---|---|---|
| D | 114,393 (41 %) | D | 115,795 (49 %) | D | 65,743 (31 %) |
| R | 146,826 (53 %) | R | 118,337 (50 %) | R | 146,163 (69 %) |
| I | 14,447 (5 %) | | | | |

## Campaign Finance

| | Receipts | Receipts from PACs | Expenditures |
|---|---|---|---|
| **1980** | | | |
| Young (R ) | $61,029 | $11,875 (19 %) | $29,313 |
| **1978** | | | |
| Young (R ) | $65,801 | $22,787 (35 %) | $57,482 |
| Christison (D ) | $128,579 | $5,600 (4 %) | $128,579 |

## Voting Studies

| Year | Presidential Support | | Party Unity | | Conservative Coalition | |
|---|---|---|---|---|---|---|
| | S | O | S | O | S | O |
| 1980 | 40 | 56 | 85 | 13 | 94 | 4 |
| 1979 | 30 | 68 | 89 | 9 | 96 | 3 |
| 1978 | 31 | 68 | 83 | 14 | 92 | 7 |
| 1977 | 44 | 48 | 84 | 7 | 83 | 5 |
| 1976 | 69 | 29 | 84 | 16 | 88 | 10 |
| 1975 | 55 | 40 | 82 | 11 | 87 | 10 |
| 1974 (Ford) | 54 | 44 | | | | |
| 1974 | 75 | 25 | 79 | 15 | 80 | 12 |
| 1973 | 63 | 31 | 79 | 16 | 78 | 15 |
| 1972 | 65 | 32 | 76 | 20 | 76 | 17 |
| 1971 | 81 | 16 | 86 | 8 | 89 | 6 |

S = Support          O = Opposition

## Key Votes

**96th Congress**

| | |
|---|---|
| Weaken Carter oil profits tax (1979) | Y |
| Reject hospital cost control plan (1979) | Y |
| Implement Panama Canal Treaties (1979) | N |
| Establish Department of Education (1979) | N |
| Approve Anti-busing Amendment (1979) | Y |
| Guarantee Chrysler Corp. loans (1979) | N |
| Approve military draft registration (1980) | Y |
| Aid Sandinista regime in Nicaragua (1980) | N |
| Strengthen fair housing laws (1980) | N |

**97th Congress**

| | |
|---|---|
| Reagan budget proposal (1981) | Y |

## Interest Group Ratings

| Year | ADA | ACA | AFL-CIO | CCUS |
|---|---|---|---|---|
| 1980 | 11 | 88 | 11 | 76 |
| 1979 | 11 | 92 | 26 | 88 |
| 1978 | 10 | 93 | 15 | 78 |
| 1977 | 10 | 83 | 17 | 94 |
| 1976 | 5 | 89 | 30 | 69 |
| 1975 | 16 | 93 | 13 | 82 |
| 1974 | 4 | 86 | 0 | 70 |
| 1973 | 16 | 92 | 27 | 82 |
| 1972 | 13 | 87 | 18 | 90 |
| 1971 | 5 | 97 | 8 | |

# 7 Sam Gibbons (D)

**Of Tampa — Elected 1962**

**Born:** Jan. 20, 1920, Tampa, Fla.
**Education:** U. of Fla., LL.B. 1947.
**Military Career:** Army, 1941-45.
**Profession:** Lawyer.
**Family:** Wife, Martha Hanley; three children.
**Religion:** Presbyterian.
**Political Career:** Fla. House, 1953-59; Fla. Senate, 1959-63.

**In Washington:** Gibbons, who fought seniority and secrecy as a House rebel in the 1960s, is focusing now on a narrower issue, but one that drives him to equal militance — free trade. He may never reach the place he wanted in the leadership, but he holds a few good cards as chairman of the Ways and Means Trade Subcommittee.

In the old days, Gibbons was one of the revolutionaries, as in a celebrated challenge to the obstreperous Adam Clayton Powell in 1966. Now he does not speak very often. As a believer in free trade, he can work for most of what he wants by doing little or nothing — sitting on protectionist bills in his subcommittee or at least taking his time with them.

Free trade is not just Gibbons' political position. It is his philosophy. "World War II had a tremendous impact on me," he has said. "I felt one reason it started was people didn't know how to work together.... My grand global goal is to make friends through commerce."

If those views were not so well known in the House, Gibbons probably would have become Trade chairman four years earlier. He was the senior Democrat on it in 1977, when it was vacant, and expected to run it. But his prospective leadership disturbed many of the committee Democrats, and Charles Vanik, D-Ohio, who had not even been on the Trade panel, exercised his full committee seniority to take it away from Gibbons. By 1981, that sort of move was impossible. Gibbons was No. 2 on all of Ways and Means, and there was nobody to block him.

In fact, Gibbons barely missed out on the full Ways and Means chairmanship in 1981. A combination of retirements and defeats left only Dan Rostenkowski of Illinois ahead of him, and Rostenkowski was interested in being majority whip instead. Gibbons quietly hoped Rostenkowski would take the whip post, then just as quietly accepted Trade when that did not happen.

He is convinced he will eventually be Ways and Means chairman no matter what happens.

Gibbons is a jovial and friendly man, but he has always seemed a bit headstrong to the more traditional Democrats in the House.

As a junior Democrat on the Education and Labor Committee in the 1960s, Gibbons crusaded to open up committee sessions to the public. He helped draft new rules to restrict unrecorded voting on the House floor and to require confirmation votes on committee chairmen. "Secrecy and seniority," he once said, "are the twin vices of this House."

Those arguments made Gibbons an ally of Arizona Democrat Morris K. Udall, who was lobbying for the same things, and Gibbons managed Udall's unsuccessful campaign for majority leader in 1971, when Hale Boggs of Louisiana won the position.

Two years later, he decided to run for majority leader himself and launched a brief and quixotic campaign that still causes him problems among the Democratic hierarchy.

Gibbons' target in that campaign was Thomas P. O'Neill Jr., the overwhelming front-runner. The two men had been allies in the earlier drive to broaden recorded voting, and Gibbons was never highly critical of O'Neill. But O'Neill felt that his own performance as whip made him the presumptive choice for leader and did not seem to understand why Gibbons would mount a

---

**7th District: West — Tampa.** Population: 595,159 (31% increase since 1970). Race: White 502,463 (84%), Black 79,592 (13%), Others 13,104 (2%). Spanish origin: 62,443 (10%).

futile campaign against him. Although Gibbons dropped out before the voting, and O'Neill won unopposed, relations between them have been cool ever since. The Speaker urged Rostenkowski to take the Ways and Means chairmanship in 1981, preferring not to have Gibbons in that sensitive role at the start of the Reagan administration.

Gibbons joined Ways and Means in 1969 and was immediately embroiled in an argument over the oil depletion allowance. He was a major player in that year's Tax Reform Act, which reduced the depletion allowance, set minimum taxes for the rich and raised the capital gains tax. In 1975, when the depletion allowance was finally eliminated for the major oil companies, Gibbons was among those leading the argument. The same year, he argued for a tough tax on gas-guzzling cars and fought quotas on imported oil.

In the late 70s, after Gibbons lost both his leadership campaign and the Trade Subcommittee, his attention seemed to wander a bit, and he played a relatively minor role on many issues as younger Democrats drew most of the attention on Ways and Means. In the 96th Congress, as chairman of an oversight subcommittee, Gibbons held months of hearings on the "underground economy" — the billions of dollars earned in the United States every year upon which no income taxes are paid.

Fifteen years earlier, as a second-term member at Education and Labor, Gibbons attracted national attention when he confronted his chairman, the flamboyant Adam Powell, over how to run the committee. Gibbons felt Powell was capricious in hiring and firing people and complained that he was often vacationing in the Caribbean when important legislation had to be handled. Gibbons once stalked out of a committee hearing, grumbling: "I'm sick of the whole thing."

With Gibbons in the lead, the committee adopted new rules that shifted power to the six subcommittee chairmen, limiting Powell's influence. Powell was "excluded" from the 90th Congress in 1967 on misconduct charges, returned in 1969, and was beaten in 1970.

Meanwhile, Gibbons was playing an active role on Education and Labor. In 1965, still in his second term, he was asked to serve as floor manager for the Johnson administration's antipoverty authorization bill. The White House thought it would help to have a white Southerner in charge, and Gibbons' credentials as a national Democrat were solid. He had backed Johnson for president in 1964 and supported most of his policies, including the Vietnam War. The bill passed, and Gibbons got an effusive telephone call from the president.

In his early years, Gibbons skirted the line between national Democratic liberalism and Southern sensibilities. He voted against the 1964 and 1968 Civil Rights acts, against school busing and for school prayer. He voted for poverty programs, the 1965 Voting Rights Act and a 1966 open housing bill that died in the Senate.

**At Home:** Gibbons is the only congressman this Hillsborough County (Tampa) district has ever had. He defeated a conservative Democrat to win it in 1962, the year it was created, then held off another conservative six years later. In recent campaigns he has been criticized by challengers as aloof from district concerns, but he has always won handsomely.

Before he came to Congress, Gibbons served 10 years in the state Legislature, where he drafted Florida's first successful urban renewal measure and supported reapportionment of the Legislature, fighting the North Florida "Pork Chop Gang" that wanted to preserve rural overrepresentation.

Gibbons finished first in the five-way 1962 Democratic congressional primary, but fell far short of a majority. His runoff opponent was retired National Guard Lt. Gen. Sumter L. Lowry, a fervid segregationist and anticommunist.

Lowry was helped by contributions from wealthy conservatives all over the South, but Gibbons picked up the support of the moderate Democrats who had failed to make the runoff, and that was more important. He defeated Lowry and won the general election handily.

After two easy re-elections, Gibbons in 1968 encountered another conservative challenge from within his party. Hillsborough County States Attorney Paul Antinori called for a hard-line approach to the war in Vietnam and crime in America. By this time, Gibbons had a solid hold on the district. He held Antinori to 39.7 percent of the primary vote.

Gibbons' support for tax revision on the Ways and Means Committee and his moderate-liberal overall record have generally endeared him to organized labor and Tampa's black community, giving him a secure political base. He lost the state AFL-CIO endorsement in 1978, when he was challenged for renomination by Richard Salem, former chairman of the Hillsborough County Democratic Committee, but still coasted in the primary with nearly 70 percent of the vote.

**The District:** Tampa, a major port city with an important manufacturing sector, disagrees fundamentally with the Republican politics of its neighbor just across the bay, St. Petersburg. The city's influential Cuban community and blue-collar orientation make it a Democratic district, different in character from most of the South.

The preference was not so strong in 1980, however, as it has been in the past. Carter had only a narrow margin in Tampa, and Reagan did well enough in the suburbs to carry Hillsborough County.

Hillsborough's disenchantment with Carter did not spread to other Democrats: Gibbons won easily, and Democratic Senate nominee Bill Gunter carried the county by more than 15,000 votes in his unsuccessful Senate campaign.

## Committees

**Ways and Means** (2nd of 23 Democrats)
Trade, chairman; Oversight.

**Joint Taxation**

## Elections

**1980 General**

| | |
|---|---|
| Sam Gibbons (D) | 132,529 (72 %) |
| Charles Jones (R) | 52,138 (28 %) |

**1978 General**

| | |
|---|---|
| Sam Gibbons (D) | Unopposed |

**Previous Winning Percentages**

| | | | |
|---|---|---|---|
| 1976 (66 %) | 1974 (100%) | 1972 (68 %) | 1970 (72 %) |
| 1968 (62 %) | 1966 (100%) | 1964 (100%) | 1962 (71 %) |

**District Vote For President**

| | 1980 | | 1976 | | 1972 |
|---|---|---|---|---|---|
| D | 82,344 (43 %) | D | 88,612 (54 %) | D | 42,349 (31 %) |
| R | 100,582 (52 %) | R | 74,570 (45 %) | R | 95,518 (69 %) |
| I | 8,726 (5 %) | | | | |

## Campaign Finance

| | Receipts | Receipts from PACs | Expenditures |
|---|---|---|---|
| **1980** | | | |
| Gibbons (D) | $93,791 | $50,050 (53 %) | $43,410 |
| Jones (R) | $100 | — (0 %) | $56 |
| **1978** | | | |
| Gibbons (D) | $89,415 | $19,750 (22 %) | $65,558 |

## Voting Studies

| | Presidential Support | | Party Unity | | Conservative Coalition | |
|---|---|---|---|---|---|---|
| Year | S | O | S | O | S | O |
| 1980 | 68 | 19 | 70 | 24 | 54 | 42 |
| 1979 | 56 | 25 | 55 | 28 | 43 | 40 |
| 1978 | 56 | 20 | 40 | 40 | 49 | 32 |
| 1977 | 66 | 23 | 55 | 38 | 45 | 49 |
| 1976 | 35 | 55 | 59 | 34 | 48 | 45 |
| 1975 | 51 | 43 | 52 | 37 | 53 | 33 |
| 1974 (Ford) | 41 | 57 | | | | |
| 1974 | 64 | 21 | 65 | 23 | 39 | 47 |
| 1973 | 38 | 53 | 73 | 19 | 30 | 62 |
| 1972 | 49 | 38 | 58 | 24 | 39 | 46 |
| 1971 | 46 | 49 | 75 | 16 | 26 | 70 |
| 1970 | 55 | 35 | 61 | 25 | 25 | 57 |
| 1969 | 49 | 38 | 71 | 13 | 29 | 53 |
| 1968 | 64 | 17 | 72 | 17 | 27 | 57 |
| 1967 | 84 | 8 | 84 | 9 | 31 | 65 |
| 1966 | 87 | 3 | 93 | 3 | 11 | 78 |
| 1965 | 80 | 13 | 74 | 20 | 22 | 73 |
| 1964 | 79 | 19 | 76 | 21 | 33 | 67 |
| 1963 | 70 | 15 | 62 | 21 | 27 | 53 |

S = Support     O = Opposition

## Key Votes

**96th Congress**

| | |
|---|---|
| Weaken Carter oil profits tax (1979) | N |
| Reject hospital cost control plan (1979) | ? |
| Implement Panama Canal Treaties (1979) | Y |
| Establish Department of Education (1979) | N |
| Approve Anti-busing Amendment (1979) | Y |
| Guarantee Chrysler Corp. loans (1979) | N |
| Approve military draft registration (1980) | Y |
| Aid Sandinista regime in Nicaragua (1980) | Y |
| Strengthen fair housing laws (1980) | Y |

**97th Congress**

Reagan budget proposal (1981)

## Interest Group Ratings

| Year | ADA | ACA | AFL-CIO | CCUS |
|---|---|---|---|---|
| 1980 | 39 | 30 | 50 | 67 |
| 1979 | 32 | 48 | 44 | 71 |
| 1978 | 10 | 67 | 26 | 67 |
| 1977 | 40 | 46 | 62 | 44 |
| 1976 | 45 | 48 | 45 | 34 |
| 1975 | 68 | 54 | 55 | 47 |
| 1974 | 52 | 21 | 82 | 56 |
| 1973 | 52 | 27 | 73 | 46 |
| 1972 | 44 | 39 | 60 | 50 |
| 1971 | 65 | 39 | 50 | - |
| 1970 | 60 | 39 | 83 | 33 |
| 1969 | 47 | 19 | 100 | - |
| 1968 | 58 | 15 | 50 | - |
| 1967 | 67 | 0 | 92 | 10 |
| 1966 | 65 | 17 | 77 | - |
| 1965 | 68 | 20 | - | 20 |
| 1964 | 60 | 26 | 73 | - |
| 1963 | - | 25 | - | - |

# 8 Andy Ireland (D)

**Of Winter Haven — Elected 1976**

**Born:** Aug. 23, 1930, Cincinnati, Ohio.
**Education:** Yale U., B.S. 1952; L.S.U. School of
Banking, graduated 1959; attended Columbia
Grad. School of Business, 1953-54.
**Profession:** Banker.
**Family:** Divorced; four children.
**Religion:** Episcopalian.
**Political Career:** Winter Haven City Commis-
sion, 1967-68; unsuccessful Democratic nomi-
nee for Fla. Senate, 1973 special election.

**In Washington:** Joking and jostling with
his Southern colleagues on "Redneck Row" at the
back of the House chamber, Ireland offers little
clue that he is a graduate of Phillips Academy and
Yale, or that he used to be the treasurer of the
Florida Bankers Association. He comes as close to
being a good old boy as anybody with his background ever will.

Whether one views Ireland as a corporate
conservative or just an old-fashioned Southern
Democrat, he leaves no doubt about his ideology.
Except for his first year, he never has voted
against the "conservative coalition" of Republicans and Southern Democrats much more than 10
percent of the time; in 1980, he voted against it 8
percent of the time. In 1981, he supported Reagan
budget proposals down the line despite strong
pressure from Democratic leaders.

On the Small Business Committee in the 96th
Congress, Ireland worked for the "Regulatory
Flexibility Act," which requires federal agencies
to weigh the effect of proposed regulations on
small businesses — and consider making exceptions for them. That bill became law in late 1980.
On the Foreign Affairs Committee, he worked on
a bill increasing protective measures for U.S.
embassies, and on new regulations for foreign
service officers. Outside his committees, he has
lobbied along with Florida citrus growers to persuade Japan to reduce barriers to the importation
of American oranges.

Ireland also has backed a bill that would
restrict the power of the Occupational Safety and
Health Administration (OSHA) to conduct inspections. The bill would exempt 91 percent of
America's work places from routine safety inspections and require OSHA to concentrate on those
businesses with poor safety records.

In most years, Ireland's legislative activity
draws less comment than his spectacular Wash-

ington fund-raiser. The Ringling Brothers and
Barnum & Bailey Circus winters in his district,
and when it comes to Washington, Ireland puts
up a tent and arranges for clowns, showgirls and
midgets to entertain his contributors before the
show begins. At $250 a ticket, it has allowed
Ireland to raise a substantial percentage of his
campaign budget.

**At Home:** Ireland had the resources to out-
class his competition in 1976, when the open 8th
District was up for grabs. The $144,000 he spent
on the effort was not an unusual amount, but it
brought him a sophisticated campaign. Expert
advice from political and advertising consultants,
a carefully-built county-by-county organization
and Ireland's own relaxed manner compensated
for his political inexperience and vagueness on
issues.

Ireland and five others sought the Democratic nomination that year when seven-term Rep.
James A. Haley announced his retirement. A
runoff between Ireland and state Rep. Ray
Mattox was expected, but Ireland won the nomination outright with 51.2 percent of the vote in
the first primary.

His general election foe was Republican state
Rep. Robert Johnson, who had served in the
Legislature for six years but was not well-known
outside his Sarasota home. Ireland won 58 percent
of the vote, a slightly higher share than veteran

---

**8th District: West central — Lake-
land, Sarasota.** Population: 646,104 (43%
increase since 1970). Race: White 555,502
(86%), Black 78,079 (12%), Others 12,523
(2%). Spanish origin: 19,659 (3%).

Democrat Haley had received in his last two elections. Ireland was unopposed in 1978 and rolled over nominal opposition in 1980.

**The District:** Ireland's political base is in Polk County, where about 275,000 people live in the Lakeland/Winter Haven metropolitan area. Polk cast more than 40 percent of the district's 1980 congressional vote, and 80 percent of it went to Ireland. The area has a high percentage of agricultural workers in numerous citrus cooperatives.

Ireland is not quite so strong on the Gulf Coast, where Manatee County (Bradenton) and a portion of Sarasota County together cast nearly half the district vote. Ireland won more than 60 percent in each of those areas in 1980.

The district's conservative nature is clearly seen in the 1980 presidential and senatorial voting. Polk, Manatee and Sarasota counties all voted for Reagan. Carter's strength was limited to Hardee County and eastern Hillsborough County, which together cast less than 10 percent of the district vote.

## Committees

**Foreign Affairs** (11th of 21 Democrats)
Asian and Pacific Affairs; International Operations.

**Small Business** (10th of 23 Democrats)
Export Opportunities and Special Small Business Problems, chairman.

## Elections

**1980 General**

| | |
|---|---|
| Andy Ireland (D ) | 151,613 (69 %) |
| Scott Nicholson (R ) | 61,820 (28 %) |

**1978 General**

| | |
|---|---|
| Andy Ireland (D ) | Unopposed |

**Previous Winning Percentage**

1976 (58 %)

**District Vote For President**

| | 1980 | | 1976 | | 1972 |
|---|---|---|---|---|---|
| D | 86,434 (36 %) | D | 93,597 (47 %) | D | 34,144 (21 %) |
| R | 142,289 (60 %) | R | 103,271 (52 %) | R | 131,853 (79 %) |
| I | 8,652 (4 %) | | | | |

## Campaign Finance

| | Receipts | Receipts from PACs | Expen- ditures |
|---|---|---|---|
| **1980** | | | |
| Ireland (D ) | $261,483 | $89,925 (34 %) | $221,103 |
| Nicholson (R ) | $12,394 | — (0 %) | $12,460 |

| **1978** | | | |
|---|---|---|---|
| Ireland (D ) | $115,297 | $29,844 (26 %) | $102,265 |

## Voting Studies

| | Presidential Support | | Party Unity | | Conservative Coalition | |
|---|---|---|---|---|---|---|
| Year | S | O | S | O | S | O |
| 1980 | 58 | 33 | 47 | 46 | 82 | 8 |
| 1979 | 46 | 44 | 42 | 46 | 76 | 12 |
| 1978 | 39 | 44 | 30 | 56 | 74 | 12 |
| 1977 | 62 | 30 | 42 | 52 | 72 | 21 |

S = Support          O = Opposition

## Key Votes

**96th Congress**

| | |
|---|---|
| Weaken Carter oil profits tax (1979) | Y |
| Reject hospital cost control plan (1979) | Y |
| Implement Panama Canal Treaties (1979) | N |
| Establish Department of Education (1979) | Y |
| Approve Anti-busing Amendment (1979) | Y |
| Guarantee Chrysler Corp. loans (1979) | Y |
| Approve military draft registration (1980) | Y |
| Aid Sandinista regime in Nicaragua (1980) | N |
| Strengthen fair housing laws (1980) | N |

**97th Congress**

| | |
|---|---|
| Reagan budget proposal (1981) | Y |

## Interest Group Ratings

| Year | ADA | ACA | AFL-CIO | CCUS |
|---|---|---|---|---|
| 1980 | 6 | 46 | 11 | 73 |
| 1979 | 16 | 50 | 11 | 71 |
| 1978 | 20 | 78 | 21 | 67 |
| 1977 | 15 | 61 | 30 | 75 |

# 9 Bill Nelson (D)

### Of Melbourne — Elected 1978

**Born:** Sept. 29, 1942, Miami, Fla.
**Education:** Yale U., B.A. 1965; U. Va., J.D. 1968.
**Military Career:** Army Reserve, 1965-71.
**Profession:** Lawyer.
**Family:** Wife, Grace Cavert; two children.
**Religion:** Episcopalian.
**Political Career:** Fla. House, 1973-79.

**In Washington:** The apple pie earnestness that made Nelson a political success in Florida made him an early curiosity among his fellow House members, some of whom began referring to him as "Mr. President" before his first term was very far along.

Nelson arrived in Washington in 1978 determined to make it to the Budget Committee as a freshman, and he made it, campaigning for the position for a solid month. As a member of the panel, he allied himself with Oklahoma's James R. Jones and the loose coalition of Democrats who fought a two-year losing battle to balance the federal budget. But he was not a major decision-maker among that group.

In the 97th Congress, he began sounding even more conservative on Budget; he voted with the panel's Democratic majority to report a resolution out of committee, but when the issue reached the House floor, he switched and sided with President Reagan and the Republicans.

Nelson's most important effort on the Budget Committee has been to eliminate revenue sharing to state governments, which he insisted were mostly in surplus and did not need it. The House dropped the program in the fiscal 1980 budget, but it was restored in conference with the Senate. Nelson then took the issue to the floor in an appropriation bill, and tried to reduce state revenue sharing money by $700 million. He was beaten overwhelmingly, 302-102. By 1980, however, he was on the winning side as the program fell victim to even stronger budget cutting pressures.

Nelson's fiscal conservatism stops at the launching pad. On the Science Committee, he has fought for the U.S. space program, much of it based in his district, with his customary zeal. When the committee gave NASA a relatively generous authorization in 1979, Nelson said he was pleased that space had "the least amount of cuts of any area in the federal budget." Later, defending the space program on the floor, he said

it would "bring us to the full sunlight of world leadership where we belong."

**At Home:** The 9th District was open in 1978, vacated by the gubernatorial campaign of Republican Rep. Louis Frey Jr., and Nelson went for it with a campaign that took on the appearance of an All-American family outing. Nelson's wife, a former college homecoming queen, and his two children accompanied him along the way. He visited nearly every community in the district during an 18-month effort.

The major obstacle he had to overcome was the seat's original occupant, Republican Edward J. Gurney. Gurney held the district for three terms before going to the Senate in 1968, but he had left politics in 1974 after being indicted on several charges, including bribery. He was acquitted of the charges following two trials and attempted a political comeback against Nelson.

Gurney's campaign presented him as a conservative, experienced legislator, and asked voters to "re-elect" him, as if he had never been away. But Nelson ran exactly the right campaign against a man who, even if wrongly, had been under suspicion for four years. Nelson avoided talking about his opponent's misfortunes but projected a "new politics" image, calling for strict financial disclosure laws and refusing to accept

---

**9th District: East central — part of Orlando, Melbourne.** Population: 567,309, (25% increase since 1970). Race: White 510,065 (90%), Black 45,928 (8%), Others 11,316 (2%). Spanish origin: 18,712 (3%).

contributions from business political action committees.

Nelson took conservative stands on economic issues and advocated more military spending, important in a district with many military and aerospace facilities.

In the end, Gurney's past image and Nelson's personal appeal combined to produce a landslide result. Thought to be narrowly ahead as the election approached, Nelson exceeded 60 percent of the vote. In 1980, he strolled to re-election.

**The District:** The growth of America's space program in the 1960's was a boon to the area surrounding NASA's Kennedy Space Center, east of Titusville. The Titusville-Cocoa-Melbourne metropolitan area on the Atlantic Coast attracted engineering and electronics industries and white-collar employment, and by 1970 it had 230,000 people. Since then, the boom has subsided. In the past decade, the 9th District has been one of the slowest-growing areas of the state.

Brevard County casts about 55 percent of the district's total vote, with the rest coming from the western portion of Orange County, which contains parts of Orlando and its suburbs. In the 1980 presidential and senatorial contests, both Orange and Brevard counties voted Republican.

## Committees

**Budget**
Task Forces: Tax Policy, chairman; Reconciliation.

**Science and Technology** (17th of 23 Democrats)
Energy Development and Applications; Space Science and Applications.

## Elections

**1980 General**

| | |
|---|---|
| Bill Nelson (D) | 139,468 (70%) |
| Stan Dowiat (R) | 58,734 (30%) |

**1978 General**

| | |
|---|---|
| Bill Nelson (D) | 89,543 (62%) |
| Edward Gurney (R) | 56,074 (39%) |

**1978 Primary**

| | |
|---|---|
| Bill Nelson (D) | 36,565 (86%) |
| Curtis Sears (D) | 5,955 (14%) |

**District Vote For President**

| | 1980 | | 1976 | | 1972 |
|---|---|---|---|---|---|
| D | 66,372 (32%) | D | 80,788 (46%) | D | 25,413 (23%) |
| R | 126,838 (62%) | R | 91,673 (52%) | R | 87,254 (77%) |
| I | 9,513 (5%) | | | | |

## Campaign Finance

| | Receipts | Receipts from PACs | Expenditures |
|---|---|---|---|
| **1980** | | | |
| Nelson (D) | $265,627 | $2,000 (1%) | $202,048 |
| Dowiat (R) | $269,045 | — (0%) | $268,979 |

| **1978** | | | |
|---|---|---|---|
| Nelson (D) | $320,591 | $1,200 (.3%) | $313,325 |
| Gurney (R) | $215,090 | $37,537 (17%) | $212,679 |

## Voting Studies

| | Presidential Support | | Party Unity | | Conservative Coalition | |
|---|---|---|---|---|---|---|
| **Year** | **S** | **O** | **S** | **O** | **S** | **O** |
| 1980 | 68 | 26 | 67 | 28 | 62 | 33 |
| 1979 | 49 | 46 | 49 | 47 | 77 | 19 |

S = Support          O = Opposition

## Key Votes

**96th Congress**

| | |
|---|---|
| Weaken Carter oil profits tax (1979) | Y |
| Reject hospital cost control plan (1979) | Y |
| Implement Panama Canal Treaties (1979) | N |
| Establish Department of Education (1979) | N |
| Approve Anti-busing Amendment (1979) | N |
| Guarantee Chrysler Corp. loans (1979) | Y |
| Approve military draft registration (1980) | Y |
| Aid Sandinista regime in Nicaragua (1980) | # |
| Strengthen fair housing laws (1980) | Y |

**97th Congress**

| | |
|---|---|
| Reagan budget proposal (1981) | Y |

## Interest Group Ratings

| Year | ADA | ACA | AFL-CIO | CCUS |
|---|---|---|---|---|
| 1980 | 33 | 46 | 37 | 82 |
| 1979 | 11 | 64 | 30 | 71 |

# 10    L. A. "Skip" Bafalis (R)

**Of Fort Myers Beach — Elected 1972**

**Born:** Sept. 28, 1929, Boston, Mass.
**Education:** St. Anselm's College, B.A. 1952.
**Military Career:** Army, 1953-56.
**Profession:** Investment banker.
**Family:** Wife, Mary Elizabeth Lund; two children.
**Religion:** Christian Church.
**Political Career:** Fla. House, 1965-67; Fla. Senate, 1967-71, minority leader, 1968; unsuccessfully sought Republican nomination for governor, 1970.

**In Washington:** Bafalis stepped out of the shadows of House politics one summer evening in 1979 when he coordinated the lobbying drive that forced a floor vote on an anti-busing amendment to the Constitution.

It took 218 signatures to force the vote, and sponsor Ron Mottl, D-Ohio, had come close before. But each time Democratic leaders had prevailed on members from their side to withdraw their names. It was Bafalis who was largely responsible on the final try for bringing in a cluster of Republican signatures all at once, raising the total to 218 without giving the Democrats a chance to react.

The amendment itself failed badly, not only missing the two-thirds vote it needed for passage but falling short even of a majority. It did force numerous Democrats into casting a politically uncomfortable vote, however, and caused some of them serious problems in the 1980 general election.

Bafalis made it to the Ways and Means Committee in his second House term, and has been a solid conservative vote there, although not an innovator. On trade matters, he has worked to protect Florida's cattle industry from foreign beef imports. And he was a bitter opponent of President Carter's program for expanded welfare support levels in 1977. "American people should be indignant, outraged, and thoroughly alarmed," he said about it. "The welfare state will have completely and fully taken over."

Bafalis has introduced his own constitutional amendment to balance the federal budget. It would require three-fourths approval of both houses of Congress in order to enact any federal deficit. The federal government would have to pay off at least 1 percent of the federal debt every year.

Bafalis is one of only a few members who frequently disqualify themselves from voting on issues related to their personal investments. A stockholder in three coal companies, he has for years voted "present" on questions dealing with clean air or mine safety. "I would like to go to bed at night," he once said, "and not have to worry about seeing my name in the headlines the next morning."

**At Home:** Bafalis has been a crusader against busing since his days in the Florida Legislature, where he organized a committee that lobbied in 38 states for a constitutional amendment against it. He was state Senate minority leader during the tenure of flamboyant Republican Gov. Claude Kirk (1967-71). Initially a strong supporter of Kirk, Bafalis came to believe that the governor's habit of provoking confrontation with the Democratic Legislature was counterproductive. Bafalis challenged Kirk in the 1970 GOP gubernatorial primary, but finished third with 13.9 percent.

That exposure helped him, however, when he campaigned in 1972 for the newly-created 10th District House seat. Bafalis faced only minor primary opposition and then won 62 percent of the general election vote. His winning total has not dropped below 65 percent since.

In 1981, some Florida Republicans began

---

**10th District: South central — Fort Pierce, Fort Myers.** Population: 878,067 (94% increase since 1970). Race: White 781,028 (89%), Black 76,358 (9%), Others 20,681 (2%). Spanish origin: 30,305 (3%).

expressing interest in another Bafalis gubernatorial campaign for 1982, and he spent the early part of the year pondering it.

**The District:** When the 10th was created, it was thought to be politically even, with the Gulf and Atlantic coastal counties favoring Republicans and the inland counties preferring conservative Democrats.

But the district population grew more than 90 percent during the past decade, and most of the growth occurred in the Republican-voting retirement communities on the Gulf Coast and urban areas north of Palm Beach on the Atlantic.

In 1980, Reagan built up overwhelming mar-

gins in the Gulf counties of Charlotte and Lee, and he did nearly as well in the Atlantic coast counties of Martin, Indian River and St. Lucie. One of Florida's four new congressional districts may be created around some of those ocean communities in the eastern half of the 10th District. Whatever happens, the area will elect a Republican to the House.

Inland, where the economy focuses on cattle, sugar and fruit, Democratic strength persists. Two inland counties, Okeechobee and Glades, stayed with Carter in 1980, but the vote in those sparsely-populated rural areas amounted to only a fraction of the district-wide total.

## Committees

**Ways and Means** (8th of 12 Republicans)
Public Assistance and Unemployment Compensation; Trade.

## Elections

**1980 General**

| | |
|---|---|
| L. A. (Skip) Bafalis (R ) | 272,393 (79 %) |
| Richard Sparkman (D ) | 72,646 (21 %) |

**1978 General**

| | |
|---|---|
| L. A. (Skip) Bafalis (R ) | Unopposed |

**Previous Winning Percentages**

1976 (66 %)    1974 (74 %)    1972 (62 %)

**District Vote For President**

| | 1980 | | 1976 | | 1972 |
|---|---|---|---|---|---|
| D | 115,382 (31 %) | D | 122,920 (45 %) | D | 41,483 (21 %) |
| R | 242,174 (64 %) | R | 146,962 (54 %) | R | 157,730 (79 %) |
| I | 15,881 (4 %) | | | | |

## Campaign Finance

| | Receipts | Receipts from PACs | Expenditures |
|---|---|---|---|
| **1980** | | | |
| Bafalis (R ) | $111,087 | — (0 %) | $128,953 |
| Sparkman (D ) | $26,997 | $5,400 (20 %) | $26,963 |
| **1978** | | | |
| Bafalis (R ) | $44,550 | $2,718 (6 %) | $22,007 |

## Voting Studies

| | Presidential Support | | Party Unity | | Conservative Coalition | |
|---|---|---|---|---|---|---|
| Year | S | O | S | O | S | O |
| 1980 | 36 | 61† | 88 | 8† | 95 | 4† |
| 1979 | 26 | 74 | 95 | 4† | 96 | 0 |

| | | | | | | |
|---|---|---|---|---|---|---|
| 1978 | 29 | 70 | 84 | 12† | 92 | 7 |
| 1977 | 40 | 55 | 92 | 6† | 94 | 2† |
| 1976 | 67 | 31† | 81 | 14† | 92 | 7† |
| 1975 | 57 | 41 | 83 | 14 | 89 | 10 |
| 1974 (Ford) | 39 | 57 | | | | |
| 1974 | 60 | 32 | 71 | 21 | 77 | 13 |
| 1973 | 66 | 28 | 79 | 16 | 83 | 16 |

†Not eligible for all recorded votes.

S = Support          O = Opposition

## Key Votes

**96th Congress**

| | |
|---|---|
| Weaken Carter oil profits tax (1979) | Y |
| Reject hospital cost control plan (1979) | Y |
| Implement Panama Canal Treaties (1979) | N |
| Establish Department of Education (1979) | N |
| Approve Anti-busing Amendment (1979) | Y |
| Guarantee Chrysler Corp. loans (1979) | N |
| Approve military draft registration (1980) | Y |
| Aid Sandinista regime in Nicaragua (1980) | N |
| Strengthen fair housing laws (1980) | N |

**97th Congress**

| | |
|---|---|
| Reagan budget proposal (1981) | Y |

## Interest Group Ratings

| Year | ADA | ACA | AFL-CIO | CCUS |
|---|---|---|---|---|
| 1980 | 6 | 95 | 11 | 76 |
| 1979 | 0 | 100 | 16 | 100 |
| 1978 | 10 | 100 | 10 | 78 |
| 1977 | 0 | 85 | 19 | 93 |
| 1976 | 5 | 89 | 27 | 58 |
| 1975 | 5 | 89 | 17 | 71 |
| 1974 | 9 | 79 | 10 | 43 |
| 1973 | 16 | 88 | 18 | 80 |

# 11 Daniel A. Mica (D)

## Of West Palm Beach — Elected 1978

**Born:** Feb. 4, 1944, Binghamton, N.Y.
**Education:** Attended U. of Fla., 1961; Fla. Atlantic U., B.A. 1966.
**Profession:** Teacher.
**Family:** Wife, Martha Fry; four children.
**Religion:** Roman Catholic.
**Political Career:** No previous office.

**In Washington:** Mica spent a decade working for Florida Democrat Paul Rogers, and when the veteran congressman decided to retire in 1978, he all but bequeathed the 11th District to his young protégé, who won it easily. But Mica is no carbon copy of Rogers, and his interests have not been those of his former boss.

Rogers was a health specialist. Mica, who joined the Foreign Affairs Committee just as thousands of immigrants were flooding into Florida from the Caribbean, has concentrated on refugee problems.

Even before the massive wave of Cuban immigrants began in 1980, Mica had expressed severe doubts about accepting large numbers of refugees. "We've gone above and beyond the call of duty," he insisted in 1979. "There is a point where people will say we've had enough." Mica also opposed doubling of admission quotas to accommodate Indochinese refugees.

Mica nearly got the chance to play a dominant role on some of these issues in the 97th Congress, but he lost out in a power struggle among Foreign Affairs Committee Democrats.

The panel's liberal Democratic bloc, dissatisfied with Pennsylvania's Gus Yatron as chairman of the Inter-American Affairs Subcommittee, organized to dump Yatron as chairman in January of 1981. Mica was next in line. As a relative hardliner on foreign policy, however, he was vulnerable to the same opposition as Yatron. He lost out on a 10-9 subcommittee vote, and the more liberal Michael Barnes of Maryland won the position.

Mica, furious at the moves, described them as a "radical-liberal revolt." He said it was "a last flicker in this House of extremist attitudes."

Mica has been a more militant anti-communist than most of the Democrats on Foreign Affairs. When the committee approved $4.8 billion in 1979 to pay for the Egypt-Israel peace agreement, Mica joined four of the panel's Republicans in a separate statement blaming the Soviet Union for the cost and charging that President Carter overlooked "the dangerous role the Soviets play in the Middle East and elsewhere.

On his second Foreign Affairs subcommittee, dealing with foreign aid, Mica has consistently favored substantial cuts in spending. In April of 1979, he voted on the House floor with most Republicans — and against most Democrats — to impose a 10 percent across-the-board cut in U.S. foreign aid. But he changed that vote later the same day, following pressure from the Carter administration and the House leadership.

**At Home:** Rogers' surprise retirement announcement came in June 1978, only a month before the candidates' filing deadline. Others scrambled to sound out their support for a race, but Mica was already hard at work.

Mica had never run for public office before and was not well-known in the district. But he had Rogers' endorsement and fund-raising contacts, and made joint appearances with the popular incumbent. Mica carefully built an organization in the district's densely-populated condominium complexes.

His principal challenger in the Democratic primary was state Rep. John J. Considine, the favorite of organized labor. A third contender, Broward County Circuit Court Clerk Robert E. Lockwood, was expected to receive enough votes to force a Mica-Considine runoff. But Mica precluded a runoff by winning an unexpectedly decisive 54.5 percent of the vote.

---

**11th District: Southeast — West Palm Beach.** Population: 843,299 (87% increase since 1970). Race: White 726,311 (86%), Black 102,412 (12%), Others 14,576 (2%). Spanish origin: 37,472 (4%).

The district's Republicans were united behind state Rep. Bill James, minority leader of the Florida House. A gregarious campaigner and effective speaker, James was seen initially as the favorite, since Mica had neither a legislative record nor a dynamic campaign style. Mica countered that he would be an effective representative because his years on Rogers' staff had taught him the nuances of congressional and bureaucratic life. Again Mica's opponents found they had underestimated him. He won by more than 20,000 votes.

The national Republican Party nevertheless saw the seat as winnable in 1980, and contributed money to Mica's challenger, attorney Al Coogler. House Minority Leader John J. Rhodes criticized Mica for failing to win a seat on Rogers' old Subcommittee on Health. Mica won 60 percent of the vote.

**The District:** The 11th is a fast-growing tourist and retirement center. It includes most of Palm Beach County, and extends into Broward County to take in Pompano Beach and part of Fort Lauderdale. Inland, there are some rural and agricultural areas around Lake Okeechobee, but the vast majority of the vote is concentrated in a narrow strip along the coast.

The district is strongly Republican in most elections, although politically active condominium residents will sometimes lend support to conservative Democrats. The importance of the growing condo vote increased dramatically in the past decade as the district's population swelled by more than 80 percent.

## Committees

**Foreign Affairs** (12th of 21 Democrats)
Inter-American Affairs; International Operations.

**Select Aging** (20th of 31 Democrats)
Health and Long-Term Care.

**Veterans' Affairs** (12th of 17 Democrats)
Hospitals and Health Care; Housing and Memorial Affairs; Oversight and Investigations.

## Elections

**1978 General**

| Dan Mica (D) | 123,346 (55%) |
|---|---|
| Bill James (R) | 99,757 (45%) |

**1978 Primary**

| Dan Mica (D) | 35,947 (55%) |
|---|---|
| John Considine (D) | 20,689 (31%) |
| Robert Lockwood (D) | 9,286 (14%) |

**District Vote For President**

| | 1980 | | 1976 | | 1972 |
|---|---|---|---|---|---|
| D | 125,797 (36%) | D | 129,016 (49%) | D | 49,270 (26%) |
| R | 197,972 (57%) | R | 130,829 (49%) | R | 140,624 (74%) |
| I | 22,713 (6%) | | | | |

## Campaign Finance

| | Receipts | Receipts from PACs | Expenditures |
|---|---|---|---|
| **1980** | | | |
| Mica (D) | $246,828 | — (0%) | $265,177 |
| Coogler (R) | $163,806 | $19,400 (12%) | $188,846 |

| **1978** | | | |
|---|---|---|---|
| Mica (D) | $159,002 | $24,299 (15%) | $158,573 |
| James (R) | $251,610 | $65,697 (26%) | $228,969 |

## Voting Studies

| | Presidential Support | | Party Unity | | Conservative Coalition | |
|---|---|---|---|---|---|---|
| Year | S | O | S | O | S | O |
| 1980 | 56 | 38 | 59 | 36 | 72 | 23 |
| 1979 | 57 | 41 | 63 | 34 | 65 | 35 |

S = Support     O = Opposition

## Key Votes

**96th Congress**

| | |
|---|---|
| Weaken Carter oil profits tax (1979) | N |
| Reject hospital cost control plan (1979) | N |
| Implement Panama Canal Treaties (1979) | Y |
| Establish Department of Education (1979) | Y |
| Approve Anti-busing Amendment (1979) | Y |
| Guarantee Chrysler Corp. loans (1979) | N |
| Approve military draft registration (1980) | Y |
| Aid Sandinista regime in Nicaragua (1980) | N |
| Strengthen fair housing laws (1980) | N |

**97th Congress**

| | |
|---|---|
| Reagan budget proposal (1981) | Y |

## Interest Group Ratings

| Year | ADA | ACA | AFL-CIO | CCUS |
|---|---|---|---|---|
| 1980 | 33 | 52 | 41 | 81 |
| 1979 | 53 | 32 | 35 | 33 |

# 12 E. Clay Shaw Jr. (R)

**Of Fort Lauderdale — Elected 1980**

**Born:** April 19, 1939, Miami, Fla.
**Education:** Stetson University, B.S. 1961, J.D. 1966; U. of Ala., M.B.A. 1963.
**Profession:** Lawyer.
**Family:** Wife, Emilie Costar; four children.
**Religion:** Roman Catholic.
**Political Career:** Fort Lauderdale assistant city attorney, 1968; chief city prosecutor, 1968-69; associate municipal judge, 1969-71; city commissioner, 1971-73; vice mayor, 1973-75; mayor, 1975-81.

**The Member:** During Shaw's tenure as Fort Lauderdale mayor, the city passed an ordinance banning the sale of drug paraphernalia. One of his primary concerns in Congress has been stemming the flow of illegal drugs funneled into America through South Florida.

As a member of the Select Narcotics task force on Law Enforcement, Shaw has called for revision of laws preventing armed forces personnel from assisting federal drug enforcement officials. He also advocates repealing the law that prohibits U.S. aid to nations that spray paraquat and similar herbicides on fields of marijuana.

As mayor, Shaw presided over Fort Lauderdale's effort to broaden its economic base beyond tourism and transform its image from a "where-the-boys-are" student beach mecca to a stylish, sophisticated "American Venice." He brags that city spending decreased (discounting inflation) each year he was mayor, without cuts in fire or police protection.

Shaw had a tough 1980 contest with Democrat Alan Becker, a former state legislator who had defeated incumbent Edward J. Stack in the Democratic primary.

**The District:** Fort Lauderdale, the dominant city in the 12th, is a bastion of traditional Republicanism, but Hollywood, the other population center along the coast, is Democratic. Inland are burgeoning condominium communities packed with retirees from the northeast, many of them Jewish and most of them lifelong liberal Democrats.

The condo vote can be troublesome for Republicans here; J. Herbert Burke, who was the GOP representative here from 1967 to 1979, never courted it effectively. But Shaw worked hard to attract the retirees, and his inroads among them, combined with his overwhelming vote in Fort Lauderdale, made him a 1980 winner.

## Committees

**Merchant Marine and Fisheries** (15th of 15 Republicans)
Coast Guard and Navigation; Merchant Marine.

**Public Works and Transportation** (17th of 19 Republicans)
Surface Transportation; Water Resources.

**Select Narcotics Abuse and Control** (7th of 8 Republicans)

## Elections

**1980 General**

| | |
|---|---|
| Clay Shaw (R) | 128,561 (54%) |
| Alan Becker (D) | 107,164 (46%) |

**District Vote For President**

| | 1980 | | 1976 | | 1972 |
|---|---|---|---|---|---|
| **D** | 90,856 (36%) | **D** | 112,277 (53%) | **D** | 51,709 (28%) |
| **R** | 140,464 (56%) | **R** | 97,868 (46%) | **R** | 130,655 (71%) |
| **I** | 19,259 (8%) | | | | |

## Campaign Finance

| | Receipts | Receipts from PACs | Expenditures |
|---|---|---|---|
| **1980** | | | |
| Shaw (R) | $433,502 | $142,216 (33%) | $423,603 |
| Becker (D) | $136,270 | $2,800 (2%) | $117,264 |

## Key Vote

**97th Congress**

| | |
|---|---|
| Reagan budget proposal (1981) | Y |

---

**12th District: Southeast — Fort Lauderdale.** Population: 638,897 (41% increase since 1970). Race: White 547,248 (86%), Black 82,946 (13%), Others 8,705 (1%). Spanish origin: 28,185 (4%).

# 13 William Lehman (D)

**Of North Miami Beach — Elected 1972**

**Born:** Oct. 5, 1913, Selma, Ala.
**Education:** U. of Ala., B.S. 1934.
**Military Career:** Army, 1942-46.
**Profession:** Teacher, Automobile dealer.
**Family:** Wife, Joan Feibelman; three children.
**Religion:** Jewish.
**Political Career:** Dade County School Board, 1966-72, chairman, 1971-72.

**In Washington:** There *is* such a thing as a shy, self-effacing used car dealer — Lehman proves it. When he gets up to talk on the House floor, smiling meekly and speaking in a soft drawl, it seems impossible to believe he once sold Buicks in Miami under the name "Alabama Bill."

Lehman has been very un-huckster-like in recent years as he has concentrated his attention on problems caused by the influx of Cubans and Haitians to Florida. But he has persisted.

As a member of the Foreign Operations Subcommittee on Appropriations, he has helped Dante Fascell, the much more voluble Miami Democrat who serves on Foreign Affairs, to lobby for federal aid to the beleaguered state. They managed to get $100 million in Cuban refugee resettlement aid added to foreign aid legislation in 1980, but the Appropriations Committee balked, objecting that a foreign aid bill was not the place for what was largely domestic relief.

Lehman did not give up. He tried for the refugee money again and again. Finally he got it attached to another appropriation, fighting the charge by M. Caldwell Butler, R-Va., that it amounted to an "election year slush fund" for President Carter to distribute to Florida.

"The people are there," Lehman insisted. "They're not going to go away."

Lehman also worked on the Haitian refugee problem, a different case because most of them were entering the country illegally. The Haitians faced deportation, but judges were reluctant to return them if it might mean reprisals by the Haitian government.

When the U.S. government seemed slow to investigate how returning refugees might be treated in Haiti, Lehman went there himself, and proposed to set up an aid program for them on his own if private charities would operate it. The charities turned him down, pointing out that any program would make it easy for Haiti's government to identify returned refugees.

On foreign aid matters, Lehman is a solid vote for generous assistance to Israel, reflecting both his strong personal views and his district, which has one of the highest Jewish constituencies in the nation. On his other Appropriations subcommittee, Transportation, he is a vote for higher mass transit funding. He believes expressways divide neighborhoods and lead to ecological "disaster."

On the House floor, Lehman generally votes with the more liberal Northern Democrats rather than with his fellow-Southerners, deviating mainly in his opposition to busing and generous welfare payments — he favors a stricter workfare system, coupled with child care facilities. He also works for increases in Social Security.

**At Home:** Lehman was a surprise winner in 1972, and fellow Democrats gave him no peace until 1976, when he finally managed to secure the district.

The 13th was brand-new for the 1972 campaign, and seven Democrats ran there. The favorite was state Sen. Lee Weissenborn, a liberal state legislator who had sponsored handgun control and a state kindergarten system.

Weissenborn finished first in the primary with 27.3 percent of the vote, but Lehman, who had gone from his successful auto business to the chairmanship of the Dade County School Board, forced a runoff by drawing 20.3 percent.

---

**13th District: Northern Miami and suburbs.** Population: 586,114 (29% increase since 1970). Race: White 409,616 (70%), Black 152,234 (26%), Others 24,264 (4%). Spanish origin: 134,624 (23%).

---

**259**

## William Lehman, D-Fla.

Lehman, more centrist than Weissenborn by reputation, said he would work in Congress for higher Social Security benefits and better rapid transit. He surprised many Democrats by winning the runoff easily with 57.1 percent of the vote. His general election victory was comfortable, although no runaway.

In 1974, Lehman was thrown into a primary runoff against Dade County Commissioner Joyce Goldberg. But as in 1972, he showed surprising strength in the second round, winning by more than 2-to-1.

The 1976 Democratic primary was also crowded, but Lehman won without a runoff and overwhelmed a Republican in the general election. That pretty much ended the serious opposi-

tion. In 1980, Republican attorney Alvin Entin mounted a highly visible campaign with help from the Moral Majority. Some conservative Protestants voted for him, but most of the district's Jewish vote went to Lehman, and he won 75 percent.

**The District:** The 13th is composed of the northern tip of Miami and portions of suburban communities like Hialeah, North Miami and North Miami Beach. It also takes in a bit of southern Broward County, with a large condominium bloc.

The Jewish population is sizable and politically active. Many residents are middle-income, retired citizens from the urban Northeast who maintain their lifelong Democratic voting habits.

## Committees

**Appropriations** (23rd of 33 Democrats)
District of Columbia; Foreign Operations; Transportation.

## Elections

**1980 General**

| | |
|---|---|
| William Lehman (D) | 127,828 (75%) |
| Alvin Entin (R) | 42,830 (25%) |

**1978 General**

| | |
|---|---|
| William Lehman (D ) | Unopposed |

**Previous Winning Percentages**

1976 (78%)    1974 (100%)    1972 (62%)

**District Vote For President**

| | 1980 | | 1976 | | 1972 |
|---|---|---|---|---|---|
| **D** | 95,384 (50%) | **D** | 130,354 (66%) | **D** | 72,957 (44%) |
| **R** | 79,330 (42%) | **R** | 65,887 (33%) | **R** | 91,015 (55%) |
| **I** | 15,235 (8%) | | | | |

## Campaign Finance

| | Receipts | Receipts from PACs | Expenditures |
|---|---|---|---|
| **1980** | | | |
| Lehman (D) | $246,065 | $52,700 (21%) | $208,900 |
| Entin (R) | $63,434 | $5,354 (8%) | $63,434 |
| **1978** | | | |
| Lehman (D) | $109,179 | $21,150 (19%) | $70,087 |

## Voting Studies

| | Presidential Support | | Party Unity | | Conservative Coalition | |
|---|---|---|---|---|---|---|
| | **S** | **O** | **S** | **O** | **S** | **O** |
| **Year** | | | | | | |
| **1980** | 79 | 12 | 91 | 6† | 18 | 77† |

| | **S** | **O** | **S** | **O** | **S** | **O** |
|---|---|---|---|---|---|---|
| 1979 | 81 | 14 | 89 | 6† | 15 | 81† |
| 1978 | 63 | 13 | 74 | 10 | 13 | 69 |
| 1977 | 75 | 19 | 84 | 9 | 11 | 81 |
| 1976 | 29 | 63 | 77 | 8 | 16 | 69 |
| 1975 | 31 | 65 | 84 | 7 | 11 | 80† |
| 1974 (Ford) | 44 | 37 | | | | |
| 1974 | 36 | 49 | 78 | 7† | 6 | 77† |
| 1973 | 29 | 63 | 86 | 8 | 16 | 80 |

S = Support          O = Opposition

†Not eligible for all recorded votes.

## Key Votes

**96th Congress**

| | |
|---|---|
| Weaken Carter oil profits tax (1979) | N |
| Reject hospital cost control plan (1979) | N |
| Implement Panama Canal Treaties (1979) | Y |
| Establish Department of Education (1979) | Y |
| Approve Anti-busing Amendment (1979) | N |
| Guarantee Chrysler Corp. loans (1979) | ? |
| Approve military draft registration (1980) | Y |
| Aid Sandinista regime in Nicaragua (1980) | Y |
| Strengthen fair housing laws (1980) | Y |

**97th Congress**

| | |
|---|---|
| Reagan budget proposal (1981) | N |

## Interest Group Ratings

| Year | ADA | ACA | AFL-CIO | CCUS |
|---|---|---|---|---|
| 1980 | 83 | 17 | 72 | 61 |
| 1979 | 89 | 8 | 80 | 17 |
| 1978 | 80 | 12 | 85 | 31 |
| 1977 | 80 | 8 | 78 | 29 |
| 1976 | 80 | 4 | 82 | 21 |
| 1975 | 95 | 8 | 100 | 19 |
| 1974 | 78 | 7 | 91 | 0 |
| 1973 | 76 | 8 | 90 | 20 |

# 14 Claude Pepper (D)

**Of Miami — Elected 1962**
Also served in U.S. Senate, 1936-51.

**Born:** Sept. 8, 1900, Chambers County, Ala.
**Education:** U. of Ala., A.B. 1921; Harvard U., LL.B. 1924.
**Profession:** Lawyer.
**Family:** Widowed.
**Religion:** Baptist.
**Political Career:** Fla. House, 1929-31; U.S. Senate, 1936-51; unsuccessfully sought Democratic nomination to U.S. Senate, 1934, 1958; unsuccessfully sought renomination to U.S. Senate, 1950.

**In Washington:** Age drives many politicians to the right and a few to the left, but it has hardly seemed to change Pepper at all. He is the same crusading liberal at 81 that he was as a freshman in the U.S. Senate at 36. Then the cause was Roosevelt and the New Deal; now it is the rights of the elderly. But all the emotion and intensity are still there.

In May of 1981, when President Reagan proposed massive cuts in Social Security benefits, Pepper called them "nothing more than a wholesale assault on the economic security of America's elderly population." Against the prevailing winds, he had already introduced his own new legislation aimed at maintaining benefits. He would create a new private pension system to add on to Social Security.

Pepper is not only the oldest member of the House, he is chairman of its Select Committee on the Aging. That panel writes no legislation, but it gives Pepper a chance to generate constant media coverage, especially through investigations of those he feels are preying upon the elderly, like unscrupulous insurance salesmen or nursing home operators.

And the publicity sometimes leads to legislation later on. In 1978, Pepper pushed through a bill raising the mandatory retirement age from 65 to 70 for workers in private industry, and banning mandatory retirement altogether for some federal workers.

Not all the crusades move a majority of members. Pepper lost out in the 96th Congress on efforts to lift age ceilings for pilots and to block a cut in disability benefits. But he is always willing to come back for another fight.

For all his energy and zeal, Pepper these days is most interesting as a reminder of the political past. His florid speeches reflect the turn-of-the-century rural South that produced him rather than the Miami district he now represents. His legislative influence is less now than it was in the Senate 40 years ago.

He was called a "fighting cock" then, and took the lead in castigating those who were not so staunch in supporting New Deal programs. He cosponsored repeal of the poll tax, even though Florida at the time was very much a Deep South state, hostile to racial change.

In the late 1930s he attended a Nuremberg conference and returned convinced that war was imminent and Hitler had to be stopped. He championed the Lend-Lease program and the draft, and was hanged in effigy on the Capitol lawn by outraged mothers.

After the war he got into trouble on foreign policy. On a 19-nation tour of Europe and the Middle East, he met Joseph Stalin in Moscow, and became convinced the Russians were disarming and wanted peace. Allying himself with former Vice President Henry A. Wallace, he split with President Truman over the Marshall Plan, opposing arms shipments to Greece and Turkey. He tried to convince Dwight Eisenhower to run as a Democrat against Truman in 1948, and when that failed, briefly put up his own name.

By 1950, McCarthyism was in full swing and Pepper was being called "Red Pepper" by fellow

---

**14th District: Central Miami and suburbs.** Population: 505,623 (12% increase since 1970). Race: White 396,942 (79%), Black 73,106 (14%), Others 35,575 (7%). Spanish origin: 277,626 (55%).

## Claude Pepper, D-Fla.

Democrat George Smathers, who defeated him for renomination. It was 12 years before Pepper made it back to Washington, as representative of a Miami constituency more supportive of his liberalism.

In the early years of his second congressional career, Pepper talked most often about crime. He became convinced organized crime was penetrating private industry and that the police were being hampered by Supreme Court decisions on the rights of the accused.

He introduced a resolution to establish a crime committee in the House in 1968. It failed then, but after Richard M. Nixon was elected president on a law-and-order campaign that year, the House changed its mind, set up the committee, and made Pepper chairman.

It turned out to have a checkered history. The Crime Committee held numerous investigations, and had some legislative achievements to point to, such as a quota on the use of amphetamines for medical purposes. But it had a tendency to chase newspaper headlines, and was widely criticized for perpetuating itself to obtain publicity. It was abolished in 1974.

Meanwhile, Pepper was accumulating seniority on the Rules Committee, where he was placed in his second term as a Southerner sympathetic to national Democratic goals. Today he is next in line for the chairmanship, and is still a reliable leadership vote on most issues, although he is stubborn and independent on any issue that concerns the interests of the elderly.

For most of his House career, Pepper continued to receive substantial income from a law practice he began in the 1950s, while he was out of office. In 1977, a House commission recommended members be limited in their outside income to 15 percent of their congressional salaries. Pepper at that time was collecting more than $100,000 a year from his law firm. He bitterly fought the limit, but he lost and the code was adopted.

Later, when a financial disclosure bill came before the Rules Committee, Pepper and several other members tried to attach an amendment to repeal the income limit. They won permission to offer it on the House floor, but it did not pass. Eventually, Pepper sold his interest in his firm to other partners.

Pepper has said that when he lost his Senate seat he found himself 50 years old, unemployed and deeply in debt, and that he will never be in that position again.

But he insists he is not thinking of leaving. He has set his retirement for the year 2000, when he will be 100 years old. The only apparent concession he has made to age is to change the color of his wig from reddish brown to gray.

**At Home:** Pepper was born in rural Alabama, went to the state university, and used his undergraduate degree as a ticket to the North. He went to law school at Harvard, and moved to Florida during its 1920s boom. He began his political career in 1929 with a term in the Florida state House.

He made a first try for the Senate in 1934, narrowly missing an upset in the Democratic runoff against incumbent Park Trammell, and made it in 1936 for a two-year term to replace Sen. Duncan U. Fletcher, who died in office.

Two years later Pepper won a full term with relative ease, but as time passed his unalloyed liberalism became more of a liability. In 1944 he narrowly avoided a runoff; by 1950 the state was ready for Smathers.

The challenger took full advantage of Pepper's reputation, adding to it by using meaningless but ominous language much of his audience did not understand. He told one group in rural Florida that Pepper "is known all over Washington as a shameless extrovert," that he "has a sister who was once a thespian," and that the senator "practiced celibacy" before his marriage. Smathers won by more than 60,000 votes.

Pepper tried to return to the Senate in 1958. He ran against Sen. Spessard Holland in the Democratic primary, but Holland won 55.9 percent of the vote.

Four years later, a new district was created in Miami, and Pepper came back to win it. His activism on behalf of the elderly has made him a perfect representative for one of the highest median-age districts in the country, and he has not been seriously threatened, although the growing number of Cubans in his district has diluted his traditional base of support.

Since 1972, Republicans have drawn their candidates from the district's expanding, mostly conservative Cuban community. Evelio S. Estrella, a Cuban immigrant active in local GOP affairs, opposed Pepper in 1972, 1976 and 1980, though he has never won as much as a third of the vote. Pepper's most serious challenge came in 1978 from Al Cardenas, a young Cuban-born attorney far more fluent in English than Estrella. Even Cardenas, however, was unable to reach 40 percent against Pepper.

**The District:** The 14th includes most of Miami itself, the central and northern parts of Miami Beach, and the city's western suburbs. The economy is service-oriented, based on tourism and retailing.

The Cuban and Latin American influx has

been responsible for the modest growth that has occurred in the 14th since 1970. Jews and blacks have traditionally been the most important political forces in the district, but the Hispanics are changing that, even though the turnout in the Hispanic community is still small. Richard M.

Nixon won this district comfortably in 1972, but four years later Jimmy Carter brought together blacks and Jewish voters to win 55.7 percent. By 1980, many of the district's elderly Jews were dissatisfied with Carter, and they helped Reagan carry the 14th with nearly 55 percent of the vote.

## Committees

**Select Aging** (Chairman)
    Health and Long-Term Care, chairman.

**Rules** (2nd of 11 Democrats)
    Rules of the House.

## Elections

**1980 General**

| | |
|---|---|
| Claude Pepper (D) | 95,820 (75%) |
| Evelio Estrella (R) | 32,027 (25%) |

**1980 Primary**

| | |
|---|---|
| Claude Pepper (D) | 26,800 (79%) |
| Douglas MacKenzie (D) | 7,012 (20%) |

**1978 General**

| | |
|---|---|
| Claude Pepper (D) | 65,202 (63%) |
| Al Cardenas (R) | 38,081 (37%) |

**Previous Winning Percentages**

| | | | |
|---|---|---|---|
| 1976 (73%) | 1974 (70%) | 1972 (68%) | 1970 (100%) |
| 1968 (77%) | 1966 (100%) | 1964 (66%) | 1962 (58%) |
| 1944*(71%) | 1938*(83%) | 1936†(100%) | |

*Senate election, † Special Senate election.*

**District Vote For President**

| | 1980 | | 1976 | | 1972 |
|---|---|---|---|---|---|
| D | 50,720 (39%) | D | 76,357 (56%) | D | 50,458 (42%) |
| R | 73,590 (55%) | R | 58,863 (43%) | R | 70,005 (58%) |
| I | 9,211 (7%) | | | | |

## Campaign Finance

| | Receipts | Receipts from PACs | Expenditures |
|---|---|---|---|
| **1980** | | | |
| Pepper (D) | $158,713 | $59,700 (38%) | $211,659 |
| Estrella (R) | $50,451 | — (0%) | $50,620 |
| **1978** | | | |
| Pepper (D) | $242,260 | $80,600 (33%) | $239,864 |
| Cardenas (R) | $243,568 | $21,774 (9%) | $242,131 |

## Voting Studies

| | Presidential Support | | Party Unity | | Conservative Coalition | |
|---|---|---|---|---|---|---|
| Year | S | O | S | O | S | O |
| 1980 | 65 | 10 | 77 | 5† | 20 | 64† |
| 1979 | 57 | 11 | 67 | 3 | 15 | 57 |
| 1978 | 67 | 17 | 77 | 9 | 18 | 70 |
| 1977 | 62 | 19 | 73 | 9 | 22 | 60 |

| Year | | | | | | |
|---|---|---|---|---|---|---|
| 1976 | 18 | 37 | 49 | 8 | 15 | 45 |
| 1975 | 38 | 48 | 78 | 10† | 22 | 67 |
| 1974 (Ford) | 39 | 52 | | | | |
| 1974 | 60 | 32 | 75 | 15 | 32 | 56 |
| 1973 | 28 | 59 | 79 | 7 | 20 | 68 |
| 1972 | 65 | 27 | 61 | 12 | 26 | 56 |
| 1971 | 61 | 32 | 69 | 16 | 33 | 58 |
| 1970 | 48 | 25 | 68 | 7 | 18 | 45 |
| 1969 | 47 | 26 | 64 | 5 | 22 | 53 |
| 1968 | 62 | 9 | 62 | 7 | 16 | 57 |
| 1967 | 76 | 6 | 83 | 1 | 19 | 67 |
| 1966 | 81 | 5 | 95 | 0 | 5 | 89 |
| 1965 | 86 | 3 | 90 | 2 | 8 | 86 |
| 1964 | 87 | 2 | 84 | 0 | 17 | 75 |
| 1963 | 86 | 4 | 93 | 0 | 13 | 67 |

S = Support        O = Opposition

*† Not eligible for all recorded votes.*

## Key Votes

**96th Congress**

| | |
|---|---|
| Weaken Carter oil profits tax (1979) | N |
| Reject hospital cost control plan (1979) | N |
| Implement Panama Canal Treaties (1979) | Y |
| Establish Department of Education (1979) | Y |
| Approve Anti-busing Amendment (1979) | N |
| Guarantee Chrysler Corp. loans (1979) | Y |
| Approve military draft registration (1980) | ? |
| Aid Sandinista regime in Nicaragua (1980) | Y |
| Strengthen fair housing laws (1980) | Y |

**97th Congress**

| | |
|---|---|
| Reagan budget proposal (1981) | N |

## Interest Group Ratings

| Year | ADA | ACA | AFL-CIO | CCUS |
|---|---|---|---|---|
| 1980 | 61 | 19 | 95 | 74 |
| 1979 | 58 | 5 | 79 | 17 |
| 1978 | 50 | 12 | 90 | 28 |
| 1977 | 55 | 8 | 86 | 6 |
| 1976 | 50 | 13 | 89 | 18 |
| 1975 | 58 | 19 | 95 | 25 |
| 1974 | 43 | 15 | 100 | 10 |
| 1973 | 56 | 9 | 100 | 27 |
| 1972 | 50 | 30 | 89 | 10 |
| 1971 | 57 | 8 | 100 | - |
| 1970 | 56 | 13 | 83 | 30 |
| 1969 | 47 | 9 | 87 | - |
| 1968 | 75 | 0 | 100 | - |
| 1967 | 67 | 4 | 100 | 10 |
| 1966 | 88 | 0 | 100 | - |
| 1965 | 74 | 4 | - | 10 |
| 1964 | 84 | 0 | 91 | - |
| 1963 | - | 0 | - | - |

# 15 Dante B. Fascell (D)

**Of Miami — Elected 1954**

**Born:** March 9, 1917, Bridgehampton, N.Y.
**Education:** U. of Miami, J.D. 1938.
**Military Career:** Army, 1941-46.
**Profession:** Lawyer.
**Family:** Wife, Jeanne-Marie Pelot; three children.
**Religion:** Protestant.
**Political Career:** Fla. House, 1951-55.

**In Washington:** Fascell has always been an impatient man, easily frustrated at the slow pace of House business and niceties of floor debate. He likes to cut through the rhetoric, get to the point of an argument, outline a compromise, and move on to the next issue.

But he is one of the most effective operators within the system that frustrates him. Shrewd and combative, he is one of the most respected of veteran Democrats, a small man who can be loud and tough when he wants to. In the days when Wayne Hays of Ohio was the House bully, Fascell faced him down in a cloakroom shouting match over a campaign finance bill.

Most of Fascell's efforts, however, are directed toward foreign policy. As the Foreign Affairs Committee's senior expert on Latin America, he has been an aggressive anti-communist, vehement in opposing anyone who suggests that the U.S. move toward close relations with the Castro regime in Cuba. Many of Fascell's constituents are exiled Cubans who have fled the Castro government.

But Fascell has not uniformly opposed U.S. friendship toward leftist governments in Latin America. He has argued that we can "no longer blindly support" dictators such as Nicaragua's now-deposed Anastasio Somoza, and that it is not helpful to see revolutionary change only in terms of a creeping "red menace." In 1980, in spite of some opposition in his district, he supported U.S. assistance to the leftist Sandinista regime that had ousted Somoza.

"It's so easy to hate communists," he has said, "to say we don't do business with communists. But it gives us no chance. We better try to do something before it gets to that state."

In the mid-70s, Fascell chaired the Foreign Affairs subcommittee dealing with Latin America; he gave up that panel in 1977 to head one with direct jurisdiction over the State Department. But he has remained the dominant presence on Latin American issues.

Fascell has been strongly allied with his committee's human rights approach of recent years, but has been more insistent than some members on applying it to the Soviet Union. He serves as chairman of the Helsinki Commission, set up by Congress to monitor compliance with earlier agreements governing East-West relations in Europe.

In the past two years, Fascell has spent much of his time trying to deal with the impact of Cuban and Haitian newcomers in Florida. In 1980, he added an amendment to the foreign aid authorization bill giving state and local governments extra funds to replace tax money used to care for their refugees. Technically, Fascell's amendment had no business in the foreign aid bill (some colleagues privately derided it as "foreign aid for Miami"), but Fascell pushed it anyway and won some relief from the financial pressure on south Florida governments.

Outside foreign policy, Fascell has specialized in changing House procedures he has considered less than modern.

He spent a decade lobbying to open House committee meetings to the public. It was his amendment, adopted by the Democratic Caucus in 1973, which required the sessions to be open unless a committee voted in public to close them. Later he moved successfully for the opening of House-Senate conferences.

> **15th District: South Miami and suburbs.** Population: 644,764 (43% increase since 1970). Race: White 558,489 (86%), Black 63,258 (10%), Others 25,017 (4%). Spanish origin: 177,767 (27%).

As a member of the Government Operations Committee, he played a key role in enactment of legislation which opened executive agency meetings to the public. Long before it was required by law, he issued his own personal financial disclosure — one that included such facts as his part-ownership of a horse that ran in the Kentucky Derby. He is still arguing for more complete disclosure of foreign travel expenses by members of Congress.

During recent terms on Government Operations, Fascell backed a federal Consumer Protection Agency and a new Department of Education. Earlier in his career, in 1965, he managed the legislation that created the Department of Housing and Urban Development.

During the Nixon era, Fascell used his membership on both Government Operations and Foreign Affairs to oppose what he saw as usurpation of power by the president. He helped write the War Powers Act, defining a congressional role in the commitment of U.S. troops abroad, and sponsored a bill curbing the use of executive privilege. In 1973, presiding over the House, he cast the deciding vote in a 206-205 decision making it easier for Congress to force the executive branch to spend appropriated funds.

Fascell also has a strong law and order streak. He had little sympathy for the peace demonstrators or urban rioters of the 1960s. He sponsored legislation setting stiff penalties for inciting a riot. He has favored the death penalty for hijackers.

Over the years, Fascell has done more than his share of lobbying for federal help for his district and state. He has moved to get federal money to stop beach erosion, assist the Florida lobster industry, and help Florida tomato growers faced with competition from Mexico.

**At Home:** Like many of the people he represents, Fascell is not a native Southerner. He was brought to Florida from Long Island by his parents when was eight, and got his law degree from the University of Miami before leaving to fight in World War II.

After the war, he used the Dade County Young Democrats and the Italian-American club as an entry into politics, then ran for the state Legislature in 1950.

Four years later, U.S. Rep. William Lantaff announced his retirement. With the slogan "Ring the bell for Dante Fascell," the 37-year-old lawyer won a majority in the five-man primary, and was unopposed in the general election.

His first significant challenge was in 1962, from Democratic state Rep. David C. Eldredge, a segregationist. Eldredge criticized Fascell as a consistent supporter of an intrusive federal government and hinted that the incumbent was sympathetic to communism.

When President Kennedy spoke at a Democratic fund-raiser in Miami Beach, he made a point of endorsing Fascell. That hurt Eldredge; he protested Kennedy's intervention, but faded to receive only 35.3 percent of the primary vote.

In the 1966 and 1968 elections, Fascell was attacked equally hard by Republican Mike Thompson, a journalist and advertising agent. Thompson criticized Fascell's proposal to convert an offshore island to a national monument, arguing that the island's potential to generate tax revenue should not be relinquished to the federal government.

Thompson won 43.1 percent of the vote in 1966 and was given a chance to defeat Fascell two years later. But he was unable to improve on his first showing.

Fascell won without difficulty in 1970, and his 1972 Republican foe, lawyer Ellis Rubin, was written off as a perennial office-seeker who had been unsuccessful in a half-dozen campaigns for state and local office. But Rubin attracted attention by campaiging against busing and promised to end television blackouts of local football games. To the surprise of many, he won 43.2 percent of the vote, holding Fascell to the lowest percentage of his career.

In his past four re-election campaigns, Fascell has won with the ease expected of a veteran incumbent. His Republican opponent in 1978 and 1980, Herbert J. Hoodwin, did not reach 35 percent of the vote.

**The District:** From his first election until redistricting in 1962, Fascell represented the most populous congressional district in the country — more than a million people in Dade and Monroe counties at Florida's southern tip. That district was a blend of Miami urban and Everglades rural, with significant concentrations of blacks, Jews and Cubans.

The 15th still includes all of Monroe County and most of Dade, but much of Miami and Miami Beach have been transferred to adjoining districts. Downtown Miami's office and commercial buildings remain in the 15th, plus the southern tip of Miami Beach, a poor section filled with elderly people who depend on Social Security checks to make ends meet.

The district now is mostly suburban, although it includes poor and middle-class black neighborhoods and a large Cuban community as well as affluent residential areas. Fascell still has some farm constituents, too, around the southern Dade County towns of Homestead and Florida City.

## Committees

**Foreign Affairs** (3rd of 21 Democrats)
International Operations, chairman; International Security and Scientific Affairs.

**Government Operations** (3rd of 23 Democrats)
Legislation and National Security.

## Elections

**1980 General**

| | |
|---|---|
| Dante Fascell (D) | 132,952 (65%) |
| Herbert Hoodwin (R) | 70,433 (35%) |

**1978 General**

| | |
|---|---|
| Dante Fascell (D) | 108,837 (74%) |
| Herbert Hoodwin (R) | 37,897 (26%) |

**Previous Winning Percentages**

| | | | |
|---|---|---|---|
| 1976 (70%) | 1974 (71%) | 1972 (57%) | 1970 (72%) |
| 1968 (57%) | 1966 (57%) | 1964 (64%) | 1962 (65%) |
| 1954 100%) | 1956 (61%) | 1958 (100%) | 1960 (71%) |

**District Vote For President**

| | 1980 | | 1976 | | 1972 |
|---|---|---|---|---|---|
| D | 73,306 (34%) | D | 108,295 (53%) | D | 60,483 (37%) |
| R | 119,415 (55%) | R | 91,053 (45%) | R | 104,864 (63%) |
| I | 21,491 (10%) | | | | |

## Campaign Finance

| | Receipts | Receipts from PACs | Expenditures |
|---|---|---|---|
| **1980** | | | |
| Fascell (D) | $61,032 | $13,475 (22%) | $73,971 |
| Hoodwin (R) | $19,418 | $600 (3%) | $18,606 |
| **1978** | | | |
| Fascell (D) | $48,499 | $9,825 (20%) | $47,724 |
| Hoodwin (R) | $70,066 | $5,800 (8%) | $69,590 |

## Voting Studies

| | Presidential Support | | Party Unity | | Conservative Coalition | |
|---|---|---|---|---|---|---|
| **Year** | **S** | **O** | **S** | **O** | **S** | **O** |
| 1980 | 86 | 9 | 90 | 6 | 21 | 75 |
| 1979 | 83 | 11 | 89 | 6 | 18 | 73 |
| 1978 | 78 | 13 | 88 | 6 | 14 | 80 |
| 1977 | 78 | 18 | 90 | 8 | 14 | 85 |
| 1976 | 25 | 69 | 91 | 6 | 17 | 80 |
| 1975 | 40 | 57 | 85 | 12 | 17 | 81 |
| 1974 (Ford) | 50 | 50 | | | | |
| 1974 | 49 | 47 | 87 | 11 | 23 | 77 |
| 1973 | 31 | 64 | 89 | 8 | 17 | 80 |
| 1972 | 62 | 32 | 84 | 12 | 20 | 76 |
| 1971 | 47 | 47 | 80 | 14 | 20 | 76 |
| 1970 | 58 | 32 | 68 | 17 | 16 | 57 |
| 1969 | 32 | 19 | 44 | 7 | 16 | 47 |
| 1968 | 82 | 10 | 70 | 11 | 29 | 59 |
| 1967 | 87 | 6 | 90 | 4 | 30 | 65 |
| 1966 | 93 | 4 | 99 | 0 | 8 | 92 |
| 1965 | 93 | 5 | 92 | 5 | 16 | 84 |
| 1964 | 92 | 8 | 94 | 5 | 17 | 75 |
| 1963 | 84 | 4 | 83 | 3 | 27 | 60 |
| 1962 | 67 | 15 | 70 | 11 | 31 | 56 |
| 1961 | 82 | 12 | 74 | 17 | 43 | 43 |

S = Support          O = Opposition

## Key Votes

**96th Congress**

| | |
|---|---|
| Weaken Carter oil profits tax (1979) | N |
| Reject hospital cost control plan (1979) | N |
| Implement Panama Canal Treaties (1979) | Y |
| Establish Department of Education (1979) | Y |
| Approve Anti-busing Amendment (1979) | N |
| Guarantee Chrysler Corp. loans (1979) | Y |
| Approve military draft registration (1980) | Y |
| Aid Sandinista regime in Nicaragua (1980) | Y |
| Strengthen fair housing laws (1980) | Y |

**97th Congress**

| | |
|---|---|
| Reagan budget proposal (1981) | N |

## Interest Group Ratings

| Year | ADA | ACA | AFL-CIO | CCUS |
|---|---|---|---|---|
| 1980 | 83 | 25 | 83 | 59 |
| 1979 | 74 | 4 | 68 | 18 |
| 1978 | 65 | 17 | 85 | 29 |
| 1977 | 80 | 8 | 78 | 12 |
| 1976 | 75 | 4 | 77 | 20 |
| 1975 | 89 | 11 | 95 | 25 |
| 1974 | 87 | 13 | 100 | 0 |
| 1973 | 88 | 7 | 91 | 27 |
| 1972 | 81 | 17 | 91 | 11 |
| 1971 | 81 | 8 | 82 | 9 |
| 1970 | 56 | 17 | 86 | 30 |
| 1969 | 53 | 13 | 89 | - |
| 1968 | 75 | 4 | 75 | - |
| 1967 | 60 | 0 | 83 | 10 |
| 1966 | 76 | 4 | 92 | - |
| 1965 | 63 | 7 | - | 20 |
| 1964 | 76 | 11 | 82 | - |
| 1963 | - | 0 | - | - |
| 1962 | 63 | 39 | 91 | - |
| 1961 | 70 | - | - | - |

# Georgia

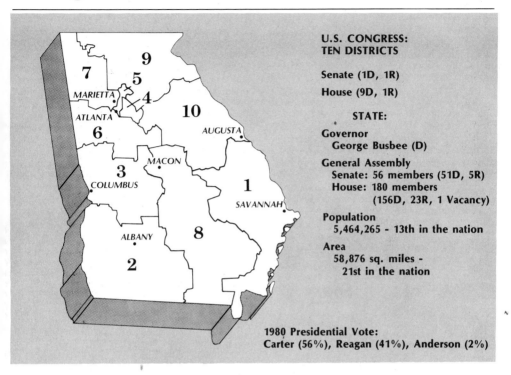

**U.S. CONGRESS:
TEN DISTRICTS**

Senate (1D, 1R)

House (9D, 1R)

**STATE:**

Governor
George Busbee (D)

General Assembly
Senate: 56 members (51D, 5R)
House: 180 members
(156D, 23R, 1 Vacancy)

Population
5,464,265 - 13th in the nation

Area
58,876 sq. miles -
21st in the nation

1980 Presidential Vote:
Carter (56%), Reagan (41%), Anderson (2%)

## ...Carter's Accomplishment

Whatever history finally says about Jimmy Carter's role in American politics, it will mark him as a significant figure in his home state, the governor who all but eliminated race as an overt political issue. Succeeding segregationist Lester Maddox, who gained fame by brandishing ax handles to drive away black customers from his chicken restaurant, Carter is the symbol of modern times in Georgia politics.

"The time for racial discrimination is over," Carter declared at his gubernatorial inauguration. He went on to hang a portrait of Martin Luther King Jr. in the statehouse and appoint blacks to high positions in Georgia government.

Ten years later, when he returned home after one term in the White House, Carter found his state governed by a moderate Democrat, George Busbee, with a world view not too different from his own. He also found signs of the Republican breakthrough that was aborted in the Maddox

and Carter years.

The Republican Party has had an unusual history in modern Georgia. Resentful over the civil rights policies of the Kennedy and Johnson administrations, the state voted for Barry Goldwater in 1964 and elected Republican Howard (Bo) Callaway to Congress. Two years later, Callaway actually won a plurality of the vote for governor, but since he did not have a majority, the contest was thrown into the Legislature, and Maddox was elected. Also in 1966, two Republicans won House seats in the Atlanta area.

That seemed to presage a Republican awakening like the one taking place in other Southern states. But it took awhile longer for Republicans to take advantage of their opening. The growing black vote aided Democratic candidates. Rural and small town whites, a large bloc in a state of five million people, tended to hold fast to the party of their ancestors. And native son Jimmy

**267**

Carter's rise to national prominence within the Democratic Party kept many Georgians loyal to their traditional party.

Republican Rep. Fletcher Thompson was beaten in his 1972 Senate try by Democrat Sam Nunn. Watergate did grave damage to the GOP, and by 1974, the party was in dreadful shape. Its Senate and gubernatorial candidates failed to draw more than 30 percent of the vote, and it lost its only House seat, in suburban Atlanta.

But there are signs of change once more. Republican Newt Gingrich again gave the GOP a seat in Georgia's U.S. House delegation in 1978, and in 1980, Mack Mattingly won the most important prize. He unseated the state's senior senator, Herman E. Talmadge, who had been formally "denounced" by the Senate for financial improprieties. The influx of Northerners, especially businessmen, made itself felt more and more as the decade advanced. Taking advantage of votes in suburban Atlanta and the state's other growing urban areas, Mattingly edged Talmadge even though Carter was managing to carry his home state at the presidential level.

# A Political Tour

**Atlanta Area.** The heavy traffic in and out of the huge Atlanta Airport testifies to the role the city plays in the Sun Belt.

Ravaged by the Civil War, Atlanta quickly sprang back to become an early center of trade and commerce in the South, home to Coca-Cola, Delta Airlines and other big corporations. Business people — not an old-line aristocracy — have been the power brokers of modern-day Atlanta.

Atlanta' business and trade outlook imbued it with a spirit of political moderation. Under Mayor Ivan Allen in the 1960s, the city escaped many of the racial troubles found elsewhere in the South and gave itself the booster-ish title: "The City Too Busy to Hate."

Since 1970, Atlanta has had a black majority. In 1972, it elected Andrew Young as the Deep South's first black congressman in the 20th century. In 1973, it elected its first black mayor, Maynard Jackson. It is the city of Martin Luther King Jr. and the largest center of black higher education in the world.

It is also a city that in recent years has had to live with a reputation for random violence and with the string of murders of black children that brought national attention in 1980 and 1981.

Blacks live in the southern part of the city. The northern end of Atlanta is wealthy, white and generally Republican. The city lost 14 percent of its overall population, and 43 percent of the white population, during the 1970s.

Meanwhile, the Atlanta suburbs lead the state in population growth. Gwinnett, Rockdale and Fayette counties, once small agricultural counties on the outer fringes of the Atlanta area, more than doubled in population from 1970 to 1980. Office complexes have sprung up around I-285, the beltway ringing Atlanta, bringing white-collar jobs closer to those living in the suburbs.

Blacks predominate in the some suburbs of southern Fulton County, and blue-collar whites live near the airport, also south of the city. But other parts of suburban Fulton County are affluent and very Republican. Communities such as Sandy Springs and Roswell north of Atlanta vote Republican in line with the suburbs of Cobb, Douglas, Fayette, Clayton, DeKalb, Rockdale and Gwinnett counties. In 1980, Reagan carried all of those counties save DeKalb, and Republican Mattingly won every county in the Atlanta area — including Fulton — in his narrow victory over veteran Democrat Talmadge.

The strongest Republican areas ring Atlanta on the north. In Cobb and Gwinnett, Mattingly topped Talmadge by better than 2-to-1. Cobb County, the site of a large Lockheed aircraft plant, is the home of many engineers and other technical people. They have elected Republicans to many local offices, still an unfamiliar habit even in other areas of suburban Atlanta.

**Black Belt.** Across the broad mid-section of the state runs flat country that once was Plantation Georgia. Later, tenant farmers toiled there. And still later, it was the starting place for much of the black migration to the North.

But today, the exodus has slowed, and in some places, reversed. For instance, Peach County, one of 18 in the region with a black majority, grew by 20 percent in the 1970s.

Agriculture still dominates the economic activity of the Black Belt, where Carter's famed peanuts and cotton are the dominant crops. In black-majority Washington County, the extraction of white clay, used in printing, fine china and pill casings, is the main industry.

Until the Voting Rights Act of 1965, white minorities in some counties controlled the politics of the area. In 1968, black candidates took over Hancock County government, and black participation has increased since then throughout the area. In 1968, Macon's white mayor, Ronnie Thompson, told a policeman half-jokingly that he should have test-fired his submachinegun in the black neighborhoods. Since then, blacks have won a third of the Macon's council seats and helped elect a sympathetic white mayor.

The Democratic primary is still the election that counts in most parts of the Black Belt, but pockets of Republican strength exist. Managers brought in with new industries clustered around Macon, along with the community around Robins Air Force Base, have made one such pocket in Bibb County.

There is also some Republican strength in Muscogee County (Columbus) and Richmond County (Augusta), on opposite sides of the state. Mattingly carried both counties in 1980, thanks largely to the Republican-oriented military populations in both areas. Columbus, an old textile town, is near the basic training center in Fort Benning, also the location of many Army schools.

**South Georgia.** This is redneck Georgia, the home of former Gov. Eugene Talmadge's "wool hats" and the area where George Wallace performed his best in 1968.

Other than 1968 and the McGovern year of 1972, this section of the state stays in the Democratic column. In 1980, Carter took everything here, except for Lowndes County (Valdosta), which has Moody Air Force Base.

Republicans do their best in the coastal counties. Mattingly captured Savannah (Chatham County) and the plush St. Simons Island resort area (Glynn County). But usually, conservative Democrats prevail along the coast.

Best known outside the state for its colonial elegance, Savannah is a strongly unionized port city which has traditionally yielded a moderate Democratic vote. It was the only area of any size outside of Atlanta to go for Humphrey in 1968.

**North Georgia.** This is the Appalachian end of the state, where moonshine and mountain Republicans can still be found. James Dickey set his novel about the isolated hill people, *Deliverance*, in North Georgia.

Textiles are an important industry, and their arrival led to an influx of Northern managers who vote Republican, joining natives of the area who had been doing that since the Civil War. As a result, Republicans have historically been stronger here than in any other region in the state. But they have not been strong enough, at least until recently, to elect many candidate beyond the individual county level. The mountain-based 9th District has often elected Democrats to the House in the 20th century.

Reagan won four of the north Georgia counties along the Tennessee border. Six of the 10 counties Nixon captured from Wallace in 1968 were in north Georgia.

# Redrawing the Lines

Georgia's population grew by 19 percent in the past decade. That was not enough to give it an additional seat in Congress, but more than enough to require noticeable shifts in district boundaries.

The fastest-growing counties are clustered in north Georgia. Except for a few counties, growth in south Georgia did not keep pace with the statewide average. The only north Georgia district that is far short of the new ideal population is Atlanta's 5th, in which blacks now constitute a slight majority.

At midyear, many redistricting options were being discussed, but no consensus had emerged.

# Governor
# George Busbee (D)

**Born:** Aug. 7, 1927, Vienna, Ga.
**Home:** Albany, Ga.
**Education:** U. of Georgia, B.B.A. 1949; U. of Georgia Law School, LL.B. 1952.
**Military Career:** Navy, World War II.
**Profession:** Lawyer.
**Family:** Wife, Mary Beth; four children.
**Religion:** Baptist.
**Political Career:** Georgia House, 1957-75; assistant floor leader, 1963-65; floor leader, 1966; majority leader, 1967-75; elected governor 1974, 1978; term expires Jan. 1983.

# Sam Nunn (D)

**Of Perry — Elected 1972**

**Born:** Sept., 8, 1938, Perry, Ga.
**Education:** Emory U., A.B. 1960, LL.B. 1962.
**Military Career:** Coast Guard, 1959-60; Coast
Guard Reserve, 1960-68.
**Profession:** Lawyer, farmer.
**Family:** Wife, Colleen Ann O'Brien; two
children.
**Religion:** United Methodist.
**Political Career:** Ga. House, 1969-72.

**In Washington:** Knowledge made Nunn a
power in the Senate in a remarkably short time,
and it is maintaining him as one now that he is a
member of the minority. There is little partisan
difference of opinion about him; Republicans as
well as Democrats turn to Nunn as an authority
on military manpower, strategy, tactics and weapons. He is a strong-willed conservative without
being an ideologue, and much of his credibility
rests on his reputation for open-mindedness.

Other Democrats have lost a considerable
portion of their clout with the Republican takeover of committee and subcommittee chairmanships. Nunn's influence, however, has not depended on formal position. Even when he was in
the majority, four Democrats outranked him on
Armed Services, and three on his other panel,
Governmental Affairs.

Eventually, however seniority is likely to be
very important to Nunn. He is 24 years younger
than any of the Democrats ahead of him on
Armed Services, and assuming Democratic control of the Senate at some point in the next 20
years, Nunn is the presumptive chairman.

It was almost inevitable than Nunn would
specialize in defense. He is the grand-nephew of
the late Georgia Democrat Carl Vinson, longtime
chairman of the House Armed Services Committee, and he occupies the Senate seat once held by
the revered Sen. Richard Russell, who chaired
Senate Armed Services.

Nunn did not leave the matter of committee
assignments to chance when he came to Washington. He teamed up with his great-uncle Vinson,
then retired, and visited all the major Senate
power brokers, starting with then-Armed Services
Chairman John Stennis, D-Miss. Nunn got the
Armed Services assignment he wanted, and he
also made a favorable impression on Stennis and
Sen. Henry Jackson, D-Wash., another senior
committee member. Both men helped Nunn along
over the years.

Within the committee, Nunn soon began
warning of the need for more attention and more
spending on national defense. During the Carter
years, he consistently raised the issue of massive
Soviet military preparations, and in 1979 he was
in the vanguard of those who demanded and got a
commitment from Carter for substantially increased military expenditures over the next five
years.

That commitment was a part of the price
Nunn sought as he weighed a decision on the now-
derailed strategic arms limitation treaty, SALT
II. The Georgia Democrat had helped Carter
enormously in 1978 by supporting the unpopular
Panama Canal treaties, and he was seen by many
as the crucial undecided vote on SALT. It was
thought that his vote — whether for or against —
would sway a significant number of others who
were uncommitted. As it happened, the treaty was
withdrawn in the wake of the Soviet invasion of
Afghanistan, and Nunn never declared his intentions. But he repeatedly insisted that the United
States needed to undertake a major arms buildup
with or without a SALT II treaty, both in its
strategic arsenal and in its conventional forces.

Nunn is probably the most forceful and persistent critic of the volunteer army and lobbyist
for a return to the draft. He would revamp
conscription procedures to eliminate past inequities, but he is convinced the current army could
not win a war if forced into one, and could not
easily be expanded at a time of crisis. "Present
military manpower problems are so severe," Nunn
said in 1979, "that our armed forces would not be
capable of meeting a national security emergency
that required a rapid, major increase in present
force levels."

The senator has repeatedly used the Pentagon's own data to demonstrate the recruitment
and retention problems of the volunteer Army,

and has scolded both the Carter and Reagan administrations for failing to face up to the issue. He concedes there is no consensus in favor of resuming the draft, but says, "You don't get consensus in this country until you get leadership."

President Reagan's defense views are more to Nunn's liking than Carter's were, but Nunn has quarreled with some of the specifics of the proposed Reagan military buildup and warned the Pentagon to be realistic in estimating the costs — or risk a loss of public support. "What is going to happen to the consensus built on defense when, six or eight months from now, this budget goes straight up?" Nunn asked Defense Secretary Caspar Weinberger at the start of the 97th Congress.

Nunn tends to see public policy issues in a long-range perspective, and to worry about the pressure to make decisions based on short-term political considerations. "We're in for a long, long tedious relationship with the Soviet Union," he warned after a 1978 trip to Moscow. He was one of the first in Congress to urge the sale of military-related items to the People's Republic of China, arguing that "a China strong enough to resist Soviet expansion and domination is in the interest of the United States."

In recent years, Nunn has been branching out beyond defense issues more than he did in his first term. He drafted an alternative version of the Kemp-Roth tax bill, one which called for substantial tax cuts but tied them to spending restraints. This measure passed the Senate in 1978 but died in conference with the House.

Nunn generally votes with business and against organized labor on economic and tax issues, although with occasional exceptions — such as his 1979 vote in favor of a windfall profits tax on oil. He votes with most Southern Democrats and against his party's majority on social issues, but there are some departures here too. He supported full voting representation in Congress for the District of Columbia, and votes against restrictions on federal funding of abortions.

Although he was on cordial terms with fellow Georgian Jimmy Carter, Nunn was never close to him; he won his Senate seat in 1972 by defeating the man then-Gov. Carter had appointed to it. Nunn was far enough to the right of Carter philosophically to be suggested by some Republicans in 1980 as a possible Reagan running mate, but the idea never went very far.

In contrast to many of his colleagues in the Senate, Nunn seems genuinely disinterested in higher office. "The legislative process has never frustrated me," he said. "I guess it depends on your expectations. I never had executive experience. My background and interests have always been in legislative matters."

**At Home:** Nunn was an ideal candidate in 1972 against David H. Gambrell, the wealthy and urbane Atlanta lawyer whom Carter named to the Senate after Russell's death. Nunn was a lawyer and state legislator himself, and not exactly poor, but his central Georgia roots allowed him to run as a old-fashioned rural Democrat, related to Carl Vinson and as suspicious of Atlanta as the rest of the state. He called Gambrell a "fake conservative" allied to Sen. George McGovern, the Democratic presidential nominee, and pursued the issue despite Gambrell's denials of any link to McGovern.

Gambrell finished first in the initial primary, but he was forced into a runoff with second-place finisher Nunn, who intensified his attacks on the incumbent, all but saying his wealthy family had bought the seat by contributing to Carter's gubernatorial campaign. It was more than enough to sink Gambrell.

The focus shifted in the general election, when Nunn encountered Republican Rep. Fletcher Thompson. This time, it was Thompson who used the McGovern issue.

But Nunn countered this by his adroit use of George C. Wallace, the governor in neighboring Alabama, who maintained high popularity in rural Georgia. Nunn journeyed to Montgomery, the Alabama capital, to receive Wallace's blessing. He said he would write in the governor's name for president.

Despite his vehement opposition to busing and "welfare loafers," Nunn also got the support of black leaders, including state Rep. Julian Bond. They figured that Nunn represented a better choice for blacks than Thompson, who they claimed had not spoken to a black audience in four years —even though 40 percent of his Atlanta district was non-white.

Further big-name help for Nunn came from Democratic Sen. Herman Talmadge, at the time an institution in state politics. Fearful that McGovern's unpopularity would tip the Senate to the Republicans and that he would lose his Agriculture Committee chairmanship, Talmadge broke his practice of campaigning only for himself, and provided critical support for Nunn in rural areas.

Another liability cropped up for Thompson when he sent out his House newsletter statewide, arousing press complaints that he had abused the frank. As a result of this flap, President Nixon omitted a public endorsement of Thompson on an Atlanta visit — an embarrassing incident for the

Republican.

Nunn ran well against Thompson in the rural counties, offsetting his opponent's strength in the Atlanta suburbs, and defeated him by 93,000 votes.

Six years later, Nunn's fiscal conservatism and support for the military had put him in such good position that no serious challenger emerged.

The luckless Republican who did take on Nunn, former U.S. Attorney John Stokes, made no headway condemning Nunn's vote for the Panama Canal treaties. Stokes had little money and ran a near-invisible campaign. Nunn's 83 percent was the highest vote any Senate candidate in the country received that fall against a major party opponent.

## Committees

**Armed Services** (5th of 8 Democrats)
Manpower and Personnel; Sea Power and Force Projection; Strategic and Theater Nuclear Forces.

**Government Affairs** (4th of 8 Democrats)
Intergovernmental Relations; Permanent Subcommittee on Investigations.

**Small Business** (Ranking Democrat)
Capital Formation and Retention.

## Elections

**1978 General**

| | |
|---|---|
| Sam Nunn (D ) | 536,320 (83 %) |
| John Stokes (R ) | 108,808 (17 %) |

**1978 Primary**

| | |
|---|---|
| Sam Nunn (D ) | 525,703 (80 %) |
| Jack Dorsey (D ) | 71,223 (11 %) |
| Other (D ) | 60,361 (9 %) |

**Previous Winning Percentage**

1972   (54%

## Campaign Finance

| | Receipts | Receipts from PACs | Expenditures |
|---|---|---|---|
| 1978 | | | |
| Nunn (D ) | $708,417 | $135,145 (19 %) | $548,814 |

## Voting Studies

| | Presidential Support | | Party Unity | | Conservative Coalition | |
|---|---|---|---|---|---|---|
| Year | S | O | S | O | S | O |
| 1980 | 72 | 20 | 52 | 45 | 91 | 8 |

| Year | S | O | S | O | S | O |
|---|---|---|---|---|---|---|
| 1979 | 66 | 25 | 62 | 31† | 72 | 22† |
| 1978 | 52 | 46 | 36 | 60 | 83 | 13 |
| 1977 | 73 | 25 | 41 | 52 | 80 | 14 |
| 1976 | 64 | 36 | 49 | 48 | 75 | 23 |
| 1975 | 70 | 27 | 40 | 59 | 91 | 9 |
| 1974 (Ford) | 62 | 35 | | | | |
| 1974 | 65 | 35 | 35 | 63 | 87 | 10 |
| 1973 | 56 | 40 | 46 | 51 | 85 | 13 |

S = Support       O = Opposition
† Not eligible for all recorded votes.

## Key Votes

**96th Congress**

| | |
|---|---|
| Maintain relations with Taiwan (1979) | N |
| Reduce synthetic fuel development funds (1979) | N |
| Impose nuclear plant moratorium (1979) | N |
| Kill stronger windfall profits tax (1979) | N |
| Guarantee Chrysler Corp. loans (1979) | N |
| Approve military draft registration (1980) | Y |
| End Revenue Sharing to the states (1980) | Y |
| Block Justice Dept. busing suits (1980) | Y |

**97th Congress**

| | |
|---|---|
| Restore urban program funding cuts (1981) | N |

## Interest Group Ratings

| Year | ADA | ACA | AFL-CIO | CCUS-1 | CCUS-2 |
|---|---|---|---|---|---|
| 1980 | 56 | 54 | 26 | 58 | |
| 1979 | 11 | 40 | 32 | 55 | 67 |
| 1978 | 25 | 67 | 26 | 78 | |
| 1977 | 20 | 64 | 37 | 82 | |
| 1976 | 20 | 62 | 60 | 33 | |
| 1975 | 11 | 68 | 27 | 69 | |
| 1974 | 14 | 78 | 36 | 90 | |
| 1973 | 30 | 66 | 40 | 78 | |

# Mack Mattingly (R)

**Of St. Simons Island — Elected 1980**

**Born:** Jan. 7, 1931, Anderson, Ind.
**Education:** Indiana University, B.S. 1957.
**Military Career:** Air Force, 1951-55.
**Profession:** Electronics company executive.
**Family:** Wife, Carolyn Longcamp; two children.
**Religion:** Methodist.
**Political Career:** Unsuccessful Republican nominee for U.S. House, 1966.

**The Member:** In a year of political upsets, Mattingly may have accomplished the greatest one of all. Democratic Sen. Herman Talmadge was a Georgia institution, if a tarnished one by 1980. Mattingly defeated him by overcoming the country club image that has hurt the GOP among Georgia Democrats in past years. He is the first Republican senator elected by popular vote in Georgia history, and the state's first GOP senator since Reconstruction.

None of it would have been possible without Talmadge's burden of personal troubles: his turbulent divorce, his hospitalization for alcoholism, and especially the decision of the Senate to "denounce" him in 1979 for financial misconduct. In the campaign, Mattingly treaded lightly but skillfully on the personal issues. He worked to convince business leaders around Atlanta that the scandals diminished Talmadge's influence and made him a less useful ally. Meanwhile, Mattingly proclaimed himself to be as reliably conservative as his opponent.

Mattingly now sits on the committee that played a part in Talmadge's demise — the Select Ethics Committee. There, he has learned that senators expect delicate handling of ethics cases.

The Ethics Committee voted May 5 to investigate Democratic Sen. Harrison A. Williams Jr., who was convicted of bribery and conspiracy in connection with the FBI's Abscam investigation. Afterwards, Mattingly said Williams "should not be afforded" the opportunity to vote on the floor until the probe was completed. The committee did not embrace Mattingly's suggestion, and he retracted it later, explaining he did not want to appear to prejudice committee deliberations.

As chairman of the Legislative Appropriations subcommittee, Mattingly rankled some members with his call for a 10 percent cut in Senate committee expenditures. Party leaders were amenable to a 10 percent reduction in committee *budgets*, a cut requiring less sacrifice than Mattingly's proposal, since few committees spend as much as their budget allows.

Mattingly grew up in Indiana and began his business career there. But he moved to Georgia in 1959 to become a corporate executive with IBM. The 1964 Goldwater presidential campaign sparked his interest in politics, and he ran for the U.S. House in 1966. Then he went into GOP organizational work, serving as state party chairman from 1975 to 1977.

## Committees

**Appropriations** (13th of 15 Republicans)
Legislative Branch, chairman; Agriculture and Related Agencies; Energy and Water Development; Military Construction; Treasury, Postal Service, General Government.

**Governmental Affairs** (8th of 9 Republicans)
Congressional Operations and Oversight, chairman; Energy, Nuclear Proliferation and Government Processes; Intergovernmental Relations.

**Joint Economic**
Economic Goals and Intergovernmental Policy; International Trade, Finance and Security Economics.

**Select Ethics** (3rd of 3 Republicans)

## Elections

| 1980 General | |
|---|---|
| Mack Mattingly (R) | 803,677 (51%) |
| Herman Talmadge (D) | 776,025 (49%) |
| **1980 Primary** | |
| Mack Mattingly (R) | 28,191 (60%) |
| E.J. Bagley (R) | 6,082 (13%) |
| Other | 12,865 (27%) |

## Campaign Finance

| | Receipts | Receipts from PACs | Expenditures |
|---|---|---|---|
| **1980** | | | |
| Mattingly (R) | $509,178 | $105,787 (21%) | $482,295 |
| Talmadge (D) | $2,158,504 | $557,419 (26%) | $2,199,352 |

## Key Votes

**97th Congress**
Restore urban program funding cuts (1981)     N

# 1 Bo Ginn (D)

**Of Millen — Elected 1972**

**Born:** May, 31, 1934, Morgan Ga.
**Education:** Ga. Southern College, B.S. 1955.
**Profession:** Congressional Aide.
**Family:** Wife, Gloria Averitt; three children.
**Religion:** Baptist.
**Political Career:** No previous office.

**In Washington:** Ginn rarely speaks on the floor, introduces few bills, and is scarcely recognized outside the House chamber. But in the trenches of the Appropriations Committee, where a good legislator can bring his district millions of extra federal dollars every year, he is recognized as one of the best.

Ginn's skills are the kinds that have always paid off in Appropriations politics: establishing personal rapport, backing a project in another state in exchange for help later on, and knowing which bureaucrat to call in which federal agency when the money is not being spent.

On the Appropriations Committee's Military Construction Subcommittee, Ginn takes good care of Stewart-Hunter Air Force Base in Savannah and the Kings Bay Submarine Support Base, East Coast home of the new Trident submarine. In the 97th Congress they are likely to get even better care than usual, because Ginn is the subcommittee's chairman. It took him only two years on Appropriations to get that job; the man ahead of him, Utah Democrat Gunn McKay, was beaten in 1980. At the same time Ginn took over Military Construction, he joined the Subcommittee on Defense, giving him a chance to pursue his issues globally as well as locally.

He began as Military Construction chairman by complaining that housing and pay for enlisted men had declined to the point of disgrace. "We have sadly neglected our people," he said. "We've got sailors at Kings Bay who are selling their blood on weekends to make ends meet." He said his subcommittee would look into spending more for day-care and "family guidance centers" on military bases.

Ginn has also been able to use the Appropriations Committee to follow up on the projects he pushed early in his career, at Public Works, where an admiring colleague once described him as having done everything but "pave his district in concrete."

One of Ginn's continuing interests is the port of Savannah, and the amount of money the fed-eral government spends on widening it. Ginn helped authorize the widening as a member of Public Works, and he continues to speak up for it on the House floor. He argued in 1979 that it would cost only $8 million to complete, and that the revenue generated for the federal government by the project would more than pay for the cost of the work.

"To say that these projects are pure pork," he told the House, "does a great disservice to this Congress." Ginn also worked on the Merchant Marine Committee in earlier years to help the fishing industry off the Georgia coast.

On broader issues, Ginn is an important voice within the Georgia delegation, one who often votes with the more liberal House leadership when it is politically "safe," and sometimes brings along most of his eight Democratic colleagues in the delegation. In 1981 he joined the Steering and Policy Committee, which makes Democratic committee assignments.

**At Home:** Ginn had to run against his old boss to make it to Congress, but once that act of audacity paid off, he had himself a good Democratic seat that his political skills could make absolutely secure. He has been virtually unopposed since 1972.

Ginn was a livestock farmer and businessman in the southeast Georgia town of Millen when he challenged Democratic Rep. G. Elliott Hagan in

---

**1st District: Southeast — Savannah, Brunswick.** Population: 527,732 (16% increase since 1970). Race: White 342,026 (65%), Black 180,225 (34%), Others 5,481 (1%). Spanish origin: 6,451 (1%).

1972. But in the 1960s, he had spent six years as Hagan's administrative assistant, before moving to Sen. Herman E. Talmadge's staff.

Ginn picked a good time to make his move. Accused repeatedly of absenteeism in Congress, Hagan had been the target of previous primary and general election challenges. The 1972 redistricting added several coastal counties to the district, increasing his problems.

Renewing the absentee issue and calling his old boss incompetent, Ginn enlisted several former Hagan allies, including an ex-campaign manager. The challenger promised to open more congressional offices around the district and to maintain a 90 percent voting participation rate.

Hagan ran narrowly ahead in the first round of the primary, drawing 43 percent to Ginn's 39 percent. But Ginn took the runoff with 55 percent, and he has been home free ever since.

**The District:** The 1st District includes all of Georgia's Atlantic coast, but it also runs about 100 miles inland into the state's black belt.

The major coastal communities are Savannah and Brunswick, both seaports of growing importance. Savannah, largest city in Georgia until the Civil War, was a declining cotton town from the end of the 19th century until after World War II, when new industries began to filter in.

The major coastal counties — Chatham (Savannah) and Glynn (Brunswick) — often vote Republican. But most of the rural counties are still loyally Democratic. Former Sen. Talmadge carried many of them by 2-to-1 in his unsuccessful 1980 Senate race.

## Committees

**Appropriations** (22nd of 33 Democrats)
Military Construction, chairman; Defense.

## Elections

**1980 General**

Bo Ginn (D )                                           Unopposed

**1978 General**

Bo Ginn (D )                                           Unopposed

**Previous Winning Percentages**

1976 (100%)    1974 (86 %)    1972 (100%)

**District Vote For President**

| | 1980 | | 1976 | | 1972 |
|---|---|---|---|---|---|
| D | 79,860 (55 %) | D | 88,992 (64 %) | D | 29,768 (25 %) |
| R | 61,810 (43 %) | R | 49,282 (36 %) | R | 90,218 (75 %) |
| I | 2,349 (2 %) | | | | |

## Campaign Finance

| | Receipts | Receipts from PACs | Expenditures |
|---|---|---|---|
| **1980** | | | |
| Ginn (D ) | $27,778 | $20,550 (74 %) | $32,902 |
| **1978** | | | |
| Ginn (D ) | $99,233 | $11,525 (12 %) | $58,340 |

## Voting Studies

| | Presidential Support | | Party Unity | | Conservative Coalition | |
|---|---|---|---|---|---|---|
| Year | S | O | S | O | S | O |
| 1980 | 59 | 36 | 64 | 30 | 71 | 23 |
| 1979 | 60 | 37 | 64 | 32 | 80 | 19 |
| 1978 | 53 | 46 | 53 | 46 | 82 | 18 |
| 1977 | 65 | 32 | 53 | 43 | 76 | 19 |
| 1976 | 53 | 47 | 44 | 54 | 86 | 11 |
| 1975 | 36 | 61 | 48 | 49 | 75 | 22 |
| 1974 (Ford) | 41 | 52 | | | | |
| 1974 | 49 | 51 | 52 | 46 | 73 | 27 |
| 1973 | 41 | 58 | 56 | 44 | 74 | 25 |

S = Support          O = Opposition

## Key Votes

**96th Congress**

| | |
|---|---|
| Weaken Carter oil profits tax (1979) | Y |
| Reject hospital cost control plan (1979) | Y |
| Implement Panama Canal Treaties (1979) | Y |
| Establish Department of Education (1979) | Y |
| Approve Anti-busing Amendment (1979) | Y |
| Guarantee Chrysler Corp. loans (1979) | # |
| Approve military draft registration (1980) | Y |
| Aid Sandinista regime in Nicaragua (1980) | N |
| Strengthen fair housing laws (1980) | N |

**97th Congress**

| | |
|---|---|
| Reagan budget proposal (1981) | Y |

## Interest Group Ratings

| Year | ADA | ACA | AFL-CIO | CCUS |
|---|---|---|---|---|
| 1980 | 33 | 30 | 44 | 70 |
| 1979 | 21 | 48 | 45 | 61 |
| 1978 | 20 | 63 | 55 | 56 |
| 1977 | 20 | 62 | 52 | 59 |
| 1976 | 15 | 61 | 43 | 69 |
| 1975 | 11 | 62 | 43 | 59 |
| 1974 | 26 | 67 | 45 | 50 |
| 1973 | 40 | 56 | 64 | 73 |

# 2 Charles Hatcher (D)

Of Albany — Elected 1980

**Born:** July 1, 1939, Colquitt County, Ga.
**Education:** Ga. Southern U., B.S. 1965; U. of Ga., J.D. 1969.
**Military Career:** Air Force, 1958-62.
**Profession:** Lawyer.
**Family:** Wife, Ellen Wilson; three children.
**Religion:** Episcopalian.
**Political Career:** Ga. House, 1973-81.

The Member: In his 1980 campaign, Hatcher promised to pursue a generally conservative line in Congress and watch over his district's agricultural interests.

Like many congressmen from farming districts, Hatcher has had to move in different fiscal directions to fulfill his campaign promise. He was one of only four freshman Democrats who voted for the Reagan-endorsed Gramm-Latta budget plans. But in the Agriculture Committee, Hatcher supported an increase in peanut price supports. Those supports were partially responsible for pushing costs in the initial version of the committee's farm bill over the limit set by Gramm-Latta.

Hatcher brought strong legislative experience to the House: he served as assistant floor leader of the Georgia House. When Democratic Rep. Dawson Mathis announced he would try for the Senate in 1980, Hatcher immediately became the front-runner to succeed him.

But he had a more difficult time than expected in winning the seat. He had to turn back a stiff challenge in the Democratic primary and runoff from Julian Holland, who was Mathis' chief legislative aide. The Republican nominee sought to brand Hatcher as a liberal because he refused to back the teaching of "divine creationism." But Hatcher seemed conservative enough to the voters, and he won convincingly.

The District: Agriculture is the mainstay of the 2nd District, with peanuts, soybeans and cotton the basic crops. There is also a significant vegetable-growing area.

The 27 mostly rural counties have two urban centers — Albany and Valdosta — whose economies are largely centered around serving the agricultural interests of the area. There is a significant black population which can make a difference in a close Democratic primary race.

The military also plays an important role in the district's economy, with Moody Air Force Base in Valdosta as well as a Marine Corps supply center and a naval air station.

## Committees

**Agriculture** (23rd of 24 Democrats)
Cotton, Rice and Sugar; Livestock, Dairy and Poultry; Tobacco and Peanuts.
**Small Business** (17th of 23 Democrats)
Energy, Environment and Safety Issues Affecting Small Business; SBA and SBIC Authority, Minority Enterprise and General Small Business Problems.

## Elections

| | |
|---|---|
| **1980 General** | |
| Charles Hatcher (D ) | 92,264 (74 %) |
| Jack Harrell Jr. (R ) | 33,107 (26 %) |
| **1980 Primary Runoff** | |
| Charles Hatcher (D ) | 49,144 (53 % ) |
| Julian Holland (D ) | 44,397 (47 % ) |
| **1980 Primary** | |
| Charles Hatcher (D ) | 40,315 (38 % ) |
| Julian Holland (D ) | 15,976 (15 % ) |
| Hanson Carter (D) | 15,747 (15 % ) |
| J. David Halstead (D ) | 13,119 (12 % ) |

**District Vote For President**

| | 1980 | | 1976 | | 1972 |
|---|---|---|---|---|---|
| **D** | 78,073 (57 %) | **D** | 88,250 (69 %) | **D** | 20,745 (20 % |
| **R** | 57,604 (42 %) | **R** | 39,456 (31 %) | **R** | 80,769 (80 % |

## Campaign Finance

| | Receipts | Receipts from PACs | Expenditure |
|---|---|---|---|
| **1980** | | | |
| Hatcher (D ) | $193,142 | $74,656 (39 %) | $242,96 |
| Harrell (R ) | $23,609 | — (0 %) | $23,47 |

## Key Vote

**97th Congress**
Reagan budget proposal (1981)

---

**2nd District: Southwest — Albany.**
Population: 522,952 (16% increase since 1970). Race: White 342,026 (65%), Black 180,225 (34%), Others 5,481 (1%). Spanish origin: 6,451 (1%).

# 3  Jack Brinkley (D)

**Of Columbus — Elected 1966**

**Born:** Dec. 22, 1930, Faceville, Ga.
**Education:** Young Harris College, B.A. 1949; U. of Ga., J.D. 1959.
**Military Career:** Air Force, 1951-56.
**Profession:** Lawyer.
**Family:** Wife, Alma Lois Kite, two children.
**Religion:** Baptist.
**Political Career:** Ga. House, 1965-67.

**In Washington:** Brinkley is an enthusiastic ally of the Pentagon who still has a boyish curiosity about airplanes and other new military equipment. His district includes the Robins Air Force Base, as well as Fort Benning, and he ran for Congress in 1966 claiming he was the only candidate who could serve the district's military needs in the tradition of Georgia's legendary Armed Services chairman, Carl Vinson, who had retired two years before.

To no one's surprise, Brinkley joined Armed Services when he arrived on Capitol Hill in 1967. He has served there ever since, not so much an initiator of policy as an advocate of various new types of military hardware.

A former Air Force pilot, he once took the controls of the Army's Cheyenne helicopter as it swooped down over Shirley Highway in northern Virginia. He later described it on the House floor as having "the dexterity of a purple martin with the sting of a red wasp." He was an enthusiastic advocate of the helicopter even after the Defense Department canceled the contract because of persistent malfunctions.

Nearly all of Brinkley's work is tied to his district in one way or another. He keeps a close eye on army personnel matters, looking out for Fort Benning, the Army's massive training center located just south of his hometown of Columbus. At the start of 1981, Brinkley became chairman of the Armed Services Subcommittee on Military Installations.

Brinkley seldom speaks on the House floor and rarely involves himself in any legislation outside Armed Services and the Veterans' Affairs Committee, where he also serves. Quiet and modest, he sometimes spends hours showing constituents around the Capitol. His voting record is solidly conservative, as it has been from his first term, when he opposed civil rights, food stamps, rent supplements, and other elements of the Johnson Great Society program.

**At Home:** A close friend of Jimmy Carter, whose hometown is in the 3rd District, Brinkley ran for Congress in 1966 when Carter passed up a House campaign to run for governor.

Brinkley had launched his political career only two years earlier by winning a seat in the state Legislature. But Carter's decision left a clear congressional field for him. The district was open; Republican incumbent Howard Callaway was running for governor himself in 1966.

Well known for his involvement in Columbus civic affairs, Brinkley narrowly led in the first primary over Earl Cocke Jr, a former national commander of the American Legion and World Bank director. In the runoff, Cocke was hurt by his ties to the Johnson administration and the fact that he had moved to the district only two years before. Brinkley won the runoff easily.

He had little trouble in the fall against Billy Mixon, a former football star at the University of Georgia, who had been Callaway's campaign manager in 1964. Mixon tried to set up a referendum on the Johnson policies, but Brinkley defused the issue by criticizing Great Society waste and "bottomless foreign aid programs."

Brinkley has been impregnable since then. He has never had a primary challenge and only twice — in 1974 and 1976 — has he faced GOP opposition. He won both times by margins of more than 4-to-1.

---

**3rd District: West Central — Columbus.** Population: 500,941 (9% increase since 1970). Race: White 319,484 (64%), Black 173,936 (35%), Others 7,521 (2%). Spanish origin: 8,345 (2%).

**The District:** The 3rd has a giant military installation at each end — Fort Benning on the west and Robins Air Force Base on the east.

In between, the land is rather poor and sparsely populated, producing some cotton, tobacco, peaches, pecans and peanuts. The rural counties are still loyally Democratic, and the district went for native son Carter easily in 1980.

The two most populous counties, Muscogee (Columbus) and Houston (Warner Robins), are turning Republican. Columbus, the second-largest city in Georgia, has a large textile industry.

## Committees

**Armed Services** (6th of 25 Democrats)
Military Installations and Facilities, chairman; Investigations.

**Veterans' Affairs** (4th of 17 Democrats)
Compensation, Pension and Insurance; Housing and Memorial Affairs.

## Elections

**1980 General**

| | |
|---|---|
| Jack Brinkley (D ) | Unopposed |

**1978 General**

| | |
|---|---|
| Jack Brinkley (D ) | Unopposed |

**Previous Winning Percentages**

| | | | |
|---|---|---|---|
| 1976 (89 %) | 1974 (88 %) | 1972 (100%) | 1970 (100%) |
| 1968 (100%) | 1966 (61 %) | | |

**District Vote For President**

| | 1980 | | 1976 | | 1972 |
|---|---|---|---|---|---|
| D | 77,017 (60 %) | D | 82,639 (69 %) | D | 23,534 (22 %) |
| R | 47,356 (37 %) | R | 36,878 (31 %) | R | 81,300 (78 %) |
| I | 2,173 (2 %) | | | | |

## Campaign Finance

| | Receipts | Receipts from PACs | Expenditures |
|---|---|---|---|
| **1980** | | | |
| Brinkley (D ) | $52,033 | $26,225 (50 %) | $29,043 |
| **1978** | | | |
| Brinkley (D ) | $45,843 | $18,260 (40 %) | $14,531 |

## Voting Studies

| | Presidential Support | | Party Unity | | Conservative Coalition | |
|---|---|---|---|---|---|---|
| Year | S | O | S | O | S | O |
| 1980 | 50 | 44 | 51 | 45 | 86 | 11 |
| 1979 | 50 | 48 | 46 | 50 | 87 | 10 |
| 1978 | 43 | 54 | 38 | 60 | 82 | 15 |
| 1977 | 54 | 41 | 42 | 54 | 84 | 13 |
| 1976 | 43 | 43 | 28 | 66 | 85 | 8 |
| 1975 | 44 | 54 | 36 | 60 | 84 | 15 |
| 1974 (Ford) | 43 | 56 | | | | |
| 1974 | 49 | 47 | 40 | 55 | 75 | 20 |
| 1973 | 54 | 46 | 42 | 57 | 85 | 14 |
| 1972 | 51 | 46 | 37 | 63 | 82 | 17 |
| 1971 | 74 | 26 | 38 | 61 | 82 | 16 |
| 1970 | 68 | 32 | 38 | 63 | 98 | 2 |
| 1969 | 40 | 60 | 25 | 75 | 98 | 2 |
| 1968 | 50 | 49 | 30 | 67 | 92 | 6 |
| 1967 | 49 | 44 | 33 | 61 | 87 | 2 |

S = Support          O = Opposition

## Key Votes

**96th Congress**

| | |
|---|---|
| Weaken Carter oil profits tax (1979) | Y |
| Reject hospital cost control plan (1979) | Y |
| Implement Panama Canal Treaties (1979) | Y |
| Establish Department of Education (1979) | Y |
| Approve Anti-busing Amendment (1979) | N |
| Guarantee Chrysler Corp. loans (1979) | Y |
| Approve military draft registration (1980) | Y |
| Aid Sandinista regime in Nicaragua (1980) | N |
| Strengthen fair housing laws (1980) | ? |

**97th Congress**

| | |
|---|---|
| Reagan budget proposal (1981) | Y |

## Interest Group Ratings

| Year | ADA | ACA | AFL-CIO | CCUS |
|---|---|---|---|---|
| 1980 | 11 | 59 | 28 | 66 |
| 1979 | 16 | 57 | 30 | 71 |
| 1978 | 15 | 70 | 35 | 56 |
| 1977 | 15 | 67 | 43 | 71 |
| 1976 | 10 | 67 | 50 | 69 |
| 1975 | 11 | 74 | 43 | 63 |
| 1974 | 9 | 87 | 36 | 60 |
| 1973 | 24 | 67 | 27 | 73 |
| 1972 | 19 | 77 | 18 | 80 |
| 1971 | 16 | 62 | 42 | - |
| 1970 | 4 | 74 | 14 | 80 |
| 1969 | 7 | 82 | 30 | - |
| 1968 | 0 | 83 | 0 | - |
| 1967 | 7 | 68 | 18 | 70 |

# 4 Elliott H. Levitas (D)

### Of Atlanta — Elected 1974

**Born:** Dec. 26, 1930, Atlanta, Ga.
**Education:** Emory U., B.A. 1952, J.D. 1956;
Rhodes Scholar, Oxford U., England, B.A.
1953, M.A. 1958.
**Military Career:** Air Force, 1955-62.
**Profession:** Lawyer.
**Family:** Wife, Barbara Hillman; three children.
**Religion:** Jewish.
**Political Career:** Ga. House, 1967-75.

**In Washington:** Levitas has seized on one issue and ridden it to public reputation, frustrating House leaders and most of the executive branch of government, but forcing even his critics to deal on his terms.

His issue — some say his obsession — has been the legislative veto, his effort to rein in the people he calls "faceless bureaucrats" by giving Congress the power to reject rules and regulations of the federal government.

He has attached legislative veto amendments relentlessly to bills on virtually every subject. When he is not allowed to offer them, he is sometimes willing to block action on the legislation itself. That does not make Levitas one of the more popular House members. But there is no sign that popularity is one of his major goals.

He was constantly at odds with President Carter, whom he described as a Georgia friend but related to more like an enemy. The Carter administration called Levitas' legislative veto idea "unconstitutional," arguing that it violates the principle of separation of powers.

Levitas has been trying for several years to wrap his entire movement into one comprehensive law which would make all federal regulations subject to the veto. His bill, carefully labeled HR 1776, has been sitting for more than two years in the Rules Committee, which has held hearings on it, but never tried to move it to the floor. The House leadership has argued that a legislative veto might shift the blame for regulations from bureaucrats to Congress, and some committee chairmen think reviewing all the regulations would increase their workload enormously.

In the absence of any action on his major bill, Levitas has waged his battle piecemeal, attaching legislative veto provisions one at a time to bills dealing with individual federal agencies. In the anti-bureaucracy climate of recent years, he has nearly always had the votes to win in the House, but until 1980, at least, the Senate refused to go along, and the resulting dispute tied up some pieces of legislation for months.

The argument prevented passage of an authorization bill for the Federal Trade Commission for four years, until a compromise was reached in 1980, after the agency had had to shut down operations briefly for lack of statutory authority. Throughout the dispute, Levitas remained adamant that FTC rulings should be subject to a one-house congressional veto. "There will be a legislative veto on the FTC bill," Levitas insisted at one point, "or there will be no FTC bill." The compromise that finally broke the deadlock called for a veto, but required action in both House and Senate for it to take effect.

When Carter proposed his own legislation to streamline the entire federal regulatory process Levitas insisted that the veto provision be attached.

A Judiciary subcommittee tried in 1979 to design a modified general veto, requiring a vote of both houses plus the signature of the president to stop a regulation. Levitas was angry. "It's nothing," he said. "It's totally unsatisfactory." He threatened to prevent the subcommittee from meeting unless he was promised a chance to offer his own amendment on the floor, and he got that promise. Eventually, however, the administration decided the entire issue was not worth the fight, and the bill never reached the floor.

Levitas has waged many of his veto fights

---

**4th District: Atlanta area — DeKalb, Rockdale counties.** Population: 543,954 (18% increase since 1970). Race: White 384,771 (71%), Black 150,798 (28%), Others 8,385 (2%). Spanish origin: 8,145 (1%).

from his place on the Government Operations Committee, where he has served during his entire House career. In 1977, when Carter's proposed consumer protection agency had to go through Government Operations, Levitas led the fight against it. Legislation creating the agency made it out of committee by one vote, despite Levitas' efforts, but he rounded up 100 Democratic votes to help kill it on the House floor, leading Ralph Nader to call him "a total big business lackey." Levitas responded that Nader was "frustrated because I did not bow down and kiss his ring and worship him and his monument, the Consumer Protection Agency."

On his other committee, Public Works, Levitas fought still another battle with the Carter administration, over deregulating the airlines. On this issue, Levitas was on the side of much of the airline industry, in favor of preserving more of a federal role and preventing unchecked competition.

The initial Carter deregulation plan had a strong "automatic entry" provision, allowing airlines to take on new routes with less government clearance. Levitas was against that, and stunned the administration by persuading the Public Works Aviation Subcommittee to replace it with a substitute leaving most of the regulatory structure in place.

Eventually the full Public Works Committee agreed on a compromise bill including modest automatic entry provisions, and Levitas voted for it on the House floor.

Levitas' voting record has surprised many Democrats who remember him as the liberal state legislator from Atlanta who fought Gov. Lester Maddox. Levitas has lived up to his early reputation as a reformer, but most of his reforms have pleased the right rather than the left. In 1980, he voted with the "conservative coalition" of Republicans and Southern Democrats 71 percent of the time in the House, and against it 20 percent.

**At Home:** The impact of Watergate was revealed as dramatically here in 1974 as it was anywhere in the nation. Republican Ben B. Blackburn plummeted from 76 percent of the vote in 1972 to a losing 45 percent two years later.

The beneficiary was Levitas, a veteran state legislator who began the campaign as a distinct underdog but scored points by attacking Blackburn's die-hard support for President Nixon.

The son of Jewish immigrants, Levitas was raised in Atlanta and earned a Rhodes scholarship to Oxford University. He was considered one of the sharpest minds in the state Legislature, where he allied himself with moderate urban interests. He worked for a modest gun control bill and promoted a "Baby ERA," to protect women from credit discrimination.

Levitas' more conservative record in Congress has earned him some criticism from old liberal allies, but his move to the right has been effective for him in his affluent suburban district.

He has also had some good luck. Blackburn scuttled his chance for a rematch in 1976 by performing ineptly during Senate hearings into his nomination to the Federal Home Loan Bank Board. Blackburn was criticized for insensitivity to the rights of minorities, and his answers failed to satisfy a committee majority, which killed the nomination.

Instead of having to fight off Blackburn, Levitas had an easy time in 1976 against state Sen. George T. Warren II. He had an even easier time in 1978.

In 1980, Republicans mounted a better-financed challenge behind Barry E. Billington, a Decatur attorney who had Moral Majority support. But Levitas demonstrated his vote-getting appeal again, winning by a margin of more than 2-1.

**The District:** The middle- and upper-class suburbs of DeKalb County dominate the 4th District, which is the leading bastion of Republicanism in Georgia, Levitas notwithstanding.

DeKalb alone gave Republican Sen. Mack Mattingly a 65,000-vote majority in 1980, more than twice his statewide margin against Democratic incumbent Herman E. Talmadge. The county is one of the few areas of Georgia that regularly elects Republicans to the state Legislature.

About 90 percent of the district population is concentrated in DeKalb, with the rest in the eastern section of Atlanta, which includes prestigious Emory University, and in tiny Rockdale County.

## Committees

**Government Operations** (10th of 23 Democrats)
Intergovernmental Relations and Human Resources; Legislation and National Security.

**Public Works and Transportation** (6th of 25 Democrats)
Investigations and Oversight, chairman; Aviation; Public Buildings and Grounds.

## Elections

**1980 General**

| | |
|---|---|
| Elliott Levitas (D ) | 117,091 (69 %) |
| Barry Billington (R ) | 51,546 (31 %) |

**1978 General**

| | |
|---|---|
| Elliott Levitas (D) | 60,284 (81 %) |
| Homer Cheung (R ) | 14,221 (19 %) |

**Previous Winning Percentages**

1976 (68 %)    1974 (55 %)

**District Vote For President**

| | 1980 | | 1976 | | 1972 |
|---|---|---|---|---|---|
| D | 90,213 (50 %) | D | 94,920 (57 %) | D | 33,043 (23 %) |
| R | 80,860 (45 %) | R | 70,912 (43 %) | R | 110,574 (77 %) |
| I | 7,560 (4 %) | | | | |

## Campaign Finance

| | Receipts | Receipts from PACs | Expenditures |
|---|---|---|---|
| **1980** | | | |
| Levitas (D ) | $132,758 | $70,004 (53 %) | $142,342 |
| Billington (R ) | $83,922 | $1,600 (2 %) | $84,355 |
| **1978** | | | |
| Levitas (D ) | $95,240 | $29,499 (31 %) | $94,745 |

## Voting Studies

| | Presidential Support | | Party Unity | | Conservative Coalition | |
|---|---|---|---|---|---|---|
| Year | S | O | S | O | S | O |
| 1980 | 57 | 36 | 54 | 43 | 71 | 20 |
| 1979 | 59 | 39 | 53 | 44 | 72 | 27 |
| 1978 | 58 | 41 | 50 | 49 | 62 | 35 |
| 1977 | 65 | 35 | 49 | 50 | 71 | 28 |
| 1976 | 43 | 55 | 40 | 55 | 67 | 31 |
| 1975 | 36 | 62 | 58 | 41 | 55 | 44 |

S = Support          O = Opposition

## Key Votes

**96th Congress**

| | |
|---|---|
| Weaken Carter oil profits tax (1979) | Y |
| Reject hospital cost control plan (1979) | Y |
| Implement Panama Canal Treaties (1979) | N |
| Establish Department of Education (1979) | Y |
| Approve Anti-busing Amendment (1979) | Y |
| Guarantee Chrysler Corp. loans (1979) | N |
| Approve military draft registration (1980) | Y |
| Aid Sandinista regime in Nicaragua (1980) | N |
| Strengthen fair housing laws (1980) | Y |

**97th Congress**

| | |
|---|---|
| Reagan budget proposal (1981) | Y |

## Interest Group Ratings

| Year | ADA | ACA | AFL-CIO | CCUS |
|---|---|---|---|---|
| 1980 | 28 | 48 | 47 | 79 |
| 1979 | 21 | 46 | 37 | 50 |
| 1978 | 20 | 65 | 60 | 39 |
| 1977 | 30 | 63 | 43 | 53 |
| 1976 | 40 | 54 | 52 | 50 |
| 1975 | 32 | 54 | 57 | 53 |

# 5 Wyche Fowler (D)

### Of Atlanta — Elected 1977

**Born:** Oct. 6, 1940, Atlanta, Ga.
**Education:** Davidson College, B.A. 1962; Emory U., LL.B. 1969.
**Military Career:** U.S. Army, 1962-63.
**Profession:** Lawyer.
**Family:** Divorced; one child.
**Religion:** Presbyterian.
**Political Career:** Atlanta Board of Aldermen, 1970-74; president, Atlanta City Council, 1974-77.

**In Washington:** Fowler often expresses the "less is more" environmentalism once associated with California Gov. Jerry Brown. He believes in the virtues of a simpler society, stripped of technological gadgetry and energy waste. He can work himself into a rage over an electric toothbrush.

Many of Fowler's ideas for societal change stretch beyond any legislative agenda. But he has tried to implement some of them from his position on the Ways and Means Committee, which he assumed in his second term in 1979.

Like some other environmentalists, Fowler has been interested in using the tax system — the only area under Ways and Means' jurisdiction — to promote energy conservation. He made a last-minute effort in 1980 to amend the conference report on the oil windfall profits tax bill with a variety of new tax credits for conservation. "Ten percent or 12 percent or 11 percent of an energy tax bill for energy conservation credits can't be too much," Fowler said. But the House was less favorably disposed toward the credits than the Senate, and Fowler's proposal would have required House conferees to go back and accept Senate language they had just succeeded in stripping from the bill. The attempt failed, and Fowler's role in it ruffled some feathers at Ways and Means, which is always skeptical about adding Senate language on the House floor.

He used the energy conservation issue in 1979 to try and win an argument over the future of U.S. passenger railroads. The Carter administration called for massive cutbacks in Amtrak passenger service, and Fowler proposed a one-year moratorium on the cutbacks pending further study. Instead of pleading equal treatment for his area of the country — the real motivation for most supporters of the moratorium — Fowler talked about energy conservation. "What we are trying to look at," he insisted, "is not only transportation, not

only trains, but something called energy." The moratorium failed, but a compromise retained much of the service originally set for elimination.

Fowler also is a charter member of the Intelligence Committee, where he is working on a bill to make it a crime to reveal publicly the names of U.S. spies overseas without violating the First Amendment rights of news outlets at home.

**At Home.** When Fowler was elected in 1977 to succeed Andrew Young, it marked the first time since 1900 that a white candidate had won a House seat previously held by a black.

Fowler, who had cultivated a reputation as a moderate reformer in city politics, defeated black civil rights leader John Lewis in a special election whose campaign was gentle but whose result divided along racial lines. Fowler ran ahead of the crowded field in the first round of voting and drew a nearly unanimous white vote to win the runoff over Lewis with 62 percent. Since then, he has not been seriously challenged.

Fowler began his political career in the mid-1960s as an aide to Rep. Charles Weltner, a liberal Atlanta Democrat who retired from Congress after two terms in 1966 rather than run on the same ticket with gubernatorial candidate Lester Maddox.

Following Weltner's retirement, Fowler won a seat on the Atlanta City Council. He tried for Congress in 1972 but lost to Young by a margin of

---

**5th District: Atlanta.** Population: 420,474 (9% decrease since 1970). Race: White 204,450 (49%), Black 211,634 (50%), Others 4,390 (1%). Spanish origin: 5,715 (1%).

nearly 2-1 in the Democratic primary.

Fowler bounced back the following year by easily winning the city council presidency over civil rights activist Hosea Williams. While on the council, Fowler initiated Atlanta's "government in the sunshine" ordinance, which banned all closed-door and executive sessions of city government agencies. He opposed a 1977 strike by city garbage workers and applauded efforts to fire the strikers.

**The District.** The 5th District comprises most of Atlanta — the business district that serves as commercial center for the Southeastern United States, the predominantly black neighborhoods of the inner city and the more affluent areas of northern Atlanta and suburban Fulton County. Eight colleges are in the district, including Georgia Tech and several prominent black schools. In Georgia politics, the 5th is a bastion of liberalism. It gave George McGovern 48 percent of the vote in 1972, his highest share in the Deep South, and the same year became the first Georgia district in this century to elect a black to Congress.

But redistricting may alter the 5th significantly. The population of Georgia grew by 18 percent in the last decade, but with a heavy migration from the inner city to the suburban counties, the 5th lost population in the 1970s, the only district in the Deep South to do so.

## Committees

**Select Intelligence** (6th of 9 Democrats)
Legislation; Oversight and Evaluation.

**Ways and Means** (16th of 23 Democrats)
Oversight; Select Revenue Measures.

## Elections

**1980 General**

| | |
|---|---|
| Wyche Fowler (D) | 101,646 (74 %) |
| F. William Dowda (R ) | 35,640 (26 %) |

**1980 Primary**

| | |
|---|---|
| Wyche Fowler (D ) | 52,547 (86 %) |
| Doug Steele (D ) | 8,760 (14 %) |

**1978 General**

| | |
|---|---|
| Wyche Fowler (D) | 52,739 (76 %) |
| Thomas Bowles (R ) | 17,132 (24 %) |

**Previous Winning Percentage**

**1977\*** (62 %)

*\* Special election*

**District Vote For President**

| | 1980 | | 1976 | | 1972 |
|---|---|---|---|---|---|
| **D** | 88,548 (60 %) | **D** | 98,102 (68 %) | **D** | 62,894 (48 %) |
| **R** | 51,201 (35 %) | **R** | 47,202 (32 %) | **R** | 68,409 (52 %) |
| **I** | 5,883 (4 %) | | | | |

## Campaign Finance

| | Receipts | Receipts from PACs | Expenditures |
|---|---|---|---|
| **1980** | | | |
| Fowler (D ) | $149,978 | $50,965 (34 %) | $141,037 |
| Dowda (R ) | $51,982 | $8,269 (16 %) | $48,856 |
| **1978** | | | |
| Fowler (D ) | $165,267 | $23,650 (14 %) | $142,684 |
| Bowles (R ) | $30,283 | $2,650 (9 %) | $27,374 |

## Voting Studies

| | Presidential Support | | Party Unity | | Conservative Coalition | |
|---|---|---|---|---|---|---|
| Year | S | O | S | O | S | O |
| 1980 | 62 | 23 | 63 | 25 | 42 | 40 |
| 1979 | 71 | 22 | 75 | 19 | 42 | 51 |
| 1978 | 70 | 25 | 62 | 30 | 43 | 48 |
| 1977 | 73 | 25† | 63 | 34† | 51 | 45† |

†Not eligible for all recorded votes.

S = Support          O = Opposition

## Key Votes

**96th Congress**

| | |
|---|---|
| Weaken Carter oil profits tax (1979) | N |
| Reject hospital cost control plan (1979) | N |
| Implement Panama Canal Treaties (1979) | Y |
| Establish Department of Education (1979) | Y |
| Approve Anti-busing Amendment (1979) | N |
| Guarantee Chrysler Corp. loans (1979) | Y |
| Approve military draft registration (1980) | Y |
| Aid Sandinista regime in Nicaragua (1980) | Y |
| Strengthen fair housing laws (1980) | Y |

**97th Congress**

| | |
|---|---|
| Reagan budget proposal (1981) | N |

## Interest Group Ratings

| Year | ADA | ACA | AFL-CIO | CCUS |
|---|---|---|---|---|
| 1980 | 61 | 48 | 71 | 71 |
| 1979 | 68 | 27 | 65 | 28 |
| 1978 | 45 | 36 | 58 | 33 |
| 1977 | 63 | 43 | 53 | 36 |

# 6 Newt Gingrich (R)

## Of Carrollton — Elected 1978

**Born:** June 17, 1943, Harrisburg, Pa.
**Education:** Emory U., B.A. 1965; Tulane U., M.A. 1968, Ph.D. 1971.
**Profession:** History professor.
**Family:** Divorced; two children.
**Religion:** Baptist.
**Political Career:** Unsuccessful Republican nominee for U.S. House, 1974, 1976.

**In Washington:** Brash newcomers are no longer a novelty in the House of Representatives, but this history professor managed to set a few precedents during a tempestuous first term in which he regularly offered strategy advice to his party's leadership and plotted out scenarios for Republican political dominance in crayon on a board in his office.

Eager to talk politics and history with colleagues, reporters, or nearly anyone else around, Gingrich brought a new supply of intellectual vitality to a House GOP bloc that had been accused of lacking it in the past. He also drew generous amounts of press attention, and hostility from some older conservatives who felt his ideas amounted to personal fantasy.

Gingrich's initial argument centered on the need for confrontation in the House between the Republicans and the Democratic majority. At the start of the 96th Congress, with the GOP contingent outnumbered by nearly 2-to-1, he told party leaders that they should forget about compromising to improve Democratic legislation, and start using the chamber as a political forum to express opposition and build electoral support, the way European parties do when they are in the opposition. To hear Gingrich tell it, often becoming more animated as he continued, he wanted to see guerrilla theater on the floor.

Two years later, with Ronald Reagan in the White House and Republicans already in charge in the Senate, Gingrich was advising his leaders to keep up the pressure, making a political case against House Democrats rather than an accommodation.

These political ideas attracted more of Gingrich's time during the 96th Congress than his two relatively modest committee assignments, Public Works and House Administration. He did play a prominent role on the floor early in his first year by calling for the expulsion of Charles C. Diggs Jr., the Michigan Democrat who had already been convicted on kickback charges. The House later censured Diggs.

Much of Gingrich's legislative work was on the budget, which he sought to use as a political weapon for the 1980 election. Gingrich and several junior colleagues helped design a campaign in which the minority's "budget of hope" contrasted with the Democrats' higher-deficit "budget of despair." They persuaded House GOP leader John J. Rhodes to bring in political consultants and public relations specialists, and to send GOP "truth squads" into Democratic districts to whip up sentiment against the incumbents on the budget issue. Later in 1980, he was active in the effort to bring Reagan and more than 100 House GOP candidates together for a unity rally on the Capitol steps.

Although he was relatively quiet on the Public Works Committee during the first term, he has a useful spot on the panel's Aviation Subcommittee, where he can deal with bills affecting the huge Atlanta Airport, located in his district.

**At Home:** Like many other Southern Republicans, Gingrich employed persistence and modern campaign techniques to capture a district accustomed to old-fashioned Democratic control.

Gingrich's spirited 1974 campaign, his first political candidacy, used professional polling and a hired staff, commodities rarely seen before in rural Georgia congressional contests. He surprised veteran Democratic Rep. John J. Flynt Jr., and

---

**6th District: West central — Atlanta suburbs.** Population: 626,354 (37% increase since 1970). Race: White 474,512 (76%), Black 146,991 (23%), Others 4,851 (1%). Spanish origin: 5,730 (1%).

came within 2,800 votes of victory.

Two years later, Gingrich had to contend with a beefed-up Flynt campaign and Georgian Jimmy Carter heading the Democratic ticket. He lost again, but still drew more than 48 percent.

Flynt retired in 1978, leaving Gingrich as the best-known contender. In a campaign that cost each candidate more than $200,000, Gingrich swept the northern portion of the district to defeat the Democratic nominee, wealthy state Sen. Virginia Shapard, by 7,600 votes.

In his earlier campaigns, Gingrich had been considered relatively liberal for a Georgia Republican. But in 1978 he relied on the tax cut issue, using an empty shopping cart to emphasize his concern about inflation. He also stressed opposition to U.S. transfer of the Panama Canal.

Gingrich raised more than half a million dollars for his 1980 re-election campaign, helping him defeat his Democratic challenger by nearly 3-to-2.

Gingrich spent his childhood in various military bases around the world before his family moved to Fort Benning, Ga. After receiving a graduate degree in European history, he took a teaching post at West Georgia College in the 6th District.

**The District:** The 6th District includes booming Atlanta suburbs and miles of west Georgia piney woods, running all the way to the Alabama border. Both the suburban and rural portions of the district are conservative in their voting habits. Most of the population growth in the last decade has been in the Atlanta suburbs, and that has helped Gingrich. Together, suburban Clayton and Douglas counties and the 6th District suburban portion of Fulton County cast about half the vote. In 1980, Gingrich carried all three.

Textile mills are scattered throughout the rest of the district. Cattle, pecans and peaches have replaced cotton as the major farm interests.

## Committees

**House Administration** (4th of 8 Republicans)
Contracts and Printing.

**Public Works and Transportation** (8th of 19 Republicans)
Aviation; Investigations and Oversight; Surface Transportation.

**Joint Library**

**Joint Printing**

## Elections

**1980 General**

| | |
|---|---|
| Newt Gingrich (R ) | 96,071 (59 %) |
| Dock Davis (D ) | 66,606 (41 %) |

**1978 Primary**

| | |
|---|---|
| Newt Gingrich (R ) | 47,078 (54 %) |
| Virginia Shapard (D ) | 39,451 (46 %) |

**1978 General**

| | |
|---|---|
| Newt Gingrich (R ) | 4,597 (76 %) |
| David Barrow (R ) | 952 (16 %) |
| Michael Esther (R ) | 535 (9 %) |

**District Vote For President**

| | 1980 | | 1976 | | 1972 |
|---|---|---|---|---|---|
| D | 95,262 (55 %) | D | 106,430 (68 %) | D | 24,574 (20 %) |
| R | 73,700 (42 %) | R | 51,183 (32 %) | R | 95,709 (80 %) |
| I | 3,389 (2 %) | | | | |

## Campaign Finance

| | Receipts | Receipts from PACs | Expenditures |
|---|---|---|---|
| **1980** | | | |
| Gingrich (R ) | $507,209 | $96,110 (19 %) | $397,557 |

| | | | |
|---|---|---|---|
| Davis (D ) | $73,057 | $15,830 (22 %) | $72,962 |
| **1978** | | | |
| Gingrich (R ) | $225,863 | $38,567 (17 %) | $219,336 |
| Shapard (D ) | $318,035 | $35,258 (11 %) | $313,056 |

## Voting Studies

| | Presidential Support | | Party Unity | | Conservative Coalition | |
|---|---|---|---|---|---|---|
| Year | S | O | S | O | S | O |
| 1980 | 35 | 56 | 79 | 13 | 91 | 7 |
| 1979 | 33 | 65 | 83 | 12 | 85 | 8 |

S = Support     O = Opposition

## Key Votes

**96th Congress**

| | |
|---|---|
| Weaken Carter oil profits tax (1979) | Y |
| Reject hospital cost control plan (1979) | Y |
| Implement Panama Canal Treaties (1979) | N |
| Establish Department of Education (1979) | Y |
| Approve Anti-busing Amendment (1979) | Y |
| Guarantee Chrysler Corp. loans (1979) | N |
| Approve military draft registration (1980) | Y |
| Aid Sandinista regime in Nicaragua (1980) | N |
| Strengthen fair housing laws (1980) | N |

**97th Congress**

| | |
|---|---|
| Reagan budget proposal (1981) | Y |

## Interest Group Ratings

| Year | ADA | ACA | AFL-CIO | CCUS |
|---|---|---|---|---|
| 1980 | 11 | 91 | 10 | 79 |
| 1979 | 11 | 92 | 0 | 89 |

# 7 Larry P. McDonald (D)

**Of Marietta — Elected 1974**

**Born:** April 1, 1935, Atlanta, Ga.
**Education:** Emory U., M.D. 1957.
**Military Career:** Navy, 1959-61.
**Profession:** Physician.
**Family:** Wife, Kathryn Jackson; three children.
**Religion:** Methodist.
**Political Career:** Sought Democratic nomination for U.S. House from Ga., 1972.

**In Washington:** McDonald's militant conservatism places him far outside both parties in the House, a free-lance conservative whose real allegiance is to the national politics of the New Right.

His membership in the Democratic Caucus is a symbol of how meaningless that designation is; in 1980 he voted against a majority of Democrats 87 percent of the time, more often than all but a few Republicans. When the 97th Congress convened in 1981 he was not present to cast the routine party-line vote for Democrat O'Neill as Speaker, and later in the day cast the only vote from the majority side of the aisle in favor of a Republican alternative to the Democratic rules package for the Congress to come.

McDonald is a member of the John Birch Society and the Moral Majority. He is argumentatively anti-communist, anti-abortion, anti-homosexual, and pro-gun. His influence is limited generally to rhetoric, which he offers in huge quantities in the *Congressional Record*, where he inserts long statements and research by conservatives on various topics. He is a senior Democrat on Armed Services now, but not a major presence on it.

His floor amendments are usually simple and direct. In 1980 he offered one to block funding for any trade between the United States and the Soviet Union, losing 284-124.

But he struck a sensitive chord later in the year with an appropriations amendment to bar the use of Legal Aid funds to defend homosexuals. That was a difficult vote for dozens of members who felt it was unconstitutional but did not want to be on record in favor of homosexuality. The amendment passed the House easily, 290-113, and was dropped in conference with the Senate.

McDonald forced a floor vote in 1979 on his demand for the impeachment of Andrew Young, President Carter's U.N. ambassador. He was beaten on that, 293 to 82. He called for the impeachment of Federal Judge Nauman S. Scott when Scott ordered desegregation of Louisiana schools.

McDonald also set out in 1980 to help a fellow member of the John Birch Society, Nelson Bunker Hunt, who was buying up silver for investment. McDonald led a successful effort in Congress to block sales of silver from the government's strategic stockpile. Had the silver been released, as the Pentagon suggested, the price would have dropped and threatened Hunt's investment.

**At Home:** McDonald has to fight regularly for his political survival. Conservatism is popular in small-town Georgia, but McDonald's strident qualities guarantee him a steady supply of determined enemies. Still, a loyal band of supporters and effective national fund-raising has allowed him to hold on since 1974.

McDonald was a urologist and member of the John Birch Society's national council when he first ran for Congress in 1972. He made a surprisingly strong debut, drawing 48 percent against veteran Rep. John Davis in the Democratic primary.

Peppering the incumbent as a liberal advocate of big government, McDonald won the rematch in 1974 with 52 percent of the vote. In his TV ads, the challenger wore Mickey Mouse ears to urge voters to get rid of "Mickey Mouse"

---

**7th District: Northwest — Rome, Atlanta suburbs.** Population: 605,720 (32% increase since 1970). Race: White 561,510 (93%), Black 40,086 (7%), Others 4,124 (1%). Spanish origin: 4,711 (1%).

government, and dressed as an Indian at the Boston Tea Party.

The general election was even closer. State and national Republican officials provided help to their candidate, former Vietnam prisoner of war Quincy Collins. With Collins urging Davis supporters to defect, McDonald won by only 543 votes in the traditionally Democratic district.

In 1978, after considering and rejecting a try for the Senate, he was nearly beaten for renomination. Wealthy carpet manufacturer Smith Foster mounted an aggressive campaign, complaining that McDonald was an ineffective congressman more concerned with advancing right-wing views than serving his constituents.

Building a coalition of anti-McDonald forces that included labor, environmental and educational groups, Foster came within 1,000 votes in the initial Democratic primary. Then McDonald rallied his national support, and waged an effective media campaign that led to his victory in the runoff by 2,600 votes.

**The District:** The 7th District extends from the suburbs of Atlanta on the south to the outskirts of Chattanooga, Tennessee, on the north. The Appalachian Mountains pass in between, sheltering a collection of farms and small textile towns.

More than half the ballots in the 7th are cast in the rapidly growing suburban communities of Cobb County (Marietta), the site of Dobbins Air Force Base and a large Lockheed Aircraft plant. In recent years, Cobb County has emerged as a GOP stronghold, although McDonald carries it.

# Committees

**Armed Services** (14th of 25 Democrats)
Research and Development; Seapower and Strategic and Critical Materials.

# Elections

**1980 General**

| | |
|---|---|
| Larry McDonald (D ) | 115,892 (68 %) |
| Richard Castellucis (R ) | 54,242 (32 %) |

**1980 Primary**

| | |
|---|---|
| Larry McDonald (D ) | 67,463 (68 %) |
| Jake Bade (D ) | 31,729 (32 %) |

**1978 General**

| | |
|---|---|
| Larry McDonald (D ) | 47,090 (66 %) |
| Ernie Norsworthy (R ) | 23,698 (34 %) |

**Previous Winning Percentages**

1976 (55 %)    1974 (50 %)

**District Vote For President**

| | 1980 | | 1976 | | 1972 |
|---|---|---|---|---|---|
| D | 89,552 (49 %) | D | 102,107 (64 %) | D | 18,686 (17 %) |
| R | 85,149 (47 %) | R | 56,812 (36 %) | R | 91,275 (83 %) |
| I | 4,435 (2 %) | | | | |

# Campaign Finance

| | Receipts | Receipts from PACs | Expenditures |
|---|---|---|---|
| **1980** | | | |
| McDonald (D ) | $260,555 | $59,505 (23 %) | $276,449 |
| Castellucis (R ) | $6,298 | $300 (5 %) | $6,292 |
| **1978** | | | |
| McDonald (D ) | $344,150 | $58,961 (17 %) | $331,925 |
| Norsworthy (R ) | $8,788 | $400 (5 %) | $9,767 |

# Voting Studies

| | Presidential Support | | Party Unity | | Conservative Coalition | |
|---|---|---|---|---|---|---|
| Year | S | O | S | O | S | O |
| 1980 | 26 | 69 | 5 | 87 | 88 | 4 |
| 1979 | 17 | 81 | 4 | 94 | 93 | 5 |
| 1978 | 14 | 72 | 3 | 82 | 80 | 1 |
| 1977 | 24 | 73 | 4 | 94 | 97 | 2 |
| 1976 | 75 | 24 | 5 | 84 | 86 | 2 |
| 1975 | 62 | 37 | 7 | 92 | 95 | 5 |

S = Support          O = Opposition

# Key Votes

**96th Congress**

| | |
|---|---|
| Weaken Carter oil profits tax (1979) | Y |
| Reject hospital cost control plan (1979) | Y |
| Implement Panama Canal Treaties (1979) | N |
| Establish Department of Education (1979) | N |
| Approve Anti-busing Amendment (1979) | Y |
| Guarantee Chrysler Corp. loans (1979) | N |
| Approve military draft registration (1980) | Y |
| Aid Sandinista regime in Nicaragua (1980) | N |
| Strengthen fair housing laws (1980) | N |

**97th Congress**

| | |
|---|---|
| Reagan budget proposal (1981) | Y |

# Interest Group Ratings

| Year | ADA | ACA | AFL-CIO | CCUS |
|---|---|---|---|---|
| 1980 | 6 | 100 | 5 | 56 |
| 1979 | 5 | 100 | 5 | 94 |
| 1978 | 15 | 100 | 5 | 91 |
| 1977 | 5 | 100 | 9 | 94 |
| 1976 | 0 | 96 | 17 | 94 |
| 1975 | 0 | 96 | 4 | 94 |

# 8 Billy Lee Evans (D)

**Of Macon — Elected 1976**

**Born:** Nov. 10, 1941, Tifton, Ga.
**Education:** U. of Ga., A.B. 1963, LL.B. 1965.
**Profession:** Lawyer.
**Family:** Divorced; three children.
**Religion:** Christian Church.
**Political Career:** Ga. House, 1969-77; unsuccessful nominee for Macon City Council, 1967.

**In Washington:** Evans has neither played nor sought a leadership role among Southern Democrats in his three House terms, generally remaining in the background and following the lead of senior conservatives from his state.

He breaks ranks occasionally to cast a pro-labor vote, reflecting the union support that was crucial to his first election in 1976. As he completed his second term, he was still scoring above 50 in AFL-CIO ratings although he has disappointed labor on some critical votes, notably common site picketing in 1977 and labor law revision in 1978.

Evans briefly attracted news attention in 1980 when, after a trip to Southeast Asia against State Department advice, he called for normal relatons between the United States and Vietnam as the only way of preserving American influence in the region. He also looked into Asian issues as a member of the Select Committee on Narcotics Abuse and Control, to which he has devoted a considerable amount of his time. Evans has supported a bill providing stiffer penalties for trafficking in marijuana and opposed one to lift stringent restrictions on the use of marijuana in treating cancer patients.

On the Public Works Committe, Evans has generally been an ally of the airlines. He supported federal subsidies to help them comply with noise control regulations and voted to soften the airline deregulation bill favored by the Carter administration. A compromise airline deregulation bill became law in 1978.

In 1979, Evans found himself in an argument with Common Cause over the lobby group's charge that he had been influenced to vote against hospital cost controls by contributions from the American Medical Association. "If anybody expects a vote based on a contribution to me, they're crazy as hell," Evans insisted. "Contributions don't have a damn thing to do with the way I vote. I don't have any respect for Common Cause at all

because of the way they try to twist everything. . . ." Evans said his ties to the AMA went back to his work on malpractice bills in the Georgia Legislature.

**At Home.** The son of Georgia tenant farmers, Evans worked his way through law school, then opened a general law practice in Macon that eventually earned him a six-figure yearly income.

His political debut was less successful; he lost his bid in 1967 for a seat on the Macon City Council. But he recouped the following year, winning a seat in the state House of Representatives.

In the early stages of his political career, Evans was a Republican. But in 1974, when his state legislative district was redrawn, he sought re-election as a Democrat and won.

Two years later Democratic Rep. W. S. Stuckey decided to retire. Evans ran behind state Rep. Wash Larsen in the initial primary, but his strong base in Macon, the district's population center, gave him 26 percent of the vote and a place in the runoff.

In the second round, Evans combined his Macon vote with support from blacks and labor and endorsements from the two candidates eliminated in the primary. He won the runoff with 52 percent over Larsen, who was backed by Stuckey.

The fall election proved anticlimatic. Evans overwhelmed Republican Billy Adams, an ex-

---

**8th District: South central — Macon, Waycross.** Population: 508,028 (11% increase since 1970). Race: White 349,339 (69%), Black 156,721 (31%), Others 1,968 (0.3%). Spanish origin: 4,162 (1%).

state senator and petroleum distributor, by a margin of more than 2-1. Since 1976, the incumbent has had no primary opposition and only one Republican rival, in 1980, whom he defeated handily.

In 1980, an Evans campaign committee was fined $400 by the Federal Election Commission for accepting $900 in illegal corporate contributions and $15,000 in illegal loans in 1976 and 1977. Evans insisted he was not involved in the transactions and that they had been honest mistakes by his supporters.

**The District.** From the city of Macon in central Georgia, the 8th District extends through the heart of Georgia's Black Belt to the Florida border. It is one of the poorest areas of the state.

It is also one of the most loyally Democratic,

regularly providing landslide margins for Democratic candidates. In 1980, both Carter and Sen. Herman E. Talmadge easily carried all 26 counties in the district.

The only pocket of Republican strength is around Macon, an old textile and railroad town which is the site of Robins Air Force Base. Evans won his seat in the Legislature as a Republican from a district in the city, and for two terms Macon's mayor was the eccentric "Machine Gun" Ronnie Thompson, a law-and-order Republican who won the GOP gubernatorial nomination in 1974.

Bibb County, which includes the city, has about 30 percent of the district population. The rest live in the other 25 counties, where cotton, tobacco and peanuts are major crops.

## Committees

**Judiciary** (13th of 16 Democrats)
Administrative Law and Governmental Relations; Monopolies and Commercial Law.

**Public Works and Transportation** (14th of 25 Democrats)
Surface Transportation; Water Resources.

**Select Narcotics Abuse and Control** (6th of 11 Democrats)

**Small Business** (12th of 23 Democrats)
Tax, Access to Equity Capital and Business Opportunities.

## Elections

**1980 General**

| | |
|---|---|
| Billy Lee Evans (D ) | 91,103 (75 %) |
| Darwin Carter (R ) | 31,033 (25 %) |

**1978 General**

| | |
|---|---|
| Billy Lee Evans (D ) | Unopposed |

**Previous Winning Percentage**

1976 (70 %)

**District Vote For President**

| | 1980 | | 1976 | | 1972 |
|---|---|---|---|---|---|
| **D** | 100,073 (64 %) | **D** | 110,789 (75 %) | **D** | 26,033 (22 %) |
| **R** | 53,197 (34 %) | **R** | 37,348 (25 %) | **R** | 91,338 (78 %) |

## Campaign Finance

| | Receipts | Receipts from PACs | Expenditures |
|---|---|---|---|
| **1980** | | | |
| Evans (D ) | $118,466 | $61,474 (52 %) | $107,743 |
| Carter (R ) | $43,446 | — (0 %) | $44,034 |

| | | | |
|---|---|---|---|
| 1978 | | | |
| Evans (D ) | $194,037 | $48,165 (25 %) | $186,027 |

## Voting Studies

| | Presidential Support | | Party Unity | | Conservative Coalition | |
|---|---|---|---|---|---|---|
| **Year** | **S** | **O** | **S** | **O** | **S** | **O** |
| 1980 | 50 | 42 | 45 | 49 | 71 | 25 |
| 1979 | 54 | 34 | 49 | 36 | 71 | 19 |
| 1978 | 44 | 46 | 40 | 51 | 70 | 24 |
| 1977 | 57 | 33 | 47 | 43 | 74 | 18 |

S = Support          O = Opposition

## Key Votes

**96th Congress**

| | |
|---|---|
| Weaken Carter oil profits tax (1979) | Y |
| Reject hospital cost control plan (1979) | Y |
| Implement Panama Canal Treaties (1979) | Y |
| Establish Department of Education (1979) | Y |
| Approve Anti-busing Amendment (1979) | Y |
| Guarantee Chrysler Corp. loans (1979) | Y |
| Approve military draft registration (1980) | Y |
| Aid Sandinista regime in Nicaragua (1980) | N |
| Strengthen fair housing laws (1980) | N |

**97th Congress**

| | |
|---|---|
| Reagan budget proposal (1981) | Y |

## Interest Group Ratings

| Year | ADA | ACA | AFL-CIO | CCUS |
|---|---|---|---|---|
| 1980 | 6 | 70 | 53 | 78 |
| 1979 | 21 | 41 | 28 | 59 |
| 1978 | 15 | 65 | 32 | 56 |
| 1977 | 10 | 48 | 35 | 59 |

# 9 Ed Jenkins (D)

**Of Jasper — Elected 1976**

**Born:** Jan. 4, 1933, Young Harris, Ga.
**Education:** Young Harris College, A.A. 1951; U. of Ga., LL.B. 1959.
**Military Career:** Coast Guard, 1952-55.
**Profession:** Lawyer.
**Family:** Wife, Jo Thomasson, two children.
**Religion:** Baptist.
**Political Career:** No previous office.

**In Washington:** Jenkins has the "textile seat" on the Ways and Means Committee, the one relinquished to him by his predecessor and political mentor, Phil Landrum, in 1977. And when called upon, he has used it the way Landrum did, to argue for protection of Southern textile interests and against foreign competition. But he has played a broader role on the committee as a moderate conservative whose votes sometimes tilt toward the Republican right and sometimes toward his party leaders.

In the 96th Congress, Jenkins staked out a clear set of economic priorities — in favor of sharp reductions in federal spending and against the massive tax cuts called for by Republicans. He introduced his own constitutional amendment that would limit spending to a percentage of the gross national product. But he refused to back one mandating a balanced budget; he insisted it was too rigid.

In 1981, he went along with the Reagan spending cuts on the House floor, while expressing skepticism about a full three-year Kemp-Roth tax cut in committee. A quiet man with a folksy manner, he chooses his issues carefully and so far has shown some influence most of the times he has wanted to use it.

One major parochial concern in the 96th Congress involved the tariff treatment of crude feathers and down, an issue of little importance to people outside the Southern textile belt. Cheap down-filled coats had been coming from overseas in huge numbers, hurting firms that manufacture similar apparel in the United States. Jenkins threatened to have the material in the coats reclassified at a higher tariff rate, giving the American companies a significant boost. His threat generated negotiations with Hong Kong, Taiwan and Korea, the major exporters, and he declared victory without offering the legislation.

On another Ways and Means issue, Jenkins moved successfully to extend the investment tax credit to poultry houses, another important district interest.

On some issues, Jenkins retains faint traces of Southern populism. He is a supporter of the Employee Stock Ownership Plan, for years promoted by Louisiana Sen. Russell B. Long. And as a legislator from a state without an oil industry, he kept more distance from oil companies in the 1979 windfall tax argument than most Southern Democrats. But he eventually voted to weaken the tax on the House floor, supporting the version introduced by his usual Ways and Means ally, James R. Jones, D-Okla.

**At Home.** As a former Landrum aide and law partner of the veteran congressman's son, Jenkins had a relatively easy time winning this district in northeast Georgia.

When Landrum announced his retirement in 1976, the early favorite to succeed him was Lt. Gov. Zell Miller. But Miller decided not to run, and Jenkins' major hurdle was eliminated. Benefiting from the Landrum connection, the Jasper lawyer finished first in a crowded Democratic primary field with 28 percent of the vote. Opponents complained that Jenkins should not have been practicing law and working for Landrum at the same time. But many voters knew Jenkins personally as Landrum's field representative and disregarded the criticism.

---

**9th District: Northeast — Gainesville.** Population: 660,892 (45% increase since 1970). Race: White 625,552 (95%), Black 31,414 (5%), Others 3,926 (1%). Spanish origin: 4,626 (1%).

---

Jenkins took the runoff with 55 percent over an older opponent, J. Albert Minish, a conservative dentist from Commerce. He overwhelmed token Republican opposition in the general election.

In 1978, Jenkins faced a primary challenge launched by a county official from suburban Atlanta, a section of the district far from his political base. But with his strength in the rural counties, Jenkins won renomination by a margin of nearly 2-1. He did not have a serious primary or general election challenge in 1980.

**The District.** Tucked away in the mountains of northeastern Georgia, the 9th District has long relished its title as the "poultry capital of the world."

But the district's traditional focus on agriculture and small textile mills is being threatened by a population boom. The 9th grew by 45 percent in the last decade, the sharpest gain of any Georgia district.

Most of the growth was concentrated in the suburbs of Atlanta, at the southern end of the district, and of Chattanooga, Tenn., at the western end. With the attraction of new industries, Gwinnett County near Atlanta doubled its population in the 1970s. Gwinnett is now the most populous county in the 9th and casts more than a quarter of the district vote.

The population increase also threatens to change the political complexion of the district. Although there are some traditional Republican strongholds, the 9th has long been a fixture in the Democratic column. But the fast-growing suburbs could spawn a new two-party system. Both Gwinnett and Catoosa County (near Chattanooga) voted for Reagan and GOP Sen. Mack Mattingly in 1980.

## Committees

**Ways and Means** (12th of 23 Democrats)
Select Revenue Measures; Trade.

## Elections

**1980 General**

| | |
|---|---|
| Ed Jenkins (D ) | 115,576 (68 %) |
| David Ashworth (R ) | 54,341 (32 %) |

**1978 General**

| | |
|---|---|
| Ed Jenkins (D ) | 47,264 (77 %) |
| David Ashworth (R ) | 14,172 (23 %) |

**Previous Winning Percentage**

1976 (79 %)

**District Vote For President**

| | 1980 | | 1976 | | 1972 |
|---|---|---|---|---|---|
| D | 106,322 (55 %) | D | 117,447 (71 %) | D | 19,459 (18 %) |
| R | 82,957 (43 %) | R | 48,178 (29 %) | R | 89,005 (82 %) |
| I | 3,736 (2 %) | | | | |

## Campaign Finance

| | Receipts | Receipts from PACs | Expenditures |
|---|---|---|---|
| **1980** | | | |
| Jenkins (D ) | $108,461 | $71,225 (66 %) | $107,212 |
| **1978** | | | |
| Jenkins (D ) | $128,237 | $49,060 (38 %) | $127,124 |

| | | | |
|---|---|---|---|
| Ashworth (R ) | $16,182 | $400 (2 %) | $16,163 |

## Voting Studies

| | Presidential Support | | Party Unity | | Conservative Coalition | |
|---|---|---|---|---|---|---|
| Year | S | O | S | O | S | O |
| 1980 | 50 | 42 | 43 | 52 | 81 | 13 |
| 1979 | 54 | 38 | 47 | 46 | 81 | 16 |
| 1978 | 44 | 34 | 36 | 44 | 59 | 12 |
| 1977 | 51 | 33 | 43 | 47 | 77 | 13 |

S = Support    O = Opposition

## Key Votes

**96th Congress**

| | |
|---|---|
| Weaken Carter oil profits tax (1979) | Y |
| Reject hospital cost control plan (1979) | Y |
| Implement Panama Canal Treaties (1979) | Y |
| Establish Department of Education (1979) | Y |
| Approve Anti-busing Amendment (1979) | Y |
| Guarantee Chrysler Corp. loans (1979) | Y |
| Approve military draft registration (1980) | Y |
| Aid Sandinista regime in Nicaragua (1980) | N |
| Strengthen fair housing laws (1980) | N |

**97th Congress**

| | |
|---|---|
| Reagan budget proposal (1981) | Y |

## Interest Group Ratings

| Year | ADA | ACA | AFL-CIO | CCUS |
|---|---|---|---|---|
| 1980 | 6 | 60 | 33 | 68 |
| 1979 | 11 | 64 | 44 | 61 |
| 1978 | 5 | 73 | 18 | 43 |
| 1977 | 15 | 65 | 30 | 75 |

# 10 Doug Barnard Jr. (D)

**Of Augusta — Elected 1976**

**Born:** March 20, 1922, Augusta, Ga.
**Education:** Mercer U., B.A. 1943, LL.B. 1948.
**Military Career:** Army, 1943-45.
**Profession:** Banker.
**Family:** Wife, Naomi Elizabeth Holt; three children.
**Religion:** Baptist.
**Political Career:** No previous office.

**In Washington:** Barnard occupies the Banking Committee position long held by his influential Georgia predecessor, Robert G. Stephens Jr. So far, he has not shown Stephens' penchant for trading votes and making and unmaking coalitions. Instead, as a banker by profession, he has focused on arcane industry details that most committee members prefer to ignore in favor of issues with more political appeal.

In the last Congress, Barnard was the only banker among 18 members of the Financial Institutions Subcommittee, where he spent much of his time. That subcommittee wrote an important piece of legislation during these years, one that altered the delicate balance between banks and their competitors, savings and loan institutions. Barnard turned out to be a banking industry ally most of the time, but occasionally disappointed banking lobbyists who expected him to side with them as a matter of course.

The American Bankers Association (ABA) supported a phaseout of Regulation Q, the Federal Reserve rule that placed a ceiling on the interest rate banks could pay on savings accounts. The House initially passed a bank deregulation bill leaving Regulation Q intact, but the Senate added a phaseout, and Barnard supported the effort, introducing his own separate House bill with a phaseout provision. Eventually a conference committee substantially accepted the Senate approach, to the satisfaction of most of the banking industry.

But on Federal Reserve rules, Barnard and the ABA did not always agree. The ABA wanted to maintain the existing voluntary reserve requirements for national banks; Barnard favored mandatory requirements, the position that eventually won out in the committee.

Barnard is only an infrequent participant in House floor debate, and one of the most consistent conservative votes in Democratic ranks. He introduced his own legislation to create tougher

work requirements for welfare recipients, and was one of the Democratic names on a bill to revive the House Committee on Internal Security.

**At Home:** When Barnard won the House seat vacated by Stephens in 1976, he became the first member of Congress from the city of Augusta in this century, even though Augusta is the district's population center.

That campaign marked his debut in elective politics after an extensive career in state government. As executive secretary to former Gov. Carl Sanders (1963-67), Barnard was one of the most influential men in Georgia. He was active in Sanders' comeback attempt in 1970, but Jimmy Carter won the nomination. Barnard then turned to business, serving as executive vice president of the Georgia Railroad Bank in Augusta.

Barnard had years' worth of contacts to call upon when Stephens' retirement opened the district in 1976. He was not helped in the district's rural counties by his ties to the Atlanta legal and business community, but he was well-financed and had a strong base in Augusta to call upon.

Barnard ran ahead of the large primary field with 27 percent of the vote, then took the runoff over Mike Padgett, a former aide to Gov. Lester Maddox, by 2,800 votes. Barnard was unopposed in the general election. He has not had a close race since then.

**The District:** Barnard's district is primarily

---

**10th District: North central — Athens, Augusta.** Population: 547,218 (18% increase since 1970). Race: White 359,005 (66%), Black 181,003 (33%), Others 7,210 (1%). Spanish origin: 7,682 (1%).

---

rural, but it is anchored on either end by its two population centers.

On the east is the pre-Revolutionary War city of Augusta, the capital of Georgia for a decade in the late 18th century. Augusta has a diverse array of industries now, although it is best known nationally as the site of the Masters golf tournament.

About 80 miles across the Piedmont plateau to the northwest is the small city of Athens, founded nearly two centuries ago as the site of the University of Georgia. Together, Richmond County (Augusta) and Clarke County (Athens) cast nearly half the district vote.

Although they are frequently in the Republican column, the urban areas are often outvoted by the poorer, traditionally Democratic counties in between, most of which have large black populations. Cotton is still the major crop in the rural areas, but it is declining in importance. Forests and clay deposits provide other economic resources.

## Committees

**Banking, Finance and Urban Affairs** (18th of 25 Democrats)
Domestic Monetary Policy; Financial Institutions Supervision, Regulation and Insurance; General Oversight and Renegotiation; International Trade, Investment and Monetary Policy.

**Government Operations** (19th of 23 Republicans)
Commerce, Consumer, and Monetary Affairs.

## Elections

**1980 General**

| | |
|---|---|
| Doug Barnard (D ) | 102,177 (80 %) |
| Bruce Neubauer (R ) | 25,194 (20 %) |

**1978 General**

| | |
|---|---|
| Doug Barnard (D ) | Unopposed |

**Previous Winning Percentage**

1976 (100%)

**District Vote For President**

| | 1980 | | 1976 | | 1972 |
|---|---|---|---|---|---|
| D | 86,035 (57 %) | D | 89,733 (66 %) | D | 30,014 (27 %) |
| R | 60,334 (40 %) | R | 46,493 (34 %) | R | 81,220 (73 %) |
| I | 3,099 (2 %) | | | | |

## Campaign Finance

| | Receipts | Receipts from PACs | Expenditures |
|---|---|---|---|
| **1980** | | | |
| Barnard (D ) | $132,061 | $73,770 (56 %) | $57,866 |
| Neubauer (R ) | $4,396 | — (0 %) | $4,431 |
| **1978** | | | |
| Barnard (D ) | $65,168 | $12,675 (19 %) | $41,709 |

## Voting Studies

| | Presidential Support | | Party Unity | | Conservative Coalition | |
|---|---|---|---|---|---|---|
| Year | S | O | S | O | S | O |
| 1980 | 53 | 41 | 47 | 44 | 79 | 13 |
| 1979 | 46 | 49 | 42 | 53 | 87 | 8 |
| 1978 | 40 | 46 | 32 | 57 | 77 | 12 |
| 1977 | 51 | 37 | 47 | 48 | 79 | 17 |

S = Support          O = Opposition

## Key Votes

**96th Congress**

| | |
|---|---|
| Weaken Carter oil profits tax (1979) | Y |
| Reject hospital cost control plan (1979) | Y |
| Implement Panama Canal Treaties (1979) | N |
| Establish Department of Education (1979) | Y |
| Approve Anti-busing Amendment (1979) | Y |
| Guarantee Chrysler Corp. loans (1979) | N |
| Approve military draft registration (1980) | Y |
| Aid Sandinista regime in Nicaragua (1980) | N |
| Strengthen fair housing laws (1980) | N |

**97th Congress**

| | |
|---|---|
| Reagan budget proposal (1981) | Y |

## Interest Group Ratings

| Year | ADA | ACA | AFL-CIO | CCUS |
|---|---|---|---|---|
| 1980 | 11 | 63 | 16 | 86 |
| 1979 | 5 | 72 | 6 | 76 |
| 1978 | 10 | 75 | 5 | 67 |
| 1977 | 20 | 69 | 35 | 88 |

# Hawaii

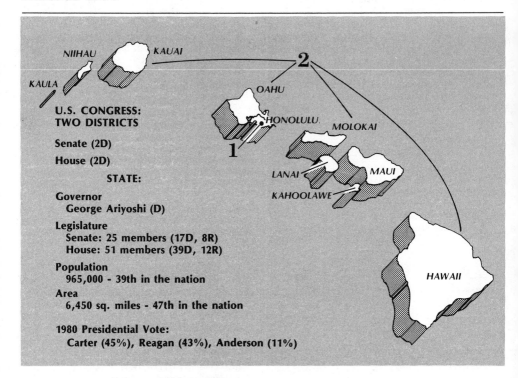

NIIHAU
KAUAI
KAULA

**2**

OAHU
HONOLULU
MOLOKAI

**U.S. CONGRESS:
TWO DISTRICTS**

**1**

Senate (2D)

House (2D)

LANAI
MAUI

KAHOOLAWE

**STATE:**

**Governor**
George Ariyoshi (D)

**Legislature**
Senate: 25 members (17D, 8R)
House: 51 members (39D, 12R)

**Population**
965,000 - 39th in the nation

**Area**
6,450 sq. miles - 47th in the nation

HAWAII

**1980 Presidential Vote:**
Carter (45%), Reagan (43%), Anderson (11%)

## ...Coping with Paradise

Hawaii strikes most people as an excellent place to live, and not just because of the climate and scenery. Unemployment is generally low, and the state has enjoyed explosive economic growth, mainly because of its booming tourist industry. Tourism contributes $2.5 billion yearly to the state's economy.

But the development that has accommodated all that tourism has brought other problems. Population has grown 60 percent in the last 20 years, bringing a quality of urban sprawl to much of the Honolulu area. Hawaii has to import 92 percent of its energy, and growth has strained the energy supply, causing the cost of living to soar. The crime rate has jumped. In 1980, soaring jet fares and the sagging mainland economy caused Hawaii's first decline in tourism in decades.

For years, Hawaii boasted of the cooperation between Oriental, Caucasian and Polynesian that exemplified its "aloha spirit." The spirit is being tested now by the demands of ethnic Hawaiians (those with pure or part Hawaiian blood, who make up about 19 percent of the state's population) for economic and political equality. While Caucasians (around 40 percent of the state population) hold the economic reins and Japanese (35 percent) much of the political power, the descendants of the islands' original inhabitants have little of either.

Whoever the state chooses to handle its promise and problems in the 1980s, Democrats are likely to remain dominant politically. Over the past 20 years, only Massachusetts and Rhode Island have been rivals to Hawaii for partisan consistency.

During the territorial days, Hawaii was run by a Republican Party dominated by the "Big Five" corporate interests based in Honolulu. After World War II, a strong labor union movement gave impetus to the growth of the Democratic

Party. Democrats embraced the interests of the Japanese and Chinese and gained majority status. In recent years, the Japanese have dominated politics, with Sen. Daniel K. Inouye and Gov. George Ariyoshi the leading figures.

Hiram Fong, the state's GOP senator from 1959 to 1977, is the only Republican who has ever served in Congress from Hawaii. Democratic presidential candidates have carried the state in five of the six elections since statehood — only George McGovern lost it.

## A Political Tour

**Honolulu County.** Honolulu County on the island of Oahu has four-fifths of the state's people. The hotels of Waikiki and natural wonders like Diamond Head draw millions of tourists each year. Pearl Harbor is on Oahu, giving the military an important role on the island. The state government, in Honolulu, is a major employer. Pineapples and sugar cane grow on Oahu, and Honolulu is a major trading center.

It is axiomatic in Hawaii that to win the state one must do well on Oahu Island. Although the island is predominantly Democratic, the concentration of economic power and wealth causes Oahu to be more competitive politically than the other islands. Reagan actually carried the Honolulu-based 1st District in 1980, but most statewide Democratic candidates still win the area easily.

Much of the GOP vote comes from the managerial group involved with the major Honolulu corporations. There is a Republican-leaning military vote and a fairly large group of Republican-voting Mormons who are connected with the Hawaii branch of Brigham Young University.

**Hawaii County.** Hawaii Island is the "big island" at the southeastern end of the chain. Taking up almost two-thirds of the state's land area, it is the second most populous, but has only an eighth of the population of Oahu. Hilo, the main city on the island, is the state's third largest.

Agriculture is the backbone of Hawaii Island's economy, with sugar cane the main crop. Cattle, macadamia nuts, coffee beans and orchids are also part of the island's agricultural economy.

**Maui and Kauai Counties.** The "other islands" of the Hawaiian chain contribute to the island's agricultural wealth but play only a minor political role.

The three populated islands of Maui County make up the state's richest pineapple-growing land. Sugar cane and beef cattle are also prevalent there and in Kauai County, the lightly populated group of islands at the the northernmost end of the archipelago.

## Redrawing the Lines

Population in Hawaii's two districts varies substantially. A Democratic-controlled nine-member commission was assigned to move about 60,000 Oahu Island voters from the 2nd District to the 1st. Because the 2nd District includes many residents of military bases who do not vote in the state, districts are drawn using voter registration figures, not the census headcount.

## Governor
## George Ariyoshi (D)

**Born:** March 12, 1926, Honolulu, Hawaii.
**Home:** Honolulu, Hawaii.
**Education:** Michigan State U., B.A. 1949; U. of Michigan, J.D. 1952.
**Military Career:** Army, 1945-46.
**Profession:** Lawyer.
**Family:** Wife, Jean; three children.
**Religion:** Protestant.
**Political Career:** Hawaii territorial House, 1954-58; territorial Senate, 1958-59; Hawaii Senate 1959-70; majority leader, 1965-66, 1969-70; lieutenant governor, 1970-73; acting governor, 1973-74 when Gov. John Burns became ill; elected governor 1974, 1978; term expires Dec. 1982.

# Daniel K. Inouye (D)

**Of Honolulu — Elected 1962**

**Born:** Sept. 7, 1924, Honolulu, Hawaii.
**Education:** U. of Hawaii, A.B. 1950; George Washington U., J.D. 1952.
**Military Career:** Army, 1943-47.
**Profession:** Lawyer.
**Family:** Wife, Margaret Shinobu Awamura; one child.
**Religion:** Methodist.
**Political Career:** Hawaii Territorial House, 1954-58, majority leader; Hawaii Territorial Senate, 1958-59; U.S. House, 1959-63.

**In Washington:** Inouye, a four-term veteran with a seat secure enough to qualify for Civil Service status, is a pillar of what remains of the old Senate Democratic "establishment." Although he has never chaired a standing committee, he has always been the ally and confidant of senior Democrats who, until 1981, occupied positions of power.

Throughout his congressional career, first in the House and now in the Senate, Inouye has gravitated toward a series of influential mentors — the late House Speaker Sam Rayburn, Lyndon B. Johnson, Hubert H. Humphrey and former Majority Leader Mike Mansfield. In the 1960s, Mansfield frequently touted him for a place on a future Democratic national ticket. The closest he came was a flurry of speculation in 1968 and a consolation prize: he was keynote speaker at the Democratic National Convention that year.

With this encouragement and support, Inouye has held a variety of minor leadership posts within the Senate Democratic hierarchy. He headed the Democratic Senatorial Campaign Committee in 1970. He is presently secretary of the Democratic Conference, the third-ranking minority leadership position. He has had the job since 1977. He has never tried to move up, however, apparently satisfied to let others have the top leadership posts without challenge.

Inouye's one period of national prominence came in 1973, when Mansfield named him to the Senate Watergate Committee, an assignment he had sought to avoid. Inouye argued that he already had too much committee work and was up for re-election the next year. "But, how can you say no to Mike Mansfield?" Inouye said later. "He's such a decent person." Inouye's polite but probing interrogation of key witnesses soon won him a popular following, and polls showed him with the highest nationwide "favorable" ratings of

any panel member. Millions chortled when Inouye, unaware that his microphone was still live, muttered "What a liar!" after hearing the testimony of White House aide John Ehrlichman. And support poured in for the senator when Ehrlichman's lawyer publicly called him "that little Jap."

Inouye, 5 feet 6 and the first Japanese-American ever elected to Congress, was decidedly not amused by the "little Jap" remark. It was quickly followed by an apology.

One of the reforms growing out of the Watergate era was the creation of a new Senate select committee to oversee U.S. intelligence agencies. Inouye was the first chairman of the panel, in 1976-77, and proposed a new legislative charter for the intelligence community that would prohibit the hiring of journalists and clergymen as covert agents. Inouye stepped down before the charter could become a reality; he insisted on serving just one term to avoid developing "too close a relationship" with the agencies he was charged with supervising. He noted that senior members of Congress had known about many of the abuses that led to creation of the special oversight committee, but had remained silent because they had become too cozy with the CIA and other agencies.

Inouye remains a member of the Intelligence Committee, but most of his recent legislative activity has been concentrated on the Commerce Committee, where he served during the 96th Congress as chairman of a subcommittee especially designed for him, Merchant Marine and Tourism. Both are vitally important to his island state. Over the years, Inouye has worked consistently to promote shipping interests and has been supported, in return, by both maritime unions and shippers. On one occasion, he was embarrassed by news accounts that his campaign committee received and failed to report campaign contributions from officials of a shipbuilding company.

Wearing his tourism hat, Inouye sponsored legislation in the 96th Congress to promote travel to the United States from abroad. As an early supporter of President Carter, he was annoyed at lack of support from the Carter administration, which tried to move in the opposite direction by downgrading the existing U.S. Travel Service. "This is good money waiting to be plucked," Inouye said of the $50-billion-a-year industry. But the effort to write an expanded program into law ended abruptly in 1980 when Carter pocket-vetoed a bill to create a new tourism corporation. It was reintroduced in 1981 and passed the Senate, but ran into opposition from the Reagan administration.

Inouye also had problems with a 1980 bill to try to bolster the ailing U.S. maritime industry. He wanted to speed up regulatory actions of the Federal Maritime Commission and broaden antitrust exemptions for the industry. The bill passed the Senate easily, with little discussion either in committee or on the floor. But the issue became tangled in a House jurisdictional squabble and a more ambitious version of the same bill never reached a floor vote in the House.

Republicans split the subcommittee in 1981 and created a new business, trade and tourism panel for one of their own, Larry Pressler of South Dakota.

On the Appropriations Committee, where he headed the Subcommittee on Foreign Operations until the Republican takeover of the Senate, Inouye has been in the middle of some bitter battles with the House, where foreign aid is not very popular. In 1980, Inouye's subcommittee waited in vain for the House to finish work on its version of the foreign aid budget, and never even marked up a bill of its own. For the second year in a row, aid programs were financed under stopgap appropriations without Congress taking a close look at separate projects.

Over the years, however, Inouye has generally won good marks for conducting a thorough line-by-line review of foreign aid programs before funding them. He has consistently argued against efforts to restrict the U.S. in its aid to the multilateral development banks.

**At Home:** World War II cost Inouye his right arm, but it made him a hero and built the foundation for a political career of uninterrupted success. Before the war, Inouye had wanted to become a surgeon. After he was wounded, fighting in Italy and France with the all Japanese-American 442nd Regiment, he went into law and eventually into politics. He held several party posts, was majority leader in the territorial House of Representatives and then moved to the territorial Senate.

Inouye originally planned to run for the U.S. Senate when Hawaii was granted statehood in 1959. But he withdrew from that race and went for the U.S. House instead, winning with the largest number of votes ever cast in Hawaii at the time. He explained that he wanted to "give some elder statesman in our party a clear field" for the Senate.

This patience was rewarded. When Democratic Sen. Oren E. Long announced his decision in 1962 not to seek re-election, he endorsed Inouye to succeed him and promised his support. Inouye went on to defeat Republican Benjamin F. Dillingham, a member of one of Hawaii's pioneer families, by a landslide. Since then, he never has gone below 75 percent of the vote.

## Committees

**Appropriations** (4th of 14 Democrats)
Defense; Foreign Operations; Labor, Health and Human Services, Education; Military Construction; State, Justice, Commerce, the Judiciary.

**Commerce, Science and Transportation** (4th of 8 Democrats)
Aviation; Communications; Merchant Marine.

**Select Indian Affairs** (2nd of 3 Democrats)

**Select Intelligence** (4th of 7 Democrats)
Budget; Collection and Foreign Operations.

## Elections

**1980 General**

| | |
|---|---|
| Daniel Inouye (D) | 224,485 (78%) |
| Cooper Brown (R) | 53,068 (18%) |

**1980 Primary**

| | |
|---|---|
| Daniel Inouye (D) | 198,467 (87%) |
| Kamuela Price (D) | 15,361 (7%) |
| John Fritz (D) | 12,930 (6%) |

**Previous Winning Percentages**

| | | | |
|---|---|---|---|
| 1974 (83%) | 1962 (69%) | 1960* (74%) | 1959† (68%) |

*House election.
† special House election.

## Daniel K. Inouye, D-Hawaii

### Campaign Finance

| | Receipts | Receipts from PACs | Expenditures |
|---|---|---|---|
| 1980 | | | |
| Inouye (D) | $747,213 | $101,817 (14%) | $480,113 |
| Brown (R) | $6,795 | — (0%) | $14,382 |

### Voting Studies

| Year | Presidential Support S | O | Party Unity S | O | Conservative Coalition S | O |
|---|---|---|---|---|---|---|
| Senate service | | | | | | |
| 1980 | 64 | 16 | 72 | 8 | 25 | 48 |
| 1979 | 63 | 11 | 66 | 6 | 18 | 51 |
| 1978 | 72 | 11 | 71 | 8 | 15 | 61 |
| 1977 | 68 | 10 | 74 | 11 | 18 | 68 |
| 1976 | 28 | 28 | 48 | 18 | 29 | 38 |
| 1975 | 32 | 34 | 65 | 11 | 20 | 55 |
| 1974 (Ford) | 46 | 31 | | | | |
| 1974 | 28 | 39 | 56 | 14 | 19 | 51 |
| 1973 | 32 | 56 | 73 | 11† | 23 | 65† |
| 1972 | 33 | 54 | 79 | 6 | 9 | 73 |
| 1971 | 30 | 43 | 64 | 10 | 20 | 54 |
| 1970 | 41 | 32 | 65 | 7 | 8 | 63 |
| 1969 | 43 | 36 | 75 | 11 | 20 | 64 |
| 1968 | 62 | 10 | 51 | 11 | 13 | 57 |
| 1967 | 65 | 15 | 67 | 9 | 11 | 61 |
| 1966 | 77 | 16 | 83 | 3 | 7 | 84 |
| 1965 | 83 | 10 | 92 | 6 | 15 | 85 |
| 1964 | 88 | 8 | 90 | 7 | 18 | 82 |
| 1963 | 89 | 3 | 92 | 2 | 5 | 93 |
| House service | | | | | | |
| 1962 | 90 | 2 | 88 | 0 | 0 | 94 |
| 1961 | 86 | 6 | 88 | 2 | 4 | 83 |

S = Support    O = Opposition
†Not eligible for all recorded votes.

### Key Votes

**96th Congress**

| | |
|---|---|
| Maintain relations with Taiwan (1979) | X |
| Reduce synthetic fuel development funds (1979) | N |
| Impose nuclear plant moratorium (1979) | N |
| Kill stronger windfall profits tax (1979) | N |
| Guarantee Chrysler Corp. loans (1979) | Y |
| Approve military draft registration (1980) | Y |
| End Revenue Sharing to the states (1980) | ? |
| Block Justice Dept. busing suits (1980) | N |

**97th Congress**

| | |
|---|---|
| Restore urban program funding cuts (1981) | Y |

### Interest Group Ratings

| Year | ADA | ACA | AFL-CIO | CCUS-1 | CCUS-2 |
|---|---|---|---|---|---|
| Senate service | | | | | |
| 1980 | 67 | 23 | 75 | 34 | |
| 1979 | 37 | 6 | 77 | 20 | 43 |
| 1978 | 60 | 19 | 80 | 41 | |
| 1977 | 60 | 13 | 85 | 23 | |
| 1976 | 45 | 0 | 73 | 0 | |
| 1975 | 56 | 8 | 90 | 13 | |
| 1974 | 43 | 13 | 88 | 17 | |
| 1973 | 70 | 15 | 91 | 11 | |
| 1972 | 65 | 6 | 100 | 0 | |
| 1971 | 63 | 0 | 100 | - | |
| 1970 | 72 | 0 | 100 | 0 | |
| 1969 | 72 | 0 | 91 | - | |
| 1968 | 64 | 0 | 100 | - | |
| 1967 | 62 | 0 | 89 | 33 | |
| 1966 | 75 | 0 | 100 | - | |
| 1965 | 82 | 4 | - | 10 | |
| 1964 | 75 | 0 | 90 | - | |
| 1963 | - | 0 | - | - | |
| House service | | | | | |
| 1962 | 100 | 0 | 100 | - | |
| 1961 | 100 | - | - | - | |

# Spark M. Matsunaga (D)

## Of Honolulu — Elected 1976

**Born:** Oct. 8, 1916, Kauai, Hawaii.
**Education:** U. of Hawaii, Ed.B. 1941; Harvard U., J.D. 1951.
**Military Career:** Army, 1941-45.
**Profession:** Lawyer.
**Family:** Wife, Helen Tokunaga; five children.
**Religion:** Episcopalian.
**Political Career:** Hawaii Territorial House, 1954-59; U.S. House, 1963-77.

**In Washington:** Matsunaga has never been an aggressive leader over two decades in Congress, but he has always been able to keep himself close to the center of power.

In the House, where he spent seven terms, he quickly gravitated to the Rules Committee, and rose in Democratic leadership ranks to be a national deputy whip.

Arriving in the Senate as a freshman in 1977, he won a place on the Finance Committee under Russell Long, and immediately found himself chairman of a newly created subcommittee on Tourism and Sugar — a gesture to constituent interests so obvious that it seemed to raise the question of why pineapples were left out.

It is Matsunaga's personality that has kept him close to the action for so many years. Sunny and even-tempered, he is impossible to dislike. And he has been a loyalist, generally willing to accept party positions and reluctant to challenge established procedures.

During his four years in the Senate, Matsunaga has spent much of his time as a sort of goodwill ambassador from Hawaii to the capital. He loves to display the symbols of his islands' tropical abundance. He is frequently photographed in a Hawaiian lei, and sometimes wears one to Finance Committee meetings. Bowls of macadamia nuts greet visitors to his office.

Matsunaga's primary legislative concern has been the promotion of Hawaii's economy. During markup of an energy bill on Finance, members were adding a "Christmas tree" full of amendments on subjects only tangential to energy. But Matsunaga outdid them all when he proposed a tax credit for an energy-related aspect of the macademia nut industry. It was not acted on.

While he held his Tourism and Sugar chairmanship, before the Republican Senate takeover in 1981, Matsunaga used it to try to fight for guaranteed price levels for sugar producers. But such a plan died in the House.

Past 60 when he was elected to the Senate, Matsunaga has generally maintained a lower pro-

file there than he did in the House, where he was not only involved in leadership matters but won some notable victories in foreign policy.

Many of Matsunaga's concerns were shaped by the experiences of Japanese-Americans during World War II. A veteran of the all-Nisei regiment that served in Europe during the war, Matsunaga escaped the internment camps to which many of his friends and relatives were confined. He sponsored 1971 legislation to repeal the Emergency Detention Act, which allowed the government to establish detention camps. He also pushed to return funds to Japanese-Americans whose bank accounts were confiscated during the war.

Matsunaga has been a strong backer of efforts to control the nuclear arms race. He was a critic of the Vietnam War under the Nixon administration, cosponsoring a variety of anti-war resolutions. With his large military constituency, however, Matsunaga has been an advocate of higher military pay. In 1979 he cosponsored an unsuccessful amendment to provide the military with a 10 percent across-the-board pay increase.

Matsunaga is the leading congressional advocate of a proposed "Department of Peace." He chairs a federal commission studying that idea, and a proposal for a National Academy of Peace.

**At Home:** Matsunaga's election in 1976 gave Hawaii two senators of Japanese ancestry for the first time since statehood. He succeeded Republican Hiram Fong, who retired, and he did it with surprising ease, turning back fellow House member Patsy T. Mink in the Democratic primary and overcoming Republican former Gov. William F. Quinn in the general election.

The primary was essentially a popularity contest between Matsunaga and Mink, who differed little on issues. Both had broad statewide recognition because before 1970 Hawaii elected its representatives to Congress on an at-large basis.

Mink accused the genial Matsunaga of lacking leadership qualities, but Matsunaga claimed his less militant approach would pay off better in the Senate. He had the support of Democratic Gov. George Ariyoshi and the AFL-CIO, and defeated her by more than 20,000 votes.

In Quinn, Matsunaga encountered a personable and well-financed campaigner who said the state ought to have one senator in Washington from each party. Quinn ran fairly well in Honolulu and on the island of Hawaii, but Matsunaga still carried both, and claimed the seat with slightly less than a 40,000-vote margin.

Matsunaga was an active participant in Hawaii politics before he ran for Congress. After serving as an assistant prosecutor in Honolulu, he won election to the territorial House, where he was majority leader. Running as a liberal in 1962, he won a U.S. House seat.

Matsunaga is legendary for taking Hawaiians out to lunch when they visit Washington. Almost every day, he can be found at a large table in the Senate dining room, hosting a group of Islanders. His annual luncheon tab runs to about $15,000, paid for out of re-election funds.

## Committees

**Energy and Natural Resources** (6th of 9 Democrats)
Energy and Mineral Resources; Energy Conservation and Supply; Public Land and Reserved Water.

**Finance** (4th of 9 Democrats)
International Trade; Savings, Pensions, and Investment Policy; Taxation and Debt Management.

**Veterans' Affairs** (3rd of 5 Democrats)

## Elections

**1976 General**

| | |
|---|---|
| Spark Matsunaga (D ) | 162,305 (54 %) |
| William Quinn (R ) | 122,724 (41 %) |

**1976 Primary**

| | |
|---|---|
| Spark Matsunaga (D ) | 105,731 (51 %) |
| Patsy Mink (D ) | 84,732 (41 %) |

**Previous Winning Percentages**

| | | | |
|---|---|---|---|
| 1974* (59 %) | 1972* (55 %) | 1970* (73 %) | 1968† (67 %) |
| 1966* (69 %) | 1964* (61 %) | 1962* (73 %) | |

*House elections    †Elected at large, 1962-1968

## Campaign Finance

| | Receipts | Receipts from PACs | Expenditures |
|---|---|---|---|
| **1976** | | | |
| Matsunaga (D ) | 416,775 | 92,983 (22 %) | 435,130 |
| Quinn (R ) | 417,652 | 53,462 (13 %) | 415,138 |

## Voting Studies

| | Presidential Support | | Party Unity | | Conservative Coalition | |
|---|---|---|---|---|---|---|
| Year | S | O | S | O | S | O |
| **Senate service** | | | | | | |
| 1980 | 69 | 20 | 83 | 7 | 11 | 82 |
| 1979 | 73 | 8 | 81 | 6 | 25 | 62 |
| 1978 | 82 | 14 | 88 | 7 | 13 | 80 |
| 1977 | 83 | 16 | 83 | 13 | 25 | 71 |
| **House service** | | | | | | |
| 1976 | 20 | 55 | 62 | 6 | 15 | 54 |
| 1975 | 38 | 57 | 78 | 7 | 16 | 72 |
| 1974 (Ford) | 48 | 52 | | | | |
| 1974 | 42 | 53 | 86 | 9 | 21 | 71 |
| 1973 | 33 | 63 | 92 | 7 | 20 | 79 |
| 1972 | 46 | 30 | 70 | 16 | 20 | 66 |
| 1971 | 39 | 58 | 88 | 7 | 16 | 79 |
| 1970 | 62 | 32 | 74 | 13 | 11 | 82 |
| 1969 | 60 | 36 | 93 | 4 | 11 | 82 |
| 1968 | 76 | 5 | 87 | 0 | 4 | 78 |
| 1967 | 84 | 6 | 92 | 1 | 4 | 87 |
| 1966 | 65 | 5 | 70 | 0 | 0 | 68 |
| 1965 | 89 | 4 | 90 | 1 | 2 | 96 |
| 1964 | 77 | 6 | 66 | 3 | 8 | 83 |
| 1963 | 87 | 3 | 96 | 0 | 0 | 93 |

S = Support    O = Opposition

## Key Votes

**96th Congress**

| | |
|---|---|
| Maintain relations with Taiwan (1979) | ? |
| Reduce synthetic fuel development funds (1979) | N |
| Impose nuclear plant moratorium (1979) | Y |
| Kill stronger windfall profits tax (1979) | N |
| Guarantee Chrysler Corp. loans (1979) | Y |
| Approve military draft registration (1980) | N |
| End Revenue Sharing to the states (1980) | N |
| Block Justice Dept. busing suits (1980) | N |

**97th Congress**

| | |
|---|---|
| Restore urban program funding cuts (1981) | Y |

## Interest Group Ratings

| Year | ADA | ACA | AFL-CIO | CCUS-1 | CCUS-2 |
|---|---|---|---|---|---|
| **Senate service** | | | | | |
| 1980 | 78 | 13 | 83 | 33 | |
| 1979 | 53 | 8 | 82 | 0 | 29 |
| 1978 | 70 | 5 | 89 | 29 | |
| 1977 | 80 | 4 | 85 | 29 | |
| **House service** | | | | | |
| 1976 | 65 | 9 | 91 | 0 | |
| 1975 | 68 | 20 | 91 | 12 | |
| 1974 | 87 | 0 | 100 | 13 | |
| 1973 | 84 | 7 | 90 | 30 | |
| 1972 | 75 | 9 | 82 | 0 | |
| 1971 | 59 | 16 | 91 | - | |
| 1970 | 88 | 0 | 100 | 10 | |
| 1969 | 73 | 0 | 90 | - | |
| 1968 | 92 | 0 | 100 | - | |
| 1967 | 87 | 0 | 92 | 20 | |
| 1966 | 94 | 0 | 100 | - | |
| 1965 | 89 | 0 | - | 10 | |
| 1964 | 96 | 0 | 100 | - | |
| 1963 | - | 0 | - | - | |

# 1 Cecil Heftel (D)

### Of Honolulu — Elected 1976

**Born:** Sept. 30, 1924, Cook County, Ill.
**Education:** Arizona State U., B.S. 1951.
**Military Career:** Army Air Corps, 1943-46.
**Profession:** Broadcast executive.
**Family:** Wife, Joyce Glassman; seven children.
**Religion:** Mormon.
**Political Career:** Unsuccessful Democratic candidate for U.S. Senate, 1970.

**In Washington:** Heftel is a swing vote on the Ways and Means Committee, a man of liberal inclination on many issues with a self-made millionaire's urge to cut the red tape and let private industry solve problems on its own.

Placed on the committee in 1979 at the start of his second House term, Heftel began looking for ways to use tax policy to stimulate energy independence. He introduced a variety of tax credit proposals, all of which seemed a little ambitious to most members of the committee. By the end of 1980, Heftel had sponsored legislation to provide incentives for energy from shale oil, municipal wastes, magnetic fusion, ocean thermal development and solar power.

On broader committee issues, Heftel is a man who is often willing to vote with the liberal Democratic leadership but who likes to listen to Republicans and their conservative Democratic allies. In the 96th Congress, he voted to soften the oil windfall profits tax and opposed President Carter's hospital cost containment program. He came within one vote, 13-12, of persuading the committee to change the way disability payments are made and cut off some of the money for the partially-disabled who are under 55 years old.

In the 97th Congress, liberal Democrats moved in Heftel's pro-business direction. A Ways and Means task force where he served endorsed some ideas he had championed for years, like corporate tax rate cuts, in an effort to hold conservative Democrats, attract some GOP votes and try to halt the Reagan dominance on Capitol Hill.

Heftel sharply criticized the Carter administration in 1979 for failing to support his $20 million bill providing special education for children of native Hawaiian ancestry. He accused the Department of Health, Education and Welfare of refusing to tell him in advance that they would oppose him. "This kind of backdoor dealing," Heftel said, "has become the most frustrating thing about dealing with the administration."

**At Home:** After a successful career in broadcasting, Heftel entered politics in 1970 by taking on Republican Sen. Hiram Fong, who had served since statehood in 1959. Although Hawaii was Democratic, Fong had never been in serious trouble and was expected to win with ease. Both the state's Democratic House members thought about challenging him and decided not to.

Heftel was willing, and he turned out to be a surprisingly difficult opponent. Democrat Daniel Inouye, the state's junior senator and the main influence behind Heftel's decision to run, provided important credibility. Heftel himself was already known in the Honolulu business community and was familiar to much of the public through appearances he made on his own television station. He held Fong's plurality to an embarrassingly small 7,566 votes.

That campaign established Heftel as a significant political figure in the state. Six years later he had a second opportunity to run for Congress, and this time his personal fortune, television reputation and alliance with Inouye made him a winner.

In 1976, Democratic Reps. Spark Matsunaga and Patsy Mink both decided on the Senate campaign they had turned down in 1970. With the Honolulu-based 1st District open, Heftel opted to run for the House. Despite Inouye's backing, he encountered strong primary opposition from John P. Craven, the state's former marine affairs com-

---

**1st District: Honolulu.** Population: 394,423 (9% increase since 1970). Race: White 124,060 (31%), Black 6,013 (2%), Asian and Pacific Islander 247,286 (63%), Others 17,084 (4%). Spanish origin: 16,146 (4%).

missioner, who ran with the support of Gov. George Ariyoshi. But Heftel won the nomination by 8,000 votes.

Then he faced Republican Fred Rohlfing, a respected former state legislator who had run a strong race for the seat in 1972. Rohlfing tried to establish a campaign spending limit, hoping to neutralize the Democrat's financial advantages, but no agreement was reached. Heftel won by 6,305 votes, on total expenditures for the year of $555,381. He has had no trouble holding on to the seat since then.

**The District:** Hawaii converted its two at-large House seats into two congressional districts in 1969. Heftel's 1st consists of the city of Honolulu and a small portion of its suburbs. Always Democratic, the district elected Spark Matsunaga to the House in 1970 and re-elected him until his successful run for the Senate in 1976. A diverse and cosmopolitan city with Japanese, Chinese, Filipino, Caucasian and native Hawaiian populations, Honolulu is the site of numerous military installations as well as a world tourist center. It is also the home of the University of Hawaii.

The district has grown only slightly over the past decade and is probably below the number needed for the 1982 election, even considering Hawaii's unique method of basing district population on registered voters.

## Committees

**Ways and Means** (15th of 23 Democrats)
Health; Oversight.

## Elections

**1980 General**

| | |
|---|---|
| Cecil Heftel (D ) | 98,256 (80 %) |
| Aloma Noble (R ) | 19,819 (16 %) |

**1980 Primary**

| | |
|---|---|
| Cecil Heftel (D ) | 73,162 (72 %) |
| Charles Campbell (D ) | 26,024 (26 %) |

**1978 General**

| | |
|---|---|
| Cecil Heftel (D ) | 84,552 (73 %) |
| William Spillane (R ) | 24,470 (21 %) |

**Previous Winning Percentage**

1976 (44 %)

**District Vote For President**

| | 1980 | | 1976 | | 1972 |
|---|---|---|---|---|---|
| D | 56,298 (43 %) | D | 65,216 (49 %) | D | 49,781 (38 %) |
| R | 58,045 (44 %) | R | 67,080 (50 %) | R | 82,272 (62 %) |
| I | 14,842 (11 %) | | | | |

## Campaign Finance

| | Receipts | Receipts from PACs | Expen-ditures |
|---|---|---|---|
| **1980** | | | |
| Heftel (D ) | $376,487 | $128,670 (34 %) | $312,070 |
| Noble (R ) | $7,413 | $750 (10 %) | $7,413 |

| **1978** | | | |
|---|---|---|---|
| Heftel (D ) | $175,083 | $25,516 (15 %) | $174,306 |
| Spillane (R ) | $2,860 | - (0 %) | $18,694 |

## Voting Studies

| | Presidential Support | | Party Unity | | Conservative Coalition | |
|---|---|---|---|---|---|---|
| Year | S | O | S | O | S | O |
| 1980 | 76 | 17 | 73 | 18 | 41 | 47 |
| 1979 | 68 | 23 | 68 | 19 | 45 | 45 |
| 1978 | 69 | 28 | 70 | 26 | 44 | 52 |
| 1977 | 68 | 23 | 80 | 12 | 32 | 59 |

S = Support          O = Opposition

## Key Votes

**96th Congress**

| | |
|---|---|
| Weaken Carter oil profits tax (1979) | Y |
| Reject hospital cost control plan (1979) | Y |
| Implement Panama Canal Treaties (1979) | Y |
| Establish Department of Education (1979) | Y |
| Approve Anti-busing Amendment (1979) | N |
| Guarantee Chrysler Corp. loans (1979) | Y |
| Approve military draft registration (1980) | Y |
| Aid Sandinista regime in Nicaragua (1980) | N |
| Strengthen fair housing laws (1980) | Y |

**97th Congress**

| | |
|---|---|
| Reagan budget proposal (1981) | N |

## Interest Group Ratings

| Year | ADA | ACA | AFL-CIO | CCUS |
|---|---|---|---|---|
| 1980 | 50 | 29 | 67 | 57 |
| 1979 | 42 | 13 | 65 | 44 |
| 1978 | 35 | 15 | 53 | 35 |
| 1977 | 60 | 15 | 86 | 18 |

# 2 Daniel K. Akaka (D)

**Of Honolulu — Elected 1976**

**Born:** Sept. 11, 1924, Honolulu, Hawaii.
**Education:** U. of Hawaii, B.Ed. 1952, M.Ed. 1966.
**Military Career:** Army, 1945-47.
**Profession:** Educator.
**Family:** Wife, Mary Mildred Chong; five children.
**Religion:** Congregationalist.
**Political Career:** Unsuccessfully sought Democratic nomination for Lt. Governor, 1974.

**In Washington:** If influence in the House depended on loyalty alone, Akaka would have had little trouble making it to the Appropriations Committee, where he has wanted to be for most of his House career. But to his surprise and frustration, he had a great deal of trouble getting there.

When Akaka made his move for the committee, in 1979, he was able to point to a voting record virtually no one in the House could match. In a series of crucial roll calls over more than a year, he had voted with Speaker O'Neill every single time, even on politically difficult issues like hospital cost containment and the Panama Canal treaties.

When the seat went instead to Bill Hefner of North Carolina, Akaka felt he had been treated unfairly. Hefner had a much lower loyalty score, but he also had a reputation as a man with influence in the Southern delegations. Perhaps more important, Akaka had been perceived as a passive, though compliant, member of the Agriculture Committee, his original assignment.

Akaka barely kept his anger controlled during the rest of 1980. When the 97th Congress convened in January, the leadership realized it had to do something. O'Neill supported Akaka's second try, and he made it to Appropriations easily.

On Agriculture, Akaka mainly supported the sugar industry, his state's dominant crop interest. He found himself in a difficult position in 1979 when the committee reported out a comprehensive sugar price support bill. That legislation would have set up direct payments to sugar growers, but would have limited those payments to $50,000 per grower.

Hawaii, unlike the sugar beet states of the Midwest, had 15 large growers who would have found their subsidies restricted by the limitation. "Hawaii will be priced out of the market," Akaka complained. He voted against the bill, allying himself with urban consumer interests, although for opposite reasons. The bill was ultimately beaten in the House.

**At Home:** Akaka is the only native Hawaiian ever elected to Congress. A close ally of Democratic Gov. George Ariyoshi, he came up through the Honolulu education bureaucracy before entering politics. After serving as a school principal and educational program specialist, he was picked in 1971 to head the state Office of Economic Opportunity.

In 1974, Ariyoshi picked him as his running mate for lieutenant governor in the Democratic primary. Ariyoshi won his contest, but Akaka lost the nomination to Nelson Doi. After Ariyoshi won the governorship, he appointed Akaka his special assistant for human resources.

In 1976, the 2nd District House seat opened up when Democratic Rep. Patsy Mink made an unsuccessful try for the U.S. Senate. Akaka entered the House primary with the backing of Ariyoshi and the state AFL-CIO. He faced formidable primary opposition in state Sen. Joe Kuroda, who had been planning his campaign for months and had the support of a variety of independent labor unions. Akaka pulled through with a majority of 2,015 votes. In November, he was swept in with 79.5 percent, and his margins have increased since then.

**The District:** This is the everything-but-Honolulu district. It includes all the Hawaiian

---

**2nd District: Honolulu suburbs and Outer Islands.** Population: 570,577 (40% increase since 1970). Race: White 194,568 (34%), Black 11,339 (2%), Asian and Pacific Islander 336,374 (59%), Others 28,296 (5%). Spanish origin: 50,332 (9%).

---

Islands outside of Oahu, where Honolulu is located, plus suburbs of the city on Oahu itself. The fast-growing suburbs have swelled the population of the district and will probably result in some transfer of population to the 1st District.

Since its creation for the 1970 elections, the 2nd has always gone Democratic, usually by margins greater than those of the 1st. In 1976, it gave Jimmy Carter a plurality of 9,257 votes, allowing him to lose the other district and still carry the state.

Like the 1st, the 2nd abounds in military installations. Pearl Harbor is only one of a complex of Navy, Marine and Air Force bases. In the outer islands, agriculture is predominant, especially sugar and pineapples.

## Committees

**Appropriations** (30th of 33 Democrats)
  Agriculture; Treasury-Postal Service.

**Select Narcotics Abuse and Control** (9th of 11 Democrats)

## Elections

**1980 General**

| | |
|---|---|
| Daniel Akaka (D) | 141,477 (90%) |
| Don Smith (LI) | 15,903 (10%) |

**1978 General**

| | |
|---|---|
| Daniel Akaka (D) | 118,272 (86%) |
| Charles Isaak (R) | 15,697 (11%) |

**Previous Winning Percentages**

1976 (80 %)

**District Vote For President**

| | 1980 | | 1976 | | 1972 |
|---|---|---|---|---|---|
| **D** | 79,581 (46 %) | **D** | 81,950 (52 %) | **D** | 51,415 (37 %) |
| **R** | 72,067 (42 %) | **R** | 72,693 (46 %) | **R** | 86,136 (63 %) |
| **I** | 17,179 (10 %) | | | | |

## Campaign Finance

| | Receipts | Receipts from PACs | Expenditures |
|---|---|---|---|
| **1980** | | | |
| Akaka (D ) | $135,510 | $36,457 (27 %) | $85,018 |
| **1978** | | | |
| Akaka (D ) | $210,574 | $32,615 (15 %) | $208,958 |
| Isaak (R ) | $8,317 | $800 (10 %) | $7,016 |

## Voting Studies

| | Presidential Support | | Party Unity | | Conservative Coalition | |
|---|---|---|---|---|---|---|
| Year | S | O | S | O | S | O |
| 1980 | 79 | 14 | 84 | 7 | 29 | 59 |
| 1979 | 76 | 19 | 86 | 8 | 28 | 67 |
| 1978 | 70 | 27 | 84 | 9 | 24 | 70 |
| 1977 | 68 | 22 | 89 | 6 | 18 | 75 |

S = Support          O = Opposition

## Key Votes

**96th Congress**

| | |
|---|---|
| Weaken Carter oil profits tax (1979) | Y |
| Reject hospital cost control plan (1979) | N |
| Implement Panama Canal Treaties (1979) | Y |
| Establish Department of Education (1979) | Y |
| Approve Anti-busing Amendment (1979) | N |
| Guarantee Chrysler Corp. loans (1979) | # |
| Approve military draft registration (1980) | Y |
| Aid Sandinista regime in Nicaragua (1980) | Y |
| Strengthen fair housing laws (1980) | Y |

**97th Congress**

| | |
|---|---|
| Reagan budget proposal (1981) | N |

## Interest Group Ratings

| Year | ADA | ACA | AFL-CIO | CCUS |
|---|---|---|---|---|
| 1980 | 72 | 25 | 74 | 67 |
| 1979 | 68 | 8 | 65 | 18 |
| 1978 | 55 | 7 | 80 | 25 |
| 1977 | 60 | 7 | 87 | 18 |

# Idaho

## ... Tilting to the Right

A competitive two-party state for much of the postwar period, Idaho has been moving gradually to the Republican right in recent years, an evolution symbolized by the defeat in 1980 of Sen. Frank Church, the symbol of its remaining ties to the national Democratic Party.

In many ways, the fact that Church came within 5,000 votes of winning in the Reagan presidential year seems more remarkable than his defeat. There had been warning signals in other elections for nearly 20 years. In 1964, Barry Goldwater drew 49.1 percent of the vote in Idaho, his best showing outside Arizona and the South. By 1966, the last Democratic congressman was gone, and there has not been another one since. In 1974, moderate Republican Rep. Orval Hansen lost his House seat to George Hansen, a militant conservative.

Much of this represented the same anti-Washington feeling prevalent in other Mountain states, expressed against liberal Democrats and environmentalists. What is interesting is that the attitude has not really hurt Democrats running at the state level. Cecil Andrus took the governorship for the Democrats in 1970, and by 1974 he was popular enough to win a second term by 115,000 votes, the largest margin in Idaho history. Republicans felt certain they would take the statehouse back when Andrus left in 1977 to become Presidnt Carter's secretary of the interior. But John V. Evans, Andrus' replacement, took advantage of Republican bickering to keep the governorship in Democratic hands.

So Idaho has had a decade of moderate Democratic leadership at home and, except for Church, militant conservative representation in Washington. The current congressional delegation is solidly anti-government and pro-development. Sen. Steven Symms, the conqueror of Church in 1980, has been allied with the John Birch Society. Senior Sen. James McClure, chairman of the Senate Energy Committee, was an early leader in the "Sagebrush Rebellion" against federal land control. George Hansen is a strident voice of the right on foreign policy.

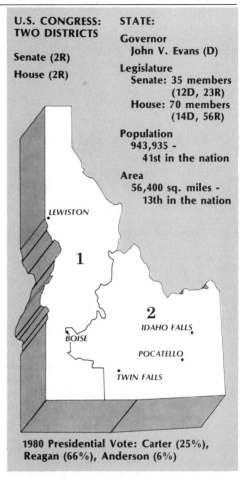

**U.S. CONGRESS: TWO DISTRICTS**

Senate (2R)
House (2R)

**STATE:**

Governor
John V. Evans (D)

Legislature
Senate: 35 members
(12D, 23R)
House: 70 members
(14D, 56R)

Population
943,935 -
41st in the nation

Area
56,400 sq. miles -
13th in the nation

**1980 Presidential Vote: Carter (25%), Reagan (66%), Anderson (6%)**

This lineup does not seem likely to change in the near future. The state's population grew by 32 percent in the 1970s, and many of the new residents were "refugees" from high taxes and urban problems in major metropolitan areas. Others were attracted by corporate jobs at the large number of businesses headquartered in Boise or by the high technology jobs becoming available as the electronics industry grows.

Idaho's natural beauty has consistently attracted environmentalists, and they are certain to remain a vocal and influential voice in the Democratic Party. But winning congressional elections may be another matter.

**305**

# A Political Tour

**Southeast Idaho.** In the mid-1800s, Mormons wandered north from Utah and founded the first settlements in what would become the state of Idaho. Today, southeastern Idaho is still Mormon. While only about a quarter of the state's residents are Mormons, almost two-thirds of the people in southeast Idaho are of the Mormon faith.

The early Mormons quickly discovered that the desert-like soils of southeast Idaho, assisted by the waters of the Snake River, were perfect for growing potatoes. Today, potatoes are the leading source of income, not only for southeast Idaho, but for the entire state.

Like their brethren elsewhere, the Mormons of southeast Idaho are generally Republicans, although Gov. Evans is a Mormon and a Democrat. GOP candidates can usually depend on comfortable margins in southeast Idaho. In Bonneville County (Idaho Falls), the region's largest, Republican presidential candidates since 1952 have averaged well over 60 percent of the vote; Ronald Reagan won 78 percent in 1980.

Idaho Falls is the state's third largest city. It is near the nuclear plant test site that pioneered commercial nuclear power in the 1950s. There is limited local opposition, but most residents are amenable to nuclear power. McClure has pressed for federal approval of a nuclear breeder reactor for Idaho Falls.

There are a few pockets of regular Democratic votes in southeastern Idaho, the greatest being Pocatello (Bannock County). Pocatello is the region's largest city with more than 40,000 people. It is a chemical industry center, specializing in phosphate fertilizers. With a heavy Democratic labor vote and a sizable student vote from Idaho State University, Bannock County gave Church a solid margin in his 1980 defeat.

But Pocatello does not cast enough votes to swing the region to Democratic candidates. Only the most popular Democrats, such as Andrus and Church in his better days, manage to carry southeast Idaho. There are few other major cities in southeast Idaho.

Twin Falls, in the "magic valley," is the third major city in this part of the state. It is in the center of a prosperous farming area that raises sugar beets and other cash crops, and it contributes to the Republican vote.

**Southwest Idaho/Boise.** The Snake River rolls on into the southwest part of the state, watering potato and sugar beet fields. The agricultural area here is almost as fertile for Republicans as it is for crops.

The hub of southwest Idaho is Boise, the state's capital and its largest city, with a population of slightly more than 100,000. The entire metropolitan area has close to a quarter million people and has been growing at a faster rate than the rest of the state.

The main reason for Boise's remarkable growth is its unusual capacity for retaining corporate headquarters. Boise inaugurated a thorough urban renewal program in the late 1960s and early 1970s to replace an aging downtown. This convinced a number of major corporations to locate or remain there.

Boise is home to Boise Cascade (the lumber and paper conglomerate), Ore-Ida (a food processing company best known for frozen french fries), J. R. Simplot Co. (a food processing and mineral development company founded and run by Idaho's "Potato King"), Albertson's (a major supermarket chain) and Morrison Knudsen (a construction firm that began a $40 million expansion of its Boise headquarters in 1980).

Although the recent influx of out-of-staters has changed Boise politics somewhat, the city is still essentially conservative and Republican. Ada County (Boise) makes up a fifth of the state vote and has given at least 56 percent to every Republican presidential candidate in the last 10 elections. The same is true of neighboring Canyon County, the state's second largest, which includes the growing cities of Caldwell and Nampa.

The rest of southwestern Idaho is made up mostly of lightly populated, Republican-voting farm counties. The Democrats in the area are mainly miners, lumbermen and Basque sheepherders, whose ancestors were among the early settlers of Idaho. This is where George Wallace scored his highest percentages in the state in 1968, winning from 15 to 23 percent in the non-urbanized counties in the region.

**The Northern Panhandle.** Idaho is divided into a clearly defined north and south by the Rocky Mountains. The south is mainly irrigated farm land, with some reasonably flat terrain and many wide-open spaces. The northern panhandle, by contrast, is mainly mountains, forests, lakes and mines. Much of it remains in wilderness. Unlike southern Idaho, the panhandle has little Mormon population.

The difference between the north and south extends into politics as well. The north has a much stronger traditional Democratic base than the south. There was considerable labor unrest in the panhandle during the late 19th and early 20th centuries, as underpaid lumbermen and miners sought to organize. Support for "free silver" also helped to establish Democrats as the party of northern Idaho.

To this day, Democratic candidates do best in the major silver mining and logging areas, although Republicans often prevail in the panhandle on the presidential level. While Church carried the panhandle by a substantial margin in 1980, Carter lost all 10 panhandle counties to Reagan.

Democrats generally do best in Shoshone County (home of the world's largest silver mine), Clearwater County and Nez Perce County. The latter contains Lewiston, the panhandle's biggest city and a major lumber center on the Snake River. The University of Idaho is also in the panhandle, at Moscow in Latah County.

The overall impact of the panhandle vote in statewide elections is limited by its relatively sparse population. Only 20 to 25 percent of Idaho's vote comes from the north.

The political complexion of the panhandle may be changing somewhat. Refugees from urban life have been settling near Coeur D'Alene, the region's second biggest city and one that is in the sphere of Spokane, Wash. Many of the new arrivals are fleeing from high taxes and city pressure; their voting habits appear to be Republican and conservative.

## Redrawing the Lines

Western Idaho's 1st District must lose roughly 21,000 people to the 2nd District. Democrats sponsored a plan to consolidate fast-growing Ada County, currently divided between two districts, into a single district. That would concentrate Ada's strong Republican vote and give Democrats a chance to win the other district.

But Republicans, who control both houses of the Legislature, favored only a minor adjustment in Ada County that would balance the districts' populations. Democratic Gov. Evans acknowledged that uniting Ada County would create an unwieldy 2nd District stretching from southeastern Idaho to the Canadian border.

## Governor
## John V. Evans (D)

**Born:** Jan. 18, 1925, Malad City, Idaho.
**Home:** Malad City, Idaho.
**Education:** Stanford U., B.A. 1951.
**Military Career:** Army, 1945-46.
**Profession:** Farmer, rancher.
**Family:** Wife, Lola; five children.
**Religion:** Mormon.
**Political Career:** Idaho Senate, 1953-59, 1967-75; mayor, Malad City, 1960-66; lieutenant governor, 1975-77; assumed governorship Jan. 1977 upon the appointment of Gov. Cecil Andrus as secretary of the interior; elected governor 1978; term expires Jan. 1983.

# James A. McClure (R)

**Of Payette — Elected 1972**

**Born:** Dec. 27, 1924, Payette, Idaho.
**Education:** U. of Idaho, J.D. 1950.
**Military Career:** Navy, 1942-46.
**Profession:** Lawyer.
**Family:** Wife, Louise Miller; three children.
**Religion:** Methodist.
**Political Career:** Payette County prosecuting attorney, 1950-56; Payette city attorney, 1953-66; Idaho Senate, 1961-67; U.S. House, 1967-73.

**In Washington:** McClure began preaching his Mountain state conservatism in the Senate long before it became a trend, fighting environmentalists and federal land policy. He continues to preach it now as a member of a large and influential coalition, and as chairman of the committee that sets much of the policy he is interested in.

Like his regional allies — Garn and Hatch of Utah, Laxalt of Nevada, and others — McClure shaped a political philosophy out of the tension between the federal custodians of the public lands and the residents who use them.

He has characterized the federal stewardship over two-thirds of Idaho as "unbalanced, extreme management to meet the needs of the few, rather than the many." To McClure, that means shutting out farmers, cattlemen, miners, loggers and drillers to suit the preservationist whims of a backpacking elite.

The 1980 election placed McClure in a good position to make the federal government more solicitous of his feelings. He is chairman not only of the Energy and Natural Resources Committee, but of the Appropriations subcommittee with jurisdiction over the Interior Department budget.

His ascent was a tonic to the energy industry. McClure has been one of the most outspoken proponents of deregulating oil and gas prices to encourage exploration. When the Carter administration proposed crude oil deregulation in 1979, McClure said it did not deregulate quickly enough. He also attempted to soften the tax on windfall profits accruing to oil companies from deregulation, calling the tax a disincentive for new production.

But he surprised some of his listeners at a luncheon in Idaho in early 1981 by accusing oil companies of "greed" after they raised wholesale prices 8-10 cents a gallon. "I am angry at what I see as a terribly foolish action," he said in a criticism of the industry. McClure is perhaps the Senate's most avid promoter of nuclear energy. He compares its economic attraction to that of hydroelectric power in his native Northwest: a huge front-end cost, but cheap operating expenses over the long run. He favors development of the nuclear breeder reactor and reprocessing of used nuclear fuel — both controversial because they produce the highly toxic weapons material, plutonium. McClure believes the risk of misplaced plutonium can be resolved by having the government control reprocessing.

In 1978, McClure announced that he had swapped his vote in support of President Carter's energy package for a commitment to continue funding a $417 million nuclear safety study in Idaho. Later he protested that Carter had reneged on the deal.

Like most Western senators, McClure supports federal public works projects for hydropower and irrigation. When the Carter administration tried to limit the amount of federally irrigated land any one landholder could control, McClure helped dismantle the proposal, calling it "part of the dogma of Marxism."

He has consistently been on the development side of land preservation fights, although until the 97th Congress, environmentalists had him outnumbered. The single largest wilderness preserve in the lower 48 states, the 2.3 million-acre River of No Return Wilderness, was created by the Senate in McClure's home state over his objection in 1980.

After becoming Energy chairman, however, McClure cautioned against expecting a repeal of the laws he had opposed. He said he expected to concentrate on making the federal government a more respectful landlord by engaging in vigorous oversight of the land-management bureaucracy.

McClure is distinguished from some of his

fellow Western conservatives by his delight in the technical minutiae of legislation. It is no accident that his chief staffer is an aerospace engineer.

On the Energy Committee, under Democratic rule, it was frequently McClure who prolonged the consideration of seemingly minor bills by dissecting them with a technician's interest. Then-chairman Henry Jackson, who preferred to follow broad policy avenues and leave the technical byways to his staff, suffered McClure's detours politely under the policy of legislation-by-consensus that has been traditional on the committee.

McClure has argued in the past that when federal regulation is called for, the way to restrain meddlesome federal bureaucrats is to write laws full of fine print. During the 1977 Clean Air Act amendments, when some conservatives were arguing that pollution standards should not be written into law, McClure disagreed. He wanted more lenient standards, but he wanted them in the statute. "I don't expect corporations voluntarily to try to achieve broad social goals," he told an interviewer.

McClure's enthusiasm for restraining federal activities spills well beyond his Energy Committee interests. He was a founder of the conservative strategy group called "The Steering Committee," and a reliable sponsor of amendments favored by the New Right.

In the 96th Congress, he offered amendments to block Internal Revenue Service restrictions on private schools, deny the Federal Trade Commission jurisdiction over doctors and lawyers, keep Legal Services Corporation lawyers from joining public interest lawsuits on environmental issues, and block federal subsidies for adoption. McClure has long been a favorite of the National Rifle Association, and a stalwart foe of any restraint on firearms. He filed suit in September, 1979, challenging the federal judgeship appointment of Abner J. Mikva, who had supported gun controls as a Democratic congressman from Illinois.

At the start of the 97th Congress, fellow conservatives campaigned successfully to make McClure chairman of the Senate Republican conference, over moderate John Heinz of Pennsylvania. The job gave him about 20 extra staffers and a voice in setting the official party line. He has built an effective public relations apparatus at the conference, providing reporters with a steady flow of information about the activities and accomplishments of the 53 Republican senators.

**At Home:** Redistricting provided McClure with his opportunity to come to Congress. Idaho's traditionally Democratic northern district was moved south in 1966 to take in Boise and its

surrounding Republican territory. That created an insurmountable problem for two-term Democrat Compton White Jr., who had nearly lost in 1964 in the old district.

McClure was a state senator. He had been a county prosecutor, and had practiced law with his father in the Snake River town of Payette, specializing in land and irrigation matters. He had gone on to the Idaho Senate in 1960, and by 1966 he was assistant majority leader.

He won the GOP nomination comfortably against Robert B. Purcell, manager of the Lewiston Chamber of Commerce, and then took on White, whom he linked to the Johnson administration's unpopular farm policies.

White focused on McClure's conservative voting record in the Legislature. He condemned McClure for once supporting the so-called Liberty Amendment, which would have abolished the federal income tax. The voters gave McClure a 4,964-vote victory.

After two easy re-elections, McClure found himself the front-runner in 1972 for the Senate seat of retiring Republican Len B. Jordan. But, despite the backing of the state Republican hierarchy, he had a tough four-way primary. His opponents attacked him for congressional absenteeism.

Heading the list of GOP competitors was George V. Hansen, a representative who had given up his seat to run unsuccessfully against Democratic Sen. Frank Church in 1968. Hansen, who later returned to the House, had a large campaign treasury and a record just as conservative as McClure's.

The other two Republicans had strong campaigns as well. Glen Wegner, a former White House aide in the Nixon administration, mounted a television blitz. Former Gov. Robert E. Smylie, the choice of party moderates, had the broadest name recognition from his three terms as Idaho's chief executive.

McClure won the nomination with a little more than a third of the vote, disappointing the second place Hansen. After the primary, Hansen disappointed McClure. He charged that officials of four Idaho corporations had tried to force him out of the race in 1971 to smooth the way for McClure.

The Democratic nominee, Idaho State University President William E. "Bud" Davis, sought to capitalize on Hansen's allegation. He appeared in newspaper ads next to a map of Idaho with "Not For Sale" stamped on it. In addition, Davis criticized McClure for favoring mining in the Sawtooth recreational area.

Davis, a genial former football coach, had the

advantage of a non-political past. But his inexperience also turned out to be a liability. He endorsed the lettuce boycott then going on in California, a seemingly harmless move but one allowing Republicans to claim he would be equally supportive of a potato boycott that might cripple Idaho's economy. His campaign never really recovered from the lettuce-potato controversy. McClure ran nearly 100,000 votes behind President Nixon statewide, but he still defeated Davis by 20,000 votes.

During his first Senate term, McClure succeeded in solidifying his base. While other Idaho conservatives became enmeshed in controversy and generated stubborn blocs of opposition, Mc-

Clure thrived on his agreeable, non-threatening manner. He managed to compile a hard-right record without alienating any major group.

In 1978, the Democrats put up journalist Dwight Jensen, a political novice who had been a television commentator in Boise. Although he was considered a competent candidate, Jensen attracted little financial support and little attention outside Boise.

Jensen blasted McClure for being too close to big corporations and insensitive to the needs of the elderly. But hardly anyone was listening. McClure essentially ignored Jensen and coasted to a second term, winning every county in the state.

## Committees

**Appropriations** (4th of 15 Republicans)
Interior, chairman; Agriculture and Related Agencies; Defense; Energy and Water Development.

**Energy and Natural Resources** (Chairman)

**Rules and Administration** (4th of 7 Republicans)

## Elections

**1978 General**

| | |
|---|---|
| James McClure (R ) | 194,412 (68 %) |
| Dwight Jensen (D ) | 89,635 (32 %) |

**Previous Winning Percentages**

1972 (52 %)    1970* (58 %)    1968* (59 %)    1966* (52 %)
* House elections.

## Campaign Finance

| | Receipts | Receipts from PACs | Expenditures |
|---|---|---|---|
| 1978 | | | |
| McClure (R ) | $378,084 | $161,873 (43 %) | $385,536 |
| Jensen (D ) | $55,163 | $17,500 (32 %) | $55,163 |

## Voting Studies

| | Presidential Support | | Party Unity | | Conservative Coalition | |
|---|---|---|---|---|---|---|
| Year | S | O | S | O | S | O |
| Senate Service | | | | | | |
| 1980 | 31 | 59 | 82 | 8 | 86 | 8 |
| 1979 | 30 | 64 | 88 | 7 | 93 | 0 |
| 1978 | 18 | 60 | 75 | 6 | 72 | 10 |
| 1977 | 42 | 50 | 81 | 5 | 83 | 3 |
| 1976 | 72 | 15 | 77 | 6 | 78 | 5 |
| 1975 | 74 | 18 | 91 | 3 | 96 | 1 |
| 1974 (Ford) | 59 | 38 | | | | |
| 1974 | 64 | 30 | 82 | 9 | 89 | 4 |

| | | | | | | |
|---|---|---|---|---|---|---|
| 1973 | 61 | 24 | 66 | 11 | 72 | 6 |
| House service | | | | | | |
| 1972 | 38 | 16 | 40 | 11 | 49 | 9 |
| 1971 | 54 | 5 | 46 | 9 | 51 | 2 |
| 1970 | 65 | 28 | 74 | 14 | 86 | 2 |
| 1969 | 40 | 47 | 80 | 15 | 87 | 2 |
| 1968 | 44 | 38 | 59 | 17 | 75 | 12 |
| 1967 | 35 | 60 | 89 | 8 | 94 | 4 |

S = Support          O = Opposition

## Key Votes

**96th Congress**

| | |
|---|---|
| Maintain relations with Taiwan (1979) | Y |
| Reduce synthetic fuel development funds (1979) | N |
| Impose nuclear plant moratorium (1979) | N |
| Kill stronger windfall profits tax (1979) | Y |
| Guarantee Chrysler Corp. loans (1979) | N |
| Approve military draft registration (1980) | N |
| End Revenue Sharing to the states (1980) | N |
| Block Justice Dept. busing suits (1980) | Y |

**97th Congress**

| | |
|---|---|
| Restore urban program funding cuts (1981) | N |

## Interest Group Ratings

| Year | ADA | ACA | AFL-CIO | CCUS-1 | CCUS-2 |
|---|---|---|---|---|---|
| Senate service | | | | | |
| 1980 | 17 | 92 | 12 | 89 | |
| 1979 | 0 | 85 | 0 | 90 | 93 |
| 1978 | 0 | 91 | 6 | 64 | |
| 1977 | 5 | 95 | 11 | 94 | |
| 1976 | 0 | 100 | 11 | 75 | |
| 1975 | 6 | 89 | 14 | 88 | |
| 1974 | 0 | 100 | 18 | 100 | |
| 1973 | 25 | 92 | 20 | 75 | |
| House service | | | | | |
| 1972 | 0 | 94 | 20 | 100 | |
| 1971 | 5 | 81 | 13 | - | |
| 1970 | 12 | 83 | 0 | 100 | |
| 1969 | 7 | 76 | 22 | - | |
| 1968 | 0 | 91 | 0 | - | |
| 1967 | 13 | 100 | 0 | 100 | |

# Steven D. Symms (R)

## Of Caldwell — Elected 1980

**Born:** April 23, 1938, Nampa, Idaho.
**Education:** University of Idaho, B.S. 1960.
**Military Career:** Marines, 1960-63.
**Profession:** Orchardist.
**Family:** Wife, Frances Stockdale; four children.
**Religion:** Methodist.
**Political Career:** U.S. House, 1973-81.

**The Member:** Symms has described himself in the past as an "individualist Republican," and that phrase reflects the strain of conservatism that has made him a success in Idaho politics.

The son of a wealthy fruit grower, he captured an open House seat in 1972 after defeating the choice of GOP regulars in a primary. He won re-election three times with relative ease, and aimed at a 1980 campaign against the state's most prestigious and durable liberal, Frank Church.

National conservative groups targeted Church for defeat, and heavy negative advertising against him took its toll early in the campaign. The incumbent proved to be a resourceful campaigner, however, and Symms had to deal with a number of side issues which emerged, including rumors that he was a womanizer, and charges that he was involved in a conflict of interest through buying silver futures while serving on a House subcommittee overseeing the Commodity Futures Trading Commission. He replied that the stories were untrue.

The conservative tide carried Symms to a narrow victory, helped along by the concession speech President Carter delivered while the polls were still open in parts of the state. The margin of victory was less than 5,000 votes.

Symms came to the Senate as a veteran of four years of guerrilla warfare in the House, where he and allies on the right used demands for roll-call votes, frequent quorum calls and numerous amendments to tie up the Democratic leadership. Symms was not the leader of the group, but he was one of its most enthusiastic participants.

Some of Symms' other forms of conservative protest brought him a reputation in the House for flamboyance — if not flakiness. In 1977, when the House was considering a plan to make voter registration easier, Symms and an accomplice forged identification cards for seven Democrats on the committee drafting the bill. Waving the cards, he said they showed how the system could lead to widespread fraud.

On another occasion, when the Judiciary Committee was considering a gun control bill that would ban "Saturday night specials," Symms appeared at a press conference armed with two revolvers. He said the bill was too broadly drawn and would affect many guns besides those it was meant to stop.

On the House Agriculture Committee, Symms fought food stamp programs but defended sugar subsidies important to Idaho's sugar beet growers. On the the Interior Committee, he fought attempts to expand wilderness areas and to establish federal land-use planning grants. In 1980 he tried to amend a wilderness bill to reduce the acreage in Idaho that would be closed to development. "When the Lord gave us resources," Symms once said, "he gave them to us with the idea that we should use them."

Since Symms sits on both the Budget and Finance Committees in the Senate, much of his time in early 1981 was taken up with deliberations over cutting taxes and reducing federal spending. He voted in the Budget Committee against Reagan's first budget resolution for fiscal 1982. Symms said the plan's projected deficits in 1983 and 1984 were too high. During Congress' Easter recess, the administration revised its spending figures so the budget would show a balance in 1984, and Symms then supported the President.

Symms chairs the transportation subcommittee on Environment and Public Works, and he co-introduced highway legislation that deviated from Reagan's plans. The Symms-backed plan continued federal funding for urban and rural roads through 1986; Reagan wanted to cut funds in that area after fiscal 1983.

**311**

## Committees

**Budget** (8th of 12 Republicans)

**Environment and Public Works** (7th of 9 Republicans)
Transportation, chairman; Environmental Pollution; Nuclear Regulation.

**Finance** (10th of 11 Republicans)
Estate and Gift Taxaton, chairman; Energy and Agricultural Taxation; International Trade.

**Joint Economic**
Economic Goals and Intergovernmental Policy; International Trade, Finance and Security Economics.

## Elections

**1980 General**

| | |
|---|---|
| Steven Symms (R) | 218,701 (50%) |
| Frank Church (D) | 214,439 (49%) |

**Previous Winning Percentages**

1978* (60%)    1976* (55%)    1974* (58%)    1972* (56%)

*House election.*

## Campaign Finance

| | Receipts | Receipts from PACs | Expenditures |
|---|---|---|---|
| **1980** | | | |
| Symms (R) | $1,790,594 | $660,419 (37%) | $1,777,942 |
| Church (D) | $1,959,789 | $212,666 (11%) | $1,923,770 |

## Voting Studies

| Year | Presidential Support | | Party Unity | | Conservative Coalition | |
|---|---|---|---|---|---|---|
| | S | O | S | O | S | O |
| **House service** | | | | | | |
| 1980 | 21 | 48 | 67 | 3 | 65 | 1 |
| 1979 | 14 | 75 | 87 | 2 | 90 | 2 |
| 1978 | 13 | 71 | 85 | 4 | 85 | 1 |
| 1977 | 24 | 66 | 87 | 2 | 90 | 1 |
| 1976 | 71 | 18 | 79 | 6 | 78 | 3 |
| 1975 | 60 | 38 | 86 | 5 | 89 | 4 |
| 1974 (Ford) | 37 | 37 | | | | |
| 1974 | 53 | 32 | 77 | 4 | 79 | 5 |
| 1973 | 58 | 34 | 84 | 12 | 84 | 10 |

S = Support          O = Opposition

## Key Votes

**97th Congress**

Restore urban program funding cuts (1981)          N

## Interest Group Ratings

| Year | ADA | ACA | AFL-CIO | CCUS |
|---|---|---|---|---|
| **House service** | | | | |
| 1980 | 0 | 83 | 13 | 74 |
| 1979 | 5 | 100 | 5 | 94 |
| 1978 | 10 | 96 | 5 | 88 |
| 1977 | 5 | 100 | 9 | 94 |
| 1976 | 0 | 100 | 9 | 94 |
| 1975 | 0 | 100 | 9 | 94 |
| 1974 | 0 | 100 | 0 | 100 |
| 1973 | 8 | 96 | 9 | 100 |

# 1 Larry E. Craig (R)

**Of Midvale — Elected 1980**
**Born:** July 20, 1945, Council, Idaho.
**Education:** U. of Idaho, B.A. 1969.
**Military Career:** National Guard, 1970-72.
**Profession:** Rancher.
**Family:** Single.
**Religion:** Methodist.
**Political Career:** Idaho Senate, 1975-81.

**The Member:** After an uphill primary campaign in 1980 against a former state attorney general, Craig's general election success seemed just about assured. But he had surprising trouble with an aggressive Democrat who charged that Craig's "Sagebrush Rebellion" sympathies might lead him to advocate selling Idaho's public lands.

On the House Interior Committee, Craig opposes new wilderness classification for areas in Idaho that have resource value. He concurs with Interior Secretary James Watt's goal of opening more federal lands to mineral development.

When the Interior Committee took the unusual step in May of ordering Watt to close three Montana wilderness areas to oil and gas drilling, Craig said the committee action would "send shock waves across the Western states."

He and other Western congressmen also asked Watt to rescind an Interior Department order banning the use of poisons on public lands. Craig says poison is the most effective method of controlling coyotes and other livestock prey.

In campaigning in 1980, Craig tied himself closely to Symms, the district's incumbent then campaigning successfully for the Senate. As a state legislator, however, he built a reputation as a pragmatist who avoided the ideological purism sometimes associated with Symms.

Craig is one of those people who seem to be on the way to Congress right from the start. He was the Future Farmers of America national vice president and head of Idaho Young Republicans before running for the state Senate.

**The District:** Once known as the more Democratic of Idaho's two districts, the 1st is now almost indistinguishable from the rest of the state in its conservative Republicanism.

The northern Panhandle counties are still a Democratic stronghold, with union members who work in the mines forming the backbone of the party's strength. But with the addition of the Boise area and other southern counties in the 1966 and 1972 redistricting, Republican strength grew and overcame the northern Democratic vote.

## Committees

**Education and Labor** (13th of 14 Republicans)
Elementary, Secondary and Vocational Education; Health and Safety.

**Interior and Insular Affairs** (11th of 17 Republicans)
Mines and Mining; Public Lands and National Parks.

**Select Aging** (19th of 23 Republicans)
Health and Long-Term Care; Human Services.

## Elections

**1980 General**

| | |
|---|---|
| Larry Craig (R ) | 116,845 (54 %) |
| Glenn Nichols (D ) | 100,697 (46 %) |

**1980 Primary**

| | |
|---|---|
| Larry Craig (R ) | 29,525 (53 %) |
| Wayne Kidwell (R ) | 26,454 (47 %) |

**District Vote For President**

| | 1980 | | 1976 | | 1972 |
|---|---|---|---|---|---|
| **D** | 66,316 (29 %) | **D** | 68,459 (39 %) | **D** | 45,597 (29 %) |
| **R** | 141,434 (62 %) | **R** | 101,793 (58 %) | **R** | 99,087 (63 %) |
| **I** | 16,754 (7 %) | | | **I** | 13,279 (8 %) |

## Campaign Finance

| | Receipts | Receipts from PACs | Expenditures |
|---|---|---|---|
| **1980** | | | |
| Craig (R ) | $290,984 | $111,104 (38 %) | $286,667 |
| Nichols (D ) | $91,114 | $34,623 (38 %) | $92,124 |

## Key Vote

**97th Congress**

| | |
|---|---|
| Reagan budget proposal (1981) | Y |

---

**1st District: North and West — Boise.** Population: 492,688 (38% increase since 1970). Race: White 473,691 (96%), Black 969 (0.1%), Others 18,028 (4%). Spanish origin: 16,421 (3%).

# 2  George Hansen (R)

**Of Pocatello — Elected 1974**
Also served 1965-69
**Born:** Sept.14, 1930, Tetonia, Idaho.
**Education:** Ricks College, B.A. 1956.
**Military Career:** Air Force, 1951-54; Naval Reserve, 1964-70.
**Profession:** Insurance executive.
**Family:** Wife, Connie Camp; five children.
**Religion:** Mormon.
**Political Career:** Mayor of Alameda, 1961-62; Pocatello City Commission, 1962-65; U.S. House, 1965-69; unsuccessful Republican nominee for U.S. Senate, 1968; unsuccessfully sought Republican nomination for U.S. Senate, 1972.

**In Washington:** Hansen leaped to international fame in 1979 after the American hostages were seized in Iran. Impatient with President Carter's refusal to confront Iran directly, he flew to Tehran, took up residence in a hotel for 10 days, and began issuing pronouncements about U.S.-Iranian relations.

He said Iranians had legitimate cause to complain about the tyranny of the former shah, that Congress could end the crisis by holding hearings on Iran's complaints, and that banker David Rockefeller should take the place of the hostages in the U.S. Embassy.

The trip brought protests from the White House, the State Department and many of Hansen's colleagues in Congress. But Hansen refused to concede that his intervention might have caused problems. He went back to Tehran a month later, for a briefer trip that went largely unnoticed.

The Iranian episode was vintage Hansen. The biggest, burliest man in Congress, he has always charged into issues impulsively, and with a sense of lonely righteousness that has led even fellow conservatives to view him as a bit erratic.

Hansen's journey to Iran was not his first effort at individual diplomacy. In July of 1979, he and Democrat Larry McDonald of Georgia traveled to Nicaragua and met with beleaguered dictator Anastasio Somoza. Although the Carter administration was then trying to persuade Somoza to give up power to moderate elements, Hansen and McDonald told Somoza that he had substantial backing in the United States. Two weeks later, Somoza fled the country and his government fell to the leftist Sandinista guerrillas.

Hansen's most famous legislative enterprise was his long guerrilla war against U.S. transfer of the Panama Canal. In 1978, during Senate consideration of the transfer treaties, Hansen argued unsuccessfully that the House should be able to vote on them. Along with other conservatives, he said the Constitution required approval of both houses of Congress for the "giveaway" of federal property such as the canal. When the Senate refused to give the House a role in the issue, Hansen accused the Senate of having "an imperious attitude reminiscent of a House of Lords."

A year later, Hansen played a major role in debate on legislation to implement the treaties. He tried to amend it to prohibit "any cost to U.S. taxpayers from the treaties," in effect requiring Panama to buy the canal. That amendment was rejected by 20 votes, but Hansen's work had its effect: the implementation bill that finally became law made several concessions to the conservative opposition, such as language providing for congressional approval of all future property transfers to Panama.

On the Banking Committee, his major assignment since 1975, Hansen has not been instrumental in many legislative decisions. But he pursued his ideas about the evils of international bankers, especially the Rockefellers.

In a series of long letters to Presidents Carter and Reagan and other top officials, Hansen alleged that actions by David Rockefeller and other important American bankers may have led to the

---

**2nd District: East — Pocatello, Idaho Falls.** Population: 451,247 (27% increase since 1970). Race: White 427,950 (95%), Black 1,747 (0.3%), Others 21,550 (5%). Spanish origin: 20,194 (4%).

takeover of the U.S. Embassy in Iran. The siege helped these bankers, Hansen said, because it forced Carter to freeze Iranian assets, thus preventing Iran from withdrawing billions of dollars of deposits from Rockefeller's Chase Manhattan Bank and other institutions.

Shortly after Reagan became president, Hansen wrote to him that "it is a grave situation indeed if American foreign policy is being manipulated by international money interests to the point of war where the nation's sons and daughters might well be called to fight and die in some foreign land for no better reason than to shore up the shaky loans of speculators in a risky market." Hansen has been unable to get the Banking Committee to look into his charges.

Letter-writing is a Hansen specialty; so is mass mailing. He has frequently used direct mail appeals to conservatives around the nation to express his opposition to abortion or his support for the government of Taiwan. On one occasion, he used it to help ease his own financial problems.

In 1977, Hansen found himself deeply in debt because of heavy personal spending in previous political campaigns. Public officials "have the same needs for financial security" as other people, he said. He asked the House ethics committee for permission to seek public contributions to ease his plight, but was refused. To get around that problem, Hansen transferred some liabilities to his wife, who then hired an advertising agency and sent out thousands of letters appealing for money. The effort reportedly raised more than $50,000.

In 1975, Hansen pleaded guilty to two misdemeanor charges of filing late and false campaign finance reports from his 1974 House primary race. He was initially sentenced to prison for two months, but that sentence was suspended and Hansen instead paid a $2,000 fine. During courtroom arguments, a federal judge said Hansen was "stupid" but not "evil."

A year later, an Idaho newspaper charged that Hansen had been delinquent in filing his federal income tax returns seven times since 1966. Hansen admitted some of his returns were late, but no action was taken against him. He later made his battle with the IRS into a political issue, claiming that the agency discriminated not only against him but against other Mormons.

**At Home:** George Hansen has roiled the politics of eastern Idaho for the past 16 years, and he shows no signs of changing to a lower profile.

He was the only Republican outside the South to unseat a Democratic representative amid the L.B.J. landslide in 1964. That year, while serving on the Pocatello City Council, he struggled through a Republican primary to win with 38.6 percent of the vote in a three-man race. In November, he beat incumbent Democratic Rep. Ralph Harding by 7,816 votes.

Hansen was easily re-elected in 1966 and set his sights on the U.S. Senate. In 1968, he challenged Democratic Sen. Frank Church, saying that in opposing the Vietnam War, Church had "played a deadly game by the extravagant use of the right to dissent." But he was outmatched by Church, who got 60 percent of the vote, his best showing in any of his five Senate races.

In 1972, Hansen made another bid for the Senate, this time for the seat of retiring Sen. Len Jordan, a Republican. But Hansen was stopped short in the Republican primary by Rep. James McClure, who beat him for the nomination by 11,000 votes, and went on to win the seat.

Two years later, Hansen found his way back to the House. He mounted a primary campaign against Republican Rep. Orval Hansen, the man who had replaced him in the House in 1968. The two men were not related, personally or politically. Orval Hansen was a moderate, low-key legislator and campaigner. George campaigned with his usual, blunt, aggressive style, and drew on his following among conservative Mormons in the towns of eastern Idaho. He ousted Orval by 2,005 votes. In November, Hansen had a to run against another near-namesake, Max Hanson, a conservative Democrat and former state legislator. This contest was not as close. Hansen reclaimed his place in Congress by nearly 15,000 votes.

In 1976, the combination of Hansen's guilty plea on campaign finance charges and the reports that he had been late filing his personal income taxes placed his political career in jeopardy. A strong Democratic candidate, state Sen. Stan Kress, came within 1,938 votes of beating him.

But Hansen has held on, defeating Kress by a much wider margin in 1978 and winning easily in 1980. He has established an unshakeable core of support through his appeal to conservative causes, his identification with Mormon concerns, and his effective campaign style. He has created an equally committed opposition, but not one strong enough so far to draw a majority of the vote.

**The District:** Taking in most of southern Idaho, the 2nd is the state's traditionally Republican congressional district. Since 1939, the only Democrat to win the seat has been Ralph Harding, who served from 1961 to 1965.

The district's conservative history has resulted partially from the high concentration of Mormons in the eastern portion of the state. They have usually backed conservative causes and candidates, and form an important element in the politics of the state.

The 1978 gubernatorial race highlighted the differences in the districts. A conservative Mormon Republican received 45.7 percent of the vote in the 2nd District but only 33.5 percent in the 1st District. In 1980, Republican Steven Symms carried the district in his campaign against incumbent Democrat Frank Church, allowing him to overcome a deficit elsewhere in the state.

## Committees

**Agriculture** (9th of 19 Republicans)
Domestic Marketing, Consumer Relations, and Nutrition; Forests, Family Farms, and Energy; Livestock, Dairy and Poultry.

**Banking, Finance and Urban Affairs** (4th of 19 Republicans)
Domestic Monetary Policy; Financial Institutions Supervision, Regulation and Insurance; International Trade, Investment and Monetary Policy.

## Elections

**1980 General**

| | |
|---|---|
| George Hansen (R ) | 116,196 (59 %) |
| Diane Bilyeu (D ) | 81,364 (41 %) |

**1980 Primary**

| | |
|---|---|
| George Hansen (R ) | 41,718 (58 %) |
| Jim Jones (R ) | 30,729 (42 %) |

**1978 General**

| | |
|---|---|
| George Hansen (R ) | 80,591 (57 %) |
| Stan Kress (D ) | 60,040 (43 %) |

**Previous Winning Percentages**

1976 (51 %)    1974 (56 %)    1966 (70 %)    1964 (52 %)

**District Vote For President**

| | 1980 | | 1976 | | 1972 |
|---|---|---|---|---|---|
| D | 43,876 (21 %) | D | 58,090 (35 %) | D | 35,229 (23 %) |
| R | 149,265 (72 %) | R | 102,358 (62 %) | R | 100,297 (66 %) |
| I | 10,304 (5 %) | | | I | 16,890 (11 %) |

## Campaign Finance

| | Receipts | Receipts from PACs | Expen-ditures |
|---|---|---|---|
| **1980** | | | |
| Hansen (R ) | $225,194 | $52,025 (23 %) | $222,447 |
| Bilyeu (D ) | $32,358 | $6,550 (20 %) | $32,355 |
| **1978** | | | |
| Hansen (R ) | $284,650 | $47,506 (17 %) | $282,203 |
| Kress (D ) | $149,817 | $71,294 (48 %) | $150,956 |

## Voting Studies

| | Presidential Support | | Party Unity | | Conservative Coalition | |
|---|---|---|---|---|---|---|
| Year | S | O | S | O | S | O |
| 1980 | 21 | 62 | 80 | 3 | 75 | 2 |
| 1979 | 14 | 77 | 88 | 3 | 85 | 2 |
| 1978 | 13 | 69 | 78 | 4 | 77 | 3 |
| 1977 | 27 | 72 | 90 | 3 | 94 | 1 |
| 1976 | 51 | 10 | 63 | 3 | 71 | 2 |
| 1975 | 57 | 34 | 85 | 5 | 89 | 2 |
| 1968 | 14 | 24 | 29 | 2 | 37 | 4 |
| 1967 | 39 | 53 | 82 | 8 | 89 | 4 |
| 1966 | 26 | 44 | 63 | 10 | 62 | 3 |
| 1965 | 32 | 64 | 90 | 5 | 98 | 2 |

S = Support          O = Opposition

## Key Votes

**96th Congress**

| | |
|---|---|
| Weaken Carter oil profits tax (1979) | Y |
| Reject hospital cost control plan (1979) | Y |
| Implement Panama Canal Treaties (1979) | N |
| Establish Department of Education (1979) | N |
| Approve Anti-busing Amendment (1979) | Y |
| Guarantee Chrysler Corp. loans (1979) | Y |
| Approve military draft registration (1980) | N |
| Aid Sandinista regime in Nicaragua (1980) | N |
| Strengthen fair housing laws (1980) | N |

**97th Congress**

| | |
|---|---|
| Reagan budget proposal (1981) | Y |

## Interest Group Ratings

| Year | ADA | ACA | AFL-CIO | CCUS |
|---|---|---|---|---|
| 1980 | 6 | 95 | 18 | 74 |
| 1979 | 0 | 95 | 5 | 100 |
| 1978 | 5 | 96 | 6 | 79 |
| 1977 | 0 | 100 | 9 | 94 |
| 1976 | 0 | 100 | 14 | 91 |
| 1975 | 0 | 96 | 5 | 94 |
| 1968 | 0 | 100 | 0 | - |
| 1967 | 7 | 89 | 8 | 90 |
| 1966 | 0 | 83 | 0 | - |
| 1965 | 5 | 100 | - | 100 |

# Illinois

**U.S. CONGRESS:**
**TWENTY-FOUR DISTRICTS**

Senate (1D, 1R)
House (10D, 14R)

**STATE:**

Governor
James R. Thompson (R)

General Assembly
Senate: 59 members (30D, 29R)
House: 177 members (86D, 91R)

Population
11,418,461 - 5th in the nation

Area
56,400 sq. miles - 24th in the nation

1980 Presidential Vote: Carter (42%),
Reagan (50%), Anderson (7%)

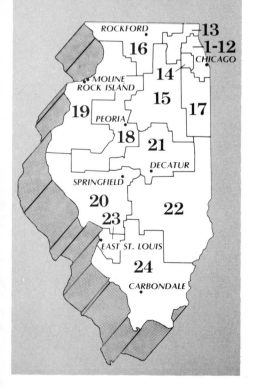

## . . . A New Balance of Power

Illinois may not be the "core America" that political observers have insisted on calling it for most of this century, but it does have more different demographic pieces than most of the big industrial states: the nation's second largest city; a suburban colossus that has come to be the single most important factor in state politics; a vast, rich, conservative section of the Corn Belt; and coal country more akin to Kentucky than to the Midwest. Other states have three of those four elements; none has all four.

What this has meant politically in recent years is a fairly even partisan split. Republicans have won 6 of the 9 presidential elections in Illinois since 1948, but two of those wins, Nixon over Humphrey in 1968 and Ford over Carter in 1976, were by less than three percentage points.

Of the nine elections for Governor since 1948, Republicans have won five, Democrats four. Republicans have won seven of 13 elections for the Senate. Over more than a quarter century between 1944 and 1972 no one of either party drew as much as 60 percent in any gubernatorial or Senate election.

The standard cliché has been that Illinois politics is a matter of Chicago vs. downstate. And to some extent it has been true. Chicago, with its huge Catholic population of Eastern Europeans and its ever-expanding black community, became a Democratic stronghold in the New Deal era. Party loyalty was inspired, maintained and often bought by Mayor Edward Kelly into the late 1940s and later Richard Daley until his death in 1976.

The big Democratic margins in Chicago were generally offset by the downstate vote, which usually supplied Republicans with healthy majorities, despite concentrations of industry (Peoria, Rock Island and Moline) and poverty (East St. Louis), and a strong Democratic vote in the southern counties.

The rough outlines of that truism still apply. Democrats still carry Chicago in virtually every statewide election, and Republicans win most of downstate. But the equation is now far more

**317**

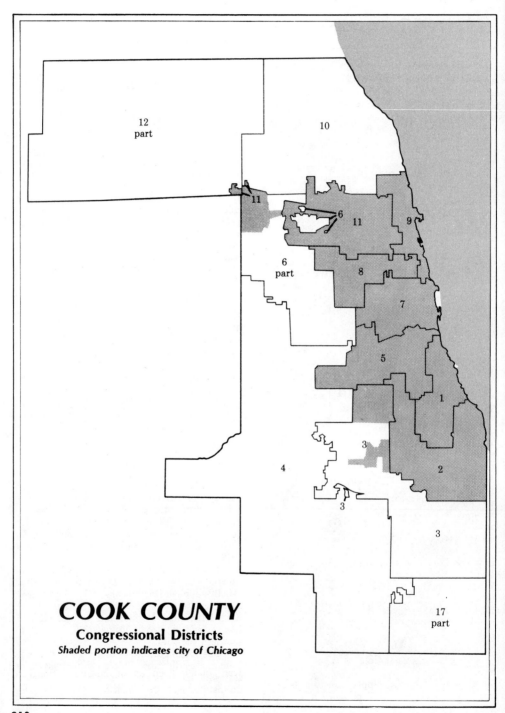

# COOK COUNTY
### Congressional Districts
*Shaded portion indicates city of Chicago*

complicated. Illinois elections are now won and lost in the Chicago suburbs.

In the 1950 Senate election, Chicago accounted for 80 percent of the Cook County vote, and 72 percent of the vote in its metropolitan area. In the 1978 Senate election, Chicago's vote amounted to 60 percent of the Cook County total, and only 44 percent of the overall Chicago metropolitan vote. Suburban Chicago, including the Cook County suburbs and the five "collar counties" (McHenry, Lake, Kane, DuPage and Will) totaled 56 percent of the Chicago metro vote and 35 percent of the state vote.

The suburban growth has been generally beneficial to the Republicans. In the newer subdivisions of the collar counties, ethnic Catholics who voted Democratic when they lived in Chicago have changed party affiliation outside the city limits. Republican Senator Charles Percy carried the Cook County suburbs with 67 percent in 1978; Republican Gov. James Thompson won with 75 percent there the same year.

Du Page, the largest of the collar counties, is the most dependable Republican territory in the state. Without Du Page, Gerald R. Ford would have lost Illinois by 10,000 votes in 1976; with it, he carried the state by 90,000.

But the growth of the suburbs has not made Illinois a GOP state, because the suburban vote is more independent than it is Republican. Sen. Adlai E. Stevenson III cut deeply into Republican suburban strength in his 1970 and 1974 victories, and in 1974 he carried two collar counties (Lake and Will) plus the Cook County suburbs.

Maverick Democrat Daniel Walker, running for governor in 1972 on a mixed platform of fiscal conservatism and political reform, used a different formula. He drew better than any Democrat in recent memory in the Corn Belt counties downstate. Walker's controversies with the Daley machine and his abrasive personality led to his defeat in a Democratic primary in 1976, but he proved what a Democrat can do downstate with the right issues.

In the 1980 Senate contest, Illinois voters had an unusual choice. The Democrat and the Republican were not only both from downstate, but both from the same small town, Belleville. Dixon was an easy winner, not only taking Chicago and most of the downstate counties but running respectably in most of the suburbs.

# A Political Tour

**Chicago.** Chicago slipped dangerously close to losing its "second city" population status to Los Angeles in 1980, but it remains first in the nation in quite a few things. It is still the heart of the nation's leading industrial area, one which is first in the production of iron and steel, electrical equipment and machinery. Chicago is still the nation's leading transportation center, with the busiest airport.

But it also has a reputation for being first in segregation among Northern cities, and its public housing projects, called "vertical ghettoes" as far back as the 1950s, are as blighted and dangerous as anything in the country. It can no longer point proudly to itself as the "city that works," as it did during the fiscally calm years under Daley. Its metropolitan transportation system lives virtually from day to day, and it has the same general money problems as any of the most troubled industrial cities.

The Daley years made permanent the Democratic Party's hold on Chicago's voters. Democrats gained local primacy at the start of the New Deal, replacing the old Republican machine, but for years Republicans managed to put up a fight within the city, and with the addition of the suburban vote, often carried Cook County in state elections. Franklin Roosevelt was held below 60 percent in Cook County in three of his four runs for president.

Since the late 1950s, the Chicago Democratic vote has been overwhelming, and most statewide Democrats who do even respectably well carry Cook County. Since Daley's first election in 1955, only one major Democratic statewide candidate has lost the city itself: Adlai Stevenson Jr. running for president in 1956. Only one other major Democrat, Senate candidate Roman Pucinski in 1972, has drawn less than 54 percent in Chicago.

Democrats are in the majority almost everywhere in Chicago. Their biggest margins are on the overwhelmingly black West Side, once the center for the city's Italian and Jewish communities. In certain West Side wards, Democrats receive over 90 percent of the vote. Some of these wards continued for years to have white party bosses who had long since moved to the suburbs, but that practice ended in the 1970s.

The South Side contains more than half of the city's population. It too is overwhelmingly black, an older, more stable community that never experienced a serious riot at the height of the racial tension in the 1960s. Dominated politically for more than 30 years by congressman William Dawson, the boss of black patronage politics in the Daley regime, the South Side has traditionally been an organization stronghold. But it has been more independent since Dawson's death in 1970. Some of the black wards broke party ranks to support Percy over Pucinski in 1972, and Democratic Rep. Ralph Metcalfe continued to win re-election to the House even after he broke with Daley in 1975. The current Democratic congressman, Harold Washington, is not a machine loyalist.

Most of the white vote on the South Side is cast by Eastern European ethnics who have remained as homeowners in the neighborhoods near the city's western border; by Irish in the "back of the yards" enclave that produced Daley and other recent political leaders; and by white-collar liberals around the University of Chicago in Hyde Park. All are Democratic in general elections, but the university community usually casts a strong anti-machine vote in primaries.

Most of the white middle class remaining in the city is on the North and Northwest Sides, but these areas too are increasingly black and Hispanic. The district represented by Ways and Means Committee Chairman Dan Rostenkowski, once was the center of Polish Chicago. Today more than half of Rostenkowski's constituents are Hispanic or black.

Chicago has lost much of its traditional influence, both in state elections and in the Legislature. Daley's immediate successor, Michael Bilandic, was not a strong party leader, and his perceived ineffectiveness led to his defeat by Byrne in 1979. But Byrne's confrontational style has hindered relations with the state Legislature and alienated much of the machine. Many Daley loyalists are lining up behind Richard Daley Jr. to challenge Byrne in 1983. Daley was elected Cook County states attorney in 1980.

If the machine is getting weaker, Chicago's Democratic slant is getting stronger. The city is now 40 percent black and 14 percent Hispanic; these communities are not fertile recruiting grounds for the GOP. In 1978, the unsuccessful Democratic candidates for governor and senator carried Chicago with 59 and 57 percent, respectively. Both Carter and Dixon took Chicago by wide margins in 1980.

But like other big cities, Chicago has lost influence because it has lost population. The city lost more than 10 percent of its population in the 1970s, and now casts only 27 percent of the state vote, down from 35 percent in 1960.

**Chicago Suburbs.** Republicans have traditionally won majorities in the Chicago suburbs, and they still do. In 1952, Eisenhower carried the Cook County suburbs of Chicago with 64 percent of the vote. In 1976, Ford carried them with 62 percent. What has changed is the size of the vote.

A generation ago, suburban Chicago for the most part meant established lakefront towns like

Evanston and Wilmette, Republican by tradition and moderate in social outlook. Now the "suburbs" extend west for miles, north almost to the Wisconsin border and south into the Corn Belt. As one moves west from Lake Michigan, into the newer developments, one finds increasing numbers of ethnic, Catholic, former Chicago Democrats. But these are prosperous communities for the most part, and strongly Republican.

From 1950 to 1978, only one major statewide Democratic candidate carried the Cook County suburbs: Adlai Stevenson III in 1970 and 1974. No major Democrat carried any of the three most solid Republican collar counties, Du Page, Kane and McHenry. The only two collar counties that sometimes vote for attractive statewide Democrats are Will, with a large blue-collar population, and Lake, which has significant black communities in Waukegan and North Chicago.

Democrats run best now in the Cook County suburbs closest to the city. Some of these, like Skokie and Glencoe are heavily Jewish, others like Evanston, have a large black vote. The 10th Congressional District, which includes Evanston and Skokie, was represented in the House by liberal Democrat Abner Mikva from 1975 to 1979.

**Central Illinois.** The agricultural heart of Illinois covers about two-thirds of the territory of the state, from the Wisconsin border almost as far south as St. Louis. There are dairy farms in the north, but mostly it is corn and soybean country. Illinois is the second leading corn-growing state in the country, the leading soybean state, and one of the leading hog states.

They also raise Republicans in central Illinois. In all but a very few counties, Republicans are in the clear majority. In many counties, statewide Republican candidates average better than 60 percent.

Perhaps the most Republican county in the state is Kendall, just southwest of metropolitan Chicago, where GOP candidates often draw over 70 percent. Even Dave O'Neal, the weak Republican Senate nominee in 1980, exceeded 60 percent. Ronald Reagan did especially well in north-central Lee County . . . he grew up there, in the town of Dixon.

There are scattered areas of Democratic voting in central Illinois. Most of these are small industrial cities, such as the farm machinery capitals of Moline and Rock Island on the Mississippi River. Democrats sometimes win in Decatur, a corn and soybean processing center. There is some blue-collar Democratic strength in Peoria and Rockford, the two largest cities in the state outside Chicago, but neither Peoria County nor Winnebago County (Rockford) goes Democratic in most elections. Rockford sent John B. Anderson to the House for 20 years as a Republican; Peoria sent Everett McKinley Dirksen to the House for 16 years before he went on to the Senate, and now is represented by Robert H. Michel, the GOP House leader.

**Southern Illinois.** The Chicago vs. downstate political equation was never thoroughly correct. Republicans did win easily in the farm country of central Illinois. But Chicago Democrats had allies far away — in southern Illinois.

Industrial towns like East St. Louis and Granite City, across the Mississippi River from St. Louis, have been Democratic for most of this century. Further south is Illinois' coal country, settled by migrants from Southern states who brought their conservative Democratic voting habits with them.

Today, southern Illinois has about 9 percent of the state population and 25 percent of the population outside metropolitan Chicago. It has a Democratic majority, but one that is narrower than in years past.

Democrats do best in St. Clair and Madison counties. St. Clair, which includes Belleville and overwhelmingly black East St. Louis, is the most heavily Democratic county in the state. Major Democratic candidates have carried it 25 of 28 times since 1950. Madison, which has Granite City, is only slightly less consistent.

East St. Louis is southern Illinois' largest city. Once a major industrial and railroad center, it has been in deep decline for decades. Unemployment and poverty are endemic. Its population declined by 21 percent in the 1970s.

The coal country is gradually dropping its partisan predictability as its voters split with the national Democratic Party. There are still strongly Democratic counties in this part of the state, such as Franklin, Gallatin and Alexander. But there are also some heavily Republican counties now, and others where serious competition between parties exists.

Some of the counties have been growing in recent years with the increased demand for coal, and these seem to be the ones where Republicans are getting stronger.

Southern Illinois demonstrated its changing politics in the 1980 congressional election, nearly unseating Paul Simon, its seemingly entrenched liberal Democratic congressman.

# Redrawing the Lines

Removing two of Illinois' 24 congressional districts is a relatively minor operation compared to eliminating 59 state House seats, as a new state constitutional amendment requires. Consequently, drafting new state legislative districts was the priority of the Illinois General Assembly during the first half of 1981.

Demographics require eliminating at least one Democratic House district from Chicago. In the seven districts located wholly within city boundaries (the 1st, 2nd, 5th, 7th, 8th, 9th and 11th), there is enough population to support only five and a half districts. Several other downstate districts also are below the ideal population.

Some black legislators said they might let Republicans draw downstate lines as they wish if the GOP supports retaining the black Chicago seats.

# Governor
# James R. Thompson (R)

**Born:** May 8, 1936, Chicago, Ill.
**Home:** Chicago, Ill.
**Education:** Washington U., B.A. 1956; Northwestern U., J.D. 1959.
**Profession:** Lawyer.
**Family:** Wife, Jayne; one child.
**Religion:** Presbyterian.
**Political Career:** U.S. attorney for the Northern District of Illinois, 1971-75; elected governor 1976, 1978; term expires Jan. 1983.

# Charles H. Percy (R)

## Of Wilmette — Elected 1966

**Born:** Sept. 27, 1919, Pensacola, Fla.
**Education:** U. of Chicago, B.A. 1941.
**Military Career:** Navy, 1943-45.
**Profession:** Business executive.
**Family:** Wife, Loraine Guyer; four children.
**Religion:** Christian Scientist.
**Political Career:** Unsuccessful Republican nominee for governor, 1964.

**In Washington:** No committee chairman in Congress made the incoming Reagan administration more nervous than Percy, who inherited the Foreign Relations Committee in the new Republican Senate. Despite his even-tempered style and relatively low profile in recent years, Percy has never surmounted the reputation for self-importance that he picked up early in his Senate career, when he was thinking about national office. He is a fixture on the Washington social circuit, but in the Senate he has been a loner, aloof from most of the personal relationships of the chamber.

On the issues, he had virtually nothing in common with the new regime. A Vietnam dove and arms control advocate, he was on record in favor of a bipartisan foreign policy, toward which Reagan was skeptical. He made the situation worse on a post-election trip to Moscow by implying to Soviet leaders that the new president was ready and eager for renewed arms limitation talks. Leaked cables from the U.S. ambassador to Moscow also indicated Percy endorsed a Palestinian state with Yasir Arafat at its head. The senator spent days modifying, correcting and qualifying his various positions.

The first few months as chairman produced some victories and some defeats. Foreign Relations was unable to act for months on the nominations of several of Reagan's State Department nominees, mostly because Republican Sen. Jesse Helms of North Carolina insisted on delaying them, and Percy was reluctant to force the issue. But on April 28, Percy went ahead without Helms, and an entire bloc of nominations was approved.

Meanwhile, Percy was succeeding in his opposition to the nomination of Ernest Lefever to be assistant secretary of state for human rights. Percy sided with Foreign Relations Democrats on that issue, considering Lefever insufficiently committed to human rights, and when the panel voted 13-4 against the nomination in May, Lefever withdrew. Percy's bipartisan approach was underscored in the committee's first major legislative debate, over a foreign aid bill. He and ranking Democrat Claiborne Pell of Rhode Island sponsored the legislation jointly.

Percy did, however, dutifully back Reagan's interventionist policy toward El Salvador, and even toned down his earlier arms control enthusiasm, saying that the "highest priority is, as Secretary Haig says, holding the Soviets to a code of international conduct."

Percy has always been as comfortable working with Democrats as with most Republicans. For years, he teamed up with Abraham Ribicoff, D-Conn., in running the Governmental Affairs Committee. They sponsored legislation creating the congressional budget process, calling for a "sunset" limitation on the life of government agencies, and proposing a new consumer protection agency.

The Governmental Affairs Committee, where he served as ranking Republican from 1975 to 1981, was friendly territory for Percy most of the time. But it was also the scene of his most uncomfortable moments in the Senate, in 1977. The Illinois senator not only drew fire from committee Democrats but also criticism from a nationwide television audience for his clumsy performance at hearings probing the finances of President Carter's old friend and budget director, Bert Lance.

Percy tried to create a role for himself as a relentless investigator determined to ferret out the truth. He drew some sympathy early in the hearings when it was disclosed that the White House leaked false information to a newspaper charging that Percy used a corporate airplane for private purposes. But Percy went on to grill Lance so mercilessly that he ended up embarrassing himself. In a sense, Percy had the last laugh, since Lance ultimately resigned. But the senator suffered painful blows to his pride and damage to his reputaton. The hearings, he said, "hurt me, and severely . . . I was depicted as a loser."

The hearings marked a sort of turning point in Percy's Senate career, ending the decade-long period in which he was a national figure who drew frequent press attention. Since 1977, he has concentrated on his Foreign Relations and Governmental Affairs assignments without attracting much publicity.

That was a role far different from the one he played as a newcomer in 1967, when it seemed only a matter of time before he sought the presidency.

He quickly established impeccable liberal credentials, voting for health care, housing and civil rights legislation, and touring the slums of Washington D.C., with television cameras close behind, to check out conditions for himself. He called for an early end to U.S. participation in Vietnam, possibly through the vehicle of an all-Asian peace conference.

Initially on good terms with President Nixon, Percy soon split with him, opposing not only his Vietnam policy but his anti-ballistic missile system, and the Supreme Court nominations of Clement Haynsworth and G. Harrold Carswell. By 1970, he had no close connections in the Nixon administration.

When the Watergate scandal unfolded, Percy was among the most vigorous advocates of a special prosecutor, and repeatedly battled Nixon over the president's attempts to invoke executive privilege in White House dealings with Congress.

Percy was actively considering his own bid for the presidency in 1976 until Nixon resigned and Gerald Ford became the obvious Republican nominee. It was clear by then, in any case, that even Ford was too liberal for many of the Republicans who attend party conventions; the GOP had moved too far right ever to accept Percy.

**At Home:** Percy's strain of liberal Republicanism has brought him labor backing, decent showings in Democratic Chicago (where he got 48.7 percent of the vote in 1972 against a congressman from the city) and three Senate victories.

He has been in the national eye since 1949, when at 29 he became the youngest man to head a major U.S. corporation — Bell & Howell, the camera and office equipment maker.

The son of a bank teller, Percy had worked his way through college managing a business he started that purchased supplies for fraternity houses and grossed $150,000 annually. Joseph McNabb, the Bell & Howell chairman, noticed the young campus entrepreneur, offered him a job upon graduation and helped him up the corporate hierarchy.

As a business leader, Percy began moving into Republican Party politics. In 1959 he chaired the Republican Committee on Program and Progress, a group whose position papers, centrist in tone, formed the basis of the 1960 party platform. Percy was chairman of the panel that wrote the platform the next year. President Eisenhower predicted a bright future for him in national politics.

As he made plans to run for governor in 1964, Percy saw that the Republican right would pose a major obstacle to his ambitions. Goldwater enthusiasts persuaded Illinois state Treasurer William J. Scott to mount a stop-Percy candidacy.

After Percy defeated Scott by a 3-2 margin in a Republican primary, he moved to pacify conservatives by supporting Goldwater as the party's presidential nominee. He even canceled a scheduled fund-raising appearance by New York Sen. Jacob Javits, who was part of a rump group of Republicans refusing to endorse Goldwater.

This gave Percy's Democratic opponent, incumbent Gov. Otto J. Kerner, the chance to call him "a political chameleon." The issue was costly to Percy, although not quite as costly as the national Democratic landslide. Percy ran 333,149 votes ahead of Goldwater in Illinois, but he lost the governorship by 179,000 votes.

Two years later, Percy came back to oust Democratic Sen. Paul H. Douglas, campaigning this time from the left. He dropped his earlier opposition to open housing legislation, and argued against the Vietnam War. Douglas, who was Percy's old college economics professor, remained a Cold War liberal — committed to civil rights and government activism but also to the U.S. presence in Indochina.

The campaign started out to be a gentlemanly affair. Percy called Douglas "a man of conviction and courage," and Douglas labeled Percy "one of the finest men in public life." Eventually, however, they quarreled over Vietnam.

In mid-September, the campaign came to a halt when Percy's 21-year-old daughter, Valerie, was brutally slain by an intruder. Both candidates suspended electioneering for 16 days, and then resumed at a subdued level. Sympathetic coverage of the Percy tragedy erased the early Douglas lead, and probably contributed to Percy's comfortable victory.

In 1972, Percy buried Democrat Roman C. Pucinski, a Chicago congressman who had made his reputation as an opponent of busing and open housing. Pucinski's clear ethnic orientation made him a weak candidate in downstate Illinois, and he suffered from massive defections among blacks in Chicago. It was the peak of Percy's political

## Charles H. Percy, R-Ill.

standing.

Republicans expected a similarly easy time in 1978, when Percy was challenged by another conservative Democrat, lawyer Alex R. Seith, a foreign policy expert aided by the Chicago organization. But it was a close contest.

Seith's campaign was rough. He portrayed Percy to Jewish voters as a friend of the Palestinians, and bought time on black radio stations implying that Percy had condoned racial slurs.

The campaign got so intense that, after a heated televised debate with Seith, Percy fainted in public. More significant, he aired a last-minute series of commercials in which he admitted that he should pay more attention to grass-roots opinion. Many Percy loyalists thought this overly apologetic for a senior senator, but it was just right to win back those who were wavering. Percy began gaining again in the final weeks and finished with a margin of nearly 250,000 votes.

## Committees

**Foreign Relations** (Chairman)
Arms Control, Oceans and International Operations, and Environment; International Economic Policy.

**Governmental Affairs** (2nd of 9 Republicans)
Energy, Nuclear Proliferation, and Government Processes, chairman; Federal Expenditures, Research, and Rules; Permanent Subcommittee on Investigations.

**Special Aging** (3rd of 8 Republicans)

## Elections

**1978 General**

| | |
|---|---|
| Charles Percy (R ) | 1,698,711 (53 %) |
| Alex Seith (D ) | 1,448,187 (46 %) |

**1978 Primary**

| | |
|---|---|
| Charles Percy (R ) | 401,409 (84 %) |
| Lar Daly (R ) | 74,739 (16 %) |

**Previous Winning Percentages**

1972 (62 %)    1966 (55 %)

## Campaign Finance

| 1978 | Receipts | Receipts from PACs | Expenditures |
|---|---|---|---|
| Percy (R ) | $2,185,153 | $217,710 (10 %) | $2,163,555 |
| Seith (D ) | $1,370,457 | $27,214 (2 %) | $1,371,485 |

## Voting Studies

| Year | Presidential Support S | O | Party Unity S | O | Conservative Coalition S | O |
|---|---|---|---|---|---|---|
| 1980 | 63 | 27 | 49 | 38 | 46 | 42 |
| 1979 | 77 | 21 | 38 | 51 | 45 | 48 |
| 1978 | 79 | 11 | 23 | 64 | 30 | 58 |
| 1977 | 63 | 20 | 41 | 45 | 49 | 38 |
| 1976 | 57 | 32 | 36 | 50 | 43 | 40 |

| | | | | | | |
|---|---|---|---|---|---|---|
| 1975 | 68 | 24 | 38 | 50 | 28 | 60 |
| 1974 (Ford) | 49 | 25 | | | | |
| 1974 | 47 | 37 | 37 | 43 | 31 | 49 |
| 1973 | 45 | 36 | 39 | 43 | 35 | 48 |
| 1972 | 46 | 48 | 33 | 44 | 26 | 50 |
| 1971 | 50 | 30 | 42 | 40 | 38 | 46 |
| 1970 | 56 | 18 | 33 | 27 | 36 | 24 |
| 1969 | 71 | 18 | 43 | 40 | 42 | 42 |
| 1968 | 55 | 15 | 40 | 30 | 30 | 44 |
| 1967 | 61 | 21 | 49 | 25 | 39 | 45 |

S = Support          O = Opposition

## Key Votes

**96th Congress**

| | |
|---|---|
| Maintain relations with Taiwan (1979) | Y |
| Reduce synthetic fuel development funds (1979) | Y |
| Impose nuclear plant moratorium (1979) | Y |
| Kill stronger windfall profits tax (1979) | N |
| Guarantee Chrysler Corp. loans (1979) | Y |
| Approve military draft registration (1980) | Y |
| End Revenue Sharing to the states (1980) | N |
| Block Justice Dept. busing suits (1980) | N |

**97th Congress**

| | |
|---|---|
| Restore urban program funding cuts (1981) | Y |

## Interest Group Ratings

| Year | ADA | ACA | AFL-CIO | CCUS-1 | CCUS-2 |
|---|---|---|---|---|---|
| 1980 | 39 | 64 | 41 | 63 | |
| 1979 | 47 | 19 | 47 | 44 | 64 |
| 1978 | 50 | 18 | 47 | 59 | |
| 1977 | 65 | 10 | 47 | 53 | |
| 1976 | 45 | 19 | 64 | 11 | |
| 1975 | 56 | 23 | 86 | 50 | |
| 1974 | 67 | 19 | 78 | 22 | |
| 1973 | 60 | 17 | 75 | 22 | |
| 1972 | 60 | 41 | 88 | 22 | |
| 1971 | 56 | 41 | 27 | - | |
| 1970 | 56 | 31 | 100 | 17 | |
| 1969 | 72 | 8 | 80 | - | |
| 1968 | 79 | 31 | 100 | - | |
| 1967 | 38 | 41 | 64 | 80 | |

# Alan J. Dixon (D)

### Of Belleville — Elected 1980

**Born:** July 7, 1927, Belleville, Ill.
**Education:** University of Illinois, B.S. 1946; Washington University, St. Louis, LL.B. 1949.
**Military Career:** Naval Air Cadet, 1945-46.
**Profession:** Lawyer.
**Family:** Wife, Joan Louise Fox; three children.
**Religion:** Presbyterian.
**Political Career:** Illinois House 1951-63; Illinois Senate, 1963-71; state treasurer, 1971-77; secretary of state, 1977-81.

**The Member:** Dixon's election to the Senate lifted him out of a thirty-year concentration on the nuts and bolts of Illinois politics into a broader forum he coveted but waited patiently to seek. He has been in politics longer than any other freshman senator, and most of the senior ones as well.

For his entire adult life, the 53-year-old Dixon has been either a state legislator, state treasurer or secretary of state. This was something of a campaign liability, since he started out unfamiliar with the major national and international issues. But by studying the issues, holding press conferences, and agreeing to debate his opponent, he managed to put the problem behind him.

He is a hard-working senator, but a quiet one with a distaste for controversy. He sits on the Agriculture and Banking committees, keeping a hand in the interests of Chicago and other Illinois cities as well as the state's sizable farming constituency.

In the Banking Committee, Dixon tried to gain more generous help for tenants whose rents are partially subsidized by the federal government. But his proposal was voted down by committee Republicans, who favored Reagan's plan to require that subsidized tenants pay up to 30 percent of their incomes for rent. Dixon has also worked with Illinois Republican Sen. Charles H. Percy on a proposal to increase inheritance tax exemptions.

Throughout his political career, Dixon has managed to stay on good terms with the party organization without being seen as a creature of it. This mixture of cooperation and independence earned him the support of a wide spectrum of voters in Illinois and made him few enemies. It served him well when bitter fighting broke out in the Chicago Democratic organization between Mayor Jane Byrne and Richard M. Daley, son of the late mayor. While Byrne and Daley fought each other, both supported Dixon's Senate candidacy.

## Committees

**Agriculture, Nutrition and Forestry** (7th of 8 Democrats)
Agricultural Production, Marketing and Stabilization of Prices; Foreign Agricultural Policy; Nutrition.

**Banking, Housing and Urban Affairs** (7th of 7 Democrats)
Consumer Affairs; Financial Institutions; Rural Housing and Development.

**Small Business** (8th of 8 Democrats)
Urban and Rural Economic Development.

## Elections

**1980 General**

| | |
|---|---|
| Alan Dixon (D) | 2,565,302 (56%) |
| David O'Neal (R) | 1,946,296 (43%) |

**1980 Primary**

| | |
|---|---|
| Alan Dixon (D) | 671,746 (67%) |
| Alex Seith (D) | 190,339 (19%) |
| Robert Wallace (D) | 64,037 (6%) |

## Campaign Finance

| | Receipts | Receipts from PACs | Expenditures |
|---|---|---|---|
| **1980** | | | |
| Dixon (D) | $2,228,868 | $294,932 (13%) | $2,178,857 |
| O'Neal (R) | $1,293,464 | $362,718 (28%) | $1,271,202 |

## Key Votes

**97th Congress**

| | |
|---|---|
| Restore urban program funding cuts (1981) | Y |

**325**

# 1 Harold Washington (D)

Of Chicago — Elected 1980

**Born:** April 15, 1922, Chicago, Ill.
**Education:** Roosevelt U., B.A. 1949; Northwestern U., J.D. 1952.
**Military Career:** Air Force, 1942-46.
**Profession:** Lawyer.
**Family:** Divorced; no children.
**Religion:** African Methodist Episcopal Zion.
**Political Career:** Ill. House, 1965-77; Ill. Senate, 1977-81; unsuccessfully sought Democratic nomination for mayor of Chicago, 1977.

**The Member:** Washington is the first congressman from this district in nearly 50 years who did not owe his initial election to the South Side's regular Democratic organization.

Washington's antipathy toward the machine was so great that even after he came to Congress, he tried to prevent Chicago Mayor Jane Byrne from appointing one of her allies to his state Senate seat. Washington refused to resign from the state Senate after being sworn into the House, and tried to persuade South Side Democrats to pick an anti-machine senator instead of the man Byrne preferred. But he eventually yielded.

At the urging of the Black Caucus, Washington tried for a seat on the Budget Committee in 1981, arguing that the panel had no other black representation. Washington's brief campaign garnered considerable support, but it lost. Washington joined the Judiciary Committee, where he strongly opposes restrictions on abortion.

In the 1980 primary, Washington easily defeated Democratic Rep. Bennett M. Stewart, a machine loyalist condemned as a party hack in the press. In 1978, Stewart had survived by only 15,000 votes against a Republican in one of the nation's most Democratic districts.

Washington traded on his reputation as an independent-minded legislator and on the publicity he drew as a mayoral candidate in 1977, when he carried five of the city's black wards.

**The District:** Despite its poverty, the predominately black South Side has a history of political stability. Democrat William L. Dawson, a classic boss, ran the district with an iron hand during nearly 30 years in Congress. It was only after Dawson's death in 1970 that the machine began to atrophy. The district changed significantly after 1970 when it absorbed much of the old 2nd, including the University of Chicago political base. The liberal university-centered 5th Ward, where most of the district's whites live, was one of the keys to Washington's success in 1980.

## Committees

**Education and Labor** (18th of 19 Democrats)
Elementary, Secondary and Vocational Education; Employment Opportunities; Health and Safety.

**Government Operations** (22nd of 23 Democrats)
Manpower and Housing.

**Judiciary** (15th of 16 Democrats)
Civil and Constitutional Rights.

## Elections

**1980 General**

| | |
|---|---|
| Harold Washington (D) | 119,562 (96%) |

**1980 Primary**

| | |
|---|---|
| Harold Washington (D) | 30,522 (48%) |
| Ralph Metcalfe Jr. (D) | 12,356 (19%) |
| Bennett Stewart (D) | 10,810 (17%) |
| John Stroger Jr. (D) | 10,284 (16%) |

**District Vote For President**

| | 1980 | | 1976 | | 1972 |
|---|---|---|---|---|---|
| **D** | 128,426 (91%) | **D** | 130,882 (91%) | **D** | 145,003 (89%) |
| **R** | 6,633 (5%) | **R** | 13,816 ( 9%) | **R** | 17,018 (10%) |
| **I** | 3,092 (2%) | | | | |

## Campaign Finance

| | Receipts | Receipts from PACs | Expenditures |
|---|---|---|---|
| **1980** | | | |
| Washington (D) | $77,672 | — (0%) | $72,716 |

## Key Vote

**97th Congress**

Reagan budget proposal (1981)                N

---

**1st District: Chicago — South Side.**
Population: 369,901 (20% decrease since 1970). Race: White 26,500 (7%), Black 338,572 (91%), Others 4,829 (1%). Spanish origin: 3,253 (1%).

# 2 Gus Savage (D)

### Of Chicago — Elected 1980

**Born:** October 30, 1925, Detroit, Michigan.
**Education:** Roosevelt U., B.A. 1951.
**Military Career:** Army, 1943-46.
**Profession:** Newspaper publisher.
**Family:** Widowed; two children.
**Religion:** Protestant.
**Political Career:** Unsuccessfully sought Democratic nomination for U.S. House, 1968 and 1970.

**The Member:** Savage was an early and emphatic opponent of President Reagan's economics. After Reagan outlined his spending and tax proposals before a joint session of Congress on Feb. 18, Savage responded: "Reagan is a reverse Robin Hood, robbing the poor and giving to the rich."

In March, Savage gained brief notoriety in Washington by accusing the D.C. police of racism after they detained his son, Thomas, for driving without a permit in a car lacking license plates and registration papers. The car was being delivered from Chicago to Washington.

Savage said the incident occurred because "it was a big black car in a black neighhborhood with a black driver." Later, he apologized for characterizing the police department as racist.

For thirty years, Savage agitated against Chicago's Democratic machine and for various liberal causes. Through the community newspapers he published on the South Side, Savage remained visible in politics and community organizing.

The Democratic organization held the district easily during the 1970s with Morgan Murphy, who was white. When Murphy retired in 1980, the machine agreed to support a black successor, Reginald Brown. But in a four-way Democratic primary that included one white candidate, Savage won with 45 percent of the vote. He is the first black to represent the district.

**The District:** Traditionally a white ethnic area centered on the South Chicago steel mills, the 2nd has seen a huge influx of blacks over the past decade. The district's population was 39.7 percent black in 1970, but blacks are now overwhelmingly in the majority. There is still a bloc of middle-income ethnic white voters, many of them of Eastern European ancestry.

## Committees

**Post Office and Civil Service** (15th of 15 Democrats)
Compensation and Employee Benefits.

**Public Works and Transportation** (22nd of 25 Democrats)
Economic Development; Investigations and Oversight; Surface Transportation.

**Small Business** (21st of 23 Democrats)
SBA and SBIC Authority, Minority Enterprise and General Small Business Problems; Tax, Access to Equity Capital and Business Opportunities.

## Elections

**1980 General**

| | |
|---|---|
| Gus Savage (D) | 129,771 (88%) |
| Marsha Harris (R) | 17,428 (12%) |

**1980 Primary**

| | |
|---|---|
| Gus Savage (D) | 28,359 (45%) |
| Reginald Brown Jr. (D) | 21,243 (33%) |
| Other | 13,993 (22%) |

**District Vote For President**

| | 1980 | | 1976 | | 1972 |
|---|---|---|---|---|---|
| **D** | 145,205 (84 %) | **D** | 137,384 (83 %) | **D** | 116,527 (65 %) |
| **R** | 20,946 (12 %) | **R** | 28,499 (17 %) | **R** | 60,220 (34 %) |
| **I** | 3,612 (2 %) | | | | |

## Campaign Finance

| | Receipts | Receipts from PACs | Expenditures |
|---|---|---|---|
| **1980** | | | |
| Savage (D ) | $72,996 | $2,200 (3 %) | $72,461 |
| Harris (R ) | $8,786 | $200 (2 %) | $8,981 |

## Key Vote

**97th Congress**

Reagan budget proposal (1981)                    N

> **2nd District: Chicago — South Side.**
> Population: 465,535 (0.2% increase since 1970). Race: White 86,438 (19%), Black 357,338 (77%), Others 21,759 (5%). Spanish origin: 35,176 (8%).

# 3 Marty Russo (D)

**Of South Holland — Elected 1974**

**Born:** Jan. 23, 1944, Chicago, Ill.
**Education:** DePaul U., B.A. 1965, J.D. 1967.
**Profession:** Lawyer.
**Family:** Wife, Karen Jorgenson; two children.
**Religion:** Roman Catholic.
**Political Career:** Assistant Cook County State's Attorney, 1971-73.

**In Washington:** Russo has made his way in the House as a protégé of Dan Rostenkowski, the influential dean of the Chicago delegation and an ally of the leadership. It has generally been a good bargain for both men.

When President Carter's hospital cost containment program was introduced in the House in 1977, it was sent to two separate panels. While Rostenkowski was refusing to guide the program through his Ways and Means Health Subcommittee in the form President Carter wanted, Russo was voting in the Commerce Committee to scuttle it altogether and replace it with an innocuous Republican substitute. Russo cast his vote after sampling opinion in his district — but also after consultation with his mentor. In 1980, when Rostenkowski turned against Chicago Mayor Jane Byrne to support Carter rather than Edward M. Kennedy for president, Russo signed on as a Carter delegate.

That history helped Russo win his own place on the Ways and Means Committee in 1980, in one of the more controversial committee assignments of recent years. Russo's overall record of voting with the leadership was not particularly high and a rival from Texas had a prior claim on the seat. But Rostenkowski went to work for Russo, talked Speaker O'Neill into endorsing him, and Russo got the job.

Russo became the center of House attention in 1979, when he won passage of an amendment blocking the Federal Trade Commission from investigating the funeral industry. Backed up by long and intense industry lobbying and with encouragement from O'Neill, Russo prevailed decisively on the House floor. When House and Senate conferees eliminated the amendment, Russo complained that they had conspired to ignore him. But having cast one public vote in favor of the funeral directors, the House was content to drop the issue.

Early in his career, as a member of the Judiciary Committee, Russo was an active proponent of gun control legislation. During his first term, in 1976, he pushed an amendment in committee that would have banned private ownership of concealable handguns. When the National Rifle Association argued that three-fourths of all existing handguns would have become illegal under the proposal, Russo held a press conference to accuse the group of a lie and a "dirty trick." A compromise version of Russo's proposal did make it out of committee that year, but the bill did not reach the floor and never has.

**At Home:** When Russo launched his House candidacy in 1974 in a district drawn to favor a Republican, his credentials seemed modest: He had served as president of the Young Democrats of Calumet Park, and he was an assistant Cook County state's attorney from 1971 to 1973. Chosen by the organization and unopposed for the Democratic nomination, he was looked upon as a long-shot candidate against freshman Republican Rep. Robert Hanrahan.

In the end, Russo pulled off one of the sleeper upsets of 1974, coming from far behind in the closing weeks of the campaign to surprise an overly confident incumbent who did little campaigning until mid-October. Russo had strong support from organized labor and the Cook County Democratic machine and the partisan advantage of the national Watergate scandal. He also benefited from an abnormally low Republi-

---

**3rd District: Chicago — Southwest suburbs.** Population: 457,236 (1% decrease since 1970). Race: White 397,567 (87%), Black 48,760 (11%), Others 10,929 (2%). Spanish origin: 16,378 (4%).

can turnout.

With constituent service and good campaign skills, Russo has managed to increase his margin in each election since 1974. By 1980, he was close to 70 percent of the vote, even though Ronald Reagan carried the district easily over Jimmy Carter in the presidential balloting.

**The District:** Before 1972, the 3rd District was centered on the southwest side of Chicago. It had been a swing district throughout the 1950s, and marginally Democratic for more than a decade after that. In 1972, a Republican redistricting plan moved it south, toward the city's southern and southwestern suburbs, leaving only a small portion of Chicago inside.

The district is heavily ethnic and Catholic, with Irish, Italian, German and Polish communities well represented. Many of the residents come from working-class families who fled Chicago and its problems as they broke into prosperity. Russo, with his Italian background, has identified himself closely with these groups to his political benefit. There is also a small Dutch settlement in the southern part of the district around South Holland. Like all Dutch-American communities, it tends to be conservative.

## Committees

**Ways and Means** (19th of 23 Democrats)
Public Assistance and Unemployment Compensation; Select Revenue Measures.

## Elections

**1980 General**

| | |
|---|---|
| Marty Russo (D ) | 137,283 (69 %) |
| Lawrence Sarsoun (R) | 61,955 (31 %) |

**1978 General**

| | |
|---|---|
| Marty Russo (D) | 95,701 (65 %) |
| Robert Dunne (R ) | 51,098 (35 %) |

**Previous Winning Percentages**

1976 (59 %)     1974 (53 %)

**District Vote For President**

| | 1980 | | 1976 | | 1972 |
|---|---|---|---|---|---|
| **D** | 87,091 (41 %) | **D** | 88,240 (42 %) | **D** | 61,653 (28 %) |
| **R** | 109,179 (52 %) | **R** | 121,448 (57 %) | **R** | 154,211 (71 %) |
| **I** | 12,594 (6 %) | | | | |

## Campaign Finance

| | Receipts | Receipts from PACs | Expenditures |
|---|---|---|---|
| **1980** | | | |
| Russo (D ) | $187,089 | $86,396 (46 %) | $180,622 |
| **1978** | | | |
| Russo (D ) | $217,245 | $89,815 (41 %) | $219,377 |
| Dunne (R ) | $115,881 | $48,151 (42 %) | $113,083 |

## Voting Studies

| | Presidential Support | | Party Unity | | Conservative Coalition | |
|---|---|---|---|---|---|---|
| Year | S | O | S | O | S | O |
| 1980 | 48 | 38 | 59 | 33 | 56 | 37 |
| 1979 | 63 | 30 | 62 | 25 | 42 | 46 |
| 1978 | 57 | 37 | 49 | 44 | 51 | 41 |
| 1977 | 63 | 27 | 59 | 33 | 42 | 47 |
| 1976 | 27 | 73 | 64 | 27 | 34 | 59 |
| 1975 | 35 | 65 | 78 | 18 | 29 | 68 |

S = Support          O = Opposition

## Key Votes

**96th Congress**

| | |
|---|---|
| Weaken Carter oil profits tax (1979) | N |
| Reject hospital cost control plan (1979) | Y |
| Implement Panama Canal Treaties (1979) | Y |
| Establish Department of Education (1979) | Y |
| Approve Anti-busing Amendment (1979) | Y |
| Guarantee Chrysler Corp. loans (1979) | Y |
| Approve military draft registration (1980) | Y |
| Aid Sandinista regime in Nicaragua (1980) | Y |
| Strengthen fair housing laws (1980) | N |

**97th Congress**

| | |
|---|---|
| Reagan budget proposal (1981) | N |

## Interest Group Ratings

| Year | ADA | ACA | AFL-CIO | CCUS |
|---|---|---|---|---|
| 1980 | 50 | 39 | 68 | 66 |
| 1979 | 53 | 20 | 70 | 35 |
| 1978 | 35 | 50 | 63 | 39 |
| 1977 | 45 | 38 | 91 | 18 |
| 1976 | 55 | 26 | 74 | 7 |
| 1975 | 79 | 25 | 87 | 18 |

# 4 Edward J. Derwinski (R)

**Of Flossmoor — Elected 1958**

**Born:** Sept. 15, 1926, Chicago, Ill.
**Education:** Loyola U., B.S. 1951.
**Military Career:** Army, 1945-46.
**Profession:** Savings and loan executive.
**Family:** Wife, Patricia Van Der Giessen; two children.
**Religion:** Roman Catholic.
**Political Career:** Ill. House, 1957-59.

**In Washington:** Two decades in the House have radically changed Derwinski's view of the world and American foreign policy, drawing him further and further from his old-time allies on the Republican right. He is as aggressive an anti-communist as he was in 1959, but in recent years he has said and done things he himself would have found suspect earlier in his career.

When he rises to speak on foreign aid these days, it is not in the tone he used in 1967, when he said that "never has the futility of foreign aid been more obvious." It is in the spirit of mild reproach he used in 1980, when he urged the House to be "responsible and international-minded," and avoid foreign aid cuts that would hurt the innocent poor in Third World countries.

Changes like that have made Derwinski a central figure on the Foreign Affairs Committee in recent years, one who dominates negotiations with committee Democrats and often eclipses the nominal Republican leader on the committee, mild-mannered William Broomfield of Michigan. He works closely with Democratic Chairman Clement J. Zablocki, a man he once attacked as the "Socialistic congressman from Milwaukee."

Those same changes, however, have blocked any chance Derwinski might have had for the leadership position he has always aspired to. A witty debater with a keen instinct for the tactics of the House floor, Derwinski is one of the shrewdest of the senior Republicans.

But when he decided to run for party conference chairman in 1979, many of the junior Republicans remembered him primarily as the man who voted to implement the Panama Canal transfer treaties and fought against cuts in foreign aid. Some of them, thinking of his penchant for one-liners on even the gravest issue, concluded he was something less than serious in his conservatism.

They would not have felt that way 20 years before, when Derwinski was a 32-year-old fresh-man, militant against communism in Eastern Eu-

rope and worried about its influence at home.

The Kennedy State Department wrote memos to its diplomats about Derwinski in the early years, warning that he was "unfriendly." Unfriendly is hardly the word. He denounced State Department officials as "a gang of fuzzy-headed idiots" and said "we could run the United Nations if we didn't have idiots like Adlai Stevenson there."

In his first year on Foreign Affairs, 1963, Derwinski won approval of his amendment requiring a minimum interest rate on international development loans. He launched his own drive to ban any aid to Yugoslavia and Poland.

That role changed very slowly. By the early 1970s, Derwinski was fighting against cuts in military aid to most regimes friendly to the U.S. In 1976, he tried to head off a move to deny economic aid to Chile, calling it a "punitive amendment that will hurt the poor and needy."

Derwinski's attitude toward left-wing governments has not changed; he has always opposed money for Syria, whose peacekeeping force in Lebanon he has described as "savage," and has been militantly against money for the Marxist Sandinistas in Nicaragua, whom he has described as "Fidel Castro 20 years later."

He has never come to accept the friendly U.S. relationship with mainland China. When Chinese Vice Premier Deng Xiaoping visited Washington, Derwinski called him a "liar," and said "we've embraced a bunch of bums." He backed President Carter's grain embargo to Russia, and

---

**4th District: Chicago suburbs — south and southwest.** Population: 540,537 (16% increase since 1970). Race: White 496,023 (92%), Black 32,283 (6%), Others 12,231 (2%). Spanish origin: 13,305 (2%).

lobbied on the floor against efforts in 1980 to end it.

But on the broader issue of U.S. policy toward most of the Third World, Derwinski takes a different line, even, as he once said, "at the risk of losing my conservative credentials." Those credentials have not been the same since he argued for transfer of the Panama Canal, resisting enormous pressure from his own party. Some of Derwinski's friends attribute the evolution to his years of extensive foreign travel, derided as junketing by many but always defended by him as a part of his education.

In earlier years, he was a frequent visitor to and ally of South Korea, and this relationship got him in the only conspicuous "trouble" of his long career. In 1977, Derwinski tried to block a congressional investigation into possible vote-buying by lobbyists for the South Korean government. Later that year, the Justice Department began looking into charges he had warned South Korea privately that one of its diplomats planned to defect to the United States. But a House ethics panel took no action and the Justice Department dropped the charges.

While traveling and changing as a member of the Foreign Affairs Committee, Derwinski has had what amounts to a second career as a member of Post Office and Civil Service. Like Democrat Morris K. Udall of Arizona, who joined in 1961, the same year he did, Derwinski has found Post Office to be a "minor" committee with major legislative opportunities for those who want to use them.

Long before he switched to his bipartisan approach on Foreign Affairs, Derwinski was working closely with Udall in trying to figure out what to do about the U.S. Post Office.

In 1970, Derwinski was the Republican floor manager of Udall's bill creating the U.S. Postal Service as a semi-private corporation, removed from politics. In the years since then, as the service has come under increasing criticism, Derwinski has held to his original idea that it should be self-sustaining. He has opposed restoring congressional control over postal rates, as well as efforts to give more responsibility to the president. "Don't saddle the president with the burden of managing the postal service," he pleaded in 1978.

That same year, Derwinski and Udall collaborated to pass President Carter's civil service bill, granting government managers more freedom to reward talent and fire the incompetent.

During much of the debate, Udall and Derwinski were on the same side against committee Democrats voicing union fears that the bill would erode job protection. At one point, Democrats complained that Udall was working more closely with Derwinski than with them.

The unity broke down briefly, when the committee added to the bill a provision modifying the Hatch Act, which bars political activity by government employees. Derwinski called that provision a "sellout" to employee unions, and threatened to drop his support for the entire proposal. But this issue was compromised on the floor, Derwinski remained on board, and the legislation became law late in the year.

**At Home:** Derwinski's progress toward a quiet, comfortable career as a suburban Chicago banker went astray when he ran for the Illinois Legislature at age 30, won in an upset, and discovered that politics was in his blood.

Derwinski's family owns a savings and loan association in the Chicago suburbs, and Derwinski was already its president in 1956. But he saw an opportunity for the Illinois House that year and waged a vigorous campaign for the GOP nomination, attracting attention with his name alone in a district where there were few Polish Republicans. Local party leaders refused to endorse him, believing that his background made him an unlikely primary winner, but he won. Two years later, he was preparing for a second term in Springfield when Republican Congressman William McVey died. The local GOP congressional committee chose Derwinski as its candidate to replace him. That year, 1958, was a bad one for Republicans and Derwinski was held to 52 percent of the vote. But his conservatism and involvement with ethnic affairs quickly made him a familiar and popular figure in the district.

He also took an interest in national ethnic issues. In 1961, he served as chairman of the Republican Big City Committee Ethnic Division. Later he was chairman of the Nationalities Division of the GOP National Committee.

**The District:** When it was created in 1948, the district swept around the southwestern portion of Cook County, combining blue-collar, white-collar, and professional and upper-class suburban communities. In 1962, some of the more Democratic areas at the southern end were attached to the 3rd, making the 4th even safer for Derwinski and most GOP statewide candidates.

Although the district has shrunk in size, it still covers basically the same area. The main ethnic groups are the same as Chicago's — Polish, German, Italian, and Irish, and there is a sizable Dutch community. The more affluent of the area's ethnics have become conservative on economic as well as social issues, and abandoned whatever ties they once had to the Democrats.

## Committees

**Foreign Affairs** (2nd of 16 Republicans)
   International Operations; International Security and Scientific
   Affairs.

**Post Office and Civil Service** (Ranking Republican)
   Investigations.

## Elections

**1980 General**

| | |
|---|---|
| Edward Derwinski (R ) | 152,377 (68 %) |
| Richard Jalovec (D ) | 71,814 (32 %) |

**1980 Primary**

| | |
|---|---|
| Edward Derwinski (R) | 40,593 (83 %) |
| Joseph Soward (R) | 8,118 (17 %) |

**1978 General**

| | |
|---|---|
| Edward Derwinski (R ) | 94,435 (67 %) |
| Andrew Thomas (D ) | 46,788 (33 %) |

**Previous Winning Percentages**

| | | | |
|---|---|---|---|
| 1976 (66 %) | 1974 (59 %) | 1972 (71 %) | 1970 (68 %) |
| 1968 (68 %) | 1966 (72 %) | 1964 (59 %) | 1962 (65 %) |
| 1960 (56 %) | 1958 (52 %) | | |

**District Vote For President**

| | 1980 | | 1976 | | 1972 |
|---|---|---|---|---|---|
| D | 76,622 (34 %) | D | 80,401 (37 %) | D | 58,453 (29 %) |
| R | 130,344 (57 %) | R | 131,103 (61 %) | R | 145,547 (71 %) |
| I | 18,017 (8 %) | | | | |

## Campaign Finance

| | Receipts | Receipts from PACs | Expen-ditures |
|---|---|---|---|
| **1980** | | | |
| Derwinski (R ) | $79,771 | $52,226 (65 %) | $98,597 |
| Jalovec (D ) | $77,973 | $2,750 (4 %) | $63,686 |
| **1978** | | | |
| Derwinski (R ) | $90,635 | $26,428 (29 %) | $72,941 |
| Thomas (D ) | $74,316 | $2,300 (3 %) | $73,437 |

## Voting Studies

| Year | Presidential Support | | Party Unity | | Conservative Coalition | |
|---|---|---|---|---|---|---|
| | S | O | S | O | S | O |
| 1980 | 42 | 45 | 70 | 22 | 64 | 24 |
| 1979 | 38 | 59 | 71 | 27 | 69 | 26 |
| 1978 | 47 | 50 | 68 | 31 | 73 | 26 |
| 1977 | 43 | 54 | 77 | 19 | 80 | 17 |

| Year | S | O | S | O | S | O |
|---|---|---|---|---|---|---|
| 1976 | 73 | 24 | 64 | 29 | 66 | 25 |
| 1975 | 74 | 19 | 71 | 23 | 74 | 19 |
| 1974 (Ford) | 46 | 31 | | | | |
| 1974 | 70 | 23 | 66 | 23 | 70 | 18 |
| 1973 | 59 | 22 | 65 | 21 | 65 | 21 |
| 1972 | 54 | 19 | 64 | 20 | 71 | 13 |
| 1971 | 49 | 12 | 39 | 7 | 43 | 4 |
| 1970 | 65 | 26 | 82 | 8 | 73 | 18 |
| 1969 | 51 | 36 | 69 | 18 | 71 | 20 |
| 1968 | 44 | 43 | 76 | 13 | 84 | 10 |
| 1967 | 36 | 45 | 72 | 8 | 63 | 17 |
| 1966 | 33 | 48 | 69 | 9 | 70 | 3 |
| 1965 | 27 | 57 | 76 | 4 | 71 | 6 |
| 1964 | 29 | 56 | 76 | 8 | 75 | 17 |
| 1963 | 15 | 63 | 84 | 2 | 67 | 20 |
| 1962 | 33 | 60 | 77 | 9 | 75 | 19 |
| 1961 | 29 | 63 | 81 | 12 | 87 | 4 |

S = Support          O = Opposition

## Key Votes

**96th Congress**

Weaken Carter oil profits tax (1979)
Reject hospital cost control plan (1979)
Implement Panama Canal Treaties (1979)
Establish Department of Education (1979)
Approve Anti-busing Amendment (1979)
Guarantee Chrysler Corp. loans (1979)
Approve military draft registration (1980)
Aid Sandinista regime in Nicaragua (1980)
Strengthen fair housing laws (1980)

**97th Congress**

Reagan budget proposal (1981)

## Interest Group Ratings

| Year | ADA | ACA | AFL-CIO | CCU |
|---|---|---|---|---|
| 1980 | 11 | 74 | 16 | 6 |
| 1979 | 11 | 73 | 40 | 8 |
| 1978 | 20 | 78 | 20 | 7 |
| 1977 | 10 | 81 | 13 | 9 |
| 1976 | 5 | 75 | 14 | 6 |
| 1975 | 0 | 79 | 26 | 9 |
| 1974 | 9 | 69 | 0 | 7 |
| 1973 | 12 | 100 | 9 | 9 |
| 1972 | 6 | 80 | 27 | 10 |
| 1971 | 11 | 100 | 11 | |
| 1970 | 20 | 89 | 0 | 10 |
| 1969 | 40 | 88 | 10 | |
| 1968 | 17 | 100 | 0 | |
| 1967 | 7 | 96 | 9 | 10 |
| 1966 | 0 | 85 | 0 | |
| 1965 | 5 | 92 | - | 10 |
| 1964 | 4 | 94 | 9 | |
| 1963 | - | 93 | - | |
| 1962 | 13 | 91 | 0 | |
| 1961 | 0 | - | 0 | |

# 5 John G. Fary (D)

**Of Chicago — Elected 1975**

**Born:** April 11, 1911, Chicago, Ill.
**Education:** Attended Loyola U.; Real Estate School of Ill.; Midwest Institute.
**Profession:** Real estate broker; tavern owner.
**Family:** Wife, Lillian Makowski; two children.
**Religion:** Roman Catholic.
**Political Career:** Ill. House, 1955-75.

**In Washington:** A decade ago there were dozens of members of the House like John Fary, aging big-city Democrats rewarded with places in Congress after an uncomplaining lifetime of party service. Today, in a chamber of issue-oriented individualists, Fary is an anachronism. But he plays his role as he was taught to play it on the South Side of Chicago a generation ago.

The Chicago Democratic Party that installed Fary in the House at age 64 expected from him loyalty rather than legislative action, and he delivers it. He delivers for Dan Rostenkowski, Ways and Means chairman and leader of the city's delegation, when the call goes out. When Speaker O'Neill needs a vote in a close situation, even on politically sensitive issues, Fary is there to comply. He is nearly always willing to cosponsor any bill introduced by his closest Chicago colleague, Frank Annunzio.

It is not a job that requires much public speaking, and one can sit in the gallery for months without hearing Fary address the House, although he is almost always nearby, reading at the back of the chamber or lingering in the House dining room over lunch with friends in the state delegation. His few entries in the *Congressional Record* are nearly all inserted without his having to deliver them in person, and deal with Lithuanian Independence celebrations or tributes to Polish patriots of earlier centuries.

On the Public Works Committee, Fary faces one issue of considerable importance to his constituents, the future of Midway Airport, located in his district. Once the nation's busiest, Midway fell into disuse in the jet era. Fary has inconspicuously worked his way up to third in seniority on the Public Works Aviation Subcommittee, and occasionally steps out of character to argue for legislative wording that would help revive Midway.

One issue on which Fary does take a strong personal stand is abortion. He opposes it whenever the opportunity comes up. "This nation cannot be taken seriously in its support for the human rights movement," he said in 1979, "as long as we allow the murder of children."

**At Home:** For more than 20 years, starting in 1955, Chicago's Southwest Side routinely re-elected a genial restaurateur and an equally genial tavern owner, both Polish-Americans, both fixtures in the city's machine. One was Congressman John C. Kluczynski, and the other was Fary, a member of the Illinois Legislature. Both labored quietly in their respective niches. Fary's main claim to fame was sponsorship of a successful drive to legalize bingo in Illinois.

In January 1975, Kluczynski died. Fary was the organization's choice to replace him in Washington. The special election campaign received some national attention after a Roman Catholic priest and former city alderman, Rev. Francis X. Lawlor, won the Republican nomination on a write-in vote. Lawlor had been active in the 1960s as leader of "block clubs" that resisted the movement of blacks into white ethnic areas.

But there was little doubt about who would win. Mayor Richard J. Daley's organization delivered 72 percent of the vote for Fary, whose saloon was located only a few blocks from the mayor's home. On victory night, Fary was declaring, "I will go to Washington to help represent Mayor Daley. For 21 years I represented the mayor in the Legislature, and he was always right."

Fary did not have another noteworthy chal-

---

**5th District: Chicago — central.** Population: 397,817 (15% decrease since 1970). Race: White 239,096 (60%), Black 118,035 (30%), Others 39,686 (10%). Spanish origin: 67,326 (17%).

**333**

lenge until 1980, three years after Mayor Daley's death, when the late Rep. Kluczynski's sister-in-law, Melanie Kluczynski, entered the Democratic primary. The organization stuck with Fary and the Kluczynski name was not enough to pull more than about a quarter of the vote.

**The District:** Long a bastion of Eastern European ethnicity, the 5th District has undergone sharp changes in the past two decades. It lost much of its economic base with the decline of the Union Stockyards, and it has changed socially as blacks have moved in from the east, often despite white resistance. The district is now nearly one-third black, and 17 percent Hispanic.

The 5th lost 15 percent of its population in the 1970s and needs to gain about 120,000 residents to meet the equal population requirement. With Chicago due to lose a congressional district and with the 5th's neighbors all needing to gain residents, the district is a prime candidate for extinction.

## Committees

**Public Works and Transportation** (11th of 25 Democrats)
Public Buildings and Grounds, chairman; Aviation; Investigations and Oversight; Water Resources.

**Small Business** (23rd of 23 Democrats)
Tax, Access to Equity Capital and Business Opportunities.

## Elections

**1980 General**

| | |
|---|---|
| John Fary (D ) | 106,142 (80 %) |
| Robert Kotowski (R ) | 27,136 (20 %) |

**1980 Primary**

| | |
|---|---|
| John Fary (D ) | 51,281 (72 %) |
| Melanie Kluczynski (D ) | 19,510 (27 %) |

**1978 General**

| | |
|---|---|
| John Fary (D ) | 98,702 (84 %) |
| Joseph Barracca (R ) | 18,802 (16 %) |

**Previous Winning Percentages**

1976 (77 %)    1975* (72 %)

*Special election

**District Vote For President**

| | 1980 | | 1976 | | 1972 |
|---|---|---|---|---|---|
| D | 106,568 (67 %) | D | 113,899 (67 %) | D | 95,943 (52 %) |
| R | 44,940 (28 %) | R | 57,147 (33 %) | R | 86,646 (47 %) |
| I | 6,096 (4 %) | | | | |

## Campaign Finance

| | | Receipts | Expen- |
|---|---|---|---|
| | Receipts | from PACs | ditures |
| **1980** | | | |
| Fary (D ) | $67,874 | $18,950 (28 %) | $58,809 |
| Kotowski (R ) | $6,927 | — (0 %) | $6,925 |

| 1978 | | | |
|---|---|---|---|
| Fary (D ) | $42,745 | $8,520 (20 %) | $37,315 |

## Voting Studies

| | Presidential Support | | Party Unity | | Conservative Coalition | |
|---|---|---|---|---|---|---|
| Year | S | O | S | O | S | O |
| 1980 | 77 | 17 | 87 | 7 | 26 | 67 |
| 1979 | 74 | 20 | 86 | 9 | 28 | 65 |
| 1978 | 66 | 21 | 75 | 14 | 26 | 65 |
| 1977 | 75 | 23 | 83 | 14 | 29 | 67 |
| 1976 | 37 | 59 | 83 | 14 | 31 | 65 |
| 1975 | 23 | 31† | 48 | 4† | 9 | 44† |

†Not eligible for all recorded votes.

S = Support        O = Opposition

## Key Votes

**96th Congress**

| | |
|---|---|
| Weaken Carter oil profits tax (1979) | N |
| Reject hospital cost control plan (1979) | X |
| Implement Panama Canal Treaties (1979) | Y |
| Establish Department of Education (1979) | Y |
| Approve Anti-busing Amendment (1979) | Y |
| Guarantee Chrysler Corp. loans (1979) | Y |
| Approve military draft registration (1980) | Y |
| Aid Sandinista regime in Nicaragua (1980) | Y |
| Strengthen fair housing laws (1980) | N |

**97th Congress**

| | |
|---|---|
| Reagan budget proposal (1981) | N |

## Interest Group Ratings

| Year | ADA | ACA | AFL-CIO | CCUS |
|---|---|---|---|---|
| 1980 | 44 | 21 | 79 | 65 |
| 1979 | 53 | 12 | 85 | 25 |
| 1978 | 40 | 22 | 80 | 31 |
| 1977 | 50 | 15 | 100 | 12 |
| 1976 | 50 | 19 | 91 | 19 |
| 1975 | 45 | 0 | 100 | 50 |

# 6   Henry J. Hyde (R)

**Of Bensenville — Elected 1974**

**Born:** April 18, 1924, Chicago, Ill.
**Education:** Georgetown U., B.S. 1947; Loyola U.,
    J.D. 1949.
**Military Career:** Navy, 1944-46.
**Profession:** Lawyer.
**Family:** Wife, Jeanne Simpson; four children.
**Religion:** Roman Catholic.
**Political Career:** Ill. House, 1967-75, majority
    leader, 1971-73; unsuccessful Republican
    nominee for U.S. House, 1962.

**In Washington:** Hyde's crusade against
federal funding for abortions has brought him
national attention most junior members only
dream of attracting. But it also has brought a
reputation for fanaticism that seems to trouble
him as he competes for a leadership role in the
House.

"When an issue develops," he said quietly
one day in 1980, "you either evade it or you
grapple with it. I grappled with it, and now it's
grappling back." Hyde would like to be known as
a thoughtful conservative who legislates with restraint. His record bears that out. But the only
subject most people want to talk about with Hyde
is abortion. And he rarely refuses to talk about it.

Hyde was a freshman when he offered his
first amendment to ban federal funding of abortions, largely at the urging of Maryland's conservative Republican, Robert E. Bauman. At that
time, the federal government was paying for between 200,000 and 300,000 abortions a year,
mostly for Medicaid recipients. The amendment
passed the House, although it was modified in the
Senate to allow payment for abortions to save the
life of the mother.

By 1981, the Hyde amendment was firmly in
place, upheld as constitutional by the Supreme
Court. It permitted abortion funding only to
save the mother's life or in cases of rape or incest.
The number of federally funded abortions has
declined to about 2,000 annually.

With that issue apparently settled, Hyde
moved on to a new crusade, to ban private abortion by federal statute. Admitting his side lacked
the votes to pass an anti-abortion Constitutional
Amendment, he introduced a new bill that would
identify conception as the beginning of life, and
might allow states to pass their own laws against
abortion.

Hyde is as much of a zealot as ever on the

subject, calling it a "civil rights issue" and referring to abortion as a descendant of slavery and
genocide. On other questions, however, he is difficult to label.

On foreign aid, for example, Hyde rises virtually every year to defend U.S. aid programs
against attacks by those who work with him on
the abortion issue. When Republicans sought to
cut funding for the Asian Development Bank by
half in 1980, Hyde accused them of trying to turn
back the clock "to the days of the early 1930s."
On another occasion, he warned them that "the
biblical injunction to give food to the hungry and
clothe the naked does not stop when we enter this
chamber."

It was Hyde who fought against a proposal to
bar strikes by Legal Services Corporation lawyers,
arguing that, as private citizens, they had a constitutional right to strike. It was a very lawyer-like
Hyde who, in 1977, pointed out that an emergency
bill to combat child pornography might be unconstitutional. "In our well-intentioned desire to attack the revolting crime of child abuse," he said,
"we have let our zeal overcome our judgment."

Hyde's more traditional conservatism shows
itself on economic issues. Taking them less seriously than he does abortion, he often unleashes
the sarcasm and debating skill he used for two
decades as a trial lawyer in Chicago. One day in
1980, when he was arguing against a new open-
ended appropriation for child welfare, Democratic

---

**6th District: Cook County — north-
west suburbs.** Population: 425,111 (8% decrease since 1970). Race: White 375,000 (88%),
Black 33,996 (8%), Others 16,115 (4%). Spanish origin: 22,759 (5%).

---

**335**

## Henry J. Hyde, R-Ill.

leaders told Hyde they disagreed with the practice in principle, but thought it was the wrong time to end it. "I understand," Hyde said. "We'll sober up tomorrow, but meanwhile pass the bottle." Hyde once introduced a bill to allow taxpayers to designate one dollar of their tax liability to be used to reduce the national debt.

In 1981, Hyde started out arguing in alliance with Southern Democrats against extension of the 1965 Voting Rights Act. He said he agreed the law discriminated against the South by making its officials pre-clear their election laws with the Justice Department. But after several weeks of hearings, Hyde, senior Republican on the Civil and Constitutional Rights Subcommittee, changed his mind. "I have learned from the hearings," Hyde said, "there still are enormous difficulties with people getting the vote in the South and other areas."

It was Hyde's reputation for debating skill, rather than his national anti-abortion following, that brought him within three votes of the Republican Conference chairmanship in a last-minute campaign in 1979. Dissatisfied with the front-running candidate, Ohio's Samuel Devine, a group of freshman members persuaded Hyde to run less than a week before the election. Hyde's 74-71 loss was seen as a moral victory by his supporters, and appeared to give him a shot at a higher leadership post later on.

Hyde was briefly a candidate for party whip in the late 1980 election for that job, but faced an impossible problem — the fact that the front-running candidate for party leader, Robert H. Michel, was a fellow-Illinoisan, and no one state has ever had the top two members of the leadership. Once Michel's election as leader began to seem certain, Hyde withdrew.

**At Home:** Hyde grew up as an Irish-Catholic Democrat in Chicago, but like Ronald Reagan, began having doubts about the Democratic Party in the late 1940s. By 1952, he had switched parties and backed Dwight D. Eisenhower for president.

After practicing law in the Chicago area for more than a decade, and serving as a GOP ward committeeman, Hyde was chosen by the Republican organization in 1962 to challenge Democratic Rep. Roman Pucinski in a northwest Chicago congressional district. The heavily ethnic district had been represented by a Republican for eight years before Pucinski won it in 1958. Hyde came within 10,000 votes of upsetting Pucinski.

Elected to the Illinois House in 1966, Hyde became one of its most active and outspoken members, and one of its most articulate debaters. He was voted "best freshman representative" in 1967, and "most effective representative" in 1972. In 1971, Hyde became majority leader; he made an unsuccessful attempt at the Speakership in 1973.

In 1974, longtime Republican Rep. Harold Collier retired from the suburban 6th Congressional District, just west of Chicago. Hyde entered the Republican primary, winning 48.7 percent of the vote in a field of six candidates. His Democratic opponent was Edward V. Hanrahan, the controversial former Cook County State's Attorney who had had a falling out with Mayor Daley's Democratic organization. Hyde bested Hanrahan by 8,000 votes at a time when Republican districts were falling to Democrats all over the country. Since then, Hyde has become politically invincible in his district, building up 2-1 margins in the last two elections.

**The District:** The 6th is a potpourri of suburban communities. It ranges from ethnic blue-collar areas practically indistinguishable from neighborhoods in the city, to old-line upper income areas and newer split-level tracts.

The district includes the old ethnic cities of Cicero and Berwyn, traditional Czech communities. Al Capone operated in Cicero in the 1920s, and racial violence occurred there in the 1960s. The 6th moves north to take in Oak Park, one of the oldest Chicago suburbs, and northwest to take in a corner of DuPage County.

The district has areas of Democratic strength along its southern border, and becomes more Republican as it moves north and west. Its Republican percentages are higher than the Illinois average in nearly every statewide election.

While parts of the area grew in the 1970s, the older towns lost population, accounting for an 8.4 percent overall decline over the past decade. Consequently, the district will have to make up a population deficit of almost 100,000 people to come up to the state average.

## Committees

**Banking, Finance and Urban Affairs** (5th of 19 Republicans)
Financial Institutions Supervision, Regulation and Insurance; International Development Institutions and Finance; International Trade, Investment and Monetary Policy.

**Judiciary** (7th of 12 Republicans)
Civil and Constitutional Rights; Monopolies and Commercial Law.

# Elections

**1980 General**

| | |
|---|---|
| Henry Hyde (R ) | 123,593 (67 %) |
| Mario Reda (D ) | 60,951 (33 %) |

**1978 General**

| | |
|---|---|
| Henry Hyde (R ) | 87,193 (66 %) |
| Jeanne Quinn (D ) | 44,543 (34 %) |

**Previous Winning Percentages**

1976 (61 %)    1974 (53 %)

**District Vote For President**

| | 1980 | | 1976 | | 1972 |
|---|---|---|---|---|---|
| D | 72,244 (38 %) | D | 77,875 (40 %) | D | 68,011 (31 %) |
| R | 98,887 (52 %) | R | 115,889 (59 %) | R | 149,989 (69 %) |
| I | 15,388 (8 %) | | | | |

# Campaign Finance

| | Receipts | Receipts from PACs | Expen-ditures |
|---|---|---|---|
| **1980** | | | |
| Hyde (R ) | $209,818 | $58,694 (28 %) | $144,469 |
| Reda (D ) | $30,558 | $15,770 (52 %) | $30,049 |
| **1978** | | | |
| Hyde (R ) | $154,079 | $44,955 (29 %) | $153,066 |
| Quinn (D ) | $5,882 | $50 (1 %) | $6,834 |

# Voting Studies

| | Presidential Support | | Party Unity | | Conservative Coalition | |
|---|---|---|---|---|---|---|
| Year | S | O | S | O | S | O |
| 1980 | 53 | 39 | 67 | 29 | 76 | 21 |
| 1979 | 42 | 50 | 71 | 25 | 78 | 19 |
| 1978 | 43 | 54 | 75 | 19 | 73 | 20 |
| 1977 | 47 | 52 | 77 | 20 | 80 | 15 |
| 1976 | 76 | 22 | 83 | 14 | 85 | 13 |
| 1975 | 79 | 20 | 82 | 15 | 85 | 14 |

S = Support          O = Opposition

# Key Votes

**96th Congress**

| | |
|---|---|
| Weaken Carter oil profits tax (1979) | Y |
| Reject hospital cost control plan (1979) | # |
| Implement Panama Canal Treaties (1979) | N |
| Establish Department of Education (1979) | N |
| Approve Anti-busing Amendment (1979) | Y |
| Guarantee Chrysler Corp. loans (1979) | Y |
| Approve military draft registration (1980) | Y |
| Aid Sandinista regime in Nicaragua (1980) | Y |
| Strengthen fair housing laws (1980) | N |

**97th Congress**

| | |
|---|---|
| Reagan budget proposal (1981) | Y |

# Interest Group Ratings

| Year | ADA | ACA | AFL-CIO | CCUS |
|---|---|---|---|---|
| 1980 | 28 | 74 | 26 | 79 |
| 1979 | 5 | 77 | 25 | 94 |
| 1978 | 10 | 70 | 5 | 94 |
| 1977 | 10 | 59 | 26 | 100 |
| 1976 | 0 | 70 | 26 | 74 |
| 1975 | 5 | 86 | 13 | 94 |

# 7 Cardiss Collins (D)

## Of Chicago — Elected 1973

**Born:** Sept. 24, 1931, St. Louis, Mo.
**Education:** Northwestern U., no degree.
**Profession:** Auditor, accountant.
**Family:** Widow of Rep. George Collins; one child.
**Religion:** Baptist.
**Political Career:** No previous office.

**In Washington:** Viewed for three terms as a relatively passive member of the Chicago delegation, loyal to the Cook County Democratic machine, Collins burst out of that stereotype in 1979 as a feisty leader of the Congressional Black Caucus and bitter critic of a Democratic president.

Collins was a novice at politics in 1973, when the Chicago organization placed her in the House as successor to her husband, George W. Collins, who was killed in an airplane crash. She was assigned to Foreign Affairs and Government Operations, and gained little attention on either one until 1977, when she led the fight for congressional endorsement of an embargo on weapons shipments to South Africa.

But unlike the two nationally-famous black women in the House, Shirley Chisholm of New York and Barbara Jordan of Texas, Collins decided to become an active participant in the Congressional Black Caucus. By 1979 she was in line for the chairmanship. She came in at a moment of increasing black disillusionment with the Carter administration, and she became a widely-quoted voice of that discontent. When caucus members went to the White House to push their legislative priorities, it was Collins who normally fired the parting shot.

When the House refused to make Martin Luther King Jr.'s birthday a legal holiday, Collins charged that "racism had a part in it," and blamed the Carter administration, which had endorsed the idea, for not working actively enough to round up votes in favor of it.

In 1980, Collins supported Sen. Ted Kennedy for president, as did many of her black colleagues, and openly attacked Carter. She said many blacks identified Carter with joblessness and inflation. After Carter's renomination, Collins said blacks were simply alienated from the campaign. "Whoever gets into office," she said," black people are in for a season of suffering."

Collins was criticized earlier in her career for spending more time on foreign policy issues than on district matters, but she muted most of that by turning down the chairmanship of the Africa Subcommittee on Foreign Affairs in 1979 in order to take over the Manpower and Housing Subcommittee on Government Operations.

There she has concentrated on public housing and public service jobs, trying to pressure federal agencies into working more efficiently. Collins' amendments for independent monitoring of CETA programs, growing out of a series of hearings, were incorporated in a 1978 law. In the 97th Congress, she held hearings to focus public attention on anti-poverty work of the Community Services Administration, threatened by a Reagan plan to shift such programs to state control.

**At Home:** George W. Collins was re-elected in 1972 in a reconstituted 7th District which promised him a safe haven for a long time. But a month later, flying home from Washington for a weekend in the district, he was killed when his airliner crashed near Chicago's Midway Airport. The Chicago organization which had built his political career picked his widow to succeed him. She has been re-elected routinely ever since.

Cardiss Collins never had been involved directly in politics before 1973, although she had absorbed some of the atmosphere from her husband, who had been a Democratic precinct captain and patronage employee in the Chicago and Cook County governments for years.

---

**7th District: Chicago — Downtown, West Side.** Population: 372,353 (20% decrease since 1970). Race: White 109,242 (29%), Black 186,659 (50%), Others 76,452 (21%). Spanish origin: 105,307 (28%).

An only child, Collins left her Detroit home for Chicago at the age of 18. She worked in a factory tying mattress springs, then got a job in state government, attended night school and earned a certificate in accounting. She worked as an auditor in the Illinois Revenue Department before her election to Congress.

**The District:** The 7th District contains some of the richest and poorest areas in Chicago.

Luxury high-rise apartment buildings line the boulevards along Lake Michigan, but the slums begin only a few blocks west, and continue for miles, almost to the city limits. Except for its

lakefront "Gold Coast," the 7th is largely a black district, although it contains communities of Hispanics and Chinese, and the remnants of the once-teeming Italian ghetto. Also in the district is Chicago's downtown office and shopping area.

Like most inner-city districts, the 7th has had a hemorrhage of population over the past decade. It lost a fifth of its residents between 1970 and 1980 and needs to gain about 150,000 new ones to reach the statewide average. With Collins as the senior black member of the Illinois delegation, however, the district seems more likely to be preserved intact than some of its neighbors.

## Committees

**Energy and Commerce** (20th of 24 Democrats)
Enery Conservation and Power; Fossil and Synthetic Fuels; Telecommunications, Consumer Protection and Finance.

**Government Operations** (7th of 23 Democrats)
Manpower and Housing, chairman.

**Select Narcotics Abuse and Control** (8th of 11 Democrats)

## Elections

**1980 General**

| | |
|---|---|
| Cardiss Collins (D ) | 80,056 (85 %) |
| Ruth Hooper (R ) | 14,041 (15 %) |

**1980 Primary**

| | |
|---|---|
| Cardiss Collins (D ) | 29,420 (78 %) |
| Mary Tuner (D ) | 8,306 (22 %) |

**1978 General**

| | |
|---|---|
| Cardiss Collins (D ) | 64,716 (86 %) |
| James Holt (R ) | 10,273 (14 %) |

**Previous Winning Percentages**

1976 (85 %)    1974 (88 %)    1973* (93 %)

*Special election*

**District Vote For President**

| 1980 | 1976 | 1972 |
|---|---|---|
| 85,999 (79 %) **D** | 91,956 (81 %) **D** | 93,318 (73 %) |
| 17,988 (17 %) **R** | 21,836 (19 %) **R** | 33,266 (26 %) |
| 3,188 (3 %) | | |

## Campaign Finance

| | Receipts | Receipts from PACs | Expenditures |
|---|---|---|---|
| **1980** | | | |
| Collins (D ) | $29,215 | $1,700 (6 %) | $19,409 |
| **1978** | | | |
| Collins (D ) | $18,925 | $7,950 (42 %) | $34,857 |
| Holt (R ) | $15,474 | $400 (3 %) | $13,610 |

## Voting Studies

| | Presidential Support | | Party Unity | | Conservative Coalition | |
|---|---|---|---|---|---|---|
| Year | S | O | S | O | S | O |
| 1980 | 52 | 28 | 66 | 5 | 2 | 68 |
| 1979 | 64 | 16 | 74 | 7 | 6 | 78 |
| 1978 | 54 | 14 | 71 | 5 | 7 | 64 |
| 1977 | 61 | 22 | 78 | 4 | 8 | 74 |
| 1976 | 24 | 57 | 82 | 3 | 6 | 71 |
| 1975 | 33 | 46 | 75 | 6 | 9 | 71 |
| 1974 (Ford) | 41 | 57 | | | | |
| 1974 | 28 | 51 | 85 | 6 | 5 | 82 |
| 1973 | 24 | 63† | 84 | 4† | 9 | 81† |

†Not eligible for all recorded votes.
S = Support          O = Opposition

## Key Votes

**96th Congress**

| | |
|---|---|
| Weaken Carter oil profits tax (1979) | N |
| Reject hospital cost control plan (1979) | N |
| Implement Panama Canal Treaties (1979) | Y |
| Establish Department of Education (1979) | ? |
| Approve Anti-busing Amendment (1979) | N |
| Guarantee Chrysler Corp. loans (1979) | Y |
| Approve military draft registration (1980) | N |
| Aid Sandinista regime in Nicaragua (1980) | Y |
| Strengthen fair housing laws (1980) | Y |

**97th Congress**

| | |
|---|---|
| Reagan budget proposal (1981) | N |

## Interest Group Ratings

| Year | ADA | ACA | AFL-CIO | CCUS |
|---|---|---|---|---|
| 1980 | 89 | 20 | 94 | 48 |
| 1979 | 79 | 5 | 100 | 20 |
| 1978 | 65 | 14 | 85 | 29 |
| 1977 | 75 | 0 | 95 | 7 |
| 1976 | 70 | 4 | 90 | 0 |
| 1975 | 100 | 4 | 95 | 29 |
| 1974 | 74 | 7 | 90 | 10 |
| 1973 | 95 | 6 | 100 | 14 |

**339**

# 8  Dan Rostenkowski (D)

**Of Chicago — Elected 1958**

**Born:** Jan. 2, 1928, Chicago, Ill.
**Education:** Attended Loyola U. , 1948-51.
**Military Career:** Army, 1946-48.
**Profession:** Insurance executive.
**Family:** Wife, LaVerne Pirkins; four children.
**Religion:** Roman Catholic.
**Political Career:** Ill. House, 1953-55; Ill. Senate, 1955-59.

**In Washington:** After more than 20 years of playing pure House politics, trading votes and committee assignments and angling for a top leadership position, Rostenkowski is now nationally famous in a role he never really wanted — haggling over the details of the revenue code as Ways and Means chairman.

It is a measure of his reputation that few colleagues ever doubted he would succeed at Ways and Means, whether he went in knowing much about it or not. Rostenkowski is always thinking. As Mayor Richard Daley's man in Washington, he quickly learned the skill of whipping a delegation into line, and he knows how to apply that to a committee. His Ways and Means predecessor, Al Ullman of Oregon, took tax policy seriously but had little political skill and found his colleagues hard to control. Running Ways and Means is essentially a political task.

For the first half of 1981, the task was to build a consensus behind a tax bill that could survive on the House floor. After watching Democratic leaders suffer a string of embarrassing defeats on the Budget, Rostenkowski wanted to make an accommodation with the Reagan administration on taxes if he could. He offered a one-year tax cut oriented toward business. But the White House insisted on a three-year, 25 percent tax cut, and persuaded a conservative Ways and Means Democrat, Kent Hance of Texas, to co-sponsor it. That left Rostenkowski with the job of trying to keep his party together behind a bill focused on lower income levels than the Reagan approach.

As attractive as the committee's chairmanship would be for almost any member, Rostenkowski thought for weeks before taking it. He was also in line to become Democratic whip, the third ranking position in the leadership and stepping-stone for the last two Speakers. Chief tax writer is a powerful office, but it is not on any conventional leadership ladder.

Rostenkowski agonized, wrung his hands, consulted friends and then took Ways and Means. His close friend Tip O'Neill and business lobbyists were equally happy at the decision: Rostenkowski is a more predictable ally for both than Sam Gibbons of Florida, an independent-minded free trader who was next in line.

Becoming Ways and Means chairman meant a major change in the tempo of Rostenkowski's life. For most of the late 1970s, he was not one of the hardest workers in the House. He had joined Ways and Means in 1965 mainly because it then made the committee assignments for all House Democrats; it offered virtually unlimited opportunities for politicking. When Ways and Means lost that function in 1975, he lost much of his interest. He chaired its Health Subcommittee for four years, but gave it up in 1979 to take a minor panel on Select Revenue Measures.

Rostenkowski is a man who likes to have a gavel in his hand. When he is not in charge on a particular subject, he sometimes prefers not to participate. He did not play an important role on the major Ways and Means legislation of the 96th Congress, the windfall profits tax on the oil industry. Over the two years of the 96th Congress, he was a noticeable presence on only two important House issues: He fought hard against public financing of House campaigns and in favor of a congressional pay raise.

The 1970s were not as successful for

---

**8th District: Chicago — North central.** Population: 429,120 (7% decrease since 1970). Race: White 211,929 (49%), Black 146,310 (34%), Others 70,881 (17%). Spanish origin: 114,879 (27%).

Rostenkowski as he had reason to hope they would be. The echoes of a miscalculation he had made in 1968 blocked what seemed to be a steady rise in the party leadership. But for a slight political lapse then, he might be Speaker today.

Rostenkowski stepped in at the command of President Johnson to restore order at the tumultuous 1968 Democratic National Convention in Chicago. He physically took the gavel from House Majority Leader Carl Albert, who had lost control of the situation. Later Rostenkowski talked openly about having done it. Albert was insulted. In 1971, Albert moved up from majority leader to Speaker of the House. Rostenkowski threw his influence behind Hale Boggs of Louisiana for majority leader, in exchange for a Boggs promise to appoint Rostenkowski as Democratic whip.

But Albert was still angry over the convention squabble, and his attitude did not improve when Rostenkowski took his time endorsing him for Speaker. Albert vetoed Rostenkowski as whip. The man chosen instead was Thomas P. O'Neill Jr.

In all the maneuvering that year, Rostenkowski also forgot to protect the position he already held, as Democratic Caucus chairman. Texans quietly rounded up the votes to elect their candidate, the late Olin E. (Tiger) Teague. Some Northern liberals cooperated with them, feeling Rostenkowski had banged his gavel a little too quickly on anti-war speakers while presiding over the House.

It took six years for Rostenkowski to make it back into the leadership. By that time, O'Neill was the newly-elected Speaker. Rostenkowski had endorsed dark horse Jim Wright of Texas for majority leader, and Wright and O'Neill agreed that a place should be found for Rostenkowski. They made him chief deputy whip.

As a member of the leadership, Rostenkowski proved generally loyal to O'Neill but was not an active lobbyist for him on most issues. He continued to spend half of every week in his district, as he had done since 1959 and as O'Neill himself did until he became Speaker. On some issues, Rostenkowski fought against the leadership position. He argued against a limit on outside earnings for House members in 1977 and tried to talk Democrats out of public financing for congressional campaigns in 1980, at the same time O'Neill was trying to talk them into it.

There are few major bills, tax or otherwise, that bear Rostenkowski's name. For most of his career, his main legislative interest has been winning federal help for Chicago and tax advantages for its businesses.

In 1972, when Mayor Daley's priority was revenue sharing, Rostenkowski worked to get it through Ways and Means. That year he also lobbied for urban mass transit subsidies, with Daley as the first witness before the Banking Committee.

As chairman of the Ways and Means Health Subcommittee in 1978, Rostenkowski was skeptical of President Carter's hospital cost control legislation. He viewed it as difficult to pass and questioned whether it was worth the effort. But he put together a compromise which would have given hospitals time to reduce their costs voluntarily, then imposed controls if they failed. The Carter administration eventually embraced this, but it did not pass.

**At Home:** If Rostenkowski's role as "Mayor Daley's man in Congress" helped make him a force in House politics, it also stamped him as a leader among Chicago Democrats at an unusually early age. He was barely 30 when the city's politicians began talking about him as a successor to Daley in City Hall — someday.

That day never came. By the time the office opened up, in 1977, Rostenkowski was a comfortable and influential 18-year House veteran. And Daley's sudden death, barely a year after his re-election, created a confusion in Chicago Democratic ranks that ultimately elevated a quiet city council, Michael J. Bilandic, to the mayoralty.

Still, Rostenkowski's political life is focused to an extraordinary degree on Chicago. Until he became Ways and Means chairman in 1981, he spent much of his time in the city, working on strategy with the regular Democratic faction that has opposed the current mayor, Jane Byrne.

It is unlikely that Rostenkowski will ever put down Chicago politics for very long. He has spent his entire adult life in it. At 24, he became the youngest member of the Illinois House. At 26, he was the youngest member of the Illinois Senate. And at 30, he was a member of Congress. When Rostenkowski went to the Legislature, Daley was Cook County clerk, and they developed the relationship that proved fruitful for both of them for a quarter-century.

It was not just youth and talent that brought Rostenkowski so far so fast; it was family. The Rostenkowskis were a sort of political elite on the city's Polish Northwest side. The congressman's father, Joseph, was a Chicago alderman and ward committeeman for 20 years and later U.S. collector of customs.

Joe Rostenkowski was influential in launching his son's political career and dissuading him from professional baseball. At one point, the younger Rostenkowski turned down an offer from Connie Mack, owner of the old Philadelphia

*Dan Rostenkowski, D-Ill.*

Athletics.

In 1958, Democratic Rep. Thomas Gordon of Chicago, chairman of the House Foreign Affairs Committee, decided to retire. Daley was mayor by then and it was his task to pick a successor. He anointed Rostenkowski. At that point, the average age of the Chicago Democratic delegation in the House was 72; Daley felt some youth was needed.

Rostenkowski was a committed loyalist, even when he was chastized, as he was by a Chicago judge in 1963 for paying constituents' traffic tickets out of Democratic Party funds.

In 1966, a year of high racial tension and strong white backlash in Chicago, Rostenkowski ran his only "scared" race. His opponent was John Leszynski, a cab driver who openly appealed to the backlash against open housing demonstrations. Rostenkowski was re-elected, but his percentage fell below 60 percent for the only time in his career. Since then, his position has been impregnable. He has exceeded 80 percent in every election since 1974.

**The District:** The traditional core of the 8th District is its middle-income ethnic residential areas. When it was drawn for the 1972 elections, it was considered the most heavily Polish-American district in the country. But it is changing rapidly. Its black and Hispanic population reached a majority by 1980.

There is some industry in the southern part of the district, particularly electronics. Zenith, Admiral, Motorola and General Electric all have plants there.

## Committees

**Ways and Means** (Chairman)
　Trade.

**Joint Taxation** (Chairman)

## Elections

**1980 General**

| | |
|---|---|
| Dan Rostenkowski (D ) | 98,524 (85 %) |
| Walter Zilke (R ) | 17,845 (15 %) |

**1980 Primary**

| | |
|---|---|
| Dan Rostenkowski (D ) | 43,081 (89 %) |
| Willie May (D ) | 5,286 (11 %) |

**1978 General**

| | |
|---|---|
| Dan Rostenkowski (D ) | 81,457 (14 %) |
| Carl Lodico (R ) | 13,302 (86 %) |

**Previous Winning Percentages**

| | | | |
|---|---|---|---|
| 1976 (81 %) | 1974 (87 %) | 1972 (74 %) | 1970 (74 %) |
| 1968 (63 %) | 1966 (60 %) | 1964 (66 %) | 1962 (61 %) |
| 1960 (67 %) | 1958 (75 %) | | |

**District Vote For President**

| | 1980 | | 1976 | | 1972 |
|---|---|---|---|---|---|
| D | 97,057 (70 %) | D | 100,267 (70 %) | D | 90,032 (55 %) |
| R | 32,694 (24 %) | R | 43,154 (30 %) | R | 71,366 (44 %) |
| I | 5,842 (4 %) | | | | |

## Campaign Finance

| | | Receipts | Expen- |
|---|---|---|---|
| | Receipts | from PACs | ditures |
| **1980** | | | |
| Rostenkowski (D ) | $301,676 | $180,975 (60 %) | $124,725 |

## Voting Studies

| | Presidential Support | | Party Unity | | Conservative Coalition | |
|---|---|---|---|---|---|---|
| Year | S | O | S | O | S | O |
| 1980 | 77 | 12 | 78 | 7 | 24 | 61 |

| | | | | | | |
|---|---|---|---|---|---|---|
| 1979 | 72 | 12 | 79 | 8 | 24 | 63 |
| 1978 | 71 | 21 | 71 | 17 | 26 | 63 |
| 1977 | 71 | 19 | 76 | 13 | 25 | 61 |
| 1976 | 27 | 55 | 71 | 10 | 22 | 57 |
| 1975 | 36 | 49 | 79 | 10 | 22 | 71 |
| 1974 (Ford) | 48 | 43 | | | | |
| 1974 | 38 | 38 | 66 | 13 | 22 | 64 |
| 1973 | 26 | 57 | 72 | 13 | 26 | 60 |
| 1972 | 54 | 30 | 76 | 15 | 23 | 63 |
| 1971 | 49 | 35 | 67 | 12 | 28 | 55 |

S = Support　　　　　O = Opposition

## Key Votes

**96th Congress**

| | |
|---|---|
| Weaken Carter oil profits tax (1979) | N |
| Reject hospital cost control plan (1979) | N |
| Implement Panama Canal Treaties (1979) | Y |
| Establish Department of Education (1979) | Y |
| Approve Anti-busing Amendment (1979) | N |
| Guarantee Chrysler Corp. loans (1979) | Y |
| Approve military draft registration (1980) | Y |
| Aid Sandinista regime in Nicaragua (1980) | Y |
| Strengthen fair housing laws (1980) | Y |

**97th Congress**

| | |
|---|---|
| Reagan budget proposal (1981) | N |

## Interest Group Ratings

| Year | ADA | ACA | AFL-CIO | CCUS |
|---|---|---|---|---|
| 1980 | 50 | 17 | 82 | 56 |
| 1979 | 63 | 4 | 80 | 29 |
| 1978 | 50 | 21 | 63 | 33 |
| 1977 | 45 | 9 | 95 | 12 |
| 1976 | 50 | 14 | 91 | 13 |
| 1975 | 58 | 9 | 100 | 14 |
| 1974 | 39 | 36 | 90 | 22 |
| 1973 | 68 | 16 | 100 | 20 |
| 1972 | 38 | 18 | 90 | 0 |
| 1971 | 62 | 23 | 80 | |

# 9 Sidney R. Yates (D)

Of Chicago — Elected 1948
Did not serve 1963-65.

**Born:** Aug. 27, 1909, Chicago, Ill.
**Education:** U. of Chicago, Ph.B. 1931, J.D. 1933.
**Military Career:** Navy, 1944-46.
**Profession:** Lawyer.
**Family:** Wife, Adeline Holleb; one child.
**Religion:** Jewish.
**Political Career:** Unsuccessful Democratic nominee for U.S. Senate, 1962.

**In Washington:** Yates has toiled on Appropriations for more than 30 years, generally working behind the scenes but occasionally stepping into the limelight with a carefully-chosen crusade — in favor of public housing in the fifties, against an SST in the seventies, and now as defender of federal support for the arts. Yates is a gentle man, but when he puts his mind to it he can be tough. He was that way in the long debate over the supersonic transport, a $1.5 billion project. It was first proposed in 1963 but sidelined until President Nixon came into office and gave it a boost in 1969.

Yates had opposed the idea from the beginning, complaining that it was an "incredible distortion of our national priorities" to spend that much public money for a private purpose. Throughout the 1960s, Yates' amendments to eliminate SST funds had been defeated regularly, always on non-recorded votes. Millions of dollars already had been spent on preliminary planning when, in 1971, the House finally confronted the issue directly.

Newly-adopted rules forced an on-the-record vote for the first time, and Yates was ready with stacks of facts and figures. Backing him up was a well organized environmental lobby and a carefully orchestrated publicity campaign.

Yates, who had never called a press conference, (and has not to this day) suddenly was quite willing to answer reporters' questions. The pending confrontation was widely publicized. When the roll finally was called on March 18, Yates won, 217-203.

Yates invested similar energy in opposing the Nixon administration plan to place anti-ballistic missiles at various sites around the country as a defense against mainland China. One would have been located outside Chicago. The plan, Yates said, represented "an unfortunate waste of vitally-needed resources." That battle was resolved

for the 1970s by the 1972 SALT I treaty limiting ABM sites to two already in existence.

Yates made it to Appropriations as a freshman in 1949. As an energetic urban liberal in the 1950s, he became a leading advocate for the government's efforts to provide aid to older cities like Chicago.

Public housing had a close call in 1953 when the Republican-controlled House sought to kill the program altogether. Yates fought back. "We need a program that will satisfy the housing needs of all Americans, of every economic level," he said, "not just those who can afford to buy their own houses...." In the end, a compromise authorized 20,000 new housing units (compared to 75,000 sought by Truman). Yates also advocated legislation in those days to make mortgage credit money more easily available.

In his second term, he took up a different kind of campaign, to convince the Navy it should promote Hyman G. Rickover to admiral. The renowned advocate of atomic submarines had been bypassed and was about to leave the service. Yates thought that was an injustice and said so, repeatedly. The resulting congressional hearings and public attention brought the desired result. Rickover was promoted, and 30 years later he was still on active duty at the age of 81.

In 1957, after Eisenhower's second victory, Yates was one of 28 House Democrats urging

---

**9th District: Chicago, northeast.**
Population: 419,088 (10% decrease since 1970). Race: White 311,939 (74%), Black 42,806 (10%), Asian and Pacific Islander 28,469 (7%), Others 35,874 (9%). Spanish origin: 58,317 (14%).

**Sidney R. Yates, D-Ill.**

senior members to endorse a comprehensive Democratic program as an alternative to GOP proposals. The list included foreign aid, civil rights, education, housing, and an end to certain tax preferences. The group was largely ignored, but much of what it advocated became the basis of New Frontier and Great Society legislation in the 1960s.

Yates was out of Congress for two years in the 1960s, the result of an unsuccessful Senate campaign. When he came back to the House in 1965, he returned to Appropriations. This time he was placed on the Transportation Subcommittee, where he was drawn into the SST fight.

Later Yates switched to the Interior Subcommittee, whose diverse jurisdiction includes the Energy Department research budget and the Natonal Endowment for the Arts. He became chairman of the panel in 1975, marking another change in his legislative life. Instead of fighting against supersonic planes, he became involved in federal subsidies to the arts and humanities, and in arguments over opening up Alaska lands to private oil exploration.

As chairman, Yates is more a manager than a policy czar. He runs his subcommittee in a bipartisan manner, deferring to others in areas of expertise, even if they happen to be Republicans. Joseph McDade, R-Pa., makes many of the funding decisions on energy; Ralph S. Regula, R-Ohio, is crucial on certain conservation issues. Yates handles the arts.

Yates likes to talk of what Congress has done for the arts and humanities. In the mid-1960s, when the endowments were created, there were 147 professional dance, theater, opera and symphony groups in the United States. In 1980, he says, there were 700.

When the Reagan administration asked Congress to cut the endowment budgets in half, Yates countered with more modest cutbacks, setting the stage for a protracted argument. In June of 1981, the subcommittee reported out a bill which would appropriate nearly as much money for the arts as had been spent in the previous year.

That bill also rejected several Reagan administration proposals to cut back on parks and environmental programs. It contained language aimed at blocking Interior Department efforts to develop controversial oil and gas reserves along the California coast.

**At Home:** Only two members of the current House entered it before Yates did in January of 1949. But he has never received the full benefits of his seniority because he made one wrong move — he left to run for the Senate against Republican leader Everett M. Dirksen in 1962. When Yates came back to the House two years later, he was at the bottom again.

Yates's Senate campaign had the backing of Chicago Mayor Richard Daley and the Democratic organization, and he made a respectable showing with 47.1 percent of the vote, more than any Democrat ever received against Dirksen.

There is still some controversy over that election. Some Democrats have always contended that President Kennedy secretly favored Dirksen, considering him the friendliest Republican Senate leader he was likely to get, and withheld backing for Yates that might have produced an upset. The Cuban missile crisis took place in the final month of the campaign, and Dirksen was consulted often and openly by the White House.

Yates said at the time he was satisfied with Kennedy's behavior, and he has expressed no grievances since then. In 1963, Kennedy appointed him U.S. Representative to the United Nations Trusteeship Council, and he served for more than a year.

In the fall of 1964, the Chicago Democratic organization suddenly found a judgeship for Rep. Edward Finnegan, whom it had chosen to replace Yates in the House. Since Finnegan had already been renominated, the local party had the right to designate a candidate for the vacancy, and to no one's surprise Yates was the choice. He had been spared the trouble of a primary, and four months later he was back in the House. He has held the seat without difficulty ever since, cordial but not quite subservient to the party regulars.

Yates had originally won his seat as a last-minute organization choice in a much different situation. Sixteen years earlier, recently returned to his Chicago law practice after World War II, Yates had been drafted to run against Republican Rep. Robert J. Twyman, who was expected to win re-election easily in a national Dewey landslide. But the Democratic ticket swept Illinois that year, and Yates came in with an 18,000 vote majority. He kept his seat narrowly in 1950 and 1952, and thereafter he was safe.

**The District:** What was once an upper-class Republican district along the Gold Coast of Chicago has been transformed over the years into a solid bastion of the Democratic Party.

The 9th was Republican until 1934, then alternated between the parties until Yates's 1948 victory. Since then redistricting has expanded it in size, and an ethnically diverse population has moved in. There are virtually no signs today of its old Republican tradition.

The 9th runs the gamut from luxurious Lake Shore Drive to middle-class ethnic neighborhoods and poorer ones with a substantial number of blacks and Hispanics. In the past, Jews have been the dominant political force, and have represented much of the area in the Illinois Legislature and on the City Council. The district lost population in the 1970s and will have to gain about 100,000 persons in the redistricting process.

## Committees

**Appropriations** (7th of 33 Democrats)
   Interior, chairman; Foreign Operations; Treasury-Postal Service.

## Elections

**1980 General**

| | |
|---|---|
| Sidney Yates (D ) | 106,543 (73 %) |
| John Andrica (R ) | 39,244 (27 %) |

**1980 Primary**

| | |
|---|---|
| Sidney Yates (D ) | 44,341 (87 %) |
| Sam Fried (D ) | 6,608 (13 %) |

**1978 General**

| | |
|---|---|
| Sidney Yates (D ) | 87,543 (75 %) |
| John Collins (R ) | 28,673 (25 %) |

**Previous Winning Percentages**

| | | | |
|---|---|---|---|
| 1976 (72 %) | 1974 (100%) | 1972 (68 %) | 1970 (76 %) |
| 1968 (64 %) | 1966 (60 %) | 1964 (64 %) | 1962 (- %) |
| 1960 (60 %) | 1958 (67 %) | 1956 (54 %) | 1954 (60 %) |
| 1952 (52 %) | 1950 (52 %) | 1948 (55 %) | |

**District Vote For President**

| | 1980 | | 1976 | | 1972 |
|---|---|---|---|---|---|
| D | 95,175 (55 %) | D | 105,492 (58 %) | D | 111,372 (54 %) |
| R | 57,063 (33 %) | R | 77,055 (42 %) | R | 93,204 (45 %) |
| I | 18,346 (11 %) | | | | |

## Campaign Finance

| | Receipts | Receipts from PACs | Expenditures |
|---|---|---|---|
| **1980** | | | |
| Yates (D ) | $74,981 | $7,909 (11 %) | $63,024 |
| Andrica (R ) | $9,359 | $4,450 (48 %) | $12,212 |
| **1978** | | | |
| Yates (D ) | $1,400 | $100 (7 %) | $14,870 |

## Voting Studies

| Year | Presidential Support S | O | Party Unity S | O | Conservative Coalition S | O |
|---|---|---|---|---|---|---|
| 1980 | 63 | 25 | 82 | 6 | 2 | 83 |
| 1979 | 77 | 18 | 91 | 6 | 7 | 92 |
| 1978 | 81 | 16 | 89 | 10 | 7 | 93 |
| 1977 | 75 | 22 | 86 | 12 | 10 | 88 |
| 1976 | 31 | 69 | 89 | 9 | 13 | 87 |
| 1975 | 39 | 60 | 89 | 7 | 8 | 86 |
| 1974 (Ford) | 41 | 56 | | | | |
| 1974 | 43 | 57 | 83 | 13 | 8 | 88 |
| 1973 | 37 | 62 | 85 | 13 | 9 | 90 |
| 1972 | 46 | 49 | 83 | 13 | 5 | 89 |
| 1971 | 30 | 70 | 92 | 8 | 1 | 99 |
| 1970 | 54 | 37 | 79 | 15 | 2 | 91 |
| 1969 | 53 | 43 | 82 | 11 | 9 | 89 |
| 1968 | 79 | 14 | 80 | 12 | 4 | 92 |
| 1967 | 83 | 8 | 85 | 8 | 7 | 89 |
| 1966 | 76 | 10 | 76 | 11 | 8 | 86 |
| 1965 | 85 | 4 | 86 | 9 | 6 | 90 |
| 1964 | - | - | - | - | - | - |
| 1963 | - | - | - | - | - | - |
| 1962 | 65 | 0 | 58 | 0 | 0 | 56 |
| 1961 | 97 | 2 | 93 | 3 | 9 | 91 |

S = Support        O = Opposition

## Key Votes

**96th Congress**

| | |
|---|---|
| Weaken Carter oil profits tax (1979) | N |
| Reject hospital cost control plan (1979) | N |
| Implement Panama Canal Treaties (1979) | Y |
| Establish Department of Education (1979) | N |
| Approve Anti-busing Amendment (1979) | N |
| Guarantee Chrysler Corp. loans (1979) | ? |
| Approve military draft registration (1980) | N |
| Aid Sandinista regime in Nicaragua (1980) | Y |
| Strengthen fair housing laws (1980) | Y |

**97th Congress**

| | |
|---|---|
| Reagan budget proposal (1981) | N |

## Interest Group Ratings

| Year | ADA | ACA | AFL-CIO | CCUS |
|---|---|---|---|---|
| 1980 | 100 | 17 | 83 | 48 |
| 1979 | 95 | 4 | 95 | 0 |
| 1978 | 100 | 7 | 85 | 22 |
| 1977 | 95 | 11 | 87 | 12 |
| 1976 | 90 | 11 | 87 | 13 |
| 1975 | 100 | 11 | 96 | 18 |
| 1974 | 100 | 0 | 100 | 20 |
| 1973 | 96 | 12 | 100 | 18 |
| 1972 | 94 | 0 | 100 | 0 |
| 1971 | 100 | 7 | 83 | - |
| 1970 | 96 | 17 | 100 | 10 |
| 1969 | 100 | 12 | 100 | - |
| 1968 | 100 | 9 | 100 | - |
| 1967 | 100 | 0 | 92 | 10 |
| 1966 | 94 | 19 | 92 | - |
| 1965 | 89 | 4 | | 10 |
| 1964 | - | - | - | - |
| 1963 | - | - | - | - |
| 1962 | 100 | 0 | 100 | - |
| 1961 | 100 | | - | - |

# 10 John E. Porter (R)

**Of Evanston — Elected 1980**

**Born:** June 1. 1935, Evanston, Ill.
**Education:** Northwestern U., B.S. and B.A.,
1957; U. of Michigan, J.D. 1961.
**Military Career:** Army Reserve, 1958-64.
**Profession:** Lawyer.
**Family:** Wife, Kathryn Cameron; five children.
**Religion:** Presbyterian.
**Political Career:** Ill. House, 1973-79; unsuc-
cessful Republican nominee for U.S. House,
1978; unsuccessful Republican nominee for
Cook County circuit court judge, 1970.

**In Washington:** Silver-haired and reserved
in manner, Porter seemed a perfect choice in 1980
not only for his moderate Republican district but
for the Banking Committee, to which he was
appointed on his arrival in the House. His style
symbolized the sort of group outsiders often expect the committee to be, rather than the raucous
collection of political eccentrics it generally is.

But a little more than a year on the committee proved to be enough for Porter. He applied for
a place on Appropriations at the start of the 97th
Congress, and he got it.

Porter has staked out a position near the
center of the GOP spectrum, moderate on most
social issues, such as the Equal Rights Amendment, which he has favored (although he opposed
the extended deadline for ratification) and
strongly oriented to corporate business on economic questions.

The first major piece of legislation Porter
introduced was a bill to make substantial cuts in
the capital gains tax, both for individuals and for
corporations. It was similar to a proposal that
Democrat Alan Cranston of California offered in
the Senate. "Venture capital has virtually dried
up in this country," Porter said.

On another occasion, Porter delivered a
scathing attack on liberal economic doctrine, especially on its willingness to accept wage and
price controls as a last resort. "It is a ham-handed
approach," Porter said on the House floor. "It
evidences not economic intellectualism but a total
surrender of policy — a bankruptcy of innovative
thinking — that most liberals normally would not
admit to."

On Banking Committee matters, Porter generally voted with the GOP's dwindling
internationalist bloc, opposing measures to restrict U.S. participation in the International Mon-

etary Fund and other world organizations. But he
has favored some cuts in U.S. contributions to
those groups.

Closer to home, Porter took the politically
sensible step of fighting airport noise and commu-
nicating that fact to a district that lives with it
continually. When conferees went to the House
floor early in 1980 with an agreement exempting
some two- and three-engine planes from some
new noise control standards, Porter spoke out
against them, even though most of the negotiating
took place before his election and the deal represented tougher standards than an earlier version.
"This is not legislating," he said. "This is a naked
attempt to circumvent the legislative process, not
to serve the interests of the people of our country,
but of a segment of a particular industry." The
House approved the conference report.

**At Home:** Porter returned this largely affluent district to Republican hands after five years
in which it had been represented by one of the
most liberal Democrats in the House. He also
appears to have ended its series of aggressively
fought, razor close, million-dollar campaigns. His
easy re-election in 1980 marked the first time
either party had won with as much as 52 percent.

Porter's predecessor, Democrat Abner J.
Mikva, had moved to the suburban 10th after
losing his seat on the South Side of Chicago in the
1972 redistricting. He was beaten in the 10th in

---

**10th District: Cook County — north-
ern suburbs.** Population: 425,595 (6% decrease since 1970). Race: White 396,950 (93%),
Black 18,099 (4%), Asian and Pacific Islander
16,002 (4%), Others 4,544 (1%). Spanish origin: 9,679 (2%).

---

1972, but came back to win in 1974 and held on tenuously until his appointment as a federal judge in 1979.

Porter had been the nominee against Mikva in 1978, and had come within 650 votes of defeating him. He was the obvious choice for the GOP nomination in the special election that followed Mikva's resignation, and won the primary with more than 70 percent of the vote. Since then, he has had little trouble.

Initially viewed as a moderate, Porter received high ratings from the liberal Independent Voters of Illinois (IVI) in his first term as an Illinois state representative (1973-75). Thereafter he became more conservative. But he had to overcome opposition from the Republican right in both his 1978 and 1979 primaries.

Porter grew up in the district he represents. He returned there to practice law after graduating from the University of Michigan law school and spending one year as an attorney in the Justice Department in Washington.

**The District:** The 10th is built around Chicago's oldest and most affluent suburbs, towns that stretch north along Lake Michigan from Evanston to Winnetka. Because it has become more densely populated, the district has continually shrunk in size since the 1950s, when it took in all of Lake County as well as the Cook County suburbs. It now includes just five townships north of Chicago — Evanston, New Trier, Northfield, Maine, and Niles.

Though the district is one of the most affluent in the nation, it has a sizable Democratic vote which allowed Mikva to win three terms. The Jewish community in Niles Township and the Northwestern University community in Evanston provide a strong base of liberal votes. In addition, some of the older affluent towns have grown more independent, willing to soften their Republican loyalties for an attractive Democratic candidate.

The newer high-income areas in the western part of the district maintain a strong Republican voting preference, however, and this is sufficient to give statewide Republican candidates good majorities in the 10th, especially if they are moderates like Porter, Gov. James R. Thompson, or Sen. Charles H. Percy.

## Committees

**Appropriations** (22nd of 22 Republicans)
District of Columbia; Foreign Operations; Labor — HHS.

## Elections

**1980 General**

| | |
|---|---|
| John Porter (R) | 137,707 (61%) |
| Robert Weinberger (D) | 89,008 (39%) |

**1980 Special Election**

| | |
|---|---|
| John Porter (R) | 36,981 (54%) |
| Robert Weinberger (D) | 30,929 (46%) |

**1979 Special Primary**

| | |
|---|---|
| John Porter (R) | 36,981 (71%) |
| John Nimrod (R) | 7,505 (29%) |

**District Vote For President**

| | 1980 | | 1976 | | 1972 |
|---|---|---|---|---|---|
| D | 78,426 (34%) | D | 89,608 (39%) | D | 89,630 (38%) |
| R | 120,146 (52%) | R | 138,449 (59%) | R | 147,305 (62%) |
| I | 28,394 (12%) | | | | |

## Campaign Finance

| | Receipts | Receipts from PACs | Expenditures |
|---|---|---|---|
| **1980*** | | | |
| Porter (R) | $644,841 | $264,354 (41%) | $650,248 |
| Weinberger (D) | $266,914 | $84,609 (32%) | $263,680 |

* Figures given are for both special and general elections.

## Voting Studies

| | Presidential Support | | Party Unity | | Conservative Coalition | |
|---|---|---|---|---|---|---|
| Year | S | O | S | O | S | O |
| 1980 | 57 | 43 | 72 | 28 | 62 | 37 |

S = Support          O = Opposition

## Key Votes

**96th Congress**

| | |
|---|---|
| Approve military draft registration (1980) | N |
| Aid Sandinista regime in Nicaragua (1980) | N |
| Strengthen fair housing laws (1980) | N |

**97th Congress**

| | |
|---|---|
| Reagan budget proposal (1981) | Y |

## Interest Group Ratings

| Year | ADA | ACA | AFL-CIO | CCUS |
|---|---|---|---|---|
| 1980 | 39 | 71 | 18 | 71 |

# 11 Frank Annunzio (D)

**Of Chicago — Elected 1964**

**Born:** Jan. 12, 1915, Chicago, Ill.
**Education:** DePaul U., B.S. 1940; M.A. 1942.
**Profession:** Teacher; labor official.
**Family:** Wife, Angeline Alesia; three children.
**Religion:** Roman Catholic.
**Political Career:** Illinois Labor Director, 1949-52.

**In Washington:** A product of Richard J. Daley's Democratic organization, Annunzio stands somewhere between the pure patronage politics of his own Chicago generation and the issue politics of his younger colleagues.

Annunzio takes himself and his issues seriously, and he has never been an easy man for the leadership or the Chicago organization to control. Intensely proud, he is a difficult vote to change on sensitive matters.

As a member of the Banking Committee and chairman of its Consumer Subcommittee, Annunzio has tried to carve out a role for himself as a sort of populist protector of the little guy. He has argued for truth-in-lending legislation, and railed against unscrupulous debt collectors, credit card abuses and high interest rates.

He thinks big business and big unions are "good for America," but has favored savings and loan associations over banks, seeing S & Ls as friends of the people, and banks as protectors of big business and profits.

In 1981, he won overwhelming passage of his bill to prevent businesses from imposing a surcharge on customers who pay with credit cards. When a small bipartisan group wrote a letter opposing the bill on the grounds that there was already too much credit buying, Annunzio blasted them on the House floor for having an "Alice in Wonderland" approach. "It is almost a necessity in this society that you have a credit card," Annunzio said, his arms waving and his voice rising to a shout. "If you allow a merchant to surcharge a credit card, you will be hurting people at all economic levels."

But as aggressive as he is on these issues, Annunzio has never approached the first rank of senior House legislators. He is more often regarded the way a Chicago columnist once described him, as "a fighter who works hard and punches well, but has nothing particularly fast — he's not quick on his feet. He can't get behind you."

Annunzio punched hard in the 96th Congress over changes in the Truth in Lending Act. Lending institutions complained that the amount of information they were required to give customers was burdensome and unnecessary, and asked Congress to change the law.

Annunzio held up changes in 1978 and 1979. In 1980, when the House considered a major banking bill, he was unable to prevent some adjustment in the law. Still, Annunzio believed he had the votes to save a section of the bill requiring a breakdown of what each loan covered and information about all charges. But House and Senate conferees voted to force the consumer to request such an itemization, and even then said the itemization need not be complete. "This guts truth in lending," Annunzio said, and he wound up voting against all the changes on the floor.

He has shown a similar stubbornness through the years on the broad issue of controls over the American economy. In 1973, when the end of the Nixon-era wage and price controls produced sudden inflation, it was Annunzio who led the fight not only to restore controls, but to roll back food prices to the levels in place nearly a year before.

The Banking Committee approved that idea, thanks in part to votes from Republicans who felt it was too extreme ever to become law. Under pressure from Democratic congressional leaders, the committee later modified the rollback to cover only a two-month period. But that also failed on

**11th District: Chicago — Northwest.** Population: 430,754 (7% decrease since 1970). Race: White 393,786 (91%), Black 1,298 (0.3%), Asian and Pacific Islander 18,626 (4%), Others 17,044 (4%). Spanish origin: 33,409 (8%).

the House floor, and controls never have been reimposed.

When Annunzio is not using his Banking Committee post to argue for consumers or the savings and loan industry, he is often using it to promote the minting of gold medals for a variety of commemorative purposes. Six gold medal bills became law in the 96th Congress. It is not a major subject, but it is one on which Annunzio has been able to establish some personal turf, and on which he nearly always wins. The House rarely turns down a gold medal for anyone, although there are always a few audible complaints about whether they are worth the expense, which was about $8,000 for a 3-inch medallion by the end of 1980.

Annunzio also serves on the House Administration Committee, whose most controversial task in the last few years has been to consider public financing of congressional campaigns. During the 96th Congress a public financing bill died in the committee, and Annunzio was on the side of those blocking the legislation. Like the other big-city machine Democrats on the committee, ones from New Jersey and Pennsylvania, Annunzio felt public financing would guarantee Republican challenges in districts that currently go Democratic by default.

Annunzio has remained a loyal, if sometimes cranky, ally of the Chicago Democratic organization. Earlier in his House career, he occasionally vied with Rep. Dan Rostenkowski for primacy in representing Daley with the Chicago delegation to Congress. Rostenkowski was more often Daley's favorite, but sometimes they differed and Annunzio took on a greater role.

In today's post-Daley era, with the Cook County machine in disarray, and Mayor Jane Byrne running the city, Annunzio is still called on frequently to help in local matters.

**At Home:** The labor movement was Annunzio's route to elective office in Chicago. More than 20 years before he was given the party's endorsement for a seat in Congress, he was already familiar in the city's politics as a strategist for the United Steelworkers of America.

By 1948, Annunzio was secretary-treasurer of the CIO's Illinois Political Action Committee. It was from that position that he was appointed director of labor for the state of Illinois. The CIO and the American Federation of Labor (AFL) were then separate organizations and bitter rivals. Both lobbied the newly elected governor, Adlai E. Stevenson, for their favorite candidate for labor director. The CIO won and Annunzio was appointed in 1949.

In 1952, Stevenson asked him to resign. Annunzio had formed his own insurance company, and suspicions arose that he might be using his state position to help his private business. Annunzio sharply denied the charges but he gave up his state job.

His political career was only beginning. Annunzio was personally close to a fellow-member of Stevenson's state Cabinet, Revenue Director Richard J. Daley. He remained active in ward politics in the 1950s, while running a personnel agency, and eventually an opportunity opened up for him.

By 1964 there were so many rumors about Democratic Rep. Roland Libonati's Mafia connections that the Cook County organizaton found him an embarrassment. Libonati gave up his 7th District House seat voluntarily, and Daley's organization turned to Annunzio to replace him. There was no primary and Annunzio was never threatened for re-election in his eight years representing the 7th District, on the city's old Near West Side.

But redistricting in 1972 caused him serious problems. Republicans wrote the plan in the Illinois Legislature, and it threw Annunzio and black U.S. Rep. George Collins into the same district. At first, Annunzio insisted he would oppose Collins in what promised to be a bloody primary. But Rep. Roman Pucinski of the 11th District had decided to run for the U.S. Senate, leaving that seat open. Daley and Democratic organization leaders convinced Annunzio to accept nomination in the 11th District, in the northwest corner of the city.

This was a harder district for a Democrat than Annunzio's old 7th. There were more Republicans in the 11th, and many of its Democrats were disaffected by their party's liberalism and the presidential candidacy of George McGovern. Annunzio held the 11th in 1972 with only 53.3 percent of the vote against a well-known Republican, Chicago Alderman John Hoellen. However, that was the closest the Republicans came. Annunzio was up to 72.4 percent in 1974 and has won by wide margins ever since.

**The District:** Located in an almost-entirely white residential area on Chicago's northwest side, the 11th District was settled before World War II by ethnic homeowners escaping the older neighborhoods closer to downtown. Poles and Germans form the main ethnic groups, although there is a substantial Jewish community.

For many years, the 11th was a swing district. Republican Rep. Timothy Sheehan represented it from 1951 to 1959. But Pucinski defeated Sheehan in 1958 and the Democrats have held on to it ever since, challenged seriously only twice, when Hoellen was the nominee in 1966 and 1972.

**349**

## Committees

**Banking, Finance and Urban Affairs** (5th of 25 Democrats)
Consumer Affairs and Coinage, chairman; Economic Stabilization; Financial Institutions Supervision, Regulation and Insurance; General Oversight and Renegotiation.
**House Administration** (2nd of 11 Democrats)
Acounts, chairman; Personnel and Police.

## Elections

**1980 General**

| | |
|---|---|
| Frank Annunzio (D ) | 121,166 (70 %) |
| Michael Zanillo (R ) | 52,417 (30 %) |

**1978 General**

| | |
|---|---|
| Frank Annunzio (D ) | 112,365 (74 %) |
| John Hoeger (R ) | 40,044 (26 %) |

**1978 Primary**

| | |
|---|---|
| Frank Annunzio (D ) | 54,403 (87 %) |
| Hugh Gallagly (D ) | 7,928 (13 %) |

**Previous Winning Percentages**

| | | | |
|---|---|---|---|
| 1976 (67 %) | 1974 (72 %) | 1972 (53 %) | 1970 (87 %) |
| 1968 (83 %) | 1966 (81 %) | 1964 (86 %) | |

**District Vote For President**

| | 1980 | | 1976 | | 1972 |
|---|---|---|---|---|---|
| D | 95,039 (47 %) | D | 103,636 (48 %) | D | 86,121 (37 %) |
| R | 91,338 (45 %) | R | 111,060 (52 %) | R | 144,360 (62 %) |
| I | 14,515 (7 %) | | | | |

## Campaign Finance

| | Receipts | Receipts from PACs | Expenditures |
|---|---|---|---|
| **1980** | | | |
| Annunzio (D ) | $108,074 | $28,300 (26 %) | $59,436 |
| **1978** | | | |
| Annunzio (D ) | $89,372 | $22,150 (25 %) | $82,201 |
| Hoeger (R ) | $6,680 | - (0 %) | $6,164 |

## Voting Studies

| | Presidential Support | | Party Unity | | Conservative Coalition | |
|---|---|---|---|---|---|---|
| Year | S | O | S | O | S | O |
| 1980 | 71 | 19 | 87 | 8 | 26 | 65 |

| | | | | | | |
|---|---|---|---|---|---|---|
| 1979 | 75 | 23 | 85 | 13 | 35 | 63 |
| 1978 | 68 | 26 | 77 | 19 | 34 | 62 |
| 1977 | 76 | 23 | 79 | 19 | 36 | 59 |
| 1976 | 35 | 65 | 81 | 16 | 31 | 65 |
| 1975 | 38 | 49 | 72 | 13 | 28 | 55 |
| 1974 (Ford) | 46 | 52 | | | | |
| 1974 | 51 | 43 | 75 | 19 | 38 | 55 |
| 1973 | 32 | 66 | 86 | 12 | 28 | 71 |
| 1972 | 46 | 35 | 74 | 8 | 26 | 56 |
| 1971 | 56 | 32 | 71 | 16 | 33 | 60 |
| 1970 | 68 | 26 | 82 | 10 | 27 | 64 |
| 1969 | 62 | 30 | 80 | 13 | 20 | 67 |
| 1968 | 88 | 6 | 98 | 0 | 4 | 92 |
| 1967 | 71 | 7 | 80 | 1 | 6 | 67 |
| 1966 | 85 | 3 | 93 | 0 | 0 | 100 |
| 1965 | 96 | 3 | 98 | 0 | 0 | 100 |

S = Support          O = Opposition

## Key Votes

**96th Congress**

| | |
|---|---|
| Weaken Carter oil profits tax (1979) | N |
| Reject hospital cost control plan (1979) | N |
| Implement Panama Canal Treaties (1979) | Y |
| Establish Department of Education (1979) | N |
| Approve Anti-busing Amendment (1979) | Y |
| Guarantee Chrysler Corp. loans (1979) | Y |
| Approve military draft registration (1980) | N |
| Aid Sandinista regime in Nicaragua (1980) | Y |
| Strengthen fair housing laws (1980) | N |

**97th Congress**

| | |
|---|---|
| Reagan budget proposal (1981) | N |

## Interest Group Ratings

| Year | ADA | ACA | AFL-CIO | CCUS |
|---|---|---|---|---|
| 1980 | 56 | 18 | 79 | 69 |
| 1979 | 63 | 12 | 90 | 11 |
| 1978 | 40 | 22 | 79 | 33 |
| 1977 | 45 | 20 | 96 | 6 |
| 1976 | 55 | 15 | 91 | 32 |
| 1975 | 47 | 23 | 95 | 12 |
| 1974 | 52 | 38 | 91 | 20 |
| 1973 | 72 | 15 | 100 | 18 |
| 1972 | 63 | 26 | 91 | 0 |
| 1971 | 68 | 12 | 100 | |
| 1970 | 60 | 14 | 100 | 10 |
| 1969 | 40 | 7 | 90 | - |
| 1968 | 92 | 0 | 100 | - |
| 1967 | 87 | 0 | 92 | 10 |
| 1966 | 100 | 0 | 100 | - |
| 1965 | 84 | 4 | - | 10 |

# 12 Philip M. Crane (R)

## Of Mt. Prospect — Elected 1969

**Born:** Nov. 3, 1930, Chicago, Ill.
**Education:** Hillsdale College, B.A. 1952; Ind. U.,
M.A. 1961, Ph.D. 1963.
**Military Career:** Army, 1954-56.
**Profession:** Educator.
**Family:** Wife, Arlene Catherine Johnson; eight
children.
**Religion:** Methodist.
**Political Career:** No previous office.

**In Washington:** Crane has always pitched
his carefully drawn conservative message beyond
the House chamber to what he has seen as a
potential national audience, frustrating his more
legislative-minded allies on the Republican right.

During his campaign for the presidency in
1980, Crane's rare appearances on the House floor
were often marked by applause from conservative
colleagues. Part of it was good-natured jest, but
part of it was comment on his long-term habit of
using the House as a platform rather than a
workplace.

Appointed to the Ways and Means Committee in 1975, he has rarely been a major participant
in its deliberations. Most of his legislative proposals have dealt with foreign affairs, especially
eliminating appropriations for aid to leftist foreign governments.

His one notable moment on the House floor
in the 96th Congress came when he proposed an
amendment that in effect would have forced the
United States to move its embassy in Israel to
Jerusalem from Tel Aviv. The Carter administration had refused to make the change on the
grounds that it would anger Egypt. Numerous
liberal Democrats found it politically difficult to
oppose the move, and the amendment was on the
verge of passage before New York Democrat Stephen Solarz arrived from the Foreign Affairs
Committee to engineer a reversal. There followed
a long debate in which Crane was accused of
seeking only to throw American foreign policy
into disarray. By that time, however, Crane had
departed.

If members question Crane's legislative diligence, however, few question his intellectual ability or his oratorical skills. Long before he made
his run for the GOP presidential nomination, he
had become a national conservative figure because of his work as president of the American
Conservative Union and his speeches on behalf of

free enterprise and national defense.

One of his most unusual initiatives was a
series of meetings with union officials in Youngstown, Ohio, in 1978, designed to see if conservatives and labor could find common political
ground. Out of those meetings, Crane introduced
three legislative proposals in the 95th Congress,
none of them differing too much with traditional
GOP economics. One provided tax incentives for
capital investment and job creation, the second
required cost-benefit analyses for new environmental regulations, and the third was designed to
block dumping of foreign products. None made
immediate legislative progress.

Crane's free enterprise views have led him
into some surprising political territory. He has
been a constant critic of the U.S. Metric Board,
arguing that government has no right to coerce
businesses into using the metric system. And
extending his doctrine to free exchange in speech,
he introduced legislation in 1978 to protect newspaper sources.

Crane's campaign for the 1980 presidential
nomination was based on what turned out to be a
faulty premise — that conservative voters would
find Ronald Reagan passé and turn to a younger
man expressing the same ideas with more vigorous eloquence. Crane spent nearly all of 1979
trying to organize support in New Hampshire for

---

**12th District: Outer Chicago sub-
urbs — Arlington Heights.** Population:
611,505 (33% increase since 1970). Race:
White 581,253 (95%), Black 6,471 (1%), Asian
and Pacific Islander 14,580 (2%), Others 9,201
(2%). Spanish origin: 20,237 (3%).

---

the March 1980 primary, but drew a hostile reception from William Loeb, the acerbic *Manchester Union-Leader* publisher and political baron, who said Crane was spoiling Reagan's chances. Loeb's newspaper printed articles accusing Crane of heavy drinking and womanizing.

Crane's wife, Arlene, was one of the dominant influences in the campaign, and she helped force a shakeup of the staff when things seemed to be going badly in the fall of 1979. But this made little difference. By the time of the New Hampshire voting Crane was considered a minor candidate, and he received only 1.8 percent of the vote. He eventually won three convention delegates, all in his home state of Illinois, but withdrew from the contest and endorsed Reagan on April 17, 1980.

**At Home:** Crane's conservative political philosophy was formed early, and the principal catalyst was his father, Dr. George W. Crane III, a psychologist and writer.

The senior Crane taught self-reliance, free enterprise and the wisdom of the Founding Fathers, and Philip believes in all three.

The Cranes sometimes are called "the Kennedys of the Right," and the analogy is worth pursuing, as long as it is not pursued too far.

Each family had a father who molded his children to be disciplined and committed. In each one, the eldest son was killed in an airplane crash. Each family was left with three remaining brothers, all of whom entered politics. Philip's younger brother, Daniel Crane, a dentist, was elected to the U.S. House from the 22nd District of Illinois in 1978. David Crane, a psychiatrist and lawyer, has lost three House races in Indiana's 6th District.

Beyond that, the differences begin to take over. In contrast to the Kennedys, the Cranes lived in modest circumstances in a working-class neighborhood on the South Side of Chicago. They were strict Methodists. And politically, they were at the opposite end of the world.

After his brother's death, Philip Crane abandoned his early career in advertising and went back to school, earning a doctorate in history from Indiana University. He went into teaching, and in 1967-68, served as director of Westminster Academy, a private conservative-oriented school north of Chicago.

In 1969, Crane entered the Republican primary in a special election held after Donald Rumsfeld resigned from Congress to become head of the Office of Economic Opportunity in the Nixon administration. Crane's meticulous organization of conservative activists brought him 22 percent of the vote and in a field of seven Republican candidates, that was enough.

Crane's Democratic opponent, Edward A. Warman, turned the election into a referendum on the Vietnam War, calling for complete withdrawal of American troops by the end of 1970 and endorsing the anti-war demonstrations held in Washington that fall. Crane supported Nixon's policy of turning over conduct of the war to the South Vietnamese.

Soft-spoken and articulate, Crane managed to refute Warman's attempt to paint him as an extremist. He won with 58.4 percent of the vote.

Crane was re-elected in 1970 with 58 percent of the vote. Then in 1972, his district was divided in half, and he ran in the more Republican portion, gaining 74.2 percent. He has had a safe seat ever since.

**The District:** Crane's original district, the old 13th, took in almost all of Cook County north of Chicago. By 1970, it had grown to the point where it had to be split in two to comply with fair districting.

The redrawn 12th District, which Crane chose to run in, consisted of newer suburbs with wealthy communities of dedicated Republican voters. Crane also gained a Republican portion of Lake County. The older suburbs to the east, including the university city of Evanston and the middle-income Jewish community of Skokie, both of which had large numbers of Democratic voters, were placed in the new 10th District, which elected a Democrat three times during the 1970s.

The 12th continued to grow through the 1970s, increasing its population by more than 30 percent, with the outer areas losing their semirural quality to encroaching suburbia. The district is now the second largest in Illinois, and was overpopulated by 85,000 people in the 1980 census.

It remains heavily Republican. In 1980, Ronald Reagan ran 93,000 votes ahead of President Carter in the district.

## Committees

**Ways and Means** (5th of 12 Republicans)
Health; Oversight; Social Security.

## Elections

**1980 General**

| | |
|---|---|
| Philip Crane (R ) | 185,080 (74 %) |
| David McCartney (D ) | 64,729 (26 %) |

**1978 General**

| | |
|---|---|
| Philip Crane (R ) | 110,503 (80 %) |
| Gilbert Bogen (D ) | 28,424 (20 %) |

**Previous Winning Percentages**

1976 (73 %)    1974 (61 %)    1972 (74 %)    1970 (58 %)
1969* (58 %)

*Special election*

**District Vote For President**

| | 1980 | | 1976 | | 1972 |
|---|---|---|---|---|---|
| D | 65,143 (26 %) | D | 70,460 (30 %) | D | 56,896 (27 %) |
| R | 158,516 (62 %) | R | 157,389 (68 %) | R | 154,690 (73 %) |
| I | 28,616 (11 %) | | | | |

## Campaign Finance

| | Receipts | Receipts from PACs | Expenditures |
|---|---|---|---|
| **1980** | | | |
| Crane (R ) | $326,509 | $3,000 (1 %) | $191,160 |
| McCartney (D ) | $9,426 | $740 (8 %) | $9,424 |
| **1978** | | | |
| Crane (R ) | $209,722 | $14,755 (7 %) | $191,075 |

## Voting Studies

| | Presidential Support | | Party Unity | | Conservative Coalition | |
|---|---|---|---|---|---|---|
| | S | O | S | O | S | O |
| Year | | | | | | |
| 1980 | 20 | 59 | 71 | 2 | 74 | 5 |

| Year | | | | | | |
|---|---|---|---|---|---|---|
| 1979 | 12 | 49 | 54 | 2 | 60 | 2 |
| 1978 | 9 | 60 | 73 | 4 | 79 | 2 |
| 1977 | 24 | 66 | 87 | 4 | 89 | 3 |
| 1976 | 71 | 20 | 84 | 7 | 87 | 4 |
| 1975 | 61 | 33 | 84 | 6 | 91 | 4 |
| 1974 (Ford) | 37 | 43 | | | | |
| 1974 | 60 | 28 | 75 | 4 | 77 | 6 |
| 1973 | 60 | 26 | 77 | 9 | 78 | 6 |
| 1972 | 35 | 46 | 80 | 15 | 83 | 12 |
| 1971 | 60 | 33 | 74 | 12 | 83 | 6 |
| 1970 | 54 | 29 | 82 | 4 | 66 | 9 |
| 1969 | 38 | 63† | 89 | 11† | 100 | 0† |

†Not eligible for all recorded votes.

S = Support            O = Opposition

## Key Votes

**96th Congress**

| | |
|---|---|
| Weaken Carter oil profits tax (1979) | Y |
| Reject hospital cost control plan (1979) | ? |
| Implement Panama Canal Treaties (1979) | N |
| Establish Department of Education (1979) | N |
| Approve Anti-busing Amendment (1979) | Y |
| Guarantee Chrysler Corp. loans (1979) | X |
| Approve military draft registration (1980) | N |
| Aid Sandinista regime in Nicaragua (1980) | N |
| Strengthen fair housing laws (1980) | N |

**97th Congress**

| | |
|---|---|
| Reagan budget proposal (1981) | Y |

## Interest Group Ratings

| Year | ADA | ACA | AFL-CIO | CCUS |
|---|---|---|---|---|
| 1980 | 6 | 95 | 8 | 64 |
| 1979 | 5 | 100 | 6 | 100 |
| 1978 | 5 | 100 | 6 | 100 |
| 1977 | 5 | 96 | 14 | 94 |
| 1976 | 5 | 96 | 14 | 94 |
| 1975 | 0 | 100 | 5 | 94 |
| 1974 | 9 | 92 | 0 | 100 |
| 1973 | 8 | 100 | 18 | 100 |
| 1972 | 0 | 100 | 18 | 100 |
| 1971 | 14 | 96 | 0 | - |
| 1970 | 8 | 100 | 0 | 100 |
| 1969 | 0 | 100 | 0 | - |

# 13 Robert McClory (R)

Of Lake Bluff — Elected 1962

**Born:** Jan. 31, 1908, Riverside, Ill.
**Education:** Attended Dartmouth College, 1926-28; Chicago-Kent Law School, LL.B. 1932.
**Military Career:** Marine Corps Reserve, 1933-37.
**Profession:** Lawyer.
**Family:** Wife, Doris Hibbard; three children.
**Religion:** Christian Scientist.
**Political Career:** Ill. House, 1951-53; Ill. Senate, 1953-63.

**In Washington:** McClory is independent and unpredictable on many issues, but he is firmly in the moderate Republican tradition that has made civil rights a bipartisan issue on the Judiciary Committee for a generation, long before he entered Congress.

As the senior GOP member on Judiciary since 1977, McClory has had relatively few chances to play a leadership role on civil rights because there have been few important bills on the subject. But he has made his presence felt at a couple of conspicuous moments.

When an anti-busing constitutional amendment came to the House floor in 1979, McClory saw it as a civil rights issue and joined with outside pressure groups in trying to persuade Republicans not to vote for it. "There is no justification for changing the law," he said, "particularly fundamental constitutional law."

The next year, he was out front again as the committee reported out an open housing bill allowing the federal government to initiate action against those it suspected of housing discrimination. When an effort was made on the House floor to weaken the legislation, McClory fought it, even though Republicans went 128-25 the other way. He also argued for a legal holiday to commemorate the birthday of the Rev. Martin Luther King Jr.

On other Judiciary issues, McClory is noted for his insistence on deliberating every issue for himself and coming up with some stubborn conclusions.

He was one of the prime Republican sponsors of the Equal Rights Amendment and fought hard to pass it through the House in 1972. But five years later, when the same ERA coalition came back requesting another five year period for ratification by the states, McClory refused to join his original allies in supporting it.

Some of them charged he was responding to the growing ERA controversy in Illinois, where the Legislature refused three times to ratify the amendment. McClory insisted he had other reasons —that extension was an unusual and unfair tactic and would set a bad precedent for other constitutional amendments.

Four years earlier, during the Judiciary Committee's impeachment proceedings against President Nixon, McClory was equally selective and very influential.

McClory was most disturbed about Nixon's refusal to honor the committee's subpoenas of taped conversations held in the Oval Office. He felt it was an attempt by the president to ignore Congress' constitutional rights and an impeachable offense in itself. None of the other committee members felt that way, but McClory insisted. He refused to support the first article of impeachment, relating to the Watergate coverup and obstruction of justice, but he was willing to support the second one, concerning "abuse of power," as long as the committee agreed to separate out a third, based on refusal to comply with subpoenas.

At that point the coalition of Republicans and Democrats supporting impeachment was a fragile one, and most of its members were willing to accept McClory's request to get him on board. Despite considerable opposition within both par-

---

**13th District: Northeast — Elgin, Waukegan.** Population: 527,004 (14% increase since 1970). Race: White 477,330 (91%), Black 30,810 (6%), Others 18,864 (4%). Spanish origin: 27,283 (5%).

ties, McClory's third article won approval in the committee on a narrow 21-17 vote and became part of the formal case against Nixon.

It was a nationally televised example of McClory's career-long march to his own drummer, one that can look heroic at times and merely willful at others.

McClory is one of the few Republicans on the committee who has consistently supported strong gun control legislation. In 1976, he voted with a Democratic majority on Judiciary as it passed a bill to ban the sale and manufacture of conceal-able weapons. Later, after considerable pressure from pro-gun forces, the committee reversed itself, 17-16. McClory refused to switch.

He did help scale it down, however, to a ban on "Saturday night specials" and similar small handguns. The committee voted to send that to the floor, but it was put aside amid the pressure of an election year and nothing resembling it has reached the floor since.

McClory has been a supporter of the Law Enforcement Assistance Administration, the federal grant program threatened during the Carter administration and marked for extinction by President Reagan. He fought to prevent elimination of LEAA grants in 1980.

McClory surprised some Judiciary allies in 1981 when he opposed a bill to reauthorize the Legal Services Corporation, an agency he had supported in the past. He said he found the office "beset with problems" and suggested Congress at least study Reagan's proposal to merge it into a social services block grant.

Outside Judiciary Committee issues, McClory is a more conservative Republican, one who votes with party majorities in favor of more funding for defense. He sits on the Intelligence Committee, where he has advocated strong penalties for those who reveal the names of CIA agents. In 1978, when the committee wrote legislation restricting the use of wiretaps in national security cases, McClory argued for relatively few limits on the government's power in dealing with foreign espionage.

**At Home:** The oldest Republican in the Illinois delegation, McClory has been under increasing challenge within his party even though he appears younger than his 73 years. He has had three serious primary opponents in his past four elections, and while he has beaten all of them, his margins seem to be narrowing; a state representative was able to roll up 40 percent of the vote against him in the 1980 primary.

McClory had a long political career before his election to the House in 1962. He was chairman of the Lake County Young Republicans as far back as the 1930s. Elected to the state House in 1950, he won a state Senate seat in 1952 and held it for a decade.

In 1962, the Illinois Legislature created a new district north of Chicago. It was clearly Republican territory, and the GOP primary drew a horde of entrants. But McClory, who already represented much of the area in the state Senate, had the inside track. He was nominated with 28 percent of the primary vote.

McClory has never had trouble in a general election. His percentage fell as low as 55 percent only once, and that was in the 1974 Watergate year. Republican turnout dropped sharply then, and McClory was criticized for hesitating briefly on the Nixon impeachment issue, although he did ultimately support it.

**The District:** The 13th twists its way along the edge of metropolitan Chicago, west and south toward central Illinois farm land and north to the Wisconsin border. Testifying to the spread of the Chicago suburbs, it has grown enough over the past decade to exceed the population norm needed for the state's districts in the 1980s.

Predominantly Republican, the district has two industrial cities: Waukegan on Lake Michigan and Elgin in Kane County. Elgin has a significant machine tool industry and blue-collar population but generally votes Republican; Waukegan, an old port city with a sizeable black and Hispanic population, is Democratic. It had considerable racial tensions in the 1960s.

## Committees

**Judiciary** (Ranking Republican)
Administrative Law and Governmental Relations; Monopolies and Commercial Law.

**Select Intelligence** (3rd of 5 Republicans)
Legislation.

## Elections

**1980 General**

| | |
|---|---|
| Robert McClory (R ) | 131,448 (72 %) |
| Michael Reese (D ) | 52,000 (28 %) |

**1980 Primary**

| | |
|---|---|
| Robert McClory (R ) | 40,335 (60 %) |
| Cal Skinner (R ) | 26,668 (40 %) |

**1978 General**

| | |
|---|---|
| Robert McClory (R ) | 64,060 (61 %) |
| Frederick Steffen (D ) | 40,675 (39 %) |

**Previous Winning Percentages**

| | | | |
|---|---|---|---|
| 1976 (67 %) | 1974 (55 %) | 1972 (62 %) | 1970 (62 %) |
| 1968 (70 %) | 1966 (69 %) | 1964 (59 %) | 1962 (64 %) |

**District Vote For President**

| | 1980 | | 1976 | | 1972 |
|---|---|---|---|---|---|
| D | 53,507 (28 %) | D | 64,623 (37 %) | D | 49,219 (30 %) |
| R | 116,322 (61 %) | R | 109,215 (62 %) | R | 113,282 (70 %) |
| I | 17,978 (9 %) | | | | |

## Campaign Finance

| | Receipts | Receipts from PACs | Expenditures |
|---|---|---|---|
| **1980** | | | |
| McClory (R ) | $112,760 | $50,807 (45 %) | $96,805 |
| **1978** | | | |
| McClory (R ) | $93,672 | $34,339 (37 %) | $111,477 |
| Steffen (D ) | $84,186 | $9,300 (11 %) | $82,216 |

## Voting Studies

| | Presidential Support | | Party Unity | | Conservative Coalition | |
|---|---|---|---|---|---|---|
| Year | S | O | S | O | S | O |
| 1980 | 44 | 48† | 63 | 29 | 60 | 28 |
| 1979 | 33 | 56 | 75 | 20 | 74 | 17 |
| 1978 | 46 | 50 | 69 | 24 | 69 | 24 |
| 1977 | 46 | 49 | 66 | 25 | 72 | 21 |
| 1976 | 82 | 18 | 68 | 27 | 69 | 24 |
| 1975 | 74 | 19 | 71 | 22 | 71 | 20 |
| 1974 (Ford) | 59 | 24 | | | | |
| 1974 | 72 | 25 | 61 | 33 | 57 | 39 |
| 1973 | 67 | 27 | 66 | 27 | 63 | 32 |
| 1972 | 70 | 16 | 66 | 29 | 62 | 33 |
| 1971 | 77 | 16 | 56 | 31 | 53 | 36 |
| 1970 | 74 | 11 | 61 | 22 | 66 | 9 |
| 1969 | 55 | 23 | 44 | 45 | 53 | 44 |
| 1968 | 52 | 29 | 52 | 27 | 53 | 33 |
| 1967 | 50 | 42 | 78 | 12 | 74 | 17 |
| 1966 | 38 | 44 | 64 | 15 | 70 | 11 |
| 1965 | 41 | 49 | 62 | 17 | 53 | 24 |
| 1964 | 25 | 58 | 63 | 10 | 58 | 0 |
| 1963 | 27 | 68 | 91 | 3 | 67 | 20 |

S = Support          O = Opposition

†Not eligible for all recorded votes.

## Key Votes

**96th Congress**

| | |
|---|---|
| Weaken Carter oil profits tax (1979) | Y |
| Reject hospital cost control plan (1979) | Y |
| Implement Panama Canal Treaties (1979) | Y |
| Establish Department of Education (1979) | N |
| Approve Anti-busing Amendment (1979) | N |
| Guarantee Chrysler Corp. loans (1979) | Y |
| Approve military draft registration (1980) | N |
| Aid Sandinista regime in Nicaragua (1980) | N |
| Strengthen fair housing laws (1980) | Y |

**97th Congress**

| | |
|---|---|
| Reagan budget proposal (1981) | Y |

## Interest Group Ratings

| Year | ADA | ACA | AFL-CIO | CCUS |
|---|---|---|---|---|
| 1980 | 17 | 67 | 21 | 73 |
| 1979 | 16 | 81 | 21 | 89 |
| 1978 | 45 | 73 | 21 | 88 |
| 1977 | 10 | 69 | 17 | 88 |
| 1976 | 20 | 63 | 5 | 76 |
| 1975 | 32 | 67 | 17 | 88 |
| 1974 | 22 | 40 | 9 | 80 |
| 1973 | 36 | 63 | 0 | 80 |
| 1972 | 38 | 45 | 18 | 75 |
| 1971 | 38 | 67 | 27 | . |
| 1970 | 24 | 58 | 29 | 78 |
| 1969 | 33 | 31 | 70 | . |
| 1968 | 25 | 65 | 75 | . |
| 1967 | 7 | 81 | 8 | 100 |
| 1966 | 6 | 80 | 0 | . |
| 1965 | 16 | 77 | . | 100 |
| 1964 | 8 | 94 | 18 | . |
| 1963 | . | 100 | . | . |

# 14 John N. Erlenborn (R)

**Of Glen Ellyn — Elected 1964**

**Born:** Feb. 8, 1927, Chicago, Ill.
**Education:** Loyola U., J.D. 1949.
**Military Career:** Navy Reserve, 1944-46.
**Profession:** Lawyer.
**Family:** Wife, Dorothy Fisher; three children.
**Religion:** Roman Catholic.
**Political Career:** Ill. House, 1957-65.

**In Washington:** The Education and Labor Committee was not a very congenial place for a conservative Republican when Erlenborn joined it in 1967, and it has changed little in all the years he has served there. Education and Labor was a bastion of liberal social policy in the Johnson years, and it is about the last refuge of labor loyalism and Great Society social policy left in Congress in the Reagan years.

The remarkable thing about Erlenborn's career on the committee has been the number of victories he has won despite the odds. Sometimes he has beaten committee Democrats on the floor after they have moved too far for a majority of the House to accept; sometimes he has maneuvered within the committee itself for a compromise *he* could accept. "He might be the best we have," Minority Leader John Rhodes once said of him. "He never got into that minority-loser frame of mind."

Despite the ideological gulf, Erlenborn managed to work with the committee's majority for six years in the struggle to enact legislation protecting benefits in private pension plans. Erlenborn was senior Republican on the Labor Subcommittee; he drafted much of the complex bill along with the subcommittee chairman, John H. Dent of Pennsylvania. "Mr. Dent and I were several miles apart when we started discussing this bill," he said after it was enacted. "Over the years, I moved a little in his direction and he moved a little in mine."

On most labor issues over the years, however, it has not worked out that way. Erlenborn has found himself militantly opposed to what the committee approved, and has fought it on the floor. For years, the words "Erlenborn substitute" had a special meaning in House politics; they represented the risk that Education and Labor Democrats ran of losing on the floor if they reported out a bill with too high a price.

When the Democrats wrote minimum wage legislation in 1972, for example, Erlenborn and his business lobbying coalition beat them. The House passed his substitute stretching out wage increases over a much longer period of years. The Senate passed a more generous minimum wage bill, but Erlenborn had the votes to prevent the House from going to conference on it, and no legislation passed at all.

The next year, the Democrats managed to defeat a similar Erlenborn substitute, with a stretch-out provision and a lower floor for teenagers, on a 218-199 vote. But President Nixon vetoed the bill, and the House sustained the veto. When a new minimum wage finally became law in 1974, after two years of struggle, it was a compromise version, raising the rate to $2.30 in three steps, one that Erlenborn and the committee's Democrats all agreed to support.

In 1977, it was confrontation again, as the new Democratic minimum wage bill included a provision for indexing — automatic future increases to compensate for inflation. Erlenborn called indexing a "mindless, thoughtless rule," and he got it knocked out of the bill on a floor amendment. He won, 223-193, and indexing was never written into the law.

Erlenborn was a consistent opponent of AFL-CIO-sponsored legislation to permit common-site picketing at construction projects. The House passed it in 1975, but President Ford vetoed it. In 1977, with President Carter poised to sign it, Erlenborn and his business coalition won a stun-

---

**14th District: Outer Chicago suburbs — Du Page County.** Population: 625,629 (35% increase since 1970). Race: White 593,031 (95%), Black 7,773 (1%), Asian and Pacific Islander 17,903 (3%), Others 6,922 (1%). Spanish origin: 15,162 (2%).

---

ning House victory, as the picketing bill lost out on a 217-205 vote.

The Erlenborn side was not nearly as successful in its efforts to stop House passage of labor law revisions aimed at making it easier for unions to organize and negotiate contracts. Erlenborn had his own "substitute" to that bill. He wanted to guarantee employers freedom to distribute anti-union views and broaden the definition of unfair labor practices. This time, the substitute got nowhere, and the Democratic bill passed on a lopsided vote. But business won in the end; a filibuster killed the legislation in the Senate.

Erlenborn also has spent 15 years on higher education subcommittees at Education and Labor, generally working more closely with the majority than he does on union issues. He has worked to curb abuses in the guaranteed student loan program, preventing students from defaulting on loans by declaring bankruptcy after they graduate. He has opposed HEW sex discrimination rules in school athletic programs, and voted to allow sex discrimination in undergraduate admissions.

On the Government Operations Committee, where he is the second Republican in seniority, Erlenborn opposed creation of a Consumer Protection Agency during the 1970s, and was adamant against President Carter' proposal for a new Department of Education, which he felt was a step toward standardized, socialized teaching. He stalled it as long as he could in committee by offering dozens of amendments, and continued the strategy on the House floor, where amendments restricting busing and affirmative action came close to defeating the measure. When President Reagan took office, Erlenborn promised to try to abolish the Education Department.

One of his few lapses in political judgment came in 1973, when he decided to challenge the man above him on Government Operations, Frank Horton of New York, for the position of ranking Republican member. Horton had voted with Democrats as often as with Republicans on Government Operations, and Erlenborn felt that gave him an opening for a successful challenge. But Horton was personally popular, and Erlenborn has never been much of a backslapper, or very kind to less talented people. Horton embarrassed him by a 100-36 vote.

Erlenborn opposed most of the poverty programs of the 1960s, and has criticized most of the jobs legislation of recent years as unrealistic. He fought attempts to give the Equal Employment Opportunity Commission strong enforcement powers, arguing that it should be restricted to suing in court. But he has defended the existence of the Legal Services program for the poor. He also surprised some of his conservative allies in 1976 by supporting a bill to ban small concealable handguns.

**At Home:** Erlenborn follows a long line of quiet, diligent conservative Republicans who have represented Du Page County in Congress during this century. Most of them have served for years with negligible opposition within the Republican Party and overwhelming victories over Democrats. The only real competition here takes place when an incumbent retires.

That was the pattern in 1964, when Erlenborn won his first term. Republican Rep. Elmer Hoffman decided to run for Illinois secretary of state, and six Republicans entered the contest to succeed him. Democrats did not even bother to hold a primary.

Erlenborn was then an eight-year veteran in the Illinois House. He had been an active member of the so-called Economy Bloc, a group of conservatives who fought against higher state spending, and had engaged in an anti-racketeering crusade. His main primary opponent was William Barr, whose name alone made him formidable: Barr's father had been a locally popular member of the Illinois Senate for 48 years. Barr led by a 3-1 margin in Will County, which was then in the district, but Erlenborn's lead in Du Page was enough to win the nomination.

Once in office, Erlenborn quickly became unassailable politically. Even in the 1974 Watergate election, the Democratic candidate was able to get only 33.4 percent of the vote.

**The District:** The district lies entirely within suburban Du Page County, the most populous of the so-called "collar counties" that surround Chicago. A generation ago Du Page still had cornfields along its western border; today it is 100 percent suburban.

Du Page is rarely outdone in its Republicanism. In 1976, it gave President Ford a margin of 100,118 votes over Jimmy Carter, an amount greater than Ford's entire statewide plurality. In 1980, Ronald Reagan carried it by an even larger amount.

The 14th now has more people than any other district in the state, and Erlenborn will have to give up nearly 100,000 of his constituents in the new redistricting. But he is certain to keep enough friendly ones to remain secure.

## Committees

**Education and Labor** (2nd of 14 Republicans)
Labor-Management Relations; Labor Standards; Post Secondary Education.

**Government Operations** (2nd of 17 Republicans)
Government Information and Individual Rights; Legislation and National Security.

## Elections

**1980 General**

| | |
|---|---|
| John Erlenborn (R ) | 202,583 (77 %) |
| LeRoy Kennel (D ) | 61,224 (23 %) |

**1980 Primary**

| | |
|---|---|
| John Erlenborn (R ) | 73,801 (81 %) |
| William Grossklas (R) | 16,938 (19 %) |

**1978 General**

| | |
|---|---|
| John Erlenborn (R ) | 118,741 (75 %) |
| James Romanyak (D ) | 39,438 (25 %) |

**Previous Winning Percentages**

| | | | |
|---|---|---|---|
| 1976 (74%) | 1974 (67%) | 1972 (73%) | 1970 (66%) |
| 1968 (71 %) | 1966 (72 %) | 1964 (59 %) | |

**District Vote For President**

| | 1980 | | 1976 | | 1972 |
|---|---|---|---|---|---|
| D | 65,736 (24 %) | D | 68,237 (28 %) | D | 54,116 (25 %) |
| R | 175,124 (64 %) | R | 168,355 (69 %) | R | 164,660 (75 %) |
| I | 28,917 (11 %) | | | | |

## Campaign Finance

| | Receipts | Receipts from PACs | Expenditures |
|---|---|---|---|
| **1980** | | | |
| Erlenborn (R ) | $79,041 | $63,800 (81 %) | $66,340 |
| **1978** | | | |
| Erlenborn (R ) | $81,821 | $35,430 (43 %) | $52,212 |

## Voting Studies

| | Presidential Support | | Party Unity | | Conservative Coalition | |
|---|---|---|---|---|---|---|
| Year | S | O | S | O | S | O |
| 1980 | 49 | 36 | 62 | 22 | 59 | 20 |
| 1979 | 50 | 46 | 65 | 30 | 67 | 26 |

| 1978 | 43 | 46 | 68 | 23 | 66 | 26 |
|---|---|---|---|---|---|---|
| 1977 | 41 | 53 | 70 | 21 | 73 | 20 |
| 1976 | 86 | 10 | 76 | 16 | 73 | 17 |
| 1975 | 81 | 13 | 71 | 17 | 72 | 15 |
| 1974 (Ford) | 76 | 17 | | | | |
| 1974 | 74 | 13 | 65 | 28 | 59 | 35 |
| 1973 | 67 | 17 | 63 | 19 | 62 | 15 |
| 1972 | 68 | 5 | 60 | 19 | 54 | 27 |
| 1971 | 86 | 7 | 69 | 15 | 71 | 19 |
| 1970 | 69 | 8 | 68 | 17 | 59 | 25 |
| 1969 | 66 | 26 | 71 | 25 | 71 | 24 |
| 1968 | 58 | 34 | 65 | 24 | 73 | 24 |
| 1967 | 52 | 35 | 64 | 18 | 61 | 20 |
| 1966 | 38 | 48 | 71 | 16 | 62 | 19 |
| 1965 | 31 | 63 | 88 | 9 | 88 | 10 |

S = Support          O = Opposition

## Key Votes

**96th Congress**

| | |
|---|---|
| Weaken Carter oil profits tax (1979) | Y |
| Reject hospital cost control plan (1979) | Y |
| Implement Panama Canal Treaties (1979) | Y |
| Establish Department of Education (1979) | N |
| Approve Anti-busing Amendment (1979) | N |
| Guarantee Chrysler Corp. loans (1979) | N |
| Approve military draft registration (1980) | Y |
| Aid Sandinista regime in Nicaragua (1980) | N |
| Strengthen fair housing laws (1980) | N |

**97th Congress**

| | |
|---|---|
| Reagan budget proposal (1981) | Y |

## Interest Group Ratings

| Year | ADA | ACA | AFL-CIO | CCUS |
|---|---|---|---|---|
| 1980 | 11 | 85 | 11 | 90 |
| 1979 | 26 | 68 | 20 | 100 |
| 1978 | 30 | 69 | 10 | 94 |
| 1977 | 15 | 80 | 22 | 100 |
| 1976 | 5 | 60 | 10 | 83 |
| 1975 | 11 | 84 | 5 | 94 |
| 1974 | 22 | 54 | 27 | 80 |
| 1973 | 20 | 60 | 0 | 100 |
| 1972 | 19 | 67 | 25 | 89 |
| 1971 | 22 | 88 | 9 | - |
| 1970 | 24 | 69 | 0 | 88 |
| 1969 | 0 | 76 | 40 | - |
| 1968 | 8 | 82 | 25 | - |
| 1967 | 13 | 84 | 8 | 90 |
| 1966 | 6 | 67 | 0 | - |
| 1965 | 16 | 96 | - | 100 |

# 15 Tom Corcoran (R)

**Of Ottawa — Elected 1976**

**Born:** May 23, 1939, Ottawa, Ill.
**Education:** U. of Notre Dame, B.A. 1961.; attended graduate school, U. of Ill., 1962; U. of Chicago, 1963; Northwestern U., 1967.
**Military Career:** Army, 1963-65.
**Profession:** Transportation executive and state government official.
**Family:** Wife, Helenmarie Anderson; five children.
**Religion:** Roman Catholic.
**Political Career:** Unsuccessfully sought Republican nomination for U.S. House, 1974.

**In Washington:** Quiet and serious, Corcoran combines a near-perfect conservative voting record with an independent streak that sometimes shows itself when colleagues least expect it.

He demonstrated that one day in 1980, when the Republican Conference met in closed session to discuss the case of Florida's Richard Kelly, the only GOP member implicated in the Abscam bribery scandal.

The House Republican leadership had agreed unanimously that Kelly should be expelled from the conference, even though the evidence was not yet public and no indictment had been handed down. But before they could put it to a vote, Corcoran raised a string of objections, implying that the session amounted to a kangaroo court and calling for delay. He was on the verge of winning his argument when Kelly made it moot by deciding to resign from the conference on his own.

Corcoran has been one of the less conspicuous Republicans on the Commerce Committee, where he is well placed on both the energy subcommittees created in 1981. He is a consistent vote against government controls on energy prices and in favor of maximum freedom for the oil and gas industries.

But Corcoran has shown an occasional willingness to take on Clarence Brown of Ohio, the committee's dominant Republican figure. He fought with Brown in the 96th Congress over the issue of nuclear waste disposal, protesting efforts to store some of the nuclear stockpile in his district, at Morris, Illinois.

He has also pushed for greater use of coal in meeting energy needs. In 1981, he introduced a bill to promote coal through softening the 1977 Clean Air Act and offering tax incentives for coal use. He has worked in concert with the railroad industry, once his employer in private life.

Corcoran is more vocal on the Post Office Committee, where he has served throughout his congressional career. He has fought consistently for a change in the rules of the U.S. Postal Service that would eliminate its governing board and once again make the postmaster general a presidential appointee subject to congressional confirmation. He argued for a congressional veto of major Postal Service actions, such as a decision to curtail Saturday mail delivery. And he was one of the relatively few committee members to express some sympathy with President Carter's ill-fated 1980 effort to save $3 billion a year by reducing government employee benefits to bring them in line with corresponding benefits in private industry.

**At Home:** In his earlier days, before he ran for Congress in a solidly conservative district, Corcoran had an image as a moderate Republican. From 1969 through 1972, he was the Washington lobbyist for Gov. Richard Ogilvie, who was beaten for re-election largely because he imposed a state income tax. In his lobbying role, Corcoran fought for an increase in Illinois' share of federal tax money and organized the state's first trade mission to the Soviet Union.

His main competition for the GOP congressional nomination in 1976 was state Rep. James Washburn, minority leader of the Illinois House

---

**15th District: North central — Aurora, DeKalb.** Population: 495,322 (7% increase since 1970). Race: White 466,866 (94%), Black 14,310 (3%), Others 14,146 (3%). Spanish origin: 23,365 (5%).

and a courthouse conservative who had the backing of most local party leaders. Corcoran was careful to stress conservative themes, attacking deficit spending, the welfare state, and government bureaucracy.

Corcoran was already well-known in the district; he had run for the nomination in 1974, losing by only 607 votes. The second time, in a field of five candidates, he finished first with 39.3 percent of the vote, running 3,000 votes ahead of Washburn.

In November, Corcoran faced Rep. Tim Lee Hall, the first Democrat in this century to win the seat. Hall's victory had come in the 1974 Watergate election, with a divided Republican Party in the district and a low turnout. Corcoran easily

returned it to Republican control in 1976, one of only two challengers in the country to oust a first-term Democrat that year.

**The District:** The 15th District is quintessential downstate Illinois — cornfields and a few small industrial cities. The district lies in the center of the Corn Belt stretching from Indiana to Nebraska, and has some of the richest farmland in the country. It also has glassworks in Ottawa and Streator, and a large Caterpillar Tractor plant in Aurora.

The area was settled by Germans and New England Yankees, and formed its Republican allegiance early. The tradition is solid, with the prosperous farmers and farm communities almost always remaining loyal to the GOP.

## Committees

**Energy and Commerce** (9th of 18 Republicans)
Energy Conservation and Power; Fossil and Synthetic Fuels.

**Post Office and Civil Service** (4th of 11 Republicans)
Human Resources; Postal Operations and Services.

## Elections

**1980 General**

| | |
|---|---|
| Tom Corcoran (R ) | 150,898 (77 %) |
| John Quillin (D ) | 45,721 (23 %) |

**1978 General**

| | |
|---|---|
| Tom Corcoran (R ) | 80,856 (62 %) |
| Tim Hall (D ) | 48,756 (38 %) |

**Previous Winning Percentages**

1976 (54 %)

**District Vote For President**

| | 1980 | | 1976 | | 1972 |
|---|---|---|---|---|---|
| **D** | 60,054 (30 %) | **D** | 78,766 (40 %) | **D** | 68,408 (34 %) |
| **R** | 123,855 (61 %) | **R** | 115,849 (59 %) | **R** | 133,071 (66 %) |
| **I** | 15,657 (8 %) | | | | |

## Campaign Finance

| | Receipts | Receipts from PACs | Expenditures |
|---|---|---|---|
| **1980** | | | |
| Corcoran (R ) | $145,693 | $63,527 (44 %) | $88,330 |
| **1978** | | | |
| Corcoran (R ) | $180,387 | $62,658 (35 %) | $180,076 |

| | | | |
|---|---|---|---|
| Hall (D ) | $21,073 | $14,400 (68 %) | $21,368 |

## Voting Studies

| Year | Presidential Support | | Party Unity | | Conservative Coalition | |
|---|---|---|---|---|---|---|
| | **S** | **O** | **S** | **O** | **S** | **O** |
| 1980 | 43 | 51 | 86 | 13 | 87 | 11 |
| 1979 | 38 | 61 | 81 | 16 | 88 | 10 |
| 1978 | 38 | 54 | 79 | 16 | 77 | 16 |
| 1977 | 42 | 58 | 87 | 10 | 93 | 6 |

S = Support        O = Opposition

## Key Votes

**96th Congress**

| | |
|---|---|
| Weaken Carter oil profits tax (1979) | Y |
| Reject hospital cost control plan (1979) | Y |
| Implement Panama Canal Treaties (1979) | N |
| Establish Department of Education (1979) | Y |
| Approve Anti-busing Amendment (1979) | Y |
| Guarantee Chrysler Corp. loans (1979) | N |
| Approve military draft registration (1980) | Y |
| Aid Sandinista regime in Nicaragua (1980) | N |
| Strengthen fair housing laws (1980) | N |

**97th Congress**

| | |
|---|---|
| Reagan budget proposal (1981) | Y |

## Interest Group Ratings

| Year | ADA | ACA | AFL-CIO | CCUS |
|---|---|---|---|---|
| 1980 | 6 | 96 | 5 | 83 |
| 1979 | 16 | 96 | 11 | 88 |
| 1978 | 25 | 88 | 10 | 81 |
| 1977 | 15 | 89 | 9 | 94 |

# 16 Lynn M. Martin (R)

**Of Rockford — Elected 1980**

**Born:** Dec. 26, 1939, Chicago, Ill.
**Education:** U. of Ill., B.A. 1960.
**Profession:** Teacher.
**Family:** Divorced; two children.
**Religion:** Roman Catholic.
**Political Career:** Winnebago County Board, 1972-76; Ill. House, 1977-79; Ill. Senate, 1979-81.

**The Member:** Martin has risen quickly in her nine-year political career, moving without interruption from county to state to federal government.

Her opportunity to serve in Washington opened up when Republican Rep. John B. Anderson announced his candidacy for the White House. It is only the second time since 1932 that the district has changed representation.

Five Republicans entered the race to succeed Anderson in 1980. But Martin's personal appeal gave her almost 50 percent of the vote. Already well-known in the Rockford area, she campaigned extensively in the rural parts of the district and did well there.

While in the Legislature, Martin fought for tax reduction and was instrumental in the passage of legislation to limit state spending. A fiscal conservative, she supports ratification of the Equal Rights Amendment.

Martin has a seat on the Budget Committee, a choice opportunity for a newcomer. She also has waged several anti-spending campaigns. She called for a limit on the number of television sets a member may buy with office funds. She found that 56 members had more than one television, and said that was excessive.

**The District:** Nestled in the northwest corner of Illinois, the 16th has been a traditional home for Yankee, German, and Scandinavian immigrants, who farmed or settled in small towns throughout the area, and became solid Republicans. The district has not elected a Democrat to the House in this century.

In the middle of the towns and farms is the industrial city of Rockford, which accounts for one-third of the district's population. It has a concentration of machine tool, textile machinery, and automotive parts plants that has spawned a considerable unionized blue-collar population. Democrats can turn out a healthy vote in Rockford, but they have not been able to overcome the traditional GOP district-wide majority.

## Committees

**Budget**
Task Forces: Human Resources and Block Grants; Reconciliation; Transportation, Research and Development, and Capitol Resources.

**House Administration** (8th of 8 Republicans)
Accounts; Contracts and Printing.

**Joint Printing**

## Elections

**1980 General**

| | |
|---|---|
| Lynn Martin (R ) | 132,905 (67 %) |
| Douglas Aurand (D) | 64,224 (33 %) |

**1980 Primary**

| | |
|---|---|
| Lynn Martin (R ) | 36,291 (45 %) |
| Don Lyon (R ) | 20,643 (26 %) |
| Dick Crosby (R ) | 9,493 (12 %) |
| Steve Anderson (R ) | 9,294 (12 %) |

**District Vote For President**

| | 1980 | | 1976 | | 1972 |
|---|---|---|---|---|---|
| D | 57,177 (28 %) | D | 76,448 (41 %) | D | 62,339 (34 %) |
| R | 108,841 (54 %) | R | 108,790 (58 %) | R | 120,432 (66 %) |
| I | 32,983 (16 %) | | | | |

## Campaign Finance

| | Receipts | Receipts from PACs | Expenditures |
|---|---|---|---|
| **1980** | | | |
| Martin (R ) | $308,224 | $145,243 (47 %) | $293,256 |
| Aurand (D ) | $41,598 | $12,715 (31 %) | $41,535 |

## Key Vote

**97th Congress**

| | |
|---|---|
| Reagan budget proposal (1981) | Y |

---

**16th District: Northwest — Rockford, Freeport.** Population: 486,845 (5 % increase since 1970). Race: White 454,518 (93 %), Black 24,523 (5 %), Others 7,804 (2 %). Spanish origin: 9,595 (2 %).

# 17 George M. O'Brien (R)

**Of Joliet — Elected 1972**

**Born:** June 17, 1917, Chicago, Ill.
**Education:** Northwestern U., A.B. 1939; Yale U., J.D. 1947.
**Military Career:** Army Air Corps, 1941-45.
**Profession:** Lawyer.
**Family:** Wife, Mary Lou Peyla; two children.
**Religion:** Roman Catholic.
**Political Career:** Will County Board of Supervisors, 1956-64; Ill. House, 1971-73; unsuccessful Republican nominee for county State's Attorney, 1964.

**In Washington:** O'Brien earned himself some uncharacteristic publicity and a little resentment from colleagues in 1979 when he made it extra hard for the House to vote itself a pay raise.

The Appropriations Committee was going through the routine of marking up a legislative funding bill when O'Brien noticed an innocuous-sounding provision calling for a "cap" of 7 percent on salary increases for top federal officials. Democratic leaders put that figure in so they could reduce it to 5.5 percent on the floor and still wind up with an increase for members as well as top-level bureaucrats.

O'Brien found himself blocked in committee, but he challenged the move on the House floor, claiming to speak for those people in the country "who do not have the opportunity to raise their own pay in the middle of their own contracts of employment." He moved to strike the whole raise.

The leadership had that one under control too. O'Brien's amendment was shouted down by voice vote, and when he asked for a record vote on the grounds that no quorum was present, the presiding officer insisted there was a quorum, even though it seemed to most of those watching that there was not.

No pay raise went through that day, because the bill to which it had been attached failed to pass. The 5.5 percent increase did become law later in the year, but it took a record vote to do it. By that time, the Illinois Republican had attracted valuable political attention as a cost-conscious public servant, if at the expense of some grumbling from members who wanted the money but did not want to go on record for it.

Most of the time, O'Brien is a bland but diligent member of Appropriations, an ally of Republican leader Robert H. Michel, his Illinois colleague. On the Appropriations Subcommittee

on Health and Human Services, he has fought for money for the handicapped; he once offered an unsuccessful floor amendment to add $225 million in aid to schools to help them remove architectural barriers for the handicapped.

On his other subcommittee — State, Justice and Commerce — he has played watchdog over the Federal Trade Commission. In 1980, he drafted legislative language seeking to influence the FTC investigation of the automobile industry, which is important in O'Brien's district. He asked that the FTC, in studying concentration in the auto industry, "devote considerable attention" to conditions in foreign countries which influence the competitive situation.

The same subcommittee has had jurisdiction over the Legal Services Corporation, and O'Brien has been more supportive of it than many of his fellow Republicans, although he has repeatedly tried to get the corporation to stop providing help to illegal aliens.

**At Home:** Years of party work paid off for O'Brien in 1972 when a new congressional district was created in the suburbs south of Chicago.

The heart of the district is Will County, and O'Brien had long been involved in Will County Republican politics. He had served on the county board of supervisors for eight years and then run a losing race for county state's attorney in 1964. Frustrated in his bid for that office, he returned

---

**17th District: Northeast — Joliet, Kankakee.** Population: 540,479 (17% increase since 1970). Race: White 460,738 (85%), Black 63,846 (12%), Others 15,895 (3%). Spanish origin: 21,823 (4%).

to his law practice in Joliet. In 1970, he was elected to the state Legislature.

When the time came to choose a candidate for the open district in 1972, Will County Republicans quickly endorsed O'Brien. With Will holding over half the district's population, it seemed futile for a candidate from outside the county to challenge O'Brien in a primary. He was unopposed for the nomination.

O'Brien went on to win the general election by a modest margin over labor-oriented Democrat John Houlihan, with some help from the Nixon presidential landslide. Two years later, he proved he could win under much more adverse circumstances, holding onto the seat in a strong Democratic year by 3,443 votes. His margins have increased ever since.

**The District:** Will County dominates the district. It consists of some suburban Chicago communities, plus the industrial city of Joliet. It is marginally Republican, with Democratic strength in Joliet offset by suburban and small-town Republican votes elsewhere in the county.

The 17th also dips south to take in Kankakee County, which has some industry in Kankakee but is more rural than Will, and Iroquois County, a more rural area.

At the northern end is a slice of southern Cook County around Chicago Heights. This is a group of ethnic, blue-collar suburban communities, many of whose residents work in nearby auto and steel plants.

## Committees

**Appropriations** (12th of 22 Republicans)
Commerce, Justice, State, and Judiciary; Labor-Health and Human Services-Education.

## Elections

**1980 General**

| | |
|---|---|
| George O'Brien (R ) | 125,806 (66 %) |
| Michael Murer (D ) | 65,305 (34 %) |

**1978 General**

| | |
|---|---|
| George O'Brien (R ) | 94,375 (71 %) |
| Clifford Sinclair (D ) | 39,260 (29 %) |

**Previous Winning Percentages**

1976 (58 %)   1974 (52 %)   1972 (56 %)

**District Vote For President**

| | 1980 | | 1976 | | 1972 |
|---|---|---|---|---|---|
| D | 72,365 (35 %) | D | 88,195 (44 %) | D | 61,854 (33 %) |
| R | 120,293 (58 %) | R | 110,999 (55 %) | R | 122,873 (66 %) |
| I | 12,138 (6 %) | | | | |

## Campaign Finance

| | Receipts | Receipts from PACs | Expenditures |
|---|---|---|---|
| **1980** | | | |
| O'Brien (R ) | $122,443 | $45,040 (37 %) | $132,147 |
| Murer (D ) | $31,260 | $11,600 (37 %) | $29,724 |
| **1978** | | | |
| O'Brien (R ) | $118,350 | $36,570 (31 %) | $112,346 |
| Sinclair (D ) | $15,984 | $2,900 (18 %) | $14,808 |

## Voting Studies

| | Presidential Support | | Party Unity | | Conservative Coalition | |
|---|---|---|---|---|---|---|
| Year | S | O | S | O | S | O |
| 1980 | 36 | 42† | 59 | 22 | 58 | 17 |
| 1979 | 36 | 48 | 63 | 21 | 72 | 15 |
| 1978 | 41 | 53 | 63 | 26 | 67 | 22 |
| 1977 | 47 | 48† | 72 | 23† | 84 | 18† |
| 1976 | 69 | 27 | 75 | 22† | 79 | 18† |
| 1975 | 69 | 24 | 69 | 19† | 75 | 13† |
| 1974 (Ford) | 50 | 43 | | | | |
| 1974 | 68 | 25 | 69 | 28† | 72 | 25 |
| 1973 | 71 | 21 | 68 | 21 | 77 | 14 |

S = Support          O = Opposition
†Not eligible for all recorded votes.

## Key Votes

**96th Congress**

| | |
|---|---|
| Weaken Carter oil profits tax (1979) | Y |
| Reject hospital cost control plan (1979) | Y |
| Implement Panama Canal Treaties (1979) | Y |
| Establish Department of Education (1979) | N |
| Approve Anti-busing Amendment (1979) | Y |
| Guarantee Chrysler Corp. loans (1979) | Y |
| Approve military draft registration (1980) | N |
| Aid Sandinista regime in Nicaragua (1980) | N |
| Strengthen fair housing laws (1980) | N |

**97th Congress**

| | |
|---|---|
| Reagan budget proposal (1981) | Y |

## Interest Group Ratings

| Year | ADA | ACA | AFL-CIO | CCUS |
|---|---|---|---|---|
| 1980 | 22 | 77 | 24 | 86 |
| 1979 | 11 | 73 | 20 | 88 |
| 1978 | 25 | 77 | 10 | 76 |
| 1977 | 15 | 73 | 18 | 94 |
| 1976 | 15 | 64 | 18 | 76 |
| 1975 | 11 | 67 | 24 | 88 |
| 1974 | 17 | 53 | 0 | 60 |
| 1973 | 16 | 68 | 27 | 80 |

# 18 Robert H. Michel (R)

**Of Peoria — Elected 1956**

**Born:** March 2, 1923, Peoria, Ill.
**Education:** Bradley U., B.S. 1948.
**Military Career:** Army, 1942-46.
**Profession:** Congressional aide.
**Family:** Wife, Corinne Woodruff; four children.
**Religion:** Apostolic Christian.
**Political Career:** No previous office.

**In Washington:** Michel won his position as Republican leader in 1981 on the same qualities that have traditionally won House GOP elections — cloakroom companionship, homespun Midwestern conservatism, an appetite for legislative detail and a knowledge of the rules.

When Republicans chose him over Michigan's Guy Vander Jagt by a 103-87 vote, they opted for Michel's "workhorse" campaign arguments against Vander Jagt's oratorical flourishes. Michel has as good a baritone voice as there is in the House, but he is not exactly an orator; his sentences often begin with volume and emphasis and end in a trail of prepositions. But Michel is at home on the House floor, where Vander Jagt has been a stranger most of his career, and in a newly conservative House, most Republicans decided strategy was preferable to speeches.

The early months of 1981 gave Michel more opportunities to plot strategy than anyone imagined, and most of them ended in victories. He managed the campaign for the Reagan budget alternative in May, holding every single Republican vote and winning over 63 Democrats. To reach unanimity on his side, he had to assure some moderate New England Republicans that he would understand if they had to vote against specific Reagan budget cuts later.

That argument meant potential problems for Michel further down the road. But it guaranteed him a smashing victory in the year's first conspicuous economic decision.

Like his two immediate predecessors as Republican leader, John J. Rhodes and Gerald R. Ford, Michel is a product of the Appropriations Committee. Like them, he has spent most of his career arguing over money and detail rather than broad policy questions. But a quarter-century on that committee has made Michel a top-flight negotiator, skilled in the trade-offs and compromises that are the hallmark of the appropriations process.

On December 16, 1980, when House-Senate haggling over an emergency spending bill was blocking congressional adjournment, Michel went to Speaker O'Neill's office in the early hours of the morning to work out a compromise that sent the institution home. "I wouldn't horse you around or pull any shenanigans," Michel told the Speaker.

The deal they arranged dropped more than 100 amendments added to the bill by the Senate, and gave liberals extra money they wanted for health care. But it kept two amendments that Michel was especially interested in — one slashing funds for public service jobs, the other restricting nursing-home programs.

That is the sort of detail work Michel did for two decades on the Appropriations Committee, usually with much less success. Concentrating on the Labor-HEW Subcommittee, he stood nearly alone for years against a working majority of liberal Democrats and Republicans. Every year when the subcommittee reported its spending bill, he took the House floor to say that it cost too much and wasted too much. But his efforts to scale back spending rarely succeeded — in committee or on the floor.

About the only exceptions came in cases where he could suggest a hint of scandal. In 1978, after the HEW inspector general issued a report showing widespread waste and fraud in Medicaid,

---

**18th District: West central — Peoria, Pekin.** Population: 486,948 (5% increase since 1970). Race: White 457,694 (94%), Black 25,799 (5%), Others 5,425 (1%). Spanish origin: 5,560 (1%).

**365**

**Robert H. Michel, R-Ill.**

Michel was able to get the House to adopt an amendment requiring the department to trim $1 billion worth of waste and fraud from its budget. HEW said it could not find that much waste, but Michel followed up the next year with a second $500 million cut.

The effort was largely symbolic, but it was not lost on presidential candidate Ronald Reagan, who made the elimination of such abuses a key part of his campaign.

Michel also anticipated Reagan in the 96th Congress by making an issue of entitlements — the programs like Social Security and Medicare that are not limited by regular congressional appropriation. Arguing that 75 percent of the domestic budget is now in this category, Michel insisted that federal spending could never be brought under control unless the rules were changed on some entitlements. In 1979, Michel introduced an amendment that successfully blocked the House from making child welfare payments a new entitlement.

Michel's conservatism is primarily fiscal. Although he is a strong opponent of abortion, he has never had much in common with the New Right social conservatives who began entering House Republican ranks in large numbers in the late 1970s.

At the beginning of 1979, when that year's aggressive class of GOP freshmen accused Rhodes of being too compliant with the majority Democrats, Michel found himself under attack as part of the Rhodes leadership. He chafed privately at talk that he was not combative enough, citing the years he had spent fighting to cut HEW budgets. But he found it difficult to defend himself without appearing to break with Rhodes.

Rhodes announced his impending retirement as party leader in December 1979, and from that time on Michel and Vander Jagt were open competitors for the leadership job.

Michel started out with a big advantage among senior members, who knew him well, and among most moderates, who found him less strident than Vander Jagt. But Vander Jagt, as chairman of the campaign committee that donated money to GOP challengers, had the edge among those first elected in 1978.

The sparring between the two candidates extended to the Republican National Convention in Detroit. When Vander Jagt was selected as keynote speaker, Michel's forces complained, and their man was made floor manager for Ronald Reagan.

In the weeks before the November election, it was clear that Michel had an edge. Vander Jagt needed the benefit of a unusually large new 1980 Republican class to have any chance.

The returns actually brought 52 new Republicans, more than Vander Jagt had even hoped for. But by installing Republican control in the White House and in the Senate, the election also helped Michel. It allowed him to argue successfully that President Reagan needed a tactician to help him move his program through the House, not a fiery speaker. Vander Jagt got his majority of the newcomers, but it was not a large enough majority to deny Michel the leadership.

**At Home:** Michel has had plenty of time to concentrate on mastering the politics of Congress; the politics of Peoria are not a problem for him. In his quarter century in elective office, he has had only one primary and few competitive general elections.

Michel was born in Peoria, the son of a French immigrant factory worker. Shortly after graduating from Bradley University in Peoria, he went to work for the district's newly-elected congressman, Republican Harold Velde.

Velde became chairman of the old House Un-American Activities Committee during the Republican-dominated 83rd Congress (1953-55) and received much publicity for his hunt for Communist subversives. Michel rose to become Velde's administrative assistant.

In 1956, Velde retired and Michel ran for the seat. Still not very well known in the district, Michel nevertheless had the support of many of the county organizations, whose only political contact he had been in Washington. He won the primary with 48 percent of the vote against four opponents.

The Democratic nominee usually draws a respectable vote, but it is nothing for Republicans to worry about in normal times. Michel's only relatively close races have been in the Democratic years of 1964 and 1974. Even then, his victory margins were 13,000 and 12,000 votes respectively.

**The District:** The 18th has been Republican throughout this century. Everett M. Dirksen represented it in the House throughout the New Deal era and on into President Truman's administration.

The one area of Democratic strength is in the industrial Peoria-Pekin area, but even there Republicans score occasional victories. Richard Carver, the mayor of Peoria and former president of the U.S. Conference of Mayors, is a Republican.

Peoria houses the headquarters of Caterpillar Tractor Co., which has numerous plants throughout northern Illinois. Most of the rest of the district consists of rich farm lands lying along the

Illinois River basin. In the western part of the district lies Knox County (Galesburg), which con-

tains Agriculture Secretary John R. Block's prosperous farm.

## Committees

**Minority Leader**

## Elections

**1980 General**

| | |
|---|---|
| Robert Michel (R ) | 125,561 (62 %) |
| John Knuppel (D ) | 76,471 (38 %) |

**1978 General**

| | |
|---|---|
| Robert Michel (R ) | 85,973 (66 %) |
| Virgil Grunkemeyer (D ) | 44,527 (34 %) |

**Previous Winning Percentages**

| | | | |
|---|---|---|---|
| 1976 (58 %) | 1974 (55 %) | 1972 (65 %) | 1970 (66 %) |
| 1968 (61 %) | 1966 (58 %) | 1964 (54 %) | 1962 (61 %) |
| 1960 (59 %) | 1958 (60 %) | 1956 (59 %) | |

**District Vote For President**

| | 1980 | | 1976 | | 1972 |
|---|---|---|---|---|---|
| D | 67,918 (33 %) | D | 88,371 (43 %) | D | 67,503 (34 %) |
| R | 124,436 (60 %) | R | 113,592 (56 %) | R | 128,247 (65 %) |
| I | 13,326 (6 %) | | | | |

## Campaign Finance

| | Receipts | Receipts from PACs | Expenditures |
|---|---|---|---|
| **1980** | | | |
| Michel (R ) | $168,068 | $104,825 (62 %) | $101,391 |
| Knuppel (D ) | $34,894 | $7,300 (21 %) | $34,483 |
| **1978** | | | |
| Michel (R ) | $72,330 | $29,707 (41 %) | $57,439 |

## Voting Studies

| | Presidential Support | | Party Unity | | Conservative Coalition | |
|---|---|---|---|---|---|---|
| Year | S | O | S | O | S | O |
| 1980 | 37 | 51 | 84 | 8 | 79 | 12 |
| 1979 | 30 | 58 | 76 | 12 | 85 | 6 |
| 1978 | 42 | 56 | 77 | 14 | 80 | 12 |
| 1977 | 44 | 44 | 75 | 10 | 82 | 4 |
| 1976 | 78 | 12 | 87 | 8 | 85 | 10 |
| 1975 | 88 | 8 | 82 | 9 | 82 | 10 |
| 1974 (Ford) | 65 | 22 | | | | |
| 1974 | 79 | 9 | 69 | 15 | 77 | 15 |
| 1973 | 75 | 17 | 84 | 7 | 86 | 5 |
| 1972 | 51 | 24 | 72 | 10 | 77 | 7 |
| 1971 | 75 | 16 | 74 | 10 | 76 | 6 |
| 1970 | 74 | 9 | 74 | 7 | 70 | 7 |
| 1969 | 64 | 28 | 69 | 20 | 80 | 11 |
| 1968 | 42 | 38 | 66 | 13 | 63 | 18 |
| 1967 | 37 | 51 | 84 | 7 | 81 | 7 |
| 1966 | 32 | 44 | 71 | 4 | 65 | 5 |
| 1965 | 27 | 54 | 76 | 10 | 76 | 12 |
| 1964 | 35 | 58 | 71 | 10 | 83 | 17 |
| 1963 | 18 | 55 | 67 | 9 | 53 | 27 |
| 1962 | 18 | 65 | 75 | 5 | 81 | 0 |
| 1961 | 22 | 60 | 69 | 14 | 78 | 9 |

S = Support          O = Opposition

## Key Votes

**96th Congress**

| | |
|---|---|
| Weaken Carter oil profits tax (1979) | Y |
| Reject hospital cost control plan (1979) | Y |
| Implement Panama Canal Treaties (1979) | N |
| Establish Department of Education (1979) | N |
| Approve Anti-busing Amendment (1979) | N |
| Guarantee Chrysler Corp. loans (1979) | N |
| Approve military draft registration (1980) | X |
| Aid Sandinista regime in Nicaragua (1980) | N |
| Strengthen fair housing laws (1980) | N |

**97th Congress**

| | |
|---|---|
| Reagan budget proposal (1981) | Y |

## Interest Group Ratings

| Year | ADA | ACA | AFL-CIO | CCUS |
|---|---|---|---|---|
| 1980 | 6 | 82 | 11 | 74 |
| 1979 | 5 | 87 | 10 | 100 |
| 1978 | 15 | 75 | 5 | 89 |
| 1977 | 15 | 88 | 9 | 94 |
| 1976 | 5 | 81 | 9 | 94 |
| 1975 | 16 | 81 | 9 | 100 |
| 1974 | 9 | 93 | 18 | 100 |
| 1973 | 0 | 88 | 0 | 100 |
| 1972 | 6 | 94 | 30 | 90 |
| 1971 | 3 | 96 | 0 | - |
| 1970 | 20 | 82 | 14 | 88 |
| 1969 | 7 | 75 | 33 | - |
| 1968 | 25 | 90 | 75 | - |
| 1967 | 7 | 89 | 0 | 100 |
| 1966 | 6 | 75 | 8 | - |
| 1965 | 0 | 84 | - | 90 |
| 1964 | 8 | 83 | 27 | - |
| 1963 | - | 100 | - | - |
| 1962 | 14 | 87 | 9 | - |
| 1961 | 0 | - | - | - |

# 19 Tom Railsback (R)

**Of Moline — Elected in 1966**

**Born:** Jan. 22, 1932, Moline, Ill.
**Education:** Grinnell College, B.A. 1954; Northwestern U. Law School, J.D. 1957.
**Military Career:** Army, 1957-59.
**Profession:** Lawyer.
**Family:** Wife, Patricia Sloan; four children.
**Religion:** Congregationalist.
**Political Career:** Ill. House, 1963-67.

**In Washington:** When the House Judiciary Committee debated President Nixon's impeachment in 1974, Railsback was at the center of the drama. He was one of a half dozen Republicans on the committee who put together a fragile bipartisan coalition that drafted obstruction of justice charges and built a majority for them.

It was a role Railsback loves to play — the judicious centrist mediating among the extreme positions. But he has played it only occasionally in the years since then. The committee went into partial eclipse after Watergate, beset by controversial social issues and limited in its legislative output, and Railsback has had a relatively low profile in the House.

By 1979, Railsback was second in seniority among committee Republicans to Robert McClory of Illinois. But he was openly dissatisfied with the way things had gone in the preceding five years. There's been "way too much partisan wrangling," he said. "Back in the old days we used to have legislation by consensus. Now it seems to me the committee is being polarized way left and way right ... we need some more moderates."

Even in a frustrating period on the Judiciary Committee, Railsback had a few chances to exercise his negotiating skills. In 1976, the panel was determined to write a gun control bill despite organized and vocal opposition. Dominated by pro-control Democrats, it narrowly passed one banning the manufacture and sale of concealable weapons.

Railsback, who supported the goal of the bill, said it was too strict ever to pass the full House. He maneuvered the legislation back to subcommittee, where it was changed to limit its application to "Saturday Night Specials" and similar handguns, lethal weapons that have relatively few loyal defenders. He said his bill offered the only chance for a "bipartisan consensus ... which can be enacted into law."

Railsback got his compromise bill through the full committee on its second consideration. But whether the consensus would have held on the floor will never be known. In the heat of an election year, with few members eager to confront the issue, it never reached the floor. Nothing has come that close since.

In 1980, Railsback took a similar position on a new open housing bill. The thrust of the bill was to give the Department of Housing and Urban Development the power to take its own action against those it felt were discriminating in the sale of property. Railsback added stronger appeal rights for those accused, helping the bill win the votes of all but five Judiciary Republicans as it was reported out of the committee. It later passed the House, in slightly altered form, but never came to a vote in the Senate.

Railsback's role as a broker between the Democrats and the more conservative wing of his own party has become even more important in the 97th Congress, as committee liberals rally to protect legislation of the past.

In the 96th Congress Railsback's most controversial legislative work was his bill restricting the role of organized contributors in congressional campaigns.

Along with Democrat David Obey of Wisconsin, Railsback brought to the floor a bill limiting to $6,000 the amount political action committees could normally give to a candidate in one election year. It had overwhelming Democratic support, but Republicans were nearly as vehement against

---

**19th District: West — Moline, Rock Island.** Population: 474,872 (3% increase since 1970). Race: White 453,330 (95%), Black 12,423 (3%), Others 9,119 (2%). Spanish origin: 13,859 (3%).

it, feeling that it limited the role conservative and business oriented groups could play in helping GOP challengers.

In the end, Railsback got 29 Republican votes, and the bill passed the House 217-198. But it added to the perception of Railsback as substantially to the left of most of his House Republican colleagues. After the bill passed, Minority Leader John J. Rhodes accused Railsback and others of insufficient party loyalty.

For much of the past decade, Railsback has struggled with a frustrating voice problem that sometimes left him unable to speak above a hoarse whisper. Explained as the result of a freak throat injury he suffered while playing paddle ball in 1973, the condition made him sound emotionally overwrought during much of the impeachment debate, adding a false note of drama to the proceedings. The problem has responded to therapy, and Railsback now suffers only from an occasional quaver in his voice.

In 1981, Railsback faced problems of a different sort — reports that he was among several Republican congressmen sharing a House in Florida for a weekend with lobbyist Paula Parkinson, who said later she traded sexual favors for members' votes. Railsback admitted he had "made a mistake" even staying in the House, but insisted "she didn't proposition me . . . I didn't touch her."

**At Home:** It took an extraordinary Democratic landslide to clear Railsback's path to Congress.

The 19th District, consistently Republican for most of this century, seemed safe in 1964 for GOP Rep. Robert McLoskey, who had taken it over just two years before. No one even entered the 1964 Democratic primary. But Gale Schisler, a 31-year-old junior high school principal, won the Democratic nomination as a write-in candidate and became the beneficiary of the Johnson presidential landslide.

Had McLoskey been re-elected in 1964, he would almost certainly have remained in office for years to come. But with his defeat, local Republicans began looking for a new face to challenge Schisler in 1966. Railsback was a 34-year-old state representative from Moline who had proved to be a popular and personable campaigner. The Republican organization settled on him as the nominee and he was unopposed in the primary. He defeated Schisler by 6,845 votes.

Since then, Railsback has had extraordinary political success. In 1968, he dispatched a highly regarded Democratic opponent by nearly 50,000 votes, and since then, Democrats have run only nominal candidates or none at all.

Railsback has proved popular with the district's blue-collar vote as well as its rural and small-town population. He has several times received the backing of the United Auto Workers, an important union in the district.

**The District:** The 19th spreads north and south along the Mississippi River from the industrial centers of Rock Island and Moline, taking in miles of corn, hogs and cattle. About one-third of the population lives in Rock Island County, center of one of the country's most intensive concentrations of the farm equipment industry.

Deere & Company is headquartered in the county, at Moline, and has several plants elsewhere in the district, as does International Harvester. It is among the blue-collar population in Rock Island County that the United Auto Workers is strong.

The Democratic vote in the Rock Island area is usually offset by the Republican vote in the remaining dozen rural and small-town counties. But unlike some of the neighboring central Illinois districts, the 19th goes Democratic reasonably often in statewide elections. Sen. Adlai E. Stevenson III received 56.7 percent of the vote in the district in 1974, and Democrat Daniel Walker carried it in his successful 1972 gubernatorial race.

## Committees

**Judiciary** (2nd of 12 Republicans)
    Courts, Civil Liberties and Administration of Justice; Monopolies and Commercial Law.

**Select Narcotics Abuse and Control** (Ranking Republican)

## Elections

**1980 General**

| | |
|---|---|
| Tom Railsback (R ) | 142,616 (73 %) |
| Thomas Hand (D ) | 51,753 (27 %) |

**1978 General**

| | |
|---|---|
| Tom Railsback (R) | Unopposed |

**Previous Winning Percentages**

| | | | |
|---|---|---|---|
| 1976 (69 %) | 1974 (65 %) | 1972 (100%) | 1970 (68 %) |
| 1968 (64 %) | 1966 (52 %) | | |

**District Vote For President**

| | 1980 | 1976 | 1972 |
|---|---|---|---|
| D | 71,381 (35 %) | 91,935 (46 %) | 77,194 (38 %) |
| R | 114,431 (57 %) | 107,012 (53 %) | 124,549 (62 %) |
| I | 13,002 (7 %) | | |

*Tom Railsback, R-Ill.*

## Campaign Finance

| | Receipts | Receipts from PACs | Expen-ditures |
|---|---|---|---|
| **1980** | | | |
| Railsback (R) | $72,297 | $14,275 (20 %) | $78,384 |
| **1978** | | | |
| Railsback (R) | $38,529 | $8,968 (23 %) | $28,647 |

## Voting Studies

| | Presidental Support | | Party Unity | | Conservative Coalition | |
|---|---|---|---|---|---|---|
| Year | S | O | S | O | S | O |
| 1980 | 49 | 34 | 49 | 35 | 44 | 39 |
| 1979 | 52 | 36 | 44 | 48 | 55 | 38 |
| 1978 | 51 | 38 | 54 | 40 | 57 | 37 |
| 1977 | 52 | 35 | 47 | 36 | 51 | 35 |
| 1976 | 51 | 43 | 49 | 43 | 61 | 31 |
| 1975 | 65 | 29 | 54 | 31 | 63 | 26 |
| 1974 (Ford) | 52 | 37 | | | | |
| 1974 | 64 | 25 | 54 | 37 | 51 | 38 |
| 1973 | 51 | 35† | 49 | 41† | 56 | 36† |
| 1972 | 76 | 8 | 52 | 34 | 51 | 32 |
| 1971 | 58 | 25 | 47 | 31 | 43 | 32 |
| 1970 | 66 | 18 | 51 | 35 | 34 | 39 |
| 1969 | 55 | 34 | 51 | 31 | 40 | 42 |
| 1968 | 58 | 28 | 56 | 30 | 53 | 39 |
| 1967 | 56 | 42 | 71 | 27 | 61 | 35 |

S = Support   O = Opposition

† Not eligible for all roll call votes.

## Key Votes

**96th Congress**

| | |
|---|---|
| Weaken Carter oil profits tax (1979) | Y |
| Reject hospital cost control plan (1979) | Y |
| Implement Panama Canal Treaties (1979) | Y |
| Establish Department of Education (1979) | N |
| Approve Anti-busing Amendment (1979) | N |
| Guarantee Chrysler Corp. loans (1979) | Y |
| Approve military draft registration (1980) | N |
| Aid Sandinista regime in Nicaragua (1980) | Y |
| Strengthen fair housing laws (1980) | Y |

**97th Congress**

| | |
|---|---|
| Reagan budget proposal (1981) | Y |

## Interest Group Ratings

| Year | ADA | ACA | AFL-CIO | CCUS |
|---|---|---|---|---|
| 1980 | 44 | 52 | 41 | 66 |
| 1979 | 26 | 50 | 55 | 82 |
| 1978 | 20 | 56 | 25 | 72 |
| 1977 | 45 | 44 | 41 | 88 |
| 1976 | 25 | 50 | 32 | 57 |
| 1975 | 42 | 54 | 58 | 71 |
| 1974 | 30 | 46 | 45 | 67 |
| 1973 | 40 | 33 | 36 | 60 |
| 1972 | 44 | 47 | 22 | 57 |
| 1971 | 46 | 54 | 36 | - |
| 1970 | 48 | 53 | 40 | 67 |
| 1969 | 40 | 29 | 80 | - |
| 1968 | 33 | 55 | 75 | - |
| 1967 | 13 | 79 | 25 | 90 |

# 20  Paul Findley (R)

### Of Pittsfield — Elected 1960

**Born:** June 23, 1921, Jacksonville, Ill.
**Education:** Ill. College, A.B. 1943.
**Military Career:** Navy, 1943-45.
**Profession:** Publisher.
**Family:** Wife, Lucille Gemme; two children.
**Religion:** Congregationalist.
**Political Career:** Sought Republican nomination for Ill. Senate, 1952.

**In Washington:** Over 20 years in the House, Findley has moved out of his initial Farm Belt conservatism into an unpredictable pattern that leaves him consorting with Palestinian rebels one day and preaching free enterprise economics the next.

He is widely respected for his independence and integrity, but his lone-wolf style and undisguised self-esteem have cost him some of the authority he might otherwise command. A Lincoln scholar who represents Lincoln's old congressional district, Findley is not averse to occasional comparisons between himself and the Rail-Splitter. When the time comes for a major decision, he once said, he tries to figure out what Lincoln would have done.

The progression of Findley's political thinking is best illustrated by his attitude toward trade with communist nations. Early in his career, Findley bitterly opposed huge wheat deals with the Soviet Union. "Trading with the enemy is bad business, whether it be wheat or electronic gear," he said in a 1963 letter to President Kennedy.

But as American farmers began to benefit from such trade, Findley changed his mind. By 1967, he was calling for diplomatic recognition of (and trade with) mainland China, and saying it was time for the United States "to shake off some outmoded, self-defeating restrictions on agricultural trade with communist countries."

It is a position consistent with Findley's free market views on agriculture in general. Militantly opposed to most government efforts to keep crop prices up, he has seized on exports as a way to solve the problem through private enterprise.

It is more difficult to find the pragmatic clue to Findley's stand on relations between the United States and the Palestine Liberation Organization. Since meeting PLO leader Yasir Arafat in 1978, Findley has maintained close contact with the PLO and suggested that the State Department do the same. "We cannot continue to

wish away the PLO's existence and still expect to move forward toward an overall peace agreement in the Middle East," he has said.

When 69 Americans were taken hostage in Iran in November 1979, Findley suggested that the PLO might be able to negotiate their release, and thereby improve its image in the United States. A subsequent PLO effort to intervene in the hostage crisis never got off the ground.

Findley told one interviewer in 1979 that he was spending up to 90 percent of his time on PLO and related Middle East issues. But he sharply reduced his public involvement with the PLO early in 1980 when political opponents made his relationship with Arafat a campaign issue.

Findley's interest in foreign affairs developed in the mid-1960s when he chaired a House Republican task force on NATO issues. In 1965 he headed a mission to Paris to investigate French President DeGaulle's complaints about NATO. As a result of that experience, Findley became an advocate of an "Atlantic Union," a loose political and economic federation of democratic nations in the North Atlantic.

Findley was one of the first House Republicans to raise questions about U.S. involvement in the Vietnam War. In March 1968, saying the failure of President Johnson's Vietnam policy was "obvious," he suggested that the United States present its case in Vietnam to the World Court, and abide by that body's decision. Findley soft-

> **20th District: West — Springfield, Quincy.** Population: 486,141 (5% increase since 1970). Race: White 460,261 (95%), Black 22,454 (5%), Others 3,426 (1%). Spanish origin: 2,719 (1%).

ened his criticism of the war once President Nixon took office, and opposed most congressional efforts in the early 1970s to cut off funds for the war.

Findley joined the House Agriculture Committee early in his first term, but left it in 1967 to take a seat on the less influential Foreign Affairs Committee. In 1970 he was given special permission to gain back his seat on Agriculture while remaining on Foreign Affairs.

Representing one of the more prosperous agricultural areas of the nation, Findley has long opposed most federal farm subsidies, arguing against them in the face of bipartisan opposition in the Agriculture Committee and seeking to reduce them on the House floor. In 1968 he wrote a book, *The Federal Farm Fable*, that skewered the programs and bureaucrats of the Department of Agriculture. In 1973, amidst reports of huge subsidy overpayments to some farmers, Findley succeeded in imposing a $20,000 annual limit on subsidies that could be paid to any farmer.

For years one of Findley's pet targets was the sugar quota, which guaranteed U.S. markets for major sugar-producing nations in exchange for limits on the amount they shipped in. He argued that the quota amounted to a government subsidy for each of those nations, including several dictatorial regimes in the Caribbean region. Opposition by Findley and others killed the quota system in 1974.

In early 1981, Findley was a strong supporter of the Reagan efforts to block a scheduled April 1st increase in dairy price supports. He said dairy price supports were costing consumers $2.7 billion a year in higher retail prices.

Findley's interest in Abraham Lincoln is a personal trademark. For years his press releases bore Lincoln's silhouette. His office is a small museum, crammed with Lincoln memorabilia.

**At Home:** In 1980, Findley's independent streak got him into one of the most difficult situations in his political career.

First, he received a serious primary challenge from Quincy Mayor David Nuessen, who came within 7,000 votes of defeating him. Then an aggressive young Democratic candidate, former state Rep. David Robinson, drew the same percentage Nuessen had — 44 percent of the vote.

The source of the problem was Findley's contacts with the PLO, and his belief in Palestinian self-determination as the way to peace in the Middle East. Both Nuessen and Robinson said Findley was spending too much time with Palestinians and not enough on the needs and interests of his district.

Findley countered with a defense of his ac-

tions but also with new emphasis on contacts with local Republican Party leaders. His personal popularity, built up over years of intensive constituent service, saw him through to another term, although not by as much as he might have hoped for in a Republican district in a solid Republican year.

Born in his district, Findley founded the *Pike Press* in Pittsfield shortly after he returned from World War II. He ran for the state Senate in 1952, but narrowly lost the primary.

In 1960, Republican Rep. Edna Simpson retired from Congress after one term. This time Findley won, drawing one-third of the vote in a four-man Republican primary and 55.6 percent in November.

Findley had a good Republican district, but he had little opportunity to rest. In 1962, redistricting combined his primarily rural territory with the district centered on Springfield, represented by a longtime Democratic incumbent, Peter Mack.

The Findley-Mack race was one of the hardest-fought in the country that year, and received national attention. Mack carried his home area in Sangamon County (Springfield) and two other counties, but Findley won the remaining 11, mostly rural counties, and the election.

That victory secured him for years. In 1964, in the face of the national Democratic landslide, Findley turned back a strong Democratic challenger by almost 21,000 votes. From then until 1980, his only close contest was in 1974, when Mack sensed the national Democratic tide and thought the moment was ripe for a comeback. Findley's margin of 14,875 votes was one of the smallest of his career, but his seat was not threatened.

**The District:** The 20th District is a combination of two historic central and western Illinois congressional districts. The western portion, from which Findley was originally elected in 1960, is one of the oldest settled areas of the state. The original residents came from below the Mason-Dixon Line and kept their Democratic allegiance. But they were also conservative, and by the 1940s, the district had fallen into Republican hands.

The other part of the district centers around Sangamon County, which contains Springfield, the state capital. This is the district Lincoln represented in Congress from 1847 to 1849. It is corn and hog country. Findley's hometown of Pittsfield likes to call itself "The Hog Capital of the World."

The three major urban centers are Springfield, Quincy, and Alton. As the state capital, Springfield has a large contingent of white-collar government workers. It is also the center of a prosperous Lincoln-oriented tourist business.

Quincy and Alton are old river ports which now manufacture machinery, glass and steel.

## Committees

**Agriculture** (2nd of 19 Republicans)
Domestic Marketing, Consumer Relations, and Nutrition; Wheat, Soybeans, and Feed Grains.

**Foreign Affairs** (3rd of 16 Republicans)
Europe and the Middle East.

## Elections

**1980 General**

| | |
|---|---|
| Paul Findley (R ) | 123,427 (56 %) |
| David Robinson (D ) | 96,950 (44 %) |

**1980 Primary**

| | |
|---|---|
| Paul Findley (R ) | 31,894 (56 %) |
| David Nuessen (R ) | 25,499 (44 %) |

**1978 General**

| | |
|---|---|
| Paul Findley (R) | 111,054 (70 %) |
| Vic Roberts (D) | 48,426 (30 %) |

**Previous Winning Percentages**

| | | | |
|---|---|---|---|
| 1976 (64 %) | 1974 (55 %) | 1972 (69 %) | 1970 (68 %) |
| 1968 (66 %) | 1966 (62 %) | | |

**District Vote For President**

| | 1980 | | 1976 | | 1972 |
|---|---|---|---|---|---|
| D | 79,942 (36 %) | D | 104,318 (47 %) | D | 77,088 (36 %) |
| R | 130,067 (58 %) | R | 114,768 (52 %) | R | 136,963 (64 %) |
| I | 10,965 (5 %) | | | | |

## Campaign Finance

| | Receipts | Receipts from PACs | Expen-ditures |
|---|---|---|---|
| **1980** | | | |
| Findley (R ) | $552,118 | $196,221 (35 %) | $530,568 |
| Robinson (D ) | $632,278 | $60,605 (10 %) | $631,098 |
| **1978** | | | |
| Findley (R ) | $126,180 | $21,760 (17 %) | $117,721 |
| Roberts (D ) | $7,320 | $500 (7 %) | $7,318 |

## Voting Studies

| | Presidential Support | | Party Unity | | Conservative Coalition | |
|---|---|---|---|---|---|---|
| Year | S | O | S | O | S | O |
| 1980 | 50 | 38 | 61 | 30 | 67 | 23 |
| 1979 | 57 | 37 | 57 | 39 | 55 | 40 |
| 1978 | 61 | 31 | 56 | 39 | 59 | 38 |
| 1977 | 46 | 51 | 56 | 41 | 54 | 40 |
| 1976 | 51 | 24 | 54 | 31 | 59 | 34 |
| 1975 | 74 | 20 | 64 | 26 | 64 | 27 |

| | | | | | | |
|---|---|---|---|---|---|---|
| 1974 (Ford) | 54 | 26 | | | | |
| 1974 | 72 | 17 | 51 | 33 | 45 | 41 |
| 1973 | 58 | 39 | 51 | 44 | 47 | 51 |
| 1972 | 65 | 11 | 73 | 18 | 65 | 27 |
| 1971 | 68 | 19 | 65 | 26 | 58 | 32 |
| 1970 | 72 | 14 | 64 | 21 | 52 | 25 |
| 1969 | 64 | 17 | 44 | 49 | 42 | 51 |
| 1968 | 60 | 32 | 66 | 24 | 73 | 22 |
| 1967 | 38 | 50 | 84 | 8 | 74 | 19 |
| 1966 | 37 | 49 | 73 | 9 | 70 | 8 |
| 1965 | 33 | 57 | 81 | 7 | 78 | 8 |
| 1964 | 29 | 71 | 95 | 2 | 92 | 8 |
| 1963 | 21 | 73 | 93 | 5 | 67 | 27 |
| 1962 | 23 | 67 | 88 | 4 | 88 | 6 |
| 1961 | 20 | 69 | 83 | 5 | 91 | 0 |

S = Support    O = Opposition

## Key Votes

**96th Congress**

| | |
|---|---|
| Weaken Carter oil profits tax (1979) | Y |
| Reject hospital cost control plan (1979) | Y |
| Implement Panama Canal Treaties (1979) | Y |
| Establish Department of Education (1979) | N |
| Approve Anti-busing Amendment (1979) | N |
| Guarantee Chrysler Corp. loans (1979) | N |
| Approve military draft registration (1980) | Y |
| Aid Sandinista regime in Nicaragua (1980) | Y |
| Strengthen fair housing laws (1980) | N |

**97th Congress**

| | |
|---|---|
| Reagan budget proposal (1981) | Y |

## Interest Group Ratings

| Year | ADA | ACA | AFL-CIO | CCUS |
|---|---|---|---|---|
| 1980 | 28 | 70 | 17 | 73 |
| 1979 | 42 | 54 | 50 | 78 |
| 1978 | 35 | 79 | 15 | 71 |
| 1977 | 45 | 59 | 27 | 81 |
| 1976 | 35 | 56 | 15 | 80 |
| 1975 | 37 | 68 | 18 | 69 |
| 1974 | 48 | 36 | 20 | 67 |
| 1973 | 56 | 58 | 27 | 64 |
| 1972 | 25 | 70 | 18 | 90 |
| 1971 | 41 | 63 | 8 | - |
| 1970 | 28 | 54 | 14 | 71 |
| 1969 | 40 | 53 | 60 | - |
| 1968 | 17 | 81 | 50 | - |
| 1967 | 13 | 93 | 0 | 100 |
| 1966 | 12 | 80 | 0 | - |
| 1965 | 0 | 88 | - | 100 |
| 1964 | 4 | 95 | 9 | - |
| 1963 | - | 100 | - | - |
| 1962 | 25 | 100 | 0 | - |
| 1961 | 0 | - | - | - |

# 21 Edward R. Madigan (R)

### Of Lincoln — Elected 1972

**Born:** Jan. 13, 1936, Lincoln, Ill.
**Education:** Lincoln College, A.A. 1955.
**Profession:** Auto leasing executive.
**Family:** Wife, Evelyn M. George; three children.
**Religion:** Roman Catholic.
**Political Career:** Ill. House, 1967-73.

**In Washington:** A quiet conservative willing to submerge his partisanship in exchange for a share in the action, Madigan has written more legislation in recent years than most members of the majority party.

Nearly all of it has been on the subject of transportation, in partnership with Democrat James J. Florio, chairman of the Commerce Transportation Subcommittee on which Madigan serves. The two men were dominant in the drafting of the 1980 railroad deregulation act, reworking it throughout the year to outmaneuver its opponents if possible, or pacify them if necessary.

In committee, Madigan kept most of the bill's basic coalition intact by winning approval of an amendment requiring railroads to prove that they faced competitive situations before they could escape government rate review. On the floor, he won agreement to extend special rate treatment to smaller shippers, keeping an important bloc on board. The bill remained in dispute until the final days of the 96th Congress, when one last compromise resulted in enactment.

Earlier in the Congress, Madigan and Florio worked together on legislation allowing the bankrupt Rock Island Railroad to maintain freight service, nine days before the service was scheduled to end.

Madigan interrupted his bipartisan approach, however, to fight Florio on the question of a "superfund" through which oil and chemical companies would finance cleanup operations at sites of dangerous spills. From the beginning of consideration, Madigan objected to the idea of forcing the companies to contribute to the fund, frequently arguing with Florio, his usual ally and supporter of a tough bill. He voted for the legislation on the House floor, but when Florio agreed in conference to a bill covering chemical but not oil spills, he tried to defeat it, and narrowly failed.

Madigan has been somewhat less visible but still active on the House Agriculture Committee, where he has been one of the few farm state Republicans willing to apply free market principles to crops that grow in his district. He fought a farm disaster aid bill that he called the "fat cat relief bill of 1977," and the next year sent a "Dear Colleague" letter to all House members urging them to reject a farm price support bill because payment levels were too high. Madigan's farm constituents, among the more prosperous in the Midwest, tolerate that approach somewhat better than counterparts in other districts.

**At Home:** Madigan was in the right place in 1972, when Republican Rep. William Springer retired. He was chairman of the state House Reapportionment Committee, charged with redrawing the district's lines. The new map had to go through a federal court, but it preserved the district's Republican leanings, and Madigan filed for Congress.

The contest for the Republican nomination was a generational affair, with Madigan representing the area's younger Republican politicians. His main competitor was Elbert Smith, 60, a downstate GOP veteran who had served as state auditor from 1957 to 1961. Madigan was an easy winner with more than 70 percent of the primary vote.

His first general election, however, was not quite as simple as had been expected. Democrats nominated Champaign County District Attorney Lawrence Johnson, one of their strongest candidates in years. Johnson was a proven vote-getter in a Republican county and was popular with the

---

**21st District: Central — Champaign, Urbana.** Population: 490,872 (6% increase since 1970). Race: White 448,796 (91%), Black 34,020 (7%), Others 8,056 (2%). Spanish origin: 4,645 (1%).

large bloc of newly-enfranchised student voters in the district. Madigan made it, but his 54 percent of the vote was not impressive at a time when President Nixon and Republican Sen. Charles H. Percy were sweeping to victory. In succeeding years, however, Madigan has easily consolidated his position.

**The District:** A prosperous central Illinois district with an agricultural base, the 21st also has several important urban centers.

The main population areas are Champaign-Urbana, with the University of Illinois and 60,000 students, and Decatur, a brass and iron manufacturing city and market center for soybeans. Bloomington is an insurance headquarters as well as home of Illinois State University.

The district is generally Republican, with some Democratic strength in Macon County (Decatur) and in the university communities.

## Committees

**Energy and Commerce** (5th of 18 Republicans)
Commerce, Transportation, and Tourism; Health and the Environment.

## Elections

**1980 General**

| | |
|---|---|
| Edward Madigan (R ) | 132,186 (68 %) |
| Penny Severns (D ) | 63,476 (32 %) |

**1978 General**

| | |
|---|---|
| Edward Madigan (R ) | 97,473 (78 %) |
| Ken Baughman (D ) | 27,054 (22 %) |

**Previous Winning Percentages**

1976 (75 %)    1974 (66 %)    1972 (55 %)

**District Vote For President**

| | 1980 | | 1976 | | 1972 |
|---|---|---|---|---|---|
| D | 66,222 (33 %) | D | 85,545 (44 %) | D | 70,046 (37 %) |
| R | 112,979 (56 %) | R | 107,154 (55 %) | R | 117,220 (62 %) |
| I | 19,334 (10 %) | | | | |

## Campaign Finance

| | Receipts | Receipts from PACs | Expenditures |
|---|---|---|---|
| **1980** | | | |
| Madigan (R ) | $147,512 | $52,605 (36 %) | $148,147 |
| Severns (D ) | $27,139 | $8,420 (31 %) | $21,439 |
| **1978** | | | |
| Madigan (R ) | $89,033 | $26,044 (29 %) | $78,219 |

## Voting Studies

| | Presidential Support | | Party Unity | | Conservative Coalition | |
|---|---|---|---|---|---|---|
| Year | S | O | S | O | S | O |
| 1980 | 40 | 50 | 78 | 15 | 74 | 13 |

| | | | | | | |
|---|---|---|---|---|---|---|
| 1979 | 50 | 43 | 59 | 31 | 72 | 21 |
| 1978 | 44 | 44 | 62 | 26 | 68 | 20 |
| 1977 | 54 | 42 | 60 | 34 | 67 | 27 |
| 1976 | 71 | 22 | 62 | 28 | 68 | 22 |
| 1975 | 65 | 27 | 65 | 28 | 71 | 23 |
| 1974 (Ford) | 56 | 35 | | | | |
| 1974 | 55 | 28 | 54 | 33 | 51 | 34 |
| 1973 | 69 | 30 | 66 | 30 | 72 | 25 |

S = Support          O = Opposition

## Key Votes

**96th Congress**

| | |
|---|---|
| Weaken Carter oil profits tax (1979) | Y |
| Reject hospital cost control plan (1979) | Y |
| Implement Panama Canal Treaties (1979) | Y |
| Establish Department of Education (1979) | Y |
| Approve Anti-busing Amendment (1979) | N |
| Guarantee Chrysler Corp. loans (1979) | Y |
| Approve military draft registration (1980) | N |
| Aid Sandinista regime in Nicaragua (1980) | N |
| Strengthen fair housing laws (1980) | N |

**97th Congress**

| | |
|---|---|
| Reagan budget proposal (1981) | Y |

## Interest Group Ratings

| Year | ADA | ACA | AFL-CIO | CCUS |
|---|---|---|---|---|
| 1980 | 11 | 76 | 24 | 68 |
| 1979 | 37 | 68 | 32 | 76 |
| 1978 | 30 | 80 | 25 | 75 |
| 1977 | 15 | 52 | 41 | 76 |
| 1976 | 20 | 68 | 18 | 76 |
| 1975 | 21 | 63 | 39 | 71 |
| 1974 | 26 | 57 | 40 | 44 |
| 1973 | 16 | 73 | 27 | 73 |

# 22 Daniel B. Crane (R)

**Of Danville — Elected 1978**

**Born:** Jan. 10, 1936, Chicago, Ill.
**Education:** Hillsdale College, B.A. 1958; Indiana
U. School of Dentistry, D.D.S. 1963.
**Military Career:** Army, 1967-70.
**Profession:** Dentist.
**Family:** Wife, Judy Van Brunt; five children.
**Religion:** Methodist.
**Political Career:** Sought Republican nomination for U.S. House, 1966.

**In Washington:** Dan Crane offers a contrast to the drive and intensity that led his older brother, Phil, who represents Illinois' 12th District, to seek the presidency in 1980. The two Cranes share a conservative political ideology, but little else.

Flippant and relaxed, Dan Crane ambles into the House chamber from the House gym most afternoons, slapping his fellow members on the back and trading stories, but rarely staying to participate in the debate.

The style was evident one day in 1979. Dan Crane made the nominating speech for his Illinois colleague, Edward J. Derwinski, who was running for Republican Conference chairman. The speech was loaded with Polish jokes about "Big Ed" and comments about other members. In the right situation, it might have been entertaining, but Derwinski already had a reputation as being a shade irreverent for an important leadership post. Crane's speech made him sound frivolous. Derwinski dropped out of the race after finishing last on the first ballot.

On the Education and Labor Committee, Crane fought hard in the 96th Congress against legislation that would allow unionization of hospital interns. While New Jersey Democrat Frank Thompson argued that anyone who works 80 to 100 hours a week "... ought to have something to say about his or her working conditions," Crane contended that collective bargaining would increase medical costs. He said the mere existence of a bargaining situation would lead the interns to ask for more benefits and more wages. "No one ever asked for fewer benefits and wages," he said.

The bill cleared the Education and Labor Committee with bipartisan support and Thompson brought it to the House floor, but Crane and other junior Republicans raised enough opposition to give it an unexpected 227-167 defeat, and

it died in the 96th Congress.

At the start of the 97th Congress, Crane became active in the drive to re-create a House committee to probe subversion and terrorism. "You can help close the door to wild revolutionaries," he said in a fund raising letter to conservatives. "I need $14,800 to kick off my anti-terrorism campaign."

**At Home:** Crane joined his brother Philip in the House in 1978 when the 22nd District became vacant on the retirement of Democratic Rep. George Shipley.

The second eldest of three living Crane brothers, Daniel had made the family's first attempt to win a House seat more than a decade before. He finished third in 1966 in a Republican primary in the 7th District of Indiana. Then he left the state for military service, eventually opening a dental practice in Danville, Illinois, just across the border from his previous home.

Shipley made it clear early that he planned to retire in 1978, and Crane announced his congressional candidacy 11 months before the election. He traded on contacts from work he had done in 1976 for Ronald Reagan's presidential campaign, and hired Richard A. Viguerie's computerized direct-mail operation. That combination gave him a substantial edge over the two other GOP contenders.

The Democrats nominated a popular state senator, Terry Bruce, and the race was considered

---

**22nd District: Southeast — Danville.** Population: 490,731 (6% increase since 1970). Race: White 479,097 (98%), Black 8,430 (2%), Others 3,204 (1%). Spanish origin: 3,128 (1%).

a tossup. But Bruce proved unable to heal the divisions created by his primary, in which he defeated Shipley's brother-in-law, and he had little success with his charge that Crane's militant anti-communism might endanger soybean sales to Eastern Europe. Crane won with nearly 55 percent of the vote and was a routine winner in 1980, when Democrats had difficulty even coming up with a candidate.

**The District:** Once a Democratic district based in southern Illinois, the 22nd has shifted northeastward over the years into more Republican territory. In 1972, it picked up seven eastern counties including Vermilion (Danville), and lost Democratic votes in rural counties and in urban Madison County (Alton).

Shipley managed to survive the change on the strength of his personal popularity. But when he retired, the Democratic margin disappeared.

The district has two distinct parts: the northern portion is good Corn Belt farmland;, the southern area is less fertile and given more to general farming. Political divisions follow the economic ones; the northern area is more Republican. It is essentially a small-town district; Danville, its main city, has 40,000 people.

## Committees

**Post Office and Civil Service** (8th of 11 Republicans)
Census and Population; Compensation and Employee Benefits.

**Small Business** (8th of 17 Republicans)
Tax, Access to Equity Capital and Business Opportunities.

## Elections

**1980 General**

| | |
|---|---|
| Daniel Crane (R ) | 146,014 (69 %) |
| Peter Voelz (D ) | 66,065 (31 %) |

**1978 General**

| | |
|---|---|
| Daniel Crane (R ) | 86,051 (54 %) |
| Terry Bruce (D ) | 73,331 (46 %) |

**1978 Primary**

| | |
|---|---|
| Daniel Crane (R ) | 15,735 (46 %) |
| Roscoe Cunningham (R ) | 12,111 (36 %) |
| Gene Stunkel (R ) | 6,183 (18 %) |

**District Vote For President**

| | 1980 | | 1976 | | 1972 |
|---|---|---|---|---|---|
| D | 76,371 (35 %) | D | 106,097 (48 %) | D | 80,804 (36 %) |
| R | 131,160 (60 %) | R | 112,582 (51 %) | R | 141,820 (64 %) |
| I | 9,135 (4 %) | | | | |

## Campaign Finance

| | | Receipts | Expen- |
|---|---|---|---|
| | Receipts | from PACs | ditures |
| **1980** | | | |
| Crane (R ) | $170,313 | $21,275 (12 %) | $165,236 |
| Voelz (D ) | $20,288 | $5,550 (27 %) | $19,691 |

| **1978** | | | |
|---|---|---|---|
| Crane (R ) | $439,305 | $107,034 (24 %) | $438,764 |
| Bruce (D ) | $109,465 | $45,117 (41 %) | $107,281 |

## Voting Studies

| | Presidential Support | | Party Unity | | Conservative Coalition | |
|---|---|---|---|---|---|---|
| Year | S | O | S | O | S | O |
| 1980 | 21 | 69 | 89 | 3 | 85 | 8 |
| 1979 | 18 | 72 | 86 | 3 | 86 | 3 |

S = Support          O = Opposition

## Key Votes

**96th Congress**

| | |
|---|---|
| Weaken Carter oil profits tax (1979) | Y |
| Reject hospital cost control plan (1979) | Y |
| Implement Panama Canal Treaties (1979) | N |
| Establish Department of Education (1979) | N |
| Approve Anti-busing Amendment (1979) | Y |
| Guarantee Chrysler Corp. loans (1979) | N |
| Approve military draft registration (1980) | N |
| Aid Sandinista regime in Nicaragua (1980) | N |
| Strengthen fair housing laws (1980) | N |

**97th Congress**

| | |
|---|---|
| Reagan budget proposal (1981) | Y |

## Interest Group Ratings

| Year | ADA | ACA | AFL-CIO | CCUS |
|---|---|---|---|---|
| 1980 | 11 | 96 | 11 | 61 |
| 1979 | 5 | 100 | 5 | 100 |

# 23 Melvin Price (D)

### Of East St. Louis — Elected 1944

**Born:** Jan. 1, 1905, East St. Louis, Ill.
**Education:** Attended St. Louis U., 1923-25.
**Military Career:** Army, 1943-44.
**Profession:** Sports writer.
**Family:** Wife, Geraldine Freelin; one child.
**Religion:** Roman Catholic.
**Political Career:** No previous office.

**In Washington:** Price owes his Armed Services chairmanship to a revolt by junior members against his two autocratic predecessors, and he has rarely tried to be a forceful leader. He plays a moderator's role while other members take the lead on major issues.

Before Price, in the days of Chairmen L. Mendel Rivers and F. Edward Hebert, junior members were told what to do and when to do it, rarely even getting the opportunity to question witnesses. Since he was installed by the Democratic Caucus in 1975 to replace Hebert, Price has bent over to be fair to all, even at the risk of diluting his own influence. He has established temporary subcommittees and handed them over to those lowest in seniority. He even set one up for Ronald V. Dellums, the California Democrat whose harangues against militarism have made him an outcast on the committee.

He also offers all committee members large doses of foreign travel. Price leads multi-country junkets two or three times a year to China, the Soviet Union, the Middle East, Africa and Europe. Flying on well-stocked Air Force jets, often taking congressional spouses, the Price delegations usually meet with civilian and military leaders in the countries they visit.

A former baseball writer who has always been awkward and halting as a public speaker, Price still finds it more comfortable to talk about the St. Louis Cardinals than the defense budget. He does not appear on television interview programs. He does not often grant interviews to newspaper reporters. He relies on staff-written speeches in the committee and on the House floor, rarely speaking extemporaneously, and his staff often guides him through legislative debate. Price gives his aides wide authority to act for him; sometimes it appears they are running the committee.

After 35 years in Congress, Price remains a labor liberal on domestic issues, one who tries harder than most Democrats on his committee to be a party loyalist. But he is in the hawkish

Armed Services tradition. In the early 1970s, he supported the war in Vietnam long after it was politically unpopular. In the late 1970s, before most other Democrats, he decried the expansion of Soviet military power. Until 1980, his committee consistently approved more military spending than the rest of the Congress was willing to pay for. Now Congress has caught up.

Price likes to support all presidents on military issues, especially Democratic ones. But his inclination to increase military spending brought him into conflict with Jimmy Carter. In 1978, Price was particularly hurt when Carter vetoed a military authorization bill, criticizing Congress' insistence on building a nuclear-powered aircraft carrier. Uncharacteristically, Price fired back at the president. "The burden of your message is that Congress does not have a place in defense policy-making except insofar as it is prepared to rubber stamp recommendations of the executive branch," he wrote. "I reject that philosophy."

Price urged the House to override Carter. "I have always worked to strengthen our national security," he said, "and I have worked in this area with every president since Harry Truman. It is not pleasant for me to have to oppose a president now. If this veto is overridden, as I hope it will be, I will greet the result not with any sense of joy, but only with the belief that we in the House have performed our duty." But Price could not con-

---

**23rd District: Southwest — East St. Louis.** Population: 441,876 (5% decrease since 1970). Race: White 357,373 (81%), Black 79,962 (18%), Others 4,541 (1%). Spanish origin: 5,249 (1%).

vince his colleagues. He did not even get a majority for the override, let alone the two-thirds required, losing 191-206.

If Price is less than aggressive on the issues, he is a zealous protector of his committee's turf. When other House committees wanted to exercise control over the nation's naval petroleum reserves, Price quickly told them to stay out. He has made sure that other committees have no say in siting military bases and facilities. When he was chairman of the now-defunct Joint Committee on Atomic Energy, Price regularly deflected efforts by some of the more environmentally oriented committees to consider bills affecting nuclear power.

Price has been one of the strongest congressional supporters of atomic power, both for military weapons and civilian purposes. He was the House sponsor of legislation passed in 1957, the Price-Anderson Act, that gave the civilian nuclear industry the subsidy it needed to get off the ground — financial liability limitation in case of accident. Price successfully fought for the controversial law's reauthorization in 1975, arguing that the nuclear industry needed the protection.

Unlike past chairmen of the Armed Services Committee, Price has not loaded his district with military bases. He has, however, been most protective of Scott Air Force Base, the one installation in the district. Scott is headquarters for the Air Force's airlift command; Price has been a powerful advocate for more transport planes, such as the C-5A.

Price's reputation for fairness led to his appointment in 1967 as chairman of the first permanent House committee on ethics. The panel was set up under public pressure in the wake of the decision to expel New York Democrat Adam Clayton Powell Jr. on charges of misusing public funds. Speaker John W. McCormack believed a committee was needed, but did not trust the chamber's most militant ethics crusader, Florida Democrat Charles E. Bennett.

Price had the perfect credentials: a reputation for integrity but a commitment to protecting the members and avoiding much controversy. The panel was relatively quiet during his seven years as chairman, ending in 1975 when he took over Armed Services.

**At Home:** One of three House members who served in Congress when Franklin D. Roosevelt was president, the quiet Price long ago ensconced himself in southern Illinois' only solidly Democratic district. Even though he was 75 and slowing down in 1980, he still had only nominal competition.

It was not that way in the beginning. In 1944, he won his first term by less than 3,000 votes; two years later, in a poor Democratic year, he held on by 2,004 votes. But a combination of redistricting and demographic change has kept him in office without much effort ever since.

Price came to Washington in 1933 as secretary to the district's new Democratic congressman, Edwin Schaefer. Schaefer had been elected in the Roosevelt landslide as the first Democrat from the district since 1912. Price had been a journalist, working for St. Louis area newspapers covering sports and politics. He served as Schaefer's secretary until his boss retired in 1942.

Republican Calvin Johnson won the seat that year; Price briefly went back to reporting and then joined the Army. He was still in uniform in 1944 when the local Democratic organization decided to run him for Congress. He was informed of his election while on K. P. duty.

After the first two close victories, Price's district was redrawn to make it more Democratic. From then on, he has had no electoral problems. Twice — in 1952 and 1960 — he vanquished Republican Phyllis Schlafly, later to become nationally known as a pro-life and anti-ERA crusader. His 1980 vote was his weakest in 34 years, but at 64.4 percent, it was scarcely a threat to him.

**The District:** A grimy industrial region across the Mississippi River from St. Louis, the 24th District takes in the communities of East St. Louis, Granite City, and Belleville. Steel, iron, glass, and petroleum refining are the principal industries. East St. Louis, a predominantly black city, has had serious economic problems and racial tensions.

Like other areas of similar makeup, the district has suffered population losses over the past decade. It needs about 75,000 additional people to come up to population equality with the state's other districts.

*Melvin Price, D-Ill.*

## Committees

**Armed Services** (Chairman)
　Research and Development, chairman; Procurement and Military Nuclear Systems.

## Elections

**1980 General**

| | |
|---|---|
| Melvin Price (D ) | 107,786 (64 %) |
| Ronald Davinroy (R ) | 59,644 (36 %) |

**1980 Primary**

| | |
|---|---|
| Melvin Price (D ) | 39,193 (86 %) |
| Vic Darnell (D ) | 4,355 (10 %) |

**1978 General**

| | |
|---|---|
| Melvin Price (D ) | 74,247 (74 %) |
| Daniel Stack (R ) | 25,858 (26 %) |

**Previous Winning Percentages**

| | | | |
|---|---|---|---|
| 1976 (79 %) | 1974 (81 %) | 1972 (75 %) | 1970 (74 %) |
| 1968 (71 %) | 1966 (72 %) | 1964 (76 %) | 1962 (74 %) |
| 1960 (72 %) | 1958 (76 %) | 1956 (68 %) | 1954 (69 %) |
| 1952 (65 %) | 1950 (65 %) | 1948 (70 %) | 1946 (51 %) |
| 1944 (51 %) | | | |

**District Vote For President**

| | 1980 | | 1976 | | 1972 |
|---|---|---|---|---|---|
| D | 82,375 (48 %) | D | 100,616 (58 %) | D | 78,164 (47 %) |
| R | 80,832 (47 %) | R | 69,486 (40 %) | R | 88,105 (53 %) |
| I | 6,836 (4 %) | | | | |

## Campaign Finance

| | Receipts | Receipts from PACs | Expenditures |
|---|---|---|---|
| **1980** | | | |
| Price (D ) | $28,222 | $23,353 (8 %) | $21,747 |
| Davinroy (R ) | $19,386 | $1,000 (5 %) | $23,683 |
| **1978** | | | |
| Price (D ) | $29,955 | $14,990 (50 %) | $42,416 |
| Stack (R ) | $12,578 | $4,000 (32 %) | $12,298 |

## Voting Studies

| | Presidential Support | | Party Unity | | Conservative Coalition | |
|---|---|---|---|---|---|---|
| Year | S | O | S | O | S | O |
| 1980 | 79 | 15 | 92 | 5 | 24 | 71 |
| 1979 | 76 | 19 | 85 | 7 | 25 | 67 |
| 1978 | 74 | 24 | 82 | 15 | 24 | 74 |

| | | | | | | |
|---|---|---|---|---|---|---|
| 1977 | 57 | 25 | 71 | 8 | 18 | 58 |
| 1976 | 33 | 67 | 89 | 11 | 23 | 77 |
| 1975 | 44 | 51 | 81 | 10 | 24 | 68 |
| 1974 (Ford) | 50 | 50 | | | | |
| 1974 | 55 | 45 | 88 | 11 | 29 | 71 |
| 1973 | 33 | 66 | 94 | 5 | 20 | 80 |
| 1972 | 70 | 30 | 89 | 11 | 17 | 83 |
| 1971 | 72 | 21 | 79 | 16 | 37 | 57 |
| 1970 | 66 | 29 | 61 | 22 | 20 | 68 |
| 1969 | 60 | 36 | 85 | 13 | 33 | 64 |
| 1968 | 86 | 9 | 89 | 4 | 6 | 86 |
| 1967 | 93 | 6 | 97 | 1 | 9 | 89 |
| 1966 | 91 | 5 | 98 | 1 | 3 | 95 |
| 1965 | 95 | 3 | 97 | 0 | 0 | 100 |
| 1964 | 98 | 2 | 97 | 0 | 8 | 92 |
| 1963 | 90 | 4 | 98 | 2 | 7 | 93 |
| 1962 | 98 | 2 | 100 | 0 | 0 | 100 |
| 1961 | 92 | 6 | 97 | 3 | 9 | 91 |

S = Support　　　　O = Opposition

## Key Votes

**96th Congress**

| | |
|---|---|
| Weaken Carter oil profits tax (1979) | N |
| Reject hospital cost control plan (1979) | N |
| Implement Panama Canal Treaties (1979) | Y |
| Establish Department of Education (1979) | Y |
| Approve Anti-busing Amendment (1979) | N |
| Guarantee Chrysler Corp. loans (1979) | Y |
| Approve military draft registration (1980) | Y |
| Aid Sandinista regime in Nicaragua (1980) | Y |
| Strengthen fair housing laws (1980) | Y |

**97th Congress**

| | |
|---|---|
| Reagan budget proposal (1981) | N |

## Interest Group Ratings

| Year | ADA | ACA | AFL-CIO | CCUS |
|---|---|---|---|---|
| 1980 | 56 | 13 | 89 | 67 |
| 1979 | 68 | 12 | 84 | 22 |
| 1978 | 45 | 23 | 85 | 22 |
| 1977 | 45 | 12 | 100 | 6 |
| 1976 | 60 | 14 | 96 | 25 |
| 1975 | 58 | 15 | 100 | 12 |
| 1974 | 43 | 13 | 100 | 10 |
| 1973 | 72 | 12 | 100 | 18 |
| 1972 | 69 | 17 | 91 | 0 |
| 1971 | 59 | 23 | 100 | - |
| 1970 | 56 | 17 | 100 | 0 |
| 1969 | 53 | 19 | 100 | - |
| 1968 | 83 | 4 | 100 | - |
| 1967 | 73 | 4 | 100 | 10 |
| 1966 | 88 | 0 | 100 | - |
| 1965 | 84 | 4 | - | 10 |
| 1964 | 92 | 0 | 100 | - |
| 1963 | - | 0 | - | - |
| 1962 | 100 | 0 | 100 | |
| 1961 | 100 | | - | |

# 24 Paul Simon (D)

**Of Carbondale — Elected 1974**

**Born:** Nov. 29, 1928, Eugene, Ore.
**Education:** Attended U. of Ore., 1945-46; Dana College, 1946-48.
**Military Career:** Army, 1951-53.
**Profession:** Publisher.
**Family:** Jeanne Hurley; two children.
**Religion:** Lutheran.
**Political Career:** Ill. House, 1955-63; Ill. Senate, 1963-69; Ill. governor, 1969-73; sought gubernatorial nomination, 1972.

**In Washington:** A disciple of Paul H. Douglas and an admirer of Hubert Humphrey, Simon arrived in Washington just as the Great Society liberalism he learned from them was coming into question.

This accident of timing has led him into a doubled-edged congressional role in which he has fought to save public jobs and child nutrition on the Education and Labor Committee while he has struggled to cut other federal spending on the Budget Committee.

In the 96th Congress, he headed a Budget task force on inflation and argued for changes in the consumer price index that would slow the growth in federal programs keyed to the cost of living. He also suggested that federal retirees should have benefits adjusted for inflation only once a year, not twice. Neither idea was very popular.

At the same time, Simon was running for Budget Committee chairman as a more traditional liberal Democrat, competing for the votes of the party's New Deal-oriented faction with David R. Obey of Wisconsin. He drew a disappointing 39 votes, dropping out after the first ballot of a contest that James R. Jones of Oklahoma eventually won.

Simon's defeat gave him more time to spend at Education and Labor, where he took over as chairman of the Postsecondary Education Subcommittee in 1981. Here he believes in a substantial role for the federal government. He fought for generous funding in the multi-year higher education bill that became law in 1980, and he worked in 1981 to forestall the drastic retrenchment proposed by President Reagan. He also tried to protect educational subsides for the handicapped, one of his traditional causes.

In 1980, Simon fought to preserve strict federal requirements that communities equip all mass transit vehicles with access for the handicapped. When the House adopted a compromise allowing alternatives like special jitney buses, he called it a "backward step."

On the Employment Opportunities Subcommittee of Education and Labor, Simon still frequently invokes the name of Humphrey. The subcommitee, chaired by Augustus Hawkins of California, is the one that wrote the Humphrey-Hawkins bill aimed at guaranteeing a job for every American willing to work. Simon was a loyal supporter of the bill and when it was diluted on the House floor to add unrelated anti-inflation and farm parity goals, he was one of those protesting most loudly.

In general, Simon has been a close labor ally on the committee, although he has broken ranks on the issue of a subminimum wage for teenagers. Simon endorsed the idea early in his House career, even though it is one of the economic proposals labor is most militantly against. He still believes in guaranteeing jobs for all, however, and has defended the CETA public jobs program against its many critics.

Simon has always believed that most of the valuable domestic programs could be retained if defense spending were kept under tighter control. This is not the form of budget cutting that most current members want to practice, but he has continued to urge it anyway. He has been a vigorous opponent of the MX missile system, and offered an amendment in 1980 to cut $500 million from a $1.6 billion MX authorization. He lost,

---

**24th District: South — Carbondale.**
Population: 517,190 (11% increase since 1970).
Race: White 490,818 (95%), Black 22,272 (4%), Others 4,100 (1%). Spanish origin: 3,112 (1%).

152-250. He fared a little better in 1981 when he convinced the House to defer MX spending at least until the whole program could be restudied. "Without SALT II," he said, "this thing is worthless."

Well-liked by nearly everyone, Simon no longer has the reputation as an aggressive leader that he carried for two decades in Illinois politics. He seems a mellower man now, conciliatory on most issues, and willing to give the benefit of the doubt to friends and foes alike. He rarely shows anger and tends to take losses philosophically. Many members feel that Simon's "almost too nice" quality was a factor against him in the 1980 budget campaign.

He was conciliatory toward the Carter administration when he lost a fight to have a new St. Louis airport located across the Mississippi in Illinois, where it would have helped some of the depressed areas around his district.

When Carter Transportation Secretary Brock Adams decided against the Illinois site, Simon wrote to his constituents, "I could have fumed and fussed and protested with statements issued to the press . . . but the facts are that while I wish Brock Adams had rendered a different decision, . . . I respect his judgment . . . and I know that the most foolish thing anyone could do . . . is to fail to recognize the facts."

**At Home:** An influential newspaper publisher by the age of 25, Simon was a prodigy in Illinois politics whose rise to the governorship seemed inevitable until he was stopped by Daniel Walker in a 1972 primary.

As editor of the *Troy Tribune* in southern Illinois in the early 1950s, Simon fought vice and political corruption in Madison and St. Clair counties. In 1954, he decided to run for the Illinois House himself. In an intensive door-to-door campaign, he defeated an organization-backed incumbent in the Democratic primary. Eight years later he went on to the state Senate.

In the Legislature, Simon established impeccable reform credentials, filing detailed financial disclosure records and receiving the "best legislator" award from the Independent Voters of Illinois seven times, more than anyone in the history of the state.

In 1968, Democratic leaders picked him as their candidate for lieutenant governor, hoping that his reform reputation would help a state ticket struggling against reported scandal and an expected Republican tide. The gubernatorial and Senate candidates lost, but Simon won, and he immediately became the premier Democratic officeholder in the state and heir-apparent to the 1972 gubernatorial nomination.

But he did not survive Walker's primary challenge. A wealthy corporate lawyer, Walker charged that Simon was a tool of Mayor Daley's Chicago Democrats — even though they were clinging to Simon rather than the other way around. Walker also seized on Simon's statement that tax increases might be necessary to finance improvements in state social services. Walker won by 40,000 votes and went on to serve one term as governor. Simon taught political science for two years at a college in Springfield.

In 1974, the southern Illinois 24th District opened up with the retirement of Democratic Rep. Kenneth Gray. Simon declared for the seat and won it easily, even though he had not technically been a resident of the district. He won new terms even more easily in 1976 and 1978.

Simon remained more liberal than most of his constituents, however, and the disparity was bound to cause him trouble eventually. In 1980 it did. Simon endorsed Ted Kennedy for president and that gave his constituents a graphic symbol of his politics, even though he had been trying to find common themes to share with them — such as criticizing federal deficits and backing greater tax encouragement for savings.

When Ronald Reagan carried the 24th District by 35,000 votes in 1980, reversing Jimmy Carter's margin there in 1976, he nearly brought Simon down. Underfinanced Republican challenger John T. Anderson (no relation to the presidential candidate) came within 2,000 votes of what would have been one of the nation's most startling upsets.

**The District:** Southern Illinois was settled out of the Deep South in the early 19th century and has retained some of its flavor. Voters tend to prefer conservative Democrats, who still predominate at the local level. Nationally, the district is not enamored of the Democratic Party, although statewide Democrats do win here a portion of the time. In 1976, when Jimmy Carter still seemed like a traditional Southerner to many voters, he carried the 24th by 18,000 votes.

The district is not strongly industrialized, but it does have an important resource — coal. The coal mines of southern Illinois have been a major source of employment in the past and are beginning to recover with the increase in coal production. Agriculturally, the area does not compare in fertility to central and northern Illinois and is devoted to general farming. Southern Illinois University's large campus is located in Carbondale.

The area gained population during the 1970s, partly because of the coal boom and partly because of the movement of people into the district from urban Madison and St.Clair counties.

## Committees

**Budget**
Task Forces: Entitlements, Uncontrollables and Indexing, chairman; National Security and Veterans; Reconciliation.

**Education and Labor** (9th of 19 Democrats)
Postsecondary Education, chairman; Employment Opportunities; Select Education.

## Elections

**1980 General**

| | |
|---|---|
| Paul Simon (D ) | 112,134 (49 %) |
| John Anderson (R ) | 110,176 (48 %) |

**1980 Primary**

| | |
|---|---|
| Paul Simon (D ) | 38,005 (73 %) |
| Edwin Arentsen (D ) | 14,183 (27 %) |

**1978 General**

| | |
|---|---|
| Paul Simon (D ) | 110,298 (66 %) |
| John Anderson (R ) | 57,763 (34 %) |

**Previous Winning Percentages**

1976 (67 %)      1974 (60 %)

**District Vote For President**

| | 1980 | | 1976 | | 1972 |
|---|---|---|---|---|---|
| D | 95,294 (40 %) | D | 127,696 (53 %) | D | 92,910 (40 %) |
| R | 131,012 (55 %) | R | 109,391 (46 %) | R | 138,435 (60 %) |
| I | 8,745 (4 %) | | | | |

## Campaign Finance

| | Receipts | Receipts from PACs | Expen-ditures |
|---|---|---|---|
| **1980** | | | |
| Simon (D ) | $74,428 | $50,125 (29 %) | $177,624 |
| Anderson (R ) | $43,412 | $4,266 (10 %) | $42,494 |

| **1978** | | | |
|---|---|---|---|
| Simon (D ) | $92,362 | $26,540 (29 %) | $99,017 |
| Anderson (R ) | $14,022 | $11,070 (79 %) | $13,998 |

## Voting Studies

| Year | Presidential Support | | Party Unity | | Conservative Coalition | |
|---|---|---|---|---|---|---|
| | S | O | S | O | S | O |
| 1980 | 65 | 21 | 80 | 7 | 13 | 78 |
| 1979 | 79 | 16 | 86 | 6 | 10 | 82 |
| 1978 | 88 | 7 | 77 | 10 | 12 | 73 |
| 1977 | 75 | 23 | 83 | 15 | 17 | 79 |
| 1976 | 25 | 67 | 85 | 10 | 15 | 82 |
| 1975 | 47 | 53 | 82 | 14 | 16 | 77 |

S = Support          O = Opposition

## Key Votes

**96th Congress**

| | |
|---|---|
| Weaken Carter oil profits tax (1979) | Y |
| Reject hospital cost control plan (1979) | N |
| Implement Panama Canal Treaties (1979) | Y |
| Establish Department of Education (1979) | Y |
| Approve Anti-busing Amendment (1979) | N |
| Guarantee Chrysler Corp. loans (1979) | # |
| Approve military draft registration (1980) | Y |
| Aid Sandinista regime in Nicaragua (1980) | Y |
| Strengthen fair housing laws (1980) | Y |

**97th Congress**

| | |
|---|---|
| Reagan budget proposal (1981) | N |

## Interest Group Ratings

| Year | ADA | ACA | AFL-CIO | CCUS |
|---|---|---|---|---|
| 1980 | 78 | 24 | 72 | 59 |
| 1979 | 74 | 0 | 72 | 17 |
| 1978 | 65 | 10 | 84 | 22 |
| 1977 | 85 | 0 | 73 | 24 |
| 1976 | 80 | 0 | 81 | 13 |
| 1975 | 89 | 18 | 91 | 12 |

# Indiana

## ... A Deep-Seated Conservatism

Of the nation's major industrial states, Indiana is probably the least typical. It is more conservative and more Republican than its counterparts. Only once since 1936 have the state's voters chosen the Democratic presidential nominee, Lyndon B. Johnson in 1964.

It is less urbanized, with a higher percentage of people living in rural areas. And it has held its own in population better than most other industrial states: its loss of one congressional seat in 1980 was the first since 1940.

Indiana's conservatism pervades both parties, and comes from a variety of factors. There is a Southern influence in the state that goes back to the early 19th century, when southern Indiana was settled by pioneers from Kentucky and Virginia. Until recently, that meant Democratic dominance in the southern part of the state. But the Democratic politics that prevailed was Southern-style. In 1976, when Southerner Jimmy Carter ran for president, 24 of the 27 Indiana counties he carried were in the southern half of the state.

Indiana has fewer Eastern and Southern European immigrants and fewer blacks than other industrial states. Ethnic and minority votes that made New Deal Democrats strong in Michigan and Illinois were not as much of a factor in Indiana. The state has only one center of major ethnic strength — Lake County, with huge steel and petrochemical industries. The small- to medium-sized industrial centers elsewhere in the state have drawn their work force from the countryside or the South. Germans, the state's most prominent ethnic group in the beginning, have for generations been largely a white-collar and professional group and a conservative political force.

Given all that, Democrats have won more than their share of elections in Indiana in recent years, thanks to a combination of good candidates and good luck.

The 1958 recession brought a Senate victory for Democrat Vance Hartke, and while he never developed much of a personal following in the state, he managed to run for re-election in two more very good years, 1964 and 1970. His luck

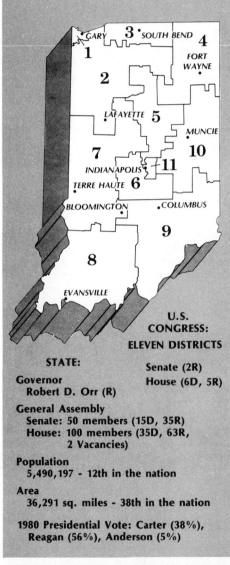

**U.S. CONGRESS: ELEVEN DISTRICTS**

**STATE:**

**Governor**
Robert D. Orr (R)

Senate (2R)
House (6D, 5R)

**General Assembly**
Senate: 50 members (15D, 35R)
House: 100 members (35D, 63R, 2 Vacancies)

**Population**
5,490,197 - 12th in the nation

**Area**
36,291 sq. miles - 38th in the nation

**1980 Presidential Vote:** Carter (38%), Reagan (56%), Anderson (5%)

finally ran out in 1976, when Republican Richard Lugar defeated him.

Meanwhile, Democrat Birch Bayh won a Senate term in 1962 on a combination of hard work and Hoosier folksiness. The same combination allowed him to survive a liberal Senate voting record in 1968 and 1974, giving the state two liberal Democratic senators for a period of 14 years — a situation it remedied fully by defeating Bayh in 1980.

Indiana is traditionally a straight-ticket state. Democrats took advantage of that in 1974 to turn a 7-4 Republican House delegation into a 9-2 Democratic delegation. Many of that year's Democratic winners proved to be good politicians, and even today Democrats have a 6-5 edge.

But those days are probably ending. Indiana Republicans redrew the district lines in early 1981 for the express purpose of unseating three Democratic congressmen, and even if they do not get all three, the 1980s appear to promise that Indiana will be voting as conservatively in Washington as it has been doing at home.

# A Political Tour

**Northern Industrial Tier.** Indiana's premier industrial region is its waterfront along Lake Michigan in the northwest corner of the state. It was here that U.S. Steel decided in 1905 to build one of the largest steel plants in the world and thus created the city of Gary, named after the company's president. The three Lake County cities of Hammond, Gary and East Chicago became an industrial strip, more like industrial Chicago, Detroit, or Cleveland than like the rest of Indiana. Lake County attracted East European immigrants and a large black community. An often-corrupt county machine regularly delivered Democratic majorities.

A growing black presence in Gary led to racial tensions in the 1960s and to the election of a black, Richard Hatcher, as Gary mayor in 1967. That weakened the hold of the Democratic machine, which unsuccessfully fought his election.

Republicans are concentrated in suburban communities in central Lake County. Some of them work in Chicago. Ronald Reagan proved attractive to these voters in 1980, and his suburban strength allowed him to come within 6,000 votes of carrying the county.

Reagan also made inroads into the ethnic Democratic vote in this area. Hurt by troubles in the steel industry and alienated by the Democratic Party's identification with liberal social causes, many steelworkers in Lake County decided to try the GOP at the presidential level, while remaining Democratic for other offices.

Moving eastward from Lake County, the density of industry declines. But there is a series of industrial communities along the railway lines that traverse northern Indiana on their way to

and from Chicago. Chief among them are South Bend and Fort Wayne.

South Bend has been heavily dependent on the transportation industry, and was badly hurt by the 1980 recession — one reason it threw 22-year veteran Democratic Rep. John Brademas out of office in November. South Bend is essentially Democratic, making St. Joseph County as a whole strongly competitive between the parties.

Fort Wayne, better diversified economically than South Bend, has been better able to maintain its economic health. Despite its industry, it has never been a strong Democratic city, partly because of its conservative German element. Most small rural counties in the area are Republican.

**The Corn Belt.** Rolling across northern and central Indiana is one of America's most productive agricultural regions, part of the Corn Belt that stretches all the way to the Missouri River. The rich soil and favorable weather conditions here have produced a prosperous, mostly conservative farm population which is usually a backbone of Republican strength.

The corn and hog economy is the underpinning of the region. In some counties, hogs outnumber people. But the area is studded with a series of small industrial cities such as Lafayette, Kokomo, Anderson, and Muncie. The cities manufacture a variety of products, but automobiles and auto parts have a large share of the employment. The strength of the United Auto Workers among the large blue-collar work force reduces the Republican vote in parts of the area. Nevertheless, Republicans are predominant in most local governments and usually carry their counties in presidential elections. They have done less well on the congressional level; much of this region has been represented by Democrats in the U.S. House during the 1970s.

**Indianapolis.** Indianapolis has managed to do something that other Northern cities have longed to do but have not accomplished: expand its boundaries to take in much of the suburban ring surrounding it. This was accomplished in 1969 with the establishment of a unified governmental structure — called Unigov — that combined Indianapolis and Marion County.

The political results of this move were significant. Republican votes in the formerly suburban part of Marion County gave the GOP control of the unified government. Before Unigov, Indianapolis was predominantly Democratic. Since Republican Mayor (now senator) Richard Lugar pushed Unigov through the state Legislature in 1967, the GOP has not lost control of City Hall.

In broader elections, Marion County generally reflects the statewide choice. In every election since 1920, it has gone for the candidate who carried Indiana. When Democrats carry the county, it is not by the margins they receive in the largest cities of other industrial states. Indianapolis has a substantial black population and some labor union strength, but it is one of the most conservative of all Midwestern cities.

**Southern Indiana.** From the Civil War to recent times, Indiana was divided politically between a Republican North and a Democratic South.

Southern Indiana was the earliest-settled area of the state, with migrants coming in from neighboring Kentucky or other Southern states. The land is not as flat or fertile as the northern Corn Belt area. There is a substantial amount of coal here, abandoned for years but now being worked because of the energy crunch.

Voters here are conservative, but have retained much of their Democratic political heritage. While the liberalism of the national Democratic Party during the 1960s and early 1970s alienated many southern Indiana Democrats, they continue to support local Democratic candidates. Most of the counties in this section of the state are controlled by Democrats and the bulk of the state's Democratic contingent in the state Legislature usually comes from this area.

Among the urban centers in this region are the old coal and railroad town of Terre Haute and the university city of Bloomington, both Democratic; Columbus, with its large white-collar engineering community; and Evansville, the state's second-largest city, an old Ohio River town trying to revitalize its economy.

Evansville and surrounding Vanderburgh County form an island of Republican strength in the rural Democratic sea. The 19th century German settlers of Evansville established the pro-Union Republican tradition. The area has maintained that flavor, with the county voting Republican in every presidential election but one since 1952.

## Redrawing the Lines

Indiana Republicans control the governorship and the Legislature, and they used their free hand to fullest advantage. The state's new district lines weave in and out of counties, concentrating Democratic voters in the districts of three Democratic incumbents and damaging the re-election prospects of the other three. The total number of districts drops from 11 to 10.

The Legislature passed the redistricting bill on April 30 and Gov. Orr signed it. Damaged most are Democrats Floyd Fithian and David W. Evans. The new map dismembers Fithian's northwest Indiana 2nd District, distributing it among four neighboring districts. Also eliminated is Evans' 6th District, which is south and west of Indianapolis. The new map has a new 6th District in GOP territory north and east of the city.

Democrat Lee H. Hamilton can retain his reconstituted 9th District by moving his home south. The new map expands the industrial 1st District, where population declined nearly 10 percent in the past decade, but Democrat Adam Benjamin Jr. should be able to retain that seat.

## Governor
## Robert D. Orr (R)

**Born:** Nov. 17, 1917, Ann Arbor, Mich.
**Home:** Indianapolis, Ind.
**Education:** Yale U., B.A. 1940; Harvard U., M.A. 1942.
**Military Career:** Army, 1942-46.
**Profession:** Recreational products manufacturer.
**Family:** Wife, Joanne; three children.
**Religion:** Presbyterian.
**Political Career:** Indiana Senate, 1969-73; lieutenant governor, 1973-81; elected governor 1980; term expires Jan. 1985.

# Richard G. Lugar (R)

**Of Indianapolis — Elected 1976**

**Born:** April, 4, 1932, Indianapolis, Ind.
**Education:** Denison U., B.A. 1954; Rhodes
Scholar, Pembroke College, Oxford, England,
B.A., 1956.
**Military Career:** Navy, 1957-60.
**Profession:** Tool company executive.
**Family:** Wife, Charlene Smeltzer; four children.
**Religion:** Methodist.
**Political Career:** Indianapolis School Board,
1964-67; mayor of Indianapolis, 1968-75; Re-
publican nominee for U.S. Senate, 1974.

**In Washington:** Lugar has been a "Howard
Baker man" throughout his Senate career, and
that alliance, combined with Lugar's reputation
as a thorough, well-briefed conservative, has kept
him at the center of major policy debate.

He is a more orthodox conservative than
Baker is, but he goes with the leadership on most
of the important issues, and he is often deputized
to take the lead on problems that Baker would
rather handle from the background.

Lugar was beginning his second year in the
Senate in 1978 when Baker turned to him to
organize the successful GOP filibuster against a
package of labor law revisions that unions badly
wanted. The Republicans won that fight against
the formidable parliamentary opposition of
Democratic leader Robert C. Byrd.

Lugar and ally Orrin G. Hatch, R-Utah,
stepped into the labor law argument at a critical
moment for Senate conservatives. Their parliamentary wizard, Alabama Democrat James B.
Allen, had died suddenly during the third week of
debate.

Baker, Lugar and Hatch met daily with the
Senate parliamentarian, looking for ways to be
ready for Byrd's maneuvers. As the argument
wore on, Lugar demonstrated a knack for organization. Under his direction, opponents of the bill
organized three teams of five to six senators each
to cover the floor in rotation, each team specializing in a particular section of the bill. Lugar's
office put out a daily "opposition bulletin" notify-
ing each team member the hours he was to be on
the floor and summarizing the previous day's
action.

The filibuster was successful. Byrd could not
muster the 60 votes he needed to shut off debate,
and the changes never became law. The next year,
Lugar managed Baker's campaign for the Republican presidential nomination — not a great claim
to fame, considering the campaign's failure, but a
symbol of their continuing alliance.

On some subjects, Lugar votes with the more
militant Senate conservatives: he opposed the
Panama Canal treaties while Baker was backing
them, and favors constitutional amendments to
balance the federal budget and prohibit abortion.
But he has little in common personally with "New
Right" Republicans like Jesse Helms of North
Carolina. Lugar is not a man of passion. He is
reserved, unemotional, and pragmatic. He insists
on observing limits in his approach to Senate
business. A few weeks after his labor law filibuster
had succeeded, he warned conservatives about
overusing the tactic in the future. "You can't keep
crying wolf," he said. "There's no point in bab-
bling on until you're blue in the face or until
people walk out on you."

The combination of Lugar's voting record
and insistence on pragmatism makes it easier for
him to get the Senate's attention. When he de-
parts from the conservative line, colleagues listen.

Despite his philosophical bent against government intervention in free enterprise, Lugar
worked out compromises that resulted in an extension of federal aid to New York City in 1978
and to Chrysler in 1980.

Lugar lists the New York and Chrysler aid
packages as his greatest Senate achievements. As
a former Indianapolis mayor, he says he "understood the problems of New York City finance."
He had a more parochial motive in the case of
Chrysler: Only Michigan has more Chrysler employees than Indiana. Lugar drew up a provision
requiring Chrysler's unions to make a pay concession to help return the company to solvency.

Lugar considers himself one of the Senate's
urban experts and he has devoted significant
amounts of energy to urban transportation, focusing his solutions on the problems of moderate-

**387**

sized cities like Indianapolis. He has fought to alter mass transit aid formulas to give more money to such cities by favoring buses over rail systems. He has also fought against changing the mass transit aid formula in ways that would favor larger cities.

After the Baker presidential campaign collapsed in early 1980, Lugar was touted as a possible Reagan running mate. He probably lost any chance he had for the vice presidency that year, however, by voting as a member of the Foreign Relations Committee to give economic aid to leftist Nicaragua. Lugar said it was worth the chance to try to save Nicaragua from a communist takeover. But Helms and others on the Republican right used that vote against Lugar during vice presidential politicking at the GOP convention.

Nevertheless, Lugar gave candidate Reagan his unconditional support, and declared as the Reagan administration took office that his goal in the 97th Congress was to "make sure the president gets a shot at whatever he wants."

True to his word, Lugar emerged as one of the administration's strongest early supporters on the Foreign Relations Committee. At the beginning of 1981, he unquestioningly backed Reagan's two most controversial State Department nominations — Secretary of State Alexander M. Haig Jr., and Deputy Secretary of State William P. Clark. In June, when Foreign Relations voted 13-4 against confirming Ernest Lefever, Reagan's choice to be assistant secretary of state for human rights, Lugar was one of the four die-hard Lefever supporters. The Indiana Republican has no problems with the Reagan administration's hard-line attitude toward the Soviet Union; he was one of the leading opponents of the SALT II treaty on Foreign Relations in 1979.

Lugar feels just as comfortable with Reagan's "supply side" economics — parts of which he has advocated himself since at least 1976. As a newly-elected senator, Lugar called for a permanent tax cut to stimulate the economy. He said he was "willing to take the gamble that the outstanding growth I think will come from this will more than make up in new revenue" the funds lost by cutting taxes.

Lugar also sits on the Agriculture and Intelligence committees — assignments he said he wanted because of his experience with a 604-acre family farm and as an intelligence briefer for the Chief of Naval Operations in the Navy.

On Agriculture, Lugar led the fight against banning nitrites used to preserve bacon and other pork products — a position that meshed both with his antipathy to government regulation and

his status as a reliable friend of Indiana's pork producers. He also has defended pesticide manufacturers in clashes with environmentally-minded committee Democrats.

In early 1981, Lugar was one of the few members of the Agriculture Committee from either party who seemed enthusiastic about cutting farm programs as much as Reagan wanted to. When the committee, after endorsing the Reagan proposals in general terms on the floor, began trying to water them down in committee, Lugar all but accused them of hypocrisy. He vowed to offer the Reagan spending cuts intact later if the committee insisted on ignoring them. Then the panel went back and agreed on a series of cuts closer to what Reagan and Lugar were demanding.

On food stamps, the Agriculture Committee wrote a bill designed to save an estimated $1.5 billion during fiscal 1982. But it rejected efforts by Helms and Lugar to go further, and restore the food stamp purchase requirement that was eliminated by the Carter administration in 1977. When the full Senate also refused to do that, Lugar cast one of the dissenting votes against the bill as it passed 77-17.

**At Home:** Lugar will never win any awards as a campaigner — he meets crowds woodenly and his style borders on lecturing — but he has always managed to impress the Indiana electorate as a man of substance, and he has prospered at the polls.

Even in 1974, running for the Senate in a Watergate-dominated year with a reputation as "Richard Nixon's favorite mayor," he came within a respectable 75,000 votes against Democrat Birch Bayh. Two years later, against a much weaker Democratic incumbent, Vance Hartke, he won going away.

If Lugar's record as mayor of Indianapolis was no help to him in 1974, it still stands as the basis of his political career. His conservative, efficiency-minded administration won him favorable notices all over Indiana, and he attracted national attention by defeating John V. Lindsay of New York City for vice president of the National League of Cities.

A Rhodes scholar, Lugar served in the Navy as a briefing officer at the Pentagon before returning home to run the family tool business. He won his first election in 1964, to the Indianapolis school board.

Three years later, he saw an opportunity to take over the mayor's office. The Democrats were divided and weak, and with the help of powerful Marion County GOP Chairman Keith Bulen, he dislodged incumbent Democrat John Barton.

Lugar's foremost accomplishment as mayor was creation of Uni-Gov — the consolidation of the city and its suburbs. He lobbied for the plan successfully before the state Legislature.

Lugar's election over Lindsay was national news because he won it in an electorate of big-city mayors, mostly Democrats. He was a spokesman for the policies of the Nixon administration, and from that time on the president began to take an interest in him.

He came to regret those ties in 1974, when he was saddled with the Nixon connection. In an attempt to deal with it, he declared that the Oval Office tape transcripts "revealed a moral tragedy" in the White House. But this alienated segments of the Republican right in Indiana, and made his campaign against Bayh even more difficult.

Still, he had come close enough to be the logical contender in 1976 against Hartke. The incumbent had nearly been beaten six years earlier, and was severely damaged by a primary challenger who charged him with foreign junketing and slavish loyalty to the telephone industry. Lugar coasted to a comfortable victory.

## Committees

**Agriculture, Nutrition and Forestry** (4th of 9 Republicans)
Agricultural Research and General Legislation, chairman; Foreign Agricultural Policy; Nutrition; Rural Development, Oversight, and Investigations.

**Banking, Housing and Urban Affairs** (5th of 8 Republicans)
Housing and Urban Affairs, chairman; Economic Policy; Financial Institutions; Rural Housing and Development.

**Foreign Relations** (5th of 9 Republicans)
European Affairs, chairman; International Economic Policy; Western Hemisphere Affairs.

**Select Intelligence** (4th of 8 Republicans)
Analysis and Production, chairman; Collection and Foreign Operations.

## Elections

**1976 General**

| | |
|---|---|
| Richard Lugar (R ) | 1,275,833 (59 %) |
| Vance Hartke (D ) | 878,522 (41 %) |

**1976 Primary**

| | |
|---|---|
| Richard Lugar (R ) | 393,064 (65 %) |
| Edgar Whitcomb (R ) | 179,203 (30 %) |

## Campaign Finance

| | Receipts | Receipts from PACs | Expenditures |
|---|---|---|---|
| **1976** | | | |
| Lugar (R ) | $742,736 | $145,366 (20 %) | $727,720 |
| Hartke (D ) | $662,389 | $275,085 (42 %) | $654,279 |

## Voting Studies

| | Presidential Support | | Party Unity | | Conservative Coalition | |
|---|---|---|---|---|---|---|
| Year | S | O | S | O | S | O |
| 1980 | 44 | 53 | 80 | 12 | 85 | 10 |
| 1979 | 43 | 57 | 90 | 10 | 90 | 10 |
| 1978 | 35 | 64 | 85 | 14 | 80 | 20 |
| 1977 | 48 | 51 | 91 | 8 | 95 | 4 |

S = Support          O = Opposition

## Key Votes

**96th Congress**

| | |
|---|---|
| Maintain relations with Taiwan (1979) | Y |
| Reduce synthetic fuel development funds (1979) | Y |
| Impose nuclear plant moratorium (1979) | N |
| Kill stronger windfall profits tax (1979) | Y |
| Guarantee Chrysler Corp. loans (1979) | Y |
| Approve military draft registration (1980) | Y |
| End Revenue Sharing to the states (1980) | N |
| Block Justice Dept. busing suits (1980) | Y |

**97th Congress**

| | |
|---|---|
| Restore urban program funding cuts (1981) | N |

## Interest Group Ratings

| Year | ADA | ACA | AFL-CIO | CCUS-1 | CCUS-2 |
|---|---|---|---|---|---|
| 1980 | 17 | 83 | 11 | 86 | |
| 1979 | 11 | 89 | 0 | 100 | 100 |
| 1978 | 10 | 92 | 11 | 89 | |
| 1977 | 10 | 81 | 10 | 94 | |

# Dan Quayle (R)

**Of Huntington — Elected 1980**

**Born:** Feb. 4, 1947, Indianapolis, Ind.
**Education:** DePauw U., B.A. 1969; Indiana University, J.D. 1974.
**Military Career:** Ind. National Guard, 1969-75.
**Profession:** Lawyer, newspaper publisher.
**Family:** Wife, Marilyn Tucker; three children.
**Religion:** Presbyterian.
**Political Career:** U.S. House, 1977-81.

**The Member:** Quayle has built a reputation as a strong supporter of conservative causes, but one who eschews the ideological purity sometimes demanded by the New Right.

Shortly after he was elected in 1976, with the help of the National Conservative Political Action Committee (NCPAC), Quayle ran afoul of the group by refusing to support a purge of liberal Republican John Anderson from the GOP leadership. The feud has continued to this day, and even after NCPAC worked to discredit his 1980 Democratic Senate opponent, Quayle publicly charged the organization with doing more harm than good and risking a backlash against its tactics.

In general, Quayle has downplayed conservative social issues while concentrating on economics and foreign policy. In 1979 he sponsored an alternative to the Chrysler bailout plan. Quayle's bill, which would have required $800 million in concessions from Chrysler's union employees, failed 296-107. He then voted for the original bill.

Quayle came closer to victory in his attempt to force the Carter administration to keep a "liaison office" in Taiwan, rather than severing all formal relations. He argued that Taiwan should be allowed the same status that the People's Republic of China enjoyed before the United States formally recognized that nation. He lost on a close 181-172 vote.

Quayle's Senate subcommittee on Employment and Productivity oversees Comprehensive Employment and Training Assistance (CETA) programs. Quayle went along with Reagan's call for drastic cuts in CETA public service jobs, but he did not embrace the President's suggestion to reduce funding for two CETA youth job training programs. The full Labor and Human Resources Committee retained money for the training programs. As a result, the budget authority it recommended for CETA was almost $1 billion above Reagan's request.

Quayle held a series of hearings in 1981 to evaluate a broad range of CETA programs. The subcommittee will consider CETA reauthorization in 1982. Quayle is expected to focus on improving, not abolishing, CETA's job training programs.

Quayle's latest idea for reviving the auto industry is to offer a $750 tax credit to encourage the purchase of new American-made cars. Since an estimated one in five residents of his state are involved in automaking, Quayle greeted favorably the announcement that Japan would limit its auto exports to the U.S. But he warned that the trade restriction will not reduce high interest rates, and offered his tax credit idea as a way to offset loan costs.

In 1980, Quayle used the slogan "A New Generation of Leadership" to unseat Democrat Birch Bayh, some 18 years after Bayh had used a similar approach against veteran Republican Sen. Homer Capehart. Quayle said Bayh was mired in the "big government" solutions of the 1960s and 1970s, suggesting that, as Bayh had said in 1962, "eighteen years in Washington is long enough for one man."

While Quayle publicly disavowed the New Right's far more shrill criticism of Bayh, many Indiana politicians believe NCPAC's "If Bayh Wins, You Lose" effort merged effectively with Quayle's television campaign to dispel the incumbent's popular image among Hoosiers. Quayle, who won by 166,452 votes, also was helped by Ronald Reagan's sweep of the state. Reagan led Carter by 411,000 votes — the second highest plurality for a Republican presidential candidate in the state's history.

Quayle's swift political climb began without the help of the regular Republican Party. The grandson of the late Eugene Pulliam, a conservative Indianapolis newspaper publisher, Quayle was a political novice in 1976, working for one of the family's newspapers. When a popular state senator chose not to make the expected congressional campaign, Quayle stepped in at the last minute and assembled his own precinct organiza-

tion, saying the local Republican organization had been ineffective. Five months after beginning his second term in the House, he became the first House member to officially declare his intention to run for the Senate in 1980.

## Committees

**Armed Services** (8th of 9 Republicans)
Manpower and Personnel; Sea Power and Force Projection; Strategic and Theater Nuclear Forces.

**Budget**

**Labor and Human Resources** (3rd of 9 Republicans)
Employment and Productivity, chairman; Education; Labor.

## Elections

**1980 General**

| | |
|---|---|
| Dan Quayle (R) | 1,182,414 (54%) |
| Birch Bayh (D) | 1,015,962 (46%) |

**1980 Primary**

| | |
|---|---|
| Dan Quayle (R) | 397,273 (77%) |
| Roger Marsh (R) | 118,273 (23%) |

**Previous Winning Percentages**

1978* (64%)   1976* (54%)

*House elections.

## Campaign Finance

| | Receipts | Receipts from PACs | Expenditures |
|---|---|---|---|
| 1980 | | | |
| Quayle (R) | $2,329,407 | $618,562 (27%) | $2,286,170 |
| Bayh (D) | $2,766,134 | $470,980 (17%) | $2,761,116 |

## Voting Studies

| | Presidential Support | | Party Unity | | Conservative Coalition | |
|---|---|---|---|---|---|---|
| Year | S | O | S | O | S | O |
| House service | | | | | | |
| 1980 | 35 | 46 | 70 | 8 | 72 | 4 |
| 1979 | 30 | 63 | 79 | 9 | 77 | 7 |
| 1978 | 43 | 47 | 80 | 13 | 79 | 13 |
| 1977 | 34 | 54 | 81 | 10 | 83 | 10 |

S = Support          O = Opposition

## Key Votes

**97th Congress**

| | |
|---|---|
| Restore urban program funding cuts (1981) | N |

## Interest Group Ratings

| Year | ADA | ACA | AFL-CIO | CCUS-1 | CCUS-2 |
|---|---|---|---|---|---|
| House service | | | | | |
| 1980 | 0 | 90 | 13 | 73 | |
| 1979 | 11 | 91 | 16 | 88 | |
| 1978 | 15 | 81 | 11 | 76 | |
| 1977 | 15 | 96 | 10 | 88 | |

# 1 Adam Benjamin Jr. (D)

**Of Hobart — Elected 1976**

**Born:** Aug. 6, 1935, Gary, Ind.
**Education:** U.S. Military Academy, B.S. 1958;
   Valparaiso U. Law School, J.D. 1966.
**Military Career:** Marine Corps, 1952-54; Army,
   1958-61.
**Profession:** Lawyer.
**Family:** Wife, Patricia Sullivan; three children.
**Religion:** Eastern Catholic.
**Political Career:** Ind. House, 1967-71; Ind.
   Senate, 1971-77; sought Democratic nomina-
   tion for U.S. House, 1972.

**In Washington:** A burly man with a rum-
pled appearance who looks like an easy-going big
city pol, Benjamin turns out on closer inspection
to be a workaholic with a passion for numbers and
a command of his subject to the minutest detail.

He was appointed to the Appropriations
Committee as a freshman in 1977, and an unusual
combination of retirements two years later gave
him his own subcommittee, on the Legislative
Branch. In 1981, another round of good fortune
made him chairman of the Transportation Appropriations Subcomittee — far ahead of the typical
seniority schedule — and he also took a place on
the Budget Committee.

Benjamin was an extraordinarily dutiful Legislative Branch chairman. Colleagues found no
dollar item small enough to escape his attention.
Some complained he was pushing too hard to hold
down expenses. But widespread publicity about
the "Billion Dollar Congress" in 1979 made Benjamin's austerity more popular. Members even
outdid him on the floor by voting a 5 percent cut
in overall legislative spending.

Benjamin's 1980 legislative bill became embroiled in a battle over a pay raise for members of
Congress, their top aides and employees of the
executive and judicial branches.

As manager of the bill, Benjamin backed
Democratic leaders, who wanted to arrange it so
the raise would go through without actually forcing House members to vote for it. The plan was to
let them vote against a higher rate, 7 percent, set
by Benjamin's committee, and thus accept a lower
rate, 5.5 percent. This would allow members to
say they had voted for economy.

When the bill finally got to the floor, bedlam
ensued — the raise was approved, but the bill was
defeated, and none passed during the year. A 5.5
percent pay raise finally cleared in an emergency

appropriation bill.

The fiscal 1981 bill passed on schedule. In it
Benjamin took a swipe at the upper-level federal
bureaucracy, moving to cancel the merit bonuses
of up to $10,000 scheduled for some members of
the Senior Executive Service. Benjamin claimed
some agencies were using the bonuses as salary to
evade ceilings voted by Congress. He tried to
place a $52,750 cap on overall executive pay. In a
compromise, Congress finally decided to limit
bonuses to no more than 25 percent of an agency's
senior executive level employees.

As Transportation chairman in 1981, Benjamin began fighting Reagan efforts to reduce funding for Conrail, Amtrak and other federal transportation programs. He helped stave off some
cuts in the Budget Committee but that proved
useless when the committee was overruled on the
floor, and a Reagan substitute budget passed.

**At Home:** Benjamin made it to the House on
his second try, defeating the man who had once
sponsored him for a West Point appointment,
House Rules chairman Ray J. Madden. The veteran Democrat called his former protégé an "un-
grateful young rat," but the voters merely saw it
as the passing of the generations and gave Benjamin a margin of more than 20,000 votes.

The passing almost took place in 1972, when
Benjamin's first challenge fell less than 5,000
votes short. He probably would have won then if
Madden had not been on the verge of promotion

---

**1st District: Northwest — Gary,
Hammond.** Population: 426,542 (10% de-
crease since 1970). Race: White 278,646 (65%),
Black 125,797 (29%), Others 22,099 (5%).
Spanish origin: 41,297 (10%).

to the Rules chairmanship, leading labor interests to work hard for his re-election. In 1974, Benjamin did not attempt a rematch.

But two years later, with Madden's powers of concentration declining a bit at age 84, Benjamin decided to try again. He mentioned few policy differences, arguing gently that the incumbent had served his district well and was ready for retirement. As in the past, Madden had help from labor plus that of the Lake County Democratic organization and the city's black mayor, Richard Hatcher. But his age was simply too much of a liability, and the result was not close.

Benjamin's congressional victory came after a long career in local and state politics in which he gained a reputation for careful and meticulous attention to duty. After serving as a zoning administrator in Gary and as executive secretary to the mayor in the mid-1960s, he was elected to the state House in 1966 and the state Senate in 1970. As a state legislator, he was known as the "great amender" — he was said to be the only one who read every bill.

**The District:** Created in 1932 to encompass the burgeoning steel-mill communities along Lake Michigan, the 1st District comprised all of Lake County until 1966, when the Supreme Court's equal population rule forced a redrawing of its lines, and the southern part of the county was removed. For 1982, the lines will change again. Indiana redistricting has extended the district beyond Lake County for the first time, bringing in parts of La Porte and Porter counties. But it is likely to be as safe for Benjamin as it has been so far. The descendants of the the Eastern and Southern Europeans who came to work in the steel mills still dominate the district, although blacks now make up nearly a third of it.

## Committees

**Appropriations** (19th of 33 Democrats)
Transportation, chairman; Energy and Water Development; Legislative.

**Budget**
Task Forces: Economic Policy and Productivity; Reconciliation; Transportation, Research and Development, and Capital Resources.

## Elections

**1980 General**

| | |
|---|---|
| Adam Benjamin Jr. (D ) | 112,016 (72 %) |
| Joseph Harkin (R ) | 43,537 (28 %) |

**1978 General**

| | |
|---|---|
| Adam Benjamin Jr. (D ) | 72,367 (80 %) |
| Owen Crumpacker (R ) | 17,419 (19 %) |

**Previous Winning Percentages**

1976 (71 %)

**District Vote For President**

| 1980 | | 1976 | | 1972 | |
|---|---|---|---|---|---|
| D | 90,660 (54 %) | D | 108,388 (61 %) | D | 82,173 (47 %) |
| R | 68,283 (41 %) | R | 68,428 (38 %) | R | 91,298 (52 %) |
| I | 6,357 (4 %) | | | | |

## Campaign Finance

| | Receipts | Receipts from PACs | Expenditures |
|---|---|---|---|
| **1980** | | | |
| Benjamin (D ) | $87,070 | $33,701 (39 %) | $73,867 |

| 1978 | | | |
|---|---|---|---|
| Benjamin (D ) | $90,186 | $30,325 (34 %) | $77,483 |
| Crumpacker (R ) | $30,378 | $400 (1 %) | $26,459 |

## Voting Studies

| | Presidential Support | | Party Unity | | Conservative Coalition | |
|---|---|---|---|---|---|---|
| Year | S | O | S | O | S | O |
| 1980 | 61 | 39 | 70 | 30 | 53 | 47 |
| 1979 | 66 | 34 | 73 | 27 | 53 | 47 |
| 1978 | 62 | 38 | 72 | 28 | 34 | 66 |
| 1977 | 59 | 39 | 73 | 26 | 31 | 67 |

S = Support      O = Opposition

## Key Votes

**96th Congress**

| | |
|---|---|
| Weaken Carter oil profits tax (1979) | Y |
| Reject hospital cost control plan (1979) | Y |
| Implement Panama Canal Treaties (1979) | N |
| Establish Department of Education (1979) | Y |
| Approve Anti-busing Amendment (1979) | N |
| Guarantee Chrysler Corp. loans (1979) | Y |
| Approve military draft registration (1980) | N |
| Aid Sandinista regime in Nicaragua (1980) | N |
| Strengthen fair housing laws (1980) | Y |

**97th Congress**

| | |
|---|---|
| Reagan budget proposal (1981) | N |

## Interest Group Ratings

| Year | ADA | ACA | AFL-CIO | CCUS |
|---|---|---|---|---|
| 1980 | 61 | 33 | 74 | 62 |
| 1979 | 47 | 19 | 80 | 44 |
| 1978 | 65 | 22 | 80 | 22 |
| 1977 | 50 | 26 | 91 | 13 |

**393**

# 2 Floyd Fithian (D)

**Of Lafayette — Elected 1974**

**Born:** Nov. 3, 1928, Vesta, Neb.
**Education:** Peru State College, B.S. 1951; U. of Neb., M.A. 1955, Ph.D. 1960.
**Military Career:** Navy, 1951-55.
**Profession:** Farmer and history professor.
**Family:** Wife, Marjorie Heim; three children.
**Religion:** Methodist.
**Political Career:** Unsuccessful campaign for Tippecanoe County Council, 1970; unsuccessful Democratic nominee for U.S. House, 1972.

**In Washington:** Fithian's formula for holding a difficult congressional district has been the same one other Indiana Democrats have used with success in recent years — clean government issues, fiscal conservatism, and a lot of attention to local problems.

His voting record has been sufficient to deny most of his critics any opportunity to call him spendthrift. He regularly voted against federal budgets and increases in the debt ceiling during the Carter years, despite urgings of House leaders. He has backed a constitutional amendment to require a balanced budget.

Meanwhile, he has sought to keep up the reform credentials he worked to establish in his early campaigns. During his first year in the House, he refused a congressional pay increase and used the money for constituent services, a practice he has continued. During his third term, he was still railing against congressional perquisites, arguing that members of Congress should not have free parking privileges. When purchasing scandals developed in the General Services Administration, he offered an amendment to deny the agency $100 million and use the money to buy American grain for the Food for Peace program.

That effort managed to tie together two of Fithian's political and legislative priorities. As a member of the Agriculture Committee, Fithian speaks for the corn and soybean growers of northern Indiana, prosperous farmers who rarely clamor for federal interference but like to hear legislators defend their interests. He has been less predictable when it comes to other crops. In 1980, when wheat growers objected to creating a wheat reserve for poor nations on the grounds that it might depress American prices, Fithian said it was needed on a humanitarian basis.

While keeping his conservative record intact, Fithian has been able to use his place on the Agriculture Committee to promote environmental issues. He has been interested in controlling the use of pesticides, and offered one amendment in 1977 guaranteeing the right of the Environmental Protection Agency to limit the use of particular chemicals to specific pests.

He has also been on the anti-pork-barrel, environmentalist side in arguments over federal water projects. It was Fithian's 1979 amendment that de-authorized 17 water projects, at an estimated savings of $2.3 billion, on the argument that the residents of the areas around the projects did not want them.

When the activities of the major oil companies became a hot political issue in the gasoline shortage of 1979, Fithian was quick to jump on it. He sponsored an energy anti-monopoly bill, which would have blocked 16 of the largest companies from acquiring any other business with assets of more than $100 million. "The oil companies have responded to the energy crisis with price gouging," he said. Some of his Indiana colleagues felt he was demagoguing the issue. But it was a popular position.

**At Home:** Many 2nd District Republicans were quietly pleased when Fithian won here in 1974. They were happy to be rid of an embarrassing Republican incumbent, and certain that a more attractive GOP newcomer could take the district back in 1976. But Fithian did not cooperate with the scenario. After two years in

---

**2nd District: Northwest — Lafayette.** Population: 571,571 (21% increase since 1970). Race: White 560,983 (98%), Black 3,130 (1%), Others 7,458 (1%). Spanish origin: 9,258 (2%).

office he was unbeatable, and he probably would have remained unbeatable in the 2nd had the Indiana Legislature not eliminated it in redistricting for 1982.

A low-key and personable history professor, Fithian became engaged in politics during Robert F. Kennedy's 1968 presidential campaign. Two years later, he made his first bid for public office — Tippecanoe County commissioner — and lost. That year he also helped manage Democrat Phil Sprague's unsuccessful congressional campaign against Republican Rep. Earl Landgrebe, the ornery and tactless trucking executive who had held the seat since 1968.

In 1972, Fithian ran himself against Landgrebe, and won 45 percent of the vote in a year when George McGovern was drawing 26 percent. His showing encouraged him to try again in 1974.

By then, Landgrebe had angered most of the district with his last-ditch defense of Nixon, even after most of the president's supporters were calling for resignation. Fithian was well organized, using computers and an intensive registration drive. He beat Landgrebe easily.

In 1976, Fithian became the first Democrat to be re-elected from the district in the 20th century. His continued victories have been a result not only of his voting record but of his toll-free telephone line, mobile office, and constant personal presence. In 1980, as Indiana was going heavily Republican for most offices, Fithian won a fourth term by nearly 20,000 votes.

**The District:** The current 2nd lies in the eastern edge of the Corn Belt, taking in several rural counties, the city of Lafayette on the south, suburbs of Gary on the north, and Porter County, a center for the steel industry.

But the district will not exist after 1982. Redistricting will scatter its counties among four other constituencies, forcing Fithian to run in unfamiliar — and heavily Republican — territory, if he does not seek statewide office.

## Committees

**Agriculture** (13th of 24 Democrats)
Conservation, Credit, and Rural Development; Department Operations, Research, and Foreign Agriculture; Wheat, Soybeans and Feed Grains.

**Government Operations** (14th of 23 Democrats)
Environment, Enegy and National Resources; Intergovernmental Relations and Human Resources.

## Elections

**1980 General**

| | |
|---|---|
| Floyd Fithian (D ) | 122,326 (54 %) |
| Ernest Niemeyer (R ) | 103,957 (46 %) |

**1978 General**

| | |
|---|---|
| Floyd Fithian (D ) | 82,402 (57 %) |
| J. Philip Oppenheim (R ) | 52,842 (36 %) |
| William Costas (I ) | 9,368 (6 %) |

**Previous Winning Percentages**

1976 (55 %)    1974 (61 %)

**District Vote For President**

| 1980 | 1976 | 1972 |
|---|---|---|
| D 66,413 (29 %) | D 83,381 (38 %) | D 53,463 (26 %) |
| R 146,560 (63 %) | R 132,805 (61%) | R 149,099 (73%) |
| I 14,348 (6 %) | | |

## Campaign Finance

| | Receipts | Receipts from PACs | Expenditures |
|---|---|---|---|
| **1980** | | | |
| Fithian (D ) | $274,591 | $121,893 (44 %) | $280,192 |
| Niemeyer (R ) | $62,865 | $10,400 (17 %) | $53,426 |
| **1978** | | | |
| Fithian (D ) | $206,213 | $79,095 (38 %) | $196,945 |

| | | | |
|---|---|---|---|
| Oppenheim (R ) | $138,223 | $26,452 (19 %) | $136,475 |

## Voting Studies

| | Presidential Support | | Party Unity | | Conservative Coalition | |
|---|---|---|---|---|---|---|
| Year | S | O | S | O | S | O |
| 1980 | 62 | 33 | 67 | 29 | 45 | 49 |
| 1979 | 70 | 26 | 73 | 24 | 44 | 53 |
| 1978 | 64 | 33 | 60 | 39 | 52 | 46 |
| 1977 | 62 | 25 | 60 | 29 | 44 | 48 |
| 1976 | 22 | 73 | 61 | 28 | 44 | 46 |
| 1975 | 28 | 69 | 69 | 24 | 37 | 55 |

S = Support          O = Opposition

## Key Votes

**96th Congress**

| | |
|---|---|
| Weaken Carter oil profits tax (1979) | N |
| Reject hospital cost control plan (1979) | Y |
| Implement Panama Canal Treaties (1979) | Y |
| Establish Department of Education (1979) | Y |
| Approve Anti-busing Amendment (1979) | Y |
| Guarantee Chrysler Corp. loans (1979) | Y |
| Approve military draft registration (1980) | N |
| Aid Sandinista regime in Nicaragua (1980) | Y |
| Strengthen fair housing laws (1980) | N |

**97th Congress**

| | |
|---|---|
| Reagan budget proposal (1981) | N |

## Interest Group Ratings

| Year | ADA | ACA | AFL-CIO | CCUS |
|---|---|---|---|---|
| 1980 | 56 | 27 | 63 | 66 |
| 1979 | 53 | 23 | 80 | 22 |
| 1978 | 25 | 58 | 50 | 33 |
| 1977 | 50 | 40 | 71 | 47 |
| 1976 | 40 | 23 | 55 | 19 |
| 1975 | 68 | 41 | 90 | 29 |

# 3 John Hiler (R)

**Of La Porte — Elected 1980**

**Born:** April 24, 1953, Chicago, Ill.
**Education:** Williams College, B.A. 1975; U. of Chicago, M.B.A. 1977.
**Profession:** Foundry executive.
**Family:** Single.
**Religion:** Roman Catholic.
**Political Career:** Republican nominee for Ind. House, 1978.

**The Member:** Hiler won his seat by blaming Congress — and specifically Majority Whip John Brademas — for most of the nation's ills. The immediate problem he cited was unemployment, which was more than 15 percent in Elkhart County. Sensing early that he was in danger, Brademas brought federal grants into the district and painted Hiler as too inexperienced and simplistic. But Hiler convinced voters that Brademas was a major architect of failed Democratic economic policies.

Hiler believes that reducing government loan and loan guarantee programs will direct more business to private lenders, who can then afford to cut interest rates. Lower interest rates will boost investment and sales in his district's construction, manufactured housing, vehicle and steel industries, Hiler says.

Hiler's political career began in 1978. Then just out of graduate school, he was working in his father's foundry when party leaders picked him to fill a last-minute vacancy in a legislative election. He came within 500 votes of winning and impressed party leaders with his strong speaking ability and hard work.

Some credited Hiler's 1980 victory to presidential coattails, but he ran ahead of Reagan in two counties and matched Reagan's 49 percent in St. Joseph County (South Bend).

**The District:** Brademas kept the 3rd in Democratic hands for 22 years, but 1981 redistricting should help Hiler hold it.

As redrawn for 1982, the 3rd will have four good Republican counties — Elkhart, La Porte, Marshall and Kosciusko. The latter two were added in redistricting.

St. Joseph County, home of Notre Dame University in South Bend, was Democratic in the past, but lately the GOP has fared well there. Redistricting also added Starke, a swing county.

Flat, fertile farmlands lie between the manufacturing towns of La Porte, South Bend, and Elkhart, whose products range from Alka-Seltzer to railroad cars.

## Committees

**Government Operations** (13th of 17 Republicans)
Commerce, Consumer, and Monetary Affairs; Environment, Energy and Natural Resources.

**Small Business** (9th of 17 Democrats)
Energy, Environment and Safety Issues Affecting Small Business; SBA and SBIC Authority, Minority Enterprise and General Small Business Problems.

## Elections

**1980 General**

| | |
|---|---|
| John Hiler (R) | 103,972 (55 %) |
| John Brademas (D) | 85,136 (45 %) |

**1980 Primary**

| | |
|---|---|
| John Hiler (R) | 23,548 (58 %) |
| Richard Pfeil (R) | 15,567 (38 %) |

**District Vote For President**

| | 1980 | | 1976 | | 1972 |
|---|---|---|---|---|---|
| D | 73,808 (39 %) | D | 84,017 (46 %) | D | 66,985 (36 %) |
| R | 101,586 (53 %) | R | 98,139 (53 %) | R | 120,430 (64 %) |
| I | 12,170 (6 %) | | | | |

## Campaign Finance

| | Receipts | Receipts from PACs | Expenditures |
|---|---|---|---|
| **1980** | | | |
| Hiler (R) | $432,001 | $130,232 (30 %) | $393,680 |
| Brademas (D) | $679,661 | $149,788 (22 %) | $666,121 |

## Key Vote

**97th Congress**

| | |
|---|---|
| Reagan budget proposal (1981) | Y |

---

**3rd District: North central — South Bend.** Population: 481,917 (2% increase since 1970). Race: White 439,303 (91%), Black 36,024 (7%), Others 6,590 (1%). Spanish origin: 6,532 (1%).

# 4 Dan Coats (R)

**Of Fort Wayne — Elected 1980**

**Born:** May 16, 1943, Jackson, Mich.
**Education:** Wheaton College, B.A. 1965; Ind. U.,
J.D. 1971.
**Military Career:** Army Corps of Engineers,
1966-68.
**Profession:** Lawyer.
**Family:** Wife, Marcia Anne Crawford; three
children.
**Religion:** Protestant.
**Political Career:** No previous office.

**The Member:** Coats is a near-carbon copy
of former Rep. Dan Quayle, and that is the way he
wants it.

As Quayle's district representative for three
years, Coats cultivated the role of surrogate congressman. He handled constituents' problems personally, and whenever Quayle was unable to attend an event, Coats stepped in for him to give a
"government is too big" address. Running for the
House the same year his boss moved to the
Senate, he had a spot on the ballot just below
Quayle and shared the highly effective political
organization both of them had helped build.

A relative newcomer to the district, Coats
had to get past a bitter GOP primary against two
candidates with much stronger local roots. But he
easily won the primary and went on to smash
Democrat John D. Walda, who was making his
second try for the seat. Winning more votes than
any previous 4th District candidate, Coats even
managed to outpoll Quayle within the district.

Since taking office, Coats has often said his
constituents expect him to vote in complete con-
cordance with President Reagan's economic
proposals.

**The District:** The 4th District is centered
around Republican Fort Wayne, Indiana's second
largest city. Fort Wayne has been a manufacturing center for the electrical products industry —
particularly General Electric — for most of the
20th century. The city accounts for about half the
district's vote.

Most of the farmers who live in the outlying
parts of the district are of German heritage. The
district has the largest concentration of German-
Americans in the state.

Except for three terms in the early 1970s, the
district has been in Republican hands since 1950.
Even when Democrat J. Edward Roush won the
seat in 1970, 1972 and 1974, Republican statewide
candidates prevailed, often by sizable margins.

## Committees

**Energy and Commerce** (17th of 18 Republicans)
Fossil and Synthetic Fuels; Oversight and Investigations.

**Select Aging** (16th of 23 Republicans)
Retirement Income and Employment.

## Elections

**1980 General**

| | |
|---|---|
| Dan Coats (R ) | 120,055 (61 %) |
| John Walda (D ) | 77,542 (39 %) |

**1980 Primary**

| | |
|---|---|
| Dan Coats (R ) | 35,138 (58 %) |
| Paul Helmke (R ) | 14,550 (24 %) |
| Elmer MacDonald (R ) | 10,808 (18 %) |

**District Vote For President**

| | 1980 | | 1976 | | 1972 |
|---|---|---|---|---|---|
| **D** | 66,137 (33 %) | **D** | 79,908 (40 %) | **D** | 63,938 (33 %) |
| **R** | 118,323 (58 %) | **R** | 118,239 (59 %) | **R** | 130,321 (67 %) |
| **I** | 15,295 (8 %) | | | | |

## Campaign Finance

| | Receipts | Receipts from PACs | Expen-ditures |
|---|---|---|---|
| **1980** | | | |
| Coats (R ) | $222,370 | $92,295 (41 %) | $205,216 |
| Walda (D ) | $114,587 | $40,350 (35 %) | $117,020 |

## Key Vote

**97th Congress**

| | |
|---|---|
| Reagan budget proposal (1981) | Y |

> **4th District: Northeast — Fort Wayne.** Population: 506,982 (7% increase since 1970). Race: White 473,781 (93%), Black 26,665 (5%), Others 6,536 (1%). Spanish origin: 6,168 (1%).

# 5 Elwood Hillis (R)

**Of Kokomo — Elected 1970**

**Born:** March 6, 1926, Kokomo, Ind.
**Education:** Ind. U., B.S. 1949, J.D. 1952.
**Military Career:** Army, 1944-46.
**Profession:** Lawyer.
**Family:** Wife, Carol Hoyne; three children.
**Religion:** Presbyterian.
**Political Career:** Ind. House, 1967-71; unsuccessful campaign for Howard County prosecutor, 1954.

**In Washington:** One of the more mild-mannered and anonymous House members for a decade, Hillis has been making considerably more noise lately as a spokesman for the auto industry, on which his district depends.

General Motors is the district's largest single employer, but Chrysler makes transmissions in Kokomo, and when the Chrysler loan guarantee came to the floor in 1979, Hillis was active in rounding up votes for it — work he does not normally specialize in.

He also became co-chairman of the Congressional Auto Task Force, made up of members who, like Hillis, need the industry for their constituents' livelihood and their own political security. In 1980, Hillis and Democratic Rep. William Brodhead of Michigan called a press conference to release the group's 64-page study of the industry's problems.

The study recommended federally imposed limits on Japanese auto imports, more favorable tax treatment on depreciation of manufacturing equipment, antitrust exemptions for new technology shared by the industry, and eased environmental and safety regulations. Hillis and Brodhead introduced their own bill to place a five-year quota on imports from Japan.

Hillis' voting record has usually responded to the unions in his district, especially but not only the United Auto Workers. In 1975, for instance, he voted for the common-site picketing bill, to expand labor's right to picket construction projects. President Ford later vetoed the legislation. In 1977, he joined the majority of his Republican colleagues in voting against it.

On Armed Services, his major committee, Hillis has normally voted a more traditionally hawkish Republican position. He has favored preparations for a military draft. As early as 1978, he introduced an amendment to beef up the Selective Service by reopening local draft offices.

"Our military is currently unable to fight a protracted conventional war," Hillis warned. "Either we will lose the war, or it will go nuclear."

The amendment was defeated on the floor. But President Carter recommended draft registration in 1980, and it was reinstituted later in the year.

**At Home:** Quiet though he is in Washington, Hillis has built up a nearly invulnerable position in his district — as he proved in 1980, when he easily beat back what had been billed as his strongest Democratic challenge in a decade. Hillis defeated Nels Ackerson, an aide to Sen. Birch Bayh, with 62 percent of the vote.

Ackerson conducted a full-time door-to-door campaign, charging that Hillis had not done enough to deal with unemployment in the district. But the incumbent had attracted attention with his participation in the Chrysler battle, and his political base in Kokomo and the surrounding rural counties was never threatened.

A member of an established Republican family in central Indiana — his father, Glen, came within 4,000 votes of the governorship in 1940 — Hillis was a two-term member of the Indiana House when Republican congressional district leaders chose him to run for Congress in 1970. GOP incumbent Richard Roudebush had been renominated, but he was later chosen by a state convention to run for the U.S. Senate. Hillis won

> **5th District: North central — Anderson, Kokomo, Marion.** Population: 501,096 (6% increase since 1970). Race: White 455,221 (91%), Black 40,640 (8%), Others 5,235 (1%). Spanish origin: 4,504 (1%).

easily in November and has continued to win without difficulty.

**The District:** The 5th is a mixture of cornfields, livestock farms and small industrial cities. Kokomo, Marion and Anderson, the three largest towns within the current district boundaries, are economically dependent on auto and auto accessory plants, and have been suffering along with the rest of the industry. The current 5th also includes a sliver of northern Indianapolis.

For 1982, redistricting will move the district north, dropping the Indianapolis portion and the city of Anderson, and also shift it west to the Illinois border. It will give Hillis a considerable amount of new territory to campaign in, but it will still be a Republican district.

## Committees

**Armed Services** (8th of 19 Republicans)
Military Personnel and Compensation; Procurement and Military Nuclear Systems; Readiness.

**Veterans' Affairs** (4th of 14 Republicans)
Hospitals and Health Care; Oversight and Investigations.

## Elections

**1980 General**

| | |
|---|---|
| Ellwood Hillis (R ) | 129,474 (62 %) |
| Nels Ackerson (D ) | 80,378 (38 %) |

**1978 Primary**

| | |
|---|---|
| Elwood Hillis (R ) | 94,950 (68 %) |
| Max Heiss (D ) | 45,479 (32 %) |

**Previous Winning Percentages**

1976 (62 %)    1974 (57 %)    1972 (64 %)    1970 (56 %)

**District Vote For President**

| | 1980 | | 1976 | | 1972 |
|---|---|---|---|---|---|
| D | 74,921 (35 %) | D | 89,307 (42 %) | D | 58,893 (30 %) |
| R | 127,867 (60 %) | R | 119,475 (57 %) | R | 135,915 (70 %) |
| I | 9,496 (4 %) | | | | |

## Campaign Finance

| | Receipts | Receipts from PACs | Expenditures |
|---|---|---|---|
| **1980** | | | |
| Hillis (R ) | $148,974 | $72,929 (49 %) | $185,414 |
| Ackerson (D ) | $115,126 | $25,026 (22 %) | $115,086 |
| **1978** | | | |
| Hillis (R ) | $102,574 | $32,125 (31 %) | $72,873 |

## Voting Studies

| | Presidential Support | | Party Unity | | Conservative Coalition | |
|---|---|---|---|---|---|---|
| Year | S | O | S | O | S | O |
| 1980 | 41 | 43† | 65 | 23† | 69 | 17 |

| Year | S | O | S | O | S | O |
|---|---|---|---|---|---|---|
| 1979 | 39 | 51 | 69 | 22 | 79 | 10 |
| 1978 | 33 | 52 | 71 | 20 | 75 | 15 |
| 1977 | 51 | 42 | 65 | 23 | 77 | 13 |
| 1976 | 57 | 29 | 60 | 29 | 72 | 16 |
| 1975 | 63 | 29 | 65 | 28 | 66 | 24 |
| 1974 | 62 | 28 | 61 | 29† | 67 | 23 |
| 1974 (Ford) | 50 | 33 | | | | |
| 1973 | 61 | 32 | 58 | 35 | 67 | 26 |
| 1972 | 65 | 14 | 51 | 28 | 57 | 26 |
| 1971 | 91 | 5 | 68 | 20 | 71 | 17 |

S = Support          O = Opposition

† Not eligible for all recorded votes.

## Key Votes

**96th Congress**

| | |
|---|---|
| Weaken Carter oil profits tax (1979) | Y |
| Reject hospital cost control plan (1979) | Y |
| Implement Panama Canal Treaties (1979) | Y |
| Establish Department of Education (1979) | Y |
| Approve Anti-busing Amendment (1979) | Y |
| Guarantee Chrysler Corp. loans (1979) | Y |
| Approve military draft registration (1980) | Y |
| Aid Sandinista regime in Nicaragua (1980) | N |
| Strengthen fair housing laws (1980) | N |

**97th Congress**

| | |
|---|---|
| Reagan budget proposal (1981) | Y |

## Interest Group Ratings

| Year | ADA | ACA | AFL-CIO | CCUS |
|---|---|---|---|---|
| 1980 | 22 | 70 | 35 | 78 |
| 1979 | 11 | 83 | 17 | 94 |
| 1978 | 10 | 69 | 35 | 56 |
| 1977 | 25 | 62 | 41 | 65 |
| 1976 | 25 | 62 | 36 | 54 |
| 1975 | 26 | 59 | 43 | 67 |
| 1974 | 26 | 50 | 40 | 75 |
| 1973 | 16 | 72 | 50 | 70 |
| 1972 | 19 | 50 | 50 | 60 |
| 1971 | 11 | 76 | 33 | - |

# 6 David W. Evans (D)

**Of Indianapolis — Elected 1974**

**Born:** Aug. 17, 1946, Lafayette, Ind.
**Education:** Ind. U., B.A. 1967.
**Profession:** Teacher.
**Family:** Wife, Darlene Ginder; one child.
**Religion:** Roman Catholic.
**Political Career:** Unsuccessful Democratic nominee for U.S. House, 1972.

**In Washington:** When Evans lent his support in 1980 to a proposal to create a memorial to the late Allard K. Lowenstein, he reminded some House colleagues of a fact easy to forget — he participated with the slain liberal leader in the anti-war movement of the 1960s, and in Lowenstein's congressional campaigns after that.

Few who have watched Evans over his six-year House career would see much reason to connect him with Lowenstein or liberalism. Elected in a conservative district in the 1974 Watergate landslide, he has taken extraordinary care not to give voters any ideological reason to turn him out of office.

By 1980, he was voting with the "conservative coalition" of Republicans and Southern Democrats 79 percent of the time on the House floor, more often than all but two other Democrats from districts outside the South. In 1981 he supported the Reagan budget over the Democratic alternative on the House floor. He has defended his voting record by arguing that "there is little room for party loyalty when important and complex and far-reaching issues and staggering amounts of money are involved."

Evans' determination to vote his district has helped him survive in hard political times, but it has probably denied him a chance to gain much influence among House Democrats, who tend to view him as being preoccupied, if not obsessed, with local opinion, and passive when it comes to drafting major legislation. When an important subcommittee chairmanship opened up on Government Operations in 1979, Evans was passed over, along with the very conservative Glenn English of Oklahoma, in favor of Toby Moffett of Connecticut.

In the 96th Congress, Evans voted for a constitutional amendment against busing. He has desribed busing as "an ill-conceived, ineffective social experiment that simply does not work." He has also backed another amendment that would ban abortion. He opposed legislation to imple-

ment the Panama Canal treaties, and to create a national minimum for welfare benefits.

In earlier Congresses, Evans had voted for common-site picketing and labor law revision, and this was used against him by Republicans at home.

Evans did vote — and work — for the 1979 Chrysler loan guarantee, which affected some automobile workers in his district, and for a liberal interpretation of trade adjustment benefits aimed at the same industry. He performed a favor for the mobile home industry by introducing an amendment, adopted in the House, allowing the industry to be classified for legislative purposes as "manufactured housing" rather than mobile homes. The new name, it was argued, would give the industry a broader public image.

**At Home:** Evans was one of the most startling of the 1974 Democratic Watergate winners. Running an underfinanced campaign against longtime GOP Rep. William Bray in a district designed to be Republican forever, Evans upset Bray by over 7,000 votes.

He had first run in 1972, losing to Bray by a wide margin. He was only 26 then, but he had been involved in politics for four years, as an aide to Lowenstein, in Robert Kennedy's campaign for president in 1968, and in John Neff's bid for Indianapolis mayor in 1971. He had also worked as a teacher and assistant high school principal in Indianapolis.

> **6th District: Central — Indianapolis suburbs.** Population: 512,727 (9% increase since 1970). Race: White 485,708 (95%), Black 22,809 (4%), Others 4,210 (1%). Spanish origin: 3,545 (1%).

Since 1974, Evans' voting record and constituent services have maintained him in office, although just barely. His opponent for three elections in a row has been Indianapolis psychiatrist David Crane, who has been trying to join his two brothers — Philip and Daniel of Illinois — in the House. Each time Evans has come out a winner, but by steadily declining margins; in 1980 his plurality was less than 1,000 votes.

That series of battles is now over. The Indiana Legislature has eliminated Evans' district for 1982, and while he may run for the House somewhere in Indiana, it will not be in the constituency he now represents.

**The District:** The current 6th is split between the city of Indianapolis and its surrounding suburbs. It includes blue-collar neighborhoods where most of the jobs are in the automobile industry, and white-collar neighborhoods where the breadwinners are state government employees.

There are also four other entire counties and parts of a fifth, with middle- and upper-income suburban areas and some farms in the outlying areas.

For 1982, this territory will be divided among three other districts, leaving Evans no recognizable constituency to run in. There is a new 6th, but it contains little of the territory Evans currently represents, and it is overwhelmingly Republican. Evans plans to run for reelection in the new 10th district, which includes about 40 percent of his old constituency. He would face another Democratic incumbent, Andy Jacobs, in the primary.

## Committees

**Banking, Finance and Urban Affairs** (12th of 25 Democrats)
Economic Stabilization; Financial Institutions Supervision, Regulation and Insurance; Housing and Community Development.

**Government Operations** (11th of 23 Democrats)
Government Activities and Transportation; Legislation and National Security.

**Select Aging** (13th of 31 Democrats)
Health and Long-Term Care; Retirement Income and Employment.

## Elections

**1980 General**

| | |
|---|---|
| David Evans (D ) | 99,089 (50 %) |
| David Crane (R ) | 98,302 (50 %) |

**1980 Primary**

| | |
|---|---|
| David Evans (D ) | 32,602 (93 %) |
| Joe Turner (D ) | 2,364 (7 %) |

**1978 General**

| | |
|---|---|
| David Evans (D ) | 66,421 (52 %) |
| David Crane (R ) | 60,630 (48 %) |

**Previous Winning Percentages**

1976 (55 %)    1974 (52 %)

**District Vote For President**

| | 1980 | | 1976 | | 1972 |
|---|---|---|---|---|---|
| **D** | 64,836 (33 %) | **D** | 80,098 (41 %) | **D** | 45,822 (26 %) |
| **R** | 123,573 (62 %) | **R** | 113,083 (58 %) | **R** | 127,747 (73 %) |
| **I** | 8,515 (4 %) | | | | |

## Campaign Finance

| | Receipts | Receipts from PACs | Expenditures |
|---|---|---|---|
| **1980** | | | |
| Evans (D ) | $311,780 | $141,033 (45 %) | $311,007 |
| Crane (R ) | $618,674 | $102,942 (17 %) | $595,637 |

| **1978** | | | |
|---|---|---|---|
| Evans (D ) | $213,048 | $108,142 (51 %) | $180,870 |
| Crane (R ) | $422,812 | $80,467 (19 %) | $431,943 |

## Voting Studies

| Year | Presidential Support | | Party Unity | | Conservative Coalition | |
|---|---|---|---|---|---|---|
| | **S** | **O** | **S** | **O** | **S** | **O** |
| 1980 | 56 | 42 | 35 | 62 | 79 | 21 |
| 1979 | 51 | 48 | 43 | 53 | 71 | 28 |
| 1978 | 45 | 52 | 40 | 57 | 67 | 28 |
| 1977 | 52 | 38 | 42 | 50 | 60 | 32 |
| 1976 | 31 | 57 | 49 | 46 | 59 | 36 |
| 1975 | 28 | 71 | 62 | 32 | 42 | 56 |

S = Support          O = Opposition

## Key Votes

**96th Congress**

| | |
|---|---|
| Weaken Carter oil profits tax (1979) | N |
| Reject hospital cost control plan (1979) | Y |
| Implement Panama Canal Treaties (1979) | N |
| Establish Department of Education (1979) | Y |
| Approve Anti-busing Amendment (1979) | Y |
| Guarantee Chrysler Corp. loans (1979) | Y |
| Approve military draft registration (1980) | Y |
| Aid Sandinista regime in Nicaragua (1980) | N |
| Strengthen fair housing laws (1980) | Y |

**97th Congress**

| | |
|---|---|
| Reagan budget proposal (1981) | Y |

## Interest Group Ratings

| Year | ADA | ACA | AFL-CIO | CCUS |
|---|---|---|---|---|
| 1980 | 28 | 63 | 53 | 52 |
| 1979 | 32 | 56 | 63 | 59 |
| 1978 | 25 | 63 | 55 | 24 |
| 1977 | 40 | 56 | 55 | 50 |
| 1976 | 50 | 41 | 55 | 33 |
| 1975 | 68 | 30 | 90 | 31 |

# 7 John T. Myers (R)

### Of Covington — Elected 1966

**Born:** Feb. 8, 1927, Covington, Ind.
**Education:** Ind. State U., B.S. 1951.
**Military Career:** Army, 1945-46.
**Profession:** Banker, farmer.
**Family:** Wife, Carol Carruthers; two children.
**Religion:** Episcopalian.
**Political Career:** No previous office.

**In Washington:** Myers' conservative folksiness and solid party loyalty symbolize the old-fashioned Republicanism that members still associate with Indiana. He is a banker, a Mason, an Elk and a Lion, and a former head of the Congressional Prayer Group. He is one of the hail fellows of GOP ranks, popular as a cloakroom comic but no leader on policy issues. He made a brief, unsuccessful bid for party whip in 1980.

Myers was a die-hard supporter of the war in Vietnam, appalled at draft dodgers and protesters. His 1977 amendment blocked funding for Carter's program of pardon for Vietnam resisters. Myers argued "amnesty for the draft dodger and deserter would be an insult to those who fought in Vietnam and the families of the men who died there." Carter was still able to end prosecution of draft dodgers, but Myers made their re-entry to the U.S. more difficult.

As a ten-year veteran of the Appropriations Committee and senior Republican on its Energy and Water Subcommittee, Myers argues strongly for dams and other public works projects.

He is as bipartisan on those issues as he is partisan on most others. When President Carter proposed to cut off funding for 18 water projects around the country, Myers was a loyal ally of Tom Bevill, D-Ala., the subcommittee chairman who fought to keep the work going. Over the years, Myers has brought his district modest but tangible public works help: water and sewer grants; a coal gasification project; money from the Economic Development Administration.

Myers' one concern about public works projects has been that they sometimes force farmers to relocate. In 1977, he introduced a bill raising benefits to farmers required to move by the federal government. He also looks out for Indiana farm interests on the Agriculture Appropriations Subcommittee. He opposed Carter's grain embargo, saying it hurt farmers rather than the Soviets.

**At Home:** When Indiana redistricted in

1966, the 7th District in the southwest part of the state found itself with no incumbent. Myers' 29 percent was enough to give him the GOP nomination over five opponents, one of whom, Daniel Crane, now serves in the House from Illinois.

As a small-town banker and farmer, Myers had long been active in the Republican Party, mostly on the local level in Covington. He also worked in Young Republican ranks.

That first nomination pretty much guaranteed Myers a district in which he would be difficult to unseat, and Democrats helped him for years by nominating candidates of limited appeal. In 1966, in the first campaign, he defeated Elden C. Tipton, a former naval officer and farmer who had already been beaten twice before. Tipton tried two more campaigns against Myers but never came close. His son, J. Elden Tipton, ran a similarly ineffective campaign against Myers in 1976.

By 1978, many Democrats in the 7th District believed Myers' only real strength was his ability to draw the Tiptons as his opposition. But since then, he has managed to discredit that theory. In both 1978 and 1980, he easily defeated opponents thought to be strong contenders. In both cases, Myers' rural support cancelled out Democratic strength in Bloomington.

**The District:** The current 7th includes urban university communities in Bloomington and

---

**7th District: West — Terre Haute, Bloomington.** Population: 506,123 (7% increase since 1970). Race: White 491,405 (97%), Black 9,571 (2%), Others 5,147 (1%). Spanish origin: 3,431 (1%).

Terre Haute, southern rural counties with a Democratic tradition, and northern rural counties with a Republican history. The makeup has worked to Myers' advantage because the Democratic support is divided between the urban and rural factions.

In redistricting for 1982, Myers loses Bloomington and picks up another university town, Lafayette, home of Purdue. The result should still be a Republican district.

## Committees

**Appropriations** (4th of 22 Republicans)
   Agriculture; Energy and Water Development.

**Standards of Official Conduct** (3rd of 6 Republicans)

## Elections

**1980 General**

| | |
|---|---|
| John Myers (R ) | 137,604 (66 %) |
| Patrick Carroll (D ) | 69,051 (33 %) |

**1978 General**

| | |
|---|---|
| John Myers (R ) | 86,955 (56 %) |
| Charlotte Zietlow (D ) | 67,469 (44 %) |

**Previous Winning Percentages**

1976 (63 %)   1974 (57 %)   1972 (62 %)   1970 (57 %)
1968 (60 %)   1966 (54 %)

**District Vote For President**

| | 1980 | | 1976 | | 1972 |
|---|---|---|---|---|---|
| D | 79,075 (37 %) | D | 100,362 (47 %) | D | 72,718 (35 %) |
| R | 119,660 (56 %) | R | 111,589 (52 %) | R | 135,270 (65 %) |
| I | 10.524 (5 %) | | | | |

## Campaign Finance

| | Receipts | Receipts from PACs | Expenditures |
|---|---|---|---|
| **1980** | | | |
| Myers (R ) | $150,229 | $5,250 (4 %) | $142,908 |
| Carroll (D ) | $53,106 | $15,003 (28 %) | $51,232 |
| **1978** | | | |
| Myers (R ) | $152,664 | $42,076 (28 %) | $136,796 |
| Zietlow (D ) | $162,265 | $500 (0 %) | $161,992 |

## Voting Studies

| | Presidential Support | | Party Unity | | Conservative Coalition | |
|---|---|---|---|---|---|---|
| Year | S | O | S | O | S | O |
| 1980 | 38 | 61 | 88 | 11 | 91 | 7 |
| 1979 | 25 | 72 | 85 | 10 | 90 | 4 |
| 1978 | 29 | 67 | 87 | 11 | 90 | 7 |
| 1977 | 35 | 57 | 82 | 12 | 90 | 3 |
| 1976 | 75 | 24 | 87 | 11 | 95 | 5 |
| 1975 | 64 | 35 | 83 | 15 | 92 | 6 |
| 1974 (Ford) | 70 | 30 | | | | |
| 1974 | 66 | 26 | 75 | 18 | 87 | 8 |
| 1973 | 71 | 21 | 74 | 19 | 86 | 10 |
| 1972 | 54 | 41 | 72 | 21 | 88 | 6 |
| 1971 | 82 | 16 | 76 | 19 | 90 | 8 |
| 1970 | 67 | 23† | 74 | 14 | 84 | 7 |
| 1969 | 58 | 42† | 87 | 11† | 96 | 0 |
| 1968 | 51 | 42 | 74 | 16 | 86 | 12 |
| 1967 | 39 | 54 | 88 | 8 | 91 | 6 |

S = Support        O = Opposition
† Not eligible for all recorded votes.

## Key Votes

**96th Congress**

| | |
|---|---|
| Weaken Carter oil profits tax (1979) | Y |
| Reject hospital cost control plan (1979) | Y |
| Implement Panama Canal Treaties (1979) | N |
| Establish Department of Education (1979) | N |
| Approve Anti-busing Amendment (1979) | Y |
| Guarantee Chrysler Corp. loans (1979) | Y |
| Approve military draft registration (1980) | N |
| Aid Sandinista regime in Nicaragua (1980) | N |
| Strengthen fair housing laws (1980) | N |

**97th Congress**

| | |
|---|---|
| Reagan budget proposal (1981) | Y |

## Interest Group Ratings

| Year | ADA | ACA | AFL-CIO | CCUS |
|---|---|---|---|---|
| 1980 | 11 | 75 | 21 | 70 |
| 1979 | 0 | 91 | 17 | 94 |
| 1978 | 10 | 81 | 10 | 72 |
| 1977 | 5 | 85 | 23 | 100 |
| 1976 | 0 | 93 | 14 | 88 |
| 1975 | 0 | 93 | 26 | 88 |
| 1974 | 0 | 79 | 9 | 90 |
| 1973 | 4 | 79 | 10 | 90 |
| 1972 | 0 | 86 | 27 | 100 |
| 1971 | 11 | 92 | 0 | - |
| 1970 | 12 | 83 | 14 | 100 |
| 1969 | 0 | 88 | 10 | - |
| 1968 | 0 | 91 | 25 | - |
| 1967 | 7 | 93 | 17 | 100 |

# 8 Joel Deckard (R)

### Of Evansville — Elected 1978

**Born:** March 7, 1942, St. Elmo, Ill.
**Education:** Attended U. of Evansville, 1962-67.
**Military Career:** National Guard, 1966-72.
**Profession:** Newsman and cable television executive.
**Family:** Divorced.
**Religion:** Protestant.
**Political Career:** Ind. House, 1967-75; unsuccessfully sought re-election to Ind. House, 1974.

**In Washington:** Deckard compiled a consistent and virtually silent conservative record on the House floor in his first term, but constituent interests drove him far from the orthodox Republican position on two environmental issues.

As a member of the Government Operations Energy Subcommittee, Deckard picked up some locally useful publicity by launching an inquiry into construction methods at a nuclear power plant on the border of his district. Five workers at the Marble Hill plant complained in 1979 that concrete being poured for the facility was riddled with flaws, hastily covered over to conceal them from federal inspectors.

Deckard flew to Indiana, interviewed the plant's workers and began warning of a local safety hazard. Federal inspectors later confirmed the existence of 170 dangerous air pockets, and the project was temporarily shut down.

Actually, Deckard's skepticism about the plant fit his broader views on energy. He had been a solar heating contractor in private life and a believer in solar rather than nuclear power as a solution to the energy shortage. He introduced legislation calling for tax credits for solar heating and continued to express anti-nuclear views. He even appeared at an anti-nuclear rally attended by Jane Fonda, the only aspect of his work on the issue that brought him much criticism or controversy.

Meanwhile, Deckard has taken an unusual position for a Midwestern Republican: against many water projects and the Army Corps of Engineers. The corps had made itself highly unpopular in western Indiana by condemning private farm land for lock and dam construction on the Ohio River. A 55-year-old widow was jailed for refusing to sell seven acres.

Deckard insisted that his district had enough water already and that the lock and dam work was beginning to cause serious soil erosion.

In early 1980, when the House voted 283-127 in favor of a $2.7 billion bill containing money for projects in about 70 percent of the nation's districts, Deckard voted against it.

**At Home:** The 8th District had four different representatives during the 1970s, and Deckard was the last of the four, returning it to GOP control after a two-term Democratic interlude.

Deckard got an early start on a political career when he was elected to the Indiana House in the Republican sweep of 1966, at the age of 24. He was re-elected three times, but was caught up in the Watergate tide in 1974, when a Democrat swept him out of office. While in the Legislature, Deckard worked to roll back property taxes and eliminate the sales tax on food items. For several years, Deckard was a newsman for radio stations in southern Illinois and Indiana. After his defeat for re-election to the Indiana Legislature, he became a division manager for a nine-state cable TV firm.

Deckard upset a moderate Evansville city councilman for the Republican congressional nomination in 1978, running a conservative-oriented campaign. He continued to stress ideology that fall in his campaign against one-term Democratic Rep. David L. Cornwell.

The incumbent was a native of tiny Paoli, far

---

**8th District: Southwest — Evansville.** Population: 508,397 (8% increase since 1970). Race: White 491,499 (97%), Black 14,235 (3%), Others 2,663 (1%). Spanish origin: 2,133 (0.4%).

from the district's population center. Deckard, an Evansville resident, started with a much stronger geographical base and took advantage of Cornwell's reputation as a man of limited substance in the House. The seat went Republican by more than 6,000 votes.

It stayed Republican in 1980, but Deckard was on shakier ground than other Indiana Republicans. His lightly-regarded Democratic challenger, state Sen. Kenneth Snider, used a helicopter to drop in on the district's small towns and complain that Deckard had not tried hard enough to have a synthetic fuel plant located in the area.

Like Cornwell before him, Snider had the liability of not being well known in Evansville. He came within a respectable 23,000 votes, indicating competition here in future years.

**The District:** The current 8th is divided between the metropolitan area of Evansville on the one hand, and 14 rural and small-town counties on the other. Many of the workers in Evansville's labor force came to Indiana from the south or from nearby rural areas. There are some identifiable remnants of the town's German population, once its dominant political force. An effort is being made to revitalize the area's shipping industry by modernizing Ohio River port facilities.

For 1982, the district's borders will change significantly. The 8th will lose two of its eastern rural counties and move north to the outskirts of Bloomington. It will still be dominated by Evansville, and its Republican framers consider it more favorable to Deckard, through still somewhat marginal.

## Committees

**Government Operations** (9th of 17 Republicans)
Environment, Energy and Natural Resources.

**Public Works and Transportation** (12th of 19 Republicans)
Aviation; Economic Development; Surface Transportation.

## Elections

**1980 General**

| | |
|---|---|
| Joel Deckard (R ) | 119,415 (55 %) |
| Kenneth Snider (D ) | 97,059 (45 %) |

**1978 General**

| | |
|---|---|
| Joel Deckard (R ) | 83,019 (52 %) |
| David Cornwell (D ) | 76,654 (48 %) |

**1978 Primary**

| | |
|---|---|
| Joel Deckard (R ) | 14,238 (49 %) |
| David Koehler (R ) | 11,591 (40 %) |
| Henry Kissling (R ) | 3,091 (11 %) |

**District Vote For President**

| | 1980 | | 1976 | | 1972 |
|---|---|---|---|---|---|
| D | 92,725 (42 %) | D | 110,693 (50 %) | D | 73,835 (35 %) |
| R | 117,505 (53 %) | R | 110,108 (50 %) | R | 138,545 (65 %) |
| I | 9,527 (4 %) | | | | |

## Campaign Finance

| | Receipts | Receipts from PACs | Expen-ditures |
|---|---|---|---|
| **1980** | | | |
| Deckard (R ) | $222,953 | $101,008 (45 %) | $209,423 |
| Snider (D ) | $137,941 | $24,000 (17 %) | $137,761 |

| **1978** | | | |
|---|---|---|---|
| Deckard (R ) | $232,433 | $64,299 (28 %) | $231,632 |
| Cornwell (D ) | $112,065 | $53,672 (48 %) | $112,985 |

## Voting Studies

| | Presidential Support | | Party Unity | | Conservative Coalition | |
|---|---|---|---|---|---|---|
| Year | S | O | S | O | S | O |
| 1980 | 45 | 49 | 66 | 22 | 73 | 19 |
| 1979 | 32 | 59 | 79 | 13 | 77 | 15 |

S = Support          O = Opposition

## Key Votes

**96th Congress**

| | |
|---|---|
| Weaken Carter oil profits tax (1979) | Y |
| Reject hospital cost control plan (1979) | Y |
| Implement Panama Canal Treaties (1979) | N |
| Establish Department of Education (1979) | N |
| Approve Anti-busing Amendment (1979) | Y |
| Guarantee Chrysler Corp. loans (1979) | Y |
| Approve military draft registration (1980) | N |
| Aid Sandinista regime in Nicaragua (1980) | N |
| Strengthen fair housing laws (1980) | N |

**97th Congress**

| | |
|---|---|
| Reagan budget proposal (1981) | Y |

## Interest Group Ratings

| Year | ADA | ACA | AFL-CIO | CCUS |
|---|---|---|---|---|
| 1980 | 22 | 74 | 11 | 68 |
| 1979 | 21 | 88 | 26 | 78 |

# 9 Lee H. Hamilton (D)

### Of Columbus — Elected 1964

**Born:** April 20, 1931, Daytona Beach, Fla.
**Education:** DePauw U., B.A. 1952; Ind. U., J.D. 1956.
**Profession:** Lawyer.
**Family:** Wife, Nancy Nelson; three children.
**Religion:** Methodist.
**Political Career:** No previous office.

**In Washington:** A man who chooses his issues carefully and times his few speeches for maximum impact, Hamilton has a reservoir of respect few members can match. But he has been reluctant to take advantage of it, and has never sought a broker's role in House politics.

Scornful of self-promotion, Hamilton approaches his job with unwavering earnestness. Every week he mails his constituents a newsletter notable because it lacks the traditional self-serving photographs and features about the incumbent. Hamilton simply explains one issue each week and sets out the major arguments on each side. Sometimes he does not even express his own opinion.

This low-key style has evolved in 15 years on the Foreign Affairs Committee, which Hamilton joined as a freshman in 1965, and on the Europe and Middle East Subcommittee, which he chairs. He is one of a handful of members who have made the once-passive Foreign Affairs Committee closer in stature to its traditionally dominant Senate counterpart.

In 1972 Hamilton sponsored the first end-the-Vietnam-War measure ever adopted by the Foreign Affairs Committee. His amendment to a foreign aid bill called for withdrawal of U.S. forces from Vietnam, contingent on release of all prisoners of war and agreement with North Vietnam on a cease-fire plan. The amendment was killed on the House floor in August 1972, but it helped set the stage for later congressional actions to end the war.

In the fall 1978 issue of *Foreign Affairs* magazine, Hamilton said Congress had been right to demand more of a foreign policy role after Vietnam. But, he said, "too often it asks what the politics are, not what the national interest is."

Hamilton frequently writes letters to top administration officials demanding explanations of policy decisions, and publishes their responses in the *Congressional Record*. He forces the State Department to brief him regularly on develop-

ments in the Middle East. When the peace treaty between Egypt and Israel in 1979 forced Congress to approve a new $4.8 billion American aid package, Hamilton managed it on the House floor and won its approval, calling it "a bargain for the United States." As subcommittee chairman, he has sought to steer a middle course between the panel's militant pro-Israel faction and its one strong Arab sympathizer, Republican Paul Findley of Illinois.

He also has pushed for more congressional supervision of intelligence agencies, even in the years since that cause has lost much of its popularity on Capitol Hill. In 1980 he resisted the softening of the law that required detailed reports on CIA covert activities to several congressional committees.

Hamilton began to build his favorable reputation early in his House career, winning election in 1965 as president of the freshman Democratic class in the 89th Congress. Later the same year, Hamilton received widespread press attention with a letter to President Johnson saying it was "time to pause" in action on Great Society social programs.

That strain of domestic conservatism has shown up in his budget voting of the last few years. Skeptical of the high-deficits the House Budget Committee has endorsed, he has sometimes voted against them on final passage. His decision to oppose the 1980 budget, calling for a

---

**9th District: Southeast — Columbus, New Albany.** Population: 544,023 (15% increase since 1970). Race: White 523,009 (98%), Black 9,145 (2%), Others 2,869 (1%). Spanish origin: 2,807 (1%).

$30 billion deficit, carried with it the votes of most of the other Indiana Democrats and helped assure the budget's defeat. Allies have frequently suggested Hamilton for the chairmanship of the Budget Committee, but he has never been willing to campaign for the position.

Much of Hamilton's time in recent years has been spent on ethics issues, as a member of the Committee on Standards of Official Conduct. In 1977, he chaired a task force which recommended new rules limiting members' outside earned income and honoraria. Most of the recommendations were adopted by the House.

By the beginning of the 96th Congress he was the dominant Democrat on the Standards Committee, doing much of the behind-the-scenes work for its mercurial chairman, Charles E. Bennett, D-Fla.

Hamilton persuaded the panel to revise the ethics rules at the start of the 96th Congress to clarify the differences between various punishments meted out in ethics cases. He worked on the committee's recommendation of censure for Michigan Democrat Charles C. Diggs Jr., convicted in a kickback scheme, and on the Abscam bribery investigations.

On Abscam, however, Hamilton broke with Bennett and most of the committee. The panel recommended that Rep. Michael "Ozzie" Myers, D-Pa., be expelled following his conviction in federal court for accepting bribes. The expulsion came to the House floor on the day the House was scheduled to recess for the 1980 election.

Hamilton said that was no time to rush to an expulsion. "Members sit here with bags packed, poised for the rush to the airport," Hamilton complained, in what was for him an unusually dramatic speech. "It is not a cool, deliberate, dispassionate atmosphere."

But the majority was on the other side, and Myers was expelled.

A veteran member of the Joint Economic Committee, Hamilton expected to become chairman in January 1981, but lost the position when a senior Democrat, Henry Reuss of Wisconsin, decided to take it. Hamilton's next chance to take over the rotating chairmanship will be in 1985.

**At Home:** The son and brother of ministers, Hamilton has a devotion to work that comes out of his traditional Methodist family. From his days in Evansville High School in 1948, when he

helped propel the basketball team to the state finals, to his race for Congress in 1964, he displayed a quiet, consistent determination.

When he graduated from DePauw University in 1952, he received an award as the outstanding senior. He accepted a scholarship to Goethe University in Germany for further study.

Hamilton practiced law for a while in Chicago, but soon decided to settle in Columbus, Indiana, where his interest in politics led him into the local Democratic Party. In 1960, he was chairman of the Bartholomew County (Columbus) Citizens for Kennedy. Two years later he managed Birch Bayh's Senate campaign in Columbus.

He was the consensus choice of the local Democratic organization for the 9th District House nomination in 1964, and won the primary with 46 percent of the vote in a field of five candidates. He went on to defeat longtime Republican Rep. Earl Wilson, a crusty fiscal watchdog who had represented the district for almost a quarter of a century.

With his widespread personal respect, Hamilton has been re-elected easily ever since. After a few years, Republicans gave up on defeating him and added Democrats to his district to give GOP candidates a better chance elsewhere in the state. In 1976, for the first time in the history of the district, the Republicans put up no candidate at all. In 1980, as Democrats were having trouble all over Indiana, Hamilton was drawing his usual percentage — nearly 65 percent of the vote.

For 1982, Hamilton has an unusual political problem. The new Republican redistricting plan is fairly kind to him, leaving most of his district intact, but it does remove his hometown of Columbus. It is generally assumed that Hamilton will establish legal residence within the new district borders, and continue to run and win.

**The District:** The current 9th is marginal in most statewide contests, although Hamilton carries it easily. It includes Columbus, home of Cummins Engine Company and a center of furniture manufacturing. The rural areas are devoted to general farming, and lack the rich soil of the state's northern corn belt.

The new 9th, without Columbus, will shift slightly to the west, taking some traditionally Democratic rural counties away from the neighboring 8th. New Albany, which stays in the district, will be the largest city.

## Committees

**Foreign Affairs** (5th of 21 Democrats)
Europe and the Middle East, chairman; International Security

and Scientific Affairs.

**Select Intelligence** (7th of 9 Democrats)
Legislation.

# Lee H. Hamilton, D-Ind.

**Joint Economic**
  Economic Goals and Intergovernmental Policy, chairman; Monetary and Fiscal Policy.

## Elections

**1980 General**

| | |
|---|---|
| Lee Hamilton (D ) | 136,574 (64 %) |
| George Meyers Jr. (R ) | 75,601 (36 %) |

**1980 Primary**

| | |
|---|---|
| Lee Hamilton (D ) | 62,160 (90 %) |
| Lendall Terry (D ) | 6,882 (10 %) |

**1978 General**

| | |
|---|---|
| Lee Hamilton (D ) | 99,727 (66 %) |
| Frank Hamilton (R ) | 52,218 (34 %) |

**Previous Winning Percentages**

| | | | |
|---|---|---|---|
| 1976 (100%) | 1974 (71 %) | 1972 (63 %) | 1970 (63 %) |
| 1968 (54 %) | 1966 (54 %) | 1964 (54 %) | |

**District Vote For President**

| | 1980 | | 1976 | | 1972 |
|---|---|---|---|---|---|
| D | 89,540 (41 %) | D | 105,561 (51 %) | D | 70,691 (36 %) |
| R | 118,182 (54 %) | R | 101,335 (49 %) | R | 123,725 (63 %) |
| I | 7,902 (4 %) | | | | |

## Campaign Finance

| | Receipts | Receipts from PACs | Expenditures |
|---|---|---|---|
| **1980** | | | |
| Hamilton (D ) | $113,260 | $34,950 (31 %) | $122,674 |
| **1978** | | | |
| L. Hamilton (D ) | $120,178 | $23,090 (19 %) | $111,793 |
| F. Hamilton (R ) | $48,786 | $3,507 (7 %) | $48,720 |

## Voting Studies

| | Presidential Support | | Party Unity | | Conservative Coalition | |
|---|---|---|---|---|---|---|
| Year | S | O | S | O | S | O |
| 1980 | 74 | 25 | 67 | 31 | 48 | 47 |
| 1979 | 76 | 23 | 71 | 29 | 44 | 56 |
| 1978 | 86 | 14 | 74 | 26 | 33 | 67 |
| 1977 | 72 | 23 | 80 | 18 | 32 | 65 |
| 1976 | 33 | 67 | 72 | 27 | 43 | 55 |
| 1975 | 51 | 48 | 69 | 29 | 45 | 54 |
| 1974 (Ford) | 65 | 35 | | | | |
| 1974 | 70 | 26 | 65 | 32 | 39 | 55 |
| 1973 | 41 | 58 | 82 | 18 | 30 | 70 |
| 1972 | 68 | 30 | 71 | 28 | 35 | 63 |
| 1971 | 42 | 54 | 85 | 12 | 17 | 78 |
| 1970 | 68 | 23 | 74 | 21 | 23 | 73 |
| 1969 | 68 | 32 | 85 | 15 | 22 | 78 |
| 1968 | 82 | 15 | 77 | 18 | 27 | 65 |
| 1967 | 85 | 12 | 79 | 19 | 44 | 52 |
| 1966 | 82 | 10 | 75 | 15 | 32 | 51 |
| 1965 | 84 | 11 | 82 | 13 | 24 | 75 |

S = Support          O = Opposition

## Key Votes

**96th Congress**

| | |
|---|---|
| Weaken Carter oil profits tax (1979) | Y |
| Reject hospital cost control plan (1979) | Y |
| Implement Panama Canal Treaties (1979) | Y |
| Establish Department of Education (1979) | N |
| Approve Anti-busing Amendment (1979) | N |
| Guarantee Chrysler Corp. loans (1979) | Y |
| Approve military draft registration (1980) | Y |
| Aid Sandinista regime in Nicaragua (1980) | Y |
| Strengthen fair housing laws (1980) | Y |

**97th Congress**

| | |
|---|---|
| Reagan budget proposal (1981) | N |

## Interest Group Ratings

| Year | ADA | ACA | AFL-CIO | CCUS |
|---|---|---|---|---|
| 1980 | 44 | 46 | 47 | 76 |
| 1979 | 53 | 27 | 70 | 50 |
| 1978 | 35 | 31 | 50 | 35 |
| 1977 | 60 | 15 | 64 | 50 |
| 1976 | 50 | 11 | 52 | 32 |
| 1975 | 68 | 43 | 74 | 29 |
| 1974 | 65 | 7 | 70 | 50 |
| 1973 | 80 | 4 | 73 | 36 |
| 1972 | 50 | 26 | 82 | 10 |
| 1971 | 89 | 7 | 75 | - |
| 1970 | 80 | 13 | 67 | 22 |
| 1969 | 53 | 13 | 90 | - |
| 1968 | 58 | 22 | 75 | - |
| 1967 | 53 | 11 | 83 | 30 |
| 1966 | 47 | 33 | 85 | - |
| 1965 | 58 | 15 | - | 10 |

# 10 Philip R. Sharp (D)

**Of Muncie — Elected 1974**

**Born:** July 15, 1942, Baltimore, Md.
**Education:** Georgetown U., B.S. 1964, Ph.D. 1974.
**Profession:** Political scientist.
**Family:** Wife, Marilyn Augburn; one child.
**Religion:** Methodist.
**Political Career:** Unsuccessful Democratic nominee for U.S. House, 1970 and 1972.

**In Washington:** Sharp's career reflects the experiences of many of the brightest members of the Democratic Class of 1974, who have changed the House modestly, but who have been changed by it substantially.

He entered Congress in 1975 as a political veteran but a legislative novice, quietly determined to overhaul what seemed to be an unresponsive process. He emerged six years later as chairman of the crucial Commerce Subcommittee on oil and gas, close to the center on most energy issues and carrying a reputation for exceptional skill at negotiation and compromise.

He began to develop that reputation in his second term, most of which he devoted to the long fight over the energy package President Carter submitted early in 1977. Strategically placed on energy subcommittees at both Commerce and Interior, Sharp was given a spot on the ad hoc panel Speaker O'Neill created to handle the legislation.

In the beginning, Sharp seemed a reliable regulatory liberal. When an effort was made on the House floor to remove price controls from natural gas, he insisted that such a move would lead to unacceptably high prices for consumers in many states. The effort was defeated.

But when it became clear in conference that the Senate insisted on decontrol, Sharp argued that a bill with decontrol was better than no bill at all. Even after the conference dropped provisions he was especially interested in, establishing new federal standards for utility rates, Sharp stayed on board.

When the conference finally reached agreement, O'Neill turned to Sharp to sell the compromise to skeptical Democrats in the younger House generation. As chairman of the Speaker's lobbying task force, he provided members with detailed briefs explaining why the product was worth voting for, and was responsible in part for its survival by one vote on the decisive roll-call.

That effort gave Sharp a useful reputation among his peers as a leadership favorite. It also moved him at least slightly to the right on energy policy. The next year, when the Commerce Committee debated controls on crude oil prices, Sharp voted in favor of dropping them — against the position of a majority of House Democrats. Some committee Republicans also credited him with influencing Commerce Chairman John D. Dingell of Michigan, who was once a vehement advocate of price controls but who has softened in recent years. Sharp has been a Dingell protégé on the committee, and when the chairman split energy jurisdiction between two subcommittees in 1981, it was no accident that Sharp got the more important of the two.

On Interior, Sharp has played a similar role as a conciliator, sometimes serving as a bridge between liberal Chairman Morris K. Udall, D-Ariz., and more conservative committee Democrats. Sharp worked on legislation in the 96th Congress to create an Energy Mobilization Board to speed up energy projects, but sought to make it difficult for the board to override existing state law.

When the House and Senate finally agreed on a compromise bill creating the board, Sharp tried to sell it on the House floor the way he had sold the gas deregulation bill — as half a loaf. "This is a bill not to be loved," he said, "but to be passed." But the House ultimately refused to do either.

---

**10th District: East — Muncie, Richmond.** Population: 487,803 (3% increase since 1970). Race: White 471,582 (97%), Black 13,083 (3%), Others 3,138 (1%). Spanish origin: 3,395 (1%).

---

## Philip R. Sharp, D-Ind.

Despite his leadership connections, Sharp has not hesitated to break with House leaders when it has been politically helpful in his marginal district. He voted against the 1980 budget, complaining that the deficit was too large, and against hospital cost containment in 1979.

He concedes that his first six years in the House affected his attitude toward government. "In many cases we've gone toward excessive regulation," he once said. "I have a greater appreciation for the market than I did when I first ran."

Some of those flirtations with the free market lead to conflict with the United Auto Workers, the strongest labor presence in Sharp's district and one seeking to move him to the left. But he and the auto workers were together in 1979 on the bill to provide loan guarantees for the Chrysler Corporation, which has several plants in the district.

Sharp has also been sympathetic to the pleas of the union and the auto industry for more lenient timetables on fuel efficiency. On public works issues, however, he has been a consistent environmentalist, voting against some water projects recommended by the Public Works Committee and routinely approved by the House.

**At Home:** Persistence paid off for Sharp in 1974, when the Watergate Democratic landslide finally gave him the House seat he had sought three times.

When he began his first campaign for Congress, in 1970, he was a 28-year-old political science professor with little campaign experience and limited contacts in the district. But he outorganized most of his six rivals that year, and won the Democratic nomination with 22 percent of the vote, edging out former Rep. John R. Walsh by 424 votes. In November, with recession worrying people in the industrial cities of central Indiana, Sharp came within 2,500 votes against Republican David W. Dennis.

His second campaign was a disappointment. Sharp was better known and even better prepared

in 1972, but President Nixon was carrying Indiana by 2-to-1, and it has never been a ticket-splitting state. Dennis' percentage rose to 57 percent.

The third time, Sharp had all the name recognition he needed, and it was the right year. Republicans were falling throughout Indiana in 1974, and Dennis hurt himself by defending Nixon during the House Judiciary Committee's impeachment investigation.

Sharp has never quite been able to make himself secure. Constituent service helped him increase his percentage in 1976, but it has declined since then, down to 53 percent in 1980. In all three re-election campaigns, he has had the same opponent — farmer William G. Frazier. Local Democrats were quietly relieved when Frazier was nominated for a third time in 1980; they felt they knew how to beat him, and had been worried about some of the Republicans who had considered running, such as Muncie lawyer Ralph Dennis, a cousin of Sharp's original rival. Dennis and other potentially strong challengers ultimately decided not to bother.

The next election will be extremely difficult for Sharp. Redistricting has altered his constituency drastically, and he is likely to be opposed by a strong Republican challenger, state Sen. Charles Bosma, who helped draw the district lines.

**The District:** The current 10th is exceptionally vulnerable to national economic trends. Automobile and auto accessory plants dot the district, and have been hurt by every recession in the past 25 years. Muncie, settled largely by Southerners, is the most populous city in the district. There is a large, generally conservative community of Quakers in Richmond.

The 10th District has been redrawn and renumbered the 2nd for the 1982 election. Sharp's home base of Muncie remains, but otherwise it is a substantially different district, with blue-collar areas removed and new Republican territory added further south.

## Committees

**Energy and Commerce** (6th of 24 Democrats)
Fossil and Synthetic Fuels, chairman.

**Interior and Insular Affairs** (11th of 23 Democrats)
Energy and the Environment.

## Elections

**1980 General**

| | |
|---|---|
| Phil Sharp (D ) | 103,083 (53 %) |
| William Frazier (R ) | 90,051 (47 %) |

**1980 Primary**

| | |
|---|---|
| Philip Sharp (D ) | 43,142 (89 %) |
| Robert Murphy (D ) | 2,773 (6 %) |

**1978 General**

| | |
|---|---|
| Philip Sharp (D ) | 73,343 (56 %) |
| William Frazier (R ) | 55,999 (43 %) |

**Previous Winning Percentages**
1976 (60 %)     1974 (54 %)

**District Vote For President**

| | 1980 | | 1976 | | 1972 |
|---|---|---|---|---|---|
| D | 69,876 (36 %) | D | 86,375 (45 %) | D | 56,978 (30 %) |
| R | 114,806 (59 %) | R | 105,448 (55 %) | R | 129,455 (69 %) |
| I | 8,730 (5 %) | | | | |

## Campaign Finance

| | Receipts | Receipts from PACs | Expenditures |
|---|---|---|---|
| **1980** | | | |
| Sharp (D ) | $159,420 | $84,951 (53 %) | $165,181 |
| Frazier (R ) | $280,355 | $46,996 (17 %) | $255,620 |
| **1978** | | | |
| Sharp (D ) | $111,761 | $51,585 (46 %) | $107,372 |
| Frazier (R ) | $127,876 | $26,119 (20 %) | $129,665 |

## Voting Studies

| | Presidential Support | | Party Unity | | Conservative Coalition | |
|---|---|---|---|---|---|---|
| Year | S | O | S | O | S | O |
| 1980 | 70 | 29 | 63 | 37 | 54 | 46 |
| 1979 | 80 | 19 | 72 | 27 | 47 | 53 |

| | | | | | | |
|---|---|---|---|---|---|---|
| 1978 | 80 | 20 | 71 | 28 | 29 | 71 |
| 1977 | 73 | 27 | 73 | 27 | 33 | 67 |
| 1976 | 33 | 67 | 73 | 26 | 42 | 57 |
| 1975 | 37 | 63 | 77 | 23 | 32 | 68 |

S = Support          O = Opposition

## Key Votes

**96th Congress**

| | |
|---|---|
| Weaken Carter oil profits tax (1979) | N |
| Reject hospital cost control plan (1979) | Y |
| Implement Panama Canal Treaties (1979) | Y |
| Establish Department of Education (1979) | Y |
| Approve Anti-busing Amendment (1979) | N |
| Guarantee Chrysler Corp. loans (1979) | Y |
| Approve military draft registration (1980) | N |
| Aid Sandinista regime in Nicaragua (1980) | Y |
| Strengthen fair housing laws (1980) | Y |

**97th Congress**

| | |
|---|---|
| Reagan budget proposal (1981) | N |

## Interest Group Ratings

| Year | ADA | ACA | AFL-CIO | CCUS |
|---|---|---|---|---|
| 1980 | 50 | 29 | 63 | 76 |
| 1979 | 53 | 28 | 70 | 39 |
| 1978 | 50 | 26 | 70 | 22 |
| 1977 | 65 | 26 | 68 | 41 |
| 1976 | 60 | 11 | 61 | 25 |
| 1975 | 89 | 18 | 78 | 24 |

# 11 Andrew Jacobs Jr. (D)

**Of Indianapolis — Elected 1964**
Did not serve 1973-75.

**Born:** Feb. 24, 1932, Indianapolis, Ind.
**Education:** Ind. U., B.S. 1954, LL.B. 1958.
**Military Career:** Marine Corps Reserve, 1949-52, active duty, 1951-52.
**Profession:** Lawyer.
**Family:** Wife, Martha Keys.
**Religion:** Roman Catholic.
**Political Career:** Ind. House, 1959-61; unsuccessful Democratic nominee for U.S. House, 1962; elected to U.S. House, 1964; unsuccessfully sought re-election, 1972; re-elected, 1974.

**In Washington:** Jacobs has carved out a niche in the House similar to the one occupied by William Proxmire of Wisconsin in the Senate — liberal on social questions, dovish on defense, outspoken to the point of showmanship in his fiscal conservatism and opposition to federal waste.

But while seniority has guaranteed Proxmire a leading role in his chamber, Jacobs remains an outsider in House politics after 15 years. He is famous for his flippant answers to the most serious questions but also for his moralistic moments on the House floor. It is a role that Jacobs seems to relish.

"I am not the best go-alonger in the House," he told his colleagues one day in 1979. "Frankly, sometimes I do not get along very well." He then complained of waiting 19 hours to offer an amendment but being "constantly bumped" by other members.

One clear source of Jacobs' loner status is his war on the perquisites of congressional office. He was instrumental in the effort to block a pay raise for House members in 1977. He introduced an amendment preventing colleagues from amassing more than $100 worth of postage stamps for their own use. Earlier in his career, he protested the chauffeured limousines made available to House leaders. He regularly returns portions of his staff allowance — and is not adverse to receiving publicity for it.

House leaders were also angry when he voted with Republicans against the Democratic rules package at the start of the 97th Congress. House Rules Chairman Richard Bolling threatened to take away Jacobs' Ways and Means assignment and his brand-new chairmanship of the Ways and Means Health Subcommittee. In the end, nothing was done, but Jacobs' loner reputation was reinforced.

Jacobs has carried his fiscal conservatism into a variety of areas. He usually votes against spending for defense and public works projects, establishing himself as a consistent tightwad to some and a consistent liberal to others. In 1978, he sought to drop three water projects budgeted at over $90 million from an appropriation bill on the grounds that they raised some of the "most serious environmental and ecological questions."

In his early congressional terms, he was best known as a critic of the Vietnam War, and his voting record was regularly criticized from the right. In recent years, he has moved onto ground usually reserved for Republicans, the balanced budget crusade. He supported efforts in 1979 to call a constitutional convention for the purpose of enacting an amendment requiring a balanced federal budget. He began offering floor amendments to balance the budget long before most Northern Democrats were sensitive to the issue. His 1978 effort, for example, lost 352-45, failing to win any significant support on either side of the aisle. But it brought him exactly the sort of public attention that has helped him prosper politically in one of the nation's most conservative cities.

In 1976, the year after he returned to the House following an involuntary two-year absence,

---

**11th District: Central — Indianapolis.** Population: 442,998 (9% decrease since 1970). Race: White 324,430 (73%), Black 113,633 (26%), Others 4,935 (1%). Spanish origin: 3,950 (1%).

---

Jacobs married Martha E. Keys, a Democratic House member from Kansas and a Ways and Means colleague. Keys lost her seat in 1978, partly on the issue of alleged inattention to her district, but Jacobs has suffered no noticeable political damage.

**At Home:** Jacobs entered politics with an old score to settle. His father, Andrew Jacobs Sr., was elected to Congress from Indianapolis in 1948 but was turned out of office after one term. The younger Jacobs began moving early toward the congressional career his father never got to carry out.

In 1958, at the age of 26, Jacobs won a seat in the state House of Representatives. Four years later he tried for Congress but was defeated by incumbent Republican Rep. Donald Bruce. In 1964, Bruce retired, and Jacobs ran again. With the help of the national Democratic landslide, he edged into office by 3,000 votes out of 295,000 cast.

It would have been difficult for Jacobs to win re-election in 1966 within the same district boundaries. But under court mandate, the lines were redrawn, and with Democrats in control in Indiana, they gave Jacobs a more favorable district. He was re-elected regularly until 1972, when Republican redistricting, combined with the Nixon presidential landslide, cost him his seat. He lost to Republican William Hudnut, a Presbyterian minister.

Jacobs did not give up, and he was able to come back to office in the 1974 Democratic Watergate surge, beating Hudnut by 7,700 votes. A year later, Hudnut was elected mayor of Indianapolis. Since 1974, Jacobs has carried his district by convincing, though not overwhelming margins.

**The District:** Until 1966, the 11th District consisted of all of Marion County. Democratic strength in the inner city of Indianapolis was usually more than counterbalanced by Republican areas further out in the county.

But with the Supreme Court's equal population edict, the county had to be divided. The Democrats drew favorable lines for themselves in 1966 and saved Jacobs from defeat. A Republican Legislature changed the lines again in 1968, but Jacobs had established enough personal popularity to win. Although the 1972 redrawing made the district slightly more Republican, Jacobs has been able to win in it four times.

Many of the Democratic votes in the district are cast by blacks, who make up about a quarter of the population, and by blue-collar workers whose jobs are in the city's auto and auto parts industries. But Republicans constitute a voting majority, with their strength coming from the large white-collar population that earns its living in state government, banking and insurance.

Republicans were in charge of redrawing the lines for 1982 and they did Jacobs a favor. The Legislature, hoping to defeat three other incumbent Indiana Democrats and considering Jacobs relatively strong, piled as many Democrats into his area as it could. Jacobs will, however, have to win a primary against another Democratic incumbent, David Evans, whose district was virtually eliminated. Evans announced in June that he would challenge Jacobs for renomination. The new 10th, clustered compactly around Indianapolis, contains more of Jacobs' old constituents than of Evans.

## Committees

**Ways and Means** (8th of 23 Democrats)
Health, chairman; Social Security.

## Elections

**1980 General**

| | |
|---|---|
| Andy Jacobs Jr. (D ) | 105,468 (57 %) |
| Sheila Suess (R ) | 78,743 (43 %) |

**1978 General**

| | |
|---|---|
| Andy Jacobs Jr. (D ) | 61,504 (57 %) |
| Charles Bosma (R ) | 45,809 (43 %) |

**Previous Winning Percentages**

| | | | |
|---|---|---|---|
| 1976 (60 %) | 1974 (53 %) | 1972 (- %) | 1970 (58 %) |
| 1968 (53 %) | 1966 (56 %) | 1964 (51 %) | |

**District Vote For President**

| | 1980 | | 1976 | | 1972 |
|---|---|---|---|---|---|
| **D** | 76,196 (41 %) | **D** | 86,624 (45 %) | **D** | 63,038 (34 %) |
| **R** | 99,311 (53 %) | **R** | 105,309 (54 %) | **R** | 123,349 (66 %) |
| **I** | 8,779 (5 %) | | | | |

## Campaign Finance

| | Receipts | Receipts from PACs | Expenditures |
|---|---|---|---|
| **1980** | | | |
| Jacobs (D ) | $39,235 | — (0 %) | $39,581 |
| Suess (R ) | $230,548 | $79,080 (34%) | $234,609 |
| **1978** | | | |
| Jacobs (D ) | $20,767 | $925 (4 %) | $18,394 |
| Bosma (R ) | $56,187 | $12,000 (21 %) | $55,971 |

## Voting Studies

| Year | Presidential Support | | Party Unity | | Conservative Coalition | |
|------|------|------|------|------|------|------|
| | S | O | S | O | S | O |
| 1980 | 45 | 50 | 29 | 66 | 67 | 29 |
| 1979 | 59 | 40 | 44 | 54 | 56 | 40 |
| 1978 | 62 | 31 | 48 | 47 | 51 | 45 |
| 1977 | 59 | 39 | 54 | 43 | 40 | 57 |
| 1976 | 27 | 67 | 58 | 32 | 35 | 59 |
| 1975 | 34 | 63 | 65 | 30 | 24 | 70 |
| 1972 | 30 | 62 | 74 | 22 | 23 | 74 |
| 1971 | 30 | 67 | 78 | 17 | 9 | 86 |
| 1970 | 51 | 42 | 67 | 24 | 11 | 82 |
| 1969 | 57 | 38 | 80 | 16 | 16 | 82 |
| 1968 | 59 | 16 | 57 | 9 | 4 | 71 |
| 1967 | 75 | 6 | 79 | 7 | 9 | 81 |
| 1966 | 75 | 3 | 79 | 1 | 3 | 86 |
| 1965 | 85 | 8 | 88 | 6 | 4 | 94 |

S = Support          O = Opposition

## Key Votes

**96th Congress**

| | |
|---|---|
| Weaken Carter oil profits tax (1979) | N |
| Reject hospital cost control plan (1979) | N |
| Implement Panama Canal Treaties (1979) | Y |
| Establish Department of Education (1979) | N |
| Approve Anti-busing Amendment (1979) | Y |
| Guarantee Chrysler Corp. loans (1979) | Y |
| Approve military draft registration (1980) | N |
| Aid Sandinista regime in Nicaragua (1980) | Y |
| Strengthen fair housing laws (1980) | Y |

**97th Congress**

| | |
|---|---|
| Reagan budget proposal (1981) | Y |

## Interest Group Ratings

| Year | ADA | ACA | AFL-CIO | CCUS |
|------|------|------|------|------|
| 1980 | 50 | 63 | 53 | 58 |
| 1979 | 68 | 60 | 55 | 56 |
| 1978 | 50 | 59 | 50 | 39 |
| 1977 | 75 | 41 | 52 | 59 |
| 1976 | 65 | 31 | 55 | 32 |
| 1975 | 74 | 36 | 70 | 41 |
| 1972 | 75 | 22 | 91 | 20 |
| 1971 | 86 | 28 | 83 | - |
| 1970 | 84 | 32 | 100 | 10 |
| 1969 | 80 | 12 | 100 | - |
| 1968 | 92 | 5 | 100 | - |
| 1967 | 73 | 4 | 100 | 0 |
| 1966 | 88 | 4 | 100 | - |
| 1965 | 84 | 7 | | 10 |

# Iowa

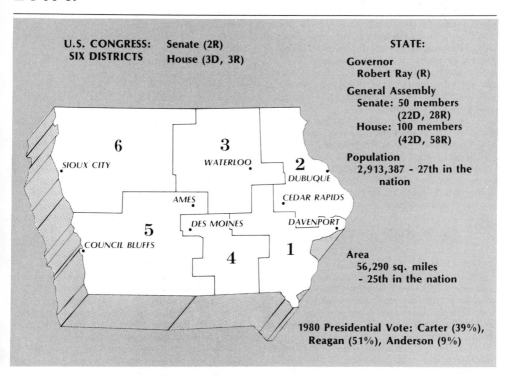

U.S. CONGRESS: Senate (2R)
SIX DISTRICTS House (3D, 3R)

STATE:

Governor
Robert Ray (R)

General Assembly
Senate: 50 members
(22D, 28R)
House: 100 members
(42D, 58R)

Population
2,913,387 - 27th in the
nation

6 — SIOUX CITY

3 — WATERLOO

2 — DUBUQUE

AMES

CEDAR RAPIDS

5 — COUNCIL BLUFFS — DES MOINES — DAVENPORT

4

1

Area
56,290 sq. miles
- 25th in the nation

1980 Presidential Vote: Carter (39%),
Reagan (51%), Anderson (9%)

## ... A Decade of Adjustment

It took most of the 1970s for the rest of the country to change its perception of Iowa. People had long thought of it as a rural conservative state, but that notion didn't square with Iowa's habit of electing liberal Democrats to Congress.

Then, just as the lesson was being learned, the state reversed its course, turning out Democratic Sens. Dick Clark and John Culver in two successive elections and ending Democratic control of the House delegation.

Like most Midwestern states, Iowa is a more complicated place than Easterners usually imagine. It has always had a base of Democratic votes in its medium-sized cities and a volatile farm population capable of springing political surprises. Iowa elected a Democratic governor three times during the Depression and twice in the lean agricultural years of the 1950s.

So it was no shock when Harold Hughes launched the state's modern Democratic resur-

gence, winning three terms as governor in the 1960s and going to the Senate in 1968. Personally popular among voters of both parties, he laid the groundwork for the two later Democratic Senate victories, by Clark in 1972 and Culver in 1974.

A predominantly Yankee-settled state, Iowa began showing interest in "clean government" around the same time as did ethnically similar states like Vermont and Oregon. This helped candidates like Hughes and Clark. In addition, labor was gaining strength in Iowa in the 1970s, with the United Auto Workers building an important base among farm implement manufacturing workers and the Amalgamated Meatcutters playing an increasing role in Waterloo and other cities.

But Iowa never became a Democratic state, even though the party's registration reached a majority for a time at mid-decade. By 1978, voters reacted against what they perceived as Clark's excessive liberalism on foreign policy and his support for abortion. He was beaten by conservative Republican Roger Jepsen essentially because blue-collar Democrats, most of them Catholic, stayed home in surprising numbers. In 1980, Culver ran for re-election as an unapologetic liberal, choosing a stance different from most Senate Democrats in similar situations. But he lost overwhelmingly to Republican Rep. Charles Grassley, a less articulate man who expressed the public sentiment that the government was simply wasting too much money.

Through all these political changes, Iowa has been governed by the same moderate Republican, Robert Ray, who replaced Hughes in 1969 and is now the senior governor in the United States. Ray does not evoke the militant support that a Clark or a Grassley does — nor the opposition either. He has won re-election four times, the last three by comfortable margins.

# A Political Tour

**Des Moines and Central Iowa.** Des Moines is Iowa's only major metropolitan area; it is looked to by the surrounding farm lands as a commercial, financial and governmental center. More than 50 insurance companies have their headquarters here, making it the nation's second largest insurance city.

Since Des Moines is the capital of Iowa, state government also contributes to the white-collar employment market. Industrial activity focuses on the manufacturing of farm machinery and tires.

Des Moines is home to two other institutions of Iowa life: one is the annual state fair; the other is the *Des Moines Register,* a newspaper of progressive reputation and statewide circulation that influences the tone and helps shape the agenda of state politics.

Democrats are strong in Des Moines and in areas north of the city in surrounding Polk County. Other suburban areas, like West Des Moines, show a preference for Republicans.

The overall Polk County vote is generally Democratic, as seen in U.S. Senate races of the past decade. Polk gave more than 58 percent to Democrats Clark and Culver in their winning Senate races of 1972 and 1974. In their unsuccessful re-election bids of 1978 and 1980, both Clark and Culver won about 56 percent of the Polk vote.

North of Des Moines in Story County is Ames, the home of Iowa State University. Since the voting age was lowered in 1971 to include college students, Story County has generally backed liberal Democrats for statewide office. But

no Democrat running for president has carried the county since Lyndon B. Johnson in 1964. Carter might have topped Reagan there in 1980, except for the independent candidacy of John B. Anderson, whose 19 percent was his fifth-best county showing in the nation.

**Eastern Iowa.** This ought to be the most Democratic part of Iowa, because it contains several medium-sized cities with manufacturing-based economies and a significant number of blue-collar voters.

Culver represented northeast Iowa in the House from 1965 to 1975; he expanded his regional political base to win the 1974 Senate election. But today his district sends a Republican to Congress, as does the 1st District immediately below it, also briefly Democratic during the 1970s. Both Republican House members now serving from this part of the state, Jim Leach and Tom Tauke, have moderate records that allow them to do well in the manufacturing cities.

The largest city in eastern Iowa is Cedar Rapids (Linn County), the second largest in the state. Politically, Linn County is evenly divided. It gave Jepsen a slight edge in 1978 but narrowly favored Culver, a hometown product, in 1980.

The next largest city is Davenport (Scott County), which recently has gone Republican. Scott was the largest county in Iowa to vote for both Jepsen in 1978 and Grassley in 1980.

The Catholic vote is important in the Mississippi River city of Dubuque in northeast Iowa. Though Dubuque County almost always votes Democratic, the pro-abortion stands that Clark and Culver took in the Senate hurt them politically. Both won more than 66 percent there in their first Senate campaigns, but barely won Dubuque County when they sought re-election.

Burlington (Des Moines County) is another Mississippi River manufacturing city. It has consistently voted for Democratic statewide candidates in the past decade, but strongly supported Republican Leach in the past two elections.

The liberal bastion in this part of the state is Johnson County, influenced by the University of Iowa vote in Iowa City. Anderson received just under 19 percent of the vote in the county.

Republicans prevail in virtually all the other counties in the eastern part of the state, where the farmers depend largely on corn, livestock and poultry for their livelihood.

**North Central Iowa.** The rich soil of the rolling prairie makes this section one of the most agriculturally productive areas of the nation.

Advances in agricultural technology have boosted crop yields here in the past generation. But farming has also become a costlier, more complex business, and many small-scale farmers have sold their land to agribusiness operations. This has eliminated farm-oriented jobs and held down population growth in the region. The 6th Congressional District, home of the state's richest farm land, lost population in the 1970s — the only district in the state with a net decline.

The farmers and small-business men in this part of the state generally vote Republican. But in some of the counties, the rural vote is balanced by blue-collar workers in farm-related manufacturing and meat packing. Labor unions have demonstrated strength in Black Hawk County (Waterloo and Cedar Falls) and Cerro Gordo County (Mason City). Both of those counties voted for a liberal Democrat for the House in 1980.

**Western Iowa.** There are only three cities of any size in the vast expanse of rural farm land that is western Iowa. Two of them — Council Bluffs and Sioux City on the Missouri River — are predominantly Republican. The third is Democratic Fort Dodge in Webster County.

With few exceptions, the small towns and farms in this part of Iowa have voted for Republicans in Senate and presidential elections during the past decade. Reagan's best showing in the state came from this area as he won more than 55 percent in most western Iowa counties.

Yet the region's two representatives in the U.S. House are both Democrats. Tom Harkin and Berkley Bedell defeated incumbent Republicans in 1974 and have since developed personal followings among rural and small-town voters. These close ties have enabled them to withstand Iowa's drift to the right in recent elections.

The soil and terrain are not as favorable to farming in the southwest quarter of Iowa as they are in other parts of the state. Iowa's southern tier counties are often hilly and rocky, especially those along the Iowa-Missouri border.

## Redrawing the Lines

In spite of their total control of state government, Republicans passed a law last year designed to make the redistricting process less political.

The law charges the state's Legislative Service Bureau with drawing a new district map, subject to the approval of the Legislature. The bureau follows certain objective guidelines but gives no consideration to partisan concerns or to the wishes of incumbents.

When the bureau's "non-partisan" map was released in April, it caused a highly partisan uproar. "It looks like a Democratic computer wrote it," said an aide to GOP Gov. Robert Ray. Two of the state's three Republican incumbents — Jim Leach and Tom Tauke — were placed in the same district. On its second try, the bureau's computer gave Leach and Tauke separate districts, but took several GOP counties from Tauke and gave him Democratic Johnson County.

State law stipulated that the bureau's first two proposals could not be amended, so the state Senate killed them. At midyear, the bureau was at work producing another map, still ignoring partisan concerns. The law allows the Legislature to change the third proposal until it satisfies a majority of members.

Iowa's overall population growth in the 1970s was only 3.1 percent, and there has been little shifting in population among districts. Leach's 1st is the largest, with 505,896 people, and Bedell's 6th is the smallest, with 464,617 people.

## Governor
## Robert Ray (R)

**Born:** Sept. 26, 1928, Des Moines, Iowa.
**Home:** Des Moines, Iowa.
**Education:** Drake U., B.A. 1952; J.D. 1954.
**Military Career:** Army, 1946-48.
**Profession:** Lawyer.
**Family:** Wife, Billie; three children.
**Religion:** Disciples of Christ.
**Political Career:** Unsuccessful campaign for Polk County attorney, 1956; unsuccessful campaign for Iowa House, 1958; elected governor 1968, 1970, 1972, 1974 and 1978; term expires Jan. 1983.

# Roger W. Jepsen (R)

**Of Davenport — Elected 1978**

**Born:** Dec. 23, 1928, Cedar Falls, Iowa.
**Education:** Ariz. State U., B.S. 1950, M.A. 1953.
**Military Career:** Army, 1946-47; Army Reserve, 1948-60.
**Profession:** Marketing executive.
**Family:** Wife, Dee Ann Delaney; six children.
**Religion:** Lutheran.
**Political Career:** Scott County Board of Supervisors, 1962-65; Iowa Senate, 1967-69; lt. governor, 1969-73.

**In Washington:** Three years in the Senate have not altered Jepsen's strong distaste for government, which he once said could best help Iowa farmers by agreeing only to "defend them, and deliver the mail, and leave them alone." But the Republican Senate majority has changed his role drastically, lifting him from junior gadfly to chairman of an important Armed Services subcommittee.

In his first term on Armed Services, Jepsen was essentially a free-lance critic of the Carter administration, which in his view was "infested" with "activists" and "social experimenters."

He criticized the Carter Defense Department for trying to promote social change in the military — stressing recruitment of women, and trying to attract the disadvantaged with enlistment bonuses.

In the 97th Congress, however, Jepsen has a forum for constructive work as head of the Subcommittee on Manpower and Personnel. He also has a hard act to follow in that chairmanship, Georgia Democrat Sam Nunn, the military specialist whose criticisms of the volunteer army more or less defined the subcommittee's work in past congresses.

Jepsen is no expert, and the approach he calls "common sense" has little similarity with Nunn's elaborate use of data and documents. In the early months of 1981, however, Jepsen sounded many of the same criticisms that Nunn had about poor quality among the current generation of Army recruits. In the closing days of the 96th Congress, he had joined Nunn in backing an amendment to restore $200 million in military personnel funds that the Appropriations Committee had tried to cut.

Jepsen's two terms on the Agriculture Committee have featured a continuing series of adjustments to the farm policies of two presidents. Although he takes a hard-line stand on defense issues, he joined many farm state Republicans in 1980 in criticizing and voting against President Carter's embargo on grain sales to the Soviet Union. He kept up the barrage in the early months of 1981 as President Reagan hesitated before lifting the embargo, and persuaded the Senate to vote 58-36 in March in favor of its removal. Reagan lifted the embargo April 24.

On farm spending matters, however, Jepsen turned out to be a Reagan loyalist, criticizing committee Republicans who wanted to continue existing farm programs at previous spending levels. Jepsen told them they were ignoring the anti-government mandate of the 1980 election. Jepsen's personal way of carrying out that mandate has been a crusade against the proposed nine-digit ZIP code, which he views as one more bureaucratic intrusion on traditional ways of doing things. He supports legislation that would block the government from adding the four extra numbers. "I walk on an airplane," Jepsen told a reporter, "and people say to me, 'If you don't do anything else but fight the ZIP code, you ought to be re-elected.'"

**At Home:** The fact that Jepsen got elected once was a surprise to most of Iowa, especially Democratic Sen. Dick Clark, who never took him very seriously. Jepsen revived a dormant political career in 1978 by enlisting a coalition of conservative groups and denouncing Clark as "the most liberal member of the United States Senate."

Abortion opponents, right-to-work advocates and gun owners enthusiastically supported Jepsen. He was also helped by direct-mail specialist Richard Viguerie, the National Conservative Political Action Committee (NCPAC) and the grass-roots organization of Terry Branstad, a conservative state senator who went on to win the lieutenant governorship in 1978.

At that point, Jepsen had been out of politics

for six years, seemingly finished by his unsuccessful attempt to mount a primary challenge to Gov. Robert Ray in 1972.

But after what he later described as a period of prayer, Jepsen decided on a comeback and defeated a moderate Ray ally in the GOP Senate primary. At that point, Clark still looked secure. But the incumbent was carrying an ADA voting record in the 90s, a serious liability even in a state with a reputation for tolerating liberal legislators. Clark tried to downplay his liberalism by stressing procedural issues like lobby registration and open government.

Despite Clark's weakness, few took Jepsen seriously even in the final weeks of the campaign. Blunt and sometimes tactless, he had been attracting controversy much of the year. He spoke sympathetically of the racial policies of the South African government during a visit to the University of Iowa, and suggested that Social Security might be better handled by private insurance companies. Jepsen persisted in his criticism of Clark's record, especially his support for the Panama Canal treaties and for abortion.

The result was a shock to both sides. A low turnout in Democratic counties, largely because of resentment at Clark's pro-abortion views, made the pre-election polling invalid. Some of Clark's supporters had rested on the assumption that he was safe, while others, like the Machinists, were angry at his support for gas deregulation. Jepsen received only 1,052 more votes than the unsuccessful Republican nominee had in 1974, but they were enough to put him in the Senate.

## Committees

**Agriculture, Nutrition and Forestry** (7th of 9 Republicans)
Soil and Water Conservation, chairman; Agricultural Credit and Rural Electrification; Foreign Agricultural Policy; Forestry, Water Resources and Environment.

**Armed Services** (7th of 9 Republicans)
Manpower and Personnel, chairman; Preparedness; Tactical Warfare.

**Joint Economic** (Vice-Chairman)
Monetary and Fiscal Policy, chairman; International Trade, Finance and Security Economics.

## Elections

**1978 General**

| | | |
|---|---|---|
| Roger Jepsen (R ) | 421,598 | (51 %) |
| Richard Clark (D ) | 395,066 | (48 %) |

**1978 Primary**

| | | |
|---|---|---|
| Roger Jepsen (R ) | 87,397 | (57 %) |
| Maurice Van Nostrand (R) | 54,189 | (36 %) |
| Joe Bertroche (R ) | 10,860 | (7 %) |

## Campaign Finance

| | Receipts | Receipts from PACs | Expenditures |
|---|---|---|---|
| **1978** | | | |
| Jepsen (R ) | $738,581 | $156,072 (21 %) | $728,268 |
| Clark (D ) | $862,635 | $214,777 (25 %) | $860,774 |

## Voting Studies

| | Presidential Support | | Party Unity | | Conservative Coalition | |
|---|---|---|---|---|---|---|
| Year | S | O | S | O | S | O |
| 1980 | 35 | 61 | 86 | 5 | 86 | 4 |
| 1979 | 29 | 60 | 87 | 4 | 87 | 1 |

S = Support     O = Opposition

## Key Votes

**96th Congress**

| | |
|---|---|
| Maintain relations with Taiwan (1979) | Y |
| Reduce synthetic fuel development funds (1979) | N |
| Impose nuclear plant moratorium (1979) | N |
| Kill stronger windfall profits tax (1979) | + |
| Guarantee Chrysler Corp. loans (1979) | N |
| Approve military draft registration (1980) | N |
| End Revenue Sharing to the states (1980) | N |
| Block Justice Dept. busing suits (1980) | Y |

**97th Congress**

| | |
|---|---|
| Restore urban program funding cuts (1981) | N |

## Interest Group Ratings

| Year | ADA | ACA | AFL-CIO | CCUS-1 | CCUS-2 |
|---|---|---|---|---|---|
| 1980 | 22 | 77 | 17 | 85 | |
| 1979 | 0 | 92 | 0 | 90 | 93 |

# Charles E. Grassley (R)

**Of New Hartford — Elected 1980**

**Born:** Sept. 17, 1933, New Hartford, Iowa.
**Education:** University of Northern Iowa, B.A. 1955, M.A. 1956.
**Profession:** Farmer.
**Family:** Wife, Barbara Ann Speicher; five children.
**Religion:** Baptist.
**Political Career:** Iowa House, 1959-75; U.S. House, 1975-8.

**The Member:** Grassley's slow and sometimes inarticulate speaking style reinforces all the Eastern stereotypes of the rural Midwest, but his congressional career suggests a man difficult to dismiss as a bumpkin. If he is no orator or legislative strategist, he is clearly a man with an instinct for the issues and the political positions on which a career can be built.

During three terms in the House, Grassley tried to cultivate his role as Republican successor to the retired and revered Iowa congressman, H. R. Gross. In each Congress, Grassley introduced Gross-like measures to reduce the federal debt, all using his predecessor's trademark bill number, HR 144.

Grassley found two ways as a representative to express constituent frustration over big and distant government. One was by criticizing New York City's request for a federal loan guarantee; the other was by fighting a proposed pay increase for members of Congress.

In 1977, when congressional salaries rose from $44,600 to $57,500, it was Grassley who led the drive for a recorded vote on the issue. By the time he obtained one, the raises were already in effect, and the other side had the votes, but Grassley drew the publicity he wanted.

When he moved into the Senate, Grassley quickly established himself as one of the most ardent budget-cutters in a Senate preoccupied with reducing federal spending.

In the Budget Committee, Grassley voted in April to scuttle the first budget resolution for fiscal 1982 — a blueprint that contained all of the elements of Reagan's economic recovery program. Two other conservative Republicans joined him, and the budget initially went down, 12-8. Grassley felt the resolution's deficits for 1981-84 broke faith with GOP pledges to balance the budget.

The admnistration then revised its spending figures for the later years, showing a balanced budget in 1984. The new plan drew a tighter rein on defense spending, predicted discovery of more waste and fraud and projected additional unspecified cuts in 1983 and 1984. Grassley seemed skeptical, but he and the other Republicans hold out changed their votes and the budget was approved.

Grassley joined the Iowa House at age 25, rose to become chairman of its Appropriations Committee and developed a reputation for personal integrity and suspicion of government.

When Gross announced his retirement from Congress in 1974, Grassley organized the district's most conservative elements, won the GOP nomination with 42 percent of the vote against four opponents and then held on against an aggressive young Democrat in a Democratic year.

When Grassley announced he was running for the Senate in 1980, conservative Republicans across Iowa began building his grass-roots organization. Against a well-financed, moderate GOP primary opponent who was endorsed by Gov. Robert Ray, Grassley won 90 of the state's 99 counties.

Then Grassley ran head-on into Democratic Sen. John C. Culver, who conducted an insistent and impassioned defense of his liberal Senate voting record. Culver characterized Grassley's legislative accomplishments as mediocre. Targeted for defeat by the Moral Majority and NCPAC, Culver lashed out at the New Right supporters in Grassley's camp, calling them a "poison in the political bloodstream."

But Grassley, an earnest, easygoing farmer, did not fit the part of a fanatic. He disassociated himself from New Right tactics without losing conservative support. He won more votes than any Senate candidate in Iowa history and outpolled Ronald Reagan by 9,000.

## Committees

**Budget** (9th of 12 Republicans)

**Finance** (11th of 11 Republicans)
Oversight of the Internal Revenue Service, chairman; Estate and Gift Taxation; International Trade.

**Judiciary** (8th of 10 Republicans)
Agency Administration, chairman; Constitution; Immigration and Refugee Policy.

**Special Aging** (7th of 8 Republicans)

## Elections

**1980 General**

| | |
|---|---|
| Charles Grassley (R) | 683,014 (54%) |
| John Culver (D) | 581,545 (46%) |

**1980 Primary**

| | |
|---|---|
| Charles Grassley (R) | 170,120 (66%) |
| Tom Stoner (R) | 89,409 (34%) |

**Previous Winning Percentages**

1978* (75%)    1976* (57%)    1974* (51%)

*House elections.

## Campaign Finance

| | Receipts | Receipts from PACs | Expen- ditures |
|---|---|---|---|
| 1980 | | | |
| Grassley (R) | $2,217,229 | $6,300 (.28%) | $,183,028 |
| Culver (D) | $1,775,398 | $79,020 (4%) | $1,750,680 |

## Voting Studies

| Year House service | Presidential Support S | O | Party Unity S | O | Conservative Coalition S | O |
|---|---|---|---|---|---|---|
| 1980 | 27 | 43 | 70 | 8 | 67 | 12 |
| 1979 | 33 | 66 | 86 | 12 | 91 | 6 |
| 1978 | 30 | 70 | 88 | 12 | 93 | 7 |
| 1977 | 34 | 66 | 92 | 8 | 91 | 9 |
| 1976 | 63 | 37 | 84 | 16 | 87 | 13 |
| 1975 | 54 | 46 | 80 | 20 | 84 | 16 |

S = Support          O = Opposition

## Key Votes

**97th Congress**

Restore urban program funding cuts (1981)          N

## Interest Group Ratings

| Year House service | ADA | ACA | AFL-CIO | CCUS-1 | CCUS-2 |
|---|---|---|---|---|---|
| 1980 | 17 | 74 | 17 | 74 | |
| 1979 | 11 | 88 | 20 | 94 | |
| 1978 | 5 | 93 | 10 | 78 | |
| 1977 | 15 | 81 | 17 | 100 | |
| 1976 | 15 | 86 | 13 | 76 | |
| 1975 | 21 | 86 | 26 | 65 | |

# 1 Jim Leach (R)

### Of Davenport — Elected 1976

**Born:** Oct. 15, 1942, Davenport, Iowa.
**Education:** Princeton U., B.A. 1964; Johns Hopkins U., M.A. 1966.
**Profession:** Propane gas marketing company executive, foreign service officer.
**Family:** Wife, Elisabeth Ann "Deba" Foxley.
**Religion:** Episcopalian.
**Political Career:** Unsuccessful Republican nominee for U.S. House, 1974.

**In Washington:** Leach is a moderate Republican whose interests have always been in foreign policy but who quickly made a reputation for himself in the House as a critic of the federal bureaucracy.

In his first term, Leach amended the 1978 Civil Service Act to place a ceiling on the number of federal workers. It was an idea that struck a popular anti-bureaucratic theme, and it sailed through the House on a 251-96 vote. It gave President Carter a year to shrink the work force to 1977 levels — a reduction of 68,000 employees. Carter, initially opposed to the amendment, later said he wanted to go even further.

Adoption of the amendment was a solid political triumph for Leach. It also made him a convenient target for the bureaucracy to use in explaining away some of its problems. When veterans' groups denounced a cutback at Veterans Administration hospitals, the Leach amendment was blamed. The General Services Administration said Leach was responsible for the slow pace of GSA investigations into contract irregularities.

From his seat on the Post Office and Civil Service Committee, Leach kept promoting the issue. He worked to place a limit on federal spending on contracts and tried to push the government to decentralize by moving more of its offices outside Washington.

All of this took Leach some distance from the international policy issues he is most interested in. In 1981, he gave up Post Office and Civil Service to take a seat on Foreign Affairs where, as the ranking Republican on the Human Rights Subcommittee, he is pressing for stronger arms controls and a total ban on the manufacture, deployment and use of chemical weapons.

Leach stayed on a second major committee, Banking, where he supports the Export-Import Bank, a tool he says is underused in helping American industry sell its products abroad. He has also introduced a bill to control the unregulated "Euro-dollar" market. Leach feared European countries were trying to depress the dollar to make oil imports, whose price is pegged to the dollar, less expensive.

As a member of Banking in 1979, Leach voted for the loan guarantee to Chrysler Corp. Before doing that, however, he persuaded the bill's managers to accept a provision spelling out the federal government's right to claim top creditor status if the company eventually went bankrupt.

**At Home:** Leach has converted this chronically-marginal district into GOP territory. His moderate voting record and high visibility have all but shut out the Democrats. In both 1978 and 1980, he won every county in the district.

Leach brought a varied background to his first campaign, in 1974, against first-term Democrat Edward Mezvinsky. He had studied at Princeton and at the London School of Economics, worked in the Office of Economic Opportunity and in the Foreign Service, was assigned to the Arms Control and Disarmament Agency, then returned to Iowa to run his family's propane gas manufacturing firm.

Leach lost to Mezvinsky in 1974 by 12,147 votes, but that was a good showing for a Republican newcomer in a Democratic year. During the next two years, he spoke regularly in the district, held his organization together and built a

---

**1st District: Southeast — Davenport, Iowa City.** Population: 505,896 (7% increase since 1970). Race: White 486,825 (96%), Black 10,463 (2%), Others 8,611 (2%). Spanish origin: 8,425 (2%).

$200,000 campaign fund.

In 1976, Leach stressed his ties to Robert Ray, Iowa's moderate Republican governor. He described himself as a "Bob Ray Republican" and called Mezvinsky "a Bella Abzug Democrat." Leach won by carrying his home base of Scott County (Davenport), which Mezvinsky had taken in 1974. The Democrat carried Iowa City, Burlington and Keokuk, but it was not enough.

Leach's 1978 opponent was Dick Myers, a truckstop operator and former mayor of Coralville. Myers campaigned actively, but by that time Leach was strong throughout the district. He had broken through in Iowa City with efforts to court the student vote. Leach outspent Myers 2-1 and drew 64 percent of the vote. It was the first time in 16 years a House candidate of either party had won more than 55 percent.

Intimidated by Leach's 1978 margin, contributors shunned Jim Larew, the 1980 Democratic nominee. A 26-year-old Harvard graduate and former aide to Sen. John Culver, Larew raised less than $50,000, one-fifth of Leach's expenditures. Larew trimmed Leach's margins slightly in the university community, but he lost by 60,747 votes.

**The District:** Davenport is Iowa's third-largest city. The city and surrounding Scott County cast about 30 percent of the 1st District vote. It is a manufacturing area (aluminum, farm implements, construction equipment) with a sizable blue-collar vote becoming increasingly Republican.

Johnson County (Iowa City), with the University of Iowa's 23,000 students, leans Democratic but not by enough to offset the vote in the strongly Republican rural counties.

## Committees

**Banking, Finance and Urban Affairs (6th of 19 Republicans)**
Financial Institutions Supervision, Regulation and Insurance; Housing and Community Development; International Trade, Investment and Monetary Policy.

**Foreign Affairs (11th of 16 Republicans)**
Asian and Pacific Affairs; Human Rights and International Organizations.

## Elections

**1980 General**

| | |
|---|---|
| Jim Leach (R ) | 133,349 (64 %) |
| Jim Larew (D ) | 72,602 (35 %) |

**1978 General**

| | |
|---|---|
| Jim Leach (R ) | 79,940 (64 %) |
| Dick Myers (D ) | 45,037 (36 %) |

**Previous Winning Percentage**

**1976 (52 %)**

**District Vote For President**

| | 1980 | | 1976 | | 1972 |
|---|---|---|---|---|---|
| D | 92,431 (41 %) | D | 104,675 (49 %) | D | 87,448 (43 %) |
| R | 105,371 (47 %) | R | 105,060 (49 %) | R | 111,577 (55 %) |
| I | 22,218 (10 %) | | | | |

## Campaign Finance

| | | Receipts | Receipts from PACs | Expenditures |
|---|---|---|---|---|
| **1980** | | | | |
| Leach (R ) | | $238,277 | $2,000 (1 %) | $235,933 |
| Larew (D ) | | $44,775 | $5,150 (12 %) | $46,834 |

| **1978** | | | | |
|---|---|---|---|---|
| Leach (R ) | | $242,314 | $3,992 (2 %) | $241,356 |
| Myers (D ) | | $123,965 | $20,200 (16 %) | $123,626 |

## Voting Studies

| | Presidental Support | | Party Unity | | Conservative Coalition | |
|---|---|---|---|---|---|---|
| Year | S | O | S | O | S | O |
| 1980 | 51 | 44 | 63 | 36 | 49 | 48 |
| 1979 | 56 | 41 | 61 | 32 | 59 | 31 |
| 1978 | 56 | 43 | 68 | 30 | 67 | 30 |
| 1977 | 51 | 49 | 67 | 31 | 64 | 33 |

S = Support          O = Opposition

†Not eligible for all recorded votes.

## Key Votes

**96th Congress**

| | |
|---|---|
| Weaken Carter oil profits tax (1979) | Y |
| Reject hospital cost control plan (1979) | Y |
| Implement Panama Canal Treaties (1979) | N |
| Establish Department of Education (1979) | Y |
| Approve Anti-busing Amendment (1979) | N |
| Guarantee Chrysler Corp. loans (1979) | Y |
| Approve military draft registration (1980) | N |
| Aid Sandinista regime in Nicaragua (1980) | Y |
| Strengthen fair housing laws (1980) | Y |

**97th Congress**

| | |
|---|---|
| Reagan budget proposal (1981) | Y |

## Interest Group Ratings

| Year | ADA | ACA | AFL-CIO | CCUS |
|---|---|---|---|---|
| 1980 | 61 | 58 | 37 | 76 |
| 1979 | 37 | 56 | 30 | 76 |
| 1978 | 35 | 63 | 25 | 78 |
| 1977 | 50 | 59 | 30 | 88 |

**423**

# 2 Tom Tauke (R)

**Of Dubuque — Elected 1978**

**Born:** Oct. 11, 1950, Dubuque, Iowa.
**Education:** Loras College, B.A. 1972; U. of Iowa, J.D. 1974.
**Profession:** Lawyer.
**Family:** Single.
**Religion:** Roman Catholic.
**Political Career:** Iowa House, 1975-79, elected in special election; Republican nominee for Iowa House, 1974.

**In Washington:** Serious and reserved, Tauke has had a middle-aged look about him from the day he arrived in the House in 1979 at age 28. He has stood out in a political way also, gaining a reputation as one of the few moderate voices in a GOP class that has tilted almost unanimously to the conservative side.

But it has not been difficult to seem like a moderate in that group without venturing very far to the left. Over his first two years in the House, Tauke actually cast his vote with the "conservative coalition" of Republicans and Southern Democrats more than 70 percent of the time.

Tauke gained much of his reputation by avoiding militant rhetoric in foreign policy and voting with other Frost Belt legislators on some federal subsidy issues. But on most matters of overall federal spending and taxation, he differed little with mainstream Republican thinking.

On the Education and Labor Committee, Tauke was one of eight Republicans to oppose unionization for hospital interns, arguing that unions would make labor strife a part of a medical education.

He was in favor of tightening the rules on student loan programs, and imposing penalties for defaulting on student loans. He offered an amendment on the House floor to waive limits on garnishment of the wages of former students who defaulted on the loans.

Like most of the Republican newcomers in the 96th Congress, Tauke pushed for stricter congressional ethics and less spending on the institution itself. Also like most of them, he had an eye for the economy move with political appeal. At one point, he tried to offer an amendment that would eliminate cheap car-washes for congressmen in the House garages. The House garage was washing and waxing cars for about $3 while a private garage would charge $16, he claimed. Tauke lost on a voice vote.

A Catholic from heavily Catholic Dubuque, Tauke has voted with anti-abortion forces on most tests in the House. But he angered some right-to-life forces at home with his endorsement of George Bush for president in 1980, although Bush won the Iowa caucuses.

**At Home:** Tauke was barely out of college when he became chairman of the Dubuque County GOP, and he won election to the state Legislature the year after he graduated from law school.

He considered a 1976 congressional bid, but decided that, at age 25, he could afford to serve another term in the Iowa House before aiming for Washington. That turned out to be a good decision. By 1978, national Republicans were ready to invest substantially in a campaign against Democratic Rep. Michael Blouin, who had won twice by unimpressive margins. Tauke was able to outspend Blouin by $100,000.

Tauke had established a following as a state legislator among anti-abortion Democrats in Dubuque. But Blouin also opposed abortion, and did not expect many defections on that issue. In 1976, he had won 61.5 percent in Dubuque County. He was counting on a similar vote for 1978.

Blouin was also depending on his labor allies in the district's two other population centers, Cedar Rapids (Linn County) and Clinton. Tauke did not enter the campaign with much name recognition in either place.

---

**2nd District: Northeast — Cedar Rapids.** Population: 484,684 (3% increase since 1970). Race: White 477,433 (99%), Black 3,802 (1%), Others 3,449 (1%). Spanish origin: 2,726 (1%).

---

But Tauke's monetary advantage and a surprisingly low Democratic turnout combined to produce an upset. In Dubuque County, Blouin was held to a mediocre 54.1 percent, and Tauke stunned him by carrying Linn and Clinton counties. The Republican padded his margin with a combined 56.7 percent in eight generally Republican rural counties.

The 1980 Democratic candidate was former state Sen. Steve Sovern, a Linn County native. His strategy against Tauke was to win convincingly in his home area, increase the Democratic percentage in Dubuque and cut his losses in Clinton and the rural areas.

But Tauke's voting record had generated no widespread dissatisfaction, and his campaign receipts exceeded $300,000, nearly three times more than Sovern had. The Democrat did improve on Blouin's 1978 showing in Dubuque County, but his margin in Linn was a meager four votes. Tauke won with a 18,412-vote plurality.

**The District:** Cedar Rapids and surrrounding Linn County cast more than 35 percent of the 2nd District's 1980 congressional vote. The second-largest city in the state, Cedar Rapids is a center for meatpacking, food processing and manufacturing of farm and radio equipment. The county has voted Democratic in some recent statewide elections, but Republican Sen. Roger Jepsen carried it narrowly in 1978, and Reagan took it easily in 1980.

The combined Dubuque city and county vote is about 20 percent of the district total. Dubuque is also a meatpacking town, and builds tractors and other farm implements. It is much more Catholic than Cedar Rapids, and more consistently Democratic. In 1980, Dubuque was the only 2nd District county that gave President Carter a plurality.

More than 10 percent of the vote comes from another local manufacturing center, Clinton County. Democrats have lost strength there during the past decade, and it now is only slightly less Republican than the district's eight rural counties, where grain, livestock and poultry are the economic staple.

## Committees

**Energy and Commerce** (13th of 18 Republicans)
Energy Conservation and Power; Fossil and Synthetic Fuels; Telecommunications, Consumer Protection, and Finance.

**Select Aging** (13th of 23 Republicans)
Human Services.

## Elections

**1980 General**

| | |
|---|---|
| Tom Tauke (R ) | 111,587 (54 %) |
| Steve Sovern (D ) | 93,175 (45 %) |

**1978 General**

| | |
|---|---|
| Tom Tauke (R ) | 72,644 (52 %) |
| Michael Blouin (D) | 65,450 (47 %) |

**District Vote For President**

| | 1980 | | 1976 | | 1972 |
|---|---|---|---|---|---|
| D | 85,681 (40 %) | D | 101,530 (49 %) | D | 86,714 (44 %) |
| R | 106,149 (50 %) | R | 103,383 (49 %) | R | 108,517 (55 %) |
| I | 20,023 (9 %) | | | | |

## Campaign Finance

| | Receipts | Receipts from PACs | Expenditures |
|---|---|---|---|
| **1980** | | | |
| Tauke (R ) | $326,406 | $49,724 (15 %) | $307,972 |
| Sovern (D ) | $131,844 | $43,612 (33 %) | $129,815 |
| **1978** | | | |
| Tauke (R ) | $250,995 | $81,843 (33 %) | $250,432 |
| Blouin (D) | $129,765 | $60,412 (47 %) | $141,533 |

## Voting Studies

| | Presidential Support | | Party Unity | | Conservative Coalition | |
|---|---|---|---|---|---|---|
| Year | S | O | S | O | S | O |
| 1980 | 52 | 43 | 78 | 19 | 72 | 24 |
| 1979 | 48 | 47 | 75 | 23 | 76 | 22 |

S = Support        O = Opposition

## Key Votes

**96th Congress**

| | |
|---|---|
| Weaken Carter oil profits tax (1979) | Y |
| Reject hospital cost control plan (1979) | Y |
| Implement Panama Canal Treaties (1979) | N |
| Establish Department of Education (1979) | N |
| Approve Anti-busing Amendment (1979) | N |
| Guarantee Chrysler Corp. loans (1979) | N |
| Approve military draft registration (1980) | N |
| Aid Sandinista regime in Nicaragua (1980) | N |
| Strengthen fair housing laws (1980) | Y |

**97th Congress**

| | |
|---|---|
| Reagan budget proposal (1981) | Y |

## Interest Group Ratings

| Year | ADA | ACA | AFL-CIO | CCUS |
|---|---|---|---|---|
| 1980 | 33 | 61 | 22 | 71 |
| 1979 | 32 | 77 | 22 | 71 |

# 3 Cooper Evans (R)

**Of Grundy Center — Elected 1980**

**Born:** May 26, 1924, Cedar Rapids, Iowa.
**Education:** Iowa State U., B.S. 1949; M.S. 1954;
Oak Ridge School of Reactor Technology,
nuclear engineering degree, 1955.
**Military Career:** Army 1943-46, 1949-65.
**Profession:** Farmer; engineer.
**Family:** Wife, Jean Marie Ruppelt; two children.
**Religion:** Methodist.
**Political Career:** Iowa House, 1975-79.

The Member: Evans is a man with the precision of an engineer and army officer and a distinct preference for working behind the scenes.

During Agriculture Committee deliberations on the 1981 farm bill, Evans successfully sponsored several land management amendments. One would offer payments to farmers who take land out of production to implement soil conservation. Another would require the Farmers Home Administration to charge higher interest on loans for projects that eliminate prime farmland.

During his Army years, Evans worked at the Pentagon and Atomic Energy Commission. He retired from the Army in 1965 and returned to Iowa. In 1974 he went to the Iowa House.

In the Legislature, Evans was interested in energy issues. He had designed nuclear plants during his years with the AEC, and favored rapid development of nuclear energy. He also invented a solar-powered grain dryer for use on his farm.

When incumbent Republican Charles E. Grassley announced his bid for the Senate in October 1979, Evans resigned from the Legislature to run for Congress. He was the clear-cut winner in a four-man GOP primary, but barely fended off Democrat Lynn Cutler in November. He won 13 of the district's 18 counties, just enough to overcome Culter's lead in the three largest cities.

The District: Since 1934, the 3rd District has elected only conservative Republicans like Grassley (1975-81) and H. R. Gross (1949-75). But the GOP claim is not undisputed. Gross won less than 60 percent of the vote in his last two elections, and Grassley had to fight two close contests before consolidating his position.

Democrats have had organizational strength in recent years in the meatpacking city of Waterloo, and have carried the district in some statewide elections. Republican margins have been large enough in most smaller towns and rural areas to keep the seat under GOP control.

## Committees

**Agriculture** (18th of 19 Republicans)
Conservation, Credit, and Rural Development; Department Operations, Research, and Foreign Agriculture; Wheat, Soybeans, and Feed Grains.

## Elections

**1980 General**

| | |
|---|---|
| Cooper Evans (R ) | 107,869 (51 %) |
| Lynn G. Cutler (D) | 101,735 (48 %) |

**1980 Primary**

| | |
|---|---|
| Cooper Evans (R ) | 26,480 (45 %) |
| Jim West (R ) | 20,460 (35 %) |
| Bill Hansen (R ) | 10,871 (18 %) |

**District Vote For President**

| | 1980 | | 1976 | | 1972 |
|---|---|---|---|---|---|
| D | 83,485 (38 %) | D | 101,443 (48 %) | D | 78,687 (39 %) |
| R | 115,682 (53 %) | R | 108,568 (51 %) | R | 119,372 (59 %) |
| I | 17,496 (8 %) | | | | |

## Campaign Finance

| | Receipts | Receipts from PACs | Expenditures |
|---|---|---|---|
| **1980** | | | |
| Evans (R ) | $576,129 | — (0 %) | $575,496 |
| Cutler (D ) | $231,592 | $75,763 (33 %) | $227,543 |

## Key Vote

**97th Congress**

| | |
|---|---|
| Reagan budget proposal (1981) | Y |

**3rd District: North central — Waterloo.** Population: 477,736 (1% increase since 1970). Race: White 464,036 (97%), Black 9,302 (2%), Others 4,398 (1%). Spanish origin: 3,207 (1%).

# 4 Neal Smith (D)

### Of Altoona — Elected 1958

**Born:** March 23, 1920, Hedrick, Iowa.
**Education:** U. of Mo., 1945-46; Syracuse U., 1946-47; Drake U., LL.B. 1950.
**Military Career:** Army Air Corps, 1942-45.
**Profession:** Farmer, lawyer.
**Family:** Wife, Beatrix Havens; two children.
**Religion:** Methodist.
**Political Career:** Unsuccessfully sought Democratic nomination for U.S. House, 1956.

**In Washington:** Smith seems almost too cautious and self-effacing to be a legislative activist, and for most of his long House career he has been outside the spotlight, tinkering with crop subsidies and dam construction on the Appropriations Committee.

But he is a man of stubbornness and quiet ambition, and at critical moments he has stepped forward to raise issues few of his colleagues have been willing to confront.

It was Smith who led the fight in the House for a tough meat inspection law, starting in 1961 and ending with passage of a bill six years later, after the *Des Moines Register* exposed scandalous conditions in meatpacking houses.

The 1967 meat inspection law did not go nearly as far as Smith wanted. He and Thomas S. Foley, D-Wash., tried to amend it on the floor to impose federal standards on the industry. That failed by six votes, and Congress eventually cleared a bill simply providing federal money for states to upgrade their facilities. But Smith's quiet persistence had been in large part responsible for forcing the issue.

During the same Congress, Smith pushed through a bill that few members really wanted banning nepotism on federal payrolls. As of 1967, more than 50 members had hired relatives as aides and paid them with federal funds. Smith's bill prevented that, although it "grandfathered" in those already employed.

To get his new rule past the House, Smith had to offer it as an amendment to a related bill, and he found a vehicle in legislation increasing federal salaries. Before most members knew what had happened, the House had passed it.

The nepotism bill required some complicated parliamentary work, and it demonstrated the fascination Smith always has had with House procedure. He has proposed a variety of rules changes over the years, including the one in 1973 that

made all committee chairmanships subject to an automatic caucus vote every two years, reducing the psychological dominance of seniority over House politics. In the 95th Congress, Smith chaired the caucus subcommittee on rules changes.

Those efforts brought him into the complex struggles over House leadership, and in these he has been less than successful. Despite his parliamentary skill and personal respect, he never has excelled at internal politics.

He tried to become House Budget chairman in 1975, but lost to Brock Adams of Washington on a 148-119 vote. In 1979, when Smith took over the State and Justice Subcommittee at Appropriations, he tried temporarily to keep his Small Business Committee chairmanship at the same time but was turned down by the Democratic Steering Committee. His efforts to keep two chairmanships at once annoyed some Democrats, especially in the Congressional Black Caucus, because Maryland's Parren Mitchell, who is black, was next in line on Small Business.

Smith allied himself in the mid-1970s with California's Phillip Burton, then campaigning for majority leader, and would have been a leadership confidante had Burton not lost by one vote.

In recent years, as he has concentrated on his Appropriations and Small Business assignments, he has waged few dramatic crusades like the ones

**4th District: South central — Des Moines.** Population: 489,070 (4% increase since 1970). Race: White 466,781 (95%), Black 14,385 (3%), Others 7,904 (2%). Spanish origin: 5,378 (1%).

over meatpacking or nepotism. But he has used Small Business to pursue his personal war against monopolies, which he insists are responsible for much of the national economic problems.

In 1980, his last year as Small Business chairman, Smith introduced a bill that followed up on two years of hearings into monopoly power in the food industry. He claimed that consumers lost $98.5 billion through concentration in the industry between 1973 and 1978. His bill would prevent any meatpacker from slaughtering more than 25 percent of the national production of cattle and hogs and bar the largest companies from operating retail food outlets.

Although Smith has never served on the Agriculture Committee, he has been close to the farm price debate throughout his years in the House. His main issue has been creation of a strategic reserve through which the government would buy up large quantities of grain, protecting the United States against future shortage but also boosting market prices.

Critics have always argued the reserve would be a permanent threat to the market and a depressing long-term influence on prices, and it has never had a full trial. But Smith believes in it.

During his two terms as Small Business chairman, Smith was frequently in conflict with the Carter administration over funding for the Small Business Administration (SBA). In 1978, Carter wanted to channel $100 million in SBA money toward loan guarantees for exporters. Smith complained that "when there is less SBA money to begin with, it is impossible to retarget loan funds to new areas." Later that year, when the committee wrote a three-year reauthorization of SBA programs, Carter vetoed it as too expensive.

**Home:** Smith's even-tempered, unaffected manner has always brought him votes beyond the normal Democratic constituency in Iowa, and he has won re-election 11 times with little strain.

But the 1980 returns implied that easy times are finally over for him. Against Republican Don Young, Smith received only 53.9 percent.

Young's strong showing capped a year in which there was an unusual amount of activity among 4th District Republicans. A three-way GOP primary attracted media attention and voter interest; Young, a Des Moines physician, emerged as the consensus choice.

With financial and organizational help from the national party, Young built a respectable campaign and raised about $250,000. He criticized Smith's voting record as too liberal and said it was unrepresentative of the prevailing philosophy in the district. He called the congressman an en-

trenched fixture in a Democratic Congress that had weakened the nation's economy and defense.

Disquieted by polls showing a sharp drop in his popularity, Smith blitzed the district with radio, television and billboard advertisements in the closing weeks of the campaign. He won just over 55 percent in Polk County (Des Moines) and Wapello County (Ottumwa), but lost two rural, small-town counties and was held to a bare majority in six others.

Until 1980, Smith had not seen tough elections since the early years of his political career. After serving as national president of the Young Democrats of America, Smith first ran for Congress in 1956, losing the Democratic primary to state Rep. William Denman, who nearly unseated GOP Rep. Paul Cunningham in the general election.

In 1958, Smith finished first in a five-man Democratic primary field. But he fell short of winning the 35 percent plurality required by state party rules, so the party's district convention was left to choose the nominee. After a three-day convention battle, in which Smith had to overcome opposition from Des Moines labor unions, he won the nomination.

Cunningham's narrow 1956 victory marked him as vulnerable in 1958, but Democratic unity had been damaged by the bitter nomination fight. Smith had to struggle to win with 52.3 percent, aided by a national Democratic tide that took three Iowa congressional seats from Republican control.

In the 1960 election, Smith was the sole survivor among the state's three first-term Democrats. His opponent, Des Moines physician Floyd Burgeson, was a forceful speaker but an inexperienced politician. Smith survived with 53 percent and won easily during the next decade.

Redistricting after the 1970 census threw Smith into the same district with Republican Rep. John Kyl. The national Democratic Party and labor groups gave Smith extra support, and he easily overcame Kyl. Smith coasted through subsequent elections until he met Republican Young in 1980.

**The District:** The 4th is dominated by Des Moines, Iowa's state capital and commercial center. The city is predominantly white, Protestant and middle-class, with much less ethnic flavor than Chicago, Omaha and other Midwestern industrial cities. Farm equipment is a crucial industry, and the United Auto Workers a significant political presence.

Metropolitan Des Moines has a population of about 330,000; the city and surrounding Polk County cast nearly two-thirds of the 4th District vote in the 1980 congressional election. Polk is one of the state's most Democratic counties, although in 1980 it gave Reagan a first-place finish with 44.6 percent of the vote.

## Committees

**Appropriations** (4th of 33 Democrats)
Commerce, Justice, State, and Judiciary, chairman; Labor-Health and Human Services-Education.

**Small Business** (2nd of 23 Democrats)
Export Opportunities and Special Small Business Problems; SBA and SBIC Authority, Minority Enterprise and General Small Business Problems.

## Elections

**1980 General**

| | |
|---|---|
| Neal Smith (D ) | 117,896 (54 %) |
| Donald Young (R ) | 100,335 (46 %) |

**1978 General**

| | |
|---|---|
| Neal Smith (D ) | 88,526 (65 %) |
| Charles Minor (R ) | 48,308 (35 %) |

**Previous Winning Percentages**

| | | | |
|---|---|---|---|
| 1976 (69 %) | 1974 (64 %) | 1972 (60 %) | 1970 (65 %) |
| 1968 (62 %) | 1966 (60 %) | 1964 (70 %) | 1962 (63 %) |
| 1960 (53 %) | 1958 (52 %) | | |

**District Vote For President**

| | 1980 | | 1976 | | 1972 |
|---|---|---|---|---|---|
| **D** | 98,326 (43 %) | **D** | 116,438 (53 %) | **D** | 92,752 (43 %) |
| **R** | 105,520 (46 %) | **R** | 98,765 (45 %) | **R** | 117,283 (55 %) |
| **I** | 21,354 (9 %) | | | | |

## Campaign Finance

| | Receipts | Receipts from PACs | Expenditures |
|---|---|---|---|
| **1980** | | | |
| Smith (D ) | $96,601 | $60,775 (63 %) | $87,813 |
| Young (R ) | $243,642 | $24,652 (10 %) | $240,518 |
| **1978** | | | |
| Smith (R ) | $47,606 | $20,600 (43 %) | $43,447 |
| Minor (D ) | $10,285 | $400 (4 %) | $9,615 |

## Voting Studies

| | Presidential Support | | Party Unity | | Conservative Coalition | |
|---|---|---|---|---|---|---|
| Year | S | O | S | O | S | O |
| 1980 | 71 | 26 | 81 | 15 | 28 | 64 |
| 1979 | 60 | 26 | 71 | 18 | 38 | 51 |
| 1978 | 71 | 27 | 79 | 18 | 33 | 65 |
| 1977 | 61 | 28 | 77 | 16 | 29 | 63 |

| | | | | | | |
|---|---|---|---|---|---|---|
| 1976 | 29 | 69 | 83 | 12 | 27 | 70 |
| 1975 | 38 | 61 | 80 | 16 | 29 | 66 |
| 1974 (Ford) | 50 | 50 | | | | |
| 1974 | 53 | 40 | 78 | 16 | 25 | 71 |
| 1973 | 38 | 58 | 77 | 15 | 26 | 63 |
| 1972 | 41 | 43 | 66 | 20 | 33 | 56 |
| 1971 | 44 | 51 | 72 | 18 | 32 | 60 |
| 1970 | 58 | 23 | 64 | 25 | 27 | 52 |
| 1969 | 60 | 36 | 73 | 16 | 31 | 60 |
| 1968 | 77 | 15 | 82 | 12 | 25 | 73 |
| 1967 | 80 | 9 | 82 | 6 | 11 | 80 |
| 1966 | 76 | 7 | 83 | 6 | 19 | 68 |
| 1965 | 82 | 7 | 88 | 7 | 14 | 78 |
| 1964 | 87 | 8 | 79 | 16 | 25 | 67 |
| 1963 | 76 | 4 | 84 | 5 | 0 | 93 |
| 1962 | 93 | 7 | 82 | 18 | 0 | 100 |
| 1961 | 89 | 6 | 90 | 2 | 9 | 87 |

S = Support          O = Opposition

## Key Votes

**96th Congress**

| | |
|---|---|
| Weaken Carter oil profits tax (1979) | Y |
| Reject hospital cost control plan (1979) | Y |
| Implement Panama Canal Treaties (1979) | N |
| Establish Department of Education (1979) | Y |
| Approve anti-busing Amendment (1979) | N |
| Guarantee Chrysler Corp. loans (1979) | Y |
| Approve military draft registration (1980) | N |
| Aid Sandinista regime in Nicaragua (1980) | Y |
| Strengthen fair housing laws (1980) | Y |

**97th Congress**

| | |
|---|---|
| Reagan budget proposal (1981) | N |

## Interest Group Ratings

| Year | ADA | ACA | AFL-CIO | CCUS |
|---|---|---|---|---|
| 1980 | 72 | 14 | 61 | 59 |
| 1979 | 42 | 21 | 53 | 56 |
| 1978 | 60 | 11 | 70 | 39 |
| 1977 | 55 | 8 | 90 | 19 |
| 1976 | 70 | 7 | 82 | 19 |
| 1975 | 63 | 15 | 90 | 18 |
| 1974 | 70 | 7 | 100 | 22 |
| 1973 | 64 | 13 | 82 | 40 |
| 1972 | 50 | 22 | 90 | 10 |
| 1971 | 62 | 19 | 75 | - |
| 1970 | 48 | 13 | 83 | 13 |
| 1969 | 60 | 18 | 78 | - |
| 1968 | 75 | 14 | 100 | - |
| 1967 | 53 | 4 | 100 | 13 |
| 1966 | 59 | 20 | 92 | - |
| 1965 | 53 | 12 | - | 20 |
| 1964 | 88 | 16 | 91 | - |
| 1963 | - | 13 | - | - |
| 1962 | 100 | 9 | 100 | - |
| 1961 | 100 | - | - | - |

# 5 Tom Harkin (D)

**Of Ames — Elected 1974**

**Born:** Nov. 19, 1939, Cumming, Iowa.
**Education:** Iowa State U., B.S. 1962; Catholic U.
Law School, J.D. 1972.
**Military Career:** Navy, 1962-67, Navy Reserve,
1968-74.
**Profession:** Lawyer.
**Family:** Wife, Ruth Raduenz; one child.
**Religion:** Roman Catholic.
**Political Career:** Democratic nominee for U.S.
House, 1972.

**In Washington:** Almost alone among the Democrats who took over conservative Midwest districts in 1974, Harkin has not moved to the right with the national political mood.

He has always been convinced that rural Iowa will accept a liberal record if it is explained with conviction, and he has rarely seemed worried about compiling one. While his Watergate classmates have been introducing balanced budget amendments and voting against the national debt, Harkin has been complaining about wasteful defense spending and taking a purist stand on human rights. And he has been winning re-election overwhelmingly.

Harkin's interest in human rights came out of an experience in 1970, when as an investigator for a House committee, he traveled to Vietnam and discovered the "tiger cages" in which prisoners of war were being kept. He has never served on the Foreign Affairs Committee, but he has always been one of the loudest voices on foreign policy issues on the House floor.

In his first term, Harkin introduced an amendment that was to become a national issue during the Carter administration. Passed in the House by voice vote, it generally barred American foreign aid to any country engaging in a consistent pattern of violations of human rights. In 1976, Harkin also got the House to appprove an amendment prohibiting Inter-American Bank loans to countries violating "internationally recognized" human rights.

That approach was exactly the one Jimmy Carter took in his 1976 campaign. But it was not the one Carter recommended as president. Three months after Carter took office, he criticized the Harkin amendment as "a mistake," and said it gave him no bargaining room. The House insisted on its earlier stand, thanks to an odd coalition of anti-foreign aid conservatives and liberals skepti-

cal of assistance to right-wing regimes. The issue was compromised in conference.

But Harkin has continued mounting various human rights crusades on the floor throughout his career, most of them without much success. He tried to cut military aid to South Korea by $45 million in 1977, but lost on a 59-24 vote. The next year he tried to prohibit any indirect aid to seven right-wing dictatorships, and lost 360-41. He has offered some futile amendments against defense budgets in an era of rising Pentagon support; his effort to cut the 1979 defense authorization by 2 percent across-the-board got 102 votes, to 252 against it.

In 1981, when President Reagan decided to send American military advisers to El Salvador, Harkin said the new administration "sees things in terms of only communism and non-communism. It reminds me of the 1950s." He joined in a court suit to block the action.

The previous year, Harkin's human rights views led him into a delicate situation, after Carter responded to the Soviet invasion of Afghanistan with an embargo on the U.S.-Soviet grain trade. Harkin supported Carter, even endorsing him in the Iowa precinct nominating caucuses while the rest of the Democratic delegation was staying neutral. Harkin introduced his own resolution in the House calling for a ban on fertilizer sales to Russia.

But by April, as farm discontent rose and

---

**5th District: Southwest — Council Bluffs.** Population: 491,384 (5% increase since 1970). Race: White 485,174 (99%), Black 1,611 (0.3%), Others 4,999 (1%). Spanish origin: 3,136 (1%).

grain prices fell, he had to back down. He complained that Carter had failed to deliver on a promise not to leave farmers "holding the bag." He called for an immediate increase in price supports, and threatened to run against the president himself in the later-stage Iowa district caucuses.

Harkin never did that, but he did try to kill the embargo with an amendment on the House floor in July. The effort had all of Harkin's passion and impulsiveness.

The amendment would have prevented the government from spending money to enforce any embargo against the Soviet Union. House Agriculture Chairman Thomas S. Foley, visibly angry at Harkin, complained that it would amount to handing the Russians a "medal of victory" and giving them unrestricted "most favored nation" status. Harkin agreed to modify his amendment to limit it to the specific 1980 grain embargo, but the modified version was beaten 279-135. When the original amendment came up, it lost 414-1, with Harkin himself voting against it.

Whatever Harkin's maverick tendencies might be on foreign policy, he is a militant and politically shrewd spokesman for Iowa livestock and corn. He voted against the 1977 farm bill when it cleared the Agriculture Committee 40-6, arguing that the support levels for corn were too low. On the floor he helped persuade Foley to raise the target price and loan rate to $2 a bushel, and ultimately voted for the bill.

In 1980, he was given an important new position on the Agriculture Committee — the chairmanship of its newly reorganized Livestock, Dairy, and Poultry Subcommittee. It was his panel that had the first word in the House on President Reagan's proposed reduction in price supports for milk. The subcommittee, with Harkin's support, voted in March for a much smaller reduction than Reagan wanted. But the full Agriculture Committee reversed that decision the next day, and when the reduction reached the House floor in late March, Harkin claimed that it was too severe and would drive thousands of dairy farmers out of business. But it passed by voice vote.

On the Science Committee, Harkin has been able to pursue his Navy pilot's interest in machines and tinkering. In the 96th Congress, he was chairman of the Science Subcommittee on Transportation, and he spent much of his time looking into the possibilities for an electric car of the future, and federal support for it. He is also part of the anti-nuclear bloc on the Science Committee; he once called the proposed Clinch River nuclear breeder reactor "an extravagant total waste of money that is not going to return anything to our energy program by the year 2000."

**At Home:** Republicans saw little cause for worry when Harkin announced for Congress in 1972 against a well-entrenched GOP incumbent in a solidly conservative district. But they soon found themselves up against one of the more resourceful Democrats in recent Iowa politics.

Harkin projected his concern for agriculture all over rural west Iowa, and drew publicity with his gimmick of "work days," spending a day at a time as a truck driver, gas station attendant, or other blue-collar occupation to persuade voters of his empathy with their concerns. Republican Rep. William Scherle defeated him, but was held to the lowest percentage of his House career.

Harkin launched his 1974 bid months before the primary, built a stronger organization and raised more money than he had the first time. Scherle, activated by his unimpressive 1972 showing, maintained a heavy schedule of appearances and tried to distance himself from the unpopular Republican administration, complaining that neither Nixon nor Ford had done enough to help farmers.

Most people assumed that Scherle's active campaign would be enough to rekindle the district's Republican voting habits. But Harkin won the election on the strength of his showing in Story County (Ames), which he took by 6,195 votes. Scherle carried 16 of the other 24 counties, but they were not enough to make up his deficit in Ames.

In 1976, Republicans thought they had a strong contender in Kenneth R. Fulk, a crusty 60-year-old conservative who had spent years as secretary of the Iowa State Fair. But Harkin had used his two years of incumbency with almost flawless skill, and embarrassed the challenger by taking 64.9 percent of the vote.

When a less visible GOP candidate held Harkin under 60 percent of the vote in 1978, Republicans decided on a major effort in 1980 behind Calvin O. Hultman, majority leader of the state Senate.

But Hultman's legislative duties delayed the start of his campaign, and staff shake-ups squandered any opportunity to build early momentum. Harkin conducted his typical high-profile campaign, traveling the district in a van and continuing the "work day" trademark.

Reagan received 55 percent of the district's presidential vote, but Harkin won re-election with 60.2 percent, renewing speculation about a possible gubernatorial campaign in 1982.

**The District:** The Democratic base in the 5th District is in Story County, which contains the city of Ames, and in Warren, Dallas and Boone counties. All those counties are in the northeast end of the district and are influenced by the nearby city of Des Moines. Together they cast more than one-third of the district vote. Story County has a significant academic vote around Iowa State University.

The most reliably Republican counties are rural Pottawattamie, Page, Montgomery, Mills and Fremont. Clustered in the southwest corner of the district, they cast about a quarter of the district vote.

Pottawattamie County is the location of Council Bluffs, the district's largest city, with 60,000 people. It stands across the Missouri River

from Omaha, the regional railroad and meat packing center.

The district's sparsely-populated central counties are almost wholly dependent on agriculture — cattle, hogs and feed grains. The small towns and farms in this area usually prefer Republicans, but Harkin's popularity has steadily increased there since 1974.

There are substantial coal deposits throughout southwest Iowa, but little mining because the coal has a high sulfur content. Researchers at Iowa State University are working on a procedure to separate sulfur-laden coal from purer coal before it is burned. If they are successful, coal extraction could boost the economy.

## Committees

**Agriculture** (10th of 24 Democrats)
   Livestock, Dairy, and Poultry, chairman; Conservation, Credit, and Rural Development; Domestic Marketing, Consumer Relations, and Nutrition.

**Science and Technology** (6th of 23 Democrats)
   Energy Development and Applications; Transportation, Aviation and Materials.

## Elections

**1980 General**

| | |
|---|---|
| Tom Harkin (D ) | 127,895 (60 %) |
| Cal Hultman (R ) | 84,472 (40 %) |

**1978 General**

| | |
|---|---|
| Tom Harkin (D ) | 82,333 (59 %) |
| Julian Garrett (R ) | 57,377 (41 %) |

**Previous Winning Percentages**

**1976 (65 %)**    **1974 (51 %)**

**District Vote For President**

| | 1980 | | 1976 | | 1972 |
|---|---|---|---|---|---|
| D | 77,523 (35 %) | D | 103,484 (48 %) | D | 74,495 (37 %) |
| R | 122,135 (55 %) | R | 107,605 (50 %) | R | 125,720 (62 %) |
| I | 19,660 (9 %) | | | | |

## Campaign Finance

| | Receipts | Receipts from PACs | Expenditures |
|---|---|---|---|
| **1980** | | | |
| Harkin (D ) | $305,814 | $101,297 (33 %) | $314,334 |
| Hultman (R ) | $310,031 | $8,525 (27 %) | $309,325 |
| **1978** | | | |
| Harkin (D ) | $140,399 | $44,300 (32 %) | $144,160 |
| Garrett (R ) | $65,948 | $8,250 (13 %) | $64,680 |

## Voting Studies

| | Presidental Support | | Party Unity | | Conservative Coalition | |
|---|---|---|---|---|---|---|
| Year | S | O | S | O | S | O |
| 1980 | 69 | 28 | 74 | 17 | 19 | 72 |
| 1979 | 66 | 28 | 71 | 20 | 27 | 65 |
| 1978 | 69 | 28 | 73 | 25 | 24 | 73 |
| 1977 | 59 | 29 | 71 | 20 | 24 | 67 |
| 1976 | 24 | 69 | 71 | 16 | 26 | 64 |
| 1975 | 27 | 67 | 78 | 16 | 18 | 76 |

S = Support          O = Opposition

## Key Votes

**96th Congress**

| | |
|---|---|
| Weaken Carter oil profits tax (1979) | Y |
| Reject hospital cost control plan (1979) | Y |
| Implement Panama Canal Treaties (1979) | Y |
| Establish Department of Education (1979) | Y |
| Approve Anti-busing Amendment (1979) | N |
| Guarantee Chrysler Corp. loans (1979) | N |
| Approve military draft registration (1980) | N |
| Aid Sandinista regime in Nicaragua (1980) | Y |
| Strengthen fair housing laws (1980) | Y |

**97th Congress**

| | |
|---|---|
| Reagan budget proposal (1981) | N |

## Interest Group Ratings

| Year | ADA | ACA | AFL-CIO | CCUS |
|---|---|---|---|---|
| 1980 | 78 | 33 | 47 | 64 |
| 1979 | 74 | 15 | 79 | 33 |
| 1978 | 60 | 26 | 70 | 22 |
| 1977 | 85 | 19 | 71 | 25 |
| 1976 | 85 | 17 | 75 | 13 |
| 1975 | 95 | 25 | 77 | 18 |

# 6 Berkley Bedell (D)

**Of Spirit Lake — Elected 1974**

**Born:** March 5, 1921, Spirit Lake, Iowa.
**Education:** Iowa State U., 1940-42, no degree.
**Military Career:** Air Force, 1942-45.
**Profession:** Fishing tackle manufacturer.
**Family:** Wife, Elinor Healy; three children.
**Religion:** Methodist.
**Political Career:** Democratic nominee for U.S. House, 1972.

**In Washington:** Cynicism develops easily in members of Congress, but it has never taken root in Bedell, who after three terms still offers a sincerity so genuine it sometimes seems naive.

Bedell has changed little since the day in 1975 when he walked up to Wayne Hays of Ohio, the bullying House Administration chairman, and said, "Everybody tells me you're an S.O.B. Are you?" But nowadays he is likely to show his personal concerns in other ways, such as visiting Agriculture Department officials to discuss crop insurance programs without mentioning that he is a member of the Agriculture Committee.

Bedell is slight and mild-mannered, but he has been willing to challenge the conventional wisdom on issues that most members handle simply by following the crowd. Early in his House career he chose to fight the Public Works Committee in its zeal for new water projects, siding with President Carter against construction of dozens of dams most members favored. He fought to impose a fee on barges and other commercial users of public waterways, and when a 6 percent user charge was passed by the House in 1977, Bedell complained that it was too low and tried to raise it.

"If it came down to a vote for a flood control project for Sioux City or a vote for good government," he said in 1978, 'I'd have to vote for good government." In 1980, when most colleagues were berating Democrat Robert Edgar for trying to cut money for new water projects, Bedell lectured them on courtesy, accusing them of impugning the motives of a colleague "because he has an opinion different from yours."

But Bedell has not built a career on moralizing. He also has had an instinct for useful political issues. In the 96th Congress he became a gasohol promoter. He began publishing a special gasohol newsletter, and pushing a bill in the House Agriculture Committee to permit farmers to devote 10 percent of their corn crop to gasohol, for a price to be guaranteed by the government. The Agricul-

ture Committee approved this, as part of a bill providing $800 million in loan guarantees for gasohol, but it never reached the floor.

On the Small Business Committee, Bedell has crusaded for reforms in the SBA Disaster Loan program, arguing that too many of them go to businesses that are not small and whose proprietors are not poor. Many of those changes were written into an SBA bill as it cleared the House in 1979, and though some later died in conference, Bedell supported the final package.

While legislating on Agriculture and Small Business, Bedell has becomed enamored with foreign policy, and looked for ways to become involved in it. He was a participant in the Law of the Sea conference, and in 1978, when the House approved a bill allowing American companies to look for minerals on the ocean floor, he fought it, implying it was imperialistic.

**At Home:** Since Bedell's first election, he has enjoyed bipartisan support and three easy re-elections in a traditionally Republican area.

His quiet political style has brought him good rapport with the farmers and small-business men in a district where he grew up and started his fishing tackle business. Bedell was once a Republican, and the personal ties he built in the GOP were not broken after his switch to the Democratic Party. Bedell's Methodist Church contacts also cut across partisan lines.

Bedell made himself a millionaire by invent-

**6th District: Northwest — Sioux City.** Population: 464,617 (1% decrease since 1970). Race: White 458,556 (99%), Black 2,140 (0.5%), Others 3,921 (1%). Spanish origin: 2,664 (1%).

ing and marketing a more durable, flexible monofilament fishing line. He has said that he entered politics because "I couldn't get the satisfaction I wanted from building a bigger and bigger fishing tackle business . . . we should concern ourselves with our fellow men and put away worship of material goods."

Bedell lost to incumbent Republican Wiley Mayne by only 9,710 votes in 1972 and handily won the 1974 rematch. Mayne, a member of the Judiciary Committee, was hurt in 1974 by his defense of President Nixon during impeachment hearings.

The GOP fielded credible challengers to Bedell in 1976 and 1978, but neither drew more than a third of the total vote. Prior to the 1980 election, there was speculation that Bedell might be weakened by a controversy involving his fish-

ing tackle business. A federal grand jury was investigating allegations that Bedell's company imported products from its Taiwan subsidiary at artificially low prices to avoid customs.

Bedell denied any wrongdoing and said the allegations were made by a disgruntled former employee. His constituents gave him the benefit of the doubt and a 57,594-vote plurality over state Sen. Clarence S. Carney.

**The District:** Most of the 6th is hogs, cattle, corn, barley, oats and soybeans. There are two urban areas on opposite sides of the district. About 85,000 people live in Sioux City, a manufacturing and meatpacking center on the Missouri River in Woodbury County. Another 30,000 people live in Fort Dodge (Webster County), a retail center near large gypsum mines in the southeast corner of the district.

## Committees

**Agriculture** (11th of 24 Democrats)
Conservation, Credit, and Rural Development; Forests, Family Farms, and Energy; Wheat, Soybeans, and Feed Grains.

**Small Business** (6th of 23 Democrats)
Energy, Environment and Safety Issues Affecting Small Business, chairman; Antitrust and Restraint of Trade Activities Affecting Small Business.

## Elections

**1980 General**

| | |
|---|---|
| Berkley Bedell (D ) | 129,460 (64 %) |
| Clarence Carney (R ) | 71,866 (36 %) |

**1978 General**

| | |
|---|---|
| Berkley Bedell (D ) | 87,139 (66 %) |
| Willis Junker (R ) | 44,320 (34 %) |

**Previous Winning Percentages**

1976 (67 %)    1974 (55 %)

**District Vote For President**

| | 1980 | | 1976 | | 1972 |
|---|---|---|---|---|---|
| D | 71,226 (34 %) | D | 92,362 (45 %) | D | 76,110 (38 %) |
| R | 121,169 (58 %) | R | 109,482 (53 %) | R | 123,738 (61 %) |
| I | 14,882 (7 %) | | | | |

## Campaign Finance

| | Receipts | Receipts from PACs | Expenditures |
|---|---|---|---|
| **1980** | | | |
| Bedell (D ) | $225,749 | $48,340 (21 %) | $200,428 |
| Carney (R ) | $256,426 | $73,131 (29 %) | $250,335 |
| **1978** | | | |
| Bedell (D ) | $98,854 | $8,749 (9 %) | $93,188 |
| Junker (R ) | $14,517 | $1,000 (7 %) | $14,477 |

## Voting Studies

| | Presidental Support | | Party Unity | | Conservative Coalition | |
|---|---|---|---|---|---|---|
| Year | S | O | S | O | S | O |
| 1980 | 71 | 22 | 72 | 21† | 24 | 69 |
| 1979 | 76 | 21 | 76 | 15 | 22 | 69 |
| 1978 | 79 | 20 | 78 | 18† | 17 | 79† |
| 1977 | 65 | 23† | 70 | 23 | 30 | 60 |
| 1976 | 25 | 75 | 75 | 22 | 35 | 63 |
| 1975 | 27 | 70 | 79 | 17 | 18 | 80 |

S = Support          O = Opposition
† Not eligible for all recorded votes.

## Key Votes

**96th Congress**

| | |
|---|---|
| Weaken Carter oil profits tax (1979) | N |
| Reject hospital cost control plan (1979) | Y |
| Implement Panama Canal Treaties (1979) | Y |
| Establish Department of Education (1979) | Y |
| Approve Anti-busing Amendment (1979) | N |
| Guarantee Chrysler Corp. loans (1979) | Y |
| Approve military draft registration (1980) | N |
| Aid Sandinista regime in Nicaragua (1980) | Y |
| Strengthen fair housing laws (1980) | Y |

**97th Congress**

| | |
|---|---|
| Reagan budget proposal (1981) | Y |

## Interest Group Ratings

| Year | ADA | ACA | AFL-CIO | CCUS |
|---|---|---|---|---|
| 1980 | 72 | 13 | 44 | 62 |
| 1979 | 79 | 23 | 70 | 44 |
| 1978 | 70 | 22 | 53 | 35 |
| 1977 | 70 | 19 | 65 | 47 |
| 1976 | 75 | 21 | 61 | 25 |
| 1975 | 89 | 12 | 74 | 25 |

# Kansas

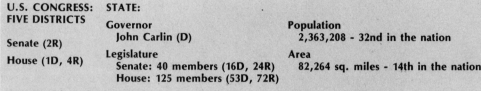

| U.S. CONGRESS: FIVE DISTRICTS | STATE: | |
|---|---|---|
| | **Governor** | **Population** |
| Senate (2R) | John Carlin (D) | 2,363,208 - 32nd in the nation |
| House (1D, 4R) | **Legislature** | **Area** |
| | Senate: 40 members (16D, 24R) | 82,264 sq. miles - 14th in the nation |
| | House: 125 members (53D, 72R) | |

1980 Presidential Vote: Carter (33%), Reagan (58%), Anderson (7%)

## ...The Rural Struggle

With nearly half its counties losing population during the 1970s and the state as a whole growing only 5.1 percent over the decade, Kansas is struggling to hold its own economically and demographically. Its farm land is still enormously productive, but family farms are disappearing in many parts of the state, yielding to agribusiness. The new farming system does not support as many residents as the old one, and many of the smaller market towns in the western part of the state are in decline.

There are however, significant growth areas. One is the urban belt along the Kansas River from Kansas City to Manhattan. Others include the Wichita area and Garden City.

Situated just north of the booming Sun Belt, Kansas is nonetheless usually thought of as a Frost Belt state. Its western portion is part of the great wheat growing area that runs from Texas up to North Dakota. In the center of the state, cattle

and hog production is the main agricultural activity. In the east, it takes in a slice of the Corn Belt.

These days, Kansas does not quite deserve the solid Republican reputation it has held for most of this century. There is no strong central party system, and energetic Democrats have a realistic chance of pushing their way into statewide office.

Democrat Robert Docking won four terms as governor beginning in 1966, and John Carlin came from far behind to take the governorship in 1978, ousting Republican Robert Bennett, whose suburban lawyer image allowed dairy farmer Carlin to score against him in the rural parts of the state. That election guaranteed Democratic control of the statehouse for 12 of the last 16 years. Democrats also captured the state House of Representatives in 1976 for the first time since 1912, but lost it in 1978.

The Democratic successes have been limited

**435**

to gubernatorial and state legislative elections. Republicans have won every Senate seat at stake since 1936. In presidential voting, the state has chosen the Republican nominee in every election but one since 1940.

# A Political Tour

**Northeast Urban Corridor.** Kansas' main growth area is the metropolitan strip in the northeastern corner of the state. The suburbs of Kansas City, Missouri, have spilled over into several eastern Kansas counties, creating a large suburban conglomeration.

Johnson and Douglas counties are the main population beneficiaries of this trend. Johnson County grew 23 percent over the past decade to reach 270,000 people, over 100,000 larger than older Wyandotte County, home of Kansas City, Kansas, a blue-collar industrial town across the river from its much larger Missouri namesake. Democrats predominate within Wyandotte, but their margins are usually overwhelmed by those of the Republican suburbs.

In 1980, Wyandotte was the only county President Carter carried in Kansas. (In 1976, when farm unrest was directed at a Republican administration, he carried 26 counties.) But Carter's margin of 9,751 votes in Wyandotte County was obliterated by Republican Ronald Reagan's 44,838-vote margin in Johnson County alone.

Further to the west, Douglas County, home of the University of Kansas at Lawrence, grew 17 percent. It, too, casts a Republican vote, diluted somewhat by Democratic votes in the university community.

Counties surrounding Topeka, the state capital, also grew at a rapid rate, although Topeka itself is losing population. At the western end of the urban strip lies Manhattan, the site of Kansas State University.

This growth corridor has been staunchly Republican in most statewide elections. However, a sizable proportion of voters are independently-minded. The 2nd District, based in this area, elected Democrats to the U.S. House four times during the 1970s.

North of the urban area lies a string of counties which are part of the Corn Belt. Like many other Kansas agricultural counties, these Republican areas are either losing population or making marginal gains.

**Wichita.** Wichita has gone through various stages as a Kansas boom town. In the early years of the century, oil was discovered and the city became a center for the state's petroleum industry. During World War II, aviation plants moved into the city and after the war the private aircraft industry continued as an important base of the city's economy. Today, Wichita is the world-leader in the production of small airplanes and jets.

The bulge in the city's population growth pattern reflects its economic ups and downs: in the 1930s it grew only 4 percent; in the next decade, it was up 46 percent, passing Kansas City for the first time as the largest city in the state; and in the 1950s it grew another 51 percent. But then the explosive growth stopped. Counties around Wichita did grow significantly in the 1970s, however, because of spillover from the Wichita suburbs.

Many Southerners, especially from Oklahoma, Texas, and Arkansas, descended upon Wichita in the 1940s and 1950s to work in the aircraft plants. Their politics were conservative Democratic and gave Wichita and surrounding Sedgwick County a more Democratic flavor than most of Kansas. While Sedgwick County usually votes Republican in presidential elections, it does so by lower margins than the average Kansas county. President Ford received 50.7 percent of the vote there in 1976 and Reagan won 51.8 percent in 1980. Wichita elected a moderate Democrat to the House in 1976, ending 42 years of Republican representation, and it has re-elected him easily twice.

**Southeast and the Balkans.** The Southeast has features not generally associated with Kansas. There are no expanses of wheat or corn fields or grazing lands, but hilly land devoted to general farming. Moreover, the area has coal, lead and zinc deposits which were mined heavily through the 1950s. As their production diminished, the area has tried to attract small industries, with some limited success.

Another feature that sets the southeast apart from the rest of this largely WASP state is its ethnic Eastern and Southern European population, descendants of immigrant miners, especially from Italy and Yugoslavia.

The area got its nickname of the Balkans for various reasons: the hilliness of the land, the ethnic makeup of the population, and a reputation for a rougher style of politics than elsewhere in the state.

The concentration of ethnic voters in the southern part of the area has given Democrats some local strength there. In 1976, Carter carried three of the southeasternmost counties of the state, including those with the small industrial cities of Pittsburg and Coffeyville.

The northern part of the area is near the

metropolitan strip and has benefited from population expansion in that section. Miami and Osage counties, bordering on the major suburban counties of Johnson and Douglas, both gained more than 10 percent in population over the past decade. Most of the remaining Balkan area made small gains, holding its own compared to the central and western part of the state, which lost population.

**The Wheat and Livestock Belt.** Stretching uniformly from Manhattan, Emporia, and Wichita to the western border with Colorado, this huge wheat growing and stock raising area represents the Kansas best known in the American mind. Altogether, it contains about two thirds of the state's land area but less than one third of its population.

As family farms have been sold to large corporate farming organizations, this area has seen a major population decline. Some small farm towns have disappeared completely as people left for larger cities or the Sun Belt. An exception has been a major growth area in the southwestern corner of the state, around Finney County (Garden City). A community that has aggressively sought new business, it landed a major asset in the 1970s — a huge beef-packing plant. Local boosters claim it is the largest plant of its kind in the world. Because of this and other efforts, Finney County grew 25 percent in population during the 1970s. Counties immediately surrounding Finney also grew, while the rest of the region declined in population.

The area's heavy dependence on the volatile agricultural economy has often meant volatile politics. While normally Republican, wheat and stock growers here have never been reluctant to dump the GOP when times are bad. Out of frustration, they support the Democratic alternative. In 1976, eighteen central and western Kansas agricultural counties voted for Carter, largely in protest against the farm policies of the Ford administration. But by 1980, they were mad at the Democratic administration and went back to the Republicans in overwhelming numbers.

## Redrawing the Lines

Remapping should not be too much of a problem in Kansas. The only districts that vary significantly from the population ideal of 472,642 are the 1st in western Kansas, which is nearly 24,000 short, and the urban belt 3rd District, which has almost 20,000 too many people.

The state's five representatives devised a plan favorable to all of them, which the state House majority leader called a "starting point." But, he said, it would not be given more weight than any other plan. A partisan redistricting plan is unlikely, since GOP control of both legislative houses is counterbalanced by the Democratic governor.

# Governor
# John Carlin (D)

**Born:** Aug. 3, 1940, Salina, Kan.
**Home:** Topeka, Kan.
**Education:** Kansas State U., B.S. 1962.
**Profession:** Dairy farmer.
**Family:** Divorced; two children.
**Religion:** Lutheran.
**Political Career:** Unsuccessful campaign for Kansas House, 1968; Kansas House, 1971-79; minority leader, 1975-77; Speaker, 1977-79; elected governor 1978; term expires Jan. 1983.

# Robert Dole (R)

**Of Russell — Elected 1968**

**Born:** July 22, 1923, Russell, Kansas.
**Education:** Washburn U., A.B. 1952, LL.B. 1952.
**Military Career:** Army, 1943-48.
**Profession:** Lawyer.
**Family:** Wife, Mary Elizabeth Hanford; one child.
**Religion:** Methodist.
**Political Career:** Kansas House, 1951-53; Russell County Attorney, 1953-61; U.S. House, 1961-69; Republican nominee for vice president, 1976.

**In Washington:** After trying for years to surmount his early reputation as a wisecracking partisan "hatchet man," Dole is finally in a position to force skeptics to take him seriously. As chairman of the Finance Committee, he is one of the most powerful members of Congress, with major influence over Reagan's program.

Dole never expected to lead the Finance Committee. Until 1979, when he became ranking minority member, he had focused most of his time and attention on the Agriculture Committee. But he has worked comfortably and amicably in the past with Sen. Russell Long, D-La., the veteran Finance chairman who is now the panel's ranking Democrat and whose help Dole still needs.

When Ronald Reagan stopped by Dole's office for a visit shortly after the 1980 election, the new chairman told him that if he had time to court senators, he ought to be courting Long. The two senators do not differ that much; both represent oil-producing states and sympathize not only with producers but with business in general.

In Dole's case, sympathy for business initially stopped short of an endorsement for the across-the-board tax cuts Reagan advocated during his campaign. Dole seemed more interested in targeted tax incentives aimed at boosting savings, investment and productivity.

But when the Finance Committee met in June of 1981 to mark up a tax bill, Dole and Reagan were on the same side. The committee voted 19-1 in favor of a three-year, 25 percent across-the-board tax cut. It did add some features of its own, including a favorite of Dole's: a provision adjusting income and capital gains taxes to future changes in the consumer price index. The Reagan administration accepted all the additions.

Dole has reason to avoid serving as a pure Reagan loyalist. He learned the hard way the dangers inherent in blind partisan loyalty. After four terms in the House, Dole began his Senate career in 1969 as the most strident GOP cheerleader for President Richard M. Nixon. In an aggressive and often abrasive fashion, he defended Nixon's Vietnam policies, his Supreme Court nominations of Clement F. Haynsworth Jr. and G. Harrold Carswell, his ABM program and virtually every other move the president made.

Dole's performance did not always sit well with his Senate colleagues, but he was rewarded in 1971 when Nixon named him Republican national chairman. He never got on well with the White House staff, however, and was pushed from the party leadership in January 1973 — a stroke of good fortune, as it turned out, since he escaped the subsequent Watergate scandal. Although he had been GOP chairman when the June 1972 burglary occurred, Dole never knew what was going on at the Nixon re-election committee. "Watergate happened on my night off," he later quipped.

Somewhat chastened by the entire experience, Dole settled down to a less visible Senate role, pressing the interests of wheat growers and cattlemen in Kansas.

On the Agriculture Committee, Dole has departed from conservative ranks to help craft and enlarge the food stamp program, popular among Kansas wheat growers as well as impoverished recipients. On that issue he regularly joined forces with South Dakota Democrat George McGovern, whom he criticized roundly in the 1972 campaign.

In 1981, when Reagan proposed drastic reductions in the food stamp program, Dole was instrumental in persuading administration officials to soften them. Then he worked with Democrat Patrick Leahy of Vermont to move the modified package through the Agriculture Committee over the objection of its chairman, Jesse Helms, R-N.C., who wanted to go even further than

Reagan. Helms tried both in committee and on the floor, and lost both times.

Dole has also been a crusader for federal aid to the handicapped. He lives with his own handicap, a virtually useless right arm and somewhat impaired left one resulting from a devastating wound sustained during combat in Italy late in World War II. The years he spent recovering left a permanent impact on his character.

Having survived real trouble, Dole seldom seems to take himself or anything else too seriously. But he has an underlying determination and fierce competitive streak. "I do try harder," he once said. "If I didn't, I'd be sitting in a rest home, in a rocker, drawing disability."

The lingering bitterness of the war came up in an unexpected and politically damaging fashion in 1976 when Dole was Gerald Ford's vice presidential running mate. In a nationally televised debate with his Democratic counterpart, Walter F. Mondale, Dole started talking of the casualties suffered in the "Democrat wars" of the 20th century — a jarring phrase and concept that drew uniformly negative reaction from the press and public. Only after days of controversy did Dole grudgingly back away from the remark and concede he really did not believe any party should be held responsible for the nation's wars. Ford had chosen Dole for the GOP ticket at the eleventh hour of the 1976 Republican National Convention. He hoped the Kansas senator could shore up weakened party support in the farm states of the Midwest, and do the bulk of the actual stumping while the president remained above the fray in the Rose Garden.

Dole did both, campaigning coast to coast in generally high spirits and good humor, but the "Democrat wars" controversy and his failure to shake off his "hatchet man" image from the Nixon era left some people feeling afterward that he was a reason for the defeat.

Dole, naturally enough, was not among them. The 1976 campaign merely whetted his appetite for national office, and in May 1979 he launched his own bid for the GOP presidential nomination.

But his campaign never got off the ground. It was plagued from the start by a lack of what he called the "Five M's" of campaigning: "money, management, manpower, momentum and media attention." While his rivals were giving speeches and shaking hands in the early primary states during the fall of 1979, Dole was in the Finance Committee room, arguing about a windfall profits tax on oil. As the senior Republican on the committee, he had a duty to be there, but his diligence left some Republicans wondering how badly he really wanted to be president.

Making weak showings in Iowa and New Hampshire, Dole withdrew from the race 10 months after he had entered it, and threw his support to Reagan.

**At Home:** Dole is today the foremost political figure in Kansas. Republicans in the state's congressional delegation defer to him out of habit. In 1980, he coasted to easy re-election.

But the road to his political security has been a bit rough. Another 982 votes in his 1960 House primary would have sent another man to Washington in his place. A swing of 2,600 would have unseated him four years later. One percentage point would have defeated him in 1974.

Dole emerged from his World War II ordeal with ambition and an ample share of discipline. Even before completing his law degree, he won a term in the Kansas House. After two years there, he became Russell County prosecutor.

Eight years later, he was a candidate for Congress, running for the Republican nomination against Keith G. Sebelius, a Republican from nearby Norton County. Dole defeated him by 982 votes, forcing Sebelius to wait eight years for a House vacancy. In the fall, Dole was an easy winner, keeping the old 6th District of western Kansas in its traditional Republican hands.

In 1962, the state's two western districts were combined, and Dole had to run against a Democratic incumbent, J. Floyd Breeding. He beat him by more than 20,000 votes.

But he had a difficult time in 1964 coping with the national Democratic landslide and with Bill Bork, a farmers' co-op official. Democrat Bork said he would be a better friend of agriculture than Dole, who he pointed out was a small-town lawyer, not a farmer. Dole won by 5,126 votes.

In 1968, Republican Frank Carlson announced his retirement from the Senate, and Dole competed with former Gov. William H. Avery for the GOP nomination to succeed him. Avery had been ousted from the statehouse two years earlier by Democrat Robert Docking, and he seemed preoccupied during much of the primary campaign with Docking rather than Dole. The result was a Dole victory by a remarkable plurality of more than 100,000 votes.

That fall, Dole also had an easy time against Democrat William I. Robinson, a Wichita attorney who criticized him for opposing federal aid to schools. Dole talked about the national social unrest of that year, and blamed much of it on the Johnson administration in Washington.

The 1974 campaign was different. Dole was weighted down with his earlier Nixon connections, which were played up, probably to an

**439**

unwise degree, by Democratic challenger William Roy, a two-term House member. Roy continued referring to Nixon and Watergate even after he had built a comfortable lead against Dole. This enabled Dole to strike back with an advertisement in which a mud-splattered poster of him was gradually wiped clean as he insisted on his honesty.

Dole came from behind in the final weeks to defeat Roy by 13,532 votes. Since then, he has had nothing to worry about. He encountered only weak opposition for a third term in 1980.

## Committees

**Agriculture, Nutrition and Forestry** (2nd of 9 Republicans)
Nutrition, chairman; Agricultural Research and General Legislation; Foreign Agricultural Policy.

**Finance** (Chairman)
Health; Oversight of the Internal Revenue Service; Social Security and Income maintenance Programs.

**Judiciary** (5th of 10 Republicans)
Courts, chairman; Criminal Law; Regulatory Reform.

**Rules and Administration** (7th of 7 Republicans)

**Joint Taxation**

## Elections

**1980 General**

| | |
|---|---|
| Robert Dole (R) | 598,686 (64%) |
| John Simpson (D) | 340,271 (36%) |

**1980 Primary**

| | |
|---|---|
| Robert Dole (R) | 201,484 (82%) |
| Jim Grainge (R) | 44,674 (18%) |

**Previous Winning Percentages**

| | | | |
|---|---|---|---|
| 1974 (51%) | 1968 (60%) | 1966* (69%) | 1964* (51%) |
| 1962* (56%) | 1960* (59%) | | |

*House elections.*

## Campaign Finance

| | Receipts | Receipts from PACs | Expenditures |
|---|---|---|---|
| **1980** | | | |
| Dole (R) | $1,275,158 | $414,471 (33%) | $1,170,268 |
| Simpson (D) | $289,848 | $62,090 (21%) | $288,204 |

## Voting Studies

| | Presidential Support | | Party Unity | | Conservative Coalition | |
|---|---|---|---|---|---|---|
| Year | S | O | S | O | S | O |
| **Senate service** | | | | | | |
| 1980 | 48 | 49 | 72 | 24 | 77 | 20 |
| 1979 | 39 | 57 | 78 | 16 | 85 | 14 |
| 1978 | 32 | 65 | 77 | 19 | 83 | 14 |
| 1977 | 53 | 44 | 85 | 12 | 89 | 8 |
| 1976 | 66 | 17 | 71 | 12 | 77 | 7 |
| 1975 | 75 | 16 | 86 | 8 | 90 | 5 |
| 1974 (Ford) | 34 | 37 | | | | |
| 1974 | 63 | 33 | 71 | 21 | 76 | 17 |
| 1973 | 71 | 27 | 83 | 14 | 89 | 10 |

| | | | | | |
|---|---|---|---|---|---|
| 1972 | 87 | 4 | 87 | 3 | 88 | 1 |
| 1971 | 80 | 13 | 80 | 9 | 87 | 4 |
| 1970 | 81 | 15 | 88 | 8 | 86 | 7 |
| 1969 | 75 | 21 | 80 | 12 | 87 | 7 |
| **House service** | | | | | | |
| 1968 | 42 | 46 | 79 | 6 | 88 | 0 |
| 1967 | 40 | 53 | 84 | 7 | 91 | 4 |
| 1966 | 37 | 63 | 90 | 10 | 100 | 0 |
| 1965 | 34 | 63 | 91 | 7 | 98 | 2 |
| 1964 | 27 | 73 | 94 | 6 | 100 | 0 |
| 1963 | 23 | 76 | 100 | 0 | 93 | 7 |
| 1962 | 33 | 65 | 93 | 5 | 94 | 0 |
| 1961 | 15 | 83 | 88 | 12 | 100 | 0 |

S = Support          O = Opposition

## Key Votes

**96th Congress**

| | |
|---|---|
| Maintain relations with Taiwan (1979) | Y |
| Reduce synthetic fuel development funds (1979) | Y |
| Impose nuclear plant moratorium (1979) | N |
| Kill stronger windfall profits tax (1979) | Y |
| Guarantee Chrysler Corp. loans (1979) | Y |
| Approve military draft registration (1980) | N |
| End Revenue Sharing to the states (1980) | Y |
| Block Justice Dept. busing suits (1980) | Y |

**97th Congress**

| | |
|---|---|
| Restore urban program funding cuts (1981) | N |

## Interest Group Ratings

| Year | ADA | ACA | AFL-CIO | CCUS-1 | CCUS-2 |
|---|---|---|---|---|---|
| **Senate service** | | | | | |
| 1980 | 22 | 77 | 28 | 90 | |
| 1979 | 21 | 64 | 21 | 73 | 75 |
| 1978 | 20 | 58 | 22 | 83 | |
| 1977 | 5 | 70 | 11 | 88 | |
| 1976 | 10 | 87 | 16 | 75 | |
| 1975 | 17 | 67 | 24 | 75 | |
| 1974 | 19 | 84 | 18 | 80 | |
| 1973 | 10 | 82 | 27 | 78 | |
| 1972 | 0 | 84 | 10 | 100 | |
| 1971 | 4 | 71 | 17 | - | |
| 1970 | 13 | 76 | 17 | 89 | |
| 1969 | 0 | 64 | 18 | - | |
| **House service** | | | | | |
| 1968 | 0 | 90 | 25 | - | |
| 1967 | 7 | 96 | 9 | 100 | |
| 1966 | 0 | 93 | 0 | - | |
| 1965 | 0 | 89 | - | 100 | |
| 1964 | 4 | 95 | 9 | - | |
| 1963 | - | 100 | - | - | |
| 1962 | 0 | 91 | 0 | - | |
| 1961 | 0 | - | - | - | |

# Nancy Landon Kassebaum (R)

Of Wichita — Elected 1978

**Born:** July 29, 1932, Topeka, Kan.
**Education:** U. of Kan., B.A. 1954; U. of Mich., M.A. 1956.
**Profession:** Broadcasting executive.
**Family:** Divorced, four children.
**Religion:** Episcopalian.
**Political Career:** Maize School Board, 1972-76.

**In Washington:** A Kansas City newspaper once described Kassebaum as looking like an "injured wren," and she still keeps an imitation of one in her home, a stained glass bird with a bandaged wing, symbolic of the fragile creature she still looks like and has worked hard in the Senate not to be.

Only three years into her late-started political career, Kassebaum still strikes colleagues as a shy woman, but she has established herself as a senator willing to handle delicate legislative chores with the public watching. She managed major railroad legislation for the Republicans in 1980, and was active in a complex and controversial airport development argument.

One bill provided federal aid for the Rock Island Railroad, vital to Kansas grain growers. She had to deal with insistence by the House that a federal subsidy for the railroad be tied to approval of separate legislation authorizing $750 million for improvements in the corridor between New York and Washington D.C. Kassebaum and the other Senate conferees were adamant against that, but she negotiated a compromise that speeded the Northeast corridor money through the Senate as a separate bill. Then the conferees met again, put the two issues back together, and voted out $90 million for the Rock Island for fiscal 1980.

The major railroad bill of the year, however, was legislation freeing the industry from many of the regulatory restrictions it has operated under in recent years. Most of this bill was written by Democrats, but Kassebaum had significant impact on it as Republican spokesman. Robert Packwood of Oregon, the senior Republican on Commerce and now its chairman, essentially left her in charge of GOP planning on railroad issues.

In the 97th Congress, as a member of the majority, Kassebaum has broader responsibilities. The Commerce Aviation Subcommittee, which she chairs, is responsble for politically sensitive airport development legislation, which past Congresses have argued endlessly over but left unsettled.

Kassebaum was far less noticeable in her first term on the Budget Committee than she was on Commerce. But she did argue consistently for revenue sharing to states, threatened by proposed Carter budget cuts in 1980. In May, the Senate approved an amendment by Kassebaum and Bill Bradley, D-N.J., to keep the revenue sharing program alive, reversing the decision of the Budget Committee. But the final conference decision at the end of the year was to cancel the grants to states, at least for the 1981 budget.

On other Budget Committee issues, Kassebaum generally voted with the panel's fiscally conservative Republican bloc throughout the 96th Congress. She supported cutbacks in the food stamp program and opposed the Chrysler loan guarantee, but also took a skeptical attitude toward some defense requests. In the early months of the 97th Congress, she generally went along with proposed Reagan spending cuts, opposing an effort by liberal Republicans to restore $1 million for urban programs.

None of Kassebaum's legislative work brought her as much attention as she attracted when she was chosen temporary chairman of the 1980 Republican National Convention. It was an honorary position, with no real decisions to make, but her selection marked the first time that a woman filled it.

Kassebaum probably could have milked the job for even more publicity if she had wanted, but she had an instinctive worry about being pushed too far too fast. When her name was presented to reporters as one of those on a list of potential candidates for vice president, she said she was not qualified for the position and asked to be removed.

**At Home:** Kassebaum can trace much of her success to her middle name — the one that links her to her father, Alfred M. Landon, the nonage-

**441**

narian ex-governor of Kansas and Republican presidential nominee in 1936.

Before 1978, Kassebaum's political activity had been confined to service on the school board in a town of 785 people, and one year as an aide to Republican Sen. James B. Pearson. Most of her adult life had been spent raising four children, and managing a radio station in Wichita.

But when Pearson announced his intention to retire in 1978, she joined a large field of aspirants to succeed him. There were nine names on the Republican primary ballot that August, and most of the other contestants, including some veteran Kansas politicians, found it difficult to attract much attention in the crowd. Kassebaum had instant name recognition, and she built upon it with a series of television ads featuring her father, then 91 years old. The result was a clear primary victory.

That fall, she faced a well-known Democratic opponent, former U.S. Rep. Bill Roy, who had come close to defeating Republican Sen. Robert Dole for re-election in 1974.

Roy, however, turned out to be a weaker nominee than many had predicted. The Watergate resentment that had helped him against Dole had disappeared, and the farm discontent aimed at a Republican administration in 1974 now focused on President Carter. Kassebaum, meanwhile, offered no record for Roy to aim at, and her gentle campaign style made attacks on her inexperience seem like bad manners. She defeated Roy much more comfortably than Dole had.

So far, Kassebaum has avoided major criticism in Kansas. Despite her views favoring legalized abortion and the Equal Rights Amendment, conservative activists have left her alone. On some issues, she has cultivated a non-partisan style that keeps Democrats off balance. In 1980, for example, she endorsed Democratic Gov. John Carlin's call for a state severance tax on state-produced oil and gas.

## Committees

**Budget** (3rd of 12 Republicans)

**Commerce, Science and Transportation** (5th of 9 Republicans)
Aviation, chairman; Science, Technology, and Space; Surface Transportation.

**Foreign Relations** (7th of 9 Republicans)
African Affairs, chairman; International Economic Policy; Western Hemisphere Affairs.

**Special Aging** (4th of 8 Republicans)

## Elections

**1978 General**

| | |
|---|---|
| Nancy Kassebaum (R ) | 403,354 (54 %) |
| William Roy (D ) | 317,602 (42 %) |

**1978 Primary**

| | |
|---|---|
| Nancy Kassebaum (R ) | 67,324 (31 %) |
| Wayne Angell (R ) | 54,161 (25 %) |
| Sam Hardage (R ) | 30,248 (14 %) |
| Jan Meyers (R ) | 20,933 (10 %) |

## Campaign Finance

| | Receipts | Receipts from PACs | Expenditures |
|---|---|---|---|
| **1978** | | | |
| Kassebaum (R ) | $864,288 | $121,721 (14 %) | $856,644 |
| Roy (D ) | $824,537 | $194,643 (24 %) | $813,754 |

## Voting Studies

| | Presidential Support | | Party Unity | | Conservative Coalition | |
|---|---|---|---|---|---|---|
| Year | S | O | S | O | S | O |
| 1980 | 52 | 41 | 63 | 26 | 59 | 28 |
| 1979 | 51 | 45 | 69 | 24 | 75 | 20 |

S = Support          O = Opposition

## Key Votes

**96th Congress**

| | |
|---|---|
| Maintain relations with Taiwan (1979) | N |
| Reduce synthetic fuel development funds (1979) | Y |
| Impose nuclear plant moratorium (1979) | N |
| Kill stronger windfall profits tax (1979) | Y |
| Guarantee Chrysler Corp. loans (1979) | N |
| Approve military draft registration (1980) | N |
| End Revenue Sharing to the states (1980) | N |
| Block Justice Dept. busing suits (1980) | Y |

**97th Congress**

| | |
|---|---|
| Restore urban program funding cuts (1981) | N |

## Interest Group Ratings

| Year | ADA | ACA | AFL-CIO | CCUS-1 | CCUS-2 |
|---|---|---|---|---|---|
| 1980 | 44 | 70 | 25 | 74 | |
| 1979 | 37 | 63 | 22 | 80 | 79 |

# 1 Pat Roberts (R)

**Of Dodge City — Elected 1980**

**Born:** April 20, 1936, Topeka, Kan.
**Education:** Kansas State University, B.A. 1958.
**Military Career:** Marine Corps, 1958-62.
**Profession:** Congressional aide.
**Family:** Wife, Franki Fann; three children.
**Religion:** Methodist.
**Political Career:** No previous office.

**The Member:** Roberts understudied the role of congressman for 12 years as the top aide to Republican Rep. Keith G. Sebelius, and when the boss announced his retirement, Roberts easily won the contest to succeed him.

During the campaign, Roberts capitalized on the popularity of Sebelius, who had endorsed him. To voters, Roberts sounded like an incumbent, with his continual references to "our record."

Roberts represents grain and livestock interests on the Agriculture Committee and adopts the customary dual view that farm-state Republicans have toward Washington — backing more agricultural aid but skeptical about most other forms of government spending.

Roberts favors government price "floors" for farm products because, he says, rising operating costs will otherwise wipe out many growers financially. He opposed the Soviet grain embargo and wants to see a more aggressive federal effort to promote agricultural exports.

After an untimely May freeze that damaged his district's wheat crop, Roberts worked to get the Department of Agriculture's disaster evaluation and payment process speeded up. He co-sponsored legislation to increase the estate tax exemption to $750,000 in order to make it easier for families to pass farms and small businesses from one generation to the next.

**The District:** The wheat-growing 1st is reliably Republican, and it has been safe over two decades for Sebelius and predecessor Robert Dole, who went on to the Senate in 1968. Sebelius had only one close call, in his initial campaign in 1968, when Democrats nominated a popular official of the state Wheat Growers.

The 1st gets bigger geographically with every census. People leave its fading grain elevator towns, and more territory has to be added to meet population standards. During the 1970s, the district covered 57 counties, and reached nearly two-thirds of the way across the state. It is certain to grow again in 1982.

## Committees

**Agriculture** (11th of 19 Republicans)
Conservation, Credit, and Rural Development; Department Operations, Research and Foreign Agriculture; Wheat, Soybeans and Feed Grains.

**Select Aging** (20th of 23 Republicans)
Health and Long-Term Care.

## Elections

**1980 General**

| | |
|---|---|
| Pat Roberts (R ) | 121,545 (62 %) |
| Phil Martin (D) | 73,586 (38 %) |

**1980 Primary**

| | |
|---|---|
| Pat Robert (R) | 37,387 (56 %) |
| Steve Pratt (R ) | 24,231 (36 %) |

**District Vote For President**

| | 1980 | | 1976 | | 1972 |
|---|---|---|---|---|---|
| **D** | 53,488 (26 %) | **D** | 91,355 (45 %) | **D** | 52,842 (27 %) |
| **R** | 134,043 (66 %) | **R** | 106,533 (53 %) | **R** | 135,605 (70 %) |
| **I** | 11,919 (6 %) | | | | |

## Campaign Finance

| | Receipts | Receipts from PACs | Expenditures |
|---|---|---|---|
| **1980** | | | |
| Roberts (R ) | $253,594 | $70,350 (28 %) | $229,593 |
| Martin (D ) | R63,387 | $615 (1 %) | $63,232 |

## Key Vote

**97th Congress**

| | |
|---|---|
| Reagan budget proposal (1981) | Y |

---

**1st District: West — Salina.** Population: 448,824 (0.2% increase since 1970). Race: White 433,373 (97%), Black 4,221 (1%), Others 11,230 (3%). Spanish origin: 14,323 (3%).

# 2 Jim Jeffries (R)

### Of Atchison — Elected 1978

**Born:** June 1, 1925, Detroit, Mich.
**Education:** Attended Mich. State U., 1946-48.
**Military Career:** Army Air Corps, 1943-45.
**Profession:** Investment consultant.
**Family:** Wife, Barbara Ann Cray; three children.
**Religion:** Presbyterian.
**Political Career:** No previous office.

**In Washington:** Jeffries is a bluff and earthy man who has strong personal opinions but has not been highly visible as a legislator.

He expressed his views in an unusual letter during his first term in office, attracting criticism and some surprise from his colleagues. Jeffries wrote to 19,000 constituents of Democratic Sen. Robert Morgan of North Carolina, urging that Morgan be defeated for not taking a strong enough stand on abortion.

Morgan was not the only target of the letter, sent on behalf of the American Life Lobby, but he made an issue of it, accusing Jeffries of "casting aspersions on the morality" of colleagues and calling for a probe by the House ethics committee.

The ethics panel found no violation of any House rule, and Jeffries said he was happy to have been able to help out the right-to-life movement. Morgan was beaten for re-election in 1980.

Given his modest committee assignments — Government Operations and District of Columbia — Jeffries was not in a position to draft much major legislation if he had tried. He opposed creation of a new Department of Education in 1979 when it cleared Government Operations by one vote. At the beginning of 1981, he switched from that committee to Public Works.

Jeffries' speeches have stressed consistently conservative themes. He spoke out against mainland Chinese participation in the 1980 Olympics, and against busing. At one point, Jeffries suggested the busing of teachers as a solution to educational problems. "If the problem is that some of the schools lack a good teacher," he said, "it would seem a lot simpler to me to move a few teachers around than it would be to move all the students around."

But Jeffries has shown a few signs of modifying his ideological approach at appropriate political times. A critic of the food stamp program, he voted to give it extra money in 1980 when it was on the verge of running out. "Many of my constituents have become excessively alarmed over the future of the food stamp program," he said. "Such a pressure-packed atmosphere is not conducive to a mature objective judgment on the merits of the legislation.

**At Home:** Opponents have belittled Jeffries' stature and credentials for public office, but they have not beaten him in several tries.

An investment counselor who moved to Kansas from Michigan, Jeffries entered active politics in 1976 as a Reagan delegate to the Republican National Convention. In 1977-78, he served as 2nd District Panama Canal Committee chairman, opposing the Panama Canal treaties.

He surprised Republicans as well as Democrats by making it to Congress in 1978. In the primary, he upset state Sen. Ron Hein, who at 28 was considered a promising new face on the Kansas Republican scene. In November, Jeffries defeated Democratic Rep. Martha Keys, reaping the political fallout from her divorce and remarriage to a House colleague, Andrew Jacobs Jr., D-Ind.

Jeffries raised $333,000 in 1978, much of it from national conservative groups, and had an effective media campaign. One of his television ads talked of high food prices and closed with a jingle, "Martha doesn't shop here any more."

By 1980, there was no shortage of challengers to Jeffries. In the Republican primary, Topeka Mayor Bill McCormick and farmer Larry Abeldt both accused him of being out of the GOP main-

---

**2nd District: Topeka, Kansas City suburbs.** Population: 448,824 (0.2% increase since 1970). Race: White 433,373 (89%), Black 36,095 (8%), Others 16,669 (4%). Spanish origin: 14,323 (3%).

stream. Together they held him under a majority of the vote, but the divided opposition allowed Jeffries to win renomination easily.

In the fall, the controversial Jeffries had to deal with Samuel Keys, his predecessor's former husband. Keys, a Kansas State professor, waged an aggressive campaign, and he was even tougher on Jeffries than Abeldt and McCormick. His commercials bluntly referred to Jeffries as an "embarrassment" to the district.

No Democrat was going to carry the 2nd District in 1980 with Ronald Reagan and Sen. Robert Dole at the top of the Republican ticket. Jeffries won a second term by over 13,000 votes.

**The District:** Located in the northeastern quadrant of Kansas, the 2nd covers the oldest settled section of the state. Topeka, the state capital, is the major city in the district. Also included are Manhattan, site of Kansas State University, and Leavenworth, home of the federal prison. At the eastern edge, the district takes in some of the Kansas City suburbs.

Like most of Kansas, the district is dependent on agriculture. The counties between the Kansas River, which flows through the southern portion of the district, and the Nebraska state line on the north, contain rich agricultural lands.

While the district is historically Republican, it has broken that tradition on occasion. In 1952, in the face of a Republican sweep, it ousted its veteran GOP incumbent in favor of a 73-year-old Democratic farmer, who campaigned against the building of a dam he said would flood a large amount of farmland. And in 1970, Democrat William Roy, a doctor and lawyer, outcampaigned complacent Republican Rep. Chester Mize to win it. When Roy ran for the Senate in 1974, Keys won the seat.

## Committees

**Public Works and Transportation** (14th of 19 Republicans)
Public Buildings and Grounds; Water Resources.

**Veterans' Affairs** (7th of 14 Republicans)
Education, Training and Employment; Oversight and Investigations.

## Elections

**1980 General**

| | |
|---|---|
| Jim Jeffries (R ) | 92,107 (54 %) |
| Sam Keys (D ) | 78,859 (46 %) |

**1980 Primary**

| | |
|---|---|
| Jim Jeffries (R ) | 26,269 (49 %) |
| Bill McCormick (R ) | 16,901 (32 %) |
| Larry Abeldt (R ) | 10,318 (19 %) |

**1978 General**

| | |
|---|---|
| Jim Jeffries (R ) | 76,419 (52 %) |
| Martha Keys (D ) | 70,460 (48 %) |

**1978 Primary**

| | |
|---|---|
| Jim Jeffries (R ) | 26,826 (58 %) |
| Ron Hein (R ) | 19,063 (42 %) |

**District Vote For President**

| | 1980 | | 1976 | | 1972 |
|---|---|---|---|---|---|
| D | 62,464 (35 %) | D | 78,881 (44 %) | D | 51,093 (29 %) |
| R | 102,325 (57 %) | R | 97,156 (54 %) | R | 119,234 (68 %) |
| I | 13,040 (7 %) | | | | |

## Campaign Finance

| | Receipts | Receipts from PACs | Expenditures |
|---|---|---|---|
| **1980** | | | |
| Jeffries (R ) | $254,171 | $63,479 (25 %) | $249,144 |
| Keys (D ) | $119,159 | $30,960 (26 %) | $117,796 |

| 1978 | | | |
|---|---|---|---|
| Jeffries (R ) | $333,902 | $88,187 (26 %) | $332,482 |
| Keys (D ) | $146,822 | $49,401 (34 %) | $145,473 |

## Voting Studies

| | Presidential Support | | Party Unity | | Conservative Coalition | |
|---|---|---|---|---|---|---|
| Year | S | O | S | O | S | O |
| 1980 | 31 | 67 | 94 | 4 | 96 | 3 |
| 1979 | 20 | 78 | 96 | 2 | 96 | 2 |

S = Support          O = Opposition

## Key Votes

**96th Congress**

| | |
|---|---|
| Weaken Carter oil profits tax (1979) | Y |
| Reject hospital cost control plan (1979) | Y |
| Implement Panama Canal Treaties (1979) | N |
| Establish Department of Education (1979) | N |
| Approve Anti-busing Amendment (1979) | Y |
| Guarantee Chrysler Corp. loans (1979) | N |
| Approve military draft registration (1980) | Y |
| Aid Sandinista regime in Nicaragua (1980) | N |
| Strengthen fair housing laws (1980) | N |

**97th Congress**

| | |
|---|---|
| Reagan budget proposal (1981) | Y |

## Interest Group Ratings

| Year | ADA | ACA | AFL-CIO | CCUS |
|---|---|---|---|---|
| 1980 | 6 | 96 | 11 | 65 |
| 1979 | 0 | 100 | 11 | 100 |

# 3 Larry Winn Jr. (R)

**Of Overland Park — Elected 1966**

**Born:** Aug. 22, 1919, Kansas City, Mo.
**Education:** U. of Kan., B.A. 1941.
**Profession:** Home builder, developer.
**Family:** Wife, Joan Elliott; five children.
**Religion:** Christian Church.
**Political Career:** No previous office.

**In Washington:** A quiet, unassuming man, Winn has assiduously avoided dramatic legislative argument during his eight terms in Congress. His voice is rarely heard outside the relatively non-controversial areas of the space program and military aid to friendly nations.

Winn has served on the House Science and Technology Committee since entering Congress and now is senior Republican on the panel. He has remained an active supporter of space programs even past the peak of enthusiasm in the 1960s, and used his position to advocate research into alternative energy sources such as gasohol and solar and wind power. Winn has also introduced a variety of measures to provide tax credits for energy efficiency and conservation.

On Foreign Affairs, Winn has steered a moderate course. Unlike most Republicans, he has voted for some politically unpopular foreign aid bills in recent years but has generally joined conservative colleagues in voting to cut or restrict the use of foreign aid money.

One of his major campaigns has been for looser restraints on arms sales abroad by weapons manufacturers. In 1980, he convinced the Foreign Affairs Committee to raise to $50 million from $25 million the amount of weapons an arms maker could sell abroad without having to go through the U.S. government. The $25 million limit, he said, was "unduly costly and burdensome to major arms exporters." In doing that, Winn was protecting the interests of his home state: Boeing, Cessna and Beechcraft aircraft companies all have plants in Kansas, and all make planes that are used for military purposes.

Winn has pleased numerous other constituents with his persistent effort to establish a Tallgrass Prairie National Reserve in Kansas and Oklahoma. But bills to create the 347,000-acre park, complete with a parkway, failed in both the 95th and 96th Congresses.

Winn received some negative publicity in April 1981, when he pleaded guilty in a Lawrence, Kan., court to a charge of driving while intoxicated and under the influence of prescription drugs. He paid a $175 fine and court costs, and was placed on probation for 30 days.

**At Home:** Winn has been the target of two strong Democratic attempts to oust him, but has managed to survive all challenges in good political shape.

He came to politics from a nationally prominent career in the home building industry, including 14 years as national director of the National Association of Home Builders. Locally, he was vice president of a Kansas City building company. The 3rd District opened up in 1966 when Republican Rep. Robert Ellsworth ran for the GOP Senate nomination. Winn entered the multi-candidate primary and defeated his nearest rival, Wayne Angell, an economist and state representative, by 1,189 votes. In November, he went on to win the seat over a strong Democratic candidate, Overland Park Mayor Marvin Rainey.

The next time the Democrats threw a major candidate at Winn was in 1970, when Kansas Lt. Gov. James DeCoursey challenged him. Winn was thought to be in trouble, but survived with 53 percent of the vote. For a decade, he was re-elected routinely. In 1980, they tried hard again with Dan Watkins, a top aide to Gov. John Carlin. But it was a Republican year in Kansas, and Winn won with 56 percent.

**The District:** The 3rd includes most of

---

**3rd District: East — Kansas City.**
Population: 492,551 (9% increase since 1970). Race: White 434,497 (88%), Black 43,570 (9%), Others 14,484 (3%). Spanish origin: 13,162 (3%).

Kansas City and three suburban counties to the southwest. Kansas City itself is essentially a suburb — a blue collar bedroom community for the much larger Kansas City, Mo. Besides its residential neighborhoods, Kansas City has an industrial base of its own in petroleum refining, auto assem-

bly and fiberglass insulation.

The suburban counties of Johnson, Douglas and Franklin have grown rapidly over the past two decades and usually cast a heavy Republican vote. However, there is a large independent vote to which Democrats often appeal.

## Committees

**Foreign Affairs** (4th of 16 Republicans)
International Operations; International Security and Scientific Affairs.

**Science and Technology** (Ranking Republican)

## Elections

**1980 General**

| | |
|---|---|
| Larry Winn Jr. (R ) | 109,294 (56 %) |
| Dan Watkins (D ) | 82,414 (42 %) |

**1978 General**

| | |
|---|---|
| Larry Winn Jr. (R ) | Unopposed |

**Previous Winning Percentages**

| | | | |
|---|---|---|---|
| 1976 (69 %) | 1974 (63 %) | 1972 (71 %) | 1970 (53 %) |
| 1968 (63 %) | 1966 (53 %) | | |

**District Vote For President**

| | 1980 | | 1976 | | 1972 |
|---|---|---|---|---|---|
| D | 70,039 (34 %) | D | 79,674 (41 %) | D | 60,787 (33 %) |
| R | 112,391 (55 %) | R | 110,289 (56 %) | R | 121,330 (65 %) |
| I | 18,272 (9 %) | | | | |

## Campaign Finance

| | Receipts | Receipts from PACs | Expenditures |
|---|---|---|---|
| **1980** | | | |
| Winn (R ) | $173,860 | $69,921 (40 %) | $199,677 |
| Watkins (D ) | $127,907 | $10,750 (8 %) | $123,494 |
| **1978** | | | |
| Winn (R ) | $13,195 | $7,500 (57 %) | $17,691 |

## Voting Studies

| | Presidential Support | | Party Unity | | Conservative Coalition | |
|---|---|---|---|---|---|---|
| Year | S | O | S | O | S | O |
| 1980 | 44 | 47† | 75 | 18 | 78 | 15 |
| 1979 | 29 | 48 | 55 | 16 | 60 | 10 |

| Year | | | | | | |
|---|---|---|---|---|---|---|
| 1978 | 34 | 56 | 71 | 18 | 79 | 14 |
| 1977 | 44 | 46 | 83 | 12 | 90 | 8 |
| 1976 | 63 | 31 | 75 | 18 | 78 | 14 |
| 1975 | 65 | 30 | 76 | 18† | 84 | 11† |
| 1974 (Ford) | 67 | 20 | | | | |
| 1974 | 85 | 15 | 79 | 17† | 78 | 19 |
| 1973 | 66 | 26 | 65 | 24 | 70 | 17 |
| 1972 | 76 | 16 | 74 | 13 | 85 | 4 |
| 1971 | 79 | 11 | 79 | 15 | 87 | 7 |
| 1970 | 65 | 20 | 64 | 17 | 82 | 0 |
| 1969 | 57 | 32 | 76 | 7 | 89 | 2 |
| 1968 | 49 | 46 | 85 | 10 | 88 | 6 |
| 1967 | 39 | 55 | 89 | 4 | 98 | 0 |

S = Support          O = Opposition

## Key Votes

**96th Congress**

| | |
|---|---|
| Weaken Carter oil profits tax (1979) | Y |
| Reject hospital cost control plan (1979) | ? |
| Implement Panama Canal Treaties (1979) | N |
| Establish Department of Education (1979) | N |
| Approve Anti-busing Amendment (1979) | Y |
| Guarantee Chrysler Corp. loans (1979) | Y |
| Approve military draft registration (1980) | Y |
| Aid Sandinista regime in Nicaragua (1980) | Y |
| Strengthen fair housing laws (1980) | N |

**97th Congress**

| | |
|---|---|
| Reagan budget proposal (1981) | Y |

## Interest Group Ratings

| Year | ADA | ACA | AFL-CIO | CCUS |
|---|---|---|---|---|
| 1980 | 11 | 79 | 14 | 83 |
| 1979 | 6 | 86 | 11 | 100 |
| 1978 | 10 | 88 | 17 | 82 |
| 1977 | 10 | 85 | 23 | 88 |
| 1976 | 10 | 75 | 23 | 76 |
| 1975 | 16 | 77 | 29 | 82 |
| 1974 | 22 | 53 | 0 | 80 |
| 1973 | 20 | 68 | 27 | 80 |
| 1972 | 0 | 76 | 10 | 89 |
| 1971 | 11 | 81 | 27 | - |
| 1970 | 4 | 72 | 14 | 89 |
| 1969 | 0 | 64 | 20 | - |
| 1968 | 0 | 83 | 25 | - |
| 1967 | 7 | 96 | 0 | 100 |

**447**

# 4 Dan Glickman (D)

**Of Wichita — Elected 1976**

**Born:** Nov. 24, 1944, Wichita, Kan.
**Education:** U. of Mich., B.A. 1966; George
   Washington U., J.D. 1969.
**Profession:** Lawyer.
**Family:** Wife, Rhoda Yura; two children.
**Religion:** Jewish.
**Political Career:** Wichita Board of Education,
   1973-76, president, 1975-76.

**In Washington:** This bright, enterprising
young legislator is a symbol of his generation in
the House; courageous when it comes to taking on
senior colleagues, but careful not to stray too far
from the political sensibilities of his district. He
makes it clear that his constituency is in Kansas,
not in Congress.

Glickman has been a visible presence in the
House since his first days there. He is known for
offering amendments to numerous bills, both
those originating within his Agriculture Committee and those coming from other committees.
Often they are politically appealing ideas other
members find it difficult to vote against, but
would prefer not to have to vote on at all. Sometimes they strike at longstanding privileges.

It was Glickman who offered an amendment
denying members a hand-bound set of the *Congressional Record* for personal use, in an effort to
save taxpayers' money. It was Glickman who
pushed a proposal to take elevator operators —
patronage employees — off most of the automatic
elevators in the Capitol, and Glickman again who
stripped an appropriation bill of an extra
$100,000 budgeted for a study of congressional
trips to parliamentary conferences in other countries. Some of these efforts have been followed up
by press releases, a practice that has not endeared
Glickman to all his brethren.

Although Glickman has sought to accommodate House Democratic leaders on some important issues, he has not voted as a traditional
Northern liberal. "I don't totally reflect my district," he said in his first term, "otherwise they
might as well send a computer to Washington.
But at some point you've got to move off your own
reflection and move to what your district thinks
unless you believe it is morally wrong."

During his first term, Glickman drew some
conservative criticism for supporting common-site
picketing and opposing development of the B-1
bomber, although he was able to point out that
one of the alternatives to the B-1 was a plane that
would be modified and repaired in Wichita. Since
he came to Congress however, Glickman has supported the "conservative coalition" — composed
of Republicans and Southern Democrats — more
often than he has opposed it.

On some politically sensitive votes, however,
he makes it clear to the leadership that he is
available "if needed." When Democratic leaders
worked in 1980 to stop an amendment adding $5
billion in defense money to the federal budget,
Glickman waited until the end of the roll-call, got
an "all clear" signal from Budget Chairman Robert N. Giaimo, and then cast a yea vote.

On the Agriculture Committee Glickman has
been a student of legislative detail. He is a close
ally of Thomas S. Foley, who was chairman until
1981, and one of the most pragmatic of the junior
Democrats on the committee. When some members argued in 1980 for a massive boost in crop
price supports, Glickman told them that "farmers
are tired of being demagogued and misled by the
administration and by us, reporting out bills that
have no chance of passing." He worked with Foley
to raise the ceiling on food stamp expenses by up
to 10 percent for 1980 and 1981, freeing the
program from cutbacks in benefits.

Glickman won important points in his district in late 1980 after national attention focused
on the explosion of a Titan II missile at a base in
Arkansas. Just a year before, Glickman had persuaded the House to accept his amendment call-

---

**4th District: Central — Wichita.** Population: 466,412 (4% increase since 1970).
Race: White 414,694 (89%), Black 33,844
(7%), Others 17,874 (4%). Spanish origin:
14,575 (3%).

ing for a study of defects in the aging missile system. With his customary flair for publicity, he told his story many times the week of the incident on TV and in the Wichita press.

**At Home:** The first Democrat elected from the Wichita district since 1940, Glickman upset GOP veteran Garner Shriver in 1976. Shriver had won easily until 1974, when his margin suddenly dropped, attracting Democratic attention.

That same year, Glickman became actively involved in state politics by serving as a regional coordinator for William Roy's Democratic Senate campaign. A member of a wealthy and prominent Wichita family, Glickman was already well-known himself as a member of the city school board, on which he had served since he was 28. He kept his name visible in the Wichita media by pushing for open board meetings and a school ombudsman. He was a top-quality challenger to the complacent

Shriver, and beat him by 3,235 votes.

Glickman was an easy re-election winner in 1978 and in 1980, when he turned down a chance to run for the Senate against Republican Bob Dole.

**The District:** Wichita, the largest city in Kansas, is an aircraft manufacturing center. Boeing is a dominant presence, but the city is also the small aircraft capital of the country. Both Cessna and Beech Aircraft companies are head-quartered there. Farm equipment and camping trailers are also important, and Wichita is an office center for Kansas' oil interests.

The Wichita area has a strong Democratic vote, but it is a conservative one. Many of the residents came from Southern states to work in the aircraft plants during World War II. Ford carried the district in 1976, but very narrowly; Reagan took it by 30,000 votes in 1980.

## Committees

**Agriculture** (16th of 24 Democrats)
Conservation, Credit, and Rural Development; Domestic Marketing, Consumer Relations and Nutrition; Wheat, Soybeans and Feed Grains.

**Judiciary** (14th of 16 Democrats)
Administrative Law and Governmental Relations.

**Science and Technology** (11th of 23 Democrats)
Transportation, Aviation and Materials, chairman.

## Elections

**1980 General**

| | |
|---|---|
| Dan Glickman (D ) | 124,014 (69 %) |
| Clay Hunter (R ) | 55,899 (31 %) |

**1978 General**

| | |
|---|---|
| Dan Glickman (D ) | 100,139 (69 %) |
| James Litsey (R ) | 43,854 (31 %) |

**Previous Winning Percentage**

**1976** (50 %)

**District Vote For President**

| | 1980 | | 1976 | | 1972 |
|---|---|---|---|---|---|
| **D** | 68,222 (37 %) | **D** | 85,681 (48 %) | **D** | 52,129 (31 %) |
| **R** | 98,143 (53 %) | **R** | 89,201 (50 %) | **R** | 110,901 (66 %) |
| **I** | 14,550 (8 %) | | | | |

## Campaign Finance

| | Receipts | Receipts from PACs | Expen-ditures |
|---|---|---|---|
| **1980** | | | |
| Glickman (D ) | $118,864 | $29,055 (24 %) | $122,894 |
| Hunter (R ) | $47,987 | $6,450 (13 %) | $42,466 |

| 1978 | | | |
|---|---|---|---|
| Glickman (D ) | $133,128 | $27,540 (21 %) | $90,827 |
| Litsey (R ) | $73,275 | $24,700 (34 %) | $73,264 |

## Voting Studies

| | Presidential Support | | Party Unity | | Conservative Coalition | |
|---|---|---|---|---|---|---|
| **Year** | **S** | **O** | **S** | **O** | **S** | **O** |
| 1980 | 68 | 28 | 61 | 36 | 52 | 43 |
| 1979 | 68 | 32 | 56 | 40 | 50 | 44 |
| 1978 | 65 | 34 | 54 | 44 | 52 | 46 |
| 1977 | 66 | 33 | 57 | 43 | 50 | 49 |

S = Support          O = Opposition

## Key Votes

**96th Congress**

| | |
|---|---|
| Weaken Carter oil profits tax (1979) | Y |
| Reject hospital cost control plan (1979) | Y |
| Implement Panama Canal Treaties (1979) | Y |
| Establish Department of Education (1979) | N |
| Approve Anti-busing Amendment (1979) | N |
| Guarantee Chrysler Corp. loans (1979) | N |
| Approve military draft registration (1980) | N |
| Aid Sandinista regime in Nicaragua (1980) | Y |
| Strengthen fair housing laws (1980) | Y |

**97th Congress**

| | |
|---|---|
| Reagan budget proposal (1981) | N |

## Interest Group Ratings

| Year | ADA | ACA | AFL-CIO | CCUS |
|---|---|---|---|---|
| 1980 | 56 | 33 | 37 | 73 |
| 1979 | 47 | 31 | 70 | 56 |
| 1978 | 50 | 48 | 50 | 39 |
| 1977 | 50 | 41 | 65 | 53 |

**449**

# 5 Bob Whittaker (R)

## Of Augusta — Elected 1978

**Born:** Sept. 18, 1939, Eureka, Kan.
**Education:** Illinois College of Optometry, B.S., D.O. 1962.
**Profession:** Optometrist.
**Family:** Wife, Marlene Faye Arnold; three children.
**Religion:** Christian Church.
**Political Career:** Kansas House, 1975-77.

**In Washington:** Whittaker focused his boyish enthusiasm on the Interior Committee during his first House term, looking out for the mining and energy production upon which the health of his depressed district often depends.

The Mining Subcommittee he served on wrote one bill making it easier for private industry to dispose of the waste produced in extracting oil from shale, and another to promote geothermal energy. Whittaker supported both. Returning for the 97th Congress, he was given a chance to pursue those issues closer to the center of policy on the Energy and Commerce Committee. He left Interior.

Meanwhile, Whittaker was attracting attention in Kansas by criticizing the Federal Aviation Administration for having faulty radar systems at airports around the country. Saying he had become interested in the issue after radar had failed on a day when he was flying to Washington, Whittaker attacked the FAA for "covering up facts about its radar" and called for a major overhaul in the system before 1985. The FAA is unpopular throughout Kansas for its proposed restrictions on the right of private planes, many of them manufactured in the state, to use commercial airports.

Whittaker broke with many Midwestern Republicans by initially supporting President Carter's embargo on U.S. grain shipments to the Soviet Union. He said he wanted to go beyond it, to a ban on all trade between the two countries. Later, after Kansas wheat farmers began complaining that they were suffering most of the harm from a policy that had achieved no noticeable result, he changed his mind and opposed the embargo.

**At Home:** With the retirement of Republican Rep. Joe Skubitz in 1978, Republicans faced a free-for-all primary to pick his successor. A former state House Speaker was one of the candidates; so was a locally prominent Pittsburg manu-

facturer. But Whittaker, a little-known two-term state representative, resigned his legislative seat in May of 1977 and began a long meticulous campaign for the seat. He campaigned door-to-door and held "work days" as a nursing home attendant, garbage collector and grain elevator worker.

His strategy paid off when he won the Republican nomination with 39 percent of the vote in a five-man field, defeating Don Johnston, the manufacturer, by nearly 3,000 votes. He went on to defeat popular Democrat Don Allegrucci, a state legislator from Pittsburg, following a campaign in which he criticized Allegrucci's opposition to capital punishment and support for liquor-by-the-drink in local restaurants. Whittaker easily confirmed his position in 1980 by trouncing his Democratic foe.

An optometrist by profession, Whittaker was a regional coordinator in 1974 for Sen. Robert Dole's re-election campaign. In the same year, he won the first of his two elections to the state House.

**The District:** Most of the 5th does not look like the sort of place people associate with Kansas. The southeastern part of the state is not a land of vast, flat wheat fields; it is hilly and agriculturally poor. It has traditionally been a mining area, especially for coal and zinc, and oil and gas wells are common near the Oklahoma border.

---

**5th District: Southeast — Emporia, Pittsburg.** Population: 480,607 (8% increase since 1970). Race: White 463,138 (96%), Black 8,397 (2%), Others 9,072 (2%). Spanish origin: 7,393 (2%).

---

Many of the voters here are descendants of Southerners who came to farm, and East Europeans who came to mine. The hilly land and ethnic mixture has earned the area the title of "The Balkans."

Before 1962, "Balkan" Kansas constituted virtually all of the 5th District. But in that year's redistricting, it spread north and west to take in more traditional Republican and wheat-growing territory. In the 1970s, the district expanded into the Wichita suburbs.

While the district has always had a large Democratic minority centered in such manufacturing and mining areas as Crawford County (Pittsburg) and Cherokee County (Baxter Springs), Republicans have usually prevailed district-wide. Democrats won here in 1958, but lost the district in 1960 and have not had it since.

## Committees

**Energy and Commerce** (12th of 18 Republicans)
Energy Conservation and Power; Health and the Environment; Oversight and Investigations.

## Elections

**1980 General**

| | |
|---|---|
| Bob Whittaker (R ) | 141,029 (74 %) |
| David Miller (D ) | 45,676 (24 %) |

**1978 General**

| | |
|---|---|
| Bob Whittaker (R ) | 86,011 (57 %) |
| Donald Allegrucci (D) | 62,402 (41 %) |

**1978 Primary**

| | |
|---|---|
| Bob Whittaker (R ) | 18,329 (39 %) |
| Don Johnston (R ) | 15,537 (33 %) |
| Pete McGill (R ) | 8,342 (18 %) |

**District Vote For President**

| | 1980 | | 1976 | | 1972 |
|---|---|---|---|---|---|
| D | 69,188 (35 %) | D | 91,782 (48 %) | D | 51,670 (28 %) |
| R | 115,470 (58 %) | R | 95,220 (50 %) | R | 128,126 (68 %) |
| I | 9,811 (5 %) | | | | |

## Campaign Finance

| | Receipts | Receipts from PACs | Expenditures |
|---|---|---|---|
| **1980** | | | |
| Whittaker (R ) | $177,078 | $74,570 (42 %) | $113,716 |
| Miller (D ) | $1,155 | (0 %) | $1,204 |

**1978**

| | | | |
|---|---|---|---|
| Whittaker (R ) | $262,337 | $69,987 (27 %) | $259,120 |
| Allegrucci (D ) | $118,256 | $41,614 (35 %) | $114,247 |

## Voting Studies

| | Presidential Support | | Party Unity | | Conservative Coalition | |
|---|---|---|---|---|---|---|
| Year | S | O | S | O | S | O |
| 1980 | 40 | 60 | 89 | 10 | 94 | 6 |
| 1979 | 33 | 66 | 86 | 13 | 95 | 5 |

S = Support          O = Opposition

## Key Votes

**96th Congress**

| | |
|---|---|
| Weaken Carter oil profits tax (1979) | Y |
| Reject hospital cost control plan (1979) | Y |
| Implement Panama Canal Treaties (1979) | N |
| Establish Department of Education (1979) | N |
| Approve Anti-busing Amendment (1979) | Y |
| Guarantee Chrysler Corp. loans (1979) | N |
| Approve military draft registration (1980) | Y |
| Aid Sandinista regime in Nicaragua (1980) | N |
| Strengthen fair housing laws (1980) | N |

**97th Congress**

| | |
|---|---|
| Reagan budget proposal (1981) | Y |

## Interest Group Ratings

| Year | ADA | ACA | AFL-CIO | CCUS |
|---|---|---|---|---|
| 1980 | 11 | 88 | 11 | 82 |
| 1979 | 0 | 96 | 10 | 100 |

# Kentucky

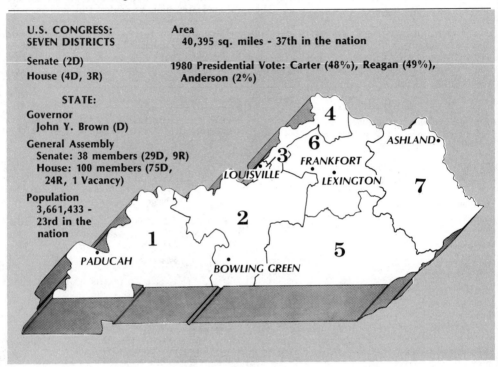

**U.S. CONGRESS:**
**SEVEN DISTRICTS**

Senate (2D)
House (4D, 3R)

**STATE:**

Governor
John Y. Brown (D)

General Assembly
Senate: 38 members (29D, 9R)
House: 100 members (75D,
24R, 1 Vacancy)

Population
3,661,433 -
23rd in the
nation

**Area**
40,395 sq. miles - 37th in the nation

1980 Presidential Vote: Carter (48%), Reagan (49%),
Anderson (2%)

ASHLAND

4

6

3  FRANKFORT

LOUISVILLE  LEXINGTON  7

2

1

5

PADUCAH

BOWLING GREEN

## ...Border Frustrations

For Republicans, Kentucky is a border state
not only in the familiar geographical sense, but in
a political sense as well. Despite a statewide
preference for conservatism and a traditional
party base in the mountain counties, Kentucky
Republicans always seem to be bordering on a
success they never achieve. They entered the
1970s holding the governorship and both U.S.
Senate seats, after years of struggle. But they
immediately began losing, and today all three
offices are solidly under Democratic control.

Democrats have managed their revival despite continuing GOP strength in national elections. Kentucky has gone Republican for president five of nine times during the postwar era.

While states further south have seen their
politics change drastically in recent years with the
coming of Sun Belt development, Kentucky, an
outer Sun Belt province, is more or less stuck in
the political patterns of the past century. This

leaves Republicans competitive, but not usually
successful at the state level.

The mountainous southeastern corner of the
state still furnishes a predictable Republican vote,
year after year, but agricultural western Kentucky
is still called "the Democratic Gibraltar," and the
coal counties along the West Virginia border
support Democrats out of residual New Deal
loyalties. For a while during the late 1960s, metropolitan Louisville seemed to be a possible source
of votes for a statewide Republican breakthrough,
but since then it has been moving back in the
other direction.

Kentucky grew moderately in the 1970s —
slightly more than the national average — but so
far it has not attracted the variety of new industries that are changing states like Arkansas and
Mississippi. The old joke that Kentucky specializes in three habit-forming commodities — tobacco, bourbon and horse racing — is still true

enough to reinforce political traditions based on old economics.

In addition, Kentucky has not had to endure a racial revolution, with all its turmoil and opportunity for political change. The state is only seven percent black, and it never had a major voting rights problem. Kentucky did give George C. Wallace 18.3 percent of its vote in 1968, more than the 13.5 percent he got nationally — but that compared to 34 percent in neighboring Tennessee. The most intense racial problem in the state during recent years was an urban problem, the result of mandatory busing in Louisville, which started in 1975.

# A Political Tour

**Jefferson County.** Although this metropolitan area has about 20 percent of the state's population, the political differences between Democratic Louisville and the generally Republican suburbs tend to cancel each other out. Jefferson supported Ronald Reagan in 1980, but gave him only about a 2,500-vote plurality.

The county lost population during the 1970s, in part due to white flight caused by the court-ordered busing. This has led to rapid growth in adjacent Bullitt and Oldham counties.

Anti-Louisville sentiment in the state's rural counties ensures that Kentucky seldom elects a governor from Jefferson County. Beyond the borders of the county, the most popular aspect of Louisville is Churchill Downs.

Louisville Republicans elected two mayors in a row during the 1960s, partly by appealing to black voters against a decayed Democratic organization. But Democrats swept back back into City Hall in 1969 and have held it since then.

Blacks, comprising almost 30 percent of the city's population, occupy most of the West End. Nearby, white liberals cluster around the University of Louisville in a neighborhood of restored Victorian houses. The affluent East End contains the Republicans. Blue-collar whites predominate in the city's southern section and usually go Democratic. Louisville is a strong union town; General Electric, Ford Motor, International Harvester and many other industrial concerns have plants in the city or just outside.

South of the city along Dixie Highway to Fort Knox stretch blue-collar suburbs like Shively and Pleasure Park Ridge, which normally favor the Democrats. Most of the Jefferson suburbs, however, are white-collar and Republican, such as St. Regis Park and St. Matthews. The suburbs, with 56.5 percent of the county's population, usually

keep county government in GOP hands.

**The Bluegrass and Ohio River Counties.** By day, the fabled grass of northern Kentucky appears no less green than any lawn in New Jersey. At dawn with the dew on it, however, the grass takes on a bluish hue.

For livestock, especially racehorses, the local grass has great nutritive value, derived from the limestone beds beneath the soil. The high phosphorous and calcium content of the grass strengthens the bones of the grazing animals.

In addition to the pasture land divided by endless white plank fences, the Bluegrass region has other types of farming. Tobacco is the main crop, with feed grains next in importance.

The Bluegrass farming counties are loyal to the Democratic Party if its candidate is not too liberal. In 1980, Jimmy Carter carried every county in the region. But in 1972, McGovern's only Bluegrass victory came in Carroll County.

Frankfort was chosen as the state capital in a 1792 compromise between competing Lexington and Louisville. But the city where Daniel Boone is buried never grew into a metropolis (1980 population 26,000), and remains a small town with picturesque old buildings. Its state government workers provide a Democratic base.

Lexington, almost eight times the size of Frankfort, is the only major urban center in Bluegrass country and the region's *de facto* capital. The University of Kentucky has attracted a burgeoning high-technology industry here, and the city's rapid growth — it almost doubled in size over the last decade — has been generated by a boom in engineering and other white-collar jobs. That boom has swung Lexington into the Republican column. Republican U.S. Rep. Larry J. Hopkins depends on it to offset the Democratic vote in the neighboring farm counties.

Along the Ohio River, the GOP usually does well in the Cincinnati suburbs, although Democrats have a good grip on local and state legislative offices. Republican strongholds include the wealthy community of Fort Thomas and the new light industrial center of Florence, where plastic bottles are made. Campbell County dropped slightly in population, but Kentucky's other two suburban Cincinnati counties, Boone and Kenton, made up for this. Run-down Newport, a speakeasy mecca in the 1920s, still retains a "sin city" flavor. It is Democratic.

**Western Kentucky.** A small aromatic mint grows luxuriantly in western Kentucky. Its name is pennyroyal, but the local pronunciation has rendered it pennyrile. It is after that plant that most of the flat and agriculturally abundant western part of the state got its name.

For the most part, Democrats hold sway in the Pennyrile, particularly in the so-called Jackson Purchase, a farm-oriented southwestern piece of the state that Andrew Jackson bought from the Chickasaw Indians. The chief city in the Purchase is Paducah, an old river town that ships tobacco, grain and coal.

In 1980, Carter carried most of the Purchase counties, which perhaps have a more Southern flavor than any place else in Kentucky. Residents of the area look toward Memphis as a major commercial center rather than more distant Louisville. Wallace did well here in 1968.

A smattering of western Kentucky counties have strong Republican legacies — Crittenden, Butler, Edmonson and Grayson. They supported Barry Goldwater in 1964 and Reagan in 1980. The Republican affinity of the eastern edge of the Pennyrile seems to have seeped down from the nearby Republican mountains of the 5th District.

North of the Pennyrile, the western coal fields fan out from Owensboro, on the Ohio River, and seldom waver from the Democrats. All the coal counties voted for Carter in 1980.

**Eastern Kentucky.** The Appalachian counties in the east have traditionally depended on what could be dug out of the rugged ground.

In the 1950s, with coal use declining, times were very hard in east Kentucky. It was a major target for the Johnson administration's War on Poverty. With coal use on the upswing in recent years, life is better. Even "up the hollers" — the poorer sections tucked away in the remotest mountain areas — such signs of modern affluence as color televisions and recreation vehicles have appeared in and next to the mobile homes.

During the Civil War, mountain disdain for the flatlanders who backed the Confederacy led many men from Appalachian Kentucky to join the Union forces. When the war ended and the Democrats took hold outside the mountains, the mountaineers embraced the Republican Party.

That Republican affiliation survives today in the core of the 5th Congressional District — the base any GOP statewide candidate must depend upon. Rockcastle, Laurel, Clay and Pulaski counties turned out well for Reagan in 1980.

To the north and east, though, the counties are more Democratic. Seven of the eight Kentucky counties McGovern carried in 1972 were from this area, which makes up the 7th District. The poverty-stricken mountains suffered a population drain for years. The recent coal boom has reversed that trend. Some mountaineers who left to work in Detroit's auto plants have returned.

The United Mine Workers has considerable influence in the easternmost counties. Harlan County, known as "Bloody Harlan," was the scene of labor violence in the 1930s. During the Evarts Coal Co. strike in 1931, five miners died.

The biggest city in eastern Kentucky is Ashland, an oil refining center and Democratic bastion.

# Redrawing the Lines

The biggest remapping chores are in underpopulated Louisville and the burgeoning east.

Louisville's 3rd District must add nearly 130,000 residents. They will be suburbanites, not the more liberal city-dwellers that 3rd District Democrat Romano L. Mazzoli counts on for his re-election every two years. Eastern Kentucky's 7th District grew 23 percent in the last decade, so it must yield counties to neighboring Republican districts in the center of the state.

# Governor
# John Y. Brown (D)

**Born:** Dec. 28, 1933, Lexington, Ky.
**Home:** Lexington, Ky.
**Education:** U. of Kentucky, B.A. 1957, LL.B. 1960.
**Military Career:** Army Reserve, 1959-65.
**Profession:** Former owner of Kentucky Fried Chicken.
**Family:** Wife, Phyllis; four children.
**Religion:** Baptist.
**Political Career:** Elected governor 1979; term expires Dec. 1983.

# Walter D. Huddleston (D)

## Of Elizabethtown — Elected 1972

**Born:** April 15, 1926, Cumberland County, Ky.
**Education:** U. of Ky., B.A. 1949.
**Military Career:** Army, 1944-46.
**Profession:** Broadcasting executive.
**Family:** Wife, Martha Jean Pearce; two children.
**Religion:** Methodist.
**Political Career:** Ky. Senate, 1966-72.

**In Washington:** Huddleston is an easygoing mainstream Democrat whose work generally stays close to the concerns of Kentucky. He is not often a legislative innovator; he is most active on the Senate floor defending the appropriation bills written in committee and making sure that no one alters the tobacco support program important to his state.

It was a threat to tobacco, in fact, that prompted one of Huddleston's rare public challenges to the White House. During the Carter administration, when he heard former HEW Secretary Joseph A. Califano Jr. was about to launch an anti-smoking campaign, Huddleston immediately went to the president and won a promise of continued support for the tobacco program.

As a senior Democrat on the Agriculture Committee, Huddleston spent much of the 96th Congress working on crop insurance legislation, creating a federal insurance program to replace the direct disaster payments that cost the government $2 billion between 1974 and 1979. The bill inspired fierce opposition from private crop insurers — who hired the now-controversial Paula Parkinson to lobby against it — but Huddleston prevailed narrowly on the floor and the program became law.

Had Democrats retained control of the Senate in 1981. Huddleston would have become chairman of Agriculture. He remains the senior minority member of both that committee, and of the Appropriations Subcommittee on Housing.

One broad issue Huddleston has spent considerable time on is espionage. As a member of the Intelligence Committee, he worked for years in behalf of a charter to define the scope of American spy operations. But defenders of the intelligence community and its covert operations have frustrated those efforts. In 1980, Huddleston finally gave up the charter idea, settling for legislation requiring the administration to report to Congress on covert intelligence acts.

But Kentucky dominates Huddleston's legislative agenda. In addition to tobacco, he has consistently promoted coal, of which his state is the nation's foremost producer. He adds pro-coal floor amendments to numerous kinds of bills, such as his successful 1979 effort to add $10 million for coal utilization programs to the budget of the Energy Department.

Kentucky is also home for major distilleries. When the Senate voted in 1979 to require health warning labels on bottles of bourbon and other distilled liquors, Huddleston said it would disrupt voluntary efforts by the industry to advertise the hazards of excessive drinking. Huddleston persuaded House and Senate conferees to substitute a study of the question for a mandatory labeling provision.

In 1980, in the midst of the flood of Cuban refugees into the United States, Huddleston waged a fight to tighten up the nation's immigration laws. He called them ineffective in limiting the numbers of both illegal and legal immigrants. "We have lost control of immigration to this country," he said. He failed to convince Congress any changes should be made. But he introduced his own large-scale immigration bill in 1981.

Huddleston shed his usually mild manner in 1980 when he bitterly criticized conservative Republican Rep. Daniel B. Crane of Illinois for lending his name to a National Conservative Political Action Committee drive against five liberal Democratic senators. Huddleston was incensed that a member of Congress would attack his own colleagues and, by implication, the institution itself.

**At Home:** Huddleston's career is bound up in large part to that of his Kentucky Democratic colleague, Wendell Ford, who is his junior in the Senate by two years but was his mentor in state politics.

A small-town radio station executive,

Huddleston was the manager of Ford's gubernatorial campaign in 1971. The next year, as state Senate majority leader, Huddleston carried out the new Ford administration's wishes. At the same time, Huddleston was preparing his campaign for the Senate seat being vacated by retiring Republican John Sherman Cooper. Ford offered his personal and factional support.

Huddleston faced only nominal primary opposition, and had a weakened opponent that fall in former Gov. Louie B. Nunn, who was hurt by memories of the unpopular sales tax enacted during his regime. Huddleston hammered on the tax theme, while Nunn tried to link the Democrat

to his party's controversial presidential nominee, George McGovern. Huddleston avoided McGovern, however, refusing to appear with him or to mention his name in public, and he managed to win statewide by 34,000 votes while Nixon was sweeping Kentucky.

Six years of attention to Kentucky concerns made Huddleston so strong by 1978 that Republicans had difficulty finding a reputable candidate to oppose him. They finally came up with an obscure state legislator, Louie Guenthner, who tried to make an issue out of Huddleston's support for the Panama Canal transfer treaties. Huddleston was an easy winner.

## Committees

**Agriculture, Nutrition and Forestry** (Ranking Democrat)
Agricultural Production, Marketing and Stabilization of Prices; Agricultural Research and General Legislation; Soil and Water Conservation.

**Appropriations** (9th of 14 Democrats)
Defense; Energy and Water Development; HUD-Independent Agencies; Interior.

**Select Intelligence** (2nd of 7 Democrats)
Collection and Foreign Operations; Legislation and the Rights of Americans.

**Small Business** (2nd of 8 Democrats)
Export Promotion and Market Development; Government Regulation and Paperwork.

## Elections

**1978 General**

| | |
|---|---|
| Walter Huddleston (D) | 290,730 (61 %) |
| Louie Guenthner (R) | 175,766 (37 %) |

**1978 Primary**

| | |
|---|---|
| Walter Huddleston (D) | 89,333 (76 %) |
| Jack Watson (D) | 13,177 (11 %) |
| William Taylor (D) | 8,710 (7 %) |
| George Tolhurst (D) | 6,921 (6 %) |

**Previous Winning Percentage**

1972 (51 %)

## Campaign Finance

| | Receipts | Receipts from PACs | Expenditures |
|---|---|---|---|
| **1978** | | | |
| Huddleston (D) | $395,557 | $152,664 (39 %) | $456,432 |
| Guenthner (R) | $77,012 | $2,750 (4 %) | $76,445 |

## Voting Studies

| | Presidential Support | | Party Unity | | Conservative Coalition | |
|---|---|---|---|---|---|---|
| Year | S | O | S | O | S | O |
| 1980 | 76 | 15 | 74 | 13 | 42 | 43 |
| 1979 | 68 | 17 | 67 | 17 | 49 | 37 |
| 1978 | 68 | 17 | 63 | 21 | 47 | 37 |
| 1977 | 75 | 16 | 57 | 29† | 52 | 34† |
| 1976 | 40 | 57 | 73 | 16 | 32 | 56 |
| 1975 | 53 | 34 | 66 | 22 | 43 | 43 |
| 1974 (Ford) | 46 | 49 | | | | |
| 1974 | 34 | 57 | 60 | 27 | 43 | 49 |
| 1973 | 30 | 58 | 74 | 10 | 25 | 60 |

S = Support          O = Opposition
† Not eligible for all recorded votes.

## Key Votes

**96th Congress**

| | |
|---|---|
| Maintain relations with Taiwan (1979) | N |
| Reduce synthetic fuel development funds (1979) | N |
| Impose nuclear plant moratorium (1979) | N |
| Kill stronger windfall profits tax (1979) | N |
| Guarantee Chrysler Corp. loans (1979) | Y |
| Approve military draft registration (1980) | Y |
| End Revenue Sharing to the states (1980) | Y |
| Block Justice Dept. busing suits (1980) | Y |

**97th Congress**

| | |
|---|---|
| Restore urban program funding cuts (1981) | Y |

## Interest Group Ratings

| Year | ADA | ACA | AFL-CIO | CCUS-1 | CCUS-2 |
|---|---|---|---|---|---|
| 1980 | 44 | 26 | 61 | 46 | |
| 1979 | 37 | 26 | 62 | 22 | 43 |
| 1978 | 30 | 27 | 67 | 50 | |
| 1977 | 45 | 19 | 80 | 28 | |
| 1976 | 55 | 23 | 84 | 11 | |
| 1975 | 50 | 17 | 60 | 25 | |
| 1974 | 52 | 26 | 70 | 10 | |
| 1973 | 55 | 15 | 82 | 22 | |

# Wendell H. Ford (D)

**Of Owensboro — Elected 1974**

**Born:** Sept. 8, 1924, Daviess County, Ky.
**Education:** Attended U. of Ky., 1942-43; graduated from Md. School of Insurance, 1947.
**Military Career:** Army, 1944-46; National Guard, 1949-62.
**Profession:** Insurance executive.
**Family:** Wife, Jean Neel; two children.
**Religion:** Baptist.
**Political Career:** Ky. Senate, 1966-68; lieutenant governor, 1968-72; Ky. governor, 1972-74.

**In Washington:** Unscathed by the GOP landslide that buried so many of his Democratic colleagues, Ford began his second term in 1981 with his political base secure and his Senate influence growing.

Seldom found in the public spotlight, the former Kentucky governor has worked hard to make his presence felt in committee, at the conference table and in the cloakroom. "Why make a speech," he once said, "when you can sit down with your colleagues and work something out?"

On the Commerce Committee, where he chaired the Consumer Subcommittee for four years, and on the Energy Committee, where he is the leading coal advocate, Ford has been one of the shrewder horse-traders in the Senate.

He does not get everything he goes after, but he almost always comes away with something. "There are no victories in Washington," according to Ford, "only varying degrees of defeat."

As Consumer chairman, Ford took a skeptical view of various kinds of federal regulation. He was the chief Senate sponsor of legislation enacted in 1980 to trim the investigative and regulatory authority of the Federal Trade Commission. In return, Ralph Nader called him "shamelessly soft on business crime." Ford's response was to suggest that Nader "get into the political arena and see if he can get elected," so that he could try Ford's job as chairman of the Consumer Subcommittee.

Ford is also a vociferous opponent of government restriction on the coal industry, a home-state interest for which he is the leading Senate advocate. He has repeatedly sought the repeal of tough federal strip mining regulations. He was a major sponsor of 1980 legislation providing utility companies with $3.6 billion over 10 years to convert to coal as a source of electricity.

Ford worked hard for deregulation of natural gas prices in the 96th Congress, finally suggesting the compromise phased-in deregulation agreed on by House and Senate conferees and speaking for it on the Senate floor.

The Kentucky Democrat sometimes seems uncomfortable with issues that defy compromise. He was a swing vote on the Panama Canal treaties, remaining uncommitted for months while both sides lobbied him furiously. He finally voted against transfer of the canal.

When there is maneuvering room, however, Ford's skills show up, allowing him to use personal relationships and friendly persuasion to cut a deal.

Ford's political skills and business contacts have endeared him to his Democratic colleagues in another area: campaign finance.

Ford has been kept on as chairman of the Democratic Senatorial Campaign Committee through three successive Congresses — the 95th, 96th and now the 97th. This party leadership post in the past has changed hands every two years, but Ford's skill at extracting contributions from business is so admired that his colleagues have been reluctant to replace him in the job.

**At Home:** Fond of calling himself "a dumb country boy with dirt between his toes," Ford displays a political shrewdness that belies the self-description. Faced with the likelihood of weak opposition in 1980, he quickly amassed a huge campaign treasury just in case a serious Republican contender came along. None did, but he conducted an exhausting campaign schedule anyway. He crushed the sacrificial Republican candidate, Mary Louise Foust, an elderly former state auditor who ran an invisible campaign.

An insurance agent, Ford started out in politics as a protégé of Democratic Gov. Bert Combs and worked for him as an aide in the statehouse from 1959 to 1963. But that relationship turned

**457**

sour. By 1971, after a term in the state Senate and one as lieutenant governor, Ford was ready for the governorship. Combs, however, decided on a comeback the same year.

Their contest for the Democratic nomination was rough. Ford said Combs was the candidate of the "fat cats and the courthouse crowd." Combs said Ford was a "punchless promiser with both hands tied behind him by special interests." Combs had his traditional base in eastern Kentucky, but Ford did better in Louisville and the counties to the west and defeated his old mentor soundly. He had little trouble in the fall against Republican Tom Emberton, a former state public service commissioner.

As governor, Ford earned widespread popularity by cutting taxes imposed under his Republican predecessor, Louie B. Nunn. This left him in good stead when he ran for the Senate in 1974

against one-term GOP incumbent Marlow W. Cook.

The Ford-Cook race was no more pleasant than the earlier gubernatorial contest. Cook accused Ford of using state contracts as governor to reward his political allies. Ford labelled Cook "marvelous Marlow, the wonderful wobbler." Cook was hurt by his earlier defense of Richard M. Nixon. It was a Democratic year, and Ford won another comfortable victory.

Ford's only serious problem in recent years has been the occasional mention of his name in connection with a state insurance scandal. His firm reportedly received $10,000 in payments from a state insurance fund after he left the governorship. He testified before a federal grand jury Dec. 4, 1980, but said he was not a target of the federal probe on the subject. He has not been accused of any wrongdoing.

## Committees

**Commerce, Science and Transportation** (5th of 8 Democrats)
Communications; Consumer; Science, Technology, and Space.

**Energy and Natural Resources** (4th of 9 Democrats)
Energy Regulation; Energy Research and Development; Water and Power.

**Rules and Administration** (Ranking Democrat)

**Joint Printing**

## Elections

**1980 General**

| | |
|---|---|
| Wendell Ford (D) | 720,891 (65%) |
| Mary Foust (R) | 386,029 (35%) |

**1980 Primary**

| | |
|---|---|
| Wendell Ford (D) | 188,047 (87%) |
| Flora Stuart (D) | 28,202 (13%) |

**Previous Winning Percentage**

1974 (54%)

## Campaign Finance

| | Receipts | Receipts from PACs | Expenditures |
|---|---|---|---|
| **1980** | | | |
| Ford (D) | $596,866 | $233,875 (39%) | $491,522 |
| Foust (R) | $7,407 | — (0%) | $7,406 |

## Voting Studies

| | Presidential Support | | Party Unity | | Conservative Coalition | |
|---|---|---|---|---|---|---|
| Year | S | O | S | O | S | O |
| 1980 | 71 | 24† | 68 | 23† | 54 | 32 |
| 1979 | 60 | 35 | 56 | 37 | 69 | 20 |
| 1978 | 49 | 42 | 46 | 46 | 65 | 28 |
| 1977 | 74 | 17 | 49 | 41 | 71 | 22 |
| 1976 | 36 | 57 | 73 | 22 | 39 | 53 |
| 1975 | 56 | 40 | 68 | 24 | 45 | 46 |

S = Support        O = Opposition
†Not eligible for all recorded votes.

## Key Votes

**96th Congress**

| | |
|---|---|
| Maintain relations with Taiwan (1979) | N |
| Reduce synthetic fuel development funds (1979) | N |
| Impose nuclear plant moratorium (1979) | Y |
| Kill stronger windfall profits tax (1979) | N |
| Guarantee Chrysler Corp. loans (1979) | Y |
| Approve military draft registration (1980) | Y |
| End Revenue Sharing to the states (1980) | N |
| Block Justice Dept. busing suits (1980) | Y |

**97th Congress**

| | |
|---|---|
| Restore urban program funding cuts (1981) | Y |

## Interest Group Ratings

| Year | ADA | ACA | AFL-CIO | CCUS-1 | CCUS-2 |
|---|---|---|---|---|---|
| 1980 | 78 | 27 | 74 | 44 | |
| 1979 | 32 | 46 | 60 | 36 | 53 |
| 1978 | 45 | 42 | 68 | 44 | |
| 1977 | 50 | 27 | 68 | 31 | |
| 1976 | 40 | 23 | 79 | 22 | |
| 1975 | 56 | 26 | 73 | 31 | |

# 1 Carroll Hubbard Jr. (D)

**Of Mayfield — Elected 1974**

**Born:** July 7, 1937, Murray, Ky.
**Education:** Georgetown College, B.S. 1959; U. of Louisville, J.D. 1962.
**Military Career:** Air National Guard, 1962-67; Army National Guard, 1968-70.
**Profession:** Lawyer.
**Family:** Wife, Joyce Lynn Hall; two children.
**Religion:** Baptist.
**Political Career:** Ky. Senate, 1968-75; gubernatorial nomination, 1979.

**In Washington:** The Panama Canal debate brought Hubbard a spate of public attention in 1979 just when he wanted it — in the middle of his off-year campaign for governor of Kentucky. The chairmanship of the Merchant Marine Committee's Panama Canal Subcommittee fell to him only a few months before the climactic House vote on legislation implementing the canal treaties.

Campaigning for governor and chairing the panel at the same time, Hubbard sometimes seemed to be talking to Kentucky rather than the people in the committee room. "I opposed the new Panama Canal treaty," he told a hearing one day. "Eighty percent of my constituency strongly opposed it, and I agreed with and represented that constituency."

Most of the legislative decisions on the bill were made by the full Merchant Marine Chairman, John M. Murphy of New York. But Hubbard had a chance to hold some well-publicized hearings. At one point, he called a meeting to investigate charges of gunrunning by Panama to Marxist guerrillas in Nicaragua. "It is time to bring up facts," Hubbard said, "that back up the views of millions of Americans who opposed the Panama Canal treaties." When the implementation bill left Merchant Marine and came to the full House, Hubbard voted against it.

Hubbard has been a member of the Banking Committee since 1975 but has not been one of its more active participants. He was on the panel's Housing Subcommittee in 1980 as it drafted a new $38 billion housing authorization, and amended the bill on the floor to restrict tenant participation in decisions made in multi-family housing projects. He said such participation discouraged investment in the projects.

On the House floor Hubbard often follows the lead of his senior Kentucky colleague, William H. Natcher, on major issues. He also uses the House floor on occasion to speak directly to constituents, an action that is technically frowned upon but allowed in practice. The House cable TV system reaches Hubbard's western Kentucky district, and he has been known to take the floor at the start of a session to make a personal comment focused on his district.

On one occasion, he rose to announce his 1980 renomination, and the fact that he had no Republican opposition for re-election. "I must admit I'm bubbling over," Hubbard said in his floor speech, "very pleased about being unopposed. . . . I would like very much to pay tribute briefly to my parents, who have been very helpful to me through the years."

**At Home:** Hubbard has established a firm grip on his western Kentucky House seat, but he has had no success expanding his appeal into the rest of the state. His gubernatorial bid failed badly.

His 1974 primary challenge to veteran Rep. Frank Stubblefield was energetic and effective. It was based on Hubbard's charge that the 67-year-old incumbent was a chronic absentee and a generally lethargic legislator. With the strong backing of organized labor, particularly the United Mine Workers, Hubbard was able to overcome Stubblefield's support from farmers and the official courthouse organizations to win by 629 votes out of nearly 60,000 cast. He defeated his

---

**1st District: West — Paducah.** Population: 517,137 (12% increase since 1970). Race: White 467,099 (90%), Black 46,332 (9%), Others 3,706 (1%). Spanish origin: 4,639 (1%).

## Carroll Hubbard Jr., D-Ky.

Republican opponent by a margin of better than 3-to-1, and has been easily re-elected since then.

But it was different in the 1979 gubernatorial contest, in which he campaigned as a conservative foe of government waste and corruption. Hubbard's personal touches were not helpful on a statewide basis, and his efforts were often lost in the confusion of a nine-candidate field, forcing him to try to use his House office to gain publicity. Without large-scale funding or the support of any significant party bloc, he was never really a factor. He finished a distant fourth with only 12 percent of the vote, carrying his home district but little else.

Hubbard had planned to follow his father into the ministry until his involvement in the 1959 Democratic gubernatorial campaign of Bert Combs changed his mind about a career. He became active in the Kentucky Young Democrats and in 1967 was elected to the state Senate, where he served until 1975.

**The District:** The 1st includes the birth-place of Jefferson Davis, and voting patterns there resemble those of the Deep South more than they do other parts of Kentucky.

Traditionally, this is the most Democratic district in the state. Democrats have held it throughout the 20th century, and Carter won it in 1976 with 66 percent of the vote, his highest share in the state.

But its tradition is also conservative. The western lowlands near the Mississippi River — where tobacco, corn, wheat and soybeans are grown — was once slaveholding territory. In 1968, four of the five counties George Wallace carried in Kentucky were in the 1st District.

While Reagan won only a handful of the district's 24 counties in 1980, he showed the greatest gains over Ford's 1976 vote in the former Wallace strongholds of the west.

Coal-mining is important in the northeastern part of the district, while relatively small factories producing textiles and chemicals are prominent in small cities like Paducah.

## Committees

**Banking, Finance and Urban Affairs** (10th of 25 Democrats)
Domestic Monetary Policy; Financial Institutions Supervision, Regulation and Insurance; Housing and Community Development.

**Merchant Marine and Fisheries** (7th of 20 Democrats)
Panama Canal and Outer Continental Shelf, chairman; Merchant Marine.

## Elections

**1980 General**

| | |
|---|---|
| Carroll Hubbard Jr. (D ) | Unopposed |

**1980 Primary**

| | |
|---|---|
| Carroll Hubbard (D ) | 35,708 (82 %) |
| Clara Humphrey (D ) | 5,046 (12 %) |
| Kenneth Rains (D ) | 2,525 (6 %) |

**1978 General**

| | |
|---|---|
| Carroll Hubbard Jr. (D ) | Unopposed |

**Previous Winning Percentages**

1976 (82 %)  1974 (78 %)

### District Vote For President

| | 1980 | | 1976 | | 1972 |
|---|---|---|---|---|---|
| D | 101,091 (54%) | D | 110,686 (66 %) | D | 51,802 (37 %) |
| R | 81,192 (44%) | R | 55,462 (33 %) | R | 87,072 (61 %) |

## Campaign Finance

| | Receipts | Receipts from PACs | Expenditures |
|---|---|---|---|
| **1980** | | | |
| Hubbard (D ) | $105,866 | $81,580 (77 %) | $85,081 |
| **1978** | | | |
| Hubbard (D ) | $120,811 | $53,013 (44 %) | $79,097 |

## Voting Studies

| | Presidential Support | | Party Unity | | Conservative Coalition | |
|---|---|---|---|---|---|---|
| Year | S | O | S | O | S | O |
| 1980 | 60 | 39 | 51 | 46 | 86 | 9 |
| 1979 | 43 | 44 | 31 | 53 | 78 | 8 |
| 1978 | 46 | 49 | 43 | 50 | 78 | 18 |
| 1977 | 54 | 43 | 47 | 51 | 80 | 17 |
| 1976 | 53 | 47 | 46 | 50 | 83 | 10 |
| 1975 | 34 | 63 | 51 | 47 | 72 | 25 |

S = Support    O = Opposition

## Key Votes

**96th Congress**

| | |
|---|---|
| Weaken Carter oil profits tax (1979) | Y |
| Reject hospital cost control plan (1979) | N |
| Implement Panama Canal Treaties (1979) | N |
| Establish Department of Education (1979) | N |
| Approve Anti-busing Amendment (1979) | Y |
| Guarantee Chrysler Corp. loans (1979) | Y |
| Approve military draft registration (1980) | Y |
| Aid Sandinista regime in Nicaragua (1980) | N |
| Strengthen fair housing laws (1980) | N |

**97th Congress**

| | |
|---|---|
| Reagan budget proposal (1981) | N |

## Interest Group Ratings

| Year | ADA | ACA | AFL-CIO | CCUS |
|---|---|---|---|---|
| 1980 | 22 | 46 | 58 | 82 |
| 1979 | 21 | 54 | 44 | 73 |
| 1978 | 10 | 68 | 63 | 50 |
| 1977 | 15 | 65 | 52 | 50 |
| 1976 | 25 | 52 | 65 | 57 |
| 1975 | 37 | 59 | 55 | 41 |

# 2 William H. Natcher (D)

**Of Bowling Green — Elected 1953**

**Born:** Sept. 11, 1909, Bowling Green, Ky.
**Education:** Western Ky. State College, A.B. 1930; Ohio State U., LL.B. 1933.
**Military Career:** Navy, 1942-45.
**Profession:** Lawyer.
**Family:** Wife, Virginia Reardon; two children.
**Religion:** Baptist.
**Political Career:** Warren County attorney, 1937-49; commonwealth attorney of Allen and Warren counties, 1951-53.

**In Washington:** Everything about Natcher is precise. He dresses carefully, votes carefully, and keeps a detailed diary of his everyday life. He steps in as the House presiding officer with even-handed precision. He speaks in his Kentucky drawl as if choosing his words with infinite care. He has never missed a vote in over 27 years in the House — an all-time record.

Members of Congress that exacting often find their way to the Appropriations Committee, and Natcher knew when he arrived that he wanted to serve there. He had to wait a year, but he is a patient man, and he was where he wanted to be. "I respect and love the House of Representatives," Natcher has said, "and I sincerely believe it is the greatest legislative body in the world."

Natcher was even more patient through 18 years as chairman of one of the least politically appealing Appropriations subcommittees, on the District of Columbia. He graduated to a more important chairmanship only in 1979, when Daniel Flood's departure gave him the panel on Labor, Health and Human Services. But through most of his years on Appropriations, Natcher has been an indispensable man. Placid but firm, he has often been the one to work out the grounds for compromise after hours of tedious argument.

In recent years, the committee has spent much of its time arguing with its Senate counterpart over emotional issues like busing, abortion, and congressional salaries. In several cases, Natcher has suggested the formulas that have allowed both sides to claim a measure of victory. In this role, Natcher deals more with mechanics — "making the trains run on time," as one colleague described it — than with legislative substance. But he is not a man to be stampeded, either by the Senate or by his more aggressive House colleagues. When he wants to, Natcher can sit in meetings day after day waiting for others to meet his terms.

Washington, D.C., officials learned this lesson to their dismay in the years Natcher headed the D.C. Appropriations Subcommittee.

The most dramatic clashes between Natcher and the city came on the issue of its proposed subway system. For three years in a row, Natcher held up final approval of the D.C. budget for months while he pressured local officials to agree to finish the highway system before going ahead with a subway. While irate local leaders fumed that Natcher must have been in the pay of the highway lobby (he was not), the congressman calmly stuck by his guns, determined to force the District to obey what he saw as a simple command of Congress — that certain roads should be built around the city. Natcher got much of what he wanted.

Most members asked to chair the D.C. Appropriations panel are delighted to turn the chore over to someone else after a term or two. Natcher, never discouraged by trivia, accepted it as a duty and spent nearly 20 years examining the budget line by line, seemingly tireless, elaborately polite and, in the end, imposing many of his own views on the city.

For years, Natcher was known in Washington by his local press clippings, which were generally unfavorable. Some of the city's liberals and black

---

**2nd District: West central — Owensboro.** Population: 541,969 (18% increase since 1970). Race: White 504,431 (93%), Black 32,239 (6%), Others 5,299 (1%). Spanish origin: 5,515 (1%).

**William H. Natcher, D-Ky.**

leaders called him a racist. When he first took over the subcommittee, he said his two main concerns were the city's crime rate and its number of illegitimate births. He said the district "should not be turned into a haven for those who roost on welfare payments."

Natcher did vote against most of the early civil rights laws, but he supported the Voting Rights Act of 1965 and most of the anti-poverty and housing programs of the Johnson administration.

In 1979, his first year as Labor-HHS chairman, Natcher attracted attention by announcing that he wanted to close the subcommittee's markup session, and then presiding over an 8-4 vote that closed it for the first time in several years. Health and labor lobbyists swarmed outside the committee room, and Natcher said it would be difficult to produce a fiscally responsible bill with them taking notes on how the members voted. In the end, Natcher claimed that the bill as drafted represented a $162 million reduction from President Carter's budget.

But despite Natcher's diligence, no Labor-HHS appropriation bill became law in either fiscal 1980 or fiscal 1981. In both years, the dispute over federal funding for abortion prevented any House-Senate agreement, and the programs were funded on a "temporary" basis. In fiscal 1981, the Senate did not even try to draft a bill, although Natcher dutifully moved his through the House with a minimum of trouble, defeating Republican efforts at reductions beyond those he had already made.

The Reagan program of budget cuts left Natcher in a difficult position in 1981, balanced between his innate fiscal conservatism and the more liberal slant of his subcommittee. In early round spending cuts, Natcher's panel went along with many Reagan recommendations for cutting labor programs, but proved more resistant when it came to education and health.

Natcher's fiscal conservatism extends to his own staff. Rather than hire the full 18 aides allowed each House member, he has less than ten, all women, none paid more than $15,000 a year.

His response to press criticism has been to ignore it. He seldom grants interviews. He politely turns aside reporters who stop him in the hall, saying he is too busy to discuss anything of substance. He transcribes his daily activities onto book-sized pages that are then bound by the Government Printing Office (at Natcher's expense). There are now 41 volumes.

Natcher does issue one press release a year. It announces the new record he has set for attendance at roll calls on the House floor. He has not

missed one since the day he was sworn in, Jan. 6, 1954. At the end of 1980, he was up to 8,201 in a row.

**At Home.** Nearly as important to Natcher as his perfect voting record is his persistent refusal to accept campaign contributions. The small political bills he incurs, seldom more than $5,000 per election, he pays himself.

The practice reflects not only Natcher's strict ethical standards, but the lack of serious opposition he has encountered over a quarter century in his Kentucky district. Since he won the seat in 1953, Republicans have come close to defeating him only once. That was in 1956, when Dwight D. Eisenhower's coattails pulled the GOP candidate within 3,000 votes of victory.

The success of Republican presidential and statewide candidates in the 2nd District has encouraged the party to make frequent bids to unseat Natcher. But since 1956, he has won re-election each time with at least 58 percent.

Natcher had congressional ambitions from the time he was a teen-ager. After serving in a number of local political offices in Warren County (Bowling Green) and as president of the Kentucky Young Democrats, he got his chance in 1953, when Democratic Rep. Garrett L. Withers died. Party leaders united behind him, and he was elected that summer without opposition in a special election.

Although Republicans have criticized him for his low profile, and reporters from outside the district have sometimes found him inaccessible, Natcher is an institution among his constituents. From his seat on the House Appropriations Committee, he has delivered millions of dollars in public works projects to the 2nd District.

During their last serious effort to win the seat, in 1976, Republicans complained that Natcher had put his attendance record and his jurisdiction over District of Columbia appropriations above the interests of the district. Natcher defused the charge by stepping up announcements of federal grants and loans which he had helped secure. He maintained his refusal to accept contributions, spent less than $10,000, and won re-election with more than 60 percent of the vote.

**The District.** The 2nd District is nearly as rural as the neighboring 1st, but not as consistently Democratic. Since 1948, the GOP has usually carried the 2nd in presidential elections, and sometimes statewide contests also. The T-shaped district is diverse, primarily agricultural but with light industry in small cities like Owensboro and Bowling Green. The district takes in some of the Bluegrass region on the east, approaches the

462

Louisville suburbs on the north and includes a portion of the western coalfields. At its southern end, it extends into the Pennyrile region of Kentucky, named after a small, locally-grown aromatic mint. The Pennyrile is rolling hill country.

## Committees

**Appropriations** (3rd of 33 Democrats)
Labor-HHS, chairman; Agriculture; District of Columbia.

## Elections

**1980 General**

| | |
|---|---|
| William Natcher (D ) | 99,670 (66 %) |
| Mark Watson (R ) | 52,110 (34 %) |

**1978 General**

| | |
|---|---|
| William Natcher (D ) | Unopposed |

**Previous Winning Percentages**

| | | | |
|---|---|---|---|
| 1976 (60 %) | 1974 (73 %) | 1972 (62 %) | 1970 (100%) |
| 1968 (56 %) | 1966 (59 %) | 1964 (68 %) | 1962 (100%) |
| 1960 (100%) | 1958 (76 %) | 1956 (52 %) | 1954 (100%) |
| 1953* (100%) | | | |
| * Special election. | | | |

**District Vote For President**

| | 1980 | | 1976 | | 1972 |
|---|---|---|---|---|---|
| D | 82,335 (47%) | D | 81,529 (55 %) | D | 46,922 (34 %) |
| R | 88,017 (50%) | R | 65,476 (44 %) | R | 88,384 (64 %) |
| I | 3,142 (2%) | | | | |

## Campaign Finance

| | Receipts | Receipts from PACs | Expenditures |
|---|---|---|---|
| **1980** | | | |
| Natcher (D ) | $3,145 | — (0 %) | $3,145 |
| Watson (R ) | $7,458 | $500 (7 %) | $7,425 |

## Voting Studies

| | Presidental Support | | Party Unity | | Conservative Coalition | |
|---|---|---|---|---|---|---|
| Year | S | O | S | O | S | O |
| 1980 | 60 | 40 | 65 | 35 | 75 | 25 |
| 1979 | 60 | 40 | 67 | 33 | 69 | 31 |
| 1978 | 66 | 34 | 77 | 23 | 43 | 57 |
| 1977 | 63 | 37 | 69 | 31 | 61 | 39 |
| 1976 | 43 | 57 | 65 | 35 | 66 | 34 |
| 1975 | 29 | 71 | 71 | 29 | 53 | 47 |
| 1974 (Ford) | 43 | 57 | | | | |
| 1974 | 60 | 40 | 71 | 29 | 56 | 44 |
| 1973 | 39 | 61 | 75 | 25 | 50 | 50 |
| 1972 | 54 | 46 | 55 | 45 | 70 | 30 |
| 1971 | 63 | 37 | 61 | 39 | 73 | 27 |
| 1970 | 66 | 34 | 61 | 39 | 73 | 27 |
| 1969 | 53 | 47 | 58 | 42 | 76 | 24 |
| 1968 | 72 | 28 | 63 | 37 | 61 | 39 |
| 1967 | 80 | 20 | 71 | 29 | 65 | 35 |
| 1966 | 73 | 27 | 71 | 29 | 54 | 46 |
| 1965 | 79 | 21 | 68 | 31 | 61 | 39 |
| 1964 | 79 | 21 | 73 | 27 | 67 | 33 |
| 1963 | 87 | 13 | 86 | 14 | 47 | 53 |
| 1962 | 87 | 13 | 84 | 16 | 19 | 81 |
| 1961 | 82 | 18 | 79 | 21 | 43 | 57 |

S = Support          O = Opposition

## Key Votes

**96th Congress**

| | |
|---|---|
| Weaken Carter oil profits tax (1979) | Y |
| Reject hospital cost control plan (1979) | Y |
| Implement Panama Canal Treaties (1979) | N |
| Establish Department of Education (1979) | Y |
| Approve Anti-busing Amendment (1979) | Y |
| Guarantee Chrysler Corp. loans (1979) | Y |
| Approve military draft registration (1980) | N |
| Aid Sandinista regime in Nicaragua (1980) | N |
| Strengthen fair housing laws (1980) | N |

**97th Congress**

| | |
|---|---|
| Reagan budget proposal (1981) | Y |

## Interest Group Ratings

| Year | ADA | ACA | AFL-CIO | CCUS |
|---|---|---|---|---|
| 1980 | 50 | 29 | 47 | 74 |
| 1979 | 42 | 15 | 50 | 44 |
| 1978 | 35 | 26 | 60 | 33 |
| 1977 | 30 | 52 | 61 | 53 |
| 1976 | 45 | 46 | 70 | 50 |
| 1975 | 42 | 39 | 91 | 29 |
| 1974 | 48 | 33 | 91 | 20 |
| 1973 | 52 | 26 | 82 | 45 |
| 1972 | 31 | 57 | 64 | 60 |
| 1971 | 30 | 48 | 75 | - |
| 1970 | 28 | 42 | 57 | 20 |
| 1969 | 27 | 59 | 50 | - |
| 1968 | 42 | 35 | 75 | - |
| 1967 | 40 | 28 | 75 | 40 |
| 1966 | 29 | 33 | 54 | - |
| 1965 | 37 | 25 | - | 30 |
| 1964 | 64 | 42 | 91 | - |
| 1963 | - | 22 | - | - |
| 1962 | 75 | 9 | 82 | - |
| 1961 | 80 | - | - | - |

# 3 Romano L. Mazzoli (D)

**Of Louisville — Elected 1970**

**Born:** Nov. 2, 1932, Louisville, Ky.
**Education:** Notre Dame U., B.S. 1954; U. of Louisville, J.D. 1960.
**Military Career:** Army, 1954-56.
**Profession:** Lawyer.
**Family:** Wife, Helen Dillon; two children.
**Religion:** Roman Catholic.
**Political Career:** Ky. Senate, 1968-70; sought Democratic nomination for mayor of Louisville, 1969.

**In Washington:** Hard-working and lawyerlike, Mazzoli is the kind of legislator who tends to the small details and leaves the posturing to others. In the 97th Congress, he serves on four legislative committees — more than any other member of the House. He has most often been heard on the House floor in recent years discussing Judiciary matters many find too technical to bother with, like bankruptcy law or changes in the antitrust act.

But he steps out of his technician's role on one issue — abortion. On that he is vocal and militant.

As co-chairman of the congressional Pro-Life Caucus, Mazzoli helped draft the "human life bill," which would redefine the word "person" to include the unborn, possibly allowing states to declare abortion murder. Mazzoli has lobbied for that appproach with the Judiciary Committee in the Senate; the one in the House, on which he serves, has been too strongly supportive of abortion to consider it.

Within the House, however, Mazzoli has attempted to chip away at legalized abortion whenever he can. In 1980, he drafted language that was added to a Legal Services Corporation bill, providing that Legal Services could handle abortion cases only when the life of the mother is involved.

In recent Congresses, much of Mazzoli's work has been on the Monopolies and Commercial Law Subcommittee. This antitrust panel has been chaired by Peter W. Rodino Jr., the full Judiciary chairman, but through 1980, at least, Rodino left most of the details to Mazzoli. In 1980, when the House passed a package of five bills designed to speed procedures in federal antitrust trials, it was Mazzoli who served as spokesman and managed the legislation on the floor.

In the 97th Congress, Mazzoli has a controversial new assignment on Judiciary, as head of its Immigration Subcommittee, where he has to steer his way between liberal efforts to increase U.S. refugee admission and conservative resentment against those newly arrived. In June, 1981, he was working on legislation that would grant amnesty to illegal aliens now in the U.S. but toughen laws to stop more illegals from coming in.

Both on the Judiciary Committee and outside it, Mazzoli has always taken an interest in congressional ethics issues. In 1976, he surprised colleagues when he rose on the floor to demand that Ohio Democrat Wayne Hays resign following disclosure that he had put his mistress on the congressional payroll. Mazzoli said he was offended at the "locker room" jokes — instead of genuine concern — that greeted the Hays affair. He felt congressional honor was at stake. "We can't sit back and wait for the ethics committee to act," he said.

Partly because of this action but also because of Mazzoli's reputation for probity, Speaker O'Neill named him in 1977 to a special committee charged with drawing up new ethics codes for members of Congress and government employees. Since then, he has worked at Judiciary on revising the federal lobbying law. When the committee wrote a lobby disclosure bill in 1979, Mazzoli tried to expand it to include "grass-roots lobbying," the kind that generates pressure on members from constituents. But he failed in the effort. No lobby bill reached the House floor in the 96th Congress.

Mazzoli has also spent three terms on the House Intelligence Committee, struggling with

---

**3rd District: Louisville and suburbs.** Population: 393,352 (15% decrease since 1970). Race: White 291,232 (74%), Black 99,210 (25%), Others 2,910 (1%). Spanish origin: 2,552 (1%).

the question of how and whether to regulate the nation's covert espionage. He has a subcommittee chairmanship on the Intelligence panel, and is using it to draft a bill which would make it a crime to disclose the names of persons working as U.S. agents in foreign countries. Mazzoli also believes the 1975 Freedom of Information Act should be made more restrictive to protect national security data.

Since 1973, Mazzoli has been on the District of Columbia Committee, choosing to keep a politically unrewarding assignment most members drop as soon as they are allowed to. He has been a strong backer of home rule and voting representation for the district.

In 1981, he added still a fourth committee — Small Business. Some of its jurisdiction overlaps with that of Judiciary, especially on one subject he is interested in — changing regulatory law. Mazzoli has worked to provide federal money to pay legal fees for small businesses which successfully challenge federal agency actions.

On most issues, Mazzoli has been a moderate Democrat, voting with the party leadership slightly more often than he has with his more conservative Kentucky colleagues. He spent his first two terms on the Education and Labor Committee, where he was usually receptive to union goals, but his voting has not been particularly oriented to labor since he left the committee. In 1972, the AFL-CIO gave Mazzoli a rating of 91; by 1980, he was down below 50.

**At Home:** Mazzoli's 211-vote victory over Republican Rep. William O. Cowger in 1970 symbolized the Democratic resurgence then beginning in city and state politics. The party has remained in power since then, and Mazzoli has held the 3rd District despite a storm of criticism over busing that threatened to end his career.

Mazzoli was a state senator in 1970, fresh from a mayoral campaign that had been unsuccessful but had increased his visibility in the city. He ran for Congress as an opponent of the Vietnam War, and developed a strong base among blacks, young liberals and blue-collar Catholics. But the decisive factor in his House victory was the bitter intraparty bickering between Cowger and Republican Gov. Louie Nunn over local patronage.

Cowger had challenged the governor to run a candidate for Congress against him in the primary. Nunn responded by saying Cowger was in need of a "psychiatric examination." The breach never healed and Mazzoli took advantage of it to win his narrow general election victory.

Redistricting strengthened Mazzoli by adding some Democratic precincts in Louisville. But his favorable political position was nearly destroyed in 1976 by the busing issue. Mazzoli at first accepted busing as a means of desegregating the Louisville schools, then switched to an anti-busing position after the city's turmoil began. But the shift in positions came too late and was too mild for vocal busing foes. He was held to 55 percent in the primary and 57 percent in the general election.

While the busing issue faded after the election, Mazzoli's problems continued when he backed the losing candidate in the 1977 Democratic mayoral primary. But his political position improved with a successful fund-raising effort and a strong vote of support from organized labor, which has dissuaded serious primary and Republican opposition. Mazzoli won re-election in 1978 and 1980 by comfortable margins.

**The District:** The 3rd encompasses the entire city of Louisville, plus several small suburbs. Louisville combines the features of an old Democratic industrial city of the North or Midwest with those of a newer Republican urban center of the South. The city contains large black and Catholic constituencies, many of the latter descendants of German immigrants who settled there in the mid-19th century.

But in its social history, Louisville has faced South. Its public places were not fully desegregated until well after World War II. In recent years busing has been a major problem, particularly in blue-collar neighborhoods on the South Side and in neighboring Shively.

Republicans, led by Cowger and Marlow Cook (later a U.S. senator) gained control of city government in the early 1960s from conservative Democratic leaders. But a more moderate group of Democrats recaptured it by the end of the decade, as the minority population was increasing. The district usually votes Democratic now in presidential and statewide races.

## Committees

**District of Columbia** (2nd of 6 Democrats)
Judiciary and Education.

**Judiciary** (8th of 16 Democrats)
Immigration, Refugees and International Law, Chairman; Mo-

nopolies and Commercial Law.

**Select Intelligence** (4th of 9 Democrats)
Legislation, Chairman.

**Small Business** (14th of 23 Democrats)
General Oversight.

# Elections

**1980 General**

| | |
|---|---|
| Romano Mazzoli (D ) | 85,873 (64 %) |
| Richard Cesler (R ) | 46,681 (35 %) |

**1980 Primary**

| | |
|---|---|
| Romano Mazzoli (D ) | 18,734 (79 %) |
| George Tolhurst (D ) | 2,142 (9 %) |
| William Gibbs (D ) | 1,852 (8 %) |

**1978 General**

| | |
|---|---|
| Romano Mazzoli (D ) | 37,346 (66 %) |
| Norbert LeVeronne (R ) | 17,785 (31 %) |

**Previous Winning Percentages**

| | | | |
|---|---|---|---|
| 1976 (57 %) | 1974 (70 %) | 1972 (62 %) | 1970 (49 %) |

**District Vote For President**

| | 1980 | | 1976 | | 1972 |
|---|---|---|---|---|---|
| D | 80,370 (56 %) | D | 79,407 (53 %) | D | 63,796 (44 %) |
| R | 56,932 (40 %) | R | 63,690 (43 %) | R | 78,143 (54 %) |
| I | 4,882 (3 %) | | | | |

# Campaign Finance

| | Receipts | Receipts from PACs | Expenditures |
|---|---|---|---|
| **1980** | | | |
| Mazzoli (D ) | $95,347 | $55,935 (59 %) | $94,674 |
| Cesler (R ) | $14,841 | $8,250 (56 %) | $18,449 |
| **1978** | | | |
| Mazzoli (D) | $119,606 | $61,670 (52 %) | $110,638 |

# Voting Studies

| | Presidential Support | | Party Unity | | Conservative Coalition | |
|---|---|---|---|---|---|---|
| Year | S | O | S | O | S | O |
| 1980 | 61 | 30 | 64 | 30 | 60 | 36 |
| 1979 | 68 | 24 | 67 | 24 | 49 | 43 |
| 1978 | 66 | 26 | 60 | 34 | 41 | 55 |
| 1977 | 70 | 23 | 72 | 22 | 37 | 56 |
| 1976 | 31 | 67 | 76 | 19 | 38 | 57 |
| 1975 | 39 | 58 | 65 | 33 | 50 | 49 |
| 1974 (Ford) | 41 | 59 | | | | |
| 1974 | 49 | 40 | 66 | 28 | 35 | 59 |
| 1973 | 45 | 54 | 71 | 29 | 36 | 64 |
| 1972 | 49 | 51 | 72 | 28 | 29 | 71 |
| 1971 | 44 | 54 | 71 | 27 | 31 | 67 |

S = Support          O = Opposition

# Key Votes

**96th Congress**

| | |
|---|---|
| Weaken Carter oil profits tax (1979) | Y |
| Reject hospital cost control plan (1979) | ? |
| Implement Panama Canal Treaties (1979) | Y |
| Establish Department of Education (1979) | N |
| Approve Anti-busing Amendment (1979) | N |
| Guarantee Chrysler Corp. loans (1979) | Y |
| Approve military draft registration (1980) | N |
| Aid Sandinista regime in Nicaragua (1980) | N |
| Strengthen fair housing laws (1980) | Y |

**97th Congress**

| | |
|---|---|
| Reagan budget proposal (1981) | Y |

# Interest Group Ratings

| Year | ADA | ACA | AFL-CIO | CCUS |
|---|---|---|---|---|
| 1980 | 33 | 33 | 46 | 62 |
| 1979 | 42 | 16 | 74 | 63 |
| 1978 | 40 | 31 | 47 | 56 |
| 1977 | 50 | 15 | 86 | 47 |
| 1976 | 65 | 11 | 74 | 38 |
| 1975 | 63 | 50 | 70 | 41 |
| 1974 | 74 | 33 | 90 | 30 |
| 1973 | 80 | 26 | 55 | 27 |
| 1972 | 63 | 26 | 91 | 60 |
| 1971 | 65 | 25 | 58 | - |

# 4 Gene Snyder (R)

**Of Brownsboro Farms — Elected 1962**
Did not serve 1965-67

**Born:** Jan. 26, 1928, Louisville, Ky.
**Education:** U. of Louisville, 1945-47; Jefferson
School of Law, LL.B. 1950.
**Profession:** Lawyer, real estate agent.
**Family:** Wife, Patricia Creighton Robertson; one
child, three stepchildren.
**Religion:** Lutheran.
**Political Career:** Jeffersontown City Attorney,
1954-58; Magistrate of Jefferson County,
1958-62; elected to U.S. House, 1962; de-
feated for re-election, 1964; re-elected to U.S.
House, 1966.

**In Washington:** Time and seniority have
transformed Snyder from the militant conservative ideologue he was as a House freshman in 1963
to the master pork-barrel politician he gradually
became over the 1970s. His voting record is as
conservative as ever, but his emphasis has narrowed from world communism and civil disorder
to the roads, dams and airports that govern life at
the Public Works Committee.

Snyder is not one of the best-liked members
of Public Works, but critics concede that he is one
of the most effective. Smart and tough, he has
gained a reputation as a man dangerous to cross.

As senior Republican on the Public Works
Aviation Subcommittee since its creation in 1975,
Snyder has been in a good position to help a
leading legislative interest, the general aviation
industry, producer of private planes. With longtime subcommittee Chairman Glenn Anderson,
D-Calif., reluctant to play a strong role, Snyder
often emerged the dominant figure on either side
of the aisle in recent years. That has changed
some now that the subcommittee chairmanship
has passed to a more active member, Norman
Mineta, D-Calif. But Snyder's presence is still
felt.

When legislation dealing with airport noise
moved through Congress in 1979, it was Snyder
who pushed the hardest to ease controls. The
agreement exempted all private two-engine
planes and many three-engine planes from strict
noise control requirements. The year before, Snyder, along with much of the airline industry,
fought unsuccessfully to block President Carter's
airline deregulation plan.

On Water Resources, Snyder's other major
Public Works subcommittee, he is a man who

knows how to get a project built in his district —
or in a friendly colleague's district. He is also
willing to fight against projects demanded by a
colleague who is not proving cooperative. Early in
his Public Works career, Snyder fought to deny
funding for a dam in the district represented by
Democrat Carl Perkins, influential dean of the
Kentucky delegation. He felt Perkins was holding
up progress on a dam Snyder wanted in northern
Kentucky. Eleven years later, Snyder was still
making cracks about Perkins' long list of public
works demands. "He takes it all," Snyder said,
"and we wrestle over the crumbs."

One of the "crumbs" Snyder wrestled hardest
over was a flood control project at Dayton, Kentucky, on the Ohio River. Carter tried to block
construction of it in early 1977, just as it was
beginning. Snyder complained bitterly that the
Carter administration was willing to ask for extra
money for a public works jobs program but that
"there's no room for long-promised assistance to a
city trying to pull itself out of the mud and keep
the river out of its living rooms." After a few
months of hesitation, the administration reversed
itself on the project.

The old ideological Snyder still turns up
occasionally. On the Merchant Marine Committee
he was vehement in his opposition to the new U.S.
policy toward Panama, and he tried repeatedly
over a period of months to block legislation imple-

---

**4th District: North — Louisville
suburbs, Newport.** Population: 534,324
(16% increase since 1970). Race: White
513,806 (96%), Black 16,542 (3%), Others
3,974 (1%). Spanish origin: 2,990 (1%).

---

menting return of the canal. Ultimately the effort was unsuccessful.

His Panama Canal rhetoric seems mild, however, in comparison to some of the remarks of his early years. In his first House term, he denounced civil rights leader Roy Wilkins as "an itinerant race agitator." In his second term, he asked congressional colleagues to explore the possibilities of a "back to Africa" movement for blacks and proposed the name of George C. Wallace for a vacancy on the U.S. Supreme Court.

He was a leading supporter of the Young Americans for Freedom, which he said was necessary against "the storm-trooper tactics of the New Left."

The rhetoric gradually began to tone down after Snyder found his home on the Public Works Committee in 1967. He was starting all over as a freshman that year, having lost his seat after one term in the 1964 Johnson landslide. Before that defeat, Snyder served on the Education and Labor Committee, part of a badly outnumbered conservative bloc that fought federal aid to education and opposed creation of a National Council on the Arts.

When he returned, he was offered his old assignment. But he declined, apparently feeling that his national orientation had cost him support. "I represent a district which has nine counties fronting on the Ohio River," he said. "I want to be in a position to work for some things I feel are necessary for the district."

**At Home:** Snyder's feisty brand of conservatism has proved popular in one of the most Republican districts in Kentucky. He had trouble in 1974, coming within 5,000 votes of losing his seat for the second time, but in all other years his margins have been comfortable.

After a brief career in Jefferson County (metropolitan Louisville) politics, Snyder was first elected to the House in 1962 on a platform that stridently opposed the "socialistic liberalism of the New Frontier."

Although he campaigned aggressively, it was strong party support that made the difference. Aided by the coattails of Republican Sen. Thruston B. Morton at the top of the ticket and the organizational strength of the new GOP administration in Louisville, Snyder narrowly unseated Democratic incumbent Frank W. Burke.

But he could not hold the seat. At that time, Snyder's district encompassed all of Jefferson County, including the city of Louisville, with its large black population. By opposing the 1964 Civil Rights Act and denouncing Roy Wilkins, Snyder alienated black voters.

The 1964 presidential contest also was a serious problem for him. When Snyder spoke up in support of Barry Goldwater, Democratic nominee Charles P. Farnsley, a former Louisville mayor, lambasted him as a candidate of the "radical right." Johnson swept the district, and Snyder lost decisively to Farnsley.

But in 1966 Snyder mounted a successful comeback, aided by redistricting and the election eve death of his Democratic opponent. His old 3rd District was reduced to the city of Louisville, and he chose to run in the redrawn 4th, which stretched along the Ohio River from the suburbs of Louisville to those of Cincinnati.

Snyder easily won the 1966 Republican primary over a more moderate rival backed by the Jefferson County organization. The fall campaign was dominated by the ill health of Snyder's Democratic rival, state Sen. John J. Moloney. Hospitalized much of the fall, Moloney died several days before the election. Democratic leaders hastily substituted Rep. Frank Chelf, the district's incumbent, who had wanted to retire after representing the area for two decades. But Snyder prevailed by 10,000 votes.

With his conservative politics favorably suited to the district, Snyder had no difficulty winning the next three times. But in 1974, Watergate and a personal controversy nearly led to his defeat.

The previous year he had divorced his wife of 22 years, who briefly considered challenging him. Then he drew considerable criticism for real estate and land deals which his opponents charged were a conflict of interest. Snyder kept up an active real estate business in Kentucky during his Washington years, working with some clients who also dealt with the federal government.

Challenged by Kyle Hubbard, the younger brother of Democratic Rep. Carroll Hubbard Jr. of the 1st District, Snyder survived narrowly by building up an 8,700-vote lead in his home base, suburban Jefferson County.

By 1976 most of the personal controversy had faded and Snyder returned to the offensive. Attacking the national Democratic Party for its failure to oppose abortion and court-ordered busing, Snyder threatened to "hang a fetus around my opponent's neck, and a bus too." He won re-election with 56 percent of the vote.

**The District:** With the exception of the mountainous 5th District, the suburban 4th is the most Republican enclave in Kentucky.

Although the district is nearly 100 miles long, the population is concentrated at the ends — the suburbs of Louisville on the west and Cincinnati on the east. Both are Republican strongholds. In between are several rural Democratic counties.

The Louisville suburbs are mostly white-collar and professional, making the 4th the most affluent district in the state. Across the river from Cincinnati, in Covington and Newport, there is a particularly large Catholic population. Anti-abortion candidate Ellen McCormack ran a close second to Carter there in the 1976 Democratic presidential primary.

## Committees

**Merchant Marine and Fisheries** (Ranking Republican)

**Public Works and Transportation** (2nd of 19 Republicans)
Aviation; Surface Transportation; Water Resources.

## Elections

**1980 General**

| | |
|---|---|
| Gene Snyder (R ) | 126,049 (67 %) |
| Phil McGary (D ) | 62,138 (33 %) |

**1978 General**

| | |
|---|---|
| Gene Snyder (R ) | 62,087 (66 %) |
| George Martin (D ) | 32,212 (34 %) |

**Previous Winning Percentages**

| | | | |
|---|---|---|---|
| 1976 (56 %) | 1974 (52 %) | 1972 (74 %) | 1970 (67 %) |
| 1968 (65 %) | 1966 (54 %) | 1962 (51 %) | |

**District Vote For President**

| | 1980 | | 1976 | | 1972 |
|---|---|---|---|---|---|
| D | 78,829 (39%) | D | 78,063 (43%) | D | 47,070 (29%) |
| R | 115,936 (57%) | R | 104,266 (57%) | R | 112,156 (69%) |
| I | 7,497 (4%) | | | | |

## Campaign Finance

| | Receipts | Receipts from PACs | Expenditures |
|---|---|---|---|
| **1980** | | | |
| Snyder (R ) | $162,655 | $106,134 (65 %) | $83,015 |
| McGary (D ) | $35,304 | $850 (2 %) | $38,005 |
| **1978** | | | |
| Snyder (R ) | $146,055 | $65,337 (45 %) | $122,834 |
| Martin (D ) | $30,384 | $1,336 (4 %) | $30,231 |

## Voting Studies

| | Presidential Support | | Party Unity | | Conservative Coalition | |
|---|---|---|---|---|---|---|
| Year | S | O | S | O | S | O |
| 1980 | 35 | 63 | 85 | 14 | 93 | 7 |
| 1979 | 26 | 72 | 85 | 14 | 97 | 3 |
| 1978 | 28 | 69 | 83 | 14 | 90 | 7 |

| | | | | | | |
|---|---|---|---|---|---|---|
| 1977 | 39 | 56 | 85 | 12 | 90 | 5 |
| 1976 | 67 | 27 | 82 | 12 | 88 | 8 |
| 1975 | 52 | 46 | 78 | 21 | 84 | 15 |
| 1974 (Ford) | 30 | 39 | | | | |
| 1974 | 57 | 38 | 66 | 21 | 78 | 13 |
| 1973 | 54 | 44 | 77 | 20 | 81 | 17 |
| 1972 | 43 | 46 | 73 | 22 | 79 | 15 |
| 1971 | 54 | 42 | 69 | 26 | 72 | 24 |
| 1970 | 49 | 29 | 57 | 24 | 66 | 7 |
| 1969 | 40 | 45 | 67 | 20 | 82 | 4 |
| 1968 | 35 | 47 | 68 | 6 | 76 | 0 |
| 1967 | 39 | 54 | 85 | 10 | 94 | 4 |
| 1964 | 27 | 71 | 74 | 11 | 75 | 17 |
| 1963 | 15 | 83 | 95 | 0 | 87 | 0 |

S = Support    O = Opposition

## Key Votes

**96th Congress**

| | |
|---|---|
| Weaken Carter oil profits tax (1979) | Y |
| Reject hospital cost control plan (1979) | Y |
| Implement Panama Canal Treaties (1979) | N |
| Establish Department of Education (1979) | N |
| Approve Anti-busing Amendment (1979) | Y |
| Guarantee Chrysler Corp. loans (1979) | N |
| Approve military draft registration (1980) | N |
| Aid Sandinista regime in Nicaragua (1980) | N |
| Strengthen fair housing laws (1980) | N |

**97th Congress**

| | |
|---|---|
| Reagan budget proposal (1981) | Y |

## Interest Group Ratings

| Year | ADA | ACA | AFL-CIO | CCUS |
|---|---|---|---|---|
| 1980 | 11 | 71 | 21 | 70 |
| 1979 | 5 | 81 | 15 | 89 |
| 1978 | 15 | 96 | 20 | 72 |
| 1977 | 10 | 81 | 27 | 82 |
| 1976 | 5 | 89 | 22 | 94 |
| 1975 | 5 | 86 | 13 | 69 |
| 1974 | 17 | 80 | 9 | 70 |
| 1973 | 20 | 85 | 27 | 82 |
| 1972 | 6 | 91 | 27 | 100 |
| 1971 | 24 | 86 | 18 | - |
| 1970 | 8 | 76 | 29 | 75 |
| 1969 | 7 | 85 | 33 | - |
| 1968 | 0 | 95 | 0 | - |
| 1967 | 13 | 89 | 17 | 70 |
| 1964 | 8 | 97 | 18 | - |
| 1963 | - | 100 | - | - |

# 5 Harold Rogers (R)

**Of Somerset — Elected 1980**

**Born:** Dec. 31, 1937, Barrier, Ky.
**Education:** U. of Ky., A.B. 1962, J.D. 1964.
**Military Career:** Army National Guard, 1956-64.
**Profession:** Lawyer.
**Family:** Wife, Shirley McDowell; three children.
**Religion:** Baptist.
**Political Career:** Commonwealth's attorney, Pulaski and Rockcastle counties, 1969-80; unsuccessful GOP nominee for lt. gov., 1979.

**The Member:** Republican freshmen selected Rogers as their representative on the panel that made GOP committee assignments for the 97th Congress. That gave Rogers a chance to do some favors for friends, and aided his own effort to get a place on Energy and Commerce, a valuable committee for a legislator from a coal-producing district.

President Reagan's proposals to trim black lung benefits and to eliminate the Applachian Regional Commission discomfited Rogers, since both those federal programs are important in his district. He promised to support Reagan's overall economizing efforts while trying to preserve the commission and prevent cuts in black lung benefits.

Rogers was a protégé of his predecessor, Republican Rep. Tim Lee Carter, who retired in 1980, and is generally identified with him as a moderate on the ideological spectrum. In 1976, when most of the Kentucky GOP backed Reagan in the state's presidential primary, Rogers ran Gerald Ford's state primary campaign.

Rogers made his name locally in the 1960s as a civic activist who promoted industrial development in Somerset. He took over as commonwealth's attorney in 1969 and continued to play a conspicuous role in politics as the prosecutor for Pulaski and Rockcastle counties. His 1979 bid for lieutenant governor was unsuccessful, but it helped build name recognition for the 1980 congressional race.

**The District:** With the lowest median family income in the state, this eastern Kentucky coal area is heavily dependent on government help. But since the Civil War, when its small farmers were hostile to slaveholding secessionist Democrats elsewhere in Kentucky, it has been the most reliably Republican area in the country. Only two of its counties, Harlan and Bell, where the United Mine Workers are active, went for Jimmy Carter in 1980.

## Committees

**Energy and Commerce** (15th of 18 Republicans)
Energy Conservation and Power; Fossil and Synthetic Fuels; Oversight and Investigations.

## Elections

| 1980 General | |
|---|---|
| Harold Rogers (R ) | 112,093 (68 %) |
| Ted Marcum (D ) | 54,027 (32 %) |

| 1980 Primary | |
|---|---|
| Harold Rogers (R) | 13,266 (23 %) |
| Tom Emberton (R) | 10,576 (19 %) |
| Gene Huff (R) | 9,595 (17 %) |
| John Rogers (R) | 7,439 (13 %) |
| Raymond Overstreet (R) | 5,171 (9 %) |
| Eddie Lovelace (R) | 3,703 (7 %) |
| Elmer Patrick (R) | 3,681 (6 %) |
| Other | 3,322 (6 %) |

**District Vote For President**

| | 1980 | | 1976 | | 1972 |
|---|---|---|---|---|---|
| **D** | 75,712 (38%) | **D** | 73,330 (43 %) | **D** | 44,287 (27 %) |
| **R** | 121,708 (60%) | **R** | 97,001 (56 %) | **R** | 117,821 (72 %) |

## Campaign Finance

| | Receipts | Receipts from PACs | Expenditures |
|---|---|---|---|
| **1980** | | | |
| Rogers (R ) | $314,233 | $97,787 (31 %) | $313,974 |
| Marcum (D ) | $7,759 | — (0 %) | $4,788 |

## Key Vote

**97th Congress**

| | |
|---|---|
| Reagan budget proposal (1981) | Y |

---

**5th District: Southeast.** Population: 559,778 (22% increase since 1970). Race: White 544,977 (97%), Black 13,137 (2%), Others 1,664 (0.2%). Spanish origin: 4,528 (1%).

# 6 Larry J. Hopkins (R)

**Of Lexington — Elected 1978**

**Born:** Oct. 25, 1933, Detroit, Mich.
**Education:** Murray State U., 1951-54; Southern Methodist U., 1959; Purdue U., 1960; no degree.
**Military Career:** Marine Corps, 1954-56.
**Profession:** Investment counselor.
**Family:** Wife, Carolyn Pennebaker; three children.
**Religion:** Methodist.
**Political Career:** Ky. House, 1972-78; Ky. Senate, 1978-79; unsuccessful Republican nominee for Fayette County Commission, 1970.

**In Washington:** A primary job of legislators from this conservative district has always been to take care of tobacco, and Hopkins, the first Republican to represent the area in half a century, has stuck close to that role. Named to the Agriculture Committee, an assignment he asked for, he lobbied the Agriculture Department virtually non-stop to continue a program that showed farmers how to save money and labor by packaging their burley tobacco in a different way. If it was a dull issue in Washington, it was a significant one at home.

Otherwise, Hopkins was relatively inconspicuous in his first term. He gained some public relations advantage from his proposal to eliminate free parking for members of Congress and their staffs, which was not done. He also pressed for a federal study of a controversial new anti-arthritis drug.

Given a seat on the Armed Services Committee in the middle of his first term, Hopkins added a quiet vote to the panel's already massive pro-Pentagon majority. He generated a major news story one day in 1980 with repeated questioning of the Joint Chiefs of Staff. The chiefs, summoned to testify on President Carter's defense budget needs, were reluctant to say openly that more money was needed. Hopkins quietly asked the same question over and over again until Joint Chiefs Chairman David Jones conceded that a little extra money would be useful, and that was enough to produce front-page stories in most papers the next morning.

Hopkins' overall approach was as conservative as his Armed Services record. He did surprise a few of his colleagues, however, by voting to place strict limits on the amount of money political action committees could contribute to congressional campaigns. Only 28 other Republicans voted with him, and all of them were later subjected to harsh criticism from Minority Leader John J. Rhodes. Hopkins received more than $124,000 from PACs in the 1978 campaign, more than any other member who voted to restrict them. The extent of the contributions had been a public issue in the latter stages of that campaign.

**At Home:** The surprising defeat of Rep. John B. Breckinridge in the 1978 Democratic primary gave Republicans and Hopkins an opportunity they had not expected.

Considering Breckinridge unbeatable, neither Hopkins nor any other formidable Republican candidates had entered the GOP primary. But after Breckinridge lost to a more liberal Democrat, Republican leaders met and substituted Hopkins for the party's token candidate, a 68-year-old former state auditor. A popular state senator from Lexington, the district's largest city, Hopkins was able to mount an expensive television campaign to make up for his late start.

Over the previous decade, he had built a strong electoral base in his hometown. After running unsuccessfully for county commissioner, he was appointed county clerk of courts and then elected to the state Legislature.

His well-organized congressional campaign aimed its appeal at conservative farmers and blue-collar workers. Hopkins portrayed his opponent, maverick state Sen. Tom Easterly, as a pawn of the unions. In return, Easterly labeled the shuffling that put Hopkins in the contest a

> **6th District: North central — Lexington, Frankfort.** Population: 548,417 (19% increase since 1970). Race: White 499,382 (91%), Black 45,538 (8%), Others 3,497 (1%). Spanish origin: 3,334 (1%).

*Larry J. Hopkins, R-Ky*

Watergate-style maneuver.

But the Democrat was unable to heal the party divisions that resulted from his campaign against Breckinridge, and Hopkins outspent him by more than 2-to-1. Winning Fayette County (Lexington) by nearly 12,000 votes, Hopkins captured the seat with 51 percent to become the first Republican to represent the district since 1930.

Easterly tried again in 1980, but the rematch with Hopkins was anticlimactic. Easterly had offended some of his 1978 supporters by attempting to mute his liberal image, and Hopkins had solidified his base by developing an efficient constituent service operation. The incumbent won re-election by nearly 3-to-2.

**The District:** The 6th encompasses the heart of the Bluegrass region. Horse-breeding is important and tobacco is the main agricultural product.

The largest urban center is rapidly growing Lexington, the site of the University of Kentucky and numerous high-technology industries. The city is Republican, and the Cincinnati suburbs at the northern end of the district, added in 1972 redistricting, lean that way most of the time.

Until 1978, a strong Democratic vote in the state capital of Frankfort and the farming counties in the center of the district usually kept the 6th in the Democratic column by a narrow margin. Those days appear to be over.

## Committees

**Agriculture** (7th of 19 Republicans)
Livestock, Dairy, and Poultry; Tobacco and Peanuts.

**Armed Services** (14th of 19 Republicans)
Investigations; Military Personnel and Compensation.

## Elections

**1980 General**

| | |
|---|---|
| Larry Hopkins (R ) | 105,376 (59 %) |
| Tom Easterly (D ) | 72,473 (41 %) |

**1978 General**

| | |
|---|---|
| Larry Hopkins (R ) | 52,092 (51 %) |
| Tom Easterly (D ) | 47,436 (46 %) |

**District Vote For President**

| | 1980 | | 1976 | | 1972 |
|---|---|---|---|---|---|
| D | 93,244 (48%) | D | 88,195 (52%) | D | 50,883 (33%) |
| R | 89,234 (46%) | R | 77,765 (46%) | R | 101,473 (65%) |
| I | 8,067 (4%) | | | | |

## Campaign Finance

| | | Receipts | Receipts from PACs | Expen-ditures |
|---|---|---|---|---|
| **1980** | | | | |
| Hopkins (R ) | $376,335 | $132,458 (35 %) | $300,296 |
| Easterly (D ) | $77,021 | $22,500 (29 %) | $79,344 |

| 1978 | | | |
|---|---|---|---|
| Hopkins (R ) | $294,354 | $124,426 (42 %) | $291,920 |
| Easterly (D ) | $137,123 | $34,400 (25 %) | $134,770 |

## Voting Studies

| | Presidential Support | | Party Unity | | Conservative Coalition | |
|---|---|---|---|---|---|---|
| Year | S | O | S | O | S | O |
| 1980 | 40 | 56 | 85 | 13 | 89 | 7 |
| 1979 | 27 | 70 | 88 | 11 | 89 | 8 |

S = Support          O = Opposition

## Key Votes

**96th Congress**

| | |
|---|---|
| Weaken Carter oil profits tax (1979) | Y |
| Reject hospital cost control plan (1979) | Y |
| Implement Panama Canal Treaties (1979) | N |
| Establish Department of Education (1979) | N |
| Approve Anti-busing Amendment (1979) | Y |
| Guarantee Chrysler Corp. loans (1979) | N |
| Approve military draft registration (1980) | Y |
| Aid Sandinista regime in Nicaragua (1980) | N |
| Strengthen fair housing laws (1980) | N |

**97th Congress**

| | |
|---|---|
| Reagan budget proposal (1981) | Y |

## Interest Group Ratings

| Year | ADA | ACA | AFL-CIO | CCUS |
|---|---|---|---|---|
| 1980 | 6 | 87 | 22 | 73 |
| 1979 | 16 | 85 | 22 | 82 |

# 7 Carl D. Perkins (D)

**Of Hindman — Elected 1948**

**Born:** Oct. 15, 1912, Hindman, Ky.
**Education:** Attended Alice Lloyd College; Lees
    College; U. of Louisville, LL.B. 1935.
**Military Career:** U.S. Army, World War II.
**Profession:** Lawyer.
**Family:** Wife, Verna Johnson; one child.
**Religion:** Baptist.
**Political Career:** Commonwealth attorney, 31st
    judicial district of Ky., 1939; Ky. Assembly,
    1940; Knott County attorney, 1941-48.

**In Washington:** It used to be said of the
late Mendel Rivers, who chaired the House
Armed Services Committee, that if he put one
more military installation in his South Carolina
district, the district would sink.

Carl Perkins is the Mendel Rivers of social
programs. There are no shipyards or Air Force
bases in the hills of eastern Kentucky, but dozens
of federal programs provide education, job training, medical care and other services for which
Perkins' district qualifies automatically by virtue
of poverty. He has created many of the programs
himself in 14 years as chairman of the Education
and Labor Committee.

Perkins is sincere and even passionate in his
New Deal liberalism, but as representative of one
of the nation's poorest constituencies, he has an
interest more immediate than long-term social
policy goals. He knows that eastern Kentucky
cannot get much poorer, and treats modern con-
cepts like cost effectiveness as a luxury Appalachia cannot afford.

When it comes time to write an education or
job training bill, committee Democrats say, only
half in jest, they first find out what "Uncle Carl"
wants for Kentucky. Then they spread the rest of
the money into enough congressional districts in
other states to guarantee majority support.

In recent years, that has been a less successful formula, as House Democrats from throughout
the country have begun to question the bread-
and-butter liberalism of Perkins' generation. "We
have to hold fast to programs we've enacted in the
past," Perkins pleaded in the 96th Congress, "to
make sure they're not hamstrung by lack of
funds." But with much of Congress questioning
not only the funding but the basic need for
Perkins-style programs, the chairman and his
committee seem on the verge of isolation in the
House these days.

It was no small thing in 1980 when Perkins
acceded to language in the budget resolution
requiring $500-million worth of cuts in spending
for the school lunch program, which he fought for
as early as 1949 and shepherded through Congress
in the years of his chairmanship.

At first, Perkins questioned the Budget Committee's right even to mandate such changes. But
he cooperated with Democratic leaders and
moved the cuts through his committee, even raising his hand to support them himself when every
other Democrat on the committee refused to do
so. And the cuts were implemented.

But he was not nearly so cooperative in 1981,
when the Reagan administration decided to make
major cuts not only in school lunch but in most of
the programs under the committee's jurisdiction.
The chairman called 24 days of hearings, summoning dozens of impoverished beneficiaries of
the programs to testify on what the Reagan reductions would do to them. Then the committee met
and blatantly rejected the whole idea, recommending that spending in its field actually be
*increased*, to a level $4 billion higher than even
President Carter had wanted.

Eventually, the full House dictated the cuts
anyway. When Perkins called a committee session
to do the job, he began it by saying that "we are
meeting with a gun pointed at our heads."

Perkins still had not given up. Among the
committee's $12 billion in spending reductions, he

---

**7th District: East — Ashland.** Population: 566,456 (23% increase since 1970). Race:
White 558,719 (99%), Black 6,492 (1%), Others 1,245 (0.2%). Spanish origin: 3,845 (1%).

---

## Carl D. Perkins, D-Ky.

deliberately included some of the most popular programs, such as Head Start. He figured they would be restored on the House floor. But Democratic leaders told him that was a dangerous assumption, and the committee went back and switched some of the reductions to public jobs programs. In the end, the House accepted even more massive Reagan-backed spending cuts.

Perkins speaks slowly and softly, and wears a perpetual grin, but it is possible to enrage him, as President Carter learned by including two Kentucky dams on his original list of federal water projects to be terminated. Carter eventually restored funding for the one in Perkins' district, the Yatesville dam, but the chairman remained bitter about the episode throughout Carter's term. He was not pleased when the Reagan administration — generally friendly to water projects — proposed terminating money for Yatesville early in 1981.

When Perkins joined the committee in the 1950s, it was controlled by a conservative Southern chairman and a coalition of Republicans and Southern Democrats that blocked social spending.

That changed in 1961, when Adam Clayton Powell of New York became chairman, but the committee produced only a limited amount of social legislation until 1965, when it was crucial to passage of most of Lyndon B. Johnson's Great Society programs. In 1965, Perkins was chairman of the General Education Subcommittee, and floor manager for the first major bill providing federal aid to primary and secondary education.

In 1967, the situation changed again. Powell had outraged congressional colleagues with his journeys to Caribbean pleasure spots at taxpayer expense, and he was denied his seat in the 90th Congress. Perkins became chairman of the full Education and Labor Committee just as it was preparing to write crucial anti-poverty bills.

Viewed by many as a hillbilly lawyer not sophisticated enough for the job, Perkins surprised colleagues by managing the legislation adroitly on the House floor. He picked off Southern Democratic votes one by one, asking favors on a personal basis or making minor concessions to hold votes. In the end, Johnson got most of his 1967 anti-poverty authorization through the House virtually intact. In the years that followed, Perkins turned the committee into an open spigot for social programs, ranging across the spectrum of problems from black lung disease and asbestos in school buildings to battered wives and youth unemployment. It was the Education and Labor Committee that fought for and eventually produced the Humphrey-Hawkins full employment program, although by the time it became law it

was reduced to an unemployment "target" of 4 percent, without any mechanism for bringing it about.

In 1979, the committee even produced a $200 billion synthetic fuels bill, largely at the insistence of Perkins, who for years has been a promoter of coal gasification (his district has large deposits of coal). It was an excellent symbol, not only of Perkins' pork barrel style and generosity with federal dollars, but of the committee's isolation in a conservative time. Many saw it as a joke, and it was soon forgotten.

**At Home:** Perkins has not had a serious challenge in a quarter century. He worked hard in the beginning to entrench himself, returning virtually every weekend to his mountainous eastern Kentucky district, and by the end of the first decade, his re-election was simply automatic. Since then, the federal help he has brought to the district has kept him impregnable. Perkins was active in local politics before he ran for Congress in 1948. The Democrats had lost the seat in 1946, when veteran Rep. A. J. May, implicated in a bribery scandal, was unseated by Republican W. Howes Meade.

Perkins quit his position as counsel for the state department of highways to make the 1948 House race. Backed by Gov. Earle C. Clements, he won the Democratic primary and had little trouble ousting Meade in the general election.

Perkins did not win his early re-election campaigns by landslide margins. But with the support of the United Mine Workers and his own defense of the tobacco industry, he soon built up his percentages. His only close call came in 1956, when Eisenhower swept the district and forced Perkins' margin down to 7,100 votes.

Until 1980, Republicans managed to field a challenger to Perkins every two years, but never a serious one. The incumbent's combined expenses in 1976 and 1978 amounted to less than $6,000.

**The District:** The 7th District stretches like an arrowhead into poverty-stricken Appalachia. Tobacco, cattle and fruit are major products in the rolling hill country of the north, with natural gas and coal found in the mountains of the southeast. A sprinkling of petrochemical and steel plants surround Ashland, the district's only population center.

While the district is one of the poorest in the nation, it ironically was the fastest-growing district in Kentucky in the 1970s. The population grew by more than 20 percent in the decade, as many former residents were lured back to their old hometowns by a revival of the coal industry and a decline in automobile industry jobs in the urban Midwest. This reversed an earlier period of heavy out-migration provoked by the failure of the coal industry in the 1950s.

With the Mine Workers a major force in politics, the 7th is a Democratic bastion. It has supported the party presidential nominee in five of the last six elections, failing only in 1972.

## Committees

**Education and Labor** (Chairman)
  Elementary, Secondary and Vocational Education; chairman.

## Elections

**1980 General**

Carl Perkins (D)                                         Unopposed

**1980 Primary**

| | |
|---|---|
| Carl Perkins (D) | 30,722 (89 %) |
| Ray Adkins (R) | 5,056 (14 %) |

**1978 General**

| | |
|---|---|
| Carl Perkins (D ) | 51,559 (76 %) |
| Granville Thomas (R) | 15,861 (24 %) |

**Previous Winning Percentages**

| | | | |
|---|---|---|---|
| 1976 (73 %) | 1974 (76 %) | 1972 (62 %) | 1970 (75 %) |
| 1968 (62 %) | 1966 (69 %) | 1964 (70 %) | 1962 (57 %) |
| 1960 (56 %) | 1958 (66 %) | 1956 (52 %) | 1954 (60 %) |
| 1952 (58 %) | 1950 (56 %) | 1948 (61 %) | |

**District Vote For President**

| | 1980 | | 1976 | | 1972 |
|---|---|---|---|---|---|
| D | 104,612 (55 %) | D | 104,133 (60 %) | D | 67,023 (42 %) |
| R | 81,826 (43 %) | R | 66,841 (39 %) | R | 92,965 (58 %) |

## Campaign Finance

| | Receipts | Receipts from PACs | Expen- ditures |
|---|---|---|---|
| **1980** | | | |
| Perkins (D ) | $0 | — (0%) | $0 |

## Voting Studies

| | Presidential Support | | Party Unity | | Conservative Coalition | |
|---|---|---|---|---|---|---|
| **Year** | **S** | **O** | **S** | **O** | **S** | **O** |
| 1980 | 55 | 41 | 70 | 27 | 54 | 43 |
| 1979 | 61 | 39 | 74 | 23 | 51 | 44 |
| 1978 | 69 | 28 | 81 | 16 | 35 | 62 |
| 1977 | 73 | 24 | 83 | 15 | 36 | 60 |
| 1976 | 37 | 63 | 85 | 14 | 35 | 65 |
| 1975 | 37 | 60 | 80 | 19 | 36 | 63 |
| 1974 (Ford) | 50 | 50 | | | | |
| 1974 | 58 | 42 | 81 | 19 | 37 | 63 |
| 1973 | 38 | 62 | 84 | 16 | 38 | 61 |
| 1972 | 51 | 43 | 78 | 16 | 32 | 65 |
| 1971 | 56 | 44 | 84 | 16 | 42 | 58 |
| 1970 | 71 | 29 | 82 | 18 | 36 | 64 |

| | | | | | |
|---|---|---|---|---|---|
| 1969 | 62 | 36 | 85 | 15 | 42 | 58 |
| 1968 | 84 | 16 | 83 | 17 | 33 | 67 |
| 1967 | 91 | 9 | 96 | 4 | 17 | 83 |
| 1966 | 94 | 6 | 99 | 1 | 11 | 89 |
| 1965 | 95 | 5 | 95 | 4 | 12 | 88 |
| 1964 | 87 | 12 | 82 | 15 | 42 | 58 |
| 1963 | 94 | 6 | 95 | 3 | 20 | 80 |
| 1962 | 88 | 12 | 91 | 9 | 19 | 81 |
| 1961 | 89 | 11 | 90 | 10 | 30 | 70 |

S = Support          O = Opposition

## Key Votes

**96th Congress**

| | |
|---|---|
| Weaken Carter oil profits tax (1979) | Y |
| Reject hospital cost control plan (1979) | N |
| Implement Panama Canal Treaties (1979) | N |
| Establish Department of Education (1979) | Y |
| Approve Anti-busing Amendment (1979) | N |
| Guarantee Chrysler Corp. loans (1979) | Y |
| Approve military draft registration (1980) | N |
| Aid Sandinista regime in Nicaragua (1980) | N |
| Strengthen fair housing laws (1980) | N |

**97th Congress**

| | |
|---|---|
| Reagan budget proposal (1981) | N |

## Interest Group Ratings

| Year | ADA | ACA | AFL-CIO | CCUS |
|---|---|---|---|---|
| 1980 | 56 | 29 | 83 | 63 |
| 1979 | 58 | 15 | 70 | 33 |
| 1978 | 45 | 23 | 67 | 33 |
| 1977 | 40 | 15 | 91 | 18 |
| 1976 | 60 | 11 | 96 | 13 |
| 1975 | 58 | 29 | 91 | 12 |
| 1974 | 43 | 20 | 100 | 10 |
| 1973 | 60 | 15 | 100 | 27 |
| 1972 | 38 | 24 | 100 | 10 |
| 1971 | 57 | 28 | 92 | - |
| 1970 | 40 | 21 | 86 | 0 |
| 1969 | 40 | 18 | 70 | - |
| 1968 | 50 | 9 | 100 | - |
| 1967 | 73 | 3 | 100 | 10 |
| 1966 | 82 | 7 | 92 | - |
| 1965 | 68 | 4 | - | 20 |
| 1964 | 80 | 11 | 100 | - |
| 1963 | - | 6 | - | - |
| 1962 | 88 | 9 | 91 | - |
| 1961 | 80 | - | - | - |

# Louisiana

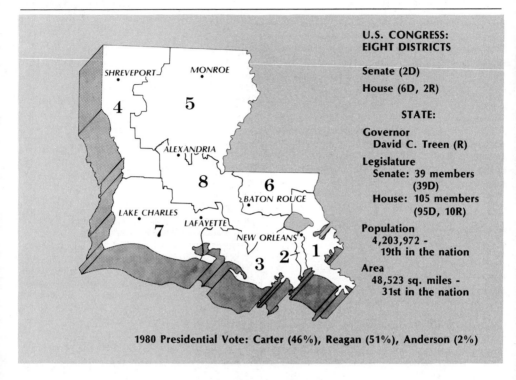

**U.S. CONGRESS:**
**EIGHT DISTRICTS**

**Senate (2D)**
**House (6D, 2R)**

**STATE:**

**Governor**
**David C. Treen (R)**

**Legislature**
**Senate: 39 members**
**(39D)**
**House: 105 members**
**(95D, 10R)**

**Population**
**4,203,972 -**
**19th in the nation**

**Area**
**48,523 sq. miles -**
**31st in the nation**

**1980 Presidential Vote: Carter (46%), Reagan (51%), Anderson (2%)**

## ...Sui Generis

It is said that Huey P. Long, seemingly fast asleep one night as a group of reporters took turns analyzing him in his hotel room, suddenly sat bolt upright and gave them some advice: "Why don't you just say I'm *sui generis* and leave it at that?" One might apply that advice to his entire state, then and now.

In other Deep South states, political divisions have occurred within a traditional Anglo-Saxon framework. The basic splits have been between poor and rich, farms and cities, lowlands and hill country. But in Louisiana, the large Catholic population of French descent has added religious and ethnic cleavages, leaving a combustible mixture that bears little resemblance to politics anywhere else in the country.

The Cajuns, as they are known, dominate south Louisiana. Anglo-Saxon Protestants dominate the northern half of the state. For years, the two regions battled fairly evenly for influence.

But in the last decade, money, population and political power have clearly moved southward.

The energy crisis in the early 1970s rekindled oil and gas exploration in Louisiana, with a boom in activity in the Gulf of Mexico off the southern coast. Attracted by high-paying jobs in oil and related industries, thousands of newcomers have flocked into mineral-rich southern Louisiana, bringing about a minor population boom.

The population movement has helped southern Louisiana voters elect the last two governors, though they have chosen two entirely different men. Edwin W. Edwards (1972-80) was a French-speaking Cajun Democrat; Republican David C. Treen represents conservative, middle-class suburban New Orleans. But neither spoke for the rural Protestant parishes of North Louisiana which dominated gubernatorial elections in the past. The north still has both U.S. senators, Bennett Johnston and Russell B. Long, but power seems to be shifting the other way, even if it is shifting in two different directions.

Treen's election in 1979 was a breakthrough for the GOP, which had no governors in this century before him. But GOP advances are still hindered by a strong Democratic coalition that includes blacks (29 percent of the voting age population), rural populists and a persistent labor movement. Republican Senate candidates have yet to draw more than 30 percent of the vote, and the GOP U.S. House representation, which reached three in 1978, fell back to two in 1980.

# A Political Tour

**New Orleans and Environs.** With a rich mixture of ethnic groups and a Mardi Gras spirit that lasts all year, New Orleans is one of the most fabled and colorful cities in the United States.

From 1820 to 1950, New Orleans was the most populous city in the South. Today, shipping and tourism are the linchpins of the local economy. Although more than 100 miles up the Mississippi River from the Gulf of Mexico, the city ranks second behind New York in value of cargo handled. Every year thousands of visitors come to hear Dixieland jazz and stroll the French Quarter.

A steady exodus of whites following integration in 1960 enabled blacks to gain a majority two decades later. The first black was elected to public office in 1967, and now the city has a black mayor, Ernest Morial.

The increasing black complexion of New Orleans has strengthened traditional Democratic voting habits. It was one of the few cities in the nation to give Jimmy Carter a higher share of the vote in 1980 (57 percent) than 1976 (55 percent).

While the population of New Orleans fell 6 percent in the last decade, white flight and the oil boom brought about swift growth in the suburban areas. The three parishes that border New Orleans on the south and west are all much more conservative than the city. All three voted for Treen in 1979 and Reagan in 1980.

Jefferson Parish on the west is the most populous with 455,000 — just 100,000 people fewer than New Orleans. It is a mix of white-collar commuters and blue-collar shipbuilders and oil workers. St. Bernard on the south and east has a growing blue-collar population that is similar to the expanding working-class neighborhoods on the marshy east side of New Orleans.

Wedged between Jefferson and St. Bernard parishes is sleepy Plaquemines, the long-time bailiwick of the legendary arch-segregationist, Leander Perez. Although it lies in New Orleans'

orbit, Plaquemines is still a lightly populated rural parish that sits on some of the richest reserves of oil, gas and sulphur in the state.

**Florida Parishes.** North from New Orleans across Lake Pontchartrain and east of the meandering Mississippi River are the eight Florida parishes, so named because they were part of Spanish Florida until 1810. Culturally, this area is more similar to neighboring Mississippi than to the rest of the Bayou State.

The population center of the region is the state capital of Baton Rouge. Growing 32 percent in the 1970s, it has eclipsed Shreveport as the second largest city in Louisiana. The politics of Baton Rouge are influenced by a large academic and blue-collar population. Louisiana State University and Southern University, the state's largest black college, provide the academic vote. The blue-collar vote comes from the unionized workers in many the refineries and petrochemical plants that line the Mississippi River.

Among the Florida Parishes, the most rapid suburban expansion has occured in Livingston and St. Tammany parishes. The latter, a popular home for New Orleans oil executives, led the state in population growth in the 1970s. Much of the rest of the region is taken over by pine forests and farm land. The large black population usually keeps the more rural parts of this area safely in the Democratic column, while some of the suburban areas are reliably Republican.

**Acadiana.** West and south of Baton Rouge is one of the most unusual areas of the Deep South — Cajun Louisiana. In a region of the country dominated by Anglo-Saxon Protestants, south Louisiana is French Catholic.

The Cajuns — a slurring of "Acadians" — are the descendants of 15,000 French settlers who moved south from Acadia (Nova Scotia) in the 18th century rather than pledge loyalty to England. Their adopted homeland became Acadiana, a triangular-shaped region with Alexandria forming the apex and the base running along the Gulf from the Mississippi River to the Texas border.

Gallic culture still permeates with French still being the primary language in some places. Although there is a sizable black population in parts of Acadiana, the heavily Catholic Cajuns have been less preoccupied with race than whites in northern Louisiana.

Nearly 30 percent of Louisiana's population lives in Acadiana, primarily in small towns and along bayous and waterways. There is no city larger than 100,000. Acadiana, though, is rich in natural resources. In the east, near the Mississippi River, most of the nation's sugar cane is raised. Central Acadiana near Lafayette is one of the nation's leading suppliers of sweet potatoes. To the west is the Louisiana rice bowl.

But the dominant feature of the economy these days is oil. With offshore oil work commanding high wages, there has been a large influx of prosperous oilworkers settling in the coastal parishes. The Cajun cultural center of Lafayette and other fast-growing coastal towns have developed GOP voting patterns in recent years.

The western part of Acadiana by east Texas is part Cajun and part cowboy. The main city is Lake Charles, a rice-exporting port with more than 30 petrochemical plants. As the most heavily unionized part of Louisiana west of the Mississippi, Calcasieu Parish (Lake Charles) has remained in the Democratic column.

**North Louisiana.** The northern half of Louisiana seems more like the Deep South than the Cajun country or New Orleans. According to an old saying, upcountry Louisiana is "nothing but poor folk, Protestants and pine trees."

Some oil and natural gas wells are located in the north, but the great boom seems to be over. The area today lacks the abundance of high-paying jobs prevalent in other parts of the South. The population growth in the upcountry has been much slower than in the rest of the state.

The economy of northern Louisiana still relies heavily on cotton, timber and livestock. Cotton is grown in the lands along the Mississippi River in the east and the Red River in the west. Both areas have some of the heaviest concentrations of blacks in the northern part of the state.

Inland, many of the early settlers were small farmers and Jacksonian Democrats. Foes of the wealthy cotton and sugar planters, they spawned the populism that early this century molded the political thinking of Huey Long, a native son.

After World War II, the north became a bulwark of states' rights and opposition to integration. In recent years, the major population centers and predominantly white parishes of the rural upcountry have been voting Republican. Only the parishes with large black constituencies have remained consistently Democratic.

The leading urban center of northern Louisiana is Shreveport, the third largest city in the state (pop. 206,000). Once a cotton market and then a center of oil and gas operations in northwest Louisiana, Shreveport has diversified in recent years.

Shreveport's strong middle-class and the military presence in nearby Bossier Parish have made the area a conservative Republican stronghold. But blacks now comprise 41 percent of the city population and industrialization has given organized labor a toehold.

# Redrawing the Lines

At midyear, one Louisiana observer said redistricting was "at the cocktail napkin stage," with legislators sketching a few ideas over drinks. The state's congressional delegation had suggested a plan that kept them safe.

The New Orleans-Jefferson County 2nd District of Rep. Lindy Boggs needs to gain 63,000 people. Growth in Baton Rouge and its suburbs bloated the 6th District into the state's largest, followed by the southern coastal 3rd and 7th Districts. North Louisiana's districts did not keep pace with the state's overall 15 percent growth.

# Governor
# David C. Treen (R)

**Born:** July 16, 1928, Baton Rouge, La.
**Home:** New Orleans, La.
**Education:** Tulane U., B.A. 1948; LL.B. 1950.
**Military Career:** Air Force, 1950-52; Counsel in courts-martial.
**Profession:** Lawyer.
**Family:** Wife, Dolores; three children.
**Religion:** Methodist.
**Political Career:** Unsuccessful campaigns for U.S. House, 1962, 1964, 1968; unsuccessful campaign for governor, 1972; U.S. House, 1973-80; elected governor 1979; term expires March 1984.

# Russell B. Long (D)

**Of Baton Rouge — Elected 1948**

**Born:** Nov. 3, 1918, Shreveport, La.
**Education:** La. State U., B.A. 1941, LL.B. 1942.
**Military Career:** Navy, 1942-45.
**Profession:** Lawyer.
**Family:** Wife, Carolyn Bason; two children.
**Religion:** Methodist.
**Political Career:** No previous office.

**In Washington:** Old habits die hard. During a roll call in the Senate Finance Committee early in the 97th Congress, it was Russell Long — not Robert Dole — who answered automatically when the clerk called out "Mr. Chairman."

The slip was scarcely surprising, for Long served 15 years as chairman of the committee before his tenure was ended by the Republican takeover of the Senate. No other outgoing chairman had held power that long, and none had used it as skillfully. Nor does any other ex-chairman retain as much operational influence as Long, who gets along famously with his successor — just as he does with nearly everyone else.

Dole and Long agree on most matters within the Finance Committee's jurisdiction and work together comfortably. Long is a crucial ally, even if he is not always an easy one to handle. "Having Russell Long on your side," a lobbyist for the Carter White House once said, "is kind of like running through a jungle being chained to a gorilla. Ain't nobody gonna bother you, but it's not an altogether pleasant journey."

Huey P. Long's son has been taking the Senate for a ride during most of the 32 years he has been in it, and it has been a fascinating trip for passengers and spectators alike.

It is not true that Long never loses; in his early days as Finance chairman, when he had to face Wilbur D. Mills of Arkansas in House-Senate tax conferences, he lost more than his share of the time. And if he had had his own way, there would have been no windfall profits tax on the oil industry in the 96th Congress.

But Long is almost never *seen* to lose. He has an almost uncanny ability to spot a nascent consensus in the Senate's maelstrom of conflicting views on any given issue, locate a center that will hold, and occupy it at precisely the right moment. There are few matters about which he feels strongly, and on those he calls in his chits. No one in recent memory has had a bigger supply. "In politics," Long says, "you must help your friends or you won't have any."

Long has always had plenty of friends to call on and not only because of past favors. Even those who bitterly oppose him find it impossible to dislike the man. He has an irrepressible sense of humor and an inexhaustible supply of down-home stories that he uses to take the steam out of an over-heated argument. He is refreshingly candid in a body where circumlocution is the norm. He can summarize a complicated issue with an instant metaphor so apt it makes one wonder what he might have been like as a writer of fiction.

It has been said that Long would give away everything but the Capitol Dome to nail down a vote and is still looking for a method to pry off the dome. That may be a slight exaggeration, but Long once did trade his father's old desk in the Senate chamber for a vote for majority whip in the 89th Congress — a race he won. "I think my father probably would have approved," he said later.

The votes he takes most seriously are those in support of programs and policies — especially tax policies — beneficial to Louisiana and its economic mainstay, the oil and gas industry. What is good for the industry is often good for Russell Long as well, since he inherited valuable oil royalties from his father. That coincidence of interests has never embarrassed him.

It was Long's fate in recent years to chair the Finance Committee at a time of public resentment against the oil industry. Success in the late 70s consisted essentially in holding off efforts to revise the generous tax treatment the industry has traditionally enjoyed.

Long has been an especially good friend of independent oil producers, now the industry's strongest force. He was unable to prevent repeal of the percentage depletion allowance for the major companies in 1975, but he protected it for

**479**

the independents. He was unable to block Congress from enacting a windfall profits tax in 1980, but he saw to it that independents were treated more favorably than the majors.

The essence of Long's career at Finance has been strategy and skillful management. He has undertaken relatively few personal legislative initiatives, especially for someone who has been in the Senate as long as he has. The ones that stand out are the voluntary tax check-off provision that provides the funds for public financing of presidential campaigns, the earned income tax credit, which benefits the working poor and the tax credit program for companies that offer employee stock ownership plans (ESOP).

Long's modus operandi as Finance chairman was nearly all carrot and no stick. At one time or another, virtually every senator discovers that the tax code is hideously unfair to some particularly important constituent who expects him to get it changed. Long has always been happy to help. "What is a loophole?" he once asked. "That is something that benefits the other guy. If it benefits you, it is tax reform." Critics have railed for years at his willingness to carve out special provisions in the code, insisting that revenue foregone through these exceptions be labeled "tax expenditures." Such semantic exercises never perturbed Long. "I've always known that what we're doing is giving government money away," he has admitted cheerfully.

He also acknowledges that tax preferences are less than a matter of ideology to him. They are the legislative tool the Finance Committee happens to possess under the rules. So he uses it. "When it comes to helping homeowners," he once said, "if I were on the Banking Committee I'd favor a loan guarantee for them because that would be in my jurisdiction, but since I'm on the Finance Committee, I favor the use of tax credits."

Tax bills, liberally festooned with favors for his fellow committee members, have always had a way of emerging from Long's committee at the last possible moment before a congressional recess or adjournment. They acquired additional ornaments on the Senate floor, as the chairman grandly announced he would be "happy to take that amendment to conference." And then the real fun began — in conference sessions with the House.

In the post-Mills era, Long has usually been the dominant force at these conferences, generously agreeing to drop Senate floor amendments he never intended to keep anyway. In many cases, he has been the one legislator who had his mind on the conference when the others were worrying

about the floor debate.

"The House sees Russell Long coming at it with a *freight car full* of, let's say, 'shinola,'" a House aide once explained, "and it gets so terrified it's going to have to eat the whole load that when it's finally presented with just a *small brown paper bag full*, it gobbles it down gratefully." But the small bag nearly always has contained virtually every provision that Long really cared about.

Loss of the chairmanship clearly put something of a crimp in Long's style, since it is Dole — not he — who took over most of the power to grant and withhold legislative favors. But Long still knows the tax code better than any other member of Congress. He is second only to Robert C. Byrd — if he is second to anyone — in his mastery of parliamentary procedure. And when it comes to senior members, at least, he still has an unmatched psychological knowledge of the tactics individual senators respond to.

Long had a period of eclipse once before, in the 1960s, for a much different reason. Elected whip in 1965, he handled the job poorly, in the opinion of many colleagues. He was drinking heavily at the time, and Democrats found him unreliable in a job that was supposed to focus on handling day-to-day details. Four years later, he lost it to Edward M. Kennedy, who in turn was beaten by Robert C. Byrd in 1971.

The current eclipse is unlikely to be more than partial. Much of the Reagan administration's economic policy is in tune with Long's own biases. Although he differs with the president over the specifics of a tax cut package, the senator shares Reagan's fundamental commitment to enlarging the American pie. Unlike his populist father, who terrified the business community with his "share the wealth" crusade, Long sees no need to play Robin Hood.

"My father was a revolutionary. I'm more of an evolutionary," he said once. "I wouldn't get there by making the rich any poorer than they are now. . . . If you're going to redistribute the wealth that way, you've got to do it with force of arms. . . . I'd simply double the wealth of the country and spread it around more evenly."

**At Home:** The senator actually was born Huey Pierce Long Jr., but his father changed the name because, he said, he did not want his son to inherit his enemies. When Russell was 16, an assassin killed Huey Long in Baton Rouge.

For most of his career, Russell Long has had the support of the conservative Louisiana business community that feared his father. Well-financed and confident of his statewide backing, he never has had to build an organization of his own.

After coming home from World War II, Long worked briefly for his uncle Earl, then preparing to run for governor. When Sen. John Overton, a Long ally, died in 1948, Russell filed as a candidate in the special election, even though he was not yet 30 years old. He took the primary narrowly over Judge Robert F. Kennon, who learned of his defeat while riding in a victory parade in New Orleans.

Five times, Long won re-election effortlessly. In 1980, however, he had a significant challenge, fueled by complaints that he had lost touch with the state and by his vote to ratify the Panama Canal treaties. State Rep. Louis (Woody) Jenkins, a conservative with the support of the Moral Majority, accused Long of failing to use his chairmanship to cut taxes and curb deficits more sharply. Long took nothing for granted and spent a vast sum on television advertising that blended references to his seniority with nostalgia for his father. Long captured all but a handful of the state's 64 parishes, although Jenkins held him to less than 60 percent of the vote — a position Long was unaccustomed to.

## Committees

**Commerce, Science and Transportation** (2nd of 8 Democrats)
Merchant Marine; Surface Transportation.

**Finance** (Ranking Democrat)
Health; Social Security and Income Maintenance Programs; Taxaton and Debt Management.

**Joint Taxation**

## Elections

**1980 Primary**

| | |
|---|---|
| Russell Long (D) | 484,770 (58%) |
| Louis Jenkins (D) | 325,922 (39%) |

* In Louisiana the primary is open to candidates of both parties. If a candidate receives 50% or more of the vote in the primary no general election is held.

**Previous Winning Percentages**

| | | | |
|---|---|---|---|
| 1974 (100%) | 1968 (100%) | 1962 (76%) | 1956 (100%) |
| 1950 (88%) | 1948* (75%) | | |

* Special election to fill an unexpired term.

## Campaign Finance

| | Receipts | Receipts from PACs | Expenditures |
|---|---|---|---|
| 1980 | | | |
| Long (D) | $2,035,347 | $445,910 (22%) | $2,166,838 |
| Jenkins (D) | $236,835 | — (0%) | $237,242 |

## Voting Studies

| | Presidential Support | | Party Unity | | Conservative Coalition | |
|---|---|---|---|---|---|---|
| Year | S | O | S | O | S | O |
| 1980 | 45 | 28 | 35 | 27 | 55 | 8 |
| 1979 | 60 | 30 | 47 | 32 | 66 | 10 |
| 1978 | 57 | 32 | 52 | 36 | 58 | 28 |
| 1977 | 59 | 32 | 39 | 46 | 72 | 12 |
| 1976 | 49 | 34 | 34 | 51 | 76 | 15 |
| 1975 | 67 | 22 | 39 | 46 | 63 | 17 |
| 1974 (Ford) | 51 | 38 | | | | |

| | | | | | | |
|---|---|---|---|---|---|---|
| 1974 | 48 | 30 | 36 | 39 | 57 | 19 |
| 1973 | 48 | 47 | 51 | 37 | 59 | 28 |
| 1972 | 67 | 20 | 35 | 48 | 68 | 16 |
| 1971 | 54 | 26 | 49 | 32 | 69 | 12 |
| 1970 | 54 | 26 | 37 | 37 | 64 | 10 |
| 1969 | 47 | 31 | 38 | 45 | 77 | 7 |
| 1968 | 36 | 38 | 48 | 23 | 57 | 19 |
| 1967 | 67 | 21 | 62 | 28 | 64 | 25 |

S = Support    O = Opposition

## Key Votes

**96th Congress**

| | |
|---|---|
| Maintain relations with Taiwan (1979) | ? |
| Reduce synthetic fuel development funds (1979) | N |
| Impose nuclear plant moratorium (1979) | ? |
| Kill stronger windfall profits tax (1979) | Y |
| Guarantee Chrysler Corp. loans (1979) | Y |
| Approve military draft registration (1980) | ? |
| End Revenue Sharing to the states (1980) | Y |
| Block Justice Dept. busing suits (1980) | Y |

**97th Congress**

| | |
|---|---|
| Restore urban program funding cuts (1981) | N |

## Interest Group Ratings

| Year | ADA | ACA | AFL-CIO | CCUS-1 | CCUS-2 |
|---|---|---|---|---|---|
| 1980 | 28 | 29 | 50 | 73 | |
| 1979 | 11 | 32 | 63 | 13 | 54 |
| 1978 | 25 | 47 | 29 | 72 | |
| 1977 | 15 | 46 | 59 | 67 | |
| 1976 | 25 | 55 | 31 | 50 | |
| 1975 | 22 | 48 | 47 | 67 | |
| 1974 | 10 | 67 | 38 | 63 | |
| 1973 | 35 | 41 | 82 | 50 | |
| 1972 | 15 | 45 | 43 | 44 | |
| 1971 | 19 | 61 | 67 | - | |
| 1970 | 13 | 67 | 25 | 50 | |
| 1969 | 0 | 67 | 10 | - | |
| 1968 | 0 | 76 | 0 | - | |
| 1967 | 23 | 23 | 36 | 60 | |

# J. Bennett Johnston (D)

## Of Shreveport — Elected 1972

**Born:** June 10, 1932, Shreveport, La.
**Education:** Attended Washington and Lee U., 1950-51 and 1952-53; attended U.S. Military Academy 1951-52; La. State U., LL.B. 1956.
**Military Career:** Army, 1956-59.
**Profession:** Lawyer.
**Family:** Wife, Mary Gunn; four children.
**Religion:** Baptist.
**Political Career:** La. House, 1964-68; La. Senate, 1968-72; sought Democratic nomination for governor, 1972.

In Washington: Johnston has been publicly overshadowed by his better-known colleague, Russell Long, but he has emerged as a Senate power in his own right, especially in the energy field.

Johnston all but ran the Energy Committee during the 96th Congress, with the consent and encouragement of former Chairman Henry M. Jackson, who was preoccupied with the SALT II treaty and other national security interests.

When the GOP won control of the Senate, Johnston had to take a back seat again, but a fair portion of his influence remains, partly because his market-oriented energy approach is in tune with the Senate's new conservative majority. He works smoothly with the new energy chairman, Republican James A. McClure of Idaho, as well as with Jackson, still his nominal Democratic superior.

In 1981, he tried to rescue Republicans from a budget dilemma over money for the strategic petroleum reserve, the giant pools of oil stored underground for emergencies. No one could figure how to budget the $3 billion spent each year to fill up the reserves. Johnston suggested a magic act: define the money as neither budget nor deficit. When it was protested that that was not exactly honest, Johnston cheerily agreed, adding it was the most "straightforwardly dishonest" solution he could think of.

In the Carter administration, Johnston worked with Republican Pete Domenici of New Mexico to push much of the president's energy program through a skeptical committee and Senate, patiently reshaping it along the way to placate a complex coterie of special interests.

An often dull public speaker, Johnston showed quick wit and persuasiveness during exhausting struggles over such programs as synthetic fuels, natural gas policy, the proposed Energy Mobilization Board and standby gas rationing. He mastered the details of energy policy and the tactics of trading votes. The bargains he struck generally left all parties with something to show for their efforts — provided they stayed alert while the deal was being cut. There is a streak of riverboat gambler in Johnston.

Although Johnston predictably looks out for the oil and gas industries, he is less closely tied to their interests than Long and other oil state senators. He is sensitive about the identification. "Oil state senator? I think that's inaccurate," Johnston said recently. "I have voted many times against the position of big oil."

Johnston has been a strong supporter of synthetic fuels development subsidies, opposed by some of the oil industry as unnecessary government intervention in the market. And he startled some colleagues in 1979 when he urged a 50-cent-a-gallon tax on gasoline as an energy conservation measure. He came back in 1981 with a new gas tax idea as an alternative to a standby gas rationing plan.

On the other hand, he was with the industry in voting against Carter's major energy bill in 1978, even though he was the one who negotiated much of the final compromise. Johnston said he voted against it because "the people in my state opposed it." The industry wanted immediate gas deregulation rather than the gradual pace in the final measure. Johnston pointed out that his vote was not needed to pass the bill anyway.

When Johnston arrived in the Senate in 1973, he hesitated about joining the Interior Committee, precursor of the Energy Committee, because aides warned him Jackson could be dictatorial and difficult. But Long persuaded his junior colleague that Louisiana needed representation on the panel, and Johnston proved to have no problems getting along with Jackson.

Johnston's influence on energy issues was somewhat enhanced in the 96th Congress because he was chairman of the Appropriations Subcommittee on Energy and Water Development. But much of his activity on that panel was devoted to fighting White House efforts to halt various water projects to which Carter objected.

On the Budget Committee, Johnston typically votes with Republicans and conservative Democrats in favor of higher defense spending and against protecting earlier, more generous outlays for social programs. In 1981, he joined a loose alliance of conservative Democrats supporting President Reagan's proposed budget cuts.

Johnston's fiscal conservatism was tested in 1979 when he served as chairman of the Senate Office Building Commission, charged with trying to hold down costs on the new Hart Building. When the project was authorized in 1972, the cost was estimated at $47.9 million. By July, 1978, the figure had risen to $174.5 million. Johnston ordered a lid of $137.7 million and threatened to fire the Capitol architect if it went higher.

For most of his career, Johnston has stayed out of the spotlight on one of the more emotional issues of recent years, court-ordered busing. Although he generally has voted against busing — quietly — he did not take a lead until busing came to Baton Rouge. Then, in the summer of 1981, Johnston stepped forth with his own anti-busing amendment tailor-made for the Louisiana case, to bar federal courts from ordering a student assigned or bused to a public school other than the one closest to home.

He called it the Neighborhood School Act and, to meet the Baton Rouge problem, drafted it to allow the attorney general to file lawsuits on behalf of students who contend they are bused in violation of federal law. At midyear, the issue still was unresolved.

One quality Johnston has always shared with Russell Long, his senior Louisiana colleague, is a desire to stay in the Senate for as many years as it takes to become a force in it. "I won't say I intend to run until they carry me out in a box," he once said, "but I would like a long career in the Senate. I find it personally satisfying."

**At Home:** Another 5,000 votes would have made Johnston governor of Louisiana in 1972. Rather than slowing him down, however, Johnston's near-miss in the Democratic runoff against Edwin Edwards brought him the public attention he needed for a successful Senate campaign a few months later.

Still, it took an unexpected turn of events to bring Johnston to Washington. After losing the governor's race, he decided on a primary challenge to veteran Sen. Allen J. Ellender, who was running for a seventh full term at 81. Ellender's age did not at first seem like a winning issue for Johnston; Ellender was a man of remarkable vigor, almost a symbol of perpetual youth. He was also chairman of the Senate Appropriations Committee and a master at providing federal money for Louisiana. But on July 27th, three weeks before the primary, Ellender died of a heart attack. Johnston had a clear path to election.

Before his 1971 campaign for governor, Johnston had been an only-moderately visible conservative state legislator from north Louisiana, and a lawyer practicing with his father in Shreveport. In the Legislature, his major issue was completion of an interstate highway linking his home city with New Orleans.

Campaigning against each other in the Democratic runoff, Johnston and Edwards differed politically, regionally and personally. Edwards, a Catholic from Cajun south Louisiana, had moderate social views and a flamboyant manner. Johnston issued calls for racial moderation, but he was more aloof in style, and as a Baptist from the Protestant north, he was universally perceived as being to Edwards' right.

Johnston attacked Edwards for absenteeism in the U.S. House, and painted him as a pawn of organized labor. Edwards blasted back at Johnston for voting to pass a series of state tax increases. Since that contest nearly a decade ago, the two men have maintained a testy relationship, which Edwards has done nothing to improve by hinting from time to time that he might try to replace Johnston in the Senate.

There was little Edwards or anyone else could do to stop Johnston once Ellender died. Former Gov. John J. McKeithen tried a last minute move to reopen filing for the August primary, but the state Democratic committee turned him down. Johnston then won the nomination by more than 6-to-1 against a little-known cotton farmer.

In the fall, McKeithen ran as an independent, making a bid for the votes of blacks and low-income whites by characterizing Johnston as the candidate of the wealthy. "He lives three strokes from the country club," said McKeithen.

The former governor had a problem, however, in the well-publicized indictments of key members of his administration. He himself was never accused of wrongdoing, but Johnston was able to campaign on the need for a return to honest government.

The Republican nominee was Ben C.

## J. Bennett Johnston, D-La.

Toledano, who had run unsuccessfully for mayor of New Orleans in 1970. Toledano sought to link Johnston to the Democratic presidential choice, George McGovern, but Johnston used his conservative voting record in the Legislature to refute any connection. Rather than hurting Johnston, Toledano and McKeithen offset each other. Johnston won his first Senate term with more than 55 percent of the vote.

By 1978, Johnston had some problems at home. He had a reputation among some local Democrats as aloof and Washington-oriented, and among others as insufficiently conservative. He drew a serious challenge from Democratic state Rep. Louis "Woody" Jenkins, who had worked for George C. Wallace in national politics.

Jenkins labeled the senator a devotee of high taxes and spending, and seemed for much of the summer to be making inroads in Johnston's popularity. But after a slow start, Johnston put on an aggressive drive for renomination. He had taken away Jenkins' best issue earlier in the year by voting against ratification of the Panama Canal treaties. Johnston won 59 percent of the primary vote, assuring him re-election under Louisiana law.

## Committees

**Appropriations** (8th of 14 Democrats)
Defense; Energy and Water Development; Foreign Operations; Interior.

**Budget** (4th of 10 Democrats)

**Energy and Natural Resources** (2nd of 9 Democrats)
Energy and Mineral Resoures; Energy Regulation; Energy Research and Development.

## Elections

**1978\* Primary**

| | |
|---|---|
| J. Bennett Johnston (D ) | 498,773 (59 %) |
| Louis Jenkins (D ) | 340,896 (41 %) |

*In Louisiana the primary is open to candidates of all parties. If a candidate wins 50% or more of the vote in the primary no general election is held.

**Previous Winning Percentage**

1972 (55 %)

## Campaign Finance

| | Receipts | Receipts from PACs | Expenditures |
|---|---|---|---|
| **1978** | | | |
| Johnston (D ) | 983,343 | 206,705 (21 %) | 857,860 |
| Jenkins (D ) | 330,015 | 17,000 (5 %) | 327,340 |

## Voting Studies

| | Presidential Support | | Party Unity | | Conservative Coalition | |
|---|---|---|---|---|---|---|
| **Year** | **S** | **O** | **S** | **O** | **S** | **O** |
| 1980 | 70 | 23 | 56 | 30 | 69 | 12 |

| | | | | | | |
|---|---|---|---|---|---|---|
| 1979 | 60 | 30 | 55 | 38 | 85 | 10 |
| 1978 | 34 | 38 | 26 | 45 | 68 | 8 |
| 1977 | 67 | 25 | 41 | 49 | 80 | 12 |
| 1976 | 45 | 43 | 42 | 47 | 72 | 16 |
| 1975 | 62 | 24 | 40 | 53 | 83 | 14 |
| 1974 (Ford) | 37 | 44 | | | | |
| 1974 | 52 | 39 | 47 | 42 | 65 | 25 |
| 1973 | 46 | 38 | 48 | 38 | 65 | 20 |

S = Support          O = Opposition

## Key Votes

**96th Congress**

| | |
|---|---|
| Maintain relations with Taiwan (1979) | N |
| Reduce synthetic fuel development funds (1979) | N |
| Impose nuclear plant moratorium (1979) | N |
| Kill stronger windfall profits tax (1979) | Y |
| Guarantee Chrysler Corp. loans (1979) | Y |
| Approve military draft registration (1980) | Y |
| End Revenue Sharing to the states (1980) | Y |
| Block Justice Dept. busing suits (1980) | Y |

**97th Congress**

| | |
|---|---|
| Restore urban program funding cuts (1981) | N |

## Interest Group Ratings

| Year | ADA | ACA | AFL-CIO | CCUS-1 | CCUS-2 |
|---|---|---|---|---|---|
| 1980 | 33 | 29 | 41 | 56 | |
| 1979 | 16 | 37 | 42 | 18 | 50 |
| 1978 | 15 | 60 | 13 | 77 | |
| 1977 | 25 | 52 | 58 | 65 | |
| 1976 | 15 | 56 | 53 | 56 | |
| 1975 | 28 | 46 | 24 | 63 | |
| 1974 | 14 | 82 | 33 | 67 | |
| 1973 | 35 | 54 | 50 | 100 | |

# 1 Bob Livingston (R)

**Of New Orleans — Elected 1977**

**Born:** April 30, 1943, Colorado Springs, Colo.
**Education:** Tulane U., B.A. 1967, J.D. 1968.
**Military Career:** Navy, 1961-63.
**Profession:** Lawyer.
**Family:** Wife, Bonnie Robichaux; three children.
**Religion:** Episcopalian.
**Political Career:** Republican nominee for U.S. House, 1976.

**In Washington:** Cautious and deliberate, this former prosecutor found himself in a prosecutorial role for much of the 96th Congress as a member of the Committee on Standards of Official Conduct. He was drafted for the assignment by Republican leaders in 1979, and it turned out to be a time-consuming job.

Livingston took a quiet interest in the details of the numerous ethics cases that came up during the Congress, often asking factual questions at the panel's open hearings. But he proved one of the harsher members of the committee, arguing strongly for the expulsion of Pennsylvania Democrat Michael O. Myers in an Abscam bribery case, and for censure of Charles H. Wilson, the California Democrat accused of several kickback charges. In the Wilson case, Livingston insisted on more action than ethics Chairman Charles E. Bennett wanted, calling for a contempt citation for a former Wilson employee who had refused to testify.

When not involved with ethics issues, Livingston worked on two committees of more interest to his district, Public Works and Merchant Marine. On the Public Works Water Resources Subcommittee, he had an opportunity to watch out for the flood control interests of his frequently threatened lowland district, although he sometimes was overshadowed by Louisiana's veteran water policy maneuverer, Democrat John Breaux. When the panel wrote a new water projects bill in 1980, Livingston offered an amendment to protect private dredging equipment manufacturers by making it illegal for the Army Corps of Engineers to sell off its used dredging equipment.

On Merchant Marine, Livingston voted the interests of his district's fishing industry. He supported a resolution to increase the tariff on imported shrimp.

At the start of the 97th Congress, Livingston left both Public Works and Merchant Marine for the Appropriations Committee.

**At Home:** The 1st District did not come close to electing a Republican to the House for a century after Reconstruction, but now that it has one, it seems quite satisfied. Livingston has had no difficulty holding the seat he won in a 1977 special election. Most of his constituents accept him as a logical replacement for his famous predecessor, Democrat F. Edward Hebert.

A prosperous New Orleans lawyer, former assistant U.S. attorney and veteran party worker, Livingston made his first bid for Congress in 1976, when Hebert stepped down. But he lost narrowly to a labor-backed Democrat, state Rep. Richard A. Tonry. The result was due in part to the independent conservative candidacy of former Democratic Rep. John R. Rarick, who drew nearly 10 percent of the vote.

Livingston did not have to wait long, however, for a second try. Tonry's 1976 primary opponent succeeded in pressing a vote fraud case against him, and Tonry resigned from the House in May 1977. He sought vindication in a second Democratic primary that June, but lost to state Rep. Ron Faucheux. Tonry subsequently pleaded guilty to several violations of federal campaign finance law and was sent to prison.

Livingston was ready to run again as soon as Tonry resigned. He mounted a well-financed campaign against Faucheux that drew significant support from blue-collar voters as well as more tradi-

---

**1st District: Southeast — New Orleans.** Population: 523,320 (15% increase since 1970). Race: White 320,741 (61%), Black 191,025 (37%), Others 11,494 (2%). Spanish origin: 18,710 (4%).

---

**485**

tional GOP voters in white-collar areas. Spending more than $500,000, Livingston launched an advertising blitz that showed him in his earlier job as a welder and as a devoted family man (in contrast to Faucheux, a young bachelor).

The Republican did not stress his party ties in the traditionally Democratic district. Instead he emphasized his background in law enforcement and claimed that he was in the conservative mainstream that had elected Hebert to Congress for 36 years.

With organized labor refusing to support Faucheux, Livingston won easily. Since then, the Democrats have not run a formidable challenger against him.

**The District:** Although the large majority of voters in the 1st are registered Democrats, the district has a history of supporting conservative candidates, especially on social issues.

Most of the district population lies within the city of New Orleans. It includes some fashionable neighborhoods along Lake Pontchartrain, as well as middle- to lower-income neighborhoods, both black and white. It has about equal numbers of Hubert Humphrey and George Wallace Democrats.

But the rest of the district is old Wallace territory — a mixture of New Orleans suburbs, rural and small-town areas and fishing communities in St. Bernard and Plaquemines parishes.

The latter was the home base of segregationist boss Leander Perez, who ruled Plaquemines Parish with autocratic control until his death in 1969, and dominated politics in the district.

Reflecting Perez' wishes, Plaquemines Parish cast more than 75 percent of its ballots for Dixiecrat Strom Thurmond in 1948, Barry Goldwater in 1964 and Wallace in 1968. But Reagan won only 54 percent of the parish vote in 1980.

## Committees

**Appropriations** (17th of 22 Republicans)
Foreign Operations; Labor-Health and Human Services-Education.

## Election

**1980 Primary***

| | |
|---|---|
| Bob Livingston (R ) | 81,777 (88 %) |
| Michael Musmeci Sr. (D ) | 8,277 (9 %) |

**1978 Primary***

| | |
|---|---|
| Bob Livingston (R ) | 89,469 (86 %) |
| Sanford Krasnoff (D ) | 14,373 (14 %) |

†Not eligible for all recorded votes.
* In Louisiana the primary is open to candidates of all parties. If a candidate wins 50% or more of the vote in the primary no general election is held.

**Previous Winning Percentages**

**1977*** (51%)
* Special Election.

**District Vote For President**

| | 1980 | | 1976 | | 1972 |
|---|---|---|---|---|---|
| D | 90,636 (46%) | D | 83,061 (50%) | D | 37,266 (28%) |
| R | 100,436(51%) | R | 78,928 (47%) | R | 88,893 (66%) |
| I | 3,794 (2%) | | | | |

## Campaign Finance

| | Receipts | Receipts from PACs | Expenditures |
|---|---|---|---|
| **1980** | | | |
| Livingston (R ) | $249,967 | $58,465 (23 %) | $138,724 |
| **1978** | | | |
| Livingston (R ) | $370,366 | $61,428 (17 %) | $347,844 |

## Voting Studies

| | Presidential Support | | Party Unity | | Conservative Coalition | |
|---|---|---|---|---|---|---|
| Year | S | O | S | O | S | O |
| 1980 | 41 | 51 | 72 | 15 | 81 | 7 |
| 1979 | 23 | 72 | 80 | 16 | 90 | 5 |
| 1978 | 30 | 67 | 82 | 11 | 88 | 5 |
| 1977 | 42 | 53† | 80 | 10† | 87 | 4† |

†Not eligible for all recorded votes.

S = Support        O = Opposition

## Key Votes

**96th Congress**

| | |
|---|---|
| Weaken Carter oil profits tax (1979) | Y |
| Reject hospital cost control plan (1979) | Y |
| Implement Panama Canal Treaties (1979) | Y |
| Establish Department of Education (1979) | N |
| Approve Anti-busing Amendment (1979) | Y |
| Guarantee Chrysler Corp. loans (1979) | N |
| Approve military draft registration (1980) | Y |
| Aid Sandinista regime in Nicaragua (1980) | N |
| Strengthen fair housing laws (1980) | N |

**97th Congress**

| | |
|---|---|
| Reagan budget proposal (1981) | Y |

## Interest Group Ratings

| Year | ADA | ACA | AFL-CIO | CCUS |
|---|---|---|---|---|
| 1980 | 11 | 83 | 5 | 84 |
| 1979 | 11 | 83 | 10 | 94 |
| 1978 | 10 | 92 | 15 | 82 |
| 1977 | 0 | 78 | 29 | 89 |

# 2 Lindy Boggs (D)

**Of New Orleans — Elected 1973**

**Born:** March 13, 1916, Brunswick Plantation, La.
**Education:** Tulane U., B.A. 1935.
**Profession:** Teacher.
**Family:** Widow of Rep. Hale Boggs; three children.
**Religion:** Roman Catholic.
**Political Career:** No previous office.

**In Washington:** Lindy Boggs' grace and even-tempered style have given her an image in Congress not too much different from the one she had for nearly 30 years as a congressional wife, campaigning and playing hostess for Hale Boggs, who was majority leader when he died in a plane crash over Alaska in 1972.

She is now a sort of unofficial hostess for the Democratic Party, presiding with equal correctness at a reception or a national convention. Well ensconced on the Appropriations Committee, she is a legislator who asks for a limited number of things, most of them for her district, but who always gets a hearing.

She has tried for years to promote legislation increasing price supports for Louisiana sugar growers, but was unable to prevent the House from killing such a bill in 1979. She has worked with Republican Paul Trible of Virginia in a new "Congressional Shipyard Coalition" that wants to stimulate the development of American ports — like New Orleans.

Boggs has spoken out on some controversial women's issues, such as bank discrimination against female borrowers, which she fought to end, but she is no militant feminist. She is uncomfortable with strategies that alienate male colleagues. She speaks of bringing "womanly attributes" to politics.

Four terms in Congress have not changed her optimistic view of the world. Once asked by an incredulous reporter whether it was true that she really liked everyone, she said yes.

She is politically cautious, given to lobbying on her issues privately among old friends such as Speaker O'Neill rather than making public statements. O'Neill has particular reason to be helpful; he is Speaker today largely because Hale Boggs appointed him majority whip in 1971, starting him along the leadership ladder. Even while rescue workers were searching for Boggs' missing plane in late 1972, Lindy gave O'Neill her blessing to begin lining up support for a campaign to succeed Hale as leader.

When she was elected to her husband's New Orleans House seat the next spring, she came in as a freshman with the contacts of a senior member. She had attended every Democratic convention since 1948; she had presided over the lavish garden parties that had brought much of the Washington Democratic community to the Boggs home in Maryland every year; she knew most of the Democrats in the House.

Since then, she has drawn more public attention for her party work than her legislative actions. In 1976, she was the first woman to chair a national convention. In 1980, while many of her House colleagues were grumbling about President Carter, she endorsed him and served on his platform-writing committee.

**At Home:** Favorable district lines in the past and weak Republican opposition have given Boggs easy election five times in the House seat her husband held for 27 years.

After Hale Boggs' near-defeat against Republican David C. Treen in 1968, Louisiana's Democratic Legislature redrew the lines to remove some conservative suburbs west of New Orleans. Since then, no Republican has come close, although redistricting could change that for 1982.

Lindy Boggs was the only major candidate in the special election that followed her husband's death. She won the five-way Democratic primary with nearly three-quarters of the vote and coasted

**2nd District: — New Orleans.** Population: 462,641 (2% increase since 1970). Race: White 264,453 (57%), Black 188,975 (41%), Others 9,213 (2%). Spanish origin: 17,649 (4%).

to an even more one-sided victory over her Republican rival. The daughter of a wealthy sugar planter, she became the first woman to be elected to the House from Louisiana.

Republicans did not mount a significant challenge against her until 1980, when the national party provided some financial support to an aggressive young lawyer, Rob Couhig, who criticized the incumbent as a liberal big spender. But with support from much of the civic leadership and strong backing among blacks, Boggs won re-election by a margin of nearly 2-1.

**The District.** Boggs' home turf is the most liberal area in Louisiana. The district includes downtown New Orleans, the French Quarter, the academic communities around Tulane, Loyola and Xavier universities and a large black community. Throughout the 1970s, the 2nd had a higher share of blacks than any other district in Louisiana.

Suburbs in Jefferson Parish to the south and west of the city are middle-income, white and conservative. But large portions of Jefferson Parish were removed from the district in 1969 redistricting, enabling the city to outvote the suburbs.

The urban advantage in the 2nd District may not last much longer. While population grew 15 percent throughout Louisiana in the last decade, it increased by only 2 percent in the 2nd, the slowest rate of growth anywhere in the state.

## Committees

**Appropriations** (18th of 33 Democrats)
Energy and Water Development; HUD-Independent Agencies.

## Elections

**1980 Primary\***

| | |
|---|---|
| Lindy Boggs (D ) | 45,091 (61 %) |
| Rob Couhig (R ) | 25,521 (34 %) |
| Clyde Bel Jr. (D ) | 3,571 (5 %) |

**1978 Primary\***

| | |
|---|---|
| Lindy Boggs (D ) | 57,056 (87 %) |
| Christine Gauvreau (I ) | 4,348 (7 %) |
| William King (I ) | 4,063 (6 %) |

*\* In Louisiana the primary is open to candidates of all parties. If a candidate wins 50% or more of the vote in the primary no general election is held.*

**Previous Winning Percentages**
1976 (93 %)    1974 (82 %)    1973 (80\* %)
*\* Special Election.*

**District Vote For President**

| | 1980 | | 1976 | | 1972 |
|---|---|---|---|---|---|
| **D** | 75,157 (52 %) | **D** | 69,774 (55 %) | **D** | 44,112 (36 %) |
| **R** | 63,701 (44 %) | **R** | 54,014 (43 %) | **R** | 67,490 (56 %) |
| **I** | 3,457 (2 %) | | | **I** | 9,784 (8 %) |

## Campaign Finance

| | Receipts | Receipts from PACs | Expenditures |
|---|---|---|---|
| **1980** | | | |
| Boggs (D ) | $264,612 | $60,875 (23 %) | $280,198 |
| **1978** | | | |
| Boggs (D ) | $75,738 | $15,205 (20 %) | $60,404 |

## Voting Studies

| | Presidential Support | | Party Unity | | Conservative Coalition | |
|---|---|---|---|---|---|---|
| **Year** | **S** | **O** | **S** | **O** | **S** | **O** |
| 1980 | 63 | 16 | 74 | 7 | 33 | 47 |

| | | | | | | |
|---|---|---|---|---|---|---|
| 1979 | 64 | 22 | 73 | 18 | 42 | 49 |
| 1978 | 64 | 32 | 71 | 25 | 42 | 54 |
| 1977 | 57 | 33 | 69 | 22 | 39 | 46 |
| 1976 | 39 | 43 | 58 | 27 | 46 | 37 |
| 1975 | 44 | 49 | 65 | 22 | 39 | 46 |
| 1974 (Ford) | 39 | 35 | | | | |
| 1974 | 75 | 19 | 63 | 25 | 41 | 42 |
| 1973 | 40 | 56† | 78 | 14† | 30 | 63† |

† Not eligible for all recorded votes.

S = Support          O = Opposition

## Key Votes

**96th Congress**

| | |
|---|---|
| Weaken Carter oil profits tax (1979) | Y |
| Reject hospital cost control plan (1979) | Y |
| Implement Panama Canal Treaties (1979) | Y |
| Establish Department of Education (1979) | N |
| Approve Anti-busing Amendment (1979) | N |
| Guarantee Chrysler Corp. loans (1979) | Y |
| Approve military draft registration (1980) | Y |
| Aid Sandinista regime in Nicaragua (1980) | Y |
| Strengthen fair housing laws (1980) | Y |

**97th Congress**

| | |
|---|---|
| Reagan budget proposal (1981) | N |

## Interest Group Ratings

| Year | ADA | ACA | AFL-CIO | CCUS |
|---|---|---|---|---|
| 1980 | 50 | 30 | 53 | 70 |
| 1979 | 42 | 20 | 61 | 50 |
| 1978 | 45 | 31 | 65 | 44 |
| 1977 | 30 | 15 | 76 | 38 |
| 1976 | 30 | 31 | 73 | 38 |
| 1975 | 47 | 24 | 77 | 41 |
| 1974 | 35 | 15 | 70 | 13 |
| 1973 | 67 | 10 | 91 | 27 |

# 3 W. J. "Billy" Tauzin (D)

**Of Thibodaux — Elected 1980**

**Born:** June 14, 1943, Chackbay, La.
**Education:** Nicholls State U., B.A. 1964; La. State U., J.D. 1967.
**Profession:** Lawyer.
**Family:** Wife, Gayle Clement; four children.
**Religion:** Roman Catholic.
**Political Career:** La. House, 1971-80.

**In Washington:** Tauzin arrived in the House in mid-1980 virtually on the arm of John Breaux, his law school classmate, state delegation dean, and overall congressional godfather. Like other South Louisiana Democrats of recent years, he is an easygoing man with a fondness for Cajun stories. Breaux, a power on the panel that makes Democratic committee assignments, sought to place Tauzin on the Energy and Commerce Committee as soon as he was sworn in, arguing that Tauzin had been an energy specialist in the Louisiana Legislature and deserved a chance to follow up on his work there.

The initial effort failed, but Tauzin returned at the start of 1981 and got what he wanted. That was partly because of Breaux, and also because Tauzin had found his way onto the assignment panel, the Democratic Steering and Policy Committee. It always helps to be in the room when the plums are handed out, and Tauzin was placed on Energy and Commerce on the first ballot.

Meanwhile, Tauzin had spent 1980 on the Public Works and Merchant Marine committees. He nearly always voted with Breaux, strongly for the oil industry and industrial development in general, but sensitive to the interests of committee and House Democratic leaders. He cosponsored a piece of legislation, backed by most Southern Democrats, which would exempt royalty holders from the oil windfall profits tax.

As chairman of the Natural Resources Committee in the Louisiana House, Tauzin concentrated on oil and gas industry problems, and wrote the state's "First Use Amendment," which taxes natural gas as it comes onshore in Louisiana. He argued that it was needed to remedy a situation in which the oil and gas industries were not paying for possible damages to the state's coastal resources.

**At Home:** Tauzin's victory in the 1980 special election restored control of the district to French-speaking, Democratic South Louisiana, after nearly a decade under a Republican from suburban New Orleans, David C. Treen.

When Treen vacated the seat after winning the governorship, he tried to pick a successor, James J. Donelon, a Democrat-turned-Republican. Former Democratic Gov. Edwin W. Edwards, who had also served in Congress, campaigned ardently for Tauzin.

Like Edwards, Tauzin is as comfortable speaking French as he is speaking English. After practicing law in the bayou towns of Houma and Thibodaux, he won a state legislative seat in 1971. He was re-elected without opposition in 1975 and with 90 percent of the vote in 1979. During eight years in the state Legislature he emerged as Edwards' protégé, serving as his floor leader in the lower chamber.

With the help of Edwards and Breaux, Tauzin finished a strong second in the first round of the special election to fill Treen's vacancy. Donelon led the four-man field, but not by a large enough margin to avoid a runoff.

The second round was bitter and expensive. Tauzin won by more than 7,000 votes, building a big lead in the Cajun parishes that offset Donelon's advantage in his home base, suburban Jefferson Parish. The unexpectedly large margin of defeat discouraged GOP leaders and they did not field a candidate against Tauzin in the general election.

**The District:** The 3rd is closely divided between the rapidly growing suburbs in Jefferson

> **3rd District: South central — New Iberia, Metairie.** Population: 570,243 (25% increase since 1970). Race: White 476,019 (83%), Black 82,294 (14%), Others 11,930 (2%). Spanish origin: 20,772 (4%).

**489**

Parish and the rural Cajun parishes to the west. The district is an oil-producing and agricultural area, with sugar cane, soybeans and rice as major crops. Commercial fishing is important also.

On many issues, the district is conservative. It gave George C. Wallace a solid plurality of the vote in 1968 and elected Treen to four terms as the first Republican congressman from Louisiana in this century.

But as a heavily Catholic district, the 3rd has also supported Catholic Democrats even when they are to the left of the state's political mainstream. The district gave John F. Kennedy 68 percent of the vote in 1960, and Edwards won a healthy 63 percent in his successful 1972 gubernatorial race against Treen.

## Committees

**Energy and Commerce** (22nd of 24 Democrats)
Fossil and Synthetic Fuels; Oversight and Investigations; Telecommunications, Consumer Protection, and Finance.

**Merchant Marine and Fisheries** (16th of 20 Democrats)
Coast Guard and Navigation; Fisheries and Wildlife Conservation and the Environment.

## Elections

**1980 Primary***

| | |
|---|---|
| W. J. Tauzin (D ) | 80,455 (85 %) |
| Bob Namer (D ) | 14,074 (15 %) |

**1980 Special Election Runoff**

| | |
|---|---|
| W. J. Tauzin (D ) | 62,108 (53 %) |
| James Donelon (R ) | 54,815 (47 %) |

**1980 Special Election**

| | |
|---|---|
| James Donelon (R ) | 37,191 (45 %) |
| W. J. Tauzin (D ) | 35,384 (43 %) |
| Anthony Guarisco (D ) | 8,827 (11 %) |

* In Louisiana the primary is open to candidates of all parties. If a candidate wins 50% or more of the vote in the primary no general election is held.

**District Vote For President**

| | 1980 | | 1976 | | 1972 |
|---|---|---|---|---|---|
| **D** | 75,364 (36%) | **D** | 75,063 (44 %) | **D** | 31,075 (22 %) |
| **R** | 125,110 (60%) | **R** | 92,350 (54 %) | **R** | 100,940 (73 %) |
| **I** | 4,500 (2%) | | | | |

## Campaign Finance

| | Receipts | Receipts from PACs | Expenditures |
|---|---|---|---|
| **1980** | | | |
| Tauzin (D ) | $555,433 | $89,040 (16 %) | $544,931 |

## Voting Studies

| | Presidential Support | | Party Unity | | Conservative Coalition | |
|---|---|---|---|---|---|---|
| **Year** | **S** | **O** | **S** | **O** | **S** | **O** |
| **1980** | 49 | 34† | 51 | 31† | 58 | 23† |

S = Support      O = Opposition

†Not eligible for all recorded votes.

## Key Votes

**96th Congress**

| | |
|---|---|
| Strengthen fair housing laws (1980) | N |

**97th Congress**

| | |
|---|---|
| Reagan budget proposal (1981) | Y |

## Interest Group Ratings

| Year | ADA | ACA | AFL-CIO | CCUS |
|---|---|---|---|---|
| **1980** | 0 | 42 | 67 | 79 |

# 4 Buddy Roemer (D)

**Of Bossier City — Elected 1980**

**Born:** October 4, 1943, Shreveport, La.
**Education:** Harvard U., B.A. 1964, M.B.A. 1967.
**Profession:** Computer executive.
**Family:** Wife, Patti Crocker; three children.
**Religion:** Methodist.
**Political Career:** No previous office.

**The Member:** Brash and articulate, Roemer launched his congressional career a few weeks early by warning Speaker Tip O'Neill in a post-election meeting that the Democratic leadership had become too closely identified with outdated liberal dogma. He threatened to vote against O'Neill's re-election as Speaker.

When Congress convened Jan. 5, Roemer did not carry through with that threat, but he did buck the party line on another loyalty test. Roemer was one of just three House Democrats to vote against the rules package proposed by Democrats. Later, in committee assignments, Roemer lost bids for the Banking and Armed Services committees.

Roemer's threat to O'Neill quieted talk that he is a bit to the left of his district. A board member of the local Urban League, Roemer has had wide appeal among blacks and young liberals. He kept critics guessing by voting for the first Gramm-Latta budget plan and against the second.

The U.S. House is Roemer's first public office. The son of a wealthy businessman and state political power broker, Roemer moved into Shreveport politics after graduating from Harvard. He ran for the 4th District seat in 1978, when it was open, but lost to Democrat Claude "Buddy" Leach in a non-partisan general election. Charges of vote-buying surfaced after the election; they led to the indictment of Rep. Leach and some allies (all were eventually acquitted), and to Leach's downfall in 1980.

**The District:** About half the district's population lives in the Shreveport area, the rest in rural parishes to the south and east. Shreveport, an oil and commercial center and the state's second largest city, shares the economic and social conservatism of other growing metropolitan areas in Texas and Louisiana.

With strong urban support, Republicans have made the district a GOP bastion in recent presidential elections. But Democrats have never lost control of the House seat, which veteran incumbent Joe D. Waggonner Jr. held until his retirement in 1978.

## Committees

**Public Works and Transportation** (23rd of 25 Democrats)
Aviation; Investigations and Oversight; Water Resources.

**Small Business** (22nd of 23 Democrats)
General Oversight; Tax, Access to Equity Capital and Business Opportunities.

## Elections

**1980 General**

| | |
|---|---|
| Buddy Roemer (D ) | 103,625 (64 %) |
| Claude Leach (D ) | 58,705 (36 %) |

**1980 Primary**

| | |
|---|---|
| Claude Leach (D ) | 35,847 (29 %) |
| Buddy Roemer (D ) | 33,049 (27 %) |
| Jimmy Wilson (R ) | 29,992 (24 %) |
| Foster Campbell (D ) | 14,666 (12 %) |
| Forrest Dunn (D ) | 8,208 (7 %) |

**District Vote For President**

| | 1980 | | 1976 | | 1972 |
|---|---|---|---|---|---|
| **D** | 78,745 (44%) | **D** | 66,125 (45 %) | **D** | 29,203 (23 %) |
| **R** | 96,750 (54%) | **R** | 78,355 (53 %) | **R** | 89,754 (72 %) |

## Campaign Finance

| | Receipts | Receipts from PACs | Expenditures |
|---|---|---|---|
| **1980** | | | |
| Roemer (D ) | $676,035 | $6,100 (1 %) | $673,324 |
| Leach (D ) | $639,518 | $26,520 (4 %) | $643,639 |

## Key Vote

**97th Congress**

| | |
|---|---|
| Reagan budget proposal (1981) | Y |

---

**4th District: Northwest - Shreveport.** Population: 508,593 (12% increase since 1970). Race: White 339,548 (67%), Black 162,166 (32%), Others 6,879 (1%). Spanish origin: 10,469 (2%).

# 5 Jerry Huckaby (D)

**Of Ringgold — Elected 1976**

**Born:** July 19, 1941, Hodge, La.
**Education:** La. State U., B.S. 1963; Ga. State U., M.B.A. 1969.
**Profession:** Farmer.
**Family:** Wife, Suzanna Woodward; two children.
**Religion:** Methodist.
**Political Career:** No previous office.

**In Washington:** Placed on both the Agriculture and Interior committees as a House freshman in 1977, Huckaby has been in a good position to defend the interests that concern him and his district — dairy farming, cotton, timber and oil.

It was Huckaby's relationship with oil that brought him brief prominence in 1979, when the Interior Committee accepted his bill opening more Alaska land to energy exploration than would have been permitted in the original version sponsored by committee Chairman Morris K. Udall, D-Ariz.

Backed by heavy lobbying from the oil industry, as well as gas and mining interests, Huckaby managed to get the amount of land barred to development — designated "wilderness" — reduced to 50 million acres from 80 million. The change allowed oil and gas exploration and drilling in the controversial Arctic Wildlife Range.

Huckaby's victory in the committee was a surprise to national environmentalists. He himself served more as the voice of the effort than as its strategist. Once the issue went to the House floor, his bill was merged with another pro-development version and he yielded his role to other pro-development forces. Eventually the House voted to reverse the committee and passed a more conservationist bill. On Agriculture, Huckaby represents the interests of the companies that harvest timber in the piney woods of north Louisiana. One of his proposals in the Forests Subcommittee was for long-term deferred payment loans to private foresters.

On other issues, Huckaby has generally been one of the most conservative of the Southern Democrats elected in recent years — which is saying a great deal. He came to the House in the last term of Joe Waggonner Jr., the wheeling-and-dealing dean of the Louisiana delegation, and during that time he followed Waggonner's lead on most important votes. In his first year, Huckaby supported the conservative coalition — Republicans and Southern Democrats — 96 percent of the time. His voting since then has been fairly close to that standard.

**At Home:** While ambitious young politicians waited for veteran Rep. Otto E. Passman to retire, Huckaby took the risk of challenging him in 1976, defeated him in the Democratic primary, and won the seat.

It was Huckaby's first campaign. But the wealthy dairy farmer mounted an aggressive, well-financed challenge that capitalized on Passman's advanced age (76) and political problems.

The 15-term incumbent had been beset with charges of irregularities in his congressional travel expenses. He had been criticized for his 1971 vote against a constitutional amendment to permit prayer in public schools.

Huckaby attacked Passman's weaknesses while promising to continue his conservative voting record. Sweeping the parishes around his home base in the western part of the district, Huckaby drew 53 percent of the primary vote.

With Passman's defeat, Republicans had high hopes of capturing the seat. Their candidate, Monroe businessman Frank Spooner, had a large treasury and was boosted by a campaign appearance on his behalf by Ronald Reagan.

But Spooner was unable to document his basic campaign theme — that Huckaby was a liberal Democrat out of step with the conservative district. Huckaby offset the Republican's 7,000-vote plurality in the district's major population

---

**5th District: North — Monroe.** Population: 507,333 (12% increase since 1970). Race: White 341,480 (67%), Black 162,886 (32%), Others 2,967 (1%). Spanish origin: 5,166 (1%).

center, Ouachita Parish (Monroe), and repeated his strong primary showing in the rural parishes to win the seat by 8,000 votes.

Some Democratic politicians within the district were annoyed that the upstart Huckaby had taken the prize so many of them had been waiting for. One of them, state Sen. James H. Brown Jr., challenged Huckaby in 1978. But Huckaby spent nearly $400,000 and won by more than 25,000 votes. He faced minimal opposition in 1980.

**The District:** The 5th District encompasses most of rural north Louisiana. Like the southern part of the state, it has a large black population. But unlike it, the 5th is dominated by fundamentalist Protestants.

This is one of the poorest areas of Louisiana. Cotton and soybeans are the dominant crops,

especially in the Mississippi delta. The district has little industry, but some oil and gas production.

While the 5th includes Winn Parish, the boyhood home of populist Huey P. Long, the district in recent years has been strictly conservative in its voting habits. Both Barry Goldwater in 1964 and George C. Wallace in 1968 drew a higher share of the vote in the 5th than in any other Louisiana district.

North Louisiana continues to support conservative Democrats on the local level. But for state office, the district has shown a preference for Protestant Republicans over Cajun Democrats. It gave Republican David C. Treen a solid 57 percent of the vote when he ran unsuccessfully for governor against Democrat Edwin W. Edwards, a Cajun, in 1972.

## Committees

**Agriculture** (15th of 24 Democrats)
Cotton, Rice and Sugar; Forests, Family Farms, and Energy; Wheat, Soybeans, and Feed Grains.

**Interior and Insular Affairs** (16th of 23 Democrats)
Energy and the Environment; Mines and Mining.

## Elections

**1980 Primary***

| | |
|---|---|
| Jerry Huckaby (D ) | 93,519 (89 %) |
| L. D. Knox (D ) | 11,748 (11 %) |

**1978 Primary***

| | |
|---|---|
| Jerry Huckaby (D) | 66,276 (52 %) |
| Jim Brown (D) | 38,969 (31 %) |
| W. C. Johnson (D) | 16,194 (13 %) |

* In Louisiana the primary is open to candidates of all parties. If a candidate wins 50% or more of the vote in the primary no general election is held.

**Previous Winning Percentage**

1976 (53 %)

**District Vote For President**

| | 1980 | | 1976 | | 1972 |
|---|---|---|---|---|---|
| **D** | 81,524 (42%) | **D** | 81,201 (48 %) | **D** | 35,213 (25 %) |
| **R** | 107,171 (55%) | **R** | 84,131 (50 %) | **R** | 97,039 (69 %) |

## Campaign Finance

| | Receipts | Receipts from PACs | Expenditures |
|---|---|---|---|
| **1980** | | | |
| Huckaby (D ) | $116,859 | $61,140 (52 %) | $60,316 |

| 1978 | | | |
|---|---|---|---|
| Huckaby (D ) | $382,825 | $95,168 (25 %) | $384,207 |
| Brown (D ) | $136,746 | $2,298 (2 %) | $117,800 |

## Voting Studies

| | Presidential Support | | Party Unity | | Conservative Coalition | |
|---|---|---|---|---|---|---|
| Year | S | O | S | O | S | O |
| 1980 | 54 | 44 | 49 | 45 | 82 | 15 |
| 1979 | 44 | 45 | 35 | 57 | 87 | 6 |
| 1978 | 28 | 52 | 24 | 58 | 74 | 10 |
| 1977 | 47 | 52 | 33 | 64 | 96 | 3 |

S = Support          O = Opposition

## Key Votes

**96th Congress**

| | |
|---|---|
| Weaken Carter oil profits tax (1979) | Y |
| Reject hospital cost control plan (1979) | Y |
| Implement Panama Canal Treaties (1979) | N |
| Establish Department of Education (1979) | Y |
| Approve Anti-busing Amendment (1979) | Y |
| Guarantee Chrysler Corp. loans (1979) | Y |
| Approve military draft registration (1980) | Y |
| Aid Sandinista regime in Nicaragua (1980) | N |
| Strengthen fair housing laws (1980) | N |

**97th Congress**

| | |
|---|---|
| Reagan budget proposal (1981) | Y |

## Interest Group Ratings

| Year | ADA | ACA | AFL-CIO | CCUS |
|---|---|---|---|---|
| 1980 | 11 | 58 | 21 | 84 |
| 1979 | 11 | 76 | 21 | 83 |
| 1978 | 25 | 88 | 35 | 63 |
| 1977 | 5 | 73 | 27 | 76 |

# 6 Henson Moore (R)

**Of Baton Rouge — Elected 1975**

**Born:** Oct. 4, 1939, Lake Charles, La.
**Education:** Louisiana State U., B.A. 1961, J.D. 1965, M.A. 1973.
**Military Career:** Army, 1965-67.
**Profession:** Lawyer.
**Family:** Wife, Carolyn Cherry; three children.
**Religion:** Episcopalian.
**Political Career:** Louisiana Republican Central Committee, 1971-75.

**In Washington:** Representing a district laced with refineries, Moore has struggled to play his obligatory role as a spokesman for oil while maintaining the flexibility to have some influence on the Ways and Means Committee.

He has done it with frequent success. In 1979, he teamed with Democrat James R. Jones of Oklahoma to weaken the windfall profits tax on the oil industry. The two lost, 19-17, in committee, but took their fight to the floor, where they managed to reverse the outcome after a well-orchestrated lobbying effort in which Moore held all but 10 of 156 Republicans, and Jones peeled off a third of the majority members.

As a result, the House took to conference a bill with a basic 60 percent tax, rather than the original 70 percent. Moore ultimately voted against the conference report — along with the entire Louisiana delegation — but his willingness to negotiate over details had a clear impact on the final product.

Much of Moore's other Ways and Means work involves protection of state economic interests. He worked for a bill in 1979 to fix rigid quotas for meat imports and restrict the extent to which they could be changed by the president if circumstances changed. That pleased Louisiana's cattlemen. The same year, he did his part for the state's sugar industry by insisting that the committee keep a provision in the new Sugar Act guaranteeing the producers a direct payment of half a cent a pound. Moore won on that, but the whole bill fell victim to consumerist arguments when it reached the House floor.

Before winning his Ways and Means assignment in 1979, Moore fought similar battles on the Agriculture and Commerce committees, also good spots given his interests. He argued against a $75 million subsidy for liquified coal production, taking on the Commerce chairman, Harley O. Staggers of West Virginia, whose district would greatly

benefit from the subsidy. He fought legislation that would have removed quotas on U.S. rice production. In 1976, as a freshman, he opposed the new Grain Inspection Act. That same year he persuaded the House to adopt a congressional veto — then a relatively new idea — for regulations issued by the Environmental Protection Agency under the Clean Air Act, but the bill died in the Senate.

**At Home.** Moore's election followed a familiar Southern pattern: victory by a Republican upon the defeat of a conservative Democratic incumbent. In Moore's case, the incumbent was the strident John R. Rarick, beaten by Baton Rouge sportscaster Jeff LaCaze in a 1974 primary.

Moore began building his campaign long before Rarick's defeat. A member of a prestigious Baton Rouge law firm and veteran party activist, he entered the race in September 1973, sending himself and his campaign manager to a California campaign school.

His preparation paid off, but not immediately. The final canvass of the November vote showed Moore the apparent victor by 44 votes out of more than 120,000 cast. LaCaze challenged the results, claiming that a voting machine malfunctioned in East Baton Rouge Parish. The Louisiana Supreme Court upheld the challenge and called for a new election in January 1975.

The rematch gave Moore a chance to focus on issues that had been obscure in their first race,

---

**6th District: East central — Baton Rouge.** Population: 577,140 (27% increase since 1970). Race: White 400,249 (69%), Black 170,911 (30%), Others 5,980 (1%). Spanish origin: 8,848 (2%).

such as LaCaze's financial help from national labor unions. Successfully courting conservative Democrats who had backed Rarick in the past, Moore swept to a comfortable 11,500-vote victory, making himself the second GOP congressman from Louisiana in this century.

Democrats have not come close to unseating him. In 1978 and 1980, he won re-election with more than 90 percent of the vote.

**The District.** The 6th is a diverse district. It extends from the state capital and academic center of Baton Rouge on the west to Bogalusa, a town known in the past for racial turmoil, on the east. The territory in between is rural, with pine forests and small farms providing the base for lumbering and agriculture.

Benefiting from Louisiana's booming oil and natural gas industry, the 6th grew at a faster rate in the last decade than any other district in the state. While most of the oil is actually pumped from fields in other parts of Louisiana, refineries and chemical plants are concentrated in the Baton Rouge area.

Baton Rouge is the GOP stronghold in the 6th. But the large academic communities at Louisiana State and Southern universities and the extensive labor activity in local industry provide the Democrats with a competitive base.

While Moore has made inroads in rural parishes, loyalty to the Democratic Party remains strong. Carter's appeal to rural and black voters enabled him to carry the 6th in both 1976 and 1980.

## Committees

**Ways and Means** (12th of 12 Republicans)
Oversight; Public Assistance and Unemployment Compensation; Select Revenue Measures.

## Elections

**1980 Primary***

| | |
|---|---|
| Henson Moore (R) | 118,540 (91 %) |
| Alice Brooks (D ) | 12,149 (9 %) |

**1978 Primary***

| | |
|---|---|
| Henson Moore (R) | 102,430 (91 %) |
| Bobby Pailette (D ) | 10,256 (9 %) |

* In Louisiana the primary is open to candidates of all parties. If a candidate wins 50% or more of the vote in the primary no general election is held

**Previous Winning Percentages**

1976 (65%)    1975* (54%)

* Special Election.

**District Vote For President**

| 1980 | 1976 | 1972 |
|---|---|---|
| D 101,252 (47%) | D 90,214 (53%) | D 36,240 (28%) |
| R 109,692 (50%) | R 74,806 (44%) | R 83,246 (65%) |
| I 4,353 (2%) | | |

## Campaign Finance

| | Receipts | Receipts from PACs | Expenditures |
|---|---|---|---|
| **1980** | | | |
| Moore (R ) | $189,635 | $74,800 (39 %) | $88,736 |
| **1978** | | | |
| Moore (R ) | $126,905 | $31,674 (25 %) | $78,686 |

## Voting Studies

| | Presidential Support | | Party Unity | | Conservative Coalition | |
|---|---|---|---|---|---|---|
| Year | S | O | S | O | S | O |
| 1980 | 38 | 56 | 80† | 16 | 88 | 8 |
| 1979 | 28 | 70 | 86 | 14 | 99 | 1 |
| 1978 | 31 | 69 | 86 | 14 | 95 | 5 |
| 1977 | 41 | 59 | 87 | 13 | 96 | 4 |
| 1976 | 75 | 25 | 86 | 13 | 92 | 8 |
| 1975 | 64 | 33 | 88 | 10 | 94 | 4 |

S = Support          O = Opposition

†Not eligible for all recorded votes.

## Key Votes

**96th Congress**

| | |
|---|---|
| Weaken Carter oil profits tax (1979) | Y |
| Reject hospital cost control plan (1979) | Y |
| Implement Panama Canal Treaties (1979) | N |
| Establish Department of Education (1979) | N |
| Approve Anti-busing Amendment (1979) | Y |
| Guarantee Chrysler Corp. loans (1979) | N |
| Approve military draft registration (1980) | N |
| Aid Sandinista regime in Nicaragua (1980) | N |
| Strengthen fair housing laws (1980) | N |

**97th Congress**

| | |
|---|---|
| Reagan budget proposal (1981) | Y |

## Interest Group Ratings

| Year | ADA | ACA | AFL-CIO | CCUS |
|---|---|---|---|---|
| 1980 | 11 | 79 | 0 | 81 |
| 1979 | 11 | 92 | 16 | 94 |
| 1978 | 5 | 96 | 0 | 78 |
| 1977 | 0 | 78 | 9 | 100 |
| 1976 | 0 | 82 | 22 | 100 |
| 1975 | 0 | 89 | 9 | 88 |

# 7 John B. Breaux (D)

**Of Crowley — Elected 1972**

**Born:** March 1, 1944, Crowley, La.
**Education:** U. of Southwestern La., B.A. 1965;
La. State U., J.D. 1967.
**Profession:** Lawyer.
**Family:** Wife, Lois Daigle; four children.
**Religion:** Roman Catholic.
**Political Career:** No previous office.

**In Washington:** Breaux had the advantage of an early start in Congress, and he has made the most of it. Elected at 28, he has become dean of the Louisiana House delegation and a major institutional power broker at an age when most of his contemporaries are still learning the legislative process.

Colleagues concede, however, that Breaux possessed more than good timing. Throughout his career, he has shown skill at legislative maneuvering and a feel for the personal relationships of the House.

Appointed in 1972 to the Merchant Marine and Fisheries Committee, he found that most members placed there pay limited attention to it. He chose to concentrate on Merchant Marine, not just for the fishing interests of his south Louisiana district but for its potential role in energy and environmental policy.

Over the years, thanks to some jurisdictional aggressiveness by Breaux and former Chairman John M. Murphy, D-N.Y., this "minor" committee has forced its way into an extraordinary number of important legislative arguments. Nearly all of these have come through Breaux's Subcommittee on Fisheries and Wildlife Conservation and the Environment, on which nearly three-fourths of the full committee serve.

In most cases, Breaux's role has been to soften the environmental constraints on energy producers, especially the oil industry, to which he is close.

In 1979, the subcommittee wrote an Alaska lands bill allowing the oil industry considerably more freedom to drill on environmentally protected land than the rival version, which passed the House but was softened in the Senate. In 1980, Breaux worked to protect oil company interests on the superfund controversy, drawing up a compromise guaranteeing that the companies would be paying strictly for the cleanup of oil spills, rather than chemical spills as well.

In the previous Congress, he was at the center of the controversy over new legislation governing energy development of the Outer Continental Shelf. A select committee was appointed to draft the legislation, with most of its members drawn from Merchant Marine and with Murphy and Breaux in the leading roles.

As it turned out, Breaux and the big oil firms fought the bill that Murphy drafted, one which increased federal regulation of the industry's exploration and contained some new bidding advantages for smaller companies. Breaux drafted his own substitute in consultation with the industry, and it was defeated by a 211-187 vote on the House floor. But over the next few days of debate, he and his allies managed to work most of the substitute into the bill by separate amendment, so that when it was over, Breaux claimed victory and voted for the bill on final passage.

On some committee issues, local interests have forced Breaux into a less predictable posture. In 1980 he sought to protect the alligator skin industry in his district. Alligators had been removed from the endangered species list, but environmentalists wanted to put them back on and Breaux worked against those efforts. But when Tennessee legislators sought an exemption to the act to complete the Tellico Dam, despite its threat to the tiny snail darter fish, he opposed that.

Breaux also uses his subcommittee the way most of its members do — to protect the particu-

---

**7th District: Southwest — Lake Charles, Lafayette.** Population: 543,235 (19% increase since 1970). Race: White 429,909 (79%), Black 109,321 (20%), Others 4,005 (1%). Spanish origin: 9,127 (2%).

lar commercial fishing interest of his area. In his case, concern for the shrimp trade between Louisiana and Japan led him to favor relatively modest restrictions on foreign fishing off the American coast. His fear was that too strict a policy would threaten the trade relationship.

Meanwhile, Breaux has used his Public Works assignment to work on flood control issues important in South Louisiana. He does not chair a subcommittee on Public Works, but he is second on its Water Resources Subcommittee behind Robert Roe of New Jersey

Beyond his committees, Breaux has shown unusual talent at the pure politics of the House — the committee assignment process. Conservative on some issues, he generally has made himself available to Democratic leaders when needed, although he voted for the Reagan budget in 1981. When Speaker Thomas P. O'Neill Jr. wanted to create a new energy committee in 1979, and the panel trying to draw one up seemed on the verge of failure, a telephone call from O'Neill's office switched Breaux's vote and brought the proposal out of committee. It died later on the floor.

Partly as a result of favors like that, Breaux has become a major player on the Steering and Policy Committee, which makes the committee selections. He has proven adept at helping junior colleagues get the assignments they want, giving them reason to do him legislative favors later on.

Candid in a roguish sort of way, Breaux makes no secret of the fact that he enjoys life as a congressman off the House floor as well as on. He was attracted to Merchant Marine initially in part because of its opportunities for foreign travel, and he has taken advantage of them. In the 96th Congress he visited Spain on committee business; in 1978 he took two trips to the Bahamas at the expense of maritime industries. In 1977 he traveled abroad five times, more than any other member of Congress not serving on a foreign policy commitee.

He was involved in some high level horse trading in 1981 as President Reagan pushed spending cuts through the Democratic House. Breaux was one of 29 Democrats who provided a close victory margin for the Republicans and, with disarming candor, he told reporters he decided to vote with Reagan after the President agreed to accept potentially costly price supports on sugar in a farm bill. "I went with the best deal," he said. When someone asked whether that meant his vote was for sale, he smiled and said no: "It can be rented."

**At Home:** Breaux learned his trade by working for one of Louisiana's master politicians, former Gov. Edwin W. Edwards. Breaux was a junior law partner of Edwards and served for four years as one of his top congressional aides.

When Edwards won the governorship in February 1972, he pushed for Breaux to be his successor in the House. With the aid of Edwards' gubernatorial campaign organization, Breaux easily paced the field of six Democratic primary candidates, then won the September runoff with a comfortable 55 percent of the vote over television newscaster Gary Tyler, the same man Edwards had defeated to win his first congressional term seven years earlier.

There was no Republican opposition. Edwards declared Breaux elected, and he was sworn in Oct. 12, 1972, as a member of the House.

Only once have Republicans mounted a serious challenge. That came in 1978, from state Rep. Mike Thompson, a former Democrat. But Breaux defeated him by nearly 2-to-1. In 1980, Breaux was the only member of the Louisiana congressional delegation to run unopposed.

**The District:** The 7th was made highly favorable for Breaux in 1972 when Lafayette, the metropolis of the Cajun country, was added to it from the 3rd.

Cajun parishes, including Acadia — the home base for both Breaux and Edwards — comprise the eastern half of the district. The western half closely resembles the industrialized southeastern portion of Texas, with a heavy emphasis on oil production and refining. The city of Lake Charles anchors the western region. Although about 30 miles inland, Lake Charles has a port connected to the Gulf of Mexico by a large waterway.

While the booming oil and natural gas industry has been responsible for a population boom in the last decade, commercial fishing and agriculture are also important in the district economy. Southwest Louisiana is one of the nation's leading rice-growing areas.

Both areas of the district have been staunchly Democratic, although the Cajun parishes bolted to Reagan in 1980 while the western parishes remained loyal to Carter.

## Committees

**Merchant Marine and Fisheries** (4th of 20 Democrats)
Fisheries and Wildlife Conservation and the Environment, chairman; Merchant Marine; Panama Canal and Outer Continental Shelf.

**Public Works and Transportation** (4th of 25 Democrats)
Surface Transportation; Water Resources.

## Elections

**1980 Primary***

| | |
|---|---|
| John Breaux (D ) | Unopposed |

**1978 Primary****

| | |
|---|---|
| John Breaux (D ) | 78,297 (60 %) |
| Mike Thompson (R ) | 42,247 (33 %) |

* In Louisiana a candidate unopposed in the primary and general elections is declared elected. His name does not appear on the ballot in either election.
** In Louisiana the primary is open to candidates of all parties. If a candidate wins 50% or more of the vote in the primary no general election is held.

**Previous Winning Percentages**

1976 (83 %)     1974 (89 %)     1972 (100%)

**District Vote For President**

| | 1980 | | 1976 | | 1972 |
|---|---|---|---|---|---|
| D | 99,322 (48 %) | D | 101,104 (59 %) | D | 41,594 (31 %) |
| R | 101,475 (49 %) | R | 65,298 (38 %) | R | 86,609 (64 %) |
| I | 4,192 (2 %) | | | | |

## Campaign Finance

| | Receipts | Receipts from PACs | Expenditures |
|---|---|---|---|
| **1980** | | | |
| Breaux (D ) | $162,698 | $73,525 (45 %) | $89,822 |
| **1978** | | | |
| Breaux (D ) | $143,515 | $48,250 (34 %) | $183,424 |
| Thompson (R ) | $123,714 | $3,050 (2 %) | $120,978 |

## Voting Studies

| Year | Presidential Support | | Party Unity | | Conservative Coalition | |
|---|---|---|---|---|---|---|
| | S | O | S | O | S | O |
| 1980 | 58 | 32 | 58 | 35 | 72 | 21 |
| 1979 | 37 | 50 | 35 | 51 | 76 | 8 |
| 1978 | 25 | 54 | 19 | 67 | 80 | 5 |
| 1977 | 39 | 44 | 39 | 48 | 76 | 13 |
| 1976 | 53 | 39 | 32 | 57 | 80 | 11 |
| 1975 | 55 | 40 | 43 | 49 | 77 | 15 |
| 1974 (Ford) | 59 | 28 | | | | |
| 1974 | 72 | 23 | 44 | 49 | 74 | 17 |
| 1973 | 37 | 45 | 50 | 33 | 57 | 23 |
| 1972 | 60 | 20† | 0 | 100† | 100 | 0† |

† Not eligible for all recorded votes.

S = Support          O = Opposition

## Key Votes

**96th Congress**

| | |
|---|---|
| Weaken Carter oil profits tax (1979) | Y |
| Reject hospital cost control plan (1979) | # |
| Implement Panama Canal Treaties (1979) | N |
| Establish Department of Education (1979) | N |
| Approve Anti-busing Amendment (1979) | Y |
| Guarantee Chrysler Corp. loans (1979) | Y |
| Approve military draft registration (1980) | Y |
| Aid Sandinista regime in Nicaragua (1980) | Y |
| Strengthen fair housing laws (1980) | N |

**97th Congress**

| | |
|---|---|
| Reagan budget proposal (1981) | Y |

## Interest Group Ratings

| Year | ADA | ACA | AFL-CIO | CCUS |
|---|---|---|---|---|
| 1980 | 11 | 48 | 28 | 77 |
| 1979 | 5 | 54 | 30 | 93 |
| 1978 | 5 | 86 | 5 | 71 |
| 1977 | 0 | 55 | 45 | 75 |
| 1976 | 10 | 64 | 43 | 88 |
| 1975 | 11 | 67 | 45 | 53 |
| 1974 | 13 | 54 | 40 | 78 |
| 1973 | 28 | 41 | 90 | 27 |
| 1972 | 0 | - | 0 | - |

# 8 Gillis W. Long (D)

**Of Alexandria — Elected 1972**
Also served 1963-1965

**Born:** May 4, 1923, Winfield, La.
**Education:** La. State U., B.A. 1949, J.D. 1951.
**Military Career:** Army, 1942-47.
**Profession:** Lawyer.
**Family:** Wife, Mary Catherine Small; two children.
**Religion:** Baptist.
**Political Career:** U.S. House, 1963-65; unsuccessfully sought renomination to U.S. House, 1964; unsuccessful candidates for Democratic gubernatorial nomination, 1963, 1971.

**In Washington:** Long is a Southern moderate with an unusual combination of interests — congressional procedure and international economics. In 1981, he won a place in the Democratic leadership as chairman of the party caucus.

Fascinated by the workings of the House, Long jumped at the chance to join the Rules Committee when he returned in 1973 after an eight-year absence. Ironically, it was a vote on expansion of the committee 10 years earlier that had led to his defeat in 1964. His primary opponent charged him with helping "pack" the Rules Committee to clear the way for liberal Kennedy legislation, and he lost his seat.

When he came back in 1973, Long also headed for the Joint Economic Committee, a sort of House-Senate think tank which studies problems but writes no legislation. Long wanted to do the sort of long-range thinking and planning impossible on House committees locked into 2-year work cycles. In recent years, he has studied such problems as U.S.-Japanese economic relations and the prospects for a North American Common Market. Thanks largely to Louisiana's strategic position as an oil and gas producer, he also has been drawn into the question of world energy supplies. A friendly, even-tempered man, Long has always been one of the more popular House members. In early 1981, he decided to cash in on some of that reputation with a campaign for caucus chairman. It was not his first foray into House politics; he had managed the 1976 campaign for majority leader by his close friend, Missouri Democrat Richard Bolling, and shared some of Bolling's ideas about the need for a stronger caucus. He was a natural candidate for party leadership, and he was an easy winner, defeating Charlie Rose of North Carolina and Matthew McHugh of New York by a lopsided margin.

Whether Long can revive the caucus as a forum for Democratic consensus remains to be seen. He views it as a place to air problems before they come up on the floor. But since the caucus has 30 to 40 members whose loyalties are more with the Reagan administration than with their own leadership, consensus seems all but impossible. Few new ideas were tried in early 1981. Long was slowed down personally by open-heart surgery early in the year, leaving him on part-time status for several months.

On Rules, Long works closely with Bolling to set the terms for debating legislation. He has worried about the long-term impact on the committee of using it to shield members by blocking the introduction of politically controversial floor amendments. "I don't think we can continue to play this role forever," he has said. "We won't be able to stand the pressure."

In 1979, when Bolling set up two new subcommittees at Rules, he gave one to Long, on the Legislative Process. Long spent most of the 96th Congress working there on "sunset" legislation, aimed at finding a way to terminate federal programs automatically unless they are specifically renewed.

"Sunset" has frightened House committee chairmen, who insist it would place an impossible burden on their workload. In 1980, Long tried to

---

**8th District: Central — Alexandria.**
Population: 511,467 (12% increase since 1970). Race: White 338,844 (66%), Black 169,685 (33%), Others 2,938 (1%). Spanish origin: 8,364 (2%).

sell them on a a different version, which dropped the automatic termination and allowed committees to set their own agendas for reviewing programs. But Long was unable to build enough support for this to move it to the House floor.

Long generally votes the moderate-liberal position of a Democratic Party loyalist. He backed all the unsuccessful Democratic budget alternatives in 1981 against the Reagan budget proposals. But he also is true to the gas and oil interests so important to his state. In 1975, he successfully amended a major energy bill to give independent oil and gas producers a higher price ceiling. In 1978, when the Carter administration wanted its energy bill brought to the floor as a single piece of legislation, Long first voted in the Rules Committee against that idea, contributing to its defeat on a tie vote. But the next day, after appeals from House leaders, he voted "present," permitting the bill to go to the floor as a single package, in which form it eventually passed.

**At Home:** Long has parlayed his famous family name into a stormy but lengthy political career.

Since 1962, he has been elected six times to the House. But because he is more liberal than most of Huey's other relatives and most of Louisiana, he has also had his political problems. Long was ousted from his congressional seat in 1964 after one term in office, and has failed in two bids for the governorship. He now keeps a large permanent campaign treasury, in an effort to ward off potential challengers tempted by his liberal voting record.

Long's early political experience was appointive. He served for a year as counsel to the Senate Small Business Committee and for eight years as counsel to the House Committee to Investigate Campaign Expenditures.

He made his first race in 1962, challenging a vulnerable House Democrat, Harold B. McSween, for renomination. McSween was closely associated with private power and lumber interests in his district, and was a target of rural cooperatives who considered him unfriendly to their cause.

McSween had been saved from political oblivion two years earlier, when former Gov. Earl Long died after defeating him in the Democratic runoff. In 1962, he had no such reprieve. Gillis Long beat him by 7,500 votes and went on to win the general election by a margin of nearly 2-1.

With the support of his cousin, Sen. Russell B. Long, Gillis sought the governorship the following year. But many other members of the Long family, including Earl's widow, backed State Public Service Commissioner John J. McKeithen, the eventual winner. Long ran third in the Democratic primary with 15 percent of the vote, although he finished within 20,000 votes of second place and a spot in the runoff.

The intra-family squabbling continued in 1964, with McKeithen and the old Earl Long faction backing former state Sen. Speedy O. Long against Gillis. Although the two Longs were cousins, their race was bitter and centered on civil rights.

Speedy accused Gillis of aiding the passage of the Civil Rights Act by voting for permanent enlargement of the House Rules Committee, thus giving the liberals an advantage. Speedy's focus on the race issue paid off with a 5,000-vote primary victory, and Gillis was out of office after only one term. He stayed in Washington as assistant director of the U.S. Office of Economic Opportunity under President Johnson.

Long sought to revive his political career in 1971 by running again for governor. He was seen as a major contender and drew strong support from the black community, finishing third in the Democratic primary with 14 percent of the vote.

That third place showing was a disappointment to Long, but it resurrected his political career. In the runoff campaign, he threw his support to Rep. Edwin W. Edwards, bringing Edwards far more votes than the 4,500 that represented his winning margin. Once in office, Edwards helped redraw the boundaries of the 8th District so that it would be favorable terrain for Gillis. Speedy announced a convenient retirement in 1972, and Gillis had no serious rivals for the seat.

Since then, he has held it without difficulty, in part because his fund-raising ability has scared away potential challengers. Although he faced a weak field of rivals in 1980, Long had more than $300,000 in cash on hand by midsummer.

**The District:** Long's current district is much friendlier to his moderate politics than the one he represented in the early 1960s. The old 8th stretched from the city of Alexandria into the Protestant and very conservative parishes to the north. The new 8th also has Alexandria, but it moves south from there into the heart of the more liberal Cajun country. Most of the parishes grow sugar and cotton, and are relatively poor. The population is one-third black.

In its present configuration, the 8th is a Democratic stronghold. It gave Carter 60 percent of the vote in 1976, his highest share in any Louisiana district.

## Committees

**Rules** (3rd of 11 Democrats)
Legislative Process, chairman.

**Joint Economic**
International Trade, Finance and Security Economics, Chairman;
Agriculture and Transportation.

## Elections

**1980 Primary***

| | |
|---|---|
| Gillis Long (D ) | 75,433 (69 %) |
| Clyde Holloway (R ) | 27,816 (25 %) |
| Robert Mitchell (R ) | 6,243 (6 %) |

**1978 Primary***

| | |
|---|---|
| Gillis Long (D ) | 80,666 (80 %) |
| Robert Mitchell (R ) | 20,547 (20 %) |

* In Louisiana the primary is open to candidates of all parties. If a candidate wins 50% or more of the vote in the primary no general election is held.

**Previous Winning Percentages**

| | | | |
|---|---|---|---|
| 1976 (94 %) | 1974 (100%) | 1972 (69 %) | 1962 (64 %) |

**District Vote For President**

| | 1980 | | 1976 | | 1972 |
|---|---|---|---|---|---|
| **D** | 106,453 (53 %) | **D** | 94,913 (60 %) | **D** | 43,439 (34 %) |
| **R** | 88,518 (44 %) | **R** | 59,564 (38 %) | **R** | 73,297 (58 %) |

## Campaign Finance

| | Receipts | Receipts from PACs | Expen-ditures |
|---|---|---|---|
| **1980** | | | |
| Long (D ) | $370,481 | $87,935 (24 %) | $223,493 |
| **1978** | | | |
| Long (D ) | $222,703 | $74,375 (33 %) | $189,507 |
| Mitchell (R ) | $7,107 | — (0 %) | $7,106 |

## Voting Studies

| Year | Presidential Support | | Party Unity | | Conservative Coalition | |
|---|---|---|---|---|---|---|
| | **S** | **O** | **S** | **O** | **S** | **O** |
| 1980 | 79 | 16 | 88 | 10 | 35 | 63 |
| 1979 | 59 | 26 | 62 | 18 | 43 | 41 |
| 1978 | 59 | 34 | 67 | 26 | 46 | 48 |
| 1977 | 58 | 34 | 71 | 24 | 47 | 48 |
| 1976 | 45 | 51 | 65 | 32 | 58 | 38 |
| 1975 | 51 | 48 | 68 | 27 | 51 | 45 |
| 1974 (Ford) | 46 | 41 | | | | |
| 1974 | 68 | 28 | 66 | 24† | 40 | 50 |
| 1973 | 42 | 54 | 74 | 22 | 46 | 52 |
| 1964 | 81 | 13 | 82 | 11 | 67 | 33 |
| 1963 | 52 | 11 | 58 | 12 | 47 | 13 |

† Not eligible for all recorded votes.

S = Support          O = Opposition

## Key Votes

**96th Congress**

| | |
|---|---|
| Weaken Carter oil profits tax (1979) | Y |
| Reject hospital cost control plan (1979) | Y |
| Implement Panama Canal Treaties (1979) | ? |
| Establish Department of Education (1979) | Y |
| Approve Anti-busing Amendment (1979) | N |
| Guarantee Chrysler Corp. loans (1979) | Y |
| Approve military draft registration (1980) | Y |
| Aid Sandinista regime in Nicaragua (1980) | Y |
| Strengthen fair housing laws (1980) | Y |

**97th Congress**

| | |
|---|---|
| Reagan budget proposal (1981) | N |

## Interest Group Ratings

| Year | ADA | ACA | AFL-CIO | CCUS |
|---|---|---|---|---|
| 1980 | 50 | 21 | 63 | 73 |
| 1979 | 26 | 24 | 50 | 57 |
| 1978 | 50 | 21 | 63 | 38 |
| 1977 | 15 | 26 | 70 | 50 |
| 1976 | 30 | 32 | 70 | 57 |
| 1975 | 47 | 32 | 74 | 29 |
| 1974 | 57 | 23 | 80 | 22 |
| 1973 | 40 | 27 | 91 | 27 |
| 1964 | 60 | 17 | 64 | - |
| 1963 | - | 14 | - | - |

# Maine

## ...The State Muskie Changed

Maine is preparing to hold its first election in 30 years in which Edmund S. Muskie will not be the leading force among state Democrats. More than any politician in almost any other state, Muskie redefined his state's politics, symbolizing its movement from traditional Yankee control toward ethnic appeals and two-party competition.

It was not so much a matter of design; Muskie came along at a moment when Maine was ripe for change. Republicans had held the reins since the Civil War, dominating the state in alliance with railroads, power companies and paper mills.

But by 1954, there was an alternative force available to seize, and Muskie seized it. He took advantage of his working-class roots to activate the state's communities, and he built a reputation for integrity that attracted many Yankee Republicans. Muskie won two terms as governor, four as senator and helped carry the state for the national Democratic ticket in 1968. By the mid-1960s, Democrats held the governorship, both U.S. House seats and periodic control of one or both houses of the state Legislature. Margaret Chase Smith, a Republican institution for 30 years, was swept out by Democrat William Hathaway in 1972.

Republicans turned much of this around in the 1970s but not with their traditional candidates. William Cohen, David Emery and Olympia Snowe, all under 35, all moderates in national GOP politics, won seats in Congress over a six-year period. Cohen defeated Hathaway for re-election to the Senate in 1978. The GOP is again a virile force in state politics, and with Muskie retired from elective office, the Republicans may be on their way to another period of dominance.

But the Democrats are unlikely to return to the famine of the pre-Muskie days. Even in the midst of the 1980 Reagan landslide, Carter lost Maine by just 4 percentage points, crippled by John Anderson's 10 percent share of the vote.

## A Political Tour

**The Industrial Core.** Southern Maine has long been the state's most densely populated

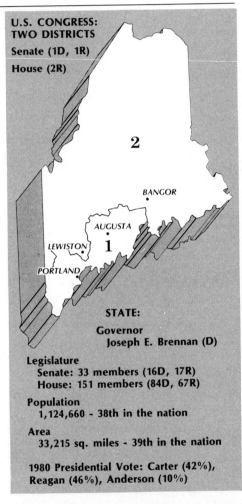

**U.S. CONGRESS: TWO DISTRICTS**

Senate (1D, 1R)

House (2R)

**STATE:**

Governor
Joseph E. Brennan (D)

Legislature
Senate: 33 members (16D, 17R)
House: 151 members (84D, 67R)

Population
1,124,660 - 38th in the nation

Area
33,215 sq. miles - 39th in the nation

1980 Presidential Vote: Carter (42%), Reagan (46%), Anderson (10%)

region. Just four southern counties — Kennebec, Androscoggin, Cumberland and York — contain half the state's population and all but one of its large cities.

The Democratic industrial core follows Interstate 95 from Biddeford in the south to Waterville in the north. Once powered by the waters of Maine's rivers, these cities originally supported major labor-intensive industries — shoes, ship building, textiles, lumber and paper.

The low wages and high unemployment afflicting this area in the 1930s and 1940s helped make southern Maine a fertile recruiting ground for Muskie and other Democrats. So did the influx of thousands of immigrants from Ireland, Poland and, especially, Quebec.

Portland, Maine's largest city with 61,000 people, has long been a shipping and business capital. It is solidly Democratic.

In current Maine politics, however, Portland is only one of six heavily Democratic cities in the region. Others are the shoe-making twin cities of Lewiston and Auburn, with a combined population slightly larger than Portland; Biddeford and Saco, along the Atlantic Coast; and, at the northern edge, Waterville, a textile city. Nearby Augusta, the state capital, has a smaller Franco-American population than any of the others and is more evenly split between factory workers and white-collar government workers.

Republican strength in southern Maine is found in towns that rely heavily on the military, like Kittery, Brunswick and Bath; in inland areas that blend into rural Maine's farms and forests; and in small coastal resorts, like Kennebunkport, that cater to the wealthy.

**The Coastal Counties.** Along the coast, contiguous to the Democratic-industrial core of Maine, is the state's Republican heartland. Lincoln, Knox, Waldo and Hancock counties consist mainly of small coastal towns that help make Maine the No. 1 lobster state, as well as the "Vacation State." There are also a number of small inland farms in these counties. The people are basically of Yankee stock.

Hancock County, with its exclusive Bar Harbour summer resorts, is one of the most Republican counties in the nation. Even Muskie, Maine's all-time Democratic vote-getter, has never won in Hancock.

**Outer Maine.** Most of Maine is rural and covered with forests that supply trees for huge lumber and paper mills. The land that is left raises apples, blueberries, corn, chickens and Maine's biggest cash crop, potatoes. The potatoes are grown largely in Aroostook County, the huge northern tract that is bigger than four states.

Yankee Republican farmers form a solid majority in rural Maine, but the chronic poverty that afflicts the area is gradually bringing more of its residents into the Democratic column as they turn to the government for assistance. Pockets of severe poverty are found in the woodlands in Aroostook County and in coastal Washington County, which lacks the tourist attraction of the more accessible coastal regions. With the help of a large Franco-American population, Democrats often prevail in Washington.

Bangor, the region's only large city and the third biggest city in the state, has a slight Democratic edge. But unlike the industrial towns further south, it occasionally votes Republican.

## Redrawing the Lines

Population in the 1st District grew nearly twice as fast as in the 2nd District during the 1970s. But the two differ in population by only 37,710, so redistricting can be accomplished with few changes. Democrats control the state House and the governor's office, but Republicans have a one-vote margin in the state Senate.

# Governor
# Joseph E. Brennan (D)

**Born:** Nov. 2, 1934, Portland, Maine
**Home:** Portland, Maine.
**Education:** Boston College, A.B. 1958; U. of Maine Law School, J.D. 1963.
**Military Career:** Army, 1953-55.
**Profession:** Lawyer.
**Family:** Divorced; two children.
**Religion:** Roman Catholic.
**Political Career:** Maine House, 1965-71; Cumberland County district attorney, 1970-72; Maine Senate, 1973-75; unsuccessful campaign for gubernatorial nomination, 1974; state attorney general, 1975-77; elected governor 1978; term expires Jan. 1983.

# William S. Cohen (R)

### Of Bangor — Elected 1978

**Born:** Aug. 28, 1940, Bangor, Maine.
**Education:** Bowdoin College, B.A. 1962; Boston
   U., LL.B. 1965.
**Profession:** Lawyer.
**Family:** Wife, Diane Dunn; two children.
**Religion:** Unitarian.
**Political Career:** Bangor City Council, 1969-72;
   mayor of Bangor, 1971-72; U.S. House, 1973-
   79.

**In Washington:** A national celebrity for
several years after his performance in the House
Judiciary Committee's 1974 impeachment debate,
Cohen has departed center stage at least temporarily since he moved to the Senate in 1978. He
has made few headlines and fewer waves while
concentrating on his committees, Armed Services
and Governmental Affairs.

At the time of the impeachment inquiry,
Cohen was a 33-year-old House freshman. Relying
on his experience as a trial lawyer, he carefully
sifted the evidence turned up in the committee's
investigation, determined, he said, to base his
decision "on something much firmer than the
shifting sands of public opinion."

Cohen's good looks, easygoing manner and
careful questioning were perfect for national television. As one of just six Republicans in favor of
impeachment, he drew unusual media attention,
nearly all of it favorable. *Time* magazine named
him one of America's 200 future leaders, and the
Jaycees called him one of 10 outstanding young
men in the nation.

During his three terms in the House, Cohen
was generally regarded as a liberal Republican.
He perceived a pressure from the party leaders to
conform, and complained about it. "In the House,
there was a purge mentality," he said a year after
he left, "a feeling that if you didn't do what was
expected, vote the way they wanted you to, you
were out."

Perhaps because he feels less pressure now, or
perhaps because his views are changing, Cohen
has moved perceptibly to the right in the Senate.
His shift is particularly evident on defense and
foreign policy issues, where his perspective has
been shaped by his work on Armed Services.
Cohen was a vigorous opponent of the SALT II
treaty and has taken a hard-line stand on Soviet
adventurism around the world.

In domestic policy, he voted against the
Chrysler loan guarantee, which many business-

oriented Republicans favored despite its departure from market economics. He was the only
member of Governmental Affairs to vote against
the new Department of Education, arguing it
would lead to greater federal control of local
schools.

On some issues there has been little percepti-
ble change. Cohen remains a strong environmentalist, fighting a prolonged battle to block the
controversial Dickey-Lincoln dam project in
northern Maine. He opposed construction of the
Tellico Dam in Tennessee because it theatened
the snail darter fish, and backed the "superfund"
bill to provide for cleanup of toxic wastes.

A Latin major in college, Cohen is the Senate's only published poet, author of a slim volume
of 36 poems entitled "Of Sons and Seasons,"
which appeared in 1978. Although the collection
received reasonably friendly reviews, Cohen is
careful to describe poetry as a "hobby." He also
kept a diary of his first year in the Senate, and
published it in early 1981.

**At Home:** Cohen all but assured himself of a
statewide political future on the day he spoke out
for President Nixon's impeachment, carving an
image not only as a Republican of conscience, but
as a man who knew how to give a good speech.
From that point on, his promotion to the Senate
was pretty much a matter of time.

If there had been no Watergate, however, the
odds are he would be in the Senate by now
anyway. His Judiciary Committee performance
merely added to the "rising star" reputation he
had carried with him most of his life, beginning in
his high school and college days on the basketball
court.

He thought about becoming a Latin scholar,
but went to law school instead and finished
among the top 10 members of his class. It was less

than a decade from law school to the Bangor mayoralty.

Cohen became mayor in 1972, after three years on the City Council. But he did not hold the job very long. Rep. William D. Hathaway was running for the Senate the same year, and his 2nd District was open. Cohen won it easily, running exceptionally well in many Democratic areas for a Republican.

After the 1974 period of celebrity, Cohen began to consider the timing for a Senate effort. He thought for nearly a year about a 1976 campaign against Maine's senior senator, Edmund S. Muskie. Private polls showed him close to Muskie, but challenging the state's most durable Democrat was no sure thing. Prudence dictated a two-year wait and a campaign against Hathaway, more liberal and less of an institution.

Knowing he was in trouble, Hathaway worked hard to save himself, but Cohen had almost no weaknesses. The personal glamour of 1974 had never really worn off, and state and national media refurbished it for the campaign. Cohen shifted slightly to the right, arguing that Hathaway was too liberal for most of Maine. He also worked for Democratic votes, concentrating his efforts in such places as Portland's Irish-Catholic Munjoy Hill section. Hathaway had not done anything in particular to offend the voters, but the challenger overwhelmed him. The Democrat was held in a three-way contest to 33.9 percent, one of the lowest figures for any Senate incumbent in recent years.

One of Cohen's few political missteps was his all-out support for Tennessee Sen. Howard H. Baker Jr. for the 1980 Republican presidential nomination. Cohen tried to engineer a straw poll victory for Baker at a statewide party gathering in late 1979, but the Tennessean lost in a surprise to George Bush.

## Committees

**Armed Services** (6th of 9 Republicans)
Sea Power and Force Projection, Chairman; Manpower and Personnel; Strategic and Theater Nuclear Forces.

**Governmental Affairs** (6th of 9 Republicans)
Oversight of Government Management, Chairman; Energy, Nuclear Proliferation, and Government Processes; Permanent Subcommittee on Investigations.

**Select Indian Affairs** (Chairman)

**Special Aging** (5th of 8 Republicans)

## Elections

**1978 General**

| | |
|---|---|
| William Cohen (R ) | 212,294 (56 %) |
| William Hathaway (D ) | 127,327 (34 %) |
| Hayes Gahagan (I) | 27,824 (7 %) |

**Previous Winning Percentages**

1976* (77 %)   1974* (71 %)   1972* (54 %)

*House elections

## Campaign Finance

| | Receipts | Receipts from PACs | Expenditures |
|---|---|---|---|
| **1978** | | | |
| Cohen (R ) | $658,254 | $157,551 (24 %) | $648,739 |
| Hathaway (D ) | $423,499 | $166,594 (39 %) | $423,027 |

## Voting Studies

| | Presidential Support | | Party Unity | | Conservative Coalition | |
|---|---|---|---|---|---|---|
| Year | S | O | S | O | S | O |
| Senate service | | | | | | |
| 1980 | 43 | 42 | 64 | 23 | 58 | 30 |
| 1979 | 55 | 37 | 62 | 34 | 55 | 38 |
| House service | | | | | | |
| 1978 | 39 | 37 | 58 | 27 | 59 | 24 |
| 1977 | 67 | 29 | 50 | 44 | 48 | 45 |
| 1976 | 43 | 57 | 41 | 58 | 50 | 50 |
| 1975 | 62 | 37 | 56 | 42 | 49 | 48 |
| 1974 (Ford) | 48 | 37 | | | | |
| 1974 | 55 | 43 | 42 | 50 | 38 | 57 |
| 1973 | 53 | 46 | 46 | 52 | 38 | 60 |

S = Support          O = Opposition

## Key Votes

**96th Congress**

| | |
|---|---|
| Maintain relations with Taiwan (1979) | Y |
| Reduce synthetic fuel development funds (1979) | Y |
| Impose nuclear plant moratorium (1979) | Y |
| Kill stronger windfall profits tax (1979) | N |
| Guarantee Chrysler Corp. loans (1979) | N |
| Approve military draft registration (1980) | N |
| End Revenue Sharing to the states (1980) | N |
| Block Justice Dept. busing suits (1980) | N |

**97th Congress**

| | |
|---|---|
| Restore urban program funding cuts (1981) | Y |

## Interest Group Ratings

| Year | ADA | ACA | AFL-CIO | CCUS-1 | CCUS-2 |
|---|---|---|---|---|---|
| Senate service | | | | | |
| 1980 | 33 | 68 | 22 | 70 | |
| 1979 | 42 | 62 | 39 | 64 | 53 |
| House service | | | | | |
| 1978 | 30 | 58 | 21 | 63 | |
| 1977 | 65 | 48 | 59 | 62 | |
| 1976 | 50 | 18 | 52 | 38 | |
| 1975 | 74 | 54 | 57 | 59 | |
| 1974 | 61 | 27 | 64 | 40 | |
| 1973 | 52 | 27 | 64 | 45 | |

# George J. Mitchell (D)

**Of Waterville — Appointed 1980**

**Born:** Aug. 20, 1933, Waterville, Maine.
**Education:** Bowdoin College, B.A. 1954; George-
town U., LL.B. 1960.
**Military Career:** Army, 1954-56.
**Profession:** Lawyer.
**Family:** Wife, Sally Heath; one child.
**Religion:** Roman Catholic.
**Political Career:** Maine Democratic chairman,
1966-68; Democratic nominee for governor,
1974; appointed to the U.S. Senate, May 8,
1980.

**In Washington:** In his first year in the
Senate Mitchell showed his colleagues a healthy
respect for facts. He has a keen memory for detail,
and he has generally seemed more comfortable
using it than staking out rhetorical positions. His
speeches are rarely loud, militant, or emotional —
just factual.

Appointed to the Senate in May of 1980,
after Edmund S. Muskie resigned to become
secretary of state, Mitchell plunged into the factual thicket immediately on the Senate Environment Committee. The panel was just starting
markup on a "superfund" bill, requiring chemical
companies to finance hazardous waste cleanup.

By the time the bill reached the Senate floor
in November, Mitchell was a specialist in the
issue. He was disappointed that the final compromise failed to compensate victims of chemical
contamination, but would allow states to be compensated for property losses. His speech expressing that disappointment attracted unusual attention on the floor.

"This Senate has made the judgment that
property is more significant than human beings,"
he said. "We are telling the people of this country
that under our value system property is worth
compensating, but a human life is not." Mitchell
said he would prepare a separate bill to compensate individual victims.

In addition to playing an environmentalist
role on his committee, Mitchell has voiced the
opposition of much of New England to the lifting
of price controls on oil. In early 1981, when
President Reagan accelerated the schedule for
decontrolling oil prices, Mitchell said Maine residents would suffer more than citizens elsewhere.

One source of energy Mitchell strongly sup-
ported in the 96th Congress was the Dickey-
Lincoln hydroelectric power project on the St.
Johns River in Maine. That placed him on the

same side as Muskie, but at odds with the current
senior senator, Republican William S. Cohen.
When Cohen tried to delete $795,000 in planning
money for Dickey-Lincoln with a 1980 floor
amendment, Mitchell fought him. "It's about
time we in the Northeast had a power project to
help us generate cheaper electricity," Mitchell
said. Cohen lost, 46-37.

Mitchell and Cohen later worked out a compromise, which would deauthorize part of the
project. The two senators jointly sponsored a bill
in May of 1981 to deauthorize the 760-megawatt
Dickey Dam, the most controversial portion of the
project. Environmentalists had complained for
years because a huge lake to be created behind
the dam would have killed wildlife and flooded
forests.

In his first year in the Senate, Mitchell also
argued for the continuation of federal revenue
sharing to states, which was deleted from the
federal budget in 1980 voting, and for keeping
programs of the Economic Development Administration, which President Reagan is trying to eliminate. In 1981, Mitchell got a seat on the Finance
Committee, which deals with revenue sharing.

**At Home:** Mitchell is a protégé of Muskie,
for whom he once worked as administrative assistant. When Muskie moved to the State Department in 1980, he pushed for the choice of Mitchell
as his successor, and Democratic Gov. Joseph
Brennan agreed. The appointment holds until
November 1982, when Mitchell must run for a full
term.

It was a broadly acceptable choice. Mitchell
had few enemies and seemed the perfect compromise, allowing Brennan to bypass the more prominent but more controversial contenders, former
Sen. William D. Hathaway and former Gov.

Kenneth M. Curtis. Mitchell had defeated Brennan in the 1974 gubernatorial primary, but that contest had left no ill feelings. Curtis, by contrast, had not had good relations with the governor, while Hathaway had the liability of a disastrously unsuccessful campaign for re-election to the Senate in 1978.

The campaign for governor in 1974 had been Mitchell's one statewide effort, and it had been a failure. Widely considered the favorite that fall, he had underestimated the independent candidacy of the late James Longley, a Lewiston businessman running on a platform of reduced state spending. Longley drew thousands of blue-collar votes that Mitchell had taken for granted, and edged the Democrat by 15,000 votes, with the Republican nominee a distant third.

Despite his relative inexperience as a candidate, Mitchell has had an extensive career in government and politics. The son of a janitor, he worked his way through law school as an insurance adjuster and spent two years in the Justice Department antitrust division before joining Muskie's staff.

After he returned to Maine to practice law in 1965, Mitchell served as Democratic state chairman and national committeeman. In the wake of the 1972 McGovern defeat, he staged an unsuccessful drive to become chairman of the Democratic National Committee. As the choice of the party's liberal faction, he lost to Robert S. Strauss of Texas.

On Muskie's recommendation, President Carter named Mitchell U.S. attorney for Maine in 1977. Two years later, the same connection won Mitchell the federal judgeship he gave up after only a few months for one more try at national politics.

## Committees

**Environment and Public Works** (6th of 7 Democrats)
Environmental Pollution; Nuclear Regulation; Regional and Community Development.

**Finance** (9th of 9 Democrats)
Economic Growth, Employment and Revenue Sharing; Energy and Agricultural Taxation; Savings, Pensions and Investment Policy.

**Veterans' Affairs** (5th of 5 Democrats)

## Voting Studies

| Year | Presidential Support | | Party Unity | | Conservative Coalition | |
|------|------|------|------|------|------|------|
| | S | O | S | O | S | O |
| 1980 | 76 | 24† | 86 | 14† | 21 | 79† |

S = Support    O = Opposition
† Not eligible for all recorded votes.

## Key Votes

**96th Congress**

| | |
|---|---|
| Approve military draft registration (1980) | N |
| End Revenue Sharing to the states (1980) | Y |
| Block Justice Dept. busing suits (1980) | N |

**97th Congress**

| | |
|---|---|
| Restore urban program funding cuts (1981) | Y |

## Interest Group Ratings

| Year | ADA | ACA | AFL-CIO | CCUS-1 | CCUS-2 |
|------|-----|-----|---------|--------|--------|
| 1980† | 67 | 18 | 78 | 48 | |

† Not eligible for all recorded votes.

# 1 David F. Emery (R)

**Of Rockland — Elected 1974**

**Born:** Sept. 1, 1948, Rockland, Maine.
**Education:** Worcester Polytechnic Institute, B.S. 1970.
**Profession:** Politician.
**Family:** Wife, Carol Rordam.
**Religion:** Congregationalist.
**Political Career:** Maine House, 1971-75.

**In Washington:** Emery has a significant position in the GOP leadership this year as chief deputy whip, but the Navy still absorbs much of his attention, reflecting the concerns of his district. The Bath Iron Works builds Navy frigates, and numerous constituents work in the Portsmouth shipyard, just across the New Hampshire border. Protecting the Bath interest is relatively easy because the yard has been delivering its ships to the Navy on time and under budget, a fact it publicizes in full-page ads in newspapers around the country.

Even when there is no local connection, however, Emery usually falls comfortably within the Armed Services Committee mainstream, backing the kind of defense spending increases that President Reagan has promised. But he is one of the more independent-minded committee members.

The clearest example of that involves the MX intercontinental missile system. Emery supports the MX, but opposes any plan to keep it secure by shuffling the missiles around hidden launching sites to avoid Soviet detection. He insists that much of the U.S. strategic force should be moved to sea — not in the small coastal submarines favored by some MX opponents, but in large, deep-sea submarines like the current Poseidon and Trident.

Emery's training as an engineer supports his interest in defense and in another field to which he has devoted some time: energy. He generally favors turning private industry loose to solve energy problems through higher production and backs new high-technology projects like synthetic fuel, tidal power and a solar satellite.

But here, too, he has shown an independent streak. After the 1979 accident at the Three Mile Island nuclear power plant in Pennsylvania, Emery called for new safeguards. He voted for a 6-month moratorium on new nuclear plant licenses.

On the Merchant Marine Committee, where he has served since 1975, Emery has worked to enact and strengthen the 200-mile U.S. fishing limit. One of his allies on Merchant Marine was Mississippi's Trent Lott; when Lott became whip in 1981, he named Emery as his deputy, not only giving Emery's career a boost but providing a place for the moderate Republican point of view.

**At Home:** Emery is something of a Superman figure in Maine politics, although he looks a lot more like Clark Kent even when he is pouncing on his Democratic opponents. Mild-mannered and inoffensive in Washington, he has been unbeatable in Maine since he was 21 years old.

From the time he was in grade school, the bookish Rockland native has been consumed by two interests: electronics and elections. At age 12, he started dropping in on local Republican headquarters, looking for things to do. During the summer between his sophomore and junior years in college, he was a page at the 1968 GOP convention. He found it so exhilarating that he decided to give up his career in electronics and "run the next time there was an election." The next time was 1970. Emery defeated a man who had been in the Legislature longer than he himself had been alive.

Four years later he took another gamble, running for Congress against four-term Democrat Peter N. Kyros. Although Kyros never was very popular within his own party, he had won his last two terms with 59 percent, and Emery was chal-

---

**1st District: South — Portland, Augusta.** Population: 581,185 (17% increase since 1970). Race: White 575,530 (99%), Black 1,649 (0.2%), Others 4,006 (1%). Spanish origin: 2,737 (0.4%).

lenging him in one of the worst Republican years in decades. But the challenger was able to keep his distance from Watergate, tying himself to Maine's GOP congressman, William Cohen, one of the House Judiciary Republicans who supported impeachment.

Kyros campaigned little, while Emery walked 600 miles around the district in a low-budget, high visibility campaign. Emery won by 679 votes.

Thinking Emery's election had been a fluke, seven Democrats entered the 1976 primary hoping for a chance to defeat him in his first bid for re-election. But by then, the young legislator had studied the art of re-election with the same devotion he once reserved for electronics. In fact, he began using electronics in politics, personally designing a computerized service operation equalled by few in the House.

Going back to Maine every weekend and supporting such locally popular measures as the 200-mile fishing limit, Emery increased his support among Democrats and Republicans alike. Since 1976 he has carried every county in his district, including some of the most Democratic in the state. His record made him a leading contender for 1982 against Democratic Sen. George Mitchell.

**The District:** Located along the coast of Maine, the 1st is slightly more Democratic than its much larger neighbor to the North and East. That is largely because it includes the city of Portland and some smaller Democratic mill towns. But Democratic congressmen have not lasted long in the 1st District. With the exception of Kyros, only two Democrats have held the seat since 1920.

## Committees

**Armed Services** (9th of 19 Republicans)
Research and Development; Seapower and Strategic and Critical Materials.

**Merchant Marine and Fisheries** (7th of 15 Republicans)
Fisheries and Wildlife Conservation and the Environment; Oceanography.

## Elections

**1980 General**

| | |
|---|---|
| David Emery (R ) | 188,667 (68 %) |
| Harold Pachios (D ) | 86,819 (32 %) |

**1978 General**

| | |
|---|---|
| David Emery (R ) | 120,791 (62 %) |
| John Quinn (D ) | 70,348 (36 %) |

**Previous Winning Percentages**

1976 (57 %)     1974 (50 %)

**District Vote For President**

| | 1980 | | 1976 | | 1972 |
|---|---|---|---|---|---|
| D | 117,613 (42 %) | D | 123,598 (48 %) | D | 85,028 (39 %) |
| R | 126,274 (45 %) | R | 127,019 (49 %) | R | 135,338 (61 %) |
| I | 30,889 (11 %) | | | | |

## Campaign Finance

| | Receipts | Receipts from PACs | Expenditures |
|---|---|---|---|
| **1980** | | | |
| Emery (R ) | $247,249 | $2,000 (1 %) | $247,509 |
| Pachios (D ) | $146,738 | $1,700 (1 %) | $141,864 |
| **1978** | | | |
| Emery (R ) | $200,514 | $100 (0 %) | $200,480 |
| Quinn (D ) | $78,424 | $19,701 (25 %) | $73,755 |

## Voting Studies

| | Presidential Support | | Party Unity | | Conservative Coalition | |
|---|---|---|---|---|---|---|
| Year | S | O | S | O | S | O |
| 1980 | 50 | 46 | 77 | 20 | 78 | 18 |
| 1979 | 33 | 47 | 64 | 19 | 67 | 15 |
| 1978 | 43 | 49 | 70 | 26 | 71 | 27 |
| 1977 | 59 | 39 | 65 | 33 | 70 | 28 |
| 1976 | 45 | 55 | 54 | 44 | 69 | 31 |
| 1975 | 49 | 51 | 61 | 35 | 54 | 41 |

S = Support          O = Opposition

## Key Votes

**96th Congress**

| | |
|---|---|
| Weaken Carter oil profits tax (1979) | Y |
| Reject hospital cost control plan (1979) | Y |
| Implement Panama Canal Treaties (1979) | N |
| Establish Department of Education (1979) | X |
| Approve Anti-busing Amendment (1979) | ? |
| Guarantee Chrysler Corp. loans (1979) | N |
| Approve military draft registration (1980) | Y |
| Aid Sandinista regime in Nicaragua (1980) | N |
| Strengthen fair housing laws (1980) | Y |

**97th Congress**

| | |
|---|---|
| Reagan budget proposal (1981) | Y |

## Interest Group Ratings

| Year | ADA | ACA | AFL-CIO | CCUS |
|---|---|---|---|---|
| 1980 | 39 | 67 | 21 | 68 |
| 1979 | 26 | 75 | 37 | 72 |
| 1978 | 25 | 69 | 35 | 59 |
| 1977 | 50 | 48 | 48 | 59 |
| 1976 | 40 | 50 | 45 | 57 |
| 1975 | 68 | 50 | 57 | 65 |

# 2 Olympia J. Snowe (R)

## Of Auburn — Elected 1978

**Born:** Feb. 21, 1947, Augusta, Maine.
**Education:** U. of Maine, B.A. 1969.
**Profession:** Public Official.
**Family:** Widow of Peter Snowe; no children.
**Religion:** Greek Orthodox.
**Political Career:** Maine House, 1973-77; Maine Senate, 1977-79.

**In Washington:** She has been called Maine's new Margaret Chase Smith, but Snowe is much more of a nuts and bolts politician than the grande dame once called the "conscience of the Senate."

A moderate Republican, Snowe spent her first term picking her issues carefully and trying to avoid spreading herself too thin. As a member of Government Operations, she concentrated her attention on the complex formulas through which federal money goes to states in programs like revenue sharing and anti-recession aid to cities.

The ultimate goal has been to change the formulas and win a bigger portion of the pie for smaller states like Maine. Her greatest victory came when she amended a $1 billion anti-recession aid bill in 1980 to place a cap of 12.5 percent on the share of the money any state could get.

The cap affected only two states, New York and California, and was bitterly fought by members of those delegations, who felt they were being treated as scapegoats. "This type of parochialism and legislating with blindness is irresponsible," said Democratic Rep. Geraldine Ferraro of New York. But Snowe correctly perceived that there are more votes in the small-state delegations than in the biggest states, if they are effectively mobilized. She put together a 4-2 advantage among Republicans and a 2-1 edge among Southern Democrats to overcome the opposition of the bill's managers.

Snowe also pushed for retaining the portion of federal revenue sharing that was earmarked for the states. The Budget Committee had voted to give revenue sharing only to city and local governments, arguing that most states were in surplus and did not need the aid.

As a member of the Aging and Small Business committees, Snowe has been able to link homestate interests, holding hearings in Maine on rural housing and government regulatory problems. In 1981, she switched from Government Operations to the Foreign Affairs Committee, a move aimed at expanding her own areas of expertise.

**At Home:** No one in Washington is likely to confuse the youthful, fashionable Snowe with her flinty Republican predecessor, but she has all of Smith's ambition and talent for winning votes.

An orphan at age nine, Snowe was raised by her aunt, who worked in a textile mill, and her uncle, a barber. Like most working-class Lewiston and Auburn families, they voted Democratic. But after working as an intern for Democratic Gov. Kenneth M. Curtis, Olympia Bouchles met Peter Trafton Snowe, a young Auburn businessman who was involved in Republican politics. She married him in 1969, adopting his partisan allegiance.

In 1973, four months after Snowe began working in the district office of Republican Rep. William S. Cohen, her husband was killed in an automobile accident while returning from Augusta, where he was serving his second term in the state House. A month later she was elected to fill his seat. After winning another term on her own, she was elected to the state Senate in 1976. At that point, Snowe began contemplating a run for the U.S. House amid rumors that Cohen planned to leave the seat to run for the Senate.

Republicans at the state and national level felt she was the ideal replacement for Cohen, and they successfully arranged for her to be the only

---

**2nd District: North — Lewiston, Auburn.** Population: 543,475 (9% increase since 1970). Race: White 534,320 (98%), Black 1,479 (0.2%), Others 7,676 (1%). Spanish origin: 2,268 (0.4%).

GOP candidate in 1978. Her Democratic opponent was Secretary of State Markham L. Gartley, who had attracted some attention because of his 1974 campaign against Cohen — in which he won only 29 percent — and because of the publicity he received for being the first prisoner of war released by the North Vietnamese.

To broaden her exposure and help soften her "Fifth Avenue" image, Snowe traded her designer clothes for a wool shirt and hiking boots and walked across the district — a tactic Cohen had been using successfully. Opposing the construction of the Dickey-Lincoln Dam and favoring "some kind" of national health insurance, Snowe appealed to many Democrats who were put off by Gartley's conservative stance. She ran far ahead of the GOP ticket in Democratic Androscoggin County (Lewiston) — her home territory — and picked up the usual Republican vote in the rest of the district to defeat Gartley handily .

Snowe managed to maintain her popularity during her first term, and Democrats made little effort to oust her in 1980. Their candidate was an independent state senator who had previously served in the Legislature as a Republican. He opposed the Equal Rights Amendment and federal funding of abortion, allowing Snowe once again to campaign as the moderate, appealing to both Democrats and Republicans.

**The District:** This is the largest district east of the Mississippi. Most of the people live in the southern end; the northern part is largely pine forest.

The district's partisan registration slightly favors Democrats, largely because of their strength in Androscoggin County. However, Democratic House candidates have rarely been successful, because of the strong Republican vote in Hancock County, located along the coast, and in Penobscot County (Bangor).

## Committees

**Foreign Affairs** (14th of 16 Republicans)
Africa; Europe and the Middle East.

**Select Aging** (9th of 23 Republicans)
Human Services.

**Small Business** (7th of 17 Republicans)
Tax, Access to Equity Capital and Business Opportunities.

## Elections

**1980 General**

| | |
|---|---|
| Olympia Snowe (R ) | 186,406 (79 %) |
| Harold Silverman (D ) | 51,026 (21 %) |

**1978 General**

| | |
|---|---|
| Olympia Snowe (R ) | 87,939 (51 %) |
| Markham Gartley (D ) | 70,691 (51 %) |
| Other | 14,424 (8 %) |

**District Vote For President**

| | 1980 | | 1976 | | 1972 |
|---|---|---|---|---|---|
| D | 103,361 (43 %) | D | 108,681 (48 %) | D | 75,556 (38 %) |
| R | 112,248 (46 %) | R | 109,301 (49 %) | R | 121,120 (62 %) |
| I | 22,438 (9 %) | | | | |

## Campaign Finance

| | Receipts | Receipts from PACs | Expen- ditures |
|---|---|---|---|
| **1980** | | | |
| Snowe (R ) | $193,025 | $58,425 (30 %) | $187,934 |
| Silverman (D ) | $20,949 | $4,000 (19 %) | $20,947 |

| 1978 | | | |
|---|---|---|---|
| Snowe (R ) | $221,594 | $61,680 (28 %) | $220,981 |
| Gartley (D ) | $132,743 | $21,200 (16 %) | $132,156 |

## Voting Studies

| | Presidential Support | | Party Unity | | Conservative Coalition | |
|---|---|---|---|---|---|---|
| Year | S | O | S | O | S | O |
| 1980 | 56 | 41 | 67 | 29 | 73 | 22 |
| 1979 | 43 | 54 | 69 | 29† | 71 | 28† |

S = Support          O = Opposition

## Key Votes

**96th Congress**

| | |
|---|---|
| Weaken Carter oil profits tax (1979) | N |
| Reject hospital cost control plan (1979) | Y |
| Implement Panama Canal Treaties (1979) | N |
| Establish Department of Education (1979) | N |
| Approve Anti-busing Amendment (1979) | N |
| Guarantee Chrysler Corp. loans (1979) | N |
| Approve military draft registration (1980) | Y |
| Aid Sandinista regime in Nicaragua (1980) | N |
| Strengthen fair housing laws (1980) | N |

**97th Congress**

| | |
|---|---|
| Reagan budget proposal (1981) | Y |

## Interest Group Ratings

| Year | ADA | ACA | AFL-CIO | CCUS |
|---|---|---|---|---|
| 1980 | 28 | 75 | 33 | 82 |
| 1979 | 39 | 62 | 60 | 72 |

# Maryland

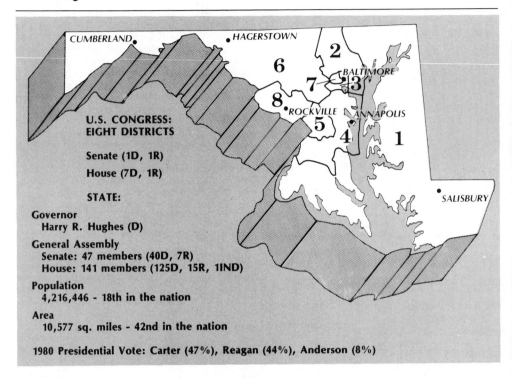

CUMBERLAND •    • HAGERSTOWN

6    2

7   BALTIMORE

8    3

• ROCKVILLE   ANNAPOLIS

5

4    1

• SALISBURY

**U.S. CONGRESS:**
**EIGHT DISTRICTS**

Senate (1D, 1R)

House (7D, 1R)

**STATE:**

**Governor**
Harry R. Hughes (D)

**General Assembly**
Senate: 47 members (40D, 7R)
House: 141 members (125D, 15R, 1IND)

**Population**
4,216,446 - 18th in the nation

**Area**
10,577 sq. miles - 42nd in the nation

**1980 Presidential Vote: Carter (47%), Reagan (44%), Anderson (8%)**

## . . . Suburbia in Control

Maryland is a little bit of everything. The ninth smallest state in the country, it manages to include within its bizarrely shaped borders a rural, traditional isolated Eastern Shore that resembles the Deep South; a mountainous northwest corner that juts into Appalachia; urban Baltimore, with the ethnicity and modern urban problems of any Northern city; and two huge, separate collections of suburbs.

But it is the suburbs that are coming to define Maryland politically. Between them, the state's two suburban Washington, D.C., counties — Montgomery and Prince George's — had more than 1.2 million people in 1980, nearly 30 percent of the population of the state. Another 638,000 live in Baltimore County, an entirely-suburban enclave just outside Baltimore, and more than 300,000 in Anne Arundel County, within commuting distance of both Baltimore and Washington.

Altogether, Maryland is now a mostly-subur-

ban constituency. But the suburbs themselves barely have more in common with each other than they do with the other parts of the state.

Baltimore County is an overwhelmingly white, blue-collar constituency, some of it Southern in orientation, conservative on social issues but loyally Democratic in most elections. Prince George's used to be something like that, but it adjoins mostly-black southeast Washington, and by 1980 it had become one-third black, moving its politics to the left but keeping its Democratic orientation.

Montgomery, on the other hand, is an upper-middle-class, white-collar area, liberal and nominally Democratic but highly independent. It strongly supports Maryland's liberal Republican senator, Charles McC. Mathias Jr.

The result of Maryland's demographic changes is a politics with little statewide coherence, in which most of the individual areas support Democrats for different reasons. Carter won it in 1980 as he was losing virtually every other state in the country. Republicans have not won the governorship since 1966, when Spiro T. Agnew was elected; they did not come close even in 1978, after Democratic incumbent Marvin Mandel had been convicted and sentenced to prison on corruption charges.

The only statewide Republican winner in the past decade has been Mathias, who has cut deeply into the Democratic vote. But there is enough of a conservative base on the Eastern Shore, in the west, and in newer suburban areas such as Anne Arundel County to convince Republicans they can win with the right candidate. They will test that theory in 1982 with a strong challenge to the junior Democratic senator, Paul S. Sarbanes.

# A Political Tour

**Baltimore.** Until recently, Baltimore's preeminence within Maryland was unquestioned. Sixty years ago, the city made up half the state's population. In 1950, when the city's population peaked at just under a million, it accounted for 40 percent of the state total. But as people fled to the suburbs, Baltimore's population plummeted. Today less than 20 percent of the state's residents live there. For the first time in the city's history, the 1980 census showed the majority of them (55 percent) were black.

Despite the population decline, however, the 1970s were a good decade for Baltimore. New construction, development and rehabilitation have boosted its morale in recent years.

Physical regeneration has been aided by innovative programs such as urban homesteading — mostly residential but some commercial as well — in which the city has sold dilapidated property for a dollar. The flashy Harbor Place shopping/commercial center in the inner-harbor area has brought new life to an otherwise deserted downtown.

Baltimore is still the nations's sixth largest port. The world's largest port of entry for cars, it also handles goods ranging from iron and steel to chemicals, grain, sugar and spices. It is becoming a major coal exporting port.

Politically, Baltimore remains the Democratic base of the state. Carter, who carried the state by 45,555 votes in 1980, did it only because he took Baltimore by 134,000.

Nearly 100,000 of that margin came from the 7th Congressional District, which is nearly 80 percent black. Represented by Democrat Parren J. Mitchell, the 7th District covers the center city

and the western side of Baltimore. It was the only district in the state to support George McGovern in 1972.

The ethnic 3rd District on the south and east sides of the city is still Democratic, but with less predictability. The Poles, Italians and other blue-collar ethnics, represented in the House by Democrat Barbara Mikulski, occasionally leaven their Democratic loyalties with a streak of social conservatism. They could not accept George McGovern in 1972; the district gave Richard Nixon 66 percent of its vote.

**Suburban Maryland.** The Baltimore suburbs are currently growing faster than those around Washington, and they are following the traditional pattern of suburban development around Northern cities. The areas closest to the city have now stopped growing. The sons and daughters of those first suburbanites are buying new homes on what was farm land a generation ago.

The Baltimore suburbs tend to be slightly less Democratic than those in the Washington area. In 1976, Gerald Ford carried all the areas closest to Baltimore, while Carter won Montgomery and Prince George's. Four years later, Carter carried Prince George's but lost both Montgomery and Baltimore counties.

Montgomery shows little real partisan affinity. In 1980, while it was going for Reagan over Carter by 20,000 votes, it gave Mathias a 136,000 vote advantage over his Democratic opponent, and re-elected its Democratic congressman by nearly 50,000 votes.

**Western Republican Panhandle.** Maryland's westernmost counties, settled by Pennsylvania Dutch and Scotch-Irish families, resemble neighboring Pennsylvania and West Virginia.

Dating back to the Civil War when the western panhandle sided with the North, the farmers of Western Maryland have been the most consistent Republican voters in the state. Registered Democrats still outnumber Republicans in all but Garrett County, but the margin does not come close to the statewide figure, and the registration edge is rarely reflected in the election returns.

The Republican strength in western Maryland is demonstrated every two years by the results in the 6th Congressional District. Reagan scored his highest percentage in the 6th in 1980. It was the only district J. Glenn Beall Jr. carried in his 1976 Senate loss to Sarbanes. And in 1974, both Mathias and losing GOP gubernatorial candidate Louise Gore ran more than 10 points ahead of their statewide percentages there. But the fact that only 7 percent of the state's voters live in the hilly panhandle permits a Democrat virtually to ignore it in favor of more densely populated areas.

**Eastern Shore.** Around the broad and shallow Chesapeake Bay, a brand of Dixie conservatism has flourished for a long time among the farmers and fishermen.

Long tied to the Democratic Party of the Civil War era, the Eastern Shore began to entertain thoughts of voting Republican after the liberal social and economic policies of the New Deal and Fair Deal challenged its conservative instincts. The voters here flirted with George Wallace's American Independent Party in 1968. Wallace won more than 20 percent of the vote in nearly every county in the region, leaving Hubert Humphrey with the lowest vote for a Democrat since the Civil War in most Eastern Shore counties. Although Carter managed to return about half of the eastern counties to the Democratic column in 1976, by 1980 all but two — Somerset and Kent — were back in GOP hands, and Reagan missed getting those two by 97 and 30 votes, respectively. By the next presidential election, two full decades will have passed since a

Democratic candidate last carried many of the old Dixie Democratic areas of the Eastern Shore.

# Redrawing the Lines

Maryland retains its eight congressional seats, but dramatic population shifts within the state make redistricting tricky. The populations of the 1st and 6th Districts, which encompass the conservative counties at the eastern and western ends of the state, have swollen to more than 600,000 each, while the two Baltimore city districts, the 3rd and the 7th, have dropped to just over 400,000.

Expanding the 7th District to preserve black Democrat Parren J. Mitchell could push Democratic incumbents in the 3rd and 2nd Districts farther from the city. As the lone GOP representative, only 4th District incumbent Marjorie S. Holt is vulnerable to a partisan gerrymander by the Democratic Legislature and governor.

## Governor
## Harry R. Hughes (D)

**Born:** Nov. 13, 1926, Easton, Md.
**Home:** Cross Key, Md.
**Education:** U. of Maryland, B.S. 1949; George Washington U. Law School, J.D. 1952.
**Military Career:** Navy Air Corps, 1944-45.
**Profession:** Lawyer.
**Family:** Wife, Patricia; two children.
**Religion:** Episcopalian.
**Political Career:** Md. House of Delegates, 1955-59; Md. Senate, 1959-71; unsuccessful campaign for U.S. House, 1964; secretary of Md. Dept. of Transportation, 1971-77; elected governor 1978; term expires Jan. 1983.

# Charles McC. Mathias Jr. (R)

**Of Frederick — Elected 1968**

**Born:** July 24, 1922, Frederick, Md.
**Education:** Haverford College, B.A. 1944; Yale U., 1943-44; U. of Md., LL.B. 1949.
**Military Career:** Navy, 1942-44.
**Profession:** Lawyer.
**Family:** Wife, Ann Hickling Bradford; two children.
**Religion:** Episcopalian.
**Political Career:** Frederick city attorney, 1954-59; Md. House, 1959-61; U.S. House, 1961-69.

**In Washington:** Mathias, one of the Senate's most liberal Republicans, galls his conservative colleagues to a degree wholly unwarranted by his actual influence.

The veteran Maryland senator is neither as abrasive as some of his fellow GOP liberals nor as skillful as others. Yet it is Mathias who generates the most anger on the right, and who alone among the dwindling band of Republican liberals has been punished for his political apostasy.

By all the normal rules of seniority, it is Mathias — not South Carolina's Strom Thurmond — who should now be chairman of the Judiciary Committee. But Senate Republicans did him out of it with a vindictiveness seldom displayed in the clubby world of the Senate.

The coup took place not in 1981, when Republicans gained control of the Senate, but in 1977, when a GOP takeover seemed little more than a distant dream. That year the ranking GOP position on Judiciary became vacant. Thurmond was next in line, but he was already ranking Republican on Armed Services and Senate rules prohibit anyone from holding that position on two major committees.

Thurmond's major legislative focus had been on Armed Services. But at the urging of his fellow conservatives, he gave up the top position there solely to block Mathias at Judiciary. Four years later he inherited the chairmanship. Again urged on by the Republican right, he then abolished the antitrust subcommittee Mathias was in line to head, and stripped the Criminal Justice Subcommittee, which Mathias did get, of much of its significant jurisdiction.

It was only through the insistence of Majority Leader Howard H. Baker Jr. that Mathias, who is seventh in seniority among Republicans, wound up with any committee chairmanship — that of the Rules Committee, which in the Senate is largely restricted to housekeeping matters.

A more aggressive and combative man than Mathias might have forestalled the conservative assaults of recent years, but Mathias, despite the hostility he has drawn, has never been much of a political infighter. His pacific nature may even encourage attacks instead of repelling them.

But what seems to provoke conservatives most is the attention — and esteem — that Mathias has always commanded from the national media and other outsiders who consider him a principled spokesman for the moderate-to-liberal wing of the Republican Party.

Ever since he entered Congress 20 years ago, Mathias has gotten excellent press. Because he is their "local" senator, the Washington newspapers in particular tend to give him heavy coverage, most of it favorable. His differences with other Republicans — on issues ranging from the Vietnam War to civil rights and civil liberties — have been highly publicized, in a way that they would not have been if he represented Wyoming, or Vermont.

Mathias was an early and ardent critic of the Nixon administration, and during the Watergate era was prominently listed on the White House "enemies list." He voted against the Haynsworth and Carswell nominations to the Supreme Court, he opposed much of Nixon's "law and order" drive, and he spoke out early against the abuses of power associated with Watergate.

After Nixon resigned, Mathias made no conspicuous effort to move to the Republican mainstream. He began complaining regularly about the party's conservative drift, and in 1978 protested the New Right's proclivity for "cannibalizing" Republicans who disagreed with conservative doctrines.

Year in and year out, Mathias has voted against the majority of his fellow Republicans in the Senate. By and large, however, that has been the extent of his offense; he has rarely been strident or abusive, and it is hard to think of a conservative stratagem that he has actively derailed.

Mathias is no workaholic. He is bored by details, and tends to be absent-minded. He seldom engages in the kind of painstaking effort needed to build coalitions in support of a particular bill or amendment, although he works assiduously to bring home the federal bacon for Maryland and succeeds nicely in that respect.

In the Senate as a whole, Mathias can seldom deliver any vote but his own. But on the Judiciary Committee, where ideological alliances have never coincided neatly with party lineups, he has often cast a crucial swing vote. In the years when major civil rights and civil liberties measures were moving through the committee, it was often Mathias who assured their approval, by lining up with the panel's liberal Democrats against his fellow Republicans and Southern Democrats.

More recently, he has been a swing vote on issues of a different sort. In 1980, for example, it was Mathias who cast the deciding vote to kill a proposed constitutional amendment requiring a balanced federal budget. He also voted against it in 1980 as the committee approved it.

Given the narrow 10-8 edge Republicans hold on Judiciary, and the tendency for Democrats on the committee to be more cohesive than in the past, Mathias can still play a critical role. He vowed early in 1981 to use his influence to defeat any move "to undo two decades of progress in assuring all Americans their civil rights and their civil liberties."

Besides Judiciary and Rules, Mathias serves on the Governmental Affairs Committee, where he chairs the subcommittee responsible for overseeing the District of Columbia. Like the Democrat he replaced, Sen. Thomas F. Eagleton, he supports self-government for the city — but stops short of allowing the district to tax Maryland and Virginia suburbanites who work in the city, as it would like to do.

At the start of the 97th Congress, Mathias voluntarily relinquished his seat on the powerful Appropriations Committee, where he was third in seniority, to take a much lower slot on Foreign Relations. That move dismayed the rest of the Maryland congressional delegation and many politicians in the state, who felt he should have remained on Appropriations to garner the maximum federal generosity possible for Maryland.

Mathias said he chose Foreign Relations over Appropriations because "the development of a consistent and coherent U.S. foreign policy remains the most vital issue confronting the nation today." His landslide 1980 re-election allows him six full years in which to smooth the feathers he ruffled by switching panels.

**At Home:** Mathias has many of the same problems among Maryland Republicans that he has among Senate Republicans, but they have never really hurt him.

He has not offered the Republican right many concessions — he refused to serve on Ronald Reagan's Maryland steering committee in 1980 — but the party's prominent conservatives have not tried to challenge him, partly for fear that any Republican who defeated Mathias for renomination would lose the general election. Former congressman Robert E. Bauman backed down from a 1980 primary challenge to Mathias for that reason.

Democrats have never presented Mathias with much of a problem; he steals away most of their natural constituency: suburban liberals, blacks, and labor. In 1974, against liberal Democrat Barbara A. Mikulski, now a House member, Mathias captured every jurisdiction in the state except Baltimore city and suburban Baltimore County. Mikulski's edge in the city, which normally gives Democrats 100,000-vote pluralities, was a mere 28,194 votes — a testament to Mathias' personal popularity.

By 1980, Mathias had the official backing — and generous campaign support — of organized labor. He became the first Republican in modern history to win every county in the state, and Baltimore city besides. He did so while Maryland voters were giving Jimmy Carter one of his few election victories.

After four years as city attorney in his hometown of Frederick, and two years in the Maryland Legislature, Mathias ran for the House in 1960 against incumbent Democrat John R. Foley, in a district that stretched from the Washington D.C. line to the West Virginia border.

Eight years later, he challenged Democratic Sen. Daniel B. Brewster, an old friend but a highly vulnerable candidate, plagued by heavy drinking and newspaper reports linking him to a mail order scandal, in which he was later tried and convicted. Even with Brewster's problems, Mathias drew only 47.8 percent of the vote; he was helped by the candidacy of George C. Mahoney, a conservative Democrat running as an independent, who drained away some of Brewster's support.

## Committees

**Foreign Relations** (6th of 9 Republicans)
International Economic Policy, chairman; African Affairs; European Affairs.

**Governmental Affairs** (4th of 9 Republicans)
Governmental Efficiency and the District of Columbia, chairman; Civil Service, Post Office, and General Services; Permanent Subcommittee on Investigations.

**Judiciary** (2nd of 10 Republicans)
Criminal Law, chairman; Juvenile Justice; Regulatory Reform.

**Rules and Administration** (Chairman)

**Joint Library**

**Joint Printing** (Chairman)

## Elections

**1980 General**

| | |
|---|---|
| Charles Mathias (R ) | 850,970 (66 %) |
| Edward Conroy (D ) | 435,118 (34 %) |

**1980 Primary**

| | |
|---|---|
| Charles Mathias (R ) | 82,430 (55 %) |
| John Brennan (R ) | 24,848 (17 %) |
| Dallas Merrell (R ) | 23,073 (15 %) |
| Roscoe Bartlett (R ) | 10,970 (7 %) |

**Previous Winning Percentages**

1974 (57 %)  1968 (48 %)  1966* (71 %)  1964* (55 %)
1962* (61 %)  1960 (52 %)

*House elections.

## Campaign Finance

| | Receipts | Receipts from PACs | Expenditures |
|---|---|---|---|
| 1980 | | | |
| Mathias (R ) | $874,995 | $296,139 (34 %) | $848,456 |
| Conroy (D ) | $166,557 | — (0 %) | $162,966 |

## Voting Studies

| | Presidential Support | | Party Unity | | Conservative Coalition | |
|---|---|---|---|---|---|---|
| Year | S | O | S | O | S | O |
| Senate service | | | | | | |
| 1980 | 48 | 17 | 16 | 55 | 10 | 61 |
| 1979 | 73 | 16 | 23 | 66 | 22 | 71 |
| 1978 | 66 | 10 | 17 | 65 | 16 | 69 |
| 1977 | 64 | 19 | 25 | 60 | 30 | 60 |
| 1976 | 40 | 42 | 20 | 59 | 20 | 64 |
| 1975 | 43 | 37 | 22 | 60 | 14 | 71 |
| 1974 (Ford) | 32 | 40 | | | | |
| 1974 | 39 | 40 | 14 | 60 | 10 | 63 |
| 1973 | 43 | 42 | 28 | 58 | 31 | 59 |
| 1972 | 41 | 50 | 35 | 53 | 33 | 59 |
| 1971 | 44 | 40 | 38 | 51 | 36 | 49 |
| 1970 | 51 | 27 | 27 | 46 | 21 | 49 |
| 1969 | 57 | 21 | 27 | 52 | 28 | 54 |
| House service | | | | | | |
| 1968 | 50 | 22 | 26 | 41 | 24 | 47 |
| 1967 | 47 | 20 | 27 | 45 | 13 | 44 |
| 1966 | 50 | 18 | 35 | 33 | 30 | 46 |
| 1965 | 48 | 22 | 34 | 48 | 27 | 55 |
| 1964 | 54 | 27 | 35 | 44 | 33 | 58 |
| 1963 | 56 | 32 | 45 | 46 | 20 | 80 |
| 1962 | 70 | 25 | 47 | 49 | 31 | 69 |
| 1961 | 57 | 42 | 66 | 34 | 52 | 48 |

S = Support          O = Opposition

## Key Votes

**96th Congress**

| | |
|---|---|
| Maintain relations with Taiwan (1979) | N |
| Reduce synthetic fuel development funds (1979) | N |
| Impose nuclear plant moratorium (1979) | N |
| Kill stronger windfall profits tax (1979) | N |
| Guarantee Chrysler Corp. loans (1979) | Y |
| Approve military draft registration (1980) | N |
| End Revenue Sharing to the states (1980) | N |
| Block Justice Dept. busing suits (1980) | ? |

**97th Congress**

| | |
|---|---|
| Restore urban program funding cuts (1981) | Y |

## Interest Group Ratings

| Year | ADA | ACA | AFL-CIO | CCUS-1 | CCUS-2 |
|---|---|---|---|---|---|
| Senate service | | | | | |
| 1980 | 72 | 8 | 100 | 46 | |
| 1979 | 63 | 15 | 79 | 18 | 33 |
| 1978 | 50 | 22 | 76 | 25 | |
| 1977 | 75 | 14 | 79 | 18 | |
| 1976 | 65 | 5 | 67 | 0 | |
| 1975 | 83 | 15 | 85 | 36 | |
| 1974 | 86 | 0 | 80 | 11 | |
| 1973 | 90 | 4 | 60 | 22 | |
| 1972 | 60 | 32 | 80 | 33 | |
| 1971 | 63 | 21 | 58 | - | |
| 1970 | 78 | 15 | 83 | 33 | |
| 1969 | 78 | 7 | 18 | - | |
| House service | | | | | |
| 1968 | 50 | 36 | 75 | - | |
| 1967 | 53 | 26 | 83 | 38 | |
| 1966 | 41 | 50 | 31 | - | |
| 1965 | 53 | 36 | - | 60 | |
| 1964 | 72 | 38 | 82 | - | |
| 1963 | - | 50 | - | - | |
| 1962 | 88 | 48 | 45 | - | |
| 1961 | 30 | - | - | - | |

# Paul S. Sarbanes (D)

### Of Baltimore — Elected 1976

**Born:** Feb. 3, 1933, Salisbury, Md.
**Education:** Princeton U., A.B. 1954; Rhodes Scholar, Balliol College, Oxford U., England, B.A. 1957; Harvard U., LL.B. 1960.
**Profession:** Lawyer.
**Family:** Wife, Christine Dunbar; three children.
**Religion:** Greek Orthodox.
**Political Career:** Md. House, 1967-71; U.S. House, 1971-77.

**In Washington:** Sarbanes is a rarity — a politician who genuinely dislikes publicity. He rarely issues news releases, avoids television appearances, and holds no press conferences. Yet he has never lost an election.

Whatever he tackles, he studies in depth — and in person, refusing to delegate responsibility to his staff. "The staff was not elected to be the senator," he says, sounding more like an old-time Republican than a modern liberal Democrat.

Because he insists on doing everything himself, Sarbanes seldom deals with more than one or two issues at a time. His style has brought him wide respect as one of the most intelligent senators, but it has also led to caricature of him as a man paralyzed by indecision, one who is still in his office pondering the nuances of an issue when he should be out taking a stand.

Sarbanes refuses to apologize for his deliberate approach. "It is quite true I don't make decisions off the top of my head," he once said. "I don't think important decisions ought to be made that way."

His thoroughness was evident when he served as floor manager for the Panama Canal treaties in 1978, doggedly defending U.S. transfer of the canal against all criticism and winning praise from treaty foes and supporters alike for the depth of his knowledge.

In characteristic fashion, Sarbanes had not actually decided to support the treaties until the eve of markup sessions in the Foreign Relations Committee, on which he serves. But once he made up his mind, he was an extremely effective advocate — and one who, for all his dislike of publicity, was willing to make himself the focus of a debate that could do him little political good.

During his six years in the House, he played one intensely visible role, during the House Judiciary Committee's 1974 impeachment proceedings against President Nixon. As usual, he took no public position before the committee began its

work. Partly for that reason, he was chosen to introduce the first, and most important, article of impeachment, charging the president with obstruction of justice. He built a tightly constructed, cogently argued lawyer's case against the embattled president, and the article was approved by the committee, 27-11.

The same year he was working on Watergate in the House, Sarbanes was plunging into the details of the House committee system, playing a key role on a panel set up to redraw the chaotic lines of committee jurisdiction. It was work that he seemed to enjoy, and much of the reform proposal eventually drafted was his work. But the idea ran into broad-scale opposition on the House floor and was defeated.

Sarbanes is cool and cerebral in most of the debates he chooses to enter. But there are issues on which he is passionate. As an American of Greek descent, he was outraged by the Turkish invasion of Cyprus in 1974, and was instrumental in forcing a cutoff of U.S. arms aid to Turkey, an embargo that was lifted against his vote and his vehement protest in 1978.

And in early 1981, he had an intense exchange with Alexander M. Haig Jr. during hearings on Haig's confirmation as secretary of state. It was Haig's role as White House chief of staff during the Watergate era that troubled Sarbanes. Dissatisfied with Haig's answers, he voted against confirmation on the Senate floor — one of just six senators to do so.

On foreign policy and on most domestic issues, Sarbanes has compiled one of the most liberal voting records in the Senate. The ADA rated him at 83 in 1980; the AFL-CIO at 95. He was outspokenly opposed to most of the cuts in domestic social spending proposed by President Reagan in 1981. In April, when the Senate voted

88-10 for $36.9 billion in budget cuts, Sarbanes cast one of the 10 votes against it.

**At Home:** Sarbanes' critics in Maryland sometimes call him "the phantom," alluding not only to his avoidance of publicity but to his less-than-zealous attitude toward routine political chores.

He puts in a great deal of time and work on Maryland matters that bring him little political profit. He personally interviewed prospects for federal judicial appointments — a time-consuming task that most senators avoid. And when Baltimore asked his help in obtaining a redevelopment grant from Washington, he subjected its proposal to a line-by-line examination. But his disdain for ordinary glad-handing is a substantial political liability.

Still, when it comes to an election he is an easy man to underestimate. He is always well organized and well financed, and he has a knack for the right issue at the right moment. He also has had the foresight to take on incumbents just when they were ripe for replacement.

The son of Greek immigrant parents, Sarbanes grew up on Maryland's Eastern Shore, attended Princeton, won a Rhodes Scholarship, and eventually took a seat in the state Legislature. In 1970, running as an anti-war, anti-machine insurgent, he defeated aging Rep. George H. Fallon for the Democratic nomination in Baltimore's multi-ethnic 4th District.

Two years later redistricting threw him together with another old-time Democrat, Rep. Edward Garmatz, but Garmatz decided to retire. Sarbanes easily defeated two party regulars who split the opposition and handed him renomination.

By 1976, Sarbanes was ready to move to the Senate, and one-term Republican J. Glenn Beall Jr. was ready to be taken. Sarbanes first had to dispose of former Sen. Joseph D. Tydings, trying for a comeback in the Democratic primary, and he did that easily, deflecting Tydings' charges that he was too liberal and had refused to move right with the times. In the fall, Beall called him an inactive legislator, and Sarbanes responded with television spots playing up his Watergate role. Sarbanes never lost his huge lead in the polls, and coasted to victory over Beall by nearly a quarter of a million votes.

The 1982 campaign will not be easy for him. In early 1981, the National Conservative Political Action Committee began airing television commercials accusing Sarbanes of working to obstruct the Reagan program and frustrate the popular will. Part of the idea was to frighten other liberal Democrats who saw the commercials on Washington D.C. television stations. But they marked a substantial threat to Sarbanes.

By mid-1981, Democrats were claiming that the negative advertising had helped create sympathy for Sarbanes. But the opposition cited polls indicating a close contest between him and the likely Republican nominee, Rep. Marjorie S. Holt.

## Committees

**Banking, Housing and Urban Affairs** (5th of 7 Democrats)
Economic Policy; Housing and Urban Affairs; Securities.

**Foreign Relations** (4th of 8 Democrats)
European Affairs; International Economic Policy; Near Eastern and South Asian Affairs.

**Joint Economic**
Investment, Jobs and Prices; Monetary and Fiscal Policy.

## Elections

**1976 General**

| | |
|---|---|
| Paul Sarbanes (D ) | 772,101 (57 %) |
| J. Glenn Beall Jr. (R ) | 530,439 (39 %) |

**1976 Primary**

| | |
|---|---|
| Paul Sarbanes (D ) | 302,983 (55 %) |
| Joseph Tydings (D ) | 191,857 (35 %) |
| Other (D ) | 52,896 (10 %) |

**Previous Winning Percentages**

1974* (84 %)   1972* (70 %)   1970* (70 %)

* House election.

## Campaign Finance

| 1976 | Receipts | Receipts from PACs | Expenditures |
|---|---|---|---|
| Sarbanes (D ) | $892,300 | $142,850 (16 %) | $891,533 |
| Beall (R ) | $578,299 | $90,825 (16 %) | $572,016 |

## Voting Studies

| | Presidential Support | | Party Unity | | Conservative Coalition | |
|---|---|---|---|---|---|---|
| Year | S | O | S | O | S | O |
| Senate service | | | | | | |
| 1980 | 73 | 25 | 87 | 11 | 4 | 92 |
| 1979 | 85 | 12 | 88 | 10 | 8 | 91 |

## Paul S. Sarbanes, D-Md.

| | | | | | | |
|---|---|---|---|---|---|---|
| 1978 | 87 | 12 | 94 | 5 | 6 | 91 |
| 1977 | 82 | 17 | 92 | 6 | 4 | 94 |
| **House service** | | | | | | |
| 1976 | 18 | 71 | 76 | 3 | 5 | 74 |
| 1975 | 37 | 60 | 92 | 7 | 6 | 92 |
| 1974 (Ford) | 41 | 57 | | | | |
| 1974 | 45 | 55 | 89 | 9 | 12 | 86 |
| 1973 | 28 | 72 | 94 | 6 | 3 | 97 |
| 1972 | 54 | 43 | 85 | 11 | 13 | 84 |
| 1971 | 28 | 67 | 81 | 11 | 6 | 86 |

S = Support          O = Opposition

## Key Votes

**96th Congress**

| | |
|---|---|
| Maintain relations with Taiwan (1979) | N |
| Reduce synthetic fuel development funds (1979) | Y |
| Impose nuclear plant moratorium (1979) | Y |
| Kill stronger windfall profits tax (1979) | N |
| Guarantee Chrysler Corp. loans (1979) | Y |
| Approve military draft registration (1980) | N |
| End Revenue Sharing to the states (1980) | N |
| Block Justice Dept. busing suits (1980) | N |

**97th Congress**

| | |
|---|---|
| Restore urban program funding cuts (1981) | Y |

## Interest Group Ratings

| Year | ADA | ACA | AFL-CIO | CCUS-1 | CCUS-2 |
|---|---|---|---|---|---|
| **Senate service** | | | | | |
| 1980 | 83 | 0 | 95 | 36 | |
| 1979 | 79 | 15 | 100 | 9 | 25 |
| 1978 | 90 | 8 | 95 | 24 | |
| 1977 | 90 | 7 | 95 | 6 | |
| **House service** | | | | | |
| 1976 | 80 | 0 | 86 | 0 | |
| 1975 | 100 | 4 | 96 | 18 | |
| 1974 | 91 | 0 | 91 | 0 | |
| 1973 | 92 | 7 | 100 | 9 | |
| 1972 | 88 | 9 | 91 | 10 | |
| 1971 | 81 | 17 | 82 | | |

# 1 Roy Dyson (D)

**Of Great Mills — Elected 1980**

**Born:** Nov. 15, 1948, Great Mills, Md.
**Education:** University of Maryland, no degree.
**Profession:** Lumber company official.
**Family:** Single.
**Religion:** Roman Catholic.
**Political Career:** Md. House, 1975-81; Democratic nominee for U.S. House, 1976.

**The Member:** Dyson seemed a sure loser to Republican Rep. Robert E. Bauman in 1980 until Bauman was charged with soliciting sex from a teen-age male. The shock of that disclosure, a few weeks before the election, gave Dyson an instant lead, which Bauman reduced in the final weeks but could not overcome. Dyson's win avenged Bauman's victory over him in 1976.

At the outset of his term, Dyson insisted Democrats needed new ideas to counter Reagan's vision of federal austerity. He became acting president of the 1980 Democratic class after suggesting that its members meet with Speaker O'Neill to call for revision of party goals.

But Dyson was under considerable political pressure to support Reagan's budget proposals. Reagan carried the conservative 1st District in 1980 and local Republicans have pledged an intensive 1982 effort to retake the seat.

In the end, Dyson was one of only four freshman Democrats who voted for the Reagan budget. He said a majority of constituents thought all previous attempts to stop inflation and limit government spending had failed. But he switched and voted with the Democrats later when specific Reagan cuts hurt Social Security.

As a member of the Merchant Marine and Fisheries Committee, Dyson argued against cuts in the National Sea Grant College program. The program sponsors research to increase the catch of fish in Chesapeake Bay.

**The District:** Despite its 3-1 Democratic registration advantage, Maryland's Eastern Shore district had sent Republicans to the House every year since 1946, except for 1958 and 1960. It is a conservative area with a large black population and a rural Southern flavor.

The 1st District also takes in three counties in southern Maryland across Chesapeake Bay and one suburban county north of Baltimore. It is economically dependent on farming, fishing and, thanks to its beaches, tourism.

## Committees

**Armed Services** (23rd of 25 Democrats)
Military Installations and Facilities; Seapower and Strategic and Critical Materials.

**Merchant Marine and Fisheries** (20th of 20 Democrats)
Coast Guard and Navigation; Fisheries and Wildlife Conservation and the Environment; Oceanography.

## Elections

**1980 General**

| | |
|---|---|
| Roy Dyson (D ) | 97,743 (52 %) |
| Robert Bauman (R ) | 91,143 (48 %) |

**1980 Primary**

| | |
|---|---|
| Roy Dyson (D ) | 26,585 (69 %) |
| Donald DeArmon (D ) | 11,833 (31 %) |

**District Vote For President**

| | 1980 | | 1976 | | 1972 |
|---|---|---|---|---|---|
| **D** | 83,894 (42 %) | **D** | 85,106 (49 %) | **D** | 42,257 (28 %) |
| **R** | 104,227 (52 %) | **R** | 87,481 (51 %) | **R** | 106,539 (71 %) |
| **I** | 11,398 (6 %) | | | | |

## Campaign Finance

| | Receipts | Receipts from PACs | Expenditures |
|---|---|---|---|
| **1980** | | | |
| Dyson (D ) | $156,700 | $73,098 (47 %) | $155,877 |
| Bauman (R ) | $365,193 | $79,710 (22 %) | $358,926 |

## Key Vote

**97th Congress**

| | |
|---|---|
| Reagan budget proposal (1981) | Y |

---

**1st District: Eastern Shore — Salisbury, Aberdeen.** Population: 609,834 (25% increase since 1970). Race: White 500,807 (82%), Black 102,373 (17%), Others 6,654 (1%). Spanish origin: 5,942 (1%).

# 2 Clarence D. Long (D)

**Of Ruxton — Elected 1962**

**Born:** Dec. 11, 1908, South Bend, Ind.
**Education:** Washington and Jefferson College, A.B. 1932, A.M. 1933; Princeton U., A.M. 1935, Ph.D. 1938.
**Military Career:** Navy, 1943-46.
**Profession:** Professor of economics, writer.
**Family:** Wife, Susanna Larter; two children.
**Religion:** Presbyterian.
**Political Career:** Unsuccessfully sought Democratic nomination for U.S. Senate, 1958.

**In Washington:** Long's view of the world is so individualistic it defies categorization. He is a foreign aid chairman hostile to most foreign aid, but militant in his support for aid to Israel. He can be a passionate spokesman for human rights, but he opposed U.S. admission of thousands of Vietnamese "boat people" on the grounds that they represented "international blackmail." In one speech in 1980, he told civil rights workers that blacks were genetically superior to whites but suggested they were unwilling to work.

Few colleagues question the judgment that Clarence Long is eccentric. Some think his iconoclasm goes beyond eccentricity. Others claim to see in his pastiche of policies a reflection of the hybrid district he represents: one that combines a large blue-collar work force, sympathetic to George Wallace in past years, and a liberal, politically active Jewish community.

Long has a position of influence as chairman of the Foreign Operations Subcommittee on Appropriations, with jurisdiction over $7 billion a year in aid programs. But he is rarely able to control the panel.

Long generally opposes aid projects that require large capital investments, such as dams, public utilities or factories. He believes they are too expensive and require technology above the heads of the poor in Third World countries. He thinks they take people from villages and deposit them in urban slums. Long favors what he calls "capital saving technology" — he would spend a smaller amount of money on simple tools usable in old-fashioned rural communities.

Because he feels this way, Long generally opposes multilateral aid funneled through sources like the World Bank, which he once called "a luxury institution, a fat cat institution, run for the benefit of the officers."

Long has frequently supported attempts by his subcommittee's ranking Republican, C. W. Bill Young of Florida, to reduce funding for the institutions and ban loans to communist countries. In recent years, that put him at odds not only with President Carter but with his own committee Democrats, and until 1981, the Senate.

As a result, Long has often been shoved aside when his bills have come to the House floor, and they have been managed by a junior Democrat on the panel, usually David R. Obey of Wisconsin.

In 1978, Obey and Matthew McHugh, D-N.Y., led a floor effort that won passage of a bill with $7.1 billion for foreign aid, 85 percent of Carter's original request. Long tried to cut multilateral assistance by $548 million, but was badly beaten.

When it comes to fighting military aid to Third World dictatorships, Long goes beyond even most human rights liberals. In 1968, he cosponsored an amendment requiring the U.S. to reduce economic aid to countries that spent money on advanced weapons. Long believes U.S. military aid is often used to shore up unconstitutional regimes in Latin America. He has taken the Reagan administration severely to task for sending military aid and advisers to El Salvador.

Long traveled to El Salvador himself in March of 1981, paying his own way because his full committee considered the trip too dangerous. He returned to Washington determined to block the administration's request for $5 million in

---

**2nd District: North — Baltimore suburbs.** Population: 521,905 (6% increase since 1970). Race: White 467,633 (90%), Black 45,758 (9%), Others 8,514 (2%). Spanish origin: 4,331 (1%).

military aid to the regime there, but he was beaten in his own subcommittee on an 8-7 vote.

Long does not feel the same way about military aid to Israel. He frequently asks the subcommittee to spend more on Israel than even some liberal Democrats want to, and wins a fair share of these battles. He rarely has to say anything about Israel on the House floor; usually, the money is already in the bill.

Long was militant in his opposition to spending money on the Vietnamese boat people. He questioned whether the tragic stories of the refugees were true or "just publicity," and suggested Americans might be "victims of international blackmail." He suggested that since China wanted trade with the U.S., it should take in the boat people to show its good faith. An angry Jack Kemp shot back that Long's statements compared to doubts about murder of Jews under the Nazis. "There's a holocaust going on and we ought to stand up and face our responsibility," Kemp said.

In fiscal 1980 and fiscal 1981, there have been no foreign aid appropriation bills; the programs have been funded at earlier levels on a "temporary" basis. That is partly because the legislation would have been difficult to pass in the political climate of the time, but it is also because of feuds between Long and his Senate counterpart, Democrat Daniel K. Inouye of Hawaii.

The feud has delayed some foreign aid bills from going to conference; in other cases, the Senate has been slow to act in the first place, given the disputes that would inevitably follow.

In domestic policy, Long has been equally stubborn and independent. He fought federal aid to urban renewal ("a real estate deal"), revenue sharing and mass transit, particularly the Washington, D.C. subway system.

He has a strong civil rights record, but in 1980 he shocked his constituency with a speech full of racial references at an NAACP dinner in Baltimore. Long said blacks are "genetically superior ... because Southern white blood flows in every black today" and said blacks suffered high unemployment because "either you are uneducated or you don't want to work."

**At Home:** There are as many elements of paradox in Long's career at home as in his career in Washington.

An economist with a doctorate from Princeton and more than a decade of experience on the faculty of Johns Hopkins University, Long has shown his greatest appeal in the blue-collar eastern end of his suburban Baltimore district.

He has generated loyalty there with a vaunted government red tape-cutting service and with an "us-against-them" populist attitude. "They" are shipping interests and other powers in the Baltimore business establishment. He has also been known for his ubiquitous presence in the district. Long returns to Baltimore County every night from Washington.

But the veteran Democrat has begun to show signs of political vulnerability. After routinely winning landslide re-election for nearly two decades, Long encountered tough primary and general election contests in 1980.

His controversial opposition to the deepening of the Baltimore port was the centerpiece of both elections, although his statements at the NAACP meeting were also an issue.

All the other candidates in the race, both Democrats and Republicans, favored deepening the port. They warned that without the project, the harbor would become too shallow for shipping and jobs would be lost. Long insisted the project was a virtual gift to Bethlehem Steel and a likely source of pollution along the bay. Long survived, but he won both the primary and general election with less than 60 percent of the vote.

Long launched his career in government in 1948, as a professor at Johns Hopkins, serving on the first Hoover Commission to Eliminate Waste in the Federal Government. After co-chairing the Maryland Volunteers for Stevenson in 1952, Long returned to government work as the senior staff member of President Eisenhower's Council of Economic Advisers.

In 1958, at age 49, Long made his debut in elective politics. He tried unsuccessfully for the Democratic U.S. Senate nomination, running fourth in the primary won by former Baltimore Mayor Thomas D'Alesandro. Then he "turned professional." He was acting chairman of the State Central Committee in 1961-62.

In 1962 he entered the campaign for the 2nd District House seat being vacated by Democrat Daniel Brewster, who was running for the Senate. With Gov. J. Millard Tawes's support, Long won an easy primary victory over three other candidates.

Long's opponent in the general election, Fife Symington, a cousin of Missouri Democratic Sen. Stuart Symington, twitted Long for accepting machine help and charged him with "ivory towerism." But Long, labeling himself a "conservative liberal," was able to rebuff the gentleman farmer's third bid for the House.

With little serious opposition in succeeding years, Long was able to entertain thoughts of higher office. But after considering a race for governor in 1966 and for the Senate in 1968, he decided to remain in the House.

**523**

## Clarence D. Long, D-Md.

**The District:** While Long's district is almost entirely suburban, it has two distinct parts. To the east and northeast of Baltimore are traditionally Democratic, blue-collar communities like Dundalk and Parkville, extensions of the ethnic neighborhoods on the east side of the city. Many residents here are employed in local factories, including the Bethlehem Steel plant at Sparrows Point, one of the largest steel mills in the nation.

To the north and northwest of Baltimore are wealthier, white-collar suburbs. While these suburbs are nominally Republican, the large Jewish element in communities like Pikesville and Randallstown provides a liberal flavor.

## Committees

**Appropriations** (6th of 33 Democrats)
    Foreign Operations, chairman; Interior; Military Construction.

## Elections

**1980 General**

| | |
|---|---|
| Clarence Long (D ) | 121,017 (57 %) |
| Helen Bentley (R ) | 89,961 (43 %) |

**1980 Primary**

| | |
|---|---|
| Clarence Long (D ) | 44,280 (57 %) |
| Thomas Kernan (D ) | 30,335 (39 %) |

**1978 General**

| | |
|---|---|
| Clarence Long (D ) | 98,601 (66 %) |
| Malcolm McKnight (R ) | 49,886 (34 %) |

**Previous Winning Percentages**

| | | | |
|---|---|---|---|
| 1976 (71 %) | 1974 (77 %) | 1972 (66 %) | 1970 (69 %) |
| 1968 (59 %) | 1966 (69 %) | 1964 (66 %) | 1962 (52 %) |

**District Vote For President**

| | 1980 | | 1976 | | 1972 |
|---|---|---|---|---|---|
| D | 102,508 (45 %) | D | 101,830 (48 %) | D | 62,755 (31 %) |
| R | 103,501 (46 %) | R | 109,176 (52 %) | R | 135,329 (67 %) |
| I | 18,928 (8 %) | | | | |

## Campaign Finance

| | Receipts | Receipts from PACs | Expenditures |
|---|---|---|---|
| **1980** | | | |
| Long (D ) | $158,280 | $35,341 (22 %) | $153,619 |
| Bentley (R ) | $253,028 | $64,076 (25 %) | $252,821 |
| **1978** | | | |
| Long (D ) | $53,331 | $8,890 (17 %) | $61,863 |
| McKnight (R) | $31,442 | $1,200 (4 %) | $30,777 |

## Voting Studies

| | Presidential Support | | Party Unity | | Conservative Coalition | |
|---|---|---|---|---|---|---|
| Year | S | O | S | O | S | O |
| 1980 | 74 | 23 | 81 | 17 | 28 | 69 |
| 1979 | 64 | 32 | 69 | 28 | 38 | 61 |
| 1978 | 62 | 36 | 68 | 28 | 38 | 60 |
| 1977 | 70 | 27 | 72 | 25 | 36 | 62 |

| | | | | | | |
|---|---|---|---|---|---|---|
| 1976 | 31 | 69 | 83 | 16 | 27 | 72 |
| 1975 | 42 | 54 | 67 | 28 | 34 | 59 |
| 1974 (Ford) | 33 | 65 | | | | |
| 1974 | 53 | 36 | 73 | 25 | 37 | 61 |
| 1973 | 30 | 68 | 73 | 23 | 35 | 62 |
| 1972 | 38 | 59 | 70 | 25 | 29 | 61 |
| 1971 | 28 | 68 | 74 | 20 | 27 | 67 |
| 1970 | 43 | 43 | 60 | 31 | 36 | 55 |
| 1969 | 51 | 47 | 76 | 20 | 27 | 60 |
| 1968 | 79 | 14 | 72 | 17 | 16 | 65 |
| 1967 | 82 | 12 | 80 | 13 | 28 | 67 |
| 1966 | 85 | 8 | 89 | 5 | 8 | 86 |
| 1965 | 85 | 10 | 81 | 10 | 4 | 88 |
| 1964 | 88 | 4 | 82 | 8 | 8 | 92 |
| 1963 | 84 | 8 | 84 | 9 | 27 | 60 |

S = Support          O = Opposition

## Key Votes

**96th Congress**

| | |
|---|---|
| Weaken Carter oil profits tax (1979) | N |
| Reject hospital cost control plan (1979) | N |
| Implement Panama Canal Treaties (1979) | Y |
| Establish Department of Education (1979) | N |
| Approve Anti-busing Amendment (1979) | N |
| Guarantee Chrysler Corp. loans (1979) | N |
| Approve military draft registration (1980) | N |
| Aid Sandinista regime in Nicaragua (1980) | Y |
| Strengthen fair housing laws (1980) | Y |

**97th Congress**

| | |
|---|---|
| Reagan budget proposal (1981) | Y |

## Interest Group Ratings

| Year | ADA | ACA | AFL-CIO | CCUS |
|---|---|---|---|---|
| 1980 | 83 | 25 | 53 | 61 |
| 1979 | 74 | 36 | 70 | 29 |
| 1978 | 40 | 37 | 47 | 39 |
| 1977 | 55 | 30 | 70 | 47 |
| 1976 | 65 | 22 | 55 | 32 |
| 1975 | 53 | 33 | 61 | 40 |
| 1974 | 57 | 29 | 82 | 30 |
| 1973 | 64 | 33 | 70 | 36 |
| 1972 | 56 | 33 | 82 | 30 |
| 1971 | 70 | 26 | 82 | - |
| 1970 | 64 | 56 | 50 | 33 |
| 1969 | 53 | 35 | 100 | - |
| 1968 | 67 | 17 | 100 | - |
| 1967 | 60 | 7 | 100 | 10 |
| 1966 | 82 | 12 | 92 | - |
| 1965 | 84 | 7 | - | 10 |
| 1964 | 88 | 6 | 82 | - |
| 1963 | - | 0 | - | - |

# 3 Barbara A. Mikulski (D)

**Of Baltimore — Elected 1976**

**Born:** July 20, 1936, Baltimore, Md.
**Education:** Mount Saint Agnes College, B.A. 1958; U. of Md. School of Social Work, M.S.W. 1965.
**Profession:** Social worker.
**Family:** Single.
**Religion:** Roman Catholic.
**Political Career:** Baltimore City Council, 1971-77; unsuccessful Democratic nominee for U.S. Senate, 1974.

**In Washington:** Tough, earthy and funny, Barbara Mikulski is not only the representative of ethnic East Baltimore but its symbol in Washington — a product of rowhouse life and clubhouse politics. Despite her affinity for consumerism, womens' rights and other causes of the modern Democratic left, she has for most of her House career been more at home with big-city organization Democrats than with the fashionable liberals who cluster around the issues she works on.

That reputation changed a little in early 1981, as Mikulski suddenly began sounding more militant, influenced by Teresa Brennan, an Australian feminist who began working in her office. For a time, new aides were hired based on their commitment to Brennan's philosophy, which stresses the inequities of patriarchal society. By mid-year, however, there were signs that the earlier Mikulski was returning to the surface.

Known in her pre-congressional days mainly as a Democratic Party reformer, she was seen on her arrival in 1977 as a likely successor to Bella Abzug as the chamber's most strident feminist voice. It did not turn out that way.

She immediately endorsed Jim Wright of Texas for majority leader over his two more liberal opponents, a move that surprised most colleagues but brought her a reputation for shrewdness when Wright won and helped her get an important committee assignment.

Mikulski's early moves were no accident. "Because of stereotypes of people," she admitted later, "I was perceived as another Bella. A lot of people expected me just to keep chewing them up." Invited to speak to a press club audience early in her first term, she delivered a witty exercise in self-deprecation, not the "barbed attack on either the president or the old-boy network" she knew they expected.

Mikulski did not get her first committee choice, Ways and Means, but she got a seat on the influential Commerce Committee and on Merchant Marine, whose jurisdiction is important to the Baltimore port.

Within a few months, Mikulski was close to achieving a reputation as a Democratic "regular." Speaker O'Neill chose her as one of a select few in 1977 to serve on an Ad Hoc Energy Committee, put together to handle the Carter energy package.

There she provided further proof that she knew how to play the legislative game. She proposed an amendment providing $65 million to help cities pay for energy conservation in municipal buildings. She badly wanted it, but she was being ignored by the president.

So she told a White House lobbyist she might have to take a walk on the critical vote before the committee — Carter's effort to prevent gas deregulation — unless she got what she wanted. At that point, Carter decided he liked her amendment, and she stayed to back him on deregulation.

Meanwhile, Mikulski was working on Merchant Marine to obtain funds for the dredging of the Chesapeake and Delaware canals and for an examination of the railroad bottleneck in the Baltimore tunnels.

In her recent terms on Commerce, Mikulski has concentrated on the Health Subcommittee, where, as a former social worker, she has backed generous federal spending on health and pushed

---

**3rd District: Baltimore south and east, Baltimore suburbs.** Population: 431,532 (12% decrease since 1970). Race: White 326,930 (76%), Black 96,852 (22%), Others 7,750 (2%). Spanish origin: 4,681 (1%).

for national health insurance. She fought in the 96th Congress for a child health assurance program and controls on hospital costs, both of which cleared the committee but neither of which became law.

At the full Commerce Committee level, Mikulski has been an active member of the consumerist Democratic faction that has favored strict regulation of the energy industry. She has voted consistently against lifting price controls on oil and supported a strong "superfund" bill forcing chemical companies to pay for the cleanup of toxic wastes.

By 1979, Mikulski was becoming disillusioned with Carter's commitment to women's rights and the poor, expressing her views in blunt East Baltimore style with the comment that Carter was pursuing a policy of "tough munchies" to the unemployed. She endorsed Edward M. Kennedy for president and campaigned with him during the Maryland primary, shocking Kennedy by telling an audience that their fathers had much in common as entrepreneurs: "My father owned a small grocery store. Your father owned Boston."

Kennedy recovered in time to ask her to make the nominating speech for him at the Democratic convention, an honor she missed when he withdrew before nominating night.

In the months since then, Mikulski has been drawn more and more into foreign affairs, leading with emotion the way she has in domestic politics. In early 1981, she went to look at conditions in Poland, her ethnic homeland, and El Salvador, which began to preoccupy her after a group of nuns from the Maryknoll order, to which she had been close, were killed in the country.

She came back from El Salvador with the conclusion that U.S. weapons were helping the army kill people in El Salvador and military aid should be stopped. "A generation of Salvadoran villagers is growing up," she said, "who will hate the sight of a U.S. symbol, because it means to them that someone is coming to shoot."

Mikulski also concluded that there should be no U.S. food aid for Poland. She called food shortage reports "greatly exaggerated" and said donations of food would encourage the Russians to come in.

**At Home.** As Mikulski has moved into the world of liberalism and social action, she has kept one foot firmly planted in the old-style ethnic politics. This has made her one of the most popular figures in Baltimore.

Mikulski is the granddaughter of Polish immigrants who settled in the city at the turn of the century. Her parents ran a grocery store in a blue-collar neighborhood in the southeastern part of town. She still lives nearby.

After graduation from a Catholic women's college, Mikulski became a social worker. She began her involvement in politics as a community organizer, leading the opposition to the construction of a controversial new highway. That work built a political power base that propelled her into the City Council in 1971 with the image of a liberal reformer.

Mikulski's energy and interest in changing the political process made her a figure in national Democratic politics while she was still on the council. She was chosen by Democratic National Chairman Jean Westwood in 1972 to serve on a commission to review the party's delegate selection rules. A year later she became chairman of the commission after United Auto Workers president Leonard Woodcock resigned.

None of Maryland's prominent Democrats showed any interest in challenging popular Republican Sen. Charles McC. Mathias Jr. in 1974. Mikulski was happy to fill the vacuum. With her Baltimore base, she took 41 percent of the vote to win a Democratic primary crowded with unfamiliar names. But Mikulski had little money for an elaborate fall campaign and had to tour the state in a camper. Mathias preempted much of her natural constituency by winning the support of the state AFL-CIO. Still, Mikulski mounted an energetic campaign that drew a respectable 43 percent of the vote. She carried Baltimore City and suburban Baltimore County.

A year later she won re-election to the City Council. But she was on the move again in 1976 when Democratic Rep. Paul S. Sarbanes left the East Baltimore 3rd District to run for the Senate. With her name identification enhanced by the 1974 Senate effort, Mikulski had little trouble winning the Democratic congressional nomination with 44 percent in a large primary field. In that urban district, her primary victory was tantamount to election, and her deep personal following has allowed her to hold the seat easily since then.

**The District.** Mikulski's district includes much of the city of Baltimore and slivers of suburban territory to the north and southwest. An increasing number of blacks moved into its ethnic enclaves during the 1970s, but it was still nearly 80 percent white in the 1980 Census.

The ethnic mix of the district is reflected in its last two representatives — Mikulski, of Polish descent, and Sarbanes, whose parents were Greek immigrants. Germans and Italians are also represented in significant numbers. Like their forebears, most of the ethnic voters are loyal Democrats. But there are limits to their support. George McGovern received less than one-third of the 3rd District ballots in 1972.

In the heart of the district are downtown Baltimore, with its revitalized Inner Harbor, and the bustling port, one of the largest on the East coast. The port of Baltimore serves a diverse array of industries, with large steel, soap and auto assembly plants nearby.

As one of three districts in Maryland that lost population in the 1970s, the 3rd District will have its boundaries substantially redrawn before 1982.

## Committees

**Energy and Commerce** (14th of 24 Democrats)
Commerce, Transportation, and Tourism; Health and the Environment.

**Merchant Marine and Fisheries** (12th of 20 Democrats)
Coast Guard and Navigation; Merchant Marine; Oceanography.

## Elections

**1980 General**

| | |
|---|---|
| Barbara Mikulski (D ) | 102,293 (76 %) |
| Russell Schaffer (R ) | 32,074 (24 %) |

**1980 Primary**

| | |
|---|---|
| Barbara Mikulski (D ) | 40,928 (75 %) |
| Others (D ) | 13,609 (25 %) |

**1978 General**

| | |
|---|---|
| Barbara Mikulski (D ) | Unopposed |

**Previous Winning Percentage**

1976 (75 %)

**District Vote For President**

| | 1980 | | 1976 | | 1972 |
|---|---|---|---|---|---|
| D | 87,965 (55 %) | D | 83,341 (52 %) | D | 53,981 (32 %) |
| R | 59,589 (37 %) | R | 78,442 (48 %) | R | 111,007 (66 %) |
| I | 10,647 (7 %) | | | | |

## Campaign Finance

| | Receipts | Receipts from PACs | Expenditures |
|---|---|---|---|
| **1980** | | | |
| Mikulski (D ) | $47,809 | $40,205 (84 %) | $39,353 |

| | | | |
|---|---|---|---|
| 1978 | | | |
| Mikulski (D ) | $40,084 | $25,250 (63 %) | $38,333 |

## Voting Studies

| | Presidential Support | | Party Unity | | Conservative Coalition | |
|---|---|---|---|---|---|---|
| Year | S | O | S | O | S | O |
| 1980 | 76 | 21 | 92 | 6 | 13 | 85 |
| 1979 | 70 | 25 | 86 | 11 | 17 | 81 |
| 1978 | 78 | 21 | 85 | 12 | 9 | 91 |
| 1977 | 76 | 22 | 89 | 7 | 13 | 85 |

S = Support        O = Opposition

## Key Votes

**96th Congress**

| | |
|---|---|
| Weaken Carter oil profits tax (1979) | N |
| Reject hospital cost control plan (1979) | N |
| Implement Panama Canal Treaties (1979) | Y |
| Establish Department of Education (1979) | N |
| Approve Anti-busing Amendment (1979) | N |
| Guarantee Chrysler Corp. loans (1979) | Y |
| Approve military draft registration (1980) | Y |
| Aid Sandinista regime in Nicaragua (1980) | Y |
| Strengthen fair housing laws (1980) | Y |

**97th Congress**

| | |
|---|---|
| Reagan budget proposal (1981) | N |

## Interest Group Ratings

| Year | ADA | ACA | AFL-CIO | CCUS |
|---|---|---|---|---|
| 1980 | 89 | 27 | 83 | 56 |
| 1979 | 84 | 12 | 100 | 22 |
| 1978 | 85 | 7 | 85 | 17 |
| 1977 | 90 | 7 | 87 | 12 |

# 4 Marjorie S. Holt (R)

### Of Severna Park — Elected 1972

**Born:** Sept. 17, 1920, Birmingham, Ala.
**Education:** Jacksonville U., B.A. 1945; U. of Fla.,
LL.B. 1949.
**Profession:** Lawyer.
**Family:** Husband, Duncan Holt; three children.
**Religion:** Presbyterian.
**Political Career:** Clerk, Anne Arundel County
Court, 1966-72.

**In Washington:** Holt's field of vision has been unusual for a woman who came to Congress direct from a county clerk's office in Maryland. She is always telling colleagues that they are not looking at problems broadly enough.

On the Budget Committee during the 95th and 96th Congresses, she argued for starting with national aggregate figures on revenue and spending, then dividing the money up by category. She introduced a bill requiring that in 1978. The committee never agreed to do it.

Holt also produced the first full-scale Republican substitute budget on the House floor, and came within five votes of seeing it passed in 1978. She never had the votes to pass one in the Carter years, but she continued to offer them, and by 1980 the substitutes had become part of a national GOP political strategy.

By the end of 1980, when she left the Budget Committee to concentrate on Armed Services, Holt had had a measurable impact on the budget process. And it seemed to have had a significant impact on her.

Identified in her first two terms as a hard-right crusader on social issues like busing and abortion, Holt seemed to grow more pragmatic and less ideological as she specialized in economics.

While most House Republicans made a policy of voting against all budget resolutions during the Carter administration, Holt swung back and forth, occasionally voting for a Democratic product if she thought the alternative seemed worse. In May of 1979, when liberal House Democrats were fighting a compromise package brought back from conference by Budget Chairman Robert N. Giaimo, D-Conn., Holt broke with the Republican majority to support it. She said that if it failed, Giaimo would change it in the direction the liberals wanted — more money for social programs and less for defense. When it failed, Giaimo did exactly that.

In 1980, Holt joined several moderate Republicans on the committee in making a bargain with Giaimo. If he produced a fiscal 1981 budget resolution drawn to be in balance, they would help report it out of committee, allowing Giaimo to override the wishes of the committee's liberals. The tactic worked, and Holt proclaimed that the GOP had gotten the best of the bargain.

When the budget reached the floor, the strategy collapsed. New economic figures showed the budget to be at least $20 billion out of balance, and Republicans deserted it in droves. Holt stuck with Giaimo.

First, however, she had a substitute to offer, drafted along with conservative freshman Democrat Phil Gramm of Texas. It added $5 billion in defense spending for 1981, and lopped off an equivalent in domestic spending. With a Democrat behind it, the substitute seemed to have a good chance of passage. But Majority Leader Jim Wright persuaded most conservative Democrats to oppose it, and Holt lost 34 Republicans, most of whom considered the domestic cuts draconian. The substitute failed by a wide margin.

Holt's budget work reflected the interest in defense that she brought with her in 1975, when she signed up for Armed Services as a freshman. She went to the Budget Committee in 1977 to be the Armed Services spokesman on it, and kept up that role for four years.

---

**4th District: Anne Arundel, Prince George's counties.** Population: 585,036 (18% increase since 1970). Race: White 440,544 (75%), Black 130,282 (22%), Others 14,210 (2%). Spanish origin: 8,458 (1%).

In 1977, the Budget Committee cut President Carter's defense request by $2.3 billion. Holt offered a floor amendment to put back $1 billion in outlays, and lost 223-184. In later years, she argued for more money to pay and house the volunteer army, citing low re-enlistment rates and substandard living conditions she said she had seen at military bases around the world.

Holt has promoted those same issues at Armed Services itself, to a considerably more sympathetic audience. She has pushed that committee to pay more attention to the budget process, asking for higher defense allotments even if it knows the Budget Committee will chop them down. "Where are we going to get additional budgetary authority," she asked Armed Services in 1980, "if we don't ask for it?"

Holt's economic pragmatism has muted her early reputation as a conservative militant, especially on busing. In 1974, she won House passage of an amendment prohibiting the federal government from withholding funds from a school district to make it comply with desegregation standards. She called the Justice Department's desegregation policy "the new racism." The amendment was watered down in conference with the Senate, and had little practical effect.

After that, Holt was quiet on the issue until 1980, when she stepped in to modify and try to save an anti-busing amendment to the Constitution. Brought to the floor by Ohio Democrat Ronald Mottl, it was clumsily drafted and appeared to ban long-distance busing for any purpose — even simple transportation. Holt cleaned up the language, but the amendment fell far short of the two-thirds majority it needed for passage.

Holt worked her way into the Republican leadership after only one term, taking over the Republican Study Committee, a legislative think tank for conservatives.

In 1981, when the chairmanship of the Republican Policy Committee, third-ranking leadership poisition, became vacant, she announced her candidacy early. For most of 1980 she had no opposition, and she made little effort to persuade colleagues to vote for her. It was a fatal mistake.

Dick Cheney of Wyoming, a highly-regarded freshman, entered the contest in the fall of 1980 and outcampaigned his senior opponent. By the time of the balloting in December, it was clear that Holt had let the office slip away from her. She carried the contest to a roll-call vote, but lost by an embarrassingly wide 99-68 margin.

**At Home:** Although Holt held the insignificant-sounding office of Anne Arundel County Court Clerk when she ran for the newly created 4th District House seat in 1972, she had earned her chance through long, hard work in the GOP vineyards.

Holt had been active in Republican politics for 13 years before running for Congress, working up from precinct leader to a key role in the Anne Arundel County campaigns of President Nixon and the late Rep. William O. Mills.

Having proved herself a good vote-getter in the 1966 and 1970 clerk's races, Holt ran with the blessing of the local party organization in 1972. She did not encounter the skepticism that party leaders had voiced when she had contemplated a congressional race a decade earlier. Nor was she hindered by other Republican contenders. "In 1972, I saw the perfect district — the timing was right," she said. "I started early, amassed support and muscled them out."

Holt overwhelmed nominal primary opposition, and in the general election benefited from the Nixon landslide to defeat her liberal Democratic opponent, former state Rep. Werner H. Fornos, by nearly 28,000 votes.

Both candidates opposed busing, an emotional issue in Prince George's County. But Holt peppered Fornos as an ally of George McGovern, whose plans for cutting the defense budget she termed "a sellout of the American people." Holt described herself as "a conservative, except where people are involved."

With her base in Anne Arundel County — the most populous part of the district — and a voting record tailored to one of Maryland's more conservative constituencies — Holt has had little difficulty winning re-election.

Her closest contest was a rematch with Fornos in 1976, and she won that by 25,000 votes. Since then, her margins have steadily increased. After the 1980 election, she announced that she was considering a race for Democrat Paul S. Sarbanes' Senate seat in 1982.

**The District:** Holt's suburban district is not one either party can take for granted in most elections. It was carried by Jimmy Carter in 1976 and Ronald Reagan in 1980, by Democratic Sen. Sarbanes in 1976 and Republican Sen. Charles McC. Mathias Jr. in both 1974 and 1980.

More than two-thirds of the district's voters live in Anne Arundel County. This is one of the fastest-growing areas of the state, with the suburbs of Baltimore extending into the northern part of the county and the suburbs of Washington, D.C., into the western part. Along Chesapeake Bay on the eastern side is the small city of Annapolis, the capital of Maryland and site of the U.S. Naval Academy.

Anne Arundel County usually votes Republican. But its vote is sometimes canceled out in statewide elections by more Democratic Prince George's County, the southern portion of which comprises the rest of the 4th District. The population numbers in this part of Prince George's have remained fairly static in recent years, but the racial complexion has changed, with low- and middle-income whites moving out as blacks from Washington, D.C., have moved in. As a result of these migrations, the 4th is now more than 20 percent black.

## Committees

**Armed Services** (6th of 19 Republicans)
Military Personnel and Compensation; Procurement and Military Nuclear Systems.

**District of Columbia** (4th of 4 Republicans)
Government Operations and Metropolitan Affairs; Judiciary and Education.

## Elections

**1980 General**

| | |
|---|---|
| Marjorie Holt (R ) | 120,985 (72 %) |
| James Riley (D ) | 47,375 (28 %) |

**1978 General**

| | |
|---|---|
| Marjorie Holt (R ) | 71,374 (62 %) |
| Sue Ward (D ) | 43,663 (38 %) |

**Previous Winning Percentages**

**1976** (58 %)    **1974** (58 %)    **1972** (59 %)

**District Vote For President**

| | 1980 | | 1976 | | 1972 |
|---|---|---|---|---|---|
| D | 80,702 (42 %) | D | 86,532 (50 %) | D | 44,937 (29 %) |
| R | 94,648 (50 %) | R | 86,352 (50 %) | R | 107,379 (70 %) |
| I | 13,422 (7 %) | | | | |

## Campaign Finance

| | Receipts | Receipts from PACs | Expenditures |
|---|---|---|---|
| **1980** | | | |
| Holt (R ) | $160,908 | $49,145 (31 %) | $147,170 |
| Riley (D ) | $9,225 | — (0 %) | $9,225 |
| **1978** | | | |
| Holt (R ) | $115,743 | $26,981 (23 %) | $107,607 |
| Ward (D ) | $39,015 | $10,445 (27 %) | $37,478 |

## Voting Studies

| | Presidential Support | | Party Unity | | Conservative Coalition | |
|---|---|---|---|---|---|---|
| Year | S | O | S | O | S | O |
| 1980 | 36 | 49† | 78 | 11 | 77 | 9 |
| 1979 | 23 | 68 | 85 | 8 | 87 | 4 |
| 1978 | 21 | 77 | 85 | 11 | 90 | 7 |
| 1977 | 30 | 57 | 86 | 8 | 92 | 3 |
| 1976 | 71 | 24 | 83 | 10 | 89 | 6 |
| 1975 | 58 | 39 | 89 | 10 | 94 | 6 |
| 1974 (Ford) | 44 | 54 | | | | |
| 1974 | 60 | 38 | 84 | 15 | 88 | 12 |
| 1973 | 69 | 30 | 85 | 14 | 94 | 5 |

S = Support          O = Opposition
†Not eligible for all recorded votes.

## Key Votes

**96th Congress**

| | |
|---|---|
| Weaken Carter oil profits tax (1979) | Y |
| Reject hospital cost control plan (1979) | Y |
| Implement Panama Canal Treaties (1979) | N |
| Establish Department of Education (1979) | N |
| Approve Anti-busing Amendment (1979) | Y |
| Guarantee Chrysler Corp. loans (1979) | X |
| Approve military draft registration (1980) | Y |
| Aid Sandinista regime in Nicaragua (1980) | N |
| Strengthen fair housing laws (1980) | N |

**97th Congress**

| | |
|---|---|
| Reagan budget proposal (1981) | Y |

## Interest Group Ratings

| Year | ADA | ACA | AFL-CIO | CCUS |
|---|---|---|---|---|
| 1980 | 6 | 86 | 16 | 72 |
| 1979 | 0 | 100 | 16 | 100 |
| 1978 | 5 | 85 | 20 | 72 |
| 1977 | 5 | 85 | 23 | 94 |
| 1976 | 5 | 84 | 18 | 76 |
| 1975 | 5 | 82 | 4 | 88 |
| 1974 | 13 | 93 | 0 | 90 |
| 1973 | 4 | 93 | 27 | 91 |

# 5 Steny Hoyer (D)

**Of Berkshire — Elected 1981**
**Born:** June 14, 1939, New York, N.Y.
**Education:** U. of Md., B.S. 1963; Georgetown U.,
   J.D. 1966.
**Profession:** Lawyer.
**Family:** Wife, Judith Pickett; three children.
**Religion:** Baptist.
**Political Career:** Md. Senate, 1967-79; Senate
   president, 1975-79; sought Democratic nomi-
   nation for lieutenant governor, 1978.

**The Member:** Hoyer has been preoccupied
with politics all his adult life, from his term as
president of Maryland Young Democrats to his
presidency of the state Senate. A losing bid for
lieutenant governor stalled his career briefly in
1978, but he made his comeback in a 1981 special
election, called because the 5th District seat of
Democratic Rep. Gladys Noon Spellman was declared vacant. The House decided that Spellman,
still semiconscious in February after an Oct. 31
heart attack, would be unable to reclaim the seat.

Hoyer entered the race to succeed Spellman,
defeated her husband and 17 others in the Democratic primary, and eased past Republican Audrey
Scott by 55.2 to 43.5 percent.

Hoyer was barely out of law school when first
elected to the state Senate in 1966. After two
terms he was chosen Senate president with the
help of Gov. Marvin Mandel. Hoyer's rise to
power coincided with the growing influence of the
Prince George's County Democratic organization,
which Hoyer helped build and lead. He made no
secret of his ambition to be governor.

Hoyer entered the 1978 gubernatorial race,
decided he lacked the support to win, and agreed
to run for lt. governor on a ticket with Acting Gov.
Blair Lee III. That team was the early favorite,
but Democrats nominated Harry R. Hughes and
Sam Bogley. Hoyer returned to private law practice, but when the Spellman seat became vacant,
he won it by reassembling most of his old coalition
of liberals, labor and blacks.

**The District.** The 5th is the less affluent,
more ethnic suburban neighbor to the prosperous
and liberal 8th District. The 5th has always had a
significant number of Catholics and an especially
high percentage of southern-oriented whites.

But in recent years, the district's in-migration has been largely black, and the black population of the 5th is now more than 30 percent. This
has made the area increasingly Democratic on
paper, but caused substantial political tensions,
and created GOP opportunities as the white residents remaining have turned more conservative.

## Committees

**Banking, Finance and Urban Affairs** (25th of 25 Democrats)
   Consumer Affairs and Coinage; Housing and Community
   Development.

**Post Office and Civil Service** (15th of 15 Democrats)
   Compensation and Employee Benefits; Human Resources.

## Elections

**1981 Special Election**

| | |
|---|---|
| Steny Hoyer (D) | 42,573 (55%) |
| Audrey Scott (R) | 33,708 (44%) |

**1981 Primary**

| | |
|---|---|
| Steny Hoyer (R) | 14,127 (30%) |
| Reuben Spellman (R) | 12,474 (27%) |
| Edward Conroy (R) | 6,190 (13%) |
| Stewart Bainum Jr. (R) | 5,882 (13%) |
| Sue Mills (R) | 4,392 (9%) |
| Thomas Patrick O'Reilly (R) | 2,526 (5%) |

**District Vote For President**

| | 1980 | | 1976 | | 1972 |
|---|---|---|---|---|---|
| **D** | 71,759 (51 %) | **D** | 82,660 (59 %) | **D** | 63,821 (43 %) |
| **R** | 55,344 (40 %) | **R** | 58,086 (41 %) | **R** | 83,579 (56 %) |
| **I** | 11,765 (8 %) | | | | |

## Campaign Finance

| | Receipts | Receipts from PACs | Expen-ditures |
|---|---|---|---|
| **1981** | | | |
| Hoyer (D) | $342,144 | $108,600 (32%) | $296,658 |
| Scott (R) | $219,196 | $55,946 (25%) | $240,912 |

**5th District: Northern Prince
Georges County.** Population: 469,179 (3Z%
decrease since 1970). Race: White 282,533
(60%), Black 166,401 (35%), Asian and Pacific
Islander 12,434 (3%), Others 7,811 (2%).
Spanish origin: 12,417 (3%).

# 6 Beverly B. Byron (D)

### Of Frederick — Elected 1978

**Born:** July 27, 1932, Baltimore, Md.
**Education:** Attended Hood College, 1963-64.
**Profession:** Civic volunteer.
**Family:** Widow of Rep. Goodloe Byron; three
children.
**Religion:** Episcopalian.
**Political Career:** No previous office.

**In Washington:** Like her late husband,
Goodloe, whom she succeeded, Beverly Byron is
one of the most conservative Northern Democrats, voting with Republicans as often as with
her own party. Her record is not a carbon copy of
his; when Democratic leaders issue an appeal for
party loyalty on a close vote in the House, she is a
little more likely to go along than he was. But the
difference is not dramatic. In 1981 she regularly
backed Republicans on budget policy.

Beverly Byron took her husband's place on
Armed Services when she arrived in 1979, and his
place on Interior two years later. Some Democratic leaders were initially hesitant about adding
her to Interior, fearing that she would not back
the environmentalist Democratic position on important issues, but she convinced them she could
be a team player. Byron is often loyal on Interior
to Phillip Burton, D-Calif., who had helped
Goodloe Byron obtain money for parkland in the
district. On Armed Services, Byron has worked
hard to learn the ropes (even test flying half a
dozen new planes) and has pressed for additional
funds for a new anti-tank fighter, the A10, which
is assembled at Hagerstown, in her district. She
also has become interested in preserving the
Army's veterinarian corps, which has been involved in chemical warfare research in Fort
Detrick, Md.

Byron had two significant floor amendments
adopted during her first term. One banned the
Occupational Safety and Health Administration
from inspecting a workplace if a state health and
safety inspector had visited the same business
within the previous six months. Byron argued
that small businesses frequently are caught in a
squeeze between state and federal inspectors. The
other banned routine OSHA inspections in businesses with fewer than 10 employees in "safe"
industries.

**At Home:** Family history repeated itself in
1978 when Beverly Byron won her husband's

House seat after he died shortly before the
election.

In 1941, Goodloe Byron's father, U.S. Rep.
William D. Byron, was killed in an airplane crash.
The elder Byron's widow won the special election
that year to fill out his term.

Goodloe Byron, who had a heart condition
but was a physical fitness buff, collapsed while
jogging along the Chesapeake and Ohio Canal
near Washington. He was 49 years old. District
Democratic leaders instantly offered her the
nomination and she accepted it within 24 hours.

The daughter of a wartime naval aide to Gen.
Dwight Eisenhower, Mrs. Byron met her husband
while she was still in high school. She got into
politics when he first ran for the Maryland House
of Delegates in 1962 because, she said, "it meant I
either stayed at home by myself or joined him."
Along with helping to organize Byron's campaigns, she shared his interest in physical fitness
and developing the national park system.

Winning the 1978 election posed little problem for her. Republican officials had not put up
an opponent against her husband, letting a perennial office-seeker, Melvin Perkins, win the GOP
line. A self-styled pauper, Perkins spent part of
the fall campaign in a jail in Baltimore County,
where he had been charged with assaulting a
woman bus driver. Mrs. Byron won by nearly 9-
to-1.

Two years later, Byron's constituent work

---

**6th District: West — Hagerstown,
Cumberland.** Population: 631,322 (28% increase since 1970). Race: White 585,199 (93%),
Black 38,171 (6%), Others 7,958 (1%). Spanish origin: 4,669 (1%).

and conservative voting record proved effective in defusing serious opposition. She triumphed easily over a lackluster primary field, and in the general election registered a landslide victory over her conservative Republican challenger, state Rep. Raymond E. Beck. Mrs. Byron carried every county in sweeping the district by a margin of better than 2-to-1.

**The District:** The elongated 6th District stretches from the Baltimore and Washington, D.C., suburbs past small towns and rolling farmland to the Appalachian Mountains. It is the fastest-growing district in Maryland, with suburban spillover from the nearby urban centers into Carroll, Frederick and Howard counties.

Rather than changing the political complexion of the district, the population boom has reinforced its Republican voting pattern. Reagan carried the district by more than 40,000 votes in 1980, his largest margin in any Maryland district.

Prior to the Byrons — whose conservatism has fit the district's mood — the GOP had a virtual lock on the congressional seat. Republicans Charles McC. Mathias Jr. and both J. Glenn Bealls (Jr. and Sr.) have all represented the district at one time or another since World War II.

About the only pocket of liberalism is the "new town" of Columbia, founded a little more than a decade ago at a spot about equidistant between Baltimore and Washington. Columbia is now the major community in Howard County, but it is outvoted by the small cities of Frederick, Hagerstown and Cumberland to the west and the large rural vote.

## Committees

**Armed Services** (16th of 25 Democrats)
Military Personnel and Compensation; Procurement and Military Nuclear Systems.

**Interior and Insular Affairs** (22nd of 23 Democrats)
Mines and Mining; Oversight and Investigations; Public Lands and National Parks.

**Select Aging** (18th of 31 Democrats)
Housing and Consumer Interests.

## Elections

**1980 General**

| | |
|---|---|
| Beverly Byron (D ) | 146,101 (70 %) |
| Raymond Beck (R ) | 62,913 (30 %) |

**1980 Primary**

| | |
|---|---|
| Beverly Byron (D ) | 38,842 (71 %) |
| Thomas Hattery (D ) | 6,388 (12 %) |
| Others (D ) | 9,439 (17 %) |

**1978 General**

| | |
|---|---|
| Beverly Byron (D ) | 126,196 (90 %) |
| Melvin Perkins (R ) | 14,545 (10 %) |

**District Vote For President**

| | 1980 | | 1976 | | 1972 |
|---|---|---|---|---|---|
| **D** | 86,833 (37 %) | **D** | 92,686 (45 %) | **D** | 52,346 (29 %) |
| **R** | 128,716 (55 %) | **R** | 112,380 (55 %) | **R** | 125,878 (69 %) |
| **I** | 17,471 (7 %) | | | | |

## Campaign Finance

| | Receipts | Receipts from PACs | Expenditures |
|---|---|---|---|
| **1980** | | | |
| Byron (D ) | $171,170 | $69,775 (41 %) | $163,168 |
| Beck (R ) | $73,207 | $11,755 (16 %) | $73,203 |

| | | | |
|---|---|---|---|
| **1978** | | | |
| Byron (D ) | $11,920 | $6,775 (57 %) | $1,542 |

## Voting Studies

| | Presidential Support | | Party Unity | | Conservative Coalition | |
|---|---|---|---|---|---|---|
| Year | S | O | S | O | S | O |
| 1980 | 55 | 41 | 41 | 53 | 83 | 13 |
| 1979 | 40 | 55 | 40 | 58 | 85 | 10 |

S = Support      O = Opposition

## Key Votes

**96th Congress**

| | |
|---|---|
| Weaken Carter oil profits tax (1979) | N |
| Reject hospital cost control plan (1979) | Y |
| Implement Panama Canal Treaties (1979) | N |
| Establish Department of Education (1979) | N |
| Approve Anti-busing Amendment (1979) | Y |
| Guarantee Chrysler Corp. loans (1979) | Y |
| Approve military draft registration (1980) | Y |
| Aid Sandinista regime in Nicaragua (1980) | N |
| Strengthen fair housing laws (1980) | N |

**97th Congress**

| | |
|---|---|
| Reagan budget proposal (1981) | Y |

## Interest Group Ratings

| Year | ADA | ACA | AFL-CIO | CCUS |
|---|---|---|---|---|
| 1980 | 22 | 65 | 32 | 73 |
| 1979 | 16 | 58 | 45 | 78 |

# 7 Parren J. Mitchell (D)

**Of Baltimore — Elected 1970**

**Born:** April 29, 1922, Baltimore, Md.
**Education:** Morgan State College, A.B. 1950;
U. of Md., M.S. 1952.
**Military Career:** Army, 1942-46.
**Profession:** College professor.
**Family:** Single.
**Religion:** Episcopalian.
**Political Career:** Unsuccessfully sought Democratic nomination for U.S. House, 1968.

**In Washington:** One can read Parren Mitchell as the angry militant he often seems to be on the House floor, lashing out at every added dollar of defense spending as an "economic dagger into the bodies of the poor."

Or one can read him the way many other members do, as a man who, once the rhetoric is stripped away, turns out to have a streak of personal conservatism and a willingness to deal pragmatically.

Mitchell made his "economic dagger" speech in April 1980, as he tried to amend the House Budget Committee's 1981 preliminary budget by adding $5 billion to domestic spending and cutting $3 billion from defense spending. He lost overwhelmingly, and cast a vote of principle against the whole budget as it was passing easily.

He was even more upset, if a little resigned, at the Reagan budget in 1981. "If we pursue this reckless, feckless course," he said on the House floor, "to that extent we pursue the further division of America in preventing us from ever becoming one nation." Like most Northern Democrats, he cast a protest vote against the entire budget.

But colleagues also remember the Mitchell of 1979, who helped provide the votes to pass the committee product and forestall something even less to his liking.

"This is not the kind of priority I would like to see established," he had said at that time, as he voted with the leadership, "but I have to look at political realities."

The rhetoric of indignation has been a Mitchell trademark throughout his decade in Congress. When his colleagues passed a series of amendments in 1977 designed to limit busing, he said they had "gone berserk" and engaged in "systemic racism." He refused to watch the final episodes of "Roots" on television, announcing that the program was leading him to lash out at

his white friends with "a vortex of primeval anger." And in 1980, when a Carter administration official remarked that black businesses were not suffering unduly from the recession, Mitchell urged a black audience to serve notice on President Carter that "no man slaps the face of the black community with impunity."

Yet there is a great deal about Mitchell that does not fit neatly into any stereotype of militance. There is, for example, his economic doctrine — a belief in the importance of a stable, limited money supply that is closer to Milton Friedman than to liberal economic orthodoxy.

Mitchell has pursued his monetarism in the last three Congresses as chairman of the Banking Committee's Monetary Policy Subcommittee. At the same time he has backed the more traditional proposals of the Congressional Black Caucus, including the Humphrey-Hawkins jobs bill, which in its full form would have required a far more expansionist economic policy than Mitchell himself called for. President Carter signed a scaled-down version of Humphrey-Hawkins in 1978, while Mitchell was Black Caucus chairman, and Mitchell praised it as a step in the right direction.

Mitchell's legislative priority, however, is in the more conservative-sounding area of minority business enterprise, which he is pursuing in the 97th Congress as Small Business chairman. He has pushed for years to guarantee that fixed percentages of federal contract jobs be reserved

---

**7th District: Baltimore — west and central.** Population: 420,492 (14% decrease since 1970). Race: White 82,409 (20%), Black 334,049 (79%), Others 4,034 (1%). Spanish origin: 3,416 (0.1%).

for minority firms. He succeeded in adding a 10 percent minority "set aside" to a 1977 public works bill.

His greatest effort has been to obtain passage of a Minority Enterprise Act, to require minority set asides on all federal projects. "If that bill gets passed," he said in 1977, "I can sit back and relax." So far it has not, and neither has he. He has continued working to attach minority enterprise language to every piece of legislation that will hold it. In 1979 he persuaded the House to authorize $1 million for the establishment of a Minority Resource Center, to promote minority involvement in foreign assistance programs.

Mitchell's defense views are easy to label. He is a pacifist, one of the few self-proclaimed pacifists in Congress, and he has voted that way. When the House passed a $157 billion defense appropriation bill for 1981, Mitchell's was one of only 42 votes against it.

But alongside that Mitchell is the one who has stood apart from some congressional liberals by refusing to take a "soft" stand on drug laws. "I can't take a public stand on the decriminalization of marijuana," he once said. "Those people, the drug traffickers, cause me to be less than a liberal."

**At Home:** Mitchell has been a crusader all his adult life, from his successful lawsuit in the early 1950s to integrate the University of Maryland graduate school to his election to the House in 1970 as Maryland's first black congressman.

He comes from one of Baltimore's most prominent black families. His brother, Clarence Mitchell Jr., was chief lobbyist for the NAACP; a nephew served in the state Legislature and ran for mayor.

Mitchell's early career was spent as a probation officer in Baltimore, then as supervisor of the city's probation department. From 1963 to 1965, he headed the state Human Rights Commission, which enforced Maryland's new public accommodations law, before he returned to Baltimore to lead the city's anti-poverty program. Mitchell stayed in that post until 1968, when he became professor of sociology at his alma mater, Morgan State University, and an assistant director of the school's Urban Studies Institute.

That was also the year Mitchell made his political debut, challenging machine Democrat Samuel N. Friedel, who had held the 7th Congressional District since its creation in 1952. The district then covered the western portion of the city and its adjoining suburbs. It was the center of Baltimore's Jewish community, although a steady influx of blacks into formerly white neighborhoods was loosening Friedel's grip on the seat.

Helped by the presence of a peace candidate who split the opposition, Friedel defeated Mitchell in the 1968 Democratic primary by about 5,500 votes out of 42,000 cast. Mitchell carried the city portion of the district but was overwhelmed in the white suburbs.

Two years later, Mitchell ran again. There were no other liberal candidates to drain votes away from Mitchell, and at 72, Friedel was becoming vulnerable on the age issue. Even though the incumbent had the endorsement of his old friend, Democratic Gov. Marvin Mandel, Mitchell narrowly defeated him by 38 votes out of nearly 69,000 cast. Many Jewish voters were unhappy about Friedel's defeat that fall, but enough supported Mitchell to allow him to win the general election with 59 percent of the vote.

Redistricting in 1971 removed the white suburbs, creating a heavily black, urban district. That removed the prospect of any serious Republican challenge, but it did not protect Mitchell from primary opposition. He received a stiff challenge in 1972 from Baltimore Solicitor George L. Russell Jr., a member of a rival black faction, who was angered that Mitchell had not supported his unsuccessful mayoral bid the previous year. Mitchell survived, but by less than 3,000 votes out of nearly 66,000 primary ballots cast. Since then, he has had no significant primary or general election contests, allowing him to flirt with the thought of running for another office.

Claiming that a black should be in at least one of the top city offices, Mitchell briefly challenged Mayor William Schaefer for re-election in 1975. But he dropped his bid in midsummer after less than two months in the race, and has expressed his intent since then to remain in Congress. "It is clear," he has said, "that this is where the damage is going to be."

**The District:** Mitchell's Baltimore district is almost unanimously Democratic. It gave Jimmy Carter 85 percent of its vote in 1980; had it not been for the 7th, Carter would have lost Maryland by nearly 50,000 votes.

The old Jewish neighborhoods of northwest Baltimore have become overwhelmingly black in the past two decades as the former residents have moved to the suburbs. In the 1960s, the 7th District extended into these suburbs in Baltimore County. But redistricting in 1971 brought in the district boundaries back to the city limits.

Now the lines have to be substantially redrawn again. The 1980 census showed that the population of the 7th declined 14 percent during the 1970s, the sharpest drop in any Maryland district.

*Parren J. Mitchell, D-Md.*

## Committees

**Banking, Finance and Urban Affairs** (6th of 25 Democrats)
Domestic Monetary Policy; General Oversight and Renegotiation; Housing and Community Development.

**Small Business** (Chairman)
SBA and SBIC Authority, Minority Enterprise and General Small Business Problems, chairman.

**Joint Economic**
Investment, Jobs and Prices; Trade, Productivity and Economic Growth.

## Elections

**1980 General**

| | |
|---|---|
| Parren Mitchell (D ) | 97,104 (89 %) |
| Victor Clark Jr. (R ) | 12,650 (12 %) |

**1980 Primary**

| | |
|---|---|
| Parren Mitchell (D ) | 33,747 (81 %) |
| Edward Makowski (D ) | 7,681 (19 %) |

**1978 General**

| | |
|---|---|
| Parren Mitchell (D ) | 51,996 (89 %) |
| Debra Freeman (I ) | 6,626 (11 %) |

**Previous Winning Percentages**

1976 (94 %)    1974 (100%)    1972 (80 %)    1970 (59 %)

**District Vote For President**

| | 1980 | | 1976 | | 1972 |
|---|---|---|---|---|---|
| D | 111,554 (85 %) | D | 101,341 (82 %) | D | 89,041 (73 %) |
| R | 14,103 (11 %) | R | 22,795 (18 %) | R | 32,369 (26 %) |
| I | 4,232 (3 %) | | | | |

## Campaign Finance

| | Receipts | Receipts from PACs | Expenditures |
|---|---|---|---|
| **1980** | | | |
| Mitchell (D ) | $115,037 | $23,610 (21 %) | $104,567 |
| **1978** | | | |
| Mitchell (D ) | $90,831 | $18,450 (20 %) | $93,693 |
| Freeman (I ) | $7,001 | — (0 %) | $7,052 |

## Voting Studies

| Year | Presidential Support | | Party Unity | | Conservative Coalition | |
|---|---|---|---|---|---|---|
| | S | O | S | O | S | O |
| 1980 | 62 | 25 | 80 | 4 | 2 | 81 |
| 1979 | 78 | 17 | 89 | 5† | 3 | 90 |
| 1978 | 72 | 18 | 86 | 6 | 5 | 88 |
| 1977 | 71 | 20 | 87 | 4 | 3 | 90 |
| 1976 | 25 | 75 | 93 | 2 | 6 | 88 |
| 1975 | 34 | 61 | 86 | 5 | 5 | 82 |
| 1974 (Ford) | 33 | 52 | | | | |
| 1974 | 26 | 55 | 81 | 9 | 3 | 91 |
| 1973 | 22 | 73 | 88 | 7 | 5 | 92 |
| 1972 | 41 | 46 | 85 | 3 | 1 | 89 |
| 1971 | 23 | 72 | 83 | 5 | 0 | 94 |

S = Support          O = Opposition

## Key Votes

**96th Congress**

| | |
|---|---|
| Weaken Carter oil profits tax (1979) | N |
| Reject hospital cost control plan (1979) | N |
| Implement Panama Canal Treaties (1979) | Y |
| Establish Department of Education (1979) | N |
| Approve Anti-busing Amendment (1979) | N |
| Guarantee Chrysler Corp. loans (1979) | Y |
| Approve military draft registration (1980) | N |
| Aid Sandinista regime in Nicaragua (1980) | Y |
| Strengthen fair housing laws (1980) | Y |

**97th Congress**

| | |
|---|---|
| Reagan budget proposal (1981) | N |

## Interest Group Ratings

| Year | ADA | ACA | AFL-CIO | CCUS |
|---|---|---|---|---|
| 1980 | 89 | 9 | 89 | 50 |
| 1979 | 100 | 0 | 100 | 6 |
| 1978 | 90 | 8 | 95 | 24 |
| 1977 | 90 | 4 | 96 | 6 |
| 1976 | 95 | 0 | 87 | 0 |
| 1975 | 79 | 7 | 100 | 18 |
| 1974 | 91 | 0 | 90 | 0 |
| 1973 | 100 | 4 | 91 | 9 |
| 1972 | 88 | 10 | 100 | 11 |
| 1971 | 100 | 11 | 82 | - |

# 8 Michael D. Barnes (D)

**Of Kensington — Elected 1978**

**Born:** Sept. 3, 1943, Washington, D.C.
**Education:** U. of N.C., B.A. 1965; George Washington U., J.D. 1972.
**Military Career:** Marine Corps, 1967-69.
**Profession:** Lawyer.
**Family:** Wife, Claudia Fangboner; one child.
**Religion:** Protestant.
**Political Career:** Md. Public Service Commission, 1975-78.

**In Washington:** One of the less predictable results of the 1980 Republican sweep was the election of this quiet, serious-minded liberal Democrat as chairman of the Foreign Affairs subcommittee dealing with Latin America.

Most subcommittee members agree that if the voting had not produced a Reagan presidency and a GOP Senate, they would have been much less likely to challenge Chairman Gus Yatron, a Pennsylvania Democrat modest in his legislative output but offensive to none.

Given the new political climate, however, and the arrival of Sen. Jesse Helms of North Carolina as chairman of the counterpart Senate panel, liberal Foreign Affairs Democrats launched a coup against Yatron.

The caucus of Foreign Affairs Democrats deposed Yatron on a 10-9 vote, then by an identical vote turned down the next man in line, Dan Mica of Florida, who shared Yatron's hard-line stand toward communist countries. Barnes was next in line and got the chairmanship.

During his freshman term on Foreign Affairs, Barnes had fit in well with the committee's liberals, voting regularly against military aid to authoritarian right-wing regimes. Representing a district with a large Jewish population, he had also opposed arms sales to Arab countries, especially of sophisticated fighter planes to Saudi Arabia.

Barnes no sooner took over the subcommittee than he found himself in the center of controversy about President Reagan's decision to send American military advisers to El Salvador. The new chairman joined most other liberal Democrats in opposing military aid to the regime in that country, and he held hearings on the issue.

When Barnes could not determine whether President Duarte of El Salvador had asked for the advisers, he called him on the telephone to find out. Barnes began one hearing by reporting Duarte's personal confirmation that he had asked

for the help. But he also told the subcommittee that Duarte did not want any additional American personnel in his country.

When Barnes won his Foreign Affairs chairmanship he left his other assignment on Judiciary, where he had worked in the 96th Congress on immigration issues and changes in federal lobbying law. But he has remained on the District of Columbia Committee, where he can express the wishes of his suburban constituents.

Barnes has also played to constituent interests by starting a Federal Government Service Task Force of 30 House members who want to promote interest in federal employee issues. He tried unsuccessfully in 1979 to de-couple high-level federal employees from congressional salary schedules, so they could draw cost-of-living raises even if members of Congress did not.

**At Home:** After years of splintering their allegiances among competing candidates, 8th District Democrats rallied in 1978 behind Barnes, a reform-minded member of the state's public service commission. As a result, the district elected its first Democrat in 20 years.

During Barnes's three years on the public service commission, he opened meetings to the public and usually sided with the environmentalists and consumer activists. He polished this image during the congressional campaign, complaining that Republican Rep. Newton Steers was not in the moderate GOP mold that had produced his district predecessors, Charles McC. Mathias

---

**8th District: Most of Montgomery County.** Population: 547,146 (11% increase since 1970). Race: White 472,363 (86%), Black 44,164 (8%), Asian and Pacific Islander 21,703 (4%), Others 8,916 (2%). Spanish origin: 20,826 (4%).

## Michael D. Barnes, D-Md.

Jr. and Gilbert Gude. Steers took Barnes too lightly, and lost by 4,000 votes out of nearly 160,000 cast.

Stunned by his defeat, Steers campaigned intensively for a rematch in 1980, and raised $565,000. But Barnes had cultivated a reputation as an independent-minded, energetic congressman. He was a leader of the unsuccessful movement in the summer of 1980 to "open" the Democratic National Convention so that delegates bound to President Jimmy Carter would be free to vote for someone else. His work did not shake loose many of the delegates bound to Carter, but it did not hurt Barnes a bit at home; in November, he was re-elected by nearly 50,000 votes while Reagan was carrying the district by 20,000.

Before launching his career in elective politics, Barnes was a lawyer. But he had also been active in national party affairs. He was an aide to Sen. Edmund S. Muskie's 1972 presidential cam-

paign and executive director of the 1976 National Democratic Platform Committee.

**The District:** The 8th is far above the rest of the state in median family income and percentage of white-collar workers. Many of its upper-middle and high-income families work for the federal government, or as lawyers in Washington, or for the hundreds of trade associations and other government-related groups that have sprung up in the area in the past two decades. Several electronics and computer companies operate in the inner suburban communities of Bethesda, Silver Spring and Wheaton, and others have blossomed along Interstate 270 to the northwest, in Rockville and Gaithersburg.

Despite a hefty Democratic registration advantage, the 8th has a history of quirky ticket-splitting. In 1976, Carter and Republican Steers carried the district. In 1980, it was won by Reagan and Democrat Barnes.

## Committees

**District of Columbia** (6th of 7 Democrats)
Government Operations and Metropolitan Affairs.

**Foreign Affairs** (13th of 21 Democrats)
Inter-American Affairs, chairman; Human Rights and International Organizations.

## Elections

**1980 General**

| | |
|---|---|
| Michael Barnes (D ) | 148,301 (59 %) |
| Newton Steers Jr. (R ) | 101,659 (41 %) |

**1978 General**

| | |
|---|---|
| Michael Barnes (D ) | 81,851 (51 %) |
| Newton Steers Jr. (R ) | 77,807 (49 %) |

**1978 Primary**

| | |
|---|---|
| Michael Barnes (D ) | 36,540 (72 %) |
| Alfred Muller (D ) | 6,175 (12 %) |

**District Vote For President**

| | 1980 | | 1976 | | 1972 |
|---|---|---|---|---|---|
| D | 100,946 (40 %) | D | 126,116 (52 %) | D | 96,643 (43 %) |
| R | 120,478 (47 %) | R | 117,949 (48 %) | R | 127,225 (56 %) |
| I | 31,674 (12 %) | | | | |

## Campaign Finance

| | Receipts | Receipts from PACs | Expenditures |
|---|---|---|---|
| **1980** | | | |
| Barnes (D ) | $348,801 | $113,514 (33 %) | $349,924 |
| Steers (R ) | $563,694 | $42,255 (7 %) | $565,952 |

| 1978 | | | |
|---|---|---|---|
| Barnes (D ) | $136,244 | $37,178 (27 %) | $134,588 |
| Steers (R ) | $165,669 | $49,330 (30 %) | $162,980 |

## Voting Studies

| | Presidential Support | | Party Unity | | Conservative Coalition | |
|---|---|---|---|---|---|---|
| Year | S | O | S | O | S | O |
| 1980 | 76 | 20 | 85 | 9 | 5 | 87 |
| 1979 | 80 | 20 | 93 | 6 | 6 | 93 |

S = Support          O = Opposition

## Key Votes

**96th Congress**

| | |
|---|---|
| Weaken Carter oil profits tax (1979) | N |
| Reject hospital cost control plan (1979) | N |
| Implement Panama Canal Treaties (1979) | Y |
| Establish Department of Education (1979) | N |
| Approve Anti-busing Amendment (1979) | N |
| Guarantee Chrysler Corp. loans (1979) | N |
| Approve military draft registration (1980) | N |
| Aid Sandinista regime in Nicaragua (1980) | Y |
| Strengthen fair housing laws (1980) | Y |

**97th Congress**

| | |
|---|---|
| Reagan budget proposal (1981) | N |

## Interest Group Ratings

| Year | ADA | ACA | AFL-CIO | CCUS |
|---|---|---|---|---|
| 1980 | 94 | 13 | 82 | 61 |
| 1979 | 89 | 8 | 95 | 0 |

# Massachusetts

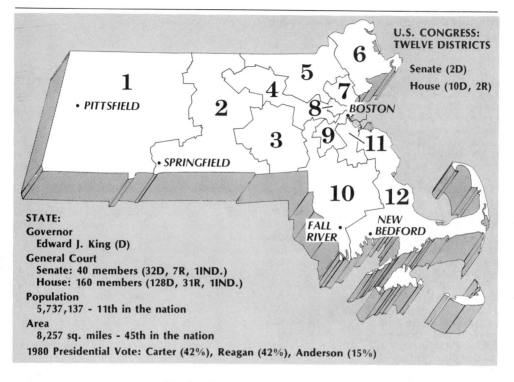

**U.S. CONGRESS: TWELVE DISTRICTS**

Senate (2D)
House (10D, 2R)

• PITTSFIELD

• SPRINGFIELD

BOSTON

FALL RIVER •

NEW • BEDFORD

**STATE:**
**Governor**
Edward J. King (D)
**General Court**
Senate: 40 members (32D, 7R, 1IND.)
House: 160 members (128D, 31R, 1IND.)
**Population**
5,737,137 - 11th in the nation
**Area**
8,257 sq. miles - 45th in the nation
**1980 Presidential Vote:** Carter (42%), Reagan (42%), Anderson (15%)

## ...Joining the Majority

"Don't blame me, I'm from Massachusetts," bumper stickers said in 1973, after things began to go wrong in the second Nixon term that all 49 other states had voted for the previous November. It was a satisfying collective smirk. But if things should go wrong in any sense in the current Republican administration, Massachusetts will have to share the blame with 43 other states. The only state to support George McGovern in 1972 went for Ronald Reagan in 1980.

Reagan's victory does not signal any pendulum swing to the right in Massachusetts. The Republican won by only 6,000 votes out of 2.5 million cast, with 42 percent of the total vote. Independent candidate John Anderson's 15 percent — his highest in the nation — greatly hurt Carter.

Yet there is an indication of growing dissatisfaction with high taxes and liberal "big government" programs. The 1978 election of conserva-

tive Gov. Edward King, who had unseated liberal incumbent Michael Dukakis in the Democratic primary, was a warning. Passage in 1980 of "Proposition, 2 1/2" placing a ceiling on local property taxes and leading to reduced services in communities all over the state, was an even more dramatic symbol that Massachusetts is more complicated than the liberal state of the Kennedys.

If the Kennedys have been the source of modern Massachusetts liberalism, they have also been the beneficiaries of broader change in the state's politics. In 1947, when John Kennedy first took a seat in Congress, Massachusetts had a Republican Governor and two Republican Senators, and the GOP held nine of the state's 14 House seats. In 1981, with Edward Kennedy nearing the end of his third full term in the Senate, his party holds the governorship, both Senate seats, and 10 of 12 House seats.

What the Kennedys did was give leadership

to issue-oriented liberals and legitimacy to a party previously associated with machine politics and corruption. They helped tame the fierce rivalry between the Yankee Protestant Republicans and Catholic Democrats.

Irish Democrats were running Boston by the turn of the century, and beginning in the 1920s, the party was competitive statewide in good national Democratic years. The Depression created a stable majority for Franklin D. Roosevelt and the New Deal. But Yankee Republicans continued to win most congressional and gubernatorial elections, helped by their increased willingness to nominate candidates from the "progressive" side of the spectrum, like Leverett Saltonstall and Henry Cabot Lodge.

When John F. Kennedy first ran for Congress in 1946, the state was nearly ready for a political upheaval, with or without him. It soon had one, symbolized not only by Kennedy's Senate victory over Lodge in 1952 but by the Democratic takeover of the legislature in 1948, which installed Thomas P. O'Neill Jr. as Speaker of the state House. The legislature has not been Republican since.

Over the following decades, Massachusetts became a national leader in state spending for welfare, unemployment insurance and other social programs. Democrats did not win every election — internecine party warfare, particularly between Irish and Italian Americans, plagued them into the 1970s — but Republican winners, such as Edward Brooke, the only black senator since Reconstruction, were progressives.

Problems developed, though. Recessions and the decline of the textile and shoe industries left many cities in a state of near-depression. Irish South Boston exploded in violence in 1975 over busing plans involving blacks from Roxbury. Catholic opposition to Massachusetts' liberal abortion laws grew. Taxes to pay for expensive social programs soared, angering millions and sending thousands packing for low-tax New Hampshire.

In 1978, angry Democrats gave a jolt to the liberal "welfare state" policies by dumping Dukakis for Edward King. That same year, Democrat Paul Tsongas unseated two-term Sen. Brooke. By 1980, Tsongas had adapted to current realities by calling for a "new liberalism" to replace what he saw as the dogma of huge spending programs and high taxes.

# Political Tour

**Boston.** Boston was getting shabby for some years after World War II. But urban renewal instituted by Mayor John Collins (1960-1968) and Kevin White (1968-    ) has transformed the city into one of the most amenable (and expensive) places in the nation to live.

The city's population, which peaked just above 800,000 in 1950, had by 1980 fallen back to where it was at the turn of the century — slightly more than 560,000. But the population slide shows signs of abating and new urban shopping precincts, such as the glittery Faneuil Hall market, have given new life to the center city.

Boston is unquestionably a Democratic city. Only three Republicans have carried it over the last two decades, all from the liberal wing of the party — John Volpe in 1966, Francis Sargent in 1970, and Brooke in 1972. But each of them also lost the city at some other time to Democrats more liberal than they. Kennedy regularly wins seven of every ten votes in the city, and in 1972, George McGovern took a healthy 66 percent — better than either of Jimmy Carter's victories there.

Boston is best defined by its various ethnic neighborhoods. South Boston is the heart of the Irish Catholic vote in the city. Although historically Democratic, South Boston supported Reagan in 1980 over Jimmy Carter. In the wake of violent anti-busing demonstrations in the 1970s, South Boston's political debate now centers on social rather than economic questions, and that favors conservative candidates. George Wallace swept South Boston in the 1976 Democratic presidential primary.

Blacks make up about a fifth of the city's population. Concentrated in Roxbury and the South End, Boston's blacks regularly give as much as 90 percent of their vote to Democratic candidates. The North End and East Boston are heavily Italian.

Thousands of college students attending Boston University, Northeastern University, and numerous smaller institutions have also had a profound effect on politics within the city. Activated by opposition to the Vietnam war and permitted to vote on campus by liberal registration laws, the student community has provided the volunteer force and votes for many liberal candidates at both the state and local level.

**Suburban Boston.** Boston has several sets of suburbs that form concentric circles around the city's north, west and south sides.

Just north of Boston are Cambridge, Watertown and Somervill, three communities that are essentially urban extensions of Boston. All have strong ethnic, blue-collar populations and are Democratic. Harvard and the Massachusetts Institute of Technology give Cambridge a more liberal flavor than the others. House Speaker O'Neill has represented Cambridge for 29 years; his early stand against the Vietnam war was popular at home even when it was controversial in national politics.

Brookline and Newton immediately to the west of Boston have large enclaves of wealthy, liberal, Jewish residents. Just south of Boston are Dedham, Milton and Quincy, where shipbuilding and other industries exist near ethnic, blue-collar neighborhoods.

The next ring of towns farther out from the Hub, as Boston is called, have been traditionally dependent on small-scale industries which have suffered in the second third of the 20th century. As shoe-making and textile work died out, the Democratic workers moved into machine factories. In turn, the machines have given way to high technology. Route 128, a ring road around Boston, has served as a magnet for numerous electronics, defense and space-related firms. With a highly-educated work force, these clean, white-collar industries have brought a new measure of economic prosperity to the area.

Route 128 is a rough dividing line between the "urban" suburbs close to Boston and those that are more countryfied. The strong Democratic vote found inside Route 128 wavers in the suburban towns further from Boston, particularly when Republicans nominate liberal candidates like Brooke and Sargent. Residential communities such as Belmont, Lexington, and Winchester support a strong GOP tradition. Further from the city, on the North Shore, Marblehead is heavily Republican but the fishing town of Gloucester and industrial Beverly are more divided between the parties. Salem, of witch trial fame, is a Democratic industrial town. Residents of these communities read Boston's newspapers and watch its television stations, but many of them have little day-to-day contact with the city.

**Northern Industrial.** Lowell, Lawrence and Haverhill are aging Massachusetts factory towns. Lowell and Lawrence were great cities of textile manufacturing; Haverhill was a leader in shoemaking. The decline of these industries set the cities back drastically but they are beginning to re-emerge as viable economic entities, bolstered by the arrival of new high-technology industry.

Large enough to qualify as a metropolitan area in its own right, the industrial region of Lawrence and Lowell is strongly Democratic. In 1978, King and Tsongas both won more than 70 percent in Lowell and Lawrence. Two years later, Carter carried both cities over Ronald Reagan, but by a less impressive margin.

Heading towards the ocean, northeast Massachusetts is dotted with small towns and fishing villages that often vote Republican.

**Southern Industrial.** Bordering on Rhode Island is Bristol County, site of two of Massachusetts' larger cities: New Bedford and Fall River. Like the cities at the northern end of the Boston sphere, New Bedford and Fall River suffered blight and high unemployment following the disappearance of major employers.

The economies of both cities were based on textiles, fishing and whaling. With the decline of all three industries, many jobs vanished and there has been little to fill the void.

Seafaring Portuguese-Americans settled in Fall River years ago and have remained an important part of the city's ethnic makeup. New Bedford also has a large Portuguese population. Both cities support Democrats regularly, although the large blue-collar constituency tends to favor moderates, such as Sen. Henry Jackson, over liberals. Jackson was an easy winner in both cities in his 1976 Democratic presidential primary bid.

**Cape Cod and Coastal Towns.** The old Yankee personality that once dominated the entire state is still alive and well on much of Cape Cod. The area is largely dependent on the thousands of tourists who come to walk on its dunes and beaches every year. It is also one of the nation's major cranberry growing areas, and fishing is still a lively industry.

Running from Cohasset and Scituate in the north to Provincetown at the tip of the Cape, and including the islands of Martha's Vineyard and Nantucket, this region is quite Republican by Massachusetts standards. The four counties that make up the area — Plymouth, Barnstable, Dukes and Nantucket — all supported Nixon in 1972 when the state went for McGovern. In 1980, Reagan carried all but Dukes County (Martha's Vineyard). On the congressional level, however, the area now sends liberal Democrat Gerry Studds to the House virtually without opposition. In the 1960s, Republican Hastings Keith won without any opposition.

This is a lightly populated region with slightly more than a half-million people in 1980. But it grew by a nearly third between 1970 and 1980, more than any other part of the state.

**Central and Western Massachusetts.** With a few notable exceptions, this is Yankee Massachusetts, where the town meeting and the village green are more reminiscent of Vermont than of Boston.

There are a few industrial centers, but most of central and western Massachusetts is taken up by the Berkshire Hills and small farms which specialize in dairy cattle, chickens, apples and cigar tobacco.

Republicans often do better among the farmers and villagers in this area than with the ethnic working-classes in the eastern part of the state. A moderate Republican, Silvio Conte, has represented western Massachusetts in Congress for 22 years.

The Democratic vote is centered in the major cities. Worcester, in east-central Massachusetts, is the state's second largest city with 162,000 people. Industry is dominant and diversified; the vote is strongly Democratic. Other industrial Democratic cities in Worcester County are Fitchburg and Leominster. The latter supported Reagan in 1980.

Springfield is the third-ranking city in the state. With 152,000 people, it is the Massachusetts focal point of the Connecticut River Valley industrial area, which also includes the cities of Holyoke and Chicopee. All the industrial cities and towns generally vote Democratic, though suburbs like West Springfield and Westfield sometimes go Republican.

There are numerous French-Canadians in the Springfield metropolitan area. They have been the largest immigrant group in the post-war era, but their numbers and political power do not compare with other ethnic groups.

A few large towns in the remainder of western Massachusetts bring mixed political results. North of Springfield are the college towns of Northampton (Smith College) and Amherst (University of Massachusetts, Amherst College), where Democrats and Republicans are fairly evenly matched. Pittsfield, in Berkshire County, has some industry, but it is neither as "ethnic" nor as Democratic as eastern Massachusetts.

# Redrawing the Lines

Sluggish overall growth during the 1970s dropped Massachusetts from the ten most populous states for the first time in history. It also cost the state its 12th seat in the House. Any one of the Boston-area districts — the 7th, 8th, 9th or 11th — could be cut. All of them lost population in the last decade and are far short of the ideal district size of 521,549. But the Boston districts are all Democratic, and instead of consolidating in Boston, Democrats at midyear were discussing carving up the overpopulated 10th District of GOP Rep. Margaret M. Heckler.

The coastal 12th District of southeastern Massachusetts far outpaced the rest of the state in population growth during the 1970s. To a lesser extent, Heckler's nearby 10th District shared in the boom, as did the 1st, 3rd and 5th Districts, which grew modestly.

## Governor
## Edward J. King (D)

**Born:** May 11, 1925, Chelsea, Mass.
**Home:** Winthrop, Mass.
**Education:** Boston College, B.A. 1948.
**Military Career:** Navy.
**Profession:** Museum administrator, Mass. Port Authority executive director, 1963-74.
**Family:** Wife, Josephine; two children.
**Religion:** Roman Catholic.
**Political Career:** Elected governor 1978; term expires Jan. 1983.

# Edward M. Kennedy (D)

**Of Boston — Elected 1962**

**Born:** Feb. 22, 1932, Boston, Mass.
**Education:** Harvard U., A.B. 1956; U. of Va., LL.B. 1959.
**Military Career:** Army, 1951-53.
**Profession:** Lawyer.
**Family:** Separated; three children.
**Religion:** Roman Catholic.
**Political Career:** Suffolk County assistant district attorney, 1962-61; south Democratic nomination for president, 1980.

**In Washington:** Kennedy has been preoccupied with national politics much of his career, but he still has been the legislator neither of his brothers ever had time to be. Over nearly 20 years, he has won his share of small battles and made symbolic issues out of the larger ones.

His cause now is the defense of social programs Reagan wants to eliminate or reduce. Many fall within the scope of the Labor and Human Resources Committee, where Kennedy has served throughout his Senate career. That was one reason he chose to take the senior Democratic position on Labor and Human Resources in 1981, rather than the one on Judiciary, which he could have chosen instead.

He has spoken out against Reagan on the full spectrum of budget and social policy issues. In June, he led the Senate as it rebuked the administration for refusing to support a worldwide campaign against the marketing of unhealthy baby formulas in Third World countries.

Still, he is a minority senator for the first time in his career, only two years after he seemed to be on the verge of real power as Judiciary chairman. When Kennedy took over at Judiciary, his tenure seemed likely to last as long as he wanted to remain in the Senate. But he did not accomplish much. By the fall of 1979, he was running for president and spending little time on committee business.

His first priority, an artful compromise with Judiciary's senior Republican, Strom Thurmond, on a bill to rewrite the U.S. criminal code, fell apart when Kennedy let his Senate duties lapse. The code never reached the floor. After the 1980 election, Kennedy returned to committee work and tried desperately to rescue an open housing bill that had already passed the House. But it failed when conservatives threatened to filibuster.

Kennedy started his Senate career without any of the leadership pressures that descended on him later. He was 30 years old, his brothers were running the country, and he voted with them while looking out for Masschusetts' interests.

In the next few years, Kennedy became a creative and often successful legislator. He was largely responsible for creating the Teacher Corps; he fought against draft deferments for college students, arguing that they were unfair to the poor, and helped bring about their elimination; he worked to draw up rules for congressional redistricting. He spoke for Hispanic farm workers in California and Indians in Alaska.

But Kennedy's strongest legislative period came in the early 1970s, following not only the Chappaquiddick tragedy in 1969 but his most embarrassing Senate defeat, his removal as majority whip in 1971.

Kennedy had been elected whip in 1969, defeating Senate Finance Chairman Russell B. Long, who had performed erratically in the post for four years. The vote was taken only months after Robert Kennedy's assassination, and the youngest Kennedy was seen as the rising liberal star.

But he was too impatient to do the odd jobs on the Senate floor that make an effective Senate leader. And that summer, his image was shattered when he drove off a bridge at Chappaquiddick and Mary Jo Kopechne drowned. When Senate Democrats met to elect their leaders in 1971, they chose Robert C. Byrd for whip, 31-24.

That led Kennedy back into the legislative process. He became chairman of the Health Subcommittee, and formed a productive partnership with his House counterpart, Florida Democrat Paul G. Rogers. Together they wrote legislation providing new federal money for research into cancer and heart and lung diseases, family planning, and doctor training. Virtually every year brought a greater federal role in health.

But there still was resistance to Kennedy's

**543**

## Edward M. Kennedy, D-Mass.

most important proposal, national health insurance. Kennedy began promoting the issue in 1969. But no comprehensive program moved close to enactment. In 1977, President Carter took office on a platform that included national health. But Carter, pleading budget constraints, eventually proposed only a limited, phased-in system, starting with catastrophic coverage. Kennedy pronounced that inadequate, and joined allies in organized labor in pressing for a more ambitious program. Neither version advanced in Congress.

Meanwhile, Kennedy was chairing the Judiciary Subcommittee on Administrative Practice and Procedure, using it to investigate everything from the Freedom of Information Act to the Food and Drug Administration. Critics said he used the panel for publicity, but the hearings he conducted sometimes led to substantive bills, such as one revising federal drug laws in 1979.

Over the years, Kennedy has taken up a myriad of causes at Judiciary. He has worked on bills to allow more refugees into the United States and provide assistance to refugees abroad. He joined with Indiana Democrat Birch Bayh in promoting the 18-year-old vote in 1980. He challenged President Nixon's habit of letting legislation die simply by refusing to act on it — casting "pocket vetoes." Kennedy argued against that practice himself in federal court, and won.

Outside his committees, Kennedy became perhaps the most outspoken Senate advocate of changes in the tax system. He coordinated the opposition to Finance Committee tax bills, taking much of the leadership away from the committee's liberals, who were reluctant to challenge Russell Long, their chairman. In 1976, when Finance wrote the most complex tax bill to emerge in 20 years, Kennedy and allies sought to change it by raising the minimum tax on the wealthy, restricting the use of corporate tax shelters, and providing an immediate credit for retirees. All those proposals lost; Kennedy voted against the bill. In recent years, Kennedy has identified himself with the issue of deregulating major industries, sometimes in alliance with free-enterprise conservatives. He tried as Judiciary chairman to bring deregulation bills under his own jurisdiction, but failed after an angry counterattack from the Commerce Committee. He was bitterly criticized on the floor by Ernest Hollings, D-S.C., a senior member of Commerce, who talked about "Kennedy hegemony."

As a chairman, Kennedy liked to hold brief hearings on a wide variety of issues, leaving legislative drafting to others. He also left quite a bit to his staff, which has always been excellent. Aides are still at his elbow constantly throughout

the day. They funnel massive amounts of information to him, and tend to the details once he has made a decision.

Kennedy himself is a quick study, but he has no patience with minor problems. Nor does he like asking anyone, including his fellow senators, for help. He is, in fact, more willing to compromise with his ideological and political enemies than to ask his friends for support. Fellow Democrats on Judiciary complained when he cut a deal with conservative Thurmond over the criminal code, rather than cajoling members of his own party into forming a united front.

It is impossible, now as in the past, to separate Ted Kennedy the legislator from Ted Kennedy the political symbol and last of the brothers. He has never been just another senator.

Kennedy's Senate office is the center of a political network that stretches coast to coast. It is not just campaign shock troops who await another call, but a remarkable array of liberal specialists in law, medicine, and academia who cheerfully respond to Kennedy's requests for a briefing or for testimony at hearings. When Kennedy travels abroad, he is received by heads of state. He has negotiated, in total secrecy at times, for the release of dissidents in the Soviet Union.

Kennedy may not be the most brilliant senator, or the smoothest. With scrambled syntax and sentences that trail off in mid-thought, he seldom gets the better of a face-to-face argument. But he is tenacious, and because he is who he is, he can transform almost any issue into front-page news merely by making it his own.

And when he is psychologically ready, he can still move an audience like no one else in American politics, as he did at the New York convention in 1980, assuring liberal loyalists that "the dream shall never die."

**At Home:** In Massachusetts, Kennedy usually has had to run against himself — or at least against his own track record. The only way for him to "win" has been to run up a lopsided margin against his modest Republican opposition, preserving his reputation for invincibility at home and his image as a national leader.

It has not always been easy to do. He set a difficult standard for himself in 1964, when he won his first full term less than a year after his brother's assassination. Bedridden following an airplane crash, and unable to campaign, he defeated Republican Howard Whitmore Jr. by the biggest margin in state history: 1,129,244 votes. It was that number, rather than GOP candidate Josiah Spaulding, that provided the real test for Kennedy in 1970. There was no way he could pass it. The Chappaquiddick accident had taken place the year before, and the national skepticism over Kennedy's handling of it had its effect even at home. Under the circumstances, his 62 percent was respectable, if no ringing vindication.

In 1976, Kennedy's stands favoring Medicaid abortions and busing in Boston seemed to pose some initial obstacles. But he had a good year. He brushed aside three anti-busing and right-to-life challengers in the primary, and then crushed Republican Michael Robertson, a businessman. He again won by a million votes.

In 1982, with an unsuccessful presidential campaign behind him and his future in national politics still unresolved, Kennedy will be up against the numbers again, seeking to establish that he still has a secure base in Massachusetts.

Things were much simpler in 1962, when he won the election to fill the remaining two years of his brother's Senate term. John Kennedy had arranged for the appointment of family friend

Benjamin A. Smith to the seat when he became president in 1961, and Smith was more than willing to step aside for the younger Kennedy the following year. Edward J. McCormack, nephew of House Speaker John W. McCormack, was not as obliging as Smith. He derided Kennedy's qualifications, pointing out his meager experience as an assistant district attorney in Boston, and uttered the now famous words in a Democratic primary debate: "If your name were Edward Moore (instead of Edward Moore Kennedy) your candidacy would be a joke." But Kennedy refused to lose his temper and the attacks created a backlash harmful to McCormack. Kennedy's slogan was simple and understated: "He Can Do More for Massachusetts."

Kennedy easily won the primary, carrying every ward in Boston and winning outstate as well. In November, he beat Republican George Cabot Lodge.

## Committees

**Judiciary** (2nd of 8 Democrats)
Immigration and Refugee Policy; Juvenile Justice.

**Labor and Human Resources** (Ranking Democrat)
Education; Employmentand Productivity; Investigations and General Oversight; Labor.

**Joint Economic**
Investment, Jobs and Prices; Trade, Productivity and Economic Growth.

## Elections

**1976 General**

| | |
|---|---|
| Edward Kennedy (D ) | 1,726,657 (69 %) |
| Michael Robertson (R ) | 722,641 (29 %) |

**Previous Winning Percentages**

| | | |
|---|---|---|
| 1970 (62 %) | 1964 (74 %) | 1962* (55 %) |

*Special election

## Campaign Finance

| | Receipts | Receipts from PACs | Expenditures |
|---|---|---|---|
| **1976** | | | |
| Kennedy (D ) | $975,601 | $104,302 (11 %) | $896,196 |
| Robertson (R ) | $169,724 | $1,800 (1 %) | $166,854 |

## Voting Studies

| | Presidential Support | | Party Unity | | Conservative Coalition | |
|---|---|---|---|---|---|---|
| **Year** | **S** | **O** | **S** | **O** | **S** | **O** |
| 1980 | 15 | 9 | 15 | 2 | 0 | 24 |
| 1979 | 73 | 7 | 72 | 5 | 2 | 88 |

| | | | | | | |
|---|---|---|---|---|---|---|
| 1978 | 80 | 12 | 88 | 5 | 5 | 88 |
| 1977 | 76 | 17 | 86 | 5 | 2 | 88 |
| 1976 | 21 | 60 | 84 | 4 | 5 | 84 |
| 1975 | 43 | 45 | 80 | 4 | 4 | 84 |
| 1974 (Ford) | 38 | 49 | | | | |
| 1974 | 31 | 61 | 78 | 8 | 4 | 80 |
| 1973 | 30 | 58 | 80 | 5 | 4 | 85 |
| 1972 | 22 | 52 | 80 | 8 | 4 | 82 |
| 1971 | 30 | 50 | 78 | 10 | 13 | 76 |

S = Support          O = Opposition

## Key Votes

**96th Congress**

| | |
|---|---|
| Maintain relations with Taiwan (1979) | N |
| Reduce synthetic fuel development funds (1979) | ? |
| Impose nuclear plant moratorium (1979) | Y |
| Kill stronger windfall profits tax (1979) | N |
| Guarantee Chrysler Corp. loans (1979) | Y |
| Approve military draft registration (1980) | N |
| End Revenue Sharing to the states (1980) | N |
| Block Justice Dept. busing suits (1980) | ? |

**97th Congress**

| | |
|---|---|
| Restore urban program funding cuts (1981) | Y |

## Interest Group Ratings

| Year | ADA | ACA | AFL-CIO | CCUS-1 | CCUS-2 |
|---|---|---|---|---|---|
| 1980 | 33 | 20 | 100 | 20 | |
| 1979 | 79 | 5 | 94 | 0 | 8 |
| 1978 | 95 | 4 | 95 | 20 | |
| 1977 | 95 | 7 | 89 | 6 | |
| 1976 | 95 | 0 | 90 | 0 | |
| 1975 | 89 | 0 | 89 | 13 | |
| 1974 | 81 | 0 | 70 | 0 | |
| 1973 | 90 | 4 | 91 | 0 | |
| 1972 | 90 | 5 | 89 | 0 | |
| 1971 | 100 | 5 | 83 | - | |

# Paul E. Tsongas (D)

**Of Lowell — Elected 1978**

**Born:** Feb. 14, 1941, Lowell, Mass.
**Education:** Dartmouth College, B.A. 1962; Yale
U., LL.B. 1967.
**Profession:** Lawyer.
**Family:** Wife, Nicola Sauvage; three children.
**Religion:** Greek Orthodox.
**Political Career:** Lowell City Council, 1969-72;
Middlesex County Commission, 1973-75; U.S.
House, 1975-79.

**In Washington:** It took only one speech,
modestly phrased and quietly delivered, to give
Tsongas a national role as public spokesman for
the new liberalism his party is trying to devise.

It was not even a speech in the Senate. It was
an address to the Americans for Democratic Action, July 3, 1980, telling the surprised group that
liberalism would become a footnote in history
unless liberals learned to be flexible and break out
of the mindset of the 1960's.

"The soul of liberalism is intact," Tsongas
said, "a conviction that government can and must
help people achieve equal opportunity and individual dignity." But he said that if liberals insisted on stressing anti-business rhetoric and ignored the need for productivity, they would "lose
the leadership of this nation."

Four months later, when Republicans took
control of the White House and the Senate,
Tsongas attained the status of a minor prophet.

He began working his "agenda for the 1980's"
into a book. Numerous interviews suggested what
the agenda would be: an emphasis on the incentives needed to fuel economic growth coupled
with a tolerant approach on social issues like
abortion and affirmative action.

The first signs of heresy in Tsongas' liberalism were evident during the 1979 debate over a
loan guarantee for Chrysler Corp. A self-proclaimed "workers' Democrat" who had been
viewed as a labor loyalist during his four-year
House career, Tsongas shocked colleagues by joining with Richard Lugar, R-Ind., to promote a
three-year wage freeze for Chrysler workers.

He later cited the debate over Chrysler —
and the intense heat he took from many liberal
groups for his stand on it — as the event that led
him to think more deeply about his own
convictions.

Tsongas made his first real Senate splash,
however, on the Alaska lands issue, when he
succeeded on the floor in substituting his own

conservation-oriented bill for one written in the
Energy Committee. Working with environmentalists on the outside, he managed to prevail in
repeated test votes not only against Ted Stevens,
Alaska's shrewd senior senator, but against his
own chairman, Henry M. Jackson, D-Wash.

Throughout that debate, Tsongas showed the
soft-voiced pragmatism and willingness to negotiate that has marked much of his political career.
He does not like to build "we and they" barricades and frequently approaches his most obstinate opponents with a compromise. On the Alaska
bill, Tsongas and Stevens ended up fighting together to end a filibuster.

Tsongas' flexibility came out again in his
shift on the issue of nuclear power. After initial
skepticism about nuclear energy, he announced in
1980 that he had changed his mind and felt
limited nuclear power — with adequate safeguards — would have to be a part of Massachusetts' energy picture. He insisted it was safer than
coal.

Tsongas is often more ideological when it
comes to foreign policy, especially American
policy towards Africa. "I would hope to be viewed
as the Africanist in the Senate," Tsongas said in
1978, and in his first year he made several impassioned speeches scoring the U.S. for its failure to
support black nationalism in Africa.

He lost out in his 1979 bid for the Foreign
Relations Committee, but he made it in 1980, and
by 1981 was playing a key role on the committee,
fighting the Reagan administration's attempts to
play down human rights in foreign policy.
Tsongas was a leader in the drive to defeat the
nomination of Ernest Lefever as assistant secretary of state for human rights. He and others said
Lefever was insensitive to the issue.

**At Home:** Once called "a classic study in

subdued ambition," Tsongas continues to puzzle old-line Massachusetts politicians. Cerebral and seemingly shy, he has few of the obvious attributes of the successful statewide politician. He has never begun a campaign as the favorite. But he has never lost an election.

Following three years in the Peace Corps, he began his political career in his economically depressed home town of Lowell. A stint on the City Council led to his successful campaign for the County Commission on a reform slate.

In 1974, with a solid clean government image, he became the first Democrat to win in his district in a century. Stressing his blue-collar roots, he took more than 60 percent of the vote against incumbent Republican Paul Cronin.

When he announced his 1978 candidacy against GOP Sen. Edward W. Brooke, the odds looked steep. More prominent Massachusetts Democrats, including Lt. Gov. Thomas P. O'Neill

III, refused to make the challenge. But a series of *Boston Globe* stories during the early part of the year disclosed that Brooke had lied about his financial worth in divorce proceedings.

Brooke's sudden vulnerability brought Tsongas a difficult primary opponent, Secretary of State Paul Guzzi, who had much of Tsongas' appeal to ethnic Democrats and was better known statewide. But Tsongas took advantage of a huge loyalty vote in his own congressional district to win the primary, even though he lost most counties.

In the fall, he scarcely had to mention Brooke's financial problems. The media kept them before the voters, and Tsongas concentrated on prying away liberal support from the incumbent, taking advantage of an endorsement from Sen. Edward Kennedy, who had never helped a Brooke opponent before. The result was an easy Tsongas win.

## Committees

**Energy and Natural Resources** (8th of 9 Democrats)
Energy Conservation and Supply; Energy Research and Development; Water and Power.

**Foreign Relations** (6th of 8 Democrats)
African Affairs; East Asian and Pacific Affairs; Western Hemisphere Affairs.

**Small Business** (7th of 8 Democrats)
Advocacy and the Future of Small Business.

## Elections

**1978 General**

| | |
|---|---|
| Paul Tsongas (D ) | 1,093,283 (55 %) |
| Edward Brooke (R ) | 890,584 (45 %) |

**1978 Primary**

| | |
|---|---|
| Paul Tsongas (D ) | 296,915 (36 %) |
| Paul Guzzi (D ) | 258,960 (31 %) |
| Kathleen Alioto (D ) | 161,036 (19 %) |
| Howard Phillips (D ) | 65,397 (8 %) |
| Elaine Noble (D) | 52,464 (6 %) |

**Previous Winning Percentages**

1976* (67 %)   1974* (61 %)

*House elections

## Campaign Finance

| | Receipts | Receipts from PACs | Expenditures |
|---|---|---|---|
| **1978** | | | |
| Tsongas (D ) | $772,513 | $45,350 (6 %) | $768,383 |
| Brooke (R ) | $957,252 | $203,767 (21 %) | $1,284,855 |

## Voting Studies

| | Presidential Support | | Party Unity | | Conservative Coalition | |
|---|---|---|---|---|---|---|
| Year | S | O | S | O | S | O |
| **Senate service** | | | | | | |
| 1980 | 72 | 22 | 79 | 10 | 7 | 75 |
| 1979 | 83 | 10 | 83 | 8 | 2 | 88 |
| **House service** | | | | | | |
| 1978 | 37 | 8 | 49 | 6 | 4 | 46 |
| 1977 | 80 | 15 | 86 | 9 | 8 | 87 |
| 1976 | 24 | 75 | 90 | 5 | 10 | 87 |
| 1975 | 34 | 66 | 91 | 7 | 5 | 92 |

S = Support          O = Opposition

## Key Votes

**96th Congress**

| | |
|---|---|
| Maintain relations with Taiwan (1979) | N |
| Reduce synthetic fuel development funds (1979) | Y |
| Impose nuclear plant moratorium (1979) | ? |
| Kill stronger windfall profits tax (1979) | N |
| Guarantee Chrysler Corp. loans (1979) | Y |
| Approve military draft registration (1980) | N |
| End Revenue Sharing to the states (1980) | N |
| Block Justice Dept. busing suits (1980) | N |

**97th Congress**

| | |
|---|---|
| Restore urban program funding cuts (1981) | Y |

## Interest Group Ratings

| Year | ADA | ACA | AFL-CIO | CCUS-1 | CCUS-2 |
|---|---|---|---|---|---|
| **Senate service** | | | | | |
| 1980 | 89 | 12 | 84 | 28 | |
| 1979 | 74 | 11 | 100 | 10 | 27 |
| **House service** | | | | | |
| 1978 | 50 | 18 | 88 | 36 | |
| 1977 | 100 | 4 | 83 | 18 | |
| 1976 | 85 | 4 | 86 | 7 | |
| 1975 | 100 | 7 | 100 | 12 | |

# 1 Silvio O. Conte (R)

Of Pittsfield — Elected 1958

**Born:** Nov. 9, 1921, Pittsfield, Mass.
**Education:** Boston College; Boston College of Law, LL.B. 1949.
**Military Career:** Navy, 1942-44.
**Profession:** Lawyer.
**Family:** Wife, Corinne Duval; four children.
**Religion:** Roman Catholic.
**Political Career:** Mass. Senate, 1951-59.

**In Washington:** Conte is too liberal ever to be a leader in House Republican ranks, but sheer seniority has given him a huge plum — the senior GOP position on Appropriations. Younger conservatives complained when Conte claimed the job in 1979, but they did not try to stop him, and he has been their titular committee leader since then, cheerfully voting against the party's majority almost two-thirds of the time.

A plain talking, cigar-smoking horse-trader, Conte in fact has as much in common with urban ethnic Democrats as with moderate Republicans of the Northeast. His politics have always caused him some trouble on the Appropriations Committee; he was muscled on to the panel as a freshman by then senior Republican Joseph W. Martin of Massachusetts, but was kept off the Labor-HEW Subcommittee for years while junior members were appointed ahead of him. When he finally got on in 1971, he had to give up seniority on his other subcommittees to do it.

Conte makes no apology for his liberalism or his close friendship with his Democratic colleague from Massachusetts, Speaker Thomas P. O'Neill Jr. Representing a district with a declining industrial base and high unemployment, Conte favors public works and public jobs measures. But he has also backed foreign aid, environmental controls, and more spending for health care programs. He incurred the wrath of the Nixon administration by opposing the invasion of Cambodia, the ABM missile system, and the SST airplane, and by crticizing the performance of Spiro T. Agnew as Nixon's vice president.

In the early days of the Reagan administration, Conte was confronted with a difficult decision, over whether to support the administration's request for funds to send American military advisers to El Salvador. Conte had serious doubts about the Reagan El Salvador policy, and his vote would have created a majority against the funding in the Foreign Operations Subcommittee on Ap-

propriations. But he ultimately went with Reagan, explaining that "this is the first foreign policy issue this administration has had out of the box," and warning that he might not vote to approve the money a second time.

But if Conte's views have isolated him among Appropriations Republicans, they have allowed him to make crucial deals with committee Democrats. When the House and Senate first became deadlocked on the abortion issue in 1976 — the House banning all federal funding of abortions, the Senate generally favoring abortion funding — Conte broke an 11-week impasse by writing compromise language to prohibit federal funding of abortions "except where the life of the mother is endangered."

In 1979, there was a deadlock over fuel assistance to the poor because Frost Belt legislators said the formula provided an unncessary "sweetener" for the warmer Southern states. Conte wrote a compromise giving 25 percent more to the Northern states, without shutting out the South. That broke the impasse.

While supporting most large-scale social spending requests, Conte has maneuvered to establish credentials as a fiscal conservative by railing at smaller budget items he says are a waste of money. Starting in the late '60s, Conte waged an annual fight to limit the size of farm subsidies. He contended that corporate giants were getting the subsidies, not family farmers. He quoted

---

**1st District: West — Berkshires, Pittsfield.** Population: 489,041 (4% increase since 1970). Race: White 472,611 (97%), Black 6,049 (1%), Others 10,381 (2%). Spanish origin: 10,545 (2%).

statistics showing that 7 percent of the farms were getting 63 percent of the money.

Conte tried repeatedly to limit individual subsidy payments to $20,000. Over the opposition of leaders on both sides, he won in the House in 1968 and 1969, only to lose in the Senate and in conference. The 1973 farm bill, however, contained a $20,000 limit for several crops included under federal price supports.

The decline of that issue, however, has not deprived Conte of fiscal windmills to tilt at. He persistently tries to cut back on the police force that patrols the Capitol building and the adjoining grounds and office buildings. Ridiculing the size of the force — two policemen for every member of Congress — Conte has said "we ought to have a workmen's compensation fund, in case they trip over each other and get hurt."

For years he attacked the "beekeeper indemnity program," inserted in appropriation bills by Oklahoma Democrat Tom Steed to protect a local interest. Steed always won, but Conte never ran out of jokes to make about the program. "There is an old Scottish song," he once told the House, "called 'I got a Bee in Ma Bonnet and Ma Honey on Ma Mind.' Too many beekeepers are running around humming, 'I Got Dead Bees in Ma Bonnet and Federal Money on Ma Mind.'"

To hear Conte screaming about fiscal injustice on the House floor, in a voice loud enough to penetrate the furthest reaches of the Capitol, one would think he is an angry man.

But Conte fights more in bluster than in anger. His face often breaks into a smile before his harangue is even finished, and as soon as it ends he is off to joke with his opponent. For Conte, the fight against waste is not only politically helpful — it is lots of fun.

But he is also capable of more serious displays of temper. When Maryland Democrat Clarence D. Long was reluctant to add money to a 1980 foreign aid bill for relief to Italian earthquake victims, Conte seemed genuinely upset. "You asked me to help out with money for Israel," Conte told Long, who represents a district with a large Jewish population, "and I bowed and scraped to the rabbis you sent over to see me. I help you — you help me. That's what this is all about. All I'm asking is a lousy $3 million."

**At Home:** Conte's anger over aid to Italy is an indication of how strongly he still feels about his ethnic roots. Both his parents were immigrants, and Conte grew up in Pittsfield's Italian neighborhood. When he came home from World War II, the Italian community put on a parade for him. Five years later, after Conte earned a law degree on the GI Bill, it was the Italian-Ameri-

cans who helped put him in the state Senate.

Since then, Conte has expanded his base of support so broadly that the 1st District is his political preserve, even though most of it is nominally Democratic. After four terms in the state Senate, where he wrote the nation's first law to extend health and accident insurance to all state and municipal employees, Conte ran in 1958 for the House seat of retiring Republican Rep. John W. Heselton. His opponent was Williams College historian James MacGregor Burns.

Burns was a close friend of then-Sen. John F. Kennedy, who was seeking re-election that year, and hoped he could ride Kennedy's coattails to the House. But even though Kennedy won 70 percent in the 1st District, Conte proved a stronger candidate than Burns. Promising to bring federal aid to towns with unemployment, and stressing his legislative record, Conte won 55 percent. Since then, no one has come close.

Part of the reason is his independent, bipartisan image. A visitor to Conte's Capitol Hill office finds as many Democrats as Republicans pictured on the walls. A 1962 campaign brochure included photographs of Conte with President Kennedy, Cabinet officers Dean Rusk and Arthur Goldberg, and Democratic House Speaker John W. McCormack. That year Conte won a higher vote than any Republican congressman in the country with Democratic opposition. It was ten years before another Democrat even filed against him.

**The District:** The 1st District is Massachusetts' largest, covering more than a third of the state. It is generally as Democratic as the state as a whole, but it has never sent a Democrat to the House. Since 1913 it has elected only three people, one of whom — the dour Allen T. Treadway — lasted from 1913 until 1945.

The district has a large concentration of first- and second-generation immigrants. French-Canadians are the largest group, followed by Poles and Italians. Most of them settled in the industrial towns and cities, such as Pittsfield. Primarily Catholic, they continue to prefer Democratic candidates for most offices. On the farms and in the villages are more-Republican Yankee voters.

As the textile and shoe industries have gradually died off, electrical manufacturing concerns have filled the void in some places. Others remain economically distressed. General Electric is the largest single employer.

The district is laced with elite private colleges, such as Amherst, Mount Holyoke, Smith, and Williams, and includes the University of Massachusetts. Because of his strong support in the university community, John Anderson carried the district in the 1980 GOP primary.

# Committees

**Appropriations** (Ranking Republican)
Labor-Health and Human Services-Education; Legislative; Transportation.

**Small Business** (2nd of 17 Republicans)
Energy, Environment and Safety Issues Affecting Small Business.

# Elections

**1980 General**

| | |
|---|---|
| Silvio Conte (R ) | 156,514 (75 %) |
| Helen Doyle (D ) | 52,457 (25 %) |

**1978 General**

| | |
|---|---|
| Silvio O. Conte (R ) | Unopposed |

**Previous Winning Percentages**

| | | | |
|---|---|---|---|
| 1976 (64 %) | 1974 (71 %) | 1972 (100%) | 1970 (100%) |
| 1968 (100%) | 1966 (100%) | 1964 (100%) | 1962 (74 %) |
| 1960 (69 %) | 1958 (55 %) | | |

**District Vote For President**

| | 1980 | | 1976 | | 1972 |
|---|---|---|---|---|---|
| D | 93,495 (43 %) | D | 124,032 (56 %) | D | 105,502 (51 %) |
| R | 85,268 (39 %) | R | 88,051 (40 %) | R | 98,861 (48 %) |
| I | 34,431 (16 %) | I | 5,840 (3 %) | | |

# Campaign Finance

| | Receipts | Receipts from PACs | Expen-ditures |
|---|---|---|---|
| **1980** | | | |
| Conte (R ) | $107,024 | $48,700 (46 %) | $80,126 |
| Doyle (D ) | $14,474 | — (0 %) | $14,464 |
| **1978** | | | |
| Conte (R ) | $21,261 | $2,400 (11 %) | $5,771 |

# Voting Studies

| | Presidential Support | | Party Unity | | Conservative Coalition | |
|---|---|---|---|---|---|---|
| Year | S | O | S | O | S | O |
| 1980 | 67 | 31 | 37 | 63 | 26 | 72 |
| 1979 | 67 | 33 | 32 | 68 | 35 | 65 |
| 1978 | 80 | 20 | 32 | 68 | 29 | 71 |
| 1977 | 72 | 27 | 34 | 61 | 32 | 61 |
| 1976 | 37 | 61 | 22 | 76 | 29 | 67 |
| 1975 | 56 | 40 | 39 | 59 | 32 | 67 |
| 1974 (Ford) | 52 | 41 | | | | |

| | | | | | | |
|---|---|---|---|---|---|---|
| 1974 | 55 | 43 | 29 | 66 | 21 | 75 |
| 1973 | 43 | 49 | 38 | 58 | 35 | 62 |
| 1972 | 54 | 32 | 33 | 53 | 23 | 63 |
| 1971 | 49 | 47 | 42 | 52 | 25 | 70 |
| 1970 | 74 | 22 | 43 | 54 | 27 | 64 |
| 1969 | 66 | 32 | 31 | 62 | 18 | 80 |
| 1968 | 69 | 16 | 41 | 46 | 31 | 61 |
| 1967 | 62 | 27 | 47 | 43 | 26 | 61 |
| 1966 | 66 | 24 | 36 | 49 | 16 | 59 |
| 1965 | 69 | 29 | 45 | 50 | 37 | 59 |
| 1964 | 69 | 31 | 56 | 40 | 33 | 67 |
| 1963 | 59 | 32 | 48 | 43 | 7 | 87 |
| 1962 | 68 | 32 | 56 | 39 | 31 | 69 |
| 1961 | 57 | 40 | 62 | 34 | 39 | 57 |

S = Support      O = Opposition

# Key Votes

**96th Congress**

| | |
|---|---|
| Weaken Carter oil profits tax (1979) | N |
| Reject hospital cost control plan (1979) | N |
| Implement Panama Canal Treaties (1979) | Y |
| Establish Department of Education (1979) | Y |
| Approve Anti-busing Amendment (1979) | N |
| Guarantee Chrysler Corp. loans (1979) | Y |
| Approve military draft registration (1980) | N |
| Aid Sandinista regime in Nicaragua (1980) | Y |
| Strengthen fair housing laws (1980) | Y |

**97th Congress**

| | |
|---|---|
| Reagan budget proposal (1981) | Y |

# Interest Group Ratings

| Year | ADA | ACA | AFL-CIO | CCUS |
|---|---|---|---|---|
| 1980 | 83 | 30 | 68 | 62 |
| 1979 | 53 | 23 | 85 | 28 |
| 1978 | 50 | 26 | 55 | 50 |
| 1977 | 65 | 12 | 78 | 29 |
| 1976 | 60 | 7 | 57 | 13 |
| 1975 | 74 | 36 | 70 | 41 |
| 1974 | 87 | 8 | 82 | 22 |
| 1973 | 60 | 22 | 50 | 60 |
| 1972 | 63 | 22 | 60 | 50 |
| 1971 | 78 | 38 | 50 | - |
| 1970 | 72 | 28 | 71 | 40 |
| 1969 | 67 | 35 | 80 | - |
| 1968 | 67 | 35 | 100 | - |
| 1967 | 60 | 33 | 64 | 70 |
| 1966 | 65 | 43 | 31 | - |
| 1965 | 53 | 44 | - | 70 |
| 1964 | 64 | 26 | 55 | - |
| 1963 | - | 41 | - | - |
| 1962 | 50 | 61 | 27 | - |
| 1961 | 50 | - | - | - |

# 2 Edward P. Boland (D)

### Of Springfield — Elected 1952

**Born:** Oct. 1, 1911, Springfield, Mass.
**Education:** Attended Boston College Law School.
**Military Career:** Army, 1942-46.
**Profession:** Government official.
**Family:** Wife, Mary Egan; four children.
**Religion:** Roman Catholic.
**Political Career:** Mass. House, 1935-41; Hampden County register of deeds, 1941-42 and 1946-52.

**In Washington:** At 70, Boland still has the jet black hair and speedy stride he brought to the House with him in 1953. And he still has the broad respect that has made him a popular member even though he is mildly ascetic and crisply aloof from much of the chamber's camaraderie. Boland has always known how to stay in touch with liberals, Southerners and big city pols, all at the same time.

It is also no small advantage to have been Thomas P. O'Neill's workweek roommate in Washington for two decades while both men were rising in influence in the House. Diametrically opposite in temperament, the two men had common backgrounds as Irish Catholics in Massachusetts politics, and common outlooks as traditional organization Democrats. The relationship has been strained occasionally in recent years, but it is still an important factor in Boland's role in the House.

Boland is a dominant presence in the housing field through his chairmanship of the HUD-Independent Agencies Subcommittee of the Appropriations Committee. It is considered a mark of his ability that the HUD appropriations usually pass without great controversy.

In 1977 O'Neill named Boland to head a Select Committee on Intelligence, formed in the aftermath of disclosures that the CIA had participated in assassination plots and had spied on American citizens. The purpose of the committee has been to oversee the CIA and be apprised of any "covert" actions the agency planned.

Boland runs the committee in a less flamboyant manner than his Senate counterparts have, characteristically avoiding attention and forcing colleagues to attend meetings at eight in the morning. Boland has said he is "less interested in . . . dragging out past abuses . . ." than he is in the present operation of the agency. In 1980, when public opinion was again calling for a strong CIA,

Boland was skeptical, insisting that the committee continue to be notified in advance of covert activities.

He fought hard in the full Appropriations Committee in 1980 for the Carter administration's draft registration proposal, although his own subcommittee had rejected it, giving him a rare defeat. Boland argued that the proposal was timely and would not lead automatically to a resumption of the draft. The committee reversed the decision, and Boland won again on the House floor. He was as much responsible as anyone in Congress when registration resumed in mid-1980.

Occasionally Boland can take a fervent dislike to a program few colleagues even notice. For years he has tried to stop funding for Project Galileo, a NASA space exploration project. Though he has yet to succeed, he continues to fight the program in every appropriations debate.

Twice during his nearly 30 years in Congress Boland had the opportunity to go for a formal leadership position in the House, and twice he hesitated, waiting for a cue from his roommate.

The first turning-point was in 1970. Speaker John McCormack, D-Mass, announced his retirement, and Majority Leader Carl Albert of Oklahoma assumed the Speakership, leaving a wide open contest to replace Albert.

Liberals Morris K. Udall of Arizona and James G. O'Hara of Michigan were both candidates, but many liberal Democrats continued

---

**2nd District: West central — Springfield.** Population: 466,126 (1% decrease since 1970). Race: White 425,713 (91%), Black 26,409 (6%), Others 14,004 (3%). Spanish origin: 17,008 (4%).

looking for a stronger challenger to the Southern favorite, Louisiana's Hale Boggs. Both O'Neill and Boland were prominently mentioned.

Boland thought about announcing his candidacy, but he and his roommate seemed unable to decide who should be the candidate and who should be the campaign manager. In the end neither one ran — Boland went to work for Udall and O'Neill for Boggs. Boggs won and appointed O'Neill whip, which turned out to be his road to the Speaker's office just six years later.

In 1978 Boland had a similar experience. That year George Mahon of Texas, longtime chairman of the Appropriations Committee, announced his retirement. Jamie Whitten of Mississippi was next in seniority, but Whitten was held in low esteem by liberals for his attacks on environmental and consumer agencies. Boland, the man with connections to the Speaker, was next after Whitten.

But once again Boland refused to announce his plans, counting instead on O'Neill to seek out the chairmanship for him. O'Neill did not know how badly Boland wanted the job. He indicated that Whitten was perfectly acceptable to him — they had once played poker together. Boland avoided his old friend for more than six months.

**At Home:** During 46 years in public life, Boland has never lost an election. Much of the time, he has not even been challenged. Seven of his 15 House terms have been won without any Republican opposition.

Lawrence J. O'Brien, Democratic organizer and Boland's lifelong friend, attributes the congressman's success to "working hard for his constituents." That work has been made easier by Boland's close association with those in high places. Besides rooming with O'Neill, Boland was often referred to as President Kennedy's "man on the Hill" in the early 1960s. In 1963 he joined Kennedy on a trip to Ireland.

A product of Springfield's poor Irish neighborhood, "Hungry Hill," Boland came from a working-class background. Both parents were immigrants from Ireland. His father, who lived until he was 92, worked on the railroads.

It was as city playground director and organizer of a sandlot baseball team that Boland built his first political organization. At age 23, with help from teen-age athletes speaking for him on street corners, Boland was elected to the state House. In 1940 he became Hampden County Recorder of Deeds, a six-year elective post. During his first term, he left Springfield to serve in the Army, returning to win a second term with both the Democratic and Republican nominations.

The closest election of Boland's career came in 1952, at the end of his second term in the county courthouse. With Democratic Rep. Foster Furcolo leaving Congress to become state treasurer, Boland decided to move up.

Because the 2nd District was located entirely within Hampden County at that time, Boland started out with a strong political base. But the Eisenhower landslide that year nearly returned the district to the Republican column — where it had been before Furcolo's victory in 1948. Eisenhower carried the district easily, as did Henry Cabot Lodge, trying to retain his Senate seat against John F. Kennedy. But Boland won by 6,577 votes.

Since then, Boland has had to mount an aggressive campaign only once, in a 1968 primary against former Springfield Mayor Charles Ryan. With 50 workers at a phone bank and volunteers going door-to-door to get out the vote, Boland easily deflated Ryan's contention that it was "time for a change."

Some Springfield Democrats joke that Boland avoided another primary challenge in 1972, when 34-year-old Mary Egan, the City Council president, was said to be interested in running against him. The 61-year-old Boland proposed marriage to her, and she accepted. They now have four children.

**The District:** This district changed its political complexion dramatically in the 1940s. Before then, like most of Massachusetts outside Boston, it was solidly Republican. But Democrats won a series of close elections just after World War II, took control, and have not yielded in three decades.

Springfield and Chicopee provide most of the Democratic vote. Nearly 80 percent of the district's vote is located in those two aging industrial centers and the surrounding suburban area. To the east are a collection of rural villages and smaller mill towns, many of which gave Ronald Reagan solid pluralities in 1980.

## Committees

**Appropriations** (2nd of 23 Democrats)
  HUD-Independent Agencies, chairman; Energy and Water Development.
**Select Intelligence** (Chairman)

## Elections

**1980 General**

| | |
|---|---|
| Edward Boland (D ) | 120,711 (67 %) |
| Thomas Swank (R ) | 38,672 (22 %) |
| John Aubuchon (I ) | 20,247 (11 %) |

**1980 Primary**

| | |
|---|---|
| Edward Boland (D ) | 38,811 (71 %) |
| Paul Kozikowski (D ) | 11,999 (22 %) |

**1978 General**

| | |
|---|---|
| Edward Boland (D ) | 101,570 (73 %) |
| Thomas Swank (R ) | 37,881 (27 %) |

**Previous Winning Percentages**

| | | | |
|---|---|---|---|
| 1976 (72 %) | 1974 (100%) | 1972 (100%) | 1970 (100%) |
| 1968 (74 %) | 1966 (100%) | 1964 (100%) | 1962 (68 %) |
| 1960 (100%) | 1958 (100%) | 1956 (61 %) | 1954 (60 %) |
| 1952 (52 %) | | | |

**District Vote For President**

| | 1980 | | 1976 | | 1972 |
|---|---|---|---|---|---|
| D | 85,152 (43 %) | D | 197,108 (59 %) | D | 97,374 (51 %) |
| R | 83,227 (42 %) | R | 74,953 (38 %) | R | 92,304 (48 %) |
| I | 27,031 (14 %) | | | | |

## Campaign Finance

| | Receipts | Receipts from PACs | Expenditures |
|---|---|---|---|
| **1980** | | | |
| Boland (D ) | $84,490 | $33,900 (40 %) | $28,553 |

## Voting Studies

| | Presidential Support | | Party Unity | | Conservative Coalition | |
|---|---|---|---|---|---|---|
| Year | S | O | S | O | S | O |
| 1980 | 72 | 21 | 84 | 11 | 24 | 68 |
| 1979 | 72 | 22 | 81 | 13 | 27 | 68 |
| 1978 | 70 | 16 | 75 | 15 | 18 | 74 |
| 1977 | 61 | 18 | 79 | 13 | 22 | 67 |
| 1976 | 25 | 75 | 89 | 7 | 20 | 75 |
| 1975 | 42 | 55 | 83 | 12 | 19 | 75 |
| 1974 (Ford) | 39 | 41 | | | | |
| 1974 | 55 | 42 | 72 | 12 | 21 | 64 |
| 1973 | 36 | 62 | 79 | 16 | 21 | 76 |
| 1972 | 54 | 41 | 83 | 11 | 13 | 82 |
| 1971 | 51 | 47 | 76 | 21 | 23 | 73 |
| 1970 | 74 | 22 | 81 | 15 | 23 | 66 |
| 1969 | 53 | 40 | 80 | 11 | 11 | 89 |
| 1968 | 71 | 8 | 72 | 6 | 4 | 75 |
| 1967 | 86 | 7 | 91 | 3 | 4 | 91 |
| 1966 | 82 | 6 | 86 | 1 | 3 | 95 |
| 1965 | 87 | 6 | 87 | 8 | 10 | 86 |
| 1964 | 85 | 8 | 74 | 11 | 17 | 83 |
| 1963 | 93 | 3 | 88 | 0 | 0 | 93 |
| 1962 | 87 | 5 | 89 | 7 | 12 | 81 |
| 1961 | 98 | 2 | 90 | 10 | 13 | 87 |

S = Support          O = Opposition

## Key Votes

**96th Congress**

| | |
|---|---|
| Weaken Carter oil profits tax (1979) | N |
| Reject hospital cost control plan (1979) | N |
| Implement Panama Canal Treaties (1979) | Y |
| Establish Department of Education (1979) | N |
| Approve Anti-busing Amendment (1979) | N |
| Guarantee Chrysler Corp. loans (1979) | Y |
| Approve military draft registration (1980) | Y |
| Aid Sandinista regime in Nicaragua (1980) | Y |
| Strengthen fair housing laws (1980) | Y |

**97th Congress**

| | |
|---|---|
| Reagan budget proposal (1981) | N |

## Interest Group Ratings

| Year | ADA | ACA | AFL-CIO | CCUS |
|---|---|---|---|---|
| 1980 | 78 | 21 | 63 | 64 |
| 1979 | 68 | 9 | 95 | 13 |
| 1978 | 50 | 15 | 75 | 29 |
| 1977 | 65 | 11 | 90 | 18 |
| 1976 | 75 | 4 | 78 | 13 |
| 1975 | 79 | 23 | 91 | 18 |
| 1974 | 65 | 0 | 100 | 0 |
| 1973 | 80 | 8 | 100 | 27 |
| 1972 | 69 | 17 | 91 | 10 |
| 1971 | 86 | 14 | 92 | - |
| 1970 | 76 | 12 | 71 | 11 |
| 1969 | 80 | 13 | 100 | - |
| 1968 | 83 | 5 | 100 | - |
| 1967 | 87 | 4 | 92 | 20 |
| 1966 | 94 | 0 | 92 | - |
| 1965 | 79 | 0 | - | 20 |
| 1964 | 92 | 0 | 100 | - |
| 1963 | - | 0 | - | - |
| 1962 | 100 | 0 | 100 | - |
| 1961 | 100 | - | - | - |

# 3 Joseph D. Early (D)

### Of Worcester — Elected 1974

**Born:** Jan. 31, 1933, Worcester, Mass.
**Education:** Holy Cross College, B.S. 1955.
**Military Career:** Navy, 1955-57.
**Profession:** Teacher and coach.
**Family:** Wife, Marilyn Powers, eight children.
**Religion:** Roman Catholic.
**Political Career:** Mass. House, 1963-75.

**In Washington:** By Massachusetts standards, Joe Early is a conservative. He is against abortion and busing and skeptical about foreign aid, like most of his blue-collar constituents in Millbury, Milford and Millville, towns whose economic declines are embedded in their names. But when it comes to labor and domestic spending, Early is solidly in the New Deal tradition, a passionate defender of federal spending for education, health, and social services.

Early was placed on the Appropriations Committee as a freshman in 1975, thanks largely to help from Massachusetts colleague Thomas P. O'Neill Jr., then the majority leader. Since then he has had plenty of opportunities to show both his liberal and conservative sides.

On the Labor-HEW Subcommittee, (now Labor, Health and Human Services) Early has fought hard against spending cuts in programs ranging from medical school grants to fuel aid for the poor. As tight budgets have put pressure on domestic programs, Early has had to give ground, but he digs in with a bulldog tenacity if it is a program affecting his district.

He has no ideological commitment to the federal government as a source of social change; he simply wants it to funnel cash into low-income areas. When the Carter adminisration sought votes for a new Department of Education, Early refused to go along. "The federal government should just supply money — not politics — for education," he argued. He was outraged when Carter tried to cut spending for grants to college students by $140 million in 1980, and even angrier at the Reagan cutbacks in 1981.

On his other subcommittee, with jurisdiction over the State Department budget, Early is stingier about spending federal money. And on foreign aid issues, outside his subcommittees, he is even more skeptical. He regularly votes to cut U.S. contributions to international organizations and aid to Third World regimes both left and right. He was reluctant to back the leadership

position favoring implementation of the Panama Canal treaties, although he finally went along.

Early does help O'Neill out on occasion, but he remains one of the more stubborn Massachusetts Democrats, one who keeps his distance from many state colleagues.

In 1978, he won an argument against both O'Neill and Sen. Edward M. Kennedy over an ambassadorship to Ireland. Early favored William Shannon, a *New York Times* columnist who grew up in Worcester. Kennedy and O'Neill each had their own candidates. Early worked through his State-Justice Appropriations Subcommittee, and President Carter eventually named Shannon to the post.

**At Home:** Well-matched to his blue-collar constituency, Early has never had much trouble staying in office. Getting to Washington, however, was slightly more troublesome.

When Democrat Harold Donohue retired in 1974 after 28 less-than-illustrious years in the House, six Democrats scrambled to take his place. Early was one of three who had held major office. During six terms in the state Legislature, he had built a solid reputation as one of the Democratic regulars, and his endorsement by the AFL-CIO was a major boost in the primary. Early won the Democratic nomination with 31.7 percent of the vote.

In the general election, against Republican state Rep. David J. Lionett, Early took the role of

---

**3rd District: Central — Worcester.**
Population: 472,767 (1% increase since 1970).
Race: White 458,045 (97%), Black 6,559 (1%),
Others 8,163 (1%). Spanish origin: 10,065
(2%).

the conservative. He opposed the state's new public campaign finance law and supported the death penalty. Lionett had developed a reputation as a liberal and reformer in the Legislature. With an independent candidate siphoning off 12 percent, Early won with the smallest plurality in the state that year. By 1976, he had entrenched himself and faced no opposition.

**The District:** This Democratic stronghold is centered on the industrial city of Worcester, which casts about a third of the vote but dominates district politics. Worcester newspapers and media outlets vie with those in nearby Boston for

the attention of the voters.

Like the neighboring 2nd District, the 3rd turned Democratic in the mid-1940s. The election of Donohue in 1946 ended 34 years of continuous Republican representation from the Worcester area. Since then, it has been favorable ground for a variety of candidates ranging from liberals like Kennedy and junior Sen. Paul Tsongas to conservatives like Gov. Edward J. King.

Worcester itself can often be counted on for a substantial liberal vote, thanks largely to the academic communities around Holy Cross, Clark University and Worcester State College.

## Committees

**Appropriations** (16th of 33 Democrats)
Commerce, Justice, State, and Judiciary; Labor-Health and Human Services—Education.

## Elections

**1980 General**

| | |
|---|---|
| Joseph Early (D ) | 141,560 (72 %) |
| David Skehan (R ) | 54,213 (28 %) |

**1978 General**

| | |
|---|---|
| Joseph Early (D ) | 119,337 (75 %) |
| Charles MacLeod (R ) | 39,259 (25 %) |

**Previous Winning Percentages**

1976 (100%)    1974 (50 %)

**District Vote For President**

| | 1980 | | 1976 | | 1972 |
|---|---|---|---|---|---|
| D | 88,322 (43 %) | D | 125,445 (59 %) | D | 108,636 (54 %) |
| R | 84,970 (42 %) | R | 80,584 (38 %) | R | 91,540 (46 %) |
| I | 29,038 (14 %) | | | | |

## Campaign Finance

| | Receipts | Receipts from PACs | Expenditures |
|---|---|---|---|
| **1980** | | | |
| Early (D ) | $76,972 | $13,805 (18 %) | $71,210 |
| **1978** | | | |
| Early (D ) | $66,451 | $12,150 (18 %) | $50,609 |
| MacLeod (R ) | $8,648 | — (0 %) | $8,645 |

## Voting Studies

| | Presidential Support | | Party Unity | | Conservative Coalition | |
|---|---|---|---|---|---|---|
| Year | S | O | S | O | S | O |
| 1980 | 52 | 35 | 60 | 30 | 33 | 57 |
| 1979 | 58 | 35 | 60 | 34 | 35 | 60 |
| 1978 | 69 | 29 | 68 | 26 | 18 | 78 |
| 1977 | 65 | 23 | 64 | 24 | 19 | 72 |
| 1976 | 25 | 71 | 81 | 11 | 17 | 78 |
| 1975 | 28 | 70 | 82 | 15 | 12 | 86 |

S = Support          O = Opposition

## Key Votes

**96th Congress**

| | |
|---|---|
| Weaken Carter oil profits tax (1979) | N |
| Reject hospital cost control plan (1979) | N |
| Implement Panama Canal Treaties (1979) | ? |
| Establish Department of Education (1979) | N |
| Approve Anti-busing Amendment (1979) | Y |
| Guarantee Chrysler Corp. loans (1979) | N |
| Approve military draft registration (1980) | N |
| Aid Sandinista regime in Nicaragua (1980) | N |
| Strengthen fair housing laws (1980) | Y |

**97th Congress**

| | |
|---|---|
| Reagan budget proposal (1981) | N |

## Interest Group Ratings

| Year | ADA | ACA | AFL-CIO | CCUS |
|---|---|---|---|---|
| 1980 | 67 | 20 | 71 | 53 |
| 1979 | 74 | 24 | 79 | 28 |
| 1978 | 70 | 23 | 68 | 24 |
| 1977 | 80 | 20 | 81 | 25 |
| 1976 | 80 | 11 | 83 | 25 |
| 1975 | 89 | 18 | 96 | 24 |

# 4 Barney Frank (D)

**Of Newton — Elected 1980**

**Born:** March 31, 1940, Bayonne, N.J.
**Education:** Harvard Univ., B.A. 1962; J.D. 1977.
**Profession:** Public official.
**Family:** Single.
**Religion:** Jewish.
**Political Career:** Massachusetts House, 1973-81.

**The Member:** Frank is the philosophical heir to predecessor Robert F. Drinan, the liberal Catholic priest who retired when the Pope decided to bar clergymen from public office.

In Congress, Frank tends the liberal fires, believing that Reagan's dismantling of the federal government will harm enough Americans to give his side a chance again.

"Banning abortions for poor people is a very popular thing," he said in 1981. "But banning all abortions for every woman in America under all circumstances is not so popular."

On the Banking Committee in 1981, Frank sponsored a measure to protect low-income tenants from being evicted if their building is purchased by a new owner. On the Judiciary Committee, he fought for the preservation of the Legal Services Corporation.

During four terms as a state legislator from Boston's Back Bay, Frank's interests ranged from support for homosexual rights to curbing wasteful spending in Boston's transit system. He won the respect of colleagues for his wit and political skill, although he frequently fought with House leaders over substantive issues.

In 1980, Frank carried endorsements from Drinan and *The Boston Globe*. He defeated a conservative primary foe, then edged past a little-known Republican in November.

**The District:** The 4th is Democratic by nature, but not generally as liberal as the people it sends to Washington. Liberals win their elections in the heavy-turnout Boston suburbs of Newton and Brookline, which cast about a third of the district's vote. Fifty-five miles to the west are the working class towns of Fitchburg and Leominster, far removed from Boston's liberal milieu. In between are more suburbs — some affluent, and some blue-collar.

Most Brookline and Newton voters are Jewish or upper-class Protestant. The other towns, largely Catholic, tend to be more conservative, especially on social issues such as abortion.

## Committees

**Banking, Finance and Urban Affairs** (22nd of 25 Democrats)
General Oversight and Renegotiation; Housing and Community Development; International Trade, Investment and Monetary Policy.

**Government Operations** (21st of 23 Democrats)
Environment, Energy and Natural Resources; Intergovernmental Relations and Human Resources.

**Judiciary** (16th of 16 Democrats)
Courts, Civil Liberties and the Administration of Justice; Immigration, Refugees and International Law.

**Select Aging** (26th of 31 Democrats)
Retirement Income and Employment.

## Elections

**1980 General**

| | |
|---|---|
| Barney Frank (D ) | 103,466 (52 %) |
| Richard Jones (R ) | 95,898 (48 %) |

**1980 Primary**

| | |
|---|---|
| Barney Frank (D ) | 42,162 (52 %) |
| Arthur Clark (D ) | 37,694 (47 %) |

**District Vote For President**

| | 1980 | | 1976 | | 1972 |
|---|---|---|---|---|---|
| **D** | 88,488 (43 %) | **D** | 117,919 (55 %) | **D** | 116,100 (55 %) |
| **R** | 83,686 (41 %) | **R** | 88,613 (42 %) | **R** | 92,341 (44 %) |
| **I** | 29,862 (15 %) | | | | |

## Campaign Finance

| | Receipts | Receipts from PACs | Expenditures |
|---|---|---|---|
| **1980** | | | |
| Frank (D ) | $446,651 | $42,362 (9 %) | $446,826 |
| Jones (R ) | $134,580 | $16,112 (12 %) | $52,481 |

## Key Vote

**97th Congress**

| | |
|---|---|
| Reagan budget proposal (1981) | N |

---

**4th District: East central — Newton, Waltham.** Population: 459,878 (4% decrease since 1970). Race: White 438,256 (95%), Black 8,804 (2%), Others 12,818 (3%). Spanish origin: 10,360 (2%).

# 5 James M. Shannon (D)

**Of Lawrence — Elected 1978**

**Born:** April 4, 1952, Lawrence, Mass.
**Education:** Johns Hopkins U., B.A. 1973; George
Washington U. Law School, J.D. 1975.
**Profession:** Lawyer.
**Family:** Wife, Silvia Castro; one child.
**Religion:** Roman Catholic.
**Political Career:** Sought Democratic nomina-
tion for Massachusetts Senate, 1976.

**In Washington:** Quickly branded as
"Speaker's Pet" at the start of the 96th Congress,
this cherubic-looking young lawyer seemed to
have little trouble coping with the attention and
pressure while reaping the political advantages.

Shannon wrote a thesis on Tip O'Neill as a
college senior in 1972, and seven years later joined
him in the Massachusetts congressional delegation. The relationship brought him a place on the
Ways and Means Committee — rare for any
freshman — and a continuing round of questions
from reporters interested in his connections as
well as his thoughts. It also brought some private
grumbling from older Democratic freshmen with
considerably more political experience but no
national press on their doorstep.

He proved to be more than a polite newcomer
on Ways and Means. Speaking for New England's
suspicions of the oil industry, Shannon was one of
the strongest voices on the committee in favor of
stiffening the windfall profits tax in 1979. When
the issue came to the House floor, it was Shannon
who offered the main liberal alternative, but his
tougher tax lost out on a 241-172 vote.

On a more parochial level, Shannon worked
for his state's shoe industry by offering and
promoting an amendment limiting exports of cattle hides. The shoe companies wanted this to
reduce the price of the material they buy, but the
cattle industry did not want it, and Shannon lost.
But he surprised veterans watching him for the
first time with a political and rhetorical skill that
belied his boyish appearance.

In 1980, though, Shannon learned the sensitivity of his role as an O'Neill favorite. The
Speaker had promised to back President Carter's
proposed oil import fee, even though it was highly
unpopular throughout New England. Shannon,
feeling no such constraint, not only worked
against the fee but conspired with Republicans to
block it — without keeping O'Neill informed of
his tactics. And Shannon's side won. It left the
Speaker wondering about the gratitude of his

protégé, and muttering to himself about the sense
of loyalty of the younger Democratic generation.
By the end of the year, however, relations seemed
to be cordial again.

As the youngest member of the 96th Congress, Shannon turned out to be ideologically
closer to O'Neill and the older New Deal liberals
than to the "sunset" Democrats of his own generation who have come to question liberal social
programs. Like David R. Obey of Wisconsin, the
unofficial leader of younger traditionalists, Shannon tends to argue that the Democratic Party has
lost ground because it has strayed from its bread-
and-butter liberal goals, not because the goals
themselves were faulty.

**At Home:** Shannon's liberalism and his district's geography have made survival in the 5th
District a challenging goal, but one he has relished. A student of politics since his elementary
school days, Shannon thrives on difficult campaigns, and he has had several of them.

After working for Democratic Rep. Michael
Harrington while in law school, Shannon lost his
first campaign in 1976. But he came within nine
votes of toppling a veteran state senator. Two
years later, rather than giving the Legislature
another try, he decided to enter the crowded field
of candidates hoping to succeed Democratic U.S.
Rep. Paul Tsongas, who was running for the
Senate.

---

**5th District: North — Lowell, Law-
rence.** Population: 495,675 (4.8% increase
since 1970). Race: White 477,005 (96%); Black
4,611 (1%); Other 14,059 (3%). Spanish origin
17,518 (4%).

---

## James M. Shannon, D-Mass.

Clearly identifying himself as a liberal, Shannon used a large cadre of college friends and other volunteers to capture a huge favorite son vote from Lawrence. That hometown majority, and a reasonble percentage of the Boston suburban vote, allowed him to overcome his meager support in Lowell, the district's largest city and rival to Lawrence. He won the nomination with 22.4 percent, or 786 votes more than the runner-up.

In November, Shannon ran against a liberal Republican sheriff and a conservative independent. Outspending both and campaigning as though he had been through dozens of elections, Shannon drew nearly twice as many votes as his nearest opponent, Republican John J. Buckley.

In 1980, Shannon had a rematch with Robert F. Hatem, a conservative Democrat who had finished a strong third in the 1978 primary. The incumbent had to overcome Hatem's strength in Lowell and an attack by a Catholic prelate against candidates who favored federal funding for abortion.

But Shannon had unified support in the liberal suburban communities, increasingly influential in the district, and had been concentrating his constituent services on Lowell. He won the primary wth 55 percent, and went on to an easy victory in November.

**The District:** Before the 5th went Democratic for Tsongas in 1974, it had elected a Republican in every election in the 20th century. The Yankee Republican vote was traditionally strong enough to override the ethnic vote in the two major mill towns, Lowell and Lawrence.

Until very recently, towns like Lexington and Concord formed the base of Republican support. That has changed in the last decade. Now these wealthy communities are dependably liberal, and the district's political battles are fought mostly in the Democratic primary.

The more rural areas at the western end of the district are still Republican, but they are too small to challenge the industrial and suburban Democratic majorities.

### Committees

**Ways and Means** (18th of 23)
  Social Security; Trade.

### Elections

**1980 General**

| | |
|---|---|
| James Shannon (D) | 136,758 (66%) |
| William Sawyer (R) | 70,547 (34%) |

**1980 Primary**

| | |
|---|---|
| James Shannon (D) | 41,207 (54%) |
| Robert Hatem (D) | 34,573 (47%) |

**1978 General**

| | |
|---|---|
| James Shannon (D) | 90,156 (52%) |
| John Buckley (R) | 48,685 (28%) |
| James Gaffney (I) | 33,835 (20%) |

**1978 Primary**

| | |
|---|---|
| James Shannon (D) | 18,529 (22%) |
| Raymond Rourke (D) | 17,743 (21%) |
| Robert Hatem (D) | 16,359 (20%) |
| John Markey (D) | 14,046 (17%) |
| Michael McLaughlin (D) | 12,644 (15%) |

**District Vote For President**

| 1980 | | 1976 | | 1972 | |
|---|---|---|---|---|---|
| D | 86,302 (39 %) | D | 125,982 (57 %) | D | 110,283 (53 %) |
| R | 97,018 (43 %) | R | 87,340 (40 %) | R | 98,541 (47 %) |
| I | 38,142 (17 %) | I | 5,199 (2 %) | | |

### Campaign Finance

| | | Receipts from PACs | Expen- ditures |
|---|---|---|---|
| | Receipts | | |
| **1980** | | | |
| Shannon (D) | $323,144 | $92,595 (29%) | $319,354 |
| Sawyer (R) | $79,402 | $1,000 (1%) | $53,045 |

| | | | |
|---|---|---|---|
| **1978** | | | |
| Shannon (D) | $180,732 | $26,350 (15%) | $180,667 |
| Buckley (R) | $109,036 | $20,773 (19%) | $97,637 |

### Voting Studies

| | Presidential Support | | Party Unity | | Conservative Coalition | |
|---|---|---|---|---|---|---|
| Year | S | O | S | O | S | O |
| 1980 | 66 | 21 | 77 | 7 | 4 | 82 |
| 1979 | 83 | 14 | 92 | 6 | 6 | 92 |

S = Support        O = Opposition

### Key Votes

**96th Congress**

| | |
|---|---|
| Weaken Carter oil profits tax (1979) | N |
| Reject hospital cost control plan (1979) | N |
| Implement Panama Canal Treaties (1979) | Y |
| Establish Department of Education (1979) | Y |
| Approve Anti-busing Amendment (1979) | N |
| Guarantee Chrysler Corp. loans (1979) | Y |
| Approve military draft registration (1980) | N |
| Aid Sandinista regime in Nicaragua (1980) | Y |
| Strengthen fair housing laws (1980) | Y |

**97th Congress**

| | |
|---|---|
| Reagan budget proposal (1981) | N |

### Interest Group Ratings

| Year | ADA | ACA | AFL-CIO | CCUS |
|---|---|---|---|---|
| 1980 | 94 | 14 | 89 | 59 |
| 1979 | 95 | 4 | 90 | 11 |

# 6 Nicholas Mavroules (D)

**Of Peabody — Elected 1978**

**Born:** Nov. 1, 1929, Peabody, Mass.
**Education:** Attended Mass. Institute of Technology, 1949-50.
**Profession:** Personnel supervisor.
**Family:** Wife, Mary Silva; three children.
**Religion:** Greek Orthodox.
**Political Career:** Peabody City Council, 1958-61 and 1964-65; Mayor of Peabody, 1967-78; unsuccessful candidate for Peabody City Council, 1955; unsuccessful candidate for Mayor of Peabody, 1961.

**In Washington:** The "team player" instincts that Mavroules learned as a minor league shortstop and small-town Massachusetts mayor helped him adjust to life in Congress in 1979, when Speaker O'Neill asked him to take a place on the Armed Services Committee.

Massachusetts wanted representation on the committee to protect its defense contracting interests, and Mavroules drew the assignment. It was not his first choice, but he accepted it with the cooperative spirit of a man who plays by the rules.

Mavroules may be a junior House Democrat, but he is an old-style Massachusetts politician. He looks after constituents personally and spends much of his week back home, where he holds office hours on Mondays and Fridays.

In addition to speaking for Massachusetts on Armed Services, Mavroules takes a more cost-conscious attitude than most committee members toward Pentagon weapons requests. He was one of only three members of the committee to oppose construction of the land-based MX missile.

Mavroules has been able to use his Armed Services seat to benefit his district's largest defense contractor, General Electric, whose plant in Lynn makes engines for the Navy's F18 attack fighters. Mavroules argued successfully in 1980 that the Navy would save money by ordering a larger number of these planes in the next fiscal year. He also kept track of Pentagon plans for the Patriot ground-to-air missile, produced by Raytheon in the neighboring 5th District.

Mavroules survived a brush with scandal in 1979 that dated back to his days as mayor of Peabody. An FBI informer claimed he had given Mavroules a $25,000 bribe to clear away legal obstacles to a restaurant liquor license. Federal prosecutors investigated the allegations, however,

and found nothing to them.

**At Home:** Mavroules has had more trouble keeping his job than most Massachusetts Democrats. Running for a second term in 1980, he showed little sign that he had expanded his base beyond the old factory towns, Peabody, Salem and Lynn, which were responsible for his initial victory. Only a 20,000-vote plurality in those three cities allowed him to overcome a strong Republican vote against him in 1980 along the more conservative North Shore.

Mavroules is an old-fashioned urban-oriented Democrat who has little in common with the Yankee elite who populate so much of his district. He learned his politics in Peabody's City Hall, where he served a total of 16 years, first on the City Council and later as mayor.

In 1978, Mavroules sensed that Democratic Rep. Michael J. Harrington had lost his rapport with working-class Democrats. There was a feeling Harrington had spent too much of his career on human rights in Chile rather than unemployment in Lynn. So Mavroules entered the primary.

Harrington, however, decided to retire rather than fight for a fifth full term. Mavroules went on to win the Democratic nomination against a state representative from Lynn and an Essex County commissioner who had Harrington's endorsement, but little else. Mavroules' victory margin was nearly equal to the plurality he won in his hometown of Peabody.

> **6th District: Northeast — Lynn, Peabody.** Population: 471,373 (1% decrease since 1970). Race: White 461,076 (98%), Black, 4,976 (1%), Other 5,321 (1%). Spanish origin: 5,680 (1%).

## Nicholas Mavroules, D-Mass.

In the 1978 general election, Mavroules faced William E. Bronson, a conservative airline pilot who was eager for a second try after holding Harrington under 55 percent in 1976. With stronger party backing, Bronson reduced his 1976 deficit of 30,000 votes to fewer than 14,000 votes. But the seat went to Mavroules.

Although Bronson wanted still another chance in 1980, he lost the Republican primary narrowly to Tom Trimarco, a moderate lawyer with Italian ethnic support. Viewed as the strongest candidate Republicans had put up in a decade, Trimarco worked hard to tie Mavroules to the Carter administration. The incumbent survived, but by only 8,200 votes, a sign that he will need at least one more election to secure the district for himself.

**The District:** For 32 years, this North Shore district was in the hands of the Republican Bates family. George J. Bates represented it from 1937 until his death in an airplane crash in 1949; his son, William H. Bates, took over and served until he died 20 years later.

The 6th has changed considerably since the Bates era, but it is still several shades more conservative than most Massachusetts districts. About half the vote is cast in wealthy coastal towns whose Republican residents represent the upper crust of Boston society.

The strongest Democratic vote is concentrated in the old leather-working towns along the southern edge of the district — Peabody, Salem and Lynn — and in Haverhill, a self-proclaimed "shoetown" along the Merrimack River. In the past decade, these communities have been strong enough to outvote the GOP-leaning North Shore in elections to the House. But not always by much.

## Committees

**Armed Services** (17th of 25 Democrats)
Investigations; Procurement and Military Nuclear Systems.

**Small Business** (15th of 23 Democrats)
Energy, Environment and Safety Issues Affecting Small Business.

## Elections

**1980 General**

| | |
|---|---|
| Nicholas Mavroules (D ) | 111,393 (51 %) |
| Thomas Trimarco (R ) | 103,192 (47 %) |

**1980 Primary**

| | |
|---|---|
| Nicholas Mavroules (D ) | 32,177 (69 %) |
| Kenneth Bellevue (D ) | 14,405 (31 %) |

**1978 General**

| | |
|---|---|
| Nicholas Mavroules (D ) | 97,099 (54 %) |
| William Bronson (R ) | 83,511 (46 %) |

**1978 Primary**

| | |
|---|---|
| Nicholas Mavroules (D ) | 34,511 (44 %) |
| James Smith (D ) | 27,600 (35 %) |
| John McKean (D ) | 16,322 (21 %) |

**District Vote For President**

| | 1980 | | 1976 | | 1972 |
|---|---|---|---|---|---|
| D | 86,256 (38 %) | D | 119,963 (53 %) | D | 116,157 (53 %) |
| R | 97,969 (44 %) | R | 97,834 (43 %) | R | 104,027 (47 %) |
| I | 38,271 (17 %) | | | | |

## Campaign Finance

| | | Receipts | Expen- |
|---|---|---|---|
| | Receipts | from PACs | ditures |
| **1980** | | | |
| Marvoules (D ) | $344,643 | $102,260 (30 %) | $347,960 |

| | | | |
|---|---|---|---|
| Trimarco (R ) | $250,908 | $28,014 (11 %) | $250,061 |
| **1978** | | | |
| Marvoules (D ) | $296,672 | $33,315 (11 %) | $290,331 |
| Bronson (R ) | $192,022 | $40,540 (21 %) | $185,029 |

## Voting Studies

| | Presidential Support | | Party Unity | | Conservative Coalition | |
|---|---|---|---|---|---|---|
| Year | S | O | S | O | S | O |
| 1980 | 64 | 26 | 74 | 10 | 15 | 65 |
| 1979 | 74 | 21 | 78 | 16 | 31 | 66 |

S = Support          O = Opposition

## Key Votes

**96th Congress**

| | |
|---|---|
| Weaken Carter oil profits tax (1979) | N |
| Reject hospital cost control plan (1979) | X |
| Implement Panama Canal Treaties (1979) | Y |
| Establish Department of Education (1979) | Y |
| Approve Anti-busing Amendment (1979) | N |
| Guarantee Chrysler Corp. loans (1979) | Y |
| Approve military draft registration (1980) | N |
| Aid Sandinista regime in Nicaragua (1980) | Y |
| Strengthen fair housing laws (1980) | ? |

**97th Congress**

| | |
|---|---|
| Reagan budget proposal (1981) | N |

## Interest Group Ratings

| Year | ADA | ACA | AFL-CIO | CCUS |
|---|---|---|---|---|
| 1980 | 72 | 15 | 78 | 61 |
| 1979 | 63 | 8 | 95 | 18 |

# 7 Edward J. Markey (D)

**Of Malden — Elected 1976**

**Born:** July 11, 1946, Malden, Mass.
**Education:** Boston College, B.A. 1968, J.D. 1972.
**Military Career:** Army Reserve, 1968-73.
**Profession:** Lawyer.
**Family:** Single.
**Religion:** Roman Catholic.
**Political Career:** Mass. House, 1973-77.

**In Washington:** A witty man with a facile mind, Markey has frequently been up against the impression that he is a shade too clever for his own good, drawn to the first available one-liner rather than to the pursuit of long-term legislative goals.

But that idea faded a bit during the 96th Congress, as Markey found in nuclear energy an issue of both constituent interest and national concern. Exceptionally well-placed in the committee system — he is on the key energy subcommittees both at Commerce and Interior — Markey showed some political skill and also some staying power.

Markey's position on nuclear energy is unequivocal; he is against it. In 1979, after the Three Mile Island nuclear accident, he began pressing for a moratorium on nuclear plant construction permits. It is as if "there is something wrong with the automobile," he said, "but rather than recall it, we are going to repair it while it is still moving."

He came within two votes of moving his moratorium through the environmentally-minded Energy Subcommittee at Interior, then brought it to the House floor for a showdown. "A single accident can kill thousands," he said there. Markey's resolution, coming several months after the Three Mile Island controversy had begun to subside, was defeated on a 254-135 vote. But it gave him an issue to proceed with.

The following year, Markey seized on the sale of American nuclear fuel to India, a country which had never signed the Nuclear Non-Proliferation Treaty. "Nuclear cooperation should be halted immediately," Markey argued, "with any country that has not agreed to give up all experiments with nuclear explosions." Markey won that fight on the House floor, although the Senate later reversed it and the shipments continued.

In his other work on the energy issue, Markey is a die-hard consumerist and critic of major oil companies. He was one of the sponsors of a successful resolution in the Democratic Caucus in 1979 to disapprove President Carter's decontrol of crude oil prices. "This is a message to the President," Markey exulted afterwards. "His policies are in conflict with the policies of his party." But the resolution went no further.

On some occasions, Markey's consumer arguments and his district's interests have matched, as they did in 1978, on a bill to regulate the shipment of liquefied natural gas. Markey wanted tighter rules for transportation of this combustible fluid, motivated in part by the location of an LNG storage facility in his district, at Everett. He spent much of the year fighting for the language he wanted, and it eventually became law in 1979.

Markey has carried his consumerist approach into most Commerce Committee business, including communications law revision, on which he worked in the 96th Congress. Allied with Ralph Nader and other consumer advocates, he fought plans to create a new AT&T subsidiary for telecommunications research, arguing that it would be a "clone" of AT&T and beyond public control. He lost in subcommittee, but the legislation itself died at the end of the Congress.

**At Home:** Any open seat in the towns north of Boston offers the promise of easy victories and prolonged tenure to the Democrat who can win it. So when the critically-ill Torbert H. MacDonald

---

**7th District: Northeast — Boston suburbs.** Population: 451,683 (5% decrease since 1970). Race: White 440,900 (98%), Black 5,045 (1%), Others 5,738 (1%). Spanish origin: 6,933 (1%).

## Edward J. Markey, D-Mass.

announced his retirement in 1976, after serving 21 years in the House, virtually everyone with any political base thought about running. By the time MacDonald died, six weeks later, there were a dozen candidates scrambling to succeed him.

It was clear that a primary with that many aspirants would be decided mostly by simple name identification. Markey already had quite a bit. Elected to the state Legislature while still in law school, he had received a fair amount of attention for his arguments with the Democratic leadership. That helped him in the primary, as did his endorsement from Michael J. Harrington, who represented the adjoining area in the House.

Markey lost three of the four largest towns in the district to favorite sons, but won his own hometown, Malden, and six of the remaining 11. That gave him 21.4 percent, considerably more than he needed to defeat runner-up Joseph Croken, a longtime administrative aide to MacDonald.

The 22,137 votes Markey received in the primary all but guaranteed his future. Since then, he has faced only two opponents — a Republican who ran as a write-in in 1976, and an obscure primary challenger who won 15 percent in 1980.

**The District:** This is the most Democratic of the districts outside Boston. It is made up of 15 towns and cities, all within Route 128, once considered the outer limit of Boston's sphere of influence. The largest communities are those along the Mystic River, close to the city limits. Malden, Medford, Revere and Everett cast more than half the vote. Although suburban, these are older, blue-collar towns, many with a strong Italian influence. They are difficult to distinguish from some of the ethnic neighborhoods within Boston. George Wallace ran second to Henry Jackson here in the 1976 presidential primary.

## Committees

**Energy and Commerce** (10th of 24 Democrats)
Energy Conservation and Power: Fossil and Synthetic Fuels; Telecommunications, Consumer Protection, and Finance.

**Interior and Insular Affairs** (12th of 23 Democrats)
Oversight and Investigations, Chairman; Energy and the Environment.

## Elections

**1980 General**

| | |
|---|---|
| Edward Markey (D ) | Unopposed |

**1980 Primary**

| | |
|---|---|
| Edward Markey (D) | 29,190 (85 %) |
| James Murphy (D ) | 5,247 (15 %) |

**1978 General**

| | |
|---|---|
| Edward Markey (D ) | 145,615 (85 %) |
| James Murphy (I ) | 26,017 (15 %) |

**Previous Winning Percentages**

1976 (77 %)

**District Vote For President**

| | 1980 | | 1976 | | 1972 |
|---|---|---|---|---|---|
| D | 91,189 (42 %) | D | 126,935 (57 %) | D | 122,026 (57 %) |
| R | 90,726 (42 %) | R | 86,572 (39 %) | R | 91,617 (43 %) |
| I | 30,656 (14 %) | | | | |

## Campaign Finance

| | Receipts | Receipts from PACs | Expenditures |
|---|---|---|---|
| **1980** | | | |
| Markey (D ) | $114,941 | $26,775 (23 %) | $67,173 |

| | | | |
|---|---|---|---|
| 1978 | | | |
| Markey (D ) | 61,508 | 12,060 (20 %) | 60,542 |

## Voting Studies

| | Presidential Support | | Party Unity | | Conservative Coalition | |
|---|---|---|---|---|---|---|
| Year | S | O | S | O | S | O |
| 1980 | 71 | 24 | 88 | 9 | 8 | 84 |
| 1979 | 83 | 14 | 88 | 10 | 8 | 90 |
| 1978 | 79 | 18 | 83 | 13 | 3 | 93 |
| 1977 | 75 | 24 | 87 | 12 | 11 | 88 |

S = Support          O = Opposition

## Key Votes

**96th Congress**

| | |
|---|---|
| Weaken Carter oil profits tax (1979) | N |
| Reject hospital cost control plan (1979) | N |
| Implement Panama Canal Treaties (1979) | Y |
| Establish Department of Education (1979) | Y |
| Approve Anti-busing Amendment (1979) | N |
| Guarantee Chrysler Corp. loans (1979) | Y |
| Approve military draft registration (1980) | N |
| Aid Sandinista regime in Nicaragua (1980) | Y |
| Strengthen fair housing laws (1980) | Y |

**97th Congress**

| | |
|---|---|
| Reagan budget proposal (1981) | N |

## Interest Group Ratings

| Year | ADA | ACA | AFL-CIO | CCUS |
|---|---|---|---|---|
| 1980 | 83 | 22 | 84 | 63 |
| 1979 | 95 | 8 | 95 | 0 |
| 1978 | 90 | 7 | 85 | 22 |
| 1977 | 90 | 8 | 78 | 18 |

# 8 Thomas P. O'Neill Jr. (D)

**Of Cambridge — Elected 1952**

**Born:** Dec. 9, 1912, Cambridge, Mass.
**Education:** Boston College, A.B. 1936.
**Profession:** Insurance broker.
**Family:** Wife, Mildred Anne Miller; five children.
**Religion:** Roman Catholic.
**Political Career:** Mass. House, 1937-53, Speaker, 1949-53; unsuccesssful candidate for Cambridge City Council, 1936.

**In Washington:** "Tip" O'Neill has emerged as a living symbol of the politics the Reagan administration wants to change.

Republicans invoke his name and even his beefy Irish face in campaigning on an anti-government theme. O'Neill himself has seemed willing to accept the role, admitting he is a big spender and talking emotionally of the "people programs" being threatened.

But it requires at least a minor rewriting of history to blame O'Neill — or credit him — for most of the government programs now under siege.

For 24 years before he was elected Speaker, O'Neill was a man interested almost exclusively in the pure politics of the House. As a member of the Rules Committee, he helped broker procedural deals that brought major bills to the floor. And he voted for them loyally. But he was no architect. He spent half of every week in Cambridge, doing personal favors for constituents the way Boston politicians always have.

O'Neill came to the House in 1953, a cigar-smoking, poker-playing Red Sox fan of 41, proud of his great success in politics. He had engineered Democratic triumphs at home and was his party's first Speaker of the Massachusetts House in the 20th century.

In Congress, O'Neill went on the Public Works Committee, to make sure Massachusetts got its share of federal jobs and projects. But he served only one term there. When Democrats reclaimed Congress after the 1954 elections, he was named to Rules. He still tells a story of meeting with Speaker Rayburn: "He says . . . you know what loyalty is. I says that's right. He says . . . I would expect you to get votes for me. I says that's party loyalty. He says you're going on the Rules Committee."

In 18 years on Rules, O'Neill nearly always supported the Speaker, whoever he happened to be, but he was seen more as a loyal soldier than as a potential House leader himself.

Along the way, however, O'Neill was performing the kind of service that wins friends and supporters for the future. He kept track of things. From his Rules seat, he knew when bills were coming up, what amendments were proposed and by whom. He could warn members of key votes and tell them when nothing of importance was scheduled. He looked out for the other Tuesday-Thursday congressmen of the urban Northeast.

Those favors alone would not have made him Speaker. Success required an unusual combination of circumstances, and two shrewd moves.

One was in foreign policy. In late 1967, O'Neill suddenly broke with President Johnson and came out publicly against the Vietnam War, which he said was "too high a price to pay for an obscure and limited objective." It angered Johnson, but it pleased students at the 22 colleges and universities in O'Neill's district. It also began to set O'Neill apart from other big-city ethnic Democrats in the minds of younger House liberals.

Three years later, O'Neill worked with that same generation of House liberals on a major reform in House procedure. As a member of the Rules Committee he sponsored the Legislative Reorganization Act of 1970, allowing recorded votes on major floor amendments for the first time. O'Neill did not initiate the changes, but he

---

**8th District: Boston and suburbs, Cambridge.** Population: 435,160 (8% decrease since 1970). Race: White 397,592 (91%), Black 17,387 (4%), Asian and Pacific Islander 12,800 (3%), Others 7,381 (2%). Spanish origin: 12,921 (3%).

fought for them and gave them credibility among more traditionalist members of the party. It contributed to O'Neill's new image as a machine Democrat with a reformist streak.

That image placed him on the leadership ladder as Democratic Whip in 1971. O'Neill had been one of the first to sign up Massachusetts Democrats in support of the man certain to be elected Speaker that year, Carl Albert. When Albert and Majority Leader Hale Boggs disagreed over whom to pick for whip, they both thought of O'Neill — loyal, popular, and by that time, a perfect choice to soothe the competing factions of young reformers and old regulars.

In October, 1972, a small plane carrying Boggs and three others disappeared into the icy wilderness of Alaska. O'Neill wanted to be certain no one moved ahead of him up the ladder to majority leader. At the same time, he did not want to appear insensitive. Boggs was listed only as missing, not dead. Finally, Mrs. Boggs (who later took her husband's seat in Congress) assured O'Neill it was all right to start lining up votes, and O'Neill went to work. By the time other Democrats thought about running, O'Neill had more than enough commitments to win.

Majority leaders nearly always become Speaker unless they do something wrong. O'Neill did nothing wrong. When Albert retired in 1976, Democrats picked him for Speaker by acclamation. O'Neill got off to a fast start in 1977 by pushing through the House a tough ethics code and by skillfully maneuvering to win passage of President Carter's package of energy conservation and oil pricing bills. He was commended as a man of sound political instincts who could handle the often delicate egos of House members. He was the strongest Speaker, it was said, since Rayburn.

In personal terms, that has remained true. O'Neill has a physical presence and a forcefulness that contrasts sharply with his two predecessors, Albert and the late John W. McCormack of Massachusetts.

But he has found himself without a real majority to command. Even in the 95th and 96th Congresses, with a nearly 2-1 partisan Democratic advantage, he was unable to prevent Republicans from drawing 50 or more Democratic votes and winning on crucial decisions. "I've got a lot of good friends out there," O'Neill said bitterly one frustrating night in 1980, "who won't even give me a vote to adjourn."

And in 1981, with the Democrats holding only a 53-seat advantage, O'Neill became a virtual captive in the Speaker's chair. No amount of personal pleading or arm-twisting was sufficient to prevent Southern Democrats from voting the Reagan position, as constituents urged them to do. The Speaker lost vote after vote on budget issues. "I have never seen anything like this in my life," he said at one point.

O'Neill has not handled the budget issue well. Never convinced that a balanced budget was very important, he declined to participate in early 1980 when other House leaders sat down with Carter administration officials to try to write one. Later he endorsed their work, but ultimately opposed a House-Senate budget compromise because it was too stingy to social programs.

In 1981 he took his usual springtime foreign tour, this one to Australia, while other Democrats were lobbying to stave off a Reagan budget victory. When he returned he announced that Reagan could not be beaten, an observation that turned out to be true but struck some colleagues as an abdication of leadership. Talk began to circulate about a retirement in 1982, although the Speaker denied it.

Beneath the frustration, though, O'Neill has seemed confident that something will snap somewhere and his old fashioned flag-waving Democratic political world will be back in style. He refuses to concede that Reagan conservatism will persist. The pendulum has swung to the right, he agrees, but it will swing back again: it has happened before.

**At Home:** Although O'Neill thrives on the politics of the House, it is politics in the Irish and Italian wards of Cambridge and Boston that brings his exuberance into full bloom. Taking his "ethnic walk" through the shops of his district or attending the wake of a constituent, O'Neill still displays the political talent that has been winning him elections in his hometown since 1936.

In the years since he replaced John F. Kennedy in the House, he has campaigned with more gusto than the political situation seemed to require. He had only token GOP opponents in his first four elections. Since then, only two Republicans have even bothered to run. One, William A. Barnstead, has become a professional O'Neill antagonist, challenging him three times in a row. But no opponent has ever received 30 percent.

O'Neill's only political defeat came in 1936, when he was a senior at Boston College. He lost a Cambridge City Council seat by 150 votes. Undeterred, he ran that fall for the state House and won. He remained there 16 years and ran an insurance business on the side. But business was secondary. Politics came first.

In 1947 he became minority leader and the following year, Democrats captured the state House for the first time in 100 years. O'Neill became Speaker. He was a tough leader, even ruthless. Tales are told on Beacon Hill of O'Neill locking the chamber doors to prevent members from "taking a walk" on crucial votes. But his firm control of the chamber resulted in the passage of social programs referred to as "The Little New Deal."

In 1951 Kennedy told O'Neill privately he planned to give up his House seat to run for the Senate. O'Neill began expanding his political base to include all of Kennedy's congressional district. To win, he had to defeat East Boston's state Sen. Michael LoPresti Sr. in the primary. It was a hard-fought campaign, centering mostly on ethnic and geographical rivalries. O'Neill's support in Cambridge gave him a narrow victory.

O'Neill's opposition to the war in Vietnam and support for Eugene McCarthy's 1968 presidential campaign earned him a loyal following on the numerous campuses in the district. But his stand was less popular in the blue-collar areas which account for a much larger portion of the vote. "My strength has always been the workmen in the back streets," O'Neill once said. "I had to sell them and I had a helluva time."

**The District:** The combination of blue-collar ethnics and university-connected liberals makes this the most solidly Democratic district in the state. The working class voters in Watertown, Somerville and the part of Cambridge furthest from Harvard Yard vote as close to a straight party line as one finds among white voters anywhere in the North. George McGovern won 65 percent of the vote here in 1972.

The district also includes a sizable portion of Boston. It has fashionable Back Bay, plus Allston and Brighton, two areas dominated by middle-class row houses and student apartments. Italian East Boston and Irish Charlestown are part of O'Neill's district as well.

## Committees

Speaker of the House

## Elections

**1980 General**

| | |
|---|---|
| Thomas O'Neill Jr. (D ) | 128,689 (78 %) |
| William Barnstead (R ) | 35,477 (22 %) |

**1978 General**

| | |
|---|---|
| Thomas O'Neill Jr. (D ) | 102,160 (75 %) |
| William Barnstead (R ) | 28,566 (21 %) |

**Previous Winning Percentages**

| | | | |
|---|---|---|---|
| 1976 (74 %) | 1974 (88 %) | 1972 (89 %) | 1970 (100%) |
| 1968 (100%) | 1966 (100%) | 1964 (100%) | 1962 (73 %) |
| 1960 (100%) | 1958 (80 %) | 1956 (75 %) | 1954 (78 %) |
| 1952 (69 %) | | | |

**District Vote For President**

| | 1980 | | 1976 | | 1972 |
|---|---|---|---|---|---|
| D | 92,707 (51 %) | D | 117,446 (62 %) | D | 127,868 (66 %) |
| R | 56,312 (31 %) | R | 62,247 (33 %) | R | 65,660 (34 %) |
| I | 28,812 (16 %) | | | | |

## Campaign Finance

| | Receipts | Receipts from PACs | Expenditures |
|---|---|---|---|
| **1980** | | | |
| O'Neill (D ) | $67,825 | $59,500 (88 %) | $62,837 |
| Barnstead (R ) | $5,445 | $200 (4 %) | $4,829 |

## Voting Studies

| | Presidential Support | | Party Unity | | Conservative Coalition | |
|---|---|---|---|---|---|---|
| Year | S | O | S | O | S | O |
| 1976 | 33 | 59 | 82 | 5 | 15 | 69 |
| 1975 | 40 | 56 | 84 | 6 | 15 | 76 |
| 1974 (Ford) | 46 | 44 | | | | |
| 1974 | 51 | 42 | 79 | 8 | 16 | 73 |
| 1973 | 31 | 63 | 86 | 8 | 21 | 74 |
| 1972 | 49 | 38 | 81 | 7 | 9 | 80 |
| 1971 | 46 | 51 | 85 | 7 | 20 | 74 |
| 1970 | 66 | 28 | 79 | 11 | 7 | 73 |
| 1969 | 53 | 36 | 84 | 7 | 13 | 84 |
| 1968 | 79 | 6 | 84 | 1 | 4 | 88 |
| 1967 | 72 | 6 | 82 | 4 | 4 | 83 |
| 1966 | 64 | 3 | 70 | 4 | 3 | 65 |
| 1965 | 80 | 5 | 84 | 5 | 4 | 86 |
| 1964 | 90 | 4 | 89 | 2 | 8 | 92 |
| 1963 | 83 | 4 | 91 | 0 | 7 | 60 |

S = Support    O = Opposition

## Interest Group Ratings

| Year | ADA | ACA | AFL-CIO | CCUS |
|---|---|---|---|---|
| 1976 | 60 | 8 | 87 | 13 |
| 1975 | 74 | 8 | 100 | 12 |
| 1974 | 65 | 8 | 100 | 11 |
| 1973 | 76 | 16 | 91 | 27 |
| 1972 | 69 | 5 | 90 | 0 |
| 1971 | 78 | 11 | 91 | - |
| 1970 | 76 | 6 | 100 | 0 |
| 1969 | 87 | 6 | 100 | - |
| 1968 | 83 | 5 | 100 | - |
| 1967 | 87 | 8 | 92 | 20 |
| 1966 | 88 | 0 | 92 | - |
| 1965 | 79 | 4 | - | 20 |
| 1964 | 88 | 0 | 100 | - |
| 1963 | - | 0 | - | - |

# 9 Joe Moakley (D)

**Of Boston — Elected 1972**

**Born:** April 27, 1927, Boston, Mass.
**Education:** Attended U. of Miami; Suffolk U., J.D. 1956.
**Military Career:** Navy, 1943-46.
**Profession:** Lawyer
**Family:** Wife, Evelyn Duffy.
**Religion:** Roman Catholic.
**Political Career:** Mass. House, 1953-65; Mass. Senate, 1965-69; Boston City Council, 1971-73; unsuccessfully sought Democratic nomination for U.S. House, 1970.

**In Washington:** "I'd like to be a Tip O'Neill-type guy if I could," Moakley said when he came to Congress in 1973. And basically, he has been. Like the Speaker, he is a party man — genial, reliable, and more concerned about politics and personalities than the fine print in the bills. If you want to know what O'Neill was like 15 years ago, some old Boston hands say, take a look at Moakley.

Fourth in seniority on the House Rules Committee, Moakley plays the lieutenant's role there that O'Neill himself played in the 1960s for an earlier Boston Speaker, John McCormack.

He spends much of his time in O'Neill's inner office in the recess of the Capitol's East Front, talking with O'Neill's aide and close friend, Leo Diehl, about politics in Massachusetts. In 1979, when the House had to hold *pro forma* sessions three times a week for a month, and O'Neill wanted to go back home, he left Moakley to wield the ceremonial gavel.

But any parallel can be carried too far. More than once in his career, Moakley has shown streaks of independence hard to reconcile with his image as a pure loyalist. As majority leader, O'Neill was determined to retain his right to appoint a party whip. He fought a move in the House Democratic Caucus to make the whip's position elective. Moakley surprised his old friend by voting for the change. "I think Tip was wrong on that," Moakley said later. "I am for an elected whip." The job remained appointive; the two men remained friends.

Moakley caused a good deal more strain in 1980 when he fought the entire leadership on an important Budget Committee bill. The Budget Committee was trying to enact a $10 billion package of spending cuts, and its chairman, Robert N. Giaimo, D-Conn., asked the Rules Commit-

tee to send his bill to the floor without permitting any amendments. Giaimo felt that allowing a vote on one amendment would make it difficult to deny others, and the entire package of cuts might unravel.

But Rules Committee Republicans, seeking to embarrass the majority, offered a motion to allow a floor vote on restoration of twice-yearly cost-of-living adjustments for federal retirees. The Budget Committee had proposed cutting back to an annual adjustment.

Moakley was one of three Democrats voting for the Republican motion, which passed 8-7, embarrassing not only Giaimo but O'Neill, who was revealed as unable to deliver the vote of one of his closest friends on a crucial issue.

But no amount of persuasion could get Moakley to change his mind. He had made a promise to a federal employee union and felt he had to stick to it. The amendment came to a floor vote and the semiannual increases were restored. Moakley was warned that, friendship aside, another such adventure off the reservation would not be well received.

Rules created permanent subcommittees for the first time in 1979, and Moakley chairs one of them, which is named the Subcommittee on the Rules of the House. So far its major controversy has been over the proposal, by Georgia Democrat

---

**9th District: Boston and suburbs.**
Population: 425,958 (10% decrease since 1970). Race: White 310,535 (73%), Black 86,889 (20%), Others 28,534 (7%). Spanish origin: 25,591 (6%).

Elliott Levitas, to allow either chamber of Congress a veto over rules proposed by regulatory agencies.

The idea is widely criticized in the executive branch as a violation of the separation-of-powers clause in the Constitution. But it has gathered strength in Congress as frustration over federal regulations has increased.

Moakley started out as neutral, but after months of hearings in the 96th Congress, he decided Congress needed some mechanism to monitor regulatory matters. He proposed creation of a Select Committee on Regulatory Affairs to oversee the agencies and look into complaints about regulations. The committee could recommend disapproval of a regulation, but both houses of Congress would have to vote for it.

As a legislator from South Boston, where busing has been the dominant political issue of the past decade, Moakley strays from his normally liberal voting pattern on that subject. In 1979, he supported an unsuccessful effort by Democrat Ronald Mottl of Ohio to win House approval of a constitutional amendment to ban busing. Moakley made an impassioned speech for the proposal on the floor, saying school systems had "squandered a fortune" on busing. "This money has been poured into an experiment that has failed to achieve its goals," he said. "Indeed, by driving white and black middle-class students out of schools, it has made its own goals unattainable," he said.

**At Home:** Moakley is from the same school of party politics as O'Neill, but it took a striking display of independence to elect him to Congress.

A champion boxer in college, he was a state representative by age 25, and knew early in his career that he would like to succeed John W. McCormack in the House. He spent 17 years in the Massachusetts Legislature, where he specialized in urban affairs and environmental legislation, and waited for McCormack to retire. But when the aged Democratic Speaker finally stepped down in 1970, Moakley found himself overmatched in the primary against the more visible Louise Day Hicks, who had nearly been elected mayor of Boston three years earlier on an anti-busing platform. Hicks took the nomination over Moakley and a black attorney with 39 percent of the primary vote.

Then things began to turn Moakley's way. Hicks lost a second try for the mayor's job in 1971, straining her reputation as a political powerhouse, and the next year the district was substantially rearranged. Much of Hicks's South Boston base was removed, and replaced with a suburban area where she was not nearly as strong. Moakley, meanwhile, regained a political forum by winning a seat on Boston's City Council.

By 1972, Hicks was one of the most vulnerable incumbents in the state. She was held to 37 percent of the primary vote, winning renomination only because five other candidates split the opposition.

Moakley was not one of the primary challengers. In the most successful political gamble of his life, he had decided to run as an independent against Hicks in the general election. Insisting that he was a lifelong Democrat, he worked to stake out a position well to the incumbent's left. Hicks said Moakley would be unable to work effectively with either party if he was elected as an independent, but the argument failed, especially in the suburban areas.

Hicks carried the part of Boston remaining in the district, but only by 192 votes, as Moakley cut into her vote in Irish neighborhoods and swept the black areas. His suburban strength gave him the seat with more than 5,000 votes to spare. Moakley never had any intention of serving as an independent in Congress. He was sworn in as a Democrat in January of 1973, and has had to expend virtually no effort to win re-election on the Democratic line every two years.

**The District:** The 9th is a sampler of traditional Democratic constituencies. In the half of Boston included in the district, one finds the heavily Italian North End, Irish working-class areas of South Boston, middle-class Jamaica Plain and Dorchester and black Roxbury. The black percentage is higher in this district than in any other in New England.

The diversity extends into the district's seven suburbs, where about 40 percent of the voters live. Needham, Dover and Westwood are filled with affluent professionals who show a strong Republican tendency. The Democrats living in this area are a liberal lot, similar to those in nearby Newton and Wellesley.

The towns extending south from the city line — Dedham, Canton, Norwood and Walpole — are white-collar communities with relatively low median incomes. Voters here are not quite as conservative as those in the white wards in Boston, but they were far more sympathetic to George Wallace and Henry Jackson in the 1976 Democratic primary than to Morris K. Udall and Birch Bayh.

## Committees

**Rules** (4th of 11 Democrats)
Rules of the House, chairman.

## Elections

**1980 General**

Joe Moakley (D )                                          Unopposed

**1978 General**

Joe Moakley (D )                                   106,805 (93 %)
Brenda Franklin (SW)                                6,794 (6 %)

**Previous Winning Percentages**

1976 (70 %)     1974 (89 %)     1972 (43 %)

**District Vote For President**

|   | 1980 | | 1976 | | 1972 |
|---|---|---|---|---|---|
| D | 73,896 (46 %) | D | 90,048 (54 %) | D | 100,437 (59 %) |
| R | 64,451 (40 %) | R | 69,631 (42 %) | R | 68,667 (40 %) |
| I | 21,695 (13 %) | | | | |

## Campaign Finance

|   | Receipts | Receipts from PACs | Expenditures |
|---|---|---|---|
| **1980** | | | |
| Moakley (D ) | $105,917 | $24,640 (28 %) | $81,938 |
| **1978** | | | |
| Moakley (D ) | $83,098 | $20,250 (24 %) | $46,217 |

## Voting Studies

| | Presidential Support | | Party Unity | | Conservative Coalition | |
|---|---|---|---|---|---|---|
| **Year** | **S** | **O** | **S** | **O** | **S** | **O** |
| 1980 | 72 | 19 | 86 | 4 | 12 | 79 |

| | | | | | | |
|---|---|---|---|---|---|---|
| 1979 | 72 | 21 | 87 | 10 | 17 | 81 |
| 1978 | 74 | 21 | 81 | 12 | 10 | 84 |
| 1977 | 71 | 23 | 84 | 10 | 11 | 81 |
| 1976 | 24 | 75 | 88 | 8 | 12 | 85 |
| 1975 | 31 | 65 | 91 | 6 | 6 | 92 |
| 1974 (Ford) | 35 | 57 | | | | |
| 1974 | 47 | 49 | 82 | 9 | 14 | 78 |
| 1973 | 27 | 71 | 92 | 8 | 6 | 92 |

S = Support          O = Opposition

## Key Votes

**96th Congress**

| | |
|---|---|
| Weaken Carter oil profits tax (1979) | N |
| Reject hospital cost control plan (1979) | N |
| Implement Panama Canal Treaties (1979) | Y |
| Establish Department of Education (1979) | Y |
| Approve Anti-busing Amendment (1979) | Y |
| Guarantee Chrysler Corp. loans (1979) | Y |
| Approve military draft registration (1980) | Y |
| Aid Sandinista regime in Nicaragua (1980) | Y |
| Strengthen fair housing laws (1980) | Y |

**97th Congress**

| | |
|---|---|
| Reagan budget proposal (1981) | N |

## Interest Group Ratings

| Year | ADA | ACA | AFL-CIO | CCUS |
|---|---|---|---|---|
| 1980 | 72 | 10 | 82 | 68 |
| 1979 | 79 | 8 | 89 | 11 |
| 1978 | 75 | 4 | 90 | 17 |
| 1977 | 80 | 8 | 81 | 6 |
| 1976 | 85 | 4 | 87 | 6 |
| 1975 | 100 | 7 | 100 | 12 |
| 1974 | 74 | 7 | 100 | 0 |
| 1973 | 88 | 11 | 100 | 9 |

# 10 Margaret M. Heckler (R)

### Of Wellesley — Elected 1966

**Born:** June 21, 1931, Flushing, N.Y.
**Education:** Albertus Magnus College, B.A. 1953;
Boston College, LL.B. 1956.
**Profession:** Lawyer.
**Family:** Husband, John Heckler; three children.
**Religion:** Roman Catholic.
**Political Career:** Wellesley Town Meeting
member, 1958-66, Governor's Council, 1962-
66.

**In Washington:** When she is engaged in a cause, Peggy O'Shaughnessy Heckler is a tough legislator, one who knows how to draw publicity, mobilize outside pressure groups, and lobby colleagues hard inside the House.

When she is not so engaged, which is much of the time, she can be lackadaisical, bored by the routine of testimony and markup. She once described Banking Committee meetings as a combination of "posturing, speechmaking and rhetoric."

Heckler has shopped around in the committee system an unusual amount in eight terms. She started out on Government Operations, went to Banking in 1971, left that for the Agriculture Committee in 1975, and switched to the Science Committee in 1981. Her only constant has been Veterans' Affairs, the focus of much of her work over the years. On the other panels, her attention has wavered.

She fought hard for a place on Agriculture so she could express consumer viewpoints, but played little role in the committee's regular work during most of the six years she was there. In typical Heckler fashion, however, she did have one dramatic victory on Agriculture — her campaign to kill legislation establishing a minimum price for sugar producers.

She has waged many fights like that, accompanied by press conferences and righteous indignation, for women's rights, help for Vietnam veterans, and day care for children. Her style has given her a "showhorse" reputation among some of her more detail-minded colleagues, but it has produced its share of successes.

She fought for the Equal Rights Amendment when it first passed the House in 1972, and was even more important several years later, when the amendment would have expired without congressional action extending the deadline for ratification by the states. In 1977, Heckler persuaded former President Gerald Ford and his wife to

lobby for the amendment among Republicans, and their arguments won over Harold Sawyer, Ford's Grand Rapids successor. When Sawyer started to back out during the Judiciary Committee meeting held to vote on the extension, Heckler grabbed his arm, led him aside, and reminded him of his commitment.

She also pushed women's issues in the Banking Committee as a junior member, arguing for a proposal to guarantee women equal rights when applying for loans, mortgages or credit.

Meanwhile, she was arguing for federal day care subsidies for children of working women. She held her own seminar on day care in her district in 1972, and spoke emotionally on the House floor when a day care bill came up later that year. When President Nixon described the legislation as "anti-family" and vetoed it, she denounced the veto as "a serious setback to the concept of child development."

Heckler parts company with most women's groups, however, on the subject of abortion. She has voted against using federal money to pay for abortions, leading the National Women's Political Caucus to withhold its endorsement of her during the 1980 election. She called the caucus a "liberal organization" and said not everyone can agree on its agenda.

On Veterans' Affairs, dominated by the World War II generation, Heckler has been a

---

**10th District: Southeast — Fall River.** Population: 523,101 (10% increase since 1970). Race: White 512,525 (98%), Black 4,542 (1%), Others 6,034 (1%). Spanish origin: 7,027 (1%).

leader among the insurgent bloc seeking to increase the amount of attention paid to those who served in Vietnam. The committee refused for seven years to approve a bill providing psychiatric counseling for Vietnam veterans, finally reversing itself and moving one through the House in 1979. Two years later, when President Reagan proposed the elimination of storefront counseling centers for Vietnam veterans, Heckler was one of the loudest voices criticizing him.

Heckler's hoped-for role as consumer voice on Agriculture never quite worked out, as she avoided most of the complex negotiating over price supports for wheat, corn, and other commodities that do not grow in Wellesley or Fall River. But sugar was different. When the committee wrote sugar price support legislation in 1979, she argued that the "American consumer now spends $1.3 billion each year to support the price of sugar."

Heckler marshaled the Consumer Federation of America and other groups to lobby with her on the bill. She held a press conference to call the bill "a shocking concession" to Cuba, which would have been given quotas for export to countries around the world, although not to the United States.

She and other critics lost their argument in committee, but they renewed it on the floor, where the bill was further troubled by a regional split among the producers themselves. Heckler argued against amendments reducing the support level, insisting that the bill should be kept as expensive as possible to make it easier to reject. Her position prevailed and the sugar bill was defeated, 249-150.

Heckler has bucked her more conservative party on countless occasions over the years; she voted against a Republican majority more than half the time in 1980. But she does not do it easily or casually. She is a nervous voter on the House floor, one who often waits to see how the tally is shaping up, and how other GOP moderates like Massachusetts' Silvio Conte have decided to go. She remained undecided for weeks before the House budget voting in May of 1981, weighing pressure from the Reagan administration against the effect of Reagan's spending cuts on the cities in her district. Ultimately she went with the Republican president, joining a unanimous corps of 190 House Republicans.

**At Home:** When Margaret Mary O'Shaughnessy was a teen-ager on Long Island, she knew she had more ambition than most of those around her. But it was not until she got to Massachusetts that she proved it — by daring to challenge a former House Speaker for renomination and then defeating him soundly.

By 1966, the year of her primary challenge to the legendary Joseph W. Martin, Heckler already had a statewide political reputation. Four years earlier she had become the first woman ever elected to the eight-member governor's council, a largely ceremonial but frequently visible state office. She had won that post against the tide in a strong Democratic year.

After winning a second term on the council, from a district covering about 60 percent of the 10th Congressional District, she decided to go after Martin. The move was unexpected and — most thought — politically unwise.

Martin, 81, had been in office since 1924 — seven years before Heckler was born. By 1966 he was in ill health and rarely attended House sessions, but he said he wanted "just one more term," and most local Republicans interested in succeeding him were prepared to oblige. They attacked Heckler for not doing likewise, but that simply enhanced her image as a spunky independent.

Heckler tried to maintain a degree of reverence toward Martin, talking most of the time about the need for "energetic, continuous, full-time representation." She used the slogan, "We Need a Heckler in Congress," and quoted from Martin's 1924 campaign, in which he ousted an 83-year-old incumbent he said had been in office too long.

With a strong vote from the Boston suburbs, Heckler drew 15,400 votes to his 12,200. Although the Democrats stepped up their effort to win the seat, the attention and momentum Heckler received from the primary and a national Republican trend elected her in the fall.

Democrats have mounted several strong campaigns against Heckler, but each has fallen far short. Box manufacturer Bertram A. Yaffe came the closest, in 1970, charging she had not been strong enough in her opposition to the war in Vietnam. He is the only candidate who has held Heckler under 60 percent since her first victory.

In 1980, Democrats thought state Sen. Robert E. McCarthy might have a chance. He raised more money than previous challengers and had a solid political base in Plymouth County. But as usual, Heckler won the Democratic city of Fall River and maintained her strength in the Boston suburbs for a comfortable victory. Then she began waiting to see whether the Democratic Legislature would leave her a district anything like the current one for 1982. She also began pondering a statewide campaign, in case the district was eliminated.

**The District:** The 10th District looks like a descendant of Gov. Elbridge Gerry's 19th century salamander-shaped creation, which has given the word "gerrymander" to the language.

Its beast-like head is in the Republican strongholds of Wellesley and Natick, west of Boston. In its substantial belly is found Taunton, an aging mill town that is solidly Democratic. On its bottom is even more Democratic Fall River, a city with a large Portuguese population that was once a major sailing and cotton mill center.

The district is Democratic on paper. It often supports statewide Democratic candidates even though the party has had little success in House contests. Only Heckler has been able to win it consistently for the Republicans.

## Committees

**Science and Technology** (9th of 17 Republicans)
Science, Research and Technology.

**Veterans Affairs'** (2nd of 14 Republicans)
Education, Training and Employment; Hospitals and Health Care.

**Joint Economic**
Agriculture and Transportation, vice-chairman; Investment, Jobs and Prices.

## Elections

**1980 General**

| | |
|---|---|
| Margaret Heckler (R ) | 131,794 (61 %) |
| Robert McCarthy (D ) | 85,629 (39 %) |

**1978 Primary**

| | |
|---|---|
| Margaret Heckler (R ) | 102,080 (61 %) |
| John Marino (D ) | 64,868 (39 %) |

**Previous Winning Percentages**

| | | | |
|---|---|---|---|
| 1976 (100%) | 1974 (64 %) | 1972 (100%) | 1970 (57 %) |
| 1968 (67 %) | 1966 (51 %) | | |

**District Vote For President**

| | 1980 | | 1976 | | 1972 |
|---|---|---|---|---|---|
| **D** | 87,030 (39 %) | **D** | 118,840 (54 %) | **D** | 102,368 (50 %) |
| **R** | 98,381 (44 %) | **R** | 95,205 (43 %) | **R** | 100,894 (49 %) |
| **I** | 34,550 (16%) | | | | |

## Campaign Finance

| | Receipts | Receipts from PACs | Expenditures |
|---|---|---|---|
| **1980** | | | |
| Heckler (R ) | $266,032 | $79,500 (30 %) | $264,688 |
| McCarthy (D ) | $155,381 | $4,335 (3 %) | $152,107 |
| **1978** | | | |
| Heckler (R ) | $200,883 | $53,350 (27 %) | $210,730 |
| Marino (D ) | $79,292 | $1,700 (2 %) | $78,848 |

## Voting Studies

| | Presidential Support | | Party Unity | | Conservative Coalition | |
|---|---|---|---|---|---|---|
| **Year** | **S** | **O** | **S** | **O** | **S** | **O** |
| **1980** | 56 | 36 | 38 | 56 | 38 | 57 |
| **1979** | 50 | 42 | 42 | 54 | 46 | 51 |
| 1978 | 58 | 26 | 41 | 51 | 34 | 57 |
| 1977 | 63 | 29 | 39 | 55 | 38 | 56 |
| 1976 | 41 | 57 | 31 | 62 | 37 | 55 |
| 1975 | 48 | 46 | 36 | 54 | 29 | 62 |
| 1974 (Ford) | 37 | 48 | | | | |
| 1974 | 43 | 34 | 20 | 68 | 18 | 68 |
| 1973 | 38 | 57 | 28 | 66 | 17 | 80 |
| 1972 | 51 | 27 | 33 | 54 | 24 | 56 |
| 1971 | 39 | 49 | 40 | 47 | 23 | 65 |
| 1970 | 65 | 26 | 25 | 60 | 9 | 70 |
| 1969 | 60 | 32 | 42 | 49 | 22 | 67 |
| 1968 | 68 | 21 | 35 | 48 | 27 | 65 |
| 1967 | 46 | 27 | 45 | 29 | 35 | 39 |

S = Support          O = Opposition

## Key Votes

**96th Congress**

| | |
|---|---|
| Weaken Carter oil profits tax (1979) | N |
| Reject hospital cost control plan (1979) | N |
| Implement Panama Canal Treaties (1979) | N |
| Establish Department of Education (1979) | Y |
| Approve Anti-busing Amendment (1979) | N |
| Guarantee Chrysler Corp. loans (1979) | Y |
| Approve military draft registration (1980) | N |
| Aid Sandinista regime in Nicaragua (1980) | # |
| Strengthen fair housing laws (1980) | Y |

**97th Congress**

| | |
|---|---|
| Reagan budget proposal (1981) | Y |

## Interest Group Ratings

| Year | ADA | ACA | AFL-CIO | CCUS |
|---|---|---|---|---|
| 1980 | 67 | 23 | 74 | 63 |
| 1979 | 47 | 38 | 75 | 39 |
| 1978 | 55 | 22 | 70 | 41 |
| 1977 | 65 | 26 | 65 | 47 |
| 1976 | 65 | 17 | 57 | 19 |
| 1975 | 74 | 33 | 71 | 31 |
| 1974 | 70 | 17 | 100 | 11 |
| 1973 | 72 | 22 | 91 | 27 |
| 1972 | 63 | 12 | 56 | 20 |
| 1971 | 73 | 33 | 73 | - |
| 1970 | 72 | 38 | 60 | 17 |
| 1969 | 60 | 38 | 80 | - |
| 1968 | 58 | 39 | 75 | - |
| 1967 | 53 | 48 | 58 | 80 |

# 11 Brian J. Donnelly (D)

**Of Dorchester — Elected 1978**

**Born:** March 2, 1947, Dorchester, Mass.
**Education:** Boston U., B.S. 1970.
**Profession:** Teacher.
**Family:** Wife, Virginia Norton; one child.
**Religion:** Roman Catholic.
**Political Career:** Mass. House, 1973-79.

**In Washington:** Donnelly's low profile and local orientation in his first term marked out a clear contrast with James M. Shannon, the other young Boston-area Democrat who came to Congress at the same time. While Shannon was cultivating a friendship with the Speaker, winning a place on Ways and Means and arguing national energy policy, Donnelly was concentrating on the Quincy shipyard and the problems of its workers.

Donnelly acquired an early reputation for being independent and slightly to the right of most Massachusetts Democrats in his generation. He showed his independence even before he was sworn in, declining to lobby for a top committee assignment with O'Neill, who had been personally close to one of his 1978 primary opponents. In the end, Donnelly was placed on the Public Works and Merchant Marine committees, second-choices for most members but useful places to pursue matters of local interest.

The dues he paid on those committees helped him in 1981, when he wanted to transfer to the Budget Committee. There were only five Democratic vacancies, but this time O'Neill pushed for Donnelly, and he got one easily.

Once there, he argued against Reagan budget cuts with the same ferocity as O'Neill and other New England Democrats. "I figure neither my wife nor I could have been educated under this budget," he said, as the debate began in his committee. He also expressed concern about an overbalance of spending toward defense and away from domestic programs.

Donnelly has worked hard for the Quincy Shipyard, especially in 1980 when it lost a crucial contract awarded by the Navy Department, costing the district numerous jobs. Donnelly and other members of the delegation successfully lobbied the Labor Department to provide Trade Adjustment Assistance payments to shipyard workers, on the grounds that foreign competition was ultimately responsible for the industry's problems.

Donnelly's conservative approach to social issues, similar to that of his blue-collar constituents, came out in his votes in favor of an anti-busing constitutional amendment. But he worked to create a positive impression in the district's sizable black community by sponsoring legislation to create a national Afro-American historic site in Boston.

**At Home:** Donnelly owes his seat in the House largely to support from James A. Burke, his Democratic predecessor, and state Sen. Joseph Timilty, an influential Dorchester Democrat. Their strong endorsements in the 1978 primary identified Donnelly as the choice of party loyalists determined to keep the district out of the hands of Patrick McCarthy, a liberal maverick.

McCarthy had challenged Burke's renomination in 1976, and the aging incumbent wanted to make sure the young "upstart" did not win on his second try.

Among the six Democrats who entered the primary to succeed Burke, Donnelly had the best base of support in the Boston part of the district. For six years, he had represented about a fifth of the Boston section of the district in the Legislature. He was assistant House majority leader for three years.

Donnelly's first endorsement came from Timilty, a locally popular legislator who had run for mayor three years before. When Burke added

---

**11th District: East — Boston, Brockton and Quincy.** Population: 461,396 (3% decrease since 1970). Race: White 406,104 (88%), Black 42,475 (9%), Others 10,817 (2%). Spanish origin: 9,297 (2%).

---

his public backing, the game was all over for McCarthy, and for the other four candidates as well. Donnelly carried the four Boston wards by a 6-1 margin and won 43 percent district-wide, to McCarthy's second-place 20 percent.

Since the 1978 primary, Donnelly has faced no opposition whatsoever. Republicans have not run a candidate in the district since 1966. Although Donnelly has yet to build up the same kind of personal loyalty that Burke enjoyed, his careful attention to constituents has achieved the same political result.

**The District:** The employment roster of the Quincy shipyard — the district's largest employer — illustrates the population of the 11th District. Many of the names are Irish, others French-Canadian and Italian. They generally vote Democratic, but prefer conservative Democrats like Gov. Edward J. King, who won 63 percent here in

the 1978 general election.

About a third of the district's voters live in the Mattapan, Hyde Park and Dorchester sections of Boston. George Wallace easily won this part of the district in the 1976 Democratic presidential primary. The rest of the district — extending south for 20 miles — was carried in that primary by Sen. Henry M. Jackson.

The towns closest to Boston — such as Milton, Braintree and Randolph — have a high percentage of commuters. Farther south, in the once-great shoe capital, Brockton, the work force works closer to home.

Before Burke's election in 1958, the district was represented for 30 years by Republican Richard B. Wigglesworth. Much earlier, this was the district that returned John Quincy Adams to Washington for 17 years after his term in the White House.

## Committees

**Budget** (16th of 18 Democrats)
Energy and the Environment; Human Resources and Block Grants; Transportation, Research and Development, and Capital Resources.

**Merchant Marine and Fisheries** (15th of 20 Democrats)
Fisheries and Wildlife Conservation and the Environment; Merchant Marine.

**Public Works and Transportation** (24th of 25 Democrats)
Economic Development; Public Buildings and Grounds; Surface Transportation.

## Elections

**1980 General**

| | |
|---|---|
| Brian Donnelly (D ) | Unopposed |

**1978 General**

| | |
|---|---|
| Brian Donnelly (D ) | 133,644 (92 %) |
| H. Graham Lowry (USL) | 12,044 (8 %) |

**1978 Primary**

| | |
|---|---|
| Brian Donnelly (D ) | 39,236 (43 %) |
| Patrick McCarthy (D ) | 18,127 (20 %) |
| James Sheets (D ) | 15,641 (17 %) |
| Margaret Dineen (D ) | 8,749 (10 %) |
| Patrick McDonough (D ) | 7,677 (8 %) |

**District Vote For President**

| | 1980 | | 1976 | | 1972 |
|---|---|---|---|---|---|
| D | 82,538 (42 %) | D | 113,549 (57 %) | D | 112,397 (56 %) |
| R | 84,624 (44 %) | R | 80,009 (40 %) | R | 86,139 (43 %) |
| I | 25,285 (13 %) | | | | |

## Campaign Finance

| | Receipts | Receipts from PACs | Expenditures |
|---|---|---|---|
| **1980** | | | |
| Donnelly (D ) | $68,978 | $24,550 (36 %) | $60,806 |
| **1978** | | | |
| Donnelly (D ) | $190,946 | $20,100 (11 %) | $184,204 |

## Voting Studies

| | Presidential Support | | Party Unity | | Conservative Coalition | |
|---|---|---|---|---|---|---|
| Year | S | O | S | O | S | O |
| 1980 | 60 | 30 | 80 | 12 | 20 | 67 |
| 1979 | 54 | 44 | 60 | 33 | 44 | 53 |

S = Support          O = Opposition

## Key Votes

**96th Congress**

| | |
|---|---|
| Weaken Carter oil profits tax (1979) | N |
| Reject hospital cost control plan (1979) | N |
| Implement Panama Canal Treaties (1979) | N |
| Establish Department of Education (1979) | N |
| Approve Anti-busing Amendment (1979) | Y |
| Guarantee Chrysler Corp. loans (1979) | Y |
| Approve military draft registration (1980) | N |
| Aid Sandinista regime in Nicaragua (1980) | Y |
| Strengthen fair housing laws (1980) | ? |

**97th Congress**

| | |
|---|---|
| Reagan budget proposal (1981) | N |

## Interest Group Ratings

| Year | ADA | ACA | AFL-CIO | CCUS |
|---|---|---|---|---|
| 1980 | 72 | 24 | 71 | 63 |
| 1979 | 63 | 28 | 74 | 11 |

# 12 Gerry E. Studds (D)

**Of Cohasset — Elected 1972**

**Born:** May 12, 1937, Mineola, N.Y.
**Education:** Yale U., B.A. 1959, M.A.T. 1961.
**Profession:** Teacher.
**Family:** Single.
**Religion:** Episcopalian.
**Political Career:** Unsuccessful Democratic nominee for U.S. House, 1970.

**In Washington:** Studds has built his congressional career on two very different pillars: a human rights approach to foreign affairs and a devotion to the fishing interests of southeastern Massachusetts.

It has been a shrewd combination. The work he has done on the Merchant Marine and Fisheries Committee has given him the political freedom he needs to be a critic of American military adventures from Vietnam to El Salvador.

In 1980, representing one of New England's more conservative districts, he voted against the "conservative coalition" 93 percent of the time and drew Ralph Nader's endorsement as the most consistent pro-consumer member of the House. He won re-election with over 70 percent of the vote.

In his first term on Merchant Marine, Studds worked hard to push through a bill extending U.S. territorial waters to a 200-mile limit, a measure the East Coast fishing industry felt was essential to fight foreign competition. Later, when the Carter administration proposed a new U.S.-Canadian fishing treaty, Studds fought in behalf of his state's fishermen, who thought it biased in favor of Canada.

As he has moved up in seniority on Merchant Marine, Studds has been in a good position to fight for the fishing industry while pursuing his own environmental values at the same time. The most conspicuous example of that has been his fight against federal leases for oil drilling in the Georges Bank, one of the world's richest fishing grounds, located near Cape Cod.

In 1980, Studds sponsored an eight-year, $848 million extension of the Coastal Zone Management Act, aimed at controlling industrial development along the ocean. He managed to add to it a new program to revitalize urban waterfronts. The Carter administration vigorously opposed the bill as too costly, but while the money was trimmed back to $805 million over five years, Studds got his new program and essentially won

the battle.

Studds' views on coastal management and other environmental issues have brought him into frequent conflict with the oil industry, and they made him an antagonist of longtime Merchant Marine Chairman John M. Murphy, D-N.Y. Studds was generally in the minority during Murphy's six-year tenure, and chafed under Murphy's leadership. That conflict ended with Murphy's re-election defeat in 1980. Now, with the mild-mannered Walter B. Jones of North Carolina chairing the panel, Studds is freer to promote his issues unimpeded.

Meanwhile, on the Foreign Affairs Committee, Studds has used his seats on the Inter-American Affairs, Europe-Middle East and Africa subcommittees to criticize U.S. military aid and arms sales abroad.

When the Reagan administration decided to send military advisers to help the regime in El Salvador, Studds introduced a bill to prohibit any such military aid. He organized a group of more than 20 House members to make floor speeches the same day denouncing the action.

Studds had supported President Carter's early policy of restraining American arms sales abroad. When Carter reversed himself and backed continued sales of billions of dollars worth of weapons to such volatile areas as the Middle East,

---

**12th District: Southeast — New Bedford, Cape Cod.** Population: 584,879 (23% increase since 1970). Race: White 560,474 (96%), Black 7,533 (1%), Others 16,872 (3%). Spanish origin: 8,098 (1%).

he became a consistent Carter antagonist.

While most committee members were becoming more hawkish in 1979 and 1980, Studds was sounding like an even more insistent dove. He attacked the administration's tendency to blame regional turmoil, in the Middle East and elsewhere, on Soviet expansionism. Poverty and nationalism are the major causes of instability in most areas, Studds insisted.

He led House opposition to Carter's sale of sophisticated AWACS radar planes to Iran in 1977, and won Foreign Affairs Committeee approval of a resolution objecting to the sale. Congress eventually approved it after Carter issued assurances about how the planes would be used.

After the shah of Iran was overthrown in 1979, Studds warned that the same thing could happen in Saudi Arabia, the major foreign source of U.S. oil and second-biggest U.S. arms customer. "Our policy of arming the shah to the teeth speaks for itself," he said. He became a militant opponent of the Reagan administration's proposed AWACS sale to Saudi Arabia in 1981.

When the House was approving a massive military aid package for Israel and Egypt as a reward for signing the 1979 peace treaty, Studds warned that the United States cannot shore up fragile regimes by sending them weapons: "We can protect our friends from communists," he said, "but we cannot protect them from their own people."

**At Home:** A decade ago, this former schoolteacher and White House aide was considered much too liberal for the most Republican district in the state. That is ancient history now. Studds himself has changed very little, but the district has moved left to meet him, and he has devoted far more effort to keeping in touch with his Cape Cod constituents than any of his predecessors ever did. He has not had a serious challenge since his first election.

The son of a Long Island architect, Studds went through a flurry of Washington jobs in the early 1960s before "retiring" to teach in an exclusive boarding school in New Hampshire.

In 1967, motivated by his opposition to the war in Vietnam, he enlisted in Eugene J. McCarthy's presidential campaign and ended up as one of the coordinators of the senator's New Hampshire primary effort. Then he moved to Massachusetts' 12th District, sensing that incumbent Republican Hastings Keith was potentially vulnerable for 1970.

A moderate state senator, William D. Weeks, also thought the conservative Keith might be an easy target and challenged him in the Republican primary. While Studds was organizing the local area's anti-war opposition into his congressional campaign force, Weeks was inadvertently helping the cause — telling Republican voters that Keith could not win the general election.

Studds won a four-way Democratic primary with a clear majority of the vote, while Keith had an ominously hard time winning renomination over Weeks. In the general election, Studds' labor support in New Bedford and anti-war loyalists on Cape Cod brought him tantalizingly close. But Keith won back just enough of Weeks' primary vote in the fall to defeat Studds by 1,522 votes out of nearly 200,000 cast.

Over the next two years, redistricting made the district slightly more Democratic. Keith decided to retire, and Weeks was unopposed for the GOP nomination. Studds never stopped campaigning. He learned Portuguese between elections to communicate better with New Bedford's largely fishing community. He began talking less about Vietnam, although he remained a "peace" candidate, and more about unemployment and the Nixon economic programs. The outcome was even closer than in 1970 — 1,118 votes — but this time Studds was on top.

By 1976, just four years after he had become the first Democrat to represent the district in more than half a century, Studds was running unopposed. In less than a decade the district had changed from safe Republican to safe Democratic.

**The District:** Although Studds no longer has trouble winning this district, it is still the most Republican one in the state. It was the only district in the state that backed Richard Nixon over George McGovern in 1972, the year of Studds' victory over Weeks. Statewide Democratic candidates usually do worse in the 12th than anyplace else in the state, even though some popular liberals, like Edward M. Kennedy, manage to carry it.

The district includes all of Cape Cod, still a Republican stronghold. Its industrial and blue-collar core is in New Bedford, the only major population center. The city has been chronically depressed ever since the textile trade died out more than a generation ago, but it is gradually being revived by a large fishing fleet and by an influx of rubber, chemical and electrical manufacturing firms. Nonetheless, unemployment remains a serious problem with the loyally Democratic voters there.

## Committees

**Foreign Affairs** (10th of 21 Democrats)
Africa; Inter-American Affairs.

**Merchant Marine and Fisheries** (5th of 20 Democrats)
Coast Guard and Navigation, chairman; Fisheries and Wildlife
Conservation and the Environment; Oceanography.

## Elections

**1980 General**

| | |
|---|---|
| Gerry Studds (D ) | 195,791 (73 %) |
| Paul Doane (R ) | 71,620 (27 %) |

**1978 General**

| | |
|---|---|
| Gerry Studds (D ) | Unopposed |

**Previous Winning Percentages**

1976 (100%)    1974 (75 %)    1972 (50 %)

**District Vote For President**

| | 1980 | | 1976 | | 1972 |
|---|---|---|---|---|---|
| D | 98,427 (36 %) | D | 132,604 (51 %) | D | 113,109 (48 %) |
| R | 130,999 (47 %) | R | 119,237 (46 %) | R | 121,406 (51 %) |
| I | 44,766 (16 %) | | | | |

## Campaign Finance

| | Receipts | Receipts from PACs | Expenditures |
|---|---|---|---|
| **1980** | | | |
| Studds (D ) | $67,923 | $15,100 (22 %) | $78,937 |
| Doane (R ) | $47,158 | $500 (1 %) | $47,490 |
| **1978** | | | |
| Studds (D ) | $25,993 | $3,775 (15 %) | $20,899 |

## Voting Studies

| Year | Presidential Support | | Party Unity | | Conservative Coalition | |
|---|---|---|---|---|---|---|
| | S | O | S | O | S | O |
| 1980 | 78 | 21 | 93 | 7 | 7 | 93 |
| 1979 | 85 | 14 | 92 | 8 | 3 | 97 |
| 1978 | 87 | 13 | 88 | 12 | 7 | 93 |
| 1977 | 78 | 22 | 89 | 10 | 10 | 90 |
| 1976 | 22 | 76 | 88 | 10 | 10 · | 87 |
| 1975 | 33 | 67 | 88 | 11 | 8 | 92 |
| 1974 (Ford) | 45 | 57 | | | | |
| 1974 | 43 | 55 | 87 | 13 | 10 | 90 |
| 1973 | 30 | 70 | 87 | 13 | 8 | 92 |

S = Support          O = Opposition

## Key Votes

**96th Congress**

| | |
|---|---|
| Weaken Carter oil profits tax (1979) | N |
| Reject hospital cost control plan (1979) | N |
| Implement Panama Canal Treaties (1979) | Y |
| Establish Department of Education (1979) | Y |
| Approve Anti-busing Amendment (1979) | N |
| Guarantee Chrysler Corp. loans (1979) | Y |
| Approve military draft registration (1980) | N |
| Aid Sandinista regime in Nicaragua (1980) | Y |
| Strengthen fair housing laws (1980) | Y |

**97th Congress**

| | |
|---|---|
| Reagan budget proposal (1981) | N |

## Interest Group Ratings

| Year | ADA | ACA | AFL-CIO | CCUS |
|---|---|---|---|---|
| 1980 | 100 | 17 | 84 | 67 |
| 1979 | 100 | 4 | 95 | 6 |
| 1978 | 95 | 7 | 90 | 22 |
| 1977 | 100 | 0 | 83 | 18 |
| 1976 | 95 | 7 | 83 | 0 |
| 1975 | 100 | 11 | 96 | 18 |
| 1974 | 100 | 7 | 100 | 0 |
| 1973 | 92 | 11 | 100 | 9 |

# Michigan

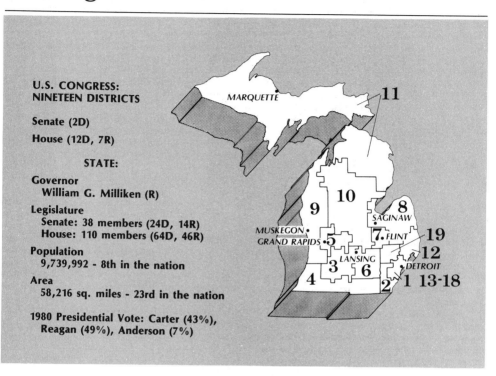

**U.S. CONGRESS:**
**NINETEEN DISTRICTS**

Senate (2D)

House (12D, 7R)

**STATE:**

Governor
William G. Milliken (R)

Legislature
Senate: 38 members (24D, 14R)
House: 110 members (64D, 46R)

Population
9,739,992 - 8th in the nation

Area
58,216 sq. miles - 23rd in the nation

1980 Presidential Vote: Carter (43%),
Reagan (49%), Anderson (7%)

MARQUETTE

11

10
9
8
SAGINAW
MUSKEGON•
GRAND RAPIDS•5    7•FLINT    19
3   LANSING    12
4    6    DETROIT
2   1  13-18

## . . . A State Divided

From its geography to its economy and politics, Michigan is a divided state. Not only is the state physically divided by the Mackinac Straits, but one part of it always seems to be arguing with another about politics, economics and social issues.

There is a basic division between the auto-manufacturing cities dominated by labor unions and the tranquil farming areas and small towns that fill the rest of the Lower Peninsula. Within that context, there is also a division between whites and blacks; Michigan has some of the most segregated housing patterns anywhere in the industrial North.

The population of Michigan is still split almost evenly between the Democratic industrial core around Detroit and the Republican "outstate" area. That has made for generations of competitive politics, with both sides struggling for the suburban "ticket splitters" who decide virtu-

ally every close election. In the 33 contests for president, Senate and governor since 1948, Democrats have won 17, Republicans 16.

The 1948 election marked a turning point in Michigan. For nearly a century, the state had been dominated by rural conservatives and Republican industrialists. But the leftward drift that began during the Depression, with the arrival of massive numbers of blue-collar workers from other parts of the country, finally made its impact in 1948. As the labor unions grew in influence and number, they joined with a group of business and university liberals to capture the moribund Democratic Party. In concert, they won the state-house behind the candidacy of soap heir G. Mennen Williams, and held it for 14 years.

When George Romney brought the GOP back into power in 1962, that party too had undergone a major transformation. It was more moderate in its approach to social and economic issues, and more diverse in its character, with suburbanites replacing the rural stalwarts. Since then, Republicans have consistently nominated moderates for statewide office, and this has enabled them to breach the basic political division and draw the independent votes they need to carry the state.

Republicans have not relinquished the governor's chair since Romney assumed it in 1963. With William G. Milliken replacing Romney in 1969, Republicans' current 18-year reign in the state exceeds that of any party in any Northern state. But Democrats have held both U.S. Senate seats since 1978.

# A Political Tour

**Inner Detroit.** In the early 20th century, Detroit was a ghetto for Eastern European immigrants lured by the offer of steady employment on the automobile assembly lines. In the Depression, it attracted a similar stream of white migrants from Kentucky, West Virginia and Tennessee. Today the children and grandchildren of those immigrants have fled to all-white suburbs, leaving behind poor housing, few jobs, and a growing black majority.

Before 1950, blacks made up about 15 percent of the city's population. But during the past two decades, two out of every three white residents have left the city and blacks have continued to move into Detroit. In 1973 or shortly thereafter, blacks began to outnumber whites. In November of 1973, the city elected its first black mayor, Coleman Young, who has remained in office ever since. Today about 63 percent of the city's 1.2 million people are black.

Few Democrats running statewide in recent years have drawn less than 60 percent of the Detroit vote. In 1980, Jimmy Carter won almost 80 percent of it.

In some of the surviving white neighborhoods, transplanted Southerners hold militantly conservative social views, backing tough law and order Democrats in primaries and occasionally Republicans in general elections. In others, where white urban homesteaders have begun to move back into the city, rehabilitating lofts and old abandoned houses, the pattern is liberal.

The glittering Renaissance Center, towering over a still-shabby downtown Detroit, is a visible symbol of the city's efforts to revitalize itself. However, the recent decline in the auto industry has hurt the city's efforts to rebound from the riots and decay of the 1960s and 1970s.

Surrounded on all sides by Detroit are two independent communities, Hamtramck and Highland Park. Both were once low-income ethnic enclaves. Today, Highland Park is nearly all black and votes as strongly Democratic as the surrounding area. Hamtramck, more than 80 percent Polish a generation ago, is increasingly black now and even more Democratic than it was in the old days.

**Suburban Detroit.** The suburban metropolis extends up to 40 miles in a semicircle from downtown Detroit. It includes more than 3.3 million people and covers a wide political spectrum.

With the city firmly in Democratic control and the outstate region generally conceded to the GOP, most close elections are decided in Macomb and Oakland counties to the north and northwest of the city, and the close-in communities in Wayne County that surround Detroit on the west and south.

To a lesser degree, the metropolitan area also extends south to Monroe County, across the Ohio border from Toledo; west to Washtenaw County, the home of the University of Michigan at Ann Arbor; and northwest into Livingston County, which was overwhelmingly rural in 1970, but has increased its population by 70 percent in the last decade, as suburbanites move still further into the countryside.

With favorable wage contracts, many auto workers who live in these areas have attained a degree of comfort in which the old social welfare values of their labor unions become secondary to the values of home, neighborhood and school. They think about black Detroit from a carefully-maintained distance, and they were more militantly opposed to busing in the early 1970s than suburbanites almost anywhere in the country. Most of the suburbs bordering on black Detroit remain intensely segregated. Ethnic working-class Warren and middle-class Dearborn and Dearborn Heights all have a black population of less than one fifth of one percent. The parts of Detroit they abut are nearly all black.

The communities just above Eight Mile Road — Detroit's northern boundary — usually vote Democratic. Some, such as Warren and East Detroit in Macomb County, preferred George Wallace to George McGovern in 1972, the peak of opposition to busing in the area. In other middle-class suburbs, such as the heavily Jewish Oak Park and Southfield, McGovern led Wallace in the 1972 Democratic presidential primary.

In the most fashionable parts of Oakland County, especially around Bloomfield Hills and Birmingham, the residents tend to be upper-income managers and executives. They vote solidly Republican. Another strongly Republican growth area is north of Warren in Sterling

Heights. Virtually all white, it has grown by 78 percent since 1970 to become the sixth largest city in the state.

**Automobile Corridor and The Thumb.** North of Detroit's metropolitan area, extending for 80 miles along Interstate 75, are four cities which owe their economic survival to General Motors. The four — Pontiac, Flint, Saginaw and Bay City are all Democratic. But the surrounding flat countryside is given over to rural Republican farmland. The combination produces a more pronounced Democratic tilt than is found in the Republican heartland further west. But the size of the Democratic vote does not begin to approach the overwhelming margins found in Detroit.

Sitting on the outer edge of the fanciest part of metropolitan Detroit in Oakland County is Pontiac. The poorest and most Democratic of the four cities in the auto corridor, it is also the most socially tense. Southern whites, blacks and Mexican-Americans — three major elements of the city's working class population — do not get along with one another very well. But each November they all vote for candidates affiliated with the Democratic Party.

Flint, the fourth largest city in the state, comes about as close to being a one-company town as any city of comparable size in the U.S. General Motors employs 74 percent of Flint's industrial work force in its Buick, Chevrolet, AC Spark Plug and Fisher Body plants. With a 41 percent black population and a strong United Auto Workers contingent, the city regularly turns in solid Democratic majorities. Genesee County, where Flint is located, was one of just three counties in Michigan's Lower Peninsula that supported Jimmy Carter in both 1976 and 1980.

Saginaw and Bay City, at the northern edge of the industrialized part of Michigan, originally were lumbering centers. Today, they too are dominated by the automobile industry, but also serve as a commercial center for the region's farmers. Bay City, the more Democratic of the two, is the only city in the auto corridor without a substantial black or foreign-born population.

Voters in the richly agricultural "Thumb" are many degrees more conservative than their city neighbors. Sanilac County, on the eastern side of the Thumb, was one of just three counties in the state that Barry Goldwater carried in 1964. With no major population centers, the countryside is devoted largely to raising beans and sugar beets, with dairy farming also important in the region's relatively healthy economy.

**Old Republican Michigan.** If one thinks of Michigan's Lower Peninsula as a mitten, the area in the palm is the state's Republican core.

Spread across this area west and north of Detroit, are seven cities, ranging in population from 36,000 to 181,000 and separated by miles of fertile farmland and hundreds of small towns.

The larger cities — Grand Rapids, Lansing and Kalamazoo — have auto manufacturing and assembly plants. But the pervasive industrial influence felt in Detroit and the other auto cities is much less pronounced in these "outstate" cities. One reason is that they all developed other economic specialties before the auto industry moved in.

The skilled Dutch craftsmen of Grand Rapids combined with Yankee businessmen to make the city a furniture capital of North America in the late 19th and early 20th century. Kalamazoo specialized in paper making. Lansing became the home of Michigan State University, and later a center for state government with a large white-collar work force.

From the chemical capital of Midland, home of the Dow Chemical Company, to Battle Creek, the breakfast cereal capital of the world, the cities in the central part of Michigan are predominantly Republican. The work force comes largely from the surrounding area rather than from European immigration or from Appalachia, the two main sources of the white Democratic vote in Detroit and the auto corridor.

The Republican heritage here goes back before the Civil War era, to the time when settlers came from Yankee New England and upstate New York. Many of the industrial workers in this part of the state are unionized now, but they rarely side with Michigan's labor-oriented Democratic Party.

The small towns interspersed throughout this area produce the strongest Republican vote in the state. The Corn Belt counties on the border with Ohio and Indiana, counties which Reagan budget director David Stockman represented in the House, are among the most solidly Republican in the Midwest.

**The Northern Lower Peninsula.** After 19th century loggers decimated the forests in the northern part of Michigan's Lower Peninsula, that part of the state was written off as an economic wasteland. It was too remote to support serious industrial growth and the land was not very good for farming. There were, however, scenic lakes and rivers for fishing which attracted summer vacationers from the cities in the southern part of the state. These people have now brought a rebirth of sorts to the region.

In the 1970s, many who once summered in the northern rural counties decided to make their retirement homes there. Auto workers leaving their jobs after 30 years in the plant were young enough to enjoy the recreational advantages of the area, and often found winterizing a summer cottage on a lake in northern Michigan more affordable than a Florida condominium. Ten rural counties in the region have grown by more than 40 percent in the last decade. One — Kalkaska County — has more than doubled its population since 1970.

With the coming of retired Democratic auto workers, along with some younger professionals seeking a quieter life, the Democratic vote in the area has jumped sharply. In 1978 a Democrat was elected to the House from this region for the first time in the 20th century. The same year, the Democratic Senate and gubernatorial candidates ran far above their statewide percentage in the area.

The western shore along Lake Michigan, however, remains firmly Republican. Settled around the same time as southern Michigan, it has always had a more favorable agricultural climate than the inland areas in the north. Cherry and apple orchards, warmed in winter by Lake Michigan, flourish alongside dairy farms.

**The Upper Peninsula.** Covering a quarter of the state's land area, the Upper Peninsula accounts for less than 4 percent of the population. Feeling detached and removed from the rest of the state, U.P. chauvinists have occasionally talked of breaking off from Michigan and becoming a separate state. But with a declining population and economic base the viability of a separate U.P. state remains dubious.

Ethnically, geographically and politically the western part of the U.P. is much closer to neighboring Wisconsin and Minnesota than to the rest of Michigan. Most of the Upper Peninsula has a strong Democratic, pro-labor orientation. Many of the iron ore miners in Gogebic and Iron counties are from the same Scandinavian background as their fellow miners on Minnesota's Iron Range — and are just as staunchly Democratic. A majority of the counties in Michigan carried by Jimmy Carter in both 1976 and 1980 were in the U.P., and Democratic candidates — even those with a strongly urban Detroit image — can bank on doing well there.

At the eastern end of the U.P. are three counties which are more agricultural and less mountainous. These are Republican counties and much more in tune with the rest of the state.

## Redrawing the Lines

When the Michigan Legislature adjourned for the summer, it had barely touched the subject of drawing new congressional boundaries.

Michigan lost one of its 19 representatives in the 1980 reapportionment. Every Detroit district lost population during the 1970s, and only three of the state's districts grew more than 15 percent — the 12th and 19th in suburban Detroit, and the 10th in central Michigan.

The two districts with the fewest people are Detroit's 1st and 13th, but both are represented by blacks, and state legislators of both parties have said they are committed to maintaining two districts dominated by black voters.

## Governor
## William G. Milliken (R)

**Born:** March 26, 1922, Traverse City, Mich.
**Home:** Traverse City, Mich.
**Education:** Yale U., B.A. 1946.
**Military Career:** Army Air Corps, World War II.
**Profession:** Retailing executive.
**Family:** Wife, Helen; two children.
**Religion:** Congregationalist.
**Political Career:** Michigan Senate, 1961-65; majority floor leader, 1963-65; lieutenant governor, 1965-69; assumed governorship Jan. 1969, upon appointment of Gov. George Romney as secretary of housing and urban development; elected governor 1970, 1974, 1978; term expires Jan. 1983.

# Donald W. Riegle Jr. (D)

**Of Flint — Elected 1976**

**Born:** Feb. 4, 1938, Flint, Mich.
**Education:** U. of Mich., B.A. 1960; Mich. State
U., M.B.A. 1961.
**Profession:** Business executive.
**Family:** Wife, Lori Hansen; three children.
**Religion:** Methodist.
**Political Career:** U.S. House, 1967-76.

**In Washington:** When Riegle was grand
marshal of a parade in Traverse City, Mich. a
couple of summers ago, he refused to ride in the
foreign car assigned to him; only after flustered
organizers of the event hastily located a Chevrolet
did the senator set forth.

Representing Michigan in the Senate means
representing Detroit, and that means representing the American automobile industry. Riegle is
devoted to both the industry and the United Auto
Workers. Whether fighting auto emission standards, promoting federal loan guarantees for a
beleaguered Chrysler Corp., or demanding curbs
on foreign car imports, Riegle goes all out for
Detroit.

Parochial Michigan interests account for
most of his departures from a consistent liberal
voting record. Some of his remaining "conservative" votes — such as his support for curbing the
powers of the Federal Trade Commission — come
out of an anti-regulatory bias carried over from
auto industry battles.

When he made his shift from the House to
the Senate in 1976, he brought with him a reputation for brashness and conceit that had been
building on the other side of the Capitol for years.
He confided to reporters soon after he arrived in
the House in 1967 that he planned to be president
someday. His public attacks on House practices
and procedures, his maverick voting record, and
his political party switch at the time of the
Watergate scandal simply fueled accusations of
opportunism.

Since his arrival in the Senate, however,
Riegle has gone far toward living down his House
reputation. If he still harbors presidential ambitions, he has learned not to show them. He has
made little effort to grab headlines, and he has
narrowed his field of interest considerably, focusing on the programs and policies vital to
Michigan.

His four Senate committee assignments —
Banking, Budget, Commerce and Labor — put

him in position to look after the varied concerns
of the industry and the workers who rely on it.
Because all four are major committees, Riegle
carries an unusually heavy workload.

In 1977, when the Clean Air Act was up for
renewal, Riegle offered the industry's principal
amendment to relax standards for carbon monox-
ide emissions from automobiles. It was turned
aside in favor of a stricter substitute version,
whose passage led Riegle to complain that "we
just cannot mandate technology that does not
exist." But Riegle had won some tangible concessions; the ultimate language was somewhat looser
than the version that had passed the Environment Committee earlier.

The same year, when President Carter's energy package came to the Senate floor, Riegle led
an effort to remove a ban on "gas-guzzler" automobiles. That was beaten on a 55-27 vote.

In 1979, Riegle's major cause was Chrysler.
He put his entire staff to work on various aspects
of the Chrysler situation, and drafted his own bill
to provide the mechanisms for a loan guarantee.
Later he backed the Carter administration's
bailout plan as it cleared the Banking Committee.
Then he helped work out a compromise that
averted a filibuster and moved the plan through
the full Senate just before the year's recess. The
compromise involved more than $500 million in
wage concessions on the part of Chrysler
employees.

In 1981, Riegle concentrated much of his
attention on the Budget Committee, where he was
one of the die-hard opponents of the Reagan
administration's budget cuts. He offered floor
amendments to continue the minimum benefit
levels under Social Security, and to restore cuts in
unemployment insurance. Later he tried to add
$1.8 billion to the overall budget for mass transit,

**581**

## Donald W. Riegle Jr., D-Mich.

education and other social programs by reducing defense spending. When that failed, 81-17, Riegle cast one of 20 votes against the full $700 billion budget as it passed the Senate.

**At Home:** Riegle has changed in many ways over 15 years in politics, but he has usually managed to be controversial — from his arrival in the House as a business-oriented Republican in 1966, through his evolution as a Vietnam dove, his switch to the Democratic Party, and his tempestuous campaign for the Senate in 1976.

Even though he developed a maverick reputation very quickly in the House, Riegle managed to stay on good terms with his party leader, Gerald R. Ford. Even after he tried to take the 1970 Michigan Senate nomination away from Lenore Romney, the choice of GOP leaders, Ford seemed to remain an ally.

The Vietnam War, however, gradually turned Riegle from maverick to full-time rebel. He was one of a small group of anti-war Republicans who backed Rep. Paul N. McCloskey Jr. of California

against President Nixon during the 1972 Republican primaries. In 1972, Riegle wrote a book about his House experiences, *O Congress*, which criticized the dominance of senior members.

By then he had burned his Republican bridges, and was winning re-election by comfortable margins mainly because he was popular among Flint's blue-collar Democratic majority. He became a Democrat in 1973, won a fifth term the next year and began a well-financed effort to win the Senate seat vacated in 1976 by Democrat Philip A. Hart. In the 1976 Democratic primary, he closed fast to upset the favorite, black Secretary of State Richard H. Austin. Riegle stressed the contrast in age between himself and Austin. He was 38, and Austin was 63.

That November, he won a comfortable victory over 10-year Republican Rep. Marvin Esch. Riegle's campaign was battered by news stories about an affair he had had with a staff member. But the revelations backfired and helped him resist a hard-hitting Esch television campaign.

## Committees

**Banking, Housing and Urban Affairs** (4th of 7 Democrats)
Economic Policy; Housing and Urban Affairs; Securities.

**Budget** (8th of 10 Democrats)

**Commerce, Science and Transportation** (6th of 8 Democrts)
Science, Technology, and Space; Surface Transportation.

**Labor and Human Resources** (6th of 7 Democrats)
Alcoholism and Drug Abuse; Labor.

## Elections

**1976 General**

| | |
|---|---|
| Donald Riegle (D ) | 1,831,031 (53 %) |
| Marvin Esch (R ) | 1,635,087 (47 %) |

**1976 Primary**

| | |
|---|---|
| Donald Riegle (D ) | 325,705 (44 %) |
| Richard Austin (D ) | 208,310 (28 %) |
| James O'Hara (D ) | 170,473 (23 %) |

**Previous Winning Percentages**

**1974\*** (65 %)   **1972\*** (70 %)   **1970\*** (69 %)   **1968\*** (61 %)
**1966\*** (54 %)

\* House elections

## Campaign Finance

| 1976 | Receipts | Receipts from PACs | Expenditures |
|---|---|---|---|
| Riegle (D ) | $849,684 | $188,710 (22 %) | $795,821 |
| Esch (R ) | $864,759 | $128,773 (15 %) | $809,564 |

## Voting Studies

| Year | Presidential Support | | Party Unity | | Conservative Coalition | |
|---|---|---|---|---|---|---|
| | S | O | S | O | S | O |
| **Senate service** | | | | | | |
| 1980 | 68 | 26 | 81 | 15 | 12 | 83 |
| 1979 | 83 | 15 | 84 | 10 | 10 | 79 |
| 1978 | 74 | 17 | 86 | 5 | 8 | 82 |
| 1977 | 60 | 25 | 75 | 11 | 4 | 84 |
| **House service** | | | | | | |
| 1976 | 10 | 47 | 29 | 2 | 3 | 27 |
| 1975 | 26 | 61 | 77 | 9 | 9 | 76 |
| 1974 (Ford) | 35 | 43 | | | | |
| 1974 | 31 | 58† | 72 | 15 | 5 | 82 |
| 1973\* | 25 | 62 | 73 | 10 | 5 | 72 |
| 1972 | 38 | 35 | 10 | 71 | 4 | 76 |
| 1971 | 32 | 54 | 26 | 58 | 14 | 76 |
| 1970 | 63 | 23 | 29 | 53 | 16 | 66 |
| 1969 | 49 | 43 | 33 | 55 | 22 | 62 |
| 1968 | 70 | 24 | 59 | 35 | 55 | 37 |
| 1967 | 56 | 37 | 64 | 29 | 61 | 37 |

S = Support       O = Opposition
\* Reigle switched from the Republican Party to the Democratic Party on Feb. 2, 1973. Scores given are for Democratic Party membership. His presidential support score for 1973 as a Republican

were S-0, O-66; party unity scores as a Republican were S-22, O-78; no conservative coalition votes occured during the time he was a Republican in 1973.

† Not eligible for all recorded votes.

## Key Votes

**96th Congress**

| | |
|---|---|
| Maintain relations with Taiwan (1979) | N |
| Reduce synthetic fuel development funds (1979) | N |
| Impose nuclear plant moratorium (1979) | Y |
| Kill stronger windfall profits tax (1979) | N |
| Guarantee Chrysler Corp. loans (1979) | Y |
| Approve military draft registration (1980) | N |
| End Revenue Sharing to the states (1980) | N |
| Block Justice Dept. busing suits (1980) | N |

**97th Congress**

| | |
|---|---|
| Restore urban program funding cuts (1981) | Y |

## Interest Group Ratings

| Year | ADA | ACA | AFL-CIO | CCUS-1 | CCUS-2 |
|---|---|---|---|---|---|
| **Senate service** | | | | | |
| 1980 | 83 | 4 | 100 | 40 | |
| 1979 | 84 | 15 | 94 | 0 | 19 |
| 1978 | 85 | 0 | 89 | 29 | |
| 1977 | 70 | 5 | 95 | 17 | |
| **House service** | | | | | |
| 1976 | 30 | 0 | 82 | 17 | |
| 1975 | 74 | 8 | 100 | 14 | |
| 1974 | 82 | 7 | 91 | 0 | |
| 1973 | 76 | 10 | 82 | 27 | |
| 1972 | 94 | 5 | 90 | 20 | |
| 1971 | 84 | 19 | 64 | - | |
| 1970 | 80 | 35 | 67 | 22 | |
| 1969 | 67 | 27 | 90 | - | |
| 1968 | 50 | 45 | 75 | - | |
| 1967 | 33 | 65 | 42 | 75 | |

# Carl Levin (D)

### Of Detroit — Elected 1978

**Born:** June 28, 1934, Detroit, Mich.
**Education:** Swarthmore College, B.A. 1956; Harvard U., LL.B. 1959.
**Profession:** Lawyer.
**Family:** Wife, Barbara Halpern; three children.
**Religion:** Jewish.
**Political Career:** Chief appellate defender for city of Detroit, 1968-69; Detroit City Council, 1970-73; Detroit City Council President, 1974-77.

**In Washington:** Levin is one of the new Senate faces being watched for evidence that Democratic liberalism is not moribund.

What has attracted attention is not so much his voting record, which shows an orthodox loyalty to his party and its programs, but his legislative skill and apparent confidence that he knows the remedy for his party's condition.

While Americans "haven't turned their backs on our goals, their stomachs have been turned by some of our methods," Levin has said. He wants costs of new regulations weighed alongside benefits, and programs canceled if they have outlived their usefulness.

In his first two years Levin won attention for his work on a compromise "legislative veto" proposal cosponsored with David L. Boren of Oklahoma. The Levin-Boren amendment, affixed to a 1980 bill extending the life of the Federal Trade Commission, allowed Congress to delay any new FTC regulation while it considered legislation to block it.

The amendment successfully headed off more drastic proposals which would have let one or both houses of Congress veto any new regulation by majority vote, without presidential approval.

The legislative veto proposal showed Levin as a tenacious lobbyist for his point of view. After winning the FTC amendment, he continued pressing to extend his veto concept government-wide, and managed to get such a bill reported from the Governmental Affairs Committee. He was still pushing the bill during the last week of the 96th's lame-duck session, when its passage before adjournment was impossible.

On the Armed Services Committee, Levin also made a favorable first impression as a quick study and a serious, persuasive debater. His first major legislative assignment was to manage a 1979 bill implementing terms of the Panama Canal treaties — a bill no other Armed Services member wanted to handle. Levin drafted the bill to Carter administration specifications and steered it through the Senate and two tricky conferences with the House.

In 1980, Levin again impressed defense observers by winning a military personnel argument with Sam Nunn, the Georgia Democrat who normally dominates that field. Nunn wanted to cut Army manpower unless the service could attract better educated recruits. The move was widely seen as a slap at the volunteer army.

Nunn won his point in the committee, but Levin, along with Ernest Hollings, D-S.C., demolished him in the full Senate. The 3-1 margin of victory was attributed to Levin's mastery of the subject, one on which Nunn rarely has much competition. Levin then joined Nunn in a face-saving compromise.

In 1981, Levin spent some of his time trying to make a case against the proposed mobile basing system for the MX missile. He offered an amendment requiring advance approval of both houses of Congress before any money could be spent on a basing mode. The amendment was tabled, 59-39.

Like other Michigan lawmakers, liberal and conservative alike, Levin is loyal to the auto industry. Along with senior Sen. Donald Riegle, he has pushed for limits on imports of foreign cars. He supported the 1979 government bailout of Chrysler, and unsuccessfully proposed a $500 million "bridge" loan to tide the company over while the larger loan was arranged.

He has also built credentials with environmentalists by fighting the slaughter of seals in the Pacific Ocean. When an International Fur Seals treaty came to the Senate floor in June of 1981, he wanted to offer an amendment to phase out any U.S. participation in commercial seal killing over a four-year period. He finally settled for language requiring studies of possible employment alternatives for Aleut natives in Alaska besides seal hunting.

"We cannot needlessly continue a vicious cycle," he said, "in which we pay Aleuts to kill seals, and we kill seals in order to have a reason to pay the Aleuts."

**At Home:** Levin's family has been winning and losing at the top levels of Michigan politics for a decade. His brother Sander was beaten twice for governor; his cousin is on the state Supreme Court.

Quiet and deliberate, Carl Levin made few long-term enemies in Michigan politics, and this helped him win consensus approval among Democrats once he became the party's nominee for the Senate in 1978. It has also kept him out of controversy during his Senate career.

Levin made his name as president of the Detroit City Council, where he teamed with Mayor Coleman A. Young, a black, to provide for demolition of thousands of abandoned buildings. The two men strayed apart at times in the late 1970s, but this probably helped Levin as a statewide candidate — it showed suburban voters that he was not inextricably tied to the city's black majority.

The real source of opportunity for Levin, however, was a major misstep by GOP Sen. Robert P. Griffin. Disappointed at losing the contest for Senate Republican leader in 1977, Griffin announced that he would retire the next year, and began skipping numerous votes on the floor. He eventually changed his mind, but not until he had missed a third of the Senate votes over an entire year. Levin said Griffin was obviously tired of the job, and the voters were not hard to convince.

## Committees

**Armed Services** (8th of 8 Democrats)
Preparedness; Tactical Warfare.

**Governmental Affairs** (8th of 8 Democrats)
Energy, Nuclear Proliferation, and Government Processes; Oversight of Government Management.

**Small Business** (6th of 8 Democrats)
Innovation and Technology.

## Elections

**1978 General**

| | |
|---|---|
| Carl Levin (D ) | 1,484,193 (52 %) |
| Robert Griffin (R ) | 1,362,165 (48 %) |

**1978 Primary**

| | |
|---|---|
| Carl Levin (D ) | 226,584 (39 %) |
| Phil Power (D ) | 115,117 (20 %) |
| Richard F. VanderVeen (D ) | 89,257 (15 %) |
| Anthony Derezinski (D ) | 53,696 (9 %) |
| John Otterbacher (D ) | 50,860 (9 %) |
| Paul Rosenbaum (D ) | 46,892 (8 %) |

## Campaign Finance

| | Receipts | Receipts from PACs | Expenditures |
|---|---|---|---|
| **1978** | | | |
| Levin (D ) | $994,439 | $206,291 (21 %) | $971,775 |
| Griffin (R ) | $1,691,534 | $307,944 (18 %) | $1,681,550 |

## Voting Studies

| | Presidential Support | | Party Unity | | Conservative Coalition | |
|---|---|---|---|---|---|---|
| Year | S | O | S | O | S | O |
| 1980 | 72 | 28 | 80 | 17 | 11 | 86 |
| 1979 | 91 | 8 | 88 | 10 | 5 | 89 |

S = Support      O = Opposition

## Key Votes

**96th Congress**

| | |
|---|---|
| Maintain relations with Taiwan (1979) | N |
| Reduce synthetic fuel development funds (1979) | N |
| Impose nuclear plant moratorium (1979) | Y |
| Kill stronger windfall profits tax (1979) | N |
| Guarantee Chrysler Corp. loans (1979) | Y |
| Approve military draft registration (1980) | N |
| End Revenue Sharing to the states (1980) | N |
| Block Justice Dept. busing suits (1980) | N |

**97th Congress**

| | |
|---|---|
| Restore urban program funding cuts (1981) | Y |

## Interest Group Ratings

| Year | ADA | ACA | AFL-CIO | CCUS-1 | CCUS-2 |
|---|---|---|---|---|---|
| 1980 | 94 | 12 | 95 | 38 | |
| 1979 | 74 | 11 | 95 | 0 | 20 |

# 1 John Conyers Jr. (D)

**Of Detroit — Elected 1964**

**Born:** May 16, 1929, Detroit, Mich.
**Education:** Wayne State U., B.A. 1957, LL.B.
1958.
**Military Career:** Army, 1950-54.
**Profession:** Lawyer.
**Family:** Single.
**Religion:** Baptist.
**Political Career:** No previous office.

**In Washington:** Conyers has carried his image as a rebel within House ranks beyond his junior years and into the period when most members have become power brokers in their own right.

An eight-term veteran at 52, Conyers has come within four places of the Judiciary Committee chairmanship. But his Crime Subcommittee moved relatively few pieces of legislation during six years under his leadership, and some of those went to the floor over his objections. In 1981, when Judiciary reorganized its subcommittees, Conyers took over the one on Criminal Justice, with authority over changes in federal criminal law.

In the past Congress, serving on another subcommittee charged with codification of the criminal code, Conyers questioned the need for such a project, arguing that a revised code might give federal prosecutors too much power. He played little role in the drafting of the bill, and voted against it in subcommittee and full committee. It did not reach the House floor.

In 1979, when Congress restructured and reauthorized the controversial Law Enforcement Assistance Administration, Conyers found himself arguing vehemently against legislation that began in his subcommittee. He said the bill, as rewritten at the full committee level by Chairman Peter W. Rodino Jr., spent too much money on a bureaucratic grant-awarding structure, money that could be used directly to help the hard-core unemployed. He opposed the extension on the House floor as well, but with the help of junior Democrats from the committee it passed anyway. Later its grant system was targeted for extinction by President Reagan and congressional budget cutters.

Gun control has been Conyers' main legislative priority over the past decade, and he continues to plead its case, although he has given up chairmanship of the panel dealing with it. In 1976

the full Judiciary panel reported out a bill banning the domestic manufacture of "Saturday Night Specials" and similar handguns. It was a weaker measure than Conyers wanted, but it had some Republican support, and it represented a tangible achievement for the gun control forces. It never reached the House floor, however, and nothing like it has in the years since. Conyers is running against the tide now, and he has made little recent progress, despite concern over the Reagan shooting.

Outside Judiciary, Conyers has a record of challenging Democratic leaders on a variety of causes. After complaining that House Democrats should have punished five Mississippi members for failing to back the party's 1968 national ticket, he became a frequent leadership critic. In 1971 he waged a symbolic campaign for Speaker against Carl Albert of Oklahoma. He received 20 votes to Albert's 200. Two years later, accusing Albert of "stagnation and reaction," he ran against Albert again. This time the score was 202-25.

He had some of the same problems with the Carter administration. Not long after Carter became president, Conyers began complaining that the White House had forgotten a 1976 campaign promise to back the Humphrey-Hawkins full employment legislation. "We're being bulldozed by a fantastically successful new administration in the White House," Conyers said in 1977, calling facetiously for a "national day of prayer" to focus

---

**1st District: Detroit — North central, Highland Park.** Population: 393,444 (16% decrease since 1970). Race: White 44,923 (11%), Black 341,928 (87%), Others 6,583 (2%). Spanish origin: 3,219 (1%).

---

national attention on the "Carter dilemma."

By the end of 1978, the situation was much worse. Conyers stalked out of a White House meeting between Carter and the Congressional Black Caucus after Carter turned down his demand for a Camp David "summit conference" on unemployment problems. The next year, he was one of five House members who broke publicly with Carter to urge that Sen. Edward M. Kennedy be drafted to run for president. Conyers stuck with Kennedy through the New York convention in 1980, but agreed to support Carter in the fall campaign against Ronald Reagan and John B. Anderson.

The congressman's role as an "elder militant" within the House and the Democratic Party is not the one many observers would have predicted in his early congressional years. Elected to the House in 1964 at age 35, he represented a new activist generation of blacks in politics and seemed to be on the verge of national leadership. "He is without question the leading Negro spokesman in the House," the *Chicago Tribune* wrote of Conyers in 1967, "and seems to be moving rapidly toward the spot of leading Negro spokesman in the country."

Conyers served on the committee that investigated misconduct charges against Adam Clayton Powell, the black representative from New York, and signed the committee report that recommended Powell's censure, cooperating with House leaders but earning the scorn of Powell, once his political hero, who called Conyers "a black Judas."

In his second term, Conyers almost single-handedly caused the defeat of a redistricting bill that would have permitted malapportioned states to delay the redrawing of congressional districts for five years. In 1968, he held back his support for Hubert H. Humphrey until late in Humphrey's fall presidential campaign, joining up in Detroit in October with a rousing speech that attracted national attention and was thought to influence a portion of the black vote in Humphrey's direction. The next year, he led seven of the nine black members of Congress to the Senate Judiciary Committee to testify against the Haynsworth nomination to the Supreme Court.

The current Conyers seems more of a legislative and political outsider than the one of a decade ago. In 1979, he missed 56 percent of all the House roll calls, more than any other healthy member. In 1980, however, he voted 80 percent of the time.

**At Home:** Conyers is no outsider in the mostly-black inner-city district he has represented since 1964. In every general election in which he has faced opposition, his winning percentage has increased over the previous time. Even the unfavorable publicity he received from his low attendance record in 1979 did not prevent him from winning his highest percentage ever in 1980.

The son of an autoworker, Conyers became interested in politics while in law school and worked loyally in the party apparatus. The creation in 1964 of a second black-majority district in Detroit gave him his first opportunity to run for office. He ran on a platform of "Equality, Jobs and Peace," pledging to strengthen the United Nations and to exempt low-income families from paying federal income tax.

Among the qualifications Conyers cited for holding office were three years as a district aide to Rep. John D. Dingell and service on a panel of lawyers picked by President Kennedy to look for ways of easing racial tensions in the South. Conyers won the primary by just 108 votes over Richard H. Austin, a Detroit accountant who has remained a political rival ever since.

Racial troubles in Conyers' district exploded in 1967, when rioting destroyed many blocks in the heart of the district. Conyers was booed when he stood atop a car telling rioters to return to their homes. Later his office was gutted by fire. But those episodes had no lasting political impact, nor did his initial reluctance to support Humphrey in 1968.

Conyers' only two primary challenges have been token affairs. Nevertheless, his relationships with Mayor Coleman A. Young and the United Auto Workers — the major political powers of Detroit — are not particularly friendly. That could cause Conyers trouble in the redistricting process. His district, like the four others that include parts of Detroit, has lost substantial population, and the state is losing one seat in the House. All other Democrats in the Detroit delegation are on much friendlier terms with Young and the UAW.

**The District:** The 1st District covers the north-central third of Detroit, which is the nation's largest black-majority city. When the district was first created in 1964, it was about 50 percent black. Now more than 80 percent of the residents are black. In every election, the 1st produces some of the highest Democratic percentages in the state.

The 1st is in better economic shape than the 13th District — Detroit's other black district. About two-thirds of the homes are owner-occupied, compared to only a third in the 13th. The median family income is higher in the 1st, as is the average number of school years completed.

**587**

But like all of Detroit, the 1st District depends on the auto industry, and unemployment is a perpetual problem.

Within the district, and surrounded by Detroit, is the city of Highland Park. Once a white ethnic bastion, it is now increasingly black, although just as middle-class as it was when dominated by Eastern Europeans and Italians. From 1968 until 1975 its mayor was the black Republican whom Conyers first defeated for his House seat in 1964.

## Committees

**Government Operatons** (6th of 23 Democrats)
Commerce, Consumer, and Monetary Affairs; Manpower and Housing.

**Juiciary** (5th of 16 Democrats)
Criminal Justice, chairman; Crime.

## Elections

**1980 General**

| | |
|---|---|
| John Conyers Jr. (D) | 123,286 (95%) |
| William Bell (R) | 6,244 (5%) |

**1978 General**

| | |
|---|---|
| John Conyers Jr. (D) | 89,646 (93%) |
| Robert Arnold (R) | 6,878 (7%) |

**Previous Winning Percentages**

| | | | |
|---|---|---|---|
| 1976 (92%) | 1974 (91%) | 1972 (88%) | 1970 (88%) |
| 1968 (100%) | 1966 (84%) | 1964 (84%) | |

**District Vote For President**

| | 1980 | | 1976 | | 1972 |
|---|---|---|---|---|---|
| D | 126,428 (92 %) | D | 128,858 (89%) | D | 137,928 (85 %) |
| R | 7,760 (6 %) | R | 14,936 (10%) | R | 22,715 (14 %) |

## Campaign Finance

| | Receipts | Receipts from PACs | Expenditures |
|---|---|---|---|
| **1980** | | | |
| Conyers (D) | $23,788 | $6,950 (30%) | $20,343 |
| **1978** | | | |
| Conyers (D) | $17,267 | $10,550 (61%) | $23,759 |

## Voting Studies

| | Presidential Support | | Party Unity | | Conservative Coalition | |
|---|---|---|---|---|---|---|
| **Year** | **S** | **O** | **S** | **O** | **S** | **O** |
| 1980 | 56 | 29 | 76 | 8 | 8 | 80 |
| 1979 | 34 | 10 | 46 | 6 | 2 | 40 |
| 1978 | 49 | 11 | 47 | 6 | 4 | 48 |

| Year | S | O | S | O | S | O |
|---|---|---|---|---|---|---|
| 1977 | 59 | 24 | 73 | 9 | 6 | 77 |
| 1976 | 8 | 61 | 60 | 7 | 7 | 62 |
| 1975 | 27 | 52 | 61 | 5 | 4 | 61 |
| 1974 (Ford) | 24 | 56 | | | | |
| 1974 | 26 | 53 | 72 | 12 | 5 | 76 |
| 1973 | 20 | 50 | 64 | 8 | 2 | 65 |
| 1972 | 41 | 43 | 74 | 9 | 5 | 84 |
| 1971 | 19 | 61 | 60 | 7 | 2 | 67 |
| 1970 | 23 | 35 | 56 | 13 | 2 | 61 |
| 1969 | 19 | 45 | 55 | 11 | 4 | 69 |
| 1968 | 40 | 7 | 43 | 5 | 2 | 55 |
| 1967 | 56 | 17 | 65 | 10 | 4 | 76 |
| 1966 | 57 | 9 | 65 | 5 | 0 | 84 |
| 1965 | 77 | 7 | 73 | 3 | 0 | 76 |

S = Support     O = Opposition

## Key Votes

**96th Congress**

| | |
|---|---|
| Weaken Carter oil profits tax (1979) | N |
| Reject hospital cost control plan (1979) | N |
| Implement Panama Canal Treaties (1979) | ? |
| Establish Department of Education (1979) | N |
| Approve Anti-busing Amendment (1979) | N |
| Guarantee Chrysler Corp. loans (1979) | Y |
| Approve military draft registration (1980) | N |
| Aid Sandinista regime in Nicaragua (1980) | ? |
| Strengthen fair housing laws (1980) | Y |

**97th Congress**

| | |
|---|---|
| Reagan budget proposal (1981) | N |

## Interest Group Ratings

| Year | ADA | ACA | AFL-CIO | CCUS |
|---|---|---|---|---|
| 1980 | 78 | 25 | 89 | 59 |
| 1979 | 79 | 13 | 100 | 8 |
| 1978 | 45 | 11 | 94 | 21 |
| 1977 | 85 | 8 | 87 | 19 |
| 1976 | 75 | 12 | 86 | 0 |
| 1975 | 79 | 9 | 89 | 25 |
| 1974 | 87 | 17 | 89 | 0 |
| 1973 | 72 | 11 | 100 | 0 |
| 1972 | 88 | 6 | 91 | 17 |
| 1971 | 76 | 17 | 78 | - |
| 1970 | 92 | 21 | 100 | 10 |
| 1969 | 100 | 29 | 100 | - |
| 1968 | 100 | 6 | 75 | - |
| 1967 | 100 | 10 | 100 | 0 |
| 1966 | 94 | 14 | 100 | - |
| 1965 | 100 | 0 | - | 10 |

# 2  Carl D. Pursell (R)

**Of Plymouth — Elected 1976**

**Born:** Dec. 19, 1932, Imlay City, Mich.
**Education:** Eastern Mich. U., B.A. 1957, M.A. 1962.
**Military Career:** Army Reserve, 1957-65.
**Profession:** Teacher, publisher, real estate agent.
**Family:** Wife, Peggy Jean Brown; three children.
**Religion:** Baptist.
**Political Career:** Wayne County Commission, 1969-71; Mich. Senate, 1971-76; unsuccessfully sought Republican nomination for Mich. Senate, 1966.

**In Washington:** Pursell's seat on the Appropriations subcommittee handling education and health gives him a chance to pursue his relatively liberal goals outside the spotlight of the House floor, where he is in a minority among his own party.

It is not always easy for GOP moderates to get on the Labor, Health and Human Services Subcommittee, but Pursell made it after one term with the help of Robert Michel of Illinois, now the party leader, who played a key role in the assignments. In his first two years on the panel, Pursell lived up to his moderate reputation, sometimes siding with the committee's Democrats but more often trying to work out bipartisan compromises.

The assignment is also politically crucial to Pursell, because it gives him a chance to influence federal help for the University of Michigan, whose 46,000 full-time students make it a dominant industry in the district. Pursell is not an uncritical vote for every federal education subsidy — he has argued for studies of waste in school aid to the poor — but he frequently speaks out against cutting the education budget.

In 1979, when President Carter tried to make deep cuts in federal grants to medical and nursing schools, Pursell was on the floor leading the opposition. He said the administration was using 7-year-old figures in deciding what to cut. "The nursing profession is not getting any input into the decision-making process," Pursell complained. "It is an insult to the nurses." Most House members were similarly persuaded, in part by a heavy lobbying campaign, and the money was restored.

Pursell has tried to persuade the Department of Education to spend more money for teaching the gifted, and for physical fitness. When the 1981 Labor-HHS bill came to the floor, he argued that plenty of money was being spent on nutrition but not enough on physical education programs.

Since Pursell's subcommittee also handles labor spending, he has been in a position to fight for the threatened trade readjustment assistance program, which provides special unemployment money to some of his district's auto workers. He favored a 1980 amendment to earmark $20 million in TRA money for retraining rather than plain compensation. "I am not sure $20 million is adequate," he said. "Perhaps it should be $50 million."

**At Home:** Pursell's moderate-to-liberal Republicanism is well-suited to a district in which academics, blue-collar workers and conservative farmers mingle in uneasy combination. His liberal social views and independence from the national GOP help with the university community at Ann Arbor. The autoworkers in the Wayne County portion of the district support Pursell for his pro-labor views. And rural Monroe County generally prefers any Republican at all to a Democrat.

Pursell took his political cues from Marvin L. Esch, the five-term Republican whom he succeeded when Esch ran unsuccessfully for the Senate in 1976. Slightly more liberal than Esch, Pursell has been able to knit together the differ-

---

**2nd District: Southeast — Ann Arbor, Livonia.** Population: 505,001 (8% increase since 1970). Race: White 461,716 (91%), Black 30,911 (6%), Others 12,374 (2%). Spanish origin: 6,778 (1%).

**Carl D. Pursell, R-Mich.**

ent parts of his district at least as well as his predecessor.

He won his first term in 1976 by 344 votes, surviving because of his strength in Wayne County, which he represented in the state Senate. He won 65 percent there, while losing the other two counties to Edward C. Pierce, a much more liberal Ann Arbor doctor.

In 1980 Pursell had another strong challenge, this one from consumer advocate Kathleen O'Reilly. By then, however, Pursell was known and liked throughout the district. Although O'Reilly came close to carrying Washtenaw County (Ann Arbor), Pursell easily won the other two parts of the district for a fairly comfortable victory.

**The District:** Despite the 2nd's nominally Democratic character, Republicans have held it in every election but one since 1932.

Although they are Democrats, the blue-collar voters in the Wayne County suburbs of Livonia, Northville and Plymouth have attained a comfortable status that tempts them into voting Republican a good deal of the time. The city of Ann Arbor, dominated by the University of Michigan and associated research facilities, is the state's foremost liberal stronghold. In between and to the south are farmers and poorer blue-collar workers, who share neither the social views of Ann Arbor's liberals nor the economic interests of Livonia's prosperous residents.

Washtenaw County has the distinction of being the only county in the nation that backed George McGovern in 1972 and Gerald Ford in 1976. In fact, in every election since 1960, the county has switched back and forth between Democratic and Republican presidential candidates.

## Committees

**Appropriations** (15th of 22 Republicans)
Labor-HHS; Transportation.

## Elections

**1980 General**

| | |
|---|---|
| Carl Pursell (R) | 115,562 (57%) |
| Kathleen O'Reilly (D) | 83,550 (41%) |

**1980 Primary**

| | |
|---|---|
| Carl Pursell (R) | 11,946 (90%) |
| Helen Gotowka (R) | 1,383 (10%) |

**1978 General**

| | |
|---|---|
| Carl Pursell (R) | 97,503 (68%) |
| Earl Greene (D) | 45,631 (32%) |

**Previous Winning Percentage**

1976 (50%)

**District Vote For President**

| | 1980 | | 1976 | | 1972 |
|---|---|---|---|---|---|
| D | 87,939 (40 %) | D | 89,584 (45%) | D | 85,093 (44 %) |
| R | 105,783 (48 %) | R | 106,374 (53%) | R | 106,154 (54 %) |
| I | 20,7500 (10 %) | | | | |

## Campaign Finance

| | Receipts | Receipts from PACs | Expenditures |
|---|---|---|---|
| **1980** | | | |
| Pursell (R) | $159,675 | $84,525 (53%) | $143,576 |
| O'Reilly (D) | $116,765 | $28,850 (25%) | $116,058 |

| 1978 | | | |
|---|---|---|---|
| Pursell (R) | $111,159 | $33,655 (30%) | $94,764 |
| Greene (D) | $27,348 | (0%) | $27,212 |

## Voting Studies

| | Presidential Support | | Party Unity | | Conservative Coalition | |
|---|---|---|---|---|---|---|
| Year | S | O | S | O | S | O |
| 1980 | 58 | 30 | 37 | 49 | 27 | 61 |
| 1979 | 50 | 37 | 38 | 47 | 48 | 42 |
| 1978 | 58 | 35 | 47 | 40 | 46 | 41 |
| 1977 | 49 | 42 | 47 | 38† | 49 | 40 |

S = Support  O = Opposition
† Not eligible for all recorded votes.

## Key Votes

**96th Congress**

| | |
|---|---|
| Weaken Carter oil profits tax (1979) | N |
| Reject hospital cost control plan (1979) | Y |
| Implement Panama Canal Treaties (1979) | N |
| Establish Department of Education (1979) | Y |
| Approve Anti-busing Amendment (1979) | Y |
| Guarantee Chrysler Corp. loans (1979) | Y |
| Approve military draft registration (1980) | N |
| Aid Sandinista regime in Nicaragua (1980) | Y |
| Strengthen fair housing laws (1980) | Y |

**97th Congress**

| | |
|---|---|
| Reagan budget proposal (1981) | Y |

## Interest Group Ratings

| Year | ADA | ACA | AFL-CIO | CCUS |
|---|---|---|---|---|
| 1980 | 89 | 36 | 71 | 72 |
| 1979 | 53 | 38 | 65 | 47 |
| 1978 | 60 | 31 | 56 | 65 |
| 1977 | 35 | 60 | 48 | 63 |

# *3 Howard Wolpe (D)

**Of Lansing — Elected 1978**

**Born:** Nov. 2, 1939, Los Angeles, Calif.
**Education:** Reed College, B.A. 1960; Mass. Institute of Technology, Ph.D. 1967.
**Profession:** Political science professor.
**Family:** Wife, C. Jeanene Taylor; one child.
**Religion:** Jewish.
**Political Career:** Kalamazoo City Commission, 1969-72; Mich. House, 1973-77; unsuccessful Democratic candidate for U.S. House, 1976.

**In Washington:** Wolpe secured a prize chairmanship in 1981 when Foreign Affairs Democrats chose him to lead the Africa Subcommittee, giving him the job over the angry opposition of committee conservatives.

An acknowledged expert on Africa, Wolpe lived in Nigeria for two years, has written two books on Nigerian politics, and taught courses on African affairs at Western Michigan University. But in his first term, he had not been one of the most active members of the Africa Subcommittee. He had participated only sporadically during subcommittee hearings in 1979 on U.S. strategic interests in Africa, and in early 1980 on the budget for U.S. foreign aid programs in Africa.

He quickly became an active chairman in 1981. He took the lead as his subcommittee voted 7-0 in May against repealing the Clark amendment, which bans aid to factions in Angola. The Reagan administration had argued for repeal, but Wolpe said such a move at that time would drive the leftist regime in power in Angola further toward Cuba and the Soviet Union.

Along with other committee liberals, Wolpe has been an outspoken critic of military aid to Zaire, the southern Africa nation ruled by dictator Mobutu Sese Seko. Wolpe has called Zaire the "most corrupt" country in Africa. During the last two years of the Carter administration, he and other critics succeeded in reducing military aid to Zaire but were unable to force a full suspension of the money.

Often Wolpe tries to persuade colleagues to look at the effects of U.S. foreign policy from an African point of view. At one hearing in 1979, for example, he said Africans view as "absurd" the competition between the United States and the Soviet Union to win the favor of African nations. "They know in advance," he said, "that if they are going to call themselves communists, they get assistance from one side; anti-communist, they get assistance from another side."

Wolpe maintained one of the more liberal voting records in the House in his first term, but he broke with most liberal Democrats in 1979 on an issue important to his district: cereal. He fought to end the Federal Trade Commission's decade-old attempt to break up what it saw as a "shared monopoly" by three cereal manufacturing companies. One of the companies, Kellogg's, is headquartered in Wolpe's district; a second, General Foods, has two plants there. Wolpe has supported congressional vetoes of all FTC regulations and backed other restrictions on the commission's ability to monitor business operations. He supports a legislative veto over other federal regulations as well.

Wolpe is also a member of the House Science and Technology Committee, where he has been a critic of the nuclear power industry. In 1979, after the Three Mile Island accident, he supported a six-month moratorium on permits for new nuclear plant construction.

**At Home:** Wolpe is only the second Democrat in the 20th century who has won this district in south central Michigan. He has done it in spite of his voting record, rather than because of it.

Wolpe's trademark — in the Kalamazoo City Council, in the Michigan Legislature, and in the House — has been constituent service, carried out with a personal touch and occasional flamboy-

---

**3rd District: South central — Kalamazoo, Battle Creek.** Population: 506,935 (8% increase since 1970). Race: White 466,302 (92%), Black 31,711 (6%), Others 8,922 (2%). Spanish origin: 7,431 (1%).

ance. After a narrow loss to Republican Rep. Garry Brown in 1976, Wolpe went into constituent service as a profession, serving as field representative for Sen. Donald Riegle for two years while preparing his second campaign.

His goal for the rematch was to reduce Brown's margin in Eaton County, a fast-growing Republican suburb of Lansing. He bought a home there and his wife joined the local Welcome Wagon to establish personal rapport with other new residents. Without losing any support in the district's other population center, Kalamazoo, Wolpe managed to win 46 percent in Eaton County, compared to 39 percent on his first try. That was enough for a narrow victory.

By 1980 Wolpe had the personal popularity to overcome a well-financed campaign by a Kalamazoo millionaire and former mayor, James Gilmore. The Republican tried in vain to exploit Wolpe's liberal voting record. But Wolpe had given the voters what they wanted on local issues, especially by fighting the Federal Trade Commission for its attacks on the cereal industry in Battle Creek. Wolpe carried Battle Creek by an increased margin in 1980, enough to offset Gilmore's support in Kalamazoo.

**The District:** The medium-sized industrial cities of Kalamazoo and Battle Creek have given Democrats a chance here in recent years, but it still takes unusual circumstances to interfere with Republican majorities.

Battle Creek, the home of Kellogg and General Foods, is the more Democratic and smaller of the two. Kalamazoo — home of The Upjohn Company and Checker Motors — has a strong conservative Dutch influence and rarely backs Democrats in statewide contests, but has gone for Wolpe. The Lansing suburbs in Eaton County, in the northern part of the district, are the most Republican areas. The Lansing-area voters have little contact with either of the district's major cities, or with the soybean, celery and peppermint farmers who occupy the flat, fertile land in between.

## Committees

**Foreign Affairs** (14th of 21 Democrats)
Africa, chairman; International Economic Policy and Trade.

**Science and Technology** (16th of 23 Democrats)
Energy Development and Applications; Energy Research and Production.

## Elections

**1980 General**

| | |
|---|---|
| Howard Wolpe (D) | 113,080 (52%) |
| James Gilmore (R) | 102,591 (47%) |

**1978 General**

| | |
|---|---|
| Howard Wolpe (D) | 83,932 (51%) |
| Garry Brown (R) | 79,572 (49%) |

**District Vote For President**

| | 1980 | | 1976 | | 1972 |
|---|---|---|---|---|---|
| D | 83,515 (35 %) | D | 80,026 (39%) | D | 71,714 (37%) |
| R | 129,069 (54 %) | R | 119,633 (59%) | R | 118,361 (61%) |
| I | 21,702 (9 %) | | | | |

## Campaign Finance

| | Receipts | Receipts from PACs | Expenditures |
|---|---|---|---|
| **1980** | | | |
| Wolpe (D) | $338,731 | $27,075 (8%) | $341,910 |
| Gilmore (R) | $724,890 | $112,832 (16%) | $702,649 |

| | | | |
|---|---|---|---|
| **1976** | | | |
| Wolpe (D) | $221,161 | $83,423 (38%) | $219,397 |
| Brown (R) | $226,170 | $137,204 (61%) | $242,768 |

## Voting Studies

| | Presidential Support | | Party Unity | | Conservative Coalition | |
|---|---|---|---|---|---|---|
| Year | S | O | S | O | S | O |
| 1980 | 70 | 27 | 85 | 15 | 17 | 81 |
| 1979 | 81 | 18 | 92 | 7 | 12 | 88 |

S = Support          O = Opposition

## Key Votes

**96th Congress**

| | |
|---|---|
| Weaken Carter oil profits tax (1979) | N |
| Reject hospital cost control plan (1979) | N |
| Implement Panama Canal Treaties (1979) | Y |
| Establish Department of Education (1979) | Y |
| Approve Anti-busing Amendment (1979) | N |
| Guarantee Chrysler Corp. loans (1979) | Y |
| Approve military draft registration (1980) | N |
| Aid Sandinista regime in Nicaragua (1980) | Y |
| Strengthen fair housing laws (1980) | Y |

**97th Congress**

| | |
|---|---|
| Reagan budget proposal (1981) | N |

## Interest Group Ratings

| Year | ADA | ACA | AFL-CIO | CCUS |
|---|---|---|---|---|
| 1980 | 94 | 30 | 79 | 71 |
| 1979 | 100 | 8 | 90 | 11 |

# 4 Mark Siljander (R)

**Of Three Rivers — Elected 1981**

**Born:** June 11, 1951, Chicago, Ill.
**Education:** Western Mich. U., B.A. 1972; M.A. 1973.
**Profession:** Public official.
**Family:** Single.
**Religion:** Non-denominational Christian.
**Political Career:** Fabius township trustee, 1973-76; Mich. House, 1977-81; Republican nominee for Mich. House, 1974.

**The Member:** Siljander kept Budget Director David Stockman from picking his successor in Michigan's always-Republican 4th District.

In a GOP primary to choose a nominee for the seat Stockman vacated, the 30-year-old Siljander unexpectedly defeated John Globensky, who was chairman of Stockman's three congressional campaigns and inherited Stockman's organization and fund-raising contacts.

Siljander's uniformly conservative values, including opposition to abortion and forced busing, endeared him to right-to-lifers and fundamentalist Christians. Disregarding polls showing Globensky comfortably ahead, Siljander kept his supporters busy planting yard signs and contacting voters by telephone. He won the GOP nomination over Globensky and five others by less than 1,000 votes.

The 4th District has not elected a Democratic representative since 1932, so Siljander was a heavy favorite over the Democratic nominee, Cass County Commisioner Johnie Rodebush. When Rodebush complained that Siljander was preoccupied with "moral issues," the Republican talked more often about his strong support for the Reagan-Stockman plan to cut taxes and the federal budget. Siljander won easily.

During his years as a state legislator, Siljander's main interest was cutting property taxes. He helped found a statewide tax revolt organization called the Tax Effeciency Association of Michigan (TEAM) and launched an unsuccessful petition drive to put a property tax limitation amendment on the 1980 Michigan ballot.

**The District:** Stretching 155 miles along Michigan's southern border and up the eastern shore of Lake Michigan for another 55 miles, the 4th is one of the most Republican districts in the nation. It is largely agricultural, with only two small population centers, one at Adrian in the east, the other at Benton Harbor and St. Joseph on the lake.

## Committees

**Small Business** (17th of 17 Republicans)
Antitrust and Restraint of Trade Activities Affecting Small Business.

**Veterans' Affairs** (13th of 14 Republicans)
Compensation, Pension and Insurance; Education, Training and Employment.

## Election

**1981 Special Election**

| | |
|---|---|
| Mark Siljander (R) | 36,046 (74%) |
| Johnie Rodebush (D) | 12,462 (26%) |

**1981 Special Primary**

| | |
|---|---|
| Mark Siljander (R) | 17,845 (40%) |
| John Globensky (R) | 16,993 (36%) |
| John Mowat (R) | 10,385 (22%) |

**District Vote For President**

| | 1980 | | 1976 | | 1972 |
|---|---|---|---|---|---|
| **D** | 62,760 (33%) | **D** | 77,086 (40%) | **D** | 55,739 (32%) |
| **R** | 112,328 (60%) | **R** | 111,830 (58%) | **R** | 116,374 (66%) |
| **I** | 10,970 (6%) | | | | |

## Campaign Finance

| | Receipts | Receipts from PACs | Expenditures |
|---|---|---|---|
| **1980*** | | | |
| Siljander (R) | $92,771 | $29,135 (31%) | $100,215 |
| Rodebush (D) | $25,494 | $5,806 (23%) | $21,473 |

*Figures include information reported by the candidates to the Federal Election Commision through May 11, 1981.

**4th District: South — Benton Harbor, Adrian.** Population: 515,197 (10% increase since 1970). Race: White 470,608 (91%), Black 36,294 (7%), Others 7,795 (2%). Spanish origin: 9,391 (2%).

# 5 Harold S. Sawyer (R)

**Of Rockford — Elected 1976**

**Born:** March 21, 1920, San Francisco, Calif.
**Education:** U. of Calif., Berkley, B.A. 1940;
Hastings Law School, J.D. 1943.
**Military Career:** Navy, 1941-45.
**Profession:** Lawyer.
**Family:** Wife, Marcia Steketee; four children.
**Religion:** Episcopalian.
**Political Career:** Kent County prosecutor,
1975-76.

**In Washington:** Sawyer probably has a more acute legal mind than the district's last Republican congressman, Gerald R. Ford, but he will never achieve Ford's easy familiarity with the personal side of the legislative process. A blunt man with a knack for public speaking, he has not been able to use that talent as effectively in Washington as he did in the courtrooms of Grand Rapids. The irreverence that reporters often find interesting and quotable occasionally puzzles his more strait-laced colleagues.

On the subject of criminal law, however, Sawyer has been an important part of the Judiciary Committee. He took an active role in the proposed revision of the federal criminal code during the 96th Congress. His personal efforts included an amendment retaining stiff penalties for possession of marijuana, and deletion of language allowing lawyers to be present in a grand jury room. The legislation did not reach the floor.

During the previous Congress, as a member of the Assassinations Committee, he disagreed with the committee's conclusion that there was a probable conspiracy to kill President Kennedy. He was an occasional source of news for the press in advance of formal release.

Sawyer also made news briefly in July of 1980, during the investigation of Billy Carter's dealings with Libya. He told reporters that President Carter had shown his brother secret diplomatic cables praising Billy's behavior during a trip to Libya. Sawyer was prominent for one hectic night on the evening news programs, but the issue died quickly.

Sawyer's four years on Judiciary have convinced nearly all his colleagues of his legal skill. But some still wonder about his political sensitivity. In 1978, when Judiciary was considering a controversial extension of the time period for ratification of the Equal Rights Amendment, Sawyer was lobbied hard by Ford and his wife,

Betty, to support it. He was the swing vote on the closely divided committee, and the Fords thought they had won his commitment.

But ERA supporters, trying to build a majority coalition, decided to settle for an extension of 39 months, rather than the previous seven years. Sawyer claimed he was unaware of any compromise and refused to support the amendment. Later Sawyer voted for the shortened extension, but by that time he had succeeded in annoying those on both sides of the issue.

When his district was hit by a Chrysler plant closing, Sawyer announced he was generally opposed to Chrysler aid, suggesting instead that states with Chrysler plants float revenue bonds for the company and lean on Chrysler suppliers to buy the bonds. He also made an issue of the UAW's $1.3 billion contract with Chrysler, arguing that the government was subsidizing a wage increase. But in the end, Sawyer wound up voting for the Chrysler bill, once again leaving neither side particularly happy with him.

**At Home:** In Grand Rapids, as in Washington, Sawyer's popularity does not equal Ford's. To win the seat in 1976, Sawyer had to rely heavily on Ford's coattails. As an appointed county prosecutor, running for his first elective office, he based most of his campaign around the incumbent Democrat's lack of support for the

---

**5th District: West central — Grand Rapids.** Population: 509,317 (9% increase since 1970). Race: White 465,810 (91%), Black 33,126 (7%), Others 10,381 (2%). Spanish origin: 9,783 (2%).

---

Ford administration. Ford's climactic Election Eve rally in Grand Rapids, with Sawyer at his side, helped generate the highest turnout the district had seen to that time.

Without Ford to help him in 1978, Sawyer was nearly beaten by Democrat Dale R. Sprik, a two-time loser for county office. Sprik held Sawyer to a margin of 1,172 votes — the smallest of any re-elected Republican in the country. Some voters were bothered by rumors of heavy drinking by Sawyer, and while that was not directly raised in the campaign, it helped Sprik make the case that the incumbent had not represented the district the way Ford had. Two years later, facing Sprik for a second time, Sawyer worked harder and won a more comfortable victory.

**The District:** This Grand-Rapids-based district has a heavy Dutch influence and a tradi-tional Republican history. From 1913 until 1973, when Ford resigned to become vice president, the area was represented by only three men, all Republicans.

Its one recent Democratic winner, Richard F. Vander Veen, who succeeded Ford in 1974, would never have won his two elections without the help of many Republicans — including Sawyer — who hoped to force President Nixon out of office by demonstrating his unpopularity in solid Republican areas. A split within the GOP allowed Vander Veen to win one full term before the district went Republican again for Sawyer in 1976.

There are a few signs of change, however. In the post-Ford era, Kent County (Grand Rapids), which accounts for nearly 90 percent of the district's vote, has sent a few more Democrats than Republicans to the state Legislature.

## Committees

**Judiciary** (9th of 12 Republicans)
Courts, Civil Liberties and the Administration of Justice; Crime.

**Veterans' Affairs** (5th of 14 Republicans)
Education, Training and Employment; Oversight and Investigations.

## Elections

**1980 General**

| | |
|---|---|
| Harold Sawyer (R) | 118,061 (53%) |
| Dale Sprik (D) | 101,737 (46%) |

**1980 Primary**

| | |
|---|---|
| Harold Sawyer (R) | 23,970 (81%) |
| Bruce Kamps (R) | 5,484 (19%) |

**1978 General**

| | |
|---|---|
| Harold Sawyer (R) | 81,794 (49%) |
| Dale Sprik (D) | 80,622 (49%) |

**Previous Winning Percentages**

1976 (53%)

**District Vote For President**

| 1980 | | 1976 | | 1972 | |
|---|---|---|---|---|---|
| D | 81,573 (35 %) | D | 67,426 (32%) | D | 75,224 (38%) |
| R | 128,106 (55 %) | R | 141,655 (67%) | R | 117,832 (60%) |
| I | 19,752 (9 %) | | | | |

## Campaign Finance

| | Receipts | Receipts from PACs | Expen-ditures |
|---|---|---|---|
| **1980** | | | |
| Sawyer (R) | $363,976 | $125,276 (34%) | $366,147 |
| Sprik (D) | $194,106 | $46,572 (19%) | $5,285 |

| **1978** | | | |
|---|---|---|---|
| Sawyer (R) | $139,056 | $27,365 (20%) | $134,454 |
| Sprik (D) | $69,710 | $11,300 (16%) | $69,641 |

## Voting Studies

| | Presidential Support | | Party Unity | | Conservative Coalition | |
|---|---|---|---|---|---|---|
| Year | S | O | S | O | S | O |
| 1980 | 50 | 50 | 81 | 16 | 84 | 13 |
| 1979 | 38 | 58 | 74 | 22 | 81 | 13 |
| 1978 | 38 | 50 | 66 | 24 | 71 | 18 |
| 1977 | 44 | 34 | 60 | 27 | 63 | 22 |

S = Support          O = Opposition

## Key Votes

**96th Congress**

| | |
|---|---|
| Weaken Carter oil profits tax (1979) | Y |
| Reject hospital cost control plan (1979) | ? |
| Implement Panama Canal Treaties (1979) | Y |
| Establish Department of Education (1979) | N |
| Approve Anti-busing Amendment (1979) | Y |
| Guarantee Chrysler Corp. loans (1979) | Y |
| Approve military draft registration (1980) | Y |
| Aid Sandinista regime in Nicaragua (1980) | N |
| Strengthen fair housing laws (1980) | N |

**97th Congress**

| | |
|---|---|
| Reagan budget proposal (1981) | Y |

## Interest Group Ratings

| Year | ADA | ACA | AFL-CIO | CCUS |
|---|---|---|---|---|
| 1980 | 11 | 83 | 24 | 79 |
| 1979 | 16 | 85 | 25 | 94 |
| 1978 | 25 | 79 | 11 | 86 |
| 1977 | 20 | 65 | 25 | 100 |

**595**

# 6 Jim Dunn (R)

Of East Lansing — Elected 1980

**Born:** July 21, 1943, Detroit, Mich.
**Education:** Mich. State U., B.A. 1967.
**Profession:** Building contractor.
**Family:** Wife, Gayle Yerkey; three children.
**Religion:** Episcopalian.
**Political Career:** No previous career.

**The Member:** A house painter who became a millionaire building contractor, Dunn is a believer in the work ethic. His business career and his political success have both been self-made, and his congressional activities reveal a streak of independence.

Dunn voted for the Reagan-endorsed budget plan, but complained that cutbacks in education were too severe and promised to work for restorations later. On the Science Committee, he resisted administration lobbying pressure and voted to terminate construction of the Clinch River nuclear breeder reactor. Dunn said one lobbyist threatened that $2 million for a cyclotron at Michigan State University would be cut if he voted against Clinch River. Reagan's chief lobbyist, Max Friedersdorf, called Dunn to say the White House did not endorse such tactics.

The major employer in the 6th District is the auto industry, and Dunn introduced legislation to eliminate or revise pollution and safety regulations. He called for tax incentives to stimulate purchase of new cars and depreciations and deductions for equipment to help the industry convert to more fuel-efficient cars.

Determination and money deserve nearly equal credit for Dunn's upset victory over Democratic Rep. Bob Carr. Carr's complacency was another factor. After increasing his margin from 647 votes in 1974 to 23,000 in 1978, Carr did not consider Dunn a threat. But Dunn began running TV ads in early 1980 to increase his recognition, and outspent Carr by nearly $200,000.

**The District:** Michigan State provides Democratic votes, but the 6th has long been a GOP stronghold. Even during Carr's three terms, it regularly backed GOP statewide candidates.

The university area and the state government enclave in Lansing are the district's most visible political communities. There is a heavy blue-collar vote in Lansing and Jackson, where large auto plants are located. But unlike Detroit's autoworkers, many of those in the 6th were raised in a rural Republican setting. They continue to reflect that background.

## Committees

**Science and Technology** (16th of 17 Republicans)
Energy Development and Applications; Transportation, Aviation and Materials.

**Veterans' Affairs** (9th of 14 Republicans)
Hospitals and Health Care; Housing and Memorial Affairs.

## Elections

**1980 General**

| | |
|---|---:|
| Jim Dunn (R) | 111,272 (51%) |
| Bob Carr (D) | 108,548 (49%) |

**1980 Primary**

| | |
|---|---:|
| Jim Dunn (R) | 21,270 (81%) |
| Aubrey Radcliffe (R) | 5,063 (19%) |

**District Vote For President**

| | 1980 | | 1976 | | 1972 |
|---|---|---|---|---|---|
| **D** | 84,771 (37%) | **D** | 84,712 (40%) | **D** | 80,875 (40%) |
| **R** | 117,384 (51%) | **R** | 120,258 (57%) | **R** | 115,811 (58%) |
| **I** | 24,499 (11%) | | | | |

## Campaign Finance

| | Receipts | Receipts from PACs | Expenditures |
|---|---|---|---|
| **1980** | | | |
| Dunn (R) | $315,354 | $38,899 (12%) | $294,366 |
| Carr (D) | $147,718 | $63,750 (43%) | $146,725 |

## Key Vote

**97th Congress**

| | |
|---|---:|
| Reagan budget proposal (1981) | Y |

---

**6th District: Central — Lansing, Jackson.** Population: 520,542 (11% increase since 1970). Race: White 473,053 (91%), Black 32,840 (6%), Others 14,649 (3%). Spanish origin: 13,155 (3%).

---

# 7 Dale E. Kildee (D)

**Of Flint — Elected 1976**

**Born:** Sept. 16, 1929, Flint, Mich.
**Education:** Sacred Heart Seminary, B.A. 1952;
U. of Detroit, teaching certificate, 1954; U. of
Mich., M.A. 1962.
**Profession:** Latin Teacher.
**Family:** Wife, Gayle Heyn; three children.
**Religion:** Roman Catholic.
**Political Career:** Mich. House, 1965-75; Mich.
Senate, 1975-77.

**In Washington:** Kildee once studied for the
priesthood, but he switched to political science,
ran for office and now is combining a message of
traditional liberalism with a sort of "Good Sa-
maritan" political style.

He has been known to fill out tax forms for
senior citizens and help fix their leaky roofs. He
has installed a special typewriter in his office so
he can communicate with deaf callers.

As a freshman congressman in 1977, Kildee
launched a crusade against "child pornography."
Revelations in his hometown of Flint about a
growing trade in obscene photos of children set off
a flurry of letters to him in Washington. He
decided to draft a bill setting heavy criminal
penalties for using children in pornographic films
and photographs.

Kildee was convinced a bill like that would be
impossible to oppose on the House floor. But to
get to the floor, it had to go through the Judiciary
Committee, where Michigan Democrat John
Conyers, chairman of the Criminal Justice Subcommittee, considered it a violation of First
Amendment rights. Kildee then rewrote the bill
so it could be considered by Education and Labor,
where he serves. He offered it as an amendment
to child abuse legislation, and it passed. Later
Conyers conceded and moved a milder bill
through his own panel. By 1981, child pornography penalties had become law.

A second Kildee priority on Education and
Labor was the National Community Education
Act of 1978. It provides federal money to encourage local school districts to keep school buildings
open after hours and in summer for community
activities. Kildee has supported strengthening
education for the disadvantaged and minorities,
particularly Indian schools and vocational education programs. He has been a militant critic of
Reagan efforts to cut back spending for school
lunches and other child nutrition programs.

Kildee is also a strong labor loyalist, and
serves on two labor-related subcommittees. One
handles minimum wage legislation; the other,
labor-management relations. Over his first four
years in the House, Kildee had an average AFL-
CIO rating of over 90. His one notable vote
against labor came in 1977, when he opposed a
cargo preference bill supported by maritime
unions. Kildee said the bill's requirement that
imported oil be shipped in U.S. vessels would
boost oil prices too much.

**At Home:** As a Democrat from the General
Motors town of Flint, Kildee draws his political
base from the labor movement he supports in
Washington.

The United Auto Workers and the AFL-CIO
have deserted him only once — when he first ran
for Congress in 1976. Trying to succeed five-term
Rep. Donald W. Riegle Jr., who was running for
the Senate, Kildee left a state senate seat he
had won only two years before. Labor, which had
worked exceptionally hard to help Kildee oust a
26-year state Senate veteran in 1974, felt he
should have served out his four-year term. But
Kildee insisted on making his move.

Winning was relatively easy, even with division in the ranks of labor. Kildee beat a local
union official in the Democratic primary with 76
percent, and went on to trounce his general election opponent. By 1980, Kildee's political
strength was so great that he drew no Republican

---

**7th District: East central — Flint.**
Population: 478,093 (3% increase since 1970).
Race: White 389,912 (82%), Black 78,966
(17%), Others 9,215 (2%). Spanish origin:
8,121 (2%).

---

opposition at all. He was the only Democratic incumbent in the delegation who had a free ride.

After giving up his plans to be a priest, Kildee spent a year studying in Pakistan, then returned to Michigan to teach Latin. By the time he arrived in the Michigan Legislature, he was a political maverick. During his brief state Senate career, he earned the animosity of some of his colleagues as self-appointed head of the "conscience caucus." He attacked the use of state funds for redecorating senators' offices. Kildee also pushed through a "truth in packaging" bill and an act to guarantee civil rights to the handicapped.

**The District:** Flint (Genesee County) has had its own congressional district only since 1964, when it was separated from Lansing. It is the most Democratic district in the state outside the Detroit area, thanks to its heavily blue-collar population.

But the 7th broke its Democratic pattern for Riegle, who won it as a brash 28-year-old GOP challenger in 1966 and held it as a liberal Republican through 1972. When Riegle became a Democrat for the 1974 campaign, the district was more than willing to switch and support him, as it has supported Kildee since 1976.

Unlike some of the other automobile towns, Flint is not an *ethnic* blue-collar area. It has been defined politically by the white Southerners who moved north to work in the auto plants a generation ago. In 1968, George Wallace won 15 percent in Genesee County, his best performance in any of Michigan's urban areas.

The district also has the largest black population outside Detroit's two inner-city districts. The white Southerners and blacks have generally agreed in their Democratic voting preferences, but the mix has also resulted in occasional racial tension.

## Committees

**Education and Labor** (13th of 19 Democrats)
Elementary, Secondary and Vocational Education; Labor-Management Relations; Labor Standards.

**Interior and Insular Affairs** (20th of 23 Democrats)
Insular Affairs; Public Lands and National Parks.

## Elections

**1980 General**

| | |
|---|---|
| Dale Kildee (D) | 147,280 (93%) |
| Dennis Berry (LIB) | 11,507 (7%) |

**1978 General**

| | |
|---|---|
| Dale Kildee (D) | 105,402 (77%) |
| Gale Cronk (R) | 29,958 (22%) |

**Previous Winning Percentage**

1976 (70%)

**District Vote For President**

| | 1980 | | 1976 | | 1972 |
|---|---|---|---|---|---|
| D | 94,834 (49 %) | D | 93,377 (52%) | D | 76,745 (45%) |
| R | 84,272 (43 %) | R | 84,998 (47%) | R | 90,776 (53%) |
| I | 12,829 (7 %) | | | | |

## Campaign Finance

| | Receipts | Receipts from PACs | Expenditures |
|---|---|---|---|
| **1980** | | | |
| Kildee (D) | $32,483 | $16,135 (50%) | $32,091 |
| **1978** | | | |
| Kildee (D ) | $50,826 | $19,550 (38 %) | $46,558 |
| Cronk (R ) | $23,504 | $600 (3 %) | $23,487 |

## Voting Studies

| | Presidential Support | | Party Unity | | Conservative Coalition | |
|---|---|---|---|---|---|---|
| Year | S | O | S | O | S | O |
| 1980 | 74 | 26 | 89 | 11 | 12 | 88 |
| 1979 | 82 | 18 | 83 | 17 | 9 | 91 |
| 1978 | 75 | 25 | 85 | 15 | 9 | 91 |
| 1977 | 73 | 27 | 83 | 17 | 13 | 87 |

S = Support          O = Opposition

## Key Votes

**96th Congress**

| | |
|---|---|
| Weaken Carter oil profits tax (1979) | N |
| Reject hospital cost control plan (1979) | N |
| Implement Panama Canal Treaties (1979) | Y |
| Establish Department of Education (1979) | Y |
| Approve Anti-busing Amendment (1979) | N |
| Guarantee Chrysler Corp. loans (1979) | Y |
| Approve military draft registration (1980) | N |
| Aid Sandinista regime in Nicaragua (1980) | Y |
| Strengthen fair housing laws (1980) | Y |

**97th Congress**

| | |
|---|---|
| Reagan budget proposal (1981) | N |

## Interest Group Ratings

| Year | ADA | ACA | AFL-CIO | CCUS |
|---|---|---|---|---|
| 1980 | 89 | 21 | 84 | 62 |
| 1979 | 89 | 12 | 95 | 0 |
| 1978 | 80 | 7 | 95 | 11 |
| 1977 | 85 | 11 | 87 | 12 |

# 8 Bob Traxler (D)

### Of Bay City — Elected 1974

**Born:** July 21, 1931, Kawkawlin, Mich.
**Education:** Mich. State U., B.A. 1953; Detroit College of Law, LL.B. 1959.
**Military Career:** Army, 1953-55.
**Profession:** Lawyer.
**Family:** Divorced, three children.
**Religion:** Episcopalian.
**Political Career:** Mich. House, 1963-74.

**In Washington:** Traxler's boisterous good humor sometimes borders on clownishness, but there is nothing frivolous about his career on the Appropriations Committee, where he has always known how to trade with his colleagues and deliver for his Michigan district.

The future promises considerable power for Traxler on the committee. As his fourth full House term began in 1981, he was already second in line on two Appropriations subcommittees, behind Jamie L. Whitten of Mississippi on Agriculture and Edward P. Boland of Massachusetts on HUD-Independent Agencies. Whitten is 71; Boland is 70.

Traxler has worked well with both men. On the HUD panel, he has been an ally of Boland not only on housing issues but on the question of funding for space and science research. He has argued against some of the strictest proposed cutbacks for NASA and the National Science Foundation.

On the Agriculture Subcommittee, he has a chance to speak up for central Michigan's sugar beet farmers, whose cause he has pleaded throughout his House career. In 1977, when President Carter considered the merits of a $240-million subsidy to sugar processors, Traxler argued help was needed to keep the industry going. "I am opposed to an OPEC-like foreign sugar cartel," he said, "that will surely come into existence if we allow the sugar beet grower to go out of business."

In the past two Congresses, however, the industry Traxler has talked about most has been the auto industry, which is crucial to the health of Bay City and Saginaw, his district's two population centers.

Along with Detroit Democrat John D. Dingell, Traxler has helped the industry fight off efforts to force the installation of air bags in new cars. In 1980, Traxler successfully amended a Transportation appropriation bill to block money from being used for the program. He said it would further hurt the competitive position of U.S. automakers.

Traxler amended another 1980 appropriation to add $119 million for faster federal purchasing of automobiles. The money, he said, would allow the government to buy 11,600 more cars in 1981. And he introduced his own bill calling for an immediate 35% cutback in foreign car imports.

**At Home:** Traxler came to Washington in 1974 amid as much attention as any House newcomer had received in years. He had turned his special election campaign into a referendum on President Nixon in the midst of the unfolding Watergate scandal. Traxler called his Republican opponent, James M. Sparling, a "stand-in for Mr. Nixon," who stumped for Sparling in the district against the advice of some local GOP leaders.

With help from organized labor, the Democrat won just enough votes in the urbanized counties to offset his opponent's strength in the rural Thumb region — the area Nixon visited in his whistle-stop tour. Traxler became the first Democrat in 42 years to represent some parts of the district.

Many thought that with Nixon gone by the next election, voters in the 8th would revert to their traditional GOP habits. But Traxler's combination of populism and gregarious constituent

---

**8th District: Bay City, Saginaw.**
Population: 505,144 (8% increase since 1970). Race: White 453,334 (90%), Black 37,183 (7%), Others 14,627 (3%). Spanish origin: 18,100 (4%).

---

## Bob Traxler, D-Mich.

relations gave him a firm lock on the district. He has steadily increased his margins in both Saginaw and Bay City, and has even won over many of the bean and sugar beet farmers in the Republican Thumb.

During 11 years representing Bay City in the Michigan House, Traxler was rated as one of the more able legislators. One of his most conspicuous crusades was for a bill to allow bingo games in churches, a successful campaign that gave him the nickname "Bingo Bob," which he still carries in the House. As the chairman of the House Judiciary Committee, he helped to modernize the state's district court system.

**The District:** Although Michigan's distinctive Thumb is the most prominent geographical feature of the 8th District, the twin industrial cities of Saginaw and Bay City and their suburbs play the greatest political role.

The two cities — old lumber towns now both devoted to the automotive industry — were not in the same district until 1972. Before then the urban Democratic vote was divided, and Republicans won easily with votes from the rural Thumb counties.

In the last decade, Saginaw and Bay City have both lost 16 percent of their population, while the suburbs and rural areas have grown by at least that much. If that trend continues, it could eventually bring about a demographic shift that would hurt Democratic candidates who rely on large pluralities from the cities to win.

## Committees

**Appropriations** (15th of 33 Democrats)
Agriculture, Rural Development and Related Agencies; HUD - Independent Agencies; Legislative.

## Elections

**1980 General**

| | |
|---|---|
| Bob Traxler (D) | 124,155 (61%) |
| Norman Hughes (R) | 77,009 (38%) |

**1978 General**

| | |
|---|---|
| Bob Traxler (D) | 103,346 (67%) |
| Norman Hughes (R) | 51,900 (33%) |

**Previous Winning Percentages**

1976 (59%)      1974 (55%)      1974* (52%)

*Special election*

**District Vote For President**

| | 1980 | | 1976 | | 1972 |
|---|---|---|---|---|---|
| D | 85,078 (40%) | D | 84,198 (44%) | D | 65,422 (37%) |
| R | 112,311 (53%) | R | 105,159 (55%) | R | 106,524 (61%) |
| I | 13,479 (6%) | | | | |

## Campaign Finance

| | Receipts | Receipts from PACs | Expenditures |
|---|---|---|---|
| **1980** | | | |
| Traxler (D) | $125,232 | $67,418 (54%) | $88,798 |
| **1978** | | | |
| Traxler (D) | $107,097 | $42,850 (40%) | $97,020 |
| Hughes (R) | $46,022 | $12,249 (27%) | $40,795 |

## Voting Studies

| | Presidential Support | | Party Unity | | Conservative Coalition | |
|---|---|---|---|---|---|---|
| Year | S | O | S | O | S | O |
| 1980 | 63 | 30 | 76 | 17 | 33 | 59 |
| 1979 | 67 | 21 | 75 | 13 | 38 | 56 |
| 1978 | 66 | 25 | 75 | 18 | 26 | 68 |
| 1977 | 56 | 27 | 70 | 20 | 33 | 57 |
| 1976 | 20 | 75 | 69 | 23 | 29 | 63 |
| 1975 | 30 | 67 | 82 | 13 | 22 | 75 |
| 1974 (Ford) | 35 | 54 | | | | |
| 1974 | 45 | 52† | 75 | 18† | 35 | 58† |

S = Support          O = Opposition
†Not eligible for all recorded votes.

## Key Votes

**96th Congress**

| | |
|---|---|
| Weaken Carter oil profits tax (1979) | N |
| Reject hospital cost control plan (1979) | Y |
| Implement Panama Canal Treaties (1979) | Y |
| Establish Department of Education (1979) | Y |
| Approve Anti-busing Amendment (1979) | Y |
| Guarantee Chrysler Corp. loans (1979) | Y |
| Approve military draft registration (1980) | N |
| Aid Sandinista regime in Nicaragua (1980) | ? |
| Strengthen fair housing laws (1980) | Y |

**97th Congress**

| | |
|---|---|
| Reagan budget proposal (1981) | N |

## Interest Group Ratings

| Year | ADA | ACA | AFL-CIO | CCUS |
|---|---|---|---|---|
| 1980 | 56 | 17 | 79 | 58 |
| 1979 | 47 | 13 | 85 | 33 |
| 1978 | 45 | 20 | 80 | 18 |
| 1977 | 60 | 22 | 77 | 19 |
| 1976 | 60 | 12 | 78 | 19 |
| 1975 | 89 | 25 | 100 | 18 |
| 1974 | 68 | 18 | 100 | 13 |

# 9 Guy Vander Jagt (R)

**Of Luther — Elected 1966**

**Born:** Aug. 26, 1931, Cadillac, Mich.
**Education:** Hope College, A.B. 1953; Yale U., B.D. 1955; U. of Mich., LL.B. 1960.
**Profession:** Lawyer.
**Family:** Wife, Carol Doorn; one child.
**Religion:** Presbyterian.
**Political Career:** Mich. Senate, 1965-66.

**In Washington:** It took Vander Jagt nearly a decade in Congress find something he could excel at, but once he discovered what it was — raising money and giving speeches for his party — he moved remarkably quickly out of the back benches.

Five years after he won his job as chairman of the GOP House campaign committee, Vander Jagt gave the keynote address at the Republican National Convention, drew public mention as a possible vice presidential nominee and came within 16 votes of the party leadership.

Vander Jagt's close run for leader against Robert H. Michel of Illinois was remarkable because it challenged a basic principle of House leadership contests: The winners are people who have proved themselves in the legislative process. Vander Jagt, by his own admission, was no parliamentary strategist; he had rarely appeared on the floor during the preceding four years, except to vote.

Vander Jagt argued that the party needed an eloquent House spokesman rather than a tactician like Michel. "We need someone who can project to the American public," he said. "...Inevitably one winds up on 'Face the Nation' or 'Meet the Press.' I think I would be a more forceful spokesman than Bob Michel." He also said he would supply "aggressive confrontation" with the Democratic majority when that was needed. That argument might have been stronger had Reagan not been elected president, obviating the need for a new party spokesman.

In the two years before that leadership vote, Vander Jagt had raised $27 million for GOP House candidates, traveling the country to rouse party audiences with florid speeches like his 1980 keynote address laced with poetry and the wisdom of political thinkers from Plato to Robert Taft.

He had built the campaign committee into a huge public relations apparatus, one that promoted Vander Jagt's own ideas and image in a glossy magazine every month.

Perhaps most important, his had been the name on the checks that his committee donated to GOP House challengers throughout the country. The 38 new Republicans elected in 1978 and the huge freshman class of 52 in 1980 provided the basis for his leadership challenge to Michel.

Before 1980, Vander Jagt's operation had been a success *only* at public relations; it had not made much progress against the Democratic House majority. Vander Jagt exuberantly predicted a Republican House gain of "76 in '76" and had to remain embarrassingly quiet for months after the "gain" turned out to be minus two. The next time around, his organization redeemed itself slightly by adding 11 new GOP seats, but Vander Jagt's critics went into 1980 wondering what all the fund raising had accomplished.

After November, those questions were largely answered. Republicans took advantage of all the expensive techniques they had been developing since 1975 — campaign schools in Washington for budding challengers, a sophisticated year-round polling operation and commercials on prime time network television — hammering home the fact that Democrats had controlled Congress for a quarter of a century. When the GOP gained 33 seats in 1980, that was as important to many Republicans as whether he had shown parliamentary skill over the years. When he lost his

**9th District: West — Muskegon.**
Population: 537,268 (15% increase since 1970).
Race: White 502,499 (94%), Black 23,437 (4%), Others 11,332 (2%). Spanish origin: 12,591 (2%).

leadership bid, he agreed to stay on as campaign chairman.

During his campaign against Michel, Vander Jagt insisted that he had performed well on the floor when he had chosen to work there and supplied examples to prove it. But the fact remained that he had never taken a great interest in the legislative process. In 1974, the year before he became campaign chairman, he was growing disillusioned with the House, spending an increasing amount of time in the gym and showing up for some of his votes in a pair of sneakers.

In those years, Vander Jagt rarely exercised his vaunted oratorical skills outside his district; he always felt it was a waste of time to deliver stemwinding speeches to an audience of empty seats and newspaper readers. But he produced a few moments of drama, especially in 1972 on the unlikely subject of sewage treatment.

Vander Jagt was known in those days primarily as a water pollution specialist. A scientist in Muskegon, the largest city in Vander Jagt's district, had invented a new sewage treatment system using earth as a "living filter," and Vander Jagt began pushing for its use in 1969.

In 1972, in debate on a water pollution bill, Vander Jagt performed the seemingly impossible — he spoke so eloquently in behalf of the new sewage system that the House voted to require the government to encourage its use even though the committee managing the bill opposed the idea.

"It is time," Vander Jagt declaimed, "that the nation was offered the environmental vision inherent in the land utilization concept of sewage treatment. The concept allows man to admit the wisdom of God and nature and to move in harmony with natural processes. To ignore this wisdom is to court environmental disaster."

There were relatively few moments like those in Vander Jagt's early congressional terms. He moved around frequently in the committee system, starting out on Science and Government Operations, taking a place on Foreign Affairs in 1971, but hoping for one on Ways and Means — which he did not get until 1975, the year his attention began to shift toward politics.

Vander Jagt was generally known in his first years as a moderate Republican in the tradition of his close friend George Romney, then Michigan's governor. His work against pollution gave him an environmentalist reputation.

But by the time he assumed the campaign chairmanship, Vander Jagt was moving to the right. The limited committee work he has done on Ways and Means since then has added to the newer image, enabling him to campaign credibly against Michel in 1980 as the conservative choice.

In 1976, he was the most vocal opponent on Ways and Means of a bill to provide $240 million in federal aid to day-care centers, helping them conform to new federal standards. The bill's passage, after one Ford veto had been sustained, required a technical waiver of the Congressional Budget Act, and Vander Jagt compared the waiver to "gang rape" of the budget process.

The next year, as senior GOP member of the Ways and Means welfare subcommittee, he was a militant opponent of President Carter's massive welfare revision proposal. He felt it offered insufficient work incentives and would have been far more expensive than Carter was willing to admit. He did vote in 1979, however, for a scaled-down Carter plan establishing a national welfare minimum for the first time. That plan contained a "sweetener" of extra federal money for Michigan and other large states with high welfare bills.

**At Home:** Traveling the country as campaign chairman is a job for someone who can afford to let his district take care of itself. Vander Jagt can. He has a safe seat. Since his first election in 1966, he has been below 60 percent only once. In 1980, he did not even have an opponent.

The son of a livestock dealer and farmer, Vander Jagt grew up on a 120-acre farm near Cadillac. He originally thought the ministry would be a good place to exercise his oratorical skills, but after earning a divinity degree he decided to be a lawyer. He paid for law school with money he made working part-time at various radio stations.

After four years practicing law in Grand Rapids with Harold Sawyer, who now represents the 5th District, Vander Jagt returned to Cadillac and easily won a state Senate seat. Two years later he realized Rep. Robert P. Griffin was a likely appointee to a Senate vacancy. He announced for Congress and had little trouble winning either the special election or the one for the full term — both held the same day. His percentage was the highest of any GOP newcomer elected that year.

**The District:** Over the past few decades the 9th has become longer and narrower, but it has remained safely in Republican hands since 1934.

It now runs 220 miles along the shores of Lake Michigan. The northern and southern ends are the areas of greatest Republican support. In the north, resorts and cherry orchards provide a profitable economic base. The southern end, around Holland, is the nation's tulip capital. As the name suggests, the Dutch influence is great.

What Democratic strength exists is in the

industrial city of Muskegon, located between the two other sections. But it is not much. Only once — in 1974 — has Vander Jagt failed to carry Muskegon County. And in most statewide contests, it favors the Republican, although by less imposing margins than the rest of the district.

## Committees

**Ways and Means** (4th of 12 Republicans)
Select Revenue Measures; Trade.

## Elections

**1980 General**

| | |
|---|---|
| Guy Vander Jagt (R) | 168,713 (97%) |
| Marshall Tuffs (AMI) | 5,985 (3%) |

**1978 General**

| | |
|---|---|
| Guy Vander Jagt (R) | 122,363 (70%) |
| Howard Leroux (D) | 53,450 (30%) |

**Previous Winning Percentages**

| | | | |
|---|---|---|---|
| 1976 (70%) | 1974 (57%) | 1972 (69%) | 1970 (64%) |
| 1968 (68%) | 1966 (67%) | 1966* (67%) | |

*Elected to a full term and also to fill an unexpired term in a special election held the same day, Vander Jagt received 67% in both elections.

**District Vote For President**

| | 1980 | | 1976 | | 1972 |
|---|---|---|---|---|---|
| D | 78,397 (32 %) | D | 78,084 (36%) | D | 64,561 (32%) |
| R | 145,274 (60 %) | R | 139,170 (63%) | R | 130,463 (65%) |
| I | 15,431 (6 %) | | | | |

## Campaign Finance

| | Receipts | Receipts from PACs | Expenditures |
|---|---|---|---|
| **1980** | | | |
| Vander Jagt (R) | $276,793 | $114,925 (42%) | $148,241 |
| **1978** | | | |
| Vander Jagt (R) | $204,418 | $79,681 (39%) | $197,290 |
| Leroux (D) | $39,483 | $15,535 (39%) | $38,498 |

## Voting Studies

| Year | Presidential Support | | Party Unity | | Conservative Coalition | |
|---|---|---|---|---|---|---|
| | S | O | S | O | S | O |
| 1980 | 39 | 42 | 67 | 16 | 66 | 17 |
| 1979 | 28 | 55 | 75 | 11 | 78 | 9 |

| | | | | | | |
|---|---|---|---|---|---|---|
| 1978 | 32 | 57 | 71 | 17 | 78 | 13 |
| 1977 | 41 | 42 | 70 | 15 | 70 | 12 |
| 1976 | 75 | 16 | 68 | 18 | 66 | 19 |
| 1975 | 70 | 18 | 71 | 17 | 76 | 15 |
| 1974 (Ford) | 52 | 37 | | | | |
| 1974 | 68 | 13 | 59 | 25 | 66 | 21 |
| 1973 | 58 | 30 | 61 | 27 | 67 | 24 |
| 1972 | 78 | 14 | 69 | 20 | 72 | 16 |
| 1971 | 61 | 21 | 60 | 23 | 66 | 23 |
| 1970 | 74 | 9 | 68 | 18 | 50 | 32 |
| 1969 | 62 | 23 | 51 | 35 | 49 | 38 |
| 1968 | 48 | 30 | 71 | 17 | 71 | 16 |
| 1967 | 56 | 39 | 71 | 22 | 70 | 26 |

S = Support          O = Opposition

## Key Votes

**96th Congress**

| | |
|---|---|
| Weaken Carter oil profits tax (1979) | Y |
| Reject hospital cost control plan (1979) | Y |
| Implement Panama Canal Treaties (1979) | N |
| Establish Department of Education (1979) | N |
| Approve Anti-busing Amendment (1979) | Y |
| Guarantee Chrysler Corp. loans (1979) | Y |
| Approve military draft registration (1980) | N |
| Aid Sandinista regime in Nicaragua (1980) | X |
| Strengthen fair housing laws (1980) | N |

**97th Congress**

| | |
|---|---|
| Reagan budget proposal (1981) | Y |

## Interest Group Ratings

| Year | ADA | ACA | AFL-CIO | CCUS |
|---|---|---|---|---|
| 1980 | 22 | 79 | 11 | 84 |
| 1979 | 5 | 88 | 26 | 94 |
| 1978 | 10 | 79 | 5 | 75 |
| 1977 | 5 | 88 | 16 | 87 |
| 1976 | 10 | 82 | 10 | 69 |
| 1975 | 16 | 88 | 9 | 88 |
| 1974 | 22 | 38 | 20 | 78 |
| 1973 | 16 | 46 | 18 | 73 |
| 1972 | 25 | 64 | 27 | 78 |
| 1971 | 24 | 72 | 20 | - |
| 1970 | 48 | 69 | 14 | 88 |
| 1969 | 27 | 42 | 78 | - |
| 1968 | 33 | 60 | 50 | - |
| 1967 | 13 | 86 | 18 | 89 |

* Not eligible for all votes.

# 10 Don Albosta (D)

## Of St. Charles — Elected 1978

**Born:** Dec. 5, 1925, Saginaw, Mich.
**Education:** Attended Delta College.
**Military Career:** Navy, 1941-45.
**Profession:** Farmer.
**Family:** Wife, Dorothy Mary Ankoviak; two children.
**Religion:** Roman Catholic.
**Political Career:** Saginaw County commissioner, 1970-74; Mich. House, 1975-77; unsuccessful Democratic nominee for Saginaw County Commission, 1968; unsuccessful Democratic nominee for U.S. House, 1976.

**In Washington:** Ruddy-faced and plain-spoken, Albosta strikes observers as a perfect match for the rural district that sent him to Congress in 1978. And he keeps his farm connections close to the surface, as he made clear when he brought a dozen Michigan farmers into Speaker O'Neill's office for an uninvited visit early in 1979.

But much of Albosta's first term was spent wooing the broader constituency he needed to get to Washington and then to stay there. In a district with a heavy population of retirees, he made an issue of his opposition to any possible taxation of Social Security benefits. He introduced legislation opposing such a tax, then offered a similar resolution in the Democratic Caucus and had little trouble obtaining a favorable caucus vote on the subject.

Many of northern Michigan's retirees are former union members, and the conservative-talking beet farmer has found himself offering an occasional vote to labor, especially the United Auto Workers. He was with them on the Chrysler loan guarantee in 1979, and at the end of that year one labor lobbyist confided quietly that Albosta had been a lot friendlier than the union had ever expected. When George Meany died, Albosta went to the floor to deliver a eulogy.

The more conservative Albosta surfaced frequently, however, on issues like gun control and fishing rights, both subjects followed closely back home. He cosponsored a bill to change an Indian treaty that was limiting sport fishing rights in Michigan waters.

Albosta came to Congress partly on the strength of his fight against chemical contamination of crops and livestock. He has struggled to keep that issue alive while representing a district that includes Dow Chemical Co. headquarters. Albosta spoke on the floor against the use of chemical weapons in Southeast Asia, but he opposed a ban on federal funds for chemical munitions. He won passage of an amendment allowing a congressional veto of EPA regulations dealing with the forced cleanup of chemical disasters by the industry.

**At Home:** A one-term state legislator, Albosta began his quest for the House with an upset primary victory in 1976, wresting the Democratic nomination from a man who had held veteran Republican Elford A. Cederberg to 54 percent in the previous election. But he found himself overmatched against Cederberg in the fall, partly because he had no political base beyond the agricultural Saginaw County area he represented in the Legislature.

Still, he decided to try again in 1978. This time, he faced behind-the-scenes opposition from party leaders who were put off by his bluntness and his publicity-conscious campaign against chemical contamination. The result was one of the most vitriolic primaries of the year.

Albosta's primary opponent was Roger Tilles, a Jewish lawyer from Long Island who was the chief aide to the Speaker of the Michigan House. When Albosta mentioned Tilles' ethnic background during the campaign, Tilles charged that Albosta was anti-Semitic. Albosta insisted he was not, and voters supported him with a 59-41 margin.

---

**10th District: North central — Midland.** Population: 580,061 (24% increase since 1970). Race: White 570,059 (98%), Black 2,345 (0.4%), Others 7,657 (1%). Spanish origin: 6,478 (1%).

Then Albosta went back to work on Cederberg, and reversed the 1976 outcome. This time he outspent the incumbent, raising more than three times what he had gathered for his first try. Cederberg was complacent, and an easy target for charges that he had ignored his district. The ranking Republican on the Appropriations Committee, Cederberg had to stay in hotels on his visits home because he no longer owned property in the district. Albosta was elected by 5,462 votes.

Michigan Republicans put Albosta at the top of their 1980 target list. But the GOP candidate, state Sen. Richard J. Allen, had the same trouble making himself known throughout the district that Albosta had faced in his first try. Allen sought to take advantage of allegations in area newspapers that Albosta had used a 1978 Small Business Administration loan to fund his campaign that year. Albosta refused to discuss the issue beyond denying any wrongdoing, and again the voters vindicated him.

**The District:** As Albosta and later Allen learned, the 23-county 10th District — 160 miles long and 110 miles wide — presents challengers with enormous problems of name recognition. To get decent media exposure in the more heavily populated southern counties, a candidate needs to buy television time in five cities — Grand Rapids, Lansing, Flint, Saginaw and Bay City — all outside the district.

Farther north the population is spread thinly among the forests, lakes and farms. Moderate Democrats do fairly well here. The only city of any size in the northern region is the Republican stronghold of Traverse City, home of Gov. William G. Milliken and former Sen. Robert P. Griffin.

In the last decade north central Michigan has experienced a significant demographic shift. Once solidly Republican, the area is becoming increasingly Democratic as union members from southern Michigan cities retire here. Drawn by the peaceful life and recreational opportunities, they are settling along scenic lakes and rivers where they once spent their vacations. These blue-collar retirees have made the 10th District one of the fastest growing rural areas in the Eastern United States.

## Committees

**Post Office and Civil Service** (8th of 15 Democrats)
Compensation and Employee Benefits; Postal Operations and Services.

**Public Works and Transportation** (20th of 25 Democrats)
Economic Development; Investigations and Oversight; Surface Transportation.

**Select Aging** (30th of 31 Democrats)
Human Services.

## Elections

**1980 General**

| | |
|---|---|
| Don Albosta (D) | 126,962 (52%) |
| Richard Allen (R) | 111,496 (46%) |

**1978 General**

| | |
|---|---|
| Don Albosta (D) | 94,913 (51%) |
| Elford Cederberg (R) | 89,451 (49%) |

**1978 Primary**

| | |
|---|---|
| Don Albosta (D) | 16,266 (59%) |
| Roger Tilles (D) | 11,374 (41%) |

**District Vote For President**

| | 1980 | | 1976 | | 1972 |
|---|---|---|---|---|---|
| D | 89,714 (36%) | D | 90,223 (41%) | D | 67,244 (35%) |
| R | 138,194 (55%) | R | 129,229 (58%) | R | 122,575 (63%) |
| I | 19,713 (8%) | | | | |

## Campaign Finance

| | Receipts | Receipts from PACs | Expenditures |
|---|---|---|---|
| **1980** | | | |
| Albosta (D) | $273,410 | $139,349 (51%) | $267,015 |
| Allen (R) | $411,018 | $86,785 (21%) | $410,995 |

| **1978** | | | |
|---|---|---|---|
| Albosta (D) | $261,407 | $14,549 (6%) | $258,244 |
| Cederberg (R) | $148,426 | $92,780 (63%) | $146,993 |

## Voting Studies

| | Presidential Support | | Party Unity | | Conservative Coalition | |
|---|---|---|---|---|---|---|
| **Year** | **S** | **O** | **S** | **O** | **S** | **O** |
| 1980 | 64 | 32 | 69 | 26 | 55 | 42 |
| 1979 | 65 | 30 | 66 | 26 | 53 | 42 |

S = Support          O = Opposition

## Key Votes

**96th Congress**

| | |
|---|---|
| Weaken Carter oil profits tax (1979) | N |
| Reject hospital cost control plan (1979) | Y |
| Implement Panama Canal Treaties (1979) | Y |
| Establish Department of Education (1979) | Y |
| Approve Anti-busing Amendment (1979) | Y |
| Guarantee Chrysler Corp. loans (1979) | Y |
| Approve military draft registration (1980) | N |
| Aid Sandinista regime in Nicaragua (1980) | Y |
| Strengthen fair housing laws (1980) | N |

**97th Congress**

| | |
|---|---|
| Reagan budget proposal (1981) | Y |

## Interest Group Ratings

| Year | ADA | ACA | AFL-CIO | CCUS |
|---|---|---|---|---|
| 1980 | 28 | 42 | 68 | 81 |
| 1979 | 58 | 12 | 80 | 44 |

# 11 Robert W. Davis (R)

**Of Gaylord — Elected 1978**

**Born:** July 31, 1932, Marquette, Mich.
**Education:** Wayne State U. College of Mortuary
Science, B.S. 1954.
**Profession:** Funeral director.
**Family:** Wife, Martha Cole; three children.
**Religion:** Episcopalian.
**Political Career:** St. Ignace City Council, 1964-
66; Mich. House, 1967-71; Mich. Senate,
1971-79.

**In Washington:** Davis spent most of his first House term catering to local interests in his marginal Upper Peninsula district.

While most members were debating the foreign policy implications of the Panama Canal treaties, Davis was looking at their impact on the fish netting industry in northern Michigan. Language in the bill implementing the treaties would have canceled import duties on fish nets, to the displeasure of the 12 firms in Davis' district that manufacture them. Davis successfully offered a floor amendment to the legislation that had the effect of restoring the duties.

Davis has had a frequent chance to talk about fishing as a member of the Merchant Marine and Fisheries Committee. Early in his first term, he entered the long-running dispute in northern Michigan between commercial fishermen and Indian tribes. Courts had ruled that the tribes had unlimited treaty rights to the catch off some Michigan waters. Davis favored legislation which would abrogate any unlimited Indian fishing rights and place the tribes under regular fish and wildlife regulations.

On other issues, he took a similar district-first position. In 1980, he voted against the $10-billion Interior appropriation bill because it contained a provision allowing the U.S. Forest Service to buy 25,000 acres of land currently owned by a private utility in his district.

The local orientation has sometimes led Davis far from the conservatism of his overall rhetoric. He is a strong supporter of the Trade Adjustment Assistance program, target of continuing criticism from most of the Republican right. The program provides extra unemployment benefits to workers laid off because of foreign competition. Davis introduced a bill in 1980 to extend the coverage to those who work for companies supplying raw materials to affected industries. That would help the Upper Peninsula iron

miners, whose already depressed industry has been hurt further by the decline in the American automobile industry's demand for steel.

Similarly, Davis' solid record of support for military spending does not extend to ELF, the proposed submarine communications system which would lay 130 miles of underground cable in the Upper Peninsula. President Carter promised Michigan voters in 1976 that he would not build it on their territory; when he asked later for a new study and $13 million for possible development, Davis denounced the entire project.

**At Home:** Davis' attention to the needs of his district has paid off — particularly his concern for the mining areas in the western end of the Upper Peninsula. In 1980, seeking his second term, he carried all 27 counties in the district. Taking Republican Rep. Philip Ruppe's place initially was more difficult. Ruppe had stepped down in 1978, planning to run for the Senate seat of retiring Republican Robert P. Griffin. When Griffin changed his mind and decided to run again, it was too late for Ruppe to get his old seat back. He sat on the sidelines and watched nine candidates — including Davis — battle for the congressional district he could have retained easily.

Davis' major problem was that he was from the Lower Peninsula, while a majority of the voters are from the Upper Peninsula (known to

---

**11th District: Upper Peninsula.** Population: 518,732 (11% increase since 1970). Race: White 504,846 (97%), Black 2,923 (1%), Others 10,963 (2%). Spanish origin: 1,964 (0.3%).

Michiganders as the UP). Even on his own turf Davis had had problems. He had been re-elected to the state Senate in 1974 by only 1,270 votes out of 80,000 cast. But his congressional campaign strategy was sound. He won the GOP primary on the strength of Lower Peninsula support, then temporarily moved to the UP and stressed his boyhood roots in that region.

Campaigning like an incumbent, Davis contrasted his experience of a dozen years in the Legislature with the record of Democrat Keith McLeod, a savings and loan executive and political neophyte. McLeod, from the Upper Peninsula, narrowly won that area, but Davis did well enough there to win a comfortable victory. It was the first time since 1888 that UP voters did not have one of their own in Washington.

Davis had been a familiar figure in the Michigan Legislature for years. In his first Senate term he was picked to be GOP whip, and later he served as the minority leader. Among his more notable accomplishments was passage of a bill that lowered the toll on the Mackinac Straits Bridge.

**The District:** This is the second largest district east of the Mississippi River. Covering 23,000 square miles — roughly the size of West Virginia — it has a tendency to favor incumbents because challengers find it difficult to make themselves known. A candidate needs to buy television time in Michigan, Minnesota and Wisconsin to reach all the voters effectively.

About 60 percent of the constituents live above the Mackinac Straits Bridge, in the UP, which until 1964 had a district of its own. The iron and copper miners who live in the remote, barren western two-thirds of the UP are, for the most part, avid Democrats. One of the two Michigan counties won by McGovern in 1972 was in the UP.

The Lower Peninsula and the three easternmost counties in the UP are more Republican. Tourism, shipping, and farming are major industries there. The migration of former city-dwellers that has transformed the 10th District is also evident in this part of the 11th, however, and may begin to swing it toward the Democrats in the 1980s.

## Committees

**Armed Services** (15th of 19 Republicans)
Investigations; Research and Development.

**Merchant Marine and Fisheries** (9th of 15 Republicans)
Coast Guard and Navigation; Fisheries and Wildlife Conservation and the Environment; Merchant Marine.

## Elections

**1980 General**

| | |
|---|---|
| Robert Davis (R) | 146,205 (66%) |
| Dan Dorrity (D) | 75,515 (34%) |

**1978 General**

| | |
|---|---|
| Robert Davis (R) | 96,351 (55%) |
| Keith McLeod (D) | 79,081 (45%) |

**1978 Primary**

| | |
|---|---|
| Robert Davis (R) | 18,520 (58%) |
| Edmund Vandette (R) | 13,478 (42%) |

**District Vote For President**

| 1980 | | 1976 | | 1972 | |
|---|---|---|---|---|---|
| D | 101,478 (42%) | D | 109,380 (48%) | D | 86,548 (42%) |
| R | 121,678 (50%) | R | 113,751 (50%) | R | 116,785 (56%) |
| I | 15,847 (7%) | | | | |

## Campaign Finance

| | Receipts | Receipts from PACs | Expenditures |
|---|---|---|---|
| **1980** | | | |
| Davis (R) | $138,895 | $71,895 (52%) | $121,198 |
| Dorrity (D) | $48,134 | $14,770 (31%) | $42,578 |

| 1978 | | | |
|---|---|---|---|
| Davis (R) | $163,423 | $55,531 (34%) | $158,755 |
| McLeod (D) | $132,777 | $52,650 (40%) | $131,304 |

## Voting Studies

| | Presidential Support | | Party Unity | | Conservative Coalition | |
|---|---|---|---|---|---|---|
| Year | S | O | S | O | S | O |
| 1980 | 50 | 44 | 63 | 31 | 58 | 29 |
| 1979 | 35 | 62 | 72 | 24† | 82 | 15† |

S = Support    O = Opposition
† Not eligible for all recorded votes.

## Key Votes

**96th Congress**

| | |
|---|---|
| Weaken Carter oil profits tax (1979) | Y |
| Reject hospital cost control plan (1979) | Y |
| Implement Panama Canal Treaties (1979) | N |
| Establish Department of Education (1979) | Y |
| Approve Anti-busing Amendment (1979) | Y |
| Guarantee Chrysler Corp. loans (1979) | Y |
| Approve military draft registration (1980) | Y |
| Aid Sandinista regime in Nicaragua (1980) | N |
| Strengthen fair housing laws (1980) | N |

**97th Congress**

| | |
|---|---|
| Reagan budget proposal (1981) | Y |

## Interest Group Ratings

| Year | ADA | ACA | AFL-CIO | CCUS |
|---|---|---|---|---|
| 1980 | 39 | 55 | 67 | 68 |
| 1979 | 6 | 76 | 35 | 89 |

# 12 David E. Bonior (D)

### Of Mount Clemens — Elected 1976

**Born:** June 6, 1945, Detroit, Mich.
**Education:** U. of Iowa, B.A., 1967; Chapman College, M.A. 1972.
**Military Career:** Air Force, 1968-72.
**Profession:** Politician.
**Family:** Separated; two children.
**Religion:** Roman Catholic.
**Political Career:** Mich. House, 1973-77.

**In Washington:** Identified with the cause of Vietnam veterans from the day of his arrival in Congress, Bonior has shown some of their restlessness in his search for an effective outlet in the House.

Early in his first House term, in 1977, Bonior was instrumental in the formation of the Vietnam Veterans congressional caucus, and he has sought ways to follow that up in other legislative battles on the House floor. One of his amendments sought to give Vietnam veterans extra preference over older veterans for civil service jobs in future years. Another resolution he introduced would provide normal disability benefits for veterans affected by Agent Orange, the chemical defoliant.

But it is difficult to build a legislative career out of those issues alone, and Bonior sought to expand into a broader role as an environmentalist. Placed, however, on the Public Works and Merchant Marine committees, he was frequently up against consistent majorities hostile to most environmental crusades. He began lobbying for a place on the Rules Committee in 1979, and finally made it two years later. On Rules, he is in more congenial company.

On Public Works, Bonior was part of the small bloc questioning the need for the multibillion-dollar water projects the panel's leadership enthusiastically promoted. In his first year on the committee, in 1977, he dissented from its overwhelming majority in favor of a $1.25 billion bill with 120 projects in it, and argued that one of them — a harbor expansion in Gulfport, Miss. — was being performed for the benefit of the du Pont chemical company. Three years later, he was one of the few Public Works members to favor a floor amendment deleting eight projects from another big water bill.

On Merchant Marine, a committee dominated by the oil and maritime industries, Bonior was also a lonely voice, frequently siding with the panel's beleaguered environmental spokesman,

Massachusetts Democrat Gerry E. Studds. In 1980, when Studds brought out a bill to extend the federal Coastal Zone Management program for eight years, Bonior successfully amended it in committee to provide $25 million in special aid for states suffering adverse environmental impact from coal shipping.

Merchant Marine dipped into the waters of foreign policy when it wrote legislation implementing the 1978 Panama Canal treaties, and Bonior was active in that fight, arguing that it was right for the United States to turn the canal over to Panama. He also spoke out for aid to the Sandinista regime in Nicaragua, without strings attached to the money.

**At Home:** While Bonior has looked for his niche in Washington, he has also looked for a way to make his blue-collar suburban district more secure politically. He has increased his percentage every time he has run, although he has not reached the normal margins of his Democratic predecessor, James G. O'Hara, who left the House in an unsuccessful try for the Senate in 1976.

Described in the Michigan press as a "textbook liberal," Bonior remains slightly to the left of majority opinion in a district preoccupied with the gloomy Detroit job situation. He showed some political daring in 1979 when he voted against an anti-busing amendment to the U.S. Constitution; the busing issue nearly unseated O'Hara in 1972. Bonior has voted for less sweeping anti-busing

> **12th District: Southeast — Macomb County, Port Huron.** Population: 544,744 (17% increase since 1970). Race: White 526,108 (97%), Black 11,596 (2%), Others 7,040 (1%). Spanish origin: 6,227 (1%).

legislation in the past.

Bonior's re-election campaigns have been supported by organized labor and the Macomb County Democratic organization, but he has not been on the closest of terms with either. In the crowded 1976 contest to find a successor to O'Hara, the unions were split and the Macomb Democratic Party favored Bonior's major primary opponent, conservative state Sen. John T. Bowman. Bonior narrowly won the primary and general election by waging an aggressive personal campaign, during which he went door-to-door handing out thousands of pine tree seedlings.

Bonior was a two-term state representative in 1976, having been elected to the Legislature only months after his return from Vietnam, where he served in the 479th tactical fighter squadron as a cook. In all his campaigns, he has sought to make the war and its veterans a more frequent subject of debate. "No one even wants to talk about the war," he once complained. "It was a disaster."

**The District.** In the last 40 years, the population of Macomb County — the heart of the 12th District, — has increased from 108,000 to about 700,000. The white flight from Detroit's center city, which is located less than 10 miles from the district's edge, brought a rapid change in Macomb's once firmly Republican voting habits.

Many of today's 12th District voters are second-generation ethnics, who joined the Democratic Party because it was their immigrant parents' traditional home. Although these blue-collar voters still back Democrats for economic reasons, they have shown a willingness to flirt with Republican candidates in years when social issues like busing dominate the discussion.

## Committees

**Rules** (10th of 11 Democrats)
Rules of the House.

## Elections

**1980 General**

| | |
|---|---|
| David Bonior (D) | 112,698 (55%) |
| Kirk Walsh (R) | 90,931 (45%) |

**1980 Primary**

| | |
|---|---|
| David Bonior (D) | 20,383 (82%) |
| Owen Love (D) | 2,399 (10%) |
| Anthony Polselli (D) | 1,842 (7%) |

**1978 General**

| | |
|---|---|
| David Bonior (D) | 82,892 (55%) |
| Kirby Holmes (R) | 68,063 (45%) |

**Previous Winning Percentage**

1976 (52%)

**District Vote For President**

| | 1980 | | 1976 | | 1972 |
|---|---|---|---|---|---|
| D | 85,473 (38%) | D | 87,787 (45%) | D | 61,017 (35%) |
| R | 122,348 (54%) | R | 104,379 (53%) | R | 110,019 (63%) |
| I | 14,804 (7%) | | | | |

## Campaign Finance

| | Receipts | Receipts from PACs | Expenditures |
|---|---|---|---|
| **1980** | | | |
| Bonior (D) | $97,734 | $58,110 (59%) | $105,574 |
| Walsh (R) | $47,295 | $23,530 (50%) | $54,140 |

| | | | |
|---|---|---|---|
| **1978** | | | |
| Bonior (D) | $121,106 | $50,366 (42%) | $119,682 |
| Holmes (R) | $69,531 | $23,181 (33%) | $69,251 |

## Voting Studies

| | Presidential Support | | Party Unity | | Conservative Coalition | |
|---|---|---|---|---|---|---|
| Year | S | O | S | O | S | O |
| 1980 | 68 | 21 | 79 | 6 | 8 | 82 |
| 1979 | 79 | 14 | 87 | 7 | 7 | 83 |
| 1978 | 79 | 15 | 86 | 10 | 7 | 86 |
| 1977 | 77 | 23 | 84 | 15 | 10 | 88 |

S = Support          O = Opposition

## Key Votes

**96th Congress**

| | |
|---|---|
| Weaken Carter oil profits tax (1979) | N |
| Reject hospital cost control plan (1979) | N |
| Implement Panama Canal Treaties (1979) | Y |
| Establish Department of Education (1979) | Y |
| Approve Anti-busing Amendment (1979) | N |
| Guarantee Chrysler Corp. loans (1979) | Y |
| Approve military draft registration (1980) | Y |
| Aid Sandinista regime in Nicaragua (1980) | Y |
| Strengthen fair housing laws (1980) | Y |

**97th Congress**

| | |
|---|---|
| Reagan budget proposal (1981) | N |

## Interest Group Ratings

| Year | ADA | ACA | AFL-CIO | CCUS |
|---|---|---|---|---|
| 1980 | 83 | 18 | 89 | 52 |
| 1979 | 89 | 0 | 95 | 6 |
| 1978 | 90 | 11 | 90 | 18 |
| 1977 | 90 | 15 | 91 | 12 |

# 13 George W. Crockett (D)

**Of Detroit — Elected 1980**
**Born:** August 10, 1909, Jacksonville, Fla.
**Education:** Morehouse College, A.B. 1931; U. of Mich., J.D. 1934.
**Profession:** Lawyer; judge.
**Family:** Wife, Harriette Clark; three children.
**Religion:** Baptist.
**Political Career:** Judge, Detroit Recorder's Court, 1966-78.

**The Member:** To those who followed Crockett's career over nearly four decades in Detroit politics, it came as little surprise when he quickly won Charles C. Diggs' endorsement for the House seat Diggs had vacated by resignation. Nor was it a surprise that Detroit Mayor Coleman A. Young, the United Auto Workers and the Shrine of the Black Madonna, a major black church in Detroit, also backed the retired judge to fill Diggs' seat.

Crockett is an elder statesman of Detroit's black community. The white-haired judge has been part of Detroit's "Black Bottom" neighborhood since he arrived in 1943 to open a fair employment practices office for the UAW. In 1952, he defended Young when the one-time union organizer was called before the House Un-American Activities Committee.

During his two six-year terms as a Recorder's Court judge, Crockett established a reputation for integrity. That was essential for a successor to Diggs, who was convicted in 1978 and censured by the House in 1979 on payroll padding charges.

Crockett joined 11 other congressmen in filing suit against the Reagan administration's decision to send military personnel into El Salvador, saying it violated the War Powers Act.

**The District:** Only one other district in the nation has lost as much population in the last decade as the 13th. Located in the heart of Detroit's inner city, it has had black representation since 1954, when Diggs first won it. The scars of riot in the 1960s are still visible. But the sight of the glimmering Renaissance Center on the Detroit River offers some measure of hope that revitalization will eventually extend into the heart of the district.

Regentrification is occurring in a few neighborhoods, but not enough for white urban homesteaders to challenge black domination. A more serious threat to continued black representation comes from redistricting. Forced nearly to double its present size, the district almost inevitably will have to move into some of the white neighborhoods that surround it.

## Committees

**Foreign Affairs** (15th of 21 Democrats)
Africa; International Operations.

**Select Aging** (31st of 31 Democrats)
Housing and Consumer Interests; Human Services.

**Small Business** (16th of 23 Democrats)
Export Opportunities and Special Small Business Problems; General Oversight.

## Elections

**1980 General**

| | |
|---|---|
| George Crockett (D) | 79,719 (92%) |
| M. Michael Hurd (R) | 6,473 (7%) |

**1980 Primary**

| | |
|---|---|
| George Crockett (D) | 8,810 (42%) |
| David Holmes (D) | 4,187 (20%) |
| Clyde Cleveland (D) | 3,373 (16%) |
| Nicholas Houd (D) | 3,364 (16%) |

**District Vote For President**

| | 1980 | | 1976 | | 1972 |
|---|---|---|---|---|---|
| **D** | 81,957 (90%) | **D** | 88,245 (86%) | **D** | 104,143 (83%) |
| **R** | 6,941 (8%) | **R** | 12,877 (13%) | **R** | 20,540 (16%) |
| **I** | 1,558 (2%) | | | | |

## Campaign Finance

| | Receipts | Receipts from PACs | Expenditures |
|---|---|---|---|
| **1980** | | | |
| Crockett (D) | $44,592 | $9,050 (20%) | $43,619 |

## Key Vote

**97th Congress**

| | |
|---|---|
| Reagan budget proposal (1981) | N |

---

**13th District: Downtown Detroit.** Population: 291,394 (37% decrease since 1970). Race: White 52,168 (18%), Black 231,027 (79%), Others 8,199 (3%). Spanish origin: 7,665 (3%).

# 14 Dennis M. Hertel (D)

**Of Detroit — Elected 1980**
**Born:** Dec. 7, 1948, Detroit, Mich.
**Education:** Eastern Mich. U., B.A., 1971; Wayne
State U., J.D. 1974.
**Profession:** Lawyer.
**Family:** Wife, Cynthia S. Grosscup; three
children.
**Religion:** Roman Catholic.
**Political Career:** Mich. House, 1975-81.

**The Member:** The three Hertel brothers
dominate politics on the northeastern side of
Detroit. Dennis Hertel spent six years in the state
Legislature. His older brother serves in the state
Senate and his younger brother was elected to
Dennis' old state House seat in 1980.

The political success of the Hertel family is a
reflection of the way their moderate, labor-oriented politics fits the area. It also is a tribute to
their grass-roots organization.

Running against a polished television figure
in 1980, Dennis Hertel assembled a volunteer
force 2,500 strong. Lacking the money and the
flair of his opponent, Hertel concentrated on one-
on-one visits with voters. He wore out four pairs
of shoes walking through the precincts.

During his three terms in the Legislature,
Hertel usually supported the Democratic leadership. Organized labor boosted his campaign for
Congress. Although his opponent and others dismissed Hertel as "a political hack," he pointed to
his successful drive to outlaw double-bottom
tankers on Michigan's highways. As co-chairman
of the Judiciary Committee, he also pushed
through a bill to require mandatory jail sentences
for criminals who use handguns.

Hertel sits on the Armed Services Committee
and has accused that panel of doing less than any
in Congress to eliminate wasteful spending.

**The District:** The 14th is an ethnically and
economically diverse district which straddles the
county line between Detroit and the blue-collar
suburbs of Macomb County.

Democratic Rep. Lucien N. Nedzi retired in
1980, and the Republican nominee, Vic Caputo,
made a strong bid for the seat. "If he can't win
that district," the state GOP chairman said, "I
don't know if a Republican ever can." Caputo fell
about 12,000 votes short.

The district includes the exclusive, upper
class Grosse Pointes. But their solidly Republican
vote is not enough to counter the strong Democratic leanings in the Polish, Belgian and Italian
neighborhoods in Detroit and its nearby suburbs.

## Committees

**Armed Services** (24th of 25 Democrats)
Procurement and Military Nuclear Systems; Seapower and Strategic and Critical Materials.

**Merchant Marine and Fisheries** (19th of 20 Democrats)
Fisheries and Wildlife Conservation and the Environment; Merchant Marine; Oceanography.

## Elections

**1980 General**

| | |
|---|---|
| Dennis Hertel (D ) | 90,362 (53 %) |
| Vic Caputo (R ) | 78,395 (46 %) |

**1980 Primary**

| | |
|---|---|
| Dennis Hertel (D ) | 20,595 (62 %) |
| John Kelly (D ) | 6,188 (19 %) |
| Walter Gajewski (D ) | 3,389 (10 %) |

**District Vote For President**

| | 1980 | | 1976 | | 1972 |
|---|---|---|---|---|---|
| **D** | 81,893 (46 %) | **D** | 87,433 (48 %) | **D** | 76,857 (39 %) |
| **R** | 83,510 (47 %) | **R** | 92,898 (51 %) | **R** | 114,564 (59 %) |
| **I** | 10,061 (6 %) | | | | |

## Campaign Finance

| | | Receipts | Expen- |
|---|---|---|---|
| | Receipts | from PACs | ditures |
| **1980** | | | |
| Hertel (D ) | $162,355 | $81,770 (50 %) | $160,600 |
| Caputo (R ) | $213,808 | $57,160 (27 %) | $211,590 |

## Key Vote

**97th Congress**
Reagan budget proposal (1981)                     N

---

**14th District: Detroit suburbs —
Grosse Pointe.** Population: 412,245 (12%
decrease since 1970). Race: White 346,235
(84%), Black 59,420 (14%), Others 6,590
(2%). Spanish origin: 4,167 (1%).

---

# 15 William D. Ford (D)

**Of Taylor — Elected in 1964**

**Born:** Aug. 6, 1927, Detroit, Mich.
**Education:** Wayne State U., 1947-48; U. of Denver, B.S. 1949. LL.B. 1951.
**Military Career:** Navy, 1944-46; Air Force Reserve, 1950-58.
**Profession:** Lawyer.
**Family:** Wife, Martha Cook; three children.
**Religion:** United Church of Christ.
**Political Career:** Taylor Township Justice of the Peace, 1955-57; Melvindale City Attorney, 1957-59; Taylor Township Attorney, 1957-64, Mich. Senate, 1963-65.

**In Washington:** "Nobody's too rich or too poor to get help from Uncle Sam," Bill Ford once said, and it is a rule he has lived by throughout his House career. He has spent most of two decades inventing and trying to protect various forms of federal generosity, and learning the parliamentary skills to do it.

But in 1981, after 16 years of having his way on most jobs and education bills in the Education and Labor Committee, Ford had to confront a Reagan administration intent on changing them.

The new era began just as Ford was making a career change, taking over as chairman of the full Post Office and Civil Service Committee. To accept that chairmanship, he had to give up the leadership of the Education and Labor Subcommittee on Higher Education, his specialty through most of the 1970s.

Ford never had any doubt that Reagan was wrong in trying to trim back federal government programs. He said he would rather shut down 10,000 post offices than accede to some of the Reagan budget demands. But there was little he could do.

"I don't think any of these cuts are warranted," Ford said as his committee reluctantly marked off $5.1 billion in postal and civil service reductions to meet the Reagan budget for 1981. "These are unfortunate cuts and probably not sound public policy."

While the budget was forcing those changes in civil service spending, it was doing something even more devastating to Ford in education, challenging his proudest achievement, the 1980 Higher Education bill. That legislation, argued over for two years in both House and Senate, provided generous aid for students, young and old, who wanted to continue their schooling. As 1981 began, colleges and universities were getting nearly half of all federal education funds — thanks in part to Ford — and they were targeted for the deepest Reagan cuts.

The 1980 bill grew out of Ford's effort to head off growing support for tax credits to pay for private school tuition. He insisted these would be tilted too far in favor of upper-middle-income parents. They also would be under the control of the congressional tax-writing committees in Congress — not the education committees.

The 1980 law, managed by Ford in the House and Claiborne Pell of Rhode Island in the Senate, expanded the program of Basic Education Opportunity Grants that provided money directly to students. It broadened eligibility for guaranteed loans to all students, including those from upper-middle-income families.

Ford is also on the Education and Labor subcommittee that handles elementary and secondary school programs. Here he argued loudly in 1981 against Reagan-backed efforts to consolidate into block grants the money Congress had carefully earmarked for specific programs. But the House ultimately voted for most of the block grants.

Ford has had a hand in virtually every piece of education legislation passed during the last decade and a half. "Over the years there's been a phenomenal change," he once said. "The American people now support federal education as

**15th District: Southwestern Wayne County.** Population: 521,598 (12% increase since 1970). Race: White 479,382 (92%), Black 32,895 (6%), Others 9,621 (2%). Spanish origin: 8,336 (2%).

something they expect the government to do. They put it almost on a par with national defense."

On Education and Labor, and in his campaigns, Ford has always been a favorite of teacher groups. He has also been a favorite of organized labor, especially the United Auto Workers, but other unions as well. As a member of the Labor-Management Relations Subcommittee throughout the 1970s, he sometimes stepped in to handle controversial labor bills, like those dealing with common-site picketing and labor law revision, when Chairman Frank Thompson of New Jersey was absent.

On Post Office and Civil Service, Ford has spoken up for the unions that represent federal employees. He was labor's negotiator on President Carter's Civil Service revision bill in 1978, expressing the fears of the unions that the merit incentives written into the bill would weaken job protection. Ultimatley he reached a compromise in behalf of the unions with the administration and with the chief sponsor of the bill, Arizona Democrat Morris K. Udall.

In 1977, Ford used his role on Post Office and Civil Service to help enact substantial pay raises for federal officials, including $13,000 increases for members of Congress. Critics wanted a recorded vote in the House on the raises, but Speaker O'Neill sent them to a special Ford subcommittee, knowing that the Michigan Democrat would dispose of the issue quietly. His subcommittee held hearings on the raises, then tabled all efforts to block them on a voice vote. Ford has never had serious political problems at home; he could afford to be on the pro pay-raise side, and he took that position openly.

The one issue that Ford has been careful about at home is busing. He supported all civil rights bills in the 1960s and all of President Johnson's anti-poverty programs, but he drew the line when federal courts ordered busing in the Detroit area in the early 1970s. He has signed congressional petitions against busing, held hearings against it and voted for anti-busing measures.

Even that record has not spared him criticism. In 1972, when he balked at an effort to pry an anti-busing constitutional amendment out of the Judiciary Committee, demonstrators marched around his Michigan office, chanting, "Sign or Resign" and "The old Bill Ford isn't what he used to be." Ford insisted he simply did not like stripping a committee of its jurisdiction over a major issue, but the groups were not appeased. In 1979, Ford voted for an anti-busing constitutional amendment on the House floor.

Ford also has joined other Michigan representatives in voting for delays and weakening of auto emission control standards in the Clean Air Act. He supported the Chrysler bailout in 1979 and favors relief for the auto companies through restrictions on imports by Japan.

**At Home:** An energetic, true-believing Democrat in a Democratic district, Ford has never had any serious trouble winning election to anything.

He put in seven years as a political apprentice in township politics on the western side of Wayne County, then went to the state Senate in 1962. It was an easy move because he had the blessing of the man who was retiring.

Taking the U.S. House seat two years later was almost as easy. The newly created 15th District had no incumbent, and most local party leaders agreed that Ford was the logical choice. His only significant primary opposition came from another local township politician, William Faust, who later became majority leader of the state Senate. Ford defeated Faust 45 to 36 percent, with the rest of the vote split among three others.

Ever since then, the Democrat has tended to his district and voted in accord with its wishes. As a senior legislator on education, he invites city and school officials from Detroit to come to Washington every year for a conference on how to get money from the federal government. He has been rewarded with routine elections. In nine campaigns, his percentage has fallen below 70 percent only three times.

Ford's 1980 election drew more attention than usual because of his opponent, Gerald Carlson. The Republican openly stated his white supremacist views and his former ties to the Ku Klux Klan and American Nazi Party. Ford got 68 percent, which was about normal.

**The District:** Anyone who drives into Detroit from the airport along the Industrial Freeway gets a good view of the 15th District. Large automobile and chemical plants line the highway, with suburban tract houses visible in the distance. Except for the town of Inkster, where most of the district's blacks live, the 15th District is dominated by white ethnics, generally loyal Democrats.

The 15th is the most middle class of the close-in districts that ring the Motor City. It is situated geographically and economically between the poorer and more polluted 16th District, and the areas to the north where the auto companies' white-collar employees and executives live.

The district went Republican for Richard M. Nixon in 1972, but the national Democratic ticket prevailed in 1976. Regan won it in 1980 by 3 percentage points. Only in the Lyndon Johnson landslide of 1964 did the Democratic presidential nominee come close to Ford's margin.

## Committees

**Education and Labor** (3rd of 19 Democrats)
Elementary, Secondary and Vocational Education; Labor-Management Relations; Postsecondary Education.

**Post Office and Civil Service** (Chairman)
Investigations, chairman.

## Elections

**1980 General**

| | |
|---|---|
| William Ford (D ) | 113,492 (68 %) |
| Gerald Carlson (R ) | 53,046 (32 %) |

**1978 General**

| | |
|---|---|
| William Ford (D ) | 95,137 (77 %) |
| Edgar Nieten (R ) | 23,177 (19 %) |

**Previous Winning Percentages**

| | | | |
|---|---|---|---|
| 1976 (74 %) | 1974 (78 %) | 1972 (66 %) | 1970 (80 %) |
| 1968 (71 %) | 1966 (68 %) | 1964 (71 %) | |

**District Vote For President**

| | 1980 | | 1976 | | 1972 |
|---|---|---|---|---|---|
| D | 85,328 (45 %) | D | 91,018 (52 %) | D | 61,803 (39 %) |
| R | 90,973 (48 %) | R | 81,165 (46 %) | R | 94,812 (59 %) |
| I | 11,976 (6 %) | | | | |

## Campaign Finance

| | Receipts | Receipts from PACs | Expenditures |
|---|---|---|---|
| **1980** | | | |
| Ford (D ) | $90,022 | $72,965 (8 %) | $83,295 |
| **1978** | | | |
| Ford (D ) | $56,137 | $34,545 (62 %) | $61,157 |

## Voting Studies

| | Presidental Support | | Party Unity | | Conservative Coalition | |
|---|---|---|---|---|---|---|
| Year | S | O | S | O | S | O |
| 1980 | 65 | 20 | 75 | 6 | 11 | 69 |
| 1979 | 70 | 17 | 76 | 5 | 15 | 71 |
| 1978 | 69 | 15 | 79 | 5 | 10 | 76 |
| 1977 | 63 | 13 | 77 | 5 | 12 | 70 |

| | | | | | |
|---|---|---|---|---|---|
| 1976 | 22 | 65 | 83 | 5 | 9 | 79 |
| 1975 | 29 | 55 | 76 | 8 | 12 | 75 |
| 1974 (Ford) | | | | | | |
| 1974 | 30 | 58 | 80 | 7 | 12 | 75 |
| 1973 | 28 | 66 | 87 | 8 | 8 | 89 |
| 1972 | 46 | 35 | * | 10 | 15 | 67 |
| 1971 | 25 | 61 | 82 | 7 | 8 | 77 |
| 1970 | 49 | 34 | 72 | 10 | 0 | 75 |
| 1969 | 49 | 45 | 80 | 2 | 4 | 84 |
| 1968 | 64 | 13 | 71 | 2 | 0 | 80 |
| 1967 | 78 | 9 | 90 | 3 | 0 | 96 |
| 1966 | 82 | 6 | 85 | 3 | 0 | 86 |
| 1965 | 90 | 6 | 95 | 2 | 2 | 98 |

* Data not available

S = Support          O = Opposition

## Key Votes

**96th Congress**

| | |
|---|---|
| Weaken Carter oil profits tax (1979) | N |
| Reject hospital cost control plan (1979) | N |
| Implement Panama Canal Treaties (1979) | ? |
| Establish Department of Education (1979) | Y |
| Approve Anti-busing Amendment (1979) | Y |
| Guarantee Chrysler Corp. loans (1979) | Y |
| Approve military draft registration (1980) | N |
| Aid Sandinista regime in Nicaragua (1980) | Y |
| Strengthen fair housing laws (1980) | Y |

**97th Congress**

| | |
|---|---|
| Reagan budget proposal (1981) | N |

## Interest Group Ratings

| Year | ADA | ACA | AFL-CIO | CCUS |
|---|---|---|---|---|
| 1980 | 78 | 5 | 95 | 59 |
| 1979 | 68 | 8 | 88 | 24 |
| 1978 | 60 | 14 | 100 | 12 |
| 1977 | 50 | 8 | 95 | 12 |
| 1976 | 60 | 7 | 90 | 8 |
| 1975 | 89 | 8 | 100 | 13 |
| 1974 | 57 | 21 | 100 | 10 |
| 1973 | 80 | 19 | 100 | 9 |
| 1972 | 75 | 12 | 88 | 0 |
| 1971 | 78 | 8 | 82 | - |
| 1970 | 92 | 6 | 100 | - |
| 1969 | 93 | 7 | 100 | 13 |
| 1968 | 94 | 0 | 100 | - |
| 1967 | 100 | 0 | - | 10 |

# 16 John D. Dingell (D)

**Of Trenton — Elected 1955**

**Born:** July 8, 1926, Colorado Springs, Colo.
**Education:** Georgetown U., B.S. 1949, LL.B. 1952.
**Military Career:** Army, 1945-46.
**Profession:** Lawyer.
**Family:** Wife, Deborah Insley; four children.
**Religion:** Roman Catholic.
**Political Career:** Assistant Wayne County Prosecutor, 1953-55.

**In Washington:** Dingell, the new chairman of the Energy and Commerce Committee, is a complex man, stubborn and vindictive on occasion, self-confident to the point of arrogance, a skilled legislative craftsman and one of the most effective House members.

His skill at moving bills through Congress is freely acknowledged and even admired. He has assembled one of the best technical staffs on the Hill. He works hard. He can mold diverse factions into a majority when he really wants to.

But he badgers witnesses, ties up conferences for weeks and bullies colleagues. He once made Sen. Pete Domenici so angry that Domenici refused to be in the same room with him.

"Occasionally," Dingell once said, "I'm going to have to do ugly things that hurt me politically.... But I was sent here to win."

Commerce today is an octopus of a committee, with jurisdiction not only over energy but over health, communications, transportation and numerous regulatory agencies. Dingell is involved in them all.

When he wants to shape legislation, he manages somehow to get along with both his committee's conservative Republicans and the bright young Democrats who have moved into leadership positions on Commerce subcommittees.

During the early stages of a bill's development Dingell can be a flexible bargainer. But once he has reached a position he is convinced is right, his mind closes like a steel trap.

In 1981, in his capacity as full Commerce chairman, Dingell fought to block the proposed Reagan budget cuts in his jurisdiction and replace them with a Democratic alternative. The committee deadlocked on the issue, 21-21, and was unable to recommend either version.

Dingell then unilaterally sent his own proposal to the House floor, where he won, even though Republicans managed to knock out every other committee's Democratic suggestions and replace them with Reagan's. Republicans feared that if they fought for Reagan's Commerce spending cuts, which included reductions in Medicaid and low income fuel assistance, they might lose. Dingell fared better than in the overall debacle than any other chairman in the House.

Despite Dingell's skill, House leaders have sometimes tried to work around him because his personality is so difficult. When President Carter offered his major energy legislation in 1977, it was sent to a specially-created ad hoc committee, partly to keep it out of Dingell's control at Commerce. Even so, Dingell, as a member of the ad hoc panel, managed to cause problems. When the Senate added a provision deregulating the price of natural gas, he tied up the House-Senate conference for months. Eventually the two sides compromised on language phasing out the controls gradually.

It is not easy to categorize Dingell on energy policy. Members who have worked with him over the years generally say he is more interested in winning than in pursuing any rigid ideology. Through most of the 1970s, he supported controls on energy prices, but he gradually seemed to change his mind on the issue, influenced by younger committee Democrats like Phil Sharp of Indiana. In 1979, when President Carter proposed to deregulate crude oil prices, Dingell voted against an effort to block him, in opposition to

---

**16th District: Dearborn, South Detroit and suburbs.** Population: 397,937 (15% decrease since 1970). Race: White 350,574 (88%), Black 33,192 (8%), Others 14,171 (4%). Spanish origin 19,154 (5%).

most of his committee's Democrats. He said the effort was futile. But he remains a persistent critic of the oil industry, berating it for stockpiling and high prices.

Dingell has been a strong supporter of conservation and solar development. He is skeptical of synthetic fuels. He is cautious about nuclear power, feeling problems should be worked out before much more money is spent.

Overall, Dingell has been a liberal national Democrat, supporting civil rights, Great Society programs, and expansion in the role of the federal government. He was an early consumer advocate, working on truth-in-advertising and Federal Trade Commission laws.

As a senior member of the Merchant Marine and Fisheries Committee, he has won awards from conservationists for measures to protect endangered species and establish a National Wildlife System. He helped create the Council on Environmental Quality, and require environmental impact statements in new federal laws.

But there is also the Dingell who infuriates some environmentalists with his militant pro-gun views, expressed in alliance with the National Rifle Association. And there is the one who has defended Detroit's auto industry against the Clean Air Act. He has been the single most powerful force for weakening auto emission controls, delaying installation of air bags for safety and allowing the automakers longer periods to meet gas mileage requirements.

In 1972, Ralph Nader called Dingell the consumer's friend. A profile by Nader's organization said, "His record on consumer protection is excellent." In 1980, Nader had a different view. "Given his position, his power, his drive, his corporate allies and his Machiavellian skills," Nader declared, "Dingell can now be considered the number one enemy of consumers on Capitol Hill."

Dingell can be as hard-nosed in fighting colleagues he does not like as he is in fighting the Clean Air Act. In recent years, he has barely been on speaking terms with James H. Scheuer, the New York Democrat who headed the Commerce Consumer Subcommittee in the 96th Congress. Scheuer wanted to require the use of air bags in new cars over Dingell's violent objection. When Dingell won the chairmanship of the full committee in 1981, he immediately abolished Scheuer's subcommittee, leaving him without a chairmanship even though he is the No. 2 ranking Democrat on Commerce.

Dingell is equally forceful when protecting his own turf. In 1974, a special panel headed by Missouri Democrat Richard Bolling proposed reorganizing House committees to create a single energy and environment panel, built around the Interior Committee, not Commerce. Much of Dingell's jurisdiction would have been wiped out. Dingell came to the floor with over 300 amendments, and said he would offer them all if necessary. Because of his efforts and those of others similarly affected, Bolling's plan was defeated.

Six years later, another reform panel recommended the same thing — a single energy committee to consolidate jurisdictional sprawl. Dingell vigorously fought it. It too failed.

**At Home:** The Dingell family has represented Detroit in Congress since 1932. For 23 years, John D. Dingell Sr., a New Deal champion of national health insurance, served from the west side of the city. When he died suddenly in 1955, while undergoing a routine physical examination, his 29-year-old son stepped into his place.

Young John literally had grown up on Capitol Hill as a House page. It was only when he received his law degree, and went to work as an assistant prosecutor, that he learned the intricacies of Detroit politics. But after three years as "my father's ears and eyes," he was ready for the 1955 special election. With backing from organized labor, he trounced a dozen Democratic candidates in the primary and went on to overwhelm his 26-year-old GOP opponent.

Since then, Dingell has had to worry about re-election only once, in 1964, when part of his district was combined with a larger part of the district held by Democratic Rep. John Lesinski Jr., who had also succeeded his father in the House. The primary between Dingell and Lesinski received national attention because it was thought to be a measure of "white backlash" over recent civil rights legislation. Dingell, whose old district was about a third black, had voted for the 1964 Civil Rights Act. Lesinski, whose district was nearly all white, was one of four Northern Democrats who had voted against it. The issue was not brought up in the campaign, but both sides knew it was the primary reason Dingell received such strong help from labor, civil rights groups, and the state Democratic Party. Dingell won with 55 percent and has not had any problems since.

**The District:** More than any other in the country, this district is devoted to the automobile. Along with the Ford headquarters, there are nearly 20 manufacturing and assembly plants located in it. It is, according to one Detroit *News* article a few years ago, "the most polluted congressional district in the nation: the air stinks, the waters are technicolor, and the sky is filled with smoke and debris."

There has been a massive loss of population in the district since 1970. Dearborn, the district's largest town and still one of the most livable areas in the district, has lost 13 percent of its population. The Delray section of Detroit and the downriver towns of Ecorse and Wyandotte lost more. As a result, the district's borders are likely to be expanded into the western suburbs of Wayne County by the next election. That may slightly reduce the district's Democratic margins, which currently are exceeded in the state only by the largely black 1st and 13th Districts.

## Committees

**Energy and Commerce** (Chairman)
Oversight and Invedstigations, chairman.

## Elections

**1980 General**

| | |
|---|---|
| John Dingell (D ) | 105,844 (70 %) |
| Pamela Seay (R ) | 42,735 (28 %) |

**1980 Primary**

| | |
|---|---|
| John Dingell (D ) | 21,780 (88 %) |
| Malcolm Beaton (D ) | 2,906 (12 %) |

**1978 General**

| | |
|---|---|
| John Dingell (D ) | 93,387 (77 %) |
| Melvin Heuer (R) | 26,827 (22 %) |

**Previous Winning Percentages**

| | | | |
|---|---|---|---|
| 1976 (76 %) | 1974 (78 %) | 1972 (68 %) | 1970 (79 %) |
| 1968 (74 %) | 1966 (63 %) | 1964 (73 %) | 1962 (83 %) |
| 1960 (79 %) | 1958 (79 %) | 1956 (74 %) | 1955* (76 %) |

*\* Special election.*

**District Vote For President**

| | 1980 | | 1976 | | 1972 |
|---|---|---|---|---|---|
| **D** | 82,483 (50 %) | **D** | 94,331 (54 %) | **D** | 82,436 (45 %) |
| **R** | 70,905 (43 %) | **R** | 75,797 (44 %) | **R** | 95,685 (53 %) |
| **I** | 10,190 (6 %) | | | | |

## Campaign Finance

| | Receipts | Receipts from PACs | Expenditures |
|---|---|---|---|
| **1980** | | | |
| Dingell (D ) | $144,116 | $89,005 (62 %) | $115,821 |
| Seay (R ) | $1,630 | — (0 %) | $1,541 |
| **1978** | | | |
| Dingell (D ) | $90,071 | $53,425 (59 %) | $61,246 |

## Voting Studies

| | Presidential Support | | Party Unity | | Conservative Coalition | |
|---|---|---|---|---|---|---|
| Year | S | O | S | O | S | O |
| 1980 | 68 | 21 | 81 | 7 | 21 | 62 |
| 1979 | 67 | 23 | 72 | 14 | 26 | 62 |
| 1978 | 63 | 25 | 74 | 18 | 27 | 63 |
| 1977 | 71 | 22 | 80 | 13 | 24 | 66 |
| 1976 | 16 | 76 | 81 | 11 | 19 | 76 |
| 1975 | 34 | 58 | 81 | 11 | 23 | 65 |

| | | | | | |
|---|---|---|---|---|---|
| 1974 (Ford) | 33 | 59 | | | |
| 1974 | 36 | 55 | 72 | 16 | 24 | 59 |
| 1973 | 21 | 60 | 76 | 12 | 20 | 67 |
| 1972 | 46 | 41 | 69 | 10 | 20 | 65 |
| 1971 | 46 | 51 | 81 | 10 | 24 | 69 |
| 1970 | 54 | 31 | 63 | 8 | 16 | 61 |
| 1969 | 49 | 34 | 82 | 9 | 20 | 73 |
| 1968 | 69 | 14 | 80 | 11 | 14 | 75 |
| 1967 | 78 | 9 | 85 | 7 | 9 | 78 |
| 1966 | 89 | 5 | 88 | 6 | 8 | 84 |
| 1965 | 82 | 7 | 86 | 7 | 6 | 90 |
| 1964 | 77 | 0 | 71 | 2 | 0 | 75 |
| 1963 | 80 | 0 | 84 | 0 | 0 | 73 |
| 1962 | 85 | 3 | 77 | 2 | 0 | 88 |
| 1961 | 89 | 6 | 86 | 10 | 0 | 96 |

S = Support          O = Opposition

## Key Votes

**96th Congress**

| | |
|---|---|
| Weaken Carter oil profits tax (1979) | N |
| Reject hospital cost control plan (1979) | N |
| Implement Panama Canal Treaties (1979) | Y |
| Establish Department of Education (1979) | N |
| Approve Anti-busing Amendment (1979) | Y |
| Guarantee Chrysler Corp. loans (1979) | Y |
| Approve military draft registration (1980) | Y |
| Aid Sandinista regime in Nicaragua (1980) | ? |
| Strengthen fair housing laws (1980) | N |

**97th Congress**

| | |
|---|---|
| Reagan budget proposal (1981) | N |

## Interest Group Ratings

| Year | ADA | ACA | AFL-CIO | CCUS |
|---|---|---|---|---|
| 1980 | 67 | 18 | 76 | 63 |
| 1979 | 58 | 17 | 80 | 35 |
| 1978 | 50 | 25 | 90 | 24 |
| 1977 | 70 | 16 | 91 | 18 |
| 1976 | 70 | 15 | 91 | 6 |
| 1975 | 63 | 15 | 95 | 18 |
| 1974 | 52 | 23 | 100 | 10 |
| 1973 | 80 | 12 | 100 | 10 |
| 1972 | 63 | 15 | 89 | 0 |
| 1971 | 76 | 22 | 83 | - |
| 1970 | 68 | 12 | 100 | 0 |
| 1969 | 80 | 25 | 100 | - |
| 1968 | 75 | 5 | 67 | - |
| 1967 | 67 | 4 | 92 | 10 |
| 1966 | 82 | 8 | 92 | - |
| 1965 | 79 | 4 | . | 10 |
| 1964 | 96 | 0 | 91 | - |
| 1963 | . | 0 | . | - |
| 1962 | 100 | 0 | 100 | - |
| 1961 | 100 | | - | - |

# 17 William M. Brodhead (D)

**Of Detroit — Elected 1974**

**Born:** Sept. 12, 1941, Cleveland, Ohio.
**Education:** Wayne State U., A.B. 1965; U. of Mich., J.D. 1967.
**Profession:** Lawyer.
**Family:** Wife, Kathleen Garlock; two children.
**Religion:** Roman Catholic.
**Political Career:** Mich. House, 1971-75.

**In Washington:** Viewed over three terms as a traditional labor liberal, Brodhead took over in 1981 as head of the Democratic Study Group, center for liberal strategy in the House, and surprised colleagues with some very unorthodox ideas.

"The old Humphrey-Johnson liberal — the more of everything for everybody liberal — is becoming extinct," he said shortly after becoming DSG chairman. "The new liberals believe in balanced budgets. We're pick-and-choose kind of people, though we still want to protect those who can't look out for themselves."

What was even more surprising was the bill Brodhead introduced at the Ways and Means Committee in 1981 reducing the minimum tax on unearned income from 70 percent to 50 percent. It was exactly the sort of idea that the committee's Democrats have derided in the past as special pleading for the rich, but Brodhead argued that if that kind of tax cut was needed to stimulate investment, it ought to be considered. The Reagan administration was considering the same thing at the same time.

In the past, Brodhead's presence on the Ways and Means Committee had been viewed primarily as an asset for the United Auto Workers at a moment when the union was fighting critical economic battles.

Brodhead arrived at Ways and Means in 1977, in time to participate in its rewrite of the trade adjustment assistance program designed to compensate workers in industries hit by foreign competition. The bill stalled in the Senate in both 1978 and 1979, but Brodhead took the issue to the House Budget Committee, where he also served, arguing that spending projections should include funds for the program. At one point he linked his support for the 1981 budget resolution to $100 million for trade adjustment assistance. When he got the money, he broke with most liberal Democrats and voted to report the budget out of committee.

When the Chrysler loan guarantee came to the House floor in 1979, Brodhead was an active lobbyist for the UAW position in favor of the legislation. It was his idea to write to members of the New York City delegation reminding them that Michigan legislators had backed a loan guarantee for New York in the previous Congress. The New York City bloc ended up voting 14-1 for the Chrysler loan.

On other issues, Brodhead has occasionally sought to establish some distance from the UAW. The union backed President Carter's 1978 plan for "real wage insurance," a scheme to provide bonuses to workers whose employers stayed within wage increase guidelines. Brodhead took a conspicuous position against real wage insurance and helped prevent its passage in committee.

His personal legislative interest, however, is in the areas of health and welfare. On those issues, he has been a classic liberal. Brodhead's district predecessor, Martha Griffiths, was for many years the key House sponsor of comprehensive national health insurance, and Brodhead has now assumed a similar role.

Brodhead fought in the Budget Committee to preserve funding for a new child health assurance program. He was a close ally of California Democrat James Corman as Corman's Ways and Means Public Assistance Subcommittee wrote a bill in 1979 to set up a uniform national welfare standard for the first time. Neither the health nor the

> **17th District: Northwest Detroit and suburbs.** Population: 453,057 (3% decrease since 1970). Race: White 307,386 (68%), Black 137,961 (30%), Others 7,710 (2%). Spanish origin: 4,952 (1%).

welfare bill became law, however.

Brodhead did have a major success in 1980 with the enactment of legislation providing federal adoption subsidies to reduce the number of children under foster care.

**At Home:** Brodhead has had only one difficult campaign, for his first House term in 1974. He was trading in his four years in the state Legislature on a try at the House seat Griffiths was giving up, and there was a free-for-all in the Democratic primary.

Running as an outspoken liberal, Brodhead faced the conservative vice president of the Detroit Board of Education, Patrick A. McDonald. With the help of an unusually early endorsement from the AFL-CIO and an active volunteer force, Brodhead managed to overcome McDonald's anti-busing campaign with just 256 votes to spare.

Brodhead's volunteers came largely from the ranks of the Liberal Conference, a local organization of anti-war Democrats formed in the 1960s. Conference founder Patricia Thornton had been responsible for attracting Brodhead into politics in the first place. Her group, strong on issues but weak on candidates, was delighted in 1968 when

the articulate 26-year-old lawyer agreed to help in Eugene McCarthy's presidential bid. Two years later, Brodhead was the conference candidate for a seat in the Legislature from Detroit's northwest side, and he won.

**The District:** Drawn up in 1952, the 17th was the only Republican district in Detroit when it was created. Two years later it joined its neighbors in going Democratic, as Griffiths defeated GOP Rep. Charles Oakman on her second try.

In the 1972 redistricting, the constituency expanded into southern Oakland County. A little more than half the district's vote still comes from Detroit, but the percentage has been steadily decreasing, because the population growth is outside the city. The increasingly-black western end of Detroit, located in the district, may be removed in 1982 as a result of redistricting. That would further enhance the suburban character of Brodhead's district.

The Oakland County part of the district is white-collar suburbia. The district as a whole has the highest percentage of white-collar workers in the state and includes a large Jewish community.

## Committees

**Ways and Means** (11th of 23 Democrats)
  Oversight; Public Assistance and Unemployment Compensation.

## Elections

**1980 General**

| | |
|---|---|
| William Brodhead (D ) | 127,525 (73 %) |
| Alfred Patterson (R ) | 44,313 (25 %) |

**1978 General**

| | |
|---|---|
| William Brodhead (D ) | 106,303 (95 %) |
| Hector M. McGregor (AM I) | 5,341 (5 %) |

**Previous Winning Percentages**

1976 (64 %)    1974 (70 %)

**District Vote For President**

| | 1980 | | 1976 | | 1972 |
|---|---|---|---|---|---|
| D | 95,422 (51 %) | D | 92,438 (49 %) | D | 77,659 (39 %) |
| R | 77,825 (41 %) | R | 94,131 (50 %) | R | 118,347 (59 %) |
| I | 12,426 (7 %) | | | | |

## Campaign Finance

| | Receipts | Receipts from PACs | Expenditures |
|---|---|---|---|
| **1980** | | | |
| Brodhead (D ) | $36,941 | $18,305 (50 %) | $18,539 |
| **1978** | | | |
| Brodhead (D ) | $25,028 | $13,225 (53 %) | $12,158 |

## Voting Studies

| | Presidential Support | | Party Unity | | Conservative Coalition | |
|---|---|---|---|---|---|---|
| Year | S | O | S | O | S | O |
| 1980 | 77 | 20 | 91 | 5 | 6 | 91 |
| 1979 | 82 | 17 | 91 | 7 | 8 | 91 |
| 1978 | 86 | 13 | 93 | 6 | 2 | 98 |
| 1977 | 78 | 20 | 90 | 7 | 5 | 94 |
| 1976 | 20 | 78 | 87 | 6 | 6 | 87 |
| 1975 | 27 | 70 | 90 | 7 | 8 | 90 |

S = Support          O = Opposition

## Key Votes

**96th Congress**

| | |
|---|---|
| Weaken Carter oil profits tax (1979) | N |
| Reject hospital cost control plan (1979) | N |
| Implement Panama Canal Treaties (1979) | Y |
| Establish Department of Education (1979) | Y |
| Approve Anti-busing Amendment (1979) | N |
| Guarantee Chrysler Corp. loans (1979) | Y |
| Approve military draft registration (1980) | N |
| Aid Sandinista regime in Nicaragua (1980) | Y |
| Strengthen fair housing laws (1980) | Y |

**97th Congress**

| | |
|---|---|
| Reagan budget proposal (1981) | N |

## Interest Group Ratings

| Year | ADA | ACA | AFL-CIO | CCUS |
|---|---|---|---|---|
| 1980 | 94 | 4 | 89 | 63 |
| 1979 | 100 | 4 | 95 | 0 |
| 1978 | 85 | 7 | 100 | 6 |
| 1977 | 80 | 11 | 91 | 12 |
| 1976 | 85 | 0 | 86 | 0 |
| 1975 | 100 | 7 | 96 | 6 |

# 18 James J. Blanchard (D)

**Of Pleasant Ridge — Elected 1974**

**Born:** Aug. 8, 1942, Detroit, Mich.
**Education:** Mich. State U., B.A. 1964, M.B.A. 1965; U. of Minn., J.D. 1968.
**Profession:** Lawyer.
**Family:** Wife, Paula Parker; one child.
**Religion:** Unitarian.
**Political Career:** No previous office.

**In Washington:** The near-bankruptcy of Chrysler in 1979 cast Blanchard in a role that surprised his colleagues and himself. Over a period of six months, he became the leading House spokesman for the $3.6 billion loan guarantee that kept the firm in business.

"Chrysler was no two-bit problem that some kid congressman could accomplish on his own," Speaker O'Neill said afterward, arguing that Blanchard's real achievement had been his relentless pursuit and persuasion of senior Democrats in Congress and on the outside. All sides gave him high marks for that.

And when the 97th Congress started, and the chairmanship of the Banking Committee's crucial Economic Stabilization Subcommittee opened up, Blanchard got it — something that might not have happened without Chrysler. Now he has formal jurisdiction — and considerable control — over future financial aid not only to Chrysler but to New York City and other federal supplicants.

Before 1979, Blanchard had picked up a reputation for diligence but had no public image to draw on in the House. A Vietnam-era liberal, he had not been particularly close to the auto industry, but he had been close to the United Auto Workers, which wanted the loan guarantee as much as Chrysler did. And he was the only person from Michigan on the Banking Committee.

The route from virtual conscription as Chrysler's spokesman to successful passage of the loan guarantee led through a series of roadblocks, including skepticism from Banking Chairman Henry Reuss in the House, outright opposition from his Senate counterpart, William Proxmire, a hedge from the Treasury Department and a proposed employee wage freeze that threatened to alienate the UAW at the last minute. Throughout this melodrama, Blanchard seemed to be everywhere — on the House floor, on television, and in the newspapers — repeating his basic lobbying theme: Chrysler is no longer making gas guzzlers,

Chrysler can be competitive if it gets the money. In the end, with House leaders joining in the campaign, the Chrysler bill made it through the House by a 271-136 vote.

On other issues, Blanchard has kept some distance from traditional New Deal thinking. He drafted his own "sunset" bill, calling for periodic review of all federal programs, and spoke for it in the Rules Committee and in the Democratic Caucus. Blanchard would include review of tax expenditures as well as direct legislative subsidies, which makes it more acceptable to labor but less acceptable to business.

On some issues, however, Blanchard is a Kennedy-style Democrat. He favors wage and price controls and tried to add them in 1980 to a bill extending the Council on Wage and Price Stability.

**At Home:** Blanchard's work on behalf of Chrysler and the UAW has not gone unnoticed in his district, which includes two Chrysler plants and many Chrysler employees. It has made his already secure district even safer. He has never been under 59 percent of the vote, even in his first campaign, in 1974, when he ousted one-term Republican Rep. Robert J. Huber.

When he ran for the House that year, Blanchard was a 32-year-old attorney who had never before sought public office. He had worked

---

**18th District: Detroit suburbs — Warren.** Population: 489,346 (5% increase since 1970). Race: White 470,142 (96%), Black 8,693 (2%), Others 10,511 (2%). Spanish origin: 4,409 (1%).

on several campaigns, however, including the 1968 McCarthy presidential campaign, and was a protégé of Attorney General Frank J. Kelley, one of the state's most successful Democratic politicians.

In a district where anti-busing demonstrations had made national news, Blanchard was viewed as a moderate as he sought the Democratic nomination against two anti-busing leaders. Although he pledged to oppose busing, Blanchard did not emphasize the issue, and he won the primary when his two opponents split the anti-busing vote.

Huber, the Republican incumbent, had been elected in a 1972 upset on the strength of the busing furor. By 1974, a court decision against an earlier busing order had blunted his major campaign issue. Blanchard swept him away in the tide that resulted from the Watergate scandal.

**The District:** The 18th straddles the Oak-land-Macomb County line, just north of Detroit. On the western side, in Oakland County, are middle-class communities like Oak Park and Huntington Woods, with large Jewish populations. There is real ambivalence here over racial issues, particularly among families whose stores in downtown Detroit were damaged or destroyed during the 1967 riots. Further north in Oakland County is Troy, a WASPish Republican area with larger homes and higher incomes. In 1980, Reagan carried some precincts in Troy by better than a 4-to-1 margin.

The Macomb County side, which makes up about a little more than 30 percent of the district's vote, is more blue-collar and Catholic. It is slightly more Democratic than the Oakland County part, but voters here frequently opt for the more conservative candidate when the leading campaign issue is social rather than economic, as in 1972.

## Committees

**Banking, Finance and Urban Affairs** (9th of 25 Democrats)
Economic Stabilization, chairman; Domestic Monetary Policy; Housing and Community Development.

**Science and Technology** (8th of 23 Democrats)
Energy Development and Applications; Natural Resources, Agriculture Research and Environment.

## Elections

**1980 General**

| | |
|---|---|
| James Blanchard (D ) | 135,705 (65 %) |
| Betty Suida (R ) | 68,575 (33 %) |

**1978 General**

| | |
|---|---|
| James Blanchard (D ) | 113,037 (75 %) |
| Robert Salloum (R ) | 36,913 (24 %) |

**Previous Winning Percentages**

1976 (66 %)    1974 (59 %)

**District Vote For President**

| | 1980 | | 1976 | | 1972 |
|---|---|---|---|---|---|
| D | 88,556 (40 %) | D | 93,225 (45 %) | D | 69,958 (36 %) |
| R | 111,164 (51 %) | R | 109,064 (53 %) | R | 118,376 (62 %) |
| I | 16,830 (8 %) | | | | |

## Campaign Finance

| | Receipts | Receipts from PACs | Expenditures |
|---|---|---|---|
| **1980** | | | |
| Blanchard (D ) | $95,894 | $51,530 (54 %) | $101,378 |
| **1978** | | | |
| Blanchard (D ) | $95,215 | $44,769 (47 %) | $89,842 |

## Voting Studies

| | Presidential Support | | Party Unity | | Conservative Coalition | |
|---|---|---|---|---|---|---|
| Year | S | O | S | O | S | O |
| 1980 | 78 | 19 | 88 | 6 | 18 | 74 |
| 1979 | 80 | 16 | 92 | 5 | 9 | 85 |
| 1978 | 80 | 17 | 85 | 12 | 15 | 82 |
| 1977 | 76 | 23 | 87 | 12 | 18 | 81 |
| 1976 | 29 | 71 | 86 | 11 | 15 | 83 |
| 1975 | 34 | 66 | 90 | 10 | 15 | 85 |

S = Support          O = Opposition

## Key Votes

**96th Congress**

| | |
|---|---|
| Weaken Carter oil profits tax (1979) | N |
| Reject hospital cost control plan (1979) | N |
| Implement Panama Canal Treaties (1979) | Y |
| Establish Department of Education (1979) | Y |
| Approve Anti-busing Amendment (1979) | Y |
| Guarantee Chrysler Corp. loans (1979) | Y |
| Approve military draft registration (1980) | N |
| Aid Sandinista regime in Nicaragua (1980) | Y |
| Strengthen fair housing laws (1980) | Y |

**97th Congress**

| | |
|---|---|
| Reagan budget proposal (1981) | N |

## Interest Group Ratings

| Year | ADA | ACA | AFL-CIO | CCUS |
|---|---|---|---|---|
| 1980 | 72 | 13 | 89 | 70 |
| 1979 | 79 | 8 | 90 | 11 |
| 1978 | 65 | 15 | 95 | 17 |
| 1977 | 60 | 19 | 87 | 18 |
| 1976 | 70 | 0 | 83 | 6 |
| 1975 | 95 | 14 | 96 | 18 |

# 19 William S. Broomfield (R)

**Of Birmingham — Elected 1956**

**Born:** April 28, 1922, Royal Oak, Mich.
**Education:** Attended Mich. State U., 1951.
**Military Career:** Army Air Corps, 1943.
**Profession:** Insurance executive.
**Family:** Wife, Jane Smith Thompson; three children.
**Religion:** Presbyterian.
**Political Career:** Mich. House, 1949-55; Mich. Senate, 1955-57.

**In Washington:** After two decades of cautious Republican orthodoxy on the Foreign Affairs Committee, Broomfield has found himself in an unorthodox role in recent years, helping Democrats stave off massive reductions in foreign aid bills.

Lacking a constituency among American voters "back in the district," foreign aid legislation has hovered on the edge of rejection in the House in recent years, often passing only with sizable cuts and with riders forbidding aid to communist governments.

Broomfield, rarely an outspoken leader on the committee, has emerged as a compromiser — unwilling to spend all the money Democratic committee leaders seek, but reluctant to cut as much as the new generation of conservative Republicans insists on.

In 1980, when Republican Robert Bauman of Maryland offered an amendment to cut the 1981 foreign aid level by 25 percent, Broomfield offered a compromise reduction of 10 percent, which carried. The previous year, when Bauman wanted a 10 percent across-the-board cut, Broomfield successfully offered a 5 percent cut that protected the Food for Peace program, aid to Egypt and Israel and other priorities.

Broomfield also supported the Carter administration in 1979 on maintaining "unofficial" relations with Taiwan, rather than establishing an official "liaison office" as favored by most Republicans. He was one of only 13 Republicans to back the president.

On most questions, however, Broomfield is still a hard-line anti-communist. He voted against aid to the Sandinista government in Nicaragua, despite the urgings of the House Democratic leadership, and is a strong backer of South Korea. He also tried to force Carter to set a specific date for lifting sanctions against the white regime in Zimbabwe-Rhodesia. He is a loyal supporter of Israel.

The one political issue that might have hurt Broomfield was one he was skillful enough not to become trapped in — school busing. In the early 1970s, when busing became an emotional and volatile issue in the Detroit area, several of the area's incumbents suffered for their tardiness in responding to constituent feelings. Broomfield took the lead against busing. He won approval on the House floor of his 1971 amendment to delay the effect of federal court orders on busing until all appeals had been exhausted.

There is one problem, however, on which nearly all Michigan congressmen are united — the need to help the American auto industry. Broomfield has cosponsored all auto bail-out legislation and has used the power of his committee seniority to gain access to the Reagan White House and urge pressure on the foreign automakers to cut exports.

**At Home:** Broomfield's longevity at home has little to do with his work on Foreign Affairs. It is a result of his ability to project himself to his suburban district as a genial, service-oriented Republican.

Servicing constituent requests and flooding the district with newsletters over a quarter-century have made Broomfield all but untouchable, as frustrated Democrats in the area admit. His "nice guy" image is likened to that of popular GOP Gov. William G. Milliken.

Broomfield's only political struggles have

---

**19th District: Parts of Oakland, Livingston counties.** Population: 577,989 (24% increase since 1970). Race: White 533,899 (92%), Black 32,252 (6%), Others 11,838 (2%). Spanish origin: 10,437 (2%).

come within his own party. But at the two critical junctures in his political career, when he seemed to be up against unfavorable odds, Broomfield has managed to be on the popular side of locally sensitive issues.

The first time was 1956, when he challenged a more senior state senator for the succession to retiring Republican George A. Dondero, who had served in Congress from suburban Detroit since 1932. The major issue was construction of a toll road through a residential section of Oakland County. Broomfield's opponent, George N. Higgins, supported it. Broomfield, who had fought it in the state Legislature, argued that any new highway should go through the more rural part of the county. Most of Oakland County's voters shared Broomfield's view, and he narrowly won the primary. The highway was never built.

Sixteen years later, Broomfield faced his second political crisis, following the realignment of Oakland County's congressional districts. Since 1964, he had been winning re-election easily in the eastern, more densely populated part of the county. But in 1972, when this area was attached to a blue-collar section of Macomb County, Broomfield decided he would have better luck in western Oakland County, even though that meant running against another Republican incumbent, Jack H. McDonald.

McDonald was already representing most of the district they were fighting over, but again

Broomfield had the paramount issue on his side: busing. His House amendment had put him in the forefront of the opposition to federally-mandated busing. Even though McDonald was just as firmly opposed to busing, Broomfield was the man whose opposition voters had been hearing about. He won the primary with 59 percent.

**The District:** This is probably the most Republican district in Michigan. In 1972, it gave Nixon his highest statewide percentage.

Although the district contains a small part of Livingston County, the affluent suburban areas of Oakland County form its political and geographical center. Exclusive communities such as Bloomfield Hills and Birmingham are populated by auto company executives who live in postwar ranch homes and more stately mansions of the 1920s. There are also suburban tract developments in parts of the district that were farmland when Broomfield first went to Washington in 1957.

The district's only poor community is the grimy town of Pontiac, which accounts for nearly a fifth of its population. A mix of Southern whites, blacks and Mexican-Americans — all employed in the auto plants there — make it a Democratic town. Many of the white voters are social conservatives. George C. Wallace drew 51 percent in Pontiac in the 1972 presidential primary, compared to 30 percent for George McGovern.

## Committees

**Foreign Affairs** (Ranking Republican)
    International Security and Scientific Affairs.

**Small Business** (4th of 17 Republicans)
    Export Opportunities and Special Small Business Problems.

## Elections

**1980 General**

| | |
|---|---|
| William Broomfield (R ) | 168,530 (73 %) |
| Wayne Daniels (D ) | 60,100 (26 %) |

**1978 General**

| | |
|---|---|
| William Broomfield (R) | 117,122 (71 %) |
| Betty Collier (D) | 47,165 (29 %) |

**Previous Winning Percentages**

| | | | |
|---|---|---|---|
| 1976 (67 %) | 1974 (63 %) | 1972 (70 %) | 1970 (65 %) |
| 1968 (60 %) | 1966 (68 %) | 1964 (60 %) | 1962 (60 %) |
| 1960 (56 %) | 1958 (53 %) | 1956 (57 %) | |

**District Vote For President**

| | 1980 | | 1976 | | 1972 |
|---|---|---|---|---|---|
| **D** | 79,959 (32 %) | **D** | 76,909 (36 %) | **D** | 57,620 (31 %) |
| **R** | 143,717 (58 %) | **R** | 132,349 (62 %) | **R** | 123,286 (67 %) |
| **I** | 19,927 (8 %) | | | | |

## Campaign Finance

| | Receipts | Receipts from PACs | Expenditures |
|---|---|---|---|
| **1980** | | | |
| Broomfield (R ) | $94,000 | $51,530 (55 %) | $83,608 |
| Daniels (D ) | $9,786 | $2,100 (21 %) | $9,608 |
| **1978** | | | |
| Broomfield (R ) | $58,234 | $6,504 (11 %) | $41,916 |

## Voting Studies

| | Presidential Support | | Party Unity | | Conservative Coalition | |
|---|---|---|---|---|---|---|
| Year | S | O | S | O | S | O |
| 1980 | 45 | 49 | 79 | 15 | 74 | 20 |
| 1979 | 45 | 51 | 73 | 22 | 78 | 17 |
| 1978 | 36 | 50 | 76 | 16 | 74 | 14 |
| 1977 | 52 | 44 | 75 | 18 | 77 | 17 |
| 1976 | 65 | 24 | 65 | 23 | 69 | 18 |
| 1975 | 67 | 19 | 67 | 21 | 73 | 18 |
| 1974 (Ford) | 63 | 26 | | | | |
| 1974 | 66 | 28 | 59 | 27 | 65 | 21 |
| 1973 | 65 | 29 | 67 | 26 | 68 | 23 |

## William S. Broomfield, R-Mich.

| | | | | | | |
|------|----|----|----|----|----|----|
| 1972 | 54 | 11 | 45 | 8  | 54 | 5  |
| 1971 | 72 | 26 | 65 | 31 | 67 | 32 |
| 1970 | 66 | 22 | 56 | 21 | 45 | 27 |
| 1969 | 64 | 26 | 55 | 35 | 62 | 33 |
| 1968 | 64 | 21 | 50 | 27 | 53 | 33 |
| 1967 | 29 | 18 | 39 | 11 | 30 | 9  |
| 1966 | 40 | 44 | 71 | 16 | 65 | 19 |
| 1965 | 54 | 39 | 62 | 29 | 61 | 35 |
| 1964 | 56 | 37 | 50 | 39 | 33 | 58 |
| 1963 | 48 | 42 | 64 | 24 | 53 | 47 |
| 1962 | 62 | 32 | 63 | 30 | 44 | 50 |
| 1961 | 45 | 48 | 76 | 17 | 78 | 22 |

S = Support          O = Opposition

## Key Votes

**96th Congress**

| | |
|---|---|
| Weaken Carter oil profits tax (1979) | Y |
| Reject hospital cost control plan (1979) | Y |
| Implement Panama Canal Treaties (1979) | N |
| Establish Department of Education (1979) | N |
| Approve Anti-busing Amendment (1979) | Y |
| Guarantee Chrysler Corp. loans (1979) | Y |
| Approve military draft registration (1980) | N |
| Aid Sandinista regime in Nicaragua (1980) | N |
| Strengthen fair housing laws (1980) | N |

**97th Congress**

| | |
|---|---|
| Reagan budget proposal (1981) | Y |

## Interest Group Ratings

| Year | ADA | ACA | AFL-CIO | CCUS |
|------|-----|-----|---------|------|
| 1980 | 11 | 75 | 17 | 76 |
| 1979 | 16 | 76 | 32 | 94 |
| 1978 | 10 | 76 | 5 | 82 |
| 1977 | 15 | 70 | 26 | 100 |
| 1976 | 15 | 65 | 23 | 76 |
| 1975 | 11 | 75 | 9 | 88 |
| 1974 | 22 | 43 | 22 | 38 |
| 1973 | 20 | 71 | 9 | 100 |
| 1972 | 6 | 54 | 33 | 75 |
| 1971 | 22 | 82 | 17 | - |
| 1970 | 32 | 50 | 33 | 89 |
| 1969 | 13 | 46 | 40 | - |
| 1968 | 42 | 57 | 75 | - |
| 1967 | 27 | 75 | 18 | 100 |
| 1966 | 12 | 75 | 8 | - |
| 1965 | 26 | 65 | - | 100 |
| 1964 | 40 | 53 | 36 | - |
| 1963 | - | 63 | - | - |
| 1962 | 43 | 57 | 9 | - |
| 1961 | 20 | - | - | - |

# Minnesota

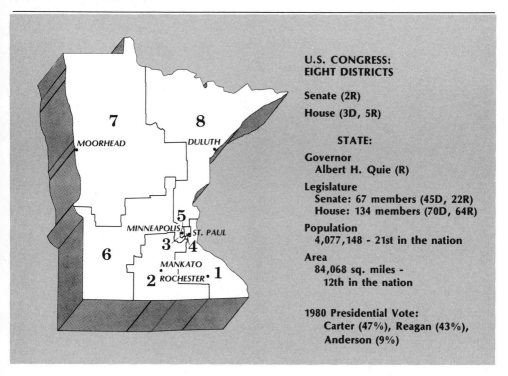

**U.S. CONGRESS:
EIGHT DISTRICTS**

Senate (2R)

House (3D, 5R)

STATE:

Governor
   Albert H. Quie (R)

Legislature
   Senate: 67 members (45D, 22R)
   House: 134 members (70D, 64R)

Population
   4,077,148 - 21st in the nation

Area
   84,068 sq. miles -
      12th in the nation

1980 Presidential Vote:
   Carter (47%), Reagan (43%),
   Anderson (9%)

## ...Textbook Politics

Politics in Minnesota comes as close to the civic textbook model as politics anywhere in the country. The turnout is often highest in the nation. There is an active, two-party system, but an unusual number of independent-minded voters. Whichever party is in power at a given moment, the state's political leaders tend to draw a degree of constituent respect rarely found in the more cynical states east of the Mississippi or the individualist ones further west. With a well-educated and well-informed electorate, Minnesota has the resources for a democratic consensus.

One of those resources is homogeneity. Minnesota is an ethnic state, but the vast majority of its ethnics come from northern Europe. First settled by Republican Yankees, the state attracted a large influx of Germans, followed by heavy Scandinavian immigration. Geographically, the Europeans settled in the same configuration as they had in the homeland. The German influ-

ence is felt most strongly in the southern part of the state, which is also the most Republican area. In the Scandinavian north, from east to west, more or less, are Finns, Swedes, and Norwegians.

Republicans — first the Yankee variety, then liberal Scandinavians — dominated the state in its early years. But heavy-handed tactics by a Republican governor in 1918 to squash the socialist-minded Non-Partisan League cost the GOP the backing of the Scandinavian wheat farmers, who liked the NPL's farm policies. They formed the Farmer-Labor Party which came to power during the Depression and later merged with the urban ethnic Catholics from the Democratic Party.

For most of the postwar years, Minnesota has been Democratic with a large "D" as well as a small one. Built in the late 1940s and 1950s under Hubert H. Humphrey's leadership, Democratic-Farmer-Labor Party control was so complete by

**625**

1975 that it seemed to be part of the culture.

That illusion ended abruptly however in 1978, the year of Humphrey's death, when Republicans took the governorship and both U.S. Senate seats after more than a decade without any of them. Those election results reflected Humphrey's absence and the fact that all those positions had been held by Democratic appointees — one an unpopular self-appointee. But they also reflected skepticism about the welfare state politics associated with the entire Democratic-Farmer-Labor Party in Minnesota. That reaction came late to Minnesota, but it came.

Whether the 1978 election was a fluke or the beginning of a major shift in direction remains to be seen. All of the Republicans who came to power in 1978 — Gov. Albert H. Quie and Sens. Rudy Boschwitz and David Durenberger — are at least a shade left of center in the national Republican Party. And in 1980 the state voted Democratic for president again, thanks largely to the presence of Walter F. Mondale as Jimmy Carter's running mate. But Carter missed a majority of the state's presidential vote, and Republicans gained a fifth House seat and held their own in the legislative elections.

# A Political Tour

**Twin Cities Area.** Half of Minnesota's population lives in the metropolitan area around the twin cities of Minneapolis and St. Paul. Straddling the Mississippi River, the cities are fraternal, not identical twins.

St. Paul, sitting on the eastern bank and facing south, was settled by German and Irish Catholics. It is a blue-collar city with strong unions, strong church influence and solid Democratic voting habits. It is smaller than Minneapolis by 100,000.

Located mostly on the western bank and facing east, Minneapolis has the well-scrubbed, Scandinavian polish that was spotlighted in the opening scenes of each segment of television's *Mary Tyler Moore Show*. A banking and financial center for the northern Midwest, Minneapolis has a sophistication that is missing in St. Paul.

Minneapolis voters are less Democratic but more liberal than those in St. Paul. As they demonstrated in 1978, they prefer a moderate Republican like Durenberger over a conservative Democrat like businessman Robert Short.

The combined 640,000 population of Minneapolis and St. Paul in 1980 represented a decline of 103,000 from 1970. St. Paul's population peaked in 1960; Minneapolis reached its highest

mark in 1950. The Twin Cities now make up less than a third of the metropolitan area's total population, which, thanks to suburban growth, has increased by 300,000 in the last decade.

Suburbanization in Minnesota is not what it is in Detroit, Cleveland and Chicago. Whites are not fleeing from center city blacks because there simply are not that many blacks in Minneapolis (8 percent) and St. Paul (5 percent) to flee from. Instead, young professional workers are leaving the older residents and blue-collar workers behind, in search of more trees and more space in the suburbs. Also, families moving to the area now settle more often in the suburbs than in the city.

The political pattern of the suburbs is Republican around Minneapolis and Democratic closer to St. Paul. The population growth has been much greater on the more affluent Minneapolis side. Bloomington, just south of Minneapolis, is now the fourth largest city in the state.

**Agricultural South.** Farm land covers most of the southern third of Minnesota. Corn and hogs predominate, but there are numerous dairy farms and hundreds of acres devoted to soybeans and oats. Worthington, in the southwestern corner, claims to be the "Turkey Capital of the World."

Germans are the predominant ethnic group throughout the area from St. Cloud south to the Iowa border. Divided between Catholic and Lutheran communities, they tend to be more conservative and Republican than the rest of the state. The highest percentages for the 1978 Republican statewide candidates and for Ronald Reagan in 1980 came from this region.

The only Democratic areas here are in the meat packing center of Austin and along the South Dakota border near the headwaters of the Minnesota River. This less-fertile land was settled by Swedes rather than Germans, and some farmers there have their roots in the Farmer-Labor Party and the populist Farmers Union. In 1972 George McGovern ran exceptionally well in this part of southern Minnesota.

Although St. Cloud used to be a Democratic city, it has been trending Republican in recent years as abortion and social issues have begun to influence its political choices. Reagan's victory in Stearns County (St. Cloud) marked the first time since 1956 that a Republican presidential candidate had won the county.

Rochester, a prosperous farm center in the southeast corner, also manufactures IBM computers and is the home of the Mayo Clinic. It regularly tops the list of Republican counties, usually giving well over 65 percent to the GOP.

The population in the eastern farming regions has continued to grow during the 1970s, but west of Mankato, nearly every county has lost, as the larger farms require fewer hands.

**Red River Valley of the North.** Not to be confused with the river that separates Texas from Oklahoma, the Red River of the North flows into Lake Winnipeg in Canada, forming the boarder between Minnesota and North Dakota. Like its namesake, the northern Red River crosses a major wheat growing area in the prairies.

Politically, this area fluctuates between Democrats and Republicans, depending largely on agricultural conditions. The diversity of crops is not very great; the price of wheat contributes significantly to farmers' interest in keeping or replacing the party in power.

Moorhead, the twin city of Fargo, N.D., is the only town of any size in the area, and one that recently has been voting Republican. North of Moorhead, rural counties like Red Lake and Mahnomen usually side with the Democrats, but they are surrounded by Republican territory. Both went for McGovern in 1972 and were the only two in the area to support the incumbent Democratic governor, Rudy Perpich, in 1978.

People have been leaving these bitterly cold plains, where winter lasts from November through April. The only growth areas in the Red River Valley are centered around winter-related industries, such as snowmobile manufacturing. But two successive winters with little snow have put those industries into a steep decline. The population boom in Pennington and Roseau counties, where two major snowmobile plants prospered in the 1970s, may now be over.

**The Iron Range.** The northeastern wedge of Minnesota is where most of the nation's iron ore once came from. Nearly all of the natural ore veins were depleted during World War II, and the steel industry began to look elsewhere for raw materials. But mining remains the mainstay of the area's faltering economy.

Settled by Finns and Swedes, and by Minnesota's only substantial East European population, the Iron Range is the most predictably Democratic region in the state. Although political battles are not uncommon, they take place within the Democratic Party or between labor and management, rather than between Democrats and Republicans.

Except for lightly-populated Cook County on the shore of Lake Superior, the entire northeastern part of the state voted for Jimmy Carter in 1980. Two years earlier, it was the only region in the state to support both Democratic U.S. Senate candidates — conservative Robert Short and liberal Wendell Anderson.

Duluth, the only city in the state outside the Twin Cities that has more than 50,000 people, is the unofficial capital of the Iron Range. The westernmost Atlantic Ocean port (thanks to the St. Lawrence Seaway), Duluth has a large blue-collar population and is reliably Democratic.

# Redrawing the Lines

The three districts clustered in the Minneapolis-St. Paul area are underpopulated and surrounded by four overpopulated districts that fan out from the Twin Cities to the edges of the state.

The GOP representatives in the outlying 6th and 7th districts received less than 55 percent of the vote in 1980, but suggestions in early 1981 that the Democratic-controlled Legislature might try to make those districts more Democratic provoked warnings of a gubernatorial veto.

## Governor
## Albert H. Quie (R)

**Born:** Sept. 18, 1923, Wheeling, Minn.
**Home:** Denison, Minn.
**Education:** Olaf College, B.S. 1950.
**Military Career:** Navy, World War II.
**Profession:** Dairy farmer.
**Family:** Wife, Gretchen; five children.
**Religion:** Lutheran.
**Political Career:** Unsuccessful campaign for Minnesota House, 1952; Minnesota Senate 1955-59; U.S. House, 1959-79; elected governor 1978; term expires Jan. 1983.

*Minnesota - Senior Senator*

# David F. Durenberger (R)

**Of Minneapolis — Elected 1978**

**Born:** Aug. 19, 1934, St. Cloud, Minn.
**Education:** St. John's U., B.A. 1955; U. of Minn.,
J.D. 1959.
**Military Career:** Army Reserve, 1956-63.
**Profession:** Lawyer.
**Family:** Wife, Gilda Beth "Penny" Baran; four
children.
**Religion:** Roman Catholic.
**Political Career:** No previous office.

**In Washington:** When Durenberger won
this seat in 1978, ending 20 years of Democratic
control, he brought a change not only in party but
in personality. Watching him puff on his pipe at a
committee meeting, quietly questioning the logic
behind a tax subsidy, it is hard to imagine anyone
less like the seat's former occupant, Hubert H.
Humphrey. Durenberger after Humphrey is like
chamber music after Tchaikovsky.

The ideological difference is not enormous.
Durenberger votes a more liberal line than a
majority of his party, frequently joining the
Democrats in support of social programs and civil
rights measures. But Humphrey was an effusive,
passionate liberal of the heart. Durenberger,
good-humored but analytical, rarely lets his emo-
tions show.

The closest he has come to a passion is his
dogged promotion of a plan to rebuild the American health care system through tax incentives.

Durenberger's health bill, a Republican answer to Democratic proposals for national health
insurance and hospital cost controls, would use
tax incentives to induce employers to offer their
workers a choice of health insurance plans. The
competition, Durenberger contends, would force
doctors and hospitals to offer better care at a
more reasonable price.

Durenberger's proposal, which grew out of
the success of prepaid health plans in the Minneapolis-St. Paul area, attracted him a modest
amount of attention in the 96th Congress. In the
97th, he is getting more — the new Republican
Senate majority made him chairman of the Finance subcommittee governing health.

Durenberger's second major preoccupation
on Finance during his first two years was a
defense of the revenue-sharing system. He was
the ranking Republican on the Finance subcommittee handling revenue-sharing, and a prominent defender of no-strings-attached grants to
state governments.

In 1980, Durenberger got the Senate to vote
down a House requirement that states which
accept revenue-sharing give up other federal aid,
dollar-for-dollar. At House insistence, this
tradeoff concept was later restored.

On the Governmental Affairs Committee,
Durenberger has proved more amenable than
most Republicans toward preservation of the federal regulatory system. In the 96th Congress, he
supported a measure to subsidize consumers who
want to participate in regulatory agency hearings.
He also sided with supporters of a strong bill to
regulate lobbyists. When that bill was foundering
on the question of whether lobby groups should
be forced to disclose their corporate financial
backers, Durenberger crafted a compromise requiring them to reveal the names of supporting
organizations, but not the amount of the backing;
his amendment narrowly failed, and the bill died
with it.

Outside of his committees, Durenberger's
most visible activity has been fighting the Postal
Service's attempt to expand the ZIP code from
five to nine digits.

In 1980 he won passage of a Senate amendment to an appropriation bill barring the nine-
digit ZIP. Despite the protests of the bill's sponsors, he demanded a roll-call vote, saying it would
help the Senate's case in conference with the
House. The sponsors gave him his roll call (90 to
0), then dropped his amendment in conference
anyway. In 1981 he reintroduced his full bill to
block the longer ZIP, but he lost on the Senate
floor and the Postal Service went ahead with it.

**At Home:** The 1978 political year did not
turn out exactly as Durenberger planned, but it
was more successful for him than most Minnesota
Republicans ever thought it could be. When the
year began, he was preparing a gubernatorial
challenge that seemed to be going nowhere. When

it ended, he was the state's senior senator.

Durenberger had hovered on the periphery of public office for years, as chief aide to GOP Gov. Harold Levander during the late 1960s and as a well-connected Minneapolis lawyer after that. But he was politically untested, and he was given little chance to take the nomination for governor away from popular Rep. Albert H. Quie.

When interim Sen. Muriel Humphrey announced that she would not run for the remaining four years of her late husband's term, Republican leaders asked Durenberger to switch contests. He was easy to persuade.

Democratic disunity aided Durenberger immensely. The party's endorsed candidate, Rep. Donald M. Fraser, was defeated in a primary by Bob Short, a blustery conservative whose campaign against environmentalists alienated much

of the Democratic left. Some Democrats chose not to vote in the general election, but even more deserted to Durenberger, who had the endorsement of the Americans for Democratic Action. As a result, the Republican won a solid victory.

Durenberger remains popular among most segments of the Minnesota electorate, although his moderate views have antagonized some in the Republicans' conservative wing. At the 1980 state GOP convention, a group of conservative activists, mainly from southern Minnesota, warned him to move right if he wanted their backing for re-election in 1982. Whether he will need their help is not clear. One potential problem on the Democratic side disappeared when former Vice President Walter F. Mondale, a senator from 1964 to 1976, announced in early 1981 that he would not seek the seat.

## Committees

**Finance** (8th of 11 Republicans)
Health, chairman; Energy and Agricultural Taxation; Social Security and Income Maintenance Programs.

**Governmental Affairs** (7th of 9 Republicans)
Intergovernmental Relations, chairman; Energy, Nuclear Proliferation, and Government Processes; Federal Expenditures, Research, and Rules.

**Select Intelligence** (6th of 8 Republicans)
Analysis and Production; Budget; Collection and Foreign Operations.

**Special Aging** (8th of 8 Republicans)

## Elections

**1978 Special Election**

| | |
|---|---|
| David Durenberger (R ) | 957,908 (61 %) |
| Robert Short (D ) | 538,675 (35 %) |

**1978 Special Primary**

| | |
|---|---|
| David Durenberger (R ) | 139,187 (67 %) |
| Malcolm Moos (R ) | 32,314 (16 %) |
| Ken Nordstrom (R ) | 14,635 (7 %) |
| Will Lundquist (R ) | 12,261 (6 %) |

## Campaign Finance

| | Receipts | Receipts from PACs | Expenditures |
|---|---|---|---|
| **1978** | | | |
| Durenberger (R ) | $1,073,135 | $250,448 (23 %) | $1,062,271 |
| Short (D ) | $1,982,442 | $40,295 (2 %) | $1,972,060 |

## Voting Studies

| | Presidential Support | | Party Unity | | Conservative Coalition | |
|---|---|---|---|---|---|---|
| Year | S | O | S | O | S | O |
| 1980 | 54 | 42 | 54 | 38 | 42 | 49 |
| 1979 | 68 | 30 | 50 | 43 | 33 | 59 |

S = Support          O = Opposition

## Key Votes

**96th Congress**

| | |
|---|---|
| Maintain relations with Taiwan (1979) | Y |
| Reduce synthetic fuel development funds (1979) | N |
| Impose nuclear plant moratorium (1979) | Y |
| Kill stronger windfall profits tax (1979) | Y |
| Guarantee Chrysler Corp. loans (1979) | N |
| Approve military draft registration (1980) | Y |
| End Revenue Sharing to the states (1980) | N |
| Block Justice Dept. busing suits (1980) | N |

**97th Congress**

| | |
|---|---|
| Restore urban program funding cuts (1981) | Y |

## Interest Group Ratings

| Year | ADA | ACA | AFL-CIO | CCUS-1 | CCUS-2 |
|---|---|---|---|---|---|
| 1980 | 44 | 72 | 33 | 77 | |
| 1979 | 53 | 36 | 67 | 45 | 50 |

# Rudy Boschwitz (R)

**Of Plymouth — Elected 1978**

**Born:** Nov. 7, 1930, Berlin, Germany.
**Education:** N.Y.U., B.S. 1950, LL.B. 1953.
**Military Career:** Army, 1954-55.
**Profession:** Owner of plywood and home improvement company.
**Family:** Wife, Ellen Lowenstein; four children.
**Religion:** Jewish.
**Political Career:** Republican National Committeeman from Minnesota, 1971-79.

**In Washington:** Friendly, garrulous and impulsive, Boschwitz has worked hard in the Senate to restrain his gadfly instincts and find an issue to focus on. The Republican Senate takeover in 1981 made that job somewhat easier: it gave Boschwitz a chance to chair three different subcommittees, all dealing one way or another with international trade.

On the Agriculture Committee, Boschwitz has a subcommittee on foreign agricultural policy, and has been using it to promote U.S. farm exports. He can follow up on that issue with his Small Business panel on Export Promotion and Market Development. More important, he took over the Foreign Relations Subcommittee on Near Eastern and South Asian Affairs, and plunged immediately into the debate over the sale of arms to Saudi Arabia.

On that issue, his position is clear. He opposed the sale of advanced AWACS jets to the Saudis, and the enhancement of F-15 planes the Carter administration agreed to sell them in 1978. "They wish to have them become offensive weapons," he said in March of 1981, "rather than just being defensive weapons as they were originally intended to be."

On Agriculture, he cast a nervous vote in favor of President Reagan's plan to cancel a scheduled April 1 increase in dairy price supports. He refused to join three Democratic holdouts, even though Minnesota is the nation's fourth leading dairy state. "I told the people of Minnesota to hang in there with President Reagan," he said later, "and I hope they hang in with me."

Boschwitz spent a frustrating two years on the Budget Committee in the 96th Congress, finding its economic uncertainties unlike anything he was used to in the plywood business. Budget ceilings would be set and then broken; inflation estimates would be set and then raised; the schedule seemed haphazard, the votes unpredictable. Boschwitz, a balanced budget man, found himself voting with liberal Democrats in 1980 against a balanced budget proposal by then-chairman Edmund S. Muskie because it called for higher taxes rather than lower spending.

He worked closely with Muskie, however, in a "Frost Belt" alliance in 1979 aimed at changing a fuel aid allocation formula to make it more favorable to Northern states. Boschwitz threatened to filibuster unless an adjustment was made. A Muskie-Boschwitz amendment was defeated, but the effort brought about a compromise formula slightly more acceptable to Minnesota and Maine. Minnesota wound up with 3.6 percent of $7 billion available over two years instead of 2.6 percent in the earlier version.

Boschwitz generally votes with the more moderate Senate Republicans. He was one of the first to endorse Sen. Howard H. Baker Jr. for president in 1980, prompting an angry reaction from an old political ally and Reagan supporter in Minnesota. Boschwitz shrugged. "I do my own thing," he said. "In these kinds of situations, I'm not the kind of guy to hesitate."

**At Home:** When a folksy, flannel-shirted Boschwitz began appearing in television ads for his plywood business more than a decade ago, some Minnesota politicians suspected he might be thinking of selling more than do-it-yourself home furnishings. They were right.

Elected a Republican national committeeman in 1971, he waited patiently for the opportune time to run for office. At the start of each election year he was on everyone's list as a Senate or gubernatorial contender, but until 1978 he always passed up the chance. By then, Boschwitz had a dedicated corps of political allies and a face well-known to the public. He started talking about inflation rather than plywood.

Boschwitz picked the right year, and the right opponent — Sen. Wendell R. Anderson, who as governor had arranged to have himself named to the Senate in late 1976 when Walter F. Mondale resigned to become Jimmy Carter's vice president. Anderson felt he could perform well enough in the job to overcome the jinx that follows most "self-appointed" senators to Washington. But he could not overcome it.

In the campaign, Boschwitz endorsed standard GOP campaign themes, but said little that was controversial. It was a campaign of personalities rather than issues, and Boschwitz had the advantage over the more reserved Anderson.

Boschwitz had been on the move much of his life. Born in Berlin, he fled Nazi Germany with his parents when he was two, moving first to Czechoslovakia, then to Switzerland, the Netherlands, England and the United States. He was educated in New York and practiced law there. But he grew tired of that, moved to Minnesota and made $5 million with his Plywood Minnesota business, which grew to include 67 outlets throughout the upper Midwest.

## Committees

**Agriculture, Nutrition and Forestry** (6th of 9 Republicans)
Foreign Agricultural Policy, chairman; Agricultural Production, Marketing and Stabilization of Prices; Agricultural Research and General Legislation; Rural Development, Oversight, and Investigations.

**Budget** (4th of 12 Republicans)

**Foreign Relations** (8th of 9 Republicans)
Near Eastern and South Asian Affairs, chairman; East Asian and Pacific Affairs; European Affairs.

**Small Business** (5th of 9 Republicans)
Export Promotion and Market Development, chairman; Capital Formation and Retention.

## Elections

**1978 General**

| | |
|---|---|
| Rudy Boschwitz (R ) | 894,092 (57 %) |
| Wendell Anderson (D ) | 638,375 (40 %) |

**1978 Primary**

| | |
|---|---|
| Rudy Boschwitz (R ) | 185,393 (87 %) |
| Harold Stassen (R) | 28,170 (13 %) |

## Campaign Finance

| | Receipts | Receipts from PACs | Expenditures |
|---|---|---|---|
| **1978** | | | |
| Boschwitz (R ) | $1,902,861 | $261,257 (14 %) | $1,870,163 |
| Anderson (D ) | $1,155,562 | $198,847 (17 %) | $1,154,351 |

## Voting Studies

| | Presidential Support | | Party Unity | | Conservative Coalition | |
|---|---|---|---|---|---|---|
| Year | S | O | S | O | S | O |
| 1980 | 53 | 45† | 74 | 23 | 67 | 33† |
| 1979 | 50 | 49 | 73 | 27 | 64 | 36 |

† Not eligible for all recorded votes.

S = Support    O = Opposition

## Key Votes

**96th Congress**

| | |
|---|---|
| Maintain relations with Taiwan (1979) | Y |
| Reduce synthetic fuel development funds (1979) | Y |
| Impose nuclear plant moratorium (1979) | Y |
| Kill stronger windfall profits tax (1979) | Y |
| Guarantee Chrysler Corp. loans (1979) | N |
| Approve military draft registration (1980) | Y |
| End Revenue Sharing to the states (1980) | N |
| Block Justice Dept. busing suits (1980) | N |

**97th Congress**

| | |
|---|---|
| Restore urban program funding cuts (1981) | N |

## Interest Group Ratings

| Year | ADA | ACA | AFL-CIO | CCUS-1 | CCUS-2 |
|---|---|---|---|---|---|
| 1980 | 28 | 96 | 11 | 86 | |
| 1979 | 21 | 63 | 21 | 73 | 75 |

# 1 Arlen Erdahl (R)

**Of West St. Paul — Elected 1978**
**Born:** Feb. 27, 1931, Blue Earth, Minn.
**Education:** St. Olaf College, B.A. 1953; Harvard U., M.P.A. 1966.
**Military Career:** Army, 1954-56.
**Profession:** Farmer.
**Family:** Wife, Ellen Syrdal; six children.
**Religion:** Lutheran.
**Political Career:** Minn. House, 1963-71; Minn. Sec. of State, 1971-75; sought Republican nomination for U.S. House, 1974; Republican nominee for Minn. Sec. of State, 1974.

**In Washington:** Erdahl took the place on Education and Labor that was held for nearly 20 years by Albert H. Quie, whose election as governor of Minnesota brought Erdahl to the House. It was not an easy place to fill, because Quie's integrity and knowledge of education gave him a special reputation. But Erdahl quietly set about his apprenticeship.

Like Quie, Erdahl has been one of the less partisan Republicans on what has traditionally been a highly partisan committee. "Just because Carter or the Democrats propose something," he said in his first term, "I'm not automatically going to be against that." In 1980, Erdahl voted with the Democratic president 55 percent of the time, compared to an average of 40 percent for all House Republicans.

One of those occasions was the vote on creation of a new Department of Education, which Carter badly wanted but which Republicans opposed in the House by a margin of three-to-one, arguing mostly that it would be a threat to local and state control of schools. Erdahl favored the department and played an important role in the debate, winning adoption of his amendment directing the department to permit voluntary prayer in schools.

He was also the only Republican on a House-Senate conference committee to support reauthorization of ACTION, the volunteer agency, without imposing severe restrictions on its activities. Most GOP members criticized ACTION Director Sam Brown for what they saw as his efforts at political organization of the poor.

On labor-related issues, Erdahl has proved to be a more orthodox Republican. When the Education and Labor Committee gave bipartisan support in 1979 to a bill permitting unionization of medical interns, Erdahl joined a rump group of nine Republicans who fought it successfully on the House floor, arguing that interns are students and should not be treated as wage earners.

**At Home:** After Erdahl suffered double defeats in 1974, few thought he would hold major office again, let alone break Quie's vote-getting record in the 1st District.

But when Erdahl won his second term in 1980 with 72 percent of the vote, he amassed a higher percentage than the popular Quie attained in 20 years of representing southern Minnesota. Ronald Reagan was part of the reason, but Erdahl ran 50,000 votes ahead of Reagan in the district.

Erdahl made his comeback in 1978 on the slogan "he fits the district," and he does. His farming background and later residence in the Twin Cities area allows him to claim he understands the values of the district's two major segments. He is not a dynamic campaigner, but he is a pleasant one: the *Minneapolis Tribune* once described him as a "chatty, inquisitive, mild-mannered product of the Gerald Ford school of moderate Republican conservatism."

Erdahl served four terms in the state Legislature, where he was chairman of the Labor Relations Committee and maintained good contacts with the other side of the aisle. In 1970 he was elected secretary of state, the last election he was to win for eight years.

In 1974, claiming residence at his Blue Earth farm in the 2nd District, Erdahl ran for the House, expecting a relatively easy time. He was defeated for the GOP nomination on the 20th ballot at a convention by state Rep. Tom Hage-

---

**1st District: Southeast — Rochester, Winona.** Population: 538,276 (14% increase since 1970). Race: White 530,694 (99%), Black 1,511 (0.3%), Others 6,071 (1%). Spanish origin: 3,834 (1%).

dorn. Embarrassed by that defeat, Erdahl tried to win a second term as secretary of state, but lost the general election badly.

Out of office, he managed to gain appointment by Democratic governors to the state Public Service Commission. This helped keep him in the public arena, and paved the way for his 1978 comeback.

That year, running in the state's easternmost district — not his original home — he was able to win the GOP endorsement. He defeated state Sen. Mel Frederick on the fifth ballot and went on to carry every county in November against Democratic state Sen. Gerry Sikorski. Although Erdahl's major base of support was in the farming communities, he also ran ahead of Sikorski in the Twin Cities' suburbs. Two years later, Democrats were so pessimistic about their chances that they did not even officially endorse their candidate.

**The District:** Extending from the southern edge of St. Paul down to the Iowa border, the 1st is arguably Minnesota's most Republican territory. It has not elected a Democratic representative since 1892.

Agriculture's domination of the district decreased somewhat in 1971 redistricting, when three rural counties were removed in exchange for working-class suburban areas near the Twin Cities. But the majority of the vote is still cast in the nine farming counties centered around the heavily Republican city of Rochester. The only place in the nine-county area where Republican strength is slightly weaker is the heavily Polish town of Winona along the Mississippi River.

For a Democrat to carry the district, he needs to run exceptionally well in the St. Paul suburbs in Washington and Dakota counties. In 1980, Carter's 8,000-vote edge there was not nearly enough to overcome the 60 percent Reagan received in the rest of the district.

## Committees

**Education and Labor** (7th of 14 Republicans)
Elementary, Secondary and Vocational Education; Postsecondary Education; Select Education.

**Foreign Affairs** (12th of 16 Republicans)
Africa; International Economic Policy and Trade.

## Elections

**1980 General**

| | |
|---|---|
| Arlen Erdahl (R ) | 171,099 (72 %) |
| Russell Smith (D ) | 67,279 (28 %) |

**1978 General**

| | |
|---|---|
| Arlen Erdahl (R ) | 110,090 (56 %) |
| Gerry Sikorski (D ) | 83,271 (43 %) |

**1978 Primary**

| | |
|---|---|
| Arlen Erdahl (R ) | 26,768 (74 %) |
| R. H. Campbell (R ) | 4,338 (12 %) |
| David Drummond (R ) | 3,937 (11 %) |

**District Vote For President**

| 1980 | | 1976 | | 1972 | |
|---|---|---|---|---|---|
| D | 88,663 (37 %) | D | 120,282 (49 %) | D | 82,155 (39 %) |
| R | 120,820 (51 %) | R | 117,565 (48 %) | R | 122,534 (59 %) |
| I | 21,763 (9 %) | | | | |

## Campaign Finance

| | Receipts | Receipts from PACs | Expenditures |
|---|---|---|---|
| **1980** | | | |
| Erdahl (R ) | $129,545 | $49,512 (38 %) | $100,261 |

| **1978** | | | |
|---|---|---|---|
| Erdahl (R ) | $199,142 | $59,365 (30 %) | $194,363 |
| Sikorski (D ) | $151,893 | $61,444 (40 %) | $149,089 |

## Voting Studies

| | Presidential Support | | Party Unity | | Conservative Coalition | |
|---|---|---|---|---|---|---|
| Year | S | O | S | O | S | O |
| 1980 | 55 | 43 | 69 | 27 | 49 | 46 |
| 1979 | 41 | 54 | 72 | 24 | 71 | 23 |

S = Support          O = Opposition

## Key Votes

**96th Congress**

| | |
|---|---|
| Weaken Carter oil profits tax (1979) | Y |
| Reject hospital cost control plan (1979) | Y |
| Implement Panama Canal Treaties (1979) | N |
| Establish Department of Education (1979) | Y |
| Approve Anti-busing Amendment (1979) | N |
| Guarantee Chrysler Corp. loans (1979) | N |
| Approve military draft registration (1980) | N |
| Aid Sandinista regime in Nicaragua (1980) | Y |
| Strengthen fair housing laws (1980) | Y |

**97th Congress**

| | |
|---|---|
| Reagan budget proposal (1981) | Y |

## Interest Group Ratings

| Year | ADA | ACA | AFL-CIO | CCUS |
|---|---|---|---|---|
| 1980 | 56 | 54 | 21 | 79 |
| 1979 | 32 | 76 | 17 | 88 |

**633**

# 2    Tom Hagedorn (R)

### Of Truman — Elected 1974

**Born:** Nov. 27, 1943, Blue Earth, Minn.
**Education:** Graduated from Blue Earth H.S., 1961.
**Military Career:** Navy, 1961.
**Profession:** Farmer.
**Family:** Separated; three children.
**Religion:** Lutheran.
**Political Career:** Minn. House, 1971-75.

**In Washington:** Much of Hagedorn's legislative career has been built around two issues: bacon and Davis-Bacon.

One is the kind that people eat at breakfast, the kind that is produced at Hormel and Wilson meatpacking plants in Hagedorn's district, and comes from hogs fed on corn from the surrounding countryside. When federal authorities considered a ban on nitrites during the 1970s, citing the meat preservation ingredient as possibly carcinogenic, Hagedorn was among those most active in trying to head it off. In 1978, he introduced legislation to delay any federal nitrite ban for two years. He labeled it the Breakfast Preservation Act of 1978.

Davis-Bacon is the law that requires contractors to pay locally "prevailing" wage rates for federal construction projects. In practice that generally means union wage rates, and conservatives have sought for years to repeal it on grounds that it forces up wage rates for private industry in communities where the government is involved.

For the past several years, the leading House critic of Davis-Bacon has been Tom Hagedorn. He has sought on some occasions to limit its applicability to specific projects, and on others to dispense with it altogether. He has not been successful so far.

Otherwise, Hagedorn is a low-key, amiable legislator with a district orientation but with personal ties to the national conservative movement. He is militantly anti-abortion; he introduced an amendment in 1978 that would have blocked the U.S. Civil Rights Commission from studying or recommending any action on the subject. In 1977, he tried to prevent the Legal Services Corp. from intervening in court cases except in behalf of individual clients. He was angered by the role that legal services lawyers played in defending the University of California against a "reverse discrimination" suit brought by medical student Allan Bakke.

**At Home:** When Hagedorn left his grain and livestock farm and his state legislative seat in 1974 to run for the House, many thought he was too young and too conservative for the district. It did not turn out to be the case.

Hagedorn has encountered only one major obstacle in a political career that began when he volunteered to work for Barry Goldwater in 1964. That was when he had to wrest the Republican congressional endorsement from then-Secretary of State Arlen Erdahl in 1974. Although Erdahl was better known, older and the favorite going into the district convention, Hagedorn worked harder, and he was the choice of retiring Rep. Ancher Nelsen.

Doggedly rounding up delegates from around the district, Hagedorn showed surprising strength on the early ballots. In one of the state's most grueling conventions of recent years, Hagedorn went on to take the endorsement from Erdahl on the 20th ballot. Since then, the boyish, blond-haired conservative has had few difficulties. Hagedorn's margin in 1974 was lower than any of Nelsen's, but in subsequent years he has been as strong as his predecessor.

Hagedorn runs well in the farm areas and in the well-to-do suburbs of Minneapolis, in the northern part of the district. He is weaker in the heavily unionized meatpacking town of Austin, which he lost in 1980.

---

**2nd District: South central — Mankato.** Population: 548,682 (15% increase since 1970). Race: White 541,265 (99%), Black 1,517 (0.2%), Others 5,900 (1%). Spanish origin: 3,950 (1%).

**The District:** The 2nd District follows the fertile Minnesota River valley from the outskirts of Minneapolis to the tiny village of Franklin, 80 miles west. Most of the territory in between is covered with hog and dairy farms and endless miles of cornfields. Politically and geographically, the district resembles rural Iowa, just across the border to the south.

Conservative German Catholics settled in Mankato and other nearby towns in the 19th Century, and have influenced politics in much of the area since then, although Lutherans are also important. The Scandinavian influence, felt more heavily in northern Minnesota, exists in the 2nd district, but is far less noticeable.

The Democratic vote in the district is concentrated in the southeastern corner, where meatpacking plants account for a high percentage of union workers.

In 1972 the district gained two predominantly Republican suburban areas near the Twin Cities — the southwest corner of Hennepin County and the western part of Dakota County. They account for about a quarter of the district's vote and gave Ronald Reagan 56 percent in 1980, compared to just under 50 percent district-wide.

## Committees

**Agriculture** (4th of 19 Republicans)
Livestock, Dairy and Poultry; Wheat, Soybeans and Feed Grains.

**Public Works and Transportation** (6th of 19 Republicans)
Aviation; Economic Development; Surface Transportation

## Elections

**1980 General**

| | |
|---|---|
| Tom Hagedorn (R ) | 158,082 (61 %) |
| Harold Bergquist (D ) | 102,586 (39 %) |

**1978 General**

| | |
|---|---|
| Tom Hagedorn (R ) | 145,415 (70 %) |
| John Considine (D ) | 61,173 (30 %) |

**Previous Winning Percentages**

1976 (60 %)    1974 (53 %)

**District Vote For President**

| 1980 | | 1976 | | 1972 | |
|---|---|---|---|---|---|
| D | 108,381 (40 %) | D | 125,616 (49 %) | D | 88,633 (40 %) |
| R | 134,627 (50 %) | R | 123,435 (48 %) | R | 129,532 (58 %) |
| I | 22,119 (8 %) | | | | |

## Campaign Finance

| | Receipts | Receipts from PACs | Expenditures |
|---|---|---|---|
| **1980** | | | |
| Hagedorn (R ) | $187,965 | $40,900 (22 %) | $196,870 |
| Bergquist (D ) | $100,677 | $16,600 (16 %) | $99,762 |
| **1978** | | | |
| Hagedorn (R ) | $177,974 | $19,000 (11 %) | $172,482 |
| Considine (D ) | $22,085 | $7,540 (34 %) | $22,086 |

## Voting Studies

| | Presidential Support | | Party Unity | | Conservative Coalition | |
|---|---|---|---|---|---|---|
| Year | S | O | S | O | S | O |
| 1980 | 41 | 55 | 79 | 11 | 82 | 11 |
| 1979 | 29 | 64 | 84 | 8 | 88 | 4 |
| 1978 | 22 | 62 | 79 | 8 | 84 | 5 |
| 1977 | 41 | 57 | 86 | 10 | 90 | 6 |
| 1976 | 71 | 25 | 85 | 10 | 87 | 8 |
| 1975 | 61 | 35 | 85 | 10 | 88 | 8 |

S = Support          O = Opposition

## Key Votes

**96th Congress**

| | |
|---|---|
| Weaken Carter oil profits tax (1979) | Y |
| Reject hospital cost control plan (1979) | Y |
| Implement Panama Canal Treaties (1979) | N |
| Establish Department of Education (1979) | N |
| Approve Anti-busing Amendment (1979) | Y |
| Guarantee Chrysler Corp. loans (1979) | N |
| Approve military draft registration (1980) | Y |
| Aid Sandinista regime in Nicaragua (1980) | N |
| Strengthen fair housing laws (1980) | N |

**97th Congress**

| | |
|---|---|
| Reagan budget proposal (1981) | Y |

## Interest Group Ratings

| Year | ADA | ACA | AFL-CIO | CCUS |
|---|---|---|---|---|
| 1980 | 11 | 68 | 21 | 81 |
| 1979 | 0 | 100 | 5 | 100 |
| 1978 | 5 | 92 | 0 | 82 |
| 1977 | 5 | 85 | 17 | 100 |
| 1976 | 0 | 89 | 13 | 85 |
| 1975 | 16 | 88 | 9 | 88 |

# 3 Bill Frenzel (R)

**Of Golden Valley — Elected 1970**

**Born:** July 31, 1928, St. Paul, Minn.
**Education:** Dartmouth College, B.A. 1950,
M.B.A. 1951.
**Military Career:** Naval Reserve, 1951-54.
**Profession:** Warehouse company executive.
**Family:** Wife, Ruth Purdy; three children.
**Political Career:** Minn. House, 1963-71.

**In Washington:** One of the most articulate Republican spokesmen on the House floor, Frenzel would likely be a party leader today if he did not carry the burden of a moderate-to-liberal image built on his arrival, when he was a dues-paying member of Common Cause and printed his news releases on recycled paper.

Frenzel has not made any major changes in his political beliefs, but most of his recent work has been in a more conservative direction, especially on the sensitive subject of campaign finance. Still, when he ran in 1979 for the stepping-stone post of House GOP policy chairman, he was beaten in an upset by the abrasive but dogged E. G. "Bud" Shuster of Pennsylvania. Some colleagues felt afterwards that Frenzel had been harmed by the perception, correct or not, that he was left of center in a Republican Conference moving rapidly to the right.

That perception may seem odd to those who have watched Frenzel in recent years attacking the Federal Election Commission (FEC) and ridiculing efforts to finance congressional elections with federal money. He is the leading congressional exponent of the view that the growth of corporate political action committees symbolizes the health of the political system, not its corruption.

Early in 1979, Frenzel argued loudly and successfully in the House Administration Committee against the public financing bill demanded by Speaker O'Neill. Later in the year, when Democrats tried to limit the amount of money political action committees could give to congressional candidates, Frenzel denounced the legislation as "a bill they had to have to protect their incumbents." It passed the House but died in the Senate amid threats of a filibuster.

Frenzel has become a strenuous critic of the FEC, the agency he worked hard to launch in the mid-70s. He introduced a bill to create the FEC in 1974 and steered it to passage in the House over the acerbic and personal opposition of Wayne L.

Hays, D-Ohio, the House Administration chairman. But by 1978, Frenzel was on the other side of the issue. "The FEC is remorseless in trying to stifle politics," he complained. "If it continues to be so picky, it might find itself with a good deal less authority." At the beginning of 1980, Frenzel and House Administration Democrats cooperated on a bill that eliminated some of the campaign finance reporting requirements candidates had most often complained about, reducing the number of written reports filed every two years from 24 to nine.

Frenzel also has taken an interest in congressional ethics. He served on the special panel that wrote an ethics code in 1977 and helped generate Republican support for it, although he disagreed with Chairman David R. Obey, D-Wis., on many of the particulars. Frenzel opposed the provision in the bill giving members an extra $5,000 in office account money in exchange for dropping the customary practice of having unofficial, untraceable private office funds.

While keeping his campaign finance role, Frenzel has become an activist on Ways and Means and a key member of its Trade Subcommittee. He has sought to push the panel away from most forms of tariff protection and toward more world trade.

Frenzel was an enthusiastic supporter of the 1979 trade expansion bill, introduced his own legislation to convert the Commerce Department

---

**3rd District: Minneapolis suburbs.**
Population: 486,954 (3% increase since 1970).
Race: White 473,655 (97%), Black 4,758 (1%),
Others 8,541 (2%). Spanish origin: 3,016 (1%).

into a department of Commerce and International Trade and expressed private doubts about the 1980 Olympic boycott on grounds that it would hamper future trade opportunities with the Soviet Union. Free trade is good politics in a state whose economy improves with substantial grain sales abroad; it also appears to be a tenet of Frenzel's ideology.

On other Ways and Means issues, Frenzel's voting record is generally in line with GOP low-tax orthodoxy. He played an important role in the coalition that reduced the capital gains tax in 1978 and sought, along with the panel's other Republicans, to soften the windfall profits tax bill in 1979.

On the Budget Committee, however, Frenzel has tried to play a moderating role among GOP members. When the first 1981 budget resolution moved through the committee, he advocated a coalition with moderate and conservative Democrats to produce a balanced budget. Chairman Robert N. Giaimo, D-Conn., went along with the idea, and all but one of the committee's Republicans supported Giaimo, allowing him to prevail over an angry bloc of liberal Democrats.

But by the time the budget reached the floor, new figures showed it to be out of balance. Still, Frenzel maintained his bargain, even though Republicans turned against the compromise by a vote of 131-22.

**At Home:** Frenzel made a critical career decision in 1978 when he opted to seek a fifth House term in his safe suburban district, declining to run for an open Senate seat he probably could have won. The choice reflected Frenzel's cautious side, not always evident in House politics but part of his makeup nevertheless.

He seemed somewhat bolder in 1970, when he first ran for Congress. An executive in his family's warehousing business, Frenzel had run for the state Legislature in 1962 and served four terms there. He was part of the "Hennepin County mafia" that sought a moderate image for the state's Republican Party and an ally of Attorney General Douglas Head, the GOP gubernatorial nominee in 1970.

Frenzel announced that year for the open House seat in suburban Minneapolis, challenging Republican front-runner Robert A. Forsythe, a former state party chairman and 1966 Senate candidate. Forsythe was better known, but Frenzel took advantage of Head's organization to win the regular party endorsement on the first convention ballot.

In the general election that year, Democrats felt they had a good chance to win the district back after 10 years of Republican control. They nominated George Rice, a local commentator on the most widely watched television station in the Twin Cities. Again, Frenzel was at a disadvantage in name identification. He stepped up his personal campaign, ringing more than 15,000 doorbells and making numerous late-night visits to bowling alleys, where he claimed he met another 10,000 voters.

But it was Frenzel's August fact-finding trip to the Middle East that seemed to change the situation. It placed his name in the headlines, and when Rice refused Frenzel's challenge to make a similar trip, it created a campaign issue. A larger than usual Jewish vote on the Republican side helped provide Frenzel with the 2,780-vote margin by which he defeated Rice. Nearly 220,000 votes were cast, the highest number ever for a Minnesota congressional race in a non-presidential year.

Frenzel's moderate brand of Republicanism quickly became popular with his suburban constituents, and they have consistently returned him to office with more than 60 percent of the vote. In 1978, when Frenzel was toying with the idea of running for the Senate, a potentially strong Democrat decided on a House campaign in the 3rd District. He was Michael O. Freeman, the son of Orville L. Freeman, former governor and Agriculture secretary. But when Frenzel decided to run again, Freeman's chances evaporated quickly, and the Republican finished with his usual large plurality.

**The District:** Shaped like the letter "C," the 3rd District surrounds Minneapolis from the west. It is a young, affluent and transient white-collar district, with a ticket-splitting electorate. Hubert H. Humphrey and former Gov. Wendell Anderson always ran well here, even when Frenzel was winning by nearly 2-1 margins.

The top part of the "C" is the most Democratic area and is currently represented in the state Senate by Hubert H. (Skip) Humphrey III. As one travels south to fashionable Minnetonka and Edina, the Republican vote solidifies. Even Mondale's presence on the Democratic ticket did not salvage Carter in this area in 1980; their ticket won less than 25 percent in some precincts. The Democratic vote is stronger in the towns of Bloomington and Richfield, at the bottom part of the "C."

Throughout the district are the nicely landscaped facilities of high technology businesses, such as Control Data and Honeywell, which hire a significant part of the district's employment force.

## Committees

**Budget**
Taskforces: Human Resources and Block Grants; Transportation, Research and Development and Capital Resources.

**House Administration** (Ranking Republican)
Accounts; Taskforce on Committee Organization.

**Ways and Means** (6th of 12 Republicans)
Trade.

## Elections

**1980 General**

| | |
|---|---|
| Bill Frenzel (R ) | 179,393 (76 %) |
| Joel Saliterman (D ) | 57,868 (24 %) |

**1980 Primary**

| | |
|---|---|
| Bill Frenzel (R ) | 12,111 (91 %) |
| Rodger Rose (R ) | 1,143 (9 %) |

**1978 General**

| | |
|---|---|
| Bill Frenzel (R ) | 128,759 (66 %) |
| Michael Freeman (D ) | 67,120 (34 %) |

**Previous Winning Percentages**

1976 (66 %)    1974 (60 %)    1972 (63 %)    1970 (51 %)

**District Vote For President**

| | 1980 | | 1976 | | 1972 |
|---|---|---|---|---|---|
| D | 114,029 (43 %) | D | 120,340 (48 %) | D | 89,867 (40 %) |
| R | 119,037 (45 %) | R | 124,539 (50 %) | R | 130,063 (58 %) |
| I | 27,710 (10 %) | | | | |

## Campaign Finance

| | Receipts | Receipts from PACs | Expen-ditures |
|---|---|---|---|
| **1980** | | | |
| Frenzel (R ) | $144,113 | $56,670 (39 %) | $112,308 |
| **1978** | | | |
| Frenzel (R ) | $188,387 | $33,345 (18 %) | $179,807 |
| Freeman (D ) | $154,840 | $33,160 (21 %) | $154,738 |

## Voting Studies

| | Presidential Support | | Party Unity | | Conservative Coalition | |
|---|---|---|---|---|---|---|
| Year | S | O | S | O | S | O |
| 1980 | 43 | 53 | 71 | 23 | 71 | 26 |
| 1979 | 45 | 47 | 65 | 23 | 61 | 26 |
| 1978 | 52 | 43 | 67 | 24 | 71 | 21 |
| 1977 | 44 | 37 | 63 | 27 | 65 | 27 |
| 1976 | 73 | 25 | 62 | 28 | 56 | 34 |
| 1975 | 76 | 19 | 69 | 25 | 66 | 29 |
| 1974 (Ford) | 65 | 35 | | | | |
| 1974 | 60 | 28 | 47 | 45 | 35 | 51 |
| 1973 | 58 | 33 | 53 | 41 | 45 | 51 |
| 1972 | 68 | 27 | 57 | 33 | 43 | 48 |
| 1971 | 56 | 30 | 54 | 32 | 44 | 46 |

S = Support          O = Opposition

## Key Votes

**96th Congress**

| | |
|---|---|
| Weaken Carter oil profits tax (1979) | Y |
| Reject hospital cost control plan (1979) | Y |
| Implement Panama Canal Treaties (1979) | N |
| Establish Department of Education (1979) | N |
| Approve Anti-busing Amendment (1979) | N |
| Guarantee Chrysler Corp. loans (1979) | N |
| Approve military draft registration (1980) | N |
| Aid Sandinista regime in Nicaragua (1980) | N |
| Strengthen fair housing laws (1980) | N |

**97th Congress**

| | |
|---|---|
| Reagan budget proposal (1981) | Y |

## Interest Group Ratings

| Year | ADA | ACA | AFL-CIO | CCUS |
|---|---|---|---|---|
| 1980 | 22 | 70 | 12 | 77 |
| 1979 | 21 | 64 | 25 | 100 |
| 1978 | 35 | 64 | 20 | 82 |
| 1977 | 25 | 72 | 27 | 80 |
| 1976 | 25 | 54 | 9 | 63 |
| 1975 | 53 | 70 | 13 | 76 |
| 1974 | 61 | 17 | 56 | 71 |
| 1973 | 52 | 44 | 9 | 82 |
| 1972 | 63 | 32 | 18 | 80 |
| 1971 | 65 | 50 | 25 | |

# 4 Bruce F. Vento (D)

**Of St. Paul — Elected 1976**

**Born:** Oct. 7, 1940, St. Paul, Minn.
**Education:** Wis. State U., B.S. 1965.
**Profession:** Science teacher.
**Family:** Wife, Mary Jean Moore; three children.
**Religion:** Roman Catholic.
**Political Career:** Minn. House, 1971-77.

**In Washington:** Vento has developed a sort of direct-action legislative style, one that seeks to overcome the slow congressional pace with a flurry of floor amendments, public statements, letters and even a formal petition to a federal agency.

Sometimes they are outside his regular committee interests, and often they generate more controversy than action. But there have been some achievements too, as well as valuable publicity back home.

In his first term, Vento officially intervened before the Interstate Commerce Commission in a successful effort to force the Burlington and Northern Railroad to cut back its coal hauling rates to Minnesota utilities.

Later, he read a newspaper article about federally financed cosmetic surgery for military personnel and decided to introduce an amendment to bar funds from the Department of Defense appropriation bill for such operations. It was accepted on a voice vote.

When stories surfaced in Minneapolis and St. Paul about foreign students living in subsidized rental housing, Vento prepared amendments — again accepted by the House — to cut off federal aid to apartment projects renting to such students.

One of his free-lance efforts attracted serious opposition from senior members of the Armed Services Committee. It was an attempt to block the Defense Department from providing veterinary care for the pets of military personnel. When he saw he would certainly lose, he withdrew the amendment.

On the Banking Committee, Vento is generally a labor ally. He has worked to strengthen public and subsidized housing and helped draft legislation to create the solar and the consumer cooperative banks — both threatened in 1981 by Reagan budget cuts. He was an early and enthusiastic backer of synthetic fuel development.

On the Interior Committee, Vento was in the thick of a Minnesota fight in 1978 over the

Boundary Waters Canoe Area. Canoeists were urging Congress to pass a bill to restrict motorboats on the area's 1,060 lakes. Resort operators were on the other side.

Vento, as the only Minnesotan on Interior, was pulled in both directions by two strong-willed Democrats in his state delegation. James Oberstar, whose district includes Boundary Waters, favored motorboats; Donald M. Fraser of Minneapolis feared heavy motor traffic would threaten the wildness of the area.

In the end, Vento came up with a compromise that phased out motorboats on all but 24 percent of the water area by the year 2000. Among Minnesota congressmen, only Oberstar voted no.

Vento's weakness is his speaking style. When he starts talking at a committee hearing or markup session, he can continue long after those listening have lost the train of his thought. The Minneapolis Tribune once called him "windy." Others say he connects clauses in a pell mell style that can be very difficult to decipher.

**At Home:** Vento has the right personal and political background to represent this labor-dominated district.

The son of a Machinists official, he was a union steward at a plastics plant, then worked in a brewery and on a refrigerator assembly line before becoming a junior high school teacher and state representative.

During his three terms in the Legislature he

---

**4th District: St. Paul.** Population: 457,422 (4% decrease since 1970). Race: White 424,903 (93%), Black 14,708 (3%), Others 17,811 (4%). Spanish origin: 9,289 (2%).

## Bruce F. Vento, D-Minn.

echoed the interests of the working-class residents of St. Paul's Phalen Park. And as a loyal team player he was rewarded with the assistant majority leader post under Speaker Martin Olav Sabo, now his Minnesota congressional colleague.

When nine-term House veteran Joseph E. Karth decided to retire in 1976, he endorsed Vento for the seat. Karth's backing and labor support were enough to give him the party endorsement.

Nonetheless, Vento faced four opponents in the Democratic primary. Two were significant: St. Paul attorney John S. Connolly, running as an even more liberal alternative to Vento, and 27-year-old state auditor Robert W. Mattson, who had twice defeated party-endorsed candidates. But Vento had too many factors working in his favor. He won a convincing primary victory with 52 percent. The November election was just as easy for Vento as it usually had been for Karth.

**The District:** St. Paul is both solidly Democratic and determinedly "down home." Minnesota's capital city does not have the shiny gloss of Minneapolis' central business district, although some of its residential areas are as pleasant and tree-lined as those on the west side of the Mississippi River.

About two-thirds of the district's voters live in St. Paul. The other third reside in the rapidly growing suburbs directly to the north. This area tends to vote about 10 percent more Republican than St. Paul, but except for Roseville and fashionable North Oaks, the suburbs still usually favor Democrats.

## Committees

**Banking, Finance and Urban Affairs** (17th of 25 Democrats)
Economic Stabilization; Financial Institutions Supervision, Regulation and Insurance; Housing and Community Development.

**Interior and Insular Affairs** (15th of 23 Democrats)
Energy and the Environment; Public Lands and National Parks.

**Select Aging** (25th of 31 Democrats)
Human Services; Retirement Income and Employment.

## Elections

**1980 General**

| | |
|---|---|
| Bruce Vento (D ) | 119,182 (59 %) |
| John Berg (R ) | 82,537 (41 %) |

**1978 General**

| | |
|---|---|
| Bruce Vento (D ) | 95,989 (58 %) |
| John Berg (R ) | 69,396 (42 %) |

**Previous Winning Percentage**

1976 (66 %)

**District Vote For President**

| | 1980 | | 1976 | | 1972 |
|---|---|---|---|---|---|
| D | 124,166 (54 %) | D | 133,051 (59 %) | D | 107,924 (52 %) |
| R | 78,432 (34 %) | R | 85,922 (38 %) | R | 95,201 (46 %) |
| I | 23,081 (10 %) | | | | |

## Campaign Finance

| | Receipts | Receipts from PACs | Expenditures |
|---|---|---|---|
| **1980** | | | |
| Vento (D ) | $148,682 | $97,972 (66 %) | $115,022 |
| Berg (R ) | $324,422 | $104,433 (32 %) | $318,545 |

| 1978 | | | |
|---|---|---|---|
| Vento (D ) | $92,083 | $48,874 (53 %) | $80,225 |
| Berg (R ) | $77,689 | $10,190 (13 %) | $76,705 |

## Voting Studies

| | Presidential Support | | Party Unity | | Conservative Coalition | |
|---|---|---|---|---|---|---|
| Year | S | O | S | O | S | O |
| 1980 | 66 | 20 | 83 | 7 | 3 | 83 |
| 1979 | 84 | 14 | 91 | 8 | 12 | 88 |
| 1978 | 76 | 17 | 86 | 9 | 7 | 89 |
| 1977 | 81 | 19 | 90 | 6 | 4 | 94 |

S = Support      O = Opposition

## Key Votes

**96th Congress**

| | |
|---|---|
| Weaken Carter oil profits tax (1979) | N |
| Reject hospital cost control plan (1979) | N |
| Implement Panama Canal Treaties (1979) | Y |
| Establish Department of Education (1979) | Y |
| Approve Anti-busing Amendment (1979) | N |
| Guarantee Chrysler Corp. loans (1979) | Y |
| Approve military draft registration (1980) | N |
| Aid Sandinista regime in Nicaragua (1980) | Y |
| Strengthen fair housing laws (1980) | Y |

**97th Congress**

| | |
|---|---|
| Reagan budget proposal (1981) | N |

## Interest Group Ratings

| Year | ADA | ACA | AFL-CIO | CCUS |
|---|---|---|---|---|
| 1980 | 100 | 9 | 84 | 59 |
| 1979 | 95 | 4 | 95 | 6 |
| 1978 | 65 | 7 | 95 | 17 |
| 1977 | 90 | 0 | 87 | 6 |

# 5 Martin Olav Sabo (D)

**Of Minneapolis — Elected 1978**

**Born:** Feb. 28, 1938, Crosby, N.D.
**Education:** Augsburg College, B.A. 1959.
**Profession:** Public official.
**Family:** Wife, Sylvia Ann Lee; two children.
**Religion:** Lutheran.
**Political Career:** Minn. House, 1961-79, Speaker, 1973-79.

**In Washington:** Sabo was quieter during his first term than most people expected a former Minnesota House Speaker to be, but he showed some skill at using the appropriations process, as well as a stubborn streak that sometimes baffled his own delegation.

He immediately sought and won a seat on Appropriations, forsaking the more conspicuous issue committees for a share in control of the federal purse strings. Placed on the HUD Subcommittee, he persuaded it to add $10 million to a housing rehabilitation loan program that was widely used in Minneapolis. On the Transportation Subcommittee, he lobbied in 1979 for more money for buses as opposed to more expensive rail mass transit systems. The panel agreed to a $200 million funding shift in that direction. At the full committee level, he was a spokesman for the Frost Belt states in their effort to shift emergency fuel assistance money from warm-weather Sun Belt states.

Sabo vigorously fought the Carter administration, the Democratic leadership and his own Appropriations subcommittee chairman, Edward P. Boland of Massachusetts, when Carter proposed draft registration in 1980. He teamed up with Republican Lawrence Coughlin of Pennsylvania to argue that registration without a draft would have no effect on military preparedness. They managed to block the program on a 6-6 tie vote in subcommittee, but it cleared the full committee and eventually became law.

On another occasion, Sabo took on his own delegation and another surprised committee chairman. He successfully persuaded the Appropriations Committee to scale down the number of beds in a proposed Veterans Administration hospital at Fort Snelling in Minnesota. Veterans' Affairs Committee Chairman Ray Roberts, D Texas, threatened to "kill the damn project, if that's the way they feel about it." Roberts' committee had approved a VA plan to replace an existing hospital with a new 845-bed facility, at a cost of $221 million. Sabo argued that the new, larger hospital would lead to a surplus of beds in the community. He successfully urged the committee to impose a 649-bed limit when approving $15 million for planning.

A legislator trying to cut funds for his own state is a rare thing, and Sabo riled his Minnesota colleagues by doing it. Five of the eight members of the Minnesota delegation immediately fired off a "Dear Colleague" letter vowing a fight to restore money for the larger hospital on the House floor. They did and won.

Sabo calls himself a "liberal decentralist," meaning that he favors federal help in solving social problems but wants the programs administered locally. So far, he is high on the liberal scale; he averaged a 97 rating from the Americans for Democratic Action for his first two years in Congress.

**At Home:** Sabo has never been a flashy campaigner, but he has been a significant presence in Minnesota politics virtually all his adult life.

When Democratic Rep. Donald Fraser left the House for his unsuccessful try at the Senate in 1978, nearly a dozen candidates began maneuvering to succeed him. But when Sabo announced he wanted the job, nearly all of them bowed out of the contest. Those who remained were cleared out either at the endorsing convention or in Sabo's 81 percent primary victory.

> **5th District: Minneapolis.** Population: 414,674 (14% decrease since 1970). Race: White 366,975 (88%), Black 28,127 (7%), Indian 9,012 (2%), Others 10,560 (3%). Spanish origin: 4,907 (1%).

*Martin Olav Sabo, D-Minn.*

One of the reasons for Sabo's strength has been his amazing combination of youth and longevity. Elected to the state Legislature at 22, he had been in the public spotlight for 18 years and served as Speaker for six years before running for Congress. He was seen by most voters as the logical liberal successor to Fraser.

Sabo's first Republican opponent, dentist Mike Till, conducted a much more visible campaign than most Republicans wage in this overwhelmingly Democratic district. When conservative businessman Robert E. Short defeated Fraser in a bitter Senate primary, Till hoped some of the animosity liberals felt toward Short would rub off on Sabo. But Sabo carefully avoided making any connection between his campaign and Short's, which was a wise move: Short received less than 24 percent in the 5th District.

Sabo's winning percentage in 1978 was not quite up to what Fraser had been receiving. But by his second election, he had achieved solid support throughout the area, even in the communities where he was weakest against Till.

**The District:** Avowed liberals continue to do well in Minneapolis, whatever their problems elsewhere in the country. The 5th District awarded Fraser large pluralities every time he ran — and after his Senate try, elected him mayor. It backed George McGovern for president in 1972, and was the only Minnesota district carried by Democrat Wendell Anderson in his campaign for the Senate in 1978.

Much of the district's liberal vote is cast in affluent white-collar neighborhoods, and in the University of Minnesota community. There are also poor black and American Indian neighborhoods surrounding the glimmering downtown area. In northeast Minneapolis, east of the Mississippi River, are more traditional blue-collar Democrats.

Around the lakes in the southern end of the district, voters tend to be slightly more prosperous, and not quite as solidly Democratic. The same is true for the small part of the district located just north of Minneapolis in Anoka County.

## Committees

**Appropriations** (25th of 33 Democrats)
HUD-Independent Agencies; Transportation.

## Elections

**1980 General**

| | |
|---|---|
| Martin Sabo (D ) | 126,451 (70 %) |
| John Doherty (R ) | 48,200 (27 %) |

**1978 General**

| | |
|---|---|
| Martin Sabo (D ) | 91,673 (62 %) |
| Michael Till (R ) | 55,412 (38 %) |

**1978 Primary**

| | |
|---|---|
| Martin Sabo (D) | 47,515 (31 %) |
| Les Betts (D) | 5,826 (10 %) |
| Willis Trueblood (D) | 5,184 (9 %) |

**District Vote For President**

| | 1980 | | 1976 | | 1972 |
|---|---|---|---|---|---|
| **D** | 144,179 (60 %) | **D** | 134,367 (61 %) | **D** | 116,090 (54 %) |
| **R** | 62,439 (26 %) | **R** | 77,440 (35 %) | **R** | 92,951 (44 %) |
| **I** | 26,450 (11 %) | | | | |

## Campaign Finance

| | Receipts | Receipts from PACs | Expenditures |
|---|---|---|---|
| **1980** | | | |
| Sabo (D ) | $97,972 | $40,292 (41 %) | $83,547 |
| **1978** | | | |
| Sabo (D ) | $87,906 | $28,674 (33 %) | $84,652 |
| Till (R ) | $129,740 | $34,763 (27 %) | $129,487 |

## Voting Studies

| Year | Presidential Support | | Party Unity | | Conservative Coalition | |
|---|---|---|---|---|---|---|
| | S | O | S | O | S | O |
| 1980 | 84 | 15 | 95 | 4 | 7 | 93 |
| 1979 | 81 | 18 | 89 | 8 | 11 | 88 |

S = Support    O = Opposition

## Key Votes

**96th Congress**

| | |
|---|---|
| Weaken Carter oil profits tax (1979) | N |
| Reject hospital cost control plan (1979) | N |
| Implement Panama Canal Treaties (1979) | Y |
| Establish Department of Education (1979) | N |
| Approve Anti-busing Amendment (1979) | N |
| Guarantee Chrysler Corp. loans (1979) | Y |
| Approve military draft registration (1980) | N |
| Aid Sandinista regime in Nicaragua (1980) | Y |
| Strengthen fair housing laws (1980) | Y |

**97th Congress**

| | |
|---|---|
| Reagan budget proposal (1981) | N |

## Interest Group Ratings

| Year | ADA | ACA | AFL-CIO | CCUS |
|---|---|---|---|---|
| 1980 | 94 | 9 | 79 | 58 |
| 1979 | 100 | 8 | 90 | 11 |

# 6 Vin Weber (R)

## Of Slayton — Elected 1980

**Born:** July 24, 1952, Slayton, Minn.
**Education:** U. of Minn., no degree.
**Profession:** Newspaper publisher.
**Family:** Wife, Jeanie Lorenz.
**Religion:** Roman Catholic.
**Political Career:** Unsuccessful Republican nominee for Minn. Senate, 1976.

**The Member:** Weber is a House version of Minnesota's junior U.S. senator, Rudy Boschwitz. He shares Boschwitz' frenetic approach to campaigns as well as legislation, a similarity that is not surprising because Weber ran Boschwitz' successful 1978 campaign and later worked for him in Washington.

Running in 1980 for the seat of Democrat Richard Nolan, who retired, Weber set a state record for House campaign spending. He put so much money into television advertising that to many voters he seemed like an incumbent by November.

Weber said at the outset of his term that a freshman should serve as a good soldier for the party leadership. But his distaste for government intervention in the energy marketplace persuaded him to violate the loyalty rule at least once. In the Science Committee, he bucked the administration and supported an amendment to delete funding for construction of the Clinch River breeder reactor.

Weber won the 1980 GOP nomination on the 10th ballot of a bruising district convention. In November, he faced a former Nolan aide. Weber carried St. Cloud, where he had strong support from anti-abortion forces and German Catholics, and added votes from prosperous farmers and suburbanites to counter Democratic strength in poorer agricultural areas.

**The District:** The 6th is dominated by agriculture, but its representation is determined increasingly by suburban voters in the 60-mile corridor from St. Cloud to the outskirts of Minneapolis. More than 40 percent of the district vote comes from this four-county region.

Farms and small towns dot the rest of the 6th. St. Cloud, the largest city, is heavily German and nominally Democratic, but conservative. The liberal Nolan won in 1974 mostly because of Watergate-inspired anger toward the GOP. Usually the area sends Republicans to the House.

## Committees

**Science and Technology** (11th of 17 Republicans)
Energy Development and Applications; Science, Research and Technology.

**Small Business** (11th of 17 Republicans)
Tax, Access to Equity Capital and Business Opportunities.

## Elections

**1980 General**

| | |
|---|---|
| Vin Weber (R ) | 140,402 (53 %) |
| Archie Baumann (D ) | 126,173 (47 %) |

**1980 Primary**

| | |
|---|---|
| Vin Weber (R ) | 18,154 (87 %) |
| Francis Brunton (R ) | 2,655 (13 %) |

**District Vote For President**

| | 1980 | | 1976 | | 1972 |
|---|---|---|---|---|---|
| **D** | 115,780 (43 %) | **D** | 140,420 (55 %) | **D** | 102,231 (46 %) |
| **R** | 131,735 (48 %) | **R** | 104,667 (41 %) | **R** | 114,196 (51 %) |
| **I** | 18,627 (7 %) | | | | |

## Campaign Finance

| | Receipts | Receipts from PACs | Expenditures |
|---|---|---|---|
| **1980** | | | |
| Weber (R ) | $554,448 | $166,207 (30 %) | $488,304 |
| Baumann (D ) | $179,885 | $78,959 (44 %) | $177,231 |

## Key Vote

**97th Congress**

| | |
|---|---|
| Reagan budget proposal (1981) | Y |

> **6th District: Southwest and central — St. Cloud.** Population: 554,522 (16% increase since 1970). Race: White 548,647 (99%), Black 680 (0.1%), Others 5,195 (1%). Spanish origin: 2,348 (0.4%).

# 7 Arlan Stangeland (R)

**Of Barnesville — Elected 1977**

**Born:** Feb. 8, 1930, Fargo, N.D.
**Education:** Moorhead H.S., 1948 graduate.
**Profession:** Farmer.
**Family:** Wife, Virginia Trowbridge; 7 children.
**Religion:** Lutheran.
**Political Career:** Minn. House, 1967-75; Republican nominee for Minn. House, 1974.

**In Washington:** Elected in 1977 with critical help from national New Right organizations, Stangeland has sought to satisfy them without straying too far from the more traditional rural Republicanism his district normally prefers.

In general, he has succeeded. At the end of his first three years in the House, Stangeland had a 94 percent rating from the American Conservative Union, one that included support for the free enterprise position on nearly every major issue. On Minnesota-related matters, however, he has sometimes proved to be the sort of project-oriented Republican of whom the ideological right tends to be skeptical.

On the Public Works Committee, Stangeland has played the traditional role of seeking federal money for his district, especially for flood control. He tried unsuccessfully to win committee approval of a $500,000 project for the Red River valley, near the North Dakota border, and was given consolation by language making the area eligible for agriculture conservation funds. In his first year, Stangeland lobbied his fellow conservatives to vote for higher feed grain price supports, although he was not a member of the Agriculture Committee, and was later credited by some farm organizations as having been partially responsible for the increase.

Like Ronald Reagan, Stangeland is a believer in the North American partnership idea; he testified in 1979 in favor of a U.S.-Canadian-Mexican energy summit conference. Although he comes from a Frost Belt district rather than an energy-producing Sun Belt area, he has generally voted on the producer side against consumers and environmentalists when issues have broken along those lines. "The idea that every river or stream has to be fishable or swimmable is unrealistic," he said in 1980, criticizing the Water Pollution Act of 1972.

In the 96th Congress, Stangeland spent considerable time on a matter of little interest in rural Minnesota, but important in the House. He argued for a change in the Republican committee assignment system. Traditionally, a few senior GOP members from large states have all but dictated who gets the important assignments. Stangeland persuaded GOP leaders to let one small-state member play a similar broker's role. The change is likely to mean a few more rural Republicans on panels like Rules, Ways and Means and Appropriations in coming years.

**At Home:** Democrats were astonished when Stangeland won the 1977 special election held to replace Bob Bergland, who had become President Carter's Agriculture Secretary. Only four months before, Bergland had won 72 percent in the district. But in retrospect, they realized they had given away a safe Democratic seat by running the wrong candidate.

The Democratic nominee, former Mondale aide Mike Sullivan, ran on the slogan, "He's in the Bergland tradition." But it was clear to the district's Norwegian Lutheran farmers that Sullivan, an Irish Catholic, was not part of their tradition. Stangeland — a farmer whose parents were Norwegian immigrants — clearly was.

Stangeland's family still lives in the district, and he returns there nearly every weekend to keep up his ties. But in the years since 1977, his image as a country farmer has come under attack by a Democrat far better suited to the district than Sullivan.

Gene Wenstrom, a former state legislator, teacher and farmer from Elbow Lake, ran against Stangeland in 1978 and 1980 and came close to

---

**7th District: Northwest — Moorhead.** Population: 554,522 (16% increase since 1970). Race: White 548,647 (99%), Black 680 (0.1%), Others 5,195 (1%). Spanish origin: 2,348 (0.4%).

beating him both times. In 1980, he said that Stangeland's voting record and list of campaign contributors exposed him as a friend of agribusiness and major oil companies. Stangeland said Wenstrom's campaign was one of "innuendo, distortions and twistings of the truth."

Wenstrom's attacks on Stangeland helped in the northern and eastern parts of the district, which are more Democratic. There Wenstrom ran as much as 7 percent better than on his first try. But elsewhere voters did not perceive Stangeland to be the villain Wenstrom suggested. The villain to many farmers was President Carter, whose grain embargo earlier in the year had devastated the district's wheat growers. The Carter vote plummeted from its 1976 levels in the central part of the district, and brought Wenstrom's vote

down as well. That allowed Stangeland to hold on for a second full term by 11,000 votes.

**The District:** Although it has swung back and forth between the parties over the past 25 years, the 7th was labeled Democratic during most of the 1970s. At the end of the decade, however, it began backing GOP statewide candidates with some regularity. Republican senators Durenberger and Boschwitz and Governor Quie all carried the district in 1978. In 1980, Reagan's percentage here was exceeded in only one Minnesota district. The 7th covers 40 percent of the state's land area. Some of the stronger Republican counties are in the grain-growing Red River valley; farther from the river, the soil is poorer, and lumbering is a main occupation. Tourism is also important in the district.

## Committees

**Agriculture** (10th of 19 Republicans)
Cotton, Rice and Sugar; Forests, Family Farms, and Energy; Wheat, Soybeans and Feed Grains.

**Public Works and Transportation** (7th of 19 Republicans)
Investigations and Oversight; Public Buildings and Grounds; Surface Transportation.

## Elections

**1980 General**

| | |
|---|---|
| Arlan Stangeland (R ) | 135,084 (52 %) |
| Gene Wenstrom (D ) | 124,026 (48 %) |

**1978 General**

| | |
|---|---|
| Arlan Stangeland (R ) | 109,456 (52 %) |
| Gene Wenstrom (D ) | 93,055 (45 %) |

**Previous Winning Percentage**

1977* (58%)
*Special Election

**District Vote For President**

| | 1980 | | 1976 | | 1972 |
|---|---|---|---|---|---|
| **D** | 108,610 (41 %) | **D** | 135,192 (55 %) | **D** | 100,410 (45 %) |
| **R** | 132,532 (51 %) | **R** | 102,502 (42 %) | **R** | 118,727 (53 %) |
| **I** | 16,503 (6 %) | | | | |

## Campaign Finance

| | Receipts | Receipts from PACs | Expenditures |
|---|---|---|---|
| **1980** | | | |
| Stangeland (R ) | $289,302 | $102,001 (35 %) | $267,705 |
| Wenstrom (D ) | $260,308 | $74,581 (29 %) | $239,372 |
| **1978** | | | |
| Stangeland (R ) | $212,291 | $62,257 (29 %) | $192,034 |
| Wenstrom (D ) | $114,729 | $34,980 (30 %) | $112,549 |

## Voting Studies

| | Presidential Support | | Party Unity | | Conservative Coalition | |
|---|---|---|---|---|---|---|
| Year | S | O | S | O | S | O |
| 1980 | 38 | 62 | 85 | 12 | 83 | 16 |
| 1979 | 31 | 66 | 90 | 8 | 94 | 5 |
| 1978 | 27 | 70 | 86 | 9 | 90 | 6 |
| 1977 | 36 | 53† | 84 | 12† | 88 | 5† |

S = Support          O = Opposition

†Not eligible for all recorded votes.

## Key Votes

**96th Congress**

| | |
|---|---|
| Weaken Carter oil profits tax (1979) | Y |
| Reject hospital cost control plan (1979) | Y |
| Implement Panama Canal Treaties (1979) | N |
| Establish Department of Education (1979) | N |
| Approve Anti-busing Amendment (1979) | Y |
| Guarantee Chrysler Corp. loans (1979) | Y |
| Approve military draft registration (1980) | Y |
| Aid Sandinista regime in Nicaragua (1980) | N |
| Strengthen fair housing laws (1980) | N |

**97th Congress**

| | |
|---|---|
| Reagan budget proposal (1981) | Y |

## Interest Group Ratings

| Year | ADA | ACA | AFL-CIO | CCUS |
|---|---|---|---|---|
| 1980 | 0 | 79 | 21 | 76 |
| 1979 | 5 | 88 | 25 | 100 |
| 1978 | 5 | 91 | 0 | 83 |
| 1977 | 0 | 88 | 13 | 94 |

# 8 James L. Oberstar (D)

### Of Chisholm — Elected 1974

**Born:** Sept. 10, 1934, Chisholm, Minn.
**Education:** College of St. Thomas, B.A. 1956;
College of Europe, M.A. 1957.
**Profession:** Congressional aide.
**Family:** Wife, Marilynn Jo Garlick; four
children.
**Religion:** Roman Catholic.
**Political Career:** No previous office.

**In Washington:** Once described by a Minnesota newspaper as part scholar and part streetfighter, Oberstar has managed to use both sides of his personality in arguing about dams and economic development on the Public Works Committee.

Few members find much opportunity for theorizing on Public Works; it is a road-building, channel-dredging institution that tends to dig first and ask questions later. But Oberstar, a political scientist and amateur linguist, can go on for hours about the proper balance of public works policy. He is always beseeching the committee to "rise above" pork-barrel thinking and study innovative ways to handle the nation's problems. He says an impending Western water shortage demands planning rather than more projects.

On the other hand, he has rarely been known to turn down a new project for northern Minnesota. Part of his approach to water problems is the argument that industry, with its heavy water requirements, should be located where the water already is, preferably around the Great Lakes — perhaps Duluth.

Oberstar knows how to use the committee to bring Duluth and the Mesabi Iron Range their share of the public works pie. He was an aide and protégé to John Blatnik, the Minnesota Democrat who chaired Public Works until 1974, when he retired and Oberstar won his seat.

When an air base near Duluth was closed, Oberstar won approval of an amendment providing $40 million to help people thrown out of work by military installation closings. Even Republicans in the state delegation look to Oberstar for help on projects; one of them, Arlen Erdahl, went to him in 1979 on a flood control project and wound up with $78.3 million for a dam in his district. On the Merchant Marine Committee, Oberstar has the same local orientation as the panel's other members. He works to promote the

Great Lakes shipping industry based in Duluth.

In the 97th Congress, however, Oberstar is talking less about water and shipping than about jobs. He took over in 1981 as chairman of the Public Works Economic Development Subcommittee, just in time to plunge into battle with the Reagan administration over its plans to eliminate the Economic Development Administration. That argument has brought out the combative streak that he has always shown in the House.

Oberstar brought OMB Director David Stockman before his subcommittee and raked him over the coals. Oberstar said EDA was one program that created permanent jobs in the private sector and brought in more money in taxes than the government invested. He claimed the $4.7 billion the agency had spent brought back $9 billion in jobs.

Stockman insisted EDA was a "shell game" that simply moved jobs around the country, but Oberstar refused to accept that, and few of the Republicans on Public Works did either. Duluth had received some $20.4 million in grants from EDA and its predecessor since 1963.

Taking on Republicans was something of a luxury for Oberstar, after a career in which he has frequently fought other Democrats, both in Minnesota politics and in the politics of the House.

In 1978, Oberstar took on two House Democrats from the Minneapolis area, Donald Fraser and Bruce Vento, in a fight over the Boundary

---

**8th District: Northeast — Duluth.**
Population: 556,150 (16% increase since 1970).
Race: White 544,455 (98%), Black 1,551
(0.2%), Others 10,144 (2%). Spanish origin:
2,354 (0.4%).

Waters area in Oberstar's district.

The Boundary Waters, which stretch up to Canada, contain 1,060 lakes that wind among virgin forests. Fraser and Vento wanted to restrict the use of motorboats and snowmobiles in the area, a move Oberstar said would hurt resort and fishing lodge owners. Strong House-passed restrictions were eventually watered down by the Senate, but Oberstar was not satisfied with the compromise, and has never forgiven Fraser. When Fraser ran for the Senate later in 1978, Oberstar's 8th District provided the votes that denied him the nomination.

The Boundary Waters dispute pointed up the nature of Oberstar's liberalism: he is a jobs and labor Democrat, in the tradition of Sen. Henry M. Jackson of Washington, skeptical of some environmental restraints and limits on growth. He has voted for relaxing auto pollution standards, for example, and supported the development-oriented version of the Alaska lands legislation. Oberstar is also one of the most militant opponents of abortion in the House. He has consistently voted against federal funds to pay for any abortions, except to save the life of the mother. He supports an anti-abortion amendment to the Constitution.

**At Home:** From the standpoint of party control, Oberstar has nothing to worry about. He inherited a solidly Democratic district in 1974 from John A. Blatnik, his employer and predecessor, and he has had only one token Republican challenger since then.

But within the district's dominant Democratic party, life is far from tranquil. For years there has been a feud between the Blatnik wing of the Democratic Party and the faction headed by the three Perpich brothers, whose leader, Rudy, was lieutenant governor of Minnesota for six years and acting governor in 1977 and 1978.

The battle between the two sides broke out into the open in 1974, and flared up again in 1980. In 1974 Blatnik tried to anoint Oberstar as his successor, but the result was an acrimonious party endorsing convention lasting 30 ballots. Eventu-

ally Blatnik and Oberstar lost, and the party's endorsement went to state Sen. A. J. "Tony" Perpich.

Blatnik then threw all his prestige and political power behind Oberstar in the Democratic primary, and Oberstar won with 50,493 votes to Perpich's 29,899.

Six years later, Oberstar faced a second Perpich. This time it was Tony's younger brother, George. When the oldest brother, Rudy, was elected lieutenant governor in 1970, George took his seat in the Senate, and carried on the liberal Perpich crusade against the mining companies and abortion foes.

At the 1980 nominating convention, George tried to keep the party endorsement out of the incumbent's hands, arguing for a neutral stand in the second Oberstar-Perpich match-up. But Oberstar won the endorsement with just one-third of a vote more than the 60 percent needed. Perpich decided not to force a primary.

Even so, the nominating contest was far from over. A conservative veterinarian from Duluth, Thomas E. Dougherty, challenged Oberstar in the primary and won 44 percent. Concentrating his campaign in the northern part of the district where unemployment was high, Dougherty picked up votes from Perpich supporters out to express a protest. Oberstar was saved by his backing in the southern end of the district, which is in the Twin Cities media area.

**The District:** Located in Minnesota's rugged Mesabi Iron Range, this is a working-class Democratic district. The hunters and fishermen here were responsible for defeating environmentalist Fraser in the 1978 Democratic Senate primary.

Mining remains the principal economic activity among the Swedes, Finns and Eastern Europeans whose ancestors settled here at the turn of the 20th century. Duluth, the district's major city, is also a large shipping center. Redistricting since 1960 has moved the district closer to the Twin Cities, including suburban communities in Anoka County.

## Committees

**Merchant Marine and Fisheries** (10th of 20 Democrats)
Coast Guard and Navigation; Fisheries and Wildlife Conservation and the Environment.

**Public Works and Transportation** (7th of 25 Democrats)
Economic Development, chairman; Aviation; Water Resources.

## Elections

**1980 General**

| | |
|---|---|
| James Oberstar (D ) | 182,228 (70 %) |
| Edward Fiore (R ) | 72,350 (28 %) |

**1980 Primary**

| | |
|---|---|
| James Oberstar (D ) | 38,450 (56 %) |
| Thomas Dougherty (D ) | 30,618 (44 %) |

**1978 General**

| | |
|---|---|
| James Oberstar (D ) | 171,125 (87 %) |
| John Hull (AM) | 25,015 (13 %) |

**Previous Winning Percentages**

| | |
|---|---|
| 1976 (100%) | 1974 (62%) |

## James L. Oberstar, D-Minn.

<table>
<tr><td colspan="3">

**District Vote For President**

</td><td>1977</td><td>73</td><td>27</td><td>92</td><td>8</td><td>12</td><td>88</td></tr>
</table>

**District Vote For President**

|  | 1980 |  | 1976 |  | 1972 |
|---|---|---|---|---|---|
| D | 150,366 (56 %) | D | 161,172 (64 %) | D | 115,622 (54 %) |
| R | 93,646 (35 %) | R | 83,325 (33 %) | R | 95,536 (44 %) |
| I | 18,744 (7 %) | | | | |

| Year | S | O | S | O | S | O | S | O |
|---|---|---|---|---|---|---|---|---|
| 1977 | 73 | 27 | 92 | 8 | 12 | 88 | | |
| 1976 | 24 | 76 | 94 | 6 | 8 | 92 | | |
| 1975 | 35 | 65 | 97 | 2 | 6 | 92 | | |

S = Support          O = Opposition

## Key Votes

**96th Congress**

| | |
|---|---|
| Weaken Carter oil profits tax (1979) | N |
| Reject hospital cost control plan (1979) | X |
| Implement Panama Canal Treaties (1979) | Y |
| Establish Department of Education (1979) | Y |
| Approve Anti-busing Amendment (1979) | N |
| Guarantee Chrysler Corp. loans (1979) | Y |
| Approve military draft registration (1980) | N |
| Aid Sandinista regime in Nicaragua (1980) | Y |
| Strengthen fair housing laws (1980) | Y |

**97th Congress**

| | |
|---|---|
| Reagan budget proposal (1981) | N |

## Campaign Finance

|  | Receipts | Receipts from PACs | Expenditures |
|---|---|---|---|
| **1980** | | | |
| Oberstar (D ) | $168,185 | $88,905 (53 %) | $188,096 |
| Fiore (R ) | $18,675 | $98 (1 %) | $18,673 |
| **1978** | | | |
| Oberstar (D ) | $56,698 | $19,775 (35 %) | $64,117 |

## Voting Studies

| | Presidential Support | | Party Unity | | Conservative Coalition | |
|---|---|---|---|---|---|---|
| Year | S | O | S | O | S | O |
| 1980 | 69 | 31 | 92 | 8 | 16 | 84 |
| 1979 | 83 | 16 | 92 | 7 | 13 | 85 |
| 1978 | 75 | 25 | 89 | 11 | 15 | 85 |

## Interest Group Ratings

| Year | ADA | ACA | AFL-CIO | CCUS |
|---|---|---|---|---|
| 1980 | 83 | 17 | 89 | 59 |
| 1979 | 79 | 4 | 95 | 18 |
| 1978 | 70 | 7 | 85 | 6 |
| 1977 | 85 | 4 | 96 | 12 |
| 1976 | 90 | 0 | 87 | 13 |
| 1975 | 100 | 0 | 96 | 6 |

# Mississippi

## ... Beyond
## Black and White

Mississippi has dropped its preoccupation with race and joined the American political mainstream.

For nearly a century after the Civil War, it was the nation's isolated backwater, the poorest state in a poverty-stricken region. Obsessed with white supremacy like no other state, Mississippi had a "lily white" social and political structure nailed in place by discriminatory Jim Crow laws and a rigid caste system. The first criterion for any successful candidate was to be a segregationist.

Although integration was federally imposed and grudgingly accepted, Mississippi's segregated society has unraveled. Before the Voting Rights Act of 1965, less than 7 percent of Mississippi blacks were registered to vote. By 1975, more than two-thirds were registered. In less than a decade, blacks were transformed from the oratorical "whipping boy" of state politics into a heavily courted source of votes.

But the relegation of race to the background is just one element of Mississippi's changing mosaic. The rural, cotton-dominated economy has given way to increasing urbanization and industrialization. And with the growing manufacturing base and easing racial friction, the population — stagnant from 1940 to 1970 as more than 900,000 blacks and 200,000 whites left the state — surged upward by 14 percent in the 1970s.

The registration of large numbers of blacks and an expanding urban middle-class have had a hand in encouraging the growth of a two-party system.

The 1964 landslide for Republican Barry Goldwater in Mississippi brought the state its first GOP member of Congress since reconstruction. And in 1978, Republicans elected their first U.S. senator in this century.

In the last two decades, the Democratic presidential candidate has carried Mississippi only once — in 1976, and then just barely. Republicans have developed a strong base among white voters in the growing urban and suburban areas, and this bodes well for GOP prospects in the 1980s.

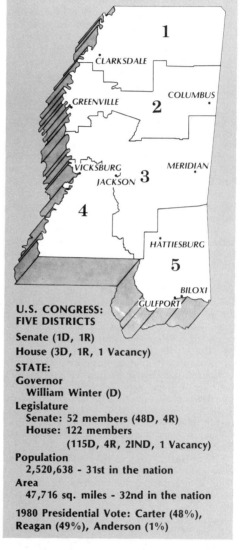

**U.S. CONGRESS:**
**FIVE DISTRICTS**
Senate (1D, 1R)
House (3D, 1R, 1 Vacancy)
**STATE:**
**Governor**
  William Winter (D)
**Legislature**
  Senate: 52 members (48D, 4R)
  House: 122 members
          (115D, 4R, 2IND, 1 Vacancy)
**Population**
  2,520,638 - 31st in the nation
**Area**
  47,716 sq. miles - 32nd in the nation

**1980 Presidential Vote: Carter (48%),**
**Reagan (49%), Anderson (1%)**

In contrast, the Democrats are still in the throes of transforming themselves from a "lily white" Dixiecrat party — defiantly at odds with Washington — into a biracial organization in tune with the national party. Dissatisfied at times with the alliance, blacks have frequently run on their own as independents — a ploy that cost the Democrats a House seat in 1980.

But with moderate candidates like Cliff Finch and William Winter, the party has been able to hold the governorship. Both candidates built winning coalitions that included blacks and poor whites. And the political awakening of the state's black population virtually guarantees a viable Democratic Party in the 1980s — if not always a winning one.

# A Political Tour

**Greater Jackson.** Although Mississippi's Delta looks to Memphis and its Gulf Coast to New Orleans, Jackson is the center of government, finance and commerce in the state. The only city over 50,000 in population, Jackson has been the state capital since 1821. But it was only after World War II that it became a major urban area. Jackson grew by almost a third in the 1970s, and now has 203,000 inhabitants. The neighboring suburban counties of Madison and Rankin increased at an even faster pace, so that today the 360,000 residents of the Greater Jackson area (Hinds, Rankin and Madison counties) account for 15 percent of the state's population. The city has been successful in attracting major manufacturing firms, with Allis-Chalmers and General Motors both establishing plants in Jackson in recent years. Jackson also has drawn some research and development firms which have helped swell the middle-class base.

Hinds and Rankin counties are now reliably Republican in national elections. Hinds has not voted for a Democratic presidential candidate since 1956, while suburban Rankin was the only Mississippi county in 1980 to support Ronald Reagan by a margin of better than 2-to-1. Predominantly black Madison County tends to vote Democratic.

**The Delta.** Only a few miles away from Jackson, but in many ways a world apart, is the Delta, a rural region that stretches north along the Mississippi from Vicksburg to the Tennessee border.

It is a flat region of rich farm land, historically one of the nation's great cotton producing areas. In recent years, Delta farmers have diversified, turning more to soybeans, oats and rice.

The Delta is a region of contrast. The white landowners still put on debutante balls and practice the gentility of the Old South. Nearby are poor blacks, many thrown out of work by the increasing mechanization of the farms.

With little manufacturing in the Delta, the population has been steadily declining as many blacks head North or to large cities in the South. In the 1970s, the Delta was the only region of the state to lose population.

An old river port and cotton market, Greenville is the largest city in the Delta, and one of the few areas in the region to gain population in the 1970s. It has a reputation as one of the most racially tolerant communities in the state.

The predominance of black voters makes the Delta Democratic territory in the absence of a strong black independent candidate.

**Southwest.** South from Vicksburg to the Louisiana border, the soil is less fertile than in the Delta. The economy of the region is based on cattle, forest products and the development of oil and natural gas deposits.

As in the Delta, though, the population is heavily black. Jefferson County, located along the Mississippi River between Natchez and Vicksburg, is 82 percent black — the highest proportion of any county in the state. From 1969 until 1981, the mayor of Fayette in Jefferson County was Charles Evers, brother of slain civil rights activist Medgar Evers.

Vicksburg and Natchez are two of the most historic cities in the state and rely heavily on the tourist trade. Vicksburg is a powerful Southern symbol; its fall to Union forces marked the beginning of the end for the Confederacy. Natchez had its heyday before the Civil War as a cotton trading center. Known for its antebellum homes, it has blossomed recently with light manufacturing and as a center for local oil activity.

Like most urban areas in Mississippi, Adams (Natchez) and Warren (Vicksburg) counties usually vote Republican. Most of the rural areas remain Democratic.

**The Hill Country and the Northeast.** In the early 20th century, the great political skirmishes in Mississippi were fought between the genteel planters of the Delta and the "redneck" farmers of the Hill Country.

Both favored segregation, but on economic issues they were poles apart. The planters, owning the richest soil in the state, espoused conservative positions. The rednecks, eking out a living on their smaller, less fertile plots, were economic populists.

The Hill Country was a bastion of support for the legendary Sen. Theodore G. Bilbo, (1935-47), who combined a shrill segregationist pitch with support for New Deal programs.

Sectional rivalries have diminished in recent years and the region's economic base has changed. Like the Delta, this area has diversified from its early dependence on cotton. Corn, poultry and cattle are all produced in abundance. And increasing industrialization has provided many farmers with more reliable incomes.

Columbus and Tupelo are the major towns. With an Air Force base and some diversified industry, the Columbus area was one of the few parts of the state to grow during Mississippi's stagnant period between 1940 and 1970. Tupelo was the first town to receive electric power from the Tennessee Valley Authority (TVA) and enjoyed an industrial boom after that. In the 1980s, construction of the Tennessee-Tombigbee Waterway is expected to again boost the area's economy.

Although relatively few blacks live in the region, all the territory except the Columbus-Starkville area is still Democratic.

**Piney Woods.** Mississippi's Piney Woods takes in roughly the southeastern quadrant of the state minus the Gulf Coast. As its name implies, much of the area is covered by scrub pine which has provided the backbone of the region's economy through production of wood products.

While there is some farming, the soil is not very fertile and there has been an increasing emphasis on beef cattle and poultry.

The Piney Woods region was one of the first areas of Mississippi to shed old Democratic loyalties. The cities of Laurel and Hattiesburg helped elect Republican Rep. Trent Lott to Congress in 1972. Meridian, an old industrial and railroad town second only to Jackson as a population center, is also increasingly Republican.

**Gulf Coast.** Mississippi's 70-mile strip along the Gulf of Mexico contrasts with the rest of the state. With a diverse economy and population, the Gulf Coast has a cosmopolitan atmosphere not found elsewhere.

In spite of a significant ethnic Catholic population, it is a conservative Republican stronghold. Reagan carried each of the three Gulf Coast counties by at least 15 percentage points in 1980. Tourism, fishing, shipbuilding, oil and chemical refining, and dollars from government and military installations contribute to the vibrant local economy.

The largest Gulf Coast city, Biloxi, stands in the center of a three-county region that contains 300,000 residents — one-eighth of the state population. Even in the period when the state as a whole was not growing, the population of the Gulf Coast was swelled by new industry and retirees from the military. The growth continued in the 1970s.

# Redrawing the Lines

The two districts that legislators must trim down are the Gulf Coast 5th and the south-central 3rd, where the population since 1970 grew 22 percent and 15 percent respectively.

In the opening stages of redistricting, there was much debate over creating a black-majority "Delta district." The current 1st, 2nd and 3rd Districts contain many heavily black counties, but each district stretches across the state to white-dominated eastern counties, thereby diluting the potential political influence of Delta blacks.

# Governor
# William Winter (D)

**Born:** Feb. 21, 1923, Grenada County, Miss.
**Home:** Jackson, Miss.
**Education:** U. of Mississippi, B.A. 1943; LL.B., 1949.
**Military Career:** Army, World War II.
**Profession:** Lawyer.
**Family:** Wife, Elise; three children.
**Religion:** Presbyterian.
**Political Career:** Mississippi House, 1948-56; state tax collector, 1956-64; state treasurer, 1964-68; unsuccessful campaign for gubernatorial nomination, 1967, 1975; lieutenant governor, 1972-76; elected governor 1979; term expires Jan. 1984.

# John C. Stennis (D)

**Of De Kalb — Elected 1947**

**Born:** Aug. 3, 1901, Kemper County, Miss.
**Education:** Miss. State U., B.S. 1923; U. of Va.
LL.B. 1928.
**Profession:** Lawyer.
**Family:** Wife, Coy Hines; two children.
**Religion:** Presbyterian.
**Political Career:** Miss. House, 1928-32; prosecuting attorney, 16th Judicial District, 1931-37; circuit judge, 1937-47.

**In Washington:** Stennis is largely an elder statesman now, respected and even revered by his younger colleagues, but no longer at the center of the action.

He remains senior Democrat on Armed Services, and on the Defense Appropriations Subcommittee, but the Democratic defeat in 1980 cost him a great deal. For the two years of the 96th Congress, he had chaired both, giving him control over the authorization of military requests and then over the actual spending. He was the first senator since Georgia's Richard Russell in the 1960s to enjoy that combination of power. Now he does not have either half of it.

Stennis is the dean of senators, and the oldest. If the nation and the Senate have changed almost beyond recognition over the long years of his tenure, Stennis remains what he has always been — a conservative, a patriot and a gentleman.

Overshadowed by other, more aggressive Southern senators early in his career, Stennis reached the peak of his prestige and influence in the late 1960s and early 1970s. Part of his power stemmed from seniority and its fruits — he was chairman of the Armed Services Committee from 1969 to 1981. But much of it flowed from his unique reputation for fairness and integrity.

Time and again during the past three decades, the Senate turned to Stennis for a verdict when its members or its customs were under suspicion, and an impartial assessment seemed vital. From the McCarthy era to Watergate, Stennis applied judicial skills and temperament acquired during ten years on the bench in Mississippi.

He served on the committee inquiring into the conduct of Wisconsin Sen. Joseph R. McCarthy in 1954 and was the first Democrat to take the Senate floor to denounce him. Charging that McCarthy had poured "slush and slime" on the Senate, Stennis said that condoning such conduct would mean "something big and fine has gone out of this chamber, and something of a wrong character, something representing a wrong course, a wrong approach, will have entered. . . ." The tone was set; McCarthy was censured.

A little more than a decade later, in 1965, Stennis chaired the Select Committee on Standards and Conduct formed in the aftermath of the Bobby Baker scandal. He had not even favored establishing the committee, but he was the unanimous choice to head it, and he supervised the inquiry that led to censure of the late Sen. Thomas J. Dodd, D-Conn., for misuse of campaign funds. The panel also prepared the way for the Senate's first code of ethics.

In 1973 President Nixon took advantage of Stennis' reputation in his effort to hold the Senate Watergate Committee and the courts at bay. Nixon said he would allow Stennis to hear tapes of White House conversations and authenticate their written summaries, provided no further effort was made by federal prosecutors to obtain the tapes themselves.

Key senators, accustomed to trusting Stennis, agreed to the deal, even though Stennis was recovering from gunshot wounds and there was some doubt about his hearing ability. Special prosecutor Archibald Cox did not agree — and was fired for his defiance in the infamous "Saturday Night Massacre." Stennis later said he had not been told the intent was to block the courts from obtaining the Watergate tapes — and would not knowingly have been party to such a deal.

On Armed Services, Stennis has always tried to give presidents the benefit of the doubt, most notably in national security and defense. As Armed Services chairman during the final years of the Vietnam War, he vigorously supported Nixon's policies and defense spending requests, even when a majority of his colleagues did not. Later, when President Carter resisted Pentagon requests for higher funding levels, Stennis tried to accommodate himself to that too, although he would have preferred a tougher posture.

On balance, Stennis has been a friend of the Pentagon over the years, one inclined to trust its leadership when the value of a particular weapons system is questioned. But he has never been willing to sign a blank check for defense spending requests, and he has demanded careful and detailed scrutiny of every proposed outlay. "I was raised to believe that waste was a sin," he said once. "To support military readiness, a senator does not have to be a wastrel," he observed on another occasion.

Stennis' most dramatic display of independence in the national security field was his advocacy of restrictions on the power of the executive to make war. In 1971, he introduced one of several versions of the war powers legislation enacted into law two years later over Nixon's veto, requiring congressional approval of sustained American military action. "The decision to make war is too big a decision for one mind to make and too awesome a responsibility for one man to bear," Stennis declared. "There must be a collective judgment given and a collective responsibility shared."

At one time, Stennis seemed almost invincible to other senators on security issues, but in the late 1970s, that ceased to be true. In 1975, his fellow Democrats rebuffed him when they set up a special committee to probe abuses by the Central Intelligence Agency and take over the oversight functions that a Stennis subcommittee had previously performed. In 1979, his own committee —in a revolt led by Sen. Henry M. Jackson, D-Wash. — embarrassed Stennis by issuing a report highly critical of President Carter's proposed strategic arms limitation treaty (SALT II), a treaty Stennis hinted he would probably support.

Nonetheless, Stennis has won far more of such battles than he has lost, and his loyalty to his committee has never wavered. At the start of the 97th Congress, when Democrats lost the Senate, he had his choice of the ranking minority post on either Armed Services or the even more powerful Appropriations Committee. He stuck with Armed Services, saying his concern for national security convinced him it was "my duty."

Duty is an old-fashioned notion Stennis takes seriously; so is responsibility. In a 1980 speech, he observed that "we seldom hear the words 'personal responsibility.' The thought should be proclaimed every time the word 'rights' is used, and their dependence always clearly emphasized."

The "rights" most rankling to Stennis have been, of course, the civil rights promoted and protected by a stream of Supreme Court decisions and acts of Congress over the past quarter of a century. The Mississippi Democrat has never been a demagogue on racial matters, but he stood with the rest of the old-time Southerners in opposition to every civil rights bill to come through the Congress. He has not budged an inch in that regard.

At the start of the last decade, Stennis took the lead in taunting his Northern colleagues about *de facto* segregation created by housing patterns; he even teamed up with Connecticut Democrat Abraham Ribicoff to push through the Senate a measure requiring the government to apply the same standards North and South in determining whether to cut off federal education aid to segregated school districts.

For all his gentleness, Stennis can be remarkably tenacious over an issue important to him or Mississippi. He has been that way in his support for the Tennessee-Tombigbee waterway, the massive public works project he has lobbied for most of his Senate career. It is his main priority on the Energy and Water Subcommittee at Appropriations, and he has argued ceaselessly against complaints either that it is environmentally wasteful or too expensive to complete.

With most of his political contemporaries retired or dead, and with his chairmanships now in the hands of Republicans, Stennis is an increasingly anachronistic figure in the Senate. But he retains the dignity and serenity of one who has chosen a path and followed it. "I want to plow a straight furrow right down to the end of my row," he said when he became a senator nearly 35 years ago. And so he has.

**At Home:** Throughout his career, Stennis has shown little concern for Mississippi political affairs. He has had little need to. His personal reputaton and his state's one-party politics have combined to make re-election a mere formality.

Democrat James O. Eastland, Stennis' senior colleague until his 1978 retirement, was always the man to see in Washington for home state political favors. Stennis has tended to avoid these things. There is no "Stennis organization" in Mississippi. In 1978, when his son ran for a Mississippi House seat, the senator campaigned actively for him. But John Hampton Stennis lost decisively to a Republican.

As Stennis has grown older, there has been periodic speculation that a strong primary challenger could defeat him. But none has tried. Former Gov. William Waller contemplated running against him in 1976, but decided against it.

Stennis was born on a cotton and cattle farm in Kemper County. He came from a long line of country doctors, although his father was a farmer and merchant. After returning home from college to practice law, Stennis served in the state House, as district attorney and as a circuit judge.

In 1947, Stennis ran in a special election held after the death of Sen. Theodore Bilbo, Mississippi's legendary race-baiting demagogue. Two of the five candidates — Forrest B. Jackson and U.S. Rep. John E. Rankin — copied Bilbo's white supremacist style. Stennis campaigned as a dignified Southern gentleman and generally avoided mentioning the racial issue. He insisted only that he was a segregationist and would preserve "the Southern way of life," and then went on to talk about farm policy. He came in first with 26.9 percent of the vote.

## Committees

**Appropriations** (2nd of 14 Democrats)
Agriculture and Related Agencies; Defense; Energy and Water Development; HUD- Independent Agencies; Transportation.

**Armed Services** (Ranking Democrat)

## Elections

**1976 General**

| | |
|---|---|
| John Stennis (D ) | Unopposed |

**Previous Winning Percentages**

1970 (88 %) 1964 (100%) 1958 (100%) 1952 (100%)
1947* (27 %)

*Special election*

## Campaign Finance

| | Receipts | Receipts from PACs | Expenditures |
|---|---|---|---|
| **1976** | | | |
| Stennis (D ) | $119,852 | $2,380 (2%) | $119,852 |

## Voting Studies

| | Presidential Support | | Party Unity | | Conservative Coalition | |
|---|---|---|---|---|---|---|
| Year | S | O | S | O | S | O |
| 1980 | 65 | 22 | 51 | 30 | 67 | 11 |
| 1979 | 55 | 30 | 52 | 34 | 76 | 8 |
| 1978 | 31 | 46 | 27 | 52 | 65 | 12 |
| 1977 | 56 | 30 | 27 | 51 | 71 | 4 |
| 1976 | 66 | 17 | 20 | 61 | 75 | 3 |
| 1975 | 65 | 20 | 27 | 60 | 83 | 2 |
| 1974 (Ford) | 68 | 26 | | | | |
| 1974 | 64 | 29 | 27 | 66 | 85 | 7 |
| 1973 | 22 | 2 | 8 | 16 | 29 | 0 |
| 1972 | 78 | 22 | 24 | 72 | 95 | 1 |
| 1971 | 68 | 26 | 33 | 59 | 94 | 0 |
| 1970 | 58 | 27 | 31 | 55 | 79 | 7 |
| 1969 | 56 | 40 | 38 | 55 | 88 | 3 |
| 1968 | 44 | 52 | 38 | 58 | 94 | 3 |
| 1967 | 54 | 36 | 44 | 50 | 96 | 2 |
| 1966 | 50 | 46 | 42 | 53 | 94 | 3 |
| 1965 | 45 | 51 | 36 | 61 | 92 | 5 |
| 1964 | 51 | 42 | 50 | 41 | 84 | 4 |
| 1963 | 38 | 38 | 51 | 40 | 79 | 2 |
| 1962 | 42 | 49 | 52 | 34 | 85 | 12 |
| 1961 | 37 | 61 | 45 | 54 | 98 | 2 |

S = Support          O = Opposition

## Key Votes

**96th Congress**

| | |
|---|---|
| Maintain relations with Taiwan (1979) | N |
| Reduce synthetic fuel development funds (1979) | N |
| Impose nuclear plant moratorium (1979) | N |
| Kill stronger windfall profits tax (1979) | N |
| Guarantee Chrysler Corp. loans (1979) | N |
| Approve military draft registration (1980) | Y |
| End Revenue Sharing to the states (1980) | Y |
| Block Justice Dept. busing suits (1980) | Y |

**97th Congress**

| | |
|---|---|
| Restore urban program funding cuts (1981) | N |

## Interest Group Ratings

| Year | ADA | ACA | AFL-CIO | CCUS-1 | CCUS-2 |
|---|---|---|---|---|---|
| 1980 | 17 | 43 | 38 | 57 | |
| 1979 | 11 | 46 | 35 | 30 | 57 |
| 1978 | 10 | 73 | 6 | 73 | |
| 1977 | 5 | 78 | 12 | 81 | |
| 1976 | 0 | 81 | 28 | 88 | |
| 1975 | 0 | 59 | 32 | 58 | |
| 1974 | 5 | 94 | 20 | 90 | |
| 1973 | 0 | 100 | 25 | 100 | |
| 1972 | 0 | 77 | 0 | 90 | |
| 1971 | 7 | 77 | 42 | · | |
| 1970 | 9 | 80 | 20 | 83 | |
| 1969 | 6 | 88 | 9 | · | |
| 1968 | 0 | 68 | 0 | | |
| 1967 | 0 | 78 | 8 | 70 | |
| 1966 | 0 | 69 | 8 | | |
| 1965 | 0 | 72 | · | 90 | |
| 1964 | 5 | 82 | 20 | | |
| 1963 | | 67 | · | | |
| 1962 | 0 | 70 | 9 | | |
| 1961 | 20 | · | · | | |

# Thad Cochran (R)

**Of Jackson — Elected 1978**

**Born:** Dec. 7, 1937, Pontotoc County, Miss.
**Education:** U. of Miss., B.A. 1959, J.D. 1965.
**Military Career:** Navy, 1959-61.
**Profession:** Lawyer.
**Family:** Wife, Rose Clayton; two children.
**Religion:** Baptist.
**Political Career:** U.S. House, 1973-78.

**In Washington:** Few Republicans gained more than Cochran when the party took over Senate control after the 1980 election.

After two quiet years on the Judiciary and Agriculture committees, he not only moved to Appropriations, but to the chairmanship of its crucial Agriculture Subcommittee. In a chamber filled with Republicans of short tenure, his two years were enough to bring him a position that in the past had required decades of apprenticeship. Cochran had a reputation as one of the most thoughtful new Republicans in the 96th Congress, but he was no renegade. As a Judiciary member, he voted with his party in favor of reimposing the death penalty and against strengthening open housing laws and antitrust restrictions.

He joined with Republican and Southern Democratic colleagues to support language preventing the Justice Department from filing school desegregation suits that could lead to court-ordered busing.

On some Judiciary matters, however, he showed an independent streak. When the committee considered revision of the federal criminal code, the two parties split on a provision to keep the federal government from prosecuting cases involving alleged extortion during labor disputes. Most Republicans wanted to allow prosecution, but Cochran, seeing an intrusion by the federal government, disagreed, and voted with the Democratic majority.

Some of Cochran's most conspicuous work during the 96th Congress came on a soft drink bottling bill he sponsored along with Indiana Democrat Birch Bayh. The bill was written to give new protection from antitrust liability to certain soft drink bottling franchises, and much of the bottling industry lobbied for it vigorously. When it reached the Senate floor, Cochran joined Bayh in an unusual filibuster designed to prevent Ohio Democrat Howard M. Metzenbaum from attaching a controversial and unrelated amendment. The tactic worked and the bill became law.

Another Cochran bill, which also became law

in 1980, overrode state usury laws on business and agricultural loans over $25,000. Cochran said it was necessary to ensure availability of credit in states that were limiting the amount of interest a bank could charge on loans.

Although Cochran has always run for office and generally voted as a conservative Republican, many of his personal contacts have been with GOP moderates. When he was in the House, he quietly belonged to the Wednesday Group, the informal moderate Republican organization. On his arrival in the Senate, in 1979, he backed moderates John Heinz, R-Pa., and Bob Packwood, R-Ore., for leadership posts over conservative opposition.

At the start of the 97th Congress, however, he voted with conservatives in the key leadership contest, backing James McClure of Idaho over Heinz for chairman of the Republican conference.

Cochran's three-term House career was relatively quiet. He spent most of his committee time on Public Works, where he joined the panel's majority in favor of heavy spending for highways and water projects. He was one of six Republicans on the panel that drafted a new ethics code for the chamber in 1977.

**At Home:** Cochran's election as the first Republican senator from Mississippi in 100 years made him a symbol of GOP success in the South.

It also made him titular head of the state's Republican Party, which has been divided in recent years into moderate and militantly conservative factions. Cochran, clearly labeled a moderate, has been on the prevailing side more than his share of the time.

In 1976, the Mississippi party was beset by an internal struggle between supporters of Gerald R. Ford and Ronald Reagan for the Republican presidential nomination. Cochran sided with Ford at the GOP convention in Kansas City, and the

**655**

## Thad Cochran, R-Miss.

delegation voted 30-0 for Ford's position in the critical rules fight that played a large role in ending Reagan's chances. Despite considerable anger within the delegation at the time, Cochran emerged with no lasting political damage.

He had already shown a considerable talent for making friends across the political spectrum. Despite his conservative House voting record, Cochran drew significant support in most of his campaigns from blacks, who made up more than 40 percent of his 4th District. After a close first election in 1972, when he succeeded retiring Democrat Charles R. Griffin, he drew over 70 percent both in 1974 and 1976.

His election to the Senate was made possible in part, however, by an independent black cam-

paign that siphoned off votes from the Democratic nominee, ex-Columbia Mayor Maurice Dantin. Democrat James O. Eastland retired in 1978 after 36 years in the Senate, and endorsed Dantin to succeed him. But a flamboyant campaign by Fayette Mayor Charles Evers, the veteran black activist, drew more attention than Cochran and Dantin combined.

In a state where Democrats need the black vote to win, Evers virtually guaranteed Republican success. Cochran drew only 45.1 percent statewide, but he finished nearly 80,000 votes ahead of Dantin. Cochran swept his 4th District, and carried the Gulf Coast and the Jackson area. He made inroads into the Democratic hill country in northern Mississippi, where he was born.

## Committees

**Agriculture, Nutrition and Forestry** (5th of 9 Republicans)
Agricultural Production, Marketing and Stabilization of Prices, chairman; Foreign Agricultural Policy; Soil and Water Conservation.

**Appropriations** (8th of 15 Republicans)
Agriculture and Related Agencies, chairman; Energy and Water Development; Interior; State, Justice, Commerce, and the Judiciary; Transportation.

## Elections

**1978 General**

| | |
|---|---|
| Thad Cochran (R ) | 263,089 (45 %) |
| Maurice Dantin (D ) | 185,454 (32 %) |
| Charles Evers (I ) | 133,646 (23 %) |

**1978 Primary**

| | |
|---|---|
| Thad Cochran (R ) | 51,212 (69 %) |
| Charles Pickering (R) | 22,949 (31 %) |

**Previous Winning Percentages**

1976 * (76%)    1974* (70%)   1972* (48%)

*House elections

## Campaign Finance

| 1978 | Receipts | Receipts from PACs | Expen-ditures |
|---|---|---|---|
| Cochran (R ) | $1,201,259 | $185,230 (15 %) | $1,052,303 |
| Dantin (D ) | $874,590 | $64,705 (7 %) | $873,518 |

## Voting Studies

| | Presidential Support | | Party Unity | | Conservative Coalition | |
|---|---|---|---|---|---|---|
| Year | S | O | S | O | S | O |
| Senate service | | | | | | |
| 1980 | 39 | 54 | 74 | 20 | 80 | 14 |
| 1979 | 48 | 47 | 75 | 17 | 75 | 8 |
| House service | | | | | | |
| 1978 | 13 | 30 | 45 | 8 | 47 | 5 |
| 1977 | 28 | 65 | 81 | 17 | 94 | 4 |
| 1976 | 63 | 33 | 81 | 17 | 90 | 6 |
| 1975 | 61 | 38 | 80 | 15 | 89 | 5 |
| 1974 (Ford) | 57 | 37 | | | | |
| 1974 | 70 | 23 | 73 | 20 | 77 | 11 |
| 1973 | 65 | 30 | 78 | 16 | 86 | 6 |

S = Support          O = Opposition

## Key Votes

**96th Congress**

| | |
|---|---|
| Maintain relations with Taiwan (1979) | Y |
| Reduce synthetic fuel development funds (1979) | Y |
| Impose nuclear plant moratorium (1979) | N |
| Kill stronger windfall profits tax (1979) | Y |
| Guarantee Chrysler Corp. loans (1979) | N |
| Approve military draft registration (1980) | Y |
| End Revenue Sharing to the states (1980) | N |
| Block Justice Dept. busing suits (1980) | Y |

**97th Congress**

| | |
|---|---|
| Restore urban program funding cuts (1981) | N |

## Interest Group Ratings

| Year | ADA | ACA | AFL-CIO | CCUS-1 | CCUS-2 |
|---|---|---|---|---|---|
| Senate service | | | | | |
| 1980 | 22 | 88 | 17 | 85 | |
| 1979 | 5 | 70 | 17 | 91 | 93 |
| House service | | | | | |
| 1978 | 0 | 83 | 7 | 71 | |
| 1977 | 0 | 74 | 18 | 88 | |
| 1976 | 5 | 77 | 35 | 80 | |
| 1975 | 5 | 81 | 29 | 88 | |
| 1974 | 17 | 85 | 11 | 88 | |
| 1973 | 8 | 81 | 9 | 100 | |

# 1 Jamie L. Whitten (D)

**Of Charleston — Elected 1941**

**Born:** April 18, 1910, Cascilla, Miss.
**Education:** Attended U. of Miss., 1926-31.
**Profession:** Lawyer.
**Family:** Wife, Rebecca Thompson; two children.
**Religion:** Presbyterian.
**Political Career:** Miss. House, 1932-33.

**In Washington:** The dean of all House members, Whitten finally has the Appropriations chairmanship that has guaranteed power on Capitol Hill for a century. But in a curious way, he probably has less actual influence than he had a decade ago, as an autocratic subcommittee chairman, feared by the Agriculture Department, farm lobbyists, environmentalists and consumers.

In the 38 years it took him to reach the top at Appropriations, the chairmanship itself lost much of its magic, and he remains presiding officer at the pleasure of his party leaders, more a master of ceremonies than an old fashioned chairman.

His one solid power base is the position he has had for all but two years since 1949, the chairmanship of the Agriculture Appropriations Subcommittee, where it long ago became a cliché to call him the "permanent secretary of agriculture."

Even there, however, it is not like it was in the old days, when it was possible for Whitten to rail against integration and social programs and dictate spending on a variety of crop subsidies without a great deal of pressure either inside or outside the institution. Subcommittees are still the source of power on Appropriations, but they are no longer protected from public comment.

It was a different committee in 1971, when a power shuffle on Appropriations gave Whitten's Agriculture panel jurisdiction over the Environmental Protection Agency, Food and Drug Administration and Federal Trade Commission.

Whitten made it clear how he felt about the agencies. He called environmentalists a "small, vocal group of extremists" and said "those people at EPA have been given more money than they can possiby use. . . ." He reiterated his skepticism about controls on pesticides, first set out in a 1966 book, "That We May Live."

Whitten's views on these subjects have not noticeably changed. But one has to listen hard to hear them. Since 1974, all Appropriations subcommittee chairmen have had to stand for reelection each two years in the Democratic Caucus. The year that rule was introduced, liberal

caucus Democrats wanted to strip Whitten of his chairmanship. They were talked out of the effort by the full Appropriations chairman, George H. Mahon of Texas, who came up with a compromise: take environmental and consumer jurisdiction away from the subcommittee, and let Whitten keep Agriculture. That was the decision reached.

Four years later, Mahon retired, and Whitten was in line to take over the full committee. Again there was a flurry of interest by liberal Democrats in bypassing him, and giving the panel to Edward Boland, D-Mass., longtime roommate of Speaker O'Neill. But O'Neill had always been on good personal terms with Whitten — they played poker together in the 1950s — and the Speaker was reluctant to breach seniority, even for an old roommate. Whitten got the chairmanship.

And O'Neill got a loyal and unobtrusive chairman, one who backs national Democratic party goals far more often than he did earlier in his career. The man who voted against Medicare, expansion of food stamp benefits, and anti-poverty programs has modified his behavior as a member of the leadership, subject to periodic confirmation. At times, he has backed the leadership even at the risk of political controversy back home. Repeatedly during the 96th Congress, Whitten worked with House Democratic leaders to find a compromise position on federal funding for abortions, and refused to go as far in outlawing

---

**1st District: North — Clarksdale.**
Population: 495,709 (14% increase since 1970). Race: White 345,823 (70%), Black 148,229 (30%), Others 1,657 (0.3%). Spanish origin: 3,993 (1%).

it as national right-to-life forces wanted. For that, he earned some hostility in his district.

Whitten was an avowed segregationist for most of his House career, a signer of the 1956 Southern Manifesto, saying the 1954 Supreme Court decision had started the nation "on the downhill road to integration, amalgamation and ruin." He opposed all major civil rights bills in the 1960s.

Today Whitten represents a district with a 30 percent black population — a smaller percentage than in the past, but one which votes in significant numbers. He is as free of rhetoric on race-related issues as the younger Southern members who joined him in the 1970s. He has black aides on his congressional staff.

His few conspicuous arguments tend to be with the Budget Committee, which has challenged the once-sacred right of Appropriations to control spending in every area of the federal budget.

Whitten served as co-chairman of the select committee that formulated the present budget process, but his skepticism about the process is evident now. In 1980 he balked at a Budget Committee instruction to halt funding for Saturday mail deliveries to save $500 million.

Budget Committee Chairman Robert Giaimo, D-Conn., who also served on Appropriations, was furious. "Appropriations can't live in its own little world and not work with us and Congress and the leadership," Giaimo stormed.

In early 1981, he began calling for a full-scale investigation of military procurement practices. He called defective military equipment "a catastrophic exercise in incompetency," and said "wasteful spending in the name of defense is frightening because it might lead the president to believe we are much stronger than we are."

That recalled a Whitten crusade that few of his colleagues remember: against wasteful Army-Navy competition in the years after World War II. He found the Navy planning an ambitious construction program while the Army had vacant buildings. His investigation persuaded the Army to allow its rival branch of the service to make use of them.

**At Home:** Whitten has accrued four decades of seniority with barely a scent of opposition in his rural, northern Mississippi district.

Between 1941, when he first won his House seat, and 1978, the year he inherited the Appropriations chairmanship, he faced Republican opposition only twice. Neither challenger reached 20 percent of the vote. Only in the last two elections has Mississippi's resurgent Republican Party managed to offer some spirited competition, and

so far even that has featured more spirit than competition.

Nor has there been much challenge inside the Democratic Party. The only real threat was in 1962, when redistricting forced Whitten to battle Rep. Frank Smith for the Democratic nomination.

The son of a Tallahatchie County farmer, Whitten has spent his entire adult life in politics. He was elected to the Mississippi House at age 21, and two years later was chosen district attorney. At 31 he was elected to Congress to succeed Wall Doxey, who had been elected to the Senate. For the next two decades he ran virtually unopposed. But in 1962, Mississippi lost one House seat in reapportionment. The state Legislature solved the problem by combining the two districts of the northern delta region, forcing a showdown between Whitten and Smith.

Their campaign was bitter. The two had been on opposite sides during the 1960 presidential election, in which Smith backed Democratic nominee John F. Kennedy while Whitten supported an unpledged slate of segregationist electors.

The population of the new district was more than one-half black, but virtually none of the blacks voted. Each congressman tried to outdo the other in support of segregation.

Smith had had a reputation as a populist on economic issues, and Whitten claimed that he cooperated with Northern liberals and the Kennedy administration rather than working to "preserve the Southern way of life." Smith retaliated that Whitten was more of a "prima donna" than an effective champion of Southern rights.

Building a huge lead in the counties of his old constituency, Whitten won easily with 60 percent of the vote. In appreciation of his national party loyalty, Smith was appointed by President Kennedy to the board of the TVA.

In 1978, Whitten was confronted by his first primary challenge since 1966. He defeated his major rival, young District Attorney Gerald W. Chatham, by a margin of 2-to-1. But for the first time, Whitten's age was a major campaign issue.

That fall, he faced his first GOP challenge since 1966. Whitten drew 68 percent of the vote to win his 20th term over Tupelo lawyer T. K. Moffett. Two years later, while Ronald Reagan was carrying Mississippi — but not the 1st District — against Jimmy Carter, Moffett was increasing his share of the vote to 37 percent.

**The District:** In Mississippi's evolving two-party system, the rural 1st has remained the most staunchly Democratic district in the state. It gave Carter a higher share of the vote in 1976 and 1980 than any other Mississippi district.

Whitten's constituency stretches east from the heavily black Mississippi delta to the hill country bordering Alabama. After losing population for decades, the district grew by nearly 14 percent in the 1970s with the attraction of new industry. The most rapid growth was in the Memphis (Tenn.) suburbs in DeSoto County. But there was also a substantial population boom in the eastern portion of the district, where construction of the Tennessee-Tombigbee waterway has generated new jobs.

## Committees

**Appropriations** (Chairman)
Agriculture, Rural Development and Related Agencies, chairman.

## Elections

**1980 General**

| | |
|---|---|
| Jamie Whitten (D ) | 104,269 (63 %) |
| T. K. Moffett (R ) | 61,292 (37 %) |

**1978 General**

| | |
|---|---|
| Jamie Whitten (D ) | 57,358 (67 %) |
| T. K. Moffett (R ) | 26,734 (31 %) |

**Previous Winning Percentages**

| | | | |
|---|---|---|---|
| 1976 (100%) | 1974 (88 %) | 1972 (100%) | 1970 (87 %) |
| 1968 (100%) | 1966 (84 %) | 1964 (100%) | 1962 (100%) |
| 1960 (100%) | 1958 (100%) | 1956 (100%) | 1954 (100%) |
| 1952 (100%) | 1950 (100%) | 1948 (100%) | 1946 (100%) |
| 1944 (99 %) | 1942 (100%) | 1941* (69 %) | |

* *Special election.*

**District Vote For President**

| | 1980 | | 1976 | | 1972 |
|---|---|---|---|---|---|
| **D** | 97,730 (55 %) | **D** | 91,615 (60 %) | **D** | 23,058 (19 %) |
| **R** | 74,191 (42 %) | **R** | 56,794 (37 %) | **R** | 92,680 (78 %) |
| **I** | 3,073 (2 %) | | | | |

## Campaign Finance

| | Receipts | Receipts from PACs | Expenditures |
|---|---|---|---|
| **1980** | | | |
| Whitten (D ) | $139,452 | $116,487 (84 %) | $67,794 |
| Moffett (R ) | $81,548 | $1,000 (1 %) | $75,353 |
| **1978** | | | |
| Whitten (D ) | $100,902 | $35,471 (35 %) | $87,331 |
| Moffett (R ) | $72,164 | $4,860 (7 %) | $71,620 |

## Voting Studies

| | Presidential Support | | Party Unity | | Conservative Coalition | |
|---|---|---|---|---|---|---|
| Year | S | O | S | O | S | O |
| 1980 | 56 | 39 | 46 | 40 | 76 | 15 |
| 1979 | 44 | 52 | 50 | 43 | 78 | 19 |
| 1978 | 40 | 48 | 39 | 45 | 73 | 13 |
| 1977 | 46 | 48 | 41 | 53 | 85 | 12 |
| 1976 | 53 | 43 | 32 | 61 | 87 | 9 |
| 1975 | 47 | 44 | 33 | 57 | 77 | 11 |

| | | | | | | |
|---|---|---|---|---|---|---|
| 1974 (Ford) | 67 | 33 | | | | |
| 1974 | 57 | 38 | 37 | 60 | 83 | 14 |
| 1973 | 59 | 34 | 34 | 62 | 87 | 8 |
| 1972 | 49 | 51 | 28 | 65 | 85 | 12 |
| 1971 | 68 | 26 | 30 | 49 | 75 | 8 |
| 1970 | 52 | 40 | 32 | 46 | 68 | 2 |
| 1969 | 45 | 45 | 27 | 64 | 84 | 7 |
| 1968 | 40 | 49 | 22 | 65 | 86 | 4 |
| 1967 | 49 | 46 | 37 | 58 | 85 | 6 |
| 1966 | 22 | 50 | 13 | 61 | 78 | 0 |
| 1965 | 29 | 63 | 23 | 67 | 86 | 6 |
| 1964 | 42 | 56 | 32 | 60 | 92 | 0 |
| 1963 | 24 | 48 | 26 | 52 | 80 | 7 |
| 1962 | 23 | 52 | 28 | 56 | 75 | 6 |
| 1961 | 34 | 62 | 34 | 59 | 96 | 4 |

S = Support          O = Opposition

## Key Votes

**96th Congress**

| | |
|---|---|
| Weaken Carter oil profits tax (1979) | Y |
| Reject hospital cost control plan (1979) | Y |
| Implement Panama Canal Treaties (1979) | N |
| Establish Department of Education (1979) | Y |
| Approve Anti-busing Amendment (1979) | Y |
| Guarantee Chrysler Corp. loans (1979) | Y |
| Approve military draft registration (1980) | Y |
| Aid Sandinista regime in Nicaragua (1980) | N |
| Strengthen fair housing laws (1980) | N |

**97th Congress**

| | |
|---|---|
| Reagan budget proposal (1981) | N |

## Interest Group Ratings

| Year | ADA | ACA | AFL-CIO | CCUS |
|---|---|---|---|---|
| 1980 | 28 | 57 | 29 | 77 |
| 1979 | 16 | 36 | 35 | 71 |
| 1978 | 20 | 55 | 39 | 43 |
| 1977 | 10 | 56 | 43 | 82 |
| 1976 | 15 | 71 | 48 | 57 |
| 1975 | 16 | 77 | 35 | 63 |
| 1974 | 26 | 71 | 18 | 80 |
| 1973 | 12 | 74 | 30 | 90 |
| 1972 | 6 | 91 | 30 | 80 |
| 1971 | 8 | 80 | 33 | - |
| 1970 | 4 | 71 | 29 | 70 |
| 1969 | 13 | 88 | 20 | - |
| 1968 | 17 | 80 | 0 | - |
| 1967 | 7 | 67 | 17 | 60 |
| 1966 | 0 | 89 | 8 | - |
| 1965 | 0 | 85 | - | 100 |
| 1964 | 12 | 72 | 0 | - |
| 1963 | - | 86 | - | - |
| 1962 | 13 | 81 | 0 | - |
| 1961 | 0 | - | - | - |

# 2 David R. Bowen (D)

**Of Cleveland — Elected 1972**

**Born:** Oct. 21, 1932, Houston, Miss.
**Education:** Harvard U., B.A. 1954; Oxford, M.A. 1956.
**Military Career:** Army, 1957-58.
**Profession:** Political science professor.
**Family:** Single.
**Religion:** Baptist.
**Political Career:** No previous office.

**In Washington:** Bowen's district concentrates on cotton, but his Washington career focuses at least as much on foreign policy and the diplomatic community.

Bowen was only in his second House term when he fell into a chairmanship the average Southern Democrat would covet — the Cotton Subcommittee on Agriculture. But while protecting his crop interests, Bowen has always wanted to spend personal time on foreign policy. Since he arrived in 1973 as a bachelor with a Rhodes Scholar background, he has been a fixture on the city's international social circuit.

For most of his congressional career, Bowen has sought committee assignments that would allow him to deal with some of the countries whose diplomats he knows personally. The Merchant Marine Committee, with its jurisdiction over international fishing, provided some of those opportunities, but Bowen also fought for a place on Foreign Affairs, and won it in 1979.

As a member of Merchant Marine, he played a key role in building support for implementation of the Panama Canal treaties. It was not a popular position in Mississippi, and it required him to break with the rest of his delegation. But he was an effective lobbyist for the transfer, placing House leaders in his debt for some time to come. He led a six-member delegation to Panama on the eve of a committee vote on the issue, and returned with a warning that if the U.S. did not transfer the canal, Panama might seize it.

Bowen's visit to the Canal Zone was one of many foreign missions he has undertaken for Merchant Marine, Foreign Affairs, and Agriculture in recent years, causing him political trouble at home. His five trips abroad during his first year on Foreign Affairs provoked sniping from critics; Bowen called them a "clear-cut part of my responsibility." He also deflected criticism of his ties to Korean rice dealer Tongsun Park, who had distributed large sums of money to members of Congress. Bowen said he had attended parties for Park, and saw no reason to apologize for it.

Meanwhile, as Cotton Subcommittee chairman, Bowen was refereeing some of the disputes between Deep South cotton growers and the increasingly vocal cotton contingent from the Southwest. During floor consideration of the 1977 farm bill, he negotiated an agreement under which cotton farmers would be allowed to qualify their land for "set-aside" subsidies much in the way wheat and feed grain farmers do. That was a response to complaints from California and Arizona that the previous cotton subsidy system was tailored to Mississippi and other traditional growing states.

**At Home.** Bowen has been an inviting target for Republicans since he first won the 2nd District in 1972. But so far they have been unable to mount an effective challenge against him.

Bowen has faced a series of political newcomers long on aggressiveness but short on money. In 1976 and 1978, his opponent was a veterinarian; in 1980, a school administrator who did not live in the district. Still, in a state where popular incumbents often win nearly unanimous re-election, Bowen has never exceeded 70 percent.

Before running for Congress, Bowen taught history and political science at colleges in Mississippi, worked as Southeastern coordinator for the O.E.O. and was a staff associate for the U.S. Chamber of Commerce. From 1968 to 1972, he served as an aide to Gov. John Bell Williams.

With the retirement of veteran Democratic

---

**2nd District: North central — Greenville, Columbus.** Population: 460,780 (5% increase since 1970). Race: White 249,364 (54%), Black 208,514 (45%), Others 2,902 (1%). Spanish 4,655 (1%).

Rep. Thomas G. Abernethy in 1972, Bowen joined the long list of aspirants to replace him. Bowen had to compete for votes in his native Delta region with former Rep. Frank E. Smith, but his 15 percent of the primary vote edged him past Smith to win a spot in the runoff against Tom Cook, former superintendent of the state prison.

Despite Bowen's unimpressive initial vote, he consolidated opposition to the controversial Cook — who had been fired from his prison post by Gov. William Waller — to win the runoff with a comfortable 57 percent. Drawing strong black support, Bowen won the general election handily.

**The District.** Like the 1st District, the rural 2nd runs across the state from east to west. The heavily black delta portion is solidly Democratic, enabling the party's candidates to carry the district in recent state and presidential races. Within the delta region are the Mississippi River port of Greenville, the largest population center, and Sunflower County, the home base of former Sen. James O. Eastland.

In the predominantly white hill country to the east are more Republican areas, such as Lowndes and Oktibbeha counties. Columbus is the seat of Lowndes County. An Air Force base and new industry have attracted GOP voters from the North and Midwest.

## Committees

**Agriculture** (6th of 24 Democrats)
Cotton, Rice and Sugar, chairman; Conservation, Credit, and Rural Development; Department Operations, Research and Foreign Agriculture.

**Foreign Affairs** (21st of 21 Democrats)

**Merchant Marine and Fisheries** (6th of 20 Democrats)
Fisheries and Wildlife Conservation and the Environment; Panand Canal and Outer Continental Shelf.

## Elections

**1980 General**

| | |
|---|---|
| David Bowen (D ) | 96,750 (70 %) |
| Frank Drake (R ) | 42,300 (30 %) |

**1978 General**

| | |
|---|---|
| David Bowen (D ) | 57,678 (62 %) |
| Roland Byrd (R ) | 35,730 (38 %) |

**Previous Winning Percentages**

1976 (63 %)    1974 (66 %)    1972 (62 %)

**District Vote For President**

| | 1980 | | 1976 | | 1972 |
|---|---|---|---|---|---|
| D | 79,717 (52 %) | D | 69,152 (51 %) | D | 24,633 (22 %) |
| R | 70,194 (46 %) | R | 61,511 (46 %) | R | 84,346 (76 %) |

## Campaign Finance

| | Receipts | Receipts from PACs | Expenditures |
|---|---|---|---|
| **1980** | | | |
| Bowen (D ) | $99,702 | $66,850 (67 %) | $56,912 |
| Drake (R ) | $22,900 | $250 (1 %) | $21,573 |
| **1978** | | | |
| Bowen (D ) | $78,174 | $41,257 (53 %) | $90,850 |
| Byrd (R ) | $90,455 | $6,874 (8 %) | $91,580 |

## Voting Studies

| Year | Presidential Support | | Party Unity | | Conservative Coalition | |
|---|---|---|---|---|---|---|
| | S | O | S | O | S | O |
| 1980 | 69 | 22 | 55 | 26 | 58 | 26 |
| 1979 | 58 | 35 | 47 | 44 | 68 | 24 |
| 1978 | 38 | 61 | 32 | 63 | 87 | 9 |
| 1977 | 47 | 46 | 45 | 48 | 83 | 11 |
| 1976 | 51 | 45 | 33 | 61 | 84 | 9 |
| 1975 | 53 | 40 | 39 | 54 | 82 | 11 |
| 1974 (Ford) | 52 | 43 | | | | |
| 1974 | 64 | 34 | 42 | 52 | 81 | 12 |
| 1973 | 58 | 37 | 42 | 55 | 85 | 12 |

S = Support          O = Opposition

## Key Votes

**96th Congress**

| | |
|---|---|
| Weaken Carter oil profits tax (1979) | Y |
| Reject hospital cost control plan (1979) | Y |
| Implement Panama Canal Treaties (1979) | Y |
| Establish Department of Education (1979) | Y |
| Approve Anti-busing Amendment (1979) | Y |
| Guarantee Chrysler Corp. loans (1979) | N |
| Approve military draft registration (1980) | Y |
| Aid Sandinista regime in Nicaragua (1980) | Y |
| Strengthen fair housing laws (1980) | N |

**97th Congress**

| | |
|---|---|
| Reagan budget proposal (1981) | Y |

## Interest Group Ratings

| Year | ADA | ACA | AFL-CIO | CCUS |
|---|---|---|---|---|
| 1980 | 28 | 43 | 24 | 78 |
| 1979 | 11 | 70 | 26 | 93 |
| 1978 | 15 | 88 | 20 | 89 |
| 1977 | 5 | 70 | 35 | 76 |
| 1976 | 20 | 70 | 48 | 67 |
| 1975 | 16 | 75 | 39 | 69 |
| 1974 | 26 | 46 | 20 | 70 |
| 1973 | 24 | 56 | 27 | 82 |

**661**

# 3 G. V. "Sonny" Montgomery (D)

**Of Meridian — Elected 1966**

**Born:** Aug. 5, 1920, Meridian, Miss.
**Education:** Miss. State U., B.S. 1943.
**Military Career:** Army, 1943-46; National Guard, 1946-80, active duty 1951-52.
**Profession:** Insurance agent.
**Family:** Single.
**Religion:** Episcopalian.
**Political Career:** Miss. Senate, 1956-66.

**In Washington:** Vietnam has dominated Sonny Montgomery's congressional career, not only during the years of fighting, but after the ceasefire as well, when most other members were no longer thinking much about it.

Montgomery ran for Congress in 1966 pledging to "bring the boys home" in honor. He spent every Christmas for the next several years visiting soldiers at the front. When the conflict finally drew to a close, he served on two committees seeking facts on men missing in action. Now, as chairman of the Veterans' Affairs Committee, he has to struggle with the question of benefits for those who served in Vietnam.

It is the career focus his personal life prepared him for. He spent most of his adult years in the military on active duty in World War II and Korea, and in the Mississippi National Guard until 1980. He headed immediately for Veterans' Affairs as a House freshman in 1967, and added a place on Armed Services four years later.

He is a member whom colleagues usually listen to, not necessarily because they agree with him but because they like him. Firmly within the tradition of soft-spoken Southern grace, Montgomery is rarely disagreeable even to those who have never agreed with him on defense issues. Many of his friendships were developed on the paddleball court in the House gym; others on Washington's dinner party circuit, where Montgomery has long been a bachelor much in demand.

Like most Mississippi Democrats, Montgomery came to Washington with the firm belief that the national Democratic party had moved too far to the left for him to support it very often.

He was one of only three House diehards to stick by President Nixon even after the House Judiciary Committee voted in favor of impeachment. These days he votes with his own leadership only about a third of the time, and House Republicans refer to him casually as "one of us."

At times in the past, GOP members interested in building a bipartisan conservative coalition to take formal House control have sought him out as a potential leader. But he has never talked seriously of bolting the Democratic Party — not so long as it controls the levers of power in the House. In 1981, Montgomery helped start the Conservative Democratic Forum, the group that lobbies for conservative positions within the Democratic Party.

Montgomery began traveling to Vietnam in his first year on Capitol Hill, initially at Agriculture Committee expense, inspecting Food for Peace programs. Later, he went on Veterans' Committee business, reviewing VA facilities. But mostly, Montgomery went because he wanted to see the military and the war firsthand.

As a result, he became an acknowledged expert on the war, although his support for it drove him far from majority opinion in the House in the early 1970s. "The time is past when we can discuss whether this is the wrong war," he said in 1967. "Our flag is committed." Three years later, he was still defending the ability of American troops to help the South Vietnamese win the war. "The morale of the American fighting man is quite high," he said then. "The one thing that seems to disturb him most is the continued anti-

**3rd District: South central — Meridian.** Population: 514,218 (15% increase since 1970). Race: White 314,027 (61%), Black 194,713 (38%), Others 5,458 (1%). Spanish origin: 4,575 (1%).

war demonstrations."

But while the House moved far from Mongomery's hawkish approach in the ensuing years, it saw him as the logical man after the war to set up a committee to find out whether U.S. servicemen were being held prisoner by the North Vietnamese.

Montgomery's committee, known formally as the Select Committee on U.S. Involvement in Southeast Asia, went to Vietnam and to Europe to meet with representatives of the communist regime in Hanoi. It finally concluded, in December 1976, that there were no Americans still imprisoned in North Vietnam.

Montgomery resisted pleas from fellow conservatives to continue pressing Hanoi for more information. He was the bearer of bad news: There was no hard evidence, he said, that any of the missing men were still alive.

Again the next year, Montgomery was called for Vietnam duty when President Carter sent a special commission to Vietnam, headed by labor leader Leonard Woodcock. Again Montgomery presented a report that did not please his conservative colleagues. He and the commission advised the president to explore the possibility of normal diplomatic relations with what had become the Socialist Republic of Vietnam.

On the Armed Services Committee, Montgomery has spoken for years in behalf of military reserve units and the National Guard. It is a subject other members treat with only intermittent attention, but Montgomery has made a specialty of it, does his homework and often gets his way. He is largely responsible, for example, for the new planes the Air National Guard is able to obtain in each year's defense authorization.

Montgomery has been less successful in his long fight to reinstate the draft. As someone who worries about the ability of American forces to fight a protracted war, he has continually questioned the merits of the all-volunteer army. Most of the Armed Services Committee agrees with him, but they have made little progress in moving the House toward a peacetime draft, although peacetime registration was reinstituted in 1980.

As Montgomery took over the Veterans' Committee in 1981, there were few major changes. The committee has been dominated by members close to traditional lobbying groups such as the American Legion and Veterans of Foreign Wars. Many of the members themselves are World War II veterans.

This 1940s orientation has set up a conflict with younger members who want to see more benefits enacted for Vietnam-era veterans. They posed a potential challenge for Montgomery as he set out in 1981 to write a new GI Bill for men and women now in the service. Montgomery has expressed a desire to increase benefits to attract more qualified persons to military service.

**At Home.** For years Montgomery has had the best of both worlds — a personal popularity in Congress and bipartisan support back home.

Not since 1968 has he won a primary or general election with less than 90 percent of the vote. "Sonny Montgomery votes with us," explained former state Republican Chairman Clarke Reed in 1974. "We don't have any issues against him except party."

Montgomery was a state senator and prominent National Guard officer when he first ran for the House in 1966. The 3d District had gone Republican on a fluke in 1964, electing little-known chicken farmer Prentiss Walker, the only Republican who had bothered to file for Congress anywhere in the state that year. Barry Goldwater carried Mississippi easily in his 1964 presidential campaign, and he carried Walker into office with him. Two years later Walker ran unsuccessfully for the Senate — he would have been beaten for re-election to the House anyway — and Montgomery found the field clear.

There were three other candidates for the Democratic nomination in 1966, but Montgomery was an easy winner. He drew 50.1 percent of the primary vote, avoiding even the necessity of a runoff.

His general election campaign was easier. Describing himself as "a conservative Mississippi Democrat," Montgomery said he opposed the new, big-spending Great Society programs but favored older ones like Social Security and rural electrification. He claimed that his Republican opponent, state Rep. L.L. McAllister Jr., was against all federal programs, and linked McAllister with the national GOP, which he called the "party of Reconstruction, Depression and 'me-too' liberalism." Sweeping every county, Montgomery won the seat with 65 percent of the vote.

He had little trouble holding it in 1968, drawing 85 percent of the primary vote against a black civil rights activist and 70 percent in the fall against Walker, who was trying to regain the seat. The Republican had lost his Senate race to veteran Democrat James O. Eastland by a margin of more than 2-1, and ran almost as poorly in his comeback attempt against Montgomery. He carried only one county.

That crushing defeat seemed to remove any remaining Republican interest in contesting Montgomery. Opposition has been negligible since 1968.

**The District.** Like the two northern Mississippi districts, the T-shaped 3rd is predominantly rural. But it is far more Republican than they are in voting behavior.

The reason is the presence of two major population centers — Lauderdale and Rankin counties — which cast more than a quarter of the vote and regularly turn in substantial GOP majorities. Rankin County includes the eastern suburbs of Jackson. Lauderdale County includes Meridian, the district's largest city. Located in the midst of the Piney Woods, Meridian has several lumber-related industries, Lockheed and General Motors plants and a Navy base.

Democratic strength is concentrated in the heavily black, cotton-growing Delta region at the western end of the district. The rest of the 22-county district tends to be more marginal in its voting habits.

## Committees

**Armed Services** (9th of 25 Democrats)
Military Installations and Facilities; Military Personnel and Compensation.

**Veterans' Affairs** (Chairman)
Oversight and Investigations, chairman; Compensation, Pension and Insurance.

## Elections

**1980 General**

| | |
|---|---|
| G.V. Montgomery (D ) | Unopposed |

**1978 General**

| | |
|---|---|
| G.V. Montgomery (D ) | 101,685 (92 %) |
| Dorothy N. Cleveland (R ) | 8,408 (8 %) |

**Previous Winning Percentages**

| | | | |
|---|---|---|---|
| 1976 (94 %) | 1974 (100%) | 1972 (100%) | 1970 (100%) |
| 1968 (70 %) | 1966 (65 %) | | |

**District Vote For President**

| | 1980 | | 1976 | | 1972 |
|---|---|---|---|---|---|
| D | 85,930 (45 %) | D | 79,021 (48 %) | D | 28,941 (20 %) |
| R | 99,014 (52 %) | R | 82,515 (50 %) | R | 110,710 (78 %) |
| I | 2,307 (1 %) | | | | |

## Campaign Finance

| | Receipts | Receipts from PACs | Expenditures |
|---|---|---|---|
| **1980** | | | |
| Montgomery (D ) | $15,895 | $7,320 (46 %) | $9,909 |
| **1978** | | | |
| Montgomery (D ) | $69,297 | $27,625 (40 %) | $45,478 |

## Voting Studies

| | Presidential Support | | Party Unity | | Conservative Coalition | |
|---|---|---|---|---|---|---|
| Year | S | O | S | O | S | O |
| 1980 | 45 | 53 | 31 | 68 | 95 | 4 |
| 1979 | 30 | 65 | 19 | 75 | 92 | 3 |
| 1978 | 30 | 65 | 23 | 73 | 91 | 6 |
| 1977 | 33 | 56 | 20 | 71 | 89 | 4 |
| 1976 | 73 | 27 | 13 | 84 | 97 | 1 |
| 1975 | 57 | 37 | 17 | 77 | 91 | 1 |
| 1974 (Ford) | 57 | 37 | | | | |
| 1974 | 70 | 23 | 20 | 73 | 92 | 1 |
| 1973 | 60 | 39 | 24 | 74 | 94 | 5 |
| 1972 | 57 | 41 | 20 | 71 | 88 | 6 |
| 1971 | 70 | 18 | 14 | 60 | 82 | 2 |
| 1970 | 46 | 29 | 24 | 58 | 80 | 2 |
| 1969 | 38 | 40 | 15 | 73 | 84 | 2 |
| 1968 | 41 | 58 | 24 | 74 | 94 | 4 |
| 1967 | 41 | 52 | 21 | 73 | 93 | 2 |

S = Support          O = Opposition

## Key Votes

**96th Congress**

| | |
|---|---|
| Weaken Carter oil profits tax (1979) | Y |
| Reject hospital cost control plan (1979) | Y |
| Implement Panama Canal Treaties (1979) | N |
| Establish Department of Education (1979) | Y |
| Approve Anti-busing Amendment (1979) | Y |
| Guarantee Chrysler Corp. loans (1979) | N |
| Approve military draft registration (1980) | Y |
| Aid Sandinista regime in Nicaragua (1980) | N |
| Strengthen fair housing laws (1980) | N |

**97th Congress**

| | |
|---|---|
| Reagan budget proposal (1981) | Y |

## Interest Group Ratings

| Year | ADA | ACA | AFL-CIO | CCUS |
|---|---|---|---|---|
| 1980 | 0 | 58 | 6 | 73 |
| 1979 | 5 | 87 | 5 | 100 |
| 1978 | 5 | 85 | 15 | 78 |
| 1977 | 0 | 92 | 14 | 93 |
| 1976 | 5 | 100 | 13 | 88 |
| 1975 | 0 | 89 | 9 | 88 |
| 1974 | 0 | 86 | 0 | 90 |
| 1973 | 4 | 85 | 18 | 91 |
| 1972 | 0 | 100 | 11 | 100 |
| 1971 | 0 | 78 | 27 | - |
| 1970 | 0 | 87 | 20 | 78 |
| 1969 | 7 | 86 | 10 | - |
| 1968 | 0 | 87 | 0 | - |
| 1967 | 0 | 81 | 0 | 90 |

# 4 Wayne Dowdy (D)

## Of McComb — Elected 1981

**Born:** July 27, 1943, Fitzgerald, Ga.
**Education:** Millsaps College, B.A. 1965; Jackson School of Law, LL.B. 1968.
**Military Career:** Miss. National Guard.
**Profession:** Lawyer.
**Family:** Wife, Susan Tenney; three children.
**Religion:** Methodist.
**Political Career:** mayor of McComb, 1978-81; city judge 1970-74.

**The Member:** Dowdy's energetic country-boy style and careful manipulation of the issues brought him an upset Democratic victory in 1981 in a Mississippi district Republicans had controlled for eight years. He managed to unite blacks and rural whites in a coalition that past Democrats had failed to hold together.

Dowdy replaced Jon Hinson, who resigned April 13 after being charged with attempted oral sodomy. The mayor of McComb, Dowdy won a July 7 runoff against Republican Liles Williams. In first-round voting two weeks earlier, Williams led Dowdy but failed to gain a majority.

To black audiences, Dowdy stressed his support for renewing the Voting Rights Act. To rural whites, he stressed old fashioned populist themes. "I'm running against the White House, the United States Chamber of Commerce and every oil company in the world," he said. Dowdy portrayed Williams as a tool of the big oil companies that contributed to his campaign. Williams, a businessman from metropolitan Jackson, far outspent Dowdy.

Hoping to help Williams win among conservative whites, President Reagan called Williams to wish him well in the presence of local media. But Dowdy won nine of the district's 12 counties.

Voter turnout in the runoff was about 25 percent higher than in first-round voting, an unusual occurrence traceable to enthusiasm for Dowdy among blacks, who make up 45.4 percent of the district's population. In previous elections, independent black candidates siphoned votes from white Democratic nominees.

**The District.** The 4th has voted Republican in most recent elections. President Ford carried it 1976, as he was losing Mississippi to Carter, and Reagan won it in 1980.

Democrats represented the 4th in Congress until 1972, when Republican Thad Cochran won the seat. Cochran moved to the Senate in 1978 and Hinson took his place.

The center of GOP politics in the district and the state is Jackson, a governmental, financial and commercial center. The GOP builds its margins in Hinds County, which includes Jackson and most of its suburbs and casts about half the 4th District vote.

## Committees

No committees assigned as of Aug. 1, 1981.

## Election

**1981 Special Election Runoff**

| | |
|---|---|
| Wayne Dowdy (D) | 55,656 (50%) |
| Liles Williams (R) | 54,744 (50%) |

**1981 Special Election ***

| | |
|---|---|
| Liles Williams (R) | 39,456 (45%) |
| Wayne Dowdy (D) | 22,166 (25%) |
| Others | 24,297 (28%) |

* Non-partisan election

**District Vote For President**

| | 1980 | | 1976 | | 1972 |
|---|---|---|---|---|---|
| **D** | 88,623 (47%) | **D** | 70,260 (44%) | **D** | 32,496 (24%) |
| **R** | 94,345 (50%) | **R** | 86,002 (54%) | **R** | 101,007 (74%) |

## Campaign Finance

| | Receipts | Receipts from PACs | Expenditures |
|---|---|---|---|
| **1981 *** | | | |
| Dowdy (D) | $136,691 | $4,500 (3%) | $157,578 |
| Williams (R) | $279,126 | $54,814 (20%) | $211,379 |

* Includes information reported by candidates to the Federal Election Commission through July 17, 1981.

---

**4th District: Southwest — Jackson, Vicksburg.** Population: 500,329 (13% increase since 1970). Race: White 271,043 (54%), Black 227,013 (45%), Others 2,273 (0.4%). Spanish origin 4,313 (1%).

# 5 Trent Lott (R)

**Of Pascagoula — Elected 1972**

**Born:** Oct. 9, 1941, Grenada, Miss.
**Education:** U. of Miss., B.P.A., 1963, J.D. 1967.
**Profession:** Lawyer.
**Family:** Wife, Tricia Thompson; two children.
**Religion:** Baptist.
**Political Career:** No previous office.

**In Washington:** Good manners and friendliness can take people quite a distance in the House, and they took Lott all the way to the minority whip's office at the start of the 97th Congress. He lacked the aggressiveness of his major opponent, Pennsylvania's E. G. "Bud" Shuster, and he did not have Shuster's record as a legislative activist. But unlike his rival, he did not have an enemy in the House — or at least not one that could be easily found. The contest was close, but Lott won it, 96-90, becoming the first Deep South Republican ever to rise that high in the party leadership and making him a contender for the Speakership one day — if he remains in the House long enough.

Before 1981, Lott served as chairman of the Republican Research Committee, a group that prepares position papers on various national issues. As third-ranking minority member on the Rules Committee, he had a relatively light workload, and seemed easy-going in his legislative style.

In his early months as whip, however, Lott turned out to be something of an innovator in his efforts to reorganize the party whip system and promote the Reagan legislative program. He appointed a moderate Republican, David Emery of Maine, to be chief deputy whip and hired former Rep. Robert E. Bauman of Maryland, defeated by personal scandal in 1980, as a strategy adviser and "coach" to new GOP members.

Along with the new Republican leader, Robert Michel of Illinois, Lott concentrated much of his effort on wooing conservative Democrats. He expanded the use of computers to track Democratic voting records and to look for issues that offered common ground. He and Michel instituted a "buddy system," assigning Republicans to solicit help from Democratic friends one-on-one. Texas Republican Tom Loeffler was assigned to be a sort of full-time ambassador to the Democratic Forum, an organization of about 40 conservative Democrats.

Lott's first job as whip was a ticklish one. He had to convince Republicans to vote for an increase in the federal debt limit, necessary for the federal government to continue meeting its obligations. During the Carter administration, Republicans had voted solidly against increases and had succeeded frequently in delaying them. Now, Lott had to ask them to forget their past records and vote for an increase so Reagan could get on to other matters. He got 150 of 186 Republicans to go along.

Lott also offered the standard Republican package of rules changes designed to help the minority by, among other things, banning proxy voting in committees and requiring that committee membership ratios follow the full House party breakdown. Democrats have long used proxies to report legislation out of committees, even with few members present. And the most important committees have more Democrats on them than full House percentages would allow. But Lott's ideas were defeated on party-line votes at the start of the Congress, as is routine.

Lott had plenty of opportunity to study House rules before he was a member. He was administrative assistant to Mississippi Democrat William Colmer, the Rules chairman from 1967 to 1973. He wanted a place on the Rules Committee when he arrived, but settled for Judiciary and Merchant Marine, which he gave up when he got his Rules appointment in 1975.

He took part on Judiciary in the historic

---

**5th District: Southeast — Biloxi, Hattiesburg.** Population: 549,602 (22% increase since 1970). Race: White 434,933 (79%), Black 108,737 (20%), Others 5,932 (1%). Spanish origin: 7,195 (1%).

impeachment proceedings of 1973 and 1974. Lott was a staunch defender of President Nixon, a position that was not a liability for him back home. Nixon was still well-liked by many Gulf Coast conservatives in the summer of 1974 when his political support was eroding elsewhere in the country.

Merchant Marine was a logical choice for Lott, because his district relies heavily on shipbuilding. Litton Industries' shipbuilding yard at Pascagoula is the largest private employer in the state. The district also is home port for many Gulf shrimpers and fishermen. On Merchant Marine, Lott introduced and won passage of a bill to help fishermen by reducing the initial investment required to build or recondition a fishing vessel.

In his years on Rules, Lott has been a consistently partisan Republican, looking for ways to use procedure to frustrate the 2-1 edge Democrats have on the committee.

In 1980, when Democrats were trying to put off consideration of a final budget resolution until after the election because the "balanced" budget they had approved in the spring had produced a $27 billion deficit, Lott tried to use his place on Rules to outmaneuver them.

A little-used procedure allows any member of the committee to call up any resolution seven days or more after it has cleared the committee. Lott decided to call up a minor bill dealing with the National Visitors Center in Washington, then seek to amend it on the floor to force consideration of the federal budget.

It was an interesting try, and he had the Republicans with him almost unanimously, but few Democrats wanted to be saddled with a budget vote a few weeks before the election. Lott lost on a party-line vote, 246-144.

Earlier in the 96th Congress, Lott had worked with Democrats Phil Gramm of Texas and James R. Jones of Oklahoma in trying to attach to a debt-limit bill an amendment making a balanced budget a precondition for increasing the debt limit in the future. That move also failed, though it forced the Democratic leadership to promise it would look at balanced-budget procedures.

**At Home.** Lott came late to the party he is leading in the House; he did not become a Republican until the eve of his first campaign.

As Colmer's administrative assistant, he had remained a nominal Democrat. But when the venerable Rules chairman decided to retire in 1972 at age 82, Lott filed in the GOP primary, saying he was "tired of the Muskies and the Kennedys and the Humphreys and the whole lot.... I will fight against the ever-increasing efforts of the so-called liberals," he concluded, "to concentrate more power in the government in Washington."

The wisdom of Lott's switch was soon confirmed. Running that fall against Democrat Ben Stone, chairman of the state Senate Banking Committee, Lott was able to stay on the offensive by linking Stone with the national Democratic Party. Aided by the Nixon landslide and an endorsement from Colmer, Lott swept into the House with 55 percent of the vote. He carried all but two of the district's 12 counties.

With the Gulf Coast developing into a Republican stronghold, Lott has had little trouble winning re-election. The Democrats mounted their most concerted challenge in 1976, when state Rep. Gerald H. Blessey brought in Jimmy Carter to campaign for him. But the incumbent won re-election with 68 percent of the vote, increasing his reputation as a future statewide candidate.

In 1980, with no re-election problems of his own, Lott was able to serve as Ronald Reagan's Mississippi campaign manager, a position that increased his name recognition across the state.

**The District.** The Republican vote in Mississippi increases as one moves south. The 5th, covering the Gulf Coast and nine counties to the north, is the most Republican district in the state. Had it not been for a 26,000-vote plurality here, Ronald Reagan would have lost Mississippi to Jimmy Carter in 1980.

One factor in the district's Republicanism is its relatively small black population. Another is the influx of new voters from outside the South attracted by the favorable climate, burgeoning industry and the arrival of government agencies such as the Naval Oceanographic Office, which recently left the Washington, D.C., area for Bay St. Louis on the Gulf.

Together, the three Gulf Coast counties, which include the cities of Gulfport, Biloxi and Pascagoula, cast about half the district vote. While the Gulf Coast is a rapidly growing industrial, military and resort area, shrimping and other forms of commercial fishing are also vital to the local economy.

Inland, the district encompasses much of the poorer Piney Woods area, where lumber-related industries are a major source of jobs. Like the Gulf Coast, the small cities of Laurel and Hattiesburg usually vote Republican in national elections. The rural areas of the district are more marginal in their voting behavior.

## Committees

**Rules** (3rd of 5 Republicans)
Legislative Process; Rules of the House.

## Elections

**1980 General**

| | |
|---|---|
| Trent Lott (R) | 131,559 (74%) |
| Jimmy McVeay (D) | 46,416 (26%) |

**1978 General**

| | |
|---|---|
| Trent Lott (R) | Unopposed |

**Previous Winning Percentages**

1976 (68%)    1974 (73%)    1972 (55%)

**District Vote For President**

| | 1980 | | 1976 | | 1972 |
|---|---|---|---|---|---|
| D | 77,281 (42%) | D | 71,261 (46%) | D | 17,654 (13%) |
| R | 103,345 (56%) | R | 80,024 (51%) | R | 116,382 (85%) |
| I | 2,500 (1%) | | | | |

## Campaign Finance

| | Receipts | Receipts from PACs | Expen-ditures |
|---|---|---|---|
| **1980** | | | |
| Lott (R) | $194,270 | $71,815 (37%) | $163,118 |
| McVeay (D) | $73,242 | — (0%) | $73,054 |
| **1978** | | | |
| Lott (R) | $43,900 | $27,575 (63%) | $32,708 |

## Voting Studies

| | Presidential Support | | Party Unity | | Conservative Coalition | |
|---|---|---|---|---|---|---|
| Year | S | O | S | O | S | O |
| 1980 | 35 | 59 | 84 | 10 | 95 | 1 |
| 1979 | 26 | 68 | 86 | 10 | 95 | 0 |
| 1978 | 29 | 66 | 86 | 12 | 96 | 3 |
| 1977 | 32 | 63 | 86 | 10 | 93 | 3 |
| 1976 | 59 | 37 | 81 | 10 | 91 | 1 |
| 1975 | 52 | 42 | 79 | 15 | 92 | 4 |
| 1974 (Ford) | 52 | 43 | | | | |
| 1974 | 74 | 23 | 78 | 15 | 90 | 4 |
| 1973 | 69 | 29 | 81 | 14 | 92 | 1 |

S = Support          O = Opposition

## Key Votes

**96th Congress**

| | |
|---|---|
| Weaken Carter oil profits tax (1979) | Y |
| Reject hospital cost control plan (1979) | Y |
| Implement Panama Canal Treaties (1979) | N |
| Establish Department of Education (1979) | Y |
| Approve Anti-busing Amendment (1979) | Y |
| Guarantee Chrysler Corp. loans (1979) | N |
| Approve military draft registration (1980) | Y |
| Aid Sandinista regime in Nicaragua (1980) | N |
| Strengthen fair housing laws (1980) | N |

**97th Congress**

| | |
|---|---|
| Reagan budget proposal (1981) | Y |

## Interest Group Ratings

| Year | ADA | ACA | AFL-CIO | CCUS |
|---|---|---|---|---|
| 1980 | 6 | 83 | 12 | 81 |
| 1979 | 0 | 92 | 0 | 100 |
| 1978 | 10 | 93 | 25 | 78 |
| 1977 | 0 | 89 | 23 | 88 |
| 1976 | 0 | 85 | 41 | 82 |
| 1975 | 0 | 79 | 13 | 88 |
| 1974 | 0 | 85 | 0 | 88 |
| 1973 | 4 | 84 | 10 | 100 |

# Missouri

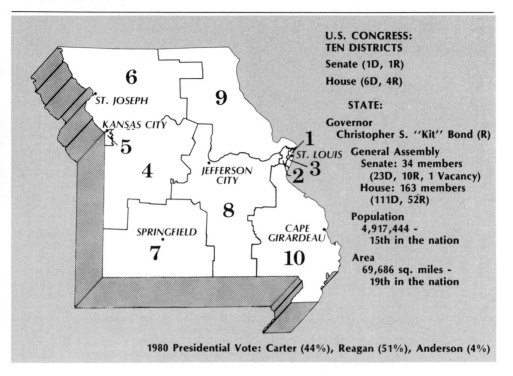

**U.S. CONGRESS:**
**TEN DISTRICTS**

Senate (1D, 1R)

House (6D, 4R)

**STATE:**

Governor
   Christopher S. "Kit" Bond (R)

General Assembly
   Senate: 34 members
      (23D, 10R, 1 Vacancy)
   House: 163 members
      (111D, 52R)

Population
   4,917,444 -
      15th in the nation

Area
   69,686 sq. miles -
      19th in the nation

1980 Presidential Vote: Carter (44%), Reagan (51%), Anderson (4%)

## ... Republicans Against Tradition

The 1980 election offered Missouri Republicans some fresh hope that they might soon shake the state free of the traditional Democratic loyalties that often take precedence over any of the issues of the day.

Besides voting for Ronald Reagan for President, Missouri elected Christopher S. Bond as governor, reversing his 1976 defeat at the hands of Democrat Joseph Teasdale, and doubled its GOP representation in the U.S. House — to four of ten seats.

Reagan demonstrated broad appeal in many parts of rural Missouri, winning 99 of the state's 114 counties, even traditional Democratic ones in Little Dixie and the Bootheel. If Republicans have made a breakthrough there, future Democratic presidential nominees will be hard-pressed to win the state.

While other border states began going Republican in past years, Missouri showed few signs of breaking out of its Civil War voting patterns. Without substantial growth to disrupt its political habits or a major statewide racial crisis to turn white voters to the right, it kept most of its Democratic habits. For most of the 1970s, only one of its U.S. House members was a Republican. Several of its most conservative rural counties even backed George McGovern for president in 1972.

Democrats have needed rural votes because their urban constituency is shrinking. In 1948, St. Louis cast 22 percent of the statewide presidential vote. In 1980, St. Louis and Kansas City together cast only 15 percent. In early 1981, when a liberal Democratic bloc dominated by Kansas City legislators organized to control the Missouri Senate, they found themselves outvoted by a rival coalition including conservative Republicans (and some Democrats) from suburban St. Louis and Democrats from the Bootheel, Little Dixie and other rural regions.

The suburbs around St. Louis and Kansas City continue to grow and to show more affection for the GOP. In 1980, Reagan won not only in normally Republican St. Louis County, outside the city, but in suburban Kansas City (Jackson County), which Carter carried in 1976.

# A Political Tour

**St. Louis.** Much has been written about the decline of this once-great city, which has fewer residents today than it did at the turn of the century. Since 1950, nearly half of its people have fled, both black and white, the well-off to distant suburbia and the less affluent to neighborhoods just outside the city. Numerous factories and businesses have closed.

Auto and truck assembly and aerospace manufacturing, mostly outside the city limits, have come to play a more important role than traditional St. Louis industries such as shoe and apparel manufacturing and brewing. But the transportation industry has been an uneven performer in the past decade. Rising gasoline prices and Japanese imported cars hurt the domestic automakers. Demand for commercial jetliners fluctuated, and the NASA space program proceeded sluggishly.

With the exodus of people and jobs from the inner city has come a corresponding loss of political influence. St. Louis cast only 8 percent of the statewide presidential vote in 1980.

St. Louis today is two distinct communities. The northern half is two-thirds black and has seen the most precipitous population decline in the city. Jimmy Carter won nearly 90 percent of the 1980 vote here. The southern part of St. Louis is an accumulation of older blue-collar, heavily German and Italian neighborhoods with few blacks and a slowly declining population. Reagan won 44 percent and Carter 52 percent in south St. Louis in 1980.

About 60 percent of the St. Louis vote is cast in the southern part of the city, where there is still meaningful partisan competition. But the overwhelming Democratic majorities in north St. Louis have given presidential candidates Kennedy, Humphrey and Carter a steady 66 percent of the overall city vote in elections since 1960.

**St. Louis Suburbs and the Missouri River Valley.** St. Louis County surrounds St. Louis on the north, west and south, but is a jurisdiction separate and independent from the city. The county has grown steadily in the postwar era, and Republicans have been the majority party for more than a decade.

In the 1960 presidential election, St. Louis County went narrowly for Kennedy, casting about 20,000 more votes than the city. In 1980, the county cast 314,000 more votes than the city, and it gave Reagan a victory margin of 14 percentage points. Nearly a quarter of Missouri's vote is now cast in this single county.

North and south St. Louis County have a significant blue-collar element, while the western part of the county is more affluent and white-collar.

The only parts of the county that Carter won in 1980 were the liberal academic community around Washington University and an area just outside north St. Louis where the neighborhoods are settled by poorer St. Louis emigrants. John B. Anderson drew a higher vote in the Washington University area than anywhere in the state except Boone County, home of the University of Missouri.

Reagan won St. Charles, Jefferson and Franklin counties, which contain outlying suburbs of St. Louis. Jefferson County gained the symbolic distinction in 1980 of being the geographic center of the nation's population — the first time that spot has been located west of the Mississippi River.

Proceeding beyond metropolitan St. Louis along the Missouri River, the southern river valley counties of Gasconade, Osage and Cole are as reliably Republican as the suburbs. Much of this area was settled in the early 19th century by pioneers of German ancestry. The immigrants lined up against the politically dominant Democratic planters and slaveholders north of the river and since then have seldom swerved from the GOP path.

In recent years, Republican dominance has crept north of the river into Warren and Montgomery counties, giving the GOP control over a swath of territory beginning in St. Louis County and stretching westward to the state capital, Jefferson City, in the center of the state.

**Southwestern Missouri — The Ozarks.** The Osage River flows into Missouri at Vernon County and meanders across the southwestern part of the state until it empties into the Missouri River just east of Jefferson City. Nearly every county south of the Osage is in the traditionally Republican-voting Ozark Mountain region.

Long a poor, isolated, Appalachian-like area, the scenic Ozarks have now been discovered by tourists, retirees and developers. The tourist presence is most obvious near Table Rock Reservoir in Taney County (near the Arkansas border) and along the Lake of the Ozarks in west-central Missouri.

But development has not altered the basic character of the Ozarks. Scotch-Irish mountaineers from western Virginia, eastern Tennessee and Kentucky settled much of this region. As a rule, they kept to themselves, and there are still many small, isolated communities.

Ozarks residents had no use for slavery, were strongly pro-Union in the Civil War and voted Republican thereafter. That pattern shows no signs of abating: Reagan's 1980 margins in the Ozarks were higher than Ford's in 1976.

Springfield, becoming less Republican in recent years, and Joplin, an old lead and zinc mining town, are the largest cities in the area. The non-tourist economy these days revolves mostly around dairy and chicken farms, light industry and religious publishing by several fundamentalist denominations with headquarters in the region.

**Metropolitan Kansas City (Jackson County).** Though it has not suffered a massive, St. Louis-like flight of people and businesses, Kansas City has many of the problems of older industrial cities.

After growing in population until 1970, the city shrank to less than 457,000 by 1980, fewer than lived in Kansas City 30 years earlier. The proportion of blacks in the 5th Congressional Disrict (Kansas City and a small part of Jackson County outside the city) grew from 24 to 31 percent in the past decade as whites moved outside the city limits.

Although the suburbs in Jackson County are growing as the city population shrinks, Kansas City still casts a solid majority (between 55 and 60 percent) of the overall county vote.

Kansas City is the financial and distribution point for a surrounding six-state agricultural region. The stockyards are less economically important than they were in the city's cowtown heyday, but meat packing continues, along with auto assembly, steel manufacturing, and production of Hallmark greeting cards and electronic equipment.

In earlier days, Kansas City was known as a western-oriented, wide open town. Its jazz, gambling and the reknowned Democratic Pendergast machine gave it a much different image than it has today. There has always been a sizable GOP minority, but urban economic problems have kept the city in the Democratic camp. Jimmy Carter won 60 percent of the Kansas City vote in both 1976 and 1980.

Carter lost the suburbs in Jackson County by eight percentage points in 1980, but emerged with a 54 to 42 percent countywide win thanks to his urban strength. Overall, Jackson County cast 12 percent of the statewide presidential vote in 1980.

In addition to Jackson County, the Kansas City metropolitan area includes Platte, Clay and Ray counties to the north and Cass County to the south. Like most of the counties in west-central Missouri, these four have generally voted Democratic in the past. But in 1980, Republicans Reagan and Bond carried Platte, Clay and Cass and several other often-Democratic counties.

**North of the Missouri River: Little Dixie and the Iowa Border.** Among the state's first settlers were westward-moving Tidewater and Piedmont Virginians and bluegrass Kentuckians who found the rich northeastern Missouri soil to their liking. They planted their Southern roots here, tried to pull Missouri into the Confederacy and have voted Democratic into the modern era.

Conservative Little Dixie's Democratic allegiance is a political anachronism, since the party has been tilting towards cities, labor and minorities since the New Deal. But there are relatively few blacks in Little Dixie, so natives have never been confronted with many of the social tensions that led to party shifts elsewhere in the country.

George McGovern scared nearly all of Missouri's conservative Democrats away from the party in 1972, but even then McGovern won Monroe County, in the heart of Little Dixie. Carter brought the rest of the region back to the party fold in 1976. But in 1980, Reagan took all but two Little Dixie counties, a hint that the area may finally be deciding that the conservatism it preaches is best-protected by the GOP.

Topographically and economically, parts of northern Missouri are similar to Iowa. The closest thing Missouri has to a Yankee influence is found in Putnam, Mercer and a few other counties on or near the Iowa border. Ohio and Iowa farmers moved into the area long ago, and for years it has rivaled the Ozarks for fidelity to the GOP.

Moving west toward the Kansas and Nebraska borders, partisan lines blur somewhat. Republicans are still preferred, but Democrat Eagleton won most northwest Missouri counties in 1980. Buchanan County (St. Joseph) is the region's most populous and is politically marginal. Democrat Teasdale won the county by 66 votes in 1976, and Republican Bond took 50.9 percent there in 1980.

**Southeast Missouri and The Bootheel.** The southeast is philosophically very conservative, but partisan allegiances are in a state of flux. There have been recent Republican gains. Generally speaking, Republicans are a majority or a near-majority in the northernmost and western-most counties of this region. There is a wedge of strongly Democratic counties in the central part of the area.

In the extreme southeast corner of the state lies the Bootheel, a cluster of Mississippi River counties that look and vote like the Old South. The Bootheel is today more entrenched in Democratic voting patterns than Little Dixie.

But Bootheel partisan traditions go back only to 1924, when cotton planters from the lower Mississippi moved into Missouri to escape the boll weevil blight that had ruined their crops further to the south. Black sharecroppers arrived to work the fields, and in no time the Bootheel looked like typical post-plantation South.

George Wallace in 1968 won more than 20 percent of the vote in the Bootheel counties of New Madrid, Mississippi, Dunklin, Scott and Pemiscot. But Democratic traditions were so strong that Hubert Humphrey still won a plurality in all those counties except Pemiscot.

Reagan in 1980 gained 10 to 15 points over Ford's 1976 Bootheel showing, but he still fell short of defeating Carter. If Reagan could not win the Bootheel, it is hard to imagine what sort of Republican could have.

# Redrawing the Lines

"They wore all their crayolas down to the nub," said one observer of the Missouri Legislature's efforts to come up with a redistricting plan. Despite intensive efforts to find an acceptable way to trim the delegation from ten to nine members, the Legislature reached its mandatory June 15 adjournment date without a new map.

Democratic leaders pushed for a plan to eliminate one of four districts held by Republicans, perhaps forcing freshman GOP Reps. Bill Emerson and Wendell Bailey to run against each other in the same southeast Missouri district. That would have taken some clever mapping, since both men's districts are overpopulated and cover large amounts of territory.

A coalition of Republicans and some Democrats sought to combine parts of two under-populated St. Louis districts, the 1st and the 3rd. That plan would have put black William Clay up against fellow Democrat Richard Gephardt in a white-majority district.

The two sides could not find common ground. Even if the Democrats had managed to push through a plan, it would likely have been vetoed by GOP Gov. Christopher Bond.

At midyear, it seemed unlikely that Bond would call the Democratic-controlled Legislature into special session for another try. Some Missourians discussed the possibility of having the federal courts draw a redistricting plan, as happened in 1972. Others suggested holding at-large congressional elections in 1982.

All of Missouri's urban districts lost population during the 1970s, including the Kansas City 5th, where Democrat Richard Bolling must pick up more than 145,000 new constituents. All the non-urban districts scored significant population gains, with the most growth occurring in southern Missouri's 7th, 8th and 10th Districts.

# Governor
# Christopher S. Bond (R)

**Born:** March 6, 1939, St. Louis, Mo.
**Home:** Kansas City, Mo.
**Education:** Princeton U., A.B. 1960; U. of Virginia Law School, LL.B. 1963.
**Profession:** Lawyer.
**Family:** Wife, Carolyn.
**Religion:** Presbyterian.
**Political Career:** Unsuccessful campaign for U.S. House, 1968; assistant attorney general, 1969-70; Missouri state auditor, 1971-73; chairman, Republican Governors Association, 1975; unsuccessful campaign for governor, 1976; elected governor 1972, 1980; term expires Jan. 1985.

# Thomas F. Eagleton (D)

**Of St. Louis — Elected 1968**

**Born:** Sept. 4, 1929, St. Louis, Mo.
**Education:** Amherst College, B.A. 1950; Harvard
U., LL.B. 1953.
**Military Career:** Navy, 1948-49.
**Profession:** Lawyer.
**Family:** Wife, Barbara Ann Smith; two children.
**Religion:** Roman Catholic.
**Political Career:** St. Louis circuit attorney,
1956-60; Mo. attorney general, 1961-65; Mo.
Lt. Governor, 1965-69; Democratic nominee
for vice president, 1972 (withdrew before
election).

**In Washington:** It has taken years for
Eagleton to lose the celebrity image he gained in a
few days as George McGovern's running mate in
1972, but he has gradually done it, settling back
into the quiet career of workaday productivity
that he was building before his psychological
history became a national issue.

It has been a career of steadily accumulating
influence, built up not only through seniority but
through a willingness to take on some of the more
tedious tasks of Senate life.

Eagleton was only two years into his freshman term when he reluctantly agreed to assume
the chairmanship of the Senate District of Columbia Committee, a politically unrewarding job most
senators avoid like the plague. He took it seriously. Within two years, Eagleton had been instrumental in pushing for D.C. home rule legislation, restoring limited self-government to the
nation's capital after a century of congressional
control.

The District Committee was abolished in
1977, folded into the larger Governmental Affairs
panel, another unglamorous spot where Eagleton
has done much of his legislative work. He would
have been Governmental Affairs chairman in 1981
if the Democrats had held the Senate; as it is, he
remains an important voice on the committee, one
the Reagan administration will find crucial if it
decides to do much dismantling of the federal
bureaucracy.

On some issues, Eagleton and the Republican
right have a surprising amount in common. Like
Reagan, Eagleton has his doubts about the Department of Energy. He supported its creation in
1977, but has publicly said the department was a
mistake and called it the government's worst
bureaucracy.

That issue reflects an important aspect of
Eagleton's style: his habit of digging into an issue

over several years and coming out some distance
from where he entered. He voted against direct
election of the president in 1979, even though he
had supported a version of it in 1970. He gradually dropped his support of "sunset" legislation to
force periodic review of government programs,
saying the measure he himself had cosponsored
"ought to go bye-bye permanently." He drafted
much of the original Senate war powers bill but
voted against the final version of the landmark
act in 1973. He had concluded that the 30-day
deadline given to a president to ask for a declaration of war amounted to a license to make war on
his own within that time.

As a member of the Labor and Appropriations committees in addition to Governmental
Affairs, Eagleton played a significant — although
not always publicized — role in much of the social
legislation of the past decade. He was largely
responsible for establishment of the National Institute of Aging, and for the expansion of the
services available to the elderly under the Older
Americans Act.

He has been a strong union supporter on
most Labor Committee issues, but has split with
the unions on occasion. He opposed the Lockheed
loan guarantee and the supersonic transport
plane, both of which labor supported. But he went
to bat for the Chrysler loan guarantee in 1979,
and on such "litmus test" issues as the ill-fated
common-site picketing and labor law revision
measures of the late 1970s, Eagleton voted the
AFL-CIO position.

On several emotional social issues, he has
voted conservatively in recent years, neutralizing
some potential opposition in Missouri. He has
always been against busing and is militantly opposed to abortion. He attracted attention and won
some friends on the right with his long-running
libertarian opposition to mandatory seat belts in

automobiles. He also began sounding fiscally conservative themes during budget and spending debates in the late 1970s.

In three terms on the Defense Appropriations Subcommittee, Eagleton has been able to pursue many of the foreign and military policy issues that interest him. As a freshman senator, before he had any defense committee assignment, he took on and defeated John Stennis, chairman of the Armed Services Committee, in a scrap over plans for the Main Battle Tank, which Eagleton opposed.

Eagleton consistently opposed U.S. involvement in Indochina, and was the sponsor of the successful 1973 appropriations amendment cutting off funds for the bombing of Cambodia. He was the chief Senate advocate of the 1974 Turkish arms embargo, imposed after Turkey used American-supplied weapons in its invasion of Cyprus. He has consistently opposed resumption of arms sales to Turkey, given that nation's continued presence on Cyprus, although the embargo was lifted in 1978. When the Senate approved a 1979 aid grant, he referred to it acidly as "our annual award for Turkish intransigence."

Eagleton opposed the volunteer army, fearing that only the poor would serve in the absence of conscription. In 1980, he voted against resumption of male-only draft registration although he supported an unsuccessful proposal to register both men and women.

For years, all of Eagleton's arguments and votes were obscured by the traumatic period in which he was dropped as McGovern's vice presidential running mate, only a few days after he admitted that he had undergone psychiatric treatment and been hospitalized three times in the 1960s for depression.

After first declaring he was "1,000 percent" behind Eagleton and would have chosen him even had he known of his mental health history, McGovern did an about-face and forced Eagleton from the ticket.

Although Eagleton subsequently campaigned vigorously for McGovern and his second running mate, R. Sargent Shriver, the episode left permanently bruised feelings on both sides, McGovern never quite forgave Eagleton for failing to mention his health history prior to his selection for the national ticket; Eagleton, convinced that the storm of public controversy could have been weathered, resented McGovern's withdrawal of support.

It has never been clear precisely how much the Eagleton affair contributed to McGovern's landslide defeat in November. Eagleton himself insisted it was no more than "one rock in the landslide." McGovern felt otherwise.

**At Home:** When Eagleton made his first Senate campaign in 1968, he was carrying a reputation as Missouri's liberal "boy wonder." Three years out of law school he had been elected circuit attorney in St. Louis. Four years later he became state attorney general, and he celebrated his 35th birthday in 1964 by winning election as lieutenant governor with nearly 65 percent of the vote.

By 1968, the logical move was for the Senate, even though it required running against an incumbent Democrat, Edward V. Long. The incumbent was saddled with allegations that he had improperly received fees from a St. Louis attorney while in office, and charges that he had doctored specifications for a St. Louis housing project to benefit a local union that had contributed to his campaign. He was also a supporter of the Johnson administration and its Vietnam War policy. Eagleton's themes were consistently liberal: he opposed the bombing of North Vietnam, recommended cutting the defense budget and called for more federal aid to cities.

The primary was close, but Eagleton took it by 26,000 votes, and went on to the general election campaign against Republican Rep. Thomas B. Curtis, an influential veteran of the House Ways and Means Committee. Eagleton criticized him for voting against the 1968 Civil Rights Act and Medicare, and renewed his call for an end to the bombing. Both candidates were St. Louis-based, but Eagleton had the natural Democratic advantage in outlying parts of the state, and campaigned more effectively there than the urbane, bow-tied tax lawyer he was running against.

Eagleton's misfortune as McGovern's temporary running mate in 1972 created strong sympathy for him in his home state. When he came up for re-election in 1974, the focus was not on any of his policy positions, but on his candor and personal courage, and on the way a Missourian had been treated in national politics. Curtis was again the Republican nominee, but at 63 and three terms out of Congress, he was not a serious threat. Eagleton won the rematch by more than a quarter-million votes.

Eagleton's 1980 Republican opponent, St. Louis County Executive Gene McNary, began with little recognition outside his home base, but launched a statewide media campaign with money from business and conservative groups. Meanwhile, Eagleton's campaign was bothered by publicity over an extortion attempt made by his niece, Elizabeth Weigand, and her attorney. They threatened to release information damaging to him unless he bowed to her wishes in a stock control dispute in the family business, Missouri Pipe Fittings Co. Weigand and her attorney were convicted of extortion on Oct. 25, shortly before the election. No "damaging information" was ever substantiated.

McNary faulted Eagleton's support for the Panama Canal treaties and the SALT II accord and promised to stop federal encroachment on local governments. Eagleton pointed often to the highways and other public works projects his Appropriations Committee seniority had helped bring the state.

Eagleton's move toward the political center had been helpful. Reagan carried Missouri, and the GOP took the governorship and two previously-Democratic congressional seats. But while McNary received nearly 48 percent of the vote, Eagleton prevailed.

## Committees

**Appropriations** (6th of 14 Democrats)
Agriculture and Related Agencies; Defense; Labor, Health and Human Services, Education; Transportation.

**Governmental Affairs** (Ranking Democrat)
Governmental Efficiency and the District of Columbia.

**Labor and Human Resources** (5th of 7 Democrats)
Aging, Family and Human Services; Education; Handicapped.

**Select Ethics** (3rd of 3 Democrats)

## Elections

**1980 General**

| | |
|---|---|
| Thomas Eagleton (D ) | 1,074,859 (52 %) |
| Gene McNary (R ) | 985,399 (48 %) |

**1980 Primary**

| | |
|---|---|
| Thomas Eagleton (D ) | 553,392 (86 %) |
| Lee Sutton (D ) | 53,280 (8 %) |
| Herb Fillmore (D ) | 38,677 (6 %) |

**Previous Winning Percentages**

1974 (60 %)    1968 (51 %)

## Campaign Finance

| | Receipts | Receipts from PACs | Expenditures |
|---|---|---|---|
| 1980 | | | |
| Eagleton (D ) | $1,267,476 | $382,570 (30 %) | $1,385,764 |
| McNary (R ) | $1,180,342 | $206,599 (18 %) | $1,173,161 |

## Voting Studies

| | Presidential Support | | Party Unity | | Conservative Coalition | |
|---|---|---|---|---|---|---|
| Year | S | O | S | O | S | O |
| 1980 | 56 | 28 | 65 | 13 | 24 | 52 |
| 1979 | 73 | 12 | 74 | 12 | 30 | 54 |

| | | | | | | |
|---|---|---|---|---|---|---|
| 1978 | 76 | 13 | 82 | 10 | 20 | 69 |
| 1977 | 82 | 13 | 72 | 19 | 39 | 55 |
| 1976 | 36 | 51 | 85 | 8 | 13 | 78 |
| 1975 | 47 | 40 | 82 | 9 | 16 | 75 |
| 1974 (Ford) | 24 | 60 | | | | |
| 1974 | 36 | 55 | 74 | 13 | 17 | 69 |
| 1973 | 33 | 58 | 89 | 3 | 7 | 83 |
| 1972 | 28 | 59 | 79 | 5 | 8 | 72 |
| 1971 | 41 | 49 | 78 | 6 | 18 | 63 |
| 1970 | 43 | 45 | 76 | 5 | 6 | 77 |
| 1969 | 47 | 38 | 82 | 10 | 17 | 72 |

S = Support          O = Opposition

## Key Votes

**96th Congress**

| | |
|---|---|
| Maintain relations with Taiwan (1979) | N |
| Reduce synthetic fuel development funds (1979) | N |
| Impose nuclear plant moratorium (1979) | ? |
| Kill stronger windfall profits tax (1979) | N |
| Guarantee Chrysler Corp. loans (1979) | Y |
| Approve military draft registration (1980) | N |
| End Revenue Sharing to the states (1980) | Y |
| Block Justice Dept. busing suits (1980) | N |

**97th Congress**

| | |
|---|---|
| Restore urban program funding cuts (1981) | Y |

## Interest Group Ratings

| Year | ADA | ACA | AFL-CIO | CCUS-1 | CCUS-2 |
|---|---|---|---|---|---|
| 1980 | 78 | 8 | 89 | 39 | |
| 1979 | 58 | 19 | 93 | 0 | 29 |
| 1978 | 50 | 9 | 79 | 35 | |
| 1977 | 60 | 15 | 80 | 35 | |
| 1976 | 60 | 8 | 88 | 0 | |
| 1975 | 72 | 4 | 85 | 19 | |
| 1974 | 71 | 18 | 89 | 25 | |
| 1973 | 90 | 8 | 80 | 0 | |
| 1972 | 70 | 21 | 90 | 0 | |
| 1971 | 89 | 24 | 67 | - | |
| 1970 | 91 | 4 | 100 | 0 | |
| 1969 | 94 | 0 | 100 | - | |

# John C. Danforth (R)

**Of Flat — Elected 1976**

**Born:** Sept. 5, 1936, St. Louis, Mo.
**Education:** Princeton U., A.B. 1958; Yale U., B.D., LL.B. 1963.
**Profession:** Lawyer.
**Family:** Wife, Sally Dobson; five children.
**Religion:** Episcopalian.
**Political Career:** Mo. Attorney General, 1969-76; Republican nominee for U.S. Senate, 1970.

**In Washington:** Danforth is self-confident and thoughtful, persistent and sometimes stubborn, the combination of qualities one might expect in someone who is a lawyer and an Episcopal priest, and heir to a cereal fortune besides.

Danforth's background makes him even more distinctive in the Senate than the snow-white patch he has had in the front of his hair since before his 40th birthday. He is still a part-time minister at a church in Washington. When President Reagan was shot, he led the Senate in prayer.

As it happens, Danforth is a key man on issues important to the Reagan administration as chairman of the Finance Subcommittee handling international trade. He has some clear ideas about trade, especially about how to help the automobile industry, an important part of Missouri's economy.

At the start of the 97th Congress, Danforth and Lloyd Bentsen of Texas, the senior Democrat on the subcommittee, cosponsored a bill to try and force Japan to cut back the number of cars exported to the United States by 1.6 million over three years.

Danforth said he believed in a free world market but the condition of the auto industry was serious enough to force an exception. "I'm playing the part of the tortoise," he said, "the administration is the hare. I'd just as soon see the administration take over and negotiate an orderly marketing agreement. But if the hare goes to sleep, the tortoise — me — will keep right on going."

Danforth is a leader in the moderate Republican bloc that was becoming an important influence on Finance even before the GOP Senate takeover in 1981. Like GOP colleagues Packwood of Oregon, Durenberger of Minnesota, and Chafee of Rhode Island, he has combined a general support for tax cuts with an interest in using the revenue code to accomplish some social goals.

His career at Finance has been an alternating series of quarrels and accommodations with Russell Long of Louisiana, the panel's Democratic chairman until 1981. Danforth was open in expressing his admiration for Long when he joined the committee, but he was Long's greatest antagonist when Finance wrote a windfall profits tax on the oil industry in 1979. Danforth stepped in regularly to challenge the chairman on one item after another, complaining about Long's obviously greater enthusiasm for handing out tax credits than for raising money. With that attitude, Danforth warned at one point, "We're going to wind up with a tax of zero and expenditures of $200 billion."

The tax as written in committee turned out to be considerably more than zero. But Danforth enraged Long on the floor with his effort to extend the windfall profits tax to state-owned wells, a help to consuming states like Missouri and a drain on producing states like Louisiana of about $10.5 billion over 10 years.

When the bill reached the Senate floor, Long stood there with his version of a filibuster, a handful of more than 100 amendments that he promised would be followed by 100 more amendments if the Senate showed any sign of accepting the Danforth amendment. It never did. Danforth lost 65-28. A sympathetic colleague hailed the Missouri Republican as "bloody but unbowed."

Early in his Senate career he attracted an outspoken critic in Ralph Nader, who said Danforth as senator had sided with big business against the workers and consumers he once defended as attorney general. Among other misdeeds, Nader charged Danforth, then senior Republican on the Commerce Consumer Subcommittee, with a "dedicated attempt" to cripple the Federal Trade Commission.

The two met in a radio debate. "Mr. Nader," said Danforth, "has followed a practice of continually misrepresenting what I have done ... mistakes are chronic.... His methods are characterized by name-calling...." Danforth said his efforts on the Commerce Committee to allow a limited congressional veto over FTC rulings helped save the commission from more rigid restrictions.

Still, it is hard to avoid the conclusion that Danforth is less the consumer advocate in Washington than he was in Missouri. It was his amendment in 1980 that barred the White House Office of Consumer Affairs from intervening on behalf of consumers in federal agency proceedings.

The office had allied itself with consumers who had gone to the Federal Communications Commission to protest telephone rate increases. Danforth said that amounted to having the president appoint a federal consumer agency after Congress refused to create one. He won that argument, 42-36, with the U.S. Chamber of Commerce and the Grocery Manufacturers of America lobbying on his side. But the provision was deleted in conference.

When the Commerce Committee wrote an airline deregulation bill, Danforth was a spokesman for Trans World Airlines, one of Missouri's largest employers and a leading opponent of the bill. He feared the bill would hurt TWA's competitive situation. Danforth eventually voted for the measure but only after amending it to protect workers in deregulated industry.

A look at Danforth's legislative record reveals wide-ranging interests. He cosponsored the Paperwork Reduction Act of 1980. He amended a truck deregulation bill the same year to give truckers greater pricing flexibility. He fought a bill for waterway user fees because he feared it threatened the Missouri barge industry. He has been a leader in efforts to bring worldwide pressure on the government in Cambodia to let international agencies relieve starvation there.

His ultimate goal is less government — somehow. "The federal government has reached a point," he has said, "where it does more to the American people than it does for them." But in his first major vote of the 97th Congress, on a proposal by Chafee to restore $1 billion of the proposed Reagan cuts in areas like primary education, mass transit, and low-income fuel aid,

Danforth voted for the restorations and against Reagan.

**At Home:** Danforth, heir to the Ralston-Purina cereal fortune, left a Wall Street law practice in 1966 to return to his native St. Louis. Two years later he ran for state attorney general, vowing to rid the office of deadwood that had accumulated during a succession of Democratic administrations.

He accomplished more than that. He revived the Missouri Republican Party. Danforth's election as attorney general in 1968 made him the first Republican in 22 years to win statewide office. As attorney general, he brought in bright young lawyers and specialized in consumer protection and the environment.

In 1970, Danforth was the GOP's only hope to dislodge Democratic Sen. Stuart Symington, who was seeking a fourth term. In an expensive campaign that introduced Missouri to modern media-oriented politics, Danforth lost by less than three percentage points. Two years later he was returned as attorney general by more than 450,000 votes, and awaited his next chance.

It came, as expected, when Symington decided to retire in 1976. Democrats appeared to seize the momentum again by nominating U.S. Rep. Jerry Litton, described by a state political observer as "one of the most exciting political personalities to come along in years." But that enthusiasm was tragically brief. Litton died in a primary-night plane crash, and Danforth was suddenly the favorite in a contest that had been looking bleak for him.

The state Democratic committee chose as its nominee former Gov. Warren Hearnes (1965-73), who had finished a poor second to Litton in the primary. Against Litton, Danforth would have had a difficult contest; against Hearnes, he won easily.

But the party rank-and-file has never been entirely comfortable with his moderate philosophy. In 1976, Danforth backed Gerald R. Ford for renomination and was denied a seat is Missouri's Reaganite national convention delegation. In 1980, Danforth was an early supporter of Sen. Howard H. Baker Jr.'s presidential bid. Reagan was the favorite of most Missouri Republicans.

## Committees

**Commerce, Science and Transportation** (4th of 9 Republicans)
Surface Transportation, chairman; Aviation; Consumer.

**Finance** (4th of 11 Republicans)
International Trade, chairman; Social Security and Income
Maintenance Progams; Taxation and Debt Management.

**Governmental Affairs** (5th of 9 Republicans)
Federal Expenditures, Research, and Rules, chairman; Intergovernmental Relations; Permanent Subcommittee on Investigations.

## Elections

**1976 General**

| | |
|---|---|
| John Danforth (R ) | 1,090,067 (57 %) |
| Warren Hearnes (D ) | 813,571 (43 %) |

**1976 Primary**

| | |
|---|---|
| John Danforth (R ) | 284,025 (93 %) |
| Gregory Hansman (D ) | 19,796 (7 %) |

## Campaign Finance

| | Receipts | Receipts from PACs | Expenditures |
|---|---|---|---|
| **1976** | | | |
| Danforth (R) | *$748,115 | $71,106 (10 %) | $741,465 |
| Hearnes (D) | **$662,737 | $44,013 (7 %) | $660,953 |

*Receipts do not include pledges that were reported as committee receipts.
**Receipts include a $125,000 transfer from his gubernatorial committee.

## Voting Studies

| | Presidential Support | | Party Unity | | Conservative Coalition | |
|---|---|---|---|---|---|---|
| Year | S | O | S | O | S | O |
| 1980 | 55 | 40 | 68 | 26 | 66 | 29 |
| 1979 | 76 | 22 | 54 | 44 | 68 | 29 |
| 1978 | 74 | 24 | 41 | 57 | 62 | 37 |
| 1977 | 63 | 31 | 76 | 20 | 83 | 14 |

S = Support          O = Opposition

## Key Votes

**96th Congress**

| | |
|---|---|
| Maintain relations with Taiwan (1979) | Y |
| Reduce synthetic fuel development funds (1979) | N |
| Impose nuclear plant moratorium (1979) | N |
| Kill stronger windfall profits tax (1979) | Y |
| Guarantee Chrysler Corp. loans (1979) | Y |
| Approve military draft registration (1980) | N |
| End Revenue Sharing to the states (1980) | N |
| Block Justice Dept. busing suits (1980) | N |

**97th Congress**

| | |
|---|---|
| Restore urban program funding cuts (1981) | Y |

## Interest Group Ratings

| Year | ADA | ACA | AFL-CIO | CCUS-1 | CCUS-2 |
|---|---|---|---|---|---|
| 1980 | 50 | 48 | 39 | 70 | |
| 1979 | 16 | 52 | 42 | 40 | 67 |
| 1978 | 25 | 38 | 32 | 71 | |
| 1977 | 25 | 56 | 30 | 82 | |

# 1 William Clay (D)

### Of St. Louis — Elected 1968

**Born:** April 30, 1931, St. Louis, Mo.
**Education:** St. Louis U., B.S. 1953.
**Military Career:** Army, 1953-55.
**Profession:** Real estate broker.
**Family:** Wife, Carol Ann Johnson; three children.
**Religion:** Roman Catholic.
**Political Career:** St. Louis Board of Aldermen, 1959-64; St. Louis Democratic committeemen, 1964-67.

**In Washington:** Clay came to Congress with a reputation as a tough-minded black activist willing to go to jail rather than compromise principle. He has remained an angry man for more than a decade in the House, aiming his rhetoric at colleagues, Republican administrations, the congressional disciplinary process, and the press.

In his first term, Clay quoted an old LBJ remark that GOP leader Gerald R. Ford had played football too long without a helmet. He accused the Nixon administration of racism, and referred to the vice president as "Zero" Agnew.

He is still sounding militant. When the House took up the Reagan budget in 1981, Clay was on his feet. "The course the House is proceeding on," he said, "is economically, politically and morally wrong, and we in the Congressional Black Caucus will not support this insanity. We would rather lose in a cause that is morally right."

Clay was a founder of the Congressional Black Caucus. In 1971, he was largely responsible for turning an informal luncheon gathering of black House members into an organized group. He warned that without structure they would become merely a "A Kongressional Koffee Klatch Klub."

Clay's legislative work has always flowed from the combination of black interests and the backing of organized labor. "I don't represent all people," he told reporters in 1981. "Some people have too much representation. The primary purpose of government is to represent the interest of those who can't represent themselves."

Clay has been a valued labor ally on both the Education and Labor and Post Office and Civil Service committees. He spoke for unions in 1978 against President Carter's civil service revision bill, claiming that it would undermine job protections for government workers.

Clay's longest-running legislative battle has been to revise the Hatch Act, which restricts political activity by government workers. Federal employee unions have agitated for years to get it changed. Clay managed to get Hatch Act revision through the House in 1975, but President Ford vetoed the bill, and the House sustained the veto.

In 1978, when the Post Office Committee took up Carter's civil service bill, Clay sought to include his Hatch Act changes as part of the package. They had passed the House a second time, in 1977, but stalled in the Senate. He got his language attached to the civil service legislation in committee, but when the bill reached the floor, sponsors of the legislation argued that Clay's addition would jeopardize the entire package. Clay refused to withdraw it, and charged that the debate on civil service revision had been deliberately set for a time when leaders of federal employee unions would be out of town. Finally, after several days (and the return of the unionists), Clay backed down, but only after receiving a letter from Carter urging prompt Senate action on a separate Hatch Act bill. In the end, the civil service changes became law, but Clay's measure never passed the Senate.

In 1980, Clay succeeded in amending a jobs bill in the House to earmark $5 million for training ex-prisoners. When the Senate refused to go along, Clay elicited a promise from the House Appropriations Committee that money for the

---

**1st District: North St. Louis and Western suburbs.** Population: 347,192 (26% decrease since 1970). Race: White 117,464 (34%), Black 226,277 (65%), Others 3,451 (1%). Spanish origin: 3,188 (1%).

program would be made available anyway. He also added language to allow National Endowment for the Arts money to go directly to city arts councils, such as the one in St. Louis.

In recent years, some of Clay's harshest rhetoric has been used against the House ethics committee. In 1980, when the committee recommended censure of his close friend, Charles H. Wilson of California, he called the panel a "kangaroo court" that was "perverted" and "devoid of fairness, justice and equity." He spoke equally sharply of the press, referring to reporters as "bloodthirsty scribes . . . awaiting the carnage."

Clay and Wilson had been allies for years on the Postal Operations Subcommittee, taking numerous foreign trips together to inspect mail facilities around the world. In 1980, Clay replaced him as Postal Operations chairman.

Clay himself has been in frequent controversy over ethics issues. He was accused at one point of billing the House for trips home he did not take. His administrative assistant went to jail for fraudulently placing a sister-in-law on the federal payroll. The Justice Department spent months scrutinizing Clay's tax returns and campaign finances.

But Clay has survived it all. No charges have ever been filed against him. He settled the House travel account by repaying some of the money, insisting that there had been a bookkeeping error. The Justice Department dropped its probe and Clay charged that it had been politically motivated.

**At Home:** Clay's career has thrived on confrontation. His own campaign literature once noted that he had been "arrested, convicted of contempt of court (and) served 110 days in jail" for demonstrating at a St. Louis bank.

That incident took place years before his election to the House in 1968. But it was one of a string of such confrontations that gave him a reputation as a civil rights activist and built his political career. In 1954, while going through military training at Fort McClellan, in Alabama, Clay found the post swimming pool and barber shop closed to blacks, and the NCO club off-limits when there were white women present. He led blacks to swim *en masse* in the pool, boycott haircuts and picket the club.

After returning to St. Louis, Clay became active in the NAACP and CORE. He was elected to the city's Board of Aldermen in 1959 and became an official in the politically active Pipefitters union in 1966. While keeping his identification as a civil rights militant, he moved closer over the years to the patronage politics of the local Democratic Party.

Redistricting by the Missouri Legislature in 1967 placed most of St. Louis' 257,000 blacks in the 1st District, ending years of fragmentation of the black vote. Democrat Frank M. Karsten, the 1st District congressman for 22 years, decided to retire.

Clay and four others sought the Democratic nomination. The party split along racial lines, with most local black leaders endorsing Clay and most white leaders favoring former state Treasurer Milton Carpenter, who was white.

There was speculation that Teamsters official Ernest Calloway, the only other black in the race, might pull enough votes from Clay to give the nomination to Carpenter. But Calloway finished a weak third and Clay won a 47.6 percent plurality.

In the general election, Clay ran on a platform geared to the district's 55 percent black majority. He called for more federal money for jobs, housing, health and education, and for changes in police agencies and the court system to eliminate bias against blacks.

The Republican candidate, also black, was Curtis C. Crawford, former director of the legal aid society of St. Louis and St. Louis County. Crawford suggested that Clay's talent was militant protest, not lawmaking. But the district was too strongly Democratic for Crawford to be a serious threat. Clay won 64.1 percent to become Missouri's first black congressman.

Since then, Clay has overcome a string of challengers who have complained that he expends too much of his effort on confrontation. He usually loses in the St. Louis County portion of the district, which is predominantly white, but wins 85 percent or more in heavily black North St. Louis.

Clay escaped a tough fight in 1978 with St. Louis Sheriff Benjamin C. Goins, his longtime rival for leadership of the city's North Side blacks. Goins' Democratic primary challenge folded when he was convicted for tax evasion and accepting bribes in office.

**The District:** Like inner-city districts in New York, Detroit and Cleveland, the 1st District has seen its population decline sharply since 1970. Less than 350,000 people live there today, a drop of 25.8 percent in 10 years.

When Missouri's state Legislature redraws congressional district boundaries, it may be difficult to ensure Clay a base of support. Clay's territory will likely expand into suburban areas, and he has not run well in the suburban areas of his current district.

The current 1st is the most consistently Democratic area of the state; George McGovern won 68.8 percent of the vote in 1972, and Jimmy Carter's percentage improved from 70 percent in 1976 to 72.3 percent in his losing 1980 campaign.

## Committees

**Education and Labor** (6th of 19 Democrats)
Employment Opportunities; Labor-Management Relations.

**Post Office and Civil Service** (3rd of 15 Democrats)
Postal Operations and Services, chairman; Civil Service; Investigations; Postal Personnel and Modernization.

## Elections

**1980 General**

| | |
|---|---|
| William Clay (D ) | 91,272 (70 %) |
| Bill White (R ) | 38,667 (30 %) |

**1980 Primary**

| | |
|---|---|
| William Clay (D ) | 37,611 (72 %) |
| Melvin Smotherson (D ) | 6,643 (13 %) |
| Elsa Hill (D ) | 4,900 (9 %) |
| David Grace (D ) | 2,893 (6 %) |

**1978 General**

| | |
|---|---|
| William Clay (D ) | 65,950 (67 %) |
| Bill White (R ) | 30,995 (31 %) |

**Previous Winning Percentages**

| | | | |
|---|---|---|---|
| 1976 (66 %) | 1974 (68 %) | 1972 (64 %) | 1970 (91 %) |
| 1968 (64 %) | | | |

**District Vote For President**

| | 1980 | | 1976 | | 1972 |
|---|---|---|---|---|---|
| D | 95,726 (72 %) | D | 96,305 (70 %) | D | 100,797 (69 %) |
| R | 30,918 (23 %) | R | 39,084 (28 %) | R | 45,409 (31 %) |
| I | 5,097 (4 %) | | | | |

## Campaign Finance

| | Receipts | Receipts from PACs | Expenditures |
|---|---|---|---|
| **1980** | | | |
| Clay (D ) | $108,560 | $51,580 (48 %) | $102,908 |
| **1978** | | | |
| Clay (D ) | $96,983 | $50,025 (52 %) | $91,254 |
| White (R ) | $40,671 | $7,250 (18 %) | $40,834 |

## Voting Studies

| | Presidential Support | | Party Unity | | Conservative Coalition | |
|---|---|---|---|---|---|---|
| Year | S | O | S | O | S | O |
| 1980 | 62 | 21 | 74 | 8 | 3 | 78 |
| 1979 | 70 | 17 | 87 | 3 | 3 | 88 |
| 1978 | 70 | 13 | 84 | 4 | 4 | 82 |
| 1977 | 53 | 13 | 75 | 2 | 3 | 73 |
| 1976 | 12 | 47 | 62 | 3 | 5 | 62 |
| 1975 | 34 | 62 | 89 | 3 | 2 | 86 |
| 1974 (Ford) | 33 | 54 | | | | |
| 1974 | 32 | 45 | 68 | 4 | 1 | 68 |
| 1973 | 26 | 66 | 79 | 4 | 3 | 79 |
| 1972 | 22 | 30 | 45 | 1 | 0 | 59 |
| 1971 | 12 | 51 | 62 | 2 | 0 | 61 |
| 1970 | 31 | 25 | 50 | 8 | 0 | 70 |
| 1969 | 28 | 38 | 65 | 5 | 4 | 80 |

S = Support     O = Opposition

## Key Votes

**96th Congress**

| | |
|---|---|
| Weaken Carter oil profits tax (1979) | N |
| Reject hospital cost control plan (1979) | N |
| Implement Panama Canal Treaties (1979) | Y |
| Establish Department of Education (1979) | Y |
| Approve anti-busing Amendment (1979) | N |
| Guarantee Chrysler Corp. loans (1979) | Y |
| Approve military draft registration (1980) | N |
| Aid Sandinista regime in Nicaragua (1980) | Y |
| Strengthen fair housing Laws (1980) | ? |

**97th Congress**

| | |
|---|---|
| Reagan budget proposal (1981) | N |

## Interest Group Rating

| Year | ADA | ACA | AFL-CIO | CCUS |
|---|---|---|---|---|
| 1980 | 83 | 16 | 89 | 53 |
| 1979 | 100 | 4 | 95 | 11 |
| 1978 | 85 | 12 | 95 | 24 |
| 1977 | 75 | 0 | 95 | 0 |
| 1976 | 75 | 0 | 88 | 9 |
| 1975 | 100 | 4 | 100 | 18 |
| 1974 | 61 | 0 | 100 | 0 |
| 1973 | 92 | 8 | 100 | 10 |
| 1972 | 81 | 7 | 88 | 14 |
| 1971 | 78 | 0 | 75 | - |
| 1970 | 84 | 7 | 100 | 10 |
| 1969 | 100 | 15 | 100 | - |

# 2 Robert A. Young (D)

**Of Maryland Heights — Elected 1976**

**Born:** Nov. 27, 1923, St. Louis, Mo.
**Education:** Attended McBride and Normandy High Schools.
**Military Career:** Army, 1943-45.
**Profession:** Pipefitter.
**Family:** Wife, Irene Slawson; three children.
**Religion:** Roman Catholic.
**Political Career:** Mo. House, 1957-63; Mo. Senate, 1963-77.

**In Washington:** Young is a labor Democrat not by political choice, as some of his colleagues are, but by his deepest personal roots. Craggy and plain-spoken, he was a working member of the Pipefitters Union in St. Louis until his election to the House in 1976.

To no one's surprise, he is also a reliable AFL-CIO vote on most issues of importance; in his first House term, he helped out by backing common-site picketing and labor law revision, the two dominant labor issues of that Congress. He has broken with the AFL-CIO on some of the social issues of less emotional concern to unions, but still averaged an 83 COPE rating for his first three years in the House.

Meanwhile, however, Young has been working carefully to keep up his good relations with the St. Louis business community. As a member of Public Works and its Aviation Subcommittee, he has been in excellent position to serve McDonnell Douglas, the giant aircraft maker that is by far the district's largest single employer. He was on the subcommittee in 1978, when it considered airline deregulation. He cast an initial vote against the "automatic entry" provision designed to create greater competition in the industry, then switched to favor it. On the floor, however, he voted against an amendment making it easier for airlines to establish new routes.

Young is also on the Public Works Water Resources Subcommittee, and there he argued the case vehemently for the Meramec Dam, a project once proposed for central Missouri that was heavily backed by organized labor but opposed by environmentalists. His 1977 floor amendment to prevent the withholding of money for the dam failed on a 302-108 vote.

Young's other major issue is abortion. He has campaigned emotionally against it and favors a constitutional amendment to stop it. In the 95th Congress, he also sought to amend a foreign aid bill to provide that none of the money in it could be used by other countries to promote sterilization. The amendment was softened on the floor to take most of the force out of it, and then passed.

**At Home:** Young was the blue-collar candidate in a 1976 Democratic primary held to replace Rep. James Symington, who was running for the Senate. His opponent, state Rep. Jack J. Schramm, was a liberal, suburban-oriented lawyer identified with environmental protection and tax relief for the elderly.

It was a bitter contest. Young and Schramm took opposing sides on the abortion issue, and their supporters argued it on personal terms, with Young's pro-life stand drawing volunteer help in some of the district's communities. Young won the nomination by 1,060 votes.

In the general election campaign, abortion was not an important issue — both Young and his opponent, House GOP leader Robert O. Snyder, opposed it. Young emphasized the need for a balanced budget, and suggested that budget-trimming begin at HEW. But he supported national health insurance and the Humphrey-Hawkins full employment bill. Young's superior organization and labor backing made the difference in a close contest; he received 51.1 percent of the vote in defeating Snyder.

Two years later, Republicans nominated Bob Chase, a former television newsman in St. Louis, who called Young a free-spending liberal. Young

---

**2nd District: St. Louis suburbs.** Population: 467,710 (0.2% decrease since 1970). Race: White 410,636 (88%), Black 50,691 (11%), Others 6,383 (1%). Spanish origin: 3,955 (1%).

responded that he had voted for programs that helped his constituents, like Social Security and defense appropriations carrying money for McDonnell Douglas. Young's plurality jumped to 23,000 votes, and two years later it was up to 66,000 against much weaker opposition.

**The District:** The 2nd contains high- and middle-income suburbs of St. Louis, a significant blue-collar population and a few low-income neighborhoods.

The partisan preference tilts toward the GOP in statewide elections, but Young's philosophical admixture has won him support across socioeconomic and ethnic lines. He had some trouble among Jewish voters against Schramm, who was Jewish, but does not encounter it any more.

The Republican vote is strongest in the south-central portion of the district, in wealthy townships like LaDue and Creve Coeur. The northern and southern ends of the district are largely blue-collar.

In addition to McDonnell Douglas, General Dynamics, Emerson Electric, Chrysler, Ford and Monsanto are important employers in the district.

## Committees

**Public Works and Transportation** (12th of 25 Democrats)
Aviation; Surface Transportation; Water Resources.

**Science and Technology** (13th of 23 Democrats)
Energy Development and Applications; Energy Research and Production.

## Elections

**1980 General**

| | |
|---|---|
| Robert Young (D ) | 148,227 (64 %) |
| John Shields (R ) | 81,762 (36 %) |

**1980 Primary**

| | |
|---|---|
| Robert Young (D ) | 51,325 (86 %) |
| Edward Roche (D ) | 8,175 (14 %) |

**1978 General**

| | |
|---|---|
| Robert Young (D ) | 102,911 (56 %) |
| Bob Chase (R ) | 79,495 (44 %) |

**1978 Primary**

| | |
|---|---|
| Robert Young (D ) | 49,916 (85 %) |
| Edward Roche (D ) | 8,765 (15 %) |

**Previous Winning Percentage**

**1976** (51 %)

**District Vote For President**

| | 1980 | | 1976 | | 1972 |
|---|---|---|---|---|---|
| D | 91,972 (39 %) | D | 95,108 (43 %) | D | 75,201 (37 %) |
| R | 128,423 (55 %) | R | 124,204 (56 %) | R | 126,412 (63 %) |
| I | 12,853 (6 %) | | | | |

## Campaign Finance

| | Receipts | Receipts from PACs | Expenditures |
|---|---|---|---|
| **1980** | | | |
| Young (D ) | $152,823 | $87,105 (57 %) | $149,633 |
| Shields (R ) | $94,812 | $2,491 (3 %) | $94,811 |

| **1978** | | | |
|---|---|---|---|
| Young (D ) | $178,220 | $83,565 (47 %) | $158,326 |
| Chase (R ) | $150,323 | $39,933 (27 %) | $148,440 |

## Voting Studies

| | Presidential Support | | Party Unity | | Conservative Coalition | |
|---|---|---|---|---|---|---|
| Year | S | O | S | O | S | O |
| 1980 | 72 | 27 | 80 | 17 | 41 | 57 |
| 1979 | 63 | 29 | 68 | 21 | 43 | 45 |
| 1978 | 54 | 43 | 63 | 33 | 46 | 48 |
| 1977 | 68 | 29 | 72 | 25 | 48 | 49 |

S = Support          O = Opposition

## Key Votes

**96th Congress**

| | |
|---|---|
| Weaken Carter oil profits tax (1979) | N |
| Reject hospital cost control plan (1979) | Y |
| Implement Panama Canal Treaties (1979) | Y |
| Establish Department of Education (1979) | Y |
| Approve Anti-busing Amendment (1979) | Y |
| Guarantee Chrysler Corp. loans (1979) | Y |
| Approve military draft registration (1980) | Y |
| Aid Sandinista regime in Nicaragua (1980) | Y |
| Strengthen fair housing laws (1980) | N |

**97th Congress**

| | |
|---|---|
| Reagan budget proposal (1981) | Y |

## Interest Group Ratings

| Year | ADA | ACA | AFL-CIO | CCUS |
|---|---|---|---|---|
| 1980 | 50 | 33 | 56 | 68 |
| 1979 | 53 | 16 | 82 | 40 |
| 1978 | 25 | 48 | 75 | 44 |
| 1977 | 35 | 30 | 91 | 29 |

# 3 Richard A. Gephardt (D)

**Of St. Louis — Elected 1976**

**Born:** Jan. 31, 1941, St. Louis, Mo.
**Education:** Northwestern U., B.S. 1962; U. of Mich., J.D. 1965.
**Military Career:** Air National Guard, 1965-71.
**Profession:** Lawyer.
**Family:** Wife, Jane Byrnes; three children.
**Religion:** Baptist.
**Political Career:** St. Louis Board of Aldermen, 1971-77.

**In Washington:** It is as difficult to label Gephardt as it is to define the new brand of liberalism that he and some of his junior Democratic allies seem to want to create.

In the course of one term, his second, he led the fight to block President Carter's hospital cost control program, worked for the maximum politically feasible tax on oil company profits, voted against a bipartisan budget compromise because its social spending levels were too low and supported a constitutional amendment to outlaw busing.

At the start of the 97th Congress, chosen to draft a statement outlining Democratic alternatives in economic policy, Gephardt recommended new business tax incentives and regulatory relief but also federal intervention to restrain wage and price increases. "Some of it is liberal, some is conservative," he explained when the statement was released. "But it's different from the Republicans."

Gephardt's combination of legislative ideas is no more striking than his roster of political allies, which has included House Rules Chairman Richard Bolling, his liberal House mentor, and David Stockman, with whom he drafted a health care bill intended as an alternative to Carter's. While Gephardt was killing President Carter's hospital cost control scheme on the House floor in 1979, he was also serving as the president's re-election campaign chairman in Missouri.

It was Bolling who provided Gephardt with an important break at the start of his congressional career, insisting that he be given a spot on the Ways and Means Committee. "I fought, bled and died to get him on there," Bolling recalled later. Once seated, Gephardt proved to have an aptitude for detail that set him apart from many of the other junior Democrats on that panel. Earnest and well-organized, he sometimes gives other members the impression of a student coun-

cil president grown up and only slightly changed. After one term on Ways and Means, he had become a major player in nearly all the committee's important decisions.

Gephardt designed and eventually sold to the committee a scheme to extricate the House from its endless round of voting on the federal debt ceiling. Until 1979, both chambers of Congress had to approve each increase in the ceiling, made necessary every few months by inflation. Raising the debt limit is a politically difficult vote, and on occasion it has taken the House several weeks and as many as six roll calls to muster a majority. Gephardt promoted a bill that made the debt increases an automatic part of each year's budget, so House members could vote for them without being politically conspicuous. That has not yet ended the tedious debt ceiling arguments, but once firmly in place, it may.

The other major Gephardt issue on Ways and Means has been Social Security. Throughout his time on the committee, he has sought major reductions in Social Security payroll taxes. In 1978, he offered an amendment to allow taxpayers a credit against their income taxes equal to 5 percent of their Social Security payroll taxes; it was defeated, 24-11. In 1980, when tax reduction became the major economic issue in Congress, Gephardt's suggestion was a payroll tax cut twice the size of the one he asked for in 1978, combined with some other cuts aimed at improving business

---

**3rd District: South St. Louis and suburbs.** Population: 407,947 (13% decrease since 1970). Race: White 375,417 (92%), Black 28,043 (7%), Others 4,514 (1%). Spanish origin: 5,095 (1%).

productivity.

Appointed to the Budget Committee in 1979, Gephardt joined a bloc that included California's Leon Panetta and Colorado's Timothy E. Wirth, all Democrats who have struggled to mix budget cutting and broader liberal priorities. All three worked with Chairman Robert N. Giaimo of Connecticut in 1980 to produce a budget they thought was in balance and got it through the committee over the opposition of more traditional liberal Democrats, led by Wisconsin's David R. Obey. But when Giaimo, in conference with the Senate, accepted a compromise calling for higher defense spending and deeper domestic cuts, Gephardt and his allies fought it. "Maybe we all just ought to go out and enlist," he said sarcastically at one point in the negotiation. The insurgents managed to defeat the compromise on the House floor, although they accepted a later version that differed from it only slightly.

Another Gephardt crusade has been for the abolition of the Law Enforcement Assistance Administration, which he insists is a useless federal agency, spending money to supply local police with hardware that has no impact on crime. He offered a floor amendment to cut off funding for LEAA grants several times in his first three years and finally won out in the Budget Committee in 1980. The Senate voted to provide some LEAA grant money, but Gephardt's side prevailed in the conference, leaving LEAA supporters in search of a new means of reviving the program.

**At Home:** Gephardt was elected to Congress in 1976 on the strength of his reputation as a young activist on the machine-dominated St. Louis Board of Aldermen.

As an alderman, Gephardt sponsored zoning laws designed to preserve ethnic neighborhoods, building a constituency among German-American working-class communities on the city's south side, an important segment of the 3rd District electorate.

Much of Gephardt's 1976 campaign focused on urban problems. He called for increased federal loans to home-buyers and for creation of a national neighborhood commission to recommend urban assistance programs to federal authorities. He also announced his support for a constitutional amendment to restrict abortions.

In the Democratic primary, Gephardt faced state Sen. Donald J. Gralike, head of an electrical workers local. Gralike was endorsed by most of the Democratic clubs in the district's suburban townships, but Gephardt was stronger within the city. He also ran a media campaign that Gralike could not match. Benefiting from a 16,000 vote advantage in the city wards, Gephardt won 56 percent of the primary vote.

Gephardt's general election opponent was Republican Joseph L. Badaracco, who had served eight years as alderman, six of those as board president. Although he had lost a primary race for lieutenant governor in 1972 and a mayoralty bid the next year, Badaracco was a veteran politician with broad name recognition. He was given an outside chance to defeat Gephardt.

Badaracco ran no television commercials, relying instead on personal appearances and his network of friends. He stressed his reputation for honesty in city politics and tried to persuade voters that Gephardt was really a rich downtown lawyer groomed for Congress by the pinstriped establishment. Gephardt responded by insisting his voting record would be similar to that of the popular Democratic incumbent, Leonor K. Sullivan, who was retiring.

Gephardt won by 2-to-1 in the city of St. Louis and received nearly 60 percent of the St. Louis County vote to defeat Badaracco handily.

Two easy re-elections to the House stirred talk that Gephardt might run against GOP Sen. John C. Danforth in 1982. But on Feb. 23, 1981, Gephardt announced he would not challenge Danforth in the next election.

Gephardt said that campaigning and raising enough money to challenge the wealthy Danforth would take too much time away from his congressional work. His early decision signaled the Missouri Legislature not to carve up his territory in 1982 redistricting, which will reduce Missouri's House delegation by one member.

**The District:** The 3rd includes the offices and commercial buildings of downtown St. Louis, middle-class South Side neighborhoods and the suburban townships of Concord, Lemay and Gravois in St. Louis County.

Its population is 92 percent white, about half Catholic and one-third over age 65. Slightly less than 60 percent of the district's vote is cast in the city of St. Louis, the remainder in St. Louis County.

The ethnic, working-class neighborhoods of South St. Louis, once firmly rooted in the New Deal coalition, today are increasingly concerned about taxes, government spending, abortion and busing. But they remain essentially Democratic.

Many of the voters in the suburban portion of the district grew up on the South Side and moved out when they made enough money. These areas are more inclined to vote Republican than the rest of the district.

The Anheuser-Busch brewery is the district's largest employer. Many other residents work in area food processing, chemical and automotive industries.

The district's population decline since 1970 has been significant — 60,000 people — but that is only half the loss experienced by the neighboring 1st District in North St. Louis.

## Committees

**Budget**
Task Forces: Human Resources and Block Grants, chairman; Reconciliation.

**Ways and Means** (13th of 23 Democrats)
Social Security.

## Elections

**1980 General**

| | |
|---|---|
| Richard Gephardt (D ) | 143,132 (78 %) |
| Robert Cedarburg (R ) | 41,277 (22 %) |

**1978 General**

| | |
|---|---|
| Richard Gephardt (D ) | 121,565 (82 %) |
| Lee Buchschacher (R ) | 26,881 (18 %) |

**Previous Winning Percentage**

1976 (64 %)

**District Vote For President**

| 1980 | | 1976 | | 1972 | |
|---|---|---|---|---|---|
| D | 82,382 (44 %) | D | 87,586 (48 %) | D | 73 406 (41 %) |
| R | 95,554 (51 %) | R | 91,967 (50 %) | R | 103,808 (58 %) |
| I | 8,191 (4 %) | | | | |

## Campaign Finance

| | Receipts | Receipts from PACs | Expenditures |
|---|---|---|---|
| **1980** | | | |
| Gephardt (D ) | $177,695 | $92,560 (52 %) | $177,785 |
| **1978** | | | |
| Gephardt (D ) | $116,605 | $44,850 (38 %) | $113,977 |

## Voting Studies

| Year | Presidential Support S | O | Party Unity S | O | Conservative Coalition S | O |
|---|---|---|---|---|---|---|
| 1980 | 79 | 17 | 80 | 17 | 33 | 62 |
| 1979 | 74 | 21 | 74 | 20 | 39 | 55 |
| 1978 | 74 | 26 | 64 | 33 | 40 | 55 |
| 1977 | 72 | 28 | 75 | 24 | 36 | 63 |

S = Support          O = Opposition

## Key Votes

**96th Congress**

| | |
|---|---|
| Weaken Carter oil profits tax (1979) | N |
| Reject hospital cost control plan (1979) | Y |
| Implement Panama Canal Treaties (1979) | Y |
| Establish Department of Education (1979) | N |
| Approve Anti-busing Amendment (1979) | Y |
| Guarantee Chrysler Corp. loans (1979) | Y |
| Approve military draft registration (1980) | Y |
| Aid Sandinista regime in Nicaragua (1980) | Y |
| Strengthen fair housing laws (1980) | N |

**97th Congress**

| | |
|---|---|
| Reagan budget proposal (1981) | N |

## Interest Group Ratings

| Year | ADA | ACA | AFL-CIO | CCUS |
|---|---|---|---|---|
| 1980 | 56 | 33 | 61 | 64 |
| 1979 | 74 | 16 | 85 | 24 |
| 1978 | 35 | 48 | 75 | 22 |
| 1977 | 50 | 30 | 70 | 29 |

# 4 Ike Skelton (D)

**Of Lexington — Elected 1976**

**Born:** Dec. 20, 1931, Lexington, Mo.
**Education:** U. of Missouri, B.A. 1953; LL.B. 1956.
**Profession:** Lawyer.
**Family:** Wife, Susan Anding; three children.
**Religion:** Disciples of Christ.
**Political Career:** Chairman, Lafayette County Democratic Committee, 1962-66; Mo. Senate, 1971-77.

**In Washington:** Searching for an issue to use in building a legislative career, Skelton quickly found one in civil defense, and he has spent most of his four congressional years working on it.

There are 150 reasons why that is a good issue for Skelton — 150 Minuteman missiles that fan out from Whiteman Air Force Base through the hills and cornfields of his district. For Skelton, civil defense is constituent service.

"Western Missouri is a potential holocaust," he warned in 1979. "These people didn't ask to have missiles put in their backyards ... to be sitting ducks for the benefit of 200 million other Americans."

Every chance he gets, Skelton lobbies for a national plan that would include either local blast shelters able to withstand nuclear attack or a sophisticated new evacuation system. His successes so far have been mixed. He was able in 1979 to win House approval of a proposed $990 million, five-year civil defense plan, but the plan was later modified, and the House Appropriations Committee cut the first year's spending from a planned $167 million to $100 million. Skelton, after trying and failing to get the other $67 million restored, managed to gain acceptance of a compromise figure of $123 million.

Along with other legislators from rural Missouri, Skelton has voted much like a Southern Democrat on many issues. He grew incensed in 1980 at the behavior of some of the Cuban refugees in the United States, and offered a resolution calling for the expulsion of any Cubans who participated in riots. A coalition of members from both ends of the political spectrum warned Skelton that the vagueness of the resolution might lead to the arrest of innocent people. He finally agreed to limit it to those who had been convicted of specific crimes, but even the milder version failed to be approved.

A childhood polio victim who went on to graduate from a military academy, Skelton has a general interest in military issues. He began trying for a place on the Armed Services Committee soon after he arrived in Washington, hoping to use it as a forum for his civil defense campaign. The assignment he got — Agriculture — limited his role on that issue. Late in 1980, however, a place on Armed Services finally opened up for Skelton.

**At Home:** As he began his 1976 campaign to succeed retiring Democrat William Randall, Skelton was a rural state legislator with a narrow political base. Only two counties in his state Senate district were within the borders of the 4th Congressional District. And his major rivals for the Democratic nomination, Jack Gant and Don Manford, were state senators from the Kansas City suburbs, which cast about 40 percent of the district's vote.

Skelton chose to emphasize that he was the only major candidate from the rural part of the district, and campaigned actively for farm and small-town support. It was a successful strategy. He ran third in the suburbs, but his rural vote brought him the nomination with 40.3 percent overall.

Independence Mayor Richard A. King was the Republican nominee. A protégé of Republican Gov. Christopher Bond, King tied his general election campaign to the GOP ticket of Bond and

---

**4th District: Kansas City, Independence.** Population: 541,810 (16% increase since 1970). Race: White 525,808 (97%), Black 10,069 (2%), Others 5,933 (1%). Spanish origin: 4,982 (1%).

# Ike Skelton, D-Mo.

senatorial candidate John C. Danforth, hoping to benefit from their coattails. Skelton continued to emphasize his farm background and fiscal conservatism. He said his vote against a pay raise for state legislators illustrated his frugality.

King was not greatly helped by the top of the Republican ticket; Danforth carried the 4th, but Bond lost it. Skelton defeated King by 24,350 votes.

Since then, Republicans have had a difficult time finding a strong challenger. Real estate broker Bill Baker did not reach even a third of the vote as the nominee in both 1978 and 1980.

**The District:** The 4th District stretches south and east from suburban Kansas City into rolling farm land.

In the Jackson County communities closest to the city, blue-collar workers are employed in the railroad, auto assembly and steel industries. But there is also a sizable white-collar vote.

Most of the corn- and livestock-growing counties to the east are reliably Democratic for Congress, although their voting behavior in other elections is hard to predict. There are several traditionally Republican rural counties on the eastern and southern fringes of the district, but their combined vote is less than 15 percent of the district total.

## Committees

**Armed Services** (19th of 25 Democrats)
Military Personnel and Compensation; Readiness.

**Small Business** (11th of 23 Democrats)
Export Opportunities and Special Small Business Problems.

## Elections

**1980 General**

| | |
|---|---|
| Ike Skelton (D ) | 151,459 (68 %) |
| William Baker (R ) | 71,869 (32 %) |

**1980 Primary**

| | |
|---|---|
| Ike Skelton (D ) | 63,567 (89 %) |
| William Biggs (D ) | 8,036 (11 %) |

**1978 General**

| | |
|---|---|
| Ike Skelton (D ) | 120,748 (73 %) |
| William Baker (R ) | 45,116 (27 %) |

**Previous Winning Percentages**

**1976** (56 %)

**District Vote For President**

| | 1980 | | 1976 | | 1972 |
|---|---|---|---|---|---|
| **D** | 98,000 (43 %) | **D** | 108,479 (51 %) | **D** | 60,306 (31 %) |
| **R** | 120,769 (53 %) | **R** | 100,517 (48 %) | **R** | 137,109 (69 %) |
| **I** | 7,736 (3 %) | | | | |

## Campaign Finance

| | | Receipts | | |
|---|---|---|---|---|
| | Receipts | Receipts from PACs | | Expenditures |
| **1980** | | | | |
| Skelton (D ) | $131,957 | $56,670 (43 %) | | $115,981 |
| Baker (R ) | $2,600 | $914 (35 %) | | $1,921 |

**1978**

| | | | |
|---|---|---|---|
| Skelton (D ) | $158,789 | $66,390 (42 %) | $149,080 |

## Voting Studies

| | Presidential Support | | Party Unity | | Conservative Coalition | |
|---|---|---|---|---|---|---|
| Year | S | O | S | O | S | O |
| 1980 | 60 | 32† | 59 | 34 | 69 | 23 |
| 1979 | 54 | 37 | 57 | 35 | 72 | 21 |
| 1978 | 48 | 41 | 49 | 44 | 60 | 27 |
| 1977 | 62 | 33 | 55 | 39 | 67 | 27 |

S = Support  O = Opposition

†Not eligible for all recorded votes.

## Key Votes

**96th Congress**

| | |
|---|---|
| Weaken Carter oil profits tax (1979) | N |
| Reject hospital cost control plan (1979) | Y |
| Implement Panama Canal Treaties (1979) | N |
| Establish Department of Education (1979) | # |
| Approve Anti-busing Amendment (1979) | Y |
| Guarantee Chrysler Corp. loans (1979) | Y |
| Approve military draft registration (1980) | Y |
| Aid Sandinista regime in Nicaragua (1980) | N |
| Strengthen fair housing laws (1980) | N |

**97th Congress**

| | |
|---|---|
| Reagan budget proposal (1981) | Y |

## Interest Group Ratings

| Year | ADA | ACA | AFL-CIO | CCUS |
|---|---|---|---|---|
| 1980 | 17 | 42 | 58 | 66 |
| 1979 | 32 | 26 | 56 | 50 |
| 1978 | 20 | 68 | 61 | 28 |
| 1977 | 30 | 56 | 71 | 53 |

# 5 Richard Bolling (D)

**Of Kansas City — Elected 1948**

**Born:** May 17, 1916, New York, N.Y.
**Education:** U. of the South, B.A. 1937, M.A. 1939.
**Military Career:** Army, 1941-46.
**Profession:** Teacher, writer.
**Family:** Widowed; three children.
**Religion:** Episcopalian.
**Political Career:** No previous office.

**In Washington:** Bolling will never reach the Speakership he aspired to, but he has probably influenced the House more than any member of his generation, assembling coalitions to pass major domestic programs and serving as intellectual father of the reform movement that changed the institution in the 1970s.

He has been protégé, confidant and adviser — in that order — to Speakers Rayburn, Albert and O'Neill. He has been the master strategist for generations of House liberals who have not understood the rules the way he has.

But the brilliance that made that role possible has been accompanied by a penchant for openly criticizing the people and practices he cannot abide. He has never been patient with House members he considers less intelligent than he is, and that is most of them. His open contempt for Speaker McCormack in the 1960s forced him into a 10-year "exile" from the center of House power.

He is not a modest man. "I like Dick," a Missouri colleague once said, " but if I told him they had just found a bomb in the basement of the Capitol, he would say, 'Yes, I knew it was there all the time and I told them to do something about it years ago.' "

Those qualities contributed to Bolling's failure to win leadership elections in 1962, when Albert defeated him for majority leader, and in 1976, when he fell three votes short in a contest eventually won by Jim Wright of Texas.

But the defeats left him in position to claim the job many colleagues feel he is best suited for, the chairmanship of the Rules Committee.

In that capacity, he has been among the angriest critics of Reagan administration economics and tactics, charging the administration with "attempting to tyrannize a whole Congress, a whole people." Bolling said Reagan was using the budget process, meant to set overall federal spending targets, to sneak through detailed changes in the scope of government. But Bolling's rule requiring specific votes on six Reagan spending cuts was beaten by six votes on the floor, allowing all the cuts to be made at one stroke.

Bolling has been on the Rules Committee since 1955, when he was named to serve as loyal lieutenant to Speaker Rayburn, plotting strategy against the Republicans and conservative Democrats who had effective control of the committee in the 1950s. In the battles over civil rights and labor legislation, it was Bolling who coordinated the outside lobbying coalitions that House liberals needed to be successful.

Bolling received an education in power in his early days on Rules. He watched Chairman Howard Smith of Virginia bottle up legislation simply by not holding meetings, or by bringing bills to the floor under procedures barring amendment. Bolling realized sincerity was not enough for liberals to win legislative battles. He made himself into a parliamentary expert, once defeating Smith by invoking a rule that allowed the committee to meet in the absence of the chairman.

In 1961, with John Kennedy in the White House pushing an ambitious legislative agenda, Bolling and fellow liberals talked Rayburn into leading a dramatic battle to expand Rules from 12 to 15 members, so newly-appointed Kennedy supporters could help outvote the old conservatives, 8-7.

When Rayburn died later that year, and

---

**5th District: Kansas City.** Population: 400,953 (14% decrease since 1970). Race: White 265,406 (66%), Black 123,796 (31%), Others 11,751 (3%). Spanish origin: 13,580 (3%).

McCormack became Speaker, Bolling began a long period of introspection. He wrote two books offering ways a strong Speaker could take control of the House, using the Democratic Caucus to shape party programs and impose discipline. Many of the ideas later became party reforms of the 1970s.

Bolling remained a key man on Rules in the 1960s, especially on passage of the 1964 civil rights bill. But while continuing to assert his liberalism, he became a critic of Lyndon Johnson and the Great Society, which he said was characterized by sloppy legislating that ended in federal waste. "All the right titles passed," he said, "but the bills were lousy."

Things changed quickly for Bolling in 1971. Albert replaced McCormack as Speaker, and Bolling was welcome again in the inner circle. The next few years marked one of the most creative periods in his career.

Bolling persuaded Albert to set up a special panel to redraw lines of committee jurisdiction. The panel spent a year on the task and recommended massive changes. In the end it failed on the House floor, victimized in part by personal jealousies and turf wars and in part by Bolling's own decision to take on some tough enemies. He infuriated his old AFL-CIO friends, for example, by proposing to split Education and Labor, with which unions felt comfortable.

At the same time, Bolling was designing the new federal budget process, the one which has ended the old system in which spending bills were routinely passed one by one without concern for their effect on the overall economy.

Bolling has always been a student of economics, and has served on the Joint Economic Committee for 24 years. He generally believes there can be a healthy economy through federal planning, but he also warned of the dangers of inflation before most other liberals were sensitive to the issue.

In 1976, Bolling was nearing the top of the Rules Committee and it seemed unlikely he would ever make another leadership campaign. But he tried once more, and came close. His main antagonist was Phillip Burton of California, who had fought him to the end on committee reform. "Burton wanted to be Speaker," Bolling said afterward, explaining his own candidacy. "I didn't want him to be Speaker."

Besides being personal rivals, the two men genuinely disagreed about the way power should be used in the House. Bolling believed it should be centralized in a strong Speaker and a majority caucus with control over legislative committees. Burton preferred a decentralized body in which

dozens of subcommittees and hundreds of legislators shared power and bargained in the legislative marketplace.

Bolling campaigned as a centrist between Burton on the left and Wright on the moderate right. He probably could have beaten Burton one-on-one if he had had a chance. But he fell three short of making the runoff — some said because Burton forces had given a few extra votes to Wright in the belief he would be easier to defeat. Wright then beat Burton in the runoff by one vote.

For years, Bolling made all major political moves in consultation with his wife, Jim, a shrewd, earthy Texan whom he married in 1964. She died suddenly in 1978, and Bolling went through a difficult period personally, at one point checking himself into an alcohol treatment unit, stunning friends who had never noticed any sign of a problem. By the end of 1980, however, Bolling seemed eager to involve himself in public issues again. He started writing a book about power and urging creation of a new federal commission to reorganize the federal government.

**At Home:** Bolling had been in Kansas City less than three years when he launched his campaign for Congress in 1948 as an alternative to the "political machine hacks" of the Pendergast Democratic organization.

Bolling went to Missouri as veterans' affairs director at the University of Kansas City, and became Midwest director of the Americans for Democratic Action and national vice chairman of the American Veterans Committee.

The 5th District was uncharacteristically in Republican hands in 1948. Democrats had been badly split in 1946 between a candidate backed by the Pendergast forces and one loyal to President Truman, and Albert Reeves became the first GOP winner there in 16 years. Democratic bickering was still going on two years later, allowing Bolling to move in and take the party's nomination as a reformer.

Despite the district's Democratic makeup, Reeves was favored. But Truman won Missouri by more than 260,000 votes, carrying Bolling in with 55.9 percent of the vote.

Bolling's popularity increased throughout the next decade. The Pendergast organization broke apart, and while few of its loyalists liked Bolling's reform politics, some of them accepted him because he drew labor and veterans' support that helped elect other local Democrats.

But in 1964, there was a serious primary challenge. Bolling had divorced his wife of 18 years and remarried five days later. His opponents in Kansas City Democratic politics decided to use the divorce as an issue to try to unseat him.

Five local party leaders united behind challenger Hunter H. Phillips, a Jackson County administrative judge. They controlled a strong patronage-based vote; even some ward leaders from predominantly black precincts deserted Bolling, despite his years of commitment to civil rights.

Bolling responded aggressively, appealing for money and volunteer workers and mobilizing his liberal grass-roots support. He said it was highhanded for factional leaders to assume their whims would be obeyed by the voters. By the time it was over, the reformer had taught the ward leaders a lesson in practical politics. He won more than two-thirds of the vote.

Since then, Bolling has brushed aside a succession of opponents. Despite a mild heart attack in 1977 and period of hospitalization for alcohol-related problems in 1979, he won his 17th term in 1980 with 70 percent of the vote.

**The District:** The 5th is an urban district, 30 percent black, and usually Democratic in national politics. It contains most of downtown Kansas City plus suburban Grandview and the western part of Raytown. Kansas City's blue-collar workers work in the city's auto assembly, steel and meatpacking industries. It is the only city in the country where the second-largest employer is a greeting card company. Hallmark employs more than 7,000 people in the 5th District.

## Committees

**Rules** (Chairman)

**Joint Economic**

Agriculture and Transportation; Economic Goals and Intergovernmental Policy.

## Elections

**1980 General**

| | |
|---|---|
| Richard Bolling (D ) | 110,957 (70 %) |
| Vincent Baker (R ) | 47,309 (30 %) |

**1980 Primary**

| | |
|---|---|
| Richard Bolling (D ) | 40,656 (82 %) |
| Bert Naberhaus (D ) | 9,110 (18 %) |

**1978 General**

| | |
|---|---|
| Richard Bolling (D ) | 82,140 (72 %) |
| Steven Walter (R ) | 30,360 (27 %) |

**Previous Winning Percentages**

| | | | |
|---|---|---|---|
| 1976 (68 %) | 1974 (69 %) | 1972 (63 %) | 1970 (61 %) |
| 1968 (65 %) | 1966 (61 %) | 1964 (68 %) | 1962 (59 %) |
| 1960 (61 %) | 1958 (70 %) | 1956 (57 %) | 1954 (59 %) |
| 1952 (56 %) | 1950 (55 %) | 1948 (56 %) | |

**District Vote For President**

| | 1980 | | 1976 | | 1972 |
|---|---|---|---|---|---|
| D | 94,430 (59 %) | D | 87,802 (58 %) | D | 71,448 (49 %) |
| R | 56,842 (35 %) | R | 60,310 (40 %) | R | 74,486 (51 %) |
| I | 8,175 (5 %) | | | | |

## Campaign Finance

| | Receipts | Receipts from PACs | Expenditures |
|---|---|---|---|
| **1980** | | | |
| Bolling (D ) | $173,017 | $103,400 (60 %) | $113,299 |
| Baker (R ) | $7,457 | — (0 %) | $11,388 |

## Voting Studies

| | Presidential Support | | Party Unity | | Conservative Coalition | |
|---|---|---|---|---|---|---|
| Year | S | O | S | O | S | O |
| 1980 | 82 | 8 | 86 | 4 | 14 | 77 |
| 1979 | 41 | 4 | 56 | 2 | 8 | 45 |
| 1978 | 74 | 8 | 75 | 8 | 12 | 70 |
| 1977 | 67 | 13 | 73 | 1 | 5 | 71 |
| 1976 | 20 | 67 | 79 | 5 | 13 | 68 |
| 1975 | 49 | 46 | 85 | 9 | 25 | 70 |
| 1974 (Ford) | 48 | 33 | | | | |
| 1974 | 55 | 36 | 74 | 13 | 20 | 69 |
| 1973 | 38 | 43 | 62 | 14 | 18 | 52 |
| 1972 | 46 | 41 | 70 | 15 | 18 | 67 |
| 1971 | 53 | 46 | 78 | 10 | 21 | 71 |

S = Support          O = Opposition

## Key Votes

**96th Congress**

| | |
|---|---|
| Weaken Carter oil profits tax (1979) | ? |
| Reject hospital cost control plan (1979) | N |
| Implement Panama Canal Treaties (1979) | ? |
| Establish Department of Education (1979) | ? |
| Approve Anti-busing Amendment (1979) | ? |
| Guarantee Chrysler Corp. loans (1979) | Y |
| Approve military draft registration (1980) | Y |
| Aid Sandinista regime in Nicaragua (1980) | Y |
| Strengthen fair housing Laws (1980) | Y |

**97th Congress**

| | |
|---|---|
| Reagan budget proposal (1981) | N |

## Interest Group Rating

| Year | ADA | ACA | AFL-CIO | CCUS |
|---|---|---|---|---|
| 1980 | 72 | 23 | 83 | 65 |
| 1979 | 53 | 7 | 57 | 8 |
| 1978 | 65 | 9 | 94 | 19 |
| 1977 | 75 | 4 | 95 | 6 |
| 1976 | 75 | 7 | 95 | 17 |
| 1975 | 79 | 11 | 96 | 13 |
| 1974 | 70 | 0 | 100 | 0 |
| 1973 | 52 | 9 | 90 | 44 |
| 1972 | 75 | 17 | 90 | 11 |
| 1971 | 65 | 11 | 90 | - |

# 6 E. Thomas Coleman (R)

**Of Kansas City — Elected 1976**

**Born:** May 29, 1943, Kansas City, Mo.
**Education:** William Jewell College, B.A. 1965;
New York U., M.P.A. 1966; Washington U.,
J.D. 1969.
**Profession:** Lawyer.
**Family:** Wife, Marilyn Anderson; three children.
**Religion:** Protestant.
**Political Career:** Mo. House, 1973-76; un-
successful campaign for Clay County clerk,
1970.

**In Washington:** There is nothing very rural
or agricultural about Coleman, a Kansas City
lawyer with a public administration degree from
New York University, but he headed straight for
the Agriculture Committee when he arrived in the
House in 1977. He has used it more to promote his
conservative skepticism about federal social
spending than to practice the committee's standard price support politics.

His most conspicuous arguments have been
about the food stamp program, which he has
criticized as wasteful and has sought to restrict.
At various times during his House career, he has
emphasized several different approaches in trying
to scale down the program.

In 1977, Coleman offered an amendment in
committee to deny food stamps for a year to
anyone convicted of fraud in connection with the
program. It failed on a vote of 12-5, and Coleman
did not take it to the floor.

Two years later, his idea was to place an
absolute limit on food stamp spending — in this
case, $6.2 billion for fiscal 1980. He said better
efficiency in detecting ineligible applicants could
hold costs to that level without wiping out any
legitimate benefits. But Agriculture Committee
Democrats insisted the best way to deal with food
stamp waste was in separate legislation, and they
held Coleman off by a bare majority of 18-16.

In 1980, Coleman's idea was to end the dupli-
cation between food stamps and the school lunch
program, limiting a family to one or the other. In
some cases, Coleman said, "we are giving money
to a family and we are never really sure whether it
is going to the child or not." He tried that
proposal on the House floor, but it failed, 269-134,
winning a slim majority on the Republican side
but few Democratic votes.

Coleman was one of the most vocal critics of
President Carter's 1980 grain embargo, and he

tried to stop it with an amendment that was as
many parts politics as it was foreign policy.

In July 1980, after the House had rejected
several attempts to end the embargo outright,
Coleman offered one providing simply that it
expire on Oct. 1 of that year unless reaffirmed by
the administration.

The purpose was to force Carter into a situation in which it would be embarrassing for him to
renew the embargo. "Frankly," Coleman said, "I
do not think that he will do so on Oct. 1, one
month before the election, when he is going to
American farmers trying to get their support."
The House chose not to press the issue; it defeated Coleman's amendment by voice vote.

**At Home:** Coleman was running what
seemed like a hopeless effort in 1976, but he was
in the right place at the right time. His opponent's
campaign collapsed overnight, and he inherited
thousands of Democratic votes.

Morgan Maxfield, a millionaire Texan transplanted to Kansas City, had won the Democratic
primary with the help of an expensive media
barrage, and he was outspending Coleman 3-1 on
the general election.

But less than a month before the voting, the
*Kansas City Star* reported that Maxfield had lied
about his early life, marital status and educational
degrees. His campaign chairman resigned and
criticized him. All Coleman had to do was wait for
the election, and when it was over, he had swept

**6th District: Northwest — St. Jo-
seph.** Population: 508,848 (8% increase since
1970). Race: White 496,912 (98%), Black 6,913
(1%), Others 5,023 (1%). Spanish origin: 5,443
(1%).

to a 37,214-vote victory in a district that had not gone Republican in a quarter of a century. He entered the House immediately, filling the vacancy caused by the death of Democrat Jerry Litton, who had been killed in an airplane crash in August on the day he was nominated for the Senate.

Running for re-election in 1978, Coleman was challenged by Democrat Phil Snowden, a 12-year veteran of the state Legislature. Snowden shared most of Coleman's conservative views and had some difficulty finding an issue to use against the incumbent. As an ex-football star at the University of Missouri, he ran commercials featuring former Missouri Coach Dan Devine.

In the two preceding years, Coleman had worked hard to add rural support to his Kansas City base. He operated a mobile office that roamed through the district's rural counties, and he assured conservative Democrats that he voiced their philosophy in the House.

Snowden won only one county. Coleman carried everything else in the district. He coasted to re-election in 1980.

**The District:** Most of the vote in this sprawling, 23-county district is in Clay, Platte and Buchanan counties, north of Kansas City.

In Clay and Platte, many residents work in the metropolitan area's industries and businesses. The city of St. Joseph, a flour-milling and meatpacking center, is in Buchanan County.

The rest of the counties are rural and generally conservative, gradually shedding Democratic voting habits. Most of them went for Reagan in 1980, as he carried the district overall by 19,000 votes. The rolling prairies here are among the most fertile agricultural areas in the state.

## Committees

**Agriculture** (5th of 19 Republicans)
Conservation, Credit and Rural Development; Domestic Marketing, Consumer Relations and Nutrition.

**Education and Labor** (5th of 14 Republicans)
Elementary, Secondary and Vocational Education; Human Resources; Postsecondary Education

## Elections

**1980 General**

| | |
|---|---|
| Thomas Coleman (R ) | 149,281 (71 %) |
| Vernon King (D ) | 62,048 (29 %) |

**1978 General**

| | |
|---|---|
| Thomas Coleman (R ) | 96,574 (56 %) |
| Phil Snowden (D ) | 76,061 (44 %) |

**Previous Winning Percentages**

**1976*** (59 %)

*Elected to fill a vacancy and at the same time elected to the 95th Congress.*

**District Vote For President**

| | 1980 | | 1976 | | 1972 |
|---|---|---|---|---|---|
| D | 93,933 (43 %) | D | 108,777 (52 %) | D | 65,754 (33 %) |
| R | 112,712 (52 %) | R | 99,618 (47 %) | R | 134,977 (67 %) |
| I | 8,233 (4 %) | | | | |

## Campaign Finance

| | Receipts | Receipts from PACs | Expenditures |
|---|---|---|---|
| **1980** | | | |
| Coleman (R ) | $225,917 | $79,237 (35 %) | $188,403 |
| King (D ) | $22,750 | — (0 %) | $22,751 |

| 1978 | | | |
|---|---|---|---|
| Coleman (R ) | $286,807 | $84,374 (29 %) | $274,804 |
| Snowden (D ) | $282,713 | $33,150 (12 %) | $280,118 |

## Voting Studies

| | Presidential Support | | Party Unity | | Conservative Coalition | |
|---|---|---|---|---|---|---|
| Year | S | O | S | O | S | O |
| 1980 | 41 | 56 | 85 | 11 | 94 | 2 |
| 1979 | 34 | 59 | 82 | 12 | 89 | 5 |
| 1978 | 32 | 65 | 81 | 16 | 90 | 9 |
| 1977 | 44 | 54 | 80 | 17 | 87 | 13 |

S = Support          O = Opposition

## Key Votes

**96th Congress**

| | |
|---|---|
| Weaken Carter oil profits tax (1979) | Y |
| Reject hospital cost control plan (1979) | Y |
| Implement Panama Canal Treaties (1979) | N |
| Establish Department of Education (1979) | N |
| Approve Anti-busing Amendment (1979) | Y |
| Guarantee Chrysler Corp. loans (1979) | N |
| Approve military draft registration (1980) | Y |
| Aid Sandinista regime in Nicaragua (1980) | N |
| Strengthen fair housing laws (1980) | N |

**97th Congress**

| | |
|---|---|
| Reagan budget proposal (1981) | Y |

## Interest Group Ratings

| Year | ADA | ACA | AFL-CIO | CCUS |
|---|---|---|---|---|
| 1980 | 6 | 87 | 11 | 73 |
| 1979 | 11 | 96 | 10 | 94 |
| 1978 | 20 | 93 | 11 | 61 |
| 1977 | 15 | 81 | 17 | 88 |

**693**

# 7 Gene Taylor (R)

**Of Sarcoxie — Elected 1972**

**Born:** Feb. 10, 1928, Sarcoxie, Mo.
**Education:** Southwest Mo. State College, 1945-47.
**Military Career:** National Guard, 1948-49.
**Profession:** Automobile dealer.
**Family:** Wife, Dorothy Wooldridge; two children.
**Religion:** Methodist.
**Political Career:** Sarcoxie Board of Education, 1954-64; mayor of Sarcoxie, 1954-60.

**In Washington:** Taylor is a joke-telling, back-slapping good ol' boy from the Ozarks, who listens to party leaders and is careful not to cause any trouble. He makes few speeches, preferring to do business informally behind the rail of the House chamber.

It was precisely those qualities that won him a Rules Committee seat in 1980 when the less-than-docile John B. Anderson left the committee to run for president. There were two far more outspoken contenders, Henry Hyde of Illinois, nationally famous as an opponent of abortion, and Bill Thomas of California, an aggressive freshman interested in the internal workings of the House. But both were ambitious and independent, and Taylor was a solid leadership vote. The GOP Committee on Committees picked Taylor.

To accept the Rules assignment, Taylor had to give up a committee where he was perfectly content, Public Works and Transportation, a useful spot for a behind-the-scenes operator like Taylor. He worked on airline deregulation, accepting it reluctantly but warning that small communities would be losers. He used the committee to try and bring federal plums to Missouri. He remained on Post Office and Civil Service where he had been fairly quiet, although he led the opposition to a bill that would have created a national holiday on the birthday of Martin Luther King Jr.

Taylor said a new national holiday would cost $212 million in federal wages lost and $3 billion in state, local and private wages. He said King's birthday should be commemorated on a Sunday. "Is it not true," he asked, "that we celebrate Easter on Sunday? How do we rise any higher than that?" The House voted for Sunday observance, and the bill's supporters then withdrew it from consideration.

But now, Taylor is happy on Rules. Eventually, every committee chairman comes there seeking help, and he can still bargain for homestate interests. Rules also is less time-consuming than legislative committees, which suits Taylor's schedule. He still spends every weekend at home.

**At Home:** Taylor has the one solid Republican district in Missouri, and he has taken it easily five times, encountering trouble only in 1974.

He won his first term in 1972 with the help of Durward G. Hall, the retiring Republican incumbent, who endorsed him for the nomination. Besides running his Ford dealership in Sarcoxie, Taylor had been in local politics for a decade. He was Missouri's GOP national committeeman.

Despite his connections, Taylor had trouble getting past John Ashcroft in the 1972 GOP primary. Ashcroft, who is now Missouri's attorney general, won 44.7 percent of the primary vote. But Taylor was an easy winner that fall against Springfield teacher William Thomas.

Two years later, Democrat Richard L. Franks gave Taylor the only other scare of his career. An irreverent young magistrate judge from Greene County, Franks campaigned extensively, complaining that farmers were being squeezed by inflation under a Republican president. Franks won Greene and adjoining Webster County, but Taylor took the district's 16 other counties to emerge the winner with 52.3 percent overall.

**The District:** The 7th is Missouri's mountain district, originally settled by pioneers from the Appalachian highlands. It has been predomi-

---

**7th District: Southwest — Springfield.** Population: 570,244 (22% increase since 1970). Race: White 559,665 (98%), Black 4,467 (1%), Others 6,112 (1%). Spanish origin: 3,544 (1%).

nantly Republican since the 19th century. GOP candidates usually win about 65 percent of the vote there. Beef and dairy cattle and timber

sawmills are important in the Ozark economy. The area's lakes make it a popular resort and retirement area.

## Committees

**Post Office and Civil Service** (2nd of 11 Republicans)
Civil Service; Postal Operations and Services.

**Rules** (4th of 5 Republicans)
Legislative Process; Rules of the House.

## Elections

**1980 General**

| | |
|---|---|
| Gene Taylor (R ) | 161,668 (68 %) |
| Ken Young (D ) | 76,844 (32 %) |

**1978 General**

| | |
|---|---|
| Gene Taylor (R ) | 104,566 (61 %) |
| Jim Thomas (D ) | 66,351 (39 %) |

**Previous Winning Percentages**

1976 (62 %)     1974 (52 %)     1972 (64 %)

**District Vote For President**

| | 1980 | | 1976 | | 1972 |
|---|---|---|---|---|---|
| D | 88,807 (36 %) | D | 103,297 (47 %) | D | 57,616 (27 %) |
| R | 146,971 (60 %) | R | 114,881 (52 %) | R | 153,239 (73 %) |
| I | 6,335 (3 %) | | | | |

## Campaign Finance

| | Receipts | Receipts from PACs | Expenditures |
|---|---|---|---|
| **1980** | | | |
| Taylor (R ) | $177,363 | $71,100 (41 %) | $99,889 |
| **1978** | | | |
| Taylor (R ) | $113,273 | $35,649 (31 %) | $104,612 |
| Thomas (D ) | $26,104 | $1,000 (4 %) | $25,037 |

## Voting Studies

| | Presidential Support | | Party Unity | | Conservative Coalition | |
|---|---|---|---|---|---|---|
| Year | S | O | S | O | S | O |
| 1980 | 29 | 67 | 86 | 8 | 92 | 3 |
| 1979 | 26 | 66 | 86 | 7 | 94 | 1 |
| 1978 | 26 | 74 | 86 | 12 | 96 | 4 |
| 1977 | 29 | 66 | 91 | 6 | 94 | 2 |
| 1976 | 73 | 25 | 91 | 9 | 96 | 3 |
| 1975 | 58 | 35 | 85 | 9 | 94 | 2 |
| 1974 (Ford) | 48 | 31 | | | | |
| 1974 | 66 | 28 | 81 | 10 | 89 | 4 |
| 1973 | 60 | 31 | 77 | 9 | 76 | 5 |

S = Support          O = Opposition

## Key Votes

**96th Congress**

| | |
|---|---|
| Weaken Carter oil profits tax (1979) | Y |
| Reject hospital cost control plan (1979) | Y |
| Implement Panama Canal Treaties (1979) | N |
| Establish Department of Education (1979) | N |
| Approve Anti-busing Amendment (1979) | Y |
| Guarantee Chrysler Corp. loans (1979) | N |
| Approve military draft registration (1980) | Y |
| Aid Sandinista regime in Nicaragua (1980) | N |
| Strengthen fair housing laws (1980) | N |

**97th Congress**

| | |
|---|---|
| Reagan budget proposal (1981) | Y |

## Interest Group Ratings

| Year | ADA | ACA | AFL-CIO | CCUS |
|---|---|---|---|---|
| 1980 | 11 | 88 | 16 | 66 |
| 1979 | 0 | 100 | 11 | 100 |
| 1978 | 10 | 96 | 20 | 83 |
| 1977 | 0 | 89 | 9 | 94 |
| 1976 | 0 | 96 | 13 | 100 |
| 1975 | 0 | 89 | 5 | 88 |
| 1974 | 4 | 79 | 0 | 100 |
| 1973 | 4 | 87 | 18 | 91 |

# 8 Wendell Bailey (R)

**Of Willow Springs — Elected 1980**

**Born:** July 30, 1940, Willow Springs, Mo.
**Education:** Southwest Mo. State U., B.S. 1962.
**Profession:** Automobile dealer.
**Family:** Wife, Jane Ann Bray; three children.
**Religion:** Baptist.
**Political Career:** Willow Springs City Council, 1970-72, mayor pro-tempore, 1971-72; Mo. House, 1973-81.

**The Member:** A car dealer and down-home legislator from rural Missouri, Bailey said during the campaign that he would win because "I'm genuine." After the election, visiting Washington prior to his swearing-in, he told a reporter: "I'm green as a gourd. I've been to Washington three times in my life."

In 1981, Bailey has worked to amend federal bankruptcy laws to allow prompt removal of grain from elevators of a storage company that goes bankrupt. The issue of grain access cropped up in 1981 when a Missouri storage company went bankrupt and farmers were not allowed to remove perishable grain stocks.

In the state Legislature, Bailey was an "open government" advocate who cast votes with a close eye on his constituents' preferences. Elected chairman of the House Republican Caucus in 1974, he pushed to have its meetings opened to the public. His office published a booklet on lobbyists to aid legislators and the press.

Bailey initially supported the Equal Rights Amendment, but changed his mind in deference to local opinion. In his congressional campaign, he referred to the Salt II treaty as "a delusion and a sham" and called for a halt to "social engineering" by federal agencies.

Bailey's conservative stands and small-town background won him votes among rural Democrats who had supported Democratic Rep. Richard H. Ichord for 20 years until he retired in 1980.

**The District:** Shaped like a warped version of the letter "Y", the 8th sprawls all over eastern and southern Missouri and cuts across numerous political and demographic boundaries. Boone County, near the center of the state, is the home of the University of Missouri, and is dependably Democratic. Bailey's Howell County base is far to the south, on the Arkansas-Missouri border. In the district's northeastern corner are the St. Louis suburbs, where the Republican vote is growing. The conservative rural counties that formed Ichord's bastion fill in the center of the district.

## Committees

**Education and Labor** (14th of 14 Republicans)
Labor Standards; Postsecondary Education; Select Education.

**Government Operations** (15th of 17 Republicans)
Government Activities and Transportation; Government Information and Individual Rights.

## Elections

**1980 General**

| | |
|---|---:|
| Wendell Bailey (R ) | 127,675 (57 %) |
| Steve Gardner (D ) | 95,751 (43 %) |

**1980 Primary**

| | |
|---|---:|
| Wendell Bailey (R ) | 17,741 (34 %) |
| Paul Dietrich (R ) | 14,081 (27 %) |
| Larry Marshall (R ) | 10,017 (19 %) |
| Don Meyer (R ) | 7,735 (15 %) |
| Janice Noland (R ) | 2,475 (5 %) |

**District Vote For President**

| | 1980 | | 1976 | | 1972 |
|---|---|---|---|---|---|
| D | 88,696 (38 %) | D | 93,354 (46 %) | D | 58,036 (32 %) |
| R | 131,676 (57 %) | R | 105,449 (52 %) | R | 124,585 (68 %) |
| I | 8,735 (4 %) | | | | |

## Campaign Finance

| | Receipts | Receipts from PACs | Expenditures |
|---|---:|---:|---:|
| **1980** | | | |
| Bailey (R ) | 320,501 | 129,990 (41 %) | 230,176 |
| Gardner (D ) | 139,596 | 41,980 (30 %) | 138,074 |

## Key Vote

**97th Congress**

| | |
|---|---:|
| Reagan budget proposal (1981) | Y |

---

**8th District: Central — Columbia, Jefferson City.** Population: 563,716 (21% increase since 1970). Race: White 538,823 (96%), Black 17,214 (3%), Others 7,679 (1%). Spanish origin: 5,157 (1%).

---

# 9 Harold L. Volkmer (D)

### Of Hannibal — Elected 1976

**Born:** April 4, 1931, Jefferson City, Mo.
**Education:** U. of Missouri, LL.B. 1955.
**Military Career:** Army, 1955-57.
**Profession:** Lawyer.
**Family:** Wife, Shirley Braskett; three children.
**Religion:** Roman Catholic.
**Political Career:** Marion County prosecuting
attorney, 1960-66; Mo. House, 1967-77.

**In Washington:** Volkmer is a man of curiosity and creativity, but his urge to speak out and offer amendments on dozens of major House issues has not helped his popularity in a chamber where members are expected to stay out of each other's way. The House is not kind to legislative busybodies, and Volkmer is not kind to the many colleagues who tell him to mind his own affairs. But he is indefatigable, easily noticed in the chamber as he hunches down over a microphone, waiting as long as necessary for a chance to jump into the debate.

One day in 1979, Volkmer asked John Burton, the eccentric California Democrat, how long he planned to keep talking. If Burton talked much longer, Volkmer said, he would go back to his office. "I think I could probably get unanimous consent," Burton responded, "for the gentleman to go back to his office for the rest of the evening."

Volkmer was active in 1980 in House Judiciary consideration of a revised federal criminal code. He tried to make operating a prostitution business a federal crime, and favored abolition of parole and increased prison terms for felons. The previous year, he was the lone vote on Judiciary against bolstering the Immigration and Naturalization Service.

When Judiciary wrote open housing legislation in 1980, Volkmer led the fight on the Democratic side to soften its enforcement provisions and make it more difficult for the federal government to proceed on its own in suspected discrimination cases. His amendment, offered with Republican F. James Sensenbrenner Jr. of Wisconsin, failed by one vote. Later the bill died on the House floor.

Volkmer has long been opposed to abortion and in 1979 attached the first successful anti-abortion amendment to an authorization bill. Previously such efforts had focused on appropriations bills. His amendment to the Child Health

Assurance bill prohibited federal funding of Medicaid abortions except if the life of the mother was in danger.

Volkmer is also an activist against gun control. In the 97th Congress he is promoting a bill to repeal some of the provisions of the 1968 gun control law, including the power to inspect records of gun dealers.

One of Volkmer's first votes in Congress was against the common-site picketing bill, a vote that angered construction unions in his district who had contributed to his campaign. But Volkmer snapped back that a contribution "doesn't buy my vote" and went to to say, "If they oppose me in both the primary and the general election, they will have a hard time getting in to see me."

**At Home:** Volkmer is a lawyer from the Mississippi River town of Hannibal, and his strength in rural areas won him the 9th District seat in 1976.

When Democratic Rep. William L. Hungate announced he would retire that year, Volkmer and 10 other Democrats sought to succeed him. Volkmer, then an influential member of the Missouri House, far outpaced the primary field, finishing 17,877 votes ahead of the second place candidate.

The Republican nominee, J. H. Frappier, had solid name recognition in the southern part of the district, near St. Louis, where he already repre-

---

**9th District: Northeast — Florissant.** Population: 553,948 (18% increase since 1970). Race: White 528,196 (95%), Black 22,259 (4%), Others 3,493 (1%). Spanish origin: 3,557 (1%).

sented about half the 9th District voters in his state Senate constituency.

Volkmer and Frappier ran nearly even in suburban St. Charles County and in the portion of St. Louis County in the district. But Volkmer took more than 60 percent in the rural portion of the district and won 55.9 percent of the total vote.

Volkmer won easily in 1978, but he had a tougher time in 1980 against Republican John W. Turner, a college professor who resigned his teaching post to run for Congress. Turner had help from the National Republican Congressional Committee, and from St. Louis County business interests. He managed to outspend Volkmer. But the incumbent campaigned tirelessly, and took 56 percent.

**The District:** The 9th reaches out from St. Louis' northern suburbs to rural northeast Missouri. Several counties in the center of the district are the heart of traditionally Democratic "Little Dixie," a corn- and cattle-raising area first settled by pro-slavery planters from Virginia and Kentucky.

Republican strength is in St. Charles County, a fast-growing area northwest of St. Louis which casts nearly a quarter of the district's vote. GOP candidates also fare well in counties to the west of St. Charles along the Missouri River.

The St. Louis County portion of the district is a middle-class suburban area whose many blue-collar residents work in plants like McDonnell Douglas Electronics.

## Committees

**Agriculture** (22nd of 24 Democrats)
Department Operations, Research and Foreign Agriculture; Livestock, Dairy and Poultry; Wheat, Soybeans and Feed Grains.

**Science and Technology** (15th of 23 Democrats)
Energy Development and Applications; Energy Research and Production; Investigations and Oversight.

## Elections

**1980 General**

| | |
|---|---|
| Harold Volkmer (D ) | 135,905 (56 %) |
| John Turner (R ) | 104,835 (44 %) |

**1980 Primary**

| | |
|---|---|
| Harold Volkmer (D ) | 73,258 (86 %) |
| Hiram King (D ) | 11,495 (14 %) |

**1978 General**

| | |
|---|---|
| Harold Volkmer (D ) | 135,170 (75 %) |
| Jerry Dent (R ) | 45,795 (25 %) |

**Previous Winning Percentage**

1976 (56 %)

**District Vote For President**

| | 1980 | | 1976 | | 1972 |
|---|---|---|---|---|---|
| **D** | 101,589 (41 %) | **D** | 108,189 (49 %) | **D** | 69,389 (35 %) |
| **R** | 136,090 (55 %) | **R** | 109,684 (50 %) | **R** | 129,397 (65 %) |
| **I** | 7,942 (3 %) | | | | |

## Campaign Finance

| | Receipts | Receipts from PACs | Expenditures |
|---|---|---|---|
| **1980** | | | |
| Volkmer (D ) | $172,159 | $83,185 (48 %) | $177,237 |
| Turner (R ) | $192,250 | $24,300 (13 %) | $190,027 |

| | | | |
|---|---|---|---|
| **1978** | | | |
| Volkmer (D ) | $107,190 | $43,339 (40 %) | $101,375 |

## Voting Studies

| | Presidential Support | | Party Unity | | Conservative Coalition | |
|---|---|---|---|---|---|---|
| Year | S | O | S | O | S | O |
| 1980 | 68 | 29 | 64 | 35 | 62 | 35 |
| 1979 | 68 | 30 | 58 | 40 | 65 | 35 |
| 1978 | 59 | 40 | 54 | 45 | 55 | 43 |
| 1977 | 66 | 29 | 58 | 40 | 47 | 52 |

S = Support          O = Opposition

## Key Votes

**96th Congress**

| | |
|---|---|
| Weaken Carter oil profits tax (1979) | N |
| Reject hospital cost control plan (1979) | Y |
| Implement Panama Canal Treaties (1979) | N |
| Establish Department of Education (1979) | Y |
| Approve Anti-busing Amendment (1979) | N |
| Guarantee Chrysler Corp. loans (1979) | Y |
| Approve military draft registration (1980) | Y |
| Aid Sandinista regime in Nicaragua (1980) | Y |
| Strengthen fair housing laws (1980) | N |

**97th Congress**

| | |
|---|---|
| Reagan budget proposal (1981) | Y |

## Interest Group Ratings

| Year | ADA | ACA | AFL-CIO | CCUS |
|---|---|---|---|---|
| 1980 | 39 | 29 | 58 | 63 |
| 1979 | 37 | 38 | 58 | 56 |
| 1978 | 45 | 54 | 65 | 29 |
| 1977 | 60 | 48 | 68 | 53 |

# 10 Bill Emerson (R)

**Of De Soto — Elected 1980**

**Born:** Jan. 1, 1938, St. Louis, Mo.
**Education:** Westminster College, B.A. 1959; U. of Baltimore, LL.B. 1964.
**Military Career:** Air Force Reserves, 1964-present.
**Profession:** Government relations consultant.
**Family:** Wife, Jo Ann Hermann; three children.
**Religion:** Presbyterian.
**Political Career:** No previous office.

**The Member:** Emerson's limited campaign experience masks years in the background of politics. He first came to Washington in 1953 and has spent nearly all his adult life working as a congressional aide or lobbyist.

Emerson was a page in the 83rd and 84th Congresses, returned home to attend college, and six years later was back, working as a special assistant to Kansas GOP Rep. Bob Ellsworth and later for Charles McC. Mathias Jr., then a House member and now Maryland's senior senator.

In the 1970s, Emerson was a lobbyist and consultant for defense and energy-related private companies. He moved back to Missouri only when he began preparing his 1980 campaign against Democratic Rep. Bill D. Burlison.

In the House, Emerson has introduced a bill to impose a moratorium on foreign acquisition of American mining companies. His attention was drawn to this issue when a Canadian mining company expressed interest in buying the St. Joe Minerals Corp., a zinc and lead mining business that is a major 10th District employer.

Along with 8th District Republican Rep. Wendell Bailey, Emerson sponsored legislation in 1981 to revise federal bankruptcy laws to allow farmers prompt grain removal rights. An elevator in Emerson's district had just gone bankrupt, barring local farmers from removing their perishable stocks from the company's elevators.

**The District:** Most people know the 10th as the district with "The Bootheel," a rural and Southern-oriented Democratic bastion in the corner of southeast Missouri. But the Bootheel cast only 15 percent of the total district vote in 1980. By contrast, 25 percent of the vote was cast in Jefferson County, just south of St. Louis. Suburban voters there helped Emerson take the county with 55 percent. He also won handily in Cape Girardeau and several other counties in the south-central part of the district.

## Committees

**Agriculture** (12th of 19 Republicans)
Cotton, Rice and Sugar; Department Operations, Research and Foreign Agriculture; Wheat, Soybeans and Feed Grains.

## Elections

**1980 General**

| | |
|---|---|
| Bill Emerson (R ) | 116,167 (55%) |
| Bill Burlison (D ) | 94,465 (45%) |

**1980 Primary**

| | |
|---|---|
| Bill Emerson (R ) | 18,758 (77 %) |
| Jim Weir (R ) | 5,573 (23 %) |

**District Vote For President**

| | 1980 | | 1976 | | 1972 |
|---|---|---|---|---|---|
| **D** | 95,288 (44 %) | **D** | 108,223 (57 %) | **D** | 57,754 (34 %) |
| **R** | 113,704 (53 %) | **R** | 80,655 (43 %) | **R** | 111,777 (66 %) |
| **I** | 4,561 (2 %) | | | | |

## Campaign Finance

| | Receipts | Receipts from PACs | Expenditures |
|---|---|---|---|
| **1980** | | | |
| Emerson (R ) | 283,847 | 84,866 (30 %) | 282,494 |
| Burlison (D ) | 167,439 | 75,900 (45 %) | 210,444 |

## Key Vote

**97th Congress**

| | |
|---|---|
| Reagan budget proposal (1981) | Y |

---

**10th District: Southeast — Cape Girardeau, the Bootheel.** Population: 555,049 (19% increase since 1970). Race: White 527,940 (95%), Black 24,545 (4%), Others 2,564 (0.4%). Spanish origin: 3,146 (1%).

---

# Montana

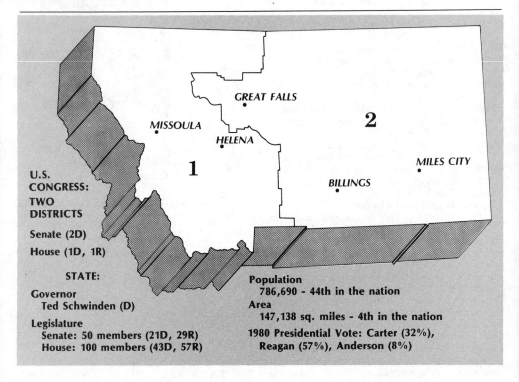

U.S.
CONGRESS:
TWO
DISTRICTS

Senate (2D)

House (1D, 1R)

STATE:

Governor
  Ted Schwinden (D)

Legislature
  Senate: 50 members (21D, 29R)
  House: 100 members (43D, 57R)

Population
  786,690 - 44th in the nation
Area
  147,138 sq. miles - 4th in the nation
1980 Presidential Vote: Carter (32%),
  Reagan (57%), Anderson (8%)

## ... The Legacy of Copper

Montana is the closest thing to a Democratic state anywhere in the Rockies, and for that the party can thank, among others, the Anaconda Copper Company.

During the early years of the century, Anaconda controlled Montana politics. Together with its ally, the Montana Power Company, it handpicked candidates for public office, paid off state legislators and controlled the major newspapers.

The business establishment once split its support between the two parties, but eventually became identified with Republicans. But by the 1920s, progressive Democrats led by Sens. Burton K. Wheeler and Thomas Walsh had disrupted the corporate-imposed harmony, creating a farmer-labor coalition that bucked the mining and power companies. Mine workers in the west and rural cooperatives in the east became the basis of a

strong Democratic Party that still retains power.

On national issues, however, Montana voters are no less conservative than voters in other Mountain states, and they have no reluctance to vote GOP in national elections. Only one Democrat has carried the state for president since 1948. But it is still difficult for a Republican to win statewide office in Montana.

In 56 years of popular Senate elections, there has been only one Republican winner, Zales Ecton in 1946. He was turned out of office by Mike Mansfield in 1952. Democrats have held the governorshp since 1968.

In recent years, coal mining and oil drilling have come to Montana, changing the state the way they have changed other parts of the West. Montana grew 13 percent in the 1970s, its fastest growth in recent decades, with population surges in small towns near the new oil and coal fields.

700

# A Political Tour

**Eastern Plains.** This is flat country — a land of sizzling summer heat and numbing winter cold, given over to wheat growing, cattle raising and, more recently, energy development. Covering three-quarters of the state, the plains usually favors Republicans.

Billings, with a population of 67,000, is the state's largest city. Originally a farming center today Billings is headquarters for the many energy ventures sprouting across the plains. Billings is a Republican town.

Coal discoveries in Rosebud County, east of Billings, have brought in many newcomers. The county grew 64 percent in the last decade, the largest increase of any county in the state. The political result has been to render this former GOP bastion into a marginal political area.

The sparsely populated ranching counties in the southeast corner of the state, most of which are losing population, are among the most Republican in the state. This area went for Barry Goldwater in 1964 and backed losing Republican state candidates through the 1970s.

In the northeast part of the state, between the Canadian border and the Missouri River, are the eight wheat-growing "High Line" counties. While they usually vote Republican in presidential contests, the wheat farmers of the region still side with Democratic statewide candidates.

**Western Mountains.** As the plains climb up into the Rocky Mountains the electorate becomes more heavily unionized and more Democratic.

The two most predictably Democratic counties in the state sit on the Divide, just south of the state capital, Helena. Silver Bow (Butte) and neighboring Deer Lodge (Anaconda) counties were the only two in the state to vote for the Democratic presidential candidates in 1972 and 1980. Dependent upon the copper mines, both counties are heavily unionized. But as huge shovels continue to dig away the copper, zinc and lead from "the richest hill on earth," the manpower needs continue to shrink, forcing many miners out of work. Deer Lodge County lost 20 percent of its population in the 1970s; Silver Bow, 9 percent.

Great Falls, the largest city in the western half of the state, has a large blue-collar population which often yields Democratic majorities, except at the presidential level. The wheat and livestock farmers nearby vote Republican, offsetting the city's Democratic majority.

Missoula is a university and lumbering town. The political strength of the university community often gives the county of a Democratic bent. Although Carter did not win the county in 1980, it was one of the few in Montana where Reagan received less than 50 percent of the vote.

North of Missoula is a mixture of Democratic logging areas and Republican counties devoted to ranching and growing cherries. The counties south of Missoula tend to be Democratic.

# Redrawing the Line

The line that divides Montana's two districts will be redrawn in 1983 by a redistricting commission that has three Democrats and two Republicans. Only minor adjustments are needed. Democrat Pat Williams' western 1st District must give about 16,700 people to Republican Ron Marlenee's eastern 2nd District.

# Governor
# Ted Schwinden (D)

**Born:** Aug. 31, 1925, Wolf Point, Mont.
**Home:** Helena, Mont.
**Education:** Montana School of Mines, 1946-47; U. of Mont., B.A. 1949, M.A. 1950; U. of Minn., 1950-54.
**Military Career:** Army, 1943-46.
**Profession:** Rancher, grain farmer.
**Family:** Wife, Jean; three children.
**Religion:** Lutheran.
**Political Career:** Montana House, 1959-61; commissioner of state lands, 1969-76; lieutenant governor, 1977-81; elected governor 1980; term expires Jan. 1985.

# John Melcher (D)

### Of Forsyth — Elected 1976

**Born:** Sept. 6, 1924, Sioux City, Iowa.
**Education:** Iowa State U., D.V.M. 1950.
**Military Career:** Army, 1943-45.
**Profession:** Veterinarian.
**Family:** Wife, Ruth Klein; five children.
**Religion:** Roman Catholic.
**Political Career:** Forsyth Board of Aldermen, 1953-55; mayor of Forsyth, 1955-61; Mont. House, 1961-63, 1969; Mont. Senate, 1963-67; U.S. House, 1969-77; Democratic nominee for U.S. House, 1966.

**In Washington:** Melcher is a man with all the blunt stubbornness of the Montana plains, but with an instinct for the political center.

His Senate work, like his earlier House career, has focused on wheat, forestry and mining, the issues of Montana's livelihood, and Melcher can defend any of them with a long-winded tenacity, even past the point when the fight is lost.

Early in 1981, as President Reagan and Congress slashed at the federal budget, Melcher introduced an omnibus farm bill that would have added at least a dollar a bushel to the price of wheat, and was generally far more costly than the farm program about to be cut.

"America's farmers and ranchers simply needed more income," Melcher told the Senate. He admitted that some might find his bill inflationary. "To that," he added, "I say, nuts."

But when his Agriculture or Energy Committee crafts a compromise, he rarely says nuts. He likes to be in on it. He has managed to compile a record on forestry issues pragmatic enough to keep him on friendly terms with both the timber industry and the Sierra Club.

In 1976, Melcher's last year in the House, he was the manager of the Land Policy and Management Act, which set standards for the use of 450 million acres of federal land. That bill drew criticism from conservationists, who said it was drawn to the wishes of mining and grazing interests, and from free-enterprise conservatives, who thought it would mean too many restriction. But Melcher defended it as rational conservation, and he had the votes to get it through, although just barely.

Melcher worked in both the House and Senate on strip-mine legislation, requiring operators to return mined land to its former condition. Montana, with the nation's largest coal reserves, had the strictest state mining laws. Without federal law, the state was at a disadvantage compared with those that gave operators greater leeway.

While Melcher was in the House, two strip-mine bills cleared Congress but were vetoed by President Ford. In 1977, his first year in the Senate, the legislation finally became law. Melcher's main Senate contribution was an amendment allowing strip mining in Western river valleys only if it did not disrupt farming or water supplies. That language was tougher on mine operators than the original Senate language, but milder than the earlier House bill. Like much of what he proposes, Melcher described it as a "middle ground," and it passed, 58-13.

In 1980, Melcher and environmentalists took on Democratic leader Robert C. Byrd of West Virginia, who wanted to weaken the 1977 measure. Melcher threatened a filibuster against Byrd's scheme. He was unable to block Senate approval of the changes, but they later died in the House.

When he is not working on mining or forests, Melcher likes to pursue the issue of animal health. As the only veterinarian in Congress, he rarely misses a chance to press for more money for animal health research, expressing his own values and pleasing ranchers who benefit from it. In 1980 he also took up a religious freedom issue, steering a bill through Congress that delighted Seventh-day Adventists — and angered some elements of labor. Melcher's bill allowed Adventists and other workers with religious objections to ignore federal labor laws requiring employees of a union shop to join the union and pay its dues. Workers have to donate to charity the money that would have gone for union dues.

**At Home:** Long regarded as the heir-apparent to Democratic Sen. Mike Mansfield, Melcher got his chance when Mansfield retired in 1976.

He had little trouble defeating conservative Republican Stanley C. Burger, thus keeping the Democratic record of success intact. Republicans have won only one Senate contest in Montana since the first popular election in 1914.

Burger spoke the conservatism that Montana often expresses in national elections, but Melcher's personal popularity was an insurmountable obstacle. Melcher's militance in behalf of wheat growers has always helped him in normally-Republican eastern Montana, which he represented in the House, and his work on strip-mine legisla-

tion had brought him a wide reputation in the western part of the state. He had strong support from the AFL-CIO and Mine Workers.

Beginning his political career on the Forsyth City Council, Melcher moved up to mayor and then went to the state Legislature. After losing a campaign for Congress in 1966, he came back to win a special election in June, 1969, when 1st District Republican James Battin resigned to become a judge. He barely won that contest, but has exceeded 60 percent in each campaign since then.

## Committees

**Agriculture, Nutrition and Forestry** (4th of 8 Democrats)
Agricultural Production, Marketing and Stabilization of Prices; Forestry, Water Resoures, and Environment; Nutrition.

**Energy and Natural Resources** (7th of 9 Democrats)
Energy Regulation; Public Lands and Reserved Water; Water and Power.

**Select Indian Affairs** (Ranking Democrat)

**Special Aging** (3rd of 7 Democrats)

## Elections

**1976 General**

| | |
|---|---|
| John Melcher (D ) | 206,232 (64 %) |
| Stanley Burger (R ) | 115,213 (36 %) |

**1976 Primary**

| | |
|---|---|
| John Melcher (D ) | 89,413 (89 %) |
| Roy Gulick (D ) | 11,593 (11 %) |

**Previous Winning Percentages**

1974* (63 %)   1972* (76 %)   1970* (64 %)   1969† (51%)

*House elections.
†Special House election.

## Campaign Finance

| | Receipts | Receipts from PACs | Expenditures |
|---|---|---|---|
| **1976** | | | |
| Melcher (D ) | $321,596 | $143,535 (45 %) | *$311,101 |
| Burger (R ) | $578,826 | $61,652 (11 %) | $563,543 |

*Expenditures do not include $6,043 in transfers to his office account and $1,122 in contributions to various local party committees.

## Voting Studies

| | Presidential Support | | Party Unity | | Conservative Coalition | |
|---|---|---|---|---|---|---|
| Year | S | O | S | O | S | O |
| **Senate service** | | | | | | |
| 1980 | 45 | 47 | 59 | 26 | 31 | 53 |
| 1979 | 57 | 35 | 66 | 28 | 41 | 55 |

| Year | S | O | S | O | S | O |
|---|---|---|---|---|---|---|
| 1978 | 53 | 40 | 57 | 37 | 44 | 53 |
| 1977 | 72 | 23 | 54 | 36 | 52 | 39 |
| **House service** | | | | | | |
| 1976 | 29 | 65 | 64 | 24 | 39 | 50 |
| 1975 | 31 | 61 | 77 | 17 | 35 | 57 |
| **1974 (Ford)** | 44 | 41 | | | | |
| 1974 | 47 | 51 | 81 | 14 | 26 | 72 |
| 1973 | 29 | 58 | 76 | 12 | 26 | 64 |
| 1972 | 51 | 27 | 67 | 12 | 20 | 60 |
| 1971 | 37 | 54 | 78 | 12 | 18 | 75 |
| 1970 | 62 | 31 | 74 | 15 | 20 | 68 |
| 1969 | 56 | 41† | 91 | 7† | 22 | 75† |

S = Support          O = Opposition
*Not eligible for all recorded votes.

## Key Votes

**96th Congress**

| | |
|---|---|
| Maintain relations with Taiwan (1979) | N |
| Reduce synthetic fuel development funds (1979) | N |
| Impose nuclear plant moratorium (1979) | Y |
| Kill stronger windfall profits tax (1979) | Y |
| Guarantee Chrysler Corp. loans (1979) | Y |
| Approve military draft registration (1980) | N |
| End Revenue Sharing to the states (1980) | N |
| Reagan budget proposal (1981) | Y |

**97th Congress**

| | |
|---|---|
| Restore urban program funding cuts (1981) | Y |

## Interest Group Ratings

| Year | ADA | ACA | AFL-CIO | CCUS-1 | CCUS-2 |
|---|---|---|---|---|---|
| **Senate service** | | | | | |
| 1980 | 50 | 13 | 88 | 46 | |
| 1979 | 58 | 15 | 89 | 18 | 33 |
| 1978 | 45 | 39 | 63 | 8 | |
| 1977 | 65 | 15 | 84 | 24 | |
| **House service** | | | | | |
| 1976 | 75 | 15 | 74 | 40 | |
| 1975 | 74 | 22 | 86 | 18 | |
| 1974 | 65 | 33 | 82 | 30 | |
| 1973 | 76 | 19 | 82 | 40 | |
| 1972 | 50 | 20 | 82 | 0 | |
| 1971 | 78 | 19 | 83 | - | |
| 1970 | 68 | 35 | 71 | 11 | |
| 1969 | 78† | 29† | 75† | - | |

†Not eligible for all recorded votes.

*Montana - Junior Senator*

# Max Baucus (D)

**Of Missoula — Elected 1978**

**Born:** Dec.11, 1941, Helena, Mont.
**Education:** Stanford U., B.A. 1964, LL.B. 1967.
**Profession:** Lawyer.
**Family:** Wife, Ann Gerascimos; one child.
**Religion:** United Church of Christ.
**Political Career:** Mont. House, 1973-75; U.S. House, 1975-79.

**In Washington:** Baucus' concern for Montana interests has dominated his career in the Senate, as it did in the House, helping him at home but limiting his visibility at the national level.

He has always managed good committee assignments — Appropriations in his first House term, Finance as a freshman senator — and used them to help encourage federal investment in Montana. That orientation has allowed him to compile a relatively liberal overall voting record without serious electoral difficulty so far.

As a member of the Senate Judiciary Committee, Baucus has managed to please the American Civil Liberties Union and other groups normally placed on the political left. But he has always tempered his voting record with fiscal conservatism and a concern for business. In the House, he was labeled one of the most frugal legislators by the National Taxpayers Union, an award he used to advantage in his Senate contest.

Voting on the oil windfall profits tax in 1979 as a member of the Senate Finance Committee, he generally allied himself with producer interests, and with Russell Long of Louisiana, then the panel's chairman. When Republicans introduced a compromise amendment in committee providing a limited tax exemption for small-scale "stripper" oil wells, Baucus joined Long in voting for it, against the majority of committee Democrats. When the windfall issue reached the Senate floor, he successfully sponsored an amendment to extend tax credits to companies producing natural gas from so-called "tight sand" — an energy source considered hard to get.

But Baucus' major effort in the Finance Committee during the 96th Congress involved health insurance. He sponsored a new program of federal certification for private insurance policies sold to supplement Medicare. Like most of Baucus' legislative work, this had a Montana connection. Senior citizens in the state had complained to him about misleading insurance promotions. The insurance industry fought his plan, but he moved it through to enactment.

At the same time, Baucus was promoting legislation to maintain the bankrupt Chicago, Milwaukee, St. Paul and Pacific Railroad, which serves Montana, and arguing for higher wheat price supports. As a House member, he once showed colleagues a movie on wheat farming made by Montana college students.

On the Judiciary Committee, Baucus is ranking minority member of the Separation of Powers Subcommittee. In April of 1981, when subcommittee Chairman John P. East, R-N.C., decided to hold hearings on an anti-abortion bill, Baucus criticized him for refusing to include pro-abortion witnesses among those testifying.

Baucus declined even to attend the first hearing.

Then, after private discussions with East and some help from Republican senators, Baucus won his point, and the subcommittee held extensive hearings on abortion.

In the 96th Congress, Baucus was one of the most active members of a special Judiciary panel investigating Billy Carter's ties with Libya.

**At Home:** The son of a wealthy Helena ranching family, Baucus used his good looks and personal charm to rise rapidly in Montana politics. After working in Washington as a lawyer for the Securities and Exchange Commission, he returned home to serve as coordinator of the state constitutional convention in 1972. The same year, he won his state legislative seat.

In 1974, Baucus moved up to the U.S. House, dislodging Republican Richard G. Shoup, who was trying for a third term. To gain publicity for the race, Baucus walked 631 miles across his congressional district. He managed to impress the labor-oriented Democrats who dominate the party in western Montana, and he did little to antagonize Republicans. He was a comfortable winner over Shoup in 1974, and an easy winner for re-election in 1976.

Meanwhile, he was focusing on the Senate. His hopes were temporarily frustrated in early 1978 by Democratic Gov. Thomas L. Judge, a political rival. After the death of veteran Democrat Lee Metcalf, the governor bypassed Baucus and appointed Paul Hatfield, chief justice of the Montana Supreme Court, to succeed Metcalf in the Senate.

But Baucus had already begun his 1978 Senate campaign, and he did not step aside for Hatfield. The newly appointed senator could not match his head start in organizing, and hurt himself by voting for the Panama Canal treaties. Baucus did not oppose the treaties, but he did not have to vote on the issue. He won their primary easily.

That fall, he had a hard-nosed Republican competitor in financier Larry Williams, who castigated him as too liberal and ridiculed his awards from the Taxpayers Union as meaningless. Baucus was hurt by charges of outside liberal influence in his campaign, and Williams seemed on the verge of overtaking him by early October.

Then Baucus' Democratic allies released their "bombshell" — a picture of the "conservative" Williams in long hair and love beads, taken before he moved from California to Montana to launch his campaign. Baucus kept his distance from the issue, but the AFL-CIO made sure the picture was all over Montana in the weeks before the election. The final result was not close.

## Committees

**Environment and Public Works** (7th of 7 Democrats)
Nuclear Regulation; Toxic Substances and Environmental Oversight; Water Resources.

**Finance** (6th of 9 Democrats)
Health; International Trade; Oversight of the Internal Revenue Service.

**Judiciary** (7th of 8 Democrats)
Agency Administration; Courts; Separation of Powers.

**Small Business** (5th of 8 Democrats)
Productivity and Competition.

## Elections

**1978 General**

| | |
|---|---|
| Max Baucus (D ) | 160,353 (56 %) |
| Larry Williams (R ) | 127,589 (44 %) |

**1978 Primary**

| | |
|---|---|
| Max Baucus (D ) | 87,085 (65 %) |
| Paul Hatfield (D ) | 25,789 (19 %) |
| John Driscoll (D ) | 18,184 (14 %) |

**Previous Winning Percentages**

1976* (66 %)   1974* (55 %)

*House elections

## Campaign Finance

| | Receipts | Receipts from PACs | Expenditures |
|---|---|---|---|
| **1978** | | | |
| Baucus (D ) | $668,189 | $168,220 (25 %) | $653,756 |
| Williams (R ) | $352,848 | $84,216 (24 %) | $346,721 |

## Voting Studies

| | Presidential Support | | Party Unity | | Conservative Coalition | |
|---|---|---|---|---|---|---|
| Year | S | O | S | O | S | O |
| **Senate service** | | | | | | |
| 1980 | 78 | 17 | 83 | 12 | 14 | 83 |
| 1979 | 65 | 25 | 78 | 13 | 24 | 68 |
| **House service** | | | | | | |
| 1978 | 52 | 26 | 55 | 23 | 29 | 51 |
| 1977 | 66 | 29 | 80 | 14 | 25 | 69 |
| 1976 | 25 | 73 | 80 | 15 | 31 | 65 |
| 1975 | 26 | 70 | 86 | 11 | 19 | 79 |

S = Support       O = Opposition

## Key Votes

**96th Congress**

| | |
|---|---|
| Maintain relations with Taiwan (1979) | N |
| Reduce synthetic fuel development funds (1979) | Y |
| Impose nuclear plant moratorium (1979) | ? |
| Kill stronger windfall profits tax (1979) | N |
| Guarantee Chrysler Corp. loans (1979) | Y |
| Approve military draft registration (1980) | Y |
| End Revenue Sharing to the states (1980) | Y |
| Block Justice Dept. busing suits (1980) | N |

**97th Congress**

| | |
|---|---|
| Restore urban program funding cuts (1981) | N |

## Interest Group Ratings

| Year | ADA | ACA | AFL-CIO | CCUS-1 | CCUS-2 |
|---|---|---|---|---|---|
| **Senate service** | | | | | |
| 1980 | 72 | 16 | 82 | 35 | |
| 1979 | 63 | 12 | 89 | 18 | 31 |
| **House service** | | | | | |
| 1978 | 40 | 35 | 79 | 33 | |
| 1977 | 65 | 23 | 65 | 24 | |
| 1976 | 75 | 19 | 74 | 19 | |
| 1975 | 74 | 18 | 91 | 12 | |

# 1 Pat Williams (D)

### Of Helena — Elected 1978

**Born:** Oct. 30, 1937, Helena, Mont.
**Education:** U. of Denver, B.A. 1961.
**Military Career:** Army, 1960-61; National Guard, 1962-69.
**Profession:** Educational administrator.
**Family:** Wife, Carol Griffith; three children.
**Religion:** Roman Catholic.
**Political Career:** Mont. House, 1967-71; Unsuccessfully sought Democratic nomination for U.S. House, 1974.

**In Washington:** The godfather of one of Pat Williams' children is a Montana labor leader, and that relationship symbolizes the political ties that helped bring Williams to Congress and keep him in office. Williams has not disappointed his union allies often on major issues, although his AFL-CIO rating dropped to 67 during the 1980 election year.

When he arrived in 1979, Williams put together committee assignments that fit his interests and his district. He took Education and Labor as his first choice, and then signed up for Interior, which oversees mining legislation, parks and wilderness areas critical to Montana.

Most of his work on education has been defensive, trying to stop the Carter and Reagan administrations from cutting school aid, especially child nutrition programs. Williams has argued that both school breakfast and lunch programs should continue without cutbacks.

He also defends the Occupational Safety and Health Administration, a favorite target of critics who say it has overregulated business and burdened it with too many detailed forms and requirements. To Williams, the agency is a basic protection against dangerous work. He also favors a strong Mine Safety and Health Administration.

Williams' philosphical differences with the Reagan administration were dramatized in 1981 when he and Labor Secretary Raymond J. Donovan got into a shouting match at a committee hearing. Williams said the past Democratic administrations deserved credit for making the distribution of national wealth more equal." "No," said Donovan, "that is what Russia is all about."

On Interior, Williams has a chance to deal with issues related to the state's mining boom. Like most Mountain State legislators of both parties, he has been critical of synthetic fuels development, citing possible environmental damage and excessive use of limited water supplies.

Synthetic fuels also would compete with coal, whose interests he tries to protect.

Williams was one of only 25 members who voted against President Carter's synfuels program when it passed the House in 1979. The next year, after it had been modified only slightly by a conference committee, he voted for it, although still warning that it represented "a full-speed, breakneck attitude toward the development of an energy technology yet unproven."

Williams backed one 1980 floor amendment favorable to the mining industry but criticized by environmentalists. It suspended federal regulation of less-toxic mineral production wastes, such as smelting slag.

He has generally sided with environmentalists, however, on the issue of creating wilderness areas. In 1981, he sponsored a resolution in Interior ordering the Reagan Interior Department to withdraw 1.5 million acres of national forest in Montana from mineral leasing. "The oil companies are physically poised 20 yards from this great wilderness complex," Williams warned.

**At Home:** While districts all over the mountain West were voting Republican in 1978, Williams was able to win a comfortable victory over a strong Republican opponent, keeping the open 1st District in Democratic hands.

Williams had been active in Montana politics for a decade before coming to Congress. His political career was temporarily derailed in 1974,

---

**1st District: Missoula, Butte.** Population: 410,071 (18% increase since 1970). Race: White 392,202 (96%), Black 448 (0.1%), Indian 14,091 (4%), Others 3,330 (1%). Spanish origin: 3,978 (1%).

when he lost the Democratic congressional nomination to Max Baucus, but when Baucus ran for the Senate in 1978, Williams had another shot at the House. He entered a multi-candidate primary, blessed with strong labor backing. Williams campaigned on the need for more jobs in western Montana, but also on the need to keep the district's industry clean. He won the nomination with 40.7 percent of the vote.

Before 1978, Williams had filled a variety of positions besides serving two terms in the state Legislature. He was Montana director of Hubert Humphrey's presidential campaign in 1968 and chairman of the Carter campaign in western Montana in 1976. He spent two years on Capitol Hill as an aide to Democrat John Melcher, then representing Montana's other district in the House, now the state's senior senator.

**The District:** Montana's mountainous 1st District is the center of the state's mining industry. The mines attracted a large Irish Catholic population whose influence is still felt in the district's politics, helping Democratic candidates like Williams.

Since 1918, when Montana was split into two congressional districts, Republicans have won the western 1st only five times — in 1920, 1938, 1940, 1970 and 1972. However, Democratic dominance is not overwhelming, and Republicans usually manage to attract a strong minority vote.

In national politics, there is no real Democratic advantage at all. In both 1976 and 1980, the 1st has gone Republican at the presidential level by about the same margin as the eastern district.

## Committees

**Education and Labor** (15th of 19 Democrats)
  Elementary, Secondary and Vocational Education; Human Resources; Labor Standards.

**Interior and Insular Affairs** (19th of 23 Democrats)
  Energy and the Environment; Public Lands and National Parks.

## Elections

**1980 General**

| | |
|---|---|
| Pat Williams (D) | 112,866 (61%) |
| John McDonald (R) | 70,874 (39%) |

**1980 Primary**

| | |
|---|---|
| Pat Williams (D) | 56,532 (75%) |
| Bill Hand (D) | 18,620 (25%) |

**1978 General**

| | |
|---|---|
| Pat Williams (D) | 86,016 (57%) |
| Jim Waltermire (R) | 64,093 (43%) |

**1978 Primary**

| | |
|---|---|
| Pat Williams (D) | 29,966 (41%) |
| Dorothy Bradley (D) | 20,381 (28%) |
| John Lynch (D) | 7,853 (11%) |
| George Turman (D) | 5,472 (7 %) |
| Gary Kimble (D) | 5,232 (7 %) |
| John Bartlett (D) | 4,769 (6 %) |

**District Vote For President**

| | 1980 | | 1976 | | 1972 |
|---|---|---|---|---|---|
| D | 64,393 (33%) | D | 77,885 (46%) | D | 65,384 (40%) |
| R | 107,574 (55%) | R | 90,124 (53%) | R | 92,166 (56%) |
| I | 16,316 (8%) | | | | |

## Campaign Finance

| | Receipts | Receipts from PACs | Expenditures |
|---|---|---|---|
| **1980** | | | |
| Williams (D) | $151,034 | $74,487 (49%) | $144,030 |
| McDonald (R) | $35,731 | $1,354 (4 %) | $35,717 |

| 1978 | | | |
|---|---|---|---|
| Williams (D) | $177,712 | $40,379 (23%) | $177,536 |
| Waltermire (R) | $244,129 | $41,759 (17%) | $241,888 |

## Voting Studies

| | Presidental Support | | Party Unity | | Conservative Coalition | |
|---|---|---|---|---|---|---|
| Year | S | O | S | O | S | O |
| 1980 | 59 | 29 | 67 | 21 | 33 | 61 |
| 1979 | 56 | 40 | 67 | 26 | 36 | 63 |

S = Support          O = Opposition

## Key Votes

**96th Congress**

| | |
|---|---|
| Weaken Carter oil profits tax (1979) | N |
| Reject hospital cost control plan (1979) | N |
| Implement Panama Canal Treaties (1979) | N |
| Establish Department of Education (1979) | N |
| Approve Anti-busing Amendment (1979) | N |
| Guarantee Chrysler Corp. loans (1979) | Y |
| Approve military draft registration (1980) | Y |
| Aid Sandinista regime in Nicaragua (1980) | N |
| Strengthen fair housing laws (1980) | ? |

**97th Congress**

| | |
|---|---|
| Reagan budget proposal (1981) | N |

## Interest Group Ratings

| Year | ADA | ACA | AFL-CIO | CCUS |
|---|---|---|---|---|
| 1980 | 72 | 18 | 67 | 66 |
| 1979 | 79 | 25 | 80 | 33 |

# 2 Ron Marlenee (R)

### Of Scobey — Elected 1976

**Born:** Aug. 8, 1935, Scobey, Mont.
**Education:** Attended Mont. State U. and U. of Mont.
**Profession:** Rancher.
**Family:** Wife, Cynthia Tiemann; three children.
**Religion:** Lutheran.
**Political Career:** No previous office.

**In Washington:** Like most of the Western Republicans on the Interior Committee, Marlenee brings to his work a deeply rooted resentment of federal government control over most of his state's land.

An individualist by temperament as well as belief, Marlenee has not been a coalition builder on Interior, or a strategist for Republican forces. But he has rarely left much doubt about his point of view.

He is a true believer in the Sagebrush Rebellion, and a critic of the Interior Department's Bureau of Land Management (BLM). In 1980, when the House considered a bill establishing new rules for the preservation of farmland, Marlenee saw it as more interference by BLM, which he calls the largest and most flagrant abuser of federal land.

"What is needed is simple," he insisted, "local control, not the federal government running around telling the local people how to manage their land."

In the 96th Congress, he offered a successful floor amendment exempting some rural communities from new federal restrictions on the open dumping of solid waste. He worked for legislation to ease federal regulations on rural Montana hospitals.

On the Agriculture Committee, however, Marlenee has been militant in his pleas for relief for his district's farmers, even if the source is the federal government. During his first year in the House, he was one of six members of the Agriculture Committee to vote against omnibus farm legislation on the grounds that its wheat price supports were too low.

Two years later, when the committee raised the target price for wheat to $3.63 a bushel, Marlenee offered an amendment to make it $4.00 a bushel, despite the Carter administration's promise to veto any bill with a price that high. When the bill reached the House floor, where it passed by voice vote, Marlenee scorned it as a pittance that would be of little use to farmers facing ruinous credit conditions.

**At Home:** Marlenee ran for Congress as a successful rancher from the northeastern corner of Montana. He started farming in 1953 with 320 acres of leased land, and built a successful wheat and Hereford cattle operation known as "Marlenee's Big Sky Ranch." As his ranch grew, he began working with the Montana Stockgrowers, with the state political arm of the American Farm Bureau Federation, and with the Montana Grain Growers.

He was also a familiar name in Republican Party circles, but he had never run for office before making his 1976 congressional bid. So he started early, announcing before incumbent Democrat John Melcher had indicated his own intention to run for the Senate. Marlenee had to work against the fact that he came from a rural area remote from most of the district's population, while his major primary opponent, former state legislator John Cavan, came from Billings, the district's largest city.

But Marlenee overcame Cavan, and went on to win in the fall against Democrat Tom Towe, whose family banking fortune allowed him to run a well-financed campaign, but whose populist approach disturbed some of the district's more conservative Democrats. Marlenee has been re-elected twice by comfortable but not overwhelming margins.

---

**2nd District: East — Billings, Great Falls.** Population: 376,619 (9% increase since 1970). Race: White 347,946 (92%), Black 1,338 (0.3%), Indian 23,179 (6%), Others 4,156 (1%). Spanish origin: 5,996 (2%).

---

**The District:** Covering the vast expanse of eastern Montana, the 2nd is the largest district in any state that has districts. It is the traditionally Republican of the state's two constituencies, a predominantly agricultural area dominated by wheat farming and stock raising.

The city of Great Falls is generally Democratic, and Billings, the largest city, has a signifi-cant Democratic vote, but any Democrat must break into the rural Republican strength to win. John Melcher, Marlenee's House predecessor and the current U.S. senator, was able to do that very well.

The district did not grow as much as the western 1st during the past decade and needs to gain about 15,000 people in redistricting.

## Committees

**Agriculture** (6th of 19 Republicans)
Forests, Family Farms, and Energy; Wheat, Soybeans and Feed Grains.

**Interior and Insular Affairs** (6th of 17 Republicans)
Oversight and Investigations; Public Lands and National Parks.

## Elections

**1980 General**

| | |
|---|---|
| Ron Marlenee (R ) | 91,431 (59 %) |
| Tom Monahan (D ) | 63,370 (41 %) |

**1978 General**

| | |
|---|---|
| Ron Marlenee (R ) | 75,766 (57 %) |
| Tom Monahan (D ) | 57,480 (43 %) |

**Previous Winning Percentage**

1976 (55 %)

**District Vote For President**

| | 1980 | | 1976 | | 1972 |
|---|---|---|---|---|---|
| D | 53,639 (32%) | D | 71,374 (45%) | D | 54,813 (36%) |
| R | 99,240 (59%) | R | 83,579 (53%) | R | 91,810 (60%) |
| I | 12,965 (8%) | | | | |

## Campaign Finance

| | Receipts | Receipts from PACs | Expenditures |
|---|---|---|---|
| **1980** | | | |
| Marlenee (R ) | $239,309 | $65,344 (27 %) | $214,917 |
| Monahan (D ) | $36,702 | $17,500 (48 %) | $36,699 |

| 1978 | | | |
|---|---|---|---|
| Marlenee (R ) | $298,774 | $52,837 (18 %) | $286,863 |
| Monahan (D ) | $27,020 | $11,950 (44 %) | $27,019 |

## Voting Studies

| | Presidential Support | | Party Unity | | Conservative Coalition | |
|---|---|---|---|---|---|---|
| Year | S | O | S | O | S | O |
| 1980 | 34 | 58 | 83 | 10 | 86 | 7 |
| 1979 | 30 | 62 | 75 | 18 | 81 | 12 |
| 1978 | 25 | 65 | 68 | 25 | 77 | 20 |
| 1977 | 34 | 58 | 67 | 20 | 77 | 14 |

S = Support          O = Opposition

## Key Votes

**96th Congress**

| | |
|---|---|
| Weaken Carter oil profits tax (1979) | Y |
| Reject hospital cost control plan (1979) | Y |
| Implement Panama Canal Treaties (1979) | N |
| Establish Department of Education (1979) | N |
| Approve Anti-busing Amendment (1979) | Y |
| Guarantee Chrysler Corp. loans (1979) | Y |
| Approve military draft registration (1980) | N |
| Aid Sandinista regime in Nicaragua (1980) | N |
| Strengthen fair housing laws (1980) | N |

**97th Congress**

| | |
|---|---|
| Reagan budget proposal (1981) | Y |

## Interest Group Ratings

| Year | ADA | ACA | AFL-CIO | CCUS |
|---|---|---|---|---|
| 1980 | 22 | 83 | 32 | 68 |
| 1979 | 21 | 92 | 32 | 72 |
| 1978 | 25 | 85 | 26 | 76 |
| 1977 | 20 | 73 | 19 | 80 |

# Nebraska

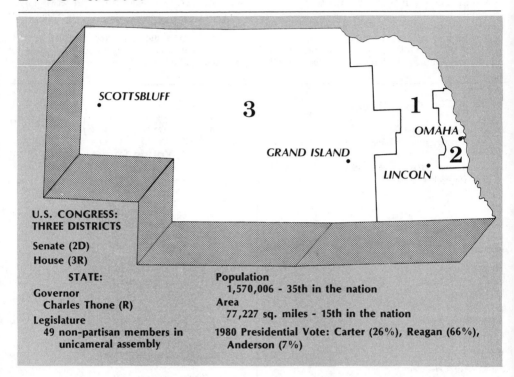

SCOTTSBLUFF
•

3

1

OMAHA
•

GRAND ISLAND
•

2

LINCOLN
•

**U.S. CONGRESS:**
**THREE DISTRICTS**

**Senate (2D)**
**House (3R)**

**STATE:**
**Governor**
**Charles Thone (R)**
**Legislature**
**49 non-partisan members in**
**unicameral assembly**

**Population**
**1,570,006 - 35th in the nation**
**Area**
**77,227 sq. miles - 15th in the nation**

**1980 Presidential Vote: Carter (26%), Reagan (66%),**
**Anderson (7%)**

## ... A Taste for the Stubborn

Nebraska knows what it likes in politics — stubborn, independent, common sense conservatives — and lately it has not worried too much about which party they belong to.

In national elections, Nebraska has been the most consistent Republican stronghold of modern times. Only one Democrat has carried it for president in the last 44 years. And for most of the postwar years, Nebraska behaved pretty much the same way in voting for Congress. From 1934 to 1976, it did not elect a single Democrat to the Senate.

Some would say it did not elect one in 1976 either. The Democratic nominee that year was Edward J. Zorinsky, the mayor of Omaha and a lifelong Republican. Zorinsky filed for the Democratic nomination only because Omaha congressman John Y. McCollister had the Republican primary sewed up. But once on the general election ballot, Zorinsky was an easy winner, and he

serves in the Senate today as a Democrat.

In 1978, the other Senate seat switched parties for Gov. J. James Exon, a legitimate Democrat but one nearly as conservative as Zorinsky. That meant two Nebraska Democrats in the Senate for the first time in the state's history.

As Zorinsky proved, party is not very strong these days in Nebraska, the only state with a non-partisan Legislature. He and Exon both spoke for the low tax, low deficit philosophy of the state's farmers and ranchers, and of the increasingly conservative Omaha middle class. Both express their irritation at big government with a crankiness that goes over well all over the state. Candidates who carry that message can win on any ticket.

It was different in the early part of this century, when the two best-known Nebraska politicians were the populist William Jennings Bryan and the progressive George Norris. Bryan and

Norris depended on struggling family farmers who sought to make a living on marginal land and usually found themselves dependent on the federal government for help. By World War II, most of this constituency had simply left. Nebraska suffered a net loss of more than 50,000 people between 1930 and 1950, while most other states were gaining, and the people remaining tended to be the more prosperous and conservative residents.

Nebraska is gaining population again now, although its 5.7 percent increase during the 1970s was smaller than the average gain nationwide. But it remains an overwhelmingly agricultural state. Agriculture provides employment, directly or indirectly, for over 80 percent of its 1,570,000 residents. Nebraska is one of the national leaders in beef cattle, corn, wheat and hogs. Its leading industries, meatpacking and food processing, are farm-related.

# A Political Tour

**Omaha.** Omaha is Nebraska's dominant city. Located on the state's eastern border, across the Missouri River from Council Bluffs, Iowa, the city itself has 312,000 residents. More than 30 percent of the state's population, almost half a million people, lives in the Nebraska portion of the Omaha metropolitan area, which includes Douglas and Sarpy counties.

Omaha is famous for its stockyards that serve the cattle, hog and sheep growers of Nebraska. Although meat packing, dairy products and food processing are the major industries, the economy is diversified. Omaha is an insurance center and the headquarters of the Union Pacific Railroad.

Although Omaha is an ethnic industrial city and nominal Democratic territory, it votes for conservatives. The blue-collar population, heavily Irish and Slavic, resembles that of ethnic areas in other Midwestern cities but has weaker Democratic Party ties. Omaha does have a substantial black community, which boosts the Democratic vote.

In gubernatorial contests, Democrats usually do well in Omaha. They have carried it and surrounding Douglas County in seven of the last eight elections. But the county has gone Republican for president every time but once in the post-Roosevelt era, and has had Republican representation in the House for all but four of the past 30 years. It elected Democrat John J. Cavanaugh to the House in 1976 and 1978, but when he retired in 1980, the Omaha-based 2nd District reverted to Republican control.

**Lincoln.** Lincoln is Nebraska's capital and second largest city, with 172,000 residents in the city and another 25,000 in the surrounding Lancaster County metropolitan area.

Republicans hold a majority in Lincoln, but there is a significant Democratic vote based around the university and the state government. Democrats here tend to be white-collar workers and more liberal than the ones in Omaha.

With the help of a strong showing in Lincoln, George McGovern beat Hubert Humphrey in the 1972 Nebraska Democratic primary. But in 1980, Lincoln stayed with Jimmy Carter rather than taking the liberal alternative provided by Sen. Edward M. Kennedy.

In recent years Lancaster County has been slightly more Republican than Omaha in statewide elections, although Democrats have carried it in six of the last 10 gubernatorial contests. The present GOP governor, Charles Thone, who comes from Lincoln, carried it with 60 percent in 1978.

In presidential elections, Lincoln remains staunchly Republican. Republicans have won 10 of the last 11 presidential races in Lincoln, losing only with Barry Goldwater in 1964. Since World War II, GOP presidential candidates have averaged almost 60 percent of the vote in Lancaster County.

**Rural Nebraska.** Nebraska's farmers raise corn, hogs and dairy cattle in the east, feed beef cattle in the the arid north-central "Sand Hills," and grow wheat in the west and south, in fields irrigated by the Platte and Niobrara rivers.

Rural Nebraska has just over half of the state's population, about 800,000 people. Nebraska's small country towns sprang up along the Platte River system or along the rail lines that spread across the state. With the further mechanization of farming, rural residents have been leaving their farms and moving into these towns.

The largest city outside Omaha and Lincoln is Grand Island. Located 90 miles west of Lincoln, Grand Island is an industrial city and trading center of 33,000 people. Most of the other cities of any size are enlarged market towns that service the surrounding farmland.

Of the 90 counties in rural Nebraska, 58 have fewer than 10,000 residents. Four counties in the Sand Hills ranching region have less than 1,000 people.

Republicans normally carry the whole of rural Nebraska comfortably. GOP candidates do well in the small cities and even better on the farms.

The most Republican county in the state is

Hooker County (pop. 990) in the Sand Hills. Richard Nixon took 88 percent of the Hooker County vote in 1968 and 1972. Barry Goldwater won 71 percent in 1964. No postwar Democrat has carried Hooker County in a major statewide race.

Rural Nebraska was once a major breeding ground of populism, but that was long ago. However, the farmers still occasionally express their anger at the ballot box. In the 1980 Democratic primary, Kennedy ran best in the farming counties, largely because of the farmers' anger over President Carter's Soviet grain embargo rather than for any endorsement of Kennedy's liberal views.

There are a few pockets of regular Democratic votes in rural Nebraska. The largest is Saline County, southwest of Lincoln, with a population of 13,000. Others are Butler County, adjoining Lancaster County on the northwest, and a lightly populated tri-county area in central Nebraska — Greeley, Sherman and Howard counties.

# Redrawing the Lines

The disparity between Nebraska's most populous district (the Omaha 2nd) and its least populous (the western 3rd) is only 12,414 people. Republicans at first suggested that district boundaries be left as they are. But when Democrats threatened to file suit in federal court demanding equalization of populations, the GOP proposed a remap that involved only two counties and did no harm to the three Republican representatives.

The new map, signed into law May 28, 1981, by Gov. Thone, moves the western half of Cass County from the 2nd District to the 1st and shifts Thayer County from the 1st district to the 3rd.

## Governor
## Charles Thone (R)

**Born:** Jan. 4, 1924, Hartington, Neb.
**Home:** Lincoln, Neb.
**Education:** U. of Nebraska College of Law, LL.B. 1950.
**Military Career:** Army, 1942-45.
**Profession:** Lawyer.
**Family:** Wife, Ruth; three children.
**Religion:** Presbyterian.
**Political Career:** Assistant U.S. district attorney in Lincoln, 1952-54; administrative assistant to former U.S. Sen. Roman Hruska, 1954-59; unsuccessful campaign for lieutenant governor, 1964; U.S. House, 1971-79; elected governor 1978; term expires Jan. 1983.

# Edward Zorinsky (D)

**Of Omaha — Elected 1976**

**Born:** Nov. 11, 1928, Omaha, Neb.
**Education:** U. of Neb., B.S. 1949.
**Military Career:** Army Reserve, 1952-66.
**Profession:** Candy and tobacco wholesaler.
**Family:** Wife, Cece Rottman; three children.
**Religion:** Jewish.
**Political Career:** Omaha Public Power District
Board, 1968-73; Mayor of Omaha, 1973-77.

**In Washington:** Zorinsky is unpredictable.
He is a lifelong Republican who switched to run
as a Democrat for the Senate and considered
switching again when Republicans gained control
in 1981. He threatened to quit the Senate in
frustration six weeks after he arrived but announced a year in advance that he wanted a
second term.

It would not have taken much work for
Zorinsky to return to his old party for the 97th
Congress. Senate Majority Leader Howard H.
Baker Jr. phoned him the morning after the
election, offering him the GOP label. The idea
interested him. Over four years in the Senate he
had voted with the Republicans most of the time
anyway — more often, in fact, than any other
Democrat except Harry F. Byrd Jr., who hardly
counts because he runs in Virginia as an
independent.

But Zorinsky's second conversion failed to
work out. Nebraska Republicans said they did not
want him and Zorinsky promptly backed away.
"I'm not accustomed to going to parties I'm not
invited to," he said.

So Zorinsky remains a nominal Democrat and
a member of the minority on Foreign Relations.
His most unusual battle there has been on behalf
of aid for Nicaragua, in which he became interested as chairman of the Western Hemisphere
Subcommittee in the 96th Congress. He argued
that U.S. financial aid would shore up Nicaragua's
economy, encouraging the left-wing Sandinista
government to hold open elections. An aid cutoff,
he warned, would force the Sandinistas into the
arms of the communists.

Fellow conservatives disputed Zorinsky's
view, arguing the Sandinista rebels were communists already. When Reagan moved into the
White House and concluded the Sandinistas were
allowing arms to reach leftist guerrillas in neighboring El Salvador, Zorinsky backed off and
agreed that aid should be suspended.

Zorinsky's decision to join Foreign Relations
was something of a surprise in 1979. Not long
before, he had shunned a trip to Red China with a
wisecrack ("Offhand, I can't think of one person
in Mainland China who voted for me in the last
election....") But once on the committee, he
changed his mind about foreign travel and made
China his first stop.

Zorinsky has cultivated an image as a fiscal
conservative, although he has been selective about
it. One of his first acts as a member of the
Agriculture Committee was to write a letter to
President Carter urging higher price supports for
wheat. In his one term on the Commerce Committee, he threatened to oppose deregulation of the
airlines because he felt the bill being considered
would spend too much money protecting the jobs
of airline employees.

Zorinsky likes to make conspicuous application of his fiscal principles in operating his office.
He mails out no newsletters, saying he can make
his views known through press releases printed
free in Nebraska newspapers. He refuses to hire
the maximum staff allowed or to pay them the
maximum salary. For a while he had an aide
steaming uncanceled stamps from incoming mail
and reusing them, until he learned that was
against the law.

**At Home:** Zorinsky's conversion from the
Republican Party, his home of 20 years, had a lot
to do with pique.

In late 1975, he was the mayor of Omaha and
wanted to move to the Senate. But retiring Republican Sen. Roman L. Hruska had anointed
Rep. John Y. McCollister as his successor. Frustrated, Zorinsky switched to the Democrats — a
move that was not too surprising, as he never had
been strongly identified with either party. As
mayor, Zorinsky prided himself on his non-partisan image.

He won a bitter Democratic senatorial primary against that party's former state chairman, Hess Dyas. At first, Dyas and many of his liberal supporters in the university and state government community around Lincoln were angry about the victory of this outsider.

But tempers cooled after the May primary. By midsummer, Dyas was saying that although Zorinsky was an "S.O.B.," nevertheless, "he is our S.O.B.," and preferable to McCollister. Zorinsky also had the active backing of Democratic Gov. J. James Exon, later a senator.

Zorinsky's nomination took McCollister by surprise, and he never recovered from it. The Republican had been preparing to run against a liberal Democrat, not a conservative one. He tried in vain to link Zorinsky to liberalism, pointing to the Democrat's endorsement by organized labor.

McCollister's district encompassed Omaha, the state's largest city. But this Republican advantage was neutralized when the Democrats nominated the Omaha mayor.

A major share of Zorinsky's victory came from Omaha, which is Democratic, though conservative. As mayor, he became very popular there for his handling of twin disasters in 1975 — a tornado and later a blizzard, which wrecked parts of the city. A tobacco wholesaler, he brought business management techniques to City Hall that earned him wide praise.

Criticism for party-switching does not appear to bother Zorinsky. He once joked that when Republicans called him turncoat and Democrats called him opportunist, "I told them they both were right."

## Committees

**Agriculture, Nutrition and Forestry** (3rd of 8 Democrats)
Agricultural Credit and Rural Electrification; Agricultural Production, Marketing and Stabilization of Prices; Foreign Agricultural Policy.

**Foreign Relations** (5th of 8 Democrats)
Arms Control, Oceans and International Operations, and Environment; European Affairs; Western Hemisphere Affairs.

## Elections

**1976 General**

| | |
|---|---|
| Edward Zorinsky (D ) | 313,809 (52 %) |
| John McCollister (R ) | 284,284 (48 %) |

**1976 Primary**

| | |
|---|---|
| Edward Zorinsky (D ) | 79,988 (49 %) |
| Hess Dyas (D) | 77,384 (47 %) |

## Campaign Finance

| | Receipts | Receipts from PACs | Expenditures |
|---|---|---|---|
| **1976** | | | |
| Zorinsky (D ) | $240,904 | $52,963 (22 %) | $237,613 |
| McCollister (R ) | $391,289 | $113,083 (29 %) | $391,287 |

## Voting Studies

| | Presidential Support | | Party Unity | | Conservative Coalition | |
|---|---|---|---|---|---|---|
| Year | S | O | S | O | S | O |
| 1980 | 53 | 44 | 35 | 62 | 87 | 10 |
| 1979 | 53 | 47 | 37 | 63 | 70 | 30 |
| 1978 | 45 | 53 | 39 | 60 | 69 | 29 |
| 1977 | 66 | 33 | 40 | 57 | 75 | 22 |

S = Support          O = Opposition

## Key Votes

**96th Congress**

| | |
|---|---|
| Maintain relations with Taiwan (1979) | N |
| Reduce synthetic fuel development funds (1979) | N |
| Impose nuclear plant moratorium (1979) | N |
| Kill stronger windfall profits tax (1979) | Y |
| Guarantee Chrysler Corp. loans (1979) | N |
| Approve military draft registration (1980) | Y |
| End Revenue Sharing to the states (1980) | Y |
| Block Justice Dept. busing suits (1980) | Y |

**97th Congress**

| | |
|---|---|
| Restore urban program funding cuts (1981) | N |

## Interest Group Ratings

| Year | ADA | ACA | AFL-CIO | CCUS-1 | CCUS-2 |
|---|---|---|---|---|---|
| 1980 | 22 | 62 | 32 | 79 | |
| 1979 | 21 | 63 | 37 | 73 | 69 |
| 1978 | 25 | 74 | 16 | 72 | |
| 1977 | 25 | 69 | 40 | 67 | |

# J. James Exon (D)

### Of Lincoln — Elected 1978

**Born:** Aug., 9, 1921, Geddes, S.D.
**Education:** Attended U. of Omaha, 1939-41.
**Military Career:** Army, 1942-45.
**Profession:** Office equipment dealer.
**Family:** Wife, Patricia Ann Pros; three children.
**Religion:** Episcopalian.
**Political Career:** Neb. Governor, 1971-79.

**In Washington:** When Commerce Secretary Malcolm Baldrige appeared before the Senate Commerce Committee in confirmation hearings, Exon chided him for a serious error in judgment — having the bad sense to leave Nebraska.

That is a move Exon has never come close to making, not even in spirit. His perspective in Congress remains that of a small-business man from the Grain Belt, which he used to be. He is a conservative who questions federal programs — except for some that are sacred in his home state — with a homespun skepticism that has always appealed to Nebraskans.

Exon's common-sense manner has survived terms on the Armed Services and Budget committees, panels which sometimes convert their members into technicians. On both those committees, and on Commerce, his third assignment, he is regarded as a backbencher, but an attentive one.

The Budget Committee has given Exon a chance to demonstrate the anti-tax, anti-spending philosophy that carried him into the Nebraska statehouse.

In 1980, he sponsored an unsuccessful amendment in committee to drastically reduce the budget for federally assisted housing. But the Budget Committee agreed to an Exon amendment reducing its target for government operating expenses by 5 percent. In order to win liberal support, Exon specifically included the Defense Department in his across-the-board cutback. Like other conservatives, however, he later supported additions to the Defense budget which more than made up for it.

In 1981, Exon proved skeptical of President Reagan's massive tax cut proposals; he tried to interest the Budget Committee in a scheme to make second- and third-year tax reductions contingent on success in reducing the federal deficit.

Despite his relative hard line on defense issues, Exon has not become an automatic vote on the Armed Services Committee for weapons requests. He does not have an insider's mastery of, or fascination with, the language, theories and hardware of national security. In the committee's public hearings, Exon asks the questions of a well-prepared amateur.

In the 96th Congress, Exon was assigned by the Armed Services Committee to study airlift and sealift components of President Carter's proposed Rapid Deployment Force. He decided the administration's proposed C-X transport, meant to move forces quickly to trouble spots, was inadequate and overpriced. But the committee overrode his objections and granted most of the funding request for the plane.

The committee also rejected his suggestion for a resolution reaffirming limits on presidential power to commit troops. But after Carter sent an abortive rescue mission to Iran, Exon was able to sell his resolution in the full Senate.

Exon is solicitous of the grain industry, which makes up a substantial portion of his constituency. On the Commerce Committee, he is best known for cosponsoring, with Republican Nancy Kassebaum of Kansas, an amendment to the 1980 rail deregulation bill protecting farmers from shipping rates that would rise and fall with demand. Exon also swallowed his fiscal austerity and offered an amendment to a synthetic fuels bill nearly doubling the subsidy for gasohol, produced from grain.

Exon had continual problems with President Carter over farm policy, and declined to endorse him for renomination because he thought the administration had not done enough for farmers. He initially defended Carter's decision to stop grain sales to the Soviet Union, in response to the invasion of Afghanistan, saying the embargo was "a whole lot better than sending boys over to enforce what we think is right." But by October of 1980, the embargo had become violently unpopular with farmers, and Exon voted for a rider that

**715**

sought to reopen the grain trade.

**At Home:** Exon has had a paradoxical political career. A partisan Democratic governor in a Republican state, he bickered continually with the nominally non-partisan but GOP-controlled Legislature. Yet he achieved a popularity that few Nebraska governors ever have attained, chiefly by keeping a tight hold on state spending and speaking up for the state's farmers.

Born in South Dakota, Exon went into the office supply business in Lincoln, Nebraska, in the 1950s, and began doing local Democratic Party chores. By the mid-1960s he was one of the better-known Democratic functionaries in a state that has never had an abundance of them. He was state coordinator of Lyndon B. Johnson's 1964 presidential campaign, and in 1968 he became Democratic national committeeman.

In 1970, public disenchantment over the newly enacted state income and sales taxes gave Exon his big break. The tax issue crippled Republican incumbent Norbert T. Tiemann's bid for a second term. Tiemann was nearly unseated by a primary challenger, and Exon took advantage of the same issues in ,the fall to oust him by 46,558 votes.

Exon had no problem turning back Republican state Sen. Richard D. Marvel in 1974. His fiscal austerity produced a state government surplus that year, and while Republicans could argue about how the money might be spent, they could not prevent their own voters from crossing party lines to endorse the governor's policies.

The 1978 Senate campaign was nearly as easy. Republican Carl T. Curtis chose to retire after four terms, and his former aide, Donald E. Shasteen, was overmatched against Exon from the start. Desperate for attention, Shasteen attracted quite a bit of it by charging that the Exon administration had used improper influence to help the governor's office equipment firm. Exon denounced the charges as "the slime of Shasteen," and they were never documented. The Democrat drew two-thirds of the vote.

## Committees

**Armed Services** (7th of 8 Democrats)
Manpower and Personnel; Military Construction; Strategic and Theater Nuclear Forces.

**Budget** (10th of 10 Democrats)

**Commerce, Science and Transportation** (7th of 8 Democrats)
Aviation; Business, Trade, and Tourism.

## Elections

**1978 General**

| | |
|---|---|
| J. James Exon (D ) | 334,276 (68 %) |
| Donald Shasteen (R ) | 159,806 (32 %) |

## Campaign Finance

| | Receipts | Receipts from PACs | Expenditures |
|---|---|---|---|
| **1978** | | | |
| Exon (D ) | $262,404 | $63,250 (24 %) | $234,862 |
| Shasteen (R ) | $222,190 | $16,349 (7 %) | $218,148 |

## Voting Studies

| | Presidential Support | | Party Unity | | Conservative Coalition | |
|---|---|---|---|---|---|---|
| Year | S | O | S | O | S | O |
| 1980 | 67 | 33 | 51 | 48 | 90 | 10 |
| 1979 | 68 | 32 | 59 | 34 | 54 | 31 |

S = Support          O = Opposition

## Key Votes

**96th Congress**

| | |
|---|---|
| Maintain relations with Taiwan (1979) | N |
| Reduce synthetic fuel development funds (1979) | N |
| Impose nuclear plant moratorium (1979) | N |
| Kill stronger windfall profits tax (1979) | N |
| Guarantee Chrysler Corp. loans (1979) | N |
| Approve military draft registration (1980) | Y |
| End Revenue Sharing to the states (1980) | Y |
| Block Justice Dept. busing suits (1980) | Y |

**97th Congress**

| | |
|---|---|
| Restore urban program funding cuts (1981) | N |

## Interest Group Ratings

| Year | ADA | ACA | AFL-CIO | CCUS-1 | CCUS-2 |
|---|---|---|---|---|---|
| 1980 | 39 | 44 | 37 | 50 | |
| 1979 | 21 | 39 | 38 | 36 | 40 |

# 1 Douglas K. Bereuter (R)

**Of Utica — Elected 1978**

**Born:** Oct. 6, 1939, York, Neb.
**Education:** U. of Neb., B.A. 1961; Harvard U., M.C.P. 1963, M.P.A. 1973.
**Military Career:** Army, 1963-65.
**Profession:** Urban planner; automobile and hardware dealer.
**Family:** Wife, Louise Anna Meyer; two children.
**Religion:** Lutheran.
**Political Career:** Neb. Senate, 1975-79.

**In Washington:** An urban moderate with an interest in city planning, Bereuter spent much of his first House term arguing about rural land issues on the Interior Committee. Then he found the spot he wanted on Banking, which authorizes most of the urban and housing legislation in Congress.

Bereuter remains a member of the Energy Subcommittee at Interior, where he has taken an interest in nuclear power. He is neither rigidly opposed nor enthusiastically in favor. He voted to support a moratorium on new nuclear plant licenses following the Three Mile Island accident in 1979 but opposed killing off the Clinch River breeder reactor as requested by Carter.

On Interior, he also played a role in one of the committee's most controversial fights of 1980, over changes in a 1902 reclamation law designed to help small farmers by limiting federally subsidized water to large agribusiness concerns.

Lobbied heavily by agribusiness groups, Interior at first rejected proposals to place a limit of 1,600 acres on the amount of land a farmer could lease and still draw federal subsidies. Bereuter was among the majority against the limit. But the following week he reversed himself, and his vote helped create a narrow majority for a compromise at 2,400 acres. The bill cleared committee but, plagued by dissent among its sponsors and opposition from the White House, it never reached the floor.

As a professional urban planner, Bereuter had been anxious to get on Banking since he first arrived on Capitol Hill, but had to wait his turn until May of 1981. He joined the committee the day it was voting on a housing bill and, except for one minor amendment, consistently supported Reagan administration spending cuts and housing policy changes. He offered one amendment of his own — to rescue a comprehensive planning program for small communities by shifting it to community development block grants.

In the 96th Congress, Bereuter fought to stop the federal government from gathering detailed information on the cost of hospital care. He became involved after a hospital official from his district complained the data collection was costly and unnecessary. Waving a 600-page manual, Bereuter said the system would only add to hospital and patient costs. He convinced the House to kill the plan by denying the money to carry it out.

Although Bereuter voted with his party's conservative House majority much of the time during his first term, he established his closest contacts with the small moderate faction among junior GOP members. He joined the Wednesday Group, which has long been the spiritual home for moderate House Republicans.

On a few crucial 1980 votes, Bereuter showed an independent streak. He differed with Republican majorities, for example, by opposing some cutbacks in foreign aid and refusing to weaken a proposed new open housing law.

**At Home:** Bereuter's background is unusual for a Nebraska politician. He took an early interest in urban affairs, and held the state's top city planning post under moderate Republican Gov. Norbert Tiemann from 1969 to 1971.

While he used conservative rhetoric during his 1978 congressional campaign, he was still looked upon as a moderate because of his

---

**1st District: East central — Lincoln.**
Population: 525,386 (6% increase since 1970). Race: White 511,727 (97%), Black 4,023 (1%), Others 9,636 (2%). Spanish origin: 4,807 (1%).

## Douglas K. Bereuter, R-Neb.

Tiemann connections. That helped him among Lincoln voters in the Republican primary, in which he had to defeat state Sen. Loran Schmit, a militant conservative oriented toward the rural areas of the district. Bereuter beat Schmit only by carrying Lancaster County (Lincoln) overwhelmingly. He lost the rest of the district. In November, he had an easier time, drawing united Republican support and a large independent vote. He was an easy winner again in 1980.

**The District:** The state capital and university town of Lincoln gives a moderate urban flavor to the 1st, which is otherwise solid Corn Belt country, prosperous and Republican. Lincoln is essentially a white-collar town, dominated by the academic and governmental communities, although there are also meatpacking and rubber products industries.

The other towns in the district, such as York, Norfolk and Beatrice, are mostly market centers closely tied to agriculture.

The last two presidential elections have been no contest in the 1st. Ford, a native Nebraskan and a moderate-sounding Republican, drew 57 percent of the vote against Jimmy Carter. By 1980, Carter had virtually no appeal in the rural parts of the district, and Reagan did even better — 61 percent.

## Committees

**Interior and Insular Affairs** (9th of 17 Republicans)
Energy and the Environment; Insular Affairs; Water and Power Resources.

**Banking, Finance and Urban Affairs** (19th of 19 Republicans)
Economic Stabilization; General Oversight and Renegotiation; Housing and Community Development.

## Elections

**1980 General**

| | |
|---|---|
| Douglas Bereuter (R ) | 160,705 (79 %) |
| Rex Story (D ) | 43,605 (21 %) |

**1978 General**

| | |
|---|---|
| Douglas Bereuter (R ) | 99,013 (58 %) |
| Hess Dyas (D ) | 71,311 (42 %) |

**1978 Primary**

| | |
|---|---|
| Douglas Bereuter (R ) | 34,790 (52 %) |
| Loran Schmit (R ) | 31,559 (48 %) |

**District Vote For President**

| | 1980 | | 1976 | | 1972 |
|---|---|---|---|---|---|
| D | 61,954 (29 %) | D | 82,586 (40 %) | D | 66,018 (33 %) |
| R | 133,971 (62 %) | R | 117,192 (57 %) | R | 133,300 (67 %) |
| I | 17,612 (8 %) | | | | |

## Campaign Finance

| | Receipts | Receipts from PACs | Expenditures |
|---|---|---|---|
| **1980** | | | |
| Bereuter (R ) | $187,343 | $59,474 (32 %) | $175,876 |
| Story (D ) | $14,592 | $7,800 (53 %) | $14,592 |

| 1978 | | | |
|---|---|---|---|
| Bereuter (R ) | $172,896 | $61,053 (35 %) | $167,688 |
| Dyas (D ) | $164,452 | $39,165 (24 %) | $164,227 |

## Voting Studies

| | Presidential Support | | Party Unity | | Conservative Coalition | |
|---|---|---|---|---|---|---|
| Year | S | O | S | O | S | O |
| 1980 | 53 | 44 | 76 | 23 | 72 | 26 |
| 1979 | 46 | 53 | 75 | 25 | 78 | 22 |

S = Support        O = Opposition

## Key Votes

**96th Congress**

| | |
|---|---|
| Weaken Carter oil profits tax (1979) | Y |
| Reject hospital cost control plan (1979) | Y |
| Implement Panama Canal Treaties (1979) | N |
| Establish Department of Education (1979) | N |
| Approve Anti-busing Amendment (1979) | N |
| Guarantee Chrysler Corp. loans (1979) | Y |
| Approve military draft registration (1980) | Y |
| Aid Sandinista regime in Nicaragua (1980) | Y |
| Strengthen fair housing laws (1980) | Y |

**97th Congress**

| | |
|---|---|
| Reagan budget proposal (1981) | Y |

## Interest Group Ratings

| Year | ADA | ACA | AFL-CIO | CCUS |
|---|---|---|---|---|
| 1980 | 33 | 74 | 32 | 79 |
| 1979 | 32 | 73 | 25 | 89 |

# 2 Hal Daub (R)

**Of Omaha — Elected 1980**

**Born:** April 23, 1941, Omaha, Neb.
**Education:** Washington University, St. Louis, B.S. 1963; University of Nebraska, J.D. 1966.
**Military Career:** Army, 1966-68.
**Profession:** Lawyer; feed company executive.
**Family:** Wife, Cindy Shin; three children.
**Religion:** Presbyterian.
**Political Career:** Douglas County Republican chairman, 1974-77; unsuccessful Republican nominee for U.S. House, 1978.

**The Member:** Daub's single-minded pursuit of Democratic Rep. John J. Cavanaugh ended suddenly in December of 1979, when the 35-year-old incumbent announced he was retiring to spend more time with his large family. With Cavanaugh out of the way, Daub could concentrate on the much easier task of winning an open seat in a Republican year. He won comfortably, defeating an experienced Democrat who matched his conservatism on many issues.

In 1981, Daub has opposed efforts to eliminate the federal impact aid program, which provides financial assistance to school districts in federally affected areas. His district contains the Strategic Air Command headquarters at Offut Air Force Base, and elimination of impact aid would cost his area about $6 million in federal money.

Daub gradually deepened his involvement in local GOP politics over a decade in which most of his time was spent building a business career.

After law school and the Army, Daub joined an Omaha law firm. In 1971, he switched to the Standard Chemical Manufacturing Company, for which he was vice president and general counsel.

Meanwhile, he became Douglas County Republican party treasurer (1970-73) and chairman (1974-77). He initially said he would not run for office until he was financially secure. But in 1978, a bit ahead of schedule, he took on Cavanaugh and drew 47.7 percent, more than had been expected.

**The District:** With about 70 percent of the district's population, Omaha dominates the 2nd politically. An old railroad and meatpacking center, it has expanded to become an insurance capital as well. While the city is considered Democratic, that label means little in congressional elections. Many of the city's Irish and East European ethnics, especially those who have left the inner city, have been voting Republican for a generation. Cavanaugh's election in 1976 marked the first time a Democrat won the seat since 1948.

## Committees

**Government Operations** (12th of 17 Republicans)
Commerce, Consumer, and Monetary Affairs; Government Activities and Transportation.

**Select Aging** (18th of 23 Republicans)
Health and Long-Term Care.

**Small Business** (12th of 17 Republicans)
Antitrust and Restraint of Trade Activities Affecting Small Business; SBA and SBIC Authority, Minority Enterprise and General Small Business Problems.

## Elections

**1980 General**

| | |
|---|---|
| Hal Daub (R ) | 107,736 (53 %) |
| Richard Fellman (D ) | 88,843 (44 %) |

**1980 Primary**

| | |
|---|---|
| Hal Daub (R ) | 33,306 (61 %) |
| Mike Albert (R ) | 17,874 (33 %) |

**District Vote For President**

| | 1980 | | 1976 | | 1972 |
|---|---|---|---|---|---|
| **D** | 61,632 (30 %) | **D** | 76,075 (39 %) | **D** | 56,211 (31 %) |
| **R** | 125,029 (61 %) | **R** | 115,237 (59 %) | **R** | 124,823 (69 %) |
| **I** | 16,000 (8 %) | | | | |

## Campaign Finance

| | Receipts | Receipts from PACs | Expenditures |
|---|---|---|---|
| **1980** | | | |
| Daub (R ) | $362,135 | $188,591 (52 %) | $360,333 |
| Fellman (D ) | $164,460 | $34,700 (21 %) | $153,539 |

## Key Vote

**97th Congress**

| | |
|---|---|
| Reagan budget proposal (1981) | Y |

> **2nd District: East - Omaha.** Population: 528,517 (7% increase since 1970). Race: White 473,053 (89%), Black 43,686 (8%), Others 11,778 (2%). Spanish origin: 10,771 (2%).

# 3 Virginia Smith (R)

**Of Chappell — Elected 1974**
**Born:** June 30, 1911, Randolph, Iowa.
**Education:** U. of Neb., B.A. 1934.
**Profession:** Farmer.
**Family:** Husband, Haven Smith.
**Religion:** Methodist.
**Political Career:** No previous office.

**In Washington:** Smith has spent her House career marching in a different direction from most of her female colleagues.

Already 63 when she was elected, she initially wanted to be known not as "Virginia" but as Mrs. Haven Smith, using the first name of the Nebraska wheat farmer to whom she had been married for 43 years. While other women have been using their House offices to promote affirmative action and other feminist causes, Smith has consistently reflected old-fashioned Nebraska values, speaking up in her high-pitched, grandmotherly voice for wheat and cattle, and for a new dam in her district.

Occasionally there has been common ground. When the 1976 tax law included a "carry-over provision" effectively increasing inheritance taxes on farmland, Smith lobbied for its repeal among the other women members, telling them the law would be catastrophic for the widows who usually inherit the property. Eventually 14 of 16 signed.

Mostly, however, Smith is interested in meat. She was on the National Cattle and Livestock Board in the 1950s, and normally says what the Nebraska cattle producers are saying. At one point, she attacked a Carter administration agriculture appointee for being "an avowed vegetarian." In 1978, when the House passed a bill making it more difficult for the president to lift meat import quotas, Smith argued that the bill's 10-year life span was too short, and that the change should be permanent. The House agreed to do that.

Besides defending farm interests on the Agriculture Appropriations Subcommittee, Smith has tried to protect a major Nebraska dam, the O'Neill unit of the Missouri Basin project. the dam may be in trouble. It routinely clears the Energy and Water Appropriations Subcommittee, on which Smith sits, but it has been having increasing difficulty on the floor. In 1980, both of Nebraska's other congressmen tried to drop money for the project, on the argument that it would eventually cost $200 million and help only 480 farms. Smith's side won, but only by 211-202.

In the 96th Congress, Smith was also on the Appropriatons panel dealing with foreign aid. There she reflected traditional Midwest Republican skepticism about spending money abroad. In 1978, she argued against the year's foreign aid bill on the issue of pure constituent feeling. "It's their money," she said. The next year, she offered an amendment to reduce the American contribution to the African Development Fund from $43 million to $26 million, but the amendment lost.

**At Home:** For a quarter of a century, Smith was an inveterate clubwoman, active not only in Nebraska but in national farm politics and Republican affairs. She spent 20 years on the board of directors of the American Farm Bureau Federation, and was chairman of its leading women's group. She was a county GOP chairman at home and a delegate to Republican national conventions.

So name recognition was no problem for her when she ran for Congress in 1974, even though she had held no public office. She survived two virtually even contests to become the first woman elected to the House from Nebraska.

Incumbent Republican Rep. Dave Martin retired that year, causing a wide-open GOP primary. Eight candidates entered, with Smith's main competition coming from Don Blank, a dentist and former mayor of McCook, and state Sen. Gerald Stromer, former president of the Nebraska Young Republicans. The finish between

---

**3rd District: Central and West — Grand Island, Hastings.** Population: 516,103 (4% increase since 1970). Race: White 505,789 (98%), Black 680 (0.1%), Others 9,634 (2%). Spanish origin: 12,442 (2%).

Smith and Blank was so close that a recount was necessary. Smith emerged the victor by 141 votes.

Democrats chose former state Sen. Wayne Ziebarth as their nominee. Ziebarth had run a statewide race for the Democratic Senate nomination in 1972 and was well-known throughout the district. And 1974 was a good Democratic year, even in Nebraska. But toward the end of the campaign Ziebarth made a fatal mistake: he remarked that women do not belong in politics. The statement rebounded against him and probably cost him the election. Smith won by only 737 votes out of over 160,000 cast. With that first victory behind her, Smith has sailed through her re-election bids with ease.

**The District:** Smith's district consists of three-quarters of the state's land area. It includes part of the corn belt in the eastern portion, then slowly shifts to wheat and ranching as it progresses westward to the Wyoming and Colorado borders. The area's few small cities, such as Grand Island and Hastings, are service centers for the surrounding agricultural population.

The district has a Republican tradition, but the marginal nature of the land and weather makes the area vulnerable to economic decline, and a bad year can turn the voters in a radical direction quickly. Democrats turned out incumbent Republican representatives in both 1958 and 1964.

## Committees

Appropriations (13th of 22 Republicans)
Agriculture; Energy and Water Development

## Elections

**1980 General**

| | |
|---|---|
| Virginia Smith (R ) | 182,887 (84 %) |
| Stan Ditus (D ) | 34,967 (16 %) |

**1978 General**

| | |
|---|---|
| Virginia Smith (R ) | 141,597 (80 %) |
| Marilyn Fowler (D ) | 35,371 (20 %) |

**Previous Winning Percentages**

1976 (73 %)    1974 (50 %)

**District Vote For President**

| | 1980 | | 1976 | | 1972 |
|---|---|---|---|---|---|
| D | 43,104 (20 %) | D | 75,031 (36 %) | D | 47,762 (24 %) |
| R | 160,712 (74 %) | R | 127,276 (61 %) | R | 148,175 (76 %) |
| I | 11,383 (5 %) | | | | |

## Campaign Finance

| | Receipts | Receipts from PACs | Expenditures |
|---|---|---|---|
| **1980** | | | |
| Smith (R ) | $113,009 | $34,158 (30 %) | $93,496 |
| Ditus (D ) | $16,482 | $2,000 (12 %) | $15,970 |
| **1978** | | | |
| Smith (R ) | $66,731 | $16,775 (25 %) | $66,795 |
| Fowler (D ) | $41,554 | $2,550 (6 %) | $40,313 |

## Voting Studies

| | Presidential Support | | Party Unity | | Conservative Coalition | |
|---|---|---|---|---|---|---|
| Year | S | O | S | O | S | O |
| 1980 | 43 | 55 | 82 | 16 | 92 | 8 |
| 1979 | 30 | 68 | 86 | 10 | 90 | 7 |
| 1978 | 29 | 59 | 82 | 11 | 88 | 6 |
| 1977 | 43 | 56 | 83 | 12 | 91 | 7 |
| 1976 | 71 | 27 | 89 | 7 | 87 | 6 |
| 1975 | 64 | 31 | 90 | 8 | 94 | 5 |

S = Support          O = Opposition

## Key Votes

**96th Congress**

| | |
|---|---|
| Weaken Carter oil profits tax (1979) | Y |
| Reject hospital cost control plan (1979) | Y |
| Implement Panama Canal Treaties (1979) | N |
| Establish Department of Education (1979) | N |
| Approve Anti-busing Amendment (1979) | Y |
| Guarantee Chrysler Corp. loans (1979) | N |
| Approve military draft registration (1980) | Y |
| Aid Sandinista regime in Nicaragua (1980) | N |
| Strengthen fair housing laws (1980) | N |

**97th Congress**

| | |
|---|---|
| Reagan budget proposal | Y |

## Interest Group Ratings

| Year | ADA | ACA | AFL-CIO | CCUS |
|---|---|---|---|---|
| 1980 | 11 | 78 | 6 | 85 |
| 1979 | 11 | 96 | 15 | 88 |
| 1978 | 10 | 78 | 5 | 76 |
| 1977 | 10 | 85 | 17 | 94 |
| 1976 | 0 | 82 | 14 | 78 |
| 1975 | 5 | 93 | 9 | 94 |

# Nevada

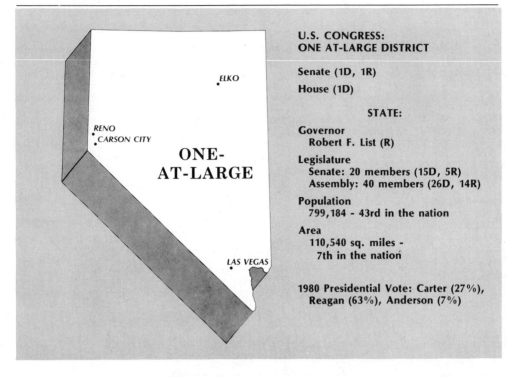

**U.S. CONGRESS:**
**ONE AT-LARGE DISTRICT**

Senate (1D, 1R)

House (1D)

**STATE:**

Governor
   Robert F. List (R)

Legislature
   Senate: 20 members (15D, 5R)
   Assembly: 40 members (26D, 14R)

Population
   799,184 - 43rd in the nation

Area
   110,540 sq. miles -
   7th in the nation

1980 Presidential Vote: Carter (27%),
   Reagan (63%), Anderson (7%)

ELKO

RENO
CARSON CITY

ONE-
AT-LARGE

LAS VEGAS

## ... Games and Politics

The importance of gambling to Nevada is hard to overemphasize. The gambling industry accounts directly or indirectly for 65 percent of the jobs in Nevada. It brings approximately $2.5 billion into the state each year. When fire gutted the MGM Grand Hotel in Las Vegas in 1980, killing 84 people and laying off the hotel's workforce, the state's unemployment rate jumped by 1.4 percentage points.

Nevada in 1931 was mainly cattle ranches and abandoned silver mines, home to only 91,058 people. Today, fifty years after the legalization of gambling, it is a thriving Sun Belt state with 800,000 residents and the second highest per capita income in the country.

Until the 1950s, Nevada politics was dominated by Reno and the older communities in the northern part of the state. It was generally Democratic but more so because Democrats were the traditional party of silver interests than for any

modern reason.

Both of those traditions began to change with gambling and prosperity. Clark County (Las Vegas) overtook Washoe County (Reno) in population in 1960, and by 1980, it had nearly three times as many people. In the 1980s, Nevada will have two congressional districts for the first time in its history; Clark County is populous enough now to support one district entirely within its borders.

Las Vegas came of age in Nevada politics in 1958, when Howard Cannon, running as a self-proclaimed liberal Democrat, became the city's first U.S. senator. Cannon has changed with Nevada over the years and now votes conservatively, the only way Democrats can vote and survive very long representing the state.

Cannon's first re-election in 1964 was by 48 votes over Republican Paul Laxalt, then the lieutenant governor. In the years since then, Laxalt has won the governorship and two U.S. Senate terms, symbolizing the newest and strongest strain in Nevada politics — opposition to the federal government. The government owns a vast majority of the state's land, and its policies have generated a "Sagebrush Rebellion" to which Laxalt and most Nevada politicians adhere.

The land resentment has erased what was left of Nevada's old Democratic tradition in national elections. Carter drew an embarrassing 26.9 percent of the vote in 1980.

## A Political Tour

**Clark County/Las Vegas.** In forty years Las Vegas has developed from a sleepy town of 10,000 to a neon extravaganza with 165,000 full-time residents. Clark County, including Las Vegas and the surrounding area, has almost 60 percent of the state's population.

Clark County is more diverse demographically than many outsiders realize. It has a substantial Catholic population, more than 40,000 blacks and a large blue-collar community.

Clark County is still reliable territory for most Democrats. Carter carried it by about 3,000 votes against Gerald R. Ford in 1976, although he lost it by a resounding margin to Reagan.

There is a large Mormon community in Clark County, and it provides Republican votes. There is also a strong Republican contingent near Nellis Air Force Base north of the city.

**Reno and Vicinity.** Though dwarfed now by Las Vegas, Reno still has over 100,000 people and is the heart of the northwestern part of the state that includes the state capital of Carson City and Lake Tahoe, a major resort center.

The northern cities of Reno and Sparks and the Lake Tahoe area provide Republicans with their greatest margins in Nevada. If the turnout in Clark County is low or if the contest is close there, the Republican vote in this populated part of the northwest is usually strong enough to swing a statewide election to the GOP.

**The Cow Counties.** The 15 percent of Nevada's people who do not live near Reno or Las Vegas live in the the the Cow Counties — a huge expanse of desert and sagebrush that occupies most of the state.

Cattle raising is the main economic interest there, but silver and gold mining have been making a comeback.

These are old populist Democratic areas, gradually turning Republican in frustration over land and water policies of Democratic administrations. Laxalt is highly popular in the Cow Counties. He carried nearly all of them in his 1974 Senate comeback, and their vote, although light, enabled him to win the 624 vote statewide victory that launched his career in Washington.

## Drawing the Lines

Regional interests triumphed over partisan politics in deciding where to put Nevada's newly-acquired second House district. Northern Nevada Democrats ignored the wishes of Las Vegas Democrats who wanted to anchor both districts in Clark County. Instead they teamed with Republicans to pass a map in June that put the new district in the northern part of the state, where both parties have a chance to win. The southern Nevada district, which includes most of Clark County, is a Democratic stronghold.

## Governor
## Robert F. List (R)

**Born:** Sept. 1, 1936, Visalia, Calif.
**Home:** Carson City, Nev.
**Education:** Utah State U., B.S. 1959; Hastings School of Law, U. of California, LL.D. 1962.
**Profession:** Lawyer.
**Family:** Wife, Kathy; three children.
**Religion:** Presbyterian.
**Political Career:** District attorney, Carson City, 1967-71; state attorney general, 1971-79; elected governor 1978; term expires Jan. 1983.

# Howard W. Cannon (D)

## Of Las Vegas — Elected 1958

**Born:** Jan. 26, 1912, St. George, Utah.
**Education:** Ariz. State Teachers College, B.E. 1933; U. of Ariz., LL.B. 1937.
**Military Career:** Army Air Corps, 1941-46; Air Force Reserve, 1946-75.
**Profession:** Lawyer.
**Family:** Wife, Dorothy Pace; two children.
**Religion:** Mormon.
**Political Career:** Washington County (Utah) Attorney, 1940-41; Las Vegas City Attorney, 1949-58.

**In Washington:** The class of 1958 changed the Senate as few others have in the 20th century, and some of its famous Democratic names — Muskie, McCarthy, Philip Hart — influenced the chamber's debate for years to come. Few would place Howard Cannon in their category. But he has outlasted them all, evolving from the self-proclaimed liberal he was in 1958 to a senator who votes with Republicans and Southern Democrats most of the time. And he has quietly written as much legislation as any member of the class.

Barely known outside his home state, Cannon made himself one of the chamber's pure power brokers, and kept up the role until the 1980 election cost him the Commerce Committee chairmanship. He presided over enactment of an exceptional array of aviation, trucking, railroad, maritime, communications and consumer legislation. Even if his minority status in the 97th Congress limits his impact on bills to come, he has shaped modern transportation policy with the ones already enacted. Some of the most significant economic deregulation measures since the New Deal became law in large part because of Cannon's support.

When he went to conference on transportation bills with the House, sitting alone across from several members of the other body, he had proxies to keep him company — proxies that let him speak unilaterally for the entire Senate. "I don't want to take issue with Howard Cannon unless I have to," Sen. Russell Long once said.

In the 96th Congress, when Cannon announced that trucking deregulation would not move very far in the form President Carter proposed, it did not move. When he changed his mind and told the Interstate Commerce Commission to halt its own deregulation efforts until Congress acted, the ICC backed off and the bill went through.

Cannon is a believer in the politics of compromise, both in dealing with other senators and with the House. When he defeated Long on an important trucking deregulation amendment — the sort of experience few senators have — he kept on working to draft language that Long could claim was at least a partial victory.

Cannon is also a senator who will take what he can get, even if it is substantially short of total victory. He has tried repeatedly, for example, to help the airlines by giving them more flexibility in meeting noise regulations. In 1978, he pushed a bill through the Senate essentially exempting all two-and three-engine planes from strict noise requirements. When the House balked at that, he went along with an exemption for most two-engine planes and a delay for some of the others, and took it back to the Senate as "an acceptable compromise considering the extreme difference in opinion." Airplanes have been a dominant issue in Cannon's career, not only because they are commercially important to Nevada, but because they are personally important to him — he was a decorated fighter pilot in World War II.

On the Armed Services Committee, Cannon has been a consistent advocate of increased defense spending, but especially of spending on the Air Force. Early in his career, he also worked on military personnel issues. The first major legislation he managed on the Senate floor was a $1.2 billion military pay raise in 1963.

Most of Cannon's attention, however, has been on the Commerce Committee. He was a principal author of the 1963 bill providing federal aid for mass transit construction, accepting amendments on the floor that reduced the scope of the bill from $500 million to $375 million, so that it would have the votes to pass. He gradually gained seniority and influence on Commerce through the 1960s and early 1970s, generally helping airlines and other transportation interests but siding with consumers on some major issues: he supported a federal consumer protection agency and a consumer cooperative bank, and he has opposed a legislative veto over FTC regulations. Cannon took over the Commerce chairmanship in late 1977, when Warren G. Magnuson, D-Wash., left it to become chairman of Appropriations. The Nevada Democrat inherited the committee at a time when President Carter was focusing much of his domestic policy on deregulating the transportation industries. Most of Cannon's success in these years were Carter successes as well, although not all the deregulation went as far as Carter originally wanted. The result in 1980 was a transportation network based significantly more on the free market than it was in 1977, and less on federal rules.

Cannon had supported airline deregulation as chairman of the Aviation Subcommittee before there were many other votes for it on Commerce as a whole. He argued for it against the position of most of the airline industry. But he had his doubts about trucking deregulation, and became an active supporter of it only when he feared the ICC would try to do the job on its own.

He was generally favorable to railroad deregulation, which came up in the 97th Congress. His problem was to pacify Long and others who feared its effect on "captive shippers, " public utilities and others who had to use railroads and might be subjected to price gouging. Cannon had the votes on that issue, including a majority of his committee's Republican votes, and Long essentially gave up. The bill did ultimately contain language asking the government to consider the nation's energy needs in looking at the rate structure.

Elements of Cannon's earlier liberal reputation persisted into the 1970s. He managed to win a place on President Nixon's "hit list" following his opposition to the former president's Supreme Court nominations and the initial anti-ballistic missile plan. But he is now one of the most conservative of the Senate's Northern Democrats. In 1980, he backed the "conservative coalition" more than twice as often as he opposed it.

Cannon's reputation suffered in 1980 from implications that he had acted unethically in handling trucking deregulation. Newspapers reported that he was under investigation by federal authorities to determine whether there was a link between his handling of trucking deregulation and his attempt to acquire an interest in a plot of land owned by the a Teamsters union pension fund. The Teamsters were militantly against deregulation. In 1981, Teamsters President Roy

Williams was indicted for trying to bribe Cannon on the issue. But it was never charged that Cannon accepted the bribe, and no action was taken against the senator.

The Senate Ethics Committee cleared him on allegations raised in a *New York Times* article that indicated Cannon had used his position to promote government actions enhancing the value of his property holdings. Cannon called the allegations "a classic example of reckless and irresponsible reporting."

**At Home:** Cannon's ascendancy coincided with the rise of Las Vegas in Nevada politics. The city's vote won him the 1958 election, breaking northern Nevada's traditional hold on the congressional delegation, and allowed him to survive by 48 votes in 1964 against Republican Paul Laxalt.

The only son of a rancher who had emigrated from England, Cannon became a lawyer and dabbled in local politics in Utah before World War II.

The war made him a hero: Germans shot down the airplane he was piloting over the Netherlands, and he spent 42 days behind enemy lines before allied troops liberated the area.

After the war he moved to Las Vegas, became the city attorney, and remained in the job for ten years. He tried for Nevada's at-large House seat in 1956, and while he lost to Walter Baring in the primary, made a decent showing.

Two years later he decided to try for the Senate, and narrowly won the Democratic nomination over Fred Anderson, a Reno physician who had been favored. Cannon drew labor support and campaigned as the more liberal of the two. When he filed for the Senate, Eleanor Roosevelt canceled plans to raise money for Anderson.

The general election was relatively easy for him against incumbent Republican George "Molly" Malone, who had previously won only in good Republican years — 1946 and 1952. Cannon assailed Malone for his isolationism.

Six years later, Cannon was hurt by reports of his close ties to Bobby Baker, the scandal-plagued Senate secretary. And he had a strong challenger in Laxalt, now his Senate colleague. But he had a good issue against Laxalt in Republican presidential nominee Barry Goldwater. Cannon declared that Goldwater and Laxalt would "set this nation back 50 to 100 years." Lyndon Johnson took 58 percent of the vote against Goldwater in Nevada, and Cannon held on by 48 votes against Laxalt, who did not make it to the Senate for another decade.

The full force of Vice President Spiro T. Agnew's law-and-order campaign descended on Cannon as he sought a third term in 1970. Republican William Raggio, the Washoe County district attorney, brought in Agnew to criticize the Nevada press and link Cannon with "ultra-liberals" guilty of "permissiveness." But the tactic backfired as the state's suspicions turned against Agnew rather than Cannon. The Democrat won his third term by a decisive margin.

Cannon had his easiest time in 1976 against former Republican congressman David Towell, who had lost his House seat after one term two years earlier. Towell came from a sparsely settled "cow county" and had no base in either Reno or Las Vegas. Cannon campaigned on his seniority and influence and took 63 percent of the vote.

# Committees

**Armed Services** (3rd of 8 Democrats)
Military Construction; Strategic and Theater Nuclear Forces; Tactical Warfare.

**Commerce, Science and Transportation** (Ranking Democrat)
Aviation.

**Rules and Administration** (2nd of 5 Democrats)

**Joint Printing**

# Elections

**1976 General**

| | |
|---|---|
| Howard Cannon (D ) | 127,295 (63 %) |
| David Towell (R ) | 63,471 (31 %) |

**1976 Primary**

| | |
|---|---|
| Howard Cannon (D ) | 61,407 (86 %) |
| Other | 10,141 (14 %) |

**Previous Winning Percentages**

1970 (58 %)   1964 (50 %)   1958 (58 %)

# Campaign Finance

| | Receipts | Receipts from PACs | Expenditures |
|---|---|---|---|
| **1976** | | | |
| Cannon (D ) | $422,203 | $85,442 (20 %) | $405,380 |
| Towell (R ) | $54,842 | $3,500 (6 %) | $54,842 |

# Voting Studies

| | Presidential Support | | Party Unity | | Conservative Coalition | |
|---|---|---|---|---|---|---|
| Year | S | O | S | O | S | O |
| 1980 | 63 | 23 | 51 | 25 | 48 | 23 |
| 1979 | 60 | 28 | 68 | 24 | 62 | 33 |
| 1978 | 46 | 44 | 45 | 50 | 62 | 30 |
| 1977 | 66 | 20 | 56 | 36 | 58 | 34 |
| 1976 | 49 | 42 | 57 | 36 | 53 | 37 |
| 1975 | 56 | 28 | 55 | 32 | 58 | 29 |
| 1974 (Ford) | 38 | 53 | | | | |
| 1974 | 47 | 41 | 61 | 33 | 51 | 41 |
| 1973 | 42 | 48 | 64 | 25 | 42 | 48 |
| 1972 | 54 | 17 | 48 | 30 | 46 | 34 |
| 1971 | 56 | 30 | 57 | 35 | 76 | 18 |
| 1970 | 41 | 30 | 37 | 31 | 43 | 22 |
| 1969 | 42 | 42 | 52 | 20 | 45 | 29 |
| 1968 | 54 | 38 | 51 | 34 | 57 | 24 |
| 1967 | 61 | 20 | 55 | 21 | 45 | 25 |
| 1966 | 54 | 33 | 53 | 36 | 56 | 36 |
| 1965 | 69 | 18 | 69 | 22 | 41 | 44 |
| 1964 | 41 | 21 | 44 | 23 | 35 | 31 |
| 1963 | 67 | 21 | 67 | 12 | 32 | 65 |
| 1962 | 62 | 23 | 59 | 23 | 71 | 26 |
| 1961 | 73 | 23 | 76 | 19 | 38 | 54 |

S = Support          O = Opposition

# Key Votes

**96th Congress**

| | |
|---|---|
| Maintain relations with Taiwan (1979) | # |
| Reduce synthetic fuel development funds (1979) | N |
| Impose nuclear plant moratorium (1979) | N |
| Kill stronger windfall profits tax (1979) | N |
| Guarantee Chrysler Corp. loans (1979) | Y |
| Approve military draft registration (1980) | # |
| End Revenue Sharing to the states (1980) | ? |
| Block Justice Dept. busing suits (1980) | Y |

**97th Congress**

| | |
|---|---|
| Restore urban program funding cuts (1981) | Y |

# Interest Group Ratings

| Year | ADA | ACA | AFL-CIO | CCUS-1 | CCUS-2 |
|---|---|---|---|---|---|
| 1980 | 33 | 39 | 41 | 53 | |
| 1979 | 21 | 24 | 61 | 18 | 50 |
| 1978 | 30 | 43 | 33 | 60 | |
| 1977 | 30 | 60 | 61 | 47 | |
| 1976 | 40 | 38 | 78 | 33 | |
| 1975 | 28 | 41 | 60 | 31 | |
| 1974 | 33 | 32 | 40 | 10 | |
| 1973 | 35 | 27 | 82 | 22 | |
| 1972 | 25 | 45 | 44 | 0 | |
| 1971 | 41 | 39 | 75 | - | |
| 1970 | 19 | 50 | 83 | 25 | |
| 1969 | 50 | 54 | 56 | - | |
| 1968 | 29 | 61 | 100 | - | |
| 1967 | 38 | 29 | 36 | 30 | |
| 1966 | 35 | 43 | 67 | - | |
| 1965 | 59 | 42 | - | 30 | |
| 1964 | 51 | 21 | 60 | - | |
| 1963 | | 5 | - | - | |
| 1962 | 36 | 18 | 100 | - | |
| 1961 | 80 | - | - | - | |

# Paul Laxalt (R)

## Of Carson City — Elected 1974

**Born:** Aug. 2, 1922, Reno, Nev.
**Education:** U. of Denver, B.S., LL.B. 1949.
**Military Career:** Army, 1943-45.
**Profession:** Lawyer.
**Family:** Wife, Carol Wilson; seven children.
**Religion:** Roman Catholic.
**Political Career:** Ormsby County District Attorney, 1951-54; Carson City Attorney, 1954-55; Nevada Lt. Governor, 1963-67; Governor, 1967-71; Unsuccessful Republican nominee for U.S. Senate, 1964.

**In Washington:** Threading his way skillfully through a minefield of political etiquette, Laxalt has maintained his special relationship with President Reagan without trampling on the official prerogatives or tender egos of the Senate's elected Republican leaders.

The Nevada senator, one of Reagan's closest friends, is serving as an unofficial but extremely influential liaison between the White House and Capitol Hill, and doing so with the easygoing tact and charm that have made him one of the most popular members of the Senate. Laxalt tells the president what he needs to know about the personalities and politics of the Senate, and then conveys Reagan's thinking to his Capitol Hill colleagues with the unquestioned authority of a genuine White House "insider."

Throughout the early months of the Reagan administration, the man most threatened by this arrangement, Senate Majority Leader Howard H. Baker Jr., has had nothing but praise for his conservative colleague. "Paul has invented a role for himself that is unique and is playing it exquisitely," Baker said at one point.

Laxalt not only rejected the overtures of fellow conservatives who wanted him to oppose Baker for the leader's job, but nominated Baker himself. When there was some conservative restlessness after Baker insisted that social issues like abortion and busing be held off until Reagan's economic program was enacted, Laxalt quickly let it be known that both he and the president agreed with Baker.

Reagan and Laxalt met when both were supporting Sen. Barry Goldwater's 1964 presidential campaign. They later became friends while serving as governors of their neighboring states. Laxalt was chairman of Reagan's 1976 and 1980 presidential campaigns, and acted as his Washington representative during the intervening years.

When Reagan was wounded by a gunman on March 30, 1981, Laxalt was one of the first to reach Reagan at the hospital — and it was Laxalt whom Reagan sought to reassure with the words, "Don't worry about me. I'll make it." The next morning, it was Laxalt who told reporters that Reagan would not let the shooting turn him into a "prisoner" in the White House.

The Nevada Republican takes his conservative politics seriously, but never personally — which is why he is universally liked. He fought long and hard against ratification of the Panama Canal treaties in 1978, leading the opposition to the pacts, which were finally approved with only one vote to spare. Yet even the most ardent advocates of ratification had nothing but praise for Laxalt's conduct and character. "I have made it a point never to let political differences become personal," the senator explained later.

For all that, it is probably fair to call Laxalt an ideologue. He was one of only three U.S. senators to draw a 100 percent rating in 1980 from the conservative Americans for Constitutional Action; the others were Jesse Helms and Barry Goldwater. He is against busing, abortion and gun control; for the death penalty, higher defense spending and a hard line in foreign policy. He believes in a minimum of government regulation and taxation, and a maximum of individual and corporate freedom.

That does not always make Laxalt a vote for business in the Senate. If the subject is large corporations, he is likely to be as hostile as some of the more militant senators on the Democratic left. He considers corporate business selfish and dependent on the federal government for help.

"Thumb your noses at big business," he told an audience in 1977. "You can't count on this sector — at least right now — to represent free

727

enterprise and the things you believe in.... If tomorrow it was announced that all government intervention in business were ended, there would be coronaries in every boardroom."

During his first term in the Senate, Laxalt did considerable committee-hopping, serving on Labor and Public Welfare and the Energy Committee before settling on Appropriations and Judiciary. But he has never devoted much of his effort or time to the accumulation of legislative expertise; the nuts and bolts of running a subcommittee do not fascinate him.

He does have subcommittee chairmanships, however. He heads the Judiciary panel on Regulatory Reform and the Appropriations Military Construction Subcommittee. Early in the 97th Congress, he introduced a bill aimed at reducing federal regulation by requiring federal agencies to make cost-benefit studies before they issue new rules. On that issue, he has worked closely with the subcommittee's senior Democrat, Patrick J. Leahy of Vermont.

When he arrived in the Senate in 1975, Laxalt quickly aligned himself with the Steering Committee, an unofficial caucus of the chamber's New Right Republicans. Like others in that group, he has tended to place a premium on ideological purity, especially within the Republican Party, and to scorn some of the traditional "half-a-loaf" negotiations that characterize the legislative process.

There are signs, however, that Laxalt has started to bend a bit with a friend in the White House and Republicans in control of the Senate. When Baker made his statement about delaying action on social issues, Laxalt defended it with the remark that "we're not on any political kamikaze trips." One of the most ambitious conservative efforts on social issues is his own Family Protection Act, a collection of 38 diverse titles whose subjects range from abortion to school prayer and tax advantages for families. Laxalt has not demanded any instant action on it either from Baker or Reagan.

One of the most sensitive issues for Laxalt has been the MX missile and the proposed basing system that would place it on tracks and send it shuttling back and forth across the Western desert. Laxalt supported development of the MX throughout the Carter years but criticized the mobile basing. He has insisted that a better basing system could be devised.

When Laxalt does differ with standard conservative thought, constituent feeling is often the reason. During the 1979 gasoline shortage in his state, Laxalt — normally a supporter of a free hand for the oil industry — angrily demanded an independent audit of the oil companies to determine whether the shortages were real or contrived. He also suggested that Nevada set up legal machinery that would allow it to buy its own gasoline supplies on the world market.

**At Home:** Laxalt attributes his outlook to the fierce independence of his father, a Basque immigrant sheepherder. The elder Laxalt insisted on speaking French at home, and his son did not know much English before he went to school. But the senator's mother ran a small hotel in Carson City, the state capital, and he listened to years of legislative gossip.

Following law school, Laxalt was elected Ormsby County district attorney, and later he was city attorney in Carson City. In 1962 he ran for lieutenant governor, fighting the year's statewide Democratic trend. Republicans were beaten for governor and for the U.S. Senate, but Laxalt managed to win.

Two years later, he was a candidate for the Senate himself, challenging Democrat Howard Cannon's campaign for a second term. His Goldwater-style conservatism was not the asset then that it is now. Lyndon Johnson ran far ahead in Nevada, and Laxalt had to defend himself against Cannon's charges that he was nothing but a Goldwater troglodyte.

Laxalt responded by avoiding charges of creeping socialism and referring instead to the need for more defense installations in Nevada. Despite the Goldwater liability, he lost to Cannon by only 48 votes out of 134,624 cast, then the second closest Senate election in the history of popular voting. His downfall was Democratic Clark County (Las Vegas), Cannon's home and political base.

In 1966, Laxalt came back to seek the governorship against two-term Democrat Grant Sawyer. He quickly disposed of the extremism issue, leading a drive to expel John Birch Society members from the state party, and began taking advantage of public reluctance to keep the same man in power for 12 years. Laxalt contended the Sawyer administration suffered from "tired blood," repeating the charge Sawyer had used himself in his 1958 defeat of two-term Republican Charles H. Russell.

Laxalt cut his losing margin in Clark from 13,636 votes in 1964 to 487 in 1966, and defeated Sawyer statewide by nearly 6,000 votes.

As governor, Laxalt worked to rid the state's gambling industry of organized crime. He encouraged the reclusive billionaire Howard Hughes, with whom he communicated by telephone and memorandum, to buy some of the state's largest casinos. In the same vein, he pushed through legislation allowing major corporations into the gaming business. But his support for gambling itself remained strong. In 1968, he complained about presidential candidate Robert F. Kennedy's earlier Justice Department probes of Nevada casino operators. Two years later, he retired as governor and entered the casino business himself.

But by 1974 he was back in politics, campaigning for the state's open Senate seat. Running against Democratic Lt. Gov. Harry Reid, Laxalt campaigned as a thoroughgoing conservative, calling for drastic reductions in the U.S. foreign aid program. He refused to criticize President Ford's pardon of Richard M. Nixon, even though he likened it to "a hundred pound weight around my neck."

Reid took Clark County by 15,076 votes — more than Cannon did in 1964. But Laxalt was far more popular in northern Nevada than he had been a decade earlier. He edged Reid statewide by 624 votes.

In 1980, Laxalt's position was far more solid, although he failed to clear 60 percent of the vote. Helped by his skepticism about the MX missile basing, he turned back Democrat Mary Gojack, a former state senator. She denounced him for preoccupation with national concerns at Nevada's expense. Gojack, a Reno resident, was little-known in Clark County, and Laxalt carried Clark for the first time in any of his Senate efforts.

## Committees

**Appropriations** (5th of 15 Republicans)
Military Construction, chairman; HUD-Independent Agencies; Interior; State, Justice, Commerce, and the Judiciary; Treasury, Postal Service, and General Government.

**Judiciary** (3rd of 10 Republicans)
Regulatory Reform, chairman; Agency Administration; Criminal Law.

## Elections

**1980 General**

| | |
|---|---|
| Paul Laxalt (R) | 144,224 (59%) |
| Mary Gojack (D) | 92,129 (37%) |

**1980 Primary**

| | |
|---|---|
| Paul Laxalt (R) | 45,857 (90%) |
| Richard Gilster (R) | 2,509 (5%) |
| Other (R) | 2,401 (5%) |

**Previous Winning Percentage**

1974 (47%)

## Campaign Finance

| | Receipts | Receipts from PACs | Expen-ditures |
|---|---|---|---|
| 1980 | | | |
| Laxalt (R) | $1,196,599 | $182,102 (15%) | $1,126,826 |
| Gojack (D) | $286,073 | $69,270 (24%) | $285,619 |

## Voting Studies

| | Presidential Support | | Party Unity | | Conservative Coalition | |
|---|---|---|---|---|---|---|
| Year | S | O | S | O | S | O |
| 1980 | 28 | 65 | 81 | 9 | 86 | 7 |
| 1979 | 28 | 62 | 82 | 5 | 80 | 3 |
| 1978 | 11 | 82 | 84 | 6 | 76 | 10 |
| 1977 | 36 | 47 | 85 | 7 | 88 | 4 |
| 1976 | 53 | 15 | 68 | 4 | 76 | 3 |
| 1975 | 72 | 16 | 88 | 5 | 92 | 5 |

S = Support          O = Opposition

## Key Votes

**96th Congress**

| | |
|---|---|
| Maintain relations with Taiwan (1979) | Y |
| Reduce synthetic fuel development funds (1979) | Y |
| Impose nuclear plant moratorium (1979) | N |
| Kill stronger windfall profits tax (1979) | Y |
| Guarantee Chrysler Corp. loans (1979) | N |
| Approve military draft registration (1980) | Y |
| End Revenue Sharing to the states (1980) | Y |
| Block Justice Dept. busing suits (1980) | Y |

**97th Congress**

| | |
|---|---|
| Restore urban program funding cuts (1981) | N |

## Interest Group Ratings

| Year | ADA | ACA | AFL-CIO | CCUS-1 | CCUS-2 |
|---|---|---|---|---|---|
| 1980 | 11 | 100 | 5 | 85 | |
| 1979 | 5 | 91 | 13 | 100 | 100 |
| 1978 | 5 | 81 | 18 | 88 | |
| 1977 | 5 | 92 | 6 | 88 | |
| 1976 | 5 | 95 | 6 | 100 | |
| 1975 | 22 | 87 | 29 | 93 | |

# AL Jim Santini (D)

**Of Las Vegas — Elected 1974**

**Born:** Aug. 13, 1937, Reno, Nev.
**Education:** U. of Nev., B.S. 1959; U. of Calif,
Hastings College of Law, J.D. 1962.
**Military Career:** Army, 1963-66.
**Profession:** Lawyer.
**Family:** Wife, Ann Crane; six children.
**Religion:** Roman Catholic.
**Political Career:** Clark County District Court
Judge, 1972-74; Clark County Justice of the
Peace, 1970-72; Clark County Public Defend-
er, 1968-70.

**In Washington:** Mining is Santini's preoccupation, and it is a subject he often dominates
through his chairmanship of the Interior Committee's Mines and Mining Subcommittee. Few
members have any political reason to be interested in it, and those who are generally share
Santini's belief in more freedom for private mineral exploration.

The argument Santini makes most often is
that the United States is running dangerously low
in minerals, risks dependence on unstable foreign
sources, and needs a national minerals policy that
encourages new production. In his view, backed
by the mining industry, we are on the verge of a
crisis.

In early 1980, Santini announced that the
Soviet Union, already self-sufficient in strategic
materials, had begun buying them from other
countries — possibly to shut the United States
out of future markets. Later in the year, he visited
three African countries and returned with the
warning that future American supplies of chro-
mium and cobalt could run short.

When the Alaska lands bill passed the House
in 1978, and again in 1979, Santini won approval
of his amendment calling for a study of the state's
mineral deposits. He then backed the more development-oriented Alaska bill against the environmentalist version, again raising the argument
of declining strategic mineral stocks.

Santini's role as a mining industry spokesman generally places him in a broader pro-development coalition on most energy bills. But not
always. He has been opposed to coal slurry pipeline bills, reflecting the concern in Nevada that
pipeline construction would rob the state of precious water. Santini introduced his own bill stat-
ing that the pipelines may impair the national
interest, and providing strong state controls over
the right to build them.

Similar local concerns led Santini to fight the
Energy Mobilization Board President Carter
hoped would speed up new energy projects. He
tried twice to persuade the Commerce Committee
to delete language allowing the board a right to
override state and local law, although he was
willing to accept an override of federal law. Failing at that, he and other worried Western state
legislators formed a coalition with national environmental groups that forced the bill's sponsors
to reverse themselves on the House floor and
remove the override provision. The board itself
never became law.

Santini was less successful in his argument
against Carter's plans for construction of the MX
missile. Insisting he favored the concept of the
MX, Santini tried to get the House to mandate
that no more than a quarter of it could be housed
in any one state. Plans at the time called for 70
percent of it to be placed in Nevada. "Where's the
water going to come from," Santini asked, raising
a now familiar point. But the House crushed him
by a 284-89 vote.

In general, Santini has become more conservative since he entered the House in 1975, in
keeping with his state's increasing frustration at
the federal government. In his first term, he
supported federal aid to the states for land use
planning; now his rhetoric seems closer to the
language of the Sagebrush Rebellion.

---

**At-Large District: Entire State.** Population: 799,184 (64% increase since 1970).
Race: White 699,377 (88%), Black 50,791
(6%), Others 49,016 (6%). Spanish origin:
53,786 (7%).

---

**At Home:** Santini is an almost ideal candidate for his vast constituency — a southern Nevadan with roots in the northern part of the state.

His popularity in the south stems from his highly visible career as a Las Vegas public defender and judge. But he grew up in the north, in Reno, where his father was a prominent banker and his grandfather was president of the University of Nevada.

When he first ran for the House in 1974, Santini was a Clark County district judge, and he campaigned on efficiency rather than any ideology. His northern background gave him the votes to defeat his primary rival, Clark County Commissioner Myron Leavitt, by 10,000 votes.

In the fall, Santini faced Republican David Towell, who had won the seat unexpectedly two years earlier, helped by the the Nixon landslide and a bitter Democratic primary in which veteran incumbent Walter Baring was defeated. Towell did not have either of his 1972 assets the second time, and Santini won by more than 30,000 votes.

He has been re-elected easily since then. In both 1976 and 1978, the line marked "None of these candidates" drew more Republican primary votes than any of the real entrants.

In early 1981, Santini began considering a campaign for the Senate seat held by veteran Democrat Howard W. Cannon.

## Committees

**Energy and Commerce** (9th of 24 Democrats)
Commerce, Transportation, and Tourism; Oversight and Investigations.

**Interior and Insular Affairs** (7th of 23 Democrats)
Mines and Mining, chairman; Public Lands and National Parks.

**Select Aging** (12th of 31 Democrats)
Housing and Consumer Interests.

## Elections

**1980 General**

| | |
|---|---|
| James Santini (D ) | 165,107 (68 %) |
| Vince Saunders (R ) | 63,163 (26 %) |
| Other | 16,317 (6 %) |

**1980 Primary**

| | |
|---|---|
| James Santini (D ) | 54,495 (79 %) |
| Lloyd Williams (D ) | 8,407 (12 %) |

**1978 General**

| | |
|---|---|
| James Santini (D ) | 132,513 (70 %) |
| Bill O'Mara (R ) | 44,425 (23 %) |
| Other | 13,705 (7 %) |

**Previous Winning Percentages**

1976 (77 %)    1974 (56 %)

**District Vote For President**

| | 1980 | | 1976 | | 1972 |
|---|---|---|---|---|---|
| **D** | 66,666 (27 %) | **D** | 92,479 (46 %) | **D** | 66,016 (36 %) |
| **R** | 155,017 (63 %) | **R** | 101,273 (50 %) | **R** | 115,750 (64 %) |
| **I** | 17,651 (7 %) | | | | |

## Campaign Finance

| | Receipts | Receipts from PACs | Expenditures |
|---|---|---|---|
| **1980** | | | |
| Santini (D ) | $515,791 | $187,949 (36 %) | $392,583 |
| Saunders (R ) | $39,331 | $300 (1 %) | $38,410 |

**1978**

| | | | |
|---|---|---|---|
| Santini (D ) | $251,040 | $73,095 (29 %) | $204,389 |
| O'Mara (R ) | $34,543 | $2,300 (7 %) | $34,543 |

## Voting Studies

| | Presidential Support | | Party Unity | | Conservative Coalition | |
|---|---|---|---|---|---|---|
| Year | S | O | S | O | S | O |
| 1980 | 38 | 38 | 32 | 45 | 64 | 15 |
| 1979 | 38 | 49 | 36 | 51 | 69 | 20 |
| 1978 | 46 | 45 | 42 | 44 | 52 | 31 |
| 1977 | 46 | 32 | 57 | 36 | 51 | 40 |
| 1976 | 35 | 53 | 58 | 33 | 57 | 33 |
| 1975 | 30 | 65 | 55 | 37 | 51 | 39 |

S = Support          O = Opposition

## Key Votes

**96th Congress**

| | |
|---|---|
| Weaken Carter oil profits tax (1979) | Y |
| Reject hospital cost control plan (1979) | Y |
| Implement Panama Canal Treaties (1979) | N |
| Establish Department of Education (1979) | Y |
| Approve Anti-busing Amendment (1979) | Y |
| Guarantee Chrysler Corp. loans (1979) | N |
| Approve military draft registration (1980) | Y |
| Aid Sandinista regime in Nicaragua (1980) | N |
| Strengthen fair housing laws (1980) | ? |

**97th Congress**

| | |
|---|---|
| Reagan budget proposal (1981) | Y |

## Interest Group Ratings

| Year | ADA | ACA | AFL-CIO | CCUS |
|---|---|---|---|---|
| 1980 | 17 | 58 | 38 | 60 |
| 1979 | 16 | 61 | 30 | 75 |
| 1978 | 5 | 65 | 35 | 56 |
| 1977 | 25 | 44 | 50 | 65 |
| 1976 | 30 | 46 | 43 | 54 |
| 1975 | 26 | 50 | 65 | 35 |

# New Hampshire

## ...Untaxed New England

U.S. CONGRESS:
TWO DISTRICTS
Senate (2R)
House (1D, 1R)
STATE:
Governor
Hugh Gallen (D)

New Hampshire has always been a sort of political paradox. Demographically, the state has a resemblance to Massachusetts, Connecticut and Rhode Island, with their large ethnic and Catholic populations and industrial economies. Politically, however, New Hampshire has voted like Maine and Vermont, its long Republican tradition broken only sporadically.

But modern New Hampshire politics is unlike that of any of the other New England states. It tends to the idiosyncratic — even the bizarre. It is the only state best known nationally for its presidential primary, a media circus often dominated by William Loeb, publisher of the *Manchester Union Leader.* Loeb's paper is the only statewide daily and reaches about 25 percent of New Hampshire's people, who are offered large doses of Loeb's belligerent anti-communism and caustic nicknames for politicians he does not like. President Ford was "Jerry the Jerk"; Nelson Rockefeller was "Rocky the Wifeswapper."

Loeb's role in national politics is quadrennial. But for much of the 1970s, he had a year-in, year-out influence over state politics — a legacy, odd as it sounds, of the feuding that followed the death of the Republican boss, Sen. Styles Bridges, in 1961.

For years after Bridges died, there was constant factional warfare in the GOP over nominations for Congress and the governorship. Loeb stepped into what amounted to a vacuum in the party, and by the early 1970s he had the ability to influence the outcome of key primaries by endorsing one candidate and blasting another. In 1972, he managed to get his favorites nominated in both parties, eventually bringing about the election of his true favorite, militant conservative publisher Meldrim Thomson Jr., who went on to serve three terms in the statehouse.

But neither Loeb nor Thomson could have done any of this without the issue of taxes. Thomson won because he was seen as the man best suited to defend the people of New Hampshire from what they consider deadly broad-based taxes. New Hampshire is the only state with no

General Court
Senate: 24 members
(10D, 13R, 1 Vacancy)
House: 400 members
(160D, 238R, 2 Vacancies)
Population
920,610 - 42nd in the nation
Area
9,304 sq. miles - 44th in the nation
1980 Presidential Vote: Carter (28%),
Reagan (58%), Anderson (13%)

state income or sales tax, and although it has one of the lowest social service spending levels in the nation, serious candidates for governor have had to take "the pledge" not to advocate broad-based taxes. Since Thomson's 1972 primary victory over Gov. Walter Peterson, who had favored a broad-based tax, few serious candidates for governor have tried to campaign on anything but an anti-tax platform.

Ironically, Thomson was beaten at his own game in 1978. His pet project, the controversial Seabrook nuclear power plant, was in financial trouble, and Thomson allowed the utilities to pass on the increased construction costs to consumers. Democrat Hugh Gallen convinced voters that Thomson was socking them with a hidden tax and won the gubernatorial election by a narrow margin. In 1980, Gallen crushed Thomson's comeback attempt at the same time that Ronald Reagan was running up 58 percent in the state.

What Democrats did manage to do well through most of the 1960s and 1970s was run for the Senate. Without the tax issue dominating the campaigns, moderate-to-conservative Democrats have had a better chance of mobilizing the state's blue-collar vote in congressional campaigns. Thomas J. McIntyre won three Senate terms, taking advantage of the post-Bridges Republican bickering; John Durkin won a shortened term in 1975, when he beat Republican Louis Wyman in a rematch after the Senate found itself unable to determine the true winner of their first meeting in November of 1974. For almost four years, the state had two Democratic senators, and one Democrat out of two in the U.S. House.

But that period seems to be over. McIntyre lost his seat in 1978 to airline pilot Gordon Humphrey, backed by New Right assistance and the most sophisticated media campaign — the only real one — the state had ever seen. In 1980, Durkin lost badly to moderate Republican Warren Rudman.

# A Political Tour

**Industrial New Hampshire — The Boston Rim.** Throughout the state's history, southern New Hampshire — Hillsborough, Rockingham and Strafford counties and part of Merrimack — has been the center of population and industry. The recent, rapid influx of people and business has given this region even greater prominence, not only to the state, but to all of New England.

The population of New Hampshire has grown by more than 300,000 in the past 20 years, and most of the new residents have settled in southern New Hampshire. Today, 70 percent of the population lives there. So many of the emigrés are from Massachusetts that parts of the region are re-garded as outer suburbs of Boston.

The new residents are sometimes referred to as "refugees" from high taxes elsewhere. So are the many manufacturers of electronic goods, machinery and other sophisticated products, who filled the void left by the decline in the textile and shoe-making industries. As businessmen and new residents see it, they have the best of both worlds; lower taxes and proximity to Boston.

What impact the new residents will have on New Hampshire's politics is uncertain. Though mainly from "liberal" Massachusetts, most new residents left to escape taxes and are unlikely to rock the conservative boat. They helped Durkin defeat Wyman in 1975, but they also helped Humphrey defeat McIntyre in 1978.

Most of the state's Democratic vote is in this region. The strongest Democratic area has long been the Merrimack River Valley, New Hampshire's industrial heartland and home to thousands of French-Canadians, Irish and other immigrants. But most New Hampshire Democrats are anti-tax, and "Democrat" does not usually mean "liberal" in New Hampshire.

Manchester, the state's largest city with 91,000 people, used to provide a fairly dependable Democratic vote. The influence of Loeb's *Union Leader* and the growing conservative bent of the city's many French-Canadians have turned Manchester in a Republican direction.

On either side of Manchester along the Merrimack River are Nashua, to the south, and Concord, the state capital, to the north. Nashua (pop. 68,000) is a heavily industrialized city and the fastest growing in the state. It commonly gives New Hampshire Democrats their greatest margins. Democrats in Concord (pop. 30,000) do almost as well, and here there is considerable sentiment for low-growth, environmentally oriented positions. John Anderson received more than 10 percent of the vote in Concord in 1980; Meldrim Thomson never got more than 38 percent there.

Rockingham County, in the southeast corner of the state, was a Republican bastion until the explosive growth of recent years. An example: Salem, a sleepy, Republican town of 4,000 in 1950, is now a city of 24,000 that is split between Democrats and Republicans. Many of the new residents turn to Boston, especially the Boston *Globe,* for information, rather than to Manchester.

Rockingham County contains New Hampshire's 13-mile coastline, and the city of Portsmouth (pop. 26,000), a blue-collar town heavily dependent on the military (Portsmouth Navy Yard). It votes strongly Democratic. But the city vote is offset by the Republican vote in the

**733**

numerous small towns and villages.

Strafford County, like Hillsborough, has traditionally provided a slim Democratic majority, thanks to industrial cities like Somersworth, Dover and Rochester. Durham, the home of University of New Hampshire, is also heavily Democratic. The western part of the county is rural and Republican.

**Southwestern New Hampshire.** Sullivan and Cheshire counties are mainly farms and woods, but there are several industrial cities that make Democrats competitive there. Keene (pop. 21,000) in Cheshire County and Claremont (pop. 15,000) in Sullivan both usually provide Democrats with a solid majority of the vote. Most of the non-urban areas are heavily Republican.

**Lake and Mountain Country.** The middle of New Hampshire is known for its forests, mountains and lakes. The region, which includes large Lake Winnipesaukee, is a vacation mecca that helps make tourism New Hampshire's second biggest industry. The primary industry of most of this region is centered around paper and lumber mills.

Though lightly populated — the counties of Belknap, Carroll and Grafton make up just 15 percent of the state population — this is New Hampshire's most staunchly Republican area. GOP candidates often run up impressive figures here. In 1980, Carroll was the only county in the state to support Thomson's unsuccessful comeback try.

There are several Democratic-voting cities that slightly limit Republican margins in Belknap and Grafton counties. Grafton has Lebanon, a mill town, and Hanover, home of Dartmouth College. Laconia, an industrial and trading center for Belknap County, has 16,000 residents who split their political preferences fairly evenly between Democrats and Republicans.

**The Northern Tip.** Coos County forms the northern end of New Hampshire. Forests cover almost all of the land area and provide a living for most of the workers. Many French-Canadians moved here from nearby Quebec, and Democrats have carried Coos County in most statewide elections in the past 20 years.

Though New Hampshire's largest county in land area, Coos has only 35,000 people — less than 4 percent of the state population. It was the only county in the state that did not experience significant population growth in the 1970s.

About a third of the county's residents live in Berlin, easily one of New Hampshire's most Democratic areas. Even George McGovern carried it in the 1972 general election, while losing all the other major Democratic industrial cities further south. Berlin (pronounced with the emphasis on the first syllable) is a city of pulp and paper mills to which Democratic presidential candidates make a traditional pilgrimage every four years.

# Redrawing the Line

Population in both of New Hampshire's congressional districts grew more than 20 percent in the 1970s, so only minor adjustments are needed to make them equal. The 1st District, represented by Democrat Norman E. D'Amours, must lose 10,600 people to the 2nd District, now represented by freshman Republican Judd Gregg.

## Governor
## Hugh Gallen (D)

**Born:** July 30, 1924, Portland, Ore.
**Home:** Littleton, N.H.
**Education:** Medford High School.
**Profession:** President of automobile dealership.
**Family:** Wife, Irene; three children.
**Religion:** Roman Catholic.
**Political Career:** Democratic state chairman, 1971-72; New Hampshire House, 1973-75; unsuccessful campaigns for Democratic gubernatorial nomination, 1974, 1976; elected governor 1978, 1980; term expires Jan. 1983.

# Gordon J. Humphrey (R)

**Of Sunapee — Elected 1978**

**Born:** Oct. 9, 1940, Bristol, Conn.
**Education:** Attended U. of Md., 1960-61; George Washington U., 1962-63; Burnside-Ott Aviation Inst., 1965.
**Military Career:** Air Force, 1958-62.
**Profession:** Airline Pilot.
**Family:** Wife, Patricia Greene.
**Religion:** Baptist.
**Political Career:** No previous office.

**In Washington:** Humphrey's early years in the Senate have been an on-the-job training course in the art of politics. Utterly new to the field when he ran for the Senate in 1978, he has struggled to overcome his lack of experience in government and national issues.

He also had to fight a reputation as a man without much sense of humor. His image of severity has minimized his influence, even in a Senate increasingly sympathetic to his conservative views. In early 1981, when Senate Labor abolished its Health Subcommittee, committee aides told reporters that Chairman Orrin Hatch, R-Utah, had abolished the panel to keep it out of Humphrey's hands. Both senators later denied it, but the rumor's wide initial acceptance reflected the strain between Humphrey and others on the Republican right.

Humphrey came to Washington in 1979 vowing to be the "toughest skinflint in the Senate." But political pressures have led him to be careful in choosing his targets.

Early in his first year in office, for example, Humphrey opposed a veterans' health bill that he said was too expensive. His stand received considerable attention in New Hampshire, and upset state veterans' groups.

But only a few months later, Humphrey led a floor fight against cuts in veterans' programs, quoting the World War I poem, "In Flanders Fields" during floor debate. In 1980, he offered an amendment to add $700 million to the veterans' budget, taking the money from jobs programs.

Humphrey was also a critic of President Reagan's 1981 proposal to reduce Social Security benefits for early retirees. "I think it was ill-advised and I'm sure by now he realizes it," Humphrey said after the idea was rejected by the Senate 96-0. "You can't change overnight the ground rules by which people run their lives."

On one issue Humphrey has been consistent and very vocal: his opposition to federal interference in traditional family matters.

In addition to supporting limitations on federal funding of abortions, he sponsored an amendment to prohibit Legal Services lawyers from participating in abortion cases. He threatened to filibuster a bill providing federal aid to shelters for the victims of family violence, and that threat was enough to kill it. The measure was opposed by conservative pro-family activists.

On the Armed Services Committee, Humphrey's sentiments have been with those who applauded the Reagan suggestions for increasing defense spending. But he opposes the MX missile, which he says would be too expensive and environmentally questionable.

With the Republican Senate takeover, Humphrey became chairman of the Armed Services Readiness Subcommittee. That puts him in charge of monitoring military operations and maintenance, one-third of the defense budget.

**At Home:** Humphrey's militant conservatism has taken him a great distance in a stunningly short time. A co-pilot for Allegheny Airlines, he moved to New Hampshire only in 1974, and had no political involvement before the day in 1977 when he walked into a meeting of the state Conservative Caucus and was named coordinator.

That post allowed him to develop connections to national New Right figures, who later helped him raise large sums for his Senate race. Humphrey remained at his airline job for the rest of the year, but he devoted increasing amounts of attention to conservative causes, especially fighting the Panama Canal treaties.

In 1978, Humphrey set his sights on Democratic Sen. Thomas J. McIntyre, a supporter of the Panama accords who had been in the Senate since 1962. Few New Hampshire politicians took the challenger seriously at first, but he fought his

**735**

way to attention in the Republican primary field with a meticulous organization and a set of carefully timed press releases.

The primary provided the first clue to what a stranger could do in New Hampshire politics with ideological loyalists, money and skill. Humphrey drew more than twice as many votes as either of his moderate Republican rivals, a former mayor of Keene and a veteran state senator.

Still, McIntyre saw little reason to panic. In both 1966 and 1972, he had easily defeated conservative Republicans by ridiculing them as tools of the far right. Neither of those challengers, however, had Humphrey's campaign organization, and neither had the money to buy advertising on Boston television — which reached 85 percent of the New Hampshire electorate.

Humphrey attacked McIntyre's canal votes and called for tax reductions, an effective appeal to the voters just across the Massachusetts border who came to New Hampshire specifically to avoid high taxes. The incumbent continued to portray

his challenger as a shrill ideologue, even though that notion seemed at variance with his quiet style. The one tactic likely to discredit Humphrey — an all-out attack on him as an opportunist — was not tried because Democrats considered it unnecessary.

On election night they found out otherwise. Humphrey built a surprising lead in early returns, and while McIntyre narrowed it as the night went on, he fell 5,800 votes short.

Humphrey's independent style in office soon brought him into conflict with some of his state's Republican leaders. The arch-conservative *Manchester Union-Leader*, which had endorsed Humphrey in 1978, condemned him for opposing the paper's choice in the 1980 GOP gubernatorial primary. An editorial blasted him as "the meddling junior senator."

Since then Humphrey has worked hard to keep up intraparty relations. He campaigned extensively for GOP Senate nominee Warren Rudman in 1980.

## Committees

**Armed Services** (5th of 9 Republicans)
Preparedness, chairman; Military Construction; Sea Power and Force Projection.

**Energy and Natural Resources** (7th of 11 Republicans)
Energy Regulation, chairman; Energy and Mineral Resources; Energy Conservation and Supply.

**Labor and Human Resources** (7th of 9 Republicans)
Alcoholism and Drug Abuse, chairman; Aging, Family and Human Services; Investigations and General Oversight.

## Elections

**1978 General**

| | |
|---|---|
| Gordon Humphrey (R ) | 133,745 (51 %) |
| Thomas McIntyre (D ) | 127,945 (49 %) |

**1978 Primary**

| | |
|---|---|
| Gordon Humphrey (R ) | 35,503 (50 %) |
| James Masiello (R ) | 18,371 (26 %) |
| Alf Jacobson (R ) | 13,619 (19 %) |

## Campaign Finance

| | Receipts | Receipts from PACs | Expenditures |
|---|---|---|---|
| **1978** | | | |
| Humphrey (R ) | $366,632 | $89,126 (24 %) | $357,107 |
| McIntyre (D ) | $298,608 | $102,450 (34 %) | $289,628 |

## Voting Studies

| Year | Presidential Support | | Party Unity | | Conservative Coalition | |
|---|---|---|---|---|---|---|
| | S | O | S | O | S | O |
| 1980 | 30 | 65 | 90 | 5 | 93 | 1 |
| 1979 | 28 | 71 | 94 | 4 | 91 | 7 |

S = Support          O = Opposition

## Key Votes

**96th Congress**

| | |
|---|---|
| Maintain relations with Taiwan (1979) | Y |
| Reduce synthetic fuel development funds (1979) | Y |
| Impose nuclear plant moratorium (1979) | N |
| Kill stronger windfall profits tax (1979) | Y |
| Guarantee Chrysler Corp. loans (1979) | N |
| Approve military draft registration (1980) | Y |
| End Revenue Sharing to the states (1980) | Y |
| Block Justice Dept. busing suits (1980) | Y |

**97th Congress**

| | |
|---|---|
| Restore urban program funding cuts (1981) | N |

## Interest Group Ratings

| Year | ADA | ACA | AFL-CIO | CCUS-1 | CCUS-2 |
|---|---|---|---|---|---|
| 1980 | 6 | 96 | 6 | 93 | |
| 1979 | 5 | 93 | 11 | 100 | 94 |

# Warren B. Rudman (R)

**Of Nashua — Elected 1980**

**Born:** May 18, 1930, Boston, Mass.
**Education:** Syracuse University, B.S. 1952; Boston College, LL.B. 1960.
**Military Career:** Army, 1952-54.
**Profession:** Lawyer.
**Family:** Wife, Shirley Wahl; three children.
**Religion:** Jewish.
**Political Career:** New Hampshire attorney general, 1970-76.

**The Member:** While there is little doubt that Rudman leans to the right side of the political spectrum, he is closer to the center than most freshman GOP legislators.

When national conservative leaders Phyllis Schlafly and Howard Phillips came before an Appropriations subcommittee and roundly criticized the Legal Services Corporation, Rudman rebuked both of them. Rudman told Schlafly that he had dealt with the LSC as state attorney general and that her statement was "grossly inaccurate and incorrect."

On economic issues, Rudman solidly supports Reagan's plan to shift spending responsibility to the states. But he has warned New Hampshire residents, who pay no sales tax or income tax, that their state may suffer withdrawal pains when federal aid is reduced.

His maiden speech in the Senate stressed the need to strengthen the national defense and favored Reagan's higher defense outlays. At the same time, however, Rudman expressed concern over the military's "fascination with high-technology weaponry." Cost overruns and production backlogs on high technology weapons render them obsolete upon deployment, he said.

Rudman came to Washington with no experience in elective politics, but he built a reputation as an activist during six years as New Hampshire attorney general.

He overhauled the little-noticed office in the early 1970s by creating a consumer protection division, and he successfully fought the legalization of gambling in New Hampshire. That gave him the statewide recognition he used in his contest for the Senate against Democratic incumbent John A. Durkin. Rudman proved to be an aggressive campaigner, interspersing political argument with stories of his days as a platoon commander in Korea.

Rudman almost made it to Washington, D.C., in 1976, when he was nominated by President Gerald R. Ford to chair the Interstate Commerce Commission. But Durkin reportedly worked behind the scenes to block the nomination, and Rudman subsequently withdrew his name. Bad blood had developed between the two politicians in 1974, when Rudman was a member of the state panel that overturned the certification of Durkin's election in a virtually even contest with Republican Louis C. Wyman. That forced the 1975 special election which Durkin won.

## Committees

**Appropriations** (14th of 15 Republicans)
Defense; Foreign Operations; Interior; Labor, Health and Human Services, Education; State, Justice, Commerce, the Judiciary.

**Governmental Affairs** (9th of 9 Republicans)
Governmental Efficiency and the District of Columbia; Oversight of Government Management; Permanent Subcommittee on Investigations.

**Small Business** (8th of 9 Republicans)
Innovation and Technology, chairman; Advocacy and the Future of Small Business.

## Elections

**1980 General**

| | |
|---|---|
| Warren Rudman (R) | 195,559 (52%) |
| John Durkin (D) | 179,455 (48%) |

**1980 Primary**

| | |
|---|---|
| Warren Rudman (R) | 20,206 (20%) |
| John Sununu (R) | 16,885 (17%) |
| Others | 59,361 (59%) |

## Campaign Finance

| | Receipts | Receipts from PACs | Expenditures |
|---|---|---|---|
| **1980** | | | |
| Rudman (R) | $637,610 | $9,000 (1%) | $585,926 |
| Durkin (D) | $659,135 | $329,410 (50%) | $657,310 |

## Key Votes

**97th Congress**

| | |
|---|---|
| Restore urban program funding cuts (1981) | N |

# 1 Norman E. D'Amours (D)

**Of Manchester — Elected 1974**

**Born:** Oct. 14, 1937, Holyoke, Mass.
**Education:** Assumption College, B.A. 1960, Boston U., LL.B. 1963.
**Military Career:** Army Reserves, 1964-67.
**Profession:** Lawyer.
**Family:** Wife, Helen Manning; three children.
**Religion:** Roman Catholic.
**Political Career:** No previous office.

**In Washington:** House leaders were startled one day in early 1980 when D'Amours, normally one of the quieter Democrats, burst into a leadership press conference demanding that Speaker O'Neill guarantee him a floor vote on energy tax credits. D'Amours wanted to amend the windfall profits tax to provide credits for wood-burning stoves and other conservation measures. The Senate had approved the idea but the House never considered it. D'Amours wanted to offer a motion to accept the Senate language; he decided to approach O'Neill in the most direct way possible.

The confrontation may have seemed rude to some of those present, especially since O'Neill was already sympathetic to the D'Amours plan. But it reflected the sensitivity to local needs that has helped D'Amours survive four straight elections in a largely Republican district.

At the time he confronted O'Neill, D'Amours was being attacked in the hostile *Manchester Union-Leader* as a free-spending pawn of the Democratic leadership, a lackey of Tip O'Neill and a supporter of a new gasoline tax. D'Amours wanted to show his constituents — preoccupied with steadily rising fuel costs — he was for tax credits, not tax increases.

As it turned out, O'Neill scheduled a vote on D'Amours' 1980 tax credit amendment, but it lost by seven votes. D'Amours shifted his campaign to the Banking Committee, however, eventually providing liberalized loan authority for woodstoves in a package of bills setting up a solar and energy conservation bank.

Although he can never hope to satisfy the conservative Manchester paper, D'Amours does try to be fiscally and personally conservative. He refuses junkets and declines pay raises in the session in which they are voted. In 1979, he cast the lone Democratic vote in his Banking subcommittee against bailing out the Chrysler Corp. He said the company should scale down its operations before getting federal help.

Early in his career, D'Amours was tapped by O'Neill to serve on a commission to straighten out House accounting and expense procedures. D'Amours attempted to get the commission to eliminate such fringe benefits as free picture framing, an annual storage trunk allotment and decorative potted plants; he did not succeed.

In 1981, D'Amours became chairman of the Oceanography Subcommittee of the Merchant Marine and Fisheries Subcommittee — just in time to hear the Reagan administration recommend dismantling a number of sea grant and coastal energy programs. D'Amours promptly held hearings and recommended some cuts but urged that the programs remain.

**At Home.** D'Amours parlayed a French name, a background in criminal law and a bitter GOP primary to win this district for the Democrats in 1974, for only the second time in 30 years.

His French ancestry was a political plus in Manchester, the center of New Hampshire's Franco-American population. He had spent two years as city prosecutor there. But he also received a boost from the Republicans.

While D'Amours was quietly winning the Democratic nomination, Republicans were sharply divided between David Banks, an auto dealer and ally of *Union-Leader* publisher William Loeb, and John F. Bridges, son of the late

---

**1st District: East — Manchester.**
Population: 470,924 (28% increase since 1970). Race: White 465,368 (99%), Black 2,197 (0.4%), Others 3,359 (1%). Spanish origin: 3,065 (1%).

and legendary GOP Sen. Styles Bridges. Banks won, but the party was in disarray, and D'Amours won by 4,778 votes.

Republicans frittered away a chance to unseat D'Amours in 1976 by nominating an unemployed former Massachusetts legislator named John Adams, who did no campaigning. Drawing 68 percent of the vote, D'Amours held his opponent to a lower percentage than any Republican in the district since the Civil War.

The GOP mounted more spirited opposition in 1978 and 1980, but D'Amours was too strong. He won both contests with more than 60 percent, beating a former Speaker of the state House in 1980.

**The District.** D'Amours' constituency includes blue-collar Manchester, the Portsmouth naval shipyard, and fast-growing Rockingham County, which is becoming an outer suburb of Boston.

Manchester is New Hampshire's largest city. Heavily ethnic, the old textile mill city usually supports the conservative preferences of the *Union-Leader*. Once a Democratic stronghold, Manchester turned in heavy majorities for Republican Gov. Meldrim Thomson Jr. in the 1970s and backed GOP newcomer Gordon J. Humphrey over Democratic Sen. Thomas J. McIntyre in 1978.

To the east is Rockingham, which besides its Boston suburbs has smaller colonial towns like Exeter, Hampton and Portsmouth, and New Hampshire's only portion of seacoast. North along the Maine border is Strafford County, which includes Durham, the site of the University of New Hampshire. With a large influx of newcomers in recent years, both counties are now less conservative in their politics than Manchester.

## Committees

**Banking, Finance and Urban Affairs** (13th of 25 Democrats)
Economic Stabilization; Financial Institutions Supervision, Regulation and Insurance; Housing and Community Development.

**Merchant Marine and Fisheries** (9th of 20 Democrats)
Oceanography, chairman; Fisheries and Wildlife Conservation and the Environment.

## Elections

**1980 General**

| | |
|---|---|
| Norman D'Amours (D ) | 114,061 (61 %) |
| Marshall Cobleigh (R ) | 73,565 (39 %) |

**1978 General**

| | |
|---|---|
| Norman D'Amours (D ) | 82,697 (62 %) |
| Daniel Hughes (R ) | 49,131 (37 %) |

**Previous Winning Percentages**

1976 (68 %)    1974 (52 %)

**District Vote For President**

| | 1980 | | 1976 | | 1972 |
|---|---|---|---|---|---|
| D | 53,617 (27 %) | D | 72,778 (43 %) | D | 54,375 (33 %) |
| R | 118,160 (60 %) | R | 95,003 (56 %) | R | 111,167 (66 %) |
| I | 23,754 (12 %) | | | | |

## Campaign Finance

| | Receipts | Receipts from PACs | Expenditures |
|---|---|---|---|
| **1980** | | | |
| D'Amours (D ) | $117,734 | $52,212 (44 %) | $100,417 |
| Cobleigh (R ) | $70,411 | $33,427 (48 %) | $66,062 |
| **1978** | | | |
| D'Amours (D ) | $78,828 | $21,412 (23 %) | $92,791 |
| Hughes (R ) | $49,520 | $13,742 (28 %) | $48,897 |

## Voting Studies

| Year | Presidential Support | | Party Unity | | Conservative Coalition | |
|---|---|---|---|---|---|---|
| | S | O | S | O | S | O |
| 1980 | 70 | 26 | 70 | 27 | 46 | 53 |
| 1979 | 61 | 34 | 65 | 27 | 42 | 51 |
| 1978 | 61 | 37 | 58 | 38 | 43 | 54 |
| 1977 | 71 | 29 | 74 | 22 | 35 | 62 |
| 1976 | 20 | 76 | 81 | 18 | 34 | 64 |
| 1975 | 28 | 71 | 75 | 24 | 32 | 66 |

S = Support          O = Opposition

## Key Votes

**96th Congress**

| | |
|---|---|
| Weaken Carter oil profits tax (1979) | N |
| Reject hospital cost control plan (1979) | N |
| Implement Panama Canal Treaties (1979) | Y |
| Establish Department of Education (1979) | # |
| Approve Anti-busing Amendment (1979) | Y |
| Guarantee Chrysler Corp. loans (1979) | N |
| Approve military draft registration (1980) | Y |
| Aid Sandinista regime in Nicaragua (1980) | Y |
| Strengthen fair housing laws (1980) | Y |

**97th Congress**

| | |
|---|---|
| Reagan budget proposal (1981) | N |

## Interest Group Ratingsufz

| Year | ADA | ACA | AFL-CIO | CCUS |
|---|---|---|---|---|
| 1980 | 56 | 38 | 58 | 62 |
| 1979 | 63 | 31 | 85 | 11 |
| 1978 | 45 | 42 | 80 | 6 |
| 1977 | 70 | 33 | 74 | 29 |
| 1976 | 75 | 14 | 70 | 6 |
| 1975 | 63 | 36 | 78 | 18 |

**739**

# 2 Judd Gregg (R)

Of Greenfield — Elected 1980

**Born:** Feb. 14, 1947, Nashua, N.H.
**Education:** Columbia U., A.B. 1969; Boston U., J.D. 1972; LL.M. 1975.
**Profession:** Lawyer.
**Family:** Wife, Katherine McLellan; two children.
**Religion:** Protestant.
**Political Career:** N.H. Governor's Executive Council, 1979-81.

**The Member:** Like many New England Republicans, Gregg is a fiscal conservative who takes moderate positions on social and environmental issues. He claims to practice "a mainstream philosophy" designed to get government under control.

On the Science Committee in 1981, Gregg voted against a $250 million coal demonstration project that was to be engineered by a New Hampshire company. The project, part of a larger research effort to convert coal to oil, failed by an 11-13 vote. House GOP Leader Robert H. Michel and the Reagan administration opposed the project and praised Gregg siding with them against the interests of a firm in his own state.

The administration was not so happy with Gregg when he and two other freshmen on the Science Committee led an effort to cut construction funding for the Clinch River nuclear breeder reactor in Tennessee. The White House lobbied to save Clinch River, but it lost that round, 18-22.

Gregg is the youngest son in an old New Hampshire political family. His father, former Gov. Hugh Gregg (1953-55), headed Reagan's 1976 New Hampshire primary campaign and George Bush's 1980 campaign in the state.

Gregg's name helped him rise quickly in New Hampshire politics. In 1978 he launched his political career by unseating a Democratic incumbent on the state Executive Council. Soon afterward, he began campaigning to succeed Republican Rep. James C. Cleveland, who retired.

**The District:** The 2nd is more Yankee and small-town oriented than New Hampshire's other distrtict, and historically more Republican. It has not sent a Democrat to Congress since 1912.

Although in recent years there has been a population boom in the Nashua area along the Massachusetts border, the bulk of the vote is still in tradition-minded towns to the north and west. They helped Cleveland win nine elections by comfortable margins and enabled Gregg to swamp his 1980 Democratic opponent, Nashua Mayor Maurice L. Arel, by a margin of nearly 2-to-1.

## Committees

**Government Operations** (17th of 17 Republicans)
Environment, Energy and Natural Resources.
**Science and Technology** (12th of 17 Republicans)
Energy Development and Applications; Science, Research and Technology.
**Select Aging** (15th of 23 Republicans)
Retirement Income and Employment.

## Elections

**1980 General**

| | |
|---|---|
| Judd Gregg (R ) | 113,304 (64 %) |
| Maurice Arel (D ) | 63,350 (36 %) |

**1980 Primary**

| | |
|---|---|
| Judd Gregg (R ) | 16,603 (34 %) |
| Susan McLane (R ) | 12,064 (25 %) |
| Charles Bass (R ) | 10,689 (22 %) |
| Robert Sweet Jr. (R ) | 3,495 (7 %) |

**District Vote For President**

| | 1980 | | 1976 | | 1972 |
|---|---|---|---|---|---|
| D | 55,247 (30 %) | D | 74,857 (44 %) | D | 62,060 (37 %) |
| R | 103,545 (56 %) | R | 90,932 (54 %) | R | 102,557 (62 %) |
| I | 25,939 (14 %) | | | | |

## Campaign Finance

| | Receipts | Receipts from PACs | Expenditures |
|---|---|---|---|
| **1980** | | | |
| Gregg (R ) | $138,942 | $48,215 (35 %) | $122,167 |
| Arel (D ) | $100,955 | $25,550 (25 %) | $100,144 |

## Key Vote

**97th Congress**

| | |
|---|---|
| Reagan budget proposal (1981) | Y |

---

**2nd District: West — Nashua, Concord.** Population: 449,686 (21% increase since 1970). Race: White 444,731 (99%), Black 1,793 (0.3%), Others 3,163 (1%). Spanish origin: 2,522 (1%).

# New Jersey

## ... An Identity Problem

Outsiders tend to think of New Jersey as a monolith and not a very nice one. They remember the stinking refineries along the turnpike, the Mafia hitmen in the movies, and the politicians indicted for corruption. Woody Allen was only reflecting the popular view when he wrote that "a certain intelligence governs our universe except in certain parts of New Jersey."

But New Jersey is not all the same. In the Legislature, crowded North Jersey and less-populous South Jersey have been fighting for decades. There is an urbanized, industrial corridor along the New Jersey Turnpike, anchored by Newark on one end and Camden on the other, but there are rural and suburban Republican areas on either side. New Jersey votes Republican for president more often than practically any other industrial state: seven out of nine times since World War II.

The Democratic New Jersey is one of city neighborhoods, ethnic fraternities and large labor unions. The Republican New Jersey offers green suburbs, country clubs and corporate headquarters. Liberals and labor unions have a strong influence within the Democratic Party, while New Jersey Republicans tend to be moderate. The most conservative GOP candidates, like 1978 Senate nominee Jeffrey Bell, usually lose general elections.

Dominated by New York City in the north and Philadelphia in the south, New Jersey has another problem — identity. Because it lacks its own commercial television station or statewide newspaper, its people are oriented to the two out-of-state metropolises, their sports teams, cultural life and politics.

Schoolchildren in Bergen County, for instance, often can name the mayor of New York but not the governor of New Jersey. To help remedy this situation, New Jersey office-holders have sought, so far in vain, to force a big-city TV station to move into the state.

Since the Civil War, political dominance has passed between the parties in cycles of a decade or two. Since World War II, waning partisanship

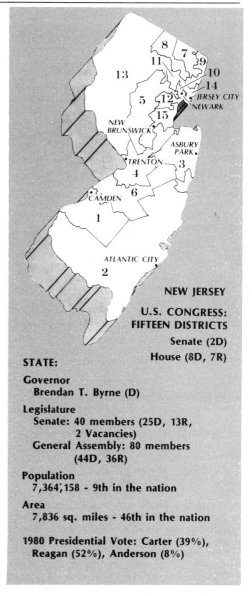

**NEW JERSEY**

**U.S. CONGRESS: FIFTEEN DISTRICTS**

Senate (2D)

House (8D, 7R)

**STATE:**

**Governor**
Brendan T. Byrne (D)

**Legislature**
Senate: 40 members (25D, 13R, 2 Vacancies)
General Assembly: 80 members (44D, 36R)

**Population**
7,364,158 - 9th in the nation

**Area**
7,836 sq. miles - 46th in the nation

**1980 Presidential Vote:** Carter (39%), Reagan (52%), Anderson (8%)

and growing suburbanization have made most state elections difficult to predict, with contests hinging on who could capture the large independent vote. The growth of the suburbs has helped

Republicans more in New Jersey even than in other states, because the Democratic cities to which its suburbs are attached vote in other states — Pennsylvania and New York.

In the 1920s and 1930s, Hudson County Democratic boss Frank ("I am the law") Hague frequently determined who would be governor. While the county machines remain an active force in local elections, they have lost their hold on statewide politics, as seen by the huge number of candidates in the 1981 gubernatorial primary (21) — an unmanageable situation Hague would not have tolerated.

A "reform" spirit long has been a factor in New Jersey politics and has contributed to the weakening of the county party organizations. This began as far back as 1911 under Gov. Woodrow Wilson, when a new law required party committee members to be elected by public vote. In 1977, nominees for governor received state financing, and in 1981 this was extended to primary candidates and helped create the huge field.

Aggressive federal prosecutors have also hurt the political machines. In the past two decades, they have exposed a pervasive system of corruption featuring kickbacks, extortion and Mafia infiltration of municipal government. Newark Mayor Hugh Addonizio, Rep. Cornelius E. Gallagher, Hudson County Democratic Chairman John V. Kenny and Jersey City Mayor Thomas J. Whelan were among scores of officials sent to prison.

Reaction to all this enabled one previously obscure jurist, Brendan T. Byrne, to become governor in 1973, simply because his honesty was incontrovertible. Byrne won a landslide victory thanks to publicity from a taped wiretap of racketeer Angelo (Gyp) DeCarlo complaining that the judge could not be bribed. Byrne won a second term in 1977.

# A Political Tour

**The Urban Core.** Newark, Elizabeth, Paterson and Jersey City began this century as humming manufacturing citadels. Close to ports on the Hudson River and to New York, they were ideally located for shipping. Immigrants landing on nearby Ellis Island found work there.

In the years since World War II, though, many of the white residents of these cities have left for the suburbs. Blacks and Hispanics moved in to replace them, but found that numerous factories had fled as well, mostly to the Sun Belt. Paterson, now heavily Hispanic, has lost almost its entire textile industry.

High unemployment and scarce opportunities helped generate the anger that led to a spate of riots in the 1960s. The worst occurred in Newark in 1967, where 26 people died and the central business district was gutted. Today, minorities live in uneasy coexistence with the remaining blue-collar whites, who are largely of Italian extraction.

In the Italian-American North Ward of Newark, one man has built a political career out of racial tension. Anthony Imperiale, who heads a vigilante patrol, won repeated elections to the state Assembly with his law-and-order appeal. "I represent your fears," he was quoted as saying in his unsuccessful 1981 campaign for governor.

The urban core includes all of Hudson and parts of other counties — eastern Essex County (Newark), eastern Union (Elizabeth) and southern Passaic (Paterson). The other half of those counties are suburban and in a different world.

This industrial area still has a loyalty to the Democrats, although a declining population base and a weakening of the once-potent machines have diminished its statewide clout.

Hudson is one continuous urban area, with Jersey City, Bayonne, Hoboken, Weehawken and the other towns blending into each other. Once the state's premier Democratic county, Hudson used to have a major impact upon any state election. In 1960, nearly 300,000 people voted in Hudson County, and they gave John F. Kennedy a 60,000-vote plurality — almost three times his statewide margin. By 1980, 100,000 fewer votes were cast in the county, and there was a serious slippage in the Democratic vote. White ethnic dissatisfaction with Jimmy Carter reduced the Democratic margin in the county to only 4,000 votes.

The strong and unified Hague machine has passed away, but the Hudson organization, despite some factional fighting, still can deliver a good Democratic vote when the candidate is more popular than Carter.

Newark does not have as strong a machine vote as the Hudson County towns. Nevertheless, the large black population there (58 percent) is predictably Democratic. Newark Mayor Kenneth Gibson, a black, has his own political apparatus, which no rival in his city can match.

Elizabeth, a dingy city marred by air pollution from refineries and chemical plants, seldom wavers from its partisan Democratic inclinations. The same can be said for Paterson, site of bloody labor strife in the 19th and early 20th centuries. **The New York Suburban Ring.** Wrapped around the urban core is an immense suburban area of generally Republican sympathies. This crescent begins in Bergen County in the north, and sweeps down on the western edge of the urban core to encompass northern Passaic, and all of Morris and Somerset counties. It ends in Middlesex County on the south. Well-to-do western Essex and Union counties are also included.

In the typical demographic pattern nationally, the outer suburbs are growing, while the inner ones have remained stable or lost population. From 1970 to 1980, New Jersey's New Milford in close-in Bergen dropped 12 percent, while Plainboro in the distant reaches of southern Middlesex more than doubled in size.

A large number of suburban corporate executives commute daily to jobs in New York City. But for others, the jobs have come to them. In the 1960s and 1970s, many companies decided to move their headquarters out of Manhattan and into the New Jersey greenery, where rents are cheaper and commutes are shorter. New Jersey's extensive research industry has flourished here, starting with Thomas Edison's Menlo Park lab, where the phonograph and the light bulb were invented in the late 19th century. Close by is the modern-day equivalent, Bell Labs.

The Democrats' strength in the more blue-collar parts of Middlesex, Union and Essex counties have prevented many Republican victories there. GOP totals are higher in the other, more homogenous suburban counties.

Bergen, with such wealthy towns as Upper Saddle River and Alpine, remains New Jersey's Republican stronghold. It gave Ronald Reagan his biggest plurality in the state in 1980, almost 100,000 votes. Morris, home of lush estates and fox hunts, went for Reagan by 2-1.

In general, suburban New Jersey Republicans prefer moderate GOP candidates. They have elected four of them to the House in the 97th Congress: Bergen's Marge Roukema and Harold C. Hollenbeck, Union's Matthew J. Rinaldo and Millicent Fenwick from Somerset. The suburbs were unenthusiastic about the conservative Jeffrey Bell, who ran against Democrat Bill Bradley for senator in 1978; they either supported Bell by small margins or went for Bradley.

**The Rural Northwest.** Here the customary New Jersey flatness gives way to the rolling foothills of the Ramapo Mountains. Composed of Hunterdon, Warren and Sussex counties, the northwest is bounded by the Delaware River. Nestled within the hills are farms and small towns with a firm GOP tradition.

The most distinctive town in this part of the state is Flemington, a quaint-looking place where the Lindbergh kidnapping trial took place and

where 90 corporations once located because of its low property taxes. The biggest municipality in the northwest is Phillipsburg (pop. 16,600), an old milltown and an enclave of Democrats. The rest of the area tends to be heavily Republican.

**Industrial South Jersey.** From Trenton south along the Delaware River, there is a proliferation of towns and smokestacks. Beginning in Mercer County (Trenton), this area forms an arc around Philadelphia and includes Burlington, Camden, Gloucester, Salem and Cumberland counties.

Its two major cities are Trenton, the state capital, and Camden. Of the two, Trenton stays in somewhat better economic and physical shape, thanks to the big state government complex. Parts of poverty-stricken Camden look like Dresden after the World War II fire bombing. Heavily black and Hispanic, the city stays alive with the help of the Campbell Soup headquarters and a huge RCA plant.

Moving south, the river water and the air get dirtier as one comes to the chemical works of Gloucester, the glass plants of Salem and the garment factories of Cumberland.

Inland are settled middle-class suburbs and, beyond that, tract housing where there once was farm land. This is not high-toned suburbia. Apart from such well-off towns as Cherry Hill and Haddonfield, much of suburban South Jersey contains lower-middle-class families, emigrants from rowhouse Philadelphia.

Before post-war suburbanization, the countryside had vegetable farms and Republican votes in ample supply. While tomatoes remain an important crop locally, feeding the Campbell's plant, farm acreage has dwindled and with it, the GOP voting bloc.

Industrial South Jersey is mostly Democratic territory, especially near the river. Enough Republican votes exist in the suburbs to make for competitive elections, although many expatriate Philadelphians there retain Democratic loyalties. The lone GOP outpost is Burlington County, which still has a lot of farm land; an old guard Republicanism holds sway there, and Republican Edwin B. Forsythe occupies its House seat.

Despite the region's partisan orientation, Reagan showed enough blue-collar appeal to capture five of the area's six counties in 1980. Mercer, owing to its many state workers, opted for Carter.

Politics in industrial South Jersey is tough and, as in the urban northern part of the state, has an aroma of corruption. In 1980, Camden Mayor Angelo Errichetti was caught up in the Abscam affair and convicted of bribery and conspiracy.

**The Shore.** Tourism makes up a healthy chunk of the New Jersey economy. For the most part, the tourists go to the Jersey Shore, a 126-mile coastline stretching from the Sandy Hook peninsula in the north to Victorian Cape May in the south. It covers Monmouth, Ocean, Atlantic and Cape May counties.

The Shore can be divided according to the origins of its visitors. Bagels and New York accents abound in the north; scrapple and Philadelphia accents in the south. The visitors not only come from different cities, but from different classes within those cities. The roller coasters and ring-toss games of Asbury Park coexist with mansions and quiet elegance in Deal.

The Shore's dominant attraction is Atlantic City, the old resort built on "ocean, emotion and promotion," as local boosters used to say. Nowadays, the faded dowager has gotten a face-lift with the introduction of casino gambling.

In recent years, many of the summer visitors to the Jersey Shore have stayed to live year-round. Ocean County had a 66 percent surge in population over the past decade, making it the fastest growing county in New Jersey. Many of the newcomers are prosperous retirees. Others still work and commute long-distance to white-collar jobs in New York or Philadelphia. Together with the longstanding residents, the newcomers give the Shore a decidedly Republican cast.

Conservative values persist in the rural inland vicinity known as the Pine Barrens. Federal and state efforts to protect the fragile ecology of the vast evergreen forest have met with resistance from pro-development local people.

Democratic strength can be found in communities with sizable black concentrations, notably Atlantic City and Asbury Park, and in old blue-collar Monmouth County towns like Keansburg. Some of the new arrivals to Monmouth have kept up Democratic affiliations, making that a swing county. The other Shore counties are more reliably Republican.

# Redrawing the Lines

The 1970s were a boom time for the south Jersey shore's 2nd District, the rural northwest's 13th District and the south-central 6th District. Population in each expanded in the 20 percent range. But while those areas grew, population in nine other New Jersey districts declined, and the state lost one of its 15 House seats in the 1980 reapportionment.

Democrats control the Legislature and the governorship, and they talked in the first half of 1981 about dropping a seat by mapping two Republicans into the same district. Marge Roukema's 7th District and Matthew J. Rinaldo's 12th were the most under-populated of the Republican districts. But neither had the population deficit found in Newark's 10th District or Jersey City's 14th. Both those urban core areas are represented by Democrats and need to gain more than 100,000 people to reach the ideal size of 526,000.

## Governor
## Brendan T. Byrne (D)

**Born:** April 1, 1924, West Orange, N.J.
**Home:** Princeton, N.J.
**Education:** Princeton U., A.B. 1949; Harvard Law School, LL.B. 1951.
**Military Career:** Army Air Corps, 1943-45.
**Profession:** Lawyer, judge.
**Family:** Wife, Jean; seven children.
**Religion:** Roman Catholic.
**Political Career:** Essex County prosecutor, 1959-68; superior court judge, 1970-73; elected governor 1973, 1977; term expires Jan. 1982.

# Harrison A. Williams Jr. (D)

**Of Bedminster — Elected 1958**

**Born:** Dec. 19, 1919, Plainfield, N.J.
**Education:** Oberlin College, A.B. 1941; Columbia U., LL.B. 1948.
**Military Career:** Navy Reserve, 1942-46.
**Profession:** Lawyer.
**Family:** Wife, Jeanette Smith; four children.
**Religion:** Presbyterian.
**Political Career:** U.S. House, 1953-57; unsuccessful Democratic nominee for N.J. Assembly, 1951; unsuccessful candidate for Plainfield City Council, 1952; unsuccessfully sought re-election to U.S. House, 1956.

**In Washington:** When the FBI's Abscam net trapped Williams and a New Jersey congressman, Frank Thompson, *The Washington Post* headlined: "Jolt for Congress: The 'White Hats' Touched by Taint."

If a long record of support for liberal causes is a white-hat credential, Williams is entitled to wear one. For 25 years, he has been originator or cosponsor of bills to help education, health care for the elderly, urban housing, and public transit. He has supported environmental protection, anti-poverty programs, coal mine safety, aid to the handicapped, and reform of private pensions.

In recent years, though, Williams has been identified less as a liberal crusader than as a solid labor man. During nearly a decade as chairman of the Labor and Human Resources Committee, he had taken most of his cues from the AFL-CIO and other labor organizations. The AFL-CIO rated him at 95 in 1979 and 94 in 1980; labor was instrumental in his last Senate re-elections. There has always been criticism of Williams as a man who simply follows a labor agenda and carries it out with the assistance of a large and skilled staff. He speaks with feeling, however, on many of his issues, and he has an even-tempered style that sometimes proves an even-advantage in the final stages of a legislative fight, when other tempers have begun to fray. Occasionally he has stepped in with a saving compromise.

Williams' long career is anchored by two Republican eras. He came to the House in the Republican 83d Congress; he remains today, despite his conviction on Abscam bribery charges, in the Republican 97th Senate. In between, however, the Democrats have been firmly in control and firmly of the view — espoused enthusiastically by Williams — that social problems can be solved by an activist government.

"We Democrats," he said early in his career, "have been instructed by the voters to live up to the great liberal tradition which was nourished and brought to a high tide of achievement by those giants in our century — Franklin Roosevelt and Harry Truman."

Williams arrived in Washington the year Truman left. As a World War II veteran and graduate of the Georgetown foreign service school, he spent his three years in the House as something of an internationalist. When Democrats regained control after the 1954 election, he won a seat on the Foreign Affairs Committee, where he argued for peaceful relations with the Soviet Union and became a supporter of reciprocal trade.

Williams sponsored a bill to end the restrictive national origins immigration policy. With Sen. John F. Kennedy, he cosponsored legislation to help businesses and aid workers hurt by competition from imports.

After he arrived in the Senate in 1959, Williams began to take on a lasting identity as a valuable ally for organized labor. He endorsed repeal of the Taft-Hartley Act's right-to-work section, common-site picketing and extension of the minimum wage to migrant workers.

Working with Kennedy on the old Labor and Public Welfare Committee, Williams was a leader in the effort to provide health care for the elderly. That eventually became Medicare. In 1960, however, it was a Kennedy presidential campaign issue. A modest health care plan passed in a special session after the Democratic convention.

As he worked his way up in seniority on the Labor Committee, he left a trail of social legislation behind him — coal mine safety, pension reform, public jobs, higher unemployment compensation, steadily increasing minimum wages,

**745**

and the Occupational Safety and Health Act. When federal officials seemed slow to enforce OSHA regulations, Williams held hearings dramatizing accidents in unsafe mines. "That publicity should tighten up things in a hurry," he said.

The one notable defeat of recent years came in 1977 on labor law revision, which was beaten on the Senate floor by a Republican filibuster, coordinated with an unprecedented grass-roots business lobbying campaign on the outside.

Meanwhile, Williams was also moving up on the Banking Committee, where for nearly 20 years he was chairman of the Securities Subcommittee, working to overhaul stock market procedures. He was nearly as good a friend of the securities industry as he was of unions. His campaigns have drawn on friendships with Wall Street.

The Banking Committee writes urban affairs legislation in the Senate, and Williams sought a role as an urban expert, taking the lead in promoting federal subsidies for public housing, and mass transit. He wrote legislation that poured billions of dollars into subways and city bus systems, and moved beyond capital construction grants to operating subsidies for the first time. In 1968, he wrote a book on urban problems and suggested the Senate create a separate housing committee.

In 1981, scarred by Abscam and outnumbered by Republicans, Williams turned over the senior Democratic slot on Labor and Human Resources to Edward M. Kennedy, preferring to stick with urban issues as ranking Democrat on Banking. But much of his time was spent in federal courtrooms.

**At Home:** Abscam has ended Williams' near-invulnerability in New Jersey politics. Before news of the scandal broke in early 1980, he even contemplated finishing off his career with a term as governor. He had overwhelmed a Republican opponent in his 1976 Senate contest, and would have been the overwhelming favorite to win the Democratic gubernatorial nomination if he wanted it. But the Abscam case forced him to step aside and cast a cloud over his entire political future. He is up for a fifth Senate term in 1982.

A Brooklyn jury found Williams guilty May 1, 1981, of bribery and conspiracy in connection with efforts to secure federal contracts for a titanium mine owned by friends. FBI agents posing as wealthy Arabs promised to bankroll the venture with a $100 million loan. An FBI videotape showed the senator accepting stock in the corporation.

On the witness stand, Williams claimed he was simply playing along to aid his friends and called his taped statements "baloney." Refusing to resign from the Senate during his appeal, he protested the prosecution had entrapped him. Defense lawyers said convicted swindler Melvin Weinberg, who worked undercover for the FBI, "coached" Williams to boast of his influence.

Until Abscam, Williams had an image of integrity in a state plagued by an image of Mafia and machine rule. He had overcome a bout with alcoholism that might have destroyed his career ten years earlier. The New Jersey NAACP denounced him in 1968 for "behavior not becoming a U.S. senator" when he showed up drunk for a major speech. His second wife, Jeanette, then working as one of his Senate committee aides, helped him beat the drinking problem, and by the time of his 1970 re-election campaign he won overwhelming support from all sides.

Williams had a rocky political start. He lost a 1951 bid for the state Assembly and a 1952 election for the Plainfield City Council. But he ran for the U.S. House against the odds in 1953 and won a special election in a traditionally Republican district, replacing GOP Rep. Clifford P. Case, who had resigned.

Williams' House career ended in the 1956 Eisenhower landslide, but in 1958 he was back, the personal choice of Democratic Gov. Robert B. Meyner to run for the Senate seat given up by Republican H. Alexander Smith. Williams won a tough primary fight against Hoboken Mayor John J. Grogan, a labor union president backed by the Hudson County machine of John V. Kenny. Williams then made peace with the Hudson faction and carried the county in the fall as he defeated GOP Republican Robert W. Kean, winning a place in the huge Democratic Senate class of 1959.

Williams was predictably strong in the Democratic year of 1964, as he trounced Republican Bernard M. Shanley, President Eisenhower's former appointments secretary.

But 1970 could not help but be difficult for him. He began it by announcing his recovery from alcoholism, hoping to defuse what would otherwise be the most potent issue against him. Then he had to deal with a significant primary opponent, state Sen. Frank Guarini, a power in Hudson County politics. Guarini accused the senator of being soft on crime. The Hudson County organization was not strong enough at that point to threaten Williams' renomination.

Republicans still considered Williams highly vulnerable that year. They nominated their former state chairman, Nelson Gross, a political professional who had managed the successful 1968 campaign for President Nixon in the state. Gross echoed the law-and-order theme that Republicans were using against Democratic senators all over the country that year. But New Jersey seemed more interested in the rising unemployment rate, and responded to Williams' efforts to link the economic problems to the Nixon administration. Labor gave Williams much of the backing he needed, and he survived comfortably, although his 54 percent represented a decline from 1964.

In 1976, there were no problems. By that time, Williams' legislative record and attention to labor interests had made him so strong that no prominent Republican dared take him on. David Norcross, a young state election official, decided to try it to boost his name recognition for the future. Norcross gained something from the effort; he was made state GOP chairman. But he never came close to Williams.

## Committees

**Banking, Housing and Urban Affairs** (Ranking Democrat)
 Financial Institutions; Housing and Urban Affairs; International
 Finance and Monetary Policy.

**Labor and Human Resources** (3rd of 7 Democrats)
 Alcoholism and Drug Abuse; Handicapped; Labor.

**Rules and Administration** (5th of 5 Democrats)

**Joint Library**

## Elections

**1976 General**

| | |
|---|---|
| Harrison Williams (D) | 1,681,140 (61 %) |
| David Norcross (R ) | 1,054,508 (38 %) |

**1976 Primary**

| | |
|---|---|
| Harrison Williams (D ) | 378,553 (85 %) |
| Stephen J. Foley (D ) | 66,178 (15 %) |

**Previous Winning Percentages**

| | | | |
|---|---|---|---|
| 1970 (54%) | 1964 (62%) | 1958 (51%) | 1954* (56%) |
| 1953† (51%) | | | |

* House election. † Special House election.

## Campaign Finance

| | Receipts | Receipts from PACs | Expenditures |
|---|---|---|---|
| **1976** | | | |
| Williams (D ) | $690,781 | $268,390 (39 %) | $610,090 |
| Norcross (R ) | $74,023 | — (0 %) | $73,499 |

## Voting Studies

| | Presidential Support | | Party Unity | | Conservative Coalition | |
|---|---|---|---|---|---|---|
| Year | S | O | S | O | S | O |
| 1980 | 72 | 25 | 84 | 9 | 4 | 86 |
| 1979 | 81 | 9 | 84 | 6 | 4 | 84 |
| 1978 | 85 | 11 | 88 | 6 | 8 | 83 |
| 1977 | 80 | 14 | 86 | 10 | 11 | 86 |
| 1976 | 30 | 62 | 76 | 10 | 18 | 68 |
| 1975 | 49 | 48 | 88 | 6 | 6 | 90 |
| 1974 (Ford) | 46 | 43 | | | | |
| 1974 | 34 | 57 | 81 | 11 | 9 | 83 |

| | | | | | |
|---|---|---|---|---|---|
| 1973 | 29 | 54 | 81 | 5 | 7 | 82 |
| 1972 | 28 | 57 | 77 | 6 | 4 | 83 |
| 1971 | 34 | 60 | 79 | 10 | 13 | 77 |
| 1970 | 36 | 40 | 77 | 5 | 7 | 70 |
| 1969 | 51 | 39 | 79 | 10 | 7 | 81 |
| 1968 | 74 | 16 | 88 | 6 | 7 | 87 |
| 1967 | 74 | 13 | 77 | 5 | 4 | 77 |
| 1966 | 68 | 15 | 81 | 4 | 1 | 89 |
| 1965 | 80 | 10 | 81 | 6 | 8 | 80 |
| 1964 | 72 | 12 | 72 | 20 | 10 | 82 |
| 1963 | 84 | 7 | 78 | 9 | 5 | 88 |
| 1962 | 81 | 10 | 83 | 11 | 24 | 68 |
| 1961 | 79 | 13 | 83 | 9 | 5 | 94 |

S = Support          O = Opposition

## Key Votes

**96th Congress**

| | |
|---|---|
| Maintain relations with Taiwan (1979) | N |
| Reduce synthetic fuel development funds (1979) | # |
| Impose nuclear plant moratorium (1979) | Y |
| Kill stronger windfall profits tax (1979) | N |
| Guarantee Chrysler Corp. loans (1979) | Y |
| Approve military draft registration (1980) | Y |
| End Revenue Sharing to the states (1980) | N |
| Block Justice Dept. busing suits (1980) | N |

**97th Congress**

| | |
|---|---|
| Restore urban program funding cuts (1981) | ? |

## Interest Group Ratings

| Year | ADA | ACA | AFL-CIO | CCUS-1 | CCUS-2 |
|---|---|---|---|---|---|
| 1980 | 72 | 13 | 94 | 24 | |
| 1979 | 74 | 0 | 95 | 0 | 15 |
| 1978 | 80 | 9 | 89 | 35 | |
| 1977 | 85 | 7 | 85 | 11 | |
| 1976 | 85 | 0 | 80 | 0 | |
| 1975 | 89 | 7 | 95 | 19 | |
| 1974 | 90 | 0 | 89 | 0 | |
| 1973 | 80 | 0 | 91 | 13 | |
| 1972 | 85 | 5 | 100 | 0 | |
| 1971 | 93 | 5 | 92 | - | |
| 1970 | 94 | 5 | 100 | 0 | |
| 1969 | 94 | 7 | 100 | - | |
| 1968 | 86 | 8 | 100 | - | |
| 1967 | 77 | 0 | 100 | 30 | |
| 1966 | 95 | 8 | 100 | - | |
| 1965 | 82 | 4 | - | 10 | |
| 1964 | 92 | 0 | 90 | - | |
| 1963 | - | 0 | - | - | |
| 1962 | 83 | 4 | 100 | - | |
| 1961 | 100 | - | - | - | |

# Bill Bradley (D)

### Of Denville — Elected 1978

**Born:** July 28, 1943, Crystal City, Mo.
**Education:** Princeton U., A.B. 1965; Rhodes Scholar, Oxford U., England, M.A. 1968.
**Military Career:** Air Force Reserve, 1967-78.
**Profession:** Basketball player.
**Family:** Wife, Ernestine Schlant; one child.
**Religion:** Protestant.
**Political Career:** No previous office.

**In Washington:** Bill Bradley was no showman during his ten years with the New York Knicks, and he has not been one in the Senate, where his limited speaking ability has led him to concentrate most of his effort behind the scenes. But he has had a successful start. Diligent and professional, and sensitive to the civilities of Senate life, he has earned considerable respect.

In early 1981, when Senate Democrats needed someone to chair a task force aimed at developing a counteroffensive to the Reagan economic program, Minority Leader Robert C. Byrd chose Bradley. It was a flattering assignment for a newcomer who already had a pair of good ones, on the Finance and Energy committees.

By late spring, Bradley's task force had issued some recommendations. It said budget reductions should be limited to those that promote growth or cut inflation, and should not be used to implement a new philosophy of government. It said the dominant economic problem was still U.S. dependence on foreign oil. The Democrats seemed no closer to a consensus, but Bradley had outlined the strategy he planned to follow.

When the Finance Committee wrote a tax bill in June, Bradley had his own set of ideas, most of them geared toward focusing the tax cut on lower- and middle-income people, rather than the wealthy. He offered amendments to do that, and to make Reagan's proposed third-year tax cut contingent on economic progress in the first two years. When none of his amendments were adopted, Bradley cast the only vote in committee against the overall bill, which he called "inflationary and inequitable."

Despite his interest in broad economic issues, Bradley made his first major speech and successful floor fight in 1979 on a very parochial issue — forcing the Navy to grant a $500 million contract for the overhaul of the aircraft carrier *Saratoga* at the Philadelphia Navy Yard. Getting the contract for Philadelphia, instead of Newport News, Virginia, where the Navy wanted to rehabilitate the

ship, meant several thousand jobs for New Jersey residents who commute to the yard across the Delaware River.

As a member of Finance in the 96th Congress, Bradley supported a stiff windfall profits tax on oil producers. Along with several other senators from consumer-oriented states, he moved successfully on the floor to raise the basic rate on recently-discovered "new oil" to 75 percent from 60 percent. That led some oil state senators to threaten a filibuster against the entire tax, but they did not carry one out.

Bradley believes in conservation as a long-term energy solution, and has supported a variety of conservation tax credits. He fought to use a portion of the windfall profits tax receipts to help poor people defray energy costs.

Before Republicans took over the Senate in 1981, Bradley chaired the Revenue Sharing Subcommittee at Finance, and used it to try to keep the revenue sharing program alive.

In 1980, he managed legislation reauthorizing revenue sharing to state and local governments. He wanted to include in it special anti-recession money for economically distressed cities. That move was unsuccessful. Bradley did win on the basic issue of providing continued authority for revenue sharing to states for three more years, but no funds for this were included in the budget for 1981 or 1982.

On the Energy Committee, Bradley's main interest has been the strategic petroleum reserve. In 1980, along with Republican Robert Dole of Kansas, he won a floor fight to require the government to put 100,000 barrels of oil per day in the strategic reserve — or else stop oil production at Elk Hills in California and Teapot Dome in Wyoming. These two federal oil holdings bring in $2 billion a year in revenues.

**At Home:** Bradley was looking ahead to

politics during most of the 10 years he spent playing forward for the New York Knicks. During the off-season, he spoke at Democratic Party gatherings, worked as a reading teacher in Harlem and spent a summer doing administrative work in the federal Office of Economic Opportunity in Washington.

His interest in politics came early, nurtured by his Republican banker father in Crystal City, Missouri, and by his days at Princeton, where he wrote his senior thesis on Harry S Truman's 1940 Senate campaign.

There was talk that Bradley would return to Missouri to seek office, but marriage to a New Jersey college professor and years of television exposure in the New York metropolitan area convinced him to run in the Garden State. To finance his Senate bid, he relied on some of his own wealth, then valued at nearly $1.6 million, and on fund-raising events by such prominent friends as singer Paul Simon and actor Robert Redford.

With superior name recognition, Princeton and Oxford degrees and a clean-cut reputation, he scored an easy Democratic primary victory over Gov. Brendan T. Byrne's candidate, former state Treasurer Richard C. Leone.

Bradley drew as his general election opponent Jeffrey Bell, a former campaign aide to Ronald Reagan. Bell had ousted four-term Sen. Clifford P. Case in the Republican primary, and his campaign had split the GOP badly. Without the liberal Case on the general election ballot, labor and minorities felt free to go with Bradley, who proved remarkably wooden as a campaigner but won comfortably nevertheless.

Despite his dull speaking style, Bradley retains a celebrity appeal that has kept his popularity intact. He periodically stands up for New Jersey in public when detractors ridicule it as a swamp of crime, pollution and tackiness. He is pushing to get the state its first commercial television franchise, and to keep the Army at Fort Dix, the basic training center which helps much of central New Jersey by catering to the purchasing power of 3,200 permanent staff and 6,000 recruits.

## Committees

**Energy and Natural Resources** (9th of 9 Democrats)
Energy and Mineral Resources; Energy Conservation and Supply; Water and Power.

**Finance** (8th of 9 Democrats)
Energy and Agricultural Taxation; Health; International Trade.

**Special Aging** (5th of 7 Democrats)

## Elections

**1978 General**

| | |
|---|---|
| Bill Bradley (D ) | 1,082,960 (55 %) |
| Jeffrey Bell (R ) | 844,200 (43 %) |

**1978 Primary**

| | |
|---|---|
| Bill Bradley (D ) | 217,502 (59 %) |
| Richard Leone (D ) | 97,667 (26 %) |
| Alexander Menza (D ) | 32,386 (9 %) |
| Other (D ) | 21,698 (6 %) |

## Campaign Finance

| | Receipts | Receipts from PACs | Expenditures |
|---|---|---|---|
| 1978 | | | |
| Bradley (D ) | $1,689,975 | $192,896 (11 %) | $1,688,499 |
| Bell (R ) | $1,432,924 | $166,263 (12 %) | $1,418,931 |

## Voting Studies

| | Presidential Support | | Party Unity | | Conservative Coalition | |
|---|---|---|---|---|---|---|
| Year | S | O | S | O | S | O |
| 1980 | 65 | 23 | 72 | 12 | 6 | 75 |
| 1979 | 88 | 10 | 87 | 9 | 11 | 85 |

S = Support    O = Opposition

## Key Votes

**96th Congress**

| | |
|---|---|
| Maintain relations with Taiwan (1979) | N |
| Reduce synthetic fuel development funds (1979) | N |
| Impose nuclear plant moratorium (1979) | Y |
| Kill stronger windfall profits tax (1979) | N |
| Guarantee Chrysler Corp. loans (1979) | Y |
| Approve military draft registration (1980) | N |
| End Revenue Sharing to the states (1980) | N |
| Block Justice Dept. busing suits (1980) | N |

**97th Congress**

| | |
|---|---|
| Restore urban program funding cuts (1981) | Y |

## Interest Group Ratings

| Year | ADA | ACA | AFL-CIO | CCUS-1 | CCUS-2 |
|---|---|---|---|---|---|
| 1980 | 72 | 0 | 100 | 38 | |
| 1979 | 68 | 4 | 95 | 0 | 25 |

# 1 James J. Florio (D)

## Of Camden — Elected 1974

**Born:** Aug. 29, 1937, Brooklyn, N.Y.
**Education:** Trenton State College, B.A. 1962; Rutgers U. Law School, LL.B. 1967.
**Military Career:** Navy, 1955-58, Naval Reserve, 1958-74.
**Profession:** Lawyer.
**Family:** Wife, Maryanne Spaeth; three children.
**Religion:** Roman Catholic.
**Political Career:** N.J. Assembly, 1970-74; Democratic nominee for U.S. House, 1972; sought Democratic gubernatorial nomination, 1977; Democratic nominee for governor, 1981.

**In Washington:** Florio sought and won the Democratic nomination for governor of New Jersey in 1981 on a solid six-year record of legislative accomplishment, built without resort to some of the social amenities that help other members succeed in Congress.

Florio managed an enormous workload in recent years as his Commerce Subcommittee on Transportation generated a series of major bills, substantially rewriting the regulatory code for railroads and prescribing rules for cleaning up hazardous waste dumping sites.

It has generally been an impressive performance, even though Florio has not been one of the more amiable or popular House members. Intense and serious, he likes to control legislative situations himself, consulting few others. He has sometimes left Democratic committee colleagues wondering what he was up to from day to day. But he has always been careful to work with the subcommittee's influential Republican, Edward Madigan of Illinois, and normally they have brought the bills to passage without massive change.

In 1980, Florio and Madigan produced a railroad deregulation bill encouraging competition in the industry by allowing the railroads greater rate setting freedom. It provoked lobbying opposition from certain shippers, particularly utilities and agricultural producers, who were afraid the railroads were being turned loose to charge them excessively high rates.

Florio stuck to his guns, and at first it seemed he would prevail easily on the House floor. But he was gradually undermined by another Commerce Committee Democrat, Bob Eckhardt of Texas, who wanted stricter controls on the railroads and complained that Florio had been unwilling even to talk to him about the issue.

At one point, Eckhardt managed to win narrow passage of an amendment seriously weakening deregulation, and the bill's future seemed in doubt. Florio then negotiated a compromise, failing to win over Eckhardt but satisfying most of the bill's other critics, including the utility industry. The bill passed the House easily in its modified form, and became law later in the year.

Florio had an even harder time with his bill creating a "superfund," through which chemical companies would pay to clean up hazardous waste sites. The issue was how much the companies would have to contribute to the fund, and there was concerted industry opposition.

Florio's bill provided for a \$1.3 billion "superfund," with the chemical industry providing 75 percent of the money and the federal government 25 percent. In order to get the bill approved by the full Commerce Committee, Florio had to scale the fund down to \$600 million and have the cost split 50-50 by industry and government.

On the House floor, however, the Commerce Committee version was merged with a stronger superfund bill from the Ways and Means Committee, one which even much of the industry was persuaded to accept. The legislation was weak-

---

**1st District: Southwest — Camden.**
Population: 524,125 (10% increase since 1970). Race: White 427,820 (82%), Black 76,064 (15%), Others 20,241 (4%). Spanish origin: 21,348 (4%).

ened somewhat in the Senate, but the bill that became law in December was relatively close to what Florio wanted — a second major victory for him in the space of a few months.

At times, Florio wins on sheer tenacity. Determined to provide $750 million in 1980 to upgrade service in the Northeast rail corridor, he attached the money to an emergency bill needed to continue freight movement over a bankrupt Rock Island line. The Senate was outraged, but Florio held the Rock Island bill hostage until he got the Northeast corridor money.

The year before, when the Public Works Committee had tried in conference with the Senate to weaken an airport noise control bill, exempting smaller planes from its provisions, Florio held up the proceedings of the conference. He urged President Carter to veto the bill if enacted in weakened form. The threat ultimately resulted in a new compromise with fewer exemptions than the Public Works Committee had proposed.

**At Home:** "Driven" is the word most often associated with Florio. He has climbed to political prominence rung by rung, finally attaining the Democratic nomination for governor on his second try in 1981.

He had been in the House only two years when he first ran for governor, in 1977, challenging Gov. Brendan T. Byrne for renomination. Florio was never really a threat in that contest; he was not widely known outside his Camden-area congressional district, and he did not have the financial resources to expand his recognition. He finished fourth out of ten Democratic candidates with 15 percent of the vote as Byrne won nomination for a second term.

The 1981 campaign was different. A new state campaign finance system provided public money for gubernatorial candidates, and it helped Florio air effective television commercials all over the state, stressing the work he had done on toxic waste and mass transit. Florio was careful to campaign as a moderate Democrat. Some voters who might have questioned his relatively liberal House voting record were reassured by his primary endorsement from the National Rifle Association.

Florio ran well even in some of the northern counties where his main rival, U.S. Rep. Robert A. Roe of Passaic County, had expected to score heavily. Florio took 25.7 percent of the vote, finishing far ahead of the second-place Roe, who had 15.5 percent. That set up a general election contest for November of 1981 between Florio and Republican Thomas Kean.

Born in Brooklyn, Florio worked his way through Rutgers University law school, serving as night watchman at the Camden County courthouse, a patronage job. He was a protégé of Angelo Errichetti, the mayor of Camden, who helped him become a state assemblyman.

Florio failed in his first try for Congress in 1972 against Republican Rep. John E. Hunt, but broke through two years later with the help of Watergate. Hunt hurt himself by remaining a stalwart defender of President Nixon.

Soon after his election to Congress, Florio drifted apart from Errichetti, who was convicted in 1980 on Abscam bribery charges. Florio himself turned down an Abscam bribe, and received valuable publicity for it all over New Jersey in the months before his second gubernatorial campaign.

**The District:** Benjamin Franklin once compared New Jersey to a barrel that empties at either end, New York or Philadelphia. The Philadelphia spigot is Camden, which has been greatly influenced by the metropolis across the Delaware River. Many of the 1st District voters came originally from Philadelphia.

Near the river are old factories and oil tanks. The aged, run-down city of Camden still houses large industries like Campbell Soup Co. and RCA, but many businesses and residents have fled, leaving block after block of boarded-up houses, crime and poverty. Blacks are the dominant group in the city, followed by Hispanics.

East of Camden, the towns are increasingly Republican, but enough Democratic sympathies remain to place many of them in the swing category.

Camden, Gloucester and the blue-collar suburbs near them have provided reliable Democratic votes for Florio, although not always for other Democratic candidates. Before Florio came along, in fact, the district had had Republican representation throughout this century. It went for Reagan in 1980.

---

## Committees

**Energy and Commerce** (7th of 24 Democrats)
Commerce, Transportation, and Tourism, chairman; Health and the Environment.

**Interior and Insular Affairs** (10th of 23 Democrats)
Oversight and Investigations; Public Lands and National Parks.

**Select Aging** (8th of 31 Democrats)
Health and Long-Term Care; Human Services.

# Elections

**1980 General**

| | |
|---|---|
| James Florio (D) | 147,352 (77%) |
| Scott Sibert (R) | 42,154 (22%) |

**1978 General**

| | |
|---|---|
| James Florio (D) | 106,096 (79%) |
| Robert Deitch (R) | 26,853 (20%) |

**Previous Winning Percentages**

1976 (70%)    1974 (58%)

**District Vote For President**

| | 1980 | | 1976 | | 1972 |
|---|---|---|---|---|---|
| D | 84,465 (43 %) | D | 112,400 (56%) | D | 74,821 (39%) |
| R | 92,376 (47 %) | R | 82,661 (42%) | R | 112,632 (59%) |
| I | 16,867 (9 %) | | | | |

# Campaign Finance

| | Receipts | Receipts from PACs | Expenditures |
|---|---|---|---|
| **1980** | | | |
| Florio (D) | $165,185 | $119,825 (73%) | $132,363 |
| Sibert (R) | $23,187 | $356 (2%) | $23,165 |
| **1978** | | | |
| Florio (D) | $88,384 | $77,372 (88%) | $76,026 |

# Voting Studies

| | Presidential Support | | Party Unity | | Conservative Coalition | |
|---|---|---|---|---|---|---|
| Year | S | O | S | O | S | O |
| 1980 | 74 | 23 | 85 | 11 | 19 | 73 |
| 1979 | 75 | 19 | 85 | 12 | 19 | 75 |
| 1978 | 66 | 29 | 75 | 22 | 29 | 68 |
| 1977 | 57 | 20 | 60 | 16 | 17 | 59 |
| 1976 | 24 | 73 | 82 | 11 | 21 | 71 |
| 1975 | 28 | 69 | 80 | 13 | 16 | 76 |

S = Support    O = Opposition

# Key Votes

**96th Congress**

| | |
|---|---|
| Weaken Carter oil profits tax (1979) | N |
| Reject hospital cost control plan (1979) | N |
| Implement Panama Canal Treaties (1979) | Y |
| Establish Department of Education (1979) | N |
| Approve Anti-busing Amendment (1979) | N |
| Guarantee Chrysler Corp. loans (1979) | Y |
| Approve military draft registration (1980) | Y |
| Aid Sandinista regime in Nicaragua (1980) | Y |
| Strengthen fair housing laws (1980) | Y |

**97th Congress**

| | |
|---|---|
| Reagan budget proposal (1981) | N |

# Interest Group Ratings

| Year | ADA | ACA | AFL-CIO | CCUS |
|---|---|---|---|---|
| 1980 | 72 | 13 | 89 | 64 |
| 1979 | 84 | 12 | 95 | 6 |
| 1978 | 55 | 22 | 75 | 33 |
| 1977 | 50 | 32 | 91 | 13 |
| 1976 | 75 | 8 | 83 | 13 |
| 1975 | 68 | 17 | 95 | 12 |

# 2 William J. Hughes (D)

**Of Ocean City — Elected 1974**

**Born:** Oct. 17, 1932, Salem, N.J.
**Education:** Rutgers U., A.B. 1955, J.D. 1958.
**Profession:** Lawyer.
**Family:** Wife, Nancy Lucille Gibson; four children.
**Religion:** Episcopalian.
**Political Career:** Assistant prosecutor, Cape May County, 1960-70; Ocean City Solicitor, 1970-74; unsuccessful Democratic nominee for U.S. House, 1970.

**In Washington:** Patient, thorough, and conservative by instinct, Hughes has a reputation as a man willing to help out the party and its leaders when needed.

As a member of the Merchant Marine Committee, he helped the Carter administration in its fight to win approval of legislation implementing the Panama Canal treaties. When the panel held hearings on charges that Panama was running guns to the Sandinista rebels in Nicaragua, Hughes spoke up for the administration side. He argued that, despite a vivid display of guns in the hearing room, treaty opponents were a long way from establishing a connection between the weapons and the Sandinista regime. Later he supported the legislation on the House floor.

Hughes was also on Carter's side during the 96th Congress on the issue of the legislative veto. The Judiciary Committee, on which Hughes serves, was writing a regulatory reform bill, and the administration was vigorously fighting language that would allow Congress a veto over a wide range of new federal regulations. Carter called Hughes with a personal appeal to vote against the legislative veto in the Administrative Law Subcommittee, where it was defeated on a close 5-4 vote.

On the Judiciary Committee, Hughes has focused on antitrust matters; in his first term he promoted a bill requiring large corporations to give advance notice of mergers to the federal government. On Merchant Marine, he has argued for strict laws regulating offshore oil drilling, and for an end to the dumping of waste in the ocean. At the start of the 97th Congress, he reintroduced his earlier bill placing a surcharge on public utilities with nuclear plants to help pay for the cost of the Three Mile Island nuclear accident.

He has also won some conspicuous victories on the issue of gasohol, which is of some impor-

tance to his vegetable-growing district. In 1979, Hughes succeeded in amending Defense and Postal Service authorization bills to direct those two departments to buy and use gasohol in operating their vehicles. Hughes said the two agencies account for 7.5 million barrels of oil or 80 percent of the oil purchased by the government.

**At Home:** Hughes has a sizable number of Republican constituents to please, and his generally conservative voting record has pleased them enough to keep him in office for four terms. He was Ocean City solicitor in 1974 when he challenged four-term Republican Rep. Charles W. Sandman Jr. He had challenged Sandman once before, in 1970, and come within 6,000 votes. The second time he began in a stronger position, because Sandman had hurt himself badly with his slashing attacks on President Nixon's detractors during the 1974 impeachment debate. The result was as much a decision on Sandman as it was a triumph for Hughes, but it was overwhelming — the incumbent drew only 41.3 percent of the vote.

Hughes has worked hard to cultivate this sprawling district. His mobile van constantly tours the area, looking for people in need of help. That effort has had an especially big payoff in normally Republican Ocean County, which is filled with retirees who have Social Security problems.

The congressman has become visible on nu-

---

**2nd District: South — Atlantic City, Vineland.** Population: 610,529 (28% increase since 1970). Race: White 521,289 (85%), Black 71,689 (12%), Others 17,551 (3%). Spanish origin: 24,546 (4%).

merous local issues. He helped get military uniform contracts for the ailing garment industry in Cumberland County, pushed for higher gasoline allocations to help seashore tourism during the 1979 energy crunch and fought against local storage of nuclear waste from the Salem atomic generating plants.

Hughes has won comfortably each time. His 1980 Republican foe tried to paint him as too close to President Carter, but Hughes triumphed easily.

**The District:** Atlantic City, the aged resort now dependent on casino gambling, is the district's focal point and a center of Democratic

strength.

That marks a turnabout from the days when the city and surrounding Atlantic County were dominated by the Republican organization of the late state Sen. Frank S. "Hap" Farley. Farley, whose name is immortalized by a rest stop on the Atlantic City Expressway, ruled from the late 1940s to the early 1970s.

Two other sources of Democratic votes are Salem and Cumberland counties, where garment, chemical and glass industry workers live. But the increasingly populous seaside towns in Cape May and Ocean counties weight the district toward Republicans in most contests.

## Committees

**Judiciary** (9th of 16 Democrats)
Crime, chairman; Monopolies and Commercial Law.

**Merchant Marine and Fisheries** (11th of 20 Democrats)
Coast Guard and Navigation; Fisheries and Wildlife Conservation and the Environment; Oceanography.

**Select Aging** (10th of 31 Democrats)
Human Services.

## Elections

**1980 General**

| | |
|---|---|
| William Hughes (D) | 135,437 (57%) |
| Beech Fox (R) | 97,072 (41%) |

**1978 General**

| | |
|---|---|
| William Hughes (D) | 112,768 (66%) |
| James Biggs (R) | 56,997 (34%) |

**Previous Winning Percentages**

1976 (62%)     1974 (57%)

**District Vote For President**

| | 1980 | | 1976 | | 1972 |
|---|---|---|---|---|---|
| D | 94,184 (37 %) | D | 123,127 (50%) | D | 73,018 (34%) |
| R | 141,469 (55 %) | R | 120,895 (49%) | R | 138,957 (64%) |
| I | 17,210 (7 %) | | | | |

## Campaign Finance

| | Receipts | Receipts from PACs | Expenditures |
|---|---|---|---|
| **1980** | | | |
| Hughes (D) | $117,960 | $24,100 (20%) | $101,246 |
| Fox (R) | $131,909 | $7,925 (6%) | $132,376 |

| | | | |
|---|---|---|---|
| **1978** | | | |
| Hughes (D) | 128,501 | $14,745 (11%) | $108,703 |

## Voting Studies

| | Presidential Support | | Party Unity | | Conservative Coalition | |
|---|---|---|---|---|---|---|
| **Year** | **S** | **O** | **S** | **O** | **S** | **O** |
| 1980 | 66 | 31 | 63 | 35 | 56 | 40 |
| 1979 | 67 | 30 | 66 | 32 | 44 | 52 |
| 1978 | 71 | 27 | 60 | 38 | 41 | 55 |
| 1977 | 63 | 32 | 61 | 34 | 42 | 53 |
| 1976 | 24 | 76 | 71 | 26 | 39 | 58 |
| 1975 | 35 | 65 | 70 | 27 | 38 | 58 |

S = Support     O = Opposition

## Key Votes

**96th Congress**

| | |
|---|---|
| Weaken Carter oil profits tax (1979) | N |
| Reject hospital cost control plan (1979) | Y |
| Implement Panama Canal Treaties (1979) | Y |
| Establish Department of Education (1979) | Y |
| Approve Anti-busing Amendment (1979) | N |
| Guarantee Chrysler Corp. loans (1979) | Y |
| Approve military draft registration (1980) | Y |
| Aid Sandinista regime in Nicaragua (1980) | N |
| Strengthen fair housing laws (1980) | Y |

**97th Congress**

| | |
|---|---|
| Reagan budget proposal (1981) | N |

## Interest Group Ratings

| Year | ADA | ACA | AFL-CIO | CCUS |
|---|---|---|---|---|
| 1980 | 61 | 42 | 53 | 65 |
| 1979 | 58 | 27 | 80 | 28 |
| 1978 | 55 | 35 | 68 | 17 |
| 1977 | 50 | 44 | 78 | 53 |
| 1976 | 60 | 36 | 61 | 19 |
| 1975 | 79 | 39 | 82 | 19 |

# 3 James J. Howard (D)

**Of Spring Lake Heights — Elected 1964**

**Born:** July 24, 1927, Irvington, N.J.
**Education:** St. Bonaventure U., B.A. 1952; Rutgers U., M.Ed. 1958.
**Military Career:** Navy, 1944-46.
**Profession:** Teacher.
**Family:** Wife, Marlene Vetrano; three children.
**Religion:** Roman Catholic.
**Political Career:** No previous office.

**In Washington:** The leading road builder in the House during the past decade, Howard has to worry about dams, airport development, and coal slurry pipelines this year as chairman of the full Public Works Committee. But highways remain his first love.

Over 15 years at Public Works, Howard's sheer nervous energy and determination have made him an effective highway advocate with a key role in developing legislation worth hundreds of billions of dollars. He has been a favorite of highway builders and users, who contribute to his campaigns and invite him to speak at meetings. A look at some of his supporters reveals names like the National Limestone Institute, the Outdoor Advertising Council and the American Road and Transportation Builders Association.

In the early years at Public Works, Howard loved highways considerably more than the mass transit projects that compete with them for federal money. But that seemed to change slowly after 1975, when Howard took over the old Public Works Roads Subcommittee, renamed the Subcommittee on Surface Transportation. By 1978, aware of growing competition for federal dollars from urban transit advocates, Howard was ready to put highways and transit together in one bill for the first time. He figured he could balance Western support for highways with Eastern demands for mass transit and keep everyone happy.

The result was a $54 billion measure. It did not go nearly as far as the Carter administration wanted to go toward ending competition between highways and mass transit for the same money, but it did give local governments some new flexibility in using their funds, and provided for 80 percent federal funding for most mass transit capital projects.

Howard's handling of the 1978 bill represented a major success for his high-pressure, everywhere-at-once style. He shepherded the bill closely from start to finish, adding amendments as bargaining chips, negotiating with the Senate, arguing with the White House, and nagging House leaders. When it finally cleared Congress, the bill contained special projects for special people — a bridge study for Washington state, a transit project in rural Texas, a toll bridge in West Virginia, and an extra piece of interstate highway in northern California.

At the very last minute, as the bill sat on President Carter's desk threatened by veto because of its cost, Howard was still cutting deals. Carter's long-sought energy bill was due on the House floor the next day and the vote was expected to be close. Howard told White House aides that if the transportation bill was not signed, he would vote no on energy and take three other New Jersey Democrats with him. Within hours, Carter was on the phone to Speaker O'Neill with a promise the highway bill would be signed into law. Howard and six other New Jersey Democrats voted with the administration as the energy package survived its key test on a 207-206 vote.

In 1981, as the highway law approached its expiration, Howard challenged Reagan administration efforts to cut back on federal highway spending. He argued for increased funding for the interstate highway system and other roads simply to keep the federal system in decent repair, and called for increased highway taxes to pay for it. The full Public Works Committee reported a bill in May that basically preserved the 1978 law

---

**3rd District: Central coast — Long Branch, Asbury Park.** Population: 525,767 (11% increase since 1970). Race: White 468,514 (89%), Black 45,382 (9%), Others 11,871 (2%). Spanish origin: 15,220 (3%).

against proposed Reagan cutbacks, but only for one year. Howard also pushed the committee to approve an amendment that could block federal aid to states that do not enforce the 55 mph speed limit, which he strongly supports.

Howard had tried in 1980 to extend mass transit legislation through 1985, but it fell victim to a Senate filibuster in the closing days of the Congress. Howard and other transit specialists had hoped to get the extension out of the way before President Reagan took office, but Senate Republicans wanted to wait.

Howard did have one conspicuous victory in 1980 — his management of a bill deregulating the trucking industry. The legislation was a major priority for the Carter administration, but Howard at first shared the skepticism of the American Trucking Associations. By the spring of 1980, however, he had decided to work for a compromise bill, arranged one with Senate Commerce Chairman Howard W. Cannon, and moved it through the House on a 367-13 vote. The administration supported the compromise, and most of the industry was willing to accept it. The Teamsters were the only major holdout as the bill became law. As passed, it removes barriers to entering the trucking business, in an effort to make it more competitive.

Howard has been a transportation man since he entered Congress in 1965, declaring highways the lifeblood of New Jersey. He lobbied to get on the Public Works Committee even before he was sworn in, going to his state's senior Democrats for help and even asking New Jersey's governor to write a letter to President Johnson for him.

Almost immediately, Howard started working on fulfillment of his campaign promise for a limited access highway connecting his Jersey shore district and Trenton. When Congress took up the 1967 highway bill, Howard was there with his own amendment. It took some rejiggering of interstate highway formulas (to give New Jersey more than its share), but Howard managed to win authorization of the highway. In recent years, he has worked on mass transit ideas appealing to his district, such as a hydrofoil or other water transportation that would connect it with New York City.

Howard has always been able to maintain close ties with all the Democratic factions in the chamber. He is a friend and occasional junketing companion of Speaker O'Neill, and can often be found joking with other members and staff outside the Speaker's office. He also was an early ally of Arizona Democrat Morris K. Udall in efforts toward procedural reform in the House, and a booster of Udall's 1976 presidential candidacy.

For several years he was a member of Udall's Interior Committee, to which he contributed mainly by giving Udall his proxy on important votes. He was rarely there himself. Howard's career has been free from scandal, even when the FBI's Abscam operation tried to entice him into accepting a bribe. Howard was only slightly amused when a hometown newspaper put his photo below a banner headline proclaiming that nine congressmen had been named in the FBI case. In small type under his picture, the paper wrote "not ninth man."

**At Home:** Howard seldom has an easy time winning in his Monmouth County district, which was reliably Republican until he captured it narrowly in the Lyndon Johnson landslide of 1964.

In his eight campaigns since then, Howard has cleared 60 percent only twice. His closest call came in 1980, when he faced a determined challenger in Republican state Assemblywoman Marie Sheehan Muhler. The New Jersey Education Association helped save Howard, a former teacher and school administrator.

Howard's growing power on the Public Works Committee has not always helped him at home. In recent years, he has had to face complaints about the decrepit commuter trains that trudge through the district far behind schedule. Opponents have said a man in Howard's position should be able to do something.

But Howard says that his congressional stature has made possible at least an upgrading of the line. In addition, he points to his successful efforts to help keep the Army from cutting jobs at Fort Monmouth, a major local employer.

Howard remains independent of the Monmouth County Democratic organization and its internal warfare. As a result, he has stayed popular with all of its factions. He made a strong recovery from a 1978 heart attack and is visible on weekends in the district throughout the year.

**The District:** Monmouth County's beaches and other recreational attractions have produced a surge in its population during the past two decades, bringing in Democrats from New York, Newark and Jersey City who have turned a once solid Republican area into marginal territory.

The county, nearly identical with the congressional district, can be divided into three parts. In the north are longstanding Democratic bastions — working-class towns like Keansburg and aging resorts like Long Branch, home to sizable black and ethnic Italian populations.

Along the coast to the south are a chain of wealthy shore communities typified by Sea Girt, with its elegant houses and fine lawns. Thanks to affluent retirees, these are year-round communities and firmly Republican.

The inland central section of Monmouth is a political tossup. Democrats have made advances there, winning local elections in Freehold, Marlboro and other medium-sized towns. Republicans remain ahead in affluent places like Colt's Neck.

Technologically oriented Fort Monmouth, in the county's central section, has spawned a large civilian electronics industry, which has brought in a contingent of Republican professional people.

## Committees

**Public Works and Transportation** (Chairman)

## Elections

**1980 General**

| | |
|---|---|
| James Howard (D) | 106,269 (50%) |
| Marie Muhler (R) | 104,184 (49%) |

**1978 General**

| | |
|---|---|
| James Howard (D) | 83,349 (56%) |
| Bruce Coe (R) | 64,730 (44%) |

**Previous Winning Percentages**

1976 (62%)   1974 (69%)   1972 (53%)   1970 (55%)
1968 (58%)   1966 (53%)   1964 (50%)

**District Vote For President**

| | 1980 | | 1976 | | 1972 |
|---|---|---|---|---|---|
| D | 74,709 (33 %) | D | 93,256 (43%) | D | 65,028 (32%) |
| R | 129,419 (57 %) | R | 118,717 (55%) | R | 133,270 (67%) |
| I | 18,136 (8 %) | | | | |

## Campaign Finance

| | Receipts | Receipts from PACs | Expenditures |
|---|---|---|---|
| **1980** | | | |
| Howard (D) | $228,366 | $80,225 (35%) | $208,253 |
| Muhler (R) | $436,110 | $50,431 (12%) | $163,436 |
| **1978** | | | |
| Howard (D) | $150,559 | $62,208 (41%) | $123,220 |
| Coe (R) | $145,179 | $300 (.2%) | $145,048 |

## Voting Studies

| | Presidential Support | | Party Unity | | Conservative Coalition | |
|---|---|---|---|---|---|---|
| Year | S | O | S | O | S | O |
| 1980 | 75 | 15 | 92 | 5 | 14 | 82 |
| 1979 | 73 | 23 | 90 | 6 | 15 | 80 |
| 1978 | 71 | 13 | 81 | 5 | 10 | 77 |
| 1977 | 81 | 9 | 82 | 4 | 9 | 81 |
| 1976 | 22 | 71 | 89 | 4 | 8 | 84 |
| 1975 | 31 | 64 | 92 | 3 | 8 | 88 |
| 1974 (Ford) | 22 | 43 | | | | |
| 1974 | 26 | 45 | 63 | 6 | 10 | 57 |
| 1973 | 20 | 71 | 87 | 8 | 6 | 89 |
| 1972 | 49 | 38 | 88 | 9 | 10 | 84 |
| 1971 | 25 | 67 | 83 | 7 | 5 | 83 |
| 1970 | 66 | 31 | 86 | 7 | 11 | 82 |
| 1969 | 43 | 40 | 75 | 5 | 4 | 84 |
| 1968 | 75 | 13 | 70 | 5 | 2 | 80 |
| 1967 | 87 | 6 | 85 | 3 | 7 | 80 |
| 1966 | 69 | 4 | 69 | 3 | 3 | 70 |
| 1965 | 92 | 3 | 94 | 2 | 0 | 96 |

S = Support          O = Opposition

## Key Votes

**96th Congress**

| | |
|---|---|
| Weaken Carter oil profits tax (1979) | N |
| Reject hospital cost control plan (1979) | N |
| Implement Panama Canal Treaties (1979) | Y |
| Establish Department of Education (1979) | Y |
| Approve Anti-busing Amendment (1979) | N |
| Guarantee Chrysler Corp. loans (1979) | Y |
| Approve military draft registration (1980) | Y |
| Aid Sandinista regime in Nicaragua (1980) | Y |
| Strengthen fair housing laws (1980) | Y |

**97th Congress**

| | |
|---|---|
| Reagan budget proposal (1981) | N |

## Interest Group Ratings

| Year | ADA | ACA | AFL-CIO | CCUS |
|---|---|---|---|---|
| 1980 | 83 | 14 | 79 | 55 |
| 1979 | 79 | 8 | 95 | 0 |
| 1978 | 60 | 9 | 84 | 7 |
| 1977 | 70 | 9 | 95 | 7 |
| 1976 | 85 | 4 | 87 | 0 |
| 1975 | 89 | 0 | 91 | 12 |
| 1974 | 65 | 9 | 100 | 17 |
| 1973 | 88 | 4 | 100 | 18 |
| 1972 | 75 | 5 | 91 | 10 |
| 1971 | 86 | 4 | 82 | - |
| 1970 | 76 | 11 | 86 | 0 |
| 1969 | 80 | 8 | 100 | - |
| 1968 | 83 | 5 | 100 | - |
| 1967 | 87 | 0 | 91 | 10 |
| 1966 | 82 | 12 | 100 | - |
| 1965 | 84 | 4 | - | 10 |

# 4 Christopher H. Smith (R)

### Of Old Bridge — Elected 1980

**Born:** March 4, 1953, Rahway, N.J.
**Education:** Trenton State College, B.A. 1975.
**Profession:** Salesman.
**Family:** Wife, Marie Hahn; two children.
**Religion:** Roman Catholic.
**Political Career:** Unsuccessful Republican nominee for U.S. House, 1978.

**The Member:** Smith's second try against Rep. Frank Thompson Jr. was a long shot until the veteran Democrat became enmeshed in Abscam. In 1978, Thompson, the leading House labor spokesman and chairman of the House Administration Committee, had taken more than 60 percent of the vote against Smith.

But Thompson was damaged fatally by his summer 1980 indictment for allegedly accepting a $50,000 bribe from a phony Arab sheik. After first soft-pedaling Abscam, Smith eventually demanded that Thompson release copies of FBI videotapes showing him discussing the scheme. Thompson refused. Smith won every town in the district except Trenton and three smaller communities.

Smith takes the standard Republican stance on federal spending — he wants less of it. He has said that making federal loan guarantees to Chrysler is simply government underwriting bankruptcy. On the Small Business Committee, however, Smith opposed a plan to increase the interest rate charged on federal loans to the handicapped. He also tried to make sure that a $500,000 housing project for his district did not fall prey to budget-cutting.

Smith is a militant opponent of abortion. He once served as the executive director of the state's Right to Life Committee.

**The District:** Industrial Mercer County, anchored by the city of Trenton, is solidly Democratic, and was sufficient until 1980 to keep Thompson comfortably in office. Mercer was one of only three New Jersey counties to support Jimmy Carter in November 1980.

Beyond Mercer, however, the towns become steadily more Republican. Most of the reliably Republican votes in the 4th come from northern Burlington County.

## Committees

**Small Business** (14th of 17 Republicans)
General Oversight; SBA and SBIC Authority, Minority Enterprise and General Small Business Problems.

**Veterans' Affairs** (10th of 14 Republicans)
Hospitals and Health Care; Housing and Memorial Affairs.

## Elections

**1980 General**

| | |
|---|---|
| Christopher Smith (R) | 95,447 (57%) |
| Frank Thompson Jr. (D) | 68,480 (41%) |

**1980 Primary**

| | |
|---|---|
| Christopher Smith (R) | 8,121 (83%) |
| John Scalamonti (R) | 1,676 (17%) |

**District Vote For President**

| | 1980 | | 1976 | | 1972 |
|---|---|---|---|---|---|
| **D** | 80,235 (44 %) | **D** | 96,930 (53%) | **D** | 74,902 (42%) |
| **R** | 85,645 (47 %) | **R** | 83,640 (45%) | **R** | 102,704 (57%) |
| **I** | 14,360 (8 %) | | | | |

## Campaign Finance

| | Receipts | Receipts from PACs | Expenditures |
|---|---|---|---|
| **1980** | | | |
| Smith (R) | $79,075 | $40,272 (51%) | $79,069 |
| Thompson (D) | $181,019 | $102,700 (57%) | $169,065 |

## Key Vote

**97th Congress**

| | |
|---|---|
| Reagan budget proposal (1981) | Y |

---

**4th District: Central — Trenton.**
Population: 487,962 (2% increase since 1970).
Race: White 403,584 (83%), Black 68,843 (14%), Others 15,535 (3%). Spanish origin: 16,839 (3%).

# 5 Millicent Fenwick (R)

**Of Bernardsville — Elected 1974**

**Born:** Feb. 25, 1910, New York, N.Y.
**Education:** Attended Columbia U., 1933; attended New School for Social Research, 1942.
**Profession:** Editor.
**Family:** Divorced; two children.
**Religion:** Protestant.
**Political Career:** Bernardsville Borough Council, 1958-64; N.J. Assembly, 1970-72.

**In Washington:** Millicent Fenwick regularly walks onto the House floor with her pipe in her hand and bangs the bowl against a brass rail in the back of the chamber. The noise — especially on a quiet day when few are present — is startling, and members jump out of their seats and turn around. Fenwick never notices the effect, and proceeds as if nothing has happened.

It is not a bad symbol for the career of this elegant, outspoken woman who has never quite seemed to inhabit the same world as her colleagues, either personally or politically. In her fourth term in Congress, she is likely as ever to be shocked and surprised by things legislators have been doing since legislatures existed. When they engage in procedural skulduggery, she lectures them like a lovable, eccentric aunt.

In 1978, when House members took advantage of some complicated maneuvering to give themselves a pay raise without directly voting on it, Fenwick took the floor to quote Jefferson, reminding them that "we are not princes. We are public servants." She fought the raise, not because of the money but because of the "dishonest" way it was enacted. She said the action "justified the contempt people have" for Congress.

Fenwick has managed to avoid that contempt, although her popularity outside the House exceeds her effectiveness within it. The model for Rep. Lacey Davenport in the comic strip "Doonesbury," she is a heroine to feminist groups, human rights organizations and good government causes. But though she spends a lot of time on the House floor, and regularly speaks out on behalf of those causes, she has yet to learn the technicalities of addressing the chair or introducing an amendment — a small matter to some, but the mark of a professional to others. Of broader political strategy, compromise and coalition building, she remains largely unaware.

But if her procedural knowledge is limited, her legislative interests are wide-ranging. On the Foreign Affairs Committee, she worked to create the Helsinki Commission to maintain pressure for human rights. She introduced a bill to end the "marriage penalty" in tax law, and sponsored legislation to keep the food stamp program from having its funding cut. She visited Vietnam in 1975, but opposed military aid to that country. She favors the ERA and federal abortion funding.

Sometimes she is ahead of public perceptions. She began calling for truck deregulation years before it became a popular cause, and introduced her own bill at the start of her House career, although she was not directly involved in drafting the legislation that became law in 1980.

And occasionally, with her innocence and honesty, she will drive to the heart of a matter in a way that members find difficult to ignore. During debate on an expensive synthetic fuels program in 1979, she implored colleagues to back it. "Our constituents want action on energy," she said in her throaty, emotional voice. "They don't really care how much it costs."

**At Home:** Fenwick comes from a wealthy New Jersey family. Her father was a successful banker and her mother's family once owned 500 acres of land along the Hudson. She went to Foxcroft, a fashionable girls school in Virginia, but her formal education was interrupted when she was 15 and her father became ambassador to Spain. She returned to the United States during

> **5th District: North Central — Morristown, Princeton.** Population: 473,351 (1% decrease since 1970). Race: White 440,977 (93%), Black 20,084 (4%), Asian and Pacific Islander 9,013 (2%), Others 3,277 (1%). Spanish origin: 8,766 (2%).

the 1930s and modeled for *Vogue*. In 1938, after her four-year marriage to Hugh Fenwick ended in divorce, she returned to *Vogue* as a writer, eventually writing a book on etiquette.

She entered politics as a local school board official, then went on to work for civil rights and prison reform. Before being elected to the state Assembly in 1969, she was director of consumer affairs for the state of New Jersey.

In 1974, she won her party's House nomination by 83 votes in a primary against the GOP Assembly floor leader, Thomas Kean. Her impeccable reputation for integrity made the general election easy, even in a runaway Democratic year. Since then, she has easily defeated all comers. Her wealthy Republican constituents, while dissenting from many of her views, seem to admire her style and independence. She trounced a conservative primary challenger in 1980.

**The District:** There are rolling hills, fox hunts and huge estates in the 5th, and most of all there are Republicans. The district has the highest median income in New Jersey, and one of the highest in the nation. Its small-town and rural elite long has been represented in Washington by the socially prominent. Fenwick's predecessor, who retired in 1974 after 11 terms, was Republican Peter H. B. Frelinghuysen, possessor of another old New Jersey name and descendant of four U.S. senators.

The few concentrations of Democrats in this area are around industrial Bound Brook in Manville, home of a Johns Manville asbestos plant, and in some segments of the Princeton academic community. Neither party, however, is highly organized.

## Committees

**Education and Labor** (9th of 14 Republicans)
Employment Opportunities; Labor-Management Relations; Labor Standards.

**Foreign Affairs** (9th of 16 Republicans)
Europe and the Middle East; International Economic Policy and Trade.

**Select Aging** (11th of 23 Republicans)
Health and Long-Term Care.

## Elections

**1980 General**

| | |
|---|---|
| Millicent Fenwick (R) | 156,016 (78%) |
| Kieran Pillion Jr. (D) | 41,269 (21%) |

**1980 Primary**

| | |
|---|---|
| Millicent Fenwick (R) | 23,419 (70%) |
| Larry Harverly (R) | 10,080 (30%) |

**1978 General**

| | |
|---|---|
| Millicent Fenwick (R) | 100,739 (73%) |
| John Fahy (D) | 38,108 (27%) |

**Previous Winning Percentage**

1976 (67%)    1973 (53%)

**District Vote For President**

| | 1980 | | 1976 | | 1972 |
|---|---|---|---|---|---|
| **D** | 68,841 (31 %) | **D** | 88,044 (40%) | **D** | 73,268 (34 %) |
| **R** | 124,281 (57 %) | **R** | 128,351 (58%) | **R** | 139,407 (64 %) |
| **I** | 22,533 (10 %) | | | | |

## Campaign Finance

| | Receipts | Receipts from PACs | Expenditures |
|---|---|---|---|
| **1980** | | | |
| Fenwick (R) | $46,648 | $3,187 (7%) | $32,578 |
| Pillion (D) | $7,177 | $1,700 (24%) | $7,177 |

| 1978 | | | |
|---|---|---|---|
| Fenwick (R) | $62,252 | — (0%) | $61,777 |
| Fahy (D) | $43,555 | $7,600 (17%) | 43,509 |

## Voting Studies

| | Presidential Support | | Party Unity | | Conservative Coalition | |
|---|---|---|---|---|---|---|
| **Year** | **S** | **O** | **S** | **O** | **S** | **O** |
| 1980 | 53 | 42 | 57 | 36 | 43 | 47 |
| 1979 | 70 | 26 | 46 | 50 | 38 | 60 |
| 1978 | 77 | 21 | 48 | 51 | 37 | 62 |
| 1977 | 65 | 34 | 42 | 58 | 29 | 71 |
| 1976 | 39 | 55 | 36 | 58 | 34 | 64 |
| 1975 | 65 | 21 | 51 | 40 | 36 | 51 |

S = Support        O = Opposition

## Key Votes

**96th Congress**

| | |
|---|---|
| Weaken Carter oil profits tax (1979) | Y |
| Reject hospital cost control plan (1979) | Y |
| Implement Panama Canal Treaties (1979) | Y |
| Establish Department of Education (1979) | N |
| Approve Anti-busing Amendment (1979) | N |
| Guarantee Chrysler Corp. loans (1979) | Y |
| Approve military draft registration (1980) | N |
| Aid Sandinista regime in Nicaragua (1980) | Y |
| Strengthen fair housing laws (1980) | Y |

**97th Congress**

| | |
|---|---|
| Reagan budget proposal (1981) | Y |

## Interest Group Ratings

| Year | ADA | ACA | AFL-CIO | CCUS |
|---|---|---|---|---|
| 1980 | 67 | 54 | 32 | 72 |
| 1979 | 53 | 48 | 47 | 67 |
| 1978 | 55 | 33 | 35 | 59 |
| 1977 | 85 | 37 | 52 | 59 |
| 1976 | 65 | 19 | 52 | 20 |
| 1975 | 58 | 52 | 55 | 67 |

# 6  Edwin B. Forsythe (R)

**Of Moorestown — Elected 1970**

**Born:** Jan. 17, 1916, Westtown, Pa.
**Education:** Graduated Westtown H.S., 1933.
**Profession:** Dairy executive.
**Family:** Wife, Mary McKnight; one child.
**Religion:** Quaker.
**Political Career:** Mayor of Moorestown, 1957-62; N.J. Senate, 1964-70; asst. minority leader, 1966, minority leader, 1967, Senate president, 1968; president pro tempore of N.J. Senate, 1969.

**In Washington:** Forsythe has spent a quiet decade on the Merchant Marine Committee swinging back and forth between the environmental causes to which he is sympathetic and the development interests he is reluctant to dismiss.

In 1980, when Merchant Marine considered a bill to stiffen the penalties for selling endangered species outside the country, Forsythe cosponsored an amendment to add plants to the bill. The previous year, when controversy over the tiny snail darter fish was holding up construction of the Tellico Dam, and there was considerable pressure on the committee to weaken the endangered species law, Forsythe was one of the law's defenders. He is also a "save the whales" activist.

But other issues have found him on the opposite side. As a member of a special panel to rework the policy for leasing federal oil and gas reserves on the Outer Continental Shelf, Forsythe sided with the oil industry against those arguing for the strictest state control over the leases. When the legislation was modified in 1978 to meet some of his objections, Forsythe still voted against it on the House floor, one of only 18 to do so.

And when an Alaska lands bill reached the House floor in 1979, he was staunchly in favor of the more pro-development version that Merchant Marine had reported out. When some environmentalists argued that the Merchant Marine bill did not set aside enough land as wilderness, Forsythe argued that they were wrong. "Acres of wilderness, they are there," he insisted. "They are good acres and very properly selected."

On that issue, and on others during recent Congresses, Forsythe allied himself with New York Democrat John M. Murphy, the panel's chairman until this year, and its dominant influence. When Murphy brought to the floor the 1979 legislation implementing transfer of the Panama Canal, only 25 of 157 Republicans went along with him and the Democratic majority in favor of it. Forsythe was one of the 25.

On one issue Forsythe is consistent and militant — he staunchly supports the legislative veto. He has added a two-House veto provision to several bills in committee, including one on coastal zone management and one increasing penalties for smuggling endangered species.

Forsythe rarely plays an active role on foreign policy or military questions, but his Quaker background shows up on defense votes. In both 1979 and 1980, he moved to "recommit" — kill — the defense appropriation bill just before it passed the House. He did it matter-of-factly, without any speech, and received less than 50 votes both times. In 1980, he was one of only three Republicans voting to recommit.

**At Home:** Forsythe's crew cut, bow tie and slow-talking manner have made him an appealing candidate in his thoroughly Republican district, which encompasses Philadelphia suburbs and the rural pinelands. A one-time dairy farmer as well as a former mayor of suburban Moorestown, he has knowledge of both parts of his district.

Forsythe was president pro tempore of the New Jersey Senate in 1969, when Republican Rep. William T. Cahill gave up the 6th District to become governor. Forsythe won the seat with Cahill's blessing, defeating a more conservative primary opponent. Except for the Watergate year

---

**6th District: South Central.** Population: 572,112 (20% increase since 1970). Race: White 519,530 (91%), Black 40,532 (7%), Others 12,050 (2%). Spanish origin: 9,849 (2%).

of 1974, when he was held to 52.5 percent of the vote, his constituents have re-elected him by large margins.

On the hottest local issue — protecting the pinelands from development — he favors the view of local Republican leaders, which resists federally imposed safeguards for the area.

**The District:** This band of central New Jersey stretches from the Delaware River to the Atlantic. Its heart, however, is the Philadelphia suburbs of Burlington County. While redistricting may alter the district's shape, Burlington prob-

ably will stay.

Moorestown, Mt. Holly and the bulk of the Burlington communities are reliably Republican. Democrats can be found in blue-collar Pennsauken, in the black sections of Willingboro and among Jewish voters in Cherry Hill.

Moving east from the developed areas near the river, one comes to the Pine Barrens, where cranberries and blueberries are the main crops. The major employer in the pines is Fort Dix, which the Army occasionally talks of closing, much to residents' alarm.

## Committees

**Merchant Marine and Fisheries** (3rd of 15 Republicans)
Fisheries and Wildlife Conservation and the Environment; Panama Canal and Outer Continental Shelf.

**Scince and Technology** (7th of 17 Republicans)
Energy Research and Production; Science, Research and Technology.

**Standards of Official Conduct** (4th of 6 Republicans)

## Elections

**1980 General**

| | |
|---|---|
| Edwin Forsythe (R) | 125,792 (56%) |
| Lewis Weinstein (D) | 92,227 (41%) |

**1980 Primary**

| | |
|---|---|
| Edwin Forsythe (R) | 18,768 (90%) |
| Richard Amber ($) | 2,126 (10%) |

**1978 General**

| | |
|---|---|
| Edwin Forsythe (R) | 89,446 (60%) |
| Thomas McGann (D) | 56,874 (38%) |

**Previous Winning Percentages**

| | | | |
|---|---|---|---|
| 1976 (59%) | 1974 (53%) | 1972 (63%) | 1970 (54%) |

**District Vote For President**

| | 1980 | | 1976 | | 1972 |
|---|---|---|---|---|---|
| D | 81,930 (35 %) | D | 108,251 (47%) | D | 68,091 (34 %) |
| R | 128,699 (55 %) | R | 115,806 (51%) | R | 130,276 (65 %) |
| I | 19,958 (9 %) | | | | |

## Campaign Finance

| | Receipts | Receipts from PACs | Expenditures |
|---|---|---|---|
| **1980** | | | |
| Forsythe (R) | $118,988 | $44,628 (38%) | $111,093 |
| Weinstein (D) | $75,171 | $10,300 (14%) | $78,188 |
| **1978** | | | |
| Forsythe (R) | $82,170 | $11,400 (14%) | $87,804 |
| McGann (D) | $60,546 | $2,268 (4%) | $60,647 |

## Voting Studies

| | Presidential Support | | Party Unity | | Conservative Coalition | |
|---|---|---|---|---|---|---|
| Year | S | O | S | O | S | O |
| 1980 | 45 | 52 | 70 | 29 | 68 | 29 |
| 1979 | 22 | 28 | 42 | 21 | 38 | 19 |
| 1978 | 42 | 50 | 73 | 23 | 63 | 32 |
| 1977 | 42 | 35 | 55 | 21 | 48 | 25 |
| 1976 | 67 | 25 | 61 | 27 | 59 | 29 |
| 1975 | 69 | 24 | 68 | 22 | 59 | 27 |
| 1974 (Ford) | 56 | 43 | | | | |
| 1974 | 62 | 28 | 51 | 42 | 41 | 50 |
| 1973 | 62 | 35 | 63 | 36 | 61 | 38 |
| 1972 | 68 | 16 | 58 | 33 | 60 | 29 |
| 1971 | 72 | 28 | 61 | 36 | 51 | 44 |
| 1970 | 92 | 8† | 71 | 29† | 54 | 38† |

S = Support          O = Opposition

†Not eligible for all recorded votes.

## Key Votes

**96th Congress**

| | |
|---|---|
| Weaken Carter oil profits tax (1979) | ? |
| Reject hospital cost control plan (1979) | Y |
| Implement Panama Canal Treaties (1979) | ? |
| Establish Department of Education (1979) | ? |
| Approve Anti-busing Amendment (1979) | ? |
| Guarantee Chrysler Corp. loans (1979) | Y |
| Approve military draft registration (1980) | N |
| Aid Sandinista regime in Nicaragua (1980) | N |
| Strengthen fair housing laws (1980) | N |

**97th Congress**

| | |
|---|---|
| Reagan budget proposal (1981) | Y |

## Interest Group Ratings

| Year | ADA | ACA | AFL-CIO | CCUS |
|---|---|---|---|---|
| 1980 | 50 | 83 | 28 | 76 |
| 1979 | 21 | 57 | 11 | 93 |
| 1978 | 40 | 70 | 16 | 94 |
| 1977 | 30 | 54 | 25 | 93 |
| 1976 | 25 | 48 | 17 | 64 |
| 1975 | 47 | 56 | 32 | 87 |
| 1974 | 61 | 21 | 40 | 67 |
| 1973 | 44 | 37 | 55 | 73 |
| 1972 | 50 | 36 | 30 | 80 |
| 1971 | 43 | 57 | 42 | |
| 1970* | 33 | - | - | 100 |

*Did not serve entire period covered by voting studies.*

# 7 Marge Roukema (R)

**Of Ridgewood — Elected 1980**

**Born:** Sept. 19, 1929, Newark, N.J.
**Education:** Montclair State College, B.A. 1951.
**Profession:** Teacher.
**Family:** Husband, Richard Roukema; two children.
**Religion:** Protestant.
**Political Career:** Ridgewood Board of Education, 1970-73; unsuccessful Republican nominee for U.S. House, 1978.

**The Member:** Moderate on social issues and conservative about money, Roukema is a good fit for her affluent suburban district. The corporate executives and other professionals who dominate the area responded well to her campaign calls for a stronger military and reduced federal spending. Her support for the Equal Rights Amendment and for legalized abortion helped reinforce her centrist reputation.

Many of Roukema's middle-income constituents do not look favorably upon plans to tighten eligibility standards for federal guaranteed student loans. In the Education and Labor Committee, Roukema pushed for a proposal to grant loan eligibility to people with incomes of up to approximately $35,000. She also wanted to provide a "needs test" for those with incomes over $35,000 who seek the loans. The committee established the eligibility ceiling at $25,000.

In 1978, when Roukema first challenged Democratic Rep. Andrew J. Maguire, she came within 8,815 votes of defeating him. She attacked him then for being "anti-defense" and "anti-business" — charges she repeated in 1980, helped by his well-publicized speeches against oil companies at committee hearings during the gasoline shortage of 1979. Roukema's campaign was also armed with taped commercials featuring national Republican names like Gerald R. Ford and Rep. Jack F. Kemp of New York.

**The District:** The tree-lined communities of western Bergen County are comfortable and habitually Republican. Voters tend to be well-educated and well-informed, and sensitive to clean government issues. The district has the highest median income in the state and the second highest median number of school years completed.

Democratic strength lies in the district's southern end, near Route 4, in towns like blue-collar Hackensack and largely Jewish Teaneck.

## Committees

**Banking, Finance and Urban Affairs** (16th of 19 Republicans)
Economic Stabilization; General Oversight and Renegotiation; Housing and Community Development.

**Education and Labor** (10th of 14 Republicans)
Elementary, Secondary and Vocational Education; Labor Standards †.

†*Serving ex officio for ranking Republican committee member John M. Ashbrook.*

## Elections

**1980 General**

| | |
|---|---|
| Marge Roukema (R) | 108,760 (51%) |
| Andrew Maguire (D) | 99,737 (47%) |

**District Vote For President**

| | 1980 | | 1976 | | 1972 |
|---|---|---|---|---|---|
| **D** | 71,849 (32 %) | **D** | 93,764 (41%) | **D** | 76,583 (33%) |
| **R** | 126,536 (57 %) | **R** | 129,777 (57%) | **R** | 150,619 (66%) |
| **I** | 21,619 (10 %) | | | | |

## Campaign Finance

| 1980 | Receipts | Receipts from PACs | Expenditure |
|---|---|---|---|
| Roukema (R) | $406,239 | $180,245 (44%) | $391,537 |
| Maguire (D) | $360,818 | $89,671 (25%) | $346,781 |

## Key Vote

**97th Congress**

| | |
|---|---|
| Reagan budget proposal (1981) | Y |

**7th District: North — Paramus, Hackensack.** Population: 447,619 (7% decrease since 1970). Race: White 415,842 (93%), Black 19,877 (4%), Others 11,900 (3%). Spanish origin: 13,789 (3%).

# 8 Robert A. Roe (D)

**Of Wayne — Elected 1969**

**Born:** Feb. 28, 1924, Wayne, N.J.
**Education:** Attended Ore. State U. and Wash. State U.
**Military Career:** Army, World War II.
**Profession:** Corporation Executive.
**Family:** Single.
**Religion:** Roman Catholic.
**Political Career:** Wayne Township committeeman, 1955-56; mayor of Wayne Township, 1956-61; Passaic County Freeholder, 1959-63; sought Democratic nomination for governor, 1977 and 1981.

**In Washington:** Most urban Democrats of Roe's generation share his belief in public works as a cure for economic stagnation, but few of them have pursued it with the zeal that he has, or maintained it as stubbornly in the face of formidable opposition.

It was Roe who inserted $2 billion in Public Works jobs money into President Carter's bill to expand the Economic Development Administration (EDA) in the 96th Congress. It was also Roe who jeopardized the entire package by his reluctance to accept it without the public works.

The hybrid legislation passed the House in 1979 by a wide margin, but the Senate wanted the EDA bill only. Conferences were held off and on over the following year, but Roe did not want to reach an agreement unless the public works section remained in. The Carter administration, which did not want the public works money, finally agreed. But the Senate was adamant against it.

Just before Congress recessed for the 1980 election, Roe appeared willing to bargain. But when Ronald Reagan was elected president, Republicans said they preferred to wait on the entire proposal until the new administration took office. That doomed both EDA expansion and public works jobs at the same time.

The whole scenario reflected a policy dispute that has plagued congressional Democrats for most of the past decade, between traditional New Deal loyalists and a more skeptical younger generation worried that public works sometimes add to inflation without having a noticeable impact on unemployment. Roe has been the leader of the traditional side.

In 1975, the year he took over the Economic Development Subcommittee, Roe managed his first major public works package, part of it aimed at creation of 250,000 jobs and part at stimulating investment. When critics complained about inflation, he shouted back in House debate, "It is simply absurd to assert that this $5 billion spent in the construction and materials industries will cause inflation." When the bill went to conference, he added an interesting new wrinkle — a provision, not discussed on the floor of either chamber, to make cities of 50,000 or more eligible to be economic redevelopment areas under legislation then a decade old. Roe's district is dominated by declining industrial cities of modest size. The bill was enacted in 1976 over a Ford veto.

In the next Congress, Roe brought to the House floor a bill authorizing an additional $4 billion for public works jobs, targeted mostly at New Jersey and other hard-pressed states of the Northeast. When Republican Bud Shuster of Pennsylvania sought to tilt the formula toward a larger number of states, Roe insisted the effort was "mischievous" and "diabolical." The formula was changed, but the program was expanded.

By 1978, however, critics were complaining that the traditional public works jobs programs, emphasizing capital spending, were wasteful. President Carter proposed $1 billion worth of new public works jobs, designed to be labor-intensive and focus on unemployment among the disadvantaged. Roe's solution was to approve that billion, and add his own $2-billion for capital intensive

---

**8th District: North — Paterson.** Population: 462,340 (3% decrease since 1970). Race: White 368,030 (80%), Black 59,519 (13%), Others 34,791 (7%). Spanish origin: 62,945 (14%).

jobs, which he said was needed to move Carter's program through the House. The legislation died at the end of the 95th Congress, setting the stage for the EDA-jobs fight that occupied Roe and his subcommittee most of the next two years.

Appointed to Public Works when he arrived in the House in 1969, he has concentrated on it and never served on any other major committee, although he has a secondary assignment on Science and Technology.

In the beginning, much of Roe's committee work was on water pollution. As a former state conservation commissioner, he knew something about it, and was instrumental in the writing of the 1972 Water Pollution Control Act. Labeling himself an environmentalist, he insisted that some of the language environmental groups wanted was unrealistic, and he fought amendments to give the federal government veto power over state discharge permits. But he insisted vehemently that the bill had not been weakened, simply made practical.

In 1981, as he began his primary campaign for governor of New Jersey, Roe gave up the Economic Development chairmanship to head the Public Works Water Resources Subcommittee, a crucial panel for a state that was going through a water shortage at the time.

**At Home:** Pork barrel politics has endeared Roe to his constituents, especially to the labor unions that benefit from the jobs that his programs have created.

Thanks to his public works legislation, the district has received a large number of new town halls, fire stations and other municipal structures — which have generated a lot of construction employment. Using his influence, Roe also has put together federal grants to save a failing plant and to restore the historic Great Falls area in Paterson.

Roe's strength in Passaic County has provided him with a base for his two forays into statewide politics, but not enough of one to bring him his goal — the Democratic nomination for governor. New Jersey chooses its governors in off-years for congressional elections, so its congressmen can seek the statehouse without having to give up their places in Washington.

Roe has tried twice. In 1977, he ran a strong race in the primary against incumbent Democrat Brendan T. Byrne, coming within 40,000 votes of denying Byrne renomination. That showing made him a front-runner in 1981, when his main competition came from another member of the U.S. House delegation, James Florio.

In the end, however, Florio defeated him easily. Better on television than Roe and well-enough financed to spread his commercials across the state, Florio took the nomination with more than 150,000 votes. Roe had refused public financing and tried to make an issue of the state's public financing system. It never caught on, and the decision left him underfinanced at the end of the campaign. Roe was again second, but it was a distant second.

In Passaic, however, Roe remains on top. His watchwords are caution and harmony, and whenever feuding flares among various Democratic factions, he can be counted on to play a peacemaker's role. Customarily, the disputants meet at the Brownstone House restaurant in Paterson, where the garrulous Roe acts as negotiator.

Roe habitually wins re-election by whopping margins. Republicans seldom bother to put up strong candidates against him. He often does well in the district's GOP towns, in addition to pulling his usual big vote in the blue-collar Democratic bastions.

Part of the reason for his appeal in the Republican suburbs may be that Roe is not a product of urban Paterson, the district's biggest town and a home of organization politics. He comes from suburban Wayne Township, which swings between the two parties. He likes to boast that he knows all levels of government, having served at each of them — municipal, county, state and federal.

Roe initially won the House seat in a tight 1969 special election to fill the unexpired term of Democrat Charles S. Joelson (1961-69), who became a state judge. Since then, he has won re-election with better than 60 percent of the vote.

**The District:** Passaic County is shaped like an hourglass. The upper half is suburban and Republican, containing such communities as Ringwood and West Milford. The lower half is largely urban and very Democratic.

The old mill town of Paterson, home to skilled silk-workers, was the site of labor strife in the early 1900s. Its famed Great Falls provided energy for textile and numerous other factories. Paterson developed a strong political machine in the 19th century, manned by the immigrants who had come to find work.

Since then, the old Democratic organization has decayed, allowing a moderate Republican to be chosen mayor of Paterson for much of the last decade in the city's non-partisan elections. A large proportion of Paterson's population is Hispanic.

## Committees

**Public Works and Transportation** (3rd of 25 Democrats)
Water Resources, chairman; Economic Development; Investigations and Oversight.

**Science and Technology** (2nd of 23 Democrats)
Energy Development and Applications; Energy Research and Production.

## Elections

**1980 General**

| | |
|---|---|
| Robert Roe (D) | 95,493 (67%) |
| William Cleveland (R) | 44,625 (31%) |

**1978 General**

| | |
|---|---|
| Robert Roe (D) | 69,496 (74%) |
| Thomas Melani (R) | 23,842 (26%) |

**Previous Winning Percentages**

1976 (71%)   1974 (74%)   1972 (63%)   1970 (61%)
1969* (49%)

*Special election.

**District Vote For President**

| | 1980 | | 1976 | | 1972 |
|---|---|---|---|---|---|
| D | 65,102 (40 %) | D | 79,487 (47%) | D | 65,125 (36%) |
| R | 84,715 (52 %) | R | 86,341 (51%) | R | 111,671 (62%) |
| I | 9,487 (6 %) | | | | |

## Campaign Finance

| | Receipts | Receipts from PACs | Expenditures |
|---|---|---|---|
| **1980** | | | |
| Roe (D) | $214,768 | $66,010 (31%) | $212,752 |
| Cleveland (R) | $10,386 | $500 (5%) | $15,894 |
| **1978** | | | |
| Roe (D) | $67,907 | $44,475 (65%) | $66,635 |
| Melani (R) | $5,801 | $800 (14%) | $5,800 |

## Voting Studies

| | Presidential Support | | Party Unity | | Conservative Coalition | |
|---|---|---|---|---|---|---|
| Year | S | O | S | O | S | O |
| 1980 | 66 | 23 | 81 | 12 | 32 | 59 |

| | | | | | | |
|---|---|---|---|---|---|---|
| 1979 | 68 | 26 | 81 | 16 | 34 | 60 |
| 1978 | 63 | 31 | 74 | 22 | 30 | 66 |
| 1977 | 42 | 18 | 51 | 11 | 14 | 45 |
| 1976 | 29 | 71 | 83 | 13 | 28 | 69 |
| 1975 | 33 | 67 | 80 | 16 | 25 | 72 |
| 1974 (Ford) | 39 | 50 | | | | |
| 1974 | 40 | 55 | 78 | 15 | 22 | 69 |
| 1973 | 31 | 64 | 80 | 11 | 15 | 74 |
| 1972 | 54 | 43 | 83 | 13 | 27 | 72 |
| 1971 | 44 | 51 | 73 | 20 | 27 | 69 |
| 1970 | 57 | 32 | 71 | 21 | 20 | 59 |
| 1969 | 47 | 53† | 86 | 14† | 19 | 81† |

S = Support          O = Opposition
†Not eligible for all recorded votes.

## Key Votes

**96th Congress**

| | |
|---|---|
| Weaken Carter oil profits tax (1979) | N |
| Reject hospital cost control plan (1979) | N |
| Implement Panama Canal Treaties (1979) | Y |
| Establish Department of Education (1979) | Y |
| Approve Anti-busing Amendment (1979) | N |
| Guarantee Chrysler Corp. loans (1979) | Y |
| Approve military draft registration (1980) | Y |
| Aid Sandinista regime in Nicaragua (1980) | N |
| Strengthen fair housing laws (1980) | Y |

**97th Congress**

| | |
|---|---|
| Reagan budget proposal (1981) | N |

## Interest Group Ratings

| Year | ADA | ACA | AFL-CIO | CCUS |
|---|---|---|---|---|
| 1980 | 67 | 17 | 83 | 59 |
| 1979 | 58 | 4 | 95 | 18 |
| 1978 | 35 | 19 | 85 | 22 |
| 1977 | 35 | 6 | 93 | 11 |
| 1976 | 70 | 14 | 87 | 6 |
| 1975 | 79 | 18 | 87 | 24 |
| 1974 | 65 | 21 | 90 | 13 |
| 1973 | 68 | 22 | 100 | 9 |
| 1972 | 63 | 48 | 91 | 20 |
| 1971 | 73 | 31 | 91 | - |
| 1970* | 80 | 28 | 71 | 11 |
| 1969* | 75 | 29 | 100 | - |

*Did not serve for entire period covered by voting studies.

# 9 Harold C. Hollenbeck (R)

### Of East Rutherford — Elected 1976

**Born:** Dec. 29, 1938, Passaic, N.J.
**Education:** Fairleigh Dickinson U., B.A. 1961; U. of Va. Law School, LL.B. 1964.
**Profession:** Lawyer.
**Family:** Divorced, one child.
**Religion:** Roman Catholic.
**Political Career:** East Rutherford Borough Council, 1967-69; N.J. Assembly, 1968-72; N.J. Senate, 1972-74; unsuccessful candidate for Bergen County Board of Freeholders, 1973.

**In Washington:** Hollenbeck has spent nearly full time securing his district during his three House terms, leaving him little opportunity to establish a visible presence in the House. He has had minor committee assignments for most of his career, and rarely speaks on the floor.

On the Science Committee, he has been a loyal member of the bipartisan majority that favors more money for pure research and lobbies against the funding cutbacks that the Budget Committee and the White House try to enact. During the 96th Congress, he won passage of a floor amendment restoring $2-million for an automatic manufacturing research facility, which he argued would help the nation compete with the Japanese.

Like many members who work in the science field, Hollenbeck has come to take a dim view of those who ridicule obscure-sounding research projects as a waste of taxpayers' money. He proposed in 1980 that lists of federal scientific grants carry descriptions of the ultimate goals of the research, making them a little safer against legislative attack. "One of those 'silly' grants led to the Salk vaccine," says Hollenbeck, who had a mild case of polio himself in 1952.

That is as close to a personal issue as one can find in Hollenbeck's congressional career. His mind is generally on New Jersey, and when he uses the House floor, it is normally for purposes far more parochial than saving American industry.

Like many House members, but more consistently than most, he laces the *Congressional Record* with marginal news from back home. In 1980, Hollenbeck inserted in the Record undelivered speeches paying tribute to the Sweet Adelines of Ramapo Valley and the Rutherford Babe Ruth League.

A major part of Hollenbeck's district politics is his liberal, urban-oriented voting record, one which forces him to break with House Republicans most of the time. In 1980 he voted against his party's majority on 64 percent of the roll calls, second only to New York's S. William Green among House GOP members. He was one of only five Republicans, for example, to oppose a 1980 amendment requiring people with incomes substantially above poverty levels to reimburse the federal government for food stamps they received during brief periods of need.

**At Home:** Hollenbeck had to have a considerable amount of luck to make it to Congress, but he has demonstrated the skill to stay.

In 1976, he was able to run against an incumbent Democrat, Henry J. Helstoski, who was under indictment on charges of bribery, later dropped. Helstoski's legal problems brought Hollenbeck a decisive victory in a district Republicans had been unable to win for more than a decade.

In 1978, Hollenbeck was an obvious Democratic target. He was held to under 50 percent of the vote, but kept his seat because the opposition was divided between Helstoski, running as an independent, and a Democrat from the district's small Hudson County section; Hudson politicians long have been suspect in Bergen County, which makes up the bulk of the 9th.

In 1980, there was no serious effort against

---

**9th District: North — Union City, Fort Lee.** Population: 459,966 (4% decrease since 1970). Race: White 419,623 (91%), Black 14,703 (3%), Asian and Pacific Islander 13,403 (3%), Others 12,237 (3%). Spanish origin: 58,301 (13%).

him. His Democratic challenger was weak and anti-abortion groups gave up on their plan to target Hollenbeck because both candidates turned out to hold the same views.

Hollenbeck has family advantages in Bergen County; his father was mayor of one of the towns, and a cousin is a Democratic state assemblyman. His pro-labor voting record has brought him strong support from unions, which are important in the blue-collar southern part of the district. He takes pains to have a good constituent service operation.

Hollenbeck came up through the ranks as a Republican officeholder, holding a state Senate seat before he ran for Congress. But his congressional campaigns have made only limited mention of his partisan affiliation.

**The District:** The 9th comprises the eastern half of Bergen County. Its core has been the working-class towns in the southern end of the district; they border the Hackensack Meadowlands, a marsh that is most noted for its sports stadium and horse track. East Rutherford, Carlstadt and other such communities lean Democratic, but favor Republicans often enough to be unpredictable.

The district's middle section is Democratic, as a result of the many young professionals in apartment-studded Fort Lee and Cliffside Park. The northern part is Republican, encompassing wealthy, tree-lined towns like Old Tappan and Alpine.

## Committees

**Public Works and Transportation** (11th of 19 Republicans)
Aviation; Economic Development; Investigations and Oversight.

**Science and Technology** (5th of 17 Republicans)
Energy Research and Production; Space Science and Applications; Transportation, Aviation and Materials.

**Select Aging** (7th of 23 Republicans)
Retirement Income and Employment.

## Elections

**1980 General**

| | |
|---|---|
| Harold Hollenbeck (R) | 116,128 (59%) |
| Gabriel Ambrosio (D) | 75,321 (38%) |

**1978 General**

| | |
|---|---|
| Harold Hollenbeck (R) | 73,478 (49%) |
| Nicholas Mastorelli (D) | 56,888 (38%) |
| Henry Helstoski (I) | 19,126 (13%) |

**Previous Winning Percentage**

1976 (53%)

**District Vote For President**

| | 1980 | | 1976 | | 1972 |
|---|---|---|---|---|---|
| D | 74,822 (35 %) | D | 96,933 (45%) | D | 74,851 (34%) |
| R | 117,284 (55 %) | R | 116,058 (54%) | R | 146,286 (66%) |
| I | 17,373 (8 %) | | | | |

## Campaign Finance

| | Receipts | Receipts from PACs | Expenditures |
|---|---|---|---|
| **1980** | | | |
| Hollenbeck (R) | $147,165 | $84,854 (58%) | $145,586 |
| Ambrosio (D) | $195,319 | $900 (0.4%) | $182,804 |

| 1978 | | | |
|---|---|---|---|
| Hollenbeck (R) | $75,618 | $46,919 (62%) | $84,548 |
| Mastorelli (D) | $119,367 | $4,450 (4%) | $121,447 |

## Voting Studies

| | Presidential Support | | Party Unity | | Conservative Coalition | |
|---|---|---|---|---|---|---|
| Year | S | O | S | O | S | O |
| 1980 | 62 | 32 | 29 | 64 | 24 | 73 |
| 1979 | 57 | 34 | 31 | 58 | 29 | 59 |
| 1978 | 56 | 29 | 34 | 60 | 28 | 65 |
| 1977 | 57 | 34 | 42 | 50 | 44 | 48 |

S = Support          O = Opposition

## Key Votes

**96th Congress**

| | |
|---|---|
| Weaken Carter oil profits tax (1979) | N |
| Reject hospital cost control plan (1979) | Y |
| Implement Panama Canal Treaties (1979) | N |
| Establish Department of Education (1979) | Y |
| Approve Anti-busing Amendment (1979) | N |
| Guarantee Chrysler Corp. loans (1979) | Y |
| Approve military draft registration (1980) | N |
| Aid Sandinista regime in Nicaragua (1980) | N |
| Strengthen fair housing laws (1980) | Y |

**97th Congress**

| | |
|---|---|
| Reagan budget proposal (1981) | Y |

## Interest Group Ratings

| Year | ADA | ACA | AFL-CIO | CCUS |
|---|---|---|---|---|
| 1980 | 89 | 32 | 74 | 66 |
| 1979 | 63 | 8 | 85 | 44 |
| 1978 | 50 | 22 | 75 | 29 |
| 1977 | 55 | 56 | 57 | 47 |

# 10 Peter W. Rodino Jr. (D)

**Of Newark — Elected 1948**

**Born:** June 7, 1909, Newark, N.J.
**Education:** U. of Newark (Rutgers), LL.B. 1937.
**Military Career:** Army, 1941-46.
**Profession:** Lawyer.
**Family:** Widowed; two children.
**Religion:** Roman Catholic.
**Political Career:** No previous office.

**In Washington:** Before 1974, Rodino had spent 26 inconspicuous years as the congressman from Newark, playing a loyal but less than innovative role on House Judiciary under autocratic Chairman Emanuel Celler. Since 1974, he has gradually faded into the background again as his committee has drifted from the center of political debate. But those few months of Watergate made him a celebrity, and he will be one the rest of his life.

No one was more surprised than Rodino by his sudden emergence as presiding officer in the congressional impeachment debate. It had been barely a year since he became Judiciary chairman, following Celler's defeat for renomination at age 84. Quiet and almost shy in public, Rodino was well-liked by colleagues but regarded by few of them as a worthy replacement for his tough-minded predecessor.

Being second in command on Judiciary had not always been a rewarding job; Celler simply did not delegate much responsibility. But Rodino had been involved, if not decisive, in the passage of all major civil rights bills over more than a decade, and had written portions of some of them. He drafted the fair employment practices provision of the 1964 Civil Rights Act. In 1966, he was floor manager for the year's open housing bill — but only because Celler was ill. And Rodino had been chief House manager of the Johnson administration's Immigration Reform Law in 1965, one eliminating the national origin quotas that had formed the foundation of American immigration policy for 30 years. He was also proud of his sponsorship, eventually successful, of legislation to make Columbus Day one of the 3-day holiday weekends legislated by Congress.

When it came time for the Judiciary Committee to° tackle President Nixon's impeachment, Rodino's years in the wings were an advantage. He had never been able to act unilaterally on anything, and he did not try in this case. Being new he was careful, working with Republicans to avoid the appearance of partisanship and going the extra mile to cooperate with the White House. Some liberal Democrats complained through the long months of preparation that Rodino was not aggressive enough, but in the end it was his caution and restraint that won over enough Republicans to make the final result bipartisan.

The long search for a special committee lawyer, the painstaking, even repetitious examination of the evidence, the patient quest for White House documents — all combined to remove the hostile edges of partisanship from the acts of a Democratic Congress sitting in judgment on a Republican president.

Two weeks after the committee approved three articles of impeachment by overwhelming majorities, Nixon's resignation ended the affair and precluded any floor debate on impeachment.

Television coverage of the Judiciary Committee's deliberations made Rodino an instant celebrity. His face was on the covers of *Time* and *Newsweek*. He appeared on every major television interview show, something he had never done or wanted to do. Reporters followed him through the Capitol corridors, waiting for his every word. Speaking invitations flowed in from all parts of the country. Book publishers sought him out. Jimmy Carter interviewed him in 1976 as a possible running mate.

For a while after Watergate, Rodino was a star on the lecture circuit and something of a

---

**10th District: Newark.** Population: 426,370 (11% decrease since 1970). Race: White 131,187 (31%), Black 256,260 (60%), Others 38,923 (9%). Spanish origin: 65,680 (15%).

---

hero, especially to Italian-Americans. He had emerged from the impeachment hearings as a different kind of "godfather," a sentimentally patriotic American free of ties to organized crime. Early in the Watergate inquiry, when anonymous tipsters attempted to link Rodino with the mob, he indignantly told reporters he wouldn't know a mobster if he stumbled over one. Years later, when the F.B.I. snared a number of congressmen in its Abscam bribery scandal, Rodino was outraged at reports that the federal agents had tried to trap him along with them.

In recent years, Rodino has slipped back into his role of quiet man. His wife died of cancer in December 1980, after a two-and-a-half-year-long illness. Rodino was with her most of the time, spending only a day or two a week in his Washington offices.

The Judiciary Committee, too, has slipped from prominence, partly because of Rodino's preoccupation with personal affairs and partly because of its reputation as a panel that attracts emotional issues — abortion, busing and school prayer — while providing little political advantage for its members. No new Democrat sought assignment to the committee in the 96th or 97th Congresses, a development that frustrated Rodino. He had to talk the Democratic leadership into allowing members to serve on Judiciary as an extra assignment.

Meanwhile, some of the panel's senior members, still paying tribute to Rodino's integrity and fairness, began complaining that the committee was accomplishing little. "You need a driver," said Republican M. Caldwell Butler of Virginia, "and he's just not a driver."

The committee worked on a variety of complex legal issues in 1979 and 1980, but little of the work bore fruit. One subcommittee labored for over a year to produce a new federal criminal code, but House leaders never brought the issue to the floor. A lobby disclosure bill cleared Judiciary for the third Congress in a row, but for the third time in a row no bill became law. The panel wrote an open housing bill labeled by President Carter as the most important civil rights legislation in a decade, and the House passed it in 1980. But it died in the Senate.

At the start of the 97th Congress, however, Rodino seemed more energetic than in recent years. He made sure that most of the committee's new members were liberal Democrats, interested in civil rights and skeptical of federal legislation on abortion and busing. He began playing a leading role in the effort to extend the 1965 Voting Rights Act, up for renewal in 1981.

**At Home:** As a white man representing mostly black Newark, Rodino has had a sensitive political situation to deal with for most of the past two decades. But his survival has never been in much doubt. The most serious black challenge, in 1972, fell short by 13,000 votes, and since Rodino's impeachment heroics in 1974, he has been more secure than that. A black Democrat tried for the nomination against him in 1980, but Rodino won with 62.1 percent. Republicans are irrelevant in Newark.

Apart from strong support from Newark's Italian-American community, Rodino retains substantial loyalties in the black wards. One reason is that he long has championed civil rights and antipoverty efforts. His reputation as conqueror of Nixon probably did more for him politically among blacks than among other groups.

Another advantage for Rodino is his alliance with Newark's popular mayor, Kenneth A. Gibson, a black. During the 1980 primary race, posters picturing the two of them were prominent in Newark's black areas. Rodino probably will be replaced by a black when he steps down, although the district will be changed substantially for 1982.

**The District:** The 1967 Newark riots drove out many businesses and white middle-class residents, leaving the black majority that has dominated Newark politics through the 1970s.

The Central and South Wards, hit hardest by riot, are overwhelmingly black, but some Irish and Puerto Ricans occupy neighborhoods alongside blacks in the West Ward. The East Ward (Ironbound) has seen a heavy Portuguese influx over the past decade, while Italian-Americans continue to control the North Ward.

The 10th District also includes the separate municipalities of East Orange (heavily black) and Harrison (largely Polish and Italian); both are very Democratic. An anomolous appendage is affluent, white Glen Ridge — usually Republican and always outnumbered.

In light of the city's population loss, several adjacent towns likely will be added to the 10th during redistricting. The Democratic-controlled Legislature is expected to keep the district essentially intact, which would mean a black successor to Rodino.

# Committees

**Judiciary** (Chairman)
Monopolies and Commercial Law, chairman.

**Select Narcotics Abuse and Control** (2nd of 11 Democrats)

# Elections

**1980 General**

| | |
|---|---|
| Reter Rodino Jr. (D) | 76,154 (85%) |
| Everett Jennings (R) | 11,778 (13%) |

**1980 Primary**

| | |
|---|---|
| Peter Rodino Jr. (D) | 26,943 (62%) |
| Donald Payne (D) | 9,825 (23%) |
| Golden Johnson (D) | 5,316 (12%) |

**1978 General**

| | |
|---|---|
| Peter Rodino Jr. (D) | 55,074 (86%) |
| John Pelt (R) | 8,066 (13%) |

**Previous Winning Percentages**

| | | | |
|---|---|---|---|
| **1976** (83%) | **1974** (81%) | **1972** (80%) | **1970** (70%) |
| **1968** (64%) | **1966** (64%) | **1964** (74%) | **1962** (73%) |
| **1960** (65%) | **1958** (64%) | **1956** (56%) | **1954** (63%) |
| **1952** (57%) | **1950** (61%) | **1948** (51%) | |

**District Vote For President**

| | 1980 | | 1976 | | 1972 |
|---|---|---|---|---|---|
| D | 73,860 (74 %) | D | 82,612 (71 %) | D | 78,416 (62 %) |
| R | 22,261 (22 %) | R | 31,267 (27 %) | R | 46,034 (36 %) |
| I | 3,490 (4 %) | | | | |

# Campaign Finance

| | Receipts | Receipts from PACs | Expenditures |
|---|---|---|---|
| **1980** | | | |
| Rodino (D) | $201,550 | $93,266 (46%) | $212,925 |
| **1978** | | | |
| Rodino (D) | $34,644 | $15,800 (46 %) | $46,110 |

# Voting Studies

| | Presidential Support | | Party Unity | | Conservative Coalition | |
|---|---|---|---|---|---|---|
| **Year** | **S** | **O** | **S** | **O** | **S** | **O** |
| 1980 | 51 | 20 | 59 | 5 | 0 | 65 |
| 1979 | 66 | 10 | 71 | 4 | 6 | 66 |
| 1978 | 31 | 7 | 34 | 3 | 2 | 33 |
| 1977 | 77 | 20 | 90 | 7 | 4 | 91 |

| | **S** | **O** | **S** | **O** | **S** | **O** |
|---|---|---|---|---|---|---|
| 1976 | 18 | 73 | 86 | 3 | 6 | 87 |
| 1975 | 35 | 54 | 85 | 3 | 7 | 81 |
| 1974 (Ford) | 43 | 52 | | | | |
| 1974 | 36 | 60 | 87 | 8 | 6 | 85 |
| 1973 | 28 | 70 | 90 | 8 | 5 | 92 |
| 1972 | 54 | 46 | 83 | 8 | 5 | 88 |
| 1971 | 33 | 51 | 80 | 7 | 4 | 81 |
| 1970 | 69 | 29 | 82 | 15 | 9 | 86 |
| 1969 | 49 | 38 | 87 | 7 | 7 | 84 |
| 1968 | 83 | 14 | 93 | 6 | 6 | 92 |
| 1967 | 83 | 8 | 88 | 4 | 6 | 80 |
| 1966 | 84 | 6 | 86 | 4 | 3 | 92 |
| 1965 | 91 | 3 | 96 | 1 | 0 | 98 |
| 1964 | 90 | 2 | 85 | 0 | 0 | 92 |
| 1963 | 77 | 4 | 81 | 2 | 7 | 87 |
| 1962 | 97 | 3 | 96 | 0 | 0 | 100 |
| 1961 | 88 | 5 | 83 | 7 | 0 | 87 |

S = Support          O = Opposition

# Key Votes

**96th Congress**

| | |
|---|---|
| Weaken Carter oil profits tax (1979) | N |
| Reject hospital cost control plan (1979) | N |
| Implement Panama Canal Treaties (1979) | Y |
| Establish Department of Education (1979) | ? |
| Approve Anti-busing Amendment (1979) | N |
| Guarantee Chrysler Corp. loans (1979) | Y |
| Approve military draft registration (1980) | N |
| Aid Sandinista regime in Nicaragua (1980) | Y |
| Strengthen fair housing laws (1980) | Y |

**97th Congress**

| | |
|---|---|
| Reagan budget proposal (1981) | N |

# Interest Group Ratings

| Year | ADA | ACA | AFL-CIO | CCUS |
|---|---|---|---|---|
| 1980 | 67 | 14 | 95 | 52 |
| 1979 | 63 | 0 | 100 | 0 |
| 1978 | 35 | 0 | 83 | 0 |
| 1977 | 85 | 0 | 91 | 6 |
| 1976 | 85 | 4 | 83 | 19 |
| 1975 | 84 | 5 | 95 | 18 |
| 1974 | 91 | 7 | 100 | 0 |
| 1973 | 92 | 4 | 100 | 9 |
| 1972 | 88 | 5 | 91 | 0 |
| 1971 | 86 | 7 | 91 | - |
| 1970 | 84 | 16 | 100 | 10 |
| 1969 | 80 | 12 | 100 | - |
| 1968 | 75 | 9 | 100 | - |
| 1967 | 80 | 0 | 100 | 10 |
| 1966 | 88 | 13 | 100 | - |
| 1965 | 89 | 4 | - | 10 |
| 1964 | 92 | 0 | 100 | - |
| 1963 | - | 0 | - | - |
| 1962 | 100 | 4 | 100 | - |
| 1961 | 100 | - | - | - |

# 11 Joseph G. Minish (D)

**Of West Orange — Elected 1962**

**Born:** Sept. 1, 1916, Throop, Pa.
**Education:** High school graduate.
**Military Career:** Army, 1941-45.
**Profession:** Labor union executive.
**Family:** Wife, Theresa LaCapra; three children.
**Religion:** Roman Catholic.
**Political Career:** No previous office.

**In Washington:** The son of a Pennsylvania coal miner, Minish manages at once to be an ornery champion of consumer rights and a ward politician skeptical of "reforms" in government and politics.

Minish has argued about consumer issues for a decade as a member of the Banking Committee, and at various times taken on the food industry, defense contractors, and more recently, land developers. A former official of the International Union of Electrical Workers, Minish still sometimes offers the anti-business rhetoric normally associated with labor Democrats of an earlier era.

More than a decade ago, as a junior member of the committee, Minish was a strong supporter of the original Truth-in-Lending Act. In 1979, as chairman of the Oversight Subcommittee at Banking, he railed against the recreational land sales industry, claiming the law allowed developers to use high-pressure tactics in selling worthless land to small investors. "Literally millions of consumers continue to be defrauded by land developers every year," Minish said.

When the committee reauthorized federal housing programs that year, Minish added a provision allowing the government to issue cease-and-desist orders prohibiting the sale of property by a developer who had violated the Interstate Land Sales Act. The real estate industry fought it with a floor amendment, offered by South Carolina Republican Carroll Campbell, striking the cease-and-desist powers from the bill.

Minish was indignant, his high-pitched voice rising even higher, as it always does at moments of confrontation. "All this amendment does," he said, "is it gives the unscrupulous landowners another opportunity to steal from innocent victims." But it passed the House, and the new language was removed.

At the same time, Minish was expressing nearly as much outrage against defense contractors. He was a last-ditch defender of the Renegotiation Board, a federal agency set up in 1951 to monitor profits on large-scale contracts. He lost on this issue, too; the board was abolished in 1979.

From his same oversight subcommittee, Minish has pressed the Food and Drug Administration to take a more active role in policing food additives. He favored a federal ban on cyclamates, the non-caloric sweetener accused of causing cancer. He campaigned successfully to force manufacturers into removing monosodium glutamate from baby food.

On energy issues, Minish wants more government involvement. He favors a new federal energy corporation, with the power to purchase foreign oil and lend money to nations that provide it on terms friendly to the United States. He tried twice in 1979 to amend foreign aid legislation to block funds for OPEC countries.

But when the issue is Congress itself, Minish does not ally himself with crusaders. As a member of the House Administration Committee in 1979, he helped kill a bill to provide partial public financing of congressional elections, and later in the year he opposed a plan to limit donations by political action committees to $6,000 per campaign.

In the latter case, Minish said he would vote for limits if they were stricter, and proposed his own plan to restrict PAC contributions to $1,000 per campaign. But that figure was much too low to have any chance of passage, and few colleagues treated it as a serious proposal.

---

**11th District: Essex County — Newark suburbs.** Population: 449,556 (5% decrease since 1970). Race: White 369,337 (82%), Black 66,141 (15%), Others 14,078 (3%). Spanish origin: 15,225 (3%).

Minish also has had his doubts about fighting established congressional power centers. In the early 1970s, then representing a district that was 37 percent black, he opposed challenges to John McMillan, D-S.C., chairman of the District of Columbia Committee, despite complaints from national black leaders about McMillan's longstanding opposition to civil rights. In 1975, when junior House Democrats unseated Wright Patman, D-Texas, as Banking chairman, Minish rejected the anti-seniority drive and stuck with Patman to the end.

**At Home:** Minish's political career has been built on two foundations — ethnicity and personality. A garrulous storyteller, he is a fixture at social gatherings of suburban Essex County's large Italian-American community. His name, originally Minisci, was changed a couple of generations ago. The fact that it sounds vaguely Jewish has never hurt him in the district.

Minish grew up with the labor movement. The son of a coal miner in northeastern Pennsylvania, he moved to New Jersey and worked as a machine operator before joining the staff of the Electrical Workers. He became well-known in the state's labor circles, serving as a political action director and a treasurer of the regional labor council.

When Democrat Hugh J. Addonizio (1949-62) gave up his Newark House seat to become mayor, organized labor backed Minish as his successor. With the blessing of the late Dennis Carey, powerful Essex County Democratic chairman, Minish received the nomination and went on to beat a liberal Republican.

Minish has enjoyed easy victories throughout his tenure in Congress, even though a 1972 redistricting plan written by a Republican Legislature added GOP suburbs in the county's western end and removed its dependably Democratic Newark portion.

His vote slipped below 60 percent in 1972, when former Republican state Sen. Milton A. Waldor, who was Jewish, cut into Minish's base among Jews and ran well in western Essex. But Minish has remained above the 60 percent level ever since. Since Waldor's defeat, the Republicans have not bothered to put up a strong candidate against him.

Although Minish avoids involvement in the bloody Essex political wars, he remains close to one Democratic faction, the old-line regulars from Carey's day. As a result, talk periodically crops up about a primary challenge to Minish from the party's liberal wing, which is at odds with the regulars. None of the liberals has come forward, however.

**The District:** This is the non-Newark portion of Essex County, a mix of blue-collar Democrats and white-collar Republicans.

The path of white flight from deteriorating Newark has determined the ethnic distribution in the suburbs next to the city. Belleville, which borders Newark's North Ward, is mostly Italian. South Orange, to the city's west, is largely Jewish.

Most of these close-in suburbanites have kept their Democratic heritage. To the west, communities like Caldwell and Fairfield are well-to-do and dependably Republican.

While Democrats dominate political life in the county, their unity is precarious. Right now, the reformers are on top, headed by County Executive Peter Shapiro, who won his post at age 26 in 1978 by defeating one of the regulars. In general, the Shapiro wing is concentrated in affluent western Essex, while the regulars have their base in the ethnic enclaves to the east.

Under longtime Essex Democratic leader Harry Lerner, who had inherited the position from Carey, harmony prevailed in the party. But after Lerner retired to Florida in 1977, leaving an ally in charge, internal feuding began.

## Committees

**Banking, Finance and Urban Affairs** (4th of 25 Democrats)
General Oversight and Renegotiation, chairman; Consumer Affairs and Coinage; Economic Stabilization; Financial Institutions Supervision, Regulation and Insurance.

**House Administration** (6th of 11 Democrats)
Personnel and Police, chairman; Contracts and Printing.

## Elections

**1980 General**

| | |
|---|---|
| Joseph Minish (D) | 106,155 (63%) |
| Robert Davis (R) | 57,772 (34%) |

**1978 General**

| | |
|---|---|
| Joseph Minish (D) | 88,294 (71%) |
| Julius Feld (R) | 35,642 (29%) |

**Previous Winning Percentages**

| | | | |
|---|---|---|---|
| 1976 (68 %) | 1974 (69 %) | 1972 (58 %) | 1970 (69 %) |
| 1968 (66 %) | 1966 (58 %) | 1964 (70 %) | 1962 (60 %) |

**District Vote For President**

| | 1980 | | 1976 | | 1972 |
|---|---|---|---|---|---|
| D | 77,094 (40 %) | D | 97,971 (47%) | D | 84,859 (39 %) |
| R | 95,919 (50 %) | R | 104,020 (50 %) | R | 128,378 (59 %) |
| I | 16,689 (9 %) | | | | |

*Joseph G. Minish, D-N.J.*

## Campaign Finance

| | Receipts | Receipts from PACs | Expen- ditures |
|---|---|---|---|
| **1980** | | | |
| Minish (D) | $132,169 | $36,849 (28%) | $77,750 |
| Davis (R) | $19,566 | — (0%) | $17,068 |
| **1978** | | | |
| Minish (D) | $102,932 | $22,000 (21%) | $71,900 |

## Voting Studies

| | Presidential Support | | Party Unity | | Conservative Coalition | |
|---|---|---|---|---|---|---|
| Year | S | O | S | O | S | O |
| 1980 | 72 | 25 | 78 | 14 | 24 | 69 |
| 1979 | 74 | 21 | 79 | 17 | 28 | 69 |
| 1978 | 70 | 27 | 70 | 26 | 30 | 66 |
| 1977 | 72 | 22 | 75 | 19 | 27 | 63 |
| 1976 | 24 | 75 | 84 | 15 | 30 | 70 |
| 1975 | 35 | 61 | 83 | 13 | 20 | 76 |
| 1974 (Ford) | 44 | 54 | | | | |
| 1974 | 45 | 53 | 84 | 13 | 25 | 74 |
| 1973 | 30 | 66 | 84 | 12 | 16 | 80 |
| 1972 | 57 | 41 | 84 | 13 | 15 | 83 |
| 1971 | 39 | 56 | 89 | 8 | 7 | 90 |
| 1970 | 71 | 29 | 81 | 19 | 14 | 86 |
| 1969 | 55 | 45 | 93 | 7 | 7 | 93 |
| 1968 | 77 | 15 | 84 | 4 | 6 | 80 |
| 1967 | 90 | 8 | 91 | 7 | 13 | 83 |
| 1966 | 82 | 8 | 83 | 6 | 8 | 89 |
| 1965 | 95 | 4 | 95 | 3 | 0 | 100 |
| 1964 | 96 | 4 | 94 | 5 | 0 | 100 |
| 1963 | 94 | 4 | 95 | 2 | 7 | 80 |

S = Support          O = Opposition

## Key Votes

**96th Congress**

| | |
|---|---|
| Weaken Carter oil profits tax (1979) | N |
| Reject hospital cost control plan (1979) | N |
| Implement Panama Canal Treaties (1979) | Y |
| Establish Department of Education (1979) | N |
| Approve Anti-busing Amendment (1979) | N |
| Guarantee Chrysler Corp. loans (1979) | Y |
| Approve military draft registration (1980) | Y |
| Aid Sandinista regime in Nicaragua (1980) | N |
| Strengthen fair housing laws (1980) | Y |

**97th Congress**

| | |
|---|---|
| Reagan budget proposal (1981) | N |

## Interest Group Ratings

| Year | ADA | ACA | AFL-CIO | CCUS |
|---|---|---|---|---|
| 1980 | 72 | 23 | 78 | 53 |
| 1979 | 58 | 16 | 100 | 12 |
| 1978 | 35 | 21 | 85 | 28 |
| 1977 | 55 | 16 | 86 | 20 |
| 1976 | 65 | 14 | 87 | 13 |
| 1975 | 79 | 19 | 96 | 18 |
| 1974 | 74 | 13 | 100 | 0 |
| 1973 | 84 | 22 | 100 | 10 |
| 1972 | 88 | 14 | 91 | 0 |
| 1971 | 86 | 18 | 82 | - |
| 1970 | 84 | 21 | 100 | 10 |
| 1969 | 80 | 12 | 100 | - |
| 1968 | 75 | 9 | 100 | - |
| 1967 | 80 | 0 | 100 | 10 |
| 1966 | 82 | 9 | 100 | - |
| 1965 | 89 | 4 | - | 10 |
| 1964 | 92 | 0 | 100 | - |
| 1963 | - | 0 | - | - |

# 12 Matthew J. Rinaldo (R)

### Of Union — Elected 1972

**Born:** Sept. 1, 1931, Elizabeth, N.J.
**Education:** Rutgers U., B.S. 1953; Seton Hall U.,
   M.B.A. 1959; N.Y.U., M.A. 1969, Ph.D. 1979.
**Profession:** Industrial relations consultant.
**Family:** Single.
**Religion:** Roman Catholic.
**Political Career:** Union County Board of
   Freeholders, 1963-64; N.J. Senate, 1968-72.

**In Washington:** Rinaldo is a cautious man who often waits to see how a roll call is developing before casting his vote. He may seem a little sensitive for someone who has never drawn less than 60 percent in his district. But he resolutely maintains the careful style that brought him to Congress and made him politically secure.

On the Commerce Committee, that often means forsaking his Republican colleagues in favor of positions he sees as more acceptable in urban New Jersey. Rinaldo voted against natural gas deregulation in 1977, and when oil decontrol came up in 1979, he argued that "the benefits are unsubstantiated and the costs are unacceptably high." He was the only Republican on his entire committee to vote to consider President Carter's plan for hospital cost controls in 1979. Unlike other moderate Republicans, however, he seems to have escaped widespread criticism within his party. His insistence that he is merely "voting New Jersey" has bought him a reasonable amount of leeway on his own side of the aisle.

Over the years, Rinaldo has waged several conspicuous arguments in behalf of consumer groups back home. In 1976, he won House passage of an amendment blocking the federal government from raising rents for senior citizens in subsidized housing projects whenever benefits go up. In 1980, as ranking Republican on the Commerce Consumer Subcommittee, Rinaldo worked for legislation making it easier for small businesses to obtain product liability insurance. When the insurance industry fought it, Rinaldo charged that the industry "is blinding itself to the real world."

One of Rinaldo's most aggressive moments on the House floor came in 1979, when he insisted that a plan to make every driver keep his car off the road one day a week would discriminate against his constituents. "Whole towns and communities could be thrown into their own area-wide recession," he insisted, adding that the idea

"could have the undesirable effect of reducing church attendance." Most House members needed no persuading; language encouraging a sticker system was removed from the bill.

**At Home:** Despite the Republican label, Rinaldo is a traditional big-city neighborhood politician, and that partly explains his success in Union County's blue-collar bastions like Elizabeth.

He seldom fails to make the rounds of weddings, funerals and testimonial dinners, stroking the labor leaders who have political influence. The results are apparent; in 1978, when Democrat Bill Bradley ran for senator, one union local had a "Bradley-Rinaldo" bumper sticker. The Republican receives quiet help from Elizabeth Mayor Tom Dunn, a sympathetic Democrat, and while the Union County GOP organization is more conservative than Rinaldo, it has always been supportive.

The district has many Italian-Americans, so Rinaldo's surname is an asset. In the more conservative western part of the county, his party affiliation carries him.

Because of his reputation as a Republican who attracts Democrats, Rinaldo's name is perennially mentioned for governor or senator. He considered a gubernatorial campaign in 1981, but decided against it.

---

**12th District: Union County.** Population: 443,033 (7% decrease since 1970). Race: White 358,539 (81%), Black 68,579 (15%), Others 15,915 (4%). Spanish origin: 37,980 (9%).

*Matthew J. Rinaldo, R-N.J.*

**The District:** Union County long has had an affinity for liberal, pro-labor Republicans. Republican Clifford P. Case represented it in the House from 1945 to 1953, before he left to serve four terms in the Senate. In 1956, Florence Dwyer won the seat back from Democrat Harrison A. Williams Jr., also later a senator. She retired and was succeeded by Rinaldo.

The predominantly suburban district's eastern end is heavily ethnic and Democratic. It becomes more Republican farther west, in such towns as Summit and Mountainside.

Union County's Republicans are far more harmonious than the Democrats — a fact that has helped the GOP in local elections. While conservative, the Union Republican Party also puts a premium on pragmatism. The organization was an early supporter of Ronald Reagan, but objected to the 1980 party platform as too far right for public acceptance.

## Committees

**Energy and Commerce** (7th of 18 Republicans)
Energy Conservation and Power; Telecommunications, Consumer Protection, and Finance.

**Select Aging** (Ranking Republican)
Human Services.

## Elections

**1980 General**

| | |
|---|---|
| Matthew Rinaldo (R) | 134,973 (77%) |
| Rose Monyek (D) | 36,577 (21%) |

**1978 General**

| | |
|---|---|
| Matthew Rinaldo (R) | 94,850 (73%) |
| Richard McCormack (D) | 34,423 (27%) |

**Previous Winning Percentages**

1976 (73%)   1974 (65%)   1972 (64%)

**District Vote For President**

| | 1980 | | 1976 | | 1972 |
|---|---|---|---|---|---|
| D | 73,013 (38 %) | D | 90,425 (45%) | D | 77,367 (37%) |
| R | 100,348 (53 %) | R | 105,632 (53%) | R | 130,187 (62%) |
| I | 14,213 (7 %) | | | | |

## Campaign Finance

| | Receipts | Receipts from PACs | Expen-ditures |
|---|---|---|---|
| **1980** | | | |
| Rinaldo (R) | $291,773 | $73,095 (25%) | $229,475 |
| **1978** | | | |
| Rinaldo (R) | $245,934 | $61,702 (25%) | $192,778 |
| McCormack (D) | $14,336 | $300 (2%) | $13,556 |

## Voting Studies

| | Presidential Support | | Party Unity | | Conservative Coalition | |
|---|---|---|---|---|---|---|
| Year | S | O | S | O | S | O |
| 1980 | 58 | 40 | 44 | 55 | 45 | 54 |
| 1979 | 48 | 50 | 51 | 48 | 61 | 37 |
| 1978 | 55 | 40 | 45 | 53 | 41 | 56 |
| 1977 | 63 | 34 | 46 | 52 | 47 | 49 |
| 1976 | 31 | 65 | 24 | 71 | 34 | 62 |
| 1975 | 47 | 49 | 42 | 56† | 45 | 55† |
| 1974 (Ford) | 44 | 54 | | | | |
| 1974 | 47 | 49 | 28 | 69 | 32 | 61 |
| 1973 | 48 | 51 | 43 | 56 | 38 | 60 |

S = Support          O = Opposition
†Not eligible for all recorded votes.

## Key Votes

**96th Congress**

| | |
|---|---|
| Weaken Carter oil profits tax (1979) | N |
| Reject hospital cost control plan (1979) | N |
| Implement Panama Canal Treaties (1979) | N |
| Establish Department of Education (1979) | Y |
| Approve Anti-busing Amendment (1979) | N |
| Guarantee Chrysler Corp. loans (1979) | Y |
| Approve military draft registration (1980) | N |
| Aid Sandinista regime in Nicaragua (1980) | N |
| Strengthen fair housing laws (1980) | Y |

**97th Congress**

| | |
|---|---|
| Reagan budget proposal (1981) | Y |

## Interest Group Ratings

| Year | ADA | ACA | AFL-CIO | CCUS |
|---|---|---|---|---|
| 1980 | 61 | 38 | 84 | 59 |
| 1979 | 42 | 50 | 70 | 44 |
| 1978 | 50 | 33 | 80 | 35 |
| 1977 | 55 | 44 | 71 | 24 |
| 1976 | 60 | 19 | 87 | 8 |
| 1975 | 79 | 36 | 82 | 29 |
| 1974 | 70 | 31 | 90 | 0 |
| 1973 | 48 | 44 | 91 | 27 |

# 13 Jim Courter (R)

### Of Hackettstown — Elected 1978

**Born:** Oct. 14, 1941, Montclair, N.J.
**Education:** Colgate U., B.A. 1963; Duke U., J.D. 1966.
**Profession:** Lawyer.
**Family:** Wife, Carmen McCalmen; two children.
**Religion:** Methodist.
**Political Career:** Allamuchy Township attorney, 1975-78.

**In Washington:** Courter injected himself into House energy debate in 1979 after only a few months in the chamber, and came away with a temporary but dramatic victory.

One Friday morning in October, as the chamber was considering a routine Energy Department authorization, Courter stunned the House by winning approval of his amendment lifting all federal controls on the price of gasoline. He had caught the Democratic leadership napping. When the amendment came up for a vote, there were 54 absentees, most of them pro-control Democrats. Courter won by three votes.

Eleven days later, Democrats rallied absent troops, scheduled another vote and dumped the Courter amendment by a healthy margin. It was not until more than a year later that President Reagan decontrolled gasoline prices upon taking office.

After the 1979 episode was over, Courter said he had anticipated defeat and counted it as a kind of victory: he had focused attention on a topic he thought should come before the House.

The gasoline ploy actually was unrelated to his committee work, which is concentrated on Armed Services. He asked to go there as a freshman partly because he has an interest in global military strategy, and partly because of the Picatinny Arsenal in Dover, which the Army has threatened to close at times over the years. The fate of the arsenal and its jobs has become a dominant issue in part of the 13th District.

Courter has a chance to discuss broader issues on the Armed Services subcommittee dealing with Military Nuclear Systems. He has frequently expressed his fears over Soviet advances in new weapons development. He was particularly vocal in the summer of 1980, when the Pentagon disclosed that the United States was developing a mysterious new "Stealth" bomber which would be virtually invisible to enemy radar.

Like other House Republicans, Courter said the Pentagon leak was a serious breach of security and implied that it was a politically-motivated attempt by the Carter administration to escape criticism for canceling the B-1 bomber three years earlier. Courter introduced a resolution to force a full Armed Services inquiry into the leak, but it was rejected on a party-line vote.

Courter's reputation as a hard worker helped him win election in 1981 as president of his second-term Republican class. This gave him some extra visibility at an opportune time — as Ronald Reagan was building his ties to junior Republicans in Congress. When Reagan summoned that group to the White House for a pep talk on budget cuts, it was Courter who got to be the spokesman.

**At Home:** Courter appears to have entrenched himself in a very short time. Bright, diligent and very conservative, he has been described as the perfect representative for his middle-class Republican district. He was popular enough, after just one full term, to keep the Democrats from running a strong opponent against him in 1980.

Courter's biggest hurdle was getting the nomination for the seat in 1978. His primary opponent, former state Sen. William E. Schluter, had come close to defeating Democratic Rep. Helen Meyner in 1976 and was better known than

---

**13th District: West — Phillipsburg.**
Population: 577,078 (21% increase since 1970). Race: White 558,115 (97%), Black 10,529 (2%), Others 8,434 (1%). Spanish origin: 12,007 (2%).

---

Courter. Through exhaustive campaigning, Courter closed the gap, edging Schluter by 134 votes.

Meyner, wife of former Gov. Robert B. Meyner (1954-62), had turned out Republican Joseph J. Maraziti in the Democratic Watergate sweep of 1974. Two years later, she had narrowly beaten Schluter on the strength of her efforts to keep open the Picatinny Arsenal.

Courter blasted Meyner as a big-spending liberal who did not even live in the 13th District. Despite Meyner's protests that her record was being distorted — at one point, she called Courter "a naughty, naughty boy" — the Republican prevailed by a small margin.

Unlike most other places in New Jersey, this district practices a sedate form of politics, and Courter does not have to spend much time worrying about competing factions within his party.

**The District:** The 13th District was drawn to assure that a Republican leader in the state

Legislature, Joseph J. Maraziti, would be able to run for Congress there in 1972, and win. It worked in 1972, but two years later circumstances were much different. Maraziti fell victim to his defense of President Nixon and to keeping a woman on his payroll in a no-show job, and the carefully crafted district lines were no help.

Maraziti's handiwork still shows, however, in the Republican leanings of the rural and suburban areas the 13th takes in. Speculation is rife that the Democratic controlled Legislature will carve it up, during redistricting, to diminish its GOP slant.

No one county dominates the district. It includes half of populous Morris County, but not quite enough for Morris to control its politics. The district ranks near the state median in family income. The minority Democrats are clustered around industrial Phillipsburg, and in some of the suburbs of Trenton.

## Committees

**Armed Services** (13th of 19 Republicans)
Procurement and Military Nuclear Systems; Research and Development.

**Post Office and Civil Service** (5th of 11 Republicans)
Census and Popualtion; Civil Service.

## Elections

**1980 General**

| | |
|---|---|
| Jim Courter (R) | 152,862 (72%) |
| Dave Stickle (D) | 56,251 (26%) |

**1978 General**

| | |
|---|---|
| Jim Courter (R) | 77,301 (52%) |
| Helen Meyner (D) | 71,808 (48%) |

**1978 Primary**

| | |
|---|---|
| Jim Courter (R) | 10,541 (38%) |
| William Schluter (R) | 10,407 (38%) |
| Frank Bell (R) | 3,190 (12%) |
| Joseph Warganz (R) | 1,982 (7%) |
| Ronald Williams (R) | 1,397 (5%) |

**District Vote For President**

| | 1980 | | 1976 | | 1972 |
|---|---|---|---|---|---|
| D | 67,700 (29 %) | D | 87,626 (40%) | D | 61,509 (30%) |
| R | 136,402 (59 %) | R | 127,745 (58%) | R | 141,609 (69%) |
| I | 22,025 (10 %) | | | | |

## Campaign Finance

| | Receipts | Receipts from PACs | Expenditures |
|---|---|---|---|
| **1980** | | | |
| Courter (R) | $353,265 | $259,332 (73%) | $262,786 |

| | | | |
|---|---|---|---|
| Stickle (D) | $18,770 | — (0%) | $18,474 |
| **1978** | | | |
| Courter (R) | $332,037 | $57,643 (17%) | $330,688 |
| Meyner (D) | $173,850 | $46,436 (27%) | $194,641 |

## Voting Studies

| | Presidential Support | | Party Unity | | Conservative Coalition | |
|---|---|---|---|---|---|---|
| **Year** | **S** | **O** | **S** | **O** | **S** | **O** |
| 1980 | 40 | 52 | 83 | 15 | 85 | 11 |
| 1979 | 38 | 61 | 85 | 14 | 89 | 10 |

S = Support          O = Opposition

## Key Votes

**96th Congress**

| | |
|---|---|
| Weaken Carter oil profits tax (1979) | Y |
| Reject hospital cost control plan (1979) | Y |
| Implement Panama Canal Treaties (1979) | N |
| Establish Department of Education (1979) | Y |
| Approve Anti-busing Amendment (1979) | N |
| Guarantee Chrysler Corp. loans (1979) | N |
| Approve military draft registration (1980) | Y |
| Aid Sandinista regime in Nicaragua (1980) | N |
| Strengthen fair housing laws (1980) | N |

**97th Congress**

| | |
|---|---|
| Reagan budget proposal (1981) | Y |

## Interest Group Ratings

| Year | ADA | ACA | AFL-CIO | CCUS |
|---|---|---|---|---|
| 1980 | 11 | 83 | 16 | 61 |
| 1979 | 11 | 81 | 21 | 94 |

# 14 Frank J. Guarini (D)

**Of Jersey City — Elected 1978**

**Born:** Aug. 20, 1924, Jersey City, N.J.
**Education:** Dartmouth College, B.A. 1947;
N.Y.U. Law School, J.D. 1950, LL.M. 1955.
**Military Career:** Navy, 1944-46.
**Profession:** Lawyer.
**Family:** Single.
**Religion:** Roman Catholic.
**Political Career:** N.J. Senate 1966-72; unsuc-
cessfully sought Democratic nomination for
U.S. Senate, 1970.

**In Washington:** Guarini won a place on the
Ways and Means Committee as a freshman in
1979, an achievement that used to be virtually
impossible for newcomers. Unlike fellow first-
termer James Shannon of Massachusetts, who
pulled off a similar coup, Guarini did not enjoy a
personal friendship with the Speaker of the
House. But he did have a tireless advocate in
Robert Roe, the veteran New Jersey Democrat
who made sure House leaders knew that the state
had lost its only spot on the panel two years
before, and that Guarini was a tax lawyer.

Actually, Guarini's previous practice of law
attracted more attention in the 96th Congress
than anything he did on Ways and Means. Sole
proprietor of a lucrative firm founded by his
father, Guarini reported income from attorney's
fees of $935,124 in 1979. It was all legal — House
members are prohibited from earning more than
15 percent of their salaries in outside income, but
Guarini insisted that he was simply being paid for
work he did before he took office. "I can't be
running 100 miles per hour and stop dead on Jan.
1," he said.

On Ways and Means, Guarini has been a
solid vote against tax privileges for the oil industry. He was one of the Democrats interested in
making the tax on windfall oil profits as strict as
possible.

Guarini is a reliable friend of labor on most
House issues, an old-fashioned public works
Democrat who believes in federally subsidized
jobs as part of the answer to economic stagnation.
As a member of Ways and Means, he can further
his partnership with Roe, who makes a similar
jobs argument from his perch at the Public Works
Committee.

One major tax initiative by Guarini in the
96th Congress was a bill to cut federal levies by
approximately $30 billion through simply dou-
bling the amount people could earn and still pay
no tax at all. He said the idea was to concentrate
the impact of a tax cut on those at the bottom end
of the economic scale.

**At Home:** It takes keen political instincts to
survive in the Byzantine power struggles that
never seem to end in Hudson County. Guarini,
the former Hudson Democratic chairman, appears to have those instincts.

Apart from an unsuccessful primary bid
against Democratic Sen. Harrison A. Williams Jr.
in 1970, Guarini has taken no false political steps.
He owes his seat to his talent for backing the right
faction.

In 1977, he sided with the winners in the
contest for mayor of Jersey City, the county's
largest town. The congressman at the time,
Democrat Joseph A. LeFante, was allied with the
losers and chose to retire after one term rather
than face a challenge for renomination. Guarini
had the seat all but handed to him.

With his Dartmouth education and personal
wealth, Guarini does not fit the stereotype of the
Hudson politico. Reserved and well-spoken, he is
thought to have ambitions for another try at the
Senate.

**The District:** Politics is the principal form
of entertainment in urbanized, blue-collar Hudson County. On election days, rowhouses still
sprout bunting, flags and campaign posters. Local

---

**14th District: Hudson County —
Jersey City.** Population: 428,399 (10% decrease since 1970). Race: White 310,185 (73%),
Black 68,034 (16%), Asian and Pacific Islander 13,155 (3%), Others 37,025 (9%). Spanish origin: 97,322 (23%).

---

779

politicians are local celebrities.

Hudson, once home of Democratic boss Frank "I am the law" Hague, retains one of the few strong Democratic organizations in the nation. Although its influence dimmed in the 1970s during the tenure of reform-minded Mayor Paul Jordan, the party apparatus has returned to prominence.

The reformers' ascendancy resulted from the conviction of several party figures on corruption charges in the early 1970s. Most notable was Democratic Rep. Cornelius Gallagher (1959-73), who was beaten by Dominick V. Daniels (1959-77) in 1972 when their districts were combined. Dan-

iels later retired and LeFante replaced him.

The rule of the reformers was short-lived, ending when Mayor Jordan's candidate for successor lost to Thomas F. X. Smith in 1977.

The 14th's ethnic composition has traditionally been Italian, Irish and Polish. Jersey City has had a relatively small black population, but the number of blacks in the district is growing, and Hispanics are also becoming more numerous and more influential in local politics. Hoboken and Union City are estimated to have Hispanic majorities. This decade, the district likely will be expanded geographically to make up for its population loss. It likely will stay firmly Democratic.

## Committees

**Select Narcotics Abuse and Control** (10th of 11 Democrats)

**Ways and Means** (17th of 23 Democrats)
  Social Security; Trade.

## Elections

**1980 General**

| | |
|---|---|
| Frank Guarini (D) | 86,921 (64%) |
| Dennis Teti (R) | 45,606 (34%) |

**1978 General**

| | |
|---|---|
| Frank Guarini (D) | 67,008 (64%) |
| Henry Hill (R) | 21,355 (20%) |
| Thomas McDonough (I) | 15,015 (14%) |

**1978 Primary**

| | |
|---|---|
| Frank Guarini (D) | 34,127 (82%) |
| Anthony Scalcione (D) | 4,163 (10%) |
| Raymond Connelly (D) | 3,165 (8%) |

**District Vote For President**

| | 1980 | | 1976 | | 1972 |
|---|---|---|---|---|---|
| D | 76,679 (51%) | D | 91,375 (56%) | D | 71,098 (40%) |
| R | 65,713 (44%) | R | 70,173 (43%) | R | 104,907 (59%) |
| I | 6,595 (4%) | | | | |

## Campaign Finance

| | Receipts | Receipts from PACs | Expenditures |
|---|---|---|---|
| **1980** | | | |
| Guarini (D) | $192,956 | $70,876 (37%) | $170,237 |
| Teti (R) | $59,543 | $5,800 (10%) | $59,428 |

| | | | |
|---|---|---|---|
| **1978** | | | |
| Guarini (D) | $88,727 | $10,200 (11%) | $83,325 |
| Hill (R) | $5,806 | $600 (10%) | $7,566 |

## Voting Studies

| | Presidential Support | | Party Unity | | Conservative Coalition | |
|---|---|---|---|---|---|---|
| **Year** | **S** | **O** | **S** | **O** | **S** | **O** |
| 1980 | 65 | 28 | 74 | 17 | 35 | 59 |
| 1979 | 71 | 23 | 78 | 14 | 28 | 67 |

S = Support          O = Opposition

## Key Votes

**96th Congress**

| | |
|---|---|
| Weaken Carter oil profits tax (1979) | N |
| Reject hospital cost control plan (1979) | N |
| Implement Panama Canal Treaties (1979) | Y |
| Establish Department of Education (1979) | N |
| Approve Anti-busing Amendment (1979) | N |
| Guarantee Chrysler Corp. loans (1979) | Y |
| Approve military draft registration (1980) | Y |
| Aid Sandinista regime in Nicaragua (1980) | N |
| Strengthen fair housing laws (1980) | Y |

**97th Congress**

| | |
|---|---|
| Reagan budget proposal (1981) | N |

## Interest Group Ratings

| Year | ADA | ACA | AFL-CIO | CCUS |
|---|---|---|---|---|
| 1980 | 67 | 39 | 74 | 59 |
| 1979 | 74 | 8 | 95 | 11 |

# 15 Bernard J. Dwyer (D)

**Of Edison — Elected 1980**

**Born:** Jan. 24, 1921, Perth Amboy, N.J.
**Education:** Rutgers U., Newark, no degree.
**Military Career:** Navy, 1940-45.
**Profession:** Insurance broker.
**Family:** Wife, Lilyan Sudzina; one child.
**Religion:** Roman Catholic.
**Political Career:** Edison Township Council, 1958-69; Edison mayor, 1969-73; N.J. Senate, 1974-80; Senate majority leader, 1980.

**The Member:** Quiet and bland in manner, Dwyer was known in the New Jersey Senate as a legislative tactician, one who avoided the public spotlight and preferred behind-the-scenes maneuvering.

His most notable individual accomplishments attracted little public attention. Dwyer pushed through a ban on state government purchase of imported cars and a $50 million bond issue to weatherize state buildings. Much of his work was done at the Joint Appropriations Committee, which he chaired at one point during his Senate career.

Dwyer's experience helped him bypass the House custom of placing only more senior members on the most powerful committees. Dwyer was the sole first-termer to win a seat on Appropriations.

In his 1980 campaign to succeed Democrat Edward J. Patten, who retired, Dwyer held off belligerent primary and general election opponents with the confidence born of solid organization support in a district where that still means a great deal. As the candidate of the Middlesex County Democratic organization, Dwyer let the party do most of the work for him.

But when opponents accused him of using his clout to get a no-bid Middlesex County insurance contract, Dwyer produced a letter from the state Senate Ethics Committee approving his conduct.

**The District:** Middlesex County makes this a Democratic district. Most of Middlesex is in the 15th, and Democrats have a 3-1 registration advantage there. Industrial New Brunswick, Perth Amboy and Woodbridge, in northern Middlesex, provide much of the Democratic vote.

Republicans are concentrated in the more suburban southern end of the county, and habitually win such towns as Plainsboro and Cranbury. Before the current district was created in 1961, the county had been split between two Republican districts.

## Committees

**Appropriations** (33rd of 33 Democrats)
  Commerce, Justice, state, and the Judiciary; Labor - Health and Human Services-Education.

## Elections

**1980 General**

| | |
|---|---|
| Bernard Dwyer (D) | 92,457 (53%) |
| William O'Sullivan Jr. (R) | 75,812 (44%) |

**1980 Primary**

| | |
|---|---|
| Bernard Dwyer (D) | 16,328 (32%) |
| David Schwartz (D) | 12,800 (25%) |
| George Spadoro (D) | 12,329 (24%) |
| Richard Pucci (D) | 7,720 (15%) |

**District Vote For President**

| | 1980 | | 1976 | | 1972 |
|---|---|---|---|---|---|
| **D** | 82,164 (43 %) | **D** | 102,132 (53%) | **D** | 74,752 (38%) |
| **R** | 93,570 (49 %) | **R** | 88,223 (45%) | **R** | 118,439 (60%) |
| **I** | 13,391 (7 %) | | | | |

## Campaign Finance

| | Receipts | Receipts from PACs | Expenditures |
|---|---|---|---|
| **1980** | | | |
| Dwyer (D) | $137,973 | $53,200 (39%) | $132,918 |
| O'Sullivan Jr. (R) | $55,264 | $18,450 (33%) | $53,055 |

## Key Vote

**97th Congress**

| | |
|---|---|
| Reagan budget proposal (1981) | N |

**15th District: Central — New Brunswick, Perth Amboy.** Population: 475,951 (0.4% decrease since 1970). Race: White 414,518 (87%), Black 38,550 (8%), Aisian and Pacific Islander 9,585 (2%), Others 13,298 (3%). Spanish origin: 32,050 (8%).

# New Mexico

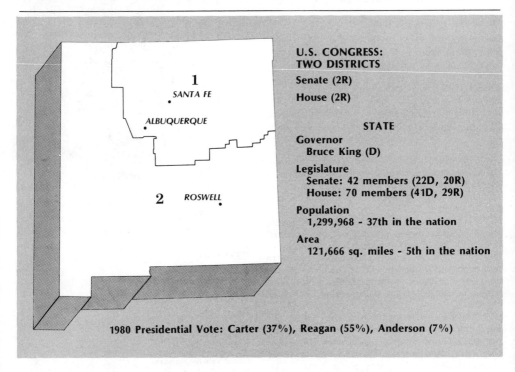

U.S. CONGRESS:
TWO DISTRICTS
Senate (2R)
House (2R)

STATE
Governor
Bruce King (D)
Legislature
Senate: 42 members (22D, 20R)
House: 70 members (41D, 29R)
Population
1,299,968 - 37th in the nation
Area
121,666 sq. miles - 5th in the nation

1980 Presidential Vote: Carter (37%), Reagan (55%), Anderson (7%)

## ... Toward an Anglo Politics

Once the exclusive domain of Hispanics and Indians, New Mexico is being increasingly "Anglocized."

For most of this century, the "Anglos" — all non-Indians or Hispanics — came to ranch, to mine or to regain their health in the sunny, dry climate. But in the boom years since World War II, the attractions have been more diverse. Some Anglos have come to develop the oil and mineral resources in New Mexico or to work in the laboratories in Los Alamos and Albuquerque uncovering the secrets of nuclear power. Others have been drawn by the mountain scenery and relaxed pace of life in the "Land of Enchantment."

Between 1940 and 1960, the population of New Mexico nearly doubled. The boom ebbed in the 1960s with a decline in defense-related jobs but revived dramatically in the 1970s when the growth in private-sector jobs spurred a population increase of 28 percent. For the first time in its

history, New Mexico will have three seats in the U.S. House after 1982.

The influx of newcomers has meant an increasingly dominant Anglo majority. Hispanics — many descendants of Spanish settlers who entered New Mexico more than 350 years ago — comprise 37 percent of the population. Indians — mostly members of the ancient Navajo or Pueblo tribes — make up 8 percent.

These groups remain the backbone of the once-dominant Democratic Party in New Mexico. With their help, the party ruled the state from the early days of the New Deal until the late 1960s.

But the defection of conservative Democrats in southeastern New Mexico ("Little Texas") and the influx of Anglos has spurred a Republican resurgence. Republicans now have both U.S. Senate and U.S. House seats. They do not hold the governor's chair or control either chamber of the state Legislature, but they were only two seats down in the state Senate after November of 1980. They lost both the 1974 and 1978 gubernatorial elections by less than 4,000 votes.

Because many of the Hispanics and Indians are poor, New Mexico ranks near the bottom tier of states in per capita income. But the economic picture will improve in the 1980s as the state's rich natural resources are developed. By the late 1970s, New Mexico was the leading state in the mining of uranium and among the top seven in the production of crude oil and natural gas.

# A Political Tour

**Albuquerque.** This is New Mexico's commercial hub and major population center. Including its Bernalillo County suburbs, the Albuquerque area is home for nearly one-third of New Mexico's 1.3 million residents.

In the post-war years, there has been an ebb and flow in defense contracts that has affected Albuquerque's growth. Originally a health spa and trade center along the Rio Grande, the city had less than 40,000 inhabitants in 1940. But 20 years later, with the coming of a lucrative military-aerospace connection, Albuquerque had more than 200,000. Growth slowed in the 1960s but with more a more diversified economy, the city surged forward again in the 1970s.

Large clothing and office machine plants have located in Albuquerque. But the real boom in recent years has been provided by electronics firms. The influx of young engineers and scientists, as well as retirees — many of them formerly with the military — have helped push Bernalillo County increasingly into the GOP column. Although its population is 37 percent Hispanic, the county has voted Republican in all but one presidential election since 1952. It has been reliably Republican in recent races for major statewide offices, but has a Democratic mayor, David Rusk, the son of former Secretary of State Dean Rusk.

**Santa Fe and the Hispanic North.** The greatest concentration of Hispanics and Democratic votes in the state is in the mountainous north.

The region is the site of some of the earliest 17th century Spanish settlements in the state, including the state capital of Santa Fe. Today, six of the state's eight predominantly Hispanic counties are in the north, with the other two in the southwest corner of the state near the Mexican border. Except for Santa Fe County, the Hispanic north is an area of slow growth.

Santa Fe is the center of the region. The evidence of its strong Hispanic and Indian culture is seen in its adobe buildings, still the most prominent architectural style in use. With nearly 50,000 residents, Santa Fe is the largest city in the state north of Albuquerque. The melding of the Spanish and Indian cultures has created an ambience attractive to young Anglos, who are migrating to Santa Fe in increasing numbers. The county grew by 38 percent in the past decade.

A colony of artists and writers has flourished in the cosmopolitan atmosphere. These people join with the Hispanics and state government workers to provide Democratic candidates with comfortable margins in Santa Fe County.

Seven different Pueblo Indian tribes live in the Rio Grande Valley north of Santa Fe. Although they usually vote Democratic, the council for the Pueblo tribes endorsed Reagan in 1980.

The rest of the Hispanic north is primarily mountainous, semi-arid grazing land, with much poverty and subsistence farming. An exception is the prosperous Anglo community of Los Alamos, where the atomic bomb was secretly developed during World War II. After the war, the gates of Los Alamos were opened, and it became a separate county. During the last three decades, Los Alamos has remained a center for the research and development of atomic energy. Its scientifically skilled, well-educated electorate is largely Republican. But voters in Los Alamos also have an independent streak, shown in 1980 when John B. Anderson received 15 percent, his highest vote in the state.

**Little Texas.** Economically, culturally and politically, the southeastern part of New Mexico is similar to the adjoining plains of Texas. That is no accident. The region was settled by Texans early this century and Anglo dominance has never been threatened. Hispanics comprise only about one-quarter of the population of Little Texas.

Most of the land is used for grazing cattle or sheep, with some suitable for dry farming crops like wheat. Irrigated farm land along the Pecos River produces cotton, vegetables and fruit.

Conservative and heavily Protestant, Little Texas was overwhelmingly Democratic for most of the century. But as the national Democratic Party moved leftward, party loyalty began to crack. In 1968, votes from Little Texas helped to send conservative Republican Ed Foreman, a former Texas congressman, to the House. Foreman lasted only one term before being unseated by conservative Democrat Harold Runnels. But in statewide contests, the region has regularly turned in GOP majorities.

Although Little Texas is not a booming area like Albuquerque, it has remained stable with oil, mining and military activity. Oil deposits are concentrated in the southern portion of Little Texas around Carlsbad, Roswell and Hobbs.

Located near the famous caverns, the town of Carlsbad is also a tourist center. Nearby are the nation's most productive potash mines where unionized miners occasionally give Democrats enough votes to carry Eddy County (Carlsbad).

Alamagordo, located just across the Sacramento Mountains from Little Texas, is culturally in step with the region. Just outside Alamagordo is the White Sands Missile Range, where the first atomic bomb was exploded in 1945.

**Mexican Highlands and Indian Country.** The western third of New Mexico is really two distinct areas. The largely Hispanic southern portion is known as the Mexican Highlands. It is a semi-arid region of desert and mountains. A wide range of mineral deposits — copper, zinc, silver, gold and lead — are located in the heart of the mountains. In the Rio Grande Valley near Las Cruces, there is irrigated farm land, where cotton, vegetables and fruit are grown.

The semi-arid high plateau to the north is Indian country. A large Navajo reservation stretches from the town of Gallup about 100 miles north to the Four Corners — the point where New Mexico, Colorado, Utah and Arizona meet. Like the Mexican Highlands, the Indian country is rich in minerals — coal and uranium — as well as oil and natural gas. Many of the energy reserves were found on Indian land, enabling them to attain a level of prosperity unmatched by other Indian tribes in New Mexico.

With the exception of Grant and Socorro counties — major mining centers in the south — the Mexican Highlands usually vote Republican. By contrast, the Indian country is predominantly Democratic. The exception is San Juan County, where a conservative Anglo population has settled in the energy-rich Four Corners area near Farmington. San Juan gave Reagan a higher share of the vote than any New Mexico county outside Little Texas.

Valencia County, the center of uranium mining activity in the 1970s, grew by 50 percent. San Juan County, one of the state's leading oil, gas and coal producing areas, grew by 54 percent. Sandoval County, which abuts Bernalillo County and drew suburban spillover from Albuquerque, had a population growth of 99 percent.

# Redrawing the Lines

The New Mexico House and Senate, both controlled by Democrats, had by midyear settled on the location of only one of the three districts.

There was general agreement that the new district the state gained as a result of its 28 percent growth would be dominated by Bernalillo County (Albuquerque). The House passed a map dividing the remaining counties into an eastern and western district. But the Senate refused to act on that plan, as many Democratic senators indicated a preference for a north-south split.

The east-west plan divides the vote of the more liberal, Spanish-speaking population in the northern counties and was supported by a coalition of Republicans and conservative Democrats.

# Governor
# Bruce King (D)

**Born:** April 6, 1924, Stanley, N.M.
**Home:** Stanley, N.M.
**Education:** U. of New Mexico, 1943-44.
**Military Career:** Army, World War II.
**Profession:** Farmer, rancher.
**Family:** Wife, Alice; two children.
**Religion:** Baptist.
**Political Career:** Sante Fe County Commission, 1954-59; New Mexico House, 1959-69; Speaker of the House, 1963-69; unsuccessful campaign for Democratic gubernatorial nomination, 1968; state Democratic chairman, 1968-69; president, state constitutional convention, 1969; governor, 1971-75; re-elected, 1978; term expires Jan. 1983.

# Pete V. Domenici (R)

**Of Albuquerque — Elected 1972**

**Born:** May 7, 1932, Albuquerque, N.M.
**Education:** U. of Albuquerque, 1950-52; U. of N.M., B.S. 1954; U. of Denver, LL.B. 1958.
**Profession:** Lawyer.
**Family:** Wife, Nancy Burk, eight children.
**Religion:** Roman Catholic.
**Political Career:** Albuquerque City Commission, 1966-70, chairman and ex-officio mayor, 1967-70; unsuccessful Republican nominee for governor, 1970.

**In Washington:** Startled when the 1980 election suddenly made him Senate Budget chairman, Domenici wasted no time in trying to implement the federal budget cuts that he had been calling for nearly as consistently as Ronald Reagan over the past few years.

Shortly after the election, Domenici sent Reagan a detailed list of spending cuts, one that budget director David Stockman later used in putting together the president's economic program. He conferred frequently with Stockman, Treasury Secretary Donald Regan and other administration officials in developing strategy.

The first few months produced a long string of successes, as Domenici's committee and the Republican Senate approved spending reductions and an overall 1982 budget tailored to Reagan's specifications, with Domenici arguing for them. The only sign of trouble came when three of the committee's most conservative Republicans balked at the 1982 budget resolution, saying it could lead to unacceptable deficits several years down the road. That dispute was quickly resolved with some new figures from Stockman outlining further cuts for 1983 and 1984. By midyear, not only the budget but the full Reagan package of spending cuts seemed well on the way to enactment.

All the harmony of the new Republican era obscured some differences in outlook between the new Budget chairman and the Reagan advisers. Domenici has never been an apostle of supply-side economics or a believer that massive tax cuts would generate enough growth to curb inflation. He has been a traditional low-deficit Republican. Domenici has argued repeatedly that there are no quick-fix solutions to the nation's economic problems. "You never heard Pete Domenici make the argument that you could balance the budget, have significant defense increases and multi-year tax

cuts simply by eliminating waste and fraud," he said in 1980.

Domenici has always insisted that inflation could be controlled only by tackling the so-called "entitlement" programs that account for 60 percent of the total federal budget. He has advocated a statutory limit on overall federal spending, saying it is needed politically to "enable the Congress to say 'no' in a manner that its members can support."

The only two budget areas Domenici has been reluctant to cut over the years are defense and energy, especially atomic energy. New Mexico relies heavily on federal spending in those fields, and the state's business leaders have gradually come to rely on Domenici as someone who can bring them federal plums. He does not like to disappoint them.

Domenici, in fact, hates to disappoint anyone. Despite his outward self-confidence and friendly, assured manner, he has a strong need for approval, from his colleagues, the press, his constituents and the general public. He was upset in 1978 when he won re-election to a second term with a mere 53 percent of the vote, instead of the 60-plus margin he had been aiming for.

Over nearly a decade in the Senate, Domenici has outgrown an early reputation for brashness and is now regarded as a thoughtful legislator, although a very stubborn one. He has been one of the more active members of the Energy and Natural Resources Committee. During the 96th Congress, he often proved to be the most forceful member on the Republican side, sometimes overshadowing the panel's current chairman, James A. McClure of Idaho.

Domenici was deeply involved in shaping most of the major energy legislation that moved through the Senate during the Carter administration. On several important bills — synthetic fuels, Energy Mobilization Board, and standby gas rationing — he teamed with his committee's dominant Democrat, J. Bennett Johnston of Louisiana, to craft compromises that could satisfy competing interests. He antagonized some independent oil producers in his home state who felt the 1978 Natural Gas Policy Act that Domenici helped to write did not move fast enough toward decontrolling natural gas prices.

Domenici's Budget chairmanship is limiting the amount of time he can spend on another issue important to him, renewal of the Clean Air Act. The New Mexico Republican is on the Environment Committee, charged with rewriting the act in the 97th Congress. He wants to loosen pollution control standards somewhat and to modify existing legal strictures against the use of natural gas to fuel power plants after 1990.

Domenici's most conspicuous past achievement on the Environment Committee was his effort to make commercial barge operators pay a user fee to support the upkeep of federally maintained inland waterways. He attached the user fee to a 1977 proposal to replace Locks and Dam 26 on the Mississippi River, and it became one of the most controversial and hotly lobbied bills of the 95th Congress. *The Washington Post* selected the bill for a case study of the legislative process, and Domenici found himself suddenly — but gratifyingly — famous for a while. By the time the barge operators and their champion, Sen. Russell Long, D-La., finished working on the measure, it bore little resemblance to the one Domenici had originally introduced. But he accepted it anyhow, as a modest first step.

**At Home:** Seeking a first term in 1972, Domenici had the advantage of speaking Spanish in a state that is 37 percent Hispanic. He also had a Hispanic-sounding surname, even though he was born Pietro Vichi Domenici, the son of an immigrant Italian grocer. He drew more votes in Hispanic northern New Mexico than Republicans normally do.

Domenici's background was in municipal government. After law school, he had made his first political foray by winning a seat on the Albuquerque City Commission, and later became chair-

man, the equivalent of mayor. As a city official, he prided himself on neighborhood meetings he held to hear residents' complaints.

Counting on his Bernalillo County (Albuquerque) base, which cast a third of the vote in the state, Domenici ran for governor in 1970. He captured the Republican nomination in a six-way race with slightly less than 50 percent of the vote. Domenici was seen as a moderate in that campaign. His closest primary rival was Stephen C. Helbing, the GOP floor leader in the state House, who advocated a crackdown on student demonstrators.

In the fall, Bernalillo County did not come through for Domenici the way he had hoped. He carried it by only 8,909 votes, not enough for him to win statewide against Democrat Bruce King, the state House Speaker. King had the party registration advantage and was better known statewide. Domenici tried to raise doubts about King by criticizing his lack of administrative experience, but with little success.

Undeterred, Domenici came back in 1972, this time running for the Senate seat being vacated by Democrat Clinton P. Anderson. His Democratic opponent was former state Rep. Jack Daniels, who had also run for governor in 1970 but lost to King in the Democratic primary.

Daniels, a wealthy banker, differed little from Domenici on the issues. But Domenici pointed out that Daniels had stood on the same platform as McGovern that year and pledged to back him as the Democratic presidential nominee. While Daniels had repudiated McGovern's call for reduced defense spending, the association hurt him.

Domenici's percentage dropped slightly in 1978. The Democratic candidate, state Attorney General Toney Anaya, was Hispanic. Domenici had taken most of the heavily Hispanic counties in 1972, but six years later he lost most of them. In addition, his 1972 plurality of 31,240 votes in Bernalillo shrank to 6,766 in 1978.

Fortunately for Domenici, Anaya did not have a united Democratic Party behind him. As chief state prosecutor, he had secured indictments against several important party figures. This aroused resentment among regulars and prompted many of them to keep their distance.

## Committees

**Budget** (Chairman)

**Energy and Natural Resources** (4th of 11 Republicans)
  Energy and Research Development, chairman; Energy Regula-

tion; Public Lands and Reserved Water.

**Environment and Public Works** (3rd of 9 Republicans)
  Nuclear Regulation; Regional and Community Development; Water Resources.

**Special Aging** (2nd of 8 Republicans)

## Elections

**1978 General**

S = Support         O = Opposition

| | |
|---|---|
| Pete V. Domenici (R ) | 183,442 (53%) |
| Toney Anaya (D ) | 160,044 (47%) |

## Key Votes

**Previous Winning Percentage**

**96th Congress**

1972 (54%)

## Campaign Finance

| Vote | |
|---|---|
| Maintain relations with Taiwan (1979) | Y |
| Reduce synthetic fuel development funds (1979) | N |
| Impose nuclear plant moratorium (1979) | N |
| Kill stronger windfall profits tax (1979) | Y |
| Guarantee Chrysler Corp. loans (1979) | N |
| Approve military draft registration (1980) | Y |
| End Revenue Sharing to the states (1980) | Y |
| Block Justice Dept. busing suits (1980) | Y |

| | Receipts | Receipts from PACs | Expen-ditures |
|---|---|---|---|
| 1978 | | | |
| Domenici (R ) | $925,622 | $150,401 (16 %) | $914,634 |
| Anaya (D ) | $175,659 | $48,505 (28 %) | $175,633 |

**97th Congress**

| Vote | |
|---|---|
| Restore urban program funding cuts (1981) | N |

## Voting Studies

## Interest Group Ratings

| | Presidential Support | | Party Unity | | Conservative Coalition | |
|---|---|---|---|---|---|---|
| Year | S | O | S | O | S | O |
| 1980 | 58 | 40 | 74 | 19 | 84 | 8 |
| 1979 | 45 | 52 | 78 | 18 | 87 | 10 |
| 1978 | 25 | 50 | 60 | 18 | 66 | 14 |
| 1977 | 57 | 39 | 84 | 8 | 89 | 3 |
| 1976 | 83 | 11 | 80 | 8 | 85 | 6 |
| 1975 | 81 | 15 | 77 | 16 | 85 | 7 |
| 1974 (Ford) | 60 | 29 | | | | |

| Year | ADA | ACA | AFL-CIO | CCUS-1 | CCUS-2 |
|---|---|---|---|---|---|
| 1980 | 17 | 71 | 22 | 88 | |
| 1979 | 5 | 69 | 26 | 55 | 73 |
| 1978 | 15 | 65 | 40 | 56 | |
| 1977 | 5 | 70 | 15 | 89 | |
| 1976 | 5 | 87 | 22 | 78 | |
| 1975 | 22 | 63 | 35 | 63 | |
| 1974 | 24 | 56 | 27 | 60 | |
| 1973 | 10 | 89 | 18 | 78 | |

# Harrison "Jack" Schmitt (R)

### Of Silver City — Elected 1976

**Born:** July 3, 1935; Santa Rita, N.M.
**Education:** Calif. Institute of Technology, B.S. 1957; U. of Oslo, Norway, (Fulbright Fellowship), 1957-58; Harvard U., Ph.D. 1964.
**Profession:** Geologist, astronaut.
**Family:** Single.
**Religion:** Methodist.
**Political Career:** No previous office.

**In Washington:** Astronaut Schmitt brought to the Senate a scientist's fascination with new technology and a conservative's faith in old virtues.

Although somewhat eclipsed by his more powerful Republican colleague from New Mexico, Pete Domenici, Schmitt has applied himself energetically to mastering the myriad of issues that come before the Senate each year.

One might almost say, too energetically. He has consistently exhausted his staff and exasperated senators who wish he would be more restrained about sharing what he has learned. In party caucuses, in committee meetings and on the floor, Schmitt loves to talk about his latest intellectual interest — whether it happens to be germane to the matter at hand or not.

Usually, it is related to science. Schmitt came to Washington fresh from a campaign in which he talked excitedly about new technologies for desalinizing water and providing rural electricity from commercial fuel cells, and he has pursued those ideas and later ones with similar enthusiasm in the years since then. He is interested these days in remote earth sensing and the colonization of space.

Schmitt brings to his chairmanship of the Senate Commerce Subcommittee on Science, Technology and Space a level of substantive expertise virtually unmatched in the Congress. Long before he became a politician, and even before he flew to the moon on Apollo 17, Schmitt was a highly respected scientist with a string of academic and professional honors.

Unlike John Glenn of Ohio, the Senate's other former astronaut, Schmitt actively sought assignment to the panel responsible for space legislation. Also unlike Glenn, he has persistently advocated a stronger U.S. commitment to space exploration. He introduced his own bill to mandate an ambitious 30-year program of space ventures. "Space spending is not inflationary," he asserts. "It's deflationary. You get a $4 to $5 return for every $1 invested over a five-year period."

Despite his identification with space, Schmitt likes to think of himself as a generalist. "I think people are getting less from the Congress just because everybody is dealing with so much detail," he once said.

Born in a small mining town in New Mexico, Schmitt retains much of the individualist conservative atttitude of the mountain West. He tends to be a libertarian conservative rather than a moral majority enthusiast; he has offended some New Right groups with his support for federal funding of abortion and for the Equal Rights Amendment.

Schmitt has been a hard-liner on Senate ethics. As vice-chairman of the chamber's Ethics Committee during its probe of former Sen. Herman Talmadge, D-Ga., he felt its decision to "denounce" Talmadge for financial misconduct was too weak. He wanted formal censure, and tried to get the panel to approve it. When he lost, 5-1, he went along with the less strict penalty of "denunciation."

It was not the only time he took a tougher stand than his colleagues on ethical questions; Schmitt was also in the minority opposing relaxation of the Senate's financial disclosure rules in 1979, and he opposed relaxation of its limit on outside earnings of members.

**At Home:** Schmitt made an impressive political debut in 1976, not only retiring two-term Democrat Joseph Montoya but winning by the largest margin any Senate Republican had achieved in the state's history.

Montoya retained the loyalty of Hispanic voters, but Schmitt, who speaks Spanish, made some inroads there, too. He defeated Montoya overwhelmingly in Albuquerque, where a third of the state's vote is cast.

Noting that his challenger had voted in Texas as late as 1972, Montoya tried to paint Schmitt as a carpetbagger, snidely referring to him as "the stranger who came down from the moon." But Schmitt chose to say little about Montoya. Indeed, he used his background as a scientist and astronaut to advantage.

While taking a conservative stance on most issues — he talked about beefing up the military and disparaged national health insurance — Schmitt intrigued audiences with his new ideas for applying scientific methods to public problems.

Montoya helped build the Republican vote total with his own personal weaknesses. Newspapers had reported that New Mexicans were disappointed in his lackluster performance on the Senate Watergate panel in 1973. Moreover, Montoya's personal integrity had been challenged. According to news reports, he had, among other things, ordered staffers to manage his business properties.

Schmitt's campaign was the realization of a political dream he had had for 15 years, since his days as a graduate student in geology at Harvard. He was not experienced at running a campaign, and many of the state's Republican regulars were suspicious of him through the fall. But his celebrity status helped him win the party endorsement easily at a state convention, and he took more than 70 percent of the vote in the primary, touring the state in a red pickup truck, and speaking Spanish in the Hispanic counties.

## Committees

**Appropriations** (7th of 15 Republicans)
Labor, Health and Human Services, Education, chairman; Defense; Energy and Water Development; HUD-Independent Agencies; Interior.

**Banking, Housing and Urban Affairs** (8th of 8 Republicans)
Rural Housing and Development, chairman; Consumer Affairs; Financial Institutions; Securities.

**Commerce, Science and Transportation** (3rd of 9 Republicans)
Science, Technology, and Space, chairman; Communications; Surface Transportation.

**Select Intelligence** (8th of 8 Republicans)
Legislation and the Rights of Americans, chairman; Collection and Foreign Operations.

## Elections

**1976 General**

| | |
|---|---|
| Harrison Schmitt (R ) | 234,681 (57 %) |
| Joseph Montoya (D ) | 176,382 (43 %) |

**1976 Primary**

| | |
|---|---|
| Harrison Schmitt (R ) | 34,074 (72 %) |
| Eugene Peirce (R ) | 10,965 (23 %) |
| Arthur Lavine (R ) | 2,481 (5 %) |

## Campaign Finance

| | Receipts | Receipts from PACs | Expenditures |
|---|---|---|---|
| **1976** | | | |
| Schmitt (R ) | $473,336 | $56,360 (12 %) | $441,309 |
| Montoya (D ) | $461,505 | $120,052 (26 %) | $451,111 |

## Voting Studies

| | Presidential Support | | Party Unity | | Conservative Coalition | |
|---|---|---|---|---|---|---|
| Year | S | O | S | O | S | O |
| 1980 | 35 | 53 | 78 | 13 | 82 | 10 |
| 1979 | 36 | 61 | 78 | 19 | 82 | 13 |
| 1978 | 26 | 70 | 80 | 13 | 77 | 16 |
| 1977 | 40 | 56† | 87 | 6† | 93 | 4 |

S = Support   O = Opposition
†Not eligible for all recorded votes.

## Key Votes

**96th Congress**

| | |
|---|---|
| Maintain relations with Taiwan (1979) | Y |
| Reduce synthetic fuel development funds (1979) | Y |
| Impose nuclear plant moratorium (1979) | N |
| Kill stronger windfall profits tax (1979) | Y |
| Guarantee Chrysler Corp. loans (1979) | Y |
| Approve military draft registration (1980) | Y |
| End Revenue Sharing to the states (1980) | Y |
| Block Justice Dept. busing suits (1980) | Y |

**97th Congress**

| | |
|---|---|
| Restore urban program funding cuts (1981) | N |

## Interest Group Ratings

| Year | ADA | ACA | AFL-CIO | CCUS-1 | CCUS-2 |
|---|---|---|---|---|---|
| 1980 | 17 | 86 | 24 | 90 | |
| 1979 | 16 | 78 | 17 | 80 | 87 |
| 1978 | 20 | 75 | 24 | 87 | |
| 1977 | 15 | 84 | 11 | 94 | |

# 1 Manuel Lujan Jr. (R)

**Of Albuquerque — Elected 1968**

**Born:** May 12, 1928, San Ildefonso, N.M.
**Education:** Attended St. Mary's College, 1946-47; College of Santa Fe, B.A. 1950.
**Profession:** Insurance broker.
**Family:** Wife, Jean Kay Couchman; four children.
**Religion:** Roman Catholic.
**Political Career:** Republican candidate for N.M. Senate 1964.

**In Washington:** When Ronald Reagan was considering his Cabinet appointments, Lujan's name came up frequently in the speculation for secretary of the interior. Lujan had been close to Reagan's pro-development position on many land issues, and he represented a chance for Hispanic representation in the Cabinet.

In the end, Reagan chose the more militant James Watt. But Lujan became ranking Republican on the House Interior Committee, where he is in position to fight for some of Watt's "Sagebrush Rebellion" positions.

Lujan is a moderate House Republican on many issues, one sometimes willing to cast a quiet vote for domestic social programs even against a majority of his party. He even voted for the environmentally oriented version of Alaska land legislation in 1979. But on the question of land use in the Mountain States, he is on the private enterprise side.

The tenets of the Sagebrush Rebellion — less federal regulation and more energy exploration on federal lands — have been part of Lujan's politics for a long time. As far back as 1970, he was arguing that federal lands should be opened up to more grazing, timber cutting and mining, as well as recreation. "I don't see why we can't all exist together," he said at the time.

In 1981, he introduced a bill providing that if the federal government takes land from a state through eminent domain, the state could acquire federal land in return. "If the time is here to reduce federal power and the federal empire," Lujan said, "this is the one way to do it."

Lujan can be temperamental at times, but he can also be a good, hard bargainer, one who does not have the disadvantage of taking himself too seriously. Republican gains in the 1980 election moved the Interior Committee a couple of votes in his direction, giving him increased bargaining power in dealing with Morris K. Udall of Arizona, the panel's Democratic chairman.

Lujan's district includes the Los Alamos nuclear laboratories, and he has been a strong supporter of nuclear energy. He has backed it not only on the Interior Committee, which regulates plant construction, but on Science and Technology, his other assignment, where he supports funding for nuclear research.

He opposed a moratorium on the licensing of nuclear power plants in the wake of the Three Mile Island incident. He did add $52 million to a Nuclear Regulatory Commission bill to improve the NRC's enforcement of safety rules, a step to assuage anti-nuclear forces.

Lujan's only dissent on nuclear issues is his effort to prevent New Mexico from becoming a nuclear waste dumping ground. He amended one bill to direct the energy secretary to give priority to already contaminated sites for future waste. Nevada Rep. Jim Santini accused Lujan of an "ill-disguised attempt to exclude consideration of his congressional district from the possibility of waste disposal."

Lujan fought to soften federal controls on strip mining, and opposed the 1977 strip mine control bill as it passed the House 241-64. He later voted for a compromise version. He worked with Democrat Udall to counter President Carter's attacks on Western water projects, especially desalinization of the Colorado River. He was an ally of agribusiness in 1980 as it fought off efforts to restrict the amount of federally subsidized

---

**1st District: Northeast — Albuquerque, Santa Fe. Population:** 664,589 (30% increase since 1970). Race: White 508,976 (77%), Black 10,950 (2%), Indian 27,879 (4%), Others 116,784 (18%). Spanish origin: 283,568 (43%).

water available for large farms.

In 1979, when the House voted for a new Energy Mobilization Board to speed up high-priority projects, Lujan worked out a compromise aimed at protecting Western water rights. He convinced Rep. John Dingell, who was managing the legislation for the Commerce Committee, to drop language allowing a waiver of state and local law. The bill as it passed the House still allowed the board to waive federal law, but the change was enough to pick up his vote on final passage.

Later, however, a House-Senate conference committee modified the arrangement slightly and the states' rights issue re-emerged. Lujan refused to sign the conference report and joined nearly all Republicans in voting to kill it on the House floor; it died on a 232-131 vote.

**At Home.** Lujan has served in Congress longer than any other Republican in New Mexico history. None of his challengers has been able to break his coalition of business-oriented Republicans and Hispanic Democrats who cross party lines to support him.

In 1980, however, Lujan slipped badly as Republicans were sweeping to victory in other areas of the West. His 5,007 vote victory over an unheralded Democratic opponent is likely to generate another serious contest for him in 1982.

Lujan comes from a prominent Hispanic family that has long been engaged in insurance and New Mexico politics. His father was mayor of Santa Fe and was the unsuccessful Republican nominee for Congress in 1944 and for governor in 1948.

After joining the family business, well known throughout northern New Mexico, Lujan launched his own career in politics by running for the state Senate in 1964. That effort ended in defeat. But after a stint as vice chairman of the state Republican Party and a move to Albuquerque to expand his business, Lujan mounted a successful House campaign in 1968. He won a crowded GOP primary with 35 percent of the vote, then unseated veteran Democratic Rep. Thomas G. Morris.

Lujan was helped by the creation of new districts in May of 1968. Previously, the state's two representatives had been elected at-large, and Morris had not run well in the Hispanic areas

comprising a large portion of the new 1st District. Lujan won the seat by 10,400 votes out of nearly 170,000 cast.

Although he has been challenged since then by some well-regarded Democrats — former state Sen. Fabian Chavez in 1970 and Lieutenant Gov. Robert Mondragon in 1974 — Lujan easily won re-election throughout the 1970s with at least 55 percent of the vote.

That made his near upset in 1980 all the more startling. It was generated by a former executive director of the state Democratic Party, Bill Richardson, who was making his first try for elective office. Outspending Lujan, Richardson campaigned aggressively, criticizing the incumbent's pro-business voting record and accusing him of absenteeism. Lujan tried to ignore the attacks — a strategy that nearly cost him his seat.

Richardson ran far stronger in Hispanic areas than previous Democratic candidates. Despite his Anglo name, he is half Mexican and speaks fluent Spanish. Lujan survived only by building a large lead in his home base, Bernalillo County (Albuquerque). Richardson has indicated that he may run again in 1982.

**The District.** Lujan's fast-growing district is about evenly divided politically. Republican strength is concentrated in Bernalillo County, which includes the state's largest city, Albuquerque, and Los Alamos County, site of the nuclear research facility staffed by well-educated, white-collar voters.

More than half of the voters in the district live in Bernalillo County, but GOP majorities there are reduced by the city's large Hispanic community. Altogether, Hispanics comprise 43 percent of the district population.

The 1st is the more liberal of New Mexico's two districts. Sen. Edward M. Kennedy carried it easily over President Jimmy Carter in the 1980 Democratic primary. In the general election, independent John B. Anderson drew three times as many votes in the 1st as he did in the more rural 2nd.

The population of Lujan's district expanded by 30 percent in the last decade. But redistricting will pare his constituency. New Mexico was awarded a third congressional seat as a result of the 1980 census.

## Committees

**Interior and Insular Affairs** (Ranking Republican)
Energy and the Environment; Water and Power Resources.

**Science and Technology** (4th of 17 Republicans)
Energy Research and Production; Investigations and Oversight.

## Elections

**1980 General**

| | |
|---|---|
| Manuel Lujan Jr. (R ) | 125,910 (51 %) |
| Bill Richardson (D ) | 120,903 (49 %) |

**1978 General**

| | |
|---|---|
| Manuel Lujan Jr. (R ) | 118,075 (62 %) |
| Robert Hawk (D ) | 70,761 (38 %) |

**Previous Winning Percentages**

1976 (72 %)  1974 (59 %)  1972 (56 %)  1970 (58 %)
1968 (53 %)

**District Vote For President**

| | 1980 | | 1976 | | 1972 |
|---|---|---|---|---|---|
| D | 97,815 (38 %) | D | 110,307 (49 %) | D | 85,996 (40 %) |
| R | 130,017 (51 %) | R | 110,951 (50 %) | R | 125,326 (58 %) |
| I | 22,201 (9 %) | | | | |

## Campaign Finance

| | Receipts | Receipts from PACs | Expenditures |
|---|---|---|---|
| **1980** | | | |
| Lujan (R ) | $185,664 | $64,100 (35 %) | $178,309 |
| Richardson (D ) | $232,478 | $35,050 (15 %) | $230,955 |
| **1978** | | | |
| Lujan (R ) | $111,322 | $24,332 (22 %) | $121,421 |
| Hawk (D ) | $49,829 | $13,700 (28 %) | $49,707 |

## Voting Studies

| | Presidential Support | | Party Unity | | Conservative Coalition | |
|---|---|---|---|---|---|---|
| | S | O | S | O | S | O |
| **Year** | | | | | | |
| 1980 | 41 | 47 | 70 | 18 | 73 | 17 |
| 1979 | 34 | 63 | 79 | 18 | 88 | 10 |
| 1978 | 18 | 53 | 63 | 14 | 66 | 12 |
| 1977 | 34 | 52 | 74 | 15 | 78 | 11 |
| 1976 | 55 | 27 | 69 | 13 | 71 | 11 |
| 1975 | 56 | 37 | 69 | 17 | 75 | 12 |
| 1974 (Ford) | 41 | 46 | | | | |
| 1974 | 60 | 26 | 58 | 24 | 62 | 21 |
| 1973 | 56 | 35 | 67 | 22 | 68 | 23 |
| 1972 | 57 | 14 | 38 | 18 | 35 | 18 |
| 1971 | 53 | 16 | 48 | 21 | 56 | 16 |
| 1970 | 52 | 14 | 51 | 13 | 39 | 16 |

S = Support          O = Opposition

## Key Votes

**96th Congress**

| | |
|---|---|
| Weaken Carter oil profits tax (1979) | Y |
| Reject hospital cost control plan (1979) | Y |
| Implement Panama Canal Treaties (1979) | N |
| Establish Department of Education (1979) | N |
| Approve Anti-busing Amendment (1979) | Y |
| Guarantee Chrysler Corp. loans (1979) | N |
| Approve military draft registration (1980) | N |
| Aid Sandinista regime in Nicaragua (1980) | N |
| Strengthen fair housing laws (1980) | N |

**97th Congress**

| | |
|---|---|
| Reagan budget proposal (1981) | Y |

## Interest Group Ratings

| Year | ADA | ACA | AFL-CIO | CCUS |
|---|---|---|---|---|
| 1980 | 28 | 58 | 26 | 73 |
| 1979 | 11 | 84 | 25 | 76 |
| 1978 | 5 | 86 | 24 | 67 |
| 1977 | 15 | 81 | 18 | 76 |
| 1976 | 15 | 91 | 20 | 67 |
| 1975 | 5 | 77 | 16 | 88 |
| 1974 | 26 | 58 | 25 | 75 |
| 1973 | 20 | 76 | 30 | 70 |
| 1972 | 13 | 50 | 40 | 83 |
| 1971 | 27 | 82 | 22 | · |
| 1970 | 36 | 69 | 17 | 67 |
| 1969 | 13 | 76 | 44 | · |

# 2 Joe Skeen (R)

Of Picacho — Elected 1980

**Born:** June 30, 1927, Roswell, N.M.
**Education:** Texas A&M U., B.S. 1950.
**Military Career:** Navy, 1945-46; Air Force Reserves, 1949-52.
**Profession:** Rancher.
**Family:** Wife, Mary Jones; two children.
**Religion:** Roman Catholic.
**Political Career:** Republican state chairman, 1962-65; N.M. Senate, 1961-71, minority leader, 1965-71; unsuccessful Republican nominee for N.M. lt. gov., 1970; unsuccessful Republican nominee for N.M. governor, 1974 and 1978.

**The Member:** After losing two carefully planned bids for governor, Skeen won a House seat without even being on the ballot. He is one of the few write-in candidates ever elected to the House.

Skeen's unusual victory came after Democratic Rep. Harold E. Runnels, who was coasting to re-election, died on Aug. 5, 1980. Runnels' death set off three months of complex maneuvering with Skeen and Runnels' widow, Dorothy, mounting court challenges to win a spot on the ballot.

When the legal efforts failed, Skeen and Runnels pursued separate write-in campaigns against the substitute Democratic nominee, David King. King was hampered by a wave of negative publicity. A former state finance commissioner, he had moved to the district only after Runnels' death, and there were complaints that his nomination was engineered by his uncle, Gov. Bruce King. Skeen's write-ins totaled 38 percent of the vote, enough to win the three-way contest.

Skeen protects the interests of his fellow sheep-ranchers on the House Agriculture Committee. He also guards the interests of the state's cattle industry and peanut growers.

**The District:** The 2nd sprawls across nearly two-thirds of the state, from the ranches and small towns in "little Texas" along the eastern border to the Indian lands in the west. In spite of its breadth, the district is politically homogeneous — rural and conservative. It has been nominally Democratic for most of its history, but in the past decade has backed only Democrats who keep their distance from national party policies.

Runnels, one of the most conservative Democrats in Congress, won re-election four times and in 1978 became the first New Mexico House member elected without opposition.

## Committees

**Agriculture** (14th of 19 Republicans)
Conservation, Credit, and Rural Development; Forests, Family Farms, and Energy; Livestock, Dairy and Poultry.

**Science and Technology** (14th of 17 Republicans)
Energy Development and Applications; Science, Research and Technology.

## Elections

**1980 General**

| | |
|---|---|
| Joe Skeen (R - write-in) | 61,564 (38 %) |
| David King (D) | 55,085 (34 %) |
| Dorothy Runnels (I - write-in) | 45,343 (28 %) |

**District Vote For President**

| | 1980 | | 1976 | | 1972 |
|---|---|---|---|---|---|
| **D** | 70,011 (35 %) | **D** | 90,841 (47 %) | **D** | 55,088 (32 %) |
| **R** | 122,762 (60 %) | **R** | 100,468 (52 %) | **R** | 110,280 (65 %) |
| **I** | 7,258 (4 %) | | | | |

## Campaign Finance

| | Receipts | Receipts from PACs | Expenditures |
|---|---|---|---|
| **1980** | | | |
| Skeen (R ) | $81,311 | $16,750 (21 %) | $73,156 |
| King (D ) | $95,982 | $9,200 (10 %) | $91,964 |

## Key Vote

**97th Congress**

| | |
|---|---|
| Reagan budget proposal (1981) | Y |

---

**2nd District: South and West — Las Cruces, Roswell.** Population: 635,379 (26% increase since 1970). Race: White 467,489 (74%), Black 13,092 (2%), Indian 76,898 (12%), Others 77,900 (12%). Spanish origin: 192,521 (30%).

# New York

**U.S. CONGRESS:**
**THIRTY-NINE DISTRICTS**

Senate (1D, 1R)

House (22D, 17R)

**STATE:**

Governor
Hugh L. Carey (D)

Legislature
Senate: 60 members
(25D, 35R)
Assembly: 150 members
(86D, 63R,
1 Vacancy)

Population
17,557,288 - 2nd in the nation

Area
49,576 sq. miles - 30th in the nation

1980 Presidential Vote:
Carter (44%), Reagan (47%), Anderson (8%)

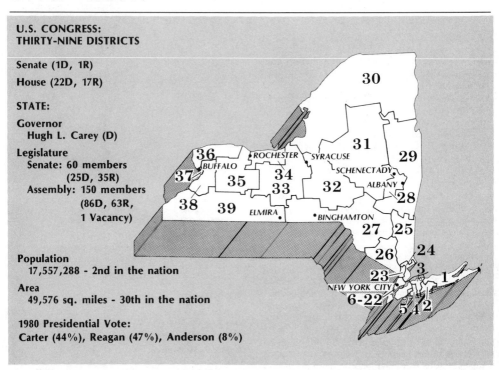

## ...The Empire in Decline

New York's loss of five congressional seats as a result of the 1980 census — the largest single loss suffered by any state in the 20th century — symbolizes the troubled times of the Empire State.

From 1810 until 1970, New York led all other states in population and congressional representation. It was the financial capital of the country. It absorbed wave after wave of immigrants seeking to transform their stagnant lives.

But in recent years, the state itself has stagnated and jobs and people have departed. New York was one of only two states, along with Rhode Island, that suffered a net population loss during the 1970s. The state has now become the "old country" for tens of thousands of emigrants searching for a better life elsewhere.

Left behind are increasing pockets of poverty, decreasing state and city services, and an insecure business community trying to decide whether to stay or move. Whether the current slide can be turned around is the central question facing New York government.

Politically, New York is also in a state of transition. The state has long had an image as a bastion of liberalism. The state elected such Democrats as Gov. Franklin D. Roosevelt, Sen. Robert F. Wagner, and Gov. Averell Harriman to public office over the past 50 years. Republicans also contributed to the image, serving as the core of their party's national liberal wing — represented by Gov. Thomas E. Dewey, Gov. Nelson A. Rockefeller, and Sen. Jacob K. Javits.

But in the 1960s, a disruptive force entered the liberal milieu. This was the Conservative Party, founded in 1962 for the express purpose of breaking the liberal monopoly on state politics. It has succeeded beyond its founders' wildest dreams. In 1970, James L. Buckley, running on the Conservative line alone, won a U.S. Senate seat in a three-way race. And in 1980, the Conservatives moved early to back Alfonse D'Amato for the Senate. He upset Javits in the Republican primary and thereby completed the reorientation of the party toward more conservative figures.

Time has also taken its toll on the state's Democratic Party. Forged by Alfred E. Smith and Franklin D. Roosevelt, the party was largely a coalition among the major immigrant groups — primarily Irish, Italians, and Jews, who were entering the middle class. But with the national Democratic Party's shift of concern from the middle class to social change and poverty programs, middle-class Democratic loyalty began to waver. Many of the Italian and Irish Catholics came to back Conservative Party candidates, while others began to switch back and forth between Democrats and Republicans. Democrats not strongly identified with "new left" issues can still win: Sen. Daniel P. Moynihan and Gov. Hugh Carey were easy general election winners in 1976 and 1978, respectively. But the Democratic left has not elected a governor or senator since Robert F. Kennedy's Senate triumph in 1964.

The growth of the suburbs around New York City in the postwar period has been the most dynamic element of the state's internal population shifts. Beginning with the construction of Levittown just after World War II, millions of New York City residents exited to the suburbs, abandoning their tenements and apartments for an individual home and a plot of green. But this movement also uprooted people from their neighborhood and traditional community, leaving them open to organization by new political machines, such as the Republican organization in Nassau County, or to independent voting habits.

The suburbs have added a third major element to the state's traditional New York City vs. upstate political alignment. The suburbs can often determine a statewide winner by leaning strongly in one direction or the other. Catholic ethnic suburbanites often cast the deciding statewide vote. The Republican county chairmen of the three major New York City suburban areas — Suffolk, Nassau, and Westchester — are all Italian-Americans.

# A Political Tour

**Long Island Suburbs.** Suffolk and Nassau counties have grown over the past four decades from an area of wealthy estates and potato farms to the epitome of American suburbia.

Like many suburbs that began growing just after World War II, Long Island has developed an economic base of its own. While many of its residents still commute to New York City, many others work in industries that have grown up on the island. Principle among these is the defense and aerospace business, represented by such giants of the industry as Grumman and Fairchild.

White-collar and professional workers predominate in the work force, many of them engineers and other technical personnel working in the defense plants and research industries.

The newcomers who populated the two counties came largely from New York City and represented a cross-section of the city's ethnic groups. Primary among them were Italian-Americans, Irish-Americans and Jews. The Nassau County Republican boss, Joseph Margiotta, has built one of the most effective political machines in the country. The area generally supports Republicans, sometimes heavily. In 1980, Ronald Reagan carried Nassau and Suffolk counties combined by a margin of 232,000 votes, considerably more than the 165,000 votes by which he carried the state.

But the island is not uniformly Republican. A large segment of voters tend to be independent and can be lured by attractive Democrats. Both counties have elected Democratic county executives. And there is a smattering of Democrats in the state legislative delegations from the area. Many residents retain some residual loyalty to the Democratic Party of their youth and the area's large Jewish population is more likely than other groups to vote Democratic.

Like other old-style suburban communities, the area shows some signs of deterioration. Nassau County lost population in the 1970s for the first time in history as residents began moving still further away from the central city. Nassau is now almost completely developed and has its own pockets of poverty, especially among black communities in the southwestern portion of the county.

**New York City.** From Manhattan's proud towers to the vast rows of apartment buildings and private homes in Brooklyn and Queens to the burned-out rubble of the South Bronx, New York City is a metropolis still containing every configuration of human life and goods.

The Democratic Party in New York City has provided the necessary margin for almost every Democratic statewide winner. The city has supported every Democratic nominee for president since 1924. However, the city's political weight has declined over the years. In 1980, it cast 31 percent of the state's presidential vote, compared to 48 percent in 1952.

New York is not thought of as an industrial city but it has always had a large blue-collar work

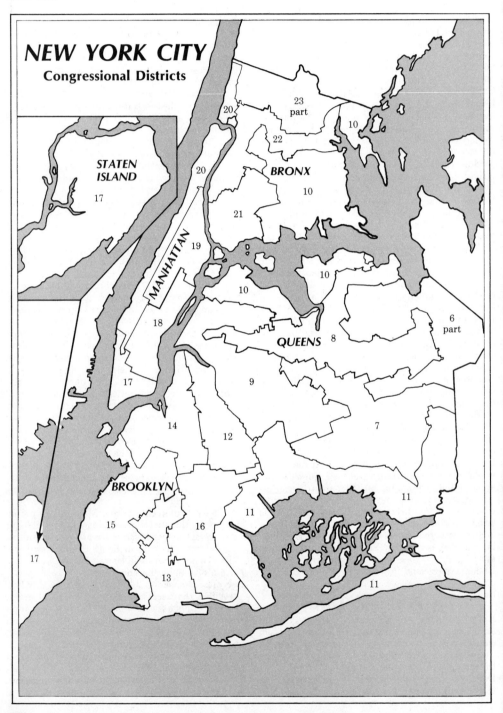

# NEW YORK CITY
## Congressional Districts

STATEN ISLAND

MANHATTAN

BRONX

QUEENS

BROOKLYN

force. Besides the numerous small industries scattered throughout the city, New York has three major industries: shipping, construction, and garment manufacturing. The unions that have grown up around these industries have had a profound impact on the city and the state. Workers in the Garment District — many of them Jewish — have traditionally backed left-wing political movements, including the Socialist Party earlier in the century, and later the American Labor and Liberal parties. The construction and dockworkers' unions have been more conservative, often dominated by Irish and Italian Catholics.

The Borough of Queens has been a political bellwether. While technically a part of New York City since 1898, the borough has long been a bedroom community rather than a core city area. As it filled up in the 1930s and 1940s, its voting patterns tended to reflect the state at large. Between 1952 and 1978, the borough voted for every winning candidate for president, governor, and U.S. Senator except one.

But in 1980, Queens twice deviated from the statewide trend by backing two Democrats, Jimmy Carter for president and Elizabeth Holtzman for senator. Their victories in the face of their statewide defeats reflected demographic changes within Queens: the decline of its middle-class population and an increasing proportion of black and Hispanic residents.

Of the city's five boroughs, Brooklyn (Kings County) is the most populous. Even with its declining population, at 2.2 million people it would be the fourth largest city in the country if it were a separate entity. Its loss of almost 400,000 residents during the 1970s will cost Brooklyn congressional and state legislative representation, but the borough will still have great political weight. Its lopsided Democratic majorities guarantee it a major say in state and city affairs.

There is still a large Jewish population in central and southern Brooklyn. Two congressional districts — the 13th and 16th — have among the heaviest proportion of Jewish residents in the country. The Bay Ridge and surrounding sections of Brooklyn near the Verrazano Narrows Bridge retain solid Italian and Irish middle-income neighborhoods and constitute one of the last bastions of Republican strength in the city.

In Brooklyn Heights, directly across the East River from Manhattan, young white professionals are moving in, refurbishing old row houses, and engaging in reform politics.

Manhattan (New York County) is perhaps the most liberal-voting county in the nation. Democrat George McGovern took 66 percent of the vote there in 1972. With the middle class being gradually squeezed out, the borough is on its way to becoming exclusively a home for the wealthy and the poor. Upper-class Jews and WASPs live in luxury apartments and renovated brownstones, while blacks and Hispanics populate run-down Harlem and parts of the dilapidated Lower East Side. And the voting pattern reflects the classic alliance sometimes found between these two groups. The borough sends a strongly liberal delegation to the City Council, state Legislature, and U.S. House. Even the Republicans are liberal; Republican U.S. Rep. S. William Green received the highest 1980 ADA rating of any Republican in the House (a score of 94 out of 100, far higher than most Democrats).

The Bronx has received national attention for its devastated southern portion. But other parts of the Bronx remained more stable. Among these are upper-class Riverdale in the northwest and middle-income ethnic neighborhoods, mostly Italian, in the north and east. The borough is solidly Democratic.

Staten Island (Richmond County), the only borough in New York City to gain population in the 1970s, remains a bastion of the middle class. It has more of the atmosphere of a town than a city, with rows of individual homes on tree-lined streets. Many Irish- and Italian-American families have moved here from the other boroughs, especially Brooklyn, in lieu of going farther out to the suburbs. The island is conservative in its voting habits and usually supports Republican candidates. President Carter received only one-third of the vote on Staten Island in 1980, compared to his citywide total of 55 percent.

**Northern Suburbs and Hudson Valley.** Traveling north from New York City through the Hudson River Valley to Albany, tightly-packed suburbs gradually give way to rich farmland and old industrial river cities. Westchester County is one of the oldest suburban areas in the New York region. Upper-class families from New York City settled in the county during the 1920s. After World War II, upwardly mobile businessmen and professionals turned the county into a stereotype of solidly Republican upper-income suburbia.

But as time passed, Westchester County saw an influx of middle-income ethnic groups, especially Italian-Americans, and some blacks. Today, the county contains a diverse population both economically and politically. While it usually goes Republican in national and statewide elections, the margins are smaller than they used to be. And Westchester has a Democratic county executive as well as two Democratic congressmen. It has become an old suburb, with a declining population.

Farther north, a new ring of suburbs has

grown up in Rockland, Orange, and Putnam counties. The population increased sharply in this area in the 1970s as people moved in from the older suburbs as well as from New York City. The voting pattern is strongly Republican.

The Hudson River shores are dotted with old industrial cities like Yonkers, Poughkeepsie, Newburgh, and further north, Troy and Albany. Back from the river, are hills and farms.

Albany is dominated by an old political machine which has retained its effectiveness, while similar organizations elsewhere have gone under. A primary reason is the popularity of the mayor, Erastus Corning, who will be 72 in 1981 and is in his 40th year in office. But Albany is also the state capital, bringing hordes of white-collar government workers to the area. Many have moved to suburban areas, especially in Saratoga County to the north and Rensselaer County to the east.

Just to the west of Albany and the upper Hudson River country lies the Mohawk Valley with its industrial cities of Schenectady and Amsterdam. Counties in this area are fairly evenly balanced between Democratic cities and Republican suburban and rural areas.

**The North Country.** A sparsely populated and economically depressed area stretching across the northern part of the state from Vermont to Lake Ontario, the North Country is a bastion of traditional Republicanism. Passing their party loyalty from generation to generation, the people of the small towns and rural areas bordering Adirondack State Park have been rock-ribbed in their Republican ways since before the Civil War. Neither depression nor scandal has had much effect on the voting strength of the party here. Besides farming, the pulp and paper industry has been a mainstay of the region's economy. The magnificent scenery of the lakes and forests has also stimulated a significant tourist industry.

There are two leavening elements in the area's Republicanism. One is the large French-Canadian element which immigrated from Quebec in the early part of the century to take advantage of the logging boom. The other is the vote on the campuses of the state university spread across the area from Plattsburgh to Oswego. They give the Democrats a respectable base in the area, but not usually enough to carry it.

**Finger Lakes Region.** The Finger Lakes Region is dominated by beautiful scenery wedged between the urban areas of Syracuse on the east and Rochester on the west.

Besides scenery, the Finger Lakes are best known for their grapes and New York state wine. The sharply-terraced hills between the long, slim lakes provide some of the best wine-growing terrain in the Eastern United States. The area was settled by Yankees early in the 19th century, around the time of the opening of the Erie Canal, and has allied itself with the Republican Party ever since its formation in the mid-1800s.

Sitting at the head of the lakes are a string of small cities — Skaneateles, Auburn, Geneva, Candandaigua — which support small industries and also serve as marketing centers for the farm communities of the region. Aside from its vineyards, the area is a center of general fruit growing, including apples, pears, and cherries.

Syracuse and Rochester have Democratic cores. But their large white-collar and technical communities outside the city limits generally offset Democratic voting strength. Syracuse also has attracted a large Italian-American population which votes conservatively, usually backing Republican or Conservative Party nominees.

Syracuse has specialized in the electronics industry, with General Electric and Bendix having plants in the area. Carrier Corp., a maker of air conditioning and heating equipment, is headquartered in Syracuse. The automobile industry is also represented in the area.

Rochester is widely known as the headquarters of the Eastman Kodak Company, which also has several plants in the area. Bausch and Lomb, makers of precision optical goods, also is headquartered here. In addition, Xerox Corp. has located several plants in and around Rochester. This modern technological base has given Rochester a relatively healthy economy, distinguishing it from other old industrial cities that have not been as successful in attracting modern industries.

**The Southern Tier.** The hilly region of the state bordering Pennsylvania from Binghamton on the east to Jamestown on the west is made up of relatively poor general farming areas and small urban centers. It has historically been a backwater, with little industrialization or population growth, but the upgrading of highways from New York City through the region has enhanced its access to the outside world.

As befits an area settled by Yankees, the region traditionally has been a Republican stronghold. But some areas have been trending Democratic in recent years. Not particularly fond of the new breed of conservative Republicans who have come to dominate the national party, some voters in this region are finding Democrats more and more attractive. Democrats have captured many of the county legislatures and state legislative seats, and now have control of both U.S. House seats in the region.

Economically, agriculture supports some of the population, especially in Chautauqua County, a grape-growing center. Otherwise, the small cities throughout the region supply jobs in a variety of industries including the Corning Glass Works in Corning and IBM in the Binghamton area.

**Western New York.** Western New York often feels alienated from the rest of the state. Hundreds of miles from New York City, it sees itself neglected by state government. Although the second largest city in the state, Buffalo is all but ignored by the colossus on the Hudson.

In many ways, Western New York is oriented toward the Midwest. Buffalo is a Great Lakes port, akin economically and ethnically to such Midwestern cities as Cleveland, Detroit and Chicago. Polish, Italian and German groups settled the city at the turn of the century. Blacks came in large numbers in the postwar period.

Proudly calling itself the Queen City of the Great Lakes, Buffalo was once the second largest railway center in the country, after Chicago. Great Lakes ships bearing iron ore and wheat came to Buffalo to unload their cargoes either for manufacture or transshipment. Flour milling was and remains a major industry. The city was built on early 20th century industries, especially steel and automobiles. With the decline of those businesses, Buffalo has suffered economically. Like other cities with similar economies and ethnic groups, Buffalo is strongly Democratic. The surrounding area has become suburbanized as Buffalo's older ethnic groups have moved out of the city. The Germans, who are strongly Republican, went first followed by the Polish-Americans, who tend to retain their Democratic allegiance.

# Redrawing the Lines

Nowhere in the nation is the redistricting task so difficult. New York must eliminate five of its 39 districts in a manner acceptable to both a Republican state Senate and a Democratic Assembly and governor.

The state currently has 17 Republican representatives and 22 Democrats. Although the greatest population losses were in districts represented by Democrats, Democratic leaders vowed from the outset to see that at least one of the eliminated seats belongs to a Republican.

The 24 districts in the New York City area have only enough population to support 20 new districts, so four seats must come from there. In doing so, legislators are required to take into consideration the Voting Rights Act of 1965, which covers much of the New York City area and demands that efforts be made to preserve minority representation when redistricting.

The act gives a stronger hand to black Democrats Shirley Chisholm of Brooklyn and Charles B. Rangel of Harlem and Hispanic Democrat Robert Garcia of the South Bronx, even though their districts — along with those of Democrats Fred Richmond in Brooklyn and Henry J. Nowak in Buffalo — suffered the greatest population losses in the state.

In addition to cutting four New York area seats, one seat will have to be removed from upstate New York. Nowak's 37th District, which encompasses Buffalo, now has a population of only 360,000, but that does not necessarily make him the redistricting victim.

# Governor
# Hugh L. Carey (D)

**Born:** April 11, 1919, Brooklyn, N.Y.
**Home:** Brooklyn, N.Y.
**Education:** St. John's College; St. John's Law School, J.D. 1951.
**Military Career:** New York National Guard, 1939-44.
**Profession:** Lawyer.
**Family:** Wife, Evangeline; 14 children by previous marriage (two deceased).
**Religion:** Roman Catholic.
**Political Career:** U.S. House, 1961-75; unsuccessful campaign for Democratic nomination, New York City Council president, 1969; elected governor 1974, 1978; term expires Jan. 1983.

# Daniel Patrick Moynihan (D)

### Of Pindars Corners — Elected 1976

**Born:** March 16, 1927, Tulsa, Okla.
**Education:** Tufts U., B.N.S. 1946, B.A. 1948;
   Fletcher School of Law and Diplomacy, M.A.
   1949, Ph.D. 1961.
**Military Career:** Navy, 1944-47.
**Profession:** Professor, writer.
**Family:** Wife, Elizabeth Brennan; three children.
**Religion:** Roman Catholic.
**Political Career:** Sought Democratic nomina-
   tion, New York City Council president, 1965.

**In Washington:** Moynihan arrived in the Senate in 1977 better known than most of his senior colleagues and globally controversial as neo-conservative thinker, scourge of the radical Third World and father of "benign neglect" towards minorities. But it is a more provincial Moynihan who has emerged since then, one most likely to offer his famous rhetoric in the cause of a few more dollars in federal aid for New York and the urban Northeast.

Shedding his reputation as a dispassionate critic of government social service programs, Moynihan has lined up emotionally with liberal Democrats in support of preserving the New Deal and Great Society. In March of 1981, when the Senate Budget Committee voted to cut federal spending by $36.4 billion, he said the panel had "undercut 30 years of social legislation in three days." Moynihan's identity as a leader of the neo-conservative wing of the Democratic Party now rests almost entirely on his foreign policy, which is as militant in its anti-communism as it was when he was criticizing the Soviet Union at the United Nations in the mid-1970s.

With his forensic reputation and his personal style — part Irish bartender, part Harvard professor — Moynihan retains substantial national popularity. For all its brilliance, however, his florid personality has not always gone over well with his more sedate colleagues in the Senate.

At times, they clearly find his erudition fascinating — moments like the ones when he interrupts routine debate with a scholarly discourse on the role of the London School of Economics, say, or the decline of private charity in Europe. In his maiden speech in the Senate, he spoke one sentence that took up half a column in the *Congressional Record*, but was grammatically correct.

But his tendency to hyperbole and personal criticism sometimes gets him into trouble with the Senate's rules of decorum. Once he attacked an amendment by Malcolm Wallop, R-Wyo., as

"inane, devoid of intellectual competence," and had to retract his remarks. Another time he mimicked the southern drawl of quiet but well-liked Kaneaster Hodges, D-Ark., bringing forth angry feelings from a number of Southern members.

Moynihan made clear his intention to bring home the goods to New York at the start of his Senate career, in his choice of a committee assignment. Eschewing the Foreign Relations Committee, a natural choice given his service as United Nations ambassador, he picked the Finance Committee, on which no New Yorker had sat for half a century.

Moynihan has generally been on good terms with the committee's conservative majority and especially with Russell B. Long, D-La., the chairman through 1980. As a member of Finance, Moynihan has used his position to focus on two issues of special importance to New York: tuition tax credits and welfare revision.

He was the chief Senate spokesman for attempts in 1978 to include private elementary and secondary school students in a bill providing tax credits for college tuition. New York has some half a million students in private, mostly Catholic, schools — far more than any other state.

The successful opposition to the private school credits was led by the public school establishment, including Moynihan's usual allies in the American Federation of Teachers. After the defeat, Moynihan wrote an article in *The Wall Street Journal* which complained of anti-Catholic bias among American opinion leaders.

As chairman of the Finance Committee's Public Assistance Subcommittee, Moynihan sought additional federal help for New York's crushing welfare burden. While the panel never got a chance to act on President Carter's two major welfare bills, Moynihan did persuade the administration to include an increase in the federal share of state welfare costs among its proposals.

As a member of the Budget Committee, Moynihan has teamed up with fellow labor Democrats Howard M. Metzenbaum of Ohio and Donald W. Riegle Jr. of Michigan, opposing cuts in domestic spending programs. He was a leader in the unsuccessful attempt to block the committee from recommending elimination of the state portion of the revenue sharing program.

Moynihan's devotion to finding money for New York has extended to the much-criticized public service jobs program of the Comprehensive Employment and Training Act (CETA). Many local governments in New York State are heavily dependent on CETA workers to perform essential services.

"Do we mean to rip apart what is left of John F. Kennedy's legacy?" he asked when Southern Democrats sought to cut CETA. CETA is also partly Moynihan's legacy, since he was an assistant to the secretary of labor when the first federal job training program was established in 1962.

Moynihan also believes New York is being shortchanged in federal money for water projects. Arguing that the projects were disproportionately concentrated in Southern and Western states, he introduced legislation to give states more authority in determining where projects will be located. New York State has a deteriorating water distribution system that needs billions of dollars for repairs.

Becoming chairman of the Environment Committee's Water Resources Subcommittee in the middle of 1980, Moynihan did not have time to push his ideas on the subject before his party lost control of the Senate.

Moynihan's chief preoccupation in foreign affairs has been with the growing military strength of the Soviet Union. In 1979, he argued at length in the *New Yorker* magazine that the U.S. had been consistently taken advantage of in arms negotiations with the Soviets.

But unlike his foreign policy ally, Henry M. Jackson, D-Wash., Moynihan did not immediately oppose the SALT II treaty with the Soviets. Instead, he used his potential vote for the treaty as a bargaining point to change what he considered a serious defect — the fact that it allowed both countries to add new strategic weapons, rather than forcing reductions. Moynihan prepared an amendment that would have voided the treaty if U.S. and Soviet negotiators did not agree on real reductions in arms levels by the end of

1981. As a result of the Soviet invasion of Afghanistan in 1979 the president withdrew the treaty from Senate consideration.

**At Home:** Moynihan's hard-line foreign policy and Democratic loyalty proved to be the right combination in New York politics in 1976.

Running for the Democratic nomination on his neo-conservative credentials, he probably could not have commanded a majority of the primary vote in any field. But with three major candidates to the left of him, his 36 per cent share was enough for a first place finish, 10,000 votes ahead of Congresswoman Bella Abzug. Once nominated, he clung to the party's working-class tradition and managed enough unity to unseat Republican James L. Buckley in the fall.

None of it would have been possible, however, without Moynihan's controversial year as American ambassador to the United Nations, where the New York media covered him in detail. His feisty defense of Israel against its enemies was crucial in giving him enough Jewish support to survive the primary, but beyond that his televised militance allowed him to begin the campaign as a celebrity, rather than just an articulate Harvard professor. "He spoke up for America," one campaign advertisement said, "He'd speak up for New York."

Moynihan's newfound reputation also enabled him to survive his weaknesses among blacks and Hispanics. As a policy adviser in the Nixon administration, he had caused himself considerable trouble when he counseled a policy of "benign neglect" toward minorities. Moynihan insisted he had been misunderstood, but the dispute only revived an issue that surfaced in 1965, when his book *Beyond the Melting Pot* attributed social problems among blacks to unstable family structure.

Moynihan's own father, a hard-drinking journalist, walked out on the family when the senator was six. His mother ran a saloon near Times Square; young Pat helped out by selling newspapers, shining shoes, tending bar and handling ships' cargo. He walked into the entrance examination for City College with a longshoreman's loading hook sticking out of his back pocket.

A life in academia followed, interspersed with periods of government service. He worked in the Labor Department in the Kennedy and Johnson administrations, as an urban affairs expert for Richard M. Nixon, and as ambassador to India under Nixon and Gerald R. Ford. He was the architect of the ill-fated Nixon "family assistance" welfare proposal, whose history he wrote a book about. In between, he taught his personal combination of economics, sociology and urban studies at Harvard, and the Harvard-M.I.T. Joint Center for Urban Studies.

In the last year of his ambassadorship in New Delhi, Moynihan began to attract increasing attention for his articles criticizing a lack of firmness in U.S. foreign policy, especially toward the Third World. His reputation made him a logical choice in 1975 for the U.N. post, whose most recent appointees had been relatively inconspicuous. His service at the U.N. helped advance his political prospects in New York, although he denied any connection at the time.

When he left the U.N. to run for the Senate, he found himself challenged not only by the equally flamboyant Abzug, but by two other well-known figures of the Democratic left: former U.S. Attorney General Ramsey Clark and New York City Council President Paul O'Dwyer.

Moynihan's chief political sponsor was Joseph Crangle, the influential Erie County (Buffalo) party chairman. Crangle pushed the state Democratic convention to guarantee ballot spots for all three liberals.

Abzug depicted Moynihan as a Buckley in Democratic clothing and quickly emerged as his main rival. But Clark and O'Dwyer took 19 percent of the vote, just enough to sink her. Moynihan split most of the New York suburbs with Abzug, won the upstate counties and captured every city borough except Manhattan.

Buckley had won the seat six years earlier as the Conservative Party candidate, taking advantage of a three-way contest involving liberal Republican incumbent Charles Goodell and liberal Democratic challenger Richard L. Ottinger. He had no such advantage in 1976.

Moynihan started with a strong lead over Buckley in the polls, and he neither said nor did anything in the fall to fracture his tenuous party harmony. He spent much of his time in Massachusetts, teaching at Harvard to protect his tenure. When he did speak out, he called Buckley a right-wing extremist out of step with the state's politics — citing Buckley's initial opposition in 1975 to federal loan guarantees for New York City.

Moynihan won all the suburban counties except Suffolk on Long Island and rolled up large margins in the city to defeat Buckley by a half-million votes.

## Committees

**Budget** (9th of 10 Democrats)

**Environment and Public Works** (5th of 7 Democrats)
Environmental Pollution; Transportation; Water Resources.

**Finance** (5th of 9 Democrats)
Economic Growth, Employment, and Revenue Sharing; International Trade; Social Security and Income Maintenance Programs.

**Select Intelligence** (Ranking Democrat)

## Elections

**1976 General**

| | |
|---|---|
| Daniel Moynihan (D) | 3,422,594 (54%) |
| James Buckley (R) | 2,836,633 (45%) |

**1976 Primary**

| | |
|---|---|
| Daniel Moynihan (D) | 333,697 (36%) |
| Bella Abzug (D) | 323,705 (35%) |
| Ramsey Clark (D) | 94,191 (10%) |
| Paul O'Dwyer (D) | 82,689 (9%) |
| Abraham Hirschfeld (D) | 82,331 (9%) |

## Campaign Finance

| | Receipts | Receipts from PACs | Expenditures |
|---|---|---|---|
| **1976** | | | |
| Moynihan (D) | $1,219,740 | $185,391 (15%) | $1,210,796 |
| Buckley (R) | $2,090,126 | $141,682 (7%) | $2,101,424 |

## Voting Studies

| Year | Presidential Support | | Party Unity | | Conservative Coalition | |
|---|---|---|---|---|---|---|
| | S | O | S | O | S | O |
| 1980 | 74 | 16 | 79 | 14 | 12 | 78 |
| 1979 | 80 | 12 | 79 | 13 | 15 | 81 |
| 1978 | 75 | 16 | 82 | 10 | 18 | 70 |
| 1977 | 75 | 17 | 79 | 13 | 19 | 73 |

S = Support     O = Opposition

## Key Votes

**96th Congress**

| | |
|---|---|
| Maintain relations with Taiwan (1979) | N |
| Reduce synthetic fuel development funds (1979) | N |
| Impose nuclear plant moratorium (1979) | N |
| Kill stronger windfall profits tax (1979) | N |
| Guarantee Chrysler Corp. loans (1979) | Y |
| Approve military draft registration (1980) | Y |
| End Revenue Sharing to the states (1980) | N |
| Block Justice Dept. busing suits (1980) | N |

**97th Congress**

| | |
|---|---|
| Restore urban program funding cuts (1981) | Y |

## Interest Group Ratings

| Year | ADA | ACA | AFL-CIO | CCUS-1 | CCUS-2 |
|---|---|---|---|---|---|
| 1980 | 72 | 8 | 100 | 33 | |
| 1979 | 47 | 15 | 100 | 0 | 21 |
| 1978 | 60 | 4 | 89 | 35 | |
| 1977 | 70 | 17 | 84 | 11 | |

# Alfonse D'Amato (R)

### Of Island Park — Elected 1980

**Born:** Aug. 1, 1937, Brooklyn, N.Y.
**Education:** Syracuse U., B.A. 1959; LL.B. 1962.
**Profession:** Lawyer.
**Family:** Wife, Penny Collenburg; four children.
**Religion:** Roman Catholic.
**Political Career:** Receiver of taxes, Town of Hempstead, 1969-71; Hempstead town supervisor, 1971-77, presiding supervisor, 1977-81.

**The Member:** D'Amato is the product of one of the last of the old-fashioned political organizations in the country — the Nassau County Republican party headed by Joseph Margiotta. He worked his way up through various local offices until he was elected presiding supervisor of Hempstead Township in 1977. Detractors ridiculed such credentials for a U.S. Senate seat. But Hempstead, with approximately 800,000 people, is the largest township in the country. It has more people than eleven states.

D'Amato's 1980 campaign was surrounded by controversy from the beginning. Starting with the the endorsement of the state's Conservative and Right-to-Life parties, he challenged liberal incumbent Jacob Javits in the Republican primary with a slashing campaign that reminded voters of the incumbent's age (76) and physical disability.

The Democratic nominee, Rep. Elizabeth Holtzman, went after D'Amato in the fall by bringing up alleged past practices of the Nassau GOP organization — such as expecting county government employees to donate a portion of their salary to the party. D'Amato denied involvement in anything unlawful.

Holtzman had to compete for the support of liberal voters with Javits, who despite his primary defeat remained on the ballot as the candidate of the Liberal party. The margin between D'Amato and Holtzman was less than 100,000 votes, with Javits a distant third.

In the Senate, D'Amato has taken a stand against rent control, something few New York politicians do, since New York City's rent controls are widely supported by apartment-dwellers there.

D'Amato successfully co-sponsored a measure in the Banking Committee that would prohibit certain federal rental assistance funds from going to cities that control rents on new or existing housing units. New York City and about 200 other cities in the country would be affected.

D'Amato said rent controls discourage investment in housing maintenance and construction.

"For too long, politicians have been pandering, supporting rent control although most would tell you that it is a hindrance," he said.

Many District of Columbia residents feared that D'Amato, who chairs the Appropriations subcommittee that oversees the city's finances, would not understand the problems of the deficit-plagued capital city. But he pushed through committee the highest-ever federal payment to the District — $300 million. Congress pays that money to D.C. in lieu of local taxes.

## Committees

**Appropriations** (12th of 15 Republicans)
District of Columbia, chairman; Defense; Foreign Operations; HUD - Independent Agencies; Transportation.

**Banking, Housing and Urban Affairs** (6th of 8 Republicans)
Securities, chairman; Consumer Affairs; Financial Institutions; Housing and Urban Affairs.

**Small Business** (9th of 9 Republicans)
Urban and Rural Economic Development, chairman; Government Regulation and Paperwork.

## Elections

**1980 General**

| | |
|---|---|
| Alfonse D'Amato (R) | 2,699,652 (45%) |
| Elizabeth Holtzman (D) | 2,618,661 (44%) |
| Jacob Javits (L) | 664,544 (11%) |

**1980 Primary**

| | |
|---|---|
| Alfonse DAmato (R) | 323,468 (56%) |
| Jacob Javits (R) | 257,433 (44%) |

## Campaign Finance

| | Receipts | Receipts from PACs | Expenditures |
|---|---|---|---|
| **1980** | | | |
| D'Amato (R) | $1,705,786 | — (0%) | $1,699,709 |
| Holtzman (D) | $2,188,891 | $185,182 (8%) | $2,173,056 |

## Key Votes

**97th Congress**

| | |
|---|---|
| Restore urban program funding cuts (1981) | N |

**803**

# 1 William Carney (R)

**Of Hauppauge — Elected 1978**

**Born:** July 1, 1942, Brooklyn, N.Y.
**Education:** Attended Fla. State U., 1960-61.
**Military Career:** Army, 1961-64
**Profession:** Sales representative.
**Family:** Wife, Barbara Ann Haverlin; two children.
**Religion:** Roman Catholic.
**Political Career:** Suffolk County Legislature, 1976-79; unsuccessful Conservative nominee for Smithtown tax receiver, 1971.

**In Washington:** Carney's penchant for wisecracks easily fits the subculture of the New York delegation, but his voting record is closer to that of New Right Republicans from the Sun Belt.

In one instance during his first term, Carney appeared to choose ideology over parochial New York concerns. He voted against a majority of his state's Republicans in opposing a 1979 welfare revision bill that carried a "sweetener" of $900 million in new federal subsidies for New York and other welfare-burdened states.

Carney has not been active on many legislative fronts, but he did play a role in final disposition of the Panama Canal issue, as a member of a special Merchant Marine Subcommittee set up to deal with the question. He argued vehemently against legislation implementing transfer of the canal from the United States to Panama. The treaties, he said, were "ill-conceived, poorly drafted and diplomatically bungled."

He charged that a House-Senate conference had removed the only significant protections the United States had in giving up the canal — the right to impose substantial costs on Panama and the requirement that Congress approve the transfer of property to that country. But the bills implementing the transfer became law in 1979.

In all, Carney sponsored only five measures during the 96th Congress. Two passed — one switching an 8-mile stretch of the Fire Island National Seashore to a more restrictive National Wilderness designation, and the other recognizing the 75th anniversary of the Order of the Sons of Italy in America.

**At Home:** Carney is the only registered member of New York's Conservative Party ever elected to Congress. His 1978 victory in a multi-candidate Republican primary was made possible by a deal between the Republican and Conservative Party leaderships in Suffolk County. The two

parties agreed on a unity slate, and Republican organization support for Carney was part of the Conservatives' asking price. Carney won the nomination with only 31.1 percent of the vote.

During his first term, the political situation at home changed radically. Much of the old Republican leadership in Suffolk County stepped down or was plagued by scandal, and the new leaders were not favorably disposed to Carney. While the GOP organization formally endorsed him for renomination in 1980 in order to preserve the party's alliance with the Conservatives, many Republican Party people worked for Carney's primary opponent. Nevertheless, Carney easily prevailed and seems to have made peace with the new Republican leadership.

Carney entered politics after a business career in which he was a sales representative for a heavy equipment firm. He won a seat in the Suffolk County Legislature in 1975 and was re-elected in 1977, with the backing of both the Republican and Conservative parties. During his time in the county Legislature, he dealt primarily with transportation and land development issues.

**The District:** Located in one of the few significant growth areas of the state, the 1st District will need to lose about 100,000 people in the redistricting process. The once-bucolic villages and potato fields of eastern Long Island have been inundated by people moving further away from New York City and its older suburbs in

---

**1st District: Eastern Long Island.**
Population: 603,787 (29% increase since 1970). Race: White 571,377 (95%), Black 21,027 (3%), Others 11,383 (2%). Spanish origin: 20,134 (3%).

Nassau County. Land use problems and attempts to save some agricultural and resort areas have been sensitive political issues. Nuclear energy and the defense industry are important, with the Brookhaven National Laboratory and a Grumman Aerospace plant located in the district. The district is generally conservative, al-though it was represented in the House for 18 years by Democrat Otis Pike, an outspoken independent whose style appealed to the district's electorate. With Pike's retirement in 1978, the district's Republican leanings reasserted themselves. In 1976, the district had given President Ford a margin of almost 20,000 votes.

## Committees

**Merchant Marine and Fisheries** (10th of 15 Republicans)
Fisheries and Wildlife Conservation and the Environment; Oceanography.

**Science and Technology** (8th of 17 Republicans)
Natural Resources, Agriculture Research and Environment; Transportation, Aviation and Materials.

## Elections

**1980 General**

| | |
|---|---|
| William Carney (R ) | 115,213 (56 %) |
| Thomas Twomey (D ) | 85,629 (42 %) |

**1980 Primary**

| | |
|---|---|
| William Carney (R ) | 15,210 (58 %) |
| John Hart (R ) | 11,102 (42 %) |

**1978 General**

| | |
|---|---|
| William Carney (R ) | 90,115 (56 %) |
| John Randolph (D ) | 67,180 (42 %) |

**1978 Primary**

| | |
|---|---|
| William Carney (R ) | 4,939 (31 %) |
| James Catterson (R ) | 3,203 (20 %) |
| John Hart (R ) | 3,085 (19 %) |
| Others (R ) | 4,665 (29 %) |

**District Vote For President**

| | 1980 | | 1976 | | 1972 |
|---|---|---|---|---|---|
| D | 71,530 (33 %) | D | 98,409 (45 %) | D | 59,420 (30 %) |
| R | 124,331 (57 %) | R | 117,277 (54 %) | R | 141,383 (70 %) |
| I | 17,756 (8 %) | | | | |

## Campaign Finance.

| | Receipts | Receipts from PACs | Expen-ditures |
|---|---|---|---|

**1980**

| | | | |
|---|---|---|---|
| Carney (R ) | $196,352 | $96,933 (49 %) | $195,878 |
| Twomey (D ) | $121,437 | $2,000 (2 %) | $120,143 |

**1978**

| | | | |
|---|---|---|---|
| Carney (R ) | $130,764 | $54,292 (42 %) | $130,642 |
| Randolph (D ) | $82,843 | $27,484 (33 %) | $76,810 |

## Voting Studies

| | Presidential Support | | Party Unity | | Conservative Coalition | |
|---|---|---|---|---|---|---|
| Year | S | O | S | O | S | O |
| 1980 | 36 | 59 | 80 | 15 | 82 | 11 |
| 1979 | 25 | 75 | 89 | 10 | 94 | 6 |

S = Support          O = Opposition

## Key Votes

**96th Congress**

| | |
|---|---|
| Weaken Carter oil profits tax (1979) | Y |
| Reject hospital cost control plan (1979) | Y |
| Implement Panama Canal Treaties (1979) | N |
| Establish Department of Education (1979) | N |
| Approve Anti-busing Amendment (1979) | Y |
| Guarantee Chrysler Corp. loans (1979) | Y |
| Approve military draft registration (1980) | Y |
| Aid Sandinista regime in Nicaragua (1980) | N |
| Strengthen fair housing laws (1980) | N |

**97th Congress**

| | |
|---|---|
| Reagan budget proposal (1981) | Y |

## Interest Group Ratings

| Year | ADA | ACA | AFL-CIO | CCUS |
|---|---|---|---|---|
| 1980 | 11 | 83 | 28 | 72 |
| 1979 | 0 | 85 | 15 | 100 |

# 2 Thomas J. Downey (D)

### Of West Islip — Elected 1974

**Born:** Jan. 28, 1949, Ozone Park, N.Y.
**Education:** Cornell U., B.S. 1970; American U.
Law School, J.D., 1979.
**Profession:** Personnel manager.
**Family:** Wife, D. Chris Milanos; one child.
**Religion:** Congregationalist.
**Political Career:** Suffolk County Legislature,
1972-75.

**In Washington:** A four-term House veteran at the remarkably early age of 31, Downey still has some of the brash irreverence he brought with him in 1975 when he looked more like a high school quarterback than a member of Congress. But beneath the surface is a serious legislator who already has made his mark on a variety of diverse issues.

For the first two Congresses, Downey was on the Armed Services Committee, where he generally joined the small dovish minority while keeping up his ties to the hawks. He was a militant critic of the B-1 bomber, but supported the neutron bomb and the cruise missile system. He also voted for money for a new nuclear aircraft carrier in opposition to a Carter veto. He found a good means of attracting publicity with his campaign to investigate cheating at West Point.

Downey became one of the most visible — and quotable — advocates of strategic arms limitation. "Listen carefully, all you hardware freaks," he said in 1980. "If you want a new MX missile, you'd better see that SALT II is ratified."

At the start of the 96th Congress, Downey switched specialties entirely, moving to the Ways and Means Committee. On a committee without any wide-ranging liberal leadership, he played as strong a role as any of the junior members in working out liberal policy options. Much of his rhetoric was against the oil companies. Even before he joined Ways and Means, he had engaged in a public shouting match with Mobil Oil, accusing the company in a letter of waging a "carefully orchestrated campaign cynically aimed at protecting the perquisites of monopoly control." As a committee member, he supported efforts to tax existing oil production at a rate as high as 85 percent, compared to the 50 percent President Carter initially recommended. Downey also worked to strengthen the "superfund" that would assess chemical companies to finance part of the cost of waste site cleanups. The committee accepted his amendments substantially increasing

the percentage of the fund the companies themselves would have to finance.

One conspicuous achievement on Ways and Means was Downey's drive to expand the trade adjustment assistance available to employees of firms hurt by foreign competition. He proposed including employees of those firms acting as suppliers of the affected companies. His Long Island district had few businesses affected directly, but many suppliers. He won his point in committee, but it did little good in the end because the legislation did not become law.

**At Home:** Downey's initial election in 1974 made him the youngest member of Congress in a decade and brought him front-page attention in *The New York Times*, which printed a picture of an unbelievably young-looking congressman-elect shooting baskets in his backyard.

But Downey had already developed a reputation for precocity. In 1971, as a 22-year-old college student, he was elected to the Suffolk County Legislature. In his three years there, he sponsored legislation to regulate sewer construction, restrict smoking in public places and impose rent control on trailer courts.

He won his congressional seat in a strongly Republican district established by the New York Legislature in 1962 and represented since then by Rep. James R. Grover. Grover's winning margins had been so large that he was thought to be

---

**2nd District: Long Island — western Suffolk County.** Population: 489,073 (5% increase since 1970). Race: White 449,101 (92%), Black 27,382 (6%), Others 12,590 (3%). Spanish origin: 33,106 (7%).

invulnerable, an opinion he shared. Even Downey's surprisingly strong showing in a debate did little to shake GOP confidence. But the election went to Downey by nearly 5,000 votes.

Once Downey took office, he practiced all the new techniques of constituent service and pioneered in some. He stayed in his office in the evening telephoning voters personally at home and held teas for them on Sundays.

His methods worked. Republicans thought they had a winner in 1976, when they nominated Peter F. Cohalan, a popular town supervisor from Islip. Cohalan described his campaign as one of "sanity" *vs.* "extreme liberalism," and complained about Downey's refusal to support an anti-busing constitutional amendment. But Dow-

ney dispatched him with suprising ease, and the GOP has not tried very hard since then.

**The District:** Downey's suburban Long Island district is populated by middle-class homeowners, many of whom are technicians or executives in the area's military and aerospace industry. Downey has fought to bring new military construction contracts to the district's predominant industry.

Downey's victories have been against the tide of sentiment that prevails in most state and national elections. Ford carried the district easily in 1976, as Reagan did in 1980. Even Republican Sen. James L. Buckley, beaten badly statewide for re-election in 1976, carried the 2nd by a comfortable margin.

## Committees

**Budget** (14th of 18 Democrats)
Task Forces: National Security and Veterans; Reconciliation.

**Select Aging** (7th of 31 Democrats)
Retirement Income and Employment.

**Ways and Means** (14th of 23 Democrats)
Trade.

## Elections

**1980 General**

| | |
|---|---|
| Thomas Downey (D ) | 84,035 (56 %) |
| Louis Modica (R ) | 65,106 (44 %) |

**1978 General**

| | |
|---|---|
| Thomas Downey (D ) | 64,807 (55 %) |
| Harold Withers (R ) | 53,332 (45 %) |

**Previous Winning Percentages**

1976 (57 %)    1974 (49 %)

### District Vote For President

| | 1980 | | 1976 | | 1972 |
|---|---|---|---|---|---|
| **D** | 52,068 (33 %) | **D** | 75,033 (45 %) | **D** | 46,571 (27 %) |
| **R** | 91,680 (58 %) | **R** | 90,243 (54 %) | **R** | 122,842 (72 %) |
| **I** | 10,830 (7 %) | | | | |

## Campaign Finance

| | Receipts | Receipts from PACs | Expenditures |
|---|---|---|---|
| **1980** | | | |
| Downey (D ) | $189,384 | $80,631 (43 %) | $190,889 |
| Modica (R ) | $72,743 | $750 (1 %) | $72,678 |
| **1978** | | | |
| Downey (D ) | $154,680 | $44,997 (29 %) | $149,400 |
| Withers (R ) | $33,763 | $6,006 (18 %) | $33,119 |

## Voting Studies

| | Presidential Support | | Party Unity | | Conservative Coalition | |
|---|---|---|---|---|---|---|
| Year | S | O | S | O | S | O |
| 1980 | 69 | 23 | 87 | 7 | 8 | 85 |
| 1979 | 75 | 17 | 86 | 7 | 10 | 84 |
| 1978 | 76 | 20 | 83 | 12 | 11 | 84 |
| 1977 | 78 | 16 | 82 | 9 | 8 | 85 |
| 1976 | 29 | 67 | 82 | 15 | 25 | 73 |
| 1975 | 33 | 66 | 88 | 11 | 9 | 90 |

S = Support          O = Opposition

## Key Votes

**96th Congress**

| | |
|---|---|
| Weaken Carter oil profits tax (1979) | N |
| Reject hospital cost control plan (1979) | N |
| Implement Panama Canal Treaties (1979) | Y |
| Establish Department of Education (1979) | Y |
| Approve Anti-busing Amendment (1979) | N |
| Guarantee Chrysler Corp. loans (1979) | Y |
| Approve military draft registration (1980) | N |
| Aid Sandinista regime in Nicaragua (1980) | Y |
| Strengthen fair housing laws (1980) | Y |

**97th Congress**

| | |
|---|---|
| Reagan budget proposal (1981) | N |

## Interest Group Ratings

| Year | ADA | ACA | AFL-CIO | CCUS |
|---|---|---|---|---|
| 1980 | 94 | 13 | 84 | 58 |
| 1979 | 89 | 0 | 88 | 11 |
| 1978 | 60 | 7 | 100 | 18 |
| 1977 | 85 | 11 | 82 | 12 |
| 1976 | 75 | 15 | 83 | 0 |
| 1975 | 100 | 14 | 91 | 18 |

# 3 Gregory W. Carman (R)

**Of Farmingdale — Elected 1980**

**Born:** Jan. 31, 1937, Farmingdale, N.Y.
**Education:** St. Lawrence U., B.A. 1958; St. Johns U., J.D. 1961.
**Military Career:** Army, 1961-64.
**Profession:** Lawyer.
**Family:** Wife, Nancy Endruschat; four children.
**Religion:** Episcopalian.
**Political Career:** Oyster Bay town councilman, 1972-81; unsuccessful Republican nominee for U.S. House, 1978.

**The Member:** A member of a prominent Long Island family, Carman fits easily into the mold of his district's respectable conservative establishment.

The son of a former district court judge, he still lives in the quiet residential community where he was born. His ancestors were among the earliest settlers of the area.

As befits a member of such a family, Carman has a long list of civic activities to his name. He is past president of the local historical society, civic association, and Rotary Club. He has been active in the Boy Scouts, volunteer fire department, and United Way.

Elected to the Oyster Bay town board three times, Carman became chairman of the committee on local government and worked on town codes and ordinances, environmental controls and transportation.

He ran a strong race for the House in 1978, winning 47.9 percent of the vote against Democratic Rep. Jerome A. Ambro. In 1980, he ran again and beat him in a close race, charging that the incumbent had voted for too much federal spending.

**The District:** Created in 1972 as a result of Long Island's population growth during the previous decade, the 3rd is split between Nassau and Suffolk counties, with a little more than 60 percent of the voters in Nassau. It was designed for a Nassau Republican, but Ambro, a Suffolk Democrat, won it in the Watergate election of 1974 and held it until 1980.

The district contains upper-class communities along the north shore of Long Island, but the bulk of the constituency comprises upper-middle-income technicians and professionals. Many of Long Island's defense industry managers and engineers live in the district. There is a predominant Catholic population, emigrants from New York City who moved into the district during the 1960s and 1970s.

## Committees

**Banking, Finance and Urban Affairs** (14th of 19 Republicans)
Consumer Affairs and Coinage; General Oversight and Renegotiation; Housing and Community Development; International Trade, Investment and Monetary Policy.

**Select Aging** (22nd of 23 Republicans)
Housing and Consumer Interests; Retirement Income and Employment.

## Elections

**1980 General**

| | |
|---|---|
| Gregory Carman (R ) | 87,952 (50 %) |
| Jerome Ambro (D ) | 83,389 (48 %) |

**District Vote For President**

| | 1980 | | 1976 | | 1972 |
|---|---|---|---|---|---|
| **D** | 63,346 (34 %) | **D** | 88,891 (46 %) | **D** | 68,602 (33 %) |
| **R** | 106,284 (57 %) | **R** | 105,322 (54 %) | **R** | 136,953 (67 %) |
| **I** | 14,895 (8 %) | | | | |

## Campaign Finance

| | | Receipts | Expen- |
|---|---|---|---|
| | Receipts | from PACs | ditures |
| **1980** | | | |
| Carman (R ) | $253,781 | $102,115 (40 %) | $249,376 |
| Ambro (D ) | $121,160 | $71,448 (59 %) | $120,061 |

## Key Vote

**97th Congress**

| | |
|---|---|
| Reagan budget proposal (1981) | Y |

---

**3rd District: Long Island — parts of Nassau and Suffolk counties.** Population: 446,948 (5% decrease since 1970). Race: White 412,076 (92%), Black 27,751 (6%), Others 7,121 (2%). Spanish origin: 11,777 (3%).

# 4 Norman F. Lent (R)

**Of East Rockaway — Elected 1970**

**Born:** March 23, 1931, Oceanside, N.Y.
**Education:** Hofstra U. B.A. 1952; Cornell U., LL.B. 1957.
**Military Career:** Navy Reserve, 1952-54.
**Profession:** Lawyer.
**Family:** Wife, Barbara Morris; three children.
**Religion:** Methodist.
**Political Career:** N.Y. Senate, 1963-71.

**In Washington:** Since his 1970 election as a challenger to "dangerous leftists," Lent has evolved toward the more moderate district-oriented politics practiced by nearly all New York area Republicans in the House.

In his early years, as social issues dominated the debate, Lent was able to mix a more aggressive conservative attitude with constituent attention. In his first term, he drafted an anti-busing amendment to the U.S. Constitution, drew 164 signatures, and saw the Rules Committee take the unusual action of prying it loose from the skeptical Judiciary Committee and clearing it for the floor. But no floor action ever took place.

As a first-term member of the Banking Committee, Lent sought to amend a housing bill to prevent the federal government from making funds for senior-citizen housing contingent on construction of housing for the poor. The Town of Hempstead was having that argument with HUD at the time.

But in recent years on the Commerce Committee, where he is now fourth in seniority, Lent has taken a greater interest in consumer issues and occasionally broken with most of the panel's Republicans. In 1979, when most Commerce Republicans were scheming to kill President Carter's hospital cost control bill, Lent voted for it in committee, after an amendment had been added giving New York State slightly more autonomy for its own program. Voting against the bill, he said, "would be politically difficult in my own district. I have a local paper that's been editorializing for it." He then voted to weaken the legislation on the floor.

Lent also supported a tough Superfund bill forcing chemical companies to pay into a fund financing cleanups at waste sites. The Commerce Committee accepted his amendment ordering the Environmental Protection Agency to begin work within 90 days compiling a list of the nation's 100 most dangerous waste sites.

In 1981, Lent became senior Republican on the Transportation Subcommittee at Commerce. When the Reagan administration proposed cuts in AMTRAK funding that would have limited rail passenger service essentially to the Northeast, Lent won subcommittee approval of a compromise aimed at keeping some semblance of a national system.

Representing a district with a large Jewish population, and frequently confronting Jewish challengers in general elections, Lent has been one of the most prolific authors of resolutions and speeches supporting the rights of Jews in the Soviet Union. He inserts frequent letters and telegrams in the *Congressional Record* urging the Soviets to release Jews they have detained.

Lent also promotes local defense contracting interests, as most Long Island legislators do. He fought for the F-14 combat plane, a contract of Long Island's Grumman Corporation, and when the House cast a 1975 vote in favor of the competing F-18, to be built elsewhere, referred to the F-18 disparagingly as "a pig in a poke."

**At Home:** Lent rose through the ranks as a satrap of the Nassau County Republican organization, headed by Joseph Margiotta. He started as an associate police justice in East Rockaway, then was elected to the state Senate in 1962. Lent was just the kind of candidate Margiotta liked: a well-behaved young lawyer, a family man, and a veteran.

---

**4th District: Long Island — eastern and southern Nassau County.** Population: 428,685 (8% decrease since 1970). Race: White 396,108 (92%), Black 24,473 (6%), Others 8,104 (2%). Spanish origin: 14,295 (3%).

In 1968, Democratic activist Allard K. Lowenstein captured the southernmost Nassau congressional district, much to the displeasure of the Republican organization. So in 1970 when lines were redrawn by the state GOP after a court order, thousands of Democrats were taken out of the district and Lent was the organization's handpicked choice to oust Lowenstein. It was a bitter contest in which Republicans implied that Lowenstein was the dupe of radical leftists, and Lowenstein responded with the hordes of outside volunteers that had become his political trademark. Lent's allies urged the district to "give up Lowenstein for Lent," and it did so decisively. The Republican has had an increasingly easy time since then.

**The District:** The 4th ranges over Nassau County from the Atlantic Coast towns in the south to some of the wealthy areas along the northern Long Island shore. The backbone of the district is the conservative Catholic middle class that left New York City for the suburbs shortly after World War II. Levittown, one of the first modern suburban communities, is in the district. The area has voted Republican for most offices since the 1970 redrawing, but not always by much.

## Committees

**Energy and Commerce** (4th of 18 Republicans)
Commerce, Transportation, and Tourism; Oversight and Investigations.

**Merchant Marine and Fisheries** (6th of 15 Republicans)
Coast Guard and Navigation; Panama Canal/Outer Continental Shelf.

## Elections

**1980 General**

| | |
|---|---|
| Norman Lent (R ) | 117,455 (67 %) |
| Charles Brennan (D ) | 58,270 (33 %) |

**1978 General**

| | |
|---|---|
| Norman Lent (R ) | 94,711 (66 %) |
| Everett Rosenblum (D ) | 46,508 (32 %) |

**Previous Winning Percentages**

| | | | |
|---|---|---|---|
| 1976 (56 %) | 1974 (54 %) | 1972 (62%) | 1970 (51 %) |

**District Vote For President**

| | 1980 | | 1976 | | 1972 |
|---|---|---|---|---|---|
| D | 65,830 (35 %) | D | 98,790 (49 %) | D | 78,366 (36 %) |
| R | 106,543 (56 %) | R | 103,663 (51 %) | R | 140,583 (64 %) |
| I | 14,164 (8 %) | | | | |

## Campaign Finance

| | Receipts | Receipts from PACs | Expenditures |
|---|---|---|---|
| **1980** | | | |
| Lent (R ) | $189,882 | $60,585 (32 %) | $150,069 |
| Brennan (D ) | $10,148 | — (0 %) | $17,159 |
| **1978** | | | |
| Lent (R ) | $116,543 | $32,849 (28 %) | $83,658 |
| Rosenblum (D ) | $12,677 | $1,900 (15 %) | $11,774 |

## Voting Studies

| | Presidential Support | | Party Unity | | Conservative Coalition | |
|---|---|---|---|---|---|---|
| Year | S | O | S | O | S | O |
| 1980 | 44 | 46 | 66 | 28 | 73 | 21 |
| 1979 | 32 | 63 | 72 | 24 | 80 | 17 |
| 1978 | 41 | 55 | 71 | 23 | 70 | 27 |
| 1977 | 46 | 41 | 72 | 18 | 78 | 15 |
| 1976 | 61 | 35 | 62 | 32 | 74 | 21 |
| 1975 | 64 | 28 | 61 | 28 | 69 | 25 |
| 1974 (Ford) | 52 | 44 | | | | |
| 1974 | 57 | 38 | 57 | 38 | 63 | 33 |
| 1973 | 61 | 28 | 60 | 29 | 58 | 31 |
| 1972 | 81 | 11 | 61 | 28 | 70 | 20 |
| 1971 | 72 | 19 | 70 | 21 | 72 | 19 |

S = Support            O = Opposition

## Key Votes

**96th Congress**

| | |
|---|---|
| Weaken Carter oil profits tax (1979) | Y |
| Reject hospital cost control plan (1979) | Y |
| Implement Panama Canal Treaties (1979) | N |
| Establish Department of Education (1979) | N |
| Approve Anti-busing Amendment (1979) | Y |
| Guarantee Chrysler Corp. loans (1979) | Y |
| Approve military draft registration (1980) | Y |
| Aid Sandinista regime in Nicaragua (1980) | N |
| Strengthen fair housing laws (1980) | N |

**97th Congress**

| | |
|---|---|
| Reagan budget proposal (1981) | Y |

## Interest Group Ratings

| Year | ADA | ACA | AFL-CIO | CCUS |
|---|---|---|---|---|
| 1980 | 17 | 61 | 33 | 70 |
| 1979 | 0 | 68 | 40 | 89 |
| 1978 | 20 | 75 | 20 | 76 |
| 1977 | 20 | 62 | 33 | 65 |
| 1976 | 20 | 54 | 35 | 63 |
| 1975 | 26 | 63 | 14 | 76 |
| 1974 | 30 | 67 | 27 | 50 |
| 1973 | 8 | 68 | 22 | 80 |
| 1972 | 13 | 53 | 44 | 100 |
| 1971 | 22 | 81 | 17 | - |

# 5 Raymond J. McGrath (R)

**Of Valley Stream — Elected 1980**

**Born:** March 27, 1942, Valley Stream, N.Y.
**Education:** State Univ. of New York, Brockport,
B.S. 1963; New York University, M.A. 1968.
**Profession:** Teacher/parks official.
**Family:** Wife, Joanne Coady; one child.
**Religion:** Roman Catholic.
**Political Career:** New York Assembly, 1977-81.

   **The Member:** McGrath was the
handpicked candidate of Nassau County Republican Chairman Joseph Margiotta to succeed Republican John W. Wydler, who retired after 18
years in the House.
   McGrath had been a loyal organization man
during his years in the Legislature, working primarily on issues of local interest to his constituents in suburban Nassau County. He labored to
end a state toll on a local parkway, and to require
the state to pay for school busing it ordered in a
Nassau County town. He helped win state approval for local hospital expansion.
   McGrath had no opposition in the 1980 primary. In the general election, he defeated Karen
Burstein, a former member of the state Public
Service Commission. She put on a spirited effort
but was overwhelmed by the local Republican
machine, the conservative trend in 1980, and
McGrath's effective campaign.
   Many of McGrath's constituents stand to
gain from Reagan's spending proposals, since
higher defense spending will mean work for
Grumman and other Long Island defense contractors. McGrath has spent some of his personal time
on a measure to coordinate federal enforcement of
arson laws.
   **The District:** The 5th is one of two districts
that lie entirely within Nassau County. As such, it
is especially important to Margiotta, who heads
one of the last effective party organizations of any
size in the country.
   Republicans have held the district ever since
it was created in 1962. Its dominant voting bloc is
made up of white-collar and middle-management
personnel who work in New York City or in the
sizable suburban economy, especially the defense
industry. There is an area in the southwestern
part of the county which includes lower-income
Democratic voters, some of them black.

## Committees

**Government Operations** (11th of 17 Republicans)
   Government Activities and Transportation; Intergovernmental
   Relations and Human Resources.

**Science and Technology** (13th of 17 Republicans)
   Energy Development and Applications; Space Science and Applications.

## Elections

**1980 General**

| | |
|---|---|
| Raymond McGrath (R ) | 105,140 (58 %) |
| Karen Burstein (D ) | 77,228 (42 %) |

**District Vote For President**

| | 1980 | | 1976 | | 1972 |
|---|---|---|---|---|---|
| D | 70,226 (36 %) | D | 100,782 (48 %) | D | 87,165 (37 %) |
| R | 106,564 (55 %) | R | 107,909 (52 %) | R | 145,115 (62 %) |
| I | 13,179 (7 %) | | | | |

## Campaign Finance

| | Receipts | Receipts from PACs | Expenditures |
|---|---|---|---|
| **1980** | | | |
| McGrath (R ) | $268,157 | $87,436 (33 %) | $265,777 |
| Burstein (D ) | $311,763 | $66,800 (21 %) | $310,158 |

## Key Vote

**97th Congress**

| | |
|---|---|
| Reagan budget proposal (1981) | Y |

> **5th District: Long Island — central
> and southwestern Nassau County.** Population: 436,801 (7% decrease since 1970).
> Race: White 370,813 (85%), Black 57,000
> (13%), Others 9,006 (2%). Spanish origin:
> 16,801 (4%).

# 6 John LeBoutillier (R)

Of Westbury — Elected 1980

**Born:** May 26, 1953, Glen Cove, N.Y.
**Education:** Harvard Univ., B.A. 1976, M.B.A 1979.
**Profession:** Author and lecturer.
**Family:** Single.
**Religion:** Episcopalian.
**Political Career:** No previous office.

**The Member:** LeBoutillier, a conservative activist since his college days, is the youngest member of the 97th Congress.

The scion of a wealthy Long Island family, he went to exclusive private schools, then to Harvard University. He gained national attention for his 1978 book *Harvard Hates America*, in which he excoriated his alma mater for being an elitist institution teaching liberal values inimical to the welfare of the United States.

Upon arriving in Washington, LeBoutillier described himself as "an angry young man . . . not the get-along, go-along type." He said he would try for a place on the House Appropriations Committee, which usually accepts no freshmen. "You don't wait your way to the top," he said.

Instead, he was assigned to Foreign Affairs. Arguing that "for too long we've been abused and bullied," LeBoutillier called for reimposition of the Soviet grain embargo, which Reagan lifted, and an expansion of trade restrictions on Russia.

LeBoutillier criticized administration plans to sell Sidewinder missiles and aerial surveillance aircraft (AWACS) to Saudi Arabia. He said the sale would endanger Israel's security.

Running in 1980 without full-scale assistance from the national GOP, LeBoutillier hit hard at Democratic Rep. Lester L. Wolff's foreign travel, calling him a junketeer. He also made an issue of Wolff's opposition to the B-1 bomber, a sensitive issue on defense-conscious Long Island.

**The District:** The 6th consists of middle- and upper-income suburbs of New York City. About half the population is technically inside the city, in the borough of Queens. But that area is more akin to the suburbs than to the lower-income areas predominant in some other parts of Queens.

On Long Island Sound are wealthy residential areas. Central Nassau County has a somewhat lower median income. There is a large concentration of Jewish voters. The 6th has voted Republican in close state and national contests — Gerald Ford carried it in 1976 — but Democrats do better here than in other Long Island districts.

## Committees

**Foreign Affairs** (15th of 16 Republicans)
Human Rights and International Organization; International Security and Scientific Affairs.

## Elections

**1980 General**

| | |
|---|---|
| John LeBoutillier (R ) | 89,762 (53 %) |
| Lester Wolff (D ) | 80,209 (47 %) |

**District Vote For President**

| | 1980 | | 1976 | | 1972 |
|---|---|---|---|---|---|
| D | 67,014 (36 %) | D | 98,146 (50 %) | D | 84,871 (38 %) |
| R | 100,023 (54 %) | R | 99,560 (50 %) | R | 140,450 (62 %) |
| I | 14,523 (8 %) | | | | |

## Campaign Finance

| | | Receipts | Expen- |
|---|---|---|---|
| | Receipts | from PACs | ditures |
| **1980** | | | |
| LeBoutillier (R ) | $497,863 | $31,049 (6 %) | $490,121 |
| Wolff (D ) | $123,218 | $54,120 (44 %) | $110,221 |

## Key Vote

**97th Congress**

| | |
|---|---|
| Reagan budget proposal (1981) | Y |

---

**6th District: Northeast Queens and northwestern Nassau counties.** Population: 432,489 (8% decrease since 1970). Race: White 388,407 (90%), Black 18,478 (4%), Asian and Pacific Islander 15,908 (4%), Others 9,696 (2%). Spanish origin: 27,510 (6%).

# 7 Joseph P. Addabbo (D)

**Of Ozone Park — Elected 1960**

**Born:** March 17, 1925, New York, N.Y.
**Education:** Attended City College of N.Y. 1942-44; St. Johns Law School, LL.B. 1946.
**Profession:** Lawyer.
**Family:** Wife, Grace Salamone; three children.
**Religion:** Roman Catholic.
**Political Career:** No previous office.

**In Washington:** A stocky, moon-faced man with a penchant for wisecracks, Addabbo looks the part of an old fashioned machine Democrat from New York City. But it is a deceptive appearance. Addabbo's interests are national, and over the last decade, he became one of the most knowledgeable and effective congressional critics of the Pentagon.

As a member of the Defense Appropriations Subcommittee since 1967 and as its chairman since 1979, Addabbo has fought a year-in, year-out struggle against what he sees as waste in the Pentagon budget. He is not so much anti-military as anti-bureaucracy: he tends to view generals as bureaucrats-in-uniform who share with their civilian counterparts an inclination toward empire-building and tunnel vision.

Throughout the 1970s, his Defense Appropriations Subcommittee routinely cut Pentagon budgets by billions of dollars, alleging specific examples of waste and inefficiency as its reason. Addabbo has always insisted the cuts could have been larger without really hurting U.S. combat power.

Addabbo speaks for a pre-Vietnam generation of liberal Democrats on defense issues. He himself supported the war throughout the Johnson years and for a while under Nixon, then changed his mind and sponsored the first anti-war resolution ever to pass the House — one cutting off funds for the bombing of Cambodia in 1973.

He is convinced that high defense spending not only absorbs scarce funds needed for domestic programs, but elicits a corresponding increase in Soviet military spending.

In the current Congress and hawkish national mood, Addabbo has few allies on his own subcommittee — even among Democrats — who will go along with him in opposing the B-1 bomber and a new nuclear aircraft carrier. But a majority on the panel is interested in rooting out waste, and Addabbo puts subcommittee staff to work through much of the year searching for it.

Addabbo says that bureaucratic biases favor the wrong kinds of weaponry — too expensive to buy enough of and too complicated to keep operable. He led the congressional fight against the B-1 in the late 70s, arguing that the cruise missile favored by President Carter had a better chance of penetrating Soviet air defenses in the 1980s. He charged that the nuclear-powered carriers favored by the Navy would be sitting ducks for Soviet cruise missiles and would absorb funds better spent on a larger number of smaller ships. With Carter supporting Addabbo's positions from the White House, they prevailed briefly in 1977 and 1978.

The situation changed in 1979. Addabbo assumed the subcommittee chairmanship that year, and with it more control over the defense spending process. But the B-1 and the nuclear carrier were picking up adherents in Congress as Addabbo was maneuvering to block them. By the end of the 96th Congress in 1980, both the B-1 and the carrier had a new lease on life, helped by widespread congressional fear of a Soviet military buildup, and contempt for what many members saw as Carter's squeamishness about the role of force in world affairs.

In other areas, however, Addabbo has been more successful in focusing attention on his views about Pentagon waste. He believes the armed services have too many duplicative weapons programs designed for the same purpose. He also

---

**7th District: Southern Queens — Ozone Park, Jamaica.** Population: 424,136 (9% decrease since 1970). Race: White 204,989 (48%), Black 189,073 (45%), Asian and Pacific Islander 11,327 (3%), Others 18,747 (4%). Spanish origin: 161,324 (38%).

thinks the services request money to begin producing weapons before they are fully tested. Both have been stated grounds for the subcommittee's funding cutbacks in recent years.

Addabbo has also argued that the services tend to squirrel away appropriated money for use at their own discretion. The subcommittee has cut funding in areas which it thinks have been used as a bank to reprogram funds for other purposes. In 1980, the subcommittee even made a small reduction in the appropriation for military pensions — hitherto politically sacrosanct — to warn the Pentagon against using that account as a slush fund.

He has used the defense appropriations bill to wage a seemingly endless campaign against federal personnel policies he considers wasteful, though not technically illegal. Frequent targets are the routine use of accumulated sick-leave before retirement and receipt of two disability pensions for the same disability.

On these issues, Addabbo generally retains bipartisan support in his subcommittee and in the House. Now, however, his panel's oversight is no longer able to yield a net cut in defense appropriations. The few billion dollars pried loose will be used for other defense programs deemed to have a higher priority.

Unlike many other members of the congressional defense establishment, Addabbo has invested a significant amount of energy in a second policy area: federal assistance to small businesses. Much of his work in this field arises out of his longtime membership on the House Small Business Committee.

He led a long battle, successful in 1980, to obtain a larger slice of the defense spending pie for Northeastern and Midwestern states. This was done by repealing the so-called Maybank amendment, a rider that had routinely been attached to every defense appropriations bill since 1953. It barred the Pentagon from buying materiel at a premium for the sake of putting contracts into areas of high unemployment.

**At Home:** Unlike most New York City congressmen, Addabbo rarely dabbles in local politics. He is a legislative-oriented House member who leaves politics to the Queens organization. He was never an insurgent and he has never tried to run for city office.

In fact, Addabbo was only modestly involved in politics before his election. As a young Queens lawyer active in civic and community affairs, he had headed Italian-American committees for the election of various candidates. But his 1960 bid for the House was his first political contest.

Throughout the 1950s, the district was represented by a Republican, Albert Bosch. Though Democratic by registration, it was made up of middle-class homeowners who went along with the Eisenhower tide in 1952 and 1956. But during that decade there was a building boom, with new residents, mostly Irish and Italian Catholics from Brooklyn, moving in.

In 1960, Bosch retired to seek a judgeship and Democrats exploited the opportunity to take the seat. Addabbo, with his Italian name and background, was able to appeal to an important segment of the district. Moreover, John F. Kennedy's drawing power for Catholic voters gave Addabbo's campaign a major boost. He took the district with 53.5 percent of the vote.

Addabbo has always been loyal to traditional organization politics, listening to constituent problems and complaints. He has held to a fairly regular liberal record. When he ran for the House in 1960, Addabbo espoused federal aid to education, assistance for the aged, and civil rights. He was a member of the National Association for the Advancement of Colored People.

Since his first election, Addabbo has had little trouble keeping his seat. The district has become a Democratic bastion, even going strongly for George McGovern in 1972. In the years since 1962, when he received 59.3 percent of the vote, Addabbo has never dropped below 60 percent. From 1974 on, he has also received the Republican nomination. Only once, in 1972, has he received a significant primary challenge, and he beat that back with 64.3 percent of the vote.

**The District:** When Addabbo was elected in 1960, his district was in transition. Today it is in a different form of transition.

In 1960, it was home for a prosperous, burgeoning middle class expanding outward from homes in the inner city. Now much of Queens is part of the inner city, and people are leaving for the outer suburbs or for the Sun Belt. The district lost nine percent of its population during the decade of the 1970s.

A large black area has grown up around the Jamaica section, where a few middle-class blacks lived when Addabbo first won. Blacks now constitute almost half of the district's population. There is a large Hispanic community.

The district will have to gain about 100,000 new residents to make it conform to the one-man, one-vote Supreme Court dictum. While New York state is losing five districts, the state legislators will probably make an effort to preserve Addabbo's district because of his power and position in the House.

## Committees

**Appropriations** (5th of 33 Democrats)
Defense, chairman; Military Construction; Treasury - Postal Service - General Government.

**Small Business** (3rd of 23 Democrats)
General Oversight; SBA and SBIC Authority, Minority Enterprise and General Small Business Problems.

## Elections

**1980 General**

| | |
|---|---|
| Joseph Addabbo (D) | 96,137 (95%) |

**1978 General**

| | |
|---|---|
| Joseph Addabbo (D) | 73,066 (95%) |

**Previous Winning Percentages**

| | | | |
|---|---|---|---|
| 1976 (95%) | 1974 (100%) | 1972 (75%) | 1970 (91%) |
| 1968 (66%) | 1966 (65%) | 1964 (70%) | 1962 (59%) |
| 1960 (54%) | | | |

**District Vote For President**

| | 1980 | | 1976 | | 1972 |
|---|---|---|---|---|---|
| D | 79,113 (64%) | D | 98,065 (73%) | D | 93,826 (59%) |
| R | 37,025 (30%) | R | 35,653 (27%) | R | 66,267 (41%) |
| I | 6,013 (5%) | | | | |

## Campaign Finance

| | Receipts | Receipts from PACs | Expenditures |
|---|---|---|---|
| **1980** | | | |
| Addabbo (D) | $108,170 | $77,175 (71%) | $105,482 |
| **1978** | | | |
| Addabbo (D) | $63,700 | $34,850 (55%) | $41,049 |

## Voting Studies

| | Presidental Support | | Party Unity | | Conservative Coalition | |
|---|---|---|---|---|---|---|
| Year | S | O | S | O | S | O |
| 1980 | 56 | 22 | 85 | 4 | 11 | 75 |
| 1979 | 66 | 22 | 80 | 12 | 18 | 72 |
| 1978 | 68 | 25 | 83 | 8 | 13 | 79 |
| 1977 | 66 | 19 | 85 | 6 | 9 | 81 |
| 1976 | 25 | 71 | 89 | 3 | 8 | 83 |
| 1975 | 35 | 61 | 88 | 4 | 5 | 86 |
| 1974 (Ford) | 46 | 52 | | | | |

| | | | | | | |
|---|---|---|---|---|---|---|
| 1974 | 32 | 62 | 85 | 9 | 11 | 85 |
| 1973 | 31 | 63 | 85 | 9 | 11 | 86 |
| 1972 | 43 | 51 | 81 | 12 | 11 | 83 |
| 1971 | 39 | 58 | 79 | 14 | 16 | 79 |
| 1970 | 54 | 35 | 75 | 15 | 5 | 84 |
| 1969 | 49 | 47 | 73 | 11 | 16 | 78 |
| 1968 | 76 | 17 | 77 | 13 | 14 | 75 |
| 1967 | 89 | 7 | 91 | 2 | 7 | 85 |
| 1966 | 81 | 8 | 85 | 9 | 11 | 76 |
| 1965 | 79 | 9 | 75 | 10 | 8 | 82 |
| 1964 | 90 | 8 | 82 | 10 | 8 | 92 |
| 1963 | 89 | 6 | 91 | 3 | 7 | 80 |
| 1962 | 78 | 17 | 77 | 14 | 12 | 81 |
| 1961 | 91 | 6 | 91 | 7 | 4 | 96 |

S = Support          O = Opposition

## Key Votes

**96th Congress**

| | |
|---|---|
| Weaken Carter oil profits tax (1979) | N |
| Reject hospital cost control plan (1979) | N |
| Implement Panama Canal Treaties (1979) | Y |
| Establish Department of Education (1979) | N |
| Approve Anti-busing Amendment (1979) | N |
| Guarantee Chrysler Corp. loans (1979) | Y |
| Approve military draft registration (1980) | N |
| Aid Sandinista regime in Nicaragua (1980) | Y |
| Strengthen fair housing laws (1980) | Y |

**97th Congress**

| | |
|---|---|
| Reagan budget proposal (1981) | N |

## Interest Group Ratings

| Year | ADA | ACA | AFL-CIO | CCUS |
|---|---|---|---|---|
| 1980 | 72 | 5 | 100 | 54 |
| 1979 | 79 | 8 | 94 | 28 |
| 1978 | 70 | 12 | 95 | 20 |
| 1977 | 80 | 4 | 91 | 6 |
| 1976 | 90 | 4 | 83 | 6 |
| 1975 | 95 | 4 | 96 | 18 |
| 1974 | 83 | 13 | 100 | 10 |
| 1973 | 80 | 20 | 100 | 27 |
| 1972 | 94 | 4 | 91 | 11 |
| 1971 | 76 | 23 | 92 | - |
| 1970 | 80 | 12 | 100 | 0 |
| 1969 | 80 | 33 | 90 | - |
| 1968 | 75 | 17 | 100 | - |
| 1967 | 80 | 4 | 100 | 10 |
| 1966 | 82 | 22 | 92 | - |
| 1965 | 68 | 8 | - | 30 |
| 1964 | 88 | 0 | 100 | - |
| 1963 | - | 11 | - | - |
| 1962 | 100 | 14 | 91 | - |
| 1961 | 100 | - | - | - |

# 8 Benjamin S. Rosenthal (D)

**Of Elmhurst — Elected 1962**

**Born:** June 8, 1923, New York, N.Y.
**Education:** Attended Long Island U. and City College; Brooklyn Law School, LL.B. 1949; N.Y.U., LL.M. 1952.
**Military Career:** Army, 1943-46.
**Profession:** Lawyer.
**Family:** Wife, Lila Moskowitz; two children.
**Religion:** Jewish.
**Political Career:** No previous office.

**In Washington:** There is a cynical quality about Rosenthal — even a sour one at times — but it has never been quite strong enough to obscure the idealistic streak that shows through.

Rosenthal has made consumer protection the central theme of his long and controversial House career. Brusk and moody but always quotable, Rosenthal seems most comfortable in verbal battle at his Government Operations subcommittee.

Government Operations is not primarily a legislative committee; its power resides in the publicity it can generate. And when it comes to publicity, Rosenthal has few peers. His hearings are media events, carefully planned and featuring special guest stars — usually ordinary citizens who have been victimized by some element of an uncaring bureaucracy or private corporation.

His staff has an uncanny ability to produce a victim with an amazing story to tell — a small child whose $10 bank deposit was entirely consumed by service charges or a black housewife who paid more for groceries in ghetto markets than people do in the affluent suburbs.

Rosenthal believes these hearings are a form of theater and ought to be designed for maximum media impact. "One congressman with a fair amount of chutzpah," he once said, "can awaken the public conscience."

His biggest legislative battle and most crushing defeat involved a 14-year effort to convince Congress and various presidents that there should be an independent federal consumer protection agency with power to intervene in government proceedings on behalf of consumers.

Rosenthal began introducing consumer agency bills in 1963 as a junior member of the Agriculture Committee. But nothing much happened until 1970. A bill passed the Senate that year but died in the House Rules Committee. In 1971 and 1974, the House passed the Rosenthal bill only to have it blocked by Senate filibusters. In 1975, the bill passed both the House and Senate by narrow margins, but congressional leaders decided they lacked the power to override an inevitable veto by President Ford; the bill never was sent to the White House.

The long crusade ended abruptly on the morning of Nov. 1, 1977, when House Speaker O'Neill pulled a Senate-passed Rosenthal bill from the House calendar. He said it could not pass. Lobbyists on Rosenthal's side, led by consumer activist Ralph Nader and President Carter's consumer adviser, Esther Peterson, still thought they had a chance to win, but O'Neill was firm. The bill died and has not been resurrected.

Those years of work and ultimate frustration have added to the supply of cynicism Rosenthal brought with him to Congress from Queens. But they have not diminished his energy. In 1980, he launched one of his classic consumer wars against the American Invsco Corp., moving to subpoena corporate records when Invsco officials balked at producing company files for the subcommittee.

Rosenthal saw a threat to the poor and elderly in the trend of converting rental apartments to condominiums. He summoned Invsco officials because their firm is the largest in the conversion business. The resulting hearings and Rosenthal's move for a contempt of Congress citation attracted newspaper and television interest and accomplished a continuing Rosenthal goal: public awareness. In 1981, he wrote a bill to give condominium owners a tax break.

---

**8th District: Central and northern Queens — Flushing.** Population: 462,896 (1% decrease since 1970). Race: White 337,530 (73%), Black 37,986 (8%), Asian and Pacific Islander 46,975 (10%), Others 40,405 (9%). Spanish origin: 100,891 (22%).

---

The Reagan administration has offered Rosenthal an especially inviting target. In 1981, angry at Reagan's efforts to trim the powers of the Federal Trade Commission, he summoned Office of Management and Budget Director David Stockman to his Commerce, Consumer and Monetary Affairs Subcommittee. Rosenthal denounced the cutback plans as "a rather nefarious shortcut" around Congress.

Not all of Rosenthal's enemies have been businessmen or bureaucrats. President Johnson disliked him for the vehemence of his anti-war stand, expressed in a midnight House session in 1969 in which he said the United States was "virtually the puppet" of South Vietnam. Speaker John McCormack thought Rosenthal disloyal for backing a challenge to him.

Rosenthal never got along with California Democrat Chet Holifield, his Government Operations chairman for four years, and later tried to dump Wisconsin's Clement J. Zablocki as chairman of Foreign Affairs, his other committee. He has always had a constituency for those fights, both inside the House and among liberal pressure groups outside it, but the effect has been to reinforce his reputation as one of the chamber's more difficult people. "I do think there are some people who think I'm abrasive," he once said. "In some ways, I think I'm abrasive. You can't change your personality."

Rosenthal got into the consumer affairs field almost by accident. When he arrived in Congress, he was assigned to the Agriculture Committee, which prompted jokes about flower pots and garden plots in Queens. But he took an interest in government food programs and was named to a Food Marketing Commission studying the impact of government on consumers. He realized he was on to an important and politically valuable issue.

In 1967, he persuaded Government Operations Chairman William Dawson to set up a consumer inquiry panel. For four years — until Holifield became chairman and killed the idea — he probed deceptive packaging, food labeling and problems of the poor. When Holifield retired in 1975 and Jack Brooks of Texas took over the committee, the panel was recreated, and Rosenthal got it back.

Rosenthal's other assignment since 1965 has been Foreign Affairs. It is secondary work for him; consumer issues are his first priority. But his Foreign Affairs membership gave him a forum for his opposition to the Vietnam War and allows him to crusade for aid to Israel.

He is one of the most militant House spokesmen for Israel and one of the angriest opponents of U.S. ties to Arab regimes. In 1979, when Carter announced plans to sell tanks and planes to several Arab nations, Rosenthal wrote to Carter to say he was violating the spirit of the law giving Congress veto power over arms sales.

In 1980, he sought to persuade Carter to grant Israel more favorable terms on $2.2 billion worth of loans made in 1979. Later, he tried to overturn the sale of 100 U.S. tanks to Jordan and opposed AWACS sales to Saudi Arabia.

**At Home:** Rosenthal's opportunity came in 1962, after Democrat Lester Holtzman resigned from the House to join the state Supreme Court. Rosenthal had been active in the Queens Democratic organization and had been president of a Democratic club in the Elmhurst section of the borough. In 1959, he had been named chairman of the Queens Democratic Party's law committee by the reigning county leader, Herbert Koehler.

When the House vacancy opened up, Rosenthal was a consensus choice among feuding factions headed by Koehler and Mayor Robert F. Wagner Jr.

But while it was a normally Democratic district, Rosenthal had unexpected trouble. Another Democrat filed in the special election, splitting the party's vote. And the Republican nominee, Thomas Galvin, found an issue in federal aid to parochial schools. The district was about 40 percent Catholic, and Catholic newspapers highlighted Galvin's stand in favor of the aid. Rosenthal stuck to his support for President Kennedy's proposal of aid to public school students only, and it cost him votes. In a small turnout, he eked out a 264-vote margin.

Once in office, Rosenthal managed to stay without difficulty. The district was redrawn later in 1962 to give him fewer Catholic constituents, and since then he has had only one primary challenge. He has maintained working relations with all sides in the Democratic Party, keeping in touch with the organization but also pleasing reformers with his policy stands.

**The District:** Sprawling through diverse neighborhoods in northern Queens, this melting-pot district is home to middle-class New Yorkers who live in a variety of housing from single-family units to high-rise apartments. There is a large Jewish population, but also Italian, Irish and German ethnic concentrations. A significant Hispanic population has moved in during the past decade.

## Committees

**Foreign Affairs** (4th of 21 Democrats)
Europe and the Middle East; Human Rights and International Organizations.

**Government Operations** (4th of 23 Democrats)
Commerce, Consumer, and Monetary Affairs, chairman; Manpower and Housing.

## Elections

**1980 General**

| | |
|---|---|
| Benjamin Rosenthal (D) | 84,273 (76%) |
| Albert Lemishow (R) | 27,156 (24%) |

**1978 General**

| | |
|---|---|
| Benjamin Rosenthal (D) | 74,872 (79%) |
| Albert Lemishow (R) | 15,165 (16%) |

**Previous Winning Percentages**

| | | | |
|---|---|---|---|
| **1976** (78%) | **1974** (79%) | **1972** (65%) | **1970** (63%) |
| **1968** (70%) | **1966** (70%) | **1964** (75%) | **1962** (66%) |
| **1962**\*(45%) | | | |

*\* Special election.*

**District Vote For President**

| | 1980 | | 1976 | | 1972 |
|---|---|---|---|---|---|
| D | 63,187 (47%) | D | 103,726 (66%) | D | 94,877 (50 %) |
| R | 58,938 (44%) | R | 51,998 (33%) | R | 93,816 (50 %) |
| I | 9,576 (7%) | | | | |

## Campaign Finance

| | Receipts | Receipts from PACs | Expen-ditures |
|---|---|---|---|
| **1980** | | | |
| Rosenthal (D) | $45,478 | $17,500 (38%) | $35,765 |
| **1978** | | | |
| Rosenthal (D) | $40,729 | $7,900 (19%) | $30,220 |

## Voting Studies

| | Presidential Support | | Party Unity | | Conservative Coalition | |
|---|---|---|---|---|---|---|
| Year | S | O | S | O | S | O |
| 1980 | 65 | 27 | 91 | 3 | 1 | 89 |
| 1979 | 65 | 15 | 68 | 4 | 0 | 72 |
| 1978 | 76 | 16 | 87 | 4 | 4 | 87 |
| 1977 | 73 | 16 | 86 | 3 | 2 | 89 |
| 1976 | 24 | 75 | 90 | 2 | 1 | 93 |
| 1975 | 27 | 61 | 89 | 4 | 3 | 91 |

| | S | O | S | O | S | O |
|---|---|---|---|---|---|---|
| 1974 (Ford) | 43 | 56 | | | | |
| 1974 | 25 | 66 | 85 | 8 | 3 | 86 |
| 1973 | 26 | 70 | 92 | 6 | 2 | 95 |
| 1972 | 43 | 49 | 87 | 10 | 2 | 90 |
| 1971 | 28 | 72 | 88 | 7 | 1 | 81 |
| 1970 | 52 | 35 | 74 | 17 | 5 | 80 |
| 1969 | 38 | 53 | 84 | 9 | 2 | 87 |
| 1968 | 66 | 11 | 71 | 5 | 0 | 86 |
| 1967 | 87 | 10 | 92 | 2 | 0 | 98 |
| 1966 | 85 | 9 | 91 | 5 | 0 | 97 |
| 1965 | 94 | 6 | 93 | 4 | 0 | 98 |
| 1964 | 92 | 6 | 92 | 3 | 0 | 100 |
| 1963 | 89 | 6 | 95 | 3 | 7 | 73 |
| 1962 | 95 | 5† | 100 | 0† | 0 | 100† |

S = Support          O = Opposition
†*Not eligible for all recorded votes.*

## Key Votes

**96th Congress**

| | |
|---|---|
| Weaken Carter oil profits tax (1979) | N |
| Reject hospital cost control plan (1979) | N |
| Implement Panama Canal Treaties (1979) | Y |
| Establish Department of Education (1979) | N |
| Approve Anti-busing Amendment (1979) | N |
| Guarantee Chrysler Corp. loans (1979) | Y |
| Approve military draft registration (1980) | N |
| Aid Sandinista regime in Nicaragua (1980) | Y |
| Strengthen fair housing laws (1980) | Y |

**97th Congress**

| | |
|---|---|
| Reagan budget proposal (1981) | N |

## Interest Group Ratings

| Year | ADA | ACA | AFL-CIO | CCUS |
|---|---|---|---|---|
| 1980 | 78 | 10 | 100 | 57 |
| 1979 | 68 | 6 | 100 | 0 |
| 1978 | 90 | 8 | 94 | 28 |
| 1977 | 90 | 0 | 86 | 13 |
| 1976 | 100 | 0 | 87 | 0 |
| 1975 | 89 | 4 | 91 | 12 |
| 1974 | 96 | 0 | 100 | 0 |
| 1973 | 100 | 12 | 100 | 10 |
| 1972 | 100 | 9 | 91 | 0 |
| 1971 | 100 | 18 | 90 | - |
| 1970 | 96 | 17 | 100 | 11 |
| 1969 | 93 | 13 | 100 | - |
| 1968 | 100 | 6 | 100 | - |
| 1967 | 93 | 4 | 100 | 10 |
| 1966 | 100 | 8 | 100 | - |
| 1965 | 100 | 4 | - | 10 |
| 1964 | 100 | 0 | 100 | - |
| 1963 | - | 0 | - | - |
| 1962 | 100 | 0 | 100 | - |

# 9 Geraldine A. Ferraro (D)

## Of Forest Hills — Elected 1978

**Born:** Aug. 26, 1935, Newburgh, N.Y.
**Education:** Marymount College, B.A. 1956; Fordham U., J.D. 1960.
**Profession:** Lawyer.
**Family:** Husband, John A. Zaccaro; three children.
**Religion:** Roman Catholic.
**Political Career:** No previous office.

**In Washington:** Unlike many female House members elected in recent years, Ferraro has generally played down feminist activism and concentrated on building alliances with senior colleagues. This approach made her one of the more influential members of her freshman class in the 96th Congress.

Brassy and irreverent, she often finds herself in the midst of a crowd when she comes to the House floor for a vote or a debate. House leaders sometimes called on her for outside speaking engagements in her first term, and at the 1980 Democratic convention, chaired by Speaker O'Neill, she was chosen to introduce the keynoter, Rep. Morris K. Udall of Arizona. At the start of her second term, she was elected secretary of the House Democratic Caucus.

Ferraro has been relatively tolerant of men who address her in less-than-liberated tones, such as the constituents who greet her by saying "hi, honey."

"I don't consider that sexual harassment," she once explained. "I've been in a male profession for 20 years as a lawyer and a prosecutor. I'm not having any problem."

Assigned to the Public Works Committee in 1979, she played a more conspicuous role in its work during the 96th Congress than most of its other 12 newcomers. She was a leader in the insurgent bloc that sought to shift highway and dam spending to urban uses. One of her arguments was that airport development funds should be used for mass transportation on the ground near congested airports. Her own New York City district is heavily affected by airport ground traffic.

Both in committee and on the floor, however, Ferraro was careful not to stray too far from the majority position. When the Public Works panel brought out a $4-billion water development bill in 1980, she called for "a shift of priorities from the new construction projects that have always dominated public works bills to rehabilitation and maintenance of existing facilities." But she voted for the bill, and against efforts to drop spending for eight controversial projects.

Ferraro's personal appeal has overshadowed a voting record surprising to many who remember the crusty Democrat who preceded her, James J. Delaney. She has shown little evidence of Delaney's conservative approach to social questions, and has been militant in her support for federal funds for abortion, arguing from her experiences as a prosecutor in Queens. Ferraro did vote for an anti-busing amendment to the Constitution in 1979.

**At Home:** Republicans felt this district was certain to fall to them with Delaney's retirement in 1978. They underestimated Ferraro, who was a political novice but a familiar figure after nearly 20 years as a lawyer in the community.

From 1961 to 1974, she was in private practice. In 1974, she joined the Queens district attorney's office, then headed by her cousin, Nicholas Ferraro. As an assistant district attorney, she headed the Special Victims Bureau, working on cases involving child abuse, domestic violence, rape, and crimes against senior citizens.

Her campaign for the House was taken lightly at first, even in her own party, which had

---

**9th District:** Population: 447,297 (4% decrease since 1970). Race: White 388,279 (81%), Black 13,343 (3%), Asian and Pacific Islander 19,522 (4%), Others 26,153 (6%). Spanish origin: 64,190 (14%).

two other strong contenders. But she ended the skepticism by winning an absolute majority in the primary. Her Italian background and relationship to the popular Nicholas Ferraro undoubtedly helped her, and she made effective use of her law and order background in a constituency sensitive about crime.

Moreover, she waged an intensive and well-financed effort, simply out-campaigning her opponents, as she went on to do against Republican Alfred Delli Bovi in the fall, denying the GOP a district it had carefully drawn to facilitate a takeover in the post-Delaney era. The 1980 election was even more decisive. Abortion stand and all, she increased her plurality to nearly 20,000 votes.

**The District:** Located on the frontiers of urban decay, the district is made up largely of middle-income Catholics of Italian and Irish background. It lies just next to devastated and abandoned areas of Brooklyn, and neighborhood preservation is a constant concern.

While the district regularly re-elected Democrat Delaney to the House, the conservative homeowners often broke traditional party ranks to oppose liberals. In 1972, 73.2 percent of the district's voters backed Nixon for president. And in 1970, when the lines were slightly different, the district backed Conservative James L. Buckley for the United States Senate with an absolute majority in a three-way race.

## Committees

**Post Office and Civil Service** (7th of 15 Democrats)
Human Resources, Chairman; Postal Operations and Services.

**Public Works and Transportation** (18th of 25 Democrats)
Aviation; Investigations and Oversight; Water Resources.

**Select Aging** (17th of 31 Democrats)
Human Services; Retirement Income and Employment.

## Elections

**1980 General**

| | |
|---|---|
| Geraldine Ferraro (D ) | 63,796 (58 %) |
| Vito Battista (R ) | 44,473 (41 %) |

**1978 General**

| | |
|---|---|
| Geraldine Ferraro (D ) | 51,350 (54 %) |
| Alfred Dellibovi (R ) | 42,108 (44 %) |

**1978 Primary**

| | |
|---|---|
| Geraldine Ferraro (D ) | 10,254 (53 %) |
| Thomas Manton (D ) | 5,499 (28 %) |
| Patrick Deignan (D ) | 3,603 (19 %) |

**District Vote For President**

| 1980 | | 1976 | | 1972 | |
|---|---|---|---|---|---|
| D | 45,916 (37 %) | D | 63,786 (46 %) | D | 46,955 (27 %) |
| R | 70,660 (57 %) | R | 75,603 (54 %) | R | 129,108 (73 %) |
| I | 6,508 (5 %) | | | | |

## Campaign Finance

| | Receipts | Receipts from PACs | Expen-ditures |
|---|---|---|---|
| **1980** | | | |
| Ferraro (D ) | $133,207 | $89,829 (67 %) | $124,743 |
| Battista (R ) | $20,341 | $500 (2 %) | $20,716 |

| 1978 | | | |
|---|---|---|---|
| Ferraro (D ) | $382,119 | $35,100 (9 %) | $382,074 |
| Dellibovi (R ) | $119,823 | $49,486 (41 %) | $110,679 |

## Voting Studies

| | Presidental Support | | Party Unity | | Conservative Coalition | |
|---|---|---|---|---|---|---|
| Year | S | O | S | O | S | O |
| 1980 | 74 | 18 | 86 | 6 | 20 | 73 |
| 1979 | 66 | 26 | 78 | 14 | 22 | 73 |

S = Support          O = Opposition

## Key Votes

**96th Congress**

| | |
|---|---|
| Weaken Carter oil profits tax (1979) | N |
| Reject hospital cost control plan (1979) | N |
| Implement Panama Canal Treaties (1979) | N |
| Establish Department of Education (1979) | N |
| Approve Anti-busing Amendment (1979) | Y |
| Guarantee Chrysler Corp. loans (1979) | Y |
| Approve military draft registration (1980) | Y |
| Aid Sandinista regime in Nicaragua (1980) | Y |
| Strengthen fair housing laws (1980) | Y |

**97th Congress**

| | |
|---|---|
| Reagan budget proposal (1981) | N |

## Interest Group Ratings

| Year | ADA | ACA | AFL-CIO | CCUS |
|---|---|---|---|---|
| 1980 | 72 | 17 | 89 | 56 |
| 1979 | 74 | 12 | 89 | 13 |

# 10 Mario Biaggi (D)

**Of The Bronx — Elected 1972**

**Born:** Oct. 26, 1917, New York, N.Y.
**Education:** N.Y.U. Law School, LL.B. 1963.
**Profession:** Lawyer, police detective.
**Family:** Wife, Marie Wassil; four children.
**Religion:** Roman Catholic.
**Political Career:** Unsuccessfully sought Democratic nomination for N.Y. Mayor, 1973.

**In Washington:** Biaggi has been a man of controversy in New York his entire political life, but he managed to keep a relatively low profile in the House for nearly a decade, until he stepped forward as the leading congressional supporter of Catholic militants in Northern Ireland.

Some colleagues thought it odd in 1977 when Biaggi, who is not Irish, formed the Ad Hoc Congressional Committee for Irish Affairs and began demanding that the British pull their troops out of Northern Ireland. But his district includes the headquarters of the Irish Northern Aid Society, an American group raising money for the Catholics in Northern Ireland. And beyond that, there has always been a streak of adventure about Biaggi, dating back to his celebrated career as a police officer in New York.

Biaggi says his only interest is peace in Ireland. He set up his committee at the request of a former head of the Ancient Order of Hibernians (an Irish-American fraternal group) to draw national attention to the civil strife.

But one of Biaggi's first moves as spokesman for the congressional Irish group was to meet with leaders of the political arm of the Irish Republican Army. He was immediately denounced for supporting continued violence, a charge he was unable to silence by pronouncing peace as his goal. Prominent American Irish-Catholics, led by House Speaker Thomas P. O'Neill Jr., Sen. Edward M. Kennedy and N.Y. Gov. Hugh Carey, felt he had gone too far. They organized a rival group, the "Friends of Ireland," and urged an end to war.

Biaggi persists, saying he is only fulfilling his own commitment to human rights. He claims credit for convincing the United States to stop shipping arms to British military units stationed in Northern Ireland. Thanks to pressure from him, Biaggi says, "We have raised the Irish issue from a position of relative obscurity to one which now enjoys national and international visibility."

Biaggi's legislative interests are eclectic. He has spent his entire House career on the Merchant Marine Committee, where he has voted consistently with maritime interests, especially unions. In the 97th Congress, he is chairman of the subcommittee which writes most of the maritime legislation, and plays a greater role in it than the relatively passive full committee chairman, Walter B. Jones of North Carolina. Biaggi considered challenging Jones for the chairmanship in 1981, but stepped aside when Jones gave him a new title, vice chairman, and a good subcommittee.

Within a few months, Biaggi's subcommittee had written a controversial piece of legislation, allowing owners of U.S. ships to buy or build vessels in foreign shipyards without losing eligibility for federal operating subsidies for those vessels. Biaggi was skeptical of the idea, but eventually voted for it after some restrictions were added. The bill pleased some ship operators, but threatened shipbuilders, who feared construction would shift away from them and into foreign yards.

In the 96th Congress, Biaggi was chairman of the Coast Guard and Navigation Subcommittee on Merchant Marine. He played a key role in writing oil spill cleanup legislation, which he initially sponsored and which Merchant Marine had joint jurisdiction over.

The legislation that implemented the Panama Canal treaties also went through Merchant Marine in the 96th Congress, and Biaggi found himself in some controversy over his floor amend-

---

**10th District: Eastern Bronx and northern Queens — Astoria, Throgs Neck.** Population: 445,159 (5% decrease since 1970). Race: White 355,564 (80%), Black 54,049 (12%), Asian and Pacific Islander 13,180 (3%), Others 19,823 (4%). Spanish origin: 41,125 (9%).

ment requiring Panama to settle all outstanding claims from American businesses before receiving canal revenues. Biaggi said 107 U.S. businesses were involved. Opponents charged that the amendment offered most of its relief to one man, shipping magnate Daniel K. Ludwig. Biaggi lost.

As chairman of the Human Services Subcommittee of the Aging Committee and as a senior member of Education and Labor, Biaggi has linked support of programs for the disabled and the elderly. He cosponsored a 1978 law authorizing $5 billion for a 4-year expansion of aid to the handicapped. In 1979 and 1980, he worked on expansion of federal loan subsidies for college students, programs he and most of the other Education and Labor Democrats began scrambling to protect as the Reagan budget won approval in Congress in 1981.

As a night school lawyer himself, Biaggi also has taken the lead in expanding opportunities for "adult non-traditional students," sponsoring new legislation to provide student aid and generally encourage older persons to go back to school.

Biaggi has sponsored repeated floor amendments to bar the Labor Department from helping illegal aliens compete for jobs with legal immigrants. He has tried and failed to add money for the Immigration and Naturalization Service to hire 1,000 more employees to crack down on those illegal aliens already holding jobs.

As a former police officer, Biaggi has introduced a bill seven times calling on local law enforcement officials to adopt an officers' "Bill of Rights." As drafted, the bill would induce cooperation by withholding federal Law Enforcement Assistance Administration aid from those who fail to adopt the new rules.

He also is trying to convince Congress to adopt his bill to shift federal elections to Sundays and close all polls at the same moment everywhere in the country. More people would vote, he says, and elections would not be influenced in the West by broadcast returns from the East.

**At Home:** It would be difficult to invent a law-and-order background as impressive as Biaggi's. Starting out in the New York City Police Department in 1942, he served 23 years, earning so many honors that he was nicknamed "America's most decorated policeman." Biaggi's limp is a constant reminder he was wounded 10 times in the line of duty. He was the only New York policeman named to the National Police Hall of Fame.

In 1960, Biaggi's career began to change. He entered New York Law School, getting his degree in 1963 at the age of 46. Then he became an assistant to the New York secretary of state. In 1965, Republican Rep. Paul A. Fino of the Bronx touted Biaggi as a fusion candidate for New York City mayor. Nothing came of it, but Biaggi received useful publicity. Later in the year, he formally left the police department and set up a private law practice.

In 1968, Fino retired from the House after 16 years and was elected to the state Supreme Court. Biaggi ran for the seat and won, asking people to "vote for law and order." With his police background and emphasis on crime at a time of riot and disruption, the Conservative Party found him attractive and backed him for Congress.

But the Conservatives' flirtation with Biaggi was a triumph of hope over reality. Biaggi has always voted in the House as a moderate, urban-oriented Democrat.

Still, the relationship between Biaggi and the Conservatives remained intact until 1973, when the party decided to back him as its candidate for mayor.

He started off the year with a seemingly good chance to be elected. But in the spring, New York City newspapers revealed Biaggi had refused to answer questions about his own finances while testifying before a federal grand jury in 1971. Biaggi hotly denied the stories, but when the transcripts were released they showed he had invoked his constitutional rights, including the Fifth Amendment's protection against self-incrimination, 16 times. The grand jury was said to be looking into reports of congressmen receiving money for introducing special immigration bills. In his own defense, Biaggi said he had refused to answer the grand jury's questions because he was angry that the panel would not let him read a prepared statement.

The revelation ruined Biaggi's mayoral campaign, although he did well enough in his Bronx constituency to run third in the Democratic primary. He already had the Conservative mayoral nomination, and so remained on the November ballot. But many Conservative leaders abandoned him and called on him to withdraw. He ran fourth in the general election.

Biaggi has put all that behind him. He has continued to win easy re-election to the House, avoiding a Democratic primary challenge and even winning the backing of the Republican Party in each election since 1972.

And in a symbolic reversal, the Conservatives have run candidates against him since 1974, while the Liberal Party, which staunchly opposed him in earlier years, gave him its nomination in both 1978 and 1980.

**The District:** The 10th is a collection of Catholic ethnic neighborhoods of the East Bronx and northern Queens, most of them Italian-American. It is a perfect district for Biaggi. These neighborhoods contain single-family homes and have strong community ties. They have remained largely intact despite the changes going on nearby. The edges of the district contain a portion of the city's black and Hispanic communities.

While strong on law and order issues and traditional moral values, 10th District Democratic voters still cling as often as they feel they can to their traditional party. They voted for Jimmy Carter for president in both 1976 and 1980.

## Committees

**Education and Labor** (7th of 19 Democrats)
Elementary, Secondary and Vocational Education; Labor-Management Relations; Select Education.

**Merchant Marine and Fisheries** (2nd of 20 Democrats)
Merchant Marine, chairman; Coast Guard and Navigation.

**Select Aging** (3rd of 31 Democrats)
Human Services, chairman.

## Elections

**1980 General**

| | |
|---|---|
| Mario Biaggi (D) | 95,322 (95%) |

**1978 General**

| | |
|---|---|
| Mario Biaggi (D) | 77,979 (95%) |

**Previous Winning Percentages**

| | | | |
|---|---|---|---|
| 1976 (92%) | 1974 (82%) | 1972 (94%) | 1970 (70%) |
| 1968 (61%) | | | |

**District Vote For President**

| | 1980 | | 1976 | | 1972 |
|---|---|---|---|---|---|
| D | 59,993 (52 %) | D | 75,985 (57 %) | D | 60,423 (37 %) |
| R | 50,555 (43 %) | R | 56,857 (43 %) | R | 103,372 (63 %) |
| I | 4,613 (4 %) | | | | |

## Campaign Finance

| | Receipts | Receipts from PACs | Expenditures |
|---|---|---|---|
| **1980** | | | |
| Biaggi (D) | $61,262 | $6,750 (11%) | $47,707 |
| **1978** | | | |
| Biaggi (D) | $78,236 | $21,550 (28%) | $71,493 |

## Voting Studies

| | Presidental Support | | Party Unity | | Conservative Coalition | |
|---|---|---|---|---|---|---|
| Year | S | O | S | O | S | O |
| 1980 | 69 | 17 | 70 | 6 | 20 | 60 |

| | | | | | | |
|---|---|---|---|---|---|---|
| 1979 | 63 | 22 | 69 | 16 | 31 | 55 |
| 1978 | 57 | 31 | 65 | 23 | 30 | 56 |
| 1977 | 66 | 22 | 67 | 19 | 27 | 62 |
| 1976 | 29 | 61 | 73 | 13 | 28 | 57 |
| 1975 | 30 | 60 | 68 | 15 | 28 | 50 |
| 1974 (Ford) | 33 | 48 | | | | |
| 1974 | 40 | 47 | 59 | 25 | 38 | 46 |
| 1973 | 24 | 51 | 65 | 14 | 23 | 63 |
| 1972 | 49 | 38 | 70 | 17 | 30 | 54 |
| 1971 | 40 | 49 | 75 | 14 | 28 | 61 |
| 1970 | 54 | 32 | 65 | 22 | 23 | 61 |
| 1969 | 49 | 51 | 71 | 18 | 31 | 67 |

S = Support          O = Opposition

## Key Votes

**96th Congress**

| | |
|---|---|
| Weaken Carter oil profits tax (1979) | N |
| Reject hospital cost control plan (1979) | N |
| Implement Panama Canal Treaties (1979) | Y |
| Establish Department of Education (1979) | N |
| Approve Anti-busing Amendment (1979) | N |
| Guarantee Chrysler Corp. loans (1979) | Y |
| Approve military draft registration (1980) | Y |
| Aid Sandinista regime in Nicaragua (1980) | ? |
| Strengthen fair housing laws (1980) | Y |

**97th Congress**

| | |
|---|---|
| Reagan budget proposal (1981) | N |

## Interest Group Ratings

| Year | ADA | ACA | AFL-CIO | CCUS |
|---|---|---|---|---|
| 1980 | 50 | 15 | 82 | 61 |
| 1979 | 63 | 13 | 88 | 12 |
| 1978 | 55 | 40 | 75 | 44 |
| 1977 | 70 | 8 | 91 | 6 |
| 1976 | 50 | 19 | 83 | 7 |
| 1975 | 47 | 28 | 82 | 24 |
| 1974 | 26 | 62 | 82 | 22 |
| 1973 | 48 | 25 | 100 | 18 |
| 1972 | 56 | 27 | 91 | 11 |
| 1971 | 65 | 32 | 83 | - |
| 1970 | 52 | 37 | 86 | 10 |
| 1969 | 80 | 40 | 80 | - |

# 11 James H. Scheuer (D)

**Of Neponsit — Elected 1964**
Did not serve 1973-75

**Born:** Feb. 6, 1920, New York, N.Y.
**Education:** Swarthmore College, A.B. 1942; Harvard Business School, M.B.A. 1943; Columbia U. Law School, LL.B. 1948.
**Military Career:** Army, 1943-45.
**Profession:** Lawyer.
**Family:** Wife, Emily Malino; four children.
**Religion:** Jewish.
**Political Career:** Unsuccessfully sought renomination to U.S. House, 1972.

**In Washington:** Scheuer, like the Consumer Protection Subcommittee he headed until 1981, has never been particularly popular in the House. Often abrasive and hot tempered, he has had to deal with a growing number of attacks on the consumer movement as it has lost favor over the past few years. Within the larger Commerce Committee, he has suffered because of a long-running feud with Michigan's John D. Dingell, now the committee chairman. For years the two men barely spoke to each other.

When Dingell took over the full committee in 1981 and decided it had too many subcommittees, there was little doubt what he meant — Scheuer's panel had to go. The deed was done over the furious objections of Scheuer himself, who said he was being punished for promoting airbags in automobiles against Dingell's opposition. "I enraged him by standing up to him," Scheuer said. But the 14-7 vote stripping him of his subcommittee also reflected his personal standing among colleagues. It left the Brooklyn Democrat, the second most senior member of Commerce, as a man without a chairmanship. He later took a less important subcommittee on Science and Technology. Scheuer won the Consumer Subcommittee in 1979 by one vote, 14-13. Once elected, he found himself embroiled in a defense of the Federal Trade Commission, an agency that was becoming increasingly irritating to Congress as it sought to regulate business activity from funeral homes to TV advertising aimed at children.

For four years, the FTC had operated without a proper authorization because the House bill to authorize it consistently included a legislative veto provision that the Senate adamantly refused to accept. Scheuer opposed both the veto and the restrictions on the agency but was forced to go along with the House veto position in conference.

The authorization finally did clear in 1980 with a limited two-house veto provision and some other restrictions on what areas the FTC could look into.

Scheuer waged a battle in the 96th Congress to preserve legislation requiring airbags in many U.S. automobiles for 1982. Here, too, Dingell was his antagonist. After the House cast a symbolic vote against airbags in 1979, Scheuer agreed to a compromise delaying their introduction for a year and restricting them at first to smaller cars. The auto industry generally accepted this, but Dingell fought it on the floor in 1980 and killed it. That left the government theoretically free to go ahead with the requirement as originally scheduled — except that the incoming Reagan administration opposed it.

Scheuer has long been interested in population problems. In 1977, he convinced the Rules Committee to establish a Select Committee on Population, which he chaired, and it produced a series of reports on world population problems during the 95th Congress. When he tried to get reauthorization in 1979, however, the House turned him down and abolished the committee.

In his earlier House career, before losing his seat in 1972, Scheuer served on the Education and Labor Committee, specializing in manpower training and programs for the elderly. He also mounted a personal campaign against international drug traffic, introducing his own bill at one

---

**11th District: Southeast Brooklyn, southern Queens.** Population: 451,889 (4% decrease since 1970). Race: White 265,203 (59%), Black 143,940 (32%), Others 43,076 (10%). Spanish origin: 66,180 (15%).

---

point providing for American aid to foreign countries to help them stop producing opium.

Wherever he has been, Scheuer has managed to keep himself in controversy. He was expelled from the Soviet Union in 1972 after an 11-day visit in which authorities said he urged Russian Jews to emigrate to Israel. Eight years earlier, in his first campaign for the House, he was among a dozen people arrested for picketing the Jordanian Pavilion at the New York World's Fair.

**At Home:** Scheuer has had one of the most peripatetic political careers of any House member in recent years. He has challenged three incumbent members of his own party for renomination and beaten two of them. He has run in four different congressional districts and won in three.

The son of a wealthy real estate man, Scheuer had a highly successful career himself in home building and construction, specializing in urban renewal. He entered politics in 1964 as part of the reform wave which swept over the Bronx that year, defeating Rep. James Healey, a Democrat allied with the traditional party organization.

He mounted a disastrous campaign for mayor of New York City in 1969, finishing last in a field of five candidates despite an expenditure of $550,000.

In 1970, when a new Hispanic district was created in the South Bronx, much of it from Scheuer's district, he moved into a neighboring district and defeated Democratic Rep. Jacob Gilbert, another organization loyalist, for renomination. Two years later, the Bronx lost a district and Scheuer was thrown in with Democratic Rep. Jonathan Bingham. This time he was not successful, and he had to retire from the House.

But Scheuer did not give up on a congressional career. Political developments in Brooklyn opened another opportunity for him. Rep. Frank Brasco of the 11th District got into legal trouble and retired in 1974. Scheuer decided to run in that district and won the primary over the candidate backed by the Brooklyn organization. Since then, he has had no electoral problems. The organization does not challenge him, and he does not bother the organization.

**The District:** The 11th is the descendant of an old east Brooklyn district that has existed for most of this century. In the 1972 redistricting, it was extended through southern Queens to the Nassau County line. There is a significant black and Hispanic population, but lower-middle- to middle-income Jewish and Catholic homeowners predominate. The location of Kennedy International Airport in the district is a constant irritant, with constituents demanding measures against noise pollution and traffic congestion.

The district's voters have been strongly Democratic, sticking with the party on almost all occasions. They did revolt in 1972, however, when President Nixon carried the district with 51.8 percent of the vote.

## Committees

**Energy and Commerce** (2nd of 24 Democrats)
Commerce, Transportation, and Tourism; Health and the Environment; Telecommunications, Consumer Protection, and Finance.

**Science and Technology** (4th of 23 Democrats)
Natural Resources, Agriculture Research and Environment, chairman.

**Select Narcotics Abuse and Control** (7th of 11 Democrats)

## Elections

**1980 General**

| | |
|---|---|
| James Scheuer (D) | 72,798 (74%) |
| Andrew Carlan (R) | 25,424 (26%) |

**1978 General**

| | |
|---|---|
| James Scheuer (D) | 58,997 (78%) |
| Kenneth Huhn (R) | 16,206 (22%) |

**Previous Winning Percentages**

| | | | |
|---|---|---|---|
| **1976** (74%) | **1974** (72%) | **1970** (72%) | **1968** (83%) |
| **1966** (84%) | **1964** 874%) | | |

**District Vote For President**

| | 1980 | | 1976 | | 1972 |
|---|---|---|---|---|---|
| **D** | 64,206 (54 %) | **D** | 92,751 (70 %) | **D** | 74,929 (48 %) |
| **R** | 48,579 (41 %) | **R** | 40,181 (30 %) | **R** | 80,690 (52 %) |
| **I** | 5,836 (5 %) | | | | |

## Campaign Finance

| | Receipts | Receipts from PACs | Expenditures |
|---|---|---|---|
| **1980** | | | |
| Scheuer (D) | $52,185 | $32,900 (63%) | $61,111 |
| **1978** | | | |
| Scheuer (D) | $42,410 | $19,750 (47%) | $24,861 |

# Voting Studies

| | Presidential Support | | Party Unity | | Conservative Coalition | |
|------|-----|-----|-----|-----|-----|------|
| Year | S | O | S | O | S | O |
| 1980 | 74 | 17 | 79 | 4 | 13 | 77† |
| 1979 | 73 | 17 | 88 | 5† | 9 | 8† |
| 1978 | 73 | 20 | 83 | 10 | 8 | 86 |
| 1977 | 80 | 16 | 88 | 7 | 4 | 92 |
| 1976 | 22 | 71 | 84 | 2 | 6 | 90 |
| 1975 | 30 | 56 | 87 | 7 | 7 | 91 |
| 1972 | 43 | 41 | 78 | 3 | 0 | 83 |
| 1971 | 30 | 65 | 87 | 9 | 5 | 87 |
| 1970 | 42 | 34 | 58 | 18 | - | 64 |
| 1969 | 36 | 47 | 75 | 9 | 2 | 78 |
| 1968 | 61 | 15 | 73 | 4 | 0 | 75 |
| 1967 | 79 | 8 | 81 | 9 | 2 | 93 |
| 1966 | 86 | 4 | 91 | 1 | 3 | 95 |
| 1965 | 92 | 5† | 90 | 8 | 0 | 100† |

S = Support     O = Opposition
† Not eligible for all recorded votes.

# Key Votes

**96th Congress**

| | |
|---|---|
| Weaken Carter oil profits tax (1979) | N |
| Reject hospital cost control plan (1979) | N |
| Implement Panama Canal Treaties (1979) | Y |
| Establish Department of Education (1979) | N |
| Approve Anti-busing Amendment (1979) | N |
| Guarantee Chrysler Corp. loans (1979) | Y |
| Approve military draft registration (1980) | Y |
| Aid Sandinista regime in Nicaragua (1980) | Y |
| Strengthen fair housing laws (1980) | Y |

**97th Congress**

| | |
|---|---|
| Reagan budget proposal (1981) | N |

# Interest Group Ratings

| Year | ADA | ACA | AFL-CIO | CCUS |
|------|-----|-----|---------|------|
| 1980 | 89 | 13 | 94 | 65 |
| 1979 | 84 | 4 | 95 | 7 |
| 1978 | 70 | 12 | 85 | 25 |
| 1977 | 85 | 15 | 91 | 12 |
| 1976 | 90 | 0 | 83 | 13 |
| 1975 | 95 | 11 | 91 | 19 |
| 1972 | 88 | 0 | 89 | 0 |
| 1971 | 86 | 18 | 83 | - |
| 1970 | 96 | 13 | 100 | 11 |
| 1969 | 100 | 14 | 100 | - |
| 1968 | 83 | 6 | 100 | - |
| 1967 | 100 | 4 | 100 | 11 |
| 1966 | 100 | 8 | 92 | - |
| 1965 | 100 | 4 | - | 10 |

# 12    Shirley Chisholm (D)

**Of Brooklyn — Elected 1968**

**Born:** Nov. 30, 1924, Brooklyn, N.Y.
**Education:** Brooklyn College, B.A. 1946; Columbia U., M.A. 1952.
**Profession:** Education consultant.
**Family:** Husband, Arthur Hardwick.
**Religion:** Methodist.
**Political Career:** N.Y. Assembly, 1965-69.

**In Washington:** The self-esteem that encouraged Chisholm to name her autobiography *Unbought and Unbossed* has made her one of the most unpredictable members for the Democratic leadership to deal with, even though she has been part of that leadership herself.

Chisholm's career history indicates that she is, if unbought and unbossed, sometimes willing to negotiate if the deal is on her terms.

Her House tenure started in controversy in 1969 when House leaders put her on the Agriculture Committee, believing they were doing her a favor because of the committee's jurisdiction over food stamps. She demanded to be taken off the committee, saying that her assignment there had no relevance to district needs, and that she did not approve of food stamps because poor people were required to pay too much of their income for them. She wanted a guaranteed minimum income instead.

She was switched to Veterans' Affairs until 1971, when she got the Education and Labor assignment she wanted. She was widely believed to have won that assignment by supporting Hale Boggs of Louisiana in his successful campaign for majority leader against the more liberal Morris K. Udall of Arizona. Chisholm has always denied any deal, contending the New York delegation demanded the assignment for her. As a member of Education and Labor, she worked on minimum wage legislation, seeking to expand its coverage. She crusaded for federal subsidies for day-care centers, which were vetoed by President Ford, and tried to amend higher education bills to focus more of the funding on students from poor families.

In 1972, Chisholm launched a campaign for the presidency, saying she hoped to "rattle the power structure." She tried to put together a coalition of blacks, feminists and other minorities, but found they were not necessarily compatible. Even her colleagues in the Congressional Black Caucus did not support her. Asked about that, she snapped, "Black males are no different than white males. Since when do I have to clear it with them." For years after that, she kept her distance from the formal activities of the Black Caucus.

Chisholm went to the 1972 convention with 24 delegates. In the end she got 151 votes, released to her by Hubert H. Humphrey and other candidates who had given up on the effort to stop George McGovern. She told the convention's black caucus, "I'm the only one among you who has the b---- to run for president." At one point, George Wallace, running in the Florida primary, told voters to vote for her if they couldn't vote for him. "At least she tells the truth unlike all those pointy-head liberals," he was quoted as saying.

In 1977, Chisholm moved closer to the power structure as a member of the House Rules Committee and secretary of the Democratic Caucus. The caucus post was mostly honorific; she had no close relationships with the top leaders. But she has used Rules on certain occasions to further her legislative goals.

Although Rules is usually considered an arm of the leadership, Chisholm has often acted independently there. In 1978 she was one of the members who voted against a rule providing for consideration of President Carter's energy plan as a single unit. The legislation had been broken into five separate sections to speed congressional action, but the leadership was determined that the final vote would be on the entire package, forcing

---

**12th District: Northeastern Brooklyn — Greenpoint.** Population: 320,886 (31% decrease since 1970). Race: White 87,218 (27%), Black 174,344 (54%), Others 59,324 (18%). Spanish origin: 100,478 (31%).

members to take it or leave it. The rule initially lost on an 8-8 tie vote. On a second vote, taken after intense lobbying of Rules Committee members, Chisholm was one of two Democrats who changed their vote from "nay" to "present," allowing the rule to be adopted.

In 1980 she again went against the leadership on Rules. The Budget Committee had called for limiting Social Security cost-of-living increases for federal retirees to once a year, rather than the previous twice a year. But Chisholm and two other Democrats joined the committee's Republicans to agree to a motion allowing a floor vote on the issue, guaranteeing that the twice-a-year payment would be restored. No amount of lobbying by Speaker O'Neill was sufficient to change her mind.

Chisholm has disappointed liberal colleagues on some issues, especially those dealing with the environment. Feeling that rigid environmental protection can be a threat to jobs, she has been reluctant to endorse some of the strictest environmental bills of recent years, although she has ended up supporting some of them, such as the Alaska lands bill of 1979. She also fought President Carter's proposed Education Department, fearing it would dilute the attention paid to special programs for minorities, and voted against it even after some of the provisions that offended her were removed.

Chisholm has opposed a reform limiting outside earned income for House members. She several times has led House members in honoraria collected for speaking engagements.

**At Home:** In 1968, Shirley Chisholm became the first black woman ever elected to Congress. At age 44, she had had a varied career in education and politics, and had struggled upward in a male-dominated public world to achieve her new position on her own.

Born Shirley St. Hill in Brooklyn, the daughter of West Indian immigrants, Chisholm spent some of her childhood years in Barbados. Returning to New York, she completed her education in Brooklyn public schools. She chose education as her first profession, serving as a nursery school teacher and director from 1946 to 1953. She then became director of a child-care center and in 1959 joined the New York City Division of Day Care as a consultant.

Chisholm entered the world of politics in 1964 when she was elected to the state Assembly. Her step up came four years later, when the Legislature created a predominantly black congressional district in Brooklyn. She narrowly defeated state Sen. William Thompson for the Democratic nomination, then went on to over-

whelm James E. Farmer, a founder and former president of the Congress of Racial Equality (CORE) in November. Farmer ran as the candidate of the Republican and Liberal parties. That was the only time Chisholm failed to receive Liberal Party backing in her congressional races.

Chisholm has been a loner in Brooklyn politics, not bothering to form an ongoing political organization of her own. At times, this has led some black politicians in the district to think she was vulnerable. She received a major primary challenge in 1976 from her archrival in Brooklyn politics, City Councilman Samuel D. Wright. Wright had built up a personal machine, based on influence in local school boards and anti-poverty programs.

But Chisholm had more power than many thought. Her energy and reputation for integrity had built a loyal following in the district without the traditional machinery. Church organizations and civic groups endorsed her and turned out the vote for her.

This support appears to leave Chisholm secure politically as long as she wants to run. She has said on several occasions that she would like to retire from the House, but when the time for decision has come, she has always gone for another term. She has never had any trouble from the Republicans.

**The District:** When the New York Legislature was forced by the Supreme Court to redraw congressional district lines in 1968, it was decided to add a second black district in New York City to the traditional one based in Harlem. By the 1960s, large areas of northern and central Brooklyn had sufficient black majorities to populate a new district.

In 1972, the lines were changed again to add even more Brooklyn blacks in Chisholm's district. The new 12th was 77.1 percent black. But in early 1974, a federal district court, applying provisions of the Voting Rights Act, held that certain New York City districts, including the 12th, were subject to the scrutiny of the Justice Department for racial fairness. This ruling and the negotiations that followed resulted in a redrawing of the 12th to place many of its blacks in the neighboring 14th District, which previously had only 23.2 percent blacks. Under the 1974 lines, Chisholm's district was reduced to a 53.9 percent black population, and the 14th was raised to 46.4 percent.

Chisholm's district lost over 150,000 people in the 1970s, according to the 1980 census results. It will have to gain almost 200,000 people in the redistricting process. With the political need to preserve a black district, there is little likelihood that the 12th will be eliminated.

## Committees

**Rules** (5th of 11 Democrats)
Legislative Process.

## Elections

**1980 General**

| | |
|---|---|
| Shirley Chisholm (D) | 35,446 (87%) |
| Charles Gibbs (R) | 3,372 (8%) |

**1980 Primary**

| | |
|---|---|
| Shirley Chisholm (D) | 9,514 (62%) |
| Louis Hernandez (D) | 2,976 (19%) |
| David Miller (D) | 2,846 (19%) |

**1978 General**

| | |
|---|---|
| Shirley Chisholm (D) | 25,697 (88%) |
| Charles Gibb (R) | 3,580 (12%) |

**Previous Winning Percentages**

1976 (87%)    1974 (80%)    1972 (88%)    1970 (82%)
1968 (68%)

**District Vote For President**

| | 1980 | | 1976 | | 1972 |
|---|---|---|---|---|---|
| **D** | 42,604 (82 %) | **D** | 49,545 (82 %) | **D** | 64,673 (84 %) |
| **R** | 8,257 (16 %) | **R** | 10,533 (18 %) | **R** | 11,949 (16 %) |
| **I** | 930 (2 %) | | | | |

## Campaign Finance

| | Receipts | Receipts from PACs | Expen- ditures |
|---|---|---|---|
| **1980** | | | |
| Chisholm (D) | $32,461 | $11,660 (36%) | $31,576 |
| **1978** | | | |
| Chisholm (D) | $14,797 | $6,750 (46%) | $14,498 |

## Voting Studies

| | Presidential Support | | Party Unity | | Conservative Coalition | |
|---|---|---|---|---|---|---|
| Year | S | O | S | O | S | O |
| 1980 | 58 | 22 | 77 | 4 | 0 | 72 |

| | | | | | | |
|---|---|---|---|---|---|---|
| 1979 | 68 | 18 | 77 | 5 | 5 | 81 |
| 1978 | 74 | 18 | 84 | 6 | 5 | 82 |
| 1977 | 67 | 20 | 87 | 2 | 2 | 89 |
| 1976 | 16 | 61 | 69 | 3 | 3 | 71 |
| 1975 | 29 | 65 | 89 | 5 | 4 | 88 |
| 1974 (Ford) | 41 | 54 | | | | |
| 1974 | 19 | 64 | 70 | 6 | 4 | 73 |
| 1973 | 23 | 64 | 78 | 7 | 4 | 80 |
| 1972 | 32 | 35 | 54 | 2 | 1 | 60 |
| 1971 | 21 | 70 | 69 | 8 | 3 | 80 |
| 1970 | 28 | 37 | 46 | 14 | 2 | 48 |
| 1969 | 21 | 47 | 51 | 16 | 11 | 67 |

S = Support          O = Opposition

## Key Votes

**96th Congress**

| | |
|---|---|
| Weaken Carter oil profits tax (1979) | N |
| Reject hospital cost control plan (1979) | X |
| Implement Panama Canal Treaties (1979) | Y |
| Establish Department of Education (1979) | N |
| Approve Anti-busing Amendment (1979) | N |
| Guarantee Chrysler Corp. loans (1979) | Y |
| Approve military draft registration (1980) | N |
| Aid Sandinista regime in Nicaragua (1980) | Y |
| Strengthen fair housing laws (1980) | Y |

**97th Congress**

| | |
|---|---|
| Reagan budget proposal (1981) | N |

## Interest Group Ratings

| Year | ADA | ACA | AFL-CIO | CCUS |
|---|---|---|---|---|
| 1980 | 78 | 15 | 95 | 55 |
| 1979 | 89 | 4 | 100 | 20 |
| 1978 | 100 | 7 | 90 | 29 |
| 1977 | 95 | 0 | 95 | 0 |
| 1976 | 80 | 5 | 86 | 0 |
| 1975 | 95 | 7 | 96 | 12 |
| 1974 | 78 | 10 | 100 | 0 |
| 1973 | 92 | 11 | 100 | 10 |
| 1972 | 69 | 7 | 73 | 13 |
| 1971 | 97 | 8 | 82 | - |
| 1970 | 80 | 25 | 100 | 22 |
| 1969 | 100 | 29 | 100 | - |

# 13 Stephen J. Solarz (D)

**Of Brooklyn — Elected 1974**

**Born:** Sept. 12, 1940, New York, N.Y.
**Education:** Brandeis U., A.B. 1962; Columbia U., M.A. 1967.
**Profession:** Political scientist.
**Family:** Wife, Nina Koldin; two children.
**Religion:** Jewish.
**Political Career:** N.Y. Assembly, 1969-75; unsuccessfully sought Democratic nomination for Brooklyn borough president, 1973.

**In Washington:** Solarz has conducted what amounts to personal diplomacy as a member of the Foreign Affairs Committee, negotiating with foreign leaders on every continent and returning with detailed assessments of what he has seen.

Solarz travels so often — 24 countries over more than six weeks in 1979 alone — that outsiders find it easy to call him a junketer. But his ambitions and output go far beyond junketing.

When he traveled to North Korea in 1980 to see Kim Il Sung, that country's dictator, traveling against the policy of the U.S. State Department, he was the first Amercian official to enter that country in more than 30 years. He returned with a report that the North Koreans were interested in improving relations with the United States.

Later in the year, after two weeks of discussions with dozens of Soviet foreign policy specialists, he held a news conference in Moscow to report on Russian attitudes toward Poland, Iraq, Afghanistan and the Persian Gulf.

Solarz' style has provoked its share of criticism from members who question why Congress needs a one-man foreign service. But it has made him an unquestioned expert on world issues and a central figure in nearly all the foreign policy arguments in the House in recent years.

Solarz represents a heavily-Jewish district, and he was drawn to the Foreign Affairs Committee initially as a defender of Israel. He has been am aggressive one throughout his four terms on the committee, arguing for more military aid and against arms sales to Arab countries. But he has been more directly responsible for policy toward Africa and East Asia. In the 96th Congress he was the Africa Subcommittee chairman; he switched to the Asian and Pacific panel in 1981.

Through years of debate over U.S. policy toward Africa, Solarz has been for placing U.S. resources behind nationalist movements, if necessary leftist ones, and phasing out help to right-wing regimes.

He fought to keep American sanctions against Zimbabwe-Rhodesia under its white supremacist regime, but once former guerrilla leader Robert Mugabe took over that country, he proclaimed that "we now have a friend in Zimbabwe." He argued to keep foreign aid to revolutionary governments in Angola and Mozambique, and to drop it for the government of Zaire, which he described as "conditioned on a system of endemic corruption." He tried to cut military aid for Morocco and Somalia.

Lobbying for Israel kept Solarz in a delicate relationship with the Carter administration. Pleased about President Carter's success in obtaining an Israeli-Egyptian peace treaty and his pressure on Syria to let Jews emigrate, Solarz endorsed Carter for renomination in 1980 as "a man of integrity and decency." But that decision was less popular later in the year after the controversial U.S. vote in the United Nations to condemn Israeli settlements on occupied Arab land. Backing Israel is only one of the ways Solarz has used to make himself conspicuous as a voice for his constituents, many of them elderly Jews who emigrated to Brooklyn from Europe.

In his first term, he introduced a floor amendment to establish a 90 percent tax credit for elderly people who insulate their homes. Later he proposed that for the federal government's purposes, any person whose principal language is other than English be counted as a member of a "minority group."

---

**13th District: Southern Brooklyn — Coney Island, Bensonhurst. Population:** 442,616 (6% decrease since 1970). Race: White 355,564 (80%), Black 54,049 (12%), Asian and Pacific Islander 13,180 (3%), Others 19,823 (4%). Spanish origin: 41,125 (9%).

On the Budget Committee in the past two Congresses, Solarz has spoken more broadly for New York and other industrial cities in the Northeast. In 1979, his first year on Budget, he mounted a lobbying campaign on the floor that reversed an earlier vote eliminating $200 million in anti-recession aid to local governments. Then he voted for the overall budget.

**At Home:** A native Brooklynite, Solarz was quick to join the ranks of reform Democrats when he returned from Brandeis and Columbia universities in the mid-1960s. In 1966, he managed the anti-war campaign of Mel Dubin, who ran for the 13th District congressional seat vacated by long-time Democratic Rep. Abraham Multer. But the organization backed state Assemblyman Bertram Podell, who won by a narrow margin.

Two years later, Solarz struck out on his own and won a seat in the Assembly. Though close to the reform movement, he maintained relatively good relations with party regulars in Albany.

In 1973, Solarz made what seemed to be a quixotic campaign as a reform candidate for Brooklyn borough president. But he did relatively well in the Democratic primary, running only 11

percentage points behind the winner, Sebastian Leone. Solarz carried the 13th Congressional District in the borough-wide primary.

The next year, Solarz got his opportunity to come to Congress. Podell had been indicted in 1973 on charges of conspiracy, bribery, perjury and conflict of interest. He protested his innocence and insisted on seeking renomination. The organization backed him, but Solarz put on a strong campaign and ousted the incumbent. Since then, Solarz has been virtually unchallenged.

**The District:** Created in 1944 to encompass the population growth in new residential areas of southern Brooklyn, the district is believed to have the largest percentage of Jewish residents of any in the country. People here have remained in their single-family homes, small apartment buildings and cooperatives while many Brooklynites have moved out to Long Island or New Jersey.

The district is still overwhelmingly white, and Democratic. It lost 6.1 percent of its people during the 1970s, and with Brooklyn due to lose a congressional district, the lines may be radically redrawn.

## Committees

**Budget**
Task Force: Transportation, Research and Development, and Capital Resources, chairman.

**Foreign Affairs** (8th of 21 Democrats)
Asian and Pacific Affairs, chairman; Africa.

## Elections

**1980 General**

| | |
|---|---|
| Stephen Solarz (D ) | 81,954 (80 %) |
| Harry DeMell (R ) | 19,536 (19 %) |

**1978 General**

| | |
|---|---|
| Stephen Solarz (D ) | 68,837 (81 %) |
| Max Carasso (R ) | 16,002 (19 %) |

**Previous Winning Percentages**

1976 (84 %)    1974 (82 %)

**District Vote For President**

| | 1980 | | 1976 | | 1972 |
|---|---|---|---|---|---|
| D | 55,370 (46 %) | D | 106,347 (70 %) | D | 97,152 (51 %) |
| R | 56,222 (47 %) | R | 44,177 (29 %) | R | 91,585 (48 %) |
| I | 6,615 (6 %) | | | | |

## Campaign Finance

| | Receipts | Receipts from PACs | Expenditures |
|---|---|---|---|
| **1980** | | | |
| Solarz (D ) | $239,472 | $26,374 (11 %) | $118,916 |
| **1978** | | | |
| Solarz (D ) | $101,872 | $15,600 (15 %) | $21,565 |

## Voting Studies

| | Presidental Support | | Party Unity | | Conservative Coalition | |
|---|---|---|---|---|---|---|
| Year | S | O | S | O | S | O |
| 1980 | 74 | 15 | 86 | 5 | 8 | 79 |
| 1979 | 77 | 17 | 91 | 5† | 3 | 91 |
| 1978 | 79 | 13 | 84 | 9 | 5 | 88 |
| 1977 | 81 | 16 | 92 | 6 | 3 | 96 |
| 1976 | 22 | 75 | 92 | 4 | 1 | 95 |
| 1975 | 38 | 54 | 82 | 8 | 11 | 79 |

S = Support          O = Opposition

† Not eligible for all recorded votes.

## Key Votes

**96th Congress**

| | |
|---|---|
| Weaken Carter oil profits tax (1979) | N |
| Reject hospital cost control plan (1979) | N |
| Implement Panama Canal Treaties (1979) | Y |
| Establish Department of Education (1979) | N |
| Approve Anti-busing Amendment (1979) | N |
| Guarantee Chrysler Corp. loans (1979) | Y |
| Approve military draft registration (1980) | Y |
| Aid Sandinista regime in Nicaragua (1980) | Y |
| Strengthen fair housing laws (1980) | Y |

**97th Congress**

| | |
|---|---|
| Reagan budget proposal (1981) | N |

## Interest Group Ratings

| Year | ADA | ACA | AFL-CIO | CCUS |
|---|---|---|---|---|
| 1980 | 78 | 20 | 89 | 52 |
| 1979 | 95 | 0 | 90 | 0 |
| 1978 | 80 | 13 | 85 | 18 |
| 1977 | 90 | 4 | 86 | 6 |
| 1976 | 95 | 0 | 87 | 0 |
| 1975 | 100 | 4 | 95 | 6 |

# 14 Fred Richmond (D)

**Of Brooklyn — Elected 1974**

**Born:** Nov. 15, 1923, Mattapan, Mass.
**Education:** Boston U., B.A. 1945.
**Military Career:** Navy, 1943-45.
**Profession:** Manufacturer.
**Family:** Divorced; one child.
**Religion:** Jewish.
**Political Career:** N.Y. City Council, 1973-75; unsuccessfully sought Democratic nomination for U.S. House, 1968.

**In Washington:** Styling himself an urbanist on the Agriculture Committee, Richmond has made a career of defending the food stamp program against its critics and helping to sell farm subsidies to big-city colleagues.

Relishing his role as a Brooklynite among farmers, he has been one of the committee's most visible members in recent years, traveling to Kansas to bail hay and arranging seminars between militant cattle ranchers and congressmen from San Francisco, Detroit and Buffalo. Sometimes he has chastised urban members for their ignorance of farm problems.

Sometimes also, his rhetoric has exceeded his influence. As chairman of the Agriculture Subcommittee on Nutrition in the 95th and 96th Congresses, he generally had to defer in strategy and debate to Thomas S. Foley, D-Wash., the full Agriculture chairman. Richmond's nervous intensity is not always effective on the House floor or in legislative bargaining.

Early in 1981, when Budget Director David Stockman proposed $3.8 billion in food stamp cuts over a two-year period, Richmond accused him of being "totally inexperienced," and "talking through his hat." Richmond said Stockman did not realize that drastic food stamp reductions would jeopardize the omnibus farm bill due at the same time.

Later, the Nutrition Subcommittee approved a modest package of food stamp cuts, far less than the administration wanted and the 1982 budget resolution called for. Richmond was frustrated as the full committee met afterward and made the cuts deeper.

Throughout his years on the Agriculture Committee, Richmond has tried to balance his role as consumer and food stamp advocate and his general sympathy with farm problems.

He staked out a position as consumer spokesman in 1975, his first year, when he proposed that half the members of a new beef promotion board

be consumer representatives. "Consumers must have a voice equal to agribusiness," he said, "anything less is an affront." The House did not agree, nor did it accept his amendment the following year to give consumers two of 20 places on a similar cotton promotion board.

But Richmond backed the emergency farm bill that reached the House floor in 1975, one raising wheat, cotton and corn price supports. When President Ford vetoed it, he voted to override the veto, against the position of most New York Democrats, and urged Congress to "stand up to the president." But the veto was sustained.

Taking over as chairman of the Nutrition Subcommittee in 1977, Richmond introduced his own legislation to repeal the purchase requirement for food stamp recipients. It was a step the Carter administration also favored, and it became law by the end of the year. But as a member of an ad hoc House subcommittee working on broader welfare issues, Richmond fought the administration's proposal to "cash out" food stamps and replace them with equivalent amounts of money. "How much blood, sweat and tears we put into a really fraud-free food stamp bill," he complained at one point. "I hate to throw it out." Congress never came close to throwing it out.

Through the 96th Congress, Richmond spent much of his time trying to keep the food stamp

---

**14th District: Northern Brooklyn — Williamsburg, Brooklyn Heights.** Population: 364,356 (22% decrease since 1970). Race: White 130,937 (36%), Black 180,545 (50%), Others 52,874 (15%). Spanish origin: 84,267 (23%).

program in business as it exceeded all the spending limits previously placed on it. Conservative House members repeatedly took the opportunity to rail against waste in the program, but most of them continued to vote for the money.

While fighting those battles, Richmond has maintained a second legislative interest as a patron of the arts. Richmond's personal art and antique collection is worth a small fortune, and he has consistently worked for higher federal subsidies to museums and creative artists. Early in his House career he proposed an income tax checkoff for support of the arts, and in 1981 he started a Congressional Arts Caucus, aimed at saving the $175 million budget for the National Endowment for the Arts from proposed Reagan-Stockman budget cuts. "Americans are 100 percent behind the arts," he insisted. "Every dollar you spend on arts generates $5 more."

**At Home:** Preparing to seek a third term in 1978, Richmond seemed as secure as anyone in the House, needing only to go through the motions of a campaign to win re-election.

It turned out to be much more complicated than that. In early 1978, he was arrested in Washington D. C. and charged with soliciting sex from a teen-aged male youth. There was talk that his political career had ended. But prosecution of the case was dropped when Richmond, as a first offender, was allowed to accept psychiatric treatment. Top New York City politicians rallied around him. And Richmond wrote to his constituents asking for their "compassion and understanding at this extremely difficult time." He had a strong primary challenge that September from Bernard Gifford, a black educator who was a former deputy chancellor of the New York City school system. Gifford insisted he was not campaigning on the morals issue, but did not repudiate a statement by Manhattan Borough President Percy Sutton, a Gifford supporter, calling Richmond an "admitted child molester."

In a contest that ultimately attracted national attention, Richmond drew 50 percent of the vote to Gifford's 32 percent. The challenger was unable to develop any issue other than Richmond's personal controversy, and Richmond had built substantial good will among his constituents, white and black.

The incumbent's most useful — and controversial —tool was the Richmond Foundation, his personal philanthropic organization. It dispenses contributions to churches, athletic associations, and YMCAs, many of them in his congressional district. Critics have always charged that the wealthy Richmond is buying the district, but his foundation has been a public relations success.

Having made a personal fortune in a variety of manufacturing ventures, Richmond became a public figure as president of the Greater New York Urban League (1959-64) and New York City Human Rights Commissioner (1964-70).

Identifying himself with the reform wing of the Democratic Party, Richmond decided in 1968 to challenge U.S. Rep. John Rooney, a fixture of the Brooklyn Democratic organization, for renomination. While he made a strong run, he could not compete with the ability of the machine to deliver the vote for the aging Rooney. Richmond then made his peace with the organization, and it sponsored him for a vacant City Council seat in 1973. When Rooney retired in 1974, the organization backed Richmond for the seat, and he won easily.

**The District:** Richmond's district is an unusual mixture of upper-income professionals, poor blacks, and a variety of ethnic groups. Many of the whites live in newly-renovated brownstones in Brooklyn Heights and Park Slope, and generally support Richmond's liberal politics.

The district lines were redrawn in 1974 because of a court decision that certain New York City districts were subject to the scrutiny of the Justice Department for racial fairness. The outcome was that the 14th District went from 23.2 percent black to 46.4 percent black, theoretically giving a black candidate a good chance to win it. But low turnout and disunity among blacks, and Richmond's cultivation of black voters, have kept the district in white hands.

The district lost over 100,000 people between 1970 and 1980 and needs to gain about 150,000 to come up to the state norm. But neighboring districts also need to gain population and Brooklyn is scheduled to lose one seat.

# Committees

**Agriculture** (8th of 24 Democrats)
Domestic Marketing, Consumer Relations, and Nutrition, Chairman; Conservation, Credit, and Rural Development; Department Operations, Research, and Foreign Agriculture.

**Small Business** (7th of 23 Democrats)
General Obersight; SBA and SBIC Authority, Minority Enterprise and General Small Business Problems.

**Joint Economic**
International Trade, Finance and Security Economics; Trade, Productivity and Economic Growth.

# Elections

**1980 General**

| | |
|---|---|
| Fred Richmond (D ) | 45,029 (76 %) |
| Christopher Lovell (R ) | 8,257 (14 %) |
| Moses Harris (I ) | 4,151 (7 %) |

**1980 Primary**

| | |
|---|---|
| Fred Richmond (D ) | 17,474 (74 %) |
| Moses Harris (D ) | 6,023 (26 %) |

**1978 General**

| | |
|---|---|
| Fred Richmond (D ) | 31,339 (77 %) |
| Arthur Bramwell (R ) | 7,516 (18 %) |

**Previous Winning Percentages**

1976 (85 %)    1974 (71 %)

**District Vote For President**

| | 1980 | | 1976 | | 1972 |
|---|---|---|---|---|---|
| D | 54,886 (74 %) | D | 63,386 (78 %) | D | 45,673 (48 %) |
| R | 14,559 (20 %) | R | 17,735 (22 %) | R | 50,225 (52 %) |
| I | 3,148 (4 %) | | | | |

# Campaign Finance

| | Receipts | Receipts from PACs | Expenditures |
|---|---|---|---|
| **1980** | | | |
| Richmond (D ) | $173,549 | $46,295 (27 %) | $199,346 |
| Lovell (R ) | $4,040 | — (0 %) | $1,622 |

| | | | |
|---|---|---|---|
| **1978** | | | |
| Richmond (D ) | $437,949 | $30,850 (7 %) | $419,663 |

# Voting Studies

| | Presidential Support | | Party Unity | | Conservative Coalition | |
|---|---|---|---|---|---|---|
| Year | S | O | S | O | S | O |
| 1980 | 62 | 21 | 80 | 3 | 1 | 81 |
| 1979 | 74 | 17 | 83 | 4 | 2 | 84 |
| 1978 | 63 | 14 | 80 | 4 | 2 | 80 |
| 1977 | 73 | 16 | 87 | 4 | 3 | 90 |
| 1976 | 18 | 73 | 89 | 2 | 3 | 90 |
| 1975 | 28 | 69 | 91 | 6 | 4 | 91 |

S = Support          O = Opposition

# Key Votes

**96th Congress**

| | |
|---|---|
| Weaken Carter oil profits tax (1979) | N |
| Reject hospital cost control plan (1979) | N |
| Implement Panama Canal Treaties (1979) | Y |
| Establish Department of Education (1979) | N |
| Approve Anti-busing Amendment (1979) | N |
| Guarantee Chrysler Corp. loans (1979) | ? |
| Approve military draft registration (1980) | N |
| Aid Sandinista regime in Nicaragua (1980) | Y |
| Strengthen fair housing laws (1980) | Y |

**97th Congress**

| | |
|---|---|
| Reagan budget proposal (1981) | N |

# Interest Group Ratings

| Year | ADA | ACA | AFL-CIO | CCUS |
|---|---|---|---|---|
| 1980 | 94 | 5 | 88 | 44 |
| 1979 | 95 | 4 | 100 | 6 |
| 1978 | 95 | 5 | 95 | 25 |
| 1977 | 95 | 0 | 91 | 6 |
| 1976 | 95 | 0 | 87 | 0 |
| 1975 | 95 | 11 | 95 | 6 |

# 15 Leo C. Zeferetti (D)

**Of Brooklyn — Elected 1974**

**Born:** July 15, 1927, Brooklyn, N.Y.
**Education:** Attended Bernard M. Baruch College of the City U. of N.Y., 1966-68. Attended N.Y.U., 1968.
**Military Career:** Navy, 1944-46.
**Profession:** Corrections officer.
**Family:** Wife, Barbara Schiebel; two children.
**Religion:** Roman Catholic.
**Political Career:** No previous office.

**In Washington:** A hard-line corrections officer elected with Conservative Party support in 1974, Zeferetti has turned out to be a conventional bread-and-butter liberal on most economic issues, loyal enough to party leaders to be trusted with a sensitive spot on the Rules Committee. He is closer in style to the old machine politics than to the ethnic conservative populism he initially seemed to reflect.

He began his congressional career as a member of the Education and Labor Committee and the Merchant Marine and Fisheries Committee. On Education and Labor, he voted with the panel's solid pro-union majority, especially on minimum wage issues affecting his working-class district. Along with most Democrats, he opposed lowering wage standards for those who regularly get tips, such as waiters and doormen. On Merchant Marine, he was close to the maritime unions whose influence over the panel has always been great.

Zeferetti's conservatism has been more apparent in legislation dealing with crime and other social issues. He voted for an anti-busing amendment to the Constitution in 1979, one of only two New York City Democrats to do so. He has also been skeptical about most proposals for congressional reform. When the overwhelming majority of his 1974 class backed public financing for congressional campaigns, Zeferetti was on the other side, reflecting his Brooklyn organization outlook rather than his House Democratic generation.

When Speaker O'Neill needed a Democrat to vote the party line on the Rules Committee in 1979, Zeferetti got the job, taking the "New York seat" on Rules that James J. Delaney had just vacated by retirement. Zeferetti has played the role expected of him, opposing the leadership on a key bill only once. That was on a 1980 budget reconciliation measure attempting to make cuts to keep the federal deficit down. Zeferetti and two of his colleagues thwarted the leadership by voting to allow an amendment on the floor that would permit twice-yearly cost-of-living increases for federal retirees.

**At Home:** Starting out as a New York prison guard, Zeferetti was elected president of the New York City Correction Officers Benevolent Association, and built a political base from that position. He also served on the New York State Crime Control Planning Board, appointed by Gov. Nelson A. Rockefeller, and as a representative to President Nixon's Conference on Correction.

In 1974, the 15th district opened up when Democratic Rep. Hugh L. Carey decided to run for governor. Zeferetti entered the race and won the primary narrowly and the election comfortably. However, he has not been able to consolidate himself in his district. He has had two problems: Republicans and reform Democrats.

In 1974, he beat anti-machine challenger Arthur Paone by only 62 votes in the Democratic primary. Two years later, Zeferetti won the Democratic primary over divided opposition with 47 percent of the vote. He has had reform-minded primary opposition in every election year, although he has not been seriously threatened since 1976.

In 1980, the Republicans and Conservatives gave Zeferetti a scare. The Conservative Party had endorsed him in all of his previous elections,

---

**15th District: Southwestern Brooklyn — Bay Ridge.** Population: 416,620 (11% decrease since 1970). Race: White 335,872 (81%), Black 26,420 (6%), Asian and Pacific Islander 11,726 (3%), Others 42,601 (10%). Spanish origin: 80,607 (19%).

but was dissatisfied with his voting record and joined with the Republicans in backing Paul Atanasio, a young Brooklyn law clerk who said Zeferetti had not taken a hawkish enough line on defense spending. Starting from far behind, the Republican closed fast toward the end of October and came within 2,200 votes, far closer than Brooklyn Democrats had expected.

**The District:** This area of southern Brooklyn contains one of the few significant Republican pockets left in New York City. Republicans repre-

sent the area on the City Council and in the state Senate.

Much of the 15th District is populated by middle-income families of Italian and Irish descent, living in one- and two-family homes. While still registered Democrats, they are conservative on social issues and many of them vote Republican in national elections.

The district needs to make up a deficit of about 100,000 people to come up to the required population average.

## Committees

**Rules** (6th of 11 Democrats)
  Legislative Process.

**Select Narcotics Abuse and Control,** Chairman

## Elections

**1980 General**

| | |
|---|---|
| Leo Zeferetti (D ) | 49,684 (50 %) |
| Paul Atanasio (R ) | 46,467 (47 %) |

**1980 Primary**

| | |
|---|---|
| Leo Zeferetti (D ) | 16,961 (71 %) |
| Peter McNeill (D ) | 6,811 (29 %) |

**1978 General**

| | |
|---|---|
| Leo Zeferetti (D ) | 49,272 (68 %) |
| Robert Whelan (R ) | 20,508 (28 %) |

**Previous Winning Percentages**

1976 (63 %)     1974 (59 %)

**District Vote For President**

| | 1980 | | 1976 | | 1972 |
|---|---|---|---|---|---|
| **D** | 46,510 (42 %) | **D** | 62,421 (50 %) | **D** | 51,107 (32 %) |
| **R** | 56,045 (51 %) | **R** | 62,787 (50 %) | **R** | 107,188 (68 %) |
| **I** | 5,613 (5 %) | | | | |

## Campaign Finance

| | Receipts | Receipts from PACs | Expenditures |
|---|---|---|---|
| **1980** | | | |
| Zeferetti (D ) | $167,716 | $83,462 (50 %) | $185,458 |
| Atanasio (R ) | $164,147 | $68,967 (42 %) | $161,803 |
| **1978** | | | |
| Zeferetti (D ) | $86,367 | $43,618 (51%) | $67,960 |
| Whelan (R ) | $16,803 | — (0 %) | $15,028 |

## Voting Studies

| | Presidental Support | | Party Unity | | Conservative Coalition | |
|---|---|---|---|---|---|---|
| Year | S | O | S | O | S | O |
| 1980 | 58 | 26 | 81 | 11 | 28 | 60 |
| 1979 | 52 | 31 | 63 | 26 | 48 | 40 |
| 1978 | 46 | 34 | 57 | 32 | 48 | 42 |
| 1977 | 66 | 16 | 61 | 26 | 39 | 47 |
| 1976 | 25 | 65 | 72 | 13 | 31 | 55 |
| 1975 | 26 | 69 | 76 | 19 | 34 | 62 |

S = Support          O = Opposition

## Key Votes

**96th Congress**

| | |
|---|---|
| Weaken Carter oil profits tax (1979) | N |
| Reject hospital cost control plan (1979) | N |
| Implement Panama Canal Treaties (1979) | Y |
| Establish Department of Education (1979) | N |
| Approve Anti-busing Amendment (1979) | Y |
| Guarantee Chrysler Corp. loans (1979) | Y |
| Approve military draft registration (1980) | Y |
| Aid Sandinista regime in Nicaragua (1980) | N |
| Strengthen fair housing laws (1980) | Y |

**97th Congress**

| | |
|---|---|
| Reagan budget proposal (1981) | N |

## Interest Group Ratings

| Year | ADA | ACA | AFL-CIO | CCUS |
|---|---|---|---|---|
| 1980 | 44 | 14 | 88 | 63 |
| 1979 | 37 | 15 | 88 | 35 |
| 1978 | 35 | 36 | 80 | 25 |
| 1977 | 45 | 19 | 95 | 18 |
| 1976 | 55 | 15 | 91 | 6 |
| 1975 | 47 | 37 | 91 | 24 |

# 16 Charles E. Schumer (D)

**Of Brooklyn — Elected 1980**

**Born:** Nov. 23, 1950, Brooklyn, N.Y.
**Education:** Harvard Univ., B.A. 1971, LL.B. 1974.
**Profession:** Lawyer.
**Family:** Wife, Iris Weinshall.
**Religion:** Jewish.
**Political Career:** N.Y. Assembly, 1975-81.

**The Member:** When Democratic Rep. Elizabeth Holtzman announced her bid for the Senate, she endorsed Schumer as her successor. Schumer is a constituency-oriented liberal who has taken particular interest in housing issues.

On the Banking Committee in 1981, he fought against a proposal that would have prevented cities with rent control laws from getting money for new housing construction or major rehabilitation. Schumer also spoke for higher public housing subsidies and for anti-redlining legislation that Holtzman had pushed.

In the New York Assembly, Schumer made personal service an all-consuming passion, keeping in constant touch with the needs of his constituency. "My district has been my life," Schumer has been quoted as saying.

Before his election to the state Legislature in 1974, Schumer worked for another Democratic assemblyman, Stephen J. Solarz. Now he has joined Solarz, a four-term House veteran, in the Brooklyn congressional delegation.

To win his House seat, Schumer had to defeat two well-known members of the New York City Council in the Democratic primary. At first it was considered a close race, but Schumer's well-organized campaign, plus Holtzman's backing gave him almost 60 percent of the vote.

**The District:** Located in central and southern Brooklyn, the 16th has been a Democratic bastion since 1922, when it sent Emanuel Celler to the House. He stayed fifty years, rising to become chairman of the House Judiciary Committee before losing the Democratic nomination to Holtzman in 1972. The district is about evenly divided between blacks and whites, with blacks having moved heavily into the northern part over the past decade. The white population is largely Jewish.

## Committees

**Banking, Finance and Urban Affairs** (21st of 25 Democrats)
Economic Stabilization; Financial Institutions Supervision, Regulation and Insurance; Housing and Community Development.

**Post Office and Civil Service** (11th of 15 Democrats)
Human Resources; Postal Personnel and Modernization.

## Elections

**1980 General**

| | |
|---|---|
| Charles Schumer (D ) | 67,343 (78 %) |
| Theodore Silverman (R ) | 17,050 (20 %) |

**1980 Primary**

| | |
|---|---|
| Charles Schumer (D ) | 23,260 (59 %) |
| Susan Alter (D ) | 7,385 (19 %) |
| Theodore Silverman (D ) | 6,041 (15 %) |
| Edward Hayes (D ) | 2,842 (7 %) |

**District Vote For President**

| | 1980 | | 1976 | | 1972 |
|---|---|---|---|---|---|
| D | 55,906 (55 %) | D | 88,533 (71 %) | D | 86,597 (54 %) |
| R | 39,496 (39 %) | R | 35,063 (28 %) | R | 74,408 (46 %) |
| I | 5,090 (5 %) | | | | |

## Campaign Finance

| | Receipts | Receipts from PACs | Expenditures |
|---|---|---|---|
| **1980** | | | |
| Schumer (D ) | $224,358 | $47,916 (21 %) | $199,805 |
| Silverman (R ) | $25,395 | $3,000 (12 %) | $23,268 |

## Key Vote

**97th Congress**

| | |
|---|---|
| Reagan budget proposal (1981) | N |

---

**16th District: Central and southern Brooklyn — Flatbush.** Population: 438,615 (6% decrease since 1970). Race: White 191,552 (44%), Black 221,430 (50%), Others 25,633 (6%). Spanish origin: 35,827 (8%).

# 17   Guy V. Molinari (R)

### Of Staten Island — Elected 1980

**Born:** Nov. 23, 1928, New York, N.Y.
**Education:** Wagner College, B.A. 1949; N. Y. U.,
LL.B. 1951.
**Military Career:** Marine Corps, 1951-53.
**Profession:** Lawyer.
**Family:** Wife, Marguerite Wing; one child.
**Religion:** Roman Catholic.
**Political Career:** N.Y. Assembly, 1975-81.

**The Member:** After serving in Congress less than three months, Molinari said he might quit to accept the GOP nomination for a Staten Island judgeship. The judgeship offered Molinari a higher salary, more job security and more influence over local patronge.

His deliberations attracted the attention of Republican leaders, including Vice President Bush. They urged Molinari to stay in Washington, reminding him that Democrats might win the 17th if he resigned. While accompanying President Reagan to New York in March, Molinari announced he would stay in Congress.

In May, Molinari met with Reagan and expressed concern that federal budget cuts would force the closing of a Staten Island public hospital. Reagan agreed to provide federal money to keep the hospital open during its transition from public to private ownership. After that meeting, Molinari pledged to vote for Reagan's budget.

In the state Assembly, Molinari led the fight to stop New York City from using large portions of Staten Island as a garbage disposal area, especially for chemical wastes. He also took a leading role in opposing reactivation of a liquefied natural gas facility on the island.

With the backing of the Conservative Party as well as GOP support, Molinari defeated Democratic Rep. John M. Murphy, who was weakened by his involvement in the FBI's Abscam investigation.

**The District:** Conservative Staten Island, with its population of middle-income homeowners, many of Italian and Irish descent, makes up two-thirds of the district. The other third consists of Lower Manhattan, a heavily Democratic area with a diverse mixture of Jews, Hispanics, Italian-Americans, and others. It includes Greenwich Village and Soho. Staten Island leans Republican, but the strong Democratic vote in Manhattan allowed Murphy to win general elections easily before his involvement in Abscam.

## Committees

**Public Works and Transportation** (16th of 19 Republicans)
Investigations and Oversight; Surface Transportation; Water Resources.

**Small Business** (16th of 17 Republicans)

## Elections

**1980 General**

| | |
|---|---|
| Guy Molinari (R ) | 69,573 (48 %) |
| John Murphy (D ) | 50,954 (35 %) |
| Mary Codd (L ) | 25,118 (17 %) |

**District Vote For President**

| | 1980 | | 1976 | | 1972 |
|---|---|---|---|---|---|
| D | 66,913 (42 %) | D | 83,302 (54 %) | D | 64,601 (38 %) |
| R | 78,115 (49 %) | R | 68,724 (45 %) | R | 105,478 (62 %) |
| I | 11,095 (7 %) | | | | |

## Campaign Finance

| | | Receipts | |
|---|---|---|---|
| | Receipts | from PACs | Expenditures |
| **1980** | | | |
| Molinari (R ) | $153,451 | $44,220 (29 %) | $148,993 |
| Murphy (D ) | $286,120 | $150,300 (53 %) | $290,108 |

## Key Vote

**97th Congress**

| | |
|---|---|
| Reagan budget proposal (1981) | Y |

---

**17th District: Staten Island, southern Manhattan.** Population: 529,299 (13% increase since 1970). Race: White 415,135 (78%), Black 38,172 (7%), Asian and Pacific Islander 47,993 (9%), Others 27,999 (5%). Spanish origin: 59,165 (11%).

# 18 S. William Green (R)

**Of Manhattan — Elected 1978**

**Born:** Oct. 16, 1929, New York, N.Y.
**Education:** Harvard College, B.A. 1950; Harvard
  Law School, J.D. 1953.
**Military Career:** Army, 1953-55.
**Profession:** Lawyer.
**Family:** Wife, Patricia Freiberg; two children.
**Religion:** Jewish.
**Political Career:** N.Y. Assembly, 1965-69.

**In Washington:** Most House Republicans
who do what Green has done — vote with the
Democrats a majority of the time, support John
Anderson for the GOP presidential nomination,
and fight the Reagan plank on women's rights at
the national convention — could expect a cold
reception from party colleagues on their return to
Washington for a new term.

But Green, as he began his second full term,
was handed a plum rather than a punishment. He
not only was placed on the Appropriations Committee, but was made ranking GOP member on its
Housing Subcommittee, the most junior Republican in the entire House to have such a position.

Part of the reason was his background. Green
spent seven years as HUD's regional administrator in New York, responsible for more than 80,000
housing units in that state alone. He is a housing
specialist.

But equally important were Green's temperament, and the politics of his district. Quiet and
agreeable, he has had a knack for casting un-
Republican votes without seeming defiant or rebellious, the way Anderson always did. And Republican leaders take Green's constituency into
account when judging him; liberal votes that
would be treasonous in a Midwesterner are written off in Green's case as simply "voting
Manhattan."

Green spent his first three years in the House
on the Banking Committee, where he arrived in
1978 just in time to participate in the debate over
a $1.6 bllion federal loan guarantee for his home
city. That particular issue has been in the background since then, but Green found plenty to do
as a housing specialist on the subcommittees rewriting the nation's housing programs in 1979 and
1980.

Green centered his concern on the dwindling
amount of rental housing available for low- and
middle-income people. He introduced a rental
housing assistance act, which provided for more

construction of rental units and rehabilitation of
older buildings, and assistance to middle-income
families as well as the poor. Some of the middle-
income provisions were incorporated in the overall housing authorization in 1980, although they
did not survive conference with the Senate.

Green also lobbied to provide subsidies to
potentially troubled state- or city-financed housing projects, and won committee approval for his
amendment to include large apartment buildings
within the scope of a Solar Bank bill, designed to
encourage use of solar heating equipment and
energy conservation.

**At Home:** Green burst into politics in February, 1978, by upsetting a legendary Manhattan
politician — Bella S. Abzug.

The confrontation between the two resulted
from the resignation of Democratic Rep. Edward
I. Koch after his election as Mayor of New York
City in 1977. That left his seat vacant and forced
a special election. Abzug, the outspoken liberal
and feminist who had previously represented
Manhattan's West Side, had moved to the East
Side for a comeback after losing bids for the U.S.
Senate and the New York mayoralty.

Green won partly on an anti-Abzug vote, but
partly because he was able to spend huge sums of
money on the campaign. He was little known to

**18th District: Manhattan — East
Side.** Population: 455,860 (3% decrease since
1970). Race: White 395,147 (87%), Black
20,948 (5%), Asian and Pacific Islander 16,055
(4%), Others 23,710 (5%). Spanish origin:
48,884 (11%).

the average voter, despite an earlier career in the state Assembly, but he is an heir to the Grand Union supermarket fortune. He invested $150,000 in radio and television commercials, mass mailings and bus ads that made him familiar very quickly.

In November, 1978, Green again defeated a strong Democratic candidate with heavy financing. His contest against Democrat Carter Burden, another millionaire, was the most expensive congressional contest in the nation. Burden spent $1.1 million; Green was far behind with a still healthy $580,000.

Before 1978, Green's professional career was exclusively in housing and urban finance. He was chief counsel to the New York Legislative Committee on Housing and Urban Development from

1961 to 1964. Then he spent four years in the New York Legislature before switching to HUD in 1970.

**The District:** Much written-about as Manhattan's "Silk Stocking District," the 18th takes in the plush town houses and apartment buildings of the affluent East Side. Originally it elected Republicans to the House, reflecting its plutocratic origins and anti-New Deal sentiments.

However, over the years the wealthy East Siders have become more liberal and the district has expanded to take in poorer Democratic areas of the lower East Side. In 1968, it went Democratic for the first time since 1936, electing Koch to the first of five terms. In 1972, it gave a healthy margin of 31,000 votes to George McGovern for president.

## Committees

**Appropriations** (18th of 22 Republicans)
District of Columbia; HUD—Independent Agencies.

## Elections

**1980 General**

| | |
|---|---|
| William Green (R ) | 91,341 (57 %) |
| Mark Green (D ) | 68,786 (43 %) |

**1978 General**

| | |
|---|---|
| William Green (R ) | 60,867 (53 %) |
| Carter Burden (D ) | 53,434 (47 %) |

**Previous Winning Percentages**

1978* (50 %)

* Special election.

**District Vote For President**

| | 1980 | | 1976 | | 1972 |
|---|---|---|---|---|---|
| D | 85,211 (50 %) | D | 108,943 (63 %) | D | 114,237 (58 %) |
| R | 63,084 (37 %) | R | 63,401 (37 %) | R | 82,529 (42 %) |
| I | 19,272 (11 %) | | | | |

## Campaign Finance

| | Receipts | Receipts from PACs | Expenditures |
|---|---|---|---|
| **1980** | | | |
| W. Green (R ) | $308,723 | $103,564 (34 %) | $315,055 |
| M. Green (D ) | $298,441 | $48,455 (16 %) | $293,020 |
| **1978** | | | |
| W. Green (R ) | $572,814 | $35,475 (6 %) | $580,463 |
| Burden (D ) | $1,139,188 | $8,200 (1 %) | $1,136,112 |

## Voting Studies

| | Presidential Support | | Party Unity | | Conservative Coalition | |
|---|---|---|---|---|---|---|
| Year | S | O | S | O | S | O |
| 1980 | 68 | 28 | 30 | 67 | 15 | 81 |
| 1979 | 64 | 33 | 38 | 60 | 20 | 78 |
| 1978 | 74 | 25† | 30 | 66† | 16 | 77† |

†Not eligible for all recorded votes.

S = Support      O = Opposition

## Key Votes

**96th Congress**

| | |
|---|---|
| Weaken Carter oil profits tax (1979) | Y |
| Reject hospital cost control plan (1979) | N |
| Implement Panama Canal Treaties (1979) | Y |
| Establish Department of Education (1979) | N |
| Approve Anti-busing Amendment (1979) | N |
| Guarantee Chrysler Corp. loans (1979) | N |
| Approve military draft registration (1980) | N |
| Aid Sandinista regime in Nicaragua (1980) | Y |
| Strengthen fair housing laws (1980) | Y |

**97th Congress**

| | |
|---|---|
| Reagan budget proposal (1981) | Y |

## Interest Group Ratings

| Year | ADA | ACA | AFL-CIO | CCUS |
|---|---|---|---|---|
| 1980 | 94 | 29 | 58 | 66 |
| 1979 | 68 | 44 | 55 | 61 |
| 1978 | 58 | 12 | 61 | 44 |

# 19 Charles B. Rangel (D)

**Of New York — Elected 1970**

**Born:** June 11, 1930, New York, N.Y.
**Education:** N.Y.U. School of Commerce, B.S.
 1957; St. John's School of Law, LL.B. 1960.
**Military Career:** Army, 1948-52.
**Profession:** Lawyer.
**Family:** Wife, Alma Carter; two children.
**Religion:** Roman Catholic.
**Political Career:** N.Y. Assembly, 1967-71; un-
 successfully sought Democratic nomination
 for N.Y. City Council president, 1969.

**In Washington:** Rangel is widely regarded as the least ideological of the senior black members of Congress, the one most likely to choose modest but tangible help for his constituents over the opportunity to express pure outrage. He has been closer to House leaders than any other member of the Congressional Black Caucus, and he may be its most effective lobbyist.

His style came out clearly in the 96th Congress, when Rangel, as chairman of the Ways and Means Health Subcommittee, kept his distance from Sen. Edward M. Kennedy's health insurance program. Rangel is an outspoken advocate of national health insurance, and the Kennedy plan was the most ambitious scheme available, but Rangel supported President Carter's more modest proposal. He eventually backed Carter over Kennedy for the Democratic presidential nomination, touring the streets of Harlem with the president before the New York primary.

Neither Carter nor Kennedy won the presidency, and national health insurance made no progress, but Rangel got what he wanted — help for two financially troubled New York City hospitals. The money was hidden deep in the federal budget, but it was enough for Rangel to keep up his support for Carter through the election year.

Hospitals were an all-consuming issue for Rangel during his term as Health Subcommittee chairman in the 96th Congress. Early in 1979, the panel approved Carter's hospital cost control bill. Although Rangel was skeptical about it, he gave the White House his support, but not until the bill was amended in subcommittee to make it more difficult for hospitals to turn away impoverished patients for financial reasons.

Meanwhile, Rangel was fighting a long-running battle to keep hospitals open in poverty areas. He held a hearing on the issue and persuaded Ways and Means to ask for $100 million in the 1981 budget for aid to distressed hospitals. When New York Mayor Edward Koch announced plans to close Sydenham Hospital in West Harlem, Rangel said Koch was "kicking poor folks around" to build middle-class political support.

Rangel has over the years made a variety of critical comments about various Democratic leaders, but has nearly always left the door open to negotiation and compromise. He was wary of President Carter in the beginning and furious when Carter fired Health, Education and Welfare Secretary Joseph Califano, with whom Rangel had worked closely. Rangel once disputed arguments that blacks needed more access to Carter. "Access has never been one of my priorities," he said. "We can cuss out the president over here as easily as we can in person."

Rangel has had an important and enduring political relationship, however, with Speaker O'Neill, a man who shares his taste for cigars and loud laughter and his preference for political infighting rather than legislative detail.

In theory, Rangel stresses the need for the Black Caucus to stay independent. "The caucus can't afford the luxury of compassion and sympathy to the Speaker because he's a friend," Rangel said in 1977. In practice, however, he has usually been willing to help O'Neill out in a crisis, and the Speaker has done what he can for Rangel. In 1978,

---

**19th District: Manhattan — Harlem.**
Population: 371,614 (20% decrease since 1970). Race: White 114,831 (31%), Black 201,434 (54%), Others 55,349 (15%). Spanish origin: 85,404 (23%).

Rangel reversed himself at the last minute and agreed to sign the conference report providing for natural gas deregulation — a top priority for both O'Neill and Carter — helping to end a stalemate that nearly killed the legislation.

Rangel joined the Ways and Means Committee in 1975 when its "New York seat" became vacant. He had to leave Judiciary, where he had lobbied for revision of the grand jury system and where he wanted to remain. The same year he became Black Caucus chairman for the 94th Congress. In that role Rangel sought to stress the possibilities for legislative trading and compromise. "We don't have to walk away from people because we don't agree with them," he once said. "We can't win fights with just 16 black votes, but we will be able to use the help to add to the 16."

On one occasion during this period, Rangel persuaded Black Caucus members to vote as a bloc against removing tobacco from the "Food for Peace" program, despite their personal feelings on the issue. The next day, members of the Virginia, North Carolina and Kentucky delegations helped provide the votes needed to approve an amendment increasing anti-recession aid to cities.

**At Home:** In 1970, Rangel gave the coup de grace to the fading political career of Harlem's flamboyant Rep. Adam Clayton Powell Jr. Accusing Powell of being an absentee, part-time representative, and promising to work full-time for his constituents, Rangel upset Powell in the Democratic primary.

Rangel had the backing of a new coalition of black politicians who were tired of Powell's behavior and wanted to elect someone who could work for tangible benefits for blacks and New York.

A high school dropout, Rangel joined the Army and fought in the Korean War. After military service, he returned to Manhattan and entered college in his mid-twenties. He got his law degree in 1960, and the next year won an appointment as assistant U.S. attorney for the Southern District of New York.

In 1966, Rangel won a seat in the New York state Assembly. Three years later, he made a quixotic bid for city-wide office by running for City Council president in the Democratic primary on a ticket headed by U.S. Rep. James Scheuer.

Rangel ran last in a field of six, but received publicity in black areas as the only city-wide black candidate.

The following year, Rangel decided to challenge Powell. The incumbent's old coalition, built around the Abyssinian Baptist Church, of which he was pastor, and the Alfred E. Isaacs Democratic Club, was no longer enough to carry the burden of his political reputation.

The veteran Democrat had been "excluded" from the 90th Congress on charges that he had misused committee funds for parties and travel to the Caribbean. The Supreme Court later ruled the exclusion unconstitutional, and Powell was seen initially as a martyr by constituents. But when he took a seat in the 91st Congress and then spent most of the following year out of the country, the situation changed.

Despite a split in Powell's opposition — there were four candidates in all — Rangel's new coalition prevailed. It was made up of younger black leaders, liberal whites and a rising power in the black community, Percy Sutton, owner of the *Amsterdam News* and later borough president of Manhattan.

Rangel has no electoral problems at home. Often he gets both the Republican and Democratic nominations.

**The District:** Created in 1944 as New York's first black district, the 19th has been represented by only two men since then — Powell and Rangel. Powell was on the New York City Council when the district was drawn up, and he was the assumed beneficiary of the new district lines.

As originally created, the district was nearly all black. But as New York has lost seats over the years, the 19th has had to expand and now takes in a large number of whites on Manhattan's West Side. When the lines were drawn in 1970, the district was only 58.7 percent black. The 1980 census figures indicate the district will have to gain about 150,000 additional constituents to come up to the state average. With few blacks in surrounding areas, the Legislature may be hard put to create a safe black district. Nevertheless, it will probably give top priority to saving a seat for Rangel, partly to preserve black representation and partly because of his influence in the House.

## Committees

**Select Narcotics Abuse and Control** (3rd of 11 Democrats)

**Ways and Means** (4th of 23 Democrats)
    Oversight, chairman; Health.

## Elections

**1980 General**

Charles Rangel (D )                    84,062 (96 %)

**1978 General**

Charles Rangel (D )                    59,731 (96 %)

**Previous Winning Percentages**

1976 (97 %)    1974 (97 %)    1972 (96 %)    1970 (87 %)

**District Vote For President**

| | 1980 | | 1976 | | 1972 |
|---|---|---|---|---|---|
| D | 87,020 (81 %) | D | 99,184 (86 %) | D | 105,600 (81 %) |
| R | 12,816 (12 %) | R | 14,661 (13 %) | R | 24,282 (19 %) |
| I | 5,565 (5 %) | | | | |

## Campaign Finance

| | Receipts | Receipts from PACs | Expenditures |
|---|---|---|---|
| **1980** | | | |
| Rangel (D ) | $95,873 | $55,450 (58 %) | $90,344 |
| **1978** | | | |
| Rangel (D ) | $52,601 | $25,350 (48 %) | $43,246 |

## Voting Studies

| | Presidential Support | | Party Unity | | Conservative Coalition | |
|---|---|---|---|---|---|---|
| Year | S | O | S | O | S | O |
| 1980 | 68 | 21 | 85 | 4 | 2 | 84 |

| | | | | | |
|---|---|---|---|---|---|
| 1979 | 76 | 18 | 86 | 4 | 3 | 87 |
| 1978 | 79 | 12 | 84 | 3 | 5 | 80 |
| 1977 | 70 | 24 | 87 | 4 | 2 | 88 |
| 1976 | 24 | 75 | 85 | 3 | 6 | 87 |
| 1975 | 35 | 56 | 84 | 2 | 5 | 85 |
| 1974 (Ford) | 37 | 56 | | | | |
| 1974 | 26 | 66 | 85 | 7 | 1 | 90 |
| 1973 | 27 | 65 | 88 | 6 | 2 | 90 |
| 1972 | 49 | 46 | 84 | 3 | 2 | 90 |
| 1971 | 18 | 63 | 79 | 7 | 1 | 81 |

S = Support          O = Opposition

## Key Votes

**96th Congress**

| | |
|---|---|
| Weaken Carter oil profits tax (1979) | ? |
| Reject hospital cost control plan (1979) | N |
| Implement Panama Canal Treaties (1979) | Y |
| Establish Department of Education (1979) | N |
| Approve Anti-busing Amendment (1979) | N |
| Guarantee Chrysler Corp. loans (1979) | Y |
| Approve military draft registration (1980) | N |
| Aid Sandinista regime in Nicaragua (1980) | # |
| Strengthen fair housing laws (1980) | Y |

**97th Congress**

| | |
|---|---|
| Reagan budget proposal (1981) | N |

## Interest Group Ratings

| Year | ADA | ACA | AFL-CIO | CCUS |
|---|---|---|---|---|
| 1980 | 78 | 14 | 95 | 56 |
| 1979 | 84 | 0 | 100 | 7 |
| 1978 | 80 | 8 | 90 | 18 |
| 1977 | 100 | 0 | 86 | 12 |
| 1976 | 95 | 0 | 87 | 0 |
| 1975 | 89 | 8 | 100 | 13 |
| 1974 | 87 | 0 | 100 | 0 |
| 1973 | 92 | 8 | 100 | 11 |
| 1972 | 94 | 4 | 90 | 11 |
| 1971 | 92 | 15 | 80 | - |

# 20 Ted Weiss (D)

**Of New York — Elected 1976**

**Born:** Sept. 17, 1927, in Hungary.
**Education:** Syracuse U., B.A. 1951, LL.B. 1952.
**Military Career:** Army, 1946-47.
**Profession:** Lawyer.
**Family:** Wife, Sonya Hoover; two children.
**Religion:** Jewish.
**Political Career:** N.Y. City Council, 1962-77; unsuccessfully sought Democrtic nomination for U.S. House, 1966 and 1968.

**In Washington:** Weiss represents one of the few districts in the country that not only tolerates liberalism but demands it, and he has filled the demand with an energy and enthusiasm that defeat never seems to quench.

He has never been quite as bellicose as Bella S. Abzug, the Democrat he replaced in 1976, but he has been about as single-minded. Born in Hungary, he sometimes seems more like a European Social Democrat than a homegrown liberal. He is a man capable of stridency and also of real personal charm.

There is no question that principle drives Ted Weiss, and often it drives him into crusades that other members tend to write off as kamikaze missions.

In the 96th Congress, Weiss tried for months to persuade the Democratic Caucus to approve a resolution calling for wage and price controls. The subject never even produced a quorum in the caucus, until the opposition finally showed up in enough numbers to vote the proposition down.

Weiss has tried over and over again to eliminate research funds for a supersonic transport plane. Initially colleagues refused to grant him a recorded vote; on recent occasions he has obtained one, but has never come close to winning. He has sought repeatedly to knock out funding for new high radiation weapons, an effort aimed at the neutron bomb.

He is universally considered a hard worker on the Education and Labor Committee, where in the 97th Congress he began fighting the Reagan cutbacks in social programs. He called the Reagan budget a "drop dead America" budget.

In earlier years on Education and Labor, he fought for the Humphrey-Hawkins full employment bill, which by the time it passed in 1978, had been watered down to expression of a government "target" of 4 percent unemployment, along with unrelated goals like full parity for farm prices. He has fought against limits on wages paid to workers in CETA public jobs programs, and tried to shift $1 billion in budget authority from defense programs to a Youth Conservation Corps. Both fights were unsuccessful.

Known to be a militant supporter of urban funding, he was placed on Government Operations by the leadership to help vote out a bill authorizing anti-recessionary aid to cities. He contributed his support in 1979 as the committee approved it on a surprisingly easy 27-12 vote. The same year, however, he battled Government Operations Chairman Jack Brooks over the creation of a new Education Department. Brooks was loyally following President Carter's request for the new agency; Weiss opposed it along with the AFL-CIO, to which he has been close.

**At Home:** A long-term survivor of the Byzantine Democratic politics of Manhattan's West Side, Weiss finally made it to the House after losing three competitive primaries.

He was a 38-year-old city councilman, allied with the reform faction of the Democratic Party, when he ran as a peace candidate against machine-backed Rep. Leonard Farbstein in the 1966 Democratic primary. Weiss appeared to have fallen 151 votes short that June, but he got

---

**20th District: Western Manhattan and Bronx — West Side, Riverdale.** Population: 456,195 (3% decrease since 1970). Race: White 258,737 (57%), Black 76,163 (17%), Asian and Pacific Islander 12,798 (3%), Others 108,497 (24%). Spanish origin: 162,927 (36%).

another chance in a special primary in September after the state Supreme Court found 1,153 invalid ballots and ordered a new election. He lost that one, however, by over 1,000 votes, and when he tried again in 1968, the organization brought Farbstein a 3,000 vote victory.

After that, it was eight years before Weiss saw an opening. When Farbstein finally did lose in 1970, it was to Abzug, and only when she decided to run for the Senate in 1976 did Weiss re-enter the picture. By then, his dues were more than paid. In an unusual show of unity for West Side politics, he won the nomination without opposition. When Abzug lost her Senate primary, some party figures suggested that Weiss accept a judgeship and let her reclaim the district. But he was not about to withdraw after ten years of waiting.

Weiss's unswerving liberal principles are popular among the majority of his constituents. His list of organization memberships reads like a litany of liberal causes: the New Democratic Coalition; Americans for Democratic Action; American Civil Liberties Union; National Association for the Advancement of Colored People; Amnesty International, U.S.A.

**The District:** The 20th is a descendant of two West Side districts which were once represented by such famous names as Franklin D. Roosevelt Jr. and Jacob K. Javits. It has a large Jewish population, along with communities of blacks and Hispanics. The West Side became increasingly chic during the 1970s, with upwardly-mobile professionals restoring the early 20th century rowhouses and apartments which had fallen on hard times. It is about the most liberal political territory in the country; the bitter factional arguments these days are not between parties, or even between reform and regular wings of the Democratic Party, but between different generations of reformers. And a generation averages about two years.

## Committees

**Education and Labor** (12th of 19 Democrats)
Employment Opportunities; Labor-Management Relations; Postsecondary Education.

**Government Operations** (15th of 23 Democrats)
Government Activities and Transportation; Government Information and Individual Rights.

## Elections

**1980 General**

| | |
|---|---|
| Ted Weiss (D ) | 86,454 (82 %) |
| James Greene (R ) | 15,350 (15 %) |

**1978 General**

| | |
|---|---|
| Ted Weiss (D ) | 64,275 (85 %) |
| Harry Torczyner (R ) | 11,661 (15 %) |

**Previous Winning Percentage**

1976 (83%)

**District Vote For President**

| 1980 | | 1976 | | 1972 | |
|---|---|---|---|---|---|
| D | 81,166 (63 %) | D | 105,988 (76 %) | D | 109,905 (65 %) |
| R | 32,635 (25 %) | R | 32,221 (23 %) | R | 57,314 (34 %) |
| I | 11,205 (9 %) | | | | |

## Campaign Finance

| | Receipts | Receipts from PACs | Expenditures |
|---|---|---|---|
| **1980** | | | |
| Weiss (D ) | $36,349 | $18,600 (51 %) | $32,092 |

| 1978 | | | |
|---|---|---|---|
| Weiss (D ) | $43,467 | $21,830 (50 %) | $37,859 |
| Torczyner (R ) | $21,463 | — (0 %) | $21,463 |

## Voting Studies

| | Presidential Support | | Party Unity | | Conservative Coalition | |
|---|---|---|---|---|---|---|
| Year | S | O | S | O | S | O |
| 1980 | 66 | 26 | 82 | 9 | 4 | 88 |
| 1979 | 72 | 22 | 83 | 8 | 0 | 93 |
| 1978 | 79 | 17 | 87 | 8 | 4 | 90 |
| 1977 | 75 | 23 | 90 | 8 | 3 | 95 |

S = Support          O = Opposition

## Key Votes

**96th Congress**

| | |
|---|---|
| Weaken Carter oil profits tax (1979) | N |
| Reject hospital cost control plan (1979) | N |
| Implement Panama Canal Treaties (1979) | Y |
| Establish Department of Education (1979) | N |
| Approve Anti-busing Amendment (1979) | N |
| Guarantee Chrysler Corp. loans (1979) | Y |
| Approve military draft registration (1980) | N |
| Aid Sandinista regime in Nicaragua (1980) | Y |
| Strengthen fair housing laws (1980) | Y |

**97th Congress**

| | |
|---|---|
| Reagan budget proposal (1981) | N |

## Interest Group Ratings

| Year | ADA | ACA | AFL-CIO | CCUS |
|---|---|---|---|---|
| 1980 | 100 | 22 | 89 | 53 |
| 1979 | 100 | 12 | 100 | 6 |
| 1978 | 100 | 8 | 90 | 29 |
| 1977 | 100 | 0 | 86 | 6 |

# 21 Robert Garcia (D)

### Of The Bronx — Elected 1978

**Born:** Jan. 9, 1933, New York, N.Y.
**Education:** Attended City College of N.Y.; Community College of N. Y.
**Military Career:** Army, 1950-53.
**Profession:** Computer engineer.
**Family:** Wife, Jane Lee; two children.
**Religion:** Protestant.
**Political Career:** N.Y. Assembly, 1965-67; N.Y. Senate, 1967-78.

**In Washington:** Managing his first major bill on the House floor in 1979, Garcia had to make a quick and painful decision. He had sponsored and shepherded legislation to create a national holiday in honor of the birthday of Martin Luther King Jr. It had been expected to pass easily. But it did not survive floor debate in the form Garcia wanted.

Republicans and conservative Democrats managed to add an amendment requiring that the celebration be on a Sunday, so federal workers would not be given an extra day off. "We celebrate Easter on Sunday," one Republican told Garcia. "How can we rise any higher than that?"

When the amendment passed overwhelmingly, Garcia had to choose between taking the bill with a provision he felt reduced the importance of the holiday, or pulling it off the floor and starting all over again. He chose to pull it. "It will be back," he announced in a burst of candor, "when we have the votes to pass it." But it never returned to the floor in the 96th Congress.

In less dramatic moments, Garcia is a junior member of the Banking and Housing Committee, where he works tirelessly on obtaining help for his blighted South Bronx district. Although a conventional liberal in most respects, he has shown a willingness to consider some unorthodox ideas; he has joined New York Republican Jack Kemp in introducing legislation to create urban "free enterprise zones." Private firms would be allowed tax breaks on investments in depressed areas like the South Bronx.

Some of the bill's Republican sponsors have tried to include provisions Garcia is skeptical about, such as a sub-minimum wage for teenagers in enterprise zones. Garcia has fought to keep these ideas out of the legislation, and argued that it should complement traditional programs, not replace them. But he has vigorously defended his decision to work with the Republican right on

the issue. "When you look around my district," he said in 1981, "the liberals failed, the conservatives failed. I thought just maybe if I can get a coalition of groups together, maybe it will work."

Garcia also pleads the South Bronx case from his position as chairman of the Post Office Subcommittee on Census and Population. He was an early critic of the 1980 census, warning that it would undercount urban blacks and Hispanics, and argued in court and at subcommittee hearings that raw census figures should be adjusted to make up for the suspected errors.

**At Home:** Garcia is the second person of Puerto Rican ancestry elected to the House from New York. He succeeded the first, his friend Herman Badillo, in a rather unusual 1978 special election.

Badillo had resigned to become deputy mayor of New York City, and the party nominees for the vacancy were selected by convention. The Democratic convention was under the control of the regular Bronx County organization, which selected State Assemblyman Louis Nine as the Democratic nominee.

Reform Democrats joined forces with the Liberal Party, which chose Garcia as its candidate. Republicans, with minimal strength in the district, also backed him. But the decisive factor was Badillo, who walked the streets of the South Bronx with Garcia, investing in him the name and

---

**21st District: South Bronx — Mott Haven, Morrisania.** Population: 233,787 (50% decrease since 1970). Race: White 55,939 (24%), Black 104,396 (45%), Others 73,452 (31%). Spanish origin: 125,902 (54%).

influence he had built up as Bronx borough president and as the first Puerto Rican elected to the House. The result was a victory for Garcia. Although he was elected only on the Republican and Liberal lines, Garcia had made it clear he would caucus with the Democrats.

Garcia and Badillo have a lot in common. Both are Protestants in a predominantly Catholic Puerto Rican community. Both have been pioneers: Badillo was the first Puerto Rican elected to Congress, Garcia the first in the New York state Senate.

**The District:** The 21st District was created in 1970 to give New York's Hispanics a constituency of their own. Its many acres of abandoned and vandalized buildings in the South Bronx have become the symbol of contemporary urban decay.

The economic problems of the district are compounded by the political weakness of the Puerto Rican community. It votes in very small numbers, limiting its influence on city and state affairs. When Garcia won his special election victory, his 7,923 votes were a majority of those cast.

Moreover, there was a mass exodus from the district during the 1970s. From a population of 467,582 persons in 1972, the population dropped to 233,787, according to the 1980 census. That makes the 21st the smallest district in the country and requires that it more than double its population to come up to the state norm.

Ordinarily, that would make it a prime candidate for elimination, since the state has to lose five seats in reapportionment. But the desire to maintain a congressional base for the city's Hispanic population should push the state legislators to try to construct a district in which Garcia can continue to win. There are enough Hispanics in adjoining areas of other districts to make this possible.

## Committees

**Banking Finance and Urban Affairs** (19th of 25 Democrats)
Economic Stabilization; Financial Institutions Supervision, Regulation and Insurance; Housing and Community Development.

**Post Office and Civil Service** (5th of 15 Democrats)
Census and Population, chairman; Investigations; Postal Personnel and Modernization.

## Elections

**1980 General**

| | |
|---|---|
| Robert Garcia (D) | 32,173 (98%) |

**1978 General**

| | |
|---|---|
| Robert Garcia (D) | 23,950 (98%) |

**Previous Winning Percentage**

1978* (55 %)

*Special election.

**District Vote For President**

| | 1980 | | 1976 | | 1972 |
|---|---|---|---|---|---|
| D | 38,695 (89 %) | D | 45,515 (90 %) | D | 59,415 (79 %) |
| R | 3,638 (8 %) | R | 4,638 (8 %) | R | 15,293 (20 %) |
| I | 639 (2 %) | | | | |

## Campaign Finance

| | Receipts | Receipts from PACs | Expenditures |
|---|---|---|---|
| **1980** | | | |
| Garcia (D) | $136,428 | $18,120 (13%) | $115,310 |

| | | | |
|---|---|---|---|
| **1978** | | | |
| Garcia (D) | $39,748 | $15,994 (40%) | $45,068 |

## Voting Studies

| | Presidential Support | | Party Unity | | Conservative Coalition | |
|---|---|---|---|---|---|---|
| Year | S | O | S | O | S | O |
| 1980 | 57 | 17 | 76 | 4 | 1 | 74 |
| 1979 | 66 | 14 | 79 | 3 | 2 | 85 |
| 1978 | 66 | 15† | 78 | 6† | 5 | 77† |

S = Support          O = Opposition

† Not eligible for all recorded votes.

## Key Votes

**96th Congress**

| | |
|---|---|
| Weaken Carter oil profits tax (1979) | N |
| Reject hospital cost control plan (1979) | N |
| Implement Panama Canal Treaties (1979) | Y |
| Establish Department of Education (1979) | N |
| Approve Anti-busing Amendment (1979) | N |
| Guarantee Chrysler Corp. loans (1979) | Y |
| Approve military draft registration (1980) | N |
| Aid Sandinista regime in Nicaragua (1980) | Y |
| Strengthen fair housing laws (1980) | ? |

**97th Congress**

| | |
|---|---|
| Reagan budget proposal (1981) | N |

## Interest Group Ratings

| Year | ADA | ACA | AFL-CIO | CCUS |
|---|---|---|---|---|
| 1980 | 72 | 14 | 94 | 46 |
| 1979 | 84 | 4 | 100 | 0 |
| 1978 | 79 | 5 | 83 | 20 |

# 22 Jonathan B. Bingham (D)

## Of The Bronx — Elected 1964

**Born:** April 24, 1914, New Haven, Conn.
**Education:** Yale U., B.A. 1936, LL.B. 1939.
**Military Career:** Army, 1943-45.
**Profession:** Lawyer, newspaper reporter.
**Family:** Wife, June Rossbach; four children.
**Religion:** United Church of Christ.
**Political Career:** Unsuccessful Democratic and
Liberal nominee for N.Y. State Senate, 1958.

**In Washington:** Bingham is one of the most fervent liberals in the House, but he is a man whose breeding has always led him to avoid passionate displays. He argues for his causes in a restrained and intellectual manner, and is usually willing to talk compromise if he cannot win outright.

Bingham's leading cause in recent years has been his opposition to nuclear power. He was the force behind the successful drive to abolish the pro-nuclear Joint Atomic Energy Committee in 1977, and transfer most nuclear jurisdiction to Interior, which is much more skeptical.

As member of Interior, Bingham had already been on an anti-nuclear crusade for several years. In 1976, he had tried to gut a bill allowing private industry to begin production of enriched uranium, the source of nuclear fission. He was beaten only when Speaker Carl Albert voted against him to break a tie. The year before, he had sought to eliminate a $560 million limit on liability for nuclear accidents.

The 96th Congress brought Bingham a seemingly endless series of nuclear issues to work on. In the wake of the Three Mile Island power plant disaster in 1979, he promoted a six-month moratorium on the issuance of construction permits for atomic power plants. In 1980, he led an effort to block the sale of nuclear fuel to India.

Bingham's nuclear views forced him in 1980 into a key role in internal House politics. A reform panel proposed the creation of a new standing committee on energy. Bingham feared the new committee would be dominated by nuclear power advocates, and he also wanted as much nuclear jurisdiction as possible to stay at Interior — where he had a seat. So he proposed a "compromise" — leave everything the way it had been but put the word "energy" in the Commerce Committee's official title. It essentially killed the original proposal, but Bingham had the right allies, not only nuclear critics but members of various com-

mittees who stood to lose their own slices of the energy issue under the original plan. Bingham won on a 300-111 vote.

A former aide to Adlai E. Stevenson at the United Nations, Bingham has specialized in foreign policy since he was elected in 1964. He chairs the International Economic Policy and Trade Subcommittee on Foreign Affairs.

He is a strong supporter of Israel and of foreign aid programs, and a severe critic of right-wing dictatorships. In 1975, along with Sen. George McGovern, Bingham attempted to lift the U.S. trade embargo against Cuba. In 1980 he opposed restoring military aid to the rightist dictatorship in the Philippines. In 1979, Bingham's subcommittee oversaw a major four-year extension of federal export control programs.

Bingham was in the forefront of the successful fight a decade ago to curb the power of the seniority system. He was among those who demanded that the members be allowed to vote on the awarding of committee chairmanships. He has also favored toughening the House ethics code.

**At Home:** Bingham inherited his twin interests in politics and foreign affairs from his father, Hiram Bingham, famous explorer, educator and U.S. senator from Connecticut (1924-33). He also has a helpful connection to New York politics through the family of his wife, niece of the late

---

**22nd District: Bronx — University Heights, Co-op City.** Population: 425,822 (9% decrease since 1970). Race: White 200,097 (47%), Black 132,483 (31%), Others 93,242 (22%). Spanish origin: 142,860 (34%).

governor and senator Herbert H. Lehman, still revered by many of the city's liberal Democrats.

Bingham's first try for elective office was an unsuccessful campaign for the New York State Senate in 1958. But in 1964, he scored a major triumph by defeating U.S. Rep. Charles Buckley for renomination. Buckley, a veteran of 30 years in the House, was chairman of the Public Works Committee, an ally of Presidents Kennedy and Johnson, and head of the powerful Bronx Democratic organization.

Buckley had long been a target of reform Democrats, and had beaten back several attempts to unseat him. Bingham, with his aristocratic background and diplomatic experience, had a natural distaste for Buckley's form of clubhouse politics. His challenge came at the right time, as reformers were beginning to unseat the old machine generation all over the city. He won the primary by nearly 4,000 votes.

Since 1964, Bingham has had only one difficult election. That was in 1972 when he and Democratic Rep. James Scheuer, who had also won a reform victory in 1964, were thrown together by redistricting. Both sides wanted to avoid a contested primary and Scheuer proposed tossing a coin. Bingham said he would abide by the decision of the district's reform clubs. But at the last minute, the Legislature drew the lines to exclude Bingham's political base from the district. He withdrew from the convention of the clubs, which then endorsed Scheuer.

Bingham then decided to fight the endorsement. Scheuer had an ethnic advantage in a district then more than half Jewish, but Bingham represented about 60 percent of the new constituency from his old district. He won the nomination by a little more than 4,000 votes.

Before his congressional career, Bingham was involved in various activities related to foreign affairs. He was an occasional correspondent for the *New York Herald Tribune* during the late 1930s in Europe, the Soviet Union, and the Far East. After World War II, he was an assistant to the secretary of state, and acting administrator of the Technical Cooperation Administration (Point Four) in 1951-53. During the Kennedy and Johnson administrations, he was on the U.S. delegation to the United Nations.

**The District:** Winding through the Bronx from the heights along the Harlem River in the west to the massive Co-op City project in the east, the district includes many communities struggling against the encroachment of urban blight. It is still one of the nation's most heavily-Jewish districts.

Most of the population lives in old walk-up apartment buildings and in Co-op City, the ten-year-old development that contains more than 40,000 residents. The district has been reliably Democratic throughout the years.

As drawn in 1972, the 22nd had a population about one-third black and Hispanic, and that proportion has remained constant over the decade. The district needs to gain 100,000 people to meet the state average. But Rep. Robert Garcia's district just to the south must gain an enormous chunk of population and the other bordering districts have smaller but pressing population needs of their own. In early 1981 there was speculation that the 22nd district might be carved up to populate the others.

## Committees

**Foreign Affairs** (6th of 21 Democrats)
International Economic Policy and Trade, chairman; International Security and Scientific Affairs.

**Interior and Insular Affairs** (5th of 23 Democrats)
Energy and the Environment; Public Lands and National Parks.

## Elections

**1980 General**

| | |
|---|---|
| Jonathan Bingham (D ) | 66,301 (84 %) |
| Robert Black (R ) | 9,943 (13 %) |

**1978 General**

| | |
|---|---|
| Jonathan Bingham (D ) | 58,727 (84 %) |
| Anthony Geidel (R ) | 11,110 (16 %) |

**Previous Winning Percentages**

| | | | |
|---|---|---|---|
| 1976 (86 %) | 1974 (85 %) | 1972 (77 %) | 1970 (76 %) |
| 1968 (72 %) | 1966 (73 %) | 1964 (71 %) | |

**District Vote For President**

| | 1980 | | 1976 | | 1972 |
|---|---|---|---|---|---|
| D | 65,231 (65 %) | D | 96,746 (76 %) | D | 101,456 (60 %) |
| R | 28,491 (29 %) | R | 29,729 (23 %) | R | 67,520 (40 %) |
| I | 4,657 (5 %) | | | | |

## Campaign Finance

| | Receipts | Receipts from PACs | Expenditures |
|---|---|---|---|
| **1980** | | | |
| Bingham (D ) | $9,135 | $1,100 (12 %) | $6,722 |

## Jonathan B. Bingham, D-N.Y.

1978

Bingham (D )          $6,040          $500 (8 %)          $6,040

## Voting Studies

| | Presidential Support | | Party Unity | | Conservative Coalition | |
|---|---|---|---|---|---|---|
| Year | S | O | S | O | S | O |
| 1980 | 72 | 25 | 90 | 5 | 3 | 93 |
| 1979 | 78 | 19 | 92 | 5 | 1 | 97 |
| 1978 | 80 | 14 | 85 | 6 | 4 | 87 |
| 1977 | 85 | 14 | 91 | 5 | 4 | 96 |
| 1976 | 24 | 75 | 95 | 1 | 3 | 94 |
| 1975 | 39 | 58 | 88 | 9 | 12 | 85 |
| 1974 (Ford) | 39 | 50 | | | | |
| 1974 | 28 | 60 | 84 | 6 | 2 | 88 |
| 1973 | 33 | 66 | 87 | 10 | 6 | 91 |
| 1972 | 51 | 46 | 66 | 10 | 5 | 77 |
| 1971 | 26 | 70 | 90 | 7 | 0 | 100 |
| 1970 | 51 | 40 | 74 | 18 | - | 93 |
| 1969 | 40 | 43 | 82 | 7 | 0 | 93 |
| 1968 | 76 | 8 | 74 | 2 | 0 | 67 |
| 1967 | 85 | 9 | 87 | 8 | 2 | 91 |
| 1966 | 93 | 4 | 98 | 1 | 0 | 100 |
| 1965 | 89 | 4 | 90 | 3 | 2 | 96 |

S = Support          O = Opposition

## Key Votes

**96th Congress**

| | |
|---|---|
| Weaken Carter oil profits tax (1979) | N |
| Reject hospital cost control plan (1979) | N |
| Implement Panama Canal Treaties (1979) | Y |
| Establish Department of Education (1979) | N |
| Approve Anti-busing Amendment (1979) | N |
| Guarantee Chrysler Corp. loans (1979) | Y |
| Approve military draft registration (1980) | N |
| Aid Sandinista regime in Nicaragua (1980) | Y |
| Strengthen fair housing laws (1980) | Y |

**97th Congress**

| | |
|---|---|
| Reagan budget proposal (1981) | N |

## Interest Group Ratings

| Year | ADA | ACA | AFL-CIO | CCUS |
|---|---|---|---|---|
| 1980 | 94 | 22 | 89 | 52 |
| 1979 | 100 | 4 | 89 | 6 |
| 1978 | 80 | 4 | 83 | 20 |
| 1977 | 95 | 4 | 87 | 12 |
| 1976 | 90 | 0 | 87 | 0 |
| 1975 | 100 | 7 | 95 | 6 |
| 1974 | 91 | 0 | 100 | 0 |
| 1973 | 100 | 0 | 91 | 27 |
| 1972 | 75 | 0 | 89 | 0 |
| 1971 | 100 | 7 | 83 | - |
| 1970 | 100 | 16 | 100 | 10 |
| 1969 | 100 | 7 | 89 | - |
| 1968 | 100 | 0 | 100 | - |
| 1967 | 100 | 3 | 100 | 10 |
| 1966 | 100 | 4 | 100 | - |
| 1965 | 100 | 4 | - | 10 |

# 23 Peter A. Peyser (D)

**Of Irvington — Elected 1970**
Did not serve, 1977-79

**Born:**Sept. 7, 1921, Cedarhurst, N.Y.
**Education:** Colgate U., B.A. 1943.
**Military Career:** Army, 1943-46; National Guard, 1946-58.
**Profession:** Life insurance executive.
**Family:** Wife, Marguerite Richards; five children.
**Religion:** Episcopalian.
**Political Career:** Mayor of Irvington, 1963-70; unsuccessfully sought Republican nomination for U.S. Senate, 1976.

**In Washington:** Peyser has served in the House as a Republican and as a Democrat. He is the only current member who can make that claim. But if his party loyalties have changed during his years in Congress, his personal style has not. Peyser is as brash, irrepressible and abrasive on the Democratic side as he was across the aisle between 1971 and 1977.

He leaps into debate on dozens of subjects, offering numerous amendments and speaking for them vociferously. His penchant for rushing into the action has earned him a maverick reputation and occasionally a stiff rebuff from colleagues. When a congressional pay raise was before the House in 1979, Peyser, who supported it, offered an amendment to deny the raise to any member who voted against it. Republican Henry Hyde said the suggestion "bordered on bribery." Democrat George Miller was more blunt. "This is the dumbest amendment I've ever seen proposed," Miller said. The amendment was shouted down.

Peyser's voting record did not change dramatically with his change in parties. He had been a moderate Republican, a consistent supporter of aid to education and the elderly, and federal housing subsidies. Redistricting in 1972 gave him an increasingly urban district, with more than 150,000 Democratic constituents in the Bronx, and he generally satisfied it.

But he is more conspicuous now as a defender of traditional Democratic programs. He heads a national campaign to fight cuts in student aid and student loans, and regularly places material in the *Congressional Record* documenting damage the reductions would do. He opposes cuts in child nutrition and the school lunch program. When the House voted for those reductions in late June, he called it a "Pearl Harbor Day" for education.

Even in 1980, before the Reagan austerity program, Peyser was adamant against $850 million worth of cuts in child nutrition and education funding forced upon his Education and Labor Committee by the House Budget Committee. When Chairman Carl Perkins suggested the panel "comply" with the demand for cutbacks, Peyser said "this may be the time for rebellion."

The spending he tries to cut is for farm subsidies. During his Republican days, Peyser sought to be a consumer advocate on the Agriculture Committee. Later, in 1979, he led a successful fight to kill legislation setting a minimum price for domestic sugar producers. He has fought unsuccessfully to prevent the United States from financing tobacco sales to foreign countries through the Food for Peace program.

Peyser was a strong supporter of President Carter's grain embargo; he accused Ronald Reagan of "hypocrisy" in opposing the embargo while taking a "get tough with the Soviets" stance.

**At Home:** Peyser began his second House career in 1979 when he returned as a Democrat, two years after leaving as a Republican.

After three terms in his first political incarnation, Peyser decided to challenge Sen. James L. Buckley in 1976 for renomination in the Republican primary. The challenge failed badly.

After his defeat, Peyser switched parties, and Democratic Gov. Hugh L. Carey nominated him

---

**23rd District: North Bronx, western Westchester County. Population:** 446,213 (5% decrease since 1970). **Race:** White 323,369 (72%), Black 95,627 (21%), Others 27,217 (6%). **Spanish origin:** 41,533 (9%).

to a post on the state public service commission. But the Republican-controlled state Senate turned down the choice, at least partly out of resentment over Peyser's decision to leave the GOP. It appeared that Peyser had brought a self-inflicted end to his political career.

However, he was fortunate. His Republican House successor decided to run for lieutenant governor in 1978, and the 23rd District was open again. Peyser entered as a Democrat, and survived a close primary and general election to win his seat back. He was returned in 1980 by a comfortable margin.

Peyser was a successful insurance man when he entered political life in 1963, winning election as mayor of Irvington, a suburban community in Westchester County. He won his first GOP campaign for the House in 1970, when Democratic incumbent Richard L. Ottinger ran for the U.S. Senate. In 1972, Ottinger tried to take the seat back but Peyser edged him by a narrow margin.

**The District:** Although Westchester County has a suburban image, Peyser's district is largely urban. Most of the city of Yonkers, an old industrial town, is within the district. There is also a chunk of the Bronx, consisting of middle-income residential areas populated in large part by people of Italian and Irish ancestry. To the north, the 23rd takes in more traditional suburban territory in central Westchester County.

## Committees

**Education and Labor** (14th of 19 Democrats)
Labor-Management Relations; Postsecondary Education.

**Government Operations** (20th of 23 Democrats)
Commerce, Consumer, and Monetary Affairs; Government Activities and Transportation.

**Post Office and Civil Service** (13th of 15 Democrats)
Census and Population; Compensation and Employee Benefits; Investigations.

## Elections

**1980 General**

| | |
|---|---|
| Peter Peyser (D ) | 85,749 (56 %) |
| Andrew Albanese (R ) | 66,771 (44 %) |

**1978 General**

| | |
|---|---|
| Peter Peyser (D ) | 66,354 (52 %) |
| Angelo Martinelli (R ) | 59,455 (46 %) |

**Previous Winning Percentages**

| | | | |
|---|---|---|---|
| 1976 (- %) | 1974 (58 %) | 1972 (50 %) | 1970 (43 %) |

**District Vote For President**

| | 1980 | | 1976 | | 1972 |
|---|---|---|---|---|---|
| D | 70,025 (41 %) | D | 90,699 (49 %) | D | 80,821 (39 %) |
| R | 85,856 (51 %) | R | 92,170 (50 %) | R | 128,392 (61 %) |
| I | 11,409 (7 %) | | | | |

## Campaign Finance

| | Receipts | Receipts from PACs | Expenditures |
|---|---|---|---|
| **1980** | | | |
| Peyser (D ) | $100,109 | $52,526 (52 %) | $70,740 |
| Albanese (R ) | $69,981 | $3,400 (5 %) | $44,031 |
| **1978** | | | |
| Peyser (D ) | $106,160 | $42,809 (40 %) | $105,552 |
| Martinelli (R ) | $143,519 | $38,579 (27 %) | $141,229 |

## Voting Studies

| | Presidential Support | | Party Unity | | Conservative Coalition | |
|---|---|---|---|---|---|---|
| Year | S | O | S | O | S | O |
| 1980 | 70 | 19 | 90 | 6 | 12 | 80 |
| 1979 | 75 | 21 | 89 | 9 | 15 | 80 |
| 1976 | 16 | 41 | 9 | 37 | 17 | 31 |
| 1975 | 44 | 42 | 23 | 60 | 27 | 57 |
| 1974 (Ford) | 44 | 44 | | | | |
| 1974 | 58 | 40 | 28 | 60 | 41 | 50 |
| 1973 | 42 | 43 | 38 | 51 | 40 | 48 |
| 1972 | 68 | 14 | 26 | 51 | 37 | 37 |
| 1971 | 77 | 16 | 50 | 37 | 56 | 26 |

S = Support          O = Opposition

## Key Votes

**96th Congress**

| | |
|---|---|
| Weaken Carter oil profits tax (1979) | Y |
| Reject hospital cost control plan (1979) | N |
| Implement Panama Canal Treaties (1979) | Y |
| Establish Department of Education (1979) | N |
| Approve Anti-busing Amendment (1979) | N |
| Guarantee Chrysler Corp. loans (1979) | Y |
| Approve military draft registration (1980) | N |
| Aid Sandinista regime in Nicaragua (1980) | Y |
| Strengthen fair housing laws (1980) | Y |

**97th Congress**

| | |
|---|---|
| Reagan budget proposal (1981) | N |

## Interest Group Ratings

| Year | ADA | ACA | AFL-CIO | CCUS |
|---|---|---|---|---|
| 1980 | 94 | 14 | 89 | 65 |
| 1979 | 79 | 12 | 95 | 22 |
| 1976 | 30 | 7 | 94 | 13 |
| 1975 | 53 | 27 | 80 | 24 |
| 1974 | 35 | 50 | 70 | 20 |
| 1973 | 40 | 35 | 82 | 55 |
| 1972 | 44 | 33 | 89 | 22 |
| 1971 | 32 | 58 | 73 | - |

# 24 Richard L. Ottinger (D)

**Of Pleasantville — Elected 1964**
Did not serve 1971-75.

**Born:** Jan. 27, 1929, New York, N.Y.
**Education:** Cornell U., B.A. 1950; Harvard Law
School, LL.B. 1953.
**Military Career:** Air Force, 1953-55.
**Profession:** Lawyer.
**Family:** Wife, Sharon Frink; four children.
**Religion:** Jewish.
**Political Career:** Unsuccessful nominee for
Westchester County Board of Supervisors,
1957, 1959; unsuccessful Democratic nominee
for U.S. Senate, 1970; unsuccessfully sought
election to U.S. House, 1972.

**In Washington:** Ottinger is a man who
works better with issues than with people. A
creative legislator with a first-rate mind, he is not
always good at selling himself or his ideas to the
rest of the House.

When Ottinger campaigned in 1979 for the
chairmanship of the Democratic Study Group, the
influential organization of House Democrats, it
was as the candidate of the party's more liberal
wing, hoping to restore the sharper, issue-oriented
approach of the group's earlier years. That style
frightened much of the DSG leadership, who felt
it risked turning the organization into a splinter
group of the left. Wisconsin Democrat David
Obey was drafted to run for the post against
Ottinger, entered a few weeks before the election,
and defeated him, 173-74.

In the 96th Congress, Ottinger was a floor
spokesman for labor and liberal Democrats on
budget matters, struggling futilely against the
climate of budget reduction that had begun in the
last two years of the Carter administration. In
1980, after President Carter hastily scrapped his
original budget proposal in favor of one with
major spending cuts, Ottinger came up with a new
idea: offer Carter's original budget with enough
new money from closing tax "loopholes" to balance the budget. It was more creative than it was
popular. Ottinger was defeated 336-70.

But on environmental issues, his specialty,
Ottinger has compiled a record of constructive
achievement. He is now third in line on Commerce and fifth on Science and Technology.

On both those committees, Ottinger's message is the same. He is convinced that the energy
resources of the planet and its ability to absorb
pollution are running out, and that only radical

conservation measures and renewable energy will
solve the problem.

Early in his career, Ottinger founded an Ad
Hoc Committee on the Environment, with 94
congressmen and 97 scientists as members. In
1975, shortly after he returned to the House
following a four-year absence, he founded the
Environmental Study Conference, a strategy and
research group which keeps members, lobbyists
and reporters posted on the status of environmental legislation.

When the Commerce Committee reorganized
in 1981, its energy jurisdiction was divided between two new subcommittees, one dealing with
oil and gas and the other with conservation.
Ottinger got the conservation panel — the less
attractive one for most members, but the one that
controls the subjects he is interested in.

Ottinger opposes raising energy prices as a
conservation tool, feeling it hurts the poor. He
was second-ranking Democrat on the Energy and
Power Subcommittee at Commerce when it
worked on President Carter's 1977 energy program and supported it as it passed the House.
Later, however, after the Senate added a provision decontrolling the price of gasoline, he turned
against the bill. He and other critics of deregulation wanted to eliminate that provision by separate vote. House leaders refused to allow a separate vote, and Ottinger accused them of "a basic

---

**24th District: Central and south-
eastern Westchester County.** Population:
441,639 (6% decrease since 1970). Race: White
355,400 (80%), Black 70,355 (16%), Others
15,884 (4%). Spanish origin: 24,923 (6%).

denial of democracy." He told other members that "the leadership of this House simply does not trust you."

Ottinger went on to oppose Carter's decision to decontrol crude oil prices in 1979 and President Reagan's decontrol of gasoline prices in 1981.

He has a chance to pursue his interest in alternative energy sources as a member of the Science Committee, where he chaired a subcommittee on Energy Development until 1981. He used it to promote federal subsidies for solar development and research on an electric car, as well as other new ideas.

For a long time, he was at odds with most of the members on Science and Technology, who rejected his militant position against nuclear power and his skepticism about funding for the space program. He has been critical of some of the private companies who benefit from federal subsidies for energy research. Even when industry has appeared to be on Ottinger's side, as when it suggested putting up solar satellites in space, Ottinger has been wary. "It's just something designed to keep the aerospace companies in business forever," he said.

In the 97th Congress, however, Ottinger seemed to be more in the mainstream on the Science Committee. He was in the majority in May as the committee voted to cut off funds for the Clinch River nuclear breeder reactor, which he had long opposed. In addition, he worked with committee Republicans on an authorization for the Nuclear Regulatory Commission that would allow temporary operating licenses for some atomic plants without formal hearings. He said the deal was necessary to head off stronger pro-nuclear moves on the floor.

**At Home:** Money and persistence have helped Ottinger overcome political odds and two major defeats to preserve his congressional career.

Ottinger is an heir to the U.S. Plywood Corp., a company founded by his father. His uncle, Albert Ottinger, was the Republican nominee for governor in 1928 and was narrowly defeated by Franklin D. Roosevelt.

Ottinger first entered politics in the late 1950s, when he ran two unsuccessful races for the Westchester County board of supervisors. In 1961, he was one of the original executives of the newly founded Peace Corps, serving as director of programs for the West Coast of South America. He resigned that position to run for the House in 1964.

The district Ottinger chose, in the western portion of suburban Westchester County, had never been represented by a Democrat, and he himself was little known. But he spent a substan-

tial amount of his own money and had the help of the 1964 Democratic landslide. Once in office, he maintained a high profile, building an environmental constituency by fighting pollution in the Hudson River.

In 1970, Ottinger entered the Democratic Senate primary and put on a $1.8 million primary campaign, borrowing $1.7 million of the money from his mother. He spent a reported $1 million on a series of six spot commercials produced by consultant David Garth, outlining his anti-war and pro-environment record and insisting that "Ottinger Delivers."

He won the nomination, but lost the three-way race in November to Conservative James L. Buckley. Much of Ottinger's potential support was drained away by Republican Charles E. Goodell, who had been appointed to the seat in 1968 after the death of Robert F. Kennedy. Goodell got the backing of the Liberal party and the support of many liberal voters who might otherwise have chosen the Democratic nominee.

Ottinger suffered another setback in 1972, when he tried to regain the House seat he had given up in 1970, challenging Republican Peter Peyser, who had taken his place. The contest was close, but 1972 was a not a good year for a Democratic comeback, and the bid failed.

In 1974, however, Ottinger got another chance. Patrician Republican Ogden R. Reid, who had represented Westchester's other district since 1963, switched parties and began a campaign for governor as a Democrat. By the time Reid discovered his effort was futile, Ottinger had begun his own well-financed campaign. Reid retired. Ottinger won the seat and has held on despite repeated strong Republican challenges.

**The District:** Once a predominantly Republican preserve of New York's well-to-do, the eastern Westchester district has changed in character both through population migration and redistricting.

The district now includes a portion of the Democratic city of Yonkers, and there is a large black community in Mount Vernon, adjacent to New York City.

Italian-Americans also form a sizable portion of the electorate. Many are Republicans, but others are swing voters, torn between a loyalty to the Democratic Party on economic issues and a preference for Republicans on social issues. The wealthier areas of the district contain a remnant of hard-core, upper-class Republicanism, but also have many independent and liberal voters whom Ottinger has courted successfully.

Like most of the older New York City suburbs, the communities of the 24th lost population during the 1970s. The district will have to gain about 75,000 people to reach the new state average.

## Committees

**Energy and Commerce** (3rd of 24 Democrats)
Energy Conservation and Power, chairman.

**Science and Technology** (5th of 23 Democrats)
Energy Development and Applications; Energy Research and Production.

## Elections

**1980 General**

| | |
|---|---|
| Richard Ottinger (D) | 100,182 (59%) |
| Joseph Christiana (R) | 66,689 (40%) |

**1978 General**

| | |
|---|---|
| Richard Ottinger (D) | 75,397 (56%) |
| Michael Edelman (R) | 57,451 (43%) |

**Previous Winning Percentages**

| | | | |
|---|---|---|---|
| 1976 (55%) | 1974 (58%) | 1968 (59%) | 1966 (55%) |
| 1964 (56%) | | | |

**District Vote For President**

| | 1980 | | 1976 | | 1972 |
|---|---|---|---|---|---|
| **D** | 68,665 (38%) | **D** | 90,227 (47%) | **D** | 82,626 (39%) |
| **R** | 93,842 (52%) | **R** | 101,587 (53%) | **R** | 127,701 (61%) |
| **I** | 14,998 (8%) | | | | |

## Campaign Finance

| | Receipts | Receipts from PACs | Expenditures |
|---|---|---|---|
| **1980** | | | |
| Ottinger (D) | $217,184 | $64,856 (30%) | $69,281 |
| Christiana (R) | $24,051 | $3,050 (13%) | $32,179 |
| **1978** | | | |
| Ottinger (D) | $85,833 | $33,925 (40%) | $85,769 |
| Edelman (R) | $63,668 | $14,461 (23%) | $64,314 |

## Voting Studies

| | Presidential Support | | Party Unity | | Conservative Coalition | |
|---|---|---|---|---|---|---|
| Year | S | O | S | O | S | O |
| 1980 | 69 | 26 | 90 | 7 | 6 | 93 |
| 1979 | 75 | 19 | 92 | 5 | 2 | 94 |
| 1978 | 79 | 18 | 84 | 12 | 4 | 93 |
| 1977 | 77 | 20 | 90 | 9 | 4 | 96 |
| 1976 | 20 | 78 | 89 | 9 | 9 | 87 |
| 1975 | 31 | 65 | 90 | 8 | 7 | 91 |
| 1970 | 12 | 26 | 40 | 7 | - | 41 |
| 1969 | 45 | 53 | 84 | 9 | 2 | 93 |
| 1968 | 74 | 21 | 68 | 20 | 12 | 82 |
| 1967 | 79 | 17 | 74 | 22 | 7 | 91 |
| 1966 | 75 | 17 | 74 | 23 | 8 | 86 |
| 1965 | 88 | 10 | 83 | 12 | 2 | 98 |

S = Support     O = Opposition

## Key Votes

**96th Congress**

| | |
|---|---|
| Weaken Carter oil profits tax (1979) | N |
| Reject hospital cost control plan (1979) | N |
| Implement Panama Canal Treaties (1979) | Y |
| Establish Department of Education (1979) | Y |
| Approve Anti-busing Amendment (1979) | N |
| Guarantee Chrysler Corp. loans (1979) | Y |
| Approve military draft registration (1980) | N |
| Aid Sandinista regime in Nicaragua (1980) | Y |
| Strengthen fair housing laws (1980) | Y |

**97th Congress**

| | |
|---|---|
| Reagan budget proposal (1981) | N |

## Interest Group Ratings

| Year | ADA | ACA | AFL-CIO | CCUS |
|---|---|---|---|---|
| 1980 | 94 | 13 | 95 | 58 |
| 1979 | 100 | 0 | 90 | 0 |
| 1978 | 80 | 4 | 89 | 22 |
| 1977 | 100 | 0 | 78 | 12 |
| 1976 | 95 | 7 | 74 | 19 |
| 1975 | 89 | 7 | 96 | 12 |
| 1970 | 84 | 7 | 100 | 0 |
| 1969 | 100 | 24 | 100 | - |
| 1968 | 92 | 23 | 75 | - |
| 1967 | 87 | 28 | 100 | 20 |
| 1966 | 82 | 31 | 85 | - |
| 1965 | 94 | 7 | - | 20 |

# 25 Hamilton Fish Jr. (R)

**Of Millbrook — Elected 1968**

**Born:** June 3, 1926, Washington, D.C.
**Education:** Harvard College, A.B. 1949; N.Y.U. Law School, LL.B. 1957.
**Military Career:** Navy Reserve, 1944-46.
**Profession:** Lawyer.
**Family:** Wife, Billy Cline; four children.
**Religion:** Episcopalian.
**Political Career:** Unsuccessful Republican nominee for U.S. House, 1966.

**In Washington:** Fish was advised early in his career to be a specialist, and generally he has followed it, sticking to Judiciary and Science bills and offering repeated floor amendments to clarify or perfect their language. Outside his subjects, he is not very visible. "Unless a bill comes out of your committee," he once told a reporter, "you don't have a lot to say about it."

On Judiciary, Fish has been an immigration specialist, generally working for a liberal policy on admissions into the United States. Over the years, he has worked to allow more Cambodian refugees into the country and require reports to Congress each year on jobs and education programs for immigrants. He has tried to maintain funding levels for the Immigration and Naturalization Service.

On the Science Committee, he has been an environmentalist and nuclear power critic. He voted against the Clinch River nuclear breeder reactor for years while the committee was authorizing money for it; he was on the winning side as it turned against the project in early 1981. He favored a moratorium on nuclear plant construction licenses and tried to cut back funding for a coal gasification plant.

Like traditional Yankee Republicans from upstate New York, Fish is a fiscal conservative and a civil rights liberal. In 1980, when Judiciary reported out a bill strengthening federal enforcement powers in housing discrimination cases, he lobbied against bipartisan efforts to weaken it. He sent a letter to other House members saying such a move would be "unthinkable."

Fish has moved onto the national stage only once. In 1974, as a member of the House Judiciary Committee, he was one of the first Republicans to announce his support for the impeachment of President Nixon. The news prompted his father to release a "My Dear Son" letter strongly critical but concluding, "I shall support you for [re-

election] as blood is thicker than water."

**At Home:** Fish came to the House with one of the most impressive pedigrees in American politics. His great-grandfather Hamilton Fish was governor of New York, U.S. senator and secretary of state. His grandfather Hamilton Fish was a U.S. representative. And his father Hamilton Fish spent 20 years in the House arguing for American business and against the New Deal.

The younger Fish had been engaged in civic activities in his ancestral Dutchess County for years when the opportunity to run for the House came in 1966. Historically Republican, the district had gone Democratic in 1964, and the GOP was determined to retake it.

Fish engaged in a highly-publicized "patrician primary" against Alexander Aldrich, cousin of Gov. Nelson A. Rockefeller. Fish won, but was beaten in November by the Democratic incumbent, Joseph Y. Resnick.

In 1968, Resnick ran for the Senate. Fish again won his primary, over a then-little known lawyer, G. Gordon Liddy. He went on to win the seat, and has held it with ease ever since.

**The District:** Fish's district has shrunk geographically since he first won it. In 1968, it comprised five entire counties straddling the Hudson River from Poughkeepsie north to the Albany area. Much of the area was rural.

The 1972 redistricting reduced it to two whole counties and parts of three others, and

**25th District: Hudson Valley — Poughkeepsie.** Population: 524,528 (12% increase since 1970). Race: White 487,290 (93%), Black 27,320 (5%), Others 9,918 (2%). Spanish origin: 11,491 (2%).

moved it south to include the northern reaches of Westchester County. It still fronts on the Hudson River from Poughkeepsie to Kingston but much of the rural territory has been removed. It is now generally a suburban district, different but still

Republican and safe for Fish. The areas in Westchester, closest to New York City, have been losing population, but the communities further out, in Putnam and Dutchess counties, have been gaining.

## Committees

**Judiciary** (3rd of 12 Republicans)
Crime; Immigration, Refugees and International Law.

**Science and Technology** (3rd of 17 Republicans)
Energy Development and Applications.

## Elections

**1980 General**

| | |
|---|---|
| Hamilton Fish Jr. (R ) | 158,936 (81 %) |
| Gunars Ozols (D ) | 37,369 (19 %) |

**1978 General**

| | |
|---|---|
| Hamilton Fish Jr. (R ) | 114,641 (78 %) |
| Gunars Ozols (D ) | 31,213 (21 %) |

**Previous Winning Percentages**

1976 (71 %) 1974 (65 %) 1972 (72 %) 1970 (71 %)
1968 (48 %)

**District Vote For President**

| | 1980 | | 1976 | | 1972 |
|---|---|---|---|---|---|
| D | 65,214 (31 %) | D | 86,387 (42 %) | D | 63,519 (30 %) |
| R | 123,685 (58 %) | R | 118,585 (58 %) | R | 148,042 (70 %) |
| I | 19,108 (9 %) | | | | |

## Campaign Finance

| | Receipts | Receipts from PACs | Expenditures |
|---|---|---|---|
| **1980** | | | |
| Fish (R ) | $96,609 | $25,015 (26 %) | $91,455 |
| **1978** | | | |
| Fish (R ) | $93,226 | $13,915 (15 %) | $82,983 |

## Voting Studies

| | Presidential Support | | Party Unity | | Conservative Coalition | |
|---|---|---|---|---|---|---|
| Year | S | O | S | O | S | O |
| 1980 | 45 | 37 | 45 | 39 | 43 | 34 |

| | | | | | | |
|---|---|---|---|---|---|---|
| 1979 | 54 | 33 | 42 | 46 | 46 | 42 |
| 1978 | 50 | 41 | 57 | 37 | 55 | 38 |
| 1977 | 51 | 37 | 56 | 34 | 58 | 33 |
| 1976 | 51 | 43 | 56 | 40 | 61 | 38 |
| 1975 | 62 | 37 | 57 | 38 | 52 | 42 |
| 1974 (Ford) | 43 | 50 | | | | |
| 1974 | 47 | 45 | 42 | 45 | 44 | 46 |
| 1973 | 49 | 41 | 44 | 50 | 34 | 58 |
| 1972 | 76 | 14 | 52 | 42 | 49 | 41 |
| 1971 | 68 | 23 | 50 | 35 | 48 | 43 |
| 1970 | 68 | 17 | 56 | 26 | 34 | 41 |
| 1969 | 62 | 32 | 51 | 40 | 44 | 47 |

S = Support          O = Opposition

## Key Votes

**96th Congress**

| | |
|---|---|
| Weaken Carter oil profits tax (1979) | Y |
| Reject hospital cost control plan (1979) | Y |
| Implement Panama Canal Treaties (1979) | Y |
| Establish Department of Education (1979) | Y |
| Approve Anti-busing Amendment (1979) | N |
| Guarantee Chrysler Corp. loans (1979) | Y |
| Approve military draft registration (1980) | N |
| Aid Sandinista regime in Nicaragua (1980) | Y |
| Strengthen fair housing laws (1980) | Y |

**97th Congress**

| | |
|---|---|
| Reagan budget proposal (1981) | Y |

## Interest Group Ratings

| Year | ADA | ACA | AFL-CIO | CCUS |
|---|---|---|---|---|
| 1980 | 61 | 52 | 41 | 68 |
| 1979 | 37 | 48 | 53 | 61 |
| 1978 | 30 | 58 | 35 | 82 |
| 1977 | 50 | 58 | 50 | 41 |
| 1976 | 35 | 48 | 35 | 38 |
| 1975 | 37 | 65 | 48 | 65 |
| 1974 | 35 | 50 | 50 | 33 |
| 1973 | 44 | 22 | 50 | 36 |
| 1972 | 38 | 29 | 55 | 50 |
| 1971 | 43 | 59 | 42 | - |
| 1970 | 48 | 68 | 14 | 77 |
| 1969 | 33 | 29 | 80 | - |

# 26 Benjamin A. Gilman (R)

### Of Middletown — Elected 1972

**Born:** Dec. 6, 1922, Poughkeepsie, N.Y.
**Education:** U. of Pa., Wharton School, B.S.
1946; N.Y.U. Law School, LL.B. 1950.
**Military Career:** Army Air Corps, 1943-45.
**Profession:** Lawyer.
**Family:** Divorced; four children.
**Religion:** Jewish.
**Political Career:** N.Y. Assembly, 1967-73.

**In Washington:** Normally quiet and inoffensive to colleagues on both sides of the aisle, Gilman surprised everyone in 1979 with an amendment that brought the Democratic leadership a week of frustration.

As a locally-oriented member with exurban constituents who drive long distances to New York City every day, Gilman decided to fight gas rationing.

House leaders brought a bill to the floor allowing the president to submit a gas rationing scheme that allowed for congressional veto only on enactment — at a time of crisis. Gilman decided to propose a congressional veto at the beginning, as soon as a rationing plan was even drawn up. As far as Speaker O'Neill was concerned, that meant no rationing plan would even make it onto the shelf.

When it first came to the floor for a vote, Gilman's amendment was adopted 232-187. Angry and stunned by the tally, House leaders quickly pulled the bill off the floor and worked feverishly to change votes. A few days later, they got it reversed, even though Gilman said Congress should not be asked to accept a standby rationing plan that amounted to a "pig in a poke." Gilman got politically valuable attention.

Most of Gilman's attention, however, is on foreign policy. On the Foreign Affairs Committee, he is a strong advocate of Israel's interests. He had an amendment adopted in a 1980 funding bill for the International Monetary Fund (IMF) that declared the United States opposed to any status in the IMF for the Palestine Liberation Organization. He also sought to overturn the sale of M-60 tanks to Jordan in 1980, because Jordan had refused to join the Mideast peace talks. That attempt failed in the House, 216-177.

Gilman has made a minor specialty of working on the release of international prisoners. He helped negotiate a three-way exchange of prisoners in 1978 between the United States, East Germany and Mozambique, and in 1980 fought to have 30 Americans freed by the Cuban government. In the latter episode, he flew to Miami to greet the prisoners after their release. He also drafted a letter in 1980 to the Iranian Parliament, signed by 186 colleagues, calling for release of the American hostages.

On the Post Office Committee in 1978, Gilman was a strenuous critic of President Carter's proposed civil service revisions, and delayed the progress of the legislation with a deluge of amendments in committee. It was never clear what the tactics accomplished; some members said Gilman's uncharacteristic militance drove them close to the Carter position. The changes eventually became law.

**At Home:** Gilman quietly worked his way through the ranks of appointive and elective office to reach the House in the 1972 election.

Shortly after receiving his law degree, he was appointed a deputy assistant attorney general of New York, and he advanced two years later to be an assistant attorney general. Later, he served as attorney for New York State's Temporary Commission on the Courts and counsel to the state Assembly's Committee on Local Finance.

Following reapportionment of the state Legislature in the mid-1960s, Gilman ran for a newly-created seat from Orange County. He served three terms (1967-73) in the Assembly and then decided

---

**26th District: Lower Hudson Valley — New City, Newburgh.** Population: 541,783 (16% increase since 1970). Race: White 491,335 (91%), Black 35,045 (6%), Others 15,403 (3%). Spanish origin: 24,675 (5%).

to challenge Democratic Rep. John G. Dow for re-election. Viewed as a moderate, Gilman had to defeat conservative builder Yale Rapkin for the Republican nomination. Strong support from his home Orange County allowed him to beat Rapkin, who was from Rockland County.

Dow had been elected in a historically Republican district in the 1964 Johnson landslide. Redistricting in 1972 had made the district even more Republican, and Gilman won comfortably even though Rapkin siphoned off 12.9 percent of the vote as Conservative Party candidate. Because of Gilman's moderate voting record, he has never received the endorsement of the Conservative Party. Nevertheless, he has won easily ever since his first election.

**The District:** The growing counties of Orange and Rockland, at the far end of the New York metropolitan area, make up most of this district. They have been among the few parts of the state to gain substantial new residents in recent years, making Gilman's district the second largest in the state in population. It must lose about 25,000 people in redistricting.

However the new lines are drawn, the district should remain predominantly Republican. Suburban middle- and upper-income areas dominate both Rockland and Orange counties, having obliterated much of the old farmland. There are small industrial cities along the Hudson River and some further inland, but their political role in the district is secondary.

## Committees

**Foreign Affairs** (5th of 16 Republicans)
Inter-American Affairs; International Economic Policy and Trade.

**Post Office and Civil Service** (3rd of 11 Republicans)
Human Resources; Postal Personnel and Modernization.

**Select Narcotics Abuse and Control** (3rd of 8 Republicans)

## Elections

**1980 General**

| | |
|---|---|
| Benjamin Gilman (R ) | 137,159 (74 %) |
| Eugene Victor (D ) | 37,475 (20 %) |

**1978 General**

| | |
|---|---|
| Benjamin Gilman (R ) | 87,059 (62 %) |
| Charles Holbrook (D ) | 41,870 (30 %) |

**Previous Winning Percentages**

**1976** (65 %)    **1974** (54 %)    **1972** (48 %)

**District Vote For President**

| | 1980 | | 1976 | | 1972 |
|---|---|---|---|---|---|
| **D** | 67,593 (33 %) | **D** | 92,098 (46 %) | **D** | 63,450 (32 %) |
| **R** | 115,086 (57 %) | **R** | 106,176 (53 %) | **R** | 133,873 (68 %) |
| **I** | 16,268 (8 %) | | | | |

## Campaign Finance

| | Receipts | Receipts from PACs | Expenditures |
|---|---|---|---|
| **1980** | | | |
| Gilman (R ) | $148,023 | $34,970 (24 %) | $120,100 |
| **1978** | | | |
| Gilman (R ) | $109,727 | $23,902 (22 %) | $92,014 |
| Holbrook (D ) | $12,588 | — (0 %) | $12,588 |

## Voting Studies

| Year | Presidential Support | | Party Unity | | Conservative Coalition | |
|---|---|---|---|---|---|---|
| | S | O | S | O | S | O |
| 1980 | 50 | 44 | 42 | 53 | 43 | 48 |
| 1979 | 50 | 45 | 44 | 53 | 45 | 51 |
| 1978 | 54 | 46 | 42 | 53 | 41 | 54 |
| 1977 | 63 | 33 | 50 | 46 | 53 | 44 |
| 1976 | 27 | 71 | 37 | 61 | 43 | 55 |
| 1975 | 52 | 46 | 46 | 51 | 44 | 54 |
| 1974 (Ford) | 46 | 46 | | | | |
| 1974 | 55 | 43 | 42 | 54 | 48 | 48 |
| 1973 | 49 | 47 | 47 | 50 | 41 | 53 |

S = Support          O = Opposition

## Key Votes

**96th Congress**

| | |
|---|---|
| Weaken Carter oil profits tax (1979) | Y |
| Reject hospital cost control plan (1979) | N |
| Implement Panama Canal Treaties (1979) | N |
| Establish Department of Education (1979) | N |
| Approve Anti-busing Amendment (1979) | N |
| Guarantee Chrysler Corp. loans (1979) | Y |
| Approve military draft registration (1980) | N |
| Aid Sandinista regime in Nicaragua (1980) | N |
| Strengthen fair housing laws (1980) | Y |

**97th Congress**

| | |
|---|---|
| Reagan budget proposal (1981) | Y |

## Interest Group Ratings

| Year | ADA | ACA | AFL-CIO | CCUS |
|---|---|---|---|---|
| 1980 | 61 | 46 | 83 | 63 |
| 1979 | 53 | 46 | 70 | 47 |
| 1978 | 55 | 38 | 75 | 39 |
| 1977 | 50 | 42 | 71 | 29 |
| 1976 | 45 | 33 | 68 | 19 |
| 1975 | 63 | 44 | 78 | 29 |
| 1974 | 26 | 40 | 73 | 20 |
| 1973 | 48 | 44 | 73 | 36 |

**859**

# 27 Matthew F. McHugh (D)

## Of Ithaca — Elected 1974

**Born:** Dec. 6, 1938, Philadelphia, Pa.
**Education:** Mount St. Mary's College, B.S. 1960; Villanova Law School, J.D. 1963.
**Profession:** Lawyer.
**Family:** Wife, Eileen Alanna Higgins; three children.
**Religion:** Roman Catholic.
**Political Career:** Tompkins County District Attorney, 1964-72

**In Washington:** McHugh's quiet, serious pragmatism has made him a major player in the appropriations process and a figure of real respect among House Democrats. A man who wears a plain black suit and a somber expression, he is not one of the more conspicuous younger members. But he has the implicit trust of most colleagues.

He has found himself in a sensitive position on the Appropriations subcommittee that handles foreign aid. A strong personal supporter of Israel, he has sometimes had to negotiate between that country's even more militant backers and the growing anti-foreign aid faction in the House.

On several occasions, merely getting the bill passed has been a difficult struggle. In 1978, McHugh's first year on the committee, he and Wisconsin Democrat David R. Obey led the successful fight for the Carter administration's $7.4 billion foreign aid request, over the objections of Clarence Long, D-Md., the Foreign Operations chairman, who wanted to slash the amount. McHugh and Obey were the winners on the floor that year; the bill passed the House with $7.1 billion in it, close to what the administration asked for, and without the restrictions on international lending that many Republicans sought.

When that bill went to conference, Long and other House negotiators were adamant against Senate language providing for aid to Syria. It finally became law after McHugh added a provision authorizing the president to approve aid to Syria only if he thought it would "serve the process of peace in the Middle East."

The next year, McHugh was defending the entire foreign aid program on the House floor against budget-cutting assaults. When Ohio Republican Clarence Miller tried to reduce the funding by a flat 5 percent across-the-board, McHugh countered with a 2 percent reduction, exempting Egypt and Israel. That compromise passed.

Outside foreign affairs, McHugh has remained committed to the reformist politics on which he and his 1974 class initially won election. In 1977, when there was discussion over a bill to provide partial public financing of House general elections, McHugh pushed for something stronger. He introduced his own bill covering primaries as well as general elections, and sharply reducing private spending levels. It attracted little support, but the more modest version never passed either. The next year, he called for a new Democratic Caucus rule requiring a vote in the caucus on whether any member disciplined by the House or convicted of a felony should retain his post. It was passed, with some modifications. Later the caucus approved a rule requiring indicted chairmen to step aside temporarily.

Beyond McHugh's personal reserve lies a reservoir of ambition. To make it to the Appropriations Committee in 1978, he had to win the support of the New York State Democratic delegation. That was a difficult task because the delegation is New York City-dominated, the seat's previous occupant was from Manhattan, and there was already an active candidate from the city, James H. Scheuer. But McHugh campaigned assiduously and defeated Scheuer, 14-11, drawing several city votes.

He was less successful in 1980, when he tried to become chairman of the House Democratic Caucus. The other candidates, Gillis W. Long and

---

**27th District: Southern Tier — Binghamton.** Population: 490,810 (5% increase since 1970). Race: White 468,490 (95%), Black 13,170 (3%), Others 9,150 (2%). Spanish origin: 8,183 (2%).

Charlie Rose, were both Southerners, and he saw an opening for a moderate liberal from the Northeast. But he started late, and in challenging Long, he was up against one of the most popular members. McHugh finished a distant third, with 41 votes to 146 for Long and 53 for Rose.

**At Home:** McHugh's victory in the 1974 Democratic sweep made him the first Democrat to represent the Binghamton area in this century. He succeeded a popular Republican, Howard W. Robison, who retired, promising to carry on in Robison's moderate tradition. He was helped in that stance by the hard-line conservative campaign of his Republican opponent, Binghamton Mayor Alfred Libous.

Before running for Congress, McHugh served as district attorney of Tompkins County, at the far western edge of the sprawling district. As district attorney, he was popular with the Cornell University community in Ithaca. He organized a local drug treatment facility and demanded peaceful handling of student protests.

Since his first victory, McHugh has consolidated his position effectively enough to turn back well-financed Republican challenges, in 1978 and 1980, both from businessman Neil Tyler Wallace.

**The District:** The district is an expanded version of one historically centered around the Southern Tier city of Binghamton. Now it stretches west to Ithaca and the Elmira suburbs and east to within a few miles of the Hudson.

Included in the district is some choice rolling farmland, devoted to dairying, as well as the resort communities in the Catskills. Near Binghamton, IBM and G.E. have large plants.

Except for McHugh, few Democrats win here district-wide. Ford carried the 27th easily in 1976, as did GOP Sen. James L. Buckley, while both lost decisively elsewhere in the state. Reagan carried it in 1980.

## Committees

**Appropriations** (21st of 33 Democrats)
Agriculture; Foreign Operations.

## Elections

**1980 General**

| | |
|---|---|
| Matthew McHugh (D ) | 103,863 (55 %) |
| Neil Wallace (R ) | 83,096 (44 %) |

**1978 General**

| | |
|---|---|
| Matthew McHugh (D) | 83,413 (56 %) |
| Neil Wallace (R ) | 66,177 (44 %) |

**Previous Winning Percentages**

1976 (67 %)    1974 (53 %)

**District Vote For President**

| | 1980 | | 1976 | | 1972 |
|---|---|---|---|---|---|
| D | 75,875 (38 %) | D | 88,715 (45 %) | D | 75,391 (37 %) |
| R | 95,553 (48 %) | R | 108,821 (51 %) | R | 126,939 (63 %) |
| I | 21,960 (11 %) | | | | |

## Campaign Finance

| | Receipts | Receipts from PACs | Expenditures |
|---|---|---|---|
| **1980** | | | |
| McHugh (D ) | $295,766 | $86,200 (29 %) | $288,061 |
| Wallace (R ) | $201,305 | $44,330 (22 %) | $199,966 |
| **1978** | | | |
| McHugh (D ) | $197,615 | $29,450 (15 %) | $199,786 |
| Wallace (R ) | $139,107 | $1,650 (1·%) | $139,043 |

## Voting Studies

| | Presidental Support | | Party Unity | | Conservative Coalition | |
|---|---|---|---|---|---|---|
| Year | S | O | S | O | S | O |
| 1980 | 76 | 20 | 88 | 8 | 11 | 84 |
| 1979 | 82 | 16 | 86 | 12 | 16 | 83 |
| 1978 | 84 | 15 | 84 | 13 | 12 | 87 |
| 1977 | 72 | 20 | 74 | 16 | 21 | 67 |
| 1976 | 24 | 75 | 87 | 11 | 18 | 77 |
| 1975 | 35 | 63 | 88 | 7 | 11 | 86 |

S = Support        O = Opposition

## Key Votes

**96th Congress**

| | |
|---|---|
| Weaken Carter oil profits tax (1979) | N |
| Reject hospital cost control plan (1979) | N |
| Implement Panama Canal Treaties (1979) | Y |
| Establish Department of Education (1979) | N |
| Approve Anti-busing Amendment (1979) | N |
| Guarantee Chrysler Corp. loans (1979) | Y |
| Approve military draft registration (1980) | N |
| Aid Sandinista regime in Nicaragua (1980) | Y |
| Strengthen fair housing laws (1980) | Y |

**97th Congress**

| | |
|---|---|
| Reagan budget proposal (1981) | N |

## Interest Group Ratings

| Year | ADA | ACA | AFL-CIO | CCUS |
|---|---|---|---|---|
| 1980 | 83 | 21 | 72 | 64 |
| 1979 | 89 | 4 | 90 | 13 |
| 1978 | 75 | 15 | 80 | 28 |
| 1977 | 70 | 10 | 80 | 33 |
| 1976 | 80 | 4 | 77 | 32 |
| 1975 | 95 | 7 | 95 | 6 |

# 28 Samuel S. Stratton (D)

### Of Amsterdam — Elected 1958

**Born:** Sept. 27, 1916, Yonkers, N.Y.
**Education:** U. of Rochester, A.B. 1937; Haverford College, M.A. 1938; Harvard U., M.A. 1940.
**Military Career:** Navy, 1942-46 and 1951-53.
**Profession:** News commentator.
**Family:** Wife, Joan Wolfe; five children.
**Religion:** Presbyterian.
**Political Career:** Schenectady City Council, 1950-56; mayor of Schenectady, 1956-59; unsuccessful Democratic nominee for N.Y. Assembly, 1950.

**In Washington:** Stratton is one of the last of the Cold War liberals — a labor Democrat who believes in wage and price controls at home but remains ferocious in his opposition to communism and his support for a strong military. He is one of the Pentagon's most combative spokesmen in Congress and a tireless critic of civilian budgeteers who meddle with military planning.

He is an advocate, rather than a legislative tactician, one who often seems just as satisfied arguing against the odds as plotting to improve them. During the Pentagon's long years in the national doghouse after Vietnam, he was a relatively lonely but undaunted lobbyist for higher defense budgets.

On broader issues, the liberalism Stratton brought with him to the House in 1958 remains — to a greater extent than many who watch him realize. He no longer scores high in ratings by the Americans for Democratic Action, but that is mainly a result of his defense views and his pro-development energy policy, which he argues is essentially a vote for national security. In the 96th Congress, Stratton voted for hospital cost controls and a national minimum welfare payment and against an anti-busing amendment to the Constitution. He cosponsored a resolution calling for wage and price controls. In the 97th Congress, he joined the Conservative Democratic Forum, the strategy group of the party's right in the House, but opposed the Reagan budget while virtually all forum members were supporting it.

But Stratton rarely attracts attention these days on anything but defense issues. He ranks third on Armed Services in the 97th Congress, and he fits in well with the panel's ideas. He wants senior military officers to tell him what they need without reference to budget or domestic politics. He has been a staunch supporter of the B-1 bomber and a new nuclear aircraft carrier.

As a member of the Investigations Subcommittee, which he chaired until 1981, he has been a tireless inquisitor. He used the subcommittee to touch off the alarms that ultimately led President Carter to reverse himself on U.S. troop withdrawals from Korea.

Within weeks of his inauguration in 1977, Carter directed the Joint Chiefs of Staff to plan for a withdrawal of the roughly 32,000 U.S. ground troops over a period of four or five years.

When Major Gen. John K. Singlaub, the third ranking U.S. Army officer in Korea, was quoted by *The Washington Post* as predicting that the withdrawal would lead to war, Carter fired him from his job, and Stratton exploited the issue.

Calling Singlaub before the Investigations Subcommittee only a few days after he was fired, Stratton tried to show that Carter had ordered the withdrawal without consulting his senior military advisers and that intelligence reports showed North Korean military strength much greater than had been estimated.

Ultimately, the new intelligence assessment was the rock on which Carter's policy foundered. It took a couple of years — during which Stratton tried unsuccessfully to block the withdrawal by legislation — but in 1979, Carter cancelled virtu-

---

**28th District: Hudson-Mohawk valleys — Albany, Schenectady.** Population: 449,019 (4% decrease since 1970). Race: White 418,868 (93%), Black 25,526 (6%), Others 3,489 (1%). Spanish origin: 5,564 (1%).

ally the entire pullout, pending a reconsideration in 1981.

**At Home:** Stratton was something of a phenomenon when he took this seat in 1958. He was the first Democrat elected from his Schenectady-Amsterdam district since 1916, and the only Democrat in the entire upstate New York House delegation outside Albany and Buffalo.

From such a precarious beginning, Stratton has gradually placed a lock on his seat. He has been re-elected 11 times and has become dean of the New York congressional delegation. To do so, he has had to survive two major redistrictings and make peace with the crusty old Albany Democratic organization.

Stratton's 1958 election was the culmination of a long political ascent against the odds. Elected to the Schenectady City Council as an anti-organization Democrat in 1949, he had to battle both the entrenched Democratic machine and a strong Republican Party. He suffered a stinging defeat in 1950 when he ran for the Assembly against GOP speaker Oswald D. Heck, one of the most powerful politicians in the state.

Stratton was re-elected to the City Council in 1953 by 125 votes, then won the mayoralty in 1955 by 282 votes, promising to "clean up" Schenectady. He fought gambling, corruption and inefficiency in the city. Because the pay from his political posts was small, Stratton supplemented his income by working for local radio and television stations, becoming a well-known announcer and newscaster. He once played a character called "Sagebrush Sam," dressed up in cowboy clothes and playing a harmonica.

In 1958, Stratton again challenged the local powers by declaring for Congress. The Democratic organizations in his five-county district supported Schenectady County Clerk Carroll "Pink" Gardner, who had run twice before. But in the primary, Stratton carried every ward and town in Schenectady County, defeating Gardner by more than 2-1 and humiliating the organization. In November, Stratton upset the traditional Republican supremacy by beating Schenectady County GOP Chairman Walter Shaw by 10,000 votes.

In 1962, Stratton went through the first of two major redistrictings. Republicans were determined to defeat him. They eliminated his district, combining Schenectady County with Albany County, where Stratton would have had little chance of defeating longtime Democratic Rep. Leo O'Brien, who was backed by the Albany regime. So he moved to another district, one stretching from Amsterdam, a small industrial city on the Mohawk River, through central New York to include the Finger Lakes cities of Auburn

and Canandaigua. The area had not elected a Democrat to the House in the 20th century. But Stratton campaigned energetically and won. He held the seat until the next major reshuffling of boundaries in 1970.

Meanwhile, Stratton attempted to expand his career to statewide politics. But his unorthodox political background and lack of an urban Democratic base doomed his efforts. In 1962, he fought for the gubernatorial nomination, but the Democratic power brokers gave it to U.S. Attorney Robert Morgenthau. In 1964, chances looked brighter for a possible U.S. Senate nomination, but U.S. Attorney General Robert F. Kennedy entered the race at the last minute and Democratic leaders flocked to him. Stratton was bitter at Kennedy's entrance and insisted on fighting him to the last vote. On the first ballot at the state convention, Kennedy smothered Stratton 968 to 153. Relations between the two were sour from then on.

In 1970, New York was forced by court order to redraw its congressional district lines once again. Stratton's district was again decimated, and he had to look for a new one. By then, Stratton's interests and those of the Albany political machine coincided. O'Brien had retired in 1966, and in a reform sweep, Republican Daniel Button was elected in his place. The Albany Democratic bosses — Mayor Erastus Corning and nonagenarian party leader "Uncle Dan" O'Connell — needed a respectable Democrat to overthrow Button. Stratton got the nomination, moved back to his old home territory and defeated Button.

**The District:** Centered on Albany, one of the few Democratic strongholds in upstate New York, Stratton's current district includes a narrow corridor to the northwest to take in the cities of Schenectady and Amsterdam.

Albany has had Democratic congressional representation for all but four years since 1922. In the 1920s, a political alliance was struck between the old-line WASP Corning family and the Irish Catholic O'Connell family. The O'Connells ran the party machinery while the Cornings held public office. Parker Corning represented the congressional district from 1923 to 1937. Another member of the family, Erastus Corning, has been mayor of Albany since 1942.

As the state capital, Albany has a large contingent of state government workers. Otherwise, it is one of a series of decayed Hudson River cities that were once industrial centers. Schenectady has a major concentration of General Electric plants. Amsterdam is an old carpet-making city, much of whose business has moved away.

# Committees

**Armed Services** (3rd of 25 Democrats)
Procurement and Military Nuclear Systems, chairman; Investigations.

# Elections

**1980 General**

| | |
|---|---|
| Samuel Stratton (D ) | 164,088 (78 %) |
| Frank Wicks (R ) | 37,504 (18 %) |

**1978 General**

| | |
|---|---|
| Samuel Stratton (D ) | 139,575 (76 %) |
| Paul Tocker (R ) | 36,017 (20 %) |

**Previous Winning Percentages**

| | | | |
|---|---|---|---|
| 1976 (79 %) | 1974 (81 %) | 1972 (80 %) | 1970 (66 %) |
| 1968 (69 %) | 1966 (66 %) | 1964 (64 %) | 1962 (55 %) |
| 1960 (62 %) | 1958 (54 %) | | |

**District Vote For President**

| | 1980 | | 1976 | | 1972 |
|---|---|---|---|---|---|
| D | 107,364 (48 %) | D | 107,602 (48 %) | D | 101,329 (43 %) |
| R | 87,325 (39 %) | R | 113,853 (51 %) | R | 134,617 (57 %) |
| I | 22,429 (10 %) | | | | |

# Campaign Finance

| | | Receipts | Expen- |
|---|---|---|---|
| | Receipts | from PACs | ditures |
| **1980** | | | |
| Stratton (D ) | $57,212 | $21,395 (37 %) | $30,635 |
| **1978** | | | |
| Stratton (D ) | $29,133 | $6,550 (22 %) | $28,057 |

# Voting Studies

| | Presidential Support | | Party Unity | | Conservative Coalition | |
|---|---|---|---|---|---|---|
| Year | S | O | S | O | S | O |
| 1980 | 58 | 36 | 62 | 31 | 52 | 40 |
| 1979 | 48 | 51 | 56 | 43 | 72 | 27 |
| 1978 | 54 | 39 | 52 | 43 | 51 | 45 |
| 1977 | 62 | 32 | 54 | 43† | 61 | 35† |
| 1976 | 43 | 43 | 64 | 27 | 50 | 44 |
| 1975 | 51 | 47 | 66 | 31 | 48 | 51 |
| 1974 (Ford) | 59 | 31 | | | | |
| 1974 | 58 | 34 | 61 | 32 | 47 | 47 |
| 1973 | 52 | 38 | 57 | 37 | 52 | 44 |
| 1972 | 78 | 16 | 62 | 37 | 51 | 48 |
| 1971 | 67 | 25 | 57 | 34 | 52 | 42 |
| 1970 | 49 | 22 | 57 | 24 | 32 | 36 |
| 1969 | 64 | 34 | 65 | 31 | 44 | 53 |
| 1968 | 62 | 19 | 43 | 27 | 35 | 45 |
| 1967 | 64 | 4 | 53 | 28 | 35 | 41 |
| 1966 | 57 | 18 | 45 | 29 | 32 | 51 |
| 1965 | 83 | 12 | 80 | 12 | 4 | 86 |
| 1964 | 90 | 4 | 87 | 6 | 17 | 83 |
| 1963 | 92 | 3 | 93 | 0 | 0 | 100 |
| 1962 | 85 | 7 | 84 | 5 | 19 | 75 |
| 1961 | 89 | 9 | 84 | 14 | 13 | 87 |

† Not eligible for all recorded votes.

S = Support          O = Opposition

# Key Votes

**96th Congress**

| | |
|---|---|
| Weaken Carter oil profits tax (1979) | Y |
| Reject hospital cost control plan (1979) | N |
| Implement Panama Canal Treaties (1979) | N |
| Establish Department of Education (1979) | N |
| Approve Anti-busing Amendment (1979) | N |
| Guarantee Chrysler Corp. loans (1979) | Y |
| Approve military draft registration (1980) | Y |
| Aid Sandinista regime in Nicaragua (1980) | N |
| Strengthen fair housing laws (1980) | N |

**97th Congress**

| | |
|---|---|
| Reagan budget proposal (1981) | N |

# Interest Group Ratings

| Year | ADA | ACA | AFL-CIO | CCUS |
|---|---|---|---|---|
| 1980 | 17 | 43 | 58 | 66 |
| 1979 | 26 | 38 | 65 | 56 |
| 1978 | 15 | 44 | 50 | 47 |
| 1977 | 30 | 41 | 81 | 35 |
| 1976 | 25 | 38 | 81 | 50 |
| 1975 | 42 | 44 | 83 | 41 |
| 1974 | 35 | 36 | 100 | 20 |
| 1973 | 36 | 31 | 100 | 27 |
| 1972 | 38 | 22 | 82 | 13 |
| 1971 | 41 | 40 | 89 | - |
| 1970 | 48 | 21 | 80 | 13 |
| 1969 | 40 | 24 | 90 | - |
| 1968 | 42 | 32 | 75 | - |
| 1967 | 33 | 35 | 45 | 25 |
| 1966 | 35 | 48 | 92 | - |
| 1965 | 79 | 12 | - | 20 |
| 1964 | 92 | 5 | 91 | - |
| 1963 | - | 0 | - | - |
| 1962 | 88 | 5 | 100 | - |
| 1961 | 90 | - | - | - |

# 29 Gerald B. H. Solomon (R)

**Of Glens Falls — Elected 1978**

**Born:** Aug. 14, 1930, Okeechobee, Fla.
**Education:** Attended Siena College, 1949-50; St.
   Lawrence U. 1952-53.
**Military Career:** Marine Corps, 1951-52.
**Profession:** Insurance broker.
**Family:** Wife, Freda Parker; five children.
**Religion:** Presbyterian.
**Political Career:** Warren County Legislature,
   1968-72; N.Y. Assembly, 1973-79.

**In Washington:** A strait-laced ex-Marine, Solomon rarely finds much to smile about on the House floor, especially when he begins talking of the majority party's fiscal profligacy and manipulation of the House rules. He is a man who takes life seriously.

As a first-term member of the 96th Congress, he was one of the junior militants who pressured GOP leader John J. Rhodes to be tougher on the Democratic opposition. "Our leaders have been absent from the floor at times they could have been creating cohesiveness," Solomon complained in 1979.

Lack of aggressiveness is not a charge that anyone could bring against Solomon. From his first days in the House, he was up and speaking about numerous issues, challenging the Democrats and harrassing them with quorum calls and demands for recorded votes on non-controversial issues.

As a second-term member in the 97th Congress, he is part of a more structured conservative Republican "watchdog" team monitoring House floor activities and questioning Democratic strategy.

He was especially aggressive about the 1979 congressional pay raise. He condemned it as an insult to American taxpayers and tried to amend it so that it would take effect only if the federal budget were balanced. He lost.

Another time, when Democrats sought to curtail oil company tax credits on foreign earnings and use the increased revenue for domestic programs, Solomon successfully amended the provision to prevent the money from being used that way. He said he agreed that the foreign tax credit should be ended but that the revenue should be used to reduce the federal deficit.

He was an active opponent of President Carter's efforts to drop U.S. treaty relations with Taiwan. His amendment to require a consular link between the two countries lost on a 225-179 vote.

Later he won approval of an amendment to bar American participation in the Asian Development Bank unless Taiwan was allowed to remain a member of the bank. Opponents of the amendment said it was unnecessary because there were no plans to expel Taiwan from the bank and, in fact, Taiwan had not borrowed money there since 1971. But Solomon persisted. In the past, Taiwan has used loans from the bank to buy nuclear power plant equipment from General Electric, which has major facilities in Solomon's district.

Solomon's watchdog style does not leave full time for his major committee, Public Works, and he does not always seem comfortable with the committee's tradition of friendly bipartisan logrolling. But he is not silent.

Solomon has fought against efforts on Public Works to force industry to pay a higher share of the cost in cleaning up water pollution. He also amended a bill in the Water Resources Subcommittee to delay dredging of pollutants from the Hudson River until all alternatives were studied. The Hudson flows through Solomon's district.

**At Home:** Running as an outspoken conservative in a solidly conservative district, Solomon took the seat away from one of the 1974 Democratic Watergate winners, Ned Pattison.

Solomon's victory was not a surprise. The surprises came in 1974 when Pattison became the

---

**29th District: Upper Hudson Valley — Saratoga Springs, Troy.** Population: 523,107 (12% increase since 1970). Race: White 508,683 (97%), Black 10,058 (2%), Others 4,366 (1%). Spanish origin: 4,478 (1%).

---

first Democrat to represent the district in the 20th century, and in 1976, when he won a second term. Two years later, however, the Democrat had to bear the burden of a candid interview in *Playboy* magazine in which he admitted that he had smoked marijuana.

Solomon had been a popular state legislator who regularly won his Assembly seat by a wide margin. His Assembly constituency lay entirely within the 29th Congressional District, so he had a good base from which to launch a congressional bid.

In addition, he was able to reconstruct the Republican-Conservative coalition. The two parties ran separate candidates in 1976, and Pattison won with less than a majority of the vote. But

Solomon was backed by both parties.

**The District:** The 29th surrounds the Albany-Schenectady area. It contains traditional upstate rural counties, the old industrial and educational city of Troy, home of Rensselaer Polytechnic Institute, and growing suburban communities near Albany, Schenectady, and Troy.

This suburban development caused the 29th to grow more than all but four other districts in the state during the 1970s. As a result, it almost exactly meets the population criterion for the state's congressional districts.

With Republicans in an overwhelmingly strong position in the district, Solomon would seem to be in a secure position no matter how the new lines are drawn.

## Committees

**Public Works and Transportation** (10th of 19 Republicans)
Investigations and Oversight; Public Buildings and Grounds; Water Resources.

**Veterans' Affairs** (6th of 14 Republicans)
Hospitals and Health Care; Oversight and Investigations.

## Elections

**1980 General**

| | |
|---|---|
| Gerald Solomon (R ) | 141,631 (67 %) |
| Rodger Hurley (D ) | 70,697 (33 %) |

**1978 General**

| | |
|---|---|
| Gerald Solomon (R ) | 99,518 (54 %) |
| Edward Pattison (D ) | 84,705 (46 %) |

**District Vote For President**

| | 1980 | | 1976 | | 1972 |
|---|---|---|---|---|---|
| D | 85,606 (37 %) | D | 86,951 (39 %) | D | 67,562 (30 %) |
| R | 119,037 (52 %) | R | 136,099 (61 %) | R | 156,802 (70 %) |
| I | 19,769 (9 %) | | | | |

## Campaign Finance

| | Receipts | Receipts from PACs | Expen- ditures |
|---|---|---|---|
| **1980** | | | |
| Solomon (R ) | $117,086 | $62,440 (53 %) | $122,581 |
| Hurley (D ) | $41,543 | $13,221 (32 %) | $40,176 |

| 1978 | | | |
|---|---|---|---|
| Solomon (R ) | $168,169 | $78,136 (46 %) | $167,723 |
| Pattison (D ) | $164,874 | $38,206 (23 %) | $155,525 |

## Voting Studies

| | Presidential Support | | Party Unity | | Conservative Coalition | |
|---|---|---|---|---|---|---|
| Year | S | O | S | O | S | O |
| 1980 | 40 | 53 | 84 | 8 | 84 | 11 |
| 1979 | 21 | 76 | 91 | 6 | 92 | 5 |

S = Support          O = Opposition

## Key Votes

**96th Congress**

| | |
|---|---|
| Weaken Carter oil profits tax (1979) | Y |
| Reject hospital cost control plan (1979) | ? |
| Implement Panama Canal Treaties (1979) | N |
| Establish Department of Education (1979) | N |
| Approve Anti-busing Amendment (1979) | Y |
| Guarantee Chrysler Corp. loans (1979) | N |
| Approve military draft registration (1980) | Y |
| Aid Sandinista regime in Nicaragua (1980) | N |
| Strengthen fair housing laws (1980) | N |

**97th Congress**

| | |
|---|---|
| Reagan budget proposal (1981) | Y |

## Interest Group Ratings

| Year | ADA | ACA | AFL-CIO | CCUS |
|---|---|---|---|---|
| 1980 | 11 | 78 | 29 | 72 |
| 1979 | 0 | 92 | 20 | 94 |

# 30 David O'B. Martin (R)

**Of Canton — Elected 1980**

**Born:** April 26, 1944, Ogdensburg, N.Y.
**Education:** University of Notre Dame, B.B.A.
1966; Albany University, J.D. 1973.
**Military Career:** Marine Corps, 1966-70.
**Profession:** Lawyer.
**Family:** Wife, DeeAnn Hedlund; three children.
**Religion:** Roman Catholic.
**Political Career:** St. Lawrence County Legislature, 1974-77; New York Assembly, 1977-81.

**The Member:** Martin follows the low-key orthodox Republicanism of his predecessor, Robert C. McEwen, who retired after serving 16 years in the House.

A Vietnam veteran, Martin entered politics in 1973 at the county level. In 1976, he received party backing for the state Legislature and moved on to Albany. A regular Republican who worked closely with the party leadership, Martin had the support of six of the seven county GOP chairmen in his bid for the congressional nomination.

Martin defeated a well-known Democrat for the House — former New York Lt. Gov. Mary Anne Krupsak. Krupsak moved into the district in order to run, but could not break the strong hold Republicans have maintained in the area.

During the campaign, Martin proposed adapting Jack Kemp's proposal for "enterprise zones," designed for high unemployment urban areas, to his district's economically suffering rural areas and small towns. In Congress, he has been a strong supporter of Reagan budget and tax proposals, objecting only to the president's method of overhauling Social Security.

**The District:** The 30th District covers the North Country from Vermont across to Lake Ontario, and is the most dependable Republican district in the state. It has not elected a Democrat to Congress in this century.

The area is not good farmland, and it has never had a solid industrial base. It includes some of the most economically depressed areas in the state. The 30th has the lowest median income of any district in the state outside the slum areas of New York City. Much of the district is also dependent on nuclear power, which has become a sensitive issue for anyone running for office.

Much of the district's limited Democratic vote is cast by French-Canadians in St. Lawrence and Franklin counties, along the Canadian border.

## Committees

**Interior and Insular Affairs** (10th of 17 Republicans)
Energy and the Environment; Mines and Mining.

## Elections

**1980 General**

| | |
|---|---|
| David Martin (R ) | 111,008 (64 %) |
| Mary Anne Krupsak (D) | 54,896 (32 %) |

**1980 Primary**

| | |
|---|---|
| David Martin (R ) | 31,661 (70 %) |
| John Zagame (R ) | 13,358 (30 %) |

**District Vote For President**

| | 1980 | | 1976 | | 1972 |
|---|---|---|---|---|---|
| **D** | 73,463 (41 %) | **D** | 75,006 (42 %) | **D** | 60,180 (33 %) |
| **R** | 90,227 (50 %) | **R** | 104,841 (58 %) | **R** | 122,127 (67 %) |
| **I** | 14,430 (8 %) | | | | |

## Campaign Finance

| | Receipts | Receipts from PACs | Expenditures |
|---|---|---|---|
| **1980** | | | |
| Martin (R ) | $236,958 | $76,654 (32 %) | $228,715 |
| Krupsak (D ) | $55,638 | $18,925 (34 %) | $54,837 |

## Key Vote

**97th Congress**

| | |
|---|---|
| Reagan budget proposal (1981) | Y |

---

**30th District: North — Plattsburgh, Watertown.** Population: 492,047 (5% increase since 1970). Race: White 482,297 (98%), Black 3,464 (1%), Others 6,286 (1%). Spanish origin: 3,398 (1%).

---

# 31 Donald J. Mitchell (R)

**Of Herkimer — Elected 1972**

**Born:** May 8, 1923, Ilion, N.Y.
**Education:** Columbia U., B.S. 1949; M.A. 1950.
**Military Career:** Navy, 1942-45, 1951-53.
**Profession:** Optometrist.
**Family:** Wife, Margaretta Levee; three children.
**Religion:** Methodist.
**Political Career:** Herkimer Town Council, 1954-56; mayor of Herkimer, 1956-59; N.Y. Assembly, 1965-73.

**In Washington:** Like a dog gnawing at a bone, Mitchell has fought relentlessly for a decade to increase federal spending on civil defense, the one relatively unpopular military cause of recent years. He is always ready to talk about what he sees as the country's need to shelter its population from a possible nuclear holocaust.

Over the objections of the House Armed Services leadership, Mitchell has gradually gained some additional committee support for civil defense. But he has had little luck convincing the rest of Congress.

Mitchell took the House floor in 1980 to complain that the Appropriations Committee was recommending only $100 million for civil defense, even though Armed Services had authorized $167 million. He came armed with large charts comparing civil defense spending in the United States and the Soviet Union, and moved to restore the $67 million. He said a $1 billion, seven-year civil defense program could save 100 million American lives.

"If we figure that on a cost-benefit ratio," he said, "that amounts to ten dollars for an American life." But even in the defense-minded summer of 1980, the House voted down Mitchell's amendment, 175-201.

A quiet congressman with little taste for grandstanding, Mitchell was not always pre-occupied with bomb shelters and evacuation plans. But in 1976, he served on a special Armed Services panel that studied the issue. He came away convinced that civil defense was being ignored.

A few other House members have advocated a renewed effort toward civil defense, but generally they have done so out of concern that their districts would be targets in a nuclear exchange. Mitchell has approached the issue from a national perspective, and he is widely credited with sensitizing his colleagues to it, although failing so far to talk them into spending more money.

Beyond that, Mitchell is not a legislative activist. Armed Services is his only assignment, and he has worked his way up to the senior GOP position on the Military Personnel Subcommittee, where he works on the mathematical minutiae of pay scales for the uniformed services. Occasionally he has a personal interest to pursue; when bonuses for military doctors were reauthorized in 1980, Mitchell tried to secure larger ones for his fellow optometrists and other specialists. But the Pentagon argued there was no need for such extra pay, and it was not approved.

**At Home:** A cautious and deliberate man, Mitchell spent more than 15 years mastering the politics of a Mohawk River town and using it to prepare for a congressional career.

After learning his trade as an optometrist, he started in politics on the Herkimer city council in 1954, placed there by appointment. He was elected to the office in 1955, and became mayor in 1956. As president of the Mohawk Valley Conference of Mayors, he brought his name a little more public visibility.

It was not until 1964 that he moved on, taking a seat in the New York Assembly. He stayed there for eight years, four of them as majority whip.

A congressional seat finally opened up in 1972, when Republican Rep. Alexander Pirnie retired after 14 years. Four candidates, including

---

**31st District: Mohawk Valley — Utica.** Population: 458,792 (2% decrease since 1970). Race: White 446,349 (97%), Black 8,668 (2%), Other 3,775 (1%). Spanish origin: 3,727 (1%).

Mitchell, entered the primary. The best known was Assemblyman John T. Buckley of Utica, a popular moderate Republican from a prominent Oneida County family.

However, two other Utica-area candidates decided to run, leaving Mitchell as the only candidate from outside Oneida County in a district with four other whole counties and parts of three more. The Oneida vote was divided, and Mitchell won the primary with 34.1 percent of the vote. After defeating fairly strong Democratic contenders in 1972 and 1974, Mitchell has had an easy time each November.

**The District:** Centered on the Mohawk Valley, the district is studded with small industrial cities. The largest are Utica and Rome, which have a substantial ethnic population, especially Irish and Italian.

But rural and small-town areas, largely Protestant, radiate to the north and south of the Mohawk Valley, and in the east, the district takes in suburban areas near Amsterdam and Schenectady. So it is predominantly Republican.

The district needs to gain about 57,000 people to reach the state average for the new congressional districts.

## Committees

**Armed Services**(5th of 19 Republicans)
Investigations; Military Installations and Facilities; Military Personnel and Compensation.

## Elections

**1980 General**

| | |
|---|---|
| Donald Mitchell (R) | 135,976 (77%) |
| Irving Schwartz (D) | 39,589 (23%) |

**1978 General**

| | |
|---|---|
| Donald Mitchell (R) | Unopposed |

**Previous Winning Percentages**

1976 (67%)    1974 (60%)    1972 (51%)

**District Vote For President**

| | 1980 | | 1976 | | 1972 |
|---|---|---|---|---|---|
| D | 76,945 (40 %) | D | 84,661 (44 %) | D | 60,942 (30 %) |
| R | 97,430 (51 %) | R | 107,363 (56 %) | R | 139,949 (70 %) |
| I | 13,370 (7 %) | | | | |

## Campaign Finance

| | Receipts | Receipts from PACs | Expenditures |
|---|---|---|---|
| **1980** | | | |
| Mitchell (R) | $102,570 | $44,300 (43%) | $78,925 |
| Schwartz (D) | $7,052 | — (0%) | $6,495 |
| **1978** | | | |
| Mitchell (R) | $75,064 | $28,629 (38%) | $44,635 |

## Voting Studies

| | Presidential Support | | Party Unity | | Conservative Coalition | |
|---|---|---|---|---|---|---|
| Year | S | O | S | O | S | O |
| 1980 | 48 | 44 | 67 | 28 | 73 | 23 |
| 1979 | 37 | 57 | 66 | 30 | 78 | 20 |
| 1978 | 45 | 49 | 61 | 33 | 70 | 26 |
| 1977 | 56 | 41 | 61 | 35 | 76 | 19 |
| 1976 | 55 | 39 | 53 | 43 | 68 | 31 |
| 1975 | 62 | 35 | 64 | 33 | 69 | 26 |
| 1974 (Ford) | 46 | 44 | | | | |
| 1974 | 58 | 40 | 65 | 33 | 76 | 23 |
| 1973 | 52 | 34 | 62 | 30 | 67 | 23 |

S = Support          O = Opposition

## Key Votes

**96th Congress**

| | |
|---|---|
| Weaken Carter oil profits tax (1979) | Y |
| Reject hospital cost control plan (1979) | Y |
| Implement Panama Canal Treaties (1979) | N |
| Establish Department of Education (1979) | N |
| Approve Anti-busing Amendment (1979) | Y |
| Guarantee Chrysler Corp. loans (1979) | Y |
| Approve military draft registration (1980) | Y |
| Aid Sandinista regime in Nicaragua (1980) | N |
| Strengthen fair housing laws (1980) | N |

**97th Congress**

| | |
|---|---|
| Reagan budget proposal (1981) | Y |

## Interest Group Ratings

| Year | ADA | ACA | AFL-CIO | CCUS |
|---|---|---|---|---|
| 1980 | 28 | 65 | 44 | 69 |
| 1979 | 21 | 68 | 40 | 56 |
| 1978 | 25 | 70 | 45 | 50 |
| 1977 | 15 | 58 | 41 | 65 |
| 1976 | 25 | 46 | 48 | 38 |
| 1975 | 26 | 61 | 41 | 76 |
| 1974 | 26 | 53 | 45 | 40 |
| 1973 | 12 | 75 | 36 | 40 |

# 32 George C. Wortley (R)

## Of Fayetteville — Elected 1980

**Born:** Dec. 8, 1926, Syracuse, N.Y.
**Education:** Syracuse U., B.S. 1948.
**Military Career:** Navy, 1945-46.
**Profession:** Publisher and printer.
**Family:** Wife, Barbara Hennessy; three children.
**Religion:** Roman Catholic.
**Political Career:** Unsuccessful Republican nominee for U.S. House, 1976.

**The Member:** Wortley has been well-known in the business and political life of Syracuse for years, but ran for office only once prior to winning his House seat in 1980. That was in 1976, when he lost to Democratic Rep. James M. Hanley. When the popular incumbent decided to retire in 1980, the seat became ripe for retaking by Republicans and Wortley was the beneficiary.

President of the Manlius Publishing Corp., which includes a group of suburban newspapers, Wortley has filled most of the standard civic positions that serve as a prelude to political office in many districts. He served on the Onondaga County civil service commission and the Town of Manlius planning board. He was vice chairman of Newspapers for Rockefeller in 1970. He was also on the National Commission on Historical Publications and Records (1977-80), appointed by President Gerald R. Ford.

The business and party contacts that Wortley made while serving in those jobs helped him when he decided to make the 1980 congressional race. He received the backing of much of the area's business community and won the GOP nomination over a candidate backed by the formal party organization.

**The District:** With a sizable white-collar professional population and an Italian-American bloc that harbors Republican sympathies, Syracuse has always leaned more to the GOP than most cities its size. Republicans were further helped when the city was divided into two districts in 1970, splitting the Democratic vote.

The 32nd consists of about half of Syracuse, some of its suburbs, and several small-town and rural counties. Despite its character, Democratic Rep. Hanley held on for eight terms with personal popularity. After his retirement, the normal Republican majority reasserted itself.

## Committees

**Banking, Finance and Urban Affairs** (15th of 19 Republicans)
Consumer Affairs and Coinage; Economic Stabilization; General Oversight and Renegotiation; Housing and Community Development.

**Select Aging** (17th of 23 Republicans)
Health and Long-Term Care; Housing and Consumer Insterests.

## Elections

### 1980 General

| | |
|---|---|
| George Wortley (R ) | 108,128 (60 %) |
| Jeffery Brooks (D ) | 56,535 (32 %) |
| Peter Del Giorno (RTL) | 11,978 (7 %) |

### 1980 Primary

| | |
|---|---|
| George Wortley (R ) | 11,521 (40 %) |
| Peter Del Giorno (R ) | 8,649 (30 %) |
| Pat Bombard (R ) | 4,459 (16 %) |
| Herbert Brewer (R ) | 4,084 (14 %) |

### District Vote For President

| | 1980 | | 1976 | | 1972 |
|---|---|---|---|---|---|
| D | 71,535 (37 %) | D | 75,658 (39 %) | D | 60,341 (30 %) |
| R | 99,489 (51 %) | R | 117,652 (61 %) | R | 138,597 (70 %) |
| I | 19,867 (10 %) | | | | |

## Campaign Finance

| | Receipts | Receipts from PACs | Expenditures |
|---|---|---|---|
| **1980** | | | |
| Wortley (R ) | $172,931 | $57,108 (33 %) | $170,106 |
| Brooks (D ) | $12,281 | $1,525 (12 %) | $15,315 |

## Key Vote

### 97th Congress

| | |
|---|---|
| Reagan budget proposal (1981) | Y |

> **32nd District: Central — Syracuse.**
> Population: 485,133 (4 % increase since 1970).
> Race: White 463,607 (96 %), Black 14,940 (3 %), Others 6,586 (1 %). Spanish origin: 3,918 (1 %).

# 33 Gary A. Lee (R)

**Of Dryden — Elected 1978**

**Born:** Aug. 18, 1933, Buffalo, N.Y.
**Education:** Colgate U., B.A. 1960
**Military Career:** Navy, 1952-56.
**Profession:** Educational administrator.
**Family:** Wife, Kathleen O'Brian; four children.
**Religion:** Christian.
**Political Career:** Corning Board of Aldermen, 1961-63; Dryden Town Council, 1965-67; Tompkins County Board of Supervisors, 1968-69; Tompkins County Legislature, 1970-74; N.Y. Assembly, 1975-79.

**In Washington:** Lee's quiet conservatism attracted less attention in his first House term than the more flamboyant tactics of some of his 1978 Republican classmates, but his high tolerance for legislative detail made him one of the more effective members of the group.

Blessed with one of the better freshman committee assignments — the Commerce Committee and its Health and Transportation subcommittees — Lee spent most of his first two years working through the legislative thicket of railroad deregulation. He became a sort of liaison with the nation's short-line railroads, who feared that the removal of rate ceilings would force them into an impossible competitive position against larger railroads.

Lee agreed to offer a floor amendment writing in special protection for the smaller carriers, and that kept the American Short Line Railroad Association on board throughout the debate, helping guarantee final passage.

On the Health Subcommittee, Lee generally went along with the free market views of the panel's dominant Republican, David A. Stockman of Michigan, now President Reagan's budget director. Lee and Stockman protested a committee bill expanding the federal role in treating mental illness, calling the added programs "frightening from a philosophical as well as a fiscal point of view." Early in the 96th Congress, Lee criticized President Carter's hospital cost containment program, arguing that similar controls in New York State had led to a $1-million deficit in a single year for a local hospital.

Lee has also become involved in the issue of Indian land claims. The Cayuga Indians claim 64,000 acres in Cayuga and Seneca counties in Lee's district. He says they are using their claims as a form of blackmail to win generous negotiated settlements and has suggested as an alternative that Congress retroactively ratify land treaties made between state governments and Indian tribes since the passage of the Non-Intercourse Act of 1790. Most Eastern Indian claims have been based on alleged violations of that act.

Lee has spoken only rarely on the House floor, but his occasional contributions leave his ideological beliefs unmistakably clear.

"Government's biggest job," he complained in his first term, "seems to be the shifting of money from those who work to those who do not, effectively killing incentive for them both. . . . We can clean the rolls of those who only want spoon-feeding."

**At Home:** Lee built the political base for his House career as a state assemblyman, using the constituent service techniques familiar in Congress. He also developed a reputation for doing his legislative homework.

He announced for Congress in 1978, on the retirement of Republican Rep. William F. Walsh of Syracuse. With the backing of all the county organizations in the district, Lee easily defeated a wealthy Syracuse businessman for the Republican nomination, even though the Syracuse area casts about half the vote in the district and Lee's home county less than a tenth.

After the primary, Syracuse interests were so

---

**33rd District: Central — Syracuse.**
Population: 470,552 (1% increase since 1970). Race: White 443,721 (94%), Black 20,918 (4%), Others 5,913 (1%). Spanish origin: 4,464 (1%).

---

eager to keep the district in local hands that one of the city's traditional Republican newspapers endorsed the Democratic nominee, Roy Bernardi the Syracuse city auditor. With that help, and with an Italian background in a city that has a large Italian community, Bernardi seemed to be a strong candidate. But thanks to a strong Republican effort throughout the district and his own effective campaigning, Lee won the election easily.

After a career in education, in which he began as a small-town schoolteacher and eventually became director of scholarships and financial aid at Cornell University, Lee entered politics on the local level in Tompkins County, at the base of the Finger Lakes region of central New York. Besides

serving in local and state government, he was Tompkins County Republican chairman from 1969 to 1974.

**The District:** Before 1970, this district was based on the Finger Lakes area, with its small lakefront cities and vineyards. The 1970 redistricting brought in a slice of Onondaga County (Syracuse). Since then the district has been divided about evenly between the two areas. The Onondaga portion includes about half the city of Syracuse, plus suburban areas to the west.

Lee is the first person from outside the Syracuse area to represent the district since the 1970 redrawing. The district is solidly Republican and only radical changes would give the Democrats a shot at winning it.

## Committees

**Energy and Commerce** (10th of 18 Republicans)
Commerce, Transportation, and Tourism; Fossil and Synthetic Fuels.

**House Administration** (6th of 8 Republicans)
Accounts; Office Systems; Personnel and Police.

## Elections

**1980 General**

| | |
|---|---|
| Gary Lee (R ) | 132,831 (76 %) |
| Dolores Reed (D ) | 39,542 (23 %) |

**1978 General**

| | |
|---|---|
| Gary Lee (R ) | 82,501 (56 %) |
| Roy Bernardi (D ) | 58,286 (40 %) |

**1978 Primary**

| | |
|---|---|
| Gary Lee (R ) | 17,936 (88 %) |
| Robert Byrne (R ) | 2,397 (12 %) |

**District Vote For President**

| | 1980 | | 1976 | | 1972 |
|---|---|---|---|---|---|
| D | 71,012 (37 %) | D | 75,268 (39 %) | D | 59,656 (30 %) |
| R | 98,664 (52 %) | R | 115,166 (60 %) | R | 137,007 (70 %) |
| I | 16,625 (9 %) | | | | |

## Campaign Finance

| | Receipts | Receipts from PACs | Expenditures |
|---|---|---|---|
| **1980** | | | |
| Lee (R ) | $202,150 | $100,750 (50 %) | $128,927 |
| Reed (D ) | $5,926 | $250 (4 %) | $5,326 |

**1978**

| | | | |
|---|---|---|---|
| Lee (R ) | $165,916 | $39,273 (24 %) | $162,725 |
| Bernardi (D ) | $69,715 | $11,657 (17 %) | $69,614 |

## Voting Studies

| | Presidential Support | | Party Unity | | Conservative Coalition | |
|---|---|---|---|---|---|---|
| Year | S | O | S | O | S | O |
| 1980 | 41 | 56 | 87 | 8 | 84 | 12 |
| 1979 | 23 | 64 | 81 | 9 | 89 | 3 |

S = Support          O = Opposition

## Key Votes

**96th Congress**

| | |
|---|---|
| Weaken Carter oil profits tax (1979) | Y |
| Reject hospital cost control plan (1979) | ? |
| Implement Panama Canal Treaties (1979) | N |
| Establish Department of Education (1979) | N |
| Approve Anti-busing Amendment (1979) | Y |
| Guarantee Chrysler Corp. loans (1979) | Y |
| Approve military draft registration (1980) | Y |
| Aid Sandinista regime in Nicaragua (1980) | N |
| Strengthen fair housing laws (1980) | N |

**97th Congress**

| | |
|---|---|
| Reagan budget proposal (1981) | Y |

## Interest Group Ratings

| Year | ADA | ACA | AFL-CIO | CCUS |
|---|---|---|---|---|
| 1980 | 11 | 90 | 19 | 70 |
| 1979 | 0 | 84 | 30 | 94 |

# 34 Frank Horton (R)

**Of Rochester — Elected 1962**

**Born:** Dec. 12, 1919, Cuero, Texas.
**Education:** La. State U., B.A. 1941; Cornell U. Law School, LL.B. 1947.
**Military Career:** Army, 1941-45.
**Profession:** Lawyer.
**Family:** Wife, Nancy Richmond Flood; two children.
**Religion:** Presbyterian.
**Political Career:** Rochester City Council, 1955-61.

**In Washington:** A liberal Republican without many partisan instincts, Horton has devoted his career to an often frustrating review of federal governmental processes — especially the burden of paperwork.

He is the senior GOP member on the Government Operations Committee and often plays the "good guy" role to Democratic Chairman Jack Brooks' "tough guy" style, defusing potential conflicts among fellow members. During the Carter administration he was sometimes more useful to Democrats than to Republicans. On several controversial issues, Horton was the swing vote that meant victory for the Democratic leadership and the Carter administration.

For instance, Horton was the only Republican on Government Operations who actively favored creation of the Department of Education, though on the final 20-19 vote, Lyle Williams, R-Ohio, was persuaded to join him. Horton also supported creating a new Department of Energy. In both cases, he avoided philosophical debates, saying he wanted only to save money and make government more efficient. He likes the idea of concentrating bureaucracy in a smaller, more manageable number of agencies.

That was the same reason Horton gave in an earlier Congress for supporting a Consumer Protection Agency when every other committee Republican opposed one. He said it made sense to consolidate the activities of a dozen or so separate consumer offices throughout the government.

Horton has been a supporter of anti-recession aid to cities, one of the few pieces of major legislation that Government Operations writes on a continuing basis. In 1978, an anti-recession aid bill promoted by the Carter administration was stalled by Brooks and L. H. Fountain of North Carolina, the chairman of the Intergovernmental Relations Subcommittee. Horton joined Speaker O'Neill and 42 other House members in writing a letter to Fountain urging him to let the bill out of the subcommittee. Ultimately the bill did emerge from committee but it died in confused maneuvering at the end of the 96th Congress.

Horton has been voting independently of his party on major issues ever since he joined the House. That record brought him a challenge in 1973, when the ranking GOP position on Government Operations opened up. The committee's second-senior Republican, John Erlenborn of Illinois, tried to elbow him aside, contending his own conservative views were more in line with the thinking of most House Republicans.

Horton insisted that on revenue sharing and other matters important to the Nixon administration, he had voted the Republican position as often as Erlenborn had. In addition, he may have had an edge in popularity over Erlenborn, one of the brightest House members but not one of the more jovial ones. Horton won, 100-36, and has had the ranking position ever since.

Much of Horton's time in recent years has been spent trying to analyze and reduce government paperwork. He steered legislation through Congress in 1975 to set up a paperwork study commission, and headed the inquiry himself. After two years, 36 reports and 770 recommendations — nearly all of them on paper — the commission went out of existence without making much of an impact on the problem it set out to conquer.

---

**34th District: West — Rochester.**
Population: 454,965 (3% decrease since 1970).
Race: White 403,847 (89%), Black 37,732 (8%), Others 13,386 (3%). Spanish origin: 12,854 (3%).

---

## Frank Horton, R-N.Y.

The Horton commission reported finding a "profusion of inconsistent and often conflicting laws, policies and practices" and recommended that government policy-makers — including Congress — consider paperwork costs when writing and implementing laws. It also suggested consolidating federal forms, writing regulations in understandable English and creating a new Cabinet agency, a Department of Administration.

Horton was able to write some of these recommendations into law later, in the 1980 Paperwork Reduction Act, which passed in the closing days of the 96th Congress. This bill had to survive an unexpected fight over computer information between Horton's House committee and the Defense Department. Once that was resolved, the bill sailed through. It set up a central office of Information and Regulatory Affairs within the Office of Management and Budget to identify and try to eliminate unnecessary paperwork. Its goal is to reduce the paperwork burden by 25 percent by 1984.

Another outgrowth of the paperwork study was a bill to set up federal information centers around the country. "This bill," Horton said as it cleared Congress, "makes it possible for every citizen to pick up the phone, dial a number and find out in one call exactly where to get (federal) information."

Horton was a founder and continues as co-chairman of the Northeast-Midwest Congressional Coalition, a group of 213 House members from Snow Belt states organized in 1976 to try to stop the flight of federal dollars to the South and West. Horton and other coalition members lobbied successfully in 1977 to rewrite the formulas by which housing and community development funds are distributed to the different regions.

Since then, the coalition has been partially successful on other regional formula issues like food stamps and fuel oil rebates. The group has generated competition from Southerners and Southwesterners, who decided in 1981 to retaliate with their own Sun Belt Council.

Horton balances his liberalism on many social measures with strong support for defense spending. He supported the war in Vietnam for most of its history. In 1967, Horton was one of the authors of a book called *How to End the Draft*, advocating an all-volunteer army. He supported the War Powers Act that strengthened the constitutional role of Congress in declaring war.

**At Home:** While thousands of people were leaving upstate New York for the Sun Belt after World War II, Horton was moving in the other direction. Born in Texas and educated in Louisiana, he headed for the snow to make his career.

After graduating from Cornell Law School, Horton settled in Rochester and became a practicing attorney. Had he remained in Texas in the 1950s, he would have found it difficult to get far in politics as a Republican. In Rochester, he fit right in.

Elected to the Rochester City Council in 1955 to fill an unexpired term, Horton was re-elected in 1957 for a four-year term. During his time on the council he was chairman of its Public Utilities and Special Services Committee. He served until 1961, when he became a casualty of a political sweep by the Democrats. It was the first time the GOP had lost control of the city government in 25 years, and Horton lost his job.

Meanwhile, he had become actively involved in minor league baseball. He was president of the Rochester Redwings and executive vice president of the International League from 1959-60.

In 1962, a Rochester-area congressional seat opened up with the illness and retirement of Republican Rep. Jessica Weis, who had been a power in the national Republican Party as New York committeewoman for 20 years.

Horton was the consensus choice of the Republican leaders in the district, and became the GOP nominee without a primary. He has never been challenged and his Democratic opposition has been minimal.

In 1976, Horton was arrested for speeding and drunk driving. He admitted his guilt, accepted a punishment of a few days in jail, and weathered the incident without political damage.

**The District:** Republicans have always been careful to keep the Democratic core of Rochester divided between two districts. As a result, the Democrats have not won a congressional election in the area since 1944.

Horton's district takes in the east side of the city, with its accompanying suburbs, and continues east to include rural Wayne County, a fruit-growing area. Unlike many old industrial cities, Rochester became an early center for high technology industries. The Eastman Kodak Company is headquartered there, and Xerox has several plants in the vicinity. The technical and professional employees of these and smaller high technology companies populate much of Horton's district. They are solidly Republican.

## Committees

**Government Operations** (Ranking Republican)
Legislation and National Security.

## Elections

**1980 General**

| | |
|---|---|
| Frank Horton (R) | 133,278 (73%) |
| James Toole (D) | 37,883 (21%) |

**1978 General**

| | |
|---|---|
| Frank Horton (R) | 122,785 (87%) |
| Others | 18,123 (13%) |

**Previous Winning Percentages**

| | | | |
|---|---|---|---|
| **1976** (66%) | **1974** (68%) | **1972** (72%) | **1970** (71%) |
| **1968** (70%) | **1966** (67%) | **1964** (56%) | **1962** (59%) |

**District Vote For President**

| | 1980 | | 1976 | | 1972 |
|---|---|---|---|---|---|
| D | 90,218 (45 %) | D | 86,580 (43 %) | D | 78,090 (37 %) |
| R | 87,091 (43 %) | R | 112,816 (56 %) | R | 131,107 (63 %) |
| I | 19,896 (10 %) | | | | |

## Campaign Finance

| | Receipts | Receipts from PACs | Expenditures |
|---|---|---|---|
| **1980** | | | |
| Horton (R) | $25,782 | $17,800 (69%) | $14,669 |
| **1978** | | | |
| Horton (R) | $24,157 | $11,350 (47%) | $8,262 |

## Voting Studies

| Year | Presidential Support S | O | Party Unity S | O | Conservative Coalition S | O |
|---|---|---|---|---|---|---|
| 1980 | 52 | 41 | 41 | 53 | 47 | 44 |
| 1979 | 57 | 36 | 37 | 55 | 53 | 41 |
| 1978 | 49 | 43 | 48 | 42 | 57 | 34 |
| 1977 | 54 | 37 | 40 | 51 | 52 | 40 |
| 1976 | 53 | 39 | 38 | 53 | 50 | 41 |
| 1975 | 63 | 28 | 40 | 44 | 41 | 36 |
| 1974 (Ford) | 54 | 41 | | | | |
| 1974 | 62 | 30 | 37 | 55 | 39 | 56 |
| 1973 | 63 | 36 | 49 | 49 | 53 | 44 |
| 1972 | 68 | 16 | 37 | 52 | 45 | 43 |
| 1971 | 65 | 30 | 38 | 50 | 41 | 47 |
| 1970 | 60 | 22 | 19 | 56 | 23 | 52 |
| 1969 | 60 | 36 | 36 | 62 | 20 | 80 |
| 1968 | 75 | 17 | 38 | 54 | 29 | 65 |
| 1967 | 64 | 27 | 43 | 48 | 31 | 61 |
| 1966 | 58 | 31 | 54 | 43 | 35 | 62 |
| 1965 | 72 | 22 | 36 | 59 | 24 | 71 |
| 1964 | 73 | 27 | 37 | 56 | 25 | 67 |
| 1963 | 46 | 54 | 67 | 28 | 67 | 27 |

S = Support          O = Opposition

## Key Votes

**96th Congress**

| | |
|---|---|
| Weaken Carter oil profits tax (1979) | Y |
| Reject hospital cost control plan (1979) | N |
| Implement Panama Canal Treaties (1979) | Y |
| Establish Department of Education (1979) | Y |
| Approve Anti-busing Amendment (1979) | N |
| Guarantee Chrysler Corp. loans (1979) | Y |
| Approve military draft registration (1980) | N |
| Aid Sandinista regime in Nicaragua (1980) | N |
| Strengthen fair housing laws (1980) | Y |

**97th Congress**

| | |
|---|---|
| Reagan budget proposal (1981) | Y |

## Interest Group Ratings

| Year | ADA | ACA | AFL-CIO | CCUS |
|---|---|---|---|---|
| 1980 | 78 | 43 | 74 | 69 |
| 1979 | 47 | 48 | 55 | 67 |
| 1978 | 55 | 33 | 55 | 53 |
| 1977 | 25 | 40 | 73 | 59 |
| 1976 | 40 | 30 | 52 | 57 |
| 1975 | 63 | 41 | 65 | 47 |
| 1974 | 52 | 23 | 70 | 33 |
| 1973 | 44 | 36 | 64 | 55 |
| 1972 | 44 | 35 | 73 | 50 |
| 1971 | 51 | 46 | 64 | - |
| 1970 | 76 | 25 | 71 | 22 |
| 1969 | 80 | 29 | 100 | - |
| 1968 | 50 | 38 | 75 | - |
| 1967 | 73 | 35 | 83 | 40 |
| 1966 | 53 | 59 | 85 | - |
| 1965 | 68 | 27 | - | 30 |
| 1964 | 52 | 33 | 64 | - |
| 1963 | - | 72 | - | - |

# 35 Barber B. Conable Jr. (R)

## Of Alexander — Elected 1964

**Born:** Nov. 2, 1922, Warsaw, N.Y.
**Education:** Cornell U., A.B. 1942, LL.B. 1948.
**Military Career:** Marine Corps, 1942-46, 1950-51, Reserves until 1972.
**Profession:** Lawyer.
**Family:** Wife, Charlotte Williams; four children.
**Religion:** Methodist.
**Political Career:** N.Y. Senate, 1963-65.

**In Washington:** After years as the witty but frustrated voice of Republican tax policy at Ways and Means, Conable finally holds some cards as he maneuvers between a popular Republican president and a divided Democratic majority in the House.

Up until now, his years as the committee's senior GOP member have been frustrating ones. He began to dominate the Republican side in 1975, just as Democrats were deciding to ignore it, making policy in closed party caucuses and letting the minority read about it in the paper. When he wanted to compromise with Democrats in exchange for a share in the decision, he found the conservative wing of his own party suspicious of him.

Conable was an angry man at the start of 1981, furious at Ways and Means Democrats for insisting on keeping their 23-12 majority on the committee even though they were no longer even close to a 2-1 advantage in the House. He argued against their move on the floor and in the press, accusing the majority of a "naked exercise of power," but got nowhere.

As angry as Democrats have made him, however, he has usually been philosophical in defeat. "What is power?" he once asked. "All it is is influence. As long as people listen when I talk, I've got influence."

People do listen when he talks. An erudite lawyer who collects antique drawings of the Capitol, Conable can speak more eloquently off the cuff than most members can from notes. He commands respect in both parties.

In the 97th Congress he also has a chance to command votes, and he is a force neither the Democrats nor the administration can afford to ignore. But he is still outnumbered in committee, and he has to balance his desire to serve the president against the doubts he and other traditional Republicans have had about some elements of Reaganomics.

Early in 1981, Conable urged the administration to send Congress a tax bill with targeted savings and investment incentives rather than the straight Kemp-Roth rate cuts. He said that would make it easier to hold most Republicans (including himself) and attract some Democrats.

But when Reagan decided on something very close to Kemp-Roth — a 25 percent across-the-board tax cut over three years — Conable loyally introduced it in committee, while stopping short of an enthusiastic endorsement and reserving the right to make "technical changes."

Conable has been on Ways and Means since 1967. He was a relatively little-known junior member during the Wilbur Mills chairmanship, when the committee met behind closed doors, but his influence on the Republican side became apparent in 1975, the year the doors opened and Mills was replaced by the vastly less imperial Al Ullman of Oregon. In 1977 Conable took over formally as ranking Republican. From 1975 to 1981, he also was on the Budget Committee.

He has usually tried to offer his own alternatives to Democratic tax measures he has opposed. Instead of trying to bail out the Social Security system with higher payroll taxes, for example, he suggested separating out Medicare and meeting its costs from general tax revenues. When Congress took up a windfall profits tax on the oil industry, he argued for a plow-back provision that

---

**35th District: West — Rochester, Batavia.** Population: 477,377 (2% increase since 1970). Race: White 432,894 (91%), Black 37,901 (8%), Others 6,582 (1%). Spanish origin 5,537 (1%).

would allow companies to escape the tax by investing profits in research and exploration.

In 1976 he won approval of legislation to straighten out the complex system for tax-exempt public charities. Previous law had been vague, denying a charity special status if it did a "substantial" amount of lobbying. Conable's bill set specific limits.

Conable has had a long-term interest in the problem of lagging U.S. productivity. Working with James R. Jones, the Oklahoma Democrat, and with the U.S. Chamber of Commerce, he drafted a bill in 1980 to provide simpler and faster depreciation for business buildings and equipment.

Conable does his share of constituent service, but that is not his primary focus. He once said he is not particularly impressed by appeals that something is good for New York. He feels his responsibility goes beyond his own area.

Still, he has done some conspicuous favors for his home state. He took the lead in supporting federal revenue sharing, partly because he believed in it but partly because New York was anxious to see the program enacted. It was Conable who tried to restore the state government portion of revenue sharing after it was cut from the 1981 budget.

Conable also walked a delicate path in 1979, when Ways and Means wrote a new welfare bill establishing minimum national benefit standards for the first time. He did not like the bill and said so on the House floor, calling it "virtually an invitation to welfare dependency in many areas of the country."

But the legislation did contain a "sweetener" provision adding $900 million in federal money to help states meet their welfare costs. This was especially important to New York, which had been driven to insolvency by its mounting welfare burden. After waiting until the very end of the roll call, Conable not only voted for the bill but brought most of his state's GOP delegation with him, saving it from defeat. It later died in the Senate.

Conable has been close to the House Republican leadership since his early years when he worked on a series of proposals to change the seniority system. In 1970 GOP leader Gerald R. Ford named him to head a special Republican task force on seniority. One of Conable's suggestions was that the position of ranking Republican, the No. 1 minority seat on each committee, be voted on every two years by all Republicans rather than going automatically to the senior person on the committee. Conable said it would make ranking members "leaders and not just survivors."

In 1971, Ford named Conable chairman of the Republican Research Committee, which is considered part of the leadership. Two years later, when Ford became vice president and new House leaders were chosen, Conable won the policy committee chairmanship, defeating the more conservative Del Clawson of California by 11 votes. But thanks to one of his own reforms, he had to give it up in 1977 when he was elected ranking Republican on Ways and Means.

Conable's days as an elected party leader are probably over. Not only is his Ways and Means position a full-time job, but his moderate conservatism does not quite fit the more militant approach taken by most of the younger GOP members in recent years. Conable is an orthodox fiscal conservative, but he has voted for federally-funded abortions, the Equal Rights Amendment and most anti-poverty bills. "I clearly consider myself a conservative," he once said. "But I don't think a conservative is worthy of the name if he sticks his head in the sand and says there are no problems."

**At Home:** Conable comes from a family dedicated to politics and the Republican Party. His father was a Wyoming County (N.Y.) judge in the 1940s, and after he retired, he and his son practied law together in Batavia, a small city in Genesee County.

The younger Conable made it to the state Senate in 1962, but he stayed only two years. When the incumbent congressman from the area, Republican Harold C. Ostertag, announced his retirement in 1964, Conable announced he would run for the seat. Conable's state Senate district covered most of Ostertag's congressional district, making it a relatively comfortable switch.

In those days upstate GOP congressmen were virtually anointed by the local county chairmen, and once the brokers of the 35th District decided to go with Conable, his career was made. He won his first term comfortably despite the Democratic landslide of 1964 and has been an easy winner ever since. The Democrats made a major effort against him in 1974 with Midge Costanza, then vice mayor of Rochester and later a Carter White House aide. But Conable still won by more than 27,000 votes.

Conable's moderate conservatism has not pleased New York's Conservative Party. The party has never endorsed him and either runs a candidate of its own or — as in 1976 and 1980 — backs the Democratic candidate.

**The District:** Once the private preserve of the Wadsworth family, with its estate overlooking the bucolic Genesee Valley, the district is now a bit more variegated but not much less Republican.

James Wadsworth Sr. held the seat from 1881 to 1885 and 1891 to 1907. James Wadsworth Jr., who was known as "the conscience of the House" and personally saved the draft in a dramatic vote on the eve of World War II, occupied it from 1933 to 1951 after serving two terms in the U.S. Senate.

The Genesee River, one of the cleaner rivers left in the country and one of the few major ones flowing northward, is the heart of a rich agricultural area. It flows into Lake Ontario at the city of Rochester, which is divided between two congressional districts in order to minimize Democratic strength.

The western Republican suburbs of Rochester are attached to the district, along with Genesee, Livingston and Wyoming counties, rural and small town areas that almost invariably vote Republican.

## Committees

**Standards of Official Conduct** (2nd of 6 Republicans)

**Ways and Means** (Ranking Republican)

**Joint Taxation**

## Elections

**1980 General**

| | |
|---|---|
| Barber Conable Jr. (R) | 127,623 (72%) |
| John Owens (D) | 44,754 (25%) |

**1978 General**

| | |
|---|---|
| Barber Conable Jr. (R) | 96,119 (69%) |
| Francis Repicci (D) | 36,428 (26%) |

**Previous Winning Percentages**

| | | | |
|---|---|---|---|
| 1976 (64%) | 1974 (57%) | 1972 (68%) | 1970 (66%) |
| 1968 (71%) | 1966 (68%) | 1964 (54%) | |

**District Vote For President**

| | 1980 | | 1976 | | 1972 |
|---|---|---|---|---|---|
| **D** | 88,257 (45 %) | **D** | 85,502 (43 %) | **D** | 69,275 (34 %) |
| **R** | 88,316 (45 %) | **R** | 111,399 (56 %) | **R** | 132,363 (66 %) |
| **I** | 15,614 (8 %) | | | | |

## Campaign Finance

| | Receipts | Receipts from PACs | Expenditures |
|---|---|---|---|
| **1980** | | | |
| Conable (R) | $32,779 | $4,050 (12%) | $34,444 |
| **1978** | | | |
| Conable (R) | $52,607 | $3,575 (7%) | $59,204 |
| Repicci (D) | $31,009 | $1,450 (5%) | $30,837 |

## Voting Studies

| | Presidential Support | | Party Unity | | Conservative Coalition | |
|---|---|---|---|---|---|---|
| **Year** | **S** | **O** | **S** | **O** | **S** | **O** |
| 1980 | 50 | 45 | 71 | 23 | 62 | 28 |
| 1979 | 43 | 45 | 63 | 25 | 56 | 31 |
| 1978 | 51 | 32 | 66 | 25 | 66 | 24 |
| 1977 | 44 | 46 | 69 | 24 | 69 | 23 |

| | S | O | S | O | S | O |
|---|---|---|---|---|---|---|
| 1976 | 80 | 8 | 66 | 21 | 66 | 29 |
| 1975 | 82 | 18 | 80 | 17 | 76 | 21 |
| 1974 (Ford) | 35 | 15 | | | | |
| 1974 | 77 | 21 | 55 | 26 | 52 | 28 |
| 1973 | 86 | 11 | 75 | 20 | 72 | 23 |
| 1972 | 89 | 11 | 80 | 14† | 77 | 19† |
| 1971 | 82 | 7 | 75 | 16 | 72 | 18 |
| 1970 | 78 | 14 | 79 | 19 | 68 | 30 |
| 1969 | 66 | 21 | 64 | 27 | 56 | 31 |
| 1968 | 67 | 21 | 56 | 33 | 45 | 41 |
| 1967 | 52 | 36 | 72 | 19 | 67 | 30 |
| 1966 | 46 | 46 | 74 | 21 | 68 | 24 |
| 1965 | 59 | 35 | 67 | 27 | 63 | 33 |

S = Support          O = Opposition

† Not eligible for all recorded votes.

## Key Votes

**96th Congress**

| | |
|---|---|
| Weaken Carter oil profits tax (1979) | Y |
| Reject hospital cost control plan (1979) | Y |
| Implement Panama Canal Treaties (1979) | N |
| Establish Department of Education (1979) | N |
| Approve Anti-busing Amendment (1979) | N |
| Guarantee Chrysler Corp. loans (1979) | N |
| Approve military draft registration (1980) | N |
| Aid Sandinista regime in Nicaragua (1980) | N |
| Strengthen fair housing laws (1980) | N |

**97th Congress**

| | |
|---|---|
| Reagan budget proposal (1981) | Y |

## Interest Group Ratings

| Year | ADA | ACA | AFL-CIO | CCUS |
|---|---|---|---|---|
| 1980 | 28 | 79 | 12 | 72 |
| 1979 | 26 | 60 | 30 | 88 |
| 1978 | 30 | 56 | 25 | 76 |
| 1977 | 20 | 82 | 19 | 87 |
| 1976 | 10 | 63 | 13 | 74 |
| 1975 | 26 | 75 | 17 | 100 |
| 1974 | 39 | 50 | 20 | 88 |
| 1973 | 20 | 63 | 0 | 100 |
| 1972 | 6 | 65 | 20 | 90 |
| 1971 | 19 | 86 | 17 | - |
| 1970 | 28 | 79 | 14 | 90 |
| 1969 | 27 | 56 | 60 | - |
| 1968 | 17 | 70 | 67 | - |
| 1967 | 7 | 85 | 8 | 90 |
| 1966 | 6 | 72 | 0 | - |
| 1965 | 11 | 59 | - | 90 |

# 36 John J. LaFalce (D)

### Of Tonawanda — Elected 1974

**Born:** Oct. 6, 1939, Buffalo, N.Y.
**Education:** Canisius College, B.S. 1961; Villa-
nova Law School, J.D. 1964.
**Military Career:** Army, 1965-67.
**Profession:** Lawyer.
**Family:** Wife, Patricia Fisher.
**Religion:** Roman Catholic.
**Political Career:** N.Y. Senate, 1971-73; N.Y.
Assembly, 1973-75.

**In Washington:** LaFalce is a blunt, intense
man who likes to argue, and he has engaged in
more than his share of arguments on the Banking
Committee, where he has served throughout his
House career. Thoughtful and well-informed, he
has nevertheless had to deal with the institution's
natural suspicion of the man who asks too many
questions about too many subjects.

But if LaFalce has not been one of the more
popular Democrats in the class of 1974, he has
been one of its more aggressive legislators. Many
of his efforts have been launched from the Small
Business Committee, where he has made ample
use of a subcommittee chairmanship. He has
pushed the issue of product liability control, arguing the case for small-business men who complain
that high liability premiums threaten to drive
them out of business, and against most insurance
companies. LaFalce's goal is a new national liability law that would supersede current state law on
the subject.

It is LaFalce's fate to represent the Love
Canal area near Buffalo. He introduced his own
bill in 1979 that would have created an industry-
financed fund to clean up chemical dumpsites like
that one, but later switched to lobbying for similar Commerce Committee legislation. He spent
much of 1980 working on the issue, testifying on it
before virtually every committee he could find
that would listen.

Visibly impatient at times with his committee colleagues, LaFalce seemed even more impatient during the 96th Congress with the way
Republicans were behaving on the House floor.
He was incensed when the House took more than
three weeks to complete work on the Department
of Education bill, largely because any germane
amendment was permitted, and GOP members
opposed to the bill insisted on introducing dozens
of them.

LaFalce wrote a personal letter to Speaker

O'Neill, urging him to adopt a get-tough policy,
limiting the number of amendments that could be
offered on the floor. "Our rules are being abused,"
he complained to the Speaker. "We are frittering
away our most valuable resource — our time."
The leadership did not announce any formal
policy change in response to LaFalce's challenge.
But most major bills after mid-1980 came to the
floor under relatively tight procedural controls,
enough of a change for LaFalce to claim partial
victory.

**At Home:** A Buffalo lawyer, LaFalce burst
onto the political scene in 1970 with an upset
victory for the state Senate in a suburban district.
Determined to cut short his political career, Republicans in the state Legislature redrew the
Senate district in 1972 to make his re-election
hopeless. So he decided to take a step down, and
run for a seat in the state Assembly. When he won
that, he secured a reputation as one of the strongest Democratic candidates in years in western
New York.

While in the Legislature, LaFalce concentrated on procedural reform, as he has done
recently in Congress. He was a strong critic of the
late Gov. Nelson A. Rockefeller and capitalized in
his campaigns on deep-seated resentments
against Rockefeller in the Buffalo area.

In 1974, when Republican Rep. Henry P.
Smith retired, LaFalce began campaigning in a
congressional district that had not been won by a

---

**36th District: West — Niagara
Falls.** Population: 446,189 (5% increase since
1970). Race: White 424,883 (95%), Black
15,770 (4%), Others 5,536 (1%). Spanish origin: 3,582 (1%).

Democrat in 62 years. Once again his aggressive style paid off — he triumphed by nearly 30,000 votes. He has easily won re-election since.

**The District:** Although relatively compact, the 36th District contains a wide variety of demographic areas. Centered on Niagara County, it dips down into Erie County to take in a small portion of the city of Buffalo and the blue-collar suburban areas of Tonawanda and Grand Island.

There is a large Italian-American community in the Erie County section of the district, and LaFalce is part of it. Niagara County combines an industrial belt along the Niagara River, some suburban areas, and rural areas to the north and east. The district also extends eastward to include all of Orleans County, a lightly-populated area of fruit farms and small towns, and a small rural portion of Monroe County.

The district is Republican in most state and national elections; Gerald R. Ford took it by more than 14,000 votes in 1976 as he was losing the state.

## Committees

**Banking, Finance and Urban Affairs** (11th of 25 Democrats)
Financial Institutions Supervision, Regulation and Insurance; Housing and Community Development; International Development Institutions and Finance; International Trade, Investment and Monetary Policy.

**Small Business** (5th of 23 Democrats)
General Oversight, chairman.

## Elections

**1980 General**

| | |
|---|---|
| John LaFalce (D ) | 122,929 (72 %) |
| William Feder (R ) | 48,428 (28 %) |

**1978 General**

| | |
|---|---|
| John LaFalce (D ) | 99,497 (74 %) |
| Francina Cartonia (R ) | 31,527 (24 %) |

**Previous Winning Percentages**

1976 (67%)    1974 (60%)

**District Vote For President**

| | 1980 | | 1976 | | 1972 |
|---|---|---|---|---|---|
| **D** | 82,034 (45 %) | **D** | 88,063 (46 %) | **D** | 78,931 (40 %) |
| **R** | 82,081 (45 %) | **R** | 102,268 (55 %) | **R** | 119,213 (60 %) |
| **I** | 14,007 (8 %) | | | | |

## Campaign Finance

| | Receipts | Receipts from PACs | Expenditures |
|---|---|---|---|
| **1980** | | | |
| LaFalce (D ) | $140,086 | $51,242 (37 %) | $66,000 |
| Feder (R ) | $34,159 | $3,061 (9 %) | $33,088 |
| **1978** | | | |
| LaFalce (D ) | $114,208 | $33,507 (29 %) | $44,407 |
| Cartonia (R ) | $9,478 | $25 (0%) | $9,476 |

## Voting Studies

| | Presidential Support | | Party Unity | | Conservative Coalition | |
|---|---|---|---|---|---|---|
| Year | S | O | S | O | S | O |
| 1980 | 75 | 16 | 74 | 15 | 19 | 64 |
| 1979 | 68 | 18 | 80 | 12 | 22 | 74 |
| 1978 | 81 | 13 | 71 | 26 | 25 | 71 |
| 1977 | 72 | 19 | 70 | 23 | 30 | 62 |
| 1976 | 27 | 55 | 71 | 19 | 29 | 59 |
| 1975 | 36 | 60 | 83 | 14 | 24 | 72 |

S = Support          O = Opposition

## Key Votes

**96th Congress**

| | |
|---|---|
| Weaken Carter oil profits tax (1979) | N |
| Reject hospital cost control plan (1979) | N |
| Implement Panama Canal Treaties (1979) | Y |
| Establish Department of Education (1979) | N |
| Approve Anti-busing Amendment (1979) | N |
| Guarantee Chrysler Corp. loans (1979) | Y |
| Approve military draft registration (1980) | Y |
| Aid Sandinista regime in Nicaragua (1980) | Y |
| Strengthen fair housing laws (1980) | Y |

**97th Congress**

| | |
|---|---|
| Reagan budget proposal (1981) | N |

## Interest Group Ratings

| Year | ADA | ACA | AFL-CIO | CCUS |
|---|---|---|---|---|
| 1980 | 56 | 25 | 82 | 65 |
| 1979 | 68 | 4 | 80 | 11 |
| 1978 | 40 | 37 | 60 | 33 |
| 1977 | 45 | 17 | 82 | 56 |
| 1976 | 50 | 15 | 70 | 44 |
| 1975 | 84 | 15 | 96 | 18 |

# 37 Henry J. Nowak (D)

**Of Buffalo — elected 1974**

**Born:** Feb. 21, 1935, Buffalo, N.Y.
**Education:** Canisius College, B.B.A. 1957; U. Of
   Buffalo, J.D. 1961.
**Military Career:** Army, 1957-62.
**Profession:** Lawyer.
**Family:** Wife, Rose Santa Lucia; two children.
**Religion:** Roman Catholic.
**Political Career:** Erie County Comptroller,
   1966-75.

**In Washington:** The Small Business Committee is a routine assignment for many of its 41 members, but it offers a useful legislative and political forum for those who want to pursue it. Nowak, an organization Democrat who rarely speaks on the House floor, has made increasingly effective use of it in the past two Congresses.

Nowak took over one of the panel's subcommittees, on Access to Capital, in 1979. Since then, he has introduced a steady stream of legislation and taken voluminous testimony at hearings. Some of them have drawn a bit of news attention — a previously rare occurrence for Nowak, one of the more retiring people in the House. One of the bills Nowak introduced in the 96th Congress would double the investment tax credit for used machinery owned by small businesses. Another would allow them to depreciate buildings over a longer period (15 years). A third one would defer the payment of federal taxes on the sale of small-business stock.

He was also a primary House sponsor of the Regulatory Flexibility Act, requiring federal agencies to weigh the impact of proposed regulations on small businesses before issuing final rules. It became law late in 1980.

When he has not been promoting small business, Nowak has been using his Public Works assignment the way nearly every other member of the committee likes to use it — to bring home some tangible federal generosity. One Public Works bill that passed the House in 1980, for example, contained $1.7 million for flood control on Cazenovia Creek in the Buffalo area, plus money for a local channel enlargement, restoration of a bridge in downtown Buffalo, and an in-depth study of the city's water supply.

**At Home:** Nowak is a solid party loyalist allied to Buffalo Democratic leader Joseph Crangle. He has rarely disappointed the Erie County organization, and it has rarely disap-

pointed him.

After serving for a year as an assistant district attorney, Nowak was plucked from obscurity by Crangle in 1965 at the age of 30, and made the Democratic nominee for Erie County comptroller. His Polish name and background as a basketball star at Canisius College made him a good choice, and a strong Democratic showing in the county that year led to his election. He proved to be a popular executive and was re-elected in 1969 and 1973.

Nowak spent nearly a decade as heir-apparent to Democratic Rep. Thaddeus J. Dulski, chairman of the House Post Office Committee. When Dulski finally decided to retire in 1974, he did it machine-style, waiting until four days before the filing deadline so nobody could mount a serious campaign against Nowak. Nobody has since, either.

**The District:** Buffalo is struggling against the same hard times as nearly all the old Northeastern industrial cities. Its steel, auto, shipping, and grain milling industries are all in decline.

In addition to most of Buffalo, the 37th District contains the grimy steel city of Lackawanna, to the south, and a few blue-collar suburbs to the east. It is a largely Polish district, whose blue-collar workers live in single-family frame homes on the east side of the city and in the suburbs across its borders. But there are also communities of Irish-Americans on the south

---

**37th District: West — Buffalo.** Population: 360,405 (23% decrease since 1970). Race: White 253,292 (70%), Black 96,413 (27%), Others 10,700 (3%). Spanish origin: 10,152 (3%).

side, Italian-Americans in the northwest, and blacks in the downtown area, about a quarter of the district's population. All vote Democratic in most elections.

Little is left of the once pervasive German ambience of Buffalo; the Germans have largely moved to the suburbs and lost much of their ethnic identity.

Buffalo has suffered a massive population decline. Once close to 600,000, it is now down to about 360,000, and the 37th district will have to gain about 150,000 new residents to come up to the state average. That means it will have to cut sharply into the surrounding surburban areas.

## Committees

**Public Works and Transportation** (8th of 25 Democrats)
Aviation; Economic Development; Surface Transportation; Water Resources.

**Small Business** (8th of 23 Democrats)
Tax, Access to Equity Capital and Business Opportunities, chairman.

## Elections

**1980 General**

| | |
|---|---|
| Henry Nowak (D ) | 94,890 (83 %) |
| Roger Heymanowski (R) | 16,560 (15 %) |

**1978 General**

| | |
|---|---|
| Henry Nowak (D ) | 70,911 (79 %) |
| Charles Roth (R ) | 17,585 (20 %) |

**Previous Winning Percentages**

1976 (78 %)    1974 (75 %)

**District Vote For President**

| | 1980 | | 1976 | | 1972 |
|---|---|---|---|---|---|
| D | 90,516 (67 %) | D | 95,814 (63 %) | D | 99,386 (57 %) |
| R | 35,329 (26 %) | R | 55,248 (36 %) | R | 74,853 (43 %) |
| I | 7,030 (5 %) | | | | |

## Campaign Finance

| | Receipts | Receipts from PACs | Expen- ditures |
|---|---|---|---|
| **1980** | | | |
| Nowak (D ) | $62,444 | $27,475 (44 %) | $40,515 |
| **1978** | | | |
| Nowak (D ) | $52,235 | $22,950 (44 %) | $37,521 |

## Voting Studies

| | Presidential Support | | Party Unity | | Conservative Coalition | |
|---|---|---|---|---|---|---|
| Year | S | O | S | O | S | O |
| 1980 | 71 | 24 | 88 | 8 | 14 | 81 |
| 1979 | 73 | 26 | 87 | 12 | 22 | 76 |
| 1978 | 78 | 21 | 81 | 19 | 19 | 80 |
| 1977 | 71 | 27 | 85 | 12 | 18 | 81 |
| 1976 | 27 | 71 | 87 | 11 | 20 | 78 |
| 1975 | 36 | 64 | 89 | 10 | 19 | 80 |

S = Support          O = Opposition

## Key Votes

**96th Congress**

| | |
|---|---|
| Weaken Carter oil profits tax (1979) | N |
| Reject hospital cost control plan (1979) | N |
| Implement Panama Canal Treaties (1979) | Y |
| Establish Department of Education (1979) | N |
| Approve Anti-busing Amendment (1979) | N |
| Guarantee Chrysler Corp. loans (1979) | Y |
| Approve military draft registration (1980) | N |
| Aid Sandinista regime in Nicaragua (1980) | Y |
| Strengthen fair housing laws (1980) | Y |

**97th Congress**

| | |
|---|---|
| Reagan budget proposal (1981) | N |

## Interest Group Ratings

| Year | ADA | ACA | AFL-CIO | CCUS |
|---|---|---|---|---|
| 1980 | 78 | 13 | 89 | 63 |
| 1979 | 79 | 12 | 95 | 11 |
| 1978 | 70 | 15 | 95 | 17 |
| 1977 | 70 | 7 | 87 | 24 |
| 1976 | 85 | 7 | 74 | 32 |
| 1975 | 89 | 7 | 100 | 12 |

# 38 Jack F. Kemp (R)

### Of Hamburg — Elected 1970

**Born:** July 13, 1935, Los Angeles, Calif.
**Education:** Occidental College, B.A. 1957.
**Military Career:** Army Reserve, 1958-62.
**Profession:** Professional football player.
**Family:** Wife, Joanne Main; four children.
**Religion:** Presbyterian.
**Political Career:** No previous office.

**In Washington:** Judged by legislative action alone, Kemp's 10-year congressional career has been nothing extraordinary. He has never had the patience to haggle over amendments or sit through long debates on the floor. Often he has not even been there.

But Kemp has done something else: absorb a grand idea, persuade himself of it beyond the slightest doubt, convert it into a national crusade, sell it to a successful presidential candidate, and defend it against a flurry of attacks from left and right.

At the beginning of 1981, as supporters of Kemp's "supply-side" economic policy were joining the Reagan administration, Kemp himself was elected to the House Republican leadership, as chairman of the party conference. That was something unusual; hardly anyone becomes a congressional leader inside the House by being a leader on the outside first.

But hardly anyone in the House has used a single issue the way Kemp has in the years since his economic conversion. As many branches of supply-side economics as there seem to be, Kemp has always expressed it in fairly simple terms: the route to national prosperity lies in lower taxes, increased incentive, and economic growth — not in redistribution of wealth. Or, to use a homily Kemp is fond of borrowing from John F. Kennedy, "a rising tide lifts all boats."

It is not far from there to the relatively simple, much-criticized Kemp-Roth bill, which he introduced with Delaware Republican Sen. William V. Roth Jr. It originally called for a 10 percent reduction in federal personal income taxes every year for three years. As of mid-1981, the Reagan administration was sticking to its support for a three-year, 25 percent reduction, not too far from the basic proposal.

Kemp defends the tax cut idea with an agressiveness that suggests he has never quite left professional sports. Debating economics seems almost to give him a physical "high" at times. He does it with an intensity that can make him seem hostile, but that has more to do with sheer competitive energy than with hostility.

Kemp has been a conservative his entire adult life, and he voted as one during his first years in the House. But he did not become a true believer until one day in 1975, when *Wall Street Journal* columnist Jude Wanniski dropped by his office for a morning interview that finally ended in Kemp's dining room at midnight.

Ever since then, Kemp has pursued his low tax and high growth philosophy with a cheerleader's enthusiasm. That has always led critics to question how much he knows about economics — even when he talks at a level of sophistication unusual for anybody in public office.

Kemp went to the 1976 Republican convention with an offer for Ronald Reagan, then contesting Gerald R. Ford for the presidential nomination. According to reports published later, Kemp and Wanniski pledged "four or five" additional delegates if Reagan would endorse the Kemp-Roth tax cut. The plan was never taken to Reagan.

But a few months later, Kemp's basic idea began showing up in Reagan's syndicated newspaper column. Kemp spent much of 1977 taking his idea on the road, and it brought in so much publicity that by the spring of 1978 the national press was full of stories about the former quarter-

---

**38th District: West — Buffalo suburbs.** Population: 498,233 (7% increase since 1970). Race: White 486,306 (98%), Black 4,818 (1%), Others 7,109 (1%). Spanish origin: 3,167 (1%).

---

back brimming with conservative zeal. Columnist James J. Kilpatrick offered his name as a likely 1980 presidential nominee.

All this happened without the actual legislation ever advancing very far in Congress. A modified Democratic version passed the Senate in 1978 but went no further. The tax cut came to a vote in the House the same year, losing on a 240-178 party-line decision. Kemp-Roth also became the centerpiece of the 1978 GOP congressional campaigns. But it was not a very effective one. Numerous Republican candidates throughout the country found it difficult to defend in debate, and Democrats insisted that it would make the federal deficit larger instead of smaller.

The 1980 election year, however, was a time of success for Kemp. Reagan endorsed the full-scale tax cut, and placed Kemp's name on a list of possible vice presidential running mates. The congressman was rapidly becoming as famous nationally as he was when he quarterbacked the Buffalo Bills. When Reagan won the presidency, several Kemp protégés were given top-level jobs in the Treasury Department.

There are still some strains in Kemp's thinking, however, that cause real conflict with traditional Republicans. Foremost among them is his attitude toward balancing the budget.

"I don't buy the argument that a balanced budget is necessarily sacrosanct," he said in 1978. Kemp's original speeches for his tax cut bill touched lightly on the need for cuts in federal spending, with the argument that lower tax rates would generate enough new revenue on their own to balance the budget eventually.

Less conspicuous was Kemp's moderate attitude on most social issues; he has never considered them very important. "In an economically healthy society," he has argued, "a lot of the social problems conservatives worry about wouldn't be problems any more."

Kemp has played down social issues partly because he has seen them as distractions in the Republican effort to build a national majority with working-class votes.

He has always complained about conservative rhetoric against unions. "This business of always calling labor 'big labor' or 'labor bosses' is wrong," he said in 1978. "We should have more respect for the American labor movement." He was saying similar things in the early days of the Reagan administration, arguing against efforts to dismantle the Occupational Safety and Health Administration and telling an audience of conservatives that "attacking the New Deal is a mistake for us." Kemp's Buffalo-area district is suburban, but it is labor oriented, and he has been careful to stay on good terms with local unions.

Kemp likes alliances that most conservatives avoid. He forged one with Rep. Robert Garcia, the Bronx Democrat of Puerto Rican background, over the issue of free-enterprise zones, which Kemp borrowed from a pair of British economists. Kemp and Garcia want to encourage development in blighted urban areas by declaring tax moratoriums and regulatory restrictions.

The one thing Kemp has in common with most conservatives is his hard-line attitude on defense. He has done little serious committee work in the House, but most of it has been on the Defense Appropriations Subcommittee, and there he has argued consistently for higher levels of military spending. In 1980, when President Carter began to sound tougher on U.S.-Soviet relations, Kemp denounced it as "the most dangerous kind of international posturing; the making of an empty threat."

In 1981, Kemp moved over to take the ranking Republican position on the Appropriations subcommittee dealing with foreign aid. In that position, he has argued strongly for Israel, defending it during the controversy over its raid on nuclear facilities in Iraq.

**At Home:** Football led Kemp to leave Southern California for the snows of Buffalo, and football gave him the publicity he needed to start a congressional career.

After playing in the American Football League as quarterback for the Buffalo Bills, and winning an award as the league's most valuable player, Kemp co-founded the AFL Players Association. He was its president from 1965 to 1970.

In 1970, Erie County Republicans were looking for a strong candidate to recapture the suburban Buffalo congressional district that the party had lost in 1964. The incumbent, Democrat Richard Max McCarthy, was running for the Senate. Kemp agreed to run.

Democrats charged that Kemp was a know-nothing football player without the background or knowledge to be an effective congressman. But he had instant appeal in Buffalo, and won by a narrow margin. Two years later, with the help of favorable redistricting, a Nixon landslide and his own hard work, Kemp won re-election by an overwhelming margin. He has never dropped below 70 percent of the vote since then.

Kemp's political success has surprised some who knew him only as an athlete, but it is no coincidence. Kemp began working in politics while he was playing in the AFL. He was a volunteer in the Nixon and Goldwater presidential campaigns, and in Ronald Reagan's gubernatorial campaign in 1966. By the late 1960s, he was working in the off-season as an assistant to Reagan's chief of staff.

Kemp has made no secret of his further political ambitions. He considered running for the U.S. Senate in 1980, but when Republican Sen. Jacob K. Javits announced for another term, Kemp decided not to challenge him in a primary. Had Javits stayed out Kemp would almost certainly have run for the post. In 1982, both the governorship and a U.S. Senate seat are up in New York.

**The District:** Located entirely within Erie County, the 38th District contains all but three of the county's townships. It is mostly suburban, although its character traverses the spectrum from blue-collar ethnic enclaves to upper income WASP areas and some rural communities.

Near the Buffalo city line, large numbers of Polish-Americans have moved into suburban parts of the district while still working in Buffalo's inner-city industries. Farther from the city are middle- to upper-income professional and managerial groups.

While the district has given Kemp overwhelming margins of victory, Democrats have a residual strength likely to show up if he is not on the House ballot.

## Committees

**Appropriations** (9th of 22 Republicans)
  Foreign Operations.

**Budget** (5th of 12 Republicans)
  Task Forces: Economic Policy and Productivity; National Security and Veterans; Tax Policy.

## Elections

**1980 General**

| | |
|---|---|
| Jack Kemp (R ) | 167,434 (82 %) |
| Gale Denn (D ) | 37,875 (18 %) |

**1978 General**

| | |
|---|---|
| Jack Kemp (R ) | 113,928 (95 %) |
| James Peck (L ) | 6,204 (5 %) |

**Previous Winning Percentages**

| | | | |
|---|---|---|---|
| 1976 (78 %) | 1974 (72 %) | 1972 (73 %) | 1970 (52 %) |

**District Vote For President**

| | 1980 | | 1976 | | 1972 |
|---|---|---|---|---|---|
| D | 92,435 (43 %) | D | 98,093 (44 %) | D | 85,344 (39 %) |
| R | 101,559 (48 %) | R | 121,992 (55 %) | R | 132,478 (61 %) |
| I | 16,489 (8 %) | | | | |

## Campaign Finance

| | Receipts | Receipts from PACs | Expenditures |
|---|---|---|---|
| **1980** | | | |
| Kemp (R ) | $172,121 | $11,980 (7 %) | $158,061 |
| **1978** | | | |
| Kemp (R ) | $76,771 | $11,160 (15 %) | $64,251 |
| Peck (L ) | $5,050 | $4,800 (95 %) | $6,418 |

## Voting Studies

| | Presidential Support | | Party Unity | | Conservative Coalition | |
|---|---|---|---|---|---|---|
| Year | S | O | S | O | S | O |
| 1980 | 37 | 52 | 76 | 15 | 71 | 14 |
| 1979 | 26 | 63 | 78 | 11 | 79 | 10 |
| 1978 | 33 | 53 | 79 | 11 | 83 | 9 |
| 1977 | 34 | 57 | 85 | 9 | 86 | 8 |
| 1976 | 73 | 22 | 91 | 5 | 91 | 5 |
| 1975 | 66 | 30 | 83 | 8 | 84 | 6 |
| 1974 (Ford) | 46 | 46 | | | | |
| 1974 | 72 | 26 | 69 | 25 | 66 | 26 |
| 1973 | 61 | 29 | 74 | 16 | 74 | 18 |
| 1972 | 76 | 22 | 69 | 24 | 74 | 18 |
| 1971 | 81 | 14 | 79 | 16 | 82 | 11 |

S = Support        O = Opposition

## Key Votes

**96th Congress**

| | |
|---|---|
| Weaken Carter oil profits tax (1979) | Y |
| Reject hospital cost control plan (1979) | Y |
| Implement Panama Canal Treaties (1979) | N |
| Establish Department of Education (1979) | N |
| Approve Anti-busing Amendment (1979) | Y |
| Guarantee Chrysler Corp. loans (1979) | N |
| Approve military draft registration (1980) | Y |
| Aid Sandinista regime in Nicaragua (1980) | N |
| Strengthen fair housing laws (1980) | N |

**97th Congress**

| | |
|---|---|
| Reagan budget proposal (1981) | Y |

## Interest Group Ratings

| Year | ADA | ACA | AFL-CIO | CCUS |
|---|---|---|---|---|
| 1980 | 6 | 86 | 12 | 75 |
| 1979 | 11 | 92 | 16 | 88 |
| 1978 | 15 | 96 | 15 | 88 |
| 1977 | 10 | 96 | 17 | 94 |
| 1976 | 5 | 85 | 22 | 82 |
| 1975 | 5 | 93 | 14 | 94 |
| 1974 | 17 | 79 | 30 | 50 |
| 1973 | 12 | 80 | 33 | 67 |
| 1972 | 25 | 70 | 36 | 89 |
| 1971 | 16 | 85 | 18 | - |

**885**

# 39 Stanley N. Lundine (D)

**Of Jamestown — Elected 1976**

**Born:** Feb. 4, 1939, Jamestown, N.Y.
**Education:** Duke U., A.B. 1961; N.Y.U., LL.B. 1964.
**Profession:** Lawyer.
**Family:** Separated; two children.
**Religion:** Protestant.
**Political Career:** Chautauqua County Public Defender, 1965-67; Mayor of Jamestown, 1969-76.

**In Washington:** Lundine believes he has a solution to many of the nation's economic problems, and he spends much of his congressional time trying to persuade his House colleagues and business and labor leaders on the outside to think about it. He is among the most single-minded legislators in the House.

The issue is better productivity, and while most politicians now pay lip service to the concept, Lundine has been more specific. His main idea is more coordination among workers, employers and the government. One of his bills in the 96th Congress would have established a new Federal Productivity Council in the government, with the budget director, Treasury secretary and labor secretary all serving as members. Another would have required the Bureau of Labor Statistics to provide more details on worker productivity in industry.

His clearest victory so far, however, came in 1978, when most of a productivity bill he had been promoting became law as an addition to jobs legislation. This idea, which Lundine called the Human Resources Development Act, provided federal aid to labor-management coordinating bodies. Lundine originally asked for $25 million, but was pleased to get $10 million authorized, thanks in part to help from New York's Republican senator, Jacob Javits. It was not until 1981, however, that any money was appropriated for the program — $1.2 million.

Another side of Lundine's productivity crusade involves employees investing in the companies they work for. Like Louisiana Democrat Russell B. Long, former chairman of the Senate Finance Committee, Lundine is a believer in ESOP — the Employee Stock Ownership Plan. When the Banking Committee voted for a loan guarantee for Chrysler Corp., in 1979, Lundine was successful in adding a variant of this approach to the bill.

Later he added an ESOP-like provision to the committee's Economic Development Act. This one required that 5 percent of all future loan guarantees be used to help employees buy their failing companies. The act did not become law.

When he is not crusading for productivity, Lundine tries to cope with the nuclear waste issue. His district has a serious waste disposal problem, and is politically sensitive about it. Lundine managed in 1980 to win approval for a new experimental disposal center for the nuclear waste located in the area.

**At Home:** Lundine stunned Republicans with his lopsided special election victory in 1976 in a district that had not gone Democratic since 1874. He defeated John T. Calkins, a former deputy counsel to President Ford and a one-time political aide to House Republicans.

A lawyer, Lundine went into government in the mid-1960s, serving as associate corporation counsel for the city of Jamestown and later as chairman of the city planning commission. Elected Mayor of Jamestown in 1969, he was re-elected three times before being tapped by Democratic congressional district leaders for the special election.

As Mayor, Lundine was active in the labor-management relations field he has pursued in the House. One of his major campaign themes was his record of bringing quarrelsome groups together

---

**39th District: Southern Tier — Chautauqua, Elmira.** Population: 471,666 (1% increase since 1970). Race: White 458,104 (97%), Black 7,412 (2%), Others 6,150 (1%). Spanish origin: 3,976 (1%).

for economic revitalization of Jamestown.

Lundine has continued to win in a traditionally Republican constituency, but not by overwhelming margins.

**The District:** Stretching across New York's Southern Tier from Elmira to Lake Erie, the district is largely an area of rolling hills and small towns. It also has a few significant industries, such as the Corning Glass Works in Corning, and plants of Westinghouse, Sperry Rand, and Bendix Corp. There are dairy farms and Taylor Wine vineyards in the countryside. However, the South-

ern Tier has generally been an economically depressed region, in the backwater of New York's economy and politics.

The area was originally settled by New Englanders early in the 19th century, and later a large Scandinavian population moved in. Lundine is a Scandinavian. The district as a whole was strongly Republican until recent years, but Democrats have been making inroads. Lundine's election in 1976 was the climax of a Democratic surge which carried the party to control of the Chautauqua County (Jamestown) Legislature in 1975.

## Committees

**Banking, Finance and Urban Affairs** (14th of 25 Democrats)
Economic Stabilization; Housing and Community Development; International Trade, Investment and Monetary Policy.

**Science and Technology** (18th of 23 Democrats)
Energy Research and Production; Science, Research and Technology.

**Select Aging** (14th of 31 Democrats)
Housing and Consumer Interests; Human Services.

## Elections

**1980 General**

| | |
|---|---|
| Stanley Lundine (D ) | 93,839 (55 %) |
| James Abdella (R ) | 75,039 (44 %) |

**1978 General**

| | |
|---|---|
| Stanley Lundine (D ) | 79,385 (58 %) |
| Crispin Maguire (R ) | 56,431 (42 %) |

**Previous Winning Percentages**

1976 (62 %)    1976*(62%)
* Special election

**District Vote For President**

| | 1980 | | 1976 | | 1972 |
|---|---|---|---|---|---|
| D | 67,886 (38 %) | D | 77,776 (42 %) | D | 63,253 (34 %) |
| R | 97,773 (54 %) | R | 106,803 (58 %) | R | 124,906 (66 %) |
| I | 12,049 (7 %) | | | | |

## Campaign Finance

| | Receipts | Receipts from PACs | Expenditures |
|---|---|---|---|
| **1980** | | | |
| Lundine (D ) | $123,759 | $49,905 (40 %) | $125,269 |
| Abdella (R ) | $81,034 | $7,500 (9 %) | $83,315 |

**1978**

| | | | |
|---|---|---|---|
| Lundine (D ) | $99,960 | $31,092 (31 %) | $92,454 |
| Maguire (R ) | $63,815 | $3,250 (5 %) | $65,508 |

## Voting Studies

| | Presidential Support | | Party Unity | | Conservative Coalition | |
|---|---|---|---|---|---|---|
| Year | S | O | S | O | S | O |
| 1980 | 69 | 21 | 77 | 12 | 16 | 67 |
| 1979 | 74 | 16 | 74 | 15 | 22 | 69 |
| 1978 | 73 | 18 | 83 | 13 | 14 | 82 |
| 1977 | 68 | 25 | 80 | 10 | 14 | 73 |
| 1976 | 36 | 59† | 82 | 11† | 17 | 71† |

† Not eligible for all recorded votes.

S = Support        O = Opposition

## Key Votes

**96th Congress**

| | |
|---|---|
| Weaken Carter oil profits tax (1979) | N |
| Reject hospital cost control plan (1979) | N |
| Implement Panama Canal Treaties (1979) | Y |
| Establish Department of Education (1979) | N |
| Approve Anti-busing Amendment (1979) | N |
| Guarantee Chrysler Corp. loans (1979) | Y |
| Approve military draft registration (1980) | N |
| Aid Sandinista regime in Nicaragua (1980) | Y |
| Strengthen fair housing laws (1980) | Y |

**97th Congress**

| | |
|---|---|
| Reagan budget proposal (1981) | N |

## Interest Group Ratings

| Year | ADA | ACA | AFL-CIO | CCUS |
|---|---|---|---|---|
| 1980 | 83 | 13 | 79 | 57 |
| 1979 | 79 | 17 | 79 | 28 |
| 1978 | 70 | 26 | 85 | 33 |
| 1977 | 75 | 15 | 71 | 44 |
| 1976 | 88 | 4 | 82 | 39 |

# North Carolina

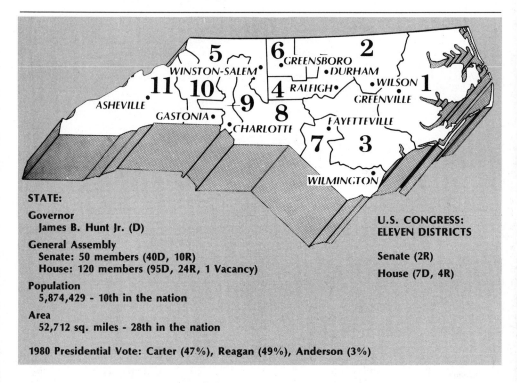

**STATE:**

**Governor**
James B. Hunt Jr. (D)

**General Assembly**
Senate: 50 members (40D, 10R)
House: 120 members (95D, 24R, 1 Vacancy)

**Population**
5,874,429 - 10th in the nation

**Area**
52,712 sq. miles - 28th in the nation

**U.S. CONGRESS:**
**ELEVEN DISTRICTS**

Senate (2R)

House (7D, 4R)

1980 Presidential Vote: Carter (47%), Reagan (49%), Anderson (3%)

## ... A Change in Image

For many years, North Carolina had the reputation of being the most progressive Southern state, thanks mostly to a tradition of clean government, economic expansion and racial peace. But "progressive" is not a word people often use in talking about North Carolina these days. Now the state is associated with Jesse Helms and John East, its two U.S. senators aligned with the "New Right" and the Moral Majority.

In many ways, North Carolina has always been a conservative state. Its business community has influenced politics more consistently and more thoroughly than has business in most Southern states. Its major industries — textiles, tobacco, and furniture — have traditionally paid low wages and bitterly fought unionization. Better paying industries have not always been welcomed.

But if North Carolina's "progressive" image was a misjudgment fostered by Northern observers on tour, its swing to the Republican right seems equally unproven. The state's Republican Party suffered through ruinous elections in 1974 and 1976, and is just now recovering. After winning the governorship and 50 state legislative seats in the 1972 Nixon landslide, the GOP found its legislative contingent reduced to 13 by 1976, as Democrats recaptured the governorship.

Republicans have rebounded somewhat since then, but still hold only 34 seats in the Legislature. Their 1980 gubernatorial candidate, I. Beverly Lake Jr., received a paltry 37 percent of the vote.

Lake, a Helms protégé, was defeated by Democratic Gov. James B. Hunt Jr., whose success in recent years has been the major obstacle to conservative control. Elected lieutenant governor in 1972, Hunt has been the state's leading Democrat ever since. He built a large political organization that was instrumental in pushing through a 1977 constitutional amendment that allowed an incumbent governor to seek re-election.

The state's industrial base is diversifying, as the state has worked hard to attract the electronics industry that boosted the economy in California, Colorado and other states in the 1970s. More than a quarter of the 29,000 new jobs created in the state in 1980 were in electronics or machinery; higher wages in these industries are helping to raise the state's average hourly manufacturing wage, which still ranks among the lowest.

# A Political Tour

**The East.** This rural area has long been the poorest and most agricultural region in North Carolina. Through much of the post-World War II era, out-migration was a serious problem: young people, especially blacks, fled the farms for urban areas.

In the past decade, the population of eastern Carolina has enjoyed an upturn. Most of the growth has been along the Atlantic Coast. Coastal resort towns such as Nags Head, Topsail Beach and Long Beach have all more than doubled their population in the last decade.

Further inland, expansion of economic opportunities has been only modest. Apparel, machinery and chemical factories are moving in, but tobacco, sweet potatoes and peanuts still pay most bills, and an Old South flavor lingers.

Many easterners trace their Democratic voting heritage to the Civil War, but they are generally more conservative than partisan. In 1968, all but a handful of eastern counties gave George Wallace a plurality in the presidential race. Helms receives a substantial crossover vote in this region from allies sometimes called "Jessecrats"; he won all four of the eastern congressional districts in 1978.

State Republican strategists hope to convert the conservative east to the GOP, but Helms is the only Republican so far who has consistently sparked defection from traditional Democratic patterns. When John East challenged Democratic Sen. Robert Morgan in 1980, East won only ten counties east of the Fall Line, the topographical divider of eastern Carolina and the Piedmont.

The most fertile ground for future Republican gains will be the more affluent coastal counties and areas where military bases are an important component in the economy. In 1980, Reagan won six coastal counties, including Onslow County, site of Camp Lejeune, a Marine Corps training center.

**The Piedmont.** Five urban centers and several large towns make up central North Carolina's Piedmont industrial crescent. The textile, tobacco and furniture manufacturing industries have prospered here.

In recent years, factories producing chemicals, computer circuits, auto parts and other transportation and electrical equipment have moved into the region, drawing from the same labor pool as the traditional economic mainstays.

The largest Piedmont urban counties are Mecklenburg (Charlotte), Guilford (Greensboro), Wake (Raleigh) and Forsyth (Winston-Salem). They have different personalities and economic bases, but their voting behavior in the presidential elections since 1968 has been remarkably similar. All four voted Republican in 1968, 1972 and 1980. Jimmy Carter won slim majorities in Mecklenburg, Guilford and Forsyth counties in 1976, but Wake County held for President Ford. In state elections, the partisan affinity breaks down. All four counties supported Republican Helms in 1978 and Democrat Hunt in 1980.

White-collar economic conservatism is the driving force of politics in these affluent counties. Three are represented by Republicans in the U.S. House.

Charlotte, the largest North Carolina city, trails only Atlanta as a Southeastern distribution, transportation and commercial center. Greensboro is the headquarters of Burlington Industries, the textile giant. Winston-Salem is the center of the state's tobacco industry and the headquarters of R. J. Reynolds. Raleigh is the seat of state government and home of North Carolina State University.

The largest Piedmont city with a still-heavy Democratic influence is Durham, which has voted Democratic in every postwar presidential election except 1972. Durham, home of Duke University, is a city of factories with a large and politically active black community.

Nearby is the Research Triangle, a collection of laboratories and other research facilities run by private firms and government agencies, and tied loosely to the state's academic institutions. In addition to Duke and N.C. State, the third point of the research triangle is at Chapel Hill in Orange County. The home of the University of North Carolina, Orange County gave Reagan only 32 percent of the vote in 1980.

Several of the rural Piedmont counties along the Virginia border are conservative Democratic, like the rural areas of the coastal plain. There is a GOP tradition in some of the hilly counties of the western Piedmont, where many of the early settlers were of German and Scotch-Irish stock.

In 1980, Reagan demonstrated great strength in medium-sized Piedmont industrial counties like Rowan (Salisbury), Alamance (Burlington), Gaston (Gastonia) and Catawba (Hickory). The bulk of textile employment is located in this area, and there was considerable apprehension that Carter-supported expansion of trade with China would flood the U.S. with inexpensive textiles.

**The West.** After a century of frustration, the North Carolina GOP in 1972 finally elected a governor. He was James E. Holshouser Jr., a moderate Republican from mountainous Watauga County in the western part of the state.

North Carolina's small Republican Party had been centered in the west since the Civil War era, when many of the region's farmers were anti-slavery and anti-secession.

Holshouser hoped to expand the party by attracting more moderates and minorities. But the rival GOP faction, led by Helms, wanted to build the party along strictly conservative lines.

When Holshouser left office in 1977, no moderate spokesman stepped in to compete with Helms, and the influence of the western moderates has declined within the party. Still, the state's westernmost congressional district elected a Republican congressman in 1980, the first in that part of the state since 1928.

Traditionally Republican highland strongholds like Watauga, Avery and Mitchell counties have become popular vacation retreats, with ski resorts and weekend homes dotting the mountainsides. Another reliably Republican area is Henderson County. Pleasant scenery and a mild climate are drawing an increasing number of well-to-do retirees there.

The only major city in the west is Asheville, in Buncombe County. Relations between Buncombe and other western counties have historically been strained. The smaller counties resent Buncombe's political clout and its position as a regional trade and distribution center.

Asheville's population declined nearly eight percent in the past decade, to 53,281, and it is considering annexing parts of Buncombe County to broaden its municipal tax base. Buncombe's electoral behavior generally parallels that of the Piedmont's urban counties. Buncombe voted for Jimmy Carter in 1976, but chose Republicans in 1968, 1972 and 1980.

Industrial activity in the west focuses on paper, pulp and textiles. A number of mountaineers commute to factories in valley towns. Though much of the terrain is steep and rocky, there is cultivation of tobacco, corn, potatoes and oats.

# Redrawing the Lines

The Democratic-controlled state Legislature spent much time in the first half of 1981 trying to draw a map to satisfy the seven Democrats in the state's 11-member delegation. But it was not an easy task, since many of the incumbents find themselves in increasingly marginal districts.

The thorniest problem involves the underpopulated 6th District, centered on Greensboro. Some legislators suggested expanding it to dilute the strength of freshman Republican Eugene Johnston. But Democrats in neighboring marginal districts were reluctant to yield any Democratic voters to Johnston.

The central Piedmont 4th District has grown nearly 24 percent since the last census and lose nearly 45,000 residents. That spawned moves to carve out a separate "Research Triangle" district in the area. At midyear, House and Senate conferees were trying to reach a consensus.

# Governor
# James B. Hunt Jr. (D)

**Born:** May 16, 1937, Greensboro, N.C.
**Home:** Lucama, N.C.
**Education:** North Carolina State U., B.S. 1959; M.S. 1962; U. of North Carolina Law School, J.D. 1964.
**Profession:** Lawyer, farmer, agricultural economist.
**Family:** Wife, Carolyn; four children.
**Religion:** Presbyterian.
**Political Career:** Lieutenant governor, 1973-77; elected governor 1976, 1980; term expires Jan. 1985.

# Jesse Helms (R)

### Of Raleigh — Elected 1972

**Born:** Oct. 18, 1922, Monroe, N.C.
**Education:** Attended Wingate Jr. College and Wake Forest College, 1941.
**Military Career:** Navy, 1942-45.
**Profession:** Editor, television commentator.
**Family:** Wife, Dorothy Jane Coble; three children.
**Religion:** Baptist.
**Political Career:** Raleigh City Council, 1957-61.

**In Washington:** Helms' ideological postures are easy enough to label and predict, but his role in the Senate has taken a series of unexpected turns since he arrived as an apostle of conservatism in 1973.

He has never been the gadfly most of his colleagues expected, content simply to play to his national movement. By mastering the rules and demonstrating a patience and timing rarely associated with ideologues, he has made himself a force in the institution.

In 1981, however, he has faced a new challenge: whether to use his skills in alliance with the Reagan administration or stay on the outside in an effort to keep the president from drifting to the center.

The first six months of the year did not quite answer that question, but they left signs that Helms would not easily abandon his role as naysayer, even if the ultimate cost might be a breach with the most conservative national administration of modern times.

"My conversations with the president indicate he has no intention of compromising his principles," Helms said early in the year. "I have believed him all these years, and I see no reason to start disbelieving him now — so we'll wait and see."

While waiting, Helms cast one of only two "no" votes on confirming Defense Secretary Caspar W. Weinberger. As a member of the Foreign Relations Committee, he began placing "holds" on Reagan's nominations for top State Department positions, blocking their committee approval. He said many of the nominees were not sufficiently aligned with Reagan's own foreign policy views.

In May, Helms' Congressional Club, his multimillion-dollar New Right fund-raising organization, opened an office in Washington to try to pressure President Reagan to name more "true" conservatives to government.

At mid-year, it was not certain what the challenges had accomplished. In May, after weeks of waiting, Foreign Relations Chairman Charles H. Percy decided to act on most of the nominations without Helms' approval, and they were approved easily.

In June, Helms was forced into a roll call on the nomination of Chester Crocker to be Reagan's assistant secretary of state for African affairs, and Crocker was confirmed, 84-7, over Helms' opposition. Helms and allies felt Crocker was insufficiently friendly to the government in South Africa.

Helms has always believed that the conservative struggle does not end with the election of a candidate, even one he admires as much as he does Reagan. He has been willing to use any available tactic to keep conservative officeholders "honest." In both the 1976 and 1980 Republican national conventions, Helms took the lead in writing militant conservative platforms, hoping to lock the candidates into position. Though platforms often are ignored, those two platform arguments did more than any other events to make Helms the spiritual leader of the hard-core conservatives within the Republican Party.

Platform writing is simply an extension of Helms' Senate interests in fighting communism abroad and promoting old-fashioned social values at home. Despite the energy he expends on foreign policy issues, Helms always seems to have plenty left over for fervent crusades on domestic questions as well. Rarely does a major piece of domestic legislation go through the Senate without Helms offering an amendment of some sort, whether it seeks to halt busing, to bar federal assistance for abortions, to remove restrictions on prayer in the public schools or to cut federal funds for welfare programs.

Some credit for this legislative skill goes to the late Sen. James B. Allen, D-Ala., who was an early Helms mentor in learning the parliamentary folkways of the Senate. Helms came to Washington with no previous legislative experience. But he sat down and read the rules and, day after day, volunteered for the least coveted duty, presiding over the Senate.

Helms provoked a few smirks in 1973 and 1974 when he won the Senate's "Golden Gavel" award for presiding more hours than anyone else. But that attitude changed when Helms started using his knowledge of parliamentary procedure to tie up the Senate on behalf of his conservate causes.

He has filibustered or threatened filibusters on dozens of bills he wanted to stop, ranging from the Panama Canal treaties and labor legislation to extension of the Legal Services Corporation.

The first eight years of Helms' guerrilla warfare in the Senate produced more symbolic victories than real ones. The Panama Canal treaties were adopted. Helms managed to attach his amendment permitting school prayer to the bill that created the new Department of Education, but it was quickly removed and inserted onto another bill that had no chance of enactment. Helms' efforts to change federal policy through budget cutting, such as his proposal to dismantle the Civil Rights Commission to save money, rarely went very far.

Still, Helms has victories to point to. He helped prevent passage of common site picketing and labor law revision, both dead now for the forseeable future. Even before Reagan took office, the Foreign Relations Committee was moving at least a few steps toward Helms' hard-line world posture and away from the arms control mentality that dominated it earlier in the 1970s. That left Helms with reason to believe he could be the dominant Republican on the committee in the Reagan years.

But the 1980 election brought Helms another role to play, as Agriculture chairman in the new Republican Senate. Helms had never shown an overriding interest in his Agriculture assignment, although he had used his position on the committee to defend tobacco and fight expansion of the food stamp program. He has sometimes voted against major farm bills purely to register his distaste for food stamp provisions.

In the early months of his chairmanship, Helms lost a key argument over the future of food stamps. The Reagan budget dictated a substantial reduction in the program, and the Agriculture Committee made one, proposing to save $1.9 billion in 1982 by removing about a milion

peopole from the food stamp rolls and reducing benefits for others. Helms wanted to go further, restoring the requirement that recipients pay a portion of their income for the stamps. "If there has ever been a federal program that cried out for reform," he said, "it is this program." But the Senate rejected his amendment on a 66-33 vote.

The arrival of new Helms allies in the Republican Senate has escalated the level of rhetoric both against the senator and in his defense.

Alan Cranston of California, the Senate Democratic whip, charged in mid-1981 that Helms "has introduced more meanness than I've seen in the Senate before."

Helms thinks that reflects his growing strength rather than his tactics. "As long as we are getting clobbered," he told a reporter, "I was just a courtly nuisance. Now that we're winning, I'm mean."

**At Home:** Helms has turned thousands of North Carolina's conservative farmers, millworkers, mechanics and other straight-ticket Democrats into "Jessecrats," switching them to the GOP column to vote for the man who speaks their mind on welfare, abortion, defense and federal spending.

For most of his adult life, Helms was a Democrat himself, even while he delivered conservative editorials for 12 years over WRAL-TV in Raleigh. He left the Democratic Party in 1970 and two years later ran for the Senate.

He was an underdog in that campaign to U.S. Rep. Nick Galifianakis, who had convincingly defeated aging Sen. B. Everett Jordan in the Democratic primary. Press accounts regularly described Helms as a "right-winger," but that label was far less dangerous to him than the liberal McGovern-Shriver presidential ticket was to Galifianakis.

Helms downplayed his rhetoric and shifted to a pro-Nixon tone. "President Nixon Needs Jesse Helms," the advertisements read, although Helms was far to the right of Nixon on most issues. A year earlier he had called the president's trip to mainland China "appeasement" of the communists. In a Republican sweep, Nixon won nearly 70 percent of the state's presidential vote. Helms defeated Galifianakis with 54 percent, and the GOP won the governorship for the first time since 1896.

Six years later, a host of Democrats sought to prove Helms' win a coattail fluke. The favorite was Luther H. Hodges Jr., a moderate banker with a well-financed campaign but a "stuffed shirt" image. Another Democrat, state Insurance Commissioner John Ingram, pledged to fight for the common man against insurance companies, banks and other monied interests he accused both Helms and Hodges of defending. Ingram was underfinanced and disorganized, but he forced Hodges into a runoff and won.

Ingram appeared to pose a threat to Helms. His populist themes had some appeal for rural and working-class conservatives who had supported Helms in 1972. But Helms had a reputation and an organization. Many of his constituents were proud that in a single Senate term he had become an articulate and nationally-known defender of the right, one who had been promoted

as a vice-presidential choice by more than 800 national convention delegates in 1976. Helms' state organization, the Congressional Club, was powerful enough to engineer Ronald Reagan's victory in the 1976 North Carolina primary.

Helms also had unprecedented amounts of money. As direct-mail solicitations brought contributions from admirers across the nation, Ingram derided the incumbent as "the six million dollar man." Helms eventually collected about $7.7 million, more than any Senate candidate in U.S. history, and won by a margin slightly larger than he had in 1972.

## Committees

**Agriculture, Nutrition and Forestry** (Chairman)
Agricultural Production, Marketing and Stabilization of Prices.

**Foreign Relations** (3rd of 9 Republicans)
Western Hemisphere Affairs, chairman; African Affairs; East Asian and Pacific Affairs; Near Eastern and South Asian Affairs.

**Rules and Administration** (5th of 7 Republicans)

**Select Ethics** (2nd of 3 Republicans)

## Elections

**1978 General**

| | |
|---|---|
| Jesse Helms (R ) | 619,151 (55 %) |
| John Ingram (D ) | 516,663 (45 %) |

**Previous Winning Percentage**

1972 (54%)

## Campaign Finance

| | Receipts | Receipts from PACs | Expenditures |
|---|---|---|---|
| 1978 | | | |
| Helms (R ) | $7,463,282 | $271,290 (4 %) | $7,460,966 |
| Ingram (D ) | $261,982 | $10,042 (4 %) | $264,088 |

## Voting Studies

| | Presidential Support | | Party Unity | | Conservative Coalition | |
|---|---|---|---|---|---|---|
| Year | S | O | S | O | S | O |
| 1980 | 34 | 66 | 92 | 7 | 98 | 2† |
| 1979 | 23 | 75 | 93 | 6 | 91 | 3 |

| | | | | | | |
|---|---|---|---|---|---|---|
| 1978 | 20 | 68 | 84 | 6 | 82 | 5 |
| 1977 | 43 | 52 | 90 | 7 | 94 | 2 |
| 1976 | 77 | 23 | 95 | 2† | 94 | 3 |
| 1975 | 68 | 28 | 90 | 7 | 94 | 1 |
| 1974 (Ford) | 60 | 33† | | | | |
| 1974 | 65 | 28 | 84 | 10† | 94 | 2 |
| 1973 | 76 | 21 | 89 | 5 | 98 | 0 |

S = Support   O = Opposition
†Not eligible for all recorded votes.

## Key Votes

**96th Congress**

| | |
|---|---|
| Maintain relations with Taiwan (1979) | Y |
| Reduce synthetic fuel development funds (1979) | Y |
| Impose nuclear plant moratorium (1979) | N |
| Kill stronger windfall profits tax (1979) | Y |
| Guarantee Chrysler Corp. loans (1979) | N |
| Approve military draft registration (1980) | Y |
| End Revenue Sharing to the states (1980) | Y |
| Block Justice Dept. busing suits (1980) | Y |

**97th Congress**

| | |
|---|---|
| Restore urban program funding cuts (1981) | N |

## Interest Group Ratings

| Year | ADA | ACA | AFL-CIO | CCUS-1 | CCUS-2 |
|---|---|---|---|---|---|
| 1980 | 11 | 100 | 5 | 83 | |
| 1979 | 5 | 100 | 5 | 100 | 86 |
| 1978 | 5 | 96 | 11 | 87 | |
| 1977 | 0 | 100 | 10 | 94 | |
| 1976 | 5 | 100 | 10 | 100 | |
| 1975 | 0 | 93 | 15 | 94 | |
| 1974 | 5 | 100 | 10 | 89 | |
| 1973 | 0 | 100 | 18 | 100 | |

# John P. East (R)

**Of Greenville — Elected 1980**

**Born:** May 5, 1931, Springfield, Ill.
**Education:** Earlham College, B.A. 1953; University of Illinois, LL.B. 1959; University of Florida, M.A. 1962, Ph.D. 1964.
**Military Career:** Marine Corps, 1953-55.
**Profession:** Political science professor.
**Family:** Wife, Priscilla Sherk; two children.
**Religion:** Christian.
**Political Career:** Unsuccessful Republican nominee for U.S. House, 1st District, 1966; unsuccessful Republican nominee for secretary of state, 1968; Republican national committeeman, 1976-  .

**The Member:** East is the philosopher among the New Right freshmen. Like the others, he calls for a restoration of "family values," but unlike most of them, East finds much of his rationale in the history of Western political thought. Some of his evidence comes from Plato, St. Thomas Aquinas and Edmund Burke, whose common ground, he says, is an anti-Utopian view. East believes that hedonism and secular humanism have weakened Western civilization.

In the less cosmic world of North Carolina Republican politics, East's political patron is Jesse Helms, the state's senior senator. Helms's political organization, the Congressional Club, recruited East and managed his 1980 campaign against Democratic incumbent Robert Morgan.

In the Senate, East wasted no time establishing himself as a philosophical soulmate of Helms. Just a few hours after Reagan took office on Jan. 20, East and Helms cast the only votes against the president's nominee for secretary of defense, Caspar Weinberger. They said Weinberger was insufficiently hawkish to run the Pentagon.

East has promoted a bill on the Judiciary Committee declaring a national policy that life begins at conception. With that policy in place, states might be able to enact anti-abortion laws. East held hearings on the bill in early 1981 in his Separation of Powers Subcommittee, but when all the initially-scheduled witnesses turned out to be oppponents of abortion, the panel's ranking Democrat, Max Baucus of Montana, sent East a protest letter. Utah Republican Sen. Orrin Hatch, whose Constitution Subcommittee was originally slated to cosponsor the hearings, withdrew. East then changed his plans and agreed to hear witnesses on both sides of the question.

The senator is a leading spokesman for legislation that would take away the Supreme Court's authority to hear cases on abortion, busing and school prayer. East thinks the Supreme Court "brought this on itself" by abusing its power of judicial review.

East contracted polio while in the Marines and is confined to a wheelchair. He is the first crippled senator since Charles E. Potter, a Michigan Republican who left office in 1959.

## Committees

**Energy and Natural Resources** (10th of 11 Republicans)
Energy Conservation and Supply; Energy Regulation; Energy Research and Development.

**Judiciary** (7th of 10 Republians)
Separation of Powers, chairman; Courts; Security and Terrorism.

**Labor and Human Resources** (9th of 9 Republicans)
Education; Handicapped; Labor.

## Elections

**1980 General**

| | |
|---|---|
| John East (R) | 898,064 (50%) |
| Robert Morgan (D) | 887,653 (49%) |

## Campaign Finance

| | Receipts | Receipts from PACs | Expenditures |
|---|---|---|---|
| **1980** | | | |
| East (R) | $1,332,565 | $168,214 (13%) | $1,176,875 |
| Morgan (D) | $649,718 | $229,355 (35%) | $948,209 |

## Key Votes

**97th Congress**

Restore urban program funding cuts (1981)                    N

# 1 Walter B. Jones (D)

**Of Farmville — Elected 1966**

**Born:** Aug. 19, 1913, Fayetteville, N.C.
**Education:** N.C. State U., B.S. 1934.
**Profession:** Office supply company executive.
**Family:** Wife, Doris Long; two children.
**Religion:** Baptist.
**Political Career:** Mayor of Farmville, N.C., 1949-53; N.C. House, 1955-59; N.C. Senate, 1965-66; unsuccessful campaign for Democratic nomination for U.S. House, 1960.

**In Washington:** Long thought of as a passive Southern Democrat whose only interest was tobacco, Jones surprised members with a methodical and successful campaign for the Merchant Marine Committee chairmanship in December of 1980.

Veteran Chairman John M. Murphy of New York had been defeated for re-election, and Jones was next in line. But he had been so unassertive in his committee work that many colleagues thought he would either yield voluntarily to Mario Biaggi of New York, the next man behind him, or assumed Biaggi would simply defeat Jones.

In recent years, Jones' image of inaction had been reinforced by a painful gout condition that had reduced his walk to a shuffle. But hardly anyone realized how much he wanted the committee chairmanship. He had been working quietly behind the scenes for weeks, telling fellow Democrats how important the subject was to North Carolina. He also told them that his 1st District predecessor, Herbert C. Bonner, had had the job, and that constituents would not understand if Jones were denied it.

His argument not only convinced most of those who listened — it convinced Speaker O'Neill. The Speaker decided there was no reason not to follow seniority, and Jones won without opposition. Biaggi got one of the Merchant Marine subcommittees, and Jones turned over his Tobacco Subcommittee on Agriculture to a fellow North Carolinian, Charlie Rose.

In his first months as Merchant Marine chairman, the committee began working on a significant change in U.S. maritime policy. It would allow owners of American ships to buy or build vessels in foreign shipyards without losing federal subsidies for operating them. Ship operators generally liked this idea, seeing it as a boon to their troubled industry. Ship builders did not care for it. "It's a radical departure from what we've

been doing," Jones admitted.

Before Jones took his chairmanship, those who viewed him as a one-issue tobacco legislator were not far wrong. In the eight years he chaired the Tobacco Subcommittee, he displayed few interests other than maintaining federal price supports for his district's most important crop. In 1977, when an attempt was made on the House floor to take tobacco out of the Food for Peace program, Jones came up with an argument some of his colleagues had never heard before. "If one is against tobacco," he said, "it is far better to export it than it is to keep it here."

Jones rarely talks in public, claiming that he is not much of an orator. But he is amusing in the private conversations that swirl around the House chamber. He once said he lived by three political rules: never say anything unkind about an opponent; never debate a challenger; and be brief.

**At Home:** Herbert Bonner, whose longtime Merchant Marine chairmanship gave Jones an issue in his own campaign for the job, would have had a much shorter tenure if Jones had had his way in the first place.

In 1960, five years after Bonner took over the committee, Jones challenged him for renomination. But Bonner won with 58 percent of the vote, and Jones had to wait until after the chairman's death in 1965 to make it to Washington, defeating John P. East, now the state's junior Republican senator. Jones won 60.3 percent against East in

---

**1st District: Northeast — Greenville, Kinston.** Population: 516,756 (12% increase since 1970). Race: White 336,087 (65%), Black 177,046 (34%), Others 3,623 (1%). Spanish origin: 4,981 (1%).

## Walter B. Jones, D-N.C.

the special election in February of 1966, and defeated him again in November by a similar margin. He has not had a significant challenge since.

**The District:** The 1st begins at the Outer Banks, passes through fishing ports and coastal swamps, and ends in flat fields of tobacco, corn and peanuts.

Industries in several inland towns process the tobacco, and also make paper. The largest city, Greenville, has less than 35,000 people.

The black population in several counties near the Virginia border is significant, but Southern-style conservative Democratic politics rules the district.

## Committees

**Agriculture** (3rd of 24 Democrats)
Tobacco and Peanuts.

**Merchant Marine and Fisheries** (Chairman)

## Elections

**1980 General**

| | |
|---|---|
| Walter Jones (D ) | Unopposed |

**1980 Primary**

| | |
|---|---|
| Walter Jones (D ) | 66,382 (79 %) |
| Joseph Hollowell Jr. (D ) | 17,170 (21 %) |

**1978 General**

| | |
|---|---|
| Walter Jones (D ) | 67,716 (80 %) |
| James Newcomb (R ) | 16,814 (20 %) |

**Previous Winning Percentages**

| | | | |
|---|---|---|---|
| 1976 (76 %) | 1974 (78 %) | 1972 (69 %) | 1970 (79 %) |
| 1968 (66 %) | 1966 (61 %) | 1966* (60 %) | |

*Special election*

**District Vote For President**

| | 1980 | | 1976 | | 1972 |
|---|---|---|---|---|---|
| D | 81,472 (52 %) | D | 79,503 (60 %) | D | 35,333 (29 %) |
| R | 72,364 (46 %) | R | 52,752 (40 %) | R | 83,557 (69 %) |
| I | 3,293 (2 %) | | | | |

## Campaign Finance

| | Receipts | Receipts from PACs | Expenditures |
|---|---|---|---|
| **1980** | | | |
| Jones (D ) | $64,858 | $35,200 (54 %) | $29,196 |
| **1978** | | | |
| Jones (D ) | $46,357 | $17,550 (38 %) | $24,067 |

## Voting Studies

| | Presidental Support | | Party Unity | | Conservative Coalition | |
|---|---|---|---|---|---|---|
| Year | S | O | S | O | S | O |
| 1980 | 50 | 31 | 56 | 24 | 61 | 23 |

| | | | | | | |
|---|---|---|---|---|---|---|
| 1979 | 45 | 35 | 52 | 34 | 76 | 10 |
| 1978 | 42 | 48 | 48 | 45 | 77 | 18 |
| 1977 | 59 | 34 | 50 | 44 | 75 | 18 |
| 1976 | 45 | 35 | 34 | 53 | 78 | 11 |
| 1975 | 35 | 60 | 49 | 45† | 72 | 21† |
| 1974 (Ford) | 28 | 24 | | | | |
| 1974 | 42 | 47 | 37 | 42 | 73 | 13 |
| 1973 | 52 | 42 | 44 | 50 | 79 | 13 |
| 1972 | 49 | 46 | 28 | 67 | 84 | 13 |
| 1971 | 67 | 28 | 38 | 52 | 76 | 14 |
| 1970 | 55 | 37 | 49 | 47 | 86 | 11 |
| 1969 | 36 | 57 | 25 | 61 | 93 | 2 |
| 1968 | 41 | 41 | 29 | 56 | 80 | 8 |
| 1967 | 46 | 47 | 28 | 60 | 83 | 6 |
| 1966 | 27 | 40† | 16 | 47† | 62 | 3 |

S = Support   O = Opposition
†Not eligible for all recorded votes.

## Key Votes

**96th Congress**

| | |
|---|---|
| Weaken Carter oil profits tax (1979) | Y |
| Reject hospital cost control plan (1979) | ? |
| Implement Panama Canal Treaties (1979) | N |
| Establish Department of Education (1979) | Y |
| Approve Anti-busing Amendment (1979) | Y |
| Guarantee Chrysler Corp. loans (1979) | Y |
| Approve military draft registration (1980) | Y |
| Aid Sandinista regime in Nicaragua (1980) | N |
| Strengthen fair housing laws (1980) | N |

**97th Congress**

| | |
|---|---|
| Reagan budget proposal (1981) | N |

## Interest Group Ratings

| Year | ADA | ACA | AFL-CIO | CCUS |
|---|---|---|---|---|
| 1980 | 22 | 38 | 50 | 75 |
| 1979 | 11 | 43 | 37 | 62 |
| 1978 | 25 | 78 | 25 | 63 |
| 1977 | 10 | 56 | 45 | 69 |
| 1976 | 10 | 86 | 45 | 77 |
| 1975 | 21 | 56 | 50 | 53 |
| 1974 | 13 | 7 | 36 | 70 |
| 1973 | 16 | 73 | 30 | 80 |
| 1972 | 19 | 83 | 18 | 80 |
| 1971 | 22 | 63 | 36 | . |
| 1970 | 12 | 79 | 43 | 60 |
| 1969 | 7 | 76 | 30 | . |
| 1968 | 8 | 73 | 0 | . |
| 1967 | 7 | 81 | 8 | 89 |

# 2 L. H. Fountain (D)

**Of Tarboro — Elected 1952**

**Born:** April 23, 1913, Leggett, N.C.
**Education:** U. of N.C., A.B. 1934, J.D. 1936.
**Military Career:** Army, 1942-46.
**Profession:** Lawyer.
**Family:** Wife, Christine Dail; one child.
**Religion:** Presbyterian.
**Political Career:** N.C. Senate, 1947-53.

**In Washington:** Fountain performs one of the more unusual balancing acts in the House: he votes a solid conservative line on the floor while playing the role of consumer activist on his Government Operations subcommittee. He rarely sides with his national party on a key vote, but he is one of Ralph Nader's favorite members of the House.

As chairman of the Intergovernmental Relations Subcommittee, Fountain doggedly pursued the Food and Drug Administration through the 1960s and into the 1970s, forcing policy changes on birth control pills, recalls of pesticides, removal of cyclamates and a ban on use of the cattle-fattening but cancer-causing hormone, DES.

He has waged all his fights without expressing much anger at his opposition. Mild-mannered and polite, he usually smiles pleasantly at people even when he is convinced they are wrong.

But it is possible to anger him — President Reagan did it in the early weeks of his term by firing all the inspectors general in the executive departments, threatening a program Fountain had worked years to create. The congressman went to the White House and asked Reagan what was going on, arguing that the inspectors general were meant to do exactly what Reagan advocated — ferret out waste and corruption in the federal government. Reagan apologized and said the ousted officials would be replaced quickly.

The inspector general system grew out of earlier Fountain committee inquiries into health research. He felt the agencies involved needed their own in-house watchdogs. There are now 18 of them in the federal government.

Fountain has chaired his subcommittee for a remarkably long time: since 1955, the year he started his second term in the House. In his second year as chairman, he hired Harvard economist Delphis Goldberg as staff director, and Goldberg has remained with him ever since, probing the federal government and making decisions with a wide range of authority from Fountain.

In fact, Fountain sometimes seems to take a back seat to his staff. He has always used aides to question witnesses, reducing his own visibility but, from his point of view, also reducing the amount of posturing by other committee members.

Fountain's self-effacing style as chairman is completely in character for him. He tends to be hesitant in all his political dealings. On the House floor, he often delays his vote until the last possible minute, mulling over the decision and waiting to see how the tally is going before committing himself. "He just has a hard time making up his mind," a colleague once said.

Despite his indecision on the floor, Fountain nearly always decides in the end to vote with the conservative coalition of Republicans and Southern Democrats. In 1980, he backed the coalition 89 percent of the time, the sixth highest record for any Democrat in the House. Earlier in his career, he was a consistent opponent of civil rights legislation.

At the same time, Fountain considers himself a loyal member of the Democratic Party. He supported the Carter-Mondale ticket both times and worked in 1980 for the re-election of Democratic Sen. Robert B. Morgan, who lost his seat to conservative Republican John P. East.

In recent years on Government Operations, Fountain found himself in the middle of a tug-of-

---

**2nd District: Northeast central — Rocky Mount, Wilson.** Population: 508,097 (11% increase since 1970). Race: White 305,582 (60%), Black 197,585 (39%), Others 4,930 (1%). Spanish origin: 4,525 (1%).

war over revenue sharing. On one side was the Democratic president, who wanted to continue the program; on the other side was Jack Brooks of Texas, the full Government Operations chairman, who felt state and local government ought to raise their own revenue and not raid an already depleted national Treasury.

Fountain had to referee this argument because revenue sharing bills start in his subcommittee. Basically, he has always liked revenue sharing. It fits in with his theory that there has been too much federal expansion — and interference — into state and local affairs. In late 1980, after months of alternating confrontation and negotiation, a bill emerged and passed that continued revenue sharing for local governments but eliminated it — at least temporarily — for states.

Fountain's subcommittee has also handled — reluctantly — legislation providing anti-recession aid to areas hard hit by unemployment. Fountain has opposed this approach and sought to reduce funding for it. Proposed originally by President Carter, the program was enacted in 1976 and lapsed in 1978. An effort to revive it in 1980 failed.

Seniority has also given Fountain the second-ranking position on another committee, Foreign Affairs. But except for an occasional overseas trip or a stint as a delegate to the United Nations, Fountain does not spend a great deal of his time with the Foreign Affairs Committee.

During the 1960s, he chaired a Foreign Affairs subcommittee on the Near East, but when members were limited in 1971 to one such chairmanship, Fountain chose to stick with Government Operations. Since then his voice has been heard only occasionally on Mideast issues.

In the recent controversy over arms sales to Saudi Arabia and other Arab nations, he has generally backed the sales. "When I look at the fact that the Saudis provide us with 21 percent of our oil," he said in 1980, "the potential danger justifies us taking a calculated risk." But he opposed the sale of AWACS jets to the shah of Iran.

Fountain is exceptionally determined when it comes to protecting the interests of eastern North Carolina. He vigorously defends all tobacco price support and loan programs, and he is just as vigorous an opponent of federal anti-smoking campaigns. He sees no inconsistency in his position on smoking and his simultaneous fight against cancer-causing drugs. He also argues that the tobacco program pays for itself and is not a drain on the federal budget.

Though Fountain seldom has been in the spotlight during his long career, he is not without

his share of ego. Now, as the senior member of the North Carolina House delegation, Fountain has quietly passed the word he would like to be addressed as "dean."

**At Home:** There was nothing indecisive or hesitant about Fountain's first campaign for Congress. As a lawyer and state legislator in 1952, he challenged his district's incumbent Democraic congressman, John H. Kerr, an octogenarian who had begun his career in North Carolina politics during the McKinley administration. Kerr had spent 30 years in the House and had not been willing to admit his time had come. Fountain defeated him easily.

After that, Fountain had an easy time in his one-party constituency until 1972, when redistricting brought Orange County (Chapel Hill) into his territory. That county is home to the University of North Carolina and the focal point of the state's liberal politics.

Chapel Hill Mayor Howard Lee challenged Fountain in the 1972 Democratic primary. Lee, the first black mayor of a predominantly white Southern town since Reconstruction, called Fountain an unyielding conservative on racial and social issues. Lee criticized some of Fountain's votes against aid to education and his opposition to free school lunches.

Race was not an issue in the campaign, but it was an obvious factor. Lee launched an extensive voter registration drive that added 18,000 new black voters to the rolls. Fountain concentrated on mobilizing rural whites in the conservative rural counties, some of whom had ceased paying much attention to his primaries because he had not needed help in years.

Lee won Orange County and ran respectably in a few others, but Fountain's broad rural base helped him take 58.8 of the overall vote.

Fountain's last serious contest was in 1976, when three Democrats tried to deny him a 13th term. It appeared for a while that Fountain might be forced into a runoff with state Sen. J. Russell Kirby, who campaigned aggressively, attacking Fountain's conservative record the way Lee had done in 1972.

But Fountain won a majority in the initial primary, helped by a surprise 600-vote plurality in Orange County, where Kirby had counted on a large vote to offset Fountain's rural strength.

**The District:** The eastern part of the 2nd lies on the edge of the coastal plain; soybeans, corn, tobacco and peanuts are important. Mechanization has reduced the argicultural workforce, but many small farmers remain. They are conservative, but usually faithfully Democratic. There are textile mills throughout the district, and they begin to predominate as one moves west, some of them employing half the residents of their communities.

Since the 1972 redistricting, however, one-fifth of the district vote has been cast in Orange County, where the university is the dominant influence. Orange went for McGovern in 1972, one of only two counties in the state that did.

In 1980, Reagan won only two counties in the 2nd: Nash and Wilson. Those counties surround Rocky Mount and Wilson, the largest cities in the eastern part of the district; both are centers for tobacco marketing and the manufacture of tobacco products.

## Committees

**Foreign Affairs** (2nd of 21 Democrats)
Europe and the Middle East; International Security and Scientific Affairs.

**Government Operations** (2nd of 23 Democrats)
Intergovernmental Relations and Human Resources, chairman.

## Elections

**1980 General**

| | |
|---|---|
| L. H. Fountain (D ) | 99,297 (73 %) |
| Barry Gardner (R ) | 35,946 (27 %) |

**1978 General**

| | |
|---|---|
| L. H. Fountain (D ) | 61,851 (78 %) |
| Barry Gardner (R ) | 15,988 (20 %) |

**Previous Winning Percentages**

| | | | |
|---|---|---|---|
| 1976 (100%) | 1974 (100%) | 1972 (72 %) | 1970 (100%) |
| 1968 (100%) | 1966 (65 %) | 1964 (100%) | 1962 (100%) |
| 1960 (88 %) | 1958 (100%) | 1956 (100%) | 1954 (100%) |
| 1952 (95 %) | | | |

**District Vote For President**

| | 1980 | | 1976 | | 1972 |
|---|---|---|---|---|---|
| D | 80,482 (55 %) | D | 81,050 (61 %) | D | 47,654 (35 %) |
| R | 60,686 (41 %) | R | 51,543 (39 %) | R | 86,006 (63 %) |
| I | 4,872 (3 %) | | | | |

## Campaign Finance

| | Receipts | Receipts from PACs | Expenditures |
|---|---|---|---|
| **1980** | | | |
| Fountain (D ) | $27,505 | $20,550 (75 %) | $18,370 |
| Gardner (R ) | $7,034 | — (0 %) | $6,919 |
| **1978** | | | |
| Fountain (D ) | $32,964 | $13,611 (41 %) | $21,984 |
| Gardner (R ) | $7,409 | — (0 %) | $7,335 |

## Voting Studies

| | Presidential Support | | Party Unity | | Conservative Coalition | |
|---|---|---|---|---|---|---|
| Year | S | O | S | O | S | O |
| 1980 | 57 | 41 | 41 | 50 | 89 | 9 |
| 1979 | 42 | 56 | 36 | 61 | 92 | 6 |
| 1978 | 41 | 54 | 29 | 62 | 88 | 5 |
| 1977 | 54 | 46 | 38 | 59 | 88 | 8 |
| 1976 | 45 | 31 | 33 | 55 | 80 | 9 |
| 1975 | 42 | 51 | 36 | 57 | 84 | 9 |
| 1974 (Ford) | 63 | 37 | | | | |

| | | | | | | |
|---|---|---|---|---|---|---|
| 1974 | 55 | 43 | 34 | 65 | 89 | 8 |
| 1973 | 47 | 50 | 40 | 58 | 83 | 16 |
| 1972 | 68 | 30 | 21 | 73 | 90 | 4 |
| 1971 | 82 | 16 | 25 | 67 | 90 | 4 |
| 1970 | 62 | 38 | 38 | 60 | 98 | - |
| 1969 | 47 | 53 | 25 | 69 | 91 | 4 |
| 1968 | 51 | 43 | 32 | 62 | 88 | 4 |
| 1967 | 28 | 34 | 18 | 48 | 56 | 0 |
| 1966 | 40 | 52 | 20 | 74 | 95 | 3 |
| 1965 | 45 | 55 | 27 | 72 | 98 | 2 |
| 1964 | 63 | 35 | 47 | 50 | 100 | 0 |
| 1963 | 56 | 42 | 50 | 46 | 93 | 0 |
| 1962 | 67 | 30 | 58 | 42 | 88 | 12 |
| 1961 | 77 | 23 | 62 | 38 | 91 | 9 |

S = Support    O = Opposition

## Key Votes

**96th Congress**

| | |
|---|---|
| Weaken Carter oil profits tax (1979) | Y |
| Reject hospital cost control plan (1979) | Y |
| Implement Panama Canal Treaties (1979) | N |
| Establish Department of Education (1979) | N |
| Approve Anti-busing Amendment (1979) | N |
| Guarantee Chrysler Corp. loans (1979) | N |
| Approve military draft registration (1980) | Y |
| Aid Sandinista regime in Nicaragua (1980) | N |
| Strengthen fair housing laws (1980) | N |

**97th Congress**

| | |
|---|---|
| Reagan budget proposal (1981) | Y |

## Interest Group Ratings

| Year | ADA | ACA | AFL-CIO | CCUS |
|---|---|---|---|---|
| 1980 | 17 | 61 | 22 | 76 |
| 1979 | 5 | 64 | 30 | 83 |
| 1978 | 15 | 88 | 10 | 71 |
| 1977 | 15 | 59 | 35 | 71 |
| 1976 | 0 | 74 | 41 | 71 |
| 1975 | 5 | 79 | 22 | 69 |
| 1974 | 13 | 67 | 27 | 50 |
| 1973 | 20 | 74 | 18 | 91 |
| 1972 | 6 | 91 | 27 | 100 |
| 1971 | 5 | 85 | 18 | - |
| 1970 | 4 | 79 | 14 | 80 |
| 1969 | 7 | 81 | 20 | - |
| 1968 | 0 | 91 | 0 | - |
| 1967 | 0 | 80 | 0 | 90 |
| 1966 | 6 | 81 | 0 | - |
| 1965 | 0 | 79 | | 100 |
| 1964 | 28 | 56 | 27 | - |
| 1963 | - | 67 | - | - |
| 1962 | 50 | 52 | 45 | - |
| 1961 | 30 | - | - | - |

# 3  Charles Whitley (D)

**Of Mt. Olive — Elected 1976**

**Born:** Jan. 3, 1927, Siler City, N.C.
**Education:** Wake Forest U., B.A. 1948, LL.B.
  1950; George Washington U., M.A. 1974.
**Military Career:** Army, 1944-46.
**Profession:** Lawyer.
**Family:** Wife, Audrey Kornegay; three children.
**Religion:** Baptist.
**Political Career:** Mt. Olive city attorney, 1951-
  57.

**In Washington:** Virtually silent in debate unless the subject is tobacco, Whitley likes to dabble in House politics behind the scenes and has gained a reputation as one of the more shrewd members of the informal Southern caucus that gathers in the back of the chamber every afternoon.

As a 15-year staff veteran in the House before his election, Whitley had a considerable amount of political sophistication when he arrived. He was given a junior leadership position as regional whip at the start of his second term, even though he had voted against Democratic majorities more often than all but three of the party's freshmen in his first Congress.

Despite his conservative voting record, he remains a useful man for the leadership, one who can occasionally deliver other North Carolina votes if he chooses. Extremely cautious even though he represents a safe district, he rarely casts a controversial vote without checking local opinion first. When he does back the leadership, other Southerners sometimes conclude it must be politically safe to do so.

Whitley served a term on Armed Services as a newcomer, but now concentrates on Agriculture, just as good from a constituent point of view. In his first term, he offered a floor amendment which kept tobacco in the Food for Peace program. Critics wanted to drop it altogether, but Whitley moved to change the language so that food products would receive priority in the program but tobacco would remain part of it. The amendment passed 260-151, with sugar, wheat and other crop interests joining Whitley in a majority coalition.

Two years later the proposal came up again, and Whitley was equally determined to head it off. "It brands a product in a way in which it should not be branded," he argued. "Tobacco is a legitimate international commodity."

When it comes to tobacco, Whitley is a devout free trader. He wants the United States to be able to ship cigarettes to Japan in unrestricted quantities, rather than shipping only tobacco leaf for Japanese processing, as is now the case.

Whitley has always been interested in the workings of the House committee system. In 1979, Speaker O'Neill appointed him to a special reform panel charged with straightening out some of its problems of overlapping jurisdiction. The panel got nowhere, but subcommittee growth was limited by action in the Democratic Caucus at the end of 1980.

**At Home:** As an aide to Democratic Rep. David Henderson, Whitley was familiar to thousands of 3rd District constituents before his 1976 campaign even began. When Henderson announced in late 1975 he would retire, Whitley immediately entered the contest and became the front-running Democrat.

But the mantle was not easily passed. State Rep. Jimmy Love of Sanford had been planning a challenge to Henderson in the Democratic primary and continued it with Whitley as the target. He waged an aggressive anti-Washington campaign, hoping to counter Whitley's image as congressman-in-waiting. Love finished 3,407 votes ahead of Whitley in the initial primary, but fell short of a majority.

In the runoff contest, Whitley used his staff experience to advantage. He stressed his familiar-

---

**3rd District: Southeast central —
Goldsboro.** Population: 520,027 (14% increase since 1970). Race: White 370,164 (71%), Black 141,411 (27%), Others 8,452 (2%). Spanish origin: 8,213 (2%).

ity with the district's problems and pointed out that his family had remained in North Carolina even when he worked in Washington. He promised to join the Armed Services Committee to argue against cutbacks at Camp Lejeune and the district's other military bases.

Whitley benefited from geography in the runoff. His home was in Wayne County (Goldsboro), the district's most populous area. Love came from Lee County, a small county at the far northwest end of the district.

Helped by a high turnout in Goldsboro, Whitley defeated Love by nearly 4,000 votes. He was an easy winner that fall against Jack Blanchard, who had been the first Republican ever elected to the state Legislature from his home district, but who had lost his seat in 1974.

Blanchard drew only 31.2 percent against Whitley, and in another try in 1978, slipped to 28.9.

**The District:** The 3rd is a largely flat, sandy, pine-covered area that includes the Marine Corps training center at Camp Lejeune in coastal Onslow County. It is a conservative region; it generally votes Democratic, but has given Republican Jesse Helms solid winning margins in his two Senate races.

The 3rd produces more tobacco than any district in the country. It also raises sweet potatoes, poultry and hogs. Goldsboro is a fast-growing tobacco market, and other small towns across the district produce textiles. Sanford calls itself the brick capital of the world.

## Committees

**Agriculture** (17th of 24 Democrats)
Cotton, Rice and Sugar; Livestock, Dairy and Poultry; Tobacco and Peanuts.

## Elections

**1980 General**

| | |
|---|---|
| Charles Whitley (D ) | 84,862 (68 %) |
| Larry Parker (R ) | 39,393 (32 %) |

**1980 Primary**

| | |
|---|---|
| Charles Whitley (D ) | 53,337 (80 %) |
| Larry Turlington (D ) | 7,127 (10 %) |
| Jimmy Hatcher (D ) | 6,578 (10 %) |

**1978 General**

| | |
|---|---|
| Charles Whitley (D ) | 54,452 (71 %) |
| Willard Blanchard (R ) | 22,150 (29 %) |

**Previous Winning Percentage**

**1976** (69 %)

**District Vote For President**

| | 1980 | | 1976 | | 1972 |
|---|---|---|---|---|---|
| **D** | 67,875 (51 %) | **D** | 68,612 (59 %) | **D** | 27,878 (26 %) |
| **R** | 63,559 (48 %) | **R** | 48,186 (41 %) | **R** | 79,431 (73 %) |
| **I** | 1,993 (2 %) | | | | |

## Campaign Finance

| | Receipts | Receipts from PACs | Expenditures |
|---|---|---|---|
| **1980** | | | |
| Whitley (D ) | $49,752 | $22,950 (46 %) | $33,267 |
| Parker (R ) | $9,874 | — (0 %) | $10,268 |

| 1978 | | | |
|---|---|---|---|
| Whitley (D ) | $56,598 | $21,013 (37 %) | $44,971 |
| Blanchard (R ) | $14,240 | $950 (7 %) | $13,583 |

## Voting Studies

| | Presidential Support | | Party Unity | | Conservative Coalition | |
|---|---|---|---|---|---|---|
| **Year** | **S** | **O** | **S** | **O** | **S** | **O** |
| 1980 | 58 | 36 | 59 | 34 | 77 | 14 |
| 1979 | 63 | 34 | 64 | 34 | 81 | 19 |
| 1978 | 38 | 52 | 33 | 49 | 80 | 9 |
| 1977 | 59 | 38 | 47 | 52 | 83 | 17 |

S = Support          O = Opposition

## Key Votes

**96th Congress**

| | |
|---|---|
| Weaken Carter oil profits tax (1979) | Y |
| Reject hospital cost control plan (1979) | Y |
| Implement Panama Canal Treaties (1979) | N |
| Establish Department of Education (1979) | Y |
| Approve Anti-busing Amendment (1979) | N |
| Guarantee Chrysler Corp. loans (1979) | Y |
| Approve military draft registration (1980) | Y |
| Aid Sandinista regime in Nicaragua (1980) | N |
| Strengthen fair housing laws (1980) | N |

**97th Congress**

| | |
|---|---|
| Reagan budget proposal (1981) | N |

## Interest Group Ratings

| Year | ADA | ACA | AFL-CIO | CCUS |
|---|---|---|---|---|
| 1980 | 28 | 39 | 53 | 81 |
| 1979 | 21 | 42 | 40 | 67 |
| 1978 | 25 | 95 | 16 | 64 |
| 1977 | 25 | 59 | 52 | 59 |

# 4 Ike Andrews (D)

### Of Siler City — Elected 1972

**Born:** Sept., 2, 1925, Bonlee, N.C.
**Education:** U. of N.C., B.S. 1950, LL.B. 1952.
**Military Career:** Army, 1943-45.
**Profession:** Lawyer.
**Family:** Wife, Patricia Wilson; two children.
**Religion:** Baptist.
**Political Career:** N.C. Senate, 1959-61; N.C. House, 1961-63, 1967-73, majority leader and speaker pro-tem., 1971-73.

**In Washington:** Andrews is known as a "country gentleman" who tells folksy stories and spends as much time in North Carolina as in Washington. He is an avid college sports fan and a faithful participant at ceremonial functions in his district. Some congressmen find such events a bore; Andrews attends with enthusiasm.

In fact, he drives back and forth to North Carolina so often — and so fast — that he accumulated 15 speeding tickets one year and had his license suspended. For a while, he tried flying, but shifted to cars again after he got his license back.

With six colleges in his district, Andrews took a seat on the House Education and Labor Committee in his first term and concentrated on higher education. It has been a quiet concentration. On the rare occasions when he issues a press statement, it nearly always concerns a grant to one of those schools or to the famed high technology Research Triangle Park at Durham.

But his subcommittee chairmanship, Human Resources, has drawn him into other areas, including Head Start, juvenile justice reforms and what remains of the Johnson antipoverty program. In 1981, Andrews went on the defensive in his low-key way against Reagan administration proposals to cut some of these programs and fold others into block grants to state and local officials. He had wide bipartisan support on Education and Labor for keeping these programs alive, even if the spending levels for them were reduced dramatically.

Andrews is a cautious voter. He supports the national Democratic Party frequently on education and most other social programs, but less often on labor or environmental legislation. With Reagan conservatism popular in North Carolina, he voted for the overall Republican budget in 1981 even though he did not support many of the specific program cuts the budget would require.

Like most North Carolina politicians, Andrews is a whole-hearted supporter of tobacco subsidies and was a vigorous opponent of the "anti-smoking" campaign waged by the Carter administration.

**At Home:** After winning narrowly in 1972, Andrews glided through three comfortable re-elections until sloppy bookkeeping cut deeply into his 1980 margin.

A 1979 Federal Election Commission audit of Andrews' campaign organization failed to find $3,000 that other groups said they had donated in 1978. After some hesitation, Andrews revealed he had cashed six contributors' checks totaling $3,000 during the 1978 campaign, used the money for personal expenses and forgot to reimburse his campaign organization.

Randolph County Commissioner Thurman Hogan, the Republican nominee in 1980, called Andrews' actions "serious violations" and demanded that he resign. Andrews countered that the money was misplaced through oversight, not malice, and he repaid the $3,000 to his campaign.

Hogan was not well known in most parts of the district, and the finance issue was not enough to produce an upset for him. But he did hold Andrews to 52.6 percent, the congressman's poorest showing since 1972.

When Andrews first ran for Congress in 1972, as a 10-year veteran of the state Legislature, he was one of six Democrats seeking to replace

---

**4th District: Central — Raleigh, Durham.** Population: 578,894 (24% increase since 1970). Race: White 436,989 (75%), Black 135,544 (23%), Others 6,361 (1%). Spanish origin: 4,417 (1%).

Democratic Rep. Nick Galifianakis, who ran for the Senate that year. State Sen. Jack Coggins finished first in the primary, but Andrews was only 879 votes behind. A runoff produced a 51.9 percent majority for Andrews.

Republican nominee Jack Hawke wrapped himself in the robes of the Nixon administration and tried to tie Andrews to George McGovern. But Andrews won by 1,100 votes.

**The District:** Andrews is a product of rural North Carolina, but 80 percent of the vote in the 4th District is cast in metropolitan Raleigh (Wake County) and Durham (Durham County), in the area around the Research Triangle, where nearly 20,000 people work in various science-related pursuits. Rural Chatham County, Andrews' original

home, casts less than 10 percent of the total vote.

In addition to the research facilities, state and federal government are major employers in Raleigh, North Carolina's capital, and surrounding Wake County still produces a considerable amount of tobacco. Wake was once solidly Democratic, but Republican sentiment is growing. Republicans Ford and Reagan won the county narrowly in the past two presidential elections.

Durham is a tobacco-processing and textile-manufacturing city with a significant black and labor vote that regularly puts Durham County in the Democratic column.

Chatham County is traditionally Democratic; Randolph County, at the western end of the district, is a GOP bastion.

## Committees

**Education and Labor** (8th of 19 Democrats)
Human Resources, chairman; Elementary, Secondary and Vocational Education; Postsecondary Education.

**Select Aging** (4th of 31 Democrats)
Health and Long-term Care.

## Elections

**1980 General**

| | |
|---|---|
| Ike Andrews (D ) | 97,167 (53 %) |
| Thurman Hogan (R ) | 84,631 (46 %) |

**1980 Primary**

| | |
|---|---|
| Ike Andrews (D ) | 58,370 (77 %) |
| Geoffrey Gadsden (D ) | 10,008 (13 %) |
| Joseph Overby (D ) | 7,809 (10 %) |

**1978 General**

| | |
|---|---|
| Ike Andrews (D ) | 74,249 (94 %) |
| Naudeen Beek (LIB) | 4,436 (6 %) |

**Previous Winning Percentages**

1976 (61 %)   1974 (65 %)   1972 (50 %)

**District Vote For President**

| | 1980 | | 1976 | | 1972 |
|---|---|---|---|---|---|
| D | 91,223 (46 %) | D | 85,541 (51 %) | D | 47,343 (30 %) |
| R | 94,339 (48 %) | R | 81,852 (49 %) | R | 107,283 (68 %) |
| I | 9,551 (5 %) | | | | |

## Campaign Finance

| | Receipts | Receipts from PACs | Expenditures |
|---|---|---|---|
| **1980** | | | |
| Andrews (D ) | $43,965 | $41,500 (94 %) | $72,446 |
| Hogan (R ) | $59,727 | $5,075 (8 %) | $59,634 |
| **1978** | | | |
| Andrews (D ) | $36,474 | $13,788 (38 %) | $27,970 |

## Voting Studies

| Year | Presidential Support | | Party Unity | | Conservative Coalition | |
|---|---|---|---|---|---|---|
| | S | O | S | O | S | O |
| 1980 | 60 | 30 | 62 | 28 | 68 | 24 |
| 1979 | 61 | 29 | 66 | 27 | 63 | 32 |
| 1978 | 58 | 35 | 50 | 42 | 66 | 25 |
| 1977 | 61 | 34 | 50 | 44 | 73 | 24 |
| 1976 | 41 | 45 | 46 | 39 | 66 | 20 |
| 1975 | 38 | 47 | 45 | 45 | 67 | 25 |
| 1974 (Ford) | 44 | 50 | | | | |
| 1974 | 53 | 36 | 42 | 40 | 65 | 20 |
| 1973 | 42 | 51 | 51 | 42 | 66 | 32 |

S = Support          O = Opposition

## Key Votes

**96th Congress**

| | |
|---|---|
| Weaken Carter oil profits tax (1979) | Y |
| Reject hospital cost control plan (1979) | Y |
| Implement Panama Canal Treaties (1979) | Y |
| Establish Department of Education (1979) | Y |
| Approve Anti-busing Amendment (1979) | N |
| Guarantee Chrysler Corp. loans (1979) | Y |
| Approve military draft registration (1980) | Y |
| Aid Sandinista regime in Nicaragua (1980) | Y |
| Strengthen fair housing laws (1980) | N |

**97th Congress**

| | |
|---|---|
| Reagan budget proposal (1981) | Y |

## Interest Group Ratings

| Year | ADA | ACA | AFL-CIO | CCUS |
|---|---|---|---|---|
| 1980 | 28 | 41 | 38 | 83 |
| 1979 | 37 | 33 | 58 | 65 |
| 1978 | 25 | 59 | 37 | 56 |
| 1977 | 25 | 44 | 48 | 65 |
| 1976 | 35 | 52 | 55 | 54 |
| 1975 | 26 | 73 | 24 | 53 |
| 1974 | 30 | 42 | 44 | 17 |
| 1973 | 48 | 50 | 45 | 73 |

# 5 Stephen L. Neal (D)

### Of Winston-Salem — Elected 1974

**Born:** Nov. 7, 1934, Winston-Salem, N.C.
**Education:** U. of Hawaii, A.B. 1959.
**Profession:** Mortgage banker, publisher.
**Family:** Wife, Rachel Miller; two children.
**Religion:** Episcopalian.
**Political Career:** No previous office.

**In Washington:** Neal's soft-spoken and politically cautious style has kept him in office longer than most politicians expected in a district used to a more clear-cut conservatism.

He has maintained his ties to the state's business community and kept his distance from the more controversial stands of the national Democratic Party, and this has given him some leeway to concentrate on a subject far from constituent interests — international finance.

A seniority gap on the Banking Committee gave Neal a valuable chairmanship while he was still in his first House term. As the head of the subcommittee on International Trade, Neal plunged into the outer reaches of monetary policy and emerged with some unusual ideas, at least for a Democrat.

Neal has turned out to be a monetarist, sharing with conservative Milton Friedman the idea that national economic health depends on a modest and steady growth in the money supply, rather than any combination of taxation and federal spending policies. Monetary policy is set by the Federal Reserve Board, and Neal's subcommittee has no control over it. But Neal has used the panel to investigate the Fed's role in the economy.

The chairmanship also carries with it the generally thankless task of managing funding bills for the Export-Import Bank and International Monetary Fund on the House floor. At a time of suspicion about foreign assistance, these usually provoke conservative warfare.

In 1978 Neal had to fight off an effort to deny Ex-Im Bank money to nations which might use it to make products that compete with ones made in the U.S.; in 1980, Republicans sought to block the United States from giving money to the IMF until the budget was balanced. Both efforts lost, but only after some sharp exchanges.

Neal's other main legislative project has been a solar energy bank, which he has pursued with a quiet obsession. He introduced his own bill in 1978 to create a $5 billion bank to loan money for

new solar projects. It cleared a Banking subcommittee in 1978 with President Carter's support, then was merged with a synthetic fuels bill and became law in 1980. It now must fight for funding in the stripped-down Reagan budget.

Neal is a true believer in energy conservation. He introduced legislation in 1979 requiring the president to set mandatory conservation targets for all 50 states, aimed at reducing the use of energy by 20 percent at the end of one year. He tried to gain Democratic Caucus approval of his plan in 1980, but the caucus did not vote on it.

Earlier, Neal was equally tenacious in fighting a local public works project. A power company wanted to dam the New River, which flows from North Carolina into Virginia. Neal fought the plan with a bill to block the project by including part of the river in the Wild and Scenic Rivers system. He personally lobbied nearly every member of the House, cajoling, bargaining and pleading that this was of critical political and esthetic importance to him. He became something of a pest, but he won.

**At Home:** Neal was one of the nation's most surprising winners in 1974 as he defeated four-term Rep. Wilmer D. Mizell, who had been seen as one of the most popular Republicans in the state. Mizell, a former National League pitcher, flirted with the idea of running for the Senate in 1974, finally deciding to keep what he and everyone else considered a safe House seat. But 1974 was not a good year to be a Republican in North

---

**5th District: Winston-Salem.** Population: 539,949 (17% increase since 1970). Race: White 458,079 (85%), Black 79,213 (15%), Others 2,657 (0.4%). Spanish origin: 3,490 (1%).

Carolina. Neal, a publisher of several suburban newspapers, linked him to the Nixon administration and the state's economic troubles and took 52 percent of the vote.

Two years later, after a brief stint as assistant secretary of commerce in the Ford administration, Mizell came back for a rematch, arguing that Neal was a liberal who had sold his property in Winston-Salem and "gone Washington." But Neal's cautious legislative record helped belie that charge, and Mizell was on his own against a strong Democratic state ticket. Neal beat him with 54.2 percent, and drew exactly the same percentage two years later.

Republicans tried hard in 1980 behind state Sen. Anne Bagnal, a militant opponent of abortion and the ERA. Reagan ran well throughout

the district, giving Bagnal a boost, and she held Neal to 51.1 percent, his worst showing ever. But she could not deny him a fourth term.

**The District:** The major city in the 5th is Winston-Salem, a tobacco-processing center that also has textile, furniture and electronics plants. Winston-Salem and surrounding Forsyth County cast more than 40 percent of the vote in the seven-county district. Forsyth County gave a narrow margin to Reagan in 1980, but Neal, who comes from Winston-Salem, carried it.

Republicans have traditionally been strong in several of the mountainous counties in the western part of the district. The GOP habits there stem from generations of antagonism toward the flatland tobacco farmers, who were wealthier, politically powerful and Democratic.

## Committees

**Banking, Finance and Urban Affairs** (7th of 25 Democrats)
International Trade, Investment and Monetary Policy, chairman; Domestic Monetary Policy; International Development Institutions and Finance.

**Government Operations** (18th of 23 Democrats)
Commerce, Consumer, and Monetary Affairs; Intergovernmental Relations and Human Resources.

## Elections

**1980 General**

| | |
|---|---|
| Stephen Neal (D ) | 99,117 (51 %) |
| Anne Bagnal (R ) | 94,894 (49 %) |

**1978 General**

| | |
|---|---|
| Stephen Neal (D ) | 68,778 (54 %) |
| Hamilton Horton (R ) | 58,161 (46 %) |

**Previous Winning Percentages**

1976 (54 %)　　1974 (52 %)

**District Vote For President**

| | 1980 | | 1976 | | 1972 |
|---|---|---|---|---|---|
| D | 83,043 (43 %) | D | 92,010 (51 %) | D | 45,830 (29 %) |
| R | 104,623 (54 %) | R | 89,368 (49 %) | R | 109,952 (69 %) |
| I | 4,510 (2 %) | | | | |

## Campaign Finance

| | Receipts | Receipts from PACs | Expenditures |
|---|---|---|---|
| **1980** | | | |
| Neal (D ) | $171,431 | $60,426 (35 %) | $169,154 |
| Bagnal (R ) | $121,075 | $33,929 (28 %) | $120,022 |

| **1978** | | | |
|---|---|---|---|
| Neal (D ) | $164,332 | $41,279 (25 %) | $166,643 |
| Horton (R ) | $122,721 | $16,619 (14 %) | $118,484 |

## Voting Studies

| | Presidential Support | | Party Unity | | Conservative Coalition | |
|---|---|---|---|---|---|---|
| Year | S | O | S | O | S | O |
| 1980 | 65 | 27 | 62 | 27 | 62 | 25 |
| 1979 | 66 | 29 | 59 | 36 | 63 | 34 |
| 1978 | 66 | 31 | 49 | 45 | 66 | 28 |
| 1977 | 66 | 25 | 55 | 37 | 56 | 37 |
| 1976 | 39 | 53 | 55 | 37 | 64 | 32 |
| 1975 | 27 | 72 | 64 | 31 | 54 | 41 |

S = Support　　　　O = Opposition

## Key Votes

**96th Congress**

| | |
|---|---|
| Weaken Carter oil profits tax (1979) | Y |
| Reject hospital cost control plan (1979) | ? |
| Implement Panama Canal Treaties (1979) | Y |
| Establish Department of Education (1979) | Y |
| Approve Anti-busing Amendment (1979) | Y |
| Guarantee Chrysler Corp. loans (1979) | N |
| Approve military draft registration (1980) | Y |
| Aid Sandinista regime in Nicaragua (1980) | Y |
| Strengthen fair housing laws (1980) | N |

**97th Congress**

| | |
|---|---|
| Reagan budget proposal (1981) | N |

## Interest Group Ratings

| Year | ADA | ACA | AFL-CIO | CCUS |
|---|---|---|---|---|
| 1980 | 44 | 50 | 31 | 83 |
| 1979 | 32 | 58 | 40 | 63 |
| 1978 | 25 | 67 | 25 | 67 |
| 1977 | 40 | 44 | 32 | 71 |
| 1976 | 45 | 46 | 52 | 36 |
| 1975 | 68 | 48 | 73 | 24 |

# 6 Eugene Johnston (R)

**Of Greensboro — Elected 1980**

**Born:** March 3, 1936, Winston-Salem, N.C.
**Education:** Wake Forest U., J.D. 1961, B.B.A.
1962.
**Military Career:** Army, 1954-57.
**Profession:** Lawyer; businessman.
**Family:** Divorced; five children.
**Religion:** Methodist.
**Political Career:** Republican nominee for N.C.
Senate, 1976 and 1978.

**The Member:** Johnston is a self-made millionaire who earned his money in several fields — law, real estate, accounting and commercial printing. His financial background helped win him a seat on the Budget Committee, where he applies his resolute conservatism to federal spending. During the 1981 spring recess, Johnston was one of the Republican congressmen who went stumping for Reagan's budget-cutting proposals in Southern districts represented by Democrats.

During Budget Committee deliberations, however, Johnston fought to preserve federal funding for tobacco support programs. He also challenged committee Democrats who talked about wasteful defense spending. "Defense is a social program," he said at one point. "It keeps people alive."

Before Johnston, the 6th District was accustomed to the manner and outlook of moderate Democratic Rep. Richardson Preyer. Preyer, used to easy elections, was not prepared for Johnston's 1980 challenge. Johnston persuaded voters that Preyer was too liberal for the district, citing votes against the B-1 bomber and in favor of food stamps for strikers. Preyer responded that Johnston was "a member of the radical right," but was never able to discredit him.

**The District:** This three-county district, a center of textile manufacturing, leans Democratic, although Guilford County (Greensboro) has developed an appreciable Republican vote with the influx of managerial personnel.

Most of the Democrats, however, are as suspicious of the national party as Democrats elsewhere in the South. The district went for Nixon in 1968 and 1972, and for Carter in 1976. In 1980, Reagan won it, capturing Guilford and Alamance counties and losing Rockingham County by a narrow margin.

## Committees

**Budget**
Task Forces: Economic Policy and Productivity; Tax Policy.

**Education and Labor** (11th of 14 Republicans)
Health and Safety; Labor-Management Relations; Labor Standards.

## Elections

**1980 General**

| | |
|---|---|
| Eugene Johnston (R ) | 80,275 (51 %) |
| Richardson Preyer (D ) | 76,957 (49 %) |

**District Vote For President**

| | 1980 | | 1976 | | 1972 |
|---|---|---|---|---|---|
| **D** | 71,266 (45 %) | D | 77,610 (53 %) | D | 38,163 (28 %) |
| **R** | 82,573 (52 %) | R | 67,483 (46 %) | R | 97,946 (71 %) |
| **I** | 5,242 (3 %) | | | | |

## Campaign Finance

| | Receipts | Receipts from PACs | Expenditures |
|---|---|---|---|
| **1980** | | | |
| Johnston (R ) | $281,906 | $38,030 (13 %) | $279,669 |
| Preyer (D ) | $168,429 | $97,040 (58 %) | $214,850 |

## Key Vote

**97th Congress**

| | |
|---|---|
| Reagan budget proposal (1981) | Y |

---

**6th District: Central — Greensboro.**
Population: 499,716 (9% increase since 1970).
Race: White 380,193 (76%), Black 115,646
(23%), Others 3,877 (1%). Spanish origin:
3,620 (1%).

# 7 Charlie Rose (D)

**Of Fayetteville — Elected 1972**

**Born:** Aug. 10, 1939, Fayetteville, N.C.
**Education:** Davidson College, B.A. 1961; U. of N.C. Law School, LL.B. 1964.
**Profession:** Lawyer.
**Family:** Wife, Sara Louise Richardson; two children.
**Religion:** Presbyterian.
**Political Career:** Chief District Court prosecutor, 12th Judicial District, 1967-71; sought Democratic nomination for U.S. House, 1970.

**In Washington:** A man with a passion for tinkering, Rose has spent a decade tinkering with computers and House politics while struggling to play a leadership role on the Agriculture Committee.

His office is an electronic village, loaded with expensive equipment that allows him to chart legislation at a glance and hold staff meetings in which computer terminals do all the talking. For years, Rose has been trying to move Congress as far into the computer age as he seems to be himself.

The House had a computer system when Rose arrived in 1973, but it was a primitive one used mainly for payrolls and retrieving information on the status of bills. Rose joined the House Administration Committee in 1973 and persuaded Chairman Wayne L. Hays to establish a computer task force.

Rose became the head of the task force, and by lobbying carefully for funds with the leadership, gradually created a House information bureaucracy that had a budget of nearly $10 million in 1980, before it was scaled back to a little more than $7 million in the 1981 climate of austerity. Some 35 percent of the budget of House Information Systems has gone directly into members' offices, giving them not only better legislative data but also the computerized mailing lists that have brought incumbents political success courting constituents in recent years.

While computerizing the institution, Rose was also putting it on television for the first time. He was instrumental in setting up the system that currently broadcasts House floor proceedings, implementing a 20-year-old idea that nobody else had been able to sell politically.

Rose had to surmount considerable fear among colleagues that TV would lead to grand-standing or show the House in a poor light, with members sleeping or reading newspapers during floor debates. Speaker O'Neill was adamantly opposed to giving commercial networks control over the cameras.

Rose softened the criticism by agreeing to let House employees monitor the cameras, and O'Neill finally accepted the idea, although he has never been happy with it. After a brief experiment with a limited closed circuit system available only in congressional offices, gavel-to-gavel coverage began on a cable network in 1979. While arguments remain about use of the videotapes in election campaigns, the system itself is clearly in to stay.

House leaders appointed Rose to the new Select Committee on Intelligence in 1977, and he is now its third-ranking Democrat. The assignment has given him a chance to explore the technology of electronic surveillance, another of his interests, and to look into what he sees as dangerous Soviet experiments in mind control.

If Rose were merely an apolitical gadgeteer, he would never have accomplished what he has so far. But he has always had a feel for the political relationships that can help him pursue his interests.

Besides becoming an early protégé of O'Neill, Rose struck an early alliance with Hays at House Administration and with California Democrat Phillip Burton, who spent years planning a 1977

> **7th District: Southeast — Fayetteville, Wilmington.** Population: 559,395 (20% increase since 1970). Race: White 349,094 (63%), Black 156,243 (28%), Indian 43,297 (8%), Others 10,761 (2%). Spanish origin: 12,102 (2%).

campaign for majority leader. When the time finally arrived, Rose was Burton's campaign manager, and the effort came agonizingly close, with Burton losing to Jim Wright of Texas by one vote.

The fallout from that bitter campaign affected Rose's contacts with the O'Neill-Wright leadership for a time, but eventually the issue subsided. In 1980, Rose hoped his ties with Burton's liberal faction of House Democrats would help him win election as chairman of the House Democratic Caucus. But he was up against another moderate Southerner, Gillis Long of Louisiana, who had all of Rose's personal popularity and fewer controversial alliances. Long won by a surprisingly lopsided vote of 146-53.

All this maneuvering has not always left Rose much time to be a leader on the Agriculture Committee, although he has had three crucial subcommittee chairmanships.

In the 95th Congress, while chairman of the Dairy and Poultry Subcommittee, Rose pushed through legislation setting minimum standards for milk in ice cream. The move was partly a reflection of his concern about food additives, but it also earned him the gratitude of the dairy industry, which has supported him politically.

In 1979, as chairman of the Livestock and Grains Subcommittee, Rose moved through his subcommittee a bill to increase target price supports for wheat and corn by 7 percent. At first he tried to link the bill to food stamp legislation to guarantee the votes for its passage; later it became clear that the farm bill would pass anyway, and it became law on its own.

At the start of 1981, Agriculture revised its subcommittee system, and Rose took a new subcommittee on Tobacco and Peanuts — the one most directly related to the crops that grow in his district.

**At Home:** Unwilling to wait for Rep. Alton Lennon to carry out his long-promised retirement, Rose went after him in a 1970 primary and came close enough that Lennon finally did retire two years later.

To run in 1970, Rose had to take leave from his work as chief prosecutor in the 12th Judicial District (Cumberland and Hoke Counties). Before he took that job, he had been an aide to Gov. Terry Sanford, (1961-65), and he was supported by many of the moderate Democrats who found

Sanford appealing. Running a well-financed, well-organized campaign that called attention to Lennon's 64 years, Rose received a respectable 43.3 percent of the vote.

Early in 1971, Rose began producing a monthly television program outlining the history of each county in the district. He said the shows were not political, but made it clear he would try again for Congress in 1972. In December, Lennon announced his retirement.

State Sen. Hector McGeachy and Fayetteville lawyer Doran Berry joined Rose in the 1972 Democratic primary. Few issues separated the three; Rose's name was better known because of his earlier campaign and because his father and grandfather had served in the Legislature.

Rose polled 48.8 percent of the vote in the initial primary, far ahead of McGeachy's 25.9 percent. Still, McGeachy demanded a runoff, and Rose won it with 55.5 percent. The general election was no problem.

Two years later, McGeachy was back again, challenging Rose with a campaign that courted the black vote. But Rose had used a mobile office during his first term to keep in touch with rural constituents, and he developed close ties with the district's business community. The incumbent took 60.5 percent in the primary, and has not had a significant primary challenge since.

Nor have Republicans been any threat. The GOP candidate in 1978, Raymond Schrump, was a former POW in Vietnam who pitched his campaign to the large military population in the district. But he barely reached 30 percent.

**The District:** The 7th District is oriented toward the military, with Fort Bragg and Pope Air Force Base both near Fayetteville, in Cumberland County. Cumberland casts about one-third of the district's total vote.

The other major city in the 7th is Wilmington (New Hanover County), an Atlantic Ocean port where Republican sentiment is considerable. New Hanover County gave a majority to Ronald Reagan in 1980, while the district's other five counties went to Carter.

Tobacco, peanuts, and soybeans dominate the farm economy. Textiles and timber are the only important industries. Nearly one-third of the district population is black; there is also a significant American Indian minority.

## Committees

**Agriculture** (7th of 24 Democrats)
Tobacco and Peanuts, chairman; Livestock, Dairy and Poultry.

**House Administration** (7th of 22 Democrats)
Policy Group on Information and Computers, chairman; Accounts; Services; Task Force on Committee Organization.

**Select Intelligence** (3rd of 9 Democrats)
Oversight and Evaluation, chairman.

## Elections

**1980 General**

| | |
|---|---|
| Charlie Rose (D ) | 88,564 (69 %) |
| Vivian Wright (R ) | 40,270 (31 %) |

**1980 Primary**

| | |
|---|---|
| Charlie Rose (D ) | 56,749 (80 %) |
| Lynn Batson (D ) | 14,029 (20 %) |

**1978 General**

| | |
|---|---|
| Charlie Rose (D ) | 53,696 (70 %) |
| Raymond Schrump (R ) | 23,146 (30 %) |

**Previous Winning Percentages**

**1976** (81 %)     **1974** (100%)     **1972** (60 %)

**District Vote For President**

| | 1980 | | 1976 | | 1972 |
|---|---|---|---|---|---|
| D | 73,710 (54 %) | D | 81,207 (66 %) | D | 30,409 (29 %) |
| R | 58,352 (43 %) | R | 40,560 (33 %) | R | 71,346 (69 %) |
| I | 3,175 (2 %) | | | | |

## Campaign Finance

| | Receipts | Receipts from PACs | Expenditures |
|---|---|---|---|
| **1980** | | | |
| Rose (D ) | $91,510 | $52,100 (57 %) | $65,576 |
| Wright (R ) | $16,996 | $192 (1 %) | $16,992 |
| **1978** | | | |
| Rose (D ) | $59,503 | $35,225 (59 %) | $57,723 |
| Schrump (R ) | $51,468 | $1,850 (4 %) | $47,933 |

## Voting Studies

| | Presidential Support | | Party Unity | | Conservative Coalition | |
|---|---|---|---|---|---|---|
| Year | S | O | S | O | S | O |
| 1980 | 59 | 21 | 67 | 19 | 45 | 35 |
| 1979 | 64 | 23 | 64 | 18 | 49 | 37 |
| 1978 | 63 | 33 | 68 | 22 | 40 | 52 |
| 1977 | 62 | 19 | 65 | 20 | 42 | 42 |
| 1976 | 43 | 53 | 60 | 26 | 51 | 35 |
| 1975 | 30 | 62 | 56 | 31 | 55 | 30 |
| 1974 (Ford) | 43 | 54 | | | | |
| 1974 | 42 | 36 | 56 | 28 | 54 | 33 |
| 1973 | 41 | 55 | 59 | 37 | 66 | 28 |

S = Support          O = Opposition

## Key Votes

**96th Congress**

| | |
|---|---|
| Weaken Carter oil profits tax (1979) | Y |
| Reject hospital cost control plan (1979) | N |
| Implement Panama Canal Treaties (1979) | Y |
| Establish Department of Education (1979) | Y |
| Approve Anti-busing Amendment (1979) | N |
| Guarantee Chrysler Corp. loans (1979) | N |
| Approve military draft registration (1980) | Y |
| Aid Sandinista regime in Nicaragua (1980) | N |
| Strengthen fair housing laws (1980) | Y |

**97th Congress**

| | |
|---|---|
| Reagan budget proposal (1981) | N |

## Interest Group Ratings

| Year | ADA | ACA | AFL-CIO | CCUS |
|---|---|---|---|---|
| 1980 | 44 | 38 | 50 | 79 |
| 1979 | 58 | 33 | 44 | 38 |
| 1978 | 50 | 43 | 53 | 35 |
| 1977 | 35 | 22 | 57 | 50 |
| 1976 | 35 | 46 | 73 | 27 |
| 1975 | 16 | 32 | 62 | 50 |
| 1974 | 35 | 58 | 56 | 67 |
| 1973 | 44 | 38 | 40 | 80 |

# 8 W. G. ''Bill'' Hefner (D)

**Of Concord — Elected 1974**

**Born:** April 11, 1930, Elora, Tenn.
**Education:** Graduated from Sardis High School, Boaz, Ala., 1948.
**Profession:** Broadcast executive.
**Family:** Wife, Nancy Hill; two children.
**Religion:** Baptist
**Political Career:** No previous office.

**In Washington:** Relatively inconspicuous on the floor, like most of his delegation, Hefner has emerged in recent years as one of the more important national Democratic loyalists from the South.

In 1979, he was instrumental in rounding up a bloc of more than 50 Southerners willing to endorse Jimmy Carter's renomination, on the grounds that Carter was the best option for any conservative who wanted to stay a Democrat.

In 1981, House leaders placed him on the Budget Committee, and he declared himself early for the budget drafted by House Democratic leaders, insisting that the massive tax cut in the Reagan budget was unwise. When Budget Chairman James R. Jones, D-Okla., decided the Democratic budget needed more defense money in order to attract a majority on the floor, Hefner offered the amendment that was designed to fill that need: an extra $6.7 billion for defense in fiscal 1982.

The amendment brought Hefner public attention that was unusual for him, but it also advertised his anti-Reagan vote at a time when Democrats from all over the South were drawing intense lobbying pressure from administration forces. Hefner's defense amendment, accepted without controversy, brought in five of the seven votes in his state delegation on the ultimate budget decision. But 46 of the 78 Southern Democrats went the other way, including three Budget Committee members who had gone along with Jones and Hefner at earlier stages.

The budget episode meant at least a slight change in Hefner's role as a member of the Democratic Forum, the organization of more than 40 conservative House Democrats who have kept up close contacts with the Reagan administration. Hefner was a charter member of that group, arguing that it could help move the party to the right. But he was perceived by others in the forum as a national Democrat on most issues, and his budget voting reinforced that perception.

Hefner's leadership connections have brought him excellent committee positions, not only on Budget but also Appropriations, and on the Steering Committee that makes assignments for all the House Democrats.

He began lobbying for a place on Appropriations early in his career, and finally made it in the summer of 1980, when the Steering Committee was split 12-12 over two other nominees. Hefner asked that his name be offered as a compromise, and was chosen. He has become a defense specialist on the committee, serving not only on the Defense Subcommittee but on Military Construction.

Before moving to Appropriations, Hefner spent a term on the Commerce Committee and a term on Public Works, where he was closely inolved in the arguments over President Carter's airline deregulation proposals. He cast an initial vote to weaken the deregulation bill at Public Works, then backed it as a compromise was worked out that eventually got it enacted.

**At Home:** Running for Congress in 1974 against the backdrop of Watergate, Hefner pledged to revive "Christian morality" in government and spiced his political speeches with renditions of his favorite hymns.

That might be seen as an incautious mixture of church and state in some parts of the country, but not in North Carolina's 8th District. Hefner's

---

**8th District: South Central — Kannapolis, Salisbury.** Population: 533,306 (17% increase since 1970). Race: White 427,534 (80%), Black 100,745 (19%), Others 5,027 (1%). Spanish origin: 3,681 (1%).

blend of inspiration, entertainment and politicking helped him soundly defeat Republican Rep. Earl B. Ruth.

Early in 1974, Ruth was not thought to be in any great danger. First elected in 1968, he had gained strength in two subsequent elections, winning more than 60 percent in 1972.

But Hefner was an exceptional candidate. As a promoter and singer of gospel music in the Carolinas and Virginia, he had made many local and statewide television appearances. He started the campaign with excellent name recognition, and gradually won back thousands of conservative Democrats who had drifted toward Ruth, allowing him to unseat the Republican with 57 percent of the vote. Hefner has kept his percentages in the high 50s since then, comfortable but not utterly safe.

**The District:** Partisan preferences in the 8th still reflect the political divisions of the 19th century. Six mountain and industrial counties in the northern part of the district voted for Reagan in 1980; five mostly agricultural counties in the southern part of the district chose Carter.

Cotton-growing was once the major economic activity in the district's southern counties, but soybeans, poultry and dairy products play an increasingly important role. Small cities and towns in the north like Kannapolis, Salisbury and Concord (Cabarrus and Rowan counties) manufacture textiles, apparel and textile machinery. On the southeast end of the district are the Sandhills resorts of Southern Pines and Pinehurst, in Moore County, a GOP enclave.

## Committees

**Appropriations** (28th of 33 Democrats)
Defense; Military Construction.

**Budget**
Task Forces: Energy and the Environment; Human Resources and Block Grants; National Security and Veterans.

## Elections

**1980 General**

| | |
|---|---|
| Bill Hefner (D ) | 95,013 (59 %) |
| Larry Harris (R ) | 67,317 (42 %) |

**1980 Primary**

| | |
|---|---|
| Bill Hefner (D ) | 45,794 (74 %) |
| Edward Sweet (D ) | 11,156 (18 %) |
| John Gray (D ) | 5,085 (9 %) |

**1978 General**

| | |
|---|---|
| Bill Hefner (D ) | 63,168 (59 %) |
| Roger Austin (R ) | 43,942 (41 %) |

**Previous Winning Percentages**

1976 (66 %)    1974 (57 %)

**District Vote For President**

| | 1980 | | 1976 | | 1972 |
|---|---|---|---|---|---|
| D | 75,483 (45 %) | D | 85,084 (55 %) | D | 37,880 (27 %) |
| R | 88,044 (52 %) | R | 69,653 (45 %) | R | 100,830 (71 %) |
| I | 3,515 (2 %) | | | | |

## Campaign Finance

| | Receipts | Receipts from PACs | Expenditures |
|---|---|---|---|
| **1980** | | | |
| Hefner (D ) | $111,117 | $25,150 (23 %) | $79,281 |
| Harris (R ) | $18,534 | — (0 %) | $18,530 |

| | | | |
|---|---|---|---|
| **1978** | | | |
| Hefner (D ) | $81,773 | $29,850 (37 %) | $74,546 |
| Austin (R ) | $23,405 | $3,876 (17 %) | $22,949 |

## Voting Studies

| Year | Presidential Support | | Party Unity | | Conservative Coalition | |
|---|---|---|---|---|---|---|
| | S | O | S | O | S | O |
| 1980 | 54 | 32 | 58 | 32† | 74 | 14 |
| 1979 | 69 | 26 | 68 | 28 | 69 | 28 |
| 1978 | 56 | 44 | 51 | 47 | 77 | 19 |
| 1977 | 62 | 34 | 55 | 41 | 68 | 26 |
| 1976 | 43 | 45 | 42 | 48 | 80 | 11 |
| 1975 | 27 | 72 | 52 | 42 | 70 | 24 |

S = Support        O = Opposition

†Not eligible for all recorded votes.

## Key Votes

**96th Congress**

| | |
|---|---|
| Weaken Carter oil profits tax (1979) | Y |
| Reject hospital cost control plan (1979) | N |
| Implement Panama Canal Treaties (1979) | Y |
| Establish Department of Education (1979) | Y |
| Approve Anti-busing Amendment (1979) | N |
| Guarantee Chrysler Corp. loans (1979) | N |
| Approve military draft registration (1980) | ? |
| Aid Sandinista regime in Nicaragua (1980) | N |
| Strengthen fair housing laws (1980) | N |

**97th Congress**

| | |
|---|---|
| Reagan budget proposal (1981) | N |

## Interest Group Ratings

| Year | ADA | ACA | AFL-CIO | CCUS |
|---|---|---|---|---|
| 1980 | 22 | 36 | 50 | 81 |
| 1979 | 42 | 36 | 47 | 47 |
| 1978 | 25 | 63 | 20 | 67 |
| 1977 | 35 | 40 | 43 | 65 |
| 1976 | 15 | 56 | 52 | 57 |
| 1975 | 32 | 58 | 48 | 41 |

# 9 James G. Martin (R)

**Of Davidson — Elected 1972**

**Born:** Dec. 11, 1935, Savannah, Ga.
**Education:** Davidson College, B.S. 1957; Princeton U., Ph.D. 1960.
**Profession:** Chemistry professor.
**Family:** Wife, Dorothy Ann McAulay; three children.
**Religion:** Presbyterian.
**Political Career:** Mecklenburg County Board of Commissioners, 1966-72, board chairman, 1967-68 and 1970-71.

**In Washington:** This soft-spoken chemistry professor pulls few surprises on the Ways and Means Committee, voting a consistently conservative position in favor of private industry. But the closer the argument gets to science, the more active he becomes — and the less predictable.

Allied with chemical companies, he played a bargaining role in 1980 as the committee drafted a "superfund" bill that would require companies to contribute to the cost of cleaning up chemical spills. He worked to scale the bill down from the level its strongest supporters wanted, and to find language the companies themselves could accept. Martin ended up supporting the combined Ways and Means-Commerce package on the floor.

Meanwhile, on another chemical issue, Martin defended saccharin, and worked against efforts to ban it on the grounds that it might cause cancer. He made numerous attempts to refute the claim that the tumors found in rats given massive doses of saccharin imply a serious risk for humans. The risk is "not great as life goes," Martin insisted at one point. "It shortens life by 23 minutes." Martin would allow the use of food additives as long as their benefits to humans were found to outweigh possible risks. Existing law requires a ban on all carcinogens.

Martin is also a strong free enterprise supporter on the health insurance issue. When hospital cost controls came up at Ways and Means in 1979, he called for a one-house congressional veto of any federal cost control regulation. Common Cause later pointed out that Martin had been the committee's top recipient of campaign contributions from medical interests in 1976, and drew a connection. Martin called the citizen's lobby group "devious and mischievous."

On issues related to pure science research, Martin sometimes parts company with Republican colleagues. In 1980, he argued against a cutback in federal support for research into some obscure and hard-to-explain subjects, such as homosexuality among seagulls. "Scientists," Martin argued, "ought to study not what we as politicians think they should study, but what their training and curiosity leads them to study."

He has argued with vehemence in the past against some water projects, putting him at odds with majority sentiment in both parties. He spoke for President Carter's 1978 veto of a public works bill loaded with funds for irrigation projects.

**At Home:** Although the 9th frequently goes Democratic in statewide contests, Charlotte Democrats have never been able to find a successful combination against Martin, and he has easily maintained the GOP dominance established by his predecessor, Charles Raper Jonas.

When Jonas announced he would retire in 1972, he delivered his organization and fund-raising contacts to Martin, a Davidson College chemistry professor and Mecklenburg County commissioner.

Martin promised to keep up Jonas' tradition of constituent service and close ties to the Charlotte business community. He said he was a civil rights moderate and a strong supporter of Nixon's policies on Vietnam and the economy.

Martin was challenged from the right in the 1972 Republican primary, but he won easily and swept to victory in the fall over Democrat Jim Beatty, a state legislator and former Olympic

---

**9th District: West central — Charlotte.** Population: 529,180 (15% increase since 1970). Race: White 397,754 (75%), Black 125,102 (24%), Others 6,320 (1%). Spanish origin: 4,822 (1%).

track star. Martin's close identification with Nixon helped him that year, but it was a minor problem for him two years later. Democratic City Councilman Milton Short, considered a sacrificial candidate by many Democrats, came within 9,645 votes.

In 1980, Martin faced an ambitious challenge from another Davidson professor, Randall Kincaid, a town commissioner in Davidson. He said Martin was too close to the oil and chemical companies that contributed to his campaign, and he criticized Martin's support for the Kemp-Roth tax cut plan.

But Kincaid, not close to Charlotte's Demo-

cratic establishment, had trouble finding money. Martin spent nearly $300,000, Kincaid only $60,000. Martin won 58.6 percent of the vote.

**The District:** The 9th is a three-county district dominated by Mecklenburg County, location of Charlotte, the largest city in either of the Carolinas. The city is the main commercial center for the populous Piedmont region surrounding it. Mecklenburg County casts three-fourths of the district's total vote, and has more Democratic voters than Martin's tenure suggests — Democratic Gov. James B. Hunt easily won the county in 1976 and 1980, and Reagan led Carter by only 1,389 votes in 1980.

## Committees

**Budget**
Task Forces: Economic Policy and Productivity; Entitlements, Uncontrollables and Indexing; Tax Policy.

**Ways and Means** (7th of 12 Republicans)
Oversight.

## Elections

**1980 General**

| | |
|---|---|
| James Martin (R ) | 101,156 (59 %) |
| Randall Kincaid (D ) | 71,504 (41 %) |

**1978 General**

| | |
|---|---|
| James Martin (R ) | 66,157 (68 %) |
| Charles Maxwell (D ) | 29,761 (31 %) |

**Previous Winning Percentages**

1976 (54 %)    1974 (54 %)    1972 (59 %)

**District Vote For President**

| | 1980 | | 1976 | | 1972 |
|---|---|---|---|---|---|
| D | 86,858 (46 %) | D | 85,955 (52 %) | D | 43,918 (29 %) |
| R | 92,319 (49 %) | R | 79,970 (48 %) | R | 102,879 (69 %) |
| I | 7,483 (4 %) | | | | |

## Campaign Finance

| | Receipts | Receipts from PACs | Expen-ditures |
|---|---|---|---|
| **1980** | | | |
| Martin (R ) | $293,774 | $115,731 (39 %) | $297,040 |
| Kincaid (D ) | $59,757 | $11,982 (20 %) | $58,955 |
| **1978** | | | |
| Martin (R ) | $255,542 | $81,005 (32 %) | $252,126 |
| Maxwell (D ) | $38,795 | $100 (0.3%) | $37,657 |

## Voting Studies

| | Presidential Support | | Party Unity | | Conservative Coalition | |
|---|---|---|---|---|---|---|
| Year | S | O | S | O | S | O |
| 1980 | 38 | 56 | 81 | 12 | 86 | 6 |
| 1979 | 26 | 67 | 82 | 12 | 87 | 6 |
| 1978 | 35 | 60 | 76 | 16 | 80 | 9 |
| 1977 | 46 | 53 | 86 | 14 | 91 | 9 |
| 1976 | 76 | 22 | 84 | 11 | 90 | 5 |
| 1975 | 63 | 31 | 84 | 12 | 85 | 9 |
| 1974 (Ford) | 56 | 39 | | | | |
| 1974 | 77 | 19 | 82 | 11 | 86 | 8 |

S = Support          O = Opposition

## Key Votes

**96th Congress**

| | |
|---|---|
| Weaken Carter oil profits tax (1979) | Y |
| Reject hospital cost control plan (1979) | Y |
| Implement Panama Canal Treaties (1979) | N |
| Establish Department of Education (1979) | N |
| Approve Anti-busing Amendment (1979) | Y |
| Guarantee Chrysler Corp. loans (1979) | N |
| Approve military draft registration (1980) | Y |
| Aid Sandinista regime in Nicaragua (1980) | N |
| Strengthen fair housing Laws (1980) | N |

**97th Congress**

| | |
|---|---|
| Reagan budget proposal (1981) | Y |

## Interest Group Ratings

| Year | ADA | ACA | AFL-CIO | CCUS |
|---|---|---|---|---|
| 1980 | 11 | 88 | 11 | 77 |
| 1979 | 5 | 88 | 5 | 100 |
| 1978 | 15 | 88 | 5 | 71 |
| 1977 | 10 | 85 | 4 | 88 |
| 1976 | 20 | 96 | 14 | 76 |
| 1975 | 5 | 88 | 5 | 94 |
| 1974 | 17 | 80 | 9 | 78 |
| 1973 | 12 | 88 | 9 | 100 |

# 10  James T. Broyhill (R)

Of Lenoir — Elected 1962

**Born:** Aug. 19, 1927, Lenoir, N.C.
**Education:** U. of N.C., B.S. 1950.
**Profession:** Furniture manufacturer.
**Family:** Wife, Louise Robbins; three children.
**Religion:** Baptist.
**Political Career:** No previous office.

**In Washington:** Watching Broyhill at a committee hearing or on the floor, silent and seemingly bored, one might draw the first impression that he is a fringe player. But first impressions are dangerous.

Behind the silence lies one of the more creative parliamentary minds in Congress, one likely to be writing a string of amendments and plotting their progress all the way through conference, or working up a four-point compromise to be presented when the first offer fails. Uninterested in publicity, Broyhill plays the inside game as well as anyone in the House.

In the 96th Congress, among other things, Broyhill plotted the defeat of President Carter's proposed hospital cost controls, fought for a limit on Federal Trade Commission authority, and tried to rewrite the Federal Communications Act in a way satisfactory to its quarrelsome constituency. Two of those three things were accomplished.

The FTC has been a Broyhill target for years. Convinced the agency was harassing legitimate business for no good reason, he won a floor amendment in 1978 guaranteeing a legislative veto of FTC orders. When the amendment was dropped in conference, the House rejected the entire authorization. The agency was able to stay in business with emergency funds.

The next year, Broyhill inserted the veto during the initial subcommittee stage at Commerce. That and the increasingly anti-regulatory political climate guaranteed its survival, and when Congress finally cleared a three-year FTC authorization in mid-1980, a version of the legislative veto was in it.

Broyhill was unable to stop hospital cost controls in 1979 the way he had stopped them before, with an amendment in committee. Heavy administration lobbying pried the legislation out of Commerce by a single vote, as Broyhill's proposal to make the entire program voluntary failed on a 21-21 count.

By the time the bill reached the House floor,

in late 1979, dissident Democrats were coordinating the opposition, and got most of the attention. But Broyhill and his Republican allies produced a 135-8 majority on their side of the aisle in favor of an amendment nearly identical to the one that lost in committee, and hospital cost controls went down to a decisive defeat.

Broyhill's role in revising the communications act was as broker rather than opponent. Through most of the two-year debate, he spoke on the side of American Telephone & Telegraph, against those who feared it would take advantage of deregulation to prey upon smaller research firms. As a compromise, Broyhill proposed requiring AT&T to set up a separate subsidiary, complete with manufacturing and research operations, for any competitive service it wanted to offer. That proposal brought the legislation successfully through the full Commerce Committee for the first time after nearly a decade of shadow boxing. But the bill never reached the House floor.

It was the marathon dispute over the Clean Air Act, in the mid-1970s, that marked Broyhill's rise to quiet prominence among Republican legislators. In that argument, Broyhill was allied with Democrat John D. Dingell of Michigan, now the Commerce chairman, against Paul Rogers, D-Fla., who chaired the panel's Health Subcommittee. Rogers wanted tough limits on auto emissions and

---

**10th District: West — Gastonia, Hickory.** Population: 548,138 (16% increase since 1970). Race: White 487,656 (89%), Black 58,194 (11%), Others 2,288 (0.4%). Spanish origin: 3,002 (1%).

strict rules on future air quality in currently clean areas; Broyhill and Dingell fought him, losing at the committee level but overturning the result on the floor.

In conference the two generally split up, with Broyhill leading the argument for leniency toward industry at some clean air sites. The end product pleased environmentalists more than it pleased industry, but the whole process helped reinforce Broyhill's reputation as a strategist.

For all his free enterprise efforts at the Commerce Committee, Broyhill still has a reputation as a centrist Republican, restrained not only in temperament and rhetoric but in ideology. He was one of seven congressional Republicans who sent an unpublicized letter to President Nixon in 1971, urging him to speed up the withdrawal of American troops from Vietnam. The same year, when then-Commerce Chairman Harley O. Staggers tried to force a contempt citation against CBS for broadcasting a critical documentary against the Pentagon, it was Broyhill who led the opposition, saying that Congress was on dangerous ground. He spoke only two minutes — a long address for Broyhill — but he carried Republicans with him by a margin of 95-76, forcing recommittal of the contempt citation by a relatively close margin.

**At Home:** Broyhill had to defeat two incumbent Democrats in 6 years to secure himself in the 10th District, but now he seems entrenched.

Although he had little political experience prior to his 1962 congressional campaign, he had no problem with name recognition. Broyhill's family owns the Broyhill furniture manufacturing company, employer of thousands of North Carolina workers.

His 1962 victory, over Democratic Rep. Hugh Q. Alexander, was helped by the Democratic Legislature. In redistricting after the 1960 census, the legislators tried to oust GOP Rep. Charles Raper Jonas by removing some Republican counties from his district and adding them to Alexander's territory. They added too many.

Broyhill launched a handshaking campaign early in 1962 and sailed past a Goldwater conservative in the primary. While his campaign was gaining momentum, Alexander was spending most of his time in Washington.

Broyhill voiced opposition to the Democratic administration's Medicare program and to increased foreign aid. He scored points with the textile industry by criticizing the Kennedy policies on foreign trade, which he said were bringing in too many low-cost cotton imports.

Alexander tried to activate the county Democratic organizations, and presented himself as the workingman's friend who had backed minimum wage and Social Security legislation. Broyhill countered with the most extensive media campaign the district had seen, and he eked out victory with 50.4 percent of the vote, becoming the second Republican in the state's delegation.

By 1966, Broyhill's share of the vote was up to 60 percent. But in 1968, redistricting threw him together with Democratic Rep. Basil L. Whitener in a new eight-county district that included traditionally Democratic Gaston and Cleveland counties, textile centers that Whitener had represented for 12 years. Only two of Broyhill's counties were included in the new district.

But Broyhill proved a more effective campaigner than Whitener, and he prevailed with 54.8 percent of the vote; in 1970, he overcame a Whitener comeback bid with 57.1 percent.

Broyhill saw his margin drop in 1974, as did all North Carolina GOP representatives, but he held on to win. In 1976, he faced a major Democratic effort, as state Rep. John Hunt tied himself closely to the popular Democratic ticket led by Jimmy Carter and gubernatorial candidate James B. Hunt.

John Hunt, known in the Legislature for his sponsorship of tax-relief legislation for low-income families, thought he could take advantage of divisions within the North Carolina GOP. But Broyhill's personal popularity brought him nearly 60 percent of the vote.

**The District:** The 10th runs from Watauga County, a popular Appalachian mountain retreat, to industrial Gaston County, on the border with South Carolina. It is the only North Carolina district in which every county gave a majority in 1980 to Republican Senate candidate John East. But presidential returns show less consistency: Carter won 54.1 percent in 1976, and Reagan won 55.2 percent in 1980.

Gaston and neighboring Cleveland County manufacture textiles, auto parts and glass. The triangle of cities in the central part of the district — Hickory, Morganton and Lenoir — are textile and furniture centers. The blue-collar Democratic vote, substantial throughout the southern and central parts of the district, is more conservative than it is partisan.

## Committees

**Energy and Commerce** (Ranking Republican)
Oversight and Investigations.

## Elections

**1980 General**

| | |
|---|---|
| James Broyhill (R ) | 120,777 (70 %) |
| James Icenhour (D ) | 52,485 (30 %) |

**1978 General**

| | |
|---|---|
| James Broyhill (R ) | Unopposed |

**Previous Winning Percentages**

| | | | |
|---|---|---|---|
| 1976 (60 %) | 1974 (54 %) | 1972 (73 %) | 1970 (57 %) |
| 1968 (55 %) | 1966 (63 %) | 1964 (55 %) | 1962 (51 %) |

**District Vote For President**

| | 1980 | | 1976 | | 1972 |
|---|---|---|---|---|---|
| D | 75,094 (42 %) | D | 90,939 (54 %) | D | 38,202 (26 %) |
| R | 97,286 (55 %) | R | 76,532 (46 %) | R | 105,093 (72 %) |
| I | 3,802 (2 %) | | | | |

## Campaign Finance

| | Receipts | Percent of Receipts from PACs | Expenditures |
|---|---|---|---|
| **1980** | | | |
| Broyhill (R ) | $279,181 | $161,875 (58 %) | $248,354 |
| Icenhour (D ) | $23,261 | — (0 %) | $18,753 |
| **1978** | | | |
| Broyhill (R ) | $29,076 | $1,207 (4 %) | $32,586 |

## Voting Studies

| | Presidential Support | | Party Unity | | Conservative Coalition | |
|---|---|---|---|---|---|---|
| Year | S | O | S | O | S | O |
| 1980 | 38 | 56 | 78 | 15 | 88 | 4 |
| 1979 | 34 | 59 | 69 | 25 | 81 | 15 |
| 1978 | 34 | 63 | 80 | 15 | 84 | 9 |
| 1977 | 44 | 51 | 80 | 15 | 88 | 8 |
| 1976 | 80 | 18 | 80 | 17 | 83 | 14 |
| 1975 | 65 | 29 | 85 | 11 | 92 | 5 |
| 1974 (Ford) | 56 | 41 | | | | |
| 1974 | 68 | 25 | 72 | 24 | 81 | 14 |
| 1973 | 66 | 30 | 77 | 21 | 88 | 10 |
| 1972 | 78 | 19 | 76 | 21 | 84 | 15 |
| 1971 | 74 | 18 | 69 | 16 | 78 | 12 |
| 1970 | 65 | 28 | 65 | 26 | 75 | 9 |
| 1969 | 60 | 40 | 71 | 27 | 84 | 13 |
| 1968 | 54 | 45 | 84 | 15 | 96 | 2 |
| 1967 | 39 | 60 | 85 | 10 | 93 | 2 |
| 1966 | 38 | 57 | 89 | 8 | 97 | 0 |
| 1965 | 32 | 63 | 86 | 12 | 92 | 8 |
| 1964 | 35 | 63 | 90 | 5 | 100 | 0 |
| 1963 | 31 | 65 | 86 | 10 | 93 | 7 |

S = Support          O = Opposition

## Key Votes

**96th Congress**

| | |
|---|---|
| Weaken Carter oil profits tax (1979) | Y |
| Reject hospital cost control plan (1979) | Y |
| Implement Panama Canal Treaties (1979) | Y |
| Establish Department of Education (1979) | N |
| Approve Anti-busing Amendment (1979) | Y |
| Gaurantee Chrysler Corp. loans (1979) | N |
| Approve Military draft registration (1980) | Y |
| Aid Sandinistas regime in Nicaragua (1980) | N |
| Strengthen Fair Housing Laws (1980) | N |

**97th Congress**

| | |
|---|---|
| Reagan budget proposal (1981) | Y |

## Interest Group Ratings

| Year | ADA | ACA | AFL-CIO | CCUS |
|---|---|---|---|---|
| 1980 | 11 | 87 | 11 | 78 |
| 1979 | 5 | 84 | 15 | 94 |
| 1978 | 20 | 88 | 5 | 83 |
| 1977 | 15 | 85 | 9 | 94 |
| 1976 | 15 | 88 | 13 | 76 |
| 1975 | 5 | 92 | 5 | 69 |
| 1974 | 17 | 79 | 0 | 67 |
| 1973 | 8 | 82 | 18 | 91 |
| 1972 | 0 | 82 | 9 | 100 |
| 1971 | 14 | 84 | 11 | - |
| 1970 | 8 | 87 | 14 | 89 |
| 1969 | 0 | 71 | 30 | - |
| 1968 | 0 | 91 | 0 | - |
| 1967 | 0 | 93 | 0 | 100 |
| 1966 | 0 | 92 | 0 | - |
| 1965 | 0 | 89 | - | 100 |
| 1964 | 4 | 95 | 0 | - |
| 1963 | - | 94 | - | - |

# 11 Bill Hendon (R)

Of Asheville — Elected 1980

**Born:** Nov. 9, 1944, Asheville, N.C.
**Education:** U. of Tenn., B.S. 1966; M.S. 1969.
**Profession:** Factory manager.
**Family:** Wife, Robbie Peters; two children.
**Religion:** Episcopalian.
**Political Career:** 11th Congressional District Republican chairman, 1979.

**The Member:** A member of an old-line local family and a leader in the Asheville Chamber of Commerce, Hendon is a favorite of the region's business community. His family owned a funeral home, which he sold to become the general manager at a local factory of a West German-owned firm, Putsch and Co. The plant makes blades to cut sugar cane.

In the House, Hendon has introduced a bill setting strict timetables for federal action on lands being considered for wilderness status. He thinks the current procedure takes too long and leaves land in limbo that could be developed. Public lands account for about 45 percent of the acreage in the 11th District, and Hendon favors more recreational use, timber harvesting, and oil drilling, as well as wilderness protection.

The first Republican to win this seat since 1928, Hendon worked doggedly to capture it. As a publicity stunt, he rode a mule-drawn wagon train through all the district's 17 counties. While conservative, he is not a close ally of the state's "New Right" senior senator, Republican Jesse Helms. He has publicly questioned the hard-hitting tactics of Helms's political organization.

Former Democratic Rep. Lamar Gudger, helped by Jimmy Carter's strong local showing in 1976, was hurt by Carter in 1980. Decrying the tax burden imposed by Washington, Hendon blamed the Carter administration and tied Gudger to it.

**The District:** Democrats lead in registration here, 60-40 percent, but Republicans have always been a potent presence. Since the Civil War, four mountainous counties — Madison, Yancey, Mitchell and Avery — have been GOP strongholds. Resort-oriented Polk and Henderson counties, in the southern part of the district, are Republican, too, due to their many out-of-state retirees.

Democratic bastions are Buncombe County, which contains Asheville, the district's sole urban center, and neighboring Haywood County. But Asheville-based Democrats frequently have to confront anti-Buncombe sentiment among the rural counties.

## Committees

**Interior and Insular Affairs** (12th of 17 Republicans)
Oversight and Investigations; Public Lands and National Parks.

**Select Aging** (22nd of 23 Republicans)
Housing and Consumer Interests; Retirement Income and Employment.

## Elections

**1980 General**

| | |
|---|---|
| Bill Hendon (R) | 104,485 (54 %) |
| Lamar Gudger (D ) | 90,789 (46 %) |

**District Vote For President**

| | 1980 | | 1976 | | 1972 |
|---|---|---|---|---|---|
| D | 89,129 (45 %) | D | 99,854 (54 %) | D | 46,095 (29 %) |
| R | 100,868 (51 %) | R | 84,061 (46 %) | R | 110,566 (69 %) |
| I | 5,364 (3 %) | | | | |

## Campaign Finance

| | Receipts | Receipts from PACs | Expenditures |
|---|---|---|---|
| **1980** | | | |
| Hendon (D ) | $248,066 | $21,016 (9 %) | $249,389 |
| Gudger (R ) | $137,175 | $62,650 (46 %) | $125,696 |

## Key Vote

**97th Congress**

| | |
|---|---|
| Reagan budget proposal (1981) | Y |

---

**11th District: West — Asheville.**
Population: 540,971 (16% increase since 1970). Race: White 503,874 (93%), Black 29,321 (5%), Others 7,776 (1%). Spanish origin: 3,754 (1%).

# North Dakota

| STATE: | Legislative Assembly | Population |
|---|---|---|
| Governor | Senate: 50 members (10D, 40R) | 652,695 - 46th in the nation |
| Allen I. Olson (R) | House: 100 members (27D, 73R) | Area |
| | | 70,665 sq. miles - 17th in the nation |

1980 Presidential Vote: Carter (26%), Reagan (64%), Anderson (8%)

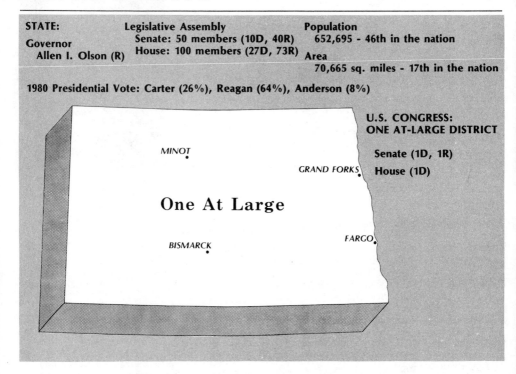

MINOT

GRAND FORKS

One At Large

BISMARCK

FARGO

**U.S. CONGRESS:
ONE AT-LARGE DISTRICT**

Senate (1D, 1R)

House (1D)

## ...Beyond Wheat and Cattle

A conservative state with a radical legacy, North Dakota is settling into a new status as a major supplier not only of the nation's food but of its energy.

For decades, North Dakota's economy revolved around wheat and cattle — and little else. About two-thirds of the state grows wheat, with cattle ranches predominant in the drier western third. But the discovery of oil in the northwest part of the state and the mining of coal in many of the western counties are changing the state's economy. Worries about the environmental and social impact have slowed the exploitation of the coal deposits, but energy resources account for an increasing share of the state's income.

A third important component of the state's economy is military. The Strategic Air Command has two major bases in the state, at Grand Forks and Minot, and there are important nuclear missile installations. If North Dakota were a separate nation, it would probably be the world's third largest nuclear power.

Much of the state's earlier agrarian radicalism remains and has become institutionalized. There is a state-owned bank, a state-owned grain mill and elevator, and state-sponsored crop insurance. All these measures, plus a workman's compensation system, were instituted in the 1910s or 1930s, during the reign of the Non-partisan League, founded to help small farmers use their collective power against railroads, grain elevators and banks.

The Non-Partisan League usually acted through the Republican Party in its early days, but it merged in 1956 with the Democrats, previously moribund in state politics. That year Quentin Burdick, son of the state's Non-Partisan League congressman, Usher Burdick, ran for the Senate as the candidate of the new alliance. The younger Burdick did not win that race, but he did win a Senate seat in 1960, and he still holds it.

Democrats also took control of the governorship in 1960 and held it for twenty years, until the second of the two Democratic governors, Arthur Link, was beaten by Republican Allen Olson. But the GOP continued to carry the state in presidential contests; since 1936, Lyndon B. Johnson is the only Democrat to have won the state.

Democratic strength comes largely from rural areas, an inheritance from the NPL. The small cities, largely marketing rather than manufacturing centers, tend to back the Republicans. In 1976, Jimmy Carter carried 22 of the state's 53 counties, all predominantly rural. Seven of the eight counties with cities of over 10,000 population supported Ford.

As in most agricultural states, the farming communities lost population in the 1970s. In all, 36 of the 53 counties suffered a net decrease in population. The growth centers were confined mostly to urban counties.

But after undergoing population declines in the censuses of 1940, 1950 and 1970, the state as a whole grew 5.6 percent during the 1970s. Its current population of 652,695, however, is still below the 1930 peak of 680,645.

## A Political Tour

**Wheat Country.** North Dakota is the second largest wheat-producing state after Kansas. The Red River of the North separates the state from Minnesota and is the center of a flat, rich, moist growing region which produces not only wheat but sugar beets and potatoes. This is the most prosperous agricultural area of the state —

the moisture in the soil allowed it to weather even the great dust storms of the 1930s. The Red River valley is also the site of two of the state's largest cities, Fargo and Grand Forks. The combination of prosperous farmers and largely service-oriented cities makes this area one of the most consistently Republican in the state.

Further west, the farms and small towns are more likely to support Democratic candidates as inheritors of the old Non-Partisan League tradition and as champions of the declining family farm. People are constantly moving out of these counties to the cities or out of state as farms become larger and larger and more mechanized.

**Cattle, Coal, and Oil.** Western North Dakota, too dry for a good wheat crop, has developed a livestock economy, newly supplemented by energy development. The dry buttes and rolling grassland attracted large cattle ranches, and this section of North Dakota is much like Wyoming, western South Dakota and Nebraska in its appearance and commercial life.

The discovery of oil in the Williston area in the 1950s and the development of long-known coal deposits throughout the West in the 1970s gave an economic boost to the area. State and local officials have tried to limit the adverse social and environmental impact of large-scale development with some success. Generally, Democrats have been the leaders of a careful, go-slow effort, while Republicans have favored more rapid development.

The West has generally supported Republicans except in time of farm depression. But popular state Democrats such as Sen. Quentin Burdick and former Gov. William Guy, (1961-75), have usually carried the region.

---

## Governor
## Allen I. Olson (R)

**Born:** Nov. 5, 1938, Rolla, N.D.
**Home:** Bismarck, N.D.
**Education:** U. of North Dakota, B.S., B.A. 1960; LL.B. 1963.
**Military Career:** Army Judge Advocate General's Corps, 1963-67.
**Profession:** Lawyer.
**Family:** Wife, Barbara; three children.
**Religion:** Presbyterian.
**Political Career:** North Dakota attorney general, 1973-81; elected governor 1980; term expires Jan. 1985.

# Quentin N. Burdick (D)

### Of Fargo — Elected 1960

**Born:** June 19, 1908, Munich, N.D.
**Education:** U. of Minn., B.A. 1931, LL.B. 1932.
**Profession:** Lawyer.
**Family:** Wife, Jocelyn Birch Peterson; six children.
**Religion:** United Church of Christ.
**Political Career:** U.S. House, 1959-60; unsuccessful candidate for N.D. State Senate, 1938; Republican nominee for lieutentnat governor, 1942; Democratic nominee for governor, 1946, and U.S. Senate, 1956.

**In Washington:** Although he is now one of its most senior members, Burdick has left only a modest imprint on the Senate during his 20 years of service.

A self-effacing, good-natured man who has concentrated largely on constituent service and protecting the interests of his home state, Burdick has never sought to play a leadership role on major national issues.

"I just want to be a good North Dakota senator. I try to represent the people of my state and hope their interests coincide with the national interest," he said in one interview.

Burdick views as his major accomplishment in Congress the 1965 authorization of the Garrison Diversion project in North Dakota, a giant public works program that later got caught up in President Carter's battles with Congress over water projects. It remains the target of environmentalist attack.

Despite his tenure, which makes him the ninth most senior Democrat in the Senate, Burdick has never chaired a standing committee — largely because he has shifted repeatedly from one panel to another, serving at various times on the Interior, Labor, Judiciary, Post Office, Public Works, Appropriations, and Environment committees.

He was in line to become chairman of the Post Office and Civil Service panel in 1977, but the Senate that year decided to fold it into the Governmental Affairs Committee as part of the first major overhaul of the Senate's committee structure in 30 years. Piqued by this development, Burdick cast the sole dissenting vote in the Senate on the reform plan.

In 1979, Burdick was dragooned into serving on the Senate Ethics Committee during its investigation into the financial affairs of Sen. Herman Talmadge of Georgia. He joined in the majority decision to denounce his fellow Democrat, then quickly got off the committee once the job was done.

Burdick has always been noted for his own rectitude and sense of ethics. In recent years, he was one of just two senators who voluntarily made public an audit of his own finances, and he once returned a $14,351 campaign contribution from a group because he disagreed with some of its policies — a task that involved writing out checks to 234 people in 32 different states.

The North Dakota Democrat has been a fairly consistent liberal throughout his congressional career. He was a staunch supporter of the Kennedy and Johnson administrations, an early critic of the Vietnam War and a strong backer of all major civil rights legislation. He was, however, one of the first Northern Democrats to criticize busing for racial balance and to support anti-busing legislation.

**At Home:** The name Burdick has been appearing on North Dakota ballots for most of the 20th century.

Quentin's father, Usher Burdick, served as a state legislator, lieutenant governor and U.S. House member. The younger Burdick ran for a string of offices unsuccessfully — lieutenant governor and governor. In 1956, he lost a challenge to Republican Sen. Milton R. Young.

Like his father, Burdick started out as a Republican. In his early races, he also ran under the banner of the old populist Non-Partisan League. But in 1946, when he tried for governor, he shifted to the Democratic label.

Burdick finally won office in 1958 — a House seat. Upon the death of the state's senior GOP senator, William Langer, he upset Republican Gov. John E. Davis in a 1960 special election for the unexpired Senate term.

This contest turned on farm issues. Burdick owed his narrow 1960 victory to his attacks on the unpopular farm policies of the Eisenhower administration and its agriculture secretary, Ezra Taft Benson. The Burdick campaign slogan that year was "Beat Benson with Burdick."

In 1964, running for a full term, it was Burdick's turn to be on the defensive. Republican businessman Thomas Kleppe, later a House member and U.S. interior secretary, criticized falling farm prices under the Kennedy administration.

But Burdick offset that by linking Kleppe to GOP presidential nominee Barry Goldwater, who advocated scrapping some farm subsidies altogether.

In a 1970 rematch, Burdick criticized the Nixon administration for refusing to back increased price supports, and benefited from resentment over Kleppe's attempts to link him with "radical liberal" Democrats. He won easily that year, and even more easily in 1976, when Republicans essentially gave up and nominated a little-known state legislator, Robert Stroup.

## Committees

**Appropriations** (10th of 14 Democrats)
 Agriculture and Related Agencies; Energy and Water Development; Interior; Labor, Health and Human Services, Education.

**Environment and Public Works** (3rd of 7 Democrats)
 Regional and Community Development; Toxic Substances and Environmental Oversight; Transportation.

**Special Aging** (6th of 7 Democrats)

## Elections

**1976 General**

| | |
|---|---|
| Quentin Burdick (D) | 175,772 (62 %) |
| Richard Stroup (R) | 103,466 (37 %) |

**Previous Winning Percentages**

1970 (61%)  1964 (58%)  1960† (50%)  1958* (50 %)

*House election    †Special Senate election*

## Campaign Finance

| 1976 | Receipts | Receipts from PACs | Expenditures |
|---|---|---|---|
| Burdick (D) | $122,605 | $59,100 (48 %) | $117,514 |
| Stroup (R) | $142,774 | $9,900 (7 %) | $136,748 |

## Voting Studies

| | Presidential Support | | Party Unity | | Conservative Coalition | |
|---|---|---|---|---|---|---|
| Year | S | O | S | O | S | O |
| 1980 | 63 | 33 | 83 | 10 | 25 | 69 |
| 1979 | 62 | 37 | 73 | 22 | 36 | 55 |
| 1978 | 54 | 39 | 61 | 31 | 41 | 50 |
| 1977 | 74 | 25 | 59 | 39 | 64 | 35 |
| 1976 | 38 | 60 | 73 | 23 | 37 | 56 |
| 1975 | 40 | 55 | 80 | 14 | 28 | 69 |
| 1974 (Ford) | 34 | 66 | | | | |
| 1974 | 37 | 63 | 83 | 15 | 16 | 83 |
| 1973 | 34 | 63 | 89 | 10† | 16 | 81† |
| 1972 | 35 | 65 | 88 | 7 | 16 | 79 |
| 1971 | 35 | 54 | 87 | 7 | 24 | 72 |
| 1970 | 45 | 41 | 71 | 15 | 22 | 62 |
| 1969 | 50 | 36 | 78 | 17 | 29 | 58 |
| 1968 | 64 | 29 | 70 | 19 | 33 | 56 |
| 1967 | 68 | 25 | 83 | 12 | 20 | 73 |
| 1966 | 58 | 30 | 67 | 14 | 11 | 70 |
| 1965 | 72 | 19 | 79 | 14 | 11 | 75 |
| 1964 | 66 | 19 | 75 | 11 | 14 | 76 |
| 1963 | 76 | 13 | 82 | 6 | 19 | 74 |
| 1962 | 69 | 18 | 82 | 2 | 6 | 71 |
| 1961 | 69 | 10 | 82 | 2 | 8 | 75 |

S = Support    O = Opposition
†Not eligible for all recorded votes.

## Key Votes

**96th Congress**

| | |
|---|---|
| Maintain relations with Taiwan (1979) | N |
| Reduce synthetic fuel development funds (1979) | N |
| Impose nuclear plant moratorium (1979) | N |
| Kill stronger windfall profits tax (1979) | N |
| Guarantee Chrysler Corp. loans (1979) | N |
| Approve military draft registration (1980) | Y |
| End Revenue Sharing to the states (1980) | Y |
| Block Justice Dept. busing suits (1980) | ? |

**97th Congress**

| | |
|---|---|
| Restore urban program funding cuts (1981) | Y |

## Interest Group Ratings

| Year | ADA | ACA | AFL-CIO | CCUS-1 | CCUS-2 |
|---|---|---|---|---|---|
| 1980 | 78 | 19 | 84 | 36 | |
| 1979 | 63 | 30 | 89 | 9 | 27 |
| 1978 | 55 | 23 | 74 | 18 | |
| 1977 | 50 | 26 | 85 | 29 | |
| 1976 | 65 | 19 | 84 | 0 | |
| 1975 | 67 | 8 | 68 | 19 | |
| 1974 | 81 | 11 | 91 | 20 | |
| 1973 | 80 | 11 | 82 | 22 | |
| 1972 | 75 | 14 | 90 | 11 | |
| 1971 | 85 | 25 | 75 | - | |
| 1970 | 84 | 22 | 100 | 0 | |
| 1969 | 83 | 20 | 90 | - | |
| 1968 | 64 | 32 | 75 | - | |
| 1967 | 62 | 27 | 75 | 10 | |
| 1966 | 90 | 23 | 92 | - | |
| 1965 | 88 | 21 | - | 10 | |
| 1964 | 88 | 13 | 90 | - | |
| 1963 | - | 4 | - | - | |
| 1962 | 91 | 0 | 100 | - | |
| 1961 | 100 | - | - | - | |

# Mark Andrews (R)

## Of Mapleton — Elected 1980

**Born:** May 19, 1926, Cass County, N.D.
**Education:** North Dakota State Univ., B.S. 1949.
**Military Career:** Army, 1944-46.
**Profession:** Farmer.
**Family:** Wife, Mary Willming; three children.
**Religion:** Episcopalian.
**Political Career:** Republican national committeeman, 1958-62; unsuccessful Republican nominee for governor, 1962; U.S. House, 1963-81.

**The Member:** "Maybe I shouldn't talk about wheat, beets and cattle in Congress," farmer Mark Andrews joked early in his House career. "I have a vested interest — but so does everybody else in my district."

In reality, Andrews has had few conflicts about representing in Congress those commodities he raises in North Dakota. He spends much of his time in committee trying to squeeze a few extra dollars for them.

Andrews arrived in the House in 1963. Rather than heading for the Agriculture Committee, as most farm-state newcomers do, Andrews set out for Appropriations, which actually spends the money, and made it a year later. "It's a whale of a lot more important than passing a bill," he once told a reporter.

Major crop support programs — loans and "target price" payments to farmers — still must be appropriated after they are authorized by the Agriculture Committee. Andrews settled into the Agriculture Appropriations Subcommittee in 1965, and eight years later was its senior minority member, giving him quiet but consistent leverage on a panel where crop interests count more than party.

In 1981, Andrews moved easily into the Senate, where he sits on both Agriculture and Appropriations, even more convenient for his interests. He has continued to press the case of commodity supports, a stance that on several occasions has put him at odds with the Reagan administration. Reagan asked Congress for broad discretion to set price support loan rates as supply and demand dictated. Minimum support levels are traditionally fixed in law, and Andrews and many others on the Agriculture Committee felt that granting such broad discretion would leave farmers too vulnerable to the budget-cutting enthusiasm of the OMB and Budget Director David Stockman. "I have confidence in the secretary [of agriculture]. "It's just the rest of those turkeys

..." Andrews joked.

Andrews was an active opponent of Reagan's effort to cancel a scheduled April 1 increase in federal milk price supports. When the Agriculture Committee voted 14-2 to skip the increase, he was the lone dissenting Republican. He later supported Reagan, however, in voting for the cancellation on the Senate floor.

He also backed a measure to restrict imports of casein, an inexpensive milk protein used in manufacturing synthetic cheese, non-dairy "creamer" and and other foods. Andrews said the import restriction would force food manufacturers to use American milk products and lessen the amount of surplus milk bought by the government.

In the House, Andrews used his Appropriations Committee seat to help with funding for water projects in dry North Dakota, especially the controversial Garrison water development project. When President Carter sought to cut back funds for Garrison in 1977, Andrews complained that it was "under attack by radical environmentalists who don't have their facts straight." Later, he warned that "Carter and company better not show up in this area."

Despite the militance of his public works rhetoric, however, Andrews is a temperate Republican on most issues, one more comfortable with the small-town prairie conservatism of a generation ago than with New Right activism.

Andrews was North Dakota's senator-in-waiting for years. As the state's only member of the House since 1972, he was the obvious candidate in 1980 to succeed Republican Sen. Milton R. Young, who retired after 36 years.

But relations between Young and Andrews were poor, with Young resentful of what he saw as Andrews' ambition to replace him. The two had tense relations in the past and at times were not on speaking terms. There was some speculation that Young ran for re-election in 1974 primarily to keep Andrews from taking the seat then.

Andrews became active politically in the late 1950s when he became North Dakota's Republican national committeeman (1958-62). In 1962, Republicans selected him as their candidate to oust Democratic Gov. William Guy. Andrews almost made it, losing by 2,007 votes. The next year he won his House seat.

## Committees

**Agriculture, Nutrition and Forestry** (9th of 9 Republicans)
Rural Development, Oversight, and Investigations, chairman; Agricultural Credit and Rural Electrification; Agricultural Production, Marketing and Stabilization of Prices; Agricultural Research and General Legislation.

**Appropriations** (9th of 15 Republicans)
Transportation, chairman; Agriculture and Related Agencies; Defense; Interior; Labor, Health and Human Services, Education.

**Budget** (7th of 12 Republicans)

**Select Indian Affairs** (3rd of 4 Republicans)

## Elections

**1980 General**

| | |
|---|---|
| Mark Andrews (R) | 210,347 (70%) |
| Kent Johanneson (D) | 86,658 (29%) |

**Previous Winning Percentages**

1978* (67%)  1976* (62%)  1974* (56%)  1972* (73%)
1970* (66%)  1968* (67%)  1966* (66%)  1964* (52%)
1963** (49%)
*House election.
**Special House election.

## Campaign Finance

| | Receipts | Receipts from PACs | Expenditures |
|---|---|---|---|
| 1980 | | | |
| Andrews (R) | $405,975 | $236,266 (58%) | $402,129 |
| Johanneson (D) | $139,249 | $6,450 (5%) | $139,203 |

## Voting Studies

| Year | Presidential Support S | O | Party Unity S | O | Conservative Coalition S | O |
|---|---|---|---|---|---|---|
| House service | | | | | | |
| 1980 | 42 | 50 | 72 | 22 | 84 | 8 |
| 1979 | 33 | 59 | 72 | 16 | 83 | 8 |
| 1978 | 35 | 60 | 69 | 27 | 79 | 18 |
| 1977 | 42 | 48 | 69 | 24 | 81 | 12 |
| 1976 | 49 | 43 | 68 | 27 | 78 | 17 |
| 1975 | 48 | 47 | 60 | 34 | 75 | 20 |
| 1974 (Ford) | 44 | 44 | | | | |
| 1974 | 53 | 38 | 48 | 47 | 61 | 31 |
| 1973 | 46 | 46 | 50 | 45 | 65 | 29 |
| 1972 | 59 | 24 | 61 | 29 | 76 | 15 |
| 1971 | 74 | 23 | 60 | 37 | 70 | 27 |
| 1970 | 60 | 22 | 47 | 31 | 45 | 23 |
| 1969 | 60 | 21 | 45 | 36 | 56 | 24 |
| 1968 | 58 | 31 | 63 | 29 | 63 | 24 |
| 1967 | 53 | 36 | 61 | 27 | 78 | 15 |
| 1966 | 46 | 46 | 73 | 21 | 92 | 3 |
| 1965 | 43 | 48 | 75 | 18 | 84 | 12 |
| 1964 | 50 | 48 | 74 | 19 | 83 | 8 |
| 1963 | 14 | 76† | 89 | 0† | 80 | 0† |

S = Support    O = Opposition
†Not eligible for all recorded votes.

## Key Votes

**97th Congress**

| | |
|---|---|
| Restore urban program funding cuts (1981) | Y |

## Interest Group Ratings

| Year | ADA | ACA | AFL-CIO | CCUS-1 | CCUS-2 |
|---|---|---|---|---|---|
| House service | | | | | |
| 1980 | 17 | 67 | 18 | 64 | |
| 1979 | 0 | 88 | 20 | 100 | |
| 1978 | 5 | 73 | 5 | 65 | |
| 1977 | 20 | 67 | 24 | 76 | |
| 1976 | 10 | 62 | 36 | 76 | |
| 1975 | 32 | 76 | 45 | 44 | |
| 1974 | 26 | 47 | 55 | 33 | |
| 1973 | 28 | 41 | 45 | 45 | |
| 1972 | 6 | 57 | 36 | 80 | |
| 1971 | 27 | 66 | 33 | - | |
| 1970 | 24 | 36 | 0 | 63 | |
| 1969 | 27 | 29 | 80 | - | |
| 1968 | 17 | 59 | 50 | - | |
| 1967 | 13 | 52 | 25 | 80 | |
| 1966 | 0 | 68 | 0 | - | |
| 1965 | 5 | 69 | - | 90 | |
| 1964 | 20 | 72 | 14 | - | |
| 1963 | | 100 | - | - | |

# AL Byron L. Dorgan (D)

**Of Bismarck — Elected 1980**

**Born:** May 14, 1942, Regent, N.D.
**Education:** U. of N. D., B.S. 1965; U. of Denver, M.B.A. 1966.
**Profession:** Public official.
**Family:** Divorced; two children.
**Religion:** Lutheran.
**Political Career:** N.D. tax commissioner, 1969-80; Democratic nominee for U.S. House, 1974.

**The Member:** While liberals were losing throughout the nation in 1980, Dorgan was wresting an open House seat from GOP control, the only candidate in the nation to do so.

A militant critic of the Vietnam War early in his career, Dorgan headed Edward M. Kennedy's presidential campaign in North Dakota in 1980. But even though the state went overwhelmingly for Ronald Reagan for president, none of Dorgan's connections seemed to hurt him. Thanks to the personal popularity he had earned as a statewide official, he decisively beat Republican Jim Smykowski, a devotee of the "New Right."

Dorgan believes that high interest rates, not high taxes, are the biggest problem facing farmers and small-business men. Congress' attention to cutting taxes instead of cutting interest rates is "like mowing your lawn when the house is burning," Dorgan says.

He is critical of the Federal Reserve Board's management of the money supply and wants to let the public judge the "tight money" philosophy of Board Chairman Paul Volcker. Dorgan introduced a bill he called "The Paul Volcker Retirement Act," which would let Congress remove the Fed chairman with a 60 percent vote of both Houses. "A little job insecurity does wonders where entrenched power is concerned," Dorgan said.

Many of Dorgan's views have roots in the prairie populism of the state's old Non-Partisan League (NPL). Suspicion of large economic interests was one standard NPL theme, and Dorgan gained public acclaim as state tax commissioner by forcing higher tax payments from out-of-state corporations with operations in North Dakota. Still, Dorgan sought in the 1980 campaign to temper his liberal reputation by supporting an anti-abortion constitutional amendment and decrying government waste, including much of the federal aid to state and local government. He opposes national health insurance because of its cost, but favors expanded federal medical care for the poor and elderly.

## Committees

**Agriculture** (24th of 24 Democrats)
Conservation, Credit, and Rural Development; Forests, Family Farms, and Energy; Wheat, Soybeans and Feed Grains.

**Small Business** (20th of 23 Democrats)
Tax, Access to Equity Capital and Business Opportunities.

**Veterans' Affairs** (17th of 17 Democrats)
Hospitals and Health Care.

## Elections

**1980 General**

| | |
|---|---|
| Byron Dorgan (D ) | 166,437 (57 %) |
| Jim Smykowski (R ) | 124,707 (43 %) |

**District Vote For President**

| | 1980 | | 1976 | | 1972 |
|---|---|---|---|---|---|
| **D** | 79,189 (26 %) | **D** | 136,078 (46 %) | **D** | 100,384 (36 %) |
| **R** | 193,695 (64 %) | **R** | 153,470 (52 %) | **R** | 174,109 (62 %) |
| **I** | 23,640 (8 %) | | | | |

## Campaign Finance

| | Receipts | Receipts from PACs | Expenditures |
|---|---|---|---|
| **1980** | | | |
| Dorgan (D ) | $199,971 | $70,078 (35 %) | $195,068 |
| Smykowski (R ) | $234,633 | $22,869 (10 %) | $226,947 |

## Key Vote

**97th Congress**

| | |
|---|---|
| Reagan budget proposal (1981) | N |

> **At-Large District: Entire state.** Population: 652,695 (6% increase since 1970). Race: White 625,536 (96%), Black 2,568 (0.3%), Indian 20,157 (3%), Others 4,434 (1%). Spanish origin: 3,903 (1%).

# *Ohio*

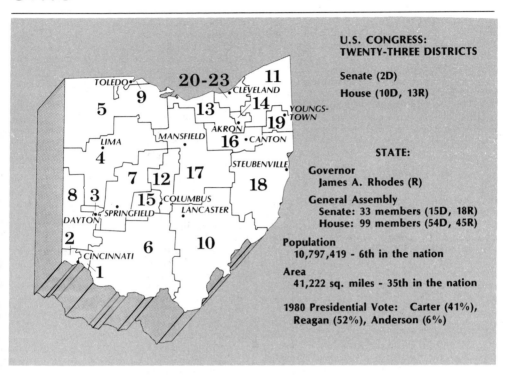

## *... An Urban Constellation*

No other major state developed the kind of urban/rural mixture that Ohio did: eight large cities scattered like stars across a field of prosperous farm land. That pattern of settlement has defined the state's politics for most of this century.

Unlike Michigan, Illinois, Missouri and Pennsylvania, each dominated by one or two huge metropolitan centers, Ohio has a dispersed urban population. Cleveland, Columbus and Cincinnati are the "Big Three," but Toledo, Akron, Dayton, Youngstown and Canton are all large enough to have their own identity. Each is a major media market with its own collection of suburbs. And each functions as an independent planet in the state's solar system.

With eight industrial cities of at least 100,000 people for most of this century — more than any other state over the same period — Ohio would seem to be traditional Democratic territory. But

the dispersion of the urban vote prevented that from happening. Several of the cities have been dominated for years by a solid Republican establishment in control of the media outlets, as well as most of the major business and industrial activity. In addition, many of these cities drew their industrial workers from nearby Republican farms rather than Eastern Europe or the deep South. Even in recent years, most of Ohio's largest cities have had Republican mayors.

None of this has prevented Cleveland, Dayton, Youngstown, Akron and Toledo from voting solidly Democratic in national elections. But there has rarely been a united Democratic front in statewide contests. Local party organizations often are so interested in promoting their own candidates for statewide office that they run figures with a strong parochial appeal who have difficulty winning outside of the local area. Even Cleveland, the largest city, accounts for only 5

**925**

percent of the state's population and rarely provides enough votes to overcome the Republican vote elsewhere.

The result of this mixture of Democratic and Republican urban areas combined with largely Republican rural counties has been a long series of close state elections and a nearly even division of winners between the two parties.

In the 32 elections for president, senator and governor held since 1948, Democrats and Republicans have won 16 apiece. And since 1970, the winner in five of those contests has received 49 percent of the vote, with the loser no more than 3 points behind.

# A Political Tour

**Cleveland, Lake Erie and the Industrial Northeast.** This is the Democratic heart of the state. From Toledo, just south of Detroit, to Youngstown, 170 miles east on the Ohio Turnpike, the area takes in the bulk of Ohio's old industrial power. Steel, rubber, glass and automobiles are the major industries of the area. All require a large blue-collar employment force, all are tied to fluctuations in the national economy, and all are now in serious trouble.

Cleveland is the most important of the region's industrial cities. Its crumbling financial base, its polluted Cuyahoga River and its riots of the 1960s combined to give Cleveland as bad a reputation as any city in the country. But even after losing nearly a quarter of its population in the last decade — mostly whites fleeing to the suburbs — Cleveland remains the basis of the Ohio Democratic vote.

With blacks on the East Side and blue-collar ethnic voters on the West Side, Cleveland is essentially two cities with differing interests and values, bound together in politics only by an allegiance to the Democratic Party. For a Democrat to win statewide, he normally needs a margin of 100,000 votes in Cuyahoga County, most of which has to come from within Cleveland proper.

The suburban areas which ring the city on all sides are politically diverse. Along the lake are the wealthiest Republican areas, towns such as Bay Village and Rocky River. South of the city are middle-class ranch homes in Parma, now the ninth largest city in the state, where the children and grandchildren of the European immigrants have settled. A few black suburban areas are beginning to emerge as black factory workers begin to move out of the East Side ghetto. Sitting on the edge of the ghetto is the heavily Jewish community of Shaker Heights, still one of the wealthiest and most liberal sections of the greater Cleveland area.

The other industrial cities in the northeast are less politically and demographically diverse, but equally important in the outcome of Ohio elections. Toledo's glass makers, Akron's rubber workers and the steel workers who remain in the depressed Youngstown/Warren area, all join with the laborers in Cleveland to form the backbone of the Democratic vote in the state. Nearly a third of Sen. Howard Metzenbaum's winning Democratic vote in 1976 came from the five counties that contain these major industrial centers.

There are exceptions to the Democratic domination of the area. In Medina and Geauga counties, Republican farmers are being displaced by Republican commuters seeking more space in suburbia. In Canton, the political tone was set long ago by the paternalistic and anti-union Timken Company, maker of roller-bearings, and by a Republican-oriented media. It still holds today.

**The Ohio River Valley and Appalachia.** This part of Ohio topographically and economically belongs in West Virginia or eastern Kentucky. Its hilly terrain makes farming an unprofitable exercise, except in a few areas near the river. But under the hills there is extensive mineral wealth. Iron ore mining was once a major industry but it has been replaced by coal mining.

At the northern end of the region — primarily Harrison, Jefferson, Belmont and Guernsey counties — extensive strip mining has leveled off the steep, forested slopes into terrain whose recent reclamation efforts resemble poorly executed plastic surgery performed on a massive scale. This area also has smoke-belching industry in Steubenville, and in Wheeling, W.Va., just across the river. The area votes heavily for Democrats, as long as they are not too liberal.

Outside the industrial and mining areas, however, the Appalachian hill people have been voting Republican for years. This was the only area in the state that re-elected a Republican congressman throughout the New Deal. The only exception to the Republican trend in this area is Athens County, home of Ohio University, which was one of just two counties in the state to go for George McGovern in 1972. Jimmy Carter in 1976 did relatively well among the state's Appalachian voters, who identified with his Southern heritage, but he lost the area badly to Reagan in 1980.

Farther west, in the counties along the Ohio and up the Scioto River, 19th century Democratic voting habits persist to varying degrees. Brown, Adams and Scioto counties will, from time to time, still support Democrats for statewide office.

Most voters in Pike County are as solidly Democratic today as they were when they sympathized with the Confederacy and against Republican Abraham Lincoln during the Civil War.

**Cincinnati and the Lower Miami River Valley.** Cincinnati is the oldest and most Republican of Ohio's major cities. A center for commerce on the Ohio River, Cincinnati was for much of the 19th century the largest city west of the Alleghenies and north of New Orleans. Its population peaked in 1950 at about a half-million and has steadily declined since, reaching 383,000 in 1980.

A cosmopolitan city and one that still has traces of German influence, Cincinnati never has seen the same degree of large-scale manufacturing that is found in the cities in the northeastern part of the state. As a result, the labor force is less black, less ethnic and more Republican. Hamilton County, which includes Cincinnati, is usually 3 to 5 percentage points more Republican than Franklin County (Columbus), and 15 to 20 points more Republican than Cuyahoga County (Cleveland).

Cincinnati's wealthy Republican establishment — including the Taft family — has exercised a great deal of influence in the city over the years. That influence is now seen more in the suburbs than in the city. Unlike suburban Cleveland, suburban Cincinnati is solidly in Republican hands. In the last 20 years, suburban sprawl has expanded in all directions, and it now practically connects Cincinnati to Dayton, 50 miles to the north.

Hamilton and Middletown in Butler County, just north of Cincinnati, started as industrial towns built on the water power of the Great Miami River. Today they are prime examples of the conservative outer reaches of a Republican city: solidly middle-class and solidly Republican. Butler County has elected some of the most conservative GOP legislators the state has seen in recent years.

**Dayton and the Upper Miami River Valley.** The "typical American voter" lives in this part of Ohio, according to Richard Scammon and Ben Wattenberg. In their book *The Real Majority*, they described the typical voter as a suburban Dayton housewife whose husband works as a machinist and whose brother-in-law is a policeman. She is also a Democrat, but is often willing to vote for Republicans.

That description probably still fits at least a few of the people living in the upper Miami Valley around Dayton. A workingman's city made strong by National Cash Register and Frigidaire, Dayton has long been a Democratic stronghold in the predominantly Republican Farm Belt. In the last decade, however, the city lost a fifth of its population and no longer has the same influence in area politics.

A large black population, settled both in the city and in the suburban townships, usually keeps Montgomery County in the Democratic column. Montgomery was the only county in the western half of the state that supported Carter in 1980.

The areas on either side of Montgomery County are politically more marginal. On the east are Springfield (Clark County) and Xenia (Greene County), both manufacturing centers. Xenia has a sizable black population. Both of these cities generally vote Democratic but not by overwhelming margins. The Republican farm vote often tips both Clark and Greene to the GOP.

To the west of Dayton is an area more heavily devoted to farming. Although most Republicans manage to carry it, an independent tradition among the farmers of German descent has given some Democrats a boost they do not find in other rural sections of Ohio.

**Columbus and the Republican Heartland.** Columbus, placed squarely in the center of the state, proudly boasts that it is the "largest small town in America." Its atmosphere and politics confirm that feeling.

Columbus is the only major city in the state to experience a population increase in the last decade — a result of its diversified economy. With the state government and Ohio State University providing a solid economic base, the city also supports a wide variety of white-collar service industries plus a fair number of manufacturing concerns.

Politically, the city's voters are usually happy to stay with the Republican Party of their parents' choosing; the city's major newspaper strongly encourages them to do so. The university community, the black East Side and the Appalachian white West Side are the only Democratic areas. Occasionally they provide enough votes to swing the city narrowly into the Democratic column in local elections. But in statewide contests, the Democratic parts of the city are outvoted by the rest of the metropolitan area. Overwhelmingly Republican suburbs on all sides ensure that in most close statewide elections, the Columbus area (Franklin County) can be counted upon to provide a 55-45 percent Republican edge.

The rich farming counties immediately to the west of Columbus are as Republican as anything in Ohio. Logan, Union, Madison, Delaware and Fayette counties usually bring in GOP percentages over 60. None of these counties have large cities, but most contain a prosperous county seat, which serves as both a farm market center and a location for the small-scale industries that dot the area. Many of the voters find time both for farming and a semi-skilled, well-paying job.

Although still Republican, the counties to the east of Columbus do not yield the same GOP margins as those to the west. Farming is not quite as good in the rolling hills that merge into the Appalachian chain. And the larger sized cities here, Newark, Lancaster and Zanesville, have a larger blue-collar vote, much of it coming from voters raised in Kentucky and West Virginia. But even so, Democrats rarely carry any of the counties in this area — John Ashbrook, a militantly conservative Republican, has represented it in the House since 1960.

**The Northern Corn Belt.** This flat part of Ohio, with its sleepy towns and miles of corn fields, is the area that links the state with the prairies and plains further west.

Excluding Toledo, this region has no major metropolitan areas. Instead it is dotted with small, well-to-do towns like Lima, Findlay, Marion and Bowling Green. All are just as Republican as the surrounding farm country.

The flat land of northwestern Ohio has some of the best soil in the state for growing corn, and just about every farmer grows some. There is also a fair amount of dairy farming and livestock production, particularly in the northwestern corner, where the land becomes hilly. Dairy farming predominates on the eastern edge of this region, around semi-industrial Mansfield.

Nowhere in the region is the Republican vote seriously threatened. Nearly every county in the northwest and north central parts of the state gave more than 60 percent of its vote to Ronald Reagan in 1980. Paulding County, the only one in the state not to vote for astronaut-hero John Glenn when he won his second Senate term as a Democrat in 1980, is located in this area, as are three of the five counties in the state which went for Republican Barry Goldwater in 1964.

During the last decade, while most of the rural areas in Ohio have continued to grow, the population in the center of the Corn Belt has seen virtually no change at all.

## Redrawing the Lines

With virtually no growth during the 1970s, Ohio lost two of its 23 districts. If the Legislature draws the lines, a compromise solution is expected as Democrats control the House, but Republicans have the Senate and the governor's office.

By midyear, however, no action had been taken as legislators waited to see if voters would approve a plan in November to remove the Legislature from the redistricting process. The alternative on the ballot calls for a non-partisan board to select a plan based on a formula for judging "compactness."

Regardless of who draws the new lines, the Cleveland area is almost certain to lose one of its four districts — all represented by Democrats — because of major population losses. The other district could come from almost anywhere in the state. There is an informal agreement among the legislators that if they draw the map, a Republican seat will be sacrificed to offset the Democratic loss in Cleveland.

## Governor
## James A. Rhodes (R)

**Born:** Sept. 13, 1909, Coalton, Ohio.
**Home:** Columbus, Ohio.
**Education:** Ohio State U.
**Profession:** Developer.
**Family:** Wife, Helen; three children.
**Religion:** Presbyterian.
**Political Career:** Columbus city auditor, 1939-43; mayor of Columbus, 1943-53; unsuccessful campaign for Republican gubernatorial nomination, 1950; Ohio state auditor, 1953-63; unsuccessful campaign for governor, 1954; governor, 1963-71; unsuccessful campaign for Republican Senate nomination, 1970; re-elected governor 1974, 1978; term expires Jan. 1983.

# John Glenn (D)

### Of Columbus — Elected 1974

**Born:** July 18, 1921, Cambridge, Ohio.
**Education:** Muskingum College, B.S. 1943.
**Military Career:** Marine Corps, 1942-65.
**Profession:** Astronaut; businessman.
**Family:** Wife, Anna Margaret Castor; two children.
**Religion:** Presbyterian.
**Political Career:** Sought Democratic nomination for U.S. Senate, 1970.

**In Washington:** Nearly 20 years after *Friendship 7*, it is still impossible for John Glenn to escape being a celebrity, and he has not tried to escape it. Each year, hundreds of visitors to the Capitol seek him out and ask for his autograph and recollections. He patiently answers the questions and signs the books, cards and scraps of paper.

What he does not do is focus his legislative career on the space program that made him world famous. Unlike Harrison Schmitt of New Mexico, the other ex-astronaut in the Senate, Glenn does not serve on the committee overseeing the National Aeronautics and Space Administration. Nor does he devote much time to its problems.

Instead, he has concentrated on energy and foreign affairs. He has served on Foreign Relations since 1977, and he has a seat on Governmental Affairs, where until 1981 he was chairman of the subcommittee that monitored the federal government's performance on energy and nuclear proliferation.

Glenn is one of the few acknowledged experts in Congress on nuclear proliferation. He was a major author and floor manager of the 1978 act that placed controls on the export of nuclear materials. He led the unsuccessful 1980 fight to block the sale of nuclear fuel to India. He has been deeply involved in the battle to regulate the disposal of nuclear wastes, although comprehensive legislation failed to clear the 96th Congress.

But despite his concern over the threat of nuclear warfare, Glenn voted against the ill-fated SALT II treaty in committee, saying he was not satisfied it would be verifiable — even though the Senate Intelligence Committee had insisted it was. His opposition, especially on those grounds, nearly drove the Carter White House to despair. Administration experts sought in vain to convince Glenn that even imperfect verification was better than none at all, which is what would exist without a treaty.

Glenn's stubborn refusal to accept that argument was characteristic. A cautious, methodical legislator, he plans, checks, and double-checks every move with the precision he learned in the Marines. But once he decides he has all the facts needed, and stakes out a position, he is unshakeable.

He is no horse-trader. When he is seeking to muster support for an amendment, he merely explains the facts and hopes they will prove persuasive — not always enough in the Senate.

Glenn has not provided many moments of excitement on the Senate floor in six years. Universally regarded as intelligent and decent, he is a soporific speaker, whose tendency to read speeches in full — even when no one is listening —often drives his colleagues to distraction. When he was selected as one of the keynote speakers for the 1976 Democratic National Convention, the senator spent three months preparing his address, only to deliver it in a monotone that contrasted poorly with the emotional rhetoric of his co-keynoter, congresswoman Barbara Jordan of Texas.

Glenn's Senate voting record is near the Democratic center. He has voted with a majority of Northern Democrats in favor of using busing as a last-resort tool in desegregation cases, and has supported federal funding of abortions. He has tilted to the hawkish side on national security matters. He backed President Carter's energy program, and supported deregulation of natural gas at the time his Ohio Democratic colleague, Howard M. Metzenbaum, was leading a filibuster against it. He voted for the Panama Canal treaties and for the 1978 Middle East arms sales package.

"I don't look at myself as being oriented in any one particular direction," Glenn has said. "I've been criticized from both ends of the spectrum, which I think is good."

Glenn does believe in spending more money on energy research leading to the development of renewable sources of fuel. He has proposed that the United States provide financial and technical aid to non-OPEC developing nations to help them explore and develop new oil and gas resources, with shared benefits.

On the Governmental Affairs Committee, Glenn has supported "sunset" legislation, which would terminate federal programs after a fixed period if they were not specifically renewed. He has fought to include tax subsidies under its provisions.

In recent years, however, most of Glenn's attention has been on foreign policy. In the 96th Congress, as chairman of the Foreign Relations subcommittee on East Asia, he endorsed Carter's normalization of relations with the People's Republic of China as a "crucial step in U.S. foreign policy." But he criticized the president for failing to obtain stronger security guarantees for Taiwan.

Glenn criticized Carter for an overall "lack of decisiveness" in foreign affairs, citing vacillation on the neutron bomb and off-again, on-again support for the shah of Iran. But when the American Embassy staff was taken hostage in Tehran after the revolution, Glenn warned against overreaction. "Let's not start World War III over this," he cautioned. He also warned that any attempt to rescue the hostages was certain to fail.

The Ohio Democrat was even more critical of the early Reagan moves in foreign policy in 1981. With Democrat Joseph Biden of Delaware, he led the fight in the Foreign Relations Committee against the nomination of Reagan's close friend and fellow Californian William P. Clark as deputy secretary of state. Glenn and his allies grilled Clark with questions on facts and details of foreign policy, seeking to demonstrate what they thought was an embarrassing ignorance in the field. But Clark was confirmed easily.

Glenn subsequently challenged Reagan's policy toward El Salvador, including the introduction of U.S. military advisers. He argued that the president should have filed a formal report with Congress on the use of advisers in a country where hostilities could break out at any time.

Glenn's celebrity status has led to speculation about a role for him in national politics almost from the day of his arrival in the Senate. But he has been characteristically cautious in responding to it. After the 1980 election, however, as talk began to turn to new faces for 1984, he started to ponder it more seriously, accepting speaking engagements in every part of the country while professing only that he is "keeping his options open."

**At Home:** Even for a national hero, politics is no easy game. Glenn began thinking about a career in the Senate almost as soon as *Friendship 7* splashed down in the Atlantic. But it took him 12 years to make it.

Not long after his historic flight, Glenn returned to Ohio to challenge 74-year-old Sen. Stephen M. Young in the 1964 Democratic primary. His space career had brought him into close contact with the Kennedys, and he was influenced by them to make his political career as a Democrat. However, he did not get very far in 1964. A bathroom fall injured his inner ear, and he had to drop out.

Following that, Glenn's political energies subsided. Instead of attending party functions, he immersed himself in business interests. He served on the boards of Royal Crown Cola and the Questor Corp., oversaw four Holiday Inn franchises he partly owned, lectured and filmed television documentaries.

In 1970, with Young retiring, Glenn decided to run for the seat, competing for the Democratic nomination against Metzenbaum, then a millionaire businessman and labor lawyer. Initially a strong favorite, Glenn found that his frequent absences from Ohio over the preceding six years had hurt him politically, giving him the image of an outsider among state Democrats. Metzenbaum had the support of the party establishment, a superb campaign organization and a budget of more than $800,000.

Through saturation television advertising, Metzenbaum erased his anonymity. By declaring that space funds should be channeled to domestic programs, he even managed to force Glenn into de-emphasizing his astronaut past. Glenn, whose celebrity status was bringing out large crowds, was overly confident. On primary day, Glenn carried 75 of the state's 88 counties but was badly beaten in the urban areas. He lost the nomination by 13,442 votes.

Metzenbaum was beaten himself in the general election by Republican Robert A. Taft Jr. Three years later, however, he made it to the Senate as an appointee, chosen by Democratic Gov. John J. Gilligan to fill a vacancy. Metzenbaum immediately began campaigning for a full term in his own right, and Glenn decided to challenge him for the nomination.

The Metzenbaum appointment outraged Glenn, and gave him an issue during their rematch in the 1974 primary. Glenn rejected Gilligan's offer to be his running mate as lieutenant governor and denounced the governor as a "boss" who practiced "machine politics." He pointed out that the state AFL-CIO and the United Auto Workers also sided with Metzenbaum.

The underdog Glenn of 1974 proved to be much tougher than the favored Glenn of 1970. He had a reputation of impeccable integrity in a year dominated by Watergate, and made an issue of Metzenbaum's long legal battle with the Internal Revenue Service, although Metzenbaum had never been charged with any wrongdoing. A Metzenbaum countercharge — that Glenn had failed to pay a state levy on his securities for one year — failed to halt Glenn's momentum.

This time, Glenn did much better in Metzenbaum's base of Cuyahoga County (Cleve-land). Coupled with his customary strength in rural areas, this allowed him to achieve a 91,000-vote primary victory.

In the fall, Glenn crushed a weak Republican opponent, Cleveland Mayor Ralph J. Perk, who was disorganized and underfinanced. Perk's situation was so bad that he had to call a press conference to deny rumors he would quit the race. The Republican lost every county in the state to Glenn, including his home of Cuyahoga.

In 1980, Glenn won by even more when the GOP put up a still weaker candidate, state Rep. James E. Betts. Party leaders had searched fruitlessly for a stronger one. Woody Hayes, the hot-tempered ex-Ohio State football coach, was one of those turning them down.

## Committees

**Foreign Relations** (3rd of 8 Democrats)
African Affairs; East Asian and Pacific Affairs; Near Eastern and South Asian Affairs.

**Governmental Affairs** (5th of 8 Democrats)
Energy, Nuclear Proliferation, and Government Processes; Permanent Subcommittee on Investigations.

**Special Aging** (2nd of 7 Democrats)

## Elections

**1980 General**

| | |
|---|---|
| John Glenn (D) | 2,770,786 (69%) |
| James Betts (R) | 1,137,695 (28%) |

**1980 Primary**

| | |
|---|---|
| John Glenn (D) | 934,230 (86%) |
| Frances Waterman (D) | 88,506 (8%) |
| Francis Hunstiger (D) | 64,270 (6%) |

**Previous Winning Percentage**

1974 (65%)

## Campaign Finance

| | Receipts | Receipts from PACs | Expenditures |
|---|---|---|---|
| **1980** | | | |
| Glenn (D) | $1,229,354 | $57,010 (5%) | $1,157,965 |
| Betts (R) | $431,344 | $58,168 (13%) | $423,060 |

## Voting Studies

| | Presidential Support | | Party Unity | | Conservative Coalition | |
|---|---|---|---|---|---|---|
| Year | S | O | S | O | S | O |
| 1980 | 72 | 21 | 77 | 16 | 29 | 58 |
| 1979 | 77 | 16 | 79 | 19 | 34 | 65 |
| 1978 | 87 | 11 | 86 | 12 | 18 | 83 |
| 1977 | 83 | 15 | 63 | 36 | 59 | 41 |
| 1976 | 53 | 38 | 79 | 13 | 28 | 64 |
| 1975 | 58 | 39 | 76 | 15 | 23 | 69 |

S = Support          O = Opposition

## Key Votes

**96th Congress**

| | |
|---|---|
| Maintain relations with Taiwan (1979) | N |
| Reduce synthetic fuel development funds (1979) | N |
| Impose nuclear plant moratorium (1979) | N |
| Kill stronger windfall profits tax (1979) | N |
| Guarantee Chrysler Corp. loans (1979) | Y |
| Approve military draft registration (1980) | Y |
| End Revenue Sharing to the states (1980) | Y |
| Block Justice Dept. busing suits (1980) | N |

**97th Congress**

| | |
|---|---|
| Restore urban program funding cuts (1981) | Y |

## Interest Group Ratings

| Year | ADA | ACA | AFL-CIO | CCUS-1 | CCUS-2 |
|---|---|---|---|---|---|
| 1980 | 67 | 17 | 72 | 38 | |
| 1979 | 53 | 4 | 84 | 0 | 31 |
| 1978 | 65 | 25 | 74 | 28 | |
| 1977 | 60 | 19 | 79 | 28 | |
| 1976 | 55 | 15 | 83 | 0 | |
| 1975 | 50 | 16 | 70 | 33 | |

# Howard M. Metzenbaum (D)

**Of Cleveland — Elected 1976**
Also served Jan.-Dec. 1974.

**Born:** June 4, 1917, Cleveland, Ohio.
**Education:** Ohio State U., B.A. 1939, LL.B. 1941.
**Profession:** Lawyer.
**Family:** Wife, Shirley Turoff; four children.
**Religion:** Jewish.
**Political Career:** Ohio House, 1943-47; Ohio Senate, 1947-51; unsuccessful Democratic nominee for U.S. Senate, 1970; unsuccessfully sought Democratic nomination for U.S. Senate, 1974.

**In Washington:** Metzenbaum has made his Senate career arguing against privileges for people and corporations as rich as he is.

A man who made a million dollars in the parking-lot business, Metzenbaum talks and votes today much like he did in the Ohio Legislature during the 1940s, when he was young and poor. He has spent much of his current term taking on the energy industry, and while he has rarely been successful in an increasingly conservative, business-oriented Senate, h.. willingness to follow issues to the point of conflict has made him a force hard to ignore.

In recent years, Metzenbaum has seemed to modify the brash and unyielding style that initially brought him into conflict with his own party's leaders. But if his style is less abrasive, his populist politics remain exactly what they were in 1977, his first full year in the Senate, when he led a two-week filibuster against the effort to lift price controls on natural gas.

Along with James Abourezk, his Democratic colleague from South Dakota, Metzenbaum brought the art of the filibuster to a new level. Debate on the gas bill had been formally cut off, so Metzenbaum and Abourezk had to use a new technique: filibuster by amendment.

Armed with some 500 amendments, the two men tried to delay the bill indefinitely by seeking roll-call votes on each one, sending the Senate into round-the-clock sessions. They might have succeeded, had Democratic leader Robert C. Byrd not forced through a cut-off of the amendments, with the aid of Vice President Walter F. Mondale.

The incident generated hard feeling all around — particularly towards Metzenbaum, who lacked Abourezk's jovial sense of humor. But even Metzenbaum's critics had to concede that he had quickly mastered Senate tactics. "I never saw a man come in here and become an ace filibusterer so fast," said Russell B. Long, D-La.

Metzenbaum has followed a similar path, with mixed success, in opposing other energy legislation. In 1978, when President Carter's energy bill came back in conference report form, he and Abourezk again used filibuster and the threat of filibuster, helping to kill a proposed crude oil equalization tax but losing out on other issues.

In 1980, without end-of-session time pressure, Metzenbaum's tactics were inadequate against another energy bill — loosening federal strip mining rules — backed by Byrd. Metzenbaum prepared hundreds of amendments, but Byrd cut him off by parliamentary maneuvering and passed the bill. It died later in the House.

Metzenbaum's other dominant concern has been federal antitrust enforcement. Before Democrats lost control of the Senate in 1980, he was chairman of the Judiciary Committee's Antitrust Subcommittee.

Here, too, the oil companies have provided him with his issue and his villain. In the 96th Congress, he concentrated on legislation to prohibit major oil producers from merging with other large corporations in the energy field. Originally, Metzenbaum and Judiciary Chairman Edward M. Kennedy had wanted a bill to block most mergers by conglomerate corporations, energy-related or otherwise. But the opposition to that broad idea proved too great, so the two Democrats settled for limiting oil company expansion. Their bill won narrow approval from the committee, but did not come to the Senate floor.

Metzenbaum was more successful in 1980 with his bill, cleared by the 96th Congress, to make antitrust trials move faster and more cheaply through the courts.

However his opposition could not stop a bill

giving soft-drink bottlers an exemption from anti-trust laws. He tried to complicate the future of the bill by adding an amendment giving consumers an expanded right to sue under antitrust laws, but was blocked by cloture.

When Republicans took over the Senate in 1981, new Judiciary Chairman Strom Thurmond decided to abolish the Antitrust Subcommitee. Metzenbaum called the move a "major mistake," but there was little he could do.

His most strident rhetoric has been reserved in recent months, however, for President Reagan's economic program. As a member of the Budget Committee, he scolded budget director David Stockman for being insensitive to the poor. "I think you've been brilliant," Metzenbaum told Stockman when the Reagan aide came to testify. "I also think you've been cruel."

When the package of budget cuts came to the Senate floor in March, Metzenbaum offered an amendment to restore $300 million for job training programs and tried to offer one to raise an additional $1.3 billion through ending various tax loopholes. Neither scheme drew much support. "This Senate really only cares about the politics of the situation," he said before he cast one of the 10 votes against the package.

Later, when Judiciary met to approve spending cuts mandated by the Reagan budget, Metzenbaum threatened to filibuster if the committee moved to abolish the U.S. Civil Rights Commission. The commission's budget was ultimately cut, but its existence was preserved.

**At Home:** An early and overwhelming success in business, Metzenbaum had to struggle through years of trial and failure in Ohio politics to make it to the Senate.

He worked his way through college selling magazines and Fuller brushes, but struck it rich soon afterward in the parking-lot business, winning franchises for the operation of parking lots at airports. He and Alva P. Bonda sold their Airport Parking Co. to International Telephone and Telegraph in 1966 for a reported $6 million. Metzenbaum also owned a 22-paper chain of suburban weeklies around Cleveland.

For a while, Metzenbaum pursued busines and politics simultaneously. In 1942, the year after he graduated from law school, he bucked the Cuyahoga County (Cleveland) Democratic organization and won a race for the state House. Later, he moved up to the state Senate. His major achievement in the Legislature came in 1949, when he won passage of a bill regulating consumer credit.

Metzenbaum left public office in 1951 to run his parking lots and practice law. His record as a labor lawyer was to help him build a political base in the 1970s.

Over the years, the liberal Metzenbaum served as a board member and financial angel for such groups as Karamu, a black cultural institution in Cleveland, and the National Council on Hunger and Malnutrition. He fought battles to integrate a number of exclusive Cleveland clubs.

Before he sought to go to Washington himself, Metzenbaum worked for other Democrats in Ohio and nationally. He was campaign manager for Stephen M. Young in his 1958 and 1964 Senate bids, backed both John and Robert Kennedy for president and supported George McGovern for the White House in 1972.

In 1970, attempting to fill the retiring Young's seat, he had to run against a national hero, astronaut John Glenn. Glenn was a household name; Metzenbaum was an obscure figure even in much of Cleveland. But the aggressive millionaire managed to place his opponent on the defensive by arguing that money should be diverted from the space program to domestic concerns. Glenn was forced to downplay his astronaut days.

To counter Glenn's celebrity, Metzenbaum aired a barrage of television ads presenting himself as an independent-minded businessman driven to run for office by the declining state of government. In addition, he distributed baseballs with the slogan "I'm a Metz fan."

Metzenbaum, with years of party work behind him, had the endorsement of most party leaders. Some of them were still resentful of Glenn's inattention following his abortive 1964 Senate candidacy. More important, Metzenbaum fielded a superior campaign organization. He won the nomination by 13,000 votes.

That fall, Metzenbaum faced another famous name, Robert A. Taft Jr., son of Ohio's dominant political figure of modern times. Metzenbaum already had beaten the younger Taft once, at least vicariously, when he managed Young's re-election in 1964. But history did not repeat itself. Taft won narrowly, taking a hard line against campus protesters and labeling the Democrat "an ultra-liberal of the McGovern-Kennedy-Bayh line." Metzenbaum called for immediate withdrawal of U.S. troops from Indochina, while Taft followed the Nixon administration on Vietnam.

Three years later, Metzenbaum suddenly found himself occupying the office he could not win in 1970. Republican Sen. William B. Saxbe resigned to become President Nixon's attorney general. Democratic Gov. John J. Gilligan, looking for support from organized labor, named

Metzenbaum to the vacancy, giving him a full year in the Senate before Saxbe's term was scheduled to expire.

Metzenbaum was also a candidate for the succeeding full term. But he found incumbency to be no advantage. Glenn came back for a rematch in 1974 and ousted his rival in the Democratic primary, partly by denouncing Gilligan as a "political boss."

Metzenbaum's wealth backfired on him in ways that he had managed to avoid in 1970. Under pressure by Glenn, he made public his tax returns — thus uncovering the politically damaging fact that he had paid no federal taxes in 1969. Metzenbaum also revealed that he had deposited $110,000 with the Internal Revenue Service to cover a back tax claim, an action which did not imply any wrongdoing but was politically controversial in a Watergate election year.

So Metzenbaum had to run as a challenger again in 1976 to realize his ambitions for a term in the Senate. With the aggressiveness that he had displayed all his adult life, he plunged ahead with still another primary campaign. This time he had an advantage in money, name recogniton and party support, and the wealth and tax issues were behind him. He easily took the nomination from the lesser-known Congressman James V. Stanton, who tried to present himself as a fresh face but had trouble attracting attention outside Cleveland.

In the fall, Metzenbaum launched a new attack on Taft's effectiveness. He claimed he had accomplished more in one year in the Senate than Taft had in six and focused on the energy issue, blaming much of America's economic problem on the oil companies. He campaigned in alliance with Jimmy Carter in 1976, positioning himself to take advantage of Carter's spring and summer popularity in Ohio. Ironically, his winning plurality of 117,000 votes was more than 10 times as great as Carter's margin in Ohio.

## Committees

**Budget** (7th of 10 Democrats)

**Energy and Natural Resources** (5th of 9 Democrats)
Energy Conservation and Supply; Energy Regulation; Public Lands and Reserved Water.

**Judiciary** (4th of 8 Democrats)
Agency Administration; Criminal Law; Juvenile Justice.

**Labor and Human Resources** (7th of 7 Democrats)
Aging, Family and Human Services; Employment and Productivity.

## Elections

**1976 General**

| | |
|---|---|
| Howard Metzenbaum (D ) | 1,941,113 (50 %) |
| Robert Taft Jr. (R ) | 1,823,774 (47 %) |

**1976 Primary**

| | |
|---|---|
| Howard Metzenbaum (D ) | 576,124 (54 %) |
| James Stanton (D ) | 400,552 (37 %) |
| James Nolan (D ) | 62,979 (6 %) |

## Campaign Finance

| | Receipts | Receipts from PACs | Expenditures |
|---|---|---|---|
| 1976 | | | |
| Metzenbaum (D ) | $1,097,337 | $125,448 (11 %) | $1,092,053 |
| Taft (R ) | $1,328,283 | $190,873 (14 %) | $1,304,207 |

## Voting Studies

| | Presidential Support | | Party Unity | | Conservative Coalition | |
|---|---|---|---|---|---|---|
| Year | S | O | S | O | S | O |
| 1980 | 71 | 22 | 84 | 13 | 12 | 85 |
| 1979 | 88 | 11 | 86 | 10 | 13 | 80 |
| 1978 | 83 | 16 | 86 | 12 | 13 | 84 |
| 1977 | 80 | 20 | 88 | 10 | 6 | 93 |
| 1974 (Ford) | 38 | 54 | | | | |
| 1974 | 24 | 60 | 71 | 10† | 7 | 75† |

† Not eligible for all recorded votes.

S = Support O = Opposition

## Key Votes

**96th Congress**

| | |
|---|---|
| Maintain relations with Taiwan (1979) | N |
| Reduce synthetic fuel development funds (1979) | N |
| Impose nuclear plant moratorium (1979) | Y |
| Kill stronger windfall profits tax (1979) | N |
| Guarantee Chrysler Corp. loans (1979) | Y |
| Approve military draft registration (1980) | N |
| End Revenue Sharing to the states (1980) | Y |
| Block Justice Dept. busing suits (1980) | N |

**97th Congress**

| | |
|---|---|
| Restore urban program funding cuts (1981) | Y |

## Interest Group Ratings

| Year | ADA | ACA | AFL-CIO | CCUS-1 | CCUS-2 |
|---|---|---|---|---|---|
| 1980 | 83 | 12 | 94 | 27 | |
| 1979 | 84 | 13 | 95 | 0 | 19 |
| 1978 | 100 | 13 | 84 | 22 | |
| 1977 | 90 | 7 | 85 | 11 | |
| 1974 | 90 | 0 | 100 | 0 | |

# 1 Bill Gradison (R)

**Of Cincinnati — Elected 1974**

**Born:** Dec. 28, 1928, Cincinnati, Ohio.
**Education:** Yale U., B.A. 1949; Harvard Business School, M.B.A. 1951; Harvard U., D.C.S. 1954.
**Profession:** Investment broker.
**Family:** Wife, Heather Jane Stirton; five children by a previous marriage.
**Religion:** Jewish.
**Political Career:** Cincinnati City Council, 1961-74; mayor of Cincinnati, 1971.

**In Washington:** Behind Gradison's quiet manner on the House floor lurks one of the party's more thoughtful legislators, one interested in bringing some intellectual coherence to conservative economic ideas.

On the Ways and Means Committee, it was Gradison who led the free-market opposition to President Carter's hospital cost containment program, arguing not against its technical provisions but against the theory that controls could work. That was an argument which most of Gradison's colleagues accepted.

But they have not always accepted his opposition to other federal business subsidies, especially tax-related ones. He voted against a Republican majority in 1980 when he supported a limit to tax-free municipal mortgage bonds. He went against a majority of both parties in 1979 when he opposed a bill to tighten up meat import quotas. Gradison argued that it was a restraint of free trade.

Four years earlier, in his first congressional term, Gradison argued vehemently against the New York City loan guarantee. "All Americans will pay for these guarantees through higher interest rates," he said, "and more inflation and less credit."

But Gradison's major legislative crusade is for indexing the federal tax system — gradually adjusting tax rates to inflation so that people are not forced into higher brackets every time their income goes up. "The federal government," Gradison says, "should not be the beneficiary of tax hikes that Congress does not levy." He tried to persuade Ways and Means to add an indexing provision to the 1978 tax bill, but lost on a 13-23 vote.

He won a surprising victory in 1978 when he got the House to send a tuition tax credit conference report back to committee, where it died. The conference report provided federal subsidies to help families meet the cost of private higher education. Gradison argued that if it was needed for college students, it ought to go to elementary and secondary school pupils as well. The House agreed with him, thanks to support from parochial school officials, and the Senate chose not to pursue the issue any further.

Despite Gradison's conservative economic record, he has always been viewed as a moderate in House GOP politics, and this may have hurt him in 1979, when he tried to become chairman of the Republican Research Committee. He split the "moderate" vote with Pennsylvania's Lawrence Coughlin, allowing the conservative Trent Lott of Mississippi to win easily, positioning himself to become party whip two years later.

**At Home:** Staying in Congress has been rather easy for Gradison. But getting there was complicated.

A member of Cincinnati's city council for fourteen years and a close friend of the Taft family, Gradison first ran for the House in a 1974 special election. As an investment broker, he had been actively involved in the redevelopment of downtown Cincinnati, and he ran a moderate, urban-oriented campaign, trying to keep his distance from the beleaguered Nixon administration. But Watergate was the central issue, and it resulted in a 4,000 vote victory for Gradison's Democratic col-

---

**1st District: Hamilton County — eastern Cincinnati and suburbs.** Population: 424,166 (8% decrease since 1970). Race: White 320,304 (76%), Black 99,593 (23%), Others 4,269 (1%). Spanish origin: 2,841 (1%).

league from the city council, Thomas A. Luken.

The two men opposed each other again in the general election that fall. By then Nixon was out of office, and Gradison had worked to win back some of the votes he had lost earlier for refusing to support a constitutional ban on abortion. A larger Republican turnout and a switch of independents back to the GOP side resulted in a 2,600 vote victory for Gradison.

Two years later, Luken recognized Gradison's popularity by deciding to run in the neighboring 2nd District, rather than competing with Gradison a third time.

**The District:** By dividing Cincinnati and its Hamilton County suburbs into eastern and western districts, Republicans have divided the Democrats and maximized their own strength.

The 1st includes the eastern half of Cincinnati and all of the eastern suburbs. With a sizable black population in Cincinnati and a few all-black suburbs, it has a larger potential Democratic vote than its neighbor to the west. But it has consistently gone Republican through the years for president, Senate and governor.

## Committees

**Ways and Means** (10th of 12 Republicans)
Health; Public Assistance and Unemployment Compensation; Social Security.

## Elections

**1980 General**

| | |
|---|---|
| Bill Gradison (R) | 124,080 (75 %) |
| Donald Zwick (D) | 38,529 (23 %) |

**1978 General**

| | |
|---|---|
| Bill Gradison (R) | 73,593 (65 %) |
| Timothy Burke (D) | 38,669 (34 %) |

**Previous Winning Percentages**

1976 (65 %)    1974 (51 %)

**District Vote For President**

| | 1980 | | 1976 | | 1972 |
|---|---|---|---|---|---|
| D | 68,356 (38 %) | D | 71,431 (40 %) | D | 63,758 (35 %) |
| R | 99,092 (55 %) | R | 103,314 (58 %) | R | 114,907 (63 %) |
| I | 9,233 (5 %) | | | | |

## Campaign Finance

| | Receipts | Receipts from PACs | Expenditures |
|---|---|---|---|
| **1980** | | | |
| Gradison (R) | $230,805 | $4,000 (2 %) | $98,441 |
| **1978** | | | |
| Gradison (R) | $105,081 | $2,734 (3 %) | $84,745 |
| Burke (D) | $13,075 | $3,566 (27 %) | $12,710 |

## Voting Studies

| | Presidential Support | | Party Unity | | Conservative Coalition | |
|---|---|---|---|---|---|---|
| Year | S | O | S | O | S | O |
| 1980 | 57 | 41 | 71 | 26 | 77 | 20 |
| 1979 | 40 | 59† | 79 | 20† | 76 | 23 |
| 1978 | 48 | 48 | 74 | 24 | 73 | 24 |
| 1977 | 46 | 41 | 77 | 20 | 78 | 18 |
| 1976 | 76 | 22 | 71 | 23 | 67 | 27 |
| 1975 | 79 | 20 | 81 | 17 | 79 | 19 |

S = Support       O = Opposition
† Not eligible for all recorded votes.

## Key Votes

**96th Congress**

| | |
|---|---|
| Weaken Carter oil profits tax (1979) | Y |
| Reject hospital cost control plan (1979) | Y |
| Implement Panama Canal Treaties (1979) | N |
| Establish Department of Education (1979) | N |
| Approve Anti-busing Amendment (1979) | Y |
| Guarantee Chrysler Corp. loans (1979) | C |
| Approve military draft registration (1980) | Y |
| Aid Sandinista regime in Nicaragua (1980) | Y |
| Strengthen fair housing laws (1980) | Y |

**97th Congress**

| | |
|---|---|
| Reagan budget proposal (1981) | Y |

## Interest Group Ratings

| Year | ADA | ACA | AFL-CIO | CCUS |
|---|---|---|---|---|
| 1980 | 22 | 67 | 17 | 76 |
| 1979 | 16 | 76 | 20 | 89 |
| 1978 | 20 | 70 | 15 | 83 |
| 1977 | 15 | 74 | 32 | 76 |
| 1976 | 15 | 72 | 19 | 50 |
| 1975 | 21 | 85 | 13 | 88 |

# 2 Thomas A. Luken (D)

**Of Cincinnati — Elected 1976**
Also served March 1974-Jan. 1975.
**Born:** July 9, 1925, Cincinnati, Ohio.
**Education:** Bowling Green U., 1943-44; Xavier U., A.B. 1947; Chase Law School, LL.B. 1950.
**Military Career:** Marine Corps, 1943-45.
**Profession:** Lawyer.
**Family:** Wife, Shirley Ast; eight children.
**Religion:** Roman Catholic.
**Political Career:** Cincinnati City Council, 1964-67, 1969-71, 1973; mayor of Cincinnati, 1971-72; elected to U.S. House in special election, March 1974; unsuccessful Democratic candidate for re-election, 1974; returned to U.S. House, 1976.

**In Washington:** Luken often finds himself a swing vote on the Commerce Committee, perched between the demands of House leaders and the interests of a Cincinnati business community to which he is attentive. It is a role he seems to relish. Stubborn and temperamental, he takes pleasure in staking out his independence on key issues.

Early in the 96th Congress, he was labeled a swing vote on President Carter's hospital cost control program, and drew heavy lobbying both from the administration and the hospital industry. By the time of decision in the Health Subcommittee, he was a firm vote on the industry side. He made the motion to table the legislation — barely unsuccessful — then tried to keep the full Commerce Committee from reporting it out.

That stance typifies the more conservative record Luken has built in the House since he returned in 1977 after losing his seat in an upset two years before. In 1974 he drew a rating of 78 from the Americans for Democratic Action; in 1977, his first year back, he drew a 40.

Some of that change is reflected in his ties to the economic interests who lobby the committee over regulatory issues. Luken worked closely with trial lawyers in 1978 against no-fault auto insurance legislation. The next year, he effectively promoted legislation to let American Cyanamid, which is a major Cincinnati employer, continue using the word "Formica" as its trademark.

When the Federal Trade Commission insisted that "Formica" should be in the public domain, Luken supported general restrictions on FTC authority, such as a legislative veto over its provisions. When conferees reached an agreement including a legislative veto, Luken said it "clearly sends the signal to the FTC that we do not want it

to run roughshod through the private sector."

But when sentiment against oil companies ran strongest, in the spring of 1979, Luken was on the consumer side against an unpopular part of the private sector. He joined the Commerce Committee's liberal Democrats in voting to restore price controls on crude oil. The idea failed by one vote and never reached the floor.

Two other strong Luken issues are abortion and tax subsidies for parochial schools, both sensitive issues in Cincinnati. Luken is militantly against abortion. He is strongly in favor of tax credits for private school tuition. In 1978 he won passage of his budget amendment calling for credits of $100 for elementary and secondary pupils, and $150 for students in private colleges. But they did not become law.

**At Home:** When Luken won a special election in the other Cincinnati district in early 1974, he said his victory was "a signal to Washington" about middle America's attitude toward the Nixon administration. Playing the role of messenger, Luken attracted help from labor and national liberal groups against Republican Bill Gradison.

Eight months later, however, running against Gradison again, Luken discovered his survival was no longer that important to many who helped him in March. He was one of four Democratic incumbents in the country who lost in 1974.

But he was determined to come back, and promptly moved into the 2nd District, just to the west. There he shed what was left of the liberal

---

**2nd District: Hamilton County — western Cincinnati and suburbs.** Population: 450,691 (3% decrease since 1970). Race: White 380,726 (84%), Black 66,408 (15%), Others 3,250 (1%). Spanish origin: 2,676 (1%).

image he had developed during the special election campaign, and before that, on the city council.

The incumbent in the 2nd District in 1976 was Republican Donald D. Clancy. Two years earlier, an unknown Democrat named Edward Wolterman had nearly defeated him in a campaign that criticized Clancy's travels and prolonged absences from the district. Luken used the same issues. Clancy outspent him, but the Democrat's strength in the urban portion of the district was enough to restore him to office by less than 5,000 votes.

Luken had a difficult time in 1978, when he was again outspent and attacked for his shifting political stance. But the Republicans had a divisive primary, and Luken once again won by a slim margin. In 1980, for the first time in five elections, he won easily, taking 65 percent in Cincinnati and 56 percent in the suburbs.

**The District:** The 2nd District, covering the western half of Cincinnati and surrounding Hamilton County, is one of the most Republican in the state. Gerald R. Ford's 62 percent showing there in 1976 was his best in any Ohio district.

Cincinnati makes up about 35 percent of the district's vote, with the rest coming from the middle-class suburbs to the north and west. There are a few solidly black wards in Cincinnati which give any Democratic candidate about 95 percent of their vote, but the dominant political bloc is the German Catholic group that has defined the personality of Cincinnati for 100 years. Once quartered in the West Side section of the city known as "Over-the-Rhine," the German-Americans have gradually moved to the suburbs.

The district also has a sizable population of Appalachian whites, who have come from the rural hills to work in Cincinnati's industries. They too tend to vote Republican.

## Committees

**Energy and Commerce** (11th of 24 Democrats)
Health and the Environment; Oversight and Investigations; Telecommunications, Consumer Protection, and Finance.

**Select Aging** (16th of 31 Democrats)
Health and Long-Term Care.

**Small Business** (9th of 23 Democrats)
Antitrust and Restraint of Trade Activities Affecting Small Business, Chairman; General Oversight.

## Elections

**1980 General**

| | |
|---|---|
| Thomas Luken (D ) | 103,423 (59 %) |
| Tom Atkins (R ) | 72,693 (41 %) |

**1978 General**

| | |
|---|---|
| Thomas Luken (D ) | 64,522 (52 %) |
| Stanley Aronoff (R ) | 58,716 (48 %) |

**Previous Winning Percentages**

1976 (51 %)  1974* (52%)

* Special election

**District Vote For President**

| 1980 | | 1976 | | 1972 | |
|---|---|---|---|---|---|
| D | 60,882 (34 %) | D | 63,640 (36 %) | D | 55,435 (30 %) |
| R | 108,150 (60 %) | R | 107,931 (62 %) | R | 124,678 (68 %) |
| I | 8,683 (5 %) | | | | |

## Campaign Finance

| | Receipts | Receipts from PACs | Expenditures |
|---|---|---|---|
| **1980** | | | |
| Luken (D ) | $294,520 | $174,872 (59 %) | $290,853 |
| Atkins (R ) | $122,513 | $5,450 (4 %) | $120,476 |
| **1978** | | | |
| Luken (D ) | $231,471 | $110,758 (48 %) | $230,690 |
| Aronoff (R ) | $275,692 | $63,752 (23 %) | $275,400 |

## Voting Studies

| | Presidential Support | | Party Unity | | Conservative Coalition | |
|---|---|---|---|---|---|---|
| Year | S | O | S | O | S | O |
| 1980 | 62 | 30 | 60 | 29 | 55 | 31 |
| 1979 | 59 | 30 | 62 | 31 | 56 | 38 |
| 1978 | 45 | 46 | 48 | 47 | 54 | 41 |
| 1977 | 61 | 30 | 57 | 36 | 49 | 46 |
| 1974 (Ford) | 26 | 46† | | | | |
| 1974 | 41 | 50† | 71 | 10† | 15 | 69† |

†Not eligible for all recorded votes.

S = Support    O = Opposition

## Key Votes

**96th Congress**

| | |
|---|---|
| Weaken Carter oil profits tax (1979) | N |
| Reject hospital cost control plan (1979) | Y |
| Implement Panama Canal Treaties (1979) | ? |
| Establish Department of Education (1979) | N |
| Approve Anti-busing Amendment (1979) | Y |
| Guarantee Chrysler Corp. loans (1979) | Y |
| Approve military draft registration (1980) | Y |
| Aid Sandinista regime in Nicaragua (1980) | Y |
| Strengthen fair housing laws (1980) | N |

**97th Congress**

| | |
|---|---|
| Reagan budget proposal (1981) | Y |

## Interest Group Ratings

| Year | ADA | ACA | AFL-CIO | CCUS |
|---|---|---|---|---|
| 1980 | 39 | 43 | 68 | 61 |
| 1979 | 37 | 32 | 89 | 61 |
| 1978 | 25 | 60 | 65 | 47 |
| 1977 | 40 | 37 | 68 | 41 |
| 1974 | 78 | 0 | 100 | 11† |

†Not eligible for all recorded votes.

# 3 Tony P. Hall (D)

**Of Dayton — Elected 1978**

**Born:** Jan. 16, 1942, Dayton, Ohio.
**Education:** Denison U., Ohio, A.B. 1964.
**Profession:** Real estate broker.
**Family:** Wife, Janet Dick; two children.
**Religion:** Presbyterian.
**Political Career:** Ohio House, 1969-73; Ohio
  Senate, 1973-79; unsuccessful Democratic
  nominee for Ohio Secretary of State, 1974.

**In Washington:** Hall traded on his reputation for diligence and party loyalty to win a place on the Rules Committee at the start of his second House term. A gregarious former football star, he has had to struggle throughout his political career against a widely-held belief that he is stronger on personality than on the issues. But House leaders saw him as a man who would help them out in key situations.

That was not the way they saw him a few months later, after he had voted with a Republican majority in favor of President Reagan's budget. Hall's decision, reached after a recess sampling opinion in his normally Democratic district, was one of the most depressing pieces of news for Speaker O'Neill and his allies. They expected to lose dozens of conservative southerners on the budget vote; they did not expect to lose Hall.

Hall's budget vote was not only a surprise in the chamber — it was a break with most of his political career. Close to labor in his heavily unionized hometown, Hall voted as a bread-and-butter liberal during his first House term. He supported President Carter on most key questions in the 96th Congress, although he criticized the president for weak leadership.

Worried about Carter's lack of popularity, Hall said he would not welcome campaign support from the president in 1980. He paid a price for that modest declaration of independence, however; Hall later complained that White House officials refused to return his telephone calls and snubbed him when announcing federal grants to his district.

A former Peace Corps volunteer, Hall headed for the Foreign Affairs Committee when he got to Washington in his first term. One of his first efforts was to prevent the Peace Corps from being moved out of ACTION, the federal agency headed by Sam Brown, controversial former anti-war activist.

He also moved early to force Carter to stick to a tough human rights policy. In March 1979, just two months after entering the House, Hall fought to reduce military aid to the Philippines, as a protest against the dictatorial regime of Ferdinand Marcos. That effort failed when the administration applied heavy pressure on the Foreign Affairs Committee. Undaunted by that losing battle, he tried it again a year later, and convinced the committee and the full House to slice $5 million from a $50 million military loan to the Philippines. But the effort was eventually rejected by a House-Senate conference committee, after more administration lobbying.

**At Home:** Hall was the clear choice of organized labor and the Montgomery County Democratic Party in 1978, when liberal Republican Rep. Charles W. Whalen decided to retire. Once a Little All-America on the football team at Denison College, Hall was well-known in Dayton as its representative in the Ohio Legislature. He had access to ample campaign funds through his father, who ran a lucrative real estate business and served as the city's major for five years.

Four years before his congressional bid, Hall had gained broader attention as the Democratic nominee for secretary of state against Republican stalwart Ted W. Brown, who had held that post for 24 years. Hall traveled around the state brandishing a rubber chicken and chastising Brown for not reporting campaign contributions from a chicken dinner fund-raising event. He came closer

---

**3rd District: Southwest — Dayton.**
Population: 425,124 (6% decrease since 1970).
Race: White 344,273 (81%), Black 74,623
(18%), Others 4,226 (1%). Spanish origin:
3,025 (1%).

to defeating Brown than anyone had in 16 years, and the campaign placed him in a good position to run for Congress.

But to reach Washington, Hall had to defeat Republican Dudley P. Kircher, a former chamber of commerce official who was considerably more conservative than Whalen. Hall emphasized his legislative experience and attacked Kircher as the "voice of big business." The Democrat made up for Kircher's $130,000 spending advantage with his strong support from organized labor. He took 70 percent of the vote in Dayton, allowing him to win narrowly district-wide.

Two years later, the national GOP showed less interest in the seat, and Hall defeated an underfinanced former state legislator by a slightly more comfortable margin. Again, Hall's victory was due to the 72 percent he received in Dayton.

**The District:** Unlike Cincinnati and Columbus, Dayton has long been a Democratic city with a large blue-collar population and a sizable number of blacks. It would almost certainly have elected a Democrat to the House during the 1970s had Whalen not been willing to vote with Democrats on most issues.

Before Whalen's election in 1966, the 3rd included considerably more suburban and rural territory, and was one of the most marginal districts in the state. From 1938 until 1950, in fact, the seat switched parties every two years.

Dayton remains a Democratic stronghold, and is an economically troubled city. With the closing of the Frigidaire plant and National Cash Register offices, the city lost 20,000 jobs between 1969 and 1979, and the population dropped more than 20 percent.

To the south are the white-collar suburbs of Kettering and Oakwood, and other Republican areas. In 1980, Reagan won 61 percent in this southern end of the district. The tier of townships north of Dayton also are largely suburban, but more blue-collar and Democratic.

## Committees

**Rules** (11th of 11 Democrats)
Rules of the House.

## Elections

**1980 General**

| | |
|---|---|
| Tony Hall (D ) | 95,558 (57 %) |
| Albert Sealy (R ) | 66,698 (40 %) |

**1978 General**

| | |
|---|---|
| Tony Hall (D ) | 62,849 (54 %) |
| Dudley Kircher (R ) | 51,833 (44 %) |

**1978 Primary**

| | |
|---|---|
| Tony Hall (D ) | 19,780 (80 %) |
| Edward Fanning (D ) | 2,946 (12 %) |
| Herbert Creech (D ) | 1,984 (8 %) |

**District Vote For President**

| | 1980 | | 1976 | | 1972 |
|---|---|---|---|---|---|
| **D** | 77,731 (48 %) | **D** | 77,872 (50 %) | **D** | 63,992 (41 %) |
| **R** | 73,192 (45 %) | **R** | 73,902 (48 %) | **R** | 88,865 (57 %) |
| **I** | 10,234 (6 %) | | | | |

## Campaign Finance

| | Receipts | Receipts from PACs | Expen-ditures |
|---|---|---|---|
| **1980** | | | |
| Hall (D ) | $169,303 | $85,850 (51 %) | $154,725 |
| Sealy (R ) | $98,389 | $25,785 (26 %) | $98,305 |

| **1978** | | | |
|---|---|---|---|
| Hall (D ) | $216,675 | $83,218 (38 %) | $216,117 |
| Kircher (R ) | $349,374 | $74,173 (21 %) | $346,193 |

## Voting Studies

| | Presidential Support | | Party Unity | | Conservative Coalition | |
|---|---|---|---|---|---|---|
| Year | S | O | S | O | S | O |
| 1980 | 74 | 21 | 85 | 10 | 19 | 75 |
| 1979 | 81 | 16 | 88 | 7 | 13 | 83 |

S = Support        O = Opposition

## Key Votes

**96th Congress**

| | |
|---|---|
| Weaken Carter oil profits tax (1979) | N |
| Reject hospital cost control plan (1979) | N |
| Implement Panama Canal Treaties (1979) | Y |
| Establish Department of Education (1979) | Y |
| Approve Anti-busing Amendment (1979) | Y |
| Guarantee Chrysler Corp. loans (1979) | Y |
| Approve military draft registration (1980) | N |
| Aid Sandinista regime in Nicaragua (1980) | Y |
| Strengthen fair housing laws (1980) | Y |

**97th Congress**

| | |
|---|---|
| Reagan budget proposal (1981) | Y |

## Interest Group Ratings

| Year | ADA | ACA | AFL-CIO | CCUS |
|---|---|---|---|---|
| 1980 | 89 | 21 | 79 | 68 |
| 1979 | 84 | 4 | 85 | 0 |

# 4 Michael Oxley (R)

**Of Findlay — Elected 1981**

**Born:** Feb. 11, 1944, Findlay, Ohio.
**Education:** Miami Univ. (Ohio), B.A. 1966; Ohio State Univ., J.D. 1969.
**Profession:** Lawyer.
**Family:** Wife, Patricia Pluguez; one child.
**Religion:** Lutheran.
**Political Career:** Ohio House, 1973-81.

**The Member:** Oxley barely defeated Democrat Dale Locker in a 1981 special election for the right to succeed the late Republican Rep. Tennyson Guyer. The 4th is considered solid GOP territory, but Locker came so close that Oxley's swearing-in was delayed for nearly a month.

Oxley, a five-term state legislator, spent about $200,000 and flooded the media with advertisements in the closing days of the campaign. He ran as a staunch supporter of Reagan's economic program, except for its recommended Social Security cutbacks. Still, he was unable to duplicate the personal following that brought Guyer 72 percent of the vote in 1980. Guyer died of a heart attack April 12.

Before his contest with Locker, Oxley survived a GOP primary in which all candidates tried to out-Reagan one another. Republican Robert J. Huffman, a Reagan backer since 1975, branded Oxley a Reagan-come-lately because Oxley had supported George Bush's 1980 drive for the GOP presidential nomination. Oxley won more than half the vote in the six-man primary field.

A former FBI agent, Oxley was ranking Republican on the Judiciary and Criminal Justice Committee in the Ohio House.

**The District:** The 4th, dominated by farms and small towns, is typical of Midwestern Republican districts. What little industry exists is widely scattered and attracts local craftsmen rather than poor migrants seeking a steady wage.

It is among the most consistent Republican districts in the state. In 1976, Democrat Howard Metzenbaum received fewer votes in the 4th District than in any other in Ohio. GOP presidential candidates have no trouble winning the district.

## Committees

No committees assigned as of Aug. 1, 1981.

## Election

**1981 Special Election**

| | |
|---|---|
| Michael Oxley (R) | 41,987 (50%) |
| Dale Locker (D) | 41,646 (50%) |

**1981 Special Primary**

| | |
|---|---|
| Michael Oxley (R) | 20,955 (51%) |
| Robert Huffman (R) | 18,512 (45%) |

**District Vote For President**

| | 1980 | | 1976 | | 1972 |
|---|---|---|---|---|---|
| D | 61,701 (32%) | D | 70,213 (39%) | D | 51,559 (68%) |
| R | 119,930 (62%) | R | 103,750 (58%) | R | 122,043 (58%) |
| I | 9,682 (5%) | | | I | 6,566 (3%) |

## Campaign Finance

| | Receipts | Receipts from PACs | Expenditures |
|---|---|---|---|
| **1981 *** | | | |
| Oxley (R) | $99,753 | $17,800 ( %) | $113,208 |
| Locker (D) | $29,360 | $2,050 ( %) | $25,974 |

* Figures include information reported by the candidates to the Federal Election Commission through June 5, 1981.

**4th District: West — Lima, Findlay.** Population: 489,043 (6% increase since 1970). Race: White 470,163 (96%), Black 15,069 (3%), Others (1%). Spanish origin 4,614 (1%).

# 5 Delbert L. Latta (R)

**Of Bowling Green — Elected 1958**

**Born:** March 5, 1920, Weston, Ohio.
**Education:** Attended Findlay College, 1938-40;
   Ohio Northern U., A.B. 1943, LL.B. 1945.
**Military Career:** Ohio National Guard (feder-
   alized), 1938-41; Marine Corps Reserve,
   1942-43.
**Profession:** Lawyer.
**Family:** Wife, Rose Mary Kiene; two children.
**Religion:** Church of Christ.
**Political Career:** Ohio Senate, 1953-59.

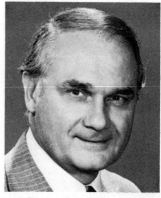

**In Washington:** Something unusual happened to Latta in the 1981 budget debate: he was
on the winning side.

Latta had been denouncing and ridiculing
Democratic budgets for most of his six years as a
senior Republican on the Budget Committee. But
he had never been able to defeat one. This time he
watched with satisfaction as the full House rejected the offerings of Budget Chairman James R.
Jones, D-Okla., on two separate occasions within
two months, and voted for Reagan-backed alternatives sponsored by himself and Phil Gramm,
the conservative Texas Democrat.

Latta is a man used to quarrels, however, and
even the sweet victory of 1981 did not come
without an argument or two. During Budget Committee deliberations, Latta had loyally offered the
original Reagan plan verbatim, and had seen it
beaten on a 17-13 party-line vote. But he was
surprised to see a second Reagan alternative mentioned from across the aisle by Gramm, who said
it was what the White House really wanted.

That alternative, basically the original Reagan figures with about $5 billion extra in spending
cuts, was the one that eventually became the
Gramm-Latta substitute on the House floor. But
Latta was angry that the White House had
reached a deal with Gramm without including
him in the discussions. The two sponsors spent an
awkward period dancing around the question of
who would get top billing before they came up
with a united front for the successful floor action.

When the budget reached the floor, Latta was
GOP manager for the substitute, flaying the opposition and traditional Democratic programs
with all the vehemence he has been noted for
over more than 20 years in the House. "About the
only people who have consistently benefited from
any of the programs instituted over the past
decade," he said, "are those who are paid good
salaries to administer them."

The making of Gramm-Latta II went more
smoothly. Attention centered on holding at least
27 of the 63 conservative Democrats who gave the
GOP a win in May. After a dramatic White House
lobbying blitz, they got 29.

The situation presented some contrasts from
the one a year before. At that time, Latta pursued
compromise with the Democratic enemy even
when most of his own Republican troops deserted
him.

It was no small thing to see Democratic
Budget Chairman Robert N. Giaimo praising
Latta on the House floor in 1980 while condemning other Republicans as mischievous. Only a year
earlier, Giaimo had accused Latta of trying to
destroy the budget process. Now he credited him
with statesmanship.

Determined to vote out a balanced budget for
the 1981 fiscal year, Giaimo had asked Latta, as
the Budget Committee's senior Republican, to
help him in a centrist coalition. Latta and his
GOP colleagues asked for a substantial tax cut as
their price of participation, but found it difficult
to turn down the offer of a balanced budget, since
deficit spending had been the basis of their opposition to previous budgets.

When the committee voted on its first budget
resolution for fiscal 1981, one which was said to
carry a $2 billion surplus, Latta brought all but
one of his Republicans along.

The committee vote turned out to be the
peak moment of budget bipartisanship in the 96th
Congress. By the time the resolution reached the
House floor in May, 1980, it was clear that costs

> **5th District: Northwest — Bowling
> Green.** Population: 513,127 (11% increase
> since 1970). Race: White 498,259 (97%), Black
> 4,466 (1%), Others 10,402 (2%). Spanish ori-
> gin: 16,167 (3%).

had been underestimated, and that the budget was not in balance after all. Latta kept his bargain with Giaimo, but most junior Republicans insisted he was leading them into a political trap. Only 21 other Republicans went along with the bipartisan approach on final clearing.

By midsummer, it was clear that the budget would be at least $30 billion in deficit, and Latta was back on the warpath. "Over the past five years," he said, "the majority party has folded, bent and mutilated the budget process any time it was needed to accommodate their pet spending programs."

That was the Latta that colleagues had grown used to. A member of the Budget Committee since its inception in 1975, he presented the same image in each of the first four years — that of a purist more interested in scolding the majority than in gaining a marginal influence over the ultimate product. He repeatedly made the same speech in committee and on the floor, warning of the growing national debt, the retreat from fiscal responsibility, and the ultimate dire consequences. Labeling all Democratic budgets as dangerous, he had consistently refused to provide Republican votes to make them a little less dangerous.

Instead of playing the traditional role as ranking committee Republican, Latta had evolved over the years into a sort of anti-chairman. He complained that the budget process had made deficit spending worse, rather than controlling it, as it was supposed to do. He said the committee was the "biggest ally" of big spenders, "an adding machine without a subtract button," arriving at a budget figure that was simply the sum of what all the other committees wanted to spend.

Whatever his role in the budget process at any given time, Latta remains as dedicated a fiscal conservative as there is in the House. He favors a constitutional amendment to require a balanced budget. He opposes most spending for welfare, environmental controls and foreign aid. He is opposed to federal aid to mass transit and government sponsored public works and public jobs programs. The only major deviation is his support for farm programs that benefit his largely rural district southwest of Toledo.

It was Latta's demonstrated Republican orthodoxy that gave him his place on the Rules Committee in 1965. Rules and Budget have been his exclusive specialties ever since, except for a brief stint on Judiciary at the height of the Nixon impeachment debate. Placed on Judiciary to serve as a tough, hard-hitting defender of the president,

he did just that until shortly before the end in 1974.

**At Home:** Like most rural Ohio Republicans, Latta has had little to worry about from Democrats and nothing to fear from his own party. He is a visible presence in his district throughout the year, but he rarely has to campaign very hard.

Since he came to the House, Latta's vote has fluctuated only from 62 percent to 73. In the last decade, only two Democrats have been willing to run against him. One has lost three times, the other, twice.

A barber's son who worked in a shoe store to get through college, Latta practiced law in Bowling Green for several years before winning a seat in the state Senate. When Republican Rep. Cliff Clevenger retired in 1958 after 20 years in the House, Latta joined six others in the Republican primary.

Latta's state Senate district included five of the nine counties then in the 5th District, which gave him an edge over candidates with more limited political bases, including Kenneth H. Adams, his own home county GOP chairman. Many Republicans were miffed at Latta for challenging his local leader, but after Latta won the primary with 34 percent and Adams finished third with 21 percent, most of the hard feelings were forgotten and Latta has had no electoral problems since.

**The District:** Located in the northwestern corner of the state, the 5th District is solidly Republican. It is a mixture of good, flat farmland and small towns. Bowling Green (pop. 25,000) is the largest town in the district.

The western counties are the most Republican and more exclusively devoted to agriculture. Packing plants operated by Heinz, Hunt, Libby and Campbell attest to the region's fine tomatoes. But the Mexican-American farm workers who live in migrant camps during harvest season have added a degree of tension to the otherwise tranquil region. A large General Motors plant in Defiance offers the major non-farm employment in the western section.

During the 22 years Latta has represented the district, its lines have changed three times, gradually gaining more territory in the east. Although not as solidly Republican, the eastern counties still provide Republicans with comfortable margins.

The region's proximity to Cleveland, Toledo, Detroit and Chicago has given it a fair number of small-scale supplier plants. As a result, union membership has been growing.

## Committees

**Budget** (Ranking Republican)

**Rules** (2nd of 5 Republicans)

## Elections

**1980 General**

| | |
|---|---|
| Delbert Latta (R ) | 137,003 (70 %) |
| James Sherck (D ) | 57,704 (30 %) |

**1978 General**

| | |
|---|---|
| Delbert Latta (R ) | 85,547 (63 %) |
| James Sherck (D ) | 51,071 (37 %) |

**Previous Winning Percentages**

| | | | |
|---|---|---|---|
| 1976 (67 %) | 1974 (63 %) | 1972 (73 %) | 1970 (71 %) |
| 1968 (71 %) | 1966 (75 %) | 1964 (66 %) | 1962 (70 %) |
| 1960 (67 %) | 1958 (54 %) | | |

**District Vote For President**

| | 1980 | | 1976 | | 1972 |
|---|---|---|---|---|---|
| D | 66,332 (32 %) | D | 83,765 (44 %) | D | 62,258 (34 %) |
| R | 122,583 (59 %) | R | 104,202 (54 %) | R | 118,680 (64 %) |
| I | 14,960 (7 %) | | | | |

## Campaign Finance

| | Receipts | Receipts from PACs | Expenditures |
|---|---|---|---|
| **1980** | | | |
| Latta (R ) | $58,780 | $43,150 (73 %) | $57,923 |
| Sherck (D ) | $17,677 | $9,560 (54 %) | $17,990 |
| **1978** | | | |
| Latta (R ) | $59,968 | $16,336 (27 %) | $45,705 |
| Sherck (D ) | $40,988 | $16,150 (39 %) | $40,249 |

## Voting Studies

| | Presidential Support | | Party Unity | | Conservative Coalition | |
|---|---|---|---|---|---|---|
| Year | S | O | S | O | S | O |
| 1980 | 32 | 58 | 86 | 8 | 86 | 8 |
| 1979 | 26 | 70 | 90 | 6 | 93 | 3 |
| 1978 | 29 | 66 | 88 | 8 | 93 | 5 |
| 1977 | 35 | 57 | 86 | 8 | 89 | 4 |
| 1976 | 84 | 14 | 92 | 7 | 95 | 3 |
| 1975 | 64 | 34 | 82 | 16 | 89 | 8 |

| 1974 (Ford) | 52 | 41 | | | | |
|---|---|---|---|---|---|---|
| 1974 | 57 | 38 | 76 | 18 | 87 | 9 |
| 1973 | 72 | 28 | 85 | 14 | 89 | 9 |
| 1972 | 70 | 30 | 89 | 10 | 94 | 5 |
| 1971 | 74 | 19 | 78 | 17 | 82 | 11 |
| 1970 | 65 | 22 | 65 | 22 | 73 | 9 |
| 1969 | 51 | 34 | 82 | 11 | 84 | 11 |
| 1968 | 52 | 40 | 85 | 9 | 84 | 8 |
| 1967 | 40 | 47 | 76 | 12 | 78 | 7 |
| 1966 | 36 | 60 | 94 | 3 | 97 | 0 |
| 1965 | 32 | 63 | 90 | 5 | 94 | 2 |
| 1964 | 31 | 67 | 89 | 6 | 92 | 0 |
| 1963 | 23 | 70 | 91 | 3 | 93 | 7 |
| 1962 | 35 | 65 | 93 | 4 | 100 | 0 |
| 1961 | 38 | 62 | 83 | 17 | 96 | 4 |

S = Support       O = Opposition

## Key Votes

**96th Congress**

| | |
|---|---|
| Weaken Carter oil profits tax (1979) | Y |
| Reject hospital cost control plan (1979) | Y |
| Implement Panama Canal Treaties (1979) | N |
| Establish Department of Education (1979) | N |
| Approve Anti-busing Amendment (1979) | Y |
| Guarantee Chrysler Corp. loans (1979) | Y |
| Approve military draft registration (1980) | N |
| Aid Sandinista regime in Nicaragua (1980) | N |
| Strengthen fair housing laws (1980) | N |

**97th Congress**

| | |
|---|---|
| Reagan budget proposal (1981) | Y |

## Interest Group Ratings

| Year | ADA | ACA | AFL-CIO | CCUS |
|---|---|---|---|---|
| 1980 | 17 | 88 | 11 | 74 |
| 1979 | 5 | 92 | 15 | 100 |
| 1978 | 5 | 89 | 5 | 65 |
| 1977 | 10 | 88 | 18 | 88 |
| 1976 | 0 | 100 | 13 | 100 |
| 1975 | 5 | 89 | 17 | 88 |
| 1974 | 9 | 86 | 0 | 70 |
| 1973 | 0 | 85 | 9 | 91 |
| 1972 | 0 | 91 | 0 | 100 |
| 1971 | 8 | 79 | 8 | - |
| 1970 | 8 | 71 | 33 | 88 |
| 1969 | 13 | 69 | 50 | - |
| 1968 | 0 | 96 | 25 | - |
| 1967 | 20 | 85 | 8 | 80 |
| 1966 | 0 | 92 | 0 | - |
| 1965 | 0 | 89 | - | 100 |
| 1964 | 4 | 89 | 18 | - |
| 1963 | - | 89 | - | - |
| 1962 | 0 | 87 | 0 | - |
| 1961 | 0 | - | - | - |

# 6 Bob McEwen (R)

**Of Hillsboro — Elected 1980**

**Born:** Jan. 12, 1950, Hillsboro, Ohio.
**Education:** U. of Miami (Fla.), B.B.A. 1972.
**Profession:** Real estate developer.
**Family:** Wife, Elizabeth Boebinger.
**Religion:** Protestant.
**Political Career:** Ohio House, 1975-81.

**The Member:** A one-time aide to Republican Rep. William H. Harsha, his 6th District predecessor, McEwen landed a seat on the Public Works Committee, where Harsha was the ranking minority member for eight years before retiring in 1981.

McEwen has been able to watch over public works projects that began during Harsha's tenure. He made sure the committee provided money for completion of a bridge in Portsmouth, and sought to establish a revolving fund for a gas centrifuge uranium enrichment plant' in Piketon. Under McEwen's plan, a revenue from sale of the enriched uranium would return to the plant and pay for its operation.

As a member of the Ohio House, McEwen spent much of his time working to get the state to dredge a flood-prone creek in his district. He also advocated abolishing the Ohio lottery.

In 1980, McEwen won an eight-candidate Republican primary in which Harsha remained publicly neutral because the field included two other candidates with whom the congressman had past political associations. A Christian Scientist, McEwen had fundamentalist Christian backing. He favors the death penalty, opposes legalization of marijuana and calls for an end to federal regulations that he says hurt industrial development.

**The District:** Until 1960, this rural southwest Ohio region was Democratic — a legacy of the Southerners who originally populated it. Harsha's election that year, though, signaled a change.

Most of the 6th is farm country and most of it now is reliably Republican. At its western edge, the Cincinnati suburbs in rapidly growing Clermont County are usually in the GOP column as well. Democrats retain influence in Scioto County, which contains industrial Portsmouth, and in adjacent Pike County.

## Committees

**Public Works and Transportation** (18th of 19 Republicans)
Economic Development; Investigations and Oversight; Surface Transportation.

**Veterans' Affairs** (8th of 14 Republicans)
Hospitals and Health Care; Housing and Memorial Affairs.

## Elections

**1980 General**

| | |
|---|---|
| Bob McEwen (R ) | 101,288 (55 %) |
| Ted Strickland (D ) | 84,235 (45 %) |

**1980 Primary**

| | |
|---|---|
| Bob McEwen (R ) | 21,360 (45 %) |
| James Christy (R ) | 8,221 (17 %) |
| Don Gingerich (R ) | 6,545 (14 %) |
| James Murray (R ) | 3,746 (8 %) |

**District Vote For President**

| | 1980 | | 1976 | | 1972 |
|---|---|---|---|---|---|
| **D** | 73,428 (37 %) | **D** | 86,444 (48 %) | **D** | 50,302 (29 %) |
| **R** | 113,219 (58 %) | **R** | 90,480 (50 %) | **R** | 117,583 (69 %) |
| **I** | 6,841 (4 %) | | | | |

## Campaign Finance

| 1980 | Receipts | Receipts from PACs | Expenditures |
|---|---|---|---|
| McEwen (R ) | $183,324 | $93,441 (51 %) | $182,388 |
| Strickland (D ) | $125,418 | $30,211 (24 %) | $80,608 |

## Key Vote

**97th Congress**

| | |
|---|---|
| Reagan budget proposal (1981) | Y |

---

**6th District: South central — Portsmouth, Chillicothe.** Population: 543,692 (17% increase since 1970). Race: White 531,144 (98%), Black 10,276 (2%), Others 2,242 (0.4%). Spanish origin: 2,509 (0.4%).

---

# 7 Clarence J. Brown (R)

**Of Urbana — Elected 1965**

**Born:** June 18, 1927, Columbus, Ohio.
**Education:** Duke U., B.A. 1947; Harvard U., M.B.A. 1949.
**Military Career:** Navy, 1951-53.
**Profession:** Newspaper editor and publisher.
**Family:** Wife, Joyce Eldridge; three children.
**Religion:** Presbyterian.
**Political Career:** No previous office.

**In Washington:** Brown has been the energy industry's primary defender through the Commerce Committee's endless regulatory arguments of recent years, and it has been a witty and resourceful defense, if often a losing one.

As energy has become the dominant domestic issue, the Commerce Subcommittee on Energy and Power has been the forum for debate, and Brown, its senior Republican, has coordinated strategy for the oil and gas companies seeking to free themselves from regulation. That has meant endless duels with Michigan Democrat John D. Dingell, now the full Commerce chairman, who has often been as determined to control prices as Brown has been to release them. But Brown has been able to make his accommodations with Dingell when necessary.

Until 1981, at least, Brown often came close, but rarely won. When President Carter submitted his first major energy legislation in 1977, Brown formed a coalition with conservative Democrats to win adoption of a gas deregulation amendment in subcommittee, 12-10. But the decision was reversed in full committee, 22-21, and the House never passed gas deregulation, although it accepted a phased-out version of it following a conference with the Senate in 1978.

By 1980, the committee seemed to be moving closer to Brown's free-enterprise views on many energy issues. But Brown was beginning to face a new set of problems from his own Republican contingent, especially the aggressive young David A. Stockman of Michigan, now President Reagan's budget director.

Brown created part of the problem by going the "wrong way" on two key energy measures. He opposed a synthetic fuels bill that sailed through Congress with bipartisan conservative support. And he fought hard for an Energy Mobilization Board to cut red tape and speed energy projects to completion. In this he was backing Dingell, who wanted the board to have the power to waive state

and federal laws that stood in the way of energy projects. The waiver was a red flag not only to environmentalists, but also to many states' rights conservatives and Westerners worried about threats to local water rights. Brown stuck with Dingell all the way, and in the end he was one of only nine Republicans to vote for the conference report on final passage. "Some things are more important than partisanship," he said on the House floor, implying that his Republican colleagues were out to kill the board simply because it was a key piece of Carter's energy package.

Meanwhile, Brown found himself on the outside as presidential candidate Ronald Reagan began searching for energy advice. A longtime supporter of Gerald R. Ford, Brown was ignored as Stockman spoke for Reagan on energy issues at the Republican National Convention and during the fall campaign.

Earlier in his career on the Commerce Committee, Brown specialized in communications issues. A newspaper publisher himself, he was outspoken in the controversy over expansion of national public television facilities, arguing that public TV should be primarily local rather than national. When the Nixon administration created an Office of Telecommunications Policy, he complained that the Federal Communications Commission was more than enough federal interference in the industry already.

---

**7th District: West central — Springfield, Marion.** Population: 474,827 (3% increase since 1970). Race: White 441,720 (93%), Black 28,450 (6%), Others 4,657 (1%). Spanish origin: 3,213 (1%).

Brown also has promoted his free-market views on the Joint Economic Committee, which by the end of the 1970s had moved far enough to the right to accept some of them. In 1979, Brown and other Republicans endorsed the committee's majority report in favor of supply-side tax cuts, an agreement that had not taken place in two previous decades of committee activity. In 1980, Brown traveled to the Far East on a Joint Economic Committee study mission, and returned with a proposal for an International Code of Business Conduct. He said American business was following strict ethical rules that were limiting it in international competition. "The price of our unique morality," Brown argued, "is lost markets, reduced economic growth and a resulting lower rate of employment."

Brown once harbored interest in a Republican leadership role, but he lost out in a climactic 1973 battle for campaign committee chairman against Robert H. Michel of Illinois. Michel went on to become whip in 1974 and party floor leader in 1981.

**At Home:** In the midst of a frustrating year in 1980, Brown sounded increasingly serious about a 1982 campaign for governor or the Senate, an event that would mark the end of an era — 44 years of continuous control in this district by the Brown family, father and son.

Clarence "Bud" Brown was only 11 years old when his father, Clarence J. Brown Sr., was elected to the House. By the time his father died of a kidney ailment in 1965, young Brown already had taken over the family-owned *Urbana Daily Citizen*, and seemed the obvious choice to assume his father's political role.

Even though he had no elective experience, Brown made his knowledge of Washington the central part of a primary campaign in which he defeated two state representatives, a former state senator and a former county prosecutor. Brown won 60 percent to 27 percent for his nearest competitor, state Rep. Charles E. Fry.

Brown continued to lean on his ties to Washington in the special runoff against the Democrat, Clark County prosecutor James A. Berry. At one point in the campaign, Brown flew to Washington to meet with House Armed Services Chairman L. Mendel Rivers about the future of the giant Wright-Patterson Air Force Base, located in the district. Brown not only promised voters he would emulate his father's conservative philosophy — he promised to rehire his father's Capitol Hill staff. He carried every county but one and won the district by an even larger percentage than his father had in 1964.

Since then Brown has won re-election eight times without falling below 60 percent. Three times Democrats have failed to put up a nominee. When they have, it has been a token effort that has received little assistance from the state party.

**The District:** There is considerable Democratic strength here on paper, but it rarely shows up in the congressional returns. Although Democrats will have a better chance next time if the Republican nominee is not named Brown, it is still difficult to imagine them winning.

Situated between Columbus and Dayton, the district is bisected by U.S. Route 40. To the north of the old National Road are four solidly Republican counties, including Champaign County, Brown's home. Casting only a third of the district's votes, this region is the more agricultural of the two. In 1980, Ronald Reagan won 62 percent in this part of the district.

The population south of Route 40 is concentrated in Springfield, Xenia and the eastern suburbs of Dayton. It is a working-class mixture of Southern whites and blacks, with Wright-Patterson Air Force Base responsible for a substantial amount of military-related employment. This area gave Reagan just 51 percent in 1980. Two years earlier, Gov. James A. Rhodes lost it while winning re-election statewide.

Over the years, redistricting has gradually shifted the district farther north. If that trend continues in 1982, it will be to the Republicans' advantage.

## Committees

**Energy and Commerce** (2nd of 18 Republicans)
Fossil and Synthetic Fuels; Health and the Environment.

**Government Operations** (3rd of 17 Republicans)
Intergovernmental Relations and Human Resources.

**Joint Economic**
Investment, Jobs and Prices.

## Elections

**1980 General**

| | |
|---|---|
| Clarence Brown (R ) | 124,137 (76 %) |
| Donald Hollister (D ) | 38,952 (24 %) |

**1978 General**

| | |
|---|---|
| Clarence Brown (R ) | Unopposed |

**Previous Winning Percentages**

| | | | |
|---|---|---|---|
| 1976 (65 %) | 1974 (61 %) | 1972 (73 %) | 1970 (69 %) |
| 1968 (64 %) | 1966 (100 %) | 1965* (60 %) | |

*Special election*

## Clarence J. Brown, R-Ohio

**District Vote For President**

| | 1980 | | 1976 | | 1972 |
|---|---|---|---|---|---|
| D | 66,366 (39 %) | D | 75,060 (45 %) | D | 52,138 (32 %) |
| R | 92,296 (54 %) | R | 86,493 (52 %) | R | 106,644 (66 %) |
| I | 9,857 (6 %) | | | | |

## Campaign Finance

| | Receipts | Receipts from PACs | Expen- ditures |
|---|---|---|---|
| **1980** | | | |
| Brown (R ) | $155,887 | $58,422 (37 %) | $205,446 |
| Hollister (D ) | $6,340 | — (0 %) | $6,028 |
| **1978** | | | |
| Brown (R ) | $58,541 | $29,155 (50 %) | $33,877 |

## Voting Studies

| | Presidential Support | | Party Unity | | Conservative Coalition | |
|---|---|---|---|---|---|---|
| Year | S | O | S | O | S | O |
| 1980 | 33 | 43 | 67 | 11 | 74 | 11 |
| 1979 | 27 | 57 | 71 | 10† | 78 | 6† |
| 1978 | 34 | 50 | 73 | 13 | 74 | 13 |
| 1977 | 39 | 56 | 81 | 11 | 83 | 10 |
| 1976 | 80 | 16 | 79 | 12 | 77 | 14 |
| 1975 | 76 | 18 | 80 | 14 | 75 | 16 |
| 1974 (Ford) | 48 | 33 | | | | |
| 1974 | 72 | 21 | 70 | 23† | 64 | 25† |
| 1973 | 62 | 17 | 66 | 22 | 65 | 21 |
| 1972 | 76 | 14 | 78 | 16 | 73 | 17 |
| 1971 | 86 | 5 | 79 | 9 | 81 | 6 |
| 1970 | 71 | 22 | 67 | 22 | 77 | 11 |
| 1969 | 66 | 26 | 65 | 20 | 78 | 13 |
| 1968 | 48 | 37 | 70 | 9 | 80 | 6 |
| 1967 | 42 | 50 | 88 | 4 | 89 | 2 |
| 1966 | 30 | 52 | 80 | 5 | 70 | 11 |

S = Support      O = Opposition

†Not eligible for all recorded votes.

## Key Votes

**96th Congress**

| | |
|---|---|
| Weaken Carter oil profits tax (1979) | Y |
| Reject hospital cost control plan (1979) | ? |
| Implement Panama Canal Treaties (1979) | N |
| Establish Department of Education (1979) | N |
| Approve Anti-busing Amendment (1979) | N |
| Guarantee Chrysler Corp. loans (1979) | N |
| Approve military draft registration (1980) | Y |
| Aid Sandinista regime in Nicaragua (1980) | N |
| Strengthen fair housing laws (1980) | N |

**97th Congress**

| | |
|---|---|
| Reagan budget proposal (1981) | Y |

## Interest Group Ratings

| Year | ADA | ACA | AFL-CIO | CCUS |
|---|---|---|---|---|
| 1980 | 11 | 67 | 27 | 74 |
| 1979 | 5 | 84 | 18 | 100 |
| 1978 | 15 | 80 | 5 | 94 |
| 1977 | 25 | 77 | 22 | 88 |
| 1976 | 15 | 76 | 13 | 94 |
| 1975 | 16 | 74 | 14 | 88 |
| 1974 | 26 | 60 | 36 | 67 |
| 1973 | 8 | 71 | 0 | 100 |
| 1972 | 19 | 57 | 27 | 89 |
| 1971 | 19 | 84 | 20 | · |
| 1970 | 24 | 56 | 17 | 75 |
| 1969 | 13 | 53 | 50 | · |
| 1968 | 8 | 91 | 50 | · |
| 1967 | 7 | 96 | 0 | 90 |
| 1966 | 6 | 81 | 0 | |

# 8 Thomas N. Kindness (R)

**Of Hamilton — Elected 1974**

**Born:** Aug. 26, 1929, Knoxville, Tenn.
**Education:** U. of Md., B.A. 1951; George Washington U., LL.B. 1953.
**Profession:** Lawyer.
**Family:** Wife, Ann Gifford; four children.
**Religion:** Presbyterian.
**Political Career:** Hamilton City Council, 1964-69; Mayor of Hamilton, 1964-67; Ohio House, 1971-75.

**In Washington:** Kindness has tried to assume the "devil's advocate" role played on Judiciary in past years by Charles Wiggins, the conservative California Republican who retired in 1978. Wiggins loved to pepper the Democrats with questions about the legal implications of their bills and warn of side effects from well-intentioned "reforms." Kindness does not put on as good a show; he lacks the Californian's forensic brilliance. But he sometimes manages to place the committee's leadership on the defensive.

He was a militant opponent of the committee's 1978 lobby disclosure bill, which he felt would impose a crushing paperwork burden on legitimate lobbyists. When the bill reached the floor, Kindness insisted on offering ten separate amendments, aimed at exempting various kinds of lobbyists and pointing out things he saw as inconsistencies in the legislation.

Lobby disclosure passed anyway, but it never became law, and in the 96th Congress did not even reach the House floor, in part because of controversies fueled by Kindness and other critics.

Kindness is one of the most consistent states' rights advocates among House conservatives; he is always asking Democrats on Judiciary why a given problem has to be handled on the federal level. In his first year in the House, 1975, he fought to allow states easier exemption from federal restrictions under the Voting Rights Act; later he opposed a "bill of rights" for institutionalized persons on the argument that it forced extra burdens on the states without giving them any resources to handle them. "It's just punishing the states," he insisted.

Kindness brought his states' rights approach to the effort in 1980 to draw up a new federal criminal code, opposing much of the additional authority the Justice Department wanted. But he ended up a supporter of the new code drawn up

by Judiciary. When that bill failed to reach the floor, Kindness introduced it again at the start of the 97th Congress.

Kindness has had leadership ambitions for much of his House career, but has never realized them. He tried to take the GOP conference chairmanship away from liberal John Anderson of Illinois in 1979, but found the top party leaders arrayed against him, and lost on an 87-55 vote. He wanted the job again two years later, when it was open, but dropped out before the balloting, which was won by Jack Kemp of New York.

**At Home:** Like many southern Ohioans, Kindness comes from below the Mason-Dixon line. He was born in Tennessee, practiced law in the District of Columbia, and moved to Hamilton, Ohio, in 1957 to become a lawyer for the Champion Paper Company. That city is where he got his start in politics and it has remained his electoral base ever since.

In 1974, when Republican Rep. Walter Powell's plainly-stated dislike for Congress led him to retire at age 43, local party leaders gave their support to Kindness, by then a two-term state representative. Kindness won the four-candidate GOP primary on the strength of his 4,000-vote plurality in Butler County (Hamilton); he lost every other part of the district.

The Democrat who had twice come close to beating Powell decided not to run again, and the party nominated T. Edward Strinko, a teacher

**8th District: Southwest — Middletown, Hamilton.** Population: 515,465 (11% increase since 1970). Race: White 482,278 (94%), Black 29,857 (6%), Others 3,330 (1%). Spanish origin: 2,810 (1%).

and former foreign service officer. The general election was complicated by the independent candidacy of Don Gingrich, a conservative who had previously managed campaigns for Powell.

With Gingrich drawing support in the rural, German Catholic areas, Kindness again had to rely on Butler County. Strinko ran ahead of him in the five other counties, but the Republican's margin at home gave him the election with less than a majority. Since then, he has won easily.

**The District:** In 1966, Ohio's Legislature created a new district — the 24th — to replace an old at-large seat and to accommodate rapid population growth in the corridor between Cincinnati and Dayton. Six years later, the 24th was renumbered as the 8th District and slightly expanded. Regardless of its precise location or number,

the district has remained essentially Republican. In the early 1970s Democrats came close to winning, but more recently Republicans — both local and statewide — have been increasing their margins.

As the suburban exodus from Cincinnati goes on, Butler and Warren counties continue to grow. These two counties — the most Republican in the district — account for 60 percent of the vote.

The Montgomery County (suburban Dayton) portion of the district tends to be more Democratic. With a few predominently black townships, it makes up about a fifth of the district's vote. While Reagan took 62 percent in Butler and Warren counties, he lost narrowly to Carter in the Montgomery County portion of the 8th District, winning just 46 percent.

## Committees

**Government Operations** (5th of 17 Republicans)
Government Information and Individual Rights.

**Judiciary** (8th of 12 Republicans)
Administrative Law and Government Relations; Criminal Justice.

## Elections

**1980 General**

| | |
|---|---|
| Thomas Kindness (R) | 139,490 (76%) |
| John Griffin (D) | 44,162 (24%) |

**1978 General**

| | |
|---|---|
| Thomas Kindness (R) | 81,156 (71%) |
| Lou Schroeder (D) | 32,493 (29%) |

**Previous Winning Percentages**

1976 (69 %)  1974 (42%)

**District Vote For President**

| | 1980 | | 1976 | | 1972 |
|---|---|---|---|---|---|
| D | 69,524 (36%) | D | 77,264 (45%) | D | 47,227 (30%) |
| R | 110,764 (58%) | R | 92,528 (54%) | R | 105,785 (67%) |
| I | 9,275 (5%) | | | | |

## Campaign Finance

| | Receipts | Receipts from PACs | Expenditures |
|---|---|---|---|
| **1980** | | | |
| Kindness (R) | $44,780 | $31,495 (70%) | $58,322 |
| **1978** | | | |
| Kindness (R) | $66,728 | $26,349 (39%) | $64,077 |
| Schroeder (D) | $15,898 | $5,300 (33%) | $15,430 |

## Voting Studies

| Year | Presidential Support | | Party Unity | | Conservative Coalition | |
|---|---|---|---|---|---|---|
| | S | O | S | O | S | O |
| 1980 | 34 | 62 | 83 | 11 | 83 | 9 |
| 1979 | 23 | 72 | 91 | 5 | 92 | 3 |
| 1978 | 22 | 69 | 84 | 10 | 90 | 5 |
| 1977 | 33 | 62 | 87 | 9 | 87 | 7 |
| 1976 | 76 | 18 | 84 | 8 | 82 | 8 |
| 1975 | 66 | 27 | 85 | 10 | 92 | 4 |

S = Support  O = Opposition

## Key Votes

**96th Congress**

| | |
|---|---|
| Weaken Carter oil profits tax (1979) | Y |
| Reject hospital cost control plan (1979) | Y |
| Implement Panama Canal Treaties (1979) | N |
| Establish Department of Education (1979) | N |
| Approve Anti-busing Amendment (1979) | Y |
| Guarantee Chrysler Corp. loans (1979) | N |
| Approve military draft registration (1980) | Y |
| Aid Sandinista regime in Nicaragua (1980) | N |
| Strengthen fair housing laws (1980) | N |

**97th Congress**

| | |
|---|---|
| Reagan budget proposal (1981) | Y |

## Interest Group Ratings

| Year | ADA | ACA | AFL-CIO | CCUS |
|---|---|---|---|---|
| 1980 | 6 | 96 | 11 | 67 |
| 1979 | 11 | 96 | 5 | 94 |
| 1978 | 5 | 93 | 5 | 83 |
| 1977 | 10 | 88 | 26 | 87 |
| 1976 | 0 | 92 | 10 | 94 |
| 1975 | 0 | 93 | 9 | 100 |

# 9 Ed Weber (R)

**Of Toledo — Elected 1980**

**Born:** July 26, 1931, Toledo, Ohio.
**Education:** Denison U., B.A. 1953; Harvard U., LL.B. 1956.
**Military Career:** Army, 1956-58.
**Profession:** Lawyer.
**Family:** Wife, Alice Hammerstrom; three children.
**Religion:** Baptist.
**Political Career:** No previous office.

**The Member:** Beyond the Toledo legal community, where he was regarded as a first-rate attorney, few knew Weber at the outset of his 1980 campaign. Even fewer thought he had a chance of defeating Democratic Rep. Thomas L. Ashley. But Weber won handily, despite the district's partisan orientation, which had kept it in the Democratic column since 1954. Weber's campaign brochure declared that "we've reached the bottom of the federal cookie jar," and his economic themes appealed to the recession-hit Toledo area.

In 1981, shortly after Reagan's budget proposals sailed through Congress in early May, Weber and a GOP colleague wrote a letter to Majority Leader Jim Wright challenging Democrats to schedule a vote on Reagan's across-the-board tax cut proposals in time for Americans to see a tax break in their July paychecks. One-hundred forty Republicans co-signed the letter.

While pushing for tax reductions, Weber has also kept an eye on his inner-city Toledo constituents. On the Banking Committee, he lobbied for more money in the Urban Development Action Grant (UDAG) program.

**The District:** A center of glass and auto manufacturing, the Great Lakes port of Toledo has long been a Democratic outpost in rural, Republican northwest Ohio. The city has dominated this district, which covers most of Lucas County. Inner-city Toledo has large numbers of Polish-Americans and blacks, and remains reliably Democratic. The blue-collar suburbs east of the city also have a Democratic orientation. Republicans are concentrated in the more affluent, white-collar suburbs to the west of Toledo, like Ottawa Hills and Maumee.

The 9th District's Democratic loyalties delivered it to George McGovern in 1972 and Jimmy Carter in 1976. Carter also won it in 1980, but barely. High unemployment — 12 percent in Toledo the month before the election — helped Reagan to run strongly and Weber to win easily.

## Committees

**Banking, Finance and Urban Affairs** (12th of 19 Republicans)
Domestic Monetary Policy; Financial Institutions Supervision, Regulation and Insurance; General Oversight and Renegotiation.

**Small Business** (14th of 17 Republicans)
Export Opportunities and Special Small Business Problems; General Oversight.

## Elections

**1980 General**

| | |
|---|---|
| Ed Weber (R) | 96,927 (56%) |
| Thomas Ashley (D) | 68,728 (40%) |

**1980 Primary**

| | |
|---|---|
| Ed Weber (R) | 16,322 (76%) |
| Vernor Wagner (R) | 5,153 (24%) |

**District Vote For President**

| | 1980 | | 1976 | | 1972 |
|---|---|---|---|---|---|
| **D** | 80,544 (45%) | **D** | 98,925 (57%) | **D** | 87,151 (50%) |
| **R** | 78,995 (45%) | **R** | 71,254 (41%) | **R** | 83,768 (48%) |
| **I** | 15,436 (9%) | | | | |

## Campaign Finance

| | Receipts | Receipts from PACs | Expenditures |
|---|---|---|---|
| **1980** | | | |
| Weber (R) | $359,025 | $91,611 (26%) | $359,050 |
| Ashley (D) | $252,782 | $142,100 (56%) | $254,264 |

## Key Vote

**97th Congress**
| | |
|---|---|
| Reagan budget proposal (1981) | Y |

**9th District: Northwest — Toledo.**
Population: 442,900 (4% decrease since 1970). Race: White 369,115 (83%), Black 63,286 (14%), Others 10,499 (2%). Spanish origin: 12,036 (3%).

# 10 Clarence E. Miller (R)

### Of Lancaster — Elected 1966

**Born:** Nov. 1, 1917, Lancaster, Ohio.
**Education:** Attended Lancaster H.S.
**Profession:** Electrical engineer.
**Family:** Wife, Helen Brown; two children.
**Religion:** Methodist.
**Political Career:** Lancaster City Council, 1957-63; mayor of Lancaster, 1963-65.

**In Washington:** Miller has made a career out of one simple amendment — the one that has led his colleagues to nickname him "5-percent Clarence." Year after year, on bill after bill, he has taken the floor to propose that appropriations be reduced by 5 percent across-the-board, or, if that seems politically impossible, 2 percent, or 5 percent with a few exemptions.

He picked up the habit initially from Frank T. Bow, the Ohio Republican who was senior GOP member on Appropriations when Miller arrived in 1967. In his first year in Congress, Miller was already standing up to endorse a 5 percent cut proposed by Bow on the expenditures for Congress itself. "If we must begin cutting our own salaries to show our sincerity," Miller said, "then let us do it."

But it took Miller several years after Bow's retirement in 1972 to claim the amendment as his personal property. It was not until 1976 that he first offered it, to an Agriculture bill, and it was badly beaten. He offered it to ten separate bills that year, and never got it passed. Even when he tried it on an unpopular foreign aid appropriation, holding up a sign to ridicule the common argument that "there are 100 other programs that could be cut, but don't cut this one," he could not get most members to take him seriously.

The next year, however, with fiscal conservatism spreading through the House, the situation began to change. Miller won his first victory in 1977, persuading the House on a 214-168 vote to cut foreign aid money by 5 percent.

In 1978, the year Proposition 13 passed in California, Miller discovered his weapon's potential — but also its limits. Modifying his strategy, he offered an amendment to cut labor, education and welfare spending by a smaller 2 percent, and found that it passed easily.

But on foreign aid, he went for too big a slice —8 percent — and lost by 15 votes. Then his 2 percent cut in agriculture spending, which seemed to have a majority on a roll-call vote, was beaten

back with some serious lobbying by the House leadership.

In retrospect, 1978 appears to have been the peak year for what Miller's critics like to call his "meat ax" approach to spending. In 1979, his 5 percent foreign aid cut was superseded by a 2 percent reduction proposed by one of the bill's managers; his HEW cut was not passed at all. At least one chairman has added enough extra money to his bill to allow for passage of a Miller amendment, and then supported him. The only changes that passed in 1980 were in the 2 percent range.

Beyond the idea of across-the-board cuts, Miller has not been one of the more active legislators. He has taken an interest in foreign aid over the years, especially in the idea of making Third World nations supply the United States with strategic materials as a condition of financial assistance. "It is important to receive something for the foreign assistance we are giving away," he once said. But he has not been successful in promoting this effort.

A more conspicuous achievement is Miller's attendance record, one of the best in the House. During most years he never misses a vote; he once introduced a resolution providing that members would lose their voting privileges if their participation fell below a certain percentage.

**At Home:** Miller's election in 1966 over

---

**10th District: Southeast — Lancaster, Zanesville.** Population: 528,320 (14% increase since 1970). Race: White 515,320 (97%), Black 9,877 (2%), Others 3,440 (1%). Spanish origin: 2,527 (0.4%).

Democratic incumbent Walter H. Moeller was due, in large part, to the long political coattails of James A. Rhodes, the district's native son. Winning re-election as governor in 1966, Rhodes carried the 10th by 34,000 votes — enough to pull Miller into office by 4,401.

Since then, Miller has kept in touch with the voters mostly through newsletters and ceremonial visits to county fairs and other gatherings. Like virtually all Appalachian districts, the 10th is sparsely populated and difficult for challengers to campaign in; Miller's opponents have been frustrated for years by their inability even to make their names known district-wide. Only once in seven re-election campaigns has Miller lost even one county — and that was removed by redistricting the following year.

In several of his campaigns, Miller has had the easy task of facing professors from Ohio University at Athens. He has been challenged by an economist, a historian and a political scientist, and none has drawn a third of the vote against him. As a countrified ex-mayor with a correspondence degree in engineering, Miller has simply fit the constituency better than they have. Since 1974, the opponents have been an accountant, an auto dealer and a hotel manager, and they have been no more of a threat.

**The District:** Larger than Connecticut, the 10th District is a part of Appalachia grafted onto a Midwestern state. During the 60s, it was stagnating economically and losing population. In the 70s, however, people began moving back to the area, in part because of the increased interest in coal mining. The 10th was second in population growth among Ohio districts during the decade.

It is also firmly Republican by tradition; the 10th is the only district in the state that did not elect a Democrat during the New Deal years. Republican Thomas Jenkins represented the area from 1924 until his retirement in 1958. Then came a flurry of close elections in which the winner never exceeded 53 percent. Democrat Moeller was elected twice, defeated in 1962, re-elected two years later, and defeated for the last time by Miller in 1966.

Athens County, the home of Ohio University, is the only predictably Democratic part of the district. It was one of just two Ohio counties to support George McGovern in 1972. The northern counties tend to be more agricultural and Republican. Many of the poorer voters along the Ohio River still call themselves Democrats as a leftover from Civil War days, but their conservative outlook usually leads them toward Republican candidates.

## Committees

**Appropriations** (6th of 22 Republicans)
  Commerce, Justice, State, and Judiciary; Treasury - Postal Service - General Government.

## Elections

**1980 General**

| | |
|---|---|
| Clarence Miller (R) | 143,403 (74%) |
| Jack Stecher (D) | 49,433 (26%) |

**1978 General**

| | |
|---|---|
| Clarence Miller (R) | 99,329 (74%) |
| James Plummer (D) | 35,039 (26 %) |

**Previous Winning Percentages**

| | | | |
|---|---|---|---|
| 1976 (69%) | 1974 (70%) | 1972 (73%) | 1970 (67%) |
| 1968 (69%) | 1966 (52%) | | |

**District Vote For President**

| | 1980 | | 1976 | | 1972 |
|---|---|---|---|---|---|
| D | 79,860 (39%) | D | 92,306 (48%) | D | 59,010 (32%) |
| R | 112,005 (55%) | R | 96,208 (50%) | R | 119,431 (65%) |
| I | 8,470 (4%) | | | | |

## Campaign Finance

| | Receipts | Receipts from PACs | Expenditures |
|---|---|---|---|
| **1980** | | | |
| Miller (R) | $41,204 | $26,225 (64%) | $32,336 |
| Stecher (D) | $7,729 | — (0%) | $7,647 |
| **1978** | | | |
| Miller (R) | $26,647 | $11,892 (45%) | $22,957 |

## Voting Studies

| | Presidential Support | | Party Unity | | Conservative Coalition | |
|---|---|---|---|---|---|---|
| Year | S | O | S | O | S | O |
| 1980 | 31 | 69 | 90 | 10 | 88 | 12 |
| 1979 | 22 | 78 | 91 | 9 | 94 | 6 |
| 1978 | 31 | 68 | 88 | 10 | 86 | 12 |
| 1977 | 35 | 65 | 89 | 11 | 88 | 12 |
| 1976 | 80 | 20 | 93 | 7 | 92 | 8 |
| 1975 | 63 | 36 | 86 | 12 | 87 | 11 |
| 1974 (Ford) | 48 | 52 | | | | |
| 1974 | 75 | 25 | 80 | 20 | 76 | 24 |

**953**

## Clarence E. Miller, R-Ohio

| Year | S | O | S | O | S | O |
|------|----|----|----|----|----|----|
| 1973 | 54 | 46 | 75 | 25 | 72 | 28 |
| 1972 | 68 | 32 | 79 | 21 | 84 | 16 |
| 1971 | 70 | 30 | 77 | 23 | 80 | 20 |
| 1970 | 69 | 31 | 74 | 26 | 73 | 27 |
| 1969 | 51 | 49 | 84 | 16 | 96 | 4 |
| 1968 | 48 | 52 | 87 | 13 | 90 | 10 |
| 1967 | 43 | 57 | 91 | 9 | 94 | 6 |

S = Support          O = Opposition

## Key Votes

**96th Congress**

| | |
|---|---|
| Weaken Carter oil profits tax (1979) | Y |
| Reject hospital cost control plan (1979) | Y |
| Implement Panama Canal Treaties (1979) | N |
| Establish Department of Education (1979) | N |
| Approve Anti-busing Amendment (1979) | Y |
| Guarantee Chrysler Corp. loans (1979) | N |
| Approve military draft registration (1980) | N |
| Aid Sandinista regime in Nicaragua (1980) | N |
| Strengthen fair housing laws (1980) | N |

**97th Congress**

| | |
|---|---|
| Reagan budget proposal (1981) | Y |

## Interest Group Ratings

| Year | ADA | ACA | AFL-CIO | CCUS |
|------|-----|-----|---------|------|
| 1980 | 11 | 75 | 16 | 79 |
| 1979 | 0 | 92 | 20 | 100 |
| 1978 | 20 | 92 | 15 | 67 |
| 1977 | 15 | 93 | 13 | 100 |
| 1976 | 5 | 93 | 13 | 100 |
| 1975 | 5 | 85 | 9 | 76 |
| 1974 | 35 | 80 | 0 | 90 |
| 1973 | 28 | 85 | 9 | 91 |
| 1972 | 6 | 87 | 0 | 100 |
| 1971 | 22 | 79 | 8 | - |
| 1970 | 40 | 68 | 14 | 90 |
| 1969 | 7 | 71 | 20 | - |
| 1968 | 0 | 91 | 0 | - |
| 1967 | 7 | 93 | 0 | 100 |

# 11 J. William Stanton (R)

**Of Painesville — Elected 1964**

**Born:** Feb. 20, 1924, Painesville, Ohio.
**Education:** Georgetown U., B.S. 1949.
**Military Career:** Army, 1942-46.
**Profession:** Automobile dealer.
**Family:** Wife, Peggy Smeeton; one child.
**Religion:** Roman Catholic.
**Political Career:** Lake County Commissioner, 1956-64.

**In Washington:** Stanton, an ex-auto dealer with close ties to financial and business leaders, has managed to walk a fine line between cooperation with the Democrats and Republican Party loyalty. His low-key, affable style has allowed him to maneuver successfully through the bickering that has dominated the Banking Committee over much of the past decade.

When he got to Congress in 1965, he wanted to serve on the Foreign Affairs Committee. But the Ohio Republican delegation was headed at that time by crusty, strong-willed Clarence Brown Sr., and Brown told Stanton he would have the "honor" of serving on Banking instead.

Stanton made the best of it. He joined Banking subcommittees dealing with international trade and financial affairs and set out on a road of selective partisanship that allowed him to give Democrats a helping hand at appropriate moments.

Early in his career, he joined a bipartisan rebel bloc that forced adoption of new committee rules, reducing the power of the autocratic Banking chairman, Wright Patman. More recently, as the dominant Republican legislator on housing issues, he worked closely with Ohio Democrat Thomas "Lud" Ashley, the Housing Subcommittee chairman until 1981. And he has fought against some of the attacks from his own side of the aisle against multinational lending institutions, such as the World Bank.

But Stanton has never wandered far from basic GOP principles. In most years, he still supports the "conservative coalition" of Republicans and Southern Democrats about two-thirds of the time on the House floor. Other Republicans see him as a pragmatist, but one who is careful about the deals he leads them into.

His pragmatism was called on in 1980 when a two-year effort to enact a new housing authorization was threatened by a dispute over "redlining" — the refusal by banks to make mortgage loans in low-income areas.

A 1975 law made redlining harder by forcing new loan disclosure requirements. The Senate had voted to make the anti-redlining law permanent and attached it to the housing bill. When the issue came to a House-Senate conference, Rep. Chalmers Wylie, R-Ohio, threatened to delete the Senate provision on the House floor as nongermane, an action likely to kill the whole law.

Stanton pulled together negotiations among both parties from both chambers, and came up with a compromise agreement to accept the Senate provision, but for only five years.

The heightened partisanship of the Reagan era has made it somewhat more difficult for Stanton to play a middleman role. When the Banking Committee considered a package of Reagan cuts in subsidized housing and community development programs, many of them programs Stanton had supported in the past, the Ohio Republican led Republican party-line votes in favor of the reductions.

Earlier, however, he tried quietly to convince Budget Director David A. Stockman to avoid major cuts in the Export-Import Bank and multilateral lending institutions.

He told Stockman that the Export-Import Bank is essential to help American companies compete in the high-priced world of aircraft sales and nuclear plants. He said nations denied funds

**11th District: Northeast — Cleveland suburbs.** Population: 525,680 (14% increase since 1970). Race: White 512,614 (98%), Black 9,151 (2%), Others 3,915 (1%). Spanish origin: 3,066 (1%).

at the international banks would appeal directly to Congress for foreign aid to make up the difference. But his arguments did little to sway Stockman or the administration.

Stanton has voted a "free enterprise" Republican position on the major loan guarantees that have preoccupied the committee in recent years — for Chrysler and for New York City. He opposed bailing out Chrysler in 1979, arguing that it would set a bad precedent, and he tried to convince House Republicans to take a formal stand against it. But party leaders refused, and nearly half the House Republicans ended up supporting the loan guarantee.

The year before, Stanton opposed a $2 billion loan guarantee for financially strapped New York City. He tried to change the bill on the House floor to make it an extension of seasonal loans to the city, rather than a guarantee, and to phase out the help after three years, rather than 15. But that move was badly beaten.

**At Home:** If there were no J. William Stanton, the 11th would more than likely be a Democratic district. But as long as he runs, voters here are likely to remain comfortable with his moderate, low-key brand of Republican politics.

Stanton's moderate image, Catholic background and prominent family ties helped him overcome the national Democratic sweep in 1964, when he first ran for the House. He has never been seriously threatened since.

It was a discussion over Christmas dinner in 1955 that led Stanton into politics. He and his father — both Ford dealers — were berating local officials for their inability to persuade Ford to locate a plant in nearby Mentor. Thinking he could do a better job, the younger Stanton ran for Lake County commissioner the next year and won. Ford eventually built the plant on the other side of Cleveland, but Stanton had a cause and a political base at the Lake County courthouse, on the same shady square as his father's bank.

After two terms promoting the rapid growth

and development of Lake County, Stanton decided in 1964 to run for the House seat being vacated by his longtime family friend, Oliver P. Bolton, who was running for Ohio's at-large House seat to publicize his name for a Senate campaign.

Stanton made it look rather easy. It required defeating three others in the Republican primary, but none of the opponents had the same financial resources or political experience as Stanton. He won easily. Against Democrat C. D. Lambros in the fall, Stanton ran a traditional Republican campaign, passing out shopping bags at county fairs and promising to curb "wasteful spending." He managed to keep his distance from the national ticket headed by Barry Goldwater, which attracted only 37 percent of the vote in the district. With strong support from Lake County, Stanton won with 55 percent.

In his first five elections, Stanton's district changed its shape four times. But losing or gaining parts of Lake, Summit and Trumbull counties never seemed to alter his healthy victory margins.

**The District:** This area gradually lost its rural and small-town character in the postwar years, and came to focus more on Cleveland.

Between 1950 and 1970 the population of Lake and Geauga counties more than doubled. The rapid growth slowed somewhat during the last decade, but the suburbs of Cleveland continue to creep further east, obliterating the truck gardens and vineyards along Lake Erie. Many of the residents of this part of the district are farmers or ethnics who have fled Cleveland. They tilt slightly to the Republican Party.

But the two eastern counties — Ashtabula and Trumbull — are more Democratic. The cities of Ashtabula and Conneaut support a fair number of industrial plants along Lake Erie. Blue-collar workers from Warren and Youngstown, just south of the district line, help to keep the Democratic vote high in the northern part of Trumbull County.

## Committees

**Banking, Finance and Urban Affairs** (Ranking Republican)
Housing and Community Development; International Development Institutions and Finance; International Trade, Investment and Monetary Policy.

**Small Business** (3rd of 17 Republicans)
General Oversight.

## Elections

**1980 General**

| | |
|---|---|
| William Stanton (R) | 128,507 (69%) |
| Patrick Donlin (D) | 51,224 (28%) |

**1978 General**

| | |
|---|---|
| William Stanton (R ) | 89,327 (68 %) |
| Patrick Donlin (D ) | 37,131 (28 %) |

**Previous Winning Percentages**

| | | | |
|---|---|---|---|
| 1976 (72%) | 1974 (61%) | 1972 (68%) | 1970 (68%) |
| 1968 (75%) | 1966 (69%) | 1964 (55%) | |

**District Vote For President**

| | 1980 | | 1976 | | 1972 |
|---|---|---|---|---|---|
| **D** | 78,781 (40%) | **D** | 92,525 (52%) | **D** | 58,172 (38%) |
| **R** | 102,888 (52%) | **R** | 83,451 (46%) | **R** | 91,525 (60%) |
| **I** | 13,654 (7%) | | | | |

## Campaign Finance

| | Receipts | Receipts from PACs | Expenditures |
|---|---|---|---|
| **1980** | | | |
| Stanton (R) | $33,562 | $2,000 (6%) | $0,501 |
| Donlin (D) | $25,994 | $3,000 (12%) | $19,871 |
| **1978** | | | |
| Stanton (R) | $28,039 | $500 (2%) | $24,816 |
| Donlin (D) | $11,880 | $3,400 (29%) | $11,671 |

## Voting Studies

| | Presidential Support | | Party Unity | | Conservative Coalition | |
|---|---|---|---|---|---|---|
| Year | S | O | S | O | S | O |
| 1980 | 56 | 39 | 57 | 38 | 62 | 31 |
| 1979 | 46 | 52 | 63 | 33 | 75 | 24 |
| 1978 | 49 | 47 | 71 | 29 | 74 | 26 |
| 1977 | 58 | 42 | 65 | 33 | 71 | 26 |
| 1976 | 80 | 18 | 66 | 34 | 69 | 31 |
| 1975 | 78 | 21 | 65 | 28 | 64 | 26 |
| 1974 (Ford) | 65 | 35 | | | | |
| 1974 | 64 | 30 | 53 | 43† | 54 | 40† |
| 1973 | 71 | 29 | 65 | 34 | 68 | 31 |
| 1972 | 76 | 14 | 66 | 25 | 65 | 24 |
| 1971 | 74 | 18 | 54 | 26 | 58 | 22 |
| 1970 | 82 | 12 | 56 | 42 | 50 | 43 |
| 1969 | 70 | 23 | 53 | 42 | 60 | 38 |
| 1968 | 74 | 18 | 50 | 48 | 43 | 53 |
| 1967 | 54 | 42 | 72 | 22 | 72 | 26 |
| 1966 | 36 | 51 | 85 | 3 | 84 | 3 |
| 1965 | 43 | 54 | 87 | 10 | 94 | 4 |

S = Support      O = Opposition
†Not eligible for all recorded votes.

## Key Votes

**96th Congress**

| | |
|---|---|
| Weaken Carter oil profits tax (1979) | Y |
| Reject hospital cost control plan (1979) | Y |
| Implement Panama Canal Treaties (1979) | N |
| Establish Department of Education (1979) | N |
| Approve Anti-busing Amendment (1979) | Y |
| Guarantee Chrysler Corp. loans (1979) | N |
| Approve military draft registration (1980) | N |
| Aid Sandinista regime in Nicaragua (1980) | Y |
| Strengthen fair housing laws (1980) | N |

**97th Congress**

| | |
|---|---|
| Reagan budget proposal (1981) | Y |

## Interest Group Ratings

| Year | ADA | ACA | AFL-CIO | CCUS |
|---|---|---|---|---|
| 1980 | 44 | 63 | 21 | 72 |
| 1979 | 16 | 68 | 35 | 89 |
| 1978 | 15 | 52 | 52 | 72 |
| 1977 | 15 | 56 | 48 | 94 |
| 1976 | 15 | 46 | 30 | 88 |
| 1975 | 26 | 60 | 35 | 71 |
| 1974 | 30 | 40 | 36 | 40 |
| 1973 | 28 | 63 | 27 | 82 |
| 1972 | 19 | 52 | 30 | 78 |
| 1971 | 24 | 65 | 50 | - |
| 1970 | 52 | 41 | 29 | 80 |
| 1969 | 27 | 35 | 80 | - |
| 1968 | 42 | 45 | 75 | - |
| 1967 | 7 | 79 | 9 | 100 |
| 1966 | 0 | 81 | 8 | - |
| 1965 | 5 | 75 | - | 90 |

# 12 Bob Shamansky (D)

**Of Bexley — Elected 1980**

**Born:** April 18, 1927, Columbus, Ohio.
**Education:** Ohio State University, B.A. 1947;
Harvard University, LL.B. 1950.
**Military Career:** Army, 1950-52.
**Profession:** Lawyer.
**Family:** Single.
**Religion:** Jewish.
**Political Career:** Unsuccessful Democratic
nominee for U.S. House, 1966.

**The Member:** This mild-mannered lawyer
pulled off a major upset in 1980 by defeating 22-
year veteran Samuel L. Devine with $90,000 of his
own money and a last-minute television and radio
blitz that took the Republican incumbent completely by surprise.

Having survived four much more visible challenges during the last decade, Devine thought he
was secure against Shamansky, whom he defeated
by nearly 2-to-1 in 1966. But in his second try,
Shamansky said Devine had a negative voting
record that consistently opposed "jobs and
progress," a motto borrowed from Republican
Gov. James A. Rhodes.

A wealthy lawyer with real estate interests in
Columbus, Shamansky is concerned with housing
problems. In Congress, he introduced legislation
to extend for two years a federal program that
partially subsidizes mortgage payments of first-
time homebuyers with incomes up to 130 percent
of the local average. A Banking subcommittee
gave the program an 18-month extension.

On Science and Technology, Shamansky
criticized Reagan's plan to sharply cut federal
funding for the National Science Foundation. He
said federally-supported research at institutions
like Ohio State expands America's technological
base and prevents loss of jobs to foreign
competitors.

**The District:** When Franklin County was
divided into two districts in 1966, Devine was
given the slightly more Republican eastern portion. The district does have most of Columbus'
black areas, but it casts little of the university
vote of Ohio State, and GOP candidates can count
on carrying wealthy areas like Bexley.

While Columbus traditionally backs Republican candidates for statewide office, Devine carried Franklin County only once in his last four
campaigns. In 1974 and 1976 he was re-elected
only because of his margins in rural Morrow and
Delaware counties. The vote there was not sufficient to save him against Shamansky in 1980.

## Committees

**Foreign Affairs** (16th of 21 Democrats)
Europe and the Middle East; International Economic Policy and Trade.

**Science and Technology** (20th of 23 Democrats)
Investigations and Oversight; Science, Research and Technology; Transportation, Aviation and Materials.

**Select Aging** (28th of 31 Democrats)
Housing and Consumer Interests.

## Elections

**1980 General**

| | |
|---|---|
| Bob Shamansky (D) | 108,690 (53%) |
| Samuel Devine (R) | 98,110 (47%) |

**District Vote For President**

| | 1980 | | 1976 | | 1972 |
|---|---|---|---|---|---|
| **D** | 83,224 (39 %) | **D** | 84,360 (43 %) | **D** | 61,510 (32 %) |
| **R** | 115,211 (54 %) | **R** | 105,978 (54 %) | **R** | 128,025 (66 %) |
| **I** | 10,253 (5 %) | | | | |

## Campaign Finance

| | Receipts | Receipts from PACs | Expen-ditures |
|---|---|---|---|
| **1980** | | | |
| Shamansky (D) | $184,064 | $10,150 (6%) | $179,321 |
| Devine (R) | $128,648 | $82,375 (64%) | $132,072 |

## Key Vote

**97th Congress**

| | |
|---|---|
| Reagan budget proposal (1981) | N |

**12th District: Central — eastern Co-
lumbus and suburbs.** Population: 515,347
(11% increase since 1970). Race: White
430,853 (84%), Black 78,583 (15%), Others
5,911 (1%). Spanish origin: 3,588 (1%).

# 13 Don J. Pease (D)

**Of Oberlin — Elected 1976**

**Born:** Sept. 26, 1931, Toledo, Ohio.
**Education:** Ohio U., B.S. 1953, M.A. 1955.
**Military Career:** Army, 1955-57.
**Profession:** Newspaper editor.
**Family:** Wife, Jeanne Wendt; one child.
**Religion:** Protestant.
**Political Career:** Oberlin City Council, 1962-64; Ohio Senate, 1965-67 and 1975-77; Ohio House, 1969-75; unsuccessfully sought re-election to Ohio Senate, 1966.

**In Washington:** Pease comes from a part of Ohio that has traditionally viewed politics as an ethical pursuit, and he has viewed it that way himself in his initial House terms, promoting clean government at home and human rights in other countries. As 1981 began, he moved to Ways and Means and shifted to tax policy.

As a member of Foreign Affairs through 1980, he spent much of his time arguing for a strong human rights position, pushing President Carter to end trade with Idi Amin's Uganda regime and trying to cut military aid to the Philippines.

In general, he reflected liberal ambivalence about sending arms to the Third World countries. He frequently said that massive military support of the Third World could lead to another Vietnam. But he favored weapons for North Yemen, saying there was no choice but to counter Soviet arms shipments. "People are fed up with being pushed around by the Soviets," he said, sounding untypically militant. "If that's the way they want to play it, that's the way we have to."

Meanwhile, Pease was worrying about keeping elections clean and limiting the influence of economic interests. In his first year in the House, when the Carter administration wanted to make it possible for voters to register at the polls on election day, Pease proposed an amendment imposing extra controls to prevent fraud. He was embarrassed in 1978 when a reporter wrote about lobbyists at his D.C. fund-raiser and vowed not to have one in 1980. He said the events probably involved "sort of an unspoken quid pro quo of some kind." Pease's political security at home made that decision relatively easy.

After one term on Foreign Affairs, Pease began negotiating for a more influential committee assignment. He started in 1979 by aiming at Appropriations. When the California delegation lobbied for one of its members, Pease offered to step aside in exchange for a promise that the Californians would back him for the next Ways and Means opening. That opening turned out to be the result of another Ohio retirement, and Pease was all but assured of it.

As part of his switch to economic issues, Pease drew up his own detailed set of budget proposals in early 1981. But the House Rules Committee would not let him offer it on the floor.

**At Home:** If it had not been for an age gap of 25 years and a difference in party labels, voters might have noticed little change in 1976 when Pease replaced Charles A. Mosher in the House.

The two liberals had been friends for years, with Pease always seeming to turn up where Mosher had been a couple of decades before. Both began their political careers on the Oberlin City Council, and both moved on to represent the same area in the Ohio Senate. When Mosher came to Washington and gave up his job as editor of the *Oberlin News-Tribune*, Pease took it over.

There have been a few complications to Pease's steady ascent. After one term in the state Senate, he was defeated for re-election. He switched to the Ohio House, spent three terms there, then made it back to the state Senate by defeating a Republican incumbent in 1974.

During his legislative career, Pease became a close ally of Ohio's teachers through his efforts as chairman of the educational review committee to

---

**13th District: (North — Lorain).**
Population: 512,747 (10% increase since 1970).
Race: White 474,275 (92%), Black 28,200 (5%), Others 10,272 (2%). Spanish origin: 14,821 (3%).

increase state funding for schools. He used their support, along with help from other labor organizations, to achieve easy victories in 1976. It also helped that his Senate district covered half of the congressional district, including about 60 percent of the population.

In his first two re-election campaigns, he faced charges from Republicans as well as Democratic primary opponents that he was too liberal and too much preoccupied with foreign affairs. His personable nature, solid labor support and clean reputation were enough to turn back these attacks easily, although his vote has been declining somewhat in his political base, Lorain County.

**The District:** Centered on Lorain and Elyria west of Cleveland, this district combines outer Cleveland suburbs, factory towns and gradually disappearing farm land.

Although the district had been in Republican hands for 40 years before Pease's election, the growing industrialization of Lorain County convinced Democrats they could win it as soon as the liberal-voting Mosher retired. They were correct. Whether the Democratic majorities will continue, however, is another question. Although Carter had an 8-point advantage over Ford in 1976, he lost the district in 1980.

The district's growth is mostly in the more Republican areas. Medina County, once sparsely populated farm land, grew by nearly 40 percent in the 1970s. Carter won only 32 percent there in 1980, although Pease managed to carry it.

## Committees

**Ways and Means** (20th of 23 Democrats)
Public Assistance and Unemployment Compensation; Trade.

## Elections

**1980 General**

| | |
|---|---|
| Don Pease (D ) | 113,439 (64 %) |
| David Armstrong (R ) | 64,296 (36 %) |

**1980 Primary**

| | |
|---|---|
| Don Pease (D ) | 41,632 (69 %) |
| John Ryan (D ) | 7,194 (12 %) |
| Peter Vander Wyden (D ) | 6,697 (11 %) |
| Norbert Dennerll Jr. (D ) | 5,192 (8 %) |

**1978 General**

| | |
|---|---|
| Don Pease (D ) | 80,875 (65 %) |
| Mark Whitfield (R ) | 43,269 (35 %) |

**Previous Winning Percentage**

1976 (66 %)

**District Vote For President**

| | 1980 | | 1976 | | 1972 |
|---|---|---|---|---|---|
| D | 76,045 (39 %) | D | 94,305 (53 %) | D | 68,413 (40 %) |
| R | 98,962 (51 %) | R | 79,357 (45 %) | R | 98,338 (57 %) |
| I | 13,471 (7 %) | | | | |

## Campaign Finance

| | Receipts | Receipts from PACs | Expenditures |
|---|---|---|---|
| **1980** | | | |
| Pease (D ) | $78,740 | $29,071 (37 %) | $5,476 |

| 1978 | | | |
|---|---|---|---|
| Pease (D ) | $46,798 | $20,657 (44 %) | $44,919 |
| Whitfield (R ) | $82,433 | $11,920 (14 %) | $81,502 |

## Voting Studies

| Year | Presidential Support | | Party Unity | | Conservative Coalition | |
|---|---|---|---|---|---|---|
| | S | O | S | O | S | O |
| 1980 | 78 | 19 | 81 | 15 | 17 | 79 |
| 1979 | 83 | 14 | 89 | 10 | 13 | 85 |
| 1978 | 79 | 17 | 76 | 22 | 20 | 77 |
| 1977 | 73 | 25 | 87 | 12 | 17 | 83 |

S = Support    O = Opposition

## Key Votes

**96th Congress**

| | |
|---|---|
| Weaken Carter oil profits tax (1979) | N |
| Reject hospital cost control plan (1979) | N |
| Implement Panama Canal Treaties (1979) | Y |
| Establish Department of Education (1979) | Y |
| Approve Anti-busing Amendment (1979) | N |
| Guarantee Chrysler Corp. loans (1979) | Y |
| Approve military draft registration (1980) | N |
| Aid Sandinista regime in Nicaragua (1980) | Y |
| Strengthen fair housing laws (1980) | Y |

**97th Congress**

| | |
|---|---|
| Reagan budget proposal (1981) | Y |

## Interest Group Ratings

| Year | ADA | ACA | AFL-CIO | CCUS |
|---|---|---|---|---|
| 1980 | 83 | 17 | 68 | 62 |
| 1979 | 84 | 12 | 85 | 11 |
| 1978 | 65 | 15 | 80 | 22 |
| 1977 | 80 | 11 | 78 | 29 |

# 14 John F. Seiberling (D)

**Of Akron — Elected 1970**

**Born:** Sept. 8, 1918, Akron, Ohio.
**Education:** Harvard U., B.A. 1941; Columbia U., LL.B. 1949.
**Military Career:** Army, 1942-46.
**Profession:** Lawyer.
**Family:** Wife, Elizabeth Behr; three children.
**Religion:** Presbyterian.
**Political Career:** President, Tri-County Regional Planning Commission, 1966-68.

**In Washington:** Seiberling is not the most popular member of Congress — he is too liberal for many and too humorless for others — but he has made himself an effective legislator by seizing a limited issue, mastering its details, and mobilizing a constituency behind it.

The issue is public lands, one that affects few districts outside the west and engages few members. Seiberling and his environmentalist allies, who are intensely interested, have been remarkably successful at convincing colleagues that they can help themselves politically at home by voting for a new wilderness area somewhere far away.

The symbol of that strategy is the Alaska lands bill, which as enacted in 1980 set aside some 104.3 million acres of that state for wilderness parks and protected areas. It doubled the nation's park and wildlife refuge systems and tripled its wilderness areas.

As chairman of the Interior Committee's Public Lands Subcommittee, Seiberling managed that legislation through a tortuous three-year struggle. Many of the ultimate decisions were made by Interior Chairman Morris K. Udall, D-Ariz., but Seiberling was the detail man, and maintained a militant environmentalist position that sometimes allowed Udall to sound a slightly more conciliatory note.

The House passed a strict Alaska bill in 1978, setting aside far more Alaska land as wilderness and closing more land to development than the Senate wanted. The two chambers never did reach agreement, however, and the issue returned at the start of the next Congress in 1979.

At that point the Carter administration had intervened on its own to set aside millions of acres of Alaska as wilderness, and Seiberling insisted throughout the second round of the battle that there would be no compromise. But when the Senate again passed a somewhat more development-oriented bill, and the prospect of a Reagan administration frightened the entire environmental movement, Seiberling was willing to accept the Senate bill and call it a day. Even the more militant among his outside coalition went along with him.

While the Alaska issue was being played out, Seiberling won passage of a smaller bill setting aside 2.2 million acres of land in Idaho as the River of No Return Wilderness. It was the same story — Mountain state members opposed the move, but they had no constituency in other areas of the country.

Also on the Interior Committee, Seiberling fought to restrict the power of a proposed Energy Mobilization Board to waive federal, state and local environmental laws. He helped engineer the board's defeat in coalition with other liberal Democrats and anti-government Republicans. Creation of the board had been one of the key components in President Carter's 1979 energy package.

Seiberling has been less conspicuous on the Judiciary Committee, but has established a consistent record as a civil libertarian willing to defend unpopular causes. He was incensed at the FBI's Abscam operation, which he considered entrapment worthy of a police state. Later in 1980, when the Judiciary Committee considered a

---

**14th District: Northeast — Akron.**
Population: 424,452 (9% decrease since 1970).
Race: White 364,955 (86%), Black 55,425 (13%), Others 4,072 (1%). Spanish origin: 2,435 (1%).

new federal criminal code, he tried to amend it to redefine entrapment and focus on the conduct of the law officer. He lost, 12-6. Still, he voted to expel Rep. Michael "Ozzie" Myers, D-Pa., convicted in the Abscam case, because he believed Myers had brought extreme discredit on the House.

The same Seiberling liberalism comes out on the civil rights and antitrust issues considered at Judiciary. He fought a provision in a 1980 housing bill that would have allowed appraisers to consider race and sex in making appraisals. He also worked out a substitute amendment to an antitrust bill limiting the exemptions for soft drink bottlers.

In 1978, Seiberling fought for a limitation on subcommittee assignments for House Democrats. He wanted a limit of four subcommittees, but his proposal was amended to allow Democrats to serve on five subcommittees.

**At Home:** Seiberling's liberalism sets him apart from his ancestors, the "rubber barons" of Akron. Long before his political debut in 1970, he had abandoned the Republican heritage of his grandfather, F. A. Seiberling — founder of both the Goodyear and Seiberling Tire and Rubber companies — and his cousin, Francis Seiberling, who represented the Akron district from 1929 to 1933.

An antitrust lawyer at Goodyear, Seiberling decided to run for office at age 51, challenging a 20-year House veteran, Republican William H. Ayres. Before that he had worked for various liberal candidates and been involved in efforts to block highway and power line projects planned for the scenic Cuyahoga River Valley.

Running on an anti-war, pro-labor, and environmentalist platform, Seiberling stood apart in the five-candidate contest for the 1970 Democratic nomination, a contest that state Sen. William B. Nye expected to win. Seiberling was helped by two unrelated events. Rubber workers went on strike at Goodyear early in the year, and Seiberling solidified his labor credentials by supporting them and refusing to cross the picket line. Later, as the campaign's most outspoken critic of President Nixon's Vietnam policy, he was helped by resentment against the U.S. invasion of Cambodia and the killing of four students at an anti-war protest at Kent State University. The shootings, which occurred the day before the primary, took place less than 15 miles from the district. Seiberling won the primary with 38 percent to Nye's 29 percent.

In the general election against Ayres,

Seiberling continued his attack on Nixon's war policy, which Ayres supported, and on the incumbent's environmental record. Ayres had been placed on the "Dirty Dozen" list of members the environmental movement wanted to defeat.

Ayres stressed his seniority and tried to identify Seiberling with student militants. Veterans for Law and Order, a group supporting Ayres, ran full-page newspaper ads showing Seiberling arm-in-arm with two long-haired students, giving a two-fingered peace salute. The photograph was taken at a University of Akron rally the day of the Kent State shootings.

Seiberling filed a complaint with the Fair Campaign Practices Committee and ran an advertisement using the same picture, explaining that he was "the man who kept the peace at The University of Akron."

The episode gave Seiberling more publicity than any of Ayres's previous opponents had been able to generate. And for the first time in 20 years, the Democrat won the endorsement of the *Akron Beacon-Journal*. Those factors, combined with a strong Democratic turnout for statewide offices, gave Seiberling 56 percent of the vote.

Seiberling has had little to worry about since then. In 1972, the Kent State area was added to his district, increasing its Democratic vote. He does not try to hide his liberalism, saying "we need every liberal we can find." In 1980, his percentage dropped below 70 percent for the first time since his initial victory, but still left him with a plurality of nearly 50,000 votes.

**The District:** The 14th District is in a part of Ohio built out of rubber — and tires in particular. Located within its confines are the corporate headquarters and major plants of the Goodyear, Goodrich, Firestone and General Tire companies. The workers in those plants are bread-and-butter Democrats, and the 14th is one of the most Democratic districts in the state. Only the largely black 21st in Cleveland gave Carter a higher percentage in 1980.

The city of Akron (population 237,000) is the most Democratic part of the district and accounts for about half the vote.

The district is also the home of Kent State University. Counting Kent State and the larger University of Akron, the student population in the district exceeds 40,000.

To the north and south of Akron are suburbs ranging from middle-class ticket-splitting areas to solidly Republican communities. Carter won 57 percent in Akron in 1980, but only 44 percent in its suburbs in Summit County.

## Committees

**Interior and Insular Affairs** (6th of 23 Democrats)
Public Lands and National Parks, chairman; Energy and the Environment; Insular Affairs.

**Judiciary** (6th of 16 Democrats)
Criminal Justice; Monopolies and Commercial Law.

## Elections

**1980 General**

| | |
|---|---|
| John Seiberling (D ) | 103,336 (65 %) |
| Louis Mangels (R ) | 55,962 (35 %) |

**1978 General**

| | |
|---|---|
| John Seiberling (D ) | 82,356 (72 %) |
| Walter Vogel (R ) | 31,311 (28 %) |

**Previous Winning Percentages**

| | | | |
|---|---|---|---|
| 1976 (74 %) | 1974 (75 %) | 1972 (74 %) | 1970 (56 %) |

**District Vote For President**

| | 1980 | | 1976 | | 1972 |
|---|---|---|---|---|---|
| D | 85,712 (51 %) | D | 103,094 (63 %) | D | 100,017 (49 %) |
| R | 68,439 (41 %) | R | 61,168 (37 %) | R | 101,028 (49 %) |
| I | 12,082 (7 %) | | | | |

## Campaign Finance

| | Receipts | Receipts from PACs | Expenditures |
|---|---|---|---|
| **1980** | | | |
| Seiberling (D ) | $31,814 | $12,275 (39 %) | $29,143 |
| Mangels (R ) | $45,171 | $1,000 (2 %) | $40,854 |
| **1978** | | | |
| Seiberling (D ) | $19,325 | $4,650 (24 %) | $20,438 |
| Vogel (R ) | $12,379 | $1,200 (10 %) | $12,352 |

## Voting Studies

| Year | Presidential Support | | Party Unity | | Conservative Coalition | |
|---|---|---|---|---|---|---|
| | S | O | S | O | S | O |
| 1980 | 79 | 19 | 90 | 7 | 6 | 94 |
| 1979 | 83 | 15 | 94 | 4 | 3 | 97 |
| 1978 | 82 | 14 | 88 | 9 | 4 | 95 |
| 1977 | 78 | 14 | 90 | 6 | 3 | 94 |
| 1976 | 25 | 71 | 91 | 7 | 7 | 92 |
| 1975 | 37 | 61 | 89 | 8 | 9 | 86 |
| 1974 (Ford) | 44 | 56 | | | | |
| 1974 | 36 | 60 | 94 | 5 | 5 | 95 |
| 1973 | 25 | 73 | 92 | 8 | 5 | 94 |
| 1972 | 43 | 46 | 84 | 7 | 1 | 94 |
| 1971 | 25 | 68 | 86 | 7 | 4 | 94 |

S = Support          O = Opposition

## Key Votes

**96th Congress**

| | |
|---|---|
| Weaken Carter oil profits tax (1979) | N |
| Reject hospital cost control plan (1979) | N |
| Implement Panama Canal Treaties (1979) | Y |
| Establish Department of Education (1979) | Y |
| Approve Anti-busing Amendment (1979) | N |
| Guarantee Chrysler Corp. loans (1979) | Y |
| Approve military draft registration (1980) | N |
| Aid Sandinista regime in Nicaragua (1980) | Y |
| Strengthen fair housing laws (1980) | Y |

**97th Congress**

| | |
|---|---|
| Reagan budget proposal (1981) | N |

## Interest Group Ratings

| Year | ADA | ACA | AFL-CIO | CCUS |
|---|---|---|---|---|
| 1980 | 100 | 13 | 79 | 70 |
| 1979 | 95 | 0 | 95 | 0 |
| 1978 | 95 | 4 | 84 | 28 |
| 1977 | 95 | 0 | 87 | 13 |
| 1976 | 95 | 4 | 86 | 13 |
| 1975 | 95 | 11 | 91 | 6 |
| 1974 | 96 | 0 | 91 | 0 |
| 1973 | 100 | 7 | 100 | 18 |
| 1972 | 100 | 5 | 100 | 0 |
| 1971 | 89 | 8 | 82 | - |

# 15 Chalmers P. Wylie (R)

**Of Columbus — Elected 1966**

**Born:** Nov. 23, 1920, Norwich, Ohio.
**Education:** Attended Otterbein College, 1939-40; Ohio State U., 1940-43; Harvard U., J.D., 1948.
**Military Career:** Army, 1943-45; Army Reserve, 1945-53. National Guard, 1958-78.
**Profession:** Lawyer.
**Family:** Wife, Marjorie Siebold; two children.
**Religion:** Methodist.
**Political Career:** Columbus City Attorney, 1954-57; Ohio House, 1961-67.

**In Washington:** Wylie represents Ohio business on the House Banking Committee pretty much as it wishes to be represented, following the lead of fellow Ohioan J. William Stanton, the committee's senior GOP member. But he can be independent and stubborn when he seizes on an issue.

In his early years on the committee, he fought to strengthen federal regulation of large one-bank holding companies, which the industry bitterly opposed. Later, he worked for an equal credit opportunity act, banning discrimination in the granting of loans, and a truth-in-leasing bill. He has been a consistent supporter of the National Consumer Cooperative Bank, created in 1978.

Those activities tend to counter the conservative reputation Wylie has gained outside the Banking Committee with his work for tough anti-obscenity laws and a constitutional amendment to return prayer to the public schools. He drew national attention in 1971 when he gathered 218 signatures on a discharge petition to pry his school prayer amendment out of House Judiciary. The issue came to a vote on the House floor, but the 240-162 margin in favor of the amendment fell short of the two-thirds needed.

Wylie embarrassed House Democrats during the 96th Congress with a surprise amendment to abolish existing thermostat controls in public buildings. He argued that the need to maintain temperatures at 65 degrees in winter and 78 in summer was ruining restaurateurs and other small-business men. The amendment passed the House easily but was dropped in conference.

He also amended a 1980 housing bill, written in the Banking Committee, to bar federal funds for middle-income housing in areas having rent control. Rent control, Wylie argued, limited private developers' profits and slowed construction of new rental housing. But the entire middle-income plan was eventually dropped. He began working in 1981 to apply a similar provision to rental housing for the poor, but lost the first round in the Banking Committee.

**At Home:** Bland and affable, Wylie is neither controversial nor celebrated in the area he has represented in the Legislature and in Congress for 20 years. But he is well-liked by the Republican voters and business community of Columbus, and he always wins with large margins.

One reason he is less than a household name is because he seldom has to campaign hard — attention is usually focused on Columbus' other district, the more marginal 12th. In four consecutive elections (1970-76), Wylie faced the same opponent, Columbus architect Manley "Mike" McGee, who campaigned on the need to have someone of his profession in the House. Wylie never received less than 61.5 percent.

Once he finished law school in 1948, Wylie began climbing carefully up the political ladder. He moved from assistant state attorney general to city attorney to state representative and then to Congress, rarely offending anyone and always making sure of his support before stepping up.

In 1964 he had the good fortune to be on the legislative committee that redrew the congressional district lines for the 1966 elections. The plan that emerged included a new district in

---

**15th District: Central — western Columbus and suburbs.** Population: 467,086 (1% increase since 1970). Race: White 404,642 (87%), Black 55,247 (12%), Others 7,197 (2%). Spanish origin: 3,495 (1%).

Columbus which had no incumbent, but included most of Wylie's legislative district. With the blessing of the county GOP chairman, Wylie ran and was easily elected.

**The District:** Of the two districts which divide Columbus, the western 15th is more Republican. Although it includes most of the student community at Ohio State, the vote there is offset by the solid Republican areas in northern Columbus and the suburbs west of the Olentangy and Scioto rivers. Upper Arlington, the most affluent suburb, gave Reagan 74 percent in 1980.

Apart from the university vote, the only other pocket of Democratic strength in the district is on the near west side of Columbus, populated by lower-income, Appalachian whites.

## Committees

**Banking, Finance and Urban Affairs** (2nd of 19 Republicans)
Consumer Affairs and Coinage; Financial Institutions Supervision, Regulation and Insurance; Housing and Community Development.

**Veterans' Affairs** (3rd of 14 Republicans)
Compensation, Pension and Insurance; Education, Training and Employment.

**Joint Economic**
Investment, Jobs and Prices; Monetary and Fiscal Policy.

## Elections

**1980 General**

| | |
|---|---|
| Chalmers Wylie (R) | 129,025 (73 %) |
| Terry Freeman (D ) | 48,708 (27 %) |

**1978 General**

| | |
|---|---|
| Chalmers Wylie (R ) | 91,023 (71 %) |
| Henry Eckhart (D ) | 37,000 (29 %) |

**Previous Winning Percentages**

| | | | |
|---|---|---|---|
| 1976 (66 %) | 1974 (62 %) | 1972 (66 %) | 1970 (71 %) |
| 1968 (73 %) | 1966 (60 %) | | |

**District Vote For President**

| | 1980 | | 1976 | | 1972 |
|---|---|---|---|---|---|
| D | 68,552 (37 %) | D | 69,123 (40 %) | D | 65,515 (35 %) |
| R | 102,639 (55 %) | R | 99,481 (57 %) | R | 119,954 (63 %) |
| I | 11,836 (6 %) | | | | |

## Campaign Finance

| | Receipts | Receipts from PACs | Expenditures |
|---|---|---|---|
| **1980** | | | |
| Wylie (R ) | $94,103 | $44,060 (47 %) | $93,073 |
| **1978** | | | |
| Wylie (R ) | $95,113 | $33,503 (35 %) | $87,741 |

## Voting Studies

| | Presidential Support | | Party Unity | | Conservative Coalition | |
|---|---|---|---|---|---|---|
| Year | S | O | S | O | S | O |
| 1980 | 46 | 47 | 76 | 21 | 74 | 21 |
| 1979 | 34 | 58 | 73 | 20 | 80 | 13 |
| 1978 | 47 | 48 | 72 | 23 | 70 | 26 |
| 1977 | 56 | 44 | 69 | 30 | 69 | 29 |
| 1976 | 69 | 20 | 70 | 19 | 67 | 18 |
| 1975 | 64 | 31 | 79 | 13 | 81 | 11 |
| 1974 (Ford) | 44 | 52 | | | | |
| 1974 | 64 | 28 | 68 | 22 | 65 | 20 |
| 1973 | 75 | 22 | 81 | 17 | 80 | 17 |
| 1972 | 70 | 22 | 82 | 11 | 82 | 12 |
| 1971 | 75 | 19 | 83 | 12 | 82 | 10 |
| 1970 | 72 | 25 | 86 | 8 | 80 | 14 |
| 1969 | 60 | 36 | 73 | 15 | 89 | 4 |
| 1968 | 57 | 37 | 78 | 12 | 80 | 14 |
| 1967 | 50 | 50 | 89 | 10 | 96 | 4 |

S = Support        O = Opposition

## Key Votes

**96th Congress**

| | |
|---|---|
| Weaken Carter oil profits tax (1979) | Y |
| Reject hospital cost control plan (1979) | N |
| Implement Panama Canal Treaties (1979) | N |
| Establish Department of Education (1979) | N |
| Approve Anti-busing Amendment (1979) | Y |
| Guarantee Chrysler Corp. loans (1979) | Y |
| Approve military draft registration (1980) | N |
| Aid Sandinista regime in Nicaragua (1980) | N |
| Strengthen fair housing laws (1980) | N |

**97th Congress**

| | |
|---|---|
| Reagan budget proposal (1981) | Y |

## Interest Group Ratings

| Year | ADA | ACA | AFL-CIO | CCUS |
|---|---|---|---|---|
| 1980 | 28 | 65 | 32 | 75 |
| 1979 | 21 | 83 | 32 | 76 |
| 1978 | 25 | 65 | 30 | 72 |
| 1977 | 35 | 56 | 27 | 82 |
| 1976 | 10 | 76 | 27 | 78 |
| 1975 | 21 | 85 | 23 | 88 |
| 1974 | 22 | 58 | 0 | 88 |
| 1973 | 24 | 74 | 27 | 91 |
| 1972 | 6 | 83 | 18 | 80 |
| 1971 | 11 | 89 | 8 | - |
| 1970 | 24 | 89 | 0 | 89 |
| 1969 | 7 | 73 | 40 | - |
| 1968 | 8 | 90 | 25 | - |
| 1967 | 7 | 93 | 8 | 100 |

**965**

# 16 Ralph Regula (R)

**Of Navarre — Elected 1972**

**Born:** Dec. 3, 1924, Beach City, Ohio.
**Education:** Mount Union College, B.A. 1948; William McKinley School of Law, LL.B. 1952.
**Military Career:** Navy, 1944-46.
**Profession:** Lawyer.
**Family:** Wife, Mary Rogusky; three children.
**Religion:** Episcopalian.
**Political Career:** Ohio House, 1965-67; Ohio Senate, 1967-73.

**In Washington:** Regula likes to work in a bipartisan setting, but he has found it hard to do that on the House Budget Committee, where the two sides traditionally line up against each other in pure partisan hostility.

In 1981, he at least found himself on the winning side, as the full House reversed the Budget Committee's Democratic leadership and endorsed the low-spending, tax-cut budget favored by President Reagan. Regula, although not viewed as a tax cut enthusiast in past years, was solidly behind the Reagan alternative both in committee and on the floor.

In earlier terms, Regula had often been the one to present the "official" Republican floor substitute for the majority budget. He never won; his closest call came in 1979, when he drew 198 votes. But Democrats always found a way to defeat him.

After his substitutes were beaten, however, and a compromise worked out in conference between House and Senate, he often urged Republicans to accept what the majority offered as a reasonable package. He always failed.

Regula worked well with Robert N. Giaimo of Connecticut, the Democrat who chaired the Budget Committee until 1981. In the 96th Congress, he and Giaimo collaborated on a proposal to establish a fixed limit on federal spending as a percentage of gross national product.

When Regula and Maryland's Marjorie Holt voted with Giaimo on a budget conference report in 1977, they became the first Republicans in the committee's history to support a Democratic budget resolution. In 1980, Regula preached cooperation throughout months of tortuous budget negotiations, but only 10 Republicans ended up supporting the year's first resolution when it was brought back from conference to the House floor. Regula was one of the 10.

Regula's style is more suited to the Appropriations Committee, his other assignment, where bipartisanship is a longstanding tradition.

On the Military Construction Subcommittee, he has continually pressed for higher contributions from America's allies in Europe toward maintenance of U.S. facilities there. In 1979, when the Pentagon wanted $57 million to build depots in Europe large enough to store supplies for a full American division, he complained that "It's their real estate, why don't the countries that are being defended feel the same urgency that we do?"

On the Interior Subcommittee, Regula has generally built a record sensitive to environmental concerns. He has sometimes been a critic of high funding levels for the National Endowment for the Arts, which that panel also deals with. At the full committee level, he has crusaded against excessive use of private consultants by federal agencies. He introduced an amendment to most of the 1981 appropriation bills requiring that contracts with consultants be open for public inspection.

One of Regula's more minor but more consistent crusades is for federal recognition of President William McKinley, his hometown's most famous product. He observes McKinley's birthday in January by passing out red carnations to his colleagues; he once persuaded the Interior Subcommittee to adopt an amendment making it illegal to rename Mount McKinley in Alaska.

---

**16th District: Northeast — Canton.**
Population: 481,871 (4% increase since 1970). Race: White 453,405 (94%), Black 25,358 (5%), Others 3,108 (1%). Spanish origin: 3,864 (1%).

---

**At Home:** Regula's re-election is as sure a thing as there is in Ohio politics. His 79 percent in 1980 made him the leading vote-getter in the congressional delegation, and marked the fourth straight time he had increased his margin.

Regula came to the House after eight years in the state Legislature, where he specialized in writing conservation bills. His state Senate constituency included a large part of Stark County, the heart of the 16th District, and when Republican Rep. Frank T. Bow retired in 1972 after 22 years in Congress, Regula won Bow's endorsement. Redistricting that year removed part of Democratic Mahoning County from the district, making it more Republican. Regula defeated Democrat Virgil Musser, who had been Bow's last opponent, with 57 percent of the vote.

**The District:** Although it has undergone a variety of changes, the 16th District has always been centered on Stark County and the city of Canton, with its industrial neighbor of Massillon a few miles away. Although it is a working-class city like Akron and Youngstown, Canton does not share in the solidly Democratic tradition of the rest of northeastern Ohio. That is partly because of the conservative mentality brought to the community by the anti-union, family-run Timken Co. — a steel and roller bearing firm that is the district's major employer. Republic Steel is also an important presence.

Canton itself has gone Democratic on occasion, but the suburbs in surrounding Stark County are solidly Republican. Since 1920, the only Democratic presidential candidates to carry the county — which accounts for 80 percent of the district — have been F.D.R. and Lyndon Johnson.

## Committees

**Appropriations** (10th of 22 Republicans)
Interior; Military Construction.

**Budget**
Task Forces: Enforcement, Credit and Multi-year Budgeting; Human Resources and Block Grants; Reconciliation.

**Select Aging** (5th of 23 Republicans)
Health and Long-Term Care.

## Elections

**1980 General**

| | |
|---|---|
| Ralph Regula (R ) | 149,960 (79 %) |
| Larry Slagle (D ) | 39,219 (21 %) |

**1978 General**

| | |
|---|---|
| Ralph Regula (R ) | 105,152 (78 %) |
| Owen Hand (D ) | 29,690 (22 %) |

**Previous Winning Percentages**

| | | |
|---|---|---|
| 1976 (67 %) | 1974 (66 %) | 1972 (57 %) |

**District Vote For President**

| | 1980 | | 1976 | | 1972 |
|---|---|---|---|---|---|
| D | 71,727 (37 %) | D | 83,776 (47 %) | D | 61,241 (34 %) |
| R | 107,794 (56 %) | R | 90,463 (51 %) | R | 113,569 (64 %) |
| I | 10,425 (5 %) | | | | |

## Campaign Finance

| | Receipts | Receipts from PACs | Expenditures |
|---|---|---|---|
| **1980** | | | |
| Regula (R ) | $14,633 | $2,000 (14 %) | $23,914 |
| Slagle (D ) | $3,605 | $2,817 (78 %) | $6,128 |
| **1978** | | | |
| Regula (R ) | $75,720 | — (0 %) | $55,300 |
| Hand (D ) | $5,375 | $1,000 (19%) | $5,309 |

## Voting Studies

| | Presidential Support | | Party Unity | | Conservative Coalition | |
|---|---|---|---|---|---|---|
| Year | S | O | S | O | S | O |
| 1980 | 49 | 49 | 77 | 23 | 84 | 14 |
| 1979 | 35 | 64 | 85 | 15 | 89 | 11 |
| 1978 | 46 | 54 | 77 | 23 | 82 | 18 |
| 1977 | 52 | 48 | 79 | 21 | 88 | 12 |
| 1976 | 71 | 25 | 71 | 27 | 77 | 21 |
| 1975 | 71 | 29 | 76 | 24† | 79 | 21† |
| 1974 (Ford) | 68 | 30 | | | | |
| 1974 | 57 | 41 | 58 | 40 | 60 | 38 |
| 1973 | 68 | 30 | 70 | 24 | 68 | 22 |

† Not eligible for all recorded votes.

S = Support    O = Opposition

## Key Votes

**96th Congress**

| | |
|---|---|
| Weaken Carter oil profits tax (1979) | Y |
| Reject hospital cost control plan (1979) | Y |
| Implement Panama Canal Treaties (1979) | N |
| Establish Department of Education (1979) | N |
| Approve Anti-busing Amendment (1979) | Y |
| Guarantee Chrysler Corp. loans (1979) | N |
| Approve military draft registration (1980) | Y |
| Aid Sandinista regime in Nicaragua (1980) | N |
| Strengthen fair housing laws (1980) | N |

**97th Congress**

| | |
|---|---|
| Reagan budget proposal (1981) | Y |

## Interest Group Ratings

| Year | ADA | ACA | AFL-CIO | CCUS |
|---|---|---|---|---|
| 1980 | 28 | 63 | 21 | 70 |
| 1979 | 21 | 73 | 25 | 83 |
| 1978 | 20 | 63 | 25 | 72 |
| 1977 | 15 | 74 | 43 | 88 |
| 1976 | 10 | 54 | 30 | 69 |
| 1975 | 21 | 64 | 35 | 71 |
| 1974 | 35 | 40 | 27 | 44 |
| 1973 | 28 | 68 | 18 | 70 |

# 17 John M. Ashbrook (R)

**Of Johnstown — Elected 1960**

**Born:** Sept. 21, 1928, Johnstown, Ohio.
**Education:** Harvard U., A.B. 1952; Ohio State U., J.D. 1955.
**Military Career:** Navy, 1946-48.
**Profession:** Lawyer, newspaper publisher.
**Family:** Wife, Jean Spencer; three children.
**Religion:** Baptist.
**Political Career:** Ohio Assembly, 1957-61.

**In Washington:** "I have never felt I had to go along with anything," Ashbrook once said, "and getting along is not important to me." He has often proved it. One of the most militant and dedicated conservatives in the House for more than 20 years, Ashbrook has placed principle not only above party, but sometimes above influence. A favorite of the readers of *Human Events* and the *National Review*, Ashbrook has always been a gadfly in the House and a maverick in the GOP. In 1972, when fellow-Rep. Paul N. McCloskey Jr. was challenging President Nixon from the left, Ashbrook was running against him from the right, complaining about Nixon's welfare proposals and moves toward detente.

His rhetoric is incendiary, and sometimes overshadows his concrete suggestions for change. He called Martin Luther King Jr. "blatantly anti-American." He said four students killed at Kent State in 1970 were "duped, stupid, foolish, unfortunate, cynical or dedicated revolutionaries," and labeled a peace group "a Trotskyist Communist organization that stands for the violent overthrow of the U.S. government."

In personal situations, Ashbrook has a boyish Midwestern charm and personal modesty that often surprises those who have heard him only in public. And as senior Republican on the Education and Labor Committee, he has worked well with the panel's Democrats on several important issues. But it is those speeches on the floor that define his reputation for most colleagues. For years, he has spent most of his time there, watching the Democrats and trying to obstruct them. Over the years, Ashbrook has harassed the majority hundreds of times with amendments, quorum calls and points of order.

"Members are constantly complaining to me when I delay a bill on a Friday afternoon and they're trying to catch a plane back to the district," he once said. "I'm sure I'm not very popular among the members and their staff, but who gives a damn."

In recent years, Ashbrook's obstructionism has not seemed as futile as it did through much of the 1960s and 1970s. Junior Republicans began to practice their own forms of guerrilla warfare on the floor, and Ashbrook's anti-government approach no longer seemed outside the national consensus.

Some Ashbrook amendments, offered in earlier years as gestures to principle, have had the votes to pass. When the House debated President Carter's proposal for a new department of education, Ashbrook managed to amend the bill to prevent the department from making rules on busing, bilingual education or sex discrimination. These changes were dropped in conference; if they had not been, the conference report would never have been approved. Ashbrook was opposed to the new department in any case.

Meanwhile, he was fighting President Carter's efforts to improve relations with mainland China and drop the U.S. alliance with Taiwan. He offered a floor amendment calling for a statement of continued "defense" relations between the United States and Taiwan, but it was defeated.

It was Nixon's visit to China in early 1972 that made Ashbrook angry enough to challenge him in three presidential primaries. He called the action a "sellout" and said Nixon had betrayed conservatives. Ashbrook did not reach 10 percent

---

**17th District: Central — Mansfield, Newark.** Population: 498,916 (8% increase since 1970). Race: White 482,817 (97%), Black 13,236 (3%), Others 2,863 (1%). Spanish origin: 3,150 (1%).

of the vote in any primary, but he won the lasting gratitude of much of the right.

Later, Ashbrook was relatively prompt in urging Nixon to resign because of Watergate. "We kept saying the other shoe had to drop soon," Ashbrook said at one point during the Watergate disclosures. "But we now find out the President is a centipede. There's a shoe a week." Ashbrook said the whole affair might not have taken place if other conservatives had joined him sooner "in criticizing the president's isolation."

Ashbrook's most emotional issue has always been domestic security. He was the senior Republican on the old Internal Security Committee before it was abolished in 1975, and would like to see the committee revived. He still believes wholeheartedly that there is a problem of domestic subversion and that the federal government should have broad powers in dealing with it. He took a seat on the Judiciary Committee when it assumed general jurisdiction over the issue, and has lobbied the committee unsuccessfully to pay more attention to it. He is also one of the committee's loudest critics of gun control; he is on the board of the National Rifle Association.

Ashbrook has spent his entire career on the Education and Labor Committee, baiting union leaders and opposing labor-backed bills.

But he is not always the militant obstructionist on the committee that he has been on the floor. He was a close personal friend of New Jersey Democrat Frank Thompson, who was the committee's dominant labor legislator until his defeat in 1980, and often cooperated with Thompson quietly. In 1979, Ashbrook surprised many colleagues by supporting Thompson's bill to allow interns and residents in hospitals to form unions. The bill was defeated on the floor after five of the committee's junior Republicans ignored Ashbrook and launched their own campaign against the bill.

During the same year, Ashbrook worked alongside Democrats in drafting a bill rewriting federal aid to higher education, despite warnings that it could add more than a billion dollars a year in new spending. "I'm hanging my hat on the hope it won't be as expensive as they say," Ashbrook explained as the bill passed the House.

**At Home:** Eleven campaigns after he began running for Congress, Ashbrook seemed finally to have his district locked up in 1980 — just as he started planning to run for the Senate in 1982.

His devotion to conservative ideology and national right-wing politics has not always helped him win re-election, and his occasional forays against the Ohio GOP establishment have caused some hard feelings at the state level. He has not

been on close terms with Gov. James Rhodes since he challenged a national convention slate pledged to Rhodes in 1968.

But in his recent campaigns, Ashbrook managed to put most of that controversy behind him. His share of the vote, which dipped down to a dangerous 52.7 percent in 1974, rose in 1980 to 73 percent — more than any candidate in the district in this century.

Ashbrook was born into politics and newspaper publishing. His father, William A. Ashbrook, founded the weekly *Johnstown Independent* in 1884 as a political springboard. A conservative Democrat and follower of Grover Cleveland, he served in the House from 1906 until his defeat in 1920. He fathered John at age 61, and six years later returned to the House. Although an arch-foe of Franklin D. Roosevelt, the elder Ashbrook remained a Democrat until his death in 1940.

Young John's first taste of conservative philosophy came from his father. But it was not until he reached Harvard that he was steered toward the Republican Party. He became friendly with classmates William Rusher, later the publisher of *National Review*, and F. Clifton White, Barry Goldwater's 1964 strategist.

As a two-term state legislator challenging Democratic Rep. Robert Levering in 1960, Ashbrook took the hard conservative line that has been his trademark ever since. Citing communism as the foremost evil, he opposed all efforts to weaken the House Un-American Activities Committee and supported loyalty oaths for students receiving federal college loans. He defeated Levering in 1960 and three more times after that.

In 1966, redistricting threw Ashbrook together with Democratic Rep. Robert T. Secrest, who had demonstrated his ability to capture Republican votes by defeating Republican incumbents in 1932, 1948 and 1962. But it was an excellent Republican year in Ohio, and with Rhodes running far ahead at the top of the ticket, Ashbrook put an end to Secrest's House career by a solid 14,000 votes.

Since then, Ashbrook has had two difficult contests. In 1974, an underfinanced and nearly unknown Democrat, David Noble, won 47 percent against him. Two years later, he drew a more sophisticated challenge from John C. McDonald, former minority leader in the Ohio House, who felt Noble had uncovered serious weaknesses in Ashbrook's support. But the strong Democratic vote in 1974 turned out to be primarily an adverse reaction to Watergate. Ashbrook had little trouble defeating McDonald.

**The District:** Since the death of William Ashbrook in 1940, Democrats have won here only once. In 1972, the district moved slightly to the west, picking up the Democratic city of Mansfield and losing Republican Wayne and Stark counties. That made little difference, however; the district still supports Republicans loyally in statewide contests. In 1974, Rhodes won 60 percent in the district — his best in the state.

Agriculture is the mainstay of the economy, although some light industry is located in Republican-oriented small towns.

## Committees

**Education and Labor** (Ranking Republican)
Labor-Management Relations.

**Judiciary** (6th of 12 Republicans)
Crime.

**Select Intelligence** (2nd of 5 Republicans)
Legislation; Oversight and Evaluation.

## Elections

**1980 General**

| | |
|---|---|
| John Ashbrook (R ) | 128,870 (73 %) |
| Donald Yunker (D ) | 47,900 (27 %) |

**1978 General**

| | |
|---|---|
| John Ashbrook (R ) | 87,010 (67 %) |
| Kenneth Grier (D ) | 42,117 (33 %) |

**Previous Winning Percentages**

| | | | |
|---|---|---|---|
| 1976 (57 %) | 1974 (53 %) | 1972 (57 %) | 1970 (62 %) |
| 1968 (65 %) | 1966 (55 %) | 1964 (52 %) | 1962 (59 %) |
| 1960 (53 %) | | | |

**District Vote For President**

| | 1980 | | 1976 | | 1972 |
|---|---|---|---|---|---|
| D | 64,651 (34 %) | D | 78,033 (44 %) | D | 50,401 (30 %) |
| R | 111,025 (59 %) | R | 92,348 (53 %) | R | 114,778 (67 %) |
| I | 9,693 (5 %) | | | | |

## Campaign Finance

| | Receipts | Receipts from PACs | Expenditures |
|---|---|---|---|
| **1980** | | | |
| Ashbrook (R ) | $150,055 | $40,675 (27 %) | $167,081 |
| Yunker (D ) | $1,697 | — (0 %) | $1,877 |
| **1978** | | | |
| Ashbrook (R ) | $180,957 | $40,918 (23 %) | $158,543 |

## Voting Studies

| | Presidential Support | | Party Unity | | Conservative Coalition | |
|---|---|---|---|---|---|---|
| Year | S | O | S | O | S | O |
| 1980 | 24 | 62 | 77 | 7 | 77 | 4 |
| 1979 | 19 | 75 | 83 | 5 | 88 | 4 |
| 1978 | 16 | 73 | 79 | 7 | 81 | 4 |
| 1977 | 29 | 66 | 89 | 5 | 88 | 6 |
| 1976 | 69 | 20 | 86 | 6 | 90 | 4 |
| 1975 | 58 | 40 | 85 | 8 | 91 | 5 |
| 1974 (Ford) | 55 | 36 | | | | |
| 1974 | 43 | 43 | 76 | 11 | 76 | 16 |
| 1973 | 55 | 36 | 67 | 11 | 69 | 11 |
| 1972 | 35 | 51 | 66 | 15 | 73 | 11 |
| 1971 | 63 | 23 | 74 | 12 | 83 | 6 |
| 1970 | 49 | 40 | 72 | 11 | 59 | 11 |
| 1969 | 34 | 43 | 65 | 11 | 69 | 11 |
| 1968 | 23 | 57 | 74 | 1 | 75 | 4 |
| 1967 | 28 | 57 | 88 | 1 | 94 | 2 |
| 1966 | 25 | 63 | 85 | 3 | 81 | 0 |
| 1965 | 26 | 58 | 75 | 3 | 75 | 0 |
| 1964 | 15 | 79 | 94 | 0 | 83 | 0 |
| 1963 | 8 | 86 | 95 | 0 | 73 | 7 |
| 1962 | 17 | 82 | 96 | 2 | 100 | 0 |
| 1961 | 18 | 82 | 91 | 5 | 100 | 0 |

S = Support    O = Opposition

## Key Votes

**96th Congress**

| | |
|---|---|
| Weaken Carter oil profits tax (1979) | Y |
| Reject hospital cost control plan (1979) | Y |
| Implement Panama Canal Treaties (1979) | N |
| Establish Department of Education (1979) | N |
| Approve Anti-busing Amendment (1979) | Y |
| Guarantee Chrysler Corp. loans (1979) | N |
| Approve military draft registration (1980) | Y |
| Aid Sandinista regime in Nicaragua (1980) | N |
| Strengthen fair housing laws (1980) | N |

**97th Congress**

| | |
|---|---|
| Reagan budget proposal (1981) | Y |

## Interest Group Ratings

| Year | ADA | ACA | AFL-CIO | CCUS |
|---|---|---|---|---|
| 1980 | 6 | 91 | 11 | 69 |
| 1979 | 5 | 100 | 15 | 94 |
| 1978 | 5 | 100 | 11 | 93 |
| 1977 | 15 | 96 | 13 | 94 |
| 1976 | 5 | 93 | 14 | 94 |
| 1975 | 5 | 89 | 4 | 94 |
| 1974 | 22 | 93 | 9 | 90 |
| 1973 | 12 | 95 | 20 | 91 |
| 1972 | 6 | 100 | 10 | 100 |
| 1971 | 8 | 93 | 10 | - |
| 1970 | 4 | 93 | 29 | 89 |
| 1969 | 13 | 100 | 20 | - |
| 1968 | 0 | 100 | 0 | - |
| 1967 | 7 | 100 | 9 | 100 |
| 1966 | 0 | 96 | 0 | - |
| 1965 | 0 | 92 | - | 100 |
| 1964 | 0 | 100 | 0 | - |
| 1963 | - | - | - | - |
| 1962 | - | 100 | 0 | - |
| 1961 | 0 | - | - | - |

# 18 Douglas Applegate (D)

**Of Steubenville — Elected 1976**

**Born:** March 27, 1928, Steubenville, Ohio.
**Education:** Steubenville H.S., graduated 1947.
**Profession:** Real estate agent.
**Family:** Wife, Betty Jean Engstrom; two children.
**Religion:** Presbyterian.
**Political Career:** Ohio House of Representatives, 1961-69; Ohio Senate, 1969-77.

**In Washington:** Successor to Wayne Hays, the fallen dictator of the House Administration Committee, Applegate is as bland as Hays was flamboyant, and as preoccupied with district issues as Hays was with the politics of the House.

Applegate has matched his predecessor's conservative voting record on most social and economic issues, and generally gone beyond it. During the dramatic week in 1979 when Speaker O'Neill was beaten on four crucial votes (the 1980 budget, an increase in the national debt ceiling, a congressional pay raise and implementation of the Panama Canal treaties) Applegate was one of a handful of Democrats to vote against him on all four. For the full 1979 year, Applegate opposed a Democratic majority in the House 60 percent of the time — more than all but one other Northern Democrat. In 1980, his opposition score was 55.

Some of Applegate's conservative economics ties in with his loyalty to the steel and coal industries, part of northeast Ohio's declining economic base. He is often a spokesman for the Ohio Steel Group, a coalition of business leaders, and a bitter critic of the national environmental movement.

Applegate sponsored legislation to delay the effective date of state requirements under the Clean Air Act. He has said that the recovery of Ohio's coal production has been held back by "overzealous environmentalists through the government bureaucracy," and has attacked "special interest groups with vast powers of influence," numbering among them the Sierra Club, the Friends of the Earth, the Solar Lobby, and the Wilderness Society.

Applegate is a strong supporter of synthetic fuels development, and badly wanted an Energy Mobilization Board to cut through environmental restrictions in development of new energy sources. He issued an angry statement after the mobilization board was defeated in 1980.

**At Home:** During much of his career in the state Legislature, Applegate was quietly planning a campaign to succeed Hays, once the redoubtable Democrat retired. Few thought that would come in 1976. But when allegations were published that Hays had kept Elizabeth Ray on the House Administration payroll solely to provide him with sex, the veteran congressman quit his campaign for a 15th term less than three months before the election. Three weeks later Hays resigned from the House to avoid an ethics committee investigation.

Because the primary had already been held, the Democratic nominee was selected by local party leaders. Applegate represented about half the district in the state Senate and was already gearing up a campaign for a third term, so he was the logical candidate to replace Hays, to whom he had been close.

Hays's resignation effectively removed him from the campaign as an issue, and Applegate had little trouble defeating both the Republican candidate and William Crabbe, the Democratic mayor of Steubenville, who earlier had launched an independent campaign aimed directly at Hays.

The first opportunity other Democrats had at this solidly Democratic district came two years later in the primary. But by then Applegate had a firm hold on the seat. Against three challengers, he took 82 percent of the Democratic primary vote. (The same day, Hays began a short-lived

---

**18th District: East — Steubenville.**
Population: 484,505 (5% increase since 1970). Race: White 474,484 (98%), Black 9,933 (2%), Others 2,088 (0.4%). Spanish origin: 1,838 (0.3%).

comeback by winning the Democratic nomination to a state House seat. After serving one term he was defeated for re-election in 1980 by a Republican.)

By 1980, Applegate had silenced all primary opposition, including Hays, who was openly thinking about trying to run for the House again. In the general election, he carried every county by a 2-to-1 margin, including the two — Tuscarawas and Noble — that he lost in 1978.

**The District:** Coal and steel give the 18th District its polluted air, its dirty rivers, its economic livelihood and its Democratic votes.

Cramped along the steep banks of the Ohio River, Steubenville — the district's largest city — has long had some of the nation's foulest atmosphere. But jobs in the smoke-belching plants along a 50-mile stretch of the Ohio take priority over the air — a fact that successful politicians quickly learn.

Although the steelworking and coal-mining Democrats of the district show strong party allegiance, they tend to shy away from liberals. In 1972 George McGovern was trounced in the district. In 1974, candidates favoring the tough strip-mining and pollution control policies of the Gilligan gubernatorial administration were outvoted by those backing Republican Gov. James A. Rhodes's "jobs and progress" platform. Jimmy Carter, who carried the district in 1976, lost it narrowly in 1980 to Ronald Reagan, who campaigned in Steubenville on the promise to end burdensome environmental regulations.

As one moves west from the Ohio River the district becomes less Democratic. Conservative Amish communities are scattered throughout Tuscarawas and Guernsey counties. As the land flattens out, the tractors of Republican farmers replace the giant shovels of Democratic coal-miners.

## Committees

**Public Works and Transportation** (17th of 25 Democrats)
Aviation; Economic Development; Surface Transportation.

**Veterans' Affairs** (8th of 17 Democrats)
Compensation, Pension and Insurance; Hospitals and Health Care.

## Elections

**1980 General**

| | |
|---|---|
| Douglas Applegate (D ) | 134,835 (76 %) |
| Gary Hammersley (R ) | 42,354 (24 %) |

**1978 General**

| | |
|---|---|
| Douglas Applegate (D ) | 71,894 (60 %) |
| Bill Ress (R ) | 48,931 (40 %) |

**Previous Winning Percentages**

1976 (63%)

**District Vote For President**

| | 1980 | | 1976 | | 1972 |
|---|---|---|---|---|---|
| D | 82,721 (45 %) | D | 106,608 (54 %) | D | 72,402 (39 %) |
| R | 88,808 (48 %) | R | 86,716 (44 %) | R | 111,452 (60 %) |
| I | 9,102 (5 %) | | | | |

## Campaign Finance

| | Receipts | Receipts from PACs | Expenditures |
|---|---|---|---|
| **1980** | | | |
| Applegate (D ) | $62,970 | $42,065 (67 %) | $44,493 |
| Hammersley (R ) | $24,025 | $500 (2 %) | $24,013 |

| 1978 | | | |
|---|---|---|---|
| Applegate (D ) | $74,214 | $31,320 (42 %) | $75,802 |
| Ress (R ) | $69,294 | $6,100 (9 %) | $69,217 |

## Voting Studies

| | Presidential Support | | Party Unity | | Conservative Coalition | |
|---|---|---|---|---|---|---|
| Year | S | O | S | O | S | O |
| 1980 | 45 | 50 | 37 | 55 | 73 | 22 |
| 1979 | 30 | 63 | 34 | 60 | 69 | 24 |
| 1978 | 46 | 46 | 54 | 40 | 57 | 37 |
| 1977 | 67 | 32 | 68 | 27 | 45 | 52 |

S = Support          O = Opposition

## Key Votes

**96th Congress**

| | |
|---|---|
| Weaken Carter oil profits tax (1979) | N |
| Reject hospital cost control plan (1979) | Y |
| Implement Panama Canal Treaties (1979) | N |
| Establish Department of Education (1979) | N |
| Approve Anti-busing Amendment (1979) | Y |
| Guarantee Chrysler Corp. loans (1979) | Y |
| Approve military draft registration (1980) | N |
| Aid Sandinista regime in Nicaragua (1980) | N |
| Strengthen fair housing laws (1980) | N |

**97th Congress**

| | |
|---|---|
| Reagan budget proposal (1981) | N |

## Interest Group Ratings

| Year | ADA | ACA | AFL-CIO | CCUS |
|---|---|---|---|---|
| 1980 | 22 | 54 | 63 | 59 |
| 1979 | 11 | 60 | 70 | 50 |
| 1978 | 20 | 46 | 55 | 50 |
| 1977 | 30 | 37 | 91 | 35 |

# 19 Lyle Williams (R)

**Of Lordstown - Elected 1978**

**Born:** Aug. 23, 1942, Philippi, W. Va.
**Education:** Molar Barber College, 1962.
**Military Career:** Army, 1960-61.
**Profession:** Barber.
**Family:** Wife, Nancie Peterson; four children.
**Religion:** Church of Christ.
**Political Career:** North Bloomfield School Board, 1970-72; Trumbull County Board of Commissioners, 1972-79.

**In Washington:** Williams has made exactly the moves any Republican has to make to hold a blue-collar constituency like his, and he has made them with sufficient skill to erase the initial perception of him as a political fluke.

He based his 1978 campaign on a promise to bring new jobs to his district, but he seemed to realize that his survival depended less on literal fulfillment of the promise than on whether he seemed to be trying. And he has always seemed to be trying something.

In his first two years, Williams had the benefit of a Democratic administration in Washington that could be held responsible for the situation. Youngstown's job hemmorhage reached epidemic levels in 1980 with massive U.S. Steel closings, but Williams was able to lead the protest and present himself as a critic of national economic policies. He joined in a federal court suit, ultimately unsuccessful, to prevent U.S. Steel from moving out.

Williams scored a major political victory on the floor of the House in 1980 by winning adoption of his amendment to an anti-recession aid bill.

The amendment involved the formula according to which the aid is distributed. Williams proposed a change to award extra money for recent increases in unemployment due to plant closings, rather than using a strict five-year average. He said something drastic had to be done to avoid tragedy in the industrial Midwest. "When the national economy begins to recover," Williams told the House, "Youngstown and her sister steel cities will be left behind as literally thousands of jobs will have disappeared forever."

The amendment was accepted by both parties and passed on a voice vote. But the legislation to which it was attached never became law.

As a member of the Government Operations Committee, Williams also found himself in a sensitive position on President Carter's proposal to create a new Department of Education. The AFL-CIO lobbied Williams against the department; the National Education Association and some of his local school boards lobbied him equally hard for it. In the end, he voted yes. The bill survived in committee by one vote, and the agency was eventually created.

**At Home:** Williams made it to Congress essentially by being in the right place at the right time. Democratic Rep. Charles J. Carney had barely won a fourth term in 1976 and appeared even more vulnerable in 1978. A former state legislator and union official, he was widely perceived as little more than an "errand boy" for organized labor, and not a very effective one at that.

As steel plants were closing in Youngstown, leaving thousands jobless, newspaper stories accused Carney of spending his time collecting more than 60,000 free surplus books from the Library of Congress, rather than fighting to keep the plants open.

In 1978 Williams was in the middle of his second four-year term on the Trumbull County Commission. He was endorsed for Congress by the 1976 GOP nominee, who chose not to run again, and coasted to an easy victory in a primary which attracted fewer than 20,000 voters. Meanwhile, Carney was renominated by 76 votes, largely because the strongest local Democrat, state Rep.

---

**19th District: Northeast — Youngstown, Warren.** Population: 449,145 (3% increase since 1970). Race: White 389,854 (87%), Black 54,198 (12%), Others 5,092 (1%). Spanish origin: 6,421 (1%).

Harry Meshel, chose to delay his candidacy until 1980.

When the inept Carney was renominated, national Republicans poured money into Williams' campaign. Labor contributions still left Carney with a spending advantage, but it did not help. Williams carried Mahoning County (Youngstown), Carney's home base, and narrowed Carney's margin in Trumbull County to just 112 votes, placing the district in Republican hands for the first time since 1936.

Meshel made his move on schedule in 1980, but he had waited too long. While Williams had not come close to fulfilling his campaign pledge of bringing 10,000 new jobs to Youngstown, voters blamed their bad fortune on the Carter administration rather than on him.

By voting with Democrats occasionally in the House, and playing down his party affiliation at home, Williams had made himself far stronger than most local politicians had expected. Meshel constantly reminded voters Williams was from

the same party as Ronald Reagan, but few seemed to care. Williams won a second term comfortably, carrying both Mahoning and Trumbull counties. Reagan lost both, with 40 and 42 percent respectively.

**The District:** Ohio's Youngstown-Warren district is one of its most depressed economically, and normally one of its most Democratic. In statewide elections, the Democratic percentage is usually just below that of the Akron and Cleveland districts.

Located on the eastern border with Pennsylvania, the area has long been a steel center serving both Pittsburgh and Cleveland. About two-thirds of the voters live in Mahoning County, with the other third in the Trumbull County cities of Warren and Niles, and in nearby suburbs. There is little political diversity within the district, although some of the suburbs south of Youngstown tend to be slightly more Republican; homes there are priced higher than most steelworkers can afford.

## Committees

**Government Operations** (8th of 17 Republicans)
Commerce, Consumer, and Monetary Affairs.

**Small Business** (6th of 17 Republicans)
Antitrust and Restraint of Trade Activities Affecting Small Business.

## Elections

**1980 General**

| | |
|---|---|
| Lyle Williams (R ) | 107,032 (58 %) |
| Harry Meshel (D ) | 77,272 (42 %) |

**1978 General**

| | |
|---|---|
| Lyle Williams (R ) | 71,890 (51 %) |
| Charles Carney (D ) | 69,977 (49 %) |

**1978 Primary**

| | |
|---|---|
| Lyle Williams (R ) | 10,516 (54 %) |
| John Hay (R ) | 5,742 (29 %) |
| Gary Van Brocklin (R ) | 2,542 (13 %) |

**District Vote For President**

| 1980 | | 1976 | | 1972 | |
|---|---|---|---|---|---|
| D | 94,569 (51 %) | D | 111,500 (60 %) | D | 88,495 (47 %) |
| R | 76,452 (41 %) | R | 69,756 (38 %) | R | 96,674 (51 %) |
| I | 13,738 (7 %) | | | | |

## Campaign Finance

| | Receipts | Receipts from PACs | Expenditures |
|---|---|---|---|
| **1980** | | | |
| Williams (R ) | $197,935 | $75,175 (38 %) | $207,760 |
| Meshel (D ) | $192,948 | $59,533 (31 %) | $192,877 |

| 1978 | | | |
|---|---|---|---|
| Williams (R ) | $107,948 | $54,438 (50 %) | $101,551 |
| Carney (D ) | $142,355 | $101,362 (71 %) | $168,257 |

## Voting Studies

| | Presidential Support | | Party Unity | | Conservative Coalition | |
|---|---|---|---|---|---|---|
| Year | S | O | S | O | S | O |
| 1980 | 48 | 42 | 48 | 43 | 61 | 27 |
| 1979 | 39 | 39 | 49 | 28 | 69 | 13 |

S = Support          O = Opposition

## Key Votes

**96th Congress**

| | |
|---|---|
| Weaken Carter oil profits tax (1979) | Y |
| Reject hospital cost control plan (1979) | Y |
| Implement Panama Canal Treaties (1979) | N |
| Establish Department of Education (1979) | Y |
| Approve Anti-busing Amendment (1979) | Y |
| Guarantee Chrysler Corp. loans (1979) | Y |
| Approve military draft registration (1980) | N |
| Aid Sandinista regime in Nicaragua (1980) | N |
| Strengthen fair housing laws (1980) | N |

**97th Congress**

| | |
|---|---|
| Reagan budget proposal (1981) | Y |

## Interest Group Ratings

| Year | ADA | ACA | AFL-CIO | CCUS |
|---|---|---|---|---|
| 1980 | 33 | 54 | 68 | 69 |
| 1979 | 16 | 59 | 45 | 71 |

# 20 Mary Rose Oakar (D)

### Of Cleveland — Elected 1976

**Born:** March 5, 1940, Cleveland, Ohio.
**Education:** Ursuline College, B.A. 1962; John Carroll U., M.A. 1966.
**Profession:** High school English and drama teacher.
**Family:** Single.
**Religion:** Roman Catholic.
**Political Career:** Cleveland City Council, 1973-77.

**In Washington:** Women's rights and Cleveland's economic survival have preoccupied Oakar since her election in 1976.

Although she serves on the Banking Committee, she has not immersed herself in the study of lending institutions or the finer details of international finance. She has treated the committee as a place to promote and defend her two causes.

During discussion of a bill to expand the Economic Development Agency in 1979, she sought to include women as a disadvantaged group, a move opponents argued would change the emphasis from economic aid to social welfare. The same year, she conditioned her support for a Chrysler loan guarantee on assurances that Chrysler would not relocate any plants in the South.

One of Oakar's crusades to help financially beleaguered Cleveland drew her into an argument with the state of Michigan over the location of a new Volkswagen assembly plant. Volkswagen had considered building a plant near Cleveland, but Michigan offered the company an unused missile plant to locate in. Oakar tried to block the 1979 legislation transferring title of the missile plant to state authorities, objecting that it was a special arrangement for Volkswagen and should not be permitted because the missile plant was funded with federal money.

Two years earlier, Oakar had tried to put money in a supplemental appropriation bill for snow removal in Indiana, Michigan, Pennsylvania and Ohio. She argued that the same bill was giving drought relief to the West. The House turned her down, 279-124, after hearing arguments that it would set a bad precedent for the federal government to take over what is normally a state function.

While Oakar is a strong supporter of women's rights, she opposes federal funding of abortions, much like her ethnic, heavily Catholic constituency. She prefers that the government encourage family planning and provide counseling to pregnant women rather than paying for abortions.

**At Home:** Oakar's efforts to help Cleveland may not always bring her legislative successes, but they have helped her win elections.

Trained as an actress by the Royal Academy of Dramatic Arts in London, Oakar knows how to communicate her achievements. During the four years she represented a largely Irish and Puerto Rican ward on Cleveland's City Council, she received considerable media attention for developing a plan to make "creative use" of vacant lots and working to outlaw the sale of airplane glue to minors.

In 1976, when Democratic Rep. James V. Stanton left the district for an unsuccessful run at the U.S. Senate, Oakar and 11 others entered the Democratic primary. Oakar's campaign focused on the fact she was the only woman running and, among the major candidates, the only one without a law degree. Although she did not mention it as much, she was also the only candidate who had been a telephone operator or a college speech and drama professor.

The power blocs in Cleveland divided their support among Oakar and three other candidates. Oakar's most significant endorsements were from a United Auto Workers local and from the Fire Fighters Union. State Sen. Anthony J. Celebrezze Jr. — now Ohio's Secretary of State — was

---

**20th District: Cleveland — Central, west, suburbs.** Population: 374,942 (19% decrease since 1970). Race: White 340,156 (91%), Black 22,484 (6%), Others 12,276 (3%). Spanish origin: 14,309 (4%).

endorsed by the *Cleveland Plain Dealer.* Former City Councilman Michael L. Climaco had the backing of the Cuyahoga County Democratic organization. City Councilman Basil Russo was supported by Republican Mayor Ralph Perk, whom Democrat Russo had endorsed the previous year. Oakar won the primary with 24 percent, to 18 percent for Celebrezze, her nearest rival.

Since then Oakar has had little to worry about. But she faces a threat in the redistricting that will probably take a House seat out of the Cleveland area; at one point she suggested enlarging the size of the House in 1982 to preserve existing urban representation.

**The District:** The line between Cleveland's 20th and 21st Districts generally divides the city's white and black population. The 20th is the white district, containing the state's largest concentration of ethnic voters. Poles, Czechs, Italians and Germans are the dominant groups, but there are dozens of other ethnic communities represented at least by a restaurant or two on the West Side.

Most of the vote is cast within Cleveland — nearly all of it west of the Cuyahoga River. The rest of the population is in suburbs close to the city which still retain an urban ethnic flavor.

The district is not as solidly Democratic as the black 21st, but it is more Democratic than either of the two suburban Cleveland districts. Richard Nixon narrowly carried it in 1972, but Jimmy Carter won it in both 1976 and 1980.

## Committees

**Banking, Finance and Urban Affairs** (15th of 25 Democrats)
Economic Stabilization; Financial Institutions Supervision, Regulation and Insurance; General Oversight and Renegotiation; Housing and Community Development; International Development Institutions and Finance.

**Post Office and Civil Service** (10th of 15 Democrats)
Compensation and Employee Benefits, Chairman; Census and Population; Postal Operations and Services.

**Select Aging** (15th of 31 Democrats)
Health and Long-Term Care; Retirement Income and Employment.

## Elections

**1980 General**

| | |
|---|---|
| Mary Oakar (D ) | Unopposed |

**1978 General**

| | |
|---|---|
| Mary Oakar (D ) | Unopposed |

**Previous Winning Percentage**

1976 (81 %)

**District Vote For President**

| | 1980 | | 1976 | | 1972 |
|---|---|---|---|---|---|
| D | 66,223 (51 %) | D | 83,947 (60 %) | D | 74,563 (47 %) |
| R | 52,315 (41 %) | R | 50,457 (36 %) | R | 79,036 (50 %) |
| I | 7,623 (6 %) | | | | |

## Campaign Finance

| | Receipts | Receipts from PACs | Expenditures |
|---|---|---|---|
| **1980** | | | |
| Oakar (D ) | $61,967 | $24,825 (40 %) | $44,603 |

| 1978 | | | |
|---|---|---|---|
| Oakar (D ) | $77,334 | $38,865 (50 %) | $77,081 |

## Voting Studies

| | Presidential Support | | Party Unity | | Conservative Coalition | |
|---|---|---|---|---|---|---|
| Year | S | O | S | O | S | O |
| 1980 | 65 | 25 | 82 | 9 | 23 | 63 |
| 1979 | 64 | 32 | 75 | 18 | 32 | 64 |
| 1978 | 60 | 28 | 65 | 20 | 21 | 62 |
| 1977 | 66 | 34 | 77 | 19 | 24 | 71 |

S = Support          O = Opposition

## Key Votes

**96th Congress**

| | |
|---|---|
| Weaken Carter oil profits tax (1979) | N |
| Reject hospital cost control plan (1979) | N |
| Implement Panama Canal Treaties (1979) | N |
| Establish Department of Education (1979) | Y |
| Approve Anti-busing Amendment (1979) | Y |
| Guarantee Chrysler Corp. loans (1979) | Y |
| Approve military draft registration (1980) | X |
| Aid Sandinista regime in Nicaragua (1980) | Y |
| Strengthen fair housing laws (1980) | Y |

**97th Congress**

| | |
|---|---|
| Reagan budget proposal (1981) | N |

## Interest Group Ratings

| Year | ADA | ACA | AFL-CIO | CCUS |
|---|---|---|---|---|
| 1980 | 67 | 13 | 89 | 63 |
| 1979 | 68 | 23 | 85 | 11 |
| 1978 | 60 | 20 | 95 | 17 |
| 1977 | 65 | 19 | 91 | 12 |

# 21 Louis Stokes (D)

**Of Cleveland — Elected 1968**

**Born:** Feb. 23, 1925, Cleveland, Ohio.
**Education:** Attended Cleveland College of Western Reserve U., 1946-48; Cleveland Marshall Law School, J.D. 1953.
**Military Career:** U.S. Army, 1943-46.
**Profession:** Lawyer.
**Family:** Wife, Jeanette Francis; four children.
**Religion:** African Methodist Episcopalian.
**Political Career:** No previous office.

**In Washington:** Stokes came to Congress in an era of black activism, and he is still an important spokesman on minority issues at the Appropriations Committee. But he has attracted more attention in recent years as a kind of troubleshooter for the House leadership.

The first assignment came in 1977, when he took over a battered committee set up to investigate the assassinations of John F. Kennedy and Martin Luther King Jr. Its original chairman, Henry Gonzalez, D-Texas, got into a nasty public fight with Richard Sprague, the Pennsylvania prosecutor who had been hired as committee counsel. The committee backed Sprague, and Gonzalez quit in a huff. Some House members wondered whether to continue the committee at all, but others argued that there had never been a fully independent study of the two assassinations, and the panel proceeded.

When Speaker O'Neill turned to Stokes, there was some criticism that a black chairman would concentrate on the King inquiry and ignore Kennedy. But Stokes insisted on a dual probe and eventually won praise for evenhandedness.

His first move was to shift the committee behind closed doors and out of the news. He conducted a restrained and disciplined inquiry, highlighted by a dramatic cross-examination of King's killer, James Earl Ray. The final report was accepted with some relief though many doubted its conclusions — that there probably were conspiracies of different kinds in both cases. Stokes emerged from the episode with his reputation enhanced.

Stokes's task at the start of the 97th Congress was much different: O'Neill asked him to take over an ethics committee criticized privately by many House members as too rigid in dealing with colleagues.

Stokes had taken an interest in ethics issues during the long debate that led to the 1979 censure of the senior black House member, Charles C. Diggs Jr., D-Mich., who had been convicted on kickback charges. Stokes acted as floor manager for Diggs but offered no specific defense to the charges. Instead, he struck a conciliatory note, commending all involved for sensitive handling of a difficult task. "The high level of debate," he concluded, "has made me very proud." Then he joined in the 414-0 vote to censure Diggs.

The following year, Stokes was named to the ethics committee himself, and dissented quietly as the committee recommended censure of Charles Wilson, D-Calif., for financial misconduct, and expulsion of Michael "Ozzie" Myers, D-Pa., following his bribery conviction arising from Abscam. John Jenrette, D-S.C., also convicted in Abscam, resigned to avoid expulsion. Stokes argued against the expulsion of Myers, tried to get Wilson off with a reprimand and voted to delay taking up Jenrette's case.

As chairman, Stokes plays a different role. He tries to approach the job in a judicial manner, leaving the sharp questioning to others. He speaks often of protecting the rights of the accused. This careful style pleases O'Neill, who sometimes appeared uncomfortable with the previous chairman, Charles E. Bennett, D-Fla., long known as a purist on ethics issues. House rules required Bennett to step down after two years in the chairmanship, and Democratic leaders took the opportu-

---

**21st District: Cleveland — East.**
Population: 351,997 (24% decrease since 1970). Race: White 68,173 (19%), Black 279,746 (79%), Others 4,078 (1%). Spanish origin: 3,889 (1%).

nity to replace him with a much less hard-line chairman.

Once in charge, Stokes endorsed a series of rules changes that would create a separate panel of members to try disciplinary cases after the ethics committee recommended action. There was some talk of delaying the Abscam investigation of Rep. Raymond Lederer, D-Pa., until after the Rules Committee acted on the proposed changes. But Stokes decided to go ahead when Rules Chairman Bolling said it would take a while. Stokes voted with the majority as the committee recommended expulsion for Lederer April 28. Lederer resigned from the House the next day.

At the same time, however, Stokes said he objected to the committee relying on Justice Department evidence prepared for court trials. He said he wanted to start his own investigations from scratch.

Stokes was the first black appointed to the Appropriations Committee and still is the only one on its HHS and HUD subcommittees. He also served three terms on the Budget Committee when it first was established, but did not play a major part in its work. In most cases, Stokes simply cast protest votes as the panel moved further and further toward an approach that emphasized spending cuts rather than social services.

Stokes's role on the Appropriations Committee changed significantly with the election of Reagan. In the past, he left much of the detail to other senior Democrats and focused his personal attention on minority-related issues. In 1981, he began spending more time at hearings, grilling administration witnesses and looking for ways to protect a broad range of domestic programs from budget cutbacks.

Stokes largely wrote the budget resolution offered by black members on the floor in 1981 as a symbolic alternative to the Reagan budget. He attacked Reagan for showing "cold and callous insensitivity" to the poor. The Reagan budget, Stokes said, "provides millions more for the most prosperous in our nation, while pennies are taken away from the poor. . . ."

He was no more gentle toward the substitute prepared by the Budget Committee and endorsed by House Democratic leaders. That budget resolution, he said, was "balanced on the backs of the people Democrats used to stand tall for. I'm ashamed of my party."

**At Home:** The Stokes family has been the dominant force in Cleveland's black politics since Louis Stokes's younger brother, Carl, first ran for mayor in the mid-1960s. Carl left politics for television after serving two terms in City Hall

(1967-71), but Louis has remained active and successful. Secure in his own re-election, he has been free to help friends and quarrel with enemies over city issues.

Louis Stokes's initial victory was won as much in the courts as in the precincts of Cleveland's East Side. He had represented a black Republican in a 1967 suit claiming the Ohio Legislature had gerrymandered the state's congressional districts. He charged they had divided the minority vote and thus prevented the election of a black candidate. Stokes won an appeal before the U.S. Supreme Court, forcing the Legislature to redraw the lines. As redrawn, the 21st District represented by white Democrat Charles A. Vanik was about 60 percent black. Vanik decided to run in a suburban district, leaving the 21st vacant.

There were 14 candidates in the district's Democratic primary in 1968 — seven blacks and seven whites. But there was little doubt about the outcome. Stokes's association with his brother and his reputation as a civil rights lawyer won him 41 percent for an easy primary victory. His closest competitor, black City Councilman Leo Jackson, had only 21 percent. Overall, the black candidates won three-fourths of the primary vote. Stokes became the first black congressman from Ohio in November of that year by defeating Charles Lucas, the Republican he had represented in the court challenge the previous year.

Over the last decade, Stokes has attempted to consolidate his power through his 21st District Congressional Caucus. He has been involved in local politics, often battling the various mayors elected since the departure of his brother, Carl.

That has led to a variety of internal struggles, as some disgruntled black politicians have accused the congressman of turning the caucus into a personal political tool. But it has not affected his popularity among rank-and-file voters; he has increased his percentage every time he has run, and has begun to develop a following even in the district's few white neighborhoods.

**The District:** Located on Cleveland's East Side, the predominantly black 21st is the most Democratic district in the state. It includes the areas devastated by riots in the late 1960s, and also more middle-class black neighborhoods farther from the downtown area. The eastern border separates the 21st District from working-class, white Euclid, as well as from heavily Jewish and liberal communities like Cleveland Heights and Shaker Heights.

Redistricting, however, may force the district into these areas or — worse for Stokes — in the other direction, across the Cuyahoga River into the ethnic neighborhoods of the West Side. During the last decade the district lost 25 percent of its population, the fifth greatest decline in the country. Adding 160,000 people to the district, wherever they come from, will undoubtedly re-duce the percentage of black voters. It probably will not, however, reduce the Democratic vote very much; most of the surrounding areas are solidly Democratic.

## Committees

**Appropriations** (10th of 33 Democrats)
District of Columbia; HUD - Independent Agencies; Labor - Health and Human Services - Education.

**Standards of Official Conduct** (Chairman)

## Elections

**1980 General**

| | |
|---|---|
| Louis Stokes (D) | 83,188 (88%) |
| Robert Woodall (R) | 11,103 (12%) |

**1978 General**

| | |
|---|---|
| Louis Stokes (D) | 58,934 (86%) |
| Bill Mack (R) | 9,533 (14%) |

**Previous Winning Percentages**

| | | | |
|---|---|---|---|
| 1976 (84%) | 1974 (82%) | 1972 (81%) | 1970 (78%) |
| 1968 (75%) | | | |

**District Vote For President**

| | 1980 | | 1976 | | 1972 |
|---|---|---|---|---|---|
| D | 97,071 (85 %) | D | 107,830 (84%) | D | 100,915 (77%) |
| R | 12,309 (11 %) | R | 17,890 (14%) | R | 27,883 (21%) |
| I | 2,982 (3 %) | | | | |

## Campaign Finance

| | Receipts | Receipts from PACs | Expenditures |
|---|---|---|---|
| **1980** | | | |
| Stokes (D) | $66,601 | $29,335 (44%) | $57,984 |
| **1978** | | | |
| Stokes (D) | $64,989 | $26,100 (40%) | $47,176 |

## Voting Studies

| | Presidential Support | | Party Unity | | Conservative Coalition | |
|---|---|---|---|---|---|---|
| Year | S | O | S | O | S | O |
| 1980 | 55 | 21 | 78 | 4 | 2 | 78 |

| | | | | | |
|---|---|---|---|---|---|
| 1979 | 78 | 14 | 90 | 3 | 3 | 92 |
| 1978 | 76 | 15 | 81 | 4 | 4 | 84 |
| 1977 | 77 | 19 | 87 | 3 | 4 | 92 |
| 1976 | 24 | 69 | 85 | 3 | 4 | 83 |
| 1975 | 30 | 62 | 88 | 3 | 3 | 84 |
| 1974 (Ford) | 41 | 52 | | | | |
| 1974 | 34 | 49 | 82 | 4 | 1 | 82 |
| 1973 | 19 | 48 | 64 | 4 | 3 | 62 |
| 1972 | 32 | 46 | 66 | 4 | 1 | 74 |
| 1971 | 21 | 58 | 72 | 3 | 0 | 85 |
| 1970 | 40 | 42 | 71 | 15 | 2 | 84 |
| 1969 | 38 | 51 | 80 | 9 | 7 | 84 |

S = Support          O = Opposition

## Key Votes

**96th Congress**

| | |
|---|---|
| Weaken Carter oil profits tax (1979) | N |
| Reject hospital cost control plan (1979) | N |
| Implement Panama Canal Treaties (1979) | Y |
| Establish Department of Education (1979) | Y |
| Approve Anti-busing Amendment (1979) | N |
| Guarantee Chrysler Corp. loans (1979) | Y |
| Approve military draft registration (1980) | N |
| Aid Sandinista regime in Nicaragua (1980) | Y |
| Strengthen fair housing laws (1980) | Y |

**97th Congress**

| | |
|---|---|
| Reagan budget proposal (1981) | N |

## Interest Group Ratings

| Year | ADA | ACA | AFL-CIO | CCUS |
|---|---|---|---|---|
| 1980 | 78 | 10 | 94 | 52 |
| 1979 | 95 | 0 | 94 | 6 |
| 1978 | 85 | 10 | 100 | 19 |
| 1977 | 90 | 0 | 91 | 7 |
| 1976 | 85 | 0 | 87 | 6 |
| 1975 | 89 | 4 | 100 | 18 |
| 1974 | 74 | 0 | 100 | 0 |
| 1973 | 68 | 10 | 100 | 9 |
| 1972 | 100 | 5 | 90 | 14 |
| 1971 | 89 | 4 | 80 | - |
| 1970 | 96 | 18 | 100 | 13 |
| 1969 | 100 | 27 | 100 | - |

# 22 Dennis E. Eckart (D)

**Of Euclid — Elected 1980**

**Born:** April 6, 1950, Cleveland, Ohio.
**Education:** Xavier U., B.A. 1971; Cleveland State U., J.D. 1973.
**Profession:** Lawyer.
**Family:** Wife, Sandra Pestotnik; one child.
**Religion:** Roman Catholic.
**Political Career:** Assistant prosecutor, Lake County, 1974; Ohio House, 1975-81.

**The Member:** Eckart was a young activist in the Ohio Legislature, a consumer affairs specialist who built much of his public reputation on a bill that gave state-subsidized tax credits to the elderly for their energy bills.

In Congress, Eckart is working toward a role as a party insider. Chosen freshman Democratic Whip, he represents the views of his fellow first-termers at caucuses of the Democratic leadership. Eckart has criticized social service funding cuts that may force closing of senior citizens' centers.

During the 1980 campaign, Eckart's liberal reputation did not hinder him in a district used to the iconoclastically liberal Charles A. Vanik, a Democrat who retired. Eckart benefited from a crack organization, much of it made up of followers of former Lieutenant Governor Richard F. Celeste.

An estimated 20 percent of the district electorate is Jewish, and Eckart is an outspoken supporter of Israel, as was Vanik. Eckart voted for a House resolution asking the president not to sell Saudi Arabia early-warning radar planes or equipment to enhance the capability of its F-15 jets.

**The District:** The Democratic leanings of this suburban area east of Cleveland are explained by ethnicity. The blue-collar workers of Polish and Slovenian descent, who fled the city for suburbs like Euclid and Mayfield have retained their Democratic allegiance, although they have an increasingly conservative cast nowadays. Jews, the other major ethnic group, predominate in Shaker Heights, and are traditionally Democratic as well.

The outlying suburbs, in Summit and Geauga counties, are mostly Republican, as are well-to-do communities nearer the city, like Chagrin Falls and Pepper Pike.

## Committees

**Education and Labor** (19th of 19 Democrats)
Postsecondary Education.

**Foreign Affairs** (19th of 21 Democrats)
Africa; International Economic Policy and Trade.

**Small Business** (19th of 23 Democrats)
Antitrust and Restraint of Trade Activities Affecting Small Business; Energy, Environment and Safety Issues Affecting Small Business.

## Elections

**1980 General**

| | |
|---|---|
| Dennis Eckart (D ) | 108,137 (55 %) |
| Joseph Nahra (R) | 80,836 (41 %) |

**1980 Primary**

| | |
|---|---|
| Dennis Eckart (D ) | 27,854 (41 %) |
| Timothy McCormack (D ) | 16,067 (23 %) |
| Anthony Calabrese Jr. (D ) | 12,313 (18 %) |
| Sheldon Schecter (D ) | 7,325 (11 %) |

**District Vote For President**

| | 1980 | | 1976 | | 1972 |
|---|---|---|---|---|---|
| **D** | 84,318 (43 %) | **D** | 99,180 (48 %) | **D** | 90,419 (42 %) |
| **R** | 92,016 (47 %) | **R** | 100,050 (49 %) | **R** | 119,412 (56 %) |
| **I** | 15,896 (8 %) | | | | |

## Campaign Finance

| | Receipts | Receipts from PACs | Expenditures |
|---|---|---|---|
| **1980** | | | |
| Eckart (D ) | $355,077 | $83,201 (23 %) | $354,048 |
| Nahra (R ) | $464,272 | $84,010 (18 %) | $466,936 |

## Key Vote

**97th Congress**
Reagan budget proposal (1981)      N

> **22nd District: Cleveland suburbs — Cleveland Heights, Euclid.** Population: 440,617 (5% decrease since 1970). Race: White 396,764 (90%), Black 38,532 (9%), Others 5,321 (1%). Spanish origin: 2,583 (1%).

# 23 Ronald M. Mottl (D)

### Of Parma — Elected 1974

**Born:** Feb. 6, 1934, Cleveland, Ohio.
**Education:** U. of Notre Dame, B.S. 1956, LL.B. 1957.
**Military Career:** Army, 1957-58.
**Profession:** Lawyer.
**Family:** Wife, Debra Budan; four children.
**Religion:** Roman Catholic.
**Political Career:** Parma City Council, 1960-66; Ohio House, 1967-69; Ohio Senate, 1969-75. Unsuccessful U.S. House candidate, 1964, 1970.

**In Washington:** Mottl's career has never been quite the same since he forced a vote in 1979 on an anti-busing amendment to the Constitution.

The amendment drew only 208 votes — far short of the two-thirds majority required — but it gave the crew-cut Cleveland Democrat some national attention and a new role as a blue-collar maverick more conservative than colleagues had realized. While he has not abandoned the economic populism standard in a district like his, he has moved far to the right on social issues.

In the months after the busing vote, his shift became increasingly clear. Mottl attended a dinner held to promote a possible future coalition between Republicans and conservative Democrats aimed at controlling the House. He cosponsored a resolution denying protected legal status to homosexuals. He wrote to 4,120 local government officials asking them to oppose strong enforcement provisions in a fair housing bill.

The last act renewed the argument between Mottl and Rep. Louis Stokes, the black Democrat from Cleveland. Stokes accused Mottl of an ethical violation because the mailing was to be financed by the National Association of Realtors. Mottl eventually picked up part of the cost himself. Stokes had previously complained Mottl was trying to restore segregation with his busing amendment.

Things had not gone smoothly for Mottl on that amendment. As initially drafted, it would have prevented local officials from assigning pupils to any school except the nearest one. That meant schools would have been restricted from making transfers needed for reasons totally unrelated to race. Mottl's amendment was finally modified to take care of the loophole, but the issue helped destroy his momentum, and exposed him to criticism as a sloppy legislator.

The whole experience seemed to drive Mottl further to the right. "Everybody is against me but the people," he said at one point. "The thing I resented most was being called a racist and a bigot. I am not."

While Mottl was becoming a national spokesman against busing, he was serving far more quietly on the Commerce Committee, where he lined up with labor and consumer groups on many energy issues. He opposed President Carter's decision to remove price controls on crude oil, and argued the consumer case against major oil companies with some vehemence at committee hearings.

Mottl's hybrid populism is also reflected in his style of life in Washington. He leaves the city promptly at the close of business every Thursday afternoon, returning the next Tuesday. While he is in town, he lives in a single, sparsely furnished room in a hotel near the Capitol. "I've never spent a weekend in Washington," he once said. "I don't like it here."

**At Home:** Mottl does feel at home in the bowling alleys of Parma and Strongsville, where his style of social conservativism is the norm. For two decades he has been a popular political figure in the ethnic suburbs of Cleveland.

Strangely, coming to Washington was one of

---

**23rd District: Cleveland suburbs.**
Population: 462,759 (no change since 1970). Race: White 453,289 (98%), Black 2,736 (1%), Others 6,734 (1%). Spanish origin: 3,896 (1%).

---

Mottl's earliest political goals. In 1964, after only two years as Parma council president, he challenged veteran Democrat Michael Feighan in the Democratic congressional primary. Six years later, midway through his first term in the state Senate, he tried for the House again. But his divorce and remarriage to an 18-year-old woman hurt him against GOP Rep. William E. Minshall.

When Minshall retired four years later, Mottl tried a third time and was narrowly successful. He had just pushed a state lottery bill through the Legislature, and it placed him first in name recognition in the six-candidate Democratic primary. He won with 42 percent over former U.S. Rep. Robert E. Sweeney, his nearest opponent.

At that point, however, Mottl's hopes were almost shattered by the candidacy of 28-year-old Cleveland Councilman Dennis J. Kucinich, later the city's embattled mayor. Two years before, running as an anti-machine Democrat, Kucinich

had nearly defeated Minshall, and then had survived the party's attempt to purge him from the council. In 1974, he decided to run as an independent and drew more than 45,000 votes, holding Mottl's margin to barely 6,000. But the Democrat won, and has won easily ever since.

**The District:** The 23rd is almost entirely suburban, surrounding Cleveland on the Republican west and the Democratic south. But except for a few affluent communities along Lake Erie, it is mostly blue-collar, middle-income territory with Eastern and Southern European ethnic elements.

The nearby steel mills and two large automobile plants located in the district give it a strong union presence. But its prevailing social conservatism makes the 23rd the least Democratic district in the Cleveland area. Nixon won nearly twice as many votes as McGovern here in 1972, and Jimmy Carter lost it both in 1976 and 1980.

## Committees

**Energy and Commerce** (15th of 24 Democrats)
Oversight and Investigations; Telecommunications, Consumer Protection, and Finance.

**Veterans' Affairs** (5th of 17 Democrats)
Hosptials and Health Care, chairman; Housing and Memorial Affairs.

## Elections

**1980 General**

| | |
|---|---|
| Ronald Mottl (D ) | Unopposed |

**1978 General**

| | |
|---|---|
| Ronald Mottl (D ) | 99,975 (75 %) |
| Homer Taft (R ) | 33,732 (25 %) |

**1978 Primary**

| | |
|---|---|
| Ronald Mottl (D ) | 24,995 (84 %) |
| Michael Normile (D ) | 4,719 (16 %) |

**Previous Winning Percentages**

1976 (73 %)    1974 (35 %)

**District Vote For President**

| | 1980 | | 1976 | | 1972 |
|---|---|---|---|---|---|
| **D** | 69,187 (35 %) | **D** | 84,525 (42 %) | **D** | 71,200 (34 %) |
| **R** | 108,387 (55 %) | **R** | 110,680 (55 %) | **R** | 131,507 (64 %) |
| **I** | 14,714 (8 %) | | | | |

## Campaign Finance

| | Receipts | Receipts from PACs | Expenditures |
|---|---|---|---|
| **1980** | | | |
| Mottl (D ) | $36,710 | $23,092 (63 %) | $62,957 |
| **1978** | | | |
| Mottl (D ) | $59,103 | $27,307 (46 %) | $40,630 |
| Taft (R ) | $11,208 | $1,100 (10 %) | $11,197 |

## Voting Studies

| | Presidential Support | | Party Unity | | Conservative Coalition | |
|---|---|---|---|---|---|---|
| Year | S | O | S | O | S | O |
| 1980 | 39 | 55 | 37 | 57 | 63 | 28 |
| 1979 | 34 | 58 | 35 | 59† | 63 | 32 |
| 1978 | 36 | 51 | 36 | 57 | 58 | 37 |
| 1977 | 56 | 39 | 44 | 52 | 53 | 42 |
| 1976 | 25 | 67 | 58 | 35 | 34 | 59 |
| 1975 | 27 | 70 | 64 | 30 | 26 | 66 |

†Not eligible for all recorded votes.

S = Support        O = Opposition

## Key Votes

**96th Congress**

| | |
|---|---|
| Weaken Carter oil profits tax (1979) | N |
| Reject hospital cost control plan (1979) | N |
| Implement Panama Canal Treaties (1979) | N |
| Establish Department of Education (1979) | Y |
| Approve Anti-busing Amendment (1979) | Y |
| Guarantee Chrysler Corp. loans (1979) | C |
| Approve military draft registration (1980) | N |
| Aid Sandinista regime in Nicaragua (1980) | N |
| Strengthen fair housing laws (1980) | N |

**97th Congress**

| | |
|---|---|
| Reagan budget proposal (1981) | Y |

## Interest Group Ratings

| Year | ADA | ACA | AFL-CIO | CCUS |
|---|---|---|---|---|
| 1980 | 33 | 46 | 72 | 59 |
| 1979 | 37 | 60 | 68 | 35 |
| 1978 | 30 | 58 | 60 | 28 |
| 1977 | 55 | 44 | 71 | 18 |
| 1976 | 55 | 37 | 74 | 25 |
| 1975 | 74 | 52 | 73 | 24 |

# Oklahoma

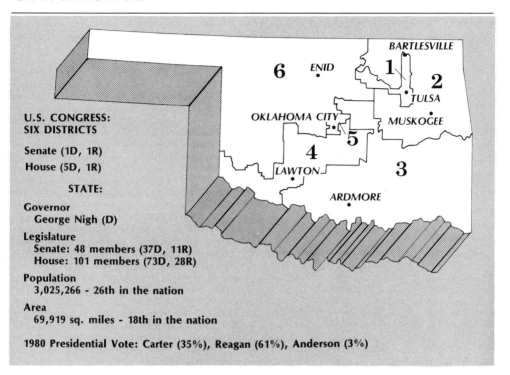

**U.S. CONGRESS:**
**SIX DISTRICTS**

Senate (1D, 1R)

House (5D, 1R)

**STATE:**

Governor
  George Nigh (D)

Legislature
  Senate: 48 members (37D, 11R)
  House: 101 members (73D, 28R)

Population
  3,025,266 - 26th in the nation

Area
  69,919 sq. miles - 18th in the nation

1980 Presidential Vote: Carter (35%), Reagan (61%), Anderson (3%)

## ... Up from the Dust Bowl

A mixture of Dixie and the Midwest, of rough hills and flat plains, of agriculture and oil, Oklahoma is emerging into prosperity and conservatism.

After a decline in the 1930s and 1940s, when Dust Bowl erosion sent much of its population fleeing west for survival, Oklahoma's population started to grow again in the 1950s, rising 4.3 percent, and then jumped 9.9 percent in the 1960s. It joined in the broader Sun Belt population growth in the 1970s by gaining 18.2 percent more people. The oil boom early in the 20th century never made the average Oklahoman prosperous or even comfortable; today's diversified economic growth is doing that, and shifting the state's politics rightward as well. The Dixie side of Oklahoma has traditionally been sufficient to guarantee Democratic domination of state politics. Admitted to the Union in 1907, the state did not elect a Republican governor until Henry

Bellmon's victory in 1962 and returned to Democratic hands in 1970. Republicans have never controlled the state Senate and have captured the state House only once, in 1920.

But in national politics, Oklahoma has gradually moved in a Republican direction in the postwar years. It backed only two Republican presidential candidates before Eisenhower in 1952, but since then it has voted for every one except Barry Goldwater in 1964. Even Southerner Jimmy Carter could not tempt Oklahoma back into the Democratic column in 1976, although he came close. Rural southeast Oklahoma still clings tenaciously to its Democratic heritage, but most of the urban areas are now consistently Republican, and they are the areas of growth.

The Southern Democratic influence in the state came from the original settlement pattern. After its Indian territory was opened up to white settlement in 1889, immigrants from Texas, Ar-

**983**

kansas, and other parts of the Deep South populated most of the state in the late 19th and early 20th centuries. Only in the northern tier of counties adjacent to Kansas did Republican-oriented settlers abound.

Today, like traditional Southern Democrats elsewhere, most Oklahomans are conservative when it comes to social issues and national defense. So even in the counties that remain largely Democratic on the local level, voters have been showing increasing disenchantment with the national Democratic Party. Even a conservative Democrat could not win a Senate seat in 1980 against an energetic young conservative Republican backed by the Moral Majority.

# A Political Tour

**Tulsa and the Northeast.** Calling itself "The Oil Capital of the World," Tulsa is a booming community with headquarters for producers and drilling equipment manufacturers as well as an aircraft and aeronautics industry. In addition, Tulsa became a deepwater port accessible to the Gulf of Mexico with the opening of the Arkansas River Navigation System in 1971.

In contrast with historically Democratic Oklahoma City, Tulsa has been the state's traditional Republican metropolitan center. It was settled primarily by Midwestern and Ozark Republicans. Between 1920 and 1980, Tulsa County went Democratic for president only twice, in 1932 and 1936. Barry Goldwater carried the county in 1964 with 55.5 percent. And the city has twice elected a Republican mayor in the 1970s.

With its long-established business community, Tulsa is more of a white-collar town than Oklahoma City. Its conservative instincts have been reinforced in recent years by its development as a center for religous fundamentalism, symbolized by the huge campus of Oral Roberts University, the city's leading tourist attraction.

In its strong Republican leanings, antagonism to rural Democratic domination of the state, and substantial white-collar migration from the North, Tulsa was a forerunner of other Sun Belt cities now catching up with it.

North of Tulsa, the counties along the Kansas border are also traditionally Republican. The thriving oil town of Bartlesville, home of Phillips 66, is located here. Washington County, which includes both Bartlesville and some Tulsa suburbs, is one of the strongest Republican counties in the state.

To the east and south of Tulsa lies Democratic territory. Hilly terrain has restricted agriculture to general farming in many areas, but cattle has become important. The Arkansas River Valley has some larger dairy and vegetable farms.

This is also Indian country. The Five Civilized Tribes were settled in eastern and central Oklahoma in the early 19th century. They took up farming and lived in towns and villages. As whites moved in, the populations mixed and today many of the region's residents have some Indian blood. The whites who moved in south of Tulsa tended to be Southern and Democratic. The Indians share their Democratic leanings. Muskogee County, the urban center of the region southeast of Tulsa, supported Carter for re-election as president in 1980 while the state as a whole was voting strongly for Reagan.

**Little Dixie.** This is the southeast quadrant of the state, settled by people from across the border in Texas and Arkansas. The area has retained a rural Southern flavor more than any other in the state. Cotton was once dominant here, especially along the Red River Valley basin, but it has since been superseded by livestock. The area does not have much oil or raise much wheat, so it has missed out on the prosperity those two commodities have brought to the rest of the state.

Democrats can still rely on majorities in most counties here, even in presidential elections. Of the 19 counties that voted for Carter in 1980, 14 were in the 3rd Congressional District, which covers most of Little Dixie. The 3rd has always remained loyal to the Democratic Party, sending Democrats to the House uninterruptedly ever since the state's admission to the Union in 1907.

This was one of the great out-migration areas during the 1930s and 1940s, when people left the land because of its failing agriculture. However, the population seems to have stabilized — every county in the region made at least a small population gain in the 1970s.

At the northern edge of Little Dixie lie Oklahoma's coal fields, some of which have been in operation since early in the century.

**Oklahoma City.** Oklahoma City contains the most famous symbols of the state's oil wealth: working wells on the state capitol grounds and the lawn of the governor's residence. Since the discovery of a large oil pool underneath the city in the 1930s, much of the economy has revolved about the oil industry. The capital also has important meat packing, trucking and aviation industries. Along with state government, the military has a significant presence, with Tinker Air Force Base located on the outskirts of the city.

For decades Oklahoma County was a Democratic center, balancing Tulsa's Republicanism. Between 1920 and 1948, the county supported a

Republican presidential nominee only once — Herbert Hoover in 1928. But the county has gradually switched its allegiance in the postwar years and now is almost as reliable in its national GOP voting habits as its rival to the northeast. Only Lyndon B. Johnson has carried it for the Democrats in a presidential election since 1952.

By 1980, Oklahoma's two major counties were voting almost exactly alike: Reagan received 66.2 percent of the vote in Tulsa County and 66.0 percent in Oklahoma County.

Surrounding Oklahoma County are burgeoning suburban communities. Of the five counties that abut Oklahoma County, even the slowest-growing shot up 28 percent in population during the 1970s; the fastest-growing jumped 75 percent. All five counties turned in large Republican margins for Reagan in 1980. The faster growing the county, the larger was the Reagan percentage.

Oklahoma City maintained itself as the largest city in the state by growing 9.5 percent over the past decade. This growth kept it about 43,000 residents ahead of Tulsa.

**The Great Plains.** Like the area of Texas immediately to the South and like Kansas to the North, most of western Oklahoma is prairie land devoted to wheat and livestock. Wheat prevails in the eastern part of the region, centered around Enid, and gradually shades into the drier cattle ranch country of the western panhandle. Water is a constant problem and schemes for transporting it from water-rich eastern Oklahoma rise and fall regularly in the state Legislature.

An individualistic conservatism prevails in the region, with a general aversion to most federal government activities — except for military expenditures and agricultural subsidies.

The northwest region of the state was a bastion of Republican strength when the state was almost uniformly Democratic. For years, it was the only area of the state sending a Republican to the U.S. House. During the leanest GOP years of the 1930s and 1940s the area provided the state Legislature with its small contingent of Republicans. In 1936, Major County, just west of Enid, was the only county in the state to vote for Republican Alfred M. Landon for president.

In 1980, every county in the northwest quadrant of the state gave Reagan a substantial majority.

## Redrawing the Lines

Through the first half of 1981, Democratic legislators concentrated on trying to stack the state's only Republican district with more GOP voters in order to strengthen neighboring Democratic incumbents.

The present 5th District (Oklahoma City), represented by Republican Mickey Edwards, grew at a slower pace during the 1970s than any other district. It must gain nearly 45,000 new residents in redistricting. At midyear, Democrats were looking for GOP-voting areas to bring into the 5th, and one plan had the new district stretching all the way to the Kansas border.

Northeast Oklahoma's 2nd District was the fastest-growing in the past decade, followed by southern Oklahoma's 4th and 3rd Districts. Population in the Tulsa 1st and the northwest 6th also grew, but both fell short of the ideal population of 504,211 and must expand in redistricting.

## Governor
# George Nigh (D)

**Born:** June 9, 1927, McAlester, Okla.
**Home:** Oklahoma City, Okla.
**Education:** East Central State Teachers College, Okla., B.A. 1950.
**Military Career:** Navy, 1946-47.
**Profession:** High school teacher.
**Family:** Wife, Donna; two children.
**Religion:** Baptist.
**Political Career:** Oklahoma House, 1951-59; lieutenant governor, 1959-63; 1967-79; governor, Jan. 6-14, 1963; unsuccessful campaign for Democratic gubernatorial nomination, 1962; elected governor 1978; term expires Jan. 1983.

# David L. Boren (D)

**Of Seminole — Elected 1978**

**Born:** April 21, 1941, Washington, D.C.
**Education:** Yale U., B.A. 1963; Rhodes Scholar, Oxford U., England, M.A. 1965; U. of Okla., J.D. 1968.
**Military Career:** National Guard, 1968-75.
**Profession:** Lawyer; professor of government.
**Family:** Wife, Molly Wanda Shi; two children.
**Religion:** Methodist.
**Political Career:** Okla. House, 1967-75; Okla. Governor, 1975-79.

**In Washington:** In the hard bargaining over the Reagan budget, Democrat Boren emerged early in 1981 as one of the Republican president's best friends. He helped save the administration from an assault led by one of its own, Republican John Chafee of Rhode Island, who wanted to restore nearly a billion dollars for urban programs.

The vice president phoned him personally, seeking help, worrying that Republican senators backing Chafee would tip the the GOP's precarious Senate balance away from Reagan. Just before the vote, Bush called again to make certain Boren and fellow conservative Democrats would vote with Reagan. They did. Some 17 Democrats voted with 42 Republicans to beat Chafee handily, even though 11 Republicans defected.

Several days later, Boren announced formation of a 12-member conservative Democratic group to work on budget cutting and other issues on which they might feel closer to Republicans than Democrats. He also warned Reagan that most of the group would not go along with a three-year 30 percent income tax cut unless targeted more specifically toward increased productivity rather than across-the-board reductions. When the Finance Committee finally began writing a tax bill in June of 1981, the Reagan-backed proposals included two of Boren's pet ideas: an exemption from the oil windfall profits tax for royalty holders, and an end to the federal inheritance tax between spouses.

Boren wants to be known as a conservative activist. Just two months after he took the oath of office in 1979, he was up on the Senate floor with an amendment to allow Taiwan to keep its Washington embassy property even though it was no longer recognized as the government of China. The action, Boren argued, was "small compensation for a long and trusted ally."

Boren later said he offered the amendment partly as a statement of his opposition to U.S. ties with mainland China — but only partly. He also wanted to win something early in his term to establish an image of effectiveness. "The appearance of having influence develops rapidly," he told an Oklahoma reporter, "and so can the appearance of not having influence."

Pale and pudgy, Boren does not look on first glance to be a power broker or even a politician. Oklahoma political cartoonists used to draw him as the Pillsbury Doughboy. But he generally is recognized as one of the brighter Senate newcomers of recent years. He figures he knows the system and how to operate within it.

He began by getting the committee assignment he wanted — Finance. When Democrats first met to hand out new committee posts in 1979, Boren was offered Armed Services and Agriculture. He went directly to Finance Chairman Russell Long, saying Oklahoma's oil-minded citizens needed a vote on the tax-writing committee. Long, always willing to have another pro-oil vote, told him to reapply for the committee. It was expanded by one to accomodate him.

Boren's ties to the oil industry are indisputable; individuals associated with it provided the largest block of contributions to his campaign. In 1979, he tried on the Senate floor to lower the basic windfall tax rate on oil company profits from 60 percent to 50 percent. That failed, but in 1981, he started all over again, with a bill to dismantle the tax altogether."To me," he has said, "being pro-oil means being pro-Oklahoma."

Boren has also sponsored bills to provide a congressional veto of federal regulations, to abolish life tenure for federal judges, and to allow states to impose strict work requirements for welfare recipients. As chairman of a Finance subcommittee on unemployment in the 96th Congress, he also promoted legislation to reduce the cost of unemployment benefits by making eligibility stricter.

**At Home:** Boren has come a long way quickly in politics by knowing how to promote the right issue at the right time.

Few Oklahoma Democrats took him seriously in 1974, when as a four-term state legislator, he decided to run for governor. A Rhodes Scholar and political science professor, he had been neither influential nor popular among insiders in the Oklahoma House. But he had a reputation as a reformer, and he exploited it skillfully in a year of scandal not only in Washington but in Oklahoma City, where Democratic Gov. David Hall was under investigation on corruption charges that were later to send him to prison.

Boren's isolation from Oklahoma's Democratic power structure was a tremendous advantage. He campaigned with a broom, promising to sweep out corruption at the state capitol, and supporting financial disclosure and open government. He edged into a spot in the primary runoff, won it easily, and had a smashing victory in November.

As governor, Boren changed focus, winning national attention as a spokesman for his state's oil producers. When he chose to run for the Senate in 1978, he was in a perfect position to seek votes and campaign support as an oil industry loyalist, and he was the favorite throughout the year. He led a seven-man primary field and went on to defeat former U.S. Rep. Ed Edmondson in a runoff.

The primary took a bizarre turn when, after a minor candidate accused the governor of being a homosexual, Boren swore on a Bible that it was not true. The accuser was discredited, and Boren suffered no lasting damage.

Boren's gubernatorial record brought him far more business support than most Democrats can expect in Oklahoma, and he had no trouble against his 1978 Republican opponent. He endorsed the Kemp-Roth tax-cut proposal and price deregulation for oil and natural gas.

Boren was the first governor to endorse Jimmy Carter for the 1976 Democratic presidential nomination, but he soured on Carter over energy issues in 1977. Boren gave Carter only lip-service support in 1980.

## Committees

**Agriculture, Nutrition and Forestry** (6th of 8 Democrats)
Agricultural Credit and Rural Electrification; Agricultural Research and General Legislation; Foreign Agricultural Policy.

**Finance** (7th of 9 Democrats)
Estate and Gift Taxation; International Trade; Social Security and Income Maintenance Programs.

## Elections

**1978 General**

| | |
|---|---|
| David Boren (D ) | 493,953 (66 %) |
| Robert Kamm (R ) | 247,857 (33 %) |

**1978 Primary Runoff**

| | |
|---|---|
| David Boren | 281,587 (60%) |
| Ed Edmondson | 184,175 (40%) |

**1978 Primary**

| | |
|---|---|
| David Boren (D ) | 252,560 (46 %) |
| Ed Edmondson (D ) | 155,626 (28 %) |
| Gene Stipe (D ) | 114,423 (21 %) |

## Campaign Finance

| | Receipts | Receipts from PACs | Expenditures |
|---|---|---|---|
| **1978** | | | |
| Boren (D ) | $779,544 | $800 (0.1 %) | $751,286 |
| Kamm (R ) | $444,734 | $31,664 (7 %) | $443,712 |

## Voting Studies

| | Presidential Support | | Party Unity | | Conservative Coalition | |
|---|---|---|---|---|---|---|
| Year | S | O | S | O | S | O |
| 1980 | 53 | 45 | 46 | 49 | 76 | 18 |
| 1979 | 47 | 47 | 33 | 59 | 81 | 10 |

S = Support          O = Opposition

## Key Votes

**96th Congress**

| | |
|---|---|
| Maintain relations with Taiwan (1979) | Y |
| Reduce synthetic fuel development funds (1979) | N |
| Impose nuclear plant moratorium (1979) | ? |
| Kill stronger windfall profits tax (1979) | Y |
| Guarantee Chrysler Corp. loans (1979) | N |
| Approve military draft registration (1980) | Y |
| End Revenue Sharing to the states (1980) | Y |
| Block Justice Dept. busing suits (1980) | Y |

**97th Congress**

| | |
|---|---|
| Restore urban program funding cuts (1981) | N |

## Interest Group Ratings

| Year | ADA | ACA | AFL-CIO | CCUS-1 | CCUS-2 |
|---|---|---|---|---|---|
| 1980 | 28 | 52 | 37 | 71 | |
| 1979 | 16 | 70 | 26 | 82 | 88 |

# Don Nickles (R)

## Of Ponca City — Elected 1980

**Born:** Dec. 6, 1948, Ponca City, Okla.
**Education:** Oklahoma State Univ., B.B.A. 1971.
**Military Career:** Army National Guard, 1970-76.
**Profession:** Machine company executive.
**Family:** Wife, Linda Lou Morrison; four children.
**Religion:** Catholic.
**Political Career:** Oklahoma Senate, 1979-81.

**The Member:** Riding a wave of support from the Moral Majority, Nickles rose from the backbenches of the Oklahoma Legislature almost overnight to become the youngest senator in the 97th Congress. His concern over what he sees as a trend toward socialism in the United States puts him at the conservative end of a conservative group of Republican newcomers. One platform in his crusade for free enterprise is the Labor and Human Resources Committee, where he chairs the subcommittee on labor.

Nickles has advocated a subminimum wage — he called it an "opportunity wage" — for young workers. He believes businesses are reluctant to hire young people at the current minimum.

But restaurateurs and other businessmen with high labor costs have complained that a youth sub-minimum might lead to an increase in the minimum wage, a move they resolutely oppose. They have not worked actively for the subminimum. When Labor Secretary Raymond J. Donovan gave only lukewarm support to the idea during subcommittee hearings in 1981, momentum for the proposal sputtered.

Another Nickles target has been the Davis-Bacon Act. It requires contractors on federally-financed construction projects to pay workers the prevailing wage rate in the area, which is usually union scale. Nickles says Davis-Bacon has had a "deadening economic effect" because government-mandated wages are too high.

Active in Republican politics over the past five years, Nickles first ran for office only in 1978, when he was elected to the state Senate. His first-term status there did not deter him from entering the 1980 Republican primary to replace Republican U.S. Sen. Henry L. Bellmon, who retired.

Nickles expressed strong belief in traditional moral values, centered around the family. The Moral Majority favored his candidacy and furnished him with invaluable aid in the form of volunteers and voter registration drives. The group found fertile soil in Oklahoma's large evangelical community and Nickles won his primary runoff by a 2-1 margin. Nickles' momentum slowed in the general election campaign, but his organization and Reagan's strength in Oklahoma pulled him to victory over Democrat Andy Coats, who was district attorney in Oklahoma City.

## Committees

**Energy and Natural Resources** (9th of 11 Republicans)
Energy Regulation; Energy Research and Development; Water and Power.

**Labor and Human Resources** (5th of 9 Republicans)
Labor, chairman; Employment and Productivity; Handicapped.

**Small Business** (7th of 9 Republicans)
Government Procurement, chairman; Productivity and Competition.

## Elections

**1980 General**

| | |
|---|---|
| Don Nickles (R) | 587,252 (54%) |
| Andy Coats (D) | 478,283 (44%) |

**1980 Primary**

| | |
|---|---|
| Don Nickles (R) | 47,879 (35%) |
| John Zink (R) | 45,914 (33%) |
| Ed Noble (R) | 39,839 (29%) |

## Campaign Finance

| | Receipts | Receipts from PACs | Expenditures |
|---|---|---|---|
| **1980** | | | |
| Nickles (R) | $762,804 | $133,457 (17%) | $666,053 |
| Coats (D) | $984,070 | $97,120 (10%) | $976,555 |

## Key Votes

**97th Congress**

| | |
|---|---|
| Restore urban program funding cuts (1981) | N |

# 1 James R. Jones (D)

**Of Tulsa — Elected 1972**

**Born:** May 5, 1939, Muskogee, Okla.
**Education:** U. of Okla., A.B. 1961; Georgetown U. Law School, LL.B. 1964.
**Military Career:** Army, 1964-65.
**Profession:** Lawyer.
**Family:** Wife, Olivia Barclay; two children.
**Religion:** Roman Catholic.
**Political Career:** Unsuccessful Democratic nominee for U.S. House, 1970.

**In Washington:** Jones's reputation as a master legislative strategist collided in 1981 with Ronald Reagan's national popularity, and Jones ended up suffering a series of punishing defeats.

After winning the Budget chairmanship early in the year with the votes of conservative Democrats from all over the South, he proved unable to hold them on the budget itself, losing 63 members of his party to the Reagan-backed substitute. Even Jones's last-minute addition of $6 billion for defense did little to bring back Democratic votes.

Then, when House committees cut $37 billion from their 1982 spending to comply with the budget, Jones took those reductions to the House floor and argued for them, only to lose to a second Reagan substitute, cutting more money from social programs. This time he lost 29 Democrats.

The second time, Jones called the whole series of events bizarre, pointing out that many of the Reagan spending cuts were not even available for scrutiny at the time of the vote. He said the whole budget process was on the verge of unraveling. But he and the Democratic leadership fell short of winning by a handful of votes.

Win or lose, however, the budget chairmanship has marked a turning point in Jones's career, ending a long period in which he sought to exploit his role as a leader of conservative Democrats while professing his permanent loyalty to the national party. Now he seems to be identified clearly as a party loyalist.

That is mildly ironic, since some of the Democratic leaders had been suspicious of him for years, considering Jones an apologist for big business who placed party loyalty at the bottom of his list. He made it to the Budget Committee in 1979 over leadership objections, and took advantage of divided opposition to win the chairmanship two years later, defeating David R. Obey of Wisconsin, 121-116, on a climactic third ballot that followed a 118-118 tie.

Few careers in the current Congress better illustrate the importance of "homework" to legislative success. A slightly built, balding man with rimless glasses and a reedy voice, Jones has achieved influence by knowing the details of legislation and the political needs of the members he has had to persuade.

He learned some of this from Lyndon Johnson, for whom he worked as appointments secretary in the White House. Observers might find it difficult to see much of LBJ in the man who brings a briefcase to the House floor and quietly answers his mail while colleagues chatter and swap jokes a few feet away. But Jones believes he learned a few things in his four White House years. "What I got from LBJ," he once said, "was an attention to detail."

It was the Ways and Means Committee's 1978 tax bill that first made Jones a major player in the House. The Carter administration initially wanted to include an increase in the capital gains tax. Jones wanted to go the other way, and when the committee stalled, he worked out a compromise with the late William A. Steiger and the committee's Republican bloc. When he felt confident of a majority, Jones took the proposal to Chairman Al Ullman, D-Ore., and Ullman bought it. The result was an overall package of $16 billion in tax cuts, including a substantial reduction in the capital gains tax. It was not close to what the

---

**1st District: North central — Tulsa.**
Population: 502,274 (18% increase since 1970).
Race: White 426,739 (85%), Black 46,653 (9%), Indian 21,257 (4%), Others 7,625 (2%).
Spanish origin: 7,909 (2%).

---

**James R. Jones, D-Okla.**

White House originally wanted, but Jones sold it as a new Democratic offering — not a product of a conservative coalition.

As a member of the Budget Committee in the 96th Congress, Jones generally cooperated in rounding up Southern votes for the leadership on budget resolutions. But he was playing a conservative opposition role on other issues. In June of 1979, for example, he teamed with Republican Henson Moore of Louisiana to weaken the oil windfall profits tax on the House floor. Jones got about a third of the Democrats on that vote, including three-fourths of the Southern Democrats, enough for a comfortable victory.

Jones spent much of the 96th Congress promoting a bill to allow accelerated depreciation on industrial plants and equipment. Drafted in consultation with the Chamber of Commerce and business lobbyist Charls Walker, it was cosponsored by Jones and Barber B. Conable Jr. of New York, the senior Republican on Ways and Means. The Reagan administration accepted much of the idea in 1981, but Jones was still faced with the prospect of selling it to a skeptical Ways and Means Committee. When the panel began working on a 1981 tax bill in June, it chose a less costly form of depreciation tax relief, called "expensing," despite Jones's vigorous objections.

His other effort was a bill to limit federal spending to a specified percentage of the gross national product. He won a promise from House leaders to allow a vote on such a bill during 1979, but no vote ever took place, and by 1980 the spending limit bill was swallowed up in the general congressional frenzy to balance the 1981 budget.

Jones has survived two incidents that earlier appeared to threaten his political career. In 1974, the Senate Watergate Committee released a memo Jones wrote when he represented the Associated Milk Producers, claiming he had persuaded President Johnson to raise milk price supports during the closing days of his administration. Jones went to work for the group shortly after Johnson left office. He said he wrote the memo as a "tall story" to prevent the group from dropping his services, and the issue subsided.

Two years later, he pleaded guilty to failing to report a $1,000 cash contribution from Gulf Oil Corp. The prosecutor said there was no evidence Jones knew where the money was coming from. Jones was fined $200.

**At Home:** A Democrat in a conservative Republican district, Jones has survived in part by developing a working relationship with the oil-and gas-oriented Tulsa business community. He rarely wins its outright support, but he manages at least to neutralize it at election time.

This has allowed him to survive in the face of huge Republican margins for other offices. In 1980, for example, President Carter drew only 28 percent of the vote in Tulsa County, the heart of the district. Jones ran 30 points ahead of him.

Jones's roots are in small-town poverty. His family lived in the black section of Muskogee, and was still paying off debts from the Depression in the 1950s. Jones worked his way through the University of Oklahoma as campus correspondent for several Oklahoma newspapers.

After law school, he went to work on Capitol Hill for Oklahoma Democratic Rep. Ed Edmondson. In 1964, while serving in the Army, Jones got an appointment as a White House military aide. The next year he joined the White House staff as a civilian and began developing the mastery of detail which has characterized his career.

When Johnson left office in 1969, Jones returned to Oklahoma, opening a law office in Tulsa. But only a year later he decided to run for Congress, challenging longtime Republican Rep. Page Belcher for re-election. Belcher won, but by taking 44 percent of the vote, Jones accomplished his major purpose — showing he was a threat to the 73-year-old Belcher's future re-election. The next year, Belcher retired.

That still forced Jones to campaign against the odds in 1972 in securely Republican territory. But Republicans had a divisive primary, and their nominee, former Tulsa Mayor James Hewgley, did not turn out to be a very aggressive candidate. Jones won comfortably against the national Nixon tide with 54.5 percent of the vote. Except in 1976, when he had strong opposition and the issue of his illegal campaign contribution, Jones has won by good margins.

**The District:** Tulsa is a corporate headquarters town with a big white-collar population and a consistent conservative outlook. It is not all oil and gas. The aerospace industry has an important foothold there, and despite its inland location, Tulsa is a port city. The dredging of the Arkansas River allows direct shipping down the Arkansas to the Mississippi and New Orleans. There is a huge fundamentalist community; Oral Roberts University is Tulsa's biggest tourist attraction.

As the prosperity of the oil and gas business has grown, Tulsa's Republicanism has grown with it. Even in 1976, when Jimmy Carter almost carried the state for president, the 1st District gave 60.8 percent of its vote to Gerald Ford.

## Committees

**Budget** (Chairman)
  Member of all Task Forces.

**Ways and Means** (7th of 23 Democrats)
  Trade.

## Elections

**1980 General**

| | |
|---|---|
| James Jones (D ) | 115,381 (58 %) |
| Richard Freeman (R ) | 82,293 (42 %) |

**1978 General**

| | |
|---|---|
| James Jones (D ) | 73,886 (60 %) |
| Paula Unruh (R ) | 49,404 (40 %) |

**Previous Winning Percentages**

**1976** (54 %)    **1974** (68 %)    **1972** (55 %)

**District Vote For President**

| | 1980 | | 1976 | | 1972 |
|---|---|---|---|---|---|
| D | 58,054 (29 %) | D | 71,288 (38 %) | D | 35,218 (21 %) |
| R | 131,885 (66 %) | R | 114,485 (61 %) | R | 133,182 (78 %) |
| I | 8,153 (4 %) | | | | |

## Campaign Finance

| | Receipts | Receipts from PACs | Expen- ditures |
|---|---|---|---|
| **1980** | | | |
| Jones (D ) | $289,666 | $145,503 (50 %) | $239,753 |
| Freeman (R ) | $141,418 | $1,321 (1 %) | $138,896 |
| **1978** | | | |
| Jones (D ) | $235,647 | $95,070 (40 %) | $210,179 |
| Unruh (R ) | $237,379 | $5,556 (2 %) | $236,437 |

## Voting Studies

| Year | Presidential Support | | Party Unity | | Conservative Coalition | |
|---|---|---|---|---|---|---|
| | S | O | S | O | S | O |
| 1980 | 63 | 32 | 66 | 31 | 65 | 33 |
| 1979 | 59 | 35 | 50 | 41 | 67 | 23 |
| 1978 | 52 | 46 | 39 | 59 | 82 | 15 |
| 1977 | 41 | 56 | 37 | 61 | 84 | 15 |
| 1976 | 51 | 43 | 32 | 60 | 80 | 11 |
| 1975 | 55 | 37 | 40 | 49† | 72 | 20† |
| 1974 (Ford) | 46 | 39 | | | | |
| 1974 | 66 | 25 | 33 | 56† | 74 | 15 |
| 1973 | 45 | 48 | 50 | 46 | 71 | 25 |

† Not eligible for all recorded votes.

S = Support        O = Opposition

## Key Votes

**96th Congress**

| | |
|---|---|
| Weaken Carter oil profits tax (1979) | Y |
| Reject hospital cost control plan (1979) | Y |
| Implement Panama Canal Treaties (1979) | Y |
| Establish Department of Education (1979) | Y |
| Approve Anti-busing Amendment (1979) | N |
| Guarantee Chrysler Corp. loans (1979) | N |
| Approve military draft registration (1980) | Y |
| Aid Sandinista regime in Nicaragua (1980) | Y |
| Strengthen fair housing laws (1980) | Y |

**97th Congress**

| | |
|---|---|
| Reagan budget proposal (1981) | N |

## Interest Group Ratings

| Year | ADA | ACA | AFL-CIO | CCUS |
|---|---|---|---|---|
| 1980 | 39 | 43 | 47 | 72 |
| 1979 | 32 | 36 | 37 | 83 |
| 1978 | 25 | 92 | 25 | 67 |
| 1977 | 5 | 72 | 38 | 76 |
| 1976 | 30 | 71 | 41 | 69 |
| 1975 | 16 | 71 | 43 | 63 |
| 1974 | 22 | 62 | 60 | 56 |
| 1973 | 28 | 54 | 55 | 70 |

# 2 Mike Synar (D)

## Of Muskogee — Elected 1978

**Born:** Oct. 17, 1950, Vinita, Okla.
**Education:** U. of Okla., B.B.A. 1972, LL.B. 1976; Northwestern U., M.A. 1973.
**Profession:** Rancher, real estate broker, lawyer.
**Family:** Single.
**Religion:** Episcopalian.
**Political Career:** No previous office.

**In Washington:** In an era when many freshman members come to Washington vowing to serve as barometer and hired hand for their demanding constituents, Synar is something of a rebel. He thinks nationally.

When *The New York Times* profiled him as a typical newcomer early in his first term, he turned out to be anything but typical. "I want to be a U.S. congressman from Oklahoma," he said, "not an Oklahoma congressman." Later he complained that parochialism in the House "causes potentially good members to be mediocre members."

As he started his second term in 1981, he publicly criticized the economic interests that contribute to campaigns and seek an influence over legislation, claiming they were a "petrifying force" in politics.

Synar's philosophy has led him into some legislative roles that many junior members, especially from the South, would have shied away from. It was his amendment, passed by one vote in 1980, that kept alive an open housing bill described by President Carter as the most important civil rights legislation of the decade.

Synar worked on that bill as a member of the House Judiciary Committee. As originally reported, it would have given the Department of Housing and Urban Development broad new enforcement powers in suspected housing discrimination cases. Critics complained that HUD would be acting as prosecutor, judge and jury. Synar's amendment transferred much of the authority to the Justice Department, nullifying the objections and keeping the bill alive to pass the House, although it died later in the Senate. Synar argued that the existing law simply made it too difficult for those discriminated against to obtain any redress of their grievances. "The current, toothless law," he said on the floor, "discourages many if not most complainants from ever filing a complaint."

The open housing fight was his one dramatic moment on the House floor during the 96th

Congress. But he cast numerous other votes that placed him closer to the national Democratic Party than to most of his regional colleagues.

He supported the implementation of the Panama Canal treaties. He backed the environmentalist version of legislation creating wilderness areas in Alaska, one that took more land out of development than most business and labor interests, particularly oil companies, preferred.

In the 97th Congress, Synar went with his Oklahoma Democratic colleague, House Budget Chairman James R. Jones, and against the Reagan-backed budget most other Southern Democrats voted for.

**At Home:** A clean-cut son of a prominent Oklahoma ranching family, Synar jumped into a congressional race in 1978, only two years after returning home from school to practice law.

Although he was inexperienced at politics, he was the right sort of challenger to Democratic Rep. Ted Risenhoover, who had become controversial because of a divorce and a reputation as a Washington playboy. The incumbent spent much of the campaign trying to refute charges that he slept in a heart-shaped waterbed in his Washington apartment. Synar campaigned intensively throughout the district and upset him by almost

---

**2nd District: Northeast — Muskogee.** Population: 542,378 (27% increase since 1970). Race: White 450,105 (83%), Black 24,842 (5%), Indian 63,979 (12%), Others 3,452 (1%). Spanish origin: 5,103 (1%).

8,000 votes. Compared to Risenhoover, Synar appeared fresh, polished, and seemly.

Synar was helped by his family name. His father and five uncles have been prominent businessmen and ranchers in the Muskogee area for over thirty years. In 1971, they were selected the "Outstanding Family" in the United States by the All-American Family Institute.

After his 1978 election, Synar set up an intensive constituent service operation. He announced that a majority of his staff would remain in Oklahoma. These steps helped protect him in 1980 when Republican nominee Gary Richardson attacked him for having a liberal voting record. Synar's percentage was down slightly from 1978, but he still held off Richardson with 14,000 votes to spare.

**The District:** Taking in the northeast corner of Oklahoma, the 2nd is a mixture of farming and ranching interests and the oil industry. It has a large and politically active Indian population, descendants of the "Five Civilized Tribes" and other groups that lived in Oklahoma before statehood. In 1980, more than 10 percent of the residents were listed by the census as Indian.

Muskogee is the historic center of the district, but Bartlesville, an increasingly Republican oil town in the northern part of the state, is now a second population center. In addition, redistricting has gradually brought the district within a few miles of Tulsa in all directions.

The southern counties have a rural, dirt-poor heritage, but have become more prosperous in recent years and more conservative. This part of the district, along with Osage County in the north, has a large Indian population, integrated into general society.

## Committees

**Energy and Commerce** (21st of 24 Democrats)
Energy Conservation and Power; Fossil and Synthetic Fuels; Oversight and Investigations.

**Government Operations** (16th of 23 Democrats)
Environment, Energy and Natural Resources.

**Judiciary** (11th of 16 Democrats)
Administrative Law and Government Relations.

**Select Aging** (22nd of 31 Democrats)
Housing and Consumer Interests; Retirement Income and Employment.

## Elections

**1980 General**

| | |
|---|---|
| Mike Synar (D ) | 101,516 (54 %) |
| Gary Richardson (R ) | 86,544 (46 %) |

**1978 General**

| | |
|---|---|
| Mike Synar (D ) | 72,583 (55 %) |
| Gary Richardson (R ) | 59,853 (45 %) |

**1978 Primary**

| | |
|---|---|
| Mike Synar (D ) | 58,397 (54 %) |
| Ted Risenhoover (D ) | 50,597 (46 %) |

**District Vote For President**

| 1980 | | 1976 | | 1972 | |
|---|---|---|---|---|---|
| **D** | 86,453 (42 %) | **D** | 101,326 (54 %) | **D** | 46,354 (26 %) |
| **R** | 113,158 (55 %) | **R** | 85,974 (46 %) | **R** | 125,232 (71 %) |
| **I** | 4,911 (2 %) | | | | |

## Campaign Finance

| | | Receipts from PACs | Expenditures |
|---|---|---|---|
| | Receipts | | |
| **1980** | | | |
| Synar (D ) | $253,511 | $11,192 (4 %) | $254,641 |
| Richardson (R ) | $200,531 | $9,300 (5 %) | $205,452 |
| **1978** | | | |
| Synar (D ) | $192,142 | $434 (0 %) | $190,050 |
| Richardson (R ) | $131,771 | $16,400 (12 %) | $130,530 |

## Voting Studies

| Year | Presidential Support | | Party Unity | | Conservative Coalition | |
|---|---|---|---|---|---|---|
| | S | O | S | O | S | O |
| 1980 | 72 | 26 | 84 | 15 | 38 | 62 |
| 1979 | 66 | 30 | 70 | 26 | 54 | 44 |

S = Support    O = Opposition

## Key Votes

**96th Congress**

| | |
|---|---|
| Weaken Carter oil profits tax (1979) | Y |
| Reject hospital cost control plan (1979) | Y |
| Implement Panama Canal Treaties (1979) | Y |
| Establish Department of Education (1979) | Y |
| Approve Anti-busing Amendment (1979) | N |
| Guarantee Chrysler Corp. loans (1979) | N |
| Approve military draft registration (1980) | Y |
| Aid Sandinista regime in Nicaragua (1980) | Y |
| Strengthen fair housing laws (1980) | Y |

**97th Congress**

| | |
|---|---|
| Reagan budget proposal (1981) | N |

## Interest Group Ratings

| Year | ADA | ACA | AFL-CIO | CCUS |
|---|---|---|---|---|
| 1980 | 61 | 26 | 44 | 63 |
| 1979 | 58 | 35 | 55 | 56 |

**993**

# 3  Wes Watkins (D)

**Of Ada — Elected 1976**

**Born:** Dec. 15, 1938, DeQueen, Ark.
**Education:** Okla. State U., B.S. 1960, M.S. 1961.
**Military Career:** Okla. Air National Guard, 1961-67.
**Profession:** Real estate broker.
**Family:** Wife, Elizabeth Lou Rogers; three children.
**Religion:** Presbyterian.
**Political Career:** Okla. Senate, 1975-77.

**In Washington:** Watkins worked hard during his first two terms to maintain his ties to the Carter administration and the House Democratic leadership without supporting either too often. It was generally a successful strategy, but it produced some uncomfortable moments.

One of them came in late 1979, at a White House meeting between President Carter and a group of nearly 100 moderate and conservative House Democrats. Watkins began complaining that members of Congress were not receiving enough attention from the president. "But you only vote with me 20 percent of the time," Carter shot back to the surprised Watkins, claiming to have documented proof on a computer in his drawer.

In 1977, Watkins' first year in the House, Carter's controversial plan to cut back on federal water projects would have eliminated two in Watkins' district, at Lukfata and McGee Creek. The freshman Democrat had little influence on his own, but he agitated against the changes and eventually became part of a coalition put together by Tom Bevill of Alabama, chairman of the Appropriations Subcommittee on Public Works, and Majority Leader Jim Wright of Texas, an irrigation enthusiast.

Watkins has been a junior-level member of the House leadership from the beginning of his congressional career. He was an assistant whip for his first four years, despite a record of opposing the leaders on many key issues. In his first year as whip, 1977, he voted with a majority of his party 31 percent of the time — the lowest score of anyone in the leadership. But he stayed on, and by 1980 was casting his vote with the party majority more than half the time. In 1981, he was given a place on the Democratic Steering and Policy Committee.

Watkins' main legislative crusade is for rural development, and he argued for it emotionally and at great length on the Banking Committee, where he served in his first two terms. He also found a way to pursue the issue through the Science Committee, his secondary assignment. He pressed for federal grants for the establishment of an Industrial Technology Research and Development Center in Durant, at the southern end of his district, and by the beginning of 1981 claimed to have attracted $900,000 in federal money.

In 1981, Watkins switched to the Appropriations Committee, and joined the Agriculture and Energy and Water subcommittees. Energy and Water funds some of the projects he fought to save several years earlier.

**At Home:** Watkins got to the House over the opposition of his famous predecessor, House Speaker Carl Albert, who retired in 1976 after 30 years representing the district.

As his successor, Albert favored his longtime chief aide, Charles Ward, and he endorsed Ward in the Democratic primary. But Watkins, who had been elected to the state Senate in 1974, had been planning a House campaign for several years. He developed the best organization among the six Democrats who entered the primary, capitalizing also on the political connections of his wife, who had served as Democratic congressional district co-chairman. Watkins ran 10,000 votes ahead of Ward in the initial primary, then trounced him in

---

**4th District: Southeast — Ardmore.**
Population: 508,801 (19% increase since 1970).
Race: White 443,047 (87%), Black 24,842 (5%), Indian 36,889 (7%), Others 4,023 (1%).
Spanish origin: 5,454 (1%).

a runoff, taking 63 percent of the vote. That was the last competitive election he has had to worry about.

Watkins had originally gone into education, completing the course work for a doctorate degree in higher education at Oklahoma State University. Then he spent three years in the OSU admissions office, and finally became a real estate developer.

**The District:** Located in the region known as "Little Dixie," named for the Deep South transplants who settled it, the 3rd has not elected a Republican in the 74 years since statehood. But it is no longer very comfortable with the national Democratic Party.

Largely rural, the district covers 23 counties and parts of two others. There is little industry, although McAlester has an Army ammunition plant and oil equipment companies furnish employment in the small urban centers. This part of the state was not favored with major oil and gas reserves.

Long a source of population outflow, the district gained about 75,000 people during the 1970s, much of it in the counties closest to Oklahoma City.

## Committees

**Appropriations** (31st of 33 Democrats)
Agriculture, Rural Development and Related Agencies; Energy and Water Development.

## Elections

**1980 General**

| | |
|---|---|
| Wes Watkins (D ) | Unopposed |

**1980 Primary**

| | |
|---|---|
| Wes Watkins (D ) | 108,478 (91 %) |
| Leland Kelly (D ) | 11,373 (9 %) |

**1978 General**

| | |
|---|---|
| Wes Watkins (D ) | Unopposed |

**Previous Winning Percentage**

1976 (82 %)

**District Vote For President**

| | 1980 | | 1976 | | 1972 |
|---|---|---|---|---|---|
| **D** | 92,068 (49 %) | **D** | 117,538 (63 %) | **D** | 49,605 (29 %) |
| **R** | 92,415 (49 %) | **R** | 66,451 (36 %) | **R** | 114,801 (68 %) |
| **I** | 3,329 (2 %) | | | | |

## Campaign Finance

| | Receipts | Receipts from PACs | Expenditures |
|---|---|---|---|
| **1980** | | | |
| Watkins (D ) | $71,788 | - (0 %) | $163,209 |
| **1978** | | | |
| Watkins (D ) | $93,415 | $4,200 (4 %) | $23,999 |

## Voting Studies

| | Presidential Support | | Party Unity | | Conservative Coalition | |
|---|---|---|---|---|---|---|
| Year | S | O | S | O | S | O |
| 1980 | 57 | 37 | 60 | 35 | 75 | 20 |
| 1979 | 31 | 66 | 31 | 63 | 92 | 4 |
| 1978 | 34 | 62 | 30 | 62 | 85 | 9 |
| 1977 | 41 | 53 | 31 | 67 | 89 | 7 |

S = Support          O = Opposition

## Key Votes

**96th Congress**

| | |
|---|---|
| Weaken Carter oil profits tax (1979) | Y |
| Reject hospital cost control plan (1979) | Y |
| Implement Panama Canal Treaties (1979) | N |
| Establish Department of Education (1979) | Y |
| Approve Anti-busing Amendment (1979) | Y |
| Guarantee Chrysler Corp. loans (1979) | N |
| Approve military draft registration (1980) | Y |
| Aid Sandinista regime in Nicaragua (1980) | Y |
| Strengthen fair housing laws (1980) | Y |

**97th Congress**

| | |
|---|---|
| Reagan budget proposal (1981) | N |

## Interest Group Ratings

| Year | ADA | ACA | AFL-CIO | CCUS |
|---|---|---|---|---|
| 1980 | 33 | 46 | 32 | 70 |
| 1979 | 0 | 68 | 11 | 89 |
| 1978 | 20 | 84 | 37 | 59 |
| 1977 | 5 | 74 | 19 | 88 |

# 4 Dave McCurdy (D)

### Of Norman — Elected 1980

**Born:** March 30, 1950, Canadian, Texas.
**Education:** U. of Okla., B.A. 1972, J.D. 1975.
**Military Career:** Air Force Reserves, 1968-72.
**Profession:** Lawyer.
**Family:** Wife, Pamela Plumb; two children.
**Religion:** Lutheran.
**Political Career:** Okla. assistant state attorney general, 1975-1977.

**The Member:** Although the 4th District gave a large majority of its 1980 vote to Reagan and has a considerable military population, McCurdy has not been afraid to challenge its sentiments in the House. He voted against Reagan's budget and has criticized the Pentagon for failing to document how it will spend the extra money Reagan wants for defense.

McCurdy said the administration's economic planners had projected an unrealistically low future inflation rate, and that any budget based on low projections would later have to be increased substantially. Despite a 45-minute session with the president and six other congressmen, McCurdy voted for the Democratic budget plan sponsored by Oklahoma Rep. Jim Jones.

"A lot of people say this vote is political suicide for me," McCurdy said, "but I still have faith the people believe they sent me to do what I think is right, not what is politically popular."

When McCurdy began his 1980 campaign, he was unknown in most of the district. He had never run for office before and had not been active in Democratic Party affairs. He built his own organization, tried to avoid any ideological label and was helped by several longtime backers of Democratic Rep. Tom Steed, who retired after serving 32 years. McCurdy narrowly defeated Republican Howard Rutledge, a retired Navy captain and former Vietnam POW who was supported by many military employees.

**The District:** The district stretches across central and southwestern Oklahoma and has three major urban centers: Shawnee, Norman, and Lawton. Before the redistricting of the 1960s, it was concentrated in the Shawnee and Stillwater areas, all east of Oklahoma City. But since, it has spread west and south to take in Norman and Lawton. The district has a strong military flavor; Altus Air Force Base and Fort Sill are located in it, and Tinker Air Force Base is in nearby Oklahoma City.

## Committees

**Armed Services** (21st of 25 Democrats)
Procurement and Military Nuclear Systems; Readiness.

**Science and Technology** (22nd of 23 Democrats)
Energy Development and Applications; Science, Research and Technology.

## Elections

| 1980 General | |
| --- | --- |
| Dave McCurdy (D ) | 74,245 (51 %) |
| Howard Rutledge (R ) | 71,339 (49 %) |
| **1980 Primary Runoff** | |
| Dave McCurdy (D ) | 33,520 (51 %) |
| James Townsend (D ) | 31,940 (49 %) |
| **1980 Primary** | |
| James Townsend (D ) | 31,104 (40 %) |
| Dave McCurdy (D ) | 26,173 (34 %) |
| Cuffie Waid (D ) | 10,722 (14 %) |
| Clifford Marshall (D ) | 7,035 (9 %) |

**District Vote For President**

| | 1980 | | 1976 | | 1972 |
| --- | --- | --- | --- | --- | --- |
| **D** | 61,333 (35 %) | **D** | 85,429 (53 %) | **D** | 37,542 (25 %) |
| **R** | 102,264 (59 %) | **R** | 73,168 (45 %) | **R** | 107,548 (72 %) |
| **I** | 7,480 (4 %) | | | | |

## Campaign Finance

| | Receipts | Receipts from PACs | Expenditures |
| --- | --- | --- | --- |
| **1980** | | | |
| McCurdy (D ) | $407,553 | $41,350 (10 %) | $229,248 |
| Rutledge (R ) | $160,323 | $29,043 (18 %) | $159,115 |

## Key Vote

**97th Congress**
Reagan budget proposal (1981)                                             N

---

**4th District: South central — Lawton, Norman.** Population: 517,352 (21% increase since 1970). Race: White 440,151 (85%), Black 37,481 (7%), Indian 22,737 (4%), Others 16,983 (3%). Spanish origin: 16,937 (3%).

# 5 Mickey Edwards (R)

**Of Oklahoma City — Elected 1976**

**Born:** July 12, 1937, Oklahoma City, Okla.
**Education:** U. of Okla., B.S. 1958; Oklahoma City U. Law School, J.D. 1969.
**Profession:** Journalist, lawyer.
**Family:** Wife, Lisa Reagan; two children.
**Religion:** Episcopalian.
**Political Career:** Unsuccessful Republican nominee for U.S. House, 1974.

**In Washington:** Edwards likes to describe himself as a "19th century liberal," rather than a conservative, and in ideological terms that may be true. But in the politics of the House he is a fixture on the Republican right, and his long-term record as an anti-government activist brought him the chairmanship of the American Conservative Union in 1980.

Edwards showed up in Congress in 1977 talking a hard-line foreign policy and an economic approach hostile to organized labor, and he immediately showed the public relations sense to attract attention to his ideas.

In his first term, he organized a "truth squad" of Republican members to speak around the country against U.S. transfer of the Panama Canal. In his second term, as the Carter administration prepared to end its close relationship with Taiwan, Edwards made a whirlwind tour of the island, said it had brought tears to his eyes, and formed a new group aimed at preserving the U.S.-Taiwan friendship treaties. He offered a floor amendment in 1979 to require congressional approval before the president could notify Taiwan that the treaties had been abrogated, but that lost on a 264-141 vote.

During four years on the Education and Labor Committee, Edwards used many of the arguments against union leaders that he had applied in Oklahoma earlier in his career. When the House debated legislation to legalize common-site picketing, badly wanted by the construction unions, Edwards tried to amend it to require a secret ballot of all employees at a construction site, both union and non-union, before picketing could begin. The amendment failed, although Edwards was on the winning side as the House unexpectedly turned down the legislation.

While Edwards has fought the unions, however, he has looked for ways to appeal to rank and file workers. In early 1978, he and Illinois Republican Philip Crane traveled to Youngstown, Ohio

to meet with union members, and Edwards came back urging that labor and the GOP begin "looking at each other as possible allies." He introduced a legislative package, offered as a solution to blue-collar economic problems. It featured new tax incentives for business, restrictions on foreign imports, and eased environmental rules.

Edwards' wooing of the workers, both in Washington and Oklahoma City, reflects an independent streak that marks him off from many of his conservative allies.

After the Three Mile Island nuclear accident, for example, he announced that he had lost his faith in nuclear power. "I became convinced," he said, "that the nuclear industry is kind of a loose cannon." He still says he could support some nuclear projects with substantial safeguards.

Edwards also tried to keep up an unorthodox position on school prayer, in line with the libertarian strain in his thinking. When religious fundamentalists asked him to sign a petition calling for a House vote on a constitutional amendment to permit prayer in public schools, he was reluctant to sign it. Then an Oklahoma minister castigated him on television, and he later signed. But he still has doubts about the amendment itself.

**At Home:** After a career in journalism, public relations and teaching, Edwards challenged Democratic Rep. John Jarman for Oklahoma City's congressional seat in 1974, and came within 3,402 votes of winning. That achievement in a

---

**5th District: Oklahoma City.** Population: 459,500 (8% increase since 1970). Race: White 375,241 (82%), Black 59,884 (13%), Indian 11,638 (3%), Others 12,737 (3%). Spanish origin: 12,132 (3%).

national Democratic year made Edwards the logical choice for 1976. Jarman switched to the Republican Party himself in 1975, but did not run again.

Edwards had been unopposed for the 1974 Republican nomination. But in 1976, with the seat open and the Republican chances obviously good, he received a primary challenge from former state Attorney General G. T. Blankenship. It was a close race, but Edwards' non-stop campaign won him the nomination by 1,087 votes.

Edwards also had a harder time in November than had been expected, with stiff competition from Democrat Tom Dunlap, a young hospital administrator and son of the popular state chancellor of higher education. Edwards won by only 3,899 votes, but he quickly established himself as a popular figure in his district and had no trouble winning in 1978 and 1980.

In addition to developing close ties with Oklahoma City's blue-collar workers, he has pursued black support more effectively than other area Republicans. In 1979, he asked the U.S. Justice Department to investigate Ku Klux Klan activity in Oklahoma, and complained about "foot-dragging" when there was no prompt response.

Before running for Congress, Edwards was a reporter and editor for the *Oklahoma City Times*, director of public relations for an advertising agency, and editor of *Private Practice* magazine, writing editorials in defense of private medicine. He was the author of *Hazardous to Your Health*, a treatise against national health insurance.

**The District:** The 5th District contains most of Oklahoma City, largely a corporate and governmental center with little major industry. Several oil companies have offices there, including headquarters for the Kerr-McGee company. State government is the major employer, so the percentage of white-collar workers in the labor force is the largest for any district in the state. Republicans consistently run better in the 5th than they do statewide.

## Committees

**Appropriations** (16th of 22 Republicans)
  Foreign Operations; Military Construction.

## Elections

**1980 General**

| | |
|---|---|
| Mickey Edwards (R ) | 90,053 (68 %) |
| David Hood (D ) | 36,815 (28 %) |

**1978 General**

| | |
|---|---|
| Mickey Edwards (R ) | 71,451 (80 %) |
| Jesse Knipp (D ) | 17,978 (20 %) |

**Previous Winning Percentages**

1976 (50 %)

**District Vote For President**

| | 1980 | | 1976 | | 1972 |
|---|---|---|---|---|---|
| D | 47,114 (28 %) | D | 68,288 (41 %) | D | 38,342 (23 %) |
| R | 109,420 (66 %) | R | 94,535 (57 %) | R | 121,906 (74 %) |
| I | 7,367 (4 %) | | | | |

## Campaign Finance

| | Receipts | Receipts from PACs | Expenditures |
|---|---|---|---|
| **1980** | | | |
| Edwards (R ) | $327,662 | $74,532 (23 %) | $300,211 |
| Hood (D ) | $38,150 | $2,163 (6 %) | $36,992 |
| **1978** | | | |
| Edwards (D ) | $252,562 | $37,694 (15 %) | $247,380 |
| Knipp (D ) | $4,505 | $700 (16 %) | $5,637 |

## Voting Studies

| | Presidential Support | | Party Unity | | Conservative Coalition | |
|---|---|---|---|---|---|---|
| Year | S | O | S | O | S | O |
| 1980 | 30 | 59 | 79 | 9 | 85 | 7 |
| 1979 | 21 | 68 | 86 | 9 | 87 | 5 |
| 1978 | 22 | 71 | 80 | 11 | 86 | 6 |
| 1977 | 28 | 72 | 90 | 7 | 94 | 4 |

S = Support          O = Opposition

## Key Votes

**96th Congress**

| | |
|---|---|
| Weaken Carter oil profits tax (1979) | Y |
| Reject hospital cost control plan (1979) | Y |
| Implement Panama Canal Treaties (1979) | N |
| Establish Department of Education (1979) | N |
| Approve Anti-busing Amendment (1979) | Y |
| Guarantee Chrysler Corp. loans (1979) | N |
| Approve military draft registration (1980) | N |
| Aid Sandinista regime in Nicaragua (1980) | N |
| Strengthen fair housing laws (1980) | N |

**97th Congress**

| | |
|---|---|
| Reagan budget proposal (1981) | Y |

## Interest Group Ratings

| Year | ADA | ACA | AFL-CIO | CCUS |
|---|---|---|---|---|
| 1980 | 17 | 83 | 6 | 78 |
| 1979 | 11 | 96 | 10 | 100 |
| 1978 | 10 | 92 | 5 | 83 |
| 1977 | 5 | 93 | 13 | 94 |

# 6 Glenn English (D)

**Of Cordell — Elected 1974**

**Born:** Nov. 30, 1940, Cordell, Okla.
**Education:** Southwestern State College, B.A. 1964.
**Military Career:** Army Reserve, 1965-71.
**Profession:** Petroleum landman.
**Family:** Wife, Jan Pangle; two children.
**Religion:** Methodist.
**Political Career:** No previous office.

**In Washington:** English has talked the language of his conservative prairie district consistently over six years in the House, and when necessary, placed its wishes over his own. It is a style that has brought him political success, but probably limited the role he can play in his party.

Viewed initially as a moderate national Democrat — he once worked for the Democrats in the California Legislature — English has been one of the most conservative of Southern members, voting against the party leadership on all but a handful of critical occasions in recent Congresses.

Declaring his district adamantly opposed to food stamp legislation, for example, he has voted against some food stamp bills. Although he has said he has no personal objections to such legislation, he has said that voting for them would have violated his philosophy of representation.

English found that philosophy costly in 1979, when the death of Leo Ryan, D-Calif., in Guyana opened up the chairmanship of a Government Operations subcommittee on energy. English was next in line for the position, but the liberal Democrats on the full Government Operations Committee decided the Oklahoman was simply too far to the right politically. Instead the plum was awarded to Connecticut's Toby Moffett, who had campaigned actively for it.

In the long-run, that may matter less to English than his continued presence on the Agriculture Committee, where he has been active, if sometimes frustrating to the committee's senior members.

Fiscally conservative on most issues, English has been an unceasing advocate of higher price support levels for his district's wheat farmers. In past years, he often tried to push those levels beyond the point that the Carter or Ford administrations were willing to accept, provoking the threat of presidential veto and forcing some farm-state colleagues into a politically difficult position.

In 1977, however, English successfully fought both the Carter administration and Agriculture Chairman Thomas S. Foley on wheat prices, insisting on a target price of $2.90 a bushel. Eventually the White House backed down, and Foley himself introduced the higher price on the House floor at the last minute.

In the 96th Congress English worked for a 7 percent "cost-of-living" increase in target prices on all feed grains for 1979. The Carter administration accepted the provision because it involved little short-term cost. English also proposed a variety of measures offering added subsidies to wheat farmers in the wake of the Carter grain embargo, bills which did not become law. He opposed the Carter administration's successful efforts to scale down farm disaster payments, which had been costing more than $400 million annually, and replace them with federal crop insurance, which farmers have to purchase.

In 1981, English voted for the Reagan budget cuts on the House floor, but said afterward that he was uncomfortable with the idea of reducing farm price supports. He said it might be desirable to strengthen controls on production in order to maintain sufficient price support levels.

**At Home:** English started his career as a petroleum landman — someone who arranges oil and gas leases. But politics soon attracted him. In

---

**6th District: West — Stillwater, Enid, the Panhandle.** Population: 494,961 (16% increase since 1970). Race: White 462,500 (93%), Black 10,956 (2%), Indian 12,964 (3%), Others 8,531 (2%). Spanish origin: 9,895 (2%).

the 1960s he went to California to be chief assistant to the Democrats in the California Legislature, at a time when dictatorial Assembly Speaker Jesse Unruh held sway. English then returned to Oklahoma and served as executive director of the Oklahoma Democratic Party from 1969 to 1973.

In 1974, English entered the Democratic primary in the 6th District, held for the previous three terms by Republican John Newbold Happy Camp, a genial and innocuous small-town banker. He was forced into a runoff against insurance agent David Hutchens, but defeated him by 9,435 votes.

In November, English conducted a town-to-town campaign across the district, contrasting his youth and energy with the barely visible effort conducted by Camp. He beat Camp by 8.8 per-

centage points and has won easily ever since.

**The District:** The 6th takes in much of the traditional Republican territory in the state — the northwestern tier of counties and the western Panhandle. These areas were settled primarily from neighboring Kansas, and the settlers brought their traditional Republicanism with them. Their descendants still display it. The southern portion of the district has a more Democratic tradition, but is conservative, like the Panhandle.

The 6th is ranching and wheat country, similar to the areas of Texas and Kansas that surround it. There is also some oil and gas, especially in the eastern part of the district around Ponca City. The district comes up to the border of Oklahoma City and takes in a small portion of it.

## Committees

**Agriculture** (12th of 24 Democrats)
Conservation, Credit, and Rural Development; Cotton, Rice and Sugar; Tobacco and Peanuts; Wheat, Soybeans, and Feed Grains.

**Government Operations** (9th of 23 Democrats)
Government Information and Individual Rights, chairman.

**Select Narcotics Abuse and Control** (5th of 11 Democrats)

## Elections

**1980 General**

| | |
|---|---|
| Glenn English (D ) | 111,694 (65 %) |
| Carol McCurley (R ) | 60,980 (35 %) |

**1978 General**

| | |
|---|---|
| Glenn English (D) | 103,512 (74 %) |
| Harold Hunter (R ) | 36,031 (26 %) |

**Previous Winning Percentages**

1976 (71 %)    1974 (53 %)

**District Vote For President**

| | 1980 | | 1976 | | 1972 |
|---|---|---|---|---|---|
| D | 55,150 (27 %) | D | 86,542 (44 %) | D | 37,994 (20 %) |
| R | 140,310 (69 %) | R | 106,437 (54 %) | R | 149,317 (78 %) |
| I | 6,607 (3 %) | | | | |

## Campaign Finance

| | Receipts | Receipts from PACs | Expenditures |
|---|---|---|---|
| **1980** | | | |
| English (D ) | $129,509 | $55,100 (43 %) | $81,837 |
| **1978** | | | |
| English (D ) | $116,866 | $38,249 (33 %) | $109,668 |

| | | | |
|---|---|---|---|
| Hunter (R ) | $65,532 | — (0 %) | $65,053 |

## Voting Studies

| | Presidential Support | | Party Unity | | Conservative Coalition | |
|---|---|---|---|---|---|---|
| Year | S | O | S | O | S | O |
| 1980 | 46 | 52 | 45 | 53 | 94 | 5 |
| 1979 | 35 | 61 | 33 | 66 | 90 | 9 |
| 1978 | 35 | 63 | 25 | 71 | 90 | 7 |
| 1977 | 34 | 66 | 30 | 68 | 91 | 8 |
| 1976 | 61 | 39 | 28 | 69 | 88 | 9 |
| 1975 | 53 | 47 | 37 | 61 | 87 | 11 |

S = Support          O = Opposition

## Key Votes

**96th Congress**

| | |
|---|---|
| Weaken Carter oil profits tax (1979) | Y |
| Reject hospital cost control plan (1979) | Y |
| Implement Panama Canal Treaties (1979) | N |
| Establish Department of Education (1979) | Y |
| Approve Anti-busing Amendment (1979) | Y |
| Guarantee Chrysler Corp. loans (1979) | N |
| Approve military draft registration (1980) | Y |
| Aid Sandinista regime in Nicaragua (1980) | N |
| Strengthen fair housing laws (1980) | N |

**97th Congress**

| | |
|---|---|
| Reagan budget proposal (1981) | Y |

## Interest Group Ratings

| Year | ADA | ACA | AFL-CIO | CCUS |
|---|---|---|---|---|
| 1980 | 6 | 63 | 26 | 65 |
| 1979 | 11 | 73 | 11 | 78 |
| 1978 | 15 | 88 | 16 | 67 |
| 1977 | 10 | 89 | 17 | 88 |
| 1976 | 25 | 79 | 39 | 69 |
| 1975 | 16 | 79 | 30 | 65 |

# Oregon

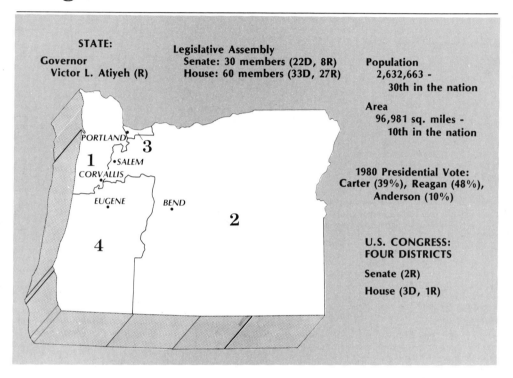

**STATE:**

Governor
Victor L. Atiyeh (R)

**Legislative Assembly**
Senate: 30 members (22D, 8R)
House: 60 members (33D, 27R)

**Population**
2,632,663 -
30th in the nation

**Area**
96,981 sq. miles -
10th in the nation

**1980 Presidential Vote:**
Carter (39%), Reagan (48%),
Anderson (10%)

**U.S. CONGRESS:**
**FOUR DISTRICTS**

Senate (2R)

House (3D, 1R)

PORTLAND
SALEM
CORVALLIS
EUGENE
BEND
1
3
2
4

## ... Ecopolitics

Oregon has spent much of this century moving in an opposite political direction from other Western states. It used to be called the "Vermont of the West" because it was so consistently Republican in national elections. Even while the states around it were going Democratic during the Depression, Oregon, like Vermont, kept up most of its GOP ties at the state level, although it did vote for Roosevelt four times.

Then in postwar years, when the Mountain states began to turn conservative and Republican, Oregon — like Vermont — moved left. Today, both states are attracting a new electorate of young professionals seeking a greener and quieter way of life. Environmental concerns have become salient political issues, and both states have begun electing moderate Republicans and liberal Democrats.

The two controversial symbols of modern Oregon politics are Wayne Morse, who was

elected to the Senate in 1944 as a progressive Republican and ended up in 1968 as an anti-war Democrat; and Tom McCall, a popular governor who urged people to visit Oregon for the scenery and then go home rather than place a permanent drain on its resources.

For most of the 1970s, Oregon sent two moderate Republicans to the U.S. Senate and four Democrats to the U.S. House. Jimmy Carter and Gerald Ford virtually tied in Oregon in 1976 — Ford ultimately won by 1,713 votes. Ronald Reagan took it in 1980, but John B. Anderson drew one of his strongest votes in the nation.

One reason Oregon does not vote much like the other Western states is that it does not have much in common with them. Settled before the Civil War, the state had a stronger Yankee strain than its neighbors. That group has been dominant for most of the state's history, although a minority group descended from Southern Democratic settlers has also had periods of power and influence.

The bulk of the state's population has always been west of the Cascade mountains, in Portland and a string of coastal and Willamette Valley towns similar in climate and temperament to San Francisco and Seattle rather than Denver and Reno.

Today, Oregon politics reflects environmental values that are distinctly in the minority in surrounding states. Most Oregonians have been jealously protective of their magnificent shorelines, valleys, mountains, rivers and forests and have sought to prevent rapid development. Though the state's population has grown by over 25 percent in the past 10 years, state environmental and zoning laws held down an even more explosive potential growth. Environmental pressures have been consistent despite the state's dependence on the timber industry, whose fortunes rose and fell periodically during the 1970s.

# A Political Tour

**Portland.** The green city of Portland dominates the state's economic activity as well as its politics. Sitting along the Willamette River, Oregon's largest city (pop. 366,000) has a reputation for being a pleasant, livable place. As the only major metropolitan area between San Francisco and Seattle, it has attracted large banks, law firms, headquarters of giant lumber firms, and a large shipping trade. Electronics firms, specialty woolen mills and some heavy industry have also located in the area. Portland has a sizable blue-collar vote.

Bisected by the Willamette, Portland is socially and politically two cities. On the west side, beyond the modern, high-rise towers of the thriving downtown area, are the affluent West Hills. Scenic parklands and quiet residential areas with magnificent views make this a favorite spot for the liberal professionals who can afford it. Politically, this is the more Republican side of town, although Jimmy Carter matched Ronald Reagan vote for vote in the area.

East of the Willamette live the majority of Portland's citizens. Poor blacks in the Albina section join blue-collar whites in the North End and the East Side's many elderly residents to give Democrats comfortable margins. Carter easily defeated Reagan in the eastern part of the city, where the vote for independent John B. Anderson was less than in the western hills.

With Mt. Hood and the Cascade mountains blocking expansion on the east, Portland's suburban growth has been pushed into Clackamas and Washington counties on the south and west. Both counties have been growing at twice the state rate, and each now has nearly a quarter-million people. Beaverton, with less than 6,000 people in 1960, had more than 30,000 residents by 1980.

The suburban vote is now nearly double that of Portland, and is predictably conservative, as white-collar management people have settled into an affluent life style. With the highest median income in the state, Washington County joined Clackamas and the part of Multnomah County outside of Portland in giving Reagan a 37,000-vote plurality in 1980. Carter's plurality in Portland was less than 24,000.

**The Willamette Valley.** Stretching 180 miles south from Portland, this 60-mile-wide valley sits comfortably between the Cascades and the Coastal mountains. With mild temperatures and fertile land, it is the state's food-basket and claims to have the potential to feed up to 12 million people. Dairy products, poultry, wheat, barley, oats, hogs, fruit and vegetables are all found in the valley. But there is more to it than farmland.

Spaced unevenly down the valley, and connected by Interstate 5, are all of Oregon's significant urban areas. From Portland on the north to Eugene and Springfield on the south, the Willamette Valley is home to two out of three Oregonians. Also in the valley are the state's two major universities — the University of Oregon at Eugene and Oregon State University at Corvallis — and enough of the state's vast timberlands to support several sawmill towns.

Willamette Valley voters register Democratic but often vote Republican. In 1980, Reagan carried every county in the valley, including Linn and Lane, the two Carter won in 1976.

Lane County, the most populous part of the Willamette Valley south of Portland, has a reputation for being the liberal heartland of Oregon. The reputation comes from Eugene, a growing city of 105,000 people. Commonly thought of as a university town, Eugene also relies heavily on the nearby fir and cedar forests for much of its non-university employment. The university vote was important in helping to pass a 1971 city referendum calling for the withdrawal of all U.S. troops from Vietnam. But workers in the lumber mills and in other diversified timber industries were the ones responsible for the defeat of a homosexual rights law seven years later. John F. Kennedy, Hubert Humphrey and George McGovern all lost Lane County to Richard Nixon.

**The Coast.** Only 25 miles wide, the Oregon coast is wet, wooded, and more reliably Democratic than any other part of the state.

With close to 130 inches of rainfall each year, it is the part of the state that brought on Gov. McCall's quip about tourists rusting on the coast's plentiful beaches. Tourism and fishing are the two economic mainstays of the coastal area, which is not as prosperous as most of the rest of the state. The two counties in the northwest corner of the state — Clatsop and Columbia — also have some fruit orchards and logging activity.

Those two counties are the most Democratic in Oregon. Columbia has voted for every Democratic presidential candidate since 1932. Neighboring Clatsop was one of the few Oregon counties to back Adlai Stevenson in 1956. It has not left the Democratic column since.

In recent years, Republicans have made some inroads in the area, particularly in the southern coastal counties. Coos County, the region's largest county, has a Democratic tradition dating back to the New Deal era, but it went Republican for president in 1980 and supported Republican Senate and gubernatorial candidates in 1978.

**Eastern and Southern Rural Oregon.** Farms, forests, and cattle ranges make up the rest of Oregon. Covering more than 70 percent of the land, it has less than 25 percent of the voters, but they are the most conservative ones.

Directly south of the Willamette Valley, in the Klamath Mountains, are a few modest-sized cities scattered among the fruit orchards and forests. Medford is the largest, with 40,000 residents. Roseburg, Klamath Falls, Grants Pass and Ashland all have about 15,000 people.

Across the Cascade mountains to the east are only two towns with more than 10,000 people (Bend and Pendleton). The rest of the population live on farms in the irrigated Columbia River Valley to the north, or in the ranch land of the Great Basin in the wide-open desert-like south.

This region is more typically "Western" than any other part of the state. Suspicion of "big government" and environmentalists has brought substantial Republican majorities in many elections. Mainstream Republicans such as Sen. Bob Packwood do well in the northernmost counties, along the Columbia, where the hilly wheat fields bring farmers a steady income.

Twenty years ago, support for public power development turned voters in the remote Wallowa Mountains toward the Democratic Party. But since then, an anti-government mood has taken over, and Union and Wallowa Counties, which supported Stevenson in 1956 and Kennedy in 1960, went overwhelmingly against Carter and veteran Democratic Rep. Al Ullman in 1980.

The most Republican county in the state is Malheur, in the southeastern corner.

# Redrawing the Lines

Population in Oregon's three congressional districts outside of Portland jumped more than 30 percent in the past decade, enough to bring the state a new congressional seat.

Democrats control both houses of the Legislature, and at midyear they were talking about creating a new seat somewhere in the Willamette Valley using parts of the current 2nd and 4th Districts. Taking too much ground from the 4th would make that southwest district friendlier territory for Republicans, but a new Willamette Valley seat should not harm incumbents in the 1st, 2nd or 3rd Districts.

---

## Governor
## Victor L. Atiyeh (R)

**Born:** Feb. 20, 1923, Portland, Ore.
**Home:** Salem, Ore.
**Education:** Attended U. of Oregon, two years.
**Profession:** President, family rug business.
**Family:** Wife, Dolores; two children.
**Religion:** Episcopalian.
**Political Career:** Oregon House, 1959-65; Oregon Senate, 1965-79; unsuccessful campaign for governor, 1974; elected governor 1978; term expires Jan. 1983.

# Mark O. Hatfield (R)

**Of Newport — Elected 1966**

**Born:** July 12, 1922, Dallas, Ore.
**Education:** Willamette U., B.A. 1943; Stanford U., A.M. 1948.
**Military Career:** Navy, 1943-46.
**Profession:** Professor.
**Family:** Wife, Antoinette Kuzmanich; four children.
**Religion:** Baptist.
**Political Career:** Ore. House, 1951-55; Ore. Senate, 1955-57; Ore. secretary of state, 1957-59; Ore. governor, 1959-67.

**In Washington:** Thanks to a knack for building personal friendship, Hatfield has steadily accumulated power in the Senate despite some views strikingly out of alignment with his party's growing conservatism.

Hatfield is well-enough regarded that his reputation as a somewhat quixotic liberal moralist presented no obstacle to the Appropriations chairmanship for which he qualified by seniority in 1981. His ascent to that job makes him the Senate's best-placed critic of defense spending and spokesman against conservative retreat from social programs.

At the same time, Hatfield's history of learning to live within the system suggests the chairmanship may tug him gradually to the right. In the first round of votes on President Reagan's budget, Hatfield was loyal to the president, opposing repeated efforts to increase domestic social spending.

The Oregon senator is best known to the public for his sallies on foreign policy and defense issues. He led the opposition to the neutron warhead and the MX missile, pressed for human rights concessions from authoritarian foreign regimes, and filibustered against reinstatement of the draft in 1980. He threatened a second filibuster if the Senate took up a bill to begin production of nerve gas weapons (it did not).

Hatfield was one of the earliest critics of the war in Vietnam on moral grounds. He has spoken for Palestinian refugees and advocated cuts in military aid to Israel as "a signal" of disapproval of Israeli bombing raids in southern Lebanon.

For years, he routinely cast his "protest vote" against spending bills for defense and foreign aid, the latter because they include gifts and sales of arms. While colleagues opposed the Salt II treaty as an unfair restriction on U.S. security, Hatfield complained that it was too weak, and did not go far enough in controlling the nuclear weapons race.

In the early defense-related confrontations of the 97th Congress, Hatfield continued to raise a lonely voice of protest. He castigated his colleagues for sparing the Pentagon budget during the siege on spending. Hatfield's suspicion of the atom extends to nuclear power; he has been one of the most active Senate opponents of the nuclear breeder reactor. His feeling is partially explained by the fact that, as a young naval officer, Hatfield was a member of the first American military team to enter Hiroshima, one month after the atom bomb demolished the city.

Hatfield has consistently supported most social programs and civil rights legislation, even such unpopular solutions as busing.

These views are rooted in a born-again religious conviction. Not to be confused with the fundamentalism of the evangelical right, Hatfield's view of the Bible places greater weight on the commitment to help the poor. Though he does not flaunt his faith during Senate debate, Hatfield courts a religious constituency with speeches and newsletters to believers, participates regularly in Capitol prayer meetings, and has written three books for religious publishing houses describing the tribulations of a Christian in politics.

Equally devout is Hatfield's belief in the freedom of the individual, a view he derives in part from Herbert Hoover, whom he greatly admired. His values help to explain his libertarian position on the draft, and his interest in volunteerism — returning responsibility for many social services to the local level. Over the years he has developed a roster of obscure bills to encourage neighborhood-based social programs, and has also preached that churches should shoulder more of the social burden.

Colleagues have been inclined to forgive Hatfield what they view as political eccentricities.

Outsiders sometimes listen to his moralistic speeches and decide he must be personally sanctimonious, but he has rarely had that problem with other senators. He has always remembered that the Senate functions on personal relationships, and he has cultivated them across lines of ideology.

A classic case is his friendship with hawkish Mississippian John Stennis, former chairman of the Armed Services Committee. Starting with a mutual interest in developing waterways and public power, the two men formed a close relationship that has survived numerous jousts on defense issues. After Stennis was shot by a burglar in 1973, Hatfield rushed to the hospital and, without identifying himself, took command of a telephone switchboard jammed with calls from newsmen and friends.

The other factor that has spared Hatfield the role of pariah has been his choice of committee assignments. During the Vietnam era, he had hoped to join the Foreign Relations Committee to exercise his interest in the problems of war and peace. But after some agonizing, he settled instead for Appropriations and Rules. Together with his seat on Energy and Natural Resources, these assignments have brought Hatfield political benefits at home (jurisdiction over public forests and rangelands, hydroelectric power and harbors) and leverage in Congress. As a member of Appropriations, he became adept at the senatorial art of *quid pro quo.*

In recent years, Hatfield has become more outspoken against federal spending, except when applied to public works and public lands programs in the Pacific Northwest. When Democrats controlled Appropriations, Hatfield once explained that he would like to cut money from the budget, but since that was impossible he was determined to steer as much of it as possible to his home state.

"There are a lot of things in the system I don't like," he said. "In the meantime, here the system is, and we have to make the best of it."

**At Home:** Hatfield has enjoyed uninterrupted success in Oregon politics — moving from state legislator to secretary of state, governor, and U.S. senator without one defeat. He has been able to appeal to liberals and labor without alienating conservatives enough to provoke a strong primary challenge.

As a member of the Oregon Senate in the 1950s, he pleased liberals with his opposition to loyalty oaths for teachers; much later he cemented that support as a critic of the Vietnam War.

Organized labor, when it has not been able to back him against a Democratic competitor, usually has remained neutral. Earlier in his career, Hatfield liked to play up his labor connections: his father, a blacksmith, belonged to the railroad brotherhood, and his father-in-law was a longshoreman.

A political science professor and university dean, Hatfield acquired Republicanism from his mother, who had been raised in the staunchly GOP territory of east Tennessee. In 1958, as secretary of state in Oregon, he blended an effective campaign style with youthful good looks to unseat Democratic Gov. Robert D. Holmes.

Holmes suffered from internal party problems; he had quarreled with Democratic legislators over taxes and patronage. Hatfield's position was enhanced when the state's Republican Party renounced its longstanding resistance to public power development, which the Democrats had used against the GOP in past elections.

As governor, Hatfield ran an administration that kept state spending down and did not raise taxes. He launched an aggressive "Sell Oregon" drive that helped spur exports. And in 1962, he withstood a strong re-election challenge from Democrat Robert Y. Thornton, the state attorney general, who was unable to mobilize the labor support he needed to defeat a popular governor.

Constitutionally forbidden to run for a third term as governor in 1966, Hatfield took aim at the Senate seat being vacated by Democrat Maurine Neuberger.

In that race, the central issue was the Vietnam War, which Hatfield opposed and his Democratic rival, Rep. Robert B. Duncan, favored. As Duncan saw it, the conflict concerned whether "Americans will die in the buffalo grass of Vietnam or the rye grass of Oregon."

Hatfield had been the lone dissenting vote on a National Governors' Conference resolution supporting the war. Afterward, in his Senate campaign, he put up billboards with the word "Courage" in large letters. He blamed the war for the state's lagging lumber industry, reasoning that the conflict had brought a downturn in home construction. Fearful of being painted as unpatriotic, however, Hatfield criticized the "inexcusable excesses of some anti-war demonstrations." Hatfield defeated Duncan, but by fewer than 25,000 votes.

Running for re-election six years later, however, he did considerably better aganst an even more militant Vietnam dove, former Sen. Wayne Morse, who was seeking a comeback as the Democratic nominee. Despite Hatfield's anti-war activities, the Nixon White House cooperated with his re-election that year, and this helped defuse conservative resentment toward him in Oregon. Morse had difficulty finding an issue to use against the Republican; in 1966, Morse had announced that he would vote for Hatfield over Duncan because of the war issue.

Morse had a built-in constituency in Oregon of at least 40 percent — people who would support him regardless of the opposition. So Hatfield could not amass a huge plurality. But he was re-elected by nearly 70,00 votes.

In 1978, Hatfield finally got an easy Senate re-election. Running against state Sen. Vern Cook, a Democrat who had a loser's reputation after two unsuccessful campaigns for the House, Hatfield won a third term by more than 200,000 votes.

## Committees

**Appropriations** (Chairman)
Energy and Water Development, chairman; Foreign Operations; Labor, Health and Human Services, Education; Legislative Branch.

**Energy and Natural Resources** (2nd of 11 Republicans)
Energy Conservation and Supply; Public Lands and Reserved Water; Water and Power.

**Rules and Administration** (2nd of 7 Republicans)

**Joint Library**

**Joint Printing**

## Elections

**1978 General**

| | |
|---|---|
| Mark Hatfield (R ) | 550,165 (62 %) |
| Vernon Cook (D ) | 341,616 (38 %) |

**1978 Primary**

| | |
|---|---|
| Mark Hatfield (R ) | 159,617 (66 %) |
| Bert Hawkins (R ) | 43,350 (18 %) |
| Robert Maxwell (R ) | 24,294 (10 %) |
| Richard Schnepel (R ) | 15,628 (6 %) |

**Previous Winning Percentages**

1972 (54 %)    1966 (52 %)

## Campaign Finance

| | Receipts | Receipts from PACs | Expenditures |
|---|---|---|---|
| **1978** | | | |
| Hatfield (R ) | $277,059 | $90,633 (33 %) | $223,874 |
| Cook (D ) | $38,977 | $6,050 (16 %) | $38,976 |

## Voting Studies

| | Presidential Support | | Party Unity | | Conservative Coalition | |
|---|---|---|---|---|---|---|
| Year | S | O | S | O | S | O |
| 1980 | 45 | 34 | 42 | 41 | 42 | 52 |

| Year | S | O | S | O | S | O |
|---|---|---|---|---|---|---|
| 1979 | 57 | 27 | 38 | 47 | 38 | 52 |
| 1978 | 62 | 18 | 21 | 62 | 31 | 51 |
| 1977 | 66 | 30 | 51 | 34 | 60 | 30 |
| 1976 | 40 | 40 | 41 | 46 | 45 | 40 |
| 1975 | 45 | 43 | 35 | 55 | 33 | 61 |
| 1974 (Ford) | 28 | 46 | | | | |
| 1974 | 29 | 47 | 28 | 53 | 21 | 56 |
| 1973 | 45 | 46 | 34 | 54 | 37 | 45 |
| 1972 | 15 | 41 | 31 | 41 | 33 | 39 |
| 1971 | 33 | 55 | 30 | 53 | 24 | 63 |
| 1970 | 46 | 31 | 27 | 47 | 21 | 54 |
| 1969 | 50 | 44 | 31 | 58 | 35 | 58 |
| 1968 | 48 | 35 | 47 | 38 | 30 | 50 |
| 1967 | 47 | 20 | 40 | 20 | 30 | 38 |

S = Support         O = Opposition

## Key Votes

**96th Congress**

| | |
|---|---|
| Maintain relations with Taiwan (1979) | Y |
| Reduce synthetic fuel development funds (1979) | N |
| Impose nuclear plant moratorium (1979) | Y |
| Kill stronger windfall profits tax (1979) | N |
| Guarantee Chrysler Corp. loans (1979) | N |
| Approve military draft registration (1980) | N |
| End Revenue Sharing to the states (1980) | + |
| Block Justice Dept. busing suits (1980) | N |

**97th Congress**

| | |
|---|---|
| Restore urban program funding cuts (1981) | N |

## Interest Group Ratings

| Year | ADA | ACA | AFL-CIO | CCUS-1 | CCUS-2 |
|---|---|---|---|---|---|
| 1980 | 50 | 65 | 47 | 59 | |
| 1979 | 58 | 40 | 63 | 11 | 46 |
| 1978 | 50 | 22 | 86 | 38 | |
| 1977 | 60 | 36 | 37 | 56 | |
| 1976 | 65 | 21 | 53 | 33 | |
| 1975 | 83 | 39 | 57 | 63 | |
| 1974 | 76 | 6 | 55 | 63 | |
| 1973 | 80 | 30 | 33 | 38 | |
| 1972 | 55 | 29 | 50 | 40 | |
| 1971 | 74 | 20 | 33 | - | |
| 1970 | 84 | 17 | 100 | 29 | |
| 1969 | 89 | 43 | 82 | - | |
| 1968 | 71 | 50 | 75 | - | |
| 1967 | 54 | 44 | 64 | 44 | |

# Bob Packwood (R)

**Of Portland — Elected 1968**

**Born:** Sept. 11, 1932, Portland, Ore.
**Education:** Willamette U., B.A. 1954; N.Y.U. School of Law, LL.B. 1957.
**Profession:** Lawyer.
**Family:** Wife, Georgie Oberteuffer; two children.
**Religion:** Unitarian.
**Political Career:** Ore. House, 1963-69.

**In Washington:** An Eastern writer once described Packwood and Oregon senior senator Mark Hatfield as the "Tweedledum and Tweedledee of Oregon politics," placing them both in the state's established moderate Republican tradition.

It is hard to imagine a more dramatic misjudgment of Packwood's legislative interests, outlook and style.

Where Hatfield is a devout right-to-lifer, Packwood early staked out a place as the Senate's foremost advocate of population control and abortion rights. He cast the only vote against Joseph Califano for HEW secretary in the Carter administration, arguing that Califano was too strongly anti-abortion to control federal health programs.

Where Hatfield is the closest thing to a pacifist in the Senate, Packwood is a strong supporter of military spending, particularly in defense of Israel. In his 1980 re-election campaign, he held fund-raising parties in heavily Jewish neighborhoods all over the country to take advantage of the popularity his position had earned him.

Where Hatfield has backed generous social spending as a member of Appropriations, Packwood has looked at the world through the eyes of the Finance Committee, and tried to use the tax system to accomplish social goals — credits for parents who send their children to private schools and incentives for business to offer employees health care.

Finally, where Hatfield has built his reputation on personal rapport and moral conviction, Packwood is a more strenuously political animal — more partisan in practice than his voting record suggests.

In 1978 he sponsored a widely noticed national conference, modeled on a successful annual meeting he started in Oregon, where Republicans spend a weekend thinking and talking about the party's future. It has become an annual and influential event.

Packwood has occupied mid-level leadership posts as chairman of the Republican senatorial campaign committee and the Republican conference. He has said he would like to succeed his friend Howard Baker as Senate GOP leader someday, if his views —particularly his out-front support for abortion — have not disqualified him.

When Packwood came to Congress in 1969, fresh from a stunning upset of Wayne Morse, *Newsweek* marked him as one of the "bright new stars" of the Senate. He made a name as a party maverick by helping Democrats defeat two of President Nixon's Supreme Court nominees, and by a series of speeches chiding the Senate as hidebound and irresponsible, especially in its practice of awarding chairmanships purely by seniority.

But scattershot interests, youthful impatience and a perennially high staff turnover contributed later to an impression that Packwood had not settled into a legislative niche, despite years of activity on the Finance and Banking committees. Packwood switched from Banking to the Commerce Committee in early 1977, but initially showed limited interest in his new assignment. In the 96th Congress, however, he assumed a more active role when the committee began to spend its time cutting back federal regulation. Now, as Commerce chairman in a Republican Senate, Packwood has a natural forum for his legislative ideas.

In 1980, his political skills were instrumental in getting the Commerce Committee to report a controversial and complex trucking deregulation bill. Packwood helped make a case that the bill would make the trucking industry more competitive, and thus less inflationary. It passed Congress despite firm opposition from the Teamsters union. He also helped round up support for passage of a plan to defederalize airports.

**1007**

Meanwhile, on Finance, Packwood was seeking to apply his enthusiasm for tax incentives to the energy industry. When Finance wrote an oil windfall profits tax bill in 1979, Packwood was prepared with tax credit proposals for virtually every new form of energy that has been suggested — solar, geothermal, wind, biomass, and others. Some of these ideas were dropped later in conference with the House, but substantial tax credit money remained in the bill, partly because of Packwood.

The junior Oregon senator earned an early reputation as an environmentalist, particularly for his fight to block dams in Hells Canyon on the Oregon-Idaho border. Later he seemed to lose some of his enthusiasm for land conservation bills, though he sponsored other environmental initiatives, such as limits on throwaway beverage containers and aerosol propellants, and whale protection legislation.

For a lawyer who spent much of his pre-political life arguing the business side of labor cases, Packwood has a surprising amount of good will among organized labor. Though his overall voting record is not rated high by unions, Packwood broke with the majority of Republicans in 1978 to support labor law revision, which would have eased union organizing, and common-site picketing, which would have expanded strike rights in the construction industry.

His flirtations with environmentalists and labor have given Packwood an up-and-down relationship with his state's major industry, timber. In recent years, the trend has been up, due to Packwood's support of cuts in capital gains taxation (private timber is taxed as a capital gain), and his 1980 bill setting up a $30 million trust fund for replanting of denuded federal forests.

**At Home:** Senate Republicans, who have twice picked Packwood to head their campaign committee, may have been impressed by his Oregon experience. He has few peers as a campaigner, organizer and fund-raiser.

Some of those skills may be in his blood. His great-grandfather was a member of the 1857 Oregon constitutional convention and held sundry political appointments; his father was a business lobbyist before the state Legislature.

As an undergraduate at Willamette University, Packwood took political science from Hatfield, then a professor. That may have colored their future relationship, which was for a long time the cordial but cool cooperation of an established senior statesman and an ambitious rival for public recognition.

As a young politician, Packwood had something of a reputation for outspokenness and boat-rocking. In 1962, he startled the party establishment by announcing that Sig Unander, that year's GOP Senate nominee against Morse, stood no chance of winning. But unlike Morse — who bolted from the Republican Party, then spent the rest of his life feuding inside the Democratic Party — Packwood has never seen himself as being at odds with the GOP. He has argued that he is a force for revitalizing it.

The Morse whom Packwood encountered in 1968 was a weaker political figure than the one who beat Unander. He had narrowly survived a rough primary with former Rep. Robert Duncan, whereas Packwood had negligible party opposition.

Packwood was to the right of Morse on several issues, including the most salient issue of the day, the Vietnam War; Packwood, while critical of the South Vietnamese government, castigated Morse for voting to cut off funds for the war.

But ideology was not the focal point of the campaign. The main issue was Morse himself. Packwood labeled Morse as ineffective, saying that the state had been harmed by the Democrat's contentious style. Other senators were reluctant to help Morse get federal projects for Oregon, he charged. Morse was 68 years old in 1968; he was feisty and vigorous, but Packwood still managed to win support on the issue of youth vs. age. Starting out far behind but building a splendid campaign organization, Packwood edged Morse by 3,293 votes out of 814,176 cast.

The 1974 contest began as a rematch between Packwood and Morse. But Morse died suddenly in midsummer, and the Democrats replaced him with state Sen. Betty Roberts.

Roberts, who had just lost the 1974 gubernatorial primary, benefited from statewide name recognition and a good campaign organization. But she also had a large debt from her bid for governor.

Packwood worked hard to insulate himself from Watergate in the year of Nixon's resignation. He was sharply critical of the departed president and objected to the pardon he received from President Ford.

In 1980, "pro-choice" advocate Packwood found himself targeted by anti-abortion groups. There was talk of a $200,000 right-to-life drive to unseat him in the primary. The immediate effect of this rumor was to mobilize support for Packwood in the women's movement. Feminist Gloria Steinem raised a half-million dollars for him with a fund-raising letter warning that he was "in danger of drowning in a virtual sea of 'right-to-life' money and zealots."

But a strong primary challenger failed to materialize as two conservative Republican opponents, Brenda Jose and Rosalie Huss, spent most of their time fighting each other. Packwood won renomination handily.

In the general election, Packwood's campaign finances became a central issue. Democrat Ted Kulongoski, a state senator, charged that Packwood was trying to buy the election and also profiting handsomely from speaking engagement fees.

But many Democratic voters found Packwood acceptable. Labor had trouble making up its mind, with the state AFL-CIO backing Kulongoski against the wishes of its executive council, which recommended no endorsement. Packwood drew the support of the building trades unions in Portland.

## Committees

**Commerce, Science and Transportation** (Chairman)
Business, Trade, and Tourism.

**Finance** (2nd of 11 Republicans)
Taxation and Debt Management, chairman; Health; Savings, Pensions, and Investment Policy.

**Small Business** (2nd of 9 Republicans)
Capital Formation and Retention, chairman; Innovation and Technology.

**Joint Taxation**

## Elections

**1980 General**

| | |
|---|---|
| Bob Packwood (R) | 594,290 (52%) |
| Ted Kulongoski (D) | 501,963 (44%) |

**1980 Primary**

| | |
|---|---|
| Bob Packwood (R) | 191,127 (62%) |
| Brenda Jose (R) | 45,973 (15%) |
| Kenneth Brown (R) | 23,599 (8%) |
| Rosalie Huss (R) | 22,929 (7%) |
| Willard Severn (R) | 22,281 (7%) |

**Previous Winning Percentages**

1974 (55%)    1968 (50%)

## Campaign Finance

| | Receipts | Receipts from PACs | Expenditures |
|---|---|---|---|
| **1980** | | | |
| Packwood (R) | $1,823,609 | $345,472 (19%) | $1,656,081 |
| Kulongoski (D) | $192,759 | $23,823 (12%) | $190,047 |

## Voting Studies

| | Presidential Support | Party Unity | Conservative Coalition |
|---|---|---|---|

| Year | S | O | S | O | S | O |
|---|---|---|---|---|---|---|
| 1980 | 65 | 29 | 40 | 43 | 35 | 55 |
| 1979 | 68 | 24 | 42 | 47 | 44 | 47 |
| 1978 | 53 | 33 | 48 | 45 | 50 | 44 |
| 1977 | 57 | 35 | 60 | 30 | 72 | 21 |
| 1976 | 64 | 26 | 55 | 34 | 61 | 28 |
| 1975 | 69 | 27 | 48 | 42 | 37 | 53 |
| 1974 (Ford) | 25 | 29 | | | | |
| 1974 | 37 | 42 | 32 | 46 | 25 | 51 |
| 1973 | 57 | 28 | 48 | 34 | 41 | 38 |
| 1972 | 65 | 15 | 69 | 25 | 68 | 24 |
| 1971 | 62 | 20 | 57 | 27 | 53 | 34 |
| 1970 | 53 | 19 | 52 | 35 | 50 | 36 |
| 1969 | 76 | 21 | 62 | 34 | 48 | 46 |

S = Support          O = Opposition

## Key Votes

**96th Congress**

| | |
|---|---|
| Maintain relations with Taiwan (1979) | Y |
| Reduce synthetic fuel development funds (1979) | Y |
| Impose nuclear plant moratorium (1979) | N |
| Kill stronger windfall profits tax (1979) | Y |
| Guarantee Chrysler Corp. loans (1979) | N |
| Approve military draft registration (1980) | N |
| End Revenue Sharing to the states (1980) | N |
| Block Justice Dept. busing suits (1980) | N |

**97th Congress**

| | |
|---|---|
| Restore urban program funding cuts (1981) | N |

## Interest Group Ratings

| Year | ADA | ACA | AFL-CIO | CCUS-1 | CCUS-2 |
|---|---|---|---|---|---|
| 1980 | 56 | 43 | 44 | 53 | |
| 1979 | 32 | 38 | 47 | 33 | 43 |
| 1978 | 45 | 41 | 69 | 44 | |
| 1977 | 45 | 42 | 63 | 50 | |
| 1976 | 45 | 40 | 25 | 22 | |
| 1975 | 72 | 41 | 45 | 60 | |
| 1974 | 62 | 19 | 70 | 25 | |
| 1973 | 50 | 36 | 20 | 67 | |
| 1972 | 45 | 55 | 40 | 43 | |
| 1971 | 30 | 60 | 20 | - | |
| 1970 | 50 | 50 | 67 | 60 | |
| 1969 | 56 | 33 | 73 | - | |

# 1 Les AuCoin (D)

## Of Forest Grove — Elected 1974

**Born:** Oct. 21, 1942, Redmond, Ore.
**Education:** Pacific U., B.A. 1969.
**Military Career:** Army, 1961-64.
**Profession:** Journalist.
**Family:** Wife, Susan Swearinger; two children.
**Religion:** Protestant.
**Political Career:** Ore. House, 1971-75, majority leader, 1973-75.

**In Washington:** One of many articulate reform-minded Democrats elected in the 1974 sweep, AuCoin chose a different approach from most of them during his first few terms, generally forsaking the turmoil of institutional politics for the intricacies of federal spending formulas. For six years AuCoin labored over housing policy as a member of the Banking Committee. In 1981 he switched to Appropriations.

Banking was a logical workplace for AuCoin because it handles housing, and housing construction helps determine the health of the forest products industry in his district and most of the state. The first year he spent much of his time on a measure to provide home mortgage subsidies for middle-income families, working to keep most of the money for new construction rather than existing units.

Two years later, AuCoin was in the thick of one of the increasingly common "formula fights," this one over how to award urban block grant money to local communities. The issue matched the urban Northeast and Midwest — advocating money to fix up old housing stock — against the South and West, which simply wanted to use income levels as the basis for the funds.

To the surprise of many members, AuCoin spoke for the older cities of the East. "I come from the West," he said. "My allegiance is to the West, but I also belong to the United States." Some observers pointed out that AuCoin's home base of Portland, although a Western city, has housing stock as old as that in some Eastern urban areas. But it was agreed that AuCoin played an important role in defeating the Sun Belt forces on the issue.

In 1980, AuCoin fought a new program of rent subsidies to middle-income families, arguing that any money available to supplement rents ought to be confined to the poor. AuCoin and Republican J. William Stanton of Ohio managed to get the full Banking Committee to vote a reduction in the program, to 32,000 units from the 120,000 units approved in subcommittee. Later it died in a House-Senate conference. AuCoin did successfully amend the 1981 housing authorization bill to provide money for rehabilitating old hotels used as low-income housing.

On the Merchant Marine Committee, AuCoin worked on legislation establishing a 200-mile U.S. fishing limit, and argued successfully for legislation to give domestic fish processors first crack at fish caught within it. He gave up the Merchant Marine assignment along with Banking to go on Appropriations in 1981.

Outside housing issues, AuCoin has normally allied himself with the "sunset" generation of House Democrats, expressing skepticism about orthodox New Deal domestic programs. He opposed the Chrysler loan guarantee, in the Banking Committee and on the floor. He cosponsored legislation calling for mandatory periodic review of federal programs.

AuCoin began speaking out more often on broader issues in 1979, when he was considering a Senate campaign against Republican Robert Packwood. An ex-newspaper reporter with a radio announcer's voice, he has always been careful to keep his name before a statewide public in Oregon, and he regularly samples public opinion outside his district. He ultimately decided not to make that challenge, though he still has statewide ambitions.

---

**1st District: Northwest — Portland and suburbs, Corvallis.** Population: 699,073 (34% increase since 1970). Race: White 669,224 (96%), Black 3,549 (1%), Others 26,300 (4%). Spanish origin: 15,098 (2%).

One key disappointment for AuCoin was his failure in 1979 to win a spot on the Budget Committee. The previous year he had voted on the House floor for several conspicuous budget-cutting amendments; this was thought to influence the more liberal Democratic leadership against his selection.

On Appropriations, AuCoin filled subcommittee vacancies on Interior and Transportation, both previously occupied by his 3rd District neighbor, Democrat Robert B. Duncan, who was beaten for renomination in 1980.

In his early months on the panel, AuCoin followed Duncan's pattern of pushing for increased investment in logging in national forests. He also has shown an interest in defending mass transit in general, and Amtrak in particular.

**At Home:** A journalist by training, AuCoin had drifted off into public relations work by 1968, when the Vietnam War motivated him to become active in politics. He campaigned for Sen. Eugene McCarthy, who won the Democratic presidential primary in Oregon.

Two years later AuCoin won a seat in the Legislature from Washington County, just west of Portland. By 1974, when Republican Wendell Wyatt decided to retire from Congress after five terms, AuCoin had risen to majority leader in the Oregon House. He was the unanimous choice for the Democratic nomination among legislators from the 1st District.

With that support and a forceful campaign leveling most of its criticism at the Nixon administration, AuCoin had little trouble winning the nomination over four lesser-known candidates.

His Republican opponent, the former director of the state Department of Environmental Quality, was equally articulate and had Wyatt's strong endorsement. But labor and education groups helped provide AuCoin with a better organization than the GOP could put together in the year of Watergate resentment. AuCoin stressed his legislative record, pointing specifically to pension reform, energy policy and tax relief measures that came out of committees he chaired. He carried every county and became the first Democrat ever to represent the district.

Since then AuCoin has performed the kinds of constituent service for which his House generation has become famous. In 1978, as part of an effort to convince voters of his bipartisan appeal, he formed a group of Republicans who supported his re-election. His opponents always claim he is too liberal for the district, but the GOP's strongest candidates have been discouraged from running by AuCoin's consistent popularity.

**The District:** This diverse constituency includes the more fashionable sections of Portland, a quickly growing suburban area west of the city, and half a dozen rural counties extending all the way to the Pacific.

The Republican leanings of suburban Washington County, which makes up a third of the district's vote, swung the district to Gerald Ford in 1976 and Ronald Reagan in 1980. Popular Democrats like AuCoin, however, have little trouble attracting ticket-splitters there.

The rural voters in the area along the Columbia River and the Pacific coast — Columbia, Clatsop and Tillamook counties — tend to be more Democratic. Logging and fishing are the primary industries in that area. Inland, along the agricultural west bank of the Willamette River, are more Republican counties — Yamhill, Polk and Benton.

## Committees

**Appropriations** (29th of 33 Democrats)
Interior; Transportation.

## Elections

**1980 General**

| | |
|---|---|
| Les AuCoin (D ) | 203,532 (66 %) |
| Lynn Engdahl (R ) | 105,083 (34 %) |

**1978 General**

| | |
|---|---|
| Les AuCoin (D ) | 158,706 (63 %) |
| Nick Bunick (R ) | 93,640 (37 %) |

**Previous Winning Percentages**
1976 (59 %)     1974 (56 %)

**District Vote For President**

| | 1980 | | 1976 | | 1972 |
|---|---|---|---|---|---|
| D | 124,003 (37%) | D | 120,319 (43%) | D | 101,749 (41%) |
| R | 158,286 (48%) | R | 150,482 (53%) | R | 137,511 (55%) |
| I | 38,597 (12%) | | | | |

## Campaign Finance

| 1980 | Receipts | Receipts from PACs | Expenditures |
|---|---|---|---|
| AuCoin (D ) | $294,491 | $122,612 (42 %) | $307,477 |
| Engdahl (R ) | $63,559 | $5,649 (9 %) | $61,045 |

## Les AuCoin, D-Ore.

**1978**

| | | | |
|---|---|---|---|
| AuCoin (D) | $252,847 | $105,411 (42 %) | $236,313 |
| Bunick (R) | $302,735 | $27,052 (9 %) | $297,719 |

## Voting Studies

| | Presidential Support | | Party Unity | | Conservative Coalition | |
|---|---|---|---|---|---|---|
| Year | S | O | S | O | S | O |
| 1980 | 62 | 26 | 20 | 13 | 21 | 62 |
| 1979 | 77 | 16 | 69 | 20 | 28 | 64 |
| 1978 | 59 | 27 | 57 | 29 | 31 | 52 |
| 1977 | 58 | 32 | 73 | 20 | 22 | 69 |
| 1976 | 29 | 53 | 57 | 22 | 30 | 48 |
| 1975 | 34 | 54 | 68 | 19 | 24 | 59 |

S = Support          O = Opposition

## Key Votes

**96th Congress**

| | |
|---|---|
| Weaken Carter oil profits tax (1979) | Y |
| Reject hospital cost control plan (1979) | Y |
| Implement Panama Canal Treaties (1979) | Y |
| Establish Department of Education (1979) | Y |
| Approve Anti-busing Amendment (1979) | N |
| Guarantee Chrysler Corp. loans (1979) | N |
| Approve military draft registration (1980) | N |
| Aid Sandinista regime in Nicaragua (1980) | N |
| Strengthen fair housing laws (1980) | Y |

**97th Congress**

| | |
|---|---|
| Reagan budget proposal (1981) | N |

## Interest Group Ratings

| Year | ADA | ACA | AFL-CIO | CCUS |
|---|---|---|---|---|
| 1980 | 83 | 25 | 39 | 54 |
| 1979 | 68 | 29 | 58 | 44 |
| 1978 | 40 | 40 | 60 | 42 |
| 1977 | 65 | 35 | 91 | 25 |
| 1976 | 70 | 22 | 61 | 25 |
| 1975 | 74 | 14 | 71 | 6 |

# 2 Denny Smith (R)

**Of Salem — Elected 1980**

**Born:** Jan. 19, 1938, Ontario, Ore.
**Education:** Willamette U., B.A. 1961.
**Military Career:** Air Force, 1958-60, 1962-67.
**Profession:** Newspaper publisher.
**Family:** Wife, Kathleen Barrett; six children.
**Religion:** Protestant.
**Political Career:** No previous office.

**The Member:** The son of a former Oregon governor and cousin to Idaho Republican Sen. Steven D. Symms, Smith has been near politics most of his life. But until he launched his year-long campaign against Democratic Rep. Al Ullman, the House Ways and Means chairman, his direct involvement in the political world was limited. Even as the owner of 16 eastern Oregon newspapers he inherited from his father, Smith's interest was on the business side rather than in the editorial content. Most of his professional life had been spent flying jets — first in Vietnam and later for Pan American Airways.

Smith's 1980 campaign was largely anti-Ullman. Spending about $700,000, a record for the state, he guaranteed near-saturation publicity for his charge that after 24 years in Washington, Ullman had lost touch with the district. As evidence, Smith pointed out that Ullman no longer owned a home in Oregon and had pushed for a nationwide value added tax most Oregonians opposed. Ullman backed off from the tax proposal in mid-1980, too late to repair its political damage.

After winning in November, Smith mailed a letter to Ullman contributors asking them to help pay off debts he had incurred in his successful challenge. Some of these contributors accused Smith of illegally culling their names from Federal Election Commission records. Smith denied that he used FEC reports, but apologized to Ullman and to about 200 Ullman supporters.

**The District:** The 2nd covers three-fourths of Oregon's land area. Before 1964, it was located entirely on the eastern side of the Cascade Range, where Ullman had built his political base. Over the last 16 years the district has become less rural, as the state capital, Salem, and some surrounding areas west of the mountains have been added.

But still there are more farmers in the 2nd than in the entire rest of the state, and the timber industry dominates the region. Overall, it votes more Republican than Oregon as a whole.

## Committees

**Interior and Insular Affairs** (15th of 17 Republicans)
Energy and the Environment; Insular Affairs.

**Veterans' Affairs** (12th of 14 Republicans)
Compensation, Pension and Insurance; Education, Training and Employment.

## Elections

**1980 General**

| | |
|---|---|
| Denny Smith (R ) | 141,854 (49 %) |
| Al Ullman (D ) | 138,089 (48 %) |

**1980 Primary**

| | |
|---|---|
| Denny Smith (R ) | 56,718 (77 %) |
| Leonard Roth (R ) | 16,884 (23 %) |

**District Vote For President**

| | 1980 | | 1976 | | 1972 |
|---|---|---|---|---|---|
| D | 107,268 (35%) | D | 118,068 (47%) | D | 81,143 (37%) |
| R | 162,767 (53%) | R | 124,597 (49%) | R | 123,722 (56%) |
| I | 25,840 (9%) | | | I | 14,652 (7%) |

## Campaign Finance

| | Receipts | Receipts from PACs | Expenditures |
|---|---|---|---|
| **1980** | | | |
| Smith (R ) | $665,151 | $143,299 (22 %) | $663,430 |
| Ullman (D ) | $645,942 | $323,550 (50 %) | $670,390 |

## Key Vote

**97th Congress**

| | |
|---|---|
| Reagan budget proposal (1981) | Y |

**2nd District: East — Salem.** Population: 706,899 (35% increase since 1970). Race: White 672,069 (95%), Black 2,515 (0.3%), Others 32,315 (5%). Spanish origin: 25,597 (4%).

# 3 Ron Wyden (D)

**Of Portland — Elected 1980**

**Born:** May 3, 1949, Wichita, Kan.
**Education:** Stanford U., A.B. 1971; U. of Ore. J.D. 1974.
**Profession:** Lawyer.
**Family:** Wife, Laurie Sue Oseran.
**Religion:** Jewish.
**Political Career:** No previous office.

**The Member:** Before Wyden announced his 1980 bid for Congress, he already had a high profile in Portland as executive director of the state's Gray Panthers, an organization promoting senior citizens' interests.

As a spokesman for the elderly in Congress, Wyden has had a field day criticizing the Social Security cuts proposed by President Reagan. Wyden said Reagan's plan breached the trust of working people relying on the federal government to help them in retirement. He orchestrated a series of floor speeches by members who share his opinions.

Wyden concurs with Reagan's belief that federal spending should be cut, but he would aim the ax at tobacco subsidies and the MX missile. He introduced a bill to authorize construction of a new lock at Bonneville Dam that he says would boost shipping and create jobs in his district.

With the votes of Portland's senior citizens, who made up a large portion of Wyden's sizable volunteer force, the young liberal ousted Rep. Robert Duncan in the 1980 Democratic primary. He charged that Duncan, elected originally from a rural district in the 1960s, was not attuned to urban needs.

**The District:** Centered around Portland, this is the most liberal of Oregon's four districts. It was the only district which gave pluralities to George McGovern for president and Wayne Morse for the U.S. Senate in 1972.

The district comprises the four-fifths of Portland lying east of the Willamette River. That is the poorer part of the city, including the black section of Portland. The working-class suburbs of eastern Multnomah County also are in the district along with about a quarter of suburban Clackamas County.

## Committees

**Energy and Commerce** (23rd of 24 Democrats)
Energy Conservation and Power; Health and the Environment; Oversight and Investigations.

**Select Aging** (29th of 31 Democrats)
Health and Long-Term Care; Retirement Income and Employment.

**Small Business** (18th of 23 Democrats)
Export Opportunities and Special Small Business Problems.

## Elections

**1980 General**

| | |
|---|---|
| Ron Wyden (D) | 156,371 (72 %) |
| Darrell R. Conger (R) | 60,940 (28 %) |

**1980 Primary**

| | |
|---|---|
| Ron Wyden (D) | 55,818 (60 %) |
| Robert Duncan (D) | 37,132 (40 %) |

**District Vote For President**

| | 1980 | | 1976 | | 1972 |
|---|---|---|---|---|---|
| **D** | 112,635 (47%) | **D** | 122,743 (53%) | **D** | 115,241 (50%) |
| **R** | 95,466 (40%) | **R** | 100,236 (43%) | **R** | 107,082 (46%) |
| **I** | 23,705 (10%) | | | | |

## Campaign Finance

| | Receipts | Receipts from PACs | Expenditures |
|---|---|---|---|
| **1980** | | | |
| Wyden (D) | $166,240 | $70,346 (42 %) | $162,157 |
| Conger (R) | $14,725 | $1,700 (12 %) | $9,724 |

## Key Vote

**97th Congress**

Reagan budget proposal (1981)                    N

---

**3rd District: Portland and suburbs.**
Population: 540,882 (4% increase since 1970).
Race: White 485,393 (90%), Black 28,891 (5%), Others 26,598 (5%). Spanish origin: 10,664 (2%).

# 4 James Weaver (D)

**Of Eugene — Elected 1974**

**Born:** Aug. 8, 1927, Brookings, S.D.
**Education:** U. of Ore., B.S. 1952.
**Military Career:** Navy, 1945-46.
**Profession:** Builder, developer.
**Family:** Divorced; three children.
**Political Career:** Unsuccessful Democratic nominee for U.S. House, 1970; sought Democratic House nomination, 1972.

**In Washington:** The House has no shortage of people who think of themselves as lonely voices of reason, but it has few who seem to relish that role as much as Weaver, the stubborn and opinionated builder from Eugene.

A man of conviction on a multitude of issues — like his grandfather, the 1892 Populist nominee for president — Weaver often responds to criticism simply by arguing more loudly.

He was that way at the end of 1980, when he single-handedly tried blocking the Northwest Power bill, designed to allocate the scarce power resources of Oregon and Washington over the next 20 years. Weaver saw the bill as a sellout to the region's utilities and aluminum companies and an endorsement of nuclear energy, which he bitterly opposes.

When the bill's managers brought it to the floor in October, Weaver assaulted it with a vengeance beyond the bounds of normal House procedure. He prepared 73 amendments to the legislation, including one that was 56 pages long and took 90 minutes to read on the House floor after Weaver objected to its routine inclusion in the *Congressional Record*.

One colleague called Weaver's behavior a "sad commentary" on the legislative process. The manager of the legislation said Weaver "certainly didn't ingratiate himself with other members." But the Oregon Democrat appeared to enjoy the scene, pointing proudly to his effort as the first filibuster by amendment in House memory.

The result was to delay passage only a month. Sponsors waited until after the November election then brought the bill back under procedures barring amendment. It passed 284-77 and became law in December. But Weaver had his moment of righteous protest, at a decisive moment in his campaign for re-election in Oregon.

He was almost that militant in 1981 against President Reagan's nomination of John Crowell to be assistant secretary of the interior with

responsibility for the Forest Service. Weaver complained in general terms that Crowell was anti-conservation and in specific terms about his role as counsel to a timber company whose subsidiary had been found guilty of price fixing by a federal court in Seattle. He said Crowell could not take the job without creating a conflict of interest.

As chairman of the Forests Subcommittee on House Agriculture, Weaver had a good forum but no real way to fight the nomination; it was the Senate's decision whether Crowell should be confirmed or not, and he was eventually, 72-25. Before that, however, Weaver tried to raise as much opposition as he could to Crowell, arguing that under his management, "the 190-million acre national forest system will suffer the same kind of abusive management that has befallen the private forests."

On most issues, he is not quite that belligerent. But he rarely gives up. He has conducted a long anti-nuclear campaign from the precincts of the Interior Committee, which is relatively sympathetic to his point of view.

"Nuclear power will bankrupt us," he said in 1979, as he offered an amendment at an Interior Subcommittee to impose a six-month moratorium on nuclear plant licensing. The amendment failed on a 16-6 vote. Later in the year he offered an amendment on the floor to deny licensing to any nuclear plant in a state that had no emergency

---

**4th District: Southwest — Eugene, Medford.** Population: 685,809 (31% increase since 1970). Race: White 663,506 (97%), Black 2,104 (0.3%), Others 20,199 (3%). Spanish origin: 14,474 (2%).

evacuation plan. That lost, 235-147.

Weaver's anti-nuclear stand is consistent with the militant environmentalism he espouses on other Interior Committee issues, to the dismay of the timber industry, which is influential in his district but which is rarely able to persuade him to argue on its behalf. Over the years, he has consistently fought the industry over creation of new wilderness areas, which he has favored, and logging in national forests, which he has opposed. He has been willing to support small-scale "set-asides" of national forest land for timber sales.

On the Agriculture Committee, Weaver is known best for his "barrels for bushels" scheme, by which the United States would withhold grain from countries that raise their oil prices beyond a specified level. He began arguing this cause in his first House term and has never stopped, despite the insistence of many farm-oriented members that Arab countries would simply buy their wheat elsewhere. In 1979, when he proposed a floor amendment requiring a minimum price of 80 percent of parity for all foreign agricultural trade, he was shouted down in a voice vote.

**At Home:** Weaver knows that major voting blocs in his district, especially the lumberjacks in the southern portion, would not vote for him even if he were unopposed. But he also knows that his liberal positions will go over well in the Eugene area — the political base which provided his victory margin in 1980.

Weaver's political career got off to a slow and difficult start, reflecting things to come. Born in South Dakota and raised in Iowa, he moved to Oregon to attend college and spent a decade as a builder and developer in Eugene before seeking elective office.

His first two campaigns for the House — the only office he has ever run for — ended in defeat. In 1970, Republican incumbent John R.

Dellenback beat him soundly. Two years later, he lost the Democratic primary by 373 votes to former Rep. Charles O. Porter, who was making one of six unsuccessful comeback tries.

But believing the district was winnable for a Democrat, Weaver tried a third time in 1974. He won the primary over a liberal university professor who had previously held office in Arizona, and a soft-spoken state legislator named Jack D. Ripper.

Running a much better-organized race in 1974 against Dellenback, Weaver tied the incumbent to the unpopular Nixon administration. By building up a 7,400-vote edge in Lane County (Eugene) and a 3,600-vote margin in coastal Coos County, Weaver overcame Dellenback's residual Republican strength in the three southern counties.

Republicans have never given up hope of unseating Weaver, but even though they have outspent him by large amounts, they still cannot cut into his base in Lane County.

**The District:** The endless forests in the southwestern part of Oregon give the area its economic livelihood, with lumber mills and paper and pulp plants the major employers in most of the seven counties in the district. If Weaver had to rely on the votes of the timber industry, the district would still be Republican.

But Lane County, the home of the University of Oregon and its 17,000 students, makes up more than 40 percent of the district's vote and substantially alters its political complexion. Eugene's reputation as a liberal haven may be somewhat exaggerated — voters in 1978 soundly repealed a city ordinance that prohibited discrimination against homosexuals — but the city does provide the major source of Democratic votes in the district.

## Committees

**Agriculture** (9th of 24 Democrats)
Forests, Family Farms, and Energy, chairman; Wheat, Soybeans, and Feed Grains.

**Interior and Insular Affairs** (8th of 23 Democrats)
Energy and the Environment; Public Lands and National Parks; Water and Power Resources.

## Elections

**1980 General**

| | |
|---|---|
| James Weaver (D ) | 158,745 (55 %) |
| Michael Fitzgerald (R ) | 130,861 (45 %) |

**1980 Primary**

| | |
|---|---|
| James Weaver (D ) | 71,388 (75 %) |
| John Newkirk (D ) | 23,758 (25 %) |

**1978 General**

| | |
|---|---|
| James Weaver (D ) | 124,745 (56 %) |
| Jerry Lausmann (R ) | 96,953 (44 %) |

**Previous Winning Percentages**

1976 (50 %)     1974 (53 %)

District Vote For President

| | 1980 | | 1976 | | 1972 |
|---|---|---|---|---|---|
| D | 112,973 (37%) | D | 129,306 (50%) | D | 94,456 (42%) |
| R | 154,512 (51%) | R | 116,717 (45%) | R | 118,007 (52%) |
| I | 24,246 (8%) | | | I | 14,261 (6%) |

| | S | O | S | O | S | O |
|---|---|---|---|---|---|---|
| 1977 | 68 | 24 | 82 | 6 | 8 | 79 |
| 1976 | 25 | 63 | 79 | 8 | 15 | 71 |
| 1975 | 29 | 69 | 89 | 9 | 11 | 87 |

S = Support          O = Opposition

## Campaign Finance

| | Receipts | Receipts from PACs | Expenditures |
|---|---|---|---|
| **1980** | | | |
| Weaver (D ) | $260,364 | $107,476 (41 %) | $224,082 |
| Fitzgerald (R ) | $356,022 | $136,274 (38 %) | $355,760 |
| **1978** | | | |
| Weaver (D ) | $177,703 | $69,747 (39 %) | $178,950 |
| Lausmann (R ) | $205,643 | $53,805 (26 %) | $206,613 |

## Key Votes

**96th Congress**

| | |
|---|---|
| Weaken Carter oil profits tax (1979) | N |
| Reject hospital cost control plan (1979) | N |
| Implement Panama Canal Treaties (1979) | Y |
| Establish Department of Education (1979) | # |
| Approve Anti-busing Amendment (1979) | N |
| Guarantee Chrysler Corp. loans (1979) | N |
| Approve military draft registration (1980) | N |
| Aid Sandinista regime in Nicaragua (1980) | Y |
| Strengthen fair housing laws (1980) | Y |

**97th Congress**

| | |
|---|---|
| Reagan budget proposal (1981) | N |

## Voting Studies

| | Presidential Support | | Party Unity | | Conservative Coalition | |
|---|---|---|---|---|---|---|
| Year | S | O | S | O | S | O |
| 1980 | 52 | 40 | 59 | 30 | 23 | 61 |
| 1979 | 64 | 26 | 68 | 25 | 24 | 63 |
| 1978 | 65 | 23 | 73 | 18 | 18 | 74 |

## Interest Group Ratings

| Year | ADA | ACA | AFL-CIO | CCUS |
|---|---|---|---|---|
| 1980 | 83 | 35 | 72 | 52 |
| 1979 | 84 | 24 | 78 | 12 |
| 1978 | 75 | 32 | 89 | 6 |
| 1977 | 85 | 8 | 95 | 7 |
| 1976 | 95 | 8 | 86 | 7 |
| 1975 | 100 | 7 | 87 | 6 |

# Pennsylvania

**U.S. CONGRESS:**
**TWENTY-FIVE DISTRICTS**
Senate (2R)
House (13D, 12R)

**STATE:**

Governor
Richard L. Thornburgh (R)
General Assembly
Senate: 50 members
(23D, 25R, 2 Vacancies)
House: 203 members (100D, 103R)

Population
11,866,728 -
4th in the nation
Area
45,333 sq. miles -
33rd in the nation

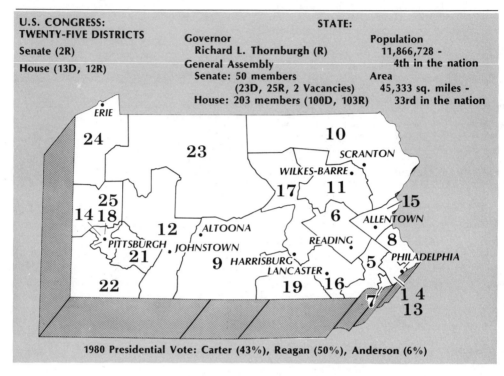

1980 Presidential Vote: Carter (43%), Reagan (50%), Anderson (6%)

## ... Yesterday's State

Pennsylvania is struggling to make the transition from the old industrial era, in which it was king, to the post-industrial society, in which it has serious problems.

Built on coal, steel, railroads, and heavy manufacturing in the 19th century, Pennsylvania was once one of the world's top economic powers all by itself. It was the focal point for America's surge to industrial primacy. The state's prosperity drew floods of immigrants, especially from Ireland, Italy and Southern and Eastern Europe.

Today, Pennsylvania is in some ways an antique. Its industries are struggling to survive. Its politics still has strong traces of old-fashioned corruption. And people are leaving for the more prosperous Sun Belt. Pennsylvania's population grew by only 0.6 percent during the 1970s, forcing loss of two congressional seats in the 1980 reapportionment.

The state is trying to find replacements for its faltering industries, but although it has attracted some new sources of employment, it has been unable so far to develop anything like Massachusetts' Research Belt or New Jersey's pharmaceutical industry. Banking, insurance, and other white-collar pursuits are holding their own at best.

The state's loss of congressional representation is symbolic of its decline in the overall American political and economic scene. The state has gone from 36 House seats in the 1920s to 23 in the 1980s. That loss is the second largest in American history, exceeded only by Virginia's loss of 14 seats between 1810 and 1870, a time in which it was split into two states.

During its years of industrial success, Pennsylvania was a rock-solid Republican state. The political machines which herded the immigrants to the polls in Philadelphia and Pittsburgh were built by Republicans instead of Democrats. Not once between 1856 and 1936 did the state vote for a Democratic presidential nominee. The impact of the Great Depression finally broke GOP dominance of the cities.

In recent years, the governorship has swung back and forth. Democrat Milton J. Shapp served two terms from 1971 to 1979 before yielding to Republican Richard L. Thornburgh. But Democrats have done poorly in Senate contests, winning the last one in 1962. Only Oregon and Kansas have gone as long without a Democratic senator.

Since the early 1960s, Republican statewide candidates have come from the moderate to liberal wing of the party, and have been able to appeal to independents and Democrats. The state's labor unions have sometimes backed Republicans for statewide office, including Richard Schweiker, who won two Senate terms as a liberal Republican before embracing Ronald Reagan, switching to conservative politics, and becoming Health and Human Services secretary in the Reagan administration.

In recent years, some of the most important divisions in Pennsylvania politics have been regional. Western Pennsylvania, particularly the Pittsburgh area, has often felt overshadowed by Philadelphia and its suburbs. The western areas have banded together in recent years to back favorite sons in primary and statewide elections, while the eastern vote has been split. Largely as a result, Pittsburgh candidates were elected to the Senate in 1976 and the governorship in 1978.

# A Political Tour

**Philadelphia.** Philadelphia is still the No. 2 city on the East Coast, but it has lost population continuously over the past thirty years, with hundreds of thousands of white residents moving away, and being only partially replaced by blacks entering the city.

Thousands of German, Irish, Italian and Polish immigrants poured into Phildelphia in the 19th and early 20th centuries, to work in steel and railroading as well as the busy dockyards and shipbuilding industries. There was also a sizable Jewish population which held many of the jobs in the city's thriving needle trade.

Today, the descendants of these immigrants still populate the area, although much of the bustle and dynamism of the earlier city has disappeared. The Germans were the first to prosper, and the bulk of them have moved out to the suburbs. Italians have established themselves in solid middle-class homes in South Philadelphia,

making a major impact on Philadelphia politics with their support for the Democratic organization and producing the city's famous "tough cop" mayor, Frank Rizzo (1972-80).

The area just north of the center city is lower-income and blue-collar, predominantly Polish and Irish. Northeast Philadelphia is a densely-populated suburban-type area, built up mostly since World War II. It contains one of the few pockets of Republican strength in the city among its middle-class population. It is also the home of much of Philadelphia's Jewish community.

Blacks are concentrated in North and West Philadelphia and part of South Philadelphia. They make up 38 percent of the city's population.

Philadelphia today is as strongly Democratic as most Northern cities, a change from the pre-Depression days when it was one of the few cities in the country dominated by a Republican machine. The city went for Republican Herbert Hoover in 1932 but by 1936 it had switched to the Democratic column. It has stayed there ever since. But the margins vary considerably. Jimmy Carter's Philadelphia plurality declined from 255,579 in 1976 to 177,145 in 1980, and his percentage dropped nearly 8 points.

Republicans held the Philadelphia city government until 1951, when Joseph Clark was elected the first Democratic mayor of the city in the 20th century. The Democrats have been in control since then, although the law-and-order ethnic bloc that supported Rizzo has quarreled violently with blacks and the liberal Democratic faction. The current mayor, William J. Green, was elected in 1979 with widespread black support after voters turned down a bid to change the city charter so that Rizzo could run for a third term.

**Philadelphia Suburbs.** Ringing Philadelphia are 2 million suburbanites living in four counties — Bucks, Delaware, Montgomery and Chester.

Along the Delaware River in Bucks County large petrochemical plants stand next to rows of suburban tract houses. In more distant parts of Bucks County, white-collar and professional areas gradually give way to affluent estates.

On the river to the south in Delaware County are oil refineries and older, grimier communities that adjoin South Philadelphia's Italian neighborhoods. Delaware County also has a large middle-income population further removed from the riverfront industry.

To the north along the Schuylkill River in Montgomery County are small steel factories and a concentration of electronics and pharmaceutical plants. But Montgomery County also is the home of Philadelphia's Main Line, the largely white,

Protestant and affluent suburban communities that grew up along the commuter route of the Pennsylvania Railroad.

The farmlands of Chester County are rapidly being turned into Philadelphia suburbs.

The four counties have voted in tandem, supporting the Republican nominee in every presidential election except one since World War II. In 1980, the four gave Ronald Reagan a combined margin of 207,830 votes, more than wiping out Carter's margin in Philadelphia.

The importance of these suburbs in Pennsylvania politics has steadily grown since World War II. In 1948, the four counties cast fewer than half as many votes as Philadelphia. The suburban vote surpassed Philadelphia's total in 1972 and the gap has continued to widen. Today the suburbs make up about a fifth of the state's vote.

**Pennsylvania Dutch Country.** This part of the state has maintained its values and traditions over a long period of time. The Pennsylvania Dutch, descendants of German Protestant dissenters, settled the area over 200 years ago. It is a rich agricultural region, and has long been a food basket for Philadelphia. Efforts are being made to preserve the farmland from encroaching suburbs and industrial development.

The area is like a flat Switzerland — peopled by hard-working Germanic families, economically prosperous, and catering to a large tourist trade. Concentrated most heavily in Lancaster County, the Pennsylvania Dutch settlers spread north to the Reading and Harrisburg areas and west to York and Gettysburg.

The Pennsylvania Dutch affiliation with the GOP has been longstanding. The people here were alienated early in this century by big city dominance of the Democratic Party. More recently they have resented the liberal social values of the national Democratic Party. Lancaster County, the wealthy heart of the region, has not sent a Democrat to Congress since the Civil War.

There are a few traditional pockets of Democratic strength, such as Reading in Berks County. An important industrial and railroad center that attracted Eastern European immigrants and spawned a strong Socialist Party, Berks County today is shifting to the right. Although it remains the most Democratic county in the Pennsylvania Dutch area, Berks went narrowly for Ford in 1976 and gave an overwhelming 22-percentage-point lead to Reagan in 1980.

**Eastern Industrial Belt.** Steel and coal have been synonymous with Pennsylvania since the 19th century, and this is one of the two regions which made that possible.

But much of the area has fallen on hard times since the anthracite (hard) coal deposits were either mined out or became uneconomical to work. That threw tens of thousands of miners out of work and made the anthracite center — Lackawanna (Scranton) and Luzerne (Wilkes-Barre) counties — chronically depressed. The two major cities were also active in the textile industry, but that has also declined under the impact of foreign and Southern competition.

Further south, in the Lehigh Valley, is a string of industrial communities. Allentown, Bethlehem, and Easton are the main cities in the heart of Pennsylvania's eastern steel-producing region. But steel is also suffering, both from aging facilities and foreign competition, giving the valley a sluggish economic climate.

Mine workers and steelworkers form the base of Democratic strength in the area. But while Democrats traditionally have been dominant, all three congressional districts in the region now are held by Republicans. As population moved out with the decline in economic prosperity, Democratic districts expanded to take in Republican rural areas, and Republicans found attractive and hard-working candidates to take advantage of Democratic complacency.

**West Central Pennsylvania.** The heart of this region is the mountain chain that runs north and south, bisecting the state. Scotch-Irish immigrants settled here in the early 19th century, and their descendants still live in the area, engaging in relatively unproductive general farming and working in light industry. On social issues, the voters have traditional values; politically, they are loyal Republicans. They remained Republican even throughout the New Deal era.

To the north and west of the mountains, the physical terrain becomes less forbidding and the political terrain less Republican. The Pennsylvania bituminous (soft) coal region takes in the western portion of this area. The miners and mining towns give a boost to Democrats in such places as Cambria (Johnstown) and Somerset counties. Altoona's traditional status as a key repair town for the Pennsylvania Railroad has declined with the railroad business. Altogether, the region is one of the lowest areas of the state in income, although the resurgence of coal provides hope for some communities.

**The Northern Tier.** The long northern border of Pennsylvania — stretching from the headwaters of the Delaware River to the shores of Lake Erie — covers a mostly rural, sometimes forested hinterland that has been a backwater of Pennsylvania politics.

In the eastern part of the region is a series of strongly Republican rural counties, settled by

Yankees from across the border in New York state. Farming is a major activity. Further west, the territory becomes more rugged, with mountains covering much of the terrain. This is hunting country and one of the strongest centers of anti-gun control sentiment in the East. There are still a significant number of oil and gas wells around Oil City and Titusville.

The western end of the Northern Tier contains Pennsylvania's outlet to the Great Lakes. The port city of Erie is a major shipment point for Great Lakes iron ore. While most of the ore goes on to the Pittsburgh area, some stops at plants in Erie and in Sharon. Erie, with a large Italian-American community, usually votes Democratic.

**Pittsburgh and the Steel Belt.** Southwestern Pennsylvania has long been a bastion of the steel industry and Democratic voting strength. Pittsburgh is the pre-eminent steel city, but the industry spreads throughout the region. Communities such as Duquesne, McKeesport, and Homestead have become synonymous with the steel industry and the labor movement. Steel mills dot the landscape throughout counties like Westmoreland, Washington, and Beaver, This is bituminous (soft) coal country as well.

The area underwent a major political change during the Depression. Its traditional Republican voting orientation was smashed by the collapse of the economy. Voters turned to the Democratic Party in droves and helped make Pennsylvania a New Deal-supporting state. With the fall of GOP strength, Pittsburgh-area Democrats became a major element of the state party.

Geographically, western Pennsylvania is cut off from the East by the mountains. Moreover, the Pittsburgh area's economy faces westward, into the Midwestern states where much of its steel is consumed. All of this leads to a feeling of political defensiveness and a heavy regionalist vote in statewide elections. In 1978, Pittsburgh native Richard L. Thornburgh carried his home county over a Philadelphian in the Republican gubernatorial primary by a ratio of 84-1.

In presidential politics, the southwestern region is Democratic. President Carter carried the eight counties of the region in 1976 by 85,998 votes, a sizable portion of his statewide margin of 123,073 votes. In 1980, Carter again carried the area, but by a reduced margin of 60,883 votes.

# Redrawing the Lines

Two seats must be cut from Pennsylvania's 25-member delegation, which now has 13 Democrats and 12 Republicans. Of the nine districts in the state that lost population during the past decade, six are in the Philadelphia area and three are in Allegheny County (Pittsburgh). Thus, those cities are the targets of district-cutters.

The Philadelphia district with the fewest residents is the 3rd, but even it is larger than Pittsburgh's 14th District, where the decade-long population decline was the most precipitous of any district in the state — down 18 percent.

Republicans have a one-vote margin in the upper house of the Legislature and a three-vote margin in the lower house. The governor also is a Republican, giving the party shaky control over the redistricting process.

---

# Governor
# Richard L. Thornburgh
# (R)

**Born:** July 16, 1932, Carnegie, Pa.
**Home:** Pittsburgh, Pa.
**Education:** Yale U., B.S. 1954; U. of Pittsburgh School of Law, LL.B. 1957.
**Profession:** Lawyer.
**Family:** Wife, Virginia; four children.
**Religion:** Protestant.
**Political Career:** Unsuccessful campaign for U.S. House, 1966; U.S. attorney for western Pennsylvania, 1969-75; assistant U.S. attorney general in charge of criminal division, 1975-77; elected governor 1978; term expires Jan. 1983.

# John Heinz (R)

**Of Pittsburgh — Elected 1976**

**Born:** Oct. 23, 1938, Pittsburgh, Pa.
**Education:** Yale U., B.A. 1960; Harvard U., M.B.A. 1963.
**Military Career:** Air Force, 1963-69.
**Profession:** Management consultant.
**Family:** Wife, Teresa Simoes-Ferreira; three children.
**Religion:** Episcopalian.
**Political Career:** U.S. House, 1971-77.

**In Washington:** Senate Republicans placed Heinz in charge of campaign fund raising in 1979, and he brought in more than $20 million, helping them immeasurably as they took over the chamber for the first time in a quarter-century. When he tried to claim what he thought was his reward, the third-ranking position in the party leadership, they turned him down.

To make matters worse, Heinz lost to a colleague, James McClure of Idaho, who already had a prize chairmanship of his own, as head of the Energy Committee. In a year in which there is a plum for nearly every Republican, Heinz has one of the smallest, as chairman of the Special Aging Committee, which writes no legislation.

There are varying explanations for the apparent ingratitude. At a time of increased conservative influence within GOP ranks, the party chose relative moderates for its first two leadership posts. Conservatives demanded someone in the hierarchy to speak for them, rather than Heinz, who had a moderate voting record. Also, Heinz simply has not been one of the more popular members. Unlike other wealthy senators who have developed a plain-folks style within the Senate, Heinz sometimes strikes colleagues as a millionaire who acts like a millionaire.

Even without a major chairmanship in the 97th Congress, Heinz has found many outlets for his legislative energy. He has two subcommittee chairmanships — International Finance and Monetary Policy on the Banking Committee, and Finance's Revenue Sharing panel. And he is chairman of the full Aging Committee, where he is studying Social Security financing and job opportunities for the elderly. He opposes any mandatory retirement age and favors long-term health care for the elderly poor under Medicaid.

Heinz has been interested in the aging for a long time. He served on the Aging Committee in the House and on a GOP task force studying problems of the elderly.

In 1980, as a member of Senate Banking, he sucessfully led the fight to prevent President Carter from expanding the Council on Wage and Price Stability. Heinz said the council's idea of using presidential purchasing authority as a weapon against price increases was an abuse of power. He also amended Carter's $3.5 billion Chrysler aid package in 1979 to require the company to double the number of stock shares so there would be no windfall profit to stockholders. Then he voted against the bill.

On Finance, Heinz has been a protectionist supporter of his state's steel industry. He introduced his own legislation to restrict foreign countries from "dumping" steel in the United States at low prices, and was one of the few senators who questioned the massive 1979 trade expansion act. Heinz said the legislation did not spell out specific enough limits on the executive branch in setting duties and subsidies. Carter aides tried to work out a compromise with Heinz, but he voted against the bill on the floor, one of only four senators to do so.

As a Vietnam-era Air Force veteran, Heinz has has taken up the Vietnam veterans' cause. He introduced legislation to give Vietnam combat veterans an extra 10 years to use their educational benefits. He has also been a leader in the effort to give federal help to victims of Agent Orange, a defoliant used in Vietnam.

**At Home:** Pennsylvania's 1976 Senate contest matched a 38-year-old Democrat with good looks and campaign skill against a Republican of the same age who had similar qualities plus a multi-million dollar fortune. The Republican won.

As attractive a candidate as Heinz was, it probably required most of the $2.39 million he spent during the year to guarantee nomination against a strong GOP primary challenger and election against the Democrat, U.S. Rep. William

J. Green.

Heinz spent $586,756 to win the primary against Arlen Specter, the former Philadelphia district attorney and now Heinz' Senate colleague. Early in the year, Heinz disclosed he had accepted $6,000 in illegal corporate campaign money from Gulf Oil while serving in the House. He returned the donations, but it cast a shadow over the primary campaign. It took extensive TV advertising to offset the negative publicity.

By fall, the issue had faded somewhat, but Heinz had a tough opponent in Green, whose base in Philadelphia matched his own in Pittsburgh.

Green said Heinz had been a tool of Richard Nixon; Heinz painted his opponent as a Democratic machine politician, and warned that Philadelphia was trying to take over the state.

Heinz cut into the labor support that Democratic statewide candidates generally receive. During five years in the House, representing a suburban Pittsburgh district with a significant blue-collar constituency, he had frequently supported union positions. The United Mine Workers gave him important support against Green, and he carried several normally Democratic mining counties in the western part of the state.

## Committees

**Banking, Housing and Urban Affairs** (3rd of 8 Republicans)
International Finance and Monetary Policy, chairman; Economic Policy; Housing and Urban Affairs; Rural Housing and Development.

**Energy and Natural Resources** (11th of 11 Republicans)
Energy and Mineral Resources; Energy Conservation and Supply; Energy Regulation.

**Finance** (6th of 11 Republicans)
Economic Growth, Employment, and Revenue Sharing, chairman; Health; International Trade.

**Special Aging** (Chairman)

## Elections

**1976 General**

| | |
|---|---|
| John Heinz (R ) | 2,381,891 (52 %) |
| William Green (D ) | 2,126,977 (47 %) |

**1976 Primary**

| | |
|---|---|
| John Heinz (R ) | 358,715 (38 %) |
| Arlen Specter (R ) | 332,513 (35 %) |
| George Packard (R ) | 160,379 (17 %) |
| C. Homer Brown (R ) | 46,828 (5 %) |

**Previous Winning Percentages**

**1974\*** (72 %)   **1972\*** (73 %)   **1971†** (67 %)
\* House election.
† Special House election

## Campaign Finance

| | Receipts | Receipts from PACs | Expenditures |
|---|---|---|---|
| **1976** | | | |
| Heinz (R ) | $3,016,731 | $51,987 (2 %) | $3,004,814 |
| Green (D ) | $1,266,375 | $256,297 (20 %) | $1,269,409 |

## Voting Studies

| | Presidential Support | | Party Unity | | Conservative Coalition | |
|---|---|---|---|---|---|---|
| Year | S | O | S | O | S | O |
| Senate service | | | | | | |
| 1980 | 56 | 41† | 57 | 38† | 50 | 42† |
| 1979 | 59 | 30 | 44 | 43 | 36 | 51 |
| 1978 | 71 | 24 | 27 | 64 | 36 | 56 |
| 1977 | 55 | 39 | 46 | 48 | 51 | 43 |
| House service | | | | | | |
| 1976 | 18 | 41 | 14 | 38 | 20 | 34 |
| 1975 | 49 | 42 | 44 | 48 | 39 | 52 |
| 1974 (Ford) | 50 | 41 | | | | |
| 1974 | 64 | 32 | 39 | 56 | 34 | 60 |
| 1973 | 51 | 45 | 51 | 48† | 45 | 54† |
| 1972 | 59 | 41 | 47 | 48 | 8 | 57 |
| 1971 | 63 | 13† | 38 | 46† | 31 | 49† |

S = Support          O = Opposition
†Not eligible for all recorded votes.

## Key Votes

**96th Congress**

| | |
|---|---|
| Maintain relations with Taiwan (1979) | Y |
| Reduce synthetic fuel development funds (1979) | Y |
| Impose nuclear plant moratorium (1979) | Y |
| Kill stronger windfall profits tax (1979) | Y |
| Guarantee Chrysler Corp. loans (1979) | N |
| Approve military draft registration (1980) | N |
| End Revenue Sharing to the states (1980) | N |
| Block Justice Dept. busing suits (1980) | N |

**97th Congress**

| | |
|---|---|
| Restore urban program funding cuts (1981) | Y |

## Interest Group Ratings

| Year | ADA | ACA | AFL-CIO | CCUS-1 | CCUS-2 |
|---|---|---|---|---|---|
| Senate service | | | | | |
| 1980 | 50 | 44 | 67 | 63 | |
| 1979 | 42 | 44 | 59 | 56 | 69 |
| 1978 | 60 | 18 | 78 | 50 | |
| 1977 | 50 | 31 | 65 | 39 | |
| House service | | | | | |
| 1976 | 30 | 15 | 67 | 20 | |
| 1975 | 68 | 41 | 74 | 40 | |
| 1974 | 57 | 14 | 82 | 30 | |
| 1973 | 60 | 30 | 56 | 40 | |
| 1972 | 63 | 9 | 55 | 20 | |
| 1971† | 67 | 44 | 100 | | |

†Not eligible for all recorded votes.

# Arlen Specter (R)

### Of Philadelphia — Elected 1980

**Born:** Feb. 12, 1930, Wichita, Kan.
**Education:** University of Pennsylvania, B.A. 1951; Yale University, LL.B. 1956.
**Military Career:** Air Force, 1951-53.
**Profession:** Lawyer.
**Family:** Wife, Joan Lois Levy; two children.
**Religion:** Jewish.
**Political Career:** Philadelphia district attorney, 1966-74; unsuccessful Republican nominee for mayor of Philadelphia, 1967; unsuccessfully sought re-election as district attorney, 1973; unsuccessfully sought Republican nomination for U.S. Senate, 1976; unsuccessfully sought Republican nomination for governor, 1978.

**The Member:** Specter adds a moderate voice from the urban Northeast to a conservative and Western-oriented Senate freshman class.

He is known as a hard worker, and he made an issue of this in his 1980 campaign, promising to be a more effective and energetic senator than his Democratic opponent, who was already burdened with a reputation as a sluggish campaigner. Specter is sometimes said to be too intense for normal political camaraderie, but he brings a careful pragmatism to the problems he works on.

One of Specter's first Senate tasks was to rescue a major program he oversees as chairman of the Judiciary subcommittee on Juvenile Justice.

The Reagan administration wanted to eliminate the federal Office of Juvenile Justice and Delinquency Prevention, placing its programs in social services block grants to the states. The Senate Budget Committee acceded to Reagan's request. But in the Judiciary Committee, Specter saved the agency at least temporarily by suggesting that its authorization be cut to $70 million annually.

Once pictured as the bright young star of Pennsylvania Republican politics, Specter began to acquire the image of a loser after his defeats for mayor of Philadelphia in 1967 and for re-election as district attorney in 1973. Then came unsuccessful primary campaigns for the Republican Senate nomination in 1976 and gubernatorial nomination in 1978. By 1980, it appeared that Specter's triumphs were behind him.

But he decided to make one more try when Republican Richard S. Schweiker announced he would leave the Senate in 1981. With the help of the two men who had defeated him in previous Republican primaries — Sen. John Heinz and Gov. Richard L. Thornburgh — Specter took the general election by running well in the Philadelphia area and keeping down the Democratic margin in the western part of the state. His opponent, former Pittsburgh Mayor Pete Flaherty, had expected to sweep the west where he is well known and popular.

## Committees

**Appropriations** (15th of 15 Republicans)
Agriculture and Related Agencies; District of Columbia; Foreign Operations; HUD-Independent Agencies; Labor, Health and Human Services, Education.

**Judiciary** (10th of 10 Republicans)
Juvenile Justice, chairman; Agency Administration; Criminal Law.

**Veterans' Affairs** (7th of 7 Republicans)

## Elections

**1980 General**

| | |
|---|---|
| Arlen Specter (R) | 2,230,404 (51%) |
| Peter Flaherty (D) | 2,122,391 (48%) |

**1980 Primary**

| | |
|---|---|
| Arlen Specter (R) | 419,372 (36%) |
| Bud Haabestad (R) | 382,281 (33%) |
| Edward Howard (R) | 148,200 (13 %) |
| Norman Bertasavage (R) | 52,408 (5%) |
| Others (R) | 149,798 (13%) |

## Campaign Finance

| | Receipts | Receipts from PACs | Expenditures |
|---|---|---|---|
| **1980** | | | |
| Specter (R) | $1,512,342 | $283,034 (19%) | $1,588,588 |
| Flaherty (D) | $635,062 | - (0%) | $633,861 |

## Key Vote

**97th Congress**

| | |
|---|---|
| Restore urban program funding cuts (1981) | Y |

# 1 Thomas M. Foglietta (D)

**Of Philadelphia — Elected 1980**

**Born:** Dec. 3, 1928, Philadelphia, Pa.
**Education:** St. Joseph's College, B.A. 1949; Temple U., J.D. 1952.
**Profession:** Lawyer.
**Family:** Single.
**Religion:** Roman Catholic.
**Political Career:** Philadelphia City Council, 1955-75; unsuccessful Republican nominee for mayor of Philadelphia, 1975.

**The Member:** Foglietta abandoned a lifelong loyalty to the Republican Party in 1980 to emerge from a complicated political situation as the representative from South Philadelphia.

To make it, he had to run as an independent, normally a guarantee of failure. But Democratic incumbent Michael "Ozzie" Myers, indicted in the Abscam bribery scandal, had managed to win renomination, leaving anti-Myers Democrats without a candidate in the general election. Foglietta became that candidate.

When Myers was convicted on bribery charges and expelled from the House Oct. 2, Foglietta gained the strength he needed to win. Once elected, he acknowledged his political debt by voting with Democrats to organize the 97th Congress.

From his seat on Armed Services, Foglietta has promoted an authorization of more than $30 million for two projects at the Philadelphia Navy Yard in his district.

Foglietta was elected to the Philadelphia City Council as a Republican at age 27, in 1955, and held the position for 20 years, serving at one time as minority floor leader. But he was considered a maverick and had good relations with many liberal Democrats in the city. As the Republican nominee for mayor in 1975, he ran a poor third.

**The District:** South Philadelphia has long been the heart of a cohesive ethnic community, primarily Italian. It was the political base for Frank L. Rizzo, the city's tough-talking "supercop" mayor of the 1970s. It is also the heart of the 1st District, although the district now stretches west and north to include large numbers of blacks. The district will have to expand even further in redistricting, perhaps to include some close-in Philadelphia suburbs.

Republicans built up the traditional political machine in Philadelphia, with South Philadelphia an important cog in the organization. It was not until 1936 that the Democrats won the seat, but they have kept it for most of the time since.

## Committees

**Armed Services** (22nd of 25 Democrats)
Military Installations and Facilities; Seapower and Strategic and Critical Materials.

**Merchant Marine and Fisheries** (17th of 20 Democrats)
Coast Guard and Navigation; Merchant Marine; Panama Canal and the Outer Continental Shelf.

## Elections

**1980 General**

| | |
|---|---|
| Thomas Foglietta (I)† | 58,737 (38 %) |
| Michael Myers (D ) | 52,956 (34 %) |
| Robert Burke (R ) | 37,893 (24 %) |

*†Caucuses with the Democrats but ran as an Independent.*

**District Vote For President**

| | 1980 | | 1976 | | 1972 |
|---|---|---|---|---|---|
| **D** | 106,823 (63 %) | **D** | 122,695 (70 %) | **D** | 109,250 (58 %) |
| **R** | 53,899 (32 %) | **R** | 50,923 (29 %) | **R** | 78,170 (41 %) |
| **I** | 8,133 (5 %) | | | | |

## Campaign Finance

| 1980 | Receipts | Receipts from PACs | Expenditures |
|---|---|---|---|
| Foglietta (I ) | $145,050 | $15,800 (11 %) | $142,835 |
| Myers (D ) | $44,156 | $19,200 (43 %) | $45,926 |

## Key Vote

**97th Congress**

Reagan budget proposal (1981)                N

---

**1st District: Philadelphia — south.**
Population: 404,943 (15% decrease since 1970). Race: White 213,165 (53%), Black 181,186 (45%), Others 11,032 (3%). Spanish origin: 5,846 (1%).

# 2 William H. Gray, III (D)

**Of Philadelphia — Elected 1978**

**Born:** Aug. 20, 1941, Baton Rouge, La.
**Education:** Franklin and Marshall College, B.A.
1963; Drew Theological Seminary, M.Div.
1966; Princeton Theological Seminary, Th.M.
1970.
**Profession:** Minister.
**Family:** Wife, Andrea Dash; three children.
**Religion:** Baptist.
**Political Career:** Unsuccessfully sought Democratic nomination for U.S. House, 1976.

**In Washington:** Gray's quiet diligence won him a place on the exclusive Budget Committee in his first year as a member, but he found almost immediately that the committee's frustrations outweighed its prestige.

Within a month of his 1978 election, he was spending much of his time working for a seat on Budget. It was a difficult task because Louis Stokes of Ohio was already on Budget, and the 17-member Black Caucus had never had two representatives on the panel before. But Gray lobbied effectively, especially among his fellow freshmen, and made it onto the committee.

It was the wrong timing for an urban-minded liberal like Gray. Although he won uniform praise as a thoughtful legislator, he found himself on the outside as committee Democrats made budget balancing their foremost priority.

By 1980, he was one of six liberal Democrats consistently voting against budget resolutions as they cleared the committee, frustrated at the bipartisan coalition organized by Chairman Robert N. Giaimo, D-Conn. "It was very clear that the Democratic leadership felt that they did not want or need the liberal vote," Gray complained, "because they were going to seek the votes on the Republican side."

Gray wanted more cuts in defense spending, and fewer on the domestic side. "I am not opposed to trying to balance the budget," he insisted. "But the way the Budget Committee did it was an unmitigated disaster." Gray was entitled to a second term on Budget in the 97th Congress, but he gave it up voluntarily for Appropriations, where he has a chance to pursue funding for housing and some of the other urban programs he is interested in.

Gray also served in the 96th Congress on the Foreign Affairs Committee, where he generally opposed spending cutbacks except in aid to countries with records of human rights violations. He voted against restoring $7.9 million in military aid to the Marcos government in the Philippines, over martial law and the imprisoning of Marcos opponents.

He was successful in winning authorization of a new African Development Foundation, aimed at filtering more U.S. aid to the village level, and worked to promote affirmative action in the Foreign Service.

**At Home:** The church, a dominant institution in black North Philadelphia, has made Gray's political career. Like his father and grandfather before him, Gray is the chief minister of the 3,000-member Bright Hope Baptist Church. On Sundays, he returns home to preach there. On election days, his parishioners are out working for him.

This religious base was vital to him in 1978, when he ousted 73-year old Robert N. C. Nix Jr., whom Gray dubbed "the phantom," charging that the older man made only infrequent visits to the district.

Nix had the allegiance of the ward leaders and organized labor, and had managed to hold off Gray by 339 votes in the 1976 Democratic primary. But Gray trounced him in 1978. Even though Nix was one of the only blacks ever to hold a significant House chairmanship — he headed the Post Office Committee — Gray received endorsements from such national black figures as

---

**2nd District: Philadelphia — west, central.** Population: 392,550 (17% decrease since 1970). Race: White 92,787 (24%), Black 293,465 (75%), Others 6,298 (2%). Spanish origin: 4,941 (1%).

Atlanta Mayor Maynard Jackson and Coretta Scott King. He also got the backing of the white Philadelphia business community.

Old-guard Nix allies still view Gray with suspicion, but his main political troubles come from young militants who say he is too close to the white power structure.

The issue flared up during the Philadelphia mayoral primary in 1979, when former Congressman William J. Green, a white liberal, opposed Charles Bowser, a black. Although Gray supported Bowser, some Bowser allies complained that he did not work effectively for their candidate. Still, Gray had no renomination problems in 1980.

**The District:** The black neighborhoods of North and West Philadelphia carry the most weight in the 2nd District. Although the most impoverished parts of the city, they nevertheless can get out the vote, as they demonstrated in a 1978 referendum on removing the two-consecutive-term limit for the mayor. Black opposition to the measure, which would have allowed law-and-order Mayor Frank L. Rizzo to run again, defeated it by a wide margin.

The integrated middle-class communities of Mt. Airy and Germantown also are important in the district, as are the white professionals living around Center City. All this territory is Democratic, giving Gray's party a 5-1 edge. There are some Republican votes in affluent white Chestnut Hill, but it too has gone for Gray.

## Committees

**Appropriations** (32nd of 33 Democrats)
Foreign Operations; Transportation.

**District of Columbia** (5th of 6 Democrats)
Government Operations and Metropolitan Affairs, chairman.

## Elections

**1980 General**

| | |
|---|---|
| William Gray III (D) | 127,106 (96 %) |

**1978 General**

| | |
|---|---|
| William Gray III (D) | 132,594 (82 %) |
| Roland Atkins (R) | 25,785 (16 %) |

**1978 Primary**

| | |
|---|---|
| William Gray III (D) | 36,506 (58 %) |
| Robert Nix (D) | 24,855 (40 %) |

**District Vote For President**

| | 1980 | | 1976 | | 1972 |
|---|---|---|---|---|---|
| D | 131,889 (81 %) | D | 128,921 (79 %) | D | 123,223 (74 %) |
| R | 22,176 (14 %) | R | 31,264 (19 %) | R | 40,817 (25 %) |
| I | 6,515 (4 %) | | | | |

## Campaign Finance

| | Receipts | Receipts from PACs | Expenditures |
|---|---|---|---|
| **1980** | | | |
| Gray III (D) | $178,850 | $42,040 (24 %) | $182,192 |

| **1978** | | | |
|---|---|---|---|
| Gray III (D) | $227,070 | $46,510 (20 %) | $225,887 |
| Atkins (D) | $34,362 | $400 (1 %) | $24,877 |

## Voting Studies

| | Presidential Support | | Party Unity | | Conservative Coalition | |
|---|---|---|---|---|---|---|
| Year | S | O | S | O | S | O |
| 1980 | 65 | 21 | 80 | 5 | 5 | 83 |
| 1979 | 79 | 14 | 94 | 2 | 2 | 92 |

S = Support          O = Opposition

## Key Votes

**96th Congress**

| | |
|---|---|
| Weaken Carter oil profits tax (1979) | N |
| Reject hospital cost control plan (1979) | N |
| Implement Panama Canal Treaties (1979) | Y |
| Establish Department of Education (1979) | N |
| Approve Anti-busing Amendment (1979) | N |
| Guarantee Chrysler Corp. loans (1979) | Y |
| Approve military draft registration (1980) | X |
| Aid Sandinista regime in Nicaragua (1980) | Y |
| Strengthen fair housing laws (1980) | Y |

**97th Congress**

| | |
|---|---|
| Reagan budget proposal (1981) | N |

## Interest Group Ratings

| Year | ADA | ACA | AFL-CIO | CCUS |
|---|---|---|---|---|
| 1980 | 72 | 19 | 95 | 62 |
| 1979 | 100 | 0 | 100 | |

# 3 Joseph F. Smith (D)

Of Philadelphia — Elected 1981

**Born:** Jan. 24, 1920, Philadelphia, Pa.
**Education:** Attended St. Joseph's College, 1940-42.
**Military Career:** U.S. Army, 1942-46.
**Profession:** Accountant.
**Family:** Wife, Regina Bukowski; one child.
**Religion:** Roman Catholic.
**Political Career:** Pa. Senate, 1971-81; unsuccessfully sought Democratic nomination for state treasurer, 1976.

**The Member:** "I live in a rowhouse, as opposed to a townhouse. The guy next to me drives a truck," says the lifelong resident of Philadelphia's blue-collar Port Richmond section. Smith is a firm friend of the party regulars who controlled the city when Frank Rizzo was mayor.

And he is an avowed enemy of the "reformers" now in charge under Rizzo's successor, former Rep. William J. Green III, (1964-77). The mayor irked many Democratic regulars with his reluctance to dispense patronage and grant political favors. For Smith, the animosity is personal. In late 1980 Green engineered Smith's ouster as minority chairman of the state Senate Appropriations Committee.

An opportunity for revenge came in the 1981 special election to replace Democrat Raymond F. Lederer, (1977-81), who resigned after his conviction on Abscam corruption charges. Green put up his protégé, Philadelphia Democratic Chairman David B. Glancey. Smith, capitalizing on the regulars' disgruntlement, took Glancey on.

Smith, after losing the Democratic nomination to Glancey in a vote of party ward leaders, continued the fight by securing the Republican nomination. Smith also ran on the independent line, and Glancey unsuccessfully challenged that move in court. Glancey stressed that he was the Democratic nominee, while Smith referred to himself as "the independent Democrat."

But Smith was better organized to get out his vote. He enjoyed substantial backing from organized labor and from rebellious Democratic ward leaders; he had seven to Glancey's 11.

**The District:** Binding this Philadelphia district together is the Frankford El, an elevated railway passing through its core, the white working class "river wards." Port Richmond, Fishtown and Bridesburg have strong ties to the Democratic Party, and the 3rd went for Jimmy Carter in 1980 by almost 2-1. Old-style organization

politics still is important in this part of the city, and Rizzo, the law-and-order former mayor, remains very popular there.

To the south, the district also takes in the well-to-do sections of Olde City, which contains historic Independence Hall, where the Declaration of Indendence was signed, and Society Hill. These elegant neighborhoods are a different world from the gritty river wards, but remain equally Democratic, although more liberal.

## Committees

No committees assigned as of Aug. 1, 1981.

## Election

**1981 Special Election**

| | |
|---|---|
| Joseph Smith (R, I)* | 29,907 (53%) |
| David Glancy (D) | 24,390 (43%) |

*\* Although Smith ran in the special election on the Republican and Independent lines, he pledged to the voters that he would caucus with the Democrats in Congress if elected.*

**District Vote For President**

| | 1980 | | 1976 | | 1972 |
|---|---|---|---|---|---|
| **D** | 86,130 (60%) | **D** | 101,997 (67%) | **D** | 87,324 (53%) |
| **R** | 46,191 (32%) | **R** | 47,471 (31%) | **R** | 76,120 (46%) |

## Campaign Finance

| | Receipts | Receipts from PACs | Expenditures |
|---|---|---|---|
| **1981 \*** | | | |
| Smith (R, I) | $18,645 | $14,000 (75%) | $13,336 |
| Glancy (D) | $121,032 | $28,700 (24%) | $58,793 |

*\* Figures include information reported by the candidates to the Federal Election Commission throught July 1, 1981.*

---

**3rd District: Philadelphia — east, central.** Population: 392,084 (17% decrease since 1970). Race: White 223,768 (57%), Black 126,832 (32%), Others 41,484 (11%). Spanish origin 45,987 (12%).

---

# 4 Charles F. Dougherty (R)

**Of Philadelphia — Elected 1978**

**Born:** June 26, 1937, Philadelphia, Pa.
**Education:** St. Joseph's College, B.S. 1959.
**Military Career:** Marine Corps, 1959-62; Marine Corps Reserve, 1957-59, 1962-79.
**Profession:** Teacher.
**Family:** Wife, Regina Lavery; six children.
**Religion:** Roman Catholic.
**Political Career:** Pa. Senate, 1973-79; unsuccessful Republican nominee for U.S. House, 1970.

**In Washington:** Dougherty arrived in Washington triumphant over the Philadelphia Democratic machine and ready to continue fighting. In his first days as a congressman, he backed constitutional amendments to ban abortion and busing, and a bill to allow tax credits for parents who send children to private schools.

As a first-term Republican, he was neither shy nor quiet. He gave short speeches on the House floor on a variety of topics, and long ones on abortion, about which he is passionate. In 1979, when Henry Hyde, R-Ill. and other abortion opponents accepted a compromise allowing federally funded abortions in cases of rape or incest, Dougherty was disgusted. "If you believe that the unborn child is nothing," he said, "just a piece of tissue, fine, vote for it. However, you are talking about human life." But the compromise passed.

Dougherty's views on abortion and busing lead some to place him on the Republican right, but when the issue is foreign aid or money for cities, he is often found voting on the Democratic side.

On 227 issues in 1980 where most Democrats opposed most Republicans, Dougherty lined up with the Democrats 51 percent of the time, more often than any other GOP newcomer. His close friends among junior Republicans have been self-described moderates like Tom Tauke of Iowa and Olympia Snowe of Maine. But he has managed to stay on good terms with his more conservative party leaders by making it clear he is willing to help them out in an "emergency."

Having upset an incumbent linked to a bribery scandal, Dougherty has been careful to present himself in office as the clean-living alternative to tainted Philadelphia Democrats. He neither drinks nor smokes. In his first financial reports, he revealed no outside income beyond a few speaking fees.

On the Armed Services Committee, where he headed in 1979 to protect Philadelphia's numerous naval installations, Dougherty clashed with a fellow Republican, Paul Trible of Virginia. The issue was whether the Navy should overhaul four aircraft carriers — a $2 billion project — in Newport News or in Philadelphia. Dougherty won, partly through help from friendly senators, but mostly because Vice President Mondale had made a 1976 campaign promise to keep Philadelphia's naval operations active. Whatever the reason, it turned out to be a political triumph for Dougherty.

**At Home:** Since the decline of the Philadelphia Republican machine in the years after World War II, Republican officeholders have been rare in the city. After Hugh Scott left the House in 1959 to go to the Senate, there were no Republican representatives from Philadelphia for 20 years.

Dougherty, the man who ended that drought, has a street-wise style more like ethnic Democratic politicians than like the genteel Hugh Scott. Thanks to his own resourcefulness and the flaws of Democratic opponents, Dougherty has restored two-party politics to the city's delegation.

Dougherty represented a part of the 4th in the state Senate when he challenged scandal-tainted Democratic Rep. Joshua Eilberg in 1978.

---

**4th District: Philadelphia — northeast.** Population: 449,684 (5% decrease since 1970). Race: White 406,877 (90%), Black 35,651 (8%), Others 7,156 (2%). Spanish origin: 6,412 (1%).

## Charles F. Dougherty, R-Pa.

Eight years before, Eilberg had beaten Dougherty easily. But the Democrat was arraigned six days before the 1978 election on charges of illegally taking money to help a Philadelphia hospital get federal funding. Dougherty was a comfortable winner. Eilberg later pleaded guilty.

In 1980, Dougherty had the good fortune to face Democrat Thomas Magrann, a controversial labor leader with a roughneck image and one-time ties to ex-Mayor Frank L. Rizzo, whose popularity had waned in the district; it was hardly a contest.

A lieutenant colonel in the Marine Reserve, Dougherty runs his campaigns and his congressional office with military precision.

His main problems are in his own party. He has been at odds with the city Republican organi-zation, led by William Meehan, and had a tight 1980 primary race against a Meehan-backed op-ponent, state Rep. Dennis O'Brien. Since then, Dougherty and Meehan have tried to patch things up.

**The District:** With its comfortable single-family homes, the sprawling Great Northeast seems more like a suburb than part of Philadelphia. Until recently, it even had a few farms.

Democrats have a wide advantage in party identification here, but voters in the Northeast are an independent bunch. Ethnic politics is usually more important than the partisan variety. Roosevelt Boulevard is the divider, with Jews to the west of it and ethnic Catholics, especially Irish, to the east.

## Committees

**Armed Services** (12th of 19 Republicans)
Military Installations and Facilities; Seapower and Strategic and Critical Materials.

**Merchant Marine and Fisheries** (11th of 15 Republicans)
Coast Guard and Navigation; Fisheries and Wildlife Conservation and the Environment; Merchant Marine.

## Elections

**1980 General**

| | |
|---|---|
| Charles Dougherty (R ) | 127,475 (63 %) |
| Thomas Magrann (D ) | 73,895 (37 %) |

**1980 Primary**

| | |
|---|---|
| Charles Dougherty (R ) | 21,923 (51 %) |
| Dennis O'Brien (R ) | 21,440 (49 %) |

**1978 General**

| | |
|---|---|
| Charles Dougherty (R ) | 110,445 (56 %) |
| Joshua Eilberg (D ) | 87,555 (44 %) |

**District Vote For President**

| | 1980 | | 1976 | | 1972 |
|---|---|---|---|---|---|
| D | 87,760 (40 %) | D | 129,639 (56 %) | D | 102,609 (43 %) |
| R | 109,437 (50 %) | R | 96,820 (42 %) | R | 132,983 (56 %) |
| I | 17,694 (8 %) | | | | |

## Campaign Finance

| | Receipts | Receipts from PACs | Expen-ditures |
|---|---|---|---|
| **1980** | | | |
| Dougherty (R ) | $242,386 | $112,292 (46 %) | $241,865 |
| Magrann (D ) | $218,649 | $61,575 (28 %) | $217,046 |

**1978**

| | | | |
|---|---|---|---|
| Dougherty (R ) | $131,650 | $50,717 (39 %) | $130,837 |
| Eilberg (D ) | $150,501 | $56,300 (37 %) | $159,904 |

## Voting Studies

| | Presidential Support | | Party Unity | | Conservative Coalition | |
|---|---|---|---|---|---|---|
| Year | S | O | S | O | S | O |
| 1980 | 56 | 27 | 35 | 51 | 40 | 46 |
| 1979 | 50 | 44 | 38 | 51 | 58 | 35 |

S = Support          O = Opposition

## Key Votes

**96th Congress**

| | |
|---|---|
| Weaken Carter oil profits tax (1979) | Y |
| Reject hospital cost control plan (1979) | Y |
| Implement Panama Canal Treaties (1979) | N |
| Establish Department of Education (1979) | Y |
| Approve Anti-busing Amendment (1979) | Y |
| Guarantee Chrysler Corp. loans (1979) | Y |
| Approve military draft registration (1980) | ? |
| Aid Sandinista regime in Nicaragua (1980) | Y |
| Strengthen fair housing laws (1980) | N |

**97th Congress**

| | |
|---|---|
| Reagan budget proposal (1981) | Y |

## Interest Group Ratings

| Year | ADA | ACA | AFL-CIO | CCUS |
|---|---|---|---|---|
| 1980 | 39 | 43 | 63 | 66 |
| 1979 | 5 | 42 | 55 | 65 |

# 5 Richard T. Schulze (R)

**Of Malvern — Elected 1974**

**Born:** Aug. 7, 1929, Philadelphia, Pa.
**Education:** Attended U. of Houston, 1949-50; Villanova U, 1952; Temple U., 1968.
**Military Career:** Army, 1951-53.
**Profession:** Owner, home appliance center.
**Family:** Wife, Nancy Lockwood; four children.
**Religion:** Presbyterian.
**Political Career:** Pa. House, 1969-75.

**In Washington:** Schulze is a protectionist Republican representing manufacturing interests of the Northeast. When many younger conservatives moved closer to free trade ideas in recent years, Schulze continued to speak up for his state's declining industrial base almost as vigorously as his predecessors did in the salad days of the Pennsylvania Manufacturers Association.

Well-ensconced on the Ways and Means Trade Subcommittee, Schulze fought to restrict the sweep of the big trade expansion bill the panel wrote in 1979. He ended up voting for it on the floor — there were only seven votes against it — but he warned against going too far. "Free trade means fair trade," Schulze said. "It is not fair if Americans play by the rules and our foreign competitors do not."

Schulze introduced his own bill in 1979 aimed at keeping a wide range of low-priced imports out of the country. The legislation was designed to prevent "dumping" — the sale of imported goods at less than fair market value. Not long afterward, he led an unsuccessful floor fight to deny most-favored-nation (MFN) trading status to Romania, on the grounds that Romania was restricting emigration. In 1980, when the House approved MFN status for China, he warned that it would "allow the Chinese to receive taxpayers' money at subsidized interest rates of between 7 and 8 percent." After the legislation passed, he complained that the Chinese were dumping mushrooms into the United States at prices that threatened the survival of domestic producers. Some of those domestic producers are in Schulze's district.

Schulze's leading legislative offering of the 96th Congress was an Individual Investors Incentive Act that would provide a 10 percent tax credit for investment in American securities. Schulze described it as a means of stimulating industrial capital formation and thus boosting productivity.

A private and sometimes taciturn man, Schulze had a middle-level GOP leadership position in the 96th Congress as chairman of the Republican Study Committee, whose staff turns out conservative fact sheets and position papers. He won that job in a three-way contest involving two more moderate competitors, one of them Lawrence Coughlin, who represents a neighboring district in the Philadelphia suburbs. At the start of the 97th Congress, Schulze was active in the unsuccessful campaign of Guy Vander Jagt of Michigan for House Republican leader.

**At Home:** A retail appliance dealer, Schulze came up through the ranks of Chester County politics, taking on such chores as chairmanship of Nixon Day festivities in 1968, and service as county register of wills. In November of 1968, he was promoted to the state Legislature.

As a dependable party man, he got his chance to run for Congress in 1974 when Republican Rep. John H. Ware III (1970-75) announced his retirement. Schulze received organization backing, but had to face a rough primary fight against four opponents.

Schulze's top competitor was Robin West, a wealthy young former aide in the Nixon White House. West had a host of volunteers and favorable publicity from a laudatory Hugh Sidey column about him in *Time* magazine. Using his personal fortune, he outspent Schulze, whom he blasted as "the machine candidate." But Schulze,

---

**5th District: Philadelphia suburbs — West Chester.** Population: 525,619 (11% increase since 1970). Race: White 493,290 (94%), Black 24,209 (5%), Others 8,120 (2%). Spanish origin: 7,590 (1%).

who reminded voters that "I don't drive a Ferrari," easily outdistanced the field. Since then, he has encountered no trouble.

**The District:** Among the rolling hills of the outer Philadelphia suburbs, new housing developments crowd up against horse pastures and colonial era farmhouses. The 5th takes in parts of Montgomery, Delaware and Chester counties — all of them firmly Republican with long-entrenched political organizations.

The county with the biggest share of the district is Chester. During much of the 1970s, its Republicans were torn by an internal revolt against the heavy-handed rule of county GOP Chairman Theodore S. A. Rubino. The strife, which spawned West's candidacy in 1974, ended when Rubino left the political scene after pleading guilty to corruption charges.

Democrats were too weak to take advantage of the GOP split. They are clustered in the few industrial towns in the district, chiefly Phoenixville and Pottstown.

## Committees

**Ways and Means** (9th of 12 Republicans)
Select Revenue Measures; Trade.

## Elections

**1980 General**

| | |
|---|---|
| Richard Schulze (R ) | 148,898 (75 %) |
| Grady Brickhouse (D ) | 47,092 (24 %) |

**1978 General**

| | |
|---|---|
| Richard Schulze (R ) | 110,565 (75 %) |
| Murray Zealor (D) | 36,704 (25 %) |

**Previous Winning Percentages**

1976 (60 %)     1974 (60 %)

**District Vote For President**

| | 1980 | | 1976 | | 1972 |
|---|---|---|---|---|---|
| D | 59,004 (29 %) | D | 77,048 (38 %) | D | 58,406 (30 %) |
| R | 126,401 (61 %) | R | 121,175 (60 %) | R | 130,761 (68 %) |
| I | 19,070 (9 %) | | | | |

## Campaign Finance

| | Receipts | Receipts from PACs | Expenditures |
|---|---|---|---|
| **1980** | | | |
| Schulze (R ) | $174,751 | $73,051 (42 %) | $133,815 |
| Brickhouse (D ) | $4,762 | $250 (5 %) | $4,761 |
| **1978** | | | |
| Schulze (R ) | $185,691 | $50,000 (27 %) | $124,390 |
| Zealor (D ) | $5,695 | — (0 %) | $5,354 |

## Voting Studies

| | Presidential Support | | Party Unity | | Conservative Coalition | |
|---|---|---|---|---|---|---|
| Year | S | O | S | O | S | O |
| 1980 | 34 | 56 | 85 | 7 | 88 | 6 |
| 1979 | 29 | 63 | 86 | 8 | 87 | 6 |
| 1978 | 24 | 64 | 82 | 8 | 82 | 9 |
| 1977 | 49 | 47 | 84 | 13 | 87 | 10 |
| 1976 | 63 | 35 | 84 | 14 | 83 | 15 |
| 1975 | 64 | 34 | 82 | 15† | 82 | 16 |

S = Support          O = Opposition

† Not eligible for all recorded votes.

## Key Votes

**96th Congress**

| | |
|---|---|
| Weaken Carter oil profits tax (1979) | Y |
| Reject hospital cost control plan (1979) | Y |
| Implement Panama Canal Treaties (1979) | N |
| Establish Department of Education (1979) | N |
| Approve Anti-busing Amendment (1979) | Y |
| Guarantee Chrysler Corp. loans (1979) | N |
| Approve military draft registration (1980) | ? |
| Aid Sandinista regime in Nicaragua (1980) | N |
| Strengthen fair housing laws (1980) | N |

**97th Congress**

| | |
|---|---|
| Reagan budget proposal (1981) | Y |

## Interest Group Ratings

| Year | ADA | ACA | AFL-CIO | CCUS |
|---|---|---|---|---|
| 1980 | 0 | 86 | 17 | 75 |
| 1979 | 5 | 92 | 15 | 100 |
| 1978 | 10 | 88 | 16 | 75 |
| 1977 | 20 | 85 | 23 | 94 |
| 1976 | 5 | 86 | 18 | 63 |
| 1975 | 16 | 86 | 17 | 82 |

# 6 Gus Yatron (D)

**Of Reading — Elected 1968**

**Born:** Oct. 16, 1927, Reading, Pa.
**Education:** Attended Kutztown State Teachers College, 1950.
**Profession:** Ice cream manufacturer.
**Family:** Wife, Millie Menzies; two children.
**Religion:** Greek Orthodox.
**Political Career:** Reading School Board, 1955-61; Penn. House, 1957-61; Penn. Senate, 1961-69.

**In Washington:** Yatron is a rarity in Congress: a subcommittee chairman who was unseated by his colleagues because they were dissatisfied with him.

In 1977, by virtue of seniority, Yatron was named chairman of the Inter-American Affairs Subcommitteee on House Foreign Affairs with jurisdiction over issues affecting Canada and Latin America. Four years later he was removed on a 10-9 vote.

Yatron called it a "political power play" on the part of the committee's liberals and that argument was reinforced when the committee also bypassed the Democrat next in line for the job, Dan Mica of Florida, in favor of the more liberal Michael Barnes of Maryland.

The anti-Yatron faction insisted the real issue was competence, that Yatron had been chairman in name only and that more dynamic members, especially Rep. Dante Fascell, D-Fla., provided the real leadership in the House on Latin American issues.

Despite several trips to Latin American nations, Yatron has never been regarded in the House as an expert on the issues of the hemisphere. He played little role in the two most controversial Latin American issues faced by Congress in recent years: the Panama Canal treaties and aid to Nicaragua.

Although the House had no constitutional role in approving the Panama Canal treaties in 1978, House members were deeply involved on both sides of the issue. Yatron chaired an eight-member panel that toured Panama in March 1978, just as the Senate was concluding consideration of the treaties. But his group made no recommendations, and Yatron was not active in the bitter 1979 House debate over legislation to implement the canal treaties.

He was similarly silent during the long controversy in the 96th Congress over economic aid to Nicaragua. President Carter argued that the United States should use financial aid to encourage moderation in the new leftist government there, but conservatives said any American money would only wind up in the hands of communists. Yatron visited Nicaragua in November 1979 as part of a House delegation, but had little to say on the subject either in committee or on the floor.

Yatron has been less sympathetic than most other Democrats on Foreign Affairs to the U.S. arms embargoes against military regimes in Chile and Argentina. In 1978, he opposed an immediate halt to all arms sales to Chile. Later that year, he criticized the Carter administration for cutting off all Export-Import loans to Argentina. In 1979, he cooperated with the Defense Department in an unsuccessful attempt to permit U.S. military training of officers from those countries, even though it was opposed by the Carter State Department.

He has compiled a generally conservative record on foreign aid issues, regularly voting with most Republicans to reduce foreign aid spending or to ban aid to leftist governments.

A Greek-American, Yatron is a member of the so-called Greek lobby on Capitol Hill, which has sought to limit arms sales and aid to Turkey since that nation's invasion of Cyprus in 1974. Greece and Turkey are longtime enemies in the Eastern Mediterranean.

---

**6th District: Southeast — Reading.**
Population: 488,524 (3% increase since 1970). Race: White 472,765 (97%), Black 8,033 (2%), Others 7,726 (2%). Spanish origin: 9,558 (2%).

---

## Gus Yatron, D-Pa.

On domestic issues, Yatron has maintained strong ties to labor unions — the AFL-CIO gave him a rating of 71 in 1980. And he has long supported trade legislation to shield U.S. metal-producing and textile industries — among the major employers in his district — from foreign competition. His overall voting record has become more conservative in recent years; since 1977 he has voted an increasing percentage of the time with Republicans and Southern Democrats.

**At Home:** Old-time Reading residents still remember how Yatron knocked out Gibraltar Joe Biacone in 1947 — in a bout that touched off a ringside brawl between the two contestants' relatives. But nothing very rough has happened to the amiable ex-boxer since he retired from the ring with a 13-2-1 record.

Through his athletic reputation and the family ice cream-making business, which he ran with his father, Yatron had enough local celebrity to launch a political career that has been highly successful. His record at the polls is 13-0-0.

Yatron may not be smooth and articulate, but he projects a down-to-earth manner that goes over well in a town where people eat pizza at private key clubs. He has a prodigious memory for names and faces, and like many members from areas close to Washington, he returns home on weekends to keep in touch. His son, George, is the Berks County (Reading) district attorney.

Yatron came up through the ranks of Berks politics, starting on the school board and eventually moving to the Legislature. When Democrat George M. Rhodes retired, he anointed Yatron as a successor and served as his campaign chairman.

Initially, Yatron had the same problem Rhodes had with Schuylkill County (Pottsville), the half of his district that is Republican. In his first election, in 1968, he won district-wide with only 51.2 percent of the vote. Since then, Yatron has extended his base from Democratic Berks, winning with more than 60 percent every outing. He devotes a great deal of time to Schuylkill, where his office specializes in solving black-lung claim problems. The Republican organization in Schuylkill no longer exerts itself on behalf of his opponents.

**The District:** The railroad workers of Reading and the miners of Schuylkill County once voted in separate districts, but they were joined in 1962 when Berks Democrat Rhodes, (1949-69), narrowly defeated Schuylkill Republican Ivor D. Fenton (1939-63).

Despite its Democratic heritage, Berks has become a swing county in statewide and national contests — although when it sides with the Republicans, the winning margin usually is small. For governor in 1970, it backed Democrat Milton Shapp with 58.8 percent; in 1978, Berks went for Republican Richard Thornburgh, who got 53.9 percent in the county.

## Committees

**Foreign Affairs** (7th of 21 Democrats)
Inter-American Affairs; International Operations.

**Post Office and Civil Service** (9th of 15 Democrats)
Census and Population; Civil Service.

## Elections

**1980 General**

| | |
|---|---|
| Gus Yatron (D ) | 117,965 (67 %) |
| George Hulshart (R ) | 57,844 (33 %) |

**1978 General**

| | |
|---|---|
| Gus Yatron (D ) | 106,431 (74 %) |
| Stephen Mazur (R ) | 37,746 (26 %) |

**Previous Winning Percentages**

1976 (74 %)   1974 (75 %)   1972 (65 %)   1970 (65 %)
1968 (51 %)

**District Vote For President**

| | 1980 | | 1976 | | 1972 |
|---|---|---|---|---|---|
| D | 65,269 (36 %) | D | 90,203 (49 %) | D | 66,793 (36 %) |
| R | 100,019 (56 %) | R | 89,194 (49 %) | R | 114,537 (62 %) |
| I | 12,240 (7 %) | | | | |

## Campaign Finance

| | Receipts | Receipts from PACs | Expenditures |
|---|---|---|---|
| **1980** | | | |
| Yatron (D ) | $72,339 | $46,750 (65 %) | $66,845 |
| Hulshart (R ) | $13,324 | — (0 %) | $13,321 |
| **1978** | | | |
| Yatron (D ) | $58,715 | $28,820 (49 %) | $55,589 |

# Voting Studies

| Year | Presidential Support | | Party Unity | | Conservative Coalition | |
|---|---|---|---|---|---|---|
| | S | O | S | O | S | O |
| 1980 | 51 | 44 | 46 | 51 | 60 | 37 |
| 1979 | 45 | 50 | 50 | 45 | 66 | 28 |
| 1978 | 51 | 45 | 49 | 47 | 57 | 38 |
| 1977 | 59 | 33 | 62 | 33 | 55 | 39 |
| 1976 | 37 | 57 | 72 | 25 | 47 | 50 |
| 1975 | 27 | 66 | 73 | 23 | 35 | 59 |
| 1974 (Ford) | 41 | 56 | | | | |
| 1974 | 43 | 45 | 71 | 22 | 40 | 53 |
| 1973 | 25 | 67 | 82 | 14 | 23 | 73 |
| 1972 | 32 | 49 | 69 | 21 | 37 | 54 |
| 1971 | 33 | 56 | 71 | 10 | 19 | 70 |
| 1970 | 62 | 32 | 69 | 17 | 16 | 70 |
| 1969 | 51 | 47 | 84 | 11 | 22 | 73 |

S = Support  O = Opposition

# Key Votes

**96th Congress**

| | |
|---|---|
| Weaken Carter oil profits tax (1979) | Y |
| Reject hospital cost control plan (1979) | Y |
| Implement Panama Canal Treaties (1979) | N |
| Establish Department of Education (1979) | Y |
| Approve Anti-busing Amendment (1979) | Y |
| Guarantee Chrysler Corp. loans (1979) | Y |
| Approve military draft registration (1980) | N |
| Aid Sandinista regime in Nicaragua (1980) | Y |
| Strengthen fair housing laws (1980) | N |

**97th Congress**

| | |
|---|---|
| Reagan budget proposal (1981) | Y |

# Interest Group Ratings

| Year | ADA | ACA | AFL-CIO | CCUS |
|---|---|---|---|---|
| 1980 | 39 | 50 | 71 | 59 |
| 1979 | 26 | 42 | 65 | 50 |
| 1978 | 40 | 44 | 60 | 39 |
| 1977 | 30 | 36 | 83 | 47 |
| 1976 | 40 | 21 | 83 | 25 |
| 1975 | 47 | 36 | 81 | 18 |
| 1974 | 48 | 20 | 90 | 11 |
| 1973 | 76 | 19 | 100 | 18 |
| 1972 | 44 | 40 | 100 | 0 |
| 1971 | 68 | 33 | 90 | - |
| 1970 | 68 | 26 | 86 | 10 |
| 1969 | 60 | 29 | 100 | - |

# 7 Robert W. Edgar (D)

### Of Broomall — Elected 1974

**Born:** May 29, 1943, Philadelphia, Pa.
**Education:** Lycoming College, B.A. 1965; Drew U. Theological School, M.Div. 1968.
**Profession:** Minister.
**Family:** Wife, Merle Deaver; three children.
**Religion:** Methodist.
**Political Career:** No previous office.

**In Washington:** Edgar has chosen a lonely role for himself as minority voice on the Public Works Committee, where a big bipartisan majority thrives on the principle of mutual pork-barrel assistance. An environmentalist who considers many dams and other public works projects to be a waste of money, the quiet Methodist minister has been an outcast on the committee.

When Public Works wrote a bill in 1980 containing $4 billion worth of water projects, Edgar was the only member of the panel to vote against it. Then he drafted 184 separate amendments for floor debate, leading one committee member to charge that he lacked "an ounce of milk of human kindness in his soul," and another to complain that he was threatening "the human rights of the people of the Appalachian region." Edgar eventually condensed most of his amendments into one calling for an end to eight of the projects in the bill. When that was defeated on a 263-117 vote, he opposed final passage.

It was Edgar's rawest confrontation with the pro-dam bloc, but it followed the pattern he had set in earlier years. During his first House term, he sought to remove money in an authorization bill for a water project in Alaska, drawing an angry comment about political etiquette from Alaska's Republican congressman, Don Young. "Those who play in other people's ballparks may be penalized," Young said, accurately predicting Edgar's future on the committee.

In the 1980 argument, Edgar also fired a few shots at the Carter administration, which was on record against many of the projects but seemed reluctant to offend some House members in an election year. "They let you get out on a limb," he complained, "and then they saw it off. Then they apologize to you for not telling you they were sawing."

Edgar did win a conspicuous public works victory at the end of the 95th Congress, when he blocked an attempt to pass a $1.4 billion water bill funding 158 projects in 46 states. Members were leaving for the October adjournment, and when Edgar demanded a roll-call vote, not enough were there to constitute a quorum. So the bill died, even though a majority of those present voted for it.

On transportation issues, another Public Works specialty, Edgar also has been in the minority, arguing for a redirection of the committee's road-building emphasis into mass transit. Early in his career, he began calling for an overall transportation trust fund, a concept anathema to most Public Works members if it meant a reduction in the Highway Trust Fund. In 1975, Edgar tried to amend an urban aid bill on the House floor to allow community development funds to be used for mass transit, but got nowhere.

Edgar has had more than his share of victories, however, in another capacity — as head of the Northeast-Midwest Congressional Coalition, an umbrella group formed to defend "Frost Belt" interests against the Southern and Western states. In 1980, Edgar issued a report in the group's behalf complaining that over the past five years the federal government had shifted $165 billion in tax money from the financially troubled East and Midwest to the comparatively healthy West and South.

The coalition has been a successful in-House lobbying operation, mobilizing effectively to win several important "formula fights" — arguments over how federal aid should be distributed. Edgar

---

**7th District: Philadelphia suburbs — Chester.** Population: 421,368 (11% decrease since 1970). Race: White 371,870 (88%), Black 44,493 (11%), Others 5,005 (1%). Spanish origin: 3,199 (1%).

himself has developed some expertise at designing amendments to bring in the broadest possible coalition. By early 1981, the group's successes had prompted formation of a rival organization, the Sun Belt Coalition.

Meanwhile, Edgar has been drawn into a wholly different subject area by his second committee assignment, Veterans' Affairs. In 1981, he became chairman of an education subcommittee charged with drafting a new GI Bill to meet the changing military needs of the '80s. The aim is to make military service more attractive to college-bound high school graduates by offering generous rewards for enlisting.

"We should not continue to play a part in switching signals on the all-volunteer force any longer," he said, defending his bill. Edgar would provide $300 a month for 36 months of college education for all who served three years on active duty. His bill would cost an estimated $1 billion or more by 1990. Edgar says it would cost more not to attract and keep trained military personnel.

With Reagan in the White House, Edgar also has been a vocal defender of existing veterans programs. In his 1982 budget, Reagan proposed trimming more than $900 million, or 3.7 percent, from the VA — mostly for hospitals. Edgar responded immediately with a vow to try to block the cuts. Among the programs he has lobbied hardest for is the network of storefront counseling centers for Vietnam veterans.

**At Home:** At his 1980 Election Night party, people wore buttons saying, "Edgar's fourth miracle." A member of the 1974 Democratic Watergate class, he represents staunchly Republican Delaware County and has had a tough fight every time. Edgar only cleared 55 percent once, in his first election — and then just barely.

When he ran in 1974, Edgar was the Protestant chaplain of Drexel University. He was making his first electoral venture. But he was able to capitalize on Delaware County's internal political situation and public distaste for the Nixon administration.

The county's once-powerful Republican machine, known as the War Board, alienated many in the party that year by dumping four-term GOP Rep. Lawrence G. Williams in favor of a state legislator, Stephen McEwen. News allegations of corruption also diminished the organization's effectiveness. The Republicans tried to regroup for November, but Edgar was ready for them. He had his own apparatus of liberal activists in place and won by 18,786 votes.

He was an obvious Republican target in 1976, but his energetic constituent service and transportation work gave him a surprising boost, and he won by 16,648. In 1978, however, he was nearly beaten by a popular and easily noticed Republican, Eugene (Sonny) Kane, the 300-pound mayor of Upper Darby. His margin dipped to 1,368.

That appeared to make Edgar a likely loser in 1980, when Republicans tried again with Dennis J. Rochford, a Delaware County councilman. Rochford was a good campaigner, and Edgar began to have serious trouble on the abortion issue; anti-abortion groups picketed some of his speeches. All but resigned himself to another razor-thin margin, Edgar surprised the local politicians with a victory by more than 12,000 votes.

**The District:** The GOP grip on Delaware County is tight. Even blue-collar towns like Upper Darby and Chester, which return big Democratic votes in national and statewide contests, usually go Republican for local offices.

Aside from industrial areas along the Delaware River, the county — which has a bigger population than the neighboring state of Delaware — is solidly suburban. The close-in Delaware County communities are filled with ethnics from Philadelphia, while the outer suburbs are more prosperous and Anglo-Saxon.

Known for its secretive ways, the War Board (officially the Delaware County Republican Board of Supervisors) ruled supreme from the 1920s to the mid-1960s under the leadership of the late John McClure. Disbanded in the mid-1970s, the War Board has been replaced by a looser Republican confederation without an individual boss.

## Committees

**Public Works and Transportation** (9th of 25 Democrats)
Economic Development; Surface Transportation; Water Resources.

**Veterans' Affairs** (6th of 17 Democrats)
Education, Training and Employment, chairman; Hospitals and Health Care.

## Elections

**1980 General**

| | |
|---|---|
| Robert Edgar (D ) | 99,381 (53 %) |
| Dennis Rochford (R ) | 87,643 (47 %) |

**1978 General**

| | |
|---|---|
| Robert Edgar (D ) | 79,771 (50 %) |
| Eugene Kane (R ) | 78,403 (49 %) |

**Previous Winning Percentages**

1976 (54 %)    1974 (55 %)

**District Vote For President**

| 1980 | | 1976 | | 1972 | |
|---|---|---|---|---|---|
| D | 69,668 (36%) | D | 93,411 (45%) | D | 73,551 (35%) |
| R | 106,245 (55%) | R | 109,433 (53%) | R | 132,991 (63%) |
| I | 15,101 (8%) | | | | |

## Campaign Finance

| | Receipts | Receipts from PACs | Expenditures |
|---|---|---|---|
| **1980** | | | |
| Edgar (D ) | $296,533 | $132,777 (45 %) | $295,529 |
| Rochford (R ) | $257,408 | $127,223 (49 %) | $253,406 |
| **1978** | | | |
| Edgar (D ) | $143,188 | $51,294 (36 %) | $142,238 |
| Kane (R ) | $216,547 | $51,441 (24 %) | $216,347 |

## Voting Studies

| | Presidential Support | | Party Unity | | Conservative Coalition | |
|---|---|---|---|---|---|---|
| Year | S | O | S | O | S | O |
| 1980 | 65 | 17 | 77 | 14 | 6 | 84 |
| 1979 | 79 | 14 | 85 | 9 | 8 | 85 |
| 1978 | 76 | 21 | 81 | 16 | 7 | 90 |
| 1977 | 75 | 18 | 84 | 13 | 8 | 90 |
| 1976 | 27 | 73 | 83 | 11 | 15 | 82 |
| 1975 | 31 | 64 | 88 | 8 | 6 | 92 |

S = Support          O = Opposition

## Key Votes

**96th Congress**

| | |
|---|---|
| Weaken Carter oil profits tax (1979) | N |
| Reject hospital cost control plan (1979) | N |
| Implement Panama Canal Treaties (1979) | Y |
| Establish Department of Education (1979) | Y |
| Approve Anti-busing Amendment (1979) | N |
| Guarantee Chrysler Corp. loans (1979) | Y |
| Approve military draft registration (1980) | N |
| Aid Sandinista regime in Nicaragua (1980) | Y |
| Strengthen fair housing laws (1980) | Y |

**97th Congress**

| | |
|---|---|
| Reagan budget proposal (1981) | N |

## Interest Group Ratings

| Year | ADA | ACA | AFL-CIO | CCUS |
|---|---|---|---|---|
| 1980 | 94 | 10 | 78 | 55 |
| 1979 | 89 | 4 | 89 | 6 |
| 1978 | 80 | 11 | 89 | 22 |
| 1977 | 100 | 11 | 86 | 13 |
| 1976 | 95 | 0 | 77 | 19 |
| 1975 | 100 | 11 | 100 | 13 |

# 8 Jim Coyne (R)

**Of Newtown — Elected 1980**

**Born:** Nov. 17, 1946, Farmville, Va.
**Education:** Yale U., B.S. 1968; Harvard U., M.B.A. 1970.
**Profession:** Chemical company president.
**Family:** Wife, Helen Mercer; two children.
**Religion:** Presbyterian.
**Political Career:** Supervisor, Upper Makefield Township, 1979-80.

**The Member:** A young businessman with degrees from Yale and Harvard, Coyne presented himself in 1980 as a moderate-to-liberal Republican, in the image of the district's popular former representative, Edward G. Biester Jr. (1967-77).

Incumbent Democrat Peter H. Kostmayer looked like a strong bet for re-election after winning 61.1 percent of the vote in 1978, but Coyne succeeded where Kostmayer's more conservative opponents had failed. He waged an aggressive person-to-person campaign against Kostmayer and had the money for both television and radio ads in the expensive Philadelphia media market.

Coyne's expertise in finance and marketing led him in 1981 to the Banking Committee, where he sponsored a bill called the First Home Financing Act. The legislation would allow an individual to set aside in a tax-exempt savings account up to $2,000 annually to be used to purchase a first home. Coyne argued that the Reagan administration should incorporate his savings incentive idea into its tax cut program.

Coyne was also head of a GOP freshman task force on committee spending that recommended an average 10 percent reduction in House committee budgets.

**The District:** Practically all of the 8th District lies within Bucks County, a Philadelphia suburban community. The county contains upper- and middle-income suburbs but has an industrial strip along the Delaware River just north of Philadelphia. It is there that most of the Democratic votes are found. Elsewhere, Democrats have to scramble for independents to have a chance of carrying the district. A small portion of the district is located in neighboring Montgomery County.

Despite a respectable Democratic vote in most elections, the district has usually sent Republicans to the House. The last time Democrats won the seat before Kostmayer's victory in 1976 was in 1936.

## Committees

**Banking, Finance and Urban Affairs** (18th of 19 Republicans)
Domestic Monetary Policy; Economic Stabilization; Housing and Community Development; International Development Institutions and Finance.

**House Administration** (7th of 8 Republicans)
Personnel and Police; Services; Policy Group on Information and Computers.

**Joint Library**

## Elections

**1980 General**

| | |
|---|---|
| Jim Coyne (R ) | 103,585 (51 %) |
| Peter Kostmayer (D ) | 99,593 (49 %) |

**District Vote For President**

| | 1980 | | 1976 | | 1972 |
|---|---|---|---|---|---|
| **D** | 66,170 (32%) | **D** | 89,931 (46 %) | **D** | 64,330 (34 %) |
| **R** | 117,511 (57 %) | **R** | 101,845 (52 %) | **R** | 118,601 (63 %) |
| **I** | 20,567 (10%) | | | | |

## Campaign Finance

| | Receipts | Receipts from PACs | Expenditures |
|---|---|---|---|
| **1980** | | | |
| Coyne (R ) | $424,653 | $118,685 (28 %) | $423,002 |
| Kostmayer (D ) | $220,862 | $75,872 (34 %) | $222,925 |

## Key Vote

**97th Congress**

| | |
|---|---|
| Reagan budget proposal (1981) | Y |

**8th District: Philadelphia suburbs — Bucks County.** Population: 542,042 (14% increase since 1970). Race: White 521,543 (96%), Black 12,930 (2%), Others 7,569 (1%). Spanish origin: 6,106 (1%).

# 9 Bud Shuster (R)

## Of Everett — Elected 1972

**Born:** Jan. 23, 1932, Glassport, Pa.
**Education:** U. of Pittsburgh, B.S. 1954; Duquesne U., M.B.A. 1960; American U., Ph.D. 1967.
**Military Career:** Army, 1954-56.
**Profession:** Electronics executive.
**Family:** Wife, Patricia Rommel; five children.
**Religion:** United Church of Christ.
**Political Career:** No previous office.

**In Washington:** Even in a chamber full of ambitious people, Shuster has always stood out as a man in a hurry. His nervous intensity and strident partisanship alienate some colleagues, but he often wins his point on sheer energy and determination.

The focus of his ambitions in the House has been a place in the Republican leadership. He was president of his 1972 Republican House class, and after three terms he decided to move for the chairmanship of the Republican Policy Committee. The front-runner for that post, Minnesota's Bill Frenzel, all but assumed it was his and did little to win. Shuster simply out-campaigned him for the job, and won it, 80-55.

Shuster immediately turned the Policy Committee into a sophisticated media operation, issuing releases on dozens of major issues and holding news conferences in the House Press Gallery to lacerate the Democratic majority. He also began firing a verbal barrage at the Democrats nearly every day on the House floor, launching a brief filibuster to protest changes in the schedule, and bringing a toy duck on the floor to complain about the "lame duck" session after the 1980 election. By mid-1980, House Budget Chairman Robert N. Giaimo was calling him "the hatchet man of the Republican Party."

But Shuster was not concerned about his image among Democrats; he was running as an avowed partisan for Republican whip in the 97th Congress. His opponent, Trent Lott of Mississippi, was virtually his opposite in style: friendly, easy-going and non-controversial. Shuster campaigned for the job for a year with all his customary single-mindedness, carefully cultivating members one by one.

Starting as a distinct underdog, he gradually gained on Lott, but not quite enough. The final score was Lott 96; Shuster, 90. Some Republicans felt the same drive and intensity that brought

Shuster so close ultimately defeated him because it raised the fear that he would be less than sympathetic to their personal needs.

While working his way up in the Republican leadership, Shuster was also becoming an important member of the Public Works Committee. He has been an ally of road builders and other highway users and a defender of the Highway Trust Fund against attempts to use it for funding mass transit. For years, he has warned that the country's highways are deteriorating and need more money for maintenance. He was chairman of the National Transportation Policy Study Committee, an ad hoc group created by Congress.

Shuster is senior Republican on the Surface Transportation Subcommittee at Public Works, and has tended to be far less partisan there than he is on the House floor. In the 96th Congress, he worked closely with New Jersey Democrat James Howard, the current Public Works chairman, to negotiate a compromise that led to enactment of a trucking deregulation bill which eased restrictions on entry into the trucking business. Smaller communities were concerned that total trucking deregulation might leave them without adequate service, and Shuster was instrumental in the agreement that truckers would have to maintain service to these areas under the new legislation.

Shuster also muted his partisanship in early 1981 when President Reagan proposed spending about $2 billion less on highways over a five-year

---

**9th District: South central — Altoona, Chambersburg.** Population: 510,690 (9% increase since 1970). Race: White 503,884 (99%), Black 4,807 (1%), Others 1,999 (0.3%). Spanish origin: 1,924 (0.3%).

period than President Carter had suggested earlier. In fact, Shuster joined with Howard in introducing a one-year bill to maintain funding at the previously planned level while future policy was being worked out.

And when Reagan proposed to eliminate federal funding after 1982 for Conrail, Shuster came out against that. "I support tightening Conrail's belt," Shuster said, "but I oppose tightening a noose around its neck."

On mass transit legislation, Shuster has wanted to shift money away from older, larger cities with established subway and bus systems and into newer cities and rural areas. He tried to do that on the mass transit authorization bill in 1980 but was beaten, 266-109.

Shuster has also been a vociferous opponent of air bags as a safety requirement for automobiles and has worked to prevent air bag regulations from going into effect. "No hard evidence exists," he has insisted, "that air-bags will actually save lives. . . . The air bag order chips away needlessly at our individual freedoms."

He has also fought requirements that buses and subways be fitted with new equipment making them accessible to handicapped people in wheelchairs. He calls such regulations "a costly failure," and wants to allow cities and transit companies to come up with an alternative system, such as special service for the handicapped. He offered an amendment on the House floor in 1980 to permit such an alternative, but was narrowly beaten, 183-181.

Shuster's style on the Public Works Committee marks a distinct contrast from the partisan aggressiveness he has shown on the Budget Committee in both the 96th and 97th Congresses. Early in 1980, he did vote for a bipartisan compromise budget drawn up to be balanced. But later in the year when it was clear the budget would produce a deficit, he resumed his barrage against the committee's Democratic leaders, accusing them of imposing "the highest tax burden in the history of our nation" and labeling the budget "a political charade."

Meanwhile, Shuster was engaging in partisan theater on the floor over the right to make one-minute speeches at the start of each session. Since early 1979, when the House began televising its proceedings, Shuster and other Republicans had been offering the short speeches to attack Democratic programs and policies, hoping excerpts might be included on the national evening news programs.

In mid-1980, Democrats tried to move the one-minute speeches to the end of the day. Shuster was almost violent in his reaction. "We were gagged," he said, "as a conscious decision of the Democratic leadership to block daytime coverage of the latest Carter-Libyan scandals." He staged his own miniature filibuster by threatening endless roll calls on a series of privileged resolutions, and eventually the Democrats gave in and restored the speeches to their original place.

**At Home:** Shuster may not be easy to love, but he is impossible to beat. His mountainous district has firm Republican loyalties, and his outspoken partisanship strikes a chord among constituents.

While he has detractors in local political circles, notably in the GOP organization of the district's most populous county, Blair (Altoona), he remains unchallenged. In 1980, he received both the Democratic and Republican nominations.

This is not to say he has escaped controversy. In the mid-70's, he was sued for alleged stock fraud in connection with the sale of securities of a company he had managed. The disgruntled stockholders, who claimed they had been shortchanged, later settled out of court. He also attracted attention when he reportedly tried to buy into a local newspaper, *The Bedford Daily Gazette*, after it criticized him.

Before entering politics, Shuster had a successful business career with the Radio Corporation of America and as an independent electronics entrepreneur. When Republican Rep. Irving Whalley, (1960-73), announced his retirement, Shuster embarked on a self-generated congressional campaign and won the GOP primary over State Sen. E. Elmer Hawbacker, who had the backing of the party committees for Bedford and Blair counties. Shuster has had an easy time winning re-election.

**The District:** To Pennsylvania Turnpike travelers, the 5th is a long winding stretch through the Appalachian Mountains, broken up by tunnels and Breezewood, the celebrated "Town of Motels." The area's semi-Appalachian character has produced a strong strain of Republicanism. Democrats are scarce in most of the rural counties.

There are Democrats to contend with in Altoona, the old railroad center that is the district's largest town. But even there, Republicans have made gains and now surpass Democrats in registration.

# Committees

**Budget**
Task Forces: Energy and the Environment; Enforcement, Credit and Multi-year Budgeting; National Security and Veterans.

**Public Works and Transportation** (4th of 19 Republicans)
Aviation; Economic Development; Surface Transportation.

# Elections

**1980 General**

| | |
|---|---|
| Bud Shuster (R ) | Unopposed |

**1978 General**

| | |
|---|---|
| Bud Shuster (R ) | 101,151 (75 %) |
| Blaine Havice (D ) | 33,882 (25 %) |

**Previous Winning Percentages**

1976 (100%)    1974 (57 %)    1972 (62 %)

**District Vote For President**

| | 1980 | | 1976 | | 1972 |
|---|---|---|---|---|---|
| D | 54,906 (33 %) | D | 66,499 (40 %) | D | 40,602 (25 %) |
| R | 104,453 (62 %) | R | 96,867 (58 %) | R | 116,170 (73 %) |
| I | 7,355 (4 %) | | | | |

# Campaign Finance

| | Receipts | Receipts from PACs | Expenditures |
|---|---|---|---|
| **1980** | | | |
| Shuster (R ) | $158,193 | $64,501 (41 %) | $156,048 |
| **1978** | | | |
| Shuster (R ) | $139,050 | $61,773 (44 %) | $146,318 |
| Havice (D ) | $26,694 | $1,500 (6 %) | $16,809 |

# Voting Studies

| Year | Presidential Support | | Party Unity | | Conservative Coalition | |
|---|---|---|---|---|---|---|
| | S | O | S | O | S | O |
| 1980 | 31 | 58 | 94 | 4 | 91 | 2 |
| 1979 | 21 | 74 | 90 | 6 | 87 | 5 |
| 1978 | 22 | 73 | 90 | 8 | 91 | 7 |
| 1977 | 39 | 61 | 90 | 10 | 96 | 4 |
| 1976 | 76 | 24 | 91 | 9 | 94 | 5 |
| 1975 | 60 | 39 | 89 | 10 | 90 | 9 |
| 1974 (Ford) | 65 | 31 | | | | |
| 1974 | 68 | 32 | 80 | 19 | 85 | 13 |
| 1973 | 66 | 34 | 88 | 12 | 95 | 5 |

S = Support          O = Opposition

# Key Votes

**96th Congress**

| | |
|---|---|
| Weaken Carter oil profits tax (1979) | Y |
| Reject hospital cost control plan (1979) | # |
| Implement Panama Canal Treaties (1979) | N |
| Establish Department of Education (1979) | N |
| Approve Anti-busing Amendment (1979) | Y |
| Guarantee Chrysler Corp. loans (1979) | N |
| Approve military draft registration (1980) | ? |
| Aid Sandinista regime in Nicaragua (1980) | N |
| Strengthen fair housing laws (1980) | N |

**97th Congress**

| | |
|---|---|
| Reagan budget proposal (1981) | Y |

# Interest Group Ratings

| Year | ADA | ACA | AFL-CIO | CCUS |
|---|---|---|---|---|
| 1980 | 6 | 91 | 11 | 77 |
| 1979 | 0 | 100 | 16 | 100 |
| 1978 | 5 | 96 | 16 | 78 |
| 1977 | 15 | 96 | 17 | 100 |
| 1976 | 0 | 86 | 13 | 94 |
| 1975 | 0 | 93 | 13 | 94 |
| 1974 | 13 | 87 | 9 | 67 |
| 1973 | 4 | 85 | 9 | 82 |

# 10 Joseph M. McDade (R)

**Of Scranton — Elected 1962**

**Born:** Sept. 29, 1931, Scranton, Pa.
**Education:** U. of Notre Dame, B.A. 1953 ; U. of Pa., LL.B. 1956.
**Profession:** Lawyer.
**Family:** Wife, Mary Theresa O'Brien; four children.
**Religion:** Roman Catholic.
**Political Career:** No previous office.

**In Washington:** McDade is a creature of the Appropriations Committee, on which he has spent all but two of his 18 years in the House, and especially of its Interior Subcommittee, on which he has served longer than its chairman, Democrat Sidney Yates of Illinois.

It is an important subcommittee, with control over most of the money the federal government spends on energy research, and McDade has had a lot to say in recent years over how the money should be spent.

One way he wants it to be spent is on synthetic fuels. In 1980, before Congress had approved President Carter's program, McDade persuaded the committee to place extra money for synfuels in the Interior Appropriation bill, to "serve notice" that Congress is serious about the issue.

Another McDade priority is exploration in Alaska. He placed in the 1981 bill some $31 million for private oil leasing in the state's National Petroleum Reserve, ignoring objections from the Interior Committee that the move was premature.

But the energy source that is most important to McDade's Scranton constituency is coal, and he is in a perfect spot to provide federal help for the coal boom he hopes will revive his depressed district. When the Carter administration tried to drop $45 million for a new commercial coal gasification plant, McDade and the subcommittee put it right back in.

The subcommittee also has control over the reclamation fund used to restore abandoned strip mines, and this is an issue McDade battled over for years on the House floor. As written initially in the Interior Committee, the landmark Strip Mine Control Act set up a reclamation fee on newly mined coal to pay for cleaning up the scarred land.

McDade objected to it as a tax that would raise the price of coal, and tried repeatedly to replace it with a fund financed through energy production on the Outer Continental Shelf. He managed to get that through the House in 1974, but the bill did not become law that year, and by 1977, when it was finally signed into law, sentiment had shifted the other way.

McDade can be energetic and excitable when he becomes involved in an issue, but over the years has taken up few causes outside the energy field, and as a result he is surprisingly inconspicuous for a man tied for ninth in seniority among all House Republicans.

In the 96th Congress, however, he went on a few unexpected crusades, with some interesting results. He complained angrily that the 1980 census was not making any distinction between legal and illegal aliens, and that states with large numbers of illegal aliens would be getting additional House representation — at the expense of states like Pennsylvania, which have few of them.

McDade offered an amendment to a 1981 appropriation bill blocking use of the Census figures for reapportionment. Many in the House viewed it as a quixotic effort, but McDade said it would make a good basis for a court challenge, and he was far from alone in his concerns. The amendment passed the House, 222-189.

The appropriation bill itself bogged down in conference with the Senate, however, and in the last days of the 96th Congress, it was replaced by

---

**10th District: Northeast — Scranton.** Population: 519,026 (10% increase since 1970). Race: White 513,959 (99%), Black 2,608 (1%), Others 2,459 (1%). Spanish origin: 2,389 (0.4%).

---

an emergency spending measure. When McDade tried to attach his reapportionment amendment to that bill, he was beaten 208-164, largely because he had lost support from members whose states stood to gain from inclusion of the aliens.

Earlier in the year, McDade took on the top officials in the federal bureaucracy, the Senior Executive Service. Members of the SES had been made eligible for large performance bonuses by a 1978 law, but McDade claimed the system was being abused, with huge bonuses being awarded routinely regardless of merit. "I think the whole system needs to be shaken out," he said, and supported a flat limit on executive pay. Congress ultimately decided to keep the bonuses but allow them for only a quarter of the SES.

For most of his career, McDade has also worked on small business issues, particularly on holding down interest rates. He amended the 1968 Truth-in-Lending Act to make loan sharking subject to federal prosecution, and he tried several times in recent years to lower or freeze interest rates on small-business loans. Those efforts have not succeeded.

On most votes, McDade is a consistent moderate Republican, one of only a handful of GOP members who vote with the Democrats roughly half the time. In both 1979 and 1980, the figure was 41 percent.

McDade was a strong supporter of civil rights during the 1960s, and one of 18 House Republicans who introduced their own civil rights bill in 1966, focusing on equal treatment for blacks in the court system. He has always been an ally of labor; the AFL-CIO gave him a 72 percent rating in 1980.

**At Home:** Times are hard in this coal-producing area, and McDade has endeared himself to constituents of both parties with his efforts to promote the region's economic development.

During the 1970s, he brought in numerous federal contracts with the help of his friend from nearby Wilkes-Barre, Rep. Daniel J. Flood, a Democratic power on the Appropriations Committee.

McDade's Republican affiliation appeals to the outlying, rural portions of the 10th, and his pro-labor voting record pleases the blue-collar Democrats in Lackawanna County (Scranton), the district's focal point. Unions regularly back McDade, and local Democratic organizations have stopped endorsing candidates to run against him.

As an Irish Catholic, he has an appeal among Lackawanna's large ethnic population that few Republicans have had in the past.

In a bid to maintain his following among Democrats, McDade avoids strong partisanship. When not campaigning for himself, he usually limits his political appearances at home to attending an annual Lincoln Day dinner. That has led to some criticism that he is not personally visible enough, but it has never been a political problem for him.

McDade is mentioned as a possibility for statewide office nearly every two years, but nothing has ever come of it. In 1966, he was offered the GOP nomination for lieutenant governor, but declined. In 1976 and 1980, he was an early Senate contender, but chose not to enter the campaign.

A lawyer and former municipal solicitor in his home city, McDade succeeded fellow Republican William W. Scranton, after whose ancestors the city is named. Scranton had served one House term and then become governor.

Handpicked by Scranton for the 1962 House nomination, McDade won an unspectacular general election victory. In 1964, his winning margin was narrower yet. By 1966, however, he had enlisted organized labor behind him. From that point on, his vote never has dipped below 60 percent.

**The District:** After World War II, the anthracite mines declined here, and as miners and railroad workers left the area, Democrats were left with a smaller base to work with. Republicans have helped themselves by nominating the kind of candidates who do well in this territory — moderates like Scranton and McDade — and they have won consistently.

The GOP has also benefited from redistricting decisions adding rural Republican territory to a constituency that, before 1950, consisted solely of coal-mining Lackawanna County, a Democratic bastion. Lackawanna still casts almost half the 10th's votes, but it habitually supports McDade, and in recent years, some statewide and national Republicans as well.

In 1976, a 15,000-vote plurality for Jimmy Carter in Lackawanna was too small for him to prevail district-wide. In 1980, Carter's Lackawanna margin shrank to 2,000 votes, and Ronald Reagan took the district handily.

## Committees

**Appropriations** (2nd of 22 Republicans)
Defense; Interior.

**Small Business** (Ranking Republican)
SBA and SBIC Authority, Minority Enterprise and General Small Business Problems.

## Elections

**1980 General**

| | |
|---|---|
| Joseph McDade (R ) | 145,703 (77 %) |
| Gene Basalyga (D ) | 43,152 (23 %) |

**1978 General**

| | |
|---|---|
| Joseph McDade (R ) | 116,003 (77 %) |
| Gene Basalyga (D ) | 35,721 (23 %) |

**Previous Winning Percentages**

| | | | |
|---|---|---|---|
| 1976 (63 %) | 1974 (65 %) | 1972 (74 %) | 1970 (65 %) |
| 1968 (67 %) | 1966 (67 %) | 1964 (51 %) | 1962 (53 %) |

**District Vote For President**

| | 1980 | | 1976 | | 1972 |
|---|---|---|---|---|---|
| D | 76,453 (39 %) | D | 97,659 (48 %) | D | 70,405 (35 %) |
| R | 107,138 (54 %) | R | 100,938 (50 %) | R | 126,032 (63 %) |
| I | 10,026 (5 %) | | | | |

## Campaign Finance

| | Receipts | Receipts from PACs | Expen-ditures |
|---|---|---|---|
| **1980** | | | |
| McDade (R ) | $72,703 | $38,950 (54 %) | $58,582 |
| **1978** | | | |
| McDade (R ) | $65,276 | $17,500 (27 %) | $66,769 |

## Voting Studies

| | Presidential Support | | Party Unity | | Conservative Coalition | |
|---|---|---|---|---|---|---|
| Year | S | O | S | O | S | O |
| 1980 | 51 | 36 | 50 | 41 | 56 | 35 |
| 1979 | 46 | 48 | 53 | 41 | 69 | 26 |
| 1978 | 42 | 41 | 49 | 40 | 50 | 37 |
| 1977 | 63 | 32 | 48 | 48 | 55 | 37 |
| 1976 | 45 | 49 | 36 | 50 | 47 | 43 |

| | | | | | | |
|---|---|---|---|---|---|---|
| 1975 | 54 | 44 | 46 | 52 | 46 | 53 |
| 1974 (Ford) | 57 | 41 | | | | |
| 1974 | 66 | 34 | 41 | 59 | 42 | 56 |
| 1973 | 40 | 54 | 38 | 55 | 40 | 55 |
| 1972 | 57 | 22 | 44 | 43 | 50 | 37 |
| 1971 | 67 | 32 | 54 | 40 | 57 | 39 |
| 1970 | 74 | 18 | 39 | 53 | 43 | 48 |
| 1969 | 70 | 30 | 44 | 55 | 42 | 56 |
| 1968 | 67 | 18 | 45 | 49 | 37 | 57 |
| 1967 | 65 | 32 | 55 | 44 | 50 | 50 |
| 1966 | 62 | 30 | 50 | 41 | 32 | 57 |
| 1965 | 70 | 29 | 46 | 50 | 37 | 53 |
| 1964 | 63 | 37 | 58 | 40 | 42 | 58 |
| 1963 | 49 | 44 | 60 | 31 | 33 | 40 |

S = Support          O = Opposition

## Key Votes

**96th Congress**

| | |
|---|---|
| Weaken Carter oil profits tax (1979) | N |
| Reject hospital cost control plan (1979) | Y |
| Implement Panama Canal Treaties (1979) | N |
| Establish Department of Education (1979) | N |
| Approve Anti-busing Amendment (1979) | N |
| Guarantee Chrysler Corp. loans (1979) | Y |
| Approve military draft registration (1980) | N |
| Aid Sandinista regime in Nicaragua (1980) | Y |
| Strengthen fair housing laws (1980) | Y |

**97th Congress**

| | |
|---|---|
| Reagan budget proposal (1981) | Y |

## Interest Group Ratings

| Year | ADA | ACA | AFL-CIO | CCUS |
|---|---|---|---|---|
| 1980 | 44 | 35 | 72 | 71 |
| 1979 | 26 | 48 | 68 | 59 |
| 1978 | 30 | 54 | 45 | 61 |
| 1977 | 40 | 42 | 87 | 29 |
| 1976 | 40 | 26 | 62 | 50 |
| 1975 | 58 | 33 | 61 | 29 |
| 1974 | 43 | 40 | 64 | 40 |
| 1973 | 48 | 22 | 82 | 36 |
| 1972 | 38 | 42 | 56 | 38 |
| 1971 | 43 | 46 | 73 | - |
| 1970 | 56 | 39 | 57 | 20 |
| 1969 | 47 | 29 | 80 | - |
| 1968 | 50 | 32 | 75 | - |
| 1967 | 57 | 52 | 67 | 50 |
| 1966 | 35 | 52 | 62 | - |
| 1965 | 32 | 30 | - | 50 |
| 1964 | 56 | 42 | 64 | - |
| 1963 | - | 53 | - | - |

# 11 James L. Nelligan (R)

**Of Forty-Fort — Elected 1980**

**Born:** Feb. 14, 1929, Wilkes-Barre, Pa.
**Education:** King's College, B.S. 1951.
**Military Career:** Army, 1946-48.
**Profession:** Accountant.
**Family:** Wife, Jean Kessler; one child.
**Religion:** Roman Catholic.
**Political Career:** Unsuccessful GOP nominee for U.S. House, special election, April 1980.

**The Member:** Nelligan probably understands the federal bureaucracy better than any other freshman in the 97th Congress. Before his 1980 election, he toiled for 28 years in various agencies and on congressional staffs, calculating and investigating the workings of the government.

Educated as an accountant, Nelligan joined the U.S. General Accounting Office in 1951 and remained there for 16 years. He then moved on to the House Government Operations Committee, the Office of Economic Opportunity, and the General Services Administration, and rounded out his government career as operations director of the House Commerce Subcommittee on Oversight.

As a congressman, Nelligan has tried to use his background to find federal aid for his economically distressed district. He persuaded the Department of Interior to release $1 million to help relocate 30 families in Centralia, Pa. Their homes had been permeated with noxious gases from a slow-burning underground mine fire.

Nelligan has also explained to local businessmen special ways in which they might win Defense Department contracts. Firms in high unemployment areas like Nelligan's district are given a 5 percent bidding advantage on defense contracts.

When Democratic Rep. Daniel J. Flood resigned in a cloud of legal complications, Nelligan ran in the 1980 special election to succeed him. He received GOP backing, but lost to Democrat Raphael Musto. In November, running with a strong statewide GOP ticket, Nelligan reversed the outcome and ended Musto's brief House career.

**The District:** Since the decline of the region's coal industry, the 11th has been beset by chronically high unemployment and has come to depend on federal largesse to aid its economy. For years, Rep. Flood provided those funds from his position on the Appropriations Committee.

The heart of the district is in the Democratic cities of Wilkes-Barre and Pittston. Republicans draw votes from suburban areas and the outlying rural counties.

## Committees

**Armed Services** (18th of 19 Republicans)
Investigations; Readiness.

## Elections

**1980 General**

| | |
|---|---|
| James Nelligan (R ) | 93,621 (52 %) |
| Raphael Musto (D ) | 86,703 (48 %) |

**1980 Primary**

| | |
|---|---|
| James Nelligan (R ) | 26,974 (54 %) |
| Robert Hudock (R ) | 13,299 (27 %) |
| Howard Williams (R ) | 5,746 (12 %) |
| Joseph Zukowsky (R ) | 3,069 (6 %) |

**District Vote For President**

| | 1980 | | 1976 | | 1972 |
|---|---|---|---|---|---|
| **D** | 80,780 (43 %) | **D** | 101,571 (54 %) | **D** | 68,764 (37 %) |
| **R** | 95,365 (51 %) | **R** | 85,292 (45 %) | **R** | 113,456 (61 %) |
| **I** | 7,605 (4 %) | | | | |

## Campaign Finance

| | Receipts | Receipts from PACs | Expenditures |
|---|---|---|---|
| **1980** | | | |
| Nelligan (R ) | $122,612 | $35,195 (29 %) | $120,366 |
| Musto (D ) | $305,032 | $67,680 (22 %) | $298,699 |

## Key Vote

**97th Congress**

| | |
|---|---|
| Reagan budget proposal (1981) | Y |

---

**11th District: Northeast — Wilkes-Barre.** Population: 481,255 (2% increase since 1970). Race: White 476,756 (99%), Black 2,600 (1%), Others 1,999 (0.4%). Spanish origin: 1,919 (0.3%).

---

# 12 John P. Murtha (D)

**Of Johnstown — Elected 1974**

**Born:** June 17, 1932, New Martinsville, W.Va.
**Education:** U. of Pittsburgh, B.A. 1962.
**Military Career:** Marine Corps, 1952-55, 1966-67.
**Profession:** Car wash operator.
**Family:** Wife, Joyce Bell; three children.
**Religion:** Roman Catholic.
**Political Career:** Pa. House, 1969-74.

**In Washington:** Murtha was a rising star in the House until Abscam cast at least a temporary shadow over his career.

He was never charged with any crime in the FBI bribery scandal, and he was able to issue a statement in mid-1980 reporting that he had been cleared. But his initial identification as one of those involved in the case hurt his public reputation, and his decision later in the year to testify against two other members raised questions about him in the minds of colleagues.

At the time Abscam broke, Murtha was making a name for himself as a "floor manager" for the Democratic leadership, a vote-counter and strategist, and a man who could deliver votes among the ethnic machine Democrats of New York, New Jersey and Pennsylvania.

Murtha rarely spoke in debate, but he was a persuasive man in tough legislative situations. More than anyone else in the House, he was responsible for the $3,200 a year congressional pay raise in 1979. He promoted it in the Appropriations Committee and saw it through to narrow enactment on the floor, keeping track of his votes by patrolling the aisles like the Marine officer he had been in Vietnam.

By early 1980, Murtha was considering a campaign for chairman of the House Democratic Caucus. Some Democrats believe Speaker O'Neill would have named him majority whip at the end of the year had the scandal not arisen.

But in February of 1980, Murtha was reported to be one of the targets of the FBI undercover agents who posed as Arab sheiks and offered members of Congress $50,000 to help them get into the United States.

Videotapes of the FBI sessions clearly show that Murtha turned down the money. "I'm not interested," he said at one point. "I'm sorry." He explained that he was on the House ethics committee and told the "sheiks" that "if you get into heat with politicians, there's no amount of money that can help."

Murtha said he only participated in the meeting to seek investments by the Arabs in coal mining operations, banks and other businesses in his district. He said pursuing such investments is a normal duty of a conscientious member of Congress, especially one representing an economically depressed area.

The tapes do, however, show Murtha discussing money for Reps. Frank Thompson, D-N.J., and John Murphy, D-N.Y. "Now these other guys are expecting, no question about it. They are expecting some, ah. . . . Let me make it very clear. The other two guys expect to be taken care of."

Murtha testified at Thompson's trial that Thompson told him about the sheiks on the House floor in October of 1979, that the Arabs had funds they wanted to invest in Murtha's district, and there would be some "walking around money" if they helped get the Arabs in the country.

"I broke no law," Murtha said. "I took no money. I was pursuing a policy of trying to attract industry to the district."

There is no question that Murtha has worked hard to bring industry to his district. It has been the focus of his career on the Appropriations Committee, and the skill that has made him politically successful at home.

On the Interior Appropriations Subcommittee, he has promoted coal as an answer to the

---

**12th District: West central — Johnstown.** Population: 491,462 (5% increase since 1970). Race: White 484,627 (99%), Black 5,160 (1%), Others 1,675 (0.3%). Spanish origin: 1,891 (0.3%).

nation's energy problems, as well as his district's economic problems. In 1979, he got an amendment attached to an energy authorization bill adding $9.5 million for a coal gasification facility in Pennsylvania.

Murtha is third-ranking Democrat on the Defense Appropriations Subcommittee, where he has generally been receptive to Pentagon spending requests. As the first Vietnam veteran elected to Congress, he also has worked for higher benefits for those who served in Vietnam. "I saw their tragedy and suffering," he once said, while everybody "in Congress was in their air-conditioned offices telling these soldiers what to do."

But for the average member, Murtha is best known as the man who engineered the 1979 pay raise, one of the hardest fought and most ingenious maneuvers in Congress in recent years.

Murtha promoted the 5.5 percent increase in the Appropriations Committee as a pay "cap," since without any action a much larger raise would have gone into effect.

When the issue first reached the House floor in June 1979, Murtha and the House leadership mustered the votes to prevent a roll call on a Republican amendment eliminating any pay raise. That left only a choice between an increase of 5.5 percent and one of 7 percent, allowing members to cast an "economy" vote for 5.5 percent. The smaller figure was approved 396-15.

But the strategy ultimately failed because a majority of members were unwilling to vote on the record for final passage of the overall Legislative Appropriation bill to which the raise had been attached. The bill was rejected, 232-186, with numerous members switching their votes to oppose it after its defeat had become clear.

Murtha was unwilling to give up. Three months later, he attached a 7 percent increase to a different appropriation bill. Again the House refused to vote on the record for the bill. Finally, after devoting weeks to lining up the votes for its passage, Murtha won approval of a 5.5 percent raise. The vote was 208-203, with Murtha, Speaker O'Neill and other House leaders lobbying

the last few votes out of hesitant Democrats in the final seconds.

**At Home:** When longtime Republican Rep. John P. Saylor died in 1973, the Cambria County (Johnstown) Democratic organization seized its chance to recapture a nominally Democratic district. They found an attractive candidate in Murtha, a personable state legislator who had won a Bronze Star and two Purple Hearts as a Marine in Vietnam.

Murtha won narrowly over Harry M. Fox, a former Saylor aide, in a 1974 special election focused on the Republican Party's Watergate problems. He easily dispatched Fox the following November and has won easily since then.

That includes 1980, when Abscam had become public. Murtha's opponent tried to make the bribery scandal an issue, but he did not succeed. Murtha's plurality was down, but he still drew 60 percent of the vote.

Murtha's argument that he was simply trying to help the district was not difficult to sell, given his record at home. Following a 1977 Johnstown flood, he took the lead in pushing for federal recovery efforts. For the many coal miners in the district, he worked to obtain a black-lung treatment clinic.

**The District:** The Johnstown vicinity has led a troubled existence. Many of its aging factories have closed, and three floods over the past 100 years have devastated it. Cambria County is a perennial supplicant to Washington.

However, this reliance on government has never turned industrial Cambria solidly Democratic. Its marginal status, combined with the Republican vote in rural counties like Indiana and Somerset, make the 12th a swing district.

Saylor, a moderate Republican, always carried Cambria, and Democratic presidential margins there have seldom been overwhelming.

The Cambria Democratic organization thrived for 36 years under the firm stewardship of its head, John Torquoto, who in 1978 was convicted on corruption charges. A Torquoto protégé has kept things running smoothly.

## Committees

**Appropriations** (14th of 33 Democrats)
Defense; Interior; Legislative.

## Elections

**1980 General**

| | |
|---|---|
| John Murtha (D ) | 106,750 (59 %) |
| Charles Getty (R ) | 72,999 (41 %) |

**1978 General**

| | |
|---|---|
| John Murtha (D ) | 104,216 (69 %) |
| Luther Elkins (R ) | 47,442 (31 %) |

**Previous Winning Percentages**

1976 (68 %)      1974 (58 %)      1974* (49 %)

*Special elections

**District Vote For President**

| | 1980 | | 1976 | | 1972 |
|---|---|---|---|---|---|
| **D** | 81,947 (45 %) | **D** | 91,243 (50 %) | **D** | 64,072 (36 %) |
| **R** | 90,454 (50 %) | **R** | 88,385 (49 %) | **R** | 112,750 (63 %) |
| **I** | 6,861 (4 %) | | | | |

## Campaign Finance

| | Receipts | Receipts from PACs | Expen-ditures |
|---|---|---|---|
| **1980** | | | |
| Murtha (D ) | $116,698 | $52,575 (45 %) | $112,357 |
| Getty (R ) | $17,675 | $200 (1 %) | $17,675 |
| **1978** | | | |
| Murtha (D ) | $49,865 | $30,000 (60 %) | $33,377 |
| Elkins (R ) | $15,176 | $400 (3 %) | $15,175 |

## Voting Studies

| | Presidential Support | | Party Unity | | Conservative Coalition | |
|---|---|---|---|---|---|---|
| Year | S | O | S | O | S | O |
| 1980 | 74 | 21 | 78 | 19 | 49 | 48 |
| 1979 | 72 | 28 | 74 | 24 | 57 | 39 |
| 1978 | 59 | 40 | 66 | 33 | 55 | 43 |
| 1977 | 66 | 29 | 61 | 28 | 54 | 38 |
| 1976 | 37 | 61 | 65 | 32 | 56 | 41 |
| 1975 | 42 | 49 | 60 | 32 | 55 | 39 |
| 1974 **(Ford)** | 44 | 52 | | | | |
| 1974 | 54 | 46† | 67 | 32† | 52 | 47† |

S = Support          O = Opposition
† Not eligible for all recorded votes.

## Key Votes

**96th Congress**

| | |
|---|---|
| Weaken Carter oil profits tax (1979) | N |
| Reject hospital cost control plan (1979) | Y |
| Implement Panama Canal Treaties (1979) | Y |
| Establish Department of Education (1979) | Y |
| Approve Anti-busing Amendment (1979) | N |
| Guarantee Chrysler Corp. loans (1979) | Y |
| Approve military draft registration (1980) | Y |
| Aid Sandinista regime in Nicaragua (1980) | Y |
| Strengthen fair housing laws (1980) | Y |

**97th Congress**

| | |
|---|---|
| Reagan budget proposal (1981) | N |

## Interest Group Ratings

| Year | ADA | ACA | AFL-CIO | CCUS |
|---|---|---|---|---|
| 1980 | 44 | 21 | 78 | 65 |
| 1979 | 37 | 8 | 79 | 47 |
| 1978 | 25 | 30 | 65 | 33 |
| 1977 | 20 | 27 | 86 | 31 |
| 1976 | 45 | 36 | 91 | 25 |
| 1975 | 42 | 48 | 95 | 36 |
| 1974 | 26 | 29 | 100 | 30 |

# 13 Lawrence Coughlin (R)

**Of Villanova — Elected 1968**

**Born:** April 11, 1929, Wilkes-Barre, Pa.
**Education:** Yale U., A.B. 1950; Harvard U.,
M.B.A. 1954; Temple U., LL.B. 1958.
**Military Career:** Marine Corps Reserve, 1948-
58, active duty, 1951-52.
**Profession:** Lawyer.
**Family:** Wife, Susan; four children.
**Religion:** Episcopalian.
**Political Career:** Pennsylvania House, 1965-67;
Pennsylvania Senate, 1967-69.

**In Washington:** Neither Coughlin nor most
of his wealthy suburban constituents have much
in common with people in inner-city Philadelphia, but Coughlin has been an urbanist on the
Appropriations Committee, pushing for the same
mass transit and housing subsidies as his colleagues from downtown Chicago, Cleveland and
New Orleans. "We can't get along without Philadelphia," he once said, "and Philadelphia can't
exist without us."

As a senior Republican on the Appropriations
subcommittee that handles housing money, he
has generally voted with the panel's Democrats to
fund programs with relative generosity. But he
has not always agreed with them about how to
distribute the money.

In 1980, when most housing programs were
reauthorized, Coughlin complained about rent
subsidies going to the middle-class, rather than to
the poor. "We cannot even provide for those who
are at the bottom of the income ladder," he said,
"so why are we providing income subsidies to
those who are well up the ladder?"

Coughlin introduced an amendment to restrict the subsidies to people with incomes below
50 percent of the median, rather than the proposed 80 percent. Most of his constituents, who
are well above 100 percent, would not have been
affected. But too many other districts would have
been. The amendment drew only 71 votes.

In the previous Congress, Coughlin had argued for an amendment to reserve 75 percent of
public housing for the elderly and handicapped,
explaining that those two groups would be better
accepted by middle-class neighborhoods than
other low-income families. That effort came close
on a 214-183 vote, but ultimately fell victim to the
argument that there was no alternative to public
housing for millions of poor people, whether they
are socially desirable neighbors or not.

Coughlin fought hard in 1980 against draft

registration, calling President Carter's proposal
"a useless gesture that sends the wrong message
to the American people — that we're doing something when we're not." Registration lost in an
Appropriations subcommittee, on a 6-6 tie vote,
but was approved in full committee by a narrow
margin.

In 1981, he gave up his senior status on the
HUD subcommittee to play a similar role on the
Transportation panel at Appropriations, where he
has strongly supported mass transit funding.

Coughlin headed a Republican task force on
congressional reform in 1977 and has regularly
tried to cut members' allowances and perks. In
1979, he tried unsuccessfully to reduce allowances
by 17 percent, charging the money was being used
for re-election purposes and merely promoted
incumbency. In 1977, in the wake of a scandal
involving House Administration Chairman
Wayne Hays, D-Ohio, he offered a Republican
package to tighten up House accounting and
allowances procedures. It narrowly lost, 199-195.
The next year, he did succeed with an amendment
requiring a GAO audit of House office accounts.

**At Home:** Coughlin looks every bit the Main
Line gentleman that he is. His bow tie and
prestigious education (Hotchkiss and Yale) are
the correct trappings for the representative from
the state's most affluent district.

Coughlin comes from a prosperous family in
upstate Wilkes-Barre. He served as an aide to

---

**13th District: Philadelphia suburbs
— eastern Montgomery County.** Population: 457,616 (3% decrease since 1970). Race:
White 423,702 (93%), Black 26,082 (6%),
Other 7,832 (2%). Spanish Oregon 3,613 (1%)

---

Marine Gen. Lewis ("Chesty") Puller, then moved to Philadelphia for a business and legal career. He dabbled in local politics and worked to elect Republican William Scranton governor in 1962.

A charter member of a group of young professionals that now controls the Montgomery County GOP, he won election to the state Legislature in the 1960s. When ally Richard S. Schweiker jumped from the House to the Senate in 1968, Coughlin took his place.

**The District:** The section of suburban Philadelphia known as the Main Line — so-called because of the railroad that runs through it — forms the core of the 13th. It is a land of estates, old money and names like Biddle and Cadwalader. It also is a Republican bastion.

The 13th takes up the more populous eastern half of Montgomery County and dips into Philadelphia to include two working-class white sections, Roxborough and Manayunk. The Democratic vote in the city, coupled with that in two blue-collar Montgomery communities, Norristown and Conshohocken, cannot offset the 3-1 GOP lead elsewhere in the district.

## Committees

**Appropriations** (7th of 22 Republicans)
District of Columbia; HUD-Independent Agencies; Transportation.

**Select Narcotics Abuse and Control** (4th of 8 Republicans)

## Elections

**1980 General**

| | |
|---|---|
| Lawrence Coughlin (R ) | 138,212 (70 %) |
| Pete Slawek (D ) | 57,745 (29 %) |

**1980 Primary**

| | |
|---|---|
| Lawrence Coughlin (R ) | 60,081 (85 %) |
| Edward Johnson (R ) | 10,243 (15 %) |

**1978 General**

| | |
|---|---|
| Lawrence Coughlin (R ) | 112,711 (71 %) |
| Alan Rubenstein (D ) | 47,151 (29 %) |

**Previous Winning Percentages**

| | | | |
|---|---|---|---|
| 1976 (63 %) | 1974 (62 %) | 1972 (67 %) | 1970 (58 %) |
| 1968 (62 %) | | | |

**District Vote For President**

| | 1980 | | 1976 | | 1972 |
|---|---|---|---|---|---|
| D | 68,587 (33 %) | D | 89,883 (42 %) | D | 77,817 (36 %) |
| R | 116,896 (56 %) | R | 120,776 (56 %) | R | 135,647 (63 %) |
| I | 20,467 (10 %) | | | | |

## Campaign Finance

| | Receipts | Receipts from PACs | Expenditures |
|---|---|---|---|
| **1980** | | | |
| Coughlin (R ) | $109,514 | $34,490 (31 %) | $103,457 |
| Slawek (D ) | $27,050 | $2,850 (11 %) | $26,533 |
| **1978** | | | |
| Coughlin (R ) | $118,032 | $22,925 (19 %) | $105,534 |
| Rubenstein (D ) | $32,282 | $1,750 (5 %) | $32,279 |

## Voting Studies

| | Presidential Support | | Party Unity | | Conservative Coalition | |
|---|---|---|---|---|---|---|
| Year | S | O | S | O | S | O |
| 1980 | 49 | 41 | 63 | 31 | 57 | 37 |
| 1979 | 46 | 46 | 61 | 30 | 66 | 26 |
| 1978 | 51 | 45 | 66 | 31 | 68 | 29 |
| 1977 | 54 | 42 | 63 | 34 | 62 | 36 |
| 1976 | 51 | 47 | 58 | 39 | 59 | 39 |
| 1975 | 67 | 29 | 58 | 38 | 50 | 46 |
| 1974 (Ford) | 46 | 46 | | | | |
| 1974 | 66 | 30 | 36 | 58 | 32 | 62 |
| 1973 | 58 | 39 | 54 | 42 | 51 | 45 |
| 1972 | 68 | 22 | 60 | 39 | 56 | 41 |
| 1971 | 61 | 37 | 55 | 38 | 42 | 49 |
| 1970 | 69 | 20 | 64 | 32 | 43 | 52 |
| 1969 | 64 | 34 | 38 | 51 | 33 | 62 |

S = Support          O = Opposition

## Key Votes

**96th Congress**

| | |
|---|---|
| Weaken Carter oil profits tax (1979) | Y |
| Reject hospital cost control plan (1979) | Y |
| Implement Panama Canal Treaties (1979) | N |
| Establish Department of Education (1979) | Y |
| Approve Anti-busing Amendment (1979) | Y |
| Guarantee Chrysler Corp. loans (1979) | Y |
| Approve military draft registration (1980) | N |
| Aid Sandinista regime in Nicaragua (1980) | Y |
| Strengthen fair housing laws (1980) | Y |

**97th Congress**

| | |
|---|---|
| Reagan budget proposal (1981) | Y |

## Interest Group Ratings

| Year | ADA | ACA | AFL-CIO | CCUS |
|---|---|---|---|---|
| 1980 | 44 | 64 | 21 | 73 |
| 1979 | 21 | 58 | 37 | 73 |
| 1978 | 25 | 56 | 21 | 78 |
| 1977 | 35 | 67 | 26 | 82 |
| 1976 | 35 | 35 | 35 | 50 |
| 1975 | 53 | 54 | 38 | 69 |
| 1974 | 65 | 20 | 60 | 11 |
| 1973 | 36 | 48 | 27 | 73 |
| 1972 | 38 | 35 | 36 | 50 |
| 1971 | 49 | 67 | 25 | . |
| 1970 | 64 | 65 | 14 | 67 |
| 1969 | 47 | 47 | 80 | . |

# 14 William J. Coyne (D)

**Of Pittsburgh — Elected 1980**

**Born:** Aug. 24, 1936, Pittsburgh, Pa.
**Education:** Robert Morris College, B.S. 1965.
**Military Career:** Army, 1955-57.
**Profession:** Public official.
**Family:** Single.
**Religion:** Roman Catholic.
**Political Career:** Pennsylvania House, 1971-73; Pittsburgh City Council, 1974-81; unsuccessfully sought Democratic nomination for Pennsylvania Senate, 1972.

**The Member:** Coyne takes a dim view of President Reagan's approach to economic recovery, and spent his first few months in the House dramatizing the effects of budget cuts on his district. He told constituents that plans to reduce federal transportation aid would increase their bus fares and force service cutbacks. He warned that across-the-board tax cuts and higher defense spending would force cutbacks in local social services.

Coyne's career has been heavily oriented toward his hometown of Pittsburgh. He still lives in the same house in the inner-city neighborhood where he was born. Before coming to Congress, he was active in Pittsburgh politics for a decade. He worked closely with the city Democratic organization and always stressed party loyalty.

Coyne was elected to the state House in 1970 but lost a bid for the state Senate in 1972. In 1973, he was elected to the City Council. While on the council, he served as city chairman of the Pittsburgh Democratic Party.

When the 14th District opened up in 1980 with the retirement of longtime Democratic Rep. William S. Moorhead, Coyne had the political connections to claim the seat. He got the backing of the organization and easily defeated Rep. Moorhead's son for the Democratic nomination. He went on to an easy win over the GOP nominee.

**The District:** The 14th is centered in downtown Pittsburgh and includes a large academic community from Duquesne University, Carnegie-Mellon University, and the University of Pittsburgh. The residential neighborhoods contain low- to middle-income families, especially of Irish, Italian and Eastern European stock. Large numbers of them are dependent on Pittsburgh's huge steel industry, which has plants in and around the district. The black population is sizable, about one quarter of the population.

## Committees

**Banking, Finance and Urban Affairs** (24th of 25 Democrats)
Economic Stabilization; Housing and Community Development; International Trade, Investment and Monetary Policy.

**House Administration** (11th of 11 Democrats)
Accounts; Policy Group on Information and Computers.

**Joint Library**

## Elections

**1980 General**

| | |
|---|---|
| William Coyne (D ) | 102,545 (69 %) |
| Stan Thomas (R ) | 44,071 (30 %) |

**1980 Primary**

| | |
|---|---|
| William Coyne (D ) | 44,142 (57 %) |
| William Moorhead Jr. (D ) | 24,209 (31 %) |
| Richard Caliguiri (D ) | 8,668 (11 %) |

**District Vote For President**

| | 1980 | | 1976 | | 1972 |
|---|---|---|---|---|---|
| **D** | 92,226 (57 %) | **D** | 98,609 (58 %) | **D** | 95,687 (51 %) |
| **R** | 54,736 (34 %) | **R** | 68,088 (40 %) | **R** | 86,912 (47 %) |
| **I** | 10,389 (6 %) | | | | |

## Campaign Finance

| | Receipts | Receipts from PACs | Expenditures |
|---|---|---|---|
| **1980** | | | |
| Coyne (D ) | $179,239 | $47,248 (26 %) | $176,005 |
| Thomas (R ) | $121,442 | $48,345 (40 %) | $126,150 |

## Key Vote

**97th Congress**

| | |
|---|---|
| Reagan budget proposal (1981) | N |

---

**14th District: Pittsburgh.** Population: 388,195 (18% decrease since 1970). Race: White 283,883 (73%), Black 98,970 (25%), Others 5,342 (1%). Spanish origin: 2,869 (1%).

# 15 Don Ritter (R)

### Of Coopersburg — Elected 1978

**Born:** Oct. 21, 1940, New York, N.Y.
**Education:** Lehigh U., B.S. 1961; M.I.T., M.S. 1963, Sc.D. 1966.
**Profession:** Metallurgist.
**Family:** Wife, Edith Duerksen; two children.
**Religion:** Unitarian.
**Political Career:** No previous office.

**In Washington:** A surprise winner in 1978 in a labor-oriented Democratic district, this former metallurgy professor has been determined to represent it on his own terms, selling a conservative voting record rather than accommodating himself to traditional union goals, as other Pennsylvania Republicans have done.

The decision has made him one of the more interesting junior members in the GOP. Usually quiet in debate, he is nevertheless a determined disciple of supply-side economics, convinced that tax breaks for the steel industry will do more to help its labor force than wage and price controls or federal social programs.

When he rose in 1980 to deliver a eulogy to George Meany, almost obligatory for any member from a blue-collar district, it was the conservative Meany he chose to remember. "No matter how sharp his comments on the business community may have been," Ritter said of the deceased labor leader, "he was dedicated to the capitalist system and the survival of free enterprise."

As a member of the congressional steel caucus, Ritter stressed a concept most of the group's Democratic members had only limited enthusiasm for — accelerated depreciation. He said faster tax write-offs would be a better tool in helping the industry to modernize than the old-fashioned protectionism increasingly popular among steel-district members. As a member of the Banking Committee in 1979, Ritter voted against the Chrysler loan guarantee, in agreement with fellow-believers Jack Kemp and David Stockman, and against many of the more traditional pro-business Republicans from industrial states. He switched in 1981 from Banking to the Energy and Commerce Committee, and its Health and Energy Conservation subcommittees.

When Ritter eulogized Meany, he referred to a second issue on which he and the labor leader would have agreed: the Soviet Union. As a metallurgist, Ritter spent a year in Moscow and came back convinced of the Soviet government's dishonorable world intentions. "I speak fluent Russian," he said on the House floor one day. "My avocation has been the study of Russian language and culture." He then went on to endorse the U.S. boycott of the 1980 Olympics, but to warn that far more would be needed to prevent further Russian adventurism in Asia. Later in the year, he inserted a statement or article in the *Congressional Record* nearly every day supporting the workers' movement in Poland and speaking out against any Soviet interference.

**At Home:** It was Ritter's extraordinary energy, rather than his political program, that brought him victory in 1978 over Democratic Rep. Fred B. Rooney, chairman of the Commerce Subcommittee on Transportation. Rooney never really made enemies in the Lehigh Valley; he simply grew less and less visible with each passing year. By 1978 he was sending telegrams to annual gatherings he had once attended.

Ritter never had run for office before and won the GOP nomination essentially because all of his primary opponents were relatively weak. But he courted some of those Democrats who wondered where Rooney was, and it paid off.

The Democratic Party felt a strong opponent could defeat Ritter in 1980, and they thought they had one in state Sen. Jeanette Reibman, a traditional labor liberal. Organized labor went all out for her, with volunteers and phone banks. Attending a United Steelworkers dinner shortly before

---

**15th District: East — Allentown, Bethlehem.** Population: 499,000 (6% increase since 1970). Race: White 481,474 (96%), Black 8,117 (2%), Others 9,409 (2%). Spanish origin: 14,124 (3%).

the election, Ritter was booed for passing out pamphlets not bearing a notation that they had been printed in a union shop.

But Ritter pressed on, ignoring union leadership and working plant gates to appeal to the rank and file. And Reibman's age — at 65, she was 10 years older than the ousted Rooney — became a liability. With the help of a strong Reagan showing in the Lehigh Valley, Ritter won decisively. He even carried Reibman's home town of Easton.

**The District:** The tale of the 15th is told in its 1976 and 1980 presidential preferences. In 1976, Jimmy Carter carried it comfortably. In 1980, with the local economy gone sour from layoffs at the Mack Truck and Bethlehem Steel plants, Ronald Reagan captured it.

The Lehigh Valley has a long history of blue-collar Democratic leanings. Northampton County, with the industrial towns of Easton and Bethlehem, is the more Democratic. Lehigh County has more of a bipartisan cast. Allentown, its major city, has a Republican mayor. The Pennsylvania Dutch influence is felt in the nearby farm communities — another source of Republican votes.

## Committees

**Energy and Commerce** (14th of 18 Republicans)
Energy Conservation and Power; Health and the Environment; Oversight and Investigations.

## Elections

**1980 General**

| | |
|---|---|
| Don Ritter (R ) | 99,874 (60 %) |
| Jeanette Reibman (D ) | 66,626 (40 %) |

**1978 General**

| | |
|---|---|
| Don Ritter (R ) | 65,986 (53 %) |
| Fred Rooney (D ) | 58,077 (47 %) |

**1978 Primary**

| | |
|---|---|
| Don Ritter (R ) | 11,057 (47 %) |
| James Feather (R ) | 3,590 (15 %) |
| John Weaver (R ) | 3,147 (13 %) |
| George Longenbach (R ) | 2,929 (12 %) |
| Harrison Moyer (R ) | 1,578 (7 %) |
| Robert Pados (R ) | 1,448 (6 %) |

**District Vote For President**

| | 1980 | | 1976 | | 1972 |
|---|---|---|---|---|---|
| D | 66,747 (39 %) | D | 89,134 (52 %) | D | 65,660 (39 %) |
| R | 86,569 (50 %) | R | 79,821 (46 %) | R | 99,845 (60 %) |
| I | 15,800 (9 %) | | | | |

## Campaign Finance

| | Receipts | Receipts from PACs | Expenditures |
|---|---|---|---|
| **1980** | | | |
| Ritter (R ) | $319,334 | $126,418 (40 %) | $318,453 |
| Reibman (D ) | $208,448 | $105,672 (51 %) | $206,516 |

| **1978** | | | |
|---|---|---|---|
| Ritter (R ) | $63,361 | $4,385 (7 %) | $63,205 |
| Rooney (D ) | $121,796 | $82,126 (67 %) | $131,005 |

## Voting Studies

| | Presidential Support | | Party Unity | | Conservative Coalition | |
|---|---|---|---|---|---|---|
| **Year** | **S** | **O** | **S** | **O** | **S** | **O** |
| 1980 | 43 | 48 | 78 | 19 | 75 | 15 |
| 1979 | 31 | 66 | 85 | 14 | 87 | 10 |

S = Support        O = Opposition

## Key Votes

**96th Congress**

| | |
|---|---|
| Weaken Carter oil profits tax (1979) | Y |
| Reject hospital cost control plan (1979) | Y |
| Implement Panama Canal Treaties (1979) | N |
| Establish Department of Education (1979) | N |
| Approve Anti-busing Amendment (1979) | Y |
| Guarantee Chrysler Corp. loans (1979) | N |
| Approve military draft registration (1980) | # |
| Aid Sandinista regime in Nicaragua (1980) | Y |
| Strengthen fair housing laws (1980) | N |

**97th Congress**

| | |
|---|---|
| Reagan budget proposal (1981) | Y |

## Interest Group Ratings

| Year | ADA | ACA | AFL-CIO | CCUS |
|---|---|---|---|---|
| 1980 | 22 | 74 | 26 | 80 |
| 1979 | 11 | 83 | 30 | 89 |

# 16 Robert S. Walker (R)

**Of East Petersburg — Elected 1976**

**Born:** Dec. 23, 1942, Bradford, Pa.
**Education:** Millersville State College, B.S. 1964; U. of Del., M.A. 1968.
**Military Career:** Pa. National Guard, 1967-73.
**Profession:** Teacher.
**Family:** Wife, Sue Albertson.
**Religion:** Presbyterian.
**Political Career:** No previous office.

**In Washington:** When Republicans need a good, loud partisan floor speech, roasting the majority as incompetent or demanding an investigation of some new Democratic scandal, they can always count on Walker to supply one on a moment's notice.

From his first days in the House in 1977, he has never tired of working to embarrass the opposition. As a first-year member, he led 20 other GOP freshmen in demanding that the House ethics committee look further into the Korean bribery affair, claiming "incontrovertible evidence" that numerous members had been bribed. Three years later, when newspaper accounts linked Billy Carter to influence buying by the Libyan government, he was the main influence behind a Republican resolution forcing more information out of the White House.

Much of Walker's aggressiveness was on display in 1978 and 1979 in debates over a new department of education, which he was militantly against in the Government Operations Committee and later on the floor. A bill creating the new department would have reached the floor in 1978, had Walker not brought the business of the chamber to a halt by demanding that a voluminous conference report preceding it on the schedule be read in full. House leaders gave up and withdrew the education bill for the rest of the year.

In 1979, President Carter finally got his Department of Education, but not before Walker and other Republican critics delayed passage for months by offering dozens of amendments, some serious and some dilatory, such as one requiring that all top department officials be working teachers. One serious amendment by Walker would have required the department to permit voluntary prayer in the public schools. It passed by a 255-122 vote, but was dropped later in conference with the Senate.

Another Walker amendment, also removed in conference, would have made it illegal to deny a pupil his right to education on the basis of racial quotas. Walker has been working on that issue his entire congressional career.

In 1977, he persuaded the House to accept language barring the use of any HEW funds "to enforce ratios, quotas or other numerical requirements." That did not become law, but he attached a similar amendment to the next year's Labor-HEW appropriation bill, blocking the use of quotas by HEW in hiring or admissions. When that was also dropped in conference, Walker tried to have the conference report sent back. He failed on a close 200-187 vote. He re-introduced his proposal in 1981.

The food stamp program is another Walker target. Since his first term, he has tried to change the program to require that only "nutritional foods" be available for purchase with the stamps. The government should insist, he said in 1977, "that people are doing something more than eating Twinkies and soda pop." He has never won on that issue.

**At Home:** Walker's media-conscious Republican politics have been successful not only among the new arrivals in burgeoning Lancaster County but among his more traditionally-minded Pennsylvania Dutch constituents. Conservatism sells well here, and Walker is a born salesman.

> **16th District: Southeast — Lancaster.** Population: 536,047 (15% increase since 1970). Race: White 503,518 (94%), Black 17,305 (3%), Others 10,224 (2%). Spanish origin: 11,390 (2%).

## Robert S. Walker, R-Pa.

When he wanted to publicize his campaign against food stamp abuse, he went to work in a grocery store. When he wanted to go after the Department of Energy, he compiled a list of its most questionable-sounding grants — for such things as a solar hotdog cooker — which was then included in Johnny Carson's monologue on the "Tonight" show.

Walker also has been in the forefront of the fight to prevent dumping of radioactive water from the damaged Three Mile Island nuclear reactor into the Susquehanna River; the plant is in the next district, but the river flows through the 16th.

After a short stint working as a teacher, Walker signed on as an aide to his congressman, Republican Edwin D. Eshleman, (1967-77), and eventually became his administrative assistant. When Eshleman decided to step down in 1976, he backed his young protégé in the 11-way primary fight for the seat.

Walker stressed his Washington experience and, with the help of Eshleman's endorsement and the top ballot position, eked out a victory with 19.5 percent of the vote. Given Lancaster's strong Republican sentiments, he has had no problems since then.

**The District:** Politics is seldom exciting in the Pennsylvania Dutch country, where Republicanism is taken for granted. The Amish and Mennonites, with their insistence on stability, set the political tone for Lancaster County, and challenges to the established order are practically non-existent.

For many years and continuing into the 1960s, the Lancaster GOP was under the patriarchal guidance of the late G. Graybill Diehm, its chairman. While power in the party is spread a little more widely nowadays — to accommodate the many newcomers in the growing region — the course of Republican rule still runs smoothly. The small Democratic vote huddles in the towns of Columbia and Coatesville.

## Committees

**Government Operations** (6th of 17 Republicans)
Government Activities and Transportation.

**Science and Technology** (6th of 17 Republicans)
Energy Development and Applications; Investigations and Oversight.

## Elections

**1980 General**

| | |
|---|---|
| Robert Walker (R) | 129,765 (77%) |
| James Woodcock (D) | 38,891 (23%) |

**1978 General**

| | |
|---|---|
| Robert Walker (R) | 91,910 (77%) |
| Charles Boohar (D) | 27,386 (23%) |

**Previous Winning Percentage**

1976 (62%)

**District Vote For President**

| | 1980 | | 1976 | | 1972 |
|---|---|---|---|---|---|
| D | 46,369 (27%) | D | 56,812 (35%) | D | 37,223 (24%) |
| R | 114,788 (66%) | R | 101,642 (63%) | R | 115,621 (74%) |
| I | 11,535 (7%) | | | | |

## Campaign Finance

| | Receipts | Receipts from PACs | Expenditures |
|---|---|---|---|
| **1980** | | | |
| Walker (R) | $27,674 | $9,075 (33%) | $23,719 |

| | | | |
|---|---|---|---|
| **1978** | | | |
| Walker (R) | $39,463 | $7,698 (20%) | $40,289 |

## Voting Studies

| | Presidential Support | | Party Unity | | Conservative Coalition | |
|---|---|---|---|---|---|---|
| Year | S | O | S | O | S | O |
| 1980 | 38 | 59 | 90 | 8 | 83 | 15 |
| 1979 | 26 | 72 | 90 | 5 | 88 | 7 |
| 1978 | 29 | 71 | 86 | 11 | 85 | 12 |
| 1977 | 37 | 57 | 86 | 8 | 86 | 10 |

S = Support          O = Opposition

## Key Votes

**96th Congress**

| | |
|---|---|
| Weaken Carter oil profits tax (1979) | Y |
| Reject hospital cost control plan (1979) | Y |
| Implement Panama Canal Treaties (1979) | N |
| Establish Department of Education (1979) | N |
| Approve Anti-busing Amendment (1979) | Y |
| Guarantee Chrysler Corp. loans (1979) | N |
| Approve military draft registration (1980) | N |
| Aid Sandinista regime in Nicaragua (1980) | N |
| Strengthen fair housing laws (1980) | N |

**97th Congress**

| | |
|---|---|
| Reagan budget proposal (1981) | Y |

## Interest Group Ratings

| Year | ADA | ACA | AFL-CIO | CCUS |
|---|---|---|---|---|
| 1980 | 17 | 92 | 11 | 76 |
| 1979 | 16 | 100 | 25 | 89 |
| 1978 | 15 | 96 | 20 | 83 |
| 1977 | 20 | 93 | 18 | 94 |

# 17 Allen E. Ertel (D)

**Of Montoursville — Elected 1976**

**Born:** Nov. 7, 1936, Williamsport, Pa.
**Education:** Dartmouth College, B.A. 1958; Thayer School of Engineering and Amos Tuck School of Business Administration, M.S. 1959; Yale Law School, LL.B. 1965.
**Military Career:** Navy, 1959-62.
**Profession:** Lawyer.
**Family:** Wife, Catharine Klepper; three children.
**Religion:** Lutheran.
**Political Career:** Lycoming County D.A., 1968-76.

**In Washington:** A good detail man who sometimes seems to enjoy arguing alone against a majority, Ertel has been an active and visible presence on the Public Works Committee during his three terms there. He has pushed to strengthen the deregulation bills that passed through Public Works on their way to enactment, and has been relatively skeptical of spending for new water projects — provided his district's own water needs are taken care of.

When Public Works wrestled with airline deregulation in 1978, Ertel wanted a strong "automatic entry" provision, allowing airlines to open up new routes without the advance permission of the Civil Aeronautics Board. The panel dropped that language, but Ertel won floor approval of an amendment requiring the federal government to assume that any new airline service was in the public interest, unless proven otherwise. He took a similar free market approach to truck deregulation in 1980, and complained when a compromise with the industry produced a modified bill. "Are we going to legislate a bad bill," he asked at one markup session, "just so we don't have to go to conference?"

Representing a district with serious flood control needs, Ertel has been careful on controversial issues in the Public Works Water Resources Subcommittee. In 1980, the committee exempted a flood control project in his district from normal cost-benefit tests, on the grounds that flooding had been exceptionally severe in the area. He argued on the House floor against amendments to take other projects out of the bill. But he won passage of his amendment de-authorizing 17 projects opposed by local residents and their representatives, at an estimated savings of $2.3 billion.

A man who prides himself on lawyerlike precision, Ertel has been known to devote weeks of personal attention to matters most of his colleagues would consider trivial. In 1979, he spoke at length in favor of his amendment to reduce former President Nixon's federal allowance, to make up for $66,614 in federal money he said Nixon spent illegally on improvements for his California home. The proposal was defeated. The year before, however, Ertel won passage of his amendment requiring the Republican Congressional Committee to move out of its space in a House office building.

At the end of 1978, Ertel pushed through a little-noticed change in Democratic Caucus rules that made a significant impact on legislative procedure. The change prevents House leaders from sending any bill with an annual cost of more than $100 million to the House floor under suspension of the rules. This has meant fewer opportunities to rush major legislation into law without full debate. One of the ironies of the change was that Ertel himself had tried such a maneuver only a few weeks before, seeking passage of a $1.4-billion bill for 158 water projects on the last day of the 95th Congress. The move failed for lack of a quorum.

**At Home:** Ertel has been able to survive and prosper in a historically Republican district. The last Democrat to represent Dauphin County (Harrisburg) before him was one-termer Guy J. Swope (1937-39).

> **17th District: Central — Harrisburg, Williamsport.** Population: 501,530 (5% increase since 1970). Race: White 462,379 (92%), Black 34,214 (7%), Others 4,937 (1%). Spanish origin: 4,660 (1%).

## Allen E. Ertel, D-Pa.

So far, Ertel has managed to better his performance with each election. He had a narrow victory in his initial bid, in 1976, when he succeeded Republican Herman T. Schneebeli, who retired. But the next two elections saw him clearing 60 percent.

Ertel's mobile van tours the elongated district, from the state capital of Harrisburg in the south to Williamsport in the north, seeking constituent problems he can solve. His work on flood control legislation has a direct political benefit at home, where the level of the Susquehanna River is often a matter of concern. Tropical Storm Agnes put large parts of Harrisburg underwater in 1972, including the governor's mansion.

Still, the disaster that commands the bulk of Ertel's attention is Three Mile Island. The close call in 1979 at the Metropolitan Edison reactor south of Harrisburg made Ertel a highly vocal critic of the Nuclear Regulatory Commission, which he says did not ensure adequate safety. He has worked to get federal loan guarantees to help the utility clean up the accident, so local residents will not have to pay so much for it.

Ertel is from the district's northern section, where he made a name as the Lycoming County (Williamsport) district attorney. He convicted Williamsport's mayor, public safety director and police chief on charges of wiretapping city workers. The case gave him additional publicity when it was discovered that allies of the mayor had tried to entrap Ertel with a prostitute.

**The District:** The oddly-shaped 17th follows the Susquehanna River, joining Lycoming and Union counties in the north to Dauphin and part of Lebanon in the south, using narrow Northumberland as connecting tissue. All the counties are Republican.

Harrisburg, the district's dominant city, has a sizable industrial workforce, but it generally retains the Republican identity found throughout the state's middle region. Steel is the district's dominant industry, but state government is its biggest employer.

## Committees

**Public Works and Transportation** (13th of 25 Democrats)
Aviation; Surface Transportation; Water Resources.

**Science and Technology** (19th of 23 Democrats)
Energy Development and Applications; Science Research and Technology.

## Elections

**1980 General**

| | |
|---|---|
| Allen Ertel (D) | 97,995 (61%) |
| Daniel Seiverling (R) | 63,790 (39%) |

**1978 Primary**

| | |
|---|---|
| Allen Ertel (D) | 79,234 (60%) |
| Thomas Rippon (R) | 53,613 (40%) |

**Previous Winning Percentage**

1976 (51%)

**District Vote For President**

| | 1980 | | 1976 | | 1972 |
|---|---|---|---|---|---|
| D | 56,536 (34%) | D | 73,024 (42%) | D | 48,248 (28 %) |
| R | 99,405 (59%) | R | 98,882 (56%) | R | 119,261 (70 %) |
| I | 10,592 (6%) | | | | |

## Campaign Finance

| | Receipts | Receipts from PACs | Expenditures |
|---|---|---|---|
| **1980** | | | |
| Ertel (D) | $141,402 | $50,150 (35%) | $97,999 |
| Seiverling (R) | $86,119 | $14,536 (17%) | $85,872 |

| 1978 | | | |
|---|---|---|---|
| Ertel (D) | $157,027 | $60,353 (38%) | $149,236 |
| Rippon (R) | $141,955 | $24,500 (17%) | $138,223 |

## Voting Studies

| | Presidential Support | | Party Unity | | Conservative Coalition | |
|---|---|---|---|---|---|---|
| Year | S | O | S | O | S | O |
| 1980 | 68 | 30 | 74 | 25 | 45 | 55 |
| 1979 | 70 | 26 | 72 | 23 | 44 | 51 |
| 1978 | 51 | 48 | 51 | 47 | 62 | 34 |
| 1977 | 70 | 28 | 58 | 38 | 50 | 46 |

S = Support      O = Opposition

## Key Votes

**96th Congress**

| | |
|---|---|
| Weaken Carter oil profits tax (1979) | Y |
| Reject hospital cost control plan (1979) | Y |
| Implement Panama Canal Treaties (1979) | Y |
| Establish Department of Education (1979) | Y |
| Approve Anti-busing Amendment (1979) | N |
| Guarantee Chrysler Corp. loans (1979) | Y |
| Approve military draft registration (1980) | N |
| Aid Sandinista regime in Nicaragua (1980) | Y |
| Strengthen fair housing laws (1980) | N |

**97th Congress**

| | |
|---|---|
| Reagan budget proposal (1981) | N |

## Interest Group Ratings

| Year | ADA | ACA | AFL-CIO | CCUS |
|---|---|---|---|---|
| 1980 | 67 | 26 | 68 | 65 |
| 1979 | 53 | 31 | 68 | 44 |
| 1978 | 30 | 50 | 56 | 47 |
| 1977 | 40 | 44 | 82 | 53 |

# 18 Doug Walgren (D)

**Of Pittsburgh — Elected 1976**

**Born:** Dec. 28, 1940, Rochester, N.Y.
**Education:** Dartmouth College, B.A. 1963; Stanford U. Law School, LL.B. 1966.
**Profession:** Lawyer.
**Family:** Wife, Carmala Vincent; one child.
**Religion:** Roman Catholic.
**Political Career:** Unsuccessful Democratic nominee for U.S House, 1970, 1972 special election and 1972 general election.

**In Washington:** This quiet, unassuming legislator has had to strike a balance between his personal background of liberal social concern and the more conservative middle-class interests of his Pittsburgh constituency.

Educated at Dartmouth and Stanford, Walgren was a legal services lawyer in the 1960s before entering politics. But while he has voted in a consistent liberal pattern in the House, he has generally associated with the ethnic Democrats of Pennsylvania rather than the younger activists with whom he seems to have more in common.

Like all western Pennsylvania Democrats, Walgren is a supporter of the steel industry, and a participant in the Steel Caucus that seeks restrictions on the introduction of imported steel products into the American market. He is also a solid vote for organized labor on most issues; in 1977, his first year in the House, he reversed himself on the issue of a sub-minimum wage for teen-agers, casting the deciding vote that killed the youth differential labor bitterly opposed.

Walgren's personal interests, however, are in the field of health, and he has pursued them, albeit inconspicuously, as a member of the Commerce Committee and its Health Subcommittee.

On these matters, Walgren's liberal outlook is clearest. In the 96th Congress, he worked on the Mental Health Systems Act, increasing federal funds for mental health programs. He promoted inclusion of language guaranteeing mental care for rape victims. Walgren also fought for money to allow the National Institutes of Health to investigate spinal cord injuries, and introduced legislation requiring that Federal Reserve Notes be redesigned to allow blind people to determine the denominations by touch.

**At Home:** It took four tries for Walgren to win his seat. Running as a Vietnam dove, he lost to three different Republicans: veteran James G. Fulton in 1970, William S. Conover in a 1972

special election after Fulton died, and John Heinz, now a U.S. senator, in the 1972 general election. Walgren's mother had been the Democratic nominee against Fulton in 1960 and 1962.

After his third defeat, Walgren settled down to practice law until Heinz left in 1976 to run for the Senate. By that time, Walgren was more than willing to run in alliance with the regular Allegheny County Democratic organization. He won the nomination in a crowded primary field that included a candidate backed by Pete Flaherty, at the time Pittsburgh's mayor.

In the 1976 general election, Walgren sounded fewer liberal themes as he faced Robert J. Casey, a public relations consultant and one of the founders of the conservative Committee for the Survival of a Free Congress.

Walgren spoke of reducing taxes and balancing the federal budget. Casey — whose GOP primary victory was aided by the similarity of his name to that of Robert P. Casey, then the popular state auditor general — dismayed many moderate Republicans and angered organized labor with his advocacy of right-to-work laws. Walgren had finally found the right circumstances, and he won easily.

In 1978, Walgren was re-elected comfortably over the Republican county chairman, who had alienated many in the local GOP hierarchy. In 1980, he rolled over token Republican opposition.

---

**18th District: Pittsburgh — northern and southwestern suburbs.** Population: 440,840 (7% decrease since 1970). Race: White 426,396 (97%), Black 10,909 (2%), Others 3,535 (1%). Spanish origin: 2,018 (0.4%).

Nowadays, he even does well in Republican areas.

Apart from his support for steel, Walgren pleased the voters by helping persuade the Carter administration to approve finishing the Allegheny Valley Expressway.

**The District:** The 18th, situated entirely in Allegheny County, has two distinct parts. In western Pittsburgh and the towns along the Allegheny River, north of the city, most of the voters are blue-collar Democrats. In the well-to-do suburbs of the North and the South Hills, like Mount

Lebanon and Fox Chapel, corporate management Republicans predominate. While the Democrats have a slight registration edge, Republicans usually surpass them in voter turnout.

The 18th was formed after the 1970 census by combining two districts that had been represented by Republicans — Fulton and Robert Corbett. Heinz captured the newly formed district in 1972 and kept the Democrats happy with his moderate voting record, which organized labor found acceptable.

## Committees

**Energy and Commerce** (12th of 24 Democrats)
Energy Conservation and Power; Health and the Environment; Oversight and Investigations.

**Science and Technology** (9th of 23 Democrats)
Science, Research and Technology, chairman; Natural Resources, Agriculture Research and Environment.

## Elections

**1980 General**

| | |
|---|---|
| Doug Walgren (D) | 127,641 (68%) |
| Steven Snyder (R) | 58,821 (32%) |

**1978 General**

| | |
|---|---|
| Doug Walgren (D) | 88,299 (57%) |
| Ted Jacob (R) | 65,088 (42%) |

**Previous Winning Percentage**

1976 (60%)

**District Vote For President**

| | 1980 | | 1976 | | 1972 |
|---|---|---|---|---|---|
| D | 81,406 (41%) | D | 90,062 (45%) | D | 74,949 (37%) |
| R | 98,677 (50%) | R | 108,001 (53%) | R | 125,938 (61%) |
| I | 13,168 (7%) | | | | |

## Campaign Finance

| | | Receipts from PACs | Expenditures |
|---|---|---|---|
| | Receipts | | |
| **1980** | | | |
| Walgren (D) | $107,457 | $54,278 (51%) | $88,133 |
| Snyder (R) | $62,962 | $9,175 (15%) | $77,232 |

**1978**

| | | | |
|---|---|---|---|
| Walgren (D) | $176,599 | $79,689 (45%) | $171,756 |
| Jacob (R) | $188,250 | $12,664 (7%) | $187,926 |

## Voting Studies

| | Presidential Support | | Party Unity | | Conservative Coalition | |
|---|---|---|---|---|---|---|
| **Year** | **S** | **O** | **S** | **O** | **S** | **O** |
| 1980 | 77 | 21 | 78 | 19 | 31 | 68 |
| 1979 | 70 | 22 | 75 | 19 | 22 | 68 |
| 1978 | 70 | 24 | 71 | 23 | 26 | 72 |
| 1977 | 67 | 23 | 74 | 20 | 24 | 71 |

S = Support          O = Opposition

## Key Votes

**96th Congress**

| | |
|---|---|
| Weaken Carter oil profits tax (1979) | N |
| Reject hospital cost control plan (1979) | N |
| Implement Panama Canal Treaties (1979) | Y |
| Establish Department of Education (1979) | N |
| Approve Anti-busing Amendment (1979) | Y |
| Guarantee Chrysler Corp. loans (1979) | Y |
| Approve military draft registration (1980) | Y |
| Aid Sandinista regime in Nicaragua (1980) | Y |
| Strengthen fair housing laws (1980) | Y |

**97th Congress**

| | |
|---|---|
| Reagan budget proposal (1981) | N |

## Interest Group Ratings

| Year | ADA | ACA | ALF-CIO | CCUS |
|---|---|---|---|---|
| 1980 | 78 | 8 | 79 | 71 |
| 1979 | 74 | 16 | 85 | 12 |
| 1978 | 56 | 26 | 80 | 22 |
| 1977 | 70 | 11 | 86 | 12 |

# 19 Bill Goodling (R)

**Of Jacobus — Elected 1974**

**Born:** Dec. 5, 1927, Loganville, Pa.
**Education:** U. of Md., B.S. 1953; Western Md. College, M.Ed. 1956.
**Military Career:** Army, 1946-48.
**Profession:** Teacher, school superintendent.
**Family:** Wife, Hilda Wright; two children.
**Religion:** Methodist.
**Political Career:** Dallastown School Board president, 1957-67.

**In Washington:** Like his father, who represented the same district for six terms before him, Goodling is a reliable conservative vote on most economic and foreign policy issues. But unlike his father, he breaks ranks when the subject is education or nutrition.

Those two matters come together at the Education and Labor Committee, where Goodling is the senior Republican on the subcommittee that handles public school legislation. Sometimes he finds himself allied with the Democratic majority rather than his GOP colleagues.

That happens most often in arguments over the school lunch program. On that issue, as a former school principal, he can sound downright liberal. In 1980, when the Carter administration tried to cut costs by reducing the school lunch subsidy to children of families above poverty level, Goodling was upset. "When we have 13 percent inflation," he argued, "we shouldn't be talking about a 10-, 15- or 20-cent increase for lower- and middle-income families."

When Reagan proposed even deeper cuts in 1981, Goodling worked with House and Senate leaders to try to negotiate a compromise and save the programs by trimming administrative costs.

In protecting child nutrition, Goodling works closely with food producers and suppliers for whom it is not simply a humanitarian issue. It is good business. This has allowed him to build a coalition that includes normally conservative groups and to win more often as a result.

Earlier in his career on Education and Labor, Goodling proposed that school districts be allowed to receive cash instead of commodities for school meals. Some could save money by buying food locally, he said. Critics insisted, however, that it would simply increase the total cost of the program, and Goodling was not successful.

On broader education issues, Goodling often is a moderating force between the strongly liberal

Democratic majority and conservative Republicans. He consistently warns committee Democrats of the futility of voting to authorize much more money for programs than they know will be approved by the Appropriations Committee.

On the Foreign Affairs Committee, and specifically the Africa Subcommittee, Goodling sticks with conservatives on most policy questions. He opposed legislation implementing the Panama Canal treaties — saying he had been unable to persuade his district to accept them — and favored an end to economic sanctions against the former all-white regime in Rhodesia.

But he has shown an independent streak. He argued in 1981 against Reagan plans to trim humanitarian aid in favor of military aid and was one of only a few in Congress to oppose the 1980 U.S. Olympic boycott. Goodling said the Olympic tradition was too important to lose, and the United States should try to move the games from Moscow rather than boycott them.

**At Home:** Goodling has made this district more securely Republican in his four House terms than his father, who won six times between 1960 and 1972, was ever able to do. George A. Goodling lived with the possibility of defeat each election year and actually lost once, in 1964; William has been over 70 percent three times in a row.

They are two different men. The elder Goodling was an indifferent speaker and disdained public appearances. His son is much more

**19th District: South central — York.**
Population: 536,129 (15% increase since 1970). Race: White 519,087 (97%), Black 11,976 (2%), Others 5,066 (1%). Spanish origin: 4,100 (1%).

outgoing and remains highly visible at home through a conspicuous schedule of public events.

Until his first run for Congress in 1974, the younger Goodling was a high school principal and had held just one elective office — on the Dallastown School Board. He was the surprise winner in a seven-way primary, outdistancing the favored John W. Eden, who had once challenged his father. Waging his first general election campaign in the Watergate year of 1974, William Goodling edged liberal Democrat Arthur L. Berger by barely 5,000 votes.

Close to the local Republican organizations, Goodling remains active on several local issues. He is an ally of neighborhood groups trying to stop a proposed chemical dump in York County.

**The District:** Until the advent of William Goodling, the 19th had the reputation of a swing district. In the 1950's, it changed hands between Republicans and Democrats every two years.

The city of York, a machinery manufacturing center, has been the bedrock of Democratic strength, but in recent years that has eroded. The blue-collar Democrats there are conservative, and the national party's direction in the last decade disturbed many of them. York County supported Democrat John F. Kennedy in 1960, but it went for Ronald Reagan in 1980.

Always reliably Republican are the district's two other counties — Adams and Cumberland (whose eastern half is in the 19th). Cumberland is dominated by the West Shore — the GOP suburbs of Harrisburg, the state capital, which lies in the adjacent 17th District.

## Committees

**Education and Labor** (4th of 14 Republicans)
Elementary, Secondary and Vocational Education.

**Foreign Affairs** (7th of 16 Republicans)
Subcommittees: Africa; Inter-American Affairs.

## Elections

**1980 General**

| | |
|---|---|
| Bill Goodling (R) | 136,873 (76%) |
| Richard Noll (D) | 41,584 (23%) |

**1978 General**

| | |
|---|---|
| Bill Goodling (R) | 105,424 (79%) |
| Rajeshwar Kumar (D) | 28,577 (21%) |

**Previous Winning Percentages**

1976 (71%)    1974 (51%)

**District Vote For President**

| | 1980 | | 1976 | | 1972 |
|---|---|---|---|---|---|
| D | 58,037 (31%) | D | 70,417 (39%) | D | 45,298 (28%) |
| R | 112,354 (61%) | R | 105,544 (59%) | R | 113,502 (70%) |
| I | 11,851 (6%) | | | | |

## Campaign Finance

| | Receipts | Receipts from PACs | Expenditures |
|---|---|---|---|
| **1980** | | | |
| Goodling (R) | $38,870 | $2,770 (7%) | $40,643 |
| Noll (D) | $11,279 | $100 (1%) | $11,274 |
| **1978** | | | |
| Goodling (R) | $41,652 | $761 (2%) | $37,067 |

## Voting Studies

| | Presidential Support | | Party Unity | | Conservative Coalition | |
|---|---|---|---|---|---|---|
| Year | S | O | S | O | S | O |
| 1980 | 43 | 44 | 80 | 14 | 68 | 20 |
| 1979 | 39 | 45 | 65 | 19 | 71 | 16 |
| 1978 | 36 | 54 | 74 | 15 | 76 | 12 |
| 1977 | 41 | 53 | 79 | 13 | 79 | 13 |
| 1976 | 65 | 29 | 82 | 14 | 84 | 11 |
| 1975 | 55 | 43 | 82 | 14 | 83 | 15 |

S = Support          O = Opposition

## Key Votes

**96th Congress**

| | |
|---|---|
| Weaken Carter oil profits tax (1979) | Y |
| Reject hospital cost control plan (1979) | ? |
| Implement Panama Canal Treaties (1979) | N |
| Establish Department of Education (1979) | ? |
| Approve Anti-busing Amendment (1979) | Y |
| Guarantee Chrysler Corp. loans (1979) | Y |
| Approve military draft registration (1980) | ? |
| Aid Sandinista regime in Nicaragua (1980) | ? |
| Strengthen fair housing laws (1980) | N |

**97th Congress**

| | |
|---|---|
| Reagan budget proposal (1981) | Y |

## Interest Group Ratings

| Year | ADA | ACA | AFL-CIO | CCUS |
|---|---|---|---|---|
| 1980 | 28 | 73 | 28 | 73 |
| 1979 | 26 | 78 | 28 | 71 |
| 1978 | 20 | 87 | 21 | 82 |
| 1977 | 10 | 81 | 29 | 100 |
| 1976 | 5 | 79 | 27 | 82 |
| 1975 | 16 | 75 | 17 | 61 |

# 20 Joseph M. Gaydos (D)

### Of McKeesport — Elected 1968

**Born:** July 3, 1926, Braddock, Pa.
**Education:** Attended Duquesne U., 1945-47; U. of Notre Dame Law School, LL.B. 1951.
**Military Career:** Naval Reserve, 1944-46.
**Profession:** Lawyer.
**Family:** Wife, Alice Gray; five children.
**Religion:** Roman Catholic.
**Political Career:** Penn. Senate, 1967-68.

**In Washington:** The United Steelworkers of America are the dominant political influence in Gaydos' district, and he focuses his career on the union's interests: occupational safety, pension rights and protection against imports.

The Occupational Safety and Health Administration is one of the Steelworkers' proudest accomplishments, and Gaydos stands guard over it as chairman of the Health and Safety Subcommittee of the Education and Labor Committee. For its entire history, the OSHA program has been a target of small businesses which find its regulations onerous, and each year brings new efforts to reduce the agency's scope.

It is Gaydos' job to defend OSHA, promising to look into complaints of overregulatory zeal but avoiding any serious efforts at revision. Labor won an additional victory in 1977 when mine safety regulations were transferred to the Labor Department, where OSHA has always been, removing them from the Interior Department, where they were subject to cross-pressures from mine owners.

One part of Gaydos' stewardship of OSHA involves the presentation of new horror stories about lax conditions in the workplace. At least once a month he inserts in the *Congressional Record* new material about a job-related fatality. One 1980 example involved a Virginia construction firm indicted for federal safety violations after two workers died in a trench collapse. "It may take criminal indictments such as this," Gaydos said, "to alert employers to their responsibility."

Gaydos also has served as chairman of the Steel Caucus, the House group seeking restrictions on steel imports into the U.S. He and the caucus were initially reluctant about the 1979 trade expansion bill, but ultimately supported it, although warning it could lead to a further decline in the steel industry if not accompanied by protective measures.

One day in 1980 Gaydos found himself the reluctant savior of major open housing legislation. The House was considering an amendment to make prosecution for bias easier under federal housing law. Open housing is one of the last things Gaydos' blue-collar constituents demand, and he voted against the amendment. But the roll call turned out to be a tie, and House leaders found Gaydos sitting in his usual spot in the "Cherokee Strip," the area of the House floor where western Pennsylvanians gather. After several rounds of badgering and appeals to party loyalty, Gaydos reluctantly cast the vote that passed the amendment and kept the bill alive. It never became law, but Gaydos made sure the leadership found someone else the next time.

**At Home:** Gaydos' stalwart defense of the steel industry has helped him politically. So have his roots in labor. Gaydos' father was a factory worker, and when he himself was a student, he held factory jobs and belonged to three unions (the Glass Workers, the Steelworkers and UAW). He later served as a United Mine Workers attorney.

In the 1968 Democratic primary, when he first ran for the seat, Gaydos used his background to counter the formal labor support claimed by his chief opponent, a Steelworkers' local president.

That year, state Sen. Gaydos had been tapped by the Allegheny County Democratic or-

---

**20th District: Southeast Allegheny County — Duquesne, McKeesport.** Population: 423,739 (10% decrease since 1970). Race: White 389,591 (92%), Black 31,269 (7%), Others 2,879 (1%). Spanish origin: 2,414 (1%).

ganization to replace U.S. Rep. Elmer Holland, whom it considered too old at 74. Holland agreed to retire, then died before his term ended.

Since his initial primary, which he won handily, Gaydos has had a virtual free ride. He has slipped below 70 percent of the vote only once.

**The District:** This is the home of Clairton, the town portrayed in the film *The Deer Hunter* as it sent its young steelworkers off to Vietnam.

A gritty mill town in the heart of the Monongahela Valley, Clairton epitomizes the 20th, which has six major steel plants. As in the movie, the ethnic pride of the Eastern and Southern Europeans is strong. So is their identification with the Democratic Party.

The district, which also takes in South Side Pittsburgh, has a smattering of Republicans, mostly in such western-end towns as Whitehall.

## Committees

**Education and Labor** (5th of 19 Democrats)
Health and Safety, chairman; Postsecondary Education.

**House Administration** (3rd of 11 Democrats)
Contracts and Printing, chairman; Accounts; Task Force on Committee Organization.

**Joint Printing**

## Elections

**1980 General**

| | |
|---|---|
| Joseph Gaydos (D) | 122,100 (73%) |
| Kathleen Meyer (R) | 46,313 (27%) |

**1978 General**

| | |
|---|---|
| Joseph Gaydos (D) | 97,745 (72%) |
| Kathleen Meyer (R) | 37,745 (28%) |

**Previous Winning Percentages**

| | | | |
|---|---|---|---|
| 1976 (75%) | 1974 (82%) | 1972 (62%) | 1970 (77%) |
| 1968* (70%) | | | |

*Elected to fill an unexpired term in a special election held the same day as the general election.*

**District Vote For President**

| | 1980 | | 1976 | | 1972 |
|---|---|---|---|---|---|
| **D** | 90,546 (50%) | **D** | 102,730 (54%) | **D** | 83,576 (42%) |
| **R** | 77,245 (43%) | **R** | 83,713 (44%) | **R** | 108,506 (55%) |
| **I** | 9,878 (5%) | | | | |

## Campaign Finance

| | Receipts | Receipts from PACs | Expenditures |
|---|---|---|---|
| **1980** | | | |
| Gaydos (D) | $108,127 | $53,700 (50%) | $98,430 |
| Meyer (R) | $1,625 | — (0%) | $1,624 |
| **1978** | | | |
| Gaydos (D) | $72,385 | $32,595 (45%) | $67,339 |

## Voting Studies

| | Presidential Support | | Party Unity | | Conservative Coalition | |
|---|---|---|---|---|---|---|
| Year | S | O | S | O | S | O |
| 1980 | 57 | 38 | 56 | 38 | 61 | 37 |

| Year | S | O | S | O | S | O |
|---|---|---|---|---|---|---|
| 1979 | 50 | 46 | 59 | 36 | 60 | 33 |
| 1978 | 57 | 40 | 64 | 32 | 49 | 49 |
| 1977 | 68 | 24 | 69 | 28 | 45 | 49 |
| 1976 | 20 | 75 | 72 | 26 | 42 | 56 |
| 1975 | 29 | 54 | 68 | 19 | 27 | 56 |
| 1974 (Ford) | 35 | 63 | | | | |
| 1974 | 43 | 57 | 72 | 27 | 41 | 58 |
| 1973 | 26 | 72 | 78 | 19 | 30 | 67 |
| 1972 | 46 | 49 | 71 | 27 | 32 | 60 |
| 1971 | 39 | 54 | 78 | 17 | 23 | 68 |
| 1970 | 54 | 29 | 72 | 11 | 11 | 61 |
| 1969 | 43 | 57 | 65 | 31 | 33 | 62 |

S = Support          O = Opposition

## Key Votes

**96th Congress**

| | |
|---|---|
| Weaken Carter oil profits tax (1979) | N |
| Reject hospital cost control plan (1979) | N |
| Implement Panama Canal Treaties (1979) | Y |
| Establish Department of Education (1979) | N |
| Approve Anti-busing Amendment (1979) | Y |
| Guarantee Chrysler Corp. loans (1979) | Y |
| Approve military draft registration (1980) | Y |
| Aid Sandinista regime in Nicaragua (1980) | N |
| Strengthen fair housing laws (1980) | Y |

**97th Congress**

| | |
|---|---|
| Reagan budget proposal (1981) | N |

## Interest Group Ratings

| Year | ADA | ACA | AFL-CIO | CCUS |
|---|---|---|---|---|
| 1980 | 33 | 48 | 94 | 56 |
| 1979 | 47 | 27 | 78 | 25 |
| 1978 | 35 | 26 | 75 | 28 |
| 1977 | 55 | 19 | 100 | 18 |
| 1976 | 65 | 14 | 96 | 19 |
| 1975 | 58 | 36 | 100 | 0 |
| 1974 | 52 | 33 | 82 | 30 |
| 1973 | 80 | 26 | 100 | 18 |
| 1972 | 63 | 41 | 90 | 0 |
| 1971 | 73 | 33 | 83 | - |
| 1970 | 72 | 21 | 100 | 0 |
| 1969 | 60 | 41 | 100 | |

# 21 Don Bailey (D)

**Of Greensburg — Elected 1978**

**Born:** July 21, 1945, Pittburgh, Pa.
**Education:** U. of Mich., B.A. 1967; Duquesne U. Law School, J.D. 1976.
**Military Career:** Army, 1967-70.
**Profession:** Lawyer.
**Family:** Single.
**Religion:** Presbyterian.
**Political Career:** No previous office.

**In Washington:** Bailey was only 33 when he came to the House in 1979, but he had more in common with the ethnic Democrats of an earlier time than with many of his contemporaries.

He is a Vietnam veteran who returned with some bitterness, not at the war, but at the American anti-war movement that he believes made fighting it more difficult. As a member of the Armed Services Committee in the 96th Congress, he was a tough and sometimes emotional supporter of higher defense spending. When the committee's leaders wanted to round up support among junior members on a crucial floor vote, they sometimes asked Bailey to do the lobbying.

At the beginning of 1981, Bailey transferred to the Ways and Means Committee.

The former football lineman is bluff and aggressive in his style, and straightforward about his desire to get money for his district. He works hard to help the steel and defense industries that employ many of his constituents, and is openly contemptuous of environmental legislation that he feels restricts business and reduces productivity.

When the House debated Alaska lands legislation in 1979, Bailey supported the more development-oriented bill. He is also an advocate of nuclear power and opposes efforts to restrict and slow down its development.

Bailey also spent one term on the Education and Labor Committee, where he succeeded 21st District predecessor John Dent, long one of organized labor's strongest allies in Congress. Bailey voted in Dent's tradition. He left the committee in 1981.

Pennsylvania has one of the more close-knit House delegations, and Bailey keeps up his ties to most of the state's House Democrats. For much of the 96th Congress, he was a political understudy to John P. Murtha, the group's unofficial spokesman and link to the House leadership. When the House decided to expel Philadelphia Democrat Michael "Ozzie" Myers, convicted of bribery in the Abscam scandal, Bailey sat next to Myers throughout the debate and argued the case against expulsion, knowing he would lose. He called the proceedings "a horrendous affront to any basic fundamental system of justice or fair play."

In the 97th Congress, Bailey took a place on the House ethics committee himself. When the panel's chief counsel recommended expulsion for Raymond Lederer, Myers' Pennsylvania colleague who was also implicated in Abscam, Bailey cast the only vote against considering the recommendation. Lederer later resigned.

**At Home:** Bailey was an upset winner in the 11-way Democratic primary that determined the successor to Dent, who retired in 1978. As a local attorney, Bailey had dabbled in politics but never had held office.

He defeated two better-known candidates: Bernard Scherer, then the Westmoreland County Democratic Chairman, and James J. Manderino, at the time the state House majority leader. Democrat Dent backed Scherer, but Bailey edged him out by 113 votes.

The young lawyer's superior organization made the difference. He had managed a local judicial campaign not long before, and Democrats who had helped in that effort worked for him for Congress. In the 1978 general election, Bailey posted a modest victory over Republican banker

---

**21st District: Southwest — Westmoreland County.** Population: 485,534 (3% increase since 1970). Race: White 469,444 (97%), Black 13,630 (3%), Others 2,460 (1%). Spanish origin: 1,625 (0.3%).

## Don Bailey, D-Pa.

Robert H. Miller, who sounded conservative economic themes. The primary had made it difficult for Bailey to unify his party behind him, but the Democratic registration advantage helped pull him through.

In the 1980 primary, he again faced Scherer, whose prospects were brightened by the defection of several former Bailey workers to his side. Nevertheless, Bailey won easily and went on to crush a weak Republican in the fall.

Bailey's aggressive manner has generated some criticism in his district. A delegation of Pittsburgh-area builders left one meeting with him complaining that he had lectured them arrogantly. But he has won new friends through his efforts to obtain federal funds for the area, and his advocacy of nuclear power and loosened environmental restrictions has proved popular.

**The District:** Steel-making Westmoreland County comprises most of the 21st, and the mills in Latrobe, Monessen and other small towns have made it a center of organized labor. Democrats, with their 2-1 registration edge, normally carry it with little trouble.

In the 1960's and through the mid-70's, the Democrats were under the control of Egidio (Gene) Cerilli, the Pennsylvania Turnpike Commission chairman. But after Cerilli was convicted on corruption charges, the party split into warring factions.

The Republicans in the district are found in the extreme eastern and western parts of Westmoreland County, and in a small slice of Allegheny County.

## Committees

**Standards of Official Conduct** (6th of 6 Democrats)

**Ways and Means** (23rd of 23 Democrats)
Public Assistance and Unemployment Compensation; Social Security.

## Elections

**1980 General**

| | |
|---|---|
| Don Bailey (D) | 112,427 (68%) |
| Dirk Matson (R) | 51,821 (32%) |

**1980 Primary**

| | |
|---|---|
| Don Bailey (D) | 48,337 (60%) |
| Bernard Scherer (D) | 27,007 (33%) |
| Eugene Saloom (D) | 5,376 (7%) |

**1978 General**

| | |
|---|---|
| Don Bailey (D) | 73,712 (53%) |
| Robert Miller (R) | 65,622 (47%) |

**1978 Primary**

| | |
|---|---|
| Don Bailey (D) | 16,671 (23%) |
| Bernard Scherer (D) | 16,558 (22%) |
| John Cicco (D) | 11,355 (15%) |
| James Manderino (D) | 6,248 (8%) |
| Joseph Petrarca (D) | 6,157 (8%) |

**District Vote For President**

| 1980 | | 1976 | | 1972 | |
|---|---|---|---|---|---|
| D | 85,062 (48%) | D | 92,450 (53%) | D | 73,049 (41%) |
| R | 81,193 (46%) | R | 78,965 (45%) | R | 99,269 (56%) |
| I | 8,341 (5%) | | | | |

## Campaign Finance

| | Receipts | Receipts from PACs | Expenditures |
|---|---|---|---|
| **1980** | | | |
| Bailey (D) | $115,061 | $16,820 (15%) | $104,761 |

| **1978** | | | |
|---|---|---|---|
| Bailey (D) | $125,800 | $40,900 (33%) | $125,146 |
| Miller (R) | $114,097 | $15,018 (13%) | $113,186 |

## Voting Studies

| | Presidential Support | | Party Unity | | Conservative Coalition | |
|---|---|---|---|---|---|---|
| Year | S | O | S | O | S | O |
| 1980 | 79 | 21 | 86 | 14 | 44 | 56 |
| 1979 | 52 | 48 | 69 | 31 | 55 | 45 |

S = Support          O = Opposition

## Key Votes

**96th Congress**

| | |
|---|---|
| Weaken Carter oil profits tax (1979) | N |
| Reject hospital cost control plan (1979) | N |
| Implement Panama Canal Treaties (1979) | Y |
| Establish Department of Education (1979) | N |
| Approve Anti-busing Amendment (1979) | Y |
| Guarantee Chrysler Corp. loans (1979) | Y |
| Approve military draft registration (1980) | Y |
| Aid Sandinista regime in Nicaragua (1980) | Y |
| Strengthen fair housing laws (1980) | Y |

**97th Congress**

| | |
|---|---|
| Reagan budget proposal (1981) | N |

## Interest Group Ratings

| Year | ADA | ACA | AFL-CIO | CCUS |
|---|---|---|---|---|
| 1980 | 50 | 21 | 79 | 59 |
| 1979 | 37 | 23 | 85 | 33 |

# 22 Austin J. Murphy (D)

**Of Charleroi — Elected in 1976**

**Born:** June 17, 1927, North Charleroi, Pa.
**Education:** Duquesne U., B.A. 1949; U. of Pittsburgh, LL.B. 1952.
**Military Career:** Marine Corps, 1944-46; Marine Corps Reserve, 1948-50.
**Profession:** Lawyer.
**Family:** Wife, Ramona McNamara; six children.
**Religion:** Roman Catholic.
**Political Career:** Pa. House, 1959-71; Pa. Senate, 1971-77.

**In Washington:** Murphy represents a steel and coal district, and he is well situated to vote its interests on the Education and Labor Committee, which handles worker pension and safety issues, and the Interior Committee, which has jurisdiction over coal issues from slurry pipelines to strip mining.

He is not a leader on either of those committees, but as far as labor is concerned he is a reliable vote on most issues, like other western Pennsylvania Democrats whose style is close to that of the big-city machine Democrats from Chicago, Philadelphia, and New Jersey. When no union issue is involved, he often casts conservative votes. The AFL-CIO gave him a 68 in 1980, but the Americans for Democratic Action rated him at only 44.

Murphy has been known to change his mind on major issues. In the Interior Committee in 1977, he cosponsored a coal slurry bill, designed to move Western coal to Eastern states through pipelines. The bill had the support of the Carter administration, plus some environmentalists and public utilities who wanted the coal. But the railroads mounted a massive lobbying campaign against it, and in 1978 Murphy voted against it in committee and on the floor.

In general, he is a pro-development vote on Interior against the positions of environmentalists who lobby the committee. But he was with environmentalists and the Carter administration in 1977 when they sought to block funding for water projects they considered environmentally damaging. When the House voted for most of the water projects anyway, Murphy supported Carter's veto of the legislation.

In 1977, Murphy was named to the Ad Hoc Energy Committee put together by Speaker O'Neill to facilitate passage of Carter's first major energy package. There he fought a proposed 2-cent gasoline tax favored by the administration. He was one of six Democrats who voted with a Republican majority against the tax, which cleared committee anyway but died on the floor.

On Education and Labor, Murphy generally votes quietly with chairman Carl Perkins and the panel's pro-labor majority. He supported common-site picketing and labor law revision in the 95th Congress. He frequently speaks for the concerns of his district's miners on black lung benefits, and on the future of the black lung trust fund.

**At Home:** The life of a politician in coal country can be a little like the life of a miner — rough. Murphy, proud of his Marine Corps past, displays a relish for combat that suits the 22nd District. In 1973, he got into a fight with motorcycle gang members who were harassing him. In 1979, after Iranians seized the American hostages, Murphy declared his willingness to rejoin the Marines and invade Tehran.

He served his time as a state legislator, waiting for Democrat Thomas E. Morgan (1945-77), chairman of the House Foreign Affairs Committee, to retire. In this district, the Democratic nomination usually means the election, so a 12-way primary ensued in 1976.

Murphy defeated, among others, the Fayette County Democratic chairman (whom Morgan backed), a former U.S. Senate aide, and a local

---

**22nd District: Southwest — Washington, Uniontown.** Population: 492,584 (5% increase since 1970). Race: White 473,953 (96%), Black 16,435 (3%), Others 2,196 (0.4%). Spanish origin: 2,590 (1%).

---

## Austin J. Murphy, D-Pa.

attorney supported by the party organization of Murphy's own Washington County. The Washington party chairman, Mike Hanna, had been feuding with Murphy since 1963, when Murphy unsuccessfully challenged him for district attorney.

In the 1978 primary, Murphy again faced the one-time Senate aide, John Hook, who accused him of corrupt dealings with a local company whose officials had raised funds for the congressman. Murphy denied the charges, and the U.S. attorney ignored them. The race also featured a court fight to remove from the ballot the name F. H. Hook — which John Hook said was placed there to siphon off his vote.

Murphy prevailed easily in that primary and had no Democratic opposition in 1980. The politics of the 22nd may have subsided.

**The District:** The southwestern corner of Pennsylvania became America's steel capital because of its supply of coal, which fires the blast furnaces of Pittsburgh. Much of the coal lies in the southern reaches of the 22nd.

Flush against the West Virginia border, the counties of Fayette and Greene are strongholds of the United Mine Workers and the Democratic Party. Equally Democratic is Washington County, a steel-producing area on the fringes of metropolitan Pittsburgh. The 22nd went for Jimmy Carter in 1980, against the state trend.

The district contains a chunk of suburban Pittsburgh in Allegheny County, which contributes the Republican vote. But the votes in Upper St. Clair and other well-to-do towns are swamped by those of the steelworkers and coal miners.

## Committees

**Education and Labor** (11th of 19 Democrats)
Select Education, chairman; Health and Safety; Labor Standards.

**Interior and Insular Affairs** (13th of 23 Democrats)
Energy and the Environment; Mines and Mining.

**Veterans' Affairs** (16th of 17 Democrats)
Compensation, Pension and Insurance.

## Elections

**1980 General**

| | |
|---|---|
| Austin Murphy (D) | 118,084 (70%) |
| Marilyn Ecoff (R) | 50,020 (30%) |

**1978 General**

| | |
|---|---|
| Austin Murphy (D) | 99,559 (72%) |
| Marilyn Ecoff (R) | 39,518 (28%) |

**Previous Winning Percentage**

1976 (55 %)

**District Vote For President**

| | 1980 | | 1976 | | 1972 |
|---|---|---|---|---|---|
| D | 92,829 (53%) | D | 103,041 (57%) | D | 72,285 (42%) |
| R | 73,735 (42%) | R | 75,161 (42%) | R | 96,023 (56%) |
| I | 7,156 (4%) | | | | |

## Campaign Finance

| | | Receipts from PACs | Expenditures |
|---|---|---|---|
| | Receipts | | |
| **1980** | | | |
| Murphy (D) | $136,364 | $46,075 (34%) | $93,663 |
| Ecoff (R) | $716 | — (0%) | $788 |

| 1978 | | | |
|---|---|---|---|
| Murphy (D) | $170,621 | $54,615 (32%) | $144,228 |

## Voting Studies

| | Presidential Support | | Party Unity | | Conservative Coalition | |
|---|---|---|---|---|---|---|
| Year | S | O | S | O | S | O |
| 1980 | 59 | 38 | 65 | 32 | 49 | 46 |
| 1979 | 52 | 48 | 60 | 40 | 66 | 34 |
| 1978 | 47 | 51 | 58 | 35 | 41 | 53 |
| 1977 | 70 | 28 | 69 | 29 | 43 | 56 |

S = Support        O = Opposition

## Key Votes

**96th Congress**

| | |
|---|---|
| Weaken Carter oil profits tax (1979) | N |
| Reject hospital cost control plan (1979) | Y |
| Implement Panama Canal Treaties (1979) | Y |
| Establish Department of Education (1979) | Y |
| Approve Anti-busing Amendment (1979) | Y |
| Guarantee Chrysler Corp. loans (1979) | Y |
| Approve military draft registration (1980) | Y |
| Aid Sandinista regime in Nicaragua (1980) | N |
| Strengthen fair housing laws (1980) | Y |

**97th Congress**

| | |
|---|---|
| Reagan budget proposal (1981) | N |

## Interest Group Ratings

| Year | ADA | ACA | AFL-CIO | CCUS |
|---|---|---|---|---|
| 1980 | 44 | 42 | 68 | 59 |
| 1979 | 42 | 38 | 70 | 50 |
| 1978 | 40 | 40 | 72 | 22 |
| 1977 | 50 | 30 | 91 | 18 |

# 23 William F. Clinger Jr. (R)

**Of Warren — Elected 1978**

**Born:** April 4, 1929, Warren, Pa.
**Education:** Johns Hopkins U., B.A. 1951; U. of
Va. Law School, LL.B. 1965.
**Military Career:** Navy, 1951-55.
**Profession:** Lawyer.
**Family:** Wife, Julia Whitla; four children.
**Religion:** Presbyterian.
**Political Career:** No previous office.

**In Washington:** An economic development
specialist, Clinger found an immediate legislative
role to play in his first term as Congress considered President Carter's proposal for a dramatic
expansion in the power and funding of the Economic Development Administration.

Clinger had been the EDA general counsel
himself during the Ford administration, and
joined the Public Works Committee in 1979
mainly because he wanted to work on redesigning
the agency. Given his background, he was brought
in on the drafting of an important piece of legislation at a point when most freshmen were still
looking for an issue. The only frustration was the
ultimate failure of the project. The bill never was
enacted, and in 1981 Clinger found himself in an
entirely different position, struggling against his
own party's efforts to dismantle the EDA
altogether.

The main reason for the failure was the
insistence of committee Democrats on including a
$2-billion public works program in the package.
That brought resistance not only from the White
House but from the Senate, and caused a stalemate that lasted through the 1980 election.

Clinger's main interest was in the proposed
expansion of EDA loan authority, and in giving
the agency new rules to use in managing all the
extra money. When the bill reached the House
floor, Clinger offered a string of amendments,
most of them placing controls on who could
receive EDA money and how the lending decision
could be made. One of his amendments would
have provided special loan funds for energy conservation projects.

In the 97th Congress, Clinger began looking
for a way to preserve some EDA role by involving
it in the creation of "enterprise zones" — areas
where the federal government would reduce business taxes to spur investment. He drafted a bill to
earmark EDA funds for public works within
zones.

Outside his speciality, Clinger was one of the
quieter members of the freshman class in the 96th
Congress, speaking out mainly in behalf of coal,
steel and other local interests. Billed as a moderate Republican when he arrived — he organized
northwest Pennsylvania for Nelson Rockefeller in
the 1968 presidential campaign — Clinger generally compiled an orthodox conservative voting
record. He did join the Wednesday Club, the
informal organization of moderate GOP House
members, and broke with his party's majority on a
few major issues, notably the Alaska lands question, on which he supported the environmentalist
position.

**At Home:** Clinger restored this seat to Republican control in 1978 after it flirted with
Democratic representation for one term. His unseating of Rep. Joseph Ammerman and his easy
win against token Democratic opposition in 1980,
appear to leave him set for a comfortable tenure
in a safe district.

The son of a local businessman, Clinger
worked in advertising for a mail order house, then
became a lawyer. Following his tour in the Economic Development Administration under Ford,
he headed home to run for office.

Ammerman had maintained a liberal voting
record and championed a consumer protection
agency, which Clinger opposed. That might have
been enough of a liability for a Democrat in a
conservative district. But in late August,

---

**23rd District: Northwest, central.**
Population: 500,405 (7% increase since 1970).
Race: White 494,439 (99%), Black 2,524 (1%),
Others 3,442 (1%). Spanish origin: 1,964
(0.3%).

Ammerman broke his hip in an automobile accident and was hospitalized for six weeks, losing valuable campaigning time.

Clinger cited his Washington experience to illustrate his campaign theme — that many federal programs did not work and needed revamping or eliminating. His victory over Ammerman was not spectacular, but it was sufficient to discourage strong opposition in 1980.

A low-key politician with a self-deprecating wit, Clinger pays far more attention to his district than did Albert Johnson, the aging Republican whom Ammerman ousted in 1976.

As a House freshman, Clinger won plaudits in his home county, Warren, for his work to get the Environmental Protection Agency to remove abandoned barrels of PCBs, a deadly substance that threatened the town of Youngsville.

**The District:** In the early 1960s, this area struck some state politicians as too remote even for the interstate highway that had been planned to cross it. "All they have up there," one of them complained, "is a bunch of bears." It was the home of many of the nation's first oil wells in the 19th century, but that part of the economy dried up long ago.

The highway has come through in the past decade, but the area remains overwhelmingly rural and agricultural, and Republican sentiments prevail. Ammerman's one term was largely the result of Johnson's political ineptness.

The district's southern portion claims the biggest population. The 23rd's Democrats can be found in this section, although they lack majorities. The strongest Democratic town is State College in Centre County, home of Penn State.

## Committees

**Government Operations** (10th of 17 Republicans)
Commerce, Consumer, and Monetary Affairs; Legislation and National Security.

**Public Works and Transportion** (9th of 19 Republicans)
Economic Development; Surface Transportaton; Water Resources.

## Elections

**1980 General**

| | |
|---|---|
| William Clinger Jr. (R) | 122,855 (74%) |
| Peter Atigan (D) | 41,033 (25%) |

**1978 General**

| | |
|---|---|
| William Clinger Jr. (R) | 73,194 (54%) |
| Joseph Ammerman (D) | 61,657 (46%) |

**1978 Primary**

| | |
|---|---|
| William Clinger Jr. (R) | 28,025 (63%) |
| Jeffrey Bower (R) | 13,082 (29%) |
| Gregory Leshock (R) | 3,378 (8%) |

**District Vote For President**

| | 1980 | | 1976 | | 1972 |
|---|---|---|---|---|---|
| D | 65,211 (38%) | D | 77,510 (45%) | D | 54,130 (33%) |
| R | 93,731 (54%) | R | 91,487 (53%) | R | 105,456 (65%) |
| I | 10,982 (6%) | | | | |

## Campaign Finance

| | Receipts | Receipts from PACs | Expenditures |
|---|---|---|---|
| **1980** | | | |
| Clinger (R) | $95,522 | $49,070 (51%) | $67,942 |

| **1978** | | | |
|---|---|---|---|
| Clinger (R) | $251,718 | $63,213 (25%) | $250,697 |
| Ammerman (D) | $172,493 | $48,262 (28%) | $174,587 |

## Voting Studies

| | Presidential Support | | Party Unity | | Conservative Coalition | |
|---|---|---|---|---|---|---|
| **Year** | **S** | **O** | **S** | **O** | **S** | **O** |
| 1980 | 57 | 43 | 69 | 31 | 77 | 23 |
| 1979 | 44 | 56† | 71 | 27† | 76 | 23† |

S = Support     O = Opposition
†Not eligible for all recorded votes.

## Key Votes

**96th Congress**

| | |
|---|---|
| Weaken Carter oil profits tax (1979) | C |
| Reject hospital cost control plan (1979) | Y |
| Implement Panama Canal Treaties (1979) | N |
| Establish Department of Education (1979) | N |
| Approve Anti-busing Amendment (1979) | N |
| Guarantee Chrysler Corp. loans (1979) | N |
| Approve military draft registration (1980) | Y |
| Aid Sandinista regime in Nicaragua (1980) | N |
| Strengthen fair housing laws (1980) | Y |

**97th Congress**

| | |
|---|---|
| Reagan budget proposal (1981) | Y |

## Interest Group Ratings

| Year | ADA | ACA | AFL-CIO | CCUS |
|---|---|---|---|---|
| 1980 | 22 | 71 | 26 | 74 |
| 1979 | 11 | 68 | 65 | 88 |

# 24 Marc L. Marks (R)

Of Sharon — Elected 1976

**Born:** Feb. 12, 1927, Farrell, Pa.
**Education:** U. of Ala., B.A. 1951; U. of Va. Law School, LL.B. 1954.
**Military Career:** Army Air Corps, 1945-46.
**Profession:** Lawyer.
**Family:** Wife, Jane London; three children.
**Religion:** Jewish.
**Political Career:** Mercer County Solicitor, 1960-66.

**In Washington:** New to politics when he arrived in the House in 1977, Marks has struggled through three difficult terms without finding a comfortable niche in the institution.

Elected as a thoughtful and independent newcomer, Marks let it be known early in his first term that he was a "swing" vote on the Commerce Committee, open to rational persuasion from all sides. Useful as that strategy sometimes is for veteran legislators, it brought the inexperienced Marks incessant pressure from nearly every interest lobbying the committee on major issues. Besieged by energy companies and consumer advocates for his vote on natural gas deregulation, he hesitated for weeks, then voted with the committee's Democrats to preserve controls, angering some Republican colleagues. But he played a similar role for most of his first term. Once, he organized a seminar on the issue of a new consumer agency to educate members who were undecided.

The 96th Congress brought a brand-new Marks, a candidate for the Senate and an outspoken liberal on a variety of issues. Marks's stepped up schedule of floor speeches made him a target of ridicule from the Republican right, which felt he was moving left simply for political reasons.

When Marks used the word "hypocrisy" in describing an anti-busing amendment to the Constitution, Maryland Republican Robert E. Bauman demanded that he retract his words. On another occasion, California's John H. Rousselot demanded a roll-call vote on a Marks amendment purely to embarrass him by demonstrating its lack of support.

By 1980, Marks had abandoned his Senate campaign and seemed willing to settle for a quieter role and a more orthodox Republican approach. His floor speeches became less frequent, and his support for the "conservative coalition," which dropped to 39 percent in 1979, rose again to 64 percent.

**At Home:** While Marks was struggling in Washington in his first two Congresses, he was generating opposition at home. For a man of moderate views and a professed desire to be reasonable, he has a remarkable tendency to anger people.

His moderate voting record — good politics for a Republican in a Democratic district — has never pleased conservatives within his own party. Some district Republicans were alienated by his interest in challenging Sen. Richard S. Schweiker, who for unrelated reasons later chose to retire. Marks's public argument with a local anti-abortion group turned the pro-life movement against him.

Both those arguments help explain his less-than-1,000-vote margin in 1980 against Democrat David DiCarlo, a state legislator. Another factor was geography. DiCarlo came from Erie, the district's population center, while Marks is from its southern end. Pluralities for Marks in his home of Mercer County, which is usually Democratic, and in Republican Crawford County, barely overcame DiCarlo's Erie County lead.

Marks had a strikingly successful start in 1976 by defeating Democrat Joseph P. Vigorito, a six-term House veteran. In this contest, and in a 1978 rematch, the articulate Marks proved a far better campaigner than Vigorito, who had a lightweight reputation. DiCarlo, on the other

---

**24th District: Northwest — Erie.**
Population: 496,948 (5% increase since 1970). Race: White 474,693 (96%), Black 18,952 (4%), Others 3,303 (1%). Spanish origin: 2,772 (1%).

hand, was Marks's match on the stump and well-thought-of as a legislator.

The 1980 contest also featured a partisan role reversal, with DiCarlo castigating Republican Marks as a big spender. Organized labor, which originally had backed DiCarlo, dropped him after he voted for a bill in the state Senate to restrict jobless benefits. The United Auto Workers endorsed Marks.

**The District:** This tri-county district is like a sandwich — with Democratic Erie County in the north, Democratic Mercer in the south and Republican Crawford in the middle. The steel mills and other heavy industrial plants of Erie and Mercer produce the blue-collar Democratic vote, while Crawford, with its dairy industry, is small-town oriented.

Despite its almost 2-1 Democratic registration edge, the 24th is a swing district. Since World War II, Republicans have won it 12 times and Democrats six. Jimmy Carter carried it in 1976 but lost it in 1980.

## Committees

**Energy and Commerce** (8th of 18 Republicans)
Oversight and Investigations; Telecommunications, Consumer Protection, and Finance.

**Select Aging** (4th of 23 Republicans)
Health and Long-Term Care.

## Elections

**1980 General**

| | |
|---|---|
| Marc Marks (R) (86) | 86,687 (50%) |
| David Dicarlo (D) | 86,567 (50%) |

**1978 General**

| | |
|---|---|
| Marc Marks (R) | 87,041 (64%) |
| Joseph Vigorito (D) | 48,894 (36%) |

**Previous Winning Percentage**

1976 (55%)

**District Vote For President**

| | 1980 | | 1976 | | 1972 |
|---|---|---|---|---|---|
| **D** | 77,440 (43%) | **D** | 95,138 (51%) | **D** | 69,480 (38%) |
| **R** | 87,842 (49%) | **R** | 87,411 (47%) | **R** | 107,896 (60%) |
| **I** | 11,691 (7%) | | | | |

## Campaign Finance

| | Receipts | Receipts from PACs | Expen-ditures |
|---|---|---|---|
| **1980** | | | |
| Marks (R) | $167,170 | $54,076 (32%) | $172,052 |
| DiCarlo (D) | $152,165 | $73,652 (48%) | $134,532 |

| | | | |
|---|---|---|---|
| **1978** | | | |
| Marks (R) | $179,277 | $49,145 (27%) | $171,653 |
| Vigorito (D) | 33,695 | $4,360 (13%) | $35,220 |

## Voting Studies

| | Presidential Support | | Party Unity | | Conservative Coalition | |
|---|---|---|---|---|---|---|
| Year | S | O | S | O | S | O |
| 1980 | 59 | 38 | 59 | 38 | 64 | 29 |
| 1979 | 76 | 17 | 22 | 67† | 39 | 50 |
| 1978 | 71 | 29 | 43 | 56 | 44 | 54 |
| 1977 | 67 | 28 | 49 | 49 | 53 | 45 |

S = Support          O = Opposition

## Key Votes

**96th Congress**

| | |
|---|---|
| Weaken Carter oil profits tax (1979) | Y |
| Reject hospital cost control plan (1979) | Y |
| Implement Panama Canal Treaties (1979) | Y |
| Establish Department of Education (1979) | Y |
| Approve Anti-busing Amendment (1979) | N |
| Guarantee Chrysler Corp. loans (1979) | Y |
| Approve military draft registration (1980) | Y |
| Aid Sandinista regime in Nicaragua (1980) | N |
| Strengthen fair housing laws (1980) | Y |

**97th Congress**

| | |
|---|---|
| Reagan budget proposal (1981) | Y |

## Interest Group Ratings

| Year | ADA | ACA | AFL-CIO | CCUS |
|---|---|---|---|---|
| 1980 | 44 | 59 | 37 | 69 |
| 1979 | 32 | 31 | 75 | 67 |
| 1978 | 50 | 38 | 55 | 44 |
| 1977 | 60 | 46 | 70 | 65 |

# 25 Eugene V. Atkinson (D)

**Of Aliquippa — Elected 1978**

**Born:** April 5, 1927, Aliquippa, Pa.
**Education:** Attended U. of Pittsburgh.
**Military Career:** Navy, 1945-46.
**Profession:** Owner of insurance agency.
**Family:** Wife, Marion Jones; one child.
**Religion:** Roman Catholic.
**Political Career:** Beaver County commissioner, 1972-78; Democratic nominee for U.S. House, 1976.

**In Washington:** The protectionist sentiment that dominates most industrial districts of the old Northeast has defined Atkinson's role in Congress right from the beginning. His job is to help the steel industry, whose ill health has turned the territory north of Pittsburgh into a depressed area.

He pursued his task with diligence but little public notice during his freshman House term in the 96th Congress. One of his projects was the Domestic Steel Industry Protection Act, which made little progress. It would have required the government to set a "trigger price" for imported steel, and if the Japanese — specifically mentioned in the bill — sold any steel in this country at a lower price, the secretary of the Treasury could take action to keep it out.

Atkinson also worked other sides of the steel "dumping" issue. He pressed the Treasury and Commerce departments for information on how much steel the Japanese were currently exporting at low prices, and what fines had been imposed. He has a background on the imports question; he was customs director of the Port of Pittsburgh for seven years.

In the 97th Congress, Atkinson found himself on both sides of the Reagan budget issue. He voted with the Republicans the first time, following a dramatic Reagan telephone call to a radio show on which he was appearing. But he switched and voted against the specific Reagan cuts known as Gramm-Latta II largely because they would sharply restrict industrial rail lines in his district. Atkinson also is opposed to block giants, a basic tenet of Reagan budgeting.

**At Home:** The son of a steelworkers' local president, Atkinson worked his way up through the ranks of Beaver County politics. At one point, he served as both county commissioner and county Democratic chairman. He got his Pittsburgh customs post in 1962, after a timely suggestion to President Kennedy from David Lawrence, Pennsylvania's Democratic governor.

That Kennedy connection may have been part of the reason Atkinson was such a vocal critic of President Carter during 1979 and 1980. He charged that the Carter administration had let down the western Pennsylvania steel industry, and endorsed Edward M. Kennedy in the 1980 Democratic presidential primary.

Atkinson failed in his first bid for Congress in 1976, losing to Republican Gary A. Myers, who had ousted Democrat Frank M. Clark two years previously. Myers ran for re-election as a "clean government" candidate, refused to take political action committee money, and portrayed Atkinson as a tool of union leaders. Atkinson did not come close.

But in 1978, Myers announced he would retire and return to his job as a steel plant foreman. After winning an 11-man Democratic primary, Atkinson barely defeated Republican Tim Shaffer, the Butler County solicitor.

Atkinson was helped by the popularity of his political ally, former Pittsburgh Mayor Pete Flaherty, then the Democratic nominee for governor. As Flaherty had in the city, Atkinson stressed fiscal prudence in county government.

**The District:** Industrial Beaver County dominates the district's politics; it provides almost half of the votes in the 25th, and they are

---

**25th District: West — New Castle.**
Population: 488,814 (3% increase since 1970).
Race: White 471,475 (96%), Black 15,252 (3%), Others 2,087 (0.4%). Spanish origin: 2,096 (0.4%).

normally Democratic votes.

Beaver County's plants concentrate on specialty steel. They have been hurt by steel mill layoffs in the last few years, although less than some of the other counties in the Pittsburgh area. Beaver went comfortably for Jimmy Carter in 1980, at a time when other blue-collar Democratic areas were defecting to the Republicans.

Lawrence County is more marginal in partisan allegiance. It has been hard hit by the closing of steel plants in nearby Youngstown, Ohio, and Carter won it only narrowly.

More rural Butler County and the northern Allegheny County suburbs are also part of the district. Their Republican margins usually are offset by the Democratic votes in Beaver.

## Committees

**Government, Operations** (17th of 23 Democrats)
Commerce, Consumer, and Monetary Affairs; Environment, Energy and Natural Resources; Manpower and Housing.

**Public Works and Transportation** (19th of 25 Democrats)
Aviation; Surface Transportation.

**Select Aging** (23rd of 31 Democrats)
Health and Long-Term Care.

## Elections

**1980 General**

| | |
|---|---|
| Eugene Atkinson (D) | 119,817 (67%) |
| Robert Morris (R) | 58,768 (33%) |

**1980 Primary**

| | |
|---|---|
| Eugene Atkinson (D) | 50,767 (75%) |
| William Kovolenko (D) | 8,706 (13%) |
| Gloriann Burick (D) | 8,041 (12%) |

**1978 General**

| | |
|---|---|
| Eugene Atkinson (D) | 68,293 (47%) |
| Jim Shaffer (R) | 62,160 (42%) |
| Robert Morris (I) | 10,588 (7%) |

**1978 Primary**

| | |
|---|---|
| Eugene Atkinson (D) | 17,044 (25%) |
| Nick Colafella (D) | 9,966 (15%) |
| Jim Ross (D) | 8,606 (13%) |
| Thomas Shumaker (D) | 8,503 (13%) |
| Ralph Pratt ((D) | 6,308 (9%) |
| John Hirt (D) | 6,238 (9%) |

**District Vote For President**

| | 1980 | | 1976 | | 1972 |
|---|---|---|---|---|---|
| **D** | 87,982 (48%) | **D** | 97,466 (53%) | **D** | 67,926 (39%) |
| **R** | 83,765 (45%) | **R** | 84,138 (46%) | **R** | 103,715 (59%) |
| **I** | 10,690 (6%) | | | | |

## Campaign Finance

| | Receipts | Receipts from PACs | Expenditures |
|---|---|---|---|
| **1980** | | | |
| Atkinson (D) | $52,234 | 735 (1%) | $51,196 |
| Morris (R) | $89,727 | $6,800 (8%) | $89,379 |
| **1978** | | | |
| Atkinson (D) | $103,432 | $825 (1 %) | $106,521 |
| Shaffer (R) | $91,432 | $10,245 (11 %) | $91,294 |

## Voting Studies

| | Presidential Support | | Party Unity | | Conservative Coalition | |
|---|---|---|---|---|---|---|
| **Year** | **S** | **O** | **S** | **O** | **S** | **O** |
| **1980** | 51 | 44 | 50 | 48 | 71 | 29 |
| **1979** | 50 | 46 | 44 | 49 | 70 | 28 |

S = Support         O = Opposition

## Key Votes

**96th Congress**

| | |
|---|---|
| Weaken Carter oil profits tax (1979) | N |
| Reject hospital cost control plan (1979) | Y |
| Implement Panama Canal Treaties (1979) | N |
| Establish Department of Education (1979) | Y |
| Approve Anti-busing Amendment (1979) | Y |
| Guarantee Chrysler Corp. loans (1979) | Y |
| Approve military draft registration (1980) | N |
| Aid Sandinista regime in Nicaragua (1980) | N |
| Strengthen fair housing laws (1980) | N |

**97th Congress**

| | |
|---|---|
| Reagan budget proposal (1981) | Y |

## Interest Group Ratings

| Year | ADA | ACA | AFL-CIO | CCUS |
|---|---|---|---|---|
| 1980 | 28 | 42 | 47 | 66 |
| 1979 | 37 | 46 | 75 | 61 |

# Rhode Island

## ...The Democratic Province

Rhode Island is not the most liberal state in the nation but is probably the most Democratic.

In the last decade, Democrats have consistently controlled the governorship and at least 70 percent of the state Legislature. In the last two decades the state supported a GOP presidential candidate only once, in 1972, and in the last 40 years, only two Republicans have been elected to Congress. Sen. John H. Chafee and Rep. Claudine Schneider, both Republicans, owe their victories to their personal skills and divided Democratic opposition.

Republicans have an image problem in Rhode Island. In this heavily Catholic, ethnic, blue-collar state, Republicans are thought of by many as being rich Protestant Yankees. The alignment was shaped by economics and deep-rooted ethnic rivalries. With little space for farming, Rhode Island developed a manufacturing-based economy early in its history. Needing workers for their factories, the Yankee mill owners encouraged a steady stream of immigrants. First the Irish, then French-Canadian, Italian and other ethnics came to Rhode Island's industrial shores during the 19th and early 20th centuries.

Although long a minority, the Yankee Republicans maintained control of the state government until the mid-1930s. But once the Democrats gained power, they kept it. Only the Italians have become a swing vote while others remain loyally Democratic, including the Irish, who occupy many of the leadership positions in the party.

Rhode Island has been buffeted economically in recent generations, first by the loss of much of its textile trade to the Southern states in the 1940s, then by the massive withdrawal of the U.S. Navy in the mid-1970s. The latter devastated the state economy, and in the last decade Rhode Island suffered its first population decline since joining the Union.

The state has begun to recoup by diversifying its economy. From an old manufacturing base dependent on the production of textiles, metals and jewelry, Rhode Island has made a major bid to attract high technology firms. Industrial parks

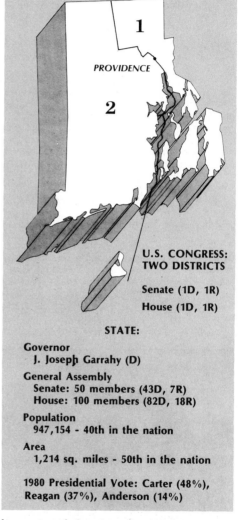

**U.S. CONGRESS: TWO DISTRICTS**

Senate (1D, 1R)

House (1D, 1R)

**STATE:**

**Governor**
J. Joseph Garrahy (D)

**General Assembly**
Senate: 50 members (43D, 7R)
House: 100 members (82D, 18R)

**Population**
947,154 - 40th in the nation

**Area**
1,214 sq. miles - 50th in the nation

1980 Presidential Vote: Carter (48%), Reagan (37%), Anderson (14%)

have sprouted along interstate highways, and the population has been moving out to the suburbs and small towns where the new jobs are.

## A Political Tour

**Greater Providence.** Nearly one-half of the population of Rhode Island lives in Providence and the towns that surround it. Providence, the state capital, remains the largest city in Rhode Island and a leading Democratic stronghold. But the city is losing its economic might to the suburbs and has steadily lost population since World War II. From a high of 268,000 in 1925, the population was down to 157,000 by 1980. As blue-collar ethnics have departed, the minority population has increased, with blacks and Hispanics making up a fifth of the city's population in 1980.

Just south of Providence along Interstates 95 and 295 are Cranston and Warwick. Both have been favorite sites for the recent development of shopping malls and new industries.

The eastern half of Cranston, abutting Providence, is indistinguishable from its neighbor. The western half is more suburban. Warwick, located to the south, is emerging as Rhode Island's leading retail center and is a separate entity away from the Providence orbit.

With a significant white-collar population — especially in Warwick — both cities are swing areas in the few closely contested statewide races.

**Blackstone Valley.** For nearly two centuries, Rhode Island's once flourishing textile industry has been centered in the Blackstone River Valley. A highly industrialized region about 15 miles long, it is anchored on the south by Pawtucket and on the north by Woonsocket, the predominantly French-Canadian, wool-manufacturing city along the Massachusetts border.

The valley is heavily ethnic and blue-collar. Although conservative on social issues, the French-Canadian and Irish voters are loyal Democrats. In 1972, three of the four cities and towns George McGovern carried in Rhode Island were in the Blackstone Valley — Central Falls, Pawtucket and Woonsocket.

**The Coastal Counties.** Rhode Island's southern flank along the ocean is split by Narragansett Bay. Although the region has two distinct parts, both are more rural, Yankee and Republican than the rest of the state.

On the west side of the bay is Washington County, which grew faster than any other part of the state in the last decade (9 percent). The growth rate would have been higher except that the population dropped by more than one-quarter in North Kingston, the site of two major naval facilities that closed in the 1970s.

Naval closings also battered the economy in Newport County on the East Bay, with Newport losing 15 percent of its population and Middletown losing 41 percent since 1970. Newport has survived by polishing its resort image.

# Redrawing the Line

During the past decade, population declined 2.6 percent in the 1st District and grew 2.1 percent in the 2nd. As a result, redistricters will move the line to the west far enough to transfer about 10,000 people into the poorer 1st District.

# Governor
# J. Joseph Garrahy (D)

**Born:** Nov. 26, 1930, Providence, R.I.
**Home:** Narragansett, R.I.
**Education:** U. of Rhode Island, U. of Buffalo.
**Military Career:** Air Force, Korean conflict.
**Profession:** Brewery sales representative.
**Family:** Wife, Margherite; five children.
**Religion:** Roman Catholic.
**Political Career:** Rhode Island Senate, 1963-69; lieutenant governor, 1969-77; State Democratic party chairman, 1967-68; elected governor 1976, 1978, 1980; term expires Jan. 1983.

# Claiborne Pell (D)

**Of Newport — Elected 1960**

**Born:** Nov. 22, 1918, New York, N.Y.
**Education:** Princeton U., A.B. 1940; Columbia
U., A.M. 1946.
**Military Career:** Coast Guard, 1941-45.
**Profession:** Investment executive.
**Family:** Wife, Nuala O'Donnell; four children.
**Religion:** Episcopalian.
**Political Career:** No previous office.

**In Washington:** This reserved, absent-minded socialite seems an incongruous spokes-man for blue-collar Rhode Island, but he has managed to play the role with political success while pursuing his personal interests in higher education, diplomacy and the arts.

Before the Republican takeover of the Senate in 1981, Pell was chairman of the Education Subcommittee of the Labor and Human Resources Committee. He was the dominant Senate voice on education issues. He also stood to become Foreign Relations chairman in the 97th Congress if the Democrats had kept control.

That accumulation of power was primarily the result of seniority. Pell possesses no notable flair for internal Senate politics or behind-the-scenes dealing with his colleagues. His aristocratic demeanor — he is the scion of a very old and wealthy family — can sometimes come across as aloofness or arrogance. Although his voting record on social and economic issues is consistently liberal, he often displays a kind of patrician distance from the concerns of ordinary folk, or even from the clubby camaraderie of the Senate.

But Pell is a proud and tenacious man who can be a very formidable critic — as Ronald Berman, former director of the National Endowment for the Humanities found out. In a controversy that attracted widespread attention in the arts community, Pell and Berman disagreed over the way NEH grants should be distributed.

Accusing Berman of elitism, Pell argued that the money should be handed out at the local level, where average citizens would have a better chance of winning a grant. Berman's defenders responded that Pell was engaging in a personal vendetta. The dispute engendered antagonism toward Pell among some writers and artists; Berman eventually lost his job.

Federal support for the arts is a personal issue for Pell, part of his interest in education in general. He has had a substantial impact on the way higher education is financed in America.

Pell's chief accomplishment was a change in federal education law that has benefited millions of low- and middle-income college students. In 1972 he pushed through, over the opposition of the House and the indifference of much of the higher education community, legislation establishing the Basic Educational Opportunity Grants (BEOG).

BEOGs quickly became the cornerstone of federal aid to students. The program marked a basic shift in policy, because it provided aid directly to students, instead of channeling it through the institutions, as early aid programs had done. The BEOG program was renamed "Pell grants" in 1980. While Pell did not publicly push for the change, associates say he sought it in private.

But 1980 was also the year of Pell's worst defeat in education legislation. The Senate rejected the conference report on the higher education reauthorization bill he had managed. Critics insisted its estimated $50-billion five-year price tag was too high. Stung by the defeat, Pell was careful to satisfy the objections before he came back with a revised second version. The second conference report, reduced in cost by about $1.4 billion, finally became law.

As a member of the Foreign Relations Committee, Pell has worked hard over the years on issues dealing with the oceans. He has been involved in the international Law of the Sea Conference, still in negotiation after nearly a decade. He was the author of a treaty, approved by Congress and ratified by numerous countries, which prohibits the placement of weapons on the ocean floor. Another Pell treaty prohibits the use of environmental modification weapons.

Pell has also taken a leading role in legislation involving the United Nations and the foreign service. He served in the foreign service himself, in Eastern Europe, and takes pride in his knowledge of the area's politics.

He has been interested in the eastern Mediterranean, and has repeatedly sponsored increases in aid to Cyprus. A strong partisan of Greece in its conflict with Turkey, he opposed the end of the embargo on arms shipments to Turkey in 1978.

Pell was not a major player when Foreign Relations debated the SALT II arms limitation treaty in 1979. He was a strong supporter of the treaty during hearings, but never developed more than a general acquaintance with it.

In the 97th Congress, with the defeat of Idaho Democrat Frank Church, Pell became the ranking Democrat on Foreign Relations. In that position, he has found himself in frequent alliance with Republican Chairman Charles H. Percy against the more conservative Republicans on the committee. Neither Pell nor Percy has been entirely successful at promoting the concept of a bipartisan foreign policy, but they have had some successes — notably the effort in June to block the nomination of Ernest Lefever as assistant secretary of state for human rights. Levever had been accused of insensitivity in human rights cases.

Pell has shown little interest in recent years in the Rules Committee, even though he chaired it during the 96th Congress. He took little active part in the panel's main work, considering measures to change Senate procedures. Majority Leader Robert C. Byrd, D-W.Va., also a committee member, handled the efforts to establish rules more favorable to the Democratic leadership.

**At Home:** Far from resenting Pell's privileged background, his blue-collar constituents have handed him landslide victories three out of four times. Only Republican John H. Chafee, now his Senate colleague, has been able to hold him under 60 percent of the vote.

Pell's pro-labor voting record has kept him in the good graces of the unions, always a potent force in Rhode Island. And while he does not have much personal rapport with the state's ethnic voters, he can communicate with them: he speaks Portuguese, Italian and French.

Pell's father, Herbert, was a Democrat who briefly represented Manhattan's Silk Stocking District in the House and served as a foreign envoy for Franklin D. Roosevelt. Claiborne Pell was born in New York, but he spent summers in the exclusive Rhode Island resort of Newport, where the Pells had been going for five generations. The family moved there permanently when

he was nine.

Following his graduation from Princeton in 1940, Pell went to Europe to try and help concentration camp inmates. The Nazis arrested him several times. He was a Coast Guard officer during World War II, and spent several years in the foreign service, stationed at the United Nations, in Czechoslovakia and Italy. Later, while working as an investment banker and publisher, he dabbled in politics, at one point serving as registration chairman for the Democratic National Committee.

Pell decided to run himself in 1960 and stunned the political community by overwhelming two former governors, Dennis J. Roberts and J. Howard McGrath, to win the Democratic nomination for the Senate. In the fall, he crushed Republican Raoul Archambault, former assistant U.S. budget director, to win his Senate seat. One of Pell's advantages that year was his relationship with John F. Kennedy, who was very popular in Rhode Island. Pell's wife, Nuala, campaigned for Kennedy in West Virginia.

Running for a second term in 1966, Pell had an equally easy time with his GOP opponent — a retired Women's Army Corps officer named Ruth M. Briggs, who insisted upon being called "colonel." She sought to make an issue out of his dovish line on the Vietnam War and to portray him as a wealthy dilettante, calling Pell "the prize entertainer of the Kennedys." But like Archambault, she failed to draw even a third of the vote.

Chafee, seeking a political comeback in 1972 after serving as Navy secretary in the Nixon administration, provided the only serious Republican opposition Pell has ever had. Starting far ahead in the polls, Chafee linked Pell to fellow anti-war Sen. George McGovern, the Democratic presidential nominee. But Pell, sensitive about the Navy's large influence in Rhode Island, deflected this by repudiating McGovern's call for cutting the defense budget. And Chafee was still carrying some of the liabilities of his support for a state income tax, which helped defeat him in his campaign for re-election as governor in 1968. As a moderate Republican, Chafee never managed to come up with a compelling reason for an overwhelmingly Democratic state to turn out an incumbent Democrat. Pell won by 32,000 votes.

Things were back to normal for Pell in 1978, when he buried Republican James G. Reynolds, a little-known bakery executive who complained that the senator was more interested in the arts than in saving jobs for Rhode Island.

## Committees

**Foreign Relations** (Ranking Democrat)

**Labor and Human Resources** (4th of 7 Democrats)
Education; Employment and Productivity.

**Rules and Administration** (3rd of 5 Democrats)

**Joint Library**

## Elections

**1978 General**

| | |
|---|---|
| Claiborne Pell (D) | 229,557 (75%) |
| James Reynolds (R) | 76,061 (25%) |

**1978 Primary**

| | |
|---|---|
| Claiborne Pell (D) | 69,729 (87%) |
| Raymond Greiner (D) | 6,076 (8%) |

**Previous Winning Percentages**

1972 (54 %)    1966 (68 %)    1960 (69 %)

## Campaign Finance

| | Receipts | Receipts from PACs | Expenditures |
|---|---|---|---|
| 1978 | | | |
| Pell (D) | $398,898 | $75,945 (19%) | $373,077 |
| Reynolds (R) | $85,615 | $5,650 (7%) | $85,614 |

## Voting Studies

| | Presidential Support | | Party Unity | | Conservative Coalition | |
|---|---|---|---|---|---|---|
| Year | S | O | S | O | S | O |
| 1980 | 69 | 16 | 73 | 10 | 19 | 65 |
| 1979 | 77 | 12 | 77 | 12 | 16 | 66 |
| 1978 | 85 | 7 | 84 | 9 | 9 | 83 |
| 1977 | 77 | 17 | 80 | 13 | 13 | 84 |
| 1976 | 34 | 51 | 79 | 12 | 19 | 70 |
| 1975 | 41 | 52 | 86 | 6 | 7 | 84 |
| 1974 (Ford) | 37 | 57 | | | | |
| 1974 | 31 | 64 | 87 | 10 | 6 | 91 |
| 1973 | 41 | 56 | 85 | 8† | 11 | 83† |
| 1972 | 26 | 48 | 68 | 5 | 5 | 60 |
| 1971 | 34 | 48 | 78 | 15 | 17 | 76 |
| 1970 | 44 | 34 | 65 | 10 | 9 | 64 |

| | | | | | | |
|---|---|---|---|---|---|---|
| 1969 | 51 | 42 | 76 | 17 | 12 | 81 |
| 1968 | 65 | 21 | 63 | 18 | 10 | 77 |
| 1967 | 69 | 20 | 78 | 10 | 9 | 77 |
| 1966 | 75 | 15 | 86 | 3 | 3 | 94 |
| 1965 | 73 | 12 | 83 | 6 | 8 | 85 |
| 1964 | 69 | 16 | 73 | 18 | 6 | 78 |
| 1963 | 80 | 13 | 84 | 9 | 9 | 90 |
| 1962 | 79 | 10 | 84 | 8 | 21 | 76 |
| 1961 | 77 | 16 | 85 | 11 | 6 | 94 |

S = Support          O = Opposition
† Not eligible for all recorded votes.

## Key Votes

**96th Congress**

| | |
|---|---|
| Maintain relations with Taiwan (1979) | N |
| Reduce synthetic fuel development funds (1979) | N |
| Impose nuclear plant moratorium (1979) | Y |
| Kill stronger windfall profits tax (1979) | N |
| Guarantee Chrysler Corp. loans (1979) | N |
| Approve military draft registration (1980) | + |
| End Revenue Sharing to the states (1980) | Y |
| Block Justice Dept. busing suits (1980) | N |

**97th Congress**

| | |
|---|---|
| Restore urban program funding cuts (1981) | Y |

## Interest Group Ratings

| Year | ADA | ACA | AFL-CIO | CCUS-1 | CCUS-2 |
|---|---|---|---|---|---|
| 1980 | 78 | 10 | 94 | 32 | |
| 1979 | 68 | 8 | 100 | 0 | 27 |
| 1978 | 75 | 4 | 89 | 19 | |
| 1977 | 80 | 8 | 80 | 11 | |
| 1976 | 90 | 0 | 88 | 0 | |
| 1975 | 89 | 0 | 91 | 19 | |
| 1974 | 86 | 6 | 80 | 0 | |
| 1973 | 80 | 7 | 100 | 0 | |
| 1972 | 75 | 16 | 88 | 0 | |
| 1971 | 89 | 23 | 75 | - | |
| 1970 | 84 | 5 | 100 | 0 | |
| 1969 | 94 | 7 | 91 | - | |
| 1968 | 79 | 14 | 100 | - | |
| 1967 | 92 | 0 | 100 | 20 | |
| 1966 | 90 | 4 | 100 | - | |
| 1965 | 94 | 4 | - | 10 | |
| 1964 | 93 | 0 | 100 | - | |
| 1963 | - | 4 | - | - | |
| 1962 | 83 | 11 | 100 | - | |
| 1961 | 100 | - | - | - | |

# John H. Chafee (R)

## Of Warwick — Elected 1976

**Born:** Oct. 22, 1922, Providence, R.I.
**Education:** Yale U., B.A. 1947; Harvard U., LL.B. 1950.
**Military Career:** Marine Corps, 1942-46, 1950-52.
**Profession:** Lawyer.
**Family:** Wife, Virginia Coates; five children.
**Religion:** Episcopalian.
**Political Career:** R.I. House, 1957-63, minority leader, 1959-63; Governor of R.I., 1963-69; unsuccessful Republican nominee for governor, 1968; unsuccessful Republican nominee for U.S. Senate, 1972.

**In Washington:** The only member of his party elected to the Senate from Rhode Island in the last 50 years, Chafee has not been particularly comfortable with the New Right approach of most of his junior GOP colleagues.

It was Chafee who offered the best-organized challenge to the Reagan budget cuts in March of 1981, drawing 40 votes with his amendment to restore $1 billion to the budget for primary education, mass transit, low-income fuel assistance, and other urban oriented programs. The White House was sufficiently worried to send Vice President Bush to the Senate in case he was needed to break a tie. Not long afterward, Chafee found himself in mostly-Democratic company on a new list of senators being considered for challenge in 1982 by the National Conservative Political Action Committee. Chafee had originally been targeted by NCPAC in November of 1980.

But notwithstanding all that, there is a considerable amount of orthodox Republicanism in Chafee's record. On the Finance Committee, he is a frequent voice for business, not only in New England but nationally. He has backed accelerated depreciation of business property and pushed to assist U.S. exporters by enacting tax breaks for Americans who work abroad. As a new member of the Banking Committee in the 97th Congress, he proposed amendments to the Foreign Corrupt Practices Act to make it easier for American firms to increase foreign sales.

Chafee has been traditional enough in his economic thinking, in fact, to publicly criticize the supply-side economics of the Reagan administration, arguing that spending reductions are generally necessary but that the massive Kemp-Roth tax cut would be inflationary. He did vote, however, for a Reagan-backed tax cut similar to Kemp-Roth when the Finance Committee considered it in June of 1981.

Chafee chose to join Finance in 1979 despite a public pledge to take the first available seat on Armed Services, where he said he would try to regain some of the naval installations Rhode Island lost under President Nixon. When the choice had to be made, Chafee thought about the importance of energy and tax issues to Rhode Island, and went back on his pledge.

As a member of Finance, Chafee has tried to balance fiscal conservatism, Republican loyalties, and his state's dependence on federal help. He was the only Republican on the committee to support President Carter's hospital cost control bill, which it defeated, 11-9. He also sought unsuccessfully to increase the basic rate on the oil windfall profits tax, which was passed in 1980.

Some of Chafee's efforts at fiscal conservatism have been carried out with an eye toward publicity in Rhode Island. The best example of that was a campaign he mounted with Republican John Danforth of Missouri — perhaps his closest ally — to try and halt construction of the new Hart Senate Office Building, which he derided as a "palace."

Chafee and Danforth tried on various occasions in 1978 and 1979 to block construction, even after the foundation had been dug and the steel frame was being erected. The effort nearly succeeded in July 1979, failing on a series of close procedural votes. "Is it right," Chafee asked rhetorically, "to proceed with this and then tell the public to save and to cut inflation . . . for us to say, 'You peasants out there must save, but not us?'"

That was criticized as demaguery by some of Chafee's colleagues, who claimed he knew the building would be built in any case. But the Rhode Island press more than made up for any criticism by giving him extensive and favorable coverage.

On the Environment and Public Works Committee, his second assignment, Chafee has been a consistent voice for environmental protection. Here too, he has demonstrated his willingness to take on formidable opponents, as he did in 1979, when he opposed Republican leader Howard Baker's plea to modify the endangered species law and build the Tellico Dam in Tennessee, which threatened the existence of the tiny snail darter fish.

Chafee also fought influential Southern colleagues with his campaign to stop the Tennessee-Tombigbee waterway in Mississippi and Alabama, a 232-mile inland barge passage for the Southeast, opposing it because of its projected multibillion-dollar cost, and on environmental grounds.

He has been less than sympathetic to exemptions for industry from hazardous waste controls. He supported strong legislation to establish a "superfund" financed by the oil and chemical industries to clean up poisons in the environment.

In foreign policy, Chafee generally has deferred to the wishes of both Carter and Reagan. He voted in favor of such Carter initiatives as ratification of the Panama Canal treaties, the sale of F-15 aircraft to Saudi Arabia and the lifting of the 1974 arms embargo against Turkey. He argued that the arms embargo had to be repealed to regain valuable U.S. posts on Turkish soil that had been used to listen in on the Soviet Union. Turkey had expelled the United States from those posts when the arms embargo was imposed.

Chafee's concern about the loss of those intelligence stations was related to his work on the Intelligence Committee, where he has been a firm friend of the CIA. The CIA director during the Carter years, Admiral Stansfield Turner, was one of Chafee's top aides when Chafee was secretary of the Navy.

Decrying assaults on CIA agents abroad who have been exposed by agency critics, Chafee has been the primary sponsor of legislation that would make it a federal crime to disclose the identity of a U.S. secret agent. He also has sponsored legislation to exempt the CIA from portions of the Freedom of Information Act, which he complains has allowed foreigners to harass the agency and get information from it.

**At Home:** Chafee's moderate-to-liberal record has enabled him to survive 20 years of politics in what is probably the nation's most Democratic state, winning most of the time and recovering easily from defeat.

A Harvard-trained lawyer, he served as state House minority leader in the early 1960s — when there was still a respectable minority to lead in Rhode Island. He ran for governor in 1962, and won by 398 votes over Democrat John A. Notte Jr., who had damaged himself by advocating a state income tax — the same issue that was to cause Chafee trouble six years later.

As a three-term governor in the 1960's, Chafee pushed for an increase in Rhode Island's social and welfare spending, calling it "a state version of the Great Society." He won re-election easily in 1964 despite a miserable Rhode Island showing by Barry Goldwater, and despite the Democratic candidate's charge that Chafee, a graduate of Deerfield and Yale, did not know "what it is like to hang around a street corner all summer long without a job."

Chafee was an easy winner again in 1966. Two years later, however, running aganst Democrat Frank Licht, he got caught on the wrong side of what turned out to be a referendum on state taxes. Chafee insisted an income tax was necessary to prevent a massive boost in the sales tax. Licht disagreed, and upset Chafee by 7,808 votes.

After his defeat, Chafee was appointed Navy secretary in the Nixon administration. That seemed likely to help the 1972 Senate campaign he was planning against Democratic Sen. Claiborne Pell. And when he left the Pentagon to begin the campaign, he seemed a likely winner.

But it did not turn out that way. Pell has always been accused of aloofness, but he knew what to do that year, purchasing superb television advertising and speaking a collection of European languages to voters in the ethnic neighborhoods of Providence and the mill towns. And the old tax issue was still a partial liability for Chafee. Even the rare Republican presidential victory in Rhode Island that fall did not help him. Pell was re-elected by 32,000 votes.

That might have been the end of Chafee's political career, had Democrats not managed to do everything but throw the state's other Senate seat at him in 1976 by fighting with each other all year.

Gov. Philip W. Noel was the front-runner for the Democratic nomination, but he crippled himself by making comments in a wire service interview that sounded like racial slurs. He had to resign as the party's national platform chairman, and went on to lose the Senate primary by 100 votes to Cadillac dealer Richard P. Lorber, who spent lavishly of his own money and accused Noel not only of racial insensitivity but of bossism.

Noel then refused to back Lorber in the general election, allowing Chafee to resurrect his old coalition of the early 1960s — Republicans, independents and dissident Democrats. Lorber tried to paint the well-to-do Chafee as an elitist, but that did not wash. Chafee won every town in the state except one.

## Committees

**Banking, Housing and Urban Affairs** (7th of 8 Republicans)
Consumer Affairs, chairman; Economic Policy; International Finance and Monetary Policy.

**Environment and Public Works** (4th of 9 Republicans)
Environmental Pollution, chairman; Regional and Community Development; Transportation.

**Finance** (5th of 11 Republicans)
Savings, Pensions, and Investment Policy, chairman; International Trade; Taxation and Development.

**Select Intelligence** (3rd of 8 Republicans)
Collection and Foreign Operations, chairman; Legislation and the Rights of Americans.

## Elections

**1976 General**

| | |
|---|---|
| John Chafee (R) | 230,329 (58%) |
| Richard Lorber (D) | 167,665 (42%) |

## Campaign Finance

| | Receipts | Receipts from PACs | Expenditures |
|---|---|---|---|
| **1976** | | | |
| Chafee (R) | 424,463 | 57,984 (14%) | 415,651 |
| Lorber (D) | 782,663 | 38,100 (5%) | 782,931 |

## Voting Studies

| | Presidential Support | | Party Unity | | Conservative Coalition | |
|---|---|---|---|---|---|---|
| Year | S | O | S | O | S | O |
| 1980 | 76 | 16 | 38 | 56 | 34 | 63 |
| 1979 | 78 | 17 | 38 | 53 | 26 | 63 |
| 1978 | 78 | 13 | 29 | 65 | 29 | 65 |
| 1977 | 56 | 26 | 53 | 34 | 61 | 29 |

S = Support          O = Opposition

## Key Votes

**96th Congress**

| | |
|---|---|
| Maintain relations with Taiwan (1979) | N |
| Reduce synthetic fuel development funds (1979) | Y |
| Impose nuclear plant moratorium (1979) | Y |
| Kill stronger windfall profits tax (1979) | Y |
| Guarantee Chrysler Corp. loans (1979) | N |
| Approve military draft registration (1980) | Y |
| End Revenue Sharing to the states (1980) | Y |
| Block Justice Dept. busing suits (1980) | N |

**97th Congress**

| | |
|---|---|
| Restore urban program funding cuts (1981) | Y |

## Interest Group Ratings

| Year | ADA | ACA | AFL-CIO | CCUS-1 | CCUS-2 |
|---|---|---|---|---|---|
| 1980 | 72 | 29 | 63 | 55 | |
| 1979 | 47 | 22 | 59 | 33 | 57 |
| 1978 | 55 | 26 | 63 | 47 | |
| 1977 | 45 | 24 | 44 | 56 | |

# 1 Fernand J. St Germain (D)

**Of Woonsocket — Elected 1960**

**Born:** Jan. 9, 1928, Blackstone, Mass.
**Education:** Providence College, Ph.B. 1948; Boston U., LL.B. 1955.
**Military Career:** Army, 1949-52.
**Profession:** Lawyer.
**Family:** Wife, Rachel O'Neill; two children.
**Religion:** Roman Catholic.
**Political Career:** Rhode Island House, 1953-61.

**In Washington:** After more than 20 years in the House, St Germain is still a mystery even to some of the members who work most closely with him. Even before he took over the full Banking Committee in 1981, he dominated key banking bills through his Financial Institutions Subcommittee. But he has always been a legislative loner, making many of the key moves on his own and consulting few colleagues.

St Germain rarely mixes in areas outside his specialty, avoids the politics of the House and maintains few social contacts with his colleagues. A flashy dresser who wears a miniature saint in his lapel, St Germain is easily noticed on the floor when he is there. But he is there very little.

It is generally agreed that he has mastered one of the most difficult of all legislative areas in the years since he took over the Financial Institutions Subcommittee in 1971. Through several difficult legislative fights, he has steered his way past competing segments of the banking community without leaving many clues about his own personal beliefs.

St Germain met with mixed success in the 96th Congress as he managed the massive banking deregulation bill that was enacted after a year of wrangling. His top priority — allowing all banks to pay interest on checking accounts — became law. St Germain called this "the most innovative consumer benefit in recent memory." But the bill also contained a provision St Germain was less happy about. That was the phase-out of "Regulation Q," which allowed savings and loan institutions to pay higher interest on savings than banks were allowed to pay.

In the previous Congress, St Germain found the political levers he needed to win approval of a different banking bill just hours before both chambers adjourned. That bill was aimed at ending the questionable banking practices that had come to light after the highly publicized failure of several large banks during the 1970s. The issue was brought into focus by the controversy surrounding Bert Lance, who was forced to resign as President Carter's budget director following questions about his private banking conduct.

Among other reforms, this 1978 legislation limited the amount of money banks could loan out to their officers and stockholders, and prevented competing banks within one community from having interlocking directorates. St Germain worked on many of these issues for more than a year, then tacked most of his 260-page bill onto a minor piece of Senate-passed legislation and got it through the House at 2:30 a.m. on the last night of the session.

After that, he raced across the Capitol to the Senate, where he had to talk Indiana Democrat Birch Bayh out of adding an unrelated health amendment that would have unraveled the compromise. St Germain prevailed, the Senate passed the bank legislation shortly before sunrise, and Congress went home.

One consistent current in St Germain's record is his interest in the consumer movement. He was the main sponsor of the National Consumer Cooperative Bank, set up in 1979 to make loans to consumer co-ops. He backed creation of a Consumer Protection Agency even after support for it had generally faded away, and voted for it

---

**1st District: East — eastern Providence, Pawtucket.** Population: 462,912 (3% decrease since 1970). Race: White 441,277 (95%), Black 11,367 (2%), Others 10,268 (2%). Spanish origin: 9,069 (2%).

## Fernand J. St Germain, D-R.I.

several times on the Government Operations Committee, his second assignment. He drafted a bill earlier in his career requiring more elaborate statements by creditors when imposing a finance charge on customers. St Germain has also used his senior position on the Banking Committee's Housing Subcommittee to blanket his district with housing projects for the elderly.

In the 97th Congress, St Germain tried in vain to protect housing programs from the Reagan budget ax. In a parliamentary sleight of hand, he had his committee add a 1-year housing extension to legislation cutting $9.1 billion as required in the belt-tightening budget process. But the St Germain plan went down to defeat along with all other House Democratic committee proposals when conservative Democrats joined Republicans to approve an alternative overall budget more to Reagan's taste.

On social issues, St Germain has always reflected some of the more conservative views of his blue-collar constituency. He sponsored a resolution that created a Federal Commission on Obscenity and Pornography, but labeled the commission's majority report a "travesty of decency" because it took a relatively permissive position. He has voted for strong anti-abortion language whenever the issue has come up. St Germain once inserted in the *Congressional Record* an article entitled "In Defense of Large Families."

**At Home:** St Germain has spent virtually his entire adult life in public office. He was elected to the state Legislature at age 24, while still a student, and eight years later he was in Congress.

St Germain came up through the machine politics that is now fading in most big cities. But his constituent service is as good as the latest techniques of the 70s generation, and he has steered millions of dollars worth of federal funds into his district. He has the further advantage of his ethnic background — he is half French and half Ukrainian, and speaks both languages fluently.

All these assets have enabled St Germain to weather a diverse range of charges over the years. One challenger referred to him as a "phantom congressman" with an inadequate attendance record. Others have called him a pawn of banks and have questioned his sources of outside income. But nobody has been able to touch him.

St Germain won his seat rather easily in 1960, when the district was opened by the retirement of veteran Democrat Aime Forand. With the endorsement of the Democratic state committee, he swept the crowded primary with 52 percent of the vote. In the general election, he swamped his Republican opponent by a margin of 2-to-1.

Since then, St Germain has rarely drawn that large a share of the vote. In seven of 10 re-election campaigns, he has won with between 56 and 63 percent. But he has not attracted serious competition in Democratic primaries.

St Germain's only real primary challenge was in 1966, when he was opposed by Eugene Gallant, a former member of the state executive council. Gallant, of French ancestry like St Germain, charged the incumbent with being a rubber stamp for President Johnson's programs. With the slogan, "A Voice, Not An Echo," Gallant held St Germain to 57 percent of the primary vote.

There has been no comparable contest since then, although in the fall of 1977 St Germain was buffeted by allegations in the Providence *Journal-Bulletin* that he played "dirty tricks" on his 1976 opponents.

The newspaper claimed that St Germain had hired a private investigator to gather information on the private lives of his Democratic primary opponent, Norman J. Jacques, and his Republican challenger, John J. Slocum Jr. Much of the information reportedly was kept in St Germain's congressional office in Washington.

St Germain denied the charges, claiming they were "contrived, conspiratorial allegations" manufactured by the *Journal-Bulletin* and his 1976 opponents. The subject was effectively neutralized in 1978 when it was disclosed that Slocum's wealthy mother had paid an investigative reporter to gather information on St Germain.

**The District:** The 1st has not elected a Republican to Congress since 1938, and has rarely supported one for governor or national office.

There is some limited Republican strength in coastal towns and small communities like Barrington and Lincoln, within commuting distance of Providence. The rest of the district is consistently Democratic, with the industrial Blackstone Valley stretching north from Pawtucket to Woonsocket often providing the heaviest majorities.

## Committees

**Banking, Finance and Urban Affairs** (Chairman)
Financial Institutions Supervision, Regulation and Insurance, chairman; Consumer Affairs and Coinage; Economic Stabilization; Housing and Community Development; International Trade, Investment and Monetary Policy.

## Elections

**1980 General**

| | |
|---|---|
| Fernand St Germain (D ) | 120,756 (68 %) |
| William Montgomery (R ) | 57,844 (32 %) |

**1980 Primary**

| | |
|---|---|
| Fernand St Germain (D ) | 23,105 (79 %) |
| Alfred Rocha (D ) | 6,121 (21 %) |

**1978 General**

| | |
|---|---|
| Fernand St Germain (D ) | 86,768 (61 %) |
| John Slocum Jr. (R ) | 54,912 (39 %) |

**Previous Winning Percentages**

| | | | |
|---|---|---|---|
| 1976 (63 %) | 1974 (73 %) | 1972 (62 %) | 1970 (61 %) |
| 1968 (60 %) | 1966 (57 %) | 1964 (66 %) | 1962 (57 %) |
| 1960 (66 %) | | | |

**District Vote For President**

| | 1980 | | 1976 | | 1972 |
|---|---|---|---|---|---|
| D | 96,144 (48 %) | D | 113,522 (57 %) | D | 98,881 (48 %) |
| R | 73,003 (37 %) | R | 85,061 (43 %) | R | 107,156 (52 %) |
| I | 28,725 (14 %) | | | | |

## Campaign Finance

| | Receipts | Receipts from PACs | Expen-ditures |
|---|---|---|---|
| **1980** | | | |
| St Germain (D ) | $135,011 | $76,241 (56 %) | $44,418 |
| **1978** | | | |
| St Germain (D ) | $135,357 | $57,875 (43 %) | $125,013 |
| Slocum (R ) | $98,944 | $50 (-0%) | $98,082 |

## Voting Studies

| Year | Presidential Support S | Presidential Support O | Party Unity S | Party Unity O | Conservative Coalition S | Conservative Coalition O |
|---|---|---|---|---|---|---|
| 1980 | 62 | 23 | 74 | 11 | 19 | 60 |
| 1979 | 75 | 20 | 78 | 12 | 19 | 73 |
| 1978 | 65 | 25 | 74 | 14 | 17 | 70 |
| 1977 | 57 | 16 | 71 | 15 | 17 | 69 |
| 1976 | 24 | 71 | 84 | 4 | 14 | 74 |
| 1975 | 31 | 65 | 84 | 10 | 14 | 79 |
| 1974 (Ford) | 43 | 52 | | | | |
| 1974 | 45 | 53 | 80 | 12 | 21 | 71 |
| 1973 | 26 | 62 | 81 | 11 | 13 | 81 |
| 1972 | 49 | 38 | 76 | 11 | 17 | 74 |
| 1971 | 40 | 56 | 84 | 12 | 17 | 79 |
| 1970 | 57 | 28 | 71 | 4 | - | 64 |
| 1969 | 43 | 47 | 78 | 7 | 7 | 82 |
| 1968 | 73 | 9 | 84 | 9 | 6 | 82 |
| 1967 | 81 | 7 | 87 | 3 | 4 | 93 |
| 1966 | 79 | 5 | 85 | 4 | 0 | 86 |
| 1965 | 83 | 9 | 81 | 8 | 2 | 90 |
| 1964 | 73 | 10 | 66 | 8 | 0 | 92 |
| 1963 | 82 | 6 | 83 | 3 | 7 | 60 |
| 1962 | 87 | 2 | 79 | 2 | 6 | 88 |
| 1961 | 80 | 6 | 78 | 14 | 9 | 87 |

S = Support    O = Opposition

## Key Votes

**96th Congress**

| | |
|---|---|
| Weaken Carter oil profits tax (1979) | N |
| Reject hospital cost control plan (1979) | N |
| Implement Panama Canal Treaties (1979) | Y |
| Establish Department of Education (1979) | Y |
| Approve Anti-busing Amendment (1979) | N |
| Guarantee Chrysler Corp. loans (1979) | Y |
| Approve military draft registration (1980) | ? |
| Aid Sandinista regime in Nicaragua (1980) | Y |
| Strengthen fair housing laws (1980) | Y |

**97th Congress**

| | |
|---|---|
| Reagan budget proposal (1981) | N |

## Interest Group Ratings

| Year | ADA | ACA | AFL-CIO | CCUS |
|---|---|---|---|---|
| 1980 | 78 | 13 | 84 | 45 |
| 1979 | 79 | 12 | 89 | 6 |
| 1978 | 65 | 15 | 85 | 18 |
| 1977 | 75 | 8 | 80 | 29 |
| 1976 | 90 | 4 | 82 | 13 |
| 1975 | 95 | 11 | 95 | 18 |
| 1974 | 78 | 14 | 90 | 0 |
| 1973 | 80 | 8 | 100 | 20 |
| 1972 | 75 | 5 | 91 | 0 |
| 1971 | 84 | 15 | 82 | - |
| 1970 | 72 | 17 | 100 | 0 |
| 1969 | 80 | 27 | 100 | - |
| 1968 | 83 | 4 | 100 | - |
| 1967 | 80 | 7 | 100 | 20 |
| 1966 | 88 | 8 | 92 | - |
| 1965 | 74 | 4 | - | 20 |
| 1964 | 84 | 7 | 100 | - |
| 1963 | - | 6 | - | - |
| 1962 | 100 | 5 | 100 | - |

# 2 Claudine Schneider (R)

Of Narragansett — Elected 1980

**Born:** March 25, 1947, Clairton, Pa.
**Education:** Windham College, B.A. 1969.
**Profession:** Environmental activist; television moderator.
**Family:** Husband, Eric Schneider.
**Religion:** Catholic.
**Political Career:** Unsuccessful Republican nominee for U.S. House, 1978.

**The Member:** The environmental movement was Schneider's springboard into politics; she led the opposition to construction of a nuclear plant near her home. And her first few months in the House brought her a major victory. She and two fellow GOP freshmen persuaded the Science and Technology Committee to delete funds for the Clinch River nuclear breeder reactor.

Schneider attacked the project on economic grounds, saying it had already cost more than twice the original estimates. She called the reactor "a notorious white elephant."

President Carter tried to kill the breeder reactor, largely because it produces plutonium that can be used to make nuclear weapons. But throughout Carter's administration, Congress funded the project. The appeal to cost-consciousness was an effective strategy with members in a budget-cutting mood. Clinch River lost in committee, 18-22, forcing advocates to try to reverse the decision on the floor.

Schneider wanted to run for governor of Rhode Island in 1978, but GOP leaders chose a better-known male to make the race. They offered Schneider the House nomination against Democratic Rep. Edward Beard. She took it, and though little-known and under-financed, showed a flair for publicity that brought her within 9,000 votes of Beard, whom she called ineffective.

Better known and better financed in 1980, she defeated Beard by a margin of 22,000 votes to become the first Republican to win either House district in Rhode Island since 1938.

**The District:** The 2nd covers the western half of the state, but most of its voters live in metropolitan Providence with its ethnic, largely Italian population. Despite Schneider's convincing win, the 2nd is predominantly Democratic.

The district's economy was severely crippled in the mid-1970's when U.S. Navy facilities at Quonset and Davisville departed. But the picture has brightened with the attraction of high technology firms from Massachusetts and oil supply industries for offshore drilling.

## Committees

**Merchant Marine and Fisheries** (14th of 15 Republicans)
Fisheries and Wildlife Conservation and the Environment; Oceanography.

**Science and Technology** (15th of 17 Republicans)
Energy Development and Applications; Natural Resources, Agriculture Research and Environment.

## Elections

**1980 General**

| | |
|---|---|
| Claudine Schneider (R ) | 115,057 (55 %) |
| Edward Beard (D ) | 92,970 (45 %) |

**District Vote For President**

| | 1980 | | 1976 | | 1972 |
|---|---|---|---|---|---|
| D | 100,951 (47 %) | D | 112,877 (54 %) | D | 94,935 (46 %) |
| R | 81,474 (38 %) | R | 95,702 (46 %) | R | 113,072 (54 %) |
| I | 30,641 (14 %) | | | | |

## Campaign Finance

| | Receipts | Receipts from PACs | Expenditures |
|---|---|---|---|
| **1980** | | | |
| Schneider (R ) | $293,167 | $117,501 (40 %) | $289,937 |
| Beard (D ) | $128,190 | $76,000 (59 %) | $126,975 |

## Key Vote

**97th Congress**

| | |
|---|---|
| Reagan budget proposal (1981) | Y |

---

**2nd District: West — western Providence, Warwick.** Population: 484,242 (2% increase since 1970). Race: White 455,415 (94%), Black 16,217 (3%), Others 12,610 (3%). Spanish origin: 10,638 (2%).

# South Carolina

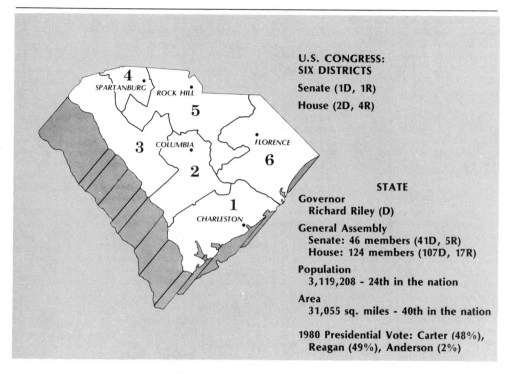

**U.S. CONGRESS:**
**SIX DISTRICTS**

Senate (1D, 1R)

House (2D, 4R)

**STATE**

Governor
  Richard Riley (D)

General Assembly
  Senate: 46 members (41D, 5R)
  House: 124 members (107D, 17R)

Population
  3,119,208 - 24th in the nation

Area
  31,055 sq. miles - 40th in the nation

1980 Presidential Vote: Carter (48%),
  Reagan (49%), Anderson (2%)

## . . . A Two-Party State

It may be only a mild surprise to most people that five of South Carolina's eight members of Congress are Republicans. But it is worth pondering that three of the four once served either in Washington or at the state level as elected Democrats. That is no coincidence. South Carolina was the first Deep South state where conservative conversion to the GOP was not only attractive, but feasible.

South Carolina has been ahead of most of its neighbors in the struggle to move from a rural, race-oriented politics to one of growth and prosperity. Its new identity as a Sun Belt industrial mecca has meant an influx of Yankee corporate managers and a lessening of racial tensions. But it has done more than change the issues in South Carolina politics. It has given the state something most of its Deep South neighbors have not achieved — a functioning two-party system.

While Republicans have been gaining in South Carolina, the growth of the black vote has guaranteed a strong built-in base for Democrats in any statewide election. South Carolina was still 30 percent black in the 1980 census, and this is a factor in every election. It helps explain why Carter came within 12,000 votes of Reagan in the state in 1980, why Republican Gov. James Edwards was replaced in 1978 by a moderate Democratic governor, Richard Riley, and most interesting of all, why Democratic Rep. John W. Jenrette Jr., convicted in an Abscam bribery case, came within 5,000 votes of re-election in the 6th District in 1980. The black population has historically been second only to that of Mississippi among American states. For most of South Carolina's history, that made race the major political issue, symbolized by the demagoguery of governors like Benjamin R. (Pitchfork Ben) Tillman in the 1890s. "I would lead a mob to lynch the Negro who ravishes a white woman," Tillman once said.

But by the 1960s, racial politics conflicted with the climate of peace and harmony that a series of governors hoped would attract business to the state. Although there were serious confrontations in the 1960s and on into the 1970s, South Carolina never developed the reputation that Mississippi and Alabama did. And it was ahead of them in economic growth. The relative racial peace succeeded as a selling card, aided by the state's low union membership (even now just 8 percent of the workforce), and its technical education system. Also helping the economic boom was the late Rep. L. Mendel Rivers, the House Armed Services chairman whose influence brought enormous numbers of defense installations into the state, especially around his district in Charleston.

# A Political Tour

**Coastal Plain.** The low country used to rule the state, and the focus of its power was Charleston, a beautiful, semitropical city of wrought-iron gates, slate roofs and open piazzas. It was the South Carolina capital until 1786, when the state government moved to centrally located Columbia.

Charleston's conservative aristocracy, living in the fabled section "south of Broad Street," controlled the city and the state for decades. The arrival of corporate newcomers from out-of-state and the increasing proportion of blacks in the city have diminished their clout somewhat. Blacks make up almost half Charleston's population.

The upper-income groups lean Republican nowadays, but there are enough blacks and white middle-class Democrats to keep the city itself Democratic. Despite the long rule by the white elite, blacks have had a profound effect on Charleston, best seen in the city's distinctive accent. Derived from the "Gullah Negroes," who were shipped as slaves from Barbados, the accent can be heard from both blue-collar worker and blueblood banker.

In the Charleston suburbs, the GOP has come on strong. North Charleston, with its air force and naval bases, is a Republican bastion, as are the white-collar communities of Hanahan and Summerville.

The beach resort areas up and down the coast from the city have taken a Republican turn, too. To the north stretches the 50-mile Grand Strand, a largely honky-tonk strip. In Beaufort County, to the south, a sizable community of military retirees supplements the Republican affiliation of wealthy year-round residents. Beaufort is the home of Hilton Head Island, an elegantly designed playground for the rich. Life is less comfortable at nearby Parris Island, a Marine training facility.

Inland, the tidewater region becomes much more agricultural, Democratic and black. The low country's white-majority counties split between Reagan and Carter in 1980, while all of the black-majority ones favored Carter.

Blacks have their biggest political pull in the Pee Dee, the northern part of the low country named after the Pee Dee River. The black vote from the area was decisive in winning a hotly contested Democratic primary for Rep. John W. Jenrette Jr. in 1980. It was not quite enough to save the Abscam-tainted congressman from defeat in the general election.

The principal inland Democratic bastion is the city of Florence, the hub of the Pee Dee. It serves the needs of the Democratic farmers from the surrounding countryside and, in addition, contains numerous industrial plants (General Electric, Union Carbide, Du Pont) that employ traditionally Democratic blue-collar workers.

The counties with white majorities — sleepy havens of courthouse politics — are conservative but usually still side with the Democratic Party. George C. Wallace ran well in them in 1968.

**Piedmont.** Socially and culturally, the foothills of the Blue Ridge Mountains are the opposite of the coastal plain. Settled by Calvinistic Scotch-Irish who owned few slaves, the Piedmont traditionally disdained the way of life in what was considered to be "hedonistic Charleston."

The textile industry left the North and settled there, building a manufacturing base that later was enlarged by plants making machinery, ball bearings, tire cord and other such items. The class of plant managers and supervisors forms the core of the Republican Party in this area, and it is here that the GOP has made its greatest gains. But the mills still generate a traditional blue-collar Democratic vote.

Republicans have made inroads in northern York County, which contains suburbs of Charlotte, N.C. The prime Republican county is Greenville, where the party does well in both local and statewide elections. Bob Jones University, a fundamentalist Christian college, provides some of the conservative fervor in Greenville. In 1976, Greenville was one of only three South Carolina counties to back Ford. In 1980, Reagan won the county by a much larger margin than Ford had.

Nearby Spartanburg is a blue-collar town and more Democratic, but it too is changing with the city's aggresive efforts to attract business with a favorable tax climate. The peach farmers in rural Spartanburg County retain a rural Democratic attitude. But they will often vote Republican, as they did in 1980 for Reagan.

Seven of the 12 counties Wallace took in 1968 were in the Piedmont. But Democratic loyalties gave 10 of the area's 14 counties to Carter in 1980.

**Midlands.** At the end of the foothills lies a central corridor separating the two worlds of the Piedmont and the coastal plains.

Popularly called "the Sand Hills," the midlands for years suffered from poor soil and slow economic growth. Many in this pine-forested region relied heavily on the woodpulp industry for their livelihood. But Sun Belt growth has arrived, bringing everything from boat manufacturers to cement makers. From 1975 to 1979, for instance, Lexington County enjoyed $264 million in new plant investment. Textiles thrive there now, also.

As in the Piedmont, the less-developed parts of the midlands are fairly dependable Democratic territory. Carter captured seven of the 12 counties in 1980. All are rural. Similar to the low country, the white-majority counties liked Wallace — Darlington, Chesterfield and Lancaster voted for both Wallace in 1968 and Carter in 1980. Rural black-majority Lee and Fairfield counties went for Carter and, in 1968, Hubert H. Humphrey.

The midlands have developed a Republican vote along Interstate 20 between Columbia, the state capital, and Augusta, Ga. The Aiken County suburbs of Augusta have moved in the GOP's direction, helped by the increasing numbers of military retirees. Significantly, Sen. Thurmond's legal residence now is in Aiken, although he was born in adjacent Edgefield, a more Democratic county. Aiken, a place of large estates and wintering wealthy families from the North, has been called "the Polo Capital of the South."

Another pocket of Republicanism exists in the winter resort town of Camden, north of Columbia. Surrounding Kershaw County has gone Republican for president since 1964, except in 1976 when it opted for Carter by a mere 85 votes.

Lexington County, which enjoys a thriving complement of new businesses, harbors the growing suburbs of Columbia. Lexington and Aiken both went for Ford in 1976.

In Richland County, across the Congaree River from Lexington, is Columbia, the state's second largest city. About 40 percent of its population is black, while only a quarter of the population in surrounding Lexington and Richland counties is black. The desegregation of Columbia's school system in the early 1970's led to white flight to the suburbs. The capital city, which lost more than a tenth of its population in the 1970s, is predictably Democratic. The booming suburbs form the conservative base of support for Republican Rep. Floyd Spence.

# Redrawing the Lines

Population in three districts grew more than 20 percent during the 1970s, and in the three others the expansion was between 13 and 20 percent. But that wasn't quite enough to win South Carolina an extra seat in Congress.

So the Democratic-controlled Legislature focused on moving people out of the 1st and 2nd Districts, where population is above the ideal of 519,868, and bringing counties into the other four districts. By midyear, redistricting committees in the state House and Senate had approved new maps that varied somewhat in the counties they shifted, but did not greatly alter the partisan balance in any district.

---

# Governor
# Richard Riley (D)

**Born:** Jan. 2, 1933, Greenville, S.C.
**Home:** Greenville, S.C.
**Education:** Furman U., A.B. 1954; U. of South Carolina Law School, LL.B. 1959.
**Military Career:** Navy, 1954-56.
**Profession:** Lawyer.
**Family:** Wife, Ann; four children.
**Religion:** Methodist.
**Political Career:** South Carolina House, 1963-67; South Carolina Senate, 1967-77; Jimmy Carter's campaign manager for South Carolina, 1976; elected governor 1978; term expires Jan. 1983.

# Strom Thurmond (R)

**Of Aiken — Elected 1954**
Did not serve April-Nov. 1956.
**Born:** Dec. 5, 1902, Edgefield, S.C.
**Education:** Clemson College, B.S. 1923.
**Military Career:** Army, 1942-46.
**Profession:** Lawyer, judge.
**Family:** Wife, Nancy Moore; four children.
**Religion:** Baptist.
**Political Career:** S.C. Senate, 1933-38; S.C. governor, 1947-51; unsuccessful States Rights nominee for U.S. president, 1948; sought Democratic nomination for U.S. Senate, 1950.

**In Washington:** Thurmond's unique capacity for survival allowed him to return to power in 1981 as the senior senator in the Republican majority, 16 years after he joined the GOP at the lowest point in its modern history.

The 1980 election was not only a personal vindication for Thurmond. It brought tangible rewards — the chairmanship of the Judiciary Committee and the position of president pro tempore of the Senate.

Being president pro tempore is ceremonial, and Democrats who have held it in recent years have largely ignored it. Thurmond relishes it, presiding personally over the opening of the Senate each day.

He is a man of ceremony. He loves playing host to the hordes of South Carolinians who visit his office, cosseting them the way a china collector cares for rare porcelain. He takes them to lunch in the senators' dining room, dragging them from table to table and introducing them to every other senator in the place. He plies them with autographed menus, ashtrays and other mementoes.

It is a part of the constituent service that has allowed Thurmond to make the transition from Dixiecrat to senior Republican in a rapidly changing state without ever losing stride. He always makes sure his state receives a steady flow of federal largess — even if he votes against the programs that provide the money.

For the last decade, as the Voting Rights Act has made blacks an important force in South Carolina politics, black communities and institutions have been conspicuous among the beneficiaries of Thurmond's constituent service and grant-promoting activities. It seems a flat contradiction of his Dixiecrat past, but he insists, "I'm not a racist, and I've done everything I could to help the people of both races throughout my lifetime."

In 1971, Thurmond became the first Southern senator to hire a black professional for his staff — a top-level aide who still runs his state office. A few years later, he sponsored the first black named to a federal judgeship in the South. He has set up scholarships at predominantly black colleges, and he has funneled a small fortune in federal grants to black day care centers, housing projects, and other community recipients.

Meanwhile, Thurmond's voting record has changed scarcely at all since the day in 1957 when he set a filibuster record (still on the books) by speaking against a civil rights bill for 24 hours and 18 minutes. He does not filibuster any more — no one does, in the old-fashioned sense — but he does not vote for civil rights bills either. The closest he has come to casting a "liberal" vote in this area was his 1978 "aye" in favor of a constitutional amendment to grant the mostly-black District of Columbia full voting representation in Congress.

Upon becoming Judiciary chairman in 1981, Thurmond said he might try to revise the landmark civil rights acts of the 1960s — a prospect that truly frightened a Washington liberal community already in despair at the shift in command from the previous chairman, Edward M. Kennedy.

"I'm going to do everything I can to keep the federal government out of jurisdictions that belong to the states," said Thurmond. "I'm not in favor of discrimination, I just don't want the federal government on the backs of the people."

Until 1977, Thurmond devoted most of his legislative attention to the Armed Services Committee, where he has served since he first came to the Senate. Despite his seniority, he has never been one of the leading powers on the committee nor specialized in particular defense issues. But he has provided constant support for the Pentagon, and has been a friendly contact for many of its senior officers.

What forced him into a new role in 1977 was the requirement under Senate rules that he choose between ranking GOP positions on Armed Services and Judiciary. He was eligible for either, but he could not have both. At the urging of fellow conservatives, he ceded Armed Services to John Tower of Texas and took Judiciary, thus preventing liberal Republican Charles Mathias of Maryland from assuming the top position there.

During four years as ranking Republican on Judiciary, Thurmond pursued many of his traditional conservative issues, opposing busing, promoting school prayer, and blocking legislation to strengthen federal enforcement in open housing cases. But he also worked closely with Kennedy to produce a new federal criminal code, just as he had worked on the same issue for years alongside John McClellan of Arkansas, a Democrat closer to his thinking. A criminal code bill passed the Senate in 1978 and a succeeding version cleared committee in 1979, but neither passed the House.

Thurmond started out as Judiciary chairman in 1981 by calling for legislation reinstating the death penalty, introducing a constitutional amendment to balance the budget, and seeking to soften the 1965 Voting Rights Act, up for renewal. By midyear, the full committee had voted 11-5 for the balanced budget amendment and 13-4 for a death penalty bill.

In taking control, Thurmond alienated some moderate Republicans by denying the second-ranking Mathias a key role in Judiciary affairs. He abolished the Antitrust Subcommittee Mathias was in line to head, and removed much of the jurisdiction from the Criminal Law panel that Mathias did get.

It was not the first time the courtly South Carolinian has been known to play rough. He has mellowed some, however, since the time in 1964 when he wrestled Texas Democrat Ralph Yarborough to the floor outside the committee room where civil rights legislation was ready for markup. Yarborough was trying to assure a committee quorum; Thurmond was trying to prevent one. The South Carolinian won the wresting match. But Yarborough, after rescue by the committee chairman, made up the quorum anyway.

**At Home:** For three decades, Thurmond has punctuated his political career with turns and reversals, and always he has managed to carry his constituents with him.

They supported him in 1948 when, as governor, he bolted the Democratic Party to run as the States Rights candidate for president. In 1964, he

announced that he was joining the GOP because the Democrats were "leading the evolution of our nation to a socialistic dictatorship." And despite the state's historic partisan leanings, he easily won re-election two years later.

Since the mid-60s, black voting strength has grown in South Carolina to 30 percent and Thurmond has adjusted again, although his efforts to help black communities has never brought much of the black vote — his long record of opposing civil rights is not that easily forgotten. He is not thought to have drawn even 10 percent of this vote in 1972 or 1978. But any little bit can help in a close election, and Thurmond tries for it.

For most white South Carolinians, Thurmond's feistiness and physical vigor remain appealing. As a 75-year-old in 1978 competing with a man barely half his age, Thurmond traveled the state with his wife and four young children in a camper called "Strom Trek," passing out family recipes, riding parade elephants and sliding down firehouse poles.

Thurmond learned politics from one of his father's friends, Democratic Sen. Benjamin "Pitchfork Ben" Tillman. Early in his career, in the state Senate and as a circuit judge, Thurmond was a populist, representing poorer white farmers against the Tidewater establishment.

In 1946, after returning from World War II service in Europe, Thurmond was elected governor. He was in his second year in office when the Democratic National Convention decided to adopt a strong civil rights plank, and Thurmond offered himself as a regional candidate for president on the States Rights Democratic ticket. He carried four states — South Carolina, Alabama, Mississippi and Louisiana.

Thurmond made a first try for the Senate in 1950, but lost the Democratic primary to incumbent Olin D. Johnston. Four years later, however, he won — the first and so far the only senator to be elected as a write-in candidate. Sen. Burnet R. Maybank had died and the 31-member State Democratic Committee froze Thurmond out by choosing state Sen. Edgar A. Brown as the party nominee. Thurmond focused his campaign on the issue of whether "31 men" or the voters should make the decision. His write-in campaign defeated Brown by nearly 60,000 votes.

True to a 1954 promise, Thurmond resigned in 1956 and ran without the benefit of incumbency. It was not very difficult for him to win, though, because no one filed against him — a happy circumstance that repeated itself in 1960, when it was time to run for a full six-year term. In 1966 and 1972, he decimated Democrats Bradley Morrah and Eugene N. Ziegler, respectively.

In 1978, Thurmond encountered a stiff re-election challenge from Charles "Pug" Ravenel, who had won the Democratic primary for governor four years before, but was ruled off the general election ballot for failure to meet residency requirements. A media-oriented "New South" politician, Ravenel tried to remind blacks of the senator's segregationist past.

But Ravenel suffered from a carpetbagger's image. He had left the state to be an investment banker in New York, returning only shortly before his 1974 gubernatorial bid. Thurmond supporters circulated a newspaper column quoting Ravenel as telling New York contributors he would "be a good senator for New York from South Carolina."

## Committees

**Armed Services** (2nd of 9 Republicans)
Military Construction, chairman; Strategic and Theater Nuclear Forces; Tactical Warfare.

**Judiciary** (Chairman)
Constitution; Courts; Immigration and Refugee Policy.

**Veterans' Affairs** (2nd of 7 Republicans)

## Elections

**1978 General**

| | |
|---|---|
| Strom Thurmond (R) | 351,733 (56%) |
| Charles Ravenel (D) | 281,119 (44%) |

**Previous Winning Percentages**

| | | | |
|---|---|---|---|
| 1972 (63%) | 1966 (62%) | 1960 (100%) | 1956* (100%) |
| 1954* (63%) | | | |

*\* Thurmond was elected as a write-in candidate in 1954. He resigned April 4, 1956, and was elected to fill the vacancy caused by his own resigntion in a 1956 special election.*

## Campaign Finance

| | Receipts | Receipts from PACs | Expen-ditures |
|---|---|---|---|
| **1978** | | | |
| Thurmond (R) | $1,753,628 | $216,890 (12%) | $2,013,431 |
| Ravenel (D) | $1,145,542 | $144,644 (13%) | $1,134,168 |

## Voting Studies

| | Presidential Support | | Party Unity | | Conservative Coalition | |
|---|---|---|---|---|---|---|
| **Year** | **S** | **O** | **S** | **O** | **S** | **O** |
| 1980 | 46 | 53 | 86 | 13 | 95 | 4 |
| 1979 | 35 | 58 | 86 | 8 | 93 | 4 |
| 1978 | 30 | 61 | 78 | 15 | 85 | 8 |
| 1977 | 55 | 39 | 81 | 10 | 89 | 2 |
| 1976 | 81 | 8 | 91 | 2 | 93 | 1 |
| 1975 | 80 | 15 | 92 | 3 | 95 | 1 |
| 1974 (Ford) | 82 | 18 | | | | |
| 1974 | 71 | 22 | 90 | 5 | 90 | 5 |
| 1973 | 76 | 16 | 92 | 3 | 94 | 1 |
| 1972 | 83 | 7 | 79 | 6 | 85 | 1 |
| 1971 | 73 | 21 | 78 | 9 | 82 | 3 |
| 1970 | 70 | 20 | 80 | 10 | 86 | 4 |
| 1969 | 63 | 26 | 78 | 11 | 87 | 1 |

| | | | | | |
|---|---|---|---|---|---|
| 1968 | 38 | 55 | 79 | 10 | 93 | 0 |
| 1967 | 44 | 45 | 81 | 10 | 89 | 2 |
| 1966 | 38 | 49 | 79 | 13 | 96 | 0 |
| 1965 | 33 | 60 | 81 | 11 | 93 | 2 |
| 1964* | 48 | 50 | 37 | 58 | 92 | 8 |
| 1963 | 17 | 75 | 22 | 72 | 88 | 2 |
| 1962 | 30 | 66 | 21 | 74 | 91 | 6 |
| 1961 | 26 | 73 | 15 | 84 | 98 | 2 |

S = Support    O = Opposition

*\* Thurmond became a Republican Sept. 16, 1964; score is based on his votes as a Democrat.*

## Key Votes

**96th Congress**

| | |
|---|---|
| Maintain relations with Taiwan (1979) | Y |
| Reduce synthetic fuel development funds (1979) | N |
| Impose nuclear plant moratorium (1979) | N |
| Kill stronger windfall profits tax (1979) | Y |
| Guarantee Chrysler Corp. loans (1979) | N |
| Approve military draft registration (1980) | Y |
| End Revenue Sharing to the states (1980) | Y |
| Block Justice Dept. busing suits (1980) | Y |

**97th Congress**

| | |
|---|---|
| Restore urban program funding cuts (1981) | N |

## Interest Group Ratings

| Year | ADA | ACA | AFL-CIO | CCUS-1 | CCUS-2 |
|---|---|---|---|---|---|
| 1980 | 17 | 88 | 11 | 88 | |
| 1979 | 5 | 83 | 0 | 73 | 81 |
| 1978 | 10 | 87 | 21 | 83 | |
| 1977 | 5 | 85 | 21 | 94 | |
| 1976 | 0 | 100 | 10 | 100 | |
| 1975 | 0 | 96 | 14 | 88 | |
| 1974 | 0 | 100 | 20 | 100 | |
| 1973 | 0 | 89 | 18 | 100 | |
| 1972 | 0 | 95 | 10 | 88 | |
| 1971 | 0 | 96 | 25 | - | |
| 1970 | 0 | 96 | 0 | 100 | |
| 1969 | 0 | 93 | 0 | - | |
| 1968 | 0 | 92 | 0 | - | |
| 1967 | 0 | 100 | 0 | 100 | |
| 1966 | 0 | 88 | 0 | - | |
| 1965 | 0 | 96 | - | 100 | |
| 1964 | 2 | 94 | 0 | - | |
| 1963 | - | 96 | - | - | |
| 1962 | 0 | 100 | 0 | - | |
| 1961 | 0 | - | - | - | |

# Ernest F. Hollings (D)

### Of Charleston — Elected 1966

**Born:** Jan. 1, 1922; Charleston, S.C.
**Education:** The Citadel, B.A. 1942; U. of S.C., LL.B. 1947.
**Military Career:** Army, 1942-45.
**Profession:** Lawyer.
**Family:** Wife, Rita Louise Liddy; four children by a previous marriage.
**Religion:** Lutheran.
**Political Career:** S.C. Assembly, 1949-55; S.C. lt. governor, 1955-59; governor, 1959-63

**In Washington:** The 1980 election marked a personal triumph for Hollings, but he had little to celebrate. While he was winning a third full term with 72 percent of the vote — his best showing ever — he was losing the Budget chairmanship that had fallen to him only seven months before.

Hollings took over the committee in May of 1980, when Edmund S. Muskie of Maine left the Senate to become President Carter's secretary of state. It was a position Hollings had long desired, and he knew what he wanted to do with it: wage his long-standing battle for more dollars for the Defense Department. That battle is still going on in the 97th Congress, but the senator who attracts most of the attention for it is Pete V. Domenici of New Mexico, who was first in line on Budget when Republicans assumed a Senate majority.

During his brief taste of the chairmanship, Hollings promoted and moved through the Senate a budget resolution drawn up to be in balance — the first such achievement in the six year history of the budget process. The task later proved even more difficult than it seemed, as recession forced on the federal government a deficit of more than $50 billion in fiscal 1981. But Hollings remained proud of the effort and sensitive to loose talk about its failure. He also used his role to stave off an across-the-board tax cut sought by Republicans as part of their 1980 election push.

Hollings has worked well with Domenici and other Republicans who share his views about defense and the need to reduce domestic spending if necessary to provide for it. But he has sometimes angered the more liberal budget writers, urban-oriented Democrats like Daniel Patrick Moynihan of New York and Howard Metzenbaum of Ohio.

He has consistently refused to press for funding for programs that they consider the lifeblood

of their constituencies — jobs, mass transit and urban development. He regards himself as a compassionate legislator and supporter of social spending — "I'm not some military nut," he once blurted out at a committee meeting — but the social programs he is willing to defend tend to be related to nutrition and income maintenance, such as food stamps and school lunches.

In 1981, after committee Democrats complained that he was going along with Domenici and the Reagan budget cuts a bit too enthusiastically, Hollings accused them of failing to accept the decision of the electorate in 1980. "I don't see how we can become a real majority party," he said, "if we don't represent the majority." When the overall Reagan budget reached the floor in 1981, Hollings voted against most attempts by other Democrats to restore domestic programs.

But he is no supply-sider on economics. Hollings was an early skeptic about the benefits of a massive three-year tax cut. He tried an amendment in May 1981 to reduce the tax cut from $53 billion to $25 billion, but got only 14 votes.

Hollings is handsome, graceful and perfectly tailored — a symbol of Southern breeding and military education. But he is not always gracious in debate. When he takes the floor to talk about budget matters, rambling about deficits and defense in his thick Tidewater accent, he can unleash a stinging sarcasm against those who have opposed him in committee. And after a long 1980 conference in which House budget writers tried to increase funding for a long series of social programs by cutting the figure for defense, Hollings said going to conference with the House was like "feeding the monkeys in the zoo."

Defense is a personal issue to Hollings, who graduated from the Citadel during World War II. It is also a constituent issue. South Carolina is home to a dozen major defense installations, many of them around Hollings' hometown of Charleston. He pursues their interests not only in budget debate but on Defense Appropriations.

But outside the basic issue of spending, Hollings has compiled a record on national security that reflects a case-by-case approach.

He opposed both the SALT I and II nuclear arms treaties on the grounds they would accord "irreversible military superiority" to the Soviet Union. He cast one of only two votes against the first SALT treaty on the Senate floor. He supports a peacetime draft.

But he also supported publication of the so-called Pentagon Papers by *The New York Times* and urged President Nixon to "come clean" and tell the nation when the Vietnam War would end. He criticized administration officials who claimed "executive privilege" and refused to answer questions about the war. He voted with the Carter administration to transfer the Panama Canal.

Hollings also has an assignment on the Commerce Committee. In the 96th Congress, he was chairman of its Subcommittee on Communications and set out on a massive effort to rewrite the Communications Act of 1934. He introduced his own bill to substitute marketplace competition for federal regulation of many aspects of the telephone, telegraph and cable TV industries, insisting that monopolies and federal regulation were ideas of the past, and "competition and diversity" were "ideas of the future."

Hollings has also threaded his way carefully through civil rights issues during his long career. Associated in earlier years with President Kennedy, Hollings voted against some major civil rights legislation as a junior senator during the Johnson years. He described the 1968 open housing bill as "ridiculous" and "discriminatory on its face." But he has consistently supported the 1965 Voting Rights Act.

He drew support in civil rights circles in 1969 when he made an inspection tour of rural areas of his state, said he had found hunger and poverty to a degree he had never realized and came out for free food stamps for the neediest. He was active in the Senate on nutrition issues in the years after that. More recently he has talked about abuses in the food stamp program, but he still votes for money to support it.

Hollings long had aspirations to the Senate leadership. When former Majority Leader Mike Mansfield announced his retirement in 1976, he announced his candidacy immediately. He later dropped out of the race, however, to give Hubert H. Humphrey of Minnesota a "clear shot" against Robert C. Byrd, D-W.Va. Humphrey eventually withdrew, and Byrd won by acclamation.

**At Home:** Hollings built his political career in South Carolina at a time of emotional argument about racial issues and succeeded in combining old-time rhetoric with a tangible record of moderation.

As a candidate in the late 1950's, he firmly espoused states' rights and condemned school integration. In his inaugural speech as governor in 1959, Hollings criticized President Eisenhower for commanding a "marching army, this time not against Berlin, but against Little Rock." But as chief executive of the state, he quietly integrated the public schools.

In fact, despite grumblings about his rhetoric, blacks provided Hollings' margin of victory in 1966, when he won his Senate seat against a more conservative Republican opponent. Since then, he never has faced a credible candidate to his left, and blacks have generally supported him.

During the Depression, the Hollings family paper business went bankrupt, so an uncle had to borrow money to send him to The Citadel, where he received an Army commission. Hollings returned home from World War II for law school and a legal career. That soon led to politics.

As a young state legislator, he attracted notice with his plan to solve the problem of inferior black schools without integration. He said a special sales tax should be imposed to upgrade the black schools.

Hollings twice won unanimous election to the state House speakership and in 1954 moved up to lieutenant governor. In 1958, Democratic Gov. George B. Timmerman was ineligible to succeed himself. Hollings won a heated three-way race for the nomination. He took a runoff from Donald S. Russell, former University of South Carolina president and a protégé of ex-Gov. James F. Byrnes. The general election was uncontested.

There were few differences among the Democratic candidates; all opposed integration. Instead, the 1958 primary turned on political alliances and geography. Hollings' base lay in Charleston and Russell's in the Piedmont.

As governor, Hollings worked hard to attract industry to the state and to strengthen its educational system, launching a technical training program and establishing a commission on higher education. In 1960, Hollings campaigned for John F. Kennedy, who carried South Carolina.

Barred from seeking a second gubernatorial term in 1962, he challenged Democratic Sen. Olin D. Johnston. Picturing himself as "a young man on the go," Hollings attacked Johnston's endorsement by the state AFL-CIO. He charged that "foreign labor bosses" were seeking to control the state through Johnston. Although Hollings ran energetically, he still failed to draw much more than a third of the vote against Johnston.

The senator died in 1965, and Donald Russell — by then governor — had himself appointed to the seat. That provided an issue for Hollings' comeback in 1966. He ousted Russell in the special primary to fill out Johnston's term.

The 1966 election year was not an ordinary one in South Carolina. The national Democratic

Party was unpopular, and Republican state Sen. Marshall Parker seized on Hollings' connections to it in an effort to defeat him. He nearly made it, but Hollings met his conservative rhetoric — and matched it — and survived by 11,758 votes.

Running for a full term two years later, Hollings had little trouble turning back Parker. Since then, he has rolled over weak Republicans — school teacher Gwenyfred Bush in 1974 and former state Rep. Marshall T. Mays in 1980.

## Committees

**Appropriations** (5th of 14 Democrats)
Defense; Energy and Water Development; Labor, Health and Human Services, Education; Legislative Branch; State, Justice, Commerce, and the Judiciary.

**Budget** (Ranking Democrat)

**Commerce, Science and Transportation** (3rd of 8 Democrats)
Communications; Science, Technology, and Space; Surface Transportation.

## Elections

**1980 General**

| | |
|---|---|
| Ernest Hollings (D) | 612,554 (70%) |
| Marshall Mays (R) | 257,946 (30%) |

**1980 Primary**

| | |
|---|---|
| Ernest Hollings (D) | 266,796 (81%) |
| Nettie Dickerson (D) | 34,720 (11%) |
| William Kreml (D) | 27,049 (8%) |

**Previous Winning Percentages**

| | | |
|---|---|---|
| 1974 (70%) | 1968 (62%) | 1966* (51%) |

*Special election.

## Campaign Finance

| 1980 | Receipts | Receipts from PACs | Expen-ditures |
|---|---|---|---|
| Hollings (D) | $975,008 | $113,040 (12%) | $733,761 |
| Mays (R) | $62,525 | — (0%) | $62,472 |

## Voting Studies

| | Presidential Support | | Party Unity | | Conservative Coalition | |
|---|---|---|---|---|---|---|
| Year | S | O | S | O | S | O |
| 1980 | 63 | 28 | 55 | 33 | 64 | 23 |
| 1979 | 57 | 37 | 62 | 31 | 75 | 20 |
| 1978 | 66 | 23 | 61 | 33 | 58 | 35 |

| 1977 | 66 | 31 | 65 | 29 | 40 | 54 |
|---|---|---|---|---|---|---|
| 1976 | 49 | 40 | 65 | 29 | 40 | 55 |
| 1975 | 48 | 45 | 61 | 32 | 56 | 36 |
| 1974 (Ford) | 43 | 50 | | | | |
| 1974 | 45 | 39 | 42 | 41 | 56 | 24 |
| 1973 | 43 | 49 | 63 | 29 | 53 | 39 |
| 1972 | 57 | 35 | 61 | 31 | 46 | 45 |
| 1971 | 43 | 29 | 53 | 35 | 63 | 28 |
| 1970 | 59 | 35 | 52 | 31 | 50 | 33 |
| 1969 | 38 | 32 | 51 | 35 | 68 | 17 |
| 1968 | 24 | 37 | 41 | 24 | 47 | 14 |
| 1967 | 54 | 35 | 47 | 37 | 61 | 13 |

S = Support          O = Opposition

## Key Votes

**96th Congress**

| | |
|---|---|
| Maintain relations with Taiwan (1979) | Y |
| Reduce synthetic fuel development funds (1979) | N |
| Impose nuclear plant moratorium (1979) | N |
| Kill stronger windfall profits tax (1979) | N |
| Guarantee Chrysler Corp. loans (1979) | ? |
| Approve military draft registration (1980) | Y |
| End Revenue Sharing to the states (1980) | N |
| Block Justice Dept. busing suits (1980) | Y |

**97th Congress**

| | |
|---|---|
| Restore urban program funding cuts (1981) | N |

## Interest Group Ratings

| Year | ADA | ACA | AFL-CIO | CCUS-1 | CCUS-2 |
|---|---|---|---|---|---|
| 1980 | 39 | 43 | 22 | 62 | |
| 1979 | 32 | 35 | 41 | 30 | 50 |
| 1978 | 30 | 52 | 39 | 59 | |
| 1977 | 30 | 52 | 56 | 61 | |
| 1976 | 40 | 28 | 80 | 25 | |
| 1975 | 44 | 33 | 42 | 27 | |
| 1974 | 24 | 60 | 50 | 75 | |
| 1973 | 45 | 44 | 60 | 67 | |
| 1972 | 25 | 40 | 40 | 20 | |
| 1971 | 44 | 39 | 75 | - | |
| 1970 | 22 | 5 | 50 | 71 | |
| 1969 | 22 | 55 | 33 | - | |
| 1968 | 14 | 56 | 75 | - | |
| 1967 | 8 | 65 | 17 | 50 | |

# 1 Thomas F. Hartnett (R)

**Of Mt. Pleasant — Elected 1980**

**Born:** Aug. 7, 1941, Charleston, S.C.
**Education:** Attended College of Charleston, 1960-62.
**Military Career:** Air Force Reserves, 1963-69.
**Profession:** Realtor.
**Family:** Wife, Bonnie Lee Kennerly; two children.
**Religion:** Roman Catholic.
**Political Career:** S.C. House, 1965-73; S.C. Senate, 1973-81; unsuccessfully sought Democratic nomination for U.S. House, 1971.

**The Member:** Hartnett is firmly in the pro-military tradition of the late South Carolina Democrat L. Mendel Rivers, who represented the district for 30 years. He landed a seat on the Armed Services Committee Rivers once chaired.

After the Reagan administration ordered cutbacks in Army Corps of Engineers personnel, Hartnett sponsored a floor amendment to keep open corps district offices in ports with major military installations. The amendment, designed to prevent the closing of the corps' Charleston office, was included in a military construction bill.

Hartnett tried and failed to get to Congress as a Democrat in a 1971 special election to replace Rivers, who died in office. But Mendel J. Davis, Rivers' godson, won the election. When Davis decided to retire in 1980 at age 38, Hartnett was in the right party at the right time. He had left the Democrats after they nominated George McGovern for president in 1972.

In the 1980 election, Hartnett edged past Democrat Charles D. "Pug" Ravenel. With his campaign slogan "because he's one of us," Hartnett pinned a carpetbagger label on Ravenel, who grew up in Charleston but spent 10 years in New York as an investment banker.

**The District:** Thanks to Rivers, the district fairly groans with military installations, ranging from the Marine Corps Recruiting Depot at Parris Island to the Charleston Naval Shipyard. An estimated 35 percent of the district's payroll depends on the Defense Department.

Republicans are predominant in the growing suburbs around Charleston, and are gaining strength in Beaufort County, location of the Hilton Head resort. Nevertheless, traditional Democratic loyalties remain. The city of Charleston has a sizable black population and tends to be Democratic. Democrats also generally carry the outlying rural counties. The district has the state's second highest share of blacks.

## Committees

**Armed Services** (19th of 19 Republicans)
Military Personnel and Compensation; Seapower and Strategic and Critical Materials.

## Elections

**1980 General**

| | |
|---|---|
| Thomas Hartnett (R ) | 81,988 (52 %) |
| Charles Ravenel (D ) | 76,743 (48 %) |

**1980 Primary**

| | |
|---|---|
| Thomas Hartnett (R ) | 10,510 (75 %) |
| Thomas Moore (R ) | 3,428 (25 %) |

**District Vote For President**

| | 1980 | | 1976 | | 1972 |
|---|---|---|---|---|---|
| **D** | 70,952 (44 %) | **D** | 70,124 (53 %) | **D** | 33,861 (31 %) |
| **R** | 85,693 (53 %) | **R** | 59,939 (46 %) | **R** | 73,480 (67 %) |
| **I** | 3,147 (2 %) | | | | |

## Campaign Finance

| | Receipts | Percent of Receipts from PACs | Expenditures |
|---|---|---|---|
| **1980** | | | |
| Hartnett (R ) | $229,423 | $106,908 (47 %) | $226,394 |
| Ravenel (D ) | $280,210 | $77,263 (28 %) | $172,933 |

## Key Vote

**97th Congress**

| | |
|---|---|
| Reagan budget proposal (1981) | Y |

---

**1st District: South — Charleston.** Population: 560,004 (27% increase since 1970). Race: White 364,032 (65%), Black 187,188 (33%), Others 8,784 (2%). Spanish origin: 9,013 (2%).

# 2 Floyd Spence (R)

**Of Lexington — Elected 1970**

**Born:** April 9, 1928, Columbia, S.C.
**Education:** U. of S.C., A.B. 1952, J.D. 1956.
**Military Career:** Navy, 1952-54.
**Profession:** Lawyer.
**Family:** Widowed; four children.
**Religion:** Lutheran.
**Political Career:** S.C. House, 1957-63; S.C. Senate, 1967-71, minority leader 1967-71; unsuccessful Republican nominee for U.S. House, 1962.

**In Washington:** Spence arrived in the House determined to serve on the Armed Services Committee, not only to protect the national security but to look after all the military installations scattered over South Carolina by the committee's longtime chairman, L. Mendel Rivers of Charleston. He got the place, but he soon had to pay for it by taking another assignment he would have preferred to avoid — the Ethics Committee.

A decade later, as the Ethics Committee's senior Republican, Spence likes to joke about the way Minority Leader Gerald R. Ford told him Ethics was a prestigious committee that would not only look good on his record, but rarely met.

At the time, Ford was telling the truth. But in the changed political climate of the past few years, the committee has met frequently and has handled one difficult assignment after another, including the Korean influence-buying scandals, the censure of two members on kickback charges and the Abscam bribery affair. Spence stays in his seat every Congress as most of the membership changes around him. Nobody else on the current committee has been there even two years.

Remarkably, given his seniority, Spence is not a dominant influence on the panel. A pleasant man with shiny golden hair and a soft-spoken manner, he is no leader in strategy or debate. But he has played a useful role. Personally well-liked and trusted by Republican colleagues, he has supported most of the tougher actions of the committee and added a measure of bipartisanship to them on the House floor.

Meanwhile, Spence has also been building seniority on the Armed Services Committee, where he is now ranking Republican on the Seapower Subcommittee. He works easily on Seapower with Chairman Charles E. Bennett, who was also his Ethics chairman in the 96th Congress. Spence generally follows Bennett's lead on naval issues and rarely challenges him with Republican alternatives.

The Armed Services Committee offers Spence a chance to look after the major military installation in his district, Fort Jackson, one of the Army's largest basic-training centers.

**At Home:** Spence has won six terms by comfortable, but not landslide, margins. With a strong base in populous Richland (Columbia) and Lexington counties, he has been able to withstand a series of Democratic challenges.

A star athlete at the University of South Carolina and later a practicing lawyer, Spence launched his political career by winning a state legislative seat as a Democrat. But he quit the Democratic Party in 1962, complaining that it was too liberal, and immediately began campaigning for Congress as a Republican.

Stressing his opposition to the "socialistic" Kennedy administration, Spence was a consensus choice for the 1962 GOP nomination in the open 2nd District. But he lost in the fall to an equally conservative Democrat, state Sen. Albert W. Watson, who edged him by 4,202 votes.

Watson himself switched parties in 1965, and in 1970 he ran for governor as a Republican. At that point, Spence made his second campaign for Congress, stressing his opposition to the busing decisions of the U.S. Supreme Court. He defeated Democrat Heyward McDonald by 6,088 votes to keep the seat in Republican hands.

---

**2nd District: Central — Columbia.**
Population: 551,344 (24% increase since 1970). Race: White 349,499 (63%), Black 195,674 (35%), Others 6,171 (1%). Spanish origin: 7,060 (1%).

## Floyd Spence, R-S.C.

Spence has not been seriously threatened since then, although he has never drawn more than 60 percent of the vote against a Democratic opponent. In 1974, he took 56 percent against Matthew Perry, the first black to be nominated for Congress by South Carolina Democrats. In 1980, his challenger was maverick state Sen. Tom Turnipseed, a onetime aide to George Wallace, whose politics shifted leftward in the 1970s.

Turnipseed blasted Spence for taking contributions from political action committees. But with superior financial resources, Spence was able to ignore Turnipseed and won 56 percent.

**The District.** Seven counties comprise the 2nd District, but most of the votes are in Richland and Lexington counties at the northern end.

Richland is dominated by the state capital of Columbia, a largely white-collar town but one with a sizable textile industry. Nearby is Fort Jackson. Across the Congaree River to the west is Lexington County, a growing suburban area.

The two counties normally vote Republican in contested state and presidential contests, although Richland is less reliable for the GOP than Lexington. Since they cast about 70 percent of the district ballots, they usually outpoll the heavily black, generally Democratic rural counties to the south.

## Committees

**Armed Services** (3rd of 19 Republicans)
Readiness; Seapower and Strategic and Critical Materials.

**Standards of Official Conduct** (Ranking Republican)

## Elections

**1980 General**

| | |
|---|---|
| Floyd Spence (R ) | 92,306 (56 %) |
| Tom Turnipseed (D ) | 73,353 (44 %) |

**1978 General**

| | |
|---|---|
| Floyd Spence (R ) | 71,208 (57 %) |
| Jack Bass (D ) | 53,021 (43 %) |

**Previous Winning Percentages**

| | | | |
|---|---|---|---|
| 1976 (58 %) | 1974 (56 %) | 1972 (100%) | 1970 (53 %) |

**District Vote For President**

| | 1980 | | 1976 | | 1972 |
|---|---|---|---|---|---|
| D | 73,940 (45 %) | D | 76,948 (52 %) | D | 38,367 (31 %) |
| R | 84,354 (52 %) | R | 69,827 (47 %) | R | 85,637 (68 %) |
| I | 2,943 (2 %) | | | | |

## Campaign Finance

| | Receipts | Receipts from PACs | Expenditures |
|---|---|---|---|
| **1980** | | | |
| Spence (R ) | $260,947 | $104,980 (40 %) | $261,613 |
| Turnipseed (D ) | $66,175 | $20,409 (31 %) | $65,624 |
| **1978** | | | |
| Spence (R ) | $164,067 | $58,439 (36 %) | $182,995 |
| Bass (D ) | $129,479 | $22,201 (17 %) | $136,959 |

## Voting Studies

| | Presidential Support | | Party Unity | | Conservative Coalition | |
|---|---|---|---|---|---|---|
| Year | S | O | S | O | S | O |
| 1980 | 43 | 56 | 87 | 12 | 96 | 3 |
| 1979 | 32 | 68 | 88 | 11 | 98 | 2 |
| 1978 | 30 | 68 | 80 | 18 | 93 | 6 |
| 1977 | 37 | 61 | 87 | 7 | 90 | 1 |
| 1976 | 75 | 25 | 87 | 11 | 94 | 3 |
| 1975 | 53 | 42 | 83 | 14 | 91 | 5 |
| 1974 (Ford) | 48 | 48 | | | | |
| 1974 | 70 | 26 | 89 | 9 | 93 | 6 |
| 1973 | 68 | 30 | 86 | 12 | 95 | 3 |
| 1972 | 62 | 35 | 82 | 8 | 90 | 2 |
| 1971 | 72 | 19 | 74 | 12 | 86 | 2 |

S = Support          O = Opposition

## Key Votes

**96th Congress**

| | |
|---|---|
| Weaken Carter oil profits tax (1979) | Y |
| Reject hospital cost control plan (1979) | Y |
| Implement Panama Canal Treaties (1979) | N |
| Establish Department of Education (1979) | Y |
| Approve Anti-busing Amendment (1979) | Y |
| Guarantee Chrysler Corp. loans (1979) | Y |
| Approve military draft registration (1980) | Y |
| Aid Sandinista regime in Nicaragua (1980) | N |
| Strengthen fair housing laws (1980) | N |

**97th Congress**

| | |
|---|---|
| Reagan budget proposal (1981) | Y |

## Interest Group Ratings

| Year | ADA | ACA | AFL-CIO | CCUS |
|---|---|---|---|---|
| 1980 | 11 | 83 | 16 | 79 |
| 1979 | 5 | 96 | 5 | 94 |
| 1978 | 15 | 89 | 20 | 72 |
| 1977 | 0 | 88 | 17 | 88 |
| 1976 | 5 | 93 | 22 | 88 |
| 1975 | 11 | 89 | 22 | 76 |
| 1974 | 9 | 93 | 0 | 100 |
| 1973 | 0 | 85 | 18 | 100 |
| 1972 | 0 | 95 | 11 | 100 |
| 1971 | 0 | 92 | 13 | |

# 3 Butler Derrick (D)

## Of Edgefield — Elected 1974

**Born:** Sept. 30, 1936, Springfield, Mass.
**Education:** U. of S.C., B.A. 1958; U. of Ga., LL.B. 1965.
**Profession:** Lawyer.
**Family:** Wife, Suzanne Mims; two children.
**Religion:** Episcopalian.
**Political Career:** S.C. House, 1969-75; Democratic candidate for S.C. House, 1966.

**In Washington:** Thoughtful, soft-spoken and pragmatic, Derrick is the sort of newcomer that House leaders point to optimistically as their model of the New South in Congress. He has been a protégé of both Speaker O'Neill and Rules Chairman Richard Bolling, and a frequent leadership lobbyist among his junior colleagues.

Like most junior members from all regions, Derrick has looked for ways to control big government and bureaucracy. He pushed hard for a "sunset" bill to require a periodic review of existing programs. And he has been willing to question some of the most deeply entrenched of those programs, such as public works projects.

Derrick is perhaps best remembered on the outside for his fight in support of President Carter's attempt to drop 18 water projects in 1977. He led that fight even though one of them — the Richard B. Russell Dam — was in his district. Derrick first argued against the projects as a member of the Budget Committee, but lost. Then he took to the floor to fight the same 18 projects and add 16 more to the list.

Derrick said opposing the dam in his district gave him credibility to take up the issue. "You can have it back," he said of the dam. "We do not want it.... The citizens who live in my district and work in the textile mills are going to be paying for these projects the rest of their lives." Derrick lost 218-194, but nine of the projects were ultimately killed.

Derrick has also specialized in nuclear waste disposal issues, and has introduced his own legislation on the subject. Some 80 percent of the nation's high level nuclear waste is stored in his district.

As an early Budget Committee appointee, Derrick has been a defender of the budget process, and favored expanding it to encompass items not directly included in the formal budget. On several crucial votes in 1979, he was O'Neill's choice to head the task force aimed at persuading younger Democrats to support the budget. But in 1981, no longer a committee member and feeling pressure from home, he voted against the leadership and for the Reagan budget.

On the Rules Committee, he has worked to produce a sunset bill more substantial than the weak version favored by most committee chairmen. Derrick wants sunset to include a review of tax deductions as well as direct spending. He sees tax deductions as a form of runaway spending.

In the 96th Congress, Derrick took on another assignment for the leadership, as a member of a select panel studying the House committee system. The panel wanted to create a permanent new Energy Committee, but nearly adjourned in chaos one day because its members could not agree on the new committee's jurisdiction. Derrick saved the proposal with a quick move for recess and a telephone call to the Speaker, who shifted a crucial vote. The panel finally brought its proposal to the floor, where neither Derrick nor anyone else was able to save it.

**At Home:** Derrick had an unusually smooth path to Congress. The 3rd District was up for grabs in 1974 with the retirement of veteran Democrat W. J. Bryan Dorn, but Derrick won it as if he were an incumbent breezing to re-election.

Derrick had been a state representative since 1969 and was a member of the influential Ways and Means Committee of the South Carolina

---

**3rd District: West — Anderson.** Population: 519,823 (20% increase since 1970). Race: White 404,837 (78%), Black 112,893 (22%), Others 2,093 (0.4%). Spanish origin: 3,574 (1%).

House. He professed fiscal conservatism, right-to-work views and hard-line support for national defense. He also identified himself publicly as a racial moderate; he had nominated the first black to a South Carolina school board.

Derrick won the Democratic primary with 65 percent of the vote over two political unknowns, sparing himself even the trouble of a runoff. In the general election, he carried all but one county to swamp former state Sen. Marshall J. Parker, twice an unsuccessful GOP candidate for the U.S. Senate, with 62 percent of the vote.

Thanks in part to a good constituent service operation, Derrick has had little difficulty holding the seat. His closest race was a rematch with Parker in 1980. Outspending the Republican by a margin of about 3-to-1, Derrick swept all 10

counties to win re-election with 60 percent.

**The District:** The small farmers and textile mill workers of the 3rd District seem gradually to be shedding their longstanding Democratic loyalties.

Republicans have made deep inroads in Aiken and Pickens counties, at either end of the district. Aiken, at the southern end, is the home base of GOP Sen. Strom Thurmond. Pickens County, on the northern border, is in the orbit of populous Greenville County, another GOP stronghold.

To the south is Anderson, one of South Carolina's major textile centers. Anderson and most of the other counties in the central part of the district went for George Wallace in 1968, but supported Jimmy Carter in both 1976 and 1980.

## Committees

**Rules** (7th of 11 Democrats)
Legislative Process.

**Select Aging** (24th of 31 Democrats)
Health and Long-term Care.

## Elections

**1980 General**

| | |
|---|---|
| Butler Derrick (D ) | 87,680 (60 %) |
| Marshall Parker (R ) | 57,840 (40 %) |

**1978 General**

| | |
|---|---|
| Butler Derrick (D ) | 81,638 (82 %) |
| Anthony Panuccio (R ) | 17,973 (18 %) |

**Previous Winning Percentages**

1976 (100%)    1974 (62 %)

**District Vote For President**

| | 1980 | | 1976 | | 1972 |
|---|---|---|---|---|---|
| D | 73,333 (50 %) | D | 78,296 (59 %) | D | 24,954 (24 %) |
| R | 70,256 (48 %) | R | 54,640 (41 %) | R | 77,547 (74 %) |
| I | 2,179 (2 %) | | | | |

## Campaign Finance

| | Receipts | Receipts from PACs | Expenditures |
|---|---|---|---|
| **1980** | | | |
| Derrick (D ) | $192,641 | $104,274 (54 %) | $188,255 |
| Parker (R ) | $67,018 | $2,535 (4 %) | $66,047 |
| **1978** | | | |
| Derrick (D ) | $90,494 | $47,050 (52 %) | $84,641 |

## Voting Studies

| | Presidential Support | | Party Unity | | Conservative Coalition | |
|---|---|---|---|---|---|---|
| Year | S | O | S | O | S | O |
| 1980 | 65 | 21 | 72 | 18 | 49 | 39 |
| 1979 | 62 | 26 | 74 | 16 | 42 | 49 |
| 1978 | 56 | 33 | 66 | 27 | 48 | 47 |
| 1977 | 57 | 30 | 60 | 28 | 47 | 39 |
| 1976 | 37 | 61 | 58 | 36 | 64 | 31 |
| 1975 | 40 | 54 | 57 | 39 | 64 | 31 |

S = Support          O = Opposition

## Key Votes

**96th Congress**

| | |
|---|---|
| Weaken Carter oil profits tax (1979) | ? |
| Reject hospital cost control plan (1979) | Y |
| Implement Panama Canal Treaties (1979) | ? |
| Establish Department of Education (1979) | Y |
| Approve Anti-busing Amendment (1979) | N |
| Guarantee Chrysler Corp. loans (1979) | Y |
| Approve military draft registration (1980) | Y |
| Aid Sandinista regime in Nicaragua (1980) | Y |
| Strengthen fair housing laws (1980) | Y |

**97th Congress**

| | |
|---|---|
| Reagan budget proposal (1981) | Y |

## Interest Group Ratings

| Year | ADA | ACA | AFL-CIO | CCUS |
|---|---|---|---|---|
| 1980 | 56 | 50 | 72 | 70 |
| 1979 | 37 | 24 | 47 | 56 |
| 1978 | 45 | 44 | 68 | 24 |
| 1977 | 35 | 32 | 52 | 53 |
| 1976 | 40 | 57 | 45 | 44 |
| 1975 | 26 | 62 | 57 | 44 |

# 4 Carroll Campbell Jr. (R)

**Of Greenville — Elected 1978**

**Born:** July 24, 1940, Greenville, S.C.
**Education:** Attended U. of S.C., 1958 and 1970.
**Profession:** Real estate broker.
**Family:** Wife, Iris Rhodes; two children.
**Religion:** Episcopalian.
**Political Career:** S.C. House, 1971-75; S.C. Senate, 1977-79; Republican nominee for lieutenant governor, 1974.

**In Washington:** Five months into his first congressional term, Campbell found himself taking some public abuse and giving some back in return.

A real estate agent by profession, Campbell was point man for the real estate industry in a complex argument about interstate land sales. Consumer advocates wanted the Department of Housing and Urban Development (HUD) to be given the power to issue cease-and-desist orders in cases where it suspected fraud. Existing law allowed HUD to investigate only after a complaint had been filed. The National Association of Realtors lobbied the issue heavily in the Banking Committee, on which Campbell served, and when it lost there, Campbell took it to the House floor.

When he and the Realtors won on the floor, 245-145, Common Cause, the citizens' lobby, issued a release noting that 203 members who voted with him had also received money from the industry in 1978. This generated local stories that Campbell had helped the Realtors "buy" the House.

So Campbell and four other House freshmen took the floor two weeks later to denounce Common Cause. He accused the group of trying to "intimidate members into trying to support public financing of congressional campaigns by slinging mud at individual members."

The campaign finance issue never seemed to leave Campbell for long during his first term. Appointed to the House Administration Committee, he was embroiled in controversy over HR 1, the public campaign finance bill supported by the Democratic leadership. He was part of a solid GOP phalanx that helped kill the bill in committee.

But after that experience, and the dispute over the Realtors' amendment, he still seemed to be looking for a campaign reform he could support. Late in 1979, Democrats tried again with a bill to limit the amounts political action committees could give to congressional candidates.

The Democrats wanted to limit an individual candidate's contributions from one PAC to $6,000 in most campaigns. Campbell wanted a limit of $70,000 on the amount a candidate could receive from all PACs combined. But he lost on that issue, and ended up voting "nay" on the second campaign bill, just as he had on the first.

Campbell is a tough, hard-driving man whose aggressiveness has not always gone over well among other members of his state's delegation. But the issue has not slowed him down in state politics or in the House. "I make no apologies for being ambitious," he told a South Carolina reporter in 1981. "... If you're not ambitious, you're not going to succeed in life."

**At Home.** Campbell has been one of the rising stars in the South Carolina Republican Party through its years of alternating hope and failure in the past decade. Before he won his House seat in 1978, he had three successful contests for the state Legislature. His campaign for lieutenant governor in 1974, while a losing one, gave him statewide exposure and a close political alliance with the victorious GOP gubernatorial candidate, James Edwards, who made Campbell his chief aide.

Campbell had his eye on the 4th District throughout the 1970s. For most of that time, the strength of the conservative Democratic incumbent, James Mann, dissuaded him from trying.

> **4th District: Northwest — Greenville, Spartanburg.** Population: 489,444 (18% increase since 1970). Race: White 394,825 (81%), Black 91,661 (19%), Others 2,980 (1%). Spanish origin: 3,831 (1%).

But Campbell began planning seriously for a 1978 campaign a year in advance, and when Mann announced his retirement, he was prepared.

At first, it seemed Democrats might keep control of the district anyway. They nominated a popular candidate in Austrian-born Max Heller, the mayor of Greenville. And they had a strong statewide ticket headed by gubernatorial nominee Richard Riley, whose home base was in the district.

But Campbell was an effective campaigner, able to capitalize on the name recognition he had built up in the past. He generated big-name campaign help — Ronald Reagan, John Connally and Jack Kemp all made appearances on his behalf. Narrowly carrying Greenville and Spartanburg counties, he won by 5,893 votes.

The 1980 election year was easy for him. He had no primary opposition and his Democratic opponent withdrew. And when the state's biggest-name Republicans, Sen. Strom Thurmond and Gov. Edwards, both endorsed Connally for presi-

dent, Campbell became Reagan's state chairman. After Reagan's easy victory in the presidential primary, Campbell was chosen to chair the South Carolina delegation at the convention in Detroit.

**The District.** Campbell's district lies in the heart of the Piedmont Plateau, an industrial region in the northwest corner of the state that began voting Republican in national elections before Campbell won his congressional seat.

Greenville is the district's largest city and a regional business center. Although the textile industry is the major employer in Greenville, the city is home base for a diverse array of industries, and has a substantial white-collar population. Greenville County has been increasingly Republican in recent years. It was one of only three South Carolina counties won by Ford in 1976, when Carter took the state easily.

Spartanburg, the other population center, is dominated more by rank-and-file textile workers and has more of a Democratic tradition. But it too is becoming more Republican.

## Committees

**Appropriations** (21st of 22 Republicans)
Commerce, Justice, State, the Judiciary; Legislative; Treasury-Postal Service.

## Elections

**1980 General**

| | |
|---|---|
| Carroll Campbell Jr. (R ) | 90,941 (93 %) |
| Thomas Waldenfels (LIB) | 6,984 (7 %) |

**1978 General**

| | |
|---|---|
| Carroll Campbell Jr. (R ) | 51,377 (52 %) |
| Max Heller (D ) | 45,484 (46 %) |

**1978 Primary**

| | |
|---|---|
| Carroll Campbell Jr. (R ) | 6,808 (88 %) |
| Robert Watkins (R) | 899 (12 %) |

**District Vote For President**

| | 1980 | | 1976 | | 1972 |
|---|---|---|---|---|---|
| D | 60,549 (43 %) | D | 63,848 (51 %) | D | 19,886 (19 %) |
| R | 76,147 (54 %) | R | 59,555 (48 %) | R | 84,401 (79 %) |
| I | 2,578 (2 %) | | | | |

## Campaign Finance

| | Receipts | Receipts from PACs | Expenditures |
|---|---|---|---|
| **1980** | | | |
| Campbell (R ) | $169,724 | $88,755 (52 %) | $153,606 |

**1978**

| | | | |
|---|---|---|---|
| Campbell (R ) | $184,933 | $60,089 (32 %) | $182,461 |
| Heller (D ) | $240,432 | $3,100 (1 %) | $240,150 |

## Voting Studies

| | Presidential Support | | Party Unity | | Conservative Coalition | |
|---|---|---|---|---|---|---|
| Year | S | O | S | O | S | O |
| 1980 | 37 | 56 | 75 | 14 | 78 | 5 |
| 1979 | 28 | 64 | 84 | 8 | 89 | 1 |

S = Support     O = Opposition

## Key Votes

**96th Congress**

| | |
|---|---|
| Weaken Carter oil profits tax (1979) | Y |
| Reject hospital cost control plan (1979) | Y |
| Implement Panama Canal Treaties (1979) | N |
| Establish Department of Education (1979) | Y |
| Approve Anti-busing Amendment (1979) | Y |
| Guarantee Chrysler Corp. loans (1979) | N |
| Approve military draft registration (1980) | Y |
| Aid Sandinista regime in Nicaragua (1980) | N |
| Strengthen fair housing laws (1980) | N |

**97th Congress**

| | |
|---|---|
| Reagan budget proposal (1981) | Y |

## Interest Group Ratings

| Year | ADA | ACA | AFL-CIO | CCUS |
|---|---|---|---|---|
| 1980 | 6 | 83 | 11 | 87 |
| 1979 | 5 | 92 | 5 | 94 |

# 5 Ken Holland (D)

**Of Gaffney — Elected 1974**

**Born:** Nov. 24, 1934, Hickory, N.C.
**Education:** U. of S.C., A.B. 1960, LL.B. 1963.
**Profession:** Lawyer.
**Family:** Wife, Diane Martin; four children.
**Religion:** Methodist.
**Political Career:** No previous office.

**In Washington:** Holland uses his position on Ways and Means to protect the textile industry, often working in alliance with Ed Jenkins, the Georgia Democrat whose district is similar to his own. He has chaired the "Congressional Textile Caucus," which was initially skeptical of the massive 1979 bill lowering trade barriers between the United States and other countries. After Robert S. Strauss, President Carter's special trade representative, promised continuing attention to the textile industry's problems, Holland and like-minded legislators finally voted for the bill.

Most of Holland's textile problems stem from competitors in Taiwan, Hong Kong and Korea, whose clothing exports are seen as a constant threat by Southern manufacturers. At one point, Holland threatened to hold trade negotiations "hostage" to resolution of the textile import issue.

On broader issues, Holland is a moderate Democrat, one of the Southerners most likely to help the leadership in a difficult situation. In the 96th Congress, for example, he voted in favor of implementing the Panama Canal treaties, against an anti-busing amendment to the Constitution and against weakening the windfall profits tax. He backed the Reagan budget proposals in 1981.

Holland became a topic of House conversation one day in 1980 when the Associated Press reported that he was sleeping on the couch in his Capitol Hill office to save money. He said he and his wife could not pay for homes in both Washington and South Carolina on his $60,700 salary. The story struck some of his colleagues as bizarre, but it reflected a concern for personal finance that has become a dominant theme in Holland's recent congressional career.

Early in 1979, he was a sponsor of a Ways and Means Committee bill to expand the business expense deduction for members of Congress, set in the 1950s at $3,000 a year. "I've voted for every pay raise," he said, "and I'm proud of it. I like serving my people, but I'm not their lackey." A few months later, he began a speech by telling colleagues that they were privileged to be hearing him for free. "Most people pay large honorariums to hear this," he said.

In October 1979 he argued vehemently against a bill to place strict new limits on contributions by political action committees. "It is laughable," he said, "to expect us to knuckle under to these so-called reformers who have never got elected to anything."

**At Home:** Holland had never run for office before his election to the House in 1974, but he was an insider in the state Democratic Party. He had been the party's legal counsel and served on its executive committee. He was a law partner of John West, who was governor from 1971 to 1975, and was a West appointee to the state highway commission.

Holland campaigned as a moderate in 1974 for the nomination to replace retiring Democrat Tom S. Gettys. He opposed the death penalty, attracting black support in a district where it is important. Holland led the seven-way primary, then won the runoff with 52 percent and easily took the general election.

But incumbency did not produce a safe seat. Holland was hurt in early 1976 when the liberal Americans for Democratic Action (ADA) rated him the most liberal member of the state delegation. That fall, he found himself in a difficult contest with Bobby Richardson, former second

---

**5th District: North central — Rock Hill.** Population: 500,296 (13% increase since 1970). Race: White 340,804 (68%), Black 156,187 (31%), Others 3,305 (1%). Spanish origin: 4,353 (1%).

## Ken Holland, D-S.C.

baseman of the New York Yankees and baseball coach at the University of South Carolina.

In Richardson, he faced an unknown quantity politically, but a household name in the district. A member of the Fellowship of Christian Athletes, Richardson projected a clean-cut, religious image, while promoting popular conservative themes. Holland barely survived, winning by less than 4,000 votes out of nearly 130,000 cast. After the election, Holland's ADA scores sank and Richardson moved out of the district.

By 1978 Holland was controversial because of a divorce, the dissatisfaction of organized labor with his more conservative voting record and charges of low House attendance. But his 1978 primary challenger, Sumner City Council member Colleen Yates, was underfinanced and not well known. Holland won renomination by a

margin of nearly 2-1. He did not have Republican opposition in either 1978 or 1980.

**The District:** Holland's district sprawls across north central South Carolina, from the low country on the southeast to the Piedmont Plateau on the west. It is a rural district, without a large city. Rock Hill, about 25 miles south of Charlotte, N.C., is the major population center.

Textile plants are the key employers in small towns around the district, with food processing and timber also important. Because of its sizable blue-collar element and nearly one-third black population, the 5th usually turns in Democratic majorities in presidential and statewide races. Jimmy Carter carried it by comfortable margins in both 1976 and 1980; Sen. Strom Thurmond is the only Republican it has supported for the U.S. Senate or governor since 1970.

## Committees

**Standards of Official Conduct** (5th of 6 Democrats)

**Ways and Means** (10th of 23 Democrats)
Health; Select Revenue Measures.

## Elections

**1980 General**

| | |
|---|---|
| Ken Holland (D ) | 99,773 (88 %) |
| Thomas Campbell (LIB) | 14,252 (12 %) |

**1978 General**

| | |
|---|---|
| Ken Holland (D ) | 63,538 (83%) |
| Harold Hough (I) | 13,251 (17%) |

**1978 Primary**

| | |
|---|---|
| Ken Holland (D ) | 46,247 (65 %) |
| Colleen Yates (D ) | 24,853 (35 %) |

**Previous Winning Percentages**

1976 (51 %)    1974 (61 %)

**District Vote For President**

| | 1980 | | 1976 | | 1972 |
|---|---|---|---|---|---|
| D | 71,387 (54 %) | D | 77,715 (60 %) | D | 32,375 (29 %) |
| R | 59,033 (44 %) | R | 50,328 (39 %) | R | 78,994 (70 %) |
| I | 1,761 (1 %) | | | | |

## Campaign Finance

| | Receipts | Receipts from PACs | Expen- ditures |
|---|---|---|---|
| **1980** | | | |
| Holland (D ) | $128,283 | $73,760 (57 %) | $93,650 |
| Campbell (R ) | $570 | — (0 %) | $60 |
| **1978** | | | |
| Holland (D ) | $133,535 | $74,953 (56 %) | $91,690 |

## Voting Studies

| | Presidential Support | | Party Unity | | Conservative Coalition | |
|---|---|---|---|---|---|---|
| Year | S | O | S | O | S | O |
| 1980 | 55 | 31 | 61 | 21 | 51 | 35 |
| 1979 | 50 | 26 | 58 | 20 | 48 | 32 |
| 1978 | 53 | 32 | 53 | 24 | 46 | 35 |
| 1977 | 41 | 25 | 46 | 26 | 42 | 24 |
| 1976 | 22 | 45 | 43 | 28 | 51 | 22 |
| 1975 | 31 | 57 | 55 | 31 | 52 | 32 |

S = Support          O = Opposition

## Key Votes

**96th Congress**

| | |
|---|---|
| Weaken Carter oil profits tax (1979) | N |
| Reject hospital cost control plan (1979) | Y |
| Implement Panama Canal Treaties (1979) | Y |
| Establish Department of Education (1979) | Y |
| Approve Anti-busing Amendment (1979) | N |
| Guarantee Chrysler Corp. loans (1979) | Y |
| Approve military draft registration (1980) | Y |
| Aid Sandinista regime in Nicaragua (1980) | N |
| Strengthen fair housing laws (1980) | N |

**97th Congress**

| | |
|---|---|
| Reagan budget proposal (1981) | Y |

## Interest Group Ratings

| Year | ADA | ACA | AFL-CIO | CCUS |
|---|---|---|---|---|
| 1980 | 22 | 41 | 60 | 77 |
| 1979 | 42 | 19 | 57 | 40 |
| 1978 | 35 | 46 | 61 | 39 |
| 1977 | 15 | 48 | 56 | 80 |
| 1976 | 35 | 57 | 52 | 39 |
| 1975 | 47 | 44 | 45 | 42 |

# 6 John L. Napier (R)

**Of Bennettsville — Elected 1980**

**Born:** May 16, 1947, Bennettsville, S.C.
**Education:** Davidson College, A.B. 1969; University of South Carolina, J.D. 1972.
**Military Career:** Army Reserve, 1969-77.
**Profession:** Lawyer.
**Family:** Wife, Pamela Caughman.
**Religion:** Presbyterian.
**Political Career:** Clio, S.C., town attorney, 1978-80.

**The Member:** Were it not for Abscam, Napier would have had a difficult time winning this rural district, where Democratic Rep. John W. Jenrette Jr. had carefully cultivated the large black community. But Jenrette's conviction on bribery charges the month before the election settled the outcome in Napier's favor, although Jenrette campaigned hard and came within 5,217 votes.

Napier, a protégé of Sen. Strom Thurmond, barely mentioned Abscam, but carefully praised voters for their "deep moral values."

Farm issues are a vital concern in the 6th District. Napier, who criticized Jenrette for leaving the House Agriculture Committee, landed a seat on that panel and serves on subcommittees dealing with tobacco, cotton and other crops grown in his district.

Napier has asked the Public Works Committee to consider funding an Army Corps of Engineers project to halt beach erosion along the "Grand Strand," a popular resort area in his district.

**The District:** The last time a Republican took this tobacco-growing Democratic district was in 1972, when Jenrette caused a Democratic split by ousting incumbent John L. McMillan in a primary. Jenrette came back to win it in 1974.

The 6th has the largest percentage of blacks in the state; there are black majorities in Williamsburg, Lee and Clarendon counties. Because they are well-organized and usually have a good turnout, blacks are a major political factor. They were the main reason Jenrette turned in a respectable showing in 1980.

The two counties in the 6th that went to Reagan in 1980 — Florence and Horry — are areas of growing GOP strength, although Democrats still win most of the local offices even there. New industry in Florence has brought an influx of managerial people, while wealthy retirees are filling the resorts on Horry's "Grand Strand."

## Committees

**Agriculture** (13th of 19 Republicans)
Conservation, Credit, and Rural Development; Cotton, Rice and Sugar; Tobacco and Peanuts.

## Elections

**1980 General**

| | |
|---|---|
| John Napier (R ) | 75,964 (52 %) |
| John Jenrette (D ) | 70,747 (48 %) |

**1980 Primary**

| | |
|---|---|
| John Napier (R ) | 3,735 (60 %) |
| Edward Young (R ) | 2,491 (40 %) |

**District Vote For President**

| | 1980 | | 1976 | | 1972 |
|---|---|---|---|---|---|
| **D** | 80,224 (54 %) | **D** | 83,876 (62 %) | **D** | 37,381 (32 %) |
| **R** | 66,358 (45 %) | **R** | 51,860 (38 %) | **R** | 76,985 (67 %) |

## Campaign Finance

| | Receipts | Receipts from PACs | Expenditures |
|---|---|---|---|
| **1980** | | | |
| Napier (R ) | $283,430 | $30,520 (11 %) | $277,856 |
| Jenrette (D ) | $169,093 | $50,095 (30 %) | $173,059 |

## Key Vote

**97th Congress**

| | |
|---|---|
| Reagan budget proposal (1981) | Y |

---

**6th District: Northeast — Florence.**
Population: 498,275 (21 % increase since 1970). Race: White 291,125 (58 %), Black 204,543 (41 %), Others 2,607 (0.5 %). Spanish origin: 5,583 (1 %).

**1105**

# South Dakota

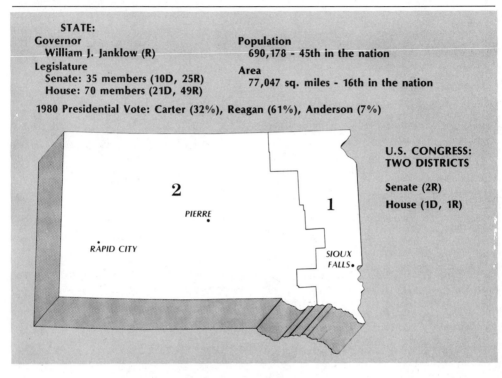

## . . . The Difference of a River

South Dakota is a Midwestern state on one side of the Missouri River and a Western state on the other. Crossing the Missouri going west means leaving the Corn Belt and entering ranching country, where in most places there is not enough water for a good crop in an average year.

There are political differences to match the geographical ones. The Corn Belt counties vote much like Iowa and Minnesota across the border — Republican but relatively tolerant of government social services. The western side is more like Wyoming — ornery, individualist and eager for government to leave it alone.

The people are mostly in the east. Throughout the 1970s, there were as many people in the 21 counties of the eastern 1st Congressional District as in the 46 counties of the western 2nd. After 1982, there will be only one district in South Dakota. The state's modest population increase of 3 percent during the past decade will cost it a

House seat and restrict it to one congressman-at-large.

The 1970s were a remarkable decade for the Democratic Party in South Dakota. After generations of consistent Republican representation, a wave of Democratic voting spread over the normally Republican state like a sudden Midwestern thunderstorm. George McGovern had led the way by building a framework of dedicated party workers beginning in the 1950s. But until 1970 only McGovern himself, who effectively aroused a populist strain in the normally staid South Dakota voter, saw much political success.

But Republicans had gradually become complacent. Their energy and organization had dissipated, and top GOP officials became embroiled in reports of scandal. In 1970, Democrats broke through, winning the governorship and both U.S. House seats. In 1972, despite McGovern's defeat for the presidency, they won the other Senate seat and control of the state Legislature.

Now it is mostly a memory for McGovern and his allies to savor as they return to private life. By the end of the 1970s, Republicans had recaptured virtually all of what they had lost. McGovern was decisively defeated in 1980 as he sought a fourth Senate term.

# A Political Tour

**East of the River.** The Corn Palace in Mitchell symbolizes the primacy of that crop in the eastern third of the state. An auditorium with mosaics wrought in various colored corn cobs on the exterior, the Corn Palace has stood as a tourist attraction and a banner of the economic foundation of the area since the last century.

The corn feeds cattle and hogs, and it provides the largest share of agricultural income in the state. Sioux Falls, the state's main metropolis, is a service center for agricultural interests, with banks, insurance companies and farm implement dealers all tied closely to the agricultural economy. There is also a large meat packing business.

Unlike other areas in the state, the Sioux Falls metropolitan area maintained a respectable growth rate in the 1970s, with surrounding Minnehaha County gaining 14.9 percent and Lincoln County, with its Sioux Falls suburbs, going up 18.5 percent. Further south, Union County — which gets some spillover from nearby Sioux City, Iowa — gained 13.4 percent. But those were the only gains over 10 percent in any South Dakota county east of the Missouri River.

The wheat-growing counties, between the eastern Corn Belt and the Missouri River, suffered the greatest loses in population, most of them declining by more than 10 percent.

At the polls, eastern South Dakota has been somewhat less staunchly Republican than the area west of the Missouri. It was in this area that George McGovern, who comes from Mitchell, molded a statewide Democratic Party and took a U.S. House seat in 1956 for the first time in twenty years. In 1976, most of the wheat and corn counties backed Carter for president, in response to unpopular Republican farm programs.

**West of the River.** On the other side of the Missouri, the towns appear less frequently. The land gradually turns from green to brown and is used for grazing. In contrast to the relatively sedate farms of the east, the west is cowboy and rodeo country.

At the western edge of South Dakota lies the state's second largest metropolitan center, Rapid City. Recovering from a devastating 1972 flood, the city has drawn federal rebuilding money and has become something of a boom town. New industries coming in, a newly constructed convention center and the prospering tourism industry have combined to attract young job-seekers to Rapid City from the farms and ranches. Adding to the population growth are retirees who come to live in the scenic Black Hills. In the area around Rapid City, many Indians have returned to the reservations from jobs that have disappeared in the industrial centers of the Midwest.

Republicans are nearly always dominant on this side of the river. In 1976, Carter carried only six counties west of the river, three of them on Indian reservations. The area sent a Democrat to the U.S. House in 1970 but reverted to its traditional Republicanism in 1972.

---

# Governor
# William J. Janklow (R)

**Born:** Sept. 13, 1939, Chicago, Ill.
**Home:** Flandreau, S.D.
**Education:** U. of South Dakota, B.S. 1964; J.D.1966.
**Military Career:** Marine Corps, 1956-59.
**Profession:** Lawyer.
**Family:** Wife, Mary; three children.
**Religion:** Lutheran.
**Political Career:** South Dakota attorney general, 1975-79; elected governor 1978; term expires Jan. 1983.

# Larry Pressler (R)

## Of Humboldt — Elected 1978

**Born:** March 29, 1942, Humboldt, S.D.
**Education:** U. of S.D., B.A. 1964; Rhodes Scholar, Oxford U., England, 1966; Harvard U., M.A. 1971, J.D. 1971.
**Military Career:** Army, 1966-68.
**Profession:** Lawyer.
**Family:** Single.
**Religion:** Roman Catholic.
**Political Career:** U.S. House, 1975-79.

**In Washington:** A born campaigner with an instinct for public relations, Pressler has had to struggle in the Senate against an impression that he is more interested in campaigning than in legislating.

He reinforced that reputation right at the start by mounting a brief and quixotic campaign for president in 1980, arguing the advantage of his youth (he was 37) and talking about the need to promote rural America. The campaign was a bust. He withdrew after 105 days in which he raised little money, failed to make the primary ballot in New Hampshire and was left out of a debate in Iowa.

But one of the aftereffects was a round of priceless publicity. Late in 1979, FBI agents posing as Arab sheiks invited Pressler to a Georgetown house to offer him a bribe, knowing that he badly neeed money for his presidential effort. It was part of the Abscam corruption probe. Pressler refused to have anything to do with the offer, and stormed out of the meeting. It briefly made him a minor hero. "I turned down an illegal contribution," he said afterward. "Where have we come to if that's considered heroic?"

On the legislative front, Pressler's most conspicuous effort in the 96th Congress was an amendment to bar the use of federal funds to enforce the Carter administration's grain embargo against the Soviet Union. The amendment, opposed by the Carter White House, was dropped later in conference between the House and Senate.

In the 97th Congress, Pressler is chairman of the Senate Commerce Subcommittee on Business, Trade and Tourism. He moved quickly on a tourism promotion bill that had passed the Senate in the previous Congress but had been vetoed by President Carter. By the end of January, Pressler had it through the Senate again. It would create a new U.S. Travel and Tourism Administration, which would prepare a detailed national tourism plan and set up offices in other countries.

But at midyear, the bill still was far from final enactment. The Reagan administration, which had been surprised by Pressler's quick move in January, opposed it.

Pressler also joined the Foreign Relations Committee in 1981. In his early months on the committee, he proved relatively independent of Reagan administration foreign policy, criticizing U.S. involvement in El Salvador and opposing Reagan's nomination of Ernest W. Lefever for assistant secretary of state for human rights.

Pressler has championed small businesses and family farms and emphasized the use of gasohol. He has offered amendments on the Senate floor to ensure adequate transportation for the elderly and rural communities, and increase airport development aid to his state. He has pushed vocational education amendments and amendments to aid needy Vietnam veterans.

**At Home:** Pressler's boyish charm swept an incumbent Democrat out of Congress in 1974, the best Democratic year of recent times, and it has kept him strong in South Dakota despite frequent charges that he is more shadow than substance.

When a 1977 *Wall Street Journal* article labeled him an image-conscious, do-little legislator, the home-state reaction was overwhelmingly in his favor. Constituents felt the Eastern press was picking on a local hero who still rode his tractor in county fair parades. The next year Pressler was elected to the Senate with more than two-thirds of the vote. That support has survived his reputation as a regular on Washington's party circuit — often damaging west of the Mississippi —and his brief foray into presidential campaigning at the end of 1979. It will not be tested again until 1984.

From the beginning, Pressler offered his state a political persona that was hard to resist: the good natured, unpretentious farm boy who succeeded early in life on sheer talent. His Rhodes Scholarship and Masters Degree from Harvard combined perfectly with his roots on the family farm in Humboldt, which is still his official residence.

Those attributes were more than enough to give Pressler his victory in 1974 over Democratic Rep. Frank Denholm, even though he filed only the day before the deadline. Pressler campaigned as a moderate Republican, noting his membership in Common Cause and criticizing South Dakota's massive Oahe irrigation project on environmental grounds. He won by nearly 15,000 votes. Two years later, he won a second term by a margin that set a state record for any House candidate facing major-party opposition.

Democratic Sen. James Abourezk chose to retire in 1978, and Pressler began the campaign year as odds-on favorite to succeed him. That situation never changed, even though Democrats nominated a competent challenger, former Rapid City Mayor Don Barnett. Pressler had built enormous good will in South Dakota through his nearly-constant presence at events all over the state, and had bolstered it with conspicuous clean government gestures, such as his decision to donate a House salary increase to charity.

Barnett was the pro-Oahe candidate that year, while Pressler called for modified development of the project. But no issue was of great importance. Pressler offered the personal qualities the electorate wanted, and there was never much doubt that he would win.

## Committees

**Commerce, Science and Transportation** (6th of 9 Republicans)
Businss, Trade and Tourism, chairman; Communications; Surface Transportation.

**Foreign Relations** (9th of 9 Republicans)
Arms Control, Oceans and International Operations, and Environment, chairman; European Affairs; Near Eastern and South Asian Affairs.

**Special Aging** (6th of 8 Republicans)

## Elections

**1978 General**

| | |
|---|---|
| Larry Pressler ( ) | 170,832 (67%) |
| Don Barnett (D) | 84,767 (33%) |

**1978 Primary**

| | |
|---|---|
| Larry Pressler (D) | 66,893 (74%) |
| Ronald Williamson (R) | 23,646 (26%) |

**Previous Winning Percentages**

1976* (80%)    1974* (55%)

*House election.

## Campaign Finance

| | Receipts | Receipts from PACs | Expenditures |
|---|---|---|---|
| **1978** | | | |
| Pressler (R) | $489,983 | $177,345 (36%) | $449,541 |
| Barnett (D) | $152,665 | $67,404 (44%) | $152,006 |

## Voting Studies

| | Presidential Support | | Party Unity | | Conservative Coalition | |
|---|---|---|---|---|---|---|
| Year | S | O | S | O | S | O |
| Senate service | | | | | | |
| 1980 | 36 | 41 | 59 | 18 | 56 | 23 |
| 1979 | 39 | 40 | 52 | 27 | 51 | 34 |
| House service | | | | | | |
| 1978 | 29 | 46 | 46 | 31 | 46 | 30 |
| 1977 | 42 | 47 | 62 | 26 | 64 | 26 |
| 1976 | 47 | 51 | 54 | 43 | 69 | 28 |
| 1975 | 40 | 58 | 58 | 39 | 66 | 31 |

S = Support        O = Opposition

## Key Votes

**96th Congress**

| | |
|---|---|
| Maintain relations with Taiwan (1979) | Y |
| Reduce synthetic fuel development funds (1979) | Y |
| Impose nuclear plant moratorium (1979) | N |
| Kill stronger windfall profits tax (1979) | Y |
| Guarantee Chrysler Corp. loans (1979) | N |
| Approve military draft registration (1980) | Y |
| End Revenue Sharing to the states (1980) | N |
| Block Justice Dept. busing suits (1980) | Y |

**97th Congress**

| | |
|---|---|
| Restore urban program funding cuts (1981) | N |

## Interest Group Ratings

| Year | ADA | ACA | AFL-CIO | CCUS-1 | CCUS-2 |
|---|---|---|---|---|---|
| Senate service | | | | | |
| 1980 | 17 | 65 | 21 | 81 | |
| 1979 | 32 | 58 | 47 | 55 | 56 |
| House service | | | | | |
| 1978 | 25 | 37 | 44 | 56 | |
| 1977 | 35 | 64 | 23 | 92 | |
| 1976 | 30 | 52 | 61 | 44 | |
| 1975 | 58 | 58 | 57 | 53 | |

# James Abdnor (R)

### Of Kennebec — Elected 1980

**Born:** Feb. 13, 1923, Kennebec, S.D.
**Education:** University of Nebraska, B.S. 1945.
**Military Career:** Army, 1942-43.
**Profession:** Farmer and rancher.
**Family:** Single.
**Religion:** Methodist.
**Political Career:** S.D. Senate, 1957-69; lieutenant governor, 1969-71; sought Republican nomination for U.S. House, 1970; U.S. House, 1973-81.

**The Member:** Abdnor's victory over Democrat George McGovern in 1980 elevated to the Senate a man who had been oriented almost exclusively to local interests during his eight-year House career. Abdnor regularly spent a large portion of his day escorting constituents on personally guided tours of the U.S. Capitol.

When he did speak out in the House, it was often to argue that South Dakota or rural America in general be given a fair share of the benefits of national legislation about to be enacted.

Appointed to the House Public Works Committee in 1973, he remained on it throughout his House career, a quiet vote nearly always available to the committee's GOP leadership. His major public works interest was the Oahe water project, located in South Dakota, which President Carter sought frequently to cut back but which Abdnor consistently defended.

In the Senate, Abdnor continues his interest in water projects. But now, as chairman of the water resources subcommittee on Environment and Public Works, he has more power to exercise and broader issues to worry about.

Abdnor took over the subcommittee at a time of a growing skepticism in Congress about federal spending for water projects. Although Abdnor supported generous funding when he was in the House, he has gone along with Senate initiatives to tighten up the authorization process for the projects in order to save money.

Abdnor's subcommittee has tried to restructure national water policy management without dealing Congress out of the decision. To oversee water problems, the subcommittee voted to eastablish a National Board of Water Policy. The Board, independent of the Interior Department, would report directly to the President and Congress. "It is essential that Congress be involved in the development of national water policy," Abdnor said.

Abdnor's concern for rural interests has on

occasion set him at odds with the administration. When Reagan proposed cancellation of an April 1 increase in dairy price supports because it was too costly, Abdnor complained that Reagan's estimates of support costs were inaccurate. Counting sales and contributions of government surplus dairy products, Abdnor said the actual cost of supports in 1980 was $314 million, not $1.3 billion as the administration estimated.

Abdnor's outlook on life and politics is largely a reflection of his upbringing in Kennebec, a tiny and close-knit agricultural community with a county courthouse overlooking one dusty street at a clearing in the fields.

Born in Kennebec, Abdnor attended school there and returned after World War II to take over the family's ranching and farming business. He served in the state Senate for 12 years, became its president pro tempore and then lieutenant governor. Never considered a political powerhouse, Abdnor made his way mainly by his frank and folksy manner and his interest in the local agricultural problems of his area.

His political career received a temporary setback in 1970 when he was upset for the GOP congressional nomination in the 2nd District. But he came back two years later to win both nomination and election in the District.

South Dakota is losing one of its two U.S. House seats in the current reapportionment, and Abdnor had his choice of running for the Senate in 1980 or facing popular Democratic Rep. Tom Daschle of the 1st District in an at-large House election in 1982. With polls showing he could beat McGovern, Abdnor made the Senate race.

The National Conservative Political Action Committee (NCPAC) played an important role in the election. Its attacks on McGovern put the incumbent on the defensive and helped frame the terms of the campaign debate, although Abdnor sought to disavow close connections with NCPAC.

Abdnor overcame a serious health problem in 1978 when he had a successful coronary bypass operation. He now jogs a mile and a half most days.

## Committees

**Appropriations** (10th of 15 Republicans)
Treasury, Postal Service, General Government, chairman; Agriculture and Related Agencies; Energy and Water Development; Labor, Health and Human Services, Education; Transportation.

**Environment and Public Works** (6th of 9 Republicans)
Water Resources, chairman; Toxic Substances and Environmental Oversight; Transportation.

**Joint Economic**
Agriculture and Transportation, chairman; Trade, Productivity and Economic Growth.

## Elections

**1980 General**

| | |
|---|---|
| James Abdnor (R) | 190,594 (58%) |
| George McGovern (D) | 129,018 (39%) |

**1980 Primary**

| | |
|---|---|
| James Abdnor (R) | 68,196 (73%) |
| Dale Bell (R) | 25,314 (27%) |

**Previous Winning Percentages**

1978* (56%)   1976* (70%)   1974* (68%)   1972* (55%)

*House election.*

## Campaign Finance

| | Receipts | Receipts from PACs | Expenditures |
|---|---|---|---|
| **1980** | | | |
| Abdnor (R) | $1,809,743 | $623,912 (34%) | $1,675,430 |
| McGovern (D) | $3,391,109 | $289,149 (9%) | $3,237,669 |

## Voting Studies

| | Presidential Support | | Party Unity | | Conservative Coalition | |
|---|---|---|---|---|---|---|
| Year | S | O | S | O | S | O |
| **House service** | | | | | | |
| 1980 | 31 | 48 | 73 | 8 | 75 | 6 |
| 1979 | 29 | 69 | 85 | 11 | 95 | 4 |
| 1978 | 27 | 61 | 75 | 16 | 79 | 8 |
| 1977 | 35 | 56 | 82 | 7 | 91 | 2 |
| 1976 | 71 | 27 | 83 | 12 | 90 | 6 |
| 1975 | 55 | 44 | 80 | 17 | 90 | 9 |
| 1974 (Ford) | 50 | 41 | | | | |
| 1974 | 58 | 36 | 72 | 24 | 82 | 14 |
| 1973 | 61 | 30 | 76 | 18 | 83 | 6 |

S = Support        O = Opposition

## Key Vote

**97th Congress**

| | |
|---|---|
| Restore urban program funding cuts (1981) | N |

## Interest Group Ratings

| Year | ADA | ACA | AFL-CIO | CCUS-1 | CCUS-2 |
|---|---|---|---|---|---|
| **House service** | | | | | |
| 1980 | 11 | 72 | 6 | 77 | |
| 1979 | 5 | 96 | 16 | 94 | |
| 1978 | 20 | 91 | 22 | 75 | |
| 1977 | 10 | 88 | 18 | 100 | |
| 1976 | 0 | 74 | 26 | 88 | |
| 1975 | 16 | 77 | 17 | 53 | |
| 1974 | 4 | 67 | 18 | 70 | |
| 1973 | 4 | 76 | 11 | 90 | |

# 1 Thomas A. Daschle (D)

**Of Aberdeen — Elected 1978**

**Born:** Dec. 9, 1947, Aberdeen, S. Dak.
**Education:** S.D. State U., B.A. 1969.
**Military Career:** Air Force, 1969-72.
**Profession:** Financial investment adviser.
**Family:** Wife, Laurie Klinkel; three children.
**Religion:** Roman Catholic.
**Political Career:** No previous office.

**In Washington:** The boyish enthusiasm that narrowly brought Daschle a South Dakota House seat in 1978 after a year of solid campaigning has helped stamp him as one of the more enterprising Democratic newcomers in the House.

By mid-1981, he had already shown unusual skill at promoting two very different issues: gasohol and Vietnam veterans' rights.

A Vietnam-era veteran, although never in combat, he joined the Veterans' Affairs Committee in 1979 and began working to move it toward the Vietnam question and away from its exclusive focus on the World War II generation. He spent a good part of his first year working for a bill to help subsidize psychiatric treatment for those who returned from Vietnam needing it. Later he introduced a bill that would create a presumption of federal liability for veterans who became ill after exposure to Agent Orange, a chemical defoliate used in Vietnam.

Daschle's Agent Orange bill passed the House in June of 1981 as part of a broader veterans' legislative package. "We have waited for years," Daschle said as the bill passed, "to be able to come home and tell these Vietnam veterans for the first time we are listening."

Daschle has worked equally hard on gasohol. Twenty percent of this fuel consists of alcohol, and nearly all the potential sources of alcohol — corn, rye, wheat and potatoes — grow in Daschle's district. He started an Alcohol Fuels Caucus and became its chairman. When the National Academy of Sciences issued a report questioning the fuel's potential, Daschle convened a hearing to counter it. Aides joked about changing the name on his door to "Daschohol."

When he has not been promoting his twin causes, Daschle has worked to reconcile the demands of his conservative constituency with his own more moderate inclinations.

Labor provided about one-third of Daschle's campaign money in 1978, and he promised in that campaign to support national repeal of state right-to-work laws. The issue cost him votes, and he told labor early in his first term that he could no longer accept the political liability of that position. But on abortion, another costly issue for him in 1978, he refused to change. He opposed amendments to bar federal funding for abortions except in cases of rape or incest.

**At Home:** Starting off as an unknown congressional aide, Daschle took this congressional district on sheer energy in 1978 and made it utterly secure by the end of his first term.

Over a period of a year, he and his wife rang more than 40,000 doorbells as they campaigned to win first the Democratic nomination over Frank Denholm, the former congressman favored to win, and then to defeat Republican nominee Leo Thorsness.

The 1st District was vacant in 1978 because incumbent Larry Pressler was running for the Senate. Early in the year, it seemed likely the district would stay Republican for Thorsness, a former prisoner of war in Vietnam who had drawn a respectable 47 percent of the statewide vote in a 1974 challenge to Sen. George McGovern.

But Daschle's non-stop campaign brought him even with Thorsness by the end of the summer, and a few weeks before the election, Daschle looked like an easy winner. At that point, however, Republicans began taking advantage of Daschle's two liabilities, his opposition to an anti-abortion amendment and his promise to vote

---

**1st District: East — Sioux Falls.**
Population: 346,631 (4% increase since 1970).
Race: White 338,042 (98%), Black 532 (0.1%), Others 8,056 (2%). Spanish origin: 1,071 (0.3%).

against right-to-work.

By Election Day, the contest was close again, and initial returns showed Thorsness an apparent winner. Only a final canvass a week later gave Daschle the seat by 139 votes. Thorsness challenged the result, but the House decided in Daschle's favor.

Daschle's 1978 campaign had considerable assistance from the remnants of Sen. James Abourezk's Democratic organization since Abourezk was not seeking re-election. Daschle became familiar with politics and legislation while working for Abourezk. He joined the senator as a legislative assistant in Washington in 1973, and was promoted to legislative director in 1975. He moved back to South Dakota in late 1976 to become field director for Abourezk and to prepare his congressional campaign.

Republicans thought they had a strong chal-

lenger in 1980 when they nominated Bart Kull, a Sioux Falls newscaster. But Daschle had been as energetic at constituent service as he was at campaigning, and he overwhelmed Kull, even as South Dakota was voting Republican by wide margins for presidential and Senate candidates (thereby ousting McGovern from the Senate).

**The District:** The 1st District is the area that began the Democratic renaissance in the state in 1956 by electing George McGovern to the House. It is an agricultural-based district, the western terminus of the American heartland's great Corn Belt. Sioux Falls, the largest city in South Dakota, is its economic and political center.

The district will be eliminated for the 1982 elections because South Dakota lost one of its two seats in the 1980 reapportionment. As a result, Daschle will have to run statewide to win another term in the House.

## Committees

**Agriculture** (19th of 24 Democrats)
Conservation, Credit, and Rural Development; Forests, Family Farms, and Energy; Wheat, Soybeans, and Feed Grains.

**Veterans' Affairs** (13th of 17 Democrats)
Education, Training and Employment; Hospitals and Health Care.

## Elections

**1980 General**

| Thomas Daschle (D) | 109,910 (66 %) |
| Bart Kull (R) | 57,155 (34%) |

**1978 General**

| Thomas Daschle (D) | 64,683 (50 %) |
| Leo Thorsness (R) | 64,544 (50 %) |

**1978 Primary**

| Thomas Daschle (D) | 21,491 (59 %) |
| Frank Denholm (D) | 14,760 (41 %) |

**District Vote For President**

| | 1980 | | 1976 | | 1972 |
|---|---|---|---|---|---|
| D | 59,684 (35 %) | D | 78,680 (50 %) D | 77,932 (49 %) |
| R | 95,170 (56 %) | R | 76,758 (49 %) R | 80,576 (51 %) |
| I | 13,181 (8 %) | | | | |

## Campaign Finance

| | Receipts | Receipts from PACs | Expenditures |
|---|---|---|---|
| **1980** | | | |
| Daschle (D) | $245,688 | $90,573 (37 %) | $204,380 |
| Kull (R) | $78,630 | $14,531 (18 %) | $83,909 |

| 1978 | | | |
|---|---|---|---|
| Daschle (D) | $225,402 | $81,216 (36 %) | $223,221 |
| Thorsness (R) | $270,367 | $83,905 (31 %) | $270,366 |

## Voting Studies

| | Presidential Support | | Party Unity | | Conservative Coalition | |
|---|---|---|---|---|---|---|
| Year | S | O | S | O | S | O |
| 1980 | 58 | 32 | 62 | 30 | 44 | 47 |
| 1979 | 65 | 33 | 72 | 25 | 36 | 63 |

S = Support    O = Opposition

## Key Votes

**96th Congress**

| | |
|---|---|
| Weaken Carter oil profits tax (1979) | N |
| Reject hospital cost control plan (1979) | Y |
| Implement Panama Canal Treaties (1979) | Y |
| Establish Department of Education (1979) | Y |
| Approve Anti-busing Amendment (1979) | N |
| Guarantee Chrysler Corp. loans (1979) | Y |
| Approve military draft registration (1980) | N |
| Aid Sandinista regime in Nicaragua (1980) | Y |
| Strengthen fair housing laws (1980) | Y |

**97th Congress**

| Reagan budget proposal (1981) | N |

## Interest Group Ratings

| Year | ADA | ACA | AFL-CIO | CCUS |
|---|---|---|---|---|
| 1980 | 72 | 35 | 74 | 68 |
| 1979 | 79 | 19 | 90 | 22 |

# 2 Clint Roberts (R)

Of Presho — Elected 1980

**Born:** Jan. 30, 1935, Presho, S.D.
**Education:** Attended Black Hills State College.
**Profession:** Rancher.
**Family:** Wife, Beverly Dittman; four children.
**Religion:** Methodist.
**Political Career:** S.D. Senate, 1973-79; Senate president 1977-79; S.D. secretary of agriculture, 1979-80; unsuccessfully sought Republican nomination for governor, 1978.

**The Member:** Most of the attention Roberts attracted in his 1980 campaign came from his reputation as a "Marlboro man" in cigarette advertisements of the past decade. Whether his face actually appeared in the ads is a matter of some controversy, but there is no question that the Marlboro image, reinforced by his role as head of the South Dakota Cowboy Hall of Fame, was a political asset. Just as helpful, however, was the decade he spent in the more mundane world of South Dakota politics and farm policy.

In Congress, Roberts seldom strays far from his field of expertise. He watches over South Dakota's interests on the Agriculture Committee, adding his name to bills like one that would set price support loan levels for commodities the government bars farmers from exporting.

A successful rancher, Roberts ventured into politics as Lyman County GOP chairman and was elected to the state Senate in 1972. He became assistant minority leader in 1975 and president pro tem in 1977. He ran for governor in 1978, coming in third in the GOP primary behind the state attorney general, William Janklow. When Janklow won the governorship, he appointed Roberts to his Cabinet as state agriculture secretary. When Republican James Abdnor left his House seat to run for the Senate in 1980, Roberts had little trouble defeating Democrat Kenneth Stofferahn. Since the 1980 census took one House seat from South Dakota, Roberts may face 1st District Democrat Tom Daschle in 1982.

**The District:** The 2nd is the more rural, Western-oriented part of South Dakota, where repeated drought has discouraged farming in many places and where once-viable crossroads villages are falling into decline. Ranching is the dominant activity. The only substantial commercial center is Rapid City, also a tourist gateway to the Black Hills and national parks further west.

Although it backed some Democratic candidates in the 1970s, the 2nd is the more conservative and Republican part of the state.

## Committees

**Agriculture** (16th of 19 Republicans)
Conservation, Credit, and Rural Development; Tobacco and Peanuts; Wheat, Soybeans, and Feed Grains.

## Elections

**1980 General**

| | |
|---|---|
| Clint Roberts (R ) | 88,991 (58 %) |
| Kenneth Stofferahn (D) | 63,447 (42 %) |

**1980 Primary**

| | |
|---|---|
| Clint Roberts (R ) | 32,984 (65 %) |
| Don Ham (R ) | 17,970 (35 %) |

**District Vote For President**

| | 1980 | | 1976 | | 1972 |
|---|---|---|---|---|---|
| **D** | 44,171 (28 %) | **D** | 68,388 (47 %) | **D** | 62,013 (42 %) |
| **R** | 103,173 (65 %) | **R** | 74,747 (52 %) | **R** | 85,900 (58 %) |
| **I** | 8,250 (5 %) | | | | |

## Campaign Finance

| | Receipts | Receipts from PACs | Expenditures |
|---|---|---|---|
| **1980** | | | |
| Roberts (R ) | $220,314 | $69,453 (32 %) | $217,765 |
| Stofferahn (D ) | $120,420 | $54,650 (45 %) | $116,776 |

## Key Vote

**97th Congress**

| | |
|---|---|
| Reagan budget proposal (1981) | Y |

---

**2nd District: Central and west — Rapid City.** Population: 343,548 (3% increase since 1970). Race: White 300,913 (88%), Black 1,612 (0.4%), Indian 38,738 (11%), Others 2,285 (1%). Spanish origin: 2,957 (1%).

---

# Tennessee

| U.S. CONGRESS: EIGHT DISTRICTS | STATE: |
| --- | --- |
| Senate (1D, 1R) | **Governor** Lamar Alexander (R) |
| House (5D, 3R) | **General Assembly** Senate: 33 members (20D, 12R, 1IND) House: 99 members (57D, 39R, 2IND, 1 Vacancy) |
| | **Population** 4,590,750 - 17th in the nation |
| | **Area** 42,244 sq. miles - 34th in the nation |

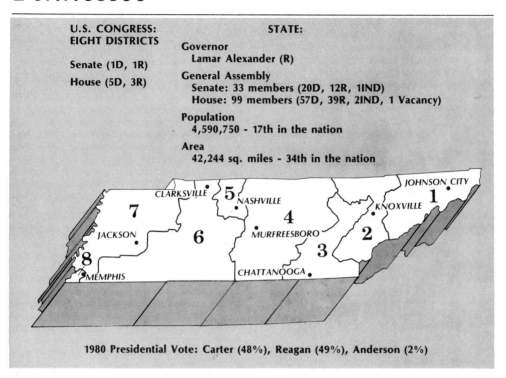

**1980 Presidential Vote: Carter (48%), Reagan (49%), Anderson (2%)**

## ...Three Southern States

Tennessee is three distinct regions, stretching 400 miles from the Appalachian highlands to the Mississippi. The different regions' politics are as different as their topography.

The farmers in the highland valleys of East Tennessee have traditionally been Republican, doggedly self-reliant and suspicious of outsiders. Middle Tennessee, where the rolling hills and bluegrass fields are well-suited to livestock and tobacco, has been the part of the state most receptive to populist Democrats. West Tennessee started as a province of "King Cotton" and slavery, and continued into the 20th century as a region of bourbon Democratic control.

More than almost anywhere else in the South, Civil War voting patterns are still the clue to politics. Pro-union sentiment was strong in the east, where the small-scale farmers owned few slaves and resented the planters in the Mississippi valley. Even though the state seceded and joined the confederacy, most of East Tennessee stayed loyal to the Union, and Republican ever after.

After the Civil War, loyalties in Middle and West Tennessee guaranteed one-party Democratic rule, over objections in the east. Memphis political boss Edward H. Crump, first elected mayor in 1909, made Tennessee his political fiefdom until after World War II. Crump controlled state Democratic primaries through a patronage network that delivered about 65,000 votes in Shelby County (Memphis) and a significant share of the outstate vote.

Voter turnout increased in the postwar years, and Crump lost control to a younger breed of progressive Democrats like Gov. Frank Clement and U.S. Senators Estes Kefauver and Albert Gore. Gore, last of those to leave public office, lost in 1970 to Republican Bill Brock.

Brock's victory was part of a GOP resurgence that elected Howard H. Baker Jr. to the Senate in

**1115**

1966 and Winfield Dunn to the governorship in 1970. Since 1970, two-party competition has flourished as it has in few other parts of the country. Democrats recaptured the governorship in 1974, but lost it in 1978. Carter beat Ford convincingly in 1976, but Reagan won narrowly in 1980. Brock lost his Senate seat in 1976 to Democrat Jim Sasser, but Baker has been re-elected comfortably twice. Republicans surged to control of the Tennessee House as early as 1968, but failed to hold it. Democrats control both houses of the state Legislature now, and have a 5-3 advantage in U.S House seats.

# A Political Tour

**East Tennessee.** The Tennessee Valley Authority's programs for flood control, electrical generation, and soil conservation lifted much of this region from rural poverty. But the TVA has shaken few natives from their historic party ties and instinctive suspicion of big government. East Tennessee is Republican territory, with rare exception.

Sullivan and Washington counties encompass northeast Tennessee's growing Tri-Cities — Kingsport, Johnson City and Bristol, an area with chemical manufacturing, paper milling, book printing and other industry.

Washington County (Johnson City) opposed secession in 1861, like most of the region, and has since regularly voted Republican.

Sullivan County (Kingsport) is one of the few eastern areas with a consistently high Democratic vote, one that goes back to its endorsement of secession in 1861. Sullivan went for Democrats Sasser and Carter in 1976, and chose Reagan over Carter only narrowly in 1980. Coal mining is an economic staple for many of the mountainous eastern counties, and in recent years exploration for oil and natural gas has boosted the economy.

Knoxville, in the center of East Tennessee, is the region's largest city and third largest in the state. TVA headquarters are there, as is the University of Tennessee's main campus. Knoxville grew up on textile and iron production and now has a larger role as regional retail and distribution center. The 1982 World's Fair will be held on a 70-acre site near the downtown area.

Despite the TVA and its association with Democratic administrations, Knoxville and surrounding Knox County remain solidly Republican. There is one enclave of Democratic support near Knoxville — among the scientific intelligentsia in Oak Ridge, the city established by the federal government during World War II to purify uranium for use in the atomic bomb.

In Tennessee's southeast corner is heavily industrialized Chattanooga, fourth largest city in the state. Steel, iron and chemicals are produced there. Former Sen. Bill Brock began building the Republican Party in Chattanooga in the early 1960s, and represented it in the U.S. House for eight years before moving to the Senate. Hamilton County, containing Chattanooga, has voted Republican in all but one presidential contest since 1952; in 1968, American Independent George Wallace finished first and Nixon second.

**Middle Tennessee.** The "capital" of Middle Tennessee is Nashville, which has also been capital of the state since 1843. Today it is a center for banking, insurance, and higher education, but it is known better regionally for religious publishing, and nationally for the country music industry.

Many Middle Tennesseans resented Crump's conservative political machine, which controlled the statehouse in Nashville by pulling strings in Memphis. Anti-Crumpism played a part in making Middle Tennessee the spawning ground for a number of the state's populist and progressive Democrats. One was Frank Clement, a Bible-thumping, evangelical-style orator who as governor (1955-59, 1963-67) enacted educational reforms, improved mental health services and vetoed several segregation bills passed by the state Legislature. Albert Gore Sr., born in north central Tennessee, championed public power and civil rights as a member of Congress.

Clement, Gore and Estes Kefauver, a liberal East Tennessee Democrat, set the political tone in Tennessee's post-Crump era and shared the spotlight at the 1956 Democratic convention: Clement was the keynoter and Gore and Kefauver vied for the vice presidential slot won eventually by Kefauver. Their larger ambitions went unrealized. The Stevenson-Kefauver ticket lost to the Republicans in 1956 and Clement failed in two later bids for the Senate. Gore was twice re-elected to the Senate, but lost in 1970 to Republican Brock. Gore's son currently represents much of Middle Tennessee in the House, and carries on the rural populist-progressive tradition, although he himself is urban in style and background.

Democratic candidates can usually depend on carrying Middle Tennessee (Reagan won only two counties in the region in 1980), but metropolitan Davidson County (Nashville) has been inclined to wander a bit in recent years. It voted for Wallace in 1968, Nixon in 1972 and Republican gubernatorial candidate Lamar Alexander in 1978.

**West Tennessee.** More than ever, the west is dominated by Memphis, whose metropolitan area is the South's seventh largest. The city's economy, born out of plantation crops, shifted its emphasis to chemicals and machinery and now attracts corporate headquarters and warehousing and distribution facilities.

Shelby County (Memphis), the bulwark of one-party rule under Crump, became the key to two-party politics in Tennessee when Crump died in 1953 and his organization crumbled. The power vacuum in Shelby County was filled partly by suburban middle-class businessmen and professionals. This group, uneasy about the Democrats' preoccupation with racial equality, found a haven in Goldwater Republicanism and extended their organization beyond Memphis to traditionally conservative rural West Tennessee.

The Shelby County GOP elected Dan Kuykendall to the Memphis congressional seat in 1966 and brought strong West Tennessee support to Baker in 1966 and Dunn and Brock in 1970. Kuykendall lost to a black Democrat in 1974, as the district's white population was declining, but upper-income whites in Shelby County continue to vote Republican in large numbers. In most parts of suburban Shelby County, Reagan won about two-thirds of the vote in 1980. Memphis itself, now heavily black, went for Carter decisively.

West Tennessee has a pocket of Republican strength in the Highland Rim area, where poor hill country farmers in counties like Hardin, Wayne, Henderson and Carroll held few slaves in antebellum days and opposed secession. Nearby Madison County (Jackson) is another area that often votes Republican.

# Redrawing the Lines

Trying to bring two more Democrats into the expanded nine-member Tennessee congressional delegation, the Democratic-controlled Legislature approved a redistricting bill in mid-June.

The state's new seat is a gangly, 23-county affair running more than 300 miles from northeastern to south-central Tennessee. To create it, Democrats made the three East Tennessee districts more compact (population in each of them grew by more than 18 percent), then attached what was left over from them to a large chunk that was split off of the strongly Democratic 4th District in midstate. The latter was 125,000 people too big.

Democrats also threw out some GOP counties from the Republican-held 6th District and shifted the boundaries westward. Located in both middle and western Tennessee, this was the state's fastest-growing area in the 1970s.

The Memphis-area district of black Democratic Rep. Harold E. Ford lost nearly 17 percent of its population in the last decade, so its boundaries had to expand further into Shelby County, taking in some areas where Ford is not likely to receive the degree of support that he does from his current constituents. None of the other incumbents were threatened by the remapping of the state.

Republican Gov. Lamar Alexander allowed the redistricting bill to become law without his signature.

# Governor
# Lamar Alexander (R)

**Born:** July 3, 1940, Blount County, Tenn.
**Home:** Nashville, Tenn.
**Education:** Vanderbilt U., B.A. 1962; New York U. School of Law, J.D. 1965.
**Profession:** Lawyer.
**Family:** Wife, Honey; four children.
**Religion:** Presbyterian.
**Political Career:** Campaign coordinator for Sen. Howard Baker Jr., 1966; Sen. Baker's legislative assistant, 1966-69; Congressional relations office in White House, 1969; manager of Winfield Dunn's gubernatorial campaign, 1970; unsuccessful campaign for governor, 1974; elected governor 1978; term expires Jan. 1983.

# Howard H. Baker Jr. (R)

**Of Huntsville — Elected 1966**

**Born:** Nov., 15, 1925, Huntsville, Tenn.
**Education:** Attended U. of the South, 1943-44;
Tulane U. 1944-45; U. of Tenn., LL.B. 1949.
**Military Career:** Navy, 1943-46.
**Profession:** Lawyer.
**Family:** Wife, Joy Dirksen; two children.
**Religion:** Presbyterian.
**Political Career:** Unsuccessful Republican
nominee for U.S. Senate, 1964.

**In Washington:** Baker wanted to be president, but many of his colleagues think he is better suited by temperament to the majority leader's position he inherited instead. His skills have always been more legislative than executive. He is a man who seeks to blur distinctions, rather than draw them, and to calm passions rather than stir them.

Despite some doubts about him on the Republican right, Baker made his shift from the minority without challenge and with the explicit blessing of Paul Laxalt, R-Nev., President Reagan's closest friend in the Senate and the only conservative who could have given Baker a run for the job.

He is regarded by colleagues in both parties as fair, reasonable and generous — qualities evident in his treatment of Minority Leader Robert C. Byrd, who found his abrupt demotion from majority leader distressing. Baker went out of his way to ease Byrd's pain, even allowing the Democratic leader to retain his Capitol office suite.

But Baker also wasted no time stamping his own mark upon the Senate. No sooner had he become majority leader than he announced he would seek authorization for televising Senate sessions — a step Byrd had vigorously resisted, even after the House inaugurated such coverage in early 1979. Baker also moved swiftly to put the Senate on a more predictable — and less grueling — routine than the occasional nights-and-Saturdays schedule Byrd had followed.

Baker's leadership skills were tested almost immediately when Reagan was forced to ask for an increase in the debt ceiling, a move Republicans have ritualistically opposed in the past. Even though he normally eschews pressure tactics, Baker leaned on recalcitrant Republicans, telling them the vote was vital not only to Reagan but to him, and he persuaded veteran conservatives to urge the freshmen to go along. All but three GOP members voted to raise the debt ceiling, and

conservatives who had planned to offer several amendments to the legislation agreed to hold off.

That display of unity across ideological lines seemed unlikely to persist very long. Baker had been a target for the New Right ever since he supported the Panama Canal treaties in 1978. He pacified some of these critics with his conciliatory attitude in early 1981, but he angered others with his plea that until the Reagan economic proposals were in place, conservative initiatives on social issues like busing, abortion and school prayer should be kept aside.

There is a certain irony to Baker's problems with the right, because it was conservatives who provided the bulk of his support when he sought the Republican leadership in 1969 and again in 1971. He narrowly lost those bids to the more liberal Hugh Scott of Pennsylvania, but came back in 1977 after Scott retired to edge Robert P. Griffin of Michigan by a single vote. In that contest, moderate and liberal Republicans generally sided with Baker; most conservatives went with Griffin.

One thing that had happened in the interim was Watergate — and Baker's often enigmatic performance as vice chairman of the Senate Watergate Committee, with his constant repetition of the question. "What did the president know, and when did he know it?"

Television audiences were impressed by Baker's charm. The press was never quite sure how to treat him, acclaiming him at first as a statesman, then suggesting, as the hearings wore on, that he might be pulling his punches. But the more lasting reaction came from some of Baker's earlier conservative supporters, who never forgave his contribution to Nixon's downfall.

The real turning point, however, was Panama, a year after he became minority leader. The canal was an emotional issue for conservatives in the Senate and outside — it was a major theme of the 1976 Reagan presidential campaign — and the New Right turned on Baker with a vengeance. Even Baker's militant opposition to the proposed SALT II treaty with the Soviet Union did not help the situation — conservative publisher Richard Viguerie helped erase him as a Reagan vice presidential contender in 1980 with a bitter attack in his magazine, Conservative Digest.

Within the Senate, however, Baker's reputation as a moderate Republican rests more on his domestic policies. As a newly elected senator in 1967, he helped defeat the efforts of his famous father-in-law, the late Minority Leader Everett M. Dirksen, to overturn the Supreme Court's one-man, one-vote ruling. The following year he persuaded Dirksen to support a compromise fair housing bill. He supported the 1970 extension of the Voting Rights Act.

Baker has favored the development of synthetic fuels and solar energy and opposed a ban on nuclear power. He has battled for years to keep Tennessee's Clinch River breeder reactor alive, arguing it represents the only virtually inexhaustible long-term energy resource.

In 1979, he joined liberals and environmentalists to oppose giving a new Energy Mobilization Board power to override state and local regulations in the name of energy conservation. That was too much, he said, though he endorsed the basic idea of a board to cut red tape and put energy development onto a "fast track." The bill never became law.

He also helped write a modified version of a 1980 "Superfund" bill to clean up contamination from poisonous wastes. The same year, he quietly amended an appropriation bill to allow the Environmental Protection Agency to use $2 million to study potential health damage from hazardous waste dump sites around Memphis.

As a member of the Environment Committee, Baker was intimately involved in drafting the Clean Air Act in 1970 and revising it in 1977. As the committee began a second rewrite in 1981, he said he wanted to protect the act from destruction, but would support some modifications.

Baker has walked a careful line on most controversial policy issues. He voted for the Equal Rights Amendment but against extending the deadline for its ratification. He opposes an anti-abortion amendment to the Constitution but voted to let the states impose tight limits on public funding of abortions for the poor.

He backed the 1973 Endangered Species Act, then fought to weaken it in 1978 so that the Tellico Dam could be built in his state. He

opposed efforts to limit presidential war powers, but reversed his field and voted to override President Nixon's veto of the War Powers Act in 1973.

Most of these votes were not contradictory, but involved the shades of gray that Baker likes to perceive and point out — whether his more passionate colleagues are worried about them or not.

**At Home:** The casual, pragmatic style that Baker displays on the Senate floor is the same one that brought him out of a small-town law office and made him Tennessee's first popularly-elected Republican senator.

Baker could have had a House seat in 1964 with little effort; his father, a seven-term Republican incumbent in the state's 2nd District, had died in office earlier in the year. But Howard Baker gambled on a campaign for the Senate, which was also open because of the death of Democrat Estes Kefauver. Baker's themes were solidly conservative; he promised to restrict federal involvement in education, then on the verge of a massive expansion. He received more votes than any Republican in Tennessee history, but lost to Democratic U.S. Rep. Ross Bass, whose pro-civil rights record earned him repute as the state's most liberal congressman.

Two years later, trying again and running against a Goldwater conservative in the Republican primary, Baker adopted a more moderate tone. "We must see that the Republican Party is so broadly based," he said, "that it can support widely divergent viewpoints and express the majority view." He told blacks he would "speak your voice and your needs" and support open-housing legislation. He won the nomination, and easily defeated Gov. Frank Clement in the general election, drawing considerably more black support than previous GOP candidates in a state that already had a significant black vote before the civil rights revolution of the 1960s.

As his 1972 re-election approached, Baker was thought to be in some trouble. A Nixon-appointed U.S. District Court judge whom Baker had sponsored handed down a desegregation order in 1971 calling for extensive busing in the Nashville-Davidson County school system. Baker had to defend his recommendation of the judge to busing foes. His Democratic opponent, U.S. Rep. Ray Blanton, stressed populist themes and claimed Baker was too closely allied with moneyed and privileged interests. Baker pointed to his backing of environmental legislation as evidence of his independence from big business.

As it turned out, Baker had little reason to be worried. His votes for open housing legislation helped him among blacks, the busing issue never seriously threatened him, and President Nixon's landslide victory in Tennessee brought thousands of extra votes into the Republican column. Baker's 61 percent stands as the highest total for a GOP Senate candidate in Tennessee history.

When the time came for a third campaign in 1978, Baker's support for the Panama Canal treaties appeared to present a problem, especially for a senator with national ambitions. Democrat Jane Eskind, who had a background as a liberal in Nashville politics, abruptly turned right as the party's Senate nominee and staked her challenge to Baker on the Panama issue.

Eskind was a competent candidate — she had engineered a statewide voter registration drive in 1976 — but her issue had largely faded by late 1978. When President Carter came to Tennessee to campaign for the Democratic ticket, he avoided criticism of Baker, whose support was crucial to the passage of the Canal treaties and other administration proposals. Carter described Eskind as "tough and competent," but his praise went no further. In an election that was seen by some as a referendum on Baker's national political possibilities, the senator won 55.5 percent.

## Committees

**Environment and Public Works** (2nd of 9 Republicans)
Nuclear Regulation; Regional and Community Development; Transportation.

**Foreign Relations** (2nd of 9 Republicans)
Arms Control, Oceans and International Operations, and Environment; East Asian and Pacific Affairs; Near Eastern and South Asian Affairs.

**Rules and Administration** (3rd of 7 Republicans)

**Joint Library**

## Elections

**1978 General**

| | |
|---|---|
| Howard Baker Jr. (R) | 642,644 (56%) |
| Jane Eskind (D) | 466,228 (40%) |

**1978 Republican Primary**

| | |
|---|---|
| Howard Baker Jr. (R) | 205,680 (83%) |
| Harvey Howard (R) | 21,154 (9%) |

**Previous Winning Percentages**

| | |
|---|---|
| 1972 (62%%) | 1966 (56%) |

## Campaign Finance

| | Receipts | Receipts from PACs | Expenditures |
|---|---|---|---|
| **1978** | | | |
| Baker (R) | $1,946,071 | $344,683 (18%) | $1,922,573 |
| Eskind (D) | $1,906,603 | $26,930 (1%) | $1,903,532 |

## Voting Studies

| | Presidential Support | | Party Unity | | Conservative Coalition | |
|---|---|---|---|---|---|---|
| Year | S | O | S | O | S | O |
| 1980 | 39 | 46 | 65 | 13 | 66 | 11 |
| 1979 | 33 | 26 | 43 | 19 | 55 | 16 |
| 1978 | 53 | 27 | 50 | 33 | 64 | 21 |
| 1977 | 55 | 35 | 71 | 19 | 82 | 11 |
| 1976 | 64 | 15 | 68 | 11 | 70 | 12 |

| | | | | | | |
|---|---|---|---|---|---|---|
| 1975 | 70 | 14 | 68 | 10 | 70 | 5 |
| 1974 (Ford) | 60 | 21 | | | | |
| 1974 | 63 | 20 | 72 | 14 | 77 | 10 |
| 1973 | 57 | 25 | 59 | 10 | 59 | 9 |
| 1972 | 63 | 4 | 58 | 3 | 57 | 3 |
| 1971 | 67 | 18 | 72 | 14 | 76 | 6 |
| 1970 | 71 | 19 | 76 | 11 | 75 | 10 |
| 1969 | 65 | 17 | 69 | 12 | 77 | 7 |
| 1968 | 35 | 40 | 72 | 4 | 76 | 6 |
| 1967 | 55 | 27 | 64 | 14 | 70 | 9 |

S = Support          O = Opposition

## Key Votes

**96th Congress**

| | |
|---|---|
| Maintain relations with Taiwan (1979) | ? |
| Reduce synthetic fuel development funds (1979) | ? |
| Impose nuclear plant moratorium (1979) | ? |
| Kill stronger windfall profits tax (1979) | Y |
| Guarantee Chrysler Corp. loans (1979) | ? |
| Approve military draft registration (1980) | Y |
| End Revenue Sharing to the states (1980) | N |
| Block Justice Dept. busing suits (1980) | Y |

**97th Congress**

| | |
|---|---|
| Restore urban program funding cuts (1981) | N |

## Interest Group Ratings

| Year | ADA | ACA | AFL-CIO | CCUS-1 | CCUS-2 |
|---|---|---|---|---|---|
| 1980 | 17 | 81 | 8 | 81 | |
| 1979 | 21 | 63 | 29 | 63 | 70 |
| 1978 | 25 | 79 | 37 | 93 | |
| 1977 | 15 | 52 | 28 | 76 | |
| 1976 | 5 | 80 | 14 | 67 | |
| 1975 | 11 | 54 | 33 | 46 | |
| 1974 | 14 | 72 | 30 | 89 | |
| 1973 | 10 | 73 | 22 | 100 | |
| 1972 | 0 | 71 | 13 | 75 | |
| 1971 | 4 | 55 | 27 | . | |
| 1970 | 13 | 89 | 20 | 70 | |
| 1969 | 11 | 36 | 33 | . | |
| 1968 | 21 | 80 | 50 | . | |
| 1967 | 23 | 65 | 33 | 100 | |

# Jim Sasser (D)

### Of Nashville — Elected 1976

**Born:** Sept. 30, 1936, Memphis, Tenn.
**Education:** Attended U. of Tenn., 1954-55; Vanderbilt U., B.A. 1958, J.D. 1961.
**Military Career:** Marine Corps Reserve, 1957-63.
**Profession:** Lawyer.
**Family:** Wife, Mary Gorman; two children.
**Religion:** Methodist.
**Political Career:** No previous office.

**In Washington:** Sasser has plugged away throughout his Senate term at a subject close to his heart and his re-election campaign — federal waste and fraud. It is what he promised to do when elected and what he is preparing to run on again in 1982. Sasser is a moderate, labor-oriented Democrat on many issues, but his public crusade is fiscal conservatism, and no level of federal spending is too trivial to complain about.

This small-scale auditing is sometimes exasperating to other senators. Late in 1980, when Sasser offered an amendment to reduce Senate staff funds by 15 percent, Budget Chairman Ernest F. Hollings of South Carolina angrily accused Sasser of playing politics. "I don't mind folks running for office," he said, "but ... the same fellows who are talking about biting the bullet are biting each other." He said the Sasser amendment would restrict a senator's ability to do his job.

But Sasser has persisted, helped until 1981 by his chairmanship of the Legislative Appropriations Subcommittee. He used that panel to fight efforts by congressional leaders to increase federal pay, and opposed a move to suspend the limit on how much money a senator could earn outside his regular salary.

Sasser persuaded the General Accounting Office to install a toll-free national hot line for citizens to call and report government fraud. He claims to have saved $2 million a year by prohibiting the use of federal funds for indoor plant watering, and $500 million by cutting the federal employee travel budget.

These funds are Sasser's proccupation not only on the Appropriations Committee but on Governmental Affairs, to which he gives most of the rest of his time. One of his projects on Governmental Affairs is a complex bill to consolidate federal grant programs and give Congress more control over them. This one passed the Senate in late 1980, mainly as a courtesy to Sasser. It was clear that there was no time for it to

become law in the 96th Congress; he wanted some momentum for a fresh start in 1981.

When Edmund S. Muskie left the Senate in 1980, Sasser inherited primary sponsorship of the long-debated "sunset bill," which would terminate any federal program automatically unless it were specifically reauthorized by Congress within a fixed period.

Once a great bipartisan hope for reining in the bureaucracy, sunset legislation passed the Senate in 1978 but failed in the House. Sasser steered it through the Governmental Affairs Committee again in 1980, but it went no further. Most senior senators were saying by then that the reauthorization task would overburden committees. "Sunset" was an idea, Thomas F. Eagleton of Missouri said, whose time had come and gone.

Sasser came to the Senate as a loyal supporter of Jimmy Carter, but cooled when the Carter administration opposed some Tennessee federal projects, such as the Tellico Dam, held up by the Endangered Species Act. Sasser said Carter simply assumed his vote on crucial issues because of past loyalty. Pressed to vote with Carter in favor of transfer of the Panama Canal, he ultimately did, but complained about the administration's attitude. "They keep expecting us to fall on our swords," Sasser said, "but there has been very little reciprocity."

As a member of the Budget Committee in the 97th Congress, Sasser has generally gone along with the Reagan-proposed cuts in federal spending, in agreement with most other Southern Democrats. But when the first round of cuts came to the Senate floor, he sought to restore $200 million for the school lunch program, an effort he had made unsuccessfully in committee. Most Democrats voted for it, but it was beaten, 54-35.

**At Home:** Sasser's 1976 Senate campaign in

## Jim Sasser, D-Tenn.

behalf of "a government that reflects our decency" bore a pronounced and deliberate similarity to Jimmy Carter's call for "a government as good as the people." When Carter won the Tennessee presidential primary that year with 77.6 percent of the vote, Sasser joked that he wanted not only to cling to Carter's coattails, but to get inside the coat.

It was a successful strategy. In November, Carter won Tennessee by nearly 200,000 votes, helping Sasser to a smaller but still comfortable victory over incumbent Republican Sen. Bill Brock, who a year earlier had been considered safe for re-election.

Sasser used his three-year chairmanship of the state Democratic Party to build a base of electoral support. He quit the party post in early 1976 to launch his Senate campaign. His chief Democratic rival was liberal Nashville business-man John J. Hooker, whose unsuccessful tries for the governorship in 1966 and 1970 had given him name recognition but a "loser" image. Sasser was endorsed by several minority and labor groups who saw him as a fresh face and a possible winner. With the support of most of the party leadership, he defeated Hooker convincingly.

Brock, a wealthy candy heir, displayed the same organizing skill that was later to make him a successful national GOP chairman. But his upper-crust image and quiet personal style contrasted unfavorably with Sasser's down-to-earth manner and ready sense of humor.

Sasser portrayed Brock as a country-club Republican, a special-interest senator who represented banks and insurance companies. It was a perfect issue in a state always susceptible to populist rhetoric, and doubly so in a year in which Carter was reinforcing Sasser's themes.

## Committees

**Appropriations** (12th of 14 Democrats)
Agriculture and Related Agencies; Energy and Water Development; HUD-Independent Agencies; Military Construction.

**Budget** (5th of 10 Democrats)

**Governmental Affairs** (6th of 8 Democrats)
Intergovernmental Relations; Permanent Subcommittee on Investigations.

**Select Small Business** (4th of 8 Democrats)
Capital Formation and Retention; Government Procurement.

## Elections

**1976 General**

| | |
|---|---|
| Jim Sasser (D) | 751,180 (53%) |
| William Brock (R) | 673,231 (47%) |

**1976 Democratic Primary**

| | |
|---|---|
| Jim Sasser (D) | 244,930 (44%) |
| John Hooker (D) | 171,716 (31%) |
| Harry Sadler (D) | 54,125 (10%) |
| David Bolin (D) | 44,056 (8%) |
| Lester Kefauver (D) | 29,864 (5%) |

## Campaign Finance

| | Receipts | Receipts from PACs | Expenditures |
|---|---|---|---|
| **1976** | | | |
| Sasser (D) | $841,644 | $119,409 (14%) | $839,379 |
| Brock (R) | $1,313,503 | $146,252 (11%) | $1,301,033 |

## Voting Studies

| | Presidential Support | | Party Unity | | Conservative Coalition | |
|---|---|---|---|---|---|---|
| Year | S | O | S | O | S | O |
| 1980 | 67 | 26 | 70 | 23 | 51 | 42 |
| 1979 | 65 | 21 | 66 | 19 | 55 | 35 |
| 1978 | 63 | 30 | 62 | 29 | 52 | 38 |
| 1977 | 75 | 23 | 74 | 19 | 30 | 65 |

S = Support          O = Opposition

## Key Votes

**96th Congress**

| | |
|---|---|
| Maintain relations with Taiwan (1979) | N |
| Reduce synthetic fuel development funds (1979) | N |
| Impose nuclear plant moratorium (1979) | N |
| Kill stronger windfall profits tax (1979) | N |
| Guarantee Chrysler Corp. loans (1979) | Y |
| Approve military draft registration (1980) | Y |
| End Revenue Sharing to the states (1980) | N |
| Block Justice Dept. busing suits (1980) | Y |

**97th Congress**

| | |
|---|---|
| Restore urban program funding cuts (1981) | N |

## Interest Group Ratings

| Year | ADA | ACA | AFL-CIO | CCUS-1 | CCUS-2 |
|---|---|---|---|---|---|
| 1980 | 67 | 23 | 68 | 43 | |
| 1979 | 37 | 29 | 53 | 10 | 36 |
| 1978 | 55 | 57 | 74 | 47 | |
| 1977 | 60 | 8 | 89 | 35 | |

# 1 James H. Quillen (R)

**Of Kingsport — Elected in 1962**

**Born:** Jan. 11, 1916, near Gate City, Va.
**Education:** Graduated from Dobyns and Bennett H.S., Kingsport, Tenn.
**Military Career:** Navy, 1942-46.
**Profession:** Newspaper publisher.
**Family:** Wife, Cecile Cox.
**Religion:** Methodist.
**Political Career:** Tenn. House, 1955-63.

**In Washington:** Quillen has never become the power broker in Washington that he has been in his home state, where he was House minority leader and still has the leverage to influence close statewide primaries by swinging his East Tennessee counties one way or the other.

Seniority has brought him the senior Republican place on the House Rules Committee, but he has never been a skillful parliamentarian, and he has not used his position to become either a policy-maker or a successful obstructionist. In the past Congress, Robert Bauman of Maryland was the dominant GOP presence on Rules; in this Congress, with party whip Trent Lott of Mississippi and former leader John J. Rhodes of Arizona serving on the committee, Quillen is still overshadowed.

His questions to witnesses before the committee are often notable for comic relief, as when he told a committee chairman that a piece of legislation appeared to be "putting the carrot before the cart."

He once broke up a hearing at Rules by putting a goldfish in his water pitcher. The hearing was on a measure softening the Endangered Species Act, which was threatening to block construction of the $119 million Tellico Dam in Tennessee because it would destroy the habitat of a small fish, the snail darter.

Quillen was a booster of the dam and an opponent of the act. He said he wanted to find out how long it would take people to notice the fish in his pitcher, and hoped to demonstrate the insignificance of the even smaller snail darter.

In 1978, Quillen used his committee position to force a floor vote on a provision to repeal the earned income limit imposed on members of Congress the previous year. A new ethics code limited outside earned income to 15 percent of salary ($8,625 at that time). Quillen, who was a board member or president of five companies, was getting considerably more than that annually in outside earned income and vigorously opposed the limit.

When a financial disclosure bill came before the committee, Quillen shocked the Democrats by coming up with enough votes to demand floor action on his amendment repealing the limit. House leaders temporarily pulled the entire bill out of consideration, then finally decided to give Quillen his chance. But the effort to repeal the limit lost by better than 2-to-1.

Like most Rules Committee Republicans, Quillen is a critic of the federal regulatory bureaucracy and defender of efforts by business to cut it back. He has been especially vehement about the Federal Trade Commission. "We shouldn't help an agency that is out to destroy free enterprise," he said in 1980. "Back home the way to kill a rattlesnake is to cut off its head. That's what we ought to do today," Quillen said.

One of the federal programs Quillen has regularly supported is revenue sharing. When the fiscal 1981 budget came to the House floor in 1980, he asked the Rules Committee to allow him to offer an amendment restoring revenue sharing money for states by cutting funds for science research, foreign aid and government overhead. That effort lost, 271-146.

The poverty of Quillen's East Tennessee district occasionally leads him to break with traditional Republican voting patterns. In 1980, when liberal Democrat David Obey proposed to amend

**1st District: Northeast — Johnson City, Kingsport.** Population: 585,624 (19% increase since 1970). Race: White 571,037 (98%), Black 12,448 (2%), Others 2,139 (0.3%). Spanish origin: 3,168 (1%).

the Budget Committee's resolution to provide an additional $1.2 billion in spending, mostly for urban and social programs, Quillen was one of only 36 Republicans who voted for it. He also voted with environmentalists in 1979 to close more of Alaska's land to development than most Republicans wanted.

**At Home:** Quillen's quarter-century of political involvement has earned him a loyal following and considerable influence in upper East Tennessee. When he campaigned actively for Ford over Reagan in his state's 1976 GOP presidential primary, the 1st District gave Ford 58.4 percent of its vote, his highest percentage in any district in the state. Ford won the statewide primary with just 50.4 percent; his 7,792-vote margin in Quillen's district was the difference.

To make it to Congress in 1962, Quillen had to survive a quarrel in his party's political dynasty. The dispute almost gave his district to a Democrat. But since then, his nine re-election campaigns have been mostly *pro forma.*

Republican Rep. B. Carroll Reece dominated 1st District politics for forty years until his death in 1961. Reece's widow served out his term, then gave her blessing to Quillen, a four-term state representative.

But four other strong Republicans jumped into the primary: a state representative, a local judge, a one-time Reece aide, and a former legislator who been a Reece protégé.

Quillen called himself a staunch conservative who opposed "wasteful spending overseas to buy friendship when friendship cannot be bought." He called for revision of tax laws and favored increasing tobacco allotments. He received only 29 percent of the primary vote, but he finished first, and in Tennessee a candidate needs only a plurality to win nomination.

Although the district had not elected a Democrat since 1878, Quillen was held to 53.9 percent in the general election. His low total was blamed partly on GOP disunity after the hard-fought primary and partly on a higher-than-usual Democratic turnout. A longstanding patronage arrangement between Reece and local Democrats had collapsed with the congressman's death.

Once in Congress, Quillen quickly learned the skills of entrenchment. He gained repute as a prodigious letter-writer, sending notes of congratulation and condolence, and all manner of other franked mailings. And he made the rounds to county courthouses during his frequent trips home, seeking for himself the kind of power Reece had long exercised.

By 1964, GOP factional fights had dissipated. Quillen won re-election with 71.7 percent and coasted through the next two elections with more than 85 percent.

Democratic attorney David B. Shine attacked Quillen on all fronts in 1970. He said the 1st District deserved more than a "pen pal" in the House and accused Quillen of opposing education, health and welfare measures that his rural constituents needed. Quillen largely ignored his opponent, and so did the voters. Shine won only 32.1 percent.

Kingsport businessman Lloyd Blevins opposed Quillen in 1974 and 1976. Blevins peaked at 41.2 percent in 1976, when Carter and Democratic Senate nominee Jim Sasser trimmed Republican margins all across the district. In 1978, Quillen's margin returned to a safe 64.5 percent, and in 1980 he had no Democratic opponent.

**The District:** Much of northeastern Tennessee is highland towns, tobacco patches and livestock clearings, but small cities have grown up around industries drawn to the region by the availability of TVA power.

Democrats often fare respectably in Sullivan County, Quillen's home, which casts a quarter of the district's vote. In 1976, Jimmy Carter won Sullivan County narrowly and Quillen carried it by only 543 votes. Sullivan's major cities are Kingsport and Bristol; chemicals, paper, and electronic and computing equipment are important manufactured goods.

The largest city in the district, however, is Johnson City, in Washington County. There and in most other parts of the district, Republican candidates rarely drop below the 55 percent level. In 1980, the 1st gave 60.9 percent to Reagan, his highest percentage in any of Tennessee's districts.

GOP allegiances are especially pronounced in the district's rugged, sparsely-populated southeastern counties. Sevier and Cocke counties, for example, each gave Quillen more than 75 percent of the vote in 1976 and more than 93 percent in 1980.

## Committees

**Rules** (Ranking Republican)

## Elections

**1980 General**

| | |
|---|---|
| James Quillen (R) | 130,296 (86%) |
| John Curtis (I) | 20,816 (14%) |

**1980 Primary**

| | |
|---|---|
| James Quillen (R) | 43,649 (77%) |
| Bill Bays (R) | 12,679 (23%) |

**1978 General**

| | |
|---|---|
| James Quillen (R) | 92,143 (65%) |
| Gordon Ball (D) | 50,694 (35%) |

**Previous Winning Percentages**

| | | | |
|---|---|---|---|
| 1976 (58%) | 1974 (64%) | 1972 (79%) | 1970 (68%) |
| 1968 (85%) | 1966 (87%) | 1964 (72%) | 1962 (54%) |

**District Vote For President**

| | 1980 | | 1976 | | 1972 |
|---|---|---|---|---|---|
| D | 70,930 (36%) | D | 83,153 (46%) | D | 31,200 (21%) |
| R | 120,203 (61%) | R | 96,233 (53%) | R | 113,840 (77%) |
| I | 5,057 (3%) | | | | |

## Campaign Finance

| | Receipts | Receipts from PACs | Expenditures |
|---|---|---|---|
| **1980** | | | |
| Quillen (R) | $143,169 | $85,625 (60%) | 146,822 |
| **1978** | | | |
| Quillen (R) | $207,868 | $72,583 (35%) | $218,151 |
| Ball (D) | $48,987 | $1,200 (2%) | $46,199 |

## Voting Studies

| | Presidential Support | | Party Unity | | Conservative Coalition | |
|---|---|---|---|---|---|---|
| Year | S | O | S | O | S | O |
| 1980 | 39 | 53† | 67 | 25† | 88 | 6 |
| 1979 | 33 | 61 | 70 | 23 | 86 | 8 |
| 1978 | 31 | 54 | 69 | 19 | 76 | 8 |
| 1977 | 33 | 43 | 67 | 16 | 76 | 5 |
| 1976 | 76 | 20 | 76 | 13 | 83 | 7 |
| 1975 | 61 | 28 | 78 | 10† | 80 | 4† |
| 1974 (Ford) | 59 | 33 | | | | |
| 1974 | 68 | 21 | 70 | 15† | 73 | 8 |
| 1973 | 69 | 24 | 73 | 16 | 80 | 7 |
| 1972 | 59 | 30 | 76 | 13 | 83 | 5 |
| 1971 | 81 | 7 | 73 | 18 | 81 | 5 |
| 1970 | 66 | 25† | 65 | 19 | 82 | 5 |
| 1969 | 55 | 41† | 77 | 15† | 84 | 7 |
| 1968 | 36 | 48† | 76 | 9 | 86 | 2 |
| 1967 | 6 | 55 | 82 | 10 | 85 | 6 |
| 1966 | 30 | 62 | 89 | 3 | 89 | 0 |
| 1965 | 30 | 59 | 84 | 10 | 92 | 6 |
| 1964 | 19 | 79 | 90 | 3 | 100 | 0 |
| 1963 | 21 | 63 | 76 | 10 | 80 | 13 |

S = Support    O = Opposition

†Not eligible for all recorded votes.

## Key Votes

**96th Congress**

| | |
|---|---|
| Weaken Carter oil profits tax (1979) | Y |
| Reject hospital cost control plan (1979) | Y |
| Implement Panama Canal Treaties (1979) | N |
| Establish Department of Education (1979) | Y |
| Approve Anti-busing Amendment (1979) | Y |
| Guarantee Chrysler Corp. loans (1979) | Y |
| Approve military draft registration (1980) | Y |
| Aid Sandinista regime in Nicaragua (1980) | N |
| Strengthen fair housing laws (1980) | N |

**97th Congress**

| | |
|---|---|
| Reagan budget proposal (1981) | Y |

## Interest Group Ratings

| Year | ADA | ACA | AFL-CIO | CCUS |
|---|---|---|---|---|
| 1980 | 17 | 57 | 16 | 63 |
| 1979 | 16 | 76 | 26 | 83 |
| 1978 | 15 | 85 | 25 | 83 |
| 1977 | 5 | 79 | 19 | 94 |
| 1976 | 10 | 88 | 13 | 88 |
| 1975 | 0 | 92 | 0 | 93 |
| 1974 | 9 | 55 | 13 | 100 |
| 1973 | 0 | 75 | 0 | 91 |
| 1972 | 6 | 85 | 9 | 100 |
| 1971 | 5 | 81 | 20 | - |
| 1970 | 4 | 94 | 0 | 90 |
| 1969 | 6 | 75 | 30 | - |
| 1968 | 0 | 100 | 25 | - |
| 1967 | 7 | 81 | 17 | 80 |
| 1966 | 0 | 96 | 0 | - |
| 1965 | 0 | 92 | - | 90 |
| 1964 | 4 | 100 | 9 | - |
| 1963 | - | 94 | - | - |

# 2 John J. Duncan (R)

## Of Knoxville — Elected 1964

**Born:** March 24, 1919, Scott County, Tenn.
**Education:** U. of Tenn., B.S. 1942; Cumberland U., LL.B. 1947.
**Military Career:** Army, 1942-45.
**Profession:** Lawyer.
**Family:** Wife, Lois Swisher; four children.
**Religion:** Presbyterian.
**Political Career:** Mayor of Knoxville, 1959-64.

**In Washington:** Duncan has remained a locally-oriented House member long after his seniority could have made him a powerful force in national economic policy. Sitting next to Barber B. Conable Jr. of New York at the head of the Republican side on the Ways and Means Committee, he says little during most committee sessions, sometimes reading letters or signing pictures for constituents.

When the subject is relevant to Tennessee, however, Duncan becomes an unyielding spokesman for his point of view, either in committee or on the floor. It was Duncan who quietly slipped language into a 1979 appropriation bill guaranteeing that the Tellico Dam, located in his district, would be completed. Environmentalists had succeeded in getting construction on the project stopped because it posed a threat to the tiny snail darter fish and violated the Endangered Species Act. President Carter vehemently opposed the exemption from the Endangered Species Act, but Duncan and the rest of the Tennessee congressional delegation prevailed.

Duncan can be dogged when it comes to the Tennessee Valley Authority, located in Knoxville, the largest city in his district, or the nuclear complex around Oak Ridge, just across the boundary, or the mining interests that operate throughout the hill counties of east Tennessee.

Duncan has been on the Ways and Means Health Subcommittee since it was created in 1975, and he has been a consistent supporter of the American Medical Association, initially in concert with his Tennessee Democratic colleague, Richard Fulton, and independently after Fulton left the committee in 1975. During the Ford administration, it was Duncan who introduced the AMA health insurance plan. It required employers to offer their employees standardized coverage through private insurers and to pay 65 percent of the premium costs.

Duncan has had one of the most conservative voting records in the House throughout his career, but it has occasionally been tempered by concern for the large number of elderly and poor in his district. He has twice amended housing bills to provide that Social Security benefits not be counted as income for the purpose of determining eligibility for federally subsidized housing. He has also voted against a majority of Republicans several times in opposing efforts to restrict the scope of the food stamp program.

**At Home:** Duncan began building his political base during five years as mayor of Knoxville. He had some difficulty winning his promotion to Congress in 1964, but since then he has averaged 76 percent of the vote in eight re-election bids.

Duncan's predecessor in the 2nd District was Howard H. Baker, father of the current Senate majority leader. When Baker died in January 1964, his widow Irene entered the special election to complete her husband's term. She won it, but by only 8,945 votes, a startlingly small margin in a district that has not elected a Democrat since 1853.

Mrs. Baker soon announced she would not seek re-election that fall, and Duncan, a political ally of the Baker family, entered the 1964 Republican primary. His chief opponent was J. Frank Qualls, an attorney from the small town of Harriman. In a contest of personalities and political networks, Duncan found 868 more friends than Qualls and won nomination with 47.5 percent.

> **2nd District: East central - Knoxville.** Population: 586,997 (19% increase since 1970). Race: White 548,568 (93%), Black 34,431 (6%), Others 3,998 (1%). Spanish origin: 3,559 (1%).

The Democrats nominated Willard Yarbrough, their earlier candidate against Mrs. Baker. Yarbrough took advantage of local anti-Goldwater sentiment: The Republican presidential nominee had campaigned in East Tennessee and suggested that the government sell the TVA. Yarbrough pledged that Democrats would keep TVA from falling into the hands of private utilities.

Goldwater won the 2nd District, but by far less than the usual Republican margins. Duncan lost two counties and won two others narrowly, but his local connections gave him a 9,909 vote margin in Knox County (Knoxville), and a 53.8 districtwide percentage against Yarbrough.

Since then, Duncan has been held under 70 percent only once. In 1976, Democrats nominated state Rep. Mike Rowland, an articulate young Knoxville lawyer. Rowland campaigned aggressively on the charge that Duncan's conservative voting habits overlooked the best interests of blue-collar workers and the poor.

It was not a conspicuously successful argument. Rowland's percentage was only 8 points higher than that of the 1974 Democratic nominee, a taxi driver whose campaign was barely visible. In the two elections since 1976, Duncan has won more than 75 percent of the vote.

Though his seat is one of the safest in the House, Duncan still travels home to Tennessee nearly every weekend. He presents flags to schools, speaks in churches on Sundays, visits county courthouses and attends weddings, funerals, dinners and rallies. Every September, at the

Tennessee Valley Fair, he sets up a refreshment stand and dispenses chilled water to thirsty fairgoers.

Against Rowland in 1976, Duncan spent nearly $156,000. Facing much weaker oposition in 1978 and 1980, he still spent more than $100,000 in each campaign. Duncan's fund-raising advantage is usually sufficient to discourage serious opposition.

**The District:** In almost every contest for national, congressional or statewide office, the 2nd is impeccably Republican.

Knox County casts nearly three-fifths of the district's vote. It is home to the University of Tennessee, serves as headquarters for the TVA and has a significant blue-collar workforce engaged in production of textiles and electronic equipment. Statewide Democratic candidates usually average about 40 percent in Knox County. Blount County is the district's second-largest, casting about 14 percent of the vote. The county is the site of huge aluminum plants in the city of Alcoa. It often votes nearly 65 percent for Republicans.

The mountainous rural counties in the northern part of the district are also faithfully Republican. Strip mining for coal has left its mark on this area's landscape; agriculture focuses on tobacco, poultry and dairying.

McMinn and Monroe counties, at the southern end of the district, gave tiny margins to Carter in 1976. But they reversed themselves in 1980, giving Reagan more than 55 percent of their vote.

## Committees

**Ways and Means** (2nd of 12 Republicans)
  Health; Oversight; Select Revenue Measures.

**Joint Taxation**

## Elections

**1980 General**

| | |
|---|---|
| John Duncan (R) | 147,949 (76%) |
| Dave Dunaway (D) | 46,578 (24%) |

**1978 General**

| | |
|---|---|
| John Duncan (R) | 125,082 (82%) |
| Margaret Francis (D) | 27,745 (18%) |

**Previous Winning Percentages**

| | | | |
|---|---|---|---|
| 1976 (63%) | 1974 (71%) | 1972 (100%) | 1970 (73%) |
| 1968 (82%) | 1966 (79%) | 1964 (54%) | |

### District Vote For President

| | 1980 | | 1976 | | 1972 |
|---|---|---|---|---|---|
| D | 79,572 (38%) | D | 94,759 (49%) | D | 40,799 (26%) |
| R | 119,858 (59%) | R | 98,032 (50%) | R | 112,505 (72%) |
| I | 6,303 (3%) | | | | |

## Campaign Finance

| | Receipts | Receipts from PACs | Expenditures |
|---|---|---|---|
| **1980** | | | |
| Duncan (R) | $155,919 | $89,200 (58%) | $109,305 |
| Dunaway (D) | $38,317 | $2,150 (6%) | $38,018 |
| **1978** | | | |
| Duncan (R) | $171,066 | $83,229 (49%) | $139,956 |

*John J. Duncan, R-Tenn.*

## Voting Studies

| Year | Presidential Support | | Party Unity | | Conservative Coalition | |
|---|---|---|---|---|---|---|
| | S | O | S | O | S | O |
| 1980 | 47 | 52 | 77 | 22 | 96 | 2 |
| 1979 | 37 | 63 | 76 | 23 | 97 | 3 |
| 1978 | 32 | 66 | 82 | 16 | 90 | 7 |
| 1977 | 51 | 49 | 82 | 18 | 94 | 5 |
| 1976 | 67 | 31 | 77 | 20 | 92 | 6 |
| 1975 | 57 | 39 | 83 | 16 | 89 | 10 |
| 1974 (Ford) | 43 | 48 | | | | |
| 1974 | 75 | 25 | 80 | 15 | 91 | 6 |
| 1973 | 66 | 34 | 82 | 17 | 93 | 6 |
| 1972 | 68 | 32 | 87 | 13 | 95 | 5 |
| 1971 | 74 | 26 | 80 | 20 | 87 | 13 |
| 1970 | 69 | 31 | 68 | 32 | 84 | 16 |
| 1969 | 53 | 47 | 85 | 15 | 96 | 4 |
| 1968 | 49 | 51 | 88 | 12 | 92 | 8 |
| 1967 | 43 | 57 | 88 | 11 | 93 | 7 |
| 1966 | 37 | 63 | 93 | 7 | 97 | 3 |
| 1965 | 29 | 71 | 94 | 5 | 100 | 0 |

S = Support          O = Opposition

## Key Votes

**96th Congress**

| | |
|---|---|
| Weaken Carter oil profits tax (1979) | Y |
| Reject hospital cost control plan (1979) | Y |
| Implement Panama Canal Treaties (1979) | N |
| Establish Department of Education (1979) | Y |
| Approve Anti-busing Amendment (1979) | Y |
| Guarantee Chrysler Corp. loans (1979) | Y |
| Approve military draft registration (1980) | Y |
| Aid Sandinista regime in Nicaragua (1980) | N |
| Strengthen fair housing laws (1980) | N |

**97th Congress**

| | |
|---|---|
| Reagan budget proposal (1981) | Y |

## Interest Group Ratings

| Year | ADA | ACA | AFL-CIO | CCUS |
|---|---|---|---|---|
| 1980 | 17 | 67 | 16 | 68 |
| 1979 | 11 | 72 | 20 | 89 |
| 1978 | 20 | 85 | 20 | 78 |
| 1977 | 0 | 67 | 17 | 94 |
| 1976 | 15 | 89 | 22 | 76 |
| 1975 | 5 | 82 | 13 | 88 |
| 1974 | 4 | 80 | 9 | 90 |
| 1973 | 12 | 85 | 18 | 82 |
| 1972 | 0 | 91 | 9 | 100 |
| 1971 | 14 | 76 | 17 | - |
| 1970 | 12 | 74 | 43 | 90 |
| 1969 | 7 | 88 | 20 | - |
| 1968 | 0 | 96 | 25 | - |
| 1967 | 13 | 79 | 17 | 80 |
| 1966 | 0 | 96 | 0 | - |
| 1965 | 0 | 96 | - | 90 |

# 3 Marilyn Lloyd Bouquard (D)

**Of Chattanooga — Elected in 1974**

**Born:** Jan. 3, 1929, Fort Smith, Ark.
**Education:** Attended Shorter College, 1958-60 and 1962-63.
**Profession:** Radio station manager.
**Family:** Husband, Joseph Bouquard; eight children.
**Religion:** Church of Christ.
**Political Career:** No previous office.

**In Washington:** Thrust into politics overnight when her husband was killed in an airplane crash while campaigning for Congress, Bouquard has developed gradually into a clever protector of her district's interests, limited in her goals but good at achieving them.

She spent most of the Carter administration defending Tennessee public works projects against White House assaults and rarely lost. This was partly because of the influence of her more senior Democratic allies, but it was partly through her own legislative infighting.

The most important project has the been the Clinch River nuclear breeder reactor, located in her district. Carter wanted to terminate the project — he said it was too expensive and would lead to the proliferation of nuclear weapons. He tried twice to end it, but both times was turned down, with Bouquard lobbying for Clinch River both in the Science Committee and on the floor.

When Carter left office, she felt she had little to fear, not only because Reagan backed Clinch River, but also because she became chairman of the Science Subcommittee that authorizes its funding. In May, however, she ran into an ambush in the full committee as environmentalists teamed with fiscal conservatives in a vote to kill the $3.2 billion project, forcing her to try to reverse the decision on the House floor. At the same time, she was drawn into the budget battle as both Democrats and Republicans, knowing of her Clinch River interest, promised to fund it. She voted for the first Reagan budget plan but switched and voted later with the Democrats, saying she objected to Reagan block grants and cuts in social services.

Equally important to Bouquard has been the Tellico Dam, once halted by the Endangered Species Act because it threatened the tiny snail darter fish. Despite Carter's threat to veto any legislation providing for further work on Tellico, the House insisted on voting money for it, and in 1979, Carter signed the bill authorizing that the dam be finished, snail darter or no snail darter. That was in large part the result of floor lobbying by Bouquard and other Tennessee and Alabama Democrats, who offered votes on other issues to members who would back them on the dam. Bouquard is at home on the House floor among the Southern Democrats who gather at the back of the chamber. She votes with them on most issues, and she has a tongue salty enough to make her "one of the boys." Her conservative record has disappointed the AFL-CIO, which provided considerable help in her early campaigns, but it has been no problem at all in her district.

**At Home:** Mort Lloyd was well-known as a Chattanooga newsman in 1974, and he had little trouble winning the 3rd District Democratic nomination. When he died a few weeks later in a plane crash, the district's county chairmen met and chose his widow as the nominee.

She had owned and operated a radio station with her husband, but had no political experience. It was generally assumed that Mort Lloyd's death ended any Democratic hopes of denying GOP Rep. Lamar Baker a third term.

But Marilyn Lloyd turned out to be surprisingly aggressive, and she found a successful combination of issues in the Watergate election year: opposition to busing, more rights for women and criticism of President Ford's pardon of former President Nixon. She unseated Baker with 51.1 percent of the vote.

---

**3rd District: Southeast — Oak Ridge, Chattanooga.** Population: 575,429 (18% increase since 1970). Race: White 506,837 (88%), Black 64,940 (11%), Others 3,652 (1%). Spanish origin: 3,982 (1%).

## Marilyn Lloyd Bouquard, D-Tenn.

In her first term, Lloyd built a following with question-and-answer town hall meetings and covered-dish suppers. Baker tried a comeback in 1976, but Lloyd defeated him by a margin of more than 2-to-1, putting an end to GOP hopes for the near term, at least. After the 1978 election, in which she drew nearly 90 percent of the vote, Lloyd married Joseph P. Bouquard, an engineer.

Bouquard's 1980 Republican opponent, dentist and physician Glen M. Byers, tied his campaign closely to Ronald Reagan and asked voters to reject the Carter-Lloyd ticket. But while Reagan was carrying the 3rd District with 56.3 percent of the vote in 1980, Lloyd won again with 61 percent — lower than the other Tennessee Democrats, but still a comfortable margin.

**The District:** More than half the district's vote is cast in Hamilton County (Chattanooga), center for textiles, chemicals and machinery. The city of Chattanooga is about one-quarter black and usually votes Democratic; the suburbs are Republican in non-congressional races.

Democrats do relatively well in neighboring Bradley County, where industrial Cleveland is surrounded by rural territory. The county casts about 10 percent of the district vote.

Most loyal to Bouquard and other Democratic candidates are the district's three northern counties — Anderson, Morgan and Roane. The Oak Ridge nuclear energy research, development and production facilities are located in Anderson and Roane; labor unions are an important voting bloc in both. Morgan is a mountainous, conservative enclave with oil drilling and strip mining.

---

## Committees

**Public Works and Transportation** (10th of 25 Democrats)
Economic Development; Public Buildings and Grounds.

**Science and Technology** (7th of 23 Democrats)
Energy Research and Production, chairman; Energy Development and Applications; Space Science and Applications.

**Select Aging** (11th of 31 Democrats)
Health and Long-Term Care.

## Elections

**1980 General**

| | |
|---|---|
| Marilyn Lloyd Bouquard (D) | 117,355 (61%) |
| Glen Byers (R) | 74,761 (39%) |

**1978 General**

| | |
|---|---|
| Marilyn Lloyd (D) | 108,282 (89%) |
| Dan East (I) | 13,535 (11%) |

**Previous Winning Percentages**

1976 (68%)    1974 (51%)

**District Vote For President**

| | 1980 | | 1976 | | 1972 |
|---|---|---|---|---|---|
| D | 82,568 (41%) | D | 96,126 (52%) | D | 41,430 (27%) |
| R | 113,363 (56%) | R | 88,578 (48%) | R | 108,187 (70%) |
| I | 4,426 (2%) | | | | |

## Campaign Finance

| | Receipts | Receipts from PACs | Expenditures |
|---|---|---|---|
| **1980** | | | |
| Bouquard (D) | $136,283 | $43,170 (32%) | $169,440 |
| Byers (R) | $26,384 | $2,773 (11%) | $43,236 |
| **1978** | | | |
| Lloyd (D) | $88,385 | $24,960 (28%) | $75,923 |

## Voting Studies

| | Presidential Support | | Party Unity | | Conservative Coalition | |
|---|---|---|---|---|---|---|
| Year | S | O | S | O | S | O |
| 1980 | 53 | 42 | 46 | 52 | 86 | 14 |
| 1979 | 49 | 47 | 51 | 46 | 83 | 12 |
| 1978 | 37 | 46 | 36 | 50 | 73 | 7 |
| 1977 | 58 | 42 | 40 | 60 | 88 | 12 |
| 1976 | 41 | 59 | 44 | 56 | 84 | 16 |
| 1975 | 29 | 71 | 53 | 47 | 74 | 26 |

S = Support          O = Opposition

## Key Votes

**96th Congress**

| | |
|---|---|
| Weaken Carter oil profits tax (1979) | Y |
| Reject hospital cost control plan (1979) | Y |
| Implement Panama Canal Treaties (1979) | N |
| Establish Department of Education (1979) | Y |
| Approve Anti-busing Amendment (1979) | Y |
| Guarantee Chrysler Corp. loans (1979) | Y |
| Approve military draft registration (1980) | Y |
| Aid Sandinista regime in Nicaragua (1980) | N |
| Strengthen fair housing laws (1980) | Y |

**97th Congress**

| | |
|---|---|
| Reagan budget proposal (1981) | Y |

## Interest Group Ratings

| Year | ADA | ACA | AFL-CIO | CCUS |
|---|---|---|---|---|
| 1980 | 22 | 54 | 53 | 72 |
| 1979 | 21 | 40 | 37 | 71 |
| 1978 | 15 | 68 | 53 | 50 |
| 1977 | 10 | 63 | 52 | 65 |
| 1976 | 10 | 61 | 65 | 50 |
| 1975 | 32 | 64 | 65 | 35 |

# 4 Albert Gore Jr. (D)

**Of Carthage — Elected 1976**

**Born:** March 31, 1948, Washington, D.C.
**Education:** Harvard U., B.A. 1969; attended
Vanderbilt School of Religion, 1972; attended
Vanderbilt Law School, 1974-76.
**Military Career:** Army, 1969-71.
**Profession:** Journalist, home builder.
**Family:** Wife, Mary Elizabeth "Tipper"
Aitcheson; three children.
**Religion:** Baptist.
**Political Career:** No previous office.

**In Washington:** Gore's combination of
Southern populist thinking and modern consumer
activism has made him one of the more visible
House members on energy and environmental
issues.

Much of the populism is a legacy of his
father, Albert Gore Sr., who spent 32 years in
Congress railing against corporate abuses and
supporting the New Deal and its legislative descendants. The elder Gore is on the other side
now, the chairman of the Island Creek Coal
Company and a director of Occidental Petroleum.
But it is the Gore of a generation ago who
sometimes seems to have reappeared on the
House floor.

Some of the younger Gore's work is vintage
anti-business rhetoric, served up in the Commerce
Committee on issues involving energy companies
and the price of oil. He was one of the strongest
defenders of oil price controls after President
Carter ordered them phased out in 1979. But
Gore's most successful efforts have been on a
different subject — the effects of untrammeled
free enterprise on the long-term public health.

He worked hard on creation of a
"superfund," a kitty financed largely by oil and
chemical companies that would help pay for
cleaning up dangerous spills and abandoned
chemical dumping grounds. Two superfund bills
passed the House by large margins in September
1980.

Earlier in the year, Gore had been the prime
mover on separate legislation giving federal environmental authorities the right to take legal action forcing cleanup of hazardous waste sites.

In most of the areas where Gore recommends
legislation, the approach is the same: write rules
for business to follow in dealing with an unwary
public, and make the offender pay substantially
when something goes wrong. He worked for one

bill to prescribe minimum nutrient levels in infant formula and another to promote certification
of private companies who sell health insurance to
the elderly.

On some of these campaigns, the media have
helped. Gore promoted his hazardous waste effort
with a public tour of a Memphis neighborhood
where chemical stockpiles had been dumped during the 1950s and where rates of serious illness
had been unusually high. He held hearings in
1980 on efforts by the contact lens industry to
discredit a simple salt-tablet preparation said to
clean the lenses as well as the industry's product.

On other Commerce Committee issues, Gore
often seems to be asking the same question: What
will it do for rural America? He pushed for a one-
year moratorium in 1979 on cutbacks in Amtrak
train service, hoping to preserve service to some of
the small towns of middle Tennessee. Working on
a rewrite of the 1934 Federal Communications
Act, he complained that some of the proposed
changes would mean higher rural telephone rates.

**At Home:** Gore's family name did not exactly scare away competition in 1976, when he
launched his campaign for Congress. Eight other
Democrats entered the contest to succeed retiring
Democrat Joe Evins. They soon found, however,
that they were opposing not only a family tradition but a born campaigner.

Gore's themes had a populist flavor. He
called for higher taxation of the rich and tighter

**4th District: Central —
Murfreesboro.** Population: 636,253 (27%
increase since 1970). Race: White 598,678
(94%), Black 34,596 (5%), Others 2,979
(0.4%). Spanish origin: 4,125 (1%).

strip mine laws, and criticized "private power trusts" who wanted to dismantle the TVA. He favored cuts in defense spending and said the government should create more public jobs.

Gore's chief rival in the crowded field was state House Majority Leader Stanley Rogers. He tried to make an issue of Gore's wealth (net worth $273,000 at the time) and claimed Gore's father was tied to energy monopolies. By stressing his legislative experience, Rogers hoped to cast Gore as a political amateur.

But Rogers' political base was in the southern part of the district, and several other candidates from that area drew votes from him. Gore was not seriously challenged in his Smith County base in the district's northern section.

Gore won 32 percent of the primary vote, finishing 3,559 votes ahead of Rogers. He was unopposed in 1978, and in 1980 the GOP candidate drew only 21 percent of the vote.

**The District:** The 4th is predominantly rural: Murfreesboro, the largest town, has less than 35,000 people. But while dairy and cattle pastureland predominates, there are also scattered small manufacturing plants producing textiles, whiskey, candy and air conditioners.

In Smyrna, a town with about 8,200 people in northwest Rutherford County, Japan's Nissan Motor Company is building a $300 million truck assembly plant. The factory is the largest single industrial-capital investment in Tennessee history and will employ more than 2,000 people.

Industrial expansion is increasing the blue-collar workforce and may reinforce the traditional Democratic ties of this middle Tennessee area. Carter carried the 4th with 56.7 percent of the vote in 1980; of the district's 25 counties, Reagan won only four.

## Committees

**Energy and Commerce** (13th of 24 Democrats)
Energy Conservation and Power; Fossil and Synthetic Fuels; Oversight and Investigations.

**Science and Technology** (12th of 23 Democrats)
Investigations and Oversight, chairman.

**Select Intelligence** (8th of 9 Democrats)
Oversight and Evaluation.

## Elections

**1980 General**

| | |
|---|---|
| Albert Gore Jr. (D) | 137,612 (79%) |
| James Seigneur (R) | 35,954 (21%) |

**1980 Primary**

| | |
|---|---|
| Albert Gore Jr. (D) | 65,886 (92%) |
| John L. Welker (D) | 5,533 (8%) |

**1978 General**

| | |
|---|---|
| Albert Gore Jr. (D) | Unopposed |

**Previous Winning Percentages**

**1976** (94%)

**District Vote For President**

| | 1980 | | 1976 | | 1972 |
|---|---|---|---|---|---|
| D | 118,739 (57%) | D | 124,267 (67%) | D | 44,719 (34%) |
| R | 85,714 (41%) | R | 58,441 (32%) | R | 82,879 (63%) |
| I | 3,734 (2%) | | | | |

## Campaign Finance

| | Receipts | Receipts from PACs | Expenditures |
|---|---|---|---|
| **1980** | | | |
| Gore (D) | $63,083 | $15,000 (24%) | $74,422 |
| Seigneur (R) | $23,761 | $363 (2%) | $13,870 |

| | | | |
|---|---|---|---|
| **1978** | | | |
| Gore (D) | $99,866 | $9,860 (10%) | $47,097 |

## Voting Studies

| | Presidential Support | | Party Unity | | Conservative Coalition | |
|---|---|---|---|---|---|---|
| Year | S | O | S | O | S | O |
| 1980 | 77 | 22 | 85 | 15 | 46 | 54 |
| 1979 | 78 | 21 | 83 | 16 | 38 | 62 |
| 1978 | 68 | 28 | 75 | 21 | 30 | 66 |
| 1977 | 77 | 23 | 77 | 22 | 35 | 64 |

S = Support      O = Opposition

## Key Votes

**96th Congress**

| | |
|---|---|
| Weaken Carter oil profits tax (1979) | N |
| Reject hospital cost control plan (1979) | N |
| Implement Panama Canal Treaties (1979) | Y |
| Establish Department of Education (1979) | Y |
| Approve Anti-busing Amendment (1979) | N |
| Guarantee Chrysler Corp. loans (1979) | Y |
| Approve military draft registration (1980) | Y |
| Aid Sandinista regime in Nicaragua (1980) | Y |
| Strengthen fair housing laws (1980) | Y |

**97th Congress**

| | |
|---|---|
| Reagan budget proposal (1981) | N |

## Interest Group Ratings

| Year | ADA | ACA | AFL-CIO | CCUS |
|---|---|---|---|---|
| 1980 | 50 | 29 | 79 | 67 |
| 1979 | 74 | 12 | 80 | 22 |
| 1978 | 65 | 15 | 70 | 22 |
| 1977 | 45 | 30 | 78 | 41 |

# 5 Bill Boner (D)

**Of Nashville — Elected 1978**

**Born:** Feb. 14, 1945, Nashville, Tenn.
**Education:** Middle Tenn. State U., B.S. 1967; George Peabody College, M.A. 1969; YMCA Night Law School, J.D. 1978.
**Profession:** Coach, bank executive.
**Family:** Wife, Betty Fowlkes; one child.
**Religion:** Methodist.
**Political Career:** Tenn. House, 1971-73, 1975-77; Tenn. Senate, 1977-79.

**In Washington:** Elected in 1978 with support from New Right political organizations, Boner immediately began moving to the center, surprising many of the ideological groups who backed him the first time. When New Right strategist Paul Weyrich was asked in late 1979 whether he was disappointed in any of the Democrats he had helped the year before, he mentioned just one — Bill Boner.

Boner is no liberal, but he has turned out to be essentially non-ideological. Although he has been willing to stake out conservative positions on highly visible issues like abortion and school prayer, he has been more interested in voting and servicing his district. And since the Nashville-based district is more than 90 percent urban and more than 20 percent black, that has meant working to bring in federal money rather than to abolish the programs that provide it.

He backed President Carter's proposed Department of Education, breaking with most conservatives but maintaining his good relations with the district's teachers, of whom he used to be a member. He took pains to inform constituents that he had helped with legislation to increase funding for public housing for the elderly, and for medical education. He stressed his backing for Meharry Medical College, with its large black enrollment. In May of 1981, when most Southern Democrats were backing the Reagan budget, Boner opposed it.

Boner was not a major legislative force among the freshmen in the 96th Congress, partly because of the time and attention he devoted to constituent service. He has claimed that his staff processed 6,000 casework requests during his first two-year term, compared to 1,500 during a similar period for his late predecessor, Clifford Allen.

Assigned to the Public Works Committee at the start of his first term, Boner did not often emerge from its backbenches. He did play a role in the committee's debates over economic aid formulas, arguing for an approach that would benefit metropolitan areas with a county-wide form of government. Nashville is such an area.

**At Home:** The 1980 election represented a vindication for Boner, who had been called the "accidental congressmen" after he won his first term largely because the incumbent Democrat died after the filing deadline.

Early in 1978, Boner was one of several Nashville Democrats interested in challenging one-term Rep. Clifford Allen. When Allen suffered a heart attack on May 26 of that year, Boner and eight others rushed into the primary.

But Allen's condition seemed to improve in the weeks that followed, and most of the strong challengers withdrew. When he died unexpectedly on June 18, Boner was the only Democrat of substance left on the ballot.

The only other Democratic candidate with any public reputation was state criminal Judge Charles Galbreath, and his was not a good one. Galbreath had been threatened with impeachment because he used court stationery to write a letter to *Hustler* magazine; the letter, reprinted in full in the magazine, was favorable to the publication and concluded with obscene language.

Boner won the primary with 52.9 percent of the vote. In the general election campaign, he took distinctly conservative stands, and received sizable contributions from medical groups and

---

**5th District: Nashville.** Population: 536,448 (9% increase since 1970). Race: White 419,389 (78%), Black 111,924 (21%), Others 6,135 (1%). Spanish origin: 4,089 (1%).

building contractors as well as from a former treasurer of the Republican National Committee.

When he won in November with 51 percent — an unimpressive figure in a heavily Democratic district — many local Democrats called him a fluke. It was assumed that he would face several opponents in the 1980 primary.

But Boner's first-term voting record proved accceptable to most Democratic voters, and his ability to untangle the federal bureaucracy for constituents earned him many friends. By the time filing came around for 1980, the opposition had melted away. Nobody even challenged his renomination.

Boner's Republican opponent was Mike Adams, a former advertising and marketing executive who had served four years as administrative assistant to Sen. Howard H. Baker Jr. Well-connected to party funding sources, Adams ran a $200,000 campaign. He complained that Boner's frequent franked mailings to constituents were thinly-disguised campaign propaganda.

Boner made the rounds to the churches, schools, shopping malls, neighborhoods and civic organizations he had frequented during two years in office. Reminding voters that he "grew up within a few blocks of the city dump" in Nashville, Boner portrayed Adams as a stuffed-shirt slicker with little understanding for the common man. Boner spent nearly $238,000 and defeated Adams convincingly.

**The District:** More than 90 percent of the 5th District vote is cast in Nashville and Davidson County, the traditional focal point of Middle Tennessee's Democratic populism. The 5th was one of three Tennessee districts carried by Carter in 1980, and it rarely supports a Republican in statewide elections.

Nashville is Tennessee's capital, and state and federal government guarantee the city a large white-collar workforce. Davidson County is home to 17 colleges and universities, and factories in the area manufacture aircraft parts, glass, textiles and tires. Nashville is also an insurance center and headquarters for the country music industry and several religious publishing firms.

## Committees

**Public Works and Transportation** (21st of 25 Democrats)
   Aviation; Investigations and Oversight; Surface Transportation.

**Veterans' Affairs** (10th of 17 Democrats)
   Education, Training and Employment; Hospitals and Health Care.

## Elections

**1980 General**

| | |
|---|---|
| Bill Boner (D) | 118,506 (65%) |
| Mike Adams (R) | 62,746 (35%) |

**1978 General**

| | |
|---|---|
| Bill Boner (D) | 68,608 (51%) |
| Bill Goodwin (R) | 47,288 (35%) |
| Henry Haile (I) | 17,674 (13%) |

**1978 Primary**

| | |
|---|---|
| Bill Boner (D) | 50,987 (53%) |
| Charles Galbreath (D) | 25,768 (27%) |

**District Vote For President**

| 1980 | | 1976 | | 1972 | |
|---|---|---|---|---|---|
| D | 114,893 (60%) | D | 110,779 (63%) | D | 53,175 (36%) |
| R | 71,628 (37%) | R | 64,543 (36%) | R | 89,046 (61%) |
| I | 5,051 (3%) | | | | |

## Campaign Finance

| | Receipts | Receipts from PACs | Expen-ditures |
|---|---|---|---|
| **1980** | | | |
| Boner (D) | $293,075 | $110,570 (38%) | $237,908 |
| Adams (R) | $194,358 | $27,185 (14%) | $194,987 |
| **1978** | | | |
| Boner (D) | $194,894 | $59,066 (30%) | $192,960 |
| Goodwin (R) | $40,492 | $4,400 (11%) | $40,494 |

## Voting Studies

| | Presidential Support | | Party Unity | | Conservative Coalition | |
|---|---|---|---|---|---|---|
| Year | S | O | S | O | S | O |
| 1980 | 58 | 34 | 62 | 33 | 73 | 22 |
| 1979 | 65 | 33 | 73 | 25 | 60 | 38 |

S = Support          O = Opposition

## Key Votes

**96th Congress**

| | |
|---|---|
| Weaken Carter oil profits tax (1979) | N |
| Reject hospital cost control plan (1979) | N |
| Implement Panama Canal Treaties (1979) | Y |
| Establish Department of Education (1979) | Y |
| Approve Anti-busing Amendment (1979) | Y |
| Guarantee Chrysler Corp. loans (1979) | Y |
| Approve military draft registration (1980) | # |
| Aid Sandinista regime in Nicaragua (1980) | N |
| Strengthen fair housing laws (1980) | N |

**97th Congress**

| | |
|---|---|
| Reagan budget proposal (1981) | N |

## Interest Group Ratings

| Year | ADA | ACA | AFL-CIO | CCUS |
|---|---|---|---|---|
| 1980 | 39 | 38 | 79 | 73 |
| 1979 | 63 | 28 | 85 | 28 |

# 6 Robin Beard Jr. (R)

**Of Franklin — Elected 1972**

**Born:** Aug. 21, 1939, Knoxville, Tenn.
**Education:** Vanderbilt U., B.A. 1961.
**Military Career:** Marine Corps, 1962-65.
**Profession:** University official.
**Family:** Wife, Catherine Rieniets; two children.
**Religion:** Methodist.
**Political Career:** No previous office.

**In Washington:** Beard's pro-military views are compatible with those of his Armed Services colleagues, but his penchant for expressing them by press release has made him a loner in a group that prefers things closely held.

Beard is a Marine Corps reserve officer who still spends two weeks on active duty every year. He credits the Marines with making a man out of him when he was younger, and they have always been a legislative constituency for him. He was widely praised within the corps in 1977, when he won House approval for an amendment barring federal benefits for Vietnam veterans whose less-than-honorable discharges were upgraded by President Carter.

Beard's style on Armed Services is acerbic and cutting. His interrogation of witnesses often turns into cross-examination, as it did in 1980, when he accused Pentagon civilian leaders of concealing serious manpower problems and told them their support for President Carter "just nauseates me." Defense Secretary Harold Brown calmly told Beard that his facts were wrong.

During the Carter administration, Beard's most frequent target was Army Secretary Clifford L. Alexander Jr. When Alexander defended the volunteer Army, Beard called him a liar.

Beard began his assaults on the volunteer army at a time when few senior committee members were willing to join him. He was happy to proceed alone. Beard's hard-working staff fed the media hot quotes, leaked documents and studies portraying a breakdown of military discipline and training. By 1980, most of Armed Services was publicly agreeing with Beard's basic premise that the voluntary system was a failure, although shying away from his incendiary rhetoric.

During his second term in the House, Beard filed a complaint against a colleague, Massachusetts Democrat Michael J. Harrington, charging that Harrington had violated House rules by releasing secret CIA information about U.S. involvement in Chile. The complaint was dismissed by the House Ethics Committee, but Beard introduced legislation making such release a criminal act.

In 1980, however, it was Beard who was accused of disclosing sensitive material after he issued a news release claiming the Soviet Union had violated a treaty by reloading its missile silos. The White House said Beard's information was highly classified. An investigation was ordered, but none was ever completed.

When Beard has not been involved in military issues, he has lobbied to protect Tennessee public works projects from the Endangered Species Act and other environmental legislation.

In 1978, when the Endangered Species Act was up for extension, Beard fought for exemptions to it. He claimed federal regulators were misusing the law to block needed water projects, including his district's controversial Columbia Dam, which was being held up because it would threaten the destruction of shellfish on the endangered list. He was also enraged that endangered woodpeckers were keeping Marine Corps tanks out of the forests on a North Carolina Marine base.

When Beard's attempts to amend the law through the normal committee system were stymied, Beard quickly went outside it. He threatened to tie up the House for days by introducing 682 amendments to a related appropriations bill. Each amendment would have dealt with a par-

---

**6th District: West central — Clarksville, part of Memphis.** Population: 659,203 (40% increase since 1970). Race: White 564,694 (86%), Black 89,355 (14%), Others 5,154 (1%). Spanish origin: 6,358 (1%).

ticular species on the endangered list, from the pink fairy armadillo to the bowhead whale.

His tactic worked. House leaders allowed him to offer his changes in the law, and he dropped his amendments to the appropriations bill. Beard's amendments passed, Columbia Dam is being built, and the Marine Corps can maneuver without worrying about woodpeckers.

**At Home:** Beard's support for the military and campaigns against environmentalist red tape have been an unqualified political success in the 6th District. Only a Democratic gerrymander or a decision on his own to run for the Senate in 1982 could alter the prospect of his prolonged tenure there.

Beard took the district in 1972 from Democrat William Anderson, a nuclear submarine commander who alienated West Tennessee conservatives by turning against the Vietnam War. Anderson's district was substantially altered in 1972, and a primary challenger took nearly 40 percent of the vote against him.

Beard, who had never run for office before, resigned as state personnel commissioner to challenge Anderson in the fall, campaigning in part on the Democrat's war views. Beard overwhelmed Anderson in the suburban Memphis part of the district and held even with him in the traditionally Democratic rural counties to take 55 percent overall. He became the first Republican ever to represent west-central Tennessee in the House.

Democrats clambered to oppose Beard in 1974, and former state Rep. Tim Schaeffer won the party's nomination. Schaeffer, a traditional middle Tennessee populist, had managed Democratic Sen. Albert Gore's 1970 re-election campaign. He criticized Beard for not speaking out earlier against the Nixon administration's role in the Watergate burglary.

But Beard reflected his constituents' conservatism. Despite a Democratic tide that swept two other Tennessee Republicans from the House, Beard won 56.7 percent, slightly higher than his 1972 margin.

In 1976, Democrats nominated former U.S. Sen. Ross Bass, who had represented most of the district in the House from 1955 to 1964. Bass, an accomplished campaigner, had the name recognition Schaeffer had lacked. But Beard was helped by a court-ordered adjustment of district lines that took 12,000 white suburban voters from the 8th District and put them in his 6th. With the new borders, Beard had a secure Republican district, and he trounced Bass even as Carter was carrying the district for president.

The 1978 Democratic candidate barely managed a quarter of the vote against Beard; in 1980 Beard was unopposed.

**The District:** Affluent, rapidly-growing suburban areas frame the 6th District on east and west. In between lie the agricultural Highland Rim counties and other rural territory where people and factories are streaming in.

Nearly a third of the district vote is cast in the suburbs of Memphis (Shelby County), where Reagan won 69 percent in 1980. The population of Germantown, one of the Shelby suburbs, has increased nearly 500 percent since 1970. Nearly 200 miles to the east, Williamson County contains some of Nashville's southern suburbs. Williamson casts about 9 percent of the district vote, and Reagan won 55 percent there in 1980.

The largest concentration of Democratic votes is in Montgomery County (Clarksville), near the Kentucky border.

Cotton, livestock and tobacco are important agricultural products, but industrialization has spread throughout the district, with plants making textiles, shoes, chemicals and other prouducts. The 6th grew forty percent in the past decade, faster than any other Tennessee district.

Redistricting could lop off the eastern end of the district. Williamson County, where Beard lives, may be attached to the territory of Democratic Rep. Albert Gore. Beard is a likely challenger to Democratic Sen. Jim Sasser in 1982.

## Committees

**Armed Services** (4th of 19 Republicans)
  Investigations; Research and Development.

**Select Narcotics Abuse and Control** (2nd of 8 Republicans)

## Elections

**1980 General**

| | |
|---|---|
| Robin Beard Jr. (R) | 127,945 (99%) |

**1978 General**

| | |
|---|---|
| Robin Beard Jr. (R) | 114,630 (75%) |
| Ron Arline (D) | 38,954 (25%) |

**Previous Winning Percentages**

| | | |
|---|---|---|
| 1976 (64 %) | 1974 (57 %) | 1972 (55 %) |

**District Vote For President**

| | 1980 | | 1976 | | 1972 |
|---|---|---|---|---|---|
| **D** | 101,836 (44%) | **D** | 104,815 (52%) | **D** | 39,799 (27%) |
| **R** | 123,782 (54%) | **R** | 94,314 (47%) | **R** | 104,742 (70%) |
| **I** | 4,730 (2%) | | | | |

## Campaign Finance

| | Receipts | Receipts from PACs | Expen-ditures |
|---|---|---|---|
| **1980** | | | |
| Beard (R) | $177,782 | $54,410 (31%) | $146,038 |
| **1978** | | | |
| Beard (R) | $192,312 | $34,525 (18%) | $156,405 |
| Arline (D) | $15,474 | $9,145 (59%) | $10,175 |

## Voting Studies

| Year | Presidential Support S | O | Party Unity S | O | Conservative Coalition S | O |
|---|---|---|---|---|---|---|
| 1980 | 32 | 56 | 80 | 9 | 83 | 4 |
| 1979 | 37 | 50 | 74 | 14 | 82 | 3 |
| 1978 | 28 | 64 | 79 | 10 | 85 | 4 |
| 1977 | 32 | 54 | 83 | 10 | 90 | 2 |
| 1976 | 82 | 18 | 88 | 7 | 94 | 2 |
| 1975 | 65 | 31 | 88 | 6 | 90 | 2 |
| 1974 (Ford) | 56 | 24 | | | | |
| 1974 | 66 | 30 | 79 | 7 | 89 | 1 |
| 1973 | 63 | 29 | 81 | 14 | 92 | 3 |

S = Support    O = Opposition

## Key Votes

**96th Congress**

| | |
|---|---|
| Weaken Carter oil profits tax (1979) | Y |
| Reject hospital cost control plan (1979) | Y |
| Implement Panama Canal Treaties (1979) | N |
| Establish Department of Education (1979) | N |
| Approve Anti-busing Amendment (1979) | Y |
| Guarantee Chrysler Corp. loans (1979) | N |
| Approve military draft registration (1980) | Y |
| Aid Sandinista regime in Nicaragua (1980) | Y |
| Strengthen fair housing laws (1980) | ? |

**97th Congress**

| | |
|---|---|
| Reagan budget proposal (1981) | Y |

## Interest Group Ratings

| Year | ADA | ACA | AFL-CIO | CCUS |
|---|---|---|---|---|
| 1980 | 11 | 91 | 19 | 75 |
| 1979 | 5 | 74 | 20 | 88 |
| 1978 | 5 | 96 | 0 | 89 |
| 1977 | 0 | 85 | 14 | 100 |
| 1976 | 5 | 93 | 14 | 94 |
| 1975 | 0 | 89 | 10 | 94 |
| 1974 | 0 | 93 | 10 | 100 |
| 1973 | 0 | 89 | 10 | 100 |

# 7 Ed Jones (D)

Of Yorkville — Elected 1969

**Born:** April 20, 1912, Yorkville, Tenn.
**Education:** U. of Tenn., B.S. 1934.
**Profession:** Agriculture agent and inspector.
**Family:** Wife, Llewellyn Wyatt; two children (one deceased).
**Religion:** Presbyterian.
**Political Career:** No previous office.

**In Washington:** Genial Ed Jones might have had the chairmanship of the Agriculture Committee in 1981, if he had wanted it badly enough. A dissident bloc on the committee was uncomfortable with the prospective chairmanship of Kika de la Garza, the sometimes-imperious Texas Democrat first in line.

Jones was next after de la Garza, and his widespread popularity gave the dissidents an issue in trying to dispose of de la Garza. But Jones himself refused to make a move, and when Speaker O'Neill made it known he wanted to follow seniority, the challenge lost by a 110-92 count.

An aggressive campaign would have been out of character, however, for the gentlemanly Tennessee dairy farmer who has quietly pursued a limited number of farm issues for a decade while ignoring most other aspects of House business.

In the early years of his career, Jones rarely strayed beyond dairy politics, treating Congress as a simple extension of the career he began by working his way through college milking cows.

In recent Congresses, however, he has been thrust into a leadership role on different issues — farm loans and disaster relief.

As chairman of the Conservation and Credit Subcommittee, Jones presided over a four-year struggle to revise the costly system of disaster relief payments. In 1977, with disaster payments and other emergency relief to farmers costing the federal government about $500 million a year, the Carter administration moved to replace it with a an expanded system of federal crop insurance. Many farmers were not pleased, but Jones introduced the administration bill and worked on it for three years, finally winning on a 202-140 vote on the House floor. To get it passed, he had to accept a larger role for private insurers, and agree to leave disaster aid intact through 1981, as the new system was phased in.

Meanwhile, Jones was managing the legislative fortunes of the Farmers Home Administra-

tion (FmHA). In 1978, he managed the bill that created $4 billion in new emergency loans by the FmHA and got it passed despite complaints that too many farmers would apply for $4 billion to cover the cost of the program. In 1980, with the initial $4 billion gone, he managed a second bill providing for an additional $2 billion over two more years.

**At Home:** Jones withstood an invasion of national political stars to win a 1969 special election and complete the term of Democratic Rep. Robert A. Everett, who died after serving 11 years.

The national GOP tried to convert the special election into a demonstration of Southern approval for President Nixon's month-old administration. House minority leader Gerald Ford and newly named party Chairman Rogers C.B. Morton came to the district to promote Jones' Republican opponent, state Rep. Leonard Dunavant.

Meanwhile, George Wallace came to speak at a district fund-raiser for American Party candidate William J. Davis. Wallace, who had carried the district easily in his 1968 presidential campaign, said electing Davis would prove that "our movement will not be defeated."

Jones shunned outside help. Because he was born and reared on a local farm and had served as Tennessee Agriculture Commissioner, Jones was able to count on strong support from the district's

---

**7th District: West — Jackson, part of Memphis.** Population: 584,542 (20% increase since 1970). Race: White 470,295 (80%), Black 110,153 (19%), Others 4,084 (1%). Spanish origin: 5,204 (1%).

farming areas and from courthouse organizations. Under Tennessee's leader-take-all system, Jones won election by taking 47.6 percent of the vote.

In the six re-election campaigns since 1969, Jones has faced only one significant challenge. In the 1976 Democratic primary, state Rep. Larry Bates faulted him as a passive legislator. Early polls indicated Jones was vulnerable, but he campaigned non-stop for more than a month prior to the primary and won 59.4 percent of the vote.

**The District:** This district is two-thirds rural, a cotton, livestock and dairy farming region, and it is nearly always Democratic except when the Democratic nominee is an unabashed liberal.

Jackson, the district's largest city, has a Bendix auto parts plant and makes Pringles for Procter and Gamble. It has a growing Republican vote. Jones is popular there, but in races for other major offices, Republicans have usually prevailed since 1970.

More than a quarter of the district's vote is cast in northern Shelby County, an industrial and suburban area near Memphis whose upwardly mobile residents usually prefer Republicans.

## Committees

**Agriculture** (4th of 24 Democrats)
Conservation, Credit, and Rural Development, chairman; Cotton, Rice and Sugar; Livestock, Dairy, and Poultry.

**House Administration** (4th of 11 Democrats)
Services, chairman; Contracts and Printing.

**Joint Printing**

## Elections

**1980 General**

| | |
|---|---|
| Ed Jones (D) | 133,606 (77%) |
| Daniel Campbell (R) | 39,227 (23%) |

**1978 General**

| | |
|---|---|
| Ed Jones (D) | 96,863 (73%) |
| Ross Cook (R) | 36,003 (27%) |

**Previous Winning Percentages**

| | | | |
|---|---|---|---|
| 1976 (100%) | 1974 (100%) | 1972 (71%) | 1970 (100%) |
| 1969* (48%) | | | |

*Special election.*

**District Vote For President**

| | 1980 | | 1976 | | 1972 |
|---|---|---|---|---|---|
| **D** | 96,419 (48%) | **D** | 100,751 (57%) | **D** | 34,241 (24%) |
| **R** | 102,092 (50%) | **R** | 73,714 (42%) | **R** | 105,072 (73%) |
| **I** | 3,282 (2%) | | | | |

## Campaign Finance

| | Receipts | Receipts from PACs | Expenditures |
|---|---|---|---|
| **1980** | | | |
| Jones (D) | $125,546 | $62,825 (50%) | $76,919 |
| **1978** | | | |
| Jones (D) | $134,369 | $65,175 (49%) | $124,445 |
| Cook (R) | $51,489 | $3,465 (7%) | $49,769 |

## Voting Studies

| | Presidential Support | | Party Unity | | Conservative Coalition | |
|---|---|---|---|---|---|---|
| **Year** | **S** | **O** | **S** | **O** | **S** | **O** |
| 1980 | 57 | 36 | 59 | 31 | 76 | 19 |
| 1979 | 61 | 36 | 59 | 34 | 74 | 19 |

| | | | | | | |
|---|---|---|---|---|---|---|
| 1978 | 40 | 48 | 48 | 42 | 67 | 22 |
| 1977 | 63 | 30 | 60 | 32 | 62 | 31 |
| 1976 | 37 | 27 | 42 | 30 | 52 | 17 |
| 1975 | 31 | 60 | 49 | 40 | 67 | 23 |
| 1974 (Ford) | 48 | 52 | | | | |
| 1974 | 40 | 32 | 37 | 36 | 55 | 15 |
| 1973 | 42 | 44 | 46 | 47 | 80 | 13 |
| 1972 | 43 | 35 | 29 | 44 | 71 | 10 |
| 1971 | 51 | 21 | 30 | 41 | 56 | 13 |
| 1970 | 42 | 35 | 49 | 33 | 57 | 18 |
| 1969 | 33 | 44† | 51 | 21† | 49† | 19† |

S = Support    O = Opposition

†Not eligible for all recorded votes.

## Key Votes

**96th Congress**

| | |
|---|---|
| Weaken Carter oil profits tax (1979) | Y |
| Reject hospital cost control plan (1979) | Y |
| Implement Panama Canal Treaties (1979) | N |
| Establish Department of Education (1979) | Y |
| Approve Anti-busing Amendment (1979) | Y |
| Guarantee Chrysler Corp. loans (1979) | Y |
| Approve military draft registration (1980) | Y |
| Aid Sandinista regime in Nicaragua (1980) | N |
| Strengthen fair housing laws (1980) | N |

**97th Congress**

| | |
|---|---|
| Reagan budget proposal (1981) | Y |

## Interest Group Ratings

| Year | ADA | ACA | AFL-CIO | CCUS |
|---|---|---|---|---|
| 1980 | 22 | 45 | 63 | 63 |
| 1979 | 32 | 23 | 55 | 67 |
| 1978 | 20 | 56 | 42 | 44 |
| 1977 | 25 | 52 | 73 | 59 |
| 1976 | 15 | 59 | 64 | 60 |
| 1975 | 11 | 63 | 73 | 44 |
| 1974 | 13 | 64 | 50 | 75 |
| 1973 | 24 | 48 | 56 | 67 |
| 1972 | 13 | 74 | 44 | 89 |
| 1971 | 22 | 48 | 45 | - |
| 1970 | 24 | 60 | 29 | 50 |
| 1969* | 33 | 36 | 56 | - |

*Member did not serve for entire period covered by voting study.

# 8 Harold E. Ford (D)

**Of Memphis — Elected 1974**

**Born:** May 20, 1945, Memphis, Tenn.
**Education:** Tenn. State U., B.S. 1967.
**Profession:** Mortician.
**Family:** Wife, Dorothy Bowles; three children.
**Religion:** Baptist.
**Political Career:** Tenn. House, 1971-75.

**In Washington:** After coming to Congress with a reputation for personal flamboyance and political activism, Ford has turned out to be a relatively quiet member of the Ways and Means Committee, and only an infrequent participant in its legislative planning.

Most of his work has focused on the Health Subcommittee. He is a defender of Medicare on Ways and Means, and fought efforts to cut back its benefits in 1981 in response to Reagan budget requirements. In May, he tried to persuade the committee to restore $71 million in Medicare cuts, but failed. In the past, he has backed legislation to expand Medicare payments to cover dentistry, chiropractic treatment, eyeglasses, and hearing aids.

Earlier in his Ways and Means career, Ford found himself in a critical position on President Carter's hospital cost control plan. Conspicuously uncommitted, he was the deciding vote in subcommittee. He was pressed hard both by the administration and by the AFL-CIO, which was afraid that strict cost controls would depress wages for hospital workers.

Ford went with Carter, infuriating labor officials who had financed more than half his 1976 re-election campaign. "You give money to your friends and you expect them to stick with you in a crisis," a labor lobbyist complained afterward. "But I can't give him a new hospital." Ford continued to support hospital cost containment through the 96th Congress, but it never passed the House.

That was a rare anti-labor vote for Ford, although he did surprise unions early in his second term by voting against a bill to legalize common-site picketing at construction projects. On most issues, Ford sticks close to the consumerism he brought with him from the Tennessee Legislature. Shortly after being sworn in, he introduced a bill to require more detailed labeling on grocery packages; he is still working on that issue, although his role is subordinate to that of New York Democrat Benjamin S. Rosenthal.

**At Home:** Ford is a member of the dominant political family in Memphis' black community. His brother John, a former city councilman, serves in the state Senate; his brother James is on the City Council now.

John Ford's reputation as a political firebrand was a sensitive issue for Harold Ford in his 1974 campaign for Congress. Then on the council, John had expressed a militance on local issues that had alienated some of the district's white electorate. Harold had demonstrated his own brand of populist rhetoric, but he went to great lengths to ensure that he was not confused with his brother. He edged past Republican Rep. Dan H. Kuykendall by 744 votes, becoming Tennessee's first black congressman.

He had begun his political career four years earlier, winning election to the Tennessee House at age 25. In his first term, he was majority whip and chaired a committee that investigated the rates and practices of utilities in the state.

Tennessee's 1972 redistricting placed Kuykendall in trouble by increasing the number of blacks in the district to 47.5 percent of the population. The Republican had won three House elections with increasing ease by taking virtually all the votes of the district's whites, but in 1972, running with the new borders for the first time, he had been held to 55.4 percent by a black Democrat who made little attempt to attract white support.

---

**8th District: Memphis.** Population: 426,254 (17% decrease since 1970). Race: White 155,580 (36%), Black 268,102 (63%), Others 2,567 (1%). Spanish origin: 3,596 (1%).

---

Ford ran a broader and more active campaign against Kuykendall. After winning a six-way Democratic primary, he reached out to white voters, stressing economic issues and promising to listen to whites as well as blacks if he were elected. He referred frequently to Kuykendall's longstanding personal friendship with Richard M. Nixon.

Before the 1976 election, a court-ordered readjustment of district lines removed 12,000 white suburban voters from his district and put them in the adjoining 6th District. The readjustment gave the 8th a black majority, and since then it has been safe for Ford.

**The District:** Like most heavily-black districts throughout the country, the 8th is reliably Democratic in good years and bad. Carter won 68

percent of its vote in 1980, considerably more than in any other Tennessee district and more than his 1976 percentage.

But the district is about to change considerably. While Tennessee's population was growing 16.9 percent in the past decade, the 8th was declining by that same percentage. Downtown Memphis has drawn new corporate headquarters and branch offices, but this growth has not arrested the decline of many urban neighborhoods. Ford's territory will almost certainly have to expand into mostly white suburban areas.

The Memphis economy is a mixture of old and new. Cotton marketing, warehousing and processing of cottonseed into oil have been important for more than a century, and still are. Major manufactured goods are farm machinery, tires and pharmaceuticals.

## Committees

**Select Aging** (9th of 31 Democrats)
Health and Long-term Care.

**Ways and Means** (9th of 23 Democrats)
Health; Oversight.

## Elections

### 1980 General

| Harold Ford (D) | Unopposed |
|---|---|

### 1980 Primary

| Harold Ford (D) | 40,825 (73%) |
|---|---|
| Minerva Johnican (D) | 11,337 (20%) |
| Mark Flanagan (D) | 2,982 (5%) |

### 1978 General

| Harold Ford (D) | 80,776 (70%) |
|---|---|
| Duncan Ragsdale (R) | 33,679 (29%) |

**Previous Winning Percentages**

1976 (61%)    1974 (50%)

**District Vote For President**

| | 1980 | | 1976 | | 1972 |
|---|---|---|---|---|---|
| D | 118,094 (68%) | D | 111,229 (64%) | D | 71,930 (42%) |
| R | 51,121 (30%) | R | 60,114 (35%) | R | 96,876 (56%) |
| I | 3,408 (2%) | | | | |

## Campaign Finance

| | Receipts | Receipts from PACs | Expenditures |
|---|---|---|---|
| **1980** | | | |
| Ford (D) | $166,956 | $54,975 (33%%) | $83,295 |
| **1978** | | | |
| Ford (D) | $198,969 | $45,740 (23%) | $179,244 |
| Ragsdale (R) | $12,913 | $723 (6%) | $12,372 |

## Voting Studies

| | Presidential Support | | Party Unity | | Conservative Coalition | |
|---|---|---|---|---|---|---|
| Year | S | O | S | O | S | O |
| 1980 | 66 | 16 | 75 | 5 | 15 | 59 |
| 1979 | 75 | 14 | 87 | 3 | 10 | 79 |
| 1978 | 66 | 17 | 80 | 7 | 14 | 67 |
| 1977 | 73 | 19 | 85 | 10 | 20 | 78 |
| 1976 | 24 | 61 | 75 | 9 | 21 | 65 |
| 1975 | 29 | 61 | 77 | 15 | 25 | 69 |

S = Support    O = Opposition

## Key Votes

**96th Congress**

| | |
|---|---|
| Weaken Carter oil profits tax (1979) | N |
| Reject hospital cost control plan (1979) | X |
| Implement Panama Canal Treaties (1979) | ? |
| Establish Department of Education (1979) | Y |
| Approve Anti-busing Amendment (1979) | N |
| Guarantee Chrysler Corp. loans (1979) | Y |
| Approve military draft registration (1980) | N |
| Aid Sandinista regime in Nicaragua (1980) | ? |
| Strengthen fair housing laws (1980) | Y |

**97th Congress**

| | |
|---|---|
| Reagan budget proposal (1981) | N |

## Interest Group Ratings

| Year | ADA | ACA | AFL-CIO | CCUS |
|---|---|---|---|---|
| 1980 | 83 | 19 | 89 | 60 |
| 1979 | 79 | 0 | 94 | 7 |
| 1978 | 70 | 12 | 90 | 19 |
| 1977 | 75 | 7 | 78 | 29 |
| 1976 | 80 | 21 | 91 | 10 |
| 1975 | 79 | 19 | 96 | 13 |

# Texas

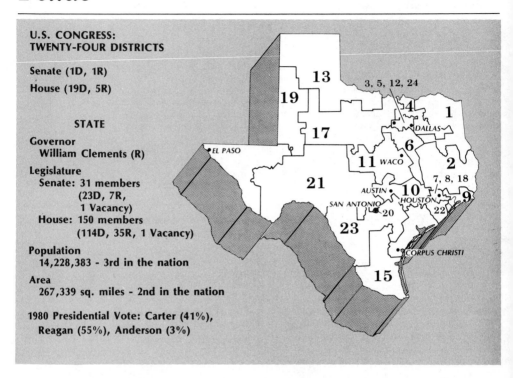

**U.S. CONGRESS:**
**TWENTY-FOUR DISTRICTS**

Senate (1D, 1R)
House (19D, 5R)

**STATE**

Governor
  William Clements (R)

Legislature
  Senate: 31 members
    (23D, 7R,
    1 Vacancy)
  House: 150 members
    (114D, 35R, 1 Vacancy)

Population
  14,228,383 - 3rd in the nation

Area
  267,339 sq. miles - 2nd in the nation

1980 Presidential Vote: Carter (41%),
  Reagan (55%), Anderson (3%)

## ... The Results of Prosperity

The spread of prosperity is changing life and politics in Texas at a rapid pace, boosting the development of a strong Republican Party and diminishing the opportunity for liberals to take the reins of state government.

The state's economy now rests on a diverse range of industries, including aerospace, defense and chemicals. Drawn by economic opportunity, newcomers have been flooding in for a generation. Since 1940, Texas' population has more than doubled. In the last decade alone, it increased by 27 percent, a rate faster than that of any other megastate except Florida.

The population boom — augmented by a large in-state migration from rural to metropolitan areas — has gradually unsettled Texas' traditional Democratic voting patterns. Much of the growth has occurred in the Republican metropolitan areas — Houston and Dallas-Fort Worth. And as Republicans gather additional support in the

oil, wheat and grazing country of west Texas, they inch closer to a majority position in state and national elections.

The new GOP coalition was strong enough in 1978 to narrowly elect William Clements, former oil executive and deputy defense secretary, as the first Republican governor since Reconstruction. The party's only post-Reconstruction senator, John Tower, was re-elected the same year, although just barely. In 1980, Ronald Reagan expanded the successful formula to carry Texas with 55 percent of the vote.

For nearly a century after the Civil War, Texas was like the rest of the South, solidly Democratic. There has always been a vocal liberal wing in the Democratic Party, but it was crippled until the 1960s by the poll tax, which restricted participation by blacks and Hispanics.

In recent years, liberals have wielded more power within the Democratic Party. But victories by the left at the primary level have sometimes meant defeat for the party in November. In 1978, liberal and moderate Democrats succeeded in defeating three-term Democratic Gov. Dolph Briscoe in his bid for renomination. That was the prelude to Clements' breakthrough in the fall.

Still, Democrats remain dominant at the grass roots. Republicans have been slow in making inroads into the huge Democratic majorities in Congress and the state Legislature. After the 1980 election, Republicans controlled less than 25 percent of the seats in the Legislature and only five of 24 U.S. House seats.

# A Political Tour

**East Texas.** Geographically and culturally, east Texas is an extension of the Deep South. It was settled prior to the Civil War by Southerners from Georgia, South Carolina and the North Carolina lowlands. They developed a cotton-based, slaveholding economy.

The region extends westward from the Louisiana line to the outskirts of metropolitan Houston, then northward to the Red River, Texas' boundary with southern Oklahoma. It is a rural region with no large cities. Small-scale cotton and dairy farms are common in the northern sector. Further south are the "Piney Woods," a timber belt. Lumber and wood finishing plants are sprinkled throughout east Texas.

But since the 1930s, farming and lumber have taken a back seat to oil. The discovery of major oil deposits in east Texas a half century ago changed the face of the entire state — from rural and agrarian into a land of opportunity and new wealth. But few people in the area profited from the oil. Except for the Hispanic Rio Grande Valley, east Texas is the poorest part of the state. It has the highest concentration of black voters, although their numbers are not as large as in the rural Black Belt areas of Mississippi and Alabama. No Texas county has a black majority.

Capitalizing on the Dixie traditions, George Wallace ran better in east Texas in 1968 than anywhere in the state. He carried virtually every county within 50 miles of the Louisiana border.

But the strong Wallace showing did not presage realignment. Rural east Texans have remained Democratic. Most of them voted against Clements in 1978 and against Reagan in 1980. Republican breakthroughs have been limited to the small population centers of the region, such as Longview and Tyler, centers for the independent oil industry.

In spite of its relative poverty, the region has been growing quickly. Most of the counties of east Texas increased their population by 20 to 40 percent in the last decade.

**Greater Houston.** Probably no part of Texas has made better use of limited geographical assets than Houston. From a small bayou town 50 miles inland from the Gulf of Mexico, it has grown into the largest city in Texas (nearly 1.6 million in 1980), the fifth-largest in the country, and the commercial center of the Southwest.

Before World War II, Houston's trade centered on the processing of local food products and the production and refining of oil. After the war, the economy diversified. Chemicals, synthetic rubber and steel became major products, and heavy industry lined the long ship channel. Air conditioning made its climate tolerable in the summer.

Although its economy hardly needed a boost, Houston and surrounding Harris County picked up another plum in the early 1960s when the city was selected as the site of the National Aeronautics and Space Administration's Manned Spacecraft Center.

The lure of wealth has attracted not only ambitious businessmen to Houston, but also aspiring politicians. Lloyd Bentsen, George Bush and John B. Connally all moved to Houston to make their fortunes and advance their political careers.

Along with the advantages of the great boom, Houston also has suffered some discomforts. The air and some of the waterways are polluted, rush hour lasts most of the day, and the area suffers from uncontrolled development. There is no zoning in Houston, and the city sprawls for miles into Harris County and beyond.

Harris County has been dabbling with Republicanism for more than a half century — it voted for Herbert Hoover in 1928. But recently, Republican voting patterns have become more pronounced. In 1968, Richard Nixon won Harris County by only four percentage points. Twelve years later, Reagan carried the county by 20 points.

Republicans have benefited from a population boom in the suburbs. While the city of Houston grew by 29 percent in the 1970s, suburban Harris County increased by 61 percent. The growth has been even more dramatic in adjacent counties that have felt the effects of Houston sprawl. Montgomery County to the north grew by 160 percent in the 1970s, while Fort Bend County to the southwest had a population boom of 150 percent. Both counties were turning in large Republican majorities in major statewide races by the end of the decade.

The brand of Republicanism in the middle- and upper-class suburbs has long been staunchly conservative. But in the inner city, the political climate is different. With the help of labor unions, an active core of liberal whites and a large minority population — 28 percent black and 18 percent Hispanic — inner Houston has been a hotbed of Texas liberalism.

Since 1972, the inner city 18th District has sent a black Democrat to Congress — first, Barbara Jordan, then Mickey Leland. The adjoining 8th District elected a white populist Democrat, Bob Eckhardt, from 1966 until 1980, when the city's massive demographic changes caught up with him, and he was beaten by a Republican in a constituency turning more suburban.

**Industrial Gulf Coast.** One of the few parts of Texas with much ethnic diversity is the industrial Gulf Coast, which extends about 300 miles from the Louisiana border to Corpus Christi.

In the northern coastal area around the major port cities of Galveston, Beaumont and Port Arthur, there is a mixture of blacks, Cajuns and blue-collar whites, many of German, Czech or Polish stock. Moving southward, the concentration of Hispanics increases. In Nueces County (Corpus Christi), they comprise nearly 50 percent of the population.

The northern coastal area is also one of the few strongholds of organized labor in Texas. Statewide, labor is not very popular; there is strong right-to-work law. But on the docks and in the oil refineries, organized labor does have clout and has helped keep the industrial Gulf Coast in the Democratic column.

Although there has been little population growth in the industrial areas, the more Republican coastal counties like Brazoria, south of Houston, have been growing quite rapidly.

Along with oil and related manufacturing and maritime industries, fishing and rice production are important to the Gulf Coast economy. The coastal prairie south of Galveston is the trading center for the state's valuable rice crop.

**Dallas-Fort Worth.** Few American cities have as controversial a reputation as Dallas. Following the assassination of President Kennedy in downtown Dallas in 1963, the city suffered with an image of frontier violence and extremism that was hard to shake. Just as that perception was fading, the television series "Dallas" came along to popularize the image of a metropolis ruled by an oligarchy of oil interests obsessed with money and power.

But Dallas is more than ostentatious wealth and unbridled conservatism. It has long been a cosmopolitan city and a financial center of the Southwest. Northerners looking for a city that fits their definition are much more likely to find it in Dallas than in newer, sloppier, more chaotic Houston.

Dallas began as a cotton and textile town in the shadow of Fort Worth. But with the opening of the east Texas oil fields, it began to boom. Many of the oil companies placed their headquarters there, and the city went on to attract a diversified array of industries, many of them high-technology electronics firms. With more than 900,000 residents, Dallas is the seventh largest city in the country.

Dallas County — which includes the city and its immediate suburbs — has been a Republican stronghold for several decades. Clements received 58 percent of the Dallas County vote in 1978, while Reagan drew 59 percent in 1980. With a minority population somewhat smaller than in Houston, Dallas is a few shades more Republican.

Thirty-three miles to the west of Dallas is the city of Fort Worth. Once the senior partner of the two, Forth Worth is now less than half the size of Dallas and declining in population.

Fort Worth has always projected more of a blue-collar image than Dallas. During the early years of the oil boom, it was headquarters for west Texas operations before they moved to Midland and Odessa in the heart of the fields. Since World War II, Fort Worth has been a major manufacturer of military and aerospace equipment.

Fort Worth has less wealth than Dallas, and in national elections, Republican majorities in surrounding Tarrant County tend to be smaller than those in Dallas County. Democrat Jim Wright, the House majority leader, has had little trouble holding his Fort Worth-based district.

Over the past three decades, the fast-growing suburbs between Dallas and Forth Worth have filled the space between the two cities. As in greater Houston, the largest growth in the Dallas-Fort Worth area in the last decade has been in adjacent suburban counties. Dallas and Tarrant counties both had growth rates of 20 percent or less in the 1970s, but Collin and Denton counties to the north both grew by at least 85 percent.

**Hill Country.** Interstate 35, which runs north-and-south through central Texas from Dallas to San Antonio, is something of a geographical dividing line. To the east is the low country and the concentration of black voters. Immediately to the west is the rolling terrain of the hill country, a rural area best suited for grazing livestock.

This is the area of Johnson City and the LBJ Ranch, as well as communities like Fredericksburg and New Braunfels, originally settled by German immigrants in the 19th century. Opposed to slavery, these Germans were an early force in the Republican Party in Texas.

The major population center in the region is Austin, the state capital. Of Texas' six largest urban centers, Travis County (Austin) is the smallest but the fastest growing. Its population increased 42 percent in the 1970s.

With a large government work force and sizable academic community affiliated with the University of Texas, it is also the least conservative politically. Travis County was the only one of the large urban counties not carried by either Clements or Reagan.

About 90 miles to the north of Austin is the region's other major city, Waco. Often called the "Baptist Rome," it is the site of numerous Baptist churches and of Baylor University, which is affiliated with the Southern Baptists. Although more conservative than Austin, Waco has not developed Republican voting patterns as strong as those of Dallas-Fort Worth or Houston.

**South Texas.** South Texas sits like the keel of a sailboat at the bottom of the state. That shape suggests the political significance the area plays in Texas politics — it provides the votes that prevent the state from tipping over into a sea of conservative predictability.

South Texas is home for most of the state's Hispanics. In the Lower Rio Grande Valley, Hispanics make up a large majority of the population. Even as far north as Bexar County (San Antonio), they comprise 47 percent of the population. Jimmy Carter received nearly 80 percent of the vote from Texas Hispanics in 1980, even though much of south Texas had voted for Sen. Edward M. Kennedy in the presidential primary that spring.

Although Hispanics have numerical superiority in the region, they have only recently begun to crack "Anglo" control of local government and commerce. While the Rio Grande Valley has large ranches and irrigated farms that produce bumper crops of cotton, vegetables and fruit, Hispanics have not shared in the prosperity. On a per capita basis, south Texas is among the poorest areas in the country, although some of the Sun Belt growth has begun to affect it, especially in the fast-growing port of Brownsville.

For much of this century, the political influence of Hispanics was curbed by the poll tax. From 1904 until the mid-1960s, Texans between the ages of 21 and 60 had to pay the tax several months before a primary in order to be eligible to vote. Throughout south Texas, Anglo bosses paid the poll taxes of many Hispanics and controlled their votes as a bloc.

Modern Hispanic political awareness dates from 1960, when Hispanics enthusiastically supported fellow Catholic John F. Kennedy for president. By 1964 the area had two Hispanic congressmen, both Democrats.

Younger, militant Hispanic activists, however, viewed the Democratic Party as an arm of the Anglo establishment and, in the early 1970s, formed a third party, La Raza Unida. The party had some early successes, winning several town elections in south Texas and drawing more than 5 percent of the statewide vote in the 1972 and 1974 gubernatorial elections. But the appeal of the party began to ebb by the end of the decade, and in 1978 Luis A. Diaz DeLeon received less than 1 percent as La Raza Unida's Senate candidate.

As the third-party effort has waned, Hispanics have begun to make inroads in Democratic Party politics in south Texas. In April 1981, 33-year-old Henry Cisneros was elected mayor of San Antonio, becoming the first Hispanic mayor of a major American city.

With nearly 800,000 residents, San Antonio is the 10th largest city in the United States. While it was founded in the early 18th century by the Spanish, San Antonio has long had an economy controlled by Anglos. Once a cattle center, the city now depends on local military bases for its prosperity. The combination of military families and descendants of German settlers have given the Republicans a strong base, particularly in suburban parts of Bexar County (pronounced "bear"). Reagan managed to carry the county in 1980.

While Bexar grew by 19 percent in the last decade, the greatest growth in south Texas was taking place in the Lower Rio Grande Valley along the Mexican border. Hidalgo County (McAllen) had a population increase of 56 percent, while neighboring Cameron County (Brownsville) along the Gulf grew by 49 percent.

**Western Plains.** The open plains of west Texas will have to be a cornerstone of any emerging Republican majority.

GOP strength in the region was long limited to the oil boom towns of Midland and Odessa and scattered wheat-growing counties in the panhandle. But in their recent statewide victories, Republicans have carried most of the counties west of Abilene.

The Texas plains are a part of America's legendary Western frontier. Grazing and farming are major sources of income in the panhandle, while ranching and oil and gas production are predominant further south.

Between 1940 and 1960, blue-collar Odessa grew from a town of less than 10,000 to more than

80,000 inhabitants. Today, at 90,000, it is mainly a white-collar city and the home for many oil executives. Both Midland and Ector (Odessa) counties gave Clements and Reagan more than 70 percent of the vote, a higher share than any other urban counties in the state.

About 120 miles to the north of Midland is Lubbock. Irrigation has enabled the Lubbock area to replace east Texas as the state's predominant cotton growing area. Although Lubbock is not in the center of any oil fields, several oil companies have established offices in the city.

Farther north is the panhandle. This windy area was devastated by the great Dust Bowl of the 1930s. Discovery of underground water supplies, however, has helped stabilize the livestock industry and farming in wheat, cotton and sorghum grains. Amarillo is the center of the agricultural region. While regularly Republican, neither Amarillo nor Lubbock turn out the huge GOP majorities that are found in Midland and Odessa.

West of the plains is the desert and ranch land of western Texas. The lone population center is El Paso, far removed from the rest of the state. Enjoying steady growth since the 1940s, it is now the fourth largest city in Texas.

With Hispanics comprising nearly two-thirds of the population, El Paso is the only major urban county in the western half of Texas that does not consistently vote Republican. Anglos, however, control the city's economy, which relies heavily on textiles produced with locally grown cotton.

## Redrawing the Lines

The task of adding three new congressional districts to the current 24 proved too complicated for the Texas Legislature to complete in its regular 1981 session.

Democrats have a large margin in both houses of the Legislature, but that will not prevent Republicans from gaining some new seats. All five districts Republicans now hold are overpopulated and can provide population for other districts with voters sympathetic to the GOP.

Rep. Bill Archer's Houston-based 7th District has grown 86 percent since 1970. Ron Paul's 22nd District south of Houston has grown 52 percent. James M. Collins' North Dallas 3rd has increased by 49 percent and Tom Loeffler's 21st outside San Antonio by 45 percent. Those four districts, combined with that of the state's other GOP representative, Jack Fields, have enough extra people to fill two full additional districts.

In May, the state House approved a plan that gave the GOP a chance to win three more seats and threatened two Democratic incumbents. The Senate passed a plan favoring incumbents that gave the GOP a shot at winning two or three more districts.

When House and Senate conferees met in late May, compromise snagged on a dispute over creating a majority black district in Dallas County. House conferees favored a black district, and GOP Gov. William P. Clements supported them. But Senate conferees said that the idea was a GOP ploy to weaken Democrats' hold on east Dallas' 5th District.

The impasse was not broken, and the Legislature adjourned as required by law. Clements said he would call a special legislative session to deal with redistricting.

Only two districts lost ground. They are San Antonio's 20th and Houston's 18th, both inner-city areas represented by Democrats.

## Governor
## William Clements (R)

**Born:** April 13, 1917, Dallas, Texas.
**Home:** Dallas, Texas.
**Education:** Southern Methodist U., 1935-36.
**Profession:** Manufacturer of oil drilling equipment.
**Family:** Wife, Rita; two children.
**Religion:** Episcopalian.
**Political Career:** Deputy secretary of defense, 1973-77; elected governor 1978; term expires Jan. 1983.

# John Tower (R)

**Of Wichita Falls — Elected 1961**

**Born:** Sept., 29, 1925, Houston, Texas.
**Education:** Southwestern U., B.A. 1948; Southern Methodist U., M.A. 1953.
**Military Career:** Navy, 1943-46.
**Profession:** Political science professor.
**Family:** Wife, Lilla Burt Cummings; three children.
**Religion:** Methodist.
**Political Career:** Republican nominee for U.S. Senate, 1960; Republican nominee for Texas House, 1954.

**In Washington:** Twenty years in the Senate have transformed Tower's reputation from playboy to powerhouse, and given him a cumulative expertise in military affairs that few in Congress can surpass. As chairman of the Armed Services Committee, he is now using that leverage to shape American defense policy to his liking.

Tower wanted the position of secretary of defense in the Reagan administration, and nearly got it. But the White House was reluctant to take a chance on losing Tower's Senate seat to a Democrat, and less than enthusiastic at the prospect of seeing Barry Goldwater, never a great workhorse, occupying the crucial Armed Services chairmanship. So Tower stayed where he was.

He began wielding the power of his chairmanship quietly, but the result was evident almost immediately, both in key Pentagon appointments and in the size and scope of the administration's first defense spending proposals. "I have made some recommendations," Tower acknowledged tersely, declining to elaborate.

That is the way Tower talks when he is operating behind the scenes. Although he is comfortable firing away at the opposition in public and partisan war games, he is tight-lipped and poker-faced when asked about his work "offstage."

Under his leadership, the Armed Services Committee is playing a more assertive role than it did under the gentle guidance of Mississippi Democrat John Stennis, who tended to defer to presidents on policy directions and to other Senate chairmen in jurisdictional disputes. Tower, never awed by executive power, holds an expansive view of his committee's turf, especially vis-à-vis the Foreign Relations Committee.

The Armed Services panel, he has said, "expects to review matters that impact on military balance that are not directly within our legislative jurisdiction." That includes weapons sales, technology transfers and security assistance requests previously handled by Foreign Relations.

The first six months of Tower's chairmanship produced general harmony between the committee and the Reagan administration — reasonable enough, considering Tower helped draft the administration's defense proposals. When most of Congress expressed skepticism about the Reagan plan to sell AWACS jets to Saudi Arabia, Tower sounded sympathetic. But he is still not a sure vote for the president or the Pentagon, as he demonstrated in April, when his committee opposed Reagan's request to reactivate a mothballed aircraft carrier.

During Tower's four years as senior Armed Services Republican, before he took over as chairman, he was already a crucial influence on the committee. In 1979, he was the driving force behind a sharply critical committee report on the SALT II treaty. The report later found its way into the papers despite the objections of Stennis, who was not opposed to the conclusions but did not want to be inconsiderate of Carter.

Tower has long advocated a major buildup of U.S. defense capabilities, with immediate emphasis on improving conventional forces. He puts no qualifiers on his commitment. "I don't think we put balancing the budget as our number one priority," he said. "We put national security as our number one priority."

In recent years, Tower has devoted nearly all of his legislative effort to defense issues. He could have chosen in 1981 to chair the Banking Committee, where he was also the ranking Republican, but never even hesitated before opting for Armed Services.

Elected in 1961 to fill Lyndon B. Johnson's seat when Johnson became vice president, Tower is now the second most senior Republican in the

Senate. There is a certain irony to such status: nearly everyone, including Tower, viewed his original election as a fluke likely to be reversed the next time Texas voters went to the polls.

Tower was noted in the early 1960s for a very active social life; if he was not going to be around long, he planned to enjoy himself while he was. Gradually, however, he settled down to serious business, and as the years and re-elections went by, his reputation changed.

Tower became chairman of the Senate's GOP Policy Committee in 1973, and transformed that once- insignificant panel into an active research and information arm of the Republican Party. The committee became a major focus for Republican alternatives to Carter policies and programs. For several years, Tower regularly appeared in the Senate Press Gallery after the weekly committee meetings to brief reporters on the latest developments within the GOP. Slouched in a chair, one leg over its side, he bantered and parried, turning aside as many questions as he answered and slipping in a few jabs of his own at the opposition.

Unlike Majority Leader Howard H. Baker Jr., who excels at conciliation, Tower has something of a tough guy reputation; if he does not actually crack heads, he manages nonetheless to convey the idea that he is capable of doing so. Within the circle of elected GOP leaders and committee chairmen, he serves as a steadying force — partly because of his experience and partly because he stays cool even when others do not.

Tower began his Senate career as an ardent conservative who all but idolized Barry Goldwater. He was the first senator to announce support for Goldwater's 1964 presidential bid, and traveled thousands of miles that year stumping for the Arizona Republican.

Four years later, while still a committed conservative, Tower helped to hold the Texas delegation and much of the South for Richard Nixon, even though many of his state's Republicans personally preferred Ronald Reagan. It was not until 1980, when he chaired the convention's platform committee, that the Texas senator was solidly aligned with Reagan.

Tower has a consistently conservative voting record in the Senate, although he has been known to bend here and there at the behest of Republican presidents. He agreed to vote for wage-price controls under Nixon, and at the urging of the Ford White House, also backed federal help for New York City. In 1981, he not only supported President Reagan's request for an increase in the federal debt ceiling, he helped whip other GOP senators in line behind the unavoidable boost.

Like most politicians, Tower votes his constituent interests over his ideological convictions some of the time; he once chided the Carter administration for insufficient support of mass transit. "I started out opposed to federal mass transit assistance, but as Texas became more urbanized, I began to see the need for assistance," Tower conceded.

**At Home:** For most of his career, Tower has been fortunate enough to run in years of national Republican strength and Democratic division in Texas. But his narrow escape in 1978 is a reminder that winning in Texas is stil no simple task for a Republican.

A political science professor and son of a strait-laced Methodist minister, Tower ran for the state Legislature as a Republican in 1954 and lost. That was his only campaign until GOP leaders chose him for a sacrificial run against Lyndon B. Johnson in 1960.

The Texas ballot that year listed Johnson twice, once for the Senate, and a second time as the Democratic vice presidential nominee. The Legislature had passed a law allowing him to seek both offices at once, but resentment over such a cozy arrangement allowed Tower to draw 41 percent of the vote. So when Johnson vacated the seat in 1961, Tower was in a good position.

The special election that year featured the biggest congressional primary field ever — 71 candidates. With a secure base of Republican support, he led the pack by drawing a third of the vote in the non-partisan primary. That set up a runoff between him and second-place finisher William A. "Dollar Bill" Blakley, a conservative Democrat who had been appointed to replace Johnson temporarily. Blakley's presence in the runoff caused a virtual boycott by liberal Democrats, and that gave Tower the election.

The phenomenon recurred in 1966, when Tower faced state Attorney General Waggoner Carr, another conservative Democrat. Liberal disaffection for Carr was made worse when Gov. John B. Connally, a Carr ally, refused to increase liberal representation on the state Democratic Committee.

Carr tried to move to the center, portraying Tower as a right-wing extremist. But the Democratic left did not see much of a difference between them. Tower won a second term with a much higher winning margin than in 1961.

In 1972, Tower faced a less conservative Democrat: Barefoot Sanders, a former Justice Department official whose country-style populist campaign reflected his first name rather than his background as a Dallas lawyer. Sanders charged that the incumbent had stood idly by while space programs economically vital to Texas were dropped from the federal budget.

Tower, though, successfully hung George McGovern on Sanders, despite his opponent's disavowal of the proposed McGovern defense budget cuts. "People are rejecting radicalism as embraced by my opponent," Tower declared.

Had Sanders been the opposition in either 1961 or 1966, he probably would have defeated Tower. But the Republican prepared himself early for a tough campaign in 1972. He far outspent his challenger, and was helped by President Nixon's easy victory in Texas. Tower won by more than 300,000 votes.

The real test, however, was 1978, when Democrats united behind a centrist, Rep. Robert

Krueger, who had been as good a friend of the oil and gas industry as Tower had been. It was a vitriolic campaign. Krueger forces called Tower a womanizer, and some Tower backers tried to imply that Krueger was a homosexual. Krueger criticized Tower for not disclosing his wife's financial holdings. Tower responded by calling Krueger, whose family owned a hosiery mill, a "little Lord Fauntleroy."

The most celebrated incident of the campaign, and a decisive one, was Tower's refusal to shake Krueger's hand when they met by accident. This display initially hurt Tower. But he turned that around with a television ad justifying his action as the only honorable course in the face of his adversary's mudslinging. Tower survived by 12,227 votes.

## Committees

**Armed Services** (Chairman)

**Banking, Housing and Urban Affairs** (2nd of 8 Republicans)
Financial Institutions, chairman; Housing and Urban Affairs; Securities.

**Budget** (6th of 12 Republicans)

## Elections

**1978 General**

| | |
|---|---|
| John Tower (R) | 1,151,376 (50%) |
| Robert Krueger (D) | 1,139,149 (49%) |

**Previous Winning Percentages**

**1972** (53%)    **1966** (56%)    **1961*** (51%)

*Special election.

## Campaign Finance

| 1978 | Receipts | Receipts from PACs | Expenditures |
|---|---|---|---|
| Tower (R) | $4,264,015 | $392,722 (9%) | $4,324,601 |
| Krueger (D) | $2,431,204 | $157,112 (6%) | $2,428,666 |

## Voting Studies

| | Presidential Support | | Party Unity | | Conservative Coalition | |
|---|---|---|---|---|---|---|
| Year | S | O | S | O | S | O |
| 1980 | 36 | 46 | 61 | 11 | 70 | 2 |
| 1979 | 39 | 55 | 78 | 14 | 76 | 10 |

| Year | S | O | | S | O | | S | O | |
|---|---|---|---|---|---|---|---|---|---|
| 1978 | 15 | 62 | | 73 | 3 | | 70 | 3 | |
| 1977 | 40 | 53 | | 83 | 7 | | 95 | 2 | |
| 1976 | 75. | 15 | | 91 | 2 | | 90 | 3 | |
| 1975 | 85 | 11 | | 92 | 5 | | 95 | 2 | |
| 1974 (Ford) | 75 | 12 | | | | | | | |
| 1974 | 71 | 19 | | 85 | 6 | | 90 | 2 | |
| 1973 | 75 | 14 | | 87 | 5 | | 93 | 3 | |
| 1972 | 72 | 4 | | 67 | 6 | | 65 | 3 | |
| 1971 | 68 | 12 | | 74 | 6 | | 81 | 1 | |

S = Support          O = Opposition

## Key Votes

**96th Congress**

| | |
|---|---|
| Maintain relations with Taiwan (1979) | Y |
| Reduce synthetic fuel development funds (1979) | Y |
| Impose nuclear plant moratorium (1979) | N |
| Kill stronger windfall profits tax (1979) | Y |
| Guarantee Chrysler Corp. loans (1979) | Y |
| Approve military draft registration (1980) | Y |
| End Revenue Sharing to the states (1980) | N |
| Block Justice Dept. busing suits (1980) | ? |

**97th Congress**

| | |
|---|---|
| Restore urban program funding cuts (1981) | N |

## Interest Group Ratings

| Year | ADA | ACA | AFL-CIO | CCUS-1 | CCUS-2 |
|---|---|---|---|---|---|
| 1980 | 6 | 91 | 13 | 94 | |
| 1979 | 11 | 88 | 0 | 100 | 100 |
| 1978 | 10 | 86 | 6 | 89 | |
| 1977 | 15 | 96 | 11 | 88 | |
| 1976 | 5 | 92 | 11 | 100 | |
| 1975 | 11 | 81 | 18 | 94 | |
| 1974 | 5 | 88 | 18 | 88 | |
| 1973 | 0 | 92 | 18 | 100 | |
| 1972 | 0 | 94 | 0 | 100 | |
| 1971 | 0 | 88 | 27 | - | |

# Lloyd Bentsen (D)

**Of Houston — Elected 1970**

**Born:** Feb. 11, 1921, Mission, Texas.
**Education:** U. of Texas, LL.B. 1942.
**Military Career:** Army Air Corps, 1942-45.
**Profession:** Lawyer; insurance executive.
**Family:** Wife, Beryl Ann "B. A." Longino; three children.
**Religion:** Presbyterian.
**Political Career:** Hidalgo County Judge, 1946-48; U.S. House, 1948-55

**In Washington:** There is a gray quality about Bentsen, and it comes not only from the elegant suits he wears and the silver in his hair, but from his record — midway between the poles on nearly any important issue — and his temperament. He is not a dour or cheerless man, but he strikes people as aloof and rather formal. Bentsen is not the kind of senator you see naturally slapping another on the back or trading funny stories. One would not pick him out of a crowd as a Texan.

Bentsen is all business. And he has devoted much of his career in the Senate to promoting American business and trying to bring it back from the doldrums it has been through in the 1970s. When he ran for president in 1976, campaigning smoothly but not very successfully, it was on a platform of economic revival through personal tax cuts and reductions in the tax on capital gains.

Those ideas are not very different from what the Reagan administration has endorsed as "supply side" economics. Bentsen has devoted the past few years to selling them in the Senate.

In the 96th Congress, as chairman of the Joint Economic Committee, Bentsen was a tireless spokesman for his view that the answers to inflation are private investment and economic growth, and that these can come through tax cuts. Both in 1979 and 1980 Bentsen was able to forge a consensus on the JEC in support of his "economics of hope" — a consensus which encompassed such divergent political views as Edward M. Kennedy and George McGovern on the left and Sen. James A. McClure, R-Idaho and Rep. John H. Rousselot, R-Calif., on the right.

Bentsen has been able to sell some of his supply-side ideas to the tax-writing Finance Committee, on which he is third-ranking Democrat. In the summer of 1980 Bentsen was instrumental in formulating a $39 billion tax cut package that the committee approved, but the Democratic leadership refused to bring to the floor.

Bentsen's biggest contribution to that bill was language providing for accelerated depreciation, which would allow businesses to write-off the cost of purchasing new factories, machinery, and equipment more quickly than under current law. Some of those ideas were incorporated by the Reagan administration in the tax bill that moved through Finance in June of 1981. During debate on that bill, Bentsen also pushed for savings tax breaks concentrated on home mortgages.

While Bentsen has concentrated on the "big picture" economic issues, he has continued to fight on the Finance Committee for the Texas oil industry, and especially independent producers.

During the debate in 1979 and 1980 over a windfall profits tax on the oil industry, Bentsen's first priority was a full exemption for the smaller independent producers. That passed the Senate, but did not end up in the final law. Still, Bentsen and his allies did manage to keep the tax on smaller producers lower than the basic rate, and later in 1980 they pushed through a partial refund on the tax for royalty holders — those who own land on which an oil well exists and receive some of the profit.

Earlier in his Senate career, Bentsen made repeated efforts to deregulate the price of natural gas. He managed to get a deregulation amendment through the Senate in 1975, on a 50-41 vote, but that language never passed the House. In 1977, he persuaded the Senate to add gas deregulation to President Carter's energy package, but the House did not include it, and when a conference committee compromised on gradual deregulation over seven years, Bentsen voted against the conference report.

Bentsen is also deeply involved in trade issues, many of which come under the purview of the Finance Committee. Soon after Congress convened in 1981, he introduced legislation with Missouri Republican John C. Danforth to limit the number of Japanese cars allowed to enter the U.S.

Bentsen plays a less prominent role on the Environment and Public Works Committee. He had a chance for the chairmanship of the important Environmental Pollution Subcommittee, vacated in 1980 when Edmund S. Muskie left to become secretary of state, but did not try for it.

Until 1981, however, Bentsen was chairman of the Environment and Public Works Subcommittee on Transportation. In that capacity, he worked on the complex formulas that govern distribution of money from the highway trust fund. In the early 1970s, he allied himself with highway users against attempts to break off trust fund money for mass transit. In 1978, the last time a major highway bill moved through Congress, Bentsen tried to keep the price tag down because he said too many commitments might threaten the solvency of the fund itself.

**At Home:** Bentsen is part of the Texas Democratic establishment that included Lyndon B. Johnson and John B. Connally, but his route into it was unique. He was elected to Congress at 27 from a rural district in South Texas, retired after three terms, moved to Houston to make a fortune in insurance, and then re-emerged in politics 15 years later as a conservative Democratic candidate for the Senate.

The Bentsen family, which is of Danish stock, has been among the conservative gentry of the lower Rio Grande Valley for most of this century. The senator's father, Lloyd Sr., was known as "Big Lloyd" around their hometown of McAllen, where he became a millionaire landowner and gave his son a lift into local politics.

Returning home from World War II, in which he had flown bombers over Europe, the younger Bentsen was elected judge in Hidalgo County at age 25. In 1948, taking advantage of family money and connections among the small group of Democrats who controlled politics in his South Texas district, he became the youngest member of the U.S. House.

As a congressman, Bentsen pleased Texas conservatives with his hard-line anti-communism. In 1950, he advocated ending the Korean War by using the atomic bomb. He represented a one-party district and was politically secure; after his first primary, he faced no opposition at all.

But by 1954, the House did not seem as attractive to Bentsen as a career in upper echelons of the Houston business community. He retired at the age of 33 and became president of Lincoln Consolidated, a holding company. By the

time Bentsen was ready for politics again in 1970, he was a millionaire.

Bentsen ran on the Democratic right in 1970 as primary challenger to veteran Sen. Ralph Yarborough, the East Texas populist who had been an enemy to the conservative wing of the party for years.

Bentsen ran against both Yarborough and the national Democratic Party. When Democratic Sens. Edmund S. Muskie of Maine and Harold Hughes of Iowa came to Texas to campaign for Yarborough, Bentsen labeled them "ultraliberal" outsiders. He ran televison commercials linking Yarborough to violent anti-war protests, and said the senator's vote against the Supreme Court nomination of G. Harrold Carswell showed he was anti-Southern.

Yarborough punched back by attacking Bentsen and his allies as "fat cats" and "reactionaries." Emphasizing his role in passing Great Society legislation, Yarborough campaigned hard to put together his old populist coalition of blacks, Hispanics, union members and rural East Texans. It was not enough to stop Bentsen, who beat Yarborough with almost 100,000 votes to spare.

After the primary, Bentsen moved to the center against GOP nominee George Bush, then a Houston congressman. The Bush-Bentsen campaign, a battle between a Houston insurance millionaire and a Houston oil millionaire, was gentle by comparison to the primary. There was little to argue about.

In the end, that helped Bentsen. He continued to promote the conservative image he had fostered in the spring, but campaigned against Nixon economic policies in the hope of winning back as many Yarborough supporters as possible. Texas was still unquestionably a Democratic state in 1970, and given a choice between two conservatives, a majority of voters preferred the Democrat.

When Bentsen won, President Nixon tried to claim the outcome as a "philosophical victory" for the Republican administration. But things did not work out that way. Over the next few years, Bentsen sought to moderate his image, looking toward a presidential campaign in 1976. Some of that moderation, such as his vote in favor of common-site picketing in 1975, outraged his more conservative 1970 supporters.

The result was a primary challenge in 1976 from Texas A&M economist Phil Gramm, now an influential member of the House. Gramm accused Bentsen of abandoning his conservative heritage in a vain bid for national office. Bentsen retained the loyalty of the party establishment and beat Gramm by more than 2-to-1, but the challenger

## Lloyd Bentsen, D-Texas

drew over 400,000 votes.

Meanwhile, Bentsen was seeking the Democratic presidential nomination, calling himself a "Harry Truman Democrat" and hoping to establish a base of support in an early Southern primary. It was a waste of effort. The combined opposition of Jimmy Carter and George C. Wallace limited Bentsen to only six delegates in his own home state, and Bentsen quickly dropped out of national politics to concentrate on his fall campaign against Republican Rep. Alan

Steelman.

That campaign turned out to be easy. Steelman took the opposite tack from Gramm, hoping to woo Yarborough liberals by calling Bentsen the captive of special interests. But Steelman ended up without a firm base in either party, and he never had the money to compete with Bentsen on an equal footing. Bentsen had a mailing list of 700,000 names, and an organization in each of the state's counties. He defeated Steelman easily.

## Committees

**Environment and Public Works** (2nd of 7 Democrats)
Regional and Community Development; Transportation; Water Resources.

**Finance** (3rd of 9 Democrats)
Energy and Agricultural Taxation; International Trade; Taxation and Debt Management.

**Select Intelligence** (7th of 7 Democrats)
Analysis and Production; Budget.

**Joint Economic**
Agriculture and Transportation; Economic Goals and Intergovernmental Policy.

## Elections

**1976 General**

| | |
|---|---|
| Lloyd Bentsen (D) | 2,199,956 (57%) |
| Alan Steelman (R) | 1,636,370 (42%) |

**1976 Primary**

| | |
|---|---|
| Lloyd Bentsen (D) | 970,983 (63%) |
| Phil Gramm (D) | 427,597 (28%) |
| Hugh Wilson (D) | 109,715 (7%) |

**Previous Winning Percentages**

| | | | |
|---|---|---|---|
| 1970 (54%) | 1952* (100%) | 1950* (100%) | 1948 (100%) |

*House elections.
†Elected in a special election and a full House election the same day.

## Campaign Finance

| | Receipts | Receipts from PACs | Expenditures |
|---|---|---|---|
| 1976 | | | |
| Bentsen (D) | $1,277,364 | $237,002 (19%) | $1,237,910 |
| Steelman (R) | $667,214 | $35,145 (5%) | $665,058 |

## Voting Studies

| | Presidential Support | | Party Unity | | Conservative Coalition | |
|---|---|---|---|---|---|---|
| Year | S | O | S | O | S | O |
| 1980 | 73 | 19 | 57 | 26 | 56 | 27 |
| 1979 | 66 | 27 | 63 | 29 | 63 | 26 |
| 1978 | 60 | 28 | 51 | 39 | 70 | 22 |
| 1977 | 63 | 32 | 41 | 49 | 78 | 15 |
| 1976 | 32 | 30 | 37 | 42 | 64 | 15 |
| 1975 | 57 | 25 | 49 | 36 | 58 | 27 |
| 1974 (Ford) | 18 | 43 | | | | |
| 1974 | 53 | 28 | 48 | 32 | 43 | 38 |
| 1973 | 44 | 47 | 59 | 35 | 57 | 36 |
| 1972 | 57 | 35 | 55 | 38 | 56 | 34 |
| 1971 | 61 | 37 | 57 | 36 | 73 | 18 |

S = Support          O = Opposition

## Key Votes

**96th Congress**

| | |
|---|---|
| Maintain relations with Taiwan (1979) | N |
| Reduce synthetic fuel development funds (1979) | N |
| Impose nuclear plant moratorium (1979) | N |
| Kill stronger windfall profits tax (1979) | Y |
| Guarantee Chrysler Corp. loans (1979) | Y |
| Approve military draft registration (1980) | Y |
| End Revenue Sharing to the states (1980) | Y |
| Block Justice Dept. busing suits (1980) | Y |

**97th Congress**

| | |
|---|---|
| Restore urban program funding cuts (1981) | N |

## Interest Group Ratings

| Year | ADA | ACA | AFL-CIO | CCUS-1 | CCUS-2 |
|---|---|---|---|---|---|
| 1980 | 39 | 43 | 41 | 59 | |
| 1979 | 26 | 38 | 47 | 45 | 67 |
| 1978 | 35 | 57 | 26 | 83 | |
| 1977 | 30 | 48 | 60 | 59 | |
| 1976 | 15 | 47 | 40 | 25 | |
| 1975 | 39 | 38 | 59 | 50 | |
| 1974 | 38 | 41 | 45 | 50 | |
| 1973 | 55 | 41 | 64 | 44 | |
| 1972 | 35 | 45 | 30 | 25 | |
| 1971 | 33 | 33 | 55 | - | |

# 1 Sam B. Hall Jr. (D)

**Of Marshall — Elected 1976**

**Born:** Jan. 11, 1924, Marshall, Texas.
**Education:** College of Marshall, B.A. 1942; Baylor U. Law School, LL.B. 1948.
**Military Career:** Air Force, 1943-45.
**Profession:** Lawyer.
**Family:** Wife, Madeleine Segal; three children.
**Religion:** Church of Christ.
**Political Career:** Unsuccessfully sought Democratic nomination for U.S. House, 1962.

**In Washington:** Hall briefly became a cause célèbre for Southern Democrats in the 96th Congress when he was twice denied a Ways and Means assignment they thought he deserved.

A defender of the oil and gas industry who has drawn considerable income from natural gas interests, Hall wanted to go on Ways and Means to work on energy issues. He was recommended for the committee in early 1979 by the Democratic Steering and Policy Committee, an instrument of the leadership, but was beaten out in the Democratic Caucus.

Most of Hall's allies took that in stride. But a year later, when a vacancy came up, they felt Hall was the obvious choice, even though his conservative voting record had left him far from the thinking of most House Democrats. When the post went instead to Marty Russo of Illinois, no party loyalist himself, many of the Southern Democrats felt they had been discriminated against. Some began talking of concerted action to improve their committee assignment influence with the leadership.

That discontent helped lead in 1981 to the Democratic Forum, the strategy and lobbying organization of the party's right. But ironically, Hall never went to Ways and Means. He could almost certainly have had a seat there in the 97th Congress, but he said he was tired of the whole argument and preferred to stay on Judiciary instead.

The previous Congress had brought Hall a significant triumph on Judiciary — passage of an antitrust exemption bill over the opposition of the chairman, Peter W. Rodino Jr. of New Jersey.

The bill protected certain exclusive bottling franchises from antitrust challenge on territorial grounds. It was lobbied heavily by the National Soft Drink Association and local bottlers throughout the country. Rodino did not want to act on it, but Hall produced more than the required 218

signatures on a petition to discharge Judiciary and bring the bill direclty to the floor. Once that happened, the chairman changed his mind and moved on it immediately, and the bill became law by the end of the year.

Hall also spent much of the 96th Congress working on the unsuccessful attempt to rewrite the federal criminal code. He fought organized labor over the section of the code dealing with extortion, arguing for more federal leeway to prosecute labor extortion cases. But he lost on that issue in committee, and the bill never reached the floor.

**At Home:** Hall is not exactly carrying on the tradition of his Democratic predecessor, Wright Patman, who fought banks and big business for 24 terms in the House as a rural populist.

Hall even tried to oust his predecessor in the 1962 Democratic primary. Although he failed, he drew a respectable 39 percent of the vote against the veteran Patman, who the following year became chairman of the House Banking Committee. That primary challenge was Hall's last political campaign before Patman died in 1976.

Hall had no legislative experience before coming to Congress. But he was well known in his hometown of Marshall as a successful lawyer and head of the school board. His strong base in the district's third largest population center helped

---

**1st District: Northeast — Texarkana.** Population: 565,829 (21% increase since 1970). Race: White 453,400 (80%), Black 105,901 (19%), Others 6,528 (1%). Spanish origin: 8,712 (2%).

him to finish first in the initial primary held after Patman's death. An extensive advertising campaign and chili feeds around the district broadened his name identification and carried him to a narrow 5,000-vote runoff victory a month later.

In a district that has been staunchly Democratic at all levels for generations, Hall had smooth sailing after his runoff victory. He coasted into the House with an easy special election triumph June 19 and increased his percentage in the November 1976 general election.

Since then he has had no primary opposition and only one general election contest — in 1978 when he defeated his Republican opponent by a margin of nearly 4-to-1.

**The District:** While Republicans have broken the barriers of Democratic domination throughout most of Texas, they are still encountering stiff resistance in the rural 1st, in the northeastern corner of the state.

Republicans have made some inroads in the district's larger towns, like Texarkana (Patman's hometown) and Marshall. Both were carried by Reagan in 1980. But the rural cotton and potato-growing counties, which dominate the large 23-county district, remain "yellow dog" Democratic.

Rural support enabled Hubert H. Humphrey to carry the district over George C. Wallace in 1968, even though the Alabama governor was sweeping some of the more urbanized counties along the Louisiana border. Strong rural support also enabled Carter to win the 1st by a big margin in 1976 and to run about even with Reagan in 1980.

## Committees

**Judiciary** (10th of 16 Democrats)
Crime; Criminal Justice; Immigration, Refugees and International Law.

**Veterans' Affairs** (7th of 17 Democrats)
Compensation, Pension and Insurance, chairman; Oversight and Investigations.

## Elections

**1980 General**

| | |
|---|---|
| Sam Hall Jr. (D) | Unopposed |

**1978 General**

| | |
|---|---|
| Sam Hall Jr. (D) | 73,708 (78%) |
| Fred Hudson (R) | 20,700 (22%) |

**Previous Winning Percentages**

1976 (84%)      1976* (72%)

*\* Special election.*

**District Vote For President**

| | 1980 | | 1976 | | 1972 |
|---|---|---|---|---|---|
| **D** | 98,029 (50 %) | **D** | 104,400 (60%) | **D** | 41,763 (29 %) |
| **R** | 95,872 (49 %) | **R** | 62,297 (40%) | **R** | 99,658 (70 %) |

## Campaign Finance

| | Receipts | Receipts from PACs | Expen- ditures |
|---|---|---|---|
| **1980** | | | |
| Hall (D) | $65,708 | $25,400 (39%) | $65,450 |
| **1978** | | | |
| Hall (D) | $84,941 | $31,134 (37%) | $44,229 |
| Hudson (R) | $76,519 | $400 (1%) | $76,520 |

## Voting Studies

| | Presidental Support | | Party Unity | | Conservative Coalition | |
|---|---|---|---|---|---|---|
| Year | S | O | S | O | S | O |
| 1980 | 46 | 50 | 34 | 65 | 96 | 3 |
| 1979 | 41 | 57 | 32 | 65 | 92 | 4 |
| 1978 | 34 | 64 | 25 | 74 | 94 | 5 |
| 1977 | 29 | 63 | 27 | 67 | 90 | 6 |
| 1976 | 65 | 35† | 29 | 68† | 95 | 3† |

S = Support          O = Opposition

*†Not eligible for all recorded votes.*

## Key Votes

**96th Congress**

| | |
|---|---|
| Weaken Carter oil profits tax (1979) | Y |
| Reject hospital cost control plan (1979) | Y |
| Implement Panama Canal Treaties (1979) | N |
| Establish Department of Education (1979) | N |
| Approve Anti-busing Amendment (1979) | Y |
| Guarantee Chrysler Corp. loans (1979) | Y |
| Approve military draft registration (1980) | Y |
| Aid Sandinista regime in Nicaragua (1980) | N |
| Strengthen fair housing laws (1980) | N |

**97th Congress**

| | |
|---|---|
| Reagan budget proposal (1981) | Y |

## Interest Group Ratings

| Year | ADA | ACA | AFL-CIO | CCUS |
|---|---|---|---|---|
| 1980 | 0 | 73 | 22 | 84 |
| 1979 | 11 | 72 | 30 | 89 |
| 1978 | 20 | 92 | 15 | 83 |
| 1977 | 5 | 85 | 19 | 82 |
| 1976 | 0 | 100 | 29 | 91 |

# 2 Charles Wilson (D)

**Of Lufkin — Elected 1972**

**Born:** June 1, 1933, Trinity, Texas.
**Education:** Attended Sam Houston State U.,
1951-52; U.S. Naval Academy, B.S. 1956.
**Military Career:** Navy, 1956-60.
**Profession:** Lumberyard manager.
**Family:** Divorced.
**Religion:** Methodist.
**Political Career:** Texas House, 1961-67; Texas
Senate, 1967-73.

**In Washington:** Wilson's reputation for
high living sometimes obscures his inside reputation as one of the better lobbyists and vote traders
in the House.

Some members who initially thought of him
only as "good time Charlie" were surprised one
day early in his second term when they listened to
him leading the defense of the percentage depletion allowance for independent oil producers. Instead of the Wilson they were used to, strutting
and wisecracking his way down the aisle, they
watched him in the well of the House presenting
charts, graphs, statistics and a flood of effective
rhetoric.

Without his amendment preserving depletion
for the independents, Wilson said, "the petroleum
industry of the United States will be controlled by
the eight men who head the eight major oil
companies in the United States."

It did not quite work. The House rejected his
amendment, 216-197. But depletion was preserved for independents in the eventual bill that
emerged from House-Senate conference, and they
have it to this day.

Meanwhile, Wilson became known as the
most persistent House defender of independent
oil interests. As public clamor against the major
oil companies has grown in recent years, the
independents have surpassed them as a lobbying
force in Congress, and as a source of money for
conservative congressional campaigns. To a certain extent, the industry's greater clout has been
Wilson's as well.

In 1979, Wilson used some of his vote trading
skill to work a deal for independents on windfall
profits tax legislation.

Late that year, House leaders were trying
desperately to round up votes for a loan guarantee
for Chrysler Corp. Wilson promised fellow-Texan
Jim Wright, the House majority leader, a bloc of
votes from Texas oil districts if their representa-

tives could be assured sympathy in the coming
windfall profits conference. The Texans wanted
an exemption from the tax for smaller producers.
"We're asking for special treatment," Wilson conceded at one point, "there's no question about
that. But we think the merits entitle us to it."

The leadership accepted the offer, and Texas
Democrats voted 16-3 to bail out Chrysler. As it
turned out, their votes were unnecessary; the
guarantee passed easily. But Wilson felt he had
bought some leverage on the issue that really
concerned him. The windfall bill that became law
the next year did provide lower rates for the
smaller independents.

As he did on the windfall issue, Wilson has
frequently played off his alliance with the Democratic leadership against his energy interests. In
the 95th Congress, as a member of the ad hoc
panel that worked on President Carter's first
energy bill, he fought for deregulation of the price
of natural gas, a move the House narrowly rejected. When the House and Senate eventually
compromised on a plan to phase out price regulation slowly over a seven-year period, he balked,
but eventually went along with Carter and
Speaker O'Neill, and signed the conference report, allowing it to reach the floor for final
approval.

In recent years, Wilson's support for oil has
broadened into a defense of Texas and other Sun
Belt states against the claims of the Frost Belt

---

**2nd District: East — Orange.** Population: 676,069 (45% increase since 1970). Race:
White 562,156 (83%), Black 99,227 (15%),
Others 14,686 (2%). Spanish origin: 22,962
(3%).

---

region that it is discriminated against in federal spending formulas. In 1981, he became the head of a new "Sun Belt Caucus" of 90 members, aimed at resisting Frost Belt arguments with counter-statistics.

Generally, however, Wilson's oil and regional lobbying has brought him less attention than his views on foreign aid, especially his defense of the Somoza regime in Nicaragua.

As a member of the Foreign Affairs Committee early in the Carter administration, Wilson sometimes made his support for overall foreign aid programs contingent upon inclusion of money for Nicaragua. In 1977, he won approval of a floor amendment adding $3.1 million to the foreign aid authorization for military assistance to that country. When the administration proved increasingly unfriendly to Somoza, Wilson became increasingly unfriendly to the program.

After leftist guerrillas seized power in Nicaragua, Wilson became a militant opponent of U.S. aid and a critic of Carter efforts to supply it. He complained bitterly in September 1979 of the way the State Department had treated the previous government. "They do not care if people are starving to death in the jungles of Nicaragua," he said, "if they do not approve of the government that is in place at that time."

But later the same year, he was working with the administration on a compromise to give the country some economic help.

A graduate of the U.S. Naval Academy, Wilson has been a foreign policy hawk his entire congressional career and spent several years on Appropriations working his way up to a place on the Defense Subcommittee. He finally made it there in 1980. During the Carter years, he was a persistent advocate of developing the neutron bomb and the B-1 bomber, both of which Carter opposed.

To make it onto Appropriations at all, Wilson had to use some of his best Texas lobbying skill. He made his move in 1977, after two House terms, challenging another applicant from the state's Democratic delegation, Richard C. White, a seven-term veteran. Texas Democrats had been recommending committee assignments on the basis of seniority for more than 40 years, and they recommended White to the leadership's Steering and Policy Committee. But Wilson campaigned for the vacancy personally among Steering and Policy members, and he won the seat. Some of the delegation was angry, but the issue eventually subsided.

Once he joined Appropriations, Wilson had to put in two terms on the District of Columbia Subcommittee, a usual starting place for new members. He was chairman of the D.C. subcommittee for a year during the 96th Congress and made frequent headlines for his verbal assaults on the city's government. "I think this city is a basket case," he said at one point. "In Washington, it takes 143 people to do what it takes 100 people to do any place else, and I aim to do something about it."

His views brought him into frequent conflict with D.C. Mayor Marion Barry, as Wilson refused to support as large a federal subsidy for the financially plagued city as Barry wanted. But he was on the district's side early in 1980, arguing against an amendment barring the use of any government funds in D.C. to pay for abortion. The amendment passed the House, but Wilson negotiated an agreement in conference limiting the ban only to federal money.

Wilson, who is divorced, has successfully managed to combine his active legislative career with the pursuit of pleasure in Washington at all hours. He has never seemed embarrassed about being labeled a playboy or a smiling Texas rogue; he seems to enjoy it. His staff is mostly female and strikingly good looking, and its members sometimes escort him around Washington socially. "I love what I'm doing," he told a reporter in 1979. "Why should I go around looking like a constipated hound dog? I'm having the time of my life."

**At Home:** A voting record that includes support for the Equal Rights Amendment and aid to New York City might seem out of place in a rural east Texas district that went for George Wallace in 1968.

But Wilson's brash, likeable personality has always helped him at home, and his loyalty to the independent oil industry has bought him some freedom on other issues. He has been unbeatable since he first won the seat in 1972.

Most of Wilson's political career has been spent somewhere to the left of his constituents. In 1960, when most Texas Democrats were backing Lyndon B. Johnson for the Democratic presidential nomination, Wilson was for John F. Kennedy. In the Texas Legislature, Wilson crusaded against high utility rates, fought for Medicaid and tax exemptions for the elderly, and sponsored bills to remove a ceiling on welfare spending. He was commonly identified as "the liberal from Lufkin," advancing his career with the help of Arthur Temple, a maverick lumber millionaire who treated him as a protégé and helped finance his campaigns.

During his successful congressional race in 1972, Wilson softened his liberalism somewhat, opposing school busing and gun control. But he still drew the support of blacks and labor and easily defeated the wife of Rep. John Dowdy in the Democratic primary. Her husband had been sentenced to prison earlier in the year for bribery, conspiracy and perjury, creating an open seat.

Wilson's penchant for high living is as well-known in Texas as it is in Washington, but it has never hindered him very much. He has always had the self-confidence to do as he pleases and depend on the electorate to accept it. The most tangible symbol of his "good time Charlie" reputation disappeared in 1979 when he sold his interest in a downtown Washington discotheque.

**The District.** Lying in the heart of the east Texas piney woods, the 2nd is one of the most rural districts in Texas. It contains no town larger than 30,000. Lumber and oil are the major industries, with much of the timberland owned by large landowners or in public hands.

But the 2nd is also one of the state's fastest growing districts. In the last decade, the Houston suburbs have spread into the district's southern portion, reinforcing the area's conservatism but changing its demographics.

Although the lines were redrawn twice in the early 1970s, the district is largely the same as in 1968, when it was the only one in Texas to vote for Wallace. But it has sometimes been hospitable to more moderate Democratic candidates willing to talk its language. Carter carried it easily in 1976 with 58 percent of the vote, although he lost it to Ronald Reagan in 1980.

## Committees

**Appropriations** (17th of 33 Democrats)
Defense; District of Columbia; Foreign Operations.

**Standards of Official Conduct** (4th of 6 Democrats)

## Elections

**1980 General**

| | |
|---|---|
| Charles Wilson (D) | 142,496 (69%) |
| F. H. Panill Sr. (R) | 60,742 (30%) |

**1980 Primary**

| | |
|---|---|
| Charles Wilson (D) | 88,557 (78%) |
| Allen Sumners (D) | 25,338 (22%) |

**1978 General**

| | |
|---|---|
| Charles Wilson (D) | 66,986 (70%) |
| Jim Dillion (R) | 28,584 (30%) |

**Previous Winning Percentages**

1976 (95%)   1974 (100%)   1972 (74%)

**District Vote For President**

| | 1980 | | 1976 | | 1972 |
|---|---|---|---|---|---|
| D | 104,390 (48 %) | D | 105,388 (58%) | D | 47,504 (32%) |
| R | 108,503 (50 %) | R | 76,350 (42%) | R | 98,598 (67%) |
| I | 3,171 (2 %) | | | | |

## Campaign Finance

| | Receipts | Receipts from PACs | Expen-ditures |
|---|---|---|---|
| **1980** | | | |
| Wilson (D) | $226,921 | $102,290 (45%) | $239,766 |
| Pannill (R) | $6,175 | $250 (4%) | $5,698 |
| **1978** | | | |
| Wilson (D) | $234,356 | $49,087 (21%) | $218,901 |
| Dillion (R) | $8,569 | $511 (6%) | $7,091 |

## Voting Studies

| | Presidential Support | | Party Unity | | Conservative Coalition | |
|---|---|---|---|---|---|---|
| Year | S | O | S | O | S | O |
| 1980 | 49 | 26 | 52 | 27 | 63 | 17 |
| 1979 | 55 | 32 | 57 | 32 | 63 | 28 |
| 1978 | 54 | 35 | 59 | 27 | 48 | 37 |
| 1977 | 49 | 33 | 65 | 21 | 45 | 41 |
| 1976 | 45 | 39 | 56 | 27 | 46 | 34 |
| 1975 | 52 | 29 | 55 | 26 | 45 | 38 |
| 1974 (Ford) | 57 | 35 | | | | |
| 1974 | 55 | 26 | 64 | 25 | 43 | 46 |
| 1973 | 29 | 58 | 71 | 20 | 38 | 53 |

S = Support       O = Opposition

## Key Votes

**96th Congress**

| | |
|---|---|
| Weaken Carter oil profits tax (1979) | Y |
| Reject hospital cost control plan (1979) | Y |
| Implement Panama Canal Treaties (1979) | N |
| Establish Department of Education (1979) | Y |
| Approve Anti-busing Amendment (1979) | N |
| Guarantee Chrysler Corp. loans (1979) | Y |
| Approve military draft registration (1980) | Y |
| Aid Sandinista regime in Nicaragua (1980) | ? |
| Strengthen fair housing laws (1980) | Y |

**97th Congress**

| | |
|---|---|
| Reagan budget proposal (1981) | Y |

## Interest Group Ratings

| Year | ADA | ACA | AFL-CIO | CCUS |
|---|---|---|---|---|
| 1980 | 17 | 43 | 39 | 67 |
| 1979 | 21 | 44 | 45 | 82 |
| 1978 | 35 | 50 | 68 | 65 |
| 1977 | 25 | 26 | 65 | 50 |
| 1976 | 20 | 40 | 71 | 54 |
| 1975 | 42 | 38 | 70 | 29 |
| 1974 | 39 | 40 | 82 | 38 |
| 1973 | 48 | 32 | 91 | 40 |

# 3 James M. Collins (R)

**Of Dallas — Elected 1968**

**Born:** April 29, 1916, Hallsville, Texas.
**Education:** Southern Methodist U., B.S.C. 1937; Northwestern U., M.B.A. 1938; American College, C.L.U. 1940; Harvard U., M.B.A. 1943.
**Military Career:** Army, 1943-46.
**Profession:** Insurance executive.
**Family:** Wife, Dorothy Dann; three children.
**Religion:** Baptist.
**Political Career:** Unsuccessful Republican nominee for U.S. House, 1966.

**In Washington:** The oil and gas industries have had no more loyal or persistent defender on the House floor over the past decade than Collins. He is ready with a one-minute speech before nearly any legislative session explaining how private enterprise could solve the energy crisis on its own, if the federal government would stop intruding with price controls and regulations.

As a gadfly rather than a strategist, however, Collins has not had a great impact on most of the major energy bills written in the Commerce Committee, where he is now third in seniority among Republicans. GOP colleagues have sometimes used Collins as a foil, allowing him to state the extreme case for private industry so their own proposals will seem more moderate.

On the floor, Collins often finds himself fighting rear-guard actions against the committee's legislative product. In 1979, he was vehement but nearly alone as he opposed legislation to strengthen regulation of interstate natural gas pipelines. "All it is going to mean," he warned, "is additional paperwork, additional regulation, and additional costs for the consumer." But it passed easily.

Occasionally, Collins' guerrilla warfare has proven more successful. In 1978, he managed to block what was supposed to be routine passage of a bill authorizing money for the EPA to begin enforcing the Toxic Substances Control Act. Collins said the act would place too great a burden on chemical companies. "If one wants more fresh air, more clean water and less noise," Collins said, "one can move back to the farm."

Prodded by Collins, the House denied the bill the two-thirds vote it needed under "suspension." It was brought back under a simple majority rule and passed.

Collins' most notable successes, however,

have been on his amendment barring the Justice Department from using federal funds to promote busing for integration. Critics insist the amendment is unconstitutional, but Collins has managed to win passage three times. It died in 1980 when President Carter vowed to veto any bill carrying it. But it passed the House again in June of 1981, and with a friendly Senate and White House, seemed likely to become law.

**At Home:** The millionaire president of an insurance business started by his family, Collins made his first bid for the House in 1966, when the 3rd District was created. At that time he was known mainly through his involvement as national president of the Southern Methodist University alumni association. Although he lost the election to veteran Democratic Rep. Joe Pool, who had won two terms previously running at-large, the Republican drew a respectable 47 percent.

When Pool died in July 1968, Collins easily defeated the congressman's widow in a special election. He has won easily since then.

Collins was burdened for years, however, by negative publicity stemming from a series of Jack Anderson articles. Anderson wrote that Collins had forced his employees to kick back part of their salaries to pay off 1968 campaign debts.

The Anderson series began in 1970 and triggered a criminal investigation, which resulted in the conviction of Collins' former administrative assistant in 1972 on charges of soliciting kick-

---

**3rd District: North central Dallas, parts of Denton, Collin counties.** Population: 696,081 (49% increase since 1970). Race: White 642,940 (92%), Black 23,144 (3%), Others 29,997 (4%). Spanish origin: 37,879 (5%).

backs. But the Justice Department announced in 1974 that it lacked sufficient evidence to prosecute Collins himself. Collins voluntarily reimbursed the government $60,000 in 1975.

**The District:** Next to the 7th in Houston, the 3rd is the most affluent district in Texas. A GOP stronghold, it became even more Republican as a result of redistricting in the early 1970s. GOP candidates carry it easily even when they lose statewide.

The 3rd includes middle and upper-income areas of Dallas and the city's northern suburbs. High technology industries are a major employer. Only two districts in the state — the 7th and the 22nd — showed a larger population gain in the 1970s.

## Committees

**Energy and Commerce** (3rd of 18 Republicans)
Energy Conservation and Power; Fossil and Synthetic Fuels; Telecommunications, Consumer Protection, and Finance.

## Elections

**1980 General**

| | |
|---|---|
| James Collins (R) | 218,228 (79%) |
| Earle Porter (D) | 49,667 (18%) |

**1978 General**

| | |
|---|---|
| James Collins (R) | Unopposed |

**Previous Winning Percentages**

| | | | |
|---|---|---|---|
| 1976 (74%) | 1974 (65%) | 1972 (73%) | 1970 (61%) |
| 1968 (59%) | 1968* (60%) | | |

*Special Election.

**District Vote For President**

| | 1980 | | 1976 | | 1972 |
|---|---|---|---|---|---|
| D | 65,057 (23 %) | D | 65,021 (27 %) | D | 39,862 (22 %) |
| R | 208,826 (73 %) | R | 172,909 (72 %) | R | 136,205 (77 %) |
| I | 10,339 (4 %) | | | | |

## Campaign Finance

| | Receipts | Receipts from PACs | Expenditures |
|---|---|---|---|
| **1980** | | | |
| Collins (R) | $305,170 | $76,550 (25%) | $303,229 |
| **1978** | | | |
| Collins (R) | $225,965 | $22,571 (10%) | $80,442 |

## Voting Studies

| | Presidential Support | | Party Unity | | Conservative Coalition | |
|---|---|---|---|---|---|---|
| Year | S | O | S | O | S | O |
| 1980 | 29 | 69 | 94 | 5 | 94 | 5 |

| | | | | | | |
|---|---|---|---|---|---|---|
| 1979 | 19 | 81 | 97 | 3 | 95 | 4 |
| 1978 | 19 | 79 | 94 | 4 | 93 | 5 |
| 1977 | 29 | 68 | 94 | 4 | 93 | 6 |
| 1976 | 78 | 22 | 92 | 5 | 94 | 3 |
| 1975 | 65 | 35 | 91 | 8 | 95 | 4 |
| 1974 (Ford) | 44 | 35 | | | | |
| 1974 | 60 | 40 | 86 | 4 | 89 | 4 |
| 1973 | 77 | 22 | 90 | 8† | 93 | 6† |
| 1972 | 68 | 24 | 84 | 13 | 88 | 9 |
| 1971 | 68 | 30 | 79 | 17 | 85 | 9 |
| 1970 | 58 | 29 | 79 | 13 | 84 | 5 |
| 1969 | 57 | 34 | 76 | 9 | 82 | 9 |

S = Support          O = Opposition
† Not eligible for all recorded votes.

## Key Votes

**96th Congress**

| | |
|---|---|
| Weaken Carter oil profits tax (1979) | Y |
| Reject hospital cost control plan (1979) | Y |
| Implement Panama Canal Treaties (1979) | N |
| Establish Department of Education (1979) | N |
| Approve Anti-busing Amendment (1979) | Y |
| Guarantee Chrysler Corp. loans (1979) | N |
| Approve military draft registration (1980) | N |
| Aid Sandinista regime in Nicaragua (1980) | N |
| Strengthen fair housing laws (1980) | N |

**97th Congress**

| | |
|---|---|
| Reagan budget proposal (1981) | Y |

## Interest Group Ratings

| Year | ADA | ACA | AFL-CIO | CCUS |
|---|---|---|---|---|
| 1980 | 11 | 96 | 11 | 67 |
| 1979 | 0 | 100 | 5 | 100 |
| 1978 | 10 | 96 | 5 | 100 |
| 1977 | 5 | 100 | 4 | 94 |
| 1976 | 0 | 96 | 13 | 94 |
| 1975 | 0 | 93 | 4 | 88 |
| 1974 | 9 | 93 | 0 | 100 |
| 1973 | 0 | 100 | 9 | 100 |
| 1972 | 6 | 91 | 9 | 100 |
| 1971 | 8 | 93 | 17 | - |
| 1970 | 0 | 84 | 14 | 90 |
| 1969 | 0 | 100 | 0 | - |

# 4 Ralph M. Hall (D)

**Of Rockwall — Elected 1980**

**Born:** May 3, 1923, Rockwall County, Texas.
**Education:** Southern Methodist U., LL.B. 1951.
**Military Career:** Navy, 1942-45.
**Profession:** Lawyer; businessman.
**Family:** Wife, Mary Ellen Murphy; three children.
**Religion:** Methodist.
**Political Career:** Rockwell County judge, 1950-62; Texas Senate, 1963-73; sought Democratic nomination for lieutenant governor, 1972.

**The Member:** Hall fits the mold of the conservative Texas Democrat who moves back and forth easily between the worlds of politics and business. He belongs to the Conservative Democratic Forum in the House and was one of four freshman Democrats who voted for the first Gramm-Latta budget resolution.

An early starter in politics, Hall was elected judge in his home county in 1950 while still in law school. After twelve years, he moved up to the state Senate, and spent a decade there, rising to become president pro tem.

In 1972, Hall made a stab at statewide politics, running for lieutenant governor on a conservative platform. But he finished third, retired from politics, and swung his career back toward business. He was the founding chairman of the Lakeside National Bank of Rockwall, former president of the Texas Aluminum Corporation, and owner of North Texas Grain and Elevator Co.

In 1980, with the retirement of Democratic Rep. Ray Roberts, Hall decided to run for the House. He defeated Jerdy Gary, the son of a former Oklahoma governor, for the Democratic nomination, and won a close contest in November.

**The District:** The 4th is the descendant of the constituency represented by former House Speaker Sam Rayburn from 1913 to his death in 1961.

Three distinct areas make up the current 4th District. The counties surrounding Dallas are beginning to feel the effects of urban sprawl. Further north are Sherman, an old cotton manufacturing town, and Denton, home of North Texas State University. In the eastern corner of the district is Tyler, a growing center for the independent oil industry. Despite its continuing Democratic congressional representation, it is a conservative district, one which sometimes goes Republican in statewide contests.

## Committees

**Energy and Commerce** (24th of 24 Democrats)
Energy Conservaton and Power; Fossil and Synthetic Fuels.

**Science and Technology** (21st of 23 Democrats)
Science, Research and Technology; Space Science and Applications; Transportation, Aviation and Materials.

## Elections

**1980 General**

| | |
|---|---|
| Ralph Hall (D) | 102,787 (52%) |
| John Wright (R) | 93,915 (48%) |

**1980 Primary**

| | |
|---|---|
| Ralph Hall (D) | 36,874 (57%) |
| Jerdy Gary (D) | 27,341 (43%) |

**District Vote For President**

| | 1980 | | 1976 | | 1972 |
|---|---|---|---|---|---|
| **D** | 79,848 (40 %) | **D** | 87,614 (51 %) | **D** | 36,736 (25 %) |
| **R** | 115,402 (58 %) | **R** | 84,834 (49 %) | **R** | 107,025 (74 %) |
| **I** | 3,309 (2 %) | | | | |

## Campaign Finance

| | Receipts | Receipts from PACs | Expenditures |
|---|---|---|---|
| **1980** | | | |
| Hall (D) | $348,285 | $46,570 (13%) | $347,903 |
| Wright (R) | $160,283 | $30,563 (19%) | $159,152 |

## Key Vote

**97th Congress**

| | |
|---|---|
| Reagan budget proposal (1981) | Y |

> **4th District: North central — Denton, Sherman.** Population: 596,579 (28% increase since 1970). Race: White 504,441 (85%), Black 77,613 (13%), Others 14,525 (2%). Spanish origin: 19,461 (3%).

# 5 Jim Mattox (D)

**Of Dallas — Elected 1976**

**Born:** Aug. 29, 1943, Dallas, Texas.
**Education:** Baylor U., B.B.A. 1965; Southern
Methodist U. Law School, J.D. 1968.
**Profession:** Lawyer.
**Family:** Single.
**Religion:** Baptist.
**Political Career:** Texas House, 1973-77.

**In Washington:** Mattox's habit of challenging symbols of authority has helped him build a following in Texas, but it has imposed an outsider's role on him in his House career.

An activist from the day he arrived in 1977, Mattox hustled his way into an assignment on the Budget Committee — an important plum. By the end of the Congress, however, his style was bringing him into conflict with the two most important members of the committee, Chairman Robert N. Giaimo of Connecticut and Majority Leader Jim Wright, whose Fort Worth district lies just a few miles from the one Mattox represents in Dallas.

One day in 1979, Wright practically leaped out of his Budget Committee seat when his fellow Texan voted with the committee's Republicans to eliminate $40-billion in borrowing authority for the proposed Panama Canal Commission. "It won't save a penny," Wright lectured Mattox. "That's a demagogue vote, Jim, and you know it."

Wright later apologized to Mattox, but the incident reflected continuing leadership attitudes toward a junior member they consider unwilling to be a team player.

A more unusual demonstration took place on a midsummer afternoon later the same year, when Mattox refused to honor the custom of wearing a tie on the House floor, then refused to leave the chamber despite orders from Speaker O'Neill. "The chair has asked the gentleman to leave the chamber," O'Neill finally said. "The gentleman from Texas is embarrassing the chair. Maybe he does not feel he is embarrassing himself."

Mattox insisted he was not embarrassed and was sure the American people "would like to see us with our shirt-sleeves rolled up and working on the energy problem."

Mattox has been on the Banking Committee during his entire House career, but has concentrated on Budget Committee work, staking out a reputation for being unpredictable and occasionally participating in coalitions with the minority. He launched several crusades against his favorite legislative target, anti-recession aid to state and local governments. In 1979, he took the issue to the floor, and won initial approval for his amendment to take the anti-recession money out of the 1980 budget, but the outcome was reversed by an intense urban lobbying campaign the next day.

On broader issues, Mattox is a moderate Democrat whose voting record reflects his district's heavy minority concentration and his own populist instincts. Despite his squabbles with Wright and O'Neill, Mattox is a more likely leadership vote on key roll calls than most members of the Texas delegation. In the 96th Congress he voted against an anti-busing amendment to the Constitution, while the delegation was voting 2-1 for it.

In 1981, he backed the Democratic leadership budget, and lashed out at fellow Southerners who broke ranks to support the Reagan alternative. "What I have seen is not pillars of courage," he said, "but scared, cowardly political animals which have been running to hide."

**At Home:** In three House elections, Mattox has won with 54, 50 and 51 percent of the vote, sometimes campaigning brilliantly and sometimes proving his own worst enemy.

Mattox's first effort in 1976 was nearly perfect. He began as soon as the Republican incumbent announced his departure and developed an

---

**5th District: Northeast — part of Dallas.** Population: 510,041 (9% increase since 1970). Race: White 376,032 (73%), Black 93,366 (18%), Others 40,643 (8%). Spanish origin: 54,932 (11%).

extensive grass-roots organization. A former dock worker, Mattox developed a strong following among the large blue-collar, black and Hispanic communities in the district. That solid base helped carry him to an easy primary victory over a former Dallas mayor and a general election triumph over a conservative Republican school board member.

But he nearly kicked away his 1978 re-election with a series of gaffes. A Mattox campaign release quoted Vice President Mondale as saying the congressman was opposed by "the ultra-right wing and the radical left," but Mondale denied saying such a thing. Mattox was further hurt when he referred to his aggressive Republican opponent, Tom Pauken, as a "young Nazi."

Mattox survived in 1978, but by less than 1,000 votes. Aided by a larger Democratic turnout two years later, he defeated Pauken in a rematch by about 2,800 votes. In early 1981, however, conservative Democrats in the Texas Legislature began working on ways to guarantee Mattox' defeat in 1982 through redistricting.

**The District.** This is one of the most diverse districts in the state. About one-fifth of the population is black, mostly in south Dallas. There are blue-collar whites in the eastern and central portions of the city. And there are wealthy, rapidly growing suburban cities like Garland and Mesquite, whose heavy GOP majorities pose a threat to the Democrats' shaky advantage.

While the district is the home of many banks, insurance companies and corporate headquarters, the 5th has not experienced a population boom as dramatic as that of its neighbor, the more affluent 3rd. While the 5th had a population of about 510,000 in 1980, the population of the 3rd had grown to nearly 700,000 in the last decade.

## Committees

**Banking, Finance and Urban Affairs** (16th of 25 Democrats)
Financial Institutions Supervision, Regulation and Insurance; General Oversight and Renegotiation; International Trade, Investment and Monetary Policy.

**Budget**
Task Forces: National Security and Veterans, Chairman; Tax Policy.

## Elections

**1980 General**

| | |
|---|---|
| Jim Mattox (D ) | 70,892 (51 %) |
| Tom Pauken (R ) | 67,848 (49 %) |

**1978 General**

| | |
|---|---|
| Jim Mattox (D ) | 35,524 (50 %) |
| Tom Pauken (R ) | 34,672 (49 %) |

**Previous Winning Percentages**

1976 (54%)

**District Vote For President**

| | 1980 | | 1976 | | 1972 |
|---|---|---|---|---|---|
| D | 64,706 (44 %) | D | 68,944 (53 %) | D | 43,359 (30 %) |
| R | 75,324 (52 %) | R | 61,251 (47 %) | R | 98,434 (69 %) |
| I | 3,479 (2 %) | | | | |

## Campaign Finance

| | Receipts | Receipts from PACs | Expenditures |
|---|---|---|---|
| **1980** | | | |
| Mattox (D ) | $542,606 | $128,115 (24 %) | $529,743 |
| Pauken (R ) | $468,744 | $177,971 (38 %) | $265,248 |
| **1978** | | | |
| Mattox (D ) | $282,547 | $78,462 (28 %) | $269,015 |
| Pauken (R ) | $252,000 | $41,454 (16 %) | $252,047 |

## Voting Studies

| | Presidential Support | | Party Unity | | Conservative Coalition | |
|---|---|---|---|---|---|---|
| Year | S | O | S | O | S | O |
| 1980 | 53 | 32 | 62 | 23 | 46 | 36 |
| 1979 | 61 | 34 | 63 | 30 | 44 | 47 |
| 1978 | 65 | 29 | 63 | 34 | 46 | 52 |
| 1977 | 66 | 33 | 71 | 27 | 35 | 63 |

S = Support          O = Opposition

## Key Votes

**96th Congress**

| | |
|---|---|
| Weaken Carter oil profits tax (1979) | Y |
| Reject hospital cost control plan (1979) | Y |
| Implement Panama Canal Treaties (1979) | Y |
| Establish Department of Education (1979) | Y |
| Approve Anti-busing Amendment (1979) | N |
| Guarantee Chrysler Corp. loans (1979) | Y |
| Approve military draft registration (1980) | Y |
| Aid Sandinista regime in Nicaragua (1980) | N |
| Strengthen fair housing laws (1980) | Y |

**97th Congress**

| | |
|---|---|
| Reagan budget proposal (1981) | N |

## Interest Group Ratings

| Year | ADA | ACA | AFL-CIO | CCUS |
|---|---|---|---|---|
| 1980 | 50 | 42 | 44 | 69 |
| 1979 | 42 | 42 | 50 | 50 |
| 1978 | 40 | 50 | 79 | 33 |
| 1977 | 60 | 30 | 65 | 35 |

# 6 Phil Gramm (D)

**Of College Station — Elected 1978**

**Born:** July 8, 1942, Fort Benning, Ga.
**Education:** U. of Ga., B.B.A., 1964, Ph.D. 1967.
**Profession:** Economist, professor.
**Family:** Wife, Wendy Lee; two children.
**Religion:** Episcopalian.
**Political Career:** Unsuccessfully sought Democratic nomination for U.S. Senate, 1976.

**In Washington:** It took only a few months for Gramm to establish himself in his first term as an influential voice of the right on energy and economics, and as a problem for the House leadership.

By the beginning of his second term, he was more than a problem. He was the most important House Democratic ally of the Reagan administration, cosponsor of the budget substitutes that reduced federal spending the way the president wanted to, rather than the way the House Democratic leadership preferred.

A close friend of Budget Director David Stockman when they served together in the 96th Congress, Gramm worked with Stockman in 1981 to implement budget recommendations they had offered without success the year before. At times, the administration seemed to be working more closely with Gramm than with Delbert Latta of Ohio, the Official Republican sponsor.

Some 63 Democrats voted for the first Gramm-Latta substitute in May, the one that set in place massive reductions in the 1982 budget and called for a three-year tax cut. That made Gramm-Latta an easy victory. It was not so easy in June, when they teamed up again to substitute a Reagan-backed package of specific spending cuts for the one Democratic leaders wanted. But 29 Democrats went along, enough for a second major triumph for Gramm over his own party.

All this isolated Gramm among House Democrats, leaving some colleagues so angry at him that he was referred to as a "traitor" when he walked into a party caucus on the Commerce Committee. It brought widespread talk that he would be stripped of his place on the Budget Committee at the end of the Congress. But it also gave him national attention, highlighting the brash self-confidence he has shown since his arrival in the House.

As a brand-new freshman in the spring of 1979, Gramm sought to attach language requiring a balanced budget to a bill raising the federal debt ceiling. Testifying for his amendment in the House Rules Committee, he challenged Chairman Richard Bolling on a point of economics. Gramm compared his academic credentials to those of Paul H. Douglas, the renowned economist who served in the Senate from Illinois for 18 years. Bolling, an economic specialist himself, was not convinced.

Gramm's amendment narrowly failed, but the incident gave him an early reputation for ego that has both helped and hurt him ever since. If he is rarely as boastful as he sounded that day in the Rules Committee, he does seem to carry an unlimited store of ideological self-assurance.

"I came here with a goal in mind," he has said, "of reversing a 30-year trend toward more and more government power."

Gramm's ambition has guaranteed conflict with Majority Leader Wright, who is forced to work hard for votes in his conservative Texas delegation, and who wants the more impressionable members of that delegation listening to him rather than a proselytizing newcomer with a Ph.D. in economics.

Gramm had fought Wright on the budget in 1980, seeking to replace the Budget Committee's resolution with his own substitute, $5 billion higher in defense and $5 billion lower in domestic spending.

Gramm drafted the proposal along with a

---

**6th District: East central — parts of Dallas, Ft. Worth.** Population: 638,044 (37% increase since 1970). Race: White 515,335 (81%), Black 93,189 (15%), Others 29,520 (5%). Spanish origin: 43,744 (7%).

Budget Committee Republican, Marjorie Holt of Maryland. Wright, fearing it would unravel a carefully constructed majority budget he felt was in balance, urged the Rules Committee to strip Gramm's name from the plan and treat Holt as its sole author.

Ultimately the amendment failed, largely because the domestic cuts it imposed were too deep at that time for most House members of both parties. But its defeat did little to erase Gramm's rebellious image.

For a brief period in early 1981, relations between Gramm and the leadership seemed to be better. In campaigning for a Budget Committee seat at the start of 1981, Gramm assured Wright he would "make every effort" to support Democratic Party policy positions. He even put it in writing. "I will work hard to perfect a budget in committee and during floor debate," Gramm wrote Wright on Jan. 8, "but as a member of the committee, I will support final passage of the budget."

When Gramm voted against the budget in committee and led the effort to defeat it on the floor, he said his actions should not have surprised anyone. "I have supported a position that I have supported since I came to Congress," he said. "Basically, the pledge I made [to Wright] was that I would represent my constituents' interests, but that I certainly would make every effort to be a team player."

On the Commerce Committee in the 96th Congress, Gramm had relatively smooth relations with the man in effective charge, Michigan's John D. Dingell. Still, he voted against Dingell and the Democrats on most issues, building bipartisan conservative coalitions with Stockman, who also served on the committee. Close to the American Medical Association, Gramm was a militant critic of President Carter's hospital cost control plan, which died in the House in 1979.

But he quietly helped Dingell out on more than one critical occasion. He went along with the chairman in behalf of the administration's second standby gas rationing scheme in 1980, arguing that the threshold for its use was so high that it might never be imposed. And he agreed to support an Energy Mobilization Board to speed up priority energy projects, siding with Dingell and against the usual conservative coalition.

Those occasional flirtations with Dingell earned Gramm a hostile reception in 1979 from *Human Events,* the conservative newspaper, which felt he was edging dangerously close to collaborationism. That sort of criticism is rarely heard any more.

**At Home:** Until 1976, Gramm's life was centered around the academic community at Texas A&M, where he taught economics. He wrote extensively on economics and energy, and established a consulting firm which performed contract research for the government and private industry in the United States, Canada and Australia.

Gramm was virtually unknown statewide when he challenged incumbent Lloyd Bentsen in the 1976 Democratic Senate primary, arguing for free market solutions to U.S. economic problems. Claiming that Bentsen had moved to the left to mount his ill-fated 1976 presidential campaign, Gramm presented himself as a conservative alternative. But he was badly under-financed, and drew only 29 percent of the vote.

Two years later, with better name recognition and financial support, Gramm sought the Democratic nomination to succeed retiring Rep. Olin E. "Tiger" Teague, challenging a Fort Worth television weatherman who was Teague's personal choice.

Gramm survived an expensive primary and runoff by building a campaign treasury of nearly half a million dollars. In the general election, his national "New Right" support pre-empted a conservative Republican challenge. Gramm coasted to an easy re-election victory in 1980.

**The District:** While the 6th District includes all or part of 11 counties, much of the population is concentrated in the Dallas-Fort Worth metropolitan area at the northern end of the district. Outside the metropolitan area, the 6th is primarily rural, containing no city larger than about 40,000 population.

The rural counties have remained loyally Democratic, providing Carter, for instance, with enough votes to carry the district narrowly in 1976. But Carter's rural support was not enough in 1980, as Reagan built up heavy majorities in the traditionally Republican Dallas-Fort Worth area and Brazos County, which includes Bryan and College Station, home of Texas A&M.

## Committees

**Budget**
   Task Forces: Energy and the Environment; Entitlements, Uncontrollables and Indexing; National Security and Veterans.

**Energy and Commerce** (16th of 24 Democrats)
   Energy Conservation and Power; Fossil and Synthetic Fuels; Health and the Environment.
**Veterans' Affairs** (15th of 17 Democrats)
   Education, Training and Employment; Hospitals and Health Care.

## Elections

**1980 General**

| | |
|---|---|
| Phil Gramm (D ) | 144,816 (71 %) |
| Dave Haskins (R ) | 59,503 (29 %) |

**1978 General**

| | |
|---|---|
| Phil Gramm (D ) | 66,025 (65 %) |
| Wes Mowery (R ) | 35,393 (35 %) |

**1978 Primary Runoff**

| | |
|---|---|
| Phil Gramm (D) | 23,762 (33 %) |
| Ron Godbey (D) | 21,169 (47 %) |

**1978 Primary**

| | |
|---|---|
| Ron Godbey (D ) | 23,540 (28 %) |
| Phil Gramm (D ) | 22,275 (27 %) |
| Thomas Edwards (D ) | 22,154 (27 %) |
| Don McNiel (D ) | 10,466 (13 %) |

**District Vote For President**

| | 1980 | | 1976 | | 1972 |
|---|---|---|---|---|---|
| D | 93,166 (43 %) | D | 95,567 (51 %) | D | 43,774 (29 %) |
| R | 118,096 (54 %) | R | 91,676 (49 %) | R | 107,759 (71 %) |
| I | 4,802 (2 %) | | | | |

## Campaign Finance

| | Receipts | Receipts from PACs | Expen- ditures |
|---|---|---|---|
| **1980** | | | |
| Gramm (D ) | $296,967 | $163,935 (55 %) | $121,215 |
| **1978** | | | |
| Gramm (D ) | $552,534 | $124,487 (23 %) | $480,778 |

| | | | |
|---|---|---|---|
| Mowery (R ) | $116,411 | $5,409 (5 %) | $116,386 |

## Voting Studies

| | Presidential Support | | Party Unity | | Conservative Coalition | |
|---|---|---|---|---|---|---|
| | S | O | S | O | S | O |
| Year | | | | | | |
| 1980 | 39 | 59 | 24 | 72 | 92 | 4 |
| 1979 | 37 | 61 | 26 | 69 | 91 | 6 |

S = Support          O = Opposition

## Key Votes

**96th Congress**

| | |
|---|---|
| Weaken Carter oil profits tax (1979) | Y |
| Reject hospital cost control plan (1979) | Y |
| Implement Panama Canal Treaties (1979) | N |
| Establish Department of Education (1979) | Y |
| Approve Anti-busing Amendment (1979) | Y |
| Guarantee Chrysler Corp. loans (1979) | N |
| Approve military draft registration (1980) | Y |
| Aid Sandinista regime in Nicaragua (1980) | N |
| Strengthen fair housing laws (1980) | N |

**97th Congress**

| | |
|---|---|
| Reagan budget proposal (1981) | Y |

## Interest Group Ratings

| Year | ADA | ACA | AFL-CIO | CCUS |
|---|---|---|---|---|
| 1980 | 0 | 71 | 11 | 78 |
| 1979 | 0 | 77 | 20 | 82 |

# 7 Bill Archer (R)

**Of Houston — Elected 1970**

**Born:** March 22, 1928, Houston, Texas.
**Education:** Attended Rice U., 1945-46; U. of Texas, B.B.A. 1948; LL.B. 1951.
**Military Career:** Air Force, 1951-53.
**Profession:** Lawyer.
**Family:** Divorced; five children.
**Religion:** Roman Catholic.
**Political Career:** Hunters Creek Village Council, 1955-62; Texas House, 1967-71.

**In Washington:** Placed on the Ways and Means Committee in 1973 after one House term, Archer has served ever since as the oil industry's unyielding voice on that panel. But sitting on the Republican side of the aisle, and showing a reluctance to compromise his basic economic principles, he has so far had limited influence over the committee's final product.

Archer's knowledge of the energy business is unquestioned, as is his willingness to explain its detailed workings to colleagues. But when the committee sits down to mark up legislation, he often is confronted by a Democratic majority that cares less about the intricacies of tertiary recovery than about meeting current public concerns.

When the oil windfall profits tax returned to the House floor after conference in 1980, it was Archer who offered the basic Republican proposal — to exempt independents who produce less than 1,000 barrels per day. It drew nearly all Republicans and most Southern Democrats, failing on a close 207-185 vote.

The real Republican coup of the windfall tax debate, however, had been engineered by a junior Ways and Means Republican, Henson Moore of Louisiana. It was Moore, working with Oklahoma Democrat James R. Jones, who put together the bipartisan coalition that softened the entire bill when it cleared the House the first time. Archer was a strong supporter of that effort, but was not the architect of it.

Archer's most conspicuous Ways and Means victory came in 1978, on that year's tax cut legislation. He offered an amendment to require indexing of capital gains taxes — adjusting them each year for inflation so that the effective rate would go up only with real income growth. Archer got this idea through the committee, with some liberal Democratic support, and it passed the House, 249-167. Archer said it was meant as a first step toward indexing the entire tax structure.

But the provision was dropped in conference with the Senate.

The year before, Archer served on the ad hoc committee that put together an energy bill to respond to the crisis that President Carter called "the moral equivalent of war." Like other Republicans, however, he complained that the majority party was freezing out any pro-industry suggestions. Ultimately Archer called that year's energy bill "a mockery of the legislative process" and sought unsuccessfully to add a floor amendment that would have added a new 10 percent tax credit for oil and gas exploration.

**At Home.** Unlike his predecessor in Congress, New England-born George Bush, Archer is a native Houstonian. Born and raised in the city, he graduated from Rice University and the University of Texas before launching his political career in 1955 as a member of the Hunters Creek Village town council.

Archer made his mark as a conservative Democrat, winning a seat in the Texas Legislature in 1966. But in 1968 he switched parties and won re-election as a Republican. Since the territory of his state legislative district closely coincided with the 7th Congressional District, Archer was the early favorite for the House seat two years later when Bush ran for the U.S. Senate.

He easily won the GOP primary, and went on to defeat a young law partner of John B. Connally

---

**7th District: Northwest Harris County.** Population: 867,727 (86% increase since 1970). Race: White 762,096 (88%), Black 51,164 (6%), Asian and Pacific Islander 26,529 (3%), Others 27,937 (3%). Spanish origin: 70,548 (8%).

in November. He has had no electoral problems since then.

**The District.** The 7th District is foremost in Texas in terms of affluence, education level and Republicanism. Much of Houston's prosperous business community lives within the district, in the upper-income neighborhoods of western Houston and its suburbs. While the 7th is primarily urban, it has little minority population. It also has a lower percentage of the very young and the very old than most Texas districts.

The influx of Northern professional people like Bush helped give the area a Republican complexion in the years after World War II. In 1976, Ford swept the presidential vote in the 7th by a nearly 3-1 margin, his best showing in any Texas district. Reagan did even better in 1980.

The population boom continued unabated in the 1970s. With an influx of more than 400,000 people in the last decade, the 7th was the state's fastest-growing district, requiring it to shed some territory in the new redistricting.

## Committees

**Ways and Means** (3rd of 12 Republicans)
Social Security; Trade.

## Elections

**1980 General**

| | |
|---|---|
| Bill Archer (R ) | 242,810 (82 %) |
| Robert Hutchings (D ) | 48,594 (16 %) |

**1978 General**

| | |
|---|---|
| Bill Archer (R ) | 128,214 (85%) |
| Robert Hutchings (D ) | 22,415 (15 %) |

**Previous Winning Percentages**

1976 (100%)  1974 (79 %)  1972 (82 %)  1970 (65 %)

**District Vote For President**

| | 1980 | | 1976 | | 1972 |
|---|---|---|---|---|---|
| D | 64,486 (22 %) | D | 66,880 (26 %) | D | 37,012 (19 %) |
| R | 220,532 (74 %) | R | 186,190 (73%) | R | 160,595 (81 %) |
| I | 11,424 (4 %) | | | | |

## Campaign Finance

| | Receipts | Receipts from PACs | Expenditures |
|---|---|---|---|
| **1980** | | | |
| Archer (R ) | $285,119 | — (0 %) | $124,687 |
| Hutchings (D ) | $3,840 | $100 (3 %) | $3,877 |
| **1978** | | | |
| Archer (R ) | $222,613 | $10,527 (5 %) | $120,720 |

## Voting Studies

| | Presidential Support | Party Unity | Conservative Coalition |
|---|---|---|---|

| Year | S | O | S | O | S | O |
|---|---|---|---|---|---|---|
| 1980 | 29 | 64 | 93 | 4 | 94 | 2 |
| 1979 | 23 | 74 | 94 | 3 | 97 | 0 |
| 1978 | 28 | 69 | 94 | 4 | 93 | 2 |
| 1977 | 30 | 67 | 96 | 2 | 96 | 4 |
| 1976 | 73 | 27 | 92 | 4 | 95 | 3 |
| 1975 | 69 | 29 | 85 | 6 | 91 | 2 |
| 1974 (Ford) | 54 | 35 | | | | |
| 1974 | 72 | 28 | 92 | 6† | 94 | 5 |
| 1973 | 63 | 34 | 86 | 13 | 89 | 11 |
| 1972 | 62 | 27 | 82 | 15 | 83 | 13 |
| 1971 | 75 | 23 | 90 | 7 | 92 | 6 |

†Not eligible for all recorded votes.

S = Support          O = Opposition

## Key Votes

**96th Congress**

| | |
|---|---|
| Weaken Carter oil profits tax (1979) | Y |
| Reject hospital cost control plan (1979) | Y |
| Implement Panama Canal Treaties (1979) | N |
| Establish Department of Education (1979) | N |
| Approve Anti-busing Amendment (1979) | Y |
| Guarantee Chrysler Corp. loans (1979) | N |
| Approve military draft registration (1980) | Y |
| Aid Sandinista regime in Nicaragua (1980) | N |
| Strengthen fair housing laws (1980) | N |

**97th Congress**

| | |
|---|---|
| Reagan budget proposal (1981) | Y |

## Interest Group Ratings

| Year | ADA | ACA | AFL-CIO | CCUS |
|---|---|---|---|---|
| 1980 | 6 | 96 | 11 | 68 |
| 1979 | 0 | 100 | 5 | 100 |
| 1978 | 10 | 100 | 0 | 89 |
| 1977 | 5 | 96 | 4 | 94 |
| 1976 | 0 | 92 | 13 | 94 |
| 1975 | 0 | 96 | 4 | 100 |
| 1974 | 0 | 100 | 0 | 100 |
| 1973 | 8 | 96 | 9 | 100 |
| 1972 | 6 | 100 | 9 | 100 |
| 1971 | 5 | 100 | 8 | - |

# 8 Jack Fields (R)

**Of Humble — Elected 1980**

**Born:** Feb. 3, 1952, Houston, Texas.
**Education:** Baylor U., B.A. 1975, LL.B. 1977.
**Profession:** Lawyer.
**Family:** Wife, Roni Sue Haddock.
**Religion:** Baptist.
**Political Career:** No previous office.

**The Member:** Fields was an utter novice at public office when he announced his 1980 candidacy against Democratic Rep. Bob Eckhardt. But he showed unusual campaign skill for a newcomer, and national Republicans and corporate contributors gave him large sums of money.

Conservatives were eager to defeat Eckhardt, for seven terms a symbol of anti-corporate populism in Congress. He had been losing rapport with his changing consituency and could not overcome Fields' meticulously organized 18-month campaign.

Fields has not betrayed the faith of his supporters. He said his support for Reagan's economic proposals was "absolute." The first bill he introduced was a tax cut package that included a provision to reduce the capital gains tax rate for individuals and corporations.

But Fields wants more federal involvement in some local affairs. He introduced a bill that would bring the Corps of Engineers into his district to build the Upper White Oak Bayou flood control project. He said local efforts to correct flooding had failed. In this case, the federal government "has an inherent repsonsibility to protect its citizens," he explained.

Fields is a rarity in a fast burgeoning metropolitan area — a fifth generation Houstonian. He started out as a campus politician, winning two terms as president of the Baylor student body, something no one had done before. After law school, he joined the family cemetery business as a vice president.

**The District:** Viewed as a labor-oriented district in the 1960s, the 8th is evolving toward conservatism as Northerners and business-oriented Republicans move in.

The district includes petrochemical, oil and shipping facilities on Houston's east side and homes of blue-collar workers who labor in those industries. But the northern part of the district has attracted thousands of middle- and upper-income families, and the Republican base grew dramatically during the 1970s. Pollsters found some new subdivisions voting Republican 9-to-1 in the 1980 presidential contest.

## Committees

**Merchant Marine and Fisheries** (13th of 15 Republicans)
Coast Guard and Navigation; Merchant Marine.

**Public Works and Transportation** (15th of 19 Republicans)
Surface Transportation; Water Resources.

## Elections

**1980 General**

| | |
|---|---|
| Jack Fields (R ) | 72,856 (52 %) |
| Bob Eckhardt (D ) | 67,921 (48 %) |

**District Vote For President**

| | 1980 | | 1976 | | 1972 |
|---|---|---|---|---|---|
| D | 72,503 (52 %) | D | 88,583 (63 %) | D | 55,946 (46 %) |
| R | 62,813 (45 %) | R | 50,435 (36 %) | R | 65,748 (54 %) |
| I | 2,722 (2 %) | | | | |

## Campaign Finance

| | Receipts | Receipts from PACs | Expenditures |
|---|---|---|---|
| **1980** | | | |
| Fields (R ) | $799,756 | $275,528 (34 %) | $794,870 |
| Eckhardt (D ) | $440,186 | $162,328 (37 %) | $440,522 |

## Key Votes

**97th Congress**

| | |
|---|---|
| Reagan budget proposal (1981) | Y |

> **8th District: Northern, eastern Harris County.** Population: 612,471 (31% increase since 1970). Race: White 410,527 (67%), Black 133,906 (22%), Others 68,038 (11%). Spanish origin: 111,361 (18%).

# 9 Jack Brooks (D)

## Of Beaumont — Elected 1952

**Born:** Dec. 18, 1922, Crowley, La.
**Education:** Attended Lamar College; U. of Texas, B.J. 1943, J.D. 1949.
**Military Career:** Marine Corps, 1942-44; Marine Corps Reserve, 1945-72.
**Profession:** Lawyer.
**Family:** Wife, Charlotte Collins; three children.
**Religion:** Methodist.
**Political Career:** Texas House, 1947-51.

**In Washington:** Brooks began his congressional career as a slightly-awed 30-year-old protégé of the legendary Sam Rayburn and stayed on to gather the power and prestige to torment — and at times awe — a long list of people from presidents of the United States to file clerks of House committees.

"I never thought being a congressman was supposed to be an easy job," he once said mildly, "and it doesn't bother me a bit to be in a good fight." It sometimes seems to bother him if he has to go very long without one. There are colleagues who consider him the meanest, most foulmouthed character they have served with since Wayne Hays of Ohio left in 1976. There are others who consider him as loyal a friend and ally as there is in politics.

Brooks has nurtured this image of a fighter, a man of strong loyalties and fierce independence, over the years. He thrives on his reputation as a hard-nosed, fast-talking, square-shooting Texan. Accuse him of being — in his words — a "mean sumbitch" and Brooks will smile sweetly, roll his eyes in blue-eyed innocence and say, "Who me?"

As chairman of the Government Operations Committee since 1975, Brooks has spent much of his time presiding over debate on the minutiae of federal spending formulas. But he has had plenty of opportunity to excercise his passion for combat. Normally restrained and decorous when he manages a bill on the floor, he can be ferocious to federal officials when they testify before his committee, and just as bad in private if he thinks someone susceptible to bullying.

Much of the current Government Operations subject matter is highly technical. In the mid-70s, Brooks began his persistent but largely unsuccessful battle against revenue sharing. It violates what he describes as one of his basic principles, accountability. In his opinion, the unit of government that raises money should be the one to spend it; state and local officials should not receive blocks of money raised by the federal government.

In the early days of the Carter administration, another Brooks principle came into play — congressional prerogatives. Carter wanted the power to reorganize executive branch agencies with a free hand. Brooks wanted to allow Congress to review all such plans before they could go into effect. Brooks threatened to block the reorganization power completely and he only gave up when it was clear Carter had the votes to beat him in his own committee.

On the most important single reorganization fight of the Carter years, however, Brooks was on the president's side. Never enthusiastic about the bill to create a separate Department of Education, Brooks nevertheless moved it out of his Government Operations Committee and managed it through weeks of debate on the House floor.

In the end, it was a matter of party loyalty for Brooks. The new department was a crucial priority for a Democratic president, and most Republicans were against it. Partisanship is one quality in which Brooks has never been lacking.

He began early. Brooks went straight to Rayburn when he arrived in Washington as the youngest Democrat in the class of 1952. He had worked hard against the Democrats-for-Eisenhower movement that swept Texas in 1952, and his strong party loyalty pleased the equally partisan

---

**9th District: East — Beaumont, Galveston, Port Arthur.** Population: 561,287 (20% increase since 1970). Race: White 413,354 (73%), Black 126,368 (23%), Others 21,565 (4%). Spanish origin: 40,020 (7%).

Rayburn, who had had to surrender the Speaker's chair that year to Republican Joseph W. Martin.

Rayburn still was House Democratic leader, however, and was able to give Brooks a helping hand. The newcomer won assignment to Judiciary and Government Operations, and two years later, when the Democrats took back the House and Rayburn took back the Speaker's job, Brooks wound up as chairman of a Government Operations subcommittee, thus beginning a long career as a scourge of federal waste and bureaucratic mismanagement.

As chairman of the Government Activities Subcommittee, Brooks tried to streamline federal agencies. He liked to call the panel the "Brooks Efficiency Subcommittee" and claimed it saved hundreds of millions of dollars.

Despite that fast start, Brooks had to wait 20 years, often impatiently, to become chairman of the full committee. By then, his natural fighting instincts were finely honed.

In his early years in the House, Brooks voted like most other Texas congressmen, in favor of the oil indusry and against many of the early civil rights bills, although he refused to sign the segregationist "Southern manifesto" in 1956 and backed federal aid to education as early as 1958. But when fellow Texan Lyndon Johnson became president, Brooks moved significantly to the left. In 1964, Brooks was one of only 11 Southern Democrats to support that year's Civil Rights Act. From then on, he voted for all of LBJ's "Great Society" legislation and for every single civil rights bill.

Brooks did not like Johnson's successor. He talked about accountability a good deal of the time during the Nixon years, especially after the Watergate scandal broke, and when the Judiciary Committee moved to take up Nixon's impeachment, Brooks was waiting. "He didn't even need to hear the evidence," an aide said later. "He was ready to impeach."

From Government Operations, Brooks challenged Nixon on another topic, federal money spent on vacation White Houses in Florida and California by the General Services Administration. Brooks was outraged at the costs, which ran into millions of dollars.

Brooks also plays a major role in the Atlantic alliance of parliamentarians from NATO countries, traveling to overseas meetings at least once a year. He is president of the group in 1981.

**At Home:** "I'm just like old man Rayburn," Brooks likes to say. "Just a Democrat, no prefix or suffix." That simple label has kept Brooks in business for a quarter-century in a district with a large union and minority population. Lately, however, there have been signs of trouble.

Critics have always portrayed Brooks as too liberal for the Gulf Coast district, but in 1980, a conservative primary challenger came within 1,000 votes of forcing him into a runoff. Veteran Democrats often find runoffs difficult to win in Texas.

A child of the Depression, Brooks was born across the state border in Crowley, La., but moved with his family to Beaumont at age five. He worked his way through the University of Texas, served in the Marine Corps in World War II, and won a seat in the state House in 1946. During four years in the Legislature, Brooks earned a law degree at the University of Texas.

Promoting himself as a lawyer and small farmer, Brooks ran for Congress in 1952, when Democratic Rep. Jesse M. Combs retired. He won, surviving a 12-way primary and a runoff.

At first, Brooks's district stretched north from his home base of Jefferson County (Beaumont) into the rural woodland of eastern Texas. But in the mid-1960s the district was changed significantly. Jefferson County remained, but the rest of his district was redrawn to stretch westward along the Gulf Coast to Galveston.

Brooks's basic constituency of labor and blacks has been strong enough to withstand repeated conservative challenges. But it nearly failed him in 1980 against Wilbur L. "Bubba" Pate, the manager of a Beaumont bus terminal. Pate said Brooks was out of step with the district. He also questioned the incumbent's bank connections and the fact that he had amassed a personal fortune while serving most of his adult life in Congress. Brooks has earned more than $50,000 in salary and director fees from Texas banks in some recent years, and in 1978 some of the banks also began paying his wife director fees, which do not count against the earned income limitation for members of Congress.

Brooks avoided a runoff by winning big in heavily unionized Galveston, but he lost his home county of Jefferson, not an encouraging sign.

**The District:** The district is dominated by the twin industrial areas of Beaumont and Port Arthur near the Louisiana border, and by Galveston, further south along the Gulf. The production, refining and distribution of petroleum and its products dominate the economy, and there is heavy unionization, with the Oil, Chemical and Atomic Workers politically active. More than one quarter of the 9th is black or Hispanic.

Usually the district votes Democratic. Jimmy Carter carried it easily in 1976 with nearly 60 percent of the vote, and narrowly won it in 1980 on the strength of victories in Galveston and

Jefferson counties. But there is also a strong conservative element which the Republicans have long tried to tap. In 1968, when the district lines were similar, although not identical, George C. Wallace drew 25 percent of the district vote for his third-party presidential campaign.

## Committees

**Government Operations** (Chairman)
Legislation and National Security, Chairman.

**Judiciary** (2nd of 16 Democrats)
Courts, Civil Liberties and Administration of Justice; Monopolies and Commercial Law.

## Elections

**1980 General**

| | |
|---|---|
| Jack Brooks (D ) | Unopposed |

**1980 Primary**

| | |
|---|---|
| Jack Brooks (D ) | 26,343 (50 %) |
| W. L. Pate (D ) | 22,188 (43 %) |
| Jack Brookshire (D ) | 3,600 (7 %) |

**1978 General**

| | |
|---|---|
| Jack Brooks (D ) | 50,792 (63 %) |
| Randy Evans (R ) | 29,473 (37 %) |

**Previous Winning Percentages**

| | | | |
|---|---|---|---|
| 1976 (100%) | 1974 (62%) | 1972 (66%) | 1970 (65%) |
| 1968 (61%) | 1966 (100%) | 1964 (63%) | 1962 (69%) |
| 1960 (70%) | 1958 (100%) | 1956 (100%) | 1954 (100%) |
| 1952 (79%) | | | |

**District Vote For President**

| | 1980 | | 1976 | | 1972 |
|---|---|---|---|---|---|
| D | 88,418 (49 %) | D | 97,800 (59 %) | D | 58,209 (40 %) |
| R | 85,646 (48 %) | R | 67,280 (41 %) | R | 86,303 (60 %) |
| I | 4,328 (2 %) | | | | |

## Campaign Finance

| | | Receipts | Expen- |
|---|---|---|---|
| | Receipts | from PACs | ditures |
| **1980** | | | |
| Brooks (D ) | $127,814 | $48,720 (38 %) | $133,569 |
| **1978** | | | |
| Brooks (D ) | $100,163 | $58,209 (58 %) | $80,171 |

## Voting Studies

| | Presidential Support | | Party Unity | | Conservative Coalition | |
|---|---|---|---|---|---|---|
| Year | S | O | S | O | S | O |
| 1980 | 54 | 20 | 74 | 15 | 43 | 43 |
| 1979 | 66 | 25 | 69 | 20 | 49 | 40 |
| 1978 | 54 | 39 | 62 | 34 | 55 | 39 |
| 1977 | 52 | 37 | 64 | 23 | 49 | 38 |
| 1976 | 33 | 61 | 64 | 29 | 54 | 33 |
| 1975 | 39 | 48 | 63 | 22 | 45 | 38 |
| 1974 (Ford) | 43 | 41 | | | | |

| | | | | | | |
|---|---|---|---|---|---|---|
| 1974 | 60 | 32 | 74 | 19† | 45 | 45 |
| 1973 | 34 | 55 | 68 | 27 | 53 | 43 |
| 1972 | 54 | 38 | 67 | 24 | 45 | 41 |
| 1971 | 54 | 37 | 61 | 30 | 57 | 32 |
| 1970 | 45 | 29 | 64 | 17 | 43 | 39 |
| 1969 | 49 | 19 | 60 | 9 | 20 | 56 |
| 1968 | 78 | 13 | 74 | 12 | 31 | 59 |
| 1967 | 85 | 4 | 96 | 1 | 13 | 80 |
| 1966 | 92 | 5 | 93 | 4 | 11 | 89 |
| 1965 | 85 | 10 | 87 | 10 | 25 | 75 |
| 1964 | 92 | 2 | 87 | 5 | 25 | 67 |
| 1963 | 92 | 1 | 91 | 0 | 0 | 80 |
| 1962 | 82 | 7 | 86 | 5 | 19 | 81 |
| 1961 | 88 | 9 | 86 | 9 | 39 | 61 |

† Not eligible for all recorded votes.
S = Support   O = Opposition

## Key Votes

**96th Congress**

| | |
|---|---|
| Weaken Carter oil profits tax (1979) | Y |
| Reject hospital cost control plan (1979) | Y |
| Implement Panama Canal Treaties (1979) | Y |
| Establish Department of Education (1979) | Y |
| Approve Anti-busing Amendment (1979) | N |
| Guarantee Chrysler Corp. loans (1979) | ? |
| Approve military draft registration (1980) | ? |
| Aid Sandinista regime in Nicaragua (1980) | Y |
| Strengthen fair housing laws (1980) | N |

**97th Congress**

| | |
|---|---|
| Reagan budget proposal (1981) | N |

## Interest Group Ratings

| Year | ADA | ACA | AFL-CIO | CCUS |
|---|---|---|---|---|
| 1980 | 28 | 21 | 50 | 69 |
| 1979 | 42 | 25 | 47 | 50 |
| 1978 | 30 | 40 | 45 | 50 |
| 1977 | 15 | 31 | 68 | 53 |
| 1976 | 30 | 33 | 77 | 38 |
| 1975 | 32 | 36 | 68 | 19 |
| 1974 | 39 | 38 | 80 | 56 |
| 1973 | 48 | 25 | 100 | 30 |
| 1972 | 25 | 35 | 90 | 22 |
| 1971 | 43 | 36 | 80 | - |
| 1970 | 36 | 29 | 86 | 25 |
| 1969 | 33 | 13 | 67 | - |
| 1968 | 58 | 0 | 100 | - |
| 1967 | 73 | 0 | 92 | 10 |
| 1966 | 82 | 11 | 100 | - |
| 1965 | 53 | 11 | - | 10 |
| 1964 | 88 | 6 | 100 | - |
| 1963 | - | 0 | - | - |
| 1962 | 63 | 9 | 91 | - |
| 1961 | 80 | - | - | - |

# 10 J. J. Pickle (D)

**Of Austin — Elected 1963**

**Born:** Oct. 11, 1913, Roscoe, Texas.
**Education:** U. of Texas, B.A. 1938.
**Military Career:** Navy, 1942-45.
**Profession:** Public relations and advertising executive.
**Family:** Wife, Beryl McCarroll; three children.
**Religion:** Methodist.
**Political Career:** No previous office.

**In Washington:** Pickle's Texas hill country twang is an instant reminder of Lyndon Johnson, who represented the same congressional district. And Pickle's legislative career suggests its own echoes of Johnson, for whom he campaigned as a young man and whose name he nearly always pronounces in reverent tones.

Like LBJ, Pickle is a man of rural populist roots who has made his accommodations with the corporate interests crucial to Texas politics. But he seems more comfortable with his role of small business protector and specialist in the problems of the Social Security system. Politically cautious, he has in the past voted against some civil rights bills and he remains a critic of busing. But he backed nearly all of Johnson's Great Society measures of the 1960s, and is amenable to persuasion from current House leaders in situations where his vote is needed.

In the 96th Congress, Pickle found himself in a somewhat uncharacteristic position, as the chief spokesman for his state's oil producers on the Ways and Means Committee. A series of retirements left him as the only Texas Democrat on Ways and Means just as the panel began markup on the windfall profits tax bill. It was Pickle who drew the assignment of trying to amend the bill to create an added tax break for oil produced through difficult and expensive "tertiary" recovery techniques. He lost that battle in committee. Later, although the legislation was softened on the House floor, he ended up casting what amounted to an obligatory vote against it.

Most of Pickle's time in the 96th Congress however, was spent on his chairmanship of the Ways and Means Social Security Subcommittee, which has been charged with the difficult task of finding ways to keep the system solvent. He has insisted that Social Security cash benefits can be financed through the existing payroll tax, despite its impact on working class incomes. He has been against switching to general treasury financing for basic benefits, although he has supported it for the Medicare trust fund.

"The Social Security tax is probably the best bargain in America today," he said in 1979, defending the old New Deal principle that working people finance their own future retirement.

In 1981, when President Reagan proposed cutting the Social Security system's early retirement benefits to keep the system solvent, Pickle was one of the few members of Congress to express some sympathy. But he hinted that Reagan should give more advance warning than the one year he suggested.

The most controversial legislation to come out of Pickle's subcommittee, however, dealt with federal disability payments. Persuaded that thousands of people were collecting too much money on disability — some making considerably more than they did at work — Pickle's panel wrote a bill limiting any disabled worker's benefits to 80 percent of previous earnings.

The bill brought a storm of protest from recipient groups, especially the organized elderly. Former HEW Secretary Wilbur J. Cohen, who served in the Johnson Cabinet, traveled to Pickle's district to attack the idea. A majority of Northern Democrats voted against it. The chairman of the Select Aging Committee, Claude Pepper, D-Fla., accused Pickle of "turning to the cripple as the source of saving revenue." But it

---

**10th District: East central — Austin.** Population: 645,490 (33% increase since 1970). Race: White 506,082 (78%), Black 77,275 (12%), Others 62,133 (10%). Spanish origin: 102,334 (16%).

passed the House easily in early 1980, thanks mostly to overwhelming Republican support.

Much of Pickle's earlier House career consisted of balancing his own New Deal instincts and LBJ's national goals against his constituents' increasing skepticism about liberal programs. He arrived in the House in December of 1963 — less than a month after Johnson's accession — and in his first two years backed both the Civil Rights Act of 1964 and the Voting Rights Act. "I caught hell in my district," he noted later. Pickle also was a strong backer of the Office of Economic Opportunity, especially its jobs programs, ones he saw as similar to those of the National Youth Administration, for which he worked in the 1930s.

But he opposed civil rights legislation in 1966 and 1968, both times on grounds that its open housing provisions were too strong. Since the end of the Johnson administration he has, like most Texas Democrats, gradually moved closer to the voting patterns of Democrats from other Southern states.

**At Home:** As a political protégé of Johnson, Pickle solidified his grip on his central Texas district during the LBJ White House years. Since then he has had few serious challenges, although in 1980 he experienced his closest race since he first won the seat.

Pickle was a congressional aide for Johnson before World War II. After the war, as a partner in a public relations agency, he served as a political adviser and helped in LBJ's successful 1948 Senate campaign.

But Pickle did not seek office himself until 1963, when he resigned from the Texas Employment Commission to run in a special election. A vacancy had been created when Democratic Rep. Homer Thornberry, the first successor to Johnson, retired to accept a federal judgeship.

Long before Pickle made his political debut, however, he had become controversial in Texas politics. He had gained the disfavor of liberal Democrats in 1954, when he worked for the re-election of Gov. Allan Shivers against the liberal favorite, Ralph Yarborough. Pickle was accused of producing a campaign film for Shivers, entitled "The Port Arthur Story," which depicted the strike-ridden city as a victim of organized labor.

Liberals supported their own candidate in the 1963 House race. But Pickle's ties to political and business interests in the district, as well as the clever marketing of his name — he handed out pickle-shaped campaign pins and recipe books — made him a formidable candidate.

Pickle ran narrowly ahead of the three-man field in the first round of voting in early November, but fell well short of the majority required. With liberals uneasy about his candidacy, he was expected to have problems winning the December runoff election against a conservative Republican opponent.

But the complexion of the campaign was changed by the Nov. 22 assassination of President Kennedy. Pickle's House race suddenly was transformed into the first test of voter support for the district's most famous citizen, President Johnson. Benefiting from a surge of party harmony, Pickle won easily.

During the height of the Johnson presidency, Pickle had no primary or Republican opposition. In 1968 he was confronted by an aggressive Republican challenger, Ray Gabler, who accused him of making a profit from land condemnation for a federally-aided reservoir project. Pickle denied any breach of ethics but was held to 62 percent of the vote.

He had no other serious challenge until 1980, when the Reagan tide in Texas and voter dissatisfaction with a court-ordered busing plan in Austin held Pickle to less than 60 percent of the vote. Pickle had been reluctant to support a constitutional amendment to ban busing, although he did vote for one on the House floor in 1979.

As in earlier races, Pickle ran better in the rural areas than in populous Austin. But he was still able to carry every county in the district.

**The District:** Although district lines have been redrawn several times since Pickle first won the seat, the 10th has for decades been dominated by the capital city of Austin. Nearly 70 percent of the district vote in 1980 was cast in Travis County (Austin).

With the state's largest academic community, the University of Texas, Austin is more liberal than other Texas cities. Travis County was the largest population center in Texas to vote for Jimmy Carter in 1980. Travis voters also gave John B. Anderson a far larger share of the vote — 6 percent — than those in any other Texas urban center.

While the 10th is traditionally Democratic, Republicans have been making inroads. Electronics industries have been locating in the Austin area in recent years, bringing an influx of new voters, many of them sympathetic to the GOP. And rural voters outside Austin have shown increasing independence. Most of the ranching and farming counties in the district went for Reagan in 1980, including Blanco County, the site of the LBJ ranch.

## Committees

**Ways and Means** (3rd of 23 Democrats)
  Social Security, chairman; Oversight.

**Joint Taxation**

## Elections

**1980 General**

| | |
|---|---|
| J. J. Pickle (D ) | 135,618 (59 %) |
| John Biggar (R ) | 88,940 (39 %) |

**1980 Primary**

| | |
|---|---|
| J. J. Pickle (D ) | 65,409 (75 %) |
| Greg Stallings (D ) | 21,271 (25 %) |

**1978 General**

| | |
|---|---|
| J. J. Pickle (D ) | 94,529 (76 %) |
| Emmett Hudspeth (R ) | 29,328 (24 %) |

**Previous Winning Percentages**

| | | | |
|---|---|---|---|
| 1976 (77 %) | 1974 (80 %) | 1972 (91 %) | 1970 (100%) |
| 1968 (62 %) | 1966 (74 %) | 1964 (76 %) | 1963* (63 %) |

*Special run-off election. Under Texas's special election law, a majority was required to win the House seat. Since no candidate had a majority in the initial special election, a run-off special election was held between the top two finishers.*

**District Vote For President**

| | 1980 | | 1976 | | 1972 |
|---|---|---|---|---|---|
| D | 108,127 (46 %) | D | 114,896 (53 %) | D | 71,652 (41 %) |
| R | 112,435 (48 %) | R | 99,798 (46 %) | R | 103,675 (59 %) |
| I | 11,413 (5 %) | | | | |

## Campaign Finance

| | Receipts | Receipts from PACs | Expenditures |
|---|---|---|---|
| **1980** | | | |
| Pickle (D ) | $375,917 | $96,600 (26 %) | $308,661 |
| Biggar (R ) | $83,047 | $1,150 (1 %) | $77,586 |
| **1978** | | | |
| Pickle (D ) | $80,966 | $28,011 (35 %) | $46,726 |
| Hudspeth (R ) | $19,266 | $400 (2 %) | $19,263 |

## Voting Studies

| | Presidential Support | | Party Unity | | Conservative Coalition | |
|---|---|---|---|---|---|---|
| Year | S | O | S | O | S | O |
| 1980 | 59 | 32 | 60 | 30 | 60 | 25 |

| | | | | | | |
|---|---|---|---|---|---|---|
| 1979 | 59 | 34 | 61 | 30 | 63 | 28 |
| 1978 | 54 | 41 | 55 | 42 | 63 | 33 |
| 1977 | 49 | 43 | 51 | 39 | 72 | 21 |
| 1976 | 53 | 39 | 52 | 42 | 69 | 26 |
| 1975 | 53 | 46 | 55 | 44 | 69 | 30 |
| 1974 (Ford) | 57 | 41 | | | | |
| 1974 | 45 | 36 | 50 | 33 | 56 | 24 |
| 1973 | 50 | 47 | 61 | 33 | 62 | 32 |
| 1972 | 51 | 41 | 58 | 37 | 60 | 38 |
| 1971 | 61 | 28 | 50 | 34 | 61 | 26 |
| 1970 | 65 | 31 | 46 | 44 | 68 | 23 |
| 1969 | 60 | 36 | 55 | 42 | 62 | 31 |
| 1968 | 60 | 13 | 46 | 20 | 37 | 31 |
| 1967 | 71 | 19 | 72 | 22 | 48 | 46 |
| 1966 | 68 | 17 | 61 | 28 | 49 | 46 |
| 1965 | 81 | 12 | 74 | 21 | 41 | 53 |
| 1964 | 79 | 19 | 73 | 24 | 83 | 17 |
| 1963 | 100 | 0† | 100 | 0† | 0 | 0 |

† Not eligible for all recorded votes.

  S = Support        O = Opposition

## Key Votes

**96th Congress**

| | |
|---|---|
| Weaken Carter oil profits tax (1979) | Y |
| Reject hospital cost control plan (1979) | Y |
| Implement Panama Canal Treaties (1979) | Y |
| Establish Department of Education (1979) | Y |
| Approve Anti-busing Amendment (1979) | Y |
| Guarantee Chrysler Corp. loans (1979) | Y |
| Approve military draft registration (1980) | ? |
| Aid Sandinista regime in Nicaragua (1980) | N |
| Strengthen fair housing laws (1980) | N |

**97th Congress**

| | |
|---|---|
| Reagan budget proposal (1981) | N |

## Interest Group Ratings

| Year | ADA | ACA | AFL-CIO | CCUS |
|---|---|---|---|---|
| 1980 | 22 | 33 | 42 | 79 |
| 1979 | 32 | 23 | 37 | 69 |
| 1978 | 45 | 65 | 50 | 50 |
| 1977 | 10 | 58 | 50 | 65 |
| 1976 | 25 | 42 | 57 | 63 |
| 1975 | 26 | 61 | 36 | 53 |
| 1974 | 17 | 38 | 63 | 88 |
| 1973 | 48 | 42 | 45 | 70 |
| 1972 | 13 | 65 | 36 | 60 |
| 1971 | 30 | 56 | 73 | - |
| 1970 | 16 | 47 | 43 | 60 |
| 1969 | 20 | 35 | 40 | - |
| 1968 | 42 | 28 | 100 | - |
| 1967 | 47 | 30 | 45 | 56 |
| 1966 | 35 | 52 | 62 | - |
| 1965 | 37 | 18 | - | 40 |
| 1964 | 62 | 33 | 80 | - |
| 1963† | - | - | - | - |

† Not eligible for all recorded votes.

# 11 Marvin Leath (D)

**Of Marlin — Elected 1978**

**Born:** May 6, 1931, Henderson, Texas.
**Education:** U. of Texas, B.B.A. 1954.
**Military Career:** Army, 1954-56.
**Profession:** Banker.
**Family:** Wife, Alta Neill; one child.
**Religion:** Presbyterian.
**Political Career:** No previous office.

**In Washington:** Along with 267 other elected Democrats, Leath pronounced the word "O'Neill" on his first day in 1979, declaring himself a member of the majority party for purposes of selecting a Speaker and organizing the House. It was about the only important vote he has cast in agreement with the national Democratic Party. He is a Republican in all but the nominal sense.

When the two parties were in disagreement during 1980, Leath was on the Republican side three times out of four. Only two other Democrats now serving — Bob Stump of Arizona and Larry McDonald of Georgia — had lower party unity scores.

Actually, Leath's closest ties are outside both major parties, among business and conservative leaders. One of his first public appearances after he arrived in Washington was a speech to a workshop organized by the conservative Committee for the Survival of a Free Congress. Leath told conservatives from around the country that the Democratic Party was as good a vehicle as any for the expression of their movement.

Leath is a devoutly religious Presbyterian, one who has shown an interest in spreading Christian gospel. Colleagues who visit Leath's home on social occasions are sometimes introduced to active evangelicals, such as Bill Bright, founder of the Campus Crusade for Christ.

Leath was not active on the House floor in his first term. He joined an effort to promote the use of gasohol, along with most farm-district members. He spoke out for his state's cellulose manufacturers against what he said was excessive regulation by the Consumer Product Safety Commission. And he backed a resolution that would earmark revenue from the windfall profits tax on the oil industry for reduction of the national debt.

**At Home.** When Democratic Rep. W. R. Poage retired in 1978 after 21 terms in the House, Republicans thought they had a good chance of winning here. But Leath's conservative campaign

neutralized the GOP offensive in the traditionally Democratic district, giving him a close first-term victory in 1978 and a free ride in 1980 — nobody on the ballot against him either in the primary or in November.

Leath displays the conservatism of a self-made man. Born into a poor east Texas family during the Depression, he went to work at the age of 12, washing dishes, driving mules and working on pipelines in the east Texas oil fields. Later he won a football scholarship to the University of Texas. After graduation he became a small-town banker, specializing in the financial needs of the farming and ranching communities of central Texas. He supported Barry Goldwater for President in 1964, but never left the Democratic Party.

Leath came to Washington in 1972 to work in Poage's office, concentrating on constituent problems and acquiring federal grants for the district. He also managed Poage's last three re-election campaigns.

When Poage decided to retire, Leath jumped into the crowded Democratic primary field. Spending heavily out of his own pocket, he ran second in the primary and qualified for the runoff. His opponent, former state Rep. Lane Denton, was a populist critic of high utility rates who two years earlier had built high name recognition in an unsuccessful race for the state railroad commission.

Consolidating the right and again spending

---

**11th District: East central — Waco.**
Population: 604,540 (30% increase since 1970). Race: White 486,093 (80%), Black 77,741 (13%), Others 40,706 (7%). Spanish origin: 57,316 (9%).

heavily, Leath won the run-off by a comfortable margin. He carried all but two of the district's 19 counties.

In the general election, Leath faced Jack Burgess, a Waco oil products distributor who two years earlier had surprised Poage by drawing 43 percent of the vote. But Leath's candidacy deprived Republicans of an effective strategy. The GOP had hoped that Denton would be the Democratic nominee, so that Burgess could make an issue of Denton's liberalism.

Burgess tried to undermine Leath's Democratic support by charging that the Democrat had failed to disclose his 1964 vote for Barry Goldwater instead of Texan Lyndon Johnson. Leath acknowledged that he voted for Goldwater, but said he returned to the Democratic Party immediately afterward.

The election was close, with Burgess carrying McLennan County (Waco) by nearly 5,000 votes. But Leath swept virtually all the smaller counties.

Altogether, his campaign cost nearly $600,000, one of the most expensive congressional efforts in 1978.

**The District.** The primarily rural 11th is evolving from a Democratic stronghold into a competitive two-party district. While Leath has at least temporarily blocked GOP progress at the congressional level, the 1980 presidential vote indicates that Republicans are making breakthroughs in both Waco and the rural counties.

Reagan easily carried Waco and ran slightly ahead of Carter in the smaller counties. Four years earlier, Carter had carried the district easily.

The 11th is one of the less affluent districts in Texas. Blacks and Hispanics together comprise about one-fifth of the population. There is little manufacturing, although oil and gas production are important. Waco serves primarily as a retail, marketing and insurance center. No other city in the 11th has a population larger than 50,000.

## Committees

**Armed Services** (20th of 25 Democrats)
Procurement and Military Nuclear Systems; Readiness.

**Veterans' Affairs** (9th of 17 Democrats)
Housing and Memorial Affairs, chairman; Education, Training and Employment; Oversight and Investigations.

## Elections

**1980 General**

| | |
|---|---|
| Marvin Leath (D) | Unopposed |

**1978 General**

| | |
|---|---|
| Marvin Leath (D) | 53,354 (52 %) |
| Jack Burgess (R) | 49,965 (48 %) |

**1978 Primary Runoff**

| | |
|---|---|
| Marvin Leath (D) | 40,261 (55 %) |
| Lane Denton (D) | 33,029 (45 %) |

**1978 Primary**

| | |
|---|---|
| Lane Denton (D) | 38,984 (40 %) |
| Marvin Leath (D) | 29,523 (30 %) |
| Lyndon Olson (D) | 22,929 (23 %) |
| Perry Ellis (D) | 6,013 (6 %) |

**District Vote For President**

| | 1980 | | 1976 | | 1972 |
|---|---|---|---|---|---|
| D | 84,009 (45 %) | D | 93,857 (57 %) | D | 40,239 (31 %) |
| R | 99,966 (53 %) | R | 70,972 (43 %) | R | 90,802 (69 %) |
| I | 3,520 (2 %) | | | | |

## Campaign Finance

| | | Receipts | Expen- |
|---|---|---|---|
| | Receipts | from PACs | ditures |
| **1980** | | | |
| Leath (D) | $249,831 | $53,700 (21 %) | $171,978 |
| **1978** | | | |
| Leath (D) | $590,482 | $68,675 (12 %) | $588,492 |
| Burgess (R) | $322,083 | $50,972 (16 %) | $320,084 |

## Voting Studies

| | Presidential Support | | Party Unity | | Conservative Coalition | |
|---|---|---|---|---|---|---|
| Year | S | O | S | O | S | O |
| 1980 | 33 | 58 | 21 | 65 | 80 | 4 |
| 1979 | 27 | 68 | 21 | 74 | 96 | 1 |

S = Support          O = Opposition

## Key Votes

**96th Congress**

| | |
|---|---|
| Weaken Carter oil profits tax (1979) | Y |
| Reject hospital cost control plan (1979) | Y |
| Implement Panama Canal Treaties (1979) | N |
| Establish Department of Education (1979) | N |
| Approve Anti-busing Amendment (1979) | Y |
| Guarantee Chrysler Corp. loans (1979) | Y |
| Approve military draft registration (1980) | Y |
| Aid Sandinista regime in Nicaragua (1980) | N |
| Strengthen fair housing laws (1980) | N |

**97th Congress**

| | |
|---|---|
| Reagan budget proposal (1981) | Y |

## Interest Group Ratings

| Year | ADA | ACA | AFL-CIO | CCUS |
|---|---|---|---|---|
| 1980 | 0 | 71 | 19 | 73 |
| 1979 | 5 | 84 | 25 | 94 |

# 12 Jim Wright (D)

**Of Fort Worth — Elected 1954**

**Born:** Dec. 22, 1922, Fort Worth, Texas.
**Education:** Attended Weatherford College; U. of Texas 1940-41.
**Military Career:** Army 1941-45.
**Profession:** Advertising executive.
**Family:** Wife, Betty Hay; four children.
**Religion:** Presbyterian.
**Political Career:** Texas House, 1947-49; Mayor of Weatherford, 1950-54.

**In Washington:** Few Democrats thought of Wright as a likely winner in 1976 when he announced for majority leader, offering himself as an alternative to the bitterly antagonistic front-runners, Richard Bolling of Missouri and Phillip Burton of California. But on the day of decision, he eliminated Bolling by three votes on the second ballot and Burton by one vote on the third.

The Texan had one enormous advantage. Unlike his two rivals, he had few enemies. He had always compromised personal differences when possible, or disagreed gently if he had to. He aimed to please — if not everyone, then as many as possible. When he had something good to say about a colleague, he went out of his way to say it.

Shortly before the 1976 balloting, Wright addressed newly-elected Democrats. With elaborate courtesy, he said something flattering about each of his opponents, and then, almost as an afterthought, suggested he might be a combination of the best in each of them.

In courting senior Democrats, he had another advantage. From his position on Public Works, he had done countless small favors, making sure there was a dam here, or a federal building there. He reminded New Yorkers he voted for federal aid to their city. He noted one-third of the House Democrats came from Southern and Southwestern states and said they deserved a spot in the leadership.

Today Wright is the day-to-day manager of House business and the presumptive heir to the Speakership some day assuming Democrats keep control. He has been a loyal O'Neill lieutenant, serving as the leadership man on the Budget Committee, and on the ad hoc panel that assembled President Carter's energy bills in the 95th Congress.

His budget role has been frustrating. Wright's winning edge for majority leader came largely from Southern Democrats, but he has been unable to persuade them to support national Democratic budget aims. In 1981, fighting against Reagan budget proposals, he consistently lost up to a dozen votes in his own Texas delegation. "I feel like the wife who was asked whether she ever considered divorce," he said. "She answered, 'Divorce, no, murder, yes.' That's how I feel about those guys."

This has not hurt Wright substantially, however, as a party leader. He still aims to please. He never misses an opportunity, for example, to say Tip O'Neill is the smartest man alive at counting votes in the House. He has even been more restrained in criticism of Reagan than other party leaders.

Wright is not modest. He sees himself as a voice of reason, an accomplished writer and a well-read and thoughtful member of Congress. He is proud of his reputation for oratory in a chamber where such talents are dying out. He is florid and sometimes theatrical, slipping unusual words into his speeches and rolling them slowly off his tongue, savoring each syllable. He is alternately loud and very soft, forcing listeners to lean forward to hear him and then surprising them by turning up the volume.

He is sometimes preachy, sometimes patronizing. "I am deeply humble and grateful.... I want the president (Reagan) to succeed very much because I want the country to succeed.... We've got to dream bold dreams.... We sat down

---

**12th District: Central, northern Tarrant County — Fort Worth.** Population: 507,160 (9% increase since 1970). Race: White 392,173 (77%), Black 81,962 (16%), Others 33,025 (7%). Spanish origin: 49,717 (10%).

and hammered upon the anvils of mutual understanding. . . ."

Some see this as trite or self-indulgent. But it can be effective. Wright changed numerous votes with his eloquent speech in 1979 against expelling Michigan Democrat Charles C. Diggs Jr., who had been convicted on kickback charges. "We do not possess the power," Wright said, "to grant to any human being the right to serve in this body. That gift is not ours to bestow."

In the exchanges of House floor debate, Wright sometimes surprises people with emotional excess. He has a hot temper. Several times during any Congress, when he is angry at an opponent, he will blurt out something unkind and be forced to apologize later. But even then the ingratiating side soon takes over. Wright's apologies are often so effusive the entire episode balances out as a compliment.

When he became majority leader, Wright had to give up Public Works, which he was in line to chair in 1977. Earlier on the committee, he had taken the lead in exposing what he called "the great highway robbery," trying to root out fraud and corruption in the massive interstate system. But he remained a strong pro-highway man.

He also defends federal water projects and has been something of a water policy specialist. At the start of the Carter administration, he played a key role in trying to to bargain with a president determined to eliminate a long list of water development projects. But he avoided criticizing Carter publicly when other Democrats were doing so.

Outside Public Works, Wright has been a strong supporter of defense spending, and especially helpful to General Dynamics, his district's leading employer and producer of the TFX fighter plane. For years, Wright exercised his oratorical skills on behalf of the much-maligned TFX, sparring with members from the state of Washington, home of Boeing, General Dynamics' chief rival. In more recent times, Wright has continued to speak up for successors to the TFX.

Wright once wrote a magazine article, "Clean Money for Congress," noting that he accepted only small campaign contributions. But in recent years, like many members, he has become dependent on larger givers. His finances have been complicated by debts he incurred in running for the Senate in 1961, and he has spent years trying to straighten them out. In 1976, he raised $132,000 at a $1,000-a-plate Washington fundraiser and used $84,000 to pay off debts still outstanding from the old Senate race. He had taken out personal loans to try and repay his contributors, and his personal and political finances had become entangled. He said he had been a poor financial manager but violated no law.

**At Home:** For most of the 1970s, Wright was secure at home and free to campaign for other Democrats across the country, gradually winning allies and accumulating power in the House. But in 1980, national GOP strategists decided to challenge him in Fort Worth, partly just to keep him there but also to see whether he had lost touch with conservative Tarrant County.

Wright had managed over more than a decade to mute the liberal image of his early years, and had proclaimed himself a centrist. But as majority leader he had to support and sometimes defend national Democratic policies. Foes started calling him a socialist. A New Right Christian group gave him a 1 percent "morality rating."

Republican Jim Bradshaw spent most of 1980 saying Wright was beholden to liberals and the Washington establishment. As a former mayor pro tempore of Fort Worth, Bradshaw was well known and collected more than $500,000 from local and national sources.

Wright pointed to his congressional influence and his ability to draw military contracts and other federal money to Fort Worth. He even sent a letter to local businessmen, telling them to back Bradshaw if they wished, but reminding them he would still be around and would remember it. Wright retained his seat by more than 40,000 votes.

For virtually his entire adult life, Wright has been immersed in politics. In 1946, shortly after returning from combat in the South Pacific, he won a seat in the Texas Legislature. He lost a re-election bid two years later but in 1950 began a four-year tenure as mayor of Weatherford, a small town about 20 miles west of Fort Worth. In 1953, he served as president of the League of Texas Municipalities.

Wright was known in those years as a liberal crusader, thanks to his support for anti-lynching legislation and for federal school aid. In 1954, he challenged conservative incumbent Wingate Lucas in the Democratic primary. Wright was opposed by much of the Fort Worth business establishment, but he turned that to his advantage by portraying himself as the candidate of the average man. He defeated Lucas by a margin of about 3-2.

Once established in the House, and recognized as a young man of talent and ambition, Wright had to decide whether to stay there. "You reach the point," he complained, "where you're not expanding your influence." The Senate beckoned, and in April 1961 he ran in a special election for the seat vacated by Vice President Johnson. The field of more than 70 candidates badly split the Democratic vote, and Texas elected its first Republican senator since Reconstruction, John G. Tower. Wright placed third, narrowly missing a runoff he probably would have won.

Wright next considered running for governor, but gave it up and began to aim for a 1966 Senate campaign. His vote the year before to repeal state "right-to-work" laws increased his following in organized labor, but it chilled his support in the Texas business community and made it difficult for him to raise money. Low on funds, he made an emotional statewide telecast appealing for $10 contributions to the half-million-dollar fund he said he would need for the race. Only $48,000 flowed in, mostly from his district, and Wright was forced to abandon his candidacy.

**The District:** When Wright first came to Congress, his district included not only Tarrant County (Fort Worth), but several rural counties to the south and west. Redistricting has pared away the rural areas, reducing the 12th to most of Fort Worth and its Tarrant County suburbs.

The district includes large minority and blue-collar populations. Wright has cultivated his constituents by helping to steer defense contracts to the district's largest industries, General Dynamics and Bell Helicopter. The 12th draws more money from the Defense Department than nearly any other district in the country.

## Committees

**Majority Leader**

**Budget**
Member of all Task Forces.

## Elections

**1980 General**

| | |
|---|---|
| Jim Wright (D ) | 99,104 (60 %) |
| Jim Bradshaw (R ) | 65,005 (39 %) |

**1980 Primary**

| | |
|---|---|
| Jim Wright (D ) | 21,186 (80 %) |
| C. R. Silcox (D ) | 5,424 (20 %) |

**1978 General**

| | |
|---|---|
| Jim Wright (D ) | 46,456 (69 %) |
| Claude Brown (R ) | 21,364 (32 %) |

**Previous Winning Percentages**

| | | | |
|---|---|---|---|
| 1976 (76 %) | 1974 (79 %) | 1972 (100%) | 1970 (100%) |
| 1968 (100%) | 1966 (200%) | 1964 (69 %) | 1962 (61 %) |
| 1960 (100%) | 1958 (100%) | 1956 (100%) | 1954 (99 %) |

**District Vote For President**

| | 1980 | | 1976 | | 1972 |
|---|---|---|---|---|---|
| D | 70,901 (46 %) | D | 74,265 (55 %) | D | 45,184 (38 %) |
| R | 78,396 (51 %) | R | 58,483 (44 %) | R | 73,669 (62 %) |
| I | 3,270 (2 %) | | | | |

## Campaign Finance

| | Receipts | Receipts from PACs | Expenditures |
|---|---|---|---|
| **1980** | | | |
| Wright (D ) | $1,185,835 | $340,475 (29 %) | $1,248,688 |
| Bradshaw (R ) | $628,120 | $80,776 (13 %) | $627,471 |

## Voting Studies

| Presidential Support | Party Unity | Conservative Coalition |
|---|---|---|

| Year | S | O | S | O | S | O |
|---|---|---|---|---|---|---|
| 1980 | 74 | 16 | 78 | 5 | 32 | 48 |
| 1979 | 69 | 14 | 77 | 9 | 35 | 52 |
| 1978 | 68 | 22 | 77 | 12 | 33 | 57 |
| 1977 | 77 | 16 | 82 | 9 | 27 | 64 |
| 1976 | 45 | 49 | 61 | 29 | 59 | 32 |
| 1975 | 52 | 45 | 64 | 31 | 59 | 36 |
| 1974 (Ford) | 50 | 26 | | | | |
| 1974 | 53 | 32 | 62 | 26 | 49 | 36 |
| 1973 | 39 | 45 | 71 | 19 | 44 | 47 |
| 1972 | 57 | 38 | 62 | 26 | 50 | 38 |
| 1971 | 67 | 19 | 43 | 27 | 48 | 23 |

S = Support   O = Opposition

## Key Votes

**96th Congress**

| | |
|---|---|
| Weaken Carter oil profits tax (1979) | Y |
| Reject hospital cost control plan (1979) | ? |
| Implement Panama Canal Treaties (1979) | Y |
| Establish Department of Education (1979) | Y |
| Approve Anti-busing Amendment (1979) | N |
| Guarantee Chrysler Corp. loans (1979) | Y |
| Approve military draft registration (1980) | Y |
| Aid Sandinista regime in Nicaragua (1980) | Y |
| Strengthen fair housing laws (1980) | Y |

**97th Congress**

| | |
|---|---|
| Reagan budget proposal (1981) | N |

## Interest Group Ratings

| Year | ADA | ACA | AFL-CIO | CCUS |
|---|---|---|---|---|
| 1980 | 39 | 29 | 71 | 73 |
| 1979 | 37 | 8 | 59 | 41 |
| 1978 | 35 | 29 | 83 | 33 |
| 1977 | 45 | 4 | 95 | 29 |
| 1976 | 30 | 19 | 86 | 50 |
| 1975 | 32 | 46 | 65 | 24 |
| 1974 | 30 | 31 | 70 | 50 |
| 1973 | 40 | 24 | 80 | 44 |
| 1972 | 19 | 41 | 80 | 33 |
| 1971 | 24 | 40 | 86 | - |

# 13 Jack Hightower (D)

**Of Vernon — Elected 1974**

**Born:** Sept. 6, 1926, Memphis, Texas.
**Education:** Baylor U., B.A. 1949, LL.B. 1951.
**Military Career:** Navy, 1944-46.
**Profession:** Lawyer.
**Family:** Wife, Colleen Ward; three children.
**Religion:** Baptist.
**Political Career:** Texas House, 1953-55; Vernon district attorney, 1955-61; Texas Senate, 1965-75; unsuccessful Democratic candidate for U.S. House, 1961 special election.

**In Washington:** Hightower came to Washington with the post-Watergate Democratic class of 1974, but had little in common with its reform-minded liberals. He has kept his conservative ranching district happy by paying close attention to local interests and maintaining only limited — though cordial — ties with the Democratic Party majority.

Most of his work deals with farm problems. First on Agriculture and later on Appropriations, Hightower has sought higher price supports for wheat and other feed grains. In 1978, he sponsored a bill requiring retailers to list on each bread wrapper the price of the raw agricultural products inside. He wanted to remind consumers that farmers were not profiting unfairly from the high cost of bread.

He also has introduced legislation increasing the amount of federal loan money available to financially strapped farmers, of which there are many in his district, and he has promoted rural community development subsidies for towns with less than 20,000 population.

By limiting his Appropriations goals to a relatively few items, Hightower has been able to establish a high batting average. Often he has been able to persuade liberal Democrats to go along with him, and sometimes he has helped them out quietly in return. He prides himself on an ability to bring opposing factions together quietly to resolve conflicts — as he did in a dispute between environmentalists, chemical companies and ranchers over federal control of pesticides.

Hightower introduces few bills of his own, and when he does they are likely to be inspired by a constituent. One such measure would limit to four years the period in which businessmen are required to keep records for most federal regulatory agencies. Another would require meatpackers

to pay ranchers more promptly for their stock.

Hightower was elected as a conservative and pretty much stays on course. In 1980 he backed the conservative coalition of Republicans and Southern Democrats 75 percent of the time, more often than all but four Democrats from Texas. He voted for the Reagan budget rather than the Democratic alternative in 1981.

Like many conservatives, Hightower has favored a proposal requiring a balanced budget, but he has opposed a constitutional amendment. He would prefer a simple resolution requiring that appropriations not exceed revenues except in times of war or national emergency.

**At Home:** The 13th is closely divided; Republican in the northern Panhandle and Democratic in the Red River Valley. But it is uniformly conservative, and Hightower's politics have satisfied it for four terms, although there were signs of trouble in 1980.

Hightower lost his first bid for the district in 1961, when he placed third in a special election to fill the vacancy created by Democratic Rep. Frank Ikard, who resigned to become an oil industry lobbyist. Hightower had quit his position as the Vernon district attorney to make the race.

Hightower, who had served one term in the Texas House in the 1950s, then ran for the state Senate in 1964, and won three times before leaving to make a second congressional bid in 1974. Stressing conservative themes that matched his

---

**13th District: Northwest — Texas Panhandle.** Population: 505,613 (8% increase since 1970). Race: White 453,213 (89%), Black 26,113 (5%), Others 26,287 (5%). Spanish origin: 42,204 (8%).

rival, Hightower ousted Republican Rep. Robert Price.

The Democrat's strength in the Wichita Falls area, which he represented in the state Legislature, offset Price's appeal in the Panhandle. Hightower defeated Price in a 1976 rematch by a margin of nearly 3-2.

The 1980 contest, against Republican Ron Slover, an Amarillo salesman, gave Hightower a disappointing margin of about 20,000 votes, the smallest of his career. The next electon will tell whether that was a warning or simply a reflection of Ronald Reagan's enormous strength in this part of Texas.

**The District:** This sprawling 33-county district was created in 1971 by combining the major portions of the old 13th and 18th districts.

The northern portion, the old 18th, is a sparsely populated ranching and wheat-growing area. Amarillo is the flour-milling, food-processing center of the region, and has a large assembly plant for atomic weapons. There is a considerable amount of natural gas exploration in the region. It is one of the state's Republican centers.

To the southeast is the area of the old 13th District, centered around Wichita Falls. It is an area of oil and gas production. The counties of the old 13th usually turn in Democratic majorities large enough to offset GOP strength in the Panhandle.

## Committees

**Appropriations** (24th of 33 Democrats)
Agriculture; Commerce, Justice, State, and Judiciary.

## Elections

**1980 General**

| | |
|---|---|
| Jack Hightower (D ) | 98,779 (55 %) |
| Ron Slover (R ) | 80,819 (45 %) |

**1978 General**

| | |
|---|---|
| Jack Hightower (D ) | 75,271 (75 %) |
| Clifford Jones (R ) | 25,275 (25 %) |

**Previous Winning Percentages**

1976 (59 %)     1974 (58 %)

**District Vote For President**

| | 1980 | | 1976 | | 1972 |
|---|---|---|---|---|---|
| **D** | 64,474 (35 %) | **D** | 85,220 (49 %) | **D** | 37,575 (24 %) |
| **R** | 113,453 (62 %) | **R** | 87,266 (50 %) | **R** | 118,004 (75 %) |
| **I** | 3,021 (2 %) | | | | |

## Campaign Finance

| | Receipts | Receipts from PACs | Expenditures |
|---|---|---|---|
| **1980** | | | |
| Hightower (D ) | $129,293 | $54,872 (42 %) | $145,292 |
| Slover (R ) | $64,715 | — (0 %) | $57,863 |
| **1978** | | | |
| Hightower (D ) | $61,825 | $25,212 (41 %) | $44,551 |
| Jones (R ) | $30,409 | $1,000 (3 %) | $30,086 |

## Voting Studies

| Year | Presidental Support | | Party Unity | | Conservative Coalition | |
|---|---|---|---|---|---|---|
| | **S** | **O** | **S** | **O** | **S** | **O** |
| 1980 | 55 | 40 | 54 | 39 | 75 | 17 |
| 1979 | 47 | 48 | 44 | 51 | 89 | 8 |
| 1978 | 41 | 53 | 45 | 51 | 79 | 16 |
| 1977 | 51 | 46 | 48 | 47 | 79 | 17 |
| 1976 | 65 | 33 | 36 | 59 | 87 | 8 |
| 1975 | 51 | 46 | 37 | 51 | 85 | 9 |

S = Support          O = Opposition

## Key Votes

**96th Congress**

| | |
|---|---|
| Weaken Carter oil profits tax (1979) | Y |
| Reject hospital cost control plan (1979) | Y |
| Implement Panama Canal Treaties (1979) | N |
| Establish Department of Education (1979) | N |
| Approve Anti-busing Amendment (1979) | Y |
| Guarantee Chrysler Corp. loans (1979) | Y |
| Approve military draft registration (1980) | Y |
| Aid Sandinista regime in Nicaragua (1980) | Y |
| Strengthen fair housing laws (1980) | N |

**97th Congress**

| | |
|---|---|
| Reagan budget proposal (1981) | Y |

## Interest Group Ratings

| Year | ADA | ACA | AFL-CIO | CCUS |
|---|---|---|---|---|
| 1980 | 17 | 43 | 35 | 82 |
| 1979 | 16 | 60 | 25 | 72 |
| 1978 | 30 | 67 | 35 | 81 |
| 1977 | 15 | 56 | 30 | 71 |
| 1976 | 15 | 64 | 35 | 69 |
| 1975 | 11 | 69 | 32 | 53 |

# 14 Bill Patman (D)

Of Ganado — Elected 1980

**Born:** March 26, 1927, Texarkana, Texas.
**Education:** U. of Texas, B.B.A., LL.B. 1953.
**Military Career:** Marine Corps, 1945-46; Air Force Reserve, 1953-66.
**Profession:** Lawyer, rancher.
**Family:** Wife, Carrin Mauritz; one child.
**Religion:** Methodist.
**Political Career:** Texas Senate, 1961-81.

**The Member:** Patman carries an instant identity in Washington as the son of Wright Patman, the populist Democrat who represented Texas in the House for 47 years and fought Wall Street as Banking chairman.

But as a state senator for 20 years, William Patman long ago passed beyond his family reputation to become a prominent Texas Democrat in his own right.

Like his father, Patman has been an outspoken foe of high interest rates. He fought the lifting of the ceiling on home loan interest rates in the Texas Legislature. Although he is sometimes labeled a liberal, he fits more appropriately into the tradition of rural populism exemplified by his father.

The younger Patman chose to make his political career in a different part of the state than his father did. Wright Patman represented the 1st District, based in Texarkana, in the northeast corner of Texas. His son was elected to the Legislature from an area along the Gulf Coast, north of Corpus Christi. In 1980, he succeeded Democratic U.S. Rep. Joe Wyatt, who retired.

**The District:** The industrial and port city of Corpus Christi constitutes about 44 percent of the population in the 14th. It has usually dominated the district politically, and the U.S. representative has nearly always come from there.

But Corpus Christi's interests also create tensions between it and the district's smaller cities, and in each of the last two elections, a non-Corpus Christi candidate has won. Patman's hometown of Ganado is in the northern part of the district. In the 1980 primary, he had the support of nearly all the areas outside of Nueces County, in which Corpus Christi is located.

## Committees

**Banking, Finance and Urban Affairs** (23rd of 25 Democrats)
Consumer Affairs and Coinage; Domestic Monetary Policy; Financial Institutions Supervision, Regulation and Insurance.

**Merchant Marine and Fisheries** (18th of 20 Democrats)
Fisheries and Wildlife Conservation and the Environment; Merchant Marine.

## Elections

| 1980 General | |
|---|---|
| Bill Patman (D ) | 93,884 (57 %) |
| Charles Concklin (R) | 71,495 (43 %) |

| 1980 Primary Runoff | |
|---|---|
| Bill Patman (D ) | 25,480 (52 %) |
| Robert Barnes (D ) | 23,923 (48 %) |

| 1980 Primary | |
|---|---|
| Bill Patman (D ) | 32,258 (35 %) |
| Robert Barnes (D ) | 28,660 (31 %) |
| Joe Salem (D ) | 21,974 (24 %) |
| Jason Luby (D ) | 8,600 (9 %) |

**District Vote For President**

| | 1980 | | 1976 | | 1972 |
|---|---|---|---|---|---|
| **D** | 80,040 (46 %) | **D** | 93,559 (58 %) | **D** | 55,264 (40 %) |
| **R** | 87,979 (51 %) | **R** | 66,425 (41 %) | **R** | 83,652 (60 %) |
| **I** | 3,406 (2 %) | | | | |

## Campaign Finance

| | Receipts | Receipts from PACs | Expenditures |
|---|---|---|---|
| **1980** | | | |
| Patman (D ) | $667,400 | $56,254 (8 %) | $665,984 |
| Concklin (R ) | $174,137 | $23,226 (13 %) | $173,902 |

## Key Vote

| 97th Congress | |
|---|---|
| Reagan budget proposal (1981) | N |

> **14th District: South Gulf Coast — Corpus Christi.** Population: 544,736 (17% increase since 1970). Race: White 441,727 (81%), Black 34,632 (6%), Others 68,377 (13%). Spanish origin: 212,551 (39%).

# 15 E. ''Kika'' de la Garza (D)

**Of Mission — Elected 1964**

**Born:** Sept. 22, 1927, Mercedes, Texas.
**Education:** St. Mary's U., LL.B. 1952.
**Military Career:** Navy, 1945-46; Army, 1950-52.
**Profession:** Lawyer.
**Family:** Wife, Lucille Alamia; three children.
**Religion:** Roman Catholic.
**Political Career:** Texas House, 1953-65.

**In Washington:** An embarrassing thing almost happened to de la Garza in 1980 as he prepared to claim the Agriculture chairmanship that seniority appeared to promise him with the departure of Thomas S. Foley, who had become majority whip.

Dissident committee Democrats, led by Berkley Bedell of Iowa and Dan Glickman of Kansas, put together a quiet but well-organized effort to have de la Garza rejected by the Democratic Caucus. Their campaign fed on perceptions that de la Garza had been condescending toward junior members of the committee, and it stressed the popularity of the next likely contender, the avuncular Ed Jones of Tennessee. Jones himself took no part in it.

The pro-de la Garza faction never realized how strong the protest was. It failed on a 110-92 vote, primarily because Foley refused to endorse it, and Speaker O'Neill made it clear he wanted to follow seniority. But it advertised tensions that had been submerged on Agriculture during Foley's six-year chairmanship.

De la Garza is a man capable of considerable personal charm, an amateur linguist and gourmet cook who converses with foreign dignitaries in their own languages. But as a descendant of Spanish land-grantees who came to south Texas in the 18th century, he sometimes displays a hauteur that is no asset in congressional relations.

On the Agriculture Committee, he has been known to ridicule the idiosyncrasies of colleagues in a manner that is meant to be funny but is taken as an insult. Outside the committee, his voting record has sometimes frustrated liberal Democrats who notice a reluctance to identify himself with liberal Hispanics of less impressive background.

"The thing about all this Chicano and Mexican-American and so forth," he once told a reporter, "is that the Spanish-speaking are members of the White race. Period. Finis."

De la Garza has never left much doubt that he is a conservative Democrat. He voted for most of the basic civil rights legislation of the 1960s, but he has always supported the "conservative coalition" of Republicans and Southern Democrats more often than he has opposed it. In 1980, he backed the coalition 65 percent of the time.

His agriculture work has been concentrated on the crops of south Texas — sugar and cotton — and on the area's water problems. Over his first decade in the House, he worked hardest to obtain a federal sugar allotment for his growers and a project to control the level of salt in the Rio Grande on the Mexican border. Salt in the river's water was making it difficult to irrigate the district's farms.

As he moved toward a senior position on Agriculture, de la Garza continued to be a spokesman for sugar growers. In 1977, when major farm legislation became law, de la Garza successfully amended it to set up a sugar price support program similar to the ones for other crops. The next year, arguing that this had not been sufficient to keep the industry prosperous, he sponsored a bill to return to the system of strict quotas and fees to limit the amount of foreign sugar entering the United States. But this was never implemented.

In 1978, when the previous year's farm legislation was adjusted, de la Garza also fought to have cotton loan rates raised to 48 cents a pound, from the previous 44 cents. That went beyond

---

**15th District: South — Brownsville.**
Population: 659,265 (41% increase since 1970).
Race: White 542,181 (82%), Black 3,038 (0.4%), Others 114,046 (17%). Spanish origin: 509,940 (77%).

Foley's earlier compromise of 46 cents, and remained in the final legislation.

Another de la Garza project in recent years was an effort to force the Agriculture Department to establish a formal soil conservation policy. He promoted a bill in 1976 to require a national soil and water resources study every five years.

He had lost a similar bill the previous year through a veto by President Ford. To get it passed the second time, he promised that it was not a land use planning measure and could not impose any conservation techniques on private farm land. "I personally oppose any form of land use legislation," de la Garza said, and the bill became law.

As chairman of the Agriculture Subcommittee on Departmental Oversight, de la Garza occasionally found himself in an awkward position on pesticide issues. In 1979, the full Agriculture Committee voted over the objections of the Environmental Protection agency to allow the use of Mirex, a chemical useful against fire ants but suspected of causing cancer. Fire ant eradication is a sensitive issue in southern Texas, and in past years de la Garza had opposed strict controls on the use of pesticides. In this case, however, he voted with Foley to reverse the committee and reimpose the ban on Mirex. "Why risk possible permanent damage to the environment for a few million acres?" he said. "I do not want that on my conscience."

Like many members of the Agriculture Committee during the 1970s, de la Garza kept up good relations with South Korea and with rice dealer Tongsun Park, its representative in Washington. In 1974, when the House considered an amendment to restrict military aid to South Korea, de la Garza criticized it as an "affront" to a friendly country. Later, de la Garza's wife told a congressional committee that the wife of the South Korean foreign minister tried to give her an envelope stuffed with money during a visit to the country. Mrs. de la Garza said she was insulted and returned the money.

**At Home.** The election of de la Garza in 1964 was a milestone of sorts for southern Texas Hispanics, who had always been the dominant population group in the 15th District but had never elected one of their own.

It was not, however, a political revolution. The new congressman was backed by the same "Anglo" business interests that had sent Democrats Lloyd Bentsen and Joe Kilgore to Congress in the 1950s. In six terms in the Texas Legislature, de la Garza had maintained a conservative voting record and had opposed passage of a state civil rights bill.

With Kilgore's retirement in 1964, the Democratic primary ended in a runoff between de la Garza and state Rep. Lindsey Rodriguez, an ardent supporter of the Johnson administration and the liberal 1964 Democratic platform. De la Garza featured a photograph of Johnson in his campaign literature, but hedged in his commitment to the platform or the Democratic administration.

Rodriguez had the support of PASO (Political Association of Spanish Speaking Organizations), which had succeeded in electing Hispanic slates in several Texas localities. He accused de la Garza, as a descendant of 18th century Spanish land-grantees, of being aloof from the problems that faced the large mass of poor Hispanics in the district. De la Garza, he complained, was no more than a puppet for the wealthy "Anglo" business establishment.

While de la Garza's business supporters were controversial, they did provide him a campaign budget that dwarfed Rodriguez', and gave him the courthouse machine backing that has always won elections here. De la Garza coasted to victory by a margin of nearly 2-to-1. That fall he won the seat over nominal Republican opposition by an even wider margin.

In one of the state's leading Democratic strongholds, de la Garza has had no trouble winning re-election. Four times since 1964 has run without GOP opposition, while the other four times he has drawn at least 65 percent of the vote. Only twice has he had primary opposition, and both times he won handily.

**The District.** The economic boom that is transforming most of the Southwest is gradually having its impact on south Texas, especially around Brownsville, which is now an area of rapid growth. But the 15th District, long a source of wealth for large "Anglo" landowners, is still one of the nation's poorest. The population is more than three-fourths Hispanic, most of it very poor.

In some of the counties, such as Duval, where Lyndon Johnson won the last few controversial votes that brought him his 1948 Senate nomination, Hispanic votes have traditionally been controlled by "Anglo" political bosses.

Although this has declined in recent years, the 15th is still a one-party district, usually voting overwhelmingly for the straight Democratic ticket. The district includes five of the eight counties in Texas that George McGovern carried in his ill-fated 1972 presidential bid. Although south Texas was the only area of the state that preferred Sen. Edward M. Kennedy over Carter in the 1980 Democratic primary, 15th District voters loyally supported Carter in both the 1976 and 1980 general elections.

Agriculture is the backbone of the district

economy. Tourism is also important and a lively foreign trade is conducted from Brownsville, a port city about 25 miles inland along the Rio Grande.

## Committees

**Agriculture** (Chairman)

## Elections

**1980 General**

| | |
|---|---|
| E. "Kika" de la Garza (D ) | 105,325 (70 %) |
| Lendy McDonald (R ) | 45,090 (30 %) |

**1978 General**

| | |
|---|---|
| E. "Kika" de la Garza (D ) | 54,560 (66 %) |
| Lendy McDonald (R ) | 27,853 (34 %) |

**Previous Winning Percentages**

| | | | |
|---|---|---|---|
| 1976 (74 %) | 1974 (100%) | 1972 (100%) | 1970 (76 %) |
| 1968 (100%) | 1966 (100%) | 1964 (69 %) | |

**District Vote For President**

| | 1980 | | 1976 | | 1972 |
|---|---|---|---|---|---|
| D | 89,487 (56 %) | D | 95,114 (65 %) | D | 53,083 (45 %) |
| R | 67,517 (42 %) | R | 49,958 (34 %) | R | 64,410 (55 %) |
| I | 2,464 (2 %) | | | | |

## Campaign Finance

| | Receipts | Receipts from PACs | Expenditures |
|---|---|---|---|
| **1980** | | | |
| de la Garza (D ) | $85,237 | $37,100 (44 %) | $66,324 |
| McDonald (R ) | $16,104 | $2,500 (16 %) | $17,639 |
| **1978** | | | |
| de la Garza (D ) | $101,453 | $28,061 (28 %) | $85,184 |
| McDonald (R ) | $31,847 | $900 (3 %) | $30,535 |

## Voting Studies

| | Presidential Support | | Party Unity | | Conservative Coalition | |
|---|---|---|---|---|---|---|
| Year | S | O | S | O | S | O |
| 1980 | 57 | 34 | 59 | 36 | 65 | 24 |
| 1979 | 39 | 46 | 31 | 53 | 77 | 9 |
| 1978 | 36 | 56 | 36 | 52 | 75 | 16 |
| 1977 | 44 | 56 | 46 | 53 | 83 | 15 |

| | | | | | | |
|---|---|---|---|---|---|---|
| 1976 | 37 | 39 | 46 | 34 | 64 | 13 |
| 1975 | 54 | 42 | 43 | 46 | 74 | 20 |
| 1974 (Ford) | 41 | 46 | | | | |
| 1974 | 60 | 17 | 37 | 39 | 63 | 19 |
| 1973 | 35 | 54 | 58 | 32 | 62 | 30 |
| 1972 | 57 | 41 | 48 | 47 | 66 | 23 |
| 1971 | 46 | 42 | 57 | 36 | 56 | 34 |
| 1970 | 51 | 26 | 46 | 32 | 52 | 25 |
| 1969 | 51 | 36 | 58 | 29 | 51 | 38 |
| 1968 | 66 | 22 | 59 | 34 | 59 | 29 |
| 1967 | 72 | 16 | 63 | 17 | 46 | 41 |
| 1966 | 69 | 17 | 65 | 23 | 51 | 35 |
| 1965 | 71 | 26 | 67 | 30 | 59 | 39 |

S = Support          O = Opposition

## Key Votes

**96th Congress**

| | |
|---|---|
| Weaken Carter oil profits tax (1979) | Y |
| Reject hospital cost control plan (1979) | ? |
| Implement Panama Canal Treaties (1979) | N |
| Establish Department of Education (1979) | N |
| Approve Anti-busing Amendment (1979) | Y |
| Guarantee Chrysler Corp. loans (1979) | N |
| Approve military draft registration (1980) | Y |
| Aid Sandinista regime in Nicaragua (1980) | N |
| Strengthen fair housing laws (1980) | Y |

**97th Congress**

| | |
|---|---|
| Reagan budget proposal (1981) | N |

## Interest Group Ratings

| Year | ADA | ACA | AFL-CIO | CCUS |
|---|---|---|---|---|
| 1980 | 22 | 52 | 40 | 71 |
| 1979 | 5 | 64 | 32 | 80 |
| 1978 | 10 | 83 | 39 | 72 |
| 1977 | 5 | 52 | 43 | 82 |
| 1976 | 25 | 57 | 71 | 34 |
| 1975 | 11 | 64 | 36 | 65 |
| 1974 | 13 | 67 | 40 | 89 |
| 1973 | 24 | 54 | 60 | 70 |
| 1972 | 13 | 55 | 60 | 25 |
| 1971 | 35 | 35 | 83 | - |
| 1970 | 28 | 40 | 83 | 50 |
| 1969 | 40 | 23 | 44 | - |
| 1968 | 37 | 29 | 75 | - |
| 1967 | 40 | 17 | 73 | 43 |
| 1966 | 29 | 33 | 54 | - |
| 1965 | 21 | 32 | 63 | 60 |

# 16 Richard C. White (D)

**Of El Paso — Elected 1964**

**Born:** April 29, 1923, El Paso, Texas.
**Education:** U. of Texas, B.A. 1946, LL.B. 1949.
**Military Career:** Marine Corps, 1942-45.
**Profession:** Lawyer.
**Family:** Wife, Kathleen Fitzgerald; seven children.
**Religion:** Episcopalian.
**Political Career:** Texas House, 1955-59.

**In Washington:** Once asked about his work on House Armed Services, White said simply, "I have watched out for the interests of my district."

That has been the basis of his career over 12 years. His district is dominated by the military — not only by the huge Army post of Fort Bliss, but by constituents who live in Texas and work across the New Mexico state line at the White Sands Missile Range. He has pursued their local issues more often than global strategy questions.

He also votes his district with extraordinary care. He polls his constituents twice a year, asking what they want him to do on major issues coming up. He then follows their advice faithfully, often explaining that he simply is serving a majority of his constituents. That almost always means voting conservatively.

White's legislative focus has been on personnel problems, both for the military and for civilian employees of the military. While working on those subjects at Armed Services, he also pursued them in the 1970s on the Post Office and Civil Service Committee, where he chaired a panel on Retirement and Employee Benefits, studying how to coordinate federal retirement programs. He left Post Office to take an Armed Services Subcommittee in 1977.

After two terms as chairman of the Armed Services Manpower Subcommittee, White now heads a panel on investigations. He made the switch partly to show himself as a man of broader interests. He is investigating the delays and cost overruns that plague new weapons systems.

White is fascinated by military gadgetry and checks out electronic equipment himself with obvious pleasure and enthusiasm.

White also is on Science and Technology, where he can look after energy research in the oil and gas producing areas in the eastern end of his district. He supports solar energy research.

**At Home.** White has drawn periodic opposition from his own party's left and from the Republican right. But with good constituent service and a conservative voting record tailored to his district's business establishment, he has had little trouble holding his El Paso-based seat.

White launched his congressional career in 1964 after establishing name identification in the state Legislature and as chairman of the El Paso County Democratic committee. He narrowly defeated a liberal Democrat in a run-off, then unseated Republican Rep. Ed Foreman to regain a traditionally Democratic constituency.

White made Foreman's militant conservatism the major issue. He accused Foreman of preaching "fear and hate," and criticized the Republican's description of a number of his House colleagues as "pinkos." White carried El Paso and most of the rural counties to win easily. Foreman later moved north across the state border and served one term in the House from New Mexico.

In 1970 and 1976, White faced primary challenges from El Paso liberals with ties to the district's large Hispanic community. But he repelled each challenge by a surprisingly large margin. His only formidable Republican opposition came in 1976 from a conservative Odessa businessman, Vic Shackelford. Then too, however, White won comfortably, building up a large lead in El Paso that the Republican could not offset elsewhere.

**The District.** While the 16th District covers most of extreme West Texas, about three-fourths

---

**16th District: West — El Paso.** Population: 599,857 (29% increase since 1970). Race: White 375,289 (63%), Black 24,071 (4%), Others 200,497 (33%). Spanish origin: 338,871 (56%).

of the population lives in the El Paso area. The largest American city along the Mexican border, El Paso has a large Hispanic population and Democratic tradition, although it occasionally backs conservative Republicans. In 1980, Ronald Reagan won El Paso County by 13,000 votes.

Hispanics have never dominated local politics, and there has been conflict with the "Anglo"

establishment. One effort by organized labor to gain unionization of a local clothing plant in the mid-1970s resulted in a two-year strike.

Outside El Paso County, most of the district is desert, although the 16th includes a large portion of the Republican oil-producing center of Odessa. Copper, nickel-smelting, textiles and meat-packing are other leading industries.

## Committees

**Armed Services** (4th of 25 Democrats)
Investigations, chairman; Military Personnel and Compensation; Research and Development.

**Science and Technology** (14th of 23 Democrats)
Energy Development and Applications; Natural Resources, Agriculture Research and Environment.

## Elections

**1980 General**

| | |
|---|---|
| Richard White (D ) | 104,734 (85 %) |
| Catherine McDivitt (LIB) | 19,010 (15 %) |

**1978 General**

| | |
|---|---|
| Richard White (D ) | 53,090 (70 %) |
| Michael Giere (R ) | 22,743 (30 %) |

**Previous Winning Percentages**

| | | | |
|---|---|---|---|
| 1976 (58 %) | 1974 (100%) | 1972 (100%) | 1970 (83 %) |
| 1968 (74 %) | 1966 (100%) | 1964 (56 %) | |

**District Vote For President**

| | 1980 | | 1976 | | 1972 |
|---|---|---|---|---|---|
| D | 51,246 (39 %) | D | 59,349 (49 %) | D | 41,326 (36 %) |
| R | 73,773 (56 %) | R | 60,264 (50 %) | R | 71,365 (63 %) |
| I | 5,547 (4 %) | | | | |

## Campaign Finance

| | Receipts | Receipts from PACs | Expenditures |
|---|---|---|---|
| **1980** | | | |
| White (D ) | $91,155 | $35,050 (38 %) | $49,964 |
| **1978** | | | |
| White (D ) | $106,839 | $42,791 (40 %) | $107,976 |
| Giere (R ) | $34,952 | $1,912 (5 %) | $34,881 |

## Voting Studies

| | Presidential Support | | Party Unity | | Conservative Coalition | |
|---|---|---|---|---|---|---|
| Year | S | O | S | O | S | O |
| 1980 | 49 | 37 | 47 | 37 | 69 | 14 |
| 1979 | 36 | 62 | 37 | 61 | 92 | 7 |

| | | | | | | |
|---|---|---|---|---|---|---|
| 1978 | 35 | 54 | 38 | 54 | 82 | 12 |
| 1977 | 52 | 47 | 43 | 53 | 90 | 10 |
| 1976 | 41 | 43 | 41 | 43 | 73 | 10 |
| 1975 | 49 | 51 | 52 | 48 | 83 | 16 |
| 1974 (Ford) | 46 | 43 | | | | |
| 1974 | 72 | 25 | 41 | 51 | 77 | 18 |
| 1973 | 38 | 54 | 57 | 38 | 71 | 26 |
| 1972 | 54 | 43 | 58 | 42 | 65 | 32 |
| 1971 | 74 | 21 | 51 | 45 | 76 | 18 |
| 1970 | 58 | 28 | 56 | 39 | 66 | 30 |
| 1969 | 62 | 38 | 58 | 40 | 67 | 31 |
| 1968 | 69 | 27 | 52 | 40 | 71 | 25 |
| 1967 | 65 | 23 | 62 | 34 | 69 | 30 |
| 1966 | 79 | 21 | 71 | 29 | 68 | 32 |
| 1965 | 64 | 35 | 55 | 43 | 71 | 27 |

S = Support          O = Opposition

## Key Votes

**96th Congress**

| | |
|---|---|
| Weaken Carter oil profits tax (1979) | Y |
| Reject hospital cost control plan (1979) | Y |
| Implement Panama Canal Treaties (1979) | N |
| Establish Department of Education (1979) | Y |
| Approve Anti-busing Amendment (1979) | Y |
| Guarantee Chrysler Corp. loans (1979) | N |
| Approve military draft registration (1980) | Y |
| Aid Sandinista regime in Nicaragua (1980) | N |
| Strengthen fair housing laws (1980) | N |

**97th Congress**

| | |
|---|---|
| Reagan budget proposal (1981) | Y |

## Interest Group Ratings

| Year | ADA | ACA | AFL-CIO | CCUS |
|---|---|---|---|---|
| 1980 | 11 | 55 | 26 | 81 |
| 1979 | 0 | 73 | 20 | 94 |
| 1978 | 25 | 80 | 20 | 71 |
| 1977 | 10 | 44 | 39 | 65 |
| 1976 | 15 | 53 | 59 | 60 |
| 1975 | 11 | 68 | 43 | 59 |
| 1974 | 9 | 67 | 18 | 90 |
| 1973 | 28 | 52 | 36 | 80 |
| 1972 | 13 | 57 | 45 | 70 |
| 1971 | 22 | 70 | 50 | . |
| 1970 | 32 | 47 | 50 | 44 |
| 1969 | 33 | 29 | 60 | . |
| 1968 | 25 | 48 | 25 | . |
| 1967 | 33 | 44 | 42 | 44 |
| 1966 | 6 | 44 | 38 | . |
| 1965 | 16 | 44 | 56 | 80 |

# 17 Charles W. Stenholm (D)

**Of Stamford — Elected 1978**

**Born:** Oct. 26, 1938, Stamford, Texas.
**Education:** Texas Tech U., B.S. 1961, M.S. 1962.
**Profession:** Cotton grower.
**Family:** Wife, Cynthia Watson; three children.
**Religion:** Lutheran.
**Political Career:** No previous office.

**In Washington:** A courteous, soft-spoken cotton grower from central Texas, Stenholm sat through a quiet first term on the Agriculture Committee showing little sign that he planned to become a leader of conservative Democrats in the House.

But after the 1980 election, he suddenly stepped forward as spokesman for more than 40 conservative Democrats pressing Speaker Thomas P. O'Neill Jr. for more influence in the party.

Observers wondered whether the pleasant Stenholm was a "front-man" for more outspoken members of the group; he insisted he was chosen mainly because he was willing to go public. Stenholm had no record of leadership to draw on, but unlike some of the others, he had no real enemies either. He had been a consistent vote against the leadership on nearly all social and economic issues during his first term, but had never been belligerent about it.

His group made its presence felt in the committee assignment process, as conservative Democrats found their way onto Budget, Ways and Means and other key committees in unusual numbers for the 97th Congress. And when the conservatives formed a permanent organization, the Conservative Democratic Forum, Stenholm became coordinator.

In that capacity, he met frequently with officials in the Reagan administration as the president lobbied for his budget proposals in 1981 in the Democratic House. Reagan did not have to worry about Stenholm's vote; the conservative Texan was with him on all major budget issues.

Before that, Stenholm was conspicuous only at the start of his first term, when dozens of his constituents, neither as courteous nor as soft-spoken as he, were using tractors to disrupt Washington traffic as part of their protest against inadequate farm prices.

Like Kent Hance of the neighboring 19th District, Stenholm was faced with a problem. He could not afford to ignore his noisy visitors from the American Agriculture Movement, but he was not inclined to have himself branded a rabble-rouser in his first month in office. "Only a few are here to cause trouble," he said. "The rest are here to ask for what's fair."

Stenholm offered only one major floor amendment during his first term, an attempt to kill a new federal crop insurance program aimed at reducing the amount the government would have to pay each year in disaster relief. Stenholm argued that the insurance would be so expensive that the farmers would not buy it and that they would end up needing relief anyway. Most of Stenholm's rural Democratic colleagues went along with him, but few others did, and he was beaten, 265-81.

**At Home.** Stenholm is a third-generation west Texan, descended from a family of Swedish immigrants who settled near his current home of Stamford. Agriculture has been the focus of his life and the basis of his political career.

He moved into politics in 1966, when the U.S. Agriculture Department made a ruling unfavorable to the cotton-growing plains section of Texas. As executive vice president of the Rolling Plains Cotton Growers Association, Stenholm made several trips to Washington to lobby against the ruling and was partially successful in changing it.

In 1977, President Carter appointed Stenholm to a panel which advises the U.S. Agricultural and Conservation Service. He resigned this position to run for the House in 1978, when

---

**17th District: West central — Abilene.** Population: 504,029 (8% increase since 1970). Race: White 448,406 (89%), Black 17,502 (3%), Others 38,121 (8%). Spanish origin: 57,525 (11%).

Democrat Omar Burleson decided to retire after 16 terms.

Stenholm had a much smaller campaign treasury than his major rival for the Democratic nomination, wealthy Abilene lawyer and businessman, A. L. "Dusty" Rhodes. But as a farmer and former member of the state Democratic executive committee, Stenholm had extensive agricultural and party ties.

Although Rhodes spent over $600,000 in an effort to win the nomination, Stenholm ran ahead of the crowded primary field and defeated Rhodes by a 2-1 margin in a run-off. He won the general election even more handily and coasted to re-election without opposition in 1980.

**The District.** The 17th District is rural, conservative and traditionally Democratic. While Republicans have made inroads in presidential voting — Reagan swept most of the 33 counties in

1980 — the GOP has made few dents into Democratic voting habits in state and local races.

Between 1966 and 1980, Republicans fielded a congressional candidate in the district just once, in 1978, when the seat was open. In 1980, Stenholm was one of only three members of the Texas congressional delegation to run unopposed. The best Republican territory is the district's lone population center, Taylor County (Abilene). Taylor and the eastern counties near Fort Worth have grown faster than other parts of the district. But the bulk of the vote is still in the normally Democratic small towns, ranches, and cotton and dairy farm areas.

Although the district itself is relatively poor, Abilene has remained fairly prosperous with the help of employment provided by Dyess Air Force Base. Military installations at Big Spring and Mineral Wells were closed in recent years.

## Committees

**Agriculture** (21st of 24 Democrats)
Cotton, Rice and Sugar; Livestock, Dairy, and Poultry; Tobacco and Peanuts; Wheat, Soybeans, and Feed Grains.

**Small Business** (13th of 23 Democrats)
Export Opportunities and Special Small Business Problems.

## Elections

**1980 General**

| Charles Stenholm (D ) | Unopposed |
| --- | --- |

**1978 General**

| Charles Stenholm (D ) | 69,030 (68 %) |
| --- | --- |
| Bill Fisher (R ) | 32,302 (32 %) |

**1978 Primary Runoff**

| Charles Stenholm (D ) | 46,599 (67 %) |
| --- | --- |
| A. L. Rhodes (D ) | 22,865 (33 %) |

**1978 Primary**

| Charles Stenholm (D ) | 36,527 (36 %) |
| --- | --- |
| A. L. Rhodes (D ) | 34,163 (34 %) |
| Jim Baum (D) | 16,622 (16 %) |
| Fike Godfrey (D ) | 6,089 (6 %) |

**District Vote For President**

| | 1980 | | 1976 | | 1972 |
| --- | --- | --- | --- | --- | --- |
| D | 77,774 (44 %) | D | 95,111 (57 %) | D | 37,811 (27 %) |
| R | 95,818 (54 %) | R | 70,621 (42 %) | R | 104,249 (73 %) |

## Campaign Finance

| | Receipts | Receipts from PACs | Expenditures |
| --- | --- | --- | --- |
| **1980** | | | |
| Stenholm (D ) | $142,550 | $44,300 (31 %) | $98,134 |
| **1978** | | | |
| Stenholm (D ) | $332,844 | $59,780 (18 %) | $331,516 |
| Fisher (R ) | $149,962 | $5,987 (4 %) | $149,705 |

## Voting Studies

| | Presidential Support | | Party Unity | | Conservative Coalition | |
| --- | --- | --- | --- | --- | --- | --- |
| Year | S | O | S | O | S | O |
| 1980 | 39 | 57 | 24 | 71 | 88 | 4 |
| 1979 | 33 | 66 | 25 | 70 | 95 | 2 |

S = Support     O = Opposition

## Key Votes

**96th Congress**

| Weaken Carter oil profits tax (1979) | Y |
| --- | --- |
| Reject hospital cost control plan (1979) | Y |
| Implement Panama Canal Treaties (1979) | N |
| Establish Department of Education (1979) | N |
| Approve Anti-busing Amendment (1979) | Y |
| Guarantee Chrysler Corp. loans (1979) | Y |
| Approve military draft registration (1980) | Y |
| Aid Sandinista regime in Nicaragua (1980) | N |
| Strengthen fair housing laws (1980) | N |

**97th Congress**

| Reagan budget proposal (1981) | Y |
| --- | --- |

## Interest Group Ratings

| Year | ADA | ACA | AFL-CIO | CCUS |
| --- | --- | --- | --- | --- |
| 1980 | 0 | 74 | 11 | 75 |
| 1979 | 0 | 83 | 20 | 94 |

**1189**

# 18 Mickey Leland (D)

Of Houston — Elected 1978

**Born:** Nov. 27, 1944, Lubbock, Texas.
**Education:** Texas Southern U., B.S. 1970.
**Profession:** Pharmacist.
**Family:** Single.
**Religion:** Roman Catholic.
**Political Career:** Texas House, 1973-79.

**In Washington:** Leland no longer uses the "black power" rhetoric that marked his style as a political activist in the 1960s, but he has remained a rebel and an outsider in his early House years, more active in national black politics than in the legislative process.

At the start of his first term, Leland founded the National Black-Hispanic Democratic Coalition and became its co-chairman, along with Rep. Robert Garcia of New York, who is of Puerto Rican background. Leland helped set up conferences in Houston, Miami and New York in 1979 and 1980, all aimed at improving the political influence of minority groups through unity.

At the same time, Leland was not a major participant at the Commerce Committee, to which he had been assigned in 1979. He did speak out there as a defender of children, particularly poor children, and a critic of those who sought to limit federal involvement in their problems.

When Republicans moved to scale down a 1979 bill to establish new subsidies for pediatric care, Leland accused them of trying to "pick on kids in the name of fiscal conservatism." When the panel voted 8-1 against a Leland amendment requiring special warnings on saccharin containers — an amendment offered by another member in his absence — he warned that "women and children are going to suffer and die." Later he said the committee had chosen "the best interests of fat people ahead of children."

Leland was reluctant to support President Carter's hospital cost containment proposal in 1979, because he felt it would limit the effectiveness of Houston hospitals already serving the poor. When he cast a deciding vote weakening the bill at the request of the Texas Medical Center, Carter administration officials complained that the legislation had been effectively gutted. Leland then changed his vote and kept hospital cost containment alive, although it died later on the House floor.

On other health legislation, Leland made an effort to guarantee the inclusion of pharmacy among subsidized services, reflecting his own background as a pharmacist in Houston. In 1980, the House modified a health professions support bill at Leland's request, so that a pharmacy school in his district could receive a subsidy.

Leland renewed his earlier, more controversial reputation with a 1979 trip to Cuba, made at Fidel Castro's invitation, to be on hand for the release of four American prisoners. That trip attracted some criticism because its $12,000 cost was borne by a wealthy Houston publisher who went along. Leland insisted he had done nothing wrong.

**At Home.** Democrat Barbara C. Jordan probably could have held the 18th District indefinitely, but she decided to retire in 1978 after only three terms in the House. Her decision was a surprise, since she had won national prominence on the House Judiciary Committee during the Nixon impeachment debate and as a keynote speaker at the 1976 Democratic National Convention.

Her retirement, though, was good news for Leland, who had thought his only chance for Congress was a federal appointment for Jordan.

Leland grew up in a poor black section of Houston and attended Texas Southern University after, he believes, he was denied entrance to the University of Houston because of his race. He became an active and often strident spokesman

---

**18th District: Central Houston.** Population: 427,491 (8% decrease since 1970). Race: White 167,074 (39%), Black 184,040 (43%), Others 76,377 (18%). Spanish origin: 132,289 (31%).

---

for civil rights and the anti-war movement. As a pharmacy student, he also took an interest in health care issues, helping to establish a free neighborhood health clinic.

When several predominantly black state legislative districts were created in Houston in 1972, Leland easily won one of them. In the Legislature, he sought to be a spokesman for a wide spectrum of black interests.

Muting the militance of his student years, he won a seat on the Democratic National Committee in 1976. But he continued to draw his basic support from liberal elements among white and Mexican-American groups and from poorer blacks. When Leland ran for Congress in 1978, these constituencies combined to give him a near-majority of the vote in the seven-way Democratic primary. In the runoff, he won by a comfortable margin over state Rep. Anthony Hall, a businessman and favorite of labor. Leland has had no serious opposition since then.

**The District.** Houston's inner-city 18th District was created by the Texas Legislature in 1971. It contains most of the city's black community and is also nearly one-third Hispanic.

The 18th is the most staunchly Democratic district in the state. It gave a higher percentage of its vote to George McGovern in 1972 and to Carter in 1976 than any district in Texas.

Besides its minority areas, the district includes downtown Houston, dotted with corporate headquarters for oil and gas industries, plus the port of Houston. Like many other urban areas around the country, the 18th decreased in population in the 1970s. It was one of only two districts in Texas to do so.

## Committees

**District of Columbia** (4th of 6 Democrats)
Judiciary and Education.

**Energy and Commerce** (18th of 24 Democrats)
Energy Conservation and Power; Fossil and Synthetic Fuels; Health and the Environment.

**Post Office and Civil Service** (6th of 15 Democrats)
Postal Personnel and Modernization, Chairman; Census and Population.

## Elections

**1980 General**

| | |
|---|---|
| Mickey Leland (D ) | 71,985 (80 %) |
| C. L. Kennedy (R ) | 16,128 (18 %) |

**1978 General**

| | |
|---|---|
| Mickey Leland (D ) | 36,783 (97 %) |

**1978 Primary Runoff**

| | |
|---|---|
| Mickey Leland (D ) | 15,587 (57 %) |
| Anthony Hall (D ) | 11,821 (43 %) |

**1978 Primary**

| | |
|---|---|
| Mickey Leland (D ) | 17,946 (48 %) |
| Anthony Hall (D ) | 9,003 (24 %) |
| Judson Robinson (D ) | 6,091 (16 %) |
| Jack Linville (D ) | 2,062 (5 %) |

**District Vote For President**

| | 1980 | | 1976 | | 1972 |
|---|---|---|---|---|---|
| D | 67,361 (72 %) | D | 82,608 (75 %) | D | 72,717 (67 %) |
| R | 23,051 (25 %) | R | 26,606 (24 %) | R | 35,701 (33 %) |
| I | 2,633 (3 %) | | | | |

## Campaign Finance

| | Receipts | Receipts from PACs | Expenditures |
|---|---|---|---|
| **1980** | | | |
| Leland (D ) | $125,554 | $63,795 (51 %) | $115,216 |
| **1978** | | | |
| Leland (D ) | $258,367 | $37,450 (14 %) | $258,366 |

## Voting Studies

| | Presidential Support | | Party Unity | | Conservative Coalition | |
|---|---|---|---|---|---|---|
| Year | S | O | S | O | S | O |
| 1980 | 62 | 21 | 78 | 6 | 4 | 84 |
| 1979 | 81 | 16 | 91 | 4 | 10 | 88 |

S = Support          O = Opposition

## Key Votes

**96th Congress**

| | |
|---|---|
| Weaken Carter oil profits tax (1979) | N |
| Reject hospital cost control plan (1979) | N |
| Implement Panama Canal Treaties (1979) | Y |
| Establish Department of Education (1979) | Y |
| Approve Anti-busing Amendment (1979) | N |
| Guarantee Chrysler Corp. loans (1979) | Y |
| Approve military draft registration (1980) | N |
| Aid Sandinista regime in Nicaragua (1980) | Y |
| Strengthen fair housing laws (1980) | Y |

**97th Congress**

| | |
|---|---|
| Reagan budget proposal (1981) | N |

## Interest Group Ratings

| Year | ADA | ACA | AFL-CIO | CCUS |
|---|---|---|---|---|
| 1980 | 83 | 5 | 100 | 67 |
| 1979 | 84 | 0 | 84 | 6 |

# 19 Kent Hance (D)

**Of Lubbock — Elected 1978**

**Born:** Nov. 14, 1942, Dimmitt, Texas.
**Education:** Texas Tech U., B.B.A. 1965; U. of
Texas Law School, LL.B. 1968.
**Profession:** Lawyer.
**Family:** Wife, Carol Hays; two children.
**Religion:** Baptist.
**Political Career:** Texas Senate, 1975-79.

**In Washington:** Hance took a political
chance in 1981 when he agreed to be the Democratic co-sponsor of President Reagan's tax bill on
the Ways and Means Committee. He brought
himself national publicity, but also earned some
resentment from his party's leaders, who placed
him on Ways and Means at the start of the year.

"It puts you on the opposite side from some
of your best friends," Hance admitted after the
decision, "and some people that have helped you.
That's unpleasant, but it can't be helped."

Hance's role as a Democratic ally of Reagan
grew out of his work with the Democratic Forum,
the organization of conservative Democrats in the
House. By backing the President's three-year, 25
percent tax cut, Hance helped build the name
recognition that could be useful to him in future
statewide Texas politics. He also gave Reagan's
tax bill the bipartisan label that the Reagan
budget had with the help of Hance's rival in the
Texas delegation, conservative Democrat Phil
Gramm.

In the previous Congress, Hance used his
down-home style to win election as president of
his Democratic freshman class, giving him a position other members have used to long-term political advantage in past years. Hance was well to the
right of most House Democrats, but the new
members elected in 1978 had a conservative tilt,
and Texas had seven people in that group, more
than any other state.

Some of those same qualities helped him two
years later, when he sought a place on Ways and
Means to defend his district's oil industry. House
leaders had promised to be more responsive to
conservatives on committee assignments, and
they gave Hance what he wanted, not quite realiz-
ing what he planned to do in the job..

Even before he made it to Ways and Means,
Hance concentrated on oil. Before the House
considered the windfall profits tax in 1979, he
wrote to his colleagues pressing the case for an
exemption for independent producers. Later he
joined other Texans in urging that royalty holders
and smaller independents, covered in the legislation as it became law, be exempted from the tax.

On the Agriculture Committee in 1979, he
joined the bloc of southerners who tempered their
fiscal conservatism with generous proposals for
agricultural relief. In the spring of 1979, under
pressure from militant west Texas wheat and
cattle growers, Hance proposed increases in feed
grain target prices higher than the 7 percent
beyond which President Carter promised a veto.
Later in the Congress, with farmers newly upset
over the president's grain embargo, Hance argued
for committee approval of his proposal to increase
price support loan rates to 65 percent of parity, a
higher figure than initially proposed. But the bill
never became law.

**At Home.** In winning this sprawling west
Texas district, Hance became only the second
man to represent it since its creation in 1934.
George Mahon, chairman of the House Appropriations Committee from 1965 to 1979, won 22
elections, most with very little opposition.

Republicans had high hopes of capturing the
district upon Mahon's retirement. Gerald R. Ford
carried it for president in 1976 with 57 percent of
the vote, and Mahon himself had been held to
54.6 percent in his final campaign that year.

But the Republicans had a bitterly divisive
nominating contest in 1978, choosing George W.
Bush, son of the current vice president, in a run-

**19th District: Northwest — Lub-
bock, Midland.** Population: 543,553 (17%
increase since 1970). Race: White 447,530
(82%), Black 30,745 (6%), Others 65,278
(12%). Spanish origin: 126,262 (23%).

off against former Odessa Mayor Jim Reese. Reese had run a surprisingly strong race against Mahon two years earlier and expected to be given the Republican nomination for a second try. He had the endorsement of Reagan.

But Bush, a young independent oil and gas producer, spent heavily. And with strong support in his home base of Midland County, he was able to offset Reese's edge in the other 16 counties.

Hance's route to the Democratic nomination was much less controversial. He defeated a fundamentalist minister from Lubbock by a margin of nearly 2-1. Hance was closely identified with district interests, having served in the state Senate as chairman of the water subcommittee. Water is an ever-present concern in the dry flatlands of west Texas.

In the general election, Bush was crippled further by his image as a wealthy outsider with an eastern background and Ivy League education. Hance, on the other hand, was born and educated in the district. It was, as one observer said, Yale against Texas Tech, and in west Texas, that is no contest.

**The District.** Hance notwithstanding, the 19th has evolved into one of the most Republican districts in Texas, with Lubbock, Midland and the district's portion of Odessa serving as the core of the GOP surge.

The Midland-Odessa area, in particular, has attracted oil entrepreneurs from outside the state who are not tied to Texas' long Democratic traditions. The area gave nearly three-quarters of its vote to Reagan in 1980 and has given similarly large shares to state and congressional GOP candidates in recent years.

While nearly always in the Republican column these days, the agricultural center of Lubbock has a larger Democratic vote. The city includes Texas Tech, and has a significant Hispanic population. One television station in the city broadcasts in Spanish.

Republicans have also made inroads in the Democratic farming and ranching counties. Carter carried most of them in in 1976, but four years later Reagan swept them all.

## Committees

**Ways and Means** (21st of 23 Democrats)
Public Assistance and Unemployment Compensation; Trade.

## Elections

**1980 General**

| | |
|---|---|
| Kent Hance (D ) | 126,632 (94 %) |
| J. D. Webster (LI) | 8,792 (6 %) |

**1978 General**

| | |
|---|---|
| Kent Hance (D ) | 54,729 (53 %) |
| George Bush (R ) | 48,070 (47 %) |

**1978 Primary**

| | |
|---|---|
| Kent Hance (D ) | 46,505 (64 %) |
| Morris Sheats (D ) | 25,791 (36 %) |

**District Vote For President**

| | 1980 | | 1976 | | 1972 |
|---|---|---|---|---|---|
| D | 48,082 (27 %) | D | 68,836 (42 %) | D | 34,307 (23 %) |
| R | 122,673 (70 %) | R | 93,983 (57 %) | R | 111,197 (76 %) |
| I | 3,461 (2 %) | | | | |

## Campaign Finance

| | Receipts | Receipts from PACs | Expenditures |
|---|---|---|---|
| **1980** | | | |
| Hance (D ) | $116,7981 | $27,543 (24 %) | $106,573 |

| **1978** | | | |
|---|---|---|---|
| Hance (D ) | $334,299 | $51,150 (15 %) | $314,110 |
| Bush (R ) | $441,518 | $40,717 (9 %) | $434,909 |

## Voting Studies

| | Presidential Support | | Party Unity | | Conservative Coalition | |
|---|---|---|---|---|---|---|
| Year | S | O | S | O | S | O |
| 1980 | 55 | 33 | 51 | 37 | 69 | 18 |
| 1979 | 37 | 61 | 32 | 63 | 91 | 5 |

S = Support          O = Opposition

## Key Votes

**96th Congress**

| | |
|---|---|
| Weaken Carter oil profits tax (1979) | Y |
| Reject hospital cost control plan (1979) | Y |
| Implement Panama Canal Treaties (1979) | N |
| Establish Department of Education (1979) | N |
| Approve Anti-busing Amendment (1979) | Y |
| Guarantee Chrysler Corp. loans (1979) | Y |
| Approve military draft registration (1980) | Y |
| Aid Sandinista regime in Nicaragua (1980) | N |
| Strengthen fair housing laws (1980) | Y |

**97th Congress**

| | |
|---|---|
| Reagan budget proposal (1981) | Y |

## Interest Group Ratings

| Year | ADA | ACA | AFL-CIO | CCUS |
|---|---|---|---|---|
| 1980 | 11 | 43 | 26 | 83 |
| 1979 | 0 | 83 | 20 | 89 |

# 20 Henry B. Gonzalez (D)

**Of San Antonio — Elected 1961**

**Born:** May 3, 1916, San Antonio, Texas.
**Education:** Attended San Antonio Junior College, 1934-37; attended U. of Texas at Austin, 1938-39; St. Mary's U. School of Law, LL.B. 1943.
**Profession:** Lawyer; probation.
**Family:** Wife, Bertha Cuellar; eight children.
**Religion:** Roman Catholic.
**Political Career:** San Antonio City Council, 1953-56; Texas Senate, 1957-61.

**In Washington:** Gonzalez has been a fighter from the beginning of his congressional career, sometimes conducting lonely crusades of principle, but more often waging what seem to be inflated personal quarrels.

Only one of them has led to violence — a 1963 dispute in which he threatened to pistol-whip a Texas colleague and then actually hit him in the shoulder on the House floor. Since then, Gonzalez has stuck to invective, but has used generous doses of it.

He used his rhetoric effectively at the start of the 97th Congress, when seniority placed him in line for the chairmanship of the important Housing Subcommittee on Banking. Some of his committee colleagues, considering Gonzalez a bit eccentric for such a sensitive job, wanted to give it to a California Democrat, Jerry Patterson.

Gonzalez hinted that if he were denied the chairmanship, he might consider bolting the Democratic Party, taking some of his Hispanic followers in Texas with him. Speaker O'Neill put down the rebellion at once.

In his early months as chairman, Gonzalez moved quickly to report a $42.5 billion housing bill out of his subcommittee. But its funding levels were far over the amount called for in the 1982 budget, and it was scaled back by $9 billion at the full committee level.

Gonzalez attracted national attention in 1977 during his brief tenure as chairman of the House Assassinations Committee, set up to investigate the Kennedy and King murders. The committee hired Richard Sprague, a respected Philadelphia prosecutor, to head the probe. But within weeks Sprague and Gonzalez were enemies. The chairman called his top aide an "unconscionable scoundrel," accused him of misusing committee funds and fired him.

A week later, with the committee in an uproar, Gonzalez himself quit, saying that the investigation could never work because "vast and powerful forces, including the country's most sophisticated crime element, won't stand for it." Gonzalez described himself as "an honest, direct man who wouldn't hold still for a transparent phony like Sprague."

A few years before, Gonzalez had been nearly as intemperate against Walter F. Mondale, then the senior senator from Minnesota. He became indignant when Mondale sent an aide to investigate school desegregation in San Antonio without informing the congressman's office. Gonzalez accused Mondale of a "grave breach of the courtesy to which I would be entitled even if I were not among your friends."

"If you want none of my friendship or support," he told Mondale, "I will be happy to accommodate you."

None of Gonzalez's later quarrels have surprised members who were present on Oct. 29, 1963, when he asked Texas Republican Rep. Ed Foreman whether he had in fact called Gonzalez a communist. Foreman replied that he had said Gonzalez's "left-wing voting record" helped serve the socialist-communist cause.

"I might pistol whip you, the way they do in Texas," Gonzalez snapped, and when Foreman challenged him to do it, Gonzalez took a swing at

**20th District: San Antonio.** Population: 423,610 (9% decrease since 1970). Race: White 309,771 (73%), Black 41,354 (10%), Others 72,485 (17%). Spanish origin: 287,330 (68%).

him. In a statement later, Gonzalez linked Foreman with "switch-blade knife wielding character assassins who are trying to spoil our way of life."

Gonzalez's last few years in the House have been quieter, but the passion has not completely disappeared. Every few weeks during the 96th Congress, when the legislative day was over and everyone else had left the House floor, Gonzalez rose to warn the empty chamber about the murder of Judge John W. Wood in San Antonio in 1979 and of his suspicions of organized crime's involvement in the killing.

"There is a joinder between the criminal element and the political, the government," he said in one speech. "You name it, organized crime is in it, and it is operating so successfully and so well that even the fronts are undetected in the main."

These speeches against the Mafia are typical of another side of Gonzalez's career — his love for crusades. A longtime Texas civil rights fighter, he arrived on the House floor for his 1962 swearing-in ceremony already carrying a bill to repeal the poll tax. In his first term he was one of a handful of members to oppose creation of a private corporation to operate a communications satellite system. And unlike the rest of them, he never gave up the issue, referring to himself for years as "the man that fought the Telstar giveaway." He waged an unceasing battle against the "Bracero" program for immigrant Mexican workers, calling it "slave labor." More recently, he has fought an uncompromising battle against nuclear power; he introduced legislation that would phase out all existing nuclear facilities.

Gonzalez wanted a spot on the Armed Services Committee when he came to Washington, but was placed on the Banking Committee instead and has been there ever since. By 1973, he was chairman of the subcommittee dealing with international finance. During most of his tenure at that subcommittee, however, he tended to defer to junior subcommittee members in preparing complex legislation on the World Bank and other lending institutions. Gonzalez has added language to foreign aid bills authorizing the government to deny U.S. loan support to nations which expropriate private American property.

Another Gonzalez amendment, to the 1974 Safe Drinking Water Act, bars federal water aid to areas with contaminated drinking supplies.

**At Home.** It took years of campaigning and frequent defeat before Gonzalez established the impregnable position he has in San Antonio politics today.

Since he won a 1961 special election, Gonzalez has had no trouble returning to the House. He has never had primary opposition, and the closest the Republicans have come was in 1964, when Gonzalez still won nearly two-thirds of the vote.

But it was different in the beginning for Gonzalez, the son of Mexican-American parents in San Antonio, who began climbing the local political ladder after military service in World War II. He ran for office while helping his father, the managing editor of a Spanish-language newspaper, operate a translation service.

Gonzalez made it to the state Senate in 1956, and quickly drew attention by filibustering against Democratic Gov. Price Daniel's bill to allow the state to close schools threatened by disturbances surrounding integration.

In 1958, Gonzalez ran as the liberal alternative to Daniel in the Democratic gubernatorial primary. He was beaten by a margin of more than 3-to-1, but the defeat only encouraged his ambition. Three years later, he sought the Senate seat vacated by Lyndon B. Johnson. While Gonzalez carried his home base, Bexar County, his statewide appeal as a Hispanic candidate was limited. But he ran sixth with 9 percent of the vote.

But he soon had another chance. Later in 1961, Democrat Paul Kilday resigned from the House to accept a judgeship, and Gonzalez emerged as the consensus Democratic candidate.

The special election presented a clear liberal-conservative choice. Gonzalez, as a member of the board of directors of the Americans for Democratic Action, was warmly endorsed by the Kennedy administration. Republican John Goode, a former GOP county chairman, had the active assistance of Barry Goldwater and Texas' newly elected Republican senator, John Tower.

With strong support in Hispanic areas, Gonzalez won with 55 percent of the vote. He became the first person of Mexican-American extraction to be elected to the House from Texas.

**The District.** Gonzalez' district has grown more compact and more Democratic during his two decades in Congress. When he was first elected in 1961, the 20th included all of Bexar County — an area that Kennedy had carried the previous year but with only 54 percent of the vote.

In 1966, redistricting pared away the rural and suburban portions of Bexar County, leaving Gonzales anchored in the heavily Hispanic and loyally Democratic city of San Antonio. Humphrey swept the district in 1968 with 71 percent of the vote, and since then Democratic candidates at all levels usually have won there easily.

The 20th District is one of the poorest in Texas, although it contains most of San Antonio's

**1195**

industry and major tourist attractions, including the Alamo. In the district or nearby are several big military bases which provide a major source of income for the city.

## Committees

**Banking, Finance and Urban Affairs** (3rd of 25 Democrats)
Housing and Community Development, chairman; Consumer Affairs and Coinage; General Oversight and Renegotiation.

**Small Business** (4th of 23 Democrats)
Antitrust and Restraint of Trade Activities Affecting Small Business; SBA and SBIC Authority, Minority Enterprise and General Small Business Problems.

## Elections

**1980 General**

| | |
|---|---|
| Henry Gonzalez (D) | 84,113 (82 %) |
| Merle Nash (R) | 17,725 (17 %) |

**1978 General**

| | |
|---|---|
| Henry Gonzalez (D) | Unopposed |

**Previous Winning Percentages**

| | | | |
|---|---|---|---|
| 1976 (100%) | 1974 (100%) | 1972 (97 %) | 1970 (100%) |
| 1968 (82 %) | 1966 (87 %) | 1964 (65 %) | 1962 (100%) |
| 1961* (55 %) | | | |

*Special election

**District Vote For President**

| | 1980 | | 1976 | | 1972 |
|---|---|---|---|---|---|
| D | 73,682 (69 %) | D | 78,572 (73 %) | D | 56,831 (60 %) |
| R | 29,400 (28 %) | R | 27,429 (26 %) | R | 37,438 (40 %) |
| I | 2,480 (2 %) | | | | |

## Campaign Finance

| | Receipts | Receipts from PACs | Expenditures |
|---|---|---|---|
| **1980** | | | |
| Gonzalez (D) | $37,296 | $14,300 (38 %) | $51,385 |
| Nash (R) | $17,170 | $425 (2 %) | $17,190 |
| **1978** | | | |
| Gonzalez (D) | $28,397 | $5,000 (18 %) | $28,703 |

## Voting Studies

| | Presidential Support | | Party Unity | | Conservative Coalition | |
|---|---|---|---|---|---|---|
| Year | S | O | S | O | S | O |
| 1980 | 76 | 20 | 90 | 5 | 22 | 73 |
| 1979 | 81 | 16 | 87 | 10 | 24 | 74 |
| 1978 | 56 | 39 | 73 | 23 | 41 | 56 |
| 1977 | 48 | 28 | 60 | 27 | 42 | 46 |

| | | | | | | |
|---|---|---|---|---|---|---|
| 1976 | 35 | 63 | 71 | 26 | 42 | 53 |
| 1975 | 34 | 52 | 61 | 26 | 41 | 45 |
| 1974 (Ford) | 37 | 59 | | | | |
| 1974 | 62 | 38 | 70 | 27 | 44 | 51 |
| 1973 | 26 | 71 | 81 | 15 | 31 | 62 |
| 1972 | 49 | 51 | 83 | 17 | 29 | 71 |
| 1971 | 60 | 39 | 81 | 18 | 37 | 62 |
| 1970 | 62 | 38 | 86 | 14 | 27 | 73 |
| 1969 | 62 | 38 | 89 | 11 | 22 | 78 |
| 1968 | 94 | 6 | 100 | 0 | 6 | 94 |
| 1967 | 88 | 11 | 99 | 1 | 6 | 94 |
| 1966 | 91 | 6 | 99 | 0 | 3 | 95 |
| 1965 | 92 | 7 | 98 | 0 | 4 | 96 |
| 1964 | 96 | 2 | 98 | 2 | 8 | 92 |
| 1963 | 93 | 3 | 98 | 0 | 13 | 73 |
| 1962 | 87 | 8 | 93 | 4† | 0 | 100 |

† Not eligible for all recorded votes.

S = Support      O = Opposition

## Key Votes

**96th Congress**

| | |
|---|---|
| Weaken Carter oil profits tax (1979) | N |
| Reject hospital cost control plan (1979) | N |
| Implement Panama Canal Treaties (1979) | ? |
| Establish Department of Education (1979) | Y |
| Approve Anti-busing Amendment (1979) | N |
| Guarantee Chrysler Corp. loans (1979) | Y |
| Approve military draft registration (1980) | Y |
| Aid Sandinista regime in Nicaragua (1980) | Y |
| Strengthen fair housing laws (1980) | Y |

**97th Congress**

| | |
|---|---|
| Reagan budget proposal (1981) | N |

## Interest Group Ratings

| Year | ADA | ACA | AFL-CIO | CCUS |
|---|---|---|---|---|
| 1980 | 72 | 17 | 79 | 56 |
| 1979 | 74 | 8 | 84 | 22 |
| 1978 | 70 | 26 | 95 | 24 |
| 1977 | 30 | 36 | 90 | 33 |
| 1976 | 50 | 37 | 90 | 21 |
| 1975 | 42 | 32 | 77 | 33 |
| 1974 | 43 | 43 | 90 | 38 |
| 1973 | 60 | 19 | 91 | 27 |
| 1972 | 56 | 26 | 100 | 22 |
| 1971 | 57 | 32 | 92 | - |
| 1970 | 64 | 11 | 100 | 0 |
| 1969 | 67 | 12 | 80 | - |
| 1968 | 100 | 0 | 100 | - |
| 1967 | 93 | 3 | 100 | 10 |
| 1966 | 88 | 7 | 100 | - |
| 1965 | 89 | 4 | 100 | 10 |
| 1964 | 96 | 0 | 100 | - |
| 1963 | - | 0 | - | - |
| 1962 | 88 | 9 | 80 | - |

# 21 Tom Loeffler (R)

**Of Hunt — Elected 1978**

**Born:** Aug. 1, 1946, Fredericksburg, Texas.
**Education:** U. of Texas, B.B.A. 1968, J.D. 1971.
**Profession:** Lawyer, rancher.
**Family:** Wife, Kathy Crawford; two children.
**Religion:** Lutheran.
**Political Career:** No previous office.

**In Washington:** Well-prepared for a House career after doing legislative work for Republican John Tower in the Senate and Gerald Ford in the White House, Loeffler was surprisingly quiet in his first two years as a junior House member.

But he was not idle. Loeffler spent much of the 96th Congress building relationships with the large bloc of conservative Texas Democrats. By the start of 1981, Republicans were relying on him as a deputy whip and liaison man across the aisle, one who could help build bipartisan conservative majorities for new Reagan programs. He played a similar role in the Ford White House, where he specialized in lobbying Southern Democrats to sustain Ford vetoes.

Loeffler has also shown some skill at going to bat for his district in critical situations.

The most important one came during floor consideration of the railroad deregulation bill in 1980. Loeffler's main goal, as it had been in markup at the Commerce Committee, was to protect San Antonio's publicly-owned power company. It had switched most of its capacity from oil to coal over three years and had seen its fuel transportation costs go up 260 percent. "A monopolistic railroad," he complained, "has absolutely gouged the consumer."

Normally among the most militant of free-enterprise advocates, Loeffler insisted on preserving enough rail regulation to keep San Antonio's future coal transit costs under control. Through weeks of haggling with the bill's manager, New Jersey Democrat James Florio, he won permission to insert language restraining future freight costs in the particular situation he was worried about. Once he had that, Loeffler went along with Florio in backing the bill, disappointing Texas Democrat Bob Eckhardt, his original ally in behalf of other state utilities.

On broader Commerce Committee issues, Loeffler's major legislative interests are the oil and gas industries, a dominant presence in much of his district. Early in 1979, he teamed with Clarence Brown, R-Ohio, on an amendment in a Commerce subcommittee to deregulate crude oil prices; it failed by only one vote. Two days later, President Carter announced his own deregulation plan, making the Republican effort moot. After that, Loeffler worked on a proposal to exempt oil royalty holders and independent producers from the already-passed windfall profits tax, a move which would delight the thousands of his constituents who collect regular checks for leasing their land to drillers. Loeffler left Commerce for Appropriations in 1981.

Loeffler's voting record is about as conservative as is possible. In his first year, he did not cast a single vote against the "conservative coalition" of Republicans and Southern Democrats.

**At Home.** Loeffler was one of the few success stories among Texas Republican House candidates in 1978. With eight open seats to aim for that year, the GOP had high hopes of making major inroads in the state's Democratic-dominated congressional delegation. But they won only one of the eight — the 21st, with Loeffler.

A native Texan, Loeffler is descended from the German immigrants who settled near San Antonio in the last century. He came to Washington after getting his law degree and went to work for Tower. From there, still in his 20s, he went on to the Ford administration.

Loeffler returned to Texas after the 1976 election, establishing himself as a rancher and

---

**21st District: South central — San Antonio, San Angelo.** Population: 678,379 (45% increase since 1970). Race: White 601,543 (89%), Black 17,002 (3%), Others 59,834 (9%). Spanish origin: 176,471 (26%).

lawyer in rural Kerr County, about 50 miles northwest of San Antonio. When Democratic Rep. Robert Krueger decided to quit the seat in order to run for the Senate, Loeffler jumped into the race to succeed him. He had little trouble winning the GOP primary in a weak field, defeating his nearest rival by better than 3-to-1.

In the general election, Loeffler stressed his Washington experience. Ford had carried the 21st easily two years earlier, and Loeffler underscored his party ties by bringing in the ex-president and Ronald Reagan to campaign for him.

The race was expensive. Both Loeffler and his Democratic rival, former state Sen. Nelson Wolff, spent more than $400,000. But the Republican won comfortably, defeating Wolff in most of the rural counties as well as the populous Republican suburbs of San Antonio. His victory broke a long Democratic hold on the 21st District seat.

Loeffler had no trouble retaining the seat in 1980, encountering no primary opposition and only a nominal Democratic challenge.

**The District.** The Republican complexion of the 21st was established in 1966, when the Bexar County suburbs of San Antonio were added to the conservative cotton-growing and ranching country to the north and west.

Redistricting since then has extended the district westward, and it is now larger than the state of Pennsylvania. But the Bexar County portion still has more than half the electorate.

Republican presidential candidates have easily swept the district in every election since 1968. But while the GOP mounted some strong challenges against Democratic House incumbents O. C. Fisher (who retired in 1974) and Krueger, the Democratic heritage of the rural counties in state and local voting prevented Republicans from capturing the seat until 1978.

## Committees

**Appropriations** (19th of 22 Republicans)
Interior; Military Construction.

## Elections

**1980 General**

| | |
|---|---|
| Tom Loeffler (R ) | 196,424 (77 %) |
| Joe Sullivan (D ) | 58,425 (23 %) |

**1978 General**

| | |
|---|---|
| Tom Loeffler (R) | 84,336 (57 %) |
| Nelson Wolff (D ) | 63,501 (43 %) |

**1978 Primary**

| | |
|---|---|
| Tom Loeffler (R ) | 8,779 (59 %) |
| Wallace Larsen (R) | 2,558 (17 %) |
| Neil Calnan (R ) | 2,007 (14 %) |
| Bobby Locke (R ) | 1,433 (10 %) |

**District Vote For President**

| | 1980 | | 1976 | | 1972 |
|---|---|---|---|---|---|
| D | 79,367 (30 %) | D | 85,953 (40 %) | D | 38,082 (24 %) |
| R | 177,764 (67 %) | R | 127,268 (59 %) | R | 121,044 (76 %) |
| I | 7,428 (3 %) | | | | |

## Campaign Finance

| | Receipts | Receipts from PACs | Expen- ditures |
|---|---|---|---|
| **1980** | | | |
| Loeffler (R ) | $488,522 | $120,925 (25 %) | $344,199 |
| Sullivan (D ) | $45,382 | $1,000 (2 %) | $45,382 |

**1978**

| | | | |
|---|---|---|---|
| Loeffler (R ) | $406,300 | $68,662 (17 %) | $402,299 |
| Wolff (D ) | $440,255 | $32,750 (7 %) | $438,013 |

## Voting Studies

| | Presidential Support | | Party Unity | | Conservative Coalition | |
|---|---|---|---|---|---|---|
| Year | S | O | S | O | S | O |
| 1980 | 32 | 67 | 93 | 7 | 96 | 4 |
| 1979 | 22 | 74 | 94 | 4 | 97 | 0 |

S = Support          O = Opposition

## Key Votes

**96th Congress**

| | |
|---|---|
| Weaken Carter oil profits tax (1979) | Y |
| Reject hospital cost control plan (1979) | Y |
| Implement Panama Canal Treaties (1979) | N |
| Establish Department of Education (1979) | N |
| Approve Anti-busing Amendment (1979) | Y |
| Guarantee Chrysler Corp. loans (1979) | X |
| Approve military draft registration (1980) | Y |
| Aid Sandinista regime in Nicaragua (1980) | N |
| Strengthen fair housing laws (1980) | N |

**97th Congress**

| | |
|---|---|
| Reagan budget proposal (1981) | Y |

## Interest Group Ratings

| Year | ADA | ACA | AFL-CIO | CCUS |
|---|---|---|---|---|
| 1980 | 0 | 92 | 11 | 73 |
| 1979 | 0 | 100 | 10 | 100 |

# 22 Ron Paul (R)

**Of Lake Jackson — Elected 1978**
Also served April 1976 - Jan. 1977.

**Born:** Aug. 20, 1935, Pittsburgh, Pa.
**Education:** Gettysburg College, B.A. 1957; Duke U. Medical School, M.D. 1961.
**Military Career:** Air Force, 1963-65.
**Profession:** Physician.
**Family:** Wife, Carol Wells; five children.
**Religion:** Episcopalian.
**Political Career:** Elected to U.S. House in special election, April 1976; unsuccessful candidate for re-election, 1976; re-elected to U.S. House, 1978.

**In Washington:** It is not always easy to tell whether Ron Paul is a conservative or a radical. His militant arguments in favor of free enterprise place him squarely in alliance with most of his GOP colleagues, but his insistence on carrying them to their ultimate conclusion leaves him with little ideological company. When he voted against the final Reagan budget in 1981 on the grounds that it did not cut spending deeply enough, he was alone among House Republicans.

For most conservatives, fiscal restraint stops at the water's edge — it does not apply to spending for defense. In Paul's opinion, it does. Bitterly anti-communist, he remains reluctant to place the full coercive power of the federal government behind an agressive foreign policy.

When the 1981 defense budget passed the House 351-42 in 1980, Paul opposed it alongside 41 dovish liberals with whom he had little else in common. Earlier, when draft registration was approved, he told conservatives they seemed more interested in registering their children than their guns. "I don't see how we as conservatives can defend the marketplace and private property," he said, "if we don't maintain that a man's life is his and not the government's."

Paul has enhanced his loner status by attacking many of the perks of congressional office, including salary increases and foreign travel. He offered a resolution to freeze salaries and then *reduce* them as the cost of living goes up and another to require three-fourths approval when a member wants to go abroad at federal expense.

Another of Paul's crusades is for gold, which he considers the only sound basis for national currency. He describes himself as "the foremost advocate of a gold dollar in Washington" and argues that current paper dollars should be legal tender only for the payment of federal taxes.

One issue on which Paul has been a conventional conservative is energy. He has long favored immediate decontrol of oil and natural gas, development of nuclear power and abolition of the "energy bureaucracy in Washington." In 1980, he cast a libertarian vote against federal help for the synthetic fuels industry. "Beside this," he said, "the federal bailouts of Lockheed and Penn Central pale into insignificance."

**At Home.** Paul's libertarian record has made it hard for him to solidify his grip on a district with a large blue-collar and minority population.

Since Democrat Bob Casey resigned in 1976 to take a seat on the Federal Maritime Commission, Paul has been in and out of Congress. He won an April 1976 special election over Democrat Bob Gammage, lost a rematch in November and then ousted Gammage in 1978. In 1980, he won re-election over Houston lawyer Mike Andrews. Each election has been close; the latter two with Gammage were decided by less than 1,500 votes.

Paul made his political debut in 1974 against the popular Casey, whose credentials were also conservative. Paul lost badly, but he made valuable conservative fund-raising contacts.

When the seat became vacant in 1976, Paul was ready. Bolstered by the effective organization assembled for Ronald Reagan's Texas primary

---

**22nd District: Southern Harris County — Fort Bend, Brazoria County.** Population: 711,212 (52% increase since 1970). Race: White 526,141 (74%), Black 123,157 (17%), Others 61,914 (9%). Spanish origin: 99,116 (14%).

## Ron Paul, R-Texas

campaign, he defeated Gammage by 8,500 votes in a run-off after narrowly trailing the Democrat in the initial race. National New Right groups helped him wage an expensive media campaign which painted the labor-backed Gammage as an ultra-liberal and an inappropriate successor to Casey.

But in November, Gammage defeated him by 268 votes, helped by strong backing from blacks and labor and a high Democratic turnout. Paul claimed voting irregularities and, after a recount, unsuccessfully appealed to the House and Texas courts. Altogether, he spent more than $550,000 to serve a few months in Congress.

Out of office, Paul became secretary of labor in a New Right shadow Cabinet. But he challenged Gammage again in 1978. Gammage had lost the support of some blacks, unions and women's groups by seeking a more centrist image. The result was a 1,200-vote victory for Paul.

Incumbency has not led to security. Paul's opposition to federal funding for the Houston Medical Center cost him the backing in 1980 of important elements of the city's business community, which endorsed his Democratic opponent. But helped by Reagan's strong vote in the district, Paul registered a narrow victory.

**The District.** The 22nd District takes in much of the urban sprawl that developed in southern Harris County (Houston) and has spread into Brazoria and Fort Bend counties as a result of the area's booming economy. The district is the home of the Manned Spacecraft Center.

As one of the most prosperous constituencies in the state, the 22nd has attracted a large influx of new voters — some from the North, others from small-town and rural parts of Texas. They are largely independent politically and open to appeals from either party. The district also contains a significant black and Hispanic element, although the bulk of Houston's minority population is in the 18th District.

## Committees

**Banking, Finance and Urban Affairs** (8th of 19 Republicans)
Domestic Monetary Policy; Economic Stabilization; General Oversight and Renegotiation.

## Elections

**1980 General**

| | |
|---|---|
| Ron Paul (R ) | 106,797 (51 %) |
| Mike Andrews (D ) | 101,094 (48 %) |

**1978 General**

| | |
|---|---|
| Ron Paul (R ) | 54,643 (51 %) |
| Bob Gammage (D ) | 53,443 (49 %) |

**Previous Winning Percentage**

1976* (56 %)

*Special election run-off

**District Vote For President**

| | 1980 | | 1976 | | 1972 |
|---|---|---|---|---|---|
| D | 81,665 (39 %) | D | 95,479 (49 %) | D | 52,290 (35 %) |
| R | 118,103 (57 %) | R | 95,998 (50 %) | R | 96,814 (65 %) |
| I | 6,320 (3 %) | | | | |

## Campaign Finance

| | Receipts | Receipts from PACs | Expen-ditures |
|---|---|---|---|
| **1980** | | | |
| Paul (R ) | $447,105 | $83,739 (19 %) | $359,558 |
| Andrews (D ) | $736,464 | $81,766 (11 %) | $729,979 |

| **1978** | | | |
|---|---|---|---|
| Paul (R ) | $323,458 | $61,870 (19 %) | $322,156 |
| Gammage (D ) | $478,044 | $153,403 (32 %) | $476,852 |

## Voting Studies

| | Presidential Support | | Party Unity | | Conservative Coalition | |
|---|---|---|---|---|---|---|
| Year | S | O | S | O | S | O |
| 1980 | 19 | 78 | 93 | 4 | 87 | 13 |
| 1979 | 22 | 76† | 90 | 9 | 85 | 15 |
| 1976 | 66 | 31† | 84 | 13† | 85 | 12† |

† Not eligible for all recorded votes.

S = Support     O = Opposition

## Key Votes

**96th Congress**

| | |
|---|---|
| Weaken Carter oil profits tax (1979) | Y |
| Reject hospital cost control plan (1979) | Y |
| Implement Panama Canal Treaties (1979) | N |
| Establish Department of Education (1979) | N |
| Approve Anti-busing Amendment (1979) | Y |
| Guarantee Chrysler Corp. loans (1979) | N |
| Approve military draft registration (1980) | N |
| Aid Sandinista regime in Nicaragua (1980) | N |
| Strengthen fair housing laws (1980) | N |

**97th Congress**

| | |
|---|---|
| Reagan budget proposal (1981) | Y |

## Interest Group Ratings

| Year | ADA | ACA | AFL-CIO | CCUS |
|---|---|---|---|---|
| 1980 | 22 | 92 | 5 | 58 |
| 1979 | 21 | 92 | 10 | 89 |
| 1976 | 14 | 94 | 6 | 86 |

**1200**

# 23 Abraham Kazen Jr. (D)

**Of Laredo — Elected 1966**

**Born:** Jan. 17, 1919, Laredo, Texas.
**Education:** Attended U. of Texas, 1937-40; Cumberland U. Law School, J.D. 1941.
**Military Career:** Air Force, 1942-45.
**Profession:** Lawyer.
**Family:** Wife, Consuelo Raymond; five children.
**Religion:** Roman Catholic.
**Political Career:** Texas House, 1947-53; Texas Senate, 1953-67.

**In Washington:** Like many Texas Democrats of his generation, Kazen started out as a Lyndon Johnson liberal. But he began moving right almost as soon as LBJ left town, and by 1980, he was voting with the "conservative coalition" 83 percent of the time. Echoes of his earlier record show up on education and housing bills that help his Hispanic constituency, but on few others.

Despite his shift to the right, Kazen has developed close ties with Speaker O'Neill by responding to occasional leadership pleas for loyalty and by filling in cheerfully as a presiding officer. After one grueling 3-day session with a foreign bill, Kazen drew a standing ovation and O'Neill gave him a gavel to keep. But he has a hot temper; in 1980, when James Weaver, D-Ore., launched a miniature filibuster on a Northwest power bill while Kazen was in the chair, the Texan became so angry that the entire issue had to be postponed for weeks.

Most of Kazen's legislative attention has been on Interior, where he works on irrigation and reclamation issues as chairman of the Water and Power Resources Subcommittee. In 1980, when his panel wrote a bill aimed at limiting federal water subsidies given to large farmers, Kazen was generally on the agribusiness side. He is a strong opponent of federal land use planning, as are most of the landowners in his district .

On Armed Services, Kazen watches matters affecting three large military facilities in his district, including Randolph Air Force Base in San Antonio, an Air Force personnel headquarters.

**At Home.** Over a 14-year career, Kazen has had as little serious opposition as any House member. No primary challenger has drawn more than a quarter of the vote against him. Republicans did not field anyone at all until 1980.

The son of a Lebanese immigrant, Kazen has held office ever since he returned from World War II. He was elected to the Texas House in 1946 and to the state Senate in 1952, where he served 14 years.

Kazen made his bid for Congress when the 23rd was created in 1966. With no incumbent running, he parlayed his name familiarity and the support of local political leaders into an easy victory.

Kazen has been criticized as insensitive to the district's large and impoverished Hispanic population, but he speaks fluent Spanish and has kept up good relations with Hispanic political leaders. A San Antonio public interest lawyer attempted to tap liberal Anglo and Hispanic dissatisfaction with Kazen in the 1980 Democratic primary, but the incumbent won by a 3-1 margin.

**The District.** The 23rd is a diverse district — ranging from conservative ranch country to liberal pockets around San Antonio. Hispanics comprise about half the population, but have not emerged as the dominant force. Most support traditional Democrats or do not vote.

About one-third of the district vote is cast in the Bexar County (San Antonio) portion. The only other population center is Laredo, a farming and livestock center on the Mexican border.

---

**23rd District: South — San Antonio, Laredo.** Population: 601,823 (29% increase since 1970). Race: White 501,255 (83%), Black 28,061 (5%), Others 72,507 (12%). Spanish origin: 319,556 (53%).

## Committees

**Armed Services** (13th of 25 Democrats)
Investigations; Military Installations and Facilities.

**Interior and Insular Affairs** (4th of 23 Democrats)
Water and Power Resources, chairman; Mines and Mining; Public Lands and National Parks.

## Elections

**1980 General**

| | |
|---|---|
| Abraham Kazen Jr. (D ) | 104,595 (70 %) |
| Bobby Locke (R ) | 45,139 (30 %) |

**1980 Primary**

| | |
|---|---|
| Abraham Kazen Jr. (D ) | 59,210 (76 %) |
| Paul Rich (D ) | 18,275 (24 %) |

**1978 General**

| | |
|---|---|
| Abraham Kazen Jr. (D ) | 69,649 (91 %) |
| Augustin Mata (LRU) | 7,185 (9 %) |

**Previous Winning Percentages**

1976 (100%)  1974 (100%)  1972 (100%)  1970 (100%)
1968 (100%)  1966 (96 %)

**District Vote For President**

| | 1980 | | 1976 | | 1972 |
|---|---|---|---|---|---|
| D | 77,745 (48 %) | D | 82,533 (59 %) | D | 44,390 (38 %) |
| R | 80,230 (50 %) | R | 56,555 (40 %) | R | 72,011 (62 %) |
| I | 3,130 (2 %) | | | | |

## Campaign Finance

| | Receipts | Receipts from PACs | Expen-ditures |
|---|---|---|---|
| **1980** | | | |
| Kazen (D ) | $333,781 | $78,402 (23 %) | $317,815 |
| Locke (R ) | $8,496 | $50 (1 %) | $8,516 |
| **1978** | | | |
| Kazen (D ) | $42,294 | $14,550 (34 %) | $55,734 |
| Mata (RU) | $3,543 | — (0 %) | $5,337 |

## Voting Studies

| Year | Presidential Support S | O | Party Unity S | O | Conservative Coalition S | O |
|---|---|---|---|---|---|---|
| 1980 | 49 | 33 | 61 | 29 | 61 | 34 |
| 1979 | 50 | 48 | 53 | 47 | 83 | 16 |
| 1978 | 38 | 55 | 40 | 49 | 74 | 16 |
| 1977 | 41 | 56 | 44 | 54 | 85 | 12 |
| 1976 | 53 | 45 | 43 | 55 | 89 | 10 |
| 1975 | 53 | 47 | 46 | 54 | 87 | 12 |
| 1974 (Ford) | 43 | 57 | | | | |
| 1974 | 57 | 32 | 52 | 37 | 60 | 22 |
| 1973 | 40 | 57 | 67 | 28 | 56 | 36 |
| 1972 | 49 | 46 | 57 | 36 | 59 | 30 |
| 1971 | 65 | 35 | 65 | 32 | 62 | 35 |
| 1970 | 58 | 38 | 69 | 26 | 59 | 36 |
| 1969 | 57 | 43 | 71 | 29 | 58 | 42 |
| 1968 | 77 | 17 | 78 | 16 | 35 | 59 |
| 1967 | 91 | 6 | 93 | 1 | 22 | 70 |

S = Support     O = Opposition

## Key Votes

**96th Congress**

| | |
|---|---|
| Weaken Carter oil profits tax (1979) | Y |
| Reject hospital cost control plan (1979) | Y |
| Implement Panama Canal Treaties (1979) | N |
| Establish Department of Education (1979) | Y |
| Approve Anti-busing Amendment (1979) | Y |
| Guarantee Chrysler Corp. loans (1979) | Y |
| Approve military draft registration (1980) | ? |
| Aid Sandinista regime in Nicaragua (1980) | Y |
| Strengthen fair housing laws (1980) | N |

**97th Congress**

| | |
|---|---|
| Reagan budget proposal (1981) | N |

## Interest Group Ratings

| Year | ADA | ACA | AFL-CIO | CCUS |
|---|---|---|---|---|
| 1980 | 22 | 30 | 44 | 62 |
| 1979 | 21 | 42 | 25 | 67 |
| 1978 | 10 | 64 | 33 | 71 |
| 1977 | 5 | 59 | 52 | 82 |
| 1976 | 15 | 68 | 61 | 57 |
| 1975 | 16 | 71 | 35 | 65 |
| 1974 | 13 | 46 | 56 | 78 |
| 1973 | 28 | 44 | 64 | 64 |
| 1972 | 13 | 45 | 64 | 40 |
| 1971 | 27 | 41 | 91 | - |
| 1970 | 28 | 39 | 71 | 30 |
| 1969 | 33 | 24 | 70 | - |
| 1968 | 58 | 5 | 100 | - |
| 1967 | 73 | 0 | 92 | 11 |

# 24 Martin Frost (D)

**Of Dallas — Elected 1978**

**Born:** Jan. 1, 1942, Glendale, Calif.
**Education:** U. of Mo., B.A. and B.J. 1964; Georgetown U. Law School, J.D. 1970.
**Military Career:** Army Reserve, 1966-72.
**Profession:** Lawyer.
**Family:** Wife, Valerie Hall; three children.
**Religion:** Jewish.
**Political Career:** Unsuccessfully sought Democratic nomination for U.S. House, 1974.

**In Washington:** When the Carter administration's hospital cost control proposal was being considered in Congress in 1979, the White House thought it had a sure vote in Frost. Regarded as bright and hard-working, he had been put on the Rules Committee as a freshman because it was expected he would go along with House leaders. And the leadership wanted the bill.

Specifically, the leadership wanted the bill sent to the floor under a closed rule — barring amendment. But Frost had his doubts about hospital cost containment. Local hospitals were fighting it, and Frost had already questioned the plan in a local newspaper column that he forwarded to the White House. When it came time to vote on the request for a closed rule, Frost and other junior Democrats balked. The bill went to the floor subject to amendment and was essentially killed by acceptance of a substitute making the entire cost control program voluntary. The episode reflected the political sensitivity that got Frost elected in 1978 and saw him returned to office in 1980 by a large margin. He has in fact been a leadership ally — and even voted with the Carter administration far more often than most Democrats — but he has managed to draw the line at his district's interests.

And he has done it without jeopardizing his relationship with Speaker O'Neill, or with Majority Leader Jim Wright, his Texas colleague. Frost is the best friend Wright has among the overwhelmingly conservative junior Texas bloc and an occasional show of independence has never hurt him.

He is also a protégé of Rules Chairman Richard Bolling, D-Mo., who backed him for his assignment over a more obstreperous Texas Democrat, Jim Mattox. Frost is exceptionally good at the "book work" other Rules members sometimes avoid. When it appeared briefly that a three-way presidential contest might be thrown into the House in 1980, Bolling assigned Frost to study the precedents and report back on how such an event might be handled.

As a junior member of the Democratic whip structure, Frost has also tried to use some of the skills he learned as a journalist in the 1960s. He has urged the top leaders to pay more attention to their image in the media.

Frost has satisfied his district's defense industry by backing higher military spending and has appealed to blue-collar communities with a hard-line attitude toward crime. But he has kept up his ties with labor and responded favorably most of the time to the liberal urban concerns of his large minority constituency. It is a complex combination. But it seems to be working, both in Texas and in the House.

**At Home:** Frost made his way to Congress in 1978 by defeating incumbent Dale Milford in a primary, something he had failed to do four years earlier.

Milford, a former television weatherman, had won the seat in 1972. But Frost was encouraged to mount a challenge in 1974 after redistricting pared away conservative suburban areas while adding black sections of Dallas much less favorable to the incumbent.

Frost complained that Milford was too supportive of President Nixon. But the incumbent withstood the challenge to win the 1974 Democratic primary with 58 percent of the vote. Frost

---

**24th District: Dallas-Fort Worth suburbs.** Population: 547,498 (17% increase since 1970). Race: White 358,904 (66%), Black 139,679 (26%), Others 48,915 (9%). Spanish origin: 64,937 (12%).

bypassed a rematch in 1976 to run Carter's campaign in north Texas. Two years later, however, he tried again, reviving complaints that Milford was too conservative. Frost added new campaign techniques for his second contest, moving beyond personal door-to-door campaigning to build an effective precinct organization.

The challenger also received the support of the state AFL-CIO and two of the largest newspapers in the Dallas-Fort Worth area. Drawing 55 percent of the vote, he ousted Milford.

Frost's Republican rival tried to turn the tables in the 1978 general election, claiming that Frost was a tool of organized labor and was too liberal for the district. The Democrat trailed in returns from Tarrant County, but offset the deficit in his home base of Dallas County to win by nearly 6,000 votes. Altogether, Frost spent nearly $350,000 in 1978 to win the seat.

Without primary opposition in 1980, Frost's re-election bid went much easier. Facing black

GOP state legislator Clay Smothers in the general election, Frost expanded his victory margin to nearly 35,000 votes.

**The District.** The 24th is a polyglot district, stretching between Fort Worth and Dallas. It includes part of Dallas' black community as well as middle-income conservative white suburbs. The district has little sense of cohesion.

Created in 1972, the 24th was transformed the following year with the removal of Republican Denton County and the addition of heavily black sections of Dallas. The changes were noticeable at the ballot box. In 1972, the 24th voted for the GOP presidential, U.S. Senate and gubernatorial candidates. In 1976, it went Democratic for all three offices.

With its current Democratic orientation and significant minority and blue-collar population, the 24th is similar to Jim Wright's neighboring 12th. As in the 12th, defense-oriented industries are major employers.

## Committees

**Rules** (9th of 11 Democrats)
Rules of the House.

## Elections

**1980 General**

| | |
|---|---|
| Martin Frost (D ) | 93,690 (61 %) |
| Clay Smothers (R ) | 59,172 (39 %) |

**1978 General**

| | |
|---|---|
| Martin Frost (D ) | 39,201 (54 %) |
| Leo Berman (R ) | 33,314 (46 %) |

**1978 Primary**

| | |
|---|---|
| Martin Frost (D ) | 22,791 (55 %) |
| Dale Milford (D ) | 18,595 (45 %) |

**District Vote For President**

| | 1980 | | 1976 | | 1972 |
|---|---|---|---|---|---|
| D | 72,529 (46 %) | D | 75,161 (55 %) | D | 53,681 (27 %) |
| R | 79,384 (50 %) | R | 60,373 (44 %) | R | 90,446 (62 %) |
| I | 3,744 (2 %) | | | | |

## Campaign Finance

| | Receipts | Receipts from PACs | Expenditures |
|---|---|---|---|
| **1980** | | | |
| Frost (D ) | $408,388 | $150,525 (37 %) | $406,096 |
| Smothers (R ) | $131,624 | $5,540 (4 %) | $126,092 |

| 1978 | | | |
|---|---|---|---|
| Frost (D ) | $348,611 | $113,795 (33 %) | $347,177 |
| Berman (R ) | $227,465 | $74,282 (33 %) | $228,740 |

## Voting Studies

| | Presidential Support | | Party Unity | | Conservative Coalition | |
|---|---|---|---|---|---|---|
| Year | S | O | S | O | S | O |
| 1980 | 66 | 23 | 67 | 15 | 44 | 43 |
| 1979 | 70 | 23 | 75 | 19 | 46 | 44 |

S = Support          O = Opposition

## Key Votes

**96th Congress**

| | |
|---|---|
| Weaken Carter oil profits tax (1979) | Y |
| Reject hospital cost control plan (1979) | Y |
| Implement Panama Canal Treaties (1979) | Y |
| Establish Department of Education (1979) | Y |
| Approve Anti-busing Amendment (1979) | N |
| Guarantee Chrysler Corp. loans (1979) | Y |
| Approve military draft registration (1980) | Y |
| Aid Sandinista regime in Nicaragua (1980) | ? |
| Strengthen fair housing laws (1980) | Y |

**97th Congress**

| | |
|---|---|
| Reagan budget proposal (1981) | N |

## Interest Group Ratings

| Year | ADA | ACA | AFL-CIO | CCUS |
|---|---|---|---|---|
| 1980 | 50 | 23 | 58 | 67 |
| 1979 | 37 | 31 | 65 | 50 |

# Utah

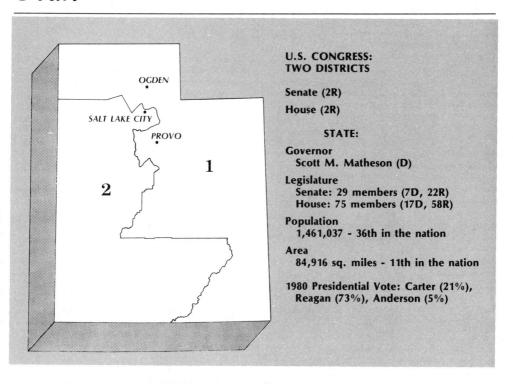

**U.S. CONGRESS:**
**TWO DISTRICTS**

Senate (2R)

House (2R)

**STATE:**

Governor
  Scott M. Matheson (D)

Legislature
  Senate: 29 members (7D, 22R)
  House: 75 members (17D, 58R)

Population
  1,461,037 - 36th in the nation

Area
  84,916 sq. miles - 11th in the nation

1980 Presidential Vote: Carter (21%),
Reagan (73%), Anderson (5%)

## ... A Hive of Conservatism

In Utah, church and state share the same symbol, which says a lot about Utah. The Church of Jesus Christ of Latter-Day Saints (LDS) founded the state and still imposes its values on everyday life.

The values are conservative ones. The common church-state symbol is the beehive, a testament to the reverence Mormons have for the industriousness of the free enterprise system. The LDS influence prevents Utah bars and restaurants from serving liquor by the drink. When Democratic Rep. Allan T. Howe was convicted in 1976 of soliciting sex from a policewoman posing as a decoy, the voters decisively turned him out of office. As late as 1978, blacks were prohibited from the LDS priesthood. Utah is the only state that still executes convicted murderers by firing squad — which was the way Gary Gilmore was put to death in 1977.

Like most of the Mountain States, Utah went through a period of flirtation with Democrats and the New Deal in the 1930s, and as late as 1948 it chose Truman in a closely contested presidential election. But Utah began its reaction against the national Democratic Party soon after that, and the reaction has been thorough. In 1980, Jimmy Carter drew an absurdly low 21 percent of the Utah vote — less even than George McGovern had drawn eight years earlier. At this point, it is hard to imagine any Democrat capable of winning the party's presidential nomination who would also have any chance to carry Utah in the fall.

Democrats, even one or two liberal ones, continued to win congressional elections in the state through the 1970s. But by 1980, Utah had thrown out the last one, Rep. Gunn McKay, who often voted with Republicans in Washington but was unable to persuade voters at home that he was sufficiently skeptical about the role of the federal government. Democratic Sen. Frank Moss worked hard to win a fourth term in 1976, waging well-publicized campaigns against smoking and alcohol, but he was swept out of office by a little-known, late starting Republican, Orrin G. Hatch. Today, the all-Republican team of Sens. Hatch and Jake Garn, and Reps. Dan Marriott and James V. Hansen may constitute the most conservative delegation in Congress.

In state politics, however, it is different. Democrats have held the governorship for 16 years, first behind conservative Calvin L. Rampton, and, since 1977, with Scott Matheson, who is more liberal but who has waged popular fights with Washington over nerve gas and the MX missile.

Utah's religious history inspires a distrust of the federal government that runs even deeper than the "Sagebrush Rebellion" taking root in all Mountain States. From 1847, when the Mormons arrived in Utah, to 1896, when the state finally gained admittance to the Union, Washington harassed the Mormon church over its practice of polygamy, which had to be abandoned before statehood could be conferred. Even the name was chosen by the federal government over "Deseret," the Mormon name.

Those experiences are not public issues anymore, but they are imbedded in Utah values. And while the church does not exercise any overt control of the political process, it remains a potent presence. Many office-holders are LDS officials as well.

# A Political Tour

Most of the people in Utah live along a narrow fertile strip at the foot of the mountainous Wasatch Range. This strip, linked by Interstate 15, is centered on Salt Lake City to the east of the Great Salt Lake and stretches south to Provo and north to Ogden. The rest of the state is sparsely populated mountains and deserts.

**Salt Lake County.** Salt Lake City was where the great cross-land migration of the Mormons ended in 1847, after they had been driven out of the East by non-believers' persecution. Mormon leader Brigham Young, the successor of founding prophet Joseph Smith, chose the site in part because its saline lake reminded him of the Dead Sea of Palestine. Over the years, the "Saints" irrigated the arid land, constructed a magnificent Temple and laid out boulevards wide enough to turn a span of oxen.

The capital of both the church and state, Salt Lake City contains enough Democratic blue-collar workers and liberal young professionals to give the more dominant suburban Republicans an occasional challenge. For governor, Salt Lake County as a whole favored Matheson in both 1976 and 1980. Both those years, however, it went against Jimmy Carter.

The city itself leans Democratic. The working-class West Side, home of the area's copper miners, votes with the Democrats, as does the central city section. In the northern hills, called The Avenues, professionals in their 20's and 30's often go Democratic, too. But in the wealthy Wasatch foothills section called the East Bench, Republicans hold sway.

More people live in the Salt Lake suburbs than in the city itself. Voters in such suburban communities as Cottonwood and Murray habitually opt for the GOP. But there are exceptions such as Sandy City, which Democrats sometimes capture.

With 42 percent of the state's population, Salt Lake County dominates Utah politically.

**The Ogden Orbit.** The Democratic stronghold in Utah is north of Salt Lake City in the railroad center of Ogden in Weber County. Originally a rough-and-ready trapping outpost in the early 19th century, Ogden was taken over by the Mormons in the middle part of the century. But the arrival of the railroad brought another influx of "Gentiles" — that is, non-Mormons. In 1869 at Promontory, north of Ogden, the Central and Union Pacific railroads were joined with the driving of a golden spike, and thus the nation's first transcontinental rail link was created.

Today, Ogden lives under the same strong Mormon influence seen elsewhere in the state. The clean-cut singing duo, Donny and Marie Osmond, were born there. Still, the city has a high number of "Jack Mormons," — those who have wandered from the church's teachings.

Weber's Democratic affiliation stems from its large blue-collar employment and union membership, a legacy of the railroad era. The county also has a sizable number of federal employees who work at Hill Air Force Base and other defense installations in the area. In both their losing efforts, Moss in 1976 and McKay in 1980 built up decent pluralities in Weber County. Carter, however, lost Weber both times he ran.

Rapidly developing Davis County sits in the corridor between Ogden and Salt Lake City. It is a politically polarized county. Its northern part, around Clearfield and Sunset, follows the lead of nearby Weber and votes Democratic. In southern Davis, towns like Bountiful are part of suburban Salt Lake and go Republican.

This partisan balance is reflected in the 1980 vote for governor. While Democrat Matheson won

Weber by more than 10,000 votes, he squeaked through in Davis with a mere 242-vote edge.

**Provo.** If an undiluted bastion of Mormonism exists in the state, Provo and surrounding Utah County is it. That is in large part because Provo is the home of Brigham Young University, established in 1875 to prepare LDS youth for school teaching and religious proselytizing. Current-day Mormons still ready themselves for missionary work at BYU and at a special church-run facility in Provo.

With few Jack Mormons and only a small blue-collar vote, the Brigham Young influence makes Utah County predictably Republican. Over the past two decades, its sole defection to the Democrats on the presidential level came when Barry Goldwater was the GOP nominee in 1964.

The northern section of the county contains Lehigh and American Forks — pockets of blue-collar workers employed at the Geneva Steelworks plant. Nevertheless, they tend to have strong Mormon beliefs and cannot be counted on as a solid Democratic bloc.

**Desert and South.** Only a quarter of the state's residents live outside the Ogden-Salt Lake-Provo strip. But the influence of the hinterlands may grow as the rugged desert and mountains of western and southern Utah experience an energy boom and accompanying growth.

The most consistent Democratic counties in the state are Carbon and Emery, where coal mining has taken off. They are the only Utah counties Carter won in 1976. This is a mostly non-Mormon area, with many ethnic residents of Greek, Italian and Mexican extraction.

In Millard County, the Inter-Mountain Power Project is under construction. This huge coal-fired generating facility will furnish electricity to cities as distant as Los Angeles. Millard was the lone Utah county that Carter carried in 1980.

The Republican stronghold in the rural areas is verdant Washington County in the southwest corner, where Brigham Young once dispatched Saints to grow cotton. Its population doubled during the 1970s as retirees and the wintering wealthy found its semitropical climate attractive.

Juab County, in the central-western section, has tar sands, and Uintah County, in the northeast, has oil shale. Both await expansion.

The biggest boom for the entire rural region could be touched off by the massive MX missile complex, which the Pentagon would like to build there. But this system would take up vast amounts of terrain, use large quantities of scarce water and bring in hordes of outsiders. The Mormon Church and most Utah politicians oppose the MX, despite their hard-line defense views.

## Redrawing the Lines

Utah won a third House seat in the 1980 reapportionment, thanks to a population expansion of nearly 38 percent during the past decade.

Republicans have a veto-proof hold on both houses of the Legislature, and they spent the first months of 1981 searching for a way to distribute Democratic voting strength among the districts as evenly as possible so the GOP can dominate them.

All the options considered by the Republicans created one district wholly within Salt Lake County, which has more than enough people for a full district. But there was less agreement on where to put the 132,000 county residents who would not fit into that district.

## Governor
## Scott M. Matheson (D)

**Born:** Jan. 8, 1929, Chicago, Ill.
**Home:** Salt Lake City, Utah.
**Education:** U. of Utah, B.S. 1950; Stanford U. Law School, LL.B. 1952.
**Profession:** Lawyer.
**Family:** Wife, Norma; four children.
**Religion:** Mormon.
**Political Career:** Elected governor 1976, 1980; term expires Jan. 1985.

# Jake Garn (R)

### Of Salt Lake City — Elected 1974

**Born:** Oct. 12, 1932, Richfield, Utah.
**Education:** U. of Utah, B.S. 1955.
**Military Career:** Navy, 1956-60; Air National Guard 1960-69.
**Profession:** Insurance executive.
**Family:** Wife, Kathleen Brewerton; six children.
**Religion:** Mormon.
**Political Career:** Salt Lake City commissioner, 1968-72; mayor of Salt Lake City, 1972-74.

**In Washington:** Garn, who has frequently bemoaned federal regulatory burdens, is trying to lighten them a little from his new interlocking power base as chairman of the Banking Committee and of the Appropriations panel handling the budget for HUD.

As soon as the 1980 election brought him his chairmanships, Garn began promising basic changes. After years of Democratic activism in the housing field, he said it was time for a period of "legislative reflection." But he was careful to quiet initial fears that he sought to dismantle housing programs altogether. "I'm an advocate of building housing," he said, "not mountains of paperwork that people can't live in."

In the first few months of his chairmanship, the Reagan administration gave Garn a chance to follow up on his ideas. In some cases he went even further than the White House wanted. Reagan asked a substantial reduction in the number of new public housing units to be built over the next two years. President Carter had proposed 260,000; Reagan suggested 175,000. Under Garn's leadership, the committee lowered it to 150,000. The administration also wanted a stricter means tests for public housing and looser urban block grants; Garn carried the ball enthusiastically for these ideas as well.

Garn disagreed on one controversial issue — he did not favor denying rent supplement aid to cities with rent controls. As a former mayor, he said the federal government should not be telling cities what policies to impose. But he went along with fellow Republicans on that question to preserve party unity.

Garn's pro-business loyalties mark a radical departure from the Banking Committee's sympathies under Democrat William Proxmire, who used the committee as a platform to champion consumer issues. That attitude left Garn so frustrated as ranking Republican that he once threatened to quit the Senate, announcing at a 1977

committee hearing: "I feel like going home and making as much money as I can before I drop dead." On another occasion, he told a group of Utah bankers that "it's too bad I don't have some hair so I could tear it out."

In those years, Garn was frank about his willingness to break with courtesies if necessary to stop liberal legislative goals. "If I'm against a bill in committee, I try to keep it there," he said in 1978. "If I can slow down a markup or find some tactic to keep it off the floor, I'll do it. . . . I don't particularly have loyalty to tradition."

Garn is generally regarded as a friend of the financial community, although he worries that a few large banks may dominate the business, which he wants to keep diversified. He deliberately moved slowly on a proposal by a presidential study commission that banks be allowed to establish branches across state lines. "I simply do not want to see develop in this country," he said, "a concentration of the financial market to where it is dominated by 10 or 12 large banks." Garn resisted early demands from the savings and loan industry that Congress slow down the planned phase-out of interest rate ceilings on bank savings accounts.

Failing industries are not likely to find Garn very sympathetic. He opposed the 1979 Chrysler aid package as "a very bad precedent," and shortly after taking command of the Banking Committee, warned Chrysler president Lee A. Iacocca that the committee would approve no further federal help.

Garn has little use for organized consumer groups, claiming they seldom know or care how much proposed legislation might cost. Indeed, he blames consumer groups for much of what he sees as excessive government regulation. He wants to soften the Truth-in-Lending law to simplify the paperwork involved in meeting federal regulations.

He is an all-business committee chairman, often demanding that meetings begin on time whether other members are there or not. He has also been determined to run the committee himself. He clashed with Indiana Republican Richard Lugar, who replaced him in 1981 as head of the Housing Subcommittee, when Lugar challenged Garn's power to name staff. Lugar wanted his own man as subcommittee staff director, but Garn objected. Lugar then threatened to resign from the committee. The chairman finally let Lugar name his own choice, but not the one he first wanted.

A hard-line conservative on defense policy, Garn was one of the leading opponents of the ill-fated SALT II treaty. He invested nearly two years of unrelenting effort into mastering its details and plotting its defeat. SALT became such a preoccupation that he even talked about it in his sleep, according to his wife.

Garn never tried to make the pact acceptable through amendments or reservations; he simply wanted to defeat it. This approach was characteristic of his general disdain for the give-a-little, get-a-little legislative style preferred by some of his congressional colleagues.

**At Home:** The basis for Garn's success in politics is his longstanding war with things governmental. His attitude toward bureaucracy and his affable campaign style brought him a narrow victory in 1974, a bad Republican year, and lifted him to a landslide re-election in 1980.

Garn has attracted many Utah voters by complaining about restrictions on state use of federal land, and others by opposing the mobile-based MX missile system, with its possible effect its construction might have on the state's limited water supply.

The son of Utah's first state director of aeronautics, Garn abandoned his career as a Navy pilot after the Korean War. From flying anti-submarine patrols in the Sea of Japan, he moved to the quiet life of an insurance agent in Salt Lake City.

Before long, however, he ran afoul of the Salt Lake City municipal government. As a Utah Air National Guard officer, he had a tough time negotiating a lease at the city airport. At one

juncture, a city commissioner snapped at him: "If you don't like the way the city is run, why don't you run for election?"

That he did in 1967, winning a term on the City Commission, where he oversaw the sewer and water systems. In 1971 he became mayor. Both were non-partisan posts.

During his tenure as mayor, Garn launched Salt Lake's downtown "beautification" project, which involved adding trees and fountains and widening streets. Although controversial at the time among local business people, who claimed all the construction work was driving off customers, the final result was widely praised later.

But Garn gained the most notice as mayor for his strident denunciations of the federal regulations he felt were weakening local government. He often referred to Washington's "dictatorship" and "police-state tactics."

Garn's Salt Lake base benefited him immeasurably in his 1974 Senate campaign, when he took on Democratic Rep. Wayne Owens, also a resident of the city. Salt Lake County casts the largest vote in the state and has a sizable number of Democrats.

Garn projected a much more mature image than the 37-year-old Owens, who looked considerably younger than he was. Owens was also a bit liberal for Utah, and the support he drew from Sen. Edward M. Kennedy and actor Robert Redford underscored that problem.

Initially, Garn was far behind Owens in the polls. But on Election Day, he broke even with the Democrat in Salt Lake County and won the mainly Republican rural areas. He defeated Owens by 24,922 votes statewide.

In 1980, Garn triumphed by the greatest percentage any Senate candidate has drawn in Utah history. The hapless loser was Dan Berman, a wealthy lawyer and former executive director of the state Democratic Party.

Berman lashed out at Garn as the puppet of special interests, noting that Garn, then ranking Republican on the Banking Committee, had received thousands of dollars in honoraria from the banking industry. Garn dismissed the attacks with good humor and refrained from issuing countercharges. Instead, he stressed his conservative record and conducted his customary door-knocking street campaign, which had proved so successful in the past.

## Committees

**Appropriations** (6th of 15 Republicans)
HUD - Independent Agencies, chairman; Defense; Energy and Water Development; Interior; Military Construction.

**Banking, Housing and Urban Affairs** (Chairman)
Financial Institutions; Housing and Urban Affairs; International Finance and Monetary Policy.

**Select Intelligence** (2nd of 8 Republicans)
Analysis and Production; Budget; Collecton and Foreign Operatons; Legislaton and the Rights of Americans.

## Elections

**1980 General**

| | |
|---|---|
| Jake Garn (R) | 437,675 (74%) |
| Dan Berman (D) | 151,454 (26%) |

**Previous Winning Percentage**

1974 (50%)

## Campaign Finance

| | Receipts | Receipts from PACs | Expen-ditures |
|---|---|---|---|
| 1980 | | | |
| Garn (R) | $1,176,104 | $287,309 (24%) | $1,048,137 |
| Berman (D) | $238,117 | $29,350 (12%) | $237,882 |

## Voting Studies

| Year | Presidential Support | | Party Unity | | Conservative Coalition | |
|---|---|---|---|---|---|---|
| | S | O | S | O | S | O |
| 1980 | 32 | 66 | 82 | 9 | 88 | 5 |
| 1979 | 29 | 69 | 93 | 3 | 89 | 4 |
| 1978 | 15 | 82 | 90 | 4 | 88 | 7 |
| 1977 | 44 | 50 | 88 | 4 | 90 | 3 |
| 1976 | 77 | 13 | 84 | 3 | 81 | 3 |
| 1975 | 74 | 16 | 87 | 4 | 87 | 2 |

S = Support          O = Opposition

## Key Votes

**96th Congress**

| | |
|---|---|
| Maintain relations with Taiwan (1979) | Y |
| Reduce synthetic fuel development funds (1979) | Y |
| Impose nuclear plant moratorium (1979) | N |
| Kill stronger windfall profits tax (1979) | Y |
| Guarantee Chrysler Corp. loans (1979) | N |
| Approve military draft registration (1980) | N |
| End Revenue Sharing to the states (1980) | N |
| Block Justice Dept. busing suits (1980) | Y |

**97th Congress**

| | |
|---|---|
| Restore urban program funding cuts (1981) | N |

## Interest Group Ratings

| Year | ADA | ACA | AFL-CIO | CCUS-1 | CCUS-2 |
|---|---|---|---|---|---|
| 1980 | 17 | 96 | 11 | 88 | |
| 1979 | 11 | 100 | 5 | 100 | 94 |
| 1978 | 5 | 95 | 5 | 94 | |
| 1977 | 10 | 100 | 11 | 89 | |
| 1976 | 0 | 96 | 10 | 88 | |
| 1975 | 11 | 84 | 25 | 94 | |

# Orrin G. Hatch (R)

**Of Salt Lake City — Elected 1976**

**Born:** March 22, 1934, Pittsburgh, Pa.
**Education:** Brigham Young U., B.S. 1959; U. of
 Pittsburgh, LL.B. 1962.
**Profession:** Lawyer.
**Family:** Wife, Elaine Hansen; six children.
**Religion:** Mormon.
**Political Career:** No previous office.

**In Washington:** Hatch's rapid rise to power
in the Senate has been accompanied by a shift
toward the political center, one that has lessened
the aura of militance that made him a "New
Right" favorite during his first years in office.

As chairman of the full Labor and Human
Resources Committee and of the Constitution
Subcommittee at Judiciary, Hatch has sounded so
conciliatory at times that those watching have
wondered what happened to him.

"If I didn't know better," a liberal House
Democrat remarked after watching Hatch during
a 1981 budget conference, "I would have thought I
heard the distinct accents of a born-again liberal."
At the time, Hatch was fighting successfully to
retain $1 billion in the budget for education and
training programs. He had just finished persuading the Reagan administration not to seek cuts in
funding for the Job Corps. It was not the labor-
baiting Republican they had come to know. Even
Hatch's personality seemed different.

Arriving in the Senate with an aggressive
attitude towards the Washington establishment
and its "soft-headed inheritors of wealth," Hatch
quickly drew a reputation as a humorless person
who did not fit well into Senate camaraderie.

"Borin' Orrin," critics called him after his
slow monotone occupied the Senate for weeks as
he mounted a successful filibuster against the
1978 labor law revision bill. That was partly sour
grapes from backers of the bill, but it reflected a
widespread perception even on his own side of the
aisle. In 1979, when he ran for the chairmanship
of the Senate GOP campaign committee, Hatch
thought he had enough commitments of support
to win. But when the vote was taken, John Heinz
of Pennsylvania had beaten him. Some senators
said afterward that Hatch's reputation as a strident conservative ideologue had cost him votes.

The perception began to change, however,
even before Republicans took control of the Senate in 1980. When the Judiciary Committee wrote
a new federal criminal code bill in 1979, Hatch
worked closely with the Democratic chairman,
Edward M. Kennedy, as well as with senior Re-

publican Strom Thurmond. He cosponsored the
bill with Kennedy and labored to find common
ground with him on more than 200 proposed
amendments.

But few expected the consensus approach he
took in his first few months as Labor chairman,
faced with a panel sharply split between conservative backers of President Reagan's economic program and liberal defenders of social programs.

The Reagan administration proposed ending
many of the existing programs and replacing them
with "block grants " to the states, at a lower level
of funding. But there was no majority for that
approach, especially with moderate Republicans
Lowell P. Weicker Jr. of Connecticut and Robert
T. Stafford of Vermont defecting to the Democratic position on most issues. Hatch labored
through the spring to find a compromise position
that could win a committee majority without
losing the support of the administration. Ultimately, he agreed to a compromise turning some
of the programs into block grants but leaving
education for the handicapped and the poor essentially unchanged.

Meanwhile, Hatch had shown considerable
skill in managing the committee through an earlier controversy, over the nomination of Raymond
J. Donovan to be secretary of labor. Donovan was
accused of having ties to organized crime but was
eventually cleared by the committee and approved by the Senate.

Despite criticism from the White House,
Hatch insisted on a vigorous investigation into
Donovan's connections. He and Kennedy, now
ranking Democrat on the committee, cooperated
privately as well as publicly, although strains
became apparent toward the end of the probe.

Hatch later got into an argument with Donovan over access to Labor Department records
involving Teamsters' union pension funds. Frus-

trated with Donovan's refusal to turn over the records, Hatch's committee issued a subpoena. Committee investigators eventually got access to the documents under a more informal procedure.

It seemed certain to many labor loyalists in 1980 that Hatch's chairmanship would guarantee angry confrontation between him and the unions. Ever since he led the 1978 labor law filibuster, Hatch was viewed by labor as its arch-enemy in the Senate. The reality has been far less cataclysmic. Hatch has sought to build bridges to labor leaders and reassure them he was not opposed to unionism.

The Utah Republican still supports a subminimum wage for teen-agers and a curb on enforcement by the Occupational Safety and Health Administration. For the first half of 1981, however, the committee was preoccupied with its deadlock over the block grant proposals and made little progress on these labor issues.

While presiding at the Labor Committee, Hatch has been playing an equally important role at Judiciary, where his job changed in 1981 from one of blocking liberal legislation to one of trying to advance conservative proposals.

Before the Republican takeover of the Senate, Hatch won a notable victory in blocking legislation to strengthen federal enforcement of open housing laws. He led a successful filibuster against the bill late in the 1980 congressional session, calling it "one of the those last-gasp ultra-liberal efforts to impose the federal government on the lives of the people."

He sought to add to the bill a requirement that the government prove that alleged violators of open housing laws had intended to discriminate in the sale or rental of housing. But last-minute negotiations broke down, and the bill died.

On becoming chairman of the Constitution Subcommittee in 1981, Hatch faced a host of controversial issues that were the object of proposed constitutional amendments — school prayer, abortion, busing and a balanced federal budget. Although all of those ideas had been pushed by conservatives for years, Hatch moved slowly. By mid-year the panel had approved only the balanced budget amendment.

As a possible alternative to other constitutional amendments, Hatch began exploring proposals to limit the jurisdiction of the Supreme Court over such social issues. But he backed off, at least temporarily, from efforts by another Judiciary Republican, John P. East of North Carolina, to limit abortions through legislation defining conception as the beginning of life. East held a Separation of Powers Subcommittee hearing in which all of the proposed witnesses were doctors

who believed that life began at conception. Hatch had originally been scheduled to cosponsor the hearing but withdrew his support, charging that the witnesses represented only one point of view.

**At Home:** Hatch's election in 1976 represented as pure an example of anti-Washington politics as the nation has seen in recent years.

Intense and serious, Hatch did not have the personal appeal of Utah's senior Republican senator, Jake Garn. Nor did he start with much name recognition; he never had run for office before. But he was able to tap the same conservative sentiment that converted the state's congressional delegation into a solid Republican phalanx during the 1970's.

Hatch's lack of government experience at any level almost certainly helped him. In his private legal practice, he had represented clients fighting federal regulations. He had the endorsement of Ronald Reagan, who played a key role in his primary effort.

Hatch was recruited for the Senate campaign against incumbent Democrat Frank E. Moss by conservative leader Ernest Wilkerson, who had challenged Moss in 1964. The campaign attracted the zeal and money of some conservatives who had been politically inactive for years.

Hatch's competitor for the Republican nomination was Jack W. Carlson, former U.S. assistant secretary of the interior. Carlson, seen as the front-runner, underscored his extensive Washington experience, arguing that it would make him a more effective senator. Besides the Interior Department, he had served with the Office of Management and Budget, the Council of Economic Advisers and the Defense Department.

That was the wrong record for Utah in 1976. Hatch, seeing that the state was fed up with federal rules, took the opposite approach. The party convention, strongly pro-Reagan, gave him 778 votes to 930 for Carlson, a Ford supporter.

In the weeks that remained before the primary, Hatch won numerous converts. The day before the voting, he reinforced his conservative credentials by running newspaper ads of the Reagan endorsement. Hatch won by almost 2-1.

The primary gave Hatch a publicity bonus that helped him catch up to Moss, who faced no party competitors. Moss, seen as a liberal by Utah standards, had helped himself at home by investigating Medicaid abuses and fighting to ban cigarette advertising from television. He stressed his seniority and the tangible benefits it had brought the state. But Hatch argued successfully that the real issue was limiting government and taxes, and that he would be more likely to do that than Moss.

## Committees

**Budget** (5th of 12 Republicans)

**Judiciary** (4th of 10 Republicans)
Constitution, chairman; Security and Terrorism; Separation of Powers.

**Labor and Human Resources** (Chairman)
Alcoholism and Drug Abuse; Employment and Productivity; Labor.

**Small Business** (3rd of 9 Republicans)
Government Regulation and Paperwork, chairman; Capital Formation and Retention.

## Elections

**1976 General**

| | |
|---|---|
| Orrin Hatch (R) | 290,221 (54%) |
| Frank Moss (D) | 241,948 (45%) |

**1976 Primary**

| | |
|---|---|
| Orrin Hatch (R) | 104,490 (65%) |
| Jack Carlson (R) | 57,249 (35%) |

## Campaign Finance

| 1976 | Receipts | Receipts from PACs | Expenditures |
|---|---|---|---|
| Hatch (R) | $393,278 | $111,208 (28%) | $370,517 |
| Moss (D) | 365,187 | $157,400 (43%) | $343,598 |

## Voting Studies

| | Presidential Support | | Party Unity | | Conservative Coalition | |
|---|---|---|---|---|---|---|
| Year | S | O | S | O | S | O |
| 1980 | 31 | 65 | 79 | 15 | 82 | 15 |
| 1979 | 27 | 68 | 90 | 3 | 90 | 3 |
| 1978 | 19 | 75 | 93 | 3 | 93 | 3 |
| 1977 | 41 | 49 | 88 | 1 | 91 | 1 |

S = Support          O = Opposition

## Key Votes

**96th Congress**

| | |
|---|---|
| Maintain relations with Taiwan (1979) | Y |
| Reduce synthetic fuel development funds (1979) | Y |
| Impose nuclear plant moratorium (1979) | N |
| Kill stronger windfall profits tax (1979) | Y |
| Guarantee Chrysler Corp. loans (1979) | N |
| Approve military draft registration (1980) | N |
| End Revenue Sharing to the states (1980) | N |
| Block Justice Dept. busing suits (1980) | Y |

**97th Congress**

| | |
|---|---|
| Restore urban program funding cuts (1981) | N |

## Interest Group Ratings

| Year | ADA | ACA | AFL-CIO | CCUS-1 | CCUS-2 |
|---|---|---|---|---|---|
| 1980 | 17 | 96 | 11 | 90 | |
| 1979 | 11 | 96 | 6 | 100 | 87 |
| 1978 | 5 | 96 | 11 | 94 | |
| 1977 | 0 | 92 | 12 | 100 | |

# 1 James V. Hansen (R)

**Of Farmington — Elected 1980**

**Born:** Aug. 14, 1932, Salt Lake City, Utah.
**Education:** U. of Utah, B.S. 1960.
**Military Career:** Navy, 1951-53.
**Profession:** Insurance agent and land developer.
**Family:** Wife, Anne Burgoyne; five children.
**Religion:** Mormon.
**Political Career:** Farmington City Council, 1963-72; Utah House, 1973-81, Speaker, 1979-81.

**The Member:** As a state legislator, Hansen was known as a pragmatic conservative adept at conciliation. He crafted a compromise among various factions over a controversial package granting tax rebates to the public and raises to state employees. Competing for the House Speakership, he defeated his rival, a Salt Lake City lawmaker, by quietly peeling away votes from the Salt Lake delegation. Democratic colleagues publicly praised him for his evenhandedness as Speaker.

Hansen takes standard conservative positions on fiscal, national security and social questions. He wants to balance the federal budget, give more money to the military and ban abortion. Hansen has been cautious in his treatment of the MX missile issue, which has become increasingly unpopular in Utah since the Mormon church publicly opposed installing it in Nevada and Utah. While still in favor of the missile itself, Hansen worked with liberal Rep. Paul Simon, D-Ill., to amend defense bills in 1981 to defer federal spending on any actual basing construction work.

Before Hansen challenged him, Democratic Rep. Gunn McKay had been surviving in Republican territory for a decade, although by decreasing margins. Aided by a strong vote for Reagan, Hansen defeated McKay by painting him as too close to the Democrats in Washington, even though McKay was Military Construction Appropriations chairman and demonstrably no liberal.

**The District:** This is the non-Salt Lake City district. It covers the eastern part of the state, and two population centers dominate it — Provo and Ogden. Provo contains Brigham Young University, with a strong Mormon Church influence, and lots of GOP votes. Ogden, an industrial and railroad town, is the home of blue-collar and government workers who tend to be Democrats. The rural counties are generally Republican.

## Committees

**Interior and Insular Affairs** (16th of 17 Republicans)
Public Lands and National Parks; Water and Power Resources.

**Standards of Official Conduct** (6th of 6 Republicans)

## Elections

**1980 General**

| | |
|---|---|
| James V. Hansen (R) | 157,111 (52 %) |
| Gunn McKay (D ) | 144,459 (48 %) |

**District Vote For President**

| | 1980 | | 1976 | | 1972 |
|---|---|---|---|---|---|
| D | 56,592 (19 %) | D | 82,493 (31 %) | D | 50,225 (21 %) |
| R | 236,439 (77 %) | R | 169,858 (64 %) | R | 166,517 (71 %) |
| I | 9,628 (3 %) | | | | |

## Campaign Finance

| | Receipts | Receipts from PACs | Expen-ditures |
|---|---|---|---|
| **1980** | | | |
| Hansen (R ) | $225,806 | $86,148 (38 %) | $222,827 |
| McKay (D ) | $275,561 | $113,295 (41 %) | $275,313 |

## Key Vote

**97th Congress**

| | |
|---|---|
| Reagan budget proposal (1981) | Y |

---

**1st District: East — Ogden, Provo.**
Population: 742,709 (40% increase since 1970).
Race: White 703,206 (95%), Black 4,965 (1%), Others 34,538 (5%). Spanish origin: 26,083 (4%).

# 2 Dan Marriott (R)

**Of Salt Lake City — Elected 1976**

**Born:** Nov. 2, 1939, Bingham, Utah.
**Education:** U. of Utah, B.S. 1967.
**Military Career:** Air National Guard, 1958-64.
**Profession:** Life insurance underwriter.
**Family:** Wife, Marilynn Tingey; four children.
**Religion:** Mormon.
**Political Career:** No previous office.

**In Washington:** Marriott has a reputation as a plodder, but he has a patient determination to master an issue and work it for his constituents. And for a Utah Republican on the Interior Committee, one issue overshadows everything else — water.

Shortly after his arrival in 1977, Marriott found the Bonneville unit of the central Utah water project was on President Carter's "hit list" of water projects the administration considered "wasteful." In an impassioned speech on the floor, Marriott pleaded with his colleagues not to "turn off the spigot, not to cut our lifeline and destroy our vital water supplies." The speech was in no way decisive, but it formed part of the case that Congress presented to Carter as it insisted on continuing with many of the threatened projects, including Bonneville.

Since then, Marriott has been equally impassioned about plans to base the "moving target" MX missile system in Utah and Nevada. Marriott favors development of the MX system, but not the Utah-Nevada basing system. In 1980, he offered an amendment barring the release of public lands for the MX missile until the government had finished studying the impact on Utah and the feasibility of putting the missile in other states. But proponents of the missile said his amendment would cause costly delay, and it was voted down, 268-135. "The people of Nevada and Utah have no idea what's coming," Marriott said. "It's like a freight train bearing down on you and you're tied to the track."

On the Interior Committee, Marriott has also been busy fighting the coal slurry pipeline bill that, like the MX, threatens to use much of the water so precious in his state. He also has worked successfully to get the federal government rather than the state to pay more of the costs of cleaning up uranium mill wastes (the state has three mills). He succeeded in amending a strip mining bill to return 50 percent of the reclamation fees paid by industry to states where the coal is mined.

**At Home.** Marriott was the beneficiary of a political accident when he won this longtime swing district in 1976. He was campaigning for the Republican nomination when incumbent Democrat Allan T. Howe was arrested for soliciting sex from a policewoman posing as a prostitute.

Marriott had never run for office before. He had been an insurance executive and had organized his own successful business, Marriott Associates, which worked primarily in business and pension consulting. At one point, he sold more than $1 million worth of insurance for seven years running, and became a lifetime member of the industry's Million Dollar Round Table.

Marriott had been troubled earlier in his life by a speech impediment. He practiced hour after hour with a tape recorder in order to overcome it, and by the time he entered politics it was no longer a problem for him.

His 1976 House campaign emphasized the survival of the free enterprise system, which he said was in danger. Well-organized and financed, he came within a few votes of winning the Republican congressional nomination outright at the state convention. He overwhelmed a Salt Lake City proctologist in the primary.

It would have been hard for Marriott to lose that fall; he had two Democratic opponents. Howe's prostitution incident had come too late for Democrats to deny him renomination, but they endorsed a write-in campaign conducted by

---

**2nd District: West — Salt Lake City.**
Population: 718,328 (36% increase since 1970).
Race: White 679,344 (95%), Black 4,260 (1%), Others 34,724 (5%). Spanish origin: 34,219 (5%).

---

Daryl McCarty, a party committeeman. In the end, Marriott drew an absolute majority of the vote, 52 percent. But Howe's surprising 40 percent indicated he could have beaten Marriott easily in the absence of scandal.

Since many Utah politicians considered his election a fluke, Marriott prepared for the 1978 contest by assembling a larger and more efficient campaign operation than had normally been seen in the state. His 1978 re-election cost more than $350,000. But the attention to detail paid off, as he swamped Democrat Edwin B. Firmage, a law professor from the University of Utah, by more than 50,000 votes. There was no major Democratic opposition in 1980.

**The District.** Although the Utah 2nd has had a variety of shapes over the last few decades, its linchpin has always been Salt Lake City, the governmental, commercial, cultural and spiritual center of the state. The city itself is dominated physically by the world headquarters of the Church of Jesus Christ of Latter-day Saints, and the church is a crucial political influence as well.

The city and its suburbs in Salt Lake County cast about 85 percent of the district ballots. The county grew by about one-third during the past decade, and with the boom has come a political change — from a fairly evenly-divided district to a Republican stronghold.

Statewide Democratic candidates generally run several percentage points better in the 2nd District than the 1st, but the decline in Democratic strength in recent years has been unmistakable. In 1960, the Democrats received 49 percent of the district's House vote and 46 percent of the presidential vote. Twenty years later, the party's share of the congressional vote was down to 30 percent, and the presidential vote to 23 percent.

## Committees

**Interior and Insular Affairs** (5th of 17 Republicans)
Energy and the Environment; Mines and Mining.

**Small Business** (5th of 17 Republicans)
Tax, Access to Equity Capital and Business Opportunities.

## Elections

**1980 General**

| | |
|---|---|
| Dan Marriott (R ) | 194,885 (67 %) |
| Arthur Monson (D ) | 87,967 (30 %) |

**1978 General**

| | |
|---|---|
| Dan Marriott (R ) | 121,492 (62 %) |
| Edwin Firmage (D ) | 68,899 (35 %) |

**Previous Winning Percentage**

1976 (52 %)

**District Vote For President**

| | 1980 | | 1976 | | 1972 |
|---|---|---|---|---|---|
| D | 67,674 (23 %) | D | 99,617 (36 %) | D | 76,059 (31 %) |
| R | 203,248 (68 %) | R | 168,050 (61 %) | R | 157,126 (64 %) |
| I | 20,656 (7 %) | | | | |

## Campaign Finance

| | Receipts | Receipts from PACs | Expen- ditures |
|---|---|---|---|
| **1980** | | | |
| Marriott (R ) | $398,044 | $126,954 (32 %) | $352,435 |
| Monson (D ) | $28,085 | $16,550 (59 %) | $27,669 |
| **1978** | | | |
| Marriott (R ) | $344,918 | $110,228 (32 %) | $353,520 |
| Firmage (D ) | $233,347 | $35,500 (15$%) | 230,760 |

## Voting Studies

| | Presidential Support | | Party Unity | | Conservative Coalition | |
|---|---|---|---|---|---|---|
| Year | S | O | S | O | S | O |
| 1980 | 37 | 55 | 75 | 17 | 80 | 15 |
| 1979 | 28 | 60 | 75 | 13 | 79 | 3 |
| 1978 | 27 | 64 | 86 | 9 | 94 | 3 |
| 1977 | 33 | 59 | 86 | 8 | 88 | 5 |

S = Support          O = Opposition

## Key Votes

**96th Congress**

| | |
|---|---|
| Weaken Carter oil profits tax (1979) | Y |
| Reject hospital cost control plan (1979) | ? |
| Implement Panama Canal Treaties (1979) | N |
| Establish Department of Education (1979) | N |
| Approve Anti-busing Amendment (1979) | ? |
| Guarantee Chrysler Corp. loans (1979) | Y |
| Approve military draft registration (1980) | N |
| Aid Sandinista regime in Nicaragua (1980) | N |
| Strengthen fair housing laws (1980) | N |

**97th Congress**

| | |
|---|---|
| Reagan budget proposal (1981) | Y |

## Interest Group Ratings

| Year | ADA | ACA | AFL-CIO | CCUS |
|---|---|---|---|---|
| 1980 | 17 | 74 | 7 | 81 |
| 1979 | 5 | 96 | 18 | 93 |
| 1978 | 5 | 100 | 15 | 94 |
| 1977 | 5 | 96 | 13 | 88 |

# Vermont

U.S. CONGRESS:
ONE AT-LARGE DISTRICT
Senate (1D, 1R)
House (1R)

STATE
Governor
  Richard A. Snelling (R)

General Assembly
  Senate: 30 members (14D, 16R)
  House: 150 members (64D, 86R)

Population
  511,456 - 48th in the nation

Area
  9,609 sq. miles - 43rd in the nation

• BURLINGTON

MONTPELIER •

ONE-
AT-LARGE

**1980 Presidential Vote: Carter (38%),
Reagan (44%), Anderson (15%)**

## ...No Longer Predictable

For most of this century, Vermont was the northern counterpart of Dixie — the state where voters marked for the GOP by habit and asked questions later.

That was mostly because it was so throughly a rural state. Even after World War II, there was little industry in Vermont that did not have to do with the state's forests or stone quarries. There were few immigrant groups and virtually no non-whites. There was little to jar traditional Yankee voting patterns.

The situation has changed in recent years; Vermont now has one of the nation's more independent electorates. But Republicans generally remain the dominant party. Unlike Republicans across the border in New Hampshire, who have pursued a policy of partisan controversy, the Vermont GOP has found centrist candidates who have been able to to blur party distinctions and appeal to the emerging independent bloc.

In the tradition of George D. Aiken, the revered Yankee who won six Senate terms, current Vermont Republicans like Sen. Robert T. Stafford and Rep. James Jeffords have considerable bipartisan appeal. Gov. Richard Snelling, branded a hard-line conservative when he ran for governor — unsuccessfully — in 1966, has won three terms in the 1970s as a moderate voice for the state and New England in national Republican politics.

Meanwhile, the Democratic Party has been changing, influenced by newcomers from New York and other states. Many of the transplants are committed environmentalists, and this has pulled Democrats to the left in some parts of Vermont, not always helping them in statewide contests.

But Vermont Democrats now know they can win with the right sort of candidate in the right year. Their current symbol of success is Sen. Patrick Leahy, who got himself elected in the Watergate year of 1974 and then held on for a second term in the much less favorable atmosphere of 1980.

And Democrats are competitive now in state

legislative politics; despite the national disaster for them in 1980, they gained four seats in the Vermont Senate, coming within two votes of controlling it.

# A Political Tour

**The Burlington Area.** Burlington, population 38,000, is the largest city in Vermont and the only one resembling a metropolitan area.

Burlington grew first as a major port and later as a manufacturing center. Recent growth in the electronics industry on the fringes of Burlington has brought some prosperity to the region, but not the city. Suffering from an acute housing shortage and high unemployment, Burlington in 1981 elected a Socialist mayor.

The home of one in every four Vermonters, Burlington and surrounding Chittenden County are essential to the success of any Democratic statewide campaign. Burlington and the French Canadian mill town of Winooski are solidly Democratic. The other towns in the Burlington orbit — Essex, Colchester, South Burlington — are less predictable, but often back Democrats. In 1980, Leahy's 5,000-vote plurality in Chittenden was nearly twice his overall statewide margin.

**North of Burlington.** Franklin and Grand Isle counties, located in the northwest corner of the state, are largely agricultural. With a sizable French Canadian population, the region is almost as Democratic as Chittenden County.

Grand Isle, a county consisting of a chain of islands in Lake Champlain, joined Chittenden County in supporting both Carter and Leahy in 1980. It is the smallest but fastest growing county in the state. Franklin County was the only county

that backed a Democrat over Snelling in the governor's 1980 landslide.

**The Northeast Kingdom.** Dubbed the "Northeast Kingdom" by Aiken when he was governor in the 1930s, Essex, Orleans and Caledonia counties are the most remote in Vermont. They are more staunchly Republican than any other region. Reagan's highest percentages came from this area.

For many years the population of this region had been dwindling. But the completion of Interstate 91 in the 1970s has made the area more accessible, and the population is now increasing faster than the statewide average. But seasonal farming remains the major economic activity, making this the poorest area in Vermont.

**The Green Mountains.** Vermont is remembered for its picturesque villages, dairy farms, ski slopes and maple syrup. All are found throughout the Green Mountains which stretch nearly the entire length of the state.

Politically, most of the small towns and villages still vote Republican. But in the last decade there has been an influx of younger, city-dwelling professionals. This new immigrant class has brought the area a new lifestyle as well as an increase in the Democratic vote.

Although most of the population is found in rural areas, a few small industrial centers are scattered around the Green Mountains. Barre, the self-proclaimed "Granite Center of the World," is heavily Democratic, as is Bellows Falls on the Connecticut River. The other small urban centers — Rutland, Brattleboro, Bennington and the state capital, Montpelier — all have some Democratic votes, but exhibit the same streak of political independence found in most of the small villages.

## Governor
# Richard A. Snelling (R)

**Born:** Feb. 18, 1927, Allentown, Pa.
**Home:** Shelburne, Vt.
**Education:** Harvard U., A.B. 1948.
**Military Career:** Army, 1944-46.
**Profession:** Founder, Shelburne Industries.
**Family:** Wife, Barbara; four children.
**Religion:** Unitarian.
**Political Career:** Vermont House, 1959-61 and 1973-77, majority leader, 1975-77; unsuccessful campaign for governor, 1966; elected governor 1976, 1978 and 1980; term expires Jan. 1983.

# Robert T. Stafford (R)

**Of Rutland — Elected 1972**
Appointed to fill a vacancy, 1971

**Born:** August 8, 1913, Rutland Vt.
**Education:** Middlebury College, B.S. 1935; U. of
 Michigan, 1936; Boston U., LL.B. 1938.
**Profession:** Lawyer/public official.
**Military Career:** Navy, 1942-46, 1951-53.
**Family:** Wife, Helen Kelley; 4 children.
**Religion:** Congregationalist.
**Political Career:** Rutland County state's attor-
 ney, 1947-51; deputy attorney general, 1953-
 55; attorney general, 1955-57; Lieutenant
 Governor, 1957-59; Governor, 1959-61; House
 of Reprsentatives, 1961-71.

**In Washington:** Stafford, the good gray
Yankee who runs the Environment Committee, is
a man with no enemies — even among those who
disagree with him.

Unassuming and considerate of others, he
generally keeps his head down and his mouth shut
unless he feels strongly about an issue. Even then,
he is never dogmatic.

That is not to say he is never stubborn. In
1981, he was largely responsible for the failure in
the Senate of President Reagan's proposals to
condense many of the existing health and education programs into a loose system of "block
grants" to local communities.

Those plans had to go through the Labor and
Human Resources Committee, where Stafford
also sits, and he quietly refused to accept them.
He said he would vote with the committee's
Democrats to prevent the changes from being
made, and since no other Republican — Lowell
Weicker of Connecticut — was willing to join him,
committee chairman Orrin Hatch, R-Utah, did
not have the votes to pass them. Ultimately
Stafford sat down with budget director David
Stockman and worked out a compromise, leaving
intact programs for the handicapped, subsidies
for low-income schoolchildren, and legal aid, all
original Reagan targets. The situation was complicated later by House passage of most of the
block grants Stafford wanted to stop.

That battle took some of Stafford's attention
away from the environmental issues he expected
to spend the year concentrating on. In fact, he
had a choice in the 97th Congress between the
Environment and Labor chairmanships. He never
hesitated. "My first choice and prime interest is
in the environment," he said.

Stafford helped write much of the anti-pollu-

tion legislation of the 1970s, laws now under
assault from industry and the Reagan administration. As the argument over renewal of the Clean
Air Act began in 1981, he said he had no intention
of backing off from his environmental position,
but would consider some of the revisions the
administration wanted. "I understand that compromise is the name of the game up here," he said.
"We have to be realistic.

He demonstrated his skill at compromise in
late 1980, in the debate over a $4.1 billion chemi-
cal cleanup bill he helped write in committee. The
bill required chemical companies to contribute
money into a "superfund" that would finance the
restoration of contaminated waste sites. After the
November elections, the bill's pro-industry critics
renewed their efforts against it, hoping it could be
held off until President Reagan and the new
Congress took office. Stafford decided to salvage
what he could. He agreed to a more modest $1.6
billion version, which was enacted into law.

Stafford calls himself a "pragmatic environmentalist," one more concerned about the goal of
environmental protection than the means of
achieving it. He has argued for a non-regulatory
approach to pollution control that would rely on
incentives and strict liability requirements rather
than setting standards in minute detail.

During much of the last decade, Stafford
teamed with former Sen. Edmund S. Muskie, D-
Maine, to build and guide a bipartisan coalition in
support of major environmental legislation. The
two New Englanders became fast friends and
effective partners despite — or perhaps because
of — their "fire and ice" temperaments. Muskie
was a master of the temper tantrum and the
frontal assault, Stafford the self-effacing voice of
sweet reason. "I wish he were here," Stafford
admitted at the start of the 97th Congress.

Like most New England Republicans,

**1219**

## Robert T. Stafford, R-Vt.

Stafford has consistently supported civil rights legislation and backed many of the urban aid programs of recent years. He generally supported President Carter in foreign policy but voted with his own party on the fiscally conservative side of most broad-scale spending issues.

**At Home:** A fixture on the Vermont political scene since the 1950s, Stafford held Vermont's single House seat from 1961, when he left the governor's office, until his appointment to the Senate a decade later. GOP Gov. Deane C. Davis named him to the seat after Republican incumbent Winston Prouty died, and he was an easy winner in the special election held the following year. It took only a modest effort for Stafford to overcome Democratic state Rep. Randolph T. Major Jr., who was little known in the state and had little money.

That gentle Senate campaign was typical of much of Stafford's career up to that point; through more than a decade as Rutland County state's attorney, lieutenant governor, and attorney general, he had rarely faced serious challenge. His only close contest was for governor in 1958, when a national Democratic trend and a local controversy over an electric generation project reduced his margin to 719 votes against Bernard J. Leddy. Two years later, when Stafford challenged one-term Democrat William Meyer for re-election to the House, he was an easy winner, and he won the rest of his House terms comfortably.

But 1976 was different. Gov. Thomas P. Salmon, the Democratic nominee, outclassed him at campaigning, which Stafford had not had to do in years. Salmon had little ideological complaint against Stafford, but said he was "intellectually and physically distant from Vermont."

Fortunately for Stafford, Salmon was past the peak of his gubernatorial popularity. His support for a state sales tax had nearly denied him the Senate nomination, and he never quite surmounted the issue.

## Committees

**Environment and Public Works** (Chairman)
Transportation.

**Labor and Human Resources** (2nd of 9 Republicans)
Education, chairman; Handicapped; Labor.

**Veterans' Affairs** (3rd of 7 Republicans)

## Elections

**1976 General**

| | |
|---|---|
| Robert Stafford (R) | 94,481 (50%) |
| Thomas Salmon (D) | 85,682 (45%) |

**1976 Primary**

| | |
|---|---|
| Robert Stafford (R) | 24,338 (69%) |
| John Welch (R) | 10,911 (31%) |

**Previous Winning Percentages**

| | | | |
|---|---|---|---|
| 1972** (64%) | 1970* (68%) | 1968* (100%) | 1966* (66%) |
| 1964* (56%) | 1962* (57%) | 1960* (57%) | |

* House election.          ** Special Senate election.

## Campaign Finance

| | Receipts | Receipts from PACs | Expenditures |
|---|---|---|---|
| **1976** | | | |
| Stafford (R) | $167,469 | $74,750 (45%) | $157,927 |
| Salmon (D) | $170,156 | $16,500 (10%) | $169,296 |

## Voting Studies

| | Presidential Support | | Party Unity | | Conservative Coalition | |
|---|---|---|---|---|---|---|
| Year | S | O | S | O | S | O |
| 1980 | 73 | 24 | 35 | 55 | 38 | 57 |
| 1979 | 63 | 22 | 28 | 51 | 29 | 54 |
| 1978 | 81 | 11 | 22 | 70 | 29 | 62 |
| 1977 | 69 | 24 | 32 | 42 | 28 | 32 |
| 1976 | 60 | 34 | 27 | 59 | 34 | 51 |
| 1975 | 55 | 39 | 33 | 63 | 30 | 69 |
| 1974 (Ford) | 60 | 26 | | | | |
| 1974 | 48 | 43 | 39 | 50 | 38 | 54 |
| 1973 | 51 | 41 | 46 | 46 | 50 | 46 |
| 1972 | 43 | 41 | 40 | 44 | 41 | 48 |
| 1971 | 56 | 28† | 60 | 38† | 58 | 38† |

S = Support          O = Opposition
† Not eligible for all recorded votes.

## Key Votes

**96th Congress**

| | |
|---|---|
| Maintain relations with Taiwan (1979) | N |
| Reduce synthetic fuel development funds (1979) | Y |
| Impose nuclear plant moratorium (1979) | N |
| Kill stronger windfall profits tax (1979) | Y |
| Guarantee Chrysler Corp. loans (1979) | Y |
| Approve military draft registration (1980) | Y |
| End Revenue Sharing to the states (1980) | Y |
| Block Justice Dept. busing suits (1980) | N |

**97th Congress**

| | |
|---|---|
| Restore urban program funding cuts (1981) | Y |

## Interest Group Ratings

| Year | ADA | ACA | AFL-CIO | CCUS-1 | CCUS-2 |
|---|---|---|---|---|---|
| 1980 | 61 | 38 | 58 | 62 | |
| 1979 | 47 | 9 | 75 | 43 | 62 |
| 1978 | 55 | 29 | 58 | 59 | |
| 1977 | 45 | 22 | 68 | 44 | |
| 1976 | 60 | 20 | 71 | 11 | |
| 1975 | 72 | 19 | 90 | 25 | |
| 1974 | 62 | 11 | 73 | 20 | |
| 1973 | 60 | 19 | 73 | 22 | |
| 1972 | 45 | 33 | 70 | 14 | |
| 1971† | 46 | 33 | 33 | - | |

† Not eligible for all recorded votes.

# Patrick J. Leahy (D)

**Of Burlington — Elected 1974**

**Born:** March 31, 1940, Montpelier, Vt.
**Education:** St. Michael's College, B.A. 1961; Georgetown U., J.D. 1964.
**Profession:** Lawyer.
**Family:** Wife, Marcelle Pomerleau; three children.
**Religion:** Roman Catholic.
**Political Career:** Chittenden County state's attorney, 1967-75.

**In Washington:** The only Vermont Democrat ever elected to the Senate by popular vote, Leahy is as respected and well-liked within the chamber as he is unknown outside it.

As the only Northeasterner on the Senate Agriculture Committee, he has been a diligent advocate of the state's dairy interests. In the early weeks of the Reagan administration, he was one of only two members of the committee to oppose the new administration's request for a cancellation in the scheduled increase in dairy prices.

He also led the fight against confirmation of John B. Crowell Jr., a Reagan nominee for assistant agriculture secretary. He said Crowell had misled the Agriculture Committee about his involvement with a timber company whose subsidiary had been held liable for price fixing. But the Senate confirmed Crowell, 72-25.

At the same time, Leahy was working closely with Bob Dole of Kansas, the committee's 2nd ranking Republican, to come up with a series of moderate reductions in food stamp spending that headed off a more draconian package of cuts sponsored by chairman Jesse Helms of North Carolina.

Leahy, a former county prosecutor, also serves on the Judiciary Committee, which he joined in 1979, and on Appropriations, where he went in 1977 after a two-year stint on Armed Services.

On Judiciary in 1979, he allied himself with labor unions in the fight over a new federal criminal code, succeeding with his amendment in committee making it more difficult for the federal government to involve itself in labor extortion cases. But the code did not become law. In 1981, as senior Democrat on a Judiciary Subcommittee handling regulatory issues, he has worked with its chairman, Nevada Republican Paul Laxalt, on a bill to force cost-benefit analysis on new regulations.

And in a departure from the usual niceties of senatorial courtesy, Leahy joined Republican Orrin Hatch in persuading the Judiciary Committee that ethical indiscretions and a lack of experience disqualified a Democratic colleague's former campaign manager from serving as a federal judge. It was the first time in 42 years that the committee had rejected a judicial nominee.

Leahy's move to Appropriations proved to be a mixed blessing; as the most junior member eligible to chair a subcommittee, he had to spend four years heading the panel responsible for the District of Columbia's budget — a job with virtualy no political benefit.

Despite his distaste for the job, and his underlying belief in home rule for the District of Columbia on budget matters, Leahy was far from reticent about scrutinizing D.C. spending requests and fighting those he considered unjustified. He called the city's proposed new convention center a "taxpayer rip-off," infuriating Mayor Marion Barry, who called Leahy "that rinky-dink senator from the state nobody's ever heard of." Leahy had his Senate softball jerseys printed up to read "Rinky Dink Senator from Vermont."

The gesture was entirely characteristic of the easygoing Leahy, a man of wry humor and little pretense whose staff and constituents call him by his first name. An Irish Catholic who sometimes seems more like a Vermont Yankee, Leahy does not approve of most of the special perquisites available to Congress. He has sought without success to do away with the exemption Congress enjoys from major health, safety and employment laws it has enacted.

**At Home:** Leahy has survived in Vermont by emphasizing his roots in the state rather than his roots in the Democratic Party. Campaigning for a second term in 1980 against the national Republican tide, he fought off a New York-born GOP challenger with a carefully-designed slogan: "Pat Leahy: Of Vermont, For Vermont."

## Patrick J. Leahy, D-Vt.

It took that slogan and all the other ingenuity Leahy could come up with to overcome the challenge from Stewart Ledbetter, former state banking and insurance commissioner. When the centrist Ledbetter won a primary victory over a more strident Republican, Leahy was placed in instant jeopardy. With financial help from national Republican groups, Ledbetter sought to convince voters that the incumbent was "out of touch with the thinking people of our state."

Ledbetter said Leahy was a free-spender and weak on defense. Leahy responded by explaining in detail why he opposed the B-1 bomber and citing cases in which he had supported the Pentagon.

It was well after midnight before the result became clear, but the last trickle of ballots gave Leahy re-election by less than 3,000 votes, preserving his record of uninterrupted success as a Democrat in a Republican state.

Leahy started that record in Burlington, the state's one major Democratic stronghold, by winning election as Chittenden County state's attorney at age 26. He revamped the office and headed a national task force of district attorneys probing the 1973-74 energy crisis.

So when he decided in 1974 to go for the Senate seat being vacated by Republican George D. Aiken, he had a solid vote in Chittenden County to build from. At 34, Leahy was still a little young to replace an 82-year-old institution in a tradition-minded state, but he was already balding and graying, and looked older than he was.

Leahy was an underdog in 1974 against U.S. Rep. Richard W. Mallary, who was widely viewed as heir-apparent, and who promised to vote in the Aiken tradition. But Mallary turned out to be a rather awkward campaigner, and Watergate had made Vermont more receptive to the heresy of voting Democratic that it had been in modern times.

## Committees

**Agriculture, Nutrition and Forestry** (2nd of 8 Democrats)
Agricultural Production, Marketing and Stabilization of Prices; Nutrition; Rural Development, Oversight, and Investigations.

**Appropriations** (11th of 14 Democrats)
District of Columbia; Foreign Operations; HUD - Independent Agencies; Interior.

**Judiciary** (6th of 8 Democrats)
Constitution; Regulatory Reform; Security and Terrorism.

**Select Intelligence** (6th of 7 Democrats)
Budget; Legislation and the Rights of Americans.

## Elections

**1980 General**

| | |
|---|---|
| Patrick Leahy (D) | 104,176 (50%) |
| Stewart Ledbetter (R) | 101,421 (49%) |

**Previous Winning Percentage**

1974 (50%)

## Campaign Finance

| | Receipts | Receipts from PACs | Expenditures |
|---|---|---|---|
| **1980** | | | |
| Leahy (D) | $525,547 | $239,317 (46%) | $434,644 |
| Ledbetter (R) | $519,824 | $139,424 (27%) | $517,664 |

## Voting Studies

| | Presidential Support | | Party Unity | | Conservative Coalition | |
|---|---|---|---|---|---|---|
| Year | S | O | S | O | S | O |
| 1980 | 64 | 22 | 72 | 16 | 13 | 75 |
| 1979 | 76 | 18 | 80 | 15 | 16 | 77 |
| 1978 | 87 | 10 | 90 | 7 | 13 | 84 |
| 1977 | 77 | 18 | 74 | 15 | 18 | 75 |
| 1976 | 36 | 51 | 91 | 5 | 7 | 89 |
| 1975 | 43 | 52 | 91 | 2 | 3 | 87 |

S = Support          O = Opposition

## Key Votes

**96th Congress**

| | |
|---|---|
| Maintain relations with Taiwan (1979) | N |
| Reduce synthetic fuel development funds (1979) | Y |
| Impose nuclear plant moratorium (1979) | Y |
| Kill stronger windfall profits tax (1979) | N |
| Guarantee Chrysler Corp. loans (1979) | Y |
| Approve military draft registration (1980) | N |
| End Revenue Sharing to the states (1980) | Y |
| Block Justice Dept. busing suits (1980) | N |

**97th Congress**

| | |
|---|---|
| Restore urban program funding cuts (1981) | Y |

## Interest Group Ratings

| Year | ADA | ACA | AFL-CIO | CCUS-1 | CCUS-2 |
|---|---|---|---|---|---|
| 1980 | 83 | 16 | 83 | 43 | |
| 1979 | 89 | 19 | 79 | 9 | 20 |
| 1978 | 65 | 21 | 79 | 24 | |
| 1977 | 80 | 15 | 80 | 17 | |
| 1976 | 85 | 8 | 85 | 0 | |
| 1975 | 94 | 0 | 71 | 0 | |

# AL James M. Jeffords (R)

### Of Rutland — Elected 1974

**Born:** May, 11, 1934, Rutland, Vt.
**Education:** Yale U., B.A. 1956; Harvard U., LL.B. 1962.
**Military Career:** Navy, 1956-59.
**Profession:** Lawyer.
**Family:** Divorced; two children.
**Religion:** Congregationalist.
**Political Career:** Vt. Senate, 1967-69; Vt. attorney general, 1969-73; candidate for Republican gubernatorial nomination, 1972.

**In Washington:** Jeffords has been a key man in the House debate over jobs and food stamps, defending the programs but demanding their overhaul. This has placed him to the left of most House Republicans, who see little value in them at all, but it has given him room to negotiate with the Democrats making most of the decisions.

In early 1981, Jeffords found himself in unusual alliance with Education and Labor Chairman Carl Perkins, urging the House to preserve the youth employment programs of the Comprehensive Employment and Training Act (CETA). The House reauthorized CETA in 1980, but President Reagan wanted to end them. Jeffords disagreed.

His alliance with Perkins, however, reflected a three-year battle to change the focus of CETA from a source of jobs in local government to a program for training young people.

When CETA came up for renewal in 1978, Jeffords surprised Democrats by winning on his amendment cutting $1 billion in public service jobs and replacing it with money for teen-age training and the Young Adult Conservation Corps. "You get almost twice as many total jobs in the youth area for the same number of dollars," he said.

Perkins abruptly withdrew the bill, but decided a few days later that Jeffords had the votes and agreed to accept most of the amendment, at a cost of about 100,000 public service jobs. Jeffords called it the first step toward changing the direction of CETA. The House and Senate later agreed to keep about half the Jeffords cuts.

Jeffords' role as CETA critic on the Education and Labor Committee is similar to his stance as food stamp critic on the Agriculture Committee. He has pursued the issue of "recoupment" — a requirement that normally prosperous people who temporarily qualify for food stamps while jobless have to reimburse the government later

with tax money. He tried this proposal in 1977 and lost, but got it through the House in 1980, although it did not survive conference.

Jeffords' was an early leader in the bipartisan Environmental Study Conference and an advocate of energy conservation. In 1975, he proposed a new $500 tax credit for woodburning stoves, which was popular in Vermont but beaten badly on the House floor. The next year he managed to add $116 million for solar energy to a spending bill.

Jeffords found himself in a difficult position in 1981 over the Reagan budget proposals. He considered the cuts in social programs too drastic, and said publicly that he might not support his party on the House floor. Under intense pressure from the White House, he solved the problem by voting for a liberal Democratic alternative budget — the only Republican to do so — and when that failed, casting a vote for the Reagan package, making the GOP count on that unanimous. Jeffords later said he was voting once for his constituents and once for his president.

**At Home:** After making one premature move for major state office, Jeffords has been waiting patiently for the right moment to run again, either for the Senate or governor's chair. His cautious approach led him to pass up a contest against Democratic Sen. Patrick J. Leahy in 1980. Many Vermont Republicans feel he could have won.

---

**At-Large District: Entire state.** Population: 511,456 (15% increase since 1970). Race: White 506,736 (99%), Black 1,135 (0.2%), Others 3,585 (1%). Spanish origin: 3,304 (1%).

Instead, Jeffords chose to campaign for a fourth House term, which he won with minor opposition. Since his election in 1974 to the seat vacated by GOP Rep. Richard Mallary, he has become one of the best-liked politicians in the state.

It was not always that easy for him. A native of Rutland, he served in the state Senate before becoming attorney general in 1969. After two terms in that office, Jeffords ran for governor.

The state GOP hierarchy viewed him as too liberal and resented his criticisms of the grandfatherly governor, Deane C. Davis. Jeffords lost the primary by less than 5,000 votes to conservative Luther Hackett. When Hackett lost the general election, some Republican leaders held Jeffords responsible, and he spent the next two years trying to restore his party role.

Running for the House in 1974, Jeffords sounded much less liberal than before, but still had to fight off two strong contenders for the GOP nomination. Although he lost the southern part of the state, he ran well enough in Rutland, Burlington and Montpelier to win the primary.

The general election against former Burlington Mayor Francis Cain was easier. Chittenden County (Burlington) was the only area Jeffords lost.

## Committees

**Agriculture** (3rd of 19 Republicans)
Conservation, Credit and Rural Development; Livestock, Dairy, and Poultry.

**Education and Labor** (3rd of 14 Republicans)
Elementary, Secondary and Vocational Education; Employment Opportunities; Select Education.

**Select Aging** (12th of 23 Republicans)
Retirement, Income and Employment.

## Elections

**1980 General**

| | |
|---|---|
| James Jeffords (R ) | 154,274 (79 %) |
| Robin Lloyd (CIT) | 24,758 (13 %) |
| Peter Diamondstone (LU) | 15,218 (8 %) |

**1978 General**

| | |
|---|---|
| James Jeffords (R ) | 90,688 (75 %) |
| S. Marie Dietz (D ) | 23,228 (19 %) |

**Previous Winning Percentages**

1976 (67 %)     1974 (53 %)

**District Vote For President**

| | 1980 | | 1976 | | 1972 |
|---|---|---|---|---|---|
| D | 81,952 (38 %) | D | 78,789 (43 %) | D | 68,174 (37 %) |
| R | 94,628 (44 %) | R | 100,387 (55 %) | R | 117,149 (63 %) |
| I | 31,761 (15 %) | | | | |

## Campaign Finance

| | Receipts | Receipts from PACs | Expenditures |
|---|---|---|---|
| **1980** | | | |
| Jeffords (R ) | $58,056 | $29,097 (50 %) | $58,781 |
| **1978** | | | |
| Jeffords (R ) | $79,064 | $6,438 (8 %) | $66,589 |
| Dietz (D ) | $8,767 | — (0 %) | $8,768 |

## Voting Studies

| | Presidential Support | | Party Unity | | Conservative Coalition | |
|---|---|---|---|---|---|---|
| Year | S | O | S | O | S | O |
| 1980 | 55 | 31 | 48 | 41 | 34 | 56 |
| 1979 | 50 | 39 | 43 | 44 | 40 | 52 |
| 1978 | 60 | 33 | 48 | 46 | 39 | 56 |
| 1977 | 68 | 25 | 43 | 51† | 36 | 57† |
| 1976 | 35 | 53 | 42 | 54 | 48 | 46 |
| 1975 | 64 | 34 | 48 | 46 | 44 | 49 |

† Not eligible for all recorded votes.

S = Support          O = Opposition

## Key Votes

**96th Congress**

| | |
|---|---|
| Weaken Carter oil profits tax (1979) | N |
| Reject hospital cost control plan (1979) | Y |
| Implement Panama Canal Treaties (1979) | N |
| Establish Department of Education (1979) | Y |
| Approve Anti-busing Amendment (1979) | N |
| Guarantee Chrysler Corp. loans (1979) | N |
| Approve military draft registration (1980) | N |
| Aid Sandinista regime in Nicaragua (1980) | Y |
| Strengthen fair housing laws (1980) | N |

**97th Congress**

| | |
|---|---|
| Reagan budget proposal (1981) | Y |

## Interest Group Rating

| Year | ADA | ACA | AFL-CIO | CCUS |
|---|---|---|---|---|
| 1980 | 67 | 30 | 18 | 79 |
| 1979 | 63 | 35 | 65 | 47 |
| 1978 | 40 | 25 | 30 | 56 |
| 1977 | 75 | 42 | 62 | 50 |
| 1976 | 55 | 33 | 48 | 32 |
| 1975 | 68 | 54 | 50 | 47 |

# Virginia

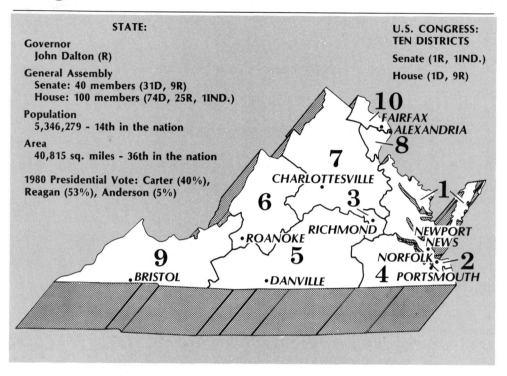

**STATE:**

Governor
  John Dalton (R)

General Assembly
  Senate: 40 members (31D, 9R)
  House: 100 members (74D, 25R, 1IND.)

Population
  5,346,279 - 14th in the nation

Area
  40,815 sq. miles - 36th in the nation

1980 Presidential Vote: Carter (40%),
Reagan (53%), Anderson (5%)

**U.S. CONGRESS:
TEN DISTRICTS**

Senate (1R, 1IND.)

House (1D, 9R)

10 FAIRFAX ALEXANDRIA 8
7 CHARLOTTESVILLE
6 3 1
ROANOKE RICHMOND NEWPORT NEWS
5 NORFOLK 2
9 4 PORTSMOUTH
BRISTOL DANVILLE

## ...The End of an Oligarchy

Few states have undergone as striking a political transformation in recent years as Virginia. From a tightly controlled "oligarchy" under the thumb of Democratic Sen. Harry F. Byrd Sr., the Old Dominion has developed into one of the nation's most fluid and chaotic political cauldrons.

The Byrd era ended in the mid-1960s with the death of the senator and the declining influence of his courthouse alliances in an increasingly urban state. The organization's demise ended nearly a century of one-party Democratic rule and more than three centuries of government by rural aristocracy.

Taking advantage of the loosening party alliances in Virginia, Republicans moved skillfully to capitalize on the upheaval. Combining conservative ideology with computer technology, they emerged as the state's dominant party in the 1970s.

But the political situation is still in flux. Virginia statutes do not favor strong party ties. There is no party registration and the party affiliation of candidates does not appear on the general election ballot.

The system encourages independents. Sen. Harry F. Byrd Jr. bolted the Democrats to win election in 1970 as an independent (a status he has maintained), and the following year an independent was elected lieutenant governor.

But the GOP has clearly been the prime beneficiary of the political turmoil. Wracked by some bitter infighting, the Democrats have not won a presidential, gubernatorial or U.S. Senate election in Virginia since 1966. And the U.S. House delegation, which had five Democratic members as recently as 1975, was reduced to one Democrat by 1981. In no other state in recent years have Democrats experienced such a political famine.

In large measure, the historic roles of the two parties in Virginia have been reversed. For a century after the Civil War, the narrow-based GOP was the more liberal of the two — urging racial moderation, election law reforms and more state spending for basic services. Virginia's conservative "Bourbon" Democrats — frequently at odds with the national party — offered balanced budgets, racial status quo and pro-business government.

But in the early 1970s, the two parties swapped roles. The Republicans were taken over by a conservative element led by the late Richard D. Obenshain, while the Democrats moved leftward with the defection of many Byrd Democrats.

The upheaval has enabled the GOP to expand its base eastward — from the Shenandoah Valley and mountainous Southwest into the one-time Byrd strongholds of the rural Piedmont, Southside and Tidewater regions, as well as the fast-growing suburbs of Washington, D.C., and Richmond. That has left the Democrats with a base large enough to be competitive but facing great difficulty in winning major statewide elections.

# A Political Tour

**Northern Virginia Suburbs.** The increasing urbanization of Virginia has transferred political power from the rural areas to the population centers — a relocation that has swelled the importance of the fast-growing Virginia suburbs of Washington, D.C.

The suburbs are home for about 20 percent of the state population. Their growth has been spurred in the last generation by the rapid expansion in the federal government and the attraction of a diverse array of white-collar industries.

A large military population, working in the Pentagon and at nearby military installations, has created a more conservative political climate than exists in suburban communities across the river in Montgomery County, Md.

Party roots are shallow in the suburbs. The rapid growth has tended not only to blur community lines but also reduce the effectiveness of local party structures. A large proportion of suburban voters are non-Virginians, and many live in the area only a few years before moving on.

The Democrats have their greatest strength in the older, inner suburbs of Alexandria and Arlington County. Both Alexandria and Arlington are much like urban areas in their settled appearance and substantial minority populations.

On the outskirts of revitalized "Old Town" Alexandria — an affluent competitor to the Georgetown section of Washington — is a large black community which comprises 22 percent of the Alexandria population. While there are fewer blacks in Arlington, the county has become a major melting pot for other nationalities. Together Asians, Hispanics and a variety of other minority groups make up 23 percent of the population. Arlington has one of the highest concentrations of Vietnamese in the nation.

To the west and south, the suburbs are newer, whiter and more Republican. And unlike Alexandria and Arlington, they are still growing rapidly. While the two inner suburbs lost population in the 1970s, the outer suburban counties grew by more than 30 percent.

In the last 40 years, Fairfax County has grown from a largely pastoral home for 40,000 residents into a sprawling suburban colossus with nearly 600,000.

More than twice as populous as any other jurisdiction in Virginia, the county has come to dominate suburban politics. With majorities in Fairfax County in 1980, the GOP regained the two suburban House seats it lost in 1974.

While Fairfax County grew by 31 percent in the last decade, the more distant suburban counties grew at an even faster pace. Commuters seeking lower housing costs and more countryside settled in Loudoun County, to the west in the Virginia "hunt" country, and Stafford and Spotsylvania counties, which lie astride Interstate 95 to the south. All had growth rates exceeding 50 percent.

**Greater Richmond.** Most of Virginia's population lives in an "urban" corridor that extends from the northern Virginia suburbs to the industrial Tidewater. At its fulcrum is Richmond and surrounding suburbs, an area that comprises 10 percent of the state population.

Blessed with a favorable location along the James River, Richmond has long been the center of Virginia commerce and government. It has been the state capital since the Revolutionary War and was the capital of the Confederacy for most of the Civil War.

Richmond was also one of the South's early manufacturing centers, originally concentrating on tobacco processing. But over the years, the economy has diversified, enabling the Richmond area to remain vibrant.

Politics in the region reflect racial divisions. Predominantly black Richmond is Democratic. The heavily white suburbs of Chesterfield and Henrico counties are conservative Republican. They have a much higher proportion of native-born Virginians than the more liberal suburbs of Washington, D.C.

The political split between Richmond and its suburbs was obvious in 1980 congressional voting. While the Republican winner, Thomas J. Bliley Jr., carried the suburbs by nearly 50,000 votes, his underfinanced Democratic opponent won the city by 3,000 votes.

And the population figures seem to favor the GOP. While Richmond lost population in the 1970s, both suburban counties gained enough new residents to exceed Richmond's population for the first time in history. Chesterfield County nearly doubled its population, growing by 84 percent in the 1970s.

**Tidewater.** The Tidewater region extends from the Potomac River on the north to the James River on the south, and from the Cheaspeake Bay on the east to the Fall Line on the west, where the coastal plain meets the Piedmont plateau.

Most of the Tidewater is rural, suited for farming and fishing. It was the center of colonial Virginia and the birthplace of the state's plantation economy. But in the 20th century the center of the region's economy has been its industrial southeastern corner.

There, in the Hampton Roads, is one of the nation's finest natural harbors. The U.S. Navy has been the linchpin of the local economy since the 19th century, building the largest constellation of naval installations on the Atlantic coast in the area. The headquarters of the Atlantic fleet is in Norfolk, while across the Hampton Roads in Newport News is one of the Navy's largest shipbuilding contractors. The Hampton Roads area is also a lively port for the shipment of coal, grains and other products from the interior of Virginia.

The heavy blue-collar element, coupled with the large black population, makes the urban Tidewater one of the few remaining bastions of Democratic strength in Virginia. The cities of Hampton, Newport News, Norfolk and Portsmouth are all at least 30 percent black.

In 1978, all four cities supported Democratic Senate nominee Andrew P. Miller in his losing campaign against Republican John W. Warner. And in 1980, all except Newport News loyally backed Jimmy Carter over Ronald Reagan.

The primary Republican base in the area is the military center and coastal resort of Virginia Beach. Through population gains and annexations it is now the second-largest city in Virginia, with 262,000 residents to Norfolk's 267,000. Virginia Beach is the only one of the Tidewater cities still experiencing a population boom, growing 52 percent in the last decade.

**Southside.** Probably the most conservative region in Virginia is rural Southside, which extends across the southern flank of the state from the Tidewater to the Blue Ridge Mountains and northward roughly as far as Richmond.

This area resembles the Deep South. It is relatively poor and has a substantial black population and an agrarian-based economy that in the 20th century has turned increasingly to textiles. The region is the leading tobacco and peanut-growing area of the state, but much of the soil was exhausted earlier this century by overproduction.

Conservatism is deeply imbued in the region's rural white population. Southside was a stronghold of the Byrd organization, the leading bastion of Virginia support for George C. Wallace for president in 1968 and a focal point of "massive resistance," the Byrd-supported attempt to stave off federally mandated school integration in the 1950s.

The heaviest concentration of blacks is in the eastern half of the region, which has remained loyally Democratic. The western half, where whites comprise a large majority of the electorate, has tended to vote Republican in recent years.

**Piedmont.** Just north of Southside is the Piedmont, a region of small towns, farms, forests and rolling hills. Like the Southside, it supported the Byrd organization and in recent years has been a part of the Republican coalition.

But with fewer blacks here, racial issues have caused less polarization. And the region has a more prosperous agricultural base, producing livestock, dairy products and fruits. A number of affluent country estates are located around Leesburg and Middleburg in the midst of the northern Virginia "hunt" country and around the bustling academic center of Charlottesville — one of the few Democratic footholds in the Piedmont.

**Shenandoah Valley.** Before Virginia became a two-party state, the Shenandoah Valley was one of the Republican Party's few strongholds. It was settled from the north in the 18th century by English, German and Scotch-Irish settlers.

The Germans established roots in the northern end of the region — in Page, Rockingham and Shenandoah counties. Foes of the Tidewater plantation aristocracy, they became the backbone of the GOP in the Valley after the Civil War.

The region's rural economy is a mixture of farming, light manufacturing and tourism. Prosperous, well-kept farms produce fruits, livestock and poultry. The small city of Winchester, at the northern end of the Valley, is the center of a large apple-growing industry and home base for the Byrd family.

**Southwest.** This region had a rough-and-tumble two-party system well before the development of the Republican Party on a statewide level. Geographically removed from the rest of the state and facing chronic economic doldrums, the mountainous region regularly bucked the Byrd organization and in the century after the Civil War was the GOP's major stronghold in Virginia.

In the party's lean years, heavy support from the poor farming and coal-producing counties of the Southwest often enabled the GOP gubernatorial candidate to draw 35 to 40 percent of the statewide vote. In 1969, mountain votes helped elect native-son Linwood Holton of Roanoke as Virginia's first Republican governor.

But as the state GOP has moved rightward in recent years and developed ties with the Richmond business establishment, it has lost part of its historic base in the Southwest. Coal-mining counties along the West Virginia border now regularly vote Democratic, as does the industrial city of Roanoke, the only major urban area in Virginia founded after the Civil War.

# Redrawing the Lines

Virginia's new congressional district boundaries do not differ markedly from the old ones, although the plan passed by the Democratic-controlled Legislature may help their party in suburban Washington's 8th District.

Former Democratic Rep. Herbert E. Harris II lost the 8th District seat to Republican Stan Parris in 1980, but the new map takes the heavily-GOP western portion of Prince William County from Parris and puts it in the 7th District, now represented by Republican J. Kenneth Robinson.

Republican Gov. John Dalton sought to realign the 8th District to make it more favorable for Parris, but the Legislature rejected his proposals in a June 8 special session. Dalton signed the remap bill June 12.

Every district in the state grew in population during the past decade, though the expansion was modest in the four southeastern districts and in the west-central 6th District.

## Governor
## John Dalton (R)

**Born:** July 11, 1931, Emporia, Va.
**Home:** Radford, Va.
**Education:** William and Mary, A.B. 1953; U. of Virginia law school, 1957.
**Military Career:** Army, 1954-56.
**Profession:** Lawyer.
**Family:** Wife, Edwina; four children.
**Religion:** Baptist.
**Political Career:** Virginia House, 1966-72; Virginia Senate, 1972-74; lieutenant governor, 1974-78; elected governor 1977; term expires Jan. 1982.

# Harry F. Byrd Jr. (I)

**Of Winchester — Elected 1966**
Appointed to fill a vacancy, 1965

**Born:** Dec. 2, 1914, Winchester, Va.
**Education:** Attended Va. Military Institute, 1931-33; U. of Va., 1933-35.
**Military Career:** Navy Reserve, 1941-46.
**Profession:** Apple grower, newspaper publisher.
**Family:** Wife, Gretchen Thomson; three children.
**Religion:** Episcopalian.
**Political Career:** Va. Senate, 1948-65.

**In Washington:** Except where the national defense is concerned, Virginia's senior senator considers nearly all federal expenditures a waste of money, and any legislation too much. His parsimony is virtually unmatched in the Senate even among conservatives.

Practicing what he preaches, he has introduced only a smattering of bills himself in the 15 years since he took over his father's old seat — and few of those have had even modest cost implications. "There are just too many laws," Byrd explained once when asked why he offered so few bills each year. He delights in asking Treasury officials at committee hearings whether they know how much the federal deficit has increased in the past week, or day, or hour. He usually knows.

His frugality extends to the operation of his own office; Byrd has regularly returned thousands of dollars in unused expense money to the U.S. Treasury, often including his own pay raises.

Although he was assigned to his father's old committees — Armed Services and Finance — and still associates with his father's old friends, such as Stennis of Mississippi and Long of Louisiana — the younger Byrd has never approached the influence of his father.

In an institution where most work is done in committee, Byrd has opted instead for a life on the floor, where he perches owlishly at the rear of the chamber for hours on end, waiting to pounce on a wayward spending proposal or to fight an extension of federal power into private enterprise. The only senator elected as an independent, he caucuses with the Democrats but votes on substantive issues with the most conservative Republicans.

His greatest legislative success came in 1971, when he pushed through an end to the embargo on chrome imports from Rhodesia that had been imposed in 1966. The embargo had been meant as punishment against that country's white supremacist regime, but Byrd said it made the United States dependent on the Soviet Union for a strategically important metal.

For six years after 1971, the "Byrd Amendment" complicated efforts of three successive administrations to win friends for the United States among black African nations. The embargo was finally reimposed in 1977, over Byrd's objections, then lifted permanently with the transition to black majority rule in Rhodesia, now Zimbabwe.

Byrd created another foreign affairs stir with his 1979 fight to require Senate approval for the termination of any mutual defense treaty, a resolution he sponsored in anger at President Carter's decision to sever relations with Taiwan. Fearing Byrd would win, Senate leaders blocked a vote. But the fight moved to the federal courts, going all the way to the Supreme Court before the president finally won.

Byrd gained national attention in 1979 for his feud with President Carter over the latter's nomination of a black state judge to a seat on the federal bench in Virginia. The nominee had not been on the list of 10 whites proposed for the judgeship by the screening committee Byrd had set up in 1978 at Carter's urging, and the senator insisted that the president — having demanded use of the selection panel in the first place — could not simply ignore its recommendations. Byrd eventually won.

One of the advocates of Virginia's "massive resistance" to school desegregation in the 1950s, Byrd has consistently opposed civil rights legislation in Congress. Angered by court-ordered busing, he has sought to require reconfirmation of federal judges every eight years.

**At Home:** A white-haired, courtly man,

**1229**

proud of his orchards in the Shenandoah Valley, Byrd offers a strong physical reminder of his father, Harry Flood Byrd Sr., who held the same seat from 1933 to 1965. It is about the only reminder he offers. The younger Byrd exercises none of the power over politics in the Old Dominion that his father did. The Byrd machine has fallen apart, with many of its stalwarts now leading the state's flourishing Republican Party. Byrd himself is remote from most of Virginia's political life.

He has survived comfortably, however, with the help of his magic family name, his proud conservatism and the tacit backing of the GOP. In 1976, after he declined the Republican nomination, that party obliged Byrd by nominating no one to oppose him.

Byrd was provoked to leave the Democratic Party in 1970 by its liberal drift, in the nation and in Virginia. A newly imposed "loyalty oath" — requiring support of the 1972 Democratic presidential nominee — was the final provocation. Perhaps more important, though, was the problem he would have had winning renomination in 1970 at a convention of the state's Democrats.

As blacks increased their role in Virginia's Democratic Party in the 1960s and as the conservative Democrats of the older generation began to depart or migrate to the GOP, Byrd increasingly found himself without much company in his father's house. In 1966, he won nomination to four

years of his father's term by less than 10,000 votes over a moderate Democrat, Armistead Boothe. When he came up again in 1970, he decided to skip the nominating process altogether and run as an independent.

Democrats responded to Byrd's declaration of independence by nominating George Rawlings, a state legislator with populist sympathies and strong support from labor and blacks. Republicans considered accepting Byrd, but moderate GOP Gov. Linwood Holton persuaded them to nominate their own candidate, state Del. Ray Garland. The election was not even close. Byrd polled an absolute majority of the vote, holding Rawlings to less than a third and Garland to an embarrassing 15 percent.

In 1976, Democrats were convinced they had a good chance to corner Byrd in a two-way contest and defeat him. Their nominee was Elmo Zumwalt, the former chief of U.S. naval operations, whose hawkish defense stand neutralized a major Byrd issue. Zumwalt called Byrd's Senate record a "monument to incompetency," but he was not a particularly effective campaigner, and his drive for Democratic unity was blunted somewhat by the decision of the Democratic senatorial campaign committee to give $5,000 to Byrd as well as $5,000 to Zumwalt.

The opposition underestimated Byrd, as it had more than once in his political career. Zumwalt failed to draw 40 percent of the vote.

## Committees

**Armed Services** (4th of 8 Democrats)
Manpower and Personnel; Sea Power and Force Protection; Tactical Warfare.

**Finance** (2nd of 9 Democrats)
Estate and Gift Taxation; International Trade; Taxation and Debt Management.

**Joint Taxation**

## Elections

**1976 General**

| | |
|---|---|
| Harry Byrd Jr. (I) | 890,778 (57%) |
| Elmo Zumwalt (D) | 596,009 (38%) |

**Previous Winning Percentages**

1970 (54%)    1966* (53%)

*Special election.*

## Campaign Finance

| | Receipts | Receipts from PACs | Expenditures |
|---|---|---|---|
| **1976** | | | |
| Byrd (I) | $809,346 | $93,268 (12%) | $802,928 |
| Zumwalt (D) | 450,229 | $107,039 (24%) | $443,107 |

## Voting Studies

| | Presidential Support | | Party Unity | | Conservative Coalition | |
|---|---|---|---|---|---|---|
| Year | S | O | S | O | S | O |
| 1980 | 46 | 51 | 29 | 67 | 96 | 2 |
| 1979 | 36 | 57 | 22 | 74 | 88 | 7 |
| 1978 | 31 | 68 | 16 | 83 | 92 | 8 |
| 1977 | 58 | 40 | 17 | 81 | 97 | 2 |
| 1976 | 75 | 21 | 14 | 81 | 89 | 6 |
| 1975 | 72 | 24 | 25 | 73 | 93 | 6 |
| 1974 (Ford) | 47 | 53 | | | | |
| 1974 | 65 | 34 | 24 | 75 | 93 | 6 |
| 1973 | 63 | 33 | 24 | 69 | 89 | 7 |
| 1972 | 83 | 17 | 30 | 68 | 92 | 7 |
| 1971 | 66 | 30 | 33 | 65 | 88 | 8 |
| 1970 | 62 | 31 | 31 | 56 | 81 | 9 |

| 1969 | 58 | 42 | 47 | 51 | 84 | 14 |
| 1968 | 43 | 55 | 31 | 61 | 80 | 16 |
| 1967 | 54 | 39 | 34 | 60 | 86 | 5 |
| 1966 | 42 | 48 | 27 | 63 | 94 | 3 |

S = Support          O = Opposition

## Key Votes

**96th Congress**

| | |
|---|---|
| Maintain relations with Taiwan (1979) | Y |
| Reduce synthetic fuel development funds (1979) | Y |
| Impose nuclear plant moratorium (1979) | N |
| Kill stronger windfall profits tax (1979) | # |
| Guarantee Chrysler Corp. loans (1979) | N |
| Approve military draft registration (1980) | Y |
| End Revenue Sharing to the states (1980) | Y |
| Block Justice Dept. busing suits (1980) | Y |

*Virginia - Senior Senator*

**97th Congress**

| | |
|---|---|
| Restore urban program funding cuts (1981) | N |

## Interest Group Ratings

| Year | ADA | ACA | AFL-CIO | CCUS-1 | CCUS-2 |
|------|-----|-----|---------|--------|--------|
| 1980 | 22 | 69 | 21 | 85 | |
| 1979 | 0 | 74 | 11 | 73 | 87 |
| 1978 | 10 | 100 | 11 | 83 | |
| 1977 | 5 | 96 | 5 | 100 | |
| 1976 | 5 | 96 | 15 | 89 | |
| 1975 | 0 | 93 | 23 | 88 | |
| 1974 | 10 | 100 | 27 | 90 | |
| 1973 | 15 | 86 | 0 | 100 | |
| 1972 | 20 | 91 | 10 | 89 | |
| 1971 | 15 | 87 | 0 | — | |
| 1970 | 22 | 87 | 17 | 78 | |
| 1969 | 11 | 88 | 0 | — | |
| 1968 | 0 | 83 | 25 | | |
| 1967 | 8 | 75 | 8 | 80 | |
| 1966 | 5 | 80 | 8 | | |

# John W. Warner (R)

## Of Middleburg — Elected 1978

**Born:** Feb. 18, 1927, Washington, D.C.
**Education:** Washington and Lee U., B.S. 1949;
U. of Va., LL.B. 1953.
**Military Career:** Navy, 1944-46, Marine Corps,
1950-52.
**Profession:** Lawyer.
**Family:** Wife, Elizabeth Taylor; three children
by a previous marriage.
**Religion:** Episcopalian.
**Political Career:** No previous office.

**In Washington:** They joked at first about
the senator who was "Mr. Elizabeth Taylor," but
Warner has confounded his critics and delighted
his friends with a record of hard work and serious-
ness of purpose.

As a former Navy secretary, Warner wanted a
place on Armed Services, and got one as a freshman in 1979. What he did not expect, however,
was that two years later a Republican Senate
majority would make him chairman of a critical
subcommittee, on Strategic Nuclear Forces.
Warner repeatedly urges a much stronger U.S.
nuclear deterrent. "We face a world situation," he
has said, "that could truly bring about the collapse of the free world as we know it."

Warner has also concentrated on personnel
issues. In 1980, he convinced the Senate to go
along with an emergency military pay raise after a
closed-door session in which he used confidential
data to paint an alarming picture of the nation's
readiness. Along with Sam Nunn, the Georgia
Democrat, Warner favored targeting the increases
toward the career military, rather than spreading
them across-the-board to attract beginning
volunteers.

On the Commerce Committee in the 96th
Congress, Warner earned a reputation as a conservative who looks at regulatory issues on a case-by-
case basis. In the 1979 debate over the future of
the Federal Trade Commission, he urged attention to the commission's views as well as those of
its critics. He supported a trial period for the use
of air bags in U.S. automobiles.

Warner has a reputation as a man who approaches even the most technical legislative topic
with a cheerful, boyish enthusiasm. His eagerness
caused a protocol problem in 1979 when, after
only two months on Capitol Hill, he invited
veteran Maryland Republican Charles McC.
Mathias Jr. to join him in Senate sponsorship of a
bill to resolve financing problems for the D.C.

subway system. What Warner failed to notice was
that Mathias already had a bill of his own.
Warner was told that if there were any cosponsoring, it would be Warner joining Mathias, not the
other way around.

After that, Warner was more careful. He
repeatedly went out of his way to work with
Democrats on issues relating to Virginia — from
Newport News shipbuilding to Appalachian coal
mining.

Through it all, Warner's basic conservatism
generally prevails. Looking at both sides of an
issue seldom convinces him that the liberal side is
correct. In his first year, Warner voted with the
"conservative coalition" of Republicans and
Southern Democrats 96 percent of the time, the
highest score in the entire Senate. In 1980, his
score was 94, which was third highest.

For the 97th Congress, Warner left the Commerce Committee, where he had struggled over air
bags and the FTC, and took a place on the Energy
Committee, where he is now chairman of a Mineral Resources Subcommittee. That panel handles
issues related to coal development, which Warner
wants to promote.

**At Home:** Warner's political career seemed
stalled at midsummer 1978. He had impressed
Virginia Republicans with his campaign for the
Senate at the state GOP convention in June, but
Richard Obenshain had been the convention
choice.

Then the state's politics and Warner's future
were reordered by an airplane accident.
Obenshain's light plane crashed Aug. 2 and he
was killed instantly. Virginia Republicans needed
a nominee, and Warner, the runner-up in June,
was the obvious choice. He had courted the convention delegates with a lavish campaign costing
nearly $500,000, and attracted enough votes to
force six ballots before being defeated. He had

also been a good loser and backed Obenshain in the weeks afterward.

Warner brought to the fall campaign the same assets he had in June: personal wealth and a statewide reputation, achieved not only as Navy secretary under Nixon and chief bicentennial planner under Ford, but as husband to Elizabeth Taylor.

He also had liabilities. Despite his Virginia roots, he was looked upon as an outsider who arrived late on the state's political scene. Some voters also saw him as a socialite and dilettante. Before he married Taylor, he was married to heiress Catherine Mellon, and received a reported $7 million from her in their divorce settlement.

But Warner's celebrity wife turned out to be a help to him. Taylor's presence on the campaign trail guaranteed large crowds, and when she proved willing to voice her enthusiasm for conservative causes, Virginia Republicans cheered her on.

The Democratic nominee, former state Attorney General Andrew Miller, was seeking to recover from a defeat in the 1977 gubernatorial primary by the state's best known liberal Democrat, Henry E. Howell. In 1978, Miller campaigned for the Senate as a conservative, but Warner tied him to the Democratic party of Howell, and Miller never managed to untie himself successfully. Warner edged Miller by fewer than 5,000 votes in the closest Senate election in Virginia history.

## Committees

**Armed Services** (3rd of 9 Republicans)
Strategic and Theater Nuclear Forces, chairman; Military Construction; Tactical Warfare.

**Energy and Natural Resources** (6th of 11 Republicans)
Energy and Mineral Resources, chairman; Energy Research and Development; Public Lands and Reserved Water.

**Rules and Administration** (6th of 7 Republicans)

**Joint Printing**

## Elections

**1978 General**

| | | |
|---|---|---|
| John Warner (R) | 613,232 | (50%) |
| Andrew Miller (D) | 608,511 | (50%) |

## Campaign Finance

| | Receipts | Receipts from PACs | Expenditures |
|---|---|---|---|
| **1978** | | | |
| Warner (R) | $2,907,073 | $108,144 (4%) | $2,897,237 |
| Miller (D) | $850,313 | $157,404 (19%) | $832,773 |

## Voting Studies

| | Presidential Support | | Party Unity | | Conservative Coalition | |
|---|---|---|---|---|---|---|
| Year | S | O | S | O | S | O |
| 1980 | 46 | 54 | 81 | 19 | 94 | 6 |
| 1979 | 41 | 59 | 90 | 10 | 96 | 4 |

S = Support          O = Opposition

## Key Votes

**96th Congress**

| | |
|---|---|
| Maintain relations with Taiwan (1979) | Y |
| Reduce synthetic fuel development funds (1979) | N |
| Impose nuclear plant moratorium (1979) | N |
| Kill stronger windfall profits tax (1979) | Y |
| Guarantee Chrysler Corp. loans (1979) | N |
| Approve military draft registration (1980) | Y |
| End Revenue Sharing to the states (1980) | Y |
| Block Justice Dept. busing suits (1980) | Y |

**97th Congress**

| | |
|---|---|
| Restore urban program funding cuts (1981) | N |

## Interest Group Ratings

| Year | ADA | ACA | AFL-CIO | CCUS-1 | CCUS-2 |
|---|---|---|---|---|---|
| 1980 | 22 | 77 | 21 | 86 | |
| 1979 | 5 | 85 | 11 | 82 | 88 |

# 1 Paul S. Trible Jr. (R)

**Of Newport News — Elected 1976**

**Born:** Dec. 29, 1946, Baltimore, Md.
**Education:** Hampden-Sydney College, B.A. 1968; Washington and Lee U. Law School, J.D. 1971.
**Profession:** Lawyer.
**Family:** Wife, Rosemary; one child.
**Religion:** Episcopalian.
**Political Career:** Commonwealth Attorney, Essex County, Va., 1974-76.

**In Washington:** Ambitious for statewide office, Trible has prepared himself for it by devoting his House career to Virginia interests. Talk of the need for a strong national defense, for example, and Trible will bring up shipbuilding. Talk of ships and he will say they should be built and cared for in Newport News.

On the Sea Power Subcommittee at Armed Services, Trible has been able to argue his broader case for a resurgent Navy. On the Military Installations Subcommittee, where he is senior Republican, he has looked after the interests of a dozen different government and military operations in the area he represents.

Trible also lent support to his area's large black population by working to make the birthday of Martin Luther King Jr. a national holiday and by creating a scholarship fund at a black college with part of a congressional salary increase.

In 1981, Trible won assignment to the House Budget Committee, the power center of spending policy. To take that post, he had to give up a seat on Merchant Marine and Fisheries, where he had pursued the interests of his area's commercial fleet for four years. He was a co-chairman of the congressional shipyard coalition, and sponsored several bills of his own aimed at supporting U.S. cargo carriers. He strengthened his ties with maritime unions by supporting the domestic cargo preference bill in 1977.

In institutional politics, Trible has generally lined up with younger Republicans willing to challenge party leaders. But he is rarely abrasive, and has stayed on good terms with senior GOP members. He is chairman of a party task force on defense policy.

Trible is often guarded in public statements, careful to avoid sounding provocative. Even in casual conversation, his words come out in neatly rounded paragraphs like a formal statement.

But he knows how to use the press to spread word of his accomplishments — like the battle to have Navy carriers overhauled at the privately-owned Newport News Shipbuilding and Drydock Co. rather than the Philadelphia Navy Yard.

Trible lost that one, but he profited by his choice of opponents: the Carter Administration had intervened directly to shift the repair operation to Philadelphia. When after years of debate (and one unsuccessful Trible court suit) the U.S.S. *Saratoga* steamed into Philadelphia, Vice President Mondale was among the dignitaries on board. It was a perfect political issue for Trible back home.

**At Home:** Republicans have expanded their influence into all corners of Virginia, but they were still weak in the heart of the Tidewater region when Trible captured the 1st District in 1976, the only Republican who has done it in this century. His own vigorous campaigning and a divisive Democratic primary combined to give him the seat vacated by veteran Rep. Thomas Downing.

As the young prosecutor of rural Essex County, Trible had a narrow political base. But he rented an apartment in the populous Hampton-Newport News area, and worked to convert Democrats to his side. During the campaign, Trible portrayed himself as a conservative defender of the middle class. Once in office, he

---

**1st District: East — Newport News, Hampton.** Population: 517,181 (11% increase since 1970). Race: White 348,861 (67%), Black 159,900 (31%), Others 8,420 (2%). Spanish origin: 6,792 (1%).

reached out to the large blue-collar and black elements in his district.

By 1978, Trible had the district locked up. He won landslide re-election over Democratic challenger Lew Puller, a Vietnam War hero and double amputee. Puller, the son of highly decorated Marine Gen. Lewis B. "Chesty" Puller, tried to blame Trible for the loss of business at the Newport News shipyard. But Trible's two years of constituent service proved more than sufficient to deflect the issue. In 1980, no Democrat even bothered to challenge him. That encouraged his thoughts about a Senate campaign in 1982, at least if independent Sen. Harry F. Byrd Jr. does not seek re-election.

**The District:** Like the rest of Virginia, the Tidewater 1st has come loose from its traditional Democratic moorings. But with a significant black and working-class population, it is no Republican stronghold.

In closely contested statewide races, the 1st has become a swing district. In 1976, Jimmy Carter carried it with 50.1 percent of the vote. Four years later, Reagan won it in a three-way contest with a similar percentage.

The southern portion of the district contains the two major cities — Hampton and Newport News. The economies of both are tied to the extensive military installations and to some of the world's largest shipbuilding facilities. Both cities frequently turn in Democratic majorities.

The center of a population boom since the end of World War II, the Hampton-Newport News area has grown from less than 50,000 residents in 1940 to more than 250,000 in 1980.

Fishing, oystering and agriculture are important in the rest of the district, where the GOP has made its deepest inroads. Republicans need a strong showing in the conservative rural counties to carry the district.

## Committees

**Armed Services** (10th of 19 Republicans)
Military Installations and Facilities; Seapower and Strategic and Critical Materials.

**Budget** (7th of 12 Republicans)
Task Forces: Entitlements, Uncontrollables and Indexing; National Security and Veterans; Tax Policy.

## Elections

**1980 General**

| | |
|---|---|
| Paul Trible Jr. (R) | 130,130 (91%) |
| Sharon Grant (I) | 13,688 (9%) |

**1978 General**

| | |
|---|---|
| Paul Trible Jr. (R) | 89,158 (72%) |
| Lewis Puller (D) | 34,578 (28%) |

**Previous Winning Percentage**

1976 (49%)

**District Vote For President**

| | 1980 | | 1976 | | 1972 |
|---|---|---|---|---|---|
| **D** | 77,510 (44%) | **D** | 80,485 (50%) | **D** | 43,069 (30%) |
| **R** | 88,022 (50%) | **R** | 75,601 (47%) | **R** | 95,400 (67%) |
| **I** | 7,324 (4%) | | | | |

## Campaign Finance

| | Receipts | Receipts from PACs | Expenditures |
|---|---|---|---|
| **1980** | | | |
| Trible (R) | $89,52 | $38,880 (44%) | $38,697 |

| 1978 | | | |
|---|---|---|---|
| Trible (R) | $254,099 | $49,990 (20%) | $257,257 |
| Puller (D) | $134,313 | $20,000 (15%) | $134,051 |

## Voting Studies

| | Presidental Support | | Party Unity | | Conservative Coalition | |
|---|---|---|---|---|---|---|
| Year | S | O | S | O | S | O |
| 1980 | 39 | 50† | 85 | 10 | 93 | 0 |
| 1979 | 34 | 64 | 81 | 14 | 96 | 3 |
| 1978 | 31 | 66 | 81 | 17 | 91 | 6 |
| 1977 | 43 | 53 | 82 | 17 | 90 | 8 |

S = Support          O = Opposition

## Key Votes

**96th Congress**

| | |
|---|---|
| Weaken Carter oil profits tax (1979) | Y |
| Reject hospital cost control plan (1979) | Y |
| Implement Panama Canal Treaties (1979) | N |
| Establish Department of Education (1979) | Y |
| Approve Anti-busing Amendment (1979) | Y |
| Guarantee Chrysler Corp. loans (1979) | N |
| Approve military draft registration (1980) | Y |
| Aid Sandinista regime in Nicaragua (1980) | N |
| Strengthen fair housing laws (1980) | N |

**97th Congress**

| | |
|---|---|
| Reagan budget proposal (1981) | Y |

## Interest Group Ratings

| Year | ADA | ACA | AFL-CIO | CCUS |
|---|---|---|---|---|
| 1980 | 6 | 79 | 16 | 74 |
| 1979 | 5 | 92 | 5 | 89 |
| 1978 | 20 | 88 | 21 | 67 |
| 1977 | 5 | 85 | 13 | 82 |

# 2 G. William Whitehurst (R)

**Of Virginia Beach — Elected 1968**

**Born:** March 12, 1925, Norfolk, Va.
**Education:** Washington and Lee U., B.A. 1950;
    U. of Va., M.A. 1951; W.Va. U., Ph.D. 1962.
**Military Career:** Navy, 1943-46.
**Profession:** History professor.
**Family:** Wife, Jennette Franks; two children.
**Religion:** Methodist.
**Political Career:** No previous office.

**In Washington:** Whitehurst combines strong support for a higher military budget with a passion for saving the lives of animals. His defense views flow naturally out of his Norfolk constituency, which includes a dozen military facilities; his concern for animals has been fostered by his wife, Jennette, who specializes in the issue as his unpaid legislative assistant.

Whitehurst was described as a political moderate in his early days in Congress, but he has gradually, almost imperceptibly, inched to the right in recent years to meet the conservatism of his party and his constituents.

In his first term, Whitehurst favored extension of the Voting Rights Act of 1965. He voted for the Equal Rights Amendment to ban discrimination by sex. He called himself a "Hatfield Republican" in those days.

But his overall voting record, especially on economic issues, has always been one of the more conservative ones in the House. In the early 1970s, Whitehurst became a leader in the campaign against school busing for racial balance, and a consistent opponent of foreign economic aid legislation. He was the only Virginian to earn a zero from the Americans for Democratic Action in 1980.

Because of the military dominance in his district, Whitehurst gravitated to the Armed Services Committee in 1969 and is now the senior Republican on its Readiness Subcommittee headed by another Virginian, Rep. Dan Daniel.

Early in 1981, he was highly critical of Navy readiness after the helicopter carrier USS *Guam* broke down in the Philadelphia River following a $23 million overhaul. "The Navy just does not get a reasonable job done in overhauls for the money expended," he said. He insisted his comments were unrelated to the fact that the *Guam* was repaired in the Philadelphia Naval Shipyard, rival to a repair firm in his area.

Whitehurst has also complained about inadequate Navy staffing; in 1979 he was outraged by reports that a fleet oiler could not go to sea because it had only two of the required 20 boilermen.

Before 1981, Whitehurst was senior Republican on another Armed Services subcommittee, dealing with Military Installations. This is the one that authorizes funding each year for the bases vital to his district.

In his other role, as a friend of animals, Whitehurst has taken the lead on enactment of the Animal Protection Act (aimed at setting humane standards for both zoos and research labs) and the Horse Protection Act (banning the practice of "soring" the hoofs of Tennessee walking horses). In the 97th Congress, the Whitehursts continued working on a bill to create a National Zoological Foundation.

**At Home:** Whitehurst stepped directly into Congress from the dean's office at Norfolk's Old Dominion College, bypassing any normal political apprenticeship.

A supporter of Democrat Lyndon B. Johnson for president in 1964, Whitehurst had not even been active behind the scenes in Republican politics before his congressional bid. But he was well known in the Norfolk area as a news analyst on a local television station.

Like Republican Paul Trible in the adjoining 1st District eight years later, Whitehurst might not have made it without a bitter primary in the

---

**2nd District: Norfolk, Virginia Beach.** Population: 494,049 (6% increase since 1970). Race: White 359,125 (73%), Black 116,278 (24%), Asian and Pacific Islander 12,960 (3%), Others 5,686 (1%). Spanish origin: 10,448 (2%).

opposing party. Veteran Democratic Rep. Porter Hardy retired in 1968, and his allies backed conservative John Rixey as his successor. But when Rixey was defeated in a primary by the liberal Frederick T. Stant, numerous conservative Democrats voted for Whitehurst in the fall, and the district went Republican with 54 percent of the vote.

Democrats have never come close to reclaiming the seat. Whitehurst's position was solidified in 1972, when redistricting removed Portsmouth and added Virginia Beach. In 1978 and 1980, Whitehurst was re-elected without Democratic opposition.

**The District.** The 2nd is composed of two cities —the young, growing and predominantly white municipality of Virginia Beach, and the older, significantly black, unionized port city of Norfolk, long the most populous in the state. Virginia Beach is Republican; Norfolk is Democratic.

Like the southern portion of the 1st District, the 2nd is heavily dependent on naval installations, shipbuilding and shipping, which are concentrated in Norfolk. But military and business-oriented newcomers have settled in Virginia Beach, changing its earlier identity as a summertime resort center.

In the past decade, while Norfolk was losing population, Virginia Beach was gaining nearly 90,000 new residents, and is now the state's second-largest city. Turnout in 1980 was higher in the Virginia Beach portion, enabling Reagan to carry the 2nd by 10 percentage points.

## Committees

**Armed Services** (2nd of 19 Republicans)
Military Installations and Facilities; Readiness.

**Select Intelligence** (4th of 5 Republicans)
Program and Budget Authorization.

## Elections

**1980 General**

| | |
|---|---|
| G. William Whitehurst (R) | 97,319 (90%) |
| Kenneth Morrison (LIB) | 11,003 (10%) |

**1978 General**

| | |
|---|---|
| G. William Whitehurst (R) | Unopposed |

**Previous Winning Percentages**

| | | | |
|---|---|---|---|
| 1976 (66%) | 1974 (60%) | 1972 (73%) | 1970 (62%) |
| 1968 (54%) | | | |

**District Vote For President**

| | 1980 | | 1976 | | 1972 |
|---|---|---|---|---|---|
| D | 57,164 (41%) | D | 62,494 (49%) | D | 35,107 (31%) |
| R | 71,129 (51%) | R | 60,261 (47%) | R | 73,828 (66%) |
| I | 7,728 (6%) | | | | |

## Campaign Finance

| | Receipts | Receipts from PACs | Expenditures |
|---|---|---|---|
| **1980** | | | |
| Whitehurst (R) | $52,162 | $17,520 (34%) | $43,672 |
| **1978** | | | |
| Whitehurst (R) | $30,600 | $7,900 (26%) | $37,796 |

## Voting Studies

| | Presidential Support | | Party Unity | | Conservative Coalition | |
|---|---|---|---|---|---|---|
| Year | S | O | S | O | S | O |
| 1980 | 38 | 50 | 76 | 12 | 93 | 0 |
| 1979 | 37 | 59 | 80 | 16 | 95 | 3 |
| 1978 | 34 | 62 | 78 | 17 | 89 | 7 |
| 1977 | 34 | 54 | 74 | 17 | 81 | 8 |
| 1976 | 71 | 20 | 77 | 13 | 84 | 8 |
| 1975 | 61 | 38 | 81 | 13 | 87 | 9 |
| 1974 (Ford) | 41 | 33 | | | | |
| 1974 | 75 | 21 | 75 | 9 | 87 | 6 |
| 1973 | 72 | 26 | 79 | 16 | 84 | 9 |
| 1972 | 73 | 24 | 83 | 8 | 89 | 5 |
| 1971 | 86 | 14 | 74 | 16† | 87 | 9† |
| 1970 | 65 | 26 | 53 | 38 | 75 | 7 |
| 1969 | 53 | 38 | 76 | 15 | 96 | 2 |

S = Support    O = Opposition

†Not eligible for all recorded votes.

## Key Votes

**96th Congress**

| | |
|---|---|
| Weaken Carter oil profits tax (1979) | Y |
| Reject hospital cost control plan (1979) | Y |
| Implement Panama Canal Treaties (1979) | N |
| Establish Department of Education (1979) | N |
| Approve Anti-busing Amendment (1979) | Y |
| Guarantee Chrysler Corp. loans (1979) | Y |
| Approve military draft registration (1980) | Y |
| Aid Sandinista regime in Nicaragua (1980) | N |
| Strengthen fair housing laws (1980) | N |

**97th Congress**

| | |
|---|---|
| Reagan budget proposal (1981) | Y |

## Interest Group Ratings

| Year | ADA | ACA | AFL-CIO | CCUS |
|---|---|---|---|---|
| 1980 | 0 | 87 | 12 | 74 |
| 1979 | 16 | 88 | 11 | 88 |
| 1978 | 15 | 89 | 25 | 78 |
| 1977 | 0 | 75 | 14 | 88 |
| 1976 | 5 | 84 | 19 | 82 |
| 1975 | 5 | 82 | 9 | 82 |
| 1974 | 4 | 93 | 0 | 70 |
| 1973 | 0 | 88 | 18 | 100 |
| 1972 | 6 | 86 | 0 | 80 |
| 1971 | 17 | 79 | 36 | - |
| 1970 | 16 | 50 | 43 | 75 |
| 1969 | 7 | 67 | 30 | - |

# 3 Thomas J. Bliley Jr. (R)

**Of Richmond — Elected 1980**

**Born:** Jan. 28, 1932, Chesterfield County, Va.
**Education:** Georgetown U., B.A. 1952.
**Military Career:** Navy, 1952-55.
**Profession:** Funeral director.
**Family:** Wife, Mary Kelley; two children.
**Religion:** Roman Catholic.
**Political Career:** Richmond City Council, 1968-77; mayor, 1970-77.

**The Member:** The 3rd District switched party control in 1980 for the first time since the 19th century, but its representation remains solidly conservative.

A Democrat when he was involved in Richmond city government, Bliley announced his conversion to the GOP only when he began launching his House campaign in early 1980. Critics claimed the switch was motivated by the district's Republican voting pattern; Bliley contended it was prompted by a leftward swing in the state Democratic leadership.

From the outset of his 1980 campaign, Bliley's near-unanimous support from the Richmond business community virtually assured his election. With a well-funded campaign, he overwhelmed his Democratic opponent.

In Congress, Bliley has been a friend of business and a proponent of President Reagan's economic proposals. When his Commerce Subcommittee began debating revisions to the Clean Air Act, Bliley tried to exempt steel plants from clean air standard deadlines; his proposal required only that they move as quickly as possible to meet the standards. The committee voted instead to let the EPA grant case-by-case exemptions of up to three years to steel plants facing 1982 cleanup deadlines.

**The District:** The 3rd District has two distinct parts — the heavily black, traditionally Democratic city of Richmond and the surrounding suburbs in Chesterfield and Henrico counties, overwhelmingly white and predominantly Republican. With most of the vote in the suburbs, the district in recent years has emerged as a GOP stronghold. Democrat David E. Satterfield III represented the 3rd from 1965 until his retirement in 1981; his conservative philosophy was acceptable to most Republicans.

## Committees

**District of Columbia** (3rd of 4 Republicans)
Fiscal Affairs and Health; Judiciary and Education.

**Energy and Commerce** (18th of 18 Republicans)
Health and the Environment; Telecommunications, Consumer Protection, and Finance.

## Elections

**1980 General**

| | |
|---|---|
| Thomas Bliley Jr. (R) | 96,524 (52%) |
| John Mapp (D) | 60,962 (33%) |
| Howard Carwile (I) | 19,549 (11%) |

**District Vote For President**

| | 1980 | | 1976 | | 1972 |
|---|---|---|---|---|---|
| D | 78,826 (40%) | D | 77,417 (42%) | D | 44,566 (27%) |
| R | 109,864 (55%) | R | 101,625 (56%) | R | 117,472 (72%) |
| I | 7,704 (4%) | | | | |

## Campaign Finance

| | Receipts | Receipts from PACs | Expenditures |
|---|---|---|---|
| **1980** | | | |
| Bliley (R) | $262,637 | $74,224 (28%) | $259,131 |

## Key Vote

**97th Congress**

| | |
|---|---|
| Reagan budget proposal (1981) | Y |

> **3rd District: Richmond and suburbs.** Population: 500,491 (8% increase since 1970). Race: White 343,399 (69%), Black 151,315 (30%), Others 5,777 (1%). Spanish origin: 4,401 (1%).

# 4 Robert W. Daniel Jr. (R)

**Of Spring Grove — Elected 1972**

**Born:** March 17, 1936, Richmond, Va.
**Education:** U. of Va., B.A. 1958; Columbia U., M.B.A. 1961.
**Military Career:** Army Reserve, 1959-66.
**Profession:** Farmer.
**Family:** Wife, Linda Hearne; five children.
**Religion:** Episcopalian.
**Political Career:** Unsuccessful Republican nominee for Va. Senate, 1971.

**In Washington:** A Virginia gentleman of inherited wealth, Daniel is reserved, proper, and conservative.

One of his few active moments on the House floor in recent years came on an unusual issue: the chamber's dress code. On that subject, he found himself in rare alignment with the Speaker, who shares neither his breeding nor his reserve.

O'Neill was being pressed on one of the hottest summer days in 1979 to abolish the House coat-and-tie requirement, especially because federal law demanded that thermostats be set at 78 or higher. But the Speaker decided to stand firm, and Daniel suddenly rose with a resolution of support for him. The issue was not comfort, Daniel said, though he found his three-piece suit comfortable enough. He argued there was a "higher consideration," the dignity of the House. The resolution was adopted, and the next evening Daniel found himself seated next to O'Neill at a formal dinner.

But that was a rare performance. Normally Daniel does not seek publicity, and when it comes, he accepts it with a kind of stoicism that seems out of character for a politician.

His interests are generally limited to military affairs and his own district, and the two often coincide. The Virginia 4th includes a cluster of Navy facilities at Portsmouth, Fort Lee and an Air Force station in Petersburg. He is on two Armed Services subcommittees, Investigations and Research and Development. On the Research Subcommittee, he is one of the strongest supporters of the MX missile, which he calls "the greatest defense need our country has today."

Daniel's office reflects his greatest interest, airplanes. It is filled with models of all the latest military planes neatly divided into two groups — the ones he has flown and the ones he has not flown.

**At Home:** Daniel is far from the most ag-gressive or charismatic campaigner in Virginia, but that has not prevented him from winning five terms in the best Democratic district in the state.

Like the district — a Wallace hotbed in 1968 — Daniel is very conservative. It was through divided opposition, however, that he gained a firm grip on the seat.

When Daniel first ran for the House in 1972, he seemed an unlikely successor to retiring Democratic Rep. Watkins M. Abbitt of Appomattox, whose hometown was moved out of the 4th by redistricting. A wealthy plantation owner and former CIA employee, Daniel had made an unsuccessful political debut the previous year when he sought the state Senate seat once held by his father, a Democrat. But the congressional campaign was different. Boosted by the Nixon landslide and a divided field of opponents, Daniel captured the House seat with barely 47 percent of the vote.

In 1974, a strong Democratic year, he was clearly vulnerable. But a locally popular black minister ran as an independent that year, allowing Daniel to slip through with the same 47 percent over Democrat Lester Schlitz.

With no independents in the race in 1976, Democrats finally achieved a unity they thought could gain them the seat. But they had waited too long. Politically entrenched after four years, Daniel won re-election by 8,500 votes, running virtually even with his opponent in the population

---

**4th District: Southeast — Portsmouth, Chesapeake.** Population: 511,154 (10% increase since 1970). Race: White 311,568 (61%), Black 192,765 (38%), Others 6,821 (1%). Spanish origin: 6,071 (1%).

centers of Portsmouth and Chesapeake, while sweeping the rural counties to the west. The Democrats have not mounted a concerted challenge against him since then.

**The District:** Redistricting in the early 1970s transformed the 4th District from a collection of old plantations and sleepy small towns into a diverse collection of urban, suburban and rural communities.

Removed from the 4th were several rural counties in the south central part of the state. Added were some suburban areas around Chesapeake, plus the city of Portsmouth.

Because of the district's large black popula-

tion and blue-collar vote in Portsmouth, the 4th has gone Democratic more consistently in recent years than any other Virginia district. In 1980, it was the only one in the state that Carter won.

Portsmouth is oriented toward the naval and shipbuilding economy of Norfolk, Hampton and Newport News. Other smaller cities in the district — Petersburg, Emporia and Suffolk — have some light industry. Rural areas produce cotton, tobacco and peanuts.

Since Martin Luther King Jr. toured the district in 1962 urging blacks to vote, black political leaders have nurtured the hope of electing one of their own to Congress from the 4th. But black candidates have not come close to victory.

## Committees

**Armed Services** (7th of 19 Republicans)
Investigations; Research and Development.

## Elections

**1980 General**

| | |
|---|---|
| Robert Daniel Jr. (R) | 92,557 (61%) |
| Cecil Jenkins (D) | 59,930 (39%) |

**1978 General**

| | |
|---|---|
| Robert Daniel Jr. (R) | Unopposed |

**Previous Winning Percentages**

1976 (53%)    1974 (47%)    1972 (47%)

**District Vote For President**

| | 1980 | | 1976 | | 1972 |
|---|---|---|---|---|---|
| D | 84,300 (50%) | D | 89,112 (57%) | D | 45,346 (34%) |
| R | 76,999 (46%) | R | 62,675 (40%) | R | 85,740 (64%) |
| I | 4,647 (3%) | | | | |

## Campaign Finance

| | Receipts | Receipts from PACs | Expenditures |
|---|---|---|---|
| **1980** | | | |
| Daniel (R) | $165,418 | $61,974 (37%) | $159,914 |
| Jenkins (D) | $85,866 | $16,102 (19%) | $84,091 |
| **1978** | | | |
| Daniel (R) | $51,628 | $16,659 (32%) | $31,644 |

## Voting Studies

| | Presidential Support | | Party Unity | | Conservative Coalition | |
|---|---|---|---|---|---|---|
| Year | S | O | S | O | S | O |
| 1980 | 32 | 64 | 92 | 6 | 98 | 0 |
| 1979 | 25 | 74 | 93 | 6 | 99 | 1 |
| 1978 | 23 | 77 | 90 | 9 | 98 | 2 |
| 1977 | 29 | 67 | 86 | 13 | 91 | 7 |
| 1976 | 76 | 24 | 88 | 9 | 96 | 3 |
| 1975 | 66 | 34 | 93 | 6† | 98 | 1† |
| 1974 (Ford) | 39 | 39 | | | | |
| 1974 | 72 | 28 | 83 | 7 | 86 | 1 |
| 1973 | 72 | 25† | 89 | 8† | 98 | 2 |

S = Support          O = Opposition

†Not eligible for all recorded votes.

## Key Votes

**96th Congress**

| | |
|---|---|
| Weaken Carter oil profits tax (1979) | Y |
| Reject hospital cost control plan (1979) | Y |
| Implement Panama Canal Treaties (1979) | N |
| Establish Department of Education (1979) | N |
| Approve Anti-busing Amendment (1979) | Y |
| Guarantee Chrysler Corp. loans (1979) | N |
| Approve military draft registration (1980) | Y |
| Aid Sandinista regime in Nicaragua (1980) | N |
| Strengthen fair housing laws (1980) | N |

**97th Congress**

| | |
|---|---|
| Reagan budget proposal (1981) | Y |

## Interest Group Ratings

| Year | ADA | ACA | AFL-CIO | CCUS |
|---|---|---|---|---|
| 1980 | 6 | 100 | 11 | 79 |
| 1979 | 0 | 100 | 10 | 100 |
| 1978 | 10 | 93 | 11 | 89 |
| 1977 | 5 | 93 | 13 | 82 |
| 1976 | 0 | 93 | 17 | 76 |
| 1975 | 0 | 93 | 5 | 94 |
| 1974 | 0 | 92 | 0 | 88 |
| 1973 | 0 | 85 | 18 | 100 |

# 5 Dan Daniel (D)

**Of Danville — Elected 1968**

**Born:** May 12, 1914, Chatham, Va.
**Education:** Attended Danville H.S.
**Military Career:** Navy, 1944.
**Profession:** Textile company executive.
**Family:** Wife, Ruby McGregor; one child.
**Religion:** Baptist.
**Political Career:** Va. House, 1959-69.

**In Washington:** Daniel has been a quiet, courtly hawk over a decade on Armed Services, voting unobtrusively for the highest possible level of defense funding. In recent years he has begun to take on a new role, as critic of Pentagon budgeting practices.

In 1978, he took over as chairman of a select subcommittee to examine "NATO standardization," the drive of Ford and Carter administration officials to reduce the number of different kinds of equipment being used to defend Europe.

The next year, his panel issued a report complaining that standardization was forcing American troops in the field to depend on inferior European equipment, and that the Pentagon should insist on top quality purchases regardless of cost.

That led Daniel into the whole issue of readiness. During the 96th Congress, he and Democrat Bob Carr of Michigan, one of the committee's handful of Pentagon critics, teamed up to demand more funds for basic maintenance in the defense budget. They argued that money was being diverted from maintenance to pay for new weapons.

In 1980, Congress enacted a Daniel-sponsored requirement that maintenance be given its own separate section in each defense authorization bill. In 1981, Daniel became chairman of a new Armed Services subcommittee established to handle that part of the bill.

Daniel has favored letting the Pentagon buy planes and missiles in large lots spread over several years. Currently, it contracts separately for each year's batch of weapons. Pentagon officials have asked for the multi-year approach, arguing it would lower the cost of weapons.

Daniel rarely talks about subjects outside the military field. Despite a friendly personal relationship with Speaker O'Neill, he seldom gives the Democratic leadership a vote on any major issue. In 1980 he voted against his party majority 70 percent of the time on the House floor, the sixth highest opposition figure for any Democrat.

**At Home:** Daniel now stands as the only obstacle to full Republican control of the Virginia congressional delegation. On legislative issues, he is no obstacle at all. He admits that his seniority among House Democrats is the main reason he has not joined the exodus himself.

Daniel has come a long way. The son of a sharecropper, he started his career at a Danville textile mill as a blue-collar worker, and ended it as assistant to the chairman of the board.

While not a dynamic force in Congress, he has cut a large figure in state and national civic organizations, serving as president of the Virginia state Chamber of Commerce and national commander of the American Legion.

A Dixiecrat in many respects, Daniel was a leader in the state's short-lived resistance to desegregation in the 1950s. In the following decade, he was a Byrd machine stalwart in the state Legislature.

Daniel came to Congress in 1968, when veteran Democratic Rep. William M. Tuck, a former governor and staunch conservative, retired and endorsed him. While George Wallace was carrying the district in the year's presidential balloting, Daniel easily outdistanced his Republican and black independent opponents with 55 percent of the vote. He faced a feeble GOP challenge in 1970 and has been unopposed for re-election since then.

**The District:** The 5th is in the heart of Virginia's rural "Southside," a largely agricultural

---

**5th District: South — Danville.** Population: 545,615 (18% increase since 1970). Race: White 399,254 (73%), Black 144,246 (26%), Others 2,115 (0.3%). Spanish origin: 3,844 (1%).

region that more closely resembles the Deep South than any other part of the state does.

The region lacks the rich soil of the Tidewater, and the 5th is one of the poorest districts in Virginia. Tobacco is the main crop. Small textile-producing cities like Danville dot the district, and there is a large black population.

Historically Democratic, the 5th continues to support conservative Democrats like Daniel. But it has long refused to vote for more liberal Democratic candidates at the state and national level. It was one of only two districts in Virginia to back Wallace in 1968, and has not voted Democratic for president in more than a quarter century. Even Barry Goldwater in 1964 carried it with 51 percent of the vote.

## Committees

**Armed Services** (8th of 25 Democrats)
Readiness, chairman; Investigations.

## Elections

**1980 General**

| Dan Daniel (D) | Unopposed |
|---|---|

**1978 General**

| Dan Daniel (D) | Unopposed |
|---|---|

**Previous Winning Percentages**

**1976** (100%)  **1974** (99%)  **1972** (100%)  **1970** (73%)
**1968** (55%)

**District Vote For President**

| | 1980 | | 1976 | | 1972 |
|---|---|---|---|---|---|
| **D** | 74,486 (40%) | **D** | 77,285 (46%) | **D** | 39,194 (27%) |
| **R** | 106,318 (56%) | **R** | 85,224 (51%) | **R** | 101,546 (71%) |
| **I** | 4,254 (2%) | | | | |

## Campaign Finance

| | Receipts | Receipts from PACs | Expenditures |
|---|---|---|---|
| **1980** | | | |
| Daniel (D) | $20,383 | $17,280 (85%) | 87,747 |
| **1978** | | | |
| Daniel (D) | 16,850 | 13,763 (82%) | 4,991 |

## Voting Studies

| | Presidential Support | | Party Unity | | Conservative Coalition | |
|---|---|---|---|---|---|---|
| Year | S | O | S | O | S | O |
| 1980 | 37 | 62 | 27 | 70 | 93 | 3 |
| 1979 | 30 | 69 | 15 | 82 | 94 | 4 |
| 1978 | 22 | 75 | 16 | 81 | 95 | 2 |
| 1977 | 33 | 66 | 19 | 81 | 97 | 3 |

| 1976 | 75 | 25 | 12 | 88 | 98 | 1 |
|---|---|---|---|---|---|---|
| 1975 | 70 | 30 | 15 | 84 | 98 | 1 |
| 1974 (Ford) | 56 | 44 | | | | |
| 1974 | 64 | 36 | 16 | 84† | 93 | 6 |
| 1973 | 66 | 34 | 19 | 81 | 100 | 0 |
| 1972 | 57 | 41 | 17 | 80 | 94 | 6 |
| 1971 | 77 | 23 | 25 | 74 | 97 | 2 |
| 1970 | 64 | 36† | 24 | 74 | 91 | — |
| 1969 | 45 | 55 | 20 | 76 | 96 | 2 |

S = Support    O = Opposition

†Not eligible for all recorded votes.

## Key Votes

**96th Congress**

| Weaken Carter oil profits tax (1979) | Y |
|---|---|
| Reject hospital cost control plan (1979) | Y |
| Implement Panama Canal Treaties (1979) | N |
| Establish Department of Education (1979) | Y |
| Approve Anti-busing Amendment (1979) | Y |
| Guarantee Chrysler Corp. loans (1979) | N |
| Approve military draft registration (1980) | Y |
| Aid Sandinista regime in Nicaragua (1980) | N |
| Strengthen fair housing laws (1980) | N |

**97th Congress**

| Reagan budget proposal (1981) | Y |
|---|---|

## Interest Group Ratings

| Year | ADA | ACA | AFL-CIO | CCUS |
|---|---|---|---|---|
| 1980 | 6 | 92 | 11 | 82 |
| 1979 | 5 | 100 | 10 | 100 |
| 1978 | 0 | 96 | 5 | 89 |
| 1977 | 0 | 93 | 9 | 94 |
| 1976 | 5 | 96 | 13 | 88 |
| 1975 | 0 | 100 | 4 | 88 |
| 1974 | 0 | 80 | 0 | 90 |
| 1973 | 4 | 85 | 18 | 100 |
| 1972 | 0 | 100 | 10 | 100 |
| 1971 | 3 | 93 | 8 | - |
| 1970 | 0 | 79 | 14 | 100 |
| 1969 | 7 | 94 | 20 | - |

# 6 M. Caldwell Butler (R)

**Of Roanoke — Elected 1972**

**Born:** June, 2, 1925, Roanoke, Va.
**Education:** U. of Richmond, B.A. 1948; U. of Va., LL.B. 1950.
**Military Career:** Navy, 1943-46.
**Profession:** Lawyer.
**Family:** Wife, June Nolde; four children.
**Religion:** Episcopalian.
**Political Career:** Va. House 1962-72, minority leader, 1968-72.

**In Washington:** No matter how long Butler serves in the House, he is unlikely to equal the dramatic effect he achieved in his very first term, the day he broke with most of the Judiciary Committee's Republicans to call for President Nixon's impeachment.

"We cannot indulge ourselves the luxury of patronizing or excusing the misconduct of our own people," he told his GOP colleagues that August afternoon, summoning up the nervous sort of eloquence that is his rhetorical style.

Butler's role in the impeachment debate gave him a reputation as a stubbornly independent man, one that he has renewed on a number of occasions since. Despite a voting record generally in line with those of his Republican colleagues, he manages frequently to go his own way.

In recent Congresses, Butler has kept up his conservative reputation by working on the Judiciary Committee to limit immigration into the United States, restrict the scope of open housing legislation, and depoliticize the Legal Services Corporation.

But he opposed President Reagan's efforts to cut out the Legal Services program entirely, and refused to go along with a constitutional amendment to ban busing. He opposed Republican efforts to establish a special prosecutor to probe President Carter's peanut warehouse. When most members of Judiciary supported a bill setting up a mechanism to create a special prosecutor in future cases involving the executive branch, he said that was unnecessary.

Sometimes ornery as well as stubborn, he can be more blunt than the average House member. In 1979, he was critical of the increasingly passive role Judiciary Chairman Peter W. Rodino Jr. was playing on the panel in the post-Watergate years. "You need a driver," Butler complained, "and he's just not a driver.... When you get right down to it, we haven't done much."

Later in the year, the committee did produce a major piece of legislation, a bill granting new enforcement powers to the Department of Housing and Urban Development in suspected discrimination cases. Butler tried unsuccessfully to strike provisions in the bill that would have changed existing law by extending its application to individual as well as investment owners of three or less rental units.

He fought a 1980 bill tripling the number of refugees the federal government would be allowed to admit, despite the certainty of its passage. He sought unsuccessfully to amend it to permit a legislative veto of presidential quota increases. Later, when the House passed an extra $100 million appropriation to deal with the refugees, Butler referred to it scornfully as an election year "slush fund."

**At Home:** As Butler's reputation has grown in Washington, opposition in his Shenandoah Valley district has virtually disappeared. He has not faced a primary or general election challenge since 1976.

Along with former Gov. Linwood Holton, the first Republican governor of Virginia in this century, Butler was an early architect of the GOP's statewide resurgence. The two men were law partners in Roanoke in the 1950s, and began by reviving the party there.

In 1958, Butler made an unsuccessful politi-

---

**6th District: West — Roanoke, Lynchburg.** Population: 501,748 (8% increase since 1970). Race: White 437,805 (87%), Black 61,322 (12%), Others 2,621 (1%). Spanish origin: 3,097 (1%).

cal debut when he sought a seat on the Roanoke City Council. But three years later he was elected to the Virginia House of Delegates. Like Holton, he was considered a moderate in state politics, and gained attention for championing abolition of the state poll tax.

In 1958, 1962 and 1964, Butler was campaign manager for Richard H. Poff, the district's Republican representative. When Poff vacated the seat in 1972 to accept a state judgeship, he threw his support to Butler. The Democratic vote was divided between the official party candidate and a liberal independent, and Butler was an easy winner.

Two years later, he again faced a fragmented field. His Judiciary Committee vote for Nixon's impeachment probably cost him some GOP votes, but the 45 percent he received was easily enough in a four-way contest.

**The District:** The 6th encompasses the lower portion of the picturesque Shenandoah Valley. It is primarily rural, but it includes the city of Roanoke, the commercial hub for mountainous southwestern Virginia.

The district has elected only Republicans Poff and Butler to the House since 1952. But in state and national elections the GOP advantage has sometimes been slim. Democrats usually carry the city of Roanoke and towns to the north like Buena Vista and Covington. Republican strength is in the Roanoke suburbs, in most of the rural counties, and in Lynchburg, the second-largest city in the district and home base for Jerry Falwell, head of the Moral Majority.

## Committees

**Government Operations** (7th of 17 Republicans)
Legislation and National Security; Manpower and Housing.

**Judiciary** (4th of 12 Republicans)
Courts, Civil Liberties and the Administration of Justice; Monopolies and Commercial Law.

## Elections

**1980 General**

| | |
|---|---|
| M. Caldwell Butler (R) | Unopposed |

**1978 General**

| | |
|---|---|
| M. Caldwell Butler (R) | Unopposed |

**Previous Winning Percentages**

1976 (62%)     1974 (45%)     1972* (55%)

*In a special election held concurrently with the general election Butler was elected to fill an unexpired term. He received 52% of the vote in the special election.*

**District Vote For President**

| | 1980 | | 1976 | | 1972 |
|---|---|---|---|---|---|
| D | 74,842 (42%) | D | 80,686 (48%) | D | 35,356 (25%) |
| R | 96,026 (53%) | R | 82,235 (49%) | R | 104,443 (73%) |
| I | 6,566 (4%) | | | | |

## Campaign Finance

| | Receipts | Receipts from PACs | Expenditures |
|---|---|---|---|
| **1980** | | | |
| Butler (R) | $43,270 | $17,750 (41%) | $114,929 |
| **1978** | | | |
| Butler (R) | $24,159 | $7,773 (32%) | $16,307 |

## Voting Studies

| | Presidential Support | | Party Unity | | Conservative Coalition | |
|---|---|---|---|---|---|---|
| Year | S | O | S | O | S | O |
| 1980 | 41 | 49 | 79 | 12 | 84 | 7 |
| 1979 | 40 | 56 | 75 | 19 | 78 | 15 |
| 1978 | 31 | 63 | 82 | 11 | 87 | 6 |
| 1977 | 37 | 63 | 81 | 16 | 88 | 8 |
| 1976 | 76 | 18 | 83 | 11 | 85 | 6 |
| 1975 | 72 | 27 | 87 | 9 | 92 | 5 |
| 1974 (Ford) | 56 | 41 | | | | |
| 1974 | 74 | 23 | 82 | 11 | 90 | 6 |
| 1973 | 75 | 23 | 88 | 10 | 95 | 5 |

S = Support          O = Opposition

## Key Votes

**96th Congress**

| | |
|---|---|
| Weaken Carter oil profits tax (1979) | Y |
| Reject hospital cost control plan (1979) | Y |
| Implement Panama Canal Treaties (1979) | Y |
| Establish Department of Education (1979) | N |
| Approve Anti-busing Amendment (1979) | N |
| Guarantee Chrysler Corp. loans (1979) | N |
| Approve military draft registration (1980) | Y |
| Aid Sandinista regime in Nicaragua (1980) | N |
| Strengthen fair housing laws (1980) | Y |

**97th Congress**

| | |
|---|---|
| Reagan budget proposal (1981) | Y |

## Interest Group Ratings

| Year | ADA | ACA | AFL-CIO | CCUS |
|---|---|---|---|---|
| 1980 | 17 | 91 | 16 | 81 |
| 1979 | 16 | 83 | 25 | 100 |
| 1978 | 10 | 96 | 0 | 100 |
| 1977 | 5 | 85 | 9 | 88 |
| 1976 | 10 | 84 | 14 | 85 |
| 1975 | 0 | 95 | 4 | 88 |
| 1974 | 9 | 87 | 9 | 100 |
| 1973 | 0 | 78 | 0 | 100 |

# 7 J. Kenneth Robinson (R)

**Of Winchester — Elected 1970**

**Born:** May 14, 1916, Winchester, Va.
**Education:** Va. Polytechnic Inst., B.S. 1937.
**Military Career:** Army, 1942-45.
**Profession:** Apple grower.
**Family:** Wife, Kathryn Rankin; six children.
**Religion:** Quaker.
**Political Career:** Va. Senate, 1966-70; unsuccessful GOP nominee for U.S. House, 1962.

**In Washington:** Robinson faithfully carries on his district's tradition of fiscal frugality and support for the armed forces, extending a philosophical line unbroken since the 1930s.

He approaches the job with caution, following party leadership on most issues, rather than striking out in any new directions. Robinson allied himself early in his career with the House Republican hierarchy and landed on two choice committees: Appropriations, where he is on the Agriculture and Defense subcommittees, and Intelligence, where he is the senior Republican.

Former Minority Leader John Rhodes once called him "the Rock of Gibraltar," a reference to his unobtrusive party loyalty as well as his stocky build. He voted with his party majority 89 percent of the time in 1980 — one of the highest scores in the House.

Robinson arrived in Washington in 1971 urging a balanced budget, a smaller federal bureaucracy and a stronger national defense. He has not wavered. He backed U.S. policies in Vietnam, opposed giving up the Panama Canal and favored continued diplomatic ties with Taiwan.

On Defense Appropriations, he has been a quiet but consistent supporter of giving the Defense Department all the funding it asks for, and has complained often in recent years that the military is not getting the equipment or maintenance it would need to fight a war.

On Intelligence, Robinson has argued for a lifting of restrictions Congress placed on covert U.S. operations in the 1970s. "We will not stand idly by," he said in 1980, "when totalitarian foreign powers send their forces or proxy forces in to destroy a legitimate government."

**At Home:** Robinson was a family friend of the late Harry F. Byrd Sr., and shared the powerful senator's conservatism and passion for apple growing. But Robinson had to buck the Byrd machine to make his political debut.

That was in 1962, when veteran Democratic

Rep. Burr P. Harrison retired from the 7th District House seat. The Republicans tapped Robinson, then the head of the Virginia Fruit Growers, as their candidate. But Byrd was still a nominal Democrat, and party took precedence over friendship. He endorsed the Democratic nominee, John O. Marsh Jr., boosting him to a 598-vote victory.

Three years later, Robinson scored his first political success, easily winning the state Senate seat vacated when Harry F. Byrd Jr. was appointed to the U.S. Senate on his father's resignation.

In 1969, many party leaders wanted Robinson to run for lieutenant governor on the Republican ticket headed by Linwood Holton. But his son was fatally ill with leukemia, and Robinson declined.

He was willing to run for Congress the following year, however, when Marsh's retirement again opened the 7th District. Facing Murat Williams, a liberal Democrat who had managed Eugene McCarthy's 1968 presidential campaign in Virginia, Robinson was an easy winner. He padded his margin in a 1972 rematch with Williams.

The Democrats came closest to unseating Robinson in the Watergate election of 1974. While the incumbent campaigned infrequently, his aggressive young Democratic opponent lambasted him for his support of the Nixon administration and for the low marks he received from education and conservation groups. Robinson managed to

---

**7th District: North — Charlottesville, Winchester.** Population: 599,915 (29% increase since 1970). Race: White 518,907 (86%), Black 76,871 (13%), Others 4,137 (1%). Spanish origin: 4,211 (8%).

defeat his challenger, Charlottesville Councilman George Gilliam, but by a margin of less than 6,000 votes.

Since then, though, the political climate has favored the incumbent, and Democrats have mounted a challenge only once, in 1978. Robinson won that year by a margin of nearly 2-to-1.

**The District:** The 7th District is Byrd country, from the northern suburbs of Richmond across the Shenandoah Mountains to Winchester, the center of the state's apple-growing industry and home of the Byrd family.

For generations, the district has been rural and conservative. But like the younger Harry Byrd, who became an independent in 1970, it has abandoned its Democratic roots and emerged as one of the state's Republican strongholds. In 1980, Reagan drew a higher share of the vote in the 7th than in any other Virginia district.

In the counties on either side of the Blue Ridge Mountains, there is a well-developed agricultural economy based on dairying and fruit production. Redistricting in 1972 added some less prosperous north central Virginia counties, traditionally rural, but becoming urbanized. With expansion of the Richmond and northern Virginia suburbs into the 7th, the district grew faster than any other in Virginia in the 1970s.

## Committees

**Appropriations** (5th of 22 Republicans)
    Agriculture; Rural Development and Related Agencies; Defense.

**Select Intelligence** (Ranking Republican)
    Program and Budget Authorization.

## Elections

**1980 General**

| | |
|---|---|
| J. Kenneth Robinson (R) | Unopposed |

**1978 General**

| | |
|---|---|
| J. Kenneth Robinson (R) | 84,517 (64%) |
| Lewis Fickett (D) | 46,950 (36%) |

**Previous Winning Percentages**

| 1976 (82%) | 1974 (53%) | 1972 (66%) | 1970 (62%) |
|---|---|---|---|

**District Vote For President**

| | 1980 | | 1976 | | 1972 |
|---|---|---|---|---|---|
| D | 74,603 (36%) | D | 79,319 (44%) | D | 39,691 (27%) |
| R | 117,538 (57%) | R | 96,884 (54%) | R | 104,720 (71%) |
| I | 9,577 (5%) | | | | |

## Campaign Finance

| | Receipts | Receipts from PACs | Expenditures |
|---|---|---|---|
| **1980** | | | |
| Robinson (R) | $60,309 | $25,800 (43%) | $33,173 |
| **1978** | | | |
| Robinson (R) | $98,348 | $25,072 (26%) | $87,087 |
| Fickett (D) | $58,506 | $20,985 (36%) | $58,493 |

## Voting Studies

| | Presidential Support | | Party Unity | | Conservative Coalition | |
|---|---|---|---|---|---|---|
| **Year** | **S** | **O** | **S** | **O** | **S** | **O** |
| 1980 | 35 | 65 | 89 | 11 | 100 | 0 |
| 1979 | 28 | 72 | 94 | 6 | 100 | 0 |

| 1978 | 23 | 76 | 88 | 8 | 95 | 2 |
|---|---|---|---|---|---|---|
| 1977 | 30 | 70 | 92 | 8 | 97 | 2 |
| 1976 | 80 | 20 | 95 | 4 | 97 | 1 |
| 1975 | 65 | 35 | 93 | 5 | 95 | 1 |
| 1974 (Ford) | 57 | 43 | | | | |
| 1974 | 72 | 28 | 93 | 6 | 98 | 2 |
| 1973 | 75 | 24 | 92 | 8 | 98 | 2 |
| 1972 | 57 | 41 | 91 | 4 | 96 | 0 |
| 1971 | 82 | 16 | 92 | 7 | 100 | 0 |

S = Support    O = Opposition

## Key Votes

**96th Congress**

| | |
|---|---|
| Weaken Carter oil profits tax (1979) | Y |
| Reject hospital cost control plan (1979) | Y |
| Implement Panama Canal Treaties (1979) | N |
| Establish Department of Education (1979) | N |
| Approve Anti-busing Amendment (1979) | Y |
| Guarantee Chrysler Corp. loans (1979) | N |
| Approve military draft registration (1980) | Y |
| Aid Sandinista regime in Nicaragua (1980) | N |
| Strengthen fair housing laws (1980) | N |

**97th Congress**

| | |
|---|---|
| Reagan budget proposal (1981) | Y |

## Interest Group Ratings

| Year | ADA | ACA | AFL-CIO | CCUS |
|---|---|---|---|---|
| 1980 | 6 | 92 | 11 | 82 |
| 1979 | 0 | 100 | 10 | 100 |
| 1978 | 10 | 93 | 10 | 82 |
| 1977 | 0 | 93 | 9 | 88 |
| 1976 | 0 | 96 | 13 | 88 |
| 1975 | 0 | 100 | 5 | 94 |
| 1974 | 0 | 93 | 0 | 100 |
| 1973 | 0 | 85 | 9 | 100 |
| 1972 | 0 | 100 | 9 | 100 |
| 1971 | 5 | 93 | 17 | |

# 8 Stan Parris (R)

**Of Woodbridge — Elected 1980**
**Also served 1973-75**

**Born:** Sept. 9, 1929, Champaign, Ill.
**Education:** U. of Illinois, B.S. 1950; George Washington U., J.D. 1958.
**Military Career:** Air Force, 1950-54.
**Profession:** Lawyer.
**Family:** Wife, Sonya Mann; three children.
**Religion:** Episcopalian.
**Political Career:** Fairfax County Board of Supervisors, 1964-67; Va. House, 1969-72; U.S. House, 1973-75; unsuccessfully sought re-election to U.S. House, 1974.

**The Member:** Swept from the House in the 1974 Democratic landslide, Parris came back in the Republican landslide of 1980. He had the satisfaction of defeating the man who unseated him, Democratic Rep. Herbert E. Harris II.

Ronald Reagan's popularity helped Parris to his narrow victory. While Reagan carried the district, Parris won by only 1,094.

When the 97th Congress was organizing, Parris pushed hard to win a seat on the Ways and Means Committee. He invoked tradition to bolster his claim; there has been at least one Virginian on that committee since 1955. Democratic Rep. Joseph Fisher, the lone Virginian on Ways and Means in the 96th Congress, lost in 1980. But there were no Republican vacancies, and Democrats refused to buy arguments that the GOP representation shuld be expanded.

Parris is chairman of the House Task Force on Economic Policy, an arm of the Republican Research Committee established in 1977 to foster support for party policy. During the 1981 debate on Reagan's budget and tax proposals, Parris broadened the Task Force's scope and lobbied to win conservative Democratic support for the administration plans.

**The District:** The 8th includes the southern portion of Virginia's Washington-area suburbs. Much of the population is mobile, affluent and less conservative than the rest of the state. But party roots are not deep and contests for important offices are usually close.

Most residents live in the inner suburbs of Alexandria and Fairfax County, but younger families seeking less expensive housing have moved to more distant Prince William and Stafford counties. Parris took advantage of support in Fairfax and the smaller counties to overcome Harris' lead in Alexandria, where a large black and young professional population nearly always votes Democratic.

## Committees

**Banking, Finance and Urban Affairs** (11th of 19 Republicans)
Economic Stabilization; Housing and Community Development; International Trade, Investment and Monetary Policy.

**District of Columbia** (2nd of 4 Republicans)
Fiscal Affairs and Health; Government Operations and Metropolitan Affairs.

## Elections

**1980 General**

| | |
|---|---|
| Stanford Parris (R) | 95,624 (49%) |
| Herbert Harris (D) | 94,530 (48%) |

**1980 Primary**

| | |
|---|---|
| Stanford Parris (R) | 9,930 (60%) |
| Robert Thoburn (R) | 6,564 (40%) |

**Previous Winning Percentage**
1972 (44%)

**District Vote For President**

| | 1980 | | 1976 | | 1972 |
|---|---|---|---|---|---|
| **D** | 67,754 (33%) | **D** | 81,501 (47%) | **D** | 54,348 (35%) |
| **R** | 113,676 (56%) | **R** | 87,858 (51%) | **R** | 100,202 (64%) |
| **I** | 18,994 (9%) | | | | |

## Campaign Finance

| | Receipts | Receipts from PACs | Expenditures |
|---|---|---|---|
| **1980** | | | |
| Parris (R) | $391,749 | $119,989 (31%) | $387,716 |
| Harris (D) | $218,600 | $108,091 (49%) | $238,680 |

## Key Vote

**97th Congress**

| | |
|---|---|
| Reagan budget proposal (1981) | Y |

---

**8th District: Northeast — Washington, D.C. suburbs, Alexandria.** Population: 587,054 (27% increase since 1970). Race: White 505,540 (86%), Black 57,737 (10%), Asian and Pacific Islander 14,961 (3%), Others 8,816 (2%). Spanish origin: 16,309 (3%).

# 9 William Wampler (R)

**Of Bristol — Elected 1966**
Also served 1953-55

**Born:** April 21, 1926, Pennington Gap, Va.
**Education:** Va. Polytechnic Institute B.S. 1948;
attended U. of Va. Law School, 1949-50.
**Military Career:** Navy, 1943-45.
**Profession:** Journalist.
**Family:** Wife, Lee McCall; two children.
**Religion:** Presbyterian.
**Political Career:** Elected to U.S. House, 1952;
unsuccessfully sought re-election to U.S.
House 1954, 1956; re-elected to U.S. House
1966.

**In Washington:** Wampler has an easy-going, low-pressure style as the Agriculture Committee's senior Republican. He takes care of cattle and tobacco interests and cooperates quietly with the Democrats, rarely pushing partisanship very far.

Much of Wampler's time is spent on food safety and on his effort to convince the federal government to spend more money on agricultural research.

In recent years, he has played a leading role in forcing the government to re-examine its ban on nitrites used to preserve meats and on herbicides used to kill weeds. He has sponsored legislation, later written into law, requiring federal officials to submit proposed bans on pesticides and food additives to an independent scientific panel.

Much of this work has been a matter of constituent interest. When tests showed traces of nitrites causing cancer in laboratory animals in the mid-1970s, Virginia producers of Smithfield hams and smoked turkeys descended on Wampler's office demanding that something be done. Without nitrites, they would be in deep economic trouble. They insisted that nitrites prevent botulism.

He began working on pesticide problems when the government moved to ban a weed-killer used in Virginia to hold down growth threatening the loblolly pine (used to make paper). Wampler thinks the government creates new problems in its zeal to protect the environment from poisonous pesticides.

At the root of most of this debate is the Delaney amendment, adopted by Congress in the 1950s to require the government to take products off the market if they cause cancer in man or animals. Wampler wants to modify the Delaney amendment; he argues that science now is capable of drawing finer distinctions between safe and unsafe foods than in the 1950s.

The drive to rewrite the Delaney amendment is largely a campaign of the American Meat Institute, of which Wampler is a close ally. The institute has written legislation which would remove the mandatory Delaney provisions and stretch out the study time periods before a product is banned.

Wampler worked several years to win congressional approval of a bill to revamp and expand the Agriculture Department's system of grants for research and teaching in agricultural science courses. He began by complaining that the department was moving away from traditional farm programs to income maintenance studies, and he introduced a bill in 1975 to double the amount of money available for research and development. Two years later, the bill was incorporated into the 1977 farm act. In 1981, concerned that the program was hurt by federal spending cutbacks, Wampler began working on a new two-year extension of the original plan.

In all of this, Wampler works easily with the committee's Democratic majority. Most bills that emerge from the Agriculture Committee are bipartisan, and Wampler is a friendly, popular

---

**9th District: Southwest — Bristol.**
Population: 554,578 (19% increase since 1970).
Race: White 539,273 (97%), Black 12,630 (2%), Others 2,675 (0.4%). Spanish origin: 3,140 (1%).

member who rarely speaks in anger, even when some of the junior Republicans on the committee would prefer that he do so.

Wampler has sometimes parted from conservative Republicans on food stamp issues. He fought President Carter's decision to make the stamps free in 1977, but was reluctant, at least until the start of the Reagan administration, to accept severe cutbacks in benefits or funding. He even defended the program against reductions recommended by his old House colleague, President Ford. When Ford wanted to raise the price of the stamps, Wampler made a floor speech in opposition. But Wampler quietly voted for Reagan's recommended cuts in 1981.

Wampler has a second, non-legislative assignment, on the Select Committee on Aging. As a member of the Aging Subcommittee on Retirement, Income and Employment, he has endorsed removing the limit on outside earnings for Social Security recipients, opposed taxing benefits and advocated a shorter waiting period for disability payments.

**At Home.** Wampler is one of only two Republicans left in the House who served there when the GOP last controlled it in the early 1950s. He was a 26-year-old newspaper reporter when he first ran for the House in 1952, taking advantage of Eisenhower's coattails to become the youngest member of the Republican 83rd Congress.

But it was only a brief encounter. In 1954, unemployment in the district's coal mines and declining farm prices made the young congressman a target of voter dissatisfaction. He lost narrowly to Democratic challenger W. Pat Jennings.

After his defeat, Wampler was appointed by the Eisenhower administration as special assistant to the general manager of the Atomic Energy Commission.

In 1956, he tried and failed to regain his House seat. But he never gave up, and the right moment finally came along in 1966. By then, the Johnson administration was even more unpopular in southwestern Virginia than it was becoming in the rest of the country. Wampler linked the liberal Jennings to controversial big-spending programs of the Great Society and beat him by nearly 7,000 votes. Jennings was elected clerk of the House of Representatives and never ran for Congress again.

While Wampler has had opposition in every election since then, Democrats have rarely come close to unseating the popular "bald eagle of the Cumberland." The only real contest was in 1974, when low cattle prices were again a source of farm discontent, and the Democratic nominee was a wealthy real estate developer, Charles Horne. The challenger spent $232,341 on his campaign but fell 2,400 votes short.

**The District.** The Appalachian district has been called the "Fighting Ninth" because of its fiercely competitive two-party system and traditional isolation from the Virginia political establishment in Richmond. In the years when Democrats routinely dominated Virginia politics, the 9th was the only district in which Republicans were consistently strong.

Mountainous southwestern Virginia was settled by Scotch-Irish and German immigrants, who had little in common with the English settlers in the Tidewater and Piedmont regions. The 9th is the poorest district in the state. In the western end, near the Kentucky and West Virginia borders, coal mining is important. Agriculture is dominant elsewhere, with corn, tobacco and dairy farming major revenue producers.

## Committees

**Agriculture** (Ranking Republican)
Department Operations, Research, and Foreign Agriculture; Tobacco and Peanuts.

**Select Aging** (2nd of 23 Republicans)
Retirement Income and Employment.

## Elections

**1980 General**

| | |
|---|---|
| William Wampler (R ) | 119,196 (69 %) |
| Roosevelt Ferguson (D ) | 52,636 (31 %) |

**1978 General**

| | |
|---|---|
| William Wampler (R ) | 76,877 (62 %) |
| Champ Clark (D ) | 47,367 (38 %) |

**Previous Winning Percentages**

| | | | |
|---|---|---|---|
| 1976 (57 %) | 1974 (51 %) | 1972 (72 %) | 1970 (61 %) |
| 1968 (60 %) | 1966 (54 %) | 1952 (52 %) | |

**District Vote For President**

| | 1980 | | 1976 | | 1972 |
|---|---|---|---|---|---|
| D | 86,013 (47 %) | D | 90,065 (51 %) | D | 44,540 (31 %) |
| R | 89,709 (49 %) | R | 79,376 (45 %) | R | 95,065 (67 %) |
| I | 4,625 (3 %) | | | | |

## Campaign Finance

| | Receipts | Receipts from PACs | Expen- ditures |
|---|---|---|---|
| **1980** | | | |
| Wampler (R ) | $121,322 | $69,420 (57 %) | $89,461 |
| Ferguson (D ) | $17,221 | - (0 %) | $17,198 |
| **1978** | | | |
| Wampler (R ) | $115,773 | $52,605 (45 %) | $112,016 |
| Clark (D ) | $62,182 | $500 (1 %) | $56,121 |

## Voting Studies

| Year | Presidental Support | | Party Unity | | Conservative Coalition | |
|---|---|---|---|---|---|---|
| | S | O | S | O | S | O |
| 1980 | 40 | 56 | 70 | 26 | 89 | 6 |
| 1979 | 32 | 61 | 72 | 22 | 90 | 3 |
| 1978 | 28 | 65 | 74 | 20 | 86 | 7 |
| 1977 | 37 | 54 | 73 | 21 | 90 | 5 |
| 1976 | 69 | 25 | 75 | 16 | 85 | 7 |
| 1975 | 60 | 33 | 80 | 13 | 89 | 2 |
| 1974 (Ford) | 52 | 43 | | | | |
| 1974 | 60 | 38 | 78 | 18 | 82 | 12 |
| 1973 | 69 | 30 | 77 | 21 | 88 | 10 |
| 1972 | 68 | 27 | 69 | 16 | 82 | 6 |
| 1971 | 77 | 19 | 76 | 19 | 87 | 8 |
| 1970 | 75 | 25 | 65 | 35 | 89 | 11 |
| 1969 | 51 | 36 | 76 | 18 | 91 | 4 |
| 1968 | 47 | 44 | 77 | 13 | 76 | 12 |
| 1967 | 50 | 46 | 80 | 16 | 83 | 13 |

S = Support          O = Opposition

## Key Votes

**96th Congress**

| | |
|---|---|
| Weaken Carter oil profits tax (1979) | Y |
| Reject hospital cost control plan (1979) | Y |
| Implement Panama Canal Treaties (1979) | N |
| Establish Department of Education (1979) | Y |
| Approve Anti-busing Amendment (1979) | Y |
| Guarantee Chrysler Corp. loans (1979) | Y |
| Approve military draft registration (1980) | Y |
| Aid Sandinista regime in Nicaragua (1980) | N |
| Strengthen fair housing laws (1980) | N |

**97th Congress**

| | |
|---|---|
| Reagan budget proposal (1981) | Y |

## Interest Group Ratings

| Year | ADA | ACA | AFL-CIO | CCUS |
|---|---|---|---|---|
| 1980 | 28 | 71 | 21 | 74 |
| 1979 | 0 | 77 | 16 | 89 |
| 1978 | 10 | 85 | 20 | 78 |
| 1977 | 5 | 65 | 13 | 88 |
| 1976 | 5 | 82 | 22 | 94 |
| 1975 | 5 | 93 | 9 | 88 |
| 1974 | 13 | 67 | 18 | 67 |
| 1973 | 4 | 78 | 18 | 91 |
| 1972 | 6 | 85 | 40 | 100 |
| 1971 | 8 | 82 | 17 | - |
| 1970 | 16 | 84 | 0 | 70 |
| 1969 | 0 | 76 | 10 | - |
| 1968 | 8 | 83 | 25 | - |
| 1967 | 7 | 88 | 27 | 78 |

# 10 Frank R. Wolf (R)

**Of Vienna — Elected 1980**
**Born:** Jan. 30, 1939, Philadelphia, Pa.
**Education:** Penn. State U., B.A. 1961; Georgetown U., LL.B. 1965.
**Military Career:** Army, 1961-62.
**Profession:** Lawyer.
**Family:** Wife, Carolyn Stover; five children.
**Religion:** Presbyterian.
**Political Career:** Unsuccessfully sought GOP nomination for U.S. House, 1976; unsuccessful GOP nominee for U.S. House, 1978.

**The Member:** Few congressional newcomers better illustrate the value of persistence than Wolf.

Barely a year after Democrat Joseph L. Fisher first won his House seat in 1974, Wolf began campaigning to defeat him. He failed to take the GOP nomination in 1976. In 1978, better known and better financed, Wolf won the Republican nomination, only to lose to Fisher by 8,911 votes. The 1980 election was the reward. With a huge campaign budget, Wolf capped five years of effort with a 4,957-vote victory.

Transportation issues have been Wolf's primary focus in Congress. He is pushing for a policy to balance passenger volume at metropolitan Washington's two federally-owned airports, National and Dulles. National now handles more than four times as many passengers as Dulles, a large, under-used facility in rural Northern Virginia. Wolf's constituents object to noise from the steady stream of jets using National, and he wants to set an annual passenger ceiling at National and impose an 11 p.m. to 7 a.m. curfew on air operations there.

Although Congress is Wolf's first elective office, he has been in Washington most of the past decade, as an aide to former Rep. Edward G. Biester Jr., R-Pa., as deputy assistant secretary of the interior, and as a lobbyist for baby food and farm implement manufacturers.

**The District:** The 10th is the most affluent district in any Southern state, but it is hardly even fair to identify it with the South. It is a set of bedroom communities for federal government employees from all regions of the country, and its voting habits resemble those of other suburban districts in the East or Midwest, except for a preoccupation with civil service issues.

Fisher held the seat for three terms by winning big in normally Democratic Arlington. But in 1980, his vote there failed to offset Wolf's lead in outlying Fairfax and Loudon counties.

## Committees

**Post Office and Civil Service** (10th of 11 Republicans)
Civil Service; Human Resources; Postal Operations and Services.

**Public Works and Transportation** (19th of 19 Republicans)
Aviation; Water Resources.

## Elections

**1980 General**

| | |
|---|---|
| Frank Wolf (R ) | 110,840 (51 %) |
| Joseph Fisher (D ) | 105,883 (49 %) |

**1980 Primary**

| | |
|---|---|
| Frank Wolf (R ) | 13,782 (75 %) |
| Martin Perper (R ) | 3,182 (17 %) |
| Harold Miller (R ) | 1,384 (8 %) |

**District Vote For President**

| | 1980 | | 1976 | | 1972 |
|---|---|---|---|---|---|
| **D** | 76,676 (34 %) | **D** | 95,532 (47 %) | **D** | 57,670 (34 %) |
| **R** | 120,328 (54 %) | **R** | 104,815 (51 %) | **R** | 110,177 (65 %) |
| **I** | 23,999 (11 %) | | | | |

## Campaign Finance

| 1980 | Receipts | Receipts from PACs | Expenditures |
|---|---|---|---|
| Wolf (R ) | $470,357 | $211,746 (45 %) | $460,504 |
| Fisher (D ) | $265,839 | $65,808 (25 %) | $270,926 |

## Key Vote

**97th Congress**
Reagan budget proposal (1981)                    Y

> **10th District: Northeast — Washington, D.C. suburbs, Arlington County.**
> Population: 534,494 (15% increase since 1970). Race: White 466,002 (87%), Black 35,247 (7%), Asian and Pacific Islander 20,838 (4%), Others 12,407 (2%). Spanish origin: 21,560 (4%).

# Washington

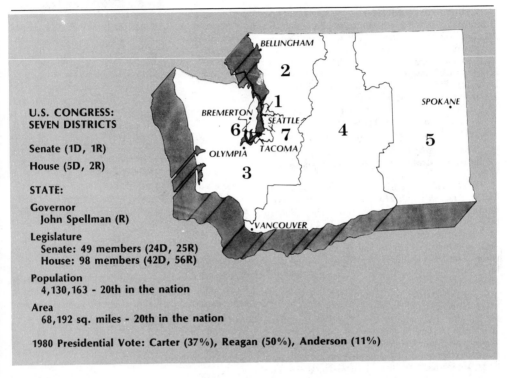

**U.S. CONGRESS:
SEVEN DISTRICTS**

Senate (1D, 1R)

House (5D, 2R)

**STATE:**

Governor
  John Spellman (R)

Legislature
  Senate: 49 members (24D, 25R)
  House: 98 members (42D, 56R)

Population
  4,130,163 - 20th in the nation

Area
  68,192 sq. miles - 20th in the nation

**1980 Presidential Vote: Carter (37%), Reagan (50%), Anderson (11%)**

## . . . Semi-Pacific

Like Oregon, Washington is divided politically by the Cascades. But unlike Oregon, it has a politics recognizable by the standards of industrial Northern states. It has a large ethnic population, a labor movement that has dominated the Democratic Party at times in the past and a rural farm bloc east of the mountains that votes more like the Midwest than the Pacific Northwest.

Many different kinds of candidates have won here in recent years, from conservative Democrat Dixy Lee Ray, who was governor from 1977 to 1981, to moderate Republicans Daniel J. Evans, who was governor for three terms before her, and John Spellman, who succeeded her.

But the clearest symbol of success is Sen. Henry M. Jackson, an easy winner for five Senate terms. Jackson's jobs-and-labor orientation has kept him popular in Seattle without really damaging his reputation as a conservationist; his hard-line foreign policy has brought him support in the

conservative east, even among people who vote Republican for most other offices.

Both of Washington's Senate seats were Democratic from 1952, when Jackson was first elected, until 1980, when Warren G. Magnuson was unseated after 36 years. Attorney General Slade Gorton, who defeated Magnuson, fits the mold of moderate Republicans who have been able to win in Washington in modern times.

Conservative Republicans in the east have not been strong enough to control GOP primaries; the Seattle-area moderates have had the votes, and they have been responsible for the election of Gorton, Evans and Spellman. This has created serious tension within the GOP. Ray won her single term as governor in 1976 mainly because she attracted votes from conservative Republicans dissatisfied with Spellman.

The Democratic Party sometimes has an opposite tension — environmentalist liberals want to move the party to the left. Ray was beaten for renomination in 1980 by psychiatrist Jim McDermott, who favored increased social spending and criticized Ray's pro-nuclear stand. When McDermott won the nomination, more traditional Democrats defected to Spellman, allowing Republicans to recapture the statehouse.

The New Deal had a profound impact on the state's political landscape. Huge federal hydroelectric projects like the Grand Coulee Dam were important to the state economically and built a constituency for activist government.

Democrats traditionally have been influenced by a strong labor movement, which organized the lumber and maritime industries. Later, union membership grew with the Seattle manufacturing complex. Aerospace dominates the economy and has made the Machinists a potent union, joining the Longshoremen and the Teamsters.

Post-war prosperity, however, has helped make Washington a swing state. Since World War II, it has gone Republican six times and Democratic three times in presidential elections. Richard Nixon narrowly carried it in 1960; Hubert Humphrey narrowly carried it in 1968. Ford edged Carter by 60,000 votes in 1976.

Washington is generally a weak-party state. It has a "blanket" primary ballot allowing voters to participate in either party's primary for each office listed.

# A Political Tour

**King County.** Made up of Seattle and its suburbs, King County provides a third of the state vote. Built on a hilly isthmus, the city of Seattle has an economy devoted to transportation — cargo trade, ship-building and airplane construction.

Boeing and the aerospace industry have played a key role in the development of the Seattle region. Aircraft-building is a cyclical industry, so the industry's slump in the early 1970s sent the local economy into a tailspin. Since then, Boeing has diversified and is strong. But aircraft remains its most important product, and the demand for planes, both civilian and military, has boosted Seattle employment.

The South Side of Seattle is blue-collar Democratic territory, with a varied ethnic population including Italian and Scandinavian communities. This area nearly always goes for Democrats at the state level, but in 1977, when the Democratic nominee in a special congressional election was a low-growth environmentalist, the voters here rebelled and chose a Republican. The following year, they replaced him with a more traditional labor-oriented Democrat.

The environmentalists are stronger in the white-collar neighborhoods of the northern part of the city. A liberal movement, combining "good government" and environmental activists, was influential in city politics throughout the 1970s. Democrat Wes Uhlman won the mayoralty in 1969 and a reputation at the time as "the John Lindsay of the West." After 10 years in office, he was succeeded by the like-minded Charles Royer.

Some of Seattle's suburbs generally cast a moderate Republican vote, favoring candidates like Evans and Spellman. But others, like Bellevue, Kirkland and Mercer Island, send conservative Republicans to the state Legislature.

With Seattle accounting for about 40 percent of King County's 1.3 million people, the partisan split between blue-collar Democrats in the city and upper-income suburban Republicans has made the county vote unpredictable. King voted Republican for president, senator and governor in 1980. Four years before, the GOP captured the county only on the presidential level, losing it in the Senate and gubernatorial races.

**Puget Sound, Eastern Shore.** Lumber has dominated life for the last 100 years in this part of the state, where most of the people are squeezed into the strip of land between the mountains and the sound.

The largest concentration of Democratic votes lies in Everett, Sen. Henry M. Jackson's hometown. Everett sprang up almost overnight in 1890, when developers realized its potential as a port and logging town. These days, Everett's timber-based economy is supplemented by a Boeing plant and the high-technology businesses associated with Boeing.

Bellingham, another timber town, is the second largest city north of the Seattle area. It and surrounding Whatcom County are closely divided in their political preferences.

The islands in the sound are Republican, as are most of the country towns in from the water. But the best ground for the GOP is in the fast-growing Seattle suburbs in southern Snohomish County, most notably Edmonds and Lynwood.

**Olympic Peninsula, Southwest Washington.** The most Democratic area in Washington, this timber-dominated region is largely rural but has four cities as anchors — Tacoma, Vancouver, Bremerton and Olympia, the state capital. All four tend to vote Democratic. In the rural logging areas, the populist heritage lives on and often produces sizable Democratic margins as well.

Although Reagan scored well statewide in 1980, Carter had his best performance in this area. The only two counties Carter captured in the state — Pacific and Grays Harbor — are along the ocean in this region.

Tacoma, the second largest city in the state with 158,000 inhabitants, is a town traditionally devoted to forest products. It is the worldwide headquarters for the Weyerhaeuser Company, one of the leading lumber companies in the world and a major landowner in the Pacific Northwest.

Vancouver is the oldest settlement in Washington. Sitting along the Columbia River on the southern edge of the state, it grew from a lumber town into an industrial complex.

Olympia is a white-collar town centered on state government, while Bremerton has a long affiliation with the Navy. Both are Democratic.

Republicans are in Olympia's suburbs and in agricultural Lewis County, to its south.

**Eastern Washington.** Part of the Inland Empire east of the Cascade Mountain Range, Republican eastern Washington covers more than half the state. Known for its wheat and its apples, this rural region casts a quarter of the state's vote.

Yakima, an agricultural center, owes its livelihood to the thousands of acres of irrigated soil surrounding it. Before the coming of federal irrigation projects in the early 1900s, the land was a sagebrush desert. The Yakima Valley produces a consistent Republican vote.

Spokane, the area's largest city, has a history of support for conservative causes, despite a strong minority element of labor Democrats. Walla Walla County, to the south, habitually has the highest vote percentages for the GOP.

The Tri-Cities — Yakima, Kennewick and Pasco — have served as homes for many blue-collar workers employed at the Hanford nuclear site. They have tended to vote Democratic. But as the three-reactor complex draws closer to completion, the construction workers are being replaced by engineers and scientists, many of whom bring Republican affiliations with them.

In similar fashion, Grant County to the north used to be Democratic because of the communities of construction workers building dams along the Columbia River. That chore is done, leaving Grant to the Republican farmers.

Logging takes place along the Canadian border, accounting for pockets of Democratic strength there, but they are minority pockets. Some of the northern counties also have a significant Indian vote, which tends to be Democratic.

# Redrawing the Lines

Rarely does a governor veto a redistricting plan passed by his own party's legislators, but that is what happened in Washington, which gains an eighth district in 1982.

The GOP-ruled Legislature passed a map April 24 that would have endangered Democrats Mike Lowry (7th District) and House Majority Whip Thomas S. Foley (5th District). But the plan also radically altered the districts of the state's two Republican incumbents — Joel Pritchard of the northern Seattle 1st District and Sid Morrison of the central 4th District.

Pritchard gave Gov. Spellman a letter signed by all seven incumbent representatives asking him to veto the bill. He did on May 18, leaving redistricting until 1982.

---

# Governor
# John Spellman (R)

**Born:** Dec. 29, 1926, Seattle, Wash.
**Home:** Seattle, Wash.
**Education:** Seattle U., B.S.S. 1949; Georgetown U. Law School, J.D. 1953.
**Military Career:** Navy, World War II.
**Profession:** Lawyer.
**Family:** Wife, Lois; six children.
**Religion:** Roman Catholic.
**Political Career:** Unsuccessful campaign for mayor of Seattle, 1965; King County commissioner, 1967-69; county executive, 1969-80; unsuccessful campaign for governor, 1976; elected governor 1980; term expires Jan. 1985.

# Henry M. Jackson (D)

**Of Everett — Elected 1952**

**Born:** May 31, 1912, Everett, Wash.
**Education:** U. of Wash., LL.B. 1935.
**Profession:** Lawyer.
**Family:** Wife, Helen Hardin; two children.
**Religion:** Presbyterian.
**Political Career:** Snohomish County Prosecuting Attorney, 1938-40; U.S. House, 1941-53.

**In Washington:** Not very long ago, it seemed the sun never set on the Jacksonian empire.

As dominant hawk on the Senate Armed Services Committee, he led an entire faction in the Democratic Party supporting a more aggressive American role in world affairs. As chairman of the Energy Committee, he handled much of the major energy and environmental legislation of the past two decades. His Permanent Subcommittee on Investigations, until he gave it up in a 1977 reorganization, allowed him to stage hearings across a wide range of controversial topics, from oil company profits to Soviet wheat sales.

As late as mid-1980 there were influential Democrats who talked seriously of Jackson as a presidential challenger. And even after the Democratic rout later in the year, his views won him a place among President Reagan's transition advisers and consideration for a Cabinet post.

But Jackson began the 97th Congress in an unfamiliar state of eclipse. The Cabinet offer never came. His chairmanships were snuffed out by a Republican majority — and with them went much of the enormous staff he had accumulated. Even his prestige in defense circles was somewhat overshadowed by new Armed Services Chairman John G. Tower and by the rise of junior stars.

During more than four decades in Congress, Jackson has come to define a type — the "Jackson Democrat" — liberal on the home front, conservative in foreign affairs.

Ironically for a man who would become watchdog over U.S.-Soviet relations, Jackson got his first national attention for his stand against red-baiting. He was a principal antagonist of Sen. Joseph McCarthy during the televised Army-McCarthy hearings in 1954.

By the 1960s, Jackson was one of a few senior Senate titans who specialized in defense. Unlike some of them, he was never fascinated by the technical detail of weapons systems and war strategy. He is a geopolitician, whose driving force has always been a consistent and deeply held mistrust

of the Soviets.

Thus he was fiercely critical of the two strategic arms limitation treaties, even calling the second agreement "appeasement." His efforts to block Senate ratification of SALT II preoccupied him during much of the 96th Congress. When Congress wrote major trade legislation in 1974, Jackson was able to combine his anti-Soviet interest with his support for Israel, the second basic theme in his foreign policy work. He wrote an amendment prohibiting favored trade status for nations restricting emigration, a device aimed at Soviet restrictions on Jewish emigration. He persuaded the Ford administration to accept it in frantic negotiations as Congress adjourned.

Jackson has been a reliable supporter of new military hardware, from the earliest nuclear submarines to the newest binary chemical weapons. He was an unyielding supporter of American participation in Vietnam, though at the very end, in 1973, he went along with efforts to end it. President Nixon so appreciated Jackson's chessboard view of the world that he offered to make him Secretary of Defense in 1968.

Jackson's clout in military circles has helped enrich his home state, where defense hardware is built (by Boeing in Seattle) or based (the Trident nuclear submarine). Over the years, Jackson has taken vast amounts of joking and serious criticism about his "junior senator from Boeing" reputation. Colleagues have generally insisted, however, that it is the Cold War that matters to Jackson, not the defense plants.

"You can never have enough security for Henry," Minnesota Democrat Eugene McCarthy once complained. "If he had his way, the sky would be black with supersonic planes."

Jackson's liberal side, his identity with the traditional Democratic ideal of an activist federal government, dates back to his first flirtation with

**Henry M. Jackson, D-Wash.**

politics, working in a local campaign for Franklin D. Roosevelt in Washington state. It has continued, with occasional lapses, in its support for the Johnson administration's "Great Society" programs, and on into the Carter years and beyond. Jackson has long been a believer in government controls on economic forces — wages, prices and energy costs.

Energy has been Jackson's principal domestic preoccupation. He helped place hydroelectric dams all along the Columbia River, and promoted nuclear power as a 30-year member of the old Joint Atomic Energy Committee. He has pressed for increased domestic petroleum exploration, while sometimes castigating big oil companies in flamboyant terms for their prices and profits.

The 1977 Senate reorganization gave Jackson unprecedented jurisdiction over almost all energy-related legislation except tax bills. He became the point man for much of President Carter's energy package, a duty he carried out methodically, though without much enthusiasm.

In the 96th Congress, Jackson was busy battling Carter on SALT II, and left much of the energy work to second-ranking J. Bennett Johnston, the Louisiana Democrat. But he took time to argue for Carter's synthetic fuels subsidy and a "mobilization board" to speed energy projects.

Jackson counts a number of environmental protection laws among his proudest achievements. He was the main force behind the 1969 National Environmental Policy Act, the symbol of the government's environmental consciousness. He has fought for bills to regulate land use and stripmining, and create parks and wilderness areas.

Neither of Jackson's two presidential campaigns was much of a success. In 1972, late-starting and under-organized, he emphasized his opposition to busing and counted on a strong showing in the Florida primary. But Florida voters found George Wallace a more satisfying outlet for their anti-busing views. Jackson finished a poor third, and his campaign was effectively over, although he remained on some primary ballots and had his name placed in nomination by Jimmy Carter.

Four years later, well-financed and seeking the presidency as a competent legislative veteran, he did somewhat better. He dealt himself into the competition by winning in Massachusetts, and emerged briefly as Jimmy Carter's most serious rival. But he did not do as well as he had predicted in New York, and Carter's victory in Pennsylvania finished him off.

At its peak, Jackson's power was enhanced beyond seniority by his close command over scores of personal and committee staffers. Some of them, such as his trusted national security aide Richard N. Perle, became influential personages in their own right under Jackson's sponsorship. His staff network enabled Jackson to keep an eye on his far flung empire even when he was personally preoccupied with an issue like SALT.

But Jackson was never imperial in his dealings with colleagues. His stewardship of the Energy Committee was an exercise in patience. Bills were rarely pushed to a roll call, and minority members were accommodated. That is helping Jackson, now that he is in the minority himself.

**At Home:** The wooden style that failed to excite voters in the 1972 and 1976 presidential contests has never been much of a problem for Jackson at home. He is no more of an orator in Washington state than he was in New Hampshire or Florida, but his energy and enthusiasm have always come through, and he has found a personal rapport with the voters in a constituency of manageable size.

Jackson is the greatest career vote getter in modern Washington history. In the 11 times he has run for Congress — six for the House, five for the Senate — he has fallen short of 55 percent just once, in the Republican year of 1946, when Jackson's seat was the only one in the state that Republicans did not capture.

The son of a Norwegian laborer who had changed his name from Gresseth, Jackson won a prize as a boy for delivering 74,880 copies of the Everett *Herald* without any customer complaints. His sister then nicknamed him "Scoop" after a reporter-cartoon character in the local paper.

After working his way through law school, and practicing briefly, Jackson won his first election, for county prosecutor, and made a reputation driving whorehouses and slot machines out of Everett, a rough timber mill town.

The job as prosecutor led him to the House in 1940, and the House led him into a 1952 challenge to Republican Sen. Harry Cain, a McCarthy-style red-baiter who called him a dupe of communists.

Cain was a good campaigner, better on a speaker's platform than Jackson. But he suffered from widespread publicity about a relationship with his secretary, and this hurt him. Jackson, ignored that issue; he hit Cain hard for voting against a Grand Coulee Dam appropriation. The upshot was a respectable victory for Jackson in another bad year for Democrats.

Going for a second term in 1958, Jackson established his reputation as an unbeatable man. With a secure Democratic base, he began courting the state's business community, joking with them about his labor loyalties but reminding them of his efforts for Boeing and other important local industries. He crushed former U.S. Attorney William Bantz that fall and has won by landslides ever since. The later GOP candidates — ex-school superintendent Lloyd Andrews in 1964, state Sen. Charles Elicker in 1970, and airline pilot George Brown in 1976 — have been sacrificial lambs.

## Committees

**Armed Services** (2nd of 8 Democrats)
Military Construction; Preparedness; Strategic and Theater Nuclear Forces.

**Energy and Natural Resources** (Ranking Democrat)

**Governmental Affairs** (2nd of 8 Democrats)
Energy, Nuclear Proliferation and Government Processes; Federal Expenditures, Research, and Rules; Permanent Subcommittee on Investigations.

**Select Intelligence** (5th of 7 Democrats)
Analysis and Production; Budget; Collection and Foreign Operations.

## Elections

**1976 General**

| | |
|---|---|
| Henry Jackson (D) | 1,071,219 (72%) |
| George Brown (R) | 361,546 (24%) |

**1976 Primary**

| | |
|---|---|
| Henry Jackson (D) | 549,974 (87%) |
| Dennis Kelley (D) | 54,470 (9%) |

**Previous Winning Percentages**

| | | | |
|---|---|---|---|
| 1970 (82%) | 1964 (72%) | 1958 (67%) | 1952 (56%) |
| 1950* (61%) | 1948* (62%) | 1946* (53%) | 1944* (60%) |
| 1942* (69%) | 1940* (57%) | | |

*House election.

## Campaign Finance

| | Receipts | Receipts from PACs | Expenditures |
|---|---|---|---|
| **1976** | | | |
| Jackson (D) | $223,322 | $12,500 (6%) | $198,375 |
| Brown (R) | $10,841 | — (0%) | $10,841 |

## Voting Studies

| | Presidential Support | | Party Unity | | Conservative Coalition | |
|---|---|---|---|---|---|---|
| Year | S | O | S | O | S | O |
| 1980 | 75 | 25 | 89 | 10 | 19 | 79 |
| 1979 | 86 | 14 | 90 | 10 | 36 | 64 |
| 1978 | 80 | 19 | 87 | 13 | 30 | 69 |
| 1977 | 77 | 23 | 86 | 12 | 18 | 82 |
| 1976 | 36 | 40 | 69 | 8 | 17 | 64 |
| 1975 | 55 | 37 | 83 | 10 | 20 | 75 |

| | | | | | |
|---|---|---|---|---|---|
| 1974 (Ford) | 41 | 56 | | | |
| 1974 | 45 | 55 | 85 | 15 | 21 | 78 |
| 1973 | 47 | 53 | 78 | 22 | 33 | 67 |
| 1972 | 61 | 15 | 42 | 29 | 38 | 37 |
| 1971 | 40 | 23 | 50 | 18 | 28 | 36 |
| 1970 | 51 | 37 | 66 | 22 | 32 | 56 |
| 1969 | 61 | 31 | 72 | 16 | 16 | 77 |
| 1968 | 77 | 16 | 82 | 12 | 29 | 67 |
| 1967 | 75 | 16 | 83 | 10 | 11 | 79 |
| 1966 | 78 | 22 | 84 | 14 | 19 | 81 |
| 1965 | 82 | 15 | 82 | 15 | 21 | 79 |
| 1964 | 56 | 29 | 55 | 25 | 16 | 69 |
| 1963 | 73 | 15 | 81 | 10 | 30 | 63 |
| 1962 | 90 | 10 | 97 | 3 | 24 | 76 |
| 1961 | 85 | 15 | 96 | 4 | 12 | 88 |

S = Support    O = Opposition

## Key Votes

**96th Congress**

| | |
|---|---|
| Maintain relations with Taiwan (1979) | N |
| Reduce synthetic fuel development funds (1979) | N |
| Impose nuclear plant moratorium (1979) | N |
| Kill stronger windfall profits tax (1979) | N |
| Guarantee Chrysler Corp. loans (1979) | Y |
| Approve military draft registration (1980) | Y |
| End Revenue Sharing to the states (1980) | Y |
| Block Justice Dept. busing suits (1980) | N |

**97th Congress**

| | |
|---|---|
| Restore urban program funding cuts (1981) | Y |

## Interest Group Ratings

| Year | ADA | ACA | AFL-CIO | CCUS-1 | CCUS-2 |
|---|---|---|---|---|---|
| 1980 | 72 | 19 | 84 | 38 | |
| 1979 | 68 | 11 | 95 | 9 | 31 |
| 1978 | 55 | 8 | 84 | 17 | |
| 1977 | 80 | 22 | 95 | 17 | |
| 1976 | 50 | 13 | 95 | 0 | |
| 1975 | 61 | 8 | 90 | 6 | |
| 1974 | 62 | 11 | 82 | 0 | |
| 1973 | 55 | 21 | 100 | 0 | |
| 1972 | 40 | 38 | 100 | 0 | |
| 1971 | 56 | 27 | 100 | - | |
| 1970 | 56 | 24 | 100 | 0 | |
| 1969 | 78 | 14 | 100 | - | |
| 1968 | 57 | 12 | 100 | - | |
| 1967 | 69 | 0 | 100 | 30 | |
| 1966 | 80 | 11 | 100 | - | |
| 1965 | 71 | 15 | - | 10 | |
| 1964 | 82 | 24 | 73 | - | |
| 1963 | - | 13 | - | - | |
| 1962 | 83- | 3 | 100 | - | |
| 1961 | 100 | - | - | - | |

# Slade Gorton (R)

### Of Olympia — Elected 1980

**Born:** Jan. 8, 1928, Chicago, Ill.
**Education:** Dartmouth College, B.A. 1950; Columbia University, LL.B. 1953.
**Military Career:** Army, 1945-46; Air Force, 1953-56.
**Profession:** Lawyer.
**Family:** Wife, Sally Jean Clark; three children.
**Religion:** Episcopalian.
**Political Career:** Washington House, 1959-69, majority leader, 1967-69; attorney general, 1969-81.

**The Member:** Gorton's moderate views on social issues mark him off from many of his fellow GOP freshman senators — he favors the Equal Rights Amendment and believes the government should maintain "neutrality" on abortion. But he is a traditional Republican on economics, and he has sounded conservative in the 97th Congress.

Gorton has been a strong supporter of indexing federal tax rates to prevent inflation from pushing people into higher brackets. He says the federal budget should be balanced and held by law at 21 or 22 percent of the gross national product.

On the Budget Committee, Gorton voted for greater reductions in subsidized housing programs than President Reagan requested, partly to make room for more money for the Export-Import Bank, which Reagan wanted to trim. The bank is a favorite of Boeing, a major employer in Washington state, because its loans help finance sales of aircraft to foreign companies.

As attorney general in his home state, Gorton mounted legal assaults on land speculators, auto dealers and drug companies, giving him the reputation of a consumer champion, but turning some in the business community against him. At the outset of his Senate candidacy, he refused to take money from political action committees, calling himself a "skinny cat" who shunned "fat cats." He later abandoned that policy when his campaign ran short of funds.

To win his seat, Gorton had to overcome a Senate institution — Democrat Warren G. Magnuson, a 44-year congressional veteran. Gorton's victory demonstrated the limits of Magnuson's legendary pork-barrel politics.

When Magnuson pushed through nearly $1 billion in federal disaster aid for his home state following the Mount St. Helens volcano eruption, some observers thought he had ensured his re-election. But Gorton charged that, as Senate Appropriations chairman, the Democrat was personally responsible for inflation. Emphasizing his contrast to the aged and slow-moving incumbent, Gorton and some of his supporters staged a 50-mile relay run to file ballot petitions with the secretary of state.

## Committees

**Budget** (12th of 12 Republicans)

**Commerce, Science and Transportation** (7th of 9 Republicans)
Merchant Marine, chairman; Science, Technology, and Space; Surface Transportation.

**Environment and Public Works** (8th of 9 Republicans)
Toxic Substances and Environmental Oversight, chairman; Environmental Pollution; Water Resources.

**Select Indian Affairs** (4th of 4 Republicans)

**Small Business** (6th of 9 Republicans)
Productivity and Competition, chairman; Government Regulation and Paperwork.

## Elections

**1980 General**

| | |
|---|---|
| Slade Gorton (R) | 936,317 (54%) |
| Warren Magnuson (D) | 792,052 (46%) |

**1980 Primary**

| | |
|---|---|
| Slade Gorton (R) | 313,560 (56%) |
| Lloyd Cooney (R) | 229,178 (41%) |

## Campaign Finance

| | Receipts | Receipts from PACs | Expenditures |
|---|---|---|---|
| **1980** | | | |
| Gorton (R) | $934,190 | $112,356 (12%) | $907,317 |
| Magnuson (D) | $1,527,786 | $319,757 (21%) | $1,614,999 |

## Key Votes

**97th Congress**

Restore urban program funding cuts (1981)   N

# 1 Joel Pritchard (R)

**Of Seattle — Elected 1972**

**Born:** May 5, 1925, Seattle, Wash.
**Education:** Attended Marietta College, 1946-48.
**Military Career:** Army, 1944-46.
**Profession:** Envelope manufacturer.
**Family:** Divorced; four children.
**Religion:** Presbyterian.
**Political Career:** Wash. House, 1959-67, Senate, 1967-71; sought GOP U.S. House nomination, 1970.

**In Washington:** Pritchard's environmentalist views place him at some distance from most House Republicans, but his easygoing irreverence and his relatively low profile on the floor have kept him out of much controversy.

One reason for Pritchard's low profile has been his committee assignments. For three terms, he did not have a major one, specializing in Seattle-related work on the Merchant Marine Committee. In 1979 he went to Foreign Affairs.

When Pritchard does step into public view, however, he often shows a surprising willingness to argue against the grain.

On Merchant Marine, Pritchard often joined fellow Republican Paul McCloskey of California in fighting the aggressive tactics of John Murphy, D-N.Y., who was chairman until 1980. In many cases, Pritchard argued the environmentalist position against Murphy and the energy and maritime industries. Murphy usually had the votes, but the opposition had an occasional triumph.

In 1977, Pritchard fought Murphy over a marine mammal bill restricting the number of dolphins that could be killed incidentally by tuna fishermen. Pritchard complained that Murphy had refused even to consider an environmentally-oriented bill favored by President Carter. He and McCloskey took the issue to the floor and got a compromise lowering the legal dolphin kill.

Pritchard was also an occasional maverick during five years on the Government Operations Committee. In 1977, when the committee was considering a bill to create a federal Consumer Protection Agency, Pritchard cast one of the panel's two GOP votes in favor, allowing it to pass, 22-21. He also cast one of 17 GOP votes for it on the floor, where it was defeated.

In his first term on Foreign Affairs, he proved quietly supportive of some foreign aid measures other Republicans criticized, and sought to act as a restraining influence on GOP budget cuts.

In 1980, Pritchard decided to take on the controversial Tennessee-Tombigbee waterway, a plan to channel a shortcut for barges from Tennessee to Mobile, Ala. Pritchard said the Army Corps of Engineers had enlarged the project without congressional approval and drastically underestimated its costs. "I have not gotten into this lightly," he said. "I have not made a career out of attacking projects . . . in eight years, I have rarely taken the well to speak."

Pritchard's amendment provoked an angry response from Appropriations Chairman Jamie Whitten, D-Miss., who said Pritchard never seemed interested in cutting any projects in the Pacific Northwest. The amendment to drop $200 million for Tennessee-Tombigbee failed, 216-196. But Pritchard came closer than anyone had ever come against the project, drawing a GOP majority on his side.

**At Home:** Pritchard came to the House after operating a successful business manufacturing envelopes, serving 12 years in the Washington Legislature, and losing a first bid for Congress. During eight years in the state House and four in the state Senate, he was a leader among the moderate GOP faction headed by Gov. Daniel Evans. In 1970, Pritchard took on Seattle's veteran Rep. Thomas Pelly in the GOP primary. Pritchard had been a protégé of Pelly early in his career, but he grew tired of the older man's

---

**1st District: Northern Seattle and suburbs.** Population: 470,418 (2% decrease since 1970). Race: White 431,266 (92%), Black 8,445 (2%), Asian and Pacific Islander 19,007 (4%), Others 11,700 (2%). Spanish origin: 9,500 (2%).

repeated promises of retirement, and ran gently on the age and enthusiasm issue. Pelly won, but Pritchard drew 46 percent, and in 1972 Pelly retired.

The succession still proved much more difficult for Pritchard than had been expected. Although the district is predominantly Republican, some of the Seattle GOP was still resentful of his 1970 challenge to Pelly. And the Democrats put up an exceptional candidate in John Hempelmann, a young and aggressive former aide to Sen. Henry M. Jackson. It took a count of absentee ballots the week after the election to determine that Pritchard had won by 2,622 votes. Since then, he has had little trouble.

Pritchard said early in his career that no member should serve more than a dozen years. If he keeps his word, he will retire in 1984.

**The District:** The 1st takes in the northern portion of Seattle and some of its surrounding suburbs. This part of the city is predominantly white-collar and middle- to upper-middle income. The suburbs are home largely to professional families involved in the city's insurance, banking, and industrial enterprises.

While the population is predominantly Republican, there is a good deal of independent voting. Many of the Republicans have not felt entirely comfortable with the conservative take-over of both the local and national GOP.

## Committees

**Foreign Affairs** (8th of 16 Republicans)
Asian and Pacific Affairs; Human Rights and International Organizations; International Operations.

**Merchant Marine and Fisheries** (4th of 15 Republicans)
Fisheries and Wildlife Conservation and the Environment; Oceanography.

## Elections

**1980 General**

| | |
|---|---|
| Joel Pritchard (R) | 180,475 (78%) |
| Robin Drake (D) | 41,830 (18%) |

**1978 General**

| | |
|---|---|
| Joel Pritchard (R) | 99,942 (64%) |
| Janice Niemi (D) | 52,706 (34%) |

**Previous Winning Percentages**

| | | |
|---|---|---|
| 1976 (72%) | 1974 (70%) | 1972 (50%) |

**District Vote For President**

| | 1980 | | 1976 | | 1972 |
|---|---|---|---|---|---|
| D | 87,148 (40%) | D | 104,738 (43%) | D | 97,852 (40%) |
| R | 92,995 (42%) | R | 126,588 (52%) | R | 137,346 (57%) |
| I | 32,085 (15%) | | | | |

## Campaign Finance

| | Receipts | Receipts from PACs | Expen-ditures |
|---|---|---|---|
| **1980** | | | |
| Pritchard (R) | $60,525 | $2,0101 (3%) | $40,045 |
| Drake (D) | $480 | — (0%) | $474 |
| **1978** | | | |
| Pritchard (R) | $115,362 | — (0%) | $125,399 |
| Niemi (D) | $60,396 | $7,772 (13%) | $60,121 |

## Voting Studies

| | Presidential Support | | Party Unity | | Conservative Coalition | |
|---|---|---|---|---|---|---|
| Year | S | O | S | O | S | O |
| 1980 | 60 | 27 | 42 | 46 | 40 | 53 |
| 1979 | 65 | 28 | 39 | 50† | 35 | 46 |
| 1978 | 64 | 29 | 50 | 43 | 49 | 43 |
| 1977 | 53 | 33 | 48 | 45 | 44 | 48 |
| 1976 | 57 | 39 | 58 | 41 | 62 | 37 |
| 1975 | 67 | 21 | 59 | 33 | 65 | 29 |
| 1974 (Ford) | 37 | 44 | | | | |
| 1974 | 62 | 36 | 38 | 47 | 26 | 67 |
| 1973 | 48 | 48 | 46 | 50 | 44 | 56 |

S = Support          O = Opposition

†Not eligible for all recorded votes.

## Key Votes

**96th Congress**

| | |
|---|---|
| Weaken Carter oil profits tax (1979) | Y |
| Reject hospital cost control plan (1979) | Y |
| Implement Panama Canal Treaties (1979) | Y |
| Establish Department of Education (1979) | Y |
| Approve Anti-busing Amendment (1979) | N |
| Guarantee Chrysler Corp. loans (1979) | N |
| Approve military draft registration (1980) | N |
| Aid Sandinista regime in Nicaragua (1980) | Y |
| Strengthen fair housing laws (1980) | Y |

**97th Congress**

| | |
|---|---|
| Reagan budget proposal (1981) | Y |

## Interest Group Ratings

| Year | ADA | ACA | AFL-CIO | CCUS |
|---|---|---|---|---|
| 1980 | 72 | 42 | 35 | 82 |
| 1979 | 32 | 46 | 30 | 82 |
| 1978 | 40 | 39 | 32 | 78 |
| 1977 | 50 | 54 | 41 | 71 |
| 1976 | 45 | 46 | 35 | 44 |
| 1975 | 47 | 43 | 55 | 63 |
| 1974 | 70 | 13 | 73 | 30 |
| 1973 | 68 | 33 | 45 | 64 |

# 2 Al Swift (D)

**Of Bellingham — Elected 1978**

**Born:** Sept. 12, 1935, Tacoma, Wash.
**Education:** Attended Whitman College, 1953-55; Central Wash. College, B.A. 1957.
**Profession:** Broadcaster.
**Family:** Wife, Paula Jackson; two children.
**Religion:** Unitarian.
**Political Career:** No previous office.

**In Washington:** Like other first-term members with congressional staff experience, Swift came to the House in 1979 knowing where the levers of power were and how to pull them. By the end of his first term he had impressed allies and opponents as a likely leader in Congresses to come.

Interested in winning a spot on the Commerce Committee — difficult for most freshmen — Swift went to see Warren G. Magnuson, the state's veteran senior senator. It was a good choice. Magnuson cornered the entire House leadership at a presidential briefing and told them to give Swift what he wanted. Swift's case was the first one brought up at the House panel that makes the assignments, and it went through unanimously.

Having won that round, Swift found himself the only legislator from his state on Commerce as it prepared to take up the Northwest power bill. The legislation, designed to allocate scarce power resources over the next two decades in Washington and Oregon, was bitterly controversial in those states but attracted little attention among legislators from other regions.

The Commerce Committee largely left it to Swift to draw up the legislation, provided he could build a regional consensus behind it. The compromise bill Swift finally moved through Commerce had the support of public and private utilities, but it displeased many environmentalists and consumer advocates, who said it allowed too great a role for nuclear power and was too generous to private power companies.

At the committee markup stage, Swift had to fight off an amendment which would have prevented regional power authorities from contracting in advance to sell their power to private utilities. But the committee members, most of them only marginally interested in the situation, went with Swift.

As a member of the Commerce Communications Subcommittee, Swift also spent much of his first term trying to draft a bill deregulating the communications industry. He supported the bill that passed the subcommittee, one aimed at establishing renewed competition in the field now dominated by AT&T under strict federal rules. But the bill ran into industry cross-pressures and never reached the floor.

Swift promoted an amendment to a hazardous wastes bill, exempting waste treatment facilities from federal regulation if they could show that local water supplies were not being contaminated. An early version of this effort was criticized by environmentalists as too sweeping; Swift modified it and won approval on the House floor.

**At Home:** Swift won his way to the House in 1978 after overcoming stiff odds in both the Democratic primary and the general election. He outcampaigned and outorganized his opposition in both cases.

Swift had served in Washington D.C. as administrative assistant to his retiring predecessor, Democratic Rep. Lloyd Meeds. But he had made a separate career back in the district as a news broadcaster in Bellingham. To secure the Democratic nomination, he had to battle Brian Corcoran, press secretary to Sen. Henry M. Jackson for 21 years. Corcoran had Jackson's good will and was able to tap the senator's traditional contributors to build a financial advantage. But Swift, more articulate and a better campaigner, came from far behind early in the year to overtake

---

**2nd District: Northwest — Bellingham, Everett.** Population: 658,046 (37% increase since 1970). Race: White 628,046 (95%), Black 4,032 (1%), Others 26,445 (4%). Spanish origin: 12,196 (2%).

## Al Swift, D-Wash.

Corcoran in the closing weeks before the primary. Swift won by 3,881 votes.

Swift's next hurdle was against Republican John Nance Garner, a distant relative and namesake of Franklin D. Roosevelt's vice president. Garner had come within 542 votes of ousting Meeds in 1976, mainly because fishermen in the district felt the incumbent had not fought hard enough against Indian fishing claims. He spent lavishly in trying to win the seat against Swift in 1978, but he no longer had the fishing rights issue; Swift took a similar position to his. The Democrat also attacked Garner's heavy spending, turning a supposed advantage into a liability. In the final result, Swift edged Garner by 3,827 votes. He consolidated his position in 1980 with a 2-to-1 victory over his Republican opponent.

**The District:** Ranging north from Seattle to the Canadian border, the 2nd contains a chunk of Seattle suburbs and several lumber, fishing and shipping cities along Puget Sound. Chief among them are Everett, which sent Henry M. Jackson to the House for six terms, and Bellingham.

The district's economy is oriented toward lumber and paper products, with Scott Paper, Weyerhaeuser, and Georgia-Pacific companies having large facilities there. The fishing industry is also critical, as Meeds was strongly reminded. And Boeing has a major aircraft plant in Everett.

## Committees

**Energy and Commerce** (17th of 24 Democrats)
Energy Conservaton and Power; Fossil amd Synthetic Fuels; Telecommunications, Consumer Protection, and Finance.

**House Administration** (10th of 11 Democrats)
Accounts; Office Systems.

**Joint Library**

## Elections

**1980 General**

| | |
|---|---|
| Al Swift (D) | 162,002 (64%) |
| Neal Snider (R) | 82,639 (33%) |

**1980 Primary**

| | |
|---|---|
| Al Swift (D) | 84,552 (92%) |
| Zell Young (D) | 7,736 (8%) |

**1978 General**

| | |
|---|---|
| Al Swift (D) | 70,620 (51%) |
| John Garner (R) | 66,793 (49%) |

**1978 Primary**

| | |
|---|---|
| Al Swift (D) | 19,057 (44%) |
| Brian Corcoran (D) | 15,176 (35%) |
| Ken St. Clair (D) | 5,812 (14%) |

**District Vote For President**

| | 1980 | | 1976 | | 1972 |
|---|---|---|---|---|---|
| D | 100,301 (37%) | D | 107,031 (47%) | D | 72,450 (37%) |
| R | 135,654 (50%) | R | 116,274 (51%) | R | 115,393 (59%) |
| I | 29,316 (11%) | | | | |

## Campaign Finance

| | Receipts | Receipts from PACs | Expenditures |
|---|---|---|---|
| **1980** | | | |
| Swift (D) | $147,339 | $77,050 (52%) | $143,100 |
| Snider (R) | $15,032 | $500 (3%) | $15,003 |

| **1978** | | | |
|---|---|---|---|
| Swift (D) | $150,818 | $39,550 (26%) | $150,435 |
| Garner (R) | $328,383 | $124,101 (38%) | $324,456 |

## Voting Studies

| | Presidential Support | | Party Unity | | Conservative Coalition | |
|---|---|---|---|---|---|---|
| Year | S | O | S | O | S | O |
| 1980 | 83 | 17 | 92 | 6 | 15 | 84 |
| 1979 | 81 | 17 | 91 | 7 | 18 | 79 |

S = Support          O = Opposition

## Key Votes

**96th Congress**

| | |
|---|---|
| Weaken Carter oil profits tax (1979) | N |
| Reject hospital cost control plan (1979) | Y |
| Implement Panama Canal Treaties (1979) | Y |
| Establish Department of Education (1979) | Y |
| Approve Anti-busing Amendment (1979) | N |
| Guarantee Chrysler Corp. loans (1979) | N |
| Approve military draft registration (1980) | N |
| Aid Sandinista regime in Nicaragua (1980) | Y |
| Strengthen fair housing laws (1980) | Y |

**97th Congress**

| | |
|---|---|
| Reagan budget proposal (1981) | N |

## Interest Group Ratings

| Year | ADA | ACA | AFL-CIO | CCUS |
|---|---|---|---|---|
| 1980 | 94 | 17 | 58 | 64 |
| 1979 | 79 | 12 | 85 | 28 |

# 3 Don Bonker (D)

**Of Olympia — Elected 1974**

**Born:** March 7, 1937, Denver, Colo.
**Education:** Lewis and Clark College, B.A. 1964.
**Military Career:** Coast Guard, 1955-59.
**Profession:** Auditor.
**Family:** Wife, Carolyn Ekern.
**Religion:** Presbyterian.
**Political Career:** Clark County Auditor, 1966-74; unsuccessful Democratic nominee for Wash. Secretary of State, 1972.

**In Washington:** The human rights era may be over in American foreign policy, but it still drives Bonker and dominates his time on the Foreign Affairs Committee. Like Oregon Sen. Mark Hatfield, he draws his liberal views from a Christian fundamentalism normally associated with the right.

In 1980, he won approval of an amendment requiring human rights courses as part of U.S. military training for officers from allied countries. He opposed restoring military aid to the Philippines because of the Marcos government's human rights violations. And when President Carter opposed a trade boycott of Uganda, then headed by dictator Idi Amin, Bonker attacked the administration for backing away from its human rights commitment. He got the House to endorse the boycott by a 377-0 vote.

Bonker was the prime mover in 1979 when the House voted to transfer the Peace Corps out of the controversial ACTION agency headed by one-time anti-war leader Sam Brown. Most House Republicans favored the move as a swipe at Brown's militant past; Bonker had a different concern. He felt the Peace Corps was getting lost in an ACTION bureaucracy more interested in domestic social change, and that it could regain some of its lost morale in a new independent agency. Bonker won on the House floor, but lost in conference.

On his other committee, Merchant Marine, Bonker has been closely allied with the minority environmentalist bloc. In 1980, he differed with Merchant Marine Chairman John M. Murphy over the issue of deep seabed mining. Murphy wanted a seabed bill giving certain investment guarantees to mining companies, despite the fact that a treaty trying to resolve seabed mining issues was being negotiated. The companies said they would not begin work without the assurances.

Elliot Richardson, the U.S. representative to the seven-year-old United Nations Law of the Sea Conference, begged Congress to hold off passing the bill until the treaty was completed. Murphy retorted that there would never be a treaty. Bonker happened to be chairman of the subcommittee with jurisdiction over the issue. Although he was not hostile to the idea of mining, he waited for several months to allow Richardson to work out an agreement. Then he reported out a bill with suggested changes by Richardson delaying commercial development until 1988. The legislation became law later in the year, essentially in that form.

Bonker has also been active on Merchant Marine in promoting U.S. exports. He is chairman of a House Export Task Force.

**At Home:** Bonker reversed an earlier defeat when he won election to the House in 1974 over the Washington secretary of state, Republican A. Ludlow Kramer. Two years earlier Bonker had tried to unseat Kramer from his state office, and had come within two percentage points of doing so.

The 1972 defeat was the only one Bonker has suffered in a precocious political career. He started as an aide to Democratic Sen. Maurine Neuberger of Oregon, then won election as Clark County auditor in 1966, at age 29. In his eight years in the auditor's office, he pioneered the use of punchcards in county elections.

---

**3rd District: Southwest — Olympia.**
Population: 695,204 (33% increase since 1970). Race: White 654,154 (94%), Black 10,996 (2%), Others 30,254 (4%). Spanish origin: 12,808 (2%).

---

## Don Bonker, D-Wash.

In 1974, Democratic Rep. Julia Butler Hansen announced her retirement and threw her support to state Sen. Robert C. Bailey, a veteran legislator who had been chairman of the Democratic Senate caucus. But Bailey was from a remote corner of the district, and Bonker had broadened his district-wide reputation in his close 1972 contest against Kramer. During the primary campaign, Bonker attracted attention by siding with small loggers against large logging companies. He defeated Bailey by 2,206 votes.

He went on to win the general election with surprising ease over Kramer, who had been hurt by his role as coordinator of a disastrous food distribution program paid for by the Hearst family in an effort to win release of their kidnapped daughter. Kramer's political career was mainly linked with Seattle; Bonker had a strong volunteer operation throughout the district.

Bonker has never been threatened for re-election, even in the 1980 Republican sweep.

**The District:** Located in the southwestern portion of the state, the 3rd traditionally included Olympia, the state capital, and Vancouver, Bonker's original political base. However, in the 1972 redistricting Vancouver was removed and the district spread north to the Tacoma and Seattle suburbs.

The district's economy is heavily oriented toward the lumber and paper industries. The misty forests of the Olympic Peninsula furnish some of America's giant paper, pulp, and lumber companies with their raw materials, and smaller logging operations are organized into milling cooperatives. Fishing is also important. The district fronts on the Pacific for 150 miles.

Historically Democratic, the district has been heavily influenced by unions associated with the lumber and paper industries.

## Committees

**Foreign Affairs** (9th of 21 Democrats)
Human Rights and International Organizations, chairman; International Economic Policy and Trade.

**Merchant Marine and Fisheries** (8th of 20 Democrats)
Coast Guard and Navigation; Fisheries and Wildlife Conservation and the Environment.

**Select Aging** (6th of 31 Democrats)
Health and Long-Term Care.

## Elections

**1980 General**

| | |
|---|---|
| Don Bonker (D) | 155,906 (63%) |
| Rod Culp (R) | 92,872 (37%) |

**1980 Primary**

| | |
|---|---|
| Don Bonker (D) | 88,001 (91%) |
| Dan Jones (D) | 8,332 (9%) |

**1978 General**

| | |
|---|---|
| Don Bonker (D) | 82,616 (59%) |
| Rick Bennett (R) | 58,270 (41%) |

**Previous Winning Percentages**
1976 (71%)    1974 (61%)

**District Vote For President**

| 1980 | | 1976 | | 1972 | |
|---|---|---|---|---|---|
| D | 99,829 (38%) | D | 113,587 (50%) | D | 82,659 (40%) |
| R | 130,003 (49%) | R | 105,441 (46%) | R | 111,965 (55%) |
| I | 26,234 (10%) | | | | |

## Campaign Finance

| | Receipts | Receipts from PACs | Expenditures |
|---|---|---|---|
| **1980** | | | |
| Bonker (D) | $91,031 | $38,883 (43%) | $96,112 |
| Culp (R) | $33,193 | $2,100 (6%) | $32,871 |

| | | | |
|---|---|---|---|
| **1978** | | | |
| Bonker (D) | $54,951 | $20,625 (38%) | $43,324 |
| Bennett (R) | $52,497 | $200 (.38%) | $51,753 |

## Voting Studies

| | Presidential Support | | Party Unity | | Conservative Coalition | |
|---|---|---|---|---|---|---|
| Year | S | O | S | O | S | O |
| 1980 | 67 | 22 | 78 | 9 | 20 | 67 |
| 1979 | 72 | 17 | 78 | 6 | 22 | 68 |
| 1978 | 71 | 16 | 73 | 10 | 18 | 65 |
| 1977 | 63 | 23 | 79 | 9 | 16 | 72 |
| 1976 | 27 | 67 | 77 | 14 | 22 | 66 |
| 1975 | 33 | 60 | 86 | 10 | 16 | 81 |

S = Support          O = Opposition

## Key Votes

**96th Congress**

| | |
|---|---|
| Weaken Carter oil profits tax (1979) | N |
| Reject hospital cost control plan (1979) | N |
| Implement Panama Canal Treaties (1979) | Y |
| Establish Department of Education (1979) | Y |
| Approve Anti-busing Amendment (1979) | N |
| Guarantee Chrysler Corp. loans (1979) | Y |
| Approve military draft registration (1980) | N |
| Aid Sandinista regime in Nicaragua (1980) | Y |
| Strengthen fair housing laws (1980) | Y |

**97th Congress**

| | |
|---|---|
| Reagan budget proposal (1981) | N |

## Interest Group Ratings

| Year | ADA | ACA | AFL-CIO | CCUS |
|---|---|---|---|---|
| 1980 | 83 | 30 | 71 | 70 |
| 1979 | 84 | 4 | 85 | 18 |
| 1978 | 65 | 21 | 89 | 22 |
| 1977 | 75 | 8 | 86 | 24 |
| 1976 | 75 | 12 | 68 | 25 |
| 1975 | 95 | 8 | 91 | 12 |

# 4 Sid Morrison (R)

**Of Zillah — Elected 1980**
**Born:** May 13, 1933, Yakima, Wash.
**Education:** Wash. State U., B.S. 1954.
**Military Career:** Army, 1954-56.
**Profession:** Orchardist.
**Family:** Wife, Marcella Britton; four children.
**Religion:** Methodist.
**Political Career:** Wash. House, 1967-75; Wash. Senate, 1975-81.

**The Member:** Morrison was known in the Washington state Legislature as a centrist, and he has spent some time in Congress trying to dilute proposals he thinks go too far.

When the Reagan administration asked Congress to cut off funds for a fusion research project at Hanford Works, an atomic power facility in the 4th District, Morrison lent his support to a House-Senate compromise that would fund the research project at least through fiscal 1982.

In the Cougar Lakes area, the administration wants to permit multiple-use development of land being considered for wilderness classification. Morrison wants to see development on part of the land and have the rest set aside as wilderness.

Morrison's 1980 campaign against Democratic Rep. Mike McCormack reflected his agricultural background. McCormack favored a water project to increase the number of salmon spawning in the Yakima River. Morrison wanted the project changed to make more water available for agricultural irrigation.

The two men found little to disagree about on the issue of nuclear power, which was a near-obsession for McCormack during his ten years in the House. Morrison takes the same pro-nuclear position his predecessor did. But the Republican did charge that McCormack had been soft on defense spending in general.

**The District:** The 4th is a north-south band stretching over the center of the state, from the Canadian border down to Oregon. Farming, aluminum and nuclear energy comprise the bulk of its economy — and define it politically.

The agricultural areas, which center around Yakima, are reliably Republican, while industrial Clark County (Vancouver), an aluminum manufacturing center, is Democratic.

The battleground is the other population center, nominally Democratic Benton County (Richland). Although the Hanford Works in Richland employs many blue-collar workers, the county went narrowly for Morrison in 1980.

## Committees

**Agriculture** (15th of 19 Republicans)
Conservation, Credit, and Rural Development; Cotton, Rice and Sugar; Forests, Family Farms, and Energy.

## Elections

**1980 General**

| | |
|---|---|
| Sid Morrison (R) | 134,691 (57%) |
| Mike McCormack (D) | 100,114 (43%) |

**1980 Primary**

| | |
|---|---|
| Sid Morrison (R) | 39,673 (59%) |
| Claude Oliver (R) | 27,547 (41%) |

**District Vote For President**

| | 1980 | | 1976 | | 1972 |
|---|---|---|---|---|---|
| **D** | 84,069 (35%) | **D** | 93,783 (44%) | **D** | 75,270 (38%) |
| **R** | 129,649 (55%) | **R** | 111,182 (52%) | **R** | 110,229 (56%) |
| **I** | 18,790 (8%) | | | | |

## Campaign Finance

| | Receipts | Receipts from PACs | Expenditures |
|---|---|---|---|
| **1980** | | | |
| Morrison (R) | $406,811 | $48,189 (12%) | $402,884 |
| McCormack (D) | $237,563 | $142,785 (60%) | $250,728 |

## Key Vote

**97th Congress**

| | |
|---|---|
| Reagan budget proposal (1981) | Y |

> **4th District: Central — Yakima, Vancover.** Population: 629,637 (32% increase since 1970). Race: White 578,297 (92%), Black 4,896 (1%), Others 46,444 (7%). Spanish origin: 40,766 (6%).

# 5 Thomas S. Foley (D)

**Of Spokane — Elected 1964**

**Born:** March 6, 1929, Spokane, Wash.
**Education:** U. of Wash., B.A. 1951, LL.B. 1957.
**Profession:** Lawyer.
**Family:** Wife, Heather Strachan.
**Religion:** Roman Catholic.
**Political Career:** No previous office.

**In Washington:** Foley's intelligence, negotiating skill and sense of detachment have allowed him to reach the top levels of the House leadership without the aggressiveness it sometimes takes to make it that far in the House.

When Foley explains the politics of a legislative situation he is involved in, he often sounds like a curious outsider, calmly perceiving the entire situation as a human comedy he happens to have wandered into.

That is a quality as useful as it is unusual. When the more militant parties to a dispute have staked out positions and are emotionally involved in maintaining them, Foley often steers them to a successful compromise, as he did as Agriculture chairman on the 1977 farm bill, the most difficult test of his career.

In some ways, Foley seems a little unusual for a politician, let alone a majority whip. He is not comfortable with the back-slapping and small-talk of a political campaign. He has never gone in for news releases or self promotion; when he became Agriculture chairman in 1975 he called reporters into his office one by one to avoid having to hold a press conference. In the six years that he ran the committee, he tried to play down partisan politics as much as possible.

So he is in an uncharacteristic position now as majority whip, playing the role of cheerleader and partisan point man for House Democrats.

Even as whip, however, Foley generally sounds like Foley. When asked whether Democratic leaders should have been tougher in trying to round up votes for their own budget and against the Reagan alternative, he said, "Well, I think getting tougher isn't the right thing we need to do. We need to present our alternatives more forcefully perhaps and more effectively to the country. . . . It was really lost in the country. It was members responding to very strong public pressure from their districts to go with the president. . . . The days when people were taken off committees or otherwise punished are gone."

Foley's preference for conciliation also represents his greatest weakness, to many colleagues. Nearly all concede that when an argument can be won without confrontation, he usually wins. But when it requires confrontation, he is less effective. Chairing a committee meeting or a party caucus, he is sometimes reluctant to bang the gavel hard even against a member who seems to be asking for it.

Foley has risen slowly and cautiously in Democratic ranks, taking advantage of his reputation as a legislative manager. In 1974 he chaired the Democratic Study Group, the strategy and research arm of liberal and moderate Democrats. In 1977 the chairmanship of the Democratic Caucus was open, and as a veteran of numerous reform battles against secrecy and seniority in the committee system, he was a logical choice. He defeated Shirley Chisholm of New York by a vote of 194-96. His four years as chairman were not a particularly active time for the caucus; it made few important decisions and Foley chose not to be an activist.

In 1981, the defeat of John Brademas of Indiana forced Speaker O'Neill to choose a new whip. Chief Deputy Whip Dan Rostenkowski of Illinois, first in line for promotion, decided instead to take over the Ways and Means Committee. Some Democrats urged O'Neill to select a whip from among the 1970s Democratic generation, but O'Neill was looking for parliamentary skill in the coming arguments with House Republicans. Foley was a parliamentary expert — he was Democratic convention parliamentarian in 1980 — and he got the job.

---

**5th District: East — Spokane, Walla Walla.** Population: 579,374 (20% increase since 1970). Race: White 543,211 (94%), Black 7,188 (1%), Others 28,975 (5%). Spanish origin: 18,314 (3%).

That required him to give up the Agriculture chairmanship, which he had won in unusual circumstances in 1975. The huge bloc of freshman Democrats was determined that year to unseat some of the aging, conservative House chairmen, and 75-year-old W. R. Poage of Texas, while popular within his own committee, was both aging and very conservative. The caucus unseated Poage by a vote of 152-133, with Foley opposing the move, and the Washington Democrat replaced him.

As chairman, Foley kept major farm bills under his own control at the full committee level, rather than parceling them out to subcommittees as most chairmen now do. He was openly bipartisan, usually managing to work out arrangements in advance with the senior committee Republican, William C. Wampler of Virginia.

His handling of the 1977 farm bill was typical. Major crop support programs and food stamp legislation were up for renewal in one package. President Carter repeatedly threatened to veto the bill as too costly. Foley painstakingly put together a compromise, balancing farm state pro-subsidy votes and urban bloc food stamp support. "Sure I want higher price supports," he said at one point. "But it won't help farmers for us to pass a bill the president won't sign."

At the last minute, Oklahoma Democrat Glenn English drafted a floor amendment to increase supports for wheat beyond what the committee had initially approved. Foley decided the amendment probably would pass, so he went back to the White House and persuaded Carter to accept it. In the end, Foley offered the English amendment himself and it went through easily.

In the 96th Congress, Foley spent much of his time arguing over funding for the food stamp program, which repeatedly exceeded the cost ceilng set for it by law. Foley has sometimes disappointed the left with his caution about liberalizing the program, but he has been a consistent supporter of it. He served as manager in 1979 and 1980 for the numerous spending additions needed to keep it going.

Earlier in his career on the Agriculture Committee, Foley was a principal author of the 1967 Meat Inspection Act, providing federal funds for states to use in imposing standards on the packing industry. He and Iowa Democrat Neal Smith narrowly failed on the House floor in an effort to make the program stronger by writing in specific federal standards.

Foley's parochial interests on the Agriculture Committee are wheat and sugar beets. He tried to win passage of a new sugar price support program in 1979, but lost badly on the floor.

For ten years, Foley also sat on the Interior Committee. There he worked on enlarging the nation's largest power plant, the Grand Coulee Dam, and protecting Northwest water from raids by California and Arizona.

In 1980, Foley was a major sponsor of the Northwest Power bill, aimed at allocating scarce energy resources in the Pacific Northwest over the rest of this century. Foley was no longer on Interior, but much of the strategy was worked out in his office. It required considerable plotting to overcome the opposition of James Weaver, the Oregon Democrat who saw the bill as too pronuclear and too generous to private power companies. A mini-filibuster by Weaver delayed passage for a month, but Foley and others ultimately moved it through on a 284-77 vote.

**At Home:** In the course of little more than a decade, Foley took over a Republican district, made himself invincible in it, and then let it slip nearly out of control. Today, as the third-ranking Democrat in the House, he has to work like a newcomer to keep from losing it.

In 1972, as President Nixon was carrying Washington easily, Foley won a fifth term with 81 percent of the vote. Six years later he held on with less than a majority in a three-way race, and in 1980 he managed to fight off the statewide Republican sweep by 7,000 votes.

Foley was at first a reluctant congressional candidate, persuaded to run in 1964 partly by the favorable political climate for Democrats and partly by Sen. Henry M. Jackson, for whom he was working at the time. Foley filed on the last possible day. He had no primary competition because no other Democrats wanted to challenge Republican Walt Horan, who had held the seat since 1942. But Horan was ailing at 66, and Foley had fund-raising help from Jackson and Sen. Warren Magnuson, as well as the advantage of the Johnson presidential landslide. He upset the incumbent in November by 12,000 votes.

Initially, Foley wanted to be a judge, as his father had been. He spent two years as deputy prosecutor in Spokane County, and a year as assistant state attorney general. But he moved to Washington D.C. in 1961 to work for Jackson as counsel to the old Senate Interior Committee.

After his 1964 victory, Foley worked hard to keep his district, and by 1970 Republicans had stopped running strong candidates against him.

But in 1976 Foley made a political mistake. Republican nominee Charles Kimball was killed in an airplane crash the month before the election, and Foley essentially stopped campaigning. That allowed Duane Alton, an unknown tire dealer from Spokane, to hold him to 58 percent of the vote.

The 1976 result convinced Republicans Foley was vulnerable, and Alton ran again in 1978. As Agriculture chairman, Foley had become a target for resentment over farm issues among his wheat-growing constituents, and his low profile in the district gave Alton another issue. Even worse for him, Indian tribal official Mel Tonasket ran as an independent and took away Democratic votes. But Alton was an inarticulate candidate, reluctant even to debate the man he was challenging, and his militant conservatism was too much for many moderate Republican voters.

Again in 1980, Republicans had high hopes. Foley's opponent this time was John Sonneland, a Spokane surgeon who had once served as state co-chairman of Common Cause. Sonneland moved to the right, calling Foley a fiscally irresponsible liberal. But the incumbent campaigned hard, stressing his more conservative ideas, such as a tax cut and congressional veto of federal rules.

This time there was no third candidate, and Foley drew back most of the vote he had lost to Tonasket in 1978. Still, the Republican tide left him with the smallest margin of his career.

**The District:** Although the 5th contains all or part of 14 counties in the eastern tier of Washington, more than half the population resides in Spokane County. Spokane is the capital of the "Inland Empire," a productive agricultural basin lying between the Cascade Range on the west and the Rocky Mountains on the east. It is a banking, marketing and commercial center, with an aluminum and forest products industry.

Wheat is the district's main crop, although there is considerable potato and vegetable farming. The Grand Coulee Dam, at the edge of the district, has helped solve the area's water and power problems since the New Deal.

The district is generally conservative and Republican, but the rural voters are quick to turn against any administration in hard times.

## Committees

**Agriculture** (2nd of 24 Democrats)

Wheat, soybeans, and Feed Grains, chairman; Cotton and Sugar; Department Operations, Research, and Foreign Agriculture; Domestic Marketing, Consumer Relations, and Nutrition; Forests, Family Farms, and Energy.

## Elections

**1980 General**

| | |
|---|---|
| Thomas Foley (D) | 120,530 (52%) |
| John Sonneland (R) | 111,705 (48%) |

**Previous Winning Percentages**

| | | | |
|---|---|---|---|
| 1978 (48%) | 1976 (58%) | 1974 (64%) | 1972 (81%) |
| 1970 (67%) | 1968 (57%) | 1966 (57%) | 1964 (54%) |

**District Vote For President**

| | 1980 | | 1976 | | 1972 |
|---|---|---|---|---|---|
| **D** | 80,554 (34%) | **D** | 91,796 (43%) | **D** | 62,692 (35%) |
| **R** | 132,936 (56%) | **R** | 114,988 (54%) | **R** | 126,121 (60%) |
| **I** | 18,973 (8%) | | | | |

## Campaign Finance

| | Receipts | Receipts from PACs | Expenditures |
|---|---|---|---|
| **1980** | | | |
| Foley (D) | $392,271 | $89,467 (23%) | $361,234 |
| Sonneland (R) | $213,675 | $32,919 (15%) | $213,853 |

## Voting Studies

| | Presidential Support | | Party Unity | | Conservative Coalition | |
|---|---|---|---|---|---|---|
| Year | S | O | S | O | S | O |
| 1980 | 76 | 21 | 85 | 12 | 38 | 60 |
| 1979 | 80 | 16 | 83 | 12 | 36 | 56 |
| 1978 | 64 | 30 | 69 | 25 | 40 | 55 |
| 1977 | 72 | 27 | 84 | 13 | 27 | 70 |
| 1976 | 37 | 61 | 78 | 19 | 36 | 59 |
| 1975 | 44 | 48 | 76 | 12 | 24 | 62 |
| 1974 (Ford) | 50 | 44 | | | | |
| 1974 | 51 | 36 | 80 | 9 | 13 | 75 |
| 1973 | 37 | 57 | 81 | 12 | 23 | 70 |
| 1972 | 68 | 32 | 78 | 18 | 22 | 73 |
| 1971 | 53 | 39 | 75 | 17 | 22 | 72 |

S = Support          O = Opposition

## Key Votes

**96th Congress**

| | |
|---|---|
| Weaken Carter oil profits tax (1979) | Y |
| Reject hospital cost control plan (1979) | Y |
| Implement Panama Canal Treaties (1979) | Y |
| Establish Department of Education (1979) | Y |
| Approve Anti-busing Amendment (1979) | N |
| Guarantee Chrysler Corp. loans (1979) | Y |
| Approve military draft registration (1980) | N |
| Aid Sandinista regime in Nicaragua (1980) | Y |
| Strengthen fair housing laws (1980) | Y |

**97th Congress**

| | |
|---|---|
| Reagan budget proposal (1981) | N |

## Interest Group Ratings

| Year | ADA | ACA | AFL-CIO | CCUS |
|---|---|---|---|---|
| 1980 | 61 | 17 | 72 | 73 |
| 1979 | 53 | 8 | 60 | 56 |
| 1978 | 30 | 22 | 65 | 33 |
| 1977 | 45 | 15 | 96 | 38 |
| 1976 | 55 | 14 | 65 | 44 |
| 1975 | 63 | 19 | 100 | 21 |
| 1974 | 78 | 0 | 100 | 11 |
| 1973 | 84 | 19 | 91 | 20 |
| 1972 | 69 | 9 | 82 | 11 |
| 1971 | 73 | 15 | 90 | |

# 6 Norman D. Dicks (D)

**Of Port Orchard — Elected 1976**

**Born:** Dec. 16, 1940, Bremerton, Wash.
**Education:** U. of Wash., B.A. 1963, J.D. 1968.
**Profession:** Lawyer.
**Family:** Wife, Suzanne Callison; two children.
**Religion:** Lutheran.
**Political Career:** No previous office.

**In Washington:** Dicks rushes into congressional action like the college linebacker he once was, aggressive and confident — or, some say, overaggressive and overconfident. He brought to the House habits he learned in the Senate as an aide to Warren G. Magnuson, the veteran Appropriations power, and he acts like an aspiring Magnuson, wheeling and dealing within the Appropriations power structure.

He wheeled and dealt exceptionally well in May of 1981, after the House, considering a supplemental money bill, cast a surprise vote against the Export-Import Bank, reducing its funding to the level recommended by President Reagan.

Export-Import funding is crucial to Boeing, which is crucial to Washington state, and Dicks coordinated the lobbying campaign that reversed the vote. Working with the Machinists' union as well as Boeing and other companies who use the bank's money, Dicks and his allies changed enough votes to convert the 231-166 decision of the previous day into a 237-162 vote to restore the money.

In the 96th Congress, Dicks was in the center of the battle over funding for the Federal Trade Commission, then headed by another old Magnuson hand, Michael J. Pertschuk. A majority of the House wanted to give Congress veto power over FTC regulations; Magnuson, Pertschuk and Dicks were all against that.

Dicks acted as self-appointed arbitrator, trying to bring together congressional critics of the FTC and the bluntly outspoken Pertschuk. The critics refused to let the FTC budget pass until some agreement was reached on the veto issue. The fight led to the shutdown of the agency for a day on two different occasions. Finally a compromise was reached providing for the veto but requiring a vote of both House and Senate to make it effective.

From his first day in the House, Dicks has displayed a brashness that has annoyed some senior members. But he has always been good at getting what he wants. He asked immediately for

assignment to Appropriations, where Magnuson had served the state of Washington so generously over the years, and he lobbied key colleagues to get it.

Since 1979, Dicks has been on the Defense Appropriations Subcommittee, where he can satisfy an interest in military manpower while looking after Boeing and the extensive Navy facilities at Bremerton. He is also on the Interior Subcommittee, where much of the national energy research is funded. His major crusade on this panel has been to get the government to stop drilling for oil on the National Petroleum Reserve in Alaska, and to allow private companies to begin.

Over his first two terms, Dicks became an increasingly frequent critic of the Carter administration and, in the summer of 1980 he was one of the organizers of a Committee for an Open Convention, widely perceived as a "Dump Carter" drive. Dicks said he only wanted to free delegates to vote their minds, and was not promoting Sen. Henry M. Jackson, D-Wash. or other possible last-minute alternatives to Carter.

**At Home:** After three years as administrative assistant to Magnuson, Dicks decided to go home in 1976 and run for Congress. He had long been planning a campaign in the 6th District for whenever incumbent Democrat Floyd Hicks chose to retire, and when Hicks was named to the state Supreme Court in 1976, Dicks began running with

---

**6th District: Puget Sound — Bremerton, Tacoma.** Population: 608,396 (27% increase since 1970). Race: White 548,226 (90%), Black 24,936 (4%), Asian and Pacific Islander 18,172 (3%), Others 17,062 (3%). Spanish origin: 14,444 (2%).

---

his usual intensity.

He had to compete with three major candidates for the nomination: a young activist state representative, a former president of Pacific Lutheran University, and the mayor of Tacoma. But Dicks's ability to tap the resources of labor and other interest groups helped him put together a winning coalition. He won the primary with 36.2 percent of the vote.

Dicks had no trouble winning against a weak Republican in 1976, and seemed to be headed for a long secure tenure. Since then, things have not looked quite so safe. His margin dropped from more than 90,000 votes in 1976 to less than 30,000 the next time against Republican James Beaver, a law professor from Tacoma, and in 1980 Beaver pressed him even further, coming within 17,000 votes.

**The District:** Stretching across the southern portion of Puget Sound, the district takes in the metropolitan areas of Tacoma and Bremerton. Both cities are linked economically to the sea, Tacoma as a port and Bremerton as a shipbuilding center. Tacoma is also associated with the wood and pulp industries, with the Weyerhaeuser Co. headquartered there. Boeing, Washington's largest employer, is also represented in the district by several plants.

The district leans Democratic, but sometimes by only a close margin. It went narrowly for Carter over Ford in 1976 in the face of a Ford victory statewide. Reagan carried it in 1980.

## Committees

**Appropriations** (20th of 33 Democrats)
Defense; Interior; Legislative.

## Elections

**1980 General**

| | |
|---|---|
| Norman Dicks (D) | 122,903 (54%) |
| Jim Beaver (R) | 106,236 (46%) |

**1980 Primary**

| | |
|---|---|
| Norman Dicks (D) | 71,407 (91%) |
| Robert Satiacum (D) | 7,059 (9%) |

**1978 General**

| | |
|---|---|
| Norman Dicks (D) | 71,057 (61%) |
| Jim Beaver (R) | 43,640 (37%) |

**Previous Winning Percentage**

**1976 (74%)**

**District Vote For President**

| | 1980 | | 1976 | | 1972 |
|---|---|---|---|---|---|
| D | 87,215 (36%) | D | 106,107 (49%) | D | 75,704 (38 %) |
| R | 121,289 (50%) | R | 103,846 (48%) | R | 115,383 (58 %) |
| I | 28,101 (12%) | | | | |

## Campaign Finance

| | Receipts | Receipts from PACs | Expenditures |
|---|---|---|---|
| **1980** | | | |
| Dicks (D) | $168,335 | $108,184 (64%) | $234,650 |
| Beaver (R) | $171,530 | $16,965 (10%) | $165,330 |

| **1978** | | | |
|---|---|---|---|
| Dicks (D) | $166,968 | $65,245 (39%) | $166,731 |
| Beaver (R) | $19,445 | $1,700 (9%) | $19,308 |

## Voting Studies

| | Presidential Support | | Party Unity | | Conservative Coalition | |
|---|---|---|---|---|---|---|
| Year | S | O | S | O | S | O |
| 1980 | 74 | 21 | 81 | 15 | 44 | 53 |
| 1979 | 75 | 18 | 82 | 9 | 33 | 64 |
| 1978 | 69 | 24 | 79 | 16 | 29 | 64 |
| 1977 | 67 | 24 | 76 | 14 | 32 | 55 |

S = Support  O = Opposition

## Key Votes

**96th Congress**

| | |
|---|---|
| Weaken Carter oil profits tax (1979) | N |
| Reject hospital cost control plan (1979) | N |
| Implement Panama Canal Treaties (1979) | Y |
| Establish Department of Education (1979) | Y |
| Approve Anti-busing Amendment (1979) | N |
| Guarantee Chrysler Corp. loans (1979) | Y |
| Approve military draft registration (1980) | Y |
| Aid Sandinista regime in Nicaragua (1980) | Y |
| Strengthen fair housing laws (1980) | Y |

**97th Congress**

| | |
|---|---|
| Reagan budget proposal (1981) | N |

## Interest Group Ratings

| Year | ADA | ACA | AFL-CIO | CCUS |
|---|---|---|---|---|
| 1980 | 67 | 26 | 76 | 71 |
| 1979 | 63 | 4 | 75 | 22 |
| 1978 | 45 | 19 | 90 | 33 |
| 1977 | 50 | 9 | 90 | 24 |

# 7 Mike Lowry (D)

**Of Mercer Island — Elected 1978**

**Born:** March 8, 1939, St. John, Wash.
**Education:** Wash. State U., B.A. 1962.
**Profession:** Public official.
**Family:** Wife, Mary Carlson; one child.
**Religion:** Baptist.
**Political Career:** King County Council, 1975-78; unsuccessful candidate for King County executive, 1973.

**In Washington:** Lowry is one of the young "old liberals" of the House, a labor loyalist closer to Speaker O'Neill in ideology than to many of the fiscally conservative Democrats of his own congressional generation. Gregarious and personally popular, he has nevertheless emerged as something of a maverick on a number of key issues.

Within his own Washington delegation, Lowry frustrated colleagues in the 96th Congress by refusing to support the bipartisan Northwest Power Bill, legislation that will create a new public authority to purchase electricity and allocate it to the region's users.

Alone among his state's House members, Lowry complained that the bill as written in the Commerce Committee was too generous to private power companies and too dependent on nuclear energy. "It is a bail-out for the private utilities and the aluminium companies," he charged at one point. That view was consistent with the feelings of the International Association of Machinists, many of whose members live in Lowry's district. There was also strong environmentalist sentiment against the nuclear provisions of the bill.

Meanwhile, Lowry was crusading against a bill that would restrict Indian rights to the salmon and steelhead fish catch in Puget Sound, arguing that it represented an abrogation of long-held treaty rights. Lowry's stand brought him the outspoken opposition of the area's politically sensitive commercial and sport fishermen, who worked against his re-election.

Lowry pursued labor interests in his first term on the Banking Committee and its Housing Subcommittee. On the House floor, he sought to amend the 1980 truck deregulation bill to provide $75 million for workers forced out of their jobs by the legislation. The Teamsters badly wanted such a provision; the American Trucking Associations vehemently opposed it. It was defeated on a voice vote.

**At Home:** A veteran of King County (Seattle) politics, Lowry took this district back in 1978 from Republican Jack Cunningham, who had won it in a 1977 special election. Talking bread-and-butter issues to blue-collar, union-oriented voters, Lowry returned the 7th to its normal Democratic representation.

Cunningham had won the contest to replace Democratic Rep. Brock Adams, who had resigned to join the Carter Cabinet. Democrats had helped Cunningham immeasurably in that campaign by nominating a candidate poorly suited to the district — an environmentalist lawyer vulnerable to charges that he was hostile to economic growth. But Lowry, as an avowed labor loyalist, had no such problem, and he was able to take advantage of Cunningham's growing reputation for arrogance in dealing with the public.

The election was thought to be nearly even in its closing days, but Lowry won by more than 8,000 votes. He was returned easily in 1980, despite a vocal challenge from Ron Dunlap, a Boeing sales manager who had promoted municipal tax limitation and had the strong support of Moral Majority forces.

Lowry had been in government a decade before he ran for Congress. He was elected to the King County Council in 1975, and was its president for one year. Before that, he had been an

---

**7th District: Southern Seattle and suburbs.** Population: 488,611 (2% increase since 1970). Race: White 394,096 (81%), Black 45,051 (9%), Asian and Pacific Islander 33,796 (7%), Others 15,668 (3%). Spanish origin: 11,952 (2%).

*Mike Lowry, D-Wash.*

aide to the Ways and Means Committee of the Washington Senate.

**The District:** Centered on the southern industrial portion of the city of Seattle and surrounding industrial blue-collar suburbs, the 7th takes in the immense Boeing headquarters and other company facilities spread throughout the area. Other prime industries include trucks, railroad equipment, shipbuilding, and steel.

The district was created in 1958 when the state Legislature eliminated the state's at-large congressional seat and divided the overpopulated Seattle district into two. Drawn to be Democratic, the district has elected a Democrat ever since its creation except in 1962 and the 1977 special election.

With people more attracted to Seattle's suburban areas than its older industrial communities, the 7th did not keep pace with the state's substantial population growth during the 1970s. As a result, the district needs to gain about 30,000 people's to meet the statewide average.

## Committees

**Banking, Finance and Urban Affairs** (20th of 25 Democrats)
Housing and Community Development; International Development Institutions and Finance; International Trade, Investment and Monetary Policy.

**Merchant Marine and Fisheries** (13th of 20 Democrats)
Coast Guard and Navigation; Fisheries and Wildlife Conservation and the Environment.

## Elections

**1980 General**

| | |
|---|---|
| Mike Lowry (D) | 112,848 (57%) |
| Ron Dunlap (R) | 84,218 (43%) |

**1980 Primary**

| | |
|---|---|
| Mike Lowry (D) | 66,209 (94%) |
| Arthur Bauder (D) | 4,092 (6%) |

**1978 General**

| | |
|---|---|
| Mike Lowry (D) | 67,450 (53%) |
| John Cunningham (R) | 59,052 (47%) |

**1978 Primary**

| | |
|---|---|
| Mike Lowry (D) | 19,601 (74%) |
| Ronn Robinson (D) | 6,713 (26%) |

**District Vote For President**

| | 1980 | | 1976 | | 1972 |
|---|---|---|---|---|---|
| D | 83,201 (43%) | D | 100,271 (48%) | D | 85,891 (42%) |
| R | 84,586 (43%) | R | 99,388 (48%) | R | 111,127 (54%) |
| I | 22,730 (12%) | | | | |

## Campaign Finance

| | Receipts | Receipts from PACs | Expenditures |
|---|---|---|---|
| **1980** | | | |
| Lowry (D) | $216,106 | $121,775 (56%) | 209,296 |
| Dunlap (R) | $221,227 | $66,202 (30%) | $221,223 |

| | | | |
|---|---|---|---|
| **1978** | | | |
| Lowry (D) | $215,806 | $56,011 (26%) | $214,609 |
| Cunningham (R) | $516,053 | $113,844 (22%) | $523,905 |

## Voting Studies

| | Presidential Support | | Party Unity | | Conservative Coalition | |
|---|---|---|---|---|---|---|
| Year | S | O | S | O | S | O |
| 1980 | 76 | 22 | 88 | 10 | 11 | 88 |
| 1979 | 79 | 19 | 92 | 7 | 15 | 84 |

S = Support          O = Opposition

## Key Votes

**96th Congress**

| | |
|---|---|
| Weaken Carter oil profits tax (1979) | N |
| Reject hospital cost control plan (1979) | N |
| Implement Panama Canal Treaties (1979) | Y |
| Establish Department of Education (1979) | Y |
| Approve Anti-busing Amendment (1979) | N |
| Guarantee Chrysler Corp. loans (1979) | N |
| Approve military draft registration (1980) | N |
| Aid Sandinista regime in Nicaragua (1980) | Y |
| Strengthen fair housing laws (1980) | Y |

**97th Congress**

| | |
|---|---|
| Reagan budget proposal (1981) | N |

## Interest Group Ratings

| Year | ADA | ACA | AFL-CIO | CCUS |
|---|---|---|---|---|
| 1980 | 100 | 17 | 68 | 59 |
| 1979 | 84 | 15 | 85 | 11 |

# West Virginia

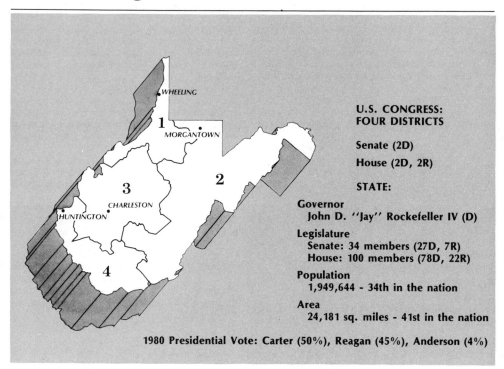

WHEELING

MORGANTOWN

1

2

3

CHARLESTON

HUNTINGTON

4

**U.S. CONGRESS:**
**FOUR DISTRICTS**

Senate (2D)

House (2D, 2R)

**STATE:**

**Governor**
John D. "Jay" Rockefeller IV (D)

**Legislature**
Senate: 34 members (27D, 7R)
House: 100 members (78D, 22R)

**Population**
1,949,644 - 34th in the nation

**Area**
24,181 sq. miles - 41st in the nation

**1980 Presidential Vote: Carter (50%), Reagan (45%), Anderson (4%)**

## ...The Importance of Coal

Coal is the symbol of West Virginia — of its decline and fall, and of its current modest reawakening.

The state has other important natural resources, including natural gas, but traditionally it has ranked first in the nation in the production of bituminous coal. It has now slipped to second place behind Kentucky. The coal industry, however, continues to be the largest single employer in the state and the largest contributor to the gross state product.

Even in the strongest coal years, before demand began to decline sharply in the 1950s, West Virginia was one of the poorest states. Most of the mine owners were not West Virginians, and few residents shared in the profits of extraction. In the postwar years, the situation gradually got worse. In 1970, the median family income of $7,414 was lower than that of all but three states, each of them in the deep South. In terms of

median school years completed, the state ranked forty-seventh.

Between 1950 and 1970, as the national population was growing by a third, West Virginia's population was declining by nearly 15 percent, and its six congressional districts were pared down to four.

That is why it is so striking that West Virginia grew by 11.8 percent during the 1970s — slightly more than the national average. Nearly all the growth was in the second half of the decade, generated by the renewed demand for coal that accompanied rising world oil prices. Charleston, the state capital, technically lost population over the ten year period, but by 1980 it had some of the appearance of an energy boom town.

The hopeful economic signs for West Virginia have had their effect on politics; in 1980 the state elected two Republicans to the U.S. House, the first ones in more than a decade. Despite those results, however, West Virginia's basic political orientation has not changed too much since the state became federally dependent and viscerally Democratic during the New Deal.

Senior Sen. Jennings Randolph survived a strong 1978 challenge and today is the only member of Congress who was serving during Franklin D. Roosevelt's "hundred days" in 1933. Robert Byrd, the Senate minority leader, is untouchable at home. Arch A. Moore Jr., who served as governor from 1969 to 1977 and nearly unseated Randolph in 1978, has been the only credible statewide Republican candidate in the last twenty years.

The dominant political figure today is Democratic Gov. John D. (Jay) Rockefeller IV. Defeated in his initial bid for the governorship but subsequently elected in 1976, he won re-election in 1980 after a campaign that advertised his name on television stations in Washington, D.C., a first for any candidate running outside the D.C. metropolitan area. At reports that he was spending almost $12 million in his re-election campaign against Moore, who was seeking a comeback, bumper stickers appeared reading, "Make him spend it all, Arch."

# A Political Tour

**Northern Panhandle.** Jutting north from the center of the state, West Virginia's northern panhandle is more like the industrialized Northeast than the rest of West Virginia. Brooke and Hancock counties at the tip of the peninsula identify more with Pittsburgh than with Charleston or Huntington.

In the four counties that make up the panhandle and in the counties just south of it, there is substantially more industrialization and urbanization than is found elsewhere in the state. And there is less poverty. The median family income in this area of the state is far above the state's average.

The prime industry in the panhandle is steel. Wheeling, often described as a "grimy steel town," is the largest city in the area (pop. 43,000) and has the same pollution problems found in most of the other steel cities located along the steep banks of the Ohio River.

The counties just south of the panhandle include some rural areas and a number of smaller cities with substantial heavy industry.

The northern panhandle and the adjacent counties make up one of the few areas in the state with significant concentrations of ethnic voters. Wheeling has a large Italian population. The ethnic voters are normally Democratic, although Republicans do well in some areas of the panhandle. A few counties south of the panhandle itself, such as Doddridge and Tyler, are solidly Republican.

Until the New Deal, this region often kept Republicans competitive in statewide elections. Moore represented much of the area in Congress from 1957 to 1969.

**The Rural East.** Relying more on agriculture than on coal, but lacking productive farm land in many places, mountainous eastern West Virginia is traditionally the poorest part of the state. It has been devoted to farming because there have been few alternatives.

The mountaineers who farm along the broad ridges here grow some corn and wheat and raise broiler chickens. There is a considerable amount of dairy farming as well.

In recent years, tourism has become increasingly important in many of the eastern counties, and raised the standard of living in some. Among the more popular sites are the baths at Berkeley Springs, the Monongalia National Forest, and historic Harper's Ferry. The three easternmost counties, known as the "eastern panhandle," are within long-range commuting distance of Washington, D.C., and have developed a community of white-collar professionals who take the train to the nation's capital every morning.

Eastern West Virginia tends to be Democratic, but there are still traces of mountain Republican tradition, and GOP candidates are competitive in some counties. Berkeley, Morgan and Grant counties are among the more Republican counties in the state.

Democrat Harley O. Staggers represented this area in Congress for sixteen terms, and until his retirement in 1980, he was the dominant political figure in the eastern part of the state. The 1980 election of Cleve Benedict, a conservative Republican, may foretell a shift in the region's political leanings.

**The Coal Counties.** The southern end of West Virginia is dominated by the coal industry and organized labor. The state as a whole is the second most unionized in the country. Boone County is the leading producer of coal in the state, with McDowell, Mingo and Logan counties not far behind. During the 1920s this area of the state was the scene of mine wars between the coal operators and their hired hands on one side, and miners and union organizers on the other. By the 1940s, thanks to New Deal legislation, the United Mine Workers had become the most powerful political force in the state, and the miners of southern West Virginia had become loyal Democrats. Those counties continue to deliver the largest Democratic margins in the state.

Historically, the coal counties of southern West Virginia have been the scene of some of the most corrupt machine politics in the country. Often with little effort to conceal it, votes have been exchanged for cash or whiskey, and corruption has been tolerated as a part of local life.

**Kanawha Valley.** If much of West Virginia seems stagnant, the Kanawha Valley is today dynamic and vigorous. The area stretches roughly from Charleston to Huntington, the manufacturing center on the Ohio River.

Charleston, in Kanawha County, is the state's financial center and the home of chemical plants belonging to a few major companies, including Union Carbide and Du Pont. In the 1970s, the area began to attract increasing numbers of young people. But Charleston also has a poor black area and considerable pollution.

Most of the voters in the area are traditional Democrats and union members, but like most West Virginians, they are strongly conservative on matters concerning God, country and family. This was demonstrated vividly in the 1974 protest over school textbooks. Fundamentalists in Kanawha County took exception to books which they charged were "un-Christian" and "pornographic." With substantial community support, they burned some offending books and temporarily shut down the schools. One textbook activist, David Michael Staton, was elected to Congress from Charleston as a Republican in 1980.

Kanawha and Cabell counties (Charleston and Huntington) account for about 20 percent of the state vote. A Republican running statewide needs to run well in this area to overcome heavy Democratic pluralities in the surrounding rural area.

## Redrawing the Lines

The 2nd District in the rural east led the state in population gain during the 1970s, increasing by nearly 20 percent. The southern 4th and western 3rd grew at about a 10 percent clip, and the northern 1st lagged behind at 5.5 percent.

Redistricting could be accomplished without greatly altering present boundaries, but in the first half of 1981, the Democratic-controlled Legislature showed interest in unseating at least one of the freshman GOP representatives and in carving out new districts that would give some state legislators a chance to run for Congress.

# Governor
# John D. Rockefeller IV
# (D)

**Born:** June 18, 1937, New York, N.Y.
**Home:** Charleston, W.Va.
**Education:** Harvard U., A.B. 1961; attended International Christian U., Tokyo, Japan, 1957-60.
**Profession:** president, West Virginia Wesleyan College.
**Family:** Wife, Sharon; four children.
**Religion:** Presbyterian.
**Political Career:** West Virginia House, 1967-69; West Virginia secretary of state, 1969-73; unsuccessful campaign for governor, 1972; elected governor 1976, 1980; term expires Jan. 1985.

# Jennings Randolph (D)

### Of Elkins — Elected 1958

**Born:** March 8, 1902, Salem, W.Va.
**Education:** Salem College, A.B. 1924.
**Profession:** Journalist; professor; airline executive.
**Family:** Widower; two children.
**Religion:** Baptist.
**Political Career:** U.S. House, 1933-47; unsuccessfully sought re-election to U.S. House, 1946.

**In Washington:** These are sad times for Randolph, one of the last of the old New Dealers and the only remaining member of Congress who served during the first 100 days of Franklin D. Roosevelt. Republicans are hard at work dismantling or diluting the projects that amount to an economic religion for him.

"I come to praise these agencies and the work they have done, not to bury them," Randolph said at a committee meeting in early 1981. He was making a vain defense of two programs the Reagan administration targeted for extinction — the Appalachian Regional Commission and the Economic Development Administration.

Randolph's public philosophy was shaped by the Depression and the poverty it brought to the mountains and hollows of West Virginia. His state came to depend on help from the federal "pork barrel" — a concept Randolph heartily endorses.

For 14 years, the West Virginia Democrat controlled the barrel as chairman of the Senate Public Works Committee (after 1977, Environment and Public Works), and he ladled out the highways and health clinics, dams and bridges, sewers and public buildings with a generous hand.

"More than $1 billion has come into our state for the sufferers of black lung disease," he said in 1978. "More than $1 billion. Isn't that wonderful? I don't begrudge a dime of it. If we have to have a deficit budget, let it be a people deficit every time."

Highways have always been pre-eminent in Randolph's affections; in West Virginia, where the hills and mountains isolate people from one another, businesses and jobs follow the highways. Randolph saw highways as a lifeline for the nation long before most other members of Congress did. As a member of the House Roads Committee in the 1940s, he held hearings on a plan for a network of transcontinental highways — a plan that evolved, in the following decade, into the interstate highway system.

The Highway Trust Fund, with its specially dedicated funds from the federal gasoline tax, was crucial to the financing of the interstate highway system, and Randolph has jealously guarded its sanctity. During the early 1970s, he fought a bruising but ultimately unsuccessful battle to keep urban lawmakers from "busting the trust" for mass transit projects. He said he never objected to federal funding for mass transit — he just wanted his highways finished first. "I only want the interstate system completed," he said in 1973, "so I can dedicate myself to work in the front ranks of mass transit."

Aviation is another major Randolph interest. He was a leading sponsor of the Civil Aeronautics Act of 1938, and the author or cosponsor of numerous other aviation measures. During his 12 years out of public office following his 1946 defeat, he was an airline vice president.

Although his Senate committee handles environmental issues as well as public works, Randolph generally concentrated on the latter and left environmental leadership to Edmund S. Muskie of Maine, who served on the committee with him for 21 years. Randolph did step forward in late 1980, however, after Muskie had left the Senate, to work with Republican Robert T. Stafford of Vermont on a compromise version of the chemical cleanup "superfund" bill. It was enacted at the end of the 96th Congress, with Randolph's support.

Randolph has been a happy warrior all these years in the Senate, confident in the perfectability of society and government's contribution to it. "Problems are truly wonderful," he once said, "because we have the opportunity to solve them."

He also has an abiding affection for his own oratory. Although Randolph does not speak often these days, he speaks at great length. Named after the silver-tongued William Jennings Bryan, he is a former public speaking teacher who uses a florid style seldom heard any more in Congress or elsewhere.

Apart from public works, his favorite cause has always been programs for the handicapped. He was the chief author of the 1936 law permitting the blind to operate vending stands in federal buildings — a measure that was copied by state and local governments around the nation, and led to the employment of thousands of handicapped Americans in an era when jobs were scarce. Randolph is the ranking Democrat on the Senate Labor Subcommittee dealing with the handicapped, and has had a hand in many of the recent legislative programs to help them.

The old New Dealer has much less use for heavy military spending, and regularly votes against foreign aid, which he considers "wasted money . . . when we have so much to do for our own people."

What he loathes most of all, however, is making a controversial decision. He has been known, during roll call votes on sensitive matters, to drop his pencil and duck down in pursuit of it just as his name is called; somehow, he seldom manages to locate the errant object until after the clerk has passed on.

The vote on the Panama Canal treaties in 1978, the year of Randolph's toughest re-election challenge, was pure agony for him. His colleague, Majority Leader Robert C. Byrd, was twisting his arm for an "aye" vote, as was President Carter. But Randolph's West Virginia mail and phone calls overwhelmingly opposed the treaties. The senator was glum, and stayed that way right through the initial call of the roll. Only after it was apparent the treaties would squeak through did he cast his "no" vote.

Randolph denied that he was prepared to vote for the Panama Canal treaties if absolutely necessary, but he readily admitted that his decision to vote "no" was based solely on constituent pressure. "They are mountain people," he said of his West Virginia voters. "Mountain people are very cautious about losing any property."

It was not the first time, nor the last, that Randolph disappointed a president of the United States. But few members of Congress have had so many chances to do so. "Presidents come and go," says the man who has served with nine of them. "I just want to keep on going."

**At Home:** Locked in the toughest Senate re-election campaign of his long career, Randolph sounded one theme in 1978 as he campaigned through his state: the bounty that his seniority and his chairmanship of the Public Works Committee had brought. At nearly every stop, he

claimed credit for a local bridge, sewage treatment plant, highway or other example of federal largess. It was enough, but just barely. Randolph defeated former Republican Gov. Arch A. Moore Jr. by 4,717 votes.

The son of a small-town mayor, Randolph worked as a reporter and taught journalism and public speaking before winning his campaign to unseat Republican congressman Frank L. Bowman in the 1932 Roosevelt sweep. Randolph served seven terms in the House, finally losing in the Republican year of 1946.

Randolph remained in Washington after his defeat, working as public relations director for Capital Airlines. But he kept his legal residence in Elkins, W.Va. When longtime Democratic Sen. Matthew M. Neely died in 1958, Randolph launched a comeback, and took the Senate primary easily over former Gov. William C. Marland, whose administration had been tainted by corruption charges.

With the strong backing of organized labor, Randolph also won comfortably in the fall over Republican John D. Hoblitzell, who had been appointed interim senator. Two years later, campaigning for a full term, he had a tougher contest against GOP Gov. Cecil H. Underwood, but still won by a comfortable 88,000 votes.

After that, there were no problems until 1978, when Moore sought to take advantage of Randolph's 76 years. A six-term House member and the first two-term governor in state history, Moore was the unquestioned leader and symbol of the state's Republican Party. His personal campaigning skills were superb; he had never lost an election. Moore criticized Randolph for indecision on the Panama Canal issue and challenged his claim of credit for the state highway system.

He treaded lightly on the age issue, even though it was the basis of Randolph's vulnerability. The senator already had been hit with that in his primary campaign, when housewife Sharon Rogers tried to call him "senile" and named her organization "the Committee to Dump the Tub of Lard."

But Moore had a critical problem of his own: he had been indicted and tried in 1976 on charges that he extorted $25,000 from a savings and loan company seeking a bank charter. In the end, he was acquitted, but the episode damaged a reputation that had gone through more than two decades in West Virginia politics without a stain.

If there had been no indictment, Moore would have been a sure winner. With it, he still came remarkably close, but Randolph survived to begin a Senate term that will end 52 years after he first took his seat in Congress.

## Committees

**Environment and Public Works** (Ranking Democrat)
Transportation.

**Labor and Human Resources** (2nd of 7 Democrats)
Education; Handicapped; Labor.

**Veterans' Affairs** (2nd of 5 Democrats)

## Elections

**1978 General**

| | |
|---|---|
| Jennings Randolph (D) | 249,034 (50%) |
| Arch Moore (R) | 244,317 (50%) |

**1978 Primary**

| | |
|---|---|
| Jennings Randolph (D) | 181,480 (80%) |
| Sharon Rogers (D) | 43,991 (20%) |

**Previous Winning Percentages**

| | | | |
|---|---|---|---|
| 1972 (66%) | 1966 (60%) | 1960 (55%) | 1958† (59%) |
| 1944* (54 %) | 1942* (50 %) | 1940* (58 %) | 1938* (55 %) |
| 1936* (60 %) | 1934* (58 %) | 1932* (53 %) | |

†Special Senate election.
*House election.

## Campaign Finance

| | Receipts | Receipts from PACs | Expenditures |
|---|---|---|---|
| 1978 | | | |
| Randolph (D) | $732,484 | $240,250 (33%) | $684,605 |
| Moore (R) | $474,218 | $111,975 (24%) | $458,823 |

## Voting Studies

| | Presidential Support | | Party Unity | | Conservative Coalition | |
|---|---|---|---|---|---|---|
| **Year** | **S** | **O** | **S** | **O** | **S** | **O** |
| 1980 | 63 | 34 | 82 | 15 | 34 | 63 |
| 1979 | 63 | 31 | 69 | 27 | 55 | 42 |
| 1978 | 54 | 35 | 55 | 34 | 47 | 43 |
| 1977 | 76 | 20 | 52 | 41 | 64 | 32 |
| 1976 | 49 | 45 | 63 | 34 | 54 | 42 |
| 1975 | 56 | 42 | 68 | 27 | 48 | 48 |
| 1974 (Ford) | 47 | 51 | | | | |
| 1974 | 41 | 54 | 68 | 23 | 35 | 56 |
| 1973 | 42 | 53 | 74 | 22 | 45 | 50 |
| 1972 | 46 | 46 | 69 | 19 | 35 | 54 |
| 1971 | 46 | 43 | 62 | 28 | 52 | 39 |
| 1970 | 60 | 34 | 68 | 22 | 39 | 54 |
| 1969 | 56 | 40 | 75 | 20 | 42 | 51 |
| 1968 | 60 | 27 | 63 | 16 | 41 | 46 |
| 1967 | 72 | 18 | 83 | 5 | 25 | 61 |
| 1966 | 63 | 26 | 69 | 14 | 20 | 73 |
| 1965 | 74 | 15 | 70 | 15 | 25 | 57 |
| 1964 | 56 | 20 | 64 | 14 | 22 | 71 |
| 1963 | 72 | 18 | 75 | 17 | 16 | 74 |
| 1962 | 86 | 11 | 85 | 10 | 38 | 56 |
| 1961 | 82 | 10 | 85 | 3 | 5 | 92 |

S = Support    O = Opposition

## Key Votes

**96th Congress**

| | |
|---|---|
| Maintain relations with Taiwan (1979) | Y |
| Reduce synthetic fuel development funds (1979) | N |
| Impose nuclear plant moratorium (1979) | Y |
| Kill stronger windfall profits tax (1979) | N |
| Guarantee Chrysler Corp. loans (1979) | Y |
| Approve military draft registration (1980) | Y |
| End Revenue Sharing to the states (1980) | N |
| Block Justice Dept. busing suits (1980) | Y |

**97th Congress**

| | |
|---|---|
| Restore urban program funding cuts (1981) | Y |

## Interest Group Ratings

| Year | ADA | ACA | AFL-CIO | CCUS-1 | CCUS-2 |
|---|---|---|---|---|---|
| 1980 | 72 | 12 | 89 | 38 | |
| 1979 | 32 | 29 | 78 | 9 | 44 |
| 1978 | 30 | 38 | 68 | 24 | |
| 1977 | 40 | 43 | 72 | 39 | |
| 1976 | 45 | 16 | 60 | 22 | |
| 1975 | 67 | 14 | 59 | 38 | |
| 1974 | 67 | 13 | 70 | 10 | |
| 1973 | 60 | 29 | 90 | 33 | |
| 1972 | 40 | 28 | 70 | 0 | |
| 1971 | 67 | 25 | 83 | - | |
| 1970 | 59 | 26 | 67 | 11 | |
| 1969 | 78 | 29 | 73 | - | |
| 1968 | 64 | 32 | 100 | - | |
| 1967 | 69 | 12 | 91 | 30 | |
| 1966 | 70 | 17 | 75 | - | |
| 1965 | 76 | 14 | - | 20 | |
| 1964 | 74 | 7 | 100 | - | |
| 1963 | - | 0 | - | - | |
| 1962 | 58 | 4 | 91 | - | |
| 1961 | 100 | | - | - | |

# Robert C. Byrd (D)

## Of Sophia — Elected 1958

**Born:** Nov. 20, 1917, North Wilkesboro, N.C.
**Education:** Beckley College, Concord College, Morris Harvey College, 1950-51; Marshall College, 1951-52; American U., J.D. 1963.
**Profession:** Public official; lawyer.
**Family:** Wife, Erma Ora James; two children.
**Religion:** Baptist.
**Political Career:** W.Va. House, 1947-51; W.Va. Senate, 1951-53; U.S. House, 1953-59.

**In Washington**: Byrd has spent a lifetime in politics making himself powerful by making himself useful. With Republicans running the Senate he no longer commands a voting majority on the floor, but on many issues he can still influence the fate of Reagan administration proposals, and when the 97th Congress began he wasted no time in proving the point.

Within Reagan's first weeks in office, the President needed Democratic votes to raise the federal debt ceiling, a routine action Republicans had traditionally opposed in order to embarrass the majority Democrats. Byrd delivered the votes Reagan needed, but not before he publicly chastised the GOP for past sins and hinted at the cooperation he could provide — or withhold.

In May, Byrd sounded surprisingly cooperative, promising to vote for the overall Reagan budget proposals because "the people want to give him a chance, so I will give him a chance." But virtually in the same breath, he delivered an ominous prophecy: "Popularity is fleeting. It comes quickly and it goes quickly."

Reagan is far from the first president to draw cryptic support from the proud and prickly West Virginian. In 1977, the year Byrd became majority leader and Jimmy Carter assumed the presidency, the senator carefully defined their relationship: "I am the president's friend," he said. "I am not the president's man."

In truth, he was a "friend" only in the most formal and professional sense, for he seemed to view Carter as an amateur with little aptitude for the exercise of power. Nonetheless, Byrd repeatedly saved the Democratic administration in difficult legislative situations — making sure that Carter knew where the credit belonged.

His most dramatic rescue operation came in 1978, when he saved the Panama Canal transfer treaties for Carter through non-stop negotiations with wavering senators, personal diplomacy with Panamanian officials and last-second language changes that finally amassed the votes needed for ratification.

But Byrd also played an indispensable role in the passage of Carter's energy program, approval of the Middle East arms sale package, lifting of the Turkish arms embargo and extension of the deadline for ratification of the Equal Rights Amendment.

While Carter's political standing diminished year by year, Byrd's own stature as a leader grew steadily. His detractors, once legion, especially on the Democratic left, gradually disappeared. His colleagues made no move to change leaders in the wake of the 1980 electoral debacle. Although there has been criticism since then that Byrd is essentially a traffic manager without much talent as a voice of opposition, his job seems secure, whether he is in the majority or the minority.

Few would have predicted such a career when Byrd was first elected to the Senate in 1958 after three terms in the House. In those days he was considered parochial in his emphasis on West Virginia issues and far to the right of most Democratic senators on others. He opposed the Civil Rights Act of 1964; he was a scourge of welfare recipients as chairman of the District of Columbia Appropriations Subcommittee, ordering inspections to see whether female welfare recipients were harboring unreported men in their homes.

But by 1967, he had a toehold on the Senate leadership ladder, defeating the veteran liberal Joseph Clark of Pennsylvania to become secretary of the Democratic Conference. Unnoticed by outsiders, Byrd set about serving his colleagues, scheduling routine business to suit their convenience and tending to countless details involved in running the Senate.

Four years later he cashed the chits he had so carefully collected and ousted a stunned Edward

M. Kennedy from the No. 2 leadership job, majority whip. Kennedy, shaken by the Chappaquiddick controversy in 1969, had been neither an active nor effective whip, but he anticipated no trouble. He went into the party caucus full of confidence and oral commitments.

Byrd, however, entered with a pocketful of due bills and a deathbed proxy from his Senate mentor, the late Richard Russell of Georgia. It was no contest.

For six years after that, Byrd was a loyal lieutenant to Majority Leader Mike Mansfield, sitting through long days of floor work while deferring to Mansfield as party spokesman and political leader.

An indefatigable worker, Byrd soon became a master of Senate rules and procedures. He studied constantly — history, philosophy, poetry and law — seeking to improve himself. (He already had a law degree, obtained in 1963 after he attended night school at American University in Washington during his first Senate term.) And he continued to perform favors, small and not so small, for his fellow senators.

When Mansfield retired, Byrd was ready. Some liberals wanted the universally beloved Hubert H. Humphrey in the top leadership job, believing he would be a more presentable and eloquent spokesman than Byrd, whom many of them still saw as a mere technician.

But Byrd once again had a long column of accounts receivable — and he called them. Humphrey, already seriously ill, withdrew before the balloting even started, and Byrd was elected by acclamation.

By the time of his accession to the leadership, Byrd had moved a considerable distance to the left ideologically. The hard-liner who broke with a majority of his party to support an anti-ballistic missile system in 1969 became strongly committed a decade later to a strategic arms limitation treaty with the Soviet Union. The bitter critic of self-government for the District of Columbia in the 1960s won Senate approval for a constitutional amendment giving the District voting representation in Congress. And the erstwhile Ku Klux Klan member who once dismissed Martin Luther King as a "self-serving rabble-rouser" fought to the very end of the 96th Congress in a vain effort to strengthen federal fair housing laws.

In a word, Byrd has gone "national." His defense of West Virginia interests, especially coal, has never ceased, but it is now seen as a piece of his record, not the dominant part of it. When he maneuvered in 1980 to get the Senate to weaken the three-year-old strip mine control act, few liberals treated it as a major offense. His right to speak for the Democratic Party in the Senate was no longer in question.

**At Home:** Byrd was born Cornelius Calvin Sale Jr. When he was 10, his mother died and his father abandoned him, and he spent his childhood with an aunt and uncle, Vlurma and Titus Byrd, in the hard-scrabble coal country of southern West Virginia.

Byrd graduated first in his high school class, but it took him 12 more years before he could afford to start college. He worked as a gas station attendant, grocery store clerk, shipyard welder and butcher before his talents as a fiddle player helped win him a seat in the state Legislature in 1946.

Friends drove Byrd around the hills and hollows, where he brought the voters out by playing "Cripple Creek" and "Rye Whiskey." From then on, he never lost an election. As he himself once put it, "There are four things people believe in in West Virginia — God Almighty, Sears Roebuck, Carters Little Liver Pills and Robert C. Byrd."

When Democrat Erland Hedrick retired in the old 6th Congressional District in 1952, Byrd was an obvious contender. But he had to surmount a serious political problem: He joined the Ku Klux Klan at age 24 and as late as 1946 wrote a letter to the imperial grand wizard urging a Klan rebirth "in every state of the Union."

When this came up publicly in 1952, his opponents and Democratic Gov. Okey L. Patteson called on him to drop out. He refused, explaining his Klan membership as a youthful indiscretion committed because of his alarm over communism, and won the election.

After three House terms, he ran for the Senate in 1958 with the support of the AFL-CIO and the United Mine Workers. He crushed his primary opposition and made a solid showing in unseating Republican Chapman Revercomb, a veteran who had been in and out of the Senate in the 1940s and won a two-year term in a comeback in 1956. Revercomb was a weak incumbent before the campaign even began, and the 1958 recession had had a serious impact in West Virginia, driving voters closer to New Deal Democratic roots. Byrd was an easy winner.

Every six years since then, West Virginians have returned him to the Senate by a greater margin. In 1964, he trounced Cooper Benedict, a former deputy assistant secretary of defense. Six years later, the Republicans put up Charleston Mayor Elmer H. Dodson, who campaigned little and suffered a humiliating defeat. In 1976, no one filed against him, and his only real contest was as a favorite son in the state's presidential primary. He won that in a landslide, defeating George C. Wallace, who was once strong in West Virginia but whose national campaign was by then close to collapse.

## Committees

**Appropriations** (3rd of 14 Democrats)
Agriculture and Related Agencies; Energy and Water Development; Interior; Labor, Health and Human Services, Education; Transportation.

**Judiciary** (3rd of 8 Democrats)
Regulatory Reform.

**Rules and Administration** (4th of 5 Democrats)

## Elections

**1976 General**

Robrt C. Byrd (D)                                                    Unopposed

**Previous Winning Percentages**

| 1970 (78%) | 1964 (68%) | 1958 (59%) | 1956 (57%) |
|---|---|---|---|
| 1954* (63%) | 1952* (56%) | | |

*House election.

## Campaign Finance

| | Receipts | Receipts from PACs | Expenditures |
|---|---|---|---|
| 1976 | | | |
| Byrd (D) | $271,124 | $64,240 (24%) | $94,335 |

## Voting Studies

| | Presidential Support | | Party Unity | | Conservative Coalition | |
|---|---|---|---|---|---|---|
| Year | S | O | S | O | S | O |
| 1980 | 73 | 26 | 87 | 12 | 42 | 58 |
| 1979 | 77 | 20 | 79 | 20 | 57 | 43 |
| 1978 | 82 | 15 | 79 | 19 | 40 | 58 |
| 1977 | 84 | 15 | 66 | 31 | 55 | 44 |
| 1976 | 47 | 53 | 73 | 26 | 42 | 57 |
| 1975 | 66 | 34 | 63 | 36 | 64 | 35 |
| 1974 (Ford) | 47 | 53 | | | | |
| 1974 | 47 | 53 | 63 | 37 | 56 | 44 |
| 1973 | 40 | 60 | 75 | 25 | 47 | 53 |
| 1972 | 67 | 30 | 68 | 31 | 50 | 48 |
| 1971 | 55 | 35 | 62 | 32 | 64 | 29 |
| 1970 | 57 | 33 | 66 | 26 | 44 | 46 |

| | | | | | | |
|---|---|---|---|---|---|---|
| 1969 | 46 | 47 | 52 | 34 | 59 | 33 |
| 1968 | 49 | 46 | 63 | 24 | 56 | 33 |
| 1967 | 65 | 27 | 68 | 24 | 71 | 23 |
| 1966 | 63 | 31 | 64 | 28 | 49 | 49 |
| 1965 | 64 | 27 | 62 | 31 | 57 | 33 |
| 1964 | 67 | 24 | 68 | 28 | 61 | 33 |
| 1963 | 75 | 12 | 85 | 11 | 32 | 58 |
| 1962 | 86 | 14 | 93 | 7 | 50 | 50 |
| 1961 | 83 | 15 | 92 | 6 | 20 | 80 |

S = Support                    O = Opposition

## Key Votes

**96th Congress**

| | |
|---|---|
| Maintain relations with Taiwan (1979) | N |
| Reduce synthetic fuel development funds (1979) | N |
| Impose nuclear plant moratorium (1979) | N |
| Kill stronger windfall profits tax (1979) | N |
| Guarantee Chrysler Corp. loans (1979) | Y |
| Approve military draft registration (1980) | Y |
| End Revenue Sharing to the states (1980) | Y |
| Block Justice Dept. busing suits (1980) | N |

**97th Congress**

| | |
|---|---|
| Restore urban program funding cuts (1981) | Y |

## Interest Group Ratings

| Year | ADA | ACA | AFL-CIO | CCUS-1 | CCUS-2 |
|---|---|---|---|---|---|
| 1980 | 56 | 15 | 58 | 33 | |
| 1979 | 53 | 26 | 58 | 18 | 33 |
| 1978 | 45 | 29 | 78 | 28 | |
| 1977 | 50 | 37 | 60 | 39 | |
| 1976 | 45 | 31 | 79 | 22 | |
| 1975 | 28 | 43 | 50 | 50 | |
| 1974 | 52 | 47 | 82 | 20 | |
| 1973 | 60 | 38 | 91 | 22 | |
| 1972 | 35 | 50 | 70 | 0 | |
| 1971 | 26 | 45 | 58 | — | |
| 1970 | 31 | 50 | 50 | 20 | |
| 1969 | 33 | 50 | 36 | — | |
| 1968 | 21 | 63 | 0 | — | |
| 1967 | 23 | 38 | 33 | 40 | |
| 1966 | 35 | 31 | 50 | — | |
| 1965 | 35 | 32 | — | 40 | |
| 1964 | 52 | 39 | 64 | — | |
| 1963 | | 8 | — | — | |
| 1962 | 67 | 7 | 91 | — | |
| 1961 | 80 | — | — | — | |

# 1 Robert H. Mollohan (D)

**Of Fairmont — Elected 1968**
Also served 1953-57

**Born:** Sept. 18, 1909, Grantsville, W.Va.
**Education:** Attended Glenville College and Shepard College, 1929-31.
**Profession:** Public official, insurance agent.
**Family:** Wife, Helen Holt; three children.
**Religion:** Baptist.
**Political Career:** U.S. House, 1953-57; unsuccessful Democratic nominee for W.Va. governor, 1956; unsuccessful Democratic nominee for U.S. House, 1958, returned to U.S. House, 1968.

**In Washington:** Mollohan is a senior member of the Armed Services Committee, but plays nothing resembling a leadership role there. In 1981, when seniority qualified him for the chairmanship of one of the panel's seven subcommittees, he declined to take one.

The Mollohan of today is far different from the aggressive young Democrat who served four years in the House during the 1950s, before leaving to run unsuccessfully for governor in 1956. He was only a junior member then, but he was an active participant, criticizing the Eisenhower administration and chairing a subcommittee with jurisdiction over the Immigration and Naturalization Service.

Mollohan eventually regained his seat after 12 years out of office. But he did not regain his enthusiasm. Since his return in 1969, he has not often strayed from the back benches of the House. Mollohan is rarely heard on the floor, either giving a speech or participating in legislative debate. He has rejected requests to substitute for an absent subcommittee chairman as manager of a bill. Most of what he does say is in praise of one constituent or another.

Occasionally Mollohan inserts a written statement in the *Congressional Record,* along with the testimony of a constituent or a news article from a West Virginia paper. In 1980, he inserted one on emergency medical services, a subject he has taken an interest in. But, apparently forgetting he had already put it in, he inserted the same speech and testimony four days later.

When the Armed Services Committee designed legislation in 1980 to provide larger bonuses to military doctors, Mollohan tried to secure more money for military dentists, at the urging of a longtime friend who represents the American Dental Association. Mollohan said military dentists needed to feel that Congress was interested in their welfare.

On his second committee, House Administration, Mollohan has been a consistent opponent of public financing for congressional elections. He provided one of the votes against a public financing bill as the committee killed it in 1979. He also has a House Administration subcommittee chairmanship, on Office Systems.

Mollohan was an active supporter of legislation enacted in 1980 to provide antitrust exemptions to soft-drink bottlers, although most of the work in Congress was done by members of the House and Senate Judiciary committees.

**At Home:** Mollohan focused early in his career on one ambition: the governorship of West Virginia. He had his chance in 1956, but he lost, and the price was 12 years out of office. When he returned to the House in 1968, it was as a man with few goals other than prolonged congressional tenure, and that he has achieved.

A protégé of the late Gov. and Sen. Matthew M. Neely, Mollohan has spent most of his adult life as a public official. After serving in the U.S. Internal Revenue Service and as a state official of the Works Progress Administration, he became superintendent of the West Virginia Industrial School for Boys in 1941. Mollohan held that

---

**1st District: North central — northern Panhandle, Wheeling.** Population: 460,542 (6% increase since 1970). Race: White 450,839 (98%), Black 7,793 (2%), Others 1,190 (0.4%). Spanish origin: 3,052 (1%).

position until 1949, when he was brought to Washington by Neely as clerk of the Senate Committee on the District of Columbia.

Three years later, with the help of the Neely organization, Mollohan won a seat in the U.S. House. After ousting Democratic incumbent Robert L. Ramsay in the primary by a margin of about 1,000 votes, he defeated former Republican Rep. Francis J. Love in the general election by a more comfortable 8,002-vote margin.

Mollohan retained his seat in 1954, defeating Ramsay again in the Democratic primary and blunting a vigorous Republican challenge in the fall from a young lawyer, Arch A. Moore Jr.

In 1956, Mollohan left his House seat to run for governor. With Neely's support, he won the Democratic nomination over a candidate supported by outgoing Gov. William C. Marland.

But in the general election against Republican Cecil H. Underwood, Mollohan was crippled by a personal scandal. It was revealed during the campaign that while Mollohan was superintendent of the state boys' school, he had received $20,000 and two cars from a Grafton coal company that obtained a contract to strip-mine on school land. The congressman denied any wrongdoing. But the issue ruined his campaign. Heavily favored during the summer, he lost to Underwood by more than 60,000 votes.

Two years later he tried a congressional comeback, but by then the Republican Moore had entrenched himself. Still tainted by the boys' school scandal, Mollohan lost by nearly 10,000 votes. He protested afterward that unsigned and unattributed campaign literature had been used against him, and filed a complaint with a special House investigating committee. A former Moore aide was indicted in 1959, but was subsequently acquitted, and Moore stayed in office.

Mollohan dropped out of the public spotlight for most of the next decade, working for various West Virginia corporations and the United Mine Workers. Private business deals made him a wealthy man.

When Moore vacated the House seat in 1968 to run for governor, Mollohan was ready to resume his political career. As the best-known candidate in a crowded Democratic field, he emerged as an easy primary winner. In the fall campaign, he won by more than 10,000 votes even though Moore was carrying the district.

Mollohan has had no serious Republican challenges since then, and only one hotly contested Democratic primary. That was in 1970, when his opponent was Robert L. "Sam" Huff, a former football star for West Virginia University and several professional teams.

Huff proved to be an effective campaigner. But Mollohan locked up the support of the United Mine Workers and local Democratic organizations and won by a margin of more than 2-to-1.

**The District:** Moore gave Republicans a foothold here during his 12-year House career, but traditional voting patterns reasserted themselves on his departure.

In 1980, both Carter and Democratic Gov. John D. "Jay" Rockefeller IV won in the 1st, with Rockefeller carrying it in his successful gubernatorial campaign against Moore by nearly 15,000 votes.

Manufacturing plants are spread throughout the 1st, but much of the heavy industry (iron and steel) is concentrated in the Panhandle. Wedged between the Pennsylvania border and the Ohio River, that region includes the cities of Wheeling and Weirton.

The Panhandle and the coal-mining country to the southeast boast significant concentrations of East European ethnics, who came to work in the mines and steel mills. These areas usually vote Democratic. The more rural counties to the southwest and the Ohio River city of Parkersburg normally vote Republican.

Although the 1st is the most prosperous district in West Virginia, the population grew by only 6 percent in the 1970s — a smaller rate than in any other district in the state.

## Committees

**Armed Services** (7th of 25 Democrats)
Investigations; Research and Development; Seapower and Strategic and Critical Materials.

**House Administration** (5th of 11 Democrats)
Office Systems, chairman; Services.

## Elections

| 1980 General | |
|---|---|
| Robert Mollohan (D ) | 107,471 (64 %) |
| Joe Bartlett (R ) | 61,438 (36 %) |

| 1978 General | |
|---|---|
| Robert Mollohan (D ) | 76,372 (63 %) |
| Gene Gaynes (R ) | 44,062 (37 %) |

**Previous Winning Percentages**

| | | | |
|---|---|---|---|
| 1976 (58 %) | 1974 (60 %) | 1972 (69 %) | 1970 (62 %) |
| 1968 (54 %) | 1954 (53 %) | 1952 (53 %) | |

**District Vote For President**

| 1980 | | 1976 | | 1972 | |
|---|---|---|---|---|---|
| D | 88,697 (48 %) | D | 105,427 (56 %) | D | 70,735 (36 %) |
| R | 85,218 (46 %) | R | 84,408 (44 %) | R | 126,902 (64 %) |
| I | 8,350 (5 %) | | | | |

## Campaign Finance

| | Receipts | Receipts from PACs | Expen-ditures |
|---|---|---|---|
| **1980** | | | |
| Mollohan (D ) | $68,401 | $34,150 (50 %) | $57,941 |
| Bartlett (R ) | $53,697 | $14,400 (27 %) | $54,696 |
| **1978** | | | |
| Mollohan (D ) | $56,375 | $26,450 (47 %) | $37,680 |
| Haynes (R ) | $14,177 | $3,250 (23 %) | $14,129 |

## Voting Studies

| | Presidential Support | | Party Unity | | Conservative Coalition | |
|---|---|---|---|---|---|---|
| Year | S | O | S | O | S | O |
| 1980 | 68 | 15 | 76 | 15 | 41 | 47 |
| 1979 | 63 | 29 | 73 | 21 | 49 | 49 |
| 1978 | 56 | 42 | 65 | 31 | 52 | 41 |
| 1977 | 63 | 32 | 68 | 28 | 54 | 43 |
| 1976 | 35 | 63 | 68 | 28 | 49 | 45 |
| 1975 | 35 | 44 | 55 | 17 | 33 | 44 |
| 1974 (Ford) | 41 | 44 | | | | |
| 1974 | 45 | 32 | 55 | 28 | 49 | 41 |
| 1973 | 35 | 51 | 67 | 24 | 48 | 44 |
| 1972 | 46 | 16 | 53 | 18 | 34 | 30 |
| 1971 | 63 | 19 | 60 | 22 | 49 | 34 |

| 1970 | 46 | 20 | 57 | 17 | 34 | 36 |
|---|---|---|---|---|---|---|
| 1969 | 57 | 38 | 76 | 16 | 40 | 49 |

S = Support            O = Opposition

## Key Votes

**96th Congress**

| | |
|---|---|
| Weaken Carter oil profits tax (1979) | N |
| Reject hospital cost control plan (1979) | Y |
| Implement Panama Canal Treaties (1979) | Y |
| Establish Department of Education (1979) | Y |
| Approve Anti-busing Amendment (1979) | Y |
| Guarantee Chrysler Corp. loans (1979) | Y |
| Approve military draft registration (1980) | Y |
| Aid Sandinista regime in Nicaragua (1980) | Y |
| Strengthen fair housing laws (1980) | N |

**97th Congress**

| | |
|---|---|
| Reagan budget proposal (1981) | N |

## Interest Group Ratings

| Year | ADA | ACA | AFL-CIO | CCUS |
|---|---|---|---|---|
| 1980 | 56 | 20 | 68 | 60 |
| 1979 | 37 | 19 | 85 | 28 |
| 1978 | 30 | 48 | 55 | 50 |
| 1977 | 25 | 41 | 87 | 38 |
| 1976 | 45 | 14 | 83 | 54 |
| 1975 | 32 | 28 | 83 | 27 |
| 1974 | 39 | 33 | 100 | 29 |
| 1973 | 40 | 24 | 100 | 27 |
| 1972 | 19 | 26 | 90 | 11 |
| 1971 | 27 | 42 | 100 | - |
| 1970 | 36 | 18 | 100 | 0 |
| 1969 | 47 | 24 | 100 | - |

# 2 Cleve Benedict (R)

**Of Lewisburg — Elected 1980**

**Born:** March 21, 1935, Harrisburg, Pa.
**Education:** Princeton U., A.B. 1957.
**Profession:** Dairy farmer.
**Family:** Wife, Ann Arthur; three children.
**Religion:** Episcopalian.
**Political Career:** Chairman, W.Va. Board of Probation and Parole, 1974-75; state commissioner of finance and administration, 1975-77; Republican State Chairman, 1976-77; Republican nominee for U.S. House, 1978.

**The Member:** Benedict took this Democratic district by projecting a folksy, down-home manner that belied his Princeton education and multimillion-dollar fortune.

Even though he is an heir to Procter & Gamble riches, Benedict campaigned as a dairy farmer who understood his rural constituents, portraying himself as a fiscal watchdog.

Since his election, he has found some Reagan spending cuts not to his liking. When the president declared that the private sector, not government, should take the lead in synfuels development, a planned $1.4 billion coal conversion project in Benedict's district was endangered. Japan, West Germany, the United States and Gulf Oil were to be partners in building the plant, but progress flagged after Reagan cut the share of federal money.

Benedict also has been trying to persuade the Interior Department to drop its opposition to construction of the Canaan Valley Dam in his district. The dam would bring jobs, tax receipts and tourism to an impoverished area, but it would inundate 7,000 acres of vegetation and wildlife.

Benedict's election in 1980 was the result of three years of energetic campaigning, including a 1978 bid against Democratic Rep. Harley O. Staggers that brought nearly 45 percent of the vote and persuaded national Republicans to take him seriously. Staggers announced his retirement in 1980, and gave only lukewarm support to the party nominee, Pat R. Hamilton, who had beaten Staggers' son in the Democratic primary.

**The District:** An incumbent can quickly make himself unbeatable in the 2nd District, because geography makes it difficult for a challenger to communicate his message. The 2nd is one of the largest districts east of the Mississippi, yet has no major media markets. Covering about half of West Virginia, it is ribbed by mountains and dotted with small towns and farms.

## Committees

**Energy and Commerce** (16th of 18 Republicans)
Energy, Conservation and Power; Fossil and Synthetic Fuels; Health and the Environment.

## Elections

**1980 General**

| | |
|---|---|
| Cleve Benedict (R ) | 102,805 (56 %) |
| Pat Hamilton (D ) | 80,940 (44 %) |

**1980 Primary**

| | |
|---|---|
| Cleve Benedict (R ) | 24,593 (62 %) |
| Edgar Heiskell (R ) | 14,778 (38 %) |

**District Vote For President**

| | 1980 | | 1976 | | 1972 |
|---|---|---|---|---|---|
| **D** | 94,094 (48 %) | **D** | 113,392 (57 %) | **D** | 66,597 (35 %) |
| **R** | 93,228 (47 %) | **R** | 86,234 (43 %) | **R** | 124,917 (65 %) |
| **I** | 9,313 (5 %) | | | | |

## Campaign Finance

| | Receipts | Receipts from PACs | Expenditures |
|---|---|---|---|
| **1980** | | | |
| Benedict (R ) | $219,046 | $147,534 (67 %) | $231,377 |
| Hamilton (D ) | $352,817 | $62,500 (18 %) | $336,554 |

## Key Vote

**97th Congress**

| | |
|---|---|
| Reagan budget proposal (1981) | Y |

**2nd District: East — Morgantown, eastern Panhandle.** Population: 522,835 (20% increase since 1970). Race: White 504,296 (96%), Black 15,405 (3%), Others 3,134 (1%). Spanish origin: 3,659 (1%).

# 3 David Michael Staton (R)

**Of South Charleston — Elected 1980**

**Born:** Feb. 11, 1940, Parkersburg, W.Va.
**Education:** Attended Concord College (W.Va.), 1961-63, no degree.
**Military Service:** Army National Guard, 1957-65.
**Profession:** Bank data processor.
**Family:** Wife, Lynn Spencer; two children.
**Religion:** Methodist.
**Political Career:** Unsuccessful Republican nominee for U.S. House, 1978 and special election, June 1980.

The Member: Persistence and good luck played nearly equal roles in Staton's emergence as the first Republican House member from this Charleston district since 1926.

It took him three tries. Largely unknown and without ties to the party or the influential Charleston business community, Staton had to mortgage his house in order to make his political debut in 1978. That campaign ended in a loss to veteran Democratic Rep. John M. Slack. But by covering the 14-county district on foot, Staton drew a respectable 41 percent of the vote.

When Slack died in early 1980, Staton was on the ballot in a special election against Democrat John Hutchinson, the Charleston mayor. Hutchinson won, but had been weakened by a bitter primary. Staton beat him in the fall by 10,000 votes.

Staton is opposed to most federal subsidies to aid ailing businesses. A devout Methodist, he was active in a local movement which protested alleged pornographic material in school textbooks.

Staton has tried to pave the way for expansion of a Volkswagen plant in his district. The company cannot expand unless allowed to acquire 4.6 acres belonging to an Army and Marine training center. During debate over the 1981 military construction bill, Staton asked that Volkswagen be allowed to obtain the land.

The District: The 3rd centers on populous Kanawha County (Charleston), which has been booming lately as a center for the reviving coal industry. Kanawha contains about half the district population. To the south are two depressed mining counties, Lincoln and Boone. To the north is more prosperous farmland.

Republican strength has been concentrated in the northern part of the district. But Staton won by outpolling Hutchinson in the Democrat's home base, Kanawha County, by more than 6,000 votes.

## Committees

**Interior and Insular Affairs** (14th of 17 Republicans)
Energy and the Environment; Mines and Mining.

**Small Business** (10th of 17 Republicans)
Export Opportunities and Special Small Business Problems; SBA and SBIC Authority, Minority Enterprise and General Small Business Problems.

## Elections

**1980 General**

| | |
|---|---|
| David Michael Staton (R) | 94,583 (53 %) |
| John Hutchinson (D ) | 84,980 (47 %) |

**1980 Primary**

| | |
|---|---|
| David Michael Staton (R) | 28,259 (74 %) |
| Richie Robb (R ) | 7,457 (20 %) |
| Tom Williams (R ) | 2,435 (6 %) |

**District Vote For President**

| | 1980 | | 1976 | | 1972 |
|---|---|---|---|---|---|
| D | 91,695 (48 %) | D | 111,688 (58 %) | D | 74,219 (37 %) |
| R | 88,693 (47 %) | R | 81,613 (42 %) | R | 122,907 (62 %) |
| I | 8,728 (5 %) | | | | |

## Campaign Finance

| | Receipts | Receipts from PACs | Expenditures |
|---|---|---|---|
| **1980** | | | |
| Staton (R ) | $156,904 | $59,253 (38 %) | $155,579 |
| Hutchinson (D ) | $237,919 | $48,215 (20 %) | $146,961 |

## Key Vote

**97th Congress**

| | |
|---|---|
| Reagan budget proposal (1981) | Y |

---

**3rd District: Central — Charleston.**
Population: 478,741 (10% increase since 1970). Race: White 461,839 (96%), Black 14,443 (3%), Others 2,459 (1%). Spanish origin: 2,561 (1%).

# 4 Nick Rahall II (D)

**Of Beckley — Elected 1976**

**Born:** May 20, 1949, Beckley, W. Va.
**Education:** Duke U., A.B. 1971.
**Profession:** Travel agent.
**Family:** Wife, Helen McDaniel; two children.
**Religion:** Presbyterian.
**Political Career:** No previous office.

**In Washington:** Reviving the nation's coal industry is more than enough work for any junior House member, and it has kept Rahall busy through his first few congressional terms. If it is an exaggeration to say he has had a one-track mind, it is only a slight one.

The chairmanship of the Coal Group, a House caucus of about 50 members with one interest in common, has given Rahall a platform from which to promote his district's leading industry. It has also given him a role to play on broader issues. In 1980, Rahall teamed with Texas Democrat Bob Eckhardt to hold up a massive railroad deregulation bill. Rahall felt, along with the coal industry, that an unrestrictive free enterprise approach to freight service might mean exorbitant rates for coal shippers. Rahall eventually accepted a slight modification, leading Eckhardt to charge "sell-out" but satisfying the industry.

The year before, when the House voted to create an Energy Mobilization Board to speed approval of new energy projects, Rahall won passage of his own pro-coal amendment. It assured priority status for power plants converting from oil or natural gas to coal. It passed the House on a 46-7 vote, but the bill itself never became law.

On the Public Works Committee, Rahall has been a solid member of the pro-development majority, backing dams and other federal generosity to his low-income district. In 1978, he successfully promoted a scheme to abolish the Water Resources Board, a unit President Carter had counted on to evaluate — and possibly slow up — future water projects. The Interior Committee passed Rahall's amendment dissolving the board, and the House approved it, but the Senate refused to go along.

Rahall has been an ally of James Howard, D-N.J., who became Public Works chairman at the start of 1981, and Howard has helped him out at home. On one occasion, the two men visited the site of a bridge over the Ohio River at Huntington, West Virginia, and shortly afterward funds for the project were authorized in an omnibus public works bill, although no discussion of the project had taken place in hearings.

**At Home:** Rahall was a little-known travel agent and radio sales manager in 1976, but he saw an opportunity and he seized it. Five years later he is a solidly entrenched member of Congress.

Rahall's chance was Democratic Rep. Ken Hechler's quixotic campaign for governor. Hechler was popular and secure in the district and could have been renominated easily. When he chose not to run, numerous Democrats decided to.

Rahall was far from the best known contender in the field, and an opponent claimed that he looked like a "25-year-old college boy," an assertion that understated his true age by only a year. But he also had family money, and he used it to conduct a media campaign none of his opponents could afford, evoking the names of Hechler, Franklin D. Roosevelt, and Sen. Robert C. Byrd, for whom he had worked briefly. Rahall won the Democratic nomination with 37 percent.

Then, after the primary was over, Hechler said it had all been a mistake, and mounted a write-in drive to retain his House seat. Rahall could never have beaten Hechler in a primary. But the write-in effort was too difficult for even a

---

**4th District: South and west — Huntington, Beckley.** Population: 487,526 (11% increase since 1970). Race: White 457,777 (94%), Black 27,410 (6%), Others 2,339 (0.4%). Spanish origin: 3,435 (1%).

popular incumbent to carry off, especially now that Rahall had Democratic organization support. The result was an easy victory for the newcomer.

The race was expensive, with both Rahall and Hechler spending about a quarter million dollars out of their own pockets. Hechler announced immediately after the election that he would challenge Rahall again in the 1978 primary.

When he did so, however, he found that incumbency had given his successor the advantages he himself once had. Rahall was bolstered by endorsements from Byrd, House Speaker Thomas P. O'Neill Jr., the National Rifle Association and the West Virginia AFL-CIO. Adding strong local party support and a late media blitz, he won renomination with 56 percent of the vote.

The margin was convincing enough for Hechler to announce that he would not try again. With the Republican Party extremely weak in the district, Rahall has had no problems since then.

**The District:** The Appalachian 4th is the most staunchly Democratic district in the state. Carter carried it in 1980 by more than 25,000 votes, even though he was unable to take any of the other districts by more than 4,000.

Democratic strength is concentrated in the mountainous southern portion of the district, the center of the state's coal-mining industry. Organized labor and local party organizations have been strong forces since the New Deal, helping to generate heavy Democratic majorities.

The district's major population center is Huntington, located along the Ohio River at the northern end of the district. It is the second largest city in West Virginia. Diversified industries, including railroading, glass, and steel, support the local economy. While surrounding Cabell County frequently votes Republican in statewide races, it is nearly always outvoted by the rest of the district.

## Committees

**Interior and Insular Affairs** (14th of 23 Democrats)
Energy and the Environment; Mines and Mining.

**Public Works and Transportation** (16th of 25 Democrats)
Aviation; Surface Transportation; Water Resources.

**Standards of Official Conduct** (2nd of 6 Democrats)

## Elections

**1980 General**

| | |
|---|---|
| Nick Rahall (D ) | 117,595 (77 %) |
| Winton Covey (R ) | 36,020 (23 %) |

**1978 General**

| | |
|---|---|
| Nick Rahall (D ) | Unopposed |

**Previous Winning Percentage**

1976 (46 %)

**District Vote For President**

| | 1980 | | 1976 | | 1972 |
|---|---|---|---|---|---|
| **D** | 92,976 (56 %) | **D** | 105,407 (63 %) | **D** | 65,884 (37 %) |
| **R** | 67,069 (40 %) | **R** | 62,505 (37 %) | **R** | 110,238 (63 %) |
| **I** | 5,300 (3 %) | | | | |

## Campaign Finance

| | Receipts | Receipts from PACs | Expenditures |
|---|---|---|---|
| **1980** | | | |
| Rahall (D ) | $143,444 | $31,545 (33 %) | $109,485 |
| **1978** | | | |
| Rahall (D ) | $243,339 | $61,175 (25 %) | $242,298 |

## Voting Studies

| | Presidential Support | | Party Unity | | Conservative Coalition | |
|---|---|---|---|---|---|---|
| Year | S | O | S | O | S | O |
| 1980 | 77 | 18 | 79 | 17 | 40 | 59 |
| 1979 | 59 | 34 | 77 | 18 | 38 | 60 |
| 1978 | 62 | 29 | 69 | 16 | 27 | 60 |
| 1977 | 67 | 25 | 70 | 24 | 42 | 53 |

S = Support          O = Opposition

## Key Votes

**96th Congress**

| | |
|---|---|
| Weaken Carter oil profits tax (1979) | Y |
| Reject hospital cost control plan (1979) | N |
| Implement Panama Canal Treaties (1979) | Y |
| Establish Department of Education (1979) | Y |
| Approve Anti-busing Amendment (1979) | N |
| Guarantee Chrysler Corp. loans (1979) | Y |
| Approve military draft registration (1980) | Y |
| Aid Sandinista regime in Nicaragua (1980) | Y |
| Strengthen fair housing laws (1980) | Y |

**97th Congress**

| | |
|---|---|
| Reagan budget proposal (1981) | N |

## Interest Group Ratings

| Year | ADA | ACA | AFL-CIO | CCUS |
|---|---|---|---|---|
| 1980 | 67 | 13 | 94 | 70 |
| 1979 | 74 | 17 | 70 | 28 |
| 1978 | 60 | 29 | 79 | 31 |
| 1977 | 55 | 30 | 78 | 35 |

# Wisconsin

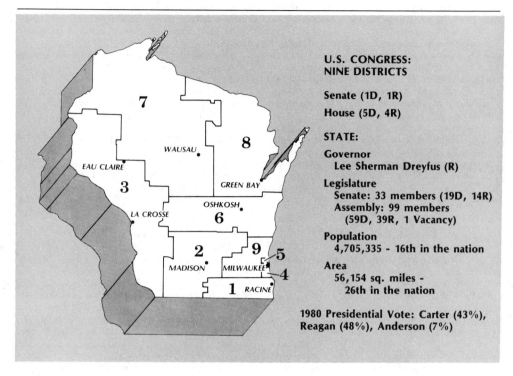

**U.S. CONGRESS:
NINE DISTRICTS**

Senate (1D, 1R)

House (5D, 4R)

**STATE:**

Governor
  Lee Sherman Dreyfus (R)

Legislature
  Senate: 33 members (19D, 14R)
  Assembly: 99 members
    (59D, 39R, 1 Vacancy)

Population
  4,705,335 - 16th in the nation

Area
  56,154 sq. miles -
    26th in the nation

1980 Presidential Vote: Carter (43%),
Reagan (48%), Anderson (7%)

## ...The Reign of Personality

Since the turn of the century, when Robert "Fighting Bob" LaFollette was first elected governor, Wisconsin has practiced an intensely personal brand of politics.

Such divergent men as LaFollette, Sens. Joseph McCarthy, William Proxmire and Gov. Lee Sherman Dreyfus have all been elected to statewide office in Wisconsin. All have owed their success in large part to the strength of their personal appeal and their ability to project an image independent of party labels.

Although most people associate the state's Progressive Party heritage with liberalism, Wisconsin is neither as Democratic nor as liberal as many assume. The Progressive philosophy that lingers in the state has been called a "mutation of old-fashioned individualism," which can just as easily manifest itself through support for government-baiting Republicans as for socially tolerant Democrats.

Another outgrowth of the old LaFollette influence is weak party identification. Abhorrence of bossism rendered party organizations essentially powerless. That in turn brought about a high degree of independent voting and a weakness for the candidate with a strong message or a flamboyant style.

While Republicans have held the upper hand in seven of the last 10 presidential contests, the governorship has traded hands regularly since the Democrats broke 20 years of GOP domination in 1958. Proxmire and Gaylord Nelson won eight consecutive Senate elections for the Democratic Party over a 23-year period until Nelson fell to Republican Robert W. Kasten in 1980.

In recent years, much of the state's liberal reputation comes from the results of its Democratic presidential primaries. The timing of the election in early April made primaries crucial for John F. Kennedy in 1960, Eugene McCarthy in

1968 and George McGovern in 1972. In each case Wisconsin boosted a liberal campaign for the Democratic nomination. But in each of those years, the state went Republican in November — for Richard M. Nixon.

Such political diversity also comes from the state's economic and ethnic mix. Wisconsin's electorate is a combination of Scandinavians, Germans and Eastern Europeans, as well as descendants of its original Yankee settlers. Its economy runs the gamut from dairy cows to beer to automobiles and heavy machinery.

Two-thirds of the state's population and most of its industry are found in the triangle described by Kenosha, south of Milwaukee in the southeast corner, Madison on the west and Green Bay in the north. The remaining four-fifths of the state's land area is lightly populated and divided between farms and woodlands.

# A Political Tour

**Milwaukee and Suburbs.** Milwaukee — the city that made Schlitz famous — is Wisconsin's only major urban center and a Democratic stronghold. With 636,000 in the city and another 761,000 in the surrounding metropolitan area, it plays a dominant but not overwhelming role in state politics.

Straddling the Menominee River, Milwaukee has two distinct personalities. North of the river is the area where many Germans settled before the Civil War. In recent decades, they have gradually moved to the suburbs, and this part of the city now contains about 80 percent of the state's black population. Overall, the city is about a quarter black.

The area south of the river was once almost exclusively Polish. Still predominantly white, it has a much greater ethnic mix now, as many of the Poles have followed other ethnic groups into suburban communities west of the city.

With its breweries (Miller, Schlitz and Pabst all have national headquarters and plants in Milwaukee), plus a wide assortment of other industrial concerns, Milwaukee has a heavily unionized blue-collar population. Although the ethnic whites and blacks have not always been on friendly terms, they usually vote the same way in November, giving Democrats a large enough base to counter the GOP areas in the rest of the county.

Surrounding Milwaukee on the north and west are Republican suburbs that extend well beyond the borders of Milwaukee County. Population growth has come to a stop in the most

exclusive communities on the northern lake front, in places like Whitefish Bay and Shorewood. But in more distant Ozaukee, Washington and Waukesha counties, new homes continue to replace fields, and suburban growth advances virtually unabated.

Ozaukee and Waukesha counties are among the strongest Republican areas in the state, with Washington just a few degrees less so. In the 1960s the John Birch Society was a dominant force in the area, but that is less true today, as more independent ex-Democrats move out of the city in greater numbers.

**Industrial Lake Front Cities.** Drawn by the convenience of shipping routes on Lake Michigan, a series of small working-class cities grew up along the shores of the lake.

With Manitowoc and Sheboygan sitting north of Milwaukee, and Racine and Kenosha sandwiched between Milwaukee and Chicago at the southern end of the state, the region is — for the most part — Democratic.

The shipbuilders of Manitowoc and auto workers at Kenosha's huge American Motors plant provide the strongest Democratic vote in the region. Both areas went for Democatic Gov. Martin Schreiber over Republican Lee Sherman Dreyfus in 1978. Racine, in spite of its 15 percent black population, often tilts slightly Republican, as does Sheboygan. Janesville and Beloit, two industrial cities west of Lake Michigan, share the same mix of blue-collar and conservative white-collar professionals. Both vote in patterns similar to those found in Racine.

Many voters in the area have supported recent Republican campaigns against the ills of Democratic "big government." Reagan carried every county in this part of the state against Carter, and, using the same theme, Kasten won four of the five counties against Nelson in 1980. Nelson had won all five by overwhelming margins in his previous re-election victory in 1974.

**Fox River Valley Cities and the Door Peninsula.** Unlike the cities along Lake Michigan, the heavily Catholic paper-mill towns in the Fox River Valley and around Lake Winnebago are Republican. They include Green Bay, the smallest city to host a professional football team; Appleton, home of Sen. Joseph McCarthy; and Oshkosh and Fond du Lac on Lake Winnebago.

At one time numerous mills prospered in these cities. Massive clearcutting long ago destroyed the lumber industry, turning the surrounding area into productive farm land. There is still, however, a relatively healthy business in paper products, especially in Appleton, where the greatest concentration of paper mills in the world is said to be found.

Germans are the most noticeable ethnic group in the area. But unlike their countrymen who settled in Milwaukee, the Fox River German descendants are Catholics who tend to be conservative. Brown County (Green Bay), which traditionally votes for Republican presidential candidates, narrowly favored John Kennedy in 1960. Otherwise, except when the Republican candidate is only of token status, the GOP usually carries the area with little difficulty.

**Dairyland.** It is the vast area covering most of the southern two-thirds of the state that justifies Wisconsin's claim as "America's Dairyland," emblazoned on the state's license plates. It has more dairy cows than any state in the union and produces as much cheese as any area of the country. Although the dairy industry is a constant throughout the region, there are certain agricultural distinctions that appear.

The southern part of Dairyland is the most strongly Republican part of the region. Richard Nixon always ran well in the rural counties here, and Gerald Ford, who lost the state in 1976, narrowly won the southern dairy counties.

The counties most thoroughly devoted to dairy farming are the ones north of La Crosse on the western side of the state. Nearly three-quarters of all the farming income is derived from the sale of dairy products. Democrats do well here, especially in the counties along the Mississippi and St. Croix Rivers that form the state's western boundary with Minnesota. But dairy farmers are not a predictable group. Jimmy Carter's narrow victory in Wisconsin in 1976 was attributed to his strong vote among dairy farmers. But four years later, he lost eight of the 14 counties he earlier had carried in the area.

The region has several urban areas of note. The most significant is Madison, the second largest city in the state. As the home of the state government and the University of Wisconsin, Madison has a reputation as being one of the most liberal cities in the United States. Since 1924, when LaFollette carried Dane County (Madison) as the Progressive Party's presidential candidate, Democrats have nearly always carried it.

Stevens Point, a heavily Polish city which also houses a branch of the University of Wisconsin, joines Eau Claire in the Democratic column, while La Crosse, on the Mississippi River, is one of the most rigidly Republican cities in the state.

**The Northwoods.** This area is similar in many ways to Michigan's Upper Peninsula on the east and Minnesota's Iron Range on the west. Once covered by great forests and iron ore deposits, the area has been fully exploited over the past several decades, leaving behind an economically depressed region. What remains are some marginal farm lands, less profitable mines and lumber mills, and Democratic voters of Scandinavian origin.

The hundreds of small lakes and clear streams and rivers, however, are providing the region with its one economic boom industry — recreation. Fishermen and campers from a wide area are being drawn to the area. Many apparently are deciding to settle there. Several of the the Northwoods counties experienced the sharpest population increases in the state during the 1970s.

Except for Vilas County, all the counties that border either Michigan or Lake Superior are solidly Democratic. Small Vilas County, the fast-

# Governor
# Lee Sherman Dreyfus (R)

**Born:** June 20, 1926, Milwaukee, Wis.
**Home:** Stevens Point, Wis.
**Education:** U. of Wisconsin, B.A. 1949; M.A. 1952; Ph.D. 1957.
**Military Career:** Navy, 1944-46.
**Profession:** University professor; chancellor, U. of Wisconsin, Stevens Point, 1972-79.
**Family:** Wife, Joyce; two children.
**Religion:** Episcopalian.
**Political Career:** Elected governor 1978; term expires Jan. 1983.

est growing in the state, owes its staunchly Republican tradition to prosperity that came from serving affluent summer residents who flock there from all across the Midwest, attracted by the county's hundreds of picturesque lakes.

The port city of Superior (Douglas County), in the far northwestern corner of the state, is the most Democratic part of the region, and the one place where the population is not expanding. With its twin city, Duluth, Superior is a major Great Lakes shipping port for iron ore and wheat.

# Redrawing the Lines

As Milwaukee County's two districts lost 90,000 people during the past decade, the city's suburban 9th District and three outstate districts enjoyed substantial gains. The 4th and 5th Districts in Milwaukee County must expand considerably, pushing the neighboring 9th westward. The overpopulated 3rd, 7th and 8th Disricts will yield territory.

# William Proxmire (D)

**Of Madison — Elected 1957**

**Born:** Nov. 11, 1915, Lake Forest, Ill.
**Education:** Yale U., B.A. 1938; Harvard U., M.B.A. 1940, M.P.A. 1940.
**Military Career:** Army, 1941-46.
**Profession:** Journalist.
**Family:** Wife, Ellen Hodges; three children.
**Religion:** Episcopalian.
**Political Career:** Wis. Assembly, 1951-53; unsuccessful Democratic nominee for governor of Wis., 1952, 1954, 1956.

**In Washington:** Proxmire's long Senate career has been a story of causes pursued to the point of obsession; slights given, received and remembered; personal eccentricities striking enough to find a place in the morning paper; and acute intelligence gradually making its impact on colleagues and public policy.

Proxmire still rises in the Senate every day to urge ratification of an international genocide convention, citing massacres on small Pacific islands and other tragedies he thinks the convention might prevent. It is as certain an event in the Senate as Proxmire's presence for the roll call, which he has answered more than 7,000 times since 1966 without a miss. And it is at least as good a symbol for the personal style of this man who sets out on a course and follows it, regardless of the opinion of those around him.

Arriving at the Senate in 1957 at the peak of Lyndon Johnson's career as majority leader, Proxmire did not hesitate to challenge Johnson directly. Within a few weeks, he was on the floor complaining about a Johnson stranglehold on the party, in a speech so seemingly self-destructive that colleagues began referring to it as "Proxmire's Farewell Address."

The senator's harsher critics have always insisted that his affinity for lost causes limited his role in the Senate, forcing him to remain a gadfly in the years when he should have become a leading power broker. There is, after all, no genocide treaty; his tirades against "pork-barrel" public works spending have had little noticeable impact, and the defense budget is going up again in the face of his continued assaults.

But as Banking chairman from 1975 to 1981, Proxmire was a gadfly with the ability to win against more orthodox opposition. The national banking community was so concerned about Proxmire's possible chairmanship in 1974 that bankers contributed generously to J. William Fulbright's re-election campaign in Arkansas, simply to avoid a string of committee changes that would make Proxmire chairman.

Disturbed over Proxmire's success several years before in winning Senate passage of truth-in-lending legislation, many bankers felt they were in for a reign of unpredictability. Some expected a series of all-out attacks on them and the Federal Reserve Board, as practiced by Wright Patman, D-Texas, who was the House Banking chairman.

But if Proxmire's six years as Banking chairman were unpredictable, they were far from a nightmare for the industry. In 1980, with most banks on his side, Proxmire secured passage of one of the most ambitious deregulation bills ever considered by Congress — the Depository Institutions Deregulation and Monetary Control Act. That legislation realized a goal Proxmire had been pursuing for more than a decade — it instructed the government gradually to lift the ceiling on the amount of interest banks and savings and loans could pay to savers.

The previous year, Proxmire had been unable to defeat the Chrysler loan guarantee, which he fought from its beginning in his committee to its final enactment, as he had other federal loan guarantees. But he did force major sacrifices from the company's lenders and workers before granting government aid. In the same 96th Congress, Proxmire pushed through Congress legislation making it illegal for American corporations to bribe foreign officials to win business contracts.

Through the years, Proxmire has continued to be cantankerous and independent on housing issues, also considered in the Banking Committee. In the Nixon-Ford years, he continually fought HUD over what he saw as the inadequate amount of money it was willing to spend on federal housing subsidies. In the 96th Congress, he nearly killed a major housing reauthorization over his opposition to rent subsidies for the middle class. He said the nation needed them "like a hole in the head." Ultimately the subsidies were dropped, and the legislation cleared.

While playing a role of major importance on these issues, however, Proxmire has not really moderated his loner approach on the Senate floor. He votes against bills everyone else favors and becomes upset about nominations no one else even wants to discuss.

In his first term, he held the Senate floor by himself for 34½ hours in protest over the nomination of Lawrence J. O'Connor Jr. to the Federal Power Commission. He no longer does that — there are few genuine filibusters on any subject — but Proxmire is still a champion nay-sayer.

He often votes against his party's majorities and with the most conservative Southern Democrats — not out of ideology, as they do, but out of specific annoyance at measures he has not liked. In early 1980, he cast the only vote in the Senate against the nomination of William French Smith to be attorney general and the only one against Malcolm Baldrige for secretary of commerce.

This still strikes many of his colleagues as nitpicking, as do some of his publicity-oriented legislative ventures, like the Limousine Limitation Act of 1979 — designed to prevent government officials from using chauffeur-driven cars to get to work.

But Proxmire has been a master at making a public issue out of waste in the Pentagon and federal bureaucracy.

The best-known ploy is the "Golden Fleece" award he gives to a federal agency very month for the "biggest, most ridiculous or most ironic waste of the taxpayer's money." Described by *The Washington Post* as "the most successful public relations device in American politics today," Proxmire's monthly fleece awards draw headlines in hundreds of newspapers across the country.

Among the more frequent recipients have been scientists on contract to the government. Proxmire was sued for libel after he awarded psychologist Ronald Hutchinson the "fleece" prize for his federally-subsidized study of agressive behavior in monkeys, performed for the National Institutes of Health. Proxmire argued that a senator's press releases and statements are exempt from normal libel laws — an opinion the court did not uphold. Proxmire paid Hutchinson $10,000 to settle the case — but the Senate paid the $124,351 bill for his defense.

Proxmire's personal style is as ascetic as it was in his years as a junior senator. He has never traveled abroad at government expense. He re-

turned over $350,000 to the Treasury during the past three years by cutting back on his personal and committee staff. He runs five miles to work each day from his Cleveland Park home to the Capitol. He dines on tuna and grapefruit, wears inexpensive suits from chain manufacturers and does his own legislative homework, assisted by a pared-down staff. His one conspicuous personal vanity is his hair transplant.

**At Home:** This driven man suffered three losses for statewide office and, spirit unbent, made a fourth attempt in a 1957 special election. That time he succeeded, becoming the first Democrat to win a Senate seat from Wisconsin in 25 years.

A tireless campaigner, he is still a regular weekend visitor back home, even though he has achieved celebrity status. Proxmire acts as if every year were an election year.

In the late 1940s, with a Harvard graduate degree in hand, Proxmire charted his political future. "I began looking around for a newspaper job that might give me political options," he once recalled. He applied to medium-sized papers in several states and became a reporter with the Madison, Wis., *Capital Times.*

Wisconsin proved a wise choice, for it then had few Democratic office-holders to stand in the way of an ambitious young man. He lost his newspaper job, but moved on to host a union-sponsored radio program, "Labor Sounds Off." After only a year in the state, he won unexpected election to the Legislature, where his career as a gadfly foreshadowed his life in the Senate.

Seeking to gain the visibility a legislative seat denied him, Proxmire took on the suicidal task of running for governor against Republican incumbent Walter J. Kohler in 1952. He lost by more than 400,000 votes. Two years later he managed to make a close election of it, but Kohler still won, and in 1956, Proxmire was beaten a third time, by state Attorney General Vernon W. Thomson.

The three defeats led to some ridicule when Proxmire campaigned in 1957 for the Senate seat left open with the death of Republican Joseph R. McCarthy. Kohler, the GOP nominee, sneered at Proxmire as a "three-time loser." Proxmire fired back by calling for the support of "all those who have ever lost in business, love, sports or politics," and asking "those lucky voters who have never lost anything" to back Kohler.

Proxmire had a united Democratic Party behind him, while Kohler suffered the ill effects of a divisive GOP primary. Proxmire won decisively.

In 1958, Republicans were together again

behind former state Supreme Court Justice Roland J. Steinle, and labor in Wisconsin was less than enchanted with Proxmire's first year in office. But Steinle lacked Proxmire's campaigning flair, and it was a national Democratic year. Proxmire did even better than he had the year before.

Proxmire was down to less than 55 percent in 1964 against a moderate Republican businessman,

Wilbur Renk, but by 1970 he was untouchable. A a crack campaign staff and a superb publicity effort allowed him to swamp John E. Erickson, general manager of the Milwaukee Bucks basketball team. In 1976, state Rep. Stanley York fared no better, although Proxmire spent nothing on media or organization. His $697 expenditure went for gas to drive around the state in a typical Proxmire blitz.

## Committees

**Appropriations** (Ranking Democrat)
Defense; HUD-Independent Agencies; Labor, Health and Human Services, Education; Treasury, Postal Sevice, and General Government.

**Banking, Housing and Urban Affairs** (2nd of 7 Democrats)
Financial Institutions; Housing and Urban Affairs; International Finance and Monetary Policy.

**Joint Economic**
International Trade, Finance and Security Economics; Trade, Productivity and Economic Growth.

## Elections

**1976 General**

| | |
|---|---|
| William Proxmire (D) | 1,396,970 (72%) |
| Stanley York (R) | 521,902 (27%) |

**Previous Winning Percentages**

1970 (71%)    1964 (53%)    1958 (57%)    1957* (56%)

*Special election.*

## Campaign Finance

| 1976 | Receipts | Receipts from PACs | Expenditures |
|---|---|---|---|
| Proxmire (D) | $25 | — (0%) | $697 |
| York (R) | $66,321 | $2,401 (4%) | $62,210 |

## Voting Studies

| | Presidential Support | | Party Unity | | Conservative Coalition | |
|---|---|---|---|---|---|---|
| Year | S | O | S | O | S | O |
| 1980 | 54 | 46 | 63 | 37 | 39 | 61 |
| 1979 | 53 | 47 | 51 | 49 | 37 | 63 |
| 1978 | 74 | 26 | 66 | 34 | 38 | 63 |
| 1977 | 64 | 36 | 82 | 18 | 17 | 83 |
| 1976 | 43 | 57 | 83 | 17 | 12 | 88 |
| 1975 | 48 | 52 | 86 | 14 | 17 | 83 |
| 1974 (Ford) | 37 | 63 | | | | |
| 1974 | 42 | 58 | 76 | 24 | 25 | 75 |
| 1973 | 41 | 59 | 86 | 14 | 11 | 89 |
| 1972 | 39 | 61 | 82 | 18 | 24 | 76 |
| 1971 | 38 | 62 | 91 | 9 | 5 | 95 |
| 1970 | 54 | 46 | 86 | 14 | 16 | 84 |
| 1969 | 47 | 53 | 85 | 15 | 19 | 81 |
| 1968 | 70 | 30 | 71 | 29 | 11 | 89 |
| 1967 | 68 | 32 | 74 | 26 | 25 | 75 |
| 1966 | 75 | 25 | 78 | 21 | 16 | 84 |
| 1965 | 78 | 21 | 87 | 13 | 5 | 95 |
| 1964 | 62 | 38 | 65 | 35 | 14 | 86 |
| 1963 | 59 | 41 | 58 | 42 | 35 | 65 |
| 1962 | 66 | 34 | 45 | 55 | 44 | 56 |
| 1961 | 81 | 19 | 76 | 22 | 23 | 75 |

S = Support    O = Opposition

## Key Votes

**96th Congress**

| | |
|---|---|
| Maintain relations with Taiwan (1979) | Y |
| Reduce synthetic fuel development funds (1979) | Y |
| Impose nuclear plant moratorium (1979) | Y |
| Kill stronger windfall profits tax (1979) | N |
| Guarantee Chrysler Corp. loans (1979) | N |
| Approve military draft registration (1980) | N |
| End Revenue Sharing to the states (1980) | Y |
| Block Justice Dept. busing suits (1980) | Y |

**97th Congress**

| | |
|---|---|
| Restore urban program funding cuts (1981) | N |

## Interest Group Ratings

| Year | ADA | ACA | AFL-CIO | CCUS-1 | CCUS-2 |
|---|---|---|---|---|---|
| 1980 | 56 | 54 | 53 | 36 | |
| 1979 | 42 | 59 | 53 | 45 | 38 |
| 1978 | 60 | 46 | 63 | 44 | |
| 1977 | 70 | 37 | 75 | 29 | |
| 1976 | 65 | 30 | 70 | 11 | |
| 1975 | 78 | 29 | 55 | 6 | |
| 1974 | 81 | 26 | 82 | 20 | |
| 1973 | 85 | 28 | 82 | 11 | |
| 1972 | 75 | 18 | 70 | 10 | |
| 1971 | 96 | 21 | 75 | - | |
| 1970 | 78 | 25 | 100 | 0 | |
| 1969 | 78 | 31 | 91 | - | |
| 1968 | 64 | 32 | 50 | - | |
| 1967 | 77 | 29 | 75 | 40 | |
| 1966 | 85 | 17 | 100 | - | |
| 1965 | 88 | 14 | - | | 20 |
| 1964 | 86 | 39 | 100 | - | |
| 1963 | - | 42 | - | - | |
| 1962 | 67 | 34 | 82 | - | |
| 1961 | 80 | - | - | - | |

# Robert W. Kasten Jr. (R)

**Of Milwaukee — Elected 1980**

**Born:** June 19, 1942, Milwaukee, Wis.
**Education:** University of Arizona, B.A. 1964; Columbia University, M.B.A. 1966.
**Military Career:** Air Force, 1967; Wisconsin Air National Guard, 1967-72.
**Profession:** Shoe company executive.
**Family:** Single.
**Religion:** Episcopalian.
**Political Career:** Unsuccessful Republican nominee for Wisconsin Assembly, 1970; served in Wisconsin Senate, 1973-75; U.S. House, 9th District, 1975-79; unsuccessfully sought Republican nomination for governor, 1978.

**The Member:** Aggressive and determined, Kasten made it to the Senate after a methodical 10-year climb in which he ran for five different offices in six elections and rebounded with surprising agility from his one major defeat.

After unexpectedly losing the GOP gubernatorial nomination in 1978, Kasten knew that another failure in 1980 would probably mark the end of his political career. But with three unimpressive candidates offering the only opposition in a GOP Senate primary, he felt it was too good an opportunity to pass up.

Kasten's 1980 campaign showed clearly that he had learned from his mistakes in 1978, when a colorful political novice, Lee Sherman Dreyfus, derailed his well-laid plans to become one of the state's youngest governors. In that race, Kasten spent so much time planning for the general election that he let the primary slip away.

Kasten's 1980 Democratic opponent, Sen. Gaylord Nelson, was one of the most successful politicians in Wisconsin history. A two-term governor and three-term senator, he had held public office continuously since 1948.

But Kasten won by 40,000 votes out of more than 2 million cast, exploiting a latent perception among voters that Nelson had lost touch with their day-to-day problems. Economic conditions played a critical role in the outcome. Many blue-collar Democrats in Milwaukee and the industrial Fox River Valley favored Kasten's less government, low tax philosophy over Nelson's more traditional liberal approach.

The first major independent regulatory agency to come up for renewal in the 97th Congress passed though Kasten's consumer subcommittee at Commerce. Despite the current anti-regulatory mood, the Consumer Products Safety Commission survived.

Reagan favored abolishing the CPSC, which issues regulations and product standards to protect consumers from unreasonable risks. As a fallback, the administration proposed to remove the CPSC's independent status and transfer it to the Commerce Department.

Kasten bucked the call to abolish the CPSC or remove its independent status. "Having a policeman, an agency, to judge products on safety is a legitimate activity," he said. He pushed for a one-year CPSC authorization in order to allow time to consider combining the CPSC with the Federal Trade Commission, which comes up for renewal in 1982.

But in the full Commerce Committee, a majority felt that a one-year authorization would leave the CPSC unsettled and demoralize its staff. The committee authorized the CPSC at $33 million for fiscal 1982 and 1983.

As chairman of the Appropriations Subcommittee on Foreign Operations, Kasten argued the case for Reagan's proposed cut in funding for the Export-Import Bank. It was a tough task, because the large corporations that receive money from the bank have subsidiaries and contractors all across the country who benefit from the export business. Kasten's own subcommittee wanted to give the bank $376 million more than Reagan requested.

Brandishing a written plea for support from OMB Director David A. Stockman, Kasten held the Appropriations Committee to approving $250 million more for the bank than Reagan had wanted.

The nephew of a Milwaukee banker, Kasten worked in a family shoe business before entering politics in the suburbs north and west of Milwaukee. After losing a state legislative election at age 28, he defeated a Republican state senator in a 1972 primary, then unseated U.S. Rep. Glenn Davis in a 1974 GOP primary.

Kasten compiled a solid conservative record in his four-year House career, straying only on environmental issues, as befits a member of the Audubon Society and the National Wildlife Federation.

As a member of the House Intelligence Committee, he played a role in a well-publicized decision to cite Secretary of State Henry Kissinger for contempt because he would not release classified documents to the committee. Later, however, Kasten became disillusioned with the committee and opposed making it permanent.

Kasten was a pivotal vote on a 1976 bill to end the federal monopoly over production of enriched uranium. After first casting the deciding vote in favor of the amendment, which would have allowed private industry to enter the field, he switched and cast the deciding vote the other way.

During his House career Kasten voted against raising Social Security taxes, against increasing the minimum wage and against a crude oil tax. He voted for strip mining controls and supported expanding the Appalachian Trail, but voted to delay imposition of tough clean air standards.

## Committees

**Appropriations** (11th of 15 Republicans)
Foreign Operations, chairman; Agriculture and Related Agencies; Defense; Energy and Water Development; Transportation.

**Budget** (10th of 12 Republicans)

**Commerce, Science and Transportation** (9th of 9 Republicans)
Consumer, chairman; Merchant Marine; Science, Technology, and Space.

**Veterans' Affairs** (4th of 7 Republicans)

## Elections

**1980 General**

| | |
|---|---|
| Robert Kasten Jr. (R) | 1,106,311 (50%) |
| Gaylord Nelson (D) | 1,065,487 (48%) |

**1980 Primary**

| | |
|---|---|
| Robert Kasten Jr. (R) | 134,586 (37%) |
| Terry Kohler (R) | 106,270 (29%) |
| Douglass Cofrin (R) | 84,355 (23%) |
| Russell Olson (R) | 40,823 (11%) |

**Previous Winning Percentages**

**1976\*** (66%)   **1974\*** (53%)

*\* House election.*

## Campaign Finance

| | Receipts | Receipts from PACs | Expenditures |
|---|---|---|---|
| **1980** | | | |
| Kasten (R) | $714,290 | $299,643 (42%) | $675,767 |
| Nelson (D) | $919,546 | $415,942 (45%) | $897,774 |

## Voting Studies

| | Presidential Support | | Party Unity | | Conservative Coalition | |
|---|---|---|---|---|---|---|
| Year | S | O | S | O | S | O |
| House service | | | | | | |
| 1978 | 21 | 29 | 44 | 11 | 38 | 12 |
| 1977 | 43 | 52 | 77 | 17 | 79 | 15 |
| 1976 | 63 | 35 | 79 | 19 | 83 | 15 |
| 1975 | 69 | 29 | 88 | 10 | 88 | 10 |

S = Support          O = Opposition

## Key Votes

**97th Congress**

| | |
|---|---|
| Restore urban program funding cuts (1981) | N |

## Interest Group Ratings

| Year | ADA | ACA | AFL-CIO | CCUS-1 | CCUS-2 |
|---|---|---|---|---|---|
| House service | | | | | |
| 1978 | 15 | 90 | 19 | 80 | |
| 1977 | 20 | 81 | 17 | 76 | |
| 1976 | 15 | 89 | 17 | 57 | |
| 1975 | 21 | 89 | 22 | 82 | |

# 1 Les Aspin (D)

### Of Racine — Elected 1970

**Born:** July, 21, 1938, Milwaukee, Wis.
**Education:** Yale U., B.A. 1960; Oxford U., England, M.A. 1962; Mass. Inst. of Technology, Ph.D. 1965.
**Military Career:** Army, 1966-68.
**Profession:** Professor of economics.
**Family:** Divorced.
**Religion:** Episcopalian.
**Political Career:** Sought Democratic nomination for Wis. treasurer, 1968.

**In Washington:** Aspin's mimeograph machine and his instinct for a good news story have brought him a national reputation, even though he chairs no committee and spends little time on the floor. His press releases have been a Washington tradition almost from the beginning of his House career.

Most congressional press releases are routinely discarded, but Aspin's usually contain at least a nugget of news, or at least a few impertinent quotes that help make headlines.

The subject is nearly always the Pentagon, which Aspin has criticized for a decade on the Armed Services Committee and for years before that in private life. But there are other topics. In May of 1981, when Speaker O'Neill seemed uncertain about how to deal with the Reagan economic program, Aspin issued a release charging that the Speaker was "in a fog" and "has no idea where to go."

Early in his career, Aspin's media reputation led to charges that he was focusing on national issues at the expense of his district. Since then, more of his publicity has been district oriented, dealing with his efforts to get a Youth Conservation Corps project for Kenosha and economic relief for American Motors, his district's largest employer. He was working on a loan guarantee for American Motors before the Chrysler bailout issue even came up; ultimately, none proved necessary.

But the Pentagon remains the focus of his legislative career. Unlike Wisconsin Sen. William Proxmire, for whom he briefly worked two decades ago, Aspin does not often complain about other agencies and rarely tries to amend bills outside the Armed Services field. He is a specialist.

Aspin has sued the Pentagon to get it to release its investigation of the My Lai massacre,

used a press release to reveal black market activities by a U.S. charity in Vietnam, and disclosed that a Coast Guard admiral took his wife and friends on a government-funded tour of the Pacific.

Despite the criticism of his media-conscious style, Aspin is generally respected for his ability to capsulize complicated issues. In 1976, he briefed Jimmy Carter on defense in preparation for the presidential campaign debate with Gerald Ford.

Aspin has launched dozens of attacks on military manpower policies, particularly the retirement system, which he claims is far too generous. In 1977, to dramatize the pension problem, Aspin offered a less-than-serious floor amendment to put servicemen under the congressional retirement program. He drew a surprising 148 votes for his proposal. Two years later, however, when the Carter administration sought changes in the retirement system, Aspin was preoccupied as chairman of an intelligence oversight subcommittee and did not play a leading role.

Aspin regularly criticizes the perquisites of the Pentagon brass. Alexander M. Haig Jr., now secretary of state, was once a favorite Aspin target. In 1973, Aspin charged Haig with "illegal money grabbing" when Haig began serving as Richard Nixon's White House chief of staff but delayed his resignation from the military to draw a bigger pension. Two years later, after Aspin

---

**1st District: Southeast — Racine, Kenosha.** Population: 515,298 (5% increase since 1970). Race: White 484,232 (94%), Black 21,952 (4%), Others 9,114 (2%). Spanish origin: 13,157 (3%).

---

disclosed that Haig's dog, Duncan, had been shipped around Europe by military plane, Haig reimbursed the government for the dog's travels.

This hounding of the Pentagon elite has been balanced somewhat by his support for rank-and-file soldiers. In 1979, the House adopted his floor amendment to secure special allowances for low-ranking servicemen stationed overseas.

Aspin came to Congress at the high point of national opposition to the Vietnam War. Having served as a Pentagon economist for Robert S. McNamara, he fought successfully for a seat on Armed Services, where he soon began his unending dispute with the panel's pro-military leadership.

In 1973, after Aspin issued a press release berating the Navy for its problems building a new ship, the late Armed Services Chairman F. Edward Hebert publicly blasted him, telling him to "put up or shut up." Aspin responded by saying that he would be happy to share his information with Hebert and that he was glad the chairman had noticed him. "It's a sign that the system is really opening up when the chairman gets into a dialogue with a very junior member," Aspin said.

Earlier in 1973, Aspin had embarrassed Hebert with a floor amendment reducing the annual defense budget by about 4 percent. Hebert and the Armed Services Committee were rarely defeated on the House floor, but Aspin put together an unlikely coalition of Democratic liberals and Republican fiscal conservatives and won adoption of the amendment, 242-163. At the beginning of the next Congress, in early 1975, Aspin was a ringleader in a House coup that dumped Hebert as committee chairman.

**At Home:** Aspin can carry on his crusade against the Pentagon with impunity back home; his district contains no military bases and few defense contractors. "I am a product of my constituency just as much as they are of theirs," Aspin once said, referring to Pentagon supporters whose districts are loaded with military installations.

Aspin insists the voters of Racine and Kenosha support his battles with the Defense Department. But his continuing electoral success probably has more to do with his local staff work and efforts to revive the area's sagging economy. He is the only Democrat ever to be elected to more than one term from the 1st District.

When the 1970 campaign year began, few would have predicted such success for a Marquette University economics professor who had just moved into the district. Aspin's academic credentials were impressive, and he had been active in statewide politics, but his ties to the district were few.

Two years earlier he had been signed up by the White House to head President Johnson's re-election effort in Wisconsin. When that effort evaporated just before the state's primary, Aspin switched to Robert F. Kennedy's campaign. That September Aspin was defeated in his first try at elective office, losing the Democratic primary for state treasurer.

Shortly afterward, he moved his family into the 1st District and became the district's Democratic chairman. The 1970 House election looked promising for an eager challenger because the incumbent Republican, Henry C. Schadeberg, had won his last two elections with just 51 percent of the vote.

To get at Schadeberg, Aspin first had to defeat former Democratic Rep. Gerald T. Flynn and chemistry professor Douglas LaFollette in the primary. Flynn posed little opposition. But LaFollette appealed to the same liberal constituency as Aspin and had a more attractive name — he was a distant relative of the state's legendary governor and U.S. senator, Robert LaFollette. Aspin appeared to lose the primary but demanded a recount and won by 20 votes.

The general election offered a clear philosophical choice. Schadeberg emphasized a "return to America's heritage of order, discipline and hard work." Aspin appealed to peace and ecology groups and, when talking with the larger middle-class segment of the electorate, stressed the need to reduce unemployment in the district. With substantial contributions from organized labor, and a well-run campaign, Aspin retired Schadeberg by winning 61 percent.

Two years later Aspin ran against Republican Merrill Stalbaum, whose brother had once held the district as a Democrat. Stalbaum called Aspin a "phony environmentalist" and attacked his campaign against the Pentagon. But by then, the Democratic incumbent had solidified his support. He won easily.

The 1978 campaign was Aspin's worst political experience of the decade. Some $27,000 in campaign contributions disappeared, taken by his campaign chairman, who later confessed he took it. And Republican William Petrie, whom Aspin had beaten easily two years before, waged a surprisingly strenuous campaign, coming within 13,000 votes of defeating him — closer than any previous challenger.

The election in 1980 turned out not to be so harrowing. Petrie refused to run for a third time without a pre-primary endorsement from the GOP, and when he bowed out, the Republican nomination went to a surprise primary winner,

Kathryn H. Canary. For the second consecutive election, Aspin lost the rural part of the district. But his vote in Racine and Kenosha improved, and his margin was up to 30,000 votes.

**The District:** The 1st has the heaviest concentration of blue-collar workers in the state, but it is far from being a solidly Democratic district. Situated between Milwaukee and Chicago, it has an industrial core along Lake Michigan in Racine and Kenosha. Johnson's Wax dominates Racine, and American Motors and Jockey Underwear are the mainstays of Kenosha's economy. Both vote Democratic; Racine is the larger and slightly less Democratic of the two.

Outside the two cities, the voting pattern changes sharply. On the district's western border are the smaller industrial towns of Janesville and Beloit, which sometimes back statewide GOP candidates. The strongest Republican vote is in Walworth County, located in the center of the district. Soybeans grow so well in this area that the Japanese Kikkoman soy sauce company built a bottling plant in Walworth.

Until Aspin's election, Democrats had won this district only twice in the 20th century — 1958 and 1964. Both times they were defeated in the following election. No Democratic presidential candidate has carried the district since Lyndon Johnson in 1964.

## Committees

**Armed Services** (10th of 25 Democrats)
Investigations; Military Personnel and Compensation.

**Budget** (12th of 18 Democrats)
Task Forces: Economic Policy and Productivity; Tax Policy; Transportation, Research and Development, and Capital Resources.

## Elections

**1980 General**

| | |
|---|---|
| Les Aspin (D ) | 126,222 (56 %) |
| Kathryn Canary (R ) | 96,047 (43 %) |

**1978 General**

| | |
|---|---|
| Les Aspin (D ) | 77,146 (55 %) |
| William Petrie (R ) | 64,437 (46 %) |

**Previous Winning Percentages**

| | | | |
|---|---|---|---|
| 1976 (65 %) | 1974 (71 %) | 1972 (64 %) | 1970 (61 %) |

**District Vote For President**

| | 1980 | | 1976 | | 1972 |
|---|---|---|---|---|---|
| D | 97,631 (42 %) | D | 106,274 (48 %) | D | 77,842 (40 %) |
| R | 115,995 (50 %) | R | 107,457 (49 %) | R | 112,221 (58 %) |
| I | 16,233 (7 %) | | | | |

## Campaign Finance

| | Receipts | Receipts from PACs | Expenditures |
|---|---|---|---|
| **1980** | | | |
| Aspin (D ) | $136,369 | $67,590 (50 %) | $139,658 |
| Canary (R ) | $75,866 | $18,465 (24 %) | $75,766 |
| **1978** | | | |
| Aspin (D ) | $76,825 | $27,450 (36 %) | $73,570 |
| Petrie (R ) | $101,733 | $9,925 (10 %) | $102,205 |

## Voting Studies

| Year | Presidential Support S | O | Party Unity S | O | Conservative Coalition S | O |
|---|---|---|---|---|---|---|
| 1980 | 82 | 13 | 85 | 9 | 21 | 77 |
| 1979 | 77 | 20 | 81 | 14 | 26 | 68 |
| 1978 | 81 | 12 | 84 | 10 | 11 | 85 |
| 1977 | 68 | 20 | 80 | 8 | 12 | 75 |
| 1976 | 29 | 59 | 80 | 8 | 13 | 76 |
| 1975 | 38 | 57 | 79 | 11 | 13 | 79 |
| 1974 (Ford) | 39 | 43 | | | | |
| 1974 | 42 | 53 | 78 | 13 | 7 | 80 |
| 1973 | 24 | 65 | 84 | 9 | 7 | 84 |
| 1972 | 46 | 43 | 83 | 11 | 13 | 83 |
| 1971 | 35 | 58 | 84 | 10 | 3 | 87 |

S = Support          O = Opposition

## Key Votes

**96th Congress**

| | |
|---|---|
| Weaken Carter oil profits tax (1979) | N |
| Reject hospital cost control plan (1979) | N |
| Implement Panama Canal Treaties (1979) | Y |
| Establish Department of Education (1979) | Y |
| Approve Anti-busing Amendment (1979) | N |
| Guarantee Chrysler Corp. loans (1979) | Y |
| Approve military draft registration (1980) | Y |
| Aid Sandinista regime in Nicaragua (1980) | Y |
| Strengthen fair housing laws (1980) | Y |

**97th Congress**

| | |
|---|---|
| Reagan budget proposal (1981) | Y |

## Interest Group Ratings

| Year | ADA | ACA | AFL-CIO | CCUS |
|---|---|---|---|---|
| 1980 | 67 | 25 | 65 | 61 |
| 1979 | 74 | 13 | 75 | 22 |
| 1978 | 60 | 12 | 85 | 28 |
| 1977 | 70 | 4 | 71 | 18 |
| 1976 | 75 | 8 | 81 | 23 |
| 1975 | 95 | 23 | 91 | 7 |
| 1974 | 96 | 7 | 100 | 25 |
| 1973 | 88 | 12 | 90 | 27 |
| 1972 | 94 | 0 | 82 | 10 |
| 1971 | 86 | 11 | 83 | - |

# 2 Robert W. Kastenmeier (D)

**Of Sun Prairie — Elected 1958**

**Born:** Jan. 24, 1924, Beaver Dam, Wis.
**Education:** U. of Wis., LL.B. 1952
**Military Career:** Army, 1943-46.
**Profession:** Lawyer.
**Family:** Wife, Dorothy Chambers; three children.
**Political Career:** Unsuccessful Democratic nominee for U.S. House, 1956.

**In Washington:** Kastenmeier does not attract the attention he did 20 years ago as a militant House liberal, but his specialties are still the same — equal rights and civil liberties.

These days, he mainly fights holding actions. As a senior member of the House Judiciary Committee, he sees his role as defender of existing rights. With Don Edwards, his fellow liberal Democrat on Judiciary, he has devised a strategy for holding off conservative demands for action. While Edwards uses his own subcommittee to stall on constitutional amendments dealing with abortion, busing, and school prayer, Kastenmeier, chairman of the Courts and Civil Liberties Subcommittee, fights efforts to strip federal courts of jurisdiction over those issues. The strategy began in the 96th Congress, when Kastenmeier tried to sit on controversial bills barring U.S. district courts and the Supreme Court from reviewing state laws on school prayer. When pro-prayer forces nearly gathered the 218 signatures they needed to pry the issue out of the Judiciary Committee, Kastenmeier agreed to hold hearings. But he took no action on the bill.

In the early months of the Reagan administration, Kastenmeier found himself playing a different role, however, defending the Legal Services Corporation against White House efforts to replace it with block grants. These could be used for any law enforcement purpose, not just for the original Legal Services commitment to providing legal aid to the poor. Kastenmeier was militant against the change.

To save the program at all, Kastenmeier had to accept several new rules restricting Legal Services lawyers, such as one barring them from filing class action suits, and a reduction in the corporation's budget. But the House voted to reauthorize the program in June of 1981, one of the few tangible victories up to that point for the liberal House critics of the Reagan administration.

Kastenmeier came to Congress as one of the small cadre of 1950s peace activists. He complained about the communist "witch hunts" of his state's former Republican senator, Joseph R. McCarthy, and said the "military-industrial complex" was out of control. With two former campaign aides, Marcus Raskin and Arthur Waskow, now well-known leftist writers, he set out to produce a manifesto to influence American foreign policy in the 1960s.

They began the Liberal Project and attracted 17 other congressmen who wanted to publish position papers on liberal issues. The 1960 election was not kind to them; 16 of the 18 were defeated. But Kastenmeier continued as head of the redrawn "Liberal Group" and a few years later published the Liberal Papers, calling for disarmament, admission of mainland China to the United Nations, and an end to the draft. Republicans labeled them "apostles of appeasement" and most Democrats ignored them. Since then, Kastenmeier has kept up a lower profile both inside the House and out.

Kastenmeier is as conservative in his personal style as he is liberal in ideology. A dull speaker with a distaste for flamboyance, he is often overshadowed on Judiciary by members who express their views more militantly.

His timing has been unusual. His opposition to the Vietnam War was so far ahead of public opinion that by the time the anti-war movement

---

**2nd District: South — Madison.** Population: 537,933 (10% increase since 1970). Race: White 523,305 (97%), Black 6,601 (1%), Others 8,027 (1%). Spanish origin: 4,423 (1%).

**Robert W. Kastenmeier, D-Wis.**

reached its peak, Kastenmeier had been through it already. He was consistent in his support for the anti-war movement, but he was never a national leader in it.

Early in his career, Kastenmeier and his allies in the Liberal Group — Don Edwards and Phillip Burton of California — worked on efforts to democratize House procedure. But here too, Kastenmeier did not play a leading role when the changes were actually made, a decade later. By then, he had turned his attention to legal work on Judiciary. He supported the procedural reforms but was not publicly associated with them by most members.

In part, that reflects Kastenmeier's reluctance to involve himself in confrontations. In recent years, at least, he has not been one of the more aggressive or conspicuous liberal Democrats in the House. Like many civil libertarians, Kastenmeier was disturbed by FBI tactics in the 1980 Abscam bribery scandal. But while he was pondering the issue, Edwards went ahead and held hearings that drew national attention to the issue of FBI entrapment.

While his friends plunged themselves into controversy during the 1970s, Kastenmeier worked on the technicalities of copyright law, producing the first comprehensive revision in that field in more than 60 years, and guiding it through nearly a decade of debate.

More recently, he has tackled the broad issue of court procedures, attempting to relieve overburdened courts and make the trial system more efficient. He was the chief sponsor of a dispute resolution law, providing federal money to help states create procedures for resolving minor disputes out of court.

Kastenmeier also serves on the Interior Committee, but he has devoted considerably less time to its work. Usually he serves as a willing liberal vote to back up Burton and Chairman Morris K. Udall on environmental issues like strip mining, creating wilderness areas in Alaska, and expansion of the California redwoods park.

Kastenmeier admits that he and other House liberals have modified the approach of 20 years ago. "We are less pretentious," he has said. "We don't presume to accomplish as much. We, in the context of the House of Representatives, ought to try to be reasonably effective. We feel we ought to be the cutting edge of American liberalism in the body politic, yet there is even a limitation to that."

**At Home:** It is no longer possible for Kastenmeier to win re-election easily on the mere strength of his opposition to the Vietnam War, or his support for the impeachment of President Nixon. In the last two elections, his percentage has declined to unsettlingly low levels. Both times he has lost every county in the district except Dane, where a solid vote from Madison has been enough to keep him in office.

Although Kastenmeier never has been very comfortable campaigning, he has stepped up his visits to the district and is beginning to do things that endangered Democrats have been doing for years. In 1980, for the first time, he hired a professional campaign manager and waged a fullfledged campaign.

By refusing to retreat from his liberal views, Kastenmeier remains vulnerable to charges that he is out of step with the new fiscal conservatism. Those attacks — made by his opponent in the last two elections, former yo-yo manufacturer James A. Wright — have particular appeal in the farming communities that surround Madison. The city's university community, however, seems to be supportive of Kastenmeier's record on civil liberties and defense issues.

Kastenmeier's first three elections were hotly contested affairs, which included accusations that Kastenmeier was sympathetic to communists. In his first campaign, in 1958, he was helped by farm discontent with the policies of the Eisenhower administration.

After 1964 redistricting removed Milwaukee's suburban Waukesha County from the district, Kastenmeier's percentages shot up. In 1970, when the old charges were updated to include criticism that Kastenmeier was "soft on radical students," the incumbent won by his highest percentage ever.

The son of a minor elected official from Dodge County, Kastenmeier took only a limited interest in politics until he was nearly 30 years old. Then he became the Democratic chairman of the second-smallest county in the district, and three years later decided to run for the seat open by Republican Glenn R. Davis, who ran for the Senate. Kastenmeier lost to GOP nominee Donald E. Tewes by a 55-45 margin. But two years later, with two of the district's most popular Democrats — William Proxmire and Gaylord Nelson — running on the statewide ticket, many Republicans stayed home in the 2nd District and Kastenmeier won.

**The District:** It is a good thing for Democrats that Dane County accounts for more than 60 percent of the district vote. Centered on Madison, the county is one of the most liberal places in the Midwest. In 1972, George McGovern carried it with 58 percent. Not only does Madison include 39,000 students at the University of Wisconsin, but its state government bureaucracy has kept many alumni in town and drawn scores of liberal voters from outside the area.

The seven other counties in the district are a different story. Their flat, rich farmland has long attracted conservative German and Scandinavian families. While McGovern was winning Dane County in 1972, Nixon was carrying the rest of the district with 62 percent.

## Committees

**Interior and Insular Affairs** (3rd of 23 Democrats)
Public Lands and National Parks.

**Judiciary** (3rd of 16 Democrats)
Courts, Civil Liberties and Administration of Justice, Chairman; Civil and Constitutional Rights; Crime.

## Elections

**1980 General**

| | |
|---|---|
| Robert Kastenmeier (D) | 142,037 (54 %) |
| James Wright (R) | 119,514 (45 %) |

**1978 General**

| | |
|---|---|
| Robert Kastenmeier (D) | 99,631 (58 %) |
| James Wright (R) | 71,412 (41 %) |

**Previous Winning Percentages**

| | | | |
|---|---|---|---|
| 1976 (66 %) | 1974 (65 %) | 1972 (68 %) | 1970 (69 %) |
| 1968 (60 %) | 1966 (58 %) | 1964 (64 %) | 1962 (53 %) |
| 1960 (53%) | 1958 (52 %) | | |

**District Vote For President**

| | 1980 | | 1976 | | 1972 |
|---|---|---|---|---|---|
| **D** | 125,446 (47 %) | **D** | 125,639 (51 %) | **D** | 111,115 (50 %) |
| **R** | 110,374 (41 %) | **R** | 113,143 (46 %) | **R** | 107,566 (49 %) |
| **I** | 25,815 (9 %) | **I** | | ( %) | |

## Campaign Finance

| | Receipts | Receipts from PACs | Expenditures |
|---|---|---|---|
| **1980** | | | |
| Kastenmeier (D ) | $220,129 | $96,559 (44 %) | $225,706 |
| Wright (R ) | $294,214 | $109,699 (37 %) | $282,348 |
| **1978** | | | |
| Kastenmeier (D ) | $39,025 | $14,540 (37 %) | $43,643 |
| Wright (R ) | $86,174 | $9,582 (11 %) | $86,041 |

## Voting Studies

| | Presidential Support | | Party Unity | | Conservative Coalition | |
|---|---|---|---|---|---|---|
| Year | S | O | S | O | S | O |
| 1980 | 71 | 26 | 89 | 10 | 9 | 87 |
| 1979 | 79 | 20 | 88 | 9† | 6 | 92 |
| 1978 | 86 | 14 | 91 | 9 | 7 | 93 |
| 1977 | 76 | 23 | 87 | 12 | 14 | 85 |
| 1976 | 33 | 67 | 89 | 10 | 18 | 81 |
| 1975 | 31 | 65 | 86 | 11 | 15 | 82 |
| 1974 (Ford) | 41 | 57 | | | | |
| 1974 | 42 | 58 | 84 | 13 | 7 | 89 |

| | | | | | | |
|---|---|---|---|---|---|---|
| 1973 | 26 | 73 | 87 | 12 | 11 | 87 |
| 1972 | 49 | 51 | 83 | 12 | 10 | 87 |
| 1971 | 26 | 72 | 88 | 9 | 2 | 94 |
| 1970 | 55 | 43 | 85 | 11 | 7 | 86 |
| 1969 | 45 | 51 | 82 | 15 | 7 | 89 |
| 1968 | 83 | 14 | 91 | 5 | 4 | 92 |
| 1967 | 80 | 16 | 87 | 9 | 2 | 96 |
| 1966 | 75 | 12 | 75 | 15 | 5 | 86 |
| 1965 | 86 | 7 | 90 | 8 | 2 | 98 |
| 1964 | 92 | 8 | 84 | 16 | 8 | 92 |
| 1963 | 84 | 13 | 81 | 15 | 7 | 93 |
| 1962 | 85 | 15 | 84 | 11 | 12 | 88 |
| 1961 | 94 | 6 | 93 | 5 | 9 | 87 |

S = Support          O = Opposition

† Not eligible for all recorded votes.

## Key Votes

**96th Congress**

| | |
|---|---|
| Weaken Carter oil profits tax (1979) | N |
| Reject hospital cost control plan (1979) | N |
| Implement Panama Canal Treaties (1979) | Y |
| Establish Department of Education (1979) | N |
| Approve Anti-busing Amendment (1979) | N |
| Guarantee Chrysler Corp. loans (1979) | Y |
| Approve military draft registration (1980) | N |
| Aid Sandinista regime in Nicaragua (1980) | Y |
| Strengthen fair housing laws (1980) | Y |

**97th Congress**

| | |
|---|---|
| Reagan budget proposal (1981) | N |

## Interest Group Rating

| Year | ADA | ACA | AFL-CIO | CCUS |
|---|---|---|---|---|
| 1980 | 100 | 13 | 79 | 58 |
| 1979 | 95 | 4 | 95 | 0 |
| 1978 | 95 | 4 | 95 | 22 |
| 1977 | 100 | 15 | 74 | 24 |
| 1976 | 90 | 11 | 83 | 0 |
| 1975 | 100 | 18 | 91 | 6 |
| 1974 | 91 | 0 | 89 | 10 |
| 1973 | 100 | 20 | 82 | 9 |
| 1972 | 100 | 9 | 91 | 0 |
| 1971 | 95 | 11 | 82 | - |
| 1970 | 92 | 11 | 100 | 10 |
| 1969 | 93 | 19 | 100 | - |
| 1968 | 100 | 0 | 75 | - |
| 1967 | 93 | 11 | 100 | 10 |
| 1966 | 94 | 20 | 100 | - |
| 1965 | 100 | 0 | - | 10 |
| 1964 | 100 | 16 | 100 | - |
| 1963 | - | 6 | - | - |
| 1962 | 88 | 4 | 91 | - |
| 1961 | 100 | - | - | - |

# 3 Steve Gunderson (R)

Of Osseo — Elected 1980

**Born:** May 10, 1951, Eau Claire, Wis.
**Education:** U. of Wis., B.S. 1973.
**Profession:** Public official.
**Family:** Single.
**Religion:** Lutheran.
**Political Career:** Wis. House, 1975-79.

**The Member:** Cows vastly outnumber people in Gunderson's district, the nation's first in dairying. His sole committee assignment is Agriculture, where he has resisted President Reagan's ideas about scaling back dairy price supports.

When the Subcommittee on Livestock, Dairy and Poultry considered Reagan's proposal to skip a scheduled April 1 increase in price supports, Gunderson and James M. Jeffords, R-Vt., actively helped Democrats try to ditch the Reagan plan in favor of a modified support program endorsed by the dairy industry. Reagan's plan eventually won out. But Gunderson continued to advocate higher dairy supports than the administration wanted.

For a man who insists his real ambition was to become a radio hockey announcer, Gunderson has done very well in politics very quickly. He won his broadcasting license at age 23, but was elected the same year to the state Legislature.

As a close associate of Republican Gov. Lee Sherman Dreyfus, Gunderson could have obtained a leadership job in the Legislature. But he quit in mid-1979 and went to work in Washington as Rep. Toby Roth's legislative director.

In six months, Gunderson was back in Wisconsin, this time to challenge Democratic Rep. Alvin Baldus. Gunderson's job-hopping stirred some complaints that his ambition exceeded his commitment to public service, but he beat Baldus by demonstrating the same energy that marked his service in the Legislature.

**The District:** Outside La Crosse and Eau Claire — the only cities in the 3rd with more than 20,000 people — most voters live on farms or in small crossroads towns. More farmers live in this district than in any other Wisconsin district.

Before Baldus' 1974 victory, the 3rd had always had GOP representation. It became slightly more Democratic in 1971, when industrial Eau Claire and several counties in the north were added. But overall, it retains its Republican nature.

## Committees

**Agriculture** (17th of 19 Republicans)
Conservation, Credit, and Rural Development; Cotton, Rice and Sugar; Livestock, Dairy, and Poultry.

## Elections

**1980 General**

| | |
|---|---|
| Steve Gunderson (R) | 132,001 (51 %) |
| Alvin Baldus (D ) | 126,859 (49 %) |

**1980 Primary**

| | |
|---|---|
| Steve Gunderson (R) | 35,710 (69 %) |
| Gary Madson (R ) | 11,515 (22 %) |
| Ward Repp (R ) | 4,487 (9 %) |

**District Vote For President**

| | 1980 | | 1976 | | 1972 |
|---|---|---|---|---|---|
| **D** | 116,758 (43 %) | **D** | 121,904 (49 %) | **D** | 85,348 (40 %) |
| **R** | 130,635 (48 %) | **R** | 119,607 (48 %) | **R** | 122,445 (58 %) |
| **I** | 19,528 (7 %) | | | | |

## Campaign Finance

| 1980 | Receipts | Receipts from PACs | Expenditures |
|---|---|---|---|
| Gunderson (R ) | $188,013 | $32,474 (17 %) | $171,267 |
| Baldus (D ) | $135,863 | $79,110 (58 %) | $136,320 |

## Key Vote

**97th Congress**

| | |
|---|---|
| Reagan budget proposal (1981) | Y |

---

**3rd District: West — La Crosse, Eau Claire.** Population: 557,065 (13% increase since 1970). Race: White 552,014 (99%), Black 861 (0.2%), Others 4,190 (1%). Spanish origin: 1,817 (0.3%).

---

# 4 Clement J. Zablocki (D)

**Of Milwaukee — Elected 1948**

**Born:** Nov. 18, 1912, Milwaukee, Wis.
**Education:** Marquette U., Ph.B. 1936.
**Military Career:** Air Force Reserve, 1956-65 (inactive).
**Profession:** Teacher.
**Family:** Widowed; two children.
**Religion:** Roman Catholic.
**Political Career:** Wis. Senate, 1943-49.

**In Washington:** Zablocki has presided benignly over the Foreign Affairs Committee in recent years as its younger members have struggled to regain some of the influence the panel lost to its Senate counterpart during the 1960s. For the most part, he has been passive, accepting the committee's activists but leaving them to do the more controversial work on their own.

Generally easygoing and anxious to avoid confrontation, Zablocki has spent much of his time trying to expedite routine committee business. Only on one issue has he been consistently aggressive: demanding that the White House notify Congress about important foreign policy decisions.

Zablocki has sometimes discouraged a foreign policy initiative favored by some of his more aggressive committee members — prohibiting aid to countries with poor human rights records. He has fought several attempts in recent years to reduce or prohibit aid to both left-wing and right-wing totalitarian regimes.

In committee, he seeks to defuse argument by suggesting that the opposing sides report the bill and then state their cases in a committee report, rather than in the actual legislation. It does not often work; few members are willing to have their proposals relegated to the fine print of committee reports that are rarely read.

Zablocki is not a master of House parliamentary maneuvering or floor debate. When managing legislation on the House floor, he tends to yield his responsibility to subcommittee chairmen and other committee members who specialize in certain subject areas.

But during the Carter administration, Zablocki's low-key style probably aided passage of some otherwise endangered bills. His reputation as a moderate lent some credibility to his support of Carter's most controversial proposals on foreign aid, the new China policy and sensitive arms sales.

He takes seriously the formal aspects of his chairmanship and relishes the opportunity to host foreign dignitaries. In January 1979, when Chinese vice-premier Deng Xiaoping made his historic visit to Washington, Zablocki impressed his guest and fellow legislators at a reception by greeting Deng with several sentences of well-spoken Chinese. He had spent hours practicing his speech in front of a mirror.

The chairman also enjoys the perquisites of his job: During the 1979 Christmas recess, he installed a massive portrait of himself at the focal point of the Foreign Affairs hearing room. The portrait displaced one of Zablocki's predecessor, Pennsylvania's Thomas E. Morgan, after whom the room is named.

Zablocki was one of a relatively few senior House committee members who faced serious opposition when the time came for elevation to his chairmanship.

In January 1977, after 18 years as second-ranking member on Foreign Affairs, Zablocki was in line to succeed Morgan. But Rep. Benjamin S. Rosenthal, D-N.Y., challenged Zablocki's qualifications to chair the committee and his credentials as a loyal Democrat. In a lengthy memo to fellow Democrats, Rosenthal criticized Zablocki's ties to right-wing regimes in South Korea and Taiwan, his somewhat conservative voting record and his record of support for the Vietnam War.

In rebuttal, Zablocki said he was being at-

---

**4th District: Southern Milwaukee.**
Population: 455,899 (7% decrease since 1970). Race: White 440,604 (97%), Black 1,445 (0.3%), Others 13,850 (3%). Spanish origin: 18,018 (4%).

tacked because of "a feeling that I'm not friendly enough toward the state of Israel." The year before, Zablocki had criticized the Ford administration's plans for a huge increase in military aid to Israel. Zablocki noted that Rosenthal is one of Israel's staunchest supporters in Congress.

Zablocki won his chairmanship on a 182-72 vote in the Democratic Caucus on Jan. 18, 1977. Two years later, active opposition to his chairmanship had evaporated.

Zablocki was chairman of the House Pacific and Asian Affairs Subcommittee during most of the 1960s, when Presidents Johnson and Nixon were prosecuting the war in Vietnam with little direct challenge from Congress. He vigorously backed the war effort and opposed all congressional attempts to cut off money for the war.

In October 1963, shortly before the overthrow of South Vietnamese President Ngo Dinh Diem, Zablocki headed a congressional study mission to Vietnam. After his trip, Zablocki expressed optimism that the South Vietnamese would be able to overcome the communist challenge.

In spite of his support for the conduct of the war under Johnson and Nixon, Zablocki has been a longtime advocate of requiring the president to consult with Congress on major foreign policy matters. In 1970, he sponsored a resolution requiring the president "whenever feasible" to notify Congress before sending troops overseas. That measure died in the Senate.

But three years later, in 1973, Zablocki sponsored the House version of the War Powers Act, passed over the vigorous opposition of President Nixon. That law set specific limits on the president's power to involve troops in foreign combat without congressional approval.

Ever since passage of the act, Zablocki has kept a close watch on adherence to it and has insisted that presidents consult with Congress before making major foreign policy moves. Zablocki criticized President Carter on two occasions for failing to consult with Congress. One was the normalization of relations with China in December 1978; the other was the unsuccessful hostage rescue attempt in Iran in April 1980.

Zablocki is one of the Foreign Affairs Committee's representatives on the House Intelligence Committee. In 1980, he helped lead a successful effort to weaken a law requiring advance notice to congressional committees of "covert activities" by the intelligence agencies.

**At Home:** Zablocki's campaign style has not changed in three decades, and it has not needed to. The former church organist and choir director has become a fact of life on Milwaukee's heavily Polish South Side.

Zablocki still keeps his political base intact by dropping in on church groups and union halls, by promptly answering constituent mail and by working to obtain federal money for Milwaukee's airport, freeways, hospitals and small businesses. Since his first election in 1948, he has never been seriously challenged at the polls.

Over the years, Zablocki's positions have earned him critics on both left and right. But the anger has usually been from outside his district and only helped to solidify his support at home. In 1962, Republican Rep. Edward J. Derwinski of Illinois came to Wisconsin and called Zablocki "the socialistic congressman from Milwaukee" because of his support for Medicare. The same year, liberals attacked Zablocki for his support of the House Un-American Activities Committee. In 1970, when a "peace" candidate challenged him in the Democratic primary, the incumbent proved how closely he mirrored his district's Vietnam policy by winning 85 percent of the vote.

A short, stocky man with a brush mustache, Zablocki has been a loyal Democratic Party worker since the 1930s, when he was a civics teacher in Milwaukee's public schools. After losing his first try for the state Senate in 1938, he was elected to it in 1942 and re-elected in 1946.

That same year Democrats denied renomination to their South Side congressman, Thaddeus B. Wasielewski, and when Wasielewski ran as a splinter candidate in November, Republican John C. Brophy was elected to the House. Two years later, Democrats united behind Zablocki, and he had little trouble winning the seat.

Zablocki made one brief effort, in 1957, to move to the Senate. But he lost a special election primary to William Proxmire and has shown no interest in leaving the House since then.

**The District:** Since the turn of the century, the South Side of Milwaukee has been home base for the city's huge Polish community. Like many of the Eastern Europeans who migrated to industrial cities, the Poles have been loyal, somewhat conservative Democrats.

Milwaukee makes up about 43 percent of the district — a share that has been steadily decreasing over the last several years. But the people living in the working-class suburbs to the south and west have a political outlook quite similar to the one still found in blue-collar neighborhoods inside the city.

Of the two Milwaukee districts, the 4th is slightly less Democratic. But Democratic presidential candidates — even George McGovern in 1972 — still manage to win pluralities there.

## Committees

**Foreign Affairs** (Chairman)
International Security and Scientific Affairs, chairman.

**Select Intelligence** (2nd of 9 Democrats)
Program and Budget Authorization.

## Elections

**1980 General**

| | |
|---|---|
| Clement Zablocki (D ) | 146,437 (70 %) |
| Elroy Honadel (R ) | 61,027 (29 %) |

**1980 Primary**

| | |
|---|---|
| Clement Zablocki (D ) | 29,411 (89 %) |
| Roman Blenski (D ) | 3,489 (11 %) |

**1978 General**

| | |
|---|---|
| Clement Zablocki (D ) | 101,575 (66 %) |
| Elroy Honadel (R ) | 52,125 (34 %) |

**Previous Winning Percentages**

| | | | |
|---|---|---|---|
| 1976 (100%) | 1974 (73 %) | 1972 (76 %) | 1970 (82 %) |
| 1968 (73 %) | 1966 (74 %) | 1964 (74 %) | 1962 (73 %) |
| 1960 (72 %) | 1958 (74 %) | 1956 (66 %) | 1954 (71 %) |
| 1952 (64 %) | 1950 (61 %) | 1948 (56 %) | |

**District Vote For President**

| | 1980 | | 1976 | | 1972 |
|---|---|---|---|---|---|
| D | 108,816 (48 %) | D | 119,386 (53 %) | D | 99,537 (49 %) |
| R | 99,267 (43 %) | R | 97,686 (44 %) | R | 96,755 (48 %) |
| I | 15,912 (7 %) | | | | |

## Campaign Finance

| | Receipts | Receipts from PACs | Expen-ditures |
|---|---|---|---|
| **1980** | | | |
| Zablocki (D ) | $17,400 | $1,345 (8 %) | $14,592 |
| Honadel (R ) | $9,720 | — (0 %) | $10,201 |
| **1978** | | | |
| Zablocki (D ) | $12,165 | $9,300 (76 %) | $10,398 |
| Honadel (R ) | $15,154 | $550 (4 %) | $14,665 |

## Voting Studies

| | Presidential Support | | Party Unity | | Conservative Coalition | |
|---|---|---|---|---|---|---|
| Year | S | O | S | O | S | O |
| 1980 | 90 | 10 | 92 | 8 | 26 | 74 |
| 1979 | 76 | 21 | 83 | 14 | 37 | 60 |
| 1978 | 73 | 27 | 78 | 22 | 33 | 67 |
| 1977 | 68 | 32 | 79 | 18 | 35 | 64 |

| | | | | | | |
|---|---|---|---|---|---|---|
| 1976 | 35 | 65 | 83 | 16 | 37 | 62 |
| 1975 | 45 | 54 | 76 | 20 | 41 | 56 |
| 1974 (Ford) | 59 | 39 | | | | |
| 1974 | 64 | 34 | 80 | 16 | 38 | 61 |
| 1973 | 44 | 56 | 80 | 20 | 41 | 59 |
| 1972 | 73 | 27 | 73 | 21 | 41 | 57 |
| 1971 | 75 | 25 | 65 | 32 | 57 | 42 |
| 1970 | 63 | 32 | 74 | 24 | 36 | 59 |
| 1969 | 53 | 47 | 82 | 16 | 36 | 64 |
| 1968 | 79 | 8 | 77 | 9 | 12 | 73 |
| 1967 | 87 | 8 | 88 | 10 | 20 | 76 |
| 1966 | 63 | 7 | 73 | 5 | 19 | 59 |
| 1965 | 89 | 6 | 88 | 6 | 8 | 86 |
| 1964 | 98 | 2 | 98 | 0 | 8 | 92 |
| 1963 | 84 | 6 | 93 | 2 | 27 | 73 |
| 1962 | 95 | 3 | 95 | 4 | 12 | 88 |
| 1961 | 89 | 6 | 93 | 2 | 17 | 74 |

S = Support          O = Opposition

## Key Votes

**96th Congress**

| | |
|---|---|
| Weaken Carter oil profits tax (1979) | N |
| Reject hospital cost control plan (1979) | N |
| Implement Panama Canal Treaties (1979) | Y |
| Establish Department of Education (1979) | N |
| Approve Anti-busing Amendment (1979) | Y |
| Guarantee Chrysler Corp. loans (1979) | Y |
| Approve military draft registration (1980) | Y |
| Aid Sandinista regime in Nicaragua (1980) | Y |
| Strengthen fair housing laws (1980) | Y |

**97th Congress**

| | |
|---|---|
| Reagan budget proposal (1981) | N |

## Interest Group Rating

| Year | ADA | ACA | AFL-CIO | CCUS |
|---|---|---|---|---|
| 1980 | 61 | 13 | 83 | 65 |
| 1979 | 53 | 12 | 79 | 18 |
| 1978 | 40 | 33 | 65 | 39 |
| 1977 | 40 | 23 | 95 | 0 |
| 1976 | 50 | 19 | 96 | 25 |
| 1975 | 58 | 32 | 96 | 12 |
| 1974 | 48 | 13 | 91 | 0 |
| 1973 | 56 | 22 | 82 | 36 |
| 1972 | 44 | 26 | 91 | 10 |
| 1971 | 38 | 38 | 100 | - |
| 1970 | 44 | 26 | 100 | 10 |
| 1969 | 53 | 24 | 100 | - |
| 1968 | 83 | 13 | 100 | - |
| 1967 | 67 | 10 | 92 | 30 |
| 1966 | 71 | 8 | 100 | - |
| 1965 | 63 | 4 | - | 10 |
| 1964 | 88 | 0 | 100 | - |
| 1963 | - | 0 | - | - |
| 1962 | 88 | 4 | 100 | - |
| 1961 | 80 | - | - | - |

# 5  Henry S. Reuss (D)

**Of Milwaukee — Elected 1954**

**Born:** Feb. 22, 1912, Milwaukee, Wis.
**Education:** Cornell U., A.B. 1933; Harvard Law
    School, LL.B. 1936.
**Military Career:** Army, 1943-45.
**Profession:** Lawyer, writer.
**Family:** Wife, Margaret Magrath; four children.
**Religion:** Episcopalian.
**Political Career:** Milwaukee School Board,
    1953-55; candidate for mayor of Milwaukee,
    1948 and 1960; unsuccessful Democratic
    nominee for Wis. attorney general, 1950;
    sought Democratic nomination for U.S. Sen-
    ate, 1952.

**In Washington:** If intelligence and influence were the same thing, Reuss would be one of
the handful of most influential House members as
he serves the last of 14 terms.

No one questions Reuss's credentials in his
specialty of international finance, which he has
always managed to discuss not only with coherence, but with relish. But as a man with an
academic style in a political institution, he has
never inspired the necessary trust among his
peers — or developed the ability to outbargain
them for what he wants.

When he retires at the end of the current
Congress, Reuss will leave behind a record of
hundreds of creative ideas proposed and many
adopted. But it will also be a record of turmoil
and frequent frustration at the Banking Committee, whose chairmanship he left in 1981 to take
over the Joint Economic Committee, which deals
in ideas and analysis, not legislation.

Reuss came to power at Banking in 1975 as
part of that year's miniature Democratic revolution, which swept aside three aging and autocratic
chairmen, including the Banking chairman,
Wright Patman of Texas. Reuss campaigned for
the chairmanship, and won it with the help of
most of that year's 75 new House Democrats.

But it was no revolution in policy. If Reuss,
unlike Patman, was mentally acute and willing to
listen to other opinions, his own views on finance
frequently coincided with Patman's. He brought
to the chairmanship the same skepticism about
the banking industry and its interests, merely
expressed with wit and intellect rather than the
hard-shell Texas populism of the 1920s.

The day he unseated Patman, Reuss began
talking freely of his priorities for the first two
years: emergency housing legislation and a credit
allocation bill to force banks to lend money for

"high productivity" investments. With Patman
out of the way, he predicted he could move both
bills out of committee in a week.

But Reuss has never been much of a vote
counter. The credit allocation bill was weakened
in committee to provide only for a reporting of
lending practices by 200 large banks, and even
that failed on the House floor. The housing bill
became law by the end of the Congress, but only
in modified form, after a veto by President Ford
and a dispute between Reuss and Housing Subcommittee Chairman Thomas L. Ashley, D-Ohio,
who felt Reuss was politically unrealistic.

Reuss's chairmanship preserved the state of
tension that had existed on the committee under
Patman, with moderate and conservative Democrats frequently joining Republicans to oppose
the generally anti-bank Democratic bloc.

Through his three terms as chairman, Reuss
remained adamant in his criticism of the industry
and the Federal Reserve Board. He has always
been free with unsolicited advice to banks. "Make
a lot of loans," he once told them, "don't charge so
much interest and make it up on volume."

Reuss sued the Fed in 1976 to block presidents of regional Federal Reserve Banks from
voting on domestic monetary policy as members
of the federal Open Market Committee. He insisted they were not federal officials and should
not make policy. Reuss has repeatedly criticized

---

**5th District: Northern Milwaukee.**
Population: 439,126 (11% decrease since
1970). Race: White 280,843 (64%), Black
146,379 (34%), Others 11,904 (3%). Spanish
origin: 10,841 (2%).

the Fed for having excessively high interest rates. In 1980, he commissioned a GAO study of the Fed's role in the economy.

He won a significant victory in 1980, after years of failure, when the broad banking deregulation that became law included a provision requiring all banks to make minimum reserve deposits with the Fed, whether they are Fed members or not.

On other economic issues, Reuss has managed to stay close to the center of policy and media attention for nearly 20 years. It was his floor amendment, in 1970, that gave President Nixon the authority to impose wage and price controls the following year, although Nixon opposed the amendment at the time. It was also Reuss who caused a brief commotion in international money markets when he endorsed the idea of allowing the dollar to float away from the price of gold. Nine days later the Nixon administration released the price of the dollar.

While fighting those battles, Reuss was pursuing his passion for urban issues as chairman of a special non-legislative Subcommittee on the City, which he created at Banking in 1977. After a year of hearings and study, he issued his own solution to the urban crisis: "forget about urban renewal programs and urban expressways which chew up neighborhoods ... terminate tax incentives to landlords to milk their properties ... stop rewarding state governments for the know-nothing waste of local land ... concentrate aid programs on the needy instead of scattering largesse almost everywhere."

That philosophy was also reflected in Reuss's early sponsorship of revenue sharing, a program normally associated with Republicans. He and Hubert Humphrey introduced their own revenue sharing bill in 1971, as the Nixon administration was preparing to move its version through Congress. Humphrey-Reuss would have focused aid to state and local governments much more directly on the poor. But Reuss voted for the Nixon-backed program as it cleared Congress.

Reuss's creativity has gone far beyond the issues of his committee work. Crusading against water pollution in 1970, he discovered an unused 1899 Refuse Act making it illegal to dump wastes into rivers. He turned in a list of 270 Wisconsin companies he said were violating it, and in the first two years after his discovery, collected more than $2,000 in "bounties," as provided by the law. He returned the money to the state.

Reuss promoted an idea similar to the Peace Corps as early as 1957, and has never ceased to offer unusual suggestions for political change. In 1974 he introduced a constitutional amendment to allow Congress a vote of "no confidence" against a president. The next year, he introduced a constitutional amendment that would give the nation two presidents at the same time, with different tasks. In 1980, concerned for the future of the Democratic Party, he proposed a Council of 300 to formulate party policy.

**At Home:** Although Reuss would occasionally shed his starched-collar image and don a pair of German lederhosen for a campaign appearance, he is not likely to miss that part of elective life. Even before winning his last term in 1980, Reuss had decided to retire in 1982 rather than face a host of new constituents after redistricting.

"I'm not a backslapper," Reuss admits readily. And it was often obvious that he did not enjoy running for re-election. But after his first campaign, he merely had to go through the motions every two years to win another term from his solidly Democratic district.

At the beginning of his career, however, winning was not that easy. Grandson of a German immigrant who became a wealthy banker, Reuss was educated in the East and worked briefly in the family bank. After serving as a combat officer in World War II, he helped administer the Marshall Plan in Paris and then returned to Milwaukee to begin a career in politics. First he ran for mayor and lost. Then, he tried to become state attorney general and lost again. His third effort came in 1952, when he wanted to challenge Sen. Joseph R. McCarthy, but lost in the Democratic primary.

He lowered his sights a bit, finally won a seat on the Milwaukee school board in 1953, and the next year beat Republican U.S. Rep. Charles J. Kersten, a House ally of McCarthy. After three terms in the House — winning by increasingly safe margins — Reuss had tired of Congress and ran for the mayor's office again. He lost again and decided to make his career in the House.

**The District:** Two-thirds of Milwaukee's population live in the 5th District. The boundaries closely follow the city limits, carefully excluding the nearby Republican areas along Lake Michigan.

Unlike voters in the heavily Polish 4th District to the south, those in northern Milwaukee are predominantly from German stock. The city's sizable black population is also located north of St. Paul Avenue, the dividing line between the two districts. Breweries and automobile plants provide employment for many of the district's blue-collar residents. They vote solidly Democratic, making this the most Democratic district in the state.

Having lost 11 percent of its population in the last decade, the 5th needs to gain more people than any other district in the state. Except for the underpopulated 4th District on the south, all the neighboring territory is Republican.

## Committees

**Banking, Finance and Urban Affairs** (2nd of 25 Democrats)
Domestic Monetary Policy; International Development Institutions and Finance.

**Joint Economic** (Chairman)
Investment, Jobs and Prices, chairman; Monetary and Fiscal Policy.

## Elections

**1980 General**

| | |
|---|---|
| Henry Reuss (D ) | 129,574 (77 %) |
| David Bathke (R ) | 37,267 (22 %) |

**1980 Primary**

| | |
|---|---|
| Henry Reuss (D ) | 20,977 (88 %) |
| Rajababu Kilaru (D) | 2,842 (12 %) |

**1978 General**

| | |
|---|---|
| Henry Reuss (D ) | 85,067 (73 %) |
| James Medina (R ) | 30,185 (26 %) |

**Previous Winning Percentages**

| | | | |
|---|---|---|---|
| 1976 (78 %) | 1974 (80 %) | 1972 (77 %) | 1970 (76 %) |
| 1968 (68 %) | 1966 (70 %) | 1964 (76 %) | 1962 (64 %) |
| 1960 (58 %) | 1958 (70 %) | 1956 (58 %) | 1954 (52 %) |

**District Vote For President**

| | 1980 | | 1976 | | 1972 |
|---|---|---|---|---|---|
| D | 117,147 (60 %) | D | 116,332 (61 %) | D | 97,596 (56 %) |
| R | 61,322 (31 %) | R | 68,240 (36 %) | R | 71,196 (41 %) |
| I | 13,972 (7 %) | | | | |

## Campaign Finance

| | Receipts | Receipts from PACs | Expenditures |
|---|---|---|---|
| **1980** | | | |
| Reuss (D ) | $70,383 | $50,475 (72 %) | $36,250 |
| Bathke (R ) | $1,692 | — (0 %) | $1,107 |
| **1978** | | | |
| Reuss (D ) | $77,597 | $39,949 (51 %) | $68,092 |
| Medina (R ) | $7,411 | $100 (1 %) | $4,952 |

## Voting Studies

| | Presidential Support | | Party Unity | | Conservative Coalition | |
|---|---|---|---|---|---|---|
| Year | S | O | S | O | S | O |
| 1980 | 56 | 19 | 78 | 3 | 3 | 76 |
| 1979 | 87 | 11 | 93 | 3 | 7 | 92 |
| 1978 | 85 | 11 | 86 | 8 | 7 | 90 |
| 1977 | 73 | 23 | 89 | 8 | 9 | 88 |
| 1976 | 25 | 75 | 93 | 3 | 10 | 86 |
| 1975 | 35 | 61 | 93 | 5 | 8 | 90 |
| 1974 (Ford) | 48 | 48 | | | | |
| 1974 | 38 | 55 | 84 | 11 | 3 | 94 |
| 1973 | 30 | 68 | 88 | 12 | 9 | 89 |
| 1972 | 46 | 54 | 90 | 10 | 6 | 94 |
| 1971 | 33 | 63 | 77 | 11 | 4 | 90 |
| 1970 | 57 | 38 | 79 | 13 | 2 | 84 |
| 1969 | 49 | 43 | 82 | 5 | 4 | 91 |
| 1968 | 85 | 5 | 84 | 7 | 4 | 92 |
| 1967 | 76 | 11 | 85 | 3 | 2 | 89 |
| 1966 | 85 | 5 | 84 | 3 | 0 | 95 |
| 1965 | 93 | 5 | 90 | 6 | 2 | 94 |
| 1964 | 92 | 4 | 87 | 3 | 0 | 100 |
| 1963 | 82 | 3 | 81 | 3 | 0 | 87 |
| 1962 | 93 | 2 | 88 | 5 | 6 | 88 |
| 1961 | 88 | 3 | 81 | 3 | 9 | 70 |

S = Support          O = Opposition

## Key Votes

**96th Congress**

| | |
|---|---|
| Weaken Carter oil profits tax (1979) | N |
| Reject hospital cost control plan (1979) | N |
| Implement Panama Canal Treaties (1979) | Y |
| Establish Department of Education (1979) | Y |
| Approve Anti-busing Amendment (1979) | N |
| Guarantee Chrysler Corp. loans (1979) | Y |
| Approve military draft registration (1980) | N |
| Aid Sandinista regime in Nicaragua (1980) | Y |
| Strengthen fair housing Laws (1980) | ? |

**97th Congress**

| | |
|---|---|
| Reagan budget proposal (1981) | N |

## Interest Group Rating

| Year | ADA | ACA | AFL-CIO | CCUS |
|---|---|---|---|---|
| 1980 | 89 | 22 | 83 | 57 |
| 1979 | 95 | 0 | 89 | 0 |
| 1978 | 80 | 8 | 90 | 22 |
| 1977 | 90 | 7 | 82 | 18 |
| 1976 | 90 | 0 | 87 | 13 |
| 1975 | 95 | 4 | 100 | 12 |
| 1974 | 96 | 0 | 100 | 20 |
| 1973 | 88 | 8 | 91 | 27 |
| 1972 | 100 | 4 | 82 | 11 |
| 1971 | 97 | 14 | 82 | - |
| 1970 | 88 | 17 | 100 | 11 |
| 1969 | 93 | 18 | 100 | - |
| 1968 | 100 | 9 | 100 | - |
| 1967 | 93 | 4 | 100 | 10 |
| 1966 | 100 | 4 | 100 | - |
| 1965 | 100 | 0 | - | 10 |
| 1964 | 100 | 0 | 100 | - |
| 1963 | - | 0 | - | - |
| 1962 | 100 | 0 | 100 | - |
| 1961 | 100 | - | - | - |

# 6 Thomas E. Petri (R)

**Of Fond du Lac — Elected 1979**

**Born:** May 28, 1940, Marinette, Wis.
**Education:** Harvard U., B.A. 1962, LLB. 1965.
**Profession:** Lawyer.
**Family:** Single.
**Religion:** Lutheran.
**Political Career:** Wis. Senate, 1973-79; unsuccessful Republican nominee for U.S. Senate, 1974.

**In Washington:** Petri is quieter and more reserved than his late predecessor, Republican William A. Steiger, who died in 1978, but he has shown some of Steiger's fondness for new ideas and challenges to tradition. Within seven months of his arrival in the House, he took on the senior members of his Education and Labor Committee and defeated them on the floor.

The issue was student loans and whether to allow recipients to work off college debts to the federal government by joining the military. Petri offered the idea as an amendment to the 1979 Higher Education bill both in subcommittee and full committee. He lost decisively.

So when the bill went to the floor, Petri quietly contacted Armed Services Committee members, arguing that his amendment would strengthen the all-volunteer Army by attracting better volunteers. By the time it came to a vote, Petri had solid support and won, 236-115. The amendment eventually became law.

He has not had similar luck with another pet idea, to require airports to provide more space for rail and bus service in order to make it more convenient for people to travel without cars. The airports themselves are opposed, but Petri has said he will take it to the floor.

Petri has been interested in problems of the elderly and serves on the Aging Committee. He sponsored legislation to phase out the earnings test on Social Security for those 65 and older. But he opposed requiring wheelchair lifts for buses, arguing it was too expensive and would discourage local communities from setting up special transit for the handicapped and elderly.

Petri has generally voted as a traditional conservative Republican, surprising some who remember him as a leader in the liberal Republican Ripon Society in earlier years. But he is not a predictable vote. He joined most of his party in 1979 in favoring a weaker windfall profits tax, but opposed most of it in voting for a moratorium on

nuclear plant licensing in the wake of the Three Mile Island incident. He voted with the Carter administration in favor of establishing the Department of Education but against bailing out the Chrysler Corp. and against a constitutional amendment to ban school busing.

**At Home:** Petri built his Wisconsin career out of the moderate Republican politics that worked for Steiger, who died of a heart attack at age 40 just a month after winning his seventh House term in 1978.

In the 1979 special election held to choose Steiger's successor, Petri campaigned on the same moderate platform Steiger had used. His campaign literature boasted of the high ratings he had received in the state Senate from the citizens' lobby, Common Cause. He noted that he had been a Peace Corps volunteer in Somalia and served as executive director of the Ripon Society.

The campaign reinforced the image Petri had created in 1974, when he was the sacrificial Republican Senate nominee against Democrat Gaylord Nelson. He drew only 35 percent of the vote against Nelson in a terrible Republican year, but brought himself some useful attention.

The earlier Senate effort made Petri the logical GOP contender for Steiger's House seat in 1979. But it did not guarantee him victory against Gary Goyke, a fellow state senator with a more forceful campaign style. Goyke made an issue of Petri's generous campaign financing and criti-

---

**6th District: East central — Oshkosh, Sheboygan. Population:** 520,319 (6% increase since 1970). **Race:** White 514,088 (99%), Black 1,225 (0.2%), Others 5,006 (1%). **Spanish origin:** 3,953 (1%).

cized him for receiving a $5,000 contribution from the American Medical Association. Petri said Goyke had his own source of political funding in organized labor.

Petri won the special election on his strength in the rural areas and his ability to cut into Goyke's vote in blue-collar cities, especially Sheboygan, which Petri narrowly carried.

Eighteen months later, there was a re-match. But the 1980 election was a pale shadow of the first contest. Goyke was still in debt from the special election and got a late start. Petri had enhanced his Steiger-like image by hiring some of Steiger's aides and taking his predecessor's place on the Education and Labor Committee. With a strong Republican tide at the statewide level, Petri carried every county in the district against Goyke the second time around.

**The District:** Although the 6th District is largely rural, it has several small blue-collar cities which usually boost the Democratic vote.

Four cities — Oshkosh, Fond du Lac, Manitowoc and Sheboygan — add up to about a third of the district's population. The rest live on farms and in Republican market towns closely linked to the region's dairy economy. The district is close in many state and national electons, but it has sent only one Democrat to Washington since 1938.

## Committees

**Education and Labor** (8th of 14 Republicans)
Elementary, Secondary and Vocational Education; Employment Opportunities; Human Resources.

**Select Aging** (14th of 23 Republicans)
Human Services.

## Elections

**1980 General**

| | |
|---|---|
| Thomas Petri (R) | 143,980 (59%) |
| Gary Goyke (D) | 98,628 (41%) |

**1979 Special Election**

| | |
|---|---|
| Thomas Petri (R) | 71,715 (50%) |
| Gary Goyke (D) | 70,492 (50%) |

**1979 Special Primary**

| | |
|---|---|
| Thomas Petri (R ) | 22,293 (35 %) |
| Tommy Thompson (R ) | 11,850 (19 %) |
| John Steinhilber (R ) | 11,810 (19 %) |
| Kenneth Benson (R) | 10,965 (17%) |
| Donald Jones (R) | 5,077 (8%) |

**District Vote For President**

| | 1980 | | 1976 | | 1972 |
|---|---|---|---|---|---|
| D | 98,007 (39%) | D | 108,920 (47%) | D | 85,778 (42%) |
| R | 131,522 (53%) | R | 118,126 (51%) | R | 114,461 (56%) |
| I | 15,699 (6%) | | | | |

## Campaign Finance

| | Receipts | Receipts from PACs | Expenditures |
|---|---|---|---|
| **1980*** | | | |
| Petri (R) | $500,726 | $188,977 (38%) | $498,854 |
| Goyke (D) | $232,366 | $115,016 (49%) | $234,563 |
| **1978** | | | |

\* Figures given are totals for both the 1979 special election and the 1980 general election.

## Voting Studies

| | Presidential Support | | Party Unity | | Conservative Coalition | |
|---|---|---|---|---|---|---|
| Year | S | O | S | O | S | O |
| 1980 | 50 | 46 | 77 | 20 | 77 | 20 |
| 1979 | 38 | 58† | 74 | 24† | 72 | 27† |

S = Support          O = Opposition
† Not eligible for all recorded votes.

## Key Votes

**96th Congress**

| | |
|---|---|
| Weaken Carter oil profits tax (1979) | Y |
| Reject hospital cost control plan (1979) | Y |
| Implement Panama Canal Treaties (1979) | N |
| Establish Department of Education (1979) | Y |
| Approve Anti-busing Amendment (1979) | N |
| Guarantee Chrysler Corp. loans (1979) | N |
| Approve military draft registration (1980) | Y |
| Aid Sandinista regime in Nicaragua (1980) | N |
| Strengthen fair housing laws (1980) | N |

**97th Congress**

| | |
|---|---|
| Reagan budget proposal (1981) | Y |

## Interest Group Ratings

| Year | ADA | ACA | AFL-CIO | CCUS |
|---|---|---|---|---|
| 1980 | 39 | 57 | 44 | 59 |
| 1979 | 39 | 71 | 37 | 69 |

# 7 David R. Obey (D)

**Of Wausau — Elected in 1969**

**Born:** Oct. 3, 1938, Okmulgee, Okla.
**Education:** U. of Wis., B.S. 1960, M.A. 1962.
**Profession:** Real estate broker.
**Family:** Wife, Joan Lepinski; two children.
**Religion:** Roman Catholic.
**Political Career:** Wis. Assembly, 1963-69.

**In Washington:** When Obey was a freshman in the House, and a subcommittee chairman ordered him to follow the custom of standing up as high ranking generals and admirals entered the room, he refused. He saw no reason why he had to defer to simple rank.

A member who starts off that way often remains an outsider, not very influential in the legislative process. But Obey, still as intense, blunt, and hot-tempered as the day he came, has proven his effectiveness time and again.

In his first 12 years in the House, Obey managed to rewrite the chamber's code of ethics; lead the drive for campaign finance reform; chair the Democratic Study Group, the research arm of House liberals; play a key role in foreign aid appropriations; and come within a single vote of the Budget Committee chairmanship.

He is at once outspoken about his liberalism and sarcastic about liberal naiveté and lack of restraint. He is a lover of the House and a critic of its procedures. Once, when the House reversed itself on four key votes in a week, he said it looked like "a national idiot."

Obey's seven-term seniority at age 42 makes it likely he will chair the Appropriations Committee some day if he stays in Congress. In his time on the committee, he has mellowed enough to be a skillful negotiator, even among the conservative Southern Democrats whose control often frustrates him. But he has not learned to curb his temper, and still sulks sometimes when he loses.

His temper was an issue in his campaign for Budget chairman at the beginning of 1981, in the closest contest the committee has ever had.

A four-year veteran on Budget, Obey was a logical successor to the retiring Robert Giaimo of Connecticut. But the national conservative sentiment expressed in November of 1980 offered an opportunity for Obey's more conservative Democratic rival, James R. Jones of Oklahoma.

Obey had the moderates and liberals and he needed and felt he had the support of Speaker O'Neill. On the first ballot, Jones and Obey tied at 100 votes apiece. The second ballot produced another tie at 118. On the third ballot Jones eked

out a victory, 121-116. Obey let it be known he thought the Speaker had failed to work for him. He remained angry at O'Neill for weeks.

Obey remains a member of the Budget Committee, where he has alternately helped and fought the Democratic leadership for four years. Initially an ally of Giaimo, Obey began to part company with him in 1979 as the chairman became a convert to fiscal conservatism and began trimming social programs to get the budgets passed.

In 1980, Giaimo was determined to produce a balanced budget resolution for fiscal 1981. Obey criticized it as too generous to defense and too stingy on social spending, and fought it both in committee and on the floor. He introduced his own floor amendment to add $700 million in domestic social spending, and surprised many colleagues by coming within 12 votes of passage, 213-201, attracting even 36 Republicans.

When President Reagan began announcing his economic program in 1981, Obey offered Democrats a simple strategy: vote for it as is, and run against it if it fails.

In May, however, Obey presented his own alternative budget for 1982. Meant as a counterpoint to the tax cutting, high deficit Reagan budget, it eliminated any deficit for 1982 by delaying any tax cut until the following year. It drew only 119 votes, all from Democrats.

The same year that Obey joined the Budget

---

**7th District: North — Wausau, Superior.** Population: 553,658 (13% increase since 1970). Race: White 544,957 (98%), Black 482 (0.08%), Others 8,219 (1%). Spanish origin: 1,890 (0.3%).

---

## David R. Obey, D-Wis.

Committee, he made an ambitious effort to impose new ethics standards on the House. It was partially successful, but at the personal cost of good relations with some members who felt he was tampering with too many established customs.

O'Neill was beginning his Speakership in 1977 in the wake of numerous scandals involving House financial practices. He chose Obey, who was tough, resourceful, and interested in the issue, to head a 15-member commission to draft new rules. The commission ultimately recommended strict disclosure of personal finances, a limit on gifts, honoraria and outside income, a ban on the use of campaign funds to pay off private debts, and an end to unofficial, privately financed, office accounts.

The most controversial recommendation limited outside earned income to 15 percent of a member's salary. Obey's relentless style and the Speaker's commitment got the package through. But when Obey returned in late 1977 with a second set of proposals to restructure administration of the House, he lost, partly because of a backlash against his tough tactics on the ethics code.

While doing all this, Obey has been a dominant influence on his Foreign Operations Appropriations Subcommittee. The chairman of the subcommittee, Democrat Clarence Long of Maryland, has only grudgingly supported multilateral aid through international lending institutions. In some recent years, Obey has simply shoved Long aside and led the fight himself for aid requested by the Carter administration and the House leadership. He has not always been successful; Republicans have managed to win passage of amendments slashing funds for the World Bank and other multilateral lenders.

On his other Appropriations subcommittee, Labor, Health and Human Services, Obey has played a different role. Most of his Democratic colleagues there favor as much spending as possible for social welfare programs, and Obey has served as a broker between them and the panel's more conservative chairman, William Natcher, D-Ky.

Obey is insistent about his belief that economic interests are buying Congress through campaign contributions. For years during the 1970s, he fought for public financing of congressional campaigns. In 1979, after a bill for partial public financing died in the House Administration Committee, Obey combined with Republican Tom Railsback of Illinois to win support for separate legislation limiting the amount a candidate can receive from political action committees. It passed

the House, but died in the Senate.

**At Home:** More than a decade ago, when the *Wall Street Journal* wanted to write about the advantages of incumbency, it sent a reporter to Obey's district, confident that he would be watching an expert. The young Democrat had been in office only a few months at the time, but his techniques were already bearing fruit. He was sending out free government publications, writing columns for local newspapers and flooding the district with newsletters, even though he admitted in one that "there hasn't been that much to talk about yet."

Obey knew that if he did not make a strong personal impression with the voters, they would return him to his Wausau real estate business. Chosen in a 1969 special election to succeed Melvin R. Laird, who had become secretary of defense, Obey was the first Democrat ever to represent the 7th District.

When Laird's seat had opened up, Obey was beginning his fourth term in the state Assembly, where he had been since he was 24. The Republican candidate, state Sen. Walter Chilsen, was a well-known former newscaster who called himself a "Laird Republican." He tried to make student violence a campaign theme. But Obey deflected that issue. He focused on discontent with the Nixon administration's low milk support prices, and on the unpopular fiscal policies of GOP Gov. Warren Knowles, to whom Chilsen was loyal.

The changed mood in rural Wisconsin farming areas turned what had been a 44,000 vote plurality for Laird in November 1968 into a 4,055-vote margin for Obey just five months later.

Obey's 1970 re-election opponent, Andre LeTendre, was a favorite of national Republicans interested in recapturing the seat. But a series of unsuccessful business dealings made him a weak candidate locally, and he got a late start. Obey won re-election by 47,000 votes — a margin Laird exceeded only twice in his career.

In 1972, redistricting placed Obey in the same district with Alvin E. O'Konski, a 30-year House veteran who was twice his age. The new district was marginally Democratic, and had more of Obey's old constituents than O'Konski's. The Republican agonized for months over whether he should retire or fight Obey. He finally decided to retire in July, only to discover it was too late to have his name removed from the ballot.

A few months later, Obey finished the job on O'Konski. The Democrat won 70 percent in the area he had previously represented — enough by itself to defeat O'Konski — and even outpolled him in the counties O'Konski had represented for years.

**The District:** The fluctuating moods of Wisconsin's dairymen and other small farmers often determine the political performance of the 7th District. Although the district supported Carter in 1976, it turned against him four years later, in a reversal of the shift that elected Obey in 1969 after years of Republican rule.

The southern part of the district is devoted largely to dairy farming, although paper mills are important and there is a considerable white-collar labor force in the insurance industry. Most of the residents are of German descent, and fairly conservative in their outlook. Around Stevens Point there is a large Polish community. A major branch of the state university is also located at Stevens Point, making it one of the most Democratic parts of the district.

To the north are mining and lumbering areas. The four counties along the shore of Lake Superior share the same solid Democratic traditions found in Minnesota's Iron Range or in the nearby western end of Michigan's Upper Peninsula.

## Committees

**Appropriations** (8th of 33 Democrats)
Foreign Operations; Labor-HHS; Treasury-Postal Service.

**Budget**
Task Forces: Economic Policy and Productivity, Chairman.

## Elections

**1980 General**

| | |
|---|---|
| David Obey (D) | 164,340 (65%) |
| Vinton Vesta (R) | 89,745 (35%) |

**1978 General**

| | |
|---|---|
| David Obey (D) | 110,874 (62%) |
| Vinton Vesta (R) | 65,750 (37%) |

**Previous Winning Percentages**

1976 (73%)    1974 (71%)    1972 (63%)    1970 (68%)
1969* (52%)

*Special election.*

**District Vote For President**

| | 1980 | | 1976 | | 1972 |
|---|---|---|---|---|---|
| D | 124,011 (46%) | D | 134,210 (55%) | D | 98,230 (45%) |
| R | 125,451 (46%) | R | 105,666 (43%) | R | 110,826 (51%) |
| I | 16,805 (6%) | | | | |

## Campaign Finance

| | Receipts | Percent of Receipts from PACs | Expenditures |
|---|---|---|---|
| **1980** | | | |
| Obey (D) | $156,095 | $58,195 (37%) | $134,287 |
| Vesta (R) | $39,803 | $650 (2%) | $38,835 |
| **1978** | | | |
| Obey (D) | $60,248 | $31,700 (53%) | $53,463 |
| Vesta (R) | $13,477 | $100 (1%) | $13,403 |

## Voting Studies

| | Presidential Support | | Party Unity | | Conservative Coalition | |
|---|---|---|---|---|---|---|
| Year | S | O | S | O | S | O |
| 1980 | 82 | 14 | 88 | 7 | 7 | 86 |
| 1979 | 73 | 22 | 87 | 7 | 9 | 86 |
| 1978 | 86 | 14 | 88 | 9 | 13 | 85 |
| 1977 | 73 | 20 | 89 | 8 | 17 | 79 |
| 1976 | 25 | 71 | 86 | 10 | 15 | 80 |
| 1975 | 43 | 57 | 87 | 11 | 17 | 81 |
| 1974 (Ford) | 59 | 41 | | | | |
| 1974 | 43 | 51 | 81 | 16 | 13 | 86 |
| 1973 | 26 | 70 | 85 | 12 | 19 | 77 |
| 1972 | 46 | 49 | 83 | 11 | 12 | 83 |
| 1971 | 33 | 67 | 90 | 7 | 3 | 93 |
| 1970 | 55 | 42 | 72 | 25 | 20 | 77 |
| 1969 | 51 | 49† | 77 | 21† | 19 | 78† |

S = Support          O = Opposition

†*Not eligible for all recorded votes.*

## Key Votes

**96th Congress**

| | |
|---|---|
| Weaken Carter oil profits tax (1979) | N |
| Reject hospital cost control plan (1979) | N |
| Implement Panama Canal Treaties (1979) | Y |
| Establish department of education (1979) | N |
| Approve Anti-busing Amendment (1979) | N |
| Guarantee Chrysler Corp. loans (1979) | Y |
| Approve military draft registration (1980) | N |
| Aid Sandinistas regime in Nicaragua (1980) | Y |
| Strengthen fair housing Laws (1980) | Y |

**97th Congress**

| | |
|---|---|
| Reagan budget proposal (1981) | N |

## Interest Group Ratings

| Year | ADA | ACA | AFL-CIO | CCUS |
|---|---|---|---|---|
| 1980 | 94 | 21 | 75 | 58 |
| 1979 | 89 | 9 | 95 | 0 |
| 1978 | 60 | 22 | 80 | 22 |
| 1977 | 85 | 0 | 76 | 33 |
| 1976 | 90 | 12 | 77 | 19 |
| 1975 | 100 | 25 | 87 | 6 |
| 1974 | 87 | 7 | 91 | 30 |
| 1973 | 96 | 19 | 70 | 36 |
| 1972 | 100 | 0 | 100 | 0 |
| 1971 | 86 | 14 | 83 | — |
| 1970 | 84 | 33 | 86 | 20 |
| 1969* | 92 | 20 | 100 | — |

* *Did not serve for entire period covered by group ratings.*

# 8 Toby Roth (R)

**Of Appleton — Elected 1978**

**Born:** Oct. 10, 1938, Strasburg, N.D.
**Education:** Marquette U., B.A. 1961.
**Military Career:** Army Reserve, 1962-69.
**Profession:** Real estate broker.
**Family:** Wife, Barbara Fischer; three children.
**Religion:** Roman Catholic.
**Political Career:** Wis. Assembly, 1973-79.

**In Washington:** Roth spent his first term building his congressional office into a potent re-election machine, and it performed admirably for him in November of 1980, bringing him a second term with nearly 70 percent of the vote. It also dominated his time, leaving him a secondary role on two minor committees, Small Business and Science and Technology. In his second term, he moved on to Foreign Affairs.

When reporters for *The Milwaukee Journal* visited Roth's office after one year, they found it mailing thousands of newspaper clippings a month to constituents whose names had appeared in local Wisconsin papers, and sending out photographs of the congressman being designated GOP "freshman of the month." "Congratulations on bagging your first deer," he wrote one woman. "I'm sure it was a great experience."

That style is not unusual for junior House members, although Roth's use of it exceeds the average, and Roth defended his approach as the oldest form of political representation. "I feel you've got to stay in touch," he said, "and there are only so many avenues you have.... You have to let the people know you're still alive."

Most of Roth's legislative work has had a clear district orientation. When the Interior Committee reported out a bill to regulate the placement of nuclear waste disposal sites, Roth threatened to object to its consideration on the floor under unanimous consent. His district contains several potential sites.

When the bill was brought up under regular procedures, he backed an amendment allowing states to veto proposed sites, and requiring a vote of both houses of Congress to overturn the veto. "The Department of Energy has been playing a real cat-and-mouse game with Wisconsin," Roth said. "Our citizens are very upset and intimidated." The amendment was defeated.

On other issues, Roth's rhetoric clearly marked him as a member of the younger and more militant Republican right. "It is time to get the freeloaders off the welfare rolls," he said in 1979. "There are many individuals receiving welfare and food stamps, in particular, who are just taking the American taxpayer for a ride."

On another occasion, he called for new legislation imposing mandatory sentences with no parole for some violent crimes. "With crime up 11 percent last year," he said, "our laws clearly do not go far enough." He introduced his own mandatory sentencing bill in 1979.

**At Home:** Roth got to the House the same way he has worked to stay there: by assembling a large and efficient volunteer organization and shaking thousands of hands. After two elections, it appears Roth has a firm grip on the district.

In 1978, when Roth decided to challenge vulnerable Democratic Rep. Robert J. Cornell, many GOP leaders were wary. He was not from Green Bay, the political center of the district. And while Roth's eager-beaver campaign style had worked well in Appleton, party veterans thought he might seem overbearing in a broader campaign against Cornell. They were wrong.

Cornell, a Roman Catholic priest, never relished running for office the way Roth does. He spent his time giving wooden campaign speeches while Roth was out at shopping centers shaking hands. In the last two weeks of the campaign, Roth claims he shook 63,000 hands. But the challenger's volunteer organization and spending advantage were probably more important. Roth outspent Cornell, $202,000-to-$72,000.

---

**8th District: Northeast — Green Bay, Appleton.** Population: 547,408 (12% increase since 1970). Race: White 533,153 (97%), Black 746 (0.1%), Others 13,509 (2%). Spanish origin: 2,492 (0.4%).

Whatever the reason, the Democrat carried only four small counties, losing both Brown and Outagamie (Green Bay and Appleton).

Two years later Roth faced former Green Bay Mayor Michael Monfils, and used the same approach. He won by an even larger margin.

**The District:** More than half of the vote in this 14-county district is in the Fox River Valley. Running the 30 miles from Appleton to Green Bay, the valley is more German and more Catholic than the industrial areas along Lake Michigan. It has made the 8th a generally Republican district.

The economy of the Fox River Valley, and the vast wooded area to the north, depends on trees and paper. In the southern, less urbanized counties and along the scenic Door County peninsula, farming is the major pursuit, with apples and cherries principal crops.

## Committees

**Foreign Affairs** (13th of 16 Republicans)
Europe and the Middle East; International Operations.

## Elections

**1980 General**

| | |
|---|---|
| Toby Roth (R) | 169,664 (68%) |
| Michael Monfils (D) | 81,043 (32%) |

**1978 General**

| | |
|---|---|
| Toby Roth (R) | 101,856 (58%) |
| Robert Cornell (D) | 73,925 (42%) |

**1978 Primary**

| | |
|---|---|
| Toby Roth (R) | 29,782 (69%) |
| Donald Haeft (R) | 13,280 (31%) |

**District Vote For President**

| | 1980 | | 1976 | | 1972 |
|---|---|---|---|---|---|
| D | 96,188 (37%) | D | 105,904 (45%) | D | 76,912 (37%) |
| R | 146,595 (56%) | R | 122,174 (52%) | R | 122,622 (60%) |
| I | 15,293 (6%) | | | | |

## Campaign Finance

| | Receipts | Receipts from PACs | Expenditures |
|---|---|---|---|
| **1980** | | | |
| Roth (R) | $151,511 | $73,894 (49%) | $144,146 |
| Monfils (D) | $23,955 | $2,300 (10%) | $20,233 |

| **1978** | | | |
|---|---|---|---|
| Roth (R) | $203,921 | $73,577 (36%) | $202,021 |
| Cornell (D) | $59,612 | $27,221 (46%) | $72,202 |

## Voting Studies

| | Presidental Support | | Party Unity | | Conservative Coalition | |
|---|---|---|---|---|---|---|
| Year | S | O | S | O | S | O |
| 1980 | 37 | 60 | 89 | 7 | 82 | 13 |
| 1979 | 26 | 68 | 88 | 8 | 92 | 6 |

S = Support          O = Opposition

## Key Votes

**96th Congress**

| | |
|---|---|
| Weaken Carter oil profits tax (1979) | Y |
| Reject hospital cost control plan (1979) | Y |
| Implement Panama Canal Treaties (1979) | N |
| Establish Department of Education (1979) | N |
| Approve Anti-busing Amendment (1979) | Y |
| Guarantee Chrysler Corp. loans (1979) | N |
| Approve military draft registration (1980) | N |
| Aid Sandinista regime in Nicaragua (1980) | N |
| Strengthen fair housing laws (1980) | N |

**97th Congress**

| | |
|---|---|
| Reagan budget proposal (1981) | Y |

## Interest Group Ratings

| Year | ADA | ACA | AFL-CIO | CCUS |
|---|---|---|---|---|
| 1980 | 22 | 75 | 11 | 67 |
| 1979 | 16 | 96 | 21 | 78 |

# 9 F. James Sensenbrenner Jr. (R)

**Of Shorewood — Elected 1978**

**Born:** June 14, 1943, Chicago, Ill.
**Education:** Stanford U., A.B. 1965; U. of Wis.
Law School, J.D. 1968.
**Profession:** Lawyer.
**Family:** Wife, Cheryl Warren.
**Religion:** Episcopalian.
**Political Career:** Wis. Assembly, 1969-75; Wis.
Senate, 1975-79.

**In Washington:** Sensenbrenner's stiff posture, nasal voice and penchant for arguing over detail give him a reputation among some colleagues as something of a stuffed-shirt. But if he appears to be pompous he is also a well-informed legislator. By the middle of his first term he had mastered procedures well enough to pose problems for the majority across the aisle.

As a freshman, he was appointed an official Republican "objector," charged with speaking for other party members who oppose certain minor bills. He expanded his territory, objecting to a raft of Democratic procedural moves both on the floor and in the Judiciary Committee.

One procedure he objected to was proxy voting in committee. When Judiciary tried to mark up a new federal criminal code, allowing absent members to vote by proxy as they usually do, Sensenbrenner insisted that large portions of the 476-page bill be read line by line. He relented only after being promised that amendments approved on proxies could be reconsidered later on.

Sensenbrenner played his objector's role with great success on the House floor when the Judiciary Committee brought out a bill offering federal money to help judges around the country reform their bail procedures. The Wisconsin freshman was the only member there to oppose the bill as it came up. But he had done his homework. The bill needed two-thirds for passage under "suspension of the rules," and Sensenbrenner produced 155 "no" votes to block its passage.

Sensenbrenner drew more votes, but was less successful, on an amendment to weaken a 1980 open housing bill. As reported by Judiciary, the bill would have allowed the federal government new power to issue cease-and-desist orders in suspected discrimination cases.

Along with Missouri Democrat Harold Volkmer, Sensenbrenner tried to rewrite it on the floor to require complainants to take action in federal court, much as under current law. But they lost by one vote, as House leaders twisted enough arms to assure passage of a minor revision in the bill and head off Sensenbrenner's challenge. In the end, the bill died in the Senate.

Another Sensenbrenner target was the Law Enforcement Assistance Administration, whose role was redefined by the Judiciary Committee in 1979 legislation. Sensenbrenner tried repeatedly to cut back on money for LEAA grants, then cast one of 54 votes against continuing the agency at all.

Sensenbrenner performed with his customary diligence and thoroughness during a term on the ethics committee, in which he generally took a hard-line attitude on cases of misconduct but avoided the grandstanding with which Republicans on the panel have sometimes been associated.

**At Home:** Sensenbrenner has held public office ever since his graduation from law school. Despite his reputation for pomposity, his personal resources and conservative views have helped him win eight victories without a defeat.

Sensenbrenner is an heir to a paper and cellulose manufacturing fortune, most of which stems from his great grandfather's invention of the sanitary napkin shortly after World War I. Marketing it under the brand name Kotex, Sensenbrenner's ancestor went on to become

---

**9th District: Milwaukee suburbs.**
Population: 578,629 (18% increase since 1970).
Race: White 569,402 (98%), Black 2,902 (1%),
Others 6,325 (1%). Spanish origin: 6,390 (1%).

chairman of the board of Kimberly Clark.

To reach Congress in 1978, Sensenbrenner had to dip into family wealth to overcome an unexpectedly strong GOP primary challenge. With Republican Robert W. Kasten Jr. leaving the 9th District to run for governor, Sensenbrenner was viewed as the obvious successor. He had been elected to four terms in the state Assembly, before moving in 1975 to the state Senate, where he quickly rose to be assistant minority leader. He had a solid political base in the older, more affluent lakeside suburbs, and his conservative stance reminded voters of the popular Kasten.

But 26-year-old Susan Shannon Engeleiter put on a strong campaign in the more middle-class western part of the district, which she represented in the state Assembly. More gregarious than Sensenbrenner, she outpolled him by 5,600 votes in the four western counties of the district. Only Sensenbrenner's familiarity in the areas along Lake Michigan — Ozaukee and the most Republican part of Milwaukee — allowed him to win the primary by 589 votes.

The Democratic nominee, Milwaukee lawyer Matthew J. Flynn, was considered one of the stronger candidates the party had fielded in the district. But he could not raise enough money to compete with Sensenbrenner on an equal footing. Sensenbrenner campaigned on his support for cutting taxes and defeated Flynn by consistently solid margins throughout the district.

**The District:** Although the nearby 4th District contains some Milwaukee suburbs, the 9th is Wisconsin's only full-fledged suburban district. Its communities range from the older, exclusive shoreline communities of Whitefish Bay and Fox Point to the more middle-class areas in Waukesha County, west of Milwaukee.

Many of the voters in the western suburbs are transplanted blue-collar workers from Milwaukee. But in the last few elections they have abandoned their Democratic leanings. In 1980, Waukesha County, home of half the district's voters, gave only 36 percent of the vote to Democratic Sen. Gaylord Nelson and just 33 percent to Carter.

## Committees

**Judiciary** (11th of 12 Republicans)
Civil and Constitutional Rights; Criminal Justice.

**Science and Technology** (10th of 17 Republicans)
Energy Development and Applications; Natural Resources, Agriculture Research and Environment.

## Elections

**1980 General**

| | |
|---|---|
| F. James Sensenbrenner Jr.(R) | 206,227 (78%) |
| Gary Benedict (D) | 56,838 (22%) |

**1978 General**

| | |
|---|---|
| F. James Sensenbrenner Jr.(R) | 118,386 (61%) |
| Matthew Flynn (D) | 75,207 (39%) |

**1978 Primary**

| | |
|---|---|
| James Sensenbrenner (R) | 29,584 (43%) |
| Susan Engeleiter (R) | 28,995 (42%) |
| Robert Brunner (R) | 9,746 (14%) |

**District Vote For President**

| 1980 | | 1976 | | 1972 | |
|---|---|---|---|---|---|
| D | 97,580 (34%) | D | 101,663 (39%) | D | 77,762 (36%) |
| R | 167,684 (58%) | R | 152,888 (59%) | R | 131,288 (61%) |
| I | 21,400 (7%) | | | | |

## Campaign Finance

| | | Receipts from PACs | Expenditures |
|---|---|---|---|
| | Receipts | | |
| **1980** | | | |
| Sensenbrenner (R) | $171,131 | $60,965 (36%) | $143,524 |

| | | | |
|---|---|---|---|
| Benedict (D) | $3,090 | $1,250 (40%) | $2,678 |
| **1978** | | | |
| Sensenbrenner (R) | $190,687 | $49,896 (26%) | $197,749 |
| Flynn (D) | $41,853 | $13,150 (31%) | $41,028 |

## Voting Studies

| | Presidential Support | | Party Unity | | Conservative Coalition | |
|---|---|---|---|---|---|---|
| Year | S | O | S | O | S | O |
| 1980 | 32 | 68 | 94 | 5 | 87 | 13 |
| 1979 | 28 | 72 | 91 | 8 | 88 | 11 |

S = Support          O = Opposition

## Key Votes

**96th Congress**

| | |
|---|---|
| Weaken Carter oil profits tax (1979) | Y |
| Reject hospital cost control plan (1979) | Y |
| Implement Panama Canal Treaties (1979) | N |
| Establish Department of Education (1979) | N |
| Approve Anti-busing Amendment (1979) | Y |
| Guarantee Chrysler Corp. loans (1979) | N |
| Approve military draft registration (1980) | N |
| Aid Sandinista regime in Nicaragua (1980) | N |
| Strengthen fair housing laws (1980) | N |

**97th Congress**

| | |
|---|---|
| Reagan budget proposal (1981) | Y |

## Interest Group Ratings

| Year | ADA | ACA | AFL-CIO | CCUS |
|---|---|---|---|---|
| 1980 | 22 | 79 | 5 | 63 |
| 1979 | 16 | 100 | 15 | 83 |

# Wyoming

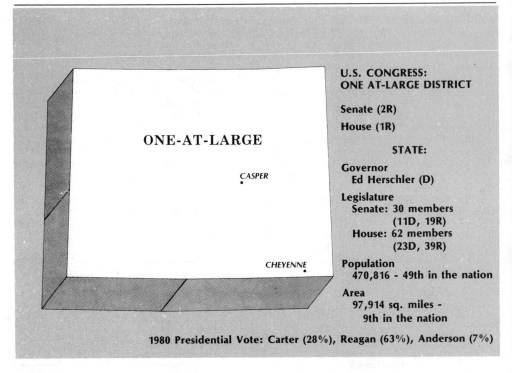

ONE-AT-LARGE

CASPER

CHEYENNE

**U.S. CONGRESS:
ONE AT-LARGE DISTRICT**

Senate (2R)

House (1R)

**STATE:**

Governor
  Ed Herschler (D)

Legislature
  Senate: 30 members
      (11D, 19R)
  House: 62 members
      (23D, 39R)

Population
  470,816 - 49th in the nation

Area
  97,914 sq. miles -
      9th in the nation

1980 Presidential Vote: Carter (28%), Reagan (63%), Anderson (7%)

## ... A Boom on the Range

Milward Simpson, Wyoming's blunt-spoken ex-governor and father of the current junior senator, once proposed a novel solution to the state's problems: build a fence around it and keep everybody else out.

Instead, Wyoming has done just the opposite: turn itself into an energy mecca wracked by development, growth, and social and political change.

The pace of the change has been staggering. Rural, arid, and insular, Wyoming was the slowest-growing state in the nation in the 1960s. In the 1970s, it was the third *fastest*-growing state, behind only Nevada and Arizona.

Credit it to, or blame it on, the energy crisis. Wyoming has oil, coal, natural gas, uranium and oil shale, all in abundance. And the boom has only just begun. Many of the resources have hardly been tapped. But the signs of change are unmistakable.

Wyoming now has nearly half a million residents, up from 332,416 in 1970. Quiet, pleasant cow towns of a decade ago are now crowded, crime-ridden boom towns, where every motel room is booked up and most of the permanent residents live in trailers.

Wyoming seems ambivalent about these changes. It is still a pro-growth state where environmental restrictions are viewed skeptically, but its residents are also leery of having their mountains torn up to provide air conditioning for the cities.

When governors of other coal states expressed their support for relaxed strip mining restrictions, Wyoming's governor, Ed Herschler, opposed them. In 1978, Democrat Herschler was re-elected in large part by proposing an increased mineral severance tax and calling his Republican opponent "a mouthpiece for the mining industry."

# A Political Tour

**Southern Wyoming.** Wyoming was always fairly easy to explain in terms of partisan politics. Democrats were competitive in the five counties along the state's southern border. North of these five — Albany, Carbon, Laramie, Sweetwater and Unita counties — they almost never won, and this made it difficult to succeed statewide.

The Democratic voting tradition in southern Wyoming goes back to the early days of the state when immigrant laborers were imported to build the Union Pacific rail line through those southern counties. The state's first coal miners followed. Many of these people were Italian immigrants; others were Oriental. Like their counterparts in other states, most of the workingmen were drawn into the Democratic Party.

Although this remains the most Democratic area in the state, today its residents are conservative on most issues and in recent years have often been siding with Republicans. Reagan easily carried all five southern counties in 1980.

The few Democrats who have won statewide in recent years — notably former Sen. Gale McGee, former U.S. Rep. Teno Roncalio and Herschler — have done so by restraining the growth of the Republican vote in the south. In 1978, when Herschler was re-elected by less than 2,400 votes statewide, he won the five southern counties by a combined margin of 8,347 votes.

Three of the four largest towns in Wyoming are in this region, including Cheyenne, the state capital, and Laramie. In 1980, slightly more than a third of the state's residents lived here.

Although the northern section as a whole has been gaining population faster than the south, a few areas, particularly Sweetwater County in the southwest, more than doubled in population during the 1970s boom. Rock Springs, an energy boom town that is the county seat, is the state's most important single source of Democratic votes.

**Northern Wyoming.** This is the Wyoming of ranch and rock. Its dry plateaus and basins accommodate the cattle ranches that make Wyoming the "Cowboy State." The mountains and valleys contain most of the state's mineral wealth.

It is conservative country that Republicans have carried in nearly every election. Ranching interests have traditionally dominated it. The population boom and gradual shift from ranching to mineral development have changed the power structure in some of these counties, but they have done little to shake the region's Republican voting habits. Converse County, the fastest-growing area in the state, gave more than 70 percent of its vote to Reagan in 1980. Over the last 60 years, Nixon in 1972 and Eisenhower in 1956 were the only GOP presidential candidates to top that figure.

Natrona County is the largest in northern Wyoming, and a solid Republican area that almost never backs Democrats. Casper, the county seat, is the state's largest city. A boom town with just over 51,000 people, Casper finally passed Cheyenne, the traditional leader, in 1980. Once mainly a trading center Casper has become the hub of Wyoming's mineral operations.

The population boom is changing the face of northern Wyoming, with new towns and subdivisions sprouting like prairie grass. Nevertheless, the people are still widely scattered. Apart from Casper, Sheridan is still the only town in northern Wyoming with more than 15,000 inhabitants.

# Governor
# Ed Herschler (D)

**Born:** Oct. 27, 1918, Kemmerer, Wyo.
**Home:** Kemmerer, Wyo.
**Education:** U. of Colorado, 1936-41; U. of Wyoming, LL.B. 1949.
**Military Career:** Marine Corps, 1942-45.
**Profession:** Lawyer.
**Family:** Wife, Kathleen; two children.
**Religion:** Episcopalian.
**Political Career:** Lincoln County prosecutor, 1951-59; Wyoming House, 1959-69; unsuccessful campaign for U.S. House nomination, 1970; elected governor 1974, 1978; term expires Jan. 1983.

# Malcolm Wallop (R)

**Of Big Horn — Elected 1976**

**Born:** Feb. 27, 1933, New York, N.Y.
**Education:** Yale U., B.A. 1954.
**Military Career:** Army, 1955-57.
**Profession:** Rancher.
**Family:** Wife, Judith Warren; four children.
**Religion:** Episcopalian.
**Political Career:** Wyo. House, 1969-73; Wyo.
Senate, 1973-77; sought Republican nomina-
tion for Wyo. governor, 1974.

**In Washington:** When Senate Republicans handed out chairmanships in 1981 as the fruits of their newly-won majority, Wallop was left with one of the few sour ones: the Ethics Committee, whose chief responsibilty is to discipline colleagues.

Wallop asked GOP leaders to make the job a little more attractive by including him in meetings of regular committee chairmen, and they agreed. But he did not seem to feel he had won a choice assignment.

On assuming command, Wallop criticized the Senate's ethics code, which the committee had been directed a year earlier to rewrite. "It is bad for the morality of the Senate," he said, "and bad for the public's perception of the Senate." He said he would seek to end the "diddly little rules that serve no public purpose and keep those that do."

Rather than telling senators not to accept gifts, for example, he said senators should merely discose annually every gift they accept. And rather than revealing personal wealth, they should be required to disclose only potential conflicts. Wallop's views prompted Common Cause, the most active outside lobbyist for ethics codes, to try to organize a counterattack with letters and calls of protest from Wallop's constituents. Wallop scaled down some of his original ideas, but not his basic position.

Wallop has plenty to do besides chairing the Ethics Committee. He heads three legislative subcommittees, notably the one at Finance on Energy and Agricultural Taxation. This has general jurisdiction over the oil windfall profits tax that Wallop opposed when it passed in 1979 as part of President Carter's energy program. During the original windfall debate in 1979, Wallop participated in a filibuster against the bill. He now supports efforts to lower the tax. He also is pushing for expansion of tax incentives for industrial energy conservation.

From the Wyoming viewpoint, Wallop's most important chairmanship may be the Public Land and Reserved Water Subcommittee of Energy and Natural Resources. With nearly half of Wyoming's land federally owned, and with water rights a vital issue, Wallop is in a position to keep an eye on every bill that would affect these subjects.

Although he is not on the Armed Services Committee, Wallop has sought a role in defense policy as part of a small group of junior senators who favor anti-missile systems rather than new offensive weapons as a primary nuclear deterrent. In 1981, he sought to add \$250 million to a defense authorization bill for research on lasers that might be used for a satellite-based missile defense. The Armed Services Committee offered \$50 million, which Wallop accepted, and the smaller amount was added by a vote of 91-3. Part of Wallop's approach is related to fears in Wyoming of what the MX offensive missile system might do to Western states if based there.

In his first two years as a senator, Wallop served as the only non-lawyer on the Senate Judiciary Committee. He spent much of his time there working on a bill to deal with kidnapping of children by their parents.

A woman constituent complained to him that her ex-husband had taken their children and fled to South America. Wallop found there was nothing he could do under existing law. So he successfully amended a criminal code bill with a provision to require federal authorities to help track down parents who snatch their own children after they lose custody. But the code bill was never enacted, and Wallop tried for months to attach his language to other, unrelated legislation. Finally, in the closing hours of the 96th Congress, he succeeded. The "child snatch" law was passed as an amendment to a bill providing Medicare reimbursement for pneumonia vaccines.

**At Home:** Wallop's Senate performance has erased differences he had earlier in his career with the more conservative wing of the Wyoming GOP.

Campaigning for the 1974 Republican gubernatorial nomination, Wallop was viewed as a moderate and drew some of his support from voters sympathetic to environmental causes. Coming from far behind, he wound up second among four candidates who finished in a virtual tie, separated by fewer than 1,500 votes.

Interesting as a statistical oddity, this primary was disastrous for Republicans, since all four felt they should have been the winner. When Wallop did not assist the eventual nominee, conservative rancher Dick Jones, many party loyalists were displeased.

But he solved that problem remarkably easily in 1976, campaigning from the right against three-term Democratic Sen. Gale W. McGee. Although oil companies and other business interests were somewhat leery about backing him, Wallop got valuable help from national conservative organizations. He depicted McGee as a proponent of big government and criticized him for not returning often enough to the state.

The challenger's television commercials were especially effective. Wallop saddled up a horse, donned a cowboy hat and urged voters to join the "Wallop Senate drive." He ridiculed environmental regulations by portraying a cowboy forced to hitch a portable toilet to his horse.

The ads helped Wallop overcome a personal background that might have been a problem. Although he was a third-generation Wyoming resident and a ten-year veteran of the state Legislature, he was born in New York City, educated at Yale, and a grandfather once sat in the House of Lords.

If Wallop sticks to a 1976 campaign plank, he will be up in 1982 for his second and final Senate term. He said when elected that all senators should serve a maximum of 12 years.

## Committees

**Energy and Natural Resources** (5th of 11 Republicans)
Public Lands and Reserved Water, chairman; Energy and Mineral Resources; Water and Power.

**Finance** (7th of 11 Republicans)
Energy and Agricultural Taxation, chairman; International Trade; Taxation and Debt Management.

**Select Ethics** (Chairman)

**Select Intelligence** (5th of 8 Republicans)
Budget, chairman; Analysis and Production.

## Elections

**1976 General**

| | |
|---|---|
| Malcolm Wallop (R) | 84,810 (55%) |
| Gale McGee (D) | 70,558 (45%) |

**1976 Primary**

| | |
|---|---|
| Malcolm Wallop (R) | 41,445 (76%) |
| Nels T. Larson (R) | 6,965 (13%) |
| Doyle Henry (R) | 5,727 (11%) |

## Campaign Finance

| | Receipts | Receipts from PACs | Expenditures |
|---|---|---|---|
| **1976** | | | |
| Wallop (R) | $305,161 | $51,560 (17%) | $301,595 |
| McGee (D) | $299,908 | $98,494 (33%) | $181,028 |

## Voting Studies

| | Presidential Support | | Party Unity | | Conservative Coalition | |
|---|---|---|---|---|---|---|
| Year | S | O | S | O | S | O |
| 1980 | 40 | 53 | 80 | 13 | 81 | 15 |
| 1979 | 35 | 60 | 80 | 9 | 82 | 7 |
| 1978 | 30 | 61 | 79 | 11 | 80 | 10 |
| 1977 | 45 | 48 | 84 | 9 | 94 | 3 |

S = Support          O = Opposition

## Key Votes

**96th Congress**

| | |
|---|---|
| Maintain relations with Taiwan (1979) | Y |
| Reduce synthetic fuel development funds (1979) | Y |
| Impose nuclear plant moratorium (1979) | - |
| Kill stronger windfall profits tax (1979) | Y |
| Guarantee Chrysler Corp. loans (1979) | N |
| Approve military draft registration (1980) | Y |
| End Revenue Sharing to the states (1980) | Y |
| Block Justice Dept. busing suits (1980) | Y |

**97th Congress**

| | |
|---|---|
| Restore urban program funding cuts (1981) | N |

## Interest Group Ratings

| Year | ADA | ACA | AFL-CIO | CCUS-1 | CCUS-2 |
|---|---|---|---|---|---|
| 1980 | 22 | 92 | 6 | 95 | |
| 1979 | 11 | 88 | 11 | 82 | 88 |
| 1978 | 10 | 78 | 11 | 80 | |
| 1977 | 0 | 96 | 20 | 94 | |

# Alan K. Simpson (R)

**Of Cody — Elected 1978**

**Born:** Sept. 2, 1931, Denver, Colo.
**Education:** U. of Wyo., B.S.L. 1954, LL.B. 1958.
**Military Career:** Army, 1954-56.
**Profession:** Lawyer.
**Family:** Wife, Ann Schroll; three children.
**Religion:** Episcopalian.
**Political Career:** Cody city attorney and U.S. Commissioner, 1959-69; Wyo. House, 1965-77.

**In Washington:** Simpson had no sooner slipped into the role of Veterans' Affairs chairman in 1981 than he was up on the Senate floor arguing against adding $330 million to the Reagan budget for veterans' programs.

He said it was a tough position to be in. "I probably shall note the sound of muffled drums somewhere on the parade grounds," he said, "as they prepare a ceremony to strip the chevrons from me after I finish these remarks." But he argued that the committee already had agreed to restore $110 million, and that was enough. He won. The amendment lost, 44-56.

If it was startling to see a new chairman fighting for less federal money in his jurisdiction, it was not out of character. Blunt, witty, and utterly individualistic, Simpson began challenging sacred cows the day he got to the Senate.

He had been in office only three weeks when he and another Republican newcomer, Gordon J. Humphrey of New Hampshire, blocked action on a $150 million package of veterans' benefits the Democrats had been working on for seven years. Simpson said he had been elected to fight inflation and "the veterans bill is as good a place as any to start." Chairman Alan Cranston, D-Calif., was forced to fall back and regroup. In the end, a bill was passed but it was trimmed to about $25 million.

Simpson also tried to put a stop to the tradition of placing new federal office buildings in the hometowns of senior members of Congress without even debating the issue. According to a 1959 law, all a congressman had to do was ask for a "study" of a new building, and the General Services Administration (GSA) would request one. Then the Public Works Committee could order it built.

Simpson stepped in one day in 1980 as his Public Works panel was conferring with its House counterpart on a bill dealing with GSA finances. He could not keep still. "Here's one old cowboy that is just tired of the old crap," he said, "This House committee has ordered up projects that are near and dear to it ... it's a ghastly way to do business."

Senate colleagues, visibly uncomfortable at Simpson's bluntness, nevertheless agreed with his argument and the conference broke up in disagreement. The bill died. The Senate took up the 1959 law in a separate bill in 1981 and voted 93-0 to repeal it.

Later, in a fuss with former Interior Secretary Cecil Andrus over a government ban on a poison used by ranchers to kill coyotes, Simpson phoned Andrus' office and said, "Let me talk to that sheep-killing bastard."

When Simpson's friends are startled at his language, he explains he is merely representing the orneriness of his Wyoming constituents. He strides through life with a perpetual half smile and says he is determined not to take himself or the Senate very seriously. "I'm trying to be the same person I've always been," he says, "and see how it works in the Senate."

Now, as chairman of the Veterans' Affairs Committee and of two other subcommittees, Simpson is in a position to play a central role in some areas that he touched only lightly in his first term.

As a freshman member of the Environment Committee, one generally sympathetic to the cause of nuclear power, Simpson fought to hold the line against efforts to slow down nuclear plant construction. Now he is chairman of the Environment Subcommittee on Nuclear Regulation, with authority to oversee the entire industry. His views could place him in conflict with the counterpart subcommittee at House Interior, which is much more skeptical toward nuclear power.

He also has charge of the Judiciary Subcommittee responsible for trying to bring some order to the chaos of U.S. immigration policy. In the 96th Congress, he served on a special presidential commission studying refugee laws, and concluded that U.S. policy is "sterile and ineffective." By mid-1981, Simpson was working on a legislative package that included proposals to expand the border patrol, penalize employers who hire illegal aliens, provide amnesty for the six million illegal aliens believed to be living in the U.S., and establish some kind of national identity card for legal immigrants.

Simpson has been a consistent conservative vote on Judiciary. He has differed with committee Democrats by arguing for easier federal prosecution of labor extortion cases, trying to soften enforcement provisions in an open housing bill, and calling for more lenient guidelines for the FBI in using informants and wiretaps.

**At Home:** The Simpsons of Wyoming have developed campaign talents that make them difficult to defeat. Like his father Milward, a former governor and U.S. senator who still practices law in Cody, Alan Simpson is at his best running an old-fashioned personal campaign, trading ranch talk and old jokes.

His friendliness was an enormous asset during his 1978 Senate campaign, in which more militant conservatives tried to persuade voters that Simpson was not really one of them.

He had spent 12 years in the state Legislature, serving at various times as chairman of the House Judiciary Committee, majority whip and majority floor leader. Had he not run for the U.S. Senate seat vacated by GOP veteran Clifford P. Hansen, he would have been Speaker of the Wyoming House.

As a state legislator, Simpson had been active in the drafting of a state land use planning law. His opponent, eccentric oilman Hugh "Bigfoot" Binford, invested in a media campaign charging that Simpson had undermined local control of land decisions. He also said Simpson was shaky in his support of state right-to-work laws.

At first ignoring the assault, Simpson eventually had to take it seriously, calling a news conference to accuse "Bigfoot" of distortion and insist he wanted to preserve local control. In the end, however, his personal acquaintance with thousands of the state's voters was probably enough to guarantee him nomination. He drew 54 percent of the vote in the primary, and coasted in November against a liberal Democratic lawyer, Raymond B. Whitaker.

## Committees

**Environment and Public Works** (5th of 9 Republicans)
Nuclear Regulation, chairman; Environmental Pollution; Toxic Substances and Environmental Oversight.

**Judiciary** (6th of 10 Republicans)
Immigration and Refugee Policy, chairman; Courts; Regulatory Reform.

**Veterans' Affairs** (Chairman)

## Elections

**1978 General**

| | |
|---|---|
| Alan Simpson (R) | 82,908 (62%) |
| Raymond Whitaker (D) | 50,456 (38%) |

**1978 Primary**

| | |
|---|---|
| Alan Simpson (R) | 37,332 (55%) |
| Hugh Binford (R) | 20,768 (30%) |
| Gordon Barrows (R) | 8,494 (12%) |

## Campaign Finance

| | Receipts | Receipts from PACs | Expenditures |
|---|---|---|---|
| **1978** | | | |
| Simpson (R) | $442,484 | $124,385 (28%) | $439,805 |
| Whitaker (D) | $143,051 | — (0%) | $143,749 |

## Voting Studies

| | Presidential Support | | Party Unity | | Conservative Coalition | |
|---|---|---|---|---|---|---|
| Year | S | O | S | O | S | O |
| 1980 | 47 | 44 | 80 | 8 | 78 | 11 |
| 1979 | 37 | 61 | 85 | 9 | 77 | 12 |

S = Support          O = Opposition

## Key Votes

**96th Congress**

| | |
|---|---|
| Maintain relations with Taiwan (1979) | Y |
| Reduce synthetic fuel development funds (1979) | Y |
| Impose nuclear plant moratorium (1979) | N |
| Kill stronger windfall profits tax (1979) | Y |
| Guarantee Chrysler Corp. loans (1979) | N |
| Approve military draft registration (1980) | Y |
| End Revenue Sharing to the states (1980) | Y |
| Block Justice Dept. busing suits (1980) | Y |

**97th Congress**

| | |
|---|---|
| Restore urban program funding cuts (1981) | N |

## Interest Group Ratings

| Year | ADA | ACA | AFL-CIO | CCUS-1 | CCUS-2 |
|---|---|---|---|---|---|
| 1980 | 17 | 91 | 6 | 88 | |
| 1979 | 11 | 81 | 0 | 90 | 100 |

# AL Dick Cheney (R)

**Of Casper — Elected 1978**

**Born:** Jan. 30, 1941, Lincoln, Neb.
**Education:** U. of Wyo., B.A. 1965; M.A. 1966.
**Profession:** Financial consultant.
**Family:** Wife, Lynne Vincent; two children.
**Religion:** Methodist.
**Political Career:** No previous office.

**In Washington:** Cheney's two years as President Ford's White House chief of staff made him something more than an ordinary freshman in 1979, and he took advantage of his reputation to play an insider's role among House Republicans throughout his first term.

By the end of that term, he was eager for a formal leadership position, even if it seemed a bit forward by traditional House standards, and announced his candidacy for the GOP policy chairmanship against Maryland Rep. Marjorie S. Holt.

Cheney seemed a decided underdog at first; Holt had already been running for several months, and was a recognized budget expert. But Cheney took advantage of the aloof reputation she had among some colleagues, her acknowledged interest in a 1982 Senate campaign and the huge bloc of junior members who wanted representation in the leadership. He defeated her, 99-68.

Cheney has managed to build an image as a pragmatic conservative, one who votes Wyoming's anti-government sentiments but negotiates with the other side on a friendly basis. When a group of Democrats led by Missouri's Richard Bolling decided to launch a bipartisan breakfast group to explore the common frustrations of House membership, Cheney was one of the first Republicans invited.

The conciliatory approach worked for him on the Interior Committee, to which he devoted much of his first-term attention. One of his interests was a historic preservation bill offering federal money to include new buildings in the National Register of Historic Places. Cheney complained that buildings should not be added to the register without the owner's permission. He threatened to hold up action on the bill at the end of the 96th Congress, but ultimately negotiated a deal that added the consent language he wanted and allowed the bill to become law.

He was less conciliatory toward the new Energy Mobilization Board President Carter wanted to create to speed up the approval of priority energy projects. That board was a sensitive issue all over the Rocky Mountain West, which feared it would override existing state law and clear the way for projects depriving the region of scarce water.

Cheney fought the board both in committee and on the floor. Managers of the legislation accepted his floor amendment blocking the board from overriding any existing state law regulating water rights. But most Westerners still found the idea dangerous and when the issue came back to the House as a conference report, Cheney joined the majority that killed the legislation outright.

Cheney also served a term on the House ethics committee, investigating the kickback case of Rep. Charles C. Diggs Jr., and the Abscam bribery charges.

More restrained than many junior Republicans, he refused to vote with a majority of them to expel Diggs at the start of the 96th Congress, after he had been convicted in federal court. When the ethics committee later recommended Diggs's censure rather than expulsion, Cheney argued the case for it on the floor, saying expulsion would deprive his constituents of their right to representation. On Abscam, he backed the committee's decision to expel Rep. Michael "Ozzie" Myers after viewing tapes of him accepting bribes from an FBI agent.

Meanwhile, Cheney was dabbling in national

> **At-Large District: Entire State.** Population: 470,816 (42% increase since 1970). Race: White 447,716 (95%), Black 3,364 (1%), Others 19,736 (4%). Spanish origin: 24,499 (5%).

politics, consulting with former boss Gerald R. Ford about whether Ford should try a second campaign for the White House in 1980. At the Republican convention in Detroit, Cheney was one of those closeted with Ford as the former president pondered whether to accept a place on Ronald Reagan's Republican ticket.

Throughout the year, Cheney retained some of his emotional loyalties from the 1976 campaign, when he was defending Ford against Reagan's challenge. Although his record matched Reagan's views on most issues, he was not one of the Californian's most enthusiastic early supporters.

**At Home:** Cheney grew up in Wyoming, but his long absence from the state while he worked in national politics subjected him to carpetbagging charges during his 1978 House campaign. He countered with literature stressing his local roots and education, and effectively played to home state pride in a Wyomingite who had served at the top in Washington.

The future of Cheney's congressional career was placed in doubt during the summer of 1978, when he suffered a mild heart attack. But he recovered quickly enough to resume a full schedule of campaigning for his party's nomination against popular state Treasurer Ed Witzenburger, who stressed that he had been a Reagan man in 1976 — the popular choice in Wyoming — while Cheney had been working for Ford. Cheney beat Witzenburger by 7,705 votes, and the general election was no contest. He won again in a landslide in 1980.

Cheney was a political science graduate student in the late 1960s when he came to Washington on a fellowship. He stayed to take a job under Donald J. Rumsfeld at the Office of Economic Opportunity, followed Rumsfeld to the Ford White House, and replaced his mentor as White House chief of staff in 1975. Cheney shared some of Rumsfeld's moderate Republican reputation during his Washington years, but he is entrenched in Wyoming now as a clear-cut Mountain conservative.

## Committees

**Interior and Insular Affairs** (7th of 17 Republicans)
Energy and the Environment; Public Lands and National Parks.

## Elections

**1980 General**

| | |
|---|---|
| Dick Cheney (R) | 116,361 (69 %) |
| Jim Rogers (D) | 53,338 (31 %) |

**1978 General**

| | |
|---|---|
| Dick Cheney (R) | 75,855 (59 %) |
| Bill Bagley (D) | 53,522 (41 %) |

**1978 Primary**

| | |
|---|---|
| Dick Cheney (R) | 28,568 (42 %) |
| Ed Witzenburger (R) | 20,863 (31 %) |
| Jack Gage (R) | 18,075 (27 %) |

**District Vote For President**

| | 1980 | | 1976 | | 1972 |
|---|---|---|---|---|---|
| D | 49,427 (28 %) | D | 62,239 (40 %) | D | 44,358 (31 %) |
| R | 110,700 (63 %) | R | 92,717 (59 %) | R | 100,464 (69 %) |
| I | 12,072 (7 %) | | | | |

## Campaign Finance

| | Receipts | Receipts from PACs | Expenditures |
|---|---|---|---|
| **1980** | | | |
| Cheney (R) | $110,949 | $65,360 (59 %) | $97,959 |
| Rogers (D) | $9,814 | $1,150 (12 %) | $8,854 |

| **1978** | | | |
|---|---|---|---|
| Cheney (R) | $220,865 | $64,900 (29 %) | $209,064 |
| Bill Bagley (D) | $175,300 | $13,100 (7 %) | $175,297 |

## Voting Studies

| | Presidential Support | | Party Unity | | Conservative Coalition | |
|---|---|---|---|---|---|---|
| **Year** | **S** | **O** | **S** | **O** | **S** | **O** |
| 1980 | 38 | 53 | 83 | 10 | 83 | 11 |
| 1979 | 30 | 66 | 86 | 8 | 85 | 6 |

S = Support          O = Opposition

## Key Votes

**96th Congress**

| | |
|---|---|
| Weaken Carter oil profits tax (1979) | Y |
| Reject hospital cost control plan (1979) | Y |
| Implement Panama Canal Treaties (1979) | N |
| Establish Department of Education (1979) | N |
| Approve Anti-busing Amendment (1979) | Y |
| Guarantee Chrysler Corp. loans (1979) | N |
| Approve military draft registration (1980) | Y |
| Aid Sandinista regime in Nicaragua (1980) | Y |
| Strengthen fair housing laws (1980) | N |

**97th Congress**

| | |
|---|---|
| Reagan budget proposal (1981) | Y |

## Interest Group Ratings

| Year | ADA | ACA | AFL-CIO | CCUS |
|---|---|---|---|---|
| 1980 | 6 | 95 | 11 | 70 |
| 1979 | 11 | 100 | 11 | 94 |

# Senate Committees, 97th Congress

The standing and select committees of the U.S. Senate are listed below in alphabetical order. The listing includes the room number, zip code, telephone number, and party ratio for each full committee. The telephone area code for Washington is 202.

Members of the majority party, Republicans, are shown in Roman type; members of the minority party, Democrats, are shown in italic type. Membership is given in order of seniority on the committee.

The word "vacancy" indicates that a committee seat had not been filled by July 1, 1981. The word "vacancy" appears for each unfilled seat as of that date.

## Agriculture, Nutrition and Forestry

*322 RSOB 20510; 224-2035*

*R 9 - D 8*

Jesse Helms, R-N.C., chairman

| | |
|---|---|
| Robert Dole, Kan. | *Walter D. Huddleston, Ky.* |
| S. I. "Sam" Hayakawa, Calif. | *Patrick J. Leahy, Vt.* |
| Richard G. Lugar, Ind. | *Edward Zorinsky, Neb.* |
| Thad Cochran, Miss. | *John Melcher, Mont.* |
| Rudy Boschwitz, Minn. | *David Pryor, Ark.* |
| Roger W. Jepsen, Iowa | *David L. Boren, Okla.* |
| Paula Hawkins, Fla. | *Alan J. Dixon, Ill.* |
| Mark Andrews, N.D. | *Howell Heflin, Ala.* |

## Appropriations

*S128 CAP 20510; 224-3471*

*R 15 - D 14*

Mark O. Hatfield, R-Ore., chairman

| | |
|---|---|
| Ted Stevens, Alaska | *William Proxmire, Wis.* |
| Lowell P. Weicker Jr., Conn. | *John C. Stennis, Miss.* |
| James A. McClure, Idaho | *Robert C. Byrd, W.Va.* |
| Paul Laxalt, Nev. | *Daniel K. Inouye, Hawaii* |
| Jake Garn, Utah | *Ernest F. Hollings, S.C.* |
| Harrison "Jack" Schmitt, N.M. | *Thomas F. Eagleton, Mo.* |
| Thad Cochran, Miss. | *Lawton Chiles, Fla.* |
| | *J. Bennett Johnston, La.* |

| | |
|---|---|
| Mark Andrews, N.D. | *Walter D. Huddleston, Ky.* |
| James Abdnor, S.D. | *Quentin N. Burdick, N.D.* |
| Robert W. Kasten Jr., Wis. | *Patrick J. Leahy, Vt.* |
| Alfonse D'Amato, N.Y. | *Jim Sasser, Tenn.* |
| Mack Mattingly, Ga. | *Dennis DeConcini, Ariz.* |
| Warren B. Rudman, N.H. | *Dale Bumpers, Ark.* |
| Arlen Specter, Pa. | |

## Armed Services

*212 RSOB 20510; 224-3871*

*R 9 - D 8*

John Tower, R-Texas, chairman

| | |
|---|---|
| Strom Thurmond, S.C. | *John C. Stennis, Miss.* |
| Barry Goldwater, Ariz. | *Henry M. Jackson, Wash.* |
| John W. Warner, Va. | *Howard W. Cannon, Nev.* |
| Gordon J. Humphrey, N.H. | *Harry F. Byrd Jr., Va.* |
| William S. Cohen, Maine | *Sam Nunn, Ga.* |
| Roger W. Jepsen, Iowa | *Gary Hart, Colo.* |
| Dan Quayle, Ind. | *J. James Exon, Neb.* |
| Jeremiah Denton, Ala. | *Carl Levin, Mich.* |

## Banking, Housing and Urban Affairs

*5300 DSOB 20510; 224-7391*

*R 8 - D 7*

Jake Garn, R-Utah, chairman

| | |
|---|---|
| John Tower, Texas | *Harrison A. Williams Jr.,* |
| John Heinz, Pa. | *William Proxmire, Wis.* |

## Senate Committees

William L. Armstrong, Colo.
Richard G. Lugar, Ind.
Alfonse D'Amato, N.Y.
John H. Chafee, R.I.
Harrison "Jack" Schmitt, N.M.

Alan Cranston, Calif.
Donald W. Riegle Jr., Mich.
Paul S. Sarbanes, Md.
Christopher J. Dodd, Conn.
Alan J. Dixon, Ill.

## Budget

203 Carroll Arms
301 First St. N.E. 20510; 224-0642

R 12 - D 10

Pete V. Domenici, R-N.M., chairman

William L. Armstrong, Colo.
Nancy Landon Kassebaum, Kan.
Rudy Boschwitz, Minn.
Orrin G. Hatch, Utah
John Tower, Texas
Mark Andrews, N.D.
Steven D. Symms, Idaho
Charles E. Grassley, Iowa
Robert W. Kasten Jr., Wis.
Dan Quayle, Ind.
Slade Gorton, Wash.

Ernest F. Hollings, S.C.
Lawton Chiles, Fla.
Joseph R. Biden Jr., Del.
J. Bennett Johnston, La.
Jim Sasser, Tenn.
Gary Hart, Colo.
Howard M. Metzenbaum, Ohio
Donald W. Riegle Jr., Mich.
Daniel Patrick Moynihan, N.Y.
J. James Exon, Neb.

## Commerce, Science and Transportation

5202 DSOB 20510; 224-5115

R 9 - D 8

Bob Packwood, R-Ore., chairman

Barry Goldwater, Ariz.
Harrison "Jack" Schmitt, N.M.
John C. Danforth, Mo.
Nancy Landon Kassebaum, Kan.
Larry Pressler, S.D.
Slade Gorton, Wash.
Ted Stevens, Alaska
Robert W. Kasten Jr., Wis.

Howard W. Cannon, Nev.
Russell B. Long, La.
Ernest F. Hollings, S.C.
Daniel K. Inouye, Hawaii
Wendell H. Ford, Ky.
Donald W. Riegle Jr., Mich.
J. James Exon, Neb.
Howell Heflin, Ala.

## Energy and Natural Resources

3106 DSOB 20510; 224-4971

R 11 - D 9

James A. McClure, R-Idaho, chairman

Mark O. Hatfield, Ore.
Lowell P. Weicker Jr., Conn.
Pete V. Domenici, N.M.
Malcolm Wallop, Wyo.
John W. Warner, Va.
Gordon J. Humphrey, N.H.
Frank H. Murkowski, Alaska
Don Nickles, Okla.
John P. East, N.C.
John Heinz, Pa.

Henry M. Jackson, Wash.
J. Bennett Johnston, La.
Dale Bumpers, Ark.
Wendell H. Ford, Ky.
Howard M. Metzenbaum, Ohio
Spark M. Matsunaga, Hawaii
John Melcher, Mont.
Paul E. Tsongas, Mass.
Bill Bradley, N.J.

## Environment and Public Works

4204 DSOB 20510; 224-6176

R 9 - D 7

Robert T. Stafford, R-Vt., chairman

Howard H. Baker Jr., Tenn.
Pete V. Domenici, N.M.
John H. Chafee, R.I.
Alan K. Simpson, Wyo.
James Abdnor, S.D.
Steven D. Symms, Idaho
Slade Gorton, Wash.
Frank H. Murkowski, Alaska

Jennings Randolph, W.Va.
Lloyd Bentsen, Texas
Quentin N. Burdick, N.D.
Gary Hart, Colo.
Daniel Patrick Moynihan, N.Y.
George J. Mitchell, Maine
Max Baucus, Mont.

## Finance

2227 DSOB 20510; 224-4515

R 11 - D 9

Robert Dole, R-Kan., chairman

Bob Packwood, Ore.
William V. Roth Jr., Del.

Russell B. Long, La.
Harry F. Byrd Jr., Va.

John C. Danforth, Mo.
John H. Chafee, R.I.
John Heinz, Pa.
Malcolm Wallop, Wyo.
David Durenberger, Minn.
William L. Armstrong, Colo.
Steven D. Symms, Idaho
Charles E. Grassley, Iowa

*Lloyd Bentsen, Texas*
*Spark M. Matsunaga, Hawaii*
*Daniel Patrick Moynihan, N.Y.*
*Max Baucus, Mont.*
*David L. Boren, Okla.*
*Bill Bradley, N.J.*
*George J. Mitchell, Maine*

Strom Thurmond, R-S.C., chairman

Charles McC. Mathias Jr., Md.
Paul Laxalt, Nev.
Orrin G. Hatch, Utah
Robert Dole, Kan.
Alan K. Simpson, Wyo.
John P. East, N.C.
Charles E. Grassley, Iowa
Jeremiah Denton, Ala.
Arlen Specter, Pa.

*Joseph R. Biden Jr., Del.*
*Edward M. Kennedy, Mass.*
*Robert C. Byrd, W.Va.*
*Howard M. Metzenbaum, Ohio*
*Dennis DeConcini, Ariz.*
*Patrick J. Leahy, Vt.*
*Max Baucus, Mont.*
*Howell Heflin, Ala.*

## Foreign Relations

*4229 DSOB 20510; 224-4651*

*R 9 - D 8*

Charles H. Percy, R-Ill., chairman

Howard H. Baker Jr., Tenn.
Jesse Helms, N.C.
S. I. "Sam" Hayakawa, Calif.
Richard G. Lugar, Ind.
Charles McC. Mathias Jr., Md.
Nancy Landon Kassebaum, Kan.
Rudy Boschwitz, Minn.
Larry Pressler, S.D.

*Claiborne Pell, R.I.*
*Joseph R. Biden Jr., Del.*
*John Glenn, Ohio*
*Paul S. Sarbanes, Md.*
*Edward Zorinsky, Neb.*
*Paul E. Tsongas, Mass.*
*Alan Cranston, Calif.*
*Christopher J. Dodd, Conn.*

## Labor and Human Resources

*4230 DSOB 20510; 224-5375*

*R 9 - D 7*

Orrin G. Hatch, R-Utah, chairman

Robert T. Stafford, Vt.
Dan Quayle, Ind.
Paula Hawkins, Fla.
Don Nickles, Okla.
Lowell P. Weicker Jr., Conn.
Gordon J. Humphrey, N.H.
Jeremiah Denton, Ala.
John P. East, N.C.

*Edward M. Kennedy, Mass.*
*Jennings Randolph, W.Va.*
*Harrison A. Williams Jr., N.J.*
*Claiborne Pell, R.I.*
*Thomas F. Eagleton, Mo.*
*Donald W. Riegle Jr., Mich.*
*Howard M. Metzenbaum, Ohio*

## Governmental Affairs

*3306 DSOB 20510; 224-4751*

*R 9 - D 8*

William V. Roth Jr., R-Del., chairman

Charles H. Percy, Ill.
Ted Stevens, Alaska
Charles McC. Mathias Jr., Md.
John C. Danforth, Mo.
William S. Cohen, Maine
David Durenberger, Minn.
Mack Mattingly, Ga.
Warren B. Rudman, N.H.

*Thomas F. Eagleton, Mo.*
*Henry M. Jackson, Wash.*
*Lawton Chiles, Fla.*
*Sam Nunn, Ga.*
*John Glenn, Ohio*
*Jim Sasser, Tenn.*
*David Pryor, Ark.*
*Carl Levin, Mich.*

## Rules and Administration

*305 RSOB 20510; 224-6352*

*R 7 - D 5*

Charles McC. Mathias Jr., R-Md., chairman

Mark O. Hatfield, Ore.
Howard H. Baker Jr., Tenn.
James A. McClure, Idaho
Jesse Helms, N.C.
John W. Warner, Va.
Robert Dole, Kan.

*Wendell H. Ford, Ky.*
*Howard W. Cannon, Nev.*
*Claiborne Pell, R.I.*
*Robert C. Byrd, W. Va.*
*Harrison A. Williams Jr., N.J.*

## Judiciary

*2226 DSOB; 224-5225*

*R 10 - D 8*

## Select Ethics

*113 Carroll Arms*
*301 First St. N.E. 20510; 224-2981*

*R 3 - D 3*

Malcolm Wallop, R-Wyo., chairman
*Howell Heflin, D-Ala., vice chairman*

Jesse Helms, N.C.
Mack Mattingly, Ga.

*David Pryor, Ark.*
*Thomas F. Eagleton, Mo.*

## Select Indian Affairs

*6313 DSOB 20510; 224-2251*

*R 4 - D 3*

William S. Cohen, R-Maine, chairman

Barry Goldwater, Ariz.
Mark Andrews, N.D.
Slade Gorton, Wash.

*John Melcher, Mont.*
*Daniel K. Inouye, Hawaii*
*Dennis DeConcini, Ariz.*

## Select Intelligence

*G308 DSOB 20510; 224-1700*

*R 8 - D 7*

Barry Goldwater, R-Ariz., chairman

Jake Garn, Utah
John H. Chafee, R.I.
Richard G. Lugar, Ind.
Malcolm Wallop, Wyo.
David Durenberger, Minn.
William V. Roth Jr., Del.
Harrison "Jack" Schmitt,
N.M.

*Daniel Patrick Moynihan,*
*N.Y.*
*Walter D. Huddleston, Ky.*
*Joseph R. Biden Jr., Del.*
*Daniel K. Inouye, Hawaii*
*Henry M. Jackson, Wash.*
*Patrick J. Leahy, Vt.*
*Lloyd Bentsen, Texas*

## Small Business

*424 RSOB 20510; 224-5175*

*R 9 - D 8*

Lowell P. Weicker Jr., R-Conn., chairman

Bob Packwood, Ore.

*Sam Nunn, Ga.*

Orrin G. Hatch, Utah
S. I. "Sam" Hayakawa,
Calif.
Rudy Boschwitz, Minn.
Slade Gorton, Wash.
Don Nickles, Okla.
Warren B. Rudman, N.H.
Alfonse D'Amato, N.Y.

*Walter D. Huddleston, Ky.*
*Dale Bumpers, Ark.*
*Jim Sasser, Tenn.*
*Max Baucus, Mont.*
*Carl Levin, Mich.*
*Paul E. Tsongas, Mass.*
*Alan J. Dixon, Ill.*

## Special Aging

*G233 DSOB 20510; 224-5364*

*R 8 - D 7*

John Heinz, R-Pa., chairman

Pete V. Domenici, N.M.
Charles H. Percy, Ill.
Nancy Landon Kassebaum,
Kan.
William S. Cohen, Maine
Larry Pressler, S.D.
Charles E. Grassley, Iowa
David Durenberger, Minn.

*Lawton Chiles, Fla.*
*John Glenn, Ohio*
*John Melcher, Mont.*
*David Pryor, Ark.*
*Bill Bradley, N.J.*
*Quentin N. Burdick, N.D.*
*Christopher J. Dodd, Conn.*

## Veterans' Affairs

*410 RSOB; 224-9126*

*R 7 - D 5*

Alan K. Simpson, R.-Wyo., chairman

Strom Thurmond, S.C.
Robert T. Stafford, Vt.
Robert W. Kasten Jr., Wis.
Jeremiah Denton, Ala.
Frank    H.    Murkowski,
Alaska
Arlen Specter, Pa.

*Alan Cranston, Calif.*
*Jennings Randolph, W.Va.*
*Spark M. Matsunaga,*
*Hawaii*
*Dennis DeConcini, Ariz.*
*George J. Mitchell, Maine*

# House Committees, 97th Congress

The standing and select committees of the U.S. House of Representatives are listed below in alphabetical order. The listing includes the room number, zip code, telephone number, and party ratio for each full committee. The telephone area code for Washington is 202.

Members of the majority party, Democrats, are shown in Roman type; members of the minority party, Republicans, are shown in italic type. Membership is given in order of seniority on the committee.

The word "vacancy" indicates that a committee seat had not been filled by July 1, 1981. The word "vacancy" appears for each unfilled seat as of that date.

## Agriculture

*1301 LHOB 20515; 225-2171*

*D 24 - R 19*

E. "Kika" de la Garza, D-Texas, chairman

| | |
|---|---|
| Thomas S. Foley, Wash. | *William C. Wampler, Va.* |
| Walter B. Jones, N.C. | *Paul Findley, Ill.* |
| Ed Jones, Tenn. | *James M. Jeffords, Vt.* |
| George E. Brown Jr., Calif. | *Tom Hagedorn, Minn.* |
| David R. Bowen, Miss. | *E. Thomas Coleman, Mo.* |
| Charlie Rose, N.C. | *Ron Marlenee, Mont.* |
| Fred Richmond, N.Y. | *Larry J. Hopkins, Ky.* |
| James Weaver, Ore. | *William M. Thomas, Calif.* |
| Tom Harkin, Iowa | *George Hansen, Idaho* |
| Berkley Bedell, Iowa | *Arlan Stangeland, Minn.* |
| Glenn English, Okla. | *Pat Roberts, Kan.* |
| Floyd Fithian, Ind. | *Bill Emerson, Mo.* |
| Leon E. Panetta, Calif. | *John L. Napier, S.C.* |
| Jerry Huckaby, La. | *Joe Skeen, N.M.* |
| Dan Glickman, Kan. | *Sid Morrison, Wash.* |
| Charles Whitley, N.C. | *Clint Roberts, S.D.* |
| Tony Coelho, Calif. | *Steve Gunderson, Wis.* |
| Thomas A. Daschle, S.D. | *Cooper Evans, Iowa* |
| Beryl Anthony Jr., Ark. | *Gene Chappie, Calif.* |
| Charles W. Stenholm, Texas | |
| Harold L. Volkmer, Mo. | |
| Charles Hatcher, Ga. | |
| Byron L. Dorgan, N.D. | |

## Appropriations

*H218 The Capitol 20515; 225-2771*

*D 33 - R 22*

Jamie L. Whitten, D-Miss., chairman

| | |
|---|---|
| Edward P. Boland, Mass. | *Silvio O. Conte, Mass.* |
| William H. Natcher, Ky. | *Joseph M. McDade, Pa.* |
| Neal Smith, Iowa | *Jack Edwards, Ala.* |
| Joseph P. Addabbo, N.Y. | *John T. Myers, Ind.* |
| Clarence D. Long, Md. | *J. Kenneth Robinson, Va.* |
| Sidney R. Yates, Ill. | *Clarence E. Miller, Ohio* |
| David R. Obey, Wis. | *Lawrence Coughlin, Pa.* |
| Edward R. Roybal, Calif. | *C. W. Bill Young, Fla.* |
| Louis Stokes, Ohio | *Jack F. Kemp, N.Y.* |
| Tom Bevill, Ala. | *Ralph Regula, Ohio* |
| Bill Chappell Jr., Fla. | *Clair W. Burgener, Calif.* |
| Bill Alexander, Ark. | *George M. O'Brien, Ill.* |
| John P. Murtha, Pa. | *Virginia Smith, Neb.* |
| Bob Traxler, Mich. | *Eldon Rudd, Ariz.* |
| Joseph D. Early, Mass. | *Carl D. Pursell, Mich.* |
| Charles Wilson, Texas | *Mickey Edwards, Okla.* |
| Lindy (Mrs. Hale) Boggs, La. | *Bob Livingston, La.* |
| Adam Benjamin Jr., Ind. | *S. William Green, N.Y.* |
| Norman D. Dicks, Wash. | *Tom Loeffler, Texas* |
| Matthew F. McHugh, N.Y. | *Jerry Lewis, Calif.* |
| Bo Ginn, Ga. | *Carroll A. Campbell Jr., S.C.* |
| William Lehman, Fla. | *John Edward Porter, Ill.* |
| Jack Hightower, Texas | |
| Martin Olav Sabo, Minn. | |
| Julian C. Dixon, Calif. | |
| Vic Fazio, Calif. | |
| W.G. "Bill" Hefner, N.C. | |
| Les AuCoin, Ore. | |
| Daniel K. Akaka, Hawaii | |
| Wes Watkins, Okla. | |
| William H. Gray III, Pa. | |
| Bernard J. Dwyer, N.J. | |

## Armed Services

2120 RHOB 20515; 225-4151

D 25 - R 19

Melvin Price, D-Ill., chairman

| | |
|---|---|
| Charles E. Bennett, Fla. | *William L. Dickinson, Ala.* |
| Samuel S. Stratton, N.Y. | *G. William Whitehurst, Va.* |
| Richard C. White, Texas | *Floyd Spence, S.C.* |
| Bill Nichols, Ala. | *Robin L. Beard, Tenn.* |
| Jack Brinkley, Ga. | *Donald J. Mitchell, N.Y.* |
| Robert H. Mollohan, W.Va. | *Marjorie S. Holt, Md.* |
| Dan Daniel, Va. | *Robert W. Daniel Jr., Va.* |
| G.V. "Sonny" Montgom-ery, Miss. | *Elwood Hillis, Ind.* |
| Les Aspin, Wis. | *David F. Emery, Maine* |
| Ronald V. Dellums, Calif. | *Paul S. Trible Jr., Va.* |
| Patricia Schroeder, Colo. | *Robert E. Badham, Calif.* |
| Abraham Kazen Jr., Texas | *Charles F. Dougherty, Pa.* |
| Antonio Borja Won Pat, Guam[1] | *Jim Courter, N.J.* |
| Larry P. McDonald, Ga. | *Larry J. Hopkins, Ky.* |
| Bob Stump, Ariz. | *Robert W. Davis, Mich.* |
| Beverly B. Byron, Md. | *Kenneth B. Kramer, Colo.* |
| Nicholas Mavroules, Mass. | *Duncan L. Hunter, Calif.* |
| Earl Hutto, Fla. | *James L. Nelligan, Pa.* |
| Ike Skelton, Mo. | *Thomas F. Hartnett, S.C.* |
| Marvin Leath, Texas | |
| Dave McCurdy, Okla. | |
| Thomas M. Foglietta, Pa. | |
| Roy Dyson, Md. | |
| Dennis M. Hertel, Mich. | |
| Vacancy | |

[1] Delegate from Guam not counted in party ratios.

## Banking, Finance and Urban Affairs

2129 RHOB 20515; 225-4247

D 25 - R 19

Fernand J. St Germain, D-R.I., chairman

| | |
|---|---|
| Henry S. Reuss, Wis. | *J. William Stanton, Ohio* |
| Henry B. Gonzalez, Texas | *Chalmers P. Wylie, Ohio* |
| Joseph G. Minish, N.J. | *Stewart B. McKinney, Conn.* |
| Frank Annunzio, Ill. | *George Hansen, Idaho* |
| Parren J. Mitchell, Md. | *Henry J. Hyde, Ill.* |
| Walter E. Fauntroy, D.C.[1] | *Jim Leach, Iowa* |
| Stephen L. Neal, N.C. | *Thomas B. Evans Jr., Del.* |
| Jerry M. Patterson, Calif. | *Ron Paul, Texas* |
| James J. Blanchard, Mich. | *Ed Bethune, Ark.* |
| Carroll Hubbard Jr., Ky. | *Norman D. Shumway, Calif.* |

| | |
|---|---|
| John J. LaFalce, N.Y. | *Stan Parris, Va.* |
| David W. Evans, Ind. | *Ed Weber, Ohio* |
| Norman E. D'Amours, N.H. | *Bill McCollum, Fla.* |
| Stanley N. Lundine, N.Y. | *Gregory W. Carman, N.Y.* |
| Mary Rose Oakar, Ohio | *George C. Wortley, N.Y.* |
| Jim Mattox, Texas | *Marge Roukema, N.J.* |
| Bruce F. Vento, Minn. | *Bill Lowery, Calif.* |
| Doug Barnard Jr., Ga. | *Jim Coyne, Pa.* |
| Robert Garcia, N.Y. | *Douglas K. Bereuter, Neb.* |
| Mike Lowry, Wash. | |
| Charles E. Schumer, N.Y. | |
| Barney Frank, Mass. | |
| Bill Patman, Texas | |
| William J. Coyne, Pa. | |
| Steny Hoyer, Md. | |

[1] Delegate from District of Columbia not counted in party ratios.

## Budget

214 HOB Annex #1 20515
(300 New Jersey Ave. S.E.); 225-7200

D 18 - R 12

James R. Jones, D-Okla., chairman

| | |
|---|---|
| Jim Wright, Texas | *Delbert L. Latta, Ohio\** |
| David R. Obey, Wis. | *Ralph Regula, Ohio* |
| Paul Simon, Ill. | *Bud Shuster, Pa.* |
| Norman Y. Mineta, Calif. | *Bill Frenzel, Minn.* |
| Jim Mattox, Texas | *Jack F. Kemp, N.Y.* |
| Stephen J. Solarz, N.Y. | *James G. Martin, N.C.* |
| Timothy E. Wirth, Colo. | *Paul S. Trible Jr., Va.* |
| Leon E. Panetta, Calif. | *Ed Bethune, Ark.* |
| Richard A. Gephardt, Mo. | *Lynn Martin, Ill.* |
| Bill Nelson, Fla. | *Albert Lee Smith Jr., Ala.* |
| Les Aspin, Wis. | *Eugene Johnston, N.C.* |
| W.G. "Bill" Hefner, N.C. | *Bobbi Fiedler, Calif.* |
| Thomas J. Downey, N.Y. | |
| Adam Benjamin Jr., Ind. | |
| Brian J. Donnelly, Mass. | |
| Beryl Anthony Jr., Ark. | |
| Phil Gramm, Texas | |

## District of Columbia

1310 LHOB 20515; 225-4457

D 7 - R 4

Ronald V. Dellums, D-Calif., chairman

| | |
|---|---|
| Walter E. Fauntroy, D.C.[1] | *Stewart B. McKinney, Conn.* |

Romano L. Mazzoli, Ky.
Fortney H. "Pete" Stark, Calif.
Mickey Leland, Texas
William H. Gray III, Pa.
Michael D. Barnes, Md.
Mervyn M. Dymally, Calif.

Stan Parris, Va.
Thomas J. Bliley Jr., Va.
Marjorie S. Holt, Md.

[1] Delegate from District of Columbia not counted in party ratios.

## Education and Labor

*2181 RHOB 20515; 225-4527*

*D 19 - R 14*

Carl D. Perkins, D-Ky., chairman

Augustus F. Hawkins, Calif.
William D. Ford, Mich.
Phillip Burton, Calif.
Joseph M. Gaydos, Pa.
William Clay, Pa.
Mario Biaggi, N.Y.
Ike F. Andrews, N.C.
Paul Simon, Ill.
George Miller, Calif.
Austin J. Murphy, Pa.
Ted Weiss, N.Y.
Baltasar Corrada, P.R.[1]
Dale E. Kildee, Mich.
Peter A. Peyser, N.Y.
Pat Williams, Mont.
William R. Ratchford, Conn.
Ray Kogovsek, Colo.
Harold Washington, Ill.
Dennis E. Eckart, Ohio

John M. Ashbrook, Ohio
John N. Erlenborn, Ill.
James M. Jeffords, Vt.
Bill Goodling, Pa.
E. Thomas Coleman, Mo.
Ken Kramer, Colo.
Arlen Erdahl, Minn.
Thomas E. Petri, Wis.
Millicent Fenwick, N.J.
Marge Roukema, N.J.
Eugene Johnston, N.C.
Larry DeNardis, Conn.
Larry E. Craig, Idaho
Wendell Bailey, Mo.

[1] Resident commissioner from Puerto Rico not counted in party ratios.

## Energy and Commerce

*2125 RHOB 20515; 225-2927*

*D 24 - R 18*

John D. Dingell, D-Mich., chairman

James H. Scheuer, N.Y.
Richard L. Ottinger, N.Y.
Henry A. Waxman, Calif.
Timothy E. Wirth, Colo.

James T. Broyhill, N.C.
Clarence J. Brown, Ohio
James M. Collins, Texas
Norman F. Lent, N.Y.

Phil Sharp, Ind.
James J. Florio, N.J.
Toby Moffett, Conn.
Jim Santini, Nev.
Edward J. Markey, Mass.
Thomas A. Luken, Ohio
Doug Walgren, Pa.
Albert Gore Jr., Tenn.
Barbara A. Mikulski, Md.
Ronald M. Mottl, Ohio
Phil Gramm, Texas
Al Swift, Wash.
Mickey Leland, Texas
Richard C. Shelby, Ala.
Cardiss Collins, Ill.
Mike Synar, Okla.
W.J. "Billy" Tauzin, La.
Ron Wyden, Ore.
Ralph M. Hall, Texas

Edward R. Madigan, Ill.
Carlos J. Moorhead, Calif.
Matthew J. Rinaldo, N.J.
Marc L. Marks, Pa.
Tom Corcoran, Ill.
Gary A. Lee, N.Y.
William E. Dannemeyer, Calif.
Bob Whittaker, Kan.
Tom Tauke, Iowa
Don Ritter, Pa.
Harold Rogers, Ky.
Cleve Benedict, W.Va.
Daniel R. Coats, Ind.
Thomas J. Bliley Jr., Va.

## Foreign Affairs

*2170 RHOB 20515; 225-5021*

*D 21 - R 16*

Clement J. Zablocki, D-Wis., chairman

L.H. Fountain, N.C.
Dante B. Fascell, Fla.
Benjamin S. Rosenthal, N.Y.
Lee H. Hamilton, Ind.
Jonathan B. Bingham, N.Y.
Gus Yatron, Pa.
Stephen J. Solarz, N.Y.

Don Bonker, Wash.
Gerry E. Studds, Mass.
Andy Ireland, Fla.
Dan Mica, Fla.
Michael D. Barnes, Md.
Howard Wolpe, Mich.
George W. Crockett Jr., Mich.
Bob Shamansky, Ohio
Sam Gejdenson, Conn.
Mervyn M. Dymally, Calif.
Dennis E. Eckart, Ohio
Tom Lantos, Calif.
David R. Bowen, Miss.

William S. Broomfield, Mich.
Edward J. Derwinski, Ill.
Paul Findley, Ill.
Larry Winn Jr., Kan.
Benjamin A. Gilman, N.Y.
Robert J. Lagomarsino, Calif.
Bill Goodling, Pa.
Joel Pritchard, Wash.
Millicent Fenwick, N.J.
Robert K. Dornan, Calif.
Jim Leach, Iowa
Arlen Erdahl, Minn.
Toby Roth, Wis.
Olympia J. Snowe, Maine
John LeBoutillier, N.Y.
Vacancy

## Government Operations

*2157 RHOB 20515; 225-5051*

*D 23 - R 17*

Jack Brooks, D-Texas, chairman

| | |
|---|---|
| L.H. Fountain, N.C. | Frank Horton, N.Y. |
| Dante B. Fascell, Fla. | John N. Erlenborn, Ill. |
| Benjamin S. Rosenthal, N.Y. | Clarence J. Brown, Ohio |
| Don Fuqua, Fla. | Paul N. McCloskey Jr., |
| John Conyers Jr., Mich. | Calif. |
| Cardiss Collins, Ill. | Thomas N. Kindness, Ohio |
| John L. Burton, Calif. | Robert S. Walker, Pa. |
| Glenn English, Okla. | M. Caldwell Butler, Va. |
| Elliott H. Levitas, Ga. | Lyle Williams, Ohio |
| David W. Evans, Ind. | H. Joel Deckard, Ind. |
| Toby Moffett, Conn. | William F. Clinger Jr., Pa. |
| Henry A. Waxman, Calif. | Raymond McGrath, N.Y. |
| Floyd Fithian, Ind. | Hal Daub, Neb. |
| Ted Weiss, N.Y. | John Hiler, Ind. |
| Mike Synar, Okla. | David Dreier, Calif. |
| Eugene V. Atkinson, Pa. | Wendell Bailey, Mo. |
| Stephen L. Neal, N.C. | Larry DeNardis, Conn. |
| Doug Barnard Jr., Ga. | Judd Gregg, N.H. |
| Peter A. Peyser, N.Y. | |
| Barney Frank, Mass. | |
| Harold Washington, Ill. | |
| Tom Lantos, Calif. | |

| | |
|---|---|
| Abraham Kazen Jr., Texas | Don Young, Alaska |
| Jonathan B. Bingham, N.Y. | Robert J. Lagomarsino, |
| John F. Seiberling, Ohio | Calif. |
| Antonio Borja Won Pat, | Dan Marriott, Utah |
| Guam[1] | Ron Marlenee, Mont. |
| Jim Santini, Nev. | Richard B. Cheney, Wyo. |
| James Weaver, Ore. | Charles Pashayan Jr., Calif. |
| George Miller, Calif. | Douglas K. Bereuter, Neb. |
| James J. Florio, N.J. | David O'B. Martin, N.Y. |
| Phil Sharp, Ind. | Larry Craig, Idaho |
| Edward J. Markey, Mass. | William M. Hendon, N.C. |
| Baltasar Corrada, P.R.[1] | Hank Brown, Colo. |
| Austin J. Murphy, Pa. | David Michael Staton, |
| Nick J. Rahall, W.Va. | W.Va. |
| Bruce F. Vento, Minn. | Denny Smith, Ore. |
| Jerry Huckaby, La. | James V. Hansen, Utah |
| Jerry M. Patterson, Calif. | Vacancy |
| Ray Kogovsek, Colo. | |
| Pat Williams, Mont. | |
| Dale E. Kildee, Mich. | |
| Tony Coelho, Calif. | |
| Beverly B. Byron, Md. | |
| Ron de Lugo, V.I.[1] | |
| Sam Gejdenson, Conn. | |

[1] Delegates from Guam and the Virgin Islands and the Resident Commissioner from Puerto Rico not counted in party ratios.

## House Administration

H 326 The Capitol 20515; 225-2061

D 11 - R 8

Augustus F. Hawkins, D-Calif., chairman

| | |
|---|---|
| Frank Annunzio, Ill. | Bill Frenzel, Minn. |
| Joseph M. Gaydos, Pa. | William L. Dickinson, Ala. |
| Ed Jones, Tenn. | Robert E. Badham, Calif. |
| Robert H. Mollohan, W.Va. | Newt Gingrich, Ga. |
| Joseph G. Minish, N.J. | William M. Thomas, Calif. |
| Charlie Rose, N.C. | Gary A. Lee, N.Y. |
| John L. Burton, Calif. | Jim Coyne, Pa. |
| William R. Ratchford, | Lynn Martin, Ill. |
| Conn. | |
| Al Swift, Wash. | |
| William J. Coyne, Pa. | |

## Interior and Insular Affairs

1324 LHOB 20515; 225-2761

D 23 - R 17

Morris K. Udall, D-Ariz., chairman

| | |
|---|---|
| Phillip Burton, Calif. | Manuel Lujan Jr., N.M. |
| Robert W. Kastenmeier, | |
| Wis. | Don H. Clausen, Calif. |

## Judiciary

2137 RHOB 20515; 225-3951

D 16 - R 12

Peter W. Rodino Jr., D-N.J., chairman

| | |
|---|---|
| Jack Brooks, Texas | Robert McClory, Ill. |
| Robert W. Kastenmeier, | Tom Railsback, Ill. |
| Wis. | Hamilton Fish Jr., N.Y. |
| Don Edwards, Calif. | M. Caldwell Butler, Va. |
| John Conyers Jr., Mich. | Carlos J. Moorhead, Calif. |
| John F. Seiberling, Ohio | John M. Ashbrook, Ohio |
| George E. Danielson, Calif. | Henry J. Hyde, Ill. |
| Romano L. Mazzoli, Ky. | Thomas N. Kindness, Ohio |
| William J. Hughes, N.J. | Harold S. Sawyer, Mich. |
| Sam B. Hall Jr., Texas | Dan Lungren, Calif. |
| Mike Synar, Okla. | F. James Sensenbrenner Jr., |
| Patricia Schroeder, Colo. | Wis. |
| Billy Lee Evans, Ga. | Bill McCollum, Fla. |
| Dan Glickman, Kan. | |
| Harold Washington, Ill. | |
| Barney Frank, Mass. | |

## Merchant Marine and Fisheries

*1334 LHOB 20515; 225-4047*

*D 20 - R 15*

Walter B. Jones, D-N.C., chairman

| | |
|---|---|
| Mario Biaggi, N.Y. | *Gene Snyder, Ky.* |
| Glenn M. Anderson, Calif. | *Paul N. McCloskey Jr., Calif.* |
| John B. Breaux, La. | *Edwin B. Forsythe, N.J.* |
| Gerry E. Studds, Mass. | *Joel Pritchard, Wash.* |
| David R. Bowen, Miss. | *Don Young, Alaska* |
| Carroll Hubbard Jr., Ky. | *Norman F. Lent, N.Y.* |
| Don Bonker, Wash. | *David F. Emery, Maine* |
| Norman E. D'Amours, N.H. | *Thomas B. Evans Jr., Del.* |
| James L. Oberstar, Minn. | *Robert W. Davis, Mich.* |
| William J. Hughes, N.J. | *William Carney, N.Y.* |
| Barbara A. Mikulski, Md. | *Charles F. Dougherty, Pa.* |
| Mike Lowry, Wash. | *Norman D. Shumway, Calif.* |
| Earl Hutto, Fla. | *Jack Fields, Texas* |
| Brian J. Donnelly, Mass. | *Claudine Schneider, R.I.* |
| W.J. "Billy" Tauzin, La. | *E. Clay Shaw Jr., Fla.* |
| Thomas M. Foglietta, Pa. | |
| Bill Patman, Texas | |
| Fofo I.F. Sunia, American Samoa[1] | |
| Dennis M. Hertel, Mich. | |
| Roy Dyson, Md. | |

[1] Delegate from American Samoa not counted in party ratios.

## Post Office and Civil Service

*309 CHOB 20515; 225-4054*

*D 15 - R 11*

William D. Ford, D-Mich., chairman

| | |
|---|---|
| Morris K. Udall, Ariz. | *Edward J. Derwinski, Ill.* |
| William Clay, Mo. | *Gene Taylor, Mo.* |
| Patricia Schroeder, Colo. | *Benjamin A. Gilman, N.Y.* |
| Robert Garcia, N.Y. | *Tom Corcoran, Ill.* |
| Mickey Leland, Texas | *Jim Courter, N.J.* |
| Geraldine A. Ferraro, N.Y. | *Charles Pashayan Jr., Calif.* |
| Don Albosta, Mich. | *William E. Dannemeyer, Calif.* |
| Gus Yatron, Pa. | |
| Mary Rose Oakar, Ohio | *Daniel B. Crane, Ill.* |
| Charles E. Schumer, N.Y. | *Wayne R. Grisham, Calif.* |
| George E. Danielson, Calif. | *Frank Wolf, Va.* |
| Ronald V. Dellums, Calif. | *Vacancy* |

Ron de Lugo, V.I.[1]
Gus Savage, Ill.
Steny Hoyer, Md.

[1] Delegate from the Virgin Islands not counted in party ratios.

## Public Works and Transportation

*2165 RHOB 20515; 225-4472*

*D 25 - R 19*

James J. Howard, D-N.J., chairman

| | |
|---|---|
| Glenn M. Anderson, Calif. | *Don H. Clausen, Calif.* |
| Robert A. Roe, N.J. | *Gene Snyder, Ky.* |
| John B. Breaux, La. | *John Paul Hammerschmidt, Ark.* |
| Norman Y. Mineta, Calif. | |
| Elliott H. Levitas, Ga. | *Bud Shuster, Pa.* |
| James L. Oberstar, Minn. | *Barry M. Goldwater Jr., Calif.* |
| Henry J. Nowak, N.Y. | |
| Robert W. Edgar, Pa. | *Tom Hagedorn, Minn.* |
| Marilyn Lloyd Bouquard, Tenn. | *Arlan Stangeland, Minn.* |
| John G. Fary, Ill. | *Newt Gingrich, Ga.* |
| Robert A. Young, Mo. | *William F. Clinger Jr., Pa.* |
| Allen E. Ertel, Pa. | *Gerald B. Solomon, N.Y.* |
| Billy Lee Evans, Ga. | *Harold C. Hollenbeck, N.J.* |
| Ronnie G. Flippo, Ala. | *H. Joel Deckard, Ind.* |
| Nick J. Rahall, W.Va. | *Wayne Grisham, Calif.* |
| Douglas Applegate, Ohio | *Jim Jeffries, Kan.* |
| Geraldine A. Ferraro, N.Y. | *Jack Fields, Texas* |
| Eugene V. Atkinson, Pa. | *Guy Molinari, N.Y.* |
| Don Albosta, Mich. | *E. Clay Shaw Jr., Fla.* |
| Bill Boner, Tenn. | *Bob McEwen, Ohio* |
| Ron de Lugo, V.I.[1] | *Frank Wolf, Va.* |
| Gus Savage, Ill. | |
| Fofo I.F. Sunia, American Samoa[1] | |
| Buddy Roemer, La. | |
| Brian J. Donnelly, Mass. | |
| Ray Kogovsek, Colo. | |

[1] Delegates from the Virgin Islands and American Samoa not counted in party ratios.

## Rules

*H313 The Capitol 20515; 225-9486*

*D 11 - R 5*

Richard Bolling, D-Mo., chairman

| | |
|---|---|
| Claude Pepper, Fla. | *James H. Quillen, Tenn.* |
| Gillis W. Long, La. | *Delbert L. Latta, Ohio* |

Joe Moakley, Mass.
Shirley Chisholm, N.Y.
Leo C. Zeferetti, N.Y.
Butler Derrick, S.C.
Anthony C. Beilenson, Calif.
Martin Frost, Texas
David E. Bonior, Mich.
Tony P. Hall, Ohio

*Trent Lott, Miss.*
*Gene Taylor, Mo.*
*John J. Rhodes, Ariz.*

## Science and Technology

*2321 RHOB 20515; 225-6371*

*D 23 - R 17*

Don Fuqua, D-Fla., chairman

Robert A. Roe, N.J.
George E. Brown Jr., Calif.
James H. Scheuer, N.Y.
Richard L. Ottinger, N.Y.
Tom Harkin, Iowa
Marilyn Lloyd Bouquard,
   Tenn.
James J. Blanchard, Mich.
Doug Walgren, Pa.
Ronnie G. Flippo, Ala.
Dan Glickman, Kan.
Albert Gore Jr., Tenn.
Robert A. Young, Mo.
Richard C. White, Texas
Harold L. Volkmer, Mo.
Howard Wolpe, Mich.
Bill Nelson, Fla.
Stanley N. Lundine, N.Y.
Allen E. Ertel, Pa.
Bob Shamansky, Ohio
Ralph M. Hall, Texas
Dave McCurdy, Okla.
Mervyn M. Dymally, Calif.

*Larry Winn Jr., Kan.*
*Barry M. Goldwater Jr.,*
   *Calif.*
*Hamilton Fish Jr., N.Y.*
*Manuel Lujan Jr., N.M.*
*Harold C. Hollenbeck, N.J.*
*Robert S. Walker, Pa.*
*Edwin B. Forsythe, N.J.*
*William Carney, N.Y.*
*Margaret M. Heckler, Mass.*
*F. James Sensenbrenner Jr.,*
   *Wis.*
*Vin Weber, Minn.*
*Judd Gregg, N.H.*
*Raymond McGrath, N.Y.*
*Joe Skeen, N.M.*
*Claudine Schneider, R.I.*
*Jim Dunn, Mich.*
*Bill Lowery, Calif.*

## Select Aging

*712 HOB Annex #1 20515*
*(300 New Jersey Ave. S.E.); 225-9375*

*D 31 - R 23*

Claude Pepper, D-Fla., chairman

Edward R. Roybal, Calif.
Mario Biaggi, Calif.
Ike Andrews, N.C.
John L. Burton, Calif.
Don Bonker, Wash.
Thomas A. Downey, N.Y.
James J. Florio, N.J.
Harold E. Ford, Tenn.
William J. Hughes, N.J.

*Matthew J. Rinaldo, N.J.*
*William C. Wampler, Va.*
*John Paul Hammerschmidt,*
   *Ark.*
*Marc L. Marks, Pa.*
*Ralph Regula, Ohio*
*Robert K. Dornan, Calif.*
*Harold C. Hollenbeck, N.J.*
*Norman D. Shumway, Calif.*

Marilyn Lloyd Bouquard,
   Tenn.
Jim Santini, Nev.
David W. Evans, Ind.
Stanley N. Lundine, N.Y.
Mary Rose Oakar, Ohio
Thomas A. Luken, Ohio
Geraldine A. Ferraro, N.Y.
Beverly B. Byron, Md.
William R. Ratchford,
   Conn.
Dan Mica, Fla.
Henry A. Waxman, Calif.
Mike Synar, Okla.
Eugene V. Atkinson, Pa.
Butler Derrick, S.C.
Bruce F. Vento, Minn.
Barney Frank, Mass.
Tom Lantos, Calif.
Robert Shamansky, Ohio
Ron Wyden, Ore.
Don Albosta, Mich.
George W. Crockett Jr.,
   Mich.

*Olympia J. Snowe, Maine*
*Dan Lungren, Calif.*
*Millicent Fenwick, N.J.*
*James M. Jeffords, Vt.*
*Tom Tauke, Iowa*
*Thomas E. Petri, Wis.*
*Judd Gregg, N.H.*
*Dan Coats, Ind.*
*George C. Wortley, N.Y.*
*Hal Daub, Neb.*
*Larry Craig, Idaho*
*Pat Roberts, Kan.*
*William M. Hendon, N.C.*
*Gregory Carman, N.Y.*
*Vacancy*

## Select Intelligence

*H405 The Capitol 20515; 225-4121*

*D 9 - R 5*

Edward P. Boland, D-Mass., chairman

Clement J. Zablocki, Wis.
Charlie Rose, N.C
Romano L. Mazzoli, Ky.
Norman Y. Mineta, Calif.
Wyche Fowler Jr., Ga.
Lee H. Hamilton, Ind.
Albert Gore Jr., Tenn.
Bob Stump, Ariz.

*J. Kenneth Robinson, Va.*
*John M. Ashbrook, Ohio*
*Robert McClory, Ill.*
*G. William Whitehurst, Va.*
*C. W. Bill Young, Fla.*

House Majority Leader Jim Wright, D-Texas and Minority Leader Robert H. Michel, R-Ill., are members *ex officio* of the full committee.

## Select Narcotics Abuse and Control

*H2-234 Annex #2 20515*
*(2nd and D Sts. S.W.); 225-1753*

*D 11 - R 8*

Leo C. Zeferetti, D-N.Y., chairman

Peter W. Rodino Jr., N.J.
Charles B. Rangel, N.Y.

*Tom Railsback, Ill.*
*Robin L. Beard, Tenn.*

Fortney H. "Pete" Stark, Calif.
Glenn English, Okla.
Billy Lee Evans, Ga.
James H. Scheuer, N.Y.
Cardiss Collins, Ill.
Daniel K. Akaka, Hawaii
Frank J. Guarini, N.J.
Robert T. Matsui, Calif.

*Benjamin A. Gilman, N.Y.*
*Lawrence Coughlin, Pa.*
*Robert K. Dornan, Calif.*
*Lawrence DeNardis, Conn.*
*E. Clay Shaw Jr., Fla.*
*Vacancy*

## Small Business

*2361 RHOB 20515; 225-5821*
*D 23 - R 17*

Parren J. Mitchell, D-Md., chairman

Neal Smith, Iowa
Joseph P. Addabbo, N.Y.
Henry B. Gonzalez, Texas
John J. LaFalce, N.Y.
Berkley Bedell, Iowa
Fred Richmond, N.Y.
Henry J. Nowak, N.Y.
Thomas A. Luken, Ohio
Andy Ireland, Fla.
Ike Skelton, Mo.
Billy Lee Evans, Ga.
Charles W. Stenholm, Texas
Romano L. Mazzoli, Ky.
Nicholas Mavroules, Mass.
George W. Crockett Jr., Mich.
Charles Hatcher, Ga.
Ron Wyden, Ore.
Dennis E. Eckart, Ohio
Byron L. Dorgan, N.D.
Gus Savage, Ill.
Buddy Roemer, La.
John G. Fary, Ill.

*Joseph M. McDade, Pa.*
*Silvio O. Conte, Mass.*
*J. William Stanton, Ohio*
*William S. Broomfield, Mich.*
*Dan Marriott, Utah*
*Lyle Williams, Ohio*
*Olympia J. Snowe, Maine*
*Daniel B. Crane, Ill.*
*John Hiler, Ind.*
*David Michael Staton, W.Va.*
*Vin Weber, Minn.*
*Hal Daub, Neb.*
*Chris Smith, N.J.*
*Ed Weber, Ohio*
*David Dreier, Calif.*
*Guy V. Molinari, N.Y.*
*Mark Siljander, Mich.*

## Standards of Official Conduct

*2360 RHOB 20515; 225-7103*

*D 6 - R 6*

Louis Stokes, D-Ohio, chairman

Nick J. Rahall, W.Va.
Bill Alexander, Ark.
Charles Wilson, Texas
Ken Holland, S.C.
Don Bailey, Pa.

*Floyd Spence, S.C.*
*Barber B. Conable Jr., N.Y.*
*John T. Myers, Ind.*
*Edwin B. Forsythe, N.J.*
*Hank Brown, Colo.*
*James V. Hansen, Utah*

## Veterans' Affairs

*335 CHOB 20515; 225-3527*
*D 17 - R 14*

G. V. "Sonny" Montgomery, D-Miss., chairman

Don Edwards, Calif.
George E. Danielson, Calif.
Jack Brinkley, Ga.
Ronald M. Mottl, Ohio
Robert W. Edgar, Pa.
Sam B. Hall Jr., Texas
Douglas Applegate, Ohio
Marvin Leath, Texas
Bill Boner, Tenn.
Richard C. Shelby, Ala.
Dan Mica, Fla.
Thomas A. Daschle, S.D.
Bob Stump, Ariz.
Phil Gramm, Texas
Austin J. Murphy, Pa.
Byron L. Dorgan, N.D.
Antonio Borja Won Pat, Guam[1]

*John Paul Hammerschmidt, Ark.*
*Margaret M. Heckler, Mass.*
*Chalmers P. Wylie, Ohio*
*Elwood Hillis, Ind.*
*Harold S. Sawyer, Mich.*
*Gerald B. Solomon, N.Y.*
*Jim Jeffries, Kan.*
*Robert C. McEwen, N.Y.*
*Jim Dunn, Mich.*
*Chris Smith, N.J.*
*Albert Lee Smith Jr., Ala.*
*Denny Smith, Ore.*
*Mark Siljander, Mich.*
*Vacancy*

[1] Delegate from Guam not counted in party ratios.

## Ways and Means

*1102 LHOB 20515; 225-3625*
*D 23 - R 12*

Dan Rostenkowski, D-Ill., chairman

Sam Gibbons, Fla.
J. J. Pickle, Texas
Charles B. Rangel, N.Y.
William R. Cotter, Conn.
Fortney H. "Pete" Stark, Calif.
James R. Jones, Okla.
Andrew Jacobs Jr., Ind.
Harold E. Ford, Tenn.
Ken Holland, S.C.
William M. Brodhead, Mich.
Ed Jenkins, Ga.
Richard A. Gephardt, Mo.
Thomas J. Downey, N.Y.
Cecil Heftel, Hawaii
Wyche Fowler Jr., Ga.
Frank J. Guarini, N.J.
James M. Shannon, Mass.
Marty Russo, Ill.
Don J. Pease, Ohio
Kent Hance, Texas
Robert T. Matsui, Calif.
Don Bailey, Pa.

*Barber B. Conable Jr., N.Y.*
*John J. Duncan, Tenn.*
*Bill Archer, Texas*
*Guy Vander Jagt, Mich.*
*Philip M. Crane, Ill.*
*Bill Frenzel, Minn.*
*James G. Martin, N.C.*
*L. A. "Skip" Bafalis, Fla.*
*Richard T. Schulze, Pa.*
*Bill Gradison, Ohio*
*John H. Rousselot, Calif.*
*W. Henson Moore, La.*

# Joint Committees, 97th Congress

The joint committees of Congress are listed below in alphabetical order. The listing includes the room number, zip code and telephone number. The telephone area code for Washington is 202.

Membership is drawn from both the Senate and House and from both parties. Membership is given in order of seniority on the committees.

In the listing, Democrats are shown on the left in Roman type; Republicans are on the right in italic. When a senator serves as chairman, the vice chairman usually is a representative, and vice versa. The chairmanship usually rotates from one chamber to the other at the beginning of each Congress.

## Economic

*G133 DSOB 20510; 224-5171*

Rep. Henry S. Reuss, D-Wis., chairman
*Sen. Roger W. Jepsen, R-Iowa, vice chairman*

### Senate Members

| | |
|---|---|
| Lloyd Bentsen, Texas | *William V. Roth Jr., Del.* |
| William Proxmire, Wis. | *James Abdnor, S.D.* |
| Edward M. Kennedy, Mass. | *Steven D. Symms, Idaho* |
| Paul S. Sarbanes, Md. | *Paula Hawkins, Fla.* |
| | *Mack Mattingly, Ga.* |

### House Members

| | |
|---|---|
| Richard Bolling, Mo. | *Clarence J. Brown, Ohio* |
| Lee H. Hamilton, Ind. | *Margaret M. Heckler, Mass.* |
| Gillis W. Long, La. | *John H. Rousselot, Calif.* |
| Parren J. Mitchell, Md. | *Chalmers P. Wylie, Ohio* |
| Fred Richmond, N.Y. | |

## Library

*415 HOB Annex #1 20515*
*(300 New Jersey Ave. S.E.); 225-0392*

Rep. Augustus F. Hawkins, D-Calif., chairman
*Sen. Charles McC. Mathias Jr., R-Md., vice chairman*

### Senate Members

| | |
|---|---|
| Claiborne Pell, R.I. | *Mark O. Hatfield, Ore.* |
| Harrison A. Williams Jr., N.J. | *Howard H. Baker Jr., Tenn.* |

### House Members

| | |
|---|---|
| Al Swift, Wash. | *Newt Gingrich, Ga.* |
| William J. Coyne, Pa. | *Jim Coyne, Pa.* |

## Printing

*S151 The Capitol 20510; 224-5241*

*Sen. Charles McC. Mathias Jr., R-Md., chairman*
Rep. Augustus F. Hawkins, D-Calif., vice chairman

### Senate Members

| | |
|---|---|
| Howard W. Cannon, Nev. | *John W. Warner, Va.* |
| Wendell H. Ford, Ky. | *Mark O. Hatfield, Ore.* |

### House Members

| | |
|---|---|
| Joseph M. Gaydos, Pa. | *Newt Gingrich, Ga.* |
| Ed Jones, Tenn. | *Lynn Martin, Ill.* |

## Taxation

*1015 LHOB 20515; 225-3621*

Rep. Dan Rostenkowski, D-Ill., chairman
*Sen. Robert Dole, R-Kan., vice chairman*

### Senate Members

| | |
|---|---|
| Russell B. Long, La. | *Bob Packwood, Ore.* |
| Harry F. Byrd Jr., Va. | *William V. Roth Jr., Del.* |

### House Members

| | |
|---|---|
| Sam Gibbons, Fla. | *Barber B. Conable Jr., N.Y.* |
| J.J. Pickle, Texas | *John J. Duncan, Tenn.* |

# Senators' Offices

The list below gives the names of senators in alphabetical order followed by the address and phone number for their Washington offices. Address abbreviations used are as follows: DSOB (Dirksen Senate Office Building), RSOB (Russell Senate Office Building). The telephone area code for Washington is 202.

**ABDNOR, JAMES (R S.D.)**
CAPITOL HILL OFFICE:
4327 DSOB 20510; 224-2321

**ANDREWS, MARK (R N.D.)**
CAPITOL HILL OFFICE:
417 RSOB 20510; 224-2043

**ARMSTRONG, WILLIAM L. (R COLO.)**
CAPITOL HILL OFFICE:
1321 DSOB 20510; 224-5941

**BAKER, HOWARD H. JR. (R TENN.)**
CAPITOL HILL OFFICE:
4123 DSOB 20510; 224-4944 (congressional office)
S-233 The Capitol 20510; 224-3135 (Majority Leader's office)

**BAUCUS, MAX (D MONT.)**
CAPITOL HILL OFFICE:
1107 DSOB 20510; 224-2651

**BENTSEN, LLOYD (D TEXAS)**
CAPITOL HILL OFFICE:
240 RSOB 20510; 224-5922

**BIDEN, JOSEPH R. JR. (D DEL.)**
CAPITOL HILL OFFICE:
456 RSOB 20510; 224-5042

**BOREN, DAVID L. (D OKLA.)**
CAPITOL HILL OFFICE:
440 RSOB 20510; 224-4721

**BOSCHWITZ, RUDY (R MINN.)**
CAPITOL HILL OFFICE:
2317 DSOB 20510; 224-5641

**BRADLEY, BILL (D N.J.)**
CAPITOL HILL OFFICE:
2107 DSOB 20510; 224-3224

**BUMPERS, DALE (D ARK.)**
CAPITOL HILL OFFICE:
3229 DSOB 20510; 224-4843

**BURDICK, QUENTIN N. (D N.D.)**
CAPITOL HILL OFFICE:
451 RSOB 20510; 224-2551

**BYRD, HARRY F. JR. (IND VA.)**
CAPITOL HILL OFFICE:
245 RSOB 20510; 224-4024

**BYRD, ROBERT C. (D W.VA.)**
CAPITOL HILL OFFICE:
133 RSOB 20510; 224-3954 (congressional office)
S-208 The Capitol 20510; 224-5556 (Minority Leader's office)

**CANNON, HOWARD W. (D NEV.)**
CAPITOL HILL OFFICE:
259 RSOB 20510; 224-6244

**CHAFEE, JOHN H. (R R.I.)**
CAPITOL HILL OFFICE:
5229 DSOB 20510; 224-2921

**CHILES, LAWTON (D FLA.)**
CAPITOL HILL OFFICE:
437 RSOB 20510; 224-5274

**COCHRAN, THAD (R MISS.)**
CAPITOL HILL OFFICE:
321 RSOB 20510; 224-5054

**COHEN, WILLIAM S. (R MAINE)**
CAPITOL HILL OFFICE:
1251 DSOB 20510; 224-2523


**CRANSTON, ALAN (D CALIF.)**
CAPITOL HILL OFFICE:
229 RSOB 20510; 224-3553 (congressional office)
S-148 The Capitol 20510; 224-2158 (Minority Whip's office)


**D'AMATO, ALFONSE (R N.Y.)**
CAPITOL HILL OFFICE:
432 RSOB 20510; 224-6542


**DANFORTH, JOHN C. (R MO.)**
CAPITOL HILL OFFICE:
460 RSOB 20510; 224-6154


**DeCONCINI, DENNIS (D ARIZ.)**
CAPITOL HILL OFFICE:
3230 DSOB 20510; 224-4521


**DENTON, JEREMIAH (R ALA.)**
CAPITOL HILL OFFICE:
5327 DSOB 20510; 224-5744


**DIXON, ALAN J. (D ILL.)**
CAPITOL HILL OFFICE:
4203 DSOB 20510; 224-2854


**DODD, CHRISTOPHER J. (D CONN.)**
CAPITOL HILL OFFICE:
404 RSOB 20510; 224-2823


**DOLE, ROBERT (R KAN.)**
CAPITOL HILL OFFICE:
2213 DSOB 20510; 224-6521


**DOMENICI, PETE V. (R N.M.)**
CAPITOL HILL OFFICE:
4239 DSOB 20510; 224-6621


**DURENBERGER, DAVID (R MINN.)**
CAPITOL HILL OFFICE:
353 RSOB 20510; 224-3244

**EAGLETON, THOMAS F. (D MO.)**
CAPITOL HILL OFFICE:
1209 DSOB 20510; 224-5721


**EAST, JOHN P. (R N.C.)**
CAPITOL HILL OFFICE:
5107 DSOB 20510; 224-3154


**EXON, J. JAMES (D NEB.)**
CAPITOL HILL OFFICE:
3313 DSOB 20510; 224-4224


**FORD, WENDELL H. (D KY.)**
CAPITOL HILL OFFICE:
363 RSOB 20510; 224-4343


**GARN, JAKE (R UTAH)**
CAPITOL HILL OFFICE:
5207 DSOB 20510; 224-5444


**GLENN, JOHN (D OHIO)**
CAPITOL HILL OFFICE:
2235 DSOB 20510; 224-3353


**GOLDWATER, BARRY (R ARIZ.)**
CAPITOL HILL OFFICE:
337 RSOB 20510; 224-2235


**GORTON, SLADE (R WASH.)**
CAPITOL HILL OFFICE:
3327 DSOB 20510; 224-2621


**GRASSLEY, CHARLES E. (R IOWA)**
CAPITOL HILL OFFICE:
232 RSOB 20510; 224-3744


**HART, GARY (D COLO.)**
CAPITOL HILL OFFICE:
221 RSOB 20510; 224-5852


**HATCH, ORRIN G. (R UTAH)**
CAPITOL HILL OFFICE:
125 RSOB 20510; 224-5251


**HATFIELD, MARK O. (R ORE.)**
CAPITOL HILL OFFICE:
463 RSOB 20510; 224-3753

**HAWKINS, PAULA (R FLA.)**
CAPITOL HILL OFFICE:
1327 DSOB 20510; 224-3041

**HAYAKAWA, S. I. "SAM" (R CALIF.)**
CAPITOL HILL OFFICE:
6217 DSOB 20510; 224-3841

**HEFLIN, HOWELL (D ALA.)**
CAPITOL HILL OFFICE:
3107 DSOB 20510; 224-4124

**HEINZ, JOHN (R PA.)**
CAPITOL HILL OFFICE:
443 RSOB 20510; 224-6324

**HELMS, JESSE (R N.C.)**
CAPITOL HILL OFFICE:
4213 DSOB 20510; 224-6342

**HOLLINGS, ERNEST F. (D S.C.)**
CAPITOL HILL OFFICE:
115 RSOB 20510; 224-6121

**HUDDLESTON, WALTER D. (D KY.)**
CAPITOL HILL OFFICE:
2121 DSOB 20510; 224-2541

**HUMPHREY, GORDON J. (R N.H.)**
CAPITOL HILL OFFICE:
6205 DSOB 20510; 224-2841

**INOUYE, DANIEL K. (D HAWAII)**
CAPITOL HILL OFFICE:
105 RSOB 20510; 224-3934

**JACKSON, HENRY M. (D WASH.)**
CAPITOL HILL OFFICE:
137 RSOB 20510; 224-3441

**JEPSEN, ROGER W. (R IOWA)**
CAPITOL HILL OFFICE:
110 RSOB 20510; 224-3254

**JOHNSTON, J. BENNETT (D LA.)**
CAPITOL HILL OFFICE:
421 RSOB 20510; 224-5824

**KASSEBAUM, NANCY LANDON (R KAN.)**
CAPITOL HILL OFFICE:
304 RSOB 20510; 224-4774

**KASTEN, ROBERT W. JR. (R WIS.)**
CAPITOL HILL OFFICE:
328 RSOB 20510; 224-5323

**KENNEDY, EDWARD M. (D MASS.)**
CAPITOL HILL OFFICE:
109 RSOB 20510; 224-4543

**LAXALT, PAUL (R NEV.)**
CAPITOL HILL OFFICE:
315 RSOB 20510; 224-3542

**LEAHY, PATRICK J. (D VT.)**
CAPITOL HILL OFFICE:
427 RSOB 20510; 224-4242

**LEVIN, CARL (D MICH.)**
CAPITOL HILL OFFICE:
140 RSOB 20510; 224-6221

**LONG, RUSSELL B. (D LA.)**
CAPITOL HILL OFFICE:
217 RSOB 20510; 224-4623

**LUGAR, RICHARD G. (R IND.)**
CAPITOL HILL OFFICE:
1113 DSOB 20510; 224-4814

**MATHIAS, CHARLES McC. JR. (R MD.)**
CAPITOL HILL OFFICE:
358 RSOB 20510; 224-4654

**MATSUNAGA, SPARK M. (D HAWAII)**
CAPITOL HILL OFFICE:
5121 DSOB 20510; 224-6361

**MATTINGLY, MACK (R GA.)**
CAPITOL HILL OFFICE:
6241 DSOB 20510; 224-3643

**McCLURE, JAMES A. (R IDAHO)**
CAPITOL HILL OFFICE:
3121 DSOB 20510; 224-2752

**MELCHER, JOHN (D MONT.)**
CAPITOL HILL OFFICE:
253 RSOB 20510; 224-2644

**METZENBAUM, HOWARD M. (D OHIO)**
CAPITOL HILL OFFICE:
347 RSOB 20510; 224-2315

**MITCHELL, GEORGE J. (D MAINE)**
CAPITOL HILL OFFICE:
344 RSOB 20510; 224-5344

**MOYNIHAN, DANIEL PATRICK (D N.Y.)**
CAPITOL HILL OFFICE:
442 RSOB 20510; 224-4451

**MURKOWSKI, FRANK H. (R ALASKA)**
CAPITOL HILL OFFICE:
2104 DSOB 20510; 224-6665

**NICKLES, DON (R OKLA.)**
CAPITOL HILL OFFICE:
6327 DSOB 20510; 224-5754

**NUNN, SAM (D GA.)**
CAPITOL HILL OFFICE:
3241 DSOB 20510; 224-3521

**PACKWOOD, BOB (R ORE.)**
CAPITOL HILL OFFICE:
145 RSOB 20510; 224-5244

**PELL, CLAIBORNE (D R.I.)**
CAPITOL HILL OFFICE:
325 RSOB 20510; 224-4642

**PERCY, CHARLES H. (R ILL.)**
CAPITOL HILL OFFICE:
4321 DSOB 20510; 224-2152

**PRESSLER, LARRY (R S.D.)**
CAPITOL HILL OFFICE:
411 RSOB 20510; 224-5842

**PROXMIRE, WILLIAM (D WIS.)**
CAPITOL HILL OFFICE:
5241 DSOB 20510; 224-5653

**PRYOR, DAVID (D ARK.)**
CAPITOL HILL OFFICE:
248 RSOB 20510; 224-2353

**QUAYLE, DAN (R IND.)**
CAPITOL HILL OFFICE:
254 RSOB 20510; 224-5623

**RANDOLPH, JENNINGS (D W.VA.)**
CAPITOL HILL OFFICE:
3203 DSOB 20510; 224-6472

**RIEGLE, DONALD W. JR. (D MICH.)**
CAPITOL HILL OFFICE:
1207 DSOB 20510; 224-4822

**ROTH, WILLIAM V. JR. (R DEL.)**
CAPITOL HILL OFFICE:
3215 DSOB 20510; 224-2441

**RUDMAN, WARREN B. (R N.H.)**
CAPITOL HILL OFFICE:
4104 DSOB 20510; 224-3324

**SARBANES, PAUL S. (D MD.)**
CAPITOL HILL OFFICE:
2327 DSOB 20510; 224-4524

**SASSER, JIM (D TENN.)**
CAPITOL HILL OFFICE:
260 RSOB 20510; 224-3344

**SCHMITT, HARRISON "JACK" (R N.M.)**
CAPITOL HILL OFFICE:
5313 DSOB 20510; 224-5521

**SIMPSON, ALAN K. (R WYO.)**
CAPITOL HILL OFFICE:
4107 DSOB 20510; 224-3424

**SPECTER, ARLEN (R PA.)**
CAPITOL HILL OFFICE:
342 RSOB 20510; 224-4254

**STAFFORD, ROBERT T. (R VT.)**
CAPITOL HILL OFFICE:
5219 DSOB 20510; 224-5141

**STENNIS, JOHN C. (D MISS.)**
CAPITOL HILL OFFICE:
205 RSOB 20510; 224-6253


**STEVENS, TED (R ALASKA)**
CAPITOL HILL OFFICE:
127 RSOB 20510; 224-3004 (congressional office)
S-229 The Capitol 20510; 224-2708 (Majority Whip's office)


**SYMMS, STEVEN D. (R IDAHO)**
CAPITOL HILL OFFICE:
452 RSOB 20510; 224-6142


**THURMOND, STROM (R S.C.)**
CAPITOL HILL OFFICE:
209 RSOB 20510; 224-5972


**TOWER, JOHN (R TEXAS)**
CAPITOL HILL OFFICE:
142 RSOB 20510; 224-2934


**TSONGAS, PAUL E. (D MASS.)**
CAPITOL HILL OFFICE:
342 RSOB 20510; 224-2742


**WALLOP, MALCOLM (R WYO.)**
CAPITOL HILL OFFICE:
204 RSOB 20510; 224-6441


**WARNER, JOHN W. (R VA.)**
CAPITOL HILL OFFICE:
405 RSOB 20510; 224-2023


**WEICKER, LOWELL P. JR. (R CONN.)**
CAPITOL HILL OFFICE:
313 RSOB 20510; 224-4041


**WILLIAMS, HARRISON A. JR. (D N.J.)**
CAPITOL HILL OFFICE:
352 RSOB 20510; 224-4744


**ZORINSKY, EDWARD (D NEB.)**
CAPITOL HILL OFFICE:
432 RSOB 20510; 224-6551

# House of Representatives' Offices

The list below gives the names of House members in alphabetical order followed by the address and phone number for their Washington offices. Address abbreviations used are as follows: CHOB (Cannon House Office Building), LHOB (Longworth House Office Building), RHOB (Rayburn House Office Building). The telephone area code for Washington is 202.

**ADDABBO, JOSEPH P. (D N.Y.—7)**
CAPITOL HILL OFFICE:
2256 RHOB 20515; 225-3461

**AKAKA, DANIEL K. (D HAWAII—2)**
CAPITOL HILL OFFICE:
1510 LHOB 20515; 225-4906

**ALBOSTA, DON (D MICH.—10)**
CAPITOL HILL OFFICE:
1318 LHOB 20515; 225-3561

**ALEXANDER, BILL (D ARK.—1)**
CAPITOL HILL OFFICE:
201 CHOB 20515; 225-4076

**ANDERSON, GLENN M. (D CALIF.—32)**
CAPITOL HILL OFFICE:
2329 RHOB 20515; 225-6676

**ANDREWS, IKE (D N.C.—4)**
CAPITOL HILL OFFICE:
2201 RHOB 20515; 225-1784

**ANNUNZIO, FRANK (D ILL.—11)**
CAPITOL HILL OFFICE:
2303 RHOB 20515; 225-6661

**ANTHONY, BERYL JR. (D ARK.—4)**
CAPITOL HILL OFFICE:
213 CHOB 20515; 225-3772

**APPLEGATE, DOUGLAS (D OHIO—18)**
CAPITOL HILL OFFICE:
435 CHOB 20515; 225-6265

**ARCHER, BILL (R TEXAS—7)**
CAPITOL HILL OFFICE:
1135 LHOB 20515; 225-2571

**ASHBROOK, JOHN M. (R OHIO—17)**
CAPITOL HILL OFFICE:
1436 LHOB 20515; 225-6431

**ASPIN, LES (D WIS.—1)**
CAPITOL HILL OFFICE:
442 CHOB 20515; 225-3031

**ATKINSON, EUGENE V. (D PA.—25)**
CAPITOL HILL OFFICE:
412 CHOB 20515; 225-2565

**AuCOIN, LES (D ORE.—1)**
CAPITOL HILL OFFICE:
2446 RHOB 20515; 225-0855

**BADHAM, ROBERT E. (R CALIF.—40)**
CAPITOL HILL OFFICE:
1108 LHOB 20515; 225-5611

**BAFALIS, L. A. "SKIP" (R FLA.—10)**
CAPITOL HILL OFFICE:
2433 RHOB 20515; 225-2536

**BAILEY, DON (D PA.—21)**
CAPITOL HILL OFFICE:
116 CHOB 20515; 225-5631

**BAILEY, WENDELL (R MO.—8)**
CAPITOL HILL OFFICE:
504 CHOB 20515; 225-5155

**BARNARD, DOUG JR. (D GA.—10)**
CAPITOL HILL OFFICE:
236 CHOB 20515; 225-4101

**BARNES, MICHAEL D. (D MD.—8)**
CAPITOL HILL OFFICE:
1607 LHOB 20515; 225-5341

**BEARD, ROBIN L. (R TENN.—6)**
CAPITOL HILL OFFICE:
229 CHOB 20515; 225-2811

**BEDELL, BERKLEY (D IOWA—6)**
CAPITOL HILL OFFICE:
2440 RHOB 20515; 225-5476

**BEILENSON, ANTHONY C. (D CALIF.—23)**
CAPITOL HILL OFFICE:
1025 LHOB 20515; 225-5911

**BENEDICT, CLEVE (R W.VA.—2)**
CAPITOL HILL OFFICE:
1229 LHOB 20515; 225-4331

**BENJAMIN, ADAM JR. (D IND.—1)**
CAPITOL HILL OFFICE:
410 CHOB 20515; 225-2461

**BENNETT, CHARLES E. (D FLA.—3)**
CAPITOL HILL OFFICE:
2107 RHOB 20515; 225-2501

**BEREUTER, DOUGLAS K. (R NEB.—1)**
CAPITOL HILL OFFICE:
1314 LHOB 20515; 225-4806

**BETHUNE, ED (R ARK.—2)**
CAPITOL HILL OFFICE:
1535 LHOB 20515; 225-2506

**BEVILL, TOM (D ALA.—4)**
CAPITOL HILL OFFICE:
2302 RHOB 20515; 225-4876

**BIAGGI, MARIO (D N.Y.—10)**
CAPITOL HILL OFFICE:
2428 RHOB 20515; 225-2464

**BINGHAM, JONATHAN B. (D N.Y.—22)**
CAPITOL HILL OFFICE:
2262 RHOB 20515; 225-4411

**BLANCHARD, JAMES J. (D MICH.—18)**
CAPITOL HILL OFFICE:
2453 RHOB 20515; 225-2101

**BLILEY, THOMAS J. JR. (R VA.—3)**
CAPITOL HILL OFFICE:
214 CHOB 20515; 225-2815

**BOGGS, LINDY (MRS. HALE) (D LA.—2)**
CAPITOL HILL OFFICE:
2353 RHOB 20515; 225-6636

**BOLAND, EDWARD P. (D MASS.—2)**
CAPITOL HILL OFFICE:
2426 RHOB 20515; 225-5601

**BOLLING, RICHARD (D MO.—5)**
CAPITOL HILL OFFICE:
2365 RHOB 20515; 225-4535

**BONER, BILL (D TENN.—5)**
CAPITOL HILL OFFICE:
118 CHOB 20515; 225-4311

**BONIOR, DAVID E. (D MICH.—12)**
CAPITOL HILL OFFICE:
1130 LHOB 20515; 225-2106

**BONKER, DON (D WASH.—3)**
CAPITOL HILL OFFICE:
434 CHOB 20515; 225-3536

**BOUQUARD, MARILYN LLOYD (D TENN.—3)**
CAPITOL HILL OFFICE:
2334 RHOB 20515; 225-3271

**BOWEN, DAVID R. (D MISS.—2)**
CAPITOL HILL OFFICE:
2421 RHOB 20515; 225-5876

**BREAUX, JOHN B. (D LA.—7)**
CAPITOL HILL OFFICE:
2159 RHOB 20515; 225-2031

1347

**BRINKLEY, JACK (D GA.—3)**
CAPITOL HILL OFFICE:
2470 RHOB 20515; 225-5901

**BRODHEAD, WILLIAM M. (D MICH.—17)**
CAPITOL HILL OFFICE:
1114 LHOB 20515; 225-4961

**BROOKS, JACK (D TEXAS—9)**
CAPITOL HILL OFFICE:
2449 RHOB 20515; 225-6565

**BROOMFIELD, WILLIAM S. (R MICH.—19)**
CAPITOL HILL OFFICE:
2306 RHOB 20515; 225-6135

**BROWN, CLARENCE J. (R OHIO—7)**
CAPITOL HILL OFFICE:
2217 RHOB 20515; 225-4324

**BROWN, GEORGE E. JR. (D CALIF.—36)**
CAPITOL HILL OFFICE:
2342 RHOB 20515; 225-6161

**BROWN, HANK (R COLO.—4)**
CAPITOL HILL OFFICE:
1319 LHOB 20515; 225-4676

**BROYHILL, JAMES T. (R N.C.—10)**
CAPITOL HILL OFFICE:
2340 RHOB 20515; 225-2576

**BURGENER, CLAIR W. (R CALIF.—43)**
CAPITOL HILL OFFICE:
343 CHOB 20515; 225-3906

**BURTON, JOHN L. (D CALIF.—5)**
CAPITOL HILL OFFICE:
1714 LHOB 20515; 225-5161

**BURTON, PHILLIP (D CALIF.—6)**
CAPITOL HILL OFFICE:
2304 RHOB 20515; 225-4965

**BUTLER, M. CALDWELL (R VA.—6)**
CAPITOL HILL OFFICE:
2330 RHOB 20515; 225-5431

**BYRON, BEVERLY B. (D MD.—6)**
CAPITOL HILL OFFICE:
1216 LHOB 20515; 225-2721

**CAMPBELL, CARROLL A. JR. (R S.C.—4)**
CAPITOL HILL OFFICE:
408 CHOB 20515; 225-6030

**CARMAN, GREGORY W. (R N.Y.—3)**
CAPITOL HILL OFFICE:
1729 LHOB 20515; 225-3865

**CARNEY, WILLIAM (R N.Y.—1)**
CAPITOL HILL OFFICE:
1113 LHOB 20515; 225-3826

**CHAPPELL, BILL JR. (D FLA.—4)**
CAPITOL HILL OFFICE:
2468 RHOB 20515; 225-4035

**CHAPPIE, GENE (R CALIF.—1)**
CAPITOL HILL OFFICE:
1730 LHOB 20515; 225-3076

**CHENEY, DICK (R WYO.—AL)**
CAPITOL HILL OFFICE:
225 CHOB 20515; 225-2311

**CHISHOLM, SHIRLEY (D N.Y.—12)**
CAPITOL HILL OFFICE:
2182 RHOB 20515; 225-6231

**CLAUSEN, DON H. (R CALIF.—2)**
CAPITOL HILL OFFICE:
2308 RHOB 20515; 225-3311

**CLAY, WILLIAM (D MO.—1)**
CAPITOL HILL OFFICE:
2264 RHOB 20515; 225-2406

**CLINGER, WILLIAM F. JR. (R PA.—23)**
CAPITOL HILL OFFICE:
1221 LHOB 20515; 225-5121

**COATS, DAN (R IND.—4)**
CAPITOL HILL OFFICE:
1427 LHOB 20515; 225-4436

**COELHO, TONY (D CALIF.—15)**
CAPITOL HILL OFFICE:
216 CHOB 20515; 225-6131

**COLEMAN, E. THOMAS (R MO.—6)**
CAPITOL HILL OFFICE:
1527 LHOB 20515; 225-7041

**COLLINS, CARDISS (D ILL.—7)**
CAPITOL HILL OFFICE:
2438 RHOB 20515; 225-5006

**COLLINS, JAMES M. (R TEXAS—3)**
CAPITOL HILL OFFICE:
2419 RHOB 20515; 225-4201

**CONABLE, BARBER B. JR. (R N.Y.—35)**
CAPITOL HILL OFFICE:
237 CHOB 20515; 225-3615

**CONTE, SILVIO O. (R MASS.—1)**
CAPITOL HILL OFFICE:
2300 RHOB 20515; 225-5335

**CONYERS, JOHN JR. (D MICH.—1)**
CAPITOL HILL OFFICE:
2313 RHOB 20515; 225-5126

**CORCORAN, TOM (R ILL.—15)**
CAPITOL HILL OFFICE:
1107 LHOB 20515; 225-2976

**COTTER, WILLIAM R. (D CONN.—1)**
CAPITOL HILL OFFICE:
2134 RHOB 20515; 225-2265

**COUGHLIN, LAWRENCE (R PA.—13)**
CAPITOL HILL OFFICE:
2467 RHOB 20515; 225-6111

**COURTER, JIM (R N.J.—13)**
CAPITOL HILL OFFICE:
325 CHOB 20515; 225-5801

**COYNE, JIM (R PA.—8)**
CAPITOL HILL OFFICE:
1513 LHOB 20515; 225-4276

**COYNE, WILLIAM J. (D PA.—14)**
CAPITOL HILL OFFICE:
511 CHOB 20515; 225-2301

**CRAIG, LARRY E. (R IDAHO—1)**
CAPITOL HILL OFFICE:
515 CHOB 20515; 225-6611

**CRANE, DANIEL B. (R ILL.—22)**
CAPITOL HILL OFFICE:
115 CHOB 20515; 225-5001

**CRANE, PHILIP M. (R ILL.—12)**
CAPITOL HILL OFFICE:
1035 LHOB 20515; 225-3711

**CROCKETT, GEORGE W. JR. (D MICH.—13)**
CAPITOL HILL OFFICE:
1531 LHOB 20515; 225-2261

**D'AMOURS, NORMAN E. (D N.H.—1)**
CAPITOL HILL OFFICE:
2242 RHOB 20515; 225-5456

**DANIEL, DAN (D VA.—5)**
CAPITOL HILL OFFICE:
2368 RHOB 20515; 225-4711

**DANIEL, ROBERT W. JR. (R VA.—4)**
CAPITOL HILL OFFICE:
2236 RHOB 20515; 225-6365

**DANIELSON, GEORGE E. (D CALIF.—30)**
CAPITOL HILL OFFICE:
2265 RHOB 20515; 225-5464

**DANNEMEYER, WILLIAM E. (R CALIF.—39)**
CAPITOL HILL OFFICE:
1032 LHOB 20515; 225-4111

**DASCHLE, THOMAS A. (D S.D.—1)**
CAPITOL HILL OFFICE:
439 CHOB 20515; 225-2801

**DAUB, HAL (R NEB.—2)**
CAPITOL HILL OFFICE:
1008 LHOB 20515; 225-4155

**DAVIS, ROBERT W. (R MICH.—11)**
CAPITOL HILL OFFICE:
1224 LHOB 20515; 225-4735

**DECKARD, JOEL (R IND.—8)**
CAPITOL HILL OFFICE:
125 CHOB 20515; 225-4636

**de la GARZA, E. "KIKA" (D TEXAS—15)**
CAPITOL HILL OFFICE:
1434 LHOB 20515; 225-2531

**DELLUMS, RONALD V. (D CALIF.—8)**
CAPITOL HILL OFFICE:
2136 RHOB 20515; 225-2661

**DeNARDIS, LAWRENCE J. (R CONN.—3)**
CAPITOL HILL OFFICE:
1429 LHOB 20515; 225-3661

**DERRICK, BUTLER (D S.C.—3)**
CAPITOL HILL OFFICE:
133 CHOB 20515; 225-5301

**DERWINSKI, EDWARD J. (R ILL.—4)**
CAPITOL HILL OFFICE:
1401 LHOB 20515; 225-3961

**DICKINSON, WILLIAM L. (R ALA.—2)**
CAPITOL HILL OFFICE:
2406 RHOB 20515; 225-2901

**DICKS, NORMAN D. (D WASH.—6)**
CAPITOL HILL OFFICE:
1122 LHOB 20515; 225-5916

**DINGELL, JOHN D. (D MICH.—16)**
CAPITOL HILL OFFICE:
2221 RHOB 20515; 225-4071

**DIXON, JULIAN C. (D CALIF.—28)**
CAPITOL HILL OFFICE:
423 CHOB 20515; 225-7084

**DONNELLY, BRIAN J. (D MASS.—11)**
CAPITOL HILL OFFICE:
1021 LHOB 20515; 225-3215

**DORGAN, BYRON L. (D N.D.—AL)**
CAPITOL HILL OFFICE:
427 CHOB 20515; 225-2611

**DORNAN, ROBERT K. (R CALIF.—27)**
CAPITOL HILL OFFICE:
332 CHOB 20515; 225-6451

**DOUGHERTY, CHARLES F. (R PA.—4)**
CAPITOL HILL OFFICE:
422 CHOB 20515; 225-8251

**DOWDY, WAYNE (D MISS.—4)**
CAPITOL HILL OFFICE:
1631 LHOB 20515; 225-5865

**DOWNEY, THOMAS J. (D N.Y.—2)**
CAPITOL HILL OFFICE:
303 CHOB 20515; 225-3335

**DREIER, DAVID (R CALIF.—35)**
CAPITOL HILL OFFICE:
1641 LHOB 20515; 225-2305

**DUNCAN, JOHN J. (R TENN.—2)**
CAPITOL HILL OFFICE:
2458 RHOB 20515; 225-5435

**DUNN, JIM (R MICH.—6)**
CAPITOL HILL OFFICE:
1630 LHOB 20515; 225-4872

**DWYER, BERNARD J. (D N.J.—15)**
CAPITOL HILL OFFICE:
437 CHOB 20515; 225-6301

**DYMALLY, MERVYN M. (D CALIF.—31)**
CAPITOL HILL OFFICE:
1116 LHOB 20515; 225-5425

**DYSON, ROY (D MD.—1)**
CAPITOL HILL OFFICE:
1020 LHOB 20515; 225-5311

**EARLY, JOSEPH D. (D MASS.—3)**
CAPITOL HILL OFFICE:
2349 RHOB 20515; 225-6101

**ECKART, DENNIS E. (D OHIO—22)**
CAPITOL HILL OFFICE:
1222 LHOB 20515; 225-6331

**EDGAR, ROBERT W. (D PA.—7)**
CAPITOL HILL OFFICE:
2442 RHOB 20515; 225-2011


**EDWARDS, DON (D CALIF.—10)**
CAPITOL HILL OFFICE:
2307 RHOB 20515; 225-3072


**EDWARDS, JACK (R ALA.—1)**
CAPITOL HILL OFFICE:
2369 RHOB 20515; 225-4931


**EDWARDS, MICKEY (R OKLA.—5)**
CAPITOL HILL OFFICE:
208 CHOB 20515; 225-2132


**EMERSON, BILL (R MO.—10)**
CAPITOL HILL OFFICE:
418 CHOB 20515; 225-4404


**EMERY, DAVID F. (R MAINE—1)**
CAPITOL HILL OFFICE:
2437 RHOB 20515; 225-6116


**ENGLISH, GLENN (D OKLA.—6)**
CAPITOL HILL OFFICE:
104 CHOB 20515; 225-5565


**ERDAHL, ARLEN (R MINN.—1)**
CAPITOL HILL OFFICE:
1518 LHOB 20515; 225-2271


**ERLENBORN, JOHN N. (R ILL.—14)**
CAPITOL HILL OFFICE:
2206 RHOB 20515; 225-3515


**ERTEL, ALLEN E. (D PA.—17)**
CAPITOL HILL OFFICE:
1211 LHOB 20515; 225-4315


**EVANS, BILLY LEE (D GA.—8)**
CAPITOL HILL OFFICE:
113 CHOB 20515; 225-6531


**EVANS, COOPER (R IOWA—3)**
CAPITOL HILL OFFICE:
317 CHOB 20515; 225-3301


**EVANS, DAVID W. (D IND.—6)**
CAPITOL HILL OFFICE:
438 CHOB 20515; 225-2276


**EVANS, THOMAS B. JR. (R DEL.—AL)**
CAPITOL HILL OFFICE:
316 CHOB 20515; 225-4165


**FARY, JOHN G. (D ILL.—5)**
CAPITOL HILL OFFICE:
1121 LHOB 20515; 225-5701


**FASCELL, DANTE B. (D FLA.—15)**
CAPITOL HILL OFFICE:
2354 RHOB 20515; 225-4506


**FAZIO, VIC (D CALIF.—4)**
CAPITOL HILL OFFICE:
1421 LHOB 20515; 225-5716


**FENWICK, MILLICENT (R N.J.—5)**
CAPITOL HILL OFFICE:
1230 LHOB 20515; 225-7300


**FERRARO, GERALDINE A. (D N.Y.—9)**
CAPITOL HILL OFFICE:
312 CHOB 20515; 225-3965


**FIEDLER, BOBBI (R CALIF.—21)**
CAPITOL HILL OFFICE:
1724 LHOB 20515; 225-5811


**FIELDS, JACK (R TEXAS—8)**
CAPITOL HILL OFFICE:
510 CHOB 20515; 225-4901


**FINDLEY, PAUL (R ILL.—20)**
CAPITOL HILL OFFICE:
2113 RHOB 20515; 225-5271


**FISH, HAMILTON JR. (R N.Y.—25)**
CAPITOL HILL OFFICE:
2227 RHOB 20515; 225-5441


**FITHIAN, FLOYD (D IND.—2)**
CAPITOL HILL OFFICE:
1210 LHOB 20515; 225-5777

**FLIPPO, RONNIE G. (D ALA.—5)**
CAPITOL HILL OFFICE:
405 CHOB 20515; 225-4801

**FLORIO, JAMES J. (D N.J.—1)**
CAPITOL HILL OFFICE:
1740 LHOB 20515; 225-6501

**FOGLIETTA, THOMAS M. (D PA.—1)**
CAPITOL HILL OFFICE:
1217 LHOB 20515; 225-4731

**FOLEY, THOMAS S. (D WASH.—5)**
CAPITOL HILL OFFICE:
1201 LHOB 20515; 225-2006

**FORD, HAROLD E. (D TENN.—8)**
CAPITOL HILL OFFICE:
2445 RHOB 20515; 225-3265

**FORD, WILLIAM D. (D MICH.—15)**
CAPITOL HILL OFFICE:
239 CHOB 20515; 225-6261

**FORSYTHE, EDWIN B. (R N.J.—6)**
CAPITOL HILL OFFICE:
2210 RHOB 20515; 225-4765

**FOUNTAIN, L. H. (D N.C.—2)**
CAPITOL HILL OFFICE:
2188 RHOB 20515; 225-4531

**FOWLER, WYCHE JR. (D GA.—5)**
CAPITOL HILL OFFICE:
1504 LHOB 20515; 225-3801

**FRANK, BARNEY (D MASS.—4)**
CAPITOL HILL OFFICE:
1609 LHOB 20515; 225-5931

**FRENZEL, BILL (R MINN.—3)**
CAPITOL HILL OFFICE:
1026 LHOB 20515; 225-2871

**FROST, MARTIN (D TEXAS—24)**
CAPITOL HILL OFFICE:
1238 LHOB 20515; 225-3605

**FUQUA, DON (D FLA.—2)**
CAPITOL HILL OFFICE:
2269 RHOB 20515; 225-5235

**GARCIA, ROBERT (D N.Y.—21)**
CAPITOL HILL OFFICE:
223 CHOB 20515; 225-4361

**GAYDOS, JOSEPH M. (D PA.—20)**
CAPITOL HILL OFFICE:
2366 RHOB 20515; 225-4631

**GEJDENSON, SAM (D CONN.—2)**
CAPITOL HILL OFFICE:
1503 LHOB 20515; 225-2076

**GEPHARDT, RICHARD A. (D MO.—3)**
CAPITOL HILL OFFICE:
218 CHOB 20515; 225-2671

**GIBBONS, SAM (D FLA.—7)**
CAPITOL HILL OFFICE:
2204 RHOB 20515; 225-3376

**GILMAN, BENJAMIN A. (R N.Y.—26)**
CAPITOL HILL OFFICE:
2160 RHOB 20515; 225-3776

**GINGRICH, NEWT (R GA.—6)**
CAPITOL HILL OFFICE:
1005 LHOB 20515; 225-4501

**GINN, BO (D GA.—1)**
CAPITOL HILL OFFICE:
2135 RHOB 20515; 225-5831

**GLICKMAN, DAN (D KAN.—4)**
CAPITOL HILL OFFICE:
1507 LHOB 20515; 225-6216

**GOLDWATER, BARRY M. JR. (R CALIF.—20)**
CAPITOL HILL OFFICE:
2240 RHOB 20515; 225-4461

**GONZALEZ, HENRY B. (D TEXAS—20)**
CAPITOL HILL OFFICE:
2252 RHOB 20515; 225-3236

**GOODLING, BILL (R PA.—19)**
CAPITOL HILL OFFICE:
109 CHOB 20515; 225-5836

**GORE, ALBERT JR. (D TENN.—4)**
CAPITOL HILL OFFICE:
1131 LHOB 20515; 225-4231

**GRADISON, BILL (R OHIO—1)**
CAPITOL HILL OFFICE:
1117 LHOB 20515; 225-3164

**GRAMM, PHIL (D TEXAS—6)**
CAPITOL HILL OFFICE:
1721 LHOB 20515; 225-2002

**GRAY, WILLIAM H. III (D PA.—2)**
CAPITOL HILL OFFICE:
429 CHOB 20515; 225-4001

**GREEN, S. WILLIAM (R N.Y.—18)**
CAPITOL HILL OFFICE:
1417 LHOB 20515; 225-2436

**GREGG, JUDD (R N.H.—2)**
CAPITOL HILL OFFICE:
503 CHOB 20515; 225-5206

**GRISHAM, WAYNE (R CALIF.—33)**
CAPITOL HILL OFFICE:
120 CHOB 20515; 225-3576

**GUARINI, FRANK J. (D N.J.—14)**
CAPITOL HILL OFFICE:
1530 LHOB 20515; 225-2765

**GUNDERSON, STEVE (R WIS.—3)**
CAPITOL HILL OFFICE:
416 CHOB 20515; 225-5506

**HAGEDORN, TOM (R MINN.—2)**
CAPITOL HILL OFFICE:
2344 RHOB 20515; 225-2472

**HALL, RALPH M. (D TEXAS—4)**
CAPITOL HILL OFFICE:
1223 LHOB 20515; 225-6673

**HALL, SAM B. JR. (D TEXAS—1)**
CAPITOL HILL OFFICE:
318 CHOB 20515; 225-3035

**HALL, TONY P. (D OHIO—3)**
CAPITOL HILL OFFICE:
1728 LHOB 20515; 225-6465

**HAMILTON, LEE H. (D IND.—9)**
CAPITOL HILL OFFICE:
2187 RHOB 20515; 225-5315

**HAMMERSCHMIDT, JOHN PAUL (R ARK.—3)**
CAPITOL HILL OFFICE:
2207 RHOB 20515; 225-4301

**HANCE, KENT (D TEXAS—19)**
CAPITOL HILL OFFICE:
1039 LHOB 20515; 225-4005

**HANSEN, GEORGE (R IDAHO—2)**
CAPITOL HILL OFFICE:
1125 LHOB 20515; 225-5531

**HANSEN, JAMES V. (R UTAH—1)**
CAPITOL HILL OFFICE:
1407 LHOB 20515; 225-0453

**HARKIN, TOM (D IOWA—5)**
CAPITOL HILL OFFICE:
2411 RHOB 20515; 225-3806

**HARTNETT, THOMAS F. (R S.C.—1)**
CAPITOL HILL OFFICE:
509 CHOB 20515; 225-3176

**HATCHER, CHARLES (D GA.—2)**
CAPITOL HILL OFFICE:
1726 LHOB 20515; 225-3631

**HAWKINS, AUGUSTUS F. (D CALIF.—29)**
CAPITOL HILL OFFICE:
2371 RHOB 20515; 225-2201

**HECKLER, MARGARET M. (R MASS.—10)**
CAPITOL HILL OFFICE:
2312 RHOB 20515; 225-4335

**HEFNER, W. G. "BILL" (D N.C.—8)**
CAPITOL HILL OFFICE:
2161 RHOB 20515; 225-3715

**HEFTEL, CECIL (D HAWAII—1)**
CAPITOL HILL OFFICE:
1030 LHOB 20515; 225-2726

**HENDON, BILL (R N.C.—11)**
CAPITOL HILL OFFICE:
212 CHOB 20515; 225-6401

**HERTEL, DENNIS M. (D MICH.-14)**
CAPITOL HILL OFFICE:
1017 LHOB 20515; 225-6276

**HIGHTOWER, JACK (D TEXAS—13)**
CAPITOL HILL OFFICE:
2348 RHOB 20515; 225-3706

**HILER, JOHN (R IND.—3)**
CAPITOL HILL OFFICE:
1338 LHOB 20515; 225-3915

**HILLIS, ELWOOD (R IND.—5)**
CAPITOL HILL OFFICE:
2336 RHOB 20515; 225-5037

**HOLLAND, KEN (D S.C.—5)**
CAPITOL HILL OFFICE:
2431 RHOB 20515; 225-5501

**HOLLENBECK, HAROLD C. (R N.J.—9)**
CAPITOL HILL OFFICE:
1526 LHOB 20515; 225-5061

**HOLT, MARJORIE S. (R MD.—4)**
CAPITOL HILL OFFICE:
2412 RHOB 20515; 225-8090

**HOPKINS, LARRY J. (R KY.—6)**
CAPITOL HILL OFFICE:
331 CHOB 20515; 225-4706

**HORTON, FRANK (R N.Y.—34)**
CAPITOL HILL OFFICE:
2229 RHOB 20515; 225-4916

**HOWARD, JAMES J. (D N.J.—3)**
CAPITOL HILL OFFICE:
2245 RHOB 20515; 225-4671

**HOYER, STENY (D MD.—5)**
CAPITOL HILL OFFICE:
1513 LHOB 20515; 225-4131

**HUBBARD, CARROLL JR. (D KY.—1)**
CAPITOL HILL OFFICE:
2244 RHOB 20515; 225-3115

**HUCKABY, JERRY (D LA.—5)**
CAPITOL HILL OFFICE:
228 CHOB 20515; 225-2376

**HUGHES, WILLIAM J. (D N.J.—2)**
CAPITOL HILL OFFICE:
436 CHOB 20515; 225-6572

**HUNTER, DUNCAN L. (R CALIF.—42)**
CAPITOL HILL OFFICE:
415 CHOB 20515; 225-5672

**HUTTO, EARL (D FLA.—1)**
CAPITOL HILL OFFICE:
330 CHOB 20515; 225-4136

**HYDE, HENRY J. (R ILL.—6)**
CAPITOL HILL OFFICE:
1203 LHOB 20515; 225-4561

**IRELAND, ANDY (D FLA.—8)**
CAPITOL HILL OFFICE:
1124 LHOB 20515; 225-5015

**JACOBS, ANDREW JR. (D IND.—11)**
CAPITOL HILL OFFICE:
1533 LHOB 20515; 225-4011

**JEFFORDS, JAMES M. (R VT.—AL)**
CAPITOL HILL OFFICE:
1524 LHOB 20515; 225-4115

**JEFFRIES, JIM (R KAN.—2)**
CAPITOL HILL OFFICE:
424 CHOB 20515; 225-6601

**JENKINS, ED (D GA.—9)**
CAPITOL HILL OFFICE:
217 CHOB 20515; 225-5211

**JOHNSTON, EUGENE (R N.C.—6)**
CAPITOL HILL OFFICE:
128 CHOB 20515; 225-3065

**JONES, ED (D TENN.—7)**
CAPITOL HILL OFFICE:
108 CHOB 20515; 225-4714

**JONES, JAMES R. (D OKLA.—1)**
CAPITOL HILL OFFICE:
203 CHOB 20515; 225-2211

**JONES, WALTER B. (D N.C.—1)**
CAPITOL HILL OFFICE:
241 CHOB 20515; 225-3101

**KASTENMEIER, ROBERT W. (D WIS.—2)**
CAPITOL HILL OFFICE:
2232 RHOB 20515; 225-2906

**KAZEN, ABRAHAM JR. (D TEXAS—23)**
CAPITOL HILL OFFICE:
2408 RHOB 20515; 225-4511

**KEMP, JACK F. (R N.Y.—38)**
CAPITOL HILL OFFICE:
2235 RHOB 20515; 225-5265

**KILDEE, DALE E. (D MICH.—7)**
CAPITOL HILL OFFICE:
314 CHOB 20515; 225-3611

**KINDNESS, THOMAS N. (R OHIO—8)**
CAPITOL HILL OFFICE:
2434 RHOB 20515; 225-6205

**KOGOVSEK, RAY (D COLO.—3)**
CAPITOL HILL OFFICE:
430 CHOB 20515; 225-4761

**KRAMER, KEN (R COLO.—5)**
CAPITOL HILL OFFICE:
114 CHOB 20515; 225-4422

**LaFALCE, JOHN J. (D N.Y.—36)**
CAPITOL HILL OFFICE:
2447 RHOB 20515; 225-3231

**LAGOMARSINO, ROBERT J. (R CALIF.—19)**
CAPITOL HILL OFFICE:
2332 RHOB 20515; 225-3601

**LANTOS, TOM (D CALIF.—11)**
CAPITOL HILL OFFICE:
1123 LHOB 20515; 225-3531

**LATTA, DELBERT L. (R OHIO—5)**
CAPITOL HILL OFFICE:
2309 RHOB 20515; 225-6405

**LEACH, JIM (R IOWA—1)**
CAPITOL HILL OFFICE:
1406 LHOB 20515; 225-6576

**LEATH, MARVIN (D TEXAS—11)**
CAPITOL HILL OFFICE:
336 CHOB 20515; 225-6105

**LeBOUTILLIER, JOHN (R N.Y.—6)**
CAPITOL HILL OFFICE:
417 CHOB 20515; 225-5956

**LEE, GARY A. (R N.Y.—33)**
CAPITOL HILL OFFICE:
322 CHOB 20515; 225-3333

**LEHMAN, WILLIAM (D FLA.—13)**
CAPITOL HILL OFFICE:
2347 RHOB 20515; 225-4211

**LELAND, MICKEY (D TEXAS—18)**
CAPITOL HILL OFFICE:
419 CHOB 20515; 225-3816

**LENT, NORMAN F. (R N.Y.—4)**
CAPITOL HILL OFFICE:
2228 RHOB 20515; 225-7896

**LEVITAS, ELLIOTT H. (D GA.—4)**
CAPITOL HILL OFFICE:
2416 RHOB 20515; 225-4272

**LEWIS, JERRY (R CALIF.—37)**
CAPITOL HILL OFFICE:
327 CHOB 20515; 225-5861

**LIVINGSTON, BOB (R LA.—1)**
CAPITOL HILL OFFICE:
206 CHOB 20515; 225-3015

**LOEFFLER, TOM (R TEXAS—21)**
CAPITOL HILL OFFICE:
1212 LHOB 20515; 225-4236

**LONG, CLARENCE D. (D MD.—2)**
CAPITOL HILL OFFICE:
2405 RHOB 20515; 225-3061

**LONG, GILLIS W. (D LA.—8)**
CAPITOL HILL OFFICE:
2311 RHOB 20515; 225-4926

**LOTT, TRENT (R MISS.—5)**
CAPITOL HILL OFFICE:
2400 RHOB 20515; 225-5772
  (congressional office)
1622 LHOB 20515; 225-0197
  (Minority Whip's office)

**LOWERY, BILL (R CALIF.—41)**
CAPITOL HILL OFFICE:
1331 LHOB 20515; 225-3201

**LOWRY, MIKE (D WASH.—7)**
CAPITOL HILL OFFICE:
1206 LHOB 20515; 225-3106

**LUJAN, MANUEL JR. (R N.M.—1)**
CAPITOL HILL OFFICE:
1323 LHOB 20515; 225-6316

**LUKEN, THOMAS A. (D OHIO—2)**
CAPITOL HILL OFFICE:
240 CHOB 20515; 225-2216

**LUNDINE, STANLEY N. (D N.Y.—39)**
CAPITOL HILL OFFICE:
231 CHOB 20515; 225-3161

**LUNGREN, DAN (R CALIF.—34)**
CAPITOL HILL OFFICE:
328 CHOB 20515; 225-2415

**MADIGAN, EDWARD R. (R ILL.—21)**
CAPITOL HILL OFFICE:
2457 RHOB 20515; 225-2371

**MARKEY, EDWARD J. (D MASS.—7)**
CAPITOL HILL OFFICE:
403 CHOB 20515; 225-2836

**MARKS, MARC L. (R PA.—24)**
CAPITOL HILL OFFICE:
1424 LHOB 20515; 225-5406

**MARLENEE, RON (R MONT.—2)**
CAPITOL HILL OFFICE:
409 CHOB 20515; 225-1555

**MARRIOTT, DAN (R UTAH—2)**
CAPITOL HILL OFFICE:
1133 LHOB 20515; 225-3011

**MARTIN, DAVID O'B. (R N.Y.—30)**
CAPITOL HILL OFFICE:
502 CHOB 20515; 225-4611

**MARTIN, JAMES G. (R N.C.—9)**
CAPITOL HILL OFFICE:
341 CHOB 20515; 225-1976

**MARTIN, LYNN (R ILL.—16)**
CAPITOL HILL OFFICE:
1208 LHOB 20515; 225-5676

**MATSUI, ROBERT T. (D CALIF.—3)**
CAPITOL HILL OFFICE:
329 CHOB 20515; 225-7163

**MATTOX, JIM (D TEXAS—5)**
CAPITOL HILL OFFICE:
1111 LHOB 20515; 225-2231

**MAVROULES, NICHOLAS (D MASS.—6)**
CAPITOL HILL OFFICE:
1204 LHOB 20515; 225-8020

**MAZZOLI, ROMANO L. (D KY.—3)**
CAPITOL HILL OFFICE:
2246 RHOB 20515; 225-5401

**McCLORY, ROBERT (R ILL.—13)**
CAPITOL HILL OFFICE:
2109 RHOB 20515; 225-5221

**McCLOSKEY, PAUL N. JR. (R CALIF.—12)**
CAPITOL HILL OFFICE:
205 CHOB 20515; 225-5411

**McCOLLUM, BILL (R FLA.—5)**
CAPITOL HILL OFFICE:
1313 LHOB 20515; 225-2176

**McCURDY, DAVE (D OKLA.—4)**
CAPITOL HILL OFFICE:
313 CHOB 20515; 225-6165

**McDADE, JOSEPH M. (R PA.—10)**
CAPITOL HILL OFFICE:
2370 RHOB 20515; 225-3731

**McDONALD, LARRY P. (D GA.—7)**
CAPITOL HILL OFFICE:
103 CHOB 20515; 225-2931

**McEWEN, BOB (R OHIO—6)**
CAPITOL HILL OFFICE:
507 CHOB 20515; 225-5705

**McGRATH, RAYMOND J. (R N.Y.—5)**
CAPITOL HILL OFFICE:
506 CHOB 20515; 225-5516

**McHUGH, MATTHEW F. (D N.Y.—27)**
CAPITOL HILL OFFICE:
306 CHOB 20515; 225-6335

**McKINNEY, STEWART B. (R CONN.—4)**
CAPITOL HILL OFFICE:
106 CHOB 20515; 225-5541

**MICA, DANIEL A. (D FLA.—11)**
CAPITOL HILL OFFICE:
131 CHOB 20515; 225-3001

**MICHEL, ROBERT H. (R ILL.—18)**
CAPITOL HILL OFFICE:
2112 RHOB 20515; 225-6201
(congressional office)
H-232 The Capitol 20515; 225-0600
(Minority Leader's office)

**MIKULSKI, BARBARA A. (D MD.—3)**
CAPITOL HILL OFFICE:
407 CHOB 20515; 225-4016

**MILLER, CLARENCE E. (R OHIO—10)**
CAPITOL HILL OFFICE:
2208 RHOB 20515; 225-5131

**MILLER, GEORGE (D CALIF.—7)**
CAPITOL HILL OFFICE:
2422 RHOB 20515; 225-2095

**MINETA, NORMAN Y. (D CALIF.—13)**
CAPITOL HILL OFFICE:
2352 RHOB 20515; 225-2631

**MINISH, JOSEPH G. (D N.J.—11)**
CAPITOL HILL OFFICE:
2162 RHOB 20515; 225-5035

**MITCHELL, DONALD J. (R N.Y.—31)**
CAPITOL HILL OFFICE:
2305 RHOB 20515; 225-3665

**MITCHELL, PARREN J. (D MD.—7)**
CAPITOL HILL OFFICE:
2367 RHOB 20515; 225-4741

**MOAKLEY, JOE (D MASS.—9)**
CAPITOL HILL OFFICE:
221 CHOB 20515; 225-8273

**MOFFETT, TOBY (D CONN.—6)**
CAPITOL HILL OFFICE:
127 CHOB 20515; 225-4476

**1357**

**MOLINARI, GUY V. (R N.Y.—17)**
CAPITOL HILL OFFICE:
501 CHOB 20515; 225-3371

**MOLLOHAN, ROBERT H. (D W.VA.—1)**
CAPITOL HILL OFFICE:
339 CHOB 20515; 225-4172

**MONTGOMERY, G. V. "SONNY"
(D MISS.—3)**
CAPITOL HILL OFFICE:
2184 RHOB 20515; 225-5031

**MOORE, HENSON (R LA.—6)**
CAPITOL HILL OFFICE:
2404 RHOB 20515; 225-3901

**MOORHEAD, CARLOS J. (R CALIF.—22)**
CAPITOL HILL OFFICE:
2346 RHOB 20515; 225-4176

**MORRISON, SID (R WASH.—4)**
CAPITOL HILL OFFICE:
1330 LHOB 20515; 225-5816

**MOTTL, RONALD M. (D OHIO—23)**
CAPITOL HILL OFFICE:
2459 RHOB 20515; 225-5731

**MURPHY, AUSTIN J. (D PA.—22)**
CAPITOL HILL OFFICE:
204 CHOB 20515; 225-4665

**MURTHA, JOHN P. (D PA.—12)**
CAPITOL HILL OFFICE:
2423 RHOB 20515; 225-2065

**MYERS, JOHN T. (R IND.—7)**
CAPITOL HILL OFFICE:
2301 RHOB 20515; 225-5805

**NAPIER, JOHN L. (R S.C.—6)**
CAPITOL HILL OFFICE:
1631 LHOB 20515; 225-3315

**NATCHER, WILLIAM H. (D KY.—2)**
CAPITOL HILL OFFICE:
2333 RHOB 20515; 225-3501

**NEAL, STEPHEN L. (D N.C.—5)**
CAPITOL HILL OFFICE:
2463 RHOB 20515; 225-2071

**NELLIGAN, JAMES L. (R PA.—11)**
CAPITOL HILL OFFICE:
1711 LHOB 20515; 225-6511

**NELSON, BILL (D FLA.—9)**
CAPITOL HILL OFFICE:
307 CHOB 20515; 225-3671

**NICHOLS, BILL (D ALA.—3)**
CAPITOL HILL OFFICE:
2417 RHOB 20515; 225-3261

**NOWAK, HENRY J. (D N.Y.—37)**
CAPITOL HILL OFFICE:
1514 LHOB 20515; 225-3306

**OAKAR, MARY ROSE (D OHIO—20)**
CAPITOL HILL OFFICE:
107 CHOB 20515; 225-5871

**OBERSTAR, JAMES L. (D MINN.—8)**
CAPITOL HILL OFFICE:
2351 RHOB 20515; 225-6211

**OBEY, DAVID R. (D WIS.—7)**
CAPITOL HILL OFFICE:
2230 RHOB 20515; 225-3365

**O'BRIEN, GEORGE M. (R ILL.—17)**
CAPITOL HILL OFFICE:
2439 RHOB 20515; 225-3635

**O'NEILL, THOMAS P. JR. (D MASS.—8)**
CAPITOL HILL OFFICE:
2231 RHOB 20515; 225-5111
(congressional office)
H-204 The Capitol 20515; 225-5414
(Speaker's Office)
H-209 The Capitol 20515; 225-2204
(Speaker's Rooms)

**OTTINGER, RICHARD L. (D N.Y.—24)**
CAPITOL HILL OFFICE:
2241 RHOB 20515; 225-6506

**OXLEY, MICHAEL (R OHIO—4)**
CAPITOL HILL OFFICE:
1724 LHOB 20515; 225-2676

**PANETTA, LEON E. (D CALIF.—16)**
CAPITOL HILL OFFICE:
431 CHOB 20515; 225-2861

**PARRIS, STAN (R VA.—8)**
CAPITOL HILL OFFICE:
428 CHOB 20515; 225-4376

**PASHAYAN, CHARLES JR. (R CALIF.—17)**
CAPITOL HILL OFFICE:
129 CHOB 20515; 225-3341

**PATMAN, BILL (D TEXAS-14)**
CAPITOL HILL OFFICE:
1408 LHOB 20515; 225-2831

**PATTERSON, JERRY M. (D CALIF.—38)**
CAPITOL HILL OFFICE:
2238 RHOB 20515; 225-2965

**PAUL, RON (R TEXAS—22)**
CAPITOL HILL OFFICE:
1234 LHOB 20515; 225-5951

**PEASE, DON J. (D OHIO—13)**
CAPITOL HILL OFFICE:
1127 LHOB 20515; 225-3401

**PEPPER, CLAUDE (D FLA.—14)**
CAPITOL HILL OFFICE:
2239 RHOB 20515; 225-3931

**PERKINS, CARL D. (D KY.—7)**
CAPITOL HILL OFFICE:
2328 RHOB 20515; 225-4935

**PETRI, THOMAS E. (R WIS.—6)**
CAPITOL HILL OFFICE:
1024 LHOB 20515; 225-2476

**PEYSER, PETER A. (D N.Y.—23)**
CAPITOL HILL OFFICE:
301 CHOB 20515; 225-5536

**PICKLE, J. J. (D TEXAS—10)**
CAPITOL HILL OFFICE:
242 CHOB 20515; 225-4865

**PORTER, JOHN EDWARD (R ILL.—10)**
CAPITOL HILL OFFICE:
1529 LHOB 20515; 225-4835

**PRICE, MELVIN (D ILL.—23)**
CAPITOL HILL OFFICE:
2110 RHOB 20515; 225-5661

**PRITCHARD, JOEL (R WASH.—1)**
CAPITOL HILL OFFICE:
2263 RHOB 20515; 225-6311

**PURSELL, CARL D. (R MICH.—2)**
CAPITOL HILL OFFICE:
1414 LHOB 20515; 225-4401

**QUILLEN, JAMES H. (R TENN.—1)**
CAPITOL HILL OFFICE:
102 CHOB 20515; 225-6356

**RAHALL, NICK J. II (D W.VA.—4)**
CAPITOL HILL OFFICE:
440 CHOB 20515; 225-3452

**RAILSBACK, TOM (R ILL.—19)**
CAPITOL HILL OFFICE:
2104 RHOB 20515; 225-5905

**RANGEL, CHARLES B. (D N.Y.—19)**
CAPITOL HILL OFFICE:
2432 RHOB 20515; 225-4365

**RATCHFORD, WILLIAM R. (D CONN.—5)**
CAPITOL HILL OFFICE:
432 CHOB 20515; 225-3822

**REGULA, RALPH (R OHIO—16)**
CAPITOL HILL OFFICE:
401 CHOB 20515; 225-3876

**REUSS, HENRY S. (D WIS.—5)**
CAPITOL HILL OFFICE:
2413 RHOB 20515; 225-3571

**RHODES, JOHN J. (R ARIZ.—1)**
CAPITOL HILL OFFICE:
2310 RHOB 20515; 225-2635

**RICHMOND, FRED (D N.Y.—14)**
CAPITOL HILL OFFICE:
1707 LHOB 20515; 225-5936

**RINALDO, MATTHEW J. (R N.J.—12)**
CAPITOL HILL OFFICE:
2338 RHOB 20515; 225-5361

**RITTER, DON (R PA.—15)**
CAPITOL HILL OFFICE:
124 CHOB 20515; 225-6411

**ROBERTS, CLINT (R S.D.-2)**
CAPITOL HILL OFFICE:
1009 LHOB 20515; 225-5165

**ROBERTS, PAT (R KAN.—1)**
CAPITOL HILL OFFICE:
1428 LHOB 20515; 225-2715

**ROBINSON, J. KENNETH (R VA.—7)**
CAPITOL HILL OFFICE:
2233 RHOB 20515; 225-6561

**RODINO, PETER W. JR. (D N.J.—10)**
CAPITOL HILL OFFICE:
2462 RHOB 20515; 225-3436

**ROE, ROBERT A. (D N.J.—8)**
CAPITOL HILL OFFICE:
2243 RHOB 20515; 225-5751

**ROEMER, BUDDY (D LA.—4)**
CAPITOL HILL OFFICE:
1725 LHOB 20515; 225-2777

**ROGERS, HAROLD (R KY.—5)**
CAPITOL HILL OFFICE:
413 CHOB 20515; 225-4601

**ROSE, CHARLIE (D N.C.—7)**
CAPITOL HILL OFFICE:
2435 RHOB 20515; 225-2731

**ROSENTHAL, BENJAMIN S. (D N.Y.—8)**
CAPITOL HILL OFFICE:
2372 RHOB 20515; 225-2601

**1360**

**ROSTENKOWSKI, DAN (D ILL.—8)**
CAPITOL HILL OFFICE:
2111 RHOB 20515; 225-4061

**ROTH, TOBY (R WIS.—8)**
CAPITOL HILL OFFICE:
215 CHOB 20515; 225-5665

**ROUKEMA, MARGE (R N.J.—7)**
CAPITOL HILL OFFICE:
226 CHOB 20515; 225-4465

**ROUSSELOT, JOHN H. (R CALIF.—26)**
CAPITOL HILL OFFICE:
2133 RHOB 20515; 225-4206

**ROYBAL, EDWARD R. (D CALIF.—25)**
CAPITOL HILL OFFICE:
2211 RHOB 20515; 225-6235

**RUDD, ELDON (R ARIZ.—4)**
CAPITOL HILL OFFICE:
1110 LHOB 20515; 225-3361

**RUSSO, MARTY (D ILL.—3)**
CAPITOL HILL OFFICE:
2464 RHOB 20515; 225-5736

**SABO, MARTIN OLAV (D MINN.—5)**
CAPITOL HILL OFFICE:
426 CHOB 20515; 225-4755

**ST GERMAIN, FERNAND J. (D R.I.—1)**
CAPITOL HILL OFFICE:
2108 RHOB 20515; 225-4911

**SANTINI, JAMES D. (D NEV.—AL)**
CAPITOL HILL OFFICE:
2429 RHOB 20515; 225-5965

**SAVAGE, GUS (D ILL.—2)**
CAPITOL HILL OFFICE:
1233 LHOB 20515; 225-0773

**SAWYER, HAROLD S. (R MICH.—5)**
CAPITOL HILL OFFICE:
123 CHOB 20515; 225-3831

**SCHEUER, JAMES H. (D N.Y.—11)**
CAPITOL HILL OFFICE:
2402 RHOB 20515; 225-5471


**SCHNEIDER, CLAUDINE (R R.I.—2)**
CAPITOL HILL OFFICE:
1431 LHOB 20515; 225-2735


**SCHROEDER, PATRICIA (D COLO.—1)**
CAPITOL HILL OFFICE:
2410 RHOB 20515; 225-4431


**SCHULZE, RICHARD T. (R PA.—5)**
CAPITOL HILL OFFICE:
2444 RHOB 20515; 225-5761


**SCHUMER, CHARLES E. (D N.Y.—16)**
CAPITOL HILL OFFICE:
126 CHOB 20515; 225-6616


**SEIBERLING, JOHN F. (D OHIO—14)**
CAPITOL HILL OFFICE:
1225 LHOB 20515; 225-5231


**SENSENBRENNER, F. JAMES JR. (R WIS.—9)**
CAPITOL HILL OFFICE:
315 CHOB 20515; 225-5101


**SHAMANSKY, BOB (D OHIO—12)**
CAPITOL HILL OFFICE:
1022 LHOB 20515; 225-5355


**SHANNON, JAMES M. (D MASS.—5)**
CAPITOL HILL OFFICE:
224 CHOB 20515; 225-3411


**SHARP, PHILIP R. (D IND.—10)**
CAPITOL HILL OFFICE:
2452 RHOB 20515; 225-3021


**SHAW, E. CLAY JR. (R FLA.—12)**
CAPITOL HILL OFFICE:
1213 LHOB 20515; 225-3026


**SHELBY, RICHARD C. (D ALA.—7)**
CAPITOL HILL OFFICE:
1705 LHOB 20515; 225-2665


**SHUMWAY, NORMAN D. (R CALIF.—14)**
CAPITOL HILL OFFICE:
1228 LHOB 20515; 225-2511


**SHUSTER, BUD (R PA.—9)**
CAPITOL HILL OFFICE:
2455 RHOB 20515; 225-2431


**SILJANDER, MARK (R MICH.—4)**
CAPITOL HILL OFFICE:
1022 LHOB 20515; 225-3761


**SIMON, PAUL (D ILL.—24)**
CAPITOL HILL OFFICE:
227 CHOB 20515; 225-5201


**SKEEN, JOE (R N.M.—2)**
CAPITOL HILL OFFICE:
1508 LHOB 20515; 225-2365


**SKELTON, IKE (D MO.—4)**
CAPITOL HILL OFFICE:
1404 LHOB 20515; 225-2876


**SMITH, ALBERT LEE JR. (R ALA.—6)**
CAPITOL HILL OFFICE:
1723 LHOB 20515; 225-4921


**SMITH, CHRISTOPHER H. (R N.J.—4)**
CAPITOL HILL OFFICE:
513 CHOB 20515; 225-3765


**SMITH, DENNY (R ORE.—2)**
CAPITOL HILL OFFICE:
1207 LHOB 20515; 225-5711


**SMITH, NEAL (D IOWA—4)**
CAPITOL HILL OFFICE:
2373 RHOB 20515; 225-4426


**SMITH, VIRGINIA (R NEB.—3)**
CAPITOL HILL OFFICE:
2202 RHOB 20515; 225-6435


**SNOWE, OLYMPIA J. (R MAINE—2)**
CAPITOL HILL OFFICE:
130 CHOB 20515; 225-6306

SNYDER, GENE (R KY.—4)
CAPITOL HILL OFFICE:
2185 RHOB 20515; 225-3465

SOLARZ, STEPHEN J. (D N.Y.—13)
CAPITOL HILL OFFICE:
1536 LHOB 20515; 225-2361

SOLOMON, GERALD B.H. (R N.Y.—29)
CAPITOL HILL OFFICE:
323 CHOB 20515; 225-5614

SPENCE, FLOYD (R S.C.—2)
CAPITOL HILL OFFICE:
2427 RHOB 20515; 225-2452

STANGELAND, ARLAN (R MINN.—7)
CAPITOL HILL OFFICE:
1519 LHOB 20515; 225-2165

STANTON, J. WILLIAM (R OHIO—11)
CAPITOL HILL OFFICE:
2466 RHOB 20515; 225-5306

STARK, FORTNEY H. "PETE" (D CALIF.—9)
CAPITOL HILL OFFICE:
1034 LHOB 20515; 225-5065

STATON, DAVID MICHAEL (R W.VA.)
CAPITOL HILL OFFICE:
425 CHOB 20515; 225-2711

STENHOLM, CHARLES W. (D TEXAS—17)
CAPITOL HILL OFFICE:
1232 LHOB 20515; 225-6605

STOKES, LOUIS (D OHIO—21)
CAPITOL HILL OFFICE:
2465 RHOB 20515; 225-7032

STRATTON, SAMUEL S. (D N.Y.—28)
CAPITOL HILL OFFICE:
2205 RHOB 20515; 225-5076

STUDDS, GERRY E. (D MASS.—12)
CAPITOL HILL OFFICE:
1501 LHOB 20515; 225-3111

STUMP, BOB (D ARIZ.—3)
CAPITOL HILL OFFICE:
211 CHOB 20515; 225-4576

SWIFT, AL (D WASH.—2)
CAPITOL HILL OFFICE:
1511 LHOB 20515; 225-2605

SYNAR, MIKE (D OKLA.—2)
CAPITOL HILL OFFICE:
1713 LHOB 20515; 225-2701

TAUKE, TOM (R IOWA—2)
CAPITOL HILL OFFICE:
319 CHOB 20515; 225-2911

TAUZIN, W. J. "BILLY" (D LA.—3)
CAPITOL HILL OFFICE:
222 CHOB 20515; 225-4031

TAYLOR, GENE (R MO.—7)
CAPITOL HILL OFFICE:
2430 RHOB 20515; 225-6536

THOMAS, WILLIAM M. (R CALIF.—18)
CAPITOL HILL OFFICE:
324 CHOB 20515; 225-2915

TRAXLER, BOB (D MICH.—8)
CAPITOL HILL OFFICE:
2448 RHOB 20515; 225-2806

TRIBLE, PAUL S. JR. (R VA.—1)
CAPITOL HILL OFFICE:
326 CHOB 20515; 225-4261

UDALL, MORRIS K. (D ARIZ.—2)
CAPITOL HILL OFFICE:
235 CHOB 20515; 225-4065

VANDER JAGT, GUY (R MICH.—9)
CAPITOL HILL OFFICE:
2409 RHOB 20515; 225-3511

VENTO, BRUCE F. (D MINN.—4)
CAPITOL HILL OFFICE:
230 CHOB 20515; 225-6631

**VOLKMER, HAROLD L. (D MO.—9)**
CAPITOL HILL OFFICE:
1007 LHOB 20515; 225-2956

**WALGREN, DOUG (D PA.—18)**
CAPITOL HILL OFFICE:
117 CHOB 20515; 225-2135

**WALKER, ROBERT S. (R PA.—16)**
CAPITOL HILL OFFICE:
1028 LHOB 20515; 225-2411

**WAMPLER, WILLIAM C. (R VA.—9)**
CAPITOL HILL OFFICE:
2407 RHOB 20515; 225-3861

**WASHINGTON, HAROLD (D ILL.—1)**
CAPITOL HILL OFFICE:
1610 LHOB 20515; 225-4372

**WATKINS, WES (D OKLA.—3)**
CAPITOL HILL OFFICE:
137 CHOB 20515; 225-4565

**WAXMAN, HENRY A. (D CALIF.—24)**
CAPITOL HILL OFFICE:
2418 RHOB 20515; 225-3976

**WEAVER, JAMES (D ORE.—4)**
CAPITOL HILL OFFICE:
1226 LHOB 20515; 225-6416

**WEBER, ED (R OHIO—9)**
CAPITOL HILL OFFICE:
512 CHOB 20515; 225-4146

**WEBER, VIN (R MINN.—6)**
CAPITOL HILL OFFICE:
514 CHOB 20515; 225-2331

**WEISS, TED (D N.Y.—20)**
CAPITOL HILL OFFICE:
132 CHOB 20515; 225-5635

**WHITE, RICHARD C. (D TEXAS—16)**
CAPITOL HILL OFFICE:
2186 RHOB 20515; 225-4831

**WHITEHURST, G. WILLIAM (R VA.—2)**
CAPITOL HILL OFFICE:
2469 RHOB 20515; 225-4215

**WHITLEY, CHARLES (D N.C.—3)**
CAPITOL HILL OFFICE:
404 CHOB 20515; 225-3415

**WHITTAKER, BOB (R KAN.—5)**
CAPITOL HILL OFFICE:
516 CHOB 20515; 225-3911

**WHITTEN, JAMIE L. (D MISS.—1)**
CAPITOL HILL OFFICE:
2314 RHOB 20515; 225-4306

**WILLIAMS, LYLE (R OHIO—19)**
CAPITOL HILL OFFICE:
1004 LHOB 20515; 225-5261

**WILLIAMS, PAT (D MONT.—1)**
CAPITOL HILL OFFICE:
1512 LHOB 20515; 225-3211

**WILSON, CHARLES (D TEXAS—2)**
CAPITOL HILL OFFICE:
1214 LHOB 20515; 225-2401

**WINN, LARRY JR. (R KAN.—3)**
CAPITOL HILL OFFICE:
2268 RHOB 20515; 225-2865

**WIRTH, TIMOTHY E. (D COLO.—2)**
CAPITOL HILL OFFICE:
2454 RHOB 20515; 225-2161

**WOLF, FRANK R. (R VA.—10)**
CAPITOL HILL OFFICE:
414 CHOB 20515; 225-5136

**WOLPE, HOWARD (D MICH.—3)**
CAPITOL HILL OFFICE:
1118 LHOB 20515; 225-5011

**WORTLEY, GEORGE C. (R N.Y.—32)**
CAPITOL HILL OFFICE:
508 CHOB 20515; 225-3701

**WRIGHT, JIM (D TEXAS—12)**
CAPITOL HILL OFFICE:
1236 LHOB 20515; 225-5071
(congressional office)
H-148 The Capitol 20515; 225-8040
(Majority Leader's office)


**WYDEN, RON (D ORE.—3)**
CAPITOL HILL OFFICE:
1440 LHOB 20515; 225-4811


**WYLIE, CHALMERS P. (R OHIO—15)**
CAPITOL HILL OFFICE:
2335 RHOB 20515; 225-2015


**YATES, SIDNEY R. (D ILL.—9)**
CAPITOL HILL OFFICE:
2234 RHOB 20515; 225-2111


**YATRON, GUS (D PA.—6)**
CAPITOL HILL OFFICE:
2267 RHOB 20515; 225-5546


**YOUNG, C. W. BILL (R FLA.—6)**
CAPITOL HILL OFFICE:
2266 RHOB 20515; 225-5961


**YOUNG, DON (R ALASKA—AL)**
CAPITOL HILL OFFICE:
2331 RHOB 20515; 225-5765


**YOUNG, ROBERT A. (D MO.—2)**
CAPITOL HILL OFFICE:
1317 LHOB 20515; 225-2561


**ZABLOCKI, CLEMENT J. (D WIS.—4)**
CAPITOL HILL OFFICE:
2183 RHOB 20515; 225-4572


**ZEFERETTI, LEO C. (D N.Y.—15)**
CAPITOL HILL OFFICE:
2436 RHOB 20515; 225-4105

# 1980 State Election Returns for President

Following are official 1980 vote returns for president compiled by Congressional Quarterly from results furnished by the secretaries of state or election boards in the 50 states. All candidates are included who were listed on the ballot. Abbreviations for party designations are: CIT (Citizens), D (Democratic), I (Independent), LIBERT (Libertarian) and R (Republican).

## ALABAMA

| | Vote Total | Per-cent |
|---|---|---|
| **President** | | |
| Ronald Reagan (R) | 654,192 | 48.8 |
| Jimmy Carter (D) | 636,730 | 47.5 |
| John B. Anderson (I) | 16,481 | 1.2 |
| Ed Clark (LIBERT) | 13,318 | 1.0 |
| Barry Commoner (CIT) | 517 | 0.0 |
| Other | 20,721 | 1.5 |

## ALASKA

| | Vote Total | Per-cent |
|---|---|---|
| **President** | | |
| Ronald Reagan (R) | 86,112 | 54.4 |
| Jimmy Carter (D) | 41,842 | 26.4 |
| John B. Anderson (I) | 11,156 | 7.0 |
| Ed Clark (LIBERT) | 18,479 | 11.7 |
| Other | 805 | 0.5 |

## ARIZONA

| | Vote Total | Per-cent |
|---|---|---|
| **President** | | |
| Ronald Reagan (R) | 529,688 | 60.6 |
| Jimmy Carter (D) | 246,843 | 28.2 |
| John B. Anderson (I) | 76,952 | 8.8 |
| Ed Clark (LIBERT) | 18,784 | 2.2 |
| Barry Commoner (write-in) | 551 | 0.1 |
| Other | 1,127 | 0.1 |

## ARKANSAS

| | Vote Total | Per-cent |
|---|---|---|
| **President** | | |
| Ronald Reagan (R) | 403,164 | 48.1 |
| Jimmy Carter (D) | 398,041 | 47.5 |
| John B. Anderson (I) | 22,468 | 2.7 |
| Ed Clark (LIBERT) | 8,970 | 1.1 |
| Barry Commoner (CIT) | 2,345 | 0.3 |
| Other | 2,594 | 0.3 |

## CALIFORNIA

| | Vote Total | Per-cent |
|---|---|---|
| **President** | | |
| Ronald Reagan (R) | 4,524,835 | 52.7 |
| Jimmy Carter (D) | 3,083,652 | 35.9 |
| John B. Anderson (I) | 739,832 | 8.6 |
| Ed Clark (LIBERT) | 148,434 | 1.7 |
| Barry Commoner (CIT) | 61,063 | 0.7 |
| Other | 29,214 | 0.4 |

## COLORADO

| | Vote Total | Per-cent |
|---|---|---|
| **President** | | |
| Ronald Reagan (R) | 652,264 | 55.0 |
| Jimmy Carter (D) | 368,009 | 31.1 |
| John B. Anderson (I) | 130,633 | 11.0 |
| Ed Clark (LIBERT) | 25,744 | 2.2 |
| Barry Commoner (CIT) | 5,614 | 0.5 |
| Other | 2,186 | 0.2 |

## CONNECTICUT

| | Vote Total | Per-cent |
|---|---|---|
| **President** | | |
| Ronald Reagan (R) | 677,210 | 48.2 |
| Jimmy Carter (D) | 541,732 | 38.5 |
| John B. Anderson (I) | 171,807 | 12.2 |
| Ed Clark (LIBERT) | 8,570 | 0.6 |
| Barry Commoner (CIT) | 6,130 | 0.4 |
| Other | 836 | 0.1 |

## DELAWARE

| | Vote Total | Per-cent |
|---|---|---|
| **President** | | |
| Ronald Reagan (R) | 111,252 | 47.2 |
| Jimmy Carter (D) | 105,754 | 44.8 |
| John B. Anderson (I) | 16,288 | 6.9 |
| Ed Clark (LIBERT) | 1,974 | 0.9 |
| Barry Commoner (write-in) | 103 | 0.0 |
| Other | 529 | 0.2 |

## FLORIDA

| | Vote Total | Per-cent |
|---|---|---|
| **President** | | |
| Ronald Reagan (R) | 2,046,951 | 55.5 |
| Jimmy Carter (D) | 1,419,475 | 38.5 |
| John B. Anderson (I) | 189,692 | 5.2 |
| Ed Clark (LIBERT) | 30,524 | 0.8 |
| Other | 285 | 0.0 |

## GEORGIA

| | Vote Total | Per-cent |
|---|---|---|
| **President** | | |
| Ronald Reagan (R) | 654,168 | 41.0 |
| Jimmy Carter (D) | 890,955 | 55.8 |
| John B. Anderson (I) | 36,055 | 2.2 |
| Ed Clark (LIBERT) | 15,627 | 1.0 |
| Barry Commoner (write-in) | 104 | 0.0 |
| Other | 8 | 0.0 |

## HAWAII

|  | Vote Total | Per- cent |
|---|---|---|
| **President** | | |
| Ronald Reagan (R) | 130,112 | 42.9 |
| Jimmy Carter (D) | 135,879 | 44.8 |
| John B. Anderson (I) | 32,021 | 10.6 |
| Ed Clark (LIBERT) | 3,269 | 1.1 |
| Barry Commoner (CIT) | 1,548 | 0.5 |
| Other | 458 | 0.1 |

## IDAHO

|  | Vote Total | Per- cent |
|---|---|---|
| **President** | | |
| Ronald Reagan (R) | 290,699 | 66.4 |
| Jimmy Carter (D) | 110,192 | 25.2 |
| John B. Anderson (I) | 27,058 | 6.2 |
| Ed Clark (LIBERT) | 8,425 | 1.9 |
| Other | 1,470 | 0.3 |

## ILLINOIS

|  | Vote Total | Per- cent |
|---|---|---|
| **President** | | |
| Ronald Reagan (R) | 2,358,094 | 49.7 |
| Jimmy Carter (D) | 1,981,413 | 41.7 |
| John B. Anderson (I) | 346,754 | 7.3 |
| Ed Clark (LIBERT) | 38,939 | 0.8 |
| Barry Commoner (CIT) | 10,692 | 0.2 |
| Other | 13,874 | 0.3 |

## INDIANA

|  | Vote Total | Per- cent |
|---|---|---|
| **President** | | |
| Ronald Reagan (R) | 1,255,656 | 56.0 |
| Jimmy Carter (D) | 844,197 | 37.6 |
| John B. Anderson (I) | 111,639 | 5.0 |
| Ed Clark (LIBERT) | 19,627 | 0.9 |
| Barry Commoner (CIT) | 4,852 | 0.2 |
| Other | 6,062 | 0.3 |

## IOWA

|  | Vote Total | Per- cent |
|---|---|---|
| **President** | | |
| Ronald Reagan (R) | 676,026 | 51.3 |
| Jimmy Carter (D) | 508,672 | 38.6 |
| John B. Anderson (I) | 115,633 | 8.8 |
| Ed Clark (LIBERT) | 13,123 | 1.0 |
| Barry Commoner (CIT) | 2,273 | 0.2 |
| Other | 1,934 | 0.1 |

## KANSAS

|  | Vote Total | Per- cent |
|---|---|---|
| **President** | | |
| Ronald Reagan (R) | 566,812 | 57.8 |
| Jimmy Carter (D) | 326,150 | 33.3 |
| John B. Anderson (I) | 68,231 | 7.0 |
| Ed Clark (LIBERT) | 14,470 | 1.5 |
| Other | 4,132 | 0.4 |

## KENTUCKY

|  | Vote Total | Per- cent |
|---|---|---|
| **President** | | |
| Ronald Reagan (R) | 635,274 | 49.0 |
| Jimmy Carter (D) | 617,417 | 47.7 |
| John B. Anderson (I) | 31,127 | 2.4 |
| Ed Clark (LIBERT) | 5,531 | 0.4 |
| Barry Commoner (CIT) | 1,304 | 0.1 |
| Other | 4,974 | 0.4 |

## LOUISIANA

|  | Vote Total | Per- cent |
|---|---|---|
| **President** | | |
| Ronald Reagan (R) | 792,853 | 51.2 |
| Jimmy Carter (D) | 708,453 | 45.8 |
| John B. Anderson (I) | 26,345 | 1.7 |
| Ed Clark (LIBERT) | 8,240 | 0.5 |
| Barry Commoner (CIT) | 1,584 | 0.1 |
| Other | 11,116 | 0.7 |

## MAINE

|  | Vote Total | Per- cent |
|---|---|---|
| **President** | | |
| Ronald Reagan (R) | 238,522 | 45.6 |
| Jimmy Carter (D) | 220,974 | 42.3 |
| John B. Anderson (I) | 53,327 | 10.2 |
| Ed Clark (LIBERT) | 5,119 | 1.0 |
| Barry Commoner (CIT) | 4,394 | 0.8 |
| Other | 675 | 0.1 |

## MARYLAND

|  | Vote Total | Per- cent |
|---|---|---|
| **President** | | |
| Ronald Reagan (R) | 680,606 | 44.2 |
| Jimmy Carter (D) | 726,161 | 47.1 |
| John B. Anderson (I) | 119,537 | 7.8 |
| Ed Clark (LIBERT) | 14,192 | 0.9 |

## MASSACHUSETTS

|  | Vote Total | Per- cent |
|---|---|---|
| **President** | | |
| Ronald Reagan (R) | 1,056,223 | 41.8 |
| Jimmy Carter (D) | 1,053,800 | 41.7 |
| John B. Anderson (I) | 382,539 | 15.2 |
| Ed Clark (LIBERT) | 22,038 | 0.9 |
| Barry Commoner (write-in) | 2,056 | 0.1 |
| Other | 7,972 | 0.3 |

## MICHIGAN

|  | Vote Total | Per- cent |
|---|---|---|
| **President** | | |
| Ronald Reagan (R) | 1,915,225 | 49.0 |
| Jimmy Carter (D) | 1,661,532 | 42.5 |
| John B. Anderson (I) | 275,223 | 7.0 |
| Ed Clark (LIBERT) | 41,597 | 1.1 |
| Barry Commoner (CIT) | 11,930 | 0.3 |
| Other | 4,218 | 0.1 |

## MINNESOTA

| | Vote Total | Per- cent |
|---|---|---|
| **President** | | |
| Ronald Reagan (R) | 873,268 | 42.6 |
| Jimmy Carter (D) | 954,173 | 46.5 |
| John B. Anderson (I) | 174,997 | 8.5 |
| Ed Clark (LIBERT) | 31,593 | 1.5 |
| Barry Commoner (CIT) | 8,406 | 0.4 |
| Other | 9,479 | 0.5 |

## MISSISSIPPI

| **President** | | |
|---|---|---|
| Ronald Reagan (R) | 441,089 | 49.4 |
| Jimmy Carter (D) | 429,281 | 48.1 |
| John B. Anderson (I) | 12,036 | 1.4 |
| Ed Clark (LIBERT) | 5,465 | 0.6 |
| Other | 4,749 | 0.5 |

## MISSOURI

| **President** | | |
|---|---|---|
| Ronald Reagan (R) | 1,074,181 | 51.2 |
| Jimmy Carter (D) | 931,182 | 44.3 |
| John B. Anderson (I) | 77,920 | 3.7 |
| Ed Clark (LIBERT) | 14,422 | 0.7 |
| Barry Commoner (write-in) | 573 | 0.0 |
| Other | 1,546 | 0.1 |

## MONTANA

| **President** | | |
|---|---|---|
| Ronald Reagan (R) | 206,814 | 56.8 |
| Jimmy Carter (D) | 118,032 | 32.4 |
| John B. Anderson (I) | 29,281 | 8.1 |
| Ed Clark (LIBERT) | 9,825 | 2.7 |

## NEBRASKA

| **President** | | |
|---|---|---|
| Ronald Reagan (R) | 419,214 | 65.6 |
| Jimmy Carter (D) | 166,424 | 26.0 |
| John B. Anderson (I) | 44,854 | 7.0 |
| Ed Clark (LIBERT) | 9,041 | 1.4 |

## NEVADA

| **President** | | |
|---|---|---|
| Ronald Reagan (R) | 155,017 | 62.5 |
| Jimmy Carter (D) | 66,666 | 26.9 |
| John B. Anderson (I) | 17,651 | 7.1 |
| Ed Clark (LIBERT) | 4,358 | 1.8 |
| Other | 4,193 | 1.7 |

## NEW HAMPSHIRE

| | Vote Total | Per- cent |
|---|---|---|
| **President** | | |
| Ronald Reagan (R) | 221,705 | 57.7 |
| Jimmy Carter (D) | 108,864 | 28.4 |
| John B. Anderson (I) | 49,693 | 12.9 |
| Ed Clark (LIBERT) | 2,064 | 0.5 |
| Barry Commoner (CIT) | 1,320 | 0.4 |
| Other | 344 | 0.1 |

## NEW JERSEY

| **President** | | |
|---|---|---|
| Ronald Reagan (R) | 1,546,557 | 52.0 |
| Jimmy Carter (D) | 1,147,364 | 38.6 |
| John B. Anderson (I) | 234,632 | 7.9 |
| Ed Clark (LIBERT) | 20,652 | 0.6 |
| Barry Commoner (CIT) | 8,203 | 0.3 |
| Other | 18,276 | 0.6 |

## NEW MEXICO

| **President** | | |
|---|---|---|
| Ronald Reagan (R) | 250,779 | 55.0 |
| Jimmy Carter (D) | 167,826 | 36.8 |
| John B. Anderson (I) | 29,459 | 6.5 |
| Ed Clark (LIBERT) | 4,365 | 0.9 |
| Barry Commoner (CIT) | 2,202 | 0.5 |
| Other | 1,606 | 0.3 |

## NEW YORK

| **President** | | |
|---|---|---|
| Ronald Reagan (R) | 2,893,831 | 46.7 |
| Jimmy Carter (D) | 2,728,372 | 44.0 |
| John B. Anderson (I) | 467,801 | 7.5 |
| Ed Clark (LIBERT) | 52,648 | 0.8 |
| Barry Commoner (CIT) | 23,186 | 0.4 |
| Other | 36,121 | 0.6 |

## NORTH CAROLINA

| **President** | | |
|---|---|---|
| Ronald Reagan (R) | 915,018 | 49.3 |
| Jimmy Carter (D) | 875,635 | 47.2 |
| John B. Anderson (I) | 52,800 | 2.9 |
| Ed Clark (LIBERT) | 9,677 | 0.5 |
| Barry Commoner (CIT) | 2,287 | 0.1 |
| Other | 416 | 0.0 |

## NORTH DAKOTA

| **President** | | |
|---|---|---|
| Ronald Reagan (R) | 193,695 | 64.2 |
| Jimmy Carter (D) | 79,189 | 26.3 |
| John B. Anderson (I) | 23,640 | 7.8 |
| Ed Clark (LIBERT) | 3,743 | 1.2 |
| Barry Commoner (CIT) | 429 | 0.2 |
| Other | 849 | 0.3 |

## OHIO

| | Vote Total | Per- cent |
|---|---|---|
| **President** | | |
| Ronald Reagan (R) | 2,206,545 | 51.5 |
| Jimmy Carter (D) | 1,752,414 | 40.9 |
| John B. Anderson (I) | 254,472 | 5.9 |
| Ed Clark (LIBERT) | 49,033 | 1.2 |
| Barry Commoner (CIT) | 8,564 | 0.2 |
| Other | 12,575 | 0.3 |

## OKLAHOMA

| | | |
|---|---|---|
| **President** | | |
| Ronald Reagan (R) | 695,570 | 60.5 |
| Jimmy Carter (D) | 402,026 | 35.0 |
| John B. Anderson (I) | 38,284 | 3.3 |
| Ed Clark (LIBERT) | 13,828 | 1.2 |

## OREGON

| | | |
|---|---|---|
| **President** | | |
| Ronald Reagan (R) | 571,044 | 48.3 |
| Jimmy Carter (D) | 456,890 | 38.7 |
| John B. Anderson (I) | 112,389 | 9.5 |
| Ed Clark (LIBERT) | 25,838 | 2.2 |
| Barry Commoner (CIT) | 13,642 | 1.2 |
| Other | 1,713 | 0.1 |

## PENNSYLVANIA

| | | |
|---|---|---|
| **President** | | |
| Ronald Reagan (R) | 2,261,872 | 49.6 |
| Jimmy Carter (D) | 1,937,540 | 42.5 |
| John B. Anderson (I) | 292,921 | 6.4 |
| Ed Clark (LIBERT) | 33,263 | 0.7 |
| Barry Commoner (CIT) | 10,430 | 0.2 |
| Other | 25,475 | 0.6 |

## RHODE ISLAND

| | | |
|---|---|---|
| **President** | | |
| Ronald Reagan (R) | 154,793 | 37.2 |
| Jimmy Carter (D) | 198,342 | 47.7 |
| John B. Anderson (I) | 59,819 | 14.4 |
| Ed Clark (LIBERT) | 2,458 | 0.6 |
| Barry Commoner (write-in) | 67 | 0.0 |
| Other | 593 | 0.1 |

## SOUTH CAROLINA

| | | |
|---|---|---|
| **President** | | |
| Ronald Reagan (R) | 441,841 | 49.4 |
| Jimmy Carter (D) | 430,385 | 48.2 |
| John B. Anderson (I) | 14,153 | 1.6 |
| Ed Clark (LIBERT) | 5,139 | 0.6 |
| Other | 2,177 | 0.2 |

## SOUTH DAKOTA

| | Vote Total | Per- cent |
|---|---|---|
| **President** | | |
| Ronald Reagan (R) | 198,343 | 60.5 |
| Jimmy Carter (D) | 103,855 | 31.7 |
| John B. Anderson (I) | 21,431 | 6.5 |
| Ed Clark (LIBERT) | 3,824 | 1.2 |
| Other | 250 | 0.1 |

## TENNESSEE

| | | |
|---|---|---|
| **President** | | |
| Ronald Reagan (R) | 787,761 | 48.7 |
| Jimmy Carter (D) | 783,051 | 48.4 |
| John B. Anderson (I) | 35,991 | 2.2 |
| Ed Clark (LIBERT) | 7,116 | 0.4 |
| Barry Commoner (CIT) | 1,112 | 0.1 |
| Other | 2,585 | 0.2 |

## TEXAS

| | | |
|---|---|---|
| **President** | | |
| Ronald Reagan (R) | 2,510,705 | 55.3 |
| Jimmy Carter (D) | 1,881,147 | 41.4 |
| John B. Anderson (I) | 111,613 | 2.5 |
| Ed Clark (LIBERT) | 37,643 | 0.8 |
| Barry Commoner (write-in) | 453 | 0.0 |
| Other | 75 | 0.0 |

## UTAH

| | | |
|---|---|---|
| **President** | | |
| Ronald Reagan (R) | 439,687 | 72.8 |
| Jimmy Carter (D) | 124,266 | 20.6 |
| John B. Anderson (I) | 30,284 | 5.0 |
| Ed Clark (LIBERT) | 7,156 | 1.2 |
| Barry Commoner (CIT) | 1,009 | 0.1 |
| Other | 1,750 | 0.3 |

## VERMONT

| | | |
|---|---|---|
| **President** | | |
| Ronald Reagan (R) | 94,628 | 44.4 |
| Jimmy Carter (D) | 81,952 | 38.4 |
| John B. Anderson (I) | 31,761 | 14.9 |
| Ed Clark (LIBERT) | 1,900 | 0.9 |
| Barry Commoner (CIT) | 2,316 | 1.1 |
| Other | 742 | 0.3 |

## VIRGINIA

| | | |
|---|---|---|
| **President** | | |
| Ronald Reagan (R) | 989,609 | 53.0 |
| Jimmy Carter (D) | 752,174 | 40.3 |
| John B. Anderson (I) | 95,418 | 5.1 |
| Ed Clark (LIBERT) | 12,821 | 0.7 |
| Barry Commoner (CIT) | 14,024 | 0.8 |
| Other | 1,986 | 0.1 |

## WASHINGTON

| President | Vote Total | Percent |
|---|---|---|
| Ronald Reagan (R) | 865,244 | 49.7 |
| Jimmy Carter (D) | 650,193 | 37.3 |
| John B. Anderson (I) | 185,073 | 10.6 |
| Ed Clark (LIBERT) | 29,213 | 1.7 |
| Barry Commoner (CIT) | 9,403 | 0.5 |
| Other | 3,268 | 0.2 |

## WEST VIRGINIA

| President | Vote Total | Percent |
|---|---|---|
| Ronald Reagan (R) | 334,206 | 45.3 |
| Jimmy Carter (D) | 367,462 | 49.8 |
| John B. Anderson (I) | 31,691 | 4.3 |
| Ed Clark (LIBERT) | 4,356 | 0.6 |

## WISCONSIN

| President | Vote Total | Percent |
|---|---|---|
| Ronald Reagan (R) | 1,088,845 | 47.9 |
| Jimmy Carter (D) | 981,584 | 43.2 |
| John B. Anderson (I) | 160,657 | 7.1 |
| Ed Clark (LIBERT) | 29,135 | 1.3 |
| Barry Commoner (CIT) | 7,767 | 0.3 |
| Other | 5,233 | 0.2 |

## WYOMING

| President | Vote Total | Percent |
|---|---|---|
| Ronald Reagan (R) | 110,700 | 62.6 |
| Jimmy Carter (D) | 49,427 | 28.0 |
| John B. Anderson (I) | 12,072 | 6.8 |
| Ed Clark (LIBERT) | 4,514 | 2.6 |

# 1980 Presidential Primary Elections

Following are the vote totals and vote percentages for all major presidential contenders in 1980 preference primaries. Figures were compiled by Congressional Quarterly from results furnished by the secretaries of state, election boards or state party committees. In the 50 states, there were 33 Democratic and 32 Republican preference contests, where voters chose directly the candidate of their choice.

Republicans in New York and Mississippi held primaries for the selection of delegates only and not for presidential preferences. Arkansas Republicans did not hold a primary, although Democrats did. Democrats in South Carolina and Mississippi did not conduct primaries.

An asterisk (*) indicates write-in votes.

| New Hampshire (2/26/80) | Votes | % |
|---|---|---|
| **Democrats** | | |
| Jimmy Carter | 52,692 | 47.1 |
| Edward M. Kennedy | 41,745 | 37.3 |
| Edmund G. Brown Jr. | 10,743 | 9.6 |
| Others | 6,750 | 6.0 |
| **Republicans** | | |
| Ronald Reagan | 72,983 | 49.6 |
| George Bush | 33,443 | 22.7 |
| Howard H. Baker Jr. | 18,943 | 12.9 |
| John B. Anderson | 14,458 | 9.8 |
| Philip M. Crane | 2,618 | 1.8 |
| John B. Connally | 2,239 | 1.5 |
| Others | 2,473 | 1.7 |

| Massachusetts (3/4/80) | | |
|---|---|---|
| **Democrats** | | |
| Kennedy | 590,362 | 65.1 |
| Carter | 260,396 | 28.7 |
| Brown | 31,498 | 3.5 |
| Others | 25,076 | 2.7 |
| **Republicans** | | |
| Bush | 124,365 | 31.0 |
| Anderson | 122,987 | 30.7 |
| Reagan | 115,334 | 28.8 |
| Baker | 19,366 | 4.8 |
| Connally | 4,714 | 1.2 |
| Crane | 4,669 | 1.2 |
| Others | 9,391 | 2.3 |

| Vermont (3/4/80) | | |
|---|---|---|
| **Democrats** | | |
| Carter | 29,015 | 73.1 |
| Kennedy | 10,135 | 25.5 |
| Brown* | 358 | 0.9 |
| Others | 195 | 0.5 |

| | Votes | % |
|---|---|---|
| **Republicans** | | |
| Reagan | 19,720 | 30.1 |
| Anderson | 19,030 | 29.0 |
| Bush | 14,226 | 21.7 |
| Baker[1] | 8,055 | 12.3 |
| Crane | 1,238 | 1.9 |
| Connally | 884 | 1.3 |
| Others | 2,458 | 3.7 |

| South Carolina (3/8/80) | | |
|---|---|---|
| **Republicans** | | |
| Reagan | 79,549 | 54.7 |
| Connally[2] | 43,113 | 29.6 |
| Bush | 21,569 | 14.8 |
| Baker | 773 | 0.5 |
| Others | 497 | 0.4 |

| Alabama (3/11/80) | | |
|---|---|---|
| **Democrats** | | |
| Carter | 193,734 | 81.6 |
| Kennedy | 31,382 | 13.2 |
| Brown | 9,529 | 4.0 |
| Others | 2,819 | 1.2 |
| **Republicans** | | |
| Reagan | 147,352 | 69.7 |
| Bush | 54,730 | 25.9 |
| Crane | 5,099 | 2.4 |
| Baker | 1,963 | 0.9 |
| Connally | 1,077 | 0.5 |
| Others | 1,132 | 0.6 |

| Florida (3/11/80) | | |
|---|---|---|
| **Democrats** | | |
| Carter | 666,321 | 60.7 |
| Kennedy | 254,727 | 23.2 |

| | Votes | % |
|---|---|---|
| Brown | 53,474 | 4.9 |
| Others | 123,481 | 11.2 |
| **Republicans** | | |
| Reagan | 345,699 | 56.2 |
| Bush | 185,996 | 30.2 |
| Anderson | 56,636 | 9.2 |
| Crane | 12,000 | 2.0 |
| Baker | 6,345 | 1.0 |
| Connally | 4,958 | 0.8 |
| Others | 3,361 | 0.6 |

## Georgia (3/11/80)

| | Votes | % |
|---|---|---|
| **Democrats** | | |
| Carter | 338,772 | 88.0 |
| Kennedy | 32,315 | 8.4 |
| Brown | 7,255 | 1.9 |
| Others | 6,438 | 1.7 |
| **Republicans** | | |
| Reagan | 146,500 | 73.2 |
| Bush | 25,293 | 12.6 |
| Anderson | 16,853 | 8.4 |
| Crane | 6,308 | 3.2 |
| Connally | 2,388 | 1.2 |
| Baker | 1,571 | 0.8 |
| Others | 1,258 | 0.6 |

## Illinois (3/18/80)

| | Votes | % |
|---|---|---|
| **Democrats** | | |
| Carter | 780,787 | 65.0 |
| Kennedy | 359,875 | 30.0 |
| Brown | 39,168 | 3.3 |
| Others | 21,237 | 1.7 |
| **Republicans** | | |
| Reagan | 547,355 | 48.4 |
| Anderson | 415,193 | 36.8 |
| Bush | 124,057 | 11.0 |
| Crane | 24,865 | 2.2 |
| Baker | 7,051 | 0.6 |
| Connally | 4,548 | 0.4 |
| Others | 7,012 | 0.6 |

## Connecticut (3/25/80)

| | Votes | % |
|---|---|---|
| **Democrats** | | |
| Kennedy | 98,662 | 46.9 |
| Carter | 87,207 | 41.5 |
| Brown | 5,386 | 2.6 |
| Others | 19,020 | 9.0 |

| | Votes | % |
|---|---|---|
| **Republicans** | | |
| Bush | 70,367 | 38.6 |
| Reagan | 61,735 | 33.9 |
| Anderson | 40,354 | 22.1 |
| Baker | 2,446 | 1.4 |
| Crane | 1,887 | 1.0 |
| Connally | 598 | 0.3 |
| Others | 4,897 | 2.7 |

## New York (3/25/80)

| | Votes | % |
|---|---|---|
| **Democrats** | | |
| Kennedy | 582,757 | 58.9 |
| Carter | 406,305 | 41.1 |

## Kansas (4/1/80)

| | Votes | % |
|---|---|---|
| **Democrats** | | |
| Carter | 109,807 | 56.6 |
| Kennedy | 61,318 | 31.6 |
| Brown | 9,434 | 4.9 |
| Others | 13,359 | 6.9 |
| **Republicans** | | |
| Reagan | 179,739 | 63.0 |
| Anderson | 51,924 | 18.2 |
| Bush | 35,838 | 12.5 |
| Baker | 3,603 | 1.3 |
| Connally | 2,067 | 0.7 |
| Crane | 1,367 | 0.5 |
| Others | 10,860 | 3.8 |

## Wisconsin (4/1/80)

| | Votes | % |
|---|---|---|
| **Democrats** | | |
| Carter | 353,662 | 56.2 |
| Kennedy | 189,520 | 30.1 |
| Brown[3] | 74,496 | 11.8 |
| Others | 11,941 | 1.9 |
| **Republicans** | | |
| Reagan | 364,898 | 40.2 |
| Bush | 276,164 | 30.4 |
| Anderson[5] | 248,623 | 27.4 |
| Baker | 3,298 | 0.4 |
| Crane[4] | 2,951 | 0.3 |
| Connally | 2,312 | 0.2 |
| Others | 9,607 | 1.1 |

## Louisiana (4/5/80)

| | Votes | % |
|---|---|---|
| **Democrats** | | |
| Carter | 199,956 | 55.7 |

**1371**

# 1980 Presidential Primaries

| | Votes | % |
|---|---|---|
| Kennedy | 80,797 | 22.5 |
| Brown | 16,774 | 4.7 |
| Others | 61,214 | 17.1 |
| **Republicans** | | |
| Reagan | 31,212 | 74.9 |
| Bush | 7,818 | 18.7 |
| Others | 2,653 | 6.4 |

## Pennsylvania (4/22/80)

| | Votes | % |
|---|---|---|
| **Democrats** | | |
| Kennedy | 736,854 | 46.0 |
| Carter | 732,332 | 45.8 |
| Brown | 37,669 | 2.3 |
| Others | 93,865 | 5.9 |
| **Republicans** | | |
| Bush | 626,759 | 51.8 |
| Reagan | 527,916 | 43.6 |
| Baker | 30,846 | 2.6 |
| Connally | 10,656 | 0.9 |
| Others | 13,645 | 1.1 |

## Texas (5/3/80)

| | Votes | % |
|---|---|---|
| **Democrats** | | |
| Carter | 770,390 | 55.9 |
| Kennedy | 314,129 | 22.8 |
| Brown | 35,585 | 2.6 |
| Others | 257,250 | 18.7 |
| **Republicans** | | |
| Reagan | 268,798 | 51.0 |
| Bush | 249,819 | 47.4 |
| Others | 8,152 | 1.6 |

## Indiana (5/6/80)

| | Votes | % |
|---|---|---|
| **Democrats** | | |
| Carter | 398,949 | 67.7 |
| Kennedy | 190,492 | 32.3 |
| **Republicans** | | |
| Reagan | 419,016 | 73.7 |
| Bush | 92,955 | 16.4 |
| Anderson | 56,344 | 9.9 |

## North Carolina (5/6/80)

| | Votes | % |
|---|---|---|
| **Democrats** | | |
| Carter | 516,778 | 70.1 |
| Kennedy | 130,684 | 17.7 |
| Brown | 21,420 | 2.9 |

| | Votes | % |
|---|---|---|
| Others | 68,380 | 9.3 |
| **Republicans** | | |
| Reagan | 113,854 | 67.6 |
| Bush | 36,631 | 21.7 |
| Anderson | 8,542 | 5.1 |
| Baker | 2,543 | 1.5 |
| Connally | 1,107 | 0.7 |
| Crane | 547 | 0.3 |
| Others | 5,167 | 3.1 |

## Tennessee (5/6/80)

| | Votes | % |
|---|---|---|
| **Democrats** | | |
| Carter | 221,658 | 75.2 |
| Kennedy | 53,258 | 18.1 |
| Brown | 5,612 | 1.9 |
| Others | 14,152 | 4.8 |
| **Republicans** | | |
| Reagan | 144,625 | 74.1 |
| Bush | 35,274 | 18.1 |
| Anderson | 8,722 | 4.4 |
| Crane | 1,574 | 0.8 |
| Others | 5,015 | 2.6 |

## Maryland (5/13/80)

| | Votes | % |
|---|---|---|
| **Democrats** | | |
| Carter | 226,528 | 47.5 |
| Kennedy | 181,091 | 38.0 |
| Brown | 14,313 | 3.0 |
| Others | 55,158 | 11.5 |
| **Republicans** | | |
| Reagan | 80,557 | 48.1 |
| Bush | 68,389 | 40.9 |
| Anderson | 16,244 | 9.7 |
| Crane | 2,113 | 1.3 |

## Nebraska (5/13/80)

| | Votes | % |
|---|---|---|
| **Democrats** | | |
| Carter | 72,120 | 46.9 |
| Kennedy | 57,826 | 37.6 |
| Brown | 5,478 | 3.5 |
| Others | 18,457 | 12.0 |
| **Republicans** | | |
| Reagan | 155,995 | 76.0 |
| Bush | 31,380 | 15.3 |
| Anderson | 11,879 | 5.8 |
| Crane | 1,062 | 0.5 |
| Others | 4,887 | 2.4 |

|  | Votes | % |
|---|---|---|

## Michigan (5/20/80)

**Democrats**
| Brown | 23,043 | 29.4 |
| Others | 55,381 | 70.6 |

**Republicans**
| Bush | 341,998 | 57.5 |
| Reagan | 189,184 | 31.8 |
| Anderson | 48,947 | 8.2 |
| Others | 15,047 | 2.5 |

## Oregon (5/20/80)

**Democrats**
| Carter | 208,693 | 58.3 |
| Kennedy | 114,651 | 32.1 |
| Brown | 34,409 | 9.6 |

**Republicans**
| Reagan | 170,449 | 54.3 |
| Bush[6] | 109,210 | 34.8 |
| Anderson | 32,118 | 10.2 |
| Crane | 2,324 | 0.7 |

## Arkansas (5/27/80)

**Democrats**
| Carter | 269,375 | 60.1 |
| Kennedy | 78,542 | 17.5 |
| Others | 100,373 | 22.4 |

## Idaho (5/27/80)

**Democrats**
| Carter | 31,383 | 62.2 |
| Kennedy | 11,087 | 22.0 |
| Brown | 2,078 | 4.1 |
| Others | 5,934 | 11.7 |

**Republicans**
| Reagan | 111,868 | 82.9 |
| Anderson | 13,130 | 9.7 |
| Bush | 5,416 | 4.0 |
| Crane | 1,024 | 0.8 |
| Others | 3,441 | 2.6 |

## Kentucky (5/27/80)

**Democrats**
| Carter | 160,819 | 66.9 |
| Kennedy | 55,167 | 23.0 |
| Others | 24,345 | 10.1 |

|  | Votes | % |
|---|---|---|

**Republicans**
| Reagan | 78,072 | 82.4 |
| Bush | 6,861 | 7.2 |
| Anderson | 4,791 | 5.1 |
| Others | 5,071 | 5.3 |

## Nevada (5/27/80)

**Democrats**
| Carter | 25,159 | 37.6 |
| Kennedy | 19,296 | 28.8 |
| Others | 22,493 | 33.6 |

**Republicans**
| Reagan | 39,352 | 83.0 |
| Bush | 3,078 | 6.5 |
| Others | 4,965 | 10.5 |

## California (6/3/80)

**Democrats**
| Kennedy | 1,507,142 | 44.8 |
| Carter | 1,266,276 | 37.7 |
| Brown | 135,962 | 4.0 |
| Others | 454,538 | 13.5 |

**Republicans**
| Reagan | 2,057,923 | 80.3 |
| Anderson | 349,315 | 13.6 |
| Bush | 125,113 | 4.9 |
| Crane | 21,465 | 0.8 |
| Others | 10,242 | 0.4 |

## Montana (6/3/80)

**Democrats**
| Carter | 66,922 | 51.5 |
| Kennedy | 47,671 | 36.6 |
| Others | 15,466 | 11.9 |

**Republicans**
| Reagan | 68,744 | 86.6 |
| Bush | 7,665 | 9.6 |
| Others | 3,014 | 3.8 |

## New Jersey (6/3/80)

**Democrats**
| Kennedy | 315,109 | 56.2 |
| Carter | 212,387 | 37.9 |
| Others | 33,412 | 5.9 |

**1373**

|  | **Votes** | **%** |  | **Votes** | **%** |
|---|---|---|---|---|---|
| **Republicans** |  |  | **Republicans** |  |  |
| Reagan | 225,959 | 81.3 | Reagan | 3,839 | 72.0 |
| Bush | 47,447 | 17.1 | Bush | 993 | 18.6 |
| Others | 4,571 | 1.6 | Others | 503 | 9.4 |

**New Mexico (6/3/80)**

**South Dakota (6/3/80)**

| **Democrats** |  |  |
|---|---|---|
| Kennedy | 73,721 | 46.3 |
| Carter | 66,621 | 41.8 |
| Others | 19,022 | 11.9 |

| **Democrats** |  |  |
|---|---|---|
| Kennedy | 33,418 | 48.6 |
| Carter | 31,251 | 45.4 |
| Others | 4,094 | 6.0 |

| **Republicans** |  |  |
|---|---|---|
| Reagan | 37,982 | 63.8 |
| Anderson | 7,171 | 12.0 |
| Bush | 5,892 | 9.9 |
| Crane | 4,412 | 7.4 |
| Others | 4,089 | 6.9 |

| **Republicans** |  |  |
|---|---|---|
| Reagan | 72,861 | 87.9 |
| Bush | 3,691 | 4.4 |
| Others | 6,353 | 7.7 |

**Ohio (6/3/80)**

**West Virginia (6/3/80)**

| **Democrats** |  |  |
|---|---|---|
| Carter | 605,744 | 51.0 |
| Kennedy | 523,874 | 44.2 |
| Others | 56,792 | 4.8 |

| **Democrats** |  |  |
|---|---|---|
| Carter | 197,687 | 62.2 |
| Kennedy | 120,247 | 37.8 |

| **Republicans** |  |  |
|---|---|---|
| Reagan | 692,288 | 80.8 |
| Bush | 164,485 | 19.2 |

| **Republicans** |  |  |
|---|---|---|
| Reagan | 115,407 | 83.6 |
| Bush | 19,509 | 14.1 |
| Others | 3,100 | 2.3 |

**Rhode Island (6/3/80)**

| **Democrats** |  |  |
|---|---|---|
| Kennedy | 26,179 | 68.3 |
| Carter | 9,907 | 25.9 |
| Brown | 310 | 0.8 |
| Others | 1,931 | 5.0 |

*1 Baker withdrew March 5.*
*2 Connally withdrew March 9.*
*3 Brown withdrew April 1.*
*4 Crane withdrew April 17.*
*5 Anderson withdrew April 24.*
*6 Bush withdrew May 26.*

# Index

# I, J

# K

# L

# U, V

# W

# X, Y, Z